82nd Association for Information Science and Technology Annual Meeting

Information...Anyone, Anywhere, Any Time, Any Way

Proceedings of the Association for Information Science and Technology Volume 56

Melbourne, Australia
19-23 October 2019

Editors:

Catherine Blake
Cecelia Brown
Lydia S. Middleton

ISBN: 978-1-7138-0601-1

Printed from e-media with permission by:

Curran Associates, Inc.
57 Morehouse Lane
Red Hook, NY 12571

Some format issues inherent in the e-media version may also appear in this print version.

Printed with permission by Curran Associates, Inc. (2020)

For permission requests, please contact Association for Information Science and Technology (ASIS&T) at the address below.

Association for Information Science and Technology (ASIS&T)
8555 16th Street, Suite 850
Silver Spring, Maryland 20910
USA

Phone: 301-495-0900
Fax: 301-495-0810

asist@asist.org

Additional copies of this publication are available from:

Curran Associates, Inc.
57 Morehouse Lane
Red Hook, NY 12571 USA
Phone: 845-758-0400
Fax: 845-758-2633
Email: curran@proceedings.com
Web: www.proceedings.com

82ND ANNUAL MEETING

ON-SITE MEETING PROGRAM

asis&t

19-23 OCTOBER 2019
CROWN CONFERENCE CENTRE
MELBOURNE, AUSTRALIA

INFORMATION...ANYONE, ANYWHERE, ANY TIME, ANY WAY

FOR MORE INFORMATION ON THIS CONFERENCE, VISIT WWW.ASIST.ORG/AM19

VOLUME 56

PROCEEDINGS EDITORS

Catherine Blake, PhD | University of Illinois - Urbana-Champaign, USA
Cecelia Brown, PhD | University of Oklahoma, USA

PUBLISHED FOR THE ASSOCIATION FOR INFORMATION SCIENCE & TECHNOLOGY

BY

JOHN WILEY & SONS, INC.

SOMERSET, NJ

Managing Editor
Lydia S. Middleton, MBA, CAE

Association for Information Science and Technology
8555 16th Street, Suite 850, Silver Spring, Maryland 20910

PROGRAM CO-CHAIRS:

Catherine Blake, PhD
University of Illinois - Urbana-Champaign, USA
Cecelia Brown, PhD
University of Oklahoma, USA

PAPER CO-CHAIRS:

Theresa Anderson, PhD
University of Technology, Sydney, Australia
VG Vinod Vydiswaran, PhD
University of Michigan, USA

PANEL & ALTERNATIVE EVENT CO-CHAIRS:

Joan Bartlett, PhD
McGill University, Canada
Dietmar Wolfram, PhD
University of Wisconsin - Milwaukee, USA

POSTER CO-CHAIRS:

Ian Ruthven, PhD
University of Strathclyde, UK
Dan Wu, PhD
Wuhan University, China

DOCTORAL COLLOQUIUM CO-CHAIRS:

Pnina Fichman, PhD
University of Indiana, USA
Howard Rosenbaum
University of Indiana, USA

ASIS&T STAFF:

Lydia Middleton, MBA, CAE
Executive Director

Cathy Nash, CMP
Director of Meetings & Events

Terrence Curtiss
Membership Manager

ASIS&T BOARD OF DIRECTORS:

President:
Elaine Toms, PhD
University of Sheffield, UK

President Elect:
Clara M. Chu, PhD
University of Illinois at Urbana-Champagne, USA

Immediate Past President:
Lisa Given, PhD
Swinburne University of Technology, Australia

Treasurer:
June Abbas
University of Oklahoma, USA

Chapter Assembly Director:
Timothy Dickey
Columbus Metropolitan Library, USA

SIG Cabinet Director:
Sarah Buchanan, PhD
University of Missouri, USA

Director:
Dania Bilal, PhD
University of Tennessee - Knoxville, USA

Director:
Emily Knox, PhD
University of Illinois - Urbana-Champaign, USA

Director:
Agnes Mainka, PhD
Heinrich Heine University, Germany

Director:
Heather O'Brien, PhD
University of British Columbia, Canada

Director:
Soo Young Rieh, PhD
University of Michigan, USA

Executive Director:
Lydia Middleton, MBA, CAE
ASIS&T, USA

Parliamentarian:
Steve Hardin
Indiana State University, USA

Gday,

Welcome to the 82nd Association for Information Science and Technology (ASIS&T) Annual Meeting. Our meeting is in Melbourne, Australia this year and we respectfully acknowledge and thank the Traditional Owners of this land, the Boon Wurrung and Woiwurrung (Wurundjeri) peoples of the Kulin Nation.

Information has been the root cause of significant changes in economic, social, scientific, political, and personal behaviors; but the benefits of such changes are only realized when information is delivered to the right group, at the right place, at the right time, and in the right way. Thus the theme of this year's conference is "INFORMATION... ANYONE, ANYWHERE, ANY TIME, ANY WAY".

The 'anyone' and 'anywhere' facets of this theme will be highlighted in the opening plenary presentation on "Mixing Reality for Cultural Proliferation', where Mikaela Jade's will share her industry experience that successfully engages indigenous women in technology. Informed by decades of experience with the multitude of information available in health care, the closing speaker, Helena Teede will highlight the importance of delivering information at the right time and in the right way in her presentation entitled 'Changing the Paradigm: Creating a Learning Health System Through Disruption Collaboration'.

The conference leadership team did an outstanding job in managing the review process and we extend a hearty thank you to the paper co-chairs VG Vinod Vydiswaran and Theresa Anderson, the poster co-chairs Ian Ruthven and Dan Wu, the panels & alternative events co-chairs Joan Bartlett and Dietmar Wolfram, and the doctoral colloquium co-chairs Pnina Fichman and Howard Rosenbaum. High-quality reviews are also critical to a good technical program and as a token of our appreciation for good reviews we instigated a best reviewer award this year that will be announced during the Opening Session, along with the best paper awards. Poster awards will be announced on Tuesday night.

Our Annual Meeting, like many conferences focus on celebrating work that is complete, but this year, the International Incubator Sessions allow you to look to the future. We have been able to secure international leaders to facilitate a discussion on several key topics and we look forward seeing the fruits of those efforts during in the next to last session of this conference, and hopefully through grants and scholarship in next year's conference.

Kind Regards,
Catherine Blake & Cecy Brown
Conference Co-Chairs

Catherine Blake, PhD

Cecy Brown, PhD

INFORMATION...ANYONE, ANYWHERE, ANY TIME, ANY WAY

This meeting will focus the creative and analytical energies of the ASIS&T community on the dramatic near horizon socio-technical shifts expected due to rapid developments in technologies such as artificial intelligence, big data analytics, virtual and augmented reality, and embedded, ubiquitous computing.

The opportunities afforded by these technologies are enormous, as are the challenges of ensuring that ethical and human-centered perspectives, including sustainability, privacy, human agency and equity, are incorporated into their design and use.

As interdisciplinary information science and technology researchers and practitioners, with more than 80 years tradition of studying and working in this rapidly evolving field, we are uniquely situated to steward and mediate this shift. ASIS&T 2019 will provide an opportunity to learn from one another and from leading experts in these emerging technologies; to discuss, critique and pose the much-needed questions; and to share perspectives grounded in our own research and practice that intersect with and provide context for current developments.

The ASIS&T Annual Meeting is a premier, peer-reviewed international conference that gathers scholars and practitioners from around the globe to share research, innovations, and insights regarding the role of information and technology in the lives of individuals, organizations and communities. We invite papers, posters and visual presentations, panel and workshop submissions that focus on the conference theme, as well as work that reflects the broader mandate of ASIS&T, regarding the creation, representation, storage, access, dissemination and use of information, media and records, and the systems, tools, and technologies associated with these processes. The conference embraces plurality in methods and theories, and encompasses research, development and practice from a broad spectrum of domains, as encapsulated in ASIS&T's many special interest groups (SIGs).

We are pleased to announce that the ASIS&T 2019 Proceedings will be published by John Wiley & Sons and will be indexed and accessible via multiple international venues.

THIS YEAR, WE WILL BE EXPLORING:

- ALGORITHMIC TRUST
- CITATION ANALYSIS
- DIGITAL CULTURAL HERITAGE
- DIGITAL YOUTH
- EVERYDAY INFORMATION BEHAVIORS
- FINDABLE, ACCESSIBLE, INTEROPERABLE, REUSABLE (FAIR)
- HEALTH INFORMATICS
- INFORMATION INTEGRATION / LINKED DATA
- INFORMATION ORGANIZATION
- INFORMATION RETRIEVAL
- INFORMATION SEEKING
- KNOWLEDGE CONSTRUCTION METRICS
- ONLINE COMMUNITIES & CITIZEN SCIENCE
- OPEN ACCESS & GOVERNMENT DATA
- PERSONAL INFORMATION MANAGEMENT
- PRIVACY & TRUST SCHOLARLY COMMUNICATION
- STUDENT INFORMATION BEHAVIORS
- TEXT ANALYTICS

WHO SHOULD ATTEND:

ASIS&T's Annual Meeting is an essential event for information science professionals.

It's ideal for:

- Information science professionals
- Faculty
- Students
- Researchers

WHY ATTEND:

- Broaden your knowledge about the latest trends and research in information science.
- Network and collaborate with your peers who are passionate about information science.
- Establish and expand on mentoring opportunities.

REVIEWERS:

343 reviewers completed 1,111 reviews for papers, panels, alternative events, posters and doctoral colloquium. Top reviewers will be recognized at the Opening Session.

June Abbas
Muhammad Abdul-Mageed
Denice Adkins
Waseem Afzal
Naresh Kumar Agarwal
Noa Aharony
Hessah Osamah Alasousi
Daniel Alemneh
David K. Allen
Robert Allen
Taghreed Alqudsi-Ghabra
Kanwal Ameen
Jiaxin An
Lu An
Theresa Dirndorfer Anderson
Tatjana Aparac
Richard Arias-Hernandez
Diana Ascher
Tariq Ashraf
Shimelis Assefa
Toluwase Victor Asubiaro
Franz Barachini
Maram Barifah
Judit Bar-Ilan
Marguerite Barry
Joan Bartlett
Syeda Batool
David Bawden
Denise Bedford
Gerald Benoit
Ofer Bergman
Dania Bilal
Wade Bishop
Catherine Blake
Maria Bonn
Jenny Bossaller
Cecelia Brown
Yi Bu
Sarah Buchanan
John Budd
Julia Bullard
Mary Burke
Jacquelyn Burkell
Kathleen Burnett
Gary Burnett
Sean Burns
Joseph Busch
Yao Cai
Jennifer Campbell-Meier
Mary Cavanagh
Hsia-Ching Chang
Tiffany Chao
Hsin-liang Chen
Pei-Ying Chen
Xiaoju Julie Chen
Ye Chen
Yi-Yun Cheng
Kahyun Choi
Wonchan Choi
Miyoung Chong
Kevin Comerford
Lynn Silipigni Connaway
Andrea Copeland
Edward Corrado
Kaitlin Costello
Mats Dahlström
Kimiz Dalkir
Peter Darch
Anubrata Das
Kate Davis
Nathan W. Davis
Shengli Deng
Andrew Dillon
Junhua Ding
Ying Ding
Ly Dinh
Jesse David Dinneen
Brian Dobreski
Isabelle Dorsch
Tina Du
Yunfei Du
Jacques du Plessis
Sanda Erdelez
Craig Evans
Tao Fan
Ixchel Faniel
Yuanyuan Feng
Katrina Fenlon
Pnina Fichman
Erin Fields
Kaja Joanna Fietkiewicz
Diana Floegel
Melodie Fox
Rob Fox
Fanch Francis
Rebecca D. Frank
Luanne Freund
Ingo Frommholz
Hengyi Fu
Henry Gabb
Jamillah Gabriel
John Gathegi
Rich Gazan
Isha Ghosh
Twyla Gibson
Sarah Ann Gilbert
Anne Gilliland
Dion Goh
Tim Gorichanaz
Juan Gorraiz
Jane Greenberg
Devon Greyson
Ekatarina Grguric
Joachim Griesbaum
Gussun Gunes
Jim Hahn
Jelina Haines
Lala Hajibayova
Leiqian Han
Yuzhe Han
Anran Hao
Noriko Hara
Jenna Hartel
Suliman Hawamdeh
Caroline Haythornthwaite
Guoxiu He
Bradley Hemminger
Sandra Hirsh
Darra Hofman
Mary Horman
Xilong Hou
Eva Hourihan Jansen
Pamela Hoyte
TsungMing Hsiao
Tzu-Kun Hsiao
Xiao Hu
Mu-hsuan Huang
Isto Huvila
Aylin Ilhan
Md Anwarul Islam
Jenna Jacobson
Hamid R. Jamali
Jim Jansen
Wei Jeng
Tao Jin
Kyle M.L. Jones
Amir Karami
Karen F. Kaufmann
Diane Kelly
Amjid Khan
Pichano Kikon
Jenna Kim
Junoh Kim
Kyung-Sun Kim
Sunyoung Kim
Youngseek Kim
Vanessa Lynn Kitzie
Emily Knox
Rick Kopak
Cindy Kröber
Chung-Huei Kuan
Pei-Yi Kuo
Kei Kurakawa
Barbara Kwasnik
Thinh Le
Chei Sian Lee
Steffen Lemke
Noah Lenstra
Dirk Lewandowski
Lei Li
Ping Li
Zack Lischer-Katz
Chang Liu
Jiqun Liu
Ying-Hsang Liu
Irene Lopatovska
Wen Lou
Chao Lu
Liuxing Lu
Pablo Lucas
Anna Lundh
Yao Lyu
Jianxia Ma
Lai Ma
Yuanye Ma
Monica Grace Maceli
Rachel Magee
Martin Ting Fung Mak
Joyline Makani
Stephann Makri
Thomas Mandl
Zinaida Manžuch
Laura Marcial
Betsy Martens
Konstantina Martzoukou
Matt Mayernik
Philipp Mayr
Dana Mckay
Pamela J. McKenzie
David McMenemy
David Melero-Fuentes
Tereza Raquel Merlo
Eric T. Meyer
Eric Matthew Meyers
Shawne Miksa
A.J. Million
Stasa Milojevic
Chao Min
Lorri Mon
Philippe Mongeon
Heather Moulaison
Angela Murillo
Mariam Nazir
Jinfang Niu
Lorraine Normore
Heather O'Brien
Melissa G. Ocepek
Fatih Oguz
Randy Oldham
Tami Oliphant
Shannon Oltmann
Peter Organisciak
Yohanan Ouaknine
Tuulevi Ovaska
Anjan Pal
Hyoungjoo Park
Anindita Paul
Isabella Peters
Vivien Petras
Heather Pfeiffer
Christina Pikas
Sarah Polkinghorne
Biliamin Oladele Popoola
Devendra Potnis
Muhammad Qayyum
Marie L. Radford
Edie Rasmussen
Diane Rasmussen Pennington
Soo Young Rieh
Marc Rittberger
Michelle Rogers
Abebe Rorissa
Howard Rosenbaum
Alan Rubel
Ellen Rubenstein
Robert Sandusky
Jayne Sappington
Steve Sawyer
Elham Sayyad Abdi
David Schiller
Paul Scifleet
Charles Senteio
Chirag Shah
Ryan Shaw
Yi Shen
Ali Shiri
Elisabeth Shook
Fei Shu
Rajesh Singh
Vivek Singh
Catherine Smith
Dagobert Soergel
Ian Song
Shijie Song
Xiaokang Song
Xiaoxuan Song
Diane Sonnenwald
Beth St. Jean
Marielle St-Germain
Wolfgang Stock
Sharon Stoerger
Emma Stuart
Besiki Stvilia
Shigeo Sugimoto
Honglei Sun
Sue Yeon Syn
Iman Tahamtan
Jian Tang
Muh-Chyun Tang
Rong Tang
Carl Taswell
Natalie Taylor
Joseph Tennis
Andrea Karoline Thomer
Cheryl Annette Thompson
Huixin Tian
Ahmet Meti Tmava
Sandra Toze
Tien-I Tsai
Giannis Tsakonas
Michael Twidale
Christine Urquhart
Nicholas Vanderschantz
Diane Velasquez
Sirje Virkus
VG Vinod Vydiswaran
Nina Wacholder
Huajin Wang
Jianqiang Wang
Lin Wang
Peiling Wang
Ping Wang
Xianwen Wang
Xiwei Wang
Xu Wang
Yukai Wang
Zhihong Wang
Julian Warner
Nicholas Weber
Rachel Williams
Rebekah Willson
Christian Wolff
Dietmar Wolfram
Christa Womser-Hacker
Adam Worrall
Dan Wu
I-Chin Wu
Shuheng Wu
Yejun Wu
Iris Xie
Hao Xu
Shenmeng Xu
Shuang Xu
Erjia Yan
Shengnan Yang
Yukun Yang
Edwin Mouda Ye
Hilary Yerbury
Kwan Yi
Ayoung Yoon
Cindy Yu
Xiajun Yuan
Chengzhi Zhang
Chenwei Zhang
Pengyi Zhang
Yi Zhang
Yuehua Zhao
Han Zheng
Lingjun Zhu
Peng Zhu
Xiaohua Zhu
Maja Zumer

TABLE OF CONTENTS >

LONG PAPERS

Putting a Price on Social Movements: A Case Study of #MeToo on Instagram 1
Tanisha Afnan, Hsiao-Ying Huang, Maria Sclafani & Masooda Bashir

How Do Parents of Children with ASD Use Information Grounds to Seek for ASD-Related Information? 10
Jiaxin An, Ying Na & Pengyi Zhang

Scientists' Data Discovery and Reuse Behavior: (Meta)data Fitness for Use and the FAIR Data Principles 21
Bradley Wade Bishop, Carolyn Hank, Joel Webster & Rebecca Howard

Information Encountering in the Humanities: Embeddedness, Temporality, and Altruism 32
Sarah A. Buchanan & Sanda Erdelez

A Comparative Study of Domestic and Cross-Country Impact of Chinese and U.S. Publications in Chemistry 43
Xiaojing Cai, Xiaozan Lyu & Ping Zhou

Definitions, Formulas, and Simulated Examples for Plagiarism Detection With FAIR Metrics 51
Adam Craig, Adarsh Ambati, Shiladitya Dutta, Arush Mehrotra, S. Koby Taswell & Carl Taswell

Dataset Bias: A Case Study for Visual Question Answering 58
Anubrata Das, Samreen Anjum & Danna Gurari

What's in People's Digital File Collections? 68
Jesse David Dinneen & Charles-Antoine Julien

Online Behavior of the Alzheimer's Disease Patient Caregivers on Croatian Online Discussion Forum 78
Sanda Erdelez, Sanjica Faletar Tanacković & Kornelija Petr Balog

The Sentiment Recognition of Online Users Based on DNNs Multimodal Fusion 89
Tao Fan, Peng Wu & Peng Zhu

How Scientists Interact With Bacteria: Creating New Knowledge 98
Giovanni Forero

Word Bibliographic Coupling: Another Way to Map Science Field and Identify Core References 107
Tsung-Ming Hsiao & Kuang-hua Chen

Who You Gonna Call? Seeking Information and Expertise for Decision Making in Local Government 117
Sally Irvine-Smith

Capturing the Change in Topical Interests of Personas Over Time 127
Bernard J. Jansen, Soon-gyo Jung & Joni Salminen

< TABLE OF CONTENTS

Teens' Everyday Information Practices on Mobile Media: "Catching Up" and "Reaching Out" . . . 137
Junoh Kimm & Jefferey Boase

The Landscape of Archived Studies in a Social Science Data Infrastructure: Investigating the ICPSR Metadata Records . . . 147
Jian-Sin Lee & Wei Jeng

Evaluating Ontology Coverage and Internal Structure to Better Align Patients With Clinical Trials . . . 157
Jooho Lee, Catherine Blake & Bridget T. McInnes

Investigation of Users' Knowledge Change Process in Learning-Related Search Tasks . . . 166
Hanrui Liu, Chang Liu & Nicholas J. Belkin

Proactive Identification of Query Failure . . . 176
Jiqun Liu & Chirag Shah

Bi-LSTM+CRF-Based Named Entity Recognition in Scientific Papers in the Field of Ecological Restoration Technology . . . 186
Jianxia Ma & Hui Yuan

Relational Privacy: Where the East and the West Could Meet . . . 196
Yuanye Ma

Understanding Early Research Experiences Through the Lens of Connected Learning . . . 206
Rachel M. Magee & Amari T. Simpson

Considering "Atmosphere" in Facilitating Information Seeking by People With Invisible Disabilities in Public Libraries . . . 216
Rebecca Muir, Kim M. Thompson & Asim Qayyum

Librarian Role-Playing as a Method for Assessing Student Information Literacy Skills . . . 227
Soo Young Rieh, Doreen Bradley, Emma Brennan-Wydra, Tori Culler, Elizabeth Hanley & Marley Kalt

Algorithmic Accountability and Digital Justice: A Critical Assessment of Technical and Sociotechnical Approaches . . . 237
Howard Rosenbaum & Pnina Fichman

Leveraging Funds of Knowledge to Manage Privacy Practices in Families . . . 245
Mega Subramaniam, Priya Kumar, Shandra Morehouse, Yuting Liao & Jessica Vitak

U.S. State and State Capital Open Government Data (OGD): A Content Examination and Heuristic Evaluation of Data Processing Capabilities of OGD Sites . . . 255
Rong Tang, Will Gregg, Sandra Hirsh & Elaine Hall

"Computer What's Your Favourite Colour?" Children's Information-Seeking Strategies in the Classroom . . . 265
Nicholas Vanderschantz & Annika Hinze

TABLE OF CONTENTS >

Searching Heterogeneous Personal Digital Traces. 276
Daniela Vianna, Varvara Kalokyri, Alexander Borgida, Amélie Marian & Thu Nguyen

Improving Explicit Term Matching With Implicit Topic Matching for Short Text Conversation . . . 286
Jianqiang Wang & Ying Sun

Combine or Connect: Practical Experiences Querying Library Linked Data 296
David M. Weigl, Deren E. Kudeki, Timothy W. Cole, J. Stephen Downie, Jacob Jett & Kevin R. Page

"You Don't Feel That You're So Far Away": Information Sharing, Technology Use, and Settlement of International Student Immigrants. 306
Adam Worrall, Erin Ballantyne & Jen Kendall

Understanding the Peer Review Endeavor 316
Shenmeng Xu, Guangyao Zhang, Yao Sun & Xianwen Wang

Performance of Citations and Altmetrics in the Social Sciences and Humanities 326
Siluo Yang & Mengxue Zheng

Research on the Impact Evaluation of Academic Journals Based on Altmetrics and Citation Indicators 336
Rongying Zhao, Xu Wang, Zhuozhu Liu, Yongkang Qi, Zhaoyang Zhang & Ruru Chang

Do I Own It? U.S. and Chinese College Students' Digital Ownership Perceptions 346
Xiaohua Zhu & Tao Yang

SHORT PAPERS

Mapping Digital Information Security Management in the University Libraries of Pakistan. 356
Maria Aslam, Ayesha Khalid, Syeda Hina Batool & Ghulam Farid

Search Is the Future? The Young Search Less for Files 360
Ofer Bergman, Tamar Israeli & Steve Whittaker

Exploration of Information Organization in Language Archives. 364
Mary Burke & Oksana Zavalina

Automated Chat Transcript Analysis Using Topic Modeling for Library Reference Services 368
Xiaoju Chen & Huajin Wang

ReTracker: Actively and Automatically Matching Retraction Metadata in Zotero 372
Yi-Yun Cheng, Nikolaus Parulian, Tzu-Kun Hsiao, Ly Dinh, Janina Sarol & Jodi Schneider

Effects of Motivation and Tool Features on Online Photo-Sharing Behavior. 377
Hyerim Cho, Josh Smith & Jin Ha Lee

Quality of Medical Advice for Chronic Pain on Social Platforms 381
Kaitlin Light Costello

Noticing the Unnoticed: Lines of Work in Everyday Life Information Practices. 386
Nicole Dalmer & Pam McKenzie

< TABLE OF CONTENTS

Systematic Examination of Pre- and Post-Retraction Citations 390
Ly Dinh, Janina Sarol, Yi-Yun Cheng, Tzu-Kun Hsiao, Nikolaus Parulian & Jodi Schneider

"A Good Intention Gone Awry": Queering Makerspaces to Support Queer Creators 395
Diana Floegel

Topics of Example Questions and Discussion at the Early Stage of Community Building for Health Q&A: A Case Study of Health Stack Exchange 399
Hengyi Fu & Sanghee Oh

How Were Science Mapping Tools Applied? The Application of Science Mapping Tools in LIS and Non-LIS Domains 404
Jiangen He, Wen Lou & Kai Li

Modeling and Representation of Intangible Cultural Heritage Knowledge Using Linked Data and Ontology 409
Xilong Hou & Xiaoguang Wang

Implications of the Embodied, Enactive Mind on Theorizing About Information Experience 413
Pamela Hoyte

Knowledge Transfer From Technology to Science: The Longevity of Paper-to-Patent Citations . . . 417
Tzu-Kun Hsiao & Vetle I. Torvik

VR Creation Experience in Cultural Heritage Education: A Preliminary Exploration 422
Xiao Hu, Jeremy Ng & Jin Ha Lee

Investigating Users' Affective Load in Collaborative Search 427
Kun Huang, Xin Yuan, Lei Li & Edwin Mouda Ye

Everyday Life Information-Seeking Behaviors of Nomadic Pastoralists in Their Oral Culture 432
Hamid R. Jamali & Fariborz Foroutan

Empowering Citizens to Manage Their Chemical Exposures Step 1 - Identify Ingredients in Consumer Products 436
Jenna Kim, Catherine Blake & Henry A. Gabb

Objectives & Key Results for Active Knowledge Sharing in IT Consulting Enterprises: A Feasibility Study 441
Natthakan Klanwaree & Songphan Choemprayong

One of a Kind: The Tail of Citizen Science Volunteers 445
Lo Lee & Peter Darch

Lack of the Normative Lens: Discussions on Research on Micro-Targeted Ads Explanation of Facebook 450
Yuanye Ma

Effects of a Gamified Learning Platform on Elementary School Students' Flow Experiences in Leisure Reading 454
Martin Ting Fung Mak, Meng Wang & Kai Wah Samuel Chu

TABLE OF CONTENTS >

Transitions and Social Interaction: Making Sense of Self and Situation Through Engagement With Others. 459
Pam McKenzie & Rebekah Willson

Relations Among Participation, Fairness and Performance in Collaborative Learning With Wiki-Based Analytics 463
Jeremy Ng, Xiao Hu, Miyu Luo & Sam K. W. Chu

Introducing Orbis: An Extendable Evaluation Pipeline for Named Entity Linking Performance Drill-Down Analyses. 468
Fabian Odoni, Adrian M. P. Braşoveanu, Philipp Kuntschik & Albert Weichselbraun

Exploring the Function of Citations in Ancient Chinese Literature 472
Fei Shu, Junping Qiu, Shibin Shu & Vincent Larivière

Facilitating Open Access to Information: A Community Approach to Open Education and Open Textbooks. 477
Adrian Stagg & Helen Partridge

Open Access to Research Artifacts: Implementing the Next Generation Data Management Plan . . . 481
Victoria Stodden, Vicki Ferrini, Margaret Gabanyi, Kerstin Lehnert, John Morton & Helen Berman

Designing Feedback Information to Encourage Users' Participation Performances in Citizen Science Projects. 486
Jian Tang, Xinxue Zhou & Meihua Yu

Cultural Barriers to Intellectual Property Ethics: A Theoretical Model 491
Tao Jin & Meihua Chen

How Do Students' Information World Maps Change While Developing Their Thesis Topics? A Longitudinal Study Using Arts-Based Elicitation Interviews. 495
Tien-I Tsai, Hsuan-Ju Chen, Chen-Hsuan Tai & Yi-Ling Chen

An Analysis on Charitable Crowdfunding in an Authoritarian Regime 499
Shengnan Yang, Chenwei Zhang & Wenjuan Sang

When Power Goes Wild Online: How Did a Voluntary Moderator's Abuse of Power Affect an Online Community?. 504
Yukun Yang

Developing a Work-Identifier Allocation Algorithm to FRBRize KORMARC Records 509
Jaehyuk Yun

Listening to the User's Voice: A Temporal Analysis of Autism-Related Questions on Quora 513
Yuehua Zhao, Chao Min, Xu Han, Sanhong Deng, Hao Wang & Jiang Li

From Free to Fee: Exploring the Factors That Influence the Askers' Switching Behavior on Online Q&A Platforms. 517
Yuxiang (Chris) Zhao, Zhouying Liu, Si Chen & Qinghua Zhu

< TABLE OF CONTENTS

PANELS AND ALTERNATIVE EVENTS

There Is a Method to It: Making Meaning in Information Research Through a Mix of Paradigms and Methods. 521
Lynn Silipigni Connaway, Ixchel M. Faniel, Bhuva Narayan & Elham Sayyed-Abdi

Exploring Card Sort Methods: Interaction and Implementation for Research, Education, and Practice 525
Lettie Y. Conrad, Andrew Demasson, Tim Gorichanaz & Amy VanScoy

Beyond the Data Management Plan: Expanding Roles for Librarians in Data Science and Open Science. 529
Lisa M. Federer & Jian Qin

Does Information Science Need History and Foundations? 532
Tim Gorichanaz, Elliott Hauser, Yazdan Mansourian, Joseph T. Tennis & Hilary Yerbury

Data Science Education in Library and Information Science Schools 536
Loni Hagen, James Andrews, Lisa Federer & Gerald Benoit

A Social Informatics Perspective on Misinformation, Disinformation, Deception and Conflict 538
Noriko Hara, Pnina Fichman, Eric T. Meyer, Yimin Chen & Soo Young Rieh

Information Behaviour and Practises Research Informing Technology and Service Design 541
Isto Huvila, Heidi Enwald, Kristina Eriksson-Backa, Ying-Hsang Liu & Noora Hirvonen

Lithium Hindsight 360: Increasing Access and Ensuring Preservation of Virtual Reality Narratives . . 546
Eugenia S. Kim

Information Experience: A Domain and Object of Study 550
Clarence Maybee, Elham Sayyad Abdi, Kate Davis & Lettie Conrad

The Convergence of Computational and Social Approaches for Unveiling Meaningful and Valuable Data 554
Angela P. Murillo, Renata G. Curty, Wei Jeng & Daqing He

Data Science Education in the iSchool Context 558
Sam Oh, Il-Yeol Song, Javed Mostafa, Yin Zhang & Dan Wu

Bridging the Library and Information Science Research – Practice Gap: A Panel Discussion. . . . 561
Helen Partridge, Lisa M. Given, Elham Sayyad Abdi, George Buchanan, Kate Bunker, Edward Luca, Dana McKay & Bhuva Narayan

Teaching Technology in Library and Information Science: Preparing Students With Diverse Needs for the Challenges of an Interconnected World 565
Danielle Pollock, Rachel Williams, Catherine Dumas, Naresh Kumar Agarwal & Sanda Erdelez

TABLE OF CONTENTS >

Technical and Policy Underpinnings of FAIR Data Principles 569
Jian Qin, Imma Subirats Coll, Marcia Lei Zeng & Brian Dobreski

Digital Equity for Marginalised and Displaced Peoples 572
Anne Gilliland, Sue McKemmish, Gregory Rolan & Barbara Reed

Data Science Research and Practice: High Time for Synergy 575
Abebe Rorissa, Lisa Federer, Loni Hagen, Jeonghyun (Annie) Kim & James Andrews

Paradigm Shift in Information Research 578
Rong Tang, Bharat Mehra, Jia Tina Du & Yuxiang (Chris) Zhao

Information Seeking at the Intersection of Search, Learning, Inquiry, and Creativity: Sharing Stories to Inform Creative Research 582
Michael Twidale & Soo Young Rieh

Information Science Education and Library and Information Studies Education: Transnational Conversations 586
Terry Weech, Clara M. Chu, Sandra Hirsh, Heidi Julien, Mary Anne Kennan, Diane L. Velasquez & Bhuva Narayan

Academic Social Networking: From Individual Acts to Institutional, Disciplinary, National, and Social Phenomena 590
Yin Zhang, Weiwei Yan, Sanghee Oh, Jongwook Lee, Keiko Kurata & Mamiko Matsubayashi

POSTERS

Toward Effective Use and Balance: Investigating Pros and Cons of Smartphone Use in an Interview Study 594
Naresh Kumar Agarwal & Wenqing Lu

Practice, Information and the Development of a Digital Platform 597
David K. Allen, Aleksandra Irnazarow & Fiona McLaughlin

Investigating Wisdom: Call for Research 599
Jeff Allen, Malak Khader & Amy Rosellini

Keeping the Human in the Data Scientist: Shaping Human-Centered Data Science Education 601
Theresa Dirndorfer Anderson & Nicola Parker

Investigating the Productive Uses of Uncertainty in Knowledge Co-Creation Practices 604
Jean Archambeault

Data for Development: The Case for Africa 607
Shimelis Assefa, Daniel Gelaw Alemneh & Abebe Rorissa

Everyday Health Information Seeking Among Millennials 609
Joan C. Bartlett, Aaron Bowen-Ziecheck, Cynthia Kumah & Jamshid Beheshti

< TABLE OF CONTENTS

A Gap Analysis of Survivorship Terminology: Knowledge Resources Versus Literature Usage . . . 612
Catherine Blake, Jenna Kim, Milind Mathur & Akanksha Aggarwal

An Integrated Framework of Patient Data Ownership . . . 615
Aaron D. Bowen-Ziecheck & Joan C. Bartlett

Machine Translation Literacy: Academic Libraries' Role . . . 618
Lynne Bowker

The Impact of a Prescribed Journal List of Disciplinary Publishing . . . 620
Jennifer Campbell-Meier, Allan Sylvester & Jacob Woods

Identifying the Contribution–Influence Gap in the Science and Technology Community . . . 622
Yu-Wei Chang, Mu-Hsuan Huang & Chung-Huei Kuan

Understanding Interactions Among Citizens, Government Authorities, Media, and NGOs on Twitter During Natural Disaster . . . 624
Sijing Chen, Jin Mao, Xiao Wang & Gang Li

Analyzing Divergent Methodologies for Political Fact Checking: United States and South Korea . . . 627
Wonchan Choi & Maria Haigh

Connective Power of the Twitter Networks: Discovering the Reverse Agenda-Setting Effects of Hashtag Activism Through Topic Modeling . . . 629
Miyoung Chong

Examination of Online Information Search Stopping Behaviors and Stopping Rules by Task Type . . 631
Dedema & Chang Liu

The Efficacy of Digital Literacy Training Initiatives Led by Local Community Organizations . . . 634
Brian Detlor, Mona Nasery & Heidi Julien

In Memoriam Boleslaw Matuszewski: The Origin of Film Librarianship . . . 636
Rubén Domínguez-Delgado & María-Ángeles López-Hernández

Are Invalid Patents Still Cited? . . . 639
Huei-Ru Dong, Dar-Zen Chen & Mu-Hsuan Huang

Tourists' Social Interactions on Social Media During a Group Trip Planning . . . 642
Jannatul Fardous & Jia Tina Du

Usability Testing of LUI: A New Human-Computer Interface for Large Displays . . . 645
Catherine Dumas, Sanda Erdelez, Jeffrey Pomerantz & Vik Parthiban

Characteristics of Collaborative Information Seeking Activities During Group Trip Planning: A Preliminary Study . . . 648
Jannatul Fardous & Jia Tina Du

The False Trade-Off of Relevance for Safety in Children's Search Systems . . . 651
Vanessa Figueiredo & Eric M. Meyers

TABLE OF CONTENTS >

When the World Ends: Study of #FakeWesteros Twitter Fan Community During the Final Season of *Game of Thrones* 654
Eric Forcier

Health Information at Intersections: Toward More Inclusive Personal Health Records for Marginalized Users 656
Amelia N. Gibson & Kristen L. Bowen

Information and Communication Research in Promoting Workplace Safety and Health: A Topic Modeling Analysis 658
Dion Hoe-Lian Goh, Han Zheng, Edmund Wei Jian Lee, Chei Sian Lee & Yin Leng Theng

Understanding the Information Landscape of Indigenous Elders' Knowledge and Cultural Practices 661
Jelina Haines, Jia Tina Du, Gus Geursen & Ellen Trevorrow

Investigating the Impacts of Family Restriction Strategy on Chinese Children's Smartphone Use Behaviors 664
Leiqian Han & Hui Yan

Book or Screen? A Preliminary Study on Preschool Children's Reading and ICT Using Behaviors 667
Yanfang Han & Hui Yan

Affording Cross-Cultural Access to Visualized Cultural Collections: A Preliminary Case Study of E-Dunhuang 669
Xiao Hu, Jia Shan, Jing Chen & J. Stephen Downie

#Cyberbullying in the Digital Age: Exploring People's Opinions With Text Mining 672
Iman Tahamtan & Li-Min Huang

How Is Knowledge Management Represented in Library and Information Science Research? 674
Md Anwarul Islam & Naresh Kumar Agarwal

Retrieval System Enhanced by Fine-Grained Knowledge Entities 677
Chuan Jiang, Dongbo Wang & Si Shen

A Clickstream Data Analysis of Users' Behavior on a Government WeChat Official Account 679
Tingting Jiang, Tianqianjin Lin, Lina Shangguan & Ying Wang

"For the Benefit of All Students": Student Trust in Higher Education Learning Analytics Practices 682
Kyle M. L. Jones & Tanisha Afnan

Put Relational Databases in Your Data Curation Toolbox 684
Jenna Jordan

< TABLE OF CONTENTS

Analyzing Public Opinion Toward the 2019 North Korea–United States Summit Through Mining Twitter. . . . 686
Jaewon Kim, Ji-young Kim & Yongjun Zhu

Toward Computational Reproducibility: A Doctoral Student's Story of Passing the Baton 688
Jenna Kim, Catherine Blake & Peter T. Darch

A Study for Categorizing Relations Between Headword and Aliases. . . . 691
Jiyoun Kim, Youngeun Koo & Yongjun Zhu

Virtual Zenana: Reimagining Small World 693
Priya Kizhakkethil & Gary Burnett

Memory Making and Documenting in a Diaspora Small World 696
Priya Kizhakkethil

Argumentation Model of WeChat Group Chat: Evidence From Content Analysis With Inductive Coding 699
Jiyao Lai, Yuzhe Han & Pengyi Zhang

A Crowdsourcing Approach to Explore Helping Motives in a Smart City: A Preliminary Analysis 701
Chei Sian Lee, Dion Hoe-Lian Goh, Sei-Ching Joanna Sin, Hamzah Osop & Yin Leng Theng

Getting Creative in Everyday Life: Investigating Arts and Crafts Hobbyists' Information Behavior 703
Lo Lee, Melissa G. Ocepek, Stephann Makri, George Buchanan & Dana McKay

Disciplinarity of Software Papers: A Preliminary Analysis. 706
Kai Li, Pei-Ying Chen & Zhichao Fang

Questions or Questioners: Factors Affecting Response Quantity on Academic Social Q&A Sites 709
Lei Li, Kun Huang, Edwin Mouda Ye & Chengzhi Zhang

How Do University Data Services Present Their Collection and Reference Service Information on the Web? 712
Chi-Shiou Lin & Yi-Yu Wang

Online News Sharing Among Taiwan's Middle-Aged and Elderly Populaces: Influencing Factors. . . . 714
Chieh Liu, Tingyu Wu & Wayland Chang

An Experimental Comparison on Reading Comprehension Effect of Visual, Audio and Dual Channels. . . . 716
Huiyun Liu, Shujin Cao & Shiyu Wu

Does Citation Content of References From Different Disciplines Demonstrate Same Distribution Pattern? 719
Lifan Liu, Yuzhuo Wang & Chengzhi Zhang

TABLE OF CONTENTS >

Understanding Formal Scholarly Communication in Information Science by Exploring Generational Evolution of Academic Writing Patterns. 722
Wen Lou, Jiao Chen & Tim Gorichanaz

Location Recommendation by Combining Geographical, Categorical, and Social Preferences With Location Popularity 725
Yaxue Ma, Jin Mao & Gang Li

Understanding the Relevance Between Text and Images in Disaster-Related Social Media Posts. . . 727
Jin Mao, Ji Zhang, Kun Lu & Gang Li

A Comparative Study of Online News Use by Young Adults in Canada and Japan. 730
Mamiko Matsubayashi & Luanne Freund

Computational Analyses of the Relation of Theme and Genre in the Writing of Aphra Behn 733
Adam Mazel & Catherine Dumas

An Exploratory GIS Prototype to Map Community Engagement in the Southern and Central Appalachian Rural Libraries 735
Bharat Mehra, Everette Scott Sikes & Vandana Singh

Toward Responsible Scholarly Communication and Innovation: A Survey of the Prevalence of Retracted Articles on Scholarly Communication Platforms 738
Shinji Mine

Identification of Citation and Cited Texts for Fine-Grained Citation Content Analysis. 740
Shiyan Ou & Hyonil Kim

Mining Knowledge Entities in mHealth Literature. 742
Min Sook Park & Hyejin Park

The Role of Data & Synthesis Centers in Convergence Research 745
Danielle Pollock, Suzie Allard, An Yan & Michelle Parker

Using Text Mining and Data Visualization to Trace the Disciplinary Boundaries of Collective Memory Studies 747
Ana Roeschley

Identifying the Collaboration Styles of Research Students 750
Harry Rolf

Library Shelf Signs Affect Users' Search Time Length: Evidence From an Experiment Using a VR Library System 752
Sho Sato, Takashi Harada, Saki Itagaki, Asuka Suehiro, Tomoka Takamura, Koji Yamashita, Ryuta Ichikawa & Katsuhiko Sukoboshi

Between Informative and Esthetic: A User Study of Content and Visualization on Government Data Dashboards 755
Liang-Yu Sie & Wei Jeng

< TABLE OF CONTENTS

Linking the Thoughts Within Scientific Papers: Construction and Visualization of Argumentation Graph. 757
Huimin Zhou, Ningyuan Song, Wanli Chang & Xiaoguang Wang

The Role of Information Cues on Users' Perceived Credibility of Online Health Rumors 760
Xiaokang Song, Yuxiang (Chris) Zhao, Shijie Song & Qinghua Zhu

What Will Influence Users' Knowledge Sharing Behavior in the Social Q&A Community? 762
Zhijun Song, Qingxing Dong, Gaohui Cao & Ye Chen

An Initial Study of Information Behavior in Pokemon Go 765
Krishna Srinivasan, Marcus Lee Kiang Tan, Derrick Chin Kiat Peh, Dion Hoe-Lian Goh & Chei Sian Lee

Moving From Assumptions to Evidence: Assessing Quality in Online Courses in a Master of Information Program 768
Sharon Stoerger & Lilia Pavlovsky

How Socio-Culture Impact the Information Behavior of Chinese Urban Newcomers 770
Honglei Sun, Jianming Zheng, Meng Wang & Ya Chen

Service Mode Selection Strategy for Resource-Constrained Content Service Providers. 773
Mengting Sun, Jingjia Ding & Xiaoqun Yuan

Professional and Institutional Support for RDM: A Case of the National Institutes of Health (NIH). 776
Sue Yeon Syn & Soojung Kim

"I'm in the Center of the Vortex": The Affective Chain of Social Media Trolling. 778
Huixin Tian & Pei-Ying Chen

"I Don't Understand It So It Can't Be Good": Users' ACG Domain Expertise and Perceived Quality of Video Tags 780
Liuyi Tong, Hui Lin & Pengyi Zhang

An Analysis of Published Journals for Papers Posted on bioR$_x$iv 783
Hiroyuki Tsunoda, Yuan Sun, Masaki Nishizawa, Xiaomin Liu & Kou Amano

Repurposing: Another R to Prioritize in Data Curation 785
Michael Twidale, Catherine Blake, Maria Souden, Jenifer Stelmack & Jenna Kim

The Use of Theory in Research Relating to Open Access: Practitioner Perspectives 788
Simon Wakeling, Stephen Pinfield, David Bawden & Lyn Robinson

Assessing the Informativeness of User Reviews on Mobile Health Applications for Chronic Diseases 790
Shengang Wang, Hyun Seung Lee & Wonchan Choi

TABLE OF CONTENTS >

Mapping the State of Community Libraries: An Empirical Study in Hubei Province 792
Chunying Wang, Zhenzhen Yuan, Ruhua Huang & Jiangping Chen

Detecting Opinion Evaluation Object Drift in Chinese Microblog Posts 794
Xiao Wang, Chao Ma & Sijing Chen

Gender Bias in Invention 796
Yukai Wang, Zhongkai Yang & Xianwen Wang

Enhancing Scholar Supportive Data: Surveying the Landscape of Information Resources for Digital Dunhuang 798
Xiaoguang Wang, Xu Tan & Qingyu Duan

A Survey of Data Science Programs and Courses in the iSchools 801
Yi-Yu Wang & Chi-Shiou Lin

Order Effect on Relevance Judgment: An Exploratory Study on the Detection of Quantum Interference 803
Zhihong Wang & Shujin Cao

Extracting Method Knowledge Elements From Scientific Literature: A Rule-Based Approach . . . 805
Zhongyi Wang, Xueying Shen, Rong Huang & Jing Huang

A Versatile Approach for Constructing a Domain Knowledge Graph for Culture 808
Jingzhu Wei & Rui Liu

Vulnerability and Meeting the Needs of People Experiencing Homelessness in Public Libraries 810
Rachel D. Williams

How Do Consumers Acquire Health Information? A Pattern Analysis on Online Health Consultation 813
Dan Wu, Hao Xu & Shu Fan

Users' Visual Attention Flow on the Search Result Page of Digital Cultural Heritage Collection . 816
Dan Wu, Shuang Xu, Xiaoyun Xu & Xi Chen

Research on Voice Search Behavior in the Last 10 Years. 819
Zhaopeng Xing, Fei Yu & Xiaojun Yuan

Using Crowdsourcing to Construct Special Collection Resources Under the Perspective of Digital Humanities 822
Xiaojuan Xu & Manli Wu

Disciplinary Comparisons of Academic Social Networking Site Use by Chinese Researchers . . . 825
Weiwei Yan & Yin Zhang

Designing Effective Knowledge Presentation Techniques for Large Digital Collections 827
Yejun Wu & Seungwon Yang

< TABLE OF CONTENTS

"Active Followers": An Emerging Role of Information Behaviour Among Group Holiday Makers 829
Edwin Mouda Ye, Jia Tina Du, Helen Ashman, Preben Hansen, Songshan (Sam) Huang & Marianna Sigala

Stages of Change in Smoking Cessation and Health Information Behavior 832
Yong Jeong Yi & Seo Jin Nam

An Analysis of Physical Characteristics of Joseon Dynasty Books Using Statistical Approaches 834
Jaehyuk Yun & Yongjun Zhu

The Antecedent and Consequence of Users' Satisfaction and Dissatisfaction With Information Seeking in Online Health Communities 836
Jinchao Zhang, Bo Luo & Fenfang Cao

Developing Community Phenotype Ontologies: Understanding Users' Preferences 838
Limin Zhang, Zuleima Cota, Hong Cui, Hsin-liang Chen, Bruce Ford, Joel Sach, Jocelyn Pender, James Macklin, Anton Reznicek & Julian Starr

Investigating Roles of Social Value Orientation and Domain Knowledge in Crowdsourced Manuscript Transcription 841
Xuanhui Zhang, Yuxiang (Chris) Zhao, Shijie Song & Qinghua Zhu

Influence of Course Type and Assignment Features on Students' Information Seeking Behaviors ... 844
Yao Zhang & Chang Liu

Exploring Older Adults' Health Information Seeking Behavior: Evidence From Urban China 847
Dongxiang Zhao

How Did People Feel During the Zika Virus Breakout? A Sentiment Analysis of Zika Virus Related Posts on Yahoo! Answers 849
Yuehua Zhao, Ye Chen, Jin Zhang, Qingxing Dong, Gaohui Cao & Zhaoyang Zhang

Scientists' Academic Disruptiveness Significantly Increased After They Moved to China 852
Zhenyue Zhao, Jiang Li, Chao Min, Yi Bu, Lele Kang & Yiyang Bian

Argument Ontology for Describing Scientific Articles: A Statistical Study Based on Articles From Two Research Areas 855
Huimin Zhou, Ningyuan Song, Hanghang Cheng & Xiaoguang Wang

Recognizing Sentences Concerning Future Research From the Full Text of JASIST 858
Zihe Zhu, Dongbo Wang & Si Shen

Putting a Price on Social Movements: A Case Study of #MeToo on Instagram

Tanisha Afnan
Indiana University-Purdue University, Indianapolis, Indiana
tafnan@iu.edu

Hsiao-Ying Huang
University of Illinois at Urbana-Champaign, Champaign, Indiana
hhuang65@illnoi.edu

Maria Sclafani
University of Illinois at Urbana-Champaign, Champaign, Indiana
mariacs2@illinois.edu

Masooda Bashir
University of Illinois at Urbana-Champaign, Champaign, Indiana
mnb@illinois.edu

ABSTRACT

Social media has enhanced the dissemination of information relating to specific social movements, allowing activists to quickly mobilize and more easily communicate. However, the practice of "hashtag activism" has unforeseen consequences; it gives users with commercial interests a great deal of control over when and how hashtags are utilized. To investigate the intersection between commodification, social movements, and social media, we examined the use of #metoo and three other #metoo-related hashtags on the popular social networking platform Instagram as a case study. The aim of the #metoo social movement, which gained traction in 2017–2018, was to raise awareness on the issue of sexual violence. We collected a sample of 200 randomly selected posts to analyze their content and relevance to the movement. Our findings not only indicate that 1 in 5 posts within our sample had a commercial aspect, but also revealed a variety of commodifying strategies employed by the users.

KEYWORDS

Human-Computer Interaction (HCI); Social Media; Social Network Site; Online Activism; Commodification

ASIS&T THESAURUS

Communities; Information Behavior; Popular Culture

INTRODUCTION

As social media platforms continue to grow in popularity, so do the variety of ways in which users may utilize them. In recent years, social movements have carved out a place for themselves within the online world of these platforms. Loosely defined, social movements can be understood as collective group action on a large scale. Typically, these movements are centered around a specific social justice or political issue (Kow, Kou, Semaan, & Cheng, 2016). While these efforts may often be premediated in nature, they also frequently emerge out of spontaneous human reactions. Individuals who participate in these movements often intend to increase widespread awareness of the issues in question, in hopes of leading to a shift in cultural norms and attitudes.

While social movements long predate human interactions online, social media outlets have begun to act as valuable tools for the rapid mobilization of newer social movements.

Existing frameworks in understanding the social psychology of social movements are typically grounded in concepts and principles that apply to movements born and built exclusively offline (Goodwin & Jasper, 2014). New emerging research is now working to track the evolution of social movements as they develop digitally, and how social media platforms may change the dynamic between the individuals participating within them.

One relatively new method that has allowed social movements to gain traction online is the practice of "hashtag activism" (Gerbaudo, 2018). Hashtag activism allows users to share information or show support for a particular cause by posting on social media platforms (e.g. Twitter, Facebook) while using a hashtag specifically coined for the movement. Although the benefits of hashtag activism in terms of its speed and reach are extraordinary, it is important to remember that the virtual spaces within which this activism exists are not always neutral. The most popular social media platforms are owned by private companies with commercial interests. Twitter has been criticized by many who argue that the platform prioritizes engagement, in the form of "tweet views" over users' physical safety and mental health (Campos, 2014). Social media platforms create virtual environments conducive to commodification because they themselves are commodities (Kuchera, 2014). The price that hashtag activists have to pay for free access to an audience of millions is to open their movements to potential commodification.

Currently, most existing literature has focused on how social media enhances online social movements, and the challenges and benefits associated with this new frontier. There are, however, no previous studies focusing on how social media users may also commodify a social movement. This study focuses on exploring the intersections between social media, social movements, and commercialization. We selected the

82nd Annual Meeting of the Association for Information Science & Technology | Melbourne, Australia | 19–23 October, 2019

DOI: 10.1002/pra2.00002

current #metoo movement, one of the most popular social movements between 2017 and 2019, for our case study (Bogost, 2017), while also narrowing our focus down onto Instagram, an image oriented platform that creates for a unique "hashtag-activist" experience as compared to other text-based social networking sites.

RELATED WORK

Role of Social Media in Social Movements

With the advent of mobile and Internet technologies, the use of Facebook, Twitter, YouTube, and other social media platforms have changed the traditional way of coordinating and mobilizing social movements. Several scholars have pointed out the importance of social media in large-scale social movements across the world, such as the Arab Spring, Occupy Wall Street and the Black Lives Matter movements (Al-Ani, Mark, Chung, & Jones, 2012). Social media platforms with massive networks and unique functions not only provide multiple information sources, but also accelerate the speed of information exchange (Cornet, Hall, Cafaro, & Brady, 2017). In addition, the immediacy and accessibility of social media also reduce the cost of participation and enable the general public to create a "shared awareness" in a short period of time (Dimond, Michaelanne, LaRose, & Bruckman, 2013).

In human–computer interaction literature, studies have found that people mainly use social media for seeking and disseminating information, framing public discourse, expressing collective solidarity, and developing counter-narratives against those produced by authoritative discourse. For instance, several studies have revealed that social media platforms like Twitter have facilitated information dissemination during times of crisis and political instability (Qu, Huang, Zhang, & Zhang, 2011). While another example may be in 2013, when approximately three-million Facebook users changed their profile picture to express their support for same-sex marriage (Adamic, 2015). A recent study by Cornet et al. (Cornet et al., 2017) further identified how Instagram users employ images to support social movements by exploring ways in which themed visual content paired with "activist" hashtags. In addition to forming and mobilizing collective action, Liu, Ford, Parnin, & Dabbish (2017) points out how social media features (e.g. hashtags, selfies) influence online participants to form their self-identity during a social movement. In other words, the personalized features on social media may also provide users an opportunity to be creative or portray an image of them.

Branding and Businesses on Social Media

Recent scholarship on branding has drawn attention to how brands utilize the user generated data provided by social media platforms in the development and implementation of marketing campaigns (Zwick, Bonsu, & Darmody, 2008). Active consumer participation is a key component of contemporary branding strategies. A study by Carah & Shaul observes how brands create opportunities, in the form of hashtags and real-world brand activation, for Instagram users to perform affective labor. By circulating and interacting with hashtags and images from brand-organized events, users both promote brands and produce data on user engagement. When users post images that contain promotional content, like brand-specific clothing, they are "incorporating them [brands] into narratives about their lives" (Carah & Shaul, 2016).

This blending of brand messages and personal narratives is common on Instagram because the platform has historically restricted paid advertising, so many brands developed strategies to interact with individual users and encourage their active participation. Marwick argues that in turn, individual users have learned from successful brands and begun to utilize the same "attention-getting techniques" to increase their own popularity. Users and brands compete for views in the "attention economy," where "page views and clicks are synonymous with success and thus online status" (Marwick, 2015). We postulate that a similar phenomenon happens on Instagram when users employ hashtags and images connected to social movements.

Instagram Functionality

Instagram is a social media platform that launched in 2010, and had already reached 800 million users by 2017 (Instagram Press, 2018). The application differs from other popular social media platforms in that it was developed for use with smartphones, and has limited functionality in a web browser. It is primarily an image-sharing application, and many of its features allow users to edit and modify images they upload before posting them.

Users can apply photographic filters that "alter the shading, temperature, feel, and presentation" of their images (Gibbs, Meese, Arnold, Nansen, & Carter, 2015). As Marwick (Marwick, 2015) notes, "compared to sites like Facebook that constrain self-presentation within a rigid profile structure, Instagram provides users with a fairly open-ended social media tool, suggesting that individuals could choose to represent themselves using a range of techniques".

Users can also cross-post on multiple platforms, tag posts with their location, write accompanying captions, interact with others by liking their content, and leave comments on other posts. Although Instagram shares many of the features common to other social media platforms, it does not allow users to embed hyperlinks in captions or comments. Users have created a workaround for this limitation by including hyperlinks in the "bio" section of their profile, a feature which allows hyperlinks, and then directing other users to their "bio" through post captions and comments.

Overview of #MeToo Movement

Though popularized online, the Me Too movement was originally born offline and created by activist Tarana Burke in 2006. After founding an organization designed to support and provide resources for adolescent girls, Burke became the confidant of many individuals looking for outlets to disclose instances of sexual assault. In order to combat the issue, Burke coined the phrase, "me too", to help empower women. Though the movement initially served to help victims of sexual assault, it exploded and evolved when it was introduced to the mainstream by actress Alyssa Milano who used the hashtag on Twitter in October of 2017. The movement then spread across other major social media platforms, including Facebook, and eventually Instagram. As the movement gained traction, culminating in the being recognized in Time Magazine, participants spread internationally across new demographics and the movement became centered around both sharing experiences of sexual violence as well as in sharing support (Dishman, 2017).

METHODS

Based on the existing literature and background, this study aims to answer the following research questions:

- What do users share by using hashtags related to the #metoo movement on Instagram?
- If commodified posts exist, what are the differences between commodified and non-commodified posts?
- Are potential commodified posts relevant to #metoo movement?
- Do different strategies of commodification exist among users on Instagram?

To begin our observation, we first searched for and identified popular hashtags associated with the movement on Instagram. In addition to the main hashtag (#metoo), we selected three other popular hashtags. These were selected based on their frequency of use on Instagram, as well as their relatedness to the original hashtag. The three additional hashtags included #metoostory, #metoomovement, and #metoomvmt.

Data Collection

Datasets for each hashtag were collected through Netlytic, "a cloud-based text and social networks analyzer", (Gruzd, 2016), from the months of January–March 2018. Netlytic uses an open API to scrape data from social media platforms, including the date and time that public posts are shared, usernames of the posters, number of followers of the posters, geographic location, and hyperlinks to each individual post. The links allowed us to manually record the number of comments and likes at the time of collection. Since Netlytic only collects the most recent posts and comments starting from the date that a dataset is first created, our data was limited to the span of a few months. The initial sets from Netlytic yielded 9,999 posts with 6,182 unique posters for #metoo, 5,265 posts with 3,270 unique posters for #metoomovement, 1,442 posts with 976 unique posters for #metoomvmt, and 2,494 messages with 795 unique posters for #metoostory. To create our sample, we used a random sample selection formula on Excel to assign a unique number to each entry without duplicates. We then used Research Randomizer (Urbaniak & Plous, 2013) to generate random samples of 50 for each hashtag to create a total sample size of 200. Additional information was then manually collected for each of the posts in our sample, including other hashtags used, and captions.

After conducting a preliminary analysis of our data, 24 foreign language posts were discovered within the original sample. Since the content of these posts were difficult to decipher they were ultimately excluded from the study sample. 24 additional posts were randomly selected from the original Netlytic datasets after filtering out all other foreign language posts. After reviewing the data, three additional posts with missing links were excluded from the analysis, resulting in a total sample size of 197 unique posts.

Data Analysis

Much of the information we could glean from our dataset was qualitative in nature, and in the form of textual and pictorial content. We leaned on a Grounded theory inspired approach (Corbin & Strauss, 1990) to observe and pinpoint phenomena within the captions. Once our dataset was finalized we first began with a selective coding process to identify and define broad categories by which we labeled individual posts as either "commodified" or "non-commodified". This initial process was conducted by three different researchers independently, who met on a regular basis to discuss updates, with an inter-rater reliability score (Cohen's kappa statistic) of 0.91.

To draw further conclusions, we analyzed a subset of posts which we categorized as commodified. We collaborated to create a set of criteria for further classifying the smaller subset of commodified posts, and utilized open and axial coding methodologies, this time referencing both images and captions, to identify and establish the recurrent themes within the posts. In our analysis of the visual content, we referenced Hand's chapter on "Visuality in Social Media" within the SAGE Handbook of Social Media Research to guide our process (Hand, 2017). After several iterative rounds of this, we utilized a closed coding process, which was conducted in group sessions, to ascertain the core variables in our data for the commodified posts (Thomas, 2006).

RESULTS

RQ 1: What Do Users Share by Using Hashtags Related to the #metoo Movement on Instagram?

We first examined the posts linked to the #metoo movement through the use of hashtags, and generated five categories of #metoo posts: commodified posts, reposted media, selfies, original media, and re-shared stories. Table 1 exhibits a detailed definition of each category. Our results show that 19.3% of posts are related to a commodity; 30.5% of them are reposted media; 17.3% are selfies; 30% of them are original media; and 3% are re-shared stories. We further analyzed the categories of posts by hashtag. As exhibited in Figure 1, the majority of posts fall in the category of original media or reposted media for all four hashtags. Interestingly, the #metoostory has more selfie posts than any of the other categories. This indicates that users may be more inclined to share their personal story with selfies when using #metoostory. In addition, approximately 66% of re-shared story posts fall in #metoomvmt.

Categories (n=197)	Definition
Commodified post (n=38)	Users post videos and images that primarily serve as advertisements for a product.
Reposted media (n=60)	Users repost memes, quotes, images, infographics or videos that were created by organizations or other individuals and recycled by user for their own post.
Selfies (n=33)	Users take photos or videos themselves as well as traditional self-portraits of individual shot by someone else.
Original media (n=59)	User create artwork, photography, quotes, or music relevant to the movement.
Re-shared stories (n=6)	Users re-share stories and/or personal confessions of others.

Table 1. Categories of posts.

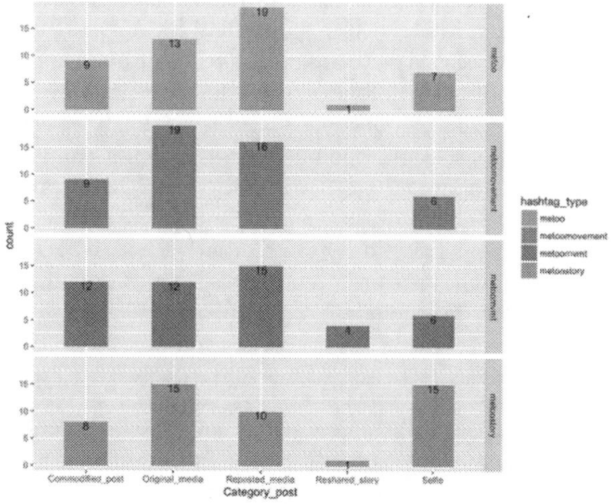

Figure 1. Distribution of posts among four hashtags.

RQ 2: If Commodified Posts Exist, What are the Differences between Commodified and Non-commodified Posts?

Our second question was to determine differences between commodified and non-commodified posts. We compared commodified and non-commodified posts in their numbers of likes, comments, and account followers by using Mann–Whitney-Wilcoxon test.

The results show no significant difference in the numbers of comments and likes between commodified and non-commercial posts. However, there is a significant difference in the number of followers. As shown in Table 2, the accounts sharing commodified posts significantly have more followers than those sharing non-commodified posts. Yet, these measures do not cover the full extent of differences between posts, as they do not account for the nuanced details that exist, and diverge, within the visual content. We hope that this variability can be addressed in future works.

	Comments		Likes		Followers	
	Mean	SE	Mean	SE	Mean	SE
Commodified posts (n=38)	15.29	3.51	773.45	537.41	26933.32	19318.43
Non-commodified posts	16.07	6.66	1461.43	1206.13	5622.70	1385.21
Wilcoxon Rank Sum Score	W=3105	p=.791	W=2928	p=.780	W=2305.5	p=.024

Table 2. Number of likes, comments, and followers of commodified and non-commodified posts.

RQ 3: Are Potential Commodified Posts Relevant to the #metoo Movement?

Our third question was to determine whether these commodified posts are related or unrelated to the #metoo movement. We defined relevance on the basis of whether the post supports or corresponds to the cause of the #metoo movement, either by helping to spread awareness on the topic of sexual violence, sharing what has become categorized in popular culture as a "me too" confession, or by referencing the culture surrounding the movement, including popular figures involved such as founder Tarana Burke. Figure 2 shows an example of relevant and irrelevant posts. According to our results, we found that 36.8% of commodified posts were irrelevant to the movement; and 63.2% of posts were relevant to the movement (see Figure 3). For the non-commodified posts, 22.6% of them were irrelevant posts and 77.4% of posts were relevant. The results indicate that commodified posts have a higher percentage of irrelevant posts than non-commodified posts.

(a) relevant post (b) irrelevant post

Figure 2. Example of commodified posts that are relevant (a) and irrelevant (b) to the movement.

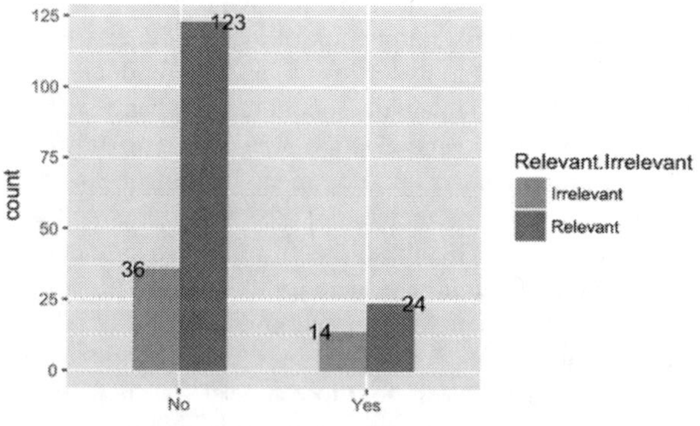

Figure 3. Overview of the commodified and non-commodified posts and their relevance to #metoo movement.

RQ 4: Do Different Strategies of Commodification Exist among Users on Instagram?

After reviewing the subset of 38 posts, we were able to identify two major strategies among these commodified posts used by individual users. We labeled these broadly as image-based and caption-based strategies.

Image-based strategy utilizes the image within the post as the primary means of product communication. We found that users used either "direct" or "indirect" approaches to display their products. The direct approach highlights the tangible product to users through the post alone, while the indirect approach requires users to take additional actions. Our results found that 68.4% (n = 26) of commodified posts used a direct image strategy, and 31.6% (n = 12) used an indirect image-based strategy.

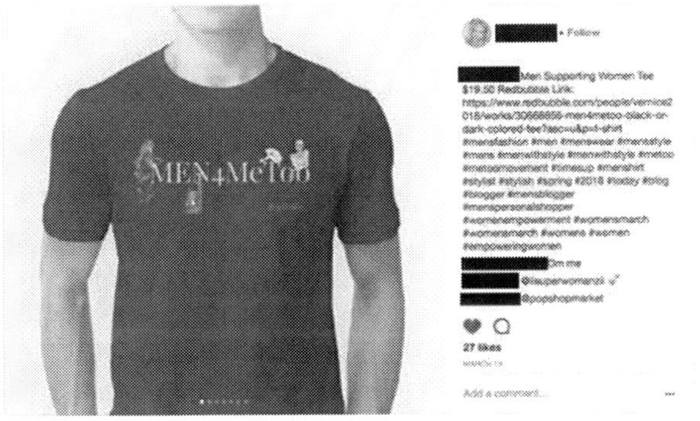

Figure 4. Direct image strategy.

Example 1

Commodified post using direct image-based strategy (as shown in Figure 4). This Instagram post appeared in our dataset for the #metoomovement dataset. It illustrates what we categorized as a direct image based strategy, with a product that could still be classified as relevant to the larger movement. A cursory glance allows a user viewing the post to identify a commercial product.

Here, very little information is provided through the caption aside from further information that guides users to the exact location in which they can purchase the pictured product, as well as the other hashtags employed to increase the post's visibility.

Figure 5. Indirect image strategy.

Example 2

This Instagram post (see Figure 5) appeared in our dataset for the #metoomvmt hashtag. It exemplifies what we categorized as an indirect image based strategy, with a product that can be classified as relevant to the larger movement. The image includes an illustration of the celebrity Oprah Winfrey. The phrase "Their time is up" is written on the award, and refers to the "Time's Up" movement, which was started in 2018 by women in the entertainment industries in response to the #metoo movement (*Time's up now*, 2017). It is not clear from either the image or the caption that this is a commercial post, however, by visiting the poster's profile page, we learned that the illustration of Winfrey is actually a pin that can be purchased from the account. In this case, the caption provides no information about the product or where it can be purchased, while the image indirectly communicates some information.

Caption based strategy, on the other hand, differs by instead leaning on the textual component of the post (i.e. the caption) as the primary means of product communication. Within the broader category of caption-based strategies, we observed three distinct approaches emerging from the posts. These include using hashtag-only captions (where no other information is provided in the caption other than hashtags), describing a personal story which ties into a product (see Figure 4), and providing advice to other users in a way that also ultimately ties into a product. 73.8% (n = 28) of posts only use hashtags in their caption; 15.7% (n = 6) describe a personal story; and 10.5% (n = 4) provided advice in the caption.

Example 3

Commodified post telling a personal story in caption. This Instagram post (see Figure 5) appeared in our dataset for the #metoomovement hashtag. The photo in the post offers little insight into whether or not a product or brand is being marketed toward the viewers, but instead stands on the textual content of the caption to serve as the primary method of information exchange. An abridged version of the caption is as follows:

> *"So, here it is. I'm finally coming out of the closet and nervously sharing something I've been working on for about a year. A while back I made a youtube video sharing a 7-step process I developed to help me heal my sexual trauma. The responses I received from women and men were mind blowing, I always knew I wanted to help people but now I know this is something I am meant to do. While the #MeToo movement was beautiful in the way it took the topic of sexual abuse and assault out of the taboo, I felt like there was one major issue with it. What's next? Now that we've taken the brave leap of sharing our broken hearts to every single person we know, now what? It wasn't until I*

moved... to escape all the people, places, and things that reminded me of my experiences that I met a man who gave me the courage to share...This is a digital product, and I've made a discount "instagram" for everyone who sees it here to get it for just $3. This is for me. This is for you."

Although the first part of the caption shares what appears to be a personal story, along the vein of the many personal confessions individuals have been able to share through the online movement, the poster eventually directs the user to a tangible product with an explicit price and discount code. By tagging their content with #metoomovement, the poster is able to promote their product to a larger user base, while their utilization of a relevant caption-based strategy that adopts the sentiments of the movement allows for it to be successful in acting in support of the movement.

Figure 6. Caption-based personal story strategy.

Example 4

Commodified post using hashtag only in caption. This Instagram post (see Figure 6) appeared in our dataset for the #metoo hashtag, and was used alongside 23 other non-associated hashtags. We classified this post as irrelevant to the larger #metoo social movement as it makes no direct references to the movement or its primary social issue. We categorized this as a caption-based strategy, in which the poster utilized a combination of tagging and hashtagging methods, or "hashtags-only", to market their product. The image is ambiguous and does not clearly communicate what good or service is being advertised to other users. The caption, however, does includes the address of a commercial establishment's location in the text, which is supplemented by the poster's use of Instagram's geotagging feature (a feature that allows users to attach a GPS location to their content). By also utilizing several other trending hashtags, both related and unrelated to the product, the poster was able to broadcast their services to a large audience.

Figure 7. Caption-based hashtag-only strategy.

Example 5

This Instagram post (see Figure 7) appeared in our dataset for the #metoostory hashtag. This poster relies on the caption to attract more followers and viewers, but does not explicitly mention tangible products or prices in the text. Here we see the use of an advice centric, caption-based strategy. Through a lengthier caption that contains empowering language, the poster directly references the #Metoo movement and ends with an open-ended question that allows for more user engagement and interaction. The logos and mottos on the pins in the photo echo the views of the caption, which, after further exploring the account, are revealed as merchandize for sale by the poster.

Figure 8. Caption-based advice strategy.

Lastly, we investigated how these different strategies were applied across both relevant and irrelevant commodified posts. As shown in Figure 9, 57.1% of irrelevant posts directly showed the product in their images, while 42.9% of them used the indirect image strategy that required users to take additional steps. For relevant commodified posts, 75% of the posts used the direct image strategy and only 25% utilized the indirect approach. This suggested that commodified posts more relevant to the movement were also more likely to use the direct image approach in comparison to their irrelevant counterparts.

An analysis of posts utilizing a caption-based strategy revealed that 85.7% of irrelevant posts used the hashtag-only method in their caption, 7.1% described a personal story, and only 7% of irrelevant posts provided some type of advice. In contrast, for relevant commodified posts, 66.7% of posts used the hashtag-only strategy, 20.8% of the posts incorporated in a personal story within their caption, and 12.5% of posts offered advice.

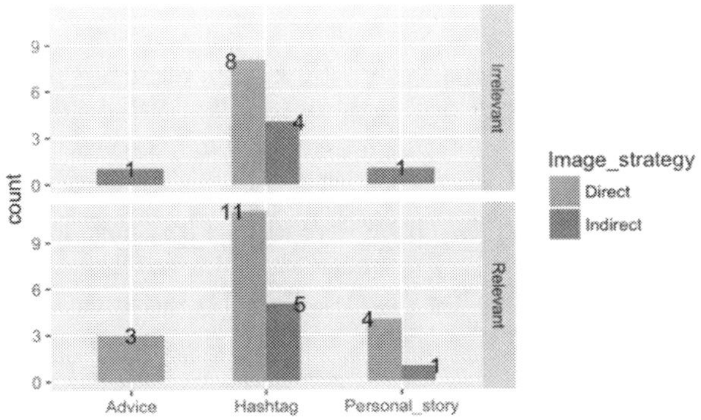

Figure 9. Distribution of "commodifying" strategies across posts.

DISCUSSION

As social media is increasingly becoming a new meeting arena for many emerging mainstream social movements, it becomes imperative to understand how and if the different ways in which the offline theoretical frameworks of social movements may explain or transform online movements. An abundance of prior research has shown how social media facilitates social movements (Olteanu, Vieweg, & Castillo, 2015), and contributes to the practice of "hashtag activism." However, the use of hashtags is a double-edged sword that affords users with commercial interests a new outlet.

Incorporating hashtags has recently become a popular way for brands and businesses to boost visibility on online social media platforms to larger audiences. Social media marketing plans, now used by major companies worldwide, have led to the development of tools such as Keyhole which work to give brands consumer insights through the use of hashtag tracking alongside other features. As the #metoo movement continued to increase in popularity, the relevant hashtags were used more frequently. "Commodified posts", or those advertising or otherwise broadcasting, products while utilizing any of the hashtags associated with the #metoo movement utilized several different strategies. Many of these commodified posts have evolved to adopt the sentiments of the movement to more successfully sell their products, while others used more simplistic approaches (i.e. hashtag-only strategy) to increase the visibility of their product through the use of a trending hashtag.

However, in the process of our study we also faced several limitations. This analysis of the #metoo movement on Instagram should act as one of the preliminary studies into the ideas surrounding the intersection of social movements and commodification on social media. We utilized a cultural analytics approach rather than a big-data approach which allowed us to manually engage with the visual and textual content of each post and perform more in-depth analyses (Hand, 2017). This, however, also restricted our ability to have a larger sample size that could be more representative of all Instagram users. Our data is also contained to the context of one social movement. Though we collected information from multiple hashtags, all our data is focused around the ideas of one social cause, which while providing insight into the attitudes surrounding the specific issue of sexual violence, might not necessarily reveal trends that apply to all other online social movements. Lastly, few freely available tools currently exist to assist in the collection of data on the platform of Instagram. This hindered our ability to collect meaningful amounts of quantitative data in regard to user demographics among other variables.

CONCLUSION

The work presented in this paper has a large scope for future research. As a case study for one specific social movement on one particular social media platform, there is still much to be learned about other hashtag heavy social media platforms that are commonly used as venues for online social movements. Instagram too, as a unique social media platform, may exhibit different tendencies when looking at different social movements. Throughout our data collection process, we made the decision to exclude several foreign language posts from our sample due to language barrier issues, but adopting those for future analysis may provide intriguing insights about international attitudes and norms. Other opportunities for consideration include researching the social media marketing strategies employed by major companies and understanding the functionality of existing marketing tools which extract information from these different social media platforms.

As we move forward with the observation of this phenomena, it will become increasingly important to understand the motivations behind the users who utilize the specific hashtags associated with social movements for increasing their brand and product visibility. As social movements and activists continue to depend more heavily on social media and other online platforms for the dissemination of information relating to specific social issues, we must recognize the ways in which the online evolution of social movements may transform the content and ideas available to the public.

REFERENCES

Adamic, L. (2015). The diffusion of support in an online social movement: Evidence from the adoption of equal-sign profile pictures. *Proceedings of the 18th ACM Conference on Computer Supported Cooperative Work & Social Computing* (pp. 1741–1750). ACM.

Al-Ani, B., Mark, G., Chung, J., & Jones, J. (2012). The Egyptian blogosphere: A counter-narrative of the revolution. *Proceedings of the ACM 2012 conference on Computer Supported Cooperative Work* (pp. 17–26). ACM.

Bogost, I. (2017). *Social apps are now a commodity.* Retrieved from https://www.theatlantic.com/technology/archive/2017/12/old-man-yells-at-snapchat/547229/

Campos, D. (2014). *The least Twitter could do.* Retrieved from https://write.danilocampos.com/the-least-twitter-could-do-6d77ba1ccc05

Carah, N., & Shaul, M. (2016). Brands and Instagram: Point, tap, swipe, glance. *Mobile Media & Communication, 4* (1), 69–84.

Castells, M. (2015). *Networks of outrage and hope: Social movements in the Internet age.* John Wiley & Sons.

Corbin, J. M., & Strauss, A. (1990). Grounded theory research: Procedures, canons, and evaluative criteria. *Qualitative sociology, 13*(1), 3–21.

Cornet, V. P., Hall, N., Cafaro, F., & Brady, E. (2017). How image-based social media websites support social movements. *Proceedings of the 2017 CHI conference extended abstracts on Human Factors in Computing Systems* (pp. 2473–2479). ACM.

Crivellaro, C., Comber, R., Bowers, J., Wright, P. C., & Olivier, P. (2014). A pool of dreams: Facebook, politics and the emergence of a social movement. In *Proceedings of the 2014 CHI Conference Extended Abstracts on Human Factors in Computing Systems* (pp. 3573–3582). ACM.

Dimond, J. P., Michaelanne, D., LaRose, D., & Bruckman, A. S. (2013). Hollaback!: the role of storytelling online in a social movement organization In *Proceedings of the 2013 conference on Computer supported cooperative work* (pp. 477–490). ACM.

Dishman, L. (2017). *This Me Too Timeline Shows Why 2017 Was A Reckoning For Sexism.* Retrieved from https://www.fastcompany.com/40504569/this-me-too-timeline shows-why-2017-was-a-reckoning-for-sexism

Gerbaudo, P. (2018). *Tweets and the streets: Social media and contemporary activism.* Pluto Press.

Gibbs, M., Meese, J., Arnold, M., Nansen, B., & Carter, M. (2015). #Funeral and Instagram: Death, social media, and platform vernacular. *Information, Communication & Society, 18*(3), 255–268.

Goodwin, J., & Jasper, J. M. (2014). *The social movements reader: Cases and concepts.* John Wiley & Sons.

Gruzd, A. (2016). *Netlytic: Software for Automated Text and Social Network Analysis.* Retrieved from http://Netlytic.org

Hand, M. (2017). Visuality in Social Media: Researching images, circulations and practices. L. Sloan & A. Quan-Haase, *The SAGE Handbook of Social Media Research Methods.* SAGE Publishing.

Hearn, A. (2008). Meat, Mask, Burden: Probing the contours of the branded self. *Journal of consumer culture, 8*(2), 197–217.

Instagram Press. 2018. *Our story.* Retrieved from https://instagram-press.com/ourstory

Kow, Y.M., Kou, Y., Semaan, B. & Cheng, W. (2016). Mediating the undercurrents: Using social media to sustain a social movement. *Proceedings of the 2016 CHI Conference on Human Factors in Computing Systems.* ACM, pp. 3883–3894.

Kuchera, B. (2014). *Twitter can fix its harassment problem, but why mess with success?* Retrieved from https://www.polygon.com/2014/7/30/5952135/twitter-harassment-problems

Liu, F., Ford, D., Parnin, C., & Dabbish, L. (2017). Selfies as social movements: Influences on participation and perceived impact on stereotypes. *Proceedings of the 2017 conference on Computer Supported Cooperative Work* (p. 72). ACM.

Lopes, A. R. (2014). The impact of social media on social movements: The new opportunity and mobilizing structure. *Journal of Political Science Research.*

Marwick, A. E. (2015). Instafame: Luxury selfies in the attention economy. *Public Culture, 27*(1), 137–160.

Monroy-Hernández, A., Kiciman, E., De Choudhury, M., Counts, S., et al. (2013). The new war correspondents: The rise of civic media curation in urban warfare. *Proceedings of the 2013 conference on Computer Supported Cooperative Work* (pp. 1443–1452). ACM.

Olteanu, A., Vieweg, S., & Castillo, C. (2015). What to expect when the unexpected happens: Social media communications across crises. *Proceedings of the 18th ACM Conference on Computer Supported Cooperative Work & Social Computing* (pp. 994–1009). ACM.

Qu, Y., Huang, C., Zhang, P., & Zhang, J. (2011). Microblogging after a major disaster in China: a case study of the 2010 Yushu earthquake. *Proceedings of the ACM 2011 conference on Computer Supported Cooperative Work* (pp. 25–34). ACM.

Shirky, C. (2011). The political power of social media: Technology, the public sphere, and political change. *Foreign affairs (2011)*, 28–41.

Shklovski, I., Palen, L. & Sutton, J. (2008). Finding community through information and communication technology in disaster response. *Proceedings of the 2008 ACM conference on Computer supported cooperative work*. ACM. pp. 127–136.

Thomas, D. R. (2006). A general inductive approach for analyzing qualitative evaluation data. *American journal of Evaluation*, *27*(2), 237–246.

Time's up now. (2017). *Time's up now*. Retrieved from https://www.timesupnow.com/#news-anchor

Urbaniak, G.C. & Plous, S. (2013). *Research Randomizer*. Retrieved from http://www.randomizer.org

Wortham, J., Sengupta, S. & Perlroth, N. (2012). *Behind Instagram's s Success, Networking the Old Way*. Retrieved from https://nyti.ms/2kLEuxt

Zwick, D., Bonsu, S. K., & Darmody, A. (2008). Putting Consumers to Work: Co-creation and new marketing govern-mentality. *Journal of consumer culture*, *8*(2), 163–196.

How Do Parents of Children with ASD Use Information Grounds to Seek for ASD-Related Information?

Jiaxin An
Department of Information Management, Peking University, Beijing, China
jiaxin.an@pku.edu.cn

Ying Na
Department of Information Management, Peking University, Beijing, China
yingn@pku.edu.cn

Pengyi Zhang
Department of Information Management, Peking University, Beijing, China
pengyi@pku.edu.cn

ABSTRACT

Parents of children with an autism spectrum disorder (ASD) have special needs about health information related to children. This research aims to understand how parents of children with ASD in China seek information in information grounds. We conducted field observations at a treatment and rehabilitation center, and interviewed 16 Chinese parents of children with ASD whose children participated in the therapy classes at this center. Results derived from qualitative coding and analysis suggest that: (1) parents' information needs evolve around improving their children's living skills, social connections are important information sources for them. (2) Parents' information grounds are closely related to their everyday life of looking after the children, such as classes and activities. Main topics of information sharing and exchange at such places include experiences of raising children with special needs, children's health status, and other child-bearing topics. (3) Factors influencing parents' information behavior in the information grounds include homogeneity, familiarity, focal activity, reward expectation, and so on. (4) Parents benefit from such information grounds to gain useful information, emotional support, and social connections. These findings provide insights on better understanding the unique needs of parents with ASD children.

KEYWORDS

Information Grounds; Parents; Children with ASD; Health Information Seeking

ASIS&T THESAURUS

Parents; Information Sharing; Qualitative Analysis

INTRODUCTION

Autism/Autism Spectrum Disorder (ASD) is a developmental disorder that affects communication and behavior, such as difficulty on communication or interaction with other people, restricted interests and repetitive behaviors (Grzadzinski, Huerta, & Lord, 2013). There are no reliable estimates of the population of people with ASD in China (Wan et al., 2013). It is believed that there are more than 10 million autistic individuals in China (Wucailu Center for Children with Autism, 2015).

Parenting a child with ASD may raise numerous challenges, ranging from obtaining a diagnosis, finding a treatment institution, getting into an appropriate education program, addressing behavior problems, to financial and emotional strains (Grzadzinski et al., 2013). In China, the recognition of "autistic tendencies" diagnosis and autism intervention centers are increasing slowly in developed areas, but ASD population in economically underdeveloped regions are still largely underserved (Zhou et al., 2014). Even in developed areas, the majority of preschool teachers lack knowledge and skills to work with ASD populations (Liu et al., 2016). As a result, most children with ASD do not attend mainstream schools, their parents are burdened with expensive training fee and high cost of living (Wucailu Center for Children with Autism, 2015). Parents also suffer from emotional pressure, which comes from cultural biases such as "having a child with a disability is shameful" (Xiang et al., 2013). Some parents put great efforts into their children's recovery even though ASD is a life-long condition that cannot be fully cured, which also adds stress on these parents (Xiang et al., 2013).

Research shows that parents are very cautious about health information related to children (Walker, 2009), they depend a lot on social networks with other parents to deal with problems when raising their children (Greyson, 2017). For parents of children with ASD, they are in huge need for information service to get access to ASD-related information including diagnosis, therapy, school programs, and so on. Their information needs change and evolve as children grow up, including physical growth, behavior management and so on. They have multiple information sources including therapists, doctors, other parents of children with ASD, national organization and so on (Gibson & Kaplan, 2015; Gibson, Kaplan, & Vardell, 2017). They also need information channels to raise the level of awareness in a community and society. However, little research has studied their information behaviors and

82nd Annual Meeting of the Association for Information Science & Technology | Melbourne, Australia | 19–23 October, 2019

DOI: 10.1002/pra2.00003

designed proper information services. This study aims to build a bridge to address this gap.

Parents of children with ASD spend too much time on their children to social with others (Rao & Beidel, 2009; Sivberg, 2002), occasions like children's classes might be important for their social activities and gaining information. This study explored their information needs and seeking behavior. In particular, we are interested in information grounds formed around children's activities. The overarching research question is: how do parents of children with ASD use information grounds to meet their needs for ASD-related information. Four sub-questions are:

1. What types of information grounds do parents of children with ASD have?
2. What topics are discussed in the information grounds?
3. What factors influence the information exchange in the information grounds?
4. What benefits do parents gain from the information grounds?

The rest of the paper is organized as follows: we first review related research in information grounds, parents' information needs and seeking behavior, and information seeking of ASD-related information. We then describe our methodology and present the results. We conclude with a summary and discussion of the findings and research limitations.

RELATED RESEARCH

Information Grounds Theory

Fisher's Information Grounds Theory provides a framework to study people's everyday information behavior (Counts & Fisher, 2008, 2010; Fisher, Durrance, & Hinton, 2004; Fisher & Landry, 2007; Fisher, Landry, & Naumer, 2007; Fisher & Naumer, 2005; Fisher, Naumer, Durrance, Stromski, & Christiansen, 2005; Pettigrew, 1999). She conducted a field study of clinic personnel and found that the clinic became a physical place for information exchange, which is based on interpersonal care and trust. Such information exchange can be triggered by events and affected by settings like seat comfort. Fisher described this phenomena as an "information grounds," "an environment temporarily created by the behavior of people who have come together to perform a given task, but from which emerges a social atmosphere that fosters the spontaneous and serendipitous sharing of information" (Pettigrew, 1999). She presented seven propositions of information grounds and summarized them as eight key concepts, including context rich, temporal setting, instrumental purpose, social interaction, social types, informal and formal information flow, alternative forms of information, and sub-contexts create grand context (Fisher et al., 2005). People can benefit along physical, social, affective, and cognitive dimensions from information grounds (Fisher et al., 2004). In the survey of college students, Fisher extracted factors of information grounds (Fisher et al., 2007). She used this framework to analyze information grounds of stay-at-home mothers and college students, finding that nearly 54% stay-at-home mothers value human-related factors like trustworthiness, diversity, similar beliefs, and common interests (Fisher & Landry, 2007), while college students value information-related factors like information relevance, information availability and unanticipated nature of obtaining information (Fisher et al., 2007).

Types of Information Grounds

Research has suggested that information grounds such as workplaces, activity groups and religious sites, are very important information sources for everyday information seeking (Counts & Fisher, 2008). People with different professions, educational backgrounds, social roles have different types of information grounds. For example, college students' information grounds include campus, restaurant and community (Fisher et al., 2007), information grounds for stay-at-home mothers include children's activities, shops, community centers and parks/playgrounds (Fisher & Landry, 2007). Information grounds can also be online in forms of online social networks (Counts & Fisher, 2010). For example, Twitter provides a "place" for IT professionals' informal and social communication, in which they keep connected socially and share information (Talip, Narayan, Edwards, & Watson, 2017). Information grounds form in physical or virtual places where people get together in temporal social settings. Information grounds can serve different roles for different groups. For example, Christians and Muslims not only share everyday information in coffee shops, but also ease conflicts and seek consensus (Rohman & Pang, 2015). Immigrants can obtain safety and belongingness while acquiring life skills in libraries (Fisher et al., 2004). Fisher pointed out that follow-up research can explore the reasons why information needs generate among individuals in information grounds, and how individuals' perception and participation of information grounds change over time (Fisher & Naumer, 2005).

Information Needs and Seeking Behavior of Parents

In general, parents are extremely cautious about health information related to children. They care about information authority and credibility, which they have their own criteria for judgment. For example, parents will assess information credibility according to information sources and their experience. They generally distrust information published by stakeholders like the government, or provided by people who have no experience on child care (Walker, 2009). Parents often triangulate information from different sources to assess and strengthen conclusions by reducing the biases of a single approach (Greyson, 2018). Meanwhile, parents are highly sensitive to negative information. When deciding whether to bring children for MMR vaccine, parents can be attracted by information of vaccination risk more easily than information of vaccination benefits, even if the risk probability is low (Gardner, Davies, McAteer, & Michie, 2010).

Research found that personal sources are usually easier and more readily accessible compared to other formal sources (Case & Given, 2007). Building a strong relationship with an expert (such as a doctor) or other parents in similar situations can raise parents' positive emotional responses, then motivate them to actively seek and exchange information (Walker, 2012). When seeking information from other people, the information seeker receives some combination of informational and relational benefits (Cross, Rice, & Parker, 2001).

Parents' health information behaviors can be influenced by their socioeconomic status, education backgrounds and states of children. Parents with lower socioeconomic status depend more on information gatekeepers, like social workers, to obtain information, while parents with higher socioeconomic status will testify information by themselves to support decision-making (Walker, 2009). Parents with higher education will actively review literature to obtain comprehensive information (Gardner et al., 2010). When children get acute illness, nearly 60% parents tend to bring children directly to the clinic for help rather than seek information by themselves (Given, Willson, Albrecht, & Scott, 2016).

ASD-Related Information Seeking

For parents of children with ASD, their health information behavior run through the whole process of raising children. Research has found that parents of younger children with ASD pay more attention to physical growth and education information, they communicate more with doctors and teachers, and their information sources decrease as their children grow up (Gibson et al., 2017). Parents of older children are more concerned about independent living ability, job training and higher education. They describe their frustration and fare about the lack of information on job training (Gibson et al., 2017). Local parental social networks are important information sources for parents. They can not only provide unavailable social activity information on official websites, but promote people to accept ASD families. Social media has become a main access for parents to obtain information. Parents can join online communities to communicate with other parents in similar situations and share experience, which they think is more labor-saving and accurate than finding information by themselves (Gibson et al., 2017; Gibson & Kaplan, 2015).

Parents of children with ASD also face great emotional and financial pressure (Gibson et al., 2017; Lai & Oei, 2014; Wang, Michaels, & Day, 2011). Mothers have higher pressure than fathers (Dabrowska & Pisula, 2010). Chinese parents of children with ASD are burdened with undeveloped service system (Zhou et al., 2014), lack of teachers with ASD knowledge (Liu et al., 2016), and social exclusion like "having disabled children is shameful" (Zhou et al., 2014). Parents' stress coping strategies can correspond to specific information behavior. Research identified two stress coping strategies: monitor and blunter. Monitors are highly sensitive to negative and dangerous information. Their stress can be reduced by offering information timely, someone with chronically illness also need emotional support. Blunters tend to shift attention from negative and dangerous information, providing information can increase their pressure (Miller, 1980). Parents of children with ASD have two most useful coping sources: problem-focused coping and social support, their use of coping strategies is influenced by demographic characters, psychological attributes, states of children and situational variables (Lai & Oei, 2014). Chinese parents of children with ASD use methods like acceptance, active coding, positive reinterpretation, growth, suppression of competing activities and planning to cope stress. And they prefer planning (Wang et al., 2011).

METHODS

The field research was conducted at *Paintings of the Innocents (PI) center*, a subordinate non-government organization (NGO) of Beijing Association for Rehabilitation of Autistic Children (BARAC). Funded by China Social Welfare Foundation, it provides various art therapy classes for children with ASD, including painting, music, and dancing. Figure 1 shows a map of PI studio where the observations and (some) interviews took place.

The first two authors were involved with the PI center as volunteers to help arrange classrooms, coordinate class activities, and clean classrooms in two music classes held in Saturday, from October 3 to December 1, 2018. Each class lasted for 1.5 hr. We gradually got familiar with the parents as volunteers. Parents has signed an informed consent with the center allowing PI to collect students' activity data including photos for management and publicity purposes. Since there is no standard IRB-like procedure required for this kind of research in China, we did not go through an IRB application process. However, we made sure that the research followed similar ethical rules to ensure participants' protection and privacy. Parents from two weekend classes were approached and recruited.

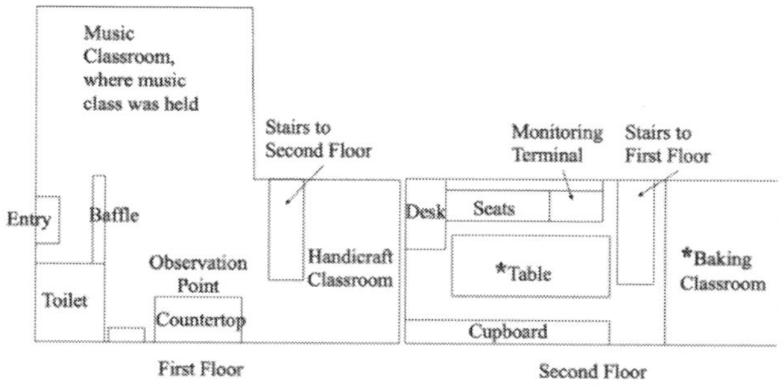

Figure 1. Map of the PI studio. (Interviews were conducted at places marked by *).

Participants were informed about the purpose of the research and provided with a protocol of the interview. If they agreed to be interviewed, they were given printed consent from, which explains the voluntary nature of the interviews, how we are going to collect and analyze the data, how we plan to protect their privacy and anonymity. After getting participants' consent, we asked them to finish a background questionnaire to collect their demographic information, status of the children, their information needs and information sources for ASD-related information. Then we conducted semi-structured interviews which lasted from 13 minutes to 86 minutes (M = 48, SD = 21.08) during November and December 2018. Interview questions are divided into 3 parts: (1) participants' experiences of seeking ASD diagnosis, treatment, and related institutions; (2) information sources and their evaluation of these sources. (3) Occasions or social settings serving as information grounds for sharing ASD-related information, in particular, topics discussed, reasons and motivations for communication, and perceived benefits in these occasions.

We interviewed 16 Chinese parents, including two couples (M1 & F1, M2 & F2) and one aunt (A1) who looks after her autistic nephew because his mother has passed away (see details in Table 1). Most participants were interviewed during class at Baking Classroom or Handicraft Classroom of the PI studio. Three parents (M5, M6 and M10) were interviewed over phone at a time of their choice, and two participants (M4 and M8) finished part of the interview face to face and the rest over phone. Participants received a box of crayons as a gift for their children.

After transcribing records, two researchers separately coded two transcripts with Nvivo 12. We counted information

Participants' relationships with children	Mother	13
	Father	2
	Aunt	1
Participants' age	35-40	1
	41-45	4
	46-50	6
	51-55	5
Annual income/ Yuan	<100k	7
	100-200k	7
	200-300k	1
	300-400k	1
Participants' education	Middle school	3
	Professional school	1
	College	4
	Bachelor	6
	Master	2
Children's gender	Male	10
	Female	4
Children's age	9-12	2
	13-17	6
	>17	6
Children's education	Mainstream school	7
	Special school	7

Table 1. Participant information.

grounds mentioned by participants, and divided them into two categories:

1. offline occasions or places such as schools, NGOs, activities for children or parents, and so on;
2. online occasions, such as social networking sites (SNS), and online support groups.

We coded topics discussed in information grounds inductively, including status of children, work opportunity,

Code	Description
People	
Educational expectation	The educational goals parents want their children to achieve, like learning skills and gaining knowledge.
Reward expectation	The rewards parents expect from participating in information grounds, like gaining useful information.
Character	For example, some parents are open to chat with others.
Familiarity	Parents tend to chat with someone familiar.
Homogeneity	Parents tend to chat with others in similar or dissimilar backgrounds.
Actor roles & social type	An actor role is parents' primary reason for being there; social type indicates parents' positions in information food chain.
Motivation	Voluntary and compulsory reasons for going to a place.
Membership size	The number of people in information grounds.
Place	
Focal activity	Activities which didn't involve information sharing primarily but bring people together in a social setting.
Conviviality	A convivial atmosphere often includes food or drink and is associated with good company and a festive mood fostering interaction among people.
Creature comfort	Factors create a relaxing climate for information exchange, like comfortable chairs.
Location & permanence	Convenience for accessing the place and maintenance of information grounds.
Privacy	The privacy level people perceived in information grounds.
Ambient noise	Ambient voice influencing people's chatting in information grounds.
Information	
Significance	Information grounds may provide information deemed important, or interesting but not vital for decision making.
Frequency discussed	Information grounds can be valued for the frequency with which particular topics occur.
How created / shared	Needs and information can encompass social interactions like conversation or passive observation.
Topics	People in information grounds are interested in purposeful information.

Table 2. Factors Influencing information grounds (Fisher et al., 2007).

experience of raising children, information sources, policy & regulation, life and entertainment, and information on organization, courses and activities. We coded benefits gained from information grounds along social, emotional and informational dimensions based on Fisher's sixth proposition (Fisher et al., 2004). We coded the factors influencing information exchange in information grounds based on Fisher's factors of information grounds, and added four codes: educational expectation, reward expectation, character and homogeneity (see Table 2 on the previous page). The first two authors coded two interview transcripts independently. The initial kappa was 0.57 between the two coders. The two coders discussed and resolved disagreements, and divided rest of the transcripts and completed the coding.

FINDINGS

Information Needs and Sources

Information Needs

When asked "what ASD-related information do you pay attention to" in the background questionnaire, the following topics are most frequent (numbers in the parenthesis indicate the number of parents who selected the topic): "independent living" (14), "puberty" (12), "language development" (9) and "policy and regulation" (9).

Independent Living. Most parents are concerned with their children's independent living when they are not able to take care of them in the future. "*As we are getting old, who will take care of our child?*" (M10). They need methods helping them to teach children basic life skills such as "shopping and cooking."

Puberty. Participants need to learn strategies to control children's (sometimes agitative) behavior during puberty. "*My son is in puberty now. He gets angry easily and attacks others.*" (M8).

Language Development. Some participants hope to improve the language ability of their children. "*My son cannot speak properly before. I learned training methods from teachers in NGOs and trained him. Now he can speak a lot.*" (M6).

Policy and regulation. Participants look for policies supporting their children's future life, including "*supports of training and recovery programs, employment, and so on.*" (M10).

Very few participants chose topics related to a typically developed child of the same age, such as "help with school works" (2) for children under 17, "sexual development/heterosexual interactions" (3) for children above 13, and "higher education/job training/employment" (2) for children above 17. Some participants think it's unnecessary for children with ASD to attend regular education programs (see F2), while some participants would still want their children to be part of the society (see M10).

> *F2: How many (Chinese) characters can children with ASD learn? To be honest, it's useless for children with ASD to attend a regular school. It's better to teach such kids some life skills like cooking so that they can take care of themselves.*

> *M10: I hope that he (the child with ASD) can live independently and be accepted by the society. It would be great if he can recover, work and contribute to the society in the future.*

Information Sources

Due to the undeveloped information service system for ASD-related information in China, parents of children with ASD lack official information sources such as national organizations and related websites (see M13).

> *M13: There is no authoritative information source in China, while many countries like Israel, UK, USA and Japan have their own institutions for ASD population. After huge efforts from China Disabled Person's Federation and parents of children with ASD, we just established one institution recently, which is unknown to many people.*

As a result, parents generally use social networking sites and tools such as WeChat (a popular social networking app in China) for ASD-related information, including WeChat group chat (15), channel subscription (10), and status of friends and connections (8).

Some WeChat groups are started by leaders of NGOs and doctors, who act as group leaders and share information on ASD-related lectures, courses, activities and so on with the group members. Other WeChat groups are organized by parents who share information with each other. "*I can get answers to my questions quickly from WeChat groups, which are also comprehensive and credible.*" (M6).

ASD-related organizations or persons can use a public channel/account (known as *Gongzhonghao*, similar to a Facebook page) to publish information. Parents of children with ASD can subscribe to these channels to obtain information. Some participants think "*Information of WeChat public accounts is timely and rich.*" (M4).

In addition, the social networking function (similar to Facebook status) allows parents to "*share information on new methods, medicines and treatments of ASD in WeChat groups*" (M10) to other parents.

For participants with high life pressure and time constraints, SNS is quite convenient (see M2).

> *M2: I have no time to collect information because I need to work. I can obtain some useful information by browsing WeChat during my commute on the bus.*

Apart from WeChat, parents depend a lot on offline social connections to obtain information, including other parents of children with ASD (15), local NGOs (12), and families or friends (9).

Other parents of children with ASD. Some participants think information from other parents are more credible (see M4).

> *M4: Information from other parents, who are not representatives of profitable organizations, might be more credible.*

Local NGOs. Teachers of NGOs or parents who attend courses held by NGOs can provide information on organizations, ASD knowledge and so on (see M3 and M7).

> *M3: The teacher of an art organization recommended PI to me, saying that PI is a better place for my child.*
>
> *M7: Beijing Association for Rehabilitation of Autistic Children (BARAC) holds lectures regularly to introduce the development of ASD treatment.*

Families or friends. Some participants get advice from their close friends. (see A1)

> *A1: My friends suggested that I should take my nephew to the gym since he was overweight. I did so and insisted for 5 years. Now my nephew's health condition is really good.*

Additionally, participants with lower income or education level expressed their difficulty in obtaining authoritative information (see F2), while participants with higher income or education have richer resources (see M5).

> *F2: I'm not professional and advanced enough to find information by myself.*
>
> *M5: I majored in medicine, and I can ask my classmates in USA or Germany for help…I am in a league for parents of children with ASD, which is held by China Association of Persons with Psychiatric Disability and their Relatives (CAPPDR), some parents in CAPPDR are national representatives, they can share authoritative information in groups.*

Overall, most participants' information needs evolve around preparing the children for independent living, controlling children's agitation during puberty, language development and policies. Their information sources included online and offline social connections, but their accessible information sources differ because of their socioeconomic status.

Types of Information Grounds

We asked participants "In what occasions or places can you get ASD-related information when communicating with others." Most information grounds are closely related to their everyday life of looking after their children, which include taking children to activities (10), classes (9) or schools (3), picking up children to home (2), and visiting teachers or friends with children (2). With little free time for social life and leisure (see M13), most participants said that they can only communicate with others in places mentioned above (see M12).

> *M13: I rarely have time to socialize with other parents, because we are so busy looking after children and elders, in addition to other responsibilities.*
>
> *M12: Only when children are attending classes or activities, parents can get together. We usually don't have time to meet in person, only keep contact on WeChat.*

Some information grounds can be without children's presence such as NGOs (6) and activities for parents (4). Some are online such as WeChat groups (4). People in WeChat groups have similar interests and topics to talk about (see A1). Some participants share information of their children's status and progress in their WeChat posts, which could catch other's attention and trigger communications (see M9).

> *A1: I can only talk about ASD-related topics with other parents of children with ASD. I won't talk about such topics with parents of normal children, because they don't know about ASD, and it's embarrassing to introduce my child's condition to them if we are not familiar with each other.*
>
> *M9: Sometimes I publish my son's paintings in my WeChat posts. Once a contact commented on how brilliant the paintings were and asked if I would be interested in taking my son to an exhibition. Then my son had a chance to show his talent and let the public know that children with ASD can do something well.*

To sum, most types of participants' information grounds are related to children. Their information grounds can be offline or online.

Topics Discussed in the Information Grounds

Most of the topics discussed in information grounds are about everyday life of children with ASD, including experiences of raising children (13), status and progress of children (13), and information on organizations, activities, and courses (10).

Experiences of Raising Children

Parents share their methods of raising children such as teaching children to ride bikes (M5), dealing with children's pickiness at mealtime (M8).

Status and Progress of Children
Parents talk about their "*children's hobbies*" (M1), "*children's study in school*" (M2) and so on.

Information on Organizations, Activities, and Courses
When seeing other children with ASD who are good at singing, painting and so on, parents will ask "*what organization or courses do you take your children to?*" (M2), exchanging their experiences at different organizations, activities, and courses.

Participants hardly talk about life and entertainments (5), policies and regulations (2) and work opportunities (1). Although they pay attention to certain topics such as children's future, someone feel stressful and try to avoid such topics (see M2).

> *M2: These topics are so sensitive that I don't want to talk about... I thought about sending my daughter to institutions as I am getting old, but such institutions charge a lot... I have no idea of my daughter's future, we are not like other parents who are rich and can afford to raise another child to take care of their brothers or sisters.*

To sum, the topics exchanged in the information grounds range widely but all evolve around the everyday life of taking care of children with ASD. Some participants might avoid stressful topics like children's future in information grounds.

Factors Influencing Information Exchange in Information Grounds

We asked "Why do you share information in such occasions or places when talking with others," participants mentioned factors about people and place.

Factors about people include "homogeneity" (15), "familiarity" (11) and expectation (10). The influence of homogeneity is two-fold:

1. Parents of children with ASD are not eager to talk to parents of a typically developed child. Most participants are willing to chat with other parents of children with ASD (see M8).

   > *M8: Because we all have such kids, we can learn from each other and relax ourselves when chatting.*

In their views, parents of non-autistic children "*do not understand children with ASD at all, let alone providing any information*" (M4), they may even "*make jokes on you*" (M12). Such views are barriers to communicate with non-autistic groups.

2. Participants whose children are high-functioning tend to communicate with parents of similar children (see M7), they have few common topics when chatting with parents whose children are low-functioning (see M4).

   > *M7: Parents with better-developed children tend to form a circle... some parents with better-developed children are unwilling to let their kids play with low-functioning ones.*

   > *M4: If children's problem is different from my child, I won't talk with their parents. I only talk with parents whose children have similar problems with my child. And I don't talk with parents whose children are higher-functioning, because we have few common topics.*

While homogeneity in parents of children with ASD promote their information exchange within the "circle," many "sub-circles" are generated based on homogeneity of children's conditions, which can be barriers for communication and information exchange.

Familiarity is another factor that motivates participants to talk with other parents of children with ASD (see M4).

> *M4: Because I've met her (a mom with an ASD child) several times before, so I chat with her more.*

Familiarity can encourage parents, especially introversive ones, to communicate with non-autistic people. For example, M5 gradually get familiar with another parent during the music class, they chat a lot (see M5).

> *M5: I came across a parent before but we haven't talked with each other. We both attend this music class. I gradually got familiar with her and we chatted a lot."*

Expectation can also motivate parents to attend courses actively for their children's enjoyment (see F2) or communicate with other parents to obtain useful information (see M7).

> *F2: I didn't want to attend the music course of PI at first, but my daughter liked the music course, so I come with her every Saturday.*

> *M7: I hope to obtain more information so that I can help my child, and I need to obtain information via communication.*

Parents' expectation for social acceptance drive them to communicate with parents of non-autistic children (see M1).

> *M1: My friends wanted to learn more about ASD. They were willing to get along with my son... I told my friends my son's characteristics at first, so that my friends would not be surprised by my son's behaviors.*

As for factors about place, participants generally mentioned "focal activities" (13) for children with ASD and their parents, like classes, performances and parties. Focal activities can bring parents of children with ASD together, increasing homogeneity in information grounds (see M10). Regular activities in fixed places can make parents meet each other frequently, then increase familiarity and promote their communication (see M2).

> *M10: In organization like PI, I can meet more parents of children with ASD, we will communicate with each other.*
>
> *M2: Including me, there are four parents accompanying their children with ASD in my daughter's class. We meet each other every day and chat if we are free.*

But focal activities can also hinder information exchange. For example, M10 are responsible for taking photos of the music class, "*So I have no free time to chat with other parents.*"

To sum, participants tend to communicate with people who are homogeneous and familiar. Focal activities like classes of children can get together parents with similar backgrounds, generating an atmosphere for information exchange in information grounds. Although parents show reluctances towards non-autistic groups, they hope to be accepted by society, which can make them jump out of their comfort zone to communicate with different groups of people.

Benefits from Information Grounds

Most participants benefit from information grounds, including information and experiences, emotional support, and social connections.

Information (4) and Experiences (10)

Parents share their raising experience with one another. Participants mentioned that they sometimes got useful experiences in raising children from other parents over a conversation (see A1).

> *A1: My own experiences are limited, but I can benefit from experiences of other parents in finding activities for my child, intervening with certain behaviors, and so on.*

Parents share information on organizations, courses, and activities. For participants with younger children, they can also know more organizations and courses from parents with older children (see M4). But participants with older children benefit less from information grounds, who already know most of the information shared in the group (see M2).

M4: We usually talk about organizations. Most organizations that I visit with my sons are introduced by other parents.

M2: I didn't benefit much. I knew almost every organization they mentioned.

Emotional Support (13)

When chatting with other parents of children with ASD, participants find a sense of belonging. "*I know that at least I'm not alone, someone have similar or even worse conditions like me.*" (M13). They release their stress by "*talking about my anxiety with other parents of children with ASD*" (M12). They are "*inspired by other parent's experiences of raising children, and hope to learn from them*" (M3).

Social Connections (6)

Some participants build long-term relationships with others (see M5).

> *M5: I've kept the relationship with parents I met in an organization for nearly 10 years, we often get together to talk about our children.*

To sum, information grounds play an important role in everyday life of parents of children with ASD. In addition to getting useful information and experiences in raising children with ASD, they also received emotional supports, and made social connections.

DISCUSSION

Compared to American parents of children with ASD (Gibson et al., 2017; Gibson & Kaplan, 2015), Chinese parents of children with ASD have similar information needs on independent living, puberty, policy and regulation, and language development. But they are in lack of official information sources such as national organizations, website and so on. As a result, they depend a lot on social networking sites and social connections to obtain information, including WeChat, other parents of children with ASD, families and so on. Their accessible information sources differ because of their socioeconomic status.

Chinese parents of children with ASD suffer from huge anxiety of their children's future due to the lack of social support (Li et al., 2015; Xiang et al., 2013). As a result, most of their information needs are about improving living skills of children. In lack of official information sources, they value information from social connections such as other parents and families of children with ASD, which they think are useful and credible. However, their lifestyle is around their children's need without little free time to build social connections with others. Therefore, information grounds such as children's classes and activities are important for them to meet more parents in similar situation, build social connections, obtain useful information and emotional support. Focal activities in these grounds can bring parents and children together, then foster an atmosphere of homogeneity and familiarity, and promote information exchange among parents in information grounds.

Nevertheless, as parents tend to communicate with others in atmosphere of high homogeneity and familiarity, they have lower motivation to communicate with people outside of ASD groups, while eagerly hoping to be acknowledged, accepted and understood by the public. More work needs to be done to solve this problem. One possible approach may include creating new information grounds to bring together not just parents of children with ASD, but parents of non-autistic children as well.

Their information exchange is also related to their stress coping strategies. As parents worry that no one can take care of their children in the future, some parents tend to be a blunter (Miller, 1980), avoiding talking about such topics. Some parents will use social support to releasing their stress (Lai & Oei, 2014), such as talking about their anxiety with other parents.

The findings from this field research lead to more open questions related to information grounds. For example, one observation we made is that more experienced parents act more as information givers, sharing their experiences and information about raising a child with ASD with unexperienced parents. What roles do parents play in information grounds and what factors influence these roles? Are parents with higher socio-economic status have advantages in information grounds? What are the differences between offline information grounds and online one like WeChat groups? Answering these questions can improve our understanding of everyday information behaviors of parents of children with ASD.

This exploratory study has limitations. First, the participants were recruited from one center in Beijing, which may not be representative of parents in other geographic and socio-economic backgrounds. Second, it focuses only on ASD-related information behavior of parents. However, like everyone else, parents of children with ASD needs a wide range of information for work, learning, leisure, and so on. Putting the seeking of ASD-related information in a bigger context may be able to better explain the findings.

CONCLUSION

Results from 16 interviews of Chinese parents of children with ASD at a treatment and rehabilitation center (the PI center), suggest:

The information needs of Chinese parents of children with ASD evolve around improving their children's living skills in the lack of social support. They obtain information from online and offline social connections including other parents, related organizations, families and friends, which they think are credible. Information grounds play an important role in their seeking and sharing of ASD related information. Most information grounds are closely related to parent's everyday life of taking care of children, such as children's classrooms and activities. They tend to communicate with each other in atmosphere of high homogeneity and familiarity, forming a unique ASD circle composed of many sub-circles based on children's different conditions. Their information exchange is related to their stress coping strategies, some parents tend to be blunters who avoid tough topics, while some parents will talk their anxiety with other parents. Parents can obtain emotional support, useful information and social connections from information grounds, while more experienced parents may benefit less. Future research can explore roles of parents in information grounds, factors influencing parents' roles and development of information grounds, and online information grounds like WeChat groups.

The findings of this study can provide insights on improving information service for ASD population and other underprivileged groups. It also calls for attention from government agencies and social organizations to provide credible information that is easily accessible, help build social support systems, and increase the awareness of the society for people with ASD.

REFERENCES

Case, D. O., & Given, L. M. (2007).*Looking for information: A survey of research on information seeking, needs, and behavior* (4th ed.). In J.-E. Mai, Bingley, England: Emerald Group Publishing Limited.

Counts, S., & Fisher, K. E. (2008). Mobile social networking: An information grounds perspective. *Proceedings of the 41st Annual Hawaii International Conference on System Sciences (HICSS 2008)*. IEEE (pp. 153–153).

Counts, S., & Fisher, K. E. (2010). Mobile social networking as information ground: A case study. *Library and Information Science Research, 32*(2), 98–115.

Cross, R., Rice, R. E., & Parker, A. (2001). Information seeking in social context: Structural influences and receipt of information benefits. *IEEE Transactions on Systems, Man, and Cybernetics, Part C (Applications and Reviews), 31*(4), 438–448.

Dabrowska, A., & Pisula, E. (2010). Parenting stress and coping styles in mothers and fathers of pre-school children with autism and Down syndrome. *Journal of Intellectual Disability Research, 54*(3), 266–280. https://doi.org/10.1111/j.1365-2788.2010.01258.x

Fisher, K. E., Durrance, J. C., & Hinton, M. B. (2004). Information grounds and the use of need-based services by immigrants in Queens, New York: A context-based, outcome evaluation approach. *Journal of the American Society for Information Science and Technology, 55*(8), 754–766.

Fisher, K. E., & Landry, C. F. (2007). Understanding the information behavior of stay-at-home mothers through affect. In N. Diane & B. Dania, *Information and emotion. The emergent affective paradigm in information behavior research and theory* (pp. 211–233). Medford, NJ: Information Today Inc.

Fisher, K. E., Landry, C. F., & Naumer, C. (2007). Social spaces, casual Interactions, meaningful exchanges: "Information ground" characteristics based on the college student experience. *Information Research, 12*(2).

Fisher, K. E., Naumer, C., Durrance, J., Stromski, L., & Christiansen, T. (2005). Something old, something new: Preliminary findings from an exploratory study about people's information habits and information grounds. *Information Research*, *10*(2), n2.

Fisher, K. E., & Naumer, C. M. (2005). Information grounds: Theoretical basis and empirical findings on information flow in soical settings. In *New directions in human information behaviour* (pp. 93–111). Dordrecht, The Netherlands: Springer.

Gardner, B., Davies, A., McAteer, J., & Michie, S. (2010). Beliefs underlying UK parents' views towards MMR promotion interventions: A qualitative study. *Psychology, Health and Medicine*, *15*(2), 220–230.

Gibson, A., Kaplan, S., & Vardell, E. (2017). A survey of information source preferences of parents of individuals with autism spectrum disorder. *Journal of Autism and Developmental Disorders*, *47*(7), 2189–2204.

Gibson, A., & Kaplan, S. J. (2015). "A family like ours": Demographic variations in information seeking behavior and community participation among parents of individuals with autism spectrum disorder (ASD). *Proceedings of the Association for Information Science and Technology*, *52*(1), 1–4. https://doi.org/10.1002/pra2.2015.145052010060

Given, L. M., Willson, R., Albrecht, L., & Scott, S. D. (2016). Information in crisis: Health & technology-related information behaviors of parents in emergency departments. *Proceedings of the Association for Information Science and Technology*, *53*(1), 1–10. https://doi.org/10.1002/pra2.2016.14505301073

Greyson, D. (2017). Health information practices of young parents. *Journal of Documentation*, *73*(5), 778–802. https://doi.org/10.1108/JD-07-2016-0089

Greyson, D. (2018). Information triangulation: A complex and agentic everyday information practice. *Journal of the Association for Information Science and Technology*, *69*(7), 869–878. https://doi.org/10.1002/asi.24012

Grzadzinski, R., Huerta, M., & Lord, C. (2013). DSM-5 and autism spectrum disorders (ASDs): An opportunity for identifying ASD subtypes. *Molecular Autism*, *4*(1), 1. https://doi.org/10.1186/2040-2392-4-12

Lai, W. W., & Oei, T. P. S. (2014). Coping in parents and caregivers of children with autism spectrum disorders (ASD): A review. *Review Journal of Autism and Developmental Disorders*, *1*(3), 207–224.

Li, W., Skora, E., Lu, M., Cai, Y., Sun, Q., Yang, G., & Wang, G. (2015). Self-esteem, social support, and life satisfaction in Chinese parents of children with autism spectrum disorder. *Research in Autism Spectrum Disorders*, *17*, 70–77. https://doi.org/10.1016/j.rasd.2015.05.003

Liu, Y., Li, J., Zheng, Q., Zaroff, C. M., Hall, B. J., Li, X., & Hao, Y. (2016). Knowledge, attitudes, and perceptions of autism spectrum disorder in a stratified sampling of preschool teachers in China. *BMC Psychiatry*, *16*(1), 1–12. https://doi.org/10.1186/s12888-016-0845-2

Miller, S. M. (1980). Monitoring versus blunting styles of coping with cancer influence the information patients want and need about their disease. *Cancer*, *76*(2), 167–177.

Pettigrew, K. E. (1999). Waiting for chiropody: Contextual results from an ethnographic study of the information behaviour among attendees at community clinics. *Information Processing and Management*, *12*(2), 12–12. https://doi.org/10.1016/S0306-4573(99)00027-8

Rao, P. A., & Beidel, D. C. (2009). The impact of children with high-functioning autism on parental stress, sibling adjustment, and family functioning. *Behavior Modification*, *33*(4), 437–451. https://doi.org/10.1177/0145445509336427

Rohman, A., & Pang, N. (2015). Seeking common ground: Coffee shops as information grounds in the context of conflict. *Proceedings of the 78th ASIS&T Annual Meeting: Information Science with Impact: Research in and for the Community, Article No. 24*. American Society for Information Science.

Sivberg, B. (2002). Family system and coping behaviors: A comparison between parents of children with autistic spectrum disorders and parents with non-autistic children. *Autism*, *6*(4), 397–409.

Talip, B. A., Narayan, B., Edwards, S. L., & Watson, J. (2017). Digital ethnography as a way to explore information grounds on Twitter. *Qualitative and Quantitative Methods in Libraries*, *5*(1), 89–105.

Walker, C. G. (2009). Seeking information: A study of the use and understanding of information by parents of young children. *The Journal of Information Literacy*, *3*(2). https://doi.org/10.11645/3.2.214

Walker, C. G. (2012). The information world of parents: A study of the use and understanding of information by parents of young children. *Library Trends*, *60*(3), 546–568. https://doi.org/10.1353/lib.2012.0000

Wan, Y., Hu, Q., Li, T., Jiang, L., Du, Y., Feng, L., … Li, C. (2013). Prevalence of autism spectrum disorders among children in China: A systematic review. *Shanghai Archives of Psychiatry*, *25*(2), 70. https://doi.org/10.3969/j.issn.1002

Wang, P., Michaels, C. A., & Day, M. S. (2011). Stresses and coping strategies of Chinese families with children with autism and other developmental disabilities. *Journal of Autism and Developmental Disorders*, *41*(6), 783–795.

Wucailu Center for Children with Autism. (2015). *Report of Chinese autism education and rehabilitation industry development status*. Beijing, China: Beijing Normal University Publishing Group.

Xiang, S., Carrie, A., Bonnie, A., Fiona, E. M., Simon, B.-C., & Brayne, C. (2013). Service provision for autism in mainland China: Preliminary mapping of service pathways. *Social Science and Medicine*, *98*, 87–94. https://doi.org/10.1016/j.socscimed.2013.08.016

Zhou, W. Z., Lu, S. J., Wei, L., Ye, A. Y., Wang, D. D., Zhao, M.-Z., … Wu, Y. Y. (2014). Statistical analysis of twenty years (1993 to 2012) of data from mainland China's first intervention center for children with autism spectrum disorder. *Molecular Autism*, *5*(1), 1–30. https://doi.org/10.1186/2040-2392-5-52

Scientists' Data Discovery and Reuse Behavior: (Meta)data Fitness for Use and the FAIR Data Principles

Bradley Wade Bishop
University of Tennessee
Knoxville, USA
wade.bishop@utk.edu

Carolyn Hank
University of Tennessee
Knoxville, USA
chank@utk.edu

Joel Webster
Texas Tech University
Lubbock, USA
joel.webster@ttu.edu

Rebecca Howard
University of Tennessee
Knoxville, USA
rhowar24@vols.utk.edu

ABSTRACT

Environmental science researchers frequently must work at regional and global scales that require them to search for, evaluate, and reuse data collected by others. This study assesses science data reusers' information-seeking behavior to determine *fitness for use*, a concept from consumer behavior research that explains how consumers define and assess product quality and compatibility to satisfy their specific needs. Using a critical incident technique, 22 researchers in earth science described their most recent data discovery resulting in reuse. An interview schedule derived from the FAIR Data Principles framed participants' information-seeking behavior along a sequence of actions, which included finding, accessing, making interoperable, and reusing data. Researchers' perspectives on how they discovered and evaluated data for reuse gives new insights into *fitness for use* of data by human consumers, and contributes to considerations for furthering work into machine-actionable data and learning.

KEYWORDS

Data Discovery; Science Data; Fitness for Use; Critical Incident Technique

ASIS&T THESAURUS

Information Reuse; Search Behavior; Earth Sciences; Interviews

INTRODUCTION

Data reuse improves and advances science permitting others to verify results; enabling the repetition of experiments; and conduct new research (Pryor, 2012). For many domain scientists in the physical sciences, the act of data discovery for reuse appears simple and straightforward—discover science data, then conduct analyses. Reuse of any data not personally collected by the individual reuser, or shared by a trusted colleague, benefits from insight provided in metadata that make data more findable, accessible, interoperable, and reusable. Any search and evaluation of science data relies on metadata. In science, data discovery may occur without human interaction or assistance if metadata and other ancillary sources provide enough information for reusers to locate and evaluate the *fitness for use* of the data. In some instances where opening up the data or reviewing the metadata does not help, domain scientists may contact the data creator or data custodian for clarification on data quality. This reliance on personal or institutional memory no longer works in today's science for several reasons. First, the data creator might not be available to provide explanation. Second, if the data is maintained in a custodial system, such as a data repository, the data custodian may not have sufficient knowledge or experience to resolve reusers' inquiries. And third, consider reuse scenarios where the reuser is a machine as opposed to a human, and the resulting need for machine-actionable data to enable machine learning in analyses. Machines as reusers require detailed metadata to enable finding, identifying, selecting, obtaining, and reusing data.

To manage scientific data deluge, additional conduits are needed to ensure that data will be findable, accessible, and interoperable for reuse for both humans and machines (Hey & Trefethen, 2003). In most sciences, but especially the disciplines discussed in this study—oceanography, geology, and hydrology—to perform research at a global scale requires sharing earth science data across organizations, institutions, agencies, and countries. Given the limited capacity of human processing power with the expanding scope, growing scale, and quickening rate of data creation, science data should be machine-actionable to unlock discoveries through analyses that are not feasible if reliant exclusively on researchers' direct, human interactions and contributions. Once found and accessed, data also needs to be interoperable with existing data types and formats used in the germane domain. A better understanding of how humans locate and evaluate science data is necessary to inform FAIR-enabled data tools and services that make data more machine-actionable as well. This study fills a gap by evaluating the perspectives of data

82nd Annual Meeting of the Association for Information Science & Technology | Melbourne, Australia | 19–23 October, 2019

DOI: 10.1002/pra2.00004

reusers' information-seeking behaviors in determining data *fitness for use*. Using a critical incident technique, 22 researchers were asked to describe their most recent search for data. An interview schedule derived from the FAIR Data Principles framed participants' behaviors in search and reuse along a sequence of actions, which included finding, accessing, making interoperable, and reusing data. This required operationalizing findability, accessibility, interoperability, and reusability from the data consumer's perspective. The following provides an overview the FAIR Data Principles, the concept of fitness for use, a selection of work on the information-seeking behaviors of scientists, and a review the method used in this study—the critical incident technique.

FAIR Data Principles

In response to the need for machine-actionable data, the Future of Research Communication and e-Scholarship (FORCE11) created the FAIR Data Principles as a guide for data stewardship and management, and applicable to various stakeholder groups, including data producers, data consumers, and data managers (Wilkinson et al., 2016). The original FAIR Data Principles publication, since cited over 1,100 times, includes fifteen foundational principles that enable reuse organized around four broad categories: Findability (F); Accessibility (A); Interoperability (I); and Re-usability (R) (2016). The FAIR acronym has gained popularity and application in a variety of domains including biology, life science, plant science, environmental science, and other data-intensive sciences (Diepenbroek et al., 2017; Rodríguez-Iglesias et al., 2016; Wolstencroft et al., 2017). In the FAIR Data Principles, the coupling of metadata and data into "(meta)data" makes clear that the principles apply to both data and metadata, and for most science data the two are indistinguishable.

Based on the principles, shown in Table 1, data is made FAIR through actions taken both before and after data creation, and relate to other factors beyond the data themselves that occur in the data lifecycle, such as information retrieval, discovery tools, and workflows. The principles build from the Joint Declaration of Data Citation Principles (JDDCP) (https://www.force11.org/group/joint-declaration-data-citation-principles-final) and other past standards in data quality like the Data Seal of Approval (DSA) (https://www.datasealofapproval.org/en/). Yet, FAIR separates itself in adoption and appeal from prior work in at least two ways: (1) simplicity, and (2) emphasis on the role of machines in the research enterprise. FAIR represents a concise, domain-independent, high-level set of principles that, *if* implemented, would supply answers for both humans and machines to discover and evaluate data prior to reuse (Wilkinson et al., 2016). "The recognition that computers must be capable of accessing a data publication autonomously, unaided by their human operators, is core to the FAIR Data Principles. Computers are now an inseparable companion in every research endeavor" (Mons et al., 2017).

The majority of the work done thus far with the FAIR Data Principles focuses on the data management role, including assessing the FAIR-ness of existing data and repositories, and the evaluation of repositories where the data are stored and made available. For example, a FAIR Metric group created ways to measure the principles. After reviewing results from focus group interviews, the FAIR Metric group discovered that both their metrics and even some principles were misunderstood (Wilkinson et al., 2018).

To be findable:	F1. (meta)data are assigned a globally unique and eternally persistent identifier. F2. data are described with rich metadata. F3. (meta)data are registered or indexed in a searchable resource. F4. metadata specify the data identifier.
To be accessible:	A1. (meta)data are retrievable by their identifier using a standardized communications protocol. A1.1 the protocol is open, free, and universally implementable. A1.2 the protocol allows for an authentication and authorization procedure, where necessary. A2 metadata are accessible, even when the data are no longer available.
To be interoperable:	I1. (meta)data use a formal, accessible, shared, and broadly applicable language for knowledge representation. I2. (meta)data use vocabularies that follow FAIR principles. I3. (meta)data include qualified references to other (meta)data.
To be re-usable:	R1. meta(data) have a plurality of accurate and relevant attributes. R1.1.(meta)data are released with a clear and accessible data usage license. R1.2.(meta)data are associated with their provenance. R1.3.(meta)data meet domain-relevant community standards.

Table 1. FAIR Data Principles.

Other research efforts consist of moving existing data toward FAIR alignment, such as the GOFAIR Project to help implement open science policy in the European Union via Horizon

2020, and the American Geophysical Union's Enabling FAIR Data Commitment Statement in the Earth, Space, and Environmental Sciences (COPDESS, n.d.; GO FAIR, n.d.).

Fitness for Use

Data should be discoverable and usable by a variety of potential reusers for effective and efficient open science. The future of science relies on the sharing and reusability of data by humans, as well as through machine-actionable data. Data sharing is not simply the release or posting of data so that others may access the information, but also the additional steps to make data discoverable. There are a variety of data sharing methods and these methods can be influenced by domain, country, journal, data type, and more (Pasquetto, Randles, & Borgman, 2017). The elements listed in the FAIR Data Principles codify the necessary details each data set needs to provide within the (meta)data itself to meet the needs of potential reusers for data discovery and subsequent evaluation of fitness for use.

To determine the suitability of data for reuse, a reuser should make some judgment on whether data are fit for their research purpose(s). The ideal set forth and codified in the FAIR Data Principles allows for the discovery and evaluation of data without consulting other sources, as data adhering to the principles should have all the metadata needed to inform appropriate reuses. *Fitness for use* is a concept from consumer behavior research to assess if a customer's needs are met by the specifications of a product (Juran, 2002). Despite some debate over the phrase, fitness for use has remained a popular term to define quality assessment of any type of product (Neely, 2005). The concept is useful for assessing the FAIR Data Principles from the reuser's perspective as there may be differences in quality expectations among data producers, data managers and data consumers, including reusers, as there exist discrepancies between suppliers and customers of all product types.

For geospatial science data, these factors to assess fitness for use might include data quality, scale, interoperability, cost, metadata, syntactic and semantic heterogeneity, and others (Chrisman, 1984; Veregin, 1999). These data specifications should appear in metadata, but even when metadata are present it may not match a reuser's specific needs due to a variety of factors. Semantics vary across domains, or there could be temporal lags between data creation and reuse. The ever-present issue of varying technical expertise of reusers may diminish the ability to make an informed evaluation (Bishop & Grubesic, 2016). In data repositories, metadata may be stored separately from the data making it harder to view and inhibiting its use to assess fitness for use. In other instances, extraneous metadata hinders a reuser's fitness for use evaluation requiring them to sift through administrative metadata that, while critical to data management and stewardship practices, may be meaningless to most reusers.

User limitations inform all fitness for use behaviors. For example a consumer assessment of any product occurs quickly based on the appearance of a product, the brand of the product, and other specifications that may be considered for its purpose, and then the evaluation is done. When purchasing melons, a consumer may thump several to inform their selection, but unfortunately there is not an equivalent for data. While the FAIR Data Principles are valuable for enabling trustworthy and interoperable access, use and reuse, data literacy is a separate issue, and potential reusers may lack the competencies when interacting with data, regardless of its FAIR-ness. Since no data are perfect, some data are good enough for reuse and reusers may take what data are available, that appear to meet basic criteria, and also come from a trusted organization (e.g., United States Geological Survey (USGS)). An informed understanding of fitness for use of science data would outline these considerations and inform the functionality and design of data, metadata, and, critically, the tools and guidance (e.g., documentation) to access both.

Critical Incident Technique and Information Seeking

In 1954, John C. Flanagan developed critical incident technique (CIT) in an attempt to understand human behaviors through direct observations in defined situations. The method has been applied to a diverse range of disciplines, including psychology, communication, nursing, job analysis, counseling, education, medicine, marketing, and social work (Butterfield, Borgen, Amundson, & Maglio, 2005). Using this method in information-seeking behavior research allows participants to recall a recent behavior and describe it (e.g., Marcella, Lockerbie, & Baxter, 2013). Context is a critical component of models resulting from role-specific information seeking behavior studies (e.g., Freund, 2014; Leckie, Pettigrew, & Sylvain, 1996). Asking participants about their most recent search allows researchers to learn patterns across a group of participants given the randomness of each participant's selection of their most recent behavior.

CIT has been applied in studies on the information-seeking behaviors of academics' scholarly communication behavior (Tenopir et al., 2003; Tenopir, King, Boyce, Grayson, & Paulson, 2005; Tenopir, King, Christian, & Volentine, 2015). Kraaijenbrink (2007) used the technique to assess 19 engineers' utilization of information from the web, identifying gaps in information identification, acquisition, and utilization. The technique has also been used in identifying information failures within information-seeking behavior (Wang & Shah, 2016). CIT has also been used as an approach to assess data sharing practices among scientists (Shen, 2018).

METHODS

Utilizing a semi-structured interview approach, this study applies CIT to better understand the perspectives of data reusers' information-seeking behavior in determining data *fitness for use*. Purposive and convenience sampling techniques were used to invite participants to take part in the study to inform future data products and tools. First, participants were recruited by contacting reusers of data in the Coastal and Marine Geology Program at two USGS Coastal and Marine Science Centers (Pacific and Woods Hole). Additional participants were discovered through snowball sampling as other seafloor geologists were interested in sharing their experience discovering and evaluating data. Ultimately, 22 reusers of data from oceanography, geology, and hydrology completed the study, with phone interviews conducted over a three-month period.

The interview schedule included questions on education and professional experience and, through prompting of a critical incident, information-seeking behavior questions. For the latter, participants were asked to "think of a recent search for data". The FAIR Data Principles design is to assess individual datasets; therefore, CIT focuses participants to focus on one search and assessment for a single dataset. The FAIR-aligned questions to determine how they discovered and evaluated that data *fitness for use* required operationalizing the FAIR Data Principles for findability, accessibility, interoperability, and reusability to a consumer perspective. Each principle addresses many different questions a reuser of data may ask in order to locate and determine fitness for use. Transposing each principle into a meaningful element required considerations outlined in a methods paper (Bishop & Hank, 2018). The resulting interview schedule is shown in Table 2.

Some FAIR principles lend themselves to dichotomous questions (e.g., either the data had an element or not) and other more complex principles require qualifiers and context to emerge from a users' explanation of their information-seeking behavior. The interview schedule followed the original order of the principles, as shown in Table 1, as participant's behaviors were also linear, from finding to accessing to assessing interoperability before commencing decisions and action regarding re-use.

The 22 completed interviews were recorded, transcribed, and analyzed in NVivo applying grounded theory application of open, axial, and selective coding (Glaser & Strauss, 1967).

RESULTS

Professional Experience

Examining position titles at face-value, most participants ($n = 16$) provided job titles that reflect their science or domain expertise, with a minority of job titles reflective of management and administration ($n = 2$) or data management and stewardship ($n = 4$). The titles are: Oceanographer/ Research Oceanographer ($n = 5$); Geophysicist/Research Geophysicist/Geologist ($n = 4$); Assistant Professor in Geology ($n = 2$); Physical Scientist ($n = 2$); Fishery Biologist; Senior Research Scientist; Deputy Center Director; Deputy Regional Manager; Database GIS Specialist; Spatial Analyst; Scientific Programmer; Metadata Management Architect; and Data Management Specialist.

Job-Related Analyses
1. What is your current job title? 2. How many years in total have you been working in your current job? 3. How many years in total have you been working with earth science data? 4. Describe your work setting? 5. Please indicate your credentials and degrees. 6. Please provide any other educational or training you have received that is applicable to performing your job.
Findability
7. How did you find the data? 8. Did the data have a persistent identifier (i.e., a long-lasting unique reference to an objects location) (e.g., DOI; PURL)? 9. Did the data have metadata? 10. Did the metadata help you find the data?
Accessibility
11. How did you access the data? 12. Was the data in an open format (e.g., Public Domain, Attribution License, and so forth)? 13. Was the data free? 14. Did the data have use constraints (e.g., limitations of use)? 15. Was the metadata accessible?
Interoperability
16. Was the data in a useable format? 17. How was the data encoded and was it using encoding common to other data used in your research (i.e., same format)? 18. Was the data using shared controlled vocabularies, data dictionaries, and/or other common ontologies? 19. Was the data machine-actionable (e.g., to be processed without humans)?
Reusability
20. Were there any issues with the data that impacted reuse of the data (e.g., resolution)? 21. Did the data geographic scale used impact reuse of the data? 22. Did the coordinate systems used impact reuse of the data? 23. Did the metadata provide sufficient information for data reuse?
Closing
24. Please provide any other feedback about this project or data fitness for use.

Table 2. Interview schedule.

Participants' time in their current positions ranged from half a year to 31 years, with about 13 years being the average. The average years spent working with science data, including all time in higher education, was almost 22 years. The interviews made it apparent that participants had experience locating science data over time and had adapted to changes in data formats and information systems.

Some participants referred to fieldwork, such as boats, cameras, and field sensors, when describing their respective work settings, but the majority described work settings with an emphasis on the hardware and software to analyze science data. Descriptions of their hardware included "heavy duty processing machines" and all types of computers, from laptops to high-performance clusters at their institution or in the cloud, to conduct simulations and run models. The most mentioned software applications were ArcGIS (n = 8); MATLAB (n = 6); Python (n = 5); Fortran (n = 3); and R (n = 2). An open standard data format created by the Society of Exploration Geophysicists (SEG), called SEG-Y, was mentioned by the seismic geologists, as well as very specialized software to view and analyze, such as SeiSee, SIOSEIS, and ECHOS. As one participant commented, "There's a lot of software we use that's more homegrown" (P020) (participants identified by number in quotations that follow).

Education and Training

Participants mentioned their most advanced degree when asked about their education. Half of the participants (n = 11) hold PhDs; including two in Oceanography, two in Geophysics, and one each in Geosciences, Marine Sciences, Biology, Civil Engineering, Aerospace Engineering, Coastal Engineering, and Astrophysics. Not all of the PhD participants mentioned their undergraduate or other graduate degrees, but those that did had other degrees within the same discipline as their terminal degree. The highest level of education for the other 11 participants were master's degrees, including a Master of Science in Oceanography, Geology, Geophysics, Marine Resource Management, Zoology, Science, and two each, respectively, in Geography and Fisheries and Wildlife. One participant held a Master's in Art.

The advanced degrees of participants demonstrate domain expertise among participants. Although all were asked about additional training received to do their jobs, only a few gave specific examples, including MATLAB workshops (n = 3), ESRI online certificates (n = 3), or Python training (n = 2). Most participants were "self-taught" and learned new skills "on the job". Nearly all mentioned gaining new skills and knowledge from online sources, including social media. As one participant mentioned, "I learn all the time from YouTube" (P001).

Critical Incidents

At the end of the job analyses questions, participants were asked to "think of a recent search for data," and told that subsequent interview questions would explore how they discovered and evaluated that data for *fitness for use*. While there was a potential limitation in study design as concerns participant recall of a specific data-seeking incident resulting in data reuse, all participants recalled and described a critical incident involving the search, evaluation, and reuse of data.

(F)AIR: Findability

The FAIR Data Principles for findability focus on metadata to make science data discoverable by humans and machines. This section of the interview began with a general question to assess how reusers of data found their data. Since the search described was a recent search for data, participants were very clear in providing step-by-step details of how they located the data, including the information systems or search engines used and, in most cases, the search terms used in their queries.

Of the 22 participants, a clear majority (n = 20) described known-item search in trusted sources. Participants mentioned specific websites and data portals at the local, state, and federal levels. As one shared, the "US Geological Survey maintains these sites and lets me look up what their URL is" (P019). Another explained: "Typically I'd be looking for government endorsed or some sort of published information" (P004). The participants that did not mention a known, trusted data collection still knew the names of trusted organizations, and utilized Google searches to locate data.

Half of participants (n = 11) mentioned that their search began with a "Google search" with specific keywords or the name of the data repository they are retrieving information from. "I start in Google and see…"shoreline," "GIS," and "download" those three keywords and see what comes up" (P006). Six participants explained how they combined and revised their search query or keywords when discovering data. Another two participants did not mention keywords, but said they conduct a "normal" search. Those information-seeking behaviors described as "normal" by participants matched the other participants use of a search engine and keywords. Web browser tools were also mentioned for facilitating findability. Four participants indicated the use of bookmarks, and a couple listed many common data repositories. One participant estimated they have 50 bookmarks: "I live by my bookmarks" (P011).

Due to the geospatial aspect of earth science data, seven participants also mentioned conducting known-location searches. This means they visit an information resource with a web-based mapping feature to allow for spatial discovery. In many searches, participants were looking for data at a particular place. "There's usually a map interface where you can look at datasets in the archive based on their map location and you know, if you were interested in one particular part of the planet, so we just go zoom into that area and look at what's available" (P015). In four interviews, state-level, governmental data resources were discussed. These searches required a combination of federal- and state-level data to determine the most appropriate dataset for their work task, as exclusive reliance on federal sources was unsatisfactory.

Eleven participants indicated their data had a persistent identifier. "The US federal stuff, there's been a lot of requirements for data releases to have persistent identifiers attached to them" and in this respect much of US federal data is FAIR compliant (P010). Unfortunately, there are still data from other sources that do not. Seven participant confirmed no—"No. [laugh] That was one of the worst parts of using that data" (P004). Four participants were unsure how to answer this question and mentioned links to data that went away, therefore, these are also likely not persistent identifiers. Of all the Findability Data Principles, this is most crucial for machine reuse even though human users can sometimes duplicate a Google search and retrieve data sources that have changed location.

A majority of participants (n = 14) indicated the data from their recent search had metadata. One participant offered a reason for this revealing that, "according to the, what we call the IOOS standards, they have to have some metadata along with their postings" (P009). Still, four participants were definitive that their data did not have metadata. "Often times you're gleaning what you can from the webpage where they're posted" (P007). The remaining four, among the 22 total participants, were unsure if their data had metadata or not. In seven instances, participants said that the metadata helped them find the data; however, 15 participants said that metadata did not help them find the data.

The FAIR Data Principles for rich metadata (F2) and that data are registered or indexed in a searchable resource (F3) concern metadata. Although metadata are essential for discovery, humans can locate data via metadata without an understanding of how metadata works. The following quotes reveal the bimodal responses to this question. "Yes, of course the metadata was used when it was ingested into data.gov and that's what allowed me to find it through the search interface that data.gov provides" (P001). The P001 participant understands how metadata works, but others seem to think metadata does not play a role in spatial data discovery. "It doesn't help me locate it, no. It does help me a bit understand it" (P009). Clearly, metadata helps both machines and humans locate data and it is interesting that humans do not acknowledge the role of metadata in their search even though they rely on keywords to find their data.

F(A)IR: Accessibility

For the FAIR Data Principles related to accessibility, nearly all participants (n = 20) described using an existing web service to download and analyze the data. Some described machine-actionable access. For example: "… some Python utilities that allow me to extract data according to my specifications. There are these, I guess they call them, methods of querying the database within my code without having to point and click through websites" (P009). For those that had download access, seven indicated that they would manually select data through a graphical user interface. The two participants that did not have easy access to data had to rely on human intervention. One contacted the original authors to get the data, and the other reported a broken download link from a website.

In regard to the principle for openness, 17 participants said the data were open and had similar comments to one from P008: "We are working with mostly folks who have open source data and even open source codes". Five mentioned the data were in the public domain. Three mentioned that the formats were open, but users would need special software for access, with one describing it as a, "bureau-specific kind of software" (P005). Two participants indicated that the data accessed were in a proprietary format, with one referencing Excel and the other a shapefile. The latter participant was not corrected, but shapefiles are an open format, and many other participants mentioned this format.

Three other participants did mentation that their data, while in an open format, had a few open access issues, such as permission to view and use the data, or that data are in an open format that is so old that few instruments in the world use it. "So, it's open, there might be even a document that describes how to read it but it might be a pain and require some custom coding or downloading some custom tool we put somewhere to read it" (P003). While the data are open format, as related by these participants, they do not adhere to the spirit of the FAIR Data Principle in that these open formats are not machine-actionable without human intervention.

While there were mixed responses on if the data was open format, all participants (n = 22) said the data were free. The protocols to access the data were likely also free.

Half of the participants (n = 11) indicated the data had no use constraints. Participant comments show that they might not understand or have considered data use constraints and permissions before. For example, as one participant put it, documentation on use was, "very generic, almost like a non-lawyer tried to write something pretending they are a lawyer" (P007). When these participants were primed through interviewer prompts with Creative Commons licenses as an example, this did not help. Eight were confident that the data had attribution licenses: "… not for commercial uses it usually says" (P014). This likely is a Creative Commons license or equivalent. Two participants mentioned unique use constraints related to oceanographic data that indicates the presence of a valuable natural resource, such as oil: "… use for planning purposes, but not to be used for navigation" (P016). One participant indicated they were restricted from publishing or even letting anyone else view the data.

When it comes to reuse and interpretation of permissions and terms of service, as evidenced from remarks from participants, human reusers do not always read licenses, and may make assumptions on access, use and reuse conditions. Some participants assumed open data and no use constraints without checking to see if there are use constraints. Machines will require some use constraint to be defined even if it is no use constraints to enable reuse. This means that, to be machine-actionable, data and/or (meta)data must have use constraints (e.g., license in the accompanying the meta(data)). In the United States, where study participants are located, the assumption that most federal science data are open and without use constraints is no longer valid in a data intensive information landscape that needs machine-actionable data.

A majority of participants (n = 16) said the metadata was accessible. Two other participants said the metadata was accessible, but had issues using it because it was not in a standard format. Although some metadata may be accessible, it is worth noting that metadata that requires humans to make sense of it is not actually machine-actionable. Four very honest participants did not know if the metadata were accessible due to never looking at it. "I'm sure there must be some metadata; I just have never used it" (P020). Accessible metadata is critical to determine fitness for use for both humans and machines.

FA(I)R: Interoperability

In consideration of FAIR Data Principles relating to interoperability, there were few issues as a recent critical incident in data search and access was a premise for the interview. The recent search for data described by most participants always stemmed from data that was reused and inherently interoperable. Eighteen of the 22 participants stated their data was in a usable format. The four participants that did not report data in a usable format were able to transform the data from how it was encoded into something usable for their purposes.

An even greater majority of participants (n = 20) indicated the data were encoded in a common format used in their discipline. The two that did not think the data were encoded in a common format likely did not know what encoding meant in this context or simply did not care to know (e.g., "I didn't actually dig deeper to find out what the underlying data representation was because I didn't care" (P001)).

When asked if the data used shared controlled vocabularies, data dictionaries, and/or other common ontologies, many participants in the study were unfamiliar with those terms. Three participants were uncertain if the data retrieved used a controlled vocabulary or not (e.g., "the metadata had some keywords, I don't know if they're controlled" (P006)). Four, while understanding the concept of controlled vocabulary, were confident that their data did not have anything like it (e.g., "Yeah, they made up their own, but it wasn't like a common or published ontology or anything" (P004)). Still, most (n = 16) indicated that yes, a controlled vocabulary was used, and that many exist in their respective domains. All five participants working in seismic geology mentioned the same data formats and metadata standards.

The final interview question in the interoperability section, Q19, did not map to a specific, discrete FAIR Data Principle. The participants had difficulty understanding and responding to this question more than any other, but whether or not data are machine-actionable is at the heart of the FAIR. The question, "Was the data machine-actionable (e.g., to be processed without humans)?," was situated under the Interoperability section because data format, encoding, and ontology questions all facilitate the processing of data by machines. Fourteen participants were confident that the data from their most recent search was machine-actionable. As one interviewee put it, "you could grab it and view it with web-services where it wouldn't have to do anything" (P006). Eight participants that stated that their data was not machine-actionable were less certain of their response. "Yeah, there might be a way to send a query to a site and get the data back, but it's not obvious to me how you would do that" (P020). Therefore, the data identified by participants in relating their critical incident are assumed to not be machine-actionable, based on participants' descriptions. More work needs to be done to implement this particular set of FAIR Data Principles. Many participants did understand the need for data to become machine-actionable. "There's been a huge push, especially by the industry to use AI or machine learning to interpret aspects of the data, such as, you know, looking at data attributes to identify oil and gas reservoirs, for example. Um...but certain aspects of that or certain aspects of processing the data, just to get the image in the first place, require human input to do that" (P018). The assertion from the participants that data and the machines would not exist without human mediation was a frequent refrain.

FAI(R): Reusability

Although the authors of FAIR debated if compliance with Findability, Accessibility, and Interoperability equaled Reusability, the authors ultimately decided that each type of data would in fact have unique reuse issues that may not relate to the other principles (L. O. Bonino da Silva Santos, personal communication, November 6, 2018). Therefore, the first question asked to participants concerned issues that impacted reuse of the data. Nine participants reported that they did not have any reuse issues. For the remaining 13 participants that did relate reuse issues, the following explains the issues, from the most to the least mentioned.

The most cited reuse issue related to precision and accuracy of data. When conducting any spatial analyses, geospatial data's accuracy (i.e., closeness of match to real-world) and precision (i.e., degree of granularity) are critical, particularly for ocean data and data about the seafloor. These aspects, mentioned by five participants, determine what can be done with data. For example, as one participant noted: "I have a survey that was designed to look at the deep crust of the Earth, I'm not going to be able to use that survey to look at the shallow sub-surface" (P018). Participants described other known limitations in working with such data. "The data may have been acquired for a specific purpose and if you're trying to use the data for a different purpose then there can be limitations in your use of that data" (P018). "It depends on the sort of degree of uncertainty you're willing to accept. For a lot of cases, like the difference between two coordinate systems will only be a matter of like 30 m, so if you're mapping something, you know, if you're mapping (a) basin map 100 kilometers wide, you can probably live with that" (P019). These human users make a judgment on acceptable margins of error and may, in some instances, calculate their inaccuracies and impreciseness, as well as explain study limitations in subsequent publications. When considering reuse from a machine perspective, the need to be programmed with potentially ambiguous parameters to arrive at an acceptable degree of uncertainty are problematic.

Version control was the second most mentioned reuse issue, identified by three participants. "Sometimes the data does change from month to month; in other words, the data you extract one month might be different the next month and we don't always know when that remote dataset has been changed or why" (P009). A human user may not know why a different version was created, and/or what changed. A machine may more easily determine the changes in a large dataset through automation but documentation would be necessary to know why a new version of data exists. This and other reuse issues relate to metadata. Metadata was specifically mentioned by three participants as an issue. The issues were either metadata were insufficient for human understanding, or absent. As one participant put it, "like in the NSF [the United States' National Science Foundation] world, PIs can load up data and claim to have filled out the metadata correctly and then when you go to use it, it's just total garbage" (P015). Metadata compliance and data management plan compliance may be barriers in making available data that aligns with the FAIR Data Principles.

Several other reuse issues were unique to the recent data search described by participants. Only two participants mentioned incomplete or missing data. "There were some gaps in the data, due to their quality control procedures, so there were some gaps" (P002). This reuse issue may appear in much of the oceanographic and hydrologic data discovered by these participants. One participant explained data must be corrected when buoy drift occurs because, "... you have posted that temperature as your best estimate, then you make corrections to it, based on whatever corrections are decided because of instrument drift and all these things" (P000). One participant said the data did not have unique identifiers (a FAIR Data Principle for findability), and stated, "... you basically have to use waterfall name to try to relate back to their original data...and that database is like an ever-changing database" (P004). One user suggested that many more data need webservices, and said, with emphasis in bold: "... many datasets don"t have existing webservices that could have existing webservices (P001). The principle for having data downloadable through webservices is explicit in FAIR within the accessibility section. Another accessibility principle, licensing, was implicated as one participant's reuse issue in that data may actually be proprietary and although their results may be shared via maps, the actual spatial data may not be shared.

There are several known data reuse issues with geospatial data used in the domains represented by participants in this study. Questions related to geographic information about scale and coordinate systems were asked. For 13 participants, the scale did not matter for data about a single point or those at continental and global scales. Scale did matter, however, for nine participants because the precision of the data impacted how it could be used. For example, one participant explained, "... if it's over a really large area, but you're trying to use it to ask very focused and specific questions in a tight region, then that will definitely limit its use or effectiveness, and vice versa" (P018). The scale data at which data are originally collected impacts reusability, but much like the next question on coordinate systems, digital data can be transformed for analyses. The reuser should account for a propagation of error when combining data collected at different scales, but this is a known data limitation of geospatial data. Seventeen of the 22 participants implied that coordinate systems did not matter because either, "... we can convert from one to the other" (P014), or in some areas there is an agreed upon coordinate system that everyone uses.

Eighteen participants did say the data had sufficient metadata for reuse. This is not a surprising result as each participant, in the critical incident shared only recent searches where they actually found and used data. Despite sentiments like, "I mean metadata is harder than data itself sometimes" (P000), most participants acknowledged satisficing; that is, the data was good enough, such as in comments like, "I mean, I am reusing it, but I did do a lot of Q&A before I accepted that fact" (P004) (Prabha, Connaway, Olszewski, & Jenkins, 2007).

Of the four participants that did not say their data had sufficient metadata, two were uncertain and two answered no. These participants did demonstrate a clearer understanding of the cognitive computing (i.e., simulate human thought via machines) implied in the FAIR Data Principles-derived questions. For example, "... there's always some problems with the metadata, when you think about it from a machine to machine perspective" (P001). The two participants that were uncertain about sufficient metadata were more measured in their assessments of sufficiency taking into account a machine's needs. A participant said, "I'm not sure I scrutinized every piece of data enough to be able to answer that" (P012). Unlike a human reuser, we can speculate that a machine actually could scrutinize every piece of data, and will need to do so to evaluate fitness for use.

DISCUSSION AND CONCLUSIONS

The critical incidents recalled in these interviews all resulted in reuse. Some other aspects of findability, accessibility, and interoperability might have emerged if the participants had been asked to describe their most recent *failed* search for data. The participants' familiarity and experience in locating science data was self-reported. Since there was no triangulation through other data collection techniques, such as transaction log analysis or direct observation, the behaviors reported may under- or over-represent participants' competence and expertise in locating and evaluating data. Another study limitation is that participants were from three domains with homogenous geospatial data. The data (e.g., seafloor) reused by these participants has fewer political boundaries than other spatial data (e.g., forest), less variety of formats (e.g., roads), and thus fewer complications in its collection and sharing than other geographic information used by other disciplines. Finally, human reusers' discovery and evaluation of data gives new insights into how scientists search and use data, but the FAIR Data Principles focus on machine-actionable data (e.g., to be processed without humans). Still, results from human participants show that some of the FAIR Data Principles are observable through automation measurement and others are not. The participants difficulty in responding to the more qualitative, subjective measures of data quality highlight the challenge machines will also have in locating and evaluating meta(data) (e.g., Q10: Did the metadata help you find the data?).

Responses to that and other metadata questions provide good illustrations of subjective measures in assessing the FAIR Data Principles. In fact, all the actionable elements of FAIR can be represented in metadata elements. In addition, the information needed to determine fitness for use is transmitted from the producer to the reuser via metadata, often with an information intermediary (i.e., data curator). The concept of metadata was not unknown to participants, but its purpose and importance in the process of sharing, accessing, and (re)using data seemed to be elusive to many. For users, even when metadata are present, they are most likely not consulted to determine fitness for use. As concerns reuse, the gap in awareness of the important role of metadata as it affects findability, accessibility and reusability is a crucial, ongoing data literacy issue. The FAIR Data Principles present a framework, but more work is needed to foster application even among highly educated and experienced communities of data reusers. As one participant pointed out, "it's like when you see a really good metadata record it's like a rare animal in the wild at times and it's really helpful" (P007).

For reusers, who are not likely to consult metadata, fitness for use may be determined simply and more quickly by using the data. While metadata could be used to assess fitness for use, metadata might overwhelm reusers with extraneous metadata to read through, or metadata might be housed separately from the data in another interface that inhibits review. In these instances, accessible metadata may not actually be legible or usable enough for human use. Additional studies should explore this intersection and resulting gaps of metadata usability.

Future work on the assessment of FAIR should also create context-dependent interview schedules that consider reusers' experiences and various, situationally relevant reuse scenarios depending on the domains studied. This study expands upon a cognitive turn for user studies to also begin to consider the user requirements of machines. Thus, machine information-seeking behavior can be anticipated (and potentially overcome through programming) by better understanding the preferences, practices, and limitations of how humans seek data. But it also demands a prerequisite, philosophical question, as succinctly captured by one participant: "What does it mean to be processed without humans? Like some non-human...somehow, some other program decides to go find it, then process it" (P021).

As machine-learning progresses, the need to understand how humans discover and evaluate science data will become more important to build into artificial intelligence. For example, branding from reputable sources is important to humans, as shared by participants in this study when discussing their selection of credible agencies for seeking out data (e.g., USGS). Do (and can) machines also apply a similar consideration to evaluate credible and authoritative sources? One participant summarized the difference between machine and human users' information needs by referring to non-scientists' information needs. "They don't want a terabyte floating point binary, number data; they just wanna know should I take my umbrella?" (P003). Yet, a machine might actually want the floating point data. This study found that indeed some data are FAIR for humans equipped with heuristics from years of training and experience, but more work must be done for the tools and data itself to be truly machine-actionable. A better understanding of how humans locate and evaluate science data is necessary to inform FAIR-enabled data tools and services that make data more machine-actionable.

ACKNOWLEDGMENTS

The authors would like to acknowledge support from the Gloria and David Sharrar Faculty Research Award 2017, administered by the University of Tennessee, those from USGS that assisted with recruitment, Fran Lightsom, Woods Hole Science Center, and Mike Frame, Core Science Analytics & Synthesis, as well as the study participants.

REFERENCES

Bishop, B. W., & Grubesic, T. H. (2016). *Geographic Information: Organization, Access, and Use*. New York, NY: Springer.

Bishop, B. W., & Hank, C. F. (2018). Measuring FAIR principles to inform fitness for use. *International Journal of Digital Curation*, *13*(1). https://doi.org/10.2218/ijdc.v13i1.630

Butterfield, L., Borgen, W., Amundson, N., & Maglio, A. (2005). Fifty years of the critical incident technique: 1954-2004 and beyond. *Qualitative Research*, *5*(4), 475–497.

Chrisman, N. R. (1984). Part 2: Issues and problems relating to cartographic data use, exchange and transfer: The role of quality information in the long-term functioning of a geographic information system. *Cartographica*, *21* (2–3), 79–88. https://doi.org/10.3138/7146-4332-6J78-0671

COPDESS. (n.d.). *Enabling FAIR data commitment statement in the Earth, Space, and Environmental Sciences*. Retrieved from http://www.copdess.org/enabling-fair-data-project/commitment-to-enabling-fair-data-in-the-earth-space-and-environmental-sciences/

Diepenbroek, M., Schindler, U., Huber, R., Pesant, S., Stocker, M., Felden, J., … Weinrebe, M. (2017). Terminology supported archiving and publication of environmental science data in PANGAEA. *Journal of Biotechnology*, *261*, 177–186. https://doi.org/10.1016/j.jbiotec.2017.07.016

Flanagan, J. C. (1954). The critical incident technique. *Psychological Bulletin*, *51*(4), 327–358.

Freund, L. (2014). Contextualizing the information-seeking behavior of software engineers. *Journal of the Association for Information Science and Technology*, *66*(8), 1594–1605.

Glaser, B. G., & Strauss, A. L. (1967). *The discovery of grounded theory: Strategies for qualitative research*. Chicago, IL: Aldine.

GO FAIR. (n.d.). *FAIRification process*. Retrieved from https://www.go-fair.org/technology/fairification-process/

Hey, A. J. G., & Trefethen, A. E. (2003). The data deluge: An e-science perspective. In F. Berman, G. C. Fox, & A. J. G. Hey, *Grid computing - making the global infrastructure a reality* (pp. 809–824). Wiley & Sons.

Joint Declaration of Data Citation Principles. (2014). *Information Standards Quarterly*, *26*(1), 28.

Juran, J. M. (2002). *Juran's quality handbook. (Juran's quality handbook.)*. Norwich, NY: Knovel.

Kraaijenbrink, J. (2007). Engineers and the web: An analysis of real life gaps in information usage. *Information Processing and Management*, *43*(5), 1368–1382.

Leckie, G. J., Pettigrew, K. E., & Sylvain, C. (1996). Modeling the information seeking of professionals: A general model derived from research on engineers, health care professionals, and lawyers. *The Library Quarterly*, *66* (2), 161–193.

Marcella, R., Lockerbie, H., & Baxter, G. (2013). Critical incident technique as a tool for gathering data as part of a qualitative study of information seeking behaviour. In I. Ramos & A. Mesquita, *Proceedings of the 12th European Conference on Research Methodology for Business and Management Studies ECRM-2013* (pp. 247–253). Guimaraes, Portugal: Academic Conferences and Publishing Limited.

Mons, B., Neylon, C., Velterop, J., Dumontier, M., da Silva Santos, L. O. B., & Wilkinson, M. D. (2017). Cloudy, increasingly FAIR; revisiting the FAIR Data guiding principles for the European Open Science Cloud. *Information Services & Use*, *37*(1), 49–56.

Neely, M. P. (2005). The product approach to data quality and fitness for use: A framework for analysis. In *Proceedings of the Tenth International Conference on Information Quality (ICIQ-05)*.

Pasquetto, I. V., Randles, B. M., & Borgman, C. L. (2017). On the reuse of scientific data. *Data Science Journal*, *16*, 8. https://doi.org/10.5334/dsj-2017-008

Prabha, C., Connaway, L. S., Olszewski, L., & Jenkins, L. R. (2007). What is enough? Satisficing information needs. *Journal of Documentation*, *63*(1), 74–89. https://doi.org/10.1108/00220410710723894

Pryor, G. (2012). Why manage research data? In G. Pryor (Ed.), *Managing research data* (pp. 1–16). London, England: Facet Publishing.

Rodríguez-Iglesias, A., Rodríguez-González, A., Irvine, A. G., Sesma, A., Urban, M., Hammond-Kosack, K. E., & Wilkinson, M. D. (2016). Publishing FAIR data: An exemplar methodology utilizing PHI-base. *Frontiers in Plant Science*, *7*, 641. https://doi.org/10.3389/fpls.2016.00641

Shen, Y. (2018). Data sharing practices, information exchange behaviors, and knowledge discovery dynamics: A study of natural resources and environmental scientists. *Environmental Systems Research*, *6*(1), 1–14.

Tenopir, C., King, D., Boyce, P., Grayson, M., Zhang, Y., & Ebuen, M. (2003). Patterns of journal use by scientists through three evolutionary phases. *D-Lib Magazine*, *9*. https://doi.org/10.1045/may2003-king

Tenopir, C., King, D., Boyce, P., Grayson, M., & Paulson, K. (2005). Relying on electronic journals: Reading patterns of astronomers. *Journal of the American Society for Information Science and Technology*, *56*(8), 786–802.

Tenopir, C., King, D., Christian, L., & Volentine, R. (2015). Scholarly article seeking, reading, and use: A continuing evolution from print to electronic in the sciences and social sciences. *Learned Publishing*, *28*(2), 93–105.

Veregin, H. (1999). Data quality parameters. In P. A. Longley, M. F. Goodchild, D. J. Maguire, & D. W. Rhind, *Geographical information systems—Volume I, Principles and technical issues* (2nd ed., pp. 177–189). New York, NY: Wiley.

Wang, Y., & Shah, C. (2016). Exploring support for the unconquerable barriers in information seeking. *Proceedings of the Association for Information Science and Technology*, *53*(1), 1–5.

Wilkinson, M. D., Dumontier, M., Aalbersberg, I. J., Appleton, G., Axton, M., Baak, A., et al. (2016). The FAIR guiding principles for scientific data management and stewardship. *Scientific Data*, *3*(160018). https://doi.org/10.1038/sdata.2016.18

Wilkinson, M. D., Sansone, S.-A., Schultes, E., Doorn, P., Bonino da Silva Santos, L. O., & Dumontier, M. (2018). A design framework and exemplar metrics for FAIRness. *Scientific Data*, *5*, 180118.

Wolstencroft, K., Krebs, O., Snoep, J. L., Stanford, N. J., Bacall, F., Golebiewski, M., … Goble, C. (2017). FAIRDOMHub: A repository and collaboration environment for sharing systems biology research. *Nucleic Acids Research*, *45*(D1), D404–D407. https://doi.org/10.1093/nar/gkw1032

Information Encountering in the Humanities: Embeddedness, Temporality, and Altruism

Sarah A. Buchanan
University of Missouri,
Columbia, MO
buchanans@missouri.edu

Sanda Erdelez
Simmons University,
Boston, MA
erdelez@simmons.edu

ABSTRACT

Humanities research informs people's movements across time and reshapes cultural worldviews. While we know that humanists integrate information resources into their research program and that serendipitous discoveries enable truly transformative knowledge creation, our picture of discovery in the humanities is unclear. There is an important role for information professionals to better support humanistic discovery as routine practice. To fully comprehend the complex research activities of humanities scholars it is necessary to expand upon existing models of information encountering (IE) by analyzing discovery episodes and the temporal and topical factors in play. We take particular interest in studying how scholars in the art history and archeology disciplines conceptualize, pursue, and often complete research projects. Ultimately we present an amended IE model that reveals intricate connections between IE, rediscovery, and altruistic collaboration mutually evolving over distinct timespans.

KEYWORDS

Serendipity; Information Encountering; Information Behavior; Humanities; Art History

ASIS&T THESAURUS

Scholars; Information Behavior; Storytelling; Information Flow; Interviews

INTRODUCTION

Scholars in the humanities dedicate long periods of time toward the pursuit of a distinct arena of research, building deep knowledge and expertise around key topics they investigate in order to answer particular questions or gaps in collective knowledge. While a scholar's way of mobilizing and crafting of evidence is highly individualized – at times even idiosyncratic – the essence of humanities scholarship is communal and collaborative owing to the vastness of available research collections and a scholar's need to be able to navigate such collections efficiently and purposefully (Trace & Karadkar, 2017). By virtue of such specialization of research topics, humanities scholars make "new" research discoveries on a regular basis but only present them as such after compiling, explaining, and contextualizing them as part of a larger chosen narrative – one that contains dozens of small discoveries which have gained meaning primarily by being presented as a coherent whole.

While serendipity has been established as a fortuitous convergence both of conditions and strategies (Copeland, 2019; Foster & Ford, 2003), there are key differences in the experience of serendipity between the humanities and the sciences that have yet to be fully articulated, partly due to a lack of comparative datasets and analyses. Yet because "the moment" remains a crucial and vital pivot point in both scientists' and creative professionals' (Makri, Blandford, Woods, Sharples, & Maxwell, 2014) productivity and one that continues to attract much public interest, there is every indication that ongoing research across disciplines is highly desired. How can serendipity be supported in humanities research? In this study we articulate the density of discovery processes that occur in the humanities disciplines of art history and archeology. We extend previous research on information encountering (IE) by providing qualitative insights on episodic components of IE as contemporary (routine) humanities research practice.

Serendipitous Information Encountering

Information encountering (IE) has been defined as the experience of serendipity in a context of human information behavior. While scholars have developed several models of serendipity varying in their degree of process or facet description, one model (Erdelez, 2000; Erdelez, 2004) uniquely focuses on the context of active search and also makes for our purposes a key distinction between foreground problem information-searching and background problem information-encountering. Additionally, since previous research focused on the practices of scholars in interdisciplinary domains (Makri & Blandford, 2012), the needs of humanities scholars when completing or forming new research projects remain proportionally less well known and thus not precisely articulated in those process-modeling conclusions. Previous research highlighted the importance of place – including the library as place – as a consequential factor for serendipitous

82nd Annual Meeting of the Association for Information Science & Technology | Melbourne, Australia | 19–23 October, 2019

DOI: 10.1002/pra2.00058

experiences and thus established a definition of "incidental serendipity" (Martin & Quan-Haase, 2016) that we chose to incorporate in our research design protocol as the *critical incident*. Alongside place, previous study of humanities scholars' typical research processes has indicated the importance of group consultation – whether fellow peers, librarians, archivists, or other experts (Siegfried, Bates, & Wilde, 1993: 284). Thus, we might make note of place and peers as two infrastructural elements already central to the study of serendipitous discovery-making. Motivated to study the experience of *serendipity* in the humanities to complement previous insights about it in the sciences, our study sought to test the applicability of the above IE model to humanities research. We pursue the research question: How can we qualitatively characterize or amend the established stages of serendipitous IE to account for humanities research via vignettes of active search?

STUDY DESIGN

Driven by an interest in studying serendipity in the context of art history and archeology, the *purpose* of our study is to evaluate the applicability of an IE model that laid out five functional elements of a typical IE episode: Noticing, Stopping, Examining, Capturing, and Returning (Erdelez, 2004). We aimed to offer original qualitative descriptions of each stage's appearance in humanities research settings. While all five elements need not be present in each IE episode, it is important to note that the latter three (Examining, Capturing, and Returning) have to do with addressing a background problem, and that in doing so, the background problem switches to become the person's foreground problem. Thus, a description of the actual experience or "moment" of serendipity should accurately focus on the particular stage of the model called Stopping, which is defined as "the interruption of the initial information seeking activity" (p. 1015). It is only once Stopping happens, that the moment becomes something more than transitory and alters the researcher's next actions. The model has been widely referenced in subsequent studies such as Makri, Ravem, and McKay (2017) and again, is a valuable building block in examining active search contexts.

Recognizing that related work which surveyed historians exclusively focused on examining their experiences in digital environments (Martin & Quan-Haase, 2017), our study invited art historians and archeologists to comment on their sum total of research experiences. Where prior work had used naturalistic observations (Makri, Bhuiya, Carthy, & Owusu-Bonsu, 2015), user tests (Martin, Greenspan, & Quan-Haase, 2017), and more rarely unstructured interviews (McCay-Peet & Toms, 2017) that asked explicitly about serendipity, we employed a different qualitative methodology: using an IE model as our underlying structure in order to gain a clearer view of the processes in play. Protocol usage gave us a structure for analysis that other work did not have.

Methodology

The study employed a qualitative methodology through protocol-based interviews, thematic coding, theoretical model reconstruction, and document analysis. We detail our sample below. As introduced above, we adopted the critical incident technique to first devise an interview protocol (Appendix A) with questions *informed* by the IE model. With protocol and interviewee communications templates in hand, our project received Exempt review status from our Institutional Review Board. Use of our protocol allowed the researchers to systematically collect interview data such that the vignettes could subsequently be subjected to comparative analysis. Interviews were scheduled in advance, usually by email, for an hour and took place in the participant's work office location. (We preferred work locations rather than home or more public locations so that the scholar would have ready access when demonstrating their tools, computer items, or personal library). Participants did not receive the interview protocol in advance but had been prompted by the researcher (first author) to be ready to discuss recent research activities, including publication trajectories.

The study sample comprises humanities researchers who hold an academic professor position with responsibilities for conducting research, teaching, and service. We provide the specific home research disciplines of our respondents in Table 1. All interviews were completed during 2018 and 2019 on the campus of a large public R1: Doctoral University located within the Central Time Zone of the U.S. An audio recording of each interview was transcribed, and subsequently two researchers performed coding on the finalized transcripts. One researcher performed initial coding into category chunks, then two researchers reviewed the contents and came to agreement. The researchers also collected artifacts that some respondents shared or pointed toward in the course of their interview (e.g., copies of publications, photographs of tools or resources) as illustrative examples of their active searches. We defined "vignette" from an information behavior perspective of a specific episode, and "critical incident" in a broadened way encompassing less-recent events, remaining mindful that responses may include one's complex negotiations of narrative identity (Singer, 2004). The researchers' deductive coding process made use of a theoretical active-search IE model (Erdelez, 2004) to identify vignettes one could say either illustrated a component of the model, or necessitated an amendment of the model. Such component analysis is reflected in the combined results and discussion structure employed below, which avoids repetition. Several instances of similar explanations for the same activity indicated that even with a sample size of six (another six participants did not respond to requests for an interview), we approached theoretical saturation and could fully explicate our revised IE model per our motivating research question. We also had to set aside many instances of simply interesting, but not immediately relevant, data. More vignettes were coded and discussed orally than appear in this paper.

Respondent, pronoun (interview minutes)	Position	Research area
P1, she (53)	Associate Professor	Medieval Art History
P2, he (88)	Assistant Professor	Roman Art and Archeology
P3, he (97)	Associate Professor	European Art History
P4, he (104)	Professor	Classical Studies: Rome
P5, he (56)	Associate Professor	Classical Studies: Greece
P6, she (70)	Professor	Greek Art and Archeology

Table 1. Respondent profile.

Noticing

Prior suggestions for creating opportunities for serendipity address the notion of capturing attention and thereby initiating divergent thinking within settings in which researchers are working. Places that provide space for brainstorming and sparking curiosity – such as (digital) libraries and, as we will see below, physical conference spaces – are an essential aspect of the first stage of IE, Noticing. In recalling where they were, several participants revealed deep immersion in their research topic: "Sometimes these projects are triggered by document finds in archives. Sometimes they're triggered by details in pictures." (P3, 1:08:07). Art historians, including P3, travel great distances to gather together copies of archival documents and published works alike as part of their sense-making research process. P3's use of the verb "triggered" matches our current understanding of encountering a piece of information that is *divergent* from their accumulations in some way. We glean here that a moment of Noticing shapes the humanities researcher's *scope* (i.e., sets up foreground and background problems). As the art historian observes, a critical incident occurs in the course of using a suite of sources and resources, and a certain combination can be so fitting that it "triggers" a radical rethink and a felicitous shift on the part of the researcher and her plan of work.

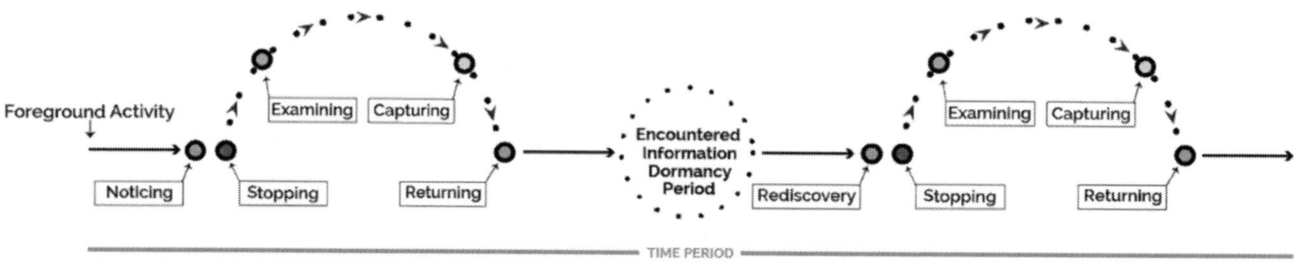

Figure 1. Expanded IE Model, with time period along the bottom and the addition of a Rediscovery component after Returning and before the second instance of Stopping.

FORMATION OF AMENDED MODEL

Though we called upon the already-known factors of place and peers when asking participants to describe encountering information, a new factor that became apparent immediately though heretofore unexamined was time – specifically the shared experience of a dormancy period after Noticing and Capturing the information nugget – which an amended IE model for humanities research must acknowledge. Vignettes compelled the addition of a Rediscovery component to capture our core contribution regarding temporal conditions of IE in the humanities. P1, as an example, accidentally rediscovered an unpublished excerpt 15 years after initially gathering it for research. We depict the item's reappearance in her work after a dormancy period, as a sixth stage occurring after one has Returned to the task it prompted: typically a publication plan now with more pieces in place. In the below sections, we analyze *and* discuss each elemental stage of the discovery process enumerated in our expanded IE model (Figure 1). Following a summary about discovery as a byproduct of one or more stages, the paper's conclusion points to areas for further investigation.

Serendipity does strike, and though no two experiences are identical, a set of humanities examples shows some commonalities. One we highlight is a degree of sensory overload, in the following scene:

> "But that's all because I was sitting at Coffee Co., the Beatles were on – I was feeling really good because they were playing nothing but Beatles stuff! I had an espresso under my belt and I was reading this piece on Carolingian manuscripts of Vergil. And it was like Bam, Bam, Bam, Bam, all these things just locked into place. And I wrote down – I'll show you the notebook – I just *wrote down* all these ideas and I came back and now I'm [thinking] this is great! This is fun! I've been *looking for a way* to make my interests in contemporary popular culture and classical antiquity in the Middle

Ages compatible. I could date it to *that moment*." (P4, 1:09:32).

While there the printed article, notebook, and aural hum were necessary resources, a narrative from an archeologist who studies material culture articulates the importance of an environment that is purposefully and by design conducive to making research discoveries:

> "I had a fellowship, and the whole idea was that I went there to write a book; they supported that. I was having trouble starting the book. My way to start, was to put out an *article* that kind of claims something, a demonstration that then I [my book] could expand on. ... Some of us would go for these long walks after lunch in the woods; some of us started a reading group and then we would get together and we'd apply it to what we were working on. ... That's where that came from. I said, 'this is what I need for it!' I think I wrote the article in a few days, the basis of it." (P6, 29:49).

This vignette punctuates, in addition to the environment, the overlapping nature of writing projects in her field: only *after* achieving the mental breakthrough of writing an exploratory journal article (in 2000) was the connective tissue of her core book-length project unlocked – so the article and the subsequent book mutually facilitated the other. The way forward for neither one had been visible before making the discovery – a discovery, again, that was uniquely realized in a collaborative research environment, with specific decisions made and conversations held among a peer group.

A third finding about Noticing in humanities contexts is *newness* on a personal level. One researcher who utilizes regional epigraphical evidence stated, "You haven't seen it before and then you see it. Always, something moves from shadow into light or from unknown into known." (P4, 22:02). That realization marks the beginning of a learning process, and deepens during the Examination stage described later. Newness in the humanities, we argue, is uniquely the product of collaborative tools, so we further interrogate how searches in a few specific scholarly tools have determined a researcher's objects of study. One for epigraphers is the Europeana network for Ancient Greek and Latin Epigraphy (EAGLE Project, Figure 2) (Liuzzo, 2018), which enables scholars to search digitized inscriptions by structured metadata fields. The classical studies professor who searches for epigraphy from Rome picks from thousands of photographed inscriptions and assembles a project around one item or around a few sorted by a particular object type (altar, tile) or inscription type (honorific, magic).

We have discussed three specific facets of Noticing in the humanities: scope, multisensory engagement, and newness. As the first stage of IE, Noticing is a determinative foundation for subsequent investments of time.

Figure 2. Screenshot of the EAGLE Project inscription basic search (in English, Greek, or Hebrew) page, a key collaborative resource-collecting tool. Not pictured are the advanced search and image search.

Stopping

Seated in an archive, the art historian described being figuratively stopped in his tracks while reading manuscripts. To him, Stopping happens thus: "I *looked* at the [national] Academy files, but while I was looking at the Academy files I noticed that there were all these *other* files that had to do with art and politics. I thought I might as well look at those too. I began thinking about relationships and then as I said [before] one thing led to another, it was unpredictable. It's kind of the *archival* version of shelf-reading, when you're in the library going 'oh that looks fun'." (P3, 55:54). Here, it is the archival setting – with its physical arrangement of the manuscripts that an archivist can present to the researcher – rather than a public coffee shop, that makes serendipity ("noticing") possible. It was a memorandum he had requested as background material (on a new-to-him topic) that he soon realized captured an act of censorship of a work of art by an exhibition committee in 1928. The vignette highlights in a clear way how the tactility of archival work, especially collections-processing, fosters discoveries.

Granted the role of collaborative tools in Noticing, it is in Stopping where we first see *collaborators* enter a serendipitous process. Stopping may in fact be most social stage (second perhaps only to Rediscovery). The art historian noted that collaborators' input was formative during an exploratory stage of research: in response to a supervisor's either/or suggestion: "I said, 'well, I'm all for controversial, cutting-edge, working on what's been neglected. So, I took that path" (P3, 22:45). Where a supervisor presented choices, the researcher chose one. Once past the exploratory stage, let us see how a researcher checks his new discovery (nugget) against the wisdom of the field. We will see how the momentum of discovery begins to slow down! The researcher found that there was "an almost unanimous scholarly consensus" that the censored painting (introduced above) is a protest against the [Great] War, however, when he took a closer look he saw something very different. Though he was not *yet* an expert ("yet" is key) he still had an experience of "seeing what people had said about this picture and realizing that it was wrong" (P3, 50:42), as a result of having happened upon the 1928 memorandum. Realization in hand though, this oldest project that was initially drafted for a graduate seminar then sat in his papers for a "looooong time," to which he was able to **return** only recently with an assured stance. "So I'm working on this article now and I've been working on it for a while, about whether this is a "queer picture," so to speak." (P3, 27:19). Such a framing was not much present in his graduate seminar, but is one he has acquired as time has passed. Emphasizing what the *passage of time* has done for the art historian's scholarship, this vignette indicates how individual humanities projects are conditioned by prevailing issues, not to mention disciplinary norms, which may make completion very tough in some years but very easy in others. Since the pressure to complete projects is a given condition of humanities research, people prioritize some and delay others.

Stopping has another element in common with Rediscovery, and that is the possibility of a *delayed reaction*:

> "When you have a topic in mind, of course when you're looking in an archive, you always look for the files that are directly related. But as we all know, historically, you may find things elsewhere. So you look for topic X, Y, or Z – clearly delineated in the find books, the archival registers. But you also look for broader categories that might be related. So, anything to do with art, I would have a look, just to see what you might find, because sometimes an unknown document will be related. Then while you're looking, you find other things! I usually take pretty, pretty systematic notes when I'm in an archive. Even if it's material that's not directly related to the given subject. ... I have voluminous reading notes .... 110 pages of reading notes typed out." (P3, 40:27).

A dedicated, painstaking, and energetic archival research process is concomitant with the "just in case" approach to topical study that characterizes art history scholarship as we explore it here. The art historian knowingly faces a vast universe of background material, and the findings from (international) archival research appear to determine when a researcher can move on from having Stopped. In this case, since the art historian knew he had not yet completed his searches, the project was delayed. It was not an easy project with clear boundaries: "I've got a single artist, but I'm not writing a working "life story." He's not the center of the universe I'm interested in, but the context and the discourse around art. In order to understand the discourse around art you have to take broad notes" (P3, 42:48). Humanities research resists containment, as illustrated here. Stopping is a *major* pivot point that many early ideas may never pass, and others only after a delay. How willing are the researchers (and their peers) to (a) move with a smaller scope, or (b) would they rather it wait as a fuller treatment? For art history, "You have to look at the picture, you have to look at the reception. I'm interested in artists as social beings, so who supported them, government files to talk about funding sources or things like that. All of these are part of a social-historical puzzle" (P3, 47:38). Archeologist P6 will offer another example of the latter, in the Rediscovery section. The issue of scope that we first encountered in Noticing, still is present in the pivot point of Stopping, and will appear in full force in Examining. We have revealed two facets of Stopping: collaborators' input and scope-related delayed reaction.

Examining

A classicist describes his item-driven process as one that compels increasing levels of curiosity: "there's moments of wonder that then must transform into moments of doing" (P4, 11:22). The researcher also works in service of today's broad, not narrow, historically-minded goals: "So if you're interested in how contemporaries in the 7th century experienced this apse, I think you have to pay more attention to the words, as well as the visual stuff, the images. So, *this project has been taking me a long time actually*, because I've been trying to think about how a 7th-century viewer would have absorbed that apse" (P4, 27:34, emphasis added). The vignette indicates how the research process in classical humanities is fundamentally molded around research questions that are open-ended, become interlocking, and that necessitate *iterative* use of examination tools for studying multimedia information nuggets in conversation with one another, in an unpredictably synergistic fashion. Curiosity at multiple levels shapes the direction of research questions and answers.

Examining is a matter of negotiating scope. When P3 published an essay on the 1928 memorandum 25 years after seeing it in an archive, the researcher's care to bound its contribution so precisely indicates how they actively set this essay as something apart from their *main* scholarly self-image. To the researcher it fulfills a personal, close-collaborator, and foundational research commitment (no less important to their continuing evolution as a productive scholar): "I was brand new; it moved me, it stuck with me" (P3, 1:20:24). Upon reflecting more broadly, the researcher stated, "That's how my career is, I started with a topic and that became a somewhat different topic than I had imagined, but it produced offshoots that become my next project, and that produces some other little offshoots. Then I decided, "well I've got this [graduate seminar] stuff that I should probably not sit on for the rest of my life." So, I started working it as a side project to the main project." (P3, 1:06:15). We see here the *embedded* nature of discovery, where an early finding remained only an interesting finding known by the researcher (his background problem), until, decades later, it could be revived as a "side project" now well-supported by the foundation of other work that was prioritized instead. We have explored the iterative levels of research with a nugget and the intellectual perspective-building which characterizes Examining in the humanities. Timing influences both.

Capturing

Humanities researchers make use of international collaborative tools as depicted in Figure 2 to capture information; in the case of epigraphy, to generate a core dataset they will subject to further analysis. Capturing and storing such information from databases is somewhat equivalent to adding a book to one's bookshelf; that is, the information is readied and assembled, though it may sit untouched as some time goes by. Such can describe projects with a defined scope, but researchers also approach reference databases or catalog records *not* with a defined goal in mind: "You take your notes sort of openendedly, but then it would help to remember things!" (P3, 46:13). We recall the approach mentioned of "starting in the archives, seeing what the archives yielded." (P3, 54:52).

Asking about a researcher's Capturing process turned out to be the most personal question in our interview protocol. Researchers' notetaking is wrapped up with their thinking strategies both for the project at hand and in general; we might illustrate two ends of this spectrum. On one end, an epigraphy researcher may consult the *ICI* (Figure 3) to define a study around a particular geographic region – this collaborative tool is considered "the nuts and bolts of working with inscriptions" (P4, 19:31) – and further to help complete a main project of studying a Roman pope's stone inscriptions in that region. Both tasks, though now firmly bounded (rather than unbounded as we will see next), proceed essentially organically:

> "The material is embedded in modern corpora and surrounded by other things. While you're looking at some Roman pope material, you might see on the next page something that catches your eye – a few phrases jump out or something like that. So that led to a study of a woman named T. Afrodite, a little. We have her epitaph, full of Vergilian language. *Who is this woman?* She's clearly Christian, but yet it's so full of what we think of as classical echoes and reminiscences" (P4, 14:30, emphasis added).

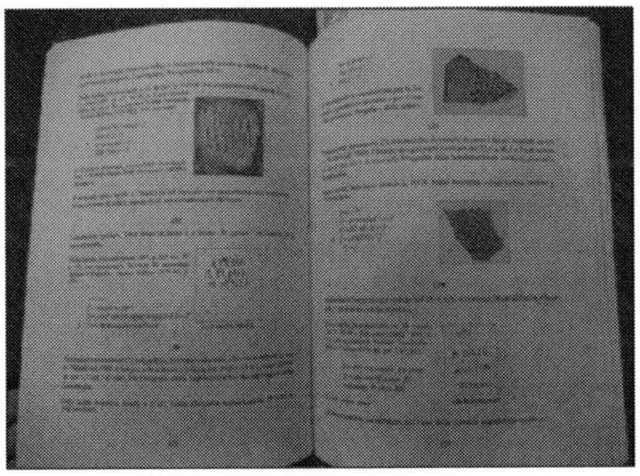

Figure 3. Critical edition of the *Inscriptions of Christian Italy* [ICI] for the city of Milan (with the text, excavation photos, commentary, and translations), part of major corpora produced in the 19th century and a key examination tool in epigraphy research.

The classical studies professor's use of the *ICI* effectively generated the source material with which to pursue his main project around the Roman pope epigrapher. Yet a high-resolution photograph of one stone surfaced (to him) the name and poem of an unfamiliar woman, and he had to pursue a biography of her (completed quickly). The trajectory of ideas illustrated hereby is ever-broadening, though he does not dwell on the mechanics. With heavy use of archival finding aids and collection guidebooks to become oriented to the content of available materials, a researcher's Capturing activities are an intricate step-by-step logbook of discoveries in progress, both mundane and profound.

Away from databases, an important part of one researcher's Capturing activities is to make regular, even daily, written contributions to a paper – portable – folder designed to collect spare notes on a particular long-term project (Figure 4). Academics who work in or adjacent to archeology, or material culture of a region, often find their research process circumscribed by the timing of summer field / study seasons located away from their home campus, even in another country or continent. Three summer months afford the opportunity to spend concentrated time among the excavated material culture of the site at hand, work that might in part or in whole sustain the other nine months of the year. Thus, year-round note-taking forms a crucial roadmap for the summer season

Figure 4. Researcher's project folder, distinguished from her others by regular use of a specific color (green). Shows one day's worth of notes, alongside Munsell Soil Book used to identify soil color anywhere.

allowing researchers to plan out day-to-day specific onsite research or study plans; writing such notes is an important aspect of plotting the trajectory of a particular project. An archeologist finds that after studying a site's material collection for decades, her task list for the summer months is increasingly intricate as the associated publication completion timeline nears (and as key collaborators age):

> "I keep a running list: 'When next there, look at this, pull this out, check this, compare these two figurines, I think they might be the same.' I see them in my sleep. There's so much material, and there's so many things that are worthy of being separate articles" (P6, 47:16).

Furthermore, since the summer field season attracts – from all over the world – students, local and non-local archeologists, specialists, and prospective team members, research is a collaborative effort and publication plans are made collectively not individually (even if subsequent writing is indeed completed individually). The Capturing stage as we have explored it is characterized by tool-based note-taking and research-team communication.

Returning

Humanities researchers not only "balance" (or one might read, keep active) multiple scholarly projects but they adroitly detailed in our interviews how the nature of their information encountering is embedded in the wider superstructure of *time* which they negotiate to conduct research. For some, projects arrive with varied time-lengths circumscribed: an art historian described three: a decade-long monograph, a medium-sized project applying a gendered analysis to a painting, and a single handwritten letter. Over two decades after discovering that letter (in 1992), the researcher commandeered an essay venue to publish his finding: "I've always wanted to talk about this … it has been one of those documents that I've never forgotten." (1:15:50). In addition to that venue, it is parsed in his forthcoming second book: "It became a full-time project in probably 2008, 2009, when I worked on it really, really hard. I had given a few talks at various places and hearing how the response was, then decided at a certain point, 'Okay. Time to actually publish something about this." (P3, 57:57). The time investment to complete the essay project in 2009 turned out not to be lengthy, but only by then were the essential pieces in place – with total focus on the task, it was soon done.

From this research narrative we see not only the embedded nature of IE within a soup of projects a humanities researcher claims at any one time, but also we see that such discoveries require both a sustained commitment and an opportune *match* to a dissemination outlet that can take years or decades to manifest. Of course, the researcher herself controls and makes choices about the kinds of venues under consideration; such choices (not to Stop) may leave the discovery lying in a dormancy period (Buchanan, Bossaller, & Erdelez, 2018) while the researcher prioritizes another project. Completion or publication of that project avails the time to Notice the dormant discovery and make it active once again. We find that the dormancy period is active rather than stagnant, and temporary rather than permanent. It is that *temporal* nature of humanities-based discovery – the time-lengths and the oblique connections to other projects so specific to one researcher – that many of our respondents' interviews have enabled us to articulate.

Rediscovery and the Role of Time Gaps

We have thus far analyzed five stages of IE identified in a framework created from a broad base of information acquisition behaviors. The model lacks one additional component that must be added to fully comprehend humanities research: Rediscovery. The original model well-depicts a single IE episode, but we have seen across multiple stages how humanities projects overlap (start, delay) due to the unnamed element of time, and cannot be understood in isolation. "For better or for worse I don't oftentimes or frequently write things up right away. *There are so many interesting things that* [get no time]. … It was something that interested me but didn't fit into anything I was doing at the time" (P3, 1:20:45, emphasis added). With time came a perfect venue for something the researcher never lost interest in. That time arrives in waves through will and effort, e.g.: "Getting a research grant for a different topic but carving out two or three days" (P3, 35:49) to gather materials *for* their main project. Deciding to focus completely on a side project does not preclude a crucial element for the person's main project from appearing; as in P3's example here of grant-funded research travel and P6's reading group breakthrough earlier, two projects can advance simultaneously.

Rediscovery can be spurred on by events seemingly far outside the researcher's control that encircle and palter with the researcher's original work such that he or she must respond in some way to stay current or retain support. Practical urgency can reveal an underpinning of student-teacher collaboration in humanities research:

> "We were all talking about ways to make our subject matter more appealing to a broader and more diverse group of people and students. Particularly when we're dealing with all these old dead white guys. I was teaching a class, so I guess it really came down to the class. … There's been a lot of work increasingly done, particularly in the UK, on the reception of Greek drama in various places. And I came across a play by Athol Fugard from South Africa called *The Island*" (10:20).

The researcher goes on to add that the next time he taught this class, he "focused on Greek drama in Africa and the African diaspora almost exclusively. I was finding things all the time. That's great. … Why is it that a Nigerian playwright would choose to use a Greek model?" (P5, 11:28). This last question opened a new line of inquiry that seeped into his teaching. We might constructively acknowledge that most humanities discoveries – even the dormant ones – are marked throughout their gestation by urgent response to a trigger that finally arrives. Teaching occurred here in a rapidly changing research environment (a college campus with activist students) that ultimately gave a scholar's work depth, import, immediacy, and resonance.

Findings suggest that Rediscovery is *stronger with* the passage of time. One researcher detailed exactly what happens after alighting on a new playwright's name:

> "Then I started thinking back: Wole Soyinka is a Nigerian playwright who's done a version of *The Bacchae*. He actually spoke here a few years ago and I'd never paid much attention to it. I went looking at that, and people who were writing about Soyinka were also writing about another Nigerian, Femi Osofisan, who's done *several* Greek dramas. So, I started reading *those* and then I realized, 'wait a minute, there's more there.' Reading one leads to another" (P5, 21:02).

Attendance at a campus colloquium in the above case was not the trigger, but out of the background it reappeared and motivated the researcher's new foreground problem. Earlier we saw humanists add books to their bookshelves, where books might then sit. In the humanities, Rediscovery is uniquely embedded in such Capturing activities in some form. The initial Capture (note) of a brilliant discovery may first take shape not as a piece of writing at all, but as a remark made during lecture: "I think the first form of recording it [my discovery] was on a syllabus for a class" (P5, 27:35). Once verbalized, that embryonic nugget of discovery seeped again into another of the researcher's scholarly efforts: an already-scheduled conference presentation (that characteristically was on a tightly related theme):

> "I came back to town [from an academic library visit] the end of February and CAMWS was in April and there I gave a talk about some of these plays I had been working on. It was really, really nice! Two attendees were just so *thrilled* – one young faculty member and one graduate student just said after, 'Why haven't we heard about this stuff and why can't we do all this [future work]?' It felt like, okay, that's exactly what I'm doing now" (P5, 28:42).

Here we see that even with his discovery only weeks old, the researcher commandeered his conference presentation (in place from active interests, thus at reduced distance from background-to-foreground) to share it in a formative stage; in doing so, he gained respect from more junior peers, affirming feedback, and an energized project. We must underscore how this collegial, very collaborative moment (between a speaker and active listeners) – in combination of course with the discovery that had happened in a library – ultimately *moved* (in a literal and affective way) the endeavor from the periphery to the center of his ongoing research program: "Okay, that's exactly what I'm doing now."

Finally, in contrast to this fast-moving vignette, another brought up the necessity of slow and careful work when Rediscovering a legacy archeological project:

> "We're integrating a limited set of new excavations with the existing archive from an excavation that I was part of originally, not too long ago in 2006-2007. Great results, but unfortunately the project kind of collapsed for various reasons and it's never been brought to proper publication. … We're eventually going to publish – it's a little challenging – both the results from the excavations in the 2000s and the current work. So, you know, I've been reaching out to former participants and staff members if they want to join" (8:59). "Starting to re-analyze and re-excavate what I did, and then parts of the site that were never (well, since the late 1800s) touched before. I know where the problems are" (P2, 49:03).

Rediscovery is a sixth stage of IE unique to the humanities, where projects are embedded rather than isolated occurrences, fully responsive to external urgencies, and move at the speed of collaboration (i.e., fast, and slow).

HUMANITIES KEY CONTRIBUTIONS: EMBEDDEDNESS, TEMPORALITY, AND SOME ALTRUISM, WITH DISCOVERY AS THEIR BYPRODUCT

The model's addition of a Rediscovery component serves as a bridge to discussing two superstructural qualities of time in our topic of humanities-based IE: embeddedness and the shape of altruism. Vignettes from the respondents capture how time-based elements of each stage appear and reappear across research projects conducted in the humanities disciplines of art history and archeology: "So for me the research process is all very organic. There's a certain serendipity involved to be sure" (P3, 39:29). We have complicated the idea of IE by surfacing *embedded support* structures that, when in place, facilitate humanities discoveries. As that same researcher later qualified, "my find was not entirely serendipitous because of course [European artist] is a major figure. There was a reason I was looking through his letters, and I talk about him in my book, even if he's not the primary focus. The result was then a [short six-page] essay." (P3, 1:04:47). Support was present in the form of Capture tools and interconnected topics whose productive overlap becomes apparent when we can map their progression through models based on Figure 1. Alternatively, one researcher offered their own topic quantification: "There are always four or five projects. That's a drag in a way, because you have to go back and forth and you have to remember what you were doing on this project before you went to that project. But it's just the reality." "Of things that are in process [the most recent] began nine months ago. I joined two other people in a project that they already had underway. Everything else is a couple of years old and in various stages." (P4, 1:28:20). Collaborative projects arise during individual work, and timing of both can be realigned. Topical scope is similarly hugely important to such projects, particularly at the pivot of moving past Stopping.

Researchers expended resources of time (scheduling days for library visits or for writing) that might trigger the discovery of a nugget the researcher could use immediately, or Capture for later. While we gathered a few vignettes of actual project completion, more frequent were vignettes of "active dormancy," where a project was ultimately pushed to the background while a foreground problem was addressed first. Depending on the iterative level of Examination in that foreground project, or perhaps collaborators' input during Capture (and jotting-down of that input since semantic memory is lossy), a second foreground project arose, or time allowed for the background-in-waiting to become foreground. Future attention by the IE and IB communities to "active dormancy" will enhance task analysis research.

Apart from the mere act of releasing scholarly writing, a more tactile instance where true altruism happens is in graduate (and undergraduate) school, between students and their professors. Like classicist P5 sharing his discovery with eager listeners at CAMWS, an archeologist willingly shares nuggets with his students: "At the fieldsite there's a very pyramidal structure; a lot of eager, junior staff members want to be assigned more. So that's where we share first. My senior colleagues coordinate these problems: 'Here's an interesting object or idea or topic or part / chunk of the site that we would like you to study.' This becomes part of the publication pipeline: it starts as individual research projects to presentations at conferences then morphs into something else." (P2, 1:20:40). While this instance of sharing takes place within a formal collaborative structure and in a vertical direction, altruistic sharing of potential research discoveries is essential to the total success of that structure. We see the supervisors "coordinating" the assignment of suspected new discoveries to particular students, who are given agency to develop deeply a topic into a reasonable direction of their choosing. Once the student's topic reaches some maturity (i.e., following conference feedback) the senior colleague returns to integrate the particular finding into the greater story of the field site. Recalling the reading group which unlocked an article and book theme for P6, the large team size of archeological fieldwork leverages the chance of making a new discovery by putting many people's individual skills and talents to use. Research altruism in the humanities – especially with ideas in embryonic form – through in-person conference interactions, graduate seminars, or seasonal teams is the momentum unlocking next discoveries. Amending the existing IE active search model with three new proposed factors of embeddedness, temporality, and altruism promises to better inform the provision of support and time allowances for researchers and their students.

CONCLUSION

Above we noted how previous research has established the importance of place and peers in fostering an IE experience. To these factors, we can add time: the "active dormancy" period that we have described occurs after Returning and before the second instance of Stopping (Figure 1), and is a unique aspect of humanities research. Overall the clearer picture we provide of what encountering new information in the humanities looks like, can be contrasted with prior work on serendipity in scientific research: humanities research operates on longer time spans, and serendipitous events occur at each stage of that time. But since it is not systematic, our pedagogical insights can raise future humanists' awareness of conditions and their own preparedness (while in the library, coffee shop, or field site) for Noticing; our findings may reconfigure how new research projects are initiated. Our work may help illumine wider research into productivity and the production of knowledge especially in the humanities. While even humanists themselves may only begrudgingly accept such time-lengths, and strive effortfully to reduce them, a final vignette drives home their control by incentives in place that structure the work: "Most of us run into reviews of things that say, 'Oh, well Joe missed that publication that came out three months before his was published.' Joe didn't miss it. Joe couldn't put it in, it's just [too late]!" (P4, 1:31:32). It exemplifies how the speed at which we – both researchers and the public – consume research is so much faster than the speed at which it is produced in the humanities.

While five stages were present in the research accounts our respondents offered, three surprising and textured qualities emerged, altering our depiction and explication of how the IE model functions: embeddedness, temporality, and altruism. A large amount of tangential storytelling and topic exploration surrounding each stage episode is unique to the humanities and was not hinted at in related literature. The background-to-foreground switch itself might be most prevalent in academic contexts – professors receive requests that "interrupt" the flow of their foreground work regularly, serendipity being one of them. In particular, we found that the embeddedness of a discovery *in the normal process of humanities work* nearly guarantees that its dormancy will only be temporary (unlike some discoveries in natural sciences that are treated as isolated disruptions). A serendipitous discovery can fuel a whole career for a humanist given enough time. It is worthy of recognition and recall.

APPENDIX: INTERVIEW PROTOCOL

Introduction

1. What is your research about?
2. Think of a situation when you stumbled upon something interesting (important, relevant) for your research?
3. What were you doing / trying to achieve?
   a. Evaluate the context of situation:

- what was the research problem/activity they were engaged in
- were they looking for something specific, browsing, exploring, routine research activity
- where were they (what was the physical setting)
- when did it happen (how long ago, time of the year, time of the day)
- who they were with (other people around)

Critical Incident

4. What caught your attention? What made this instance different from all other possible interesting things you may stumble upon (wrong color, wrong shape, triggered memory…)
5. What were you thinking/feeling when you oriented on the object/item?
6. Did you hesitate about diverting from original goal? Why yes/not?
7. Did you explore/examine what you stumbled upon? When did this happen?
8. How much time did you devote to it?
9. What were you thinking/feeling when examining it?
10. Were other people involved in this process?
11. What did you do with the nugget (find of interest)?
12. How did you record information about it? (take a photo, sketch in the journal, take measurements, etc.)
13. Did you use it in your work/research? What does using mean to you?
14. Do you plan to use it, when?
15. After devoting time to this nugget, did you return to the initial activity?
16. Did you integrate it in your research/career?

Wrap Up

17. Have you experienced similar situation before/after this event?
18. How do you develop your research agenda? (free choice, impact of advisor, funding, regional presence, organizational culture/history of department, field)
19. What's the time span of a particular project?
20. How much overlap between your projects?
21. What do you consider to be a project? (object study, publication goal, collaborative partnership)
22. Do you have flexibility in adjusting your schedule?
23. Do you tend to share hints etc. about things you stumble upon and are relevant to someone else's research?

REFERENCES

Buchanan, S. A., Bossaller, S., & Erdelez, S. (2018). Information encountering by an art historian: A methodological case study. In *Proceedings of ASIS&T*, *55*, 762–764. https://doi.org/10.1002/pra2.2018.14505501106

Copeland, S. (2019). On serendipity in science: Discovery at the intersection of chance and wisdom. *Synthese*, *196*(6), 2385–2406. https://doi.org/10.1007/s11229-017-1544-3

Erdelez, S. (2000). *Towards Understanding Information Encountering on the Web*. In *Proceedings of the 63rd Annual Meeting of ASIS* 37, 363-371.

Erdelez, S. (2004). Investigation of information encountering in the controlled research environment. *Information Processing & Management*, *40*(6), 1013–1025. https://doi.org/10.1016/j.ipm.2004.02.002

Foster, A., & Ford, N. (2003). Serendipity and information seeking: An empirical study. *Journal of Documentation*, *59*(3), 321–340. https://doi.org/10.1108/00220410310472518

Liuzzo, P. M. (2018). EAGLE continued: IDEA. The International Digital Epigraphy Association. In A. De Santis & I. Rossi, *Crossing experiences in digital epigraphy: From practice to discipline* (Vol. *17*, pp. 216–230). Warsaw, Poland: De Gruyter. https://doi.org/10.1515/9783110607208-018

Makri, S., Bhuiya, J., Carthy, J., & Owusu-Bonsu, J. (2015). Observing serendipity in digital information environments. In *Proceedings of ASIS&T* (Vol. *52*, pp. 1–10). https://doi.org/10.1002/pra2.2015.145052010019

Makri, S., & Blandford, A. (2012). Coming across information serendipitously – Part 1: A process model. *Journal of Documentation*, *68*(5), 684–705. https://doi.org/10.1108/00220411211256030

Makri, S., Blandford, A., Woods, M., Sharples, S., & Maxwell, D. (2014). "Making my own luck": Serendipity strategies and how to support them in digital information environments. *JASIST*, *65*(11), 2179–2194. https://doi.org/10.1002/asi.23200

Makri, S., Ravem, M., & McKay, D. (2017). After serendipity strikes: Creating value from encountered information. In *Proceedings of ASIS&T*, *54*, 279–288. https://doi.org/10.1002/pra2.2017.14505401031

Martin, K., Greenspan, B., & Quan-Haase, A. (2017). STAK – Serendipitous tool for augmenting knowledge: A conceptual tool for bridging digital and physical resources. *Digital Studies/le Champ Numérique*, *9*. https://doi.org/10.16995/dscn.265

Martin, K., & Quan-Haase, A. (2016). The role of agency in historians' experiences of serendipity in physical and digital information environments. *Journal of Documentation*, *72* (6), 1008–1026. https://doi.org/10.1108/JD-11-2015-0144

Martin, K., & Quan-Haase, A. (2017). "A process of controlled serendipity": An exploratory study of historians' and digital historians' experiences of serendipity in digital environments. In *Proceedings of ASIS&T*, *54*, 289–297. https://doi.org/10.1002/pra2.2017.14505401032

McCay-Peet, L., & Toms, E. G. (2015). Investigating serendipity: How it unfolds and what may influence it. *Journal of the Association for Information Science and Technology*, *66*(7), 1463–1476. https://doi.org/10.1002/asi.23273

McCay-Peet, L., & Toms, E. G. (2017). Researching serendipity in digital information environments. *Synthesis Lectures on Information Concepts, Retrieval, and Services*, *9* (6), i–91. https://doi.org/10.2200/S00790ED1V01Y201707ICR059

Siegfried, S., Bates, M. J., & Wilde, D. N. (1993, June). A profile of end-user searching behavior by humanities scholars: The Getty Online Searching Project Report No. 2. *Journal of the Association for Information Science*, *44*(5), 273–291.

Singer, J. A. (2004). Narrative identity and meaning making across the adult lifespan: An introduction. *Journal of Personality*, *72*(3), 437–460. https://doi.org/10.1111/j.0022-3506.2004.00268.x

Trace, C. B., & Karadkar, U. P. (2017). Information management in the humanities: Scholarly processes, tools, and the construction of personal collections. *Journal of the Association for Information Science and Technology*, *68*(2), 491–507. https://doi.org/10.1002/asi.23678

A Comparative Study of Domestic and Cross-Country Impact of Chinese and U.S. Publications in Chemistry

Xiaojing Cai
Zhejiang University
Hangzhou, China
cai_xj@zju.edu.cn

Xiaozan Lyu
Zhejiang University
Hangzhou, China
lvxz1991@zju.edu.cn

Ping Zhou
Zhejiang University
Hangzhou, China
pingzhou@zju.edu.cn

ABSTRACT

Based on publications in Chemistry in 2015, this paper investigated the citation impact on domestic and foreign scholarly communities of Chinese and US publications, and to what extent does such impact relate to international collaboration and government funding. First- or corresponding authorship in international collaboration is defined as dominance and is taken into consideration. Citations to publications are designated as domestic citations (Chinese or US citations), partner citations or other citations according to overlap of countries of citing and cited publications. Significant difference exists in the two countries. Most citations of Chinese publications are from domestic and partner countries, with domestic citations being the mainstay. In contrast, US papers receive more other citations than domestic or partner citations, and citations from partner countries contribute significantly. US papers have higher global impact than those of China. High domestic citation propensity is associated with non-international collaboration, dominance of focal country in international collaboration, and national funding support. Such phenomenon is more pronounced in Chinese papers. In other words, citation impact of Chinese publications is more limited in domestic community, whereas that of the US is more global.

KEYWORDS

Domestic Impact; Cross-Country Impact; Citation Impact; Evaluation

ASIS&T THESAURUS

Scientometrics; Citation Impact; Self Citation

INTRODUCTION

In bibliometrics studies, researchers tend to evaluate the research performance of nations' scientific outputs based on indicators such as mean citation counts (Albarrán, Perianes-Rodríguez, & Ruiz-Castillo, 2015), mean normalized citation indicators (De Moya-Anegon, Guerrero-Bote, Lopez-Illescas, & Moed, 2018; Herranz & Ruiz-Castillo, 2012; Marshall & Travis, 2011), shares of world citations (Gonzalez-Brambila, Reyes-Gonzalez, Veloso, & Perez-Angón, 2016), shares of highly cited papers in the world (Bornmann & Wagner, 2015; Leydesdorff, Wagner, & Bornmann, 2014; Rodríguez-Navarro & Brito, 2018), etc. Among the mass of studies, however, indicators used might be inadequate enough to reflect the global impact of national outputs, because such indicators might be biased to some extent due to the clubbing effect (Tang, Shapira, & Youtie, 2015) or so-called country over-citations (Bakare & Lewison, 2017), that is, researchers tend to cite themselves at individual, institutional or country level, thus resulting in somewhat inflated citation counts.

The existence of excessive national self-citations in many countries has been confirmed in existing studies. From the cited side (cited references), Mervis (2012) found that Asian scientists were increasingly citing Asian papers, and in the reference lists of Asian papers, the visibility of Asian references was about to equal that of EU and US references. During the period of 1980–1996, about 40% of the references and citations of European papers were other European outputs, and for US, the percentage of US references in the references of US papers were even higher (about 60%) (Larivière, Gong, & Sugimoto, 2018). From the citing side (citing articles), high percentage of citations from the same country (namely rate of country self-citation) can be observed. For example, 47% and 37% of the citations to Chinese and US papers were from their own countries (Larivière et al., 2018), and about 52% and 36%, respectively, to Chinese and US highly cited papers in nanotechnology were also detected (Tang et al., 2015). Jaffe (2011) also observed high rates of country self-citations in various countries. Furthermore, Gingras and Khelfaoui (2018) reported obvious national citation bias in both publications with or without international collaboration of the US, UK, Germany, Canada and France in selected fields, that is, publications of these countries are more visible in their own countries than their presence measured as their world shares of research output.

High rate of national self-citations is dependent on the volume of national scientific output. In general, the more papers

82nd Annual Meeting of the Association for Information Science & Technology | Melbourne, Australia | 19–23 October, 2019

DOI: 10.1002/pra2.00005

a country publishes, the more likely that authors cite domestic research output, thus leading to higher self-citation counts and self-citation rates of the country (Jaffe, 2011; Minasny, Hartemink, & McBratney, 2010). Self-citation rates at country level are also more related to research topics that favor regional studies or national interests, publication date and the applied or basic sciences (Bakare & Lewison, 2017). Language also plays a part (Egghe, Rousseau, & Yitzhaki, 1999; Ren & Rousseau, 2002). However, for a country, high self-citation rate might imply lower citation impact (Jaffe, 2011); Bornmann, Adams and Leydesdorff (2018) also found similar results that in the Netherlands and Germany, less-cited research are more likely to build on domestic research, and on the contrary, those more cited tend to base on international research. Researchers' insufficient attention on quality when citing others might be one of the possible reasons. But after all, it is not appropriate to arbitrarily equate high self-citation rates or more references to domestic literature as less influential. When assessing the global influence of a nation, we think it is better to consider citations from other nations as well. National Science Board (2018, Chapter 5) had done similarly by analyzing the share of foreign citations to selected countries or economies and relative citations among country pairs, which enhances understandings of relative impact of a country's impact to the other one or other countries. Hassan and Haddawy (2013) also considered foreign citations to compare countries' ability of attracting citations made by researchers from outside the country, so as to measure the international impact of countries. Following this idea, we will analyze the citation impact of countries combing citations from both domestic and international sources.

Among the many factors associated with domestic and international citations, there are some factors about collaboration and funding at micro level. For example, papers co-authored by researchers from different countries were more cited (Puuska, Muhonen, & Leino, 2014; Sooryamoorthy, 2009; Zhou & Glänzel, 2010). This is possibly because of better quality of internationally collaborated research, or due to the fact that the more authors, institutions, and countries, the wider audiences and higher possibilities of being cited by domestic and international researchers. Similarly, Gingras and Khelfaoui (2018) found that countries' domestic papers without international collaboration were more visible and cited more in home countries than internationally collaborative papers. Whether or not being the home country of first or corresponding author's country (i.e., international dominance) may influence the origin of citing countries: internationally collaborated publications dominated by a nation might resemble domestic publications more, thus related to higher national citation bias than those not dominated by the nation. As for funding, previous research about Chemistry publications suggests lower proportion of internationally collaborated publications in funded datasets, indicating that funding appears to be more supportive of or more effective in supporting domestic research (Zhou & Cai, 2018). In addition, there is a negative interaction effect between government funding and international collaboration in raising the citation impact for some countries (Zhou, et al., 2019). Hence, it is reasonable to predict that national funding might also show a bias toward domestic citations. In this paper we focus on National Natural Science Foundation of China (NSFC) and National Science Foundation in the US (NSF) to investigate how government funding affects the origins of citations. Such practice of focusing only one source of government funding might not be suitable. Because publications might receive funding support from multiple sources at the same time, and it may be other funding agencies rather than targeted funders that play a part; besides, effect of funding on publications may vary a lot or even not exist. Nevertheless, due to the important roles of NSFC and NSF in their focal countries, comparison between publications funded and unfunded is able to suggest the possibility of national funding's affecting the national orientation in citations.

This paper takes publications in Chemistry as research object. Chemistry is targeted due to several reasons: first, Chemistry is a traditional and mature discipline, with long history of literature and stable publishing practice and citation pattern. Second, our previous study about Chemistry research revealed higher average citation counts of Chinese internationally collaborated publications than that of US internationally collaborated publications, as well as inactivity of national funding in supporting international collaboration in both countries (Zhou & Cai, 2018). This paper will further investigate the citation distribution of China and the USA in Chemistry to enhance the understanding of Chinese and US research output.

Thus, the research questions are as follows:

- What is the distribution of domestic and cross-country impact reflected in citations of Chinese and US research output in Chemistry?
- To what extent do the domestic and cross-country impact relate to international collaboration, country of first- or corresponding authors in international collaboration, as well as the government funding?

The present study examines the above questions by comparing domestic and cross-country impact of publications with or without the above mentioned factors. More precisely, in this study we aim first, to contribute the understanding of the global influence of national output (i.e., China and the USA in this paper). Researchers usually evaluate the research production of nations via integrated citation indicators, which might reflect only limited aspects of the impact of a country's research publications. When country origins of citations are taken into consideration, we are able to consider another aspect of impact – international impact as well when assessing impact of nations.

Second, we are interested in whether and how collaborating with other countries and national government funding affects the citations of publications. Clarifying the above relationship (if exists) also help provide implications for research community and stakeholders about better international collaboration and government funding support.

METHODOLOGY

Data were downloaded from Web of Science (WoS) Clarivate Analytics. Bibliometrics data consists of two parts: first, publications (articles and reviews) in 2015 in Chemistry with affiliations in either China or the USA. Chemistry is defined by the seven Chemistry categories in JCR: Chemistry, Analytical; Chemistry, Applied; Chemistry, Inorganic & Nuclear; Chemistry, Medical; Chemistry, Multidisciplinary; Chemistry, Organic; Chemistry, Physical. Second, citing articles in 3 years since the publishing year, namely, in 2015–2017. All of the cited and citing articles are designated with one or more countries according to the addresses of authors. Taiwan of China is regarded as a separated region (in fact part of China), and meanwhile, England, Wales, North Ireland and Scotland are incorporated into UK.

Cited publications are classified bimodally into:

- Internationally collaborated publications (IC), or Non-internationally collaborated publications (NIC), according to whether co-authored by authors from 2 or more countries;
- China (or US)-dominated publications (DIC), or China (or US)-not-dominated publications (NDIC), based on whether Chinese (or US) author acts as first- or corresponding-author in IC; and
- Funded or unfunded, based on whether NSFC (or NSF) funding exists in the funding acknowledgement.

Raw citation counts in 3 years rather than normalized indicators are used in this study for two reasons. First, cited publications in this study were published in the same year and in the same discipline (although broader), therefore differences in citation behaviors among sub-disciplines exist but might be comparatively lesser. Second, we focus mainly on citations made by authors from domestic countries (China or USA), partner countries and other countries (illustrated later), and these citations are comparable and more suitable for calculating number and proportions of citations. Proportions of citations using normalized indicators are meaningless.

For publications with authors from a single country (NIC), it is easy to define domestic and cross-country citations according to the existence of the focal country in countries of citing articles. However, for internationally collaborated publications (IC), some terms of citation origins should be clearly defined in order to illustrate the distributions of citations in both countries and avoid confusion. Hence, *Domestic & Partner citations* and *Other citations* of every publication are defined as follows:

Domestic & partner citations	Domestic citations	Citations made by domestic researchers, i.e., authors from *China (or USA)*
	Partner citations	Citations made by researchers from partner countries (that co-exist with domestic country in the addresses of a cited paper)
Other citation		Citations made by researchers from other countries (that are not mentioned among the addresses of a cited paper)

Table 1. Definition of citations.

For IC, *Domestic & partner citations* are country self-citations in broader sense; for NIC, *Domestic citations* equal to *Domestic & partner citations* since there are no partner countries or partner citations for NIC. Moreover, rather than individual or institutional meaning, "self-citations" mentioned later in the paper refer to country-level citations. T test is used to compare mean citations of NIC and IC, NDIC and DIC.

RESULTS

In 2015, there were 53,899 and 28,849 Chinese and US articles in Chemistry, of which 40,114 (74%) and 9,358 (31%) were supported by NSFC and NSF funding, respectively. NIC are the majority in both countries, no matter in all or NSFC/NSF-funded datasets, especially for China (over 80%). Compared with all datasets, the shares of IC in NSFC- and NSF-datasets are 2.4% and 11.4% lower respectively. Moreover, in the NSFC/NSF-funded publications, Chinese and US DIC account for 90% and 64%, higher than that in all datasets by 17 and 21 percent points. Thus, as far as the number of the publications is concerned, NSFC and NSF are less active in supporting international collaboration, or, the roles of NSFC and NSF in supporting domestic research are more pronounced (Zhou & Cai, 2018). Similarly, both funding agencies are more domestic-oriented in supporting international collaboration reflected by higher proportions of DIC (Table 2).

		China	China NSFC	US	US NSF
Share (%)	NIC	81.3	84.7	57.5	68.9
	IC	18.7	15.3	42.5	31.1
	NDIC / IC	26.8	9.9	56.8	35.6
	DIC / IC	73.2	90.1	43.2	64.4
Citations per paper	NIC	10.2	11.2	12.2	13.7
	IC	16.4	17.0	14.6	16.5
	NDIC	19.0	22.5	13.4	15.2
	DIC	15.4	16.3	16.1	17.2
Share of HCP* (%)	NIC	1.5	1.8	2.3	2.8
	IC	4.3	4.5	3.4	4.0
	NDIC	5.8	8.4	2.8	3.4
	DIC	3.8	4.0	4.2	4.3

Table 2. Basic profile.

*HCP: ESI highly cited papers.

In general, the citation impact of IC is higher than that of NIC in both China and US, according to the mean citations per paper and shares of HCP. When only IC are considered, publications dominated by China (DIC) show a lower impact than those not, while in the US the opposite is true—US DIC exhibit higher citations than NDIC. Such result indicates obvious citation advantage of Chinese IC and China's dependence on collaborating with others in terms of average citation impact. While for the US, NIC perform only slightly inferior than IC, and, US's dominance in IC is related to higher citation impact, suggesting excellence of US in scientific research. Publications funded by NSFC in China and NSF in the US are more cited than those not funded, regardless of types of international collaboration and dominance, indicating that NSFC and NSF contribute to increasing the overall impact of national output, or relate to higher research performance (Table 2). Further, it is interesting to notice the citation gap between Chinese and US IC: although Chinese papers show lower citation impact than US in general (including IC and NIC), Chinese IC receive more citations than US IC, and it is publications dominated by partner countries (i.e., DIC) that contribute significantly to the citation gap.

International Collaboration and Citing Orientation

As far as number of citations concerned, IC in both countries show higher Total citations than NIC, yet citation gap comes from different types of citations (Figure 1a, c). Chinese IC are more cited because of overall more cites from domestic & partner, and other countries. US IC's citations advantage over NIC mainly originates from higher *Domestic & partner citations* than NIC, with *Other citations* of NIC and IC of the same level. In more details, *Domestic citations* of IC are less than that of NIC, however, *Partner citations* (in IC) offset the citation gap and greatly contribute to the IC's *Domestic & partner citations*.

According to t test, the differences between mean citations (for all the types) of NIC and IC are significant ($p < .05$) in a and c.

If higher citations of IC are resulted from better quality of internationally collaborated research, it is reasonable to expect same or similar shares of domestic and cross-country citations of IC and NIC. Therefore, we investigate further the difference between shares of domestic and cross-country citations in NIC and IC.

In Chinese case, 62% of citations to IC are *Domestic citations*, and 73% are *Domestic & partner citations*. For NIC, 70% of citations are *Domestic (& partner) citations*, significantly lower than 73% and much higher than 62%. The shares of *Other citations* in NIC and IC are almost the same (about 40%) (Figure 1b, d). From this point of view, by collaborating with other countries, China gains more visibility in partner countries. The citation advantage (raw counts) of Chinese IC over NIC results mainly from the growing *Partner citations* and *Other citations*, with *Domestic citations* fall

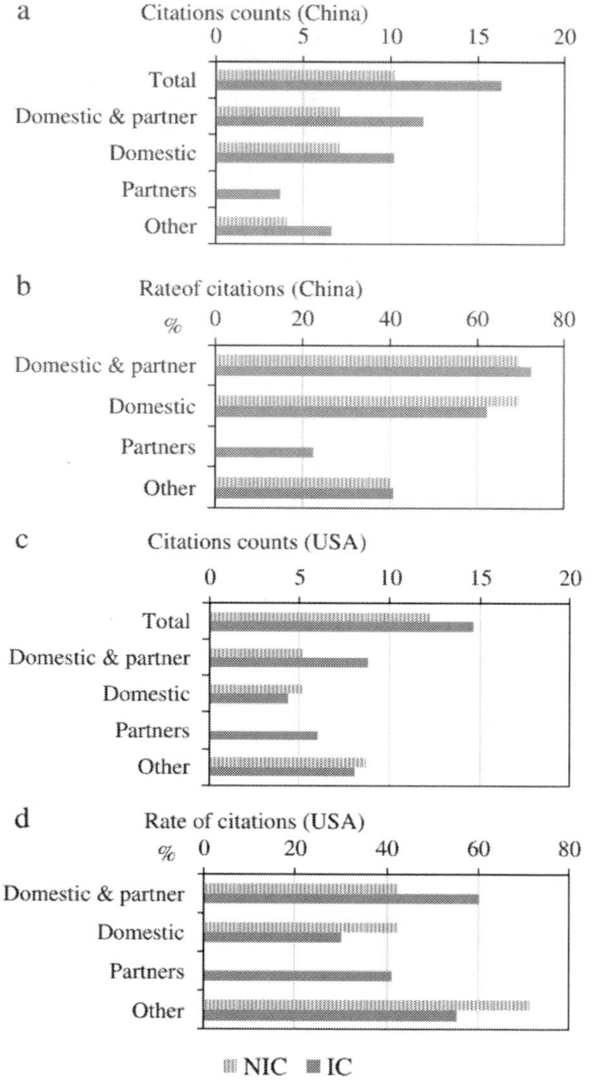

Figure 1. Numbers and shares of domestic and cross-country citations for NIC and IC.

* According to t test, the difference between mean citations of NDIC and DIC are significant ($p < .05$) except for the citations from China for Chinese NDIC and DIC.

a bit in terms of citation share. The situation in the US is somewhat different: the share of *Domestic & partner citations* of IC is 18 percent points higher than that of NIC, while the share of *Other citations* is 15 percent points lower than that of NIC. Moreover, of the high share of *Domestic & partner citations* of IC (60%), a large part (41%) is associated with *Partner citations* and only a shrinking share (30%) is *Domestic citations*. As a result, *Partners* in international collaboration are the main contributors of relatively high citations of IC compared with NIC in US, and US IC publications are less recognized by domestic researchers and other nations than NIC (Figure 1b, d).

As for "self-citations" (*Domestic & partner citations*) and *Other citations*, the majority of Chinese NIC and IC's citations are self-citations from domestic & partner countries (70%); about 90% of the IC's *Domestic & partner citations* are also China's domestic citations. Nevertheless, citations involving other countries (not mentioned among the addresses of cited publications) account for much smaller share (40%). Therefore, for Chinese papers, regardless of with or without international collaboration, citations are largely derived from China's own counterparts. For US NIC and IC, however, citations from other countries account for 71% and 56%, much higher or similar compared with shares of *Domestic & partner citations* (43% and 60%). Among the *Domestic & partner citations* of IC, 50% are generated by US citing publications and 68% are by partner countries. Hence, it seems that US publications are cited more openly and in wider range than Chinese publications: citations from partner or other countries take up a larger share of total citations, and partner countries are the main players of the *Domestic & partner citations* in IC. In view of large share of within-country citations, the global influence of Chinese papers is clearly lower than that of the US, although the average raw citations of Chinese IC have surpassed that of the US IC (Table 2).

International Dominance and Citing Orientation

The above findings are more prominent when comparing NDIC and DIC. In terms of number of citations, there is no visible difference in the *Domestic citations* between Chinese NDIC and DIC, while the *Partner citations* and *Other citations* of NDIC are higher than those of DIC, namely, IC publications that are dominated by authors from partner countries are cited more by partner countries and other countries. US DIC take the lead versus NDIC in terms of *Total*, *Domestic* and *Other citations* in IC, showing that publications dominated by US are more recognized by researchers of US and other nations. Therefore, Chinese DIC are less cited than NDIC because of relatively few citations from partner countries and other countries (foreign countries to China), whereas for the US, DIC that benefit from high US *Domestic citations* and *Other citations* are more cited than NDIC (Figure 2a, c):

As for shares of citations, DIC or NDIC's contrast between shares of *Domestic & partner citations* and *Other citation*, and contrast between shares of *Domestic citations* and *Partner citations* are similar as IC's contrast for both countries. However, there are some subtle difference. Difference between DIC and NDIC is not visible for the share of *Domestic & partner citations* for both countries though, DIC show a higher share of *Domestic citations* than NDIC, as well as a lower proportion of *Partner citations* accordingly. This indicates a greater contribution of focal countries (China or USA) to share of *Domestic & partner citations* in DIC, or more pronounced national citation propensity in DIC than in NDIC. Another point is that, *Other citations* account for even a lower share when dominated by China, but higher share in US-dominated IC (Figure 2b, d).

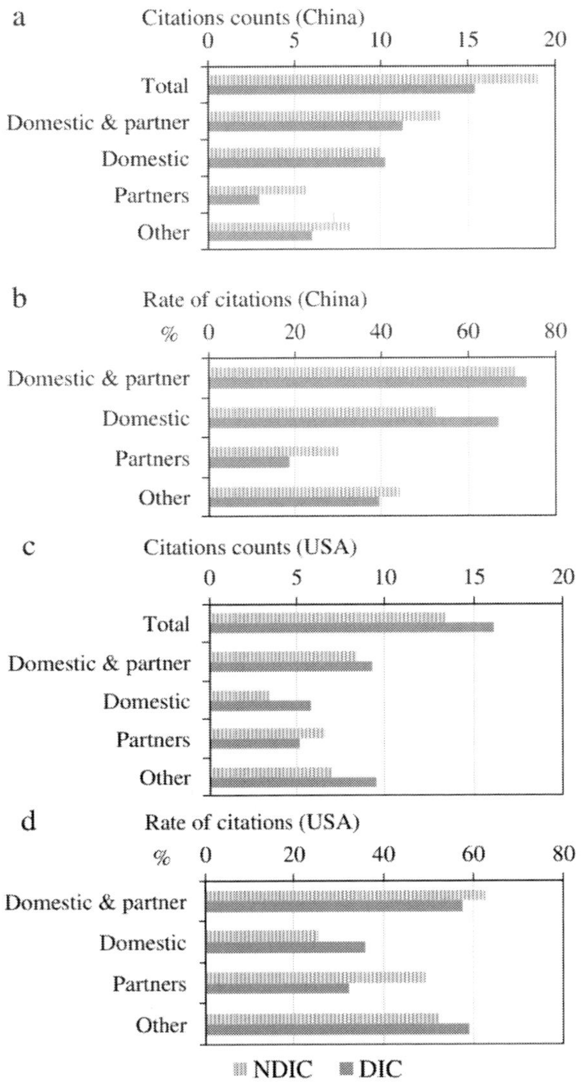

Figure 2. Numbers and shares of domestic and cross-country citations for NDIC and DIC.

In summary, Chinese DIC is more prominent of domestic orientation as reflected in forward citations, since their citing papers are mostly domestic, or occupied mainly by Chinese publications with lower share of *Partner* or *Other* citing papers. Similarly, the global impact of the US publications is higher and wider: publications especially those NIC or US-dominated IC, have higher share of *Other citations*. This result also proves that DIC resemble more like NIC according to the frequency and origins of citations in both countries. To put this another way, DIC are like domestic papers with characteristics of IC, or IC with higher domestic orientation.

National Funding and Citing Orientation

We further compare the contrasts of predictive citations of funded and unfunded publications (*contrast* for short) for NIC, DIC, and NDIC (Figures 3 and 4). In general, in both China and the USA, all types of citations of NIC, DIC, and NDIC are obviously higher when funded by NSFC (or NSF) as shown by positive contrasts of predictive margins, except for *Partner citations* of DIC and NDIC. For China, the contrasts of *Domestic & partner citations* are between 3 and 4, obviously higher than that of *Other citations* (between 1 and 2); while for US, contrasts of *Domestic & partner citations* and *Other citations* are of the same range (1–2). This result corresponds to the relative shares of citations from different sources, because the contrasts of different citations are generally proportional to the average citations of the corresponding types of citations for NIC, DIC and NDIC.

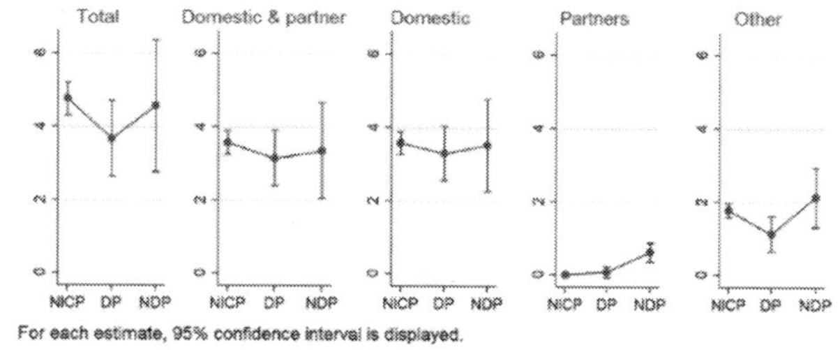

Figure 3. Contrasts of predictive margins (funded vs unfunded) of Chinese publications.

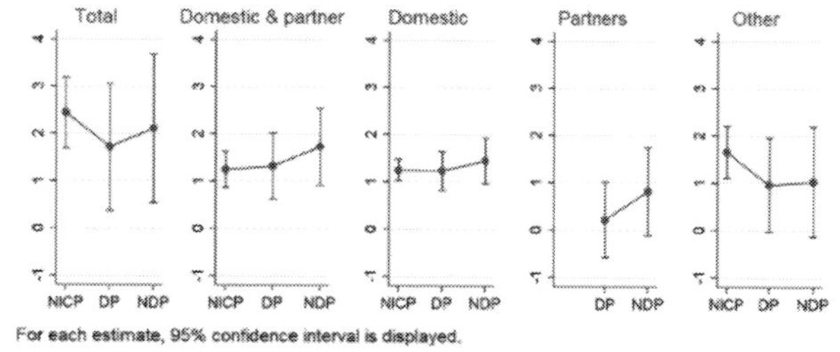

Figure 4. Contrasts of predictive margins (funded vs unfunded) of US publications.

Shares of *Domestic & partner citations* in funded datasets are generally higher than those in unfunded datasets. However, in contrasts of *Domestic & partner citations*, contrasts of *Domestic citations*, are the main contributors, thus leading to higher proportions of *Domestic citations* when funded (see Table 3). As can be seen, the proportions of *Domestic citations* in NSFC or NSF funded publications are higher than those in publications without NSFC or NSF funding, independent of the publication types (NIC, DIC, NDIC). Reversely, slightly lower shares of *Partner citations* or *Other citations* are also found especially in Chinese DIC, NDIC and US DIC. This implies national citation propensity of national funding in both countries reflected in forward citations.

			Not funded	Funded	Contrast
China	NIC	Domestic	66.8	70.4	↑
		Others	42.5	40.1	
	DIC	Domestic & partners	70.7	74.1	↑
		Domestic	61.4	67.8	↑
		Partners	22.2	17.7	↓
		Other	41.1	38.7	↓
	NDIC	Domestic & partners	70.9	71.4	
		Domestic	51.1	56.4	↑
		Partners	31.6	27.9	↓
		Other	44.2	44.7	
USA	NIC	Domestic	41.5	43.3	↑
		Others	71.1	70.6	
	DIC	Domestic & partners	56.7	58.7	↑
		Domestic	34.8	38.5	↑
		Partners	33.1	31.1	↓
		Other	58.9	58.6	
	NDIC	Domestic & partners	62.2	65.0	↑
		Domestic	23.9	30.1	↑
		Partners	49.6	48.1	
		Other	52.5	52.0	

Table 3. Shares of domestic and cross-country citations when funded or unfunded.

CONCLUSIONS AND DISCUSSIONS

In this paper we investigated the origins of citations at country level based on publications of China and the US in Chemistry, and explored whether domestic and cross-country citations to publications are related to international collaboration, dominance of focal country in international collaboration and national funding.

For the first question, results show similar findings as previous studies (Larivière et al., 2018; Tang et al., 2015): most citations of Chinese and US papers are from domestic or partner countries, and shares of *Domestic citations* of China and the US reach over 60% and 30%, respectively. Compared with *Domestic citations*, *Partner citations* (in IC) and *Other citations* are less in Chinese publications but obviously higher in US publications; this is consistent with relatively higher and lower shares of foreign citations of US and China as reported by National Science Board (2018, Chapter 5). These characteristics remain true even when factors related to international collaboration and funding are taken into account. As noted in existing studies (Jaffe, 2011; Minasny, Hartemink, & McBratney, 2010), high domestic citation rate is related to publication volume of the nations. According to distribution of categories of citing articles in this study, the citing papers for Chemistry papers in 2015 were mainly from Chemistry, followed by Materials Science. In 2015–2017, Chinese researchers published 31% and 33.5% of world output in Chemistry and Material Science, while US produced only half of Chinese output, i.e., about 16% and 17% respectively. Given the above statistics, 60%

and 30% self-citation rates of China and US mean almost equal degree of excessive self-citation at country level.

In summary, China is main beneficiary of its own research, with its citation impact mainly within the scope of the country due to high publication volume, whereas US publications show a broader impact and are more influential in the world. In this regard, although the mean raw citations of Chinese papers keep increasing, researchers should be aware that the scope of the citation influence is somewhat limited. One of the possible explanations might be that the excessive citations from Chinese researchers to domestic papers distort the measurement of impact of national research output to some extent, which leads to misunderstanding of comparative research strength of nations.

For the second question, we found that high domestic citation propensity is associated with non-international collaboration, dominance in international collaboration and national funding support. This finding is in line with our expectations. First, publications without international collaboration show lower international visibility and thus a higher national citation propensity. Second, internationally collaborated publications dominated by a country (DIC) resemble more like non-internationally collaborated publications of (NIC) the focal country than those non-dominated (NDIC), and are therefore associated with a higher national propensity in citing practice. Third, national funding support is more supportive of domestic research and domestic-dominated internationally collaborated research in terms of output, and in turn, research supported by such funding also shows domestic citation propensity in citations. Such phenomena is more pronounced in Chinese publications than US counterparts. Specifically, about 80% of Chinese publications are NIC, 73% of the IC are dominated by China, and 74% of all publications are funded by NSFC; while for US publications, the corresponding shares are 42%, 43%, and 31%. In fact, China has long been encouraging researchers to actively participate international collaboration and improving its scientific impact, its share of international collaboration is still low due to dramatically increased national output, and the dominance in IC is also high, indicating larger share of international collaboration mainly initiated by Chinese researchers. Moreover, majority of research output are sponsored by national government funding – NSFC, which are obviously domestic-oriented, thus the national output of China exhibits lower cross-country impact and higher share of domestic citations. From yet another perspective, national citation propensity of partner countries also helps increase China's international citations when China collaborates with other countries. This in fact also shows significant progress of China's international collaboration policy. For US, somewhat contrast to the situation in China, the share of international collaboration is higher with a considerably higher proportion of publications dominated by other nations, thus related to a more outward and open impact reflected by relatively lower share of domestic-citation and higher share of cross-country citations.

Results provide some implications. First, researchers should be aware of the insufficiency of citations in reflecting the influence of national output and be cautious in using related indicators in macro-level research. This doesn't mean foreign citations are superior than domestic ones, but only suggest researchers to keep an eye on the limitation of single metrics. Second, it is better to consider the shares of citations from domestic and foreign scholarly communities in country-level assessment of research performance. For example, use proportion of foreign citations or domestic citations to reflect another aspect of national impact or degree of internationalism.

ACKNOWLEDGMENTS

Authors gratefully acknowledge the grants from National Natural Science Foundation of China (#71473219, 71843012). Also thanks for the suggestion from anonymous mentor and reviewers.

REFERENCES

Albarrán, P., Perianes-Rodríguez, A., & Ruiz-Castillo, J. (2015). Differences in citation impact across countries. *Journal of the Association for Information Science and Technology*, *66*(3), 512–525.

Bakare, V., & Lewison, G. (2017). Country over-citation ratios. *Scientometrics*, *113*(2), 1199–1207.

Bornmann, L., Adams, J., & Leydesdorff, L. (2018). The negative effects of citing with a national orientation in terms of recognition: National and international citations in natural-sciences papers from Germany, The Netherlands, and the UK. *Journal of Informetrics*, *12*(3), 931–949.

Bornmann, L., & Wagner, C. S. (2015). BRICS countries and scientific excellence: A bibliometric analysis of most frequently cited papers. *Journal of the Association for Information Science and Technology*, *66*(7), 1507–1513.

De Moya-Anegon, F., Guerrero-Bote, V. P., Lopez-Illescas, C., & Moed, H. F. (2018). Statistical relationships between corresponding authorship, international co-authorship and citation impact of national research systems. *Journal of Informetrics*, *12*(4), 1251–1262.

Egghe, L., Rousseau, R., & Yitzhaki, M. (1999). The "own-language preference": Measures of relative language self-citation. *Scientometrics*, *45*(2), 217–232.

Gingras, Y., & Khelfaoui, M. (2018). Assessing the effect of the United States' "citation advantage" on other countries' scientific impact as measured in the Web of Science (WoS) database. *Scientometrics*, *114*(2), 517–532.

Gonzalez-Brambila, C. N., Reyes-Gonzalez, L., Veloso, F., & Perez-Angón, M. A. (2016). The Scientific Impact of Developing Nations. *PLoS One*, *11*(3), e0151328.

Hassan, S. U., & Haddawy, P. (2013). Measuring international knowledge flows and scholarly impact of scientific research. *Scientometrics*, *94*(1), 163–179.

Herranz, N., & Ruiz-Castillo, J. (2012). Sub-field normalization in the multiplicative case: Average-based citation indicators. *Journal of Informetrics*, *6*(4), 543–556.

Jaffe, K. (2011). Do countries with lower self-citation rates produce higher impact papers? or does humility pay. *Interciencia*, *36*(9), 694–698.

Larivière, V., Gong, K., & Sugimoto, C. R. (2018). Citations strength begins at home. *Nature*, *564*(7735), S70–S71.

Leydesdorff, L., Wagner, C. S., & Bornmann, L. (2014). The European Union, China, and the United States in the top-1% and top-10% layers of most-frequently cited publications: Competition and collaborations. *Journal of Informetrics*, *8*(3), 606–617.

Marshall, E., & Travis, J. (2011). U.K. scientific papers rank first in citations. *Science*, *334*(6055), 443.

Mervis, J. (2012). Science indicators 2012. Report notes China's influence in emerging Asian science zone. *Science*, *335*(January), 274–276.

Minasny, B., Hartemink, A. E., & McBratney, A. (2010). Individual, country, and journal self-citation in soil science. *Geoderma*, *155*(3–4), 434–438.

National Science Board. (2018). *Science & Engineering Indicators, 2018.*

Puuska, H.-M., Muhonen, R., & Leino, Y. (2014). International and domestic co-publishing and their citation impact in different disciplines. *Scientometrics*, *98*(2), 823–839.

Ren, S. L., & Rousseau, R. (2002). International visibility of Chinese scientific journals. *Scientometrics*, *53*(3), 389–405.

Rodríguez-Navarro, A., & Brito, R. (2018). Technological research in the EU is less efficient than the world average. EU research policy risks Europeans' future. *Journal of Informetrics*, *12*(3), 718–731.

Sooryamoorthy, R. (2009). Do types of collaboration change citation? collaboration and citation patterns of South African science publications. *Scientometrics*, *81* (1), 177–193.

Tang, L., Shapira, P., & Youtie, J. (2015). Is there a clubbing effect underlying Chinese research citation increases. *Journal of the Association for Information Science and Technology*, *66*(9), 1923–1932.

Zhou, P., & Cai, X. (2018). Funding, collaboration and research performance: A comparative study of leading universities in China and the USA. *23rd International Conference on Science and Technology Indicators*. Leiden.

Zhou, P., Cai, X., Xiong, W., & Lyu, X. (2019). A bibliometric perspective on the roles of government funding and international collaboration in scientific research. ISSI 2019. (Accepted)

Zhou, P., & Glänzel, W. (2010). In-depth analysis on China's international cooperation in science. *Scientometrics*, *82*(3), 597–612.

Definitions, Formulas, and Simulated Examples for Plagiarism Detection With FAIR Metrics

Adam Craig
Brain Health Alliance,
Ladera Ranch, CA, USA
acraig@bhavi.us

Adarsh Ambati
Brain Health Alliance,
Ladera Ranch, CA, USA
aambati@bhavi.us

Shiladitya Dutta
Brain Health Alliance,
Ladera Ranch, CA, USA
sdutta@bhavi.us

Arush Mehrotra
Brain Health Alliance,
Ladera Ranch, CA, USA
amerotra@bhavi.us

S. Koby Taswell
Brain Health Alliance,
Ladera Ranch, CA, USA
ktaswell@bhavi.us

Carl Taswell
Brain Health Alliance,
Ladera Ranch, CA, USA
ctaswell@brainhealthalliance.org

ABSTRACT

In prior work, we proposed a family of metrics as a tool to quantify adherence to or deviation from good citation practices in scholarly research and publishing. We called this family of metrics FAIR as an acronym for *Fair Attribution to Indexed Reports* and *Fair Acknowledgment of Information Records*, and introduced definitions for these metrics with counts of instances of correct or incorrect attribution or non-attribution in primary research articles with citations for previously published references. In the present work, we extend our FAIR family of metrics by introducing a collection of ratio-based metrics to accompany the count-based metrics described previously. We illustrate the mathematical properties of the ratio-based metrics with various simulated examples in order to assess their suitability as a means of identifying papers under peer review as more or less likely to be suspicious for plagiarism. These FAIR metrics would alert peer reviewers to prioritize low-scoring manuscripts for closer scrutiny. Finally, we outline our planned strategy for future validation of the FAIR metrics with an approach using both expert human analysts and automated algorithms for computerized analysis.

KEYWORDS

Scientometrics; Bibliometrics; FAIR Metrics; Citation Practices; Plagiarism Detection

ASIS&T THESAURUS

Scientometrics (1569); Semantic Analysis (1435); Plagiarism (176)

82nd Annual Meeting of the Association for Information Science & Technology | Melbourne, Australia | 19–23 October, 2019

DOI: 10.1002/pra2.00006

INTRODUCTION

Plagiarism continues to pose a threat to the integrity of scholarly research and publishing (Steen, 2011). While lexical comparison tools are useful for detecting exact copying or mildly obfuscated copying, they often fail to detect plagiarism of conceptual knowledge, substantive content and/or novel ideas (Meuschke & Gipp, 2013), defined by (Maurer, Kappe, & Zaka, 2006) as "using similar concept or opinion which is not common knowledge." In contrast, semantic analysis offers an alternative approach that can even detect plagiarism despite translation of the text into another language (Potthast, Barrón-Cedeño, Eiselt, Stein, & Rosso, 2010). Strategies range from using Latent Semantic Indexing (LSI) for detection of topic boundaries (Rehurek, 2008) to multi-phase processes such as those used by (Sindhu & Idicula, 2016) and (Osman & Salim, 2013). The FAIR metrics that we present here do not represent a new algorithmic approach to semantic analysis. Instead, the FAIR metrics that we expound here do provide a quantitative tool to measure the relative numbers of pairs of matching and mismatching statements found through semantic analysis. We define and formulate these metrics to quantify FAIR citing behavior for the purpose of promoting established traditional standards that repudiate plagiarism when publishing scholarly literature in general, and the medical scientific research literature in particular.

In (Craig & Taswell, 2018a), we presented core design principles for the FAIR metrics, which we explained could serve as a countervailing influence to the perverse incentive engendered by overreliance on current citation metrics that discourage some authors from citing rival authors, i.e., not adhering to the tradition of *standing on the shoulders of giants*[1] and citing other authors who previously published related work in

[1] This phrase has been attributed to Isaac Newton who wrote it in a letter to Robert Hooke in 1675, but the metaphor of dwarfs standing on the shoulders of giants has a history dating back many centuries earlier (Wikipedia, 2019).

their same research field that should be relevant to their discussion of the literature. Subsequently, we formulated a set of such metrics suitable for use with primary research articles (Craig & Taswell, 2018b) where we defined metrics based on the possible relationships between whether a statement is actually novel or not and whether the authors claim or discuss it as novel or not. In this current paper, we continue our past work on the FAIR metrics, described previously as simple counts of instances of the different types of statements, and extend it by formulating a family of four ratio-based FAIR metrics with mathematical notation and definitions for their formulas, demonstrating their numerical properties and evaluating their suitability as plagiarism detection tools via simulated examples of the underlying counts for the calculated values of the metrics.

FORMULATION OF RATIO-BASED FAIR METRICS

Following (Craig & Taswell, 2018a, 2018b), we further refined and extended our definitions of the simple count-based FAIR metrics to clarify how they interrelate with the formal notation summarized in Table 1 and explained in detail here for the ratio-based FAIR metrics.

Let $G(A)$ mean that the function G operates on set A. Let $G(A|B)$ mean that the function G operates on set A conditionally given set B, or that the function G operates on set A in comparison with set B. Let C refer to the set C of statements in a Control paper or in a Comparison Collection of papers. Let T refer to the set T of statements in a Test paper.

Now let $K(C)$ be the number K of Known, observed, original, and previously published statements found in the set C. Let $M(T \mid C)$ be the number M of Misquoted, Misattributed and/or Mistaken statements found in set T similar to known statements found in set C that have been repeated from C with incorrect citation and thus done without FAIRness. Let $Q(T \mid C)$ be the number Q of Quoted statements found in set T similar to known statements found in set C that have been repeated from C with correct citation and thus done with FAIRness. Let $P(T \mid C)$ be the number P of Paraphrased or Plagiarized statements found in set T similar to known statements found in set C that have been repeated from C without any citation and thus done without FAIRness. Let $N(T \mid C)$ be the number N of Novel or Non-plagiarized statements found in set T not similar to any known statements found in set C, ie, those that have not been repeated from C and that do not require any citation of a reference from C and thus done with FAIRness.

For the combined category counts S and R: Let $S(T \mid C) = M(T \mid C) + Q(T \mid C) + P(T \mid C) \leq K(C)$ be the total number S of Similar statements (= misquoted + quoted + plagiarized statements) found in set T repeated from and similar to known statements found in set C. Then $S(T \mid C)$ represents the *intersection* of statements found in both T and C, ie, those that have been repeated in T from C. Let $R(T \mid C) = M(T \mid C) + Q(T \mid C) + P(T \mid C) + N(T \mid C) \geq K(C)$ be the total number R of all Reported statements (=misquoted + quoted + plagiarized + novel statements) found in set T when compared to statements found in set C. Then $R(T \mid C)$ represents the *union* of statements found in both T and C, ie, both those that have and have not been repeated in T from C. Also, require the imposed condition that $0 < S(T \mid C) \leq K(C) \leq R(T \mid C)$ in order to prevent division by zero in any of the formulas for the ratio-based FAIR metrics.

We then defined formulas for the FAIR metrics as ratios of the four categories of basic counts M, Q, P and N and the two categories of combined counts S and R so that they could serve as measures of FAIRness quality independent of the size, scope and scale of the test set T in comparison with the control set C. These formulas are summarized in Table 2 and explained in detail here.

Define the first FAIR metric

$$F_1(T|C) = Q(T|C)/S(T|C) \qquad (1)$$

as the ratio of the Quoted count to Similar count. When Misquoted and Quoted counts are zero with $M(T \mid C) = Q(T \mid C) = 0$ and the Plagiarized and Similar counts are equal with $P(T \mid C) = S(T \mid C) > 0$, then $F_1(T \mid C) = 0$. When Misquoted and Plagiarized counts are zero with $M(T \mid C) = P(T \mid C) = 0$ and the Quoted and Similar counts are equal with $Q(T \mid C) = S(T \mid C) > 0$, then $F_1(T \mid C) = 1$. Observe that increasing F_1 between 0 and 1 means increasing FAIRness.

Define the second FAIR metric

$$F_2(T|C) = (Q(T|C) - M(T|C))/S(T|C) \qquad (2)$$

as the ratio of the Quoted-Misquoted difference count to Similar count. When Quoted and Plagiarized counts are zero with $Q(T \mid C) = P(T \mid C) = 0$ and the Misquoted and Similar counts are equal with $M(T \mid C) = S(T \mid C) > 0$, then $F_2(T \mid C) = -1$. When Misquoted and Plagiarized counts are zero with $M(T \mid C) = P(T \mid C) = 0$ and the Quoted and Similar counts are equal with $Q(T \mid C) = S(T \mid C) > 0$, then $F_2(T \mid C) = 1$. Observe that increasing F_2 between -1 and 1 means increasing FAIRness with a zero boundary and sign change indicating a transition when $Q(T \mid C) > M(T \mid C)$.

Define the third FAIR metric

$$F_3(T|C) = (Q(T|C) - P(T|C))/S(T|C) \qquad (3)$$

as the ratio of the Quoted-Plagiarized difference count to Similar count. When Misquoted and Quoted counts are zero with $M(T \mid C) = Q(T \mid C) = 0$ and the Plagiarized and Similar counts are equal with $P(T \mid C) = S(T \mid C) > 0$, then $F_3(T \mid C) = -1$. When Misquoted and Plagiarized counts are zero with $M(T \mid C) = P(T \mid C) = 0$ and the Quoted and Similar counts are equal with $Q(T \mid C) = S(T \mid C) > 0$, then $F_3(T \mid C) = 1$. Observe that increasing F_3 between -1 and 1 means increasing

FAIRness with a zero boundary and sign change indicating a transition when $Q(T \mid C) > P(T \mid C)$.

Define the fourth FAIR metric

$$F_4(T|C) = (Q(T|C) - N(T|C))/R(T|C) \quad (4)$$

as the ratio of the Quoted-Novel difference count to Reported count. When Misquoted and Quoted counts are zero with $M(T \mid C) = Q(T \mid C) = 0$ and the Novel and Reported counts are equal with $N(T \mid C) = R(T \mid C) > 0$, then $F_4(T \mid C) = -1$. When Misquoted, Plagiarized and Novel counts are zero with $M(T \mid C) = P(T \mid C) = N(T \mid C) = 0$ and the Quoted and Reported counts are equal with $Q(T \mid C) = R(T \mid C) > 0$, then $F_4(T \mid C) = 1$. Observe that increasing F_4 between -1 and 1 means increasing FAIRness with a zero boundary and sign change indicating a transition when $Q(T \mid C) > N(T \mid C)$.

presence of plagiarism and vice versa. All metrics in the family $F_i(T \mid C)$ for FAIRness have been designed such that increasing values correspond to increasing FAIRness. The interval of values (0, 1) for F_1 is different from the interval of values (−1, +1) for F_2, F_3, and F_4 because F_1 has a numerator with a simple count instead of the differences of counts used in the numerators for the other metrics in the family.

SIMULATED EXAMPLES OF FAIR METRICS

Table 3 lists a variety of different FAIRness metric scenarios with simulated examples of possible situations that might occur. The cases *None* through *All* illustrate the numerical stability of the metrics, which are only undefined in two obviously pathological cases: an empty paper devoid of any statements whatsoever and the *NOnly* paper consisting entirely of novel claims. In this latter hypothetical case, while the

Symbol	Definition
C	set C of statements in a Control paper or in a Comparison Collection of papers
$F_1(T\|C)$	FAIR metric scaled on interval [0,1] for T compared with C (dependent on Q and S)
$F_2(T\|C)$	FAIR metric scaled on interval [−1,+1] for T compared with C (dependent on Q, M and S)
$F_3(T\|C)$	FAIR metric scaled on interval [−1,+1] for T compared with C (dependent on Q, P and S)
$F_4(T\|C)$	FAIR metric scaled on interval [−1,+1] for T compared with C (dependent on Q, N and R)
$G(A)$	function G operates on set A
$G(A\|B)$	function G operates on set A in comparison with set B (on set A given set B)
$M(T\|C)$	number M of Misquoted (incorrectly cited) statements found in T compared with C
$N(T\|C)$	number N of Novel (uncited) statements found in T compared with C
$K(C)$	number K of Known statements found in C
$P(T\|C)$	number P of Plagiarized (uncited) statements found in T compared with C
$Q(T\|C)$	number Q of Quoted (correctly cited) statements found in T compared with C
$R(T\|C)$	number R of Reported statements found in T compared with C
$S(T\|C)$	number S of Similar statements found in T compared with C
T	set T of statements in a Test paper

Table 1. Notation for FAIR metrics.

Symbol		Formula
$F_1(T \mid C)$	=	$Q(T \mid C)/S(T \mid C)$
$F_2(T \mid C)$	=	$[Q(T \mid C) - M(T \mid C)]/S(T \mid C)$
$F_3(T \mid C)$	=	$[Q(T \mid C) - P(T \mid C)]/S(T \mid C)$
$F_4(T \mid C)$	=	$[Q(T \mid C) - N(T \mid C)]/R(T \mid C)$
$S(T \mid C)$	=	$M(T \mid C) + Q(T \mid C) + P(T \mid C) \le K(C)$
$R(T \mid C)$	=	$M(T \mid C) + Q(T \mid C) + P(T \mid C) + N(T \mid C) \ge K(C)$

Table 2. Formulas for ratio FAIR metrics with required condition $0 < S(T \mid C) \le K(C) \le R(T \mid C)$.

This ratio-based family of metrics $Fi(T \mid C)$ for FAIRness has been designed to depend on the Misquoted count $M(T \mid C)$, Quoted count $Q(T \mid C)$, Plagiarzied count $P(T \mid C)$, and Novel count $N(T \mid C)$ relative to the Similar count $S(T \mid C)$ or Reported count $R(T \mid C)$ in different ways for different scenarios that all nevertheless focus on various aspects of the definition of FAIRness for appropriately citing previously published references. In particular, note especially that the presence of novelty should not nullify nor otherwise hide the simultaneous

authors have not plagiarized any known prior work as indicated by a count of $P(T \mid C) = 0$, they have also failed to place their novel claims in the context of the existing body of knowledge found within the related field of published literature as indicated by a count of $Q(T \mid C) = 0$. For another possible explanation of this case, such a scenario might occur if the evaluation system failed to find sets of statements for any of the papers that the authors cited. This case may arise if the automated system performing the semantic analysis for the counts has incorrectly retrieved the C statements from the wrong source, such as an incorrectly identified service in the Nexus-PORTAL-DOORS-Scribe cyberinfrastructure system (Craig, Bae, Veeramacheneni, Taswell, & Taswell, 2016; Taswell, 2008, 2009, 2010), devoted to a problem-oriented domain other than the one to which the T paper relates. The rest of the cases, *GoodA* through *SplitC*, illustrate that each metric remains constant so long as the proportions of the counts remain constant. This stability implies that the metrics serve appropriately as measures of adherence to good

Name	M	Q	P	N	S	R	F_1	F_2	F_3	F_4
None	0	0	0	0	0	0	NaN	NaN	NaN	NaN
MOnly	10	0	0	0	10	10	0	-1	0	0
QOnly	0	10	0	0	10	10	1	1	1	1
POnly	0	0	10	0	10	10	0	0	-1	0
NOnly	0	0	0	10	0	10	NaN	NaN	NaN	-1
MAndQ	10	10	0	0	20	20	0.5	0	0.5	0.5
MAndP	10	0	10	0	20	20	0	-0.5	-0.5	0
MAndN	10	0	0	10	10	20	0	-1	0	-0.5
QAndP	0	10	10	0	20	20	0.5	0.5	0	0.5
QAndN	0	10	0	10	10	20	1	1	1	0
PAndN	0	0	10	10	10	20	0	0	-1	-0.5
NoN	10	10	10	0	30	30	0.33	0	0	0.33
NoP	10	10	0	10	20	30	0.5	0	0.5	0
NoQ	10	0	10	10	20	30	0	-0.5	-0.5	-0.33
NoM	0	10	10	10	20	30	0.5	0.5	0	0
All	10	10	10	10	30	40	0.33	0	0	0
GoodA	0	5	0	5	5	10	1	1	1	0
GoodB	0	10	0	10	10	20	1	1	1	0
GoodC	0	15	0	15	15	30	1	1	1	0
BadA	5	0	5	0	10	10	0	-0.5	-0.5	0
BadB	10	0	10	0	20	20	0	-0.5	-0.5	0
BadC	15	0	15	0	30	30	0	-0.5	-0.5	0
SplitA	5	5	2	2	12	14	0.42	0	0.25	0.21
SplitB	10	10	4	4	24	28	0.42	0	0.25	0.21
SplitC	15	15	6	6	36	42	0.42	0	0.25	0.21

Table 3. Examples of the effects of different combinations of zero and nonzero counts on the FAIR metrics.

citation practices independently of the scope of the work and the number of statements identified in the T paper.

Figure 1 shows how each metric varies as we vary one of the counts and hold the rest constant. $F_2(T \mid C)$ decreases most rapidly as $M(T \mid C)$ increases (upper left), reflecting its design as a measure of misattribution. $F_3(T \mid C)$ decreases most rapidly as $P(T \mid C)$ increases (lower left), showing its suitability for flagging possible instances of plagiarism. $F_1(T \mid C)$ decreases less rapidly but in response to increases in $M(T \mid C)$, $P(T \mid C)$, or both. As such, it serves as a more general measure of FAIRness. All metrics increase as $Q(T \mid C)$ increases (upper right), because proper citation of prior work is the desirable content of which we are measuring the prevalence relative to other content. Although the presence of novel statements is desired in primary research publications, $F_1(T \mid C)$, $F_2(T \mid C)$, and $F_3(T \mid C)$ remain constant as $N(T \mid C)$ increases (lower right), while $F_4(T \mid C)$ decreases. This behavior of the FAIR metrics reflects the standard expectation that scholars should place novel claims in the proper context by relating them to published knowledge and hypotheses on the topic. Not inappropriately favoring papers with novel claims also makes these FAIR metrics applicable to reproducibility and replication studies as well as review articles, which do not need to report novel findings in order to fulfill their roles in the ecosystem of scholarly literature.

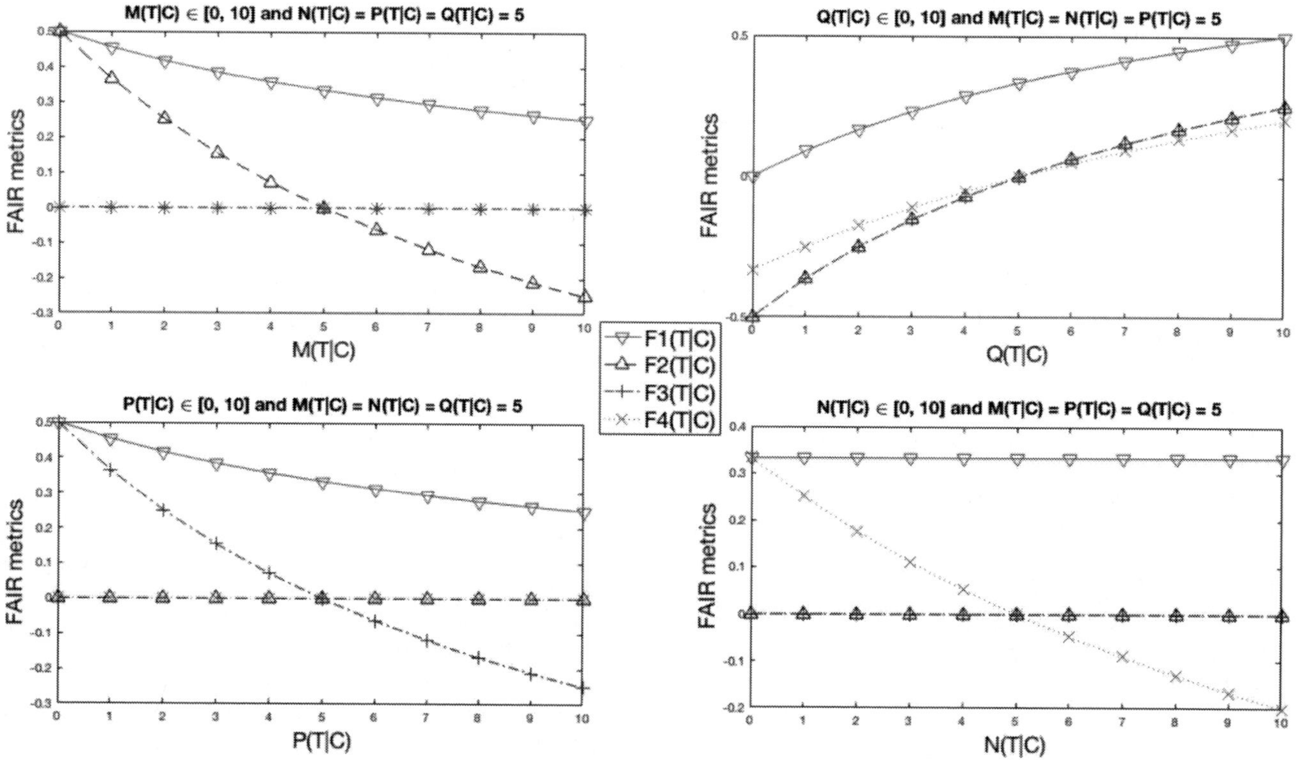

Figure 1. Effect on FAIR metrics of varying each count in turn while holding the others constant.

STRATEGY FOR VALIDATION OF FAIR METRICS

Now that we have designed and demonstrated the FAIR metrics with the requisite mathematical properties, our next step will be to test and validate them on real-world examples of papers known in advance to be plagiarizing or novel. Although automated semantic similarity detection has been improving, the capabilities of existing tools remain inferior to those of human minds (Agirre, Banea et al., 2016). Moreover, any methodology to compute the FAIR metrics, regardless of whether human guided or computer automated, will require processing several steps.

The first step extracts the most essential and significant statements from each article in a clear, concise, consistent format. Currently, methods for extracting RDF triples from free-form text still depend on the rough structure of the text in order to derive triples. These methods convert each sentence into a set of triples without regard for the importance or non-importance of the claim that each RDF triple represents within the semantic thematic content, reasoning and discussion communicated by the article analyzed (Klyne & Carroll, 2004). The second step acquires a learned summary of the statements. An example of a machine learning approach for this task appears in (Leskovec, Grobelnik, & Milic-Frayling, 2004).

The third step discerns common knowledge that does not require citation from knowledge that should require citation. The calculation framework needs to filter out common knowledge, as it is not novel but does not require citation either, meaning that it is not considered for categorization into any of the four basic counts $M(T \mid C)$, $Q(T \mid C)$, $P(T \mid C)$, or $N(T \mid C)$. Without the experience of the world that humans take for granted, automated agents must rely on compendious semantic networks, such as ConceptNet 3 (Havasi, Speer, & Alonso, 2007). Furthermore, each problem domain has its own repository of common knowledge that experts and ontology engineers must encode in a domain ontology (Fensel, 2001). Therefore, the system would need to search the relevant ontologies for equivalents to each key claim.

The fourth step compares each statement in the test paper T to potential equivalents in the set of statements from prior works C. For a human analyst, deciding whether two natural language statements are equivalent can require in-depth understanding of the concepts and relationships involved and may require careful consideration of nuance and context, leading to variance even in human-generated ratings of semantic similarity, as seen in (Agirre et al., 2016). Despite these challenges, automated semantic equivalence detection systems continue to advance, as we can see from the improvement in top scores between (Agirre, Diab, Cer, & Gonzalez-Agirre, 2012) and (Agirre et al., 2016).

Finally, the FAIR metric calculations must be evaluated for consistency across the family of results with F_1, F_2, F_3, and F_4 for a given test paper T in comparison to the control collection of papers C. While each of these requisite steps has possible computerized algorithmic solutions, none has yet achieved the equivalent of human reasoning ability. With these issues in mind, we have chosen to begin with an approach in which human analysts manually extract and compare the core claims of each text. Future results from this human expert-derived analysis will provide a best-case scenario benchmark against which to compare subsequent automated computerized solutions that calculate FAIR metrics from counts of statements analyzed via natural language processing (NLP) and concept similarity detection (CSD) tools which we are developing (Bae, Craig, & Taswell, 2017; Craig, Ambati et al., 2019; Dutta & Taswell, 2018).

DISCUSSION OF PILOT STUDY

In a preliminary pilot study, we tested the feasibility of this manual approach with eight volunteer analysts using confirmed instances of plagiarism in the fields of brain science and computer science. To keep the workload for each analyst manageable with balanced data sets, we created a text corpus consisting of collections of triples of papers with each triple consisting of one paper in each of the following three roles: a plagiarizing test paper T_p (with subscript p for plagiarizing) as a primary research article retracted for plagiarism, found through the Retraction Watch database, a comparison control paper C as the paper that T_p plagiarized according to its retraction notice, and a novel test paper T_n (with subscript n for novel) as another primary research article not known to have been retracted for plagiarism, but also with a close conceptual relationship to C, found through a Google Scholar search with a list of key terms from C.

From our pilot study, it became clear that having a control set C of prior literature consisting only of statements from a single paper meant discarding too many statements found in T_p or T_n attributed to other previously published papers because the analyst might not find them in C and thus be unable to classify them as either M or Q counts. Thus, the pilot study design produced low-biased values for these two counts, M and Q, which we knew were unrealistic and not representative of the real-world situation. When we conduct our full study with human analysts using a more labor intensive but also more realistic approach for the experimental study design, we will need to construct for each T_p and T_n a more comprehensive set C consisting of statements from all papers that we know T_p and T_n either plagiarized and/or cited. Then we should be able to obtain better estimates for all of the four basic categories of counts M, Q, P, and N.

Another important lesson that we learned from the pilot study involved the manner in which plagiarizing papers could escape detection by the FAIR metrics by changing the entities described in the claims in such a way that the statements are no longer similar enough to match as the same statements found in T compared with C. For example, (Yao et al., 2017) is nearly identical in research methodology and wording of text to (Li et al., 2015), but it substitutes ligand-receptor pair CXCL12/CXCR4 for each reference to CCL21/CXCR7 and transcription factor Twist for each instance of Slug in the text. Since these substitutions make the claims of the plagiarizing paper conceptually different from those of the original when the similarity comparison is performed without the use of weighting factors, it can achieve a relatively high FAIR metric score. Such cases fall outside of the scope of the simple FAIR metrics as currently formulated for T compared with C unless we modify them further to allow for additional weighting factors obtained from the outputs of more sophisticated analyses performed with artificial neural networks that have been trained on C.

CONCLUSION

Nevertheless, we have already shown that the simple unweighted versions of the FAIR metrics can serve to complement the lexical plagiarism detection techniques that have been effective at detecting copied text surrounding altered key terms (Meuschke & Gipp, 2013). The current unweighted FAIR metrics can also serve to alert human peer reviewers and editors who can then better decide how to make appropriate judgments when scrutinizing manuscripts with low FAIRness scores suspected of plagiarism. Our next goal for subsequent studies of the FAIR metrics with primary research articles, using collections with those which are known *a priori* with high confidence to be either plagiarizing or non-plagiarizing, will be to evaluate and establish differences in the distributions of FAIR metric scores for plagiarizing papers compared with those for non-plagiarizing papers. Acquired experience with different problem-oriented research domains will enable members of each of those scientific communities to establish thresholds for each of the FAIR metrics for sufficient FAIRness to avoid triggering alerts for possible plagiarism. While we would expect $P(T \mid C)$ ideally to be zero for correctly referenced non-plagiarizing articles and nonzero for plagiarizing articles, the presence of both mistakes by authors in their writing of manuscripts as well as flaws in the NLP extraction and semantic comparison of statements could complicate the analysis and results. Even so, we expect that the distributions of the FAIR metric scores will be sufficiently different for plagiarizing versus non-plagiarizing articles that they will serve as a useful tool for expert reviewers to prioritize papers for further examination when the FAIR metrics yield low values suspicious for plagiarism.

REFERENCES

Agirre, E., Banea, C., Cer, D., Diab, M., Gonzalez-Agirre, A., Mihalcea, R., … Wiebe, J. (2016). SemEval-2016 Task 1: Semantic textual similarity, monolingual and cross-lingual evaluation. In *Proceedings of the 10th International Workshop on Semantic Evaluation (SemEval-2016)* (pp. 497–511).

Agirre, E., Diab, M., Cer, D., & Gonzalez-Agirre, A. (2012). SemEval-2012 Task 6: A pilot on semantic textual similarity. In *Proceedings of the First Joint Conference on Lexical and Computational Semantics-Vol. 1: Proceedings of the main conference and the shared task, and Vol. 2: Proceedings of the Sixth International Workshop on Semantic Evaluation* (pp 385–393). Association for Computational Linguistics.

Bae, S. H., Craig, A. G., & Taswell, C. (2017). Expanding Nexus diristries of dementia literature with the NPDS concept-validating search engine agent. In *Proceedings of the 39th Annual International Conference of the IEEE Engineering in Medicine and Biology Society* (pp 3704–3707).

Craig, A., Ambati, A., Dutta, S., Kowshik, P., Nori, S., Taswell, S. K., … Taswell, C. (2019). DREAM principles and FAIR metrics from the PORTAL-DOORS Project for the semantic web. In *Proceedings 11th International Conference on Electronics, Computers and Artificial Intelligence (ECAI)*. IEEE. in press.

Craig, A., Bae, S. H., Veeramacheneni, T., Taswell, S. K., & Taswell, C. (2016). Web service APIs for Scribe registrars, Nexus diristries, PORTAL registries and DOORS directories in the NPD system. In *Proceedings of the 9th International SWAT4LS Conference*.

Craig, A. & Taswell, C. (2018a). The FAIR metrics of adherence to citation best practices. In *Proceedings of ASIS&T 81st Annual Meeting SIGMET Workshop*.

Craig, A. & Taswell, C. (2018b). Formulation of FAIR metrics for primary research articles. In *2018 IEEE International Conference on Bioinformatics and Biomedicine (BIBM)*. IEEE.

Dutta, S. & Taswell, C. (2018). SPARQL-based search engine and agent for finding brain literature and converting references to NPDS metadata records. In *Proceedings of the 11th International Conference on Brain Informatics*, number B277.

Fensel, D. (2001). Ontologies. In *Ontologies* (pp. 11–18). Springer.

Havasi, C., Speer, R., & Alonso, J. (2007). ConceptNet 3: A flexible, multilin-gual semantic network for common sense knowledge. In *Recent advances in natural language processing* (pp. 27–29). Citeseer.

Klyne, G. & Carroll, J. J. (2004). *Resource description framework (RDF): Concepts and abstract syntax*. Retrieved from

Leskovec, J., Grobelnik, M., & Milic-Frayling, N. (2004). Learning substructures of document semantic graphs for document summarization. In *LinkKDD*.

Li, G., Yang, Y., Xu, S., Ma, L., He, M., & Zhang, Z. (2015). Slug signaling is up-regulated by ccl21/cxcr7 to induce emt in human chondrosarcoma. *Medical Oncology*, *32*(2), 2.

Maurer, H. A., Kappe, F., & Zaka, B. (2006). Plagiarism-a survey. *Journal of Universal Computer Science*, *12*(8), 1050–1084.

Meuschke, N., & Gipp, B. (2013). State-of-the-art in detecting academic plagiarism. *International Journal for Educational Integrity*, *9*(1).

Osman, A. H. & Salim, N. (2013). An improved semantic plagiarism detection scheme based on chi-squared automatic interaction detection. In *International Conference on Computing, Electrical and Electronic Engineering (ICCEEE)* (pp. 640–647). IEEE.

Potthast, M., Barrón-Cedeño, A., Eiselt, A., Stein, B., & Rosso, P. (2010). Overview of the 2nd international competition on plagiarism detection. In *Proceedings of the 4th Workshop on Uncovering Plagiarism, Authorship, and Social Software Misuse* (pp. 1–14).

Rehurek, R. (2008). *Semantic-based plagiarism detection*. (PhD thesis), Masarykova univerzita, Fakulta informatiky.

Sindhu, L., & Idicula, S. M. (2016). A plagiarism detection system for Malayalam text based documents with full and partial copy. *Procedia Technology*, *25*, 372–377.

Steen, R. G. (2011). Retractions in the scientific literature: do authors deliberately commit research fraud? *Journal of Medical Ethics*, *37*(2), 113–117.

Taswell, C. (2008). DOORS to the semantic web and grid with a PORTAL for biomedical computing. *IEEE Transactions on Information Technology in Biomedicine*, *12*(2), 191–204. In the Special Section on Bio-Grid.

Taswell, C. (2009). The hierarchically distributed mobile metadata (HDMM) style of architecture for pervasive metadata networks. In *Proceedings of ISPAN 2009 The 10th International Symposium on Pervasive Systems, Algorithms and Networks* (pp. 315–320). IEEE.

Taswell, C. (2010). A distributed infrastructure for metadata about metadata: The HDMM architectural style and PORTAL-DOORS system. *Future Internet*, *2*(2), 156–189. In Special Issue on Metadata and Markup.

Wikipedia (2019). Standing on the shoulders of giants.

Yao, C., Li, P., Song, H., Song, F., Qu, Y., Ma, X., ... Wu, J. (2017). Retraction note to: Cxcl12/cxcr4 axis upregulates twist to induce emt in human glioblastoma. *Molecular Neurobiology*, *54*(9), 7553–7553.

Dataset Bias: A Case Study for Visual Question Answering

Anubrata Das
School of Information
University of Texas at Austin
anubrata@utexas.edu

Samreen Anjum
School of Information
University of Texas at Austin
samreen@utexas.edu

Danna Gurari
School of Information
University of Texas at Austin
danna.gurari@ischool.utexas.edu

ABSTRACT
We examine the issue of bias in datasets designed to train visual question answering (VQA) algorithms. These datasets include a collection of natural language questions about images (aka - visual questions). We consider three popular datasets that are captured by people with sight, people who are blind, and generated by computers. We first demonstrate that machine learning algorithms can be trained to recognize each dataset's bias, and so determine the source of a novel visual question. We then discuss potential risks and benefits of biased VQA datasets and corresponding machine learning algorithms that can identify the source of a visual question; e.g., whether it comes from a person with sight, a person who is blind, or bot (aka - computer). Our ultimate aim is to inspire the development of more inclusive VQA systems.

KEYWORDS
Bias in Machine Learning; Visual Question Answering; Assistive Technologies; Ethics of Artificial Intelligence

ASIS&T THESAURUS
Information Science; Data Science; Information Science; Knowledge and Information; Data; Information Science; Information Resources; Data Sets

INTRODUCTION
Large-scale datasets are essential to train modern machine learning algorithms and evaluate their performance. However, such datasets are susceptible to the presence of bias, which can have more implications for their applicability than initially understood. We aim to explore this issue for the task called visual question answering (VQA), given the recent explosion of interest in this task from the artificial intelligence community (Antol et al., 2015).

Our focus in this work is on how biases in datasets can affect specific groups/populations. Prior work has demonstrated that understanding different effects on specific groups is important for many reasons. For example, algorithms trained on a dataset representing one population typically only work

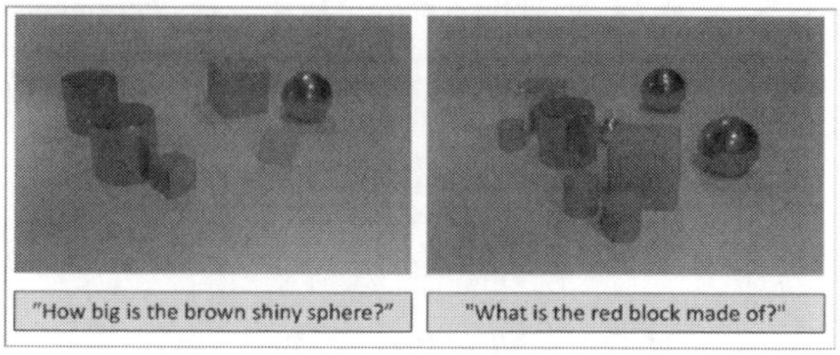

(a) CLEVR

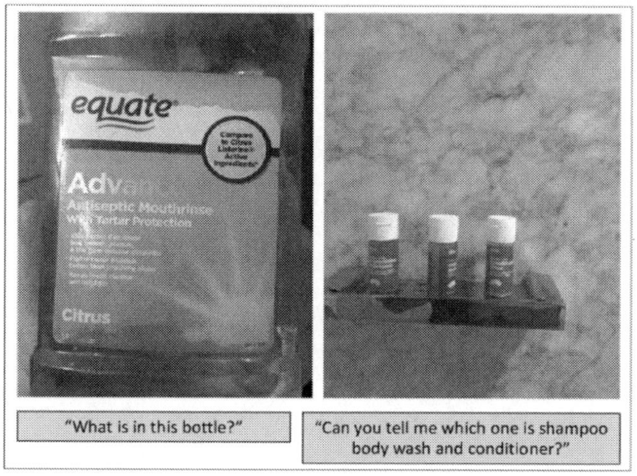

(b) VizWiz

(c) VQA_1.0

Figure 1. Example visual questions from three visual question answering datasets. Bias arises in these datasets due to them being generated from limited sources, specifically sighted people for VQA_1.0 (Antol et al., 2015), people who are blind for VizWiz (Gurari et al., 2018), and computers for CLEVR (Johnson et al., 2017). (a) CLEVR (b) VizWiz (c)VQA_1.0.

82nd Annual Meeting of the Association for Information Science & Technology | Melbourne, Australia | 19–23 October, 2019

DOI: 10.1002/pra2.00007

well for that population (Torralba & Efros, 2011); e.g., lgorithms trained on data from sighted people do not work well for data from people with visual impairments (Gurari et al., 2018). Additionally, algorithms learn to reinforce biases that are present in datasets, as exemplified in use cases such as for university admission (Dwork, Hardt, Pitassi, Reingold, & Zemel, 2012), resume search (Zehlike et al., 2017), facial recognition (Buolamwini & Gebru, 2018), and criminal sentence determination (Chouldechova, 2017) where algorithms learned to discriminate against different user groups (including with respect to gender, race and ethnicity). Finally, biased datasets representing distinct populations can be used maliciously to train algorithms to identify and subsequently discriminate against that group (Narayanan & Shmatikov, 2008; Thomas & Kovashka, 2016).

To our knowledge, no prior work has examined the issue of dataset bias for VQA. Yet, VQA is emerging in the artificial intelligence community as a premiere challenge for mimicking the ability of a sighted person to answer a natural language question about an image (aka, visual question). The popularity of the VQA problem is exemplified by the fact that over 15 VQA datasets have been proposed since 2015 (Gurari et al., 2018), with the most popular VQA dataset having been cited over 1,000 times to date (Antol et al., 2015). Exemplar visual questions are shown in Figure 1. We believe the time is ripe to examine the issue of dataset bias for VQA – before cutting-edge research algorithms are incorporated into widely used products and services.

The key contributions of our work are as follows:

1. We propose multiple machine learning algorithms that can identify whether a visual question was asked by a sighted person, a blind person, or a computer, and conduct analysis which demonstrates that such algorithms can learn to do so with minimal amounts of training data.
2. We develop a web-based tool to detect the sources of visual questions in VQA datasets, in order to raise awareness about the issue of biased datasets.
3. We discuss potential benefits and risks of biased datasets, including the ability to train algorithms that can identify the source of a visual question.

Ultimately, our aim is to raise awareness of the issues with dataset bias to catalyze the development of more inclusive VQA systems that minimize harm and benefit society.

RELATED WORK

Ethics in Machine Learning

Ethical issues in machine learning are being studied by researchers in both academia (X. Jiang, Sun, Yang, Zhuge, & Yao, 2016; Katell, 2018; Lepri, Oliver, Letouzé, Pentland, & Vinck, 2018; Nikolov, Lalmas, Flammini, & Menczer, 2018; Wilkie & Azzopardi, 2018) and industry[1,2] (Bellamy et al., 2018). The ubiquity of machine learning applications is a reason for the increasing concern. One of the prominent ethical issues is that machine learning algorithms carry or even amplify existing biases in the society (Zhao, Wang, Yatskar, Ordonez, & Chang, 2017). Presence of these biases affects the decision-making process of users (Binns, 2017). The information science community offers a rich foundation for exploring ethical aspects of systems, since this community began discussing such issues long before the discussion began in the machine learning community (Hoffmann, Roberts, Wolf, & Wood, 2018). Our work complements prior work by contributing richer understanding of the ethical implications of bias in a new context of VQA.

Visual Question Answering Datasets

Recent advancement in VQA research is predominantly driven by the advent and availability of large-scale VQA datasets. Included is a dataset from Antol et al. (2015) which contains images scraped from the web paired with questions about them from crowd workers. Gurari et al. (2018) shared visual questions from individuals with visual impairments. Johnson et al. (2017), in contrast, designed a computer algorithm to generate visual questions automatically. In response, many machine learning algorithms have been proposed to automatically answer visual questions, including those described by Lu, Yang, Batra, and Parikh (2016), Jabri, Joulin, and Van Der Maaten (2016), and Y. Jiang et al. (2018). Reviews of the artificial intelligence community's progress are discussed by Kafle and Kanan (2017) and Wu et al. (2017). To the best of our knowledge, our work is the first to examine the issues and implications of bias in VQA datasets.

Bias in Datasets

Torralba and Efros (2011) and Tommasi, Patricia, Caputo, and Tuytelaars (2017) have explored the existence of different types of biases in popular datasets such as ImageNet (Deng et al., 2009), Caltech 256 (Griffin, Holub, & Perona, 2007), PASCAL VOC (Everingham, Van Gool, Williams, Winn, & Zisserman, 2010) and LabelMe (Russell, Torralba, Murphy, & Freeman, 2008). In some cases, these dataset biases are used to the benefit of designing the prediction algorithm (McLaughlin, Del Rincon, & Miller, 2015), (Khosla, Zhou, Malisiewicz, Efros, & Torralba, 2012), (Gong, Sha, & Grauman, 2012). Although exploiting bias can increase predictive performance of algorithms, this practice impacts the original research goals of building generalized algorithms (Torralba & Efros, 2011). Our work contributes knowledge about risks and opportunities to take advantage of dataset biases when designing VQA services.

Predicting Identity from Visual Data

Our work relates to that from Thomas and Kovashka (2016), which proposes algorithms to identify the photographer of an image directly from an image. We instead propose a novel problem of training machine learning algorithms to identify

[1] IBM AI Fairness 360: https://aif360.mybluemix.net/
[2] Google Impact Challenge: https://ai.google/social-good/impact-challenge/

the source 'population' who asked the visual question directly from the visual question; i.e., whether a visual question comes from a sighted person, blind person, or bot (aka – computer).

METHODOLOGY

We approach the problem of examining bias in VQA datasets by analyzing whether a machine learning algorithm can learn to identify which visual questions come from which dataset. We do this using three datasets that represent visual questions asked by three 'populations': sighted people, blind people, and bots. Consequently, if a machine learning model can identify which among the three datasets a visual question comes from, then it can identify which among three 'populations' (i.e., sighted people, blind people, bots) produced a visual question. An overview of the machine learning systems we evaluate is shown in Figure 2, and further detail is provided below. To summarize, we begin by describing the three VQA datasets that we consider and their unique biases in terms of how the visual questions were collected. We then describe the machine learning systems to predict the sources. We include a discussion of target labels, extracted features, and classification models.

We would also like to highlight that the objective of this work is not to critique any dataset but to repurpose existing datasets to understand biases in visual question answering.

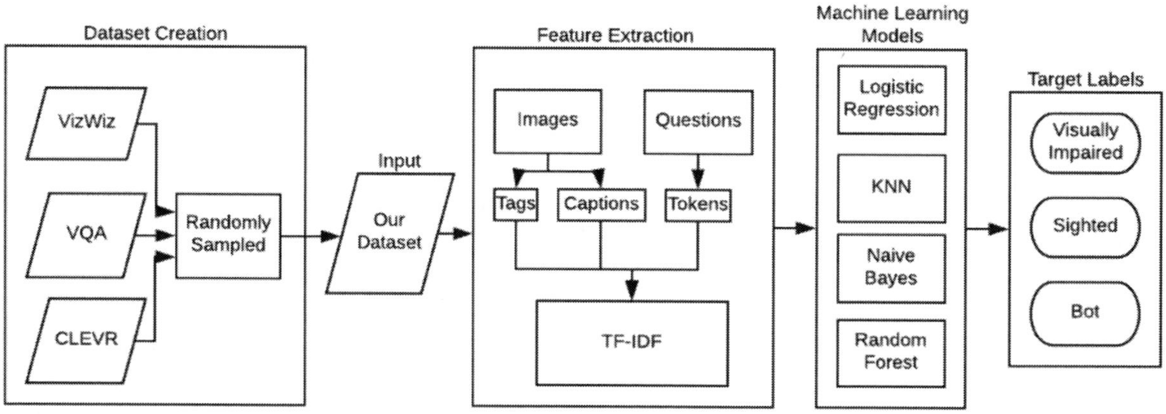

Figure 2. Flowchart describing our machine learning system pipeline.

Datasets

Visual questions from different populations can be distinct from each other in terms of how the *images* are collected or generated, how the *questions* are collected or generated, or the combination of both *images* and *questions*. We compile a random collection of samples from three popular VQA datasets (VQA, VizWiz, and CLEVR) with a balanced number of 600 per dataset. The result is a representative set of 1800 visual questions that come from sighted people, blind people, and computers respectively. We describe each dataset and its biases below.

VQA_1.0 (Antol et al., 2015)
Dataset
The original dataset is a collection of images (250,000), questions (760,000), and answers (about 10 million). It consists of images from the MSCOCO dataset (Lin et al., 2014), which were originally scraped from the photo sharing website Flickr.[3] It also contains open-ended questions about these images asked by sighted crowd workers from Amazon Mechanical Turk.

Bias
There exists a certain type of bias in this dataset as the questions are collected with an objective to stump a robot. Specifically, when curating the questions, sighted crowd workers were instructed to provide questions assuming they will be asked to a robot with the aim of stumping the robot. This method of collecting questions has the potential to incorporate the annotators' ideas of a robot and its perceived level of intelligence. For example, if a user thinks robots are not smart enough, then the questions would be too simple. In contrast, the questions could be too complex if a user thinks a robot should be able to answer complex questions about an image. VQA_1.0 also has a bias that it only contains very complex images that show scenes with multiple objects, since images were downloaded from Flickr after being found using at least two object types in the search query.

VizWiz (Gurari et al., 2018)
Dataset
The dataset is collected from users of a VQA mobile phone application (Bigham et al., 2010), which was built for people with visual impairments. Specifically, users of the application took a picture and recorded a spoken question before submitting it to the application to receive an answer. As a result, this

[3] https://www.flickr.com/

dataset largely represents real visual questions visually impaired users face in their daily lives.

Bias

Although VizWiz is a unique and useful dataset for building assistive technologies, this dataset still has its limitation in terms of bias and inclusion. Since the VizWiz dataset is prepared to address the single goal of assisting people with vision impairments, it is not inclusive in terms of the visual ability of all users, i.e., both sighted and visually impaired. Brady, Morris, Zhong, White, and Bigham (2013) characterized some patterns observed in these visual questions. For example, the users often ask identification questions to solicit assistance in recognizing objects. There is also a particular pattern present in terms of the image quality. Often the images in this dataset show a single object with lots of blur, poor lighting conditions, and poor framing of the content of interest.

CLEVR (Johnson et al., 2017)

Dataset

This dataset is fully computer-generated. It consists of images showing three basic shapes (spheres, cubes, and cylinders) in two different sizes (small and big) and eight different colors. Four spatial relationships can arise between the objects. The questions are asked about the objects present in the images and the relationship between them. For example, the questions could be about the attributes (color, size) of an object, comparison of different attributes, counting of objects, and whether or not an object exists in the image. In other words, the visual questions explore the relationship between objects in an image.

Bias

This dataset is limited in terms of representing the diversity of possible real-world scenarios and users. For example, the computer-generated images do not necessarily represent the variety of challenges for real-world images in terms of illumination, object diversity, and scene complexity. Similarly, the questions do not reflect the diversity of visual questions that would interest real users of a VQA system.

Machine Learning Pipeline

We now describe our machine learning pipeline designed to predict if a visual question has been asked by a sighted user, asked by a visually impaired user, or is computer-generated. This pipeline involves two consecutive steps: preprocessing and then training, as described below and illustrated in Figure 2. We consider classical machine learning approaches in our pipeline in order to examine the potential of off-the-shelf machine learning frameworks.

Target Labels

As discussed in the previous section, there is a clear distinction between the three datasets (VQA_1.0, VizWiz, and CLEVR) in terms of how the visual questions are collected/generated. For VizWiz, they are collected from visually impaired users, for VQA they are collected from sighted annotators, and for CLEVR they are generated automatically using algorithms. With the objective of detecting the source of sample images using these datasets, the target labels for our machine learning algorithms are (1) sighted, (2) visually impaired, and (3) bot (aka – computer).

Feature Extraction

In order to build a classifier for our multimodal machine learning problem, we first extract natural language features from each *visual question*.

We extract features for each image using Microsoft Azure Cognitive Services API.[4] We first extract "Image Captions", which are human-readable single sentence descriptions of a given image. We use the Azure Cognitive Services API to generate the captions with corresponding confidences in the predicted captions. We then use the image caption with the highest confidence for each of the images. We also extract "Image Tags", which are a collection of words generated based on objects, actions, or scene of an image. The main difference between the image captions and image tags is that tags are not limited to the central theme of the image. Tags include keywords that are related to the background, foreground, objects and their associations in the context of an image. For example, some of the tags of the rightmost image in Figure 1-c include "soccer", "boys", "ground", "grass", and "goalpost".

We also extract features for each question. We tokenize each of the questions in order to use each word in a question as a predictive feature.

Finally, we use Term Frequency-Inverse Document Frequency (TF-IDF) to represent the concatenated image and question features (Dillon, 1983). This is a simplified representation of natural language data where the structural property of the text is ignored, and every unique word and their number of occurrences are considered. It first creates a bag-of-words model for an input feature, and then transforms each resulting feature vector by down-weighting the most common features in the dataset. At the end of the feature extraction pipeline, for each visual question, we have a TF-IDF vector representation and associated target label.

Machine Learning Algorithms

In order to predict the source of a visual question, we consider four classification models described below.

Random Forest

We choose a Random Forest classifier since it is a flexible and easy to use model that tends to perform well on discrete data. Random forest algorithm searches a space of decision trees to obtain the optimal function with discrete outputs.

[4] https://azure.microsoft.com/en-us/services/cognitive-services/?v=18.44a

From a pilot study we observe that random forest performs well with 54 trees and so chose this value.

K-Nearest Neighbors
We train a KNN classifier with a K value of five. KNN determines the class by querying the K nearest neighbors in a dataset. This model provides an intuitive and interpretable classifier.

Naïve Bayes
Naïve Bayes estimates the probability of a target label occurring given the probability of the features. The naïve assumption is that each feature is independent of other features in the feature vector.

Logistic Regression
We also train a logistic regression classifier. Logistic regression is an effective algorithm for classification that generalizes well from binary to multiclass classifier problems.

EXPERIMENTS

We perform a set of experiments to measure the ability of a system to classify the source of a visual question, i.e., whether it is from a sighted person, visually impaired person, or computer. In doing so, we explore the following research questions: (1) how effective are machine learning algorithms at identifying the source of a visual question?, (2) how much data is needed to train a machine learning algorithm to recognize the source of a visual question?, and (3) what are the cues used by the machine learning algorithms in making decisions? The details of the experimental setups and results are discussed in the subsequent sections.

Experiment 1: Classification Models

We first evaluate the prediction performance of different classification algorithms in order to examine the effectiveness of simple, off-the-shelf machine learning pipelines. To do so, we compare the performance of the following trained algorithms: Naïve Bayes, K-Nearest Neighbors, Random Forest, and Logistic Regression.

Evaluation
We split the 1,800 visual questions sampled from the three datasets (VQA_1.0, VizWiz, and CLEVR) into 1,500 training examples and 300 test examples. We then tuned the hyperparameters for each classifier using 10-fold cross validation on the training set. Next, using the optimal hyperparameters, we compared each trained algorithm's predictions against the target labels using standard evaluation metrics: precision, recall, accuracy, and F1-score. For these metrics, scores range between 0 and 1, and higher scores are better. We also plot ROC curves for all classifiers to visualize the trade-off between the false positive and true positive rates. We include in this plot results for random guessing since that is the best a person can achieve today. In addition, we include the micro and macro average curves. The micro average is computed by aggregating the true positive and false positive rates across all classes and taking the average, while the macro average curve is computed by averaging the performance of each class independently.

Results
We show results in Table 1 and Figure 3.

Overall, all machine learning algorithms performed remarkably well with all performance scores at a value of 0.92 or higher (Table 1). The best scores were obtained using the logistic regression model. The ROC curves in Figure 3 illustrate the performance of the algorithms with respect to each dataset. We can observe that all four algorithms were able to predict the source of the samples from the CLEVR dataset with a perfect score. The variation in performance arises from VizWiz and VQA_1.0 datasets. Both LR and KNN performed similarly on both datasets, while NB and RF algorithms were better at predicting the samples from VizWiz than VQA_1.0.

Experiment 2: Impact of Training Dataset Size

We next examine how much training data is needed to design an effective machine learning algorithm.

	Precision	Recall	F1-Score	Accuracy
Naïve Bayes	0.93	0.92	0.92	0.92
KNN	0.94	0.94	0.94	0.94
Random forest	0.96	0.96	0.96	0.96
Logistic regression	0.99	0.99	0.99	0.99

Table 1. Performance of four machine learning algorithms with respect to four evaluation metrics. As observed across all metrics, all prediction algorithms are very good at identifying whether the visual question was asked by a sighted person, person with visual impairments, or computer.

Evaluation
We again split our dataset so that we have 300 test visual questions, and evaluate using the accuracy metric and F1-score.

Implementation
We examine the impact of the amount of training data on the performance of the top-performing logistic regression algorithm from the previous experiment. To do so, we vary the size of the training dataset using equal proportions of the three VQA datasets: VQA_1.0, VizWiz and CLEVR. We train a total of six versions of the algorithm using 300, 600, 750, 900, 1,200 and 1,500 visual questions respectively.

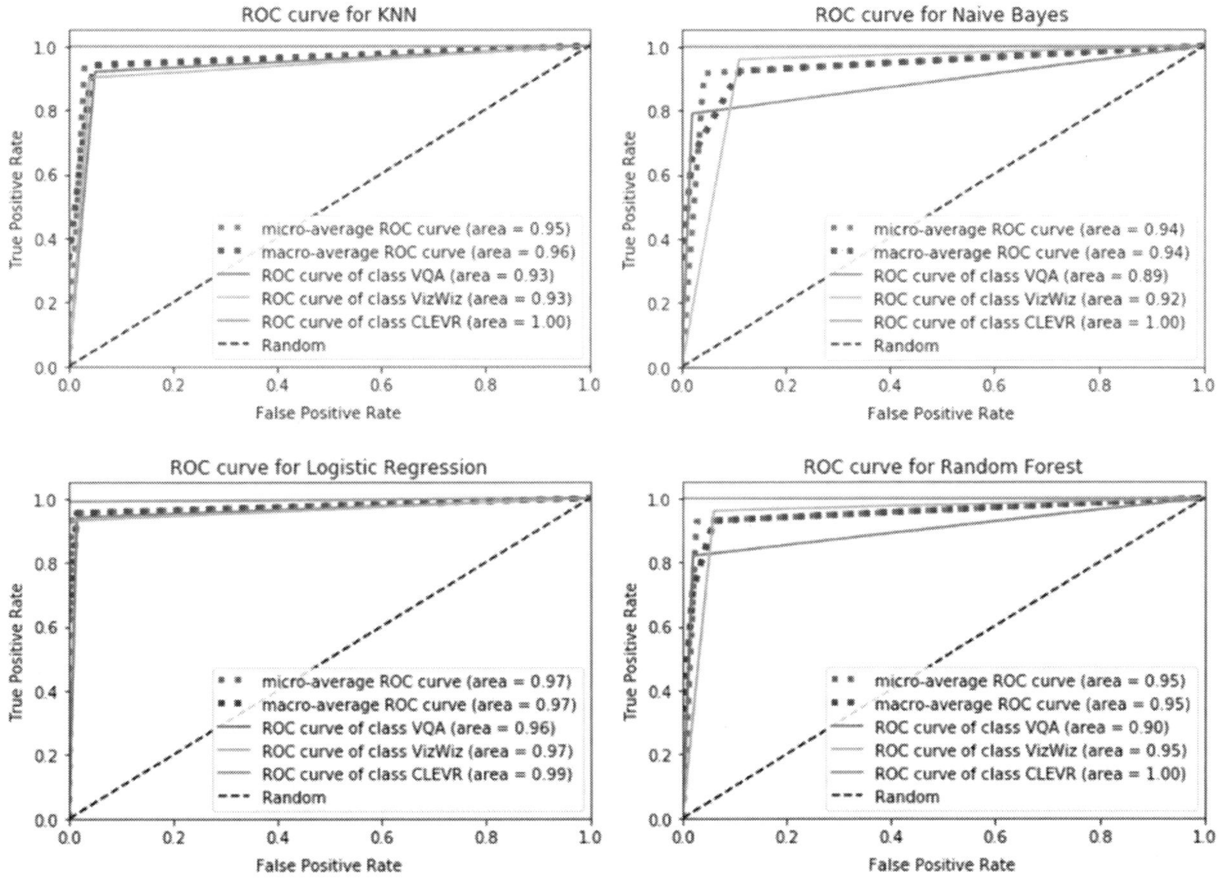

Figure 3. ROC curves for all the classifiers and the best a user can achieve today (random guessing). All four algorithms predict the source of CLEVR dataset very well. LR and KNN algorithms perform similarly on VQA and VizWiz datasets, while RF and NB perform better on VizWiz than VQA.

Results

We show results in Figure 4 and Table 2.

We can observe in Figure 4 that in general the performance improves as the size of the training dataset was increased. The model trained with 1,500 examples achieved the highest F1-score of 0.96. Of note, this is a very small portion of the available data in the visual question answering datasets. In particular, the existing training datasets for VizWiz, CLEVR, and VQA_1.0, contain over 30,000, 70,000, and 200,000 visual questions respectively. Hence, it is possible to predict the source of a visual question with a high accuracy score by using a small subset of the available training data.

Moreover, we observe that an algorithm trained with as little as 300 examples still achieves over an 85% accuracy. The trivial nature of this process to train an accurate machine learning algorithm raises a question about the implication of VQA systems in terms of the privacy of the user. Using minimal user interaction data with such systems, it is possible to easily predict the visual capabilities of the user.

In terms of individual datasets, we found that increasing the size of training dataset had the most positive impact on the VQA_1.0 and VizWiz datasets (Table 2). Specifically,

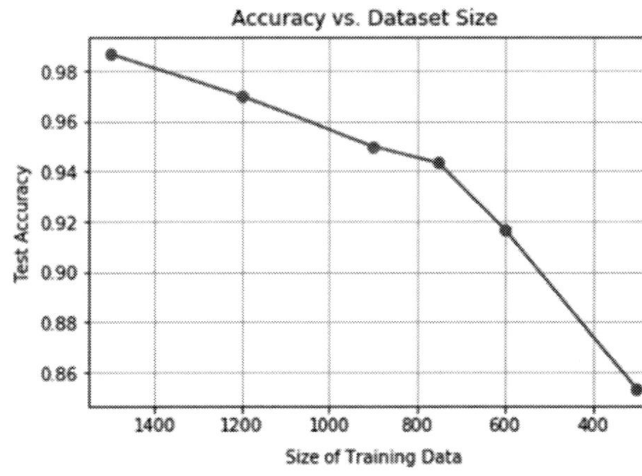

Figure 4. Performance of a Logistic Regression classification algorithm using different dataset sizes. The best performance is achieved using model with 1500 training samples.

the F1-score increased from 0.74 to 0.98 for the VQA_1.0 dataset, and from 0.81 to 0.98 for the VizWiz dataset when the training samples were increased from 300 to 1,500, respectively. In contrast, the model could predict samples from the CLEVR dataset with a 0.99 F1-score even with a training dataset of size 300.

	F1-Score (1500)	F1-Score (900)	F1-Score (300)
Bot	1.00	1.00	0.99
Sighted	0.98	0.93	0.74
Visually impaired	0.98	0.92	0.81
Avg/total	0.99	0.95	0.86

Table 2. Performance of a Logistic Regression classification algorithm using different dataset sizes for each target labels. The algorithm can predict the samples from the bot with a high accuracy even with 300 samples.

Experiment 3: Predictive Features

In the final experiment we explore the predictive power of the different features used in our machine learning system.

Evaluation

Following experiments 1 and 2, we split the dataset in order to have 1,500 training samples and 300 test samples, and evaluate using the F1-score.

Implementation

We conduct this experiment using our best performing algorithm from experiment 1, logistic regression. To explore the predictive power of the different features in our machine learning algorithm we train a model using only the features extracted from the image and another model using only the features extracted from the question.

Results

We show results in Table 3.

We notice that with a minimal feature, such as with either the questions or the image tags alone, our model can achieve a high F1-score of 0.93. We infer that using a small dataset along with a very small feature set, it is possible to identify the visual abilities of a user. The positive side is that, it is also easy for visual question answering systems to detect automatically generated visual questions and so defend their systems against bots with a high accuracy for a similar training setup.

Upon analyzing the effect of each feature across each dataset, we observed that training the model with the combination of tags and captions from images performed better than the questions. Moreover, comparing the features extracted from images, the use of tags was more beneficial than captions, specifically in the case of VizWiz and CLEVR datasets. And, using the combination of both tags and captions, the model was able to predict the source of the samples at a better rate than with the individual tags or captions.

	Questions	Images (tags + captions)	Tags	Captions
Bot	0.99	1.00	1.00	0.88
Sighted	0.90	0.93	0.90	0.90
Visually impaired	0.91	0.92	0.90	0.77
Avg/total	0.93	0.95	0.93	0.86

Table 3. Logistics Regression classifier performance (F1-Score) across different feature set. The best performance is achieved using both image tags and captions.

WEB INTERFACE

To raise awareness of bias in a VQA dataset, we develop a web-application[5] that visualizes the presence of bias in a given dataset. A developer can upload his/her dataset to this web-application to test the presence of bias. Using our model described in the previous section, we predict the sources (sighted, visually impaired, and bot) of each of the images present in the uploaded dataset. We then plot the frequency distribution of the dataset across the sources, an example of which is shown in Figure 6. In this case, we created this dataset with 300 images containing equal number of samples from sighted, visually impaired and computer-generated models. We communicate the presence of bias in the dataset by plotting a frequency distribution across different data sources. We use the Flask[6] framework for web-development and d3.js[7] for visualizations.

DISCUSSION

With the increased use of artificial intelligence in application and value sensitive areas, it is more important to be aware of the possible biases both in academia and industry. The broader goal of artificial intelligence to mimic human intelligence is sacrificed if we fail to be intentional about creating diverse datasets. We call for more research in building inclusive datasets that represent diverse populations, including for visual question answering.

Protecting the privacy of the users is an essential part of the discourse related to disabilities (Braithwaite, 1991). For assistive technologies, as Hamidi, Poneres, Massey, and Hurst (2018) argue, users recognize the trade-off involved

[5] Web-app Repo: https://bitbucket.org/ischoolml/biasvqa-web/src/master/
[6] https://flask.pocoo.org/
[7] https://d3js.org/

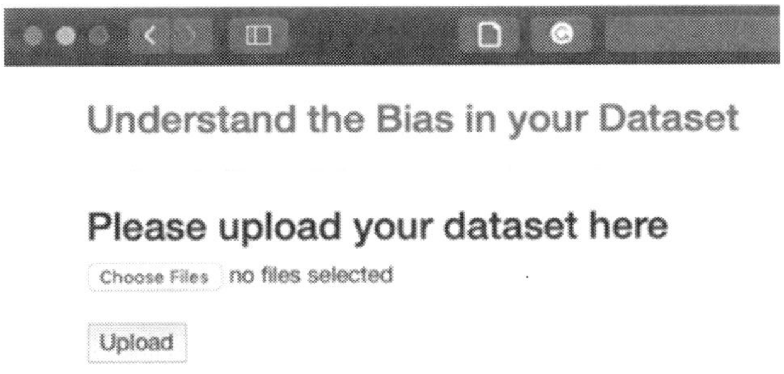

Figure 5. Web-application to upload datasets to understand bias present in them.

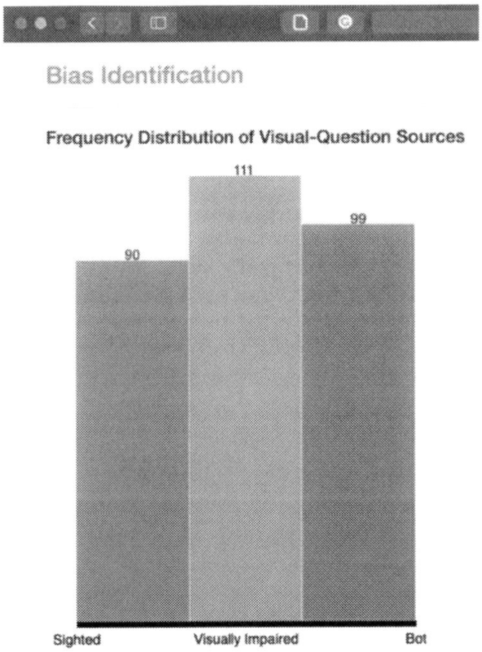

Figure 6. Frequency distribution (predicted) across image sources after uploading a dataset to the web-application.

in terms of privacy and usability of a system. Although users might be comfortable with a system using their data, it is crucial for them to understand the ways the data might be used. Consequently, we need to acknowledge that there is a privacy concern associated with the analysis presented in this work. Using social media data and photos captured by individuals, it is possible to identify the visual abilities of the users. The same also appears to be possible when using questions asked by people with different visual abilities. This information can be used and misused in areas such as targeted marketing and insurance for individuals.

Finally, online systems can be impacted by a high amount of malicious traffic directed towards these systems. For example, an online visual question answering system can be attacked by computer-generated visual questions. With an unusually high number of requests, such a system might crash. Having a preventive layer to detect if a bot is generating the requests can be useful to tackle such adversaries in advance. Another possible application of this use case would be a captcha-like scenario where users are asked to provide questions given an image. Using features from both questions and images, we show that a machine learning model can be trained to detect if a computer generates a request.

CONCLUSION

In this work, we explore and analyze the presence of bias in visual question answering. We create a machine learning based system to recognize the bias of different VQA datasets using off-the-shelf solutions. Our findings highlight that it is easy to identify the status of the visual abilities of a user based on the visual questions submitted by them. Our findings also highlight that with a minimal signal from the data, using only the image or the question, it is possible to predict the source of a visual question. We provide a web interface to help increase awareness and provide a tool for developers to understand the biases of a dataset. Our call for the community is for more research towards building inclusive datasets for VQA and minimizing the potential harm that can arise in VQA applications.

We acknowledge there are certain limitations to this work. Our focus only addresses the problem of visual question answering and may not translate directly to other problem domains. Also, we repurpose existing datasets as a surrogate for labeled data based on an individual's visual abilities. It may not be possible to repurpose existing datasets in different domains due to the availability of such existing datasets. In the future, it would be valuable to perform a qualitative analysis of awareness of the dataset bias issue, such as through interviews with academic researchers, application developers, and users of VQA services.

ACKNOWLEDGMENTS

We gratefully acknowledge funding from the National Science Foundation (IIS-1755593).

REFERENCES

Antol, S., Agrawal, A., Lu, J., Mitchell, M., Batra, D., Zitnick, C. L., & Parikh, D. (2015). VQA: Visual question answering. In *2015 IEEE International Conference on Computer Vision (ICCV)* (pp. 2425–2433). https://doi.org/10.1109/ICCV.2015.279

Bellamy, R. K., Dey, K., Hind, M., Hoffman, S. C., Houde, S., Kannan, K., … Zhang, Y. (2018). Ai fairness 360: An extensible toolkit for detecting, understanding, and mitigating unwanted algorithmic bias. *ArXiv* Preprint ArXiv 1810.01943.

Bigham, J. P., Jayant, C., Ji, H., Little, G., Miller, A., Miller, R. C., … Yeh, T. (2010). VizWiz: Nearly real-time answers to visual questions. 10.

Binns, R. (2017). Fairness in machine learning: Lessons from political philosophy. *ArXiv* Preprint ArXiv: 1712.03586.

Brady, E., Morris, M. R., Zhong, Y., White, S., & Bigham, J. P. (2013). Visual challenges in the everyday lives of blind people. In *Proceedings of the SIGCHI Conference on Human Factors in Computing Systems* (pp. 2117–2126). https://doi.org/10.1145/2470654.2481291

Braithwaite, D. O. (1991). "Just how much did that wheelchair cost?": Management of privacy boundaries by persons with disabilities. *Western Journal of Communication (Includes Communication Reports)*, *55*(3), 254–274.

Buolamwini, J., & Gebru, T. (2018). Gender shades: Intersectional accuracy disparities in commercial gender classification. In *Conference on Fairness, Accountability and Transparency* (pp. 77–91).

Chouldechova, A. (2017). Fair prediction with disparate impact: A study of bias in recidivism prediction instruments. *Big Data*, *5*(2), 153–163.

Deng, J., Dong, W., Socher, R., Li, L.-J., Li, K., & Fei-Fei, L. (2009). Imagenet: A large-scale hierarchical image database. In *Computer Vision and Pattern Recognition, 2009. CVPR 2009. IEEE Conference On* (pp. 248–255). IEEE.

Dillon, M. (1983). In G. Salton & M. McGill, *Introduction to modern information retrieval*. New York, NY: *McGraw-Hill*. pp. xv+ 448.

Dwork, C., Hardt, M., Pitassi, T., Reingold, O., & Zemel, R. (2012). Fairness through awareness. *Proceedings of the 3rd Innovations in Theoretical Computer Science Conference* (pp. 214–226). ACM.

Everingham, M., Van Gool, L., Williams, C. K. I., Winn, J., & Zisserman, A. (2010). The pascal visual object classes (VOC) challenge. *International Journal of Computer Vision*, *88*(2), 303–338. https://doi.org/10.1007/s11263-009-0275-4

Gong, B., Sha, F., & Grauman, K. (2012). Overcoming dataset bias: An unsupervised domain adaptation approach. *NIPS Workshop on Large Scale Visual Recognition and Retrieval*, *3*. Citeseer.

Griffin, G., Holub, A., & Perona, P. (2007). *Caltech-256 object category dataset*.

Gurari, D., Li, Q., Stangl, A. J., Guo, A., Lin, C., Grauman, K., … Bigham, J. P. (2018). Vizwiz grand challenge: Answering visual questions from blind people. In *Proceedings of the IEEE Conference on Computer Vision and Pattern Recognition* (pp. 3608–3617).

Hamidi, F., Poneres, K., Massey, A., & Hurst, A. (2018). Who should have access to my pointing data?: Privacy tradeoffs of adaptive assistive technologies. In *Proceedings of the 20th International ACM SIGACCESS Conference on Computers and Accessibility* (pp. 203–216). ACM.

Hoffmann, A. L., Roberts, S. T., Wolf, C. T., & Wood, S. (2018). Beyond fairness, accountability, and transparency in the ethics of algorithms: Contributions and perspectives from LIS. *Proceedings of the Association for Information Science and Technology*, *55*(1), 694–696.

Jabri, A., Joulin, A., & Van Der Maaten, L. (2016). Revisiting visual question answering baselines. In *European Conference on Computer Vision* (pp. 727–739). Springer, Cham.

Jiang, X., Sun, X., Yang, Z., Zhuge, H., & Yao, J. (2016). Exploiting heterogeneous scientific literature networks to combat ranking bias: Evidence from the computational linguistics area. *Journal of the Association for Information Science and Technology*, *67*(7), 1679–1702.

Jiang, Y., Natarajan, V., Chen, X., Rohrbach, M., Batra, D., & Parikh, D. (2018). Pythia v0. 1: The winning entry to the VQA challenge 2018. *ArXiv* Preprint ArXiv: 1807.09956.

Johnson, J., Hariharan, B., van der Maaten, L., Fei-Fei, L., Zitnick, C. L., & Girshick, R. (2017). CLEVR: A diagnostic dataset for compositional language and elementary visual reasoning. In *Computer Vision and Pattern Recognition (CVPR), 2017 IEEE Conference On* (pp. 1988–1997). IEEE.

Kafle, K., & Kanan, C. (2017). Visual Question Answering: Datasets, Algorithms, and Future Challenges. *Computer Vision and Image Understanding*, *163*, 3–20. https://doi.org/10.1016/j.cviu.2017.06.005

Katell, M. (2018). Algorithmic reputation and information equity. *Proceedings of the Association for Information Science and Technology*, *55*(1), 226–233.

Khosla, A., Zhou, T., Malisiewicz, T., Efros, A. A., & Torralba, A. (2012). Undoing the damage of dataset bias. In D. Hutchison, T. Kanade, J. Kittler, J. M. Kleinberg, F. Mattern, J. C. Mitchell, et al., *Computer vision â€ ECCV 2012* (Vol. *7572*, pp. 158–171). https://doi.org/10.1007/978-3-642-33718-5_12

Lepri, B., Oliver, N., Letouzé, E., Pentland, A., & Vinck, P. (2018). Fair, transparent, and accountable algorithmic decision-making processes. *Philosophy & Technology*, *31*(4), 611–627.

Lin, T.-Y., Maire, M., Belongie, S., Hays, J., Perona, P., Ramanan, D., … Zitnick, C. L. (2014). Microsoft COCO: Common objects in context. In D. Fleet, T. Pajdla, B. Schiele, & T. Tuytelaars, *Computer Vision – ECCV 2014* (Vol. *8693*, pp. 740–755). https://doi.org/10.1007/978-3-319-10602-1_48

Lu, J., Yang, J., Batra, D., & Parikh, D. (2016). Hierarchical question-image co-attention for visual question answering. In *Advances In Neural Information Processing Systems* (pp. 289–297).

McLaughlin, N., Del Rincon, J. M., & Miller, P. (2015). Data-augmentation for reducing dataset bias in person re-identification. *2015 12th IEEE International Conference on Advanced Video and Signal Based Surveillance (AVSS)* (pp. 1–6). https://doi.org/10.1109/AVSS.2015.7301739

Narayanan, A. & Shmatikov, V. (2008). Robust De-anonymization of Large Sparse Datasets. *2008 IEEE Symposium on Security and Privacy (Sp 2008)* (pp. 111–125). https://doi.org/10.1109/SP.2008.33

Nikolov, D., Lalmas, M., Flammini, A., & Menczer, F. (2018). Quantifying biases in online information exposure. *Journal of the Association for Information Science and Technology*.

Russell, B. C., Torralba, A., Murphy, K. P., & Freeman, W. T. (2008). LabelMe: A database and web-based tool for image annotation. *International Journal of Computer Vision*, *77*(1–3), 157–173.

Thomas, C., & Kovashka, A. (2016). Seeing behind the camera: Identifying the authorship of a photograph. *Proceedings of the IEEE Conference on Computer Vision and Pattern Recognition* (pp. 3494–3502).

Tommasi, T., Patricia, N., Caputo, B., & Tuytelaars, T. (2017). A deeper look at dataset bias. In *Domain adaptation in computer vision applications* (pp. 37–55). Springer.

Torralba, A., & Efros, A. A. (2011). Unbiased look at dataset bias. *CVPR, 2011*, 1521–1528. https://doi.org/10.1109/CVPR.2011.5995347

Vinyals, O., Toshev, A., Bengio, S., & Erhan, D. (2017). Show and tell: Lessons learned from the 2015 mscoco image captioning challenge. *IEEE Transactions on Pattern Analysis and Machine Intelligence*, *39*(4), 652–663.

Wilkie, C., & Azzopardi, L. (2018). The impact of fielding on retrieval performance and bias. *Proceedings of the Association for Information Science and Technology*, *55*(1), 564–572.

Wu, Q., Teney, D., Wang, P., Shen, C., Dick, A., & van den Hengel, A. (2017). Visual question answering: A survey of methods and datasets. *Computer Vision and Image Understanding*, *163*, 21–40.

Zehlike, M., Bonchi, F., Castillo, C., Hajian, S., Megahed, M., & Baeza-Yates, R. (2017). Fa* ir: A fair top-k ranking algorithm. *Proceedings of the 2017 ACM on Conference on Information and Knowledge Management* (pp. 1569–1578). ACM.

Zhao, J., Wang, T., Yatskar, M., Ordonez, V., & Chang, K.-W. (2017). Men also like shopping: Reducing gender bias amplification using corpus-level constraints. *ArXiv*: Preprint ArXiv 1707.09457.

What's in People's Digital File Collections?

Jesse David Dinneen
Victoria University of Wellington, New Zealand
jesse.dinneen@vuw.ac.nz

Charles-Antoine Julien
McGill University, Montreal, Canada
charles.julien@mcgill.ca

ABSTRACT
Thoughtfully designing services and rigorously testing software to support personal information management (PIM) requires understanding the relevant collections, but relatively little is known about what people keep in their file collections, especially personal collections. Complementing recent work on the structure of 348 file collections, we examine those collections' contents, how much content is duplicated, and how collections used for personal matters differ from those used for study and work. Though all collections contain many images, some intuitively common file types are surprisingly scarce. Personal collections contain more audio than others, knowledge workers' collections contain more text documents but far fewer folders, and IT collections exhibit unusual traits. Collection duplication is correlated to collections' structural traits, but surprisingly, not to collection age. We discuss our findings in light of prior works and provide implications for various kinds of information research.

KEYWORDS
Personal Information Management; Computer Files

ASIS&T THESAURUS
1577 Personal Files; 2988 Personal Documents; 1469 Personal Collections; 1524 Interfaces

INTRODUCTION
The task of managing digital files, also called file management (FM), is ubiquitous in computing: at home and at work, people create, download, copy, name, rename, organize (or leave unorganized), delete (or not), share, navigate to, and search for digital files and folders (Dinneen & Julien, 2019). The result of such activities are collections of files and folders people personally manage for personal, professional, and educational purposes. Such collections are very large, typically containing tens and even hundreds of thousands of files (Dinneen, Julien, & Frissen, 2019). But what is in these collections? What are people storing?

82nd Annual Meeting of the Association for Information Science & Technology | Melbourne, Australia | 19–23 October, 2019

DOI: 10.1002/pra2.00064

To our knowledge, only five recent (e.g., since 1999) studies have examined the contents of people's file collections, though none have examined *strictly* personal collections (i.e., those not used in work or study), and while several studies of personal information management (PIM) have suggested occupational factors likely determine users' behavior and collections, empirical data for comparing such collections has been scarce. Further, though two studies (Henderson, 2011; Hicks, Dong, Palmer, & McAlpine, 2008) found a surprising amount of duplication of contents in work collections, the causes of duplication remain unknown.

As knowledge about the contents of file collections is limited, so too is our ability to model and understand them, test and compare relevant software improvements, and ultimately support their management. For example, it is unclear what kinds of files should comprise representative test collections to be used in evaluating PIM prototype software, and without such collections it is hard to perform comparable tests of alternative interfaces and improvements. Without a thorough, baseline description of the artefact created during the process of managing files, it is difficult to model that process and the many possible determinants suggested by past studies (e.g., technological, demographic, and individual differences).

Here we examine the contents of 348 collections used for personal, work, and study activities. We provide tabular data that describe the typical composition of such collections, discuss notable differences across collection types, and examine potential causes of content duplication. We end by discussing implications for future work.

LITERATURE REVIEW AND RESEARCH QUESTIONS
PIM refers to the study and practice of individuals managing information owned by or about them *and* to individuals personally managing information, owned by them or otherwise (Jones, Dinneen, Capra, Diekema, & Pérez-Quiñones, 2017), typically with the intention of later returning to that information. PIM research has explored a broad range of contexts and activities within this scope, including the common computing phenomenon of managing digital files, where personal could mean, for example, using a private computer to backup travel photos, using a company computer to organize project files, or retrieving manuscripts previously downloaded to a laboratory computer. Beyond PIM, files have been considered important digital possessions (Cushing,

2013) and a common part of personal archives (Marshall, 2008).

Hundreds of studies have covered various topics in FM (Dinneen & Julien, 2019), like searching and navigating to files (Bergman, Tene-Rubinstein, & Shalom, 2013; Teevan, Alvarado, Ackerman, & Karger, 2004), file sharing (Capra, Vardell, & Brennan, 2014), and developing augmentations to FM software (Fitchett, Cockburn, & Gutwin, 2013). To investigate the common PIM activities of storing, organising, and retrieving (or exploiting) digital items (Jones et al., 2017; Whittaker, 2011), many studies have characterized the artefacts produced by FM activities: people's digital collections (i.e., files and folders). Specifically, studies have measured collections' *scale* (i.e., how many files users store; Boardman & Sasse, 2004; Gonçalves & Jorge, 2003), *structure* (i.e., how files and folders are organized; Bergman, Whittaker, Sanderson, Nachmias, & Ramamoorthy, 2010; Henderson & Srinivasan, 2009), and *contents* (i.e., files and their types, discussed next).

Contents of File Collections

The contents of file collections (i.e., the files a user manages on some computer) are generated or acquired by users actively storing files and folders (e.g., by creating and downloading them) or passively keeping (i.e., not deleting) files and folders (e.g., in downloaded archives; Watkins, Sellen, & Lindley, 2015). Users' files come from various sources, including the Web (Jones, Bruce, & Dumais, 2001), external devices (Capra et al., 2014), and peer-to-peer or cloud software (Marshall & Tang, 2012). Users keep files for many different purposes (e.g., personal or professional) and reasons, for example, because they are needed only briefly, or are being modified over the duration of some ongoing project, or will be needed again at some future time (Nardi, Anderson, & Erickson, 1995). In extreme cases, participants self-identifying as hoarders and minimalists have explained that they hoard because they are afraid of missing some data at a crucial moment, or do otherwise because they are reacting to or trying to prevent information overload (Vitale, Janzen, & McGrenere, 2018). The end result is that, even in typical cases, collections contain tens to hundreds of thousands of files across tens of thousands of folders (Dinneen et al., 2019), and those items necessarily compete for attention when users navigate through and retrieve them. It is therefore hard not to wonder: what are the contents of these collections?

Beyond satisfying scholarly curiosity, answering the above question also has practical implications. Evaluating PIM prototypes (e.g., those designed to improve user experience) requires test collections, and making sound comparisons across prototypes requires consistency in those collections (Gurrin et al., 2019). However, no such collections are available for testing FM prototypes, as was acknowledged a decade ago (Chernov, Demartini, Herder, Kopycki, & Nejdl, 2008). A thorough description of collections' contents is also needed for studying and modelling the many possible determinants suggested by past studies, including technological (Bergman et al., 2010; Boardman & Sasse, 2004), demographic (Khoo et al., 2007), and individual (Lansdale, 1988) differences, and to compare the FM habits and collections of particular professional or social groups to a baseline, but such modelling, study, and comparisons require a baseline of data to compare to.

Five recent (i.e., in the last two decades) studies have sought to understand the contents of people's collections, evidenced by file extensions or categorized file types. Two studies of work collections – one of eleven varied professionals (Gonçalves & Jorge, 2003) and one of seventy-three university staff (Henderson, 2009) – mostly agree in their findings: collections are, on average, approximately 30% text files, 20% image files, 10% unidentifiable, with spreadsheets, presentations, system files, source code, and extensionless files each comprising less than 10%, and audio, video, shortcuts, and other kinds of files being relatively negligible (i.e., approaching 0%). A third study, of forty engineers' collections (Hicks et al., 2008), differed in that it showed 10% less text and a considerably higher 24% unidentified files. Finally, two studies (Agrawal, Bolosky, Douceur, & Lorch, 2007; Douceur & Bolosky, 1999) observed thousands of Microsoft employees' work collections over six years, but reported the thirty most common file extensions rather than categorized file types, preventing easy comparison to the other previously mentioned works. They observed .gif files to be the most frequent (9%), *.h*, *.htm*, and *.dll* files to be slightly less frequent, and *.jpg*, *.bmp*, and *.doc* files to be infrequent (e.g., 0.6% for *.doc*), at least until extensionless files became more frequent than any single extension. However, the authors note that the presence of technical staff collections, which make up the majority, have skewed the results as some differences were present among job roles (e.g., technical staff had considerably fewer *.gif* and more *.c* files). Such differences are intuitive – it seems reasonable to assume developers keep programming files, while teachers keep presentations and documents – but while such differences have been suggested by past works (Khoo et al., 2007; Kwaśnik, 1991), they have not been explored or quantified.

Duplication in File Collections

An additional concern about the contents of file collections is content duplication (i.e., file and folder duplication). Duplication can cause confusion during navigation and search, sharing, and version control, and duplicates may occupy limited storage space. Indeed, in one study 47% of participants reported struggling with duplicate files (Henderson, 2011). Several tools have been developed to prevent and treat duplication, for example file version control and software to identify duplicate images (Bergman, Tucker, & Dahamshy,

2018), but is unclear if such tools are commonly used, and duplication nonetheless persists; additional potential causes therefore warrant consideration.

Duplication has, so far, been studied by examining the presence of repeating file and folder names, both of which appear common, ranging from 20% (Henderson, 2005, 2011) to 30% (Hicks et al., 2008) duplication in collections. The causes of duplication are unclear; participants often suggest for example, they may download the same file from an email multiple times (Henderson, 2011). But given the size of collections and the high percentage of duplication, it is unclear if incremental actions like downloading attachments could be the primary cause. Surprisingly, only four participants suggested copy and pasting folders may lead to duplication, but recent works suggests this may be a primary cause, as multiplicative actions (like copy and paste) may shape other attributes of the file system (like extreme imbalance in file classification; Dinneen et al., 2019). Some telling properties of duplication have been examined; for example, file name duplication has been seen to correlate strongly with folder name duplication, collection size (in files and folders), and the mean depth of folders within the folder tree (Henderson, 2011), but additional file system variables possibly related to duplication remain to be examined (e.g., file classification skew and the maximum depth of the folder tree) or the time required to produce duplicates (i.e., the age of the collection).

Summary and Research Questions

In short, we do not know what is in personal file collections, how work collections differ, or what causes content duplication, and these gaps in knowledge limit our ability to model FM, test improvements, and support computer users. To address these issues, in this manuscript we examine 349 collections to answer the following research questions:

RQ1. What are the typical contents of people's personal, professional, and scholarly file collections?

RQ2. How do the contents of different collection types differ?

RQ3. Do file and folder duplication correlate with other collection traits (e.g., folder depth or classification skew)?

METHODOLOGY

Recruitment and Data Collection

Various methods have been used to collect data about personal file collections, such as guided tours of users' computers (Thomson, 2015), recording participants desktops during structured tasks (Bergman et al., 2010), and taking snapshots of user's collections (e.g., Henderson, 2009). We used the last approach, employing cross-platform, open-source software called Cardinal, described and validated by Dinneen, Odoni, Frissen, and Julien (2016) and used later by Dinneen et al. (2019).

When run, Cardinal solicits a participant's demographic information and use(s) of the computer, then accesses the portions of their folder hierarchy where they have specified they manage files, and records various properties (e.g., file extensions). Known system folders were ignored unless the user explicitly stated they manage files within them, and hidden files and folders were assumed to be either actively hidden by participants (i.e., we are not meant to see them) or else unknown to participants (i.e., not managed by them), and so were ignored. Files pointing to other files (i.e., shortcuts, aliases, and symlinks) were counted as pointers rather than the kind of file they pointed to. Though no file or folder names were recorded, instances of non-unique names were noted to provide a measure of duplication.

We recruited participants[1] from February of 2016 to August of 2018 by posting calls on study recruitment Websites, online communities (e.g., Facebook, Reddit), and mailing lists (e.g., industrial, governmental, and academic). Criteria for participation were only that participants have files stored locally (i.e., not exclusively in the cloud, whether at home, work, or school) that they personally manage, and have the abilities to read English and download and run the software. Participation thus consisted of running the software, answering the questionnaires, specifying where on the computer they manage files (both active, working areas and backup locations like external drives were encouraged), and reviewing a summary of the results before choosing to let the software submit the data to the researchers. Participation was therefore remote and anonymous.

Data Analysis

To facilitate comparison with prior studies, file extensions were categorized into file types. There is currently no common taxonomy of file types nor consensus about how to categorize extensions, but the skewed distributions of extension frequency previously observed (Douceur & Bolosky, 1999) suggest that categorising the few, most common extensions will account for most files. We adapted the 18 file type categories used by Gonçalves and Jorge (2003), with some modifications: (1) the *source code* and *Web script* categories were merged into a new category, *development* files; (2) *shockwave* was merged into *video*; (3) *PDA-related* was merged into *PIM*; and (4) a *pointers* category was added to account for shortcuts and symlinks. The result was 15 categories, discussed below, which have only minor differences to the categories used by Gonçalves and Jorge (2003), Henderson (2011), and Hicks et al. (2008).

We categorized the most common extensions within each participant's collection until each collection was at least 80% categorized (excluding two outliers) and unidentified files comprised on average only 7% of a collection. This

[1] This study was approved by ethics committees at Victoria University of Wellington (HEC #25658) and McGill University (REB #75-0715).

entailed categorising 453 extensions, each of which we researched to determine the best category, and which together include all the extensions listed in the prior works discussed above. The extensions, categories, and python function to categorize them are available on GitHub.[2]

Collections were divided into those used for personal matters, work, or study, according to participants' responses. To account for potential differences in work collections (discussed above), those were further divided (using participants' stated occupations) into three broad groups: (1) knowledge workers, (2) IT staff, or (3) other. Knowledge workers included quality assurance managers, doctors, journalists, librarians, and so on, whereas IT staff included positions like programmer, system administrator, or IT technician. The *other* category included occupations that are not obviously knowledge work (e.g., tradespeople, retail associates, and artists), null values, and people unemployed at the time of participation.

Following Henderson (2011), proportions of file and folder duplication within each collection was inferred by the presence of duplicate file and folder names. Limitations to this approach are discussed below.

As in prior studies of computer files, data along most measures were highly skewed, and approximated log normal distributions even after outliers were removed using interquartile range (Wilcox, 2011). Thus, to convey the *range* of typical values and avoid overestimation, log normal medians and means – hereafter, median* and mean* – are reported when appropriate (see Limpert, Stahel, & Abbt, 2001 for more detail). Further, nonparametric tests were used: Mann–Whitney U tests assess significance (p) in differences between groups with skewed data of unequal variance, and Kendall's tau (τ) assesses correlation strength. Though such tests are often used for ordinal (rank) data, they perform well with continuous (interval or ratio) data and are more suitable for heavily skewed distributions than parametric equivalents (e.g., t tests and Pearson's rho; Chok, 2010). Differences between groups were tested pairwise (with the Mann–Whitney U test) since n-way tests like MANOVA require normal data distributions and log transformation of skewed data containing many 0 values is not straightforward.

RESULTS

We received data describing 348 collections, totalling 50 million files and nearly 8 million folders. Table 1 summarizes the samples' demographic features, uses of the collections, and operating systems.

Complete statistical descriptions of each collection type are provided on the Web[2], while in this section we present an overview of the range of file extensions, the categorized collections, how collection types contrast, and results of inferential testing of duplication and related phenomena. For brevity, after describing personal collections we present only the strongest differences between collection types rather than describing each exhaustively.

[2] https://github.com/jddinneen/file-extension-categoriser

Sample trait	**Values**
Age	Range 14–64 Mean 30 (SD 9.96)
Gender	Male: 218 (63%) Female: 123 (35%) Other: 7 (2%)
Operating system	Mac OS: 169 (48%) Windows: 135 (39%) GNU/Linux: 44 (13%)
Collection use	Work: 166 (48%) Knowledge work: 93 Other: 48 IT: 25 School: 143 (41%) Personal: 39 (11%)

Table 1. Summary of attributes of sampled participants, systems, and collections.

File Extensions

The collected data contain 85,000 unique extensions, distributed in a highly skewed and long-tailed manner as observed in prior works (Douceur & Bolosky, 1999). Thus, despite our categorization efforts accounting for less than 1% of the variety of extensions, and despite extensionless files comprising on average 10%, 83% of all files were categorized and on average only 7% of each collection was left uncategorized.

Personal Collections

Personal collections were, in typical cases, comprised of 45 thousand to 85 thousand files across 7 thousand to 21 thousand folders. The data across most file types was highly skewed, indicating great variation across the collections, but a few general claims can be made. Images and development files were the most common types at 22–29% and 4–35%, respectively (e.g., 20,000 image files and 12,000 development files, depending on collection size). Next most common were system, audio, and extensionless files at roughly 5–25% each (e.g., ~7,000 of each kind). The typical proportion of audio files varied greatly, however, from 1% to 20%. Unidentified files comprised 6–9% of collections, and text files 3–5% (e.g., ~2,000 text files). PIM and video files were relatively scarce (0–1%), and every other type (i.e., databases, spreadsheets, executables, backups, presentations, bookmarks, and pointers) was relatively non-existent (e.g., a dozen or so files each).

Differences Across Groups

Figure 1 displays treemaps of example personal, knowledge work, and IT collections that feature proportions of file types within the typical range (e.g., median* and mean*) for their respective groups. Treemapping is a method for visually displaying differences in group compositions, and originally, file system data (Shneiderman & Wattenberg, 2001). The full results tables should be consulted for discrete values and comprehensive descriptions of the composition of typical collections in each group.

On average, personal collections were smaller than all other collection types while IT collections were the largest, generally ten times larger than personal collections ($p = .059$) at 61 thousand to 829 thousand files. Knowledge workers' collections had the least folders, typically 2.5 to 14 thousand, or about half that of typical student collections ($p = .006$) and a fifth of IT collections ($p = .007$).

Most collection types had proportions of images and development files comparable to personal collections, with the most notable differences being that on average IT collections had fewer images (11–26%; $p = .019$) and more development files (up to 49% even in typical cases; $p < .001$). Knowledge workers also had smaller proportions of images than personal collections (16–24%; $p = .076$).

Personal and *other* work collections had the most system files (5–24%), whereas other groups had fewer with IT staff having the fewest (2–5%; $p = .0495$ when comparing to other). Personal collections contained the highest proportion of audio files of all collection types, with students having the second most and knowledge workers' collections having the least (0–1%; $p < .001$ when comparing to students). Although IT collections resembled personal collections in the proportion of text files, knowledge workers', students', and other workers' collections each contained almost twice as many (5–10%; $p < .001$ when comparing knowledge workers' to personal collections). In all collection types there were relatively few video files (e.g., 0–2%) and almost none (approaching 0%) of all remaining file types; for example, even knowledge workers had ~0% presentation files.

All work and student collections exhibited smaller proportions of extensionless files than personal collections did, and with much narrower ranges of typical values, but the pairwise differences were not statistically significant; for example IT collections had on average 4–6% (SD* 2.3) as compared with 2–29% in personal collections (SD* of 9.7; $p = .359$).

Duplication Results

Across all groups we observed that 23–34% of files in a collection were typically duplicated (excludes two outliers), while on average 44% (traditional mean) of folders were duplicated. IT collections exhibited the most duplication of files (40–48%), and personal collections the least (20–26%; $p = .002$ when comparing to IT), while folder duplication was greater overall but followed a similar pattern: IT collections had the most (53–60%), and personal collections had the least (33–47%; $p = .021$).

All correlations reported here were statistically significant ($p < .001$; omitted below for brevity). File and folder duplication correlated moderately ($\tau = 0.39$), and each correlated moderately with their total counts ($\tau = 0.36$ for files, 0.40 for folders). We found weak correlations between folder tree width and file and folder duplication ($\tau = 0.29$ and 0.33, respectively), and folder depth correlated moderately with file duplication ($\tau = 0.45$) and folder duplication ($\tau = 0.48$), and similarly, maximum folder tree depth (i.e., the deepest part of the tree) correlated moderately with folder duplication ($\tau = 0.45$) and weakly with file duplication ($\tau = 0.26$). We also found weak correlations between skewness in the classification of files into folders (i.e., the degree to which files are placed into relatively few folders, leaving most folders relatively empty) and file ($\tau = 0.16$) and folder duplication ($\tau = 0.29$). Duplication had no linear relationship with the age of collections whether measured by mean or maximum file age (e.g., $\tau < 0.05$).

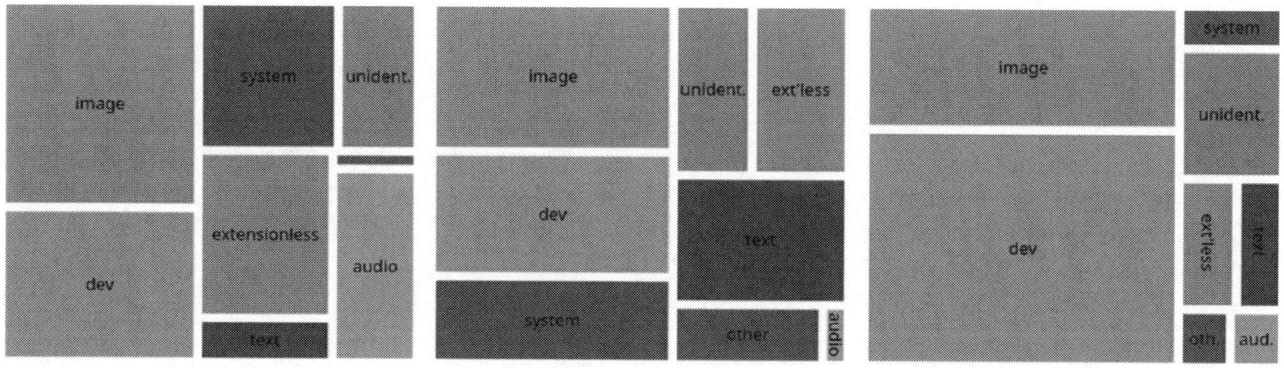

Figure 1. Treemaps showing examples of typical collections for personal use (left), knowledge work (middle), and IT work (right). All collection types typically contain many images and development files and relatively few of the rarest file types (e.g., video, databases, etc; here collectively called *other*). Personal collections contain more images and audio files, knowledge workers' collections contain more text files, and IT collections contain more development files and few system files.

DISCUSSION

Here we synthesize and discuss our results and compare them to commensurable findings from prior works.

File Extensions

We saw 85 thousand extensions, a far greater variety than reported in prior works (e.g., 623 occurring more than once; Henderson, 2009). This suggests file extension variety is growing, but the distribution of extensions remains a similar shape (e.g., following Lotka's law; Douceur & Bolosky, 1999) and consequently categorising the majority of the collection can still be done with relatively few (e.g., 450) extensions (c.f. 350; Gonçalves & Jorge, 2003).

Characterisations of Collections by Type

RQ1 asked "what are the typical contents of people's personal, professional, and scholarly file collections?" The tabular data provide an uninterpreted answer to the question, which we contextualize below by characterising and interpreting each collection type, with emphasis on differences between collection types so to answer RQ2.

Personal collections are the smallest (in terms of files), and despite containing relatively many image files (as did most collection types) they exhibit some uniqueness in their composition. They had the most audio files and system files, second most development files (behind IT), and widest range of extensionless files. While image and audio files are unsurprising given that many people keep personal music and image collections, the prevalence of system files is surprising, particularly as the data collection software scanned only user-managed folders and ignored system folders unless users specified otherwise. It is similarly unclear what caused the presence of so many development files and the occasional cases of so many extensionless files.

Personal collections also exhibited the widest range of file types, perhaps reflecting a wide variety personal computing activities that may not be reflected in PIM research focusing on professional contexts. Surprisingly, like most other collections, personal ones contained relatively few (e.g., 0.1%) file types like backups, executables, PIM files, and so on, thus suggesting the variety of file extensions are variations within the main categories (e.g., different image extensions). Personal collections also featured relatively few text files, likely reflecting the popularity of such formats (e.g., *.docx*) in knowledge work (as contrasted with personal matters). Perhaps because of their size (considered below), personal collections featured the least duplication, though still roughly 20–50%.

Knowledge workers' collections (e.g., work collections managed by doctors, teachers, librarians…) were the smallest of the work collections, and while bigger than personal collections, they nonetheless featured ~30% fewer folders, which is surprising given the popularity and many uses of folders identified in previous PIM research on knowledge workers. Such collections had the least audio files, perhaps indicating an absence of music collections on work machines, and predictably, more text files, perhaps due to reasons considered above.

The percentages of system, development, and images files observed in knowledge workers' collections are roughly consistent (i.e., within 2–3%) with prior works (Gonçalves & Jorge, 2003; Henderson, 2009; Hicks et al., 2008), suggesting no meaningful change over time, but the percentage of text files observed (7–12%) was much less than in those works, which saw 21–34%. The cause for this difference is unclear; given the data are highly skewed, it is possible that in prior works averages were inflated by outliers. That knowledge workers had relatively few archive, audio, video, shortcut, PIM, and database files also roughly aligns with the prior similar studies, but surprisingly, knowledge workers kept relatively few (e.g., <1%) of other types that are commonly associated with knowledge work, like spreadsheets and presentation files, which contrasts with those works, which found 4%–8% spreadsheets and 2–7% executable files. Such differences may be attributable to the high portion of previously uncategorized files (e.g., 24%) or to occupational differences (e.g., examining only engineers; Hicks et al., 2008).

Other work collections were generally big, but otherwise like the other work collections in most ways. However, they did feature more image and audio file percentages, comparable to personal collections, perhaps reflecting the multiple uses of machines people working in less traditional roles (e.g., whereas knowledge workers may not store many personal images on machines owned by their employers, freelance designers may work from the same machine on which they store such photos). These collections were also highly varied, which may reflect the diversity of the participants' occupations.

Students' collections resembled knowledge workers' collections, but with twice as many folders and more audio files; this may reflect that many students are knowledge workers in training (and/or that education is often knowledge work) and therefore may manage computer files similarly.

IT collections are huge and unsurprisingly contain many development files. They also contain relatively few other text files, but surprisingly, contain far fewer system files than other collections (and perhaps far fewer extensionless files, though this lacked statistical significance). Absolute values indicate the difference is not simply due to having more development files (i.e., thus lowering the proportion of system files): IT collections contain up to 5,500 system files, whereas knowledge workers' collections typically contain up to 32,000. Although in this manuscript we do not examine differences across operating systems, because IT collections were distributed no differently across the OSes than other collections (and comprised only 16% of the Linux machines) it seems unlikely OS is the main cause of the relative scarcity of system files in IT collections. It is possible that IT professionals make a concerted effort to separate their systems' files from other work files (and/or consider it routine maintenance), whereas, for example, it may be rare for knowledge workers to do so. That IT collections had 0% executables shows a decrease from 3% in 1999 (Douceur & Bolosky), and likely reflects general collection growth (e.g., in development files) over time.

RQ2 asked "How do the contents of collection types differ?" In summary, personal collections are generally smaller than work collections and contain more images and audio files, and are generally more varied than other collection types. Knowledge workers' collections contain more text files and far fewer folders than personal collections. IT collections exhibit some predictable traits like having many development files, but also some surprising ones, like having far fewer system files.

File and Folder Duplication

Results regarding duplication were broadly similar to but weaker than observations made by Henderson (2011), with the most notable exception being that we observed more duplication overall: roughly 30% for files (matching Hicks et al., 2008) and 44% for folders (as compared with ~20%). This may be attributable to general collection growth over the last decade – Henderson (2011) suggests that larger collections may have more duplication, and the results here support this – but the results here also suggest the story is more complicated. Specifically, the presence of several correlations (ranging from weak to moderate) between duplication and structural variables suggests that multiplicative actions may not just cause duplication directly (pasting causes duplicates), but also *indirectly*: multiplying parts of the tree produces a more complex structure that is harder to navigate (Julien *et al.*, 2013), which is therefore more costly to maintain. For example, users may multiply branches of the tree *downward*, thus increasing measures of file system depth, and consequently be less likely to later navigate back down to those files to address the resulting duplicates. This could explain why measures of depth are the strongest correlates with duplication, stronger even than collection size.

Surprisingly, we found no notable correlations between duplicate files or folders and the age of collections whether measuring age by the mean age of files or the oldest file in a collection. This is surprising because prior studies (e.g., Dinneen et al., 2019; Henderson, 2011) suggest that it takes time for a collection to grow, even multiplicatively, and thus older collections should exhibit greater duplication. It is possible the majority of duplication is produced near to the creation of a folder system and that only incremental duplication (i.e., downloading duplicates) happens later, though this warrants further investigation.

RQ3 asked if file and folder duplication correlate with other collection traits. In summary, duplication does appear to correlate with structural properties of the file system, especially folder depth. Given that duplication is so common despite the availability of anti-duplication tools like those mentioned above, perhaps additional strategies should be implemented to prevent and treat duplication; for example, upon a user initiating a large copy and paste action, the file manager interface could provide a dialogue to exclude some subfolders, and the OS could periodically scan for duplicates and prompt the user to resolve them.

Implications for Assessing Collections

The tabular data and characterizations of collections provided by this study can be consulted when assessing existing collections managed by particular groups of participants, and also when generating or selecting collections for use in evaluations of PIM software. For example, a study examining digital information management of administrative staff at a university could compare the contents of their collections to the knowledge workers' collections described here to assess if the participants are representative or typical (e.g., if those collections have <7% or >12% text files, they are not typical). Similarly, to increase the generalisability of evaluations of prototypes like file manager plugins or desktop search improvements, the collections used should be representative of those likely to be used in practice (e.g., in personal contexts, or by IT staff, or by general users), and this can be achieved by consulting the ranges of typical values reported here and choosing or generating only collections that fit within the ranges given.

LIMITATIONS

The present study has notable limitations, some of which are attributable to using extensions to identify file types: 23% of all files did not fit a traditional file type category, either because they had no extensions or had extensions so rare we did not categorize them (i.e., 84.5 k of the 85 k different extensions, or 99% of the variety). Categorisation is often imperfect, and some extensions fit multiple categories (e.g., *.py* is a text file, used for development, and used by the system). While the majority of extensions fit neatly into one category, studies categorising files (and extensionless files) differently may observe different results. As our categorisation method is the most comprehensive thus far, and is shared on the Web, we hope it facilitates consistency and comparison in future works.

Similar limitations are present in the collection groupings. For example, though work collections were separated from those used only for personal matters, they included collections used for both, and those used strictly for work may differ further still. Likewise, the occupation categories used (e.g., knowledge workers) here are broad; future work may find it useful to examine differences across more specific title groupings, like those provided by the International Standard Classification of Occupations.

The method used in this study and prior works to infer duplicates from name duplication is imperfect as it can detect false positives (files can share names without containing the same content) and miss duplicates (files can have different names despite containing the same content). The effect of such limitations is currently unclear, but future studies may address them by implementing purpose-built methods for detecting duplication (e.g., full-text analysis or computer vision).

Finally, the data collection method used in this study necessarily omits some information useful in interpreting the results, like users' reports of *why* they keep duplicates or particular file types, and the analyses used were intended primarily to explore basic potential differences between collection types. In future work it would be useful to complement such quantitative descriptions with qualitative reports and further analyses for nonparametric data.

CONCLUSION

Supporting people in the daily task of managing information requires understanding many dimensions of the relevant phenomena, including, for example, what is in their file collections. In this manuscript we established the contents of people's file collections, including personal, study, and work collections of various kinds, and discussed commonalities and notable differences among the broad collection types. In doing so we identified an extreme variety in file extensions, provided an updated categorisation scheme for the extensions, and discussed remaining limitations to be addressed. Trends and differences in these results across prior studies and across time were also discussed, including those related to file duplication. We also discussed the implications of the results for PIM research, and provide the statistical tables to facilitate such works. Expanding on those implications, we next consider concrete implications for both narrow and broader research.

Starting narrowly, several aspects of the data remain to be analysed, for example of duplication across file types, occupations, or operating systems (Bergman et al., 2010), and of individual differences that may pertain to FM, like age, gender, education, and individual differences. Going forward, follow-up work would benefit from more actively involving participants in data collection to add valuable context (present in many qualitative studies) to the numeric results, thus potentially overcoming persistent methodological debates about qualitative and quantitative approaches and yielding a more holistic and comprehensive understanding of the relevant phenomena.

More broadly, considering the role of files in other areas of information science is also likely to be fruitful, and is a natural fit. For example, information behavior research that examines how people "seek, manage… and use information" in wider information ecosystems (Fisher, Erdelez, & McKechnie, 2005, p. xix) and related activities like filing, archiving, and organising collected information (Meho & Tibbo, 2003) matches very closely previous characterizations of what users do with files (Boardman & Sasse, 2004; Malone, 1983). We hope the contents of people's digital collections can be useful in considering how PIM integrates into broader information behavior.

One area that may benefit from FM research is (digital) cultural heritage: it may interest cultural heritage institutions (especially digital ones) to know what is in people's collections, because the contents and (original) order of personal collections of relevant individuals influences what value can later be made of such collections (e.g., by libraries, archives and museums) and how those collections can best be preserved and accessed. Further, the way people collect and organize their personal and work collections (often with blurred boundaries between them) can have impact on areas where personal and collective meets, such as records management (because personal attitudes, practices, and habits are often mirrored in the workplace) and digital curation, for example, because the way files are curated from the point of creation directly affects their longevity and authenticity (Oliver & Harvey, 2016). When personal collections belong to people whose life and work has significance for cultural heritage sector, the way they organized, preserved and explained their collections will greatly influence the interpretation and long-term usability of such collections. Some works have considered files as part of the personal archive (Cushing, 2013; Kaye et al., 2006; Marshall, Bly, & Brun-Cottan, 2006), but fuller synthesis of the areas remains to be done.

In summary, while the present manuscript elucidates what is in people's file collections and what might cause duplication, we hope to have further stimulated researchers in and beyond PIM to consider the everyday role of FM.

ACKNOWLEDGMENTS

We thank our participants for their time and effort, and Maja Krtalić and anonymous peer reviewers for their feedback.

REFERENCES

Agrawal, N., Bolosky, W. J., Douceur, J. R., & Lorch, J. R. (2007). A five-year study of file-system metadata. *ACM Transactions on Storage (TOS)*, *3*(3), 9.

Bergman, O., Tene-Rubinstein, M., & Shalom, J. (2013). The use of attention resources in navigation versus search. *Personal and Ubiquitous Computing*, *17*(3), 583–590.

Bergman, O., Tucker, S., & Dahamshy, S. (2018). The effect of demoting near-duplicate pictures. *Proceedings of the Association for Information Science and Technology*, *55* (1), 755–756.

Bergman, O., Whittaker, S., Sanderson, M., Nachmias, R., & Ramamoorthy, A. (2010). The effect of folder structure on personal file navigation. *Journal of the American Society for Information Science and Technology*, *61*(12), 2426–2441.

Boardman, R., & Sasse, M. A. (2004). Stuff goes into the computer and doesn't come out: a cross-tool study of personal information management. In CHI '04: Proceedings of the SIGCHI Conference on Human Factors in Computing Systems (pp. 583–590). ACM.

Capra, R., Vardell, E., & Brennan, K. (2014). File synchronization and sharing: User practices and challenges. *Proceedings of the American Society for Information Science and Technology*, *51*(1), 1–10.

Chernov, S., Demartini, G., Herder, E., Kopycki, M., & Nejdl, W. (2008). Evaluating personal information management using an activity logs enriched desktop dataset. In PIM Workshop at CHI '08: the SIGCHI Conference on Human Factors in Computing Systems, Florence, Italy.

Chok, N. S. (2010). *Pearson's versus Spearman's and Kendall's correlation coefficients for continuous data* (Dissertation). University of Pittsburgh.

Cushing, A. L. (2013). "It's stuff that speaks to me": Exploring the characteristics of digital possessions. *Journal of the American Society for Information Science and Technology*, *64*(8), 1723–1734.

Dinneen, J. D., & Julien, C.-A. (2019). The ubiquitous digital file: A review of file management research. *Journal of the American Society for Information Science and Technology* AIS Reviews.

Dinneen, J. D., Julien, C.-A., & Frissen, I. (2019). The scale and structure of personal file collections. In *CHI '19: Proceedings of the 37th Annual ACM Conference on Human Factors in Computing Systems* (pp. 327:1–327:12). ACM.

Dinneen, J. D., Odoni, F., Frissen, I., & Julien, C.-A. (2016). Cardinal: novel software for studying file management behavior. In *Proceedings of the 79th Annual Meeting of the Association for Information Science and Technology* (pp. 36:1–36:10).

Douceur, J. R., & Bolosky, W. J. (1999). A large-scale study of file-system contents. *ACM SIGMETRICS Performance Evaluation Review*, *27*(1), 59–70.

Fisher, K. E., Erdelez, S., & McKechnie, L. (2005). *Theories of information behavior*. Information Today, Inc.

Fitchett, S., Cockburn, A., & Gutwin, C. (2013). Improving navigation-based file retrieval. In CHI '13: Proceedings of the SIGCHI Conference on Human Factors in Computing Systems (pp. 2329–2338). ACM.

Gonçalves, D. J., & Jorge, J. A. (2003). An empirical study of personal document spaces. In *International Workshop on Design, Specification, and Verification of Interactive Systems* (pp. 46–60). Berlin: Springer.

Gurrin, C., Schoeffmann, K., Joho, H., Munzer, B., Rami Albatal, R., Hopfgartner, F., … Dang-Nguyen, D.-T. (2019). A test collection for interactive lifelog retrieval. In I. Kompatsiaris, B. Huet, V. Mezaris, C. Gurrin, W. H. Cheng, & S. Vrochidis, *Lecture Notes in Computer Science: Vol. 11295. MultiMedia Modeling. MMM 2019* (pp. 312–324). Cham: Springer.

Henderson, S. (2005). Genre, task, topic and time: facets of personal digital document management. In Proceedings of the 6th ACM SIGCHI New Zealand Conference (pp. 75–82). ACM.

Henderson, S. (2009). *How do people manage their documents?: An empirical investigation into personal document management practices among knowledge workers* (Doctoral dissertation). University of Auckland.

Henderson, S. (2011). Document duplication: How users (struggle to) manage file copies and versions. *Proceedings of the American Society for Information Science and Technology*, *48*(1), 1–10.

Henderson, S., & Srinivasan, A. (2009). An empirical analysis of personal digital document structures. In *Symposium on Human Interface* (pp. 394–403). Berlin, Heidelberg: Springer.

Hicks, B. J., Dong, A., Palmer, R., & Mcalpine, H. C. (2008). Organizing and managing personal electronic files: A mechanical engineer's perspective. *ACM Transactions on Information Systems*, *26*(4), 23.

Jones, W., Bruce, H., & Dumais, S. (2001). Keeping found things found on the web. In Proceedings of the 10th International Conference on Information and Knowledge Management (pp. 119–126). ACM.

Jones, W., Dinneen, J. D., Capra, R., Diekema, A., & Pérez-Quiñones, M. (2017). Personal Information Management. In J. McDonald & M. Levine-Clark, *Encyclopedia of Library and Information Sciences* (4th ed., pp. 3584–3605). CRC Press.

Kaye, J., Vertesi, J., Avery, S., Dafoe, A., David, S., Onaga, L., … & Pinch, T. (2006). To have and to hold: exploring the personal archive. In CHI '06: Proceedings of the SIGCHI Conference on Human Factors in Computing Systems (pp. 275–284). ACM.

Khoo, C. S., Luyt, B., Ee, C., Osman, J., Lim, H. H., & Yong, S. (2007). How users organize electronic files on their workstations in the office environment: A preliminary study of personal information organization behaviour. *Information Research*, *11*(2), 12–12.

Kwaśnik, B. (1991). The importance of factors that are not document attributes in the organization of personal documents. *Journal of Documentation*, *47*(4), 389–398.

Lansdale, M. W. (1988). The psychology of personal information management. *Applied Ergonomics*, *19*(1), 55–66.

Limpert, E., Stahel, W. A., & Abbt, M. (2001). Log-normal distributions across the sciences: Keys and clues. *BioScience, 51*(5), 341–352.

Malone, T. W. (1983). How do people organize their desks?: Implications for the design of office information systems. *ACM Transactions on Information Systems (TOIS), 1*(1), 99–112.

Marshall, C. (2008). Rethinking personal digital archiving Part 2, implications for services, applications, and institutions. *D-Lib Magazine, 14*(3/4).

Marshall, C., Bly, S., & Brun-Cottan, F. (2006). The long term fate of our digital belongings: Toward a service model for personal archives. In *Archiving Conference* (Vol. 2006, No. 1, pp. 25–30). Society for Imaging Science and Technology.

Marshall, C., & Tang, J. C. (2012). That syncing feeling: early user experiences with the cloud. In Proceedings of the Conference on Designing Interactive Systems (pp. 544–553). ACM.

Meho, L. I., & Tibbo, H. R. (2003). Modeling the information-seeking behavior of social scientists: Ellis's study revisited. *Journal of the American society for Information Science and Technology, 54*(6), 570–587.

Nardi, B., Anderson, K., & Erickson, T. (1995). Filing and finding computer files. In Proceedings of East-West HCI. Moscow.

Oliver, G., & Harvey, R. (2016). *Digital curation*. Chicago: ALA Neal-Schuman.

Shneiderman, B., & Wattenberg, M. (2001). Ordered treemap layouts. In INFOVIS 2001: IEEE Symposium on Information Visualization (pp. 73–78). IEEE.

Teevan, J., Alvarado, C., Ackerman, M. S., & Karger, D. R. (2004). The perfect search engine is not enough: a study of orienteering behavior in directed search. In CHI '04: Proceedings of the SIGCHI Conference on Human Factors in Computing Systems (pp. 415–422).

Thomson, L. (2015). The guided tour technique in information science: explained and illustrated. In *Proceedings of the 78th Annual Meeting of the Association for Information Science and Technology* (pp. 135:1–135:5).

Vitale, F., Janzen, I., & McGrenere, J. (2018). Hoarding and minimalism: Tendencies in digital data preservation. In *CHI '18: Proceedings of the 36th Annual ACM Conference on Human Factors in Computing Systems* (pp. 587:1–587:12). ACM.

Watkins, R. D., Sellen, A., & Lindley, S. E. (2015). Digital collections and digital collecting practices. In CHI '15: Proceedings of the 33rd Annual ACM Conference on Human Factors in Computing Systems (pp. 3423–3432). ACM.

Whittaker, S. (2011). Personal information management: From information consumption to curation. *Annual Review of Information Science and Technology (ARIST), 45*(1), 1–62.

Wilcox, R. (2011). *Modern statistics for the social and behavioral sciences: A practical introduction*. CRC.

Online Behavior of the Alzheimer's Disease Patient Caregivers on Croatian Online Discussion Forum

Sanda Erdelez
Simmons University, Boston, MA, USA
sanda.erdelez@simmons.edu

Sanjica Faletar Tanacković
University of Osijek, Osijek, Croatia
sfaletar@ffos.hr

Kornelija Petr Balog
University of Osijek, Osijek, Croatia
kpetr@ffos.hr

ABSTRACT

This paper presents findings from a study which investigated the information needs of caregivers (CGs) of persons with Alzheimer's Disease (AD) in Croatia, a country where the health and social care systems for AD patients and their CGs are not fully established nor efficient. The study was conducted with the help of qualitative content analysis on the total population of initial posts (N = 83) on the Croatian Internet Forum (Forum.hr) from May 2005 through January 2019. The analysis revealed that CGs' information needs fall into the following categories: information about the disease, medication/treatment, coping with the disease, physicians, available services, general care for the AD patient, legal and financial issues, and faith. The analysis further revealed that CGs post on this online discussion list not only when they require specific information or advice, but also to describe their situation and experiences and to share practical information that they think will help others, and also to seek emotional support.

KEYWORDS

Alzheimer's Disease; Caregivers; Information Needs; Online Forum

ASIS&T THESAURUS

Older persons; Information Seeking; Information Needs

INTRODUCTION

Based on the comprehensive collection of data about the size and complexity of the challenges of dementia and practical case studies from around the world, in 2012, the World Health Organization (WHO) and Alzheimer's Disease International (ADI) called upon governments, policymakers and other stakeholders to recognize dementia as a global public health priority, implement sustained action and coordination across multiple levels and with all stakeholders, and develop national dementia plans and strategies (Dementia, 2012). The prevalence of dementia is expected to explode in the coming years with an increasingly aging population. For this reason, an urgent and serious focus on Alzheimer's Disease (AD) is required in order to make health and social care systems informed and responsive to this impending threat. It is estimated by the WHO that in 2017 worldwide around 50 million people have dementia, with nearly 10 million new cases every year (World Health Organization, 2017). Also, the percentage of people with Alzheimer's dementia increases with age: 3 percent of people ages 65–74, 17 percent of people ages 75–84, and 32 percent of people ages 85 and older have Alzheimer's dementia (Alzheimer Association, 2019). Alzheimer's Disease, an incurable neurological disease with an unknown cause, is the most common cause of dementia. This disease is not related to a particular ethnic group, social class, gender, geographic location or any other known socio-demographic characteristic. Although it is more common among elderly persons, recent data shows that younger persons can also be affected (Alzheimer's Disease International, 2016).

Alzheimer's Disease usually starts gradually with characteristic memory loss. During the course of their disease, AD patients experience severe impairment of cognitive (e.g., speaking and decision-making) and physical abilities. Eventually their daily functioning and participation in social activities becomes difficult and then impossible, requiring around-the-clock supervision and care (Alzheimer's Disease International, 2016). In countries such as Croatia where health and social care systems for AD patients and their caregivers (CGs) are not sufficiently developed (Rušac, 2016), this in most cases leads to complete dependency of AD patients on their informal CGs, unpaid non-professionals. These CGs are in most cases family members such as spouses of AD patients, partners, siblings, children, grandchildren, other relatives, and friends, who provide supervision, support and assistance with daily living activities (e.g., feeding, hygiene, therapy administration, etc.) during all stages of disease to maintain them at home (Brodaty & Donkin, 2009). In case of Croatia, Mimica et al. (2015) estimate that a total of 202,164 family members care for 80,864 AD patients. Similarly, Haley (1997) acknowledged that (unpaid) family CGs are a critically important part of long-term care of AD patients in the United States.

The need for CG supervision and presence increases over the course of the disease, and CGs often care for family members

82nd Annual Meeting of the Association for Information Science & Technology | Melbourne, Australia | 19–23 October, 2019

DOI: 10.1002/pra2.00008

diagnosed with AD for years before they die or are institutionalized. Caring for elderly member of one's family with AD is an arduous task, with cognitive impairment, progressive loss of autonomy and behavioral disorders associated with AD often leading to growing CG burden (Dauphinot et al., 2015, 2016), which may have physical, psychological, emotional, social and financial impact on the CGs (Novais et al., 2017). This is particularly true in cases when CGs do not know much about the illness, which is often stigmatized in their community, so they are ashamed to speak about it and ask for help. As care needs change over the years as patients move from initial to final stages of the disease, CGs do not know how to cope with this illness. They do not receive the required formal assistance and support, and they have poor knowledge of available services, even when they exist (Mimica et al., 2015; Rušac, 2016; Uzun et al., 2019). Interestingly though, Van der Roest et al. (2007, 2009) point out that even in Western European countries where various professional support services are available, CG needs often remain unmet because they have difficulties in finding the appropriate services, and professional care seems to be insufficiently attuned to their needs.

This study was motivated by the need to explore the information needs of AD patients' CGs in Croatia (particularly unmet needs) and their use of an online Internet forum for meeting these needs. As the literature review will show, there is to our knowledge no research about the information needs of Croatian CGs of AD patients. Notably, in a country where support for AD patients and their CGs is inadequate there is a need to investigate this phenomena in order to gain insights which may promote a global discussion of this phenomenon by all relevant bodies at a national level, and eventually facilitate the provision of appropriate services to AD patients and their CGs.

CONTEXT OF THE STUDY

Based on statistics from *Alzheimer's Disease International (ADI)* and *Alzheimer Europe*, Dološić (2016) confirms that the size of population with dementia in Croatia is similar to that in other countries. In 2012 in Croatia there were 80,864 patients with dementia (1.89% of Croatia's population) and at the same time 202,164 individuals, mainly family members, were taking care of them (Mimica et al., 2015).

Although Croatia is a relatively developed European country, its health, social, financial, and legal systems do not support AD patients and their CGs adequately. For instance, the abovementioned number of AD patients in Croatia is only an estimate because a national registry of AD patients has not yet been established. Furthermore, AD patients in Croatia are not treated adequately, i.e., with antidementia drugs. Mimica and Presečki (2010) explain that a majority of Croatia's AD patients are in reality treated with supportive (alternative) medication like gingko biloba, nootropics (piracetam), anti-inflammatories, statins, estrogens, omega-3 fatty acid, vitamin E, vitamin C, etc., and only a minority of them are receiving standard treatment (cholinesterase inhibitors [ChEI] and/or memantine) because antidementia drugs are not on the reimbursement list of the Croatian Health Insurance Fund and AD patients cannot afford to buy them, although antidementia drugs are prescribed to them (Bencarić, 2010).

Professionals such as healthcare and social workers in Croatia lack adequate education and training to work with AD patients and their CGs (Samardžija, 2013). Furthermore, palliative care for AD patients in Croatia, the goal of which is to improve the quality of life both for patients and their CGs at any stage of the illness, is underdeveloped and almost nonexistent (Dološić, 2016; S. Dološić, AD strategy, personal communication, 2019). The recent statistical data shows that there are only 62 beds reserved for patients receiving palliative care in psychiatric hospitals in the whole country. This, together with the issues related to the legal status of patients and their CGs when making decisions about the rights and interests of AD patients with the help of legal instruments (such as advance decision-making, advance directives, informed consent for medical treatment, etc.) raises both ethical and legal questions about the possible infringement of constitutional rights of AD patients in Croatia (Dološić, 2016; Dološić, Milić Babić, & Rušac, *in print*).

Although in 2014 the Croatian Society for Alzheimer's Disease and Old Age Psychiatry of the Croatian Medical Association and Alzheimer Croatia initiated drafting of a national strategy to address AD (2015-2020), this document was never officially adopted (S. Dološić, AD strategy, personal communication, 2019). In line with similar international policy documents, this strategy identified the following priorities: early diagnosis of the disease, access to treatment with antidementive drugs, and the development of comprehensive and coordinated support for AD patients and their CGs. This support included the development of a national AD registry, access to social services and financial support, the balanced regional development of centers for AD diagnosis and treatment, as well as home-care centers with specialized units for AD patients, development of palliative care for AD patients, and reducing stigmatization in the community. This document promises to establish a positive legal framework for the enforcement of the rights of AD patients and their caregivers, and thus contribute toward the development of comprehensive and responsive healthcare and social systems for mental health patients in general. There are some indications that it might finally reach the agenda of Croatian national government in 2019 (Mimica et al., 2015).

In order to contribute to a better understanding of this phenomena a 2018 research project titled *Information needs of AD patients and their caregivers* received an 18-month grant from the University of Osijek, Croatia. In this project, an interdisciplinary team of scholars from different fields (medicine, law, and information science) set out to identify information and service needs of AD patients and their CGs in

Croatia with special emphasis on understanding the barriers and challenges they face in obtaining the required information or services. The study is designed as a three-phase investigation. First, a critical description and overview of the local context with special emphasis on legislative framework, available support services, and human rights issues will be given (Dološić, 2019; *in print*). Second, the authors will explore the information and service needs of AD patients and their CGs expressed online (Erdelez et al., 2019, *in print*). Third, in-person interviews with CGs of AD patients will be conducted.

This paper builds upon preliminary results presented in Erdelez et al. (2019, *in print*) in which the patterns of online forum posting activity related to AD were explored. The analysis of the dataset, which included initial statements posted over a period of 13 years on the Croatian Internet forum *Forum.hr*, revealed that the frequency of postings varied during the studied period, but no conclusion could be made about overall trends in posting frequency. Overall, there were an average of 20.2 initial posts per year, with the largest number of posts identified in 2016 (N = 12), and the smallest number of posts in 2006, 2011 and 2017 (N = 2). Although (as in any other forum) it is believed that a certain level of passive participation at Forum.hr is present with people reading rather than contributing messages, these numbers are generally below what was expected. Interestingly, while some initial posts remained unanswered (37.3% out of 83 posts), some (18.7%) prompted multiple answers and apparently related to highly important topics. Also, this study revealed that posters were predominantly women – daughters, wives, and granddaughters of patients with AD.

In order to contribute to the emerging information science interest in AD (Erdelez, Howarth, & Gibson, 2015; Harland & Bath, 2008) and to learn how AD patients and their CGs could be better served, this quantitative study of initial posts under the topical thread Alzheimer's Disease at Forum.hr was followed by a qualitative content analysis to address the following research questions:

RQ1: What motivates the CGs of AD patients to use the online forum Forum.hr?
RQ2: What information needs do the CGs of AD patients in Croatia express online on Forum.hr?
RQ3: Which topics are covered by the posts?

LITERATURE REVIEW

The examination of relevant literature in English and Croatian reveals general agreement that AD, in the words of Marc Wortmann, is as much an economic and fiscal disaster as it is a social and health challenge, and that its impact on societies with an increasingly aging population is growing dramatically (Alzheimer's Disease International, 2012). This presumption has led scholars from around the world to address the diverse needs of AD patients and their informal CGs (Edelman et al., 2006), and also to explore unmet needs (e.g., Lai & Chung, 2007; Tatangelo et al., 2018), support and service utilization (Lethin et al., 2016), and challenges and barriers CGs experience when caring for their family members diagnosed with AD (e.g., Arévalo-Flechas et al., 2014; Brodaty & Donkin, 2009; Kucmanski et al., 2016; Rosa et al., 2009; Uzun et al., 2019; Vaingankar et al., 2013) in order to maximize service utilization by CGs and minimize their burden.

In their recent systematic review of quantitative, qualitative, and mixed-method studies into CG needs, existing need assessment instruments and the main topics of needs explored among CGs of patients with AD and related diseases, Novais et al. (2017) identified a total of 70 studies (in English and French) published between January 1980 and January 2017. Although their objective was to analyze methodologies used in these studies, based on their findings, authors point out that the main objectives of analyzed studies were to explore the experiences of CGs with caring and community services; their information, training and support needs; their satisfaction with services; and the gap between their perceived need and the proposed services. Novais et al.'s study identified the following five main areas of CG needs: information, psychological, social, psychoeducational and other needs.

CAN-D (Carer's Needs Assessment for Dementia), one of the rare validated instruments for the needs assessment of dementia CGs, was developed by a research team led by Wancata et al. (2005) who found out that a high proportion of dementia patients' CG needs in Austria were unmet or only partially met. CGs identified major problem areas such as lack of information about dementia and its treatment, lack of information about services, financial burden and legal issues. CGs also pointed out disappointment caused by illness, concerns about the patient's future and communication problems and conflicts with the patient. Special problem areas arose around issues such as not having enough time for one's self and being burned out, social isolation and conflicts within family, fear of stigmatization and discrimination, and feelings of guilt and being blamed. For every problem area stated above, a number of interventions were identified and their appropriateness and importance was rated by CGs. These interventions can range from printed information material and financial compensation for counseling and emotional support to temporary supervision of the patient at home, care for the patient in a day center, respite care, assistance with household chores and meals-on-wheels. For example, one of the most frequently found problems of CGs of dementia patients in their study was "disappointment caused by illness, concerns about patient's future" and "burnout or being overstrained by care." The intervention most frequently needed for these problem areas/needs according to the CGs was "counseling and emotional support."

Several other studies investigated the interventions available to support CGs and assessed the effectiveness of a variety of interventions on CG burden and psychological disorders. For example, Farran et al. (2004) point out that clinical trials with CGs suggest that CG skill-building interventions may be more effective than information/support interventions. In their studies, they tried to identify specific skills needed by CGs in addressing their concerns in the following areas: dealing with change, managing competing responsibilities and stressors, providing a broad spectrum of care, finding and using resources, and experiencing emotional and physical responses to care.

Whitlatch and Orsulic-Jeras (2018) describe a variety of resources, services and program models targeted to the education, information, and support needs of AD patients and their families (both individual- and family-centered), from the time of first symptoms through end-of-life care. They also highlight a variety of unmet needs and a lack of programming, in particular as related to specific groups who have fewer information and support options available to them because of geography (e.g., those living in rural areas) or minority status (e.g., marginalized groups such as LGBTQIA people).

Although scholars in information science (IS) appear to be natural partners to medicine, healthcare, economics, legal and other scholars in exploring the information needs of AD patients and their CGs, in the IS literature there is a paucity of publications and research on this topic. For example, Erdelez et al. (2015) discussed the potential for IS scholars to engage in AD research and Harland and Bath (2008) described how existing models of information behavior may improve provision of information to CGs of people with dementia.

To conclude, an overview of recent literature shows that only the focused attention of healthcare professionals, policymakers and scholars from various disciplines can facilitate AD patient home care and reduce CG burden and thus contribute to the quality of their life. Therefore, additional studies by interdisciplinary teams addressing the unique and changing information, education, coping skills, and support and service needs of AD patients and their CGs, taking into account individual characteristics and local environments, are required (Novais et al., 2017).

METHODOLOGY

In this qualitative study, authors analyzed a set of 83 primary or initial posts, i.e., statements that initiated a discussion by posting a question or a comment in an Alzheimer's Disease thread at the Croatian Internet forum *Forum.hr* (https://www.forum.hr/showthread.php?s=44194313219b1aee44fcb19d8b93503c&t=143099&page=15). The dataset (N = 83) is comprised of all initial posts from May 3, 2006 (when the discussion on AD began on this online forum) through January 31, 2019. In other words, these 83 posts are not a sample but a whole population of initial posts that were posted over a period of 13 years. Since authors were interested in learning about CG information needs, only initial posts were analyzed for this study because it was concluded that in responses posters would provide feedback and comment on questions that were posted in initial posts. The analysis of responses will be studied in the second phase of the study.

Forum.hr is available 24 hours a day and is anonymous and asynchronous. This means that users as a rule do not use their real names (which guarantees them certain level of anonymity) and they do not need to be online at the same time in order to exchange information and communicate.

Also, this study, although qualitative in nature, uses numbers and percentages, which bear no statistical importance, but are used to illustrate the obtained results.

Analysis

A multi-stage content analysis was conducted. In the first stage of the analysis, a set of initial codes was derived from the existing literature, in particular based on the coding schemes developed in Edelman et al. (2006), Kucmanski et al. (2016), Novais et al. (2017), Wackerbarth and Johnson (2001), Wancata et al. (2005), Whitlatch and Orsulic-Jeras (2018), and Zwaanswijk et al. (2013) whose coding models focused on information, service, and support needs of AD patient CGs. In our study, all initial posts (83 total) were coded using this initial coding scheme both to evaluate their value and to identify missing codes. In order to code the posts, study authors determined under which topic(s) the post belonged. Many posts were long and discussed multiple topics, and one individual post could be classified under more than one coded category. Sometimes it was easy to determine the topic(s) and sometimes it was quite a challenge. Therefore, coding was conducted independently by two coders (the authors) in order to test and ensure intercoder reliability. In conflicting cases, coders discussed each individual post against the existing code scheme until they reached agreement. In the second stage of the analysis, authors examined all posts in detail and developed a revised coding scheme closely reflecting the nature of the studied posts. In this process, some topics/codes were identified as irrelevant and therefore abandoned, and some new ones were added. Also at this stage a set of subcodes was developed in order to reflect the thematic nature of the posts more precisely. Once the coding scheme was established in this way, all posts were coded again by the same two coders, and conflicting posts were settled in a manner identical to that described earlier (i.e., coders discussed the posts until agreement was reached).

The intercoder reliability score in our study was $\kappa = 0.73$ (measured by Cohen's kappa), which gives evidence for moderate agreement. Moderate agreement means that 35–65% of the sample data can be considered reliable (McHugh, 2012).

Eventually the whole dataset was coded against two distinctive sets of codes: one referred to the loose formal category of the type of the posts and the second to the topic/theme of the post. Under the post type, the following codes were distinguished (Table 1):

- seeking factual information (poster seeks distinct piece of information; e.g., "*How can one differentiate first symptoms of AD from common forgetfulness?*")
- seeking general facts or advice (poster seeks general information or advice about what to do in their situation; e.g., "*I read a lot of posts here... When you are in a situation that you have to put your parents into home for people with AD because they cannot take care of themselves... It's not the question of money. But whenever I mention this option they do not want to listen. I am alone, I have no one... What should I do?"*)
- sharing one's experience (poster describes one's situation without stating an explicit question (e.g., "*I just got a call from home for people with AD where my aunt is placed. They said she got completely lost last night and they had major problems with her. The problem lies in the fact that she is 83, and although AD appeared 2-3 years ago doctors did not want to do anything because she is too old.*")
- expressing emotions and seeking emotional support (poster shares his emotions and feelings without stating an explicit question; e.g., (*"My heart is broken. She is my heart, my dear mom. Damn Alzheimer's!"*)
- sharing information (poster shares his personal advice and/or refers readers to external information sources which he thinks is useful; e. g. "*I found this great article on AD. Maybe it can help someone.*").

Under the post topic, the following codes were distinguished: emotions and general health of the CG, about the disease, / treatment, coping with the disease, physicians, available services, general care for the AD patient, legal and financial issues, and faith (Table 2).

FINDINGS AND DISCUSSION

AD Patient CG Motivation to Use the Online Forum Forum.hr and Their Information Needs Expressed Online

Distribution of posts (as shown in Table 1) indicate that all analyzed posts fall into either of five post types described in detail in the above section. Posters most commonly seek factual information (48.2%) and emotional support (32.5%). To a lesser degree, they share information (15.7%) and their own experience (13.3%) and seek advice (12%). Only three posts were grouped in the "Other" category because they could not be related to any other code. In this category, for example, one can find a post in which a CG shares his opinion about AD as a widespread disease awaiting all of us.

Detailed analysis of the posts suggests that not all posters at Forum.hr had a clear question or a need for distinct information when they submitted their initial post: only about half (48.2%) required specific, factual information (e.g., "*Is there a cure to AD?*"), and 12% sought general information or advice about what to do in their situation (e.g., "*I am interested in the experience of people whose parents suffer from AD. How can we help them? And us?*").

Post type	N	%
Seeking factual information	40	48.2
Seeking emotional support	27	32.5
Sharing information (without explicit question)	13	15.7
Sharing one's experience and describing one's situation (without explicit questions)	11	13.3
Seeking advice	10	12.0
Other	3	3.6

Table 1. Initial posts by type.

Over a third (39.8%) of those posters who required some kind of information and expressed a need for either distinct, factual information or general advice posted long posts (the average length of an initial post was 187.7 words, with the shortest initial post of only 4 words, and the longest being 1088 words) in which detailed descriptions of their own situation and experience preceded the question.

Interestingly, ten (12%) posters did not express any information need at all in their initial post. Their posts were solely descriptions of their situation and personal accounts of their first-hand experience of living with and caring for an AD patient. In such submissions, posters seem to be thinking aloud about their problem/situation and probably looking for feedback from others in the same position about whether what they are going through is normal. They might also be sharing their experience to show other CGs that whatever they are going through is also "normal."

> "*It's getting worse every day. Mom is moving things from one place to another and forgets where she put them. Dad is sitting in from of the TV, sleeps and eats... I just wanted to share my situation.*"

All such posts were extremely supportive and in several posts, after sharing their experience and situation, posters gave open support to the readers, i.e., to other CGs.

"It is not enough that AD takes memories of our dearest, it also wants the caregiver… I was crushed physically… It took me a year to get well. The following year my mother in law was diagnosed with AD… My physician said it is too early for me to take care of an AD patient again and that I need to seek help this time. He told me that this time I might not recover… Grandmother Ana died in the hospital… 10 days after surgery… I wish you all patience, take care…"

"This was one encouraging post; it is difficult, but we have to keep on going."

"All I can say is good luck to everyone (and myself), and take it easy."

Furthermore, some posters returned to the discussion list after some time with a new post just to give (an unsolicited) update on their personal situation, again without posting any specific question.

"I just wanted to let you know that my mom is fighting for her life. This pneumonia is taking her away from me… I have little hope."

Data indicate also that a significant portion of posters (32.5%) seek emotional support and relief through their participation in the discussion list.

"My dad suffers from AD. Today, I went to see him and it was so tough. Immensely… Mom is taking care of him. My poor mother. I lost both father and mother, at the same time. Damn, Alzheimer's… damn."

Also, some posters (15.7%) participated in the discussion list by submitting an initial post in which they just shared information about something that they thought would be useful to others (unsolicited), either by providing information about a relevant website, online support group, TV show, etc. (*"Today, at 8.15 p.m., Croatian TV Channel 2, there will be a TV a show on AD. I can't wait to see what it will about."*) or by providing practical information about new services in the community, recommending a specific medication, cosmetics, or physical exercise, etc.

"I am breaking in but maybe this will be useful for somebody. In Zagreb, close to Vrapče Marketplace, there is a day care for AD patients, with professional healthcare personnel. They do exercises and play games, physical therapy, bathing, hair dos, seasons' decoration, and they are the first in Croatia who organize visits of volunteers with dogs as a part of therapy. It is unbelievable how they open up and communicate with the dog (e.g., for Valentine's Day, dog was distributing gifts and they had to give him a cookie). There you go. I just wanted to let you know this."

The fact that posters in their initial posts did not only post questions (in order to obtain a specific answer) but used the forum to a significant degree to describe their own experience, seek emotional support and relief, and share practical information they thought would be useful to other CGs indicates that information and service needs of AD patients and their CGs in Croatia are not adequately catered for by the system, be it healthcare institutions and professionals or social and support services.

"I write this post exclusively as a token of appreciation to all those who shared their experiences and helped me understand the scope of the problem - personal, social and institutional. Your posts helped me in the moments of despair and I hope this one will also help somebody"

It also appears that the posters who actually posted questions did not look for information somewhere else (or at least they do not talk about that in their posts). They turned to other CGs through this discussion list who were in the same situation believing that they would have ready answers for their questions and advice for their situations.

"I feel completely lost, I do not know whom to turn to because Alzheimer Association exists only in Zagreb."

"I often visited this forum to find help for myself and my situation. I registered yesterday and now I want to describe my experience in fighting the mystery called Alzheimer's, maybe somebody finds it useful."

This is also well-illustrated by the abovementioned post where a poster shares information about a new day care center in the community. One would expect that health-care professionals and social services would inform CGs if such a center existed or opened in their neighborhood.

Post Topics

Table 2 illustrates the topics represented among the initial posts. Nine distinctive categories of topics were identified: emotions and general health of the CG, about the disease, medication/treatment, coping with the disease, physicians, available services, general care for the AD patient, legal and financial issues, and faith. The most numerous category is one related to the emotions and general health of CGs (32.5%) and will be discussed in detail later on. It is followed by posts in which CGs seek information about medication/treatment (19.3%) and the disease in general (16.8%). It is evident that when posters look for information about the medication or treatment, they usually look for information on traditional medication/treatment (13.3%) and less frequently on alternative methods (6.0%). Also, it is evident that posters who seek information about alternative treatment are more recent (although the first post related to alternative treatment was in 2009, the majority of other posts related to this topic appeared slightly later – in 2011, 2014 and 2016). Nine posts were categorized as "Coping with the disease" and in those posts CGs usually express their inability to cope with the disease and the way it takes away their loved ones (*"Now that I look, back I realize that her (grandmother's) health deteriorated rapidly in a very short time"*). The posters also express their experiences with physicians and offer opinions on their bedside manner, expertise and support in general. Unfortunately, in the majority of posts related to this topic CGs offer negative comments (e.g., *"Physicians didn't do anything for her, maybe because they thought she was 'ancient"; "I feel that doctors do not invest enough time, effort, etc. in AD patients"*; *"My mother was examined by a very young neurologist who was obviously completely ignorant about the AD..."; "Physicians often ask me 'What do you think we should do now?"*). Negative comments date quite early, almost from the beginning of the forum discussion (2006), whereas the few positive comments are more recent (the earliest is from 2013), which may be an indication that with the increased number of patients, physicians are becoming more familiar with the disease, side-effects of medications, various treatments, etc. However, even when the CG gives a positive opinion of the physician, there is still a problem of unsuitable treatment or medication (*"Physician was dedicated, but the medication that she prescribed... was very limited in treatment of the disease"*).

When CGs post about available services, it is usually to inquire or offer information about associations, hospitalization, day care institutions, etc. The first such inquiry dates from 2007 and the CG asks about a day care institution: *"Is there in Croatia some association, nursing home, etc. where we can leave an AD patient for a few hours during a day?"* Croatia was generally slow to react to the complex needs of AD patients and their CGs. A few posts from this category (n = 6) reveal that there are not enough institutions (nursing homes, hospitals, etc.) that can competently take care of the AD patients (*"... people in a nursing home insisted on transferring him to the hospital, and in the hospital to transferring him to a specialized institution, to a psychogeriatric ward. ... We listened to them. They restrained him there ("human fixation" is what they call it), concluded that his pain receptors in the brain were completely unresponsive; at first, he fought (he had open wounds on arms and legs, but later he stopped; ... I completely lost control over his condition because there was a visit limitation. Through a continuous "human fixation" he picked up all the possible bacterial infections and ended up at the intensive-care unit; they stabilized his condition and returned him to the psychogeriatric ward, terminal disease patients' section.... I do not judge, I just describe how this system cares for AD patients"*). To complicate the problem further, some institutions are taking only immobile AD patients; the first AD association in Croatia was located for a long time only in Zagreb, the country's capital, leaving the rest of the country's AD patients and their CGs to cope on their own.

The last three topics that received the fewest posts are dedicated to general care for the AD patient, with posters posting general inquiries about topics related to care, legal, and financial issues and faith. Legal and financial issues appear rather late in the forum discussion – the first mention was in 2013 and critical of the information available (*"Nobody mentioned what sort of rights I have as a CG – home care, transportation costs..."*), which only supports the argument that Croatia lags behind in medical, social, community, and economic care and support for AD patients and their CGs. CGs are additionally frustrated by conflicting regulations they are facing. One family did not have funds to send their patient to the nursing home and decided to take the option to give away the patient's house in return for care in the state-owned nursing home (*"... social services tell us that we must have her consent ... but I do not understand how we can get a consent from a mental patient..."*).

Faith is not very present in the forum discussions – we identified only four initial posts in which CGs made references to religious topics. (*"I can only hope that God will take him under his wing and give him strength to continue fighting the disease"; "I pray that God saves my mother from those terrible moments, I pray for myself and for all of you"; "I pray every day that my daddy forgives me"*).

Topics	N	%
Emotions and general health of CGs	27	32.5
About the disease	14	16.8
Medication / Treatment - Traditional	11	13.3
Medication / Treatment - Alternative	5	6.0
Coping with the disease	9	10.8
Physicians	9	10.8
Available services	6	7.2
General care for the AD patient	4	4.8
Legal and financial issues	4	4.8
Faith	4	4.8

Table 2. Initial post topics.

Caregivers' Emotions

As was previously discussed in this paper, one of the most prominent topics at the forum discussion analyzed here is emotions. Very often, posters' reason for going online and taking part in this forum is not to look for specific information but to alleviate some of the pain, fear, frustration, or other emotions they might be feeling at the moment. Table 3 presents categories of emotions present in our sample. The two most represented categories are the one related to the grief, pain and despair CGs feel *"... I broke down, lost all my strength! From yesterday, I'm on tranquilizers and anti-depressants... it would be easier if mother were in hospital, if I were not responsible for everything..."*) and the category related to the feelings of helplessness, tiredness and loneliness (*"It was a horror of my life... I had no life of my own."; "I don't see the point of all that if nobody will actually help me get through this stage of my life. ...I realized that the professional help for these patients is perfectly dismal and that we are left to cope with it as we know"; "It is difficult to describe some of the days, difficult to say somebody what is happening and what you are going through – only those who also have been in this situation and seen the disease up-close can understand."; "I'm alone, I don't have anybody... what should I do?"*).

Because the final stage of the disease often involves hospitalization, feelings of guilt are unavoidably present among our posters – especially those who cannot take care of the patient even in the earlier stages of the disease (*"How did you cope with that problem? I'm an only child, and this kills me psychologically. I know that we cannot take care of him... I myself have three children on my own, I cannot sleep, I wake up at night and try to comprehend, but I can't..."*). Our posters also express fear – for their loved ones who are sick, but also fear of getting the disease themselves (*"Ever since I've met the big A, I'm afraid of old age."; "I often feel a sort of existential apprehension when I look at my husband and see how, once extremely intelligent, emotional and creative man, gradually loses his dignity and key qualities that used to make him the man he was"*).

Posters in our sample see the forum as the opportunity to share their experiences, but also to receive support and help from others with similar experiences (*"Thank you for existing. I've just come across you today and cannot be happier;" Thanks for reading this"; "This writing gives me some relief"*). A few posts deal with love for the patients, hope and coming to terms with this difficult disease (*"I must say that I've just realized that the love is the greatest force because, no matter how crazy I got because of my mother's disease, my love for her won and cast a shadow over all the rage and despair I occasionally felt"; "You see, even Alzheimer's is not incurable, you just have to find the right medication"*). Interestingly, anger or frustration were not identified as frequently expressed feelings on the forum. Also, we detected two other feelings – worry about the patient and wondering about (mis)diagnosing the stage of the disease.

Again, the lack of emotional and psychological support for CGs at the system level could also be inferred based on the fact that posters frequently sought emotional support and that they found relief in writing about their situation. Several posters explicitly stated how writing on this discussion list helps them deal with their situation.

Emotions	N	%
Grief, pain, despair	15	55.6
Tiredness, loneliness, helplessness	10	37.0
Guilt	6	22.2
Fear	6	22.3
Relief, support, help	4	14.8
Hope, love, acceptance	3	11.1
Anger, frustration	2	7.4
Worry	2	7.4
Wondering	1	3.7

Table 3. Types of emotions.

CONCLUSION

The qualitative study presented in this paper aimed to contribute to the understanding of the information needs of CGs of AD patients in Croatia, a country with insufficiently developed support for AD patients and their CGs, and their use of an online Internet forum for meeting these needs. Although Croatia is a moderately developed country technology-wise, the total number of posts (N = 83) submitted over a period of 13 years under the AD thread on Forum.hr, the largest general discussion list in Croatia, is strikingly small. The small number of total posts analyzed and rather weak active post behavior are among the main limitations of this study.

The reasons behind this low activity might be that the majority of CGs of AD patients come from an age group over 50 and this age group in general lacks information literacy skills, and thus are not regular users of electronic information sources. Although information about the age of posters is not available, by studying their posts it can be concluded that posters in our study are younger people who are still working. Thus, the reason that the use of the AD discussion forum in Croatia is lower than expected may be the low level of CG computer literacy and their low use of the Internet in general. A rise in the use of electronic information resources will likely happen when members of Generation X become CGs. Because of the social stigmatization of AD, the availability of online AD discussion list may provide younger CGs an outlet for anonymously asking questions that they do not dare ask in person and for seeking emotional support from other CGs.

Analysis of the posts suggests that not all posters who posted an initial post required distinct, factual information. Although a majority of posters did seek some kind of information or advice, some posters did not express any information need at all, but gave personal accounts of their firsthand experience of caring for an AD patient and shared some practical information they thought would be useful to other CGs (e.g., announcement about a new daycare center, link to a relevant website etc.). In relation to the post topics, the analysis revealed that posters sought information relating to emotions and general health of the CG, about the disease, medication/-treatment, coping with the disease, physicians, available services, general care for the AD patient, legal and financial issues, and faith. In their posts about physicians posters most often communicated negative experience and dissatisfaction with their expertise and support. Posts in which posters inquired about available local services and support (AD associations, nursery homes, day care centers etc.) were also very common. Very often posters participated in the forum only to seek emotional support and relief, and to alleviate some of the pain, fear, frustration, or other emotions they might be feeling at the moment. This surely indicates that information, support and service needs of AD patients and their CGs in Croatia are not adequately catered to.

Previous research about information needs of Croatian CGs of AD patients is almost non-existent and the majority of research studies reported in the literature review are conducted in Western countries with developed healthcare and social support systems for people suffering from memory-related health conditions and their CGs. Due to the imposed limitations on the length of this paper, an extensive comparison of results obtained in this study and other similar international studies will be provided elsewhere and will be focus of further research.

The contribution of the study presented here is that it provides an insight into the struggles CGs experience in an environment with a limited access to information and support. The CGs who participated in the AD online discussion list on the Forum.hr turn to the forum and other CGs because they feel they do not have anyone else to ask for information. While the Croatian Society for Alzheimer's Disease makes continuous progress in increasing public awareness about AD and its challenges for both patients and CGs, practical support in local communities, especially from healthcare institutions and social services is missing, especially in smaller locations. If such support exists, the CGs who post on Forum.hr are not aware of its availability and instead rely on each other for information and emotional support. However, the low frequency of initial posts suggests that many information needs may remain unmet. The next stage of this research project will address this issue by collecting data from in-person interviews with a sample of CGs.

The results of this study are relevant and useful for all stakeholders involved in the dissemination of information and provision of support to AD patients and their CGs, such as AD associations, medical institutions, public libraries, etc., and could be used to influence public policy (government) connected to AD related decisions, and ultimately to improve the quality of life of AD patients and their CGs. Finally, the study suggests how Information Science can contribute to AD research, in particular by examining the information needs and behaviors of AD patients and their CGs.

ACKNOWLEDGMENTS

We thank Silvija Dološić who provided helpful information and comments on local AD circumstances. Authors also gratefully acknowledge the grant from the University of Osijek, Croatia.

REFERENCES

Alzheimer Association. (2019). *Alzheimer Disease Facts and Figures.* Retrieved from https://www.alz.org/media/Documents/alzheimers-facts-and-figures-2019-r.pdf

Alzheimer's Disease International. (2016). *Help for care partners of people with dementia.* Geneva, Switzerland: World Health Organization. Retrieved from https://www.alz.co.uk/adi/pdf/helpforcarepartners.pdf

Arévalo-Flechas, L. C., Gayle, J. A., Monica, E., Peter, N. B., & Sharon, L. L. (2014). Latino Alzheimer's caregivers: What is important to them? *Journal of Managerial Psychology, 29*(6), 661–684.

Bencarić, L. (2010). *Registar lijekova u Hrvatskoj.* Zagreb, Croatia: Udruga poslodavaca u zdravstvu.

Brodaty, H., & Donkin, M. (2009). Family caregivers of people with dementia. *Dialogues in Clinical Neuroscience, 11*(2), 217–228.

Dauphinot, V., Ravier, A., Novais, T., Delphin-Combe, F., Moutet, C., Xie, J., … Krolak-Salmon, P. (2016). Relationship between comorbidities in patients with cognitive complaint and caregiver burden; a cross-sectional study. *Journal of the American Medical Directors Association, 17*(3), 232–237.

Dauphinot, V., Delphin-Combe, F., Mouchoux, C., Dorey, A., Bathsavanis, A., Makaroff, Z., … Krolak-Salmon, P. (2015). Risk factors of caregiver burden among patients with Alzheimer's disease or related disorders: A cross-sectional study. *Journal Alzheimer Disorder, 44*(3), 907–906.

Dementia: A public health priority. (2012). *Alzheimer's Disease International and World Health Organization.* Retrieved from https://www.who.int/mental_health/publications/dementia_report_2012/en/

Dološić, S. (2016). *Ljudska prava oboljelih od Alzheimerove bolesti : Završni specijalistički rad.* Osijek, Croatia: Pravni fakultet. Retrieved from https://urn.nsk.hr/urn:nbn:hr:132:025098

Dološić, S., Milić Babić, M., & Rušac, S. (2019 in print). Alzheimerova bolest kroz prizmu ljudskih prava. *Socijalna psihijatrija.*

Edelman, P., Kuhn, D., Fulton, B. R., & Kyrouac, G. A. (2006). Information and service needs of persons with Alzheimer's disease and their family caregivers living in rural communities. *American Journal of Alzheimer's Disease and Other Dementias*, *21*(4), 226–233.

Erdelez, S., Howarth, L., & Gibson, T. (2015). How can Information Science contribute to Alzheimer's Disease research? *Proceedings of the Association for Information Science and Technology*, *52*(1), 1–4. https://doi.org/10.1002/pra2.2015.14505201006.

Erdelez, S., K. P. Balog, A. Ružolčić, T. Žilić, S. F. Tanackoviæ. (2019 in print). The use of online discussion forums by people with Alzheimer Disease and their caregivers. In *Proceedings of an International Conference BOBCATSSS "Information and Technology Transforming Lives: Connection, Interaction, Innovation"*, 22-24 January 2019, Osijek, Croatia.

Farran, C. J., Loukissa, D., Perraud, S., & Paun, O. (2004). Alzheimer's disease caregiving information and skills. Part II: Family caregiver issues and concerns. *Research in Nursing and Health*, *27*(1), 40–51.

Haley, W. E. (1997). The family caregiver's role in Alzheimer's disease. *Neurology*, *48*(5/6), 25–29.

Harland, J. A., & Bath, P. A. (2008). Understanding the information behaviours of carers of people with dementia: A critical review of models from information science. *Aging and Mental Health*, *12*(4), 467–477.

Kucmanski, L. S., Leoni, Z., Daniela, S. G., Valéria, S. F. M., Tatiana, G. S., & Sílvia, S. S. (2016). Alzheimer's desease: Challenges faced by family caregivers. *Revista Brasileira de Geriatria e Gerontologia*, *19*(6), 1022–1029.

Lai, C. K. Y., & Chung, J. C. C. (2007). Caregivers' informational needs on dementia and dementia care. *Asian Journal of Gerontology and Geriatrics*, *2*, 78–87.

Lethin, C., Leino-Kilpi, H., Roe, B., Soto, M. M., Saks, K., Stephan, A., … Zabalegui, A. (2016). Formal support for informal caregivers to older persons with dementia through the course of the disease: An exploratory, cross-sectional study. *BMC Geriatrics*, *16*(32), 1–15.

McHugh, M. L. (2012). Interrater reliability: Kappa statistics. *Biochemia Medica*, *22*(3), 276-282. Retrieved from https://www.ncbi.nlm.nih.gov/pmc/articles/PMC3900052/

Mimica, N., & Presečki, P. (2010). How do we treat people with dementia in Croatia? *Psychiatria Danubina*, *22*(2), 363–366.

Mimica, N., M. K. Jukić, P. Presečki, M. Ivičić, M. Braš, L. Vrbić, … K. Glamuzina. (2015). Hrvatska strategija borbe protiv Alzheimerove bolesti i drugih demencija – prijedlog nacrta uz nadopune. *Medix*, *21*(117), 111–118. Retrieved from https://bib.irb.hr/datoteka/775700.Pages_from_Medix_117_Strategija.pdf

Novais, T., Dauphinot, V., Krolak-Salmon, P., & Mouchoux, C. (2017). How to explore the needs of informal caregivers of individuals with cognitive impairment in Alzheimer's disease or related diseases? A systematic review of quantitative and qualitative studies. *BMC Geriatrics*, *17*(1), 86.

Rosa, E., Lussignoli, G., Sabbatini, F., Chiappa, A., Di Cesare, S., Lamanna, L., & Zanetti, O. (2009). Needs of caregivers of the patients with dementia. *Archives of Gerontology and Geriatrics*, *51*, 54–58.

Rušac, S. (2016). Alzheimerova bolest: Izazovi socijalnog rada. *Ljetopis socijalnog rada*, *23*(3), 439–461.

Samardžija, H. (2013). *Iskustva stručnjaka u radu s osobama oboljelim od demencije* (Diplomski rad). Sveučilište u Zagrebu, Pravni fakultet, Studijski Centar Socijalnog Rada, Zagreb.

Tatangelo, G., McCabe, M., Macleod, A., & You, E. (2018). "I just don't focus on my needs." The unmet health needs of partner and offspring caregivers of people with dementia: A qualitative study. *International Journal of Nursing Studies*, *77*, 8–14.

Uzun, S., Mimica, N., Kozumplik, O., Jukić, M. K., Laidlaw, I. T., Kalinić, D., … Požgain, I. (2019). Alzheimer's disease – influence on female caregivers' living and mental health. *Socijalna Psihijatrija*, *47*(1), 86–101.

Vaingankar, J. A., Subramaniam, M., Picco, L., Eng, G. K., Shafie, S., Sambasivam, R., … Chong, S. A. (2013). Perceived unmet needs of informal caregivers of people with dementia in Singapore. *International Psychogeriatrics*, *25*(10), 1605–1619.

Van der Roest, H. G., Meiland, F. J., Maroccini, R., Comijs, H. C., Jonker, C., & Dröes, R. M. (2007). Subjective needs of people with dementia: A review of the literature. *International Psychogeriatrics*, *19*(3), 559–592.

Van der Roest, H. G., Meiland, F. J., Comijs, H. C., Derksen, E., Jansen, A. P., van Hout, H. P., … Dröes, R. M. (2009). What do community-dwelling people with dementia need? A survey of those who are known to care and welfare services. *International Psychogeriatrics*, *21*(5), 949–965.

Wackerbarth, S. B., & Johnson, M. M. S. (2001). Essential information and support needs of family caregivers. *Patient Education and Counseling*, *47*, 95–100.

Wancata, J., Krautgartner, M., Berner, J., Alexandrowicz, R., Unger, A., Kaiser, G., … Weiss, M. (2005). The carers' needs assessment for dementia (CNA-D): Development, validity and reliability. *International Psychogeriatrics*, *17*, 393–406.

Whitlatch, C. J., & Orsulic-Jeras, S. (2018). Meeting the informational, educational, and psychosocial support needs of persons living with dementia and their family caregivers. *Gerontologist*, *58*(1), 58–73.

World Health Organization. (2017). *Dementia*. Retrieved from https://www.who.int/news-room/fact-sheets/detail/dementia

Zwaanswijk, M., Peeters, J. M., van Beek, A. P., Meerveld, J. H., & Francke, A. L. (2013). Informal caregivers of people with dementia: Problems, needs and support in the initial stage and in subsequent stages of dementia: A questionnaire survey. *The Open Nursing Journal*, *7*, 6–13.

The Sentiment Recognition of Online Users Based on DNNs Multimodal Fusion

Tao Fan
Department of Information Management, Nanjing University of Science and Technology, Nanjing No.200 Xiaolingwei Street, China
fantao0718@outlook.com

Peng Wu
Department of Information Management, Nanjing University of Science and Technology, Nanjing No.200 Xiaolingwei Street, China
wupeng@njust.edu.cn

Peng Zhu
Department of Information Management, Nanjing University of Science and Technology, Nanjing No.200 Xiaolingwei Street, China
124409867@qq.com

ABSTRACT

Online users are more willing to express their opinions and emotions on social platforms in online public opinion events, through combing texts and images rather than texts alone. Facing the change of emotional expressions, it is extremely vital to recognize the sentiments of online users in online public opinion events in an appropriate way. In this paper, we propose a novel Deep Neural Networks (DNNs) model to recognize online users' sentiments in online public opinion events by analyzing the sentiments of texts and attached images together. Also, we compare two fusion strategies, feature-level fusion and decision-level fusion, to combine the affective information from texts and images. In feature-level fusion, fine-tuned Convolutional Neural Networks (CNNs) and Bidirectional Long Short-Term Memory (BiLSTMs) are employed to extract visual and textual features respectively. Then the features are concatenated and fed to a DNNs system to complete classification. In decision-level fusion, a rule is employed to fuse the output from unimodality, generating final predicted labels. Experimental results showed that the proposed DNNs multimodal model achieved better performance than unimodal sentiment recognition model. In fusion strategy, the feature-level fusion performed better in our experiments.

KEYWORDS

Multimodal Fusion; Sentiment Recognition; Online Users; Online Public Opinion Events; Social Media

ASIS&T THESAURUS

Knowledge and Information; Data Analysis

INTRODUCTION

With the prevalence of social platforms, more and more online users are willing to share what happened around them, accelerating the propagation and flow of information. Meanwhile, online users prefer to express their emotions and feelings on topics, expecting to bring out resonance or boost the development of some event. When it comes to online public opinion events, emotions of online users appear to be particularly important.

During online public opinion events, online users usually seek emotional support by posting a blog, as it is a way to virtually bond with others, share information and demand remediation (Stephens & Malone, 2009; Wu, Shen, He, & Du, 2017). When online users with the same emotion come together, they can lead the public opinion. If the converging emotion is negative, online public opinion events may become worse and cause serious consequence. Therefore, it's extremely vital to detect online users' emotions in online public opinion events.

The research about recognizing the online users' emotions in online public opinion events are mainly based on texts. Jiang, Lin, and Qiang (2015) collected the online users' opinions about Three Gorges project from social networks sites and built a corresponding emotion lexicon to recognize the sentiment of online users. Mandel et al. (2012) trained several classifiers on the messages collected from Hurricane Irene in Twitter to recognize the sentiment of the public. However, in multimedia era, online users are more willing to post blogs attached with images to express their feelings on social platforms (Cai & Xia, 2015). Furthermore, it is insufficient to recognize online users' emotions just through analyzing the texts. When texts have different meanings, it's hard to distinguish online users' sentiments. It's necessary to combine texts and images to recognize the sentiment of online users. So far, the field of multimodal sentiment analysis has not received much attention and there is little work about recognizing sentiments of online users combing different modalities, such as texts, images, etc. in online public opinion events.

Due to the superior performance of deep learning, researchers apply it to tasks of recognizing the sentiment in texts (Tang, Qin, & Liu, 2015; Wang, Yu, Lai, & Zhang, 2016; Zhou, Sun, Liu, & Lau, 2015) and images (Gelli, Uricchio, Bertini,

82nd Annual Meeting of the Association for Information Science & Technology | Melbourne, Australia | 19–23 October, 2019

DOI: 10.1002/pra2.00009

Del Bimbo, & Chang, 2015; Jindal & Singh, 2015; Xu, Cetintas, Lee, & Li, 2014), promoting the development of affective computing. In this paper, we develop novel models based on Deep Neural Networks (DNNs), fusing visual and textual modality, to recognize the sentiment of online users in online public opinion events with different fusion strategies. Different from previous research (Poria, Chaturvedi, Cambria, & Hussain, 2016; Zadeh, Chen, Poria, Cambria, & Morency, 2017), we use visual sentiment rather than facial expressions considering the real data in online public opinion events.

In visual sentiment recognition, we employ transfer learning and fine-tune the VGG16 Net pretrained on ImageNet (Deng et al., 2009) to recognize visual sentiment. In textual sentiment recognition, the process can be divided into two steps. First, we use word embeddings techniques to vectorize the words as the representation of texts. Then the vectorized texts, as input, are fed into Bidirectional Long-Term Memory (BiLSTMs) network to operate sentiment classification. In feature fusion, we use two feature fusion strategies, which are feature-level fusion (early fusion) and decision-level fusion (late fusion). In feature-level fusion, the features extracted from the interlayer of unimodality sentiment recognition model are concatenated into a long feature vector. And the joint vectors are fed to DNNs to continue training. In decision-level fusion, the predicted results of unimodality are fused based on a rule and form a final sentiment label.

The rest of the paper is organized as follows. Section 2 describes the related work of visual sentiment recognition, textual sentiment recognition and multimodal sentiment recognition. Section 3 illustrates the unimodal sentiment recognition model and multimodal sentiment recognition model. Section 4 demonstrates the preprocess of dataset and experimental results. Finally, Section 5 summarizes the paper and outlines future work (Li & Xu, 2014; Lu, Suryanarayan, Adams, Li, Newman, & Wang, 2012, Machajdik & Hanbury, 2010; Thelwall, Buckley, & Paltoglou, 2011).

RELATED WORK

How to recognize the sentiment of online users in public opinion events refers to the sentiment recognition of blogs posted from online users. In this section, we introduce the research about visual and textual sentiment recognition. Extracting the features from unimodality and employing the techniques to fuse the unimodal features are the core of multimodal sentiment recognition. The techniques of extracting and fusing features from unimodality are described in this section.

Visual Sentiment Recognition

The sentiment recognition of visual multimedia is a growing area of research interest. The techniques of visual sentiment recognition can be divided into three broad categories: the methods based on low-level visual features (Jia et al., 2012; Yanulevskaya et al., 2012), the methods based on mid-level semantics representation (Borth, Ji, Chen, Breuel, & Chang, 2013) and the methods based on deep learning (Chen, Borth, Darrell, & Chang, 2014).

As an important branch of artificial intelligence, deep learning has been employed in visual sentiment recognition. You, Luo, Jin, and Yang (2016) introduced a 3+ million weakly labeled images of different emotions. Then a CNNs model pretrained on ImageNet was fine-tuned on the new dataset. The results showed that compared with machine learning techniques the CNNs model had certain superiority. To explore the superiority of fine-tuning techniques in visual sentiment analysis, Campos, Jou, and Giro-i-Nieto (2017) employed a pre-trained AlexNet-styled network and fine-tuned on DeepSent to evaluate the performance of visual sentiment recognition. In their experiments, through releasing different layers or adding layers for fine-tuning, they found that deep architectures can learn useful features for recognizing the visual sentiment in images and raise the performance.

Textual Sentiment Recognition

The research about analyzing the sentiment of online users has always been the focus of online public opinion research. The main methods to recognize the online users' sentiment are analyzing the texts the online users deliver on social platforms through natural language processing techniques. Conventional textual sentiment analysis techniques can be divided into two categories: rule-based methods (Hu, Tang, Gao, & Liu, 2013; Kim & Hovy, 2006; Turney, 2002) and statistics approaches with a large annotated with emotional polarity dataset (Pang, Lee, & Vaithyanathan, 2002; Wang & Manning, 2012).

Deep learning techniques accelerate the development of natural language processing and bring a promising future (Socher, Bengio, & Manning, 2012). Kim and Hovy (2006) applied CNNs to textual sentiment recognition. They used word vectors to represent texts and employed CNNs to extract textual features and recognize the sentiments. Due to sequential features of sentences, Recurrent Neural Network (RNNs) (Rumelhart, 1988) can allow the connections between neurons to form cycles, based on the network which can memorize information. Based on that, RNNs were applied to recognize the sentiments on movie review texts (Socher et al., 2013). When the gap of contextual content becomes large, RNNs cannot learn distant information. Long Short-Term Memory (LSTMs) (Gers, Schmidhuber, & Cummins, 1999). As the extension of RNNs, LSTMs can solve the long dependence problem through controlling gate and be employed to recognize the sentiments (Tai, Socher, & Manning, 2015).

Multimodal Sentiment Recognition

Multimodalities are composed of different unimodality, such as images, texts, audios, gestures etc. Multimodal sentiment recognition can be seen as a fusion of emotional information from different unimodality. There are two main fusion strategies: feature-level fusion and decision-level fusion.

Feature-level fusion combines the features extracted from the interlayer or input as a joint vector before the classification is performed. Rosas, Mihalcea, and Morency (2013) employed bag of words to represent texts and used OpenEAR to extract features from audio. And they used Okao Vision to extract facial features. Then these features were concatenated into a long vector fed into SVM. Majumder, Hazarika, Gelbukh, Cambria, and Poria (2018) proposed a novel feature-level fusion strategy which proceeds in a hierarchical fashion, first fusing the modalities two in two and only then fusing all three modalities.

In decision-level fusion, every single unimodality is modeled and classified respectively. Then the predicted results from unimodality are fused based on expert rules or simple operators to decide the final labels. Alam and Riccardi (2014) combined the features from different unimodality in decision-level and applied majority voting to finish classification. Dobrišek, Gajšek, Mihelič, Pavešić, and Štruc (2013) designed a multimodal emotion recognition system exploiting audio and video information. The system processed both source of information to produce corresponding matching scores and combined the computed matching scores to obtain a predicted label.

So far, most research about multimodal sentiment recognition in social platforms has focused on the combination of textual features and facial expressions features. However, in real environment, especially in online public events, most online users post microblogs attached with emotional images rather than facial images. Additionally, there is little work combing texts and attached images to consider the sentiments of online users in online public opinion events. In proposed study, we use visual sentiment rather than facial emotions and combine textual features to recognize the sentiment. Moreover, we employ the DNNs to recognize the fused features and make comparison with different fusion strategies.

METHOD

First, we present an empirical framework to recognize unimodal sentiment and extract visual and textual features for multimodal sentiment recognition. Then we discuss our two fusion strategies. The multimodal sentiment recognition framework is shown in Figure 1.

Unimodal Sentiment Recognition

Visual Sentiment Recognition with CNNs

Images have become an inseparable part in our social lives, which can deliver emotions that texts can't express and capture moments tied with deep affections. So how to recognize the sentiments and latent dispositions embedded in images has become more and more important. In this work, we use VGG-16 Net (Simonyan & Zisserman, 2014) as our base

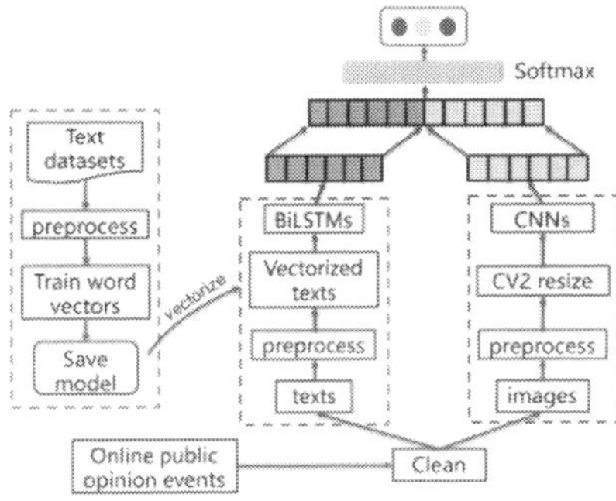

Figure 1. The framework of multimodal sentiment recognition of online users.

model for visual sentiment recognition, which was proposed by Oxford University in 2014. Due to its simplicity and practicality, VGG-16 Net becomes popular and more researchers paid attention to it. Convolutional Neural Networks (CNNs) often contain a large number of parameters that need to be learned, and also usually require large training datasets (Campos et al., 2017). Additionally, it takes a lot of time and resources to train CNNs from scratch. In visual sentiment recognition tasks, it is hard to collect a large dataset with accurate annotations on subjective reasoning. An appropriate way to avoid the disadvantages of small dataset is transfer learning.

Transfer learning performs representation learning on a different, but related, dataset and then applies the gained knowledge to the actual training phase (Pan & Yang, 2010). Fine-tuning is a practical strategy in transfer learning and made up of initializing all weights in the network except last fully-connected layers, employing the weights of pre-trained model. Given that the sentiments of ImageNet images mostly are neutral, we decide to use these images to pretrain VGG-16 model and then transfer weights and parameters. In this work, we employed a pre-trained VGG-16 model with Image-Net images in keras.[1] According to the classes of dataset sentiments, we changed last fully connected layers as is shown in Figure 2. The number of neurons that the last layer contains are always as the same as the sentiment classes of the dataset and set to 3.

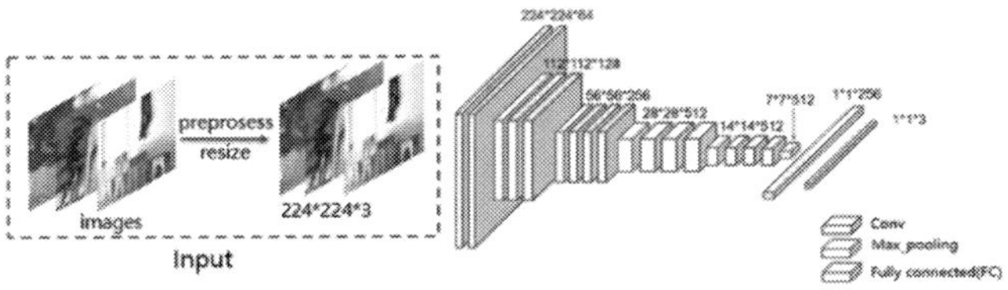

Figure 2. The adapted VGG-16 Net for visual sentiment recognition.

[1] Available at: https: //keras.io/zh/applications/#vgg16

In our experiments, the weights of new added fully connected layers are randomly initialized and the rest layers of network are initialized with the weights from pre-trained VGG-16 model. The whole training process is divided into two parts. First, in the process of warming up, we freeze the layers in network except two new added layers, which do not involve the training. The network is trained using stochastic gradient descent with momentum of 0.9 and the learning rate is set to 0.001. The training epochs is 50 using batches of 128 images. When it is finished, we begin to fine-tune the network. The last convolutional neural network is released and combined with last two fully connected layers involve in the training. The training epochs are 100 using batches of 128. To avoid overfitting, we employ oversampling by rotating, overturning and cropping the images.

Textual Sentiment Recognition with BiLSTMs

The framework of textual sentiment recognition is shown in Figure 3. We use word embeddings to represent texts as the input and employ BiLSTMs to recognize the textual sentiment.

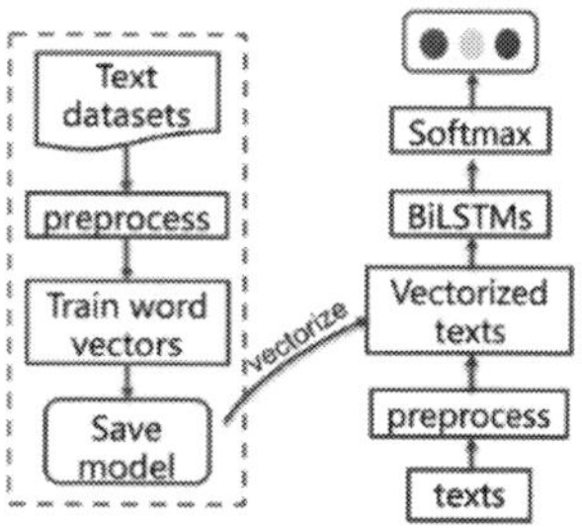

Figure 3. The framework of textual sentiment recognition.

Usually, in natural language processing, there are two methods to represent words, which are one-hot representation and distributed representation. In one-hot representation, every word is represented as a long vector resulting that the vector is too sparse and "dimension curse." As a representative of distributed representation, word embedding techniques can map words to a lower dimensional space and avoid the risk of high dimensions. And it can make semantically related words closer. Skip-gram model is one of word embedding and performs well. Intuitively, Skip-gram can predict contextual semantic units when the input word is given through unsupervised learning (Mikolov, Chen, Corrado, & Dean, 2013). As is shown in Figure 4, the word w(t) is chosen as the input, which is represented by a x-dimensional vector. When the size of skip_window is set to n, the predicted outputs are w(t − n), w(t − n − 1), …, w(t + n − 1), w(t + n) through unsupervised training. If the training corpus is huge, the trained word vectors are more representative and contain more information. In this work, we choose the Skip-gram model[2] in genism package to train word embeddings. The window_size is set to 5. The dimensions of word vectors are set to 100.

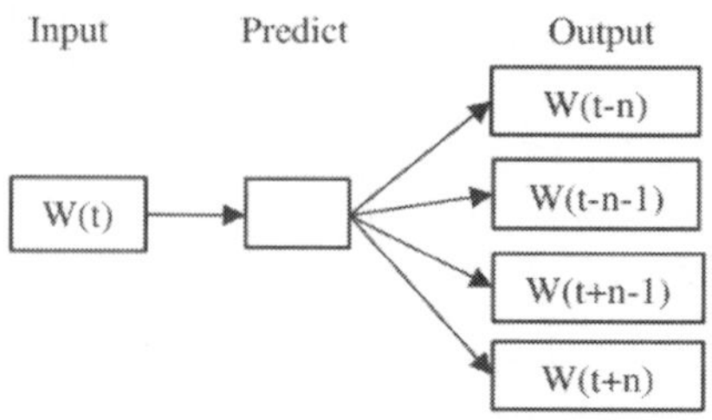

Figure 4. The basic idea behind Skip-gram model.

With success of deep learning in computer vision, more and more scholars apply deep learning techniques to natural language processing. The most representative network is Recurrent Neural Network (RNNs). However, with the gap of contexts becoming huge and the network going deeper, the gradient explosion and vanishment occur. As an extension of RNNs, Long Short-Term Memory (LSTMs) networks can advance RNNs by controlling the unique gates subtly to combine short memory with long memory and solve the gradient explosion and vanishment to some extent (Srivastava, Mansimov, & Salakhutdinov, 2015). LSTMs contain three gates, namely input gate, forget gate and output gate, and a cell state. The Forget gate controls information the history cell state should preserve. In Equation (1), the output h_{t-1} of previous word is

$$f_t = \sigma\left(w_f \cdot [h_{t-1}, x_t] + b_f\right) \tag{1}$$

taken and x_t is numerical representation of current word. w_f represents the weight matrix and b_f represents the bias vector. Through the neural network layer with its sigmoid activation function σ, it returns a vector f_t, whose elements are in the range [0, 1]. A zero represents forgetting and an one represents remembering. Input gate decides what information of input is preserved to new cell state. In Equations (2) and (3), input

$$i_t = \sigma\left(w_i \cdot [h_{t-1}, x_t] + b_i\right) \tag{2}$$

$$\widetilde{C}_t = \tanh\left(w_c \cdot [h_{t-1}, x_t] + b_c\right) \tag{3}$$

gate layer with its sigmoid activation function decides what information in cell state need to be updated and returns a vector i_t. Additionally, a neural network layer with tanh activation function returns a new vector $\widetilde{C}_t$, which represents the alternative updated information. In Equations (4) and (5),

$$C_t = f_t \odot f_{t-1} + i_t \odot \widetilde{C}_t \tag{4}$$

$$o_t = \sigma\left(w_o \cdot [h_{t-1}, x_t] + b_O\right) \tag{5}$$

we combine i_t with $\widetilde{C}_t$ and update the history cell state to a new cell state C_t. $\odot$ refers to element-wise multiplication. Based on the cell state. The output gate layer with sigmoid

[2] Available at: https://pypi.org/project/word2vec/

activation function decides the passing information and returns a vector o_t. In Equation (6), the final output h_t is

$$h_t = o_t \odot \tanh(C_t) \qquad (6)$$

element- wise multiplied by o_t and the output of the neural network with its tanh activation function.

Bidirectional LSTMs (BiLSTMs) network is combined with forward LSTMs and backward LSTMs, which can increase the amount of available contextual information and capture bidirectional semantic dependencies. In our experiments, BiLSTMs network is chosen as the classifier of textual sentiment.

Multimodal Sentiment Recognition with DNNs

Here we describe how to combine the visual and textual features to recognize the sentiment with DNNs. And we discuss the fusion strategies for using textual and visual features.

Feature-Level Fusion

Multimodal features fusion is the core of multimodal sentiment recognition. Feature-level fusion refers to extracting the features from the interlayer of unimodality and simply concatenating them to form a single long feature vector. Though the trivial method seems simple, it has shown the high accuracy (Poria, Cambria, Howard, Huang, & Hussain, 2015). Then the single long vector as the fused feature is fed to DNNs to continue training. The structure of multimodal sentiment recognition is detailed in Figure 6. In this experiment, we employ fine-tuned VGG-16 Net and BiLSTMs to extract visual features and textual features respectively. After concatenation, the fused features are fed to softmax layer to continue training and finish sentiment recognition.

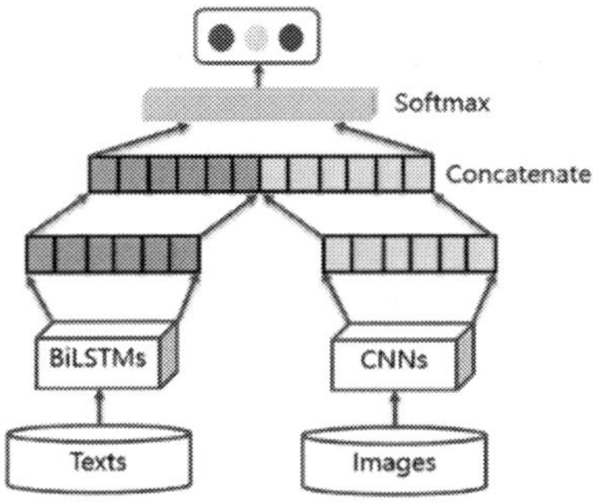

Figure 5. Feature-level fusion architecture.

Decision-Level Fusion

The structure of decision-level fusion is illustrated in Figure 7. Instead of concatenating the feature vectors extracted from the interlayer of neural networks, we obtain the final outputs from the softmax layer of above unimodal sentiment recognition models. The outputted vector is in a

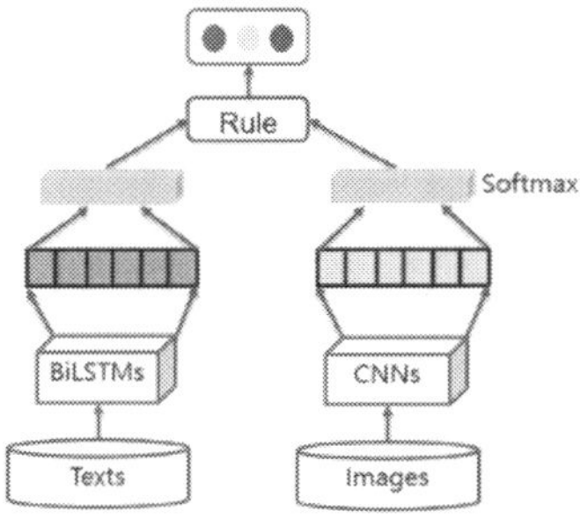

Figure 6. Decision-level fusion architecture.

form of array: $[\lambda_1, \lambda_2, \ldots, \lambda_i]$. λ_i represents the probability values of each sentiment and i denotes the number of sentiments. In this case, we get three sentiments. And the predicted probability scores of each unimodal sentiment are in a form of 3-dimensional array. Based on the decision-level fusion rule (Poria et al., 2015) below, we calculate the final label of the classification.

$$l' = argmax\left(q_1 s_i^v + q_2 s_i^t\right), \quad i = 1, 2, 3, \ldots, C$$

In this rule, q_1 and q_2 denote the weight for visual modality and textual modality. An equal-weighted scheme is adopted, so $q_1 = q_2 = 0.5$ in this case. C denotes the number of sentiments. s_i^v and s_i^t denote the probability values of each sentiment from visual and textual modality. l' denotes the final predicted sentiment label.

EXPERIMENTAL RESULTS

In this section, we first describe the dataset used in this study and show the results of different unimodal sentiment recognition. Next, to examine the advancement of multimodal fusion and compare performances of different fusion strategies, we use two fusion strategies for predicting the sentiment of multimodalities. In feature-level fusion, we extract the textual and visual features and feed the concatenated features into deep neural networks, training in a manner of end to end. In decision-level fusion, the predicted outputs from unimodalities are fused based on a rule to form a final classification label.

Experimental Dataset and Preprocessing

As there is no publicly available microblog dataset containing texts and images in online public opinion events, we have collected a series of data about online public opinion events in latest 2 years from Sina, which is the most famous microblog site in China just like twitter. The dataset includes "Chongqing bus crash incident," "40th anniversary of reform and opening up," "Typhoon Shanzhu," etc. When a blog attached with several images, we choose the only one representative image, whose emotional polarity is strongest. An example is shown in Table 1. The dataset contains 2,001 texts and images respectively. After accurate and detailed annotation, the sentiment polarities of dataset are divided into positive, neutral and negative. In annotated dataset, the numbers of positive sentiment, neutral sentiment and negative sentiment are 712, 768 and 512. In addition, we still crawl online public opinion events texts for training the word vectors, which in all are 291, 1235 from Sina microblog in latest years.

Image	Text (translated)
	The tree was strong in the wind, which was shot in lianhua mountain. In my eyes, it was the most vigorous and powerful tree after typhoon.

Table 1. An example of collected online opinion events dataset.

Before experiments, we preprocess the datasets. Usually, every single image posted in microblog has a unique watermark to show its ownership. However, it's useless for visual sentiment. By means of CV2,[3] we remove the watermarks on images. Then we set the size of image to 224*224 with three channels, adapting the input of VGG16 Net. For texts, microblog texts usually contain emoticons, which is rich of emotions. In this work, we transform them into emotional words based on corresponding affections. For example, an emoticon, , means joy and can be transformed into word, "[happiness]." Due to the irregularity and substandard in blogs, these signals are removed from texts, such as "@," "#," etc. Additionally, the operations of word segmentation and removing stop words are performed, with jieba[4] package in python and stop word lexicons.

The Results of Unimodal Sentiment Recognition

In the sentiment recognition of images, the training epochs are set to 100 using batches of 128 in fine-tuning the network. The network is trained using stochastic gradient descent with momentum of 0.9 and the learning rate is set to 0.001. To avoid overfitting, we employ oversampling by rotating, overturning and cropping the images. Relu (Dahl, Sainath, & Hinton, 2013) is adopted as the activation function for CNNs. For texts, the training epochs are 100 using batches of 128. The learning rule is Adam with standard parameters. To avoid overfitting, the dropout rate is set to 0.5 (Hinton, Srivastava, Krizhevsky, Sutskever, & Salakhutdinov, 2012). And loss function is categorical crossentropy. The top-performing results of unimodal sentiment recognition is detailed in Table 2. 80% of the dataset are for training and 20% of that are for testing. The training set and testing set are the same in unimodal sentiment recognition and multimodal sentiment recognition.

[3] Available at: https://pypi.org/project/opencv-python/
[4] Available at: https://pypi.org/project/jieba/

From Table 2, we can see that the results of textual sentiment recognition outperform that of visual sentiment recognition by a large margin. It shows that textual features may contain more emotional information than visual features and are easier to be learned by sentiment recognition model.

Modality	Precision (%)	Recall (%)	F1 (%)
V	51.589	49.377	48.798
T	**80.494**	**80.549**	**80.477**

Table 2. The results of visual sentiment recognition. V represents the visual modality and T represents the textual modality.

Feature-Level Fusion

We extract the visual and textual features from the last fully-connected layer of unimodal sentiment recognition model. The extracted features are concatenated and fed to DNNs to continue training. The result is illustrated in Table 3. From Table 3, we can find that when visual features are employed, the performance of sentiment classification improves in feature-level fusion. Combing Table 2, we can see that in evaluated metrics, the results of feature-level fusion outperform that of unimodality. It indicates that visual features play a role in the boost of sentiment recognition performance.

Modalities	Precision (%)	Recall (%)	F1 (%)
V+T	83.355	82.250	81.729

Table 3. The results of bimodal sentiment classification in feature-level fusion.

Decision-Level Fusion

In decision-level fusion experiments, we employ a rule on output extracted from the softmax layer of unimodal sentiment recognition model, producing final predicted labels. Experimental results are shown in Table 4. We find that the results outperform that of unimodality. Combined with Table 3, the performance of decision-level fusion is inferior to feature-level fusion. And when fused with visual features, the performance of fused features is superior to the unimodal features no matter what in which fusion level. It indicates that the fused features contain more emotional information and do raise the performance of sentiment classification to some extent.

Modalities	Precision (%)	Recall (%)	F1 (%)
V+T	81.563	81.031	80.601

Table 4. The results of bimodal sentiment classification in decision-level.

DISCUSSION AND ANALYSIS

Our unimodal experiments showed that in sentiment recognition task of online users, the performance of textual features is better than visual features when deep neural networks are applied. In social platforms, online users usually share what happened around them by sending texts and images. Compared to images, texts are more emotional and emotional polarity is more obvious. For example, when online users intend to criticize some behavior and express their anger, we can easily understand their emotion from text. It's difficult for us to recognize the sentiment when the image looks confusing. Maybe it's the reason why the performance of visual sentiment recognition is inferior to textual sentiment recognition.

Though the performance of visual sentiment recognition is not satisfied, we can see that when visual features are used in feature-level or decision-level fusion, the results of sentiment recognition on fused features outperform the unimodal features from Figure 8. It indicates that in the sentiment recognition of online users, the images attached to the texts do assist models to understand the mood and sentiment online users want to express. Especially in online public opinion events, online users want to condemn the initiators of the event but what they express is sometimes in a form of irony. For example, online users may send the text that "you are awesome" to express their anger and contempt and match an image that shows an upside-down thumb. Just analyzing the texts, we cannot easily recognize the sentiment that the online user wants to convey. When the image is considered with text, the sentiment the online user expresses becomes distinct because the image shows the strong emotional polarity and is helpful to understand the real sentiment. Additionally, in Figure 8, feature-level fusion outperforms decision-level fusion and unimodality in our experiments. It shows that feature-level fusion is more robust and our proposed DNNs model is more effective.

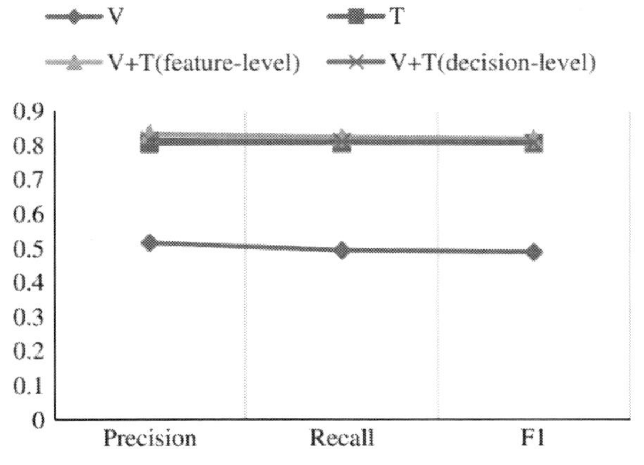

Figure 7. The results of unimodal and multimodal fusion.

In theory, aiming at the situation that texts are insufficient to recognize the sentiment of online users, we first combine texts with attached images to consider the sentiment of online users in public opinion events compared to previous related work (Jiang et al., 2015; Su et al., 2017). Additionally, considering the real mircoblogs, visual sentiment, rather than facial emotions (Poria et al., 2016; Zadeh et al., 2017), are employed as visual modality to recognize the sentiment together. In practice, we present a DNNs multimodal sentiment recognition model, containing fine-tuned CNNs and BiLSTMs and compare two feature fusion strategies. Experimental results showed that the proposed method is better than unimodal sentiment recognition model and feature-level fusion performs better.

CONCLUSIONS AND FUTURE WORK

In this paper, we have presented a DNNs multimodal sentiment recognition framework, combing texts and images, to recognize the sentiments of online users in online public opinion events. Additionally, we have presented unimodal sentiment recognition model and compared two feature fusion strategies. In terms of experimental results, we found that when visual features are fused, the results of multimodal sentiment recognition outperform that of unimodality. It indicates that visual features play a key role in multimodal sentiment recognition and boost the performance.

In future work, we plan to boost the performance of visual sentiment recognition, through expanding our dataset and improving our corresponding model. Furthermore, we still seek to improve texts sentiment classification through considering contextual content, which will further boost the accuracy of classification. Additionally, we will explore the integration of vlogs and blogs to recognize the sentiment of online users.

ACKNOWLEDGMENTS

This research was supported by the National Natural Science Foundation of China under contract No.71774084, 71503124, 71503126, The National Social Science Fund of China under contract No.15BTQ063,17ZDA291, Jiangsu "Qinlan" project [2016]15, Jiangsu Graduation Training and Innovation Project under contract No. KYCX18_0494.

REFERENCES

Alam, F., & Riccardi, G. (2014). Predicting personality traits using multimodal information. *Proceedings of the 2014 ACM Multi Media on Workshop on Computational Personality Recognition* (pp. 15–18). ACM.

Borth, D., Ji, R., Chen, T., Breuel, T., & Chang, S. F. (2013). Large-scale visual sentiment ontology and detectors using adjective noun pairs. *Proceedings of the 21st ACM International Conference on Multimedia* (pp. 223–232). ACM.

Cai, G., & Xia, B. (2015). Convolutional neural networks for multimedia sentiment analysis. *Natural language processing and chinese computing* (pp. 159–167). Cham, Switzerland: Springer.

Campos, V., Jou, B., & Giro-i-Nieto, X. (2017). From pixels to sentiment: Fine-tuning cnns for visual sentiment prediction. *Image and Vision Computing*, *65*, 15–22.

Chen, T., Borth, D., Darrell, T., & Chang, S. F. (2014). Deepsentibank: Visual sentiment concept classification with deep convolutional neural networks. *arXiv preprint arXiv*:1410.8586.

Dahl, G. E., Sainath, T. N., & Hinton, G. E. (2013, May). Improving deep neural networks for LVCSR using rectified linear units and dropout. *2013 IEEE International Conference on Acoustics, Speech and Signal Processing* (pp. 8609–8613). IEEE.

Deng, J., Dong, W., Socher, R., Li, L. J., Li, K., & Fei-Fei, L. (2009). Imagenet: A large-scale hierarchical image database. *2009 IEEE Conference on Computer Vision and Pattern Recognition* (pp. 248–255). IEEE.

Dobrišek, S., Gajšek, R., Mihelič, F., Pavešić, N., & Štruc, V. (2013). Towards efficient multi-modal emotion recognition. *International Journal of Advanced Robotic Systems*, *10*(1), 53.

Gelli, F., Uricchio, T., Bertini, M., Del Bimbo, A., & Chang, S. F. (2015). Image popularity prediction in social media using sentiment and context features. *Proceedings of the 23rd ACM International Conference on Multimedia* (pp. 907–910). ACM.

Gers, F. A., Schmidhuber, J., & Cummins, F. (1999). Learning to forget: Continual prediction with LSTM.

Hinton, G. E., Srivastava, N., Krizhevsky, A., Sutskever, I., & Salakhutdinov, R. R. (2012). Improving neural networks by preventing co-adaptation of feature detectors. *arXiv preprint arXiv:1207.0580*.

Hu, X., Tang, J., Gao, H., & Liu, H. (2013). Unsupervised sentiment analysis with emotional signals. *Proceedings of the 22nd International Conference on World Wide Web* (pp. 607–618). ACM.

Jia, J., Wu, S., Wang, X., Hu, P., Cai, L., & Tang, J. (2012). Can we understand van gogh's mood?: Learning to infer affects from images in social networks. *Proceedings of the 20th ACM International Conference on Multimedia* (pp. 857–860). ACM.

Jiang, H., Lin, P., & Qiang, M. (2015). Public-opinion sentiment analysis for large hydro projects. *Journal of Construction Engineering and Management*, *142*(2), 05015013.

Jindal, S., & Singh, S. (2015). Image sentiment analysis using deep convolutional neural networks with domain specific fine tuning. *2015 International Conference on Information Processing (ICIP)* (pp. 447–451). IEEE.

Kim, S. M., & Hovy, E. (2006). Extracting opinions, opinion holders, and topics expressed in online news media text. *Proceedings of the Workshop on Sentiment and Subjectivity in Text* (pp. 1–8). Association for Computational Linguistics.

Li, W., & Xu, H. (2014). Text-based emotion classification using emotion cause extraction. *Expert Systems with Applications*, *41*(4), 1742–1749.

Lu, X., Suryanarayan, P., Adams, R. B., Jr., Li, J., Newman, M. G., & Wang, J. Z. (2012). On shape and the computability of emotions. *Proceedings of the 20th ACM International Conference on Multimedia* (pp. 229–238). ACM.

Machajdik, J., & Hanbury, A. (2010). Affective image classification using features inspired by psychology and art theory. *Proceedings of the 18th ACM International Conference on Multimedia* (pp. 83–92). ACM.

Majumder, N., Hazarika, D., Gelbukh, A., Cambria, E., & Poria, S. (2018). Multimodal sentiment analysis using hierarchical fusion with context modeling. *Knowledge-Based Systems*, *161*, 124–133.

Mandel, B., Culotta, A., Boulahanis, J., Stark, D., Lewis, B., & Rodrigue, J. (2012). A demographic analysis of online sentiment during hurricane irene. *Proceedings of the Second Workshop on Language in Social Media* (pp. 27–36). Association for Computational Linguistics.

Mikolov, T., Chen, K., Corrado, G., & Dean, J. (2013). Efficient estimation of word representations in vector space. *arXiv preprint arXiv*:1301.3781.

Pan, S. J., & Yang, Q. (2010). A survey on transfer learning. *IEEE Transactions on Knowledge & Data Engineering*, *22*(10), 1345–1359.

Pang, B., Lee, L., & Vaithyanathan, S. (2002). Thumbs up?: Sentiment classification using machine learning techniques. *Proceedings of the ACL-02 Conference on Empirical Methods in Natural Language processing* (Vol. *10*, pp. 79–86). Association for Computational Linguistics.

Poria, S., Cambria, E., Howard, N., Huang, G. B., & Hussain, A. (2015). Fusing audio, visual and textual clues for sentiment analysis from multimodal content. *Neurocomputing*, *174*, 50–59.

Poria, S., Chaturvedi, I., Cambria, E., & Hussain, A. (2016). Convolutional MKL based multimodal emotion recognition and sentiment analysis. *2016 IEEE 16th International Conference on Data Mining (ICDM)* (pp. 439–448). IEEE.

Rosas, V. P., Mihalcea, R., & Morency, L. P. (2013). Multimodal sentiment analysis of spanish online videos. *IEEE Intelligent Systems*, *28*(3), 38–45.

Rumelhart, D. E., Hinton, G. E., & Williams, R. J. (1988). Learning representations by back-propagating errors. *Cognitive modeling*, *5*(3), 1.

Simonyan, K., & Zisserman, A. (2014). Very deep convolutional networks for large-scale image recognition. *arXiv preprint arXiv:1409.1556.*

Socher, R., Bengio, Y., & Manning, C. D. (2012). Deep learning for NLP (without magic). *Tutorial Abstracts of ACL 2012* (pp. 5–5). *Association for Computational Linguistics.*

Socher, R., Perelygin, A., Wu, J., Chuang, J., Manning, C. D., Ng, A., & Potts, C. (2013). Recursive deep models for semantic compositionality over a sentiment treebank. *Proceedings of the 2013 Conference on Empirical Methods in Natural Llanguage Processing* (pp. 1631–1642).

Srivastava, N., Mansimov, E., & Salakhutdinov, R. (2015). Unsupervised learning of video representations using lstms. *arXiv preprint arXiv*:1502.04681.

Stephens, K. K., & Malone, P. C. (2009). If the organizations won't give us information…: The use of multiple new media for crisis technical translation and dialogue. *Journal of Public Relations Research, 21*(2), 229–239.

Su, L. Y. F., Cacciatore, M. A., Liang, X., Brossard, D., Scheufele, D. A., & Xenos, M. A. (2017). Analyzing public sentiments online: Combining human-and computer-based content analysis. *Information, Communication & Society, 20*(3), 406–427.

Tai, K. S., Socher, R., & Manning, C. D. (2015). Improved semantic representations from tree-structured long short-term memory networks. *arXiv preprint arXiv:1503.00075.*

Tang, D., Qin, B., & Liu, T. (2015). Document modeling with gated recurrent neural network for sentiment classification. *Proceedings of the 2015 Conference on Empirical Methods in Natural Language Processing* (pp. 1422–1432).

Thelwall, M., Buckley, K., & Paltoglou, G. (2011). Sentiment in Twitter events. *Journal of the American Society for Information Science and Technology, 62*(2), 406–418.

Turney, P. D. (2002). Thumbs up or thumbs down?: Semantic orientation applied to unsupervised classification of reviews. *Proceedings of the 40th Annual Meeting on Association for Computational Linguistics* (pp. 417–424). Association for Computational Linguistics.

Wang, J., Yu, L. C., Lai, K. R., & Zhang, X. (2016). Dimensional sentiment analysis using a regional CNN-LSTM model. *Proceedings of the 54th Annual Meeting of the Association for Computational Linguistics* (Volume 2: Short Papers). Vol. 2 (pp. 225–230).

Wang, S., & Manning, C. D. (2012). Baselines and bigrams: Simple, good sentiment and topic classification. *Proceedings of the 50th Annual Meeting of the Association for Computational Linguistics: Short Papers* (Vol. 2, pp. 90–94). Association for Computational Linguistics.

Wu, P., Shen, S., He, D., & Du, J. T. (2017). A belief–desire–intention model for blog users' negative emotional norm compliance: Decision-making in crises. *The Electronic Library, 35*(4), 798–821.

Xu, C., Cetintas, S., Lee, K. C., & Li, L. J. (2014). Visual sentiment prediction with deep convolutional neural networks. *arXiv preprint arXiv:1411.5731.*

Yanulevskaya, V., Uijlings, J., Bruni, E., Sartori, A., Zamboni, E., Bacci, F., … Sebe, N. (2012). In the eye of the beholder: Employing statistical analysis and eye tracking for analyzing abstract paintings. *Proceedings of the 20th ACM International Conference on Multimedia* (pp. 349–358). ACM.

You, Q., Luo, J., Jin, H., & Yang, J. (2016). Building a large scale dataset for image emotion recognition: The fine print and the benchmark. *Thirtieth AAAI Conference on Artificial Intelligence.*

Zadeh, A., Chen, M., Poria, S., Cambria, E., & Morency, L. P. (2017). Tensor fusion network for multimodal sentiment analysis. *arXiv preprint arXiv: 1707.07250.*

Zhou, C., Sun, C., Liu, Z., & Lau, F. (2015). A C-LSTM neural network for text classification. *arXiv preprint arXiv: 1511.08630.*

How Scientists Interact With Bacteria: Creating New Knowledge

Giovanni Forero
University of Technology Sydney,
Sydney, Australia
giovanni.e.forero@student.uts.edu.au

ABSTRACT

This paper presents a current investigation analyzing the interactions between scientists and their objects of study, specifically bacteria, to understand the role of physical objects during informational processes of investigation and research; it focuses on the techniques that the scientists deployed in the laboratory during the course of their investigation in order to generate information and build knowledge. This investigation is carried out in a micro-biology laboratory at an Australasian university that studies particular bacteria and how they become resistant to antibiotics. This study uses Latour's Actor Network Theory (ANT) as a conceptual framework and methodological approach, in order to understand the associations and interactions enacted in the laboratory as a mechanism to produce scientific papers, and how these interactions are mediated by a range of actors including technology, practices and personal events. This study also discusses some of the implications of using ANT as a conceptual framework and methodological approach, and its potential value as a theoretical foundation for future research in information studies.

KEYWORDS

Actor Network Theory; Bacteria; Objects; Agency; Information Processes; Observer; Knowledge

ASIS&T THESAURUS

Information Science; Knowledge and Information; Data and Information Attributes

INTRODUCTION

Popular culture usually perceives scientists as experts, engaged entirely in a cognitive process, whose observation of phenomena and expertise in understanding what is observed leads to new knowledge. This approach leads, in popular culture, to the representation of the mad scientist reduced to a brain in a jar. Yet, scientists are more than their expertise and cognitive capacity. They are part of society and their laboratory can be seen as a social environment. From this social perspective, this study seeks to identify the strategies, techniques and practices that scientists use to engage with their object of study. The object of this study are bacteria, imperceptible to the naked eye, but nonetheless, living organisms. How scientists in the laboratory make sense of their discoveries and communicate them to each other is an important part of this study.

Thus, this study challenges traditional cognitive conceptions of information as a private and propositional process internal to the observer (Frohmann, 2007; Leckie, Given, & Buschman, 2010). It explores the possible participation of the bacteria and other objects in the process of information creation. The question of how the bacteria might communicate with the scientists is important, as is the question of what other entities might actively contribute to the creation of new scientific knowledge (c.f., Pickering, 1995).

The research question guiding this investigation is: How do scientists interact with bacteria to create new knowledge?

LITERATURE REVIEW

When attempting to trace the role of objects in informational processes through the literature and determine how they are described through their relations with their human observers within the processes of learning and observation, one can perceive that at best objects have been brought into the picture in a mere passive and utilitarian fashion, as **"physical lumps outside of human knowledge"** (Harman, 2009). This approach has a long tradition, evident from the work of Fairthorne, one of the founding theorists in Information Science. His work emphasized the distinction between a physical object in a library collection or a document in a repository and the information it contained, when he noted that the use of the term "information" to denote the physical object was primarily a metaphorical use of the term (Fairthorne, 1954, 1967).

Brookes (1974), saw that disciplines such as physics and biology were using information to describe physical realities beyond the documental sense and that it would be beneficial for the discipline to become conversant with these other ways in which the term information was being used that went beyond its focus on the document. Knorr Cetina (1999) and Haider and Kjellberg (2016) have taken up this challenge.

Brookes's (1980) main contribution to this debate was his cognitive approach presented in the **"fundamental**

82nd Annual Meeting of the Association for Information Science & Technology | Melbourne, Australia | 19–23 October, 2019

DOI: 10.1002/pra2.00060

equation", where he proposed that an increase in the information entering the private cognitive processes of an observer would in turn produce an increase in the knowledge state of the observer. This cognitive and behaviorist approach has been, according to authors like Olsson (2010), Frohmann (2007), Van House (2003), Leckie et al. (2010) dominant in information science for quite some time.

The cognitive approaches derived from the work of Brookes and others emphasized the individual's capacity to create knowledge, even though they might take into account the environment in which the information-bearing object was generated.

Relevant to this study is an acknowledgement of the influence of Weiner's theory of Cybernetics, and Shannon and Weaver's model of communication, which presented the brain and the human agent as processing units of physical signals (Bonnevie, 2001; Gleick, 2011). This work isolated the informational processes from the physical processes that triggered them and subsequently limited the informational processes to a private, mental and propositional exercise or physical process. The shortcoming of the model was that it operated from an engineering perspective, where problems were seen, not in terms of content or meaning, but in terms of quality of transmission. From a social sciences perspective, this was incomplete and it led to a variety of approaches that have explored the link between information, its meaning and the knowledge of an individual.

Perhaps one of the boldest recognitions of the potential role of objects in informational processes is Buckland's (1991) **"information-as-thing"** conception. Based on Briet's definition of an object as fulfilling an evidential role through a circumstantial relation with the observer, Buckland allows for these objects to be categorized as informational, provided they afford the observer an opportunity to learn from the object. However, even in this case, objects are not seen as actively participating, but passively being categorized as informative based on the observer's impression of the object.

This tension between the thing and its meaning has been explored more recently by Frohmann (2007), in his consideration of the differences between information and the document. This work suggests that in various ways, the multiplicity, materiality and agency of the document are important to documentation but could equally be of value to the field of information science. This echoes the perceptions of Latour (2005) and Harman (2009) who address the difficulty of bridging this incommensurable gap between an object, its meaning and the person making sense of it, emphasizing the seeming impossibility of the individual to step outside of their own perspective to gain a full understanding.

Latour's Actor Network Theory (ANT) is not as widely used in information studies as a conceptual framework as in other fields (Van House, 2003). However, it does seem to offer a number of tools to the researcher to understand the role of objects in information processes and to explore how human observers interact with such objects as they are associated as participants within a particular social environment.

Latour's view of objects as agents and active participants in social environments enables the researcher to understand the agency of non-human actors and how such actors have an impact on the observer's knowledge as finally recorded in an authoritative academic paper (Knorr Cetina, 1999; Van House, 2003).

ANT's novel outlook on objects offers the possibility for the researcher to circumvent long-standing debates about the nature of objects. It also offers the possibility of focussing on the concrete qualities of actors as perceived by other agents in the network, through their effect on the rest of the participants. As Latour (2005) would insist: to "follow the actors" regardless of who or what they are, could give the researcher a richer picture of the social environment in general, and the informational processes that occur and generate knowledge in particular. In addition, ANT seems to be particularly helpful in uncovering the voice of these entities that appear to surround us and inform us, but that so far have been buried under the cacophony of our own voices and anthropocentric interest.

CONCEPTUAL FRAMEWORK

From the literature review it is possible to understand that objects have for the most part been relegated to passive, or utilitarian roles in the processes that generate information, data and knowledge. It is important however for this investigation to understand whether objects of study have any impact on the processes that generate information about them when scientists interact with them to study them and if so how.

This investigation uses Latour's Actor Network Theory (ANT) to understand how scientists and objects interact with each other through the establishment of a social network within the laboratory, in which each actor contributes within the context of the network to produce a set of specific outcomes (Latour, 1996, 2005). One of the distinctive features of ANT is its position about the potential source of agency; from ANT's perspective, an actor is that which acts, irrespective of whether this actor is human or not (Latour, 2005; Wheeler, 2010). Moreover, an actor, "that which acts" is also an ontological feature of Latour's metaphysics that recognize the capacity of any entity to impact, or modify any other actor it comes into contact with; and therefore it is expected that those actors will leave traceable effects of their force or agency on others (Latour, 2005; Van House, 2003; Wheeler, 2010). ANT, thus, is viewed as an important philosophical foundation to understand if objects in general, but the bacteria in particular, have any influence, not only on their human counterparts -the scientists- but also, on the informational processes which create new knowledge framed in scientific papers.

From this perspective, it is important to highlight that ANT, due to its strong empirical background inherited from its roots in anthropology (Harman, 2009; Van House, 2003), is able to provide to the researcher a strong methodological approach. It enables the investigator to explore the social environment and record the scientists' impressions, their social interactions, and the formal artifacts produced by the laboratory through interviews, observation and document analysis.

It is also important to note that unlike the methodological approach common in anthropology, which focuses on social cultures as a result of human associations (Bryman, 2012), ANT extends the scope of the potential actors in a social network to any entity which acts during the course of events pertaining to the social environment (Latour, 2005). In addition, one of the most important advantages of ANT is that it offers researchers a set of vocabularies or a toolkit to deal with different agencies across the network. This point is important, because it allows the researcher to track how certain actors are moved from immaterial to material, displaced, translated or enroll into the network (Van House, 2003).

ANT's concept of translation is significant for this investigation, as it allows the researcher to trace how the bacteria "translate" or change the scientists' understandings and potentially to identify the moment in which an object has an impact on a scientist's informational understanding and leads to a change in a piece of authoritative knowledge (Haider & Kjellberg, 2016). Latour (2005) highlights the process of informing as one of the most important forms of translation.

In a wider sense, the methods that are usually used with ANT allow the researcher to trace the agency of objects and the actors or mediators involved within the network of associations. "Immutable mobiles", which are formal pieces of documentation, are of particular importance for the ANT framework, because they allow knowledge to achieve a material status (Latour, 2005; Van House, 2003), which solidifies it in such a way that it acquires a concrete and fixed shape. However, at the same time that these **"immutable mobiles"** become fixed, they also become extremely portable as well, in such a way that they could travel and touch other entities and achieve the transformation and enrolment of new actors into the network.

Three factors are important in understanding ANT. Actors are not explained only through social factors, they are concrete entities, revealed through their associations, which are usually seen through a network of actors and connections and there is no hierarchy making human agents more significant than other agents in the environment. Strictly speaking, there is no division between human agents and all other objects suspended in the ethos of the physical reality.

Consequently, these three factors will have an influence on the researcher's findings when analyzing the network from an ANT perspective. The final point, referred to as the principle of symmetry, is significant for this study. A human must be seen as part of a complex social environment populated by a multiplicity of actors with whom that individual interacts and negotiates. In this study, the individual is an intentional agent who responds to external factors such as the need to write scientific papers, the importance of gaining research funding and so on, as well as to other actors, and in the end these interactions and responses will have an effect on the individual's final knowledge state.

METHODOLOGY

The significance of admitting non-human actors as participants of the social environment is that the researcher accepts that they do participate, they do act, and they do influence the outcome. This is of course a philosophical position about the reality of the social context, the laboratory in this case, but it does have a methodological implication, as it will broaden the scope of observed participants to include any entity, intentional or not, that could imprint its agency onto the network. Of course, this is not a minor point, rather the opposite, as it will provide the researcher with an augmented set of influencers. Accordingly, if connections are traced with painstaking detail, it could reveal that the direction and force of the informational process might not necessarily could come from the human mind only, but emerge in a concerted partnership with the agent's environments.

ANT Methodology Implemented in this Research

The current investigation has been carried out in a microbiology laboratory at an Australasian university, with a group of scientists who study what they refer to as bacteria lifestyles. The study was approved by the Human Research Ethics Committee of the University and observations were carried out over several months in 2018, with the last interviews performed in February 2019. In order to gain access to the laboratory, the researcher was required to undergo basic training in environmental health and safety relevant to the work of the project team. The researcher was invited by the project team leader to a briefing meeting that was conducted with the whole team in order to gain general approval for the researcher to be present in the laboratory. Five of the eight team members agreed to take part in the study and individual arrangements were then made with the research scientists to observe each of them. All participants signed a consent form to participate in the research and authorized the recording of all sessions.

All participants completed two interviews, one prior to a session of observation and another one after the observation session, apart from one of the senior researchers who is currently doing bio-informatics research and did not have any laboratory experiments at the time. The observation sessions with the other four researchers involved following them through the laboratories while they were performing their experiments, manipulating the bacteria, or using different technologies but mainly microscopy. Email was also used to clarify points from the observations and discussions.

All interviews were semi-structured, with a preliminary set of questions designed to start the discussion, and to remind the interviewer to inquire about important themes, but for the most part each interviewee was encouraged to explain in depth her processes, thoughts and feelings when investigating the bacteria. In preparation for each interview, the researcher read papers written by the participants, and all sessions were audio-recorded, giving a total of over 20 hr of recordings; all interviews and observation sessions were transcribed.

Once all the recordings from the interviews and observation sessions were transcribed, the researcher interacted with the transcriptions in order to identify common themes, patterns, meanings and categories, illuminated from an ANT perspective. Four of the most prominent themes identified through the transcriptions are discussed on this paper.

FINDINGS

The work of these scientists is full of challenges, as they attempt to define their career, balance their lives and achieve scientific relevance through their work, while at the same time, as most of them explained in the interviews, helping humanity by investigating and finding new ways to counteract the rise of super-bugs or multi-resistant bacteria.

This study clearly showed that creating new knowledge was not an internal, private propositional endeavor. What the interactions with the scientists and their observation process illustrates, among other things, is that when a scientist comes to the laboratory he or she is accompanied by many interconnected entities, whether in the process of engaging in microscopy or in the stages of preparing a paper, or some other activity. These other interconnected entities are not -at least not totally- left outside the laboratory. They are, as it were, at least for a short period of time, exercising a potential agency on the way the scientist is engaged in their work.

Some of these other entities or actors that might exert an possible agency on the scientists are not fully developed through this paper, but are worth mentioning at least to set the context of an individual scientist who is not only a brain in a jar, but who is an actor who brings her whole self to the laboratory and who is susceptible to being affected by other circumstances that might have an impact on the individual observer. A couple of instances of these circumstances are for example the scientist who now has to balance the timing of the experiments with the day care of her new born baby; the consequence of this is that she cannot start a new experiment on Friday, as she will not be able to work through the weekend as she would have done before becoming a mother; and a post-doctoral researcher who needs to calibrate his investigation and papers with any prospect of scholarships and the terms and conditions of visas.

Even though, at one level, the individual scientist may be the only human actor being observed by the researcher in the social environment of the specific research study, nevertheless, from an ANT perspective, there is a large number of entities involved in the study, painting a picture that shows the complexity of information processes where an interconnected individual responds and interacts in a dynamic and complex reality populated with actors, whose own agency influences the way the individual constructs information and knowledge.

Four themes emerging from the study are presented here. Firstly, the bacteria are presented as relational information objects. Secondly, metaphors are used by scientists to explain some of their concepts and their relationships with the bacteria. Thirdly, a particular microscope is acknowledged as a key factor in the work of the research team. Finally, the notion of story-telling as fundamental to the research process and the creation and dissemination of scholarly knowledge is introduced.

The Bacteria as Relational Informational Objects

The ethos of the particular laboratory investigated through this present research places a particular emphasis on "observing" the bacteria as noted by some of the participants: ***"In the group, there's always been a love of watching, which is why we are very big in microscopy, so we always looked at bacteria, we always stare at them, because you learn a lot by … Looking … even if you, sit at a train station and you look at people doing something, you learn a lot about their behavior, you learn about how they survive, how they find this or… but you have to look at them to understand that, and in our lab we have done a lot of microscopy to do that, you just watch them forever doing something and you might understand something by just looking at them doing whatever they normally do"***.

This statement by one of the senior researchers is very telling and full of interesting themes that need to be unpacked further. Similar sentiments were expressed by other participants. From a documentalist, perspective (Buckland, 1991; Tourney, 2005), an object could be considered a document in a circumstantial or situational context when it stands in an evidential relationship with an observer and the observer learns from the object. This can lead easily to Briet's idea of considering the antelope as a primary document when observed in a zoological garden, according to her: ***"…naturally occurring phenomena such as stars, pebbles, and animals in and of themselves were not documents, until they had been observed and recorded by an individual"*** (Tourney, 2005, p. 297).

However, what is important is that the object is brought into a more central role under these perspectives. In those statements by Briet, even though the object does seem to be informational in a situational capacity, nonetheless, it does not seem to be on equal footing with its observer when it comes to agency, but is only considered from the human vantage point. The object just acquires its informational dimension under the gaze of the observer. From this perspective, the bacteria would not be informational except when under the microscope, and even then, it is not the bacteria in themselves which are informational; they only become informational under the total and complete determination of human agents.

There are a couple of things to point out here, the first one is that is important to retain the relational basis by which information is somehow attained. Latour (2005) would indicate at this point that scientists are able to perceive the qualities or accidental features of an object, due to the ability of agents to link through temporal associations. Furthermore, Harman (2009) would highlight that Latour's view about the concreteness of an object shows how objects can reveal themselves to other actors. In other words, an object is its accidental features and the two are indistinguishable, there is no obscure and undetermined essence beyond the object's relationships.

It stand to reason that unless one wants to promote some kind of solipsism, one has to admit that the observer and the object touch at a point in time, it is through the observer's interaction with her environment, that such observations somehow get translated into stabilized knowledge in the form of academic papers. The next question is if the object is only suspended in the ethos, neutral to the observer's understanding or whether the object affects such understanding through interaction, how is such an object translated into formal written pieces of information?

From this perspective, Haider and Kjellberg's (2016) statement when quoting Borgman seems to become relevant when thinking about this situation: **"Rarely can a magic moment be established when things become data"** (Haider & Kjellberg, 2016, p. 143). However, what can be established as a minimum in this case, is that there seems to be a particular sense in which the bacteria are affecting the observer in the context of a specific situation at a certain point in time. And furthermore, what the scientist learns from the bacteria is in no sense a mere private mental event in the mind of the individual, but rather a relationship framed at a particular point in time, which does certainly seem to have an effect on the private mental and knowledge state of the individual, but not as a unilateral event, with the change occurring only in the individual scientist. Knorr Cetina (1999), p. 79) points out to the relational and practical aspect of the scientist's interaction with the phenomena, that could encompass the scientist's sensory apparatus as well, and highlights how through such interaction, the phenomena themselves do affect the observer's understanding not only on a mental plane but even their feelings and experience.

Thus, it becomes clear that, as ANT proposes, objects in a social environment are not merely **"physical lumps"** outside of human knowledge (Harman, 2009), but that they do have agency. They affect other actors in the social environment, and in the words of Latour (2005): **"We are made to do things by other agencies over which we have no control and that seem plain and mundane enough"**.

Therefore, what we might expect is that the creation of information is not a siloed process happening privately, but an interactive process between the observer and the bacteria in which the bacteria might also participate and affect the observer's understanding. One of the participants expressed this indicating that such might be the case in the following statement **"I think there is not information just in my head, because the way I do something, does modify also the way they behave, so there is a bit of an exchange, so if I do, change one thing, they'll react in a different way, so I can see that as them telling me that what I did is not what I thought. ... You know, I am doing this because is going to lead to that! And they [are] like no, no, no, I am going to do this instead, so they're telling me what you just did has caused us to behave this way. So it is in a way... They don't talk to you, but it is in a way an exchange of information, so is not just me having information and thinking something**.

It is them reacting to my behavior and saying NO I am not doing that, I am doing this instead and that way, that will change my information, because then I will be like... RIGHT OK!... so, if you've done that, then you are not... you know, they can't talk and they can't tell me that but they behave differently and their behavior tell me RIGHT... this is the answer!".

As we can see through this statement, there is an effect and an interaction, and the scientist himself does not feel this is a one-way street, but instead a symbiotic process, a dance as it were, a two-way system of exchanges with both of these parties feeling affected by each other. It is probably obvious to highlight, as the scientist did in the statement above, that this process does not occur in typical communication fashion as enacted among human agents: **"...they can't talk and they can't tell me that..."**. In fact, in this particular case, humans cannot even see bacteria with their own eyes; knowledge of the bacteria is mediated through many means, but of particular importance for this investigation is the mediation of technology to reach an intangible object that otherwise would not be observable.

How, then, do the bacteria and the observer assemble during the process of creation of information if it cannot be done directly through the sensory apparatus of the scientists? Here Knorr Cetina (1999) notes the importance of the embodiment of science, this embodiment of practices, the sensing and the acting in what she calls the **"information processing machinery"**. What Knorr-Cetina seems to be indicating is the fact that knowledge might not be uniquely propositional but also performative, ingrained in the senses and practices (Knorr Cetina, 1999), reaching a deeper level of understanding. This did not happen directly through direct sensory feedback only, but can be augmented through an external sensory apparatus provided by technology, in what she refers to as exosomatic senses (Knorr Cetina, 1999).

Metaphor as a Conceptual Tool

Even though the bacteria are an intangible entity and although it would be very difficult to identify them without the use of technology or laboratory techniques, the constant interaction of the scientists with these entities allows them to have a greater awareness of the bacteria's presence, which for a lay person could go completely unnoticed. Through this interaction in the laboratory it is possible to perceive how the bacteria imprint their presence on the scientist and even -as mentioned by the scientist- the conditions, and the mood they are in. Thus, one finds that they refer to these entities in anthropomorphic terms, they use these metaphorical terms that they apply to the bacteria's states and behavior and those metaphors might be important for the scientists as they seem to use them to explain the phenomena they observe.

The very title of the over-arching research project, Bacteria Lifestyles, uses the metaphor of lifestyles to convey the sense that this project is about how communities of bacteria live and thrive and the adjustments they make, affecting their ability to survive in different environments.

Two examples from the interviews of the use of metaphor to explain microbiological processes among the bacteria through a typical human process by mapping a metaphorical structure as human communication (Lakoff, 1992) are presented below:

> ***"what we call quorum sensing, is the language, if you want, the bacteria and especially biofilm uses to communicate with each other to say, "Oh, there is an enemy here. Let's do something else to protect ourselves."***

Another scientist said:

> ***"I mean you're doing an experiment with the bacteria; you want … a really robust, happy population."***

The metaphorical sense has come up time and time again through the interviews, observation, public documentation and academic papers, as a constant and pervasive tool that may have a triple functionality: a. coming to grips with the phenomena, b. stabilizing knowledge and c. explaining concepts to others.

Second in importance for understanding the metaphorical meanings that the scientists apply to the phenomena could be the fact that this is a way in which human agents explain how the bacteria affect them. In other words, the metaphor could be a way in which the scientists employ a semantic and conceptual device to define the actual relations in which the bacteria make their presence noticeable to human agents. Lakoff (1992), in his *Theory of Metaphor*, reacts against the traditional understanding of metaphor as a poetic and merely linguistic device and explains that even though the metaphor is expressed through language, it expresses a conceptual level of experience, that the "*locus of metaphor*" is not language but thought. In other words, metaphor can refer to the reality of the world. Similarly, Knorr Cetina (1999) speaks of **"symbolic classifications"**, the use of an imaginative vocabulary that reconfigures the actors in the laboratory by placing a figurative classification layer over the rigid technical vocabulary. These **"imaginative terminological repertoires"** (1996) superimpose figurative or symbolic categories over the technical categories to express more strongly the universe of interactions occurring in the laboratory.

This point is extremely critical, when Knorr Cetina (1999) refers to the everyday categories **"extended into the scientific world"**, it is in a way expressing the metaphorical conceptual mapping that Lakoff (1992) alludes to. Even more subtly it reflects, through such identification, a level of relational process between the entities, by which a transduction process could be mapping every day concepts into laboratory experience, where the properties of one object are expressed through the properties of the second one. Harman (2018) agrees with Lakoff (1992) in that the metaphorical sense is perhaps of greater importance than traditionally accepted, and concludes that metaphors are conceptual devices rather than linguistic ones.

The Microscope as an Actor

Understanding participants' uses of microscopes was important due to the emphasis this particular laboratory places on observation of the bacteria. Most of the scientists interact frequently with a varied range of microscopes, the microscope in this case mediates between the bacteria and the observer extending the limited capabilities of the scientist's sensory apparatus to get a closer look at the bacteria. Knorr Cetina (1999) discusses at length the total engagement of scientists in the practice of learning, discovery, and drawing information. She shows that the scientist is not only a propositional machine that internally processes the flow of signals received from the external world into knowledge (Bonnevie, 2001), but she also engages all her sensory body so she is completely involved with the object; then she connects and associates with it through a process of decoding signs.

Briet used the term indexical for objects from which we learn, and this is congruent with Knorr Cetina's (1999) emphasis on signs: ***"Signs, however, cannot be eliminated completely from experimental work. Like any other science, molecular biology draws from the power of signs to represent phenomenal occurrences"***. Nevertheless, because there is a distance between the object and the observer, these signs that need to be interpreted by the observer are not being obtained directly from the bacteria, as it is obvious that there is a gap that is being bridged by the microscope.

The scientists in this study do recognize the significant value of these tools, to the point that they know that some of the knowledge acquired would be impossible to attain without recent technology: ***"You would never be able to guess that that was happening, so… [it] is so hard, but with the technology we have, we can actually follow and see what is happening."*** In this instance, the technology becomes not only a tool but a device that gives them entry to the object of their study, and thereby is held in very high regard and with such importance: ***"No, we weren't allowed [to approach the microscope unsupervised], we had a person, <name of the person>, that was only her could operate this…"***.

Even though the decision of what technology to use will depend on the type of experiment or behavior the scientists would like to do or see, these microscopes allow the scientists to control the environment in which the bacteria is observed; this includes the temperature, humidity, CO_2 and O_2, so they can work in hypoxic and non-hypoxic environments. In particular, DeltaVision OMX SR, the microscope used in one of these experiments, allows the scientist to penetrate the bacteria to a closer degree of precision, - one to 20 microns (GE Company Healthcare Life Sciences, 2015). This allows them to identify the membrane and the secretion process through a system of vesicles, a practice fundamental to the research project's objectives.

Furthermore, the microscope applies a series of transformations to present a dynamic picture of the behavior of the bacteria to the scientists, to illustrate these transformations. In other words, here, the microscope functions like another team member, providing a high-level explanation of the process and visualization of the outcome. Subsequently, the resulting representation of the bacteria's behavior is displayed on the monitor. Now, it is appropriate to note that there is a major break with traditional microscopes. The scientists acknowledge that they engage all their sensory apparatus in the process of researching, and this change in how data is presented to them seems in a way to separate them a little from the bacteria: ***"So another very difficult and different thing of this microscope compared to the other ones is that as you saw, there's no eye piece so you cannot see with your own eyes. So, you have to search for your sample using the software."***

This microscope allows them to go deeper through a series of images and representations, while collecting simultaneously a great amount of data that would have been impossible otherwise if the scientist's eyes were looking at the bacteria directly. All this data, and the signs and signals, become part of the scientist's data collection that will support their investigation; they become not only observers but sign interpreters of the phenomena, phenomena that went through a series of transformations between the microscope and the computer. This leaves to one side the experiments themselves, which require the scientists to prepare the sample for "observation". Therefore, even though the scientists do not have to understand the internal functionality of the microscope, they do need to learn the software and how to handle it, in order to be able to find the bacteria through the sample. This microscope changes radically the way in which the scientist deals with these signs: the signs are now presented in a computer's monitor, the way in which the technology changes the performative interaction of the scientists with its object of study is radical. However, the benefit of the new method allows the scientist to get, perhaps not closer, but certainly deeper into the world of the bacteria, so they accommodate to the microscope's demands.

How Actors Tell their Story

The transformations observed in this study do not start and finish here. The researcher interacts with a number of processes and techniques, as the scientists themselves comment: ***"Yes, depending on what you're looking at or what you want to – you pretty much prepare the bacteria, grow the bacteria in the way you want them to be at the end."*** The microscope enters almost at the final stage after a series of techniques, practices, plans and preparations to make sure the sample can behave as it would be under natural circumstances, and scientists can "observe" the bacteria to determine whether the original hypotheses and assumptions are confirmed or if the behaviors of the bacteria shows a different picture.

The initial hypothesis may come from any of a number of sources, including knowledge and experience built up over time, discussion with peers, reading the literature, interaction with the bacteria, something the researcher may think should be challenged or corroborated, or perhaps an assignment from the laboratory leader. In other words, even the development of their hypotheses is not a fully private process, but is a relational process between the individual and her context. Through whichever avenue the scientist arrives at the hypothesis driving her investigation, she would use her prior knowledge and experiences to start forming a story about the internal processes happening at the level of the bacteria. Through these processes, scientists interact with the available literature; this prior knowledge does have an impact on the scientists' understandings and affects the way they view these processes or even the phenomenon itself.

According to the interviews, as soon as the scientists start planning the experiments, techniques and the technology that would be more beneficial to test their hypotheses, this story, this narrative, starts to become an entity in itself. Whether the story goes as intended by the scientists is not entirely up to them, but is dependent on the number of actors -including the bacteria themselves- that came together to build the story as one component in the actor-network. Through this process there is an imperative relational factor, the set of actors and intermediaries that contribute to the final outcome of the network. Without their impact and participation, it would be impossible to achieve anything other than a fictional or imagined story, instead of a story based on observations. The final result is in effect the result of an assemblage of entities working in a particular social environment.

Below, there is an example of one of the scientists discussing a hypothesis that did not get totally validated by the data:

> ***"'So that story has been in her head for a long time. So, I think when I came in and said, 'Well, actually this isn't going to do it,' it took her a while to get her head out of***

that story because it'd been so cemented in her head. But to make your story, you have your first bit of data that you use to make your hypothesis and you could probably – a couple ideas where that story might go, and then you just have to follow the data and be like, 'Well, but that experiment suggested this.'"

The range of factors that affect the story that eventually becomes a scientific paper (Van House, 2003) is incredibly large; the more the researcher keeps penetrating the social environment the more they make themselves evident in the informational process.

CONCLUSION

What can be seen from the interviews and other data collected is, firstly, that knowledge established in scientific papers is far from being a solitary, independent human effort. Secondly, the whole of the scientist, not only her mental faculties, is engaged in the process of constructing information, but that this process is also affected by the number of actors participating in the network, including the bacteria and the microscope, and the series of transformations by which each level of abstraction gets coded to a new level of reality.

This brief overview of the micro-biological laboratory as a social environment, in which not only human participants but also other non-human agents affect the social processes that occur within the laboratory (Latour, 1996, 2005; Van House, 2003), shows that the number of actors with participatory agency during the investigation can multiply exponentially. This is contrary to the cognitive approaches to information that place the generation of information as a private affair in the mind of the observer (Brookes, 1980; Fairthorne, 1954). The findings of this study, analyzing the work of the laboratory during the investigation of bacteria, from the perspective of ANT present a different picture.

First of all, it shows that information processes in the laboratory are not merely private propositional endeavors (Harman, 2009), but instead, information construction in the laboratory is a more complex and multi-dimensional process, in which the scientist is a critical and necessary component. However, the process need not be fully dependent on the observer, it stands to reason that it is logical to think that the observer is part of multi-participatory universe of entities all associating and attempting to engage each other and in constant movement and interaction, where networks are relative and dynamic frameworks of interaction.

This study also shows that ANT makes several contributions to information studies. The first is that information is a more social process than we had imagined, and when Latour (2005) speaks of transformations, he is in large part referring to the fact that transformation only happens through connection, association and relation, by getting in contact with another entity. Therefore, it seems to be logical to think that information is a relational process, in which at least for the production of scientific papers, many entities could have an influence on the final product. Perhaps the microscope may act as a mediator in some cases, but in some others its presence, its influence is so determinant, so dominant, that it changes, transforms, the way the bacteria are seen. That the particular microscope demands great care and attention, and that prestige is attached to using it means that its agency may give the resulting scholarly text greater credibility.

The social is also found in the way the community and the hypothesis have an influence on how the story in itself, which leads to the scientific paper, starts to be formed. It is not only the scientist, but a plethora of entities forming a network of actors, all exerting a degree of influence to piece together the symbolic reality of the bacteria.

Finally, if information is the result of numerous interactions among multiple actors, this could also mean that information has a relational dimension in addition to the cognitive processes that happens at the private level. Information is not a private fact because if it were, it would be fictional, imaginary, and in order to be considered factual, it needs to be dependent not only on the observer's human interactions or propositional states, but acknowledged through relational and transformational moves as the observer engages and connects with her reality, including the norms of the wider discipline and scientists in other laboratories.

ACKNOWLEDGMENTS

I acknowledge the contribution of the researchers who gave their time to explain their work to me, and the project leader who supported my involvement in the laboratory.

REFERENCES

Bonnevie, E. (2001). Dretske's semantic information theory and meta-theories in library and information science. *Journal of Documentation*, *57*(4), 16.

Brookes, B. C. (1974). Robert Fairthorne and the Scope of Information Science. *Journal of Documentation*, *30*(2), 16.

Brookes, B. C. (1980). The foundations of information science: Part 1. Philosophical aspects. *Journal of Information Science*, *2*, 125–133.

Bryman, A. (2012). *Social research methods*. Oxford University Press.

Buckland, M. (1991). Information as thing. *Journal of the American Society for Information Science*, *42*(5), 10.

Fairthorne, A. R. (1954). The theory of communication. *Aslib Proceedings*, *6*(4), 255–267.

Fairthorne, A. R. (1967). Morphology of "information flow". *Journal of the Association for Computing Machinery*, *14* (4), 710–719.

Frohmann, B. (2007). Multiplicity, materiality, and autonomous agency of documentation. In *A document (Re) turn: Contributions from a research field in transition* (pp. 27–39).

GE Company Healthcare Life Sciences 2015, *DeltaVision OMX SR: Customer instructions, Structured Illumination.*

Gleick, J. (2011). *The information: A history, a theory, a Flood.* Sydney, Australia: HarperCollins Publishers.

Haider, J., & Kjellberg, S. (2016). Data in the making: Temporal aspects in the construction of research data. *New big science in focus 8*, chap. 8.

Harman, G. (2009). *Prince of networks: Bruno Latour and metaphysics.* Melbourne, Australia: re.press.

Harman, G. (2018). *Object-oriented ontology: A new theory of everything.* England: Penguin Random House.

Knorr Cetina, K. K. (1999). *Epistemic cultures: How the sciences make knowledge.* Harvard University Press.

Lakoff, G. (1992). The contemporary theory of metaphor. In A. Ortony, *Metaphor and thought* (2nd ed., pp. 202–251). New York, NY: Cambridge University Press.

Latour, B. (1996). On actor-network theory A few clarifications plus more than a few complications. *Danish Philosophy Journal, 25*(3), 16.

Latour, B. (2005). *Reassembling the social - An introduction to actor-network-theory.* New York, NY: Oxford University Press.

Leckie, G. J., Given, L., & Buschman, J. E. (2010). *Critical theory for library and information science.* Santa Barbara, CA: Libraries Unlimited.

Mingers, J. (2008). Management Knowledge and knowledge management: Realism and forms of truth. *Knowledge Management Research & Practice, 6.*

Olsson, M. R. (2010). Michel Foucault: Discourse, power/-knowledge, and the battle for truth. *Critical theory for library and information science: Exploring the social from across the discipline* (pp. 63–74). Libraries Unlimited.

Pickering, A. (1995). *The mangle of practice: Time, agency & science.* Chicago, IL and London, England: The University of Chicago Press.

Sokolov, A. V. (2010). Information: Concept, categories, and ambivalent nature. *Scientific and Technical Information Processing, 37*(2), 14.

Tourney, M. M. (2005). Caging virtual antelopes: Suzanne Briet's definition of documents in the context of the digital age. *Archival Science, 3*(3), 291–311.

Van House, N. A. (2003). Science and technology studies and information studies. *Annual Review of Information Science and Technology, 38*, 85.

Wheeler, W. (2010). Bruno Latour: Documenting human and nonhuman associations. *Critical theory for library and information science - exploring the social from across the discipline* (pp. 189–203). Libraries Unlimited.

Word Bibliographic Coupling: Another Way to Map Science Field and Identify Core References

Tsung-Ming Hsiao
Department of Library and Information Science,
Nation Taiwan University, Taipei, Taiwan
f03126010@ntu.edu.tw

Kuang-hua Chen
Department of Library and Information Science,
Nation Taiwan University, Taipei, Taiwan
khchen@ntu.edu.tw

ABSTRACT

This study investigates how to measure subject relationship based on bibliographic coupling strength. Since the 1960s, researchers use citation analysis methods to discover the relationship between different works and authors. However, how to apply citation-based methods in measuring the relationships between various subjects remains unknown. We propose a novel method to measure relationships between subjects based on bibliographic coupling strengths. Our dataset is composed of 7,692 articles published in 10 core information science journals from 2008 to 2017. The result shows that our method provides another viewpoint of exploring the development of science. Furthermore, our method can identify the core works in different subjects and help to judge how similar different subjects are.

KEYWORDS

Bibliometrics; Citation Analysis; Bibliographic Coupling

ASIS&T THESAURUS

Bibliometrics, Citation Analysis, Bibliographic Coupling

INTRODUCTION

Mapping scientific structure is an important issue in Scientometrics. Previous studies use different relationships to map scientific structure, including direct citation, bibliographic relationship, subject relevance, co-authorship, co-word, co-occurrence, etc. (Morris & Martens, 2008). Among these relationships, citation-based relationships play critical roles when researchers want to discover the intellectual structure of certain scientific fields. Two main citation-based methods are proposed to explore latent structures, namely bibliographic coupling (BC) and co-citation (CC) (Kessler, 1963b; Marshakove, 1973; Small, 1973). BC measures relationship based on common references in two documents. When there are lots of common references, two documents have high coupling strength and close relationship. CC measures relationship based on how many times two documents are co-cited in other documents. The more times they are co-cited, the closer relationship they have.

At first, BC and CC are applied to documents only. In 1981, White and Griffith propose to use *oeuvre* of an author as the analyzing target of CC and coin this method as author co-citation analysis (ACA) (White & Griffith, 1981, 1982). Since then, authors are regarded as alternative entities to explore scientific structures. After ACA has been widely applied over two decades, Zhao & Strotmann apply ACA's principle in BC and propose author bibliographic coupling analysis (ABCA) (Zhao & Strotmann, 2008a). In their following study, Zhao & Strontmann argue that combining ACA and ABCA will "be possible to gain a thorough view of the intellectual structure of a research field" (Zhao & Strotmann, 2008b, p. 2084).

In the bibliographic universe, Svenonius (2000) define three major types of bibliographic entities, including works, authors, and subjects. To the best of our knowledge, only two kinds of bibliographic entities, works, and authors, are applied in BC and CC until 2017. Recently, Huang, Wang, Bu, & Min propose keyword co-citation analysis (KCA). According to their study, KCA "has a good performance in mapping knowledge domains and depicting scientific intellectual structure" (Huang, Wang, Bu, & Min, 2018, p. 37). Because keywords are assigned by people to identify the subjects of certain work, KCA can be considered to be a way to check the relationship between different subjects.

Inspired by Huang et al. (2018), we propose a novel method to map scientific structure based on BC strength. Huang et al. (2018) use keywords as the analyzing targets and surrogates of the subjects of certain work. Instead of keywords only, the analyzing targets of our method are words. Words used in our method may be assigned by persons (e.g. authors) or extracted by various algorithms (e.g. based on TF-IDF). Using words as the analyzing targets brings the possibility of analyzing works without available keywords and the flexibility of using various ways to extracting topic words. The relationships between different words are measured based on BC strength. As a parallel citation-based method of CC, BC is possible to measure word relationship and provides more insights into the intellectual structure of science. Given that our method is based on BC and uses

82nd Annual Meeting of the Association for Information Science & Technology | Melbourne, Australia | 19–23 October, 2019

DOI: 10.1002/pra2.00010

words as the analyzing targets, we coin this method as word bibliographic coupling (WBC).

Hence, the present study attempts to examine the results of using BC to measure word relationship and explore the possible utilities of WBC. Ten important information science journals are included in this study. Because there are some traditional word-based methods, like keyword co-occurrence, we use keywords as analyzing targets of WBC to compare the results of keyword co-occurrence and WBC. This study is expected to enhance the understanding of citation-based methods and increase the capability of bibliometrics to provide a more comprehensive view of scientific structures.

RELATED WORKS

Mapping Intellectual Structure

Mapping can be defined as "a representation of the structure and interconnection of known elements of a system" (Morris & Martens, 2008, p. 215). Morris & Martens define five different goals of the mapping research specialties. These five goals are as follows (Morris & Martens, 2008, p. 242):

1. Mapping social structure
2. Mapping base knowledge
3. Mapping research subtopics
4. Mapping overlapping relations among the elements of the specialty
5. Mapping changes occurring in the specialty

Mapping intellectual structure has a long history. It helps people have a better understanding of human knowledge. In libraries, mapping intellectual structure is usually conducted by kinds of bibliographic tools, like bibliography, classification schema, and thesaurus (Hjørland, 2003). Using these tools, the library builds the bibliographic system, draws the map of intellectual structure, and gives guidance to explore the bibliographic universe. By providing these tools, the ultimate purposes of the library are helping their patrons to access proper resources.

With the increasing influence and importance of scientific knowledge in the 20th century, how to accelerate the scientific research process becomes a critical issue. In 1955, Garfield started to develop *Science Citation Index* and proposed it as "a bibliographic system for science literature" and "a new approach to subject control of the literature of science" (Garfield, 1955, p. 108). Based on the citation index, Price (1965) studied networks of scientific papers and proposed that citation networks show two literature practices, research front of recent works and eternal record of human knowledge. Price's study shows that citation-based relationships can be used as an effective tool to map intellectual structure and identify core literature.

In the last half of the 20th century, researchers proposed various quantitative approaches to map intellectual science. These approaches based on kinds of relationships, including direct citation, bibliographic coupling, co-citation, co-word, and co-authorship (Huang et al., 2018). Researchers not only use these methods to investigate the development of certain research field but also focus on the comparison among three citation-based approaches, namely BC, CC, and direction citations. The results in these studies show that each method may have their own pros and cons in mapping intellectual structure (Ahlgren & Jarneving, 2008; Boyack & Klavans, 2010; Jarneving, 2005; Klavans & Boyack, 2017; Yan & Ding, 2012). To sum up, multiple tools/methods are necessary when drawing the intellectual structure, no matter in traditional library science or recent quantitative analysis approaches.

The Development of Bibliographic Coupling

Kessler coined bibliographic coupling in 1963. In Kessler's preliminary study, BC showed its potential to measure the relation between two different scientific papers and cluster papers into subgroups (Kessler, 1963a). In another study, Kessler testified BC and concluded that BC may be made as a retrieval tool because its properties as follows (Kessler, 1963b, p. 11):

1. The process of BC is independent of words and language.
2. The process of BC requires no expert reading or judgment.
3. The group of papers associated with a given paper extends into the past as well as the future.
4. The classification result produced by BC is not static or permanent for a given paper.
5. For a certain paper p_O, all papers that have at least one coupling unit to p_O may be considered as the "logical references" of p_O. By utilizing these logical references, a related paper set, p_m, may be further processed.

Although BC is proposed before CC a full decade, the methodology development of BC is slower than CC. After CC proposed by Small (1973) and Marshakove (1973) separately, White and Griffith (1981, 1982) introduces ACA, a technique based on CC to analyze the intellectual structure. Other related issues of CC are also discussed during the following decades (Boyack, Small, & Klavans, 2013; Callahan, Hockema, & Eysenbach, 2010; Eom, 2008; Gmür, 2003). Compared with CC, Zhao and Strotmann (2008a) point out that the interest in applying BC is only recently resurged in 2008. In their study, Zhao & Strotmann design ABCA by combining two different propositions, Kessler's principles of BC as well as White & Griffith's *oeuvre* as a measurement unit. In another study, Zhao & Strotmann map the intellectual structure of information science by ABCA and ACA as well as compare these results. They report that ABCA provides a more realistic description within a research field and ACA reveals the external and internal as well as recent and historical influences in a research field (Zhao & Strotmann, 2008b). Therefore, both approaches, BC and CC, are necessary to obtain a more comprehensive view of the certain intellectual field.

While Zhao & Strotmann design ABCA and testify its utility, further comparisons among the results of different calculation methods of author coupling strength are not conducted. To answer this question, Ma (2012) reports the results of three different coupling strength methods, including simple method, minimum method, and combined method. Ma's study shows that minimum method is the most appropriate one in their study. The result reassures the validity of the calculation method used by Zhao and Strotmann (2008a, 2008b). In Zhao and Strotmann (2014), ACA and ABCA are applied to analyze the information science (IS) field's development from 2006 to 2010. Zhao & Strotmann not only test and confirm their previous forecast but also forecast future research trends in IS. After a series of studies, BC and ABCA have been proven as effective and capable methods to analyze the structure of the intellectual field.

Application of Different Bibliographic Entities

According to the aforementioned studies, two different citation-based quantitative methods, BC and CC, have been used to map the intellectual structure. Two kinds of bibliographic entities, document and author, are used as the analyzing targets in previous studies. However, the possibility of using the subject entity as the analyzing targets is not investigated.

In information organization, kinds of entities compose the bibliographic universe. Svenonius (2000) defines three major types of bibliographic entities, including works, authors, and subjects. Besides, Morris and Martens (2008) review the development history of mapping intellectual structure. They conclude seven different entity types, including paper journals, reference journals, paper, references, paper authors, reference authors, and index terms. The seven entity types proposed by Morris & Martens can be classified into three major entity types, namely works, authors, and subjects. Hence, there are at least three major bibliographic entity types. However, until 2017, the citation-based method is applied in work entity and author entity only.

Recently, Huang et al. (2018) propose KCA, a citation-based method, to measure the relationship between different keywords based on CC strength and map science structure. Based on the results of network analysis and MDS-measurement, they argued that KCA has a good performance in mapping intellectual structures. Because keywords are assigned by people to identify the subjects of certain work, KCA can be considered as the citation method applied in the subject entity. However, using keywords as the only analyzing targets limits KCA's possibility to apply in different types of works without people assigned keywords. Therefore, we propose to use words as analyzing targets instead of using keywords only. These words may be assigned by persons, like authors keywords, or extracted by algorithm, like TF-IDF. We also propose to measure the relationships between different words based on BC and investigate whether the results of BC provide more insights into the scientific structure.

Hence, the present study proposes a novel method, WBC, to measure the relationship between two words based on their bibliographic coupling strength. We argue that words can represent subjects of research work. Given that references used by authors should be related to these subjects, it should be reasonable to assume that references will be related to these words. The related reference r_j of a word W_i may be cited many times in different works and can be represented as a references collection R_i as

$$R_i : r_1, \ldots, r_1, r_2, \ldots, r_j, \ldots, r_j, \ldots r_n$$

where n is the number of distinct references cited by these works. If any reference r_j is re-cited m times by multiple works, there will be m appearances of r_j in this collection. Table 1 is a simple example.

Article	Word	Reference
A1	W_1	r1, r2, r3
A2	W_2	r4, r5, r6
A3	W_1, W_2, W_3	r3, r6
A4	W_1, W_2	r3, r6

Table 1. An example of references collection.

In this example, the composition of the three references collections are as follows:

1. R_1: r1, r2, r3, r3, r3, r6, r6
2. R_2: r3, r3, r4, r5, r6, r6, r6
3. R_3: r3, r6

After calculating lots of works, the references collection R_i will reveal the real concepts of W_i. In the example of Table 1, r3 is the most frequently used reference in R_1, the references collection of W_1. Therefore, it is reasonable to assume that there is a close relationship between r3 and W_1. By counting the coupling strength of two different collections, R_i and R_j, we can measure the relationship between W_i and W_j and map the intellectual structure after calculating relationship among numerous words. In the previous example, the coupling strength of R_2 and R_3 is two and we use it as a measurement for the relationship between W_2 and W_3.

The present study uses 7,692 articles published in 10 important IS journals during 2008 ~ 2017 to map the intellectual structure of the IS field and investigate the pros and cons of WBC. The article keywords are chosen to represent the subjects of each article in this study. This study also compares the differences between the results of WBC and keyword co-occurrence. Then, the following research questions can be answered:

Q1. Are there any differences between the mapping results of WBC and keyword co-occurrence?

Q2. Do the results of WBC provide different insights compared with the results of keyword co-occurrence?

Q3. Will WBC be an appropriate approach to measure the relationship between words?

METHODS

In our study, the dataset is composed of articles published in important journals of the IS research field. In previous landmark article on ACA and mapping IS field, White and McCain (1998) chosen 12 journals of information science to map IS field. In a series of studies conducted by Zhao & Strotmann, they followed White and McCain (1998) and used these 12 journals to testify ABCA and map the structure of information science. Therefore, we follow the previous studies and choose the same journals to compose our dataset. However, because *Annual Review of Information Science and Technology* has discontinued, this journal does not include in this study. Due to the lack of recent data of *Proceedings of the ASIST Annual Meeting* in *Web of Science*, our study will not include this publication either. Hence, only articles published in the remaining 10 journals, as Table 2 shows, are included in our study.

1. Electronic library
2. Information processing & management
3. Information technology and libraries
4. Journal of documentation
5. Journal of information science
6. Journal of the association for information science and technology
7. Library & information science research
8. Library resources & technical services
9. Program -- Automated library and information systems
10. Scientometrics

Table 2. Journals used to map IS field.

The dataset is composed of all articles published in the 10 journals from 2008 to 2017. Full records for these articles are downloaded from *Web of Science* in February 2019. There is a total of 9,437 records. Based on the data type of these records, we remove records whose data type is not "article". After removing unnecessary data, the number of the remaining records are 7,692. These articles are then categorized into two groups, each covering 5 years, i.e., 2008 to 2012 and 2013 to 2017. Both "author keywords" and *Web of Sciences'* "KeyWords Plus" are used as keywords to represent subjects of articles in our study.

Based on the result of Ma (2012), our study chooses minimum method to count BC strength of two different keywords. Following Rousseau (2010), if two keywords used in the same article, the references in this article will be excluded from counting BC strength. In this exploratory study, we only change each keyword to lowercase and remove punctuations. Further processes such as word sense disambiguation will not be conducted in the present study.

Both keyword co-occurrence and WBC are conducted in this study. For any two keywords, W_i and W_j, their BC strength is calculated by the following steps:

1. Build reference collections, R_i and R_j, for W_i and W_j.
2. For those articles contains both W_i and W_j as their keywords, collect their references as another reference collection R_k.
3. Let N represent the number of elements in the intersection of R_i and R_j as well as M represents the number of all elements in R_k.
4. The BC strength of Wi and W_j is equal to N minus M.

After calculating BC strength of each keyword pair, we could build BC strength matrix. Another matrix, keyword co-occurrence matrix, is built by counting how many times two keywords co-occur in the same article. We build a subset of 100 keywords according to the keyword pair's relationship strength, including BC strength and co-occurrence times. Keywords with high relationship strength are chosen first. Each keyword set contains 100 words unless there are strength ties among keywords. If so, all keywords in those tie pairs will be included. After collecting these keywords, other keywords and relationships will be excluded. We only use these important keywords and strong relationship and build the WBC matrix and co-occurrence matrix.

After constructing the matrixes, factor analysis is used to extract important factors from matrixes and identify keywords' factor loadings. Factors with eigenvalues greater than 1 are retained as important factors (Kim & Mueller, 1978). These factors are considered as sub research fields in IS and we assume that a keyword will be related to a factor if the keyword's factor loading is greater than or equal to 0.3. We conduct factor analysis with SAS 9.4 and use Gephi 0.92 to depict the word-factor relationship networks.

RESULT AND DISCUSSION

Basic Statistics

Table 3 shows the number of articles, keywords, and references. ps of articles include 3,455 and 4,237 articles published during 2008~2012 and 2013~2017, respectively. We take both author keywords and *Web of Sciences'* KeyWords Plus into consideration. The average keywords per article in 2008~2012 is about 6.62. In 2013~2017, the number slightly increases to 8.65. The number of distinct keywords also increases from 7,130 to 11,629. The increase of average keywords and distinct keywords shows that IS groups and articles concern more diverse research issues. The number of average references is also rising from 35.59 to 44.41. The growth scale of distinct references is more than 150% (from 80,138 to 122,392). These results reveal that IS researchers cite more references in an article and use more different words in their research while the concerning issues in IS fields are growing. Four sets of keywords are chosen from two groups of articles. The details for each set are listed in Table 4. Due to the range of co-occurrence frequency is much smaller than WBC, there is one relatively large set, co-occurrence of 2008~2012, with 115 keywords. Other three sets contain 100 keywords.

	2008~2012	2013~2017
Articles	3,455	4,237
Keywords/avg. keywords (distinct keywords)	22,865 / 6.62 (7,130)	36,639 / 8.65 (11,629)
References/avg. references (distinct references)	122,953 / 35.59 (80,138)	188,167 / 44.41 (122,392)

Table 3. Articles, keywords, and references in two periods.

In each period, the composition of Co-occurrence set and WBC set are similar. About 80% of the keywords appear in both sets. Important keyword pairs extracted by both methods are generally similar. It means that keyword pairs with high co-occurrence frequency usually have more common references. However, for some keyword pairs, high co-occurrence frequency does not bring high WBC. The possible reasons may be that some keywords are used frequently but lack generally recognizing related works or consistent meaning. Therefore, keyword pairs include this kind of keywords may have high co-occurrence with other keywords but low WBC strength. The result shows that WBC provides a different viewpoint to observe the intellectual structure of science.

	Keywords (Co-occurrence)	Keywords (WBC)	Words in common
2008~2012	115	100	85
2013~2017	100	100	81

Table 4. Keywords of two different methods.

Factor Analysis

Table 5 represents the result of factor analysis. About 20 factors are extracted from the results of keyword co-occurrence and total variance explained are 89%. For the results of WBC, factor analysis extracts 12~13 factors and explains 90% variance in total. Although only about 1% differences between the results of the total variance explained, the extracted factor number of keyword co-occurrence is almost twice as the number of WBC. According to Zhao and Strotmann (2008b), each factor extracted by factor analysis can be seen as a research sub-field. The result shows that using keyword co-occurrence can reveal more sub-fields than WBC.

The distribution of related keywords of each factor is another concerning question. We define a keyword having factor loading greater or equal to 0.3 as the factor's related keyword. On average, factors extracted from results of keyword co-occurrence have 8~12 related keywords. However, in WBC, factors have 14~16 related keywords on average. Figure 1 shows the distribution of factors and their related keywords. X-axis indicates the number of related keywords in the factor and Y-axis means the number of factors in this category. In both time periods, factors of keyword co-occurrence concentrate in two categories, less than 5 related keywords or 6~10 related keywords. Although most of the factors of WBC also fall in these two categories, the proportion is much less than keyword co-occurrence.

	Factor number	Total variance explained (%)
Keyword co-occurrence (2008~2012)	24	89.00
WBC (2008~2012)	13	90.47
Keyword co-occurrence (2013~2017)	19	89.27
WBC (2013~2017)	12	90.22

Table 5. Results of factor analysis.

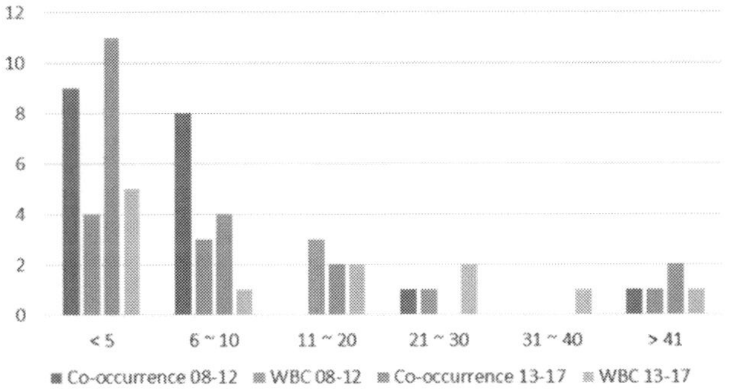

Figure 1. Number of factors of two different methods.

The results show that keyword co-occurrence reveals more sub-fields when mapping intellectual structure and WBC collects more related keywords for each factor. One possible reason is that WBC measure keyword pair's relationships based on their common related references, not based on co-occurrence frequency. It is extremely rare to use all related keywords of a subject in a single work. However, related keywords with common references should not be scare and WBC can collect these related keywords. Therefore, we argue that WBC is better in collecting related keywords of a sub-fields and keyword co-occurrence is better in showing more sub-fields.

Network Analysis

We also represent the results of factor analysis in network format. Figures 2–5 show results measured by both methods in two different periods. Light yellow nodes are keywords and light purple nodes are factors. The edge between keyword node and factor node represent factor loading and the width of the line indicates the factor loading of the keyword node. Only factor loading greater or equal to 0.3 will be shown in the graph. Based on related words of factors, we also identify possible sub-fields of those factors with at least three related words or connected with the giant network.

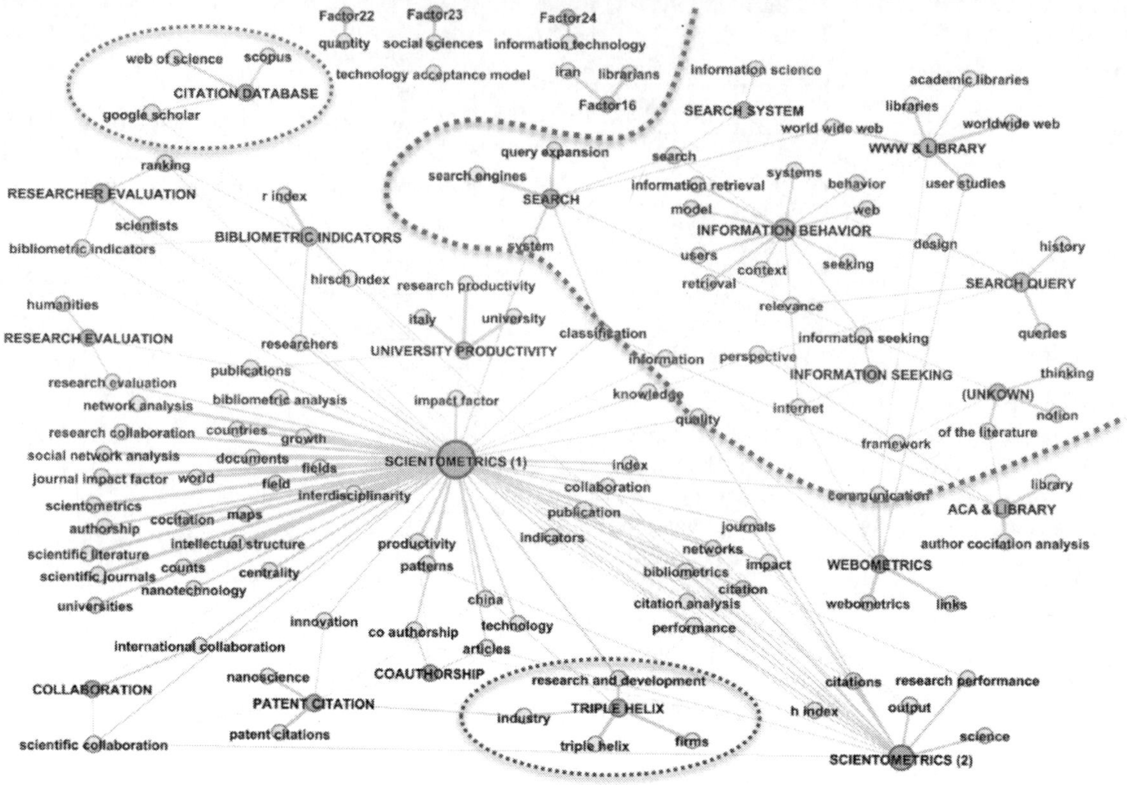

Figure 2. The network of Keyword Co-occurrence results (2008~2012).

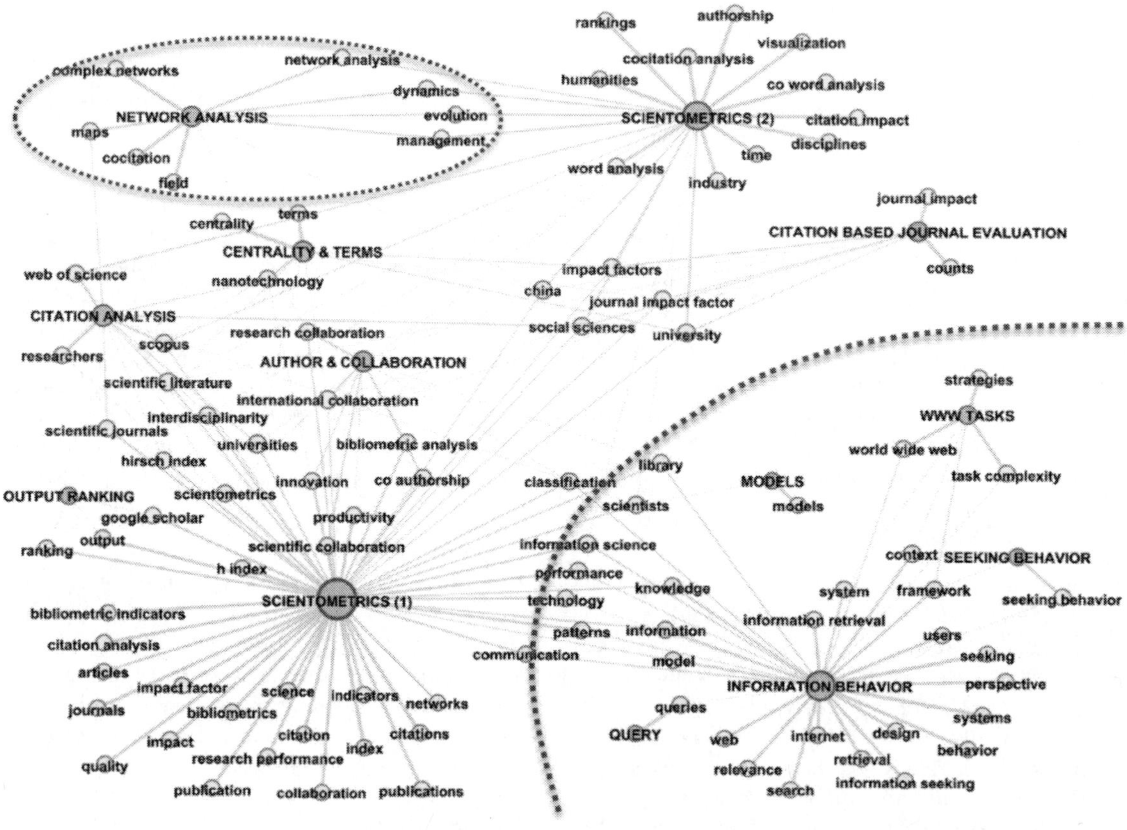

Figure 3. The network of WBC results (2008~2012).

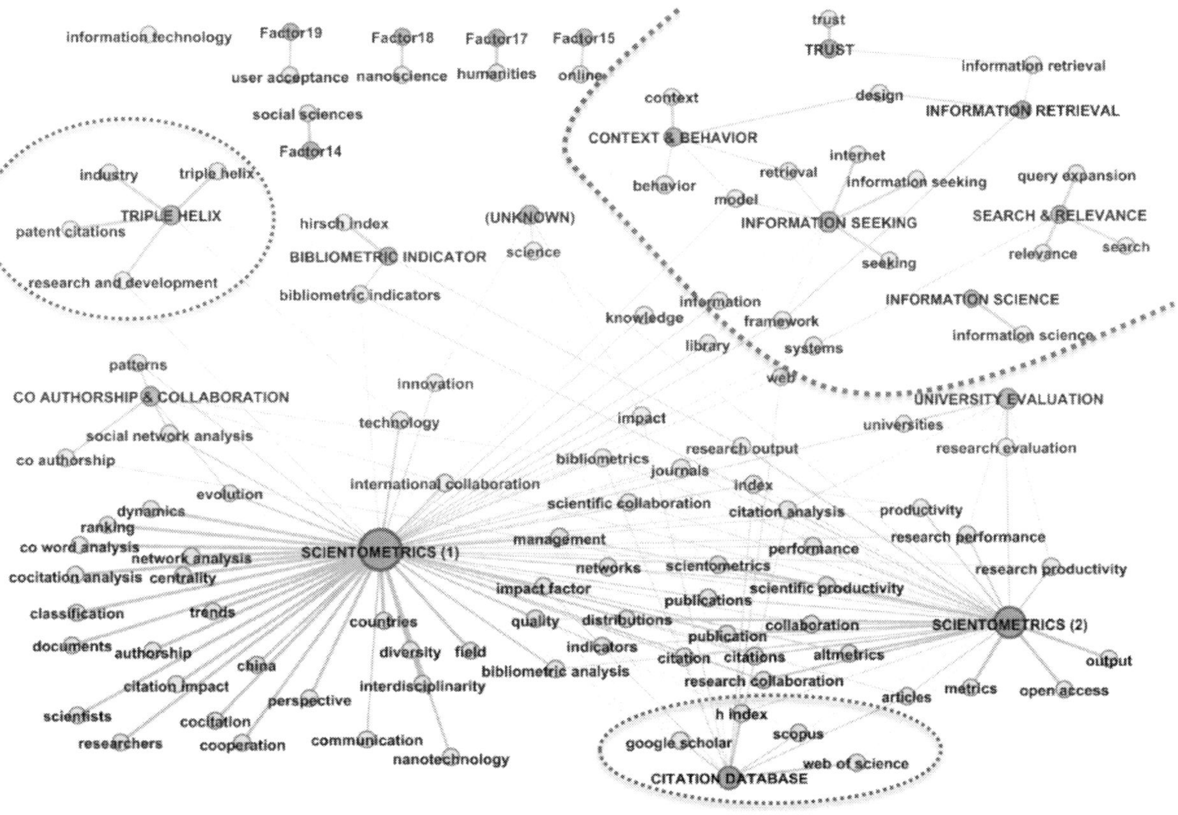

Figure 4. The network of Keyword Co-occurrence results (2013~2017).

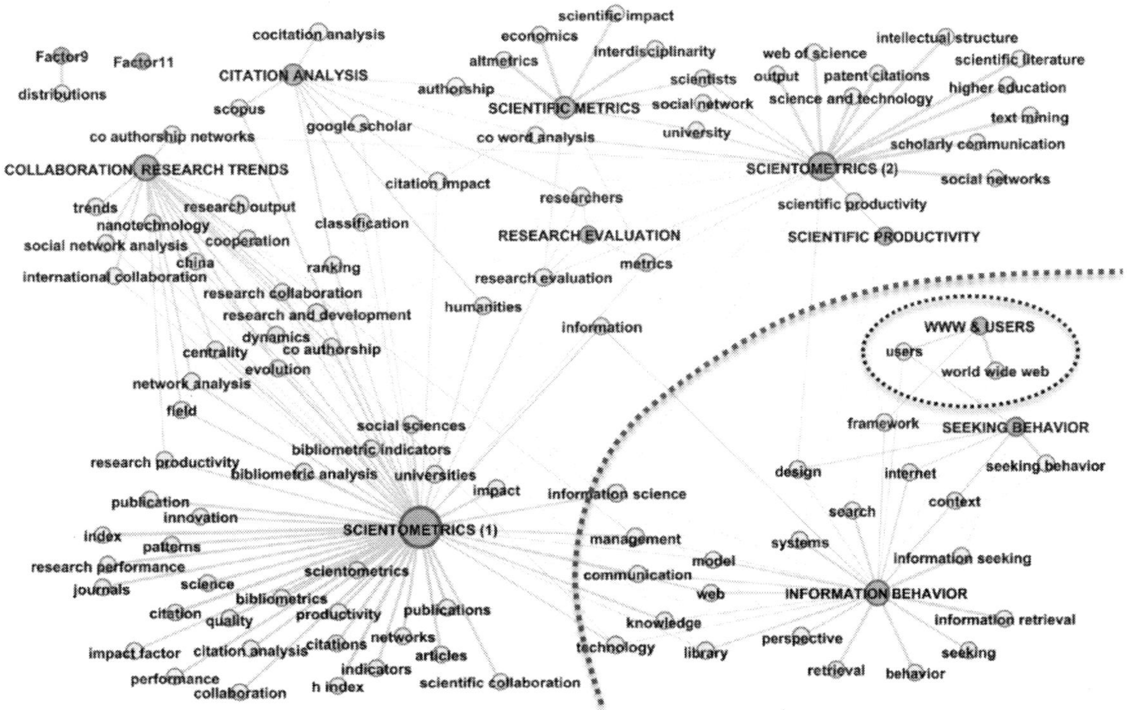

Figure 5. The network of WBC results (2013~2017).

Besides, we also identify main factors in these networks according to the average related words per factor. Table 6 shows the detail. In a helicopter view, the IS field mapped by two methods are similar. First, there are two primary types of sub-field, one is related to Scientometrics and another is about information behavior. The red dot line divides two types of sub-field in the graph. Both methods reveal similar results. Second, more main factors are related to Scientometrics in general. In all four results, only the keyword co-occurrence result of 2008 ~ 2012 does not correspond to this description.

	Average related words	Main factors	Other factors
Keyword co-occurrence (2008~2012)	8.88	2 (S) / 3 (IB)	11 (S) / 3 (IB) 1 (U) / 4 (IS)
WBC (2008~2012)	14.07	2 (S) / 1 (IB)	6 (S) / 4 (IB)
Keyword co-occurrence (2013~2017)	11	3 (S) / 1 (IB)	4 (S) / 5 (IB) 1 (U) / 4 (IS)
WBC (2013~2017)	16.25	3 (S) / 1 (IB)	4 (S) / 2 (IB) 2 (IS)

Table 6. Main factors in different results.
S = Scientometrics; IB = Information Behavior;
U = Unknown Factor; IS = Isolated Factor;

One difference between the results of the two methods is the number of isolated factors. We define a factor as an isolated factor when it does not connect with the large component in the network. In both periods, there are at least four isolated factors in each network mapped by keyword co-occurrence. In the networks of WBC, there are two isolated factors in the second-period network. Combined with the results of average related words per factor in two different networks, we argue that WBC built a more connecting network than keyword co-occurrence.

The important keywords chosen by the two methods are different to some extent. In the first period, there are 115 and 100 keywords chosen by keyword co-occurrence and WBC respectively. Near 20% of keywords chosen by WBC are not chosen by keyword co-occurrence. The tendency is similar in the second period. Between keywords chosen by WBC and keyword co-occurrence, about 15% of keywords are different. If taking synonyms into consideration, the percentage of differences are still more than 10%.

When comparing these networks, some keywords and factors in keyword co-occurrence networks are not existing in the WBC networks. One example is TRIPLE HELIX (blue circle in Figures 2 and 4). Main related keywords of TRIPLE HELIX in both periods are *triple helix*, *industry*, *technology*, and *research and development*. *Triple helix* appears in both keyword co-occurrence networks but the WBC networks in two periods do not include this keyword. Other four keywords have no common related factor or are excluded in both WBC networks. Another example is CITATION DATABASE (red circle in Figures 2 and 4). In both periods, keyword co-occurrence shows that *scopus*, *web of science*, and *google scholar* all related to this factor. In WBC, none single factor is related to all three keywords.

WBC also provides some keywords and factors that do not exist in keyword co-occurrence networks. In the first period, WBC shows NETWORK ANALYSIS (blue circle in Figure 3) with related keywords including *network analysis*, *complex networks*, *maps*, *fields*, and *cocitation*. In Figure 2, SCIENTOMETRICS (1) includes these keywords except *complex networks*. It means that keyword co-occurrence does not reveal the factor, NETWORK ANALYSIS. Another similar example is WWW & USERS (black circle) in Figure 5. In Figure 4, keyword co-occurrence does not extract *users* and *world wide web* as important related keywords, two related keywords of WWW & USERS in Figure 5.

We also compare the high factor loading keywords belonged to the main factors. In factor analysis, the factor loading means the proportion of latent factor's effect on this variable. Variables with high factor loading can represent the feature of the latent factor. We assume that keywords with high factor loading can be used to represent the important research topics in the sub-field in the present study. In the first period, there are six and three main factors in the networks of keyword co-occurrence and WBC respectively. There are 36 words with factor loading more than 0.9 and no duplicate words. In the second period, although there are some duplicate words in high factor loading words of main factors, the proportion is small, only 5.6%. The results show that the important topics revealed by two methods are different even the sub-fields are similar. These results support our argument that WBC provides a different perspective to map intellectual structure and will show a more comprehensive landscape when combining with keyword co-occurrence.

Core Literature of Keywords and Sub-Fields

Another interesting question is how to identify the core literature of different words and sub-fields. For a single word, the distribution of reference collection R_i can be used to identify core literature about W_i. Using this method, the present study identifies the core literature of three words, including *h index*, *library* and *information seeking*. Table 7 shows the top 3 frequently used references of each keyword in two periods. The frequently used references of *h index* are the same in two periods. The first article by Hirsch is the origin of *h*-index and the second article by Egghe is about *g*-index, an improvement of *h*-index. The third article introduces *R*- and *AR*-indices to eliminate some disadvantages of *h*-index. All articles are highly related to *h*-index.

	2008~2012		2013~2017	
	Reference	Freq.	Reference	Freq.
h index	Hirsch JE, 2005, P NATL ACAD SCI USA, V102, P16569	103	Hirsch JE, 2005, P NATL ACAD SCI USA, V102, P16569	94
	Egghe L, 2006, SCIENTOMETRICS, V69, P131	46	Egghe L, 2006, SCIENTOMETRICS, V69, P131	54
	Jin BH, 2007, CHINESE SCI BULL, V52, P855	34	Jin BH, 2007, CHINESE SCI BULL, V52, P855	30
Library	White HD, 1998, J AM SOC INFORM SCI, V49, P327	8	Milojevic S, 2011, J AM SOC INF SCI TEC, V62, P1933	16
	Moed H. F., 2005, CITATION ANAL RES EV	6	KUHLTHAU CC, 1991, J AM SOC INFORM SCI, V42, P361	10
	Hjorland B, 2002, J DOC, V58, P422	6	Lariviere V, 2012, J AM SOC INF SCI TEC, V63, P997	10
Information science	White HD, 1998, J AM SOC INFORM SCI, V49, P327	31	White HD, 1998, J AM SOC INFORM SCI, V49, P327	18
	WHITE HD, 1981, J AM SOC INFORM SCI, V32, P163	17	Lariviere V, 2012, J AM SOC INF SCI TEC, V63, P997	10
	HJORLAND B, 1995, J AM SOC INFORM SCI, V46, P400	13	Milojevic S, 2011, J AM SOC INF SCI TEC, V62, P1933	10

Table 7. Top 3 frequently used references.

The top 3 references of *library* are totally different in two periods. In the first period, the top frequently used references are White's article about mapping IS field, Moed's book of citation analysis in research evaluation, and Hjørland's work that introduces 11 approaches to conduct domain analysis. In the second period, all above works are excluded from the top 3. Milojević's article about the cognitive structure of the library and IS field becomes top 1. Kuhlthau's information search process work is in second place. The third is Larivière's studying of the history of the library and IS filed during the first 100 years in bibliometric methods.

The references of *information science* are similar to references of *library*. In both periods, White's article about mapping IS takes the first place. Another two frequently used references in the first period are White's article about ACA and Hjørland's article introducing domain analysis. As to the second period, Lariviere's and Milojević's articles are another two frequently used references.

These results show the possibility to use each word's reference collection as a tool to extract core literature and measure the similarity between words. Taking one step further, the intersection or union of reference collections of multiple words can reveal core references and authors among these words. We use *context* and *information seeking* as an example. In the second period, the intersection of these two words' reference collections includes authors as follows: M. J. Bates, N. J. Belkin, K. Bystrom, C. C. Kuhlthau, R., Savolainen, and T. D. Wilson. Using a similar approach, it may be an objective method to choose the core works and authors of each factor.

CONCLUSION AND FUTURE WORK

The present study proposes a novel way, WBC, to measure the relationship between words based on the similarity of their related references. WBC maps intellectual structure based on words, a bibliographic entity different from documents and authors. This method gives another viewpoint to observe the research field. After comparing with keyword co-occurrence, the results support that WBC provides a different perspective to map intellectual structures. Furthermore, reference collections can be used as a tool to find out important references and authors of these words and factors.

We need further a more comprehensive study to verify the steps of extracting important references. Also, some problems like word disambiguation and ways to extract documents' feature words will be studied in our following studies. Especially the latter one, with a more precise way to identify topic words of each document, WBC should provide more accurate results based on topic words when mapping the intellectual structure of research field. With these improvements, WBC will be researchers' another tool to analyze research field and make analyzers have a better understanding about the research field.

ACKNOWLEDGMENTS

We would like to thank the anonymous reviewers for their suggestions and comments. This research was partially supported by Ministry of Science and Technology of the Republic of China under the grant number MOST 107-2410 -H-002-203.

REFERENCES

Ahlgren, P., & Jarneving, B. (2008). Bibliographic coupling, common abstract stems and clustering: A comparison of two document-document similarity approaches in the context of science mapping. *Scientometrics, 76*(2), 273–290.

Boyack, K. W., & Klavans, R. (2010). Co-citation analysis, bibliographic coupling, and direct citation: Which citation approach represents the research front most accurately? *Journal of the American Society for Information Science and Technology, 61*(12), 2389–2404.

Boyack, K. W., Small, H., & Klavans, R. (2013). Improving the accuracy of co-citation clustering using full text. *Journal of the American Society for Information Science and Technology, 64*(9), 1759–1767.

Callahan, A., Hockema, S., & Eysenbach, G. (2010). Contextual cocitation: Augmenting cocitation analysis and its applications. *Journal of the American Society for Information Science and Technology, 61*(6), 1130–1143.

Eom, S. (2008). All author cocitation analysis and first author cocitation analysis: A comparative empirical investigation. *Journal of Informetrics, 2*(1), 53–64.

Garfield, E. (1955). Citation indexes for science: A new dimension in documentation through association of ideas. *Science, 122*(3159), 108–111.

Gmür, M. (2003). Co-citation analysis and the search for invisible colleges: A methodological evaluation. *Scientometrics, 57*(1), 27–57.

Hjørland, B. (2003). Fundamentals of knowledge organization. *Knowledge Organization, 30*(2), 87–111.

Huang, W., Wang, B., Bu, Y., & Min, C. (2018). A study on scientometrics of co-citation analysis of keywords. *Information and Documentation Services, 2018*(2), 37–42.

Jarneving, B. (2005). A comparison of two bibliometric methods for mapping of the research front. *Scientometrics, 65*(2), 245–263.

Kessler, M. (1963a). An experimental study of bibliographic coupling between technical papers (Corresp.). *IEEE Transactions on Information Theory, 9*(1), 49–51.

Kessler, M. (1963b). Bibliographic coupling between scientific papers. *American Documentation, 14*(1), 10–25.

Kim, J.-O., & Mueller, C. W. (1978). Factor analysis: statistical methods and practical issues. In *Quantitative applications in the social sciences*. London, England: SAGE Publications.

Klavans, R., & Boyack, K. W. (2017). Which type of citation analysis generates the most accurate taxonomy of scientific and technical knowledge? *Journal of the Association for Information Science and Technology, 68*(4), 984–998.

Ma, R. (2012). Author bibliographic coupling analysis: A test based on a Chinese academic database. *Journal of Informetrics, 6*(4), 532–542.

Marshakove, I. (1973). System of document connections based on references. *Nauchno-Tekhnicheskaya Informatsiya, 2*(6), 3–8.

Morris, S. A., & Martens, B. V. d. V. (2008). Mapping research specialties. *Annual Review of Information Science and Technology, 42*(1), 213–295.

Price, D. J. de S. (1965). Networks of scientific papers. *Science, 149*(3683), 510–515.

Rousseau, R. (2010). Bibliographic coupling and co-citation as dual notions. In L. Birger, *The janus faced scholar: A festschrift in Honour of Peter Ingwersen*.

Small, H. (1973). Co-citation in the scientific literature: A new measure of the relationship between two documents. *Journal of the American Society for Information Science, 24*(4), 265–269.

Svenonius, E. (2000). The intellectual foundation of information organization. In *Digital libraries and electronic publishing*. Cambridge, MA: MIT Press.

White, H. D., & Griffith, B. C. (1981). Author cocitation: A literature measure of intellectual structure. *Journal of the American Society for Information Science, 32*(3), 163–171.

White, H. D., & Griffith, B. C. (1982). Authors as markers of intellectual space: Co-citation in studies of science, technology and society. *Journal of Documentation, 38*(4), 255–272.

White, H. D., & McCain, K. W. (1998). Visualizing a discipline: An author co-citation analysis of information science, 1972–1995. *Journal of the American Society for Information Science, 49*(4), 327–355.

Yan, E., & Ding, Y. (2012). Scholarly network similarities: How bibliographic coupling networks, citation networks, cocitation networks, topical networks, coauthorship networks, and coword networks relate to each other. *Journal of the American Society for Information Science and Technology, 63*(7), 1313–1326.

Zhao, D., & Strotmann, A. (2008a). Author bibliographic coupling: Another approach to citation-based author knowledge network analysis. *Proceedings of the American Society for Information Science and Technology, 45*(1), 1–10.

Zhao, D., & Strotmann, A. (2008b). Evolution of research activities and intellectual influences in information science 1996–2005: Introducing author bibliographic-coupling analysis. *Journal of the American Society for Information Science and Technology, 59*(13), 2070–2086.

Zhao, D., & Strotmann, A. (2014). The knowledge base and research front of information science 2006–2010: An author cocitation and bibliographic coupling analysis. *Journal of the Association for Information Science and Technology, 65*(5), 995–1006.

Who You Gonna Call? Seeking Information and Expertise for Decision Making in Local Government

Sally Irvine-Smith
University of Technology Sydney,
Sydney, Australia
sally.b.irvine-smith@student.uts.edu.au

ABSTRACT

This paper analyzes the findings of a research project into the information seeking practices of local government decision-makers in terms of collaborative information seeking (CIS) and expertise seeking. It finds that the participants do collaborate in information seeking and that there is a clear preference for personal information sources. The generally accepted definition of CIS as groups collectively seeking information in the performance of common projects or tasks is found to have limited applicability in many real-life situations. Conversely, viewing expertise seeking as an individual activity in which another person is selected as an information source based on their high level of knowledge or skill does not reflect the collaborative nature of the modern organization. It is argued that neither approach adequately accounts for the full range of behaviors observed in practice, and that research into organizational information behavior would benefit from a conceptual amalgamation of CIS and expertise seeking.

KEYWORDS

Collaborative Information Seeking; CIS; Expertise Seeking; Organizational Information Behavior

ASIS&T THESAURUS

Information Behavior; Information Sharing; Information Use

INTRODUCTION: ORGANIZATIONAL INFORMATION SEEKING

Organizations, by their very nature, involve people working together. Whether working on an individual project or as part of a team, a modern organizational member is constantly communicating and sharing information with others. Information eddies and flows between members in complex ways and gathering, assimilating and creating information are increasingly recognized as group activities (Hansen & Jarvelin, 2005). Organizational decision making is intrinsically and invariably embedded in collaborative processes (c.f., Nikoi & Boateng, 2014, p. xx).

82nd Annual Meeting of the Association for Information Science & Technology | Melbourne, Australia | 19–23 October, 2019

DOI: 10.1002/pra2.00061

How people work together in organizations to find information is consequently of much interest to information researchers. Two research areas devoted to information seeking in a group setting are collaborative information seeking (CIS) and expertise seeking (Hertzum, 2017). This paper takes a new approach to analyze the information seeking practices of local government decision makers with specific reference to these areas of research. It examines the efficacy of the respective assumptions and concepts employed by both in explicating real-life practices.

Two Approaches to Collaborative Information Seeking (CIS) Research

Two broad activity-based approaches can be identified in CIS research to date. In the first the activity, defining collaborating is central to the investigation. I call this the collaboration-centric approach. In this research strand CIS is described as both an information-seeking activity involving collaboration and a collaborative activity with a goal of information seeking (Shah, 2014, p. 216). Researchers such as Shah are very concerned to describe exactly what it means to collaborate. Shah has accordingly proposed a model of collaboration in which five sets of activities – communication, contribution, coordination, cooperation and collaboration – are juxtaposed in concentric circles or sets from weakest to strongest. Thus collaboration is a superset of all four other activities, and the strongest activity in terms of interaction, intent, trust and other behavioral factors. The intention of the model is to enable various tasks and activities to be classified: scheduling a meeting, for example, is a coordinating task while two individuals carrying out different tasks for one project is an example of co-operation. Central to Shah's model, and the activity-based approach, is a strict definition of people working together "synergistically" to achieve a common goal (Shah, 2008, 2010, pp. 6–7, 12; Shah, 2014, p. 217).

The second research strand conceptualizes CIS in a more organic way and focuses on the activities of information seeking. I call this the information-centric approach. It is less concerned with a rigid definition of collaboration and instead assumes that if those activities are carried out by someone in an organization they will necessarily interact with others, either directly or indirectly, in the course of enacting those tasks (Hansen & Widen, 2017, p. 556). In early research in the field, Fidel et al defined information retrieval as collaborative when the actors involved are colleagues and are engaged in the same work practices (Fidel, Pejtersen, Cleal, & Bruce, 2004, p. 944). Hertzum argues strongly against definitions which dissociate information sharing from seeking, searching and retrieval. He conceptualizes CIS as the full range of information-seeking activities performed by actors in a group setting in addition to those contextual grounding activities which allow them to make sense of their work – a shared understanding without which they would be unable to assimilate information (Hertzum, 2008).

While seemingly eschewing Shah's strict regime for classification of work tasks, proponents of the information-centric approach are nevertheless starting to call for more robust theorizing to understand the stages and processes of CIS (Hansen & Widen, 2017, p. 558). A methodological review of 76 empirical studies involving CIS found that they suffer from a lack of model building, rarely build on each other in a cumulative manner, do not draw conclusions outside their own setting and are consequently not generalizable, and provide little data on outcomes (Hertzum & Hansen, 2019).

Expertise Seeking

There is an extraordinarily long tradition of research into expertise in such fields as psychology and *organizational behavior* and decision making (Hoffman, Shadbolt, & Burton, 1995). Investigation of seeking out people as an information source and *conceptualizing* it as an information-related activity is a comparatively recent development. The use of the term "expertise seeking" as a label for this activity is more recent still, Hertzum using it to describe the multiple studies which investigate how and why people select other people when they need information (Hertzum, 2014).

Expertise seeking research deals largely with three broad categories or themes, none of which are mutually exclusive. The first of these can be characterized as investigating the preference for people over paper – or, put more properly, studies of the relative importance of personal and documentary information sources. When, in 1994, Choo investigated information sources used by chief executives he evinced some surprise that people – subordinate managers, staff and customers – were of greater importance to his subjects than documentary sources. Choo concluded that chief executives receive so much information that they require some sure means by which it can be reduced and summarized yet remain meaningful to them: other people are, essentially, trusted distillation and filtration mechanisms (Choo, 1994). A decade later Bystrom discovered people are increasingly preferred to documentary sources as tasks increase in complexity. She found that the more information is required to perform a task, the greater the reliance on people rather than documentary sources (Bystrom, 2002). Hertzum, in a very comprehensive literature review of expertise seeking, finds that of 25 studies that ranked information sources, or investigated comparative use, people outranked documentary sources in 23 of them (Hertzum, 2014, pp. 778–780).

A second strong theme in research into expertise seeking is devoted to an examination of the source characteristics of accessibility and quality (c.f., Marton & Choo, 2002). Here, there is an underlying assumption that there must always be a trade-off between the ease of attaining the information and the quality, relevance and accuracy of the information. Lu and Yuan, for example, argue that people adjust their strategies: when their information need is low or high quality matters, but accessibility is crucial when they have medium needs (Lu & Yuan, 2011). A third area of expertise seeking research deals with the contextual and environmental factors that impact seeking information from human sources. This includes research into the importance and urgency of tasks (Agarwal, Xu, & Poo, 2011; Xu, Tan, & Yang, 2006); how factors relating to the seeker, such as experience, social ties, and gender influence source selection; and barriers to expertise seeking (Hertzum, 2002, 2014, pp. 787–789).

Hertzum, whose research interests include both CIS and expertise seeking, contends that they deal essentially with the same thing – the collaborative aspects of information seeking - yet maintain almost completely separate discourses. His bibliometric analysis of papers from both fields reveals they share only 4% of citations. He argues strongly for increased interaction between the two areas. (Hertzum, 2017)

INFORMATION SEEKING PRACTICES OF LOCAL GOVERNMENT DECISION MAKERS

This paper explores some of the findings of a research project investigating the information seeking practices of two groups of local government decision-makers: council officers (organizational employees) and elected members (councilors). The project, as a whole, adopts an approach wherein information seeking activities – active information seeking – are conceptualized as but one dimension of a broader range of practices that will include scanning, monitoring, retrieving, filtering, synthesizing, evaluating, sharing, creating and assembling (McKenzie, 2003, pp. 26–27; Talja & Hansen, 2006, p. 125).

Consequently, this study takes a different approach from many others associated with collaboration, collaborative information behavior, and expertise seeking. It is not starting from a position of investigating particular behavior as simply "collaborative information seeking" or as "expertise seeking". Neither is it specifically investigating phenomena that might be characterized as CIS or expertise seeking. Rather, the project has been designed to construct a detailed understanding of the full gamut of actions and activities by which decision makers become informed. In this paper, those activities which relate to information seeking have been extracted for particular analysis in relation to CIS and expertise seeking. This approach may provide a different perspective and instructive insights which will contribute to both fields.

Data has been collected from 15 employees of two local councils and seven elected members of five local councils in Sydney, Australia. Nine of the organizational representatives are employees of Marri, a large outer-metropolitan council; and the remaining six are employed by Ngarang, a smaller mid-suburban area (Council names being fictionalized for anonymity). The employees range from team leader to the senior executive level with the majority being professional officers or senior managers. The seven elected members represented five different local government areas in Sydney Australia, including inner-metropolitan, suburban and peri-urban localities.

The organizational officers were asked to describe daily actions activities in relation to their work; the elected members were asked to describe only those actions and activities they enacted for the purposes of being an elected member of a local council. Both sets of participants were asked about a decision they were currently making or had recently made. The interviews were designed to obtain a detailed understanding of "what people do" in accordance with the notion, described above, that people engage in a wide range of activities to become informed.

The first part of the interview did not deal specifically with information but rather asked participants to describe those routine tasks, actions, activities, conversations, movements and interactions they performed on a daily basis. The second part of the interview dealt with an examination of a decision – of the participants' own choosing – with a view to identifying the information-related activities and processes that went into its making. In this way, a detailed picture of the participants' normative information activities was assembled.

As noted above, while the research project overall was designed to elicit a rich picture of the entirety of actions and activities which contribute to a decision maker becoming informed, this paper reports only on that sub-set of information-related actions that can be categorized as information seeking. In the first instance the participants' rich description of their daily activities is analyzed in terms of habitual information sources, and the means by which they identify and access those sources. Secondly, the participants were asked direct questions about the actual information sources they used when making their decision; how they identified those sources, the mechanisms by which they accessed the information and the relative importance they gave to each source of information and their responses to these questions are analyzed. Lastly, the participants were asked if they could identify a single source of information that was more useful or important to them than any other, and these responses likewise examined in terms of the CIS and expertise seeking approaches described above.

Information Sources of Local Council Employees

Five of the 15 organizational participants are certain they cannot identify a single source of information that was more important than any other. Indeed E2 from Ngarang replied that seeking information from a single source was simply not possible: to do that you would only get one side of the story. E2's decision related to the implementation of a module relating to customer complaints in a new electronic system. She had to be aware of both "internal" and "external" expectations – those of organizational colleagues and the community - as "one side won't necessarily know about the concerns of the other". Her main source of information was comments from both staff and customers regarding failures in the current system, although she also found 5 other members of the internal implementation committee to be useful information sources, and is particularly interested in hearing "their points of view". E1, from the same council and whose interest was local property, similarly cannot identify a single source, but says his best source is a local real estate agent. He also "got a lot of information" from his Director. He does use on-line resources as well: researching buyer's agents on line and using a specialized on-line application to find the median price of property in the area.

E7, a senior manager from Marri whose decision related to parking in the city center, similarly finds it impossible to identify a single source of information that is more important than another. He obtains his information from a wide range of sources, both documentary and people. To inform himself about parking E7 speaks to members from the peak industry association, his counterparts in other councils, and also to a representative of a very well-known parking station management company. Additionally, he employs consultants to perform a physical empirical study of parking practices in the city, the data from which also informs his decision. E7 also undertakes internet searches on parking technologies, which he mentions almost in passing, but returns to at the end of the interview saying that they were equally as important as talking to people. E5 from Ngarang is looking to put driver monitoring software in the council fleet to reduce vehicular insurance claims. This is a suggestion made to him by the account manager at his insurance provider, which he develops more fully by speaking to Ngarang's Fleet Manager and his own manager. While he looks on line to see what products are available, E5 is not about to trust any claims made therein because "anybody can write anything on the Internet". He is more interested in "that first-hand experience" and consequently contacts several fleet officers from other organizations, details of whom are provided by his insurance provider. While E5 probably discusses his ideas the most with his own manager, he cannot say that one of these sources is more important than any other.

E3, a senior manager in Ngarang, is in the process of deciding the disposition of two members of staff whose current roles will be made unnecessary after an imminent change in business processes. He has a choice of terminating their employment or redeploying them elsewhere in his team. E3 assures himself that their roles will be unnecessary by the simple expedient of quantifying this on the system – it is clear that the system automates processes previously carried out by these two employees. But E3 also requires personal sources of information: he seeks information from his team leader and other staff members about the tasks they could be given, and also talks to colleagues in other councils about these work processes.

Two more participants list information sources in a chronological fashion – that is, in the order in which they were consulted. They give the information source that initially sparked the idea for their decision a particular emphasis, but also make it clear that much more information is subsequently needed. While these participants do not definitively assert that it is impossible to identify a single important source, their responses suggest that this is the case. E9, a professional officer from Marri specializing in project management, is making a decision about a developer's proposal and the people making this proposal are obviously a key source of information. But after the proposal is made E9 talks to his team, other managers, and also looks at physical details of the piece of land in question on the Geographical Information System (GIS). E10, another professional officer from Marri, speaks about a decision regarding the use of a community panel to provide strategic direction for resource allocation. She hears about the concept at a conference, and seeks out the person who presented on the issue. E10 then speaks to a colleague, and visits people at 3 other councils who have used citizens' juries and similar forms of engagement.

This is also the experience of E12, a senior manager at Marri whose decision relates to the use of local schools as after-hours child-care facilities. Like E10, E12's decision-making process is launched when she hears about the availability of grants for such services at a meeting of local government children's services managers. The idea is presented by a representative of the State government agency who distributes these grants, and E12 accordingly asserts this person is her single most important source of information. After the initial serendipitous encounter, E12 and her Business Coordinator visit the State government agency and speak to the presenter about "specifics" of the funding program. However it is clear that another significant source of information for E12, and one on whom she heavily relies, is the Business Coordinator. E12 generally depends on two members of her team for her information – the Business Coordinator and the senior HR officer – but for this decision E12 relies on the former to "do the research". This involves finding out about the funding required and the availability of grants, but also about provision of similar services elsewhere. E12's decision is not informed solely by the work of the Business Coordinator; she contacts colleagues at two other councils which she knows use school facilities for these services. E12 also uses documentary sources such as news articles about the funding program. Importantly, she knows from the reports of parent advisory committees – always an important source of information for her - that such facilities are needed and will be well-received by the community.

E12 is one of five participants who have no doubts as to their single most important information source. E4, a planning manager from Ngarang, identifies Alison, a team member who used to work in her own planning team but since transferred to the IT section. As E4's decision relates to implementation of a new system, Alison is a vital resource as she has detailed knowledge of both the needs of the planning team and system capabilities. But if Alison is the most important source, she is by no means the only one: if E4 does not know or understand something she will ask people who do. In relation to her decision E4 talks to people in another council who use the software currently being implemented, and members of an external advisory committee on which she sits. She listens to feedback from community members at a specially organized consultative event and, of course, to the other members of her team. E11, a manager leading the Governance team in Marri, is looking at letting staff buy out their council-provided mobile phones when they retire or resign. His single most important source of information is Arthur who used to work for E11 but now works in the IT team – an experience almost identical to E4's. Like E4, E11 does not depend on Arthur alone; he talks to the three staff members who wish to retain their mobile phones, and to certain key people such as the managers of the Finance, IT and Legal teams. E11 also undertakes an internet search to see if other councils have published policies on the subject – he cannot find any – but will personally contact a colleague from a neighboring council to see if he knows of any.

E13, a senior finance manager from Marri, describes the importance of a single information source in terms of the person with whom he "got the most benefit in discussing things" – in this case the Assistant General Manager (AGM). For E13 discussion with the AGM, with its attendant benefits of being able to "say things out loud", were key to informing himself during the decision-making process. E13 develops his idea for a productivity fund during discussions with the AGM, although the original idea for it comes from attendance at meetings of external professional and industry groups. E13 asks one of his team, the Corporate Planning Co-ordinator, to look at what other councils are doing, and also hires a consultant specializing in productivity. He looks at documentary sources such as Marri's financial records – these from a "cost-tracking perspective" - and also three reports on productivity produced by a major professional services organization. Similarly, E15, a planning manager at Marri, has no hesitation in naming her Community Engagement Officer as her most important source of information.

Only three of the organizational participants describe a documentary source as their main source of information, although only one of them appears to make this assessment in terms of continuous reference during the decision-making process. E6, Ngarang's team leader in the records management unit, is the most junior council officer interviewed. E6's decision relates to legal destruction of official records, and she identified the disposal instrument issued by the State's recordkeeping agency by which local government records are legally destroyed as her most important information source. It is clearly, and for obvious reasons, one upon which she relies in an operational and recurrent manner. Nevertheless, E6 does routinely discuss her disposal decisions with a single colleague who "went on an archivist (sic) course".

The other two participants citing a documentary source as the most importance do so in terms of it being the thing which sparked their decision. An executive, E8 is the most senior organizational participant interviewed. E8 seems barely to "seek" information at all – his description of his daily activities shows a picture of information coming to him, almost entirely from human sources. E8 "works hard on fraternities", by which he means that fraternizing is a major part of his role and an important way he receives information. His decision relates to an advocacy campaign and he has discussed it with local business organizations, his peers at neighboring councils and the leadership of an independent think tank. Interaction with his peers at an association of local authorities provided many ideas for his advocacy campaign but it was actually a document – a consultant's review of Marri's advocacy service – that was E8's most important source of information. Similarly E14, a manager with responsibility for sustainability, is deciding whether Marri should deliver an intensive permaculture workshop to the local community. He cites his most important, and initial, source of information as the program of the course. He had not thought of doing this until the presenter of this course, which had been delivered previously in another council area, emailed the unsolicited program, including content and costs through to him. Upon receipt of the material E14 did discuss whether or not to proceed with his coordinator, but asserts he did not get "any additional information as such" from this encounter.

E9, the professional officer from Marri, comes the closest to describing CIS as it is defined in the collaboration-centric approach. He makes certain to bring to the attention of the interviewer a decision-making tool he and his colleagues have designed, one which considers social return on investment. In this endeavor, E9 is part of a collaborative information seeking process where team members research "a lot of stuff" on decision-making and "social value" on line. E9 describes this as people doing their own research – "probably Google" – and then coming together for a discussion on what they found. This in turn identifies others in the organization with knowledge in the area.

These organizational participants tell analogous stories of their search for information – their experiences are markedly similar. The non-linear nature of the information seeking is striking: information is found, received, generated and stored in no particular order. Activities associated with information seeking – be they searching on-line, talking to colleagues, calling peers at other councils, or reading reports – happen concurrently and recurrently. Even the two participants who provide a chronology of their decision making, E9 and E10, do not describe their information seeking as a linear progression of one information source after another.

For many of those interviewed, information that was sought and found at a distance in time from the present decision making, and for quite a different purpose, was no less important to them than that more recently generated. Information seeking activities are on-going, and these decision makers call on their past knowledge in equal addition to the information they are receiving contemporaneously. Information is a reusable resource and information sought and stored for a different matter or task is routinely re-purposed for the decision on hand.

Information, for these decision makers, comes from multiple sources and even that minority of participants who could identify their most important source were sure to emphasize it was by no means their only source. Source selection was unproblematic for these people: they knew who to call. If they did not know a person who had the information, they knew someone who could find it for them. Even E11, who was unsuccessful in his search for a policy on disposal of mobile phones, was not particularly disheartened by this. He rather felt that this would be the case and is, in any case, intending to contact his counterpart at a neighboring council to see if he knows of any.

That locating multiple sources of information, both personal and documentary, is necessary to their decision-making activities is not problematic to these employees – it is simply how they work. The only person that appeared regretful of not being able to go to a single point of truth for information was E9 who had, as described above, co-developed a decision-making tool. The purpose of this tool was to allow his colleagues to ascertain if the decisions they were making had quantifiable social value. Sadly, E9's colleagues have not been particularly interested in using the tool which indicates, perhaps, that they prefer to make their own assessments and judgements.

Information Sources of Elected Members

In addition to the organizational participants, seven elected members, representing five different local councils, were interviewed using the same techniques. They include two current mayors, a former mayor and two former deputy mayors. One of the participants is nearing the end of his first four-year term and the longest serving councilor is in her 22 year. The remaining five elected members are nearing the end of their 3rd term - that is, they have all served nearly twelve years on their respective councils. They are self-selected participants in the research; that is, they had each responded positively to unsolicited emails from the researcher, who was previously unknown to them.

The information sources of the elected members can be categorized into two groups: council (both employees and fellow councilors) and community. These are predictable sources arising from the operation of the system of local government itself. Local councilors are elected by the community and generally serve that community on a part-time, voluntary basis. It is to be expected that they will get information concerning their legal and operational obligations – how they must act - from the council officers whose purpose it is, after all, to provide the elected members with pertinent information. They also get information from more experienced councilors who can "show them the ropes". Neither is it surprising that information about community expectations would come from members of the community - or at least that part of the local community that councilors believe themselves to represent. It is to be anticipated that the elected members taking part in this project will have similar types of information sources, and this was found to be the case.

All elected members interviewed in the project receive information from council officers in the form of written reports and formal briefings. It is common practice for general council meetings and meetings of committees of council to be preceded by briefings at which council officers present detailed information on decisions to be made, as well as recommendation on those decisions. Similarly, for all decisions to be made by council and its committees, detailed reports are prepared for the councilors. All participants treat this source of information as a given; it is integral to their decision-making processes, accepted as their right and due, and a normative means by which the "official" position – that arrived at by professional officers with expertise and qualifications in their fields – is communicated to them.

But no participant in this research depends solely on the information supplied to them by, or elicited from, council officers. Another common source of information for all of the elected members is their fellow councilors. C6, a mayor, describes how the councilors from his political party, the majority, meet before each meeting to talk through issues and decide on positions. C3, from another council and the other side of politics, also consults with her political colleagues on every issue. C1, another mayor, does not feel the need to be on every committee because she can "just talk to" the councilors who are on them. C7 will speak to her fellow councilors if she thinks they have "special expertise" in an area.

C4 is unusual among those interviewed in professing an interest in "historical documents", by which he means past decisions made by his council and recorded in the official minutes. However, he only knows where to look in the minutes by speaking to long-term councilors who can provide an indication of when the decision was made. He is also from the same council and political party as C6 and attends the meetings of the councilors described by the latter. C5 and C2, both political independents, similarly meet regularly with their fellow independent councilors. C5, however, does single one person out more than the rest, who tend to "factionalize". C2 is at pains to point out that they do not make joint decisions – caucusing is not allowed in the State - they meet to discuss matters and get better informed about issues.

The elected members interviewed take the responsibility to serve the community very seriously, and they perform a variety of activities to find out the views of that community. A prime source of community concerns for a majority of the councilors is the local media: C7 reads the local papers "from cover to cover"; C3 subscribes to two major dailies in addition to the locally produced papers; and C4 reads the local paper "as soon as it comes out" and also monitors social media sites like Facebook to see what people are commenting on. C5 also reads the local papers, occasionally listens to local radio, and regularly checks in on four Facebook groups devoted to her local area.

C6, a long-serving councilor and current mayor, describes a number of strategies by which he seeks out and gages community opinion. Like the other mayor interviewed, C1, he judges the depth of feeling on an issue by the number of emails he receives in relation to it and the number of people who turn up to council meetings where it is discussed. But C6 also describes a more idiosyncratic mechanism by which he elicits feedback from the community. When he is walking through the local area, which he does frequently, C6 always tries to make eye contact with people he passes. That way, if they recognize him, he can stop and have a chat and find out their concerns. Like C6, C3 feels that if the community has a pressing issue they will let her know "any way they can" - by emailing, phoning and accosting her in the supermarket. C3 greatly delights in attending community functions, at which usually "half a dozen people" will speak to her about their problems. C7 likes to be active in community groups and attend community forums and "religiously avoids" having private face-to-face meetings with residents about issues as one cannot guarantee that everyone is getting the same information in such encounters. Like C7, C5 finds community forums a good way of gaging the feelings of the community, but she finds that members of the community will seek her out to air their concerns: she receives around 3 phone calls and "easily" 3 or 4 emails a day from local residents.

When deciding the fate of a local council building C4 gets most of his information about that building from those members of the community interested enough in the issue to attend an informal meeting about it on-site at short notice. C4 forms an association with four of these local residents with whom he meets regularly while the property decision is on-going. C2 gages community opinion by the simple expedient of asking her work colleagues: she has the benefit of working in the same local area in which she lives and which she represents on council. She discusses issues with them at length, often without letting them know she is asking because of a decision to be made in council, thereby getting an unbiased opinion.

Family members are also a vital source of information to C2, she speaks regularly with her two adult sons about most of the work she does on council and clearly sets great store in their opinions and advice. Indeed, C2's sons seem to be a prime conduit by which people communicate their concerns to her. Similarly, C5 often speaks to her husband about council matters and, in relation to a particular decision she is making about tree removal, to a close family member who is a landscape architect.

The information seeking practices of the elected members interviewed are remarkably homogenous. The participants are uniformly appreciative of the professional reports and briefings provided by the professional officers from their respective councils. They all have an implicit trust in these and are secure in the knowledge that the information they receive from these official sources are accurate and within the letter of the law.

But it is clear that all the elected members interviewed believe that this is only part of the information they need. They want to be assured they are doing the right thing in legal terms, and they certainly want to know the recommendations of their employees. They are also interested in knowing which of the recommendations their officers prefer – and this the regarded rather in the way of an opinion. But if it is an opinion, it is one among many, and the councilors are equally concerned with finding out the opinions and wishes of their constituents, particularly those who have elected them.

While the mechanisms of getting information about what they community want may differ slightly – be it C2 talking to her work colleagues and her sons, C4 calling a community meeting, by attending community functions like C3, or by gaging community feeling through emails and telephone calls like C1 and C6 - all those interviewed made sure to get information from the community. What is interesting here is the very practical and pragmatic mechanisms used by elected members to elicit this information.

APPLICATION OF THE CIS AND EXPERTISE SEEKING APPROACHES

Collaborative Information Seeking (CIS) in the Local Sphere

When Shah propounds his circular C5 model of CIS (Shah, 2008, 2010, 2014, 2015) one of his purposes is to show that information seeking is not a linear progression of activities. In this respect, Shah's model does represent the real-life activities of participants in this research. But in other ways, Shah's collaboration-centric model is too restrictive to represent and explain behaviors identified in this research. Shah's model pre-supposes that CIS refers to people performing the same tasks, working toward completion of a single task, or seeking information for a common purpose. Given and Willson, in their study of scholars' research practices, found a remarkable lack of group-based information searching despite their participants engaging in a wide range of collaborative information behaviors. They conclude that a more holistic approach needs to be taken when examining CIS, and similarly argue for scrutinizing the larger context of collaborative information behavior rather than focusing on joint searching activities (Given & Willson, 2015).

The collaboration-centric research narrative is well suited to certain investigations - examinations of the use of on-line collaborative tools or system-based search applications for information retrieval, for example. But some argue that the focus on information seeking retrieval inherent in CIS necessarily results in a research agenda dealing with task-based studies. They contend that the field would benefit from a conceptual broadening to a more context-based approach (Widen & Hansen, 2012).

Certainly, taking a narrowly focused definition of what constitutes collaboration is not particularly useful for examining the full range of activities demonstrated by the officers and elected members in this research. Like the participants' of Given's and Willson's study, the participants in this research generally sought their information, and information sources, independently. Yet their behavior and activities are without a doubt collaborative. They consistently call on other people as primary sources of information, and as sources of information about where to seek further information. More than this, many of the organizational participants used conversation with other people as a mechanism for separating ideas, cementing opinions and straightening facts – in other words for generating information. Importantly, the participants in this research all work with collaborative intent. Although pursuing their own roles and decisions they are all actively working toward common goals. Both organizational officers and elected members have recognizably common goals of performing the best they can for the organization, being efficient with money and other resources, and making good decisions for their community.

I have argued above that there is another way of defining CIS, which I have called the information-centric approach. In this approach, CIS is defined as "information-seeking activities performed by actors to inform their collaborative work combined with the collaborative-grounding activities involved in making this information part of the actors' shared understanding of their work" (Hertzum, 2008, p. 958). This appears to be a more productive way to represent the real-life activities discussed in this project.

Despite its more general applicability, Hertzum and Hansen argue that the information-centric approach, while the basis for a wide range of empirical studies, suffers from the lack of a shared model to which individual studies can contribute. They urge researchers to develop models which will allow the results of disparate empirical studies to cumulate and build on each other. In particular, they emphasize the need for CIS research to more robustly discuss outcomes – what the research means for the community being studied. As a step forward they propose a "tentative" model of factors which give rise to CIS (Hertzum & Hansen, 2019). The model comprises such factors as beliefs, attitudes, systems, social norms, facilitating conditions and behavioral intention. I wonder, however, if such a model is an over-complication: if the factor that gives rise to CIS is, quite simply, that this is how people work in organizations.

The research reported herein shows people finding information by asking other people, by reading reports and documents compiled by other people, and by having conversations with other people during which the two-way communicative process allows them to generate new information or re-assess old. These are routine daily activities, business as usual; they are recurrent and on-going. They are not enacted only at those times when there is a special information need or an extraordinary problem to be solved. For CIS research to be more generalizable and to allow the better analysis of reasons, experiences and outcomes desired by Hertzum and Hansen, it needs to take more account of how collaboration, in information activities as in many others, is part of every-day life, and of the use of other people as information sources. Perhaps what is missing in CIS is, as Hertzum argues, the concerns with which expertise seeking research generally deals (Hertzum, 2017).

Knowing Who to Call: Expertise Seeking in the Local Sphere

That people extensively use other people as sources when seeking information is scarcely a novel finding (c.f. Bystrom, 2002, p. 588). While the data collected in this project can be analyzed through ideas prevalent in CIS research, they can equally be interpreted in terms of expertise seeking.

Hoffman et al describe a "practical" definition of expert*s* as people with years of experience, professional criteria such as qualifications and memberships of professional societies, and the fact that they have held down jobs in operational settings (Hoffman et al., 1995, p. 131). This would, I think, be accepted by the participants in this research as a satisfactory description of someone upon whom they would call for information.

On the whole, the participants need go to no effort to find their expert – they know who to call. In the case of council officers this is a result of being firmly part of their own organizational environment. The expert is the person who deals with the matters under consideration on a daily basis. Senior managers depend on their team members to do research, collate data and write reports, in addition to providing verbal advice. They know which members of the team to approach because they work with them every day - they see what they do, have discussions and conversations and have constant recurring opportunities to assess the quality of their work. Through this adjacency they have an excellent understanding of the areas on which each team member will be most knowledgeable and competent.

Other personal information sources are defined by their roles: if you need information on accounts you call someone in the Finance Department; if you need to know about building use you contact Planning. There is evidence in the data that people tend to seek out others at the same organizational level – if you are a manager you contact another manager. This could be interpreted as an example of simple organizational etiquette – it being inappropriate for a manager to contact a more junior employee without going through their manager – but it was common to employees of both councils. The data suggests a more likely explanation: once again, one of adjacency. Managers meet with each other frequently in formal and informal meetings, and they are often the ones who make presentations on the work their teams are doing to the rest of the organization.

External personal information sources for council officers fall into two unequal categories: those personally known to the information seeker and those contacted as an official point of enquiry. The former, and much larger, category comprised colleagues from another council. These people were often met physically through attendance at conferences or virtually via membership of professional associations and committees. They occupy a similar, if not identical, role to the inquirer and are generally at the same organizational level as the information seeker. Sources in the latter, much smaller, category were mostly representatives of State government departments and, in two cases, employees of suppliers of goods or services.

Elected members equally know which officers to call in their councils based on their roles. The majority of elected members interviewed stated that they will personally contact the manager of the relevant section if they need additional information on any particular matter. All the participants in this research come from councils where direct personal contact with senior officers is allowed, while direct contact with officers below the level of department head is generally prohibited. This convention is, for the most part, obeyed by the research participants: 3 elected members who admitted to occasionally contacting staff below this senior level professed a long-standing personal acquaintance with them, and are assured they will not be reported.

The elected members interviewed in this project actively seek out their fellow councilors, especially those with whom they share a common political view-point. Here expertise takes the form of ideological compatibility; it is evident that the councilors like to pass the professionally safe and dispassionate recommendations provided by their professional officers through the prism of opinions of like-minded people.

As discussed above many studies in the field of expertise seeking are devoted to the relative importance of personal and documentary information sources. All participants in this research use documentary sources, including on-line documents, in addition to people. However, the participants are noticeably more engaged when describing the people they talk to, and interact with, as opposed to the reports they read. Interaction and discussive two-way communication is clearly of utmost importance to these participants. Far more time is spent in the interview discussing personal sources than documentary, and participants can enumerate and describe the different people to whom they have spoken even after the passage of some time. Documentary sources are often mentioned only as an aside, or their existence inferred only through a recitation of activities such as reading. Several of the elected members assert they find face-to-face briefings by professional officers far more informative than reading the associated report.

The participants' experts are adjacent and, therefore, highly accessible. There is no indication that any trade-off in terms of quality is necessary. Those interviewed clearly believe the people they approach for information are well-informed, knowledgeable, and competent. Importantly, the participants believe themselves competent to judge and assess the information they receive – a finding particularly noticeable in the elected members. This competence comes from experience: the enactment of habitual information actions over a period of time and as part of routine every day activities. Neither is there any indication of the sufficiency principle – "satisficing" - when barely enough is good enough (Lu & Yuan, 2011, pp. 134–135). Participants in this research give every indication they seek as many sources as possible to get a good range of options, opinions, competing views – they are clearly prepared to put as much effort as is necessary into their search rather than the least.

The findings of this project can productively be interpreted in the context of expertise seeking. However, expertise seeking is generally characterized as a directed and purposive information activity enacted by an individual. It will be a richer field if it takes greater account of the social nature of the modern organization and, as Hertzum suggests, deals with the collaborative elements in expertise seeking and the information-generating interplay between seeker and source (Hertzum, 2017).

CONCLUSION

This paper discusses the findings of a research project into the information seeking practices of two groups of local government decision-makers: council officers (organizational employees) and elected members (councilors). It takes a new approach and, unlike other projects where data has been collected expressly to investigate a particular set of behaviors, it uses data which has been collected to identify the full range of routine information activities enacted by the participants. The findings show the participants' information seeking activities are highly collaborative and demonstrate that other people are a significant source of information. It seems logical, then, to examine the findings in terms of the two research areas devoted to these fields: collaborative information seeking (CIS) and expertise seeking.

The findings of the research described herein show that, for these organizational information seekers at least, collaboration and expertise seeking cannot be conceptually distinguished or treated as separate discrete behaviors. They are integral parts of information practices which are efficient, longitudinal and, above all, communicative.

Although to date these two research fields have occupied almost completely separate conceptual spaces, an amalgamation of both would strengthen information seeking research by taking into account the essentially collaborative nature of contemporary organizations. Today's organizational members interact for the purposes of finding, receiving, generating and sharing information as integral parts of every day routines. CIS research will be more generalizable and to allow the better analysis of reasons, experiences and outcomes if day-to-day collaborative information activities, particularly the use of other people as information sources, are taken into account. Expertise seeking research will be richer for taking greater account of the social nature of the modern organization and investigates both the collaborative elements inherent in this activity and the information-generating interplay occurring between seeker and source.

ACKNOWLEDGMENTS

This research is supported by an Australian Government Research Training Program Scholarship.

REFERENCES

Agarwal, N. K., Xu, Y., & Poo, D. C. C. (2011). A context-based investigation into source use by information seekers. *Journal of the American Society for Information Science and Technology*, *62*(6), 1087–1104.

Bystrom, K. (2002). Information and information sources in tasks of varying complexity. *Journal of the American Society for Information Science and Technology*, *53*(7), 581–591.

Choo, C. W. (1994). Perception and use of information sources by Chief Executives in environmental scanning. *Library & Information Science Research*, *16*(1), 23–40.

Fidel, R., Pejtersen, A. M., Cleal, B., & Bruce, H. (2004). A multidimensional approach to the study of human-information interaction: A case study of collaborative information retrieval. *Journal of the American Society for Information Science and Technology*, *55*(11), 939–953.

Given, L. M., & Willson, R. (2015). Collaboration, information seeking, and technology use: A critical examination of humanities scholars' research practices. In P. Hansen, C. Shah, & C.-P. Klas, *Collaborative information seeking: Best practices, new domains and new thoughts* (pp. 139–164). Switzerland: Springer International Publishing.

Hansen, P., & Jarvelin, K. (2005). Collaborative Information Retrieval in an information-intensive domain. *Information Processing & Management*, *41*, 1101–1119.

Hansen, P., & Widen, G. (2017). The embeddedness of collaborative information seeking in information culture. *Journal of Information Science*, *43*(4), 554–566.

Hertzum, M. (2002). The importance of trust in software engineers' assessment and choice of information sources. *Information and Organisation*, *12*, 1–18.

Hertzum, M. (2008). Collaborative information seeking: the combined activity of information seeking and collaborative grounding. *Information Processing & Management*, *44*, 957–962.

Hertzum, M. (2014). Expertise seeking: a review. *Information Processing & Management*, *50*, 775–795.

Hertzum, M. (2017). Collaborative information seeking and expertise seeking: Different discourses about similar issues. *Journal of Documentation*, *73*(5), 858–876.

Hertzum, M., & Hansen, P. (2019). Empirical studies of collaborative information seeking: A review of methodological issues. *Journal of Documentation*, *75*(1), 140–163.

Hoffman, R. R., Shadbolt, N. R., & Burton, A. M. (1995). Eliciting knowledge from experts: A methodological analysis. *Organisational Behaviour and Human Decision Processes*, *62*(2), 129–158.

Lu, L., & Yuan, Y. C. (2011). Shall I Google it or ask the competent villain down the hall? The moderating role of information need in information source selection. *Journal of the American Society for Information Science and Technology*, *62*(1), 133–145.

Marton, C., & Choo, C. W. (2002). A question of quality: The effect of source quality on information seeking by women in IT professions. *Proceedings of the American Society for Information Science and Technology*, *39*(1), 140–151.

McKenzie, P. J. (2003). A model of information practices in accounts of every-day life information seeking. *Journal of Documentation*, *59*(1), 19–40.

Nikoi, E., & Boateng, K. (2014). *Collaborative communication processes and decision making in organisations*. Hershey, PA: Business Science Reference.

Shah, C. (2008). Toward collaborative information seeking (CIS). In *Proceedings of the JCDL Workshop on Collaborative Information*. Retrieved from https://arxiv.org/pdf/0908.0709.pdf

Shah, C. (2010). Collaborative information seeking: A literature review. In *Exploring the digital frontier: Advances in librarianship* (Vol. *32*, pp. 3–33). Bingley, England: Emerald Group Publishing Ltd.

Shah, C. (2014). Collaborative information seeking. *Journal of the American Society for Information Science and Technology*, *65*(2), 215–236.

Shah, C. (2015). Collaborative information seeking: From 'What?' and 'Why?' to 'How?' and 'So What?'. In P. Hansen, C. Shah, & C.-P. Klas, *Collaborative information seeking: Best practices, new domains and new thoughts* (pp. 3–16). Switzerland: Springer International Publishing.

Talja, S., & Hansen, P. (2006). Information sharing. In A. Spink & C. Cole, *New directions in human information behaviour* (pp. 113–134). Dordrecht, Netherlands: Springer.

Widen, G., & Hansen, P. (2012). *Managing collaborative information sharing: Bridging research on information culture and collaborative information behaviour*. Information Research, *17*(4). Retrieved from http://www.informationr.net/ir/17-4/paper538.html

Xu, Y., Tan, C. Y., & Yang, L. (2006). Who will you ask? An empirical study of interpersonal task information seeking. *Journal of the American Society for Information Science and Technology*, *57*(12), 1666–1677.

Capturing the Change in Topical Interests of Personas Over Time

Bernard J. Jansen
Qatar Computing Research Institute, Doha, Qatar
jjansen@acm.org

Soon-gyo Jung
Qatar Computing Research Institute, Doha, Qatar
sjung@hbku.edu.qa

Joni Salminen
Qatar Computing Research Institute, Doha, Qatar
jsalminen@hbku.edu.qa

ABSTRACT

In this research, we collect monthly content consumption and demographic data from YouTube over two years for a large media publisher. We use automation to generate 15 personas each month and examine the consistency of the generated personas over time. We find that there are 35 unique personas in total for the entire period, reflecting the changes in the underlying audience population. For each persona, we generate topics of interest and identify the top three monthly topics for each of the 35 personas following an identical algorithmic approach each month. We then compare the sets of topical interests of the personas month-over-month for the entire two-year period. Findings show that there is an average 20.2% change in topical interests and that 68% of the personas experience more topical change than topical consistency. Findings suggest that the topical interests of online audiences are fluid and changes in the underlying audience data can occur within a relatively short period, resulting in the need for constant updating of personas using data-driven methods. The implications for organizations seeking to understand their online audience are that they should employ routine data analysis to detect changes in the audience interests and investigate ways to automate their persona generation processes.

KEYWORDS

Personas; Web Analytics; Online Data Representations

ASIS&T THESAURUS

Information Discovery; Information Behavior; Information and Data Processes

INTRODUCTION

Personas portray segments of audiences, as well as customers or users, as imaginary people (Cooper, 2004), usually within the form of a persona profile containing attributes of the segment that the fictionalized person represents (Nielsen, Hansen, Stage, & Billestrup, 2015). Personas are used widely in a variety of domains for understanding audiences, users, and customers. In this research, we employ personas to represent audience segments for a major online media organization that publishes thousands of news videos yearly.

Personas have been criticized for staling (Chapman & Milham, 2006), meaning that the underlying data from which they were created becomes invalid, resulting in outdated personas. This limitation is especially acute for organizations distributing online content, especially concerning changes in topical interests. It is this last concern, the change in topical interests of personas, that we investigate in this research. Despite the routinely stated critique of personas changing over time (Chapman, Love, Milham, Elrif, & Alford, 2008; Chapman & Milham, 2006; Salminen, Kwak, An, Jung, & Jansen, 2018), we could locate no specific research investigating whether changes in content interests of audience segments, as represented by personas, actually do become outdated. Similarly, there is a lack of research determining how frequently interests do change, if they change at all.

As such, there are several gaps in the literature. *Do topical interests of personas change over time? If so, how often do they change? What is the pace of change? How many topics change? How does one identify when topics change?* These are some of the questions that motivate our research. We could locate no previous empirical analyses of the change in personas' topical interests in any context. We are interested in examining this aspect for personas in pursuit of a larger research project to make personas more data-driven and reflective of audience analytics and segments (Jung, Salminen, An, Kwak, & Jansen, 2018; Salminen, Jansen, An, Kwak, & Jung, 2019).

In this research, we collect user data monthly during a more than two-year period for a large international YouTube content-producing organization with an audience in the hundreds of thousands. To simplify the representation of this large audience population, we generate 15 personas from each monthly dataset following an identical algorithmic methodology for data-driven persona creation (An, Kwak, Salminen, Jung, & Jansen, 2018b). Personas are deployed to represent users or customers in many domains (Friess, 2012). For our research, these generated personas represent the audience segments of the YouTube channel of a media

82nd Annual Meeting of the Association for Information Science & Technology | Melbourne, Australia | 19–23 October, 2019

DOI: 10.1002/pra2.00011

organization that currently employs the system used for creating the personas for gaining insights into their audience composition and content preferences.

Associated with the generation of these personas, we identify the top three topical interests of each persona for each month, including the top three interests in the persona profile. We then compare the changes in the topical interests of the personas by month over the entire data collection period. Our findings show that personas' topical interests do change, and these interests can change quite rapidly.

In the following sections, we present a brief literature review, research objectives, methodology, and results. We end with implications and future research directions. See Table 1 for key constructs and definitions applicable to this research.

Persona: An imaginary person created from data that represents a user segment for content, system, or product (Nielsen et al., 2015)
Persona set: The collection of one or more personas that represent the audience population for an organization. In this research, the set of personas is 15, corresponding to the relatively small number recommended in the persona literature (e.g., Goodman, Kuniavsky, & Moed, 2013)
Audience segment: Group of individuals that are similar in specific ways, such as age, gender, interests or behaviors, and usually derived from demographics (e.g., Jenkinson, 1994)
Demographics: Statistical data relating to a population or particular groups within it
Topic: Is the subject of one or more pieces of content. The topic of online content is determined via general processes of topic modeling and text classification (e.g., Xiao, Ji, Li, Zhuang, & Shi, 2018)
Topic modeling: A form of supervised or unsupervised learning where the set of possible topics is inferred from the data (e.g., Hong & Davison, 2010)

Table 1. Key terms employed in this research with definitions.

REVIEW OF LITERATURE

The availability of online content enables users to indicate their preferences for this content via views, likes, comments, and shares (Lee & Tandoc, 2017). With content being produced online, there have been efforts in development services to personalize this content to audiences based on user interests (Karimi, Jannach, & Jugovac, 2018), which requires a focus on topical preferences from audience segments (Li, Bai, Wenjun, & Xihao, 2019; Sánchez & Bellogín, 2019) or on personalization.

Personas are a common method of presenting audience segments (Goodwin & Cooper, 2009); however, there are concerns that multiple or periodic rounds of data collection may be needed to keep the personas updated (Mulder & Yaar, 2007), which can be time consuming and expensive. In fact, without periodic new data collection, end users of the personas are uncertain whether the personas are representative of their *current* target audience. This criticism, widely present in the persona literature (e.g., Chapman & Milham, 2006), is based on the assumption that there can be instability in the audience populations (Drutsa, Gusev, & Serdyukov, 2017) or, as our premise is for this research, in attributes of the current audience. This criticism of staling of the segmentation data assumes that there are periods of instability and change in the underlying populations or data from which the personas are created.

This is an acute concern for online content producers, such as news organizations, social media platforms, news services, and blog sites. The use of online data and metrics allows for the identification of important content for persona generation (Jansen, Jung, Salminen, An, & Kwak, 2017). However, we could find no prior research that would show that the content interests of personas change over time. When using personas for decision making, keeping the personas up-to-date in terms of interests and changes in these interests is of critical importance when creating online content.

For instance, there have been a variety of efforts toward personalization for the delivery of online content based on understanding the interests of audience members. As an example of these efforts, Watters and Wang (2000) extract feature phrases from news content. However, it seems that people prefer a combination of personalization and serendipitous content (Shepherd, Duffy, Watters, & Gugle, 2001), indicating, perhaps, that audiences are interested in new types of content or tire when being exposed to the same topics over time. Therefore, efforts have also focused on modeling audience preferences over time, including efforts based on similarity among audience members (Lv, Meng, & Zhang, 2017) or specific aspects of the content, such as entity identification (Zhang, Boons, & Batista-Navarro, 2019).

Personalizing the delivery of news and other online content depends on the ability to predict user interests, with tailored content being preferred by users, although declared interest and actual interest may differ (Sela, Lavie, Inbar, Oppenheim, & Meyer, 2015). Therefore, developing personalized content systems requires not only detecting and tracking current interests but also predicting what content users would be interested in the future (Mele, Bahrainian, & Crestani, 2019) or at least what related future content (Toraman & Can, 2017) a person might prefer. Although content producing organizations naturally attempt to do this, studies on online news have shown that most news content focuses on consistent themes (i.e., United States, Western Europe), although this is undergoing a change with shifts in news content to Middle Eastern, and Asian countries (Segev, Sheafer, & Shenhav, 2013).

Additionally, prior work (Kwak, An, Salminen, Jung, & Jansen, 2018) has shown that media attention and public attention are both similar and different depending on the resolution of the analysis, with strong regional similarities with both media and public attention but also a substantial number of countries where media attention and public attention are dissimilar by topical interest. In these cases, the public within these countries may be ignored by country-specific content outlets and seek other online sources to address their content needs and desires (Kwak et al., 2018). At the individual level, there has been limited prior work in examining the changes in and the diversity of news content consumption. However, previous research has noted a trend for decreasing content consumption diversity, with the degree of consumption diversity being correlated with the diversity of content available (Zhang, Zheng, & Peng, 2017). However, there is a notable gap in the research in determining the drift or change in the topical interests of an audience for online content.

This is an important research gap to address, as creating personas is not a cheap, easy, or quick process, given it has historically involved ethnography studies or focus groups (Goodwin & Cooper, 2009). When automated methods are employed (An, Kwak, Salminen, Jung, & Jansen, 2018a), there is still effort and time involved in the persona creation process. Therefore, whether or not additional rounds of data collection are needed has practical implications, notably for those organizations with large user populations, such as major online content publishers whose audiences' might fluctuate rapidly.

RESEARCH OBJECTIVES

Our research goals are twofold. First, we investigate whether the topical interests of personas change over time and, if so, how much. Secondly, we determine if the change in topical interest is associated with changes in the set of personas. In pursuit of these goals, we address the following research questions, which are:

- Research Question 01 (RQ01): *Do the topical interests of personas change over time? Is so, how?*
- Research Question 02 (RQ02): *Do the changes in the topical interests of personas vary by the changes in the set of personal? If so, how?*

Our motivation for these questions is to investigate if and how much topical interests of a set of personas change over time to provide insights for organizations concerning how frequently they need to monitor their audiences to keep up-to-date on the interests of audience segments. As audience segmentation is a common practice, we are also interested in whether there are differences in changes in topical interest specifically based on the stability of the audience segmentation, which again provides insight for organizations that use personas or related customer understanding processes.

As such, we define two concepts for this work, which are:

- *Topic Consistency* – the concept of moving from one set of topics to another set of topics within a given period. We address this topic drift by the following two measures, which are:
  - *Consistency* – the persistence in a set of topics from one period to another
  - *Change* – the difference in a set of topics from one period to another
- *Persona Stability* – the concept of the constancy of a set of personas within a given period. We address personas variance by the following two measures, which are:
  - *Stability* – the persistence in a set of personas from one period to another
  - *Instability* – the difference in a set of personas from one period to another

METHODOLOGY

We investigate these questions using data from a major publisher of YouTube content. With the increased availability of online user and customer data, there is the opportunity to use data-driven personas derived directly from a system's users or a company's customer analytics data (Vecchio, Mele, Ndou, & Secundo, 2018), with each persona representing a distinct audience segment. Personas developed from this approach can be created automatically (Jung et al., 2017), which we did for this research.

Data Collection

This organization had more than 665,404 subscribers and more than 4,800 of pieces of online content at the time of the study. As such, the organization is representative of those publishers that distribute content via major online platforms, such as other content producers, app developers, software-as-a-service (SaaS) providers, and other media outlets. These organizations typically have a large and potentially diverse audience, varied online content, and the potential for changes in the underlying audience population.

The YouTube Analytics API provides statistics for each piece of content and various user profile data, (e.g., gender, age, country location) at an aggregate level. Individual user data is not provided to safeguard users' privacy. Via the YouTube Analytics API, we collect the detailed record of content interactions by country, gender, and age group for each piece of content. We collect data for all videos of the channel published each month from October 2016 through January 2019. There was 1 month where the data collection failed, so we have 26 months of data available for this research.

System for Generating Personas

In terms of producing the personas, the applied approach for generating data-driven personas is discussed in prior work (An et al., 2018a); therefore, we only briefly present it here. The approach relies on non-negative matrix factorization (NMF) (Lee & Seung, 1999) to take the aggregated user data

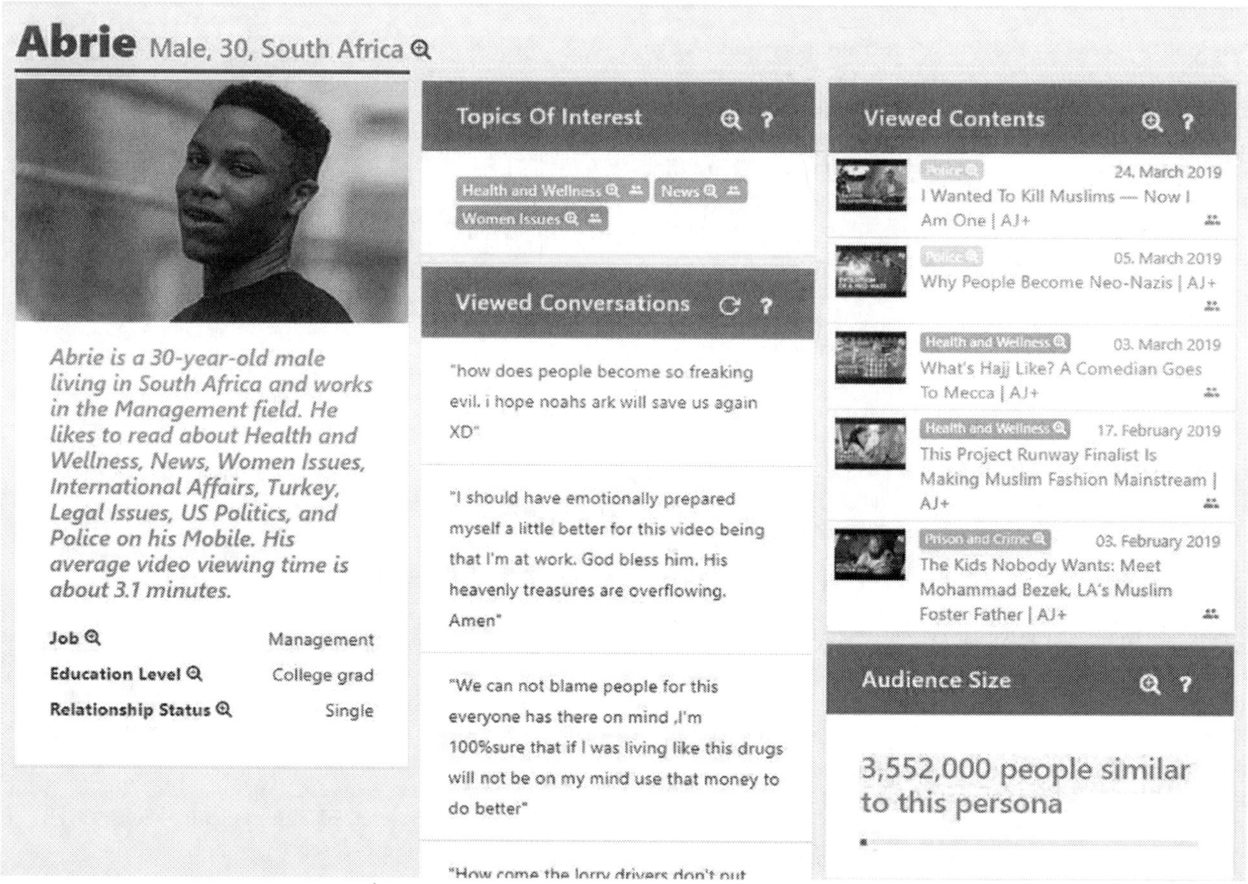

Figure 1. Example of a data-driven persona profile used in this research. The persona is created automatically from audience demographic and associated behaviors data of the organization's online content. One component of the persona profile is the Topics of Interest, which is the focus of this research. Topics of Interest are computed using the Z-score over the persona set.

and identify unique behavioral patterns (Sánchez & Bellogín, 2019), associating these unique sets of behavioral patterns, with demographic attributes, and then using other algorithmic approaches to generate a complete persona profile.

In our example, we apply NMF to the video content views retrieved from You Analytics for the organization, resulting in a set of unique view patterns. Also, using data from YouTube Analytics, each unique behavior pattern is associated with one or more set of demographics. The demographic with the highest NMF weight is associated with the behavior pattern. These are the base personas that the system then enriches with name, photo, etc. Each video is automatically topically classified, providing topics of interests for each persona. An example of a complete persona profile from the system is shown in Figure 1. This approach has several advantages, including that is responsive to interactions with both existing and new content, which is important as our datasets are cascading (i.e., existing content will get new user interactions, and new content is added that has no prior user interactions). The result of the process is the set of the most distinct personas in terms of both behavioral and demographic user attributes.

We apply the identical methodological approach to each monthly dataset, generating 15 personas each iteration. Although 15 personas are three to five times the standard number of personas (Pruitt & Grudin, 2003), we deem the higher number of personas reasonable for organizations with varied online audiences. The result of monthly data collection and repeated analysis is a series of monthly sets of organizational personas over the period. Once we have the complete series of 26 data sets, we then present the 15 top personas for each month. We use a system to automate this process and display the listings of personas, as shown in Figure 2 (i.e., a listing of multiple personas) and Figure 3 (i.e., one persona listing for readability of the topical interests).

Again, the topic classification method of automatic persona generation is explained in prior work (An et al., 2018a). However, as a brief overview, one of the benefits of using NMF for generating these personas, representing audience segments, is a clear association between the audience segments' interest and non-interest in specific digital content.

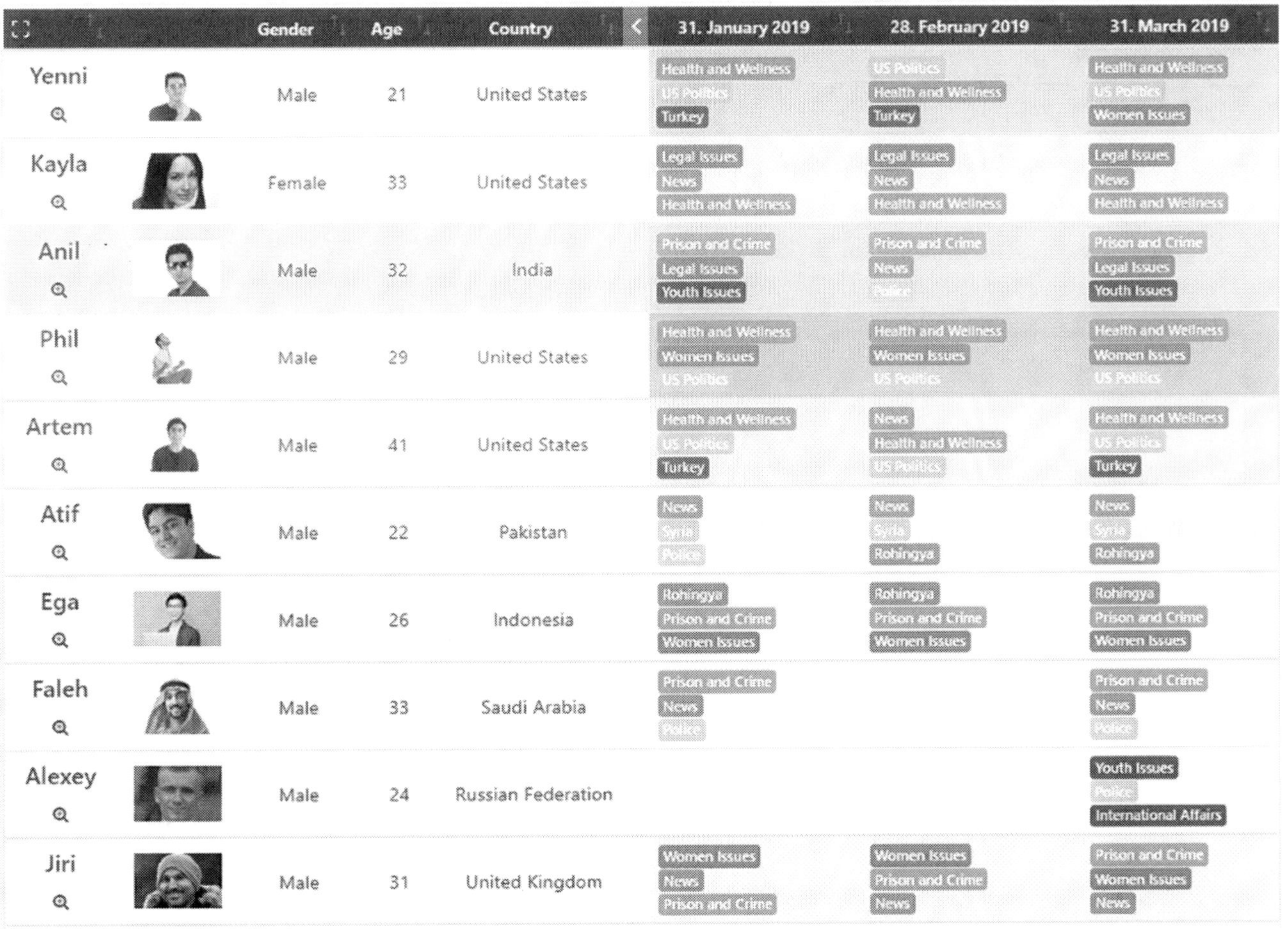

Figure 2. Screenshot of a portion of the persona sets. The left lists the specific personas. The top displays the month of the data collection. Along the right is the listing the top three topics of interest for each persona for each monthly data collection.

Figure 3. Screenshot of one persona with monthly data collection date and specific topics of interest for each period.

Beginning with this association, we can identify content that a given customer segment might be interested in even before content publication. For the problem of predicting interest in new content, the most intuitive solution is to find similar content that has already been published relative to the new content and assume that the level of interest in similar content will remain the same by a given audience segment. To compute the similarity of content in a robust way, we explicitly express the content features and how we leverage them for persona creation.

We define a matrix that captures the features of each piece of content. We then derive another matrix that represents an association between an audience segment and content features. Then, using Latent Dirichlet Allocation (LDA) (Blei, Ng, & Jordan, 2003), we cluster content into topical categories to which we assign a human interpretable label.

We quantify the topical interests for the personas by computing the Z-score for F_t^{i}. For the topic t and the persona i, as follows:

$$F_t^{i} = \frac{F_t^{i} - avg(F_t)}{\sigma} \quad (1)$$

where F_t is a set of F_t^{i} for any existing persona X, and σ is the standard deviation of the F_t. A higher Z-score means that a persona is more likely to view content belonging to a topic than the other personas. The result is a ranking of topics for each persona, as shown in Figure 4. The bars to the left indicate topics of most interest and the bars to the right indicate topics of least interest, relative to the entire set of personas generated for that monthly data collection.

In summary, we used the identical algorithmic process to generate both the personas and the topical interests of these personas for each monthly data collection. As such, the results from an identical process allowed for the comparison of topical interests across all months for each persona, which is the focus of the research we report here.

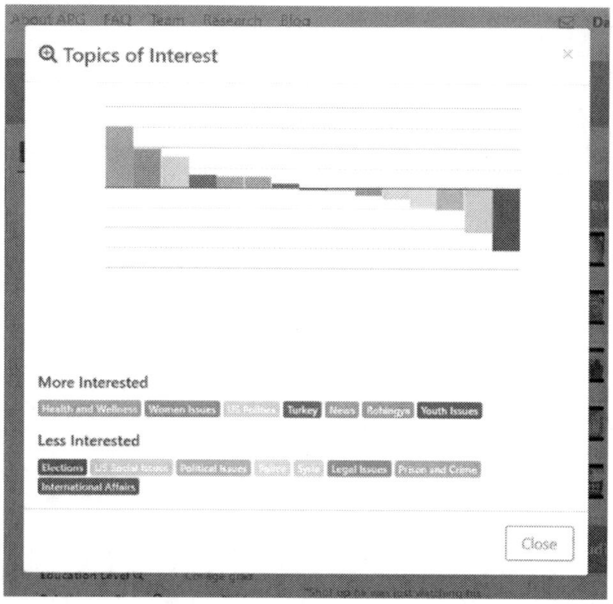

Figure 4. Screenshot of the ranking of topics by the interest for a specific persona. A similar calculation is computed for each persona for each data collection period. Note that a lower ranked topic does not imply non-interest, just less interest than a higher ranked topic.

Methodology for Comparing Topical Interest

We compare the top three topical interest of each persona month-over-month (MoM) (i.e., overlap expressed for the previous month. We selected the top three topics as this is what is presented in the persona profiles and most likely to be used by the organization for audience analysis. We did not consider the order of the three topics. Specifically, we define our consistency metric as the following:

$$\text{MoM} = (T_{PM} \Pi\, T_{CM})/T_{PM} \quad (2)$$

Where T_{PM} is the set of persona's topics in the prior month, T_{CM} is the set of persona's topics in the current month. Once we have the overlap for this metric, it is trivial to calculate the MoM change (i.e., the MoM change is one minus the MoM consistency value). Returning to our research questions, we now examine the change in topics of personas over time.

RESULTS AND DISCUSSION

Returning to our research questions, we first present overall findings and then examine RQ01 (*Do the topical interests of personas change over time?*) and RQ02 (*Do the changes in the topical interests of personas vary by the changes in the persona set?*).

Exploratory Results

Table 2 shows the aggregate distribution of topics during the 26-months of data collection. As shown in Table 2, the topics were stratified into three general clusters, a highly popular cluster (General News, Prison, and Crime, etc.), a mid-popular cluster (Women Issues, Syria, etc.), and less popular cluster (Turkey, US Politics, etc.).

	Topic	Count	%
1	General news	218	18.7
2	Prison and crime	154	13.3
3	Health and wellness	142	12.1
4	Police and law enforcement	129	11.0
5	Women issues	104	8.9
6	Syria and the syrian conflict	67	5.7
7	Youth issues	64	5.5
8	Legal issues	59	5.0
9	Refugee issues, Rohingya	59	5.0
10	Turkey MENA relations	49	4.2
11	US politics	49	4.2
12	International affairs	48	4.1
13	Elections (world)	12	1.0
14	US social issues	11	0.9
15	Political issues	5	0.4
		1170	100

Table 2. The distribution of topics over the entire data collection period of 26 months for 15 personas in each month.

Month-over-Month Change in Personas

To examine RQ01, we computed the MoM change, with findings presented in Table 3. As shown in Table 3, the average MoM change was 29.2% of topics among each set of 15 personas per month (standard deviation of 27.2%). The minimum MoM change was 0.0%, and the maximum MoM change was 82.6%. The median was 25.0%.

	MoM consistency (%)	MoM change (%)
Average	70.8	29.2
Std. dev.	72.8	27.2
Max	17.4	82.6
Min	100.0	0.0
Median	75.0	25.0

Table 3. Overall statistics for the topic of interest consistency and changes for the entire set of personas over the entire data collection period.

Table 4 shows the number of personas that experienced primarily higher months of change, higher months of consistency, and with change and consistency the same. As shown in Table 4, more than 68% of the personas experience a higher level of MoM change compared to consistency during the data collection period, and 5.7% of the personas experienced an equal amount of change.

So, returning to our RQ01, the topical interests of persona do change, and these interests can change rather rapidly. The topical interests by persona varied by approximately 29% MoM and more than 68% of the personas experienced more topical change than consistency MoM during the data collection period.

MoM	Number of Personas	%
Greater change	24	68.6
Equal	2	5.7
Greater consistency	9	25.7
	35	100.0

Table 4. MoM change and consistency of number of personas.

Change in Personas During the Entire Period

Moving to RQ02, concerning if the change in topical interest is correlated with the change in personas set, we examine the persona ordered by stability.

Table 5 shows the persistence of the personas' appearance over the period. As shown, a set of personas can be defined as: core audience, as they are always or nearly always in the audience, that are loyal customers (stability of 19–26 months); a set of customers that are generally but not always in the audience (8–12 months); and then a set of customers that stay in the audience for a short time (1–7 months).

We ran a Spearman correlation test to determine the strength and direction of the monotonic relationship between personas stability and topical consistency. Results of the test indicate that there is a significant and positive association between persona stability and topic consistency ($r_s(27) = .73$, $p < .05$). Figure 5 shows the relationship between persona stability and topical consistency. As shown, there is a positive relationship but also with outliers and some variance. So, the topical interests are affected by the stability of the persona set. The more consistent a persona is with an organization the more stable is their top interests.

Verification of Organizational Content

One factor that could have impacted the topical analysis is the content produced by the organization could have changed in a given month relative to what was published previously. To investigate this possibility, we compared the aggregated consistency of topics month-over-month for all content. We further compute the Jaccard coefficient that measures the

Months	Percentage of period (%)	Number of personas	% of personas
26	100	5	13.17
24	92	3	7.89
21	81	1	2.64
20	77	1	2.63
19	73	1	2.63
12	46	1	2.63
11	42	1	2.63
10	38	1	2.63
9	35	2	5.26
8	31	3	7.89
7	27	4	10.53
6	23	2	5.26
3	12	1	2.63
2	8	1	2.63
1	4	11	28.95
		38	100.00

Table 5. The stability of personas during the data collection period. Months is the number of months that a given persona appeared in the data set (i.e., the measure of stability).

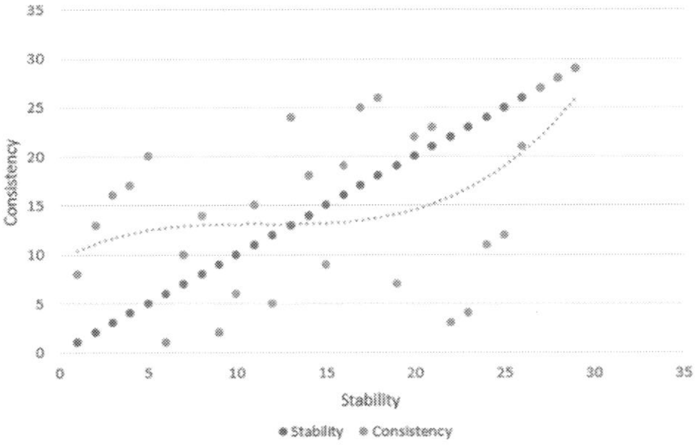

Figure 5. Plot with trend line and the equation of persona stability (x-axis) and topical consistency (y-axis).

overlap of two sets, which in our case are *set 1* = the topics in the prior month; and *set 2* = the topics in the current month. We use the first month as the starting baseline. Equation 3 shows the calculation for the Jaccard coefficient.

$$J = \frac{N_c}{N_a + N_b - N_c} \quad (3)$$

where:

N_a = Number of topics in the prior month.

N_b = Number of topics in the current month.

N_c = Number of topics in the intersection of the Prior Month and the current month.

As shown in Table 6, the average consistency was 97.0% (3.1% change). The average Jaccard coefficient was 0.93, indicating a high level of similarity among the topics published. These scores indicate further that the changes in interests noted in the topical drift of the personas were the result of changes in audience, changes in the audience preferences, or changes in both and not due to the availability of or changes in the content from the organization.

DISCUSSION AND IMPLICATIONS

In this research, we show that the topical interests of personas do change over time, confirming a central thesis in the persona literature. A key implication is that organizations using personas should engage in continuous data collection to ensure that potential changes in their audience base and interests are reflected in the personas they are using.

over time).The repeated data collection can be done via traditional means (i.e., surveys, analytics) or using automated methods, as done here. The advantage of using online data sources and algorithmic approaches for persona creation is the effortless comparison of changes over time and the use of identical methods for persona generation.

Our research also addresses the widely cited criticism of Chapman and Milham (2006) that argues *personas are beyond the scope of scientific validation* because their creative process cannot be replicated. By quantifying and standardizing the persona generation process and the attributes of the generated personas (in this case, their topics of interest), data-driven personas can be brought into the realm of scientific inquiry. While Chapman and Milham (2006) attempted this years ago, there has been little considerable progress since then regarding the longitudinal change of personas, a predisposition taken for granted in the literature. In this research, we clearly show how to quantify and measure

Month	Matching topics	Missing topics	Total topics	Consistency with prior month (%)	Jaccard coefficient with prior month
2	14	0	14	100.0	0.93
3	12	1	13	92.3	0.80
4	12	0	12	100.0	0.92
5	11	3	14	78.6	0.73
6	14	1	15	93.3	0.93
7	13	0	13	100.0	0.87
8	13	0	13	100.0	1.00
9	13	0	13	100.0	1.00
10	12	0	12	100.0	0.92
11	11	1	12	91.7	0.85
12	12	1	13	92.3	0.92
13	13	0	13	100.0	1.00
14	12	0	12	100.0	0.92
15	12	0	12	100.0	1.00
16	12	0	12	100.0	1.00
17	12	0	12	100.0	1.00
18	12	0	12	100.0	1.00
19	12	0	12	100.0	1.00
20	12	1	13	92.3	0.92
21	12	0	12	100.0	0.92
22	10	0	10	100.0	0.83
23	10	2	12	83.3	0.83
24	12	0	12	100.0	1.00
25	11	0	11	100.0	0.92
26	11	0	11	100.0	1.00
Total	300	10			
Average			12.4	97.0% (3.0% change)	0.93

Table 6. Comparison of the overall topics published by the organization MoM (with month 1 as the base). Matching topics is the number of topics in the current month that was also in the prior month. Total topics are the number of topics that occurred among all personas for the current month. Consistency is the MoM percentage of topics in the current month relative to the prior month.

Regarding online content consumption, our findings confirm and expand those reported in (Zhang et al., 2017) that noted a decrease in the consumption of content diversity over time (i.e., the content people consumed tended toward sameness

this change (consistency), finding results that validate the need for periodic updating of personas or any other customer/user profiles that are based on evolving analytics data. This novel aspect of this research, the concept of analyzing the change of audience behaviors as personas over time, is an innovative approach only made practically possible by the availability of large-scale online data that can be used for developing behavioral personas, as noted in prior work (e.g., Zhang, Brown, & Shankar, 2016).

Although there have been discussions in prior works concerning the possible change in personas (Chapman et al., 2008; Chapman & Milham, 2006), there is a subtle distinction in our research reported here, which concerns a change in content preferences, which we show is due to both (a) an underlying change in the audience and (b) some of the current audience undergoing changing preferences. For online content producing organizations, it highlights the need to monitor both large demographical changes in the audience and the more fluid fluctuations in audience preferences that have an impact on content consumption.

Future research could investigate the pace of topic change for a high-frequency content producer and a low-frequency content producer. The assumption is that the personas (i.e., audience composition) remain more stable for low-frequency content producers because no new audiences are attracted by the changing topic profile of the content. However, this assumption needs investigation.

Other future research could entail using the presented comparison approach to determine the optimal number of topical interests over a period of time, which could be the number where the period of change is minimized. This also highlights a possible limitation in our research, in that we might overestimate topic change by limiting our focus to only the top three topics. Future research could address this limitation. Finally, we could also examine the effect of detecting topical shifts on content automatically (Alkhodair, Ding, Fung, & Liu, 2019) for integration into an overall data-driven persona system. This could assist content companies in avoiding content becoming stale or having audience segments become bored with the content that is too similar to what they have consumed in the past. Online content companies could anticipate new content that would excite the audience via new content for audience segments.

CONCLUSION

We confirm that topical interests of online audiences can change over time, empirically validating a criticism of personas that their updating requires continual data collection and confirming that the underlying audience population can change. In the data set used here, there were substantial changes in topics, even within a relatively short period. This indicates that organizations incorporating personas or seeking to understand their audiences, in whatever manner the data is collected, should frequently update their audience insights, as changes are likely. Naturally, some of the answers to our research questions may vary organization to organization.

REFERENCES

Alkhodair, S. A., Ding, S. H. H., Fung, B. C. M., & Liu, J. (2019). Detecting breaking news rumors of emerging topics in social media. *Information Processing & Management.*

An, J., Kwak, H., Salminen, J., Jung, S. G., & Jansen, B. J. (2018a). Customer segmentation using online platforms: Isolating behavioral and demographic segments for persona creation via aggregated user data. *Social Network Analysis and Mining, 8*(1), 54.

An, J., Kwak, H., Salminen, J., Jung, S. G., & Jansen, B. J. (2018b). Imaginary people representing real numbers: Generating personas from online social media data. *ACM Transactions on the Web, 12*(4), 27.

Blei, D. M., Ng, A. Y., & Jordan, M. I. (2003). Latent Drichlet Allocation. *Journal of Machine Learning Research, 3*, 993–1022.

Chapman, C. N., Love, E., Milham, R. P., Elrif, P., & Alford, J. L. (2008). *Quantitative evaluation of personas as information.* In paper presented at the Proceedings of the Human Factors and Ergonomics Society Annual Meeting.

Chapman, C. N., & Milham, R. P. (2006). *The personas' new clothes: Methodological and practical arguments against a popular method.* In paper presented at the Proceedings of the Human Factors and Ergonomics Society Annual Meeting.

Cooper, A. (2004). *The inmates are running the asylum: Why high tech products drive us crazy and how to restore the sanity* (2nd ed.). Pearson Higher Education.

Drutsa, A., Gusev, G., & Serdyukov, P. (2017). Periodicity in user engagement with a search engine and its application to online controlled experiments. *ACM Transactions on the Web, 11*(2), 1–35.

Friess, E. (2012). *Personas and decision making in the design process: An ethnographic case study.* In paper presented at the Proceedings of the SIGCHI Conference on Human Factors in Computing Systems, Austin, TX.

Goodman, E., Kuniavsky, M., & Moed, A. (2013). *Observing the user experience: A practitioner's guide to user research* (2nd ed.). Morgan Kaufmann.

Goodwin, K., & Cooper, A. (2009). *Designing for the digital age: How to create human-centered products and services.* Indianapolis, IN: Wiley.

Hong, L., & Davison, B. D. (2010). *Empirical study of topic modeling in Twitter.* In paper presented at the Proceedings of the First Workshop on Social Media Analytics, Washington, DC.

Jansen, B. J., Jung, S.-G., Salminen, J., An, J., & Kwak, H. (2017). Viewed by too many or viewed too little: Using information dissemination for audience segmentation. *Proceedings of the Association for Information Science and Technology, 54*(1), 189–196.

Jenkinson, A. (1994). Beyond segmentation. *Journal of Targeting, Measurement and Analysis for Marketing, 3*(1), 60–72.

Jung, S., An, J., Kwak, H., Ahmad, M., Nielsen, L., & Jansen, B. J. (2017). *Persona Generation from Aggregated Social Media Data*. In paper presented at the ACM Conference on Human Factors in Computing Systems 2017 (CHI2017), Denver, CO.

Jung, S., Salminen, J., An, J., Kwak, H., & Jansen, B. J. (2018). *Automatically conceptualizing social media analytics data via personas*. In paper presented at the The International AAAI Conference on Web and Social Media (ICWSM 2018), San Francisco, CA.

Karimi, M., Jannach, D., & Jugovac, M. (2018). News recommender systems – Survey and roads ahead. *Information Processing & Management, 54*(6), 1203–1227.

Kwak, H., An, J., Salminen, J., Jung, S.-G., & Jansen, B. J. (2018). *What we read, what we search: Media attention and public attention among 193 countries*. In paper presented at the Proceedings of the 2018 World Wide Web Conference, Lyon, France.

Lee, D. D., & Seung, S. H. (1999). Learning the parts of objects by non-negative matrix factorization. *Nature, 401*(6755), 788–791.

Lee, E.-J., & Tandoc, E. C. (2017). When news meets the audience: How audience feedback online affects news production and consumption. *Human Communication Research, 43*(4), 436–449.

Li, C., Bai, J., Wenjun, Z., & Xihao, Y. (2019). Community detection using hierarchical clustering based on edge-weighted similarity in cloud environment. *Information Processing & Management, 56*(1), 91–109.

Lv, P., Meng, X., & Zhang, Y. (2017). FeRe: Exploiting influence of multi-dimensional features resided in news domain for recommendation. *Information Processing & Management, 53*(5), 1215–1241.

Mele, I., Bahrainian, S. A., & Crestani, F. (2019). Event mining and timeliness analysis from heterogeneous news streams. *Information Processing & Management, 56*(3), 969–993.

Mulder, S., & Yaar, Z. (2007). *A practical guide to creating and using personas for the web*. New Riders.

Nielsen, L., Hansen, K. S., Stage, J., & Billestrup, J. (2015). A template for design personas: Analysis of 47 persona descriptions from danish industries and organizations. *International Journal of Sociotechnology and Knowledge Development, 7*(1), 45–61.

Pruitt, J., & Grudin, J. (2003). *Personas: Practice and theory*. In paper presented at the Proceedings of the 2003 Conference on Designing for User Experiences, San Francisco, CA.

Salminen, J., Jansen, B. J., An, J., Kwak, H., & Jung, S. G. (2019). Automatic persona generation for online content creators: Conceptual rationale and a research agenda. In L. Nielsen (Ed.), *Personas - User focused design* (pp. 135–160).

Salminen, J., Kwak, H., An, J., Jung, S. G., & Jansen, B. J. (2018). Are personas done? Evaluating their usefulness in the age of digital analytics. *Persona Studies, 4*(2), 47–65.

Sánchez, P., & Bellogín, A. (2019). Building user profiles based on sequences for content and collaborative filtering. *Information Processing & Management, 56*(1), 192–211.

Segev, E., Sheafer, T., & Shenhav, S. R. (2013). Is the world getting flatter? A new method for examining structural trends in the news. *Journal of the American Society for Information Science and Technology, 64*(12), 2537–2547.

Sela, M., Lavie, T., Inbar, O., Oppenheim, I., & Meyer, J. (2015). Personalizing news content: An experimental study. *Journal of the Association for Information Science and Technology, 66*(1), 1–12.

Shepherd, M., Duffy, J. F., Watters, C., & Gugle, N. (2001). The role of user profiles for news filtering. *Journal of the American Society for Information Science and Technology, 52*(2), 149–160.

Toraman, C., & Can, F. (2017). Discovering story chains: A framework based on zigzagged search and news actors. *Journal of the Association for Information Science and Technology, 68*(12), 2795–2808. https://doi.org/10.1002/asi.23885

Vecchio, P. D., Mele, G., Ndou, V., & Secundo, G. (2018). Creating value from social big data: Implications for smart tourism destinations. *Information Processing & Management, 54*(5), 847–860.

Watters, C., & Wang, H. (2000). Rating news documents for similarity. *Journal of the American Society for Information Science, 51*(9), 793–804.

Xiao, D., Ji, Y., Li, Y., Zhuang, F., & Shi, C. (2018). Coupled matrix factorization and topic modeling for aspect mining. *Information Processing & Management, 54*(6), 861–873.

Zhang, H., Boons, F., & Batista-Navarro, R. (2019). Whose story is it anyway? Automatic extraction of accounts from news articles. *Information Processing & Management*.

Zhang, L., Zheng, L., & Peng, T.-Q. (2017). Structurally embedded news consumption on mobile news applications. *Information Processing & Management, 53*(5), 1242–1253.

Zhang, X., Brown, H.-F., & Shankar, A. (2016). *Data-driven personas: Constructing archetypal users with clickstreams and user telemetry*. In paper presented at the Proceedings of the 2016 CHI Conference on Human Factors in Computing Systems, San Jose, CA.

Teens' Everyday Information Practices on Mobile Media: "Catching Up" and "Reaching Out"

Junoh Kimm
University of Toronto
Toronto, Canada
junoh.kim@mail.utoronto.ca

Jefferey Boase
University of Toronto
Toronto, Canada
j.boase@utoronto.ca

ABSTRACT

Mobile media have become a central part of everyday life for many teens. We examine how teens use the media to access diverse information to maintain and reconnect with personal relationships in their personal networks. Based on semi-structured interviews with 81 teens from ethnically and economically diverse backgrounds, we find that teens generally have broad networks of ties with whom they communicate through both face-to-face interactions and mobile media. To maintain these networks, the teens in our study use information that they either unexpectedly encounter or purposely seek out on various platforms available on their mobile devices to "reach out" to dormant ties and "catch up" with active ties.

KEYWORDS

Teens; Mobile Media; Information Practices; Communication Networks

ASIS&T THESAURUS

Mobile Communications (1256); Information Behavior (805); Human Communications (972)

INTRODUCTION

Teens are now coming of age at a time when mobile media have created unprecedented access to both people and information (Rainie & Wellman, 2012). Globally, teens are not only at the forefront of adopting new information and communication technologies (International Telecommunication Union, 2017; Ling, 2010), but they are also pioneers in setting new social norms and establishing new practices in the digital world (Jenkins, Ito, & Boyd, 2016). To teens, mobile media are often an important part of their cultural, academic, and social lives, whereas to some adults, the rapid adoption of new technology and changes in everyday practices can be deeply disconcerting. To this day, research on mobile phone use has suggested contradictory findings about its implications in teens' everyday lives.

82nd Annual Meeting of the Association for Information Science & Technology | Melbourne, Australia | 19–23 October, 2019

DOI: 10.1002/pra2.00012

Concerns about the social implications of mobile media can be formalized in two contradicting hypotheses; (1) the material properties of mobile media are inherently limited in hosting genuine social interactions (Turkle, 2015; Twenge, 2017), and (2) mobile communication heightens connectivity with like-minded familiar relationships, at the expense of connections with people with diverse ideas and backgrounds (Campbell & Kwak, 2012; Habuchi, 2005; Wilken, 2009). Meanwhile, several youth media studies (e.g., Boyd, 2014; Ito et al., 2008; Livingstone & Sefton-Green, 2016; Vickery, 2017) have highlighted the possible supportive role that mobile media play in extending teens' daily participation in diverse networks as they make their way toward adulthood.

Recently, studies have indicated that smartphones can facilitate increased interaction with weak tie relationships that have the potential to provide diverse support and information (e.g., Kobayashi, Boase, Suzuki, & Suzuki, 2015; Schock, 2016). With the wide adoption of smartphones and contrary perspectives on the implications of teens' digital media engagements, there is an increasing need to understand how teens manage, reconnect, and strengthen their personal relationships using mobile media.

In this paper, we focus on the relationship between mobile media and personal networks by examining how teens use the media, as material *means*, to seek and encounter socially relevant information for staying in-touch or reconnecting with different individuals who can provide valuable support and ideas of the world around them.

For the purpose of analysis, we refer to dormant ties as those social connections that are relationally distant but can still be reached for support and information. These relationships can be thought of as those who were "present at one point in time, and absent in another, [and] may eventually return to the network" (Marin & Hampton, 2019, p. 3). Such loosely connected ties are more likely to provide information that is not readily available in one's immediate social circle (Burt, 1992; Granovetter, 1983). While interactions with close friends and family provide strong emotional support and a sense of belonging, reconnecting with dormant ties can provide new instrumental information, such as career opportunities, references, or suggestions regarding where to apply for college (Lin, 2001).

To understand teens' use of mobile media, we draw on the concept of everyday information practices (Savolainen, 1995, 2007, 2008). We understand information practices to include both active and less-directed practices (McKenzie, 2003). Recognizing that teens' use of mobile media is not always deliberate or strategic, this paper presents the ways in which teens maintain and reconnect with their personal network ties using mobile media as part of their everyday information practices.

LITERATURE REVIEW

Understanding Teens' Everyday Information Practices

Teens in this study are at a point when they need to explore and learn various ideas about themselves, others, and the world around them to make "meaningful life choices" (Agosto & Hughes-Hassell, 2006). Our approach to studying this population is different from one that assumes teens are in a transitional period characterized by rebellious behavior and a lack of reason (e.g., Hall, 1908). We recognize that adolescence is a social invention that emerged out of political, social, and economic agendas (Hine, 1999). In this research, teenage participants themselves and their daily experiences are respected as legitimate stories. This approach emphasizes a more nuanced exploration of teens' everyday experiences and practices of mobile media.

From the late 1970s, information research began looking at the mundane lived experiences of individuals (Case & Given, 2016). Reijo Savolainen argues that "everyday information practices may be understood as a set of socially and culturally established ways to identify, seek, use, and share the information available in various sources" (2008, p. 3). In contrast to work or specific task-oriented goals, everyday information is an overarching approach that encompasses diverse information engagements. This accounts for various mundane and socially embedded information practices that are both "active" and "less-directed" (McKenzie, 2003).

The transitional period of coming of age is a unique context that shapes their encountering, seeking, using, and sharing of information. Savolainen notes that "there is a need for empirical studies relating the spatial and temporal factors of information seeking" (2006). Within the body of scholarship studying human information behavior (Bates, 2010), a growing body of work has explored how different populations in transition have diverse information practices that include both active and less-direct information seeking (e.g., Allard & Caidi, 2018, on Filipino migrants' and their translocal information practices).

The exploration process of encountering, disassociating, and reconceptualising information is particularly important for individuals situated in transitional periods. People in transitional periods often face difficulty when imagining what information they need and how to find it (Allard & Caidi, 2018). With the structural limitations and social restrictions that teens experience today (Boyd, 2014; Vickery, 2017), teens are often under pressure to make their first major life-decisions without sufficient exploration and preparation. This research thus accounts for lived information experiences such as exploring, leisure activities, everyday sociality, and unanticipated information encountering from globalized diverse activities teens have on mobile media.

Personal Networks and Information

Information behavior studies have consistently found that "people choose other people as their preferred source of information" (Johnson, 2004; also see Lu, 2007; Shah, 2017). Structures of social network impact information flow, access, and use (Erickson, 1996; Haythornthwaite, 2005; Hersberger, 2003; Schutz, 2008; Veinot, 2010). Teens tend to be embedded in strong peer-based social structures and interactions because they are separated from adults for most of the day (Chudacoff, 1989).

Despite the dominance of local peer-based interactions, digital media has the potential to allow for more diverse connections by blurring the boundaries of time and space (Rainie & Wellman, 2012). However, personal networks are not fully mobilized from the constraints of time and space. Rather they take a "hybrid" form, whereby day-to-day in-person social interactions structure opportunities for future connection on mobile media (Hampton, 2016). Personal networks consist of diverse ties, such as loosely connected "weak ties" (e.g., old classmate friends on Facebook, or followers on Instagram) and closely connected "strong ties" (e.g., family and best friends).

The characteristics of personal networks exogenously condition the types of information and resources that an individual can access (Lin, 2001). Access to quality information and resources is dependent on the individual's ability to connect and develop networks of diverse social ties and communities with valuable information (Burt, 1992). This requires one to develop a robust communicative skillset for "investment in social relations" (Lin, 2001, p. 19). While the ways in which relationships facilitate information flow is relevant, teens have information priorities and practices different from adults because of their stage in life and their sociocultural spaces. Teens require a large pool of information where they can explore and experience different options to make long-term decisions, particularly where their education and careers are concerned. Meanwhile, their everyday practices are different from those of adults as they are embedded in a different type of peer-based society and culture. This study thus expands on previous work by examining how mobile media are used in everyday information practices to maintain active network ties and reactivated dormant network ties.

Mobile Media for Network Investment and Management

Having a robust personal network is important during transitional periods, such as coming of age or relocating. However, network studies consistently find people who undergo transitions typically lose about one-third to one-half of all ties who used to provide information and social support (e.g., Coleman, 1988; Ikkink & Tilburg, 1999; Small, 2017). This is particularly notable with students after graduation (Bidart & Lavenu, 2005; Roberts & Dunbar, 2011; Suitor & Keeton, 1997). These findings are consistent with more recent studies on student networks (Small, 2017; Small, Pamphile, & McMahan, 2015). The "persistent and pervasive" (Hampton, 2016) connectivity facilitated by mobile media may help to compensate for these network declines by helping teens engage their peer-networks (Boyd, 2014).

By allowing individuals to acquire and maintain an awareness of the social dynamics of ties within their networks, mobile media as a *means* may support teens in nurturing different types of relationships. Selfies or tweets shared by teens, for example, may seem unproductive or distractive activities, but they often serve a supportive role "to maintain robust learning ecologies and peer network" (Vickery, 2017). Studies on interpersonal communication have consistently found the significance of non-verbal interactions that serve to establish, maintain, and manage different social relationships and increase communication capabilities (Malinowski, 1943; Musolf, 2003; Pavlidou, 1994). The everyday practices teens have on mobile media may nurture relationships and initiate interactions with diverse ties.

Using digital media, teens share information that allows them to develop diverse social relationships (Vitak & Ellison, 2013). By feeding teens' knowledge of how others are doing, such information can lower the initial psychological and social barriers to initiate a conversation with individuals, particularly when reconnecting with dormant relationships. This paper focuses on this issue by exploring how teens understand their information practices on mobile media and the implications of these practices for maintaining and reactivating network ties.

RESEARCH QUESTIONS

The three governing questions for our exploration are:

1. How do teens use mobile media to interact with their personal networks?
2. What information practices do teens have on their mobile media to connect with their *active* social ties?
3. What information practices do teens have on their mobile media to connect with their *dormant* social ties?

METHOD

We draw on explorative and semi-structured interviews conducted in 2016 with an ethnically and economically diverse sample of 81 high school students living in the Greater Toronto Area. We interviewed this number of participants as in order to cover many other issues which were part of a larger project. We determined that we had interviewed a sufficient number of participants when saturation was reached in regards to the many topics that we covered (Corbin & Strauss, 2007). The male–female ratio held fairly even at 52 percent and 48 percent, respectively. Our 81 participants were between the ages of 15–19% and 51% of the participants reported low-income household.

The interviews were approximately 30 to 40 minutes long and held one-on-one in quiet public spaces, such as libraries and community centers. The majority of the interviews occurred in community centers where administrators provided permission to recruit teens. Some of the recruitment also occurred through word of mouth, where teens knew a participant or had seen the recruiting advertisement, and contacted the interviewers directly as a result. Interviewers focused their recruiting efforts in neighborhoods that were diverse in terms of neighborhood-level incomes and the ethnic composition of the residents. This recruiting method was designed to explore a variety of voices and perspectives during the interviews. Interviews were conducted and transcribed by a team of five trained graduate students. The first author then iteratively developed and applied codes as he immersed himself in the reading and rereading of these interviews. In this way, the codes emerged from the data, and allowed us to identify certain themes across multiple interviews. The interviews were manually transcribed to ensure the researchers would understand more nuanced information. We then iteratively developed and applied codes as we immersed ourselves in the reading and rereading of these interviews. The emergence of codes and themes that are shared by this diverse array of respondents suggests the existence of common perspectives and understandings.

The semi-structured interviews first started with a series of general questions focused on the various types of daily communication, including face-to-face and email. Drawing name generator technique (Fischer, 1982), interviewers then asked respondents to provide the first names of the following six specific types of individuals: (1) someone with whom they "enjoy socializing" (Wellman, 1979), (2) someone with whom they "discuss important matters" (Burt, 1984; Marsden, 1987), (3) someone who holds "significantly different values and beliefs" from themselves, (4) someone with whom they are "on good terms, but who is not part of their close core group" (Coser, 1975; Granovetter, 1983), (5) someone who has provided them with "information that helped accomplish something important" (McAllister & Fischer, 1978), and (6) someone who has helped them to "significantly rethink matters that are important" to them. For each of these ties, participants were asked a set of follow-up questions regarding how they communicate with them and other aspects of their relationship. At all points during these interviews, interviewers actively tried to listen to the participants and sought to understand the purposes, consequences, and stories behind their mobile media practices. As the collected data is sensitive, we use pseudonyms when quoting from the respondents.

FINDINGS

Participants

In the beginning of the interview, participants were asked to complete a short survey that included questions about their backgrounds, such as their parent's occupation and education level, the number of siblings living in the same household, activities that they do outside of school, and how they communicate using different types of media. Responses indicated that the teens in our study came from diverse socio-economic backgrounds (e.g., their parents were truck drivers, teachers, and dentists) and family structures (e.g., single parent or single child families), reflecting the economic and cultural diversity of the city. During the interviews, 12 teens mentioned their immediate family connections in China, Greece, Hong Kong, India, Jamaica, Pakistan, the Philippines, and the United States. The male–female ratio held fairly even at 52:48 and all participants were between the ages of 15 and 19. They had varying mobile data plans, while 10 participants did not have any data plan on their devices. Most participants described school and home Wi-Fi as providing their main connection to the internet. All participants were using two or more social media platforms with varying degrees of activities. While education performance was often mentioned as a daily concern, 15 participants reported that they were not satisfied with their education. Participants often had mixed feelings about school, and their feelings about it usually depended on their daily moods. Hana (18) described, "Sometimes I just have a bad day and I don't wanna be at school, and others it's like — I'm okay and happy."

An Overview: Network Information Practices

Despite varying degrees of limitations in data connectivity and accessing devices at school and home, the teens with whom we spoke described drawing on a wide range of mobile media to browse, seek, use, and share information about their networks. This information is often strategically collected, but also passively utilized to maintain relationally, culturally, and geographically diverse ties. Overall, our results indicate that mobile media are deeply embedded in teens' everyday lives as a means of obtaining information that helps them to reach out and catch up with diverse network ties.

Q1. How do teens use mobile media to interact with their personal networks?

For most teens in our study, mobile media are used to interact with friends and family. Their usage often depends on knowledge of their personal networks, and whether network ties might be attempting to contact them. When asked how often she checks her mobile phone, Jean (17) said,

> Throughout the day. Sometimes I don't always check it, like sometimes I'll check it on an hourly basis, while other days I'll check it, on like a, daily basis. So like, if I'm not expecting anybody to contact me on Facebook, then I probably won't check it until like the end of the day or the morning.

As discussed at the beginning of this paper, some scholars have argued that mobile media are incapable of fostering supportive interactions. To the contrary, the teens we interviewed are comfortably using a wide range of mobile media for both affective and instrumental interactions. Many teens explicitly described different practices associated with different mobile media, as seen in the response of Adam (17) when we asked about his daily mobile phone use.

> Different apps for different things. I'll use texting for quick messaging, see what's up, talk about homework, what's on tests, links, stuff like that. Email, check files and whatnot. For Snapchat, it is like what's going on in school — say if someone's doing a presentation we'll record them or something interesting.

Concerns that mobile media do not allow for supportive interaction often hinge on the assumption that mobile media do not provide enough social cues for successful or meaningful interactions. We find no evidence to support this view. Awareness of social cues is most notable when participants compared face-to-face interactions with mobile communication. Face-to-face communication was reported to be more phatic in nature, "random", and is often influenced by temporal and environmental factors. Lae (19) explained, "[f]or in-person, it is whatever that comes up. Usually, there are more people around so we talk about different things. Pretty random." In-person social practices generally consisted of less-goal-oriented phatic interactions with "no substance" (Jeff, 15), influenced by the temporal, "what's going on in my mind at that time" (Tin, 16), and spatial, "where we are" (Dawn, 17) factors. In contrast, teens were more strategic and purposeful with their mobile communication where they felt more "in-control" of the flow of interactions. They often strategically use mobile media, such as text messages, in a near-synchronous manner that facilitates constant continuous open-ended interactions. Uno (15) articulated why he chooses text messaging for specific types of interactions.

> Unlike talking, I think with text messages, you are looking at the words you are saying, there's a lot more review that goes into it. You can read over something and know that's going to come across weird, instead of just blurting it out.

When teens are discussing times when they have connected to people who are in a notable position in their networks or have more exclusive information, particularly regarding school and university admissions, they clearly articulate the different implicit cues associated with each type of media on their devices. Amy (17) described,

> I use email for school and like other important application stuff. It just seems formal. When you go on it, you are emailing a teacher or someone that is like in charge, right? Texting is so easy because it's always like… I guess … It just feels different. Social media is not very appropriate for these people.

Their media practices are not solely based on the content or purpose of the communication, especially as many mobile media are starting to offer similar functions (e.g., time-lapsed content sharing on Snapchat, WeChat, Instagram, and Facebook). They are rather dependent upon the nature of the relationship, such as the relational closeness or the norms of their community. Galen (15), for example, "prefer[s] calling over texting" with his "close friend" because, "texting is just kind of… you don't hear the sincerity inside their voice, and what they want to say." Meanwhile, he stated that text-based media (e.g., email, texting or WhatsApp) are his default communication channels for "not so close people" who often provide him information about university applications and volunteer works. Similarly, Elise (17) chooses WhatsApp and texting with her mentor from a summer camp to "talk about school, what's needed in school to keep it steady average, and what's needed to get a good scholarship and stuff, because that's what our camp friends use to communicate."

In short, the teens we interviewed showed a strong awareness of their mobile media use. They intentionally used a variety of mobile media – such as text messages, voice calling, etc. – and their media selection was based on a variety of factors. In many of their comments, the teens further demonstrated an awareness of social cues, and could describe how these cues factored into their use of this technology. These results are in stark opposition to the view that teens are passively manipulated by mobile media, and that mobile media use is necessarily detrimental to their relationships and day-to-day resources.

Q2. What information practices do teens have on their mobile media to connect with their active social ties?

One of the most notable practices that we observed among the teens was the extension of their daily face-to-face interactions through various mobile media, which help to keep connections active across time and space. Teens described these short and frequent interactions as "catching up." This practice of catching up helps them to maintain their active relationships with parents, classmates, siblings, and "best-friends." Indeed, our participants often reported that the majority of their calls and texts made on their devices were to coordinate their daily schedule with parents. Vishal's (16) mom is a frequent flyer and they rely heavily on mobile media for their daily interactions. He described,

> She does tell me she is going on a flight or to make sure I brush my teeth and do all the chores. Saying I love you… take care before she is going on a flight and she calls me a lot so we just talk.

These short-burst catching up practices symbolically maintain their relationships by sharing content that can vary from humorous videos, found while "randomly" browsing on social media, to mundane day-to-day activities. Rather than conveying specific information, these practices often carry more phatic messages similar to the face-to-face interactions. This reaffirms and keeps connections active across different platforms. Maya (18) described,

> On Facebook, I usually text and call her. Snapchat is like, when I wanna snap of me doing something [and] send her, and Instagram is like when I see a funny video and I will just DM [direct message] her… It's like catching up, like how are you and stuff. I'll just text a couple of words.

We find that mobile media are not only used to connect directly with ties, but they are used as part of the information practices that proceed from and shape those interactions. As part of everyday information practices, teens in our study use and share information that they encounter and seek out on various mobile media to connect with active ties. In particular, social networking media such as Facebook and Instagram are often used to obtain network information resources to genuinely connect with diverse ties and increase awareness of their relationships. Bryce (19) explains his Instagram use with his classmates as follows,

> Just like, pictures of them, like a basketball game, they would record a little bit of the basketball game. … If I see a nice picture, or if he does something good on basketball, I'll be like — "Oh, that was a nice shot."

Socially relevant information obtained from mobile media often becomes a resource to catch up with relationally weaker ties. Likemany, Hana (16) acquires information about her new classmate whom she describes as being, "not that close yet." This information then becomes an icebreaker for, "getting to know each other" better. She explains,

> I see something like the vacation they went [sic], something cool. That kind of stuff on Instagram. Then, usually [I use] Facebook message to talk about her vacation, [asking] how was it, but we usually talk about school stuff, homework, or like things the teacher said in class. Things I don't get.

With distant ties who are not part of the core social group, such as an acquaintance from work or someone from an after school program, our participants used mobile media to artfully catch up. Teens often use and share the information resources they encounter from mobile media to send friendly messages to show their interests in a tie's daily activity or hobby. Sunny (17) is not "exactly interested" in dancing, however, when she sees her friend's post about dancing practice, she responses as a way to keep on good term with this friend. She described,

> We see each other once a week in person. We usually text, "How're you doing?" [I see her] Facebook posts about 3 times a week. Usually about herself dancing. [I] don't often direct message her, but sometimes [I do] to share her dancing stuff about YouTube. We're only on social media, [we don't] text and call.

Similarly, Tony (15) connects with ties with varying degrees of closeness using mobile media. He said that social media on his smartphone is particularly useful when connecting with his classmate outside of his core group of friends. The interactions with these ties would not have been active without mobile media. He explained, "I don't know, it's just to talk to different friends, so, like, I really don't need to hear sincerity in their voice — It's awkward."

Teens articulated their mobile media as a way to extend their everyday interactions with family and friends. They use the information that they encounter on mobile media – particularly mobile based social media – during their interactions with both relationally strong and weaker ties. These catching up practices often facilitate phatic information exchanges, which reaffirm and maintain their personal networks.

Q3. What information practices do teens have on their mobile media to connect with their *dormant* social ties?

The participants in our study generally describe reconnecting with dormant ties as "reaching out." In comparison to other means, teens find mobile media are "easier" for tie reconnection. This is especially true when they use mobile media to connect with ties that help them to accomplish something important, rethink important matters, or learn something new. Most of the teens in our study shared the view that, "[mobile communication is] more convenient and just easy to reach out" (Nadia, 17).

Lorna (18) used to live in Jamaica until her family immigrated to Canada 2 years ago. The physical distance introduced by the cross-border migration has negatively impacted her personal network. As a result, her migration experience has been challenging. In fact, she struggled to think of just one close friend in Canada. Other than her parents, a large part of her network is based in Jamaica. While the two-years absence of the face-to-face interactions poses a challenge to keeping her ties intact, mobile media play a key role in reaching out to these ties that have become dormant. Reaching out to dormant ties in Jamaica gives her a sense of belonging and comfort during the challenging time. She said,

> If I have, like, myself might have problems, like that I have something I don't want to talk to anyone else [about], like [I] talk to her about it.

When discussing her experience of reaching out to a friend that she has known for 8 years, she mentioned,

> We met in grade five. She was new to the school. But, I mean, we were not really close ever since I left Jamaica but... we talk, but like once ... I asked how she's doing. She would ask me how was Canada and, like, if I find a new friend or how is has been, or when [I will] come see her, or yeah, stuff like that.

During the emotionally taxing period of resettlement, practices for reaching out on mobile media provide access to emotional support from both frequently contacted close friends, and from dormant ties back home.

Even teens who did not experience such a significant life transition like Lorna go through several network changes as they move from elementary to middle school, and middle school to high school. Most teens we spoke to had friends who were very close at one point in time, but are no longer close. Wendy (17) articulated,

> I was friends with them from elementary school. I think we were fairly close. But we are not as close [as] we're in high school now. We texted stuff like we should meet up or talking about general school stuff.

Reconnecting with ties that are not part of teens' core groups is particularly important as these ties can provide them information that is not available in immediate environments. Reaching out to dormant ties mostly occurred when teens sought information that helped them accomplish something important, such as finding a part-time job, completing a task at school, or finding extracurricular activities. Marc (15) said,

> I text my sister's friend if I'm needing help with, like homework or school. They're in university. I'm connected with her on Facebook and Snapchat. She typically posts if she's traveled somewhere.

Marc does not directly communicate with this tie after she entered university. He encounters information about what's going on in this person's life while he is "just sort of scrolling through the feed" on Snapchat. This information acquired during social media browsing becomes a social resource that he uses to start interactions when he needs help with his school work.

Most of our participants repeatedly mentioned that they always need help with their homework. Their descriptions implied that they understood that their networks contained resources, and that it was necessary to use information when reaching out to network ties to obtain these resources.

Similarly, Sergey (16) explained his Facebook use,

> I'd say I use Facebook may be 3 to 4 times a day and I only really talk to people. I don't really post anything. I don't really like browsing, but I just every now and then I browse my newsfeeds and talk to people about it. It makes the conversation less awkward sometimes. Like, how was the trip? Or like, you know, everything alright with whatever, but mostly I just talk to people who either I don't have their number or we [are] both online at the same time and typing is a little faster than texting.

Teens generally had an expectation that social networking applications, particularly Facebook, are useful for reconnecting with dormant ties. Many teens we interviewed did not share or post anything on those applications, but rather kept them as address books to reconnect with their ties in the future. Indeed, participants were only interacting with a limited number of contacts on these media. While many teens strategically use socially relevant information resources to genuinely reach out to their dormant ties for instrumental resources, some teens kept different media accounts active on their devices solely for any potential reconnections with their dormant ties. Chris (15) does not "interact [with anyone] publicly on Facebook." When we asked him in what situation he would Facebook message someone who had helped him significantly rethink matters that are important to him, he said,

> We used to be better friends but we kind of drifted apart. Maybe... If I need, like, homework. Because I don't have, like, photo-texting. So, if they're going to send me pictures of their homework. I might only get them in this way.

Teens' mobile media have two roles in facilitating their practice of reaching out. First, they provide teens a chance to encounter information about how others are doing either directly or less-directly. These information resources then become a way of starting a genuine interaction that helps them to reconnect with the dormant tie. Second, teens have general expectations that mobile media with social networking functions, particularly Facebook, act as address books. That is to say, they view them as repositories of contact information that can be used to locate and connect with dormant ties in the future. Most teens we interviewed did not have the actual phone numbers of their dormant ties, but rather they find mobile networking applications to be the "go-to" channel to reconnect.

DISCUSSION

This article examines various information practices that teens have on mobile media and the implications for maintaining and reconnecting their personal relationships. Contrary to scholarship that views mobile media as necessarily detrimental to personal relationships, we find that teens actively use mobile media to connect with a variety of ties. We describe the ways in which teens encounter socially located information about their ties on mobile media and use these media to reach out and catch up with relationally varied ties. In the discussion that follows we focus first on the findings regarding catching up with active relationships, before proceeding to discuss the findings regarding reaching out to dormant relationships.

Catching Up with Active Networks

Early mobile phones were limited in facilitating diverse information and social practices. They were largely used for social grooming and coordinating activities (Ling & Yttri, 2002). The limited calling and SMS texting functions of mobile phones contributed to the development of the tele-cocooning hypothesis (Habuchi, 2005; Kobayashi & Boase, 2014), which holds that mobile communication hinders network diversification and expansion (Campbell & Kwak, 2012). Today, mobile media allow for multiplex, spatially unbounded, and highly frequent information practices with a broad range of ties (Schrock, 2015). Despite the new technological functionality of mobile media, our participants had robust networks rooted in the offline world.

The teens in our study use mobile media to catch up and maintain their networks of active ties. With active ties, teens often send short burst signals rather than long formal communication to catch up. Licoppe (2004) refers to this type of activity as "connected presence." Catching up practices include leveraging the information they either encounter or seek, to start a conversation, or share their daily events with the activated ties. These practices promote social cohesions and intimacy. Similar to the tele-cocooning hypothesis, Ling's (2008) notion of bounded solidarity is that mobile interaction fosters intimacy, cohesion, and shared rituals within a particular social realm that insulates one's social network.

While the short catching up practices are to extend shared norms and belongingness beyond physical co-presence, we also found that these practices exist with relationally weaker ties. This finding reveals an understudied aspect of mobile interaction among teens. It run contrary to the tele-cocooning hypothesis, which assumes that constant interaction with strong ties will necessarily come at the expense of interaction with weaker ties.

Another important and understudied finding of this study is that teens maintain daily information practices through mobile social media platforms that are critical to maintaining active tie connections. Their casual browsing of social media apps provides them with information that they can use as part of catching up. Although adults may view this type of activity as unnecessary, it serves the important social function of meditating active social connections.

Reaching Out to Dormant Ties

In this paper, we found that teens often consider different relational factors, such as closeness, frequency of contact, community, and the other person's preferences when deciding how to start conversations with dormant ties. Their approach to reconnection shows that information practices are a key part of this process.

Sometimes teens purposely seek out information that they can use to reconnect with dormant ties, and other times they happen upon this information during their daily use of social media apps. The great diversity of information platforms and technologies available on mobile devices today have increased both the chance of encountering information about their network and the ability to seek out the information. This increases connectivity, convenience, and exposure to information about network ties, such as their vacations, life changes, what they like or think throughout the day. In turn, this shared information allows teens to reactivate dormant ties.

Teens reach out to ties as they identify information gaps, information needs, and information resources. When teens reach out to dormant ties, they often start by liking a person's post, poking them, or sharing culturally embedded images such as digital memes or interesting articles. These specific practices vary between the participants and they often evolve, reinvent, and recreate these practices over time. This finding does not support concerns that mobile media are manipulating teens and their use of this media is passive (Turkle, 2015; Twenge, 2017). We find that teens are using social media on their own terms, and that they are often changing these practices as needed. Teens use "tactics to negotiate" (de Certeau, 1984) the material properties of mobile media to fit in their everyday practices.

Future Research

The two information practices for network management observed in this study, reaching out and catching up, shed light on questions about the potentially positive role that mobile media can play in teen life. Nevertheless, the current study has not explored the negative consequences of these social connections. As Portes (1998) and other network scholars have pointed out, although they provide important benefits, social relationships can have downsides. Peer pressure, bullying, and other negative influences all exist within personal networks. Although this was not a theme that came out of our interviews, future researchers would do well to explore the situations in which catching up and reaching out disadvantage teens.

Another limitation of this study is the sample population and its size. We have not explored the role that mobile media play in facilitating information and network ties among other sociodemographic groups, such as teens living in low-income families, and teens in smaller urban, or rural towns. Further exploration is needed to determine whether teens in these environments use mobile media in ways that are similar to the participants in our study. Additionally, while this exploration provides insight into different practices teens have on their mobile media for their network management, a larger scale study would be required to see if these findings exist in the general population.

REFERENCES

Agosto, D. E., & Hughes-Hassell, S. (2006). Toward a model of the everyday life information needs of urban teenagers, part 1: Theoretical model. *Journal of the American Society for Information Science and Technology, 57*, 1394–1403.

Allard, D., & Caidi, N. (2018). Imagining Winnipeg: The translocal meaning making of Filipino migrants to Canada. *Journal of the Association for Information Science and Technology, 69*, 1193–1204.

Bidart, C., & Lavenu, D. (2005). Evolutions of personal networks and life events. *Social Networks, 27*(4), 359–376.

Boase, J. (2008). Personal networks and the personal communication system. *Information, Communication & Society, 11*(4), 490–508.

Boyd, d. (2014). *It's complicated : The social lives of networked teens*. New Haven, CT: Yale University Press.

Burt, R. S. (1992). *Structural holes*. Cambridge, MA: Harvard University Press.

Campbell, S. W. (2018). From Frontier to Field: Old and New Theoretical Directions in Mobile Communication Studies. *Communication Theory, 29*(1), 46–65.

Campbell, S. W., & Kwak, N. (2012). Mobile communication and strong network ties: Shrinking or expanding spheres of public discourse? *New Media and Society, 14* (2), 262–280.

Case, D. O., & Given, L. G. (2016). *Looking for information: A survey of research on information seeking, needs and behavior* (4th ed.). Bingley: Emerald.

Catman, E. A. (1996). The impoverished life world of outsiders. *Journal of the American Society for Information Science, 47*, 193–206.

Chudacoff, H. P. (1989). *How Old Are You?: Age Consciousness in American Culture*. Princeton, NJ: Princeton University Press.

Coleman, J. (1988). Social Capital in the Creation of Human Capital. *American Journal of Sociology, 94*, S95–S120.

Corbin, J. M., & Strauss, A. (2007). *Basics of qualitative research: Techniques and procedures for developing grounded theory* (3rd ed.). Los Angeles, CA: Sage Publications.

De Certeau, M. (1984). *The practice of everyday life*. Berkeley, CA: University of California Press.

Dervin, B. (1992). From the minds' eye of the user: The sensemaking qualitative quantitative methodology. In J. Glazier & R. Powell, *Qualitative research in information management* (p. 6184). Englewood, CA: Libraries Unlimited.

Erickson, B. (1996). Culture, class, and connections. *The American Journal of Sociology, 102*(1), 217–251.

Fischer, C. (1982). *To dwell among friends: Personal networks in town and city*. Chicago, IL: University of Chicago Press.

Granovetter, M. (1983). The strength of weak ties: A network theory revisited. *Sociological Theory, 1*, 210–233.

Habuchi, I. (2005). Accelerating re exivity. In M. Ito & D. Okabe, *Personal, portable, pedestrian: Mobile phones in Japanese life* (pp. 165–182). Cambridge, MA: MIT Press.

Hampton, K. N., Lee, C. J., & Her, E. J. (2011). How new media affords network diversity: Direct and mediated access to social capital through participation in local social settings. *New Media & Society, 13*, 1031–1049.

Haythornthwaite, C. (2005). Social networks and Internet connectivity effects. *Information, Communication & Society, 8*(2), 125–147.

Hersberger, J. (2003). A qualitative approach to examining information transfer via social networks among homeless populations. *The New Review of Information Behavior Research, 1*(1), 95–108.

Hine, T. (1999). *The rise and fall of the American teenager*. New York, NY: Perennial.

Ikkink, K. K., & Tilburg, T. V. (1999). Broken ties: Reciprocity and other factors affecting the termination of older adults' relationships. *Social Networks, 21*(2), 131–146.

International Telecommunication Union. (2017). *ICT facts and figures 2017*. Geneva, Switzerland.

Ito, M., Horst, H., Bittanti, M., Boyd, D., Herr-Stephenson, B., Lange, P., & Robinson, L. (2008). *Living and learning with new media: Summary of findings from the digital youth project*. Cambridge, MA: MIT Press.

Ito, M., Okabe, D., & Matsuda, M. (2005). *Personal, portable, pedestrian: Mobile phones in Japanese life*. Cambridge, MA: MIT Press.

Jenkins, H., Ito, M., & Boyd, D. (2016). Participatory culture in a networked Era: A conversation on youth, learning, commerce, and politics. *Journal of Identity and Migration Studies, 10*(2), 214.

Johnson, C.A. (2004). Choosing people: The role of social capital in information seeking behaviour. *Information Research, 10*(1), paper 201.

Kobayashi, T., & Boase, J. (2014). Tele-cocooning: Mobile texting and social scope. *Journal of Computer-Mediated Communication, 19*(3), 681–694.

Kobayashi, T., Boase, J., Suzuki, T., & Suzuki, T. (2015). Emerging from the cocoon? Revisiting the tele-cocooning hypothesis in the smartphone era. *Journal of Computer- Mediated Communication, 20*(3), 330–345.

Licoppe, C. (2004). 'Connected' presence: the emergence of a new repertoire for managing social relationships in a changing communication technoscape. *Environment and Planning D: Society and Space, 22*(1), 135–156.

Lin, N. (2001). *Social capital: A theory of social structure and action*. Cambridge, England: Cambridge University Press.

Ling, R. (2008). *New tech, new ties: How mobile communication is reshaping social cohesion*. Cambridge, MA: MIT Press.

Ling, R. (2010). Texting as a life phase phenomenon. *Journal of Computer-Mediated Communication, 15*, 2797–2292.

Livingstone, S., & Sefton-Green, J. (2016). *The class: Living and learning in the digital age*. New York, NY: NYU Press.

Lu, Y. (2007). The human in human information acquisition: Understanding gatekeeping and proposing new directions in scholarship. *Library & Information Science Research, 29*(1), 103123.

Malinowski, B. (1943). The pan-African problem of culture contact. *American Journal of Sociology, 48*(6), 649–665.

Marin, A., & Hampton, K. N. (2019). Network instability in times of stability. *Sociology Forum, 34*, 313–336.

Marsden, P. (1987). Core discussion networks of Americans. *American Sociological Review, 52*(1), 122–131.

McKenzie, P. (2003). A model of information practices in accounts of everyday-life information seeking. *Journal of Documentation, 59*(1), 19–40.

Musolf, G. (2003). *Structure and agency in everyday life : An introduction to social psychology*. Lanham, MD: Rowman & Littlefield.

Pavlidou, T. (1994). Contrasting German-Greek politeness and the consequences. *Journal of Pragmatics, 21*, 487–511.

Portes, A. (1998). Social capital: Its origins and applications in modern sociology. *Annual Review of Sociology, 24* (1), 1–24.

Portes, A., & Landolt, P. (1996). The downside of social capital. *The American Prospect*, *94*(1), 18–21.

Quan-Haase, A., Mo, G., & Wellman, B. (2017). Connected seniors: How older adults in East York exchange social support online and offline. *Information, Communication & Society*, *20*(7), 967–983.

Rainie, H., & Wellman, B. (2012). *Networked: The new social operating system*. Cambridge, MA: MIT Press.

Roberts, S., & Dunbar, R. (2011). The costs of family and friends. *Evolution and Human Behavior*, *32*(3), 186–197.

Savolainen, R. (1995). Everyday life information seeking: Approaching information seeking in the context of way of life. *Library and Information Science Research*, *17* (3), 259–294.

Savolainen, R. (2007). Information behavior and information practice: Reviewing the umbrella concepts of information-seeking studies. *Library Quarterly*, *77*(2), 109–132.

Savolainen, R. (2008). *Everyday information practices: A social phenomenological perspective*. Toronto, Canada: Scarecrow Press.

Schrock, A. (2015). Communicative affordances of mobile media: Portability, availability, locatability, and multimediality. *International Journal of Communication*, *9*(1), 1229–1246.

Schutz, J. B. (2008). Examining information behavior through social networks. *Journal of Documentation*, *65* (4), 592–631.

Shah, C. (2017). *Social information seeking: Leveraging the wisdom of the crowd*. Berlin, Germany: Springer.

Small, M., Pamphile, V., & McMahan, P. (2015). How stable is the core discussion network? *Social Networks*, *40*, 90–102.

Small, M. L. (2017). *Someone to talk to*. Oxford, England: Oxford University Press.

Suitor, J., & Keeton, S. (1997). Once a friend, always a friend? Effects of homophily on women's support networks across a decade. *Social Networks*, *19*(1), 51–62.

Twenge, J. (2017). *IGen: Why today's super-connected kids are growing up less rebellious, more tolerant, less happy and completely unprepared for adulthood (and what this means for the rest of us)*. New York, NY: Simon & Schuster.

Veinot, T. (2010). We have a lot of information to share with each other: Understanding the value of peer-based health information exchange. *Information Research*, (4), 15.

Vickery, J. (2017). *Worried about the wrong things: Youth, risk, and opportunity in the digital world*. Cambridge, MA: MIT Press.

Vitak, J., & Ellison, N. (2013). There's a network out there you might as well tap': Exploring the benefits of and barriers to exchanging informational and support-based resources on Facebook. *New Media & Society*, *15*(2), 243–259.

Wellman, B. (1979). The community question. *American Journal of Sociology*, *84*(5), 1201–1231.

Wellman, B., Hogan, B., Berg, K., Boase, J., Carrasco, J., Coté, R., … Tran, P. (2006). Connected lives: The project. In P. Purcell, *Networked neighborhoods* (pp. 161–216). Berlin, Germany: Springer.

Wells, M., & Mitchell, K. (2008). How do high-risk youth use the internet? Characteristics and implications for prevention. *Child Maltreatment*, *13*(3), 227–234.

Wilken, R. (2009). Bonds and bridges: Mobile phone use and social capital debates. In R. Ling & S. W. Campbell, *Mobile communication: Bringing us together and tearing us apart* (pp. 127–149). New Brunswick, Canada: Transaction.

The Landscape of Archived Studies in a Social Science Data Infrastructure: Investigating the ICPSR Metadata Records

Jian-Sin Lee
University of Washington,
Seattle, USA
roxine19@uw.edu

Wei Jeng
National Taiwan University,
Taipei, Taiwan
wjeng@ntu.edu.tw

ABSTRACT

Data sharing and reuse practices in social sciences have changed in the past few decades with the continuing development of cyber-infrastructures. However, little is known about how such practices chronically change over time. Via the lens of 35 years' worth of archived data on the world's largest social science data infrastructure, ICPSR, this study aims to reveal data characteristics (e.g., archived data themes and temporal distribution) that shape and represent the trend of social science data sharing and reuse. After a preliminary analysis on metadata of 10,362 studies and 159,616 associated citation records, an upward trend is found regarding the number of studies archived on ICPSR and their citation counts. We also report problems with metadata standards and the challenges of reusing data derived from these studies. Our results can be a cornerstone to investigate the roles of ICPSR as a research data infrastructure within the context of open science.

KEYWORDS

Metadata; Research Data Sharing; Data Citation; Data Curation; Social Science Data Infrastructure; ICPSR

ASIS&T THESAURUS

Metadata; Research Data Sets; Information Infrastructure

INTRODUCTION

Since the early 2000s, governments all over the world have attached great importance to open science when creating scientific research policies. Such an agenda for open science and open data is supported by mandates for data management or data sharing plans from research funding agencies, e.g., the National Science Foundation (NSF), the UK Research Councils, and the European Commission (Lyon, 2016). In order to help researchers meet these requirements, research data infrastructure (hereafter: RDI), including data repositories that are located "outside" the research environment, has been built to enable research data sharing and reuse (Latif, Limani, & Tochtermann, 2019).

82nd Annual Meeting of the Association for Information Science & Technology | Melbourne, Australia | 19–23 October, 2019

DOI: 10.1002/pra2.00062

Within the context of open science, RDI allows researchers to facilitate data reuse, encourage scientific collaboration, and achieve higher research impact through data sharing (Beitz, Groenewegen, Harboe-Ree, Macmillan, & Searle, 2014). Previous work (Jeng, He, & Chi, 2017; Mongeon et al., 2017) has also found that data citation can incentivize data sharing, as it can potentially increase research visibility or accumulate scholarly impact. Such a rewarding system, based on data metrics, is believed to have a positive influence on researchers' career development.

However, data sharing practices among different disciplines are not evenly developed (Tenopir et al., 2011). As early as the 1970s and 80s, social scientists documented that they were already reusing secondary data to validate original studies or to produce new research via re-analysis (Fienberg, Martin, & Straf, 1985). With the rapid and continuing development of cyber-infrastructures, research data sharing and reuse in social sciences has changed in the past few decades. Today, networked technologies, mandates, policies, and discipline norms all come on stage to influence individual researchers' data activities and practices. Among these determinants, the advancement of cyber-infrastructure has drastically changed how social scientists share data, in comparison to data sharing practices before the Internet was commonly used. More specifically, instead of resorting to portable storage devices such as magnetic tapes, cassettes, or hard/floppy disks to distribute data (Clubb, Austin, Geda, & Traugott, 1985), researchers now share data via certain forms of research infrastructure in the digital age (Bernard, Wutich, & Ryan, 2017).

Cragin, Palmer, Carlson, and Witt (2010) studied scholars' data sharing practices and willingness from small sciences in the 2000s. The team revealed the research infrastructure for social science disciplines, such as preferred file exchange formats, file size, and embargo time (i.e., data not published or shared until a set date or certain conditions have been met) for researchers. Based on the curation profile published on the project website (Zilinski & Lorenz, 2012; Tancheva, 2012), social science subjects such as linguistics and etymology handle very large files in a single project: each file can range from 150 MB to 3 GB. However, embargo time varies. One research team may set a 5.5-year embargo time, whereas another team may not specify a restriction. Cragin et al. (2010) found that very few scholars routinely deposit their research data into data repositories. The study also shows that although providing resources and services for shared data is considered important, no field-wide norms have been established.

In social science disciplines, different data practices can also be observed. Compared to STEM disciplines, social scientists are more likely to be concerned about data misuse by others. Tenopir et al. (2011, 2015) conducted a national investigation with social science researchers as survey participants. The survey found that social scientists are less likely to make their data electronically available to others when compared with STEM scholars. Overwhelmingly, 162 out of the 204 (79%) social scientist participants agreed or somewhat agreed that they had concerns about data being used in unintended ways.

Over the past few decades, the Internet and cloud storage technologies, as well as initiatives from governments and funding agencies, do help disseminate data. However, little is known about how data sharing and reuse practices in social sciences chronically change over time.

Robinson, Mongeon, Jeng, and Costas (2017) have explored over 6 million metadata records downloaded from DataCite, one of the most comprehensive interdisciplinary sources for open data currently available, to determine its potential to be a new source for data metrics development. They reported critical data characteristics such as resource type, geographic distribution, and publication year. The team also made recommendations for DataCite to provide better metadata standards. To echo such efforts, further studies can be conducted to investigate the landscape of social science data sharing in a longer timeframe. In doing so, the roles of an RDI in the context of open science can be mapped. Also, an RDI itself (e.g., metadata schemes) and its working mechanisms (e.g., potential influences on data citation) are likely to be improved to facilitate more data sharing and reuse practices.

Case Study: ICPSR

One of the top choices for many social scientists to archive data, the Inter-university Consortium for Political and Social Research (ICPSR) was established in 1962, and is located at the Institute of Social Research, University of Michigan, the U.S. We selected ICPSR as our study site because it supports or adopts:

1. *Historical archive, rich data collections*. For nearly 60 years (1962-), ICPSR has been the world's largest data repository of social science research. As of mid-June 2019, ICPSR hosts 11,080 studies as well as over 70,000 datasets, and indexes 82,360 unique data-related publications. According to the website's description, thematic collections on the site include research topics on "criminal justice, health & aging, substance abuse & mental health, child care, and health & medical care" (ICPSR, n.d.-a).
2. *Mature data standard development*. Metadata in data curation and reuse processes is the key to ensuring that research data can be well discovered, accessed, used, preserved, disseminated, and tracked. The Data Documentation Initiative (DDI), adopted by ICPSR, is a long-standing standard for describing data produced in social, economic, and health sciences (DDI Alliance, 2018). With over 400 items, DDI is relatively mature and has an active working group to maintain and support this standard, making it a sustainable metadata scheme that can ensure interoperability among different data sources.
3. *Metadata harvesting availability*. ICPSR hosts an Open Archive Initiative Protocol for Metadata Harvesting (OAI-PMH) service, i.e., an application programming interface (API) that has several standardized schemes available such as Dublin Core, DDI, and MARC21, in both JSON and XML formats. Utilizing the ICPSR-authorized OAI-PMH[1] service enables efficient and reliable metadata downloading.

Research Aims

As the very first step of our ultimate goal, this study aims to reveal important data characteristics and parameters of the ICPSR collections in order to shed light on data sharing and reuse practices in social sciences, and also to provide an opportunity for discovering disciplinary differences through comparison to existing work. By reviewing the metadata records of archived studies and their data-related publications indexed on ICPSR, this study explains the metadata fields and presents factual information about these records, such as their thematic and temporal distribution. We also report other descriptive statistics for data metrics, and propose inconsistencies within the metadata records and challenges of reusing the ICPSR data collections. This is done in an attempt to facilitate discussions of potential directions for improvement for such a large data repository.

In addition to disclosing factual information, this study also aims to develop a research protocol that covers data collection, cleansing, and analysis by documenting important steps, field selection criteria, and decision-making rationale. Finally, two datasets appended to this study are cleansed and publicly released to encourage data reuse practices and more relevant studies in the scientific community.

METHODOLOGY

To understand the key features and data-derived publications of the archived studies on ICPSR, we collected metadata records into two levels: the *study* level and *citation* level. A study-level record describes elements related to a study deposited on ICPSR, e.g., *study title*, *principal investigators* (PIs), *distribution date*, *study keywords*, and *funding agencies*. A citation-level record contains fields providing

[1] https://www.icpsr.umich.edu/icpsrweb/content/membership/or/metadata/oai.html

bibliographic information of a "data-related publication" that cites a certain ICPSR archived study. The fields include *citation title*, *authors*, *publisher*, etc. Appendices A and B provide details of these two levels of metadata records.

In order to gain quantitative insights from the ICPSR records and the downloaded metadata, this study adopts a content analysis approach. Before conducting data analysis, we first performed a data cleansing process to prepare our research materials. In the following sub-sections, we report the step-by-step protocol for collecting metadata records, choosing necessary fields to include, and parsing fetched data into the final datasets.

Data Collection

A Python script was used to obtain metadata records via the OAI-PMH service provided by ICPSR. Both the study-level and citation-level metadata records were downloaded as XML files, complying with DDI version 2.5. In order to convert the XML files into spreadsheets for further analysis, we used another Python script with Regular Expressions (RE) to parse a selection of study-level and citation-level metadata fields into two separate CSV files. As shown in Table 1, as of February 2019, ICPSR has provided 10,362 study records and 159,616 data-related publication records.

No.	Study level	Citation level
Records	10,362	159,616
Variables	51	25

Table 1. Numbers of records and variables included in the two ICPSR metadata datasets.

Data Cleansing Process

For the purpose of developing a research protocol to handle large-scale, complex metadata records obtained from a data repository, details of the data cleansing process for both levels are thoroughly documented and discussed in the following sub-sections. Codebooks based on our protocol are compiled and published along with the two datasets and the Python script as an Open Science Framework (OSF) project.[2] As shown in Appendices A and B, the codebooks serve as references for describing each field in the two datasets.

The Study Level

In the study-level XML files, each record, i.e., an ICPSR-archived study, contains three main elements: (1) *document description*, (2) *study description*, and (3) *file description*. Within these elements, there are approximately 54 unique child elements and their attributes that carry identifiable and meaningful information for each record. To make the dataset succinct, we discarded 21 elements/attributes according to the following criteria:

1. *Repeated elements within a single record*: In the XML string of each record, there are three elements that all indicate the ICPSR identifier of the record and two elements that both contain the study title. Therefore, after parsing two unique elements that respectively present the ICPSR identifier and the study title of the record, we discarded the other three repeated elements.
2. *Elements/attributes with same values for all records*: To avoid data redundancy, we excluded nine elements displaying the exact same values that show up in each record. For example, the value of the *producer* sub-element under the *study description* element is always *"Please see full citation"* in each record.
3. *Elements/attributes that contain free-text content*: As a preliminary exploration, we intend to first emphasize structured data that are relatively easily quantified. Therefore, we discarded nine elements with free-text content, e.g., the *abstract*, *notes*, and *sampling procedure* sub-elements.

After filtering out the aforementioned elements, a 33-field CSV file was yielded. Variables were essentially grouped into four categories as shown in the first column of Appendix A: (1) *Project Description*, (2) *Scope of Project*, (3) *Methodology*, and (4) *ICPSR-generated Metadata*. This categorization is based on the ICPSR data package submission system, where PIs fill out a form with metadata fields. According to the nature of an element in the study-level XML files, as well as captions and annotations defined by ICPSR, a qualifier was given to each variable in the second column of Appendix A. The next column illustrates the data coverage rate of each field, and the last column was the associated explanations corresponding to the qualifier. It is noteworthy that variable clusters can be identified when some of the fields have the same or close coverage rates.

Besides the four main categories, a fifth category entitled *Researcher-Derived* was given to 18 fields that we created on our own for data analysis and does not exist on the ICPSR site. Related objectives and details are discussed below:

- A *serial number* variable ranging from 1 to 10,362 was generated to provide unique and continuous identifiers for all studies. Such a variable would be more intuitive compared to the studies' original ICPSR identifiers ranging from 1 to 37,244 (i.e., missing values exist).
- The year values in the *current version date* and *original release date* fields were extracted out to be two new fields for the ease of analyzing these temporal variables on a proper scale.
- We added 13 new fields that display the counts of certain variables in the dataset such as *author*, *funding agency*, and *keyword*. It is also worth noting that a specific field was calculated based on the citation-level dataset and created to present the *citation count* of each study.
- We acquired the *version number* of each study from the end of the URL in the *holdings* field. This variable represents the number of changes in the studies made by ICPSR or per request of the PIs.

[2] https://osf.io/zds6u/?view_only=5f6b1a0064624d98aeae8e9baca3d35d

The Citation Level

From the citation-level XML files, we parsed nearly 160,000 records via the *related publication* element. In contrast to the way we addressed the study-level metadata records, none of the sub-elements were discarded because the information given by them was relatively limited (i.e., only nine unique sub-elements were included).

There are 25 variables included in our final citation-level dataset (Appendix B). The second and the third variables were parsed from the study-level XML files for reference purposes, the nine variables highlighted in light gray were obtained from the citation-level XML files, and the remaining ones were researcher-derived that are explained in the next paragraph.

In addition to the original 11 variables described above, 14 new variables were added to the citation-level dataset. Since this paper aims to provide datasets that allow further data metric analysis, most of the new variables were created either to facilitate examination on temporal and serial publication-related variables or to help filter invalid records.

- A *serial number* field describing each unique citation-to-study relationship was added, and the number of authors was also calculated as a new field.
- To obtain serial publication-related information via the *ISSN* field, we used the Serial Title API provided by Elsevier[3] and the ISSN of each citation record to access information about the serial publications to which the citing works belong. The serial publications included by Elsevier's API cover 94.2% of those citation records with an *ISSN*. From the JSON files downloaded via the Serial Title API, we parsed out the *title*, *publisher*, *ISSN*, and *eISSN* (i.e., the online ISSN) of each serial publication as four new fields in the citation-level dataset. The *ISSN* and *eISSN* fields acquired from Elsevier's API can be reference values for the original ICPSR metadata records, since whether a certain ISSN value parsed from the citation-level XML files is a print ISSN or an online ISSN is not explicitly annotated.
- The year values in the *production date* field were parsed out to be a new variable indicating each citation record's publication year. However, since this approach reported the production year for only 22.0% of all the records, we further extracted the year values from the *bibliographic reference* field. The year values captured are shown in three new fields: one displays the production year of the citing works belonging to serial publications, another displays those belonging to non-serial publications, and these two variables were merged into a third variable that ends up covering 90.6% of all the citation records' production years.
- To filter out invalid values, we created four dummy variables to mark records that have questionable values in the fields of *producer*, *production date*, *production year of serial publications*, and *production year of non-serial publications*. A value of one would be assigned if the data values are considered uncertain or invalid.

[3] https://dev.elsevier.com/documentation/SerialTitleAPI.wadl

Data Analysis

We used Python to obtain metadata records from ICPSR's OAI-PMH service, parse data values from the XML files into two CSV files, and perform cleansing work toward the final datasets. Analytic functions in the spreadsheet software were used to calculate descriptive statistics as well as to conduct exploratory data analysis. For visualization layouts, we used Tableau to filter out temporal values which are out of our analysis scope (i.e., 1984-2018) and then visualize the results.

RESULTS

Our preliminary findings are presented in three sub-sections. Firstly, we provide an overview of the temporal and thematic dimensions as well as factual information about the ICPSR-archived studies. Secondly, we report and discuss key characteristics and descriptive statistics of the citation-level records. In the third sub-section, we point out some problems encountered while performing the data cleansing process and potential challenges for researchers when reusing ICPSR data collections.

Overview of ICPSR Study-Level Metadata

In regard to the temporal distribution of data deposited on ICPSR, we examined the *original release date* variable to unveil the changes of study counts over the past 35 years (1984-2018). We found an upward trend in the quantity of studies distributed by ICPSR, with values in 1984 and 2009 being particularly high, as shown in Figure 1.

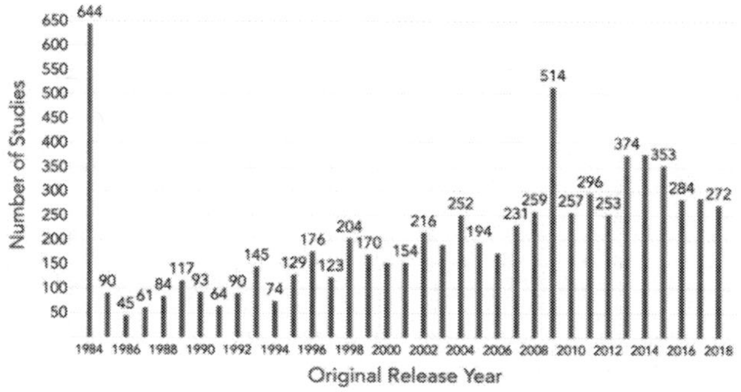

Figure 1. Number of the ICPSR-archived studies distributed by year (1984-2018).

According to its website, during the 1965-1985 period, ICPSR had been "engaging in a series of data conversion projects to digitize historical sources and make them available to the scholarly community" (ICPSR, n.d.-b). Thus, based on the evidence described above, we consider that in 1984 (the minimum in the *original release date* field), a considerable number of studies accumulated over the previous two decades are believed to be released online by ICPSR in a relatively short window.

As for the peak in 2009, this dramatic increase seems to result from the contribution of the United States Bureau of Justice Statistics (BJS) and the Federal Bureau of Investigation (FBI). Both institutions are in the top 10 list of PIs that share the most data collections on ICPSR. The BJS published 32.8% and the FBI published 18.6% of all their studies on ICPSR specifically in 2009.

Figure 2. A word cloud generated from the keyword frequency of the ICPSR-archived studies.

To explore thematic aspects, we conducted an analysis of the studies' keywords controlled by the ICPSR Subject Thesaurus. Approximately 142,000 keywords were identified in the study-level dataset. For the 10,060 studies to which keywords were given (97.1% of all the study records), there is an average of 14.1 keywords (SD = 8.7) and a median of 12 for each study. Figure 2 is a word cloud visualizing the word frequency in the *keyword* field.

Rank	Subject term	Frequency
1	Public opinion	1,957
2	Demographic characteristics	1,624
3	Economic conditions	1,340
4	Employment	1,223
5	National economy	1,066
6	Attitudes	965
7	Income	939
8	Census data	916
9	Voting behavior	855
10	Presidential performance	818

Table 2. Top 10 frequent keywords (subject terms) of the ICPSR-archived studies.

For further details, Table 2 shows the top 10 subject terms and their term frequencies of the study-level dataset. This list not only reveals focal areas of the ICPSR collections (i.e., politics, economics, etc.) but also demonstrates the nature of data attached to a certain study, with terms such as demographic characteristics and census data.

As for authorship, the *author* field can also illustrate thematic features of ICPSR studies to some extent, since the top PIs in the dataset are mainly organizations instead of individuals. In fact, the first individual researcher as a PI is in 12th place on the list. As shown in Table 3, the majority of the top 10 PIs are United States government agencies; some others are from journalism industries, and the remaining one is the Survey Research Center at the University of Michigan. As for individual PIs, they are primarily university faculty members, senior research fellows of academic associations, and scholars/staff members in research institutions. These PIs' backgrounds, judged by their affiliations, are basically consistent with previous findings of this study in regard to the disciplinary focuses derived from the analysis of study keywords, e.g., social science, criminology, and healthcare.

Rank	Data contributors	No. of studies
1	United States. Bureau of the Census	941
2	United States Department of Justice. Bureau of Justice Statistics	811
3	CBS News	668
4	ABC News	536
5	University of Michigan. Survey Research Center. Economic Behavior Program	494
6	United States Department of Health and Human Services. National Center for Health Statistics	446
7	The New York Times	399
8	The Washington Post	383
9	United States Department of Education. National Center for Education Statistics	306
10	United States Department of Justice. Federal Bureau of Investigation	208

Table 3. Top 10 PIs of the ICPSR studies.

Reviewing the thematic distribution of the data series to which the ICPSR studies belong is another way to understand the nature of the ICPSR data collections and the issues with which they are concerned. With regard to all the ICPSR studies, 6,376 (61.5%) records are found to be related to one series. Among the 251 unique series, the top five series account for over one-third (36.1%) of those records: 1) ABC News/Washington Post Poll Series, 2) CBS News/New York Times Poll Series, 3) Survey of Consumer Attitudes and Behavior Series, 4) Federal Justice Statistics Program Data Series, and 5) Census of Population and Housing Series. It can be observed that studies belonging to these top five series are led by the top 1-5, 7, and 8 PIs shown in Table 3.

In addition to the PIs, funding agencies are also important stakeholders with respect to the peaks and valleys of different disciplines' data sharing practices in a data repository. For the 4,987 studies (48.1% of all the records), the top three funding agencies are the BJS, the National Institute of Justice (NIJ), and the National Science Foundation (NSF). Respectively, they fund 26.5%, 23.5%, and 12.8% of the studies which have values in the *funding agency* field of the study-level dataset. Note that a study can be funded by more than one funding agency. It is also worth mentioning that among the over 900 unique funding agencies, there are 78 agencies

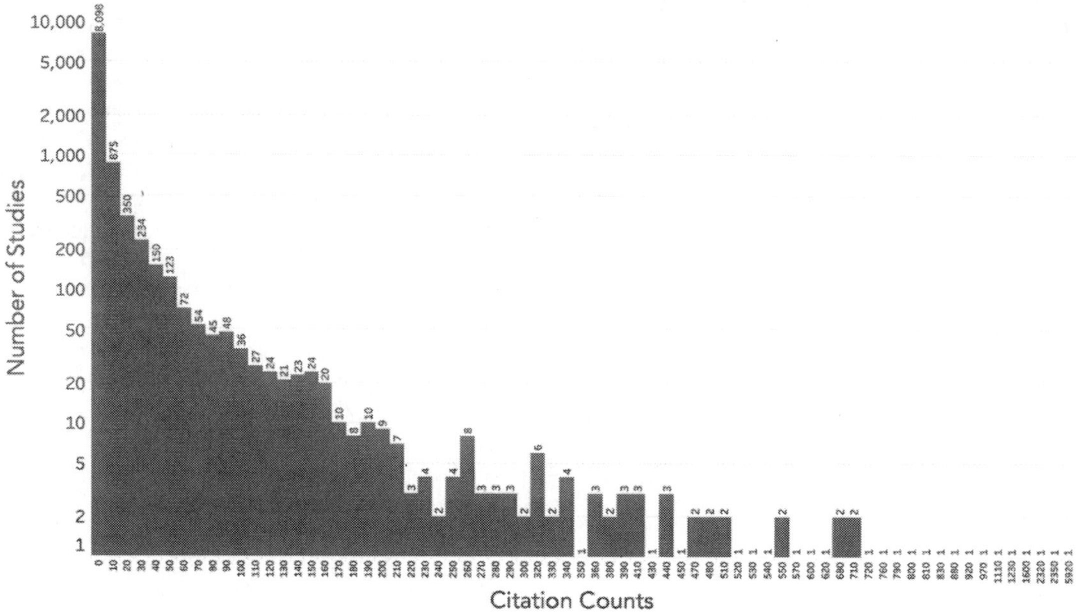

Figure 3. Frequency distribution of each ICPSR study's citation counts.

affiliated with the U.S. Department of Health and Human Services (HHS), which account for 2,065 records (41.4%) of the 4,987 studies.

In respect to data usage of ICPSR, a label of *use condition* is given by the ICPSR website for all of the study records in order to suggest their data accessibility. Specifically, 97.2% of the studies are labeled "available," with 45.1% to the general public and 52.1% only to ICPSR member institutions. On the contrary, 0.4% of the study records are labeled "unavailable," meaning temporarily inaccessible, and 2.4% of the study records are labeled "restricted," meaning no longer distributed by ICPSR. These two groups (2.8% in total) listed in the study-level dataset are now unsearchable by regular website visitors.

As for the data volume of the collections, we found that 32.2% of the study-level records have files attached, with the numbers ranging from 2 to 2,553 (mean = 21.2, SD = 77.6, and median = 4). However, after actually searching on ICPSR and observing the search results, we found that the XML files obtained via ICPSR's OAI-PMH service do not include the name of the very first file in each study. That is, null values in the *file name* field might actually mean that there is one file attached to a certain study. Therefore, if we assume that all the study records having null values in the *file name* field actually have one file attached, and add one back to those studies which originally have values in the *file name* field, then the adjusted average number of data files attached to each study becomes 24.2 (SD = 143.9, median = 5).

Nonetheless, further verification of our assumptions is needed, since at this point, it has not been proved that all the records with null values in the *file name* field in fact have one file attached. Also, we did find that in the study information pages on the ICPSR website, some of the fields that are supposed to contain the first file for download do not actually have a file attached. This can cause inaccuracies in our adjusted calculated results mentioned above.

Overview of ICPSR Citation-Level Metadata

A data-related publication on ICPSR is defined as "a work using data held in the ICPSR archive" (ICPSR, n.d.-c). These records might be able to unveil data citation practices on ICPSR as a potential main source of reusable data collections available to the scientific community. Types of data-related publications include journal articles, magazine articles, books, electronic sources, audiovisual materials, etc. In the second half of this section, we especially focus on discussing serial publications.

Figure 3 demonstrates the frequency distribution of each ICPSR study's citation counts. Note that the y-axis is plotted on a logarithmic scale and not all the tick values on the x-axis are equidistant. There are 7,195 (69.4%) study records being cited at least one time, with the cited times ranging from 0 to 5,924. On average, each ICPSR-archived study is cited 15.1 times (SD = 85.1, median = 2). Most of the top-cited studies (e.g., the six studies which are cited more than 1,000 times) are longitudinal studies or large-scale public surveys belonging to certain data series.

Regarding the temporal trend of data-related publications, we reviewed the year values of the *production year* variable extracted from the *bibliographic reference* field that cover

90.6% of all the data-related publications. As mentioned previously, the minimum original release year of the earliest studies on ICPSR is 1984 when the historical source digitization had finally reached an end. Consequently, notwithstanding the production of the earliest data-related publication in the citation-level dataset being traced back to 1849, we set 1984 as a watershed for exploring the citation benefit in terms of sharing data collections on ICPSR.

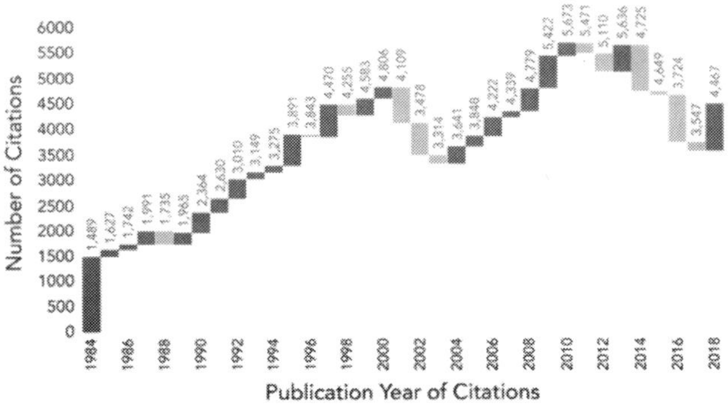

Figure 4. Total citation counts of ICPSR studies by year.

Figure 4 is a waterfall chart displaying the growth and decline of the number of all citation records indexed on ICPSR in a 35-year period (1984-2018). Bars in deep blue show growth while the orange ones represent declines. As shown in Figure 4, in general, an upward trend can be observed over time. This observation suggests that more and more publications have cited ICPSR-archived studies over the past three decades, and a continuous growth of citation counts might be expected in the next few years.

Rank	Serial publication	No. of citations
1	American Journal of Public Health	1,821
2	Public Opinion Quarterly	1,545
3	Journal of Marriage and Family	1,305
4	American Journal of Political Science	1,287
5	American Political Science Review	1,190
6	Social Science Quarterly	1,091
7	Journal of Human Resources	1,085
7	Social Forces	1,085
9	Demography	1,027
10	Criminology	1,015

Table 4. Top 10 serial publications that contribute the most citations to ICPSR studies.

To help assess the research impact of the ICPSR data collections, we reviewed the distribution of the serial publications obtained from Elsevier's Serial Title API using the ISSN values offered by ICPSR. For all the citations in our dataset, there are 91,888 (57.6%) records with an ISSN. Eventually, serial publication titles were retrieved for 87,311 (54.7%) records. Within those citation records which have values in the *serial publication title* field, 2,946 unique serial publications were identified. Each serial publication has contributed 29.4 (SD = 102.6) citations to the ICPSR studies on average. However, the mean seems to be influenced by some extreme values which account for more citations, given its median = 4.

Table 4 presents the top 10 serial publications that include the most works citing studies on ICPSR, which account for 14.4% of the citation counts with regard to those records having values in the *serial publication title* field.

Problems and Challenges of ICPSR-Archived Studies

Several issues with ICPSR studies have arisen during the data wrangling and analysis processes. In this section, we report and discuss problems with the metadata records provided by ICPSR and highlight the challenges of reusing the data collections.

Problems with the ICPSR Metadata Records

At large, ICPSR has provided relatively clean metadata records for bibliometric and data metric analysis. Most of the data fields fetched from the OAI-PMH service have a suitable coverage rate, in spite of the fact that only the *principal investigators* and *summary* fields are input-required during the data package submitting process.

However, the complex hierarchical structure of certain elements in the XML files and some field control issues may cause difficulties in parsing the records for further review. In particular, it can be difficult to parse data values from free-text fields (e.g., *summary*, *sampling procedure*, and *collection notes*) into a clean format in a labor- and time-efficient approach. The reason for this lies in how these text values are generated. When filling out the metadata fields in the data package submission system, PIs or ICPSR curators can format the text they have entered, such as defining different levels of headings or creating a list with several items. This results in an abundance of irregular markups and tags to certain elements in the XML files, which makes parsing free-text values a resource-intensive task.

As for field control issues, some data fields in essence seem to be better controlled with specific vocabularies but are still assigned as free-text fields. For example, based on values in the *geographic unit* field, a close-ended list might be more helpful for avoiding inconsistencies in letter casing and single/plural issues resulting from the free text entered, and thus can enhance the analyzability of the variables. In addition, for free-text fields that are annotated to comply with the guidelines of the ICPSR thesaurus, their data values still present in different precision levels, e.g., some values in the *geographic coverage* field indicate the country level but some report as precisely as the city level.

Lastly, variables extracted from the XML files can be easier to understand and use if the relationships between the data fields and their stakeholders are explicitly reported. Using the *cleaning operations* field as an example, the variable is used to document processing steps performed by ICPSR curators instead of the PIs. A better annotation system embedded in the XML files can help prevent misunderstandings and thus facilitate a more efficient data analysis process.

Challenges of Reusing Data Collections on ICPSR

While the XML files downloaded via ICPSR's OAI-PMH service include rich information that reveal facts and further insights, inconsistencies were found in 1) the entries displayed and 2) the naming convention practices, which can confuse users and thus impede reuse of the data collections.

First of all, we found a divergence in entries shown in the XML files and in the Research Information Systems (RIS) files. An RIS file exported from the study information pages on the ICPSR website is a text file that contains about 10 items, such as "AU" (i.e., *author*) and "TY" (i.e., *publication type*). These items are metadata fields used to describe the data-related publications. Instead of targeting general website visitors, RIS files are typically offered to individual users who are interested in analyzing the metadata records of data-related publications. The discrepancy we have identified is that not all entries displayed in the RIS files can be found in the XML files. For example, the *publication type* field in the RIS files contains values such as journal articles, books, and reports, which can help identify the specific type of data-related publications. However, this is not applicable to the citation-level XML files, as there is not a particular field which documents the publication type of the citations. Regarding citation records, we could only distinguish serial publications from non-serial publications based on whether there are ISSN values for the citation records, since extra manual verification can be time-consuming and labor-intensive.

In regard to the degree of comprehensiveness, it is also worth mentioning that even though about 28.5% of the study records carry null values in the *original release year* field of the XML files, the original release date of these study records is still viewable in the study information pages on the ICPSR websites. Further exploration is needed to discover the reason for the missing values in the XML files and determine whether there are similar issues with other variables in our datasets.

Finally, from a perspective of naming convention, for the same information shown in the XML files, RIS files, and the study information pages, some of the field names are slightly different with respect to the same content. This might still perplex users who try to draw comparisons among these information sources. For instance, the date when a study was first distributed on ICPSR is titled *original release date* on the ICPSR website but named *distDate* (i.e., distribution date) in the XML files. The date when the current version of a study was distributed on ICPSR is titled *version date* on the website while named *datestamp* in the XML files. After exploratory data analysis, we believe that the *publication year* field in the RIS files contains the same year values as the *datestamp* field in the XML files. Such inconsistencies can cause uncertainty and even misinterpretation with respect to analysis on temporal dimensions of the ICPSR-archived studies.

CONCLUSION

This study has mapped the landscape of archived studies on ICPSR, the largest social science data infrastructure worldwide. By reviewing representative parameters of two-level metadata records and conducting exploratory data analysis, we have unfolded key characteristics of the ICPSR-archived studies and their related publications, such as themes and contributors, as well as the temporal distribution of the studies and the trend of data reuse based on the citation counts of their associated publications.

Our results suggest that there is an upward trend in regard to the number of ICPSR-archived studies and their citation counts over the past 35 years. The thematic features of the ICPSR data collections are consistent with their collection development policies, which mainly focus on politics, economics, public health, behavioral science, etc. We also report problems with the metadata records themselves and the potential drawbacks in terms of reusing deposited data collections on ICPSR, including metadata field control issues and the inconsistencies in naming convention practices. Finally, the cleansed datasets are publicly released. By thoroughly documenting our data collection protocol, we aim to encourage more relevant studies and data reuse practices within the ASIS&T community.

As a leading research data infrastructure in social science disciplines, ICPSR plays an essential role in providing a platform to expand scholars' research impact through data sharing. Performing analyses on metadata records of such a platform can be a gateway to future exploration of relevant practices. More specifically, the examination of thematic features along with temporal dimensions helps reveal the growth and decline in terms of data sharing in different subdisciplines. Studies' citation counts show differences in the research impact of various research topics, PIs, funding agencies, etc. In addition, more in-depth investigation into serial publications to which the citing works belong would illustrate how the ICPSR data collections are reused by publications from highly-cited journals and magazines. A network demonstrating interdisciplinary interaction in regard to research data can also be mapped.

As the first step of these ultimate goals, this study not only provides factual information and descriptive statistics but also proposes challenges and reflections. All of these efforts can shed light on how an RDI such as ICPSR can improve its metadata integrity, consistency, and transparency, so as to build a better environment for the advancement of data metrics. Moreover, the datasets provided and operational details in our research protocol can be the most important materials to facilitate more large-scale quantitative profiling and qualitative investigations on such a large batch of social science data collections and consequently, take one more step toward open science.

FUTURE WORK

For future directions, we are continuing the data cleansing work by extending it to the free-text fields. Particularly, there are values of some variables viewable on the ICPSR website but not displayed in the XML files. Such a gap should be eliminated as one of our next steps. Additional cleaning strategies including disambiguation, verification, and removal of garbled characters are also key steps toward a fuller understanding of the metadata records.

Further analysis is also needed to reveal more insights. For instance, data mining techniques (e.g., building classifiers or predictive models to identify themes and types of highly-cited studies) can be adopted to explore free-text content, such as study descriptions or scopes of projects. Most importantly, data citation patterns in social sciences can be clarified by thoroughly examining the relationships between citations originating from different serial publications and changes in their growth over time.

ACKNOWLEDGMENTS

This work was financially supported by the Ministry of Science and Technology (MOST) in Taiwan, under #MOST 108-2636-H-002-002- and MOST 108-3017-F-002-003-, and the Center for Research in Econometric Theory and Applications (Grant no. 108L900204) from The Featured Areas Research Center Program within the framework of the Higher Education Sprout Project by the Ministry of Education (MOE) in Taiwan.

REFERENCES

DDI Alliance. (2018). *Document, discover, and interoperate*. Retrieved from https://www.ddialli-ance.org/

Beitz, A., Groenewegen, D., Harboe-Ree, C., Macmillan, W., & Searle, S. (2014). Case study 3: Monash University, a strategic approach. In G. Pryor, S. Jones, & A. Whyte, *Delivering research data management services: Fundamentals of good practice* (pp. 89–114). London, England: Facet Publishing.

Bernard, H., Wutich, A., & Ryan, W. (2017). *Analyzing qualitative data: Systematic approaches*. Los Angeles, CA: SAGE.

Clubb, J. M., Austin, E. W., Geda, C. L., & Traugott, M. W. (1985). Sharing research data in the social sciences. In S. Fienber, M. Martin, & M. Straf, *Sharing research data* (pp. 39–88). Washington, DC: National Academies Press.

Cragin, M. H., Palmer, C. L., Carlson, J. R., & Witt, M. (2010). Data sharing, small science and institutional repositories. *Philosophical Transactions. Series A, Mathematical, Physical, and Engineering Sciences, 368* (1926), 4023–4038.

Fienberg, S. E., Martin, M. E., & Straf, M. L. (1985). *Sharing research data*. National Academies Press.

ICPSR. (n.d.-a-a). *How do I access ICPSR data if I am not at a member institution?*. Retrieved April 16, 2019a from https://www.icpsr.umich.edu/icpsrweb/content/shared/ICPSR/faqs/how-do-i-access-icpsr-data-if-i-am-not.html

ICPSR. (n.d.-b-b). *The founding and early years*. Retrieved April 16, 2019b from https://www.icpsr.umich.edu/icpsrweb/content/about/history/early-years.html

ICPSR. (n.d.-c-c). *Data-related publications*. Retrieved April 16, 2019c from https://www.icpsr.umich.edu/icpsrweb/ ICPSR/citations/

Jeng, W., He, D., & Chi, Y. (2017). Social science data repositories in data deluge: A case study of ICPSR's workflow and practices. *The Electronic Library, 35*(4), 626–649.

Latif, A., Limani, F., & Tochtermann, K. (2019). A generic research data infrastructure for long tail research data management. *Data Science Journal, 18*(1), 17.

Lyon, L. (2016). Transparency: The emerging third dimension of open science and open data. *LIBER Quarterly, 25*(4), 153–171.

Robinson, N., Mongeon, P., Jeng, W., & Costas, R. (2017). DataCite as a novel bibliometric source: Coverage, strengths and limitations. *Journal of Informetrics, 11*(3), 841–854.

Tancheva, K. (2012). Linguistics - Cornell University. *Data Curation Profiles Directory, 4*, 7.

Tenopir, C., Allard, S., Douglass, K., Aydinoglu, U., Wu, L., Read, E., … Frame, M. (2011). Data sharing by scientists: Practices and perceptions. *PLoS One, 6*(6), e21101.

Tenopir, C., Dalton, E. D., Allard, S., Frame, M., Pjesivac, I., Birch, B., & Dorsett, K. (2015). Changes in data sharing and data reuse practices and perceptions among scientists worldwide. *PLoS One, 10*(8), e0134826.

Zilinski, L., & Lorenz, S. (2012). Linguistics / Etymology - University of South Florida. *Data Curation Profiles Directory, 4*, 9.

APPENDIX

Both of the study-level and citation-level datasets, as well as the two codebooks and the Python script are available online as an Open Science Framework (OSF) project.[4]

Appendix A. Metadata fields of the study-level dataset

Captions	Qualifiers	Coverage rate	Explanation
Researcher-derived	Serial Number	100.00%	Serial numbers sorted by the study ID, ranging from 1 to 10362.
ICPSR-generated	Study ID	100.00%	Unique identification numbers given by ICPSR for each study.
Project Description	Study Title	100.00%	Full authoritative title for the work.
Project Description	Study Alternative Title	12.89%	The name by which a data collection may be commonly referred. Often takes the form of a shortened (by abbreviation/acronym) version of the title.
Project Description	Principal Investigator (PI)	100.00%	The name of the Principal Investigator(s), in order of importance to the study. The Principal Investigator may be an organization.
Researcher-derived	PI Counts	100.00%	The number of principal investigators of the study.
Project Description	PI affliation	29.42%	The affiliation of the Principal Investigator(s), in order of importance to the study.
Project Description	Funding Agency	48.12%	The name of the organization(s) that supported the production and/or archiving of these data, along with associated Grant Number(s).
Researcher-derived	Funding Agency Counts	48.12%	The number of funding agencies of the study.
Project Description	Grant Number	25.04%	The grant/contract number of the project that sponsored the effort.
Researcher-derived	Citation Counts	100.00%	The number of data-related publications that cite the study.
Project Description	Distributor	71.49%	A list of organizations that distribute the study.
Researcher-derived	Distributor Counts	71.49%	The number of distributors of the study.
ICPSR-generated	Current Version Date	45.86%	Date of distribution by ICPSR for the current version of the data collection.
ICPSR-generated	Version Date	100.00%	Also known as release or edition. If there have been substantive changes in the data since their creation, this statement should be used at the appropriate level.
Researcher-derived	Version Year	100.00%	Year value extracted from the version date.
ICPSR-generated	First Version Date	71.49%	Date when the data collection was first distributed by ICPSR.
Researcher-derived	First Version Year	71.49%	Year value extracted from the first version date.
Project Description	Series Name	61.52%	The name of the series to which the study belongs.
Project Description	Series Number	61.52%	The identification numbers of the series.
Scope of Project	Study Keyword	97.08%	Relevant social science subject terms that capture the essence of the data collection. Subject terms follow guidelines specified in the ICPSR Thesaurus.
Researcher-derived	Study Keyword Counts	97.08%	The number of keywords of the study.
ICPSR-generated	Classification Field	97.83%	The classification field indicates the broad substantive topic(s) that the data cover.
Researcher-derived	Classification Field Counts	97.83%	The number of classification fields of the study.
ICPSR-generated	Controlled Vocabulary	97.83%	Specification of the controlled vocabulary in use, e.g., LCSH, MeSH, etc.
Scope of Project	Data Time Period	91.45%	The time period to which the data refer. Includes the range(s) of dates.
Scope of Project	Data Time Period (Cycle)	45.88%	Specification of the relevant cycle, wave, or round of the data time period.
Scope of Project	Data Time Period (Event)	91.34%	Specification of "start", "end", or "single" for each date entered to the data time period.
Methodology	Data Time Method	19.08%	The time method or time dimension of the data collection.
Researcher-derived	Data Time Method Counts	19.08%	The number of time methods of the study.
Scope of Project	Data Collection Date	81.84%	Date(s) the data were collected.
Scope of Project	Data Collection Date (Cycle)	51.03%	Specification of the relevant cycle, wave, or round of the data collection date.
Scope of Project	Data Collection Date (Event)	81.84%	Specification of "start", "end", or "single" for each date entered to the data collection date.
Methodology	Data Collection Methods	37.73%	The method(s) used to collect the data.
Researcher-derived	Data Collection Methods Counts	37.73%	The number of collection methods of the study.
Scope of Project	Data Types	91.38%	Information describing the kind of data included in the file.
Researcher-derived	Data Types Counts	91.38%	The number of data types of the study.
Methodology	Unit of Observation	42.90%	The major unit being analyzed in the data collection. For example: Individuals, Arrest event, Incident, Agency, Year and quarter, County within state.
Researcher-derived	Unit of Observation Counts	42.90%	The number of units of observation of the study.
Scope of Project	Geographic Coverage	95.17%	The geographic area(s) covered in the data collection. Geographic areas follow guidelines specified in the ICPSR Geographic Names Thesaurus.
Researcher-derived	Geographic Coverage Counts	95.17%	The number of geographic coverage of the study.
Methodology	Smallest Geographic Unit	23.99%	The smallest geographic unit represented in the data that can be analyzed.
Researcher-derived	Smallest Geographic Unit Counts	23.99%	The number of smallest geographic units of the study.
Scope of Project	File Names	32.19%	Contains a short title that will be used to distinguish a particular file/part from other files/parts in the data collection.
Researcher-derived	File Counts	32.19%	The number of files attached to the study.
ICPSR-generated	Data Cleaning Operations	54.37%	Methods used to "clean" the data collection (performed by ICPSR), e.g., consistency checking, wild code checking, etc.
Researcher-derived	Data Cleaning Operations Counts	54.37%	The number of data cleaning operations of the study.
ICPSR-generated	Use Conditions	100.00%	Indicates any additional information that will assist the user in understanding the access and use conditions of the data collection.
ICPSR-generated	Holdings	100.00%	Information concerning either the physical or electronic holdings of the cited work.
Researcher-derived	Holdings Version Number	100.00%	Version numbers extracted from the end of the holding URLs.
ICPSR-generated	Bibliographic Reference	99.93%	Complete bibliographic reference containing all of the standard elements of a citation that can be used to cite the work.

Appendix B. Metadata fields of the citation-level dataset

Qualifiers	Coverage rate	Explanation
Serial Number (Citation-to-Study)	100.00%	Serial numbers sorted by the study ID and then the first letter of the first PI's last name, ranging from 1 to 159616.
Study ID	100.00%	Unique identification numbers given by ICPSR for each study.
Study Title	100.00%	Full authoritative title for the study.
Citation ID	98.02%	Unique identification numbers given by ICPSR for each data-related publication.
Citation Title	98.01%	Full authoritative title for the data-related publication.
Authoring Entity	98.02%	The person, corporate body, or agency responsible for the data-related publication's substantive and intellectual content.
Authoring Entity Counts	97.07%	The number of authoring entities of the data-related publication.
Production Year (1)	21.99%	Year value extracted from the production date (non-serial publication).
Production Year (2)	90.58%	Year value extracted from the bibliographic reference (including non-serial and serial publication).
Production Year (Non-serial Publication)	33.07%	Year value extracted from the bibliographic reference (non-serial publication).
Production Year (Non-serial Publication) (*)	0.14%	The value 1 is given when there is not a year value included in the bibliographic reference (non-serial publication).
Production Year (Serial Publication)	57.55%	Year value extracted from the bibliographic reference (serial publication).
Production Year (Serial Publication) (*)	0.01%	The value 1 is given when there is not a year value included in the bibliographic reference (serial publication).
Production Date (Non-serial Publication)	22.19%	Date when the data-related publication were produced (not distributed or archived).
Production Date (Non-serial Publication) (*)	0.20%	The value 1 is given when a specific year value cannot be identified from this column (e.g., "n.d." and "unknown").
Producer (Non-serial Publication)	33.22%	The person or organization with the financial or administrative responsibility for the physical processes whereby the work was brought into existence.
Producer (Non-serial Publication) (*)	0.01%	The value 1 is given when an obvious error occurs (e.g., a year value shows in this column).
Production Place (Non-serial Publication)	27.70%	Address of the archive or organization that produced the data-related publication.
ISSN (Serial Publication)	57.57%	The ISSN of each data-related publication which belongs to a serial publication.
ISSN (Elsevier API)	53.98%	The ISSN of the serial publication to which the data-related publication belongs (parsed from Elsevier's API).
Online ISSN (Elsevier API)	42.27%	The online ISSN of the serial publication to which the data-related publication belongs (parsed from Elsevier's API).
Title (Serial Publication)	54.70%	The title of the serial publication (parsed from Elsevier's API).
Publisher (Serial Publication)	54.23%	The publisher of the serial publication (parsed from Elsevier's API).
Holdings	41.98%	Information concerning either the physical or electronic holdings of the cited work.
Bibliographic Reference	98.02%	Complete bibliographic reference containing all of the standard elements of a citation that can be used to cite the work.

[4] https://osf.io/zds6u/?view_only=5f6b1a0064624d98aeae8e9baca3d35d

Evaluating Ontology Coverage and Internal Structure to Better Align Patients With Clinical Trials

Jooho Lee
School of Information Sciences, University of Illinois, Champaign, IL, USA
lee185@illinois.edu

Catherine Blake
School of Information Sciences, University of Illinois, Champaign, IL, USA
clblake@illinois.edu

Bridget T. McInnes
Department of Computer Science, Virginia Commonwealth University, Richmond, VA, USA
btmcinnes@vcu.edu

ABSTRACT

Recruiting patients for a clinical trial is a time-consuming activity that can delay recruiting and the reporting of clinical trial results. Ontologies can be used to align the inclusion criteria of a clinical trial with candidate patients but such an approach requires that (a) the concepts within an ontology adequately cover patient characteristics that are likely to be used in a clinical trial; (b) the quantitative similarity scores decline gracefully patient characteristics become less suited to the trial protocol; and (c) the alignment must be robust despite surface level differences in how eligibility features are described. The concepts are extracted from grant proposals and eight archetype breast cancer patients are mapped as matching a breast cancer clinical trial protocol does. The Medical Subject Heading (MeSH) and National Cancer Institute Thesaurus (NCIt) are evaluated with respect to coverage, connectivity, standard similarity properties and the granularity of rankings.

KEYWORDS

Clinical Trial; Semantic Similarity; Knowledge Representation

ASIS&T THESAURUS

Biomedical Informatics; Quantitative Analysis; Knowledge Representation

INTRODUCTION

Breast cancer is the second leading cause of cancer-related death among American women. In 2018, there were an estimated 266,129 patients with 40,920 deaths in the US[1] and there are currently 1,815 clinical trials recruiting subjects.[2] Better aligning patients with ongoing clinical trials can accelerate a clinical trial by decreasing the amount of time taken to enroll the required number of participants, which in turn can enable the results of a clinical trial to be reported earlier. Manual methods that formalize inclusion criterion of a clinical trial have been explored (Weng, Tu, Sim, & Richesson, 2010), but require time and expertise that may not be available (Penberthy, Dahman, Petkov, & DeShazo, 2012). Our goal is to automatically extract key characteristics about a clinical trial protocol directly from the funded grant proposal to measure the similarity between the trial and each candidate breast cancer patient for cohort selection.

As with many medical conditions, both genetic environment and behavioral factors (hormone therapy, ionizing radiation, oral contraceptives, overweight and obesity among postmenopausal women, and alcohol consumption) have been linked to breast cancer (American Cancer Society, 2017). A patient's ethnic background can serve as a proxy for both genetic and cultural practices that influence risk. For example, Ashkenazi Jewish women have higher BRACA1 and BRACA2 genes and African American women have a disproportionately high incident of certain subtypes of breast cancer (Palmer et al., 2014). This prior knowledge about factors that influence a medical condition can be used to create patient archetypes that mirror the factors that are likely to determine if a patient is a good candidate for a clinical trial.

Mapping clinically relevant facets to an ontology can improve the process of aligning patients to a specific clinical trial. However, ontologies will only be helpful if they provide adequate coverage of the patient characteristics that used in clinical trial protocols. If coverage alone were adequate, we could count the number of concepts in common and divide by the number of requirements in the trial; however, the descriptions provided in a grant abstract may be more general or more precise than those provided by a patient. For example, if a grant targets the condition metastatic breast cancer, and the patient description includes breast cancer, the similarity score (ranging from 0 [not qualified] to 1 [perfect match]) should not be 1 (i.e. a perfect match), but the score should also not be zero because the patient may still qualify for the trial. However, the similarity score should be zero if the patient has a different condition such as lung cancer. Therefore, we must know that metastatic breast cancer is a type

82nd Annual Meeting of the Association for Information Science & Technology | Melbourne, Australia | 19–23 October, 2019

DOI: 10.1002/pra2.00014

[1] Source: https://seer.cancer.gov/statfacts/html/breast.html
[2] Search for breast cancer trials in a recruiting stage from https://clinicaltrials.gov conducted August 27, 2018.

of breast cancer, which would be captured as an IS-A relationship in an ontology.

In this paper, we evaluate an ontology-based semantic similarity measure on two widely used ontologies for cohort selection: The National Cancer Institute Thesaurus (NCIt) and the Medical Subject Headings (MeSH). We created eight patient archetypes with varying features known to influence treatment outcomes and likely to be defined in a trial protocol. We evaluate the similarity scores provided by these ontologies with respect to trials and patient characteristics.

BACKGROUND

It is difficult to fully define all characteristics of a trial in advance; however prior studies provide factors that influence treatment outcomes that are likely to be defined within a trial protocol. From a retrieval perspective these have been characterized as Patient, Intervention, Condition and Outcome (PICO) elements (J. Lin & Demner-Fushman, 2006). In clinical setting, physicians construct their clinical question in a structured way as listed in Table 1.

Population/Problem: What is the primary problem or disease? What are the characteristics of the patient (e.g., age, gender, co-existing conditions, etc.)?
Intervention: What is the main intervention (e.g., diagnostic test, medication, therapeutic procedure, etc.)?
Comparison: What is the main intervention compared to (e.g., no intervention, another drug, another therapeutic procedure, a placebo, etc.)?
Outcome: What is the effect of the intervention (e.g., symptoms relieved or eliminated, cost reduces, etc.)?
Example: Clinical question: In children [Population] with an acute febrile illness, what is the efficacy of single-medication therapy with acetaminophen [Intervention] or ibuprofen [Comparison] in reducing fever [Outcome]?

Table 1. PICO elements and entity recognition on clinical question.

Automated systems have been developed to extract these entities directly from published abstracts (Boudin et al., 2010; Hassanzadeh, Groza, & Hunter, 2014; Huang et al., 2013; Karystianis, Buchan, & Nenadic, 2014) achieving an F-score of 86.3% for P and C combined (Boudin et al., 2010); 73.9% for P (Huang et al., 2013); and 83.31% on structured and 79.34% on unstructured text for P element (Hassanzadeh et al., 2014).

Semantic similarity is a computational method, that quantifies likeness between two concepts based on their shared characteristics. The ontology-based measures can be classified as two approaches: 1. edge-based, and 2. information content (IC)-based approach. Both approaches can estimate similarity of the two concepts which belong to a same ontology. *Edge-based measures* treat an ontology as a directed graph and each concept is an edge of the graph. On this approach, the similarity is estimated by the number or distance of semantic links between concept pairs (Leacock & Chodorow, 1998; Wu & Palmer, 1994). The one problem of this approach is that it only considers the minimum number of semantic links. Because it cannot consider multiple inheritance of a concept, which is common in many ontology structures. This might cause miscalculation of similarity of a concept pair. Thus, IC-based measures try to overcome the limitations of edge-based measures by accounting the amount of information that a concept pair has in common. Similarity estimation methods exploiting the IC are proposed by several studies (Jiang & Conrath, 1997; D. Lin, 1998; McInnes & Pedersen, 2013, 2015; Resnik, 1995). In definition, the similarity between two concepts c_1 and c_2 are estimated by ICs of the two concepts and IC of the *Least Common Subsumer* (LCS) or *Most Informative Common Ancestor* (MICA). If a concept c_A is subsumer of c_B, then c_A is a parent or ancestor of c_B. LCS refers to a common ancestor of concept c_1 and c_2, which is most specific among all the shared concepts.

The critical part of similarity calculation of IC-based approach is computation of IC of a target concept. Many studies proposed IC calculation methods (Ben Aouicha & Hadj Taieb, 2016; Meng, Gu, & Zhou, 2012; Resnik, 1995; Sánchez, Batet, & Isern, 2011; Sebti & Barfroush, 2008; Seco, Veale, & Hayes, 2004, Zhou, Wang, & Gu, 2008, August). The calculation of semantic similarity is based on the evaluation of the semantic evidence observed in a knowledge source such as ontologies or domain corpora. For example, acetaminophen and ibuprofen are semantically similar to each other because they are both pain reliever drugs and therefore are co-located in an ontology.

In this work, we use the Jaccard similarity coefficient for aggregating the concepts by grant abstract and by breast cancer archetype. Previous studies have shown the adapted Jaccard similarity coefficient achieves best score on well-studied datasets among all the methods tested (Hao, Rusanov, Boland, & Weng, 2014). The Jaccard index compares the similarity and dissimilarity between two concepts (Niwattanakul, Singthongchai, Naenudorn, & Wanapu, 2013). We calculate Jaccard similarity coefficient as follows:

$$Sim_i(t_i,t_j) = \begin{cases} 0, |SF(t_i)| \; or \; |SF(t_j)| = 0 \\ \dfrac{|SF(t_i) \cap SF(t_j)|}{|SF(t_i) \cup SF(t_j)|}, otherwise \end{cases}$$

where T denotes a collection of k clinical trials ($T = \{t_1, t_i, \ldots t_j, \ldots t_k\}$). A Semantic Feature (SF) set contains the extracted concepts describing the grant or patient. The similarity score of two feature sets, $SF(t_i)$ and $SF(t_j)$, is 0 when no feature exists in either $SF(t_i)$ and $SF(t_j)$. Otherwise, we divide the intersection of $SF(t_i)$ and $SF(t_j)$ by the union of $SF(t_i)$ and

$SF(t_j)$. The basic idea is that we are counting the number of features that t_i and t_j have in common, and normalizing it based on their combined number of features.

MATERIALS AND METHOD

The impact of ontological structure on the Jaccard similarity measure is evaluated by comparing concepts from existing grants with archetype patients that reflect population and condition characteristics that are likely to influence a patient's inclusion in a trial. Grant information was downloaded from NIH RePORTER and three grants (7094759, 7190702, and 8384429) that included 'breast cancer' were selected at random.

This study focuses on the P (Population) and C (Condition) elements. We used MetaMap (Aronson & Lang, 2010) to identify population concepts using the semantic types: Age Group (T100), Family Group (T099), Patient or Disabled Group (T101), and Population Group (T098)); and condition concepts using the semantic types: Disease or Syndrome (T047), Neoplastic Process (T191), and Sign or Symptom (T184). The list of semantic types were originally from Boudin et al., and modified to exclude abstract concepts such as Pathologic Function (T046) (Boudin et al., 2010). The concepts with the semantic types reside in the high in the semantic tree are abstract and can be extracted from almost all abstracts. The input and reformatted output format of MetaMap is demonstrated in Table 2.

Sentence-level text
3824388|10|Obesity is one of the most important preventable causes of cancer and the most significant risk factor for breast cancer in postmenopausal women.
3824388|70|These findings provide a mechanistic role for adipocytes and macrophages prior to carcinogenesis that may be critical for prevention and treatment of obesity-related cancer.
Formatted output of MetaMap
Population
3824388|S|1|0|0|10|postmenopausal women|43210|P|MSH
Condition/Disease
3824388|S|1|0|6|70|treatment of obesity related cancer|877578|D|NCI
3824388|S|1|0|6|70|macrophages prior to carcinogenesis|596263|D| NCI

Table 2. Input and output of entity extraction task with MetaMap.

Application ID, Grant number		7094759, R01CA114068-01A1		7190702, R01CA125554-01		8384429, R01CA170851-01	
# of sentences		11		15		13	
# of words		332		448		361	
MeSH	P					*43157*	*Caucasians*
		43210	***Woman***	***43210***	***Woman***	***43210***	***Woman***
				1257890	***Population groups***	***85756***	***African Americans***
						15576	**Family**
	D	***6142***	***Malignant neoplasm of breast***	***6142***	***Malignant neoplasm of breast***	***6142***	***Malignant neoplasm of breast***
		18790	Cardiac Arrest	6826	Malignant neoplasms	6826	Malignant neoplasms
						27627	**Neoplasm metastasis**
				27651	***Neoplasms***	***27651***	***Neoplasms***
						877578	**Treatment related secondary malignancy**
NCIt	P	***43210***	***Woman***	***1257890***	***Population groups***	*7457*	*Caucasoid race*
		599755	*Cohort*			*27361*	*Person*
						30705	*Patients*
						43210	***Woman***
						85756	***African American***
						15576	**Family**
	D	***6142***	***Malignant neoplasm of breast***	***6142***	***Malignant neoplasm of breast***	***6142***	***Malignant neoplasm of breast***
		1512441	High-Risk Cancer	*7104*	*Carcinoma of female Breast*	**27627**	**Neoplasm metastasis**
				27651	***Neoplastic growth***	***27651***	***Neoplastic Growth***
				1519670	Tumor angiogenesis	**877578**	**Treatment related secondary malignancy**
				1519689	Tumor promotion	1306459	Primary malignant neoplasm
						1519670	Tumor Angiogenesis
						1533592	Malignant Paraganglionic Neoplasm

Table 3. MeSH and NCIt Concepts in 3 NIH abstracts. Bold depicts common concepts.

This paper considers only the concepts in MeSH and NCIt that are connected using the following relations: parent (PAR), child (CHD), broader (RB), narrower (RN), sibling (SIB), synonymous (SY) and other (RO) (U.S. National Library of Medicine, 2016). We formulate eight archetypes based on breast cancer risk factors that are likely to be considered when recruiting for a clinical trial. The text description of these archetypes was also mapped to NCIt and MeSH concepts using MetaMap as described above. We use the Jaccard similarity coefficient (described in background section) to quantify the similarity between the grant proposal and the patients using the extracted concepts as features.

RESULTS

We first describe the alignment between each facet that is reported in the grants and the MeSH and NCIt ontologies. We then create 8 patients that mirror facets that are important in the study of breast cancer and finally we compare the similarity between each study and each patient archetype.

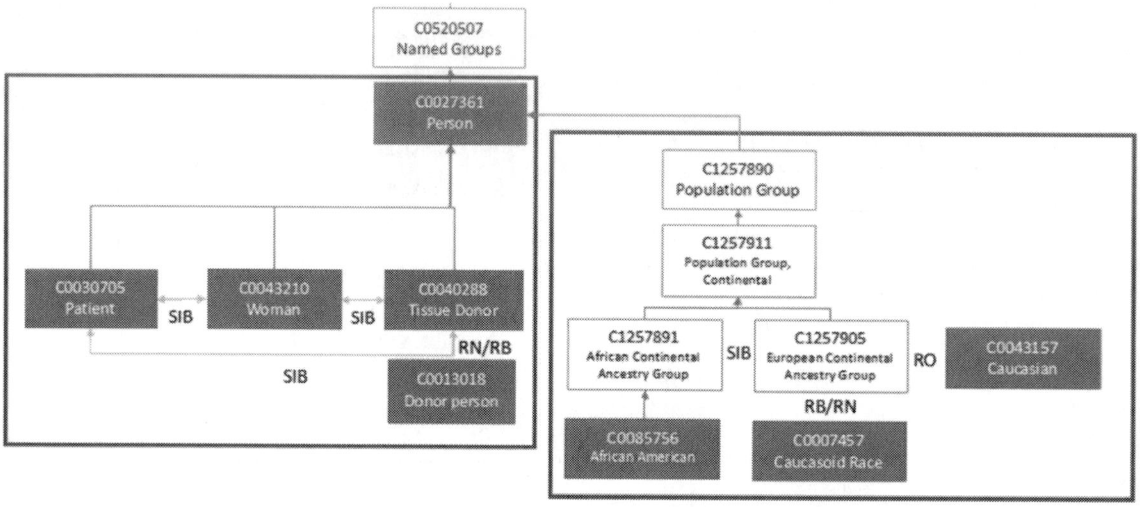

(A) Population facet in MeSH.

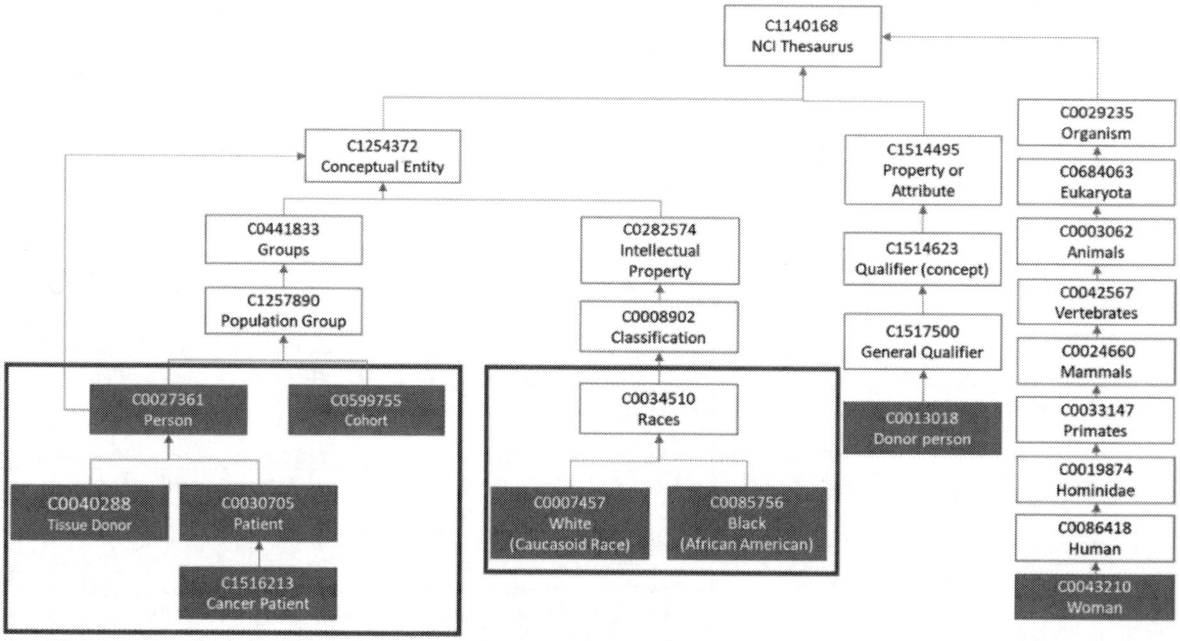

(B) Population facet in NCIt

Figure 1. Population characteristics in MeSH and NCIt. White depicts concepts that do not appear in a grant but are provided for context. Arrows point to the parent of a parent–child relationship. A. Population facet in MeSH. B. Population facet in NCIt.

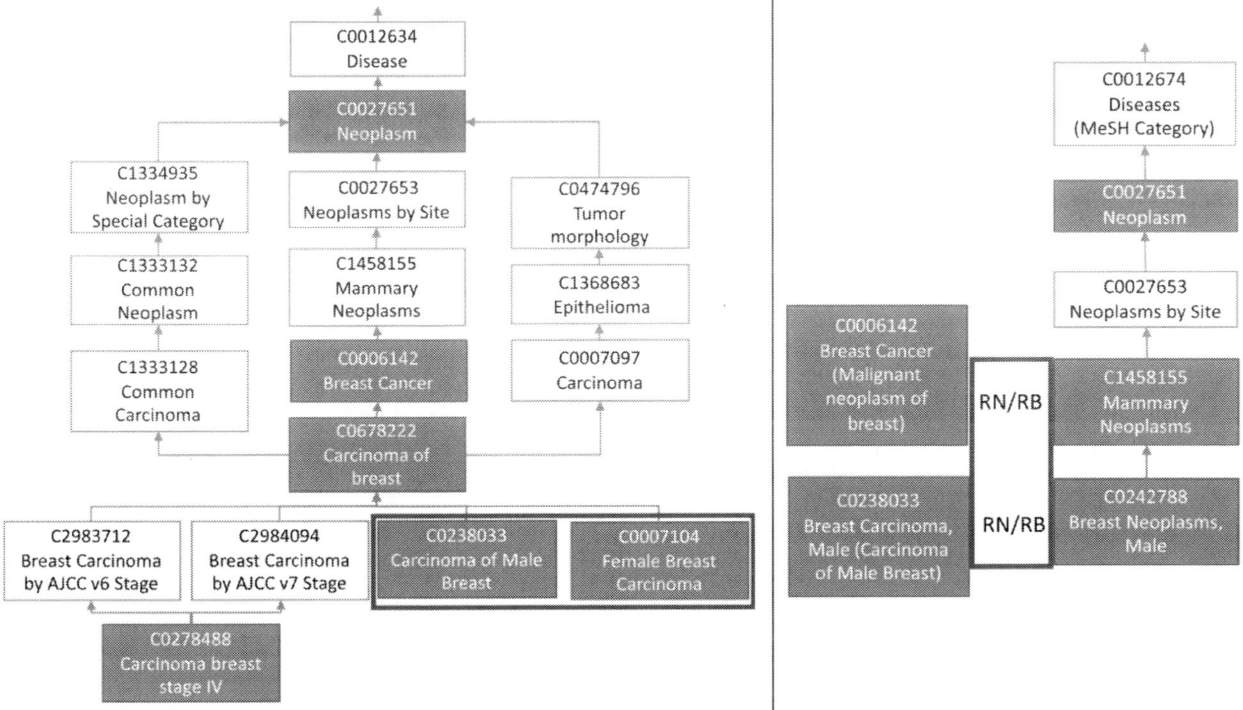

(A) Disease facet in NCIt

(B) Disease facet in MeSH

Figure 2. Disease facets. White depicts concepts that do not appear in a grant, and arrows point to the parent of a parent–child relationship. A. Disease facet in NCIt B. Disease facet in MeSH.

Identifying Concepts in Grants

There were 15 population and 34 condition MeSH concepts, and 16 population and 53 condition NCIt concepts identified from three NIH grant abstracts (see Table 3). Since all three abstracts are from the grant investigating breast cancer, many concepts overlap among them. Among 5 unique population MeSH concepts, 4 concepts are overlapped to NCIt concepts. Four of the condition MeSH concepts out of 8 also overlapped to NCIt concepts out of 10 unique concepts. NCIt had a higher coverage where the precision, recall, and F-score when evaluating the coverage for P, D, and I element were 98%, 87.5%, and 92.8%, and 97.1%, 100%, and 98.6% for MeSH and NCIt respectively.

Figures 1 and 2 illustrate how the extracted population and condition concepts are linked to each other in MeSH and NCIt ontologies. Although all the relations mentioned above are considered in constructing ontology trees, only PAR-CHD relation was shown in NCIt tree. On the contrary, MeSH tree depicts all the relation types such as PAR-CHD, RB-RN, SIB, and RO.

Population facets are captured under the *Person (C0027361)* concept in MeSH, whereas the concepts are more dispersed in NCIt (see Figure 1B). All concepts are linked by PAR-CHD relation in NCIt, but the additional relationship types (RN-RB, RO, SIB) are needed to connect these concepts in MeSH. For example, the *Caucasoid Race (C0007457)* and *Caucasian (C0043157)* concepts are not linked through the PAR-CHD relation in MeSH. The usage of relation types other than PAR-CHD might add more vocabularies to the ontology, however, it sometimes links redundant concepts to the ontology tree.

Three concepts *Patient (C0030705)*, *Woman (C0043210)*, and *Tissue donor (C0040288)* in MeSH tree are marked as siblings and shares a parent, *Person (C0027361)*. It is true that patient, woman, and tissue donor are person, but it is questionable that sibling relation exist among the three concepts. The similarity score between *Woman* and *Person* in MeSH would be larger since the concepts are closely located, on the other hand, the score would be lower in NCIt due to the remote distance of the concepts.

Additional analysis on condition facets shows that MeSH has fewer concepts than NCIt to capture the stage and the location of the cancer. The grant abstract text "metastatic breast cancer" is mapped to *Malignant neoplasm of breast (C0006142)* in MeSH and *Carcinoma breast stage IV (C0278488)* in NCIt (see Table 3). Note that breast cancer concepts *C0006142* and *C0238033* are not linked to the main

	Input text	MeSH		NCIt	
1	White female with breast cancer	43210	Women		
		7457	Caucasoid race	7457	Caucasoid race
		6142	Breast cancer	7104	Carcinoma of female breast
2	White female withmetastatic breast cancer	43210	Women	43210	Women
		7457	Caucasoid race	7457	Caucasoid race
		6142	Breast cancer	7104	Carcinoma of female breast
				278488	Stage IV breast carcinoma
3	African American female with breast cancer	43210	Women		
		85756	African americans	85756	African Americans
		6142	Breast cancer	7104	Carcinoma of female breast
4	African American female with metastatic breast cancer	43210	Women	43210	Women
		85756	African americans	85756	African American
		6142	Breast cancer	278488	Stage IV breast carcinoma
				7104	Carcinoma of female breast
5	White male with breast cancer	7457	Caucasoid race	7457	Caucasoid race
		238033	Carcinoma of male breast	238033	Carcinoma of male breast
6	White male with metastatic breast cancer	7457	Caucasoid race	7457	Caucasoid race
		238033	Carcinoma of male breast	238033	Carcinoma of male breast
				278488	Stage IV breast carcinoma
7	African American male with breast cancer	85756	African Americans	85756	African Americans
		238033	Carcinoma of male breast	238033	Carcinoma of male breast
8	African American male with metastatic breast cancer	85756	African Americans	85756	African Americans
		238033	Carcinoma of male breast	238033	Carcinoma of male breast
				278488	Stage IV breast carcinoma

Table 4. Archetype patients and the corresponding MeSH and NCIt concepts.

branch of the MeSH tree influencing the similarity calculation. The concepts linked by relations other than PAR-CHD cannot be calculated with this method given our current implementation.

Mapping from Patients to Concepts

Table 4 shows the results of mapping the eight archetype patients to the MeSH and NCIt ontologies using MetaMap. As with the grant mappings, there is not a one-to-one relationship between the facets in the archetype patients and the concepts. For example, a phrase, "White female with breast cancer" is mapped to three concepts in MeSH (woman, Caucasoid race, and breast cancer) and two concepts in NCIt (Caucasoid race, and carcinoma of female breast). The phrase "white male with breast cancer" is mapped to two concepts - Caucasoid race, and a concept that combines male and carcinoma of breast. In both examples the NCIt captures all the information about the patient into one concept. The non-existent combined concept, *Carcinoma of Female Breast*, might indicate underlying gender discrepancy in the MeSH ontology.

One factor that is critical in recruiting patients is their stage of breast cancer as different treatment strategies are used at different stages. However, only NCIt can differentiate between different stages of breast cancer such as *Stage IV Breast Carcinoma (C0278488)* (see Table 4).

Similarity Scores between Patients

A similarity measure should satisfy the following formal properties: symmetry D(A,B) = D(B,A); constancy of self-similarity D(A,A) = 0; positivity (separation) D(A,B) = 0 if and only if A = B; and the triangular inequality D(A,B) < = D(A,C) + D (B,C). From a practical perspective this means that comparing a patient that has every facet aligned with a clinical trial protocol should result in a similarity of 1 and patients that share no facets in common should be 0. More importantly, the similarity measure should gradually decline from 1 to 0 as fewer facets align between the patient and the trial.

Both MeSH and NCIt satisfy the self-similarity property for all eight patients (see Table 5). However, using MeSH does not satisfy the separation property because MeSH is unable to differentiate between the concepts breast cancer and metastatic breast cancer (see cases 1-2, 3-4, 5-6, and 7-8 in Table 5 that have a similarity of one when the concepts are different). At the other end of the spectrum MeSH resulted in a similarity score of zero for patients 3-5, 3-6, 4-5 and 4-6 even though these patients do have a disease factor in common. When differentiating between diseases both MeSH and NCIt have a composite issue where two factors (gender and disease) are combined in concept *C2380033 Carcinoma of the Male Breast*. There is no well-accepted way to account for aligning multiple separate concepts from either the grant or patient with a composite concept quantitatively.

If patients are the same except for one facet, the similarity score should be less than one, but should not be zero. Changing only gender resulted in a MeSH similarity of 0.25 which is a dramatic drop. Similarly, changing only race lowers the similarity score to 0.33–0.50. These changes produce a much smaller drop when using NCIt. Lastly, we measured the variation of the scores using standard deviation, where MeSH (0.3988) was greater deviation than NCIt (0.1640). This metric shows a gradual decline in similarity scores using NCIt.

grained distinctions between concepts, such as NCIt, are better suited for aligning eligibility features to patients.

DISCUSSION

The biomedical community has widely recognized the value of ontologies for a range of activities from providing access to biomedical literature using MeSH to capturing a medical diagnosis using SNOMED. However, it can be difficult for a user to determine which of the many ontologies available is most suited for a new application. The strategy presented in this paper shows how to create archetypes of the patients with particular conditions and then uses and widely adopted similarity measure properties to evaluate how well a given set of archetype patents align with each ontology. This enables us to quantify the alignment between task and ontology choice. Such an approach could be added to the BioPortal (https://bioportal.bioontology.org/) that already provides users with a valuable resource of ontologies. Specifically, the BioPortal could be extended so that a user could provide a sample set of archetypes patients. The BioPortal could then enable the user to interactively explore each ontological space in order to determine which ontology is best aligned to the new task. Lastly, the similarity measures can provide the user with useful information about how the internal

MeSH									NCIt							
1	2	3	4	5	6	7	8		1	2	3	4	5	6	7	8
1.00								**1**	1.00							
1.00	1.00							**2**	0.69	1.00						
0.50	0.50	1.00						**3**	0.64	0.54	1.00					
0.50	0.50	1.00	1.00					**4**	0.67	0.78	0.69	1.00				
0.25	0.25	0.00	0.00	1.00				**5**	0.87	0.56	0.63	0.55	1.00			
0.25	0.25	0.00	0.00	1.00	1.00			**6**	0.88	0.60	0.65	0.59	0.92	1.00		
0.01	0.01	0.25	0.25	0.33	0.33	1.00		**7**	0.63	0.55	0.87	0.67	0.64	0.67	1.00	
0.01	0.01	0.25	0.25	0.33	0.33	1.00	1.00	**8**	0.65	0.59	0.84	0.72	0.67	0.73	0.92	1.00
Standard deviation = 0.3988									Standard deviation = 0.1640							

Table 5. Pairwise similarity scores of archetype patients using MeSH and NCIt.

		MeSH		NCIt
7094759	3	0.5286	4	0.3794
	4	0.5286	2	0.3784
	1	0.5244	8	0.2373
	2	0.5244	6	0.2364
	7	0.0076	3	0.2231
	8	0.0076	7	0.2231
	5	0.0000	1	0.2220
	6	0.0000	5	0.2220

		MeSH		NCIt
7190702	3	0.5592	8	0.3239
	4	0.5592	6	0.3238
	1	0.3641	7	0.2739
	2	0.3641	5	0.2737
	7	0.1742	4	0.2622
	8	0.1742	2	0.2620
	5	0.0000	3	0.2324
	6	0.0000	1	0.2322

		MeSH		NCIt
8384429	3	0.3400	4	0.3431
	4	0.3400	2	0.3424
	1	0.2105	8	0.2721
	2	0.2105	6	0.2714
	7	0.1034	3	0.2682
	8	0.1034	7	0.2682
	5	0.0000	1	0.2674
	6	0.0000	5	0.2674

Table 6. Pairwise MeSH and NCIt similarity (Jaccard measure) of patients and grant abstracts.

Ranking

A gradual decline in similarity scores as patients share fewer concepts would be useful when ranking either trials to the patients, or patients to the most promising trial. MeSH is unable to provide a fine-grain level of differentiation between patients and instead generates zero or close to zero similarity scores on white male breast cancer patients (patient types 5, and 6) because the concept, *Breast Cancer of Male* is detached from MeSH tree (see Figure 2 and Table 6). An ontology that produces a similarity score that changes with respect to any change in the facets is desirable, but the MeSH score was the same when all facets other than the stage of breast cancer was the same. In contrast, the finer granularity of NCIt coverage provides a graceful decline when ranking patients. This indicates that ontologies that contain finer-

structure of the selected ontology might influence how patients are ranked.

There are more than twice as many unique concept identifiers in the 2016 version of the UMLS for MeSH as there are for the NCIt (363,050 in MeSH versus 121,764 in NCIt), but these results show that the concepts in the NCIt are much better able to capture breast cancer patient characteristics that would make them eligible for a clinical trial. The approach presented in this paper, where patient archetypes are first created that reflect important facets in biomedicine, which are then compared with candidate ontologies provides a strategy to assess the alignment between ontologies and the task requirements. Moreover, the formal criterion used to determine a good similarity measure provide another lens in which to assess how well the internal structure of the ontology can meet the needs of a given application.

Limitations

This work explored an experimental approach in recruiting patients for a clinical trial with a limited sample of three biomedical grant abstracts and one type of disease. The scope of the data should be expanded for validating our findings in future researches.

CONCLUSION

The F1-score of both the MeSH ontology and the NCIt are very high (92.8% in MeSH vs. 98.6% in NCIt), which shows that the ontologies have good coverage with respect to the grant description and patients; however, concept coverage is a necessary, but not a sufficient condition when evaluating an ontology for a given task. We show that the level of concept specificity and the internal structure of the ontology should also play a role.

This study identifies population and condition facets automatically from funded grant proposals and a set of breast cancer patients. These facets are used to prioritize clinical trials for a patient using an ontology-based semantic similarity measure. Results show that NCIt provides better coverage and that the similarity scores between patients and clinical trials gracefully decline when ranking patients for a clinical trial and vice versa. A greater level of concept specificity and a higher number of internal connections between concepts in NCIt are responsible for this fine-grain similarity measure.

In contrast to the NCIt, the semantic similarity scores from MeSH do not satisfy the separation property which is desirable in any measure of similarity because the MeSH ontology does not differentiate between 'breast cancer' and "metastatic breast cancer". MeSH also generates similarity measures of zero or very close to zero for the "white male breast cancer" patient archetype (patient types 5, and 6) because the concept, *Breast Cancer of Male* is detached from MeSH tree. For these reasons we recommend using the NCIt rather than MeSH when ranking breast cancer patients for a clinical trial or prioritizing clinical trials for a given patient.

ACKNOWLEDGMENTS

This material is based upon work supported by the National Science Foundation under Grant No. 1535167.

REFERENCES

American Cancer Society. (2017). *Breast Cancer Facts & Figures 2017–2018.*

Aronson, A. R., & Lang, F.-M. (2010). An overview of MetaMap: Historical perspective and recent advances. *Journal of the American Medical Informatics Association*, *17*(3), 229–236.

Ben Aouicha, M., & Hadj Taieb, M. A. (2016). Computing semantic similarity between biomedical concepts using new information content approach. *Journal of Biomedical Informatics*, *59*, 258–275. https://doi.org/10.1016/j.jbi.2015.12.007

Boudin, F., Nie, J.-Y., Bartlett, J. C., Grad, R., Pluye, P., & Dawes, M. (2010). Combining classifiers for robust PICO element detection. *BMC Medical Informatics and Decision Making*, *10*, 29–29. https://doi.org/10.1186/1472-6947-10-29

Hao, T., Rusanov, A., Boland, M. R., & Weng, C. (2014). Clustering clinical trials with similar eligibility criteria features. *Journal of Biomedical Informatics*, *52*, 112–120. https://doi.org/10.1016/j.jbi.2014.01.009

Hassanzadeh, H., Groza, T., & Hunter, J. (2014). Identifying scientific artefacts in biomedical literature: The Evidence Based Medicine use case. *Journal of Biomedical Informatics*, *49*, 159–170. https://doi.org/10.1016/j.jbi.2014.02.006

Huang, K.-C., Chiang, I. J., Xiao, F., Liao, C.-C., Liu, C. C.-H., & Wong, J.-M. (2013). PICO element detection in medical text without metadata: Are first sentences enough? *Journal of Biomedical Informatics*, *46*(5), 940–946. https://doi.org/10.1016/j.jbi.2013.07.009

Jiang, J. J., & Conrath, D. W. (1997). *Semantic similarity based on corpus statistics and lexical taxonomy*. Paper presented at the International Conference on Research in Computational Linguistics, ROCLING X, Taipei, Taiwan.

Karystianis, G., Buchan, I., & Nenadic, G. (2014). Mining characteristics of epidemiological studies from Medline: A case study in obesity. *Journal of Biomedical Semantics*, *5*(1), 1–11. https://doi.org/10.1186/2041-1480-5-22

Leacock, C., & Chodorow, M. (1998). Combining local context and WordNet similarity for word sense identification. *WordNet: An Electronic Lexical Database*, *49*(2), 265–283.

Lin, D. (1998). An information-theoretic definition of similarity. *Icml*, *98*, 296–304.

Lin, J., & Demner-Fushman, D. (2006). *The role of knowledge in conceptual retrieval: A study in the domain of clinical medicine*. Paper presented at the Proceedings of the 29th annual international ACM SIGIR conference on Research and development in information retrieval. Seattle, Washington, USA.

McInnes, B. T., & Pedersen, T. (2013). Evaluating measures of semantic similarity and relatedness to disambiguate terms in biomedical text. *Journal of Biomedical Informatics*, *46*(6), 1116–1124. https://doi.org/10.1016/j.jbi.2013.08.008

McInnes, B. T., & Pedersen, T. (2015). Evaluating semantic similarity and relatedness over the semantic grouping of clinical term pairs. *Journal of Biomedical Informatics*, *54*, 329–336. https://doi.org/10.1016/j.jbi.2014.11.014

Meng, L., Gu, J., & Zhou, Z. (2012). A new model of information content based on concept's topology for measuring semantic similarity in WordNet. *International Journal of Grid and Distributed Computing*, *5*(3), 81–94.

Niwattanakul, S., Singthongchai, J., Naenudorn, E., & Wanapu, S. (2013). *Using of Jaccard coefficient for keywords similarity*. Paper presented at the Proceedings of the International MultiConference of Engineers and Computer Scientists.

Palmer, J. R., Viscidi, E., Troester, M. A., Hong, C.-C., Schedin, P., Bethea, T. N., ... Ambrosone, C. B. (2014). Parity, lactation, and breast cancer subtypes in African American women: Results from the AMBER consortium. *JNCI Journal of the National Cancer Institute*, *106*(10), dju237. https://doi.org/10.1093/jnci/dju237

Penberthy, L. T., Dahman, B. A., Petkov, V. I., & DeShazo, J. P. (2012). Effort required in eligibility screening for clinical trials. *Journal of oncology practice*, *8*(6), 365–370.

Resnik, P. (1995). Using information content to evaluate semantic similarity in a taxonomy. *arXiv* preprint cmp-lg/9511007.

Sánchez, D., Batet, M., & Isern, D. (2011). Ontology-based information content computation. *Knowledge-Based Systems*, *24*(2), 297–303. https://doi.org/10.1016/j.knosys.2010.10.001

Sebti, A., & Barfroush, A. A. (2008, October). *A new word sense similarity measure in wordnet*. Paper presented at the 2008 International Multiconference on Computer Science and Information Technology.

Seco, N., Veale, T., & Hayes, J. (2004). An intrinsic information content metric for semantic similarity in WordNet. *ECAI, 16*, 1089.

U.S. National Library of Medicine. (2016). *Abbreviations Used in Data Elements - 2016AA Release*. Retrieved from https://www.nlm.nih.gov/research/umls/knowledge_sources/metathesaurus/release/abbreviations.html#REL

Weng, C., Tu, S. W., Sim, I., & Richesson, R. (2010). Formal representation of eligibility criteria: A literature review. *Journal of Biomedical Informatics*, *43*(3), 451–467. https://doi.org/10.1016/j.jbi.2009.12.004

Wu, Z., & Palmer, M. (1994). *Verbs semantics and lexical selection*. Paper presented at the Proceedings of the 32nd annual meeting on Association for Computational Linguistics.

Zhou, Z., Wang, Y., & Gu, J. (2008, December. *A New model of information content for semantic similarity in WordNet*. Paper presented at the 2008 Second International Conference on Future Generation Communication and Networking Symposia.

Investigation of Users' Knowledge Change Process in Learning-Related Search Tasks

Hanrui Liu
Peking University, People's Republic of China
lhr2013@pku.edu.cn

Chang Liu
Peking University, People's Republic of China
imliuc@pku.edu.cn

Nicholas J. Belkin
Rutgers University, New Brunswick, USA
belkin@comminfo.rutgers.edu

ABSTRACT

This study aims to examine users' knowledge change characteristics and knowledge change process, and examined factors that may influence users' knowledge change process. A user search experiment was conducted, in which participants were asked to search for two learning-related search tasks and use a mind-map to organize their thoughts during the search process. Pre- and post-search questionnaires were distributed to collect users' self-assessed topic familiarity and task difficulty. Besides the overall knowledge change process by all the users, we identified four types of knowledge change styles using a hierarchical clustering method: Early knowledge change, Medium-term knowledge change, Late knowledge change and Average knowledge change. In addition, we found that task type, task difficulty in information integration and difficulty in drawing the mind-map had significant influences on users' knowledge change styles. This study took a process perspective to characterize users' knowledge change at different stages and shed light on when and how learning occurs during the search process.

KEYWORDS

Knowledge Change Process; Learning-Related Tasks; Search as Learning; Mind-Map

ASIS&T THESAURUS

Information Behavior; Knowledge and Information; User Studies

INTRODUCTION

In recent years, "Searching as learning" has emerged as an important research area in library and information science. "Search as learning" considers search systems as learning technologies rather than merely information retrieval tools, and allows for an understanding of users' information search behavior in the broader context of human learning. Interpreting users' information search behaviors from the learning perspective is not new. Belkin's (1980) ASK model argues that users experience information needs when they realize their knowledge state is anomalous and is inadequate to achieve some goal, and their anomalous state of knowledge then changes through the search process. Marchionini (1997) described information seeking as "a process, in which humans purposefully engage in order to change their state of knowledge." Kuhlthau's ISP model (2005) examined users' emotional change and cognitive changes during the search process, and found that from the beginning to the end of the seeking process, users' cognitive state changes from fuzzy to concrete.

Research in search as learning has proposed several ways to measure the learning outcome after searching (Bhattacharya & Gwizdka, 2019; Collins-Thompson, Rieh, Haynes, & Syed, 2016; Gadiraju, Yu, Dietze, & Holtz, 2018; Wilson & Wilson, 2013; Yu et al., 2018); and the relationship between search interactions and learning performance or knowledge change (Bhattacharya & Gwizdka, 2019; Ghosh, Rath, & Shah, 2018; Liu & Song, 2018).

But one of the key challenges in search as learning, when and how does learning occur during the search process, seems not to have been fully examined in existing literature. One difficulty is how to collect users' knowledge change or learning explicitly during the search process. Research has taken users' writing behaviors during the search process as indicators of their learning (Liu & Belkin, 2012; Potthast & Hagen, 2012, 2016). However, text writing could hardly present the structure of users' knowledge and it is hard to tell how much they learn at each point of writing. Research in sense-making has examined the evolvement of their knowledge structures using think-aloud protocols, e.g., Zhang and Soergel (2016). They identified three broad classes of conceptual changes: accretion, tuning and restructuring. However, there are some problems associated with the think-aloud method, including that some subjects may have a difficult time simultaneously articulating their thoughts and completing whatever Interactive Information Retrieval (IIR) task has been assigned to them (Kelly, 2009). In our study, we explored using a mind-mapping technique to elicit users' knowledge change process during their search. The goal of this study is to investigate users' knowledge change process when they are searching for learning-related search tasks. The following three main research questions guide the current study:

82nd Annual Meeting of the Association for Information Science & Technology | Melbourne, Australia | 19–23 October, 2019

DOI: 10.1002/pra2.00063

RQ1. What are the characteristics of knowledge change in different search stages from the perspective of search process?

RQ2. Are there any different knowledge change styles among different users from the perspective of search process? If so, what are the styles?

RQ3. What factors may have influence on users' knowledge change styles?

RELATED WORK

Learning is a dynamic process and searching is an evolving process. Both knowledge change in the learning process and differences in knowledge state before and after learning are areas worth exploring. In early research in the field of information retrieval, a small number of studies have discussed knowledge change. In addition, empirical research also provides a large amount of evidence which demonstrates that knowledge change is a common phenomenon in the process of IIR (Eickhoff, Teevan, White et al. 2014; Vakkari, Pennanen & Serola, 2003; Wildemuth, 2004). Liu, Belkin, Zhang and Yuan (2013) found that a successful search process often has a tendency of growing knowledge. More recent research on knowledge change tends to compare the differences in knowledge states before and after the search. Bhattacharya and Gwizdka (2019) proposed a knowledge change measure by measuring the difference in a user's knowledge of vocabulary on the topic of the search task. They further examined how measures of users' eye-fixations and search interaction measures are related to their knowledge change measure.

There are also some studies which discuss the way knowledge changes, most of them focusing on how users integrate new with old knowledge. This kind of research is based on Piaget's Constructivist theory of learning, that the learning process is the active construction of learners based on their own existing knowledge and experience. Piaget identified two types of cognitive changes in knowledge acquisition: Assimilation, which refers to the addition of information to existing knowledge structure; and Accommodation, which refers to the modification or change of existing knowledge structures (Piaget, 1936, 1976). Following Piaget's two types of cognitive changes, Rumelhart and Norman (1978) further classified knowledge learning into three categories: accretion, tuning and restructuring. Accretion is the normal kind of fact learning and gradual addition within existing knowledge without structural change. Tuning is a more significant kind for information organizing and interpreting, or minor modification. Restructuring is a yet more significant and difficult process, which involves radical change of existing structures or creation of new structures. Restructuring rarely happens and it takes place only after considerable time and effort, since it probably requires a critical mass of information to have been accumulated first. Zhang and Soergel (2016) examined the process patterns and conceptual changes in knowledge representations during information seeking and sensemaking using a think-aloud protocol. The knowledge change in this study was extracted from users' concept map change and their think-aloud protocol. They did not examine how users' knowledge change was associated with their search. In addition, the three types of knowledge change proposed by Rumelhart and Norman (1978) could further be split into two dimensions: (1) knowledge change type, whether adding new knowledge or modifying existing knowledge; (2) knowledge structure change, whether main knowledge structure is changed or just some details in the knowledge structure is changed.

Rieh et al. (2014) suggest that information search strategy, domain knowledge, and cognitive level may affect the level of user's knowledge change or their knowledge change process. Kelly and Cool (2002) and White, Dumais, and Teevan (2009) found users' topic familiarity and domain knowledge before searching often have significant influence upon users' search interactions. Wilson and Wilson (2013) found that participants with more topic knowledge produced texts with higher quality and covered more topics in their summaries.

In light of the above, we see that past research on learning process and learning performance during search have mainly compared the overall differences between post-search and pre-search. In this work, we aim to contribute by investigating the knowledge change process through eliciting users' knowledge states during search using mind mapping. Our contribution includes that (a) we examined both the knowledge point acquisition and the structural change in users' knowledge states during search; (b) we identified four types of knowledge change styles among users and found different users have knowledge structural change at different search stages; (c) we found task difficulty, especially the difficulty to integrate different information items during search was significantly related to users' knowledge change styles.

METHOD

A user study was conducted to address our research question. We had thirty-one students from a major Chinese comprehensive university as our participants in this study. Among all the participants, there were twelve males and nineteen females, with ages between seventeen and twenty-nine. There were fourteen undergraduates and seventeen postgraduates whose majors included Information Science, Computer Science, Chemistry, Psychology, Sociology, Medical Science and Environmental Science.

User Experiment

Participants used a desktop computer in our research lab to carry out two learning-related search tasks. During the experiment, participants were first asked to complete a background questionnaire. Before the search started, participants read the task description, and then they were asked to draw a mind-map using XMind8,[1] to represent knowledge they already

[1] https://www.xmind.net/xmind8-pro/

know about the topic. XMind is a tool for supporting construction of mind-maps. The mind-map structure in XMind contains a root in the center, with main branches radiating from it. The next step was to complete the pre-search questionnaire, to elicit data like users' topic familiarity. During the search, participants could continually modify the mind-map according to what they read and learned while searching for information, and they could stop searching whenever they believed that the mind-map had represented enough knowledge needed for the task. After the search, participants were asked to write an essay in a notepad to answer the questions of the tasks, referring only to their own mind-map records. After writing the essay, participants were asked to complete the post-search questionnaire about task difficulty. After that, participants continued to work for the second search task with the same procedure as in the first search task. Finally, the participants completed a post-experiment questionnaire. The order of the two search tasks were balanced among all the participants; that is half of participants completed Task 1 first, the other half completed Task 2 first. During the search, participants' interactions with the computer were recorded by Morae Recorder 3.3.

Learning-related Search Tasks

We adopted Lee et al. (2015)'s learning classification to construct the learning-related search tasks in our experiment. Lee et al. (2015) classified learning into Receptive learning, Critical learning and Creative learning based on Bloom's cognitive complexity level (1956). Receptive learning is defined as understanding, remembering and reproducing what is taught, critical learning as criticizing and evaluating ideas from multiple perspectives, and creative learning as creating new ideas or artifacts from what is learned. Creative learning is highly demanding for users, which is difficult in an experimental environment. Therefore, we selected receptive and critical learning as task design principles.

Task 1 (Receptive learning, Topic: iPhoneX face recognition): Your brother has just entered college and wants to change to a new mobile phone. He heard that Apple has launched a very powerful face recognition technology in iPhoneX, which makes the use of mobile phones more convenient and interesting. He hopes that you can introduce him to functions and usage scenarios using face recognition technology in iPhoneX; at the same time, what the advantages and innovations are of face recognition in iPhoneX compared with previous face recognition technology. You need to search for relevant information to explain the above questions to your brother.

Task 2 (Critical learning, Topic: Bitcoin): Recently, Bitcoin has set off another wave of enthusiasm. Many students are interested in it but do not know much about it. In the "Internet Finance" course, you chose the topic of "Bitcoin" to give a presentation of about 3 minutes. You intend to introduce the differences between Bitcoin and common currency (such as RMB, USD) used in our lives. At the same time, analyze whether Bitcoin can become a currency that is generally circulated in reality, and finally give your conclusion (Yes/No). In order to complete this presentation, you need to search for relevant information and prepare a lecture material for yourself.

For both tasks, participants were told to use the mind-map to organize their ideas and information. The mind-map they drew during search would be used to help them write up their presentations after search, and it was the only source they referred to at that time.

Mind-map Drawing in this Experiment

To examine the knowledge change process, we need to choose an effective knowledge representation tool to visualize the knowledge structure hidden in users' minds. Compared to text typing, visualizations can help us better represent users' knowledge structures.

Concept map and Mind-map are two types of knowledge representation tools that have been widely used to represent people's knowledge state, and both of them are able to present the relationships among nodes as knowledge points. But there are some differences between them. The concept map is mainly used to represent the relationships between concepts in an objective knowledge system, which has correct and incorrect concepts and relationships. The mind-map technique is mainly used to represent people's thinking process in learning, and there is no absolute correct or wrong. In our research, we focus on how users would integrate the new information they collect during the search process with their existing knowledge structure to acquire new knowledge and address the information problems in the search tasks. Therefore, the mind-mapping technique is more appropriate. In addition, Mind mapping has been regarded as a creative and logical means of note-taking and note-making that literally "maps out" students' ideas, and this technique has been highly recommended by many high school teachers in China. Many Chinese college and school students therefore have experience in drawing mind-maps. Mind-mapping experience was required during recruitment, and participants' mind-mapping experience was assessed in the background questionnaire to ensure that they all had sufficient knowledge in drawing mind-maps.

Participants were asked to first draw a pre-search mind-map after they read the task description, before they filled in the pre-search questionnaire and before they conducted the search. At this point, they were asked to draw a mind-map which represented what they already knew about this search task. They were instructed that they could draw a mind map structure directly if they had a structure in mind; otherwise, it was suggested that they list as many points as possible, and that they could then choose which of them to include in the mind map structure later.

During their search, which was recommended for about 30 minutes, they were asked to search for related and useful information that could help them accomplish the task. They could modify their mind-map using the information they collected. We suggested that they use the mind-map to organize their thoughts after obtaining new information, by modifying the mind-map appropriately. They were also told that, after they were done with searching, they would be asked to write down what they planned to tell others about this task, using only their mind-map for this purpose, without returning to any webpages at that point.

Figure 1. A sample pre-search mind-map for Task 1 (S07).

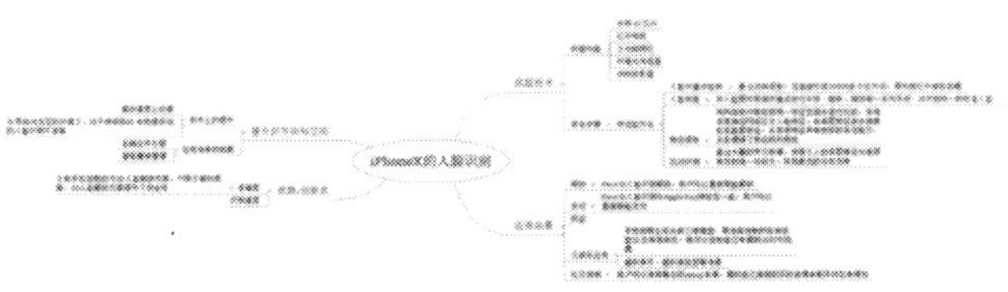

Figure 2. A sample post-search mind-map for Task 1 (S07).

An example of participants' pre-search mind-map is shown in Figure 1, and the mind-map after search is shown in Figure 2. The point of these figures is to indicate the general nature of a mind-map, and to show how the structure of such a representation could change. The actual meanings of the nodes are not at issue here. We then coded the level of each node in the mind-map in the post-search map. There was at least one knowledge tree in the mind-map, and each tree had a central node, which was the primary node and coded as level 1, and its children nodes were coded as level 2. We coded each node's level according to the above rules. An example of the coding is shown in Figure 3.

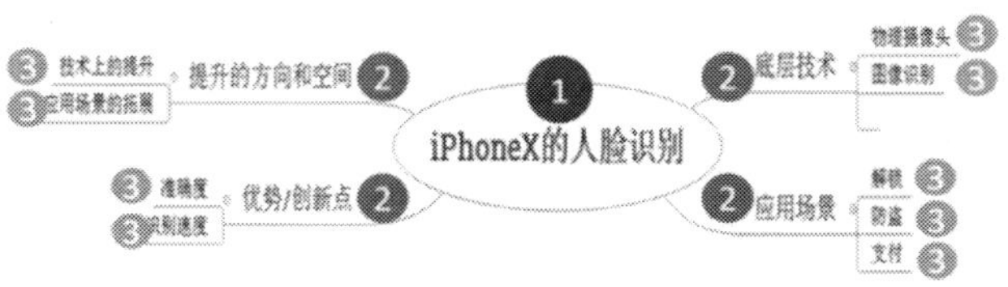

Figure 3. A coding example for node levels.

Encoding of Users' Knowledge Change

Through watching video recordings, we encoded the knowledge change process, including knowledge change types and knowledge structure change.

Knowledge change type is a way to describe user knowledge change from a new or existing knowledge perspective, which includes two major categories, ADD and OPT. ADD means add nodes to the structure, and OPT means optimization of existing nodes. Modifying node content, deleting and moving nodes all belong to OPT.

Knowledge structure change describes the user knowledge change from the viewpoint of knowledge change degree. It includes two categories, knowledge facet change (KFC) and knowledge point change (KPC). The knowledge facet change refers to modification of the level 1 and level 2 nodes, and the knowledge point change refers to the modification of the level 3 nodes and below. The former indicates the mind-map structure is adjusted, the knowledge structure has changed, and the degree of change is high. The latter means modifications about details of the content, the knowledge structure has not changed, and the degree of change is low.

Dimensions of knowledge change	Categories	Explanations
Knowledge change type	ADD	Add node(s) to the structure.
	OPT	Optimization of existing node(s), including modify or delete the content of existing node(s) etc.
Knowledge structure change	KFC	Knowledge facet change, modification of the level 1 and level 2 nodes.
	KPC	Knowledge point change, modification of the level 3 nodes and below.

Table 1. Definitions of knowledge change.

Knowledge Change Variables

We used three variables to describe users' overall knowledge change during the search process.

1. Knowledge change frequency: each time the user changed their mind-map during the search process was counted as one knowledge change, and knowledge change frequency refers to the number of times knowledge change occurs in each search session.
2. Ratio of knowledge change type frequency

As mentioned before, we classified users' knowledge change into two types, adding nodes (ADD) and optimizing the existing nodes (OPT), and then we calculated the distribution of ADD and OPT frequency in a whole session.

- Ratio of ADD = the total number of ADD in a whole session / (the total number of ADD + the total number of OPT in a whole session)
- Ratio of OPT = the total number of OPT in a whole session / (the total number of ADD + the total number of OPT in a whole session)

3. Ratio of knowledge structure change frequency

With respect to the knowledge structure change, there were knowledge facet change (KFC) and knowledge point change (KPC), as described above. Therefore, we calculated the distribution of these two types of knowledge structure change as below:

- Ratio of KFC = the total number of KFC in a whole session / (the total number of KFC + the total number of KPC in a whole session)
- Ratio of KPC = the total number of KPC in a whole session / (the total number of KFC + the total number of KPC in a whole session)

Knowledge Change Variables in Each Stage

After describing the overall knowledge change characteristics, we examined users' knowledge change from a search process perspective to see if there was any variance in different search stages. Each search session was evenly divided into three stages according to the whole searching time: early stage (first 1/3), middle stage (middle 1/3), and last stage (last 1/3).

1. Ratio of knowledge change frequency in each stage

- Ratio of knowledge change frequency [i] = knowledge change frequency in the current stage [i] / the total number of knowledge change frequency in a whole session (*i refers to the current stage.)

2. Ratio of each knowledge change type in each stage, and there are two measures:

- Ratio of ADD frequency [i] = the frequency of ADD in the current stage [i] / the total number of ADD in a whole session
- Ratio of OPT frequency [i] = the frequency of OPT in the current stage [i] / the total number of OPT in a whole session (*i refers to the current stage.)

3. Ratio of each knowledge structure change type in each stage and there are two measures:

- Ratio of KFC frequency [i] = the frequency of KFC in the current stage [i] / the total number of KFC in a whole session (*i refers to the current stage.)
- Ratio of KPC frequency [i] = the frequency of KPC in the current stage [i] / the total number of KPC in a whole session. (*i refers to the current stage.)

Our goal is to investigate characteristics of knowledge change from the process perspective, we used above five knowledge change variables in each stage to conduct hierarchical clustering analysis for knowledge change style.

Pre-search and Post-search Questionnaires

We first elicited users' topic familiarity in the pre-search questionnaire. We asked participants how much they know about each search topic after they read the task description and before they conducted the search, using a five-point Likert Scale. Higher score indicates more familiarity.

We also measured task difficulty assessment after-search. Participants were asked to assess task difficulty from seven dimensions using a five-point Likert Scale as follows. Higher score indicates the task was more difficult.

- Difficulty in Information integration (IIN):
  How difficult do you think it was to integrate new knowledge you found through search?
- Difficulty in Drawing mind-map (DMM):
  How difficult do you think it was to draw the mind-map?
- Difficulty in Gathering an amount of demanding information (GDI):
  How difficult do you think it was to gather the amount of information needed to complete the task?
- Difficulty in Query formulation (QFO):
  How difficult do you think it was to construct queries?
- Difficulty in Information understanding (IUN):
  How difficult do you think it was to understand the information you found through search?
- Difficulty in Gathering useful information (GUS):
  How difficult do you think it was to find useful information through search?
- Difficulty in Writing essays (WES):
  How difficult do you think it was to write the essay using the mind-map you constructed?

RESULTS

Overall Knowledge Change Characteristics

In this study, we have 31 participants, which yields 62 sessions. Among these sessions, participants performed an average of 35.71 knowledge changes per session, with a median of 34. The participant with the fewest knowledge changes had only 7 changes in one session, and the most knowledge change session had 118 changes.

From the process perspective, Figure 4 shows the percentages of knowledge change frequency in the three stages. In general, the second stage had most knowledge changes (35.1%), followed by the first stage (34.5%) and the third stage (30.4%).

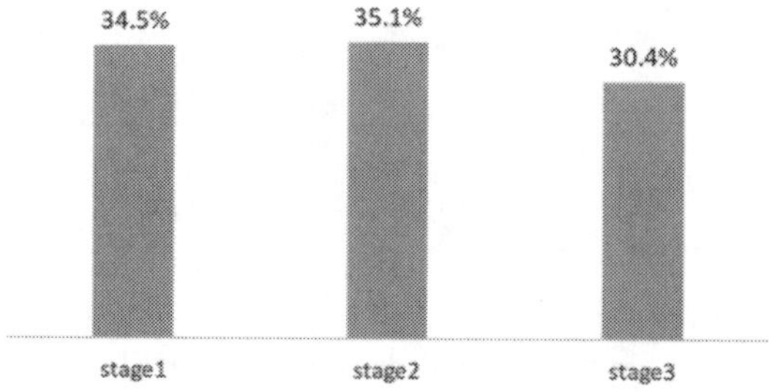

Figure 4. The percentage of knowledge change frequency in three stages.

Secondly, we examined users' knowledge change types and their distributions among all the sessions. Knowledge change types included adding nodes (ADD) and optimization of existing nodes (OPT). As shown in Figure 5, among all the

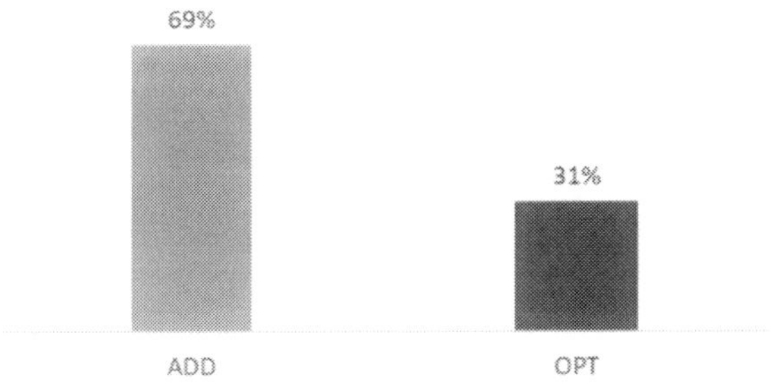

Figure 5. Ratio of knowledge change frequency.

knowledge changes in this experiment, ADD accounted for 69%, whereas OPT accounted for 31%. Therefore, users' main type of knowledge change is to add new nodes.

We then compared the ratio of each type of knowledge change from the process perspective. As shown in Figure 6, the ratio of ADD was highest in the second stage and the ratio of the OPT was highest in the first stage. Therefore, users' optimization of existing nodes mostly occurred in the first stage, and adding new nodes mainly occurred in the second stage.

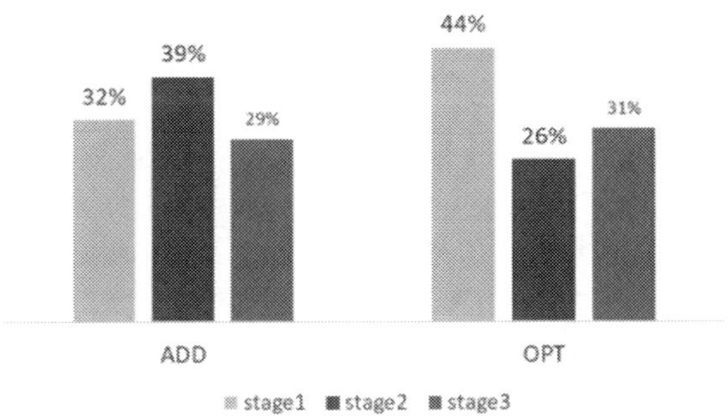

Figure 6. Percentage of each knowledge change type in each stage.

Knowledge structure change included knowledge facet change and knowledge point change. As shown in Figure 7, facet changes accounted for 18%, point changes accounted for 82%. Therefore, users were mainly adding nodes rather than changing the structure during search.

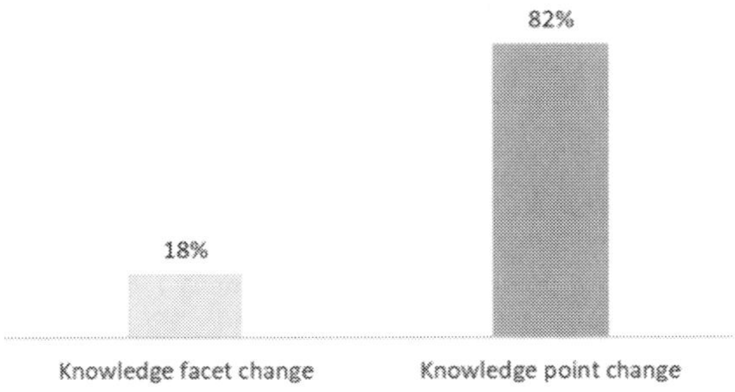

Figure 7. Ratio of knowledge structure change frequency.

From the process perspective, the ratio of knowledge point change was relatively higher in the first and second stage, and a bit lower in the third stage; the ratio of knowledge facet change was highest in the first stage, followed by the second stage, and lowest in the third stage. Therefore, users mainly adjusted their structure in the first stage, and modified lower-level nodes in the first and second stage.

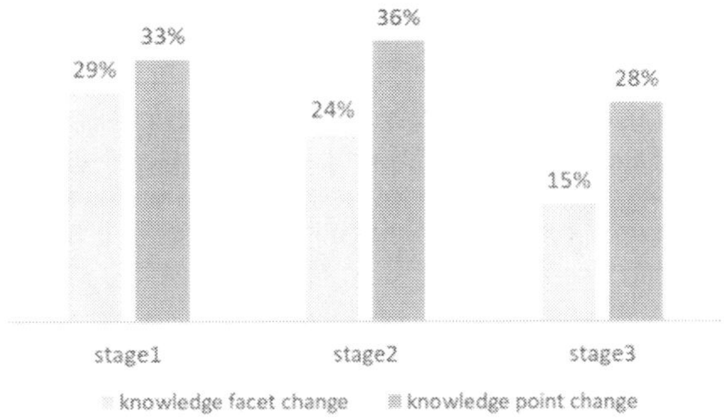

Figure 8. Percentage of each knowledge structure change in each stage.

In general, the knowledge changes varied greatly among different stages. Users mainly changed their knowledge by adding nodes, especially knowledge point notes, and they did not optimize existing nodes or modify their knowledge structure very frequently. From the search process perspective, the frequencies of knowledge change in the three search stages were relatively similar, and the third stage had the fewest changes. Specifically, the behaviors of optimizing existing nodes and adjusting the structure mainly occurred in the first stage, and adding new nodes and modifying knowledge points behaviors mainly occurred in the second stage.

Knowledge Change Styles

We then examined whether users have different styles of knowledge change in different search sessions using the hierarchical clustering analysis. We used the hclust package in R to carry out hierarchical clustering analysis, and adopted the Ward method (Joe & Ward, 1963) to calculate the distance among the clusters. According to the results of the dendrogram, four types of distinguishing clusters were identified, based on the maximization of difference, approximate equivalence of level, and scale of clusters, as shown in Figure 9.

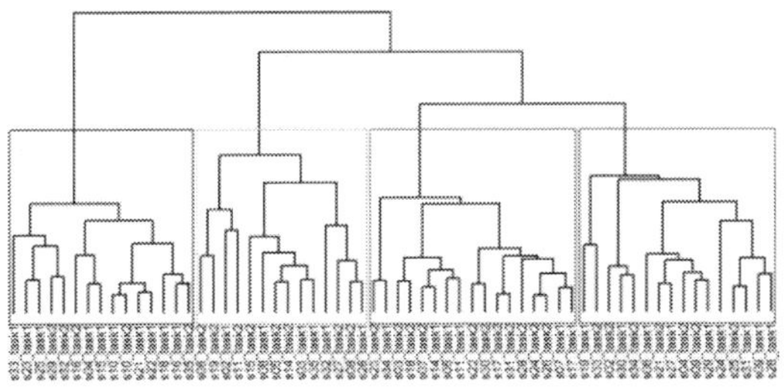

Figure 9. Knowledge change style dendrogram.

In terms of the characteristics of each cluster, we named the four knowledge change styles as follows: Early knowledge change (the cluster shown in blue outlines in Fig. 9, N = 15), Medium-term knowledge change (the cluster shown in yellow outlines in Fig. 9, N = 14), Late knowledge change (the cluster shown in purple outlines in Fig. 9, N = 16) and Average knowledge change (the cluster shown in green outlines in Fig. 9, N = 17).

Early Knowledge Change Style (E-style, N = *15)*

As shown in Figure 10, for Early knowledge change style, their knowledge changes mainly occur in the first stage, and they mainly change knowledge facets during the first stage. The frequencies of addition of knowledge nodes and modification of knowledge points in the three stages are evenly distributed.

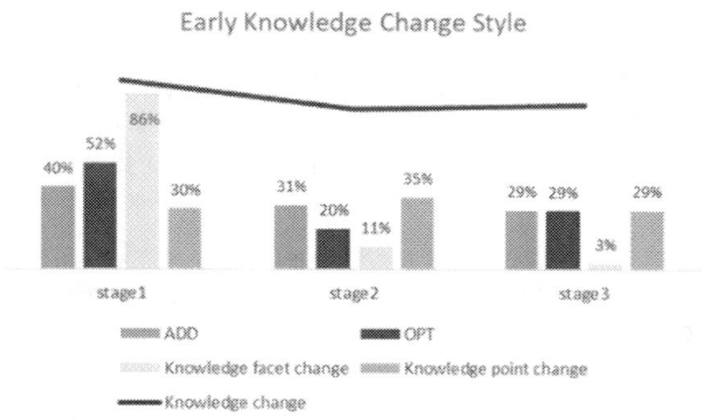

Figure 10. Early knowledge change style.

Medium-Term Knowledge Change Style (M-style, N = *14)*

As shown in Figure 11, the participants with Medium-term knowledge change style mainly change their knowledge in the second stage (middle stage), in which they would change knowledge facets and knowledge points, and add new nodes to the mind-map. They may optimize their knowledge points in the first stage, but there is a peak in the middle stage, and there is very little knowledge change in the last stage.

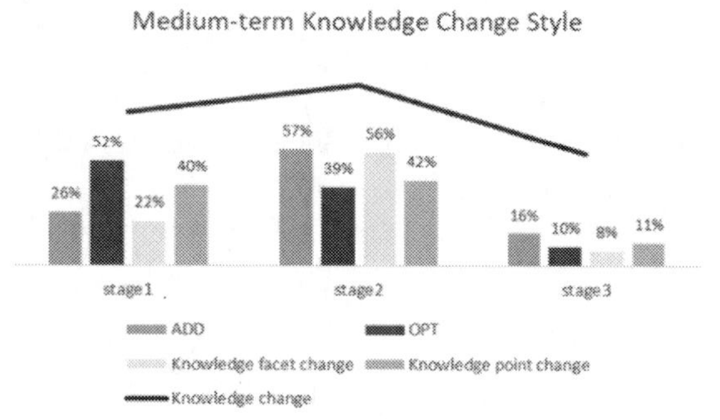

Figure 11. Medium-term knowledge change style.

Late Knowledge Change Style (L-style, N = *16)*

As shown in Figure 12, for Late knowledge change style searchers, their knowledge change frequency increases through the search process, and most of the knowledge changes occur in the last stage, in which they change the knowledge facets, add new nodes and optimize their knowledge as well.

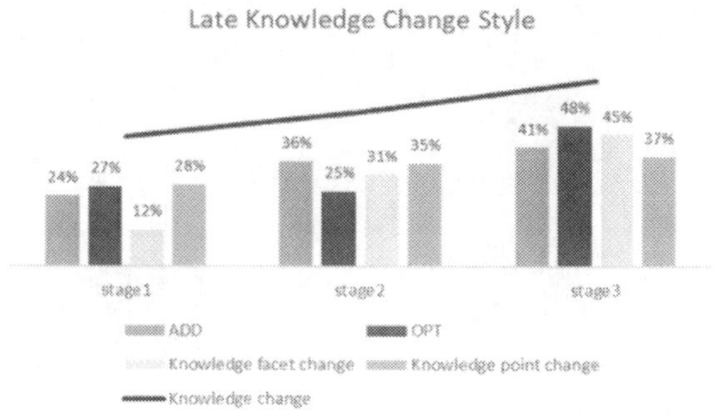

Figure 12. Late knowledge change style.

Average Knowledge Change Style (A-style, N = *17)*

As shown in Figure 13, for Average knowledge change style users, their knowledge changes occur fairly evenly in three stages, and they do not have any structural change in their mind-map, only changing knowledge points during the search process.

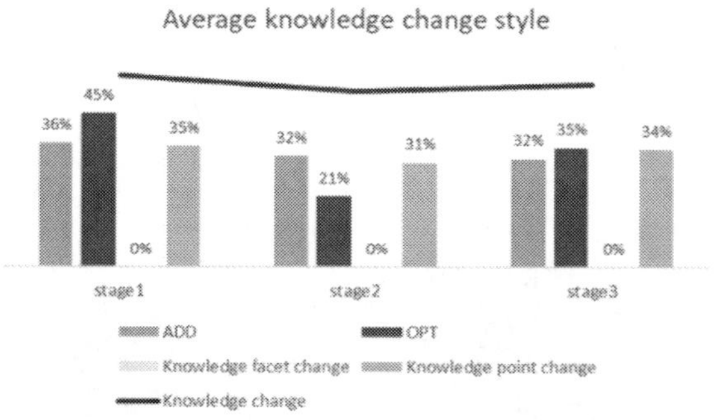

Figure 13. Average knowledge change style.

To summarize, the main differences among the four knowledge change styles are the main stage for them to have knowledge changes in mind-mapping and the main stage when they change the knowledge facets in the mind-mapping. It can be seen that these two knowledge change variables seem to be highly related; that is, whenever there are more knowledge changes in a certain stage, it is more likely that the knowledge facets would be adjusted, indicating that higher level of knowledge structure changes often require a large amount of accretion of specific knowledge points.

Influencing Factors on Knowledge Change Style

After identifying the knowledge change style, we further checked whether participants would adopt different knowledge change styles in different tasks, and what factors would influence users' knowledge change style. First, Table 2 lists users' knowledge change styles in the two tasks. It is shown that among all the 31 participants, only six users kept their knowledge change styles consistent in the two search tasks (highlighted in the table), and all the other 25 participants used different knowledge change styles in the two search tasks.

Receptive task	Critical task	Number of users
E-style (N=7)	E-style	2
	M-style	2
	L-style	3
	A-style	0
M-style (N=6)	E-style	1
	M-style	1
	L-style	3
	A-style	1
L-style (N=4)	E-style	2
	M-style	1
	L-style	1
	A-style	0
A-style (N=14)	E-style	3
	M-style	4
	L-style	5
	A-style	2

Table 2. Users' knowledge change styles in different tasks.

We then checked whether task type, task difficulty and users' pre-search topic familiarity would have any significant relationship with the usage of knowledge change styles. Figure 14 shows number of users in each knowledge change style in each of the two search tasks. More users adopted A-style in the receptive task, whereas more users adopted L-style in the critical task. Chi-square test also showed significant relationship between knowledge change style and task type ($\chi^2 = 11.470$, $p = .009$). However, from a close examination of the usage of knowledge change style, as shown in Table 2, we can see that the styles the users used were dependent upon task features, but also moderated by users' individual characteristics.

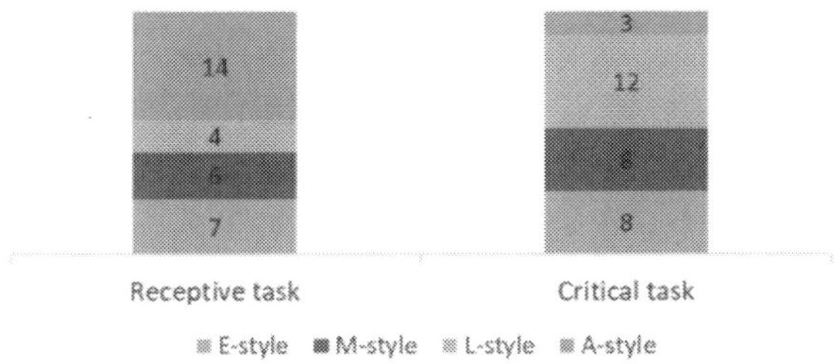

Figure 14. The distribution of knowledge change styles in two types of task.

Regarding the influence of task difficulty, as suggested in Liu, Li, and Hastings (2019), there could be many reasons why users found the tasks difficult or easy. Therefore, in our study, when assessing task difficulty, we asked participants to assess the task difficulty in seven dimensions in the post-search questionnaire, as introduced in the "Pre-search and post-search questionnaires" section. We conducted one-way ANOVA tests to analyze whether there was any significant difference in task difficulty ratings among four types of knowledge change styles. The results showed there were significant differences in two dimensions of task difficulty: the difficulty in Information integration (IIN) and the difficulty in Drawing mind-map (DMM) (Table 3).

Task difficulty dimensions	Knowledge change styles (Mean difficulty level in each style)				*p*
	E-style	M-style	L-style	A-style	
IIN	2.47	**3.00**	**3.06**	2.06	**.023***
DMM	2.13	**2.86**	**2.94**	2.06	**.014***
GDI	2.73	3.07	3.25	2.65	.264
QFO	2.13	2.43	2.69	2.53	.32
IUN	2.33	2.71	2.44	2.00	.281
GUS	2.00	2.14	2.19	2.59	.483
WES	2.07	1.93	2.19	1.82	.692

Table 3. Comparison of difficulty levels among four knowledge change styles.

Post-hoc analysis demonstrated that users who used Medium-term and Late knowledge change styles evaluated the task to be significantly more difficult than Early and Average knowledge change style users in two task difficulty dimensions: difficulty in Information integration and difficulty in Drawing mind-map for this task. Since the knowledge change style is characterized by users' mind-map modifying behaviors, it is reasonable that their knowledge change style is significantly correlated with the difficulty of drawing the mind-map for this task during search. In addition, the process of drawing a mind-map is indeed to integrate new information found through search with users' existing knowledge structure. Therefore, when they had difficulties in integrating information through searching or in mind-map drawing, they might have had to postpone their knowledge change stage, especially the change at the higher level of knowledge structure, so they are more likely to adopt Medium-term or Late knowledge change styles.

Previous studies also suggest that users' topic knowledge may affect users' search behavior and knowledge change during search process. Thus we also examined the effect of users' self-assessed topic familiarity, as the feature of users' topic knowledge, on their knowledge change style. One-way ANOVA results suggested that topic familiarity did not have a significant influence on knowledge change styles in our study ($p = .849$).

DISCUSSION

For "search as learning" research, it is very important to characterize when and how users learn new knowledge during the search process. Some previous studies (e.g., Hagen, Potthast, Völske, Gomoll, & Stein, 2016; Liu & Belkin, 2012) examined users writing behaviors during the search process. In our study, through users' mind-map drawing behaviors, we were able to examine both the content of knowledge changes and the structure of their knowledge changes. In general, users had knowledge changes in all the stages during the search process, but they mainly revised existing nodes and modified knowledge facets in the first stage, and had new nodes addition and knowledge point changes in the second stage.

We also examined users' knowledge change from the search process perspective. Studies in sensemaking process have indicated users' learning process as a sequential process, which includes accretion, tuning and radical change (Zhang & Soergel, 2016). They also suggest users often adjust the sequence of these process through evolving search. In our study, we identified four different learning processes, the so called "knowledge change styles" in the current study. Our results indicate users may have different knowledge change styles during the search process in different sessions. In some sessions, they first modify the main structure, and then add details to the knowledge structure; in some other sessions, they may optimize their existing knowledge points and postpone modifying the main structure to the medium-term or late stage of searching; and in some other cases, they do not change their main knowledge structure at all. Therefore, our study also highlights the differences among sessions in their knowledge change process. We then further investigated the influence of task type, seven dimensions of task difficulty and users' topic familiarity on users' knowledge change styles. Task type was found to have a significant effect on users' knowledge change styles, especially on Late and Average knowledge change style, moderated by users' individual characteristics. Two dimensions of task difficulty have significant influence on users' knowledge change styles: Medium-term and Late knowledge change styles had more difficulty in Information integration and Drawing the mind-map significantly than Early and Average knowledge change style ones.

It is quite surprising that users' pre-search topic familiarity was not significantly related to their knowledge change style. One possible reason is that we characterized users' knowledge change according to their interactions with mind-maps, therefore, how much they know about the topic may not be the same as how easy it is to draw the mind-map for the topic. In future studies, we will examine users' knowledge structure in users' mind-map before searching, to see if the structural characteristics, such as the complexity of mind-map would have any influence in their knowledge change styles. We will also examine how users' search interactions are related to their knowledge change process. In addition, sequential analysis will be conducted to further explore the knowledge change process to refine time granularity. More research is needed to understand the factors that influence users' knowledge change process. If the search system could detect users' knowledge change process, it could be designed to tailor search results accordingly to help users gain knowledge during search process.

CONCLUSION

Our study investigates the characteristics of users' knowledge change process during search sessions. We have identified four knowledge change styles, including: Early knowledge change style, Medium-term knowledge change style, Late knowledge change style and Average knowledge change style. For Early knowledge change style, users' knowledge change, especially knowledge structural change, often occurs in the first stage. For Medium-term knowledge style, the knowledge change frequency is the highest in the second stage, during which users change knowledge structure and knowledge points, and add nodes to the mind-map. Late knowledge change users' knowledge change frequency increases through the search process, and they mainly change the knowledge facets, add new nodes and optimize their knowledge in the last stage. Regarding Average knowledge change style, their knowledge change occurs fairly evenly in the three stages, and they usually do not change knowledge facet, but only change knowledge points. Furthermore, we divided task difficulty into seven dimensions, and examined if task difficulty would influence knowledge change style. It was found that two dimensions of task difficulty had a significant influence on knowledge change style: the difficulty in Information integration and the difficulty in Drawing mind-map. Medium-term knowledge change style users and Late knowledge change style users felt more difficult than Early knowledge change and Average knowledge change users in those two dimensions. Topic familiarity was not found to be correlated to users' knowledge change styles. Further research is needed to examine the factors that could influence users' knowledge change style in the future.

REFERENCES

Agosti, M., Fuhr, N., Toms, E., & Vakkari, P. (2014). Evaluation methodologies in information retrieval dagstuhl seminar 13441. *ACM SIGIR Forum*, *48*(1), 36–41.

Allan, J., Croft, B., Moffat, A., & Sanderson, M. (2012). Frontiers, challenges, and opportunities for information retrieval. *ACM SIGIR Forum*, *46*(1), 2–32.

Belkin, N. (1980). Anomalous states of knowledge as a basis for information retrieval. *Canadian Journal of Information and library Science*, 133–143.

Bhattacharya, N., & Gwizdka, J. (2019). Measuring learning during search: Differences in interactions, eye-gaze, and semantic similarity to expert knowledge. In *Proceedings of CHIIR'2019* (p. 9).

Bloom, B. S., Engelhart, M. D., Furst, E. J., et al. (1956). *Taxonomy of educational objectives: The classification of educational objectives of educational goals' handbook cognitive domain* (Vol. *1(15)*, pp. 58–60).

Collins-Thompson, K., Rieh, S. Y., Haynes, C. C., & Syed, R. (2016). Assessing learning outcomes in web search: A comparison of tasks and query strategies. In *ACM on Conference on Human Information Interaction and Retrieval* (pp. 163–172).

Eickhoff, C., Teevan, J., White, R., & Dumais, S. (2014). Lessons from the journey: A query log analysis of within-session learning. In *Proceedings of the 7th ACM International Conference on Web Search and Data Mining* (pp. 223–232). New York, NY: ACM Press.

Gadiraju, U., Yu, R., Dietze, S., & Holtz, P. (2018). Analyzing knowledge gain of users in informational search sessions on the web. In *Proceedings of the 2018 Conference on Human Information Interaction & Retrieval* (pp. 2–11). ACM.

Ghosh, S., Rath, M., & Shah, C. (2018). Searching as learning: Exploring search behavior and learning outcomes in learning-related tasks. In *Proceedings of the 2018 Conference on Human Information Interaction & Retrieval* (pp. 22–31). ACM.

Gwizdka, J., Hansen, P., Hauff, C., He, J., & Kando, N. (2016). *Search as Learning (SAL) Workshop 2016. International ACM SIGIR Conference on Research & Development in Information Retrieval* (pp. 1249–1250).

Hagen, M., Potthast, M., Völske, M., Gomoll, J., & Stein, B. (2016). How writers search: Analyzing the search and writing logs of non-fictional essays. In *Proceedings of the 2016 ACM on Conference on Human Information Interaction and Retrieval* (pp. 193–202). ACM.

Kelly, D. (2009). Methods for evaluating interactive information retrieval systems with users. *Foundations and Trends® in Information Retrieval*, *3*((1–2)), 1–224.

Kelly, D., & Cool, C. (2004). The effects of topic familiarity on information search behavior. In *Proceedings of the 2nd ACM/IEEE-CS Joint Conference on Digital Libraries* (pp. 74–75).

Kuhlthau, C. C. (2005). Accommodating the user's information search process: Challenges for information retrieval system designers. *Bulletin of the American Society for Information Science and Technology*, *25*(3), 12–16.

Lee, H. J., Lee, J., Makara, K. A., Fishman, B. J., & Hong, Y. I. (2015). Does higher education foster critical and creative learners? an exploration of two universities in South Korea and the USA. *Higher Education Research & Development*, *34*(1), 131–146.

Liu, C., & Song, X. (2018). How do information source selection strategies influence users' learning outcomes. In *Proceedings of the 2018 Conference on Human Information Interaction & Retrieval* (pp. 257–260). ACM.

Liu, J., & Belkin, N. J. (2012). Searching vs. writing: Factors affecting information use task performance. In *Proceedings of ASIS&T Annual Meeting* (Vol. *49(1)*, pp. 1–10).

Liu, J., Belkin, N. J., Zhang, X., & Yuan, X. (2013). Examining users' knowledge change in the task completion process. *IP&M*, *49*(5), 1058–1074.

Liu, J., Li, Y., & Hastings, S. K. (2019). Simplified scheme of search task difficulty reasons. *Journal of the JASIS&T*, *70* (5), 526–529.

Marchionini, G. (1997). *Information seeking in electronic environments (No. 9)*. Cambridge University Press.

Piaget, J. (1936). *Origins of intelligence in the child* (2nd ed.). London, England: Routledge & Kegan Paul 1952.

Piaget, J. (1974). *Origins of Intelligence in Children (p. 418). International Universities Press*. Retrieved from http://books.google.com.my/books/about/Origins_of_Intelligence_in_Children.html?id=H7MkAQAAMAAJ&pgis=1

Piaget, J. (1976). Piaget's theory. In B. Inhelder, H. H. Chipman, & C. Zwingmann, *Piaget and his school*. Heidelberg, Germany: Springer.

Potthast, M., Hagen, M., Völske, M., & Stein, B. (2013). Crowdsourcing interaction logs to understand text reuse from the web. In *Proceedings of the 51st Annual Meeting of the Association for Computational Linguistics (Volume 1: Long Papers)* (Vol. *1*, pp. 1212–1221).

Rieh, S. Y., Gwizdka, J., Freund, L., & Collins-Thompson, K. (2014). Searching as learning: Novel measures for information interaction research. In *Proceedings of the ASIST Annual Meeting* (Vol. *51*).

Rumelhart, D. E., & Norman, D. A. (1978). Accretion, tuning, and restructuring: Modes of learning. *Semantic Factors in Cognition*. Report No. 7602, 37–53.

Vakkari, P., Pennanen, M., & Serola, S. (2003). Changes of search terms and tactics while writing a research proposal: A longitudinal case study. *Information Processing & Management*, *39*(3), 445–463.

Ward, J. H., Jr. (1963). Hierarchical grouping to optimize an objective function. *Journal of the American Statistical Association*, *58*(301), 236–244.

White, R. W., Dumais, S. T., & Teevan, J. (2009). Characterizing the influence of domain expertise on web search behavior. In *ACM International Conference on Web Search & Data Mining* (p. 132).

Wildemuth, B. M. (2004). The effects of domain knowledge on search tactic formulation. *Journal of the American Society for Information Science and Technology*, *55*(3), 246–258.

Wilson, M. J., & Wilson, M. L. (2013). A comparison of techniques for measuring sensemaking and learning within participant-generated summaries. *JASIS&T*, *64* (2), 291–306.

Yu, R., Gadiraju, U., Holtz, P., Rokicki, M., Kemkes, P., & Dietze, S. (2018). Predicting user knowledge gain in informational search sessions. In *The 41st International ACM SIGIR Conference on Research & Development in Information Retrieval* (pp. 75–84).

Zhang, P., & Soergel, D. (2016). Process patterns and conceptual changes in knowledge representations during information seeking and sensemaking: A qualitative user study. *Journal of Information Science*, *42*(1), 59–78.

Proactive Identification of Query Failure

Jiqun Liu
School of Communication & Information, Rutgers University, New Brunswick, NJ
jl2033@scarletmail.rutgers.edu

Chirag Shah
School of Communication & Information, Rutgers University, New Brunswick, NJ
chirags@rutgers.edu

ABSTRACT

When a user fails to find any useful information to support the task at hand after issuing a query, the user experiences a *query failure*. Since users possess limited cognitive resources, query failures often lead to user frustration as no clear benefit is obtained from the associated search interactions. Therefore, to improve users' search experiences, we conducted a controlled-lab study with 40 participants, seeking to explore the extent to which query failures can be proactively identified *before users start examining the retrieved results*. Specifically, based on the data collected from 693 query segments generated in 80 search sessions, we used past search behaviors and current query attributes as features to build classifiers and examined the performance in capturing query failures. We report that (1) analytics algorithms utilizing past search behavioral data have significantly better performances than the baseline model in tasks of different types, and (2) The knowledge of users' search intentions can help improve the performance of the prediction model. Results pave way for developing proactive system supports for task-based search interactions.

KEYWORDS

Query Failure; Proactive Information Retrieval; Search Intention; Task-Based Information Searching

ASIS&T THESAURUS

Information Seeking; Information Retrieval; Search Behavior

INTRODUCTION

Search interaction is a major component of information-intensive tasks. Users often go through multiple rounds of search interactions in complex tasks where the needed item(s) and dimension(s) for result evaluation are not clearly defined (Liu, 2017; Liu, Mitsui, Belkin, & Shah, 2019). When a user fails to find any useful information to support the task at hand after issuing a query, the user experiences a *query failure*, which often lead to search frustration (Feild, Allan, & Jones, 2010; Smith & Kantor, 2008). Hence, to help users save their limited cognitive resources and improve their search efficiency and experience, search systems need to *proactively* capture query failures and provide useful interventions *before* users allocate time and energy to reviewing the results presented on the associated search engine result pages (SERPs).

In the past interactive information retrieval (IIR) studies on query quality evaluation, most researchers sought to infer query performance and capture low-performing queries based on the associated search behavioral features (e.g., Guo, White, Dumais, Wang, & Anderson, 2010; Kumaran & Carvalho, 2009; Wu, Kelly, & Huang, 2012). Although this approach can enhance our understanding on the connection between query performance and user behavior, the associated models were built upon the search interactions that happened *after* the target query was issued. Hence, this inference approach leaves no room for the system to help users by saving their time and energy in the current query segment. Given this problem, our study sought to provide "preventive care" for search system users by developing predictive methods to proactively identify query failures (see Figure 1).

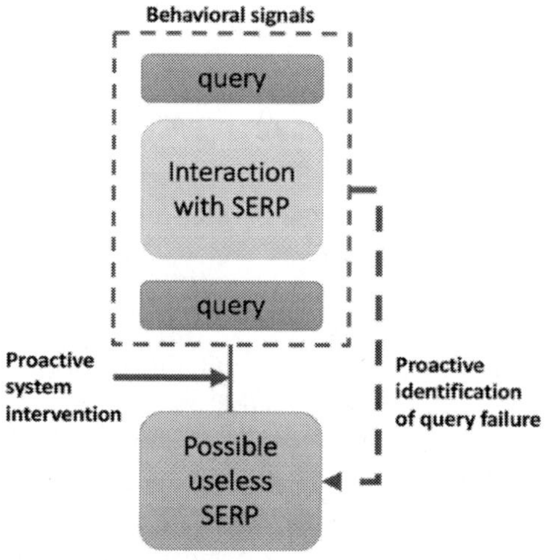

Figure 1. Proactive identification of query failure.

With respect to the operational definition, this study considers two states of query: (1) *useful query*: one or more useful documents can be identified in the associated SERP, and (2) *query failure*: no useful document is identified in the associated SERP. Based on these definitions, we adopted a machine learning approach and built classifiers to predict

82nd Annual Meeting of the Association for Information Science & Technology | Melbourne, Australia | 19–23 October, 2019

DOI: 10.1002/pra2.00015

query failure from the search interactions extracted from the previous query segment. Specifically, this study sought to answer the following research questions (RQs):

RQ1: How is a user's search interaction associated with the subsequent query state (i.e. useful query or query failure)?

RQ2: To what extent can query failure be predicted from past search behaviors?

RQ3: To what extent can we leverage the knowledge of users' query-level search intentions in predicting query failures?

By addressing the RQs above, this study has multiple contributions and implications:

- Our results reveal the underlying connection between past search interactions and the quality or performance of the subsequent query in task-based search process.
- The query failure prediction model is a critical step toward achieving comprehensive proactive supports and recommendations in interactive information retrieval.
- Methodologically, the study procedure, behavioral features and techniques employed in this study can be reused in examining and predicting other dimensions of search interactions (e.g., user interest and expectation).

RELATED WORKS

Corresponding to the RQ1 and RQ2, this section first reviews the findings from previous works on inferring and evaluating query quality. Then, to test the usefulness of search intention feature in different contexts (RQ3), this section discusses the existing research progresses made in characterizing tasks and search intentions in the context of information searching.

Inferring Query Performance

Among the IIR studies focusing on query analysis and evaluation, some of them sought to infer query quality and performance based on users' interactions with the SERP and content pages retrieved from the target query. For instance, He and Ounis (2006) focused on a series of query features in performance prediction and their TREC-based experiments indicated that many of the query-based predictors have significant association with query performance measured by the average precision of document retrieval. Similarly, Hauff, Hiemstra, and de Jong (2008) identified 22 pre-retrieval predictors based solely on query terms and assessed the prediction performance using three TREC test collections. Kumaran and Carvalho (2009) took a step forward by combining query features and the attributes of retrieved documents (i.e. IDF-based features) in building models for query quality prediction. Guo et al. (2010) used features of the query, retrieved search results, and user behavioral features (e.g., result browsing, dwell time on pages) to infer query performance. Their findings demonstrated that using interaction signals can significantly improve the performance of predicting query performance. Wang, Liu, Mandal, and Shah (2017) conducted a field study on query-level search failures and stated that users' pages visiting and dwell time on pages can significantly affect their query-level search outcomes. To understand query quality evaluation from the user side, Wu et al. (2012) conducted a controlled-lab user study, aiming to figure out how users evaluate query quality based on query features as well as their own interactions with the SERPs. They found that for exploratory search tasks, users' ratings of query quality were highly correlated with the number of relevant documents and the proportion of relevant documents viewed. Similar to previous works, Wu et al. (2012) also confirmed the importance of including search interaction features in query performance prediction.

Despite of the contributions of the previous studies discussed above, they still have limitations as they either (1) only consider query attributes, or (2) seek to infer query quality from the associated search interactions (after the retrieval step), leaving no room for proactive system interventions (although in many of these cases, the authors used the term *prediction* to label their works on *inferring* query performance). In addition, the impacts of cognitive-level search intentions and task type on query failure prediction still remains ambiguous.

Given the interactive nature of Web search, different query segments are likely to be connected within the same task context (Liu, Mitsui et al., 2019). The multi-dimensional associations between adjacent query segments can create valuable opportunities for capturing query failure from past search behaviors. Hence, to provide proactive supports for users, search systems need to combine past search behavior features with current query attributes in predicting the query performance *before the retrieval step*. The proactive identification of query failure can push us closer toward the vision of proactive information retrieval (Shah, 2018).

Task and Search Intention

The existing IIR research have shown that many facets of users' search interaction vary significantly across tasks of different types (Jiang, He, & Allan, 2014; Liu, Cole et al., 2010). Thus, the predictability of query failure in information search process may also change according to multiple task features.

IIR researchers have developed a series of frameworks and typologies to define task types. For instance, Capra, Arguello, O'Brien, Li, and Choi (2018) focused on task prior determinability (i.e. the level of uncertainty about task outcomes and processes) and argued that the variations in needed items and the clarity of dimensions for result evaluation can significantly affect the overall task determinability. Kelly, Arguello, Edwards, and Wu (2015) examined the cognitive complexity of task and adopted Bloom (1956)'s taxonomy of learning domains in characterizing different levels of task complexity. Li and Belkin (2008) took a step back and looked at the bigger picture of task. Specifically, instead of merely focusing on one aspect of task, they developed a faceted approach to characterize multiple dimensions of tasks (e.g., task product, task goal, task complexity) and tested the effects of multiple facets on users' search behavior (e.g., Liu et al., 2010). This multi-faceted scheme allows researchers to characterize tasks over multiple dimensions and conceptually supports the IIR studies focusing on how task traits affect users' cognitive states and search behaviors.

In addition to the global task context, users' search patterns are also affected by their changing cognitive spaces (Ingwersen, 1996). In some recent IIR studies, researchers have investigated the roles of query-level search intentions in local query segments. In these studies, a query segment is defined as a search session segment which starts from one issued query and ends at the next query (Mitsui, Liu, Belkin, & Shah, 2017). Ruotsalo et al. (2018) represented users' interactive intents as keywords for interaction and developed an intent extraction and visualization technique to support search interactions. Rha, Mitsui, Belkin and Shah (2016) empirically investigated the connections between search intentions and queries and found that users' search intentions in query segments are significantly associated with their query reformulation types. Hence, knowing search intentions can help researchers better understand what a user is trying to accomplish with a formulated or reformulated query. Furthermore, Liu, Mitsui et al. (2019) sought to build a multi-level framework of Web search and studied the relations between task, search intention and user behaviors. They found that (1) task features (i.e. objective task type and subjective task perception) have significant impacts on the frequencies of occurrences of different intentions, and (2) users' search evaluation is closely associated with many search intentions in query segments. Therefore, using search intentions as features in prediction models may help systems better capture query failures in task-based search interactions.

Summary

Based on the discussions above, to achieve the goal of query failure detection, it is important to combine past search interaction features with query features. In addition, researchers should also consider the roles of task types and search intentions in query failure prediction.

METHOD

To answer the proposed RQs, we conducted a controlled-lab user study and performed correlation and prediction analyses based on the collected data. The specific methods and techniques are fully explained in the following subsections.

Search Tasks and Participants

In the controlled-lab user study, we designed and assigned four work tasks, all within journalism domain, in order to control the task context: Copy editing (CPE), Story pitch (STP), Relationships (REL), and Interview preparation (INT). In addition, to control the variance in task familiarity, we recruited 40 upper-division undergraduates who have finished either one journalism writing or reporting class.

We defined four different types of search tasks based on four task facets extracted from the Li and Belkin (2008)'s faceted classification scheme, as modified by Cole, Hendahewa, Belkin, and Shah (2015): Product, Goal, Level, and Named. The values of these facets are explained in Table 1.

Each of the four task types has two different versions (i.e. different topics: coelacanths; methane clathrates and global warming). We selected these two specific topics for controlling participants' familiarity with the task topic, as our participant population was considered likely to not be familiar with either. To avoid possible biases in task types and topics, we asked each participant to do two tasks of different topics and types, in Latin Square design, pairing CPE with INT, and STP with REL. The four specific tasks for the topic of coelacanth are listed as follows. Note that the work task associated with each search task was designed as a context or cover story. Participants only need to complete the search task part in this study.

Facets	Values and definitions
Product	Intellectual: a task which produces new ideas; Factual: a task locating facts, data, or other information objects
Goal	Specific: a task with explicit and measurable goal; Amorphous: the goal of task is not explicitly defined and cannot be quantitatively measured
Level	Document level: a task for which a document as a whole is judged; Segment level: a task for which a part or parts of document are judged
Named	True: what is to be found is explicitly named; False: what is to be found is not explicitly named

Table 1. Facet values and definitions.

- **CPE** (Factual Specific Segment Named True).

Work task: You are a copy editor at a newspaper and you have only 20 minutes to check the accuracy of six italicized statements in the excerpt of a piece of news story below.

Search task: Please find and save an authoritative page that either confirms or disconfirms each statement.

- **STP** (Factual Amorphous Segment Named False).

Work task: You are planning to pitch a science story to your editor and need to identify interesting facts about the coelacanth, a fish that dates from the time of dinosaurs and was thought to be extinct.

Search task: Save pages that contain the six most interesting facts about coelacanths and/or research about their preservation.

- **REL** (Intellectual Amorphous Document Named True).

Work task: You are writing an article about coelacanths and conservation efforts. You have found an interesting article about coelacanths but in order to develop your article you need to be able to explain the relationship between key facts you have learned.

Search task: In the following, there are five italicized passages, find an authoritative Web page that explains the relationship between two of the italicized facts.

- **INT** (Intellectual Amorphous Document Named False).

Work task: You are writing an article that profiles a scientist and their research work. You are preparing to interview Mark Erdmann, a marine biologist, about coelacanths and conservation programs.

Search task: Identify and save authoritative Web pages for the following: Identify two (living) people who likely can provide some personal stories about Dr. Erdmann and his work. Find the three most interesting facts about Dr. Erdmann's research. Find an interesting potential impact of Dr. Erdmann's work.

Query Failure

Compared to the traditional relevance-based measurements, usefulness can serve as a better evaluation criterion as it considers both task success and the value of system support over the entire information seeking episodes (Cole, Liu et al., 2009). Hence, in this study, we define query state based on the notion of usefulness. Specifically, query failure refers to the query segments where users fail to find any useful document to support the task. In contrast, useful query refers to the query segments where users find at least one useful document. Built upon this operational definition of query failure, we classified query segments into the two categories and built classifiers for the query failure prediction task.

Search Intentions

In this study, search intentions are defined as the things that users seek to accomplish *within a query segment*. Knowing search intentions is likely to be helpful for proactively capturing query failures. To systematically elicit data from participants about their intentions, we adopted the typology of search intention proposed by Rha et al. (2016) and asked participants to identify their intentions for *each query segment* based on the typology. This typology is relatively comprehensive and includes 20 intentions (see Table 2). The annotation process is explained in the following section.

Category	Search intention
Keep record	Keep record of a link (KR)
Identify search information	Identifying something to start (IS); Identify something more to search (IM)
Learn	Domain knowledge (LK); Database content (LD)
Find	Find known item(s) (FK); Find specific information (FS); Find items sharing a named feature (FN); Find items without predefined criteria (FW)
Access item(s)	Access a specific item (AS); Access items with common characteristics (AC); Access a website or similar (AW)
Evaluate	Evaluate correctness of an item (EC); Evaluate usefulness of an item (EU); Pick best items from all the useful ones (EB); Evaluate specificity of an item (ES); Evaluate duplication of an item (ED) (i.e., determine whether the information in one item is the same as in others)
Obtain	Obtain specific information to highlight or copy (OS); Obtain part of an item (OP); Obtain a whole item(s) (OW)

Table 2. Search intentions in query segments.

Study Procedure

The study procedure (see Figure 2) started with a demographic questionnaire and a tutorial video on the browser interface features offered by the plugin. After finishing the demographic, participants read the task description and completed a pre-search questionnaire on topic familiarity, task experience, and estimated task difficulty. Each participant had up to 20 min to complete the assigned search task, by searching on the Web within the supplied browser. During the search process, our Firefox browser plugin automatically recorded participants' search activities (e.g., query, timestamp, URL, snippet, page type).

After completing the search task and post-search questionnaire on task perception, participants were asked to read a guidance of intention annotation task. Then, the browser plugin replayed the entire search process, query segment by query segment, asking participants to annotate their intention(s) (i.e., identify if the intention was present or absent) for each segment based on the predefined typology. Note that within each query segment, participants were allowed to select any number of intentions from the list as they might have multiple search intentions in one local step of search. Hence, if we consider the totality of all intentions as users' cognitive space during search, then the specific search intentions are essentially separate dimensions of the cognitive space, rather than different values of the same categorical variable. Figure 3 presents the post-search replay and intention annotation interface.

The same procedure (from pre-search questionnaire to intention annotation) was repeated for the second search task. The

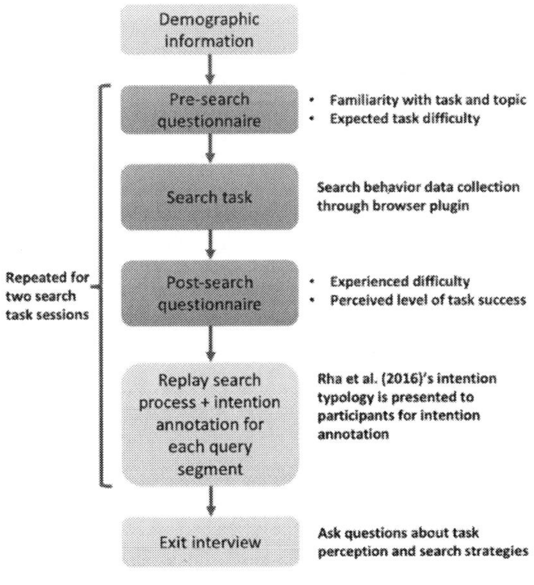

Figure 2. Study procedure.

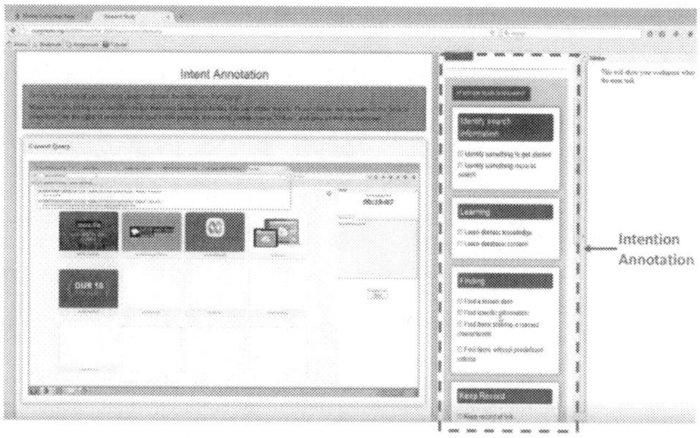

Figure 3. Intention annotation interface. When the main screen was replaying a query segment, the user can identify associated search intention(s) within the side bar on the right.

whole study session (around 2 hr in total) ended with an exit interview in which we asked questions about participants' task perceptions and search strategies.

Behavioral Measures and Data Analysis

The central research problem of this study is to proactively identify or predict query failure from past search behaviors and current query attributes. To address this problem, based on previous empirical studies on query quality prediction and evaluation, we extracted a series of behavioral features from multiple aspects of users' search interactions (see Table 3). Regarding the dwell time and open time features, dwell time on a page refers to the amount of time that a user actually spent on reading the contents on the page. In contrast, open time measures how long a page has been kept open within a query segment (Hienert, Mitsui, Mayr, Shah, & Belkin, 2018; Mitsui et al., 2017). Note that the query behavior category includes both previous query features and current query attributes. Query reformulation type includes: generalization, specialization, repeat existing query, new query, word substitution, and other reformulation types. We sought to predict query failure at the point where a query is formulated but the retrieval and result examination step is not yet executed (see Figure 1).

Types	Behavioral measurements
Query behavior	Query length, query reformulation type
Browsing	Number of clicks, number of tabs, number of pages visited, number of sources (i.e. unique Internet domains) visited
Dwell time	Mean dwell time on content page, total dwell time on content pages, total dwell time on SERP, total session elapsed time
Display/open time	Total open time on content pages, total open time on SERP

Table 3. Behavioral Measurements.

With respect to data analysis, to answer the RQ1, this study mainly used Mann-Whitney U test to examine the connection between past search behavior and current query state (binary) as none of the search behavior data was normally distributed. The statistical test for each behavior feature was conducted between the useful query group (at least one useful document bookmarked) and query failure group. To answer RQ2, we employed multiple classifiers (e.g., Logistic regression, Naïve Bayes, SVM) to predict query failure. For RQ3, we added query-level search intentions as features into the classifiers/prediction models and see to what extent we can improve the performance of query failure prediction with the knowledge of user intentions. In addition, given that users' search interactions and performances often vary across tasks of different types (Liu et al., 2010), we also ran the prediction models in separate task contexts and compared the prediction performances across different task types, aiming to enhance our understanding of the predictability of query failure. In prediction analyses, we compared the classifiers built upon a series of search features with the baseline model (ZeroR). We trained and evaluated models using 5-fold cross-validation. The results are explained in the following section.

RESULTS

To answer the proposed research questions, we collected search behavior and intention data from 693 query segments generated by 40 participants in 80 task-based sessions. Since the last query segment of each session does not have subsequent query, we did not use the search interaction data generated in these query segments. Hence, we conducted data analyses based on the search interaction and intention data extracted from 613 query segments (184 query segments in CPE tasks, 90 in STP tasks, 137 in REL tasks, and 202 in INT tasks). The results of data analyses are organized according to the RQs in the following subsections.

RQ1: Search behavior and subsequent query state

To examine the associations between search behaviors in the current query segments and subsequent query states, we ran Mann Whitney U test for most pairs of behavior measure and query state (see results shown in Table 4). To statistically test the correlations between query reformulation and subsequent query state, we adopted Pearson's Chi-square test as query reformulation type is a categorical variable.

Since this study applied nonparametric tests, Table 4 reports the medians and inter-quartile ranges (IQR) (instead of means and standard deviations) of behavior measures. In Pearson's Chi-square tests we did not find any statistically significant correlation between query reformulation type (either current or subsequent) and subsequent query state.

According to the results shown in Table 4, overall, participants who were better prepared in the current query segment were less likely to encounter query failure in the following query segment. Specifically, when a participant was more active in interacting with and extracting knowledge from current query segments (e.g., spent longer time on content pages and SERP, visited more unique Internet domains), the

Behavior measure	Useful	Failure	Mann-Whitney test
Current query length	4(3)	4(3)	z=.479, p=.632
Next query length*	**5(3)**	**4(3)**	**z=2.16, p=.029**
Number of clicks	3(4)	3(4)	z=.716, p=.474
Number of tabs	3(3)	3(2)	z=-1.84, p=.064
Number of pages	5(4)	5(3)	z=-1.48, p=.140
Number of sources*	**4(2)**	**3(3)**	**z=-2.23, p=.026**
Mean dwell time content*	**10.2(15.9)**	**8.4(13.5)**	**z=2.15, p=.031**
Total dwell time content	48.5(83.2)	39.5(81.7)	z=.949, p=.343
Total dwell time SERP*	**10.5(15.5)**	**7.2(9.3)**	**z=2.49, p=.013**
Total session elapsed time*	**6.6(7.6)**	**8.3(7.7)**	**z=-2.43, p=.015**
Total open time content	155(287)	157(341)	z=-.135, p=.892
Total open time SERP**	**39.2(33.6)**	**25.8(18.5)**	**z=2.72, p=.007**

Table 4. Correlations between current search behavior and next query state: Median (IQR) and Mann-Whitney U test. The unit of total session elapsed time is minute. *: p<.05, **: p<.01. The statistically significant correlations are boldfaced.

participant was more likely to enter into the useful query state in the subsequent query segment. This may be because when participants engaged in deeper interactions with current SERPs and results, they had a better chance to obtain more useful information and knowledge from the retrieved pages and then to use them in facilitating query formulation and result examination in the following query segment. In addition, we found that as the search session proceeded, participants were more likely to experience query failure, especially in the middle and later stages (see Figure 4). This may be because participants gradually raised the threshold for page usefulness judgment as they obtained more and more useful information along the way. Another possible reason is that in later search stages participants encountered more repeated documents which were judged as useful documents earlier and had difficulty in finding new useful pages to support the task at hand.

Based on the identified connections between current search behavior and subsequent query state, in the following subsection we employed search behavior and intention features to build classifiers for predicting query failure *before* the retrieval and SERP examination steps.

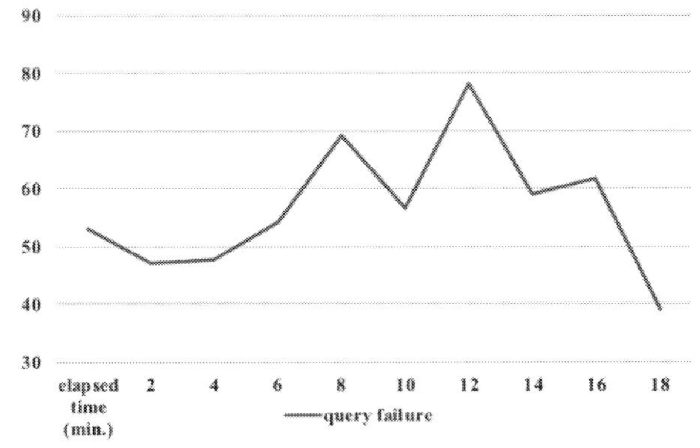

Figure 4. The frequency (%) of query failure during search.

RQ2 & RQ3: Predicting query failure

RQ2 and RQ3 speak to the problem of proactively identifying query failure in search process. Particularly, as a preparation for answering RQ3, Figure 5 reports the proportions of query segments where the intention was identified by users as present (which means the users had this intention in the associated query segments). The results regarding intention distribution indicate that for most search intentions, the proportions of the query segments where the intention was present is clearly smaller than the opposite situation (i.e. where the intention was absent). This result suggests that no search intention is ubiquitous in any of the task-based search sessions. Hence, different combinations of search intentions may correspond to largely different cognitive states, which may significantly affect users' search strategies and performances in the associated query segments.

To better compare the performances of baseline model (ZeroR), search behavior models and behavior-intention models, we report and explain the results of all prediction analyses in the same subsection. Figures 6–8 only show the performances of best classifiers in prediction for brevity. The full result tables presenting the performances of all classifiers are provided in the Tales A1–A6.

Accuracy is a way to measure overall performance improvement in a classification problem. According to the results illustrated in Figure 6, we made gains in accuracy by building prediction models based on search behavioral features (3% above the ZeroR baseline). Also, adding search intention features into the classifiers resulted in additional 5% increase in overall accuracy. Since the main focus of this study was proactively capturing query failures in search process, we also analyzed the precision of predicting query failures. The results indicate that the behavior model clearly outperforms the baseline (11% increase), and that adding intention features can obtain another 2.8% improvement.

Task type usually plays a central role in affecting users' task-based search interactions. Given that users often have different search intention patterns, search strategies, and performances in tasks of different types (Aula, Khan, & Guan,

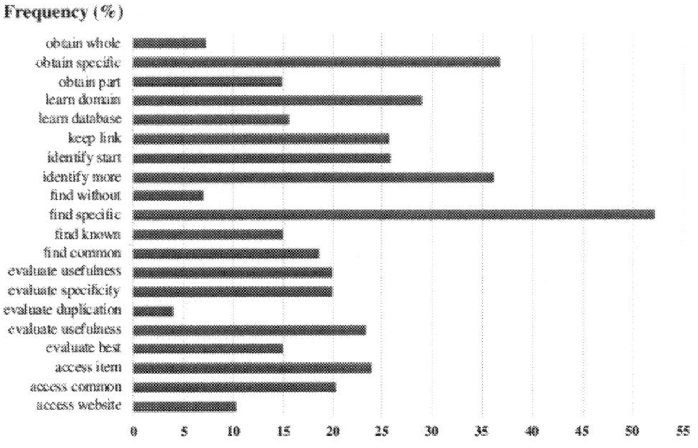

Figure 5. Intention selected in query segments (%).

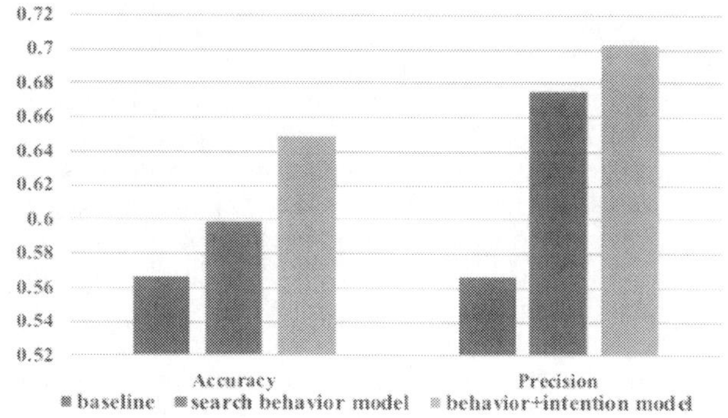

Figure 6. Prediction performance: overall accuracy and precision of predicting query failure.

2010; Liu et al., 2010; Liu, Mitsui et al., 2019), we also ran our prediction models in the four task contexts respectively.

According to the results in Figure 7, the search behavior model had better performance in the two factual tasks (CPE and STP), compared to the two intellectual tasks (REL and INT). One possible reason behind this is that the needed information items and dimensions for result evaluations were more well-defined in factual tasks than in intellectual tasks. As a result, the connection between search behavioral patterns and query states could be more predictable in factual tasks, which might make it easier to differentiate useful queries from query failures based on search behavioral features. Overall, the behavior model achieved 2%–6% increase in accuracy for the first three tasks. There is no clear improvement in accuracy for the INT task. In terms of the behavior-intention models, it is worth noting that incorporating search intention features into the classifiers led to a significant increase (11.4%) in accuracy for the INT task where search behavior model failed to achieve any major improvement. This result suggests that there might be a big gap between users' cognitive space and explicit search strategies, especially in intellectual amorphous task. In other words, in the INT tasks, search intention features still contained plenty of useful, implicit, predicative signals which could not be captured by explicit search behaviors. Perhaps more fine-grained behavioral measures or neuro-physiological signals can help capture the hidden variances and disconnections in the cognition-behavior gap.

Compared to improving the overall accuracy of query state prediction, it is more important to accurately capture potential query failures where timely system supports and interventions are badly needed. To what extent can we proactively identify query failures based on search behavior and intention features in tasks of different types? to answer this question, we looked at the precision of query failure prediction in different task contexts. According to the results in Figure 8, search behavior models achieved significant improvement (ranging from 9% to 14%) compared to the baseline model. This result proves that the classifiers built upon past search behavioral measures are

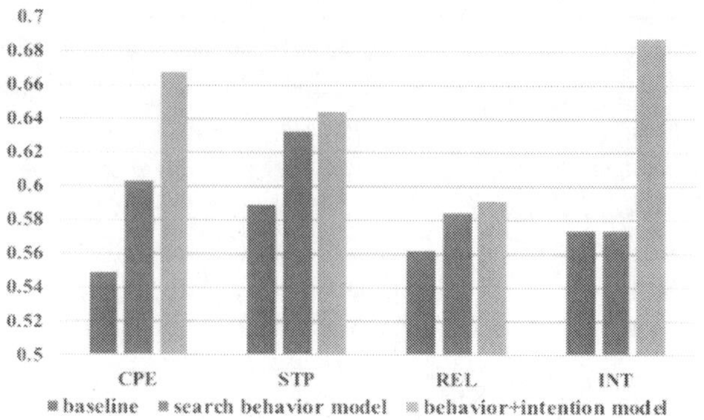

Figure 7. Results for accuracy in tasks of different types.

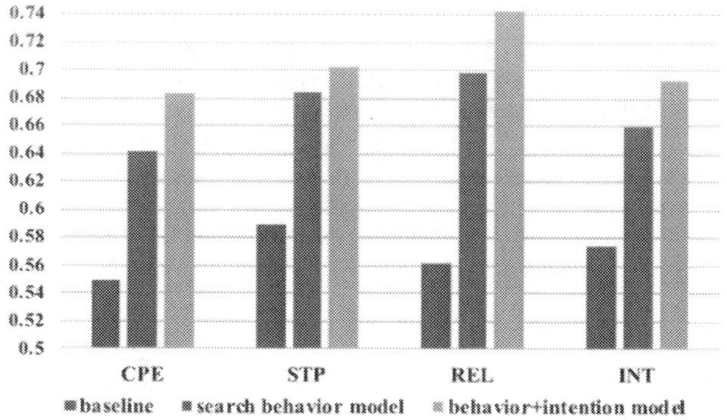

Figure 8. Precision of predicting query failure.

useful in identifying subsequent query failures and capturing the opportunities for providing proactive system interventions. Furthermore, assume we know users' intentions for the subsequent query segments. Built upon this assumption, we found that adding search intention features can help further improve the precision score in all task types, indicating that the knowledge of users' intentions in local steps can facilitate the identification of potential query failures. The search intention transitions and cognitive activities are often more active in the tasks where the goal is not clearly defined (i.e. goal-amorphous task) as users need to do more open-ended explorations when trying to define search goals and evaluate documents (Liu, Mitsui et al., 2019). As a result, compared to the goal-specific task (CPE task), search intention features might offer more useful information about users' cognitive space in goal-amorphous tasks and thereby helped achieve higher precision scores in the STP, REL, and INT tasks.

DISCUSSION

Page browsing and result examination is cognitively costly for users in search interactions. Proactively capturing queries that are very likely to be useless for the task at hand can help save a user's limited cognitive resource (e.g., working memory, visual processing system) and thereby improve his or her search efficiency and experience. To explore the possibility of offering proactive system interventions for search system users in local search steps (i.e. query segments), this study examined the extent to which we can predict query failure from search behaviors and intentions before the retrieval and result examination steps. With respect to the research questions, we have following answers.

In terms of the association between past search behaviors and subsequent query state (RQ1), we found that participants were less likely to experience query failure in the following search step if they were more active in interacting with the current search results (e.g., spent longer time on SERP and clicked content pages, visited more unique Internet domains). This result echoes Wang et al. (2017)'s field study finding that when users spent more efforts on carefully examining search results, they usually encounter less search obstacles and problems. In addition, our finding empirically confirms the underlying connections between adjacent local steps of Web search identified in previous IIR studies (e.g., Liu, Mitsui et al., 2019; Teevan, Alvarado, Ackerman, & Karger, 2004) and highlights the importance of leveraging the existing signals from search interactions to proactively identify future opportunities for task-based system support and intervention. With respect to user persuasion and education, the answer to RQ1 also supports Liu, Wang, Mandal, and Shah (2019)'s argument that encouraging deeper, fully engaged search interaction (through explicit intervention or intelligent nudging) is critical for a search system to improve users' task performances and search experiences.

Besides, we also found that participants tended to encounter query failures more frequently in the middle and late search stages compared to the early stages (see Figure 4, the two peak points in query failure frequency at 8th and 12th minutes). This could result from the effect of *threshold priming*. Specifically, when users successfully gathered many highly relevant pages in early stages, they might gradually (and unconsciously) raise their thresholds for usefulness judgment (Scholer, Kelly, Wu, Lee, & Webber, 2013). As a result, it might become more difficult for them to identify useful pages that meet their requirements in the later stages. Another possible reason is that users might use repeated keywords and queries in later search stages and encountered repeated search results, which also led to the difficulty in identifying new useful documents. This finding indicates that the usefulness judgment process in Web searching is highly dynamic and subjective in nature, and that different dimensions of usefulness judgments and their associations with users' evolving mental models still need to examined in detail.

To answer RQ2, we adopted several classification algorithms and built prediction models based on a series of search behavioral measures. Overall, our result proves that behavior-based classifiers always outperform their corresponding baseline models in search tasks of different types. Particularly, compared to the baselines, the prediction models built on past search behaviors achieved 9% to 14% improvements in the precision of query failure prediction. This result demonstrates that search behavioral signals are quite useful in proactive identifications of query failures, especially in complex, goal-amorphous tasks where search processes are not well supported and users often need to take a zigzag path toward the ultimate task goal (Capra et al., 2018; Liu, Mitsui et al., 2019). Through building a behavior-based model for predicting query failure, our study goes beyond the traditional inference approach and speaks to the issue of developing proactive supports for real-time search interactions. To further improve the performance of behavioral model, future studies can investigate more diverse, fine-grained behavioral measures that can help capture some other implicit aspects of search tactics in local steps.

For RQ3, we added search intentions as features into the prediction models and found that the behavior-intention models can further improve the overall accuracy and the precision of query failure prediction to varying degrees in tasks of different types. This finding supports Ingwersen (1996)'s argument that from a cognitive perspective, users' search interactions are affected by multiple dimensions of cognitive space. Also, it demonstrates that a deeper understanding of cognitive changes can help researcher better study search interactions and predict search outcomes. In addition, the result speaks to the practical value of predicting local-step search intentions using behavioral signals collected from search sessions (cf. Mitsui et al., 2017).

As always, there are several limitations to this study as well as needs for future research efforts. First, the size of dataset and task types are limited. Many of the potential task facet combinations defined by Li and Belkin (2008)'s framework still remained untouched in this study. To further test the predicative power and generalizability of the classifiers, we will run them on multiple, larger scale datasets generated in different task contexts. Second, search intentions as features still require participants' annotations. The findings from recent works on characterizing and inferring search intentions (e.g., Liu, Mitsui et al., 2019; Mitsui et al., 2017) can be of help for partially addressing this issue. Third, the behavioral features extracted for model building are by no means complete. Therefore, defining and extracting more fine-grained behavioral features from multiple sources (e.g., search logs, eye tracking devices) will be the next step of our future research on predicting query failures in Web search.

CONCLUSION

Few IIR research have tried to leverage the signals from past search interactions in proactively capturing future query failures. Given this research gap, we built query failure prediction models based on search behavioral features and tested them in predicting the query state (useful query or query failure) in the subsequent query segments. Furthermore, to examine the usefulness of search intention features as signals from cognitive level, we integrated intention features with behavioral features in behavior-intention models and applied the models in our research context. The results demonstrate that search behavior models always outperform the baseline models in all tasks types, and that using the knowledge of users' search intention(s) can help further improve the overall accuracy as well as the precision of query failure prediction.

The ultimate goal of this research line is to provide proactive system supports and interventions in real-time search interactions before users encounter search problems (in this case, query failure). To this end, future research needs to (1) take advantages of the findings from other relevant research and further examine different dimensions of search problem detection, such as user frustration prediction (Feild et al., 2010) and expectation disconfirmation prediction (Liu & Shah, 2019), and (2) explore the possible directions for designing proactive system recommendations and interfaces.

ACKNOWLEDGMENTS

This work is supported by the National Science Foundation (NSF) grant IIS-1717488. It also uses datasets generated as a part of the project supported by the NSF grant IIS-1423239.

REFERENCES

Aula, A., Khan, R. M., & Guan, Z. (2010). How does search behavior change as search becomes more difficult? In *Proceedings of the Conference on Human Factors in Computing Systems* (pp. 35–44). ACM.

Bloom, B. S. (1956). *Taxonomy of educational objectives Cognitive domain* (Vol. *1*, pp. 20–24). New York, NY: McKay.

Capra, R., Arguello, J., O'Brien, H., Li, Y., & Choi, B. (2018). The effects of manipulating task determinability on search behaviors and outcomes. In *the 41st International ACM SIGIR Conference on Research & Development in Information Retrieval* (pp. 445–454). ACM.

Cole, M., Liu, J., Belkin, N., Bierig, R., Gwizdka, J., Liu, C., … Zhang, X. (2009). Usefulness as the criterion for evaluation of interactive information retrieval. In *Proceedings of HCIR* (pp. 1–4).

Cole, M. J., Hendahewa, C., Belkin, N. J., & Shah, C. (2015). User activity patterns during information search. *ACM Transactions on Information Systems (TOIS)*, *33*(1), 1.

Feild, H. A., Allan, J., & Jones, R. (2010). Predicting searcher frustration. In *Proceedings of the 33rd SIGIR Conference on Research and Development in Information Retrieval* (pp. 34–41). ACM.

Guo, Q., White, R. W., Dumais, S. T., Wang, J., & Anderson, B. (2010). Predicting query performance using query, result, and user interaction features. In *Proceedings* of *Adaptivity, Personalization and Fusion of Heterogeneous Information* (pp. 198-201). ACM.

Hauff, C., Hiemstra, D., & de Jong, F. (2008). A survey of pre-retrieval query performance predictors. In *Proceedings of the 17th ACM Conference on Information and Knowledge Management* (pp. 1419–1420). ACM.

He, B., & Ounis, I. (2006). Query performance prediction. *Information Systems*, *31*(7), 585–594.

Hienert, D., Mitsui, M., Mayr, P., Shah, C., & Belkin, N. J. (2018). The role of the task topic in web search of different task types. In *Proceedings of the 2018 Conference on Human Information Interaction & Retrieval* (pp. 72–81). ACM.

Ingwersen, P. (1996). Cognitive perspectives of information retrieval interaction: Elements of a cognitive IR theory. *Journal of Documentation*, *52*(1), 3–50.

Jiang, J., He, D., & Allan, J. (2014). Searching, browsing, and clicking in a search session: Changes in user behavior by task and over time. In *Proceedings of the 37th International ACM SIGIR Conference on Research & Development in Information Retrieval* (pp. 607–616). ACM.

Kelly, D., Arguello, J., Edwards, A., & Wu, W. C. (2015). Development and evaluation of search tasks for IIR experiments using a cognitive complexity framework. In *Proceedings of the 2015 Conference on The Theory of Information Retrieval* (pp. 101–110). ACM.

Kumaran, G., & Carvalho, V. R. (2009). Reducing long queries using query quality predictors. In *Proceedings of the 32nd International ACM SIGIR Conference on Research and Development in Information Retrieval* (pp. 564–571). ACM.

Li, Y., & Belkin, N. J. (2008). A faceted approach to conceptualizing tasks in information seeking. *Information Processing and Management*, *44*(6), 1822–1837.

Liu, J. (2017). Toward a unified model of human information behavior: An equilibrium perspective. *Journal of Documentation*, *73*(4), 666–688.

Liu, J., Cole, M. J., Liu, C., Bierig, R., Gwizdka, J., Belkin, N. J., … Zhang, X. (2010). Search behaviors in different task types. In *Proceedings of the 10th Annual Joint Conference on Digital Libraries* (pp. 69–78). ACM.

Liu, J., Mitsui, M., Belkin, N. J., & Shah, C. (2019). Task, information seeking intentions, and user behavior: Toward a multi-level understanding of web search. In *Proceedings of International ACM SIGIR Conference on Human Information Interaction and Retrieval* (pp. 123–132). ACM.

Liu, J., & Shah, C. (2019). Investigating the impacts of expectation disconfirmation on web search. In *Proceedings of Conference on Human Information Interaction and Retrieval* (pp. 319–323). ACM.

Liu, J., Wang, Y., Mandal, S., & Shah, C. (2019). Exploring the immediate and short-term effects of peer advice and cognitive authority on Web search behavior. *Information Processing and Management*, *56*(3), 1010–1025.

Mitsui, M., Liu, J., Belkin, N. J., & Shah, C. (2017). Predicting information seeking intentions from search behaviors. In *Proceedings of the 40th ACM SIGIR Conference on*

Research and Development in Information Retrieval (pp. 1121–1124). ACM.

Rha, E. Y., Mitsui, M., Belkin, N. J., & Shah, C. (2016). Exploring the relationships between search intentions and query reformulations. *Proceedings of the Association for Information Science and Technology, 53*(1), 1–9.

Ruotsalo, T., Peltonen, J., Eugster, M. J., Głowacka, D., Floréen, P., Myllymäki, P., ... Kaski, S. (2018). Interactive intent modeling for exploratory search. *ACM Transactions on Information Systems (TOIS), 36*(4), 44.

Scholer, F., Kelly, D., Wu, W. C., Lee, H. S., & Webber, W. (2013). The effect of threshold priming and need for cognition on relevance calibration and assessment. In *Proceedings of the 36th International ACM SIGIR Conference on Research and Development in Information Retrieval* (pp. 623–632). ACM.

Shah, C. (2018). Information fostering-being proactive with information seeking and retrieval: Perspective paper. In *Proceedings of the 2018 Conference on Human Information Interaction & Retrieval* (pp. 62–71). ACM.

Smith, C. L., & Kantor, P. B. (2008). User adaptation: Good results from poor systems. In *Proceedings of the 31st Annual International ACM SIGIR Conference on Research and Development in Information Retrieval* (pp. 147–154). ACM.

Teevan, J., Alvarado, C., Ackerman, M. S., & Karger, D. R. (2004). The perfect search engine is not enough: A study of orienteering behavior in directed search. In *Proceedings of the SIGCHI Conference on Human Factors in Computing Systems* (pp. 415–422). ACM.

Wang, Y., Liu, J., Mandal, S., & Shah, C. (2017). Search successes and failures in query segments and search tasks: A field study. *Proceedings of the Association for Information Science and Technology, 54*(1), 436–445.

Wu, W. C., Kelly, D., & Huang, K. (2012). User evaluation of query quality. In *Proceedings of the 35th ACM SIGIR Conference on Research and Development in Information Retrieval* (pp. 215–224). ACM.

APPENDIX

Classifier	Accuracy	Precision
Logistic regression	**.599**	.621
Naïve bayes	.566	**.675**
AdaBoost	.579	.579
Support vector machine	.586	.595
Random forest	.566	.602
ZeroR (baseline)	.566	.566

Table A1. overall performance: search behavior model. The The best performers are boldfaced.

Classifier	Accuracy	Precision
Logistic regression	.625	.650
Naïve bayes	.648	**.703**
AdaBoost	.643	.654
Support vector machine	**.649**	.652
Random forest	.631	.652
ZeroR (baseline)	.566	.566

Table A2. overall performance: behavior-intention model. The best performers are boldfaced.

Classifier	CPE	STP	REL	INT
Logistic regression	.576	.589	.547	.480
Naïve bayes	.571	.556	.581	.490
AdaBoost	**.603**	.611	.518	**.574**
Support vector machine	.560	.611	.569	.545
Random forest	.594	**.633**	**.584**	.525
ZeroR (baseline)	.549	.589	.562	**.574**

Table A3. Accuracy in tasks of different types: behavior model. The best performers are boldfaced.

Classifier	CPE	STP	REL	INT
Logistic regression	.598	.654	.609	.545
Naïve bayes	.582	.659	**.698**	**.659**
AdaBoost	.619	.673	.566	.576
Support vector machine	.583	.645	.618	.575
Random forest	**.642**	**.685**	.616	.579
ZeroR (baseline)	.549	.589	.562	.574

Table A4. Precision of query failure prediction: behavior model. The best performers are boldfaced.

Classifier	CPE	STP	REL	INT
Logistic regression	.641	.578	**.591**	.584
Naïve bayes	.598	.622	.672	.545
AdaBoost	.658	**.644**	.555	**.688**
Support vector machine	.663	.589	.584	.589
Random forest	**.668**	.578	.577	.624
ZeroR (baseline)	.549	.589	.562	.574

Table A5. Accuracy in tasks of different types: behavior-intention model. The best performers are boldfaced.

Classifier	**CPE**	**STP**	**REL**	**INT**
Logistic regression	.670	.647	.624	.636
Naïve bayes	.606	**.702**	**.742**	.682
AdaBoost	**.683**	.672	.603	**.693**
Support vector machine	.679	.648	.625	.630
Random forest	.682	.642	.607	.667
ZeroR (baseline)	.549	.589	.562	.574

Table A6. Precision of query failure prediction: behavior-intention model. The best performers are boldfaced.

Bi-LSTM+CRF-Based Named Entity Recognition in Scientific Papers in the Field of Ecological Restoration Technology

Jianxia Ma
The Northwest Institute of Eco-Environment and Resources, Chinese Academy of Sciences, Lanzhou, China
majx@lzb.ac.cn

Hui Yuan
Department of Library, Information and Archives Management, University of Chinese Academy of Sciences, Beijing, China
Yuanhui@llas.ac.cn

ABSTRACT

We carried out an experiment to extract ecological-restoration-technology-related entities (i.e., entities related to the fragile ecological remediation technology of desertification, rocky desertification, water and soil erosion control areas, place entities, and time entities related to the technology performed,) from full-text documents published in the CNKI from 1978 to 2017. Based on the extraction of the time entities, place entities, and fragile ecological remediation technology entities, we analyzed the technologies with the greatest potential from among China's fragile ecological restoration technologies using the category clustering of fragile ecological restoration technologies with LDA and the place distribution and evolution of fragile ecological treatment technologies. This research shows that the proposed Bi-LSTM+CRF combined with the feature-based named entity knowledgebase can be used to perform geographical knowledge discovery from text, and it has has good prospects for applications in intelligence analysis based on text mining.

KEYWORDS

Named Entity Recognition; Deep Learning; Bi-LSTM +CRF; Ecological Restoration Technology; Geographical Knowledge Discovery from Text

ASIS&T THESAURUS

Entity Extraction; Geography; Latent Semantic Analysis; Quantitative Analysis

INTRODUCTION

The problem of global land degradation, including phenomena such as desertification, soil erosion, and rocky desertification, is becoming increasingly severe. China is among countries with the most serious ecological degradation, and it faces grave problems that threaten ecosystem functions and livelihoods, including desertification, soil erosion, and forest ecosystem degradation (Defries et al., 2012). Eco-technology plays an important role in alleviating land degradation and promoting the restoration and management of degraded land. In the 1950s, China began to carry out research, experiments, and demonstrations of key technologies and modes for the restoration and reconstruction of degraded ecosystems. The ecologically fragile zones included the upper reaches of the Yangtze River and Yellow River, the western Karst region, the arid desert region, and typical coastal zones. A large number of ecological management and restoration technologies have been developed through the implementation of major ecological projects, including Sanjiangyuan ecological management, rocky desertification treatment, Beijing-Tianjin sandstorm source control, the return of farmland to forest (grassland), and natural forest protection. However, while there is much information about the creation and usage of these useful technologies, there is no central clearinghouse for it because it appears in a wide variety of text documents, from articles to patents. There is neither a systematic summary (or a scientific evaluation of this material) nor a unified platform bringing together the information about ecological degradation problems in different ecological fragile regions and existing eco-technologies. This lack hinders the popularization and application of these technologies (G. D. Chen, 2012; Gao, 2014).

If we can use text extraction and deep learning technology to extract the name of the ecological restoration technology, the implementation time of the ecological restoration technology, and the geographical location of the implementation of the technology, we can store this information structurally; this process would allow for the analysis and visualization of the development of ecological control technology. This elucidation of the technologies would be valuable for promoting the popularization of the ecological restoration technologies accumulated in China.

Research on the automatic extraction, analysis methods, and technologies of entities, attributes, and relationships related to resources and environment is helpful for promoting the

82nd Annual Meeting of the Association for Information Science & Technology | Melbourne, Australia | 19–23 October, 2019

DOI: 10.1002/pra2.00016

research and application of text-mining-based resource and environment information analysis technology in a big data environment.

RELATED RESEARCH

Named Entity Recognition (NER) is a sub-branch of the information extraction (IE) of the whole process of text mining. It is the foundation of coreference resolution, relationship extraction, and event extraction. With the rapid growth in the available text information, many researchers conducted significant amounts of research based on NER in wide fields, especially in biomedical science. The process of populating a structured relational database from unstructured sources has received renewed interest in the database community through high-profile start-up companies (e.g., Tamr and Trifacta), established companies, like IBM (with its Watson AI) (Brown, Epstein, Murdock, & Fin, 2013; Ferrucci et al., 2010), and a variety of research efforts (Y. Chen & Wang, 2014; Li, Reiss, & Chiticariu, 2011; Weikum & Theobald, 2010). Many geoscience studies related to NER have been carried out. Peters, Zhang, and Livny (2014) developed and validated the quality of a machine reading system, PaleoDeepDive, that automatically locates and extracts data from heterogeneous text, tables, and figures in paleontological publications. C. Wang, Ma, and Chen (2018a) carried out an experiment in information extraction and knowledge graph construction from geoscience literature. Morrison, Liu, Eleish, et al. (2017) used network analysis methods to display and explore the hidden relationships among mineral species, localities, and observations.

Text mining for Chinese literature requires some preprocessing work. Word segmentation is a necessary step in this process. The methods of Chinese word segmentation have been classified as dictionary-based, statistically-based, and hybrid. L. Huang, Du, and Chen (2015a) used Conditional Random Fields (CRF) to segment geological documents written in Chinese.

In recent years, deep learning (DL) has developed rapidly in the field of Natural Language Processing(NLP). NER has also shifted from the earliest dictionaries, rules-based methods, and traditional machine learning methods to deep learning methods. The work of Collobert et al. (2011) is one of the earliest representative works that used neural networks for NER; the authors proposed two network structures, the window method and sentence method. NER research that used the cyclic neural network structure and CRF layer appeared in 2015-2016. Lample, Ballesteros, Subramanian, Kawakami, and Dyer (2016) introduced two kinds of neural network structures; the first is based on the Bi-LSTM and CRF model, and the other is based on the transformation method to construct and mark text segmentation. Z. Huang, Xu, and Yu (2015b) proposed a variety of sequence annotation models based on the LSTM, including the LSTM network model, Bi-LSTM network model, LSTM+CRF model, and Bi-LSTM+CRF model. Ma and Hovy (2016) introduced a neural network architecture that combines the Bi-LSTM, CNN, and CRF. It extracts representations from the word and character levels without feature engineering and data preprocessing. The F1 value of the named entity recognition on the CoNLL-2003 corpus is 91.21%. At present, the NN / CNN / RNN -CRF model, which combines a neural network with the CRF model, has become the mainstream model for named entity recognition. Since it inherited the advantages of the deep learning method, the NER method, based on a neural network structure, can reach the mainstream level without a large number of artificial features depending on the word vectors and character vectors. Furthermore, adding high-quality dictionary features can further enhance the model's effectiveness.

The Bi-LSTM, as a type of RNN, has achieved good results in NER. However, it also has some problems that need to be solved, including (1) the further improvement of its own structure to better fit the issue, (2) a lack of labeled data, which restrains the performance of the DL, (3) and the failure to make full use of external resources and domain knowledge.

The recognition of Chinese-named entities is more complicated than those in English. This is mainly because there is no delimiter symbol indicating the boundary of words in Chinese texts. The recognition effect of named entities is greatly affected by the results of automatic word segmentation. Research on Chinese naming recognition based on neural networks has received much attention (C. Wang, Ma, & Chen, 2018a; Zhang, Wu, Liu, et al., 2017). A Chinese named entity recognition based on deep learning (G. Y. Wang, 2015; Zhu, Yang, & Wang, 2016) has begun to emerge. The researchemerged. Research and experiments with the LSTM (Y. Wang et al., 2017; Zeng et al., 2018) on Chinese named entity recognition have been carried out.

METHOD

In this study, we applied the Bi-LSTM+CRF combined with a feature-based named entity knowledge base to extract the technology, time and place named entities related to the fragile ecological remediation for the desertification, rocky desertification, and water and soil erosion control regions from full-text documents published in the CNKI from 1978 to 2017.

The Bi-LSTM+CRF model used in this study consists of 3 layers: word embedding, Bi-LSTM (including the Tanh layer), and the CRF layer, as shown in Figure 1. When the overall structure is determined, more details about each layer must be considered, such as the (1) input layer information, the origin of the initial word vector, processing tools, and dimensions; (2) Bi-LSTM layer, including the number of units, network layers, iterations, and maximum patience value, and (3) the fact that the CRF layer assumes the role of classifier in the whole neural network structure.

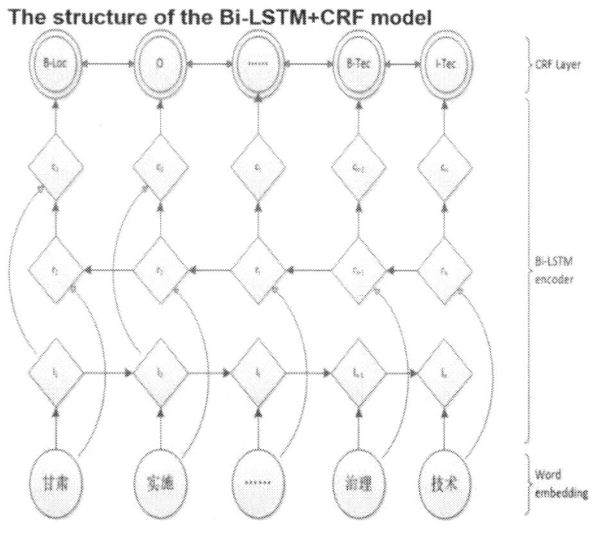

Figure 1. The structure of the Bi-LSTM+CRF model.

The Structure of the Bi-LSTM+CRF Model

The circles at the bottom of the Figure 1 represent the input layer for the embedding input layer, the diamonds represent the decisive equation of the learning input, and the concentrics represent the random variable. The information flow sends the word embedding of the input layer to the Bi-LSTM, where l (i) represents word (i) and the historical signal coming in from the left, and r (i) represents word (i) and future signals coming in from the right. The information of the 2 vectors is connected by C (i) to represent word (i).

In the word embedding layer, Word2Vec is used to embed the words in the corpus. The expression of word embedding can be purely pre-trained or fine-tuned in the training model where the effect will be better.

In the Bi-LSTM layer, 3 gates in the LSTM are used to control the input information into the memory cell and the proportion of the information forgotten in the last stage, and then the cell state is updated. Finally, the updated cell state is processed by the tanh equation, which is multiplied by sigmoid as the final output.

In the CRF layer, the final result of the deep neural network, which is taken as the feature, is connected with the CRF model.

The Implementation Procedure for the Bi-LSTM+CRF Model

The implementation procedure for the Bi-LSTM+CRF model mainly includes the model building stage and the post processing stage (as shown in Figure 2).

1. The model building stage
i. Corpus preprocessing

First, the PDF document is transformed into TXT format with PDFBox and segmented. Ansj-seg (implemented in Java by ICTCLAS,[1] Institute of Computing Technology, Chinese Academy of Sciences) was the segmentation tool used in this research. The Chinese word segmentation was implemented based on n-gram+CRF+HMM, and the word list and the part of speech of each word were obtained after the document segmentation.

ii. Annotated text

In order to distinguish the time, place, and technology entities and non-entities in the process of building the model, we used the IOB2 annotation method, where B represents the beginning of the entity, I represents the entity follow-up, and O represents the non-entity. In the IOB2 annotation system, each word is assigned a tag that can be divided into 2 parts: one part is the location tag of B, I, and O, and the other part is the entity type tag, which indicates which entity type the tagged content belongs to.

Tag	Type of entity	Tag	Function
Time	Time entity	B	The word is the starting position of a chunk
Place	Place entity	I	The word is the middle position of a chunk
Tech	Eco-technology entity	O	The word is not in any chunk

Table 1. Entity type labels and IOB2 annotation system.

We analyzed the contents of the tags. The classification and tagging methods used in this study are shown in Table 2.

The Table 3 shows some examples of the entity annotation of Chinese text corpus. the first column shows the words in the text, the second column shows the part of speech of the word, and the third column shows the entity that the word represents in the sentence.

After processing the corpus, the NER problem can be transformed into a sequence labeling problem.

iii. Named entities knowledge base

We analyzed the characteristics and classification of the time entity, place named entity, and eco-technology entity, and then constructed the corresponding named entity knowledge base as the training corpus of the neural network model and word vector to improve the overall recognition and extraction effect.

[1] NLPIR Chinese word segmentation system. http://ictclas.nlpir.org/

Symbol	O	B-Time	I-Time	B-Place	I-Place	B-Tech	I-Tech
Meaning	Non-entity	Beginning of time	Middle of time	Beginning of place	Middle of place	Beginning of tech	Middle of tech

Table 2. Entity classification and tagging.

Words in texts	Words in texts(In English)	Part of speech	IOB2 annotation
在	In	p	O
毛乌素	Maowusu	ns	B-Place
沙地	sandlot	n	I-Place
应	should	v	O
推行	carry out	v	O
灌草	bush, grass	nw	B-Tech
乔	and arbour	nr	I-Tech
相结合	combined	nz	I-Tech
以	with	p	O
……		……	……

Table 3. Entity annotation examples.

In Chinese texts, the descriptions of the ecological restoration technology names have the following characteristics:

- The ecological restoration technology names may contain the geographical named entity. The ecological restoration technology names (eco-technology) often contain the geographic location information of the technical implementation and are nested in the technical names in the form of toponymic entities, such as "deep planting of poplar in Alpine arid sandy land (高寒干旱沙地杨树深栽造林)".
- The ecological restoration technology names may include the ecosystem or ecological type. Some of the eco-technology names are named after the implementation of ecological areas or a combination of ecological areas and geographical names, such as "oasis agriculture and forestry intercropping(绿洲农林间作)" and "loess plateau terrace technology (黄土高原梯田技术)".
- The ecological restoration technology names may include the ecological degradation types. The description of the technology by technical name is usually combined with the type of ecological degradation, indicating the technology is applicable to a certain type of degradation, such as "integrated desertification control technology (荒漠化综合治理技术)".
- The ecological restoration technology names may contain trigger words. Suffixes such as "technology (技术)", "measures (措施)", and "engineering (工程)" appear in the text, and left boundary words such as "implementation (实施)", "carry out(开展)" and "adoption (采用)" are used to indicate the technical name in the text.
- There may be an indication or ellipsis of the name of the ecological restoration technology. The ecological restoration technology name may be referred to in context, such as "in the process of governance (此次治理过程中)." Other examples include "this time (此次) ", "this technology(该技术)…" and "the technology".
- Omission of the name of the ecological restoration technology. Some eco-technologies are usually described in terms of trigger vocabulary and degenerate types or technical types, without specific and complete technical names, especially for technical categories or unclear technologies. Examples of this sort include "plant measures" and "chemical measures".

We analyzed and summarized the constitutive rules of the ecological restoration technology names (including the names of places, ecosystems/regions, types of degradation, and triggers) and the constraints of the entities (such as the left and right boundary words). We summarized the rules for extracting the names of ecological control technologies in the Chinese texts. Some rule samples are shown in Table 4.

iv. Word vectors

In neural networks, words are usually represented by word vectors. Generally, in the process of training parameter initialization, the neural network model only randomly initializes the word vectors. The random initial word vectors do not carry any information. If the training corpus is too small, little information is learned by the model, so the results are poor.

Word vectors can be trained by a large-scale unlabeled corpus, and they contain abundant syntactic and semantic information in a large-scale corpus. In this study, word vectors trained by a large-scale unlabeled corpus were used to replace the initial word vectors of the neural network model, so that the rich information contained in the word vectors could be applied in the initial stage of the neural network model to improve the performance of the model. We used Google's open source word vector tool Word2Vec[2] to train the word vectors.

2. The post processing stage

The predictive corpus was pre-processed and cleaned, and the text was processed into a suitable format by word segmentation. The predictive corpus was input into the Bi-LSTM +CRF model, and the recognition results were output by the model. Then, the recognition results were acquired and post-processed.

[2] Word2vec: https://github.com/svn2github/word2vec

Type of Eco-Technology Name	Sub-class of Eco-technology name and Expression pattern	Example
Eco-technology names with auxiliary words	LeftWord	实施, 开展, 采用… (Implement, develop,adopt...)
	RightWord	技术, 措施, 工程… (Technology, Measures, Engineering...)
	Agrotype	沙地, 草甸土, 盐碱地… (Sandy land, meadow soil, saline-alkali land...)
	Ecosystem / ecological zone	黄土高原、高寒草甸… (. Loess Plateau, Alpine Meadow...)
	Ecological degradation types	荒漠化、石漠化…… (Desertification,rock desertification...)
Simple eco-technology name	TriggerWords	沙障, 防护林, 固沙剂… (Sand barrier, shelter forest, sand fixing age...)
	Eco-technology category	生物措施, 工程措施 … (Biological measures, engineering measures)
Eco-technology name with other entities	With place and Agrotype: (LeftWord) + Place + (Agrotype)+ TriggerWords + (RightWord)	柴达木沙地杨树深栽造林 (Deep-planting afforestation of Chaidamu sandy land)
	With Ecosystem / ecological zone Ecological zone + TriggerWords + (RightWord)	绿洲农林间作 (Oasis agriculture and forestry intercropping) 黄土高原梯田技术 (Terrace technology in the Loess Plateau)
	Ecological degradation types (EcoDegType); EcoDegType + (TriggerWords) + RightWord	荒漠化综合治理技术 (Desertification comprehensive treatment technology) 冻融荒漠化防治 (Freezing and thawing desertification control)
Eco-technology phrase	LeftWord + TriggerWords + (RightWord) TriggerWords + RightWord TCategory + RightWord	设置生物围栏(Set the bio fence)，采用乔灌混交技术 草方格沙障技术 (Adopting the technique of arboring and mixing technology)， 林草复合法植物/农业/工程措施 (plant / agriculture / engineering measures with forest and grass compound method)

Table 4. Examples of Extraction Rules for Ecological Restoration Technology.

The acquisition process of the three types of entities was as follows:

Step 1: The Bi-LSTM+CRF model was trained to recognize the test data, extract the identified classification tags, and convert the corresponding tags into the corresponding entity string as candidate entities.

Step 2: We then determined the relationship between different entities based on the location of the candidate entity in the text.

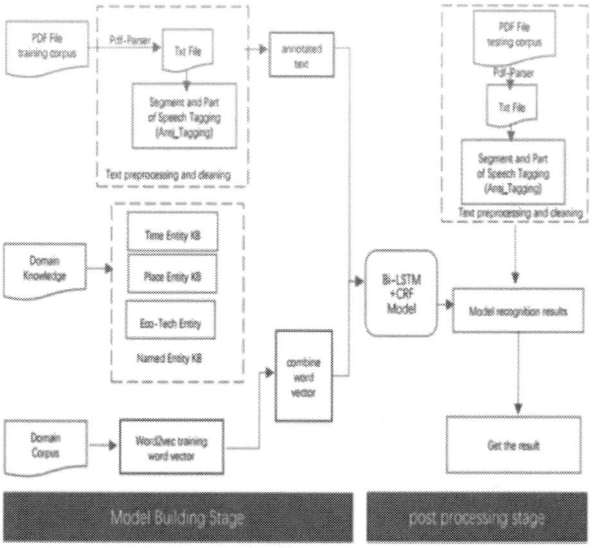

Figure 2. The implementation procedure of the Bi-LSTM +CRF model.

RESULTS

In order to compare the effect of the unlabeled corpus on the word2Vec training, the bibliographic information corpus and the entity knowledge base corpus were combined into two unlabeled sets with the CBOW model (Mikolov, Chen, Corrado, & Dean, 2013), the dimension of the word vector was set to 100 dimensions, and the context window size was 5. The sampling threshold was 1e-3, and started with a learning rate of 0.02.

The training of the named entity recognition model with a random initial word vector in the Bi-LSTM+CRF neural network was treated as the benchmark method. We then tried to replace the word vector result of the two unlabeled text sets (as shown in Table 5) trained by Word2Vec with the random initial word vector. The results produced by the different sets are compared in Table 6.

Sets	Source	The part used for word vector training
Unlabeled text sets1	634 papers	Title, keyword, and abstracts of 634 papers
Unlabeled text sets2	634 papers+entity knowledge base corpus	Title + keyword + abstract +time + place + tech of 634 papers

Table 5. The two unlabeled text sets for Word2Vec training.

Compared with the random initialization word vector, w2v-1 achieved good results, and P, R, and F1 improved by 7.57%, 34.50%, and 30.21%, respectively. W2v-2 increased by 0.76%, 0.22%, and 0.43% on the basis of the w2v-1. The two text sets are highly correlated with the extracted domain content. Experiments show that for a certain type of corpus, the larger the corpus size, the better the performance of the word vector. As a key input to neural networks, a good word vector is important.

No	Input word vector	P (%)			R (%)			F1		
		Time	Place	Tech	Time	Place	Tech	Time	Place	Tech
1	Base line	62.66%			21.69%			32.22%		
		61.85%	61.88%	40.68%	40.68%	40.68%	8.89%	40.68%	45.04%	15.68%
2	w2v-1	70.23%			56.19%			0.6243		
		79.79%	75.12%	63.84%	66.01%	52.18%	54.96%	72.25%	61.58%	59.07%
3	w2v-2	70.99%			56.41%			62.86%		
		79.14%	72.05%	69.73%	69.73%	69.73%	56.21%	69.73%	61.20%	61.24%
4	w2v-2 + MoreData	73.10%			59.94%			65.87%		
		74.16%	75.82%	70.43%	70.43%	70.43%	53.78%	70.43%	68.88%	58.04%
5	w2v-2 + MoreData+ dictionaries	**74.34%**			**64.04%**			**68.81%**		
		78.63%	82.02%	66.02%	72.20%	65.71%	58.75%	75.27%	72.97%	62.17%

(1) Baseline: a random initial word vector;
(2) W2v-1: word vector obtained by inputting unlabeled text sets1 into word2Vec
(3)W2V-2: word vector obtained by inputting unlabeled text sets2 into word2Vec
(4) Word vector + more training corpus (different scales);
(5) Word vector + more training corpus + dictionary.

Table 6. Results with different word vectors.

Our research mainly focused on the following key issues:

1. A neural network model based on Bi-LSTM and CRF was constructed, which included the following steps:

- Use Word2Vec to obtain the initial word vector;
- Transfer the word vector input to the Bi-LSTM neural network to model the context information of each word;
- At the output of the Bi-LSTM neural network, use continuous CRF tags on the sentences and annotate the entities in the sentences. Compared with the traditional machine learning method, this scheme is based on statistical probability and can make use of the lexical context dependency, so the application scenarios are more extensive.

2. Optimize the initial word vector of Word2Vec

The initial word vector is an important input of the neural network model, and the effect of the word vector is closely related to the field and size of the corpus. In this study, the model performance (F value) was improved by 30.64% by combining the title data of the training literature and the named entity knowledge base data of the related fields into Word2Vec.

3. Construct a named entity knowledge base based on the entity's characteristics.

We had access to the Chinese literature about ecological restoration technology, and summed the time, place, and ecological management technology named entities from it. Based on the analysis of the characteristics of the time entities, place entities, and eco-technology entities, a named entities knowledge base was built to be put into the model as a training corpus. In our tests, the system performance (F value) was increased by 5.95%.

EXPERIMENTAL APPLICATION

We based our work on the extraction of the time entities, place entities, and fragile ecological remediation technology entities from 634 papers searched from the CNKI document database. We carried out an analysis of the development status of China's fragile ecological restoration technologies, including the hot technologies of China's fragile ecological remediation technologies, the category clustering of fragile ecological remediation technologies, and the spatial layout and evolution of fragile ecological remediation technologies.

Analysis of the Development Trend of Ecological Restoration Technology

There were 21764 temporal entities extracted from 634 papers, with an accuracy of 78.63%. In this study, the specific time was mapped to 10-year time units, i.e., the 1950s and 1960s.

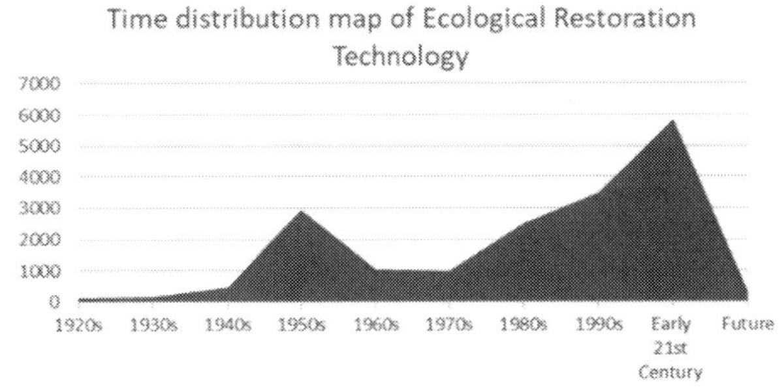

Figure 3. Time distribution map of Ecological Restoration Technology.

Desertification, rocky desertification, soil erosion, and other aspects of control in the 1950s experienced an outbreak. This outbreak occurred after the founding of the People's Republic of China because some ecological restoration programs were carried out for the northern Shaanxi ecological environment control, desertification control, soil and water conservation and rehabilitation projects, as well as the "Northern Great Desert" and other areas of development. Since the 1970s, the number of time entities has increased continuously, which shows that the attention and measures for ecological restoration in China have gradually increased. The "future" time mainly appears in the relevant sentences of governance objectives.

Regional Distribution Analysis of Ecological Restoration Technology

In order to analyze the distribution of ecological restoration technology implementation sites in the experimental data sets, 48 971 toponymic entities were classified according to provinces in 634 papers. The accuracy of the extraction of the toponymic entities was 82.02%. The geographical entities of the provincial and municipal districts were directly mapped, and the ecological regions were mapped to the main provinces including them, such as the Alxa Desert to the Inner Mongolia Autonomous Region and the Hexi Corridor to Gansu Province, while geographical entities of the trans-provincial regions, such as the Qinghai-Tibet Plateau and the Loess Plateau, were mapped to all the provinces involved. For example, the Alxa Desert and the Hexi Corridor were mapped to six provinces and regions (Tibet, Qinghai, Xinjiang, Gansu, Sichuan, and Yunnan) and the Loess Plateau was mapped to seven provinces and regions (Qinghai, Gansu, Ningxia, Inner Mongolia, Shaanxi, Shanxi, and Henan), totaling 40,246 entities.

As Figure 4 shows, ecological restoration is mainly concentrated in the Inner Mongolia Autonomous Region and Gansu Province, followed by Qinghai Province, the Xinjiang Uyghur Autonomous Region, Ningxia, Shaanxi, Beijing, and Tibet. The reasons for the concentration of the related controls in the Inner Mongolia Autonomous Region are the deserts and sandy areas, including the Alxa Desert, Ulan Buhe Desert, Kubuqi Desert, Tengger Desert, Badain Jilin Desert, and Horqin Sandy Land. Other eco-control concentrated provinces also include the ecological areas which urgently need to be controlled, such as the Loess Plateau, Qinghai-Tibet Plateau, Qaidam Basin, and Taklimakan Desert. Because of the influence of sandstorms and other extreme weather in the Inner Mongolia Autonomous Region and Beijing's strategic position as the capital city, there are many related ecological restoration measures in these regions.

Analysis of Classification of Ecological Restoration Technology

In order to analyze the main methods of eco-restoration technology in experimental data sets, the names of restoration technologies extracted from 634 data sets were sorted out.

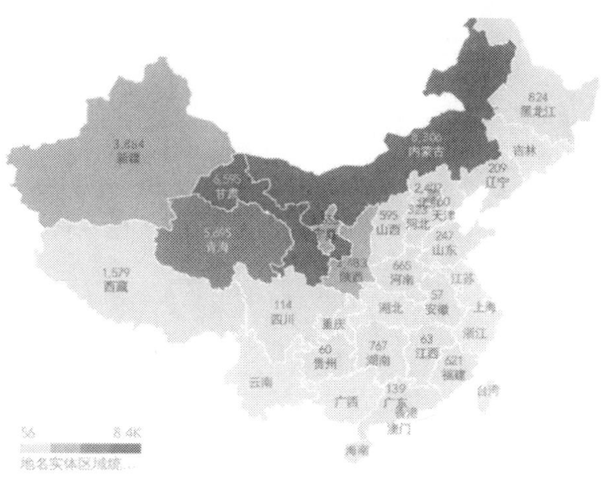

Figure 4. Regional distribution map of ecological management.

Based on frequency statistics of the names of the ecological restoration technologies identified, a word-cloud is shown in Figure 5. The words "grass checkered sand barrier", "aerial seeding afforestation", "vertical sand barrier", "shelter forest", and "fence enclosure"(草方格沙障", "飞播造林", "高立式沙障", "防护林", and "围栏封育) are prominent. These techniques are used much more frequently than other techniques. There are also new techniques, such as "anti-season afforestation of frozen seedlings", "overhead afforestation", and "containerized water afforestation" ("冷藏苗反季节造林", "顶凌造林", and "容器盛水造林").

Figure 5. Word cloud picture of ecological restoration technology.

Next, we analyzed the classification of these technologies through LDA topic clustering (see Figure 6). The topic of ecological restoration technology was clustered by LDA. Based on the analysis of the number of the eco- restoration technology names and LDA topic model results, the number of topics was determined to be 7, and the most frequent keywords under each topic (λ = 1 on the right) and the special keywords under each topic (λ = 0 on the right) were obtained.

According the topic cluster based on TDA, 7 topics were obtained: biological measures, engineering measures, physical measures, agricultural measures, management measures, plant measures, chemical measures.

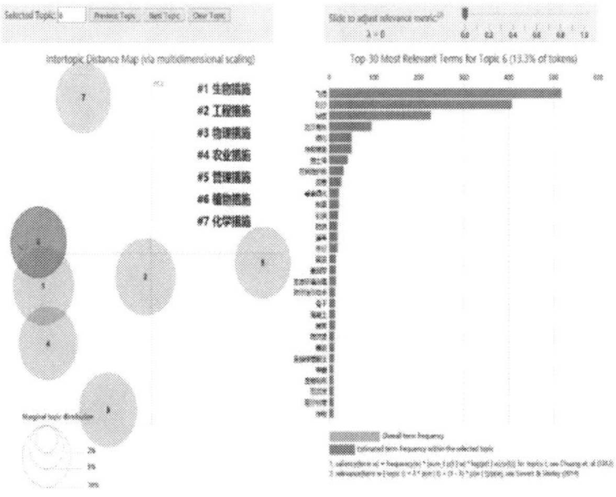

Figure 6. Topic cluster diagram of ecological restoration technology.

Analysis of the Development Trend of Different Types Ecological Restoration Technology

The proportions of the different types of ecological remediation technologies corresponding to different time periods were calculated as shown in Figure 7.

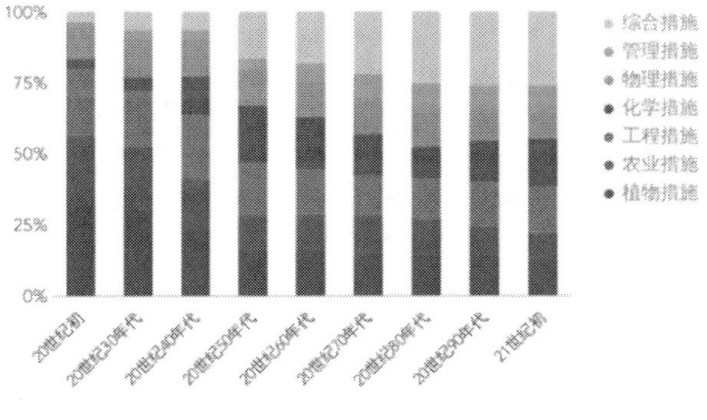

Figure 7. Development of different types of eco-restoration technology.

The proportions of comprehensive measures and management measures have been increasing, possibly due to the gradual combination of various types of measures and the management of the control areas with the development of technology and the progress of ecological restoration awareness. The proportions of plant measures, agricultural measures, and engineering measures have declined slightly in recent years, but their overall proportion has been relatively high. The chemical measures grew rapidly in the 1950s-1960s, decreased slightly in the 1970s-1980s, and then increased again after the 1990s. The reason may be that the chemical measures were developed and applied in the 1950s, but some of them may have caused negative results because of the immaturity of the technology. Negative effects reduced the use of chemical measures in the 1970s and 1980s, but with the development of the technology and the progress in the creation of better chemical agents, a new batch of chemical materials and corresponding measures appeared after the 1990s.

DISCUSSION

We used natural language processing technology and deep learning technology, the Bi-LSTM combined with CRF, to extract named entities related to ecological restoration technology in Chinese literature. We carried out the experimental application of the extraction results.

The results of our work are described below

1. The method of extracting the time, place name, and ecological control technology from Chinese literature based on the Bi-LSTM+CRF neural network model was designed and implemented

We constructed a neural network model based on the bidirectional LSTM and CRF.

2. Optimizing the Word2Vec initial word vector

In this study, the title data of the training literature and the named entity knowledge-based data of the related fields were obtained and then combined into different unannotated text sets. Through the Word2Vec training, the initial word vector improved the model's performance (F1 value) by 0.3064. The larger the corpus size, the better the performance of the word vector.

3. The knowledge base combined with the optimized Word2-Vec word vector improved the model's performance

The 89,619 training entities were obtained by annotating the time, place name, and ecological restoration technology name from the literature on ecological control technology. By summarizing the characteristics of the time, place name, and eco-governance technology names appearing in the literature, we built the knowledge base of the three entity types (including 7,703 entities). We input 97,322 entities into the model to form the training corpus. The training corpus combined with the word vector improved the system performance (F value) by 0.0595.

4. The experimental analysis based on the extracted entities was carried out

The implementation of ecological restoration technology had an outbreak in the 1950s and steadily increased after the 1970s; the implementation areas of ecological control were mainly concentrated in the northwest regions of Inner Mongolia, Gansu, Qinghai, Xinjiang, Ningxia, and Shaanxi; ecological restoration technology mainly included comprehensive plant measures, agricultural measures, and engineering measures. Seven types of measures,including, physical measures, chemical measures, and management measures et al were included in the study. Through the cross-analysis of the relationship between the time-ecological restoration technology and place-ecological restoration technology, the application of ecological restoration technology in different time periods and provincial administrative units was analyzed.

We found the Bi-LSTM+CRF neural network model can be applied to the identification of entities related to ecological restoration technology; we also found that knowledge resources in related fields can be used as a high-quality unlabeled corpus and training corpus, based on which is the better training corpus of the Word2Vec initial word vector and overall model. The accuracy rate and F value of 74.34% and 0.6881, respectively, were obtained by using this model in the Chinese literature about ecological restoration technology.

Improvements in named entity recognition research can be made to continue its advancement:

1. Develop new neural network models and mechanisms

One possible direction for research involves combining the recent development related to pretraining method such as Bert (Devlin et al., 2018). to improve the efficiency of extraction of entities.

3. Identify the relationships between entities

The recognition and judgment of the relationships between entities in this paper only used the information of the location of the entities appearing in the text, which is not ideal for practical applications. Taking into consideration more aspects of the information and characteristics of the entity relationships and identifying the relationships between the extracted entities are key research and processing directions.

ACKNOWLEDGMENTS

This work was supported by the National Key Research and Development Program of China (2016YFC0503706) and the National Natural Science Foundation of China (71376920).

REFERENCES

Brown, E, Epstein, E., Murdock, J. W., & Fin, T.-H. (2013). *Tools and methods for building Watson* (IBM Research Report). https://domino.research.ibm.com/library/cyberdig.nsf/papers/152EF31994BDC3DC85257B1F005DE78F

Chen, G. D. (2012). *Integration of ecological restoration experiment demonstration in West China*. Beijing, China: Science Press (In Chinese).

Chen, Y., & Wang, D. Z. (2014). Knowledge expansion over probabilistic knowledge bases. In *SIGMOD '14 Proceedings of the 2014 ACM SIGMOD International Conference on Management of Data*.

Collobert, R., Weston, J., Bottou, L., Karlen, M., Kavukcuoglu, K., & Kuksa, P. (2011). Natural language processing (almost) from scratch. *The Journal of Machine Learning Research*, *12*, 2493–2537.

Defries, R. S., Ellis, E. C., Chapin, F. S., Pamela, A., Matson, B. L., Turner, I. I., … Syvitski, J. (2012). Planetary opportunities: A social contract for global change science to contribute to a sustainable future. *BioScience*, *62* (6), 603–606.

Devlin, J. et al. (2018). Bert: Pre-training of deep bidirectional transformers for language understanding. arXiv preprint, Arxiv: 1810.04805.

Ferrucci, D. et al. (2010). Building Watson: An overview of the DeepQA project. AI Magazine. Retrieved from https://doi.org/10.1609/aimag.v31i3.2303

Gao, J. X. (2014). *Evaluation and restoration of a degraded ecosystem in Southwest Mountainous Area*. Beijing, China: Science Press (In Chinese).

Huang, L., Du, Y. F., & Chen, G. Y. (2015a). GeoSegmenter: A statistically learned Chinese word segmenter for the geoscience domain. *Computers & Geosciences*, *76*, 11–17.

Huang, Z., Xu, W., & Yu, K. (2015b). Bidirectional LSTM-CRF models for sequence tagging. arXiv preprint arXiv: 150801991.

Lample, G., Ballesteros, M., Subramanian, S., Kazuya, K., & Chris D. (2016). Neural architectures for named entity recognition. arXiv preprint arXiv: 160301360.

Li, Y., Reiss, F. R., & Chiticariu, L. (2011). Chiticariu. SystemT: A declarative information extraction system. In *HLT, 2011. Proceedings of the ACL-HLT 2011 System Demonstrations* (pp. 109–114).

Ma, X., & Hovy, E. (2016). End-to-end sequence labeling via bi-directional LSTM-CNNS-CRF. arXiv preprint arXiv: 160301354.

Mikolov, T., Chen, K., Corrado, G., & Jeffrey D. (2013), Efficient estimation of word representations in vector space. arXiv preprint arXiv: 13013781.

Morrison, S. M., Liu, C., Eleish, A., et al. (2017). Network analysis of mineralogical systems. *American Mineralogist*, *102*(8), 1588–1596.

Peters, S. E., Zhang, C., & Livny, M. (2014). A machine reading system for assembling synthetic paleontological databases. *PLoS ONE, 9*(12), e113523. https://doi.org/10.1371/journal.pone.0113523

Wang, G. Y (2015). *Chinese named entity recognition based on deep learning*. (Dissemination). Beijing Industry University.

Wang, Y., et al. (2017). Named entity recognition for chinese telecommunications field based on Char2Vec and Bi-LSTMs. In *Proceedings of the 12th International Conference on Intelligent Systems and Knowledge Engineering (IEEE ISKE)*.

Wang, C., Ma, X., & Chen, J. (2018a). Information extraction and knowledge graph construction from geoscience literature. *Computers & Geosciences*. https://doi.org/10.1016/j.cageo.2017.12.007

Wang, L., Xie, Y., Junsheng, Z., et al. (2018b). Segment-level Chinese named entity recognition based on neural network, *32*(3), 84–90 100.

Weikum, G., & Theobald, M. (2010). From information to knowledge: Harvesting entities and relationships from web sources. In *Proceedings of the Twenty-Ninth ACM SIGMOD-SIGACT-SIGART Symposium on Principles of Database Systems PODS'10*. June 6–11, 2010. Indianapolis, IN.

Zeng, J. et al. (2018). A two-stage Bi-LSTM model for Chinese Company name recognition. *Proceedings of the 7th International Conference on Artificial Intelligence and Mobile Services (AIMS). Vol. 2018. Lecture Notes in Computer Science*, (pp. 3–15). https://doi.org/10.1007/978-3-319-94361-9_1

Zhang, H., WU, D., LIU, Y., et al. (2017). Chinese named entity recognition based on deep neural network, *31*(4), 28–35.

Zhu, D. H., Yang, L., & Wang, D. B. (2016). Recognizing Chinese Organization names based on deep learning: A recurrent network model, Mordern Library and Information Technology, *12*(36-43).

Relational Privacy: Where the East and the West Could Meet

Yuanye Ma
University of North Carolina at
Chapel Hill,
Chapel Hill, USA
yuanye1@live.unc.edu

ABSTRACT

This paper argues that *relational privacy* can be used as a starting point for conceptualizing privacy in Eastern cultures for it aligns with an Eastern philosophical conception of person. This paper starts with one of the main conceptions of privacy as one having control over personal information, and leverages the criticisms toward control-based privacy and its foundation in individual autonomy, to introduce the concept of relational autonomy from the perspectives of feminist theory and Confucianism. It concludes by discussing the implications for conceptualizing privacy from these two foundations. The paper contributes to privacy research in that it provides an initial suggestion of how the conception of privacy might be characterized by the Western and Eastern philosophical traditions; it explicitly relates the conception of privacy to the conception of the person, and it deliberately phrases the discussion within an intercultural environment.

KEYWORDS

Privacy; Confucianism; Feminist Theory; Intercultural Information Ethics

ASIS&T THESAURUS

Information Science; Philosophy

INTRODUCTION

There is little agreement on the understandings of privacy as it could differ by culture (Moore, 2008); nevertheless, privacy has become a global concern across countries and cultures. However, privacy discussions are dominated by Western cultures, whereas thoughts from other non-Western cultures remain less seen. Meanwhile, current working conceptualizations of privacy rooted in the Western concept of *individual autonomy* as having control over personal information is increasingly falling short in helping answer many privacy questions people face in actual life. Privacy researchers have moved on and proposed *relational privacy* (Bannerman, 2018; Stoljar, 2015) as a more promising alternative to the understanding of privacy. This paper aims to begin exploring these two aspects of privacy research, i.e., how privacy is understood in Eastern culture, and how an Eastern understanding of privacy might relate to the latest conception of privacy in the Western academia. This paper strives to argue that the conception of *relational privacy* can be used as a starting point for conceptualizing an Eastern understanding of privacy. *Relational privacy* is what an Eastern conception of privacy can be characterized as for it aligns with the conception of *the person* in Eastern Confucianism as being *relational*; moreover, *relational privacy* could serve as a bridge between potential conception of privacy under Confucianism and the most recent advancement of the conception of privacy in Western feminist philosophy.

In contrast to the abundance of privacy research in Western academia, discussions of privacy in non-Western cultures are scattered and sometimes conflicting. Some have argued that the concept of privacy is completely absent in many Eastern cultures (Ess, 2005); Nakada and Tamura (2005) argued that privacy was an imported concept for Japan; similarly, it was suggested that the concept of privacy might not have existed at all in traditional Chinese culture (Wang, 2012). However, others studying privacy in Japanese culture, after constructing a more nuanced existence status of privacy in the Japanese society, came to argue that though a full equivalence of the richness of the English word privacy in the Japanese culture is less likely, it is still possible that both cultures (Japanese and American) can "share a minimal conception of privacy" (Mizutani, Dorsey, & Moor, 2004, p. 124).

However, studies of intercultural privacy research present an intriguing picture, from which two lessons for cross-cultural privacy research can be taken. Firstly, it will take more than a simple translation to compare a concept like privacy across cultures. "Any assumption that 'privacy' in Asian contexts directly translates Western notions is both mistaken and dangerously misleading" (Ess, 2005, p. 5); Secondly, to do a cross-cultural study properly, researchers would need to attend to the cultural background that gives rise to the specific concept. Since culture can be all-encompassing, perhaps choosing to focus on the most relevant concepts of the culture and relating the key concept(s) to the study of privacy is a potential way to move inter-cultural privacy research forward.

82nd Annual Meeting of the Association for Information Science & Technology | Melbourne, Australia | 19–23 October, 2019

DOI: 10.1002/pra2.00065

When trying to resolve the puzzle of comparing privacy across cultures, Mizutani, Dorsey, and Moor (2004) suggested that differences in the conception of *the self*[1] might be a key to understanding the differences of privacy in various cultures. For example, unlike the Western conception that emphasizes control and self-determination, the Japanese self can be said as not having a self, or the Japanese society "efface the self" (p. 123) because of the influence from Buddhism. In addition, even when recognizing the existence of the self, the way it is constructed in the Japanese culture can be drastically different from other cultures. Therefore, this paper will use the concept of *the person* as a key concept, and proposes that some of the unique conceptions of how *the person* is understood in a culture can be insightful for conceptualizing privacy.

The term *relational privacy* (Bannerman, 2018) is used to broadly categorize all conceptions of privacy that rest on *relational autonomy* and hence adopt a contextualized perspective. This paper argues that *relational privacy* can be used as a starting point for conceptualizing privacy in Eastern cultures for it aligns with an Eastern philosophical conception of person under Confucianism. This paper is structured as follows: it will first go through one of the main conceptions of privacy as one having control over personal information and discuss how it has been criticized. Based on these criticisms of control-based privacy, this paper then considers feminist theorists' proposal of *relational autonomy*. Two conceptions of privacy, *networked privacy* and *group privacy*, are discussed because both recognize that contextual factors need to be part of a discussion of privacy.

Afterwards, this paper introduces Confucian role ethics and draws directly from the Confucian texts to reveal how the Confucian person is considered as relational, embedded and is always learning and developing. However, it is also recognized that, despite the existence of some common ground (Li, 1994) between the Eastern Confucian philosophy and feminist philosophy, there are more to be explored in terms of how the two diverge in their consideration of technology and the conception of relation between human and technology, and finally the potential implications for understanding privacy. The paper contributes to existing privacy research in that, firstly, it provides an initial suggestion of how the conception of privacy might be characterized by the Western and Eastern philosophical traditions; second, it explicitly relates the conception of privacy to the conception of the person and considers privacy as an ethical question; and lastly, it deliberately phrases the discussion within an intercultural environment.

INDIVIDUAL AUTONOMY BASED CONCEPTUALIZATION OF PRIVACY

Privacy was defined as the *right to be let alone* in the seminal work of Warren and Brandeis (1890), it rested on this underlying belief that "the person should have protection over the liberal self" (Cohen 2012b, p. 1905). In the years subsequent to this seminal definition, discussions have explored various aspects of privacy, from whether privacy is worthy as a separate value to examinations of privacy from various perspectives (e.g., *intimacy*) (DeCew, 2018). Despite the variety of privacy research, the one understanding that has been adopted by many when thinking about and implementing privacy is to regard privacy as "having control over one's information", or "a control-based definition of privacy" (Moore, 2007, p. 812). Over the years, the *control-based definition of privacy* has evolved from the control of the communication of information to others (Westin, 1967) to an emphasis on the individual's control over the information as the basic attributes of the right to privacy (Miller, 1971). Further updates to the *control-based definition of privacy* went on to specify the scope of information that should fall under control, for example, "data about an individual that is identifiable to that individual" (Murphy, 1995, p. 2383).

The control-based definition of privacy has "remained largely unchanged since the 1970s" (Solove, 2013, p. 1880), despite that it is not without criticisms (Floridi, 2006; Moor, 1990). It has been criticized for being "counterintuitive" (Moor, 1990, p. 75), and for relying on the false assumption that information is something that can be controlled (Mai, 2016). It has also been criticized for being "misleading" (Tavani & Moor, 2001, p. 6) because although the idea of control is valuable as a necessary component for the management of privacy, when it comes to the conceptualization of privacy, *restricted access* might be a more appropriate term. In addition, the problem of conceptualizing privacy as control is that it rarely aligns with the reality of people's practice with their personal information nowadays. In particular, Schwartz (2000) has described how privacy as control over personal information has permeated privacy understanding in the U.S., from court decisions and government administration to academic scholars (p. 820–821), and has identified the "autonomy trap" as one of the flaws of the control based view.

Schwartz (2000) criticized *control-based privacy* for it can neither provide effective description of the current informational environment, nor can it provide practical guidance on what people should do to safeguard their privacy. Or, in Schwartz (2000)'s words, control-based privacy is problematic for it creates the "data seclusion deception" (p. 821). On the practical aspect, for example, sharing of personal data among third-party organizations is a common practice among commercial companies that people have no control of (Kim, 2014). More importantly, questions arise regarding what might constitute of personal information over which individuals should have control (Solove, 2002). Schwartz (2000) mentioned two practical reasons why data seclusion is not possible (including "public accountability" and "bureaucratic rationality" (p. 828)). Here, this paper could add that, control based understanding of privacy exacerbates "data seclusion deception" for it ignores how technology functions. The

[1] *The self* and *the person* are used interchangeably in this paper.

application of big data and machine learning further challenges the existence of a clear information boundary that can be used to build a clear definition of personal information. For example, it is unclear if information inferred by machine learning algorithms about a person falls within the categorization of personal information. Further, computer algorithms can conflict with existing human understanding of personal information, and it may not even be clear how they can be interpreted (Bornstein, 2016).

In addition to these practice oriented criticisms of control-based understanding of privacy, a more fundamental criticism is aimed at its conceptual foundation, *individual autonomy*. Schwartz (2000) used "autonomy trap" (p. 821) to describe how control-based understanding is problematic for it is based on unrealistic decision-making assumptions that ignores "information asymmetry" and "bounded rationality"; moreover, it ignores that autonomy can be impacted by contextual factors. The concept of *individual autonomy* has been particularly questioned by feminist theorists for presenting "a masculinist ideals of personhood" (Stoljar, 2015) though critics can from who a number of other areas including psychiatry, moral philosophy, medicine, etc. (O'Shea, 2012). Feminist theory rejects the Kantian concept of autonomy as being *atomistic* and deprived of any social relations (Stoljar, 2015), and proposed *relational autonomy* as an alternative to *individual autonomy*.

Despite these practice oriented criticisms of control-based understanding of privacy, as well as its philosophical foundation of *individual autonomy*, control based privacy went on to function as a shared foundation among studies and practices of privacy today. For instance, it has been informing privacy related policies and laws (Cohen 2012a; Mokrosinska, 2018; Richards, 1981). The world's strongest data protection regulation, according to Burgess (2018), the General Data Protection Regulation (GDPR) of the European Union, requires companies to give their users explanations about the decisions made using their personal data so that individuals can have control over their data (Baulch, 2018). Existing understandings of privacy, including those that were proposed as a counter to the control-based privacy, e.g. *restricted access*, share the same assumptions of control based understanding.

Individual autonomy conceives of *the person* as a liberal self that exists as "an autonomous core — an essential self-identifiable after the residue of influence has been subtracted" (Cohen, 2012b, p. 1905). *Intercultural information ethics* study has traced through the Western philosophy tradition to identify how the concept of privacy is associated with *individual autonomy*, or the understanding of the "subjectivity" as its "natural house" and the respect of privacy equals respecting each other's "autonomous being" (Capurro, 2005, p. 39). This way of conceiving *the person* as being individualistic, with self-government or self-direction serves as the foundation of the control-based understanding of privacy in that neither considers the relation *the person* might have with his or her environment.

Similarly, though privacy as *restricted access* was proposed as an alternative (Moor, 1990) to the control based understanding of privacy, it still phrases privacy in an individualistic and isolated manner where "*restricted access* is understood as an abstract "situation where an individual or group ... is protected from intrusion, observation, and surveillance by others" (p. 76). Still, other *restricted access* views consider privacy an abstract status as if it is something that an individual can single-mindedly decides to hold. Even the word *control* is still present in some *restricted access* oriented definitions of privacy as enumerated in Allen (1988, p. 11). For example, one *restricted access* as *selective control over access to oneself*. In other words, these reconceptualizations, despite their variation, all reside on the same foundation of *individual autonomy*.

Just to reiterate, challenges toward control-based conception of privacy are becoming harder to ignore because of the technology application like big data analytics; however, this paper would like to suggest that digital technologies are only making the problematic nature of control-based privacy understanding harder to ignore; and control-based conception is only an expression of its more foundational assumption from *individual autonomy*. In other words, this paper's question is directed toward *individual autonomy* serving as the base for the many conceptions of privacy including privacy *having-control* and as *restricted access*. Therefore, alternative conceptualizations of privacy would need to reflect not only on the definition of privacy itself; but more importantly, it needs to speak to a different conception of the person other than *individual autonomy*, and this paper proposes to discuss *relational autonomy* as a potential alternative.

Relational autonomy conceives of *the person* as *socially embedded* (Mackenzie & Stoljar, 2000). Two aspects of the understanding of relational autonomy from this perspective are especially relevant. First, *relational autonomy* recognizes the social embeddedness of the person; the person, instead of being deprived of any social relations, is influenced by all sorts of social contingencies. Second, *relational autonomy* conceives of autonomy as a *competency* that is contextualized and most importantly can be developed. These two aspects in particular can align with an Eastern conception of the person, which will be discussed later. First, we will discuss how r*elational autonomy* has inspired new understandings of privacy.

In Bannerman (2018), it was argued that relational autonomy could promote a better understanding of privacy for its richer understanding of autonomy. Two more nuanced understanding of autonomy under relational autonomy are *procedural autonomy* and *substantive autonomy*. *Procedural autonomy* indicates that realization of autonomy requires the "adoption of certain procedures"; and *substantive autonomy* requires one to "espouse certain values" (p. 5); or as Westlund expressed it, "autonomy is constitutively relational" (2009, p. 5). The procedural understanding invites the consideration of the context or environment rather than just the individual in isolation. The substantive understanding is likely to bring in a fostering capacity perspective; in order to truly achieve the substantive form of autonomy, the person shall develop the ability to "influence, and benefit from", each of his/her "choices" (p. 5).

Below we will discuss two specific examples of understanding privacy that have adopted a *relational autonomy* perspective.

1. *Networked privacy* (Marwick & boyd, 2014) in particularly describes both the contextual nature of the environment from which various understandings of privacy emerge, and the individual's different relations with the environment which could influence how one comes to understand privacy. The concept of *networked privacy* builds on the understanding of privacy as *contextual integrity* which indicates whether privacy is violated is determined by information related *norms* in that specific situation (Nissenbaum, 2004) and it criticizes *contextual integrity* for assuming that an individual can easily understand the context and norms and they are stable and readily given; instead, *networked privacy* conceives of the context and norm as not only co-constructed by participants but also are frequently shifting (Ananny, 2016). In a word, *networked privacy* considers the possibility that individuals may interpret contexts differently, that contexts may be destabilized or collapse, or that other people may have control over the context in ways that are beyond the purview of the individual (e.g. surveillance, information leakage, or data-mining). Therefore, *networked privacy* requires individuals to not only refer to some external rules/regulations but also to construct on their own a clear expectation of privacy.
2. *Group privacy* (Floridi, 2016; Mittelstadt, 2017) also aims to capture the changing information environment, and focuses on the particular challenge to understanding privacy brought by algorithms. Computer algorithms can create ad-hoc and temporary groups to which none of the existing interpretations of privacy can be applied; just to use the example from Mittelstadt (2017, p. 477): a group can be "dog owners living in Wales aged 38–40 that exercise regularly." "Being identified as a member of this group could drive a variety of automated decision-making with harmful or beneficial effects for individual members, such as a preferential rate for health insurance." The existence of such groups is essentially informational, and these informational traits are only meaningful to algorithms on the group level when multitude of individuals' information are considered together. Hence, such groups go beyond the mere collection of individuals and hence gain status as a different entity to whom a privacy right belong. *Group privacy* could help with drawing a distinction between privacy under individual and collective context, it could also help with mapping out privacy contexts across time and virtual spaces and raise questions about individual and group's relationship within different contexts.

Note that *relational privacy* is a general categorization of all conceptions of privacy leveraging *relational autonomy*, and this specific way of understanding privacy did not necessarily come posterior to the existence of the term *relational privacy*. Actually, Allen's own definition of *restricted access*, or "privacy-as-inaccessibility", took a different approach than the other understandings of privacy as *restricted access* and look at privacy "as a matter of degree rather than as an all-or-none concept" (1988, p. 18), which seems to suggest the variation of privacy by contexts.

To summarize, in this section we have discussed the conceptualization of privacy, especially how a control-based definition has been one of the dominant understandings of privacy and its reliance on *individual autonomy*. The source of frustration of privacy as having control over personal information comes from its reliance on *individual autonomy* which conceives of *the person* being *individualistic* and *autonomous* without considering the environment. For a better understanding of privacy, we have seen how based on a different conception of the person, i.e., *relational autonomy*, researchers have come up with the conception of *relational privacy*, and how two recent conceptions of privacy are constructed leveraging a relational perspective. Next, we will turn to the Eastern philosophy tradition for a continued discussion of a relational conception of the person.

THE CONCEPTION OF A RELATIONAL PERSON IN CONFUCIANISM

The East and West comparative framework has been used as a tool to form discussions and obtain understandings in many fields including philosophy, culture, psychology, all based upon this underlying understanding that there are some fundamental level differences between the Eastern and the Western ways of viewing the world. According to Hofstede (2001)'s cultural dimension model, Asian cultures, for instance, the Chinese culture, are categorized as *collectivist*, while American culture as an example of Western culture sits on the opposite direction of *collectivist*, which is *individualist*. These national cultural level differences in general align with individual level observations, where studies have found that Easterners emphasize the interdependence and situatedness and perceive more holistically a given situation, while Western people are characterized as independent and recognize more individual dispositions of a person (Choi, Nisbett, & Norenzayan, 1999; Markus & Conner, 2014; Nisbett, 2004). Since the concept of *individual autonomy* is based a Western understanding of *the person*, it would be helpful to start with looking into the opposite direction, to try to picture how *the person* might be conceived of under the Eastern culture tradition. To do so, this paper offers a brief discussion of the conception of *the person* under one of the most influential philosophy traditions across East Asian countries, Confucianism.[2]

One of the research themes of Confucian philosophy is Confucian role ethics, which "originates in and variates from the concrete family feelings that constitute the relations between children and their elders and the interdependent roles they live, and aims to explore how to live optimally within the roles and relations that constitute one" (Rosemont & Ames, 2008, p. 1). Ramsey (2016) has mapped out existing research of Confucian role ethics and identified two major divergent perspectives, a *strong* one and a *moderate* one, in how Confucianism might interpret the relation between *the person* and the social environment. The *strong* perspective argues that *the person* is fully constituted by the social roles and relationships (Hall & Ames, 1998). On the other hand, the *moderate* perspective conceives of *the person* as one capable of self-government and whose behaviors are based on meaningful personal reflections; namely, the *moderate* perspective differs from the *strong* perspective in that it not only recognizes the entitlement that *the person* is required of by one's social environment but also the person's own deliberate efforts.

The original Confucian text could offer some vivid illustrations for understanding the Confucian person in the social environment. The Confucian person in general is conceived of as going through a transformation from the relatively naive/crude status he is born with into a more learnt/civilized one; and what can signal one's learning achievement is whether one can perform rituals well. Those who can perform rituals to their best by achieving a balance between one's innate nature and social manners can be considered as having virtue.[3] More specifically, in *The Analect*,[4] *the person* is conceived as a figure who is to go through a lifelong journey of diligent pursuit of *Xue* (learn, learning, 学); the object of *Xue* is *Li* (ritual, 礼) which "encompasses both formal rituals and everyday social practices" (Berkson, 2016, p. 231).

The emphasis put on *the person* following rituals in *The Analects* might have been one of the contributing reasons for some to argue that the Chinese culture has no such idea of *individual autonomy*, and have led some to argue that under Confucianism the individual person can be insignificant compared to the group. However, as the *moderate* view pointed out above, interpretations exist which argue that in addition to obeying societal rules and learning to fulfill these roles' requirement, Confucianism also recognizes *the person*'s active efforts, "heart/mind ... has the capacity to reflect on and reshape such activities to ensure their orientation in an ethical direction" (Shun, 2004, p. 188). *The person* is putting out some deliberate efforts, however, such efforts differ from the understanding of Kantian *individual autonomy* for it is always embedded within the social environment. Confucianism emphasizes individuals' ritual practices within certain social contexts, where unique practices could emerge as a result of *the person*'s particular judgment of that context. A great example to showcase is filial piety (Xiao, 孝) which is one of the most important virtues in Confucianism. In general, it refers to an idea of younger members of the family obeying and serving the seniors in the family environment. However, when being asked about what filial piety was, in *The Analects* Confucius gave different answers to different people.[5] By actually practicing the rituals *the person* is wielding his power of self-governing, and when rituals are channeled through a person via the processes of learning and practicing, rituals turned into "embodied action – how we carry ourselves, the proper motions, gestures, etc." (Berkson, 2016, p. 232). *The person* following and practicing long-inherited rituals like Xiao is not just learning to subordinating himself to the societal expectations, but is also realizing and reviving the ritual in his own way.

So the differences in interpreting the Confucian person with or without autonomy lie in the understanding of *the person*'s relationship with rituals; in other words, how to understand *the person*'s agency in recognition of the influence of social environment. For those who take a moderate role ethics perspective and argue that there is a place of autonomy in Confucianism, social rituals are considered as something crude which need to be further processed or developed as "considerations enter into one's reflection" (Shun, 2004, p. 194). In other words, each person's fine-tuning of the general guidance of rituals is what contains *the person*'s deliberate efforts. However, such deliberate efforts, when recognized as autonomy, still bear significant difference from *individual autonomy* in Western culture as it is always specific and contextualized. It emphasizes *the person* as one situated within the environment, rather than one who is self-governing and directing regardless of the environment; hence it aligns with *relational autonomy*, rather than *individual autonomy*.

Confucian conception of the person aligns with *relational autonomy* in that firstly, the person is socially embedded.

[2] Confucianism is a school of philosophical thoughts originated in China, but the influence of this tradition spread across East Asian (Yao, 2000). Confucianism differs from Western philosophy tradition in methodology, metaphysics, epistemology, and ethics (Wong, 2017).

[3] The Master said, "Where the solid qualities are in excess of accomplishments, we have rusticity; where the accomplishments are in excess of the solid qualities, we have the manners of a clerk. When the accomplishments and solid qualities are equally blended, we then have the man of virtue." (Analects, 6.18)

[4] The Analects is an anthology of brief passages that present the words of Confucius and his disciples, it describes Confucius as a man, and recounts some of the events of his life (Eno, 2015).

[5] Confucius offered different answers to students who came with the same question about filial piety. When Meng Yi asked about filial piety, the Master said, "It is not being disobedient."; when Meng Wu asked, the Master said, "Parents are anxious lest their children should be sick."; when Zi You asked, the Master said, "The filial piety nowadays means the support of one's parents. But dogs and horses likewise are able to do something in the way of support; - without reverence, what is there to distinguish the one support given from the other?"; and when Zi Xia asked, the Master said, "The difficulty is with the countenance". (Analects, 2.5–2.8)

Secondly, autonomy is a *competency* that can be developed – in particular, the *procedural* understanding underlines that autonomy is not a default but something to be achieved. Finally, Confucianism and *relational autonomy* can find common ground in their understandings toward emotion, where both recognize that "certain emotional states and attitudes to oneself are further necessary conditions … for autonomy" (Stoljar, 2015). As summarized in Wong (2004), the society and the social environment provides the relational context as important conditions for the self-development of the Confucian person. The Confucian views autonomy as something to be achieved through *the person*'s life journey, in comparison to the typical understanding of autonomy in the West as an abstract, stable state that one is assumed from the beginning. "If such persons are autonomous, then we must say that for the Confucians, autonomy is an ethical achievement, a rare one at that, and one that must come about through the right circumstances and the help of others" (p. 426).

Seok (2017) wrote that the difference in understanding the relation of emotion and morality can be one of the reasons that explain the divergence in the conception of *the person* in the East and West. Seok (2017) leveraged the concept of moral agency to understand the different conceptions of person and recognized that the Western conception of *the person* under Kantian philosophy considers *the person* with *self-enclosed independency*. The very opposite of Kantian person is heteronomy which sees agency as entirely up to external contingencies. However, between these two extremes of the *self-governing* and *other governing* (p. 2) is what might correspond to the concept of a relational person, which Seok (2017) termed as *communal agency*. *Communal agency* is individual agency in recognition of the influence of social context, and "moral inclinations and other-regarding emotions are the essential foundations of virtue" under Confucianism (Seok, 2017, p. 4).

To summarize, understanding autonomy from a relational perspective as it recognizes that *the person* is "enabled by past and present networks of which we are a part: the people and material things with which we are connected give us the capacity to be autonomous" (Bannerman, 2018, p. 4). It is this relational perspective of *the person* that can not only serve as a valuable alternative to *individual autonomy*, but also as a connection between the Western feminist philosophy and Eastern Confucianism role ethics. Research has begun to explore the compatibility between Confucian ethics and feminist philosophy (Sullivan, 2016); however, this paper just begins to explore this topic. Within this context, we now turn to discuss the how the juxtaposition of the relational understanding of *the person* under Confucianism and feminist philosophy can contribute to the understanding of privacy.

A RELATIONAL PRIVACY UNDER RELATIONAL PERSON

A relational perspective on viewing privacy, in particular where the person is put back into his environment can potentially benefit the research of privacy in two ways. First, it frees the individual from the expectation of exerting control that he/she does not have, so that attention can be directed toward fostering the person's privacy-related capacity. It could also be redirected to focus on seeking meaning from the various potential applications of one's information. It is only when we recognize that meaningful privacy is embedded within its environment, that can we start to ask what might be within the current context that enables or disables privacy and other values we would like to protect. To learn from *relational autonomy*, "given that some network configurations foster autonomy, while others do not, what is important is individuals' ability to control, and play a role in constituting, networks of relations in such a way that makes the interdependence of the individual with the other elements of the network conducive to autonomy in a substantive sense" (Bannerman, 2018, p. 6). Second, a relational perspective can reconcile and provide a common ground between Western and Eastern traditions, which is important for researching privacy in today's cross-cultural environment. A relational perspective can offer a place where conversations can be initiated for both Eastern and Western cultural and ethical traditions. In addition, taking the relational aspect of privacy into consideration can help with the study of privacy in other non-Western cultures. For example, it has been argued that the principle of Ubuntu is "in some conflict with the idea of individual privacy as understood in the West" (Hongladarom, 2016, p. 55), whereas *Ubuntu as an* African philosophical notion indicates that "the very existence of a self is dependent with the existence of other selves that the former self is in relation with".

Adopting a relational perspective to understand privacy can potentially inspire new empirical research. Research of how privacy was talked about within certain specific environment could reveal how various aspects of privacy that might be highlighted in certain context. Yuan, Feng, and Danowski (2013) conducted a semantic network analysis on corpus extracted from the Chinese social media site Weibo, and showed that the word "privacy" in the Chinese language context is highly embedded within terms relating to social relationships. In other words, those words describing one's social roles are those that appear most frequently with the word "privacy", including "wife, superiors, friends and colleagues" (p. 1017). Recognizing that the population who had contributed the Weibo corpus are probably not representative of the entire Chinese population, further questions could ask about how understandings of privacy might vary by population and context. On the other hand, it also needs to be recognized that taking this relational perspective could also bring challenges: as Nissenbaum (2004, p. 154) notes, it can mean "painstaking analysis of details for each situation".

There are some incongruences between the understanding of privacy via the relational perspectives of Confucianism and feminist philosophy. Feminist theorists somehow still use control as a metaphor despite that they recognize the networked nature of privacy, "it is the ability to control our networked selves to achieve autonomy" (Bannerman, 2018, p. 6); in a sense, one is either going to be controlled, or to control the networked environment. Such conceptual antagonism/dichotomy between the person and his/her environment is not observed in the Confucian conception of the person. It is the feminist perspective that considers autonomy as a capacity that can find more resonance with the relational understanding of the person under Confucianism. This paper suggests that the strong substantive view of feminist *relational autonomy* corresponds to the moderate Confucian conceptions of the person in that both consider that the external environment has significant impact on autonomy, and autonomy is something that can be developed.

A second potential diverging point is that it is unclear what the relational consideration of Confucian person and *relational autonomy* under Confucian philosophy might say about the relation between human and technology. *Relational privacy* under feminist theory already explicitly recognize the *networked* nature of the self, which includes the fact that especially nowadays the self is constructed partially by networked information technologies, in addition to the relations with other people (Bannerman, 2018, p. 2). For Confucianism, on the other hand, it remains less clear how the relation with information technology might be conceptualized.

Despite these concerns, considering feminist theory and Confucianism jointly could spark research contributing to this relational understanding of privacy in three ways. First, like the ethnographic study conducted in Marwick and Boyd (2014), research could explore specific contexts to examine how context-specific privacy issues and scenarios might emerge, and how and to what extent they might deviate from a typical control-based understanding of privacy. Still following this line of inquiry, cross/intercultural comparative work can be another potentially interesting approach to examine how and where various contextual and relational factors coexist. For example, assuming a somewhat similar technological context, how might other cultural factors influence people's understanding of privacy? Second, despite the understanding that privacy norms and understandings can emerge from each specific context, are there some underlying shared social norms and understandings that might be more salient in one context/culture than the other? To explore the second line of inquiry, natural language processing techniques might be used to analyze privacy relevant texts from different contexts and cultures. Third, is there empirical evidence of how prevalent such control-based belief of privacy is among individual, corporate and/or government documents, not only in Western cultures, but in other cultures as well?

CONCLUSION

This paper continues the exploration of a relational conceptualization of privacy, and suggests that a relational understanding of privacy can serve as a valuable supplement to the existing *individual autonomy*-based understanding of privacy. *Individual autonomy* as the foundation of privacy has been questioned for its unrealistic assumption of individual-government and the lack of consideration of social context and relations. It is also questioned for its narrow conception of *the person* as *atomistic* without taking into consideration of the information environment. Then, to explore potential alternative foundations for the conceptualization of privacy, this paper discussed the concept of the relational autonomy from the perspectives of feminist theory and Confucianism. It concludes by discussing the implications for conceptualizing privacy from these two foundations.

This paper chooses to stay with this relatively general term of Western and Eastern conception of privacy, rather than conception of privacy more specific to a culture, since the influence of these two major threads of philosophical thoughts have spread their influence beyond one country/culture. And the East and the West framework could continue serving as a useful tool for future exploration of cross-culture privacy in terms of identifying more common grounds as well as divergences in understanding privacy. And by drawing on Eastern and Western philosophical traditions, this paper continues the work of *intercultural information ethics*. However, it should be noted that the paper's current discussion on *relational autonomy* is limited to feminist theorists' conception, among all possible Western philosophical theories; similarly, the paper's discussion on Confucianism is also limited within only roles ethics. With these limitations in mind, this paper still contributes to privacy research for it suggests using *relational autonomy* as the foundation for conceptualizing privacy, relates the conception of privacy to the conception of *the person*, and frames the discussion within an intercultural environment.

The lack of a simple equivalence between Western and Eastern values and concepts should continue driving future research work. For example, a detailed study of the relational self under feminist theory and Confucian role ethics could bring more clarity to the concept of relational autonomy and how it might be used to interpret privacy, and could inspire more discussions in intercultural information ethics (Capurro, 2008). For example, it was suggested that the relationality of the Confucian self, however, is not fully explained by the feminist viewpoint ..." Confucian agents are not just social beings but also broadly conceived cosmic beings (or "becomings") (Seok, 2017, p. 6). In closing, this paper is mindful of Capurro (2005)'s proposition that "intercultural information ethics needs more work, as comparing apparently similar or dissimilar concepts that were coined in different historical and cultural settings is dangerous in at least two ways. One danger is that we remain satisfied with merely juxtaposing such concepts; the second is that we thereby remain in such an early stage of an intercultural dialog, defined by what may only look like a common ground or an incompatible view ..." (p. 45).

ACKNOWLEDGMENTS

This paper would like to thank Professor Stephanie W. Haas who has provided helpful comments on previous versions of this document.

REFERENCES

Allen, A. (1988). *Uneasy access: Privacy for women in a free society*. Totowa, NJ: Rowman & Littkfield.

Allen, A. L. (2000): Privacy-as-data control: Conceptual, practical, and moral limits of the paradigm. *Connecticut Law Review*, *32*(3), 861–876.

Analects. 2006–2018. *Chinese Text Project*. Retrieved from http://ctext.org/analects

Ananny, M. (2016). Toward an ethics of algorithms: Convening, observation, probability, and timeliness. *Science, Technology, & Human Values*, *41*(1), 93–117. https://doi.org/10.1177/0162243915606523

Bannerman, S. (2018). Relational privacy and the networked governance of the self. *Information, Communication & Society*, 1–16. https://doi.org/10.1080/1369118X.2018.1478982

Baulch, K. (2018). *25 May – GDPR tightens data protection rules for companies and gives people back control. June 3, 2019, from United Kingdom - European Commission*. Retrieved from https://ec.europa.eu/unitedkingdom/news/25-may-%E2%80%93-gdpr-tightens-data-protection-rules-companies-and-gives-people-back-control_en

Berkson, M. (2016). Xunzi as a theorist and defender of ritual. In E. L. Hutton (Ed.), *Dao companion to the philosophy of Xunzi Dao Companions to Chinese Philosophy* (pp. 229–267). Dordrecht, Netherlands: Springer. https://doi.org/10.1007/978-94-017-7745-2_8

Bornstein, A. M. (2016, September). Is artificial intelligence permanently inscrutable? Nautilus. Retrieved from http://nautil.us/issue/40/learning/is-artificial-intelligence-permanently-inscrutable

Burgess, M. (2018, October). What is GDPR? The summary guide to GDPR compliance in the UK. Wired UK. Retrieved from https://www.wired.co.uk/article/what-is-gdpr-uk-eu-legislation-compliance-summary-fines-2018

Capurro, R. (2005). Privacy: An intercultural perspective. *Ethics and Information Technology*, *7*(1), 37–47.

Capurro, R. (2008). Intercultural information ethics: foundations and applications. *Journal of Information, Communication & Ethics in Society; Bingley*, *6*(2), 116–126. https://doi.org/10.1108/14779960810888347

Choi, I., Nisbett, R. E., & Norenzayan, A. (1999). Causal attribution across cultures: Variation and universality. *Psychological Bulletin*, *125*(1), 47–63. Retrieved from https://doi.org/10.1037/0033-2909.125.1.47

Cohen, J. E. (2012a). *Configuring the networked self: Law, code, and the play of everyday practice*. New Haven, CT: Yale University Press. Retrieved from http://ebookcentral.proquest.com/lib/unc/detail.action?docID=3420804

Cohen, J. E. (2012b). What privacy is for. In *SSRN Scholarly Paper ID 2175406*. Rochester, NY: Social Science Research Network. Retrieved from https://papers.ssrn.com/abstract=2175406

DeCew, J. (2018). Privacy. In E. N. Zalta (Ed.), *The Stanford encyclopedia of philosophy*. Stanford, CA: The Metaphysics Research Lab Center for the Study of Language and Information.

Eno, R. (2015). *Analects of Confucius*. Indiana University. Retrieved from http://www.indiana.edu/~p374/Analects_of_Confucius_(Eno-2015).pdf

Ess, C. (2005). "Lost in translation"?: Intercultural dialogues on privacy and information ethics (introduction to special issue on privacy and data privacy protection in Asia). *Ethics and Information Technology*, *7*(1), 1–6.

Floridi, L. (2006). Four challenges for a theory of informational privacy. *Ethics and Information Technology*, *8*(3), 109–119. Retrieved from https://doi.org/10.1007/s10676-006-9121-3

Floridi, L. (2016). Group privacy: A defence and an interpretation. In L. Taylor, B. van der Sloot, & L. Floridi, *Group privacy—new challenges of data technologies*. Berlin, Germany: Springer.

Fuchs, C. (2011). Towards an alternative concept of privacy. *Journal of Information, Communication & Ethics in Society*, *9*(4), 220–237. https://doi.org/10.1108/14779961111191039

Hall, D. L., & Ames, R. T. (1998). *Thinking from the han: Self, truth, and transcendence in Chinese and western culture*. Albany, NY: State University of New York Press.

Hofstede, G. (2001). *Culture's consequences: Comparing values, behaviors, institutions, and organizations across nations* (2nd ed.). Thousand Oaks, CA: Sage.

Hongladarom, S. (2016). Cultural attitudes toward privacy. In S. Hongladarom, *A buddhist theory of privacy* (pp. 37–56). https://doi.org/10.1007/978-981-10-0317-2_3

Kim, N. (2014). Three's crowd: Towards contextual integrity in third-party data sharing. *Harvard Journal of Law Technology*, *28*(1), 325–348.

Li, C. (1994). The confucian concept of jen and the feminist ethics of care: A comparative study. *Hypatia*, *9*(1), 70–89.

Mackenzie, C., & Stoljar, N. (2000). *Relational autonomy: Feminist perspectives on autonomy, agency, and the social self*. Cary, NC: Oxford University Press, Incorporated. Retrieved from http://ebookcentral.proquest.com/lib/unc/detail.action?docID=430598

Mai, J.-E. (2016). Three models of privacy: New perspectives on informational privacy. *Nordicom Review*, *37*, 171–175.

Markus, H. R., & Conner, A. (2014). *Clash!: How to thrive in a multicultural world* (Reprint ed.). Plume.

Marwick, A. E., & Boyd, D. (2014). Networked privacy: How teenagers negotiate context in social media. *New Media & Society*, *16*(7), 1051–1067 https://doi.org/10.1177/1461444814543995

Miller, A. R. (1971). *The assault on privacy: Computers, data banks, and dossiers*. Ann Arbor, MI. Retrieved from http://hdl.handle.net/2027/mdp.39015003835124

Mittelstadt, B. (2017). From individual to group privacy in big data analytics. *Philosophy & Technology*, *30*(4), 475–494. https://doi.org/10.1007/s13347-017-0253-7

Mizutani, M., Dorsey, J., & Moor, J. H. (2004). The internet and Japanese conception of privacy. *Ethics and Information Technology*, *6*(2), 121–128. https://doi.org/10.1023/B:ETIN.0000047479.12986.42

Mokrosinska, D. (2018). Privacy and Autonomy: On Some Misconceptions Concerning the Political Dimensions of Privacy. *Law and Philosophy*, *37*(2), 117–143. https://doi.org/10.1007/s10982-017-9307-3

Moor, J. H. (1990). The ethics of privacy protection. *Library Trends; Baltimore*, *39*(1–2), 69.

Moore, A. D. (2007). Toward informational privacy rights. *San Diego Law Review*, *44*(4), 809.

Moore, A. D. (2008). Defining Privacy. *Journal of Social Philosophy*, *39*(3), 411–428. https://ssrn.com/abstract=1980849

Murphy, R. S. (1995). Property rights in personal information: An economic defense of privacy. *Georgetown Law Journal*, *84*, 2381–2418.

Nakada, M., & Tamura, T. (2005). Japanese conceptions of privacy: An intercultural perspective. *Ethics and Information Technology*, *7*(1), 27–36. https://doi.org/10.1007/s10676-005-0453-1

Nisbett, R. (2004). *The Geography of Thought: How Asians and Westerners Think Differently-- and Why. 1st Free Press* (pbk. ed.). New York: Free Press.

Nissenbaum, H. (2004). Privacy as contextual integrity. *Washington Law Review* *79*(1), 119-158. Chicago

O'Shea, T. (2012). *Green Paper Technical Report: Critics of Autonomy*. Essex Autonomy Project. Retrieved from https://autonomy.essex.ac.uk/wp-content/uploads/2016/11/CriticsofAutonomyGPRJune2012.pdf

Ramsey, J. (2016). Confucian role ethics: A critical survey. *Philosophy Compass*, *11*(5), 235–245. https://doi.org/10.1111/phc3.12324

Reigeluth, T. (2014). Why data is not enough: Digital traces as control of self and self-control. *Surveillance & Society*, *12*(2), 243–254. https://doi.org/10.24908/ss.v12i2.4741

Richards, D. A. J. (1981). Rights and autonomy. *Ethics*, *92* (1), 3–20.

Rosemont, H., & Ames, R. T. (2008). *The Chinese classic of family reverence: A philosophical translation of the Xiaojing*. Honolulu, HI: University of Hawaii Press. Retrieved from http://ebookcentral.proquest.com/lib/-unc/detail.action?docID=3413199

Rostow, T. (2017). What happens when an acquaintance buys your data?: A new privacy harm in the age of data brokers. *Yale Journal on Regulation*, *34*(2), 667–707.

Sanchez-Burks, J., Lee, F., Choi, I., Nisbett, R., Zhao, S., & Koo, J. (2003). Conversing across cultures: East-West communication styles in work and nonwork contexts. *Journal of Personality and Social Psychology*, *85*(2), 363–372. https://doi.org/10.1037/0022-3514.85.2.363

Schwartz, P. M. (2000). Internet privacy and the state. *Connecticut Law Review*, *32*(3), 815–860.

Seok, B. (2017). Moral agency, autonomy, and heteronomy in early Confucian philosophy. *Philosophy Compass*, *12*(12), e12460. https://doi.org/10.1111/phc3.12460

Shun, K.-l. (2004). Conceptualization of the person in early confucian thought. In K.-l. Shun & D. B. Wong, *Confucian ethics: A comparative study of self, autonomy, and community* (pp. 183–199). Cambridge, MA: Cambridge University Press.

Solove, D. (2002). Conceptualizing privacy. *California Law Review*, *90*(4), 1087. https://doi.org/10.15779/Z382H8Q

Solove, D. J. (2013). Introduction: Privacy self-management and the consent dilemma. *Harvard Law Review*, *126*(7), 1880–1903.

Steijn, W., & Vedder, A. (2015). Privacy concerns, dead or misunderstood?: The perceptions of privacy amongst the young and old. *Information Polity*, *20*(4), 299–311. https://doi.org/10.3233/IP-150374

Stoljar, N. (2015). Feminist perspectives on autonomy. In E. N. Zalta, *The Stanford encyclopedia of philosophy*. Stanford, CA: The Metaphysics Research Lab Center for the Study of Language and Information.

Sullivan, I. M. (2016). Simone de beauvoir and confucian role ethics: Role-relational ambiguity and confucian mystification. *Hypatia*, *31*(3), 620–635. https://doi.org/10.1111/hypa.12262

Tavani, H. T., & Moor, J. H. (2001). Privacy protection, control of information, and privacy-enhancing technologies. *ACM SIGCAS Computers and Society*, *31*(1), 6–11. https://doi.org/10.1145/572277.572278

Wang, H. (2012). The conceptual basis of privacy standards in China and its implications for China's privacy law.

Frontiers of Law in China, *7*(1), 134–160. https://doi.org/10.3868/s050-001-012-0007-4

Warren, S. D., & Brandeis, L. D. (1890). The right to privacy. *Harvard Law Review*, *4*(5), 193–220. https://doi.org/10.2307/1321160

Westin, A. (1967). *Privacy and freedom* (1st ed.). New York, NY: Atheneum.

Westlund, A. C. (2009). Rethinking relational autonomy. *Hypatia*, *24*(4), 26–49. https://doi.org/10.1111/j.1527-2001.2009.01056.x

Wong, D. (2017). Comparative philosophy: Chinese and western. In E. N. Zalta, *The Stanford encyclopedia of philosophy*. Stanford, CA: The Metaphysics Research Lab Center for the Study of Language and Information.

Wong, D. B. (2004). Relational and autonomous selves. *Journal of Chinese Philosophy*, *31*(4), 419–432. https://doi.org/10.1111/j.1540-6253.2004.00163.x

Wong, D. B. (2015). Early confucian philosophy and the development of compassion. *Dao*, *14*(2), 157–194. https://doi.org/10.1007/s11712-015-9438-x

Yao, X. (2000). *An introduction to confucianism*. New York, NY. ProQuest Ebook Central: Cambridge University Press. Retrieved from http://ebookcentral.proquest.com/-lib/unc/detail.action?docID=217851

Yuan, E. J., Feng, M., & Danowski, J. A. (2013). "Privacy" in semantic networks on Chinese social media: The case of Sina Weibo. *Journal of Communication*, *63*(6), 1011–1031. https://doi.org/10.1111/jcom.12058

Understanding Early Research Experiences Through the Lens of Connected Learning

Rachel M. Magee
University of Illinois,
Urbana-Champaign, USA
rmmagee@illinois.edu

Amari T. Simpson
University of Illinois,
Urbana-Champaign, USA
atsimps2@illinois.edu

ABSTRACT

This paper examines the early research experiences of eighteen researchers from a variety of scholarly fields to identify key factors in effective, successful experiences. Applying thematic analysis to semi-structured interviews, and using the Connected Learning framework as a lens to examine early research experiences, we identify three factors that are common in successful experiences: exposure to key events early in researchers' lives, mentorship from a variety of sources that proactively connects early researchers to opportunities and models support, and experiences that prompt curiosity and joy, sparking the interests of those who go on to become researchers. This work has implications for the design of early research experiences and demonstrates how connecting youth to research opportunities early in their learning allows them to pursue their interests, build relationships with mentors/mentees, and access opportunities to develop as researchers and critical thinkers.

KEYWORDS

Early Research Experience; Research; Connected Learning; Informal Learning

ASIS&T THESAURUS

Learning; Public Libraries; Qualitative Analysis

INTRODUCTION

Academe and scholarly work have long been critiqued for their lack of inclusion and equity. Critics highlight the lack of support for people of color (Brunsma, Embrick, & Shin, 2017) and scholars who identify as women (Van den Brink & Benschop, 2012). Within Library and Information Science (LIS), some initiatives like the iSchool Inclusion Institute (2017) aim to support diverse students in pursuing graduate education and gaining original research experience, but many of the existing conversations focus on the needs of users and service populations (Cooke, 2016), LIS curriculum (Cooke, Sweeney, & Noble, 2016), and practitioners, such as the lack of support for women of color working in the field (Chou, Pho, & Roh, 2018). Colleges, universities, and funders have also begun to respond to inclusion issues with programs to connect individuals from nondominant and underrepresented backgrounds to opportunities and resources. The U.S. National Science Foundation Includes program works to ensure traditionally underrepresented and underserved groups are represented in the science and engineering workforce. Yet many of the programs that aim to increase access to research experiences emphasize science, technology, engineering, and math (STEM) without much attention on other forms of research and scholarship, such as the social sciences, arts & humanities, and professional disciplines. Further, many of the existing approaches that work to connect learners to early research experiences, or EREs, focus on connecting advanced students to existing college curricula, or to engage post-secondary students in the research process. Given the relevance of research and information skills to youth, as well as their capacities and openness to these kinds of experiences (Murray, Obare, & Hageman, 2016; Gazzaniga, Heatherton, & Halpern, 2016), designing EREs for youth is a key area of opportunity.

LIS is well-suited to address this opportunity. Research in this area has examined key elements of the research process, including youth information behavior (Chelton & Cool, 2004) and many professional organizations have emphasized the importance of incorporating inquiry, expanded literacies, and community engagement into library work (American Association of School Librarians, 2018; Young Adult Library Services Association, 2014, 2017). Libraries have a commitment to lifelong learning and equal access, which ideally situates them to address issues of inclusion in research activities. These institutions also aim to nurture a "well-informed citizenry," a common goal in international understandings of the purpose of libraries and librarianship (International Federation of Library Associations and Institutions, and United Nations Educational, Scientific, and Cultural Organization, 1994). Ensuring that youth have opportunities to participate in research will support them developing critical skills for assessing the research they encounter in their everyday lives.

Original research is also an interest-driven process, and libraries and youth services librarians are working to capitalize on their unique position to promote interest-driven engagement

82nd Annual Meeting of the Association for Information Science & Technology | Melbourne, Australia | 19–23 October, 2019

DOI: 10.1002/pra2.00066

through the Connected Learning framework (ConnectedLib, 2019; Ito et al., 2013). In our work here, we examine how elements of EREs can align with the Connected Learning framework to better understand the opportunities inherent in involving youth in research experiences, especially in informal settings. Given that understanding the development of successful researchers can serve in the design and implementation of initiatives that diversify future researchers (Little, Green, & Hoption, 2018), we worked with 18 active researchers to learn more about their early research experiences, addressing the following research questions:

- How do researchers describe and conceptualize their early research experiences?
- What factors contribute to the success of these experiences?
- How can these factors inform the design and implementation of early research experiences for youth?

BACKGROUND

Research and Early Research Experiences

The original research process or academic research process – what we refer to in this paper as "research" - describes the different kinds and types of investigative practices that occur within a research setting, like research universities, private research foundations, or other research institutions (Carpi, Ronan, Falconer, & Lents, 2017; Murray, Obare, & Hageman, 2016). Research is often conceptualized differently across disciplines and narrowed to a set of individuals who conduct research (Craney et al., 2011), though it can be described as a dynamic process of disseminating findings to other scholars and the public (Zhang & Swaid, 2017). Before postsecondary stages of education, research is often reduced to the scientific method in curriculum, although young people are capable of inquiry and are considered "natural-born scientists" (Murray, Obare, & Hageman, 2016, p. 5). Multiple researchers have raised concerns about when individuals have – or do not have – the opportunity to engage in research activities and who should have a chance to conduct research given the racial demographics of researchers today (Murray, Obare, & Hageman, 2016). Early experiences with research can inform the development of academic identity, and knowing more about this development process can support efforts to diversify who conducts research (Little et al., 2018).

Research and Education

Existing EREs often occur within the STEM curriculum of middle and high school through formal opportunities like independent study or science fair projects (e.g., Wasserman, 2016) and lab-based research experiences or research internships (e.g., Hernandez, 2016). Historically, underfunded schools and limited opportunities for underrepresented students have had substantial effects on the research field and workforce overall; these issues negatively impacte the future demographics of the research workforce (Murray, Obare, & Hageman, 2016b). School library practitioners explicitly argue for empowering all "learners to persist" in activities associated with EREs, including "inquiry, advanced study, enriching professional work, and community participation" in formal educational settings (American Association of School Librarians, 2018).

Undergraduate students today have a variety of opportunities to engage in research during postsecondary education, through activities like course-based undergraduate research (e.g, Mraz-Craig et al., 2018), independent study (e.g., Gilmore, Vieyra, Timmerman, Feldon, & Maher, 2015), and summer research internships (e.g., Lopatto, 2010). Recent studies capture the positive impacts and effects of research-based experiences on undergraduates' academic outcomes (Bowman & Holmes, 2018), research interests (Alderton & Manzi, 2017), research identity formation (Mraz-Craig et al., 2018), and persistence onto research-oriented careers long-term (Gilmore et al., 2015). However, there is little body of literature that explores the EREs of present-day researchers. Opening up a dialog about existing researchers' experiences can strengthen and inform the design of future opportunities, and provide an understanding of how formal and informal experiences can work together to build original research abilities.

Research and Information

The LIS field is concerned with how people interact with information, and the research processes examined in the field are significant elements of the original research process. Wilson highlighted that data is included in information, and that information behavior (IB) is "the totality of human behavior in relation to sources and channels of information" (2000, p. 49), including information seeking (Case & Given, 2016; Wilson, 2000). In LIS scholarship focused on researchers much work examines information seeking during the research process, with findings have important implications for academic librarians and information specialists to tailor services for these demographics (Hunt & Bakker, 2018; Kumar & Shukla, 2013).

LIS has a significant body of work examining how young people engage in information behaviors and information seeking (Chelton & Cool, 2004). Work has framed the interactivity, connectivity, and access of the digital information environment as prompts for extended examination of youth information seeking behavior (Dresang, 2005). Some research focuses on various youth populations' information needs, including youth from urban locations (Agosto & Hughes-Hassell, 2006) and age bounded groups like tweens (Meyers, Fisher, & Marcoux, 2009). Literacy development is another key theme of work focused on youth (e.g., Bruce, 1997), building on the field's interests in supporting learning and continually engaging with the impacts of technological change on information interactions. As with many of the concepts of information science, interest in literacy and learning straddles both formal and informal contexts (De Abreu & Mihailidis, 2013). Work on youth information behaviors in more formal academic settings includes work like information problem solving (Eisenberg & Berkowitz, 1990) and guided inquiry (Kuhlthau, 2010). Guided inquiry involves "considering a question or problem that prompts extensive investigation on the part of the student. In this sense, it is a research approach to learning" (ibid, p. 18). This approach to inquiry recognizes the value of connecting curriculum to youth experiences, including those outside of school, and serves as an important model for how formal approaches can support EREs.

Connected Learning and Libraries

Youth learning and inquiry is also important in informal contexts like public libraries, where it is now often framed through the concept of Connected Learning (CL). Ito et al. (2013) developed the CL framework for supporting youth learning within their social community for academic achievement or career success, aiming to support the "interests and needs of nondominant young people and their communities" (p. 34). They focus their attention on youth ages 12 – 18; this is a "critical time when individuals form interests and social identities" and "adolescence and early adulthood [are] periods when young people establish an orientation to schooling and learning that can carry into adulthood, and begin to make decisions that will lead them to certain job and career opportunities" (Ito et al., 2013, p. 8). This unique time of identity exploration and openness to career and learning opportunities allows for particularly impactful support and experiences. The role of adult support, including guidance and motivation, role modeling, and cultivating youth voice, is key for successful CL (Vaclavik, Sánchez, Buehler, Gray, & Rodriguez, 2017).

Libraries and librarians were quick to recognize how this framework was relevant to youth services (Connected Learning Alliance, n.d.-b), emphasizing interest-driven engagement with youth (Martin, 2015). Work examines public youth services librarians pursing CL, "giving what young people want" by focusing on their interests (Hoffman, Subramaniam, Kawas, Scaff, & Davis, 2016, p. 323). In early 2019, the ConnectedLib toolkit for practicing librarians working to incorporate CL was released (ConnectedLib, n.d.), demonstrating how the CL framework has been useful for supporting youth learning in informal settings and is increasingly used in public libraries across the United States. Given increasing emphasis on learning in informal settings like public libraries and the value of engagement with early research experiences, here we use the CL framework as a lens for understanding EREs and as a bridge to conceptualize how libraries and librarians could support these kinds of inquiry and learning experiences in more informal settings, which will complement longer standing work focused on inquiry and research in formal academic settings.

STUDY DESIGN AND METHODS

In order to examine these connections, we worked with eighteen individuals in an exploratory study to better understand how they conceptualize their early research experiences, what makes these experiences successful, and how we may apply these concepts to improve the design and implementation of EREs. As we designed our study we were informed by Tracy's (2010) criteria for excellent qualitative research, which emphasizes thinking about quality and rigor throughout the research process. Ways that we incorporated this approach included using a team based approach to the development of the study instruments, by conducting multiple interviews together to ensure a mutual approach to the study, including both authors in the full process of data collection which helped enable extended familiarization with our data, and transcription techniques that emphasized detailed fidelity and were enumerated in a style guide. Additional details about our data collection, recruiting techniques, participants, and analysis approach follow.

Data Collection

Data collection occurred from October 2018 through March 2019. We conducted individual semi-structured interviews with each participant. Interviews lasted between 36 minutes and 67 minutes, with an average length of 51 minutes, and were conducted using Skype. Interview questions asked the participants about their professional experiences as researchers, their early research experiences, and current experiences working with students and mentees. Participants were also asked to complete an online survey that included questions about educational background, race/ethnicity, gender, and professional experience. Each participant was remunerated with a $10 gift card to Starbucks or Amazon for completion of the interview and survey. The research design was approved by an ethics review board and consented to by participants.

Recruiting

We initially developed a list of 500 researchers stratified across disciplines and the four United States Census Regions (US Census Bureau, 2000). We recruited participants who worked at institutions commonly referred to as R1 institutions, that have a heavy emphasis on research (Carnegie Classification of Institutions of Higher Education, 2018). This was an exploratory study and we wanted to develop an understanding of the EREs of individuals who emphasize research in their careers. While we considered recruiting across a wider range of institutions and organizations and are doing so in later stages of this research project, we felt it was valuable to speak to individuals who had opportunities to not only learn how to research but were also engaged in instructing others in the research process, often framed through doctoral education.

We acknowledge that other institutions and organizations contribute valuable research and scholarship, but wanted to begin our work in this area with a well-scoped and defined group of participants, who have succeeded at research in a generally accepted manner (by being employed in a research focused position) and with similar work contexts as shared contexts can support saturation in analysis (Guest, Bunce, & Johnson, 2006). An equal number of invitations went to individuals from STEM (e.g., Mechanical engineering, Geophysical sciences, etc.), arts & humanities (e.g., History, English, etc.), social science (e.g. Political science, International affairs, etc.), and other disciplines, often professional fields (e.g., Counseling, Business, etc.). Due to low response rates, especially in the arts & humanities and social sciences fields, we adjusted our recruitment efforts partially through data collection. We invited participation from an additional 115 researchers in arts & humanities and social sciences at our home R1 institution, which added four to the total participant number.

Participants

Eighteen participants took part in semi-structured interviews, and seventeen participants completed the demographic survey for this paper. Ten participants identified as female and seven as male. The mean number of years doing research work (not necessarily as independent researchers) was 22 years (SD = 12.2). Participants came from across the academy, with eight from STEM fields, seven from arts & humanities, two from social sciences, and one from other disciplines. Professional titles of participants included assistant professor ($n = 5$), associate professor ($n = 8$), full professor ($n = 4$), and research professor/professor emeritus ($n = 1$). Eight participants lived in the Midwest, two in the West, two in the Northeast, and six in the South. All participants worked at R1 institutions in the United States, had an earned doctoral degree, and were currently working on a research project. Despite working to recruit participants from a wide variety of backgrounds, all participants who completed the survey identified as White, which we address in more detail in the Limitations section.

Analysis

We completed audio recordings of all interviews in addition to generating handwritten notes. Both authors participated in conducting interviews. Two interviews were conducted with both researchers present, which helped to develop a mutual approach to the process and support the rigor of our research process (Tracy, 2010). The remainder of the interviews included one participant and one of the two researchers. Using the transcribed audio recordings, we (both authors) conducted thematic analysis to identify patterns in the responses of our participants (Braun & Clarke, 2006; Terry, Hayfield, Clarke, & Braun, 2017). We employed an inductive, open coding approach and allowed for multiple codes. We used a combination of handwritten notes, Microsoft Word documents, and the Dedoose (2018) program to conduct our coding. Our process included familiarizing ourselves with the data, then iterative rounds of coding and refining codes to develop themes (including through the writing of memos), which we revised and defined, and ultimately used to inform the findings of this paper. Though we did not calculate intercoder reliability with a metric or percentage, we performed subjective intercoder agreement checks throughout the coding process (Guest, MacQueen, and Namey, 2014), typically on a weekly basis. These checks informed the development and revision of the codebook and included sharing memos and talking through subtleties of patterns and themes in the data.

FINDINGS

For the work discussed in this paper, we focused on participants' discussions of three main themes that consistently appeared in discussion. These elements were key factors in the development of an interest in research and the trajectory of a research career. Participants identified *key events* that introduced them to research, discussed the importance of experiences with *mentorship*, including elements that they work to emulate, and they highlighted the importance of *curiosity and joy* in their work. While we examine each of these areas in turn, they are interrelated and often functioned in concert for our participants.

Given this project's interest in understanding learning experiences to ultimately design effective research experiences for teens, here we employ the Connected Learning framework as a lens for understanding these main themes. The framework highlights the value of tangible, real world experiences that afford *opportunities*, of supportive *relationships* including those with mentors, and the importance of learning growing out of personal *interests* (Connected Learning Alliance, n.d.; Ito et al., 2013). By examining the experiences and perceptions of researchers through this framework, we reveal a number of opportunities with regard to developing successful EREs that promote excellent and impactful learning for youth. In order to maintain the anonymity of participants, quotes are attributed using pseudonyms assigned by the research team, and any identifying features (such as institution or location) have been modified or redacted. Each quote is shared with participants' self-identified gender, title, and field.

Key Events: Opportunities

For the participants in this study, key events connected them to opportunities to develop relevant skills and to practice them in real world settings. While the Connected Learning framework is certainly rooted in networked understandings of interaction, the experiences described by our participants directly relate to the framework's emphasis on "tangible connections to real-world career and civic opportunities" (Connected Learning Alliance, n.d.-a). When discussing their EREs, participants often focused on key events that introduced them to activities of the research process they currently use in their work. Some participants discussed structured introductions to research which typically occurred through undergraduate or graduate level programs. David (M, Associate Professor, Civil Engineering) described a National Science Foundation undergraduate research opportunity that included field work:

> *"We were able to do a, a really neat project there that pulled in people from engineering...biology...chemistry...we were going out and sampling the river over the summer and analyzing a bunch of stuff and that was fun."*

Enjoying these structured experiences was an important element for participants. Annie (unspecified gender, Associate Professor, Earth Sciences) described how despite their concerns about being placed in the geology major following higher education norms in her country of origin, this structured experience worked out well:

> *"I found I actually like it. But the reason…is because when I was a kid, I [grew] up in the, in the wildness…I was exposed to, to nature so much that when I entered the college, I was like oh wow, yeah, something I observed when I was a child and now, I can actually explain…my childhood experience… [it] directed my research direction a little bit."*

Annie's first experiences with research reconnected her to important childhood experiences. This serves as an example of a common thread in many participants' descriptions of their first experiences with research. While we had been anticipating responses about formal research experiences, many participants focused on very early learning experiences, some going back even to primary school age when discussing their first exposure to research. One participant described how an early project around the age of twelve introduced her to research processes she now uses:

> *"It has nothing to do with higher ed exactly…I had a teacher who had me do a summer project for her…over the summer where [I] could like research our town…in the summer between fifth and sixth grade…I was in a special collections department…that was kind of when I first started doing research…similar to the kind of research I do today, I work with primary sources and archives."* – Mary, F, Associate Professor, History

Mary traced her experience using sophisticated resources for scholarly work to a young age and emphasized that formal learning experiences later in life were not her first introduction to the research process. Other participants discussed somewhat unusual opportunities from their high school experience, which typically ranges from 14 – 18 years old. These still occurred before formal compulsory education was completed, and also allowed participants to develop skills they now use in their research. For one participant, though framed as missing out on the opportunity to take advanced placement biology because she wasn't "*smart enough*", a high school course introduced her to the process of data collection in the field and offered the opportunity to develop her own project:

> *"But as a consolation prize, they let me take a course called Scientific Research …the last three years of high school. I got to develop a project and I got to work with scientists nearby and it involved waking up before dawn and driving and looking at the predation effect that field voles felt when foraging for seed at night, and I loved it. I loved being outdoors and I loved doing science, and ever since then, I was pretty much hooked."* – Emily, F, Assistant Professor, Earth Sciences

Multiple participants also discussed how non-formal or informal settings and experiences were key in their development as researchers.

> *"The college art museum asked…if there were any students who were interested to work with this group of artists…It totally changed I think the trajectory of my life actually. Like doing that research with them and watching how they did it and how they interact with people and what our end result was…it was amazing."* – Tina, F, Associate Professor, Arts and Design

For the participants in this study, key events were significant experiences that connected enjoyable, interesting activities with the development of relevant skills and abilities. These key events often happened early in the participants' lives and functioned as opportunities for them start or continue in developing as a researcher.

Mentorship: Relationships

When describing the key events that prompted them down their paths to research, many participants also discussed individuals who served as mentors. These mentors often explicitly connected them to additional opportunities to continue their research experience and served as role models for their own future work as mentors. The Connected Learning framework focuses on the importance of relationships (Connected Learning Alliance, n.d.-a), highlighting the value of youth seeking out mentors and the importance of ensuring the development of intentional mentorship, which engages adults in supporting and caring for youth (Connected Learning Alliance, 2018). The participants in this study had reflections on both receiving and providing mentorship in the traditional academic advisor/advisee relationship, and also discussed informal mentors from their youth who impacted research directions. Amanda (F, Assistant Professor, Language, Literature, and Culture) described two different approaches to mentoring that resonated with multiple participants' experiences.

> *"One really helped with the writing…the other person I think is my creative mentor…[who] helped me to think about how to set up my research and how to find questions and how to really find my own voice…the two of them couldn't have done the other job…I needed both."*

Participants also highlighted how impactful providing mentorship could be:

> *"That's rewarding to me…I facilitated that process for her; I was finding out something that she's [passionate] about and that something she could, you know, make her*

career on." Zachary, M, Associate Professor, Counseling Psychology

And they discussed how they worked to emulate the mentorship experiences they felt were valuable. Bennett (M, Associate Professor, Political Science) described being inspired by his mentor in his current research practice:

> *"Anytime I have a difficult question related to advising students...I pretty much always ask myself what I think [my advisor] would do, and then I do that. And it works out."*

While these traditional research relationships were discussed by most participants, a number also described other adults who provided mentorship and guidance in their development as learners and researchers.

> *"I've had tons of mentors who influence how I do research. I'd say the first was my teacher of that class in high school. She was just so supportive of me and helped me think through my ideas and just really believed in me."* - Emily, F, Assistant Professor, Earth Sciences

In contrast to this teacher's approach to providing support, another teacher emphasized process.

> *"I had a very good physics teacher in the 12th grade and he was extremely rigorous in terms of 'this is how you set up an experiment, this is how you handle the results, this how you write a report.'...I would say he, he was one of the strictest teachers I ever had but I really appreciate that now."*- David, M, Associate Professor, Civil and Environmental Engineering

For one participant, community college faculty were key mentors, one of whom explicitly encouraged continued research experience:

> *"actually when I told [him], I was thinking about sort of applying to graduate school, he said to me, 'oh there is no question about that, you are applying to graduate school'"* Eliena, F, Full Professor, Civil & Environmental Engineering

Eliena's experience highlights how one of the important roles of mentors in EREs was to help learners connect with opportunities, many of which were described as key events. Overall, participants had a variety of mentorship relationships, and their discussions of them show that early experiences can inform later approaches to guiding and supporting newer researchers.

Curiosity and Joy: Interests

When describing their early research experiences, participants highlighted how important their enjoyment, exploration, and interest-driven learning were for their excitement about and continuation in their research career. The Connected Learning framework discusses the importance of interest guiding the experiences of learners, highlighting that "when a subject is personally interesting and relevant, learners achieve much higher-order learning outcomes" (Ito et al., 2013, p. 12). Participants consistently described their EREs as connecting them to their interests.

> *"I thought of my grandfather right away. Because he told me so many stories about the war, and his life before the war...and it made me really interested to learn more about the area where he grew up...I kind of really started reading about history and reading novels that relate to history so already bringing in that humanistic point of view as well. So that was really early."* – Amanda, F, Assistant Professor, Language, Literature, and Culture

Amanda's experience shows how even family members can influence a researcher's development. Other researchers highlighted how exciting it was to develop new knowledge through the research process.

> *"What's exciting is just learning new things, right? That by virtue of doing research, you're always having to think about things that you have not thought about before. And certainly that general notion is what attracted me to academia in the first place, to always be learning."* – Lee, M, Full Professor, English

As Dan (M, Full Professor, Theater) put it:

> *"I like the curiosity and the opportunity to discover something I didn't expect."*

Another researcher framed her focus as a drive to help ensure that research was open to news ways to what she learned:

> *"I went to college and realized that there were really different ways to tell those stories and I realized how much of history and literary interpretation was based on...a particular dominant way that story was told, and that maybe there ought to be some different ways of telling it."* – Cilla, F, Assistant Professor, English

Ultimately, having ownership in a project or research direction (following interests) was an important element of many participants' EREs. Participants described these early research experiences with bold language that emphasizes how impactful they were. In discussing multiple visits to a museum as a part of an ERE, Emily (F, Assistant Professor, Earth Sciences) stated: *"it was thrilling every time."* Eleanor (F, Assistant Professor, Food Science) highlighted how foundational this ownership was for her:

"When I started my first project, that really was like, 'well, this is something I want to do the rest of my life.'" – Eleanor, F, Assistant Professor, Food Science

These descriptions of early research experiences demonstrate how significant EREs can be for learners. When early researchers are able to connect to opportunities through key events, build relationships that provide and model mentorship, and have their interests drive their experiences, a strong basis for an understanding of research skills and potential for a research career is nurtured.

DISCUSSION

The reflections of these participants show that the components of successful early research experiences are often interrelated and co-occurring. Returning to our research questions, we set out to develop understandings of the following: How do researchers describe and conceptualize their early research experiences? What factors contribute to the success of these experiences? How can these factors inform the design and implementation of early research experiences for youth?

This work demonstrates that researchers describe and conceptualize their early research experiences as rooted in joyful discovery, learning, and curiosity. Early research experience is centered around key events that highlight the potential of interest driven inquiry to young learners, and often connect youth and young adults with mentors who provide support and model guidance practices. These elements (*key events, mentorship,* and *curiosity and joy*) are important factors in successful EREs. Further, these elements relate to crucial components of Connected Learning experiences: opportunities, relationships, and interests. With these connections, it becomes clear that the CL framework can support implementing EREs for youth and young adults. By connecting CL and EREs in informal settings like public libraries, we have the opportunity to broaden access to the original research process and encourage more diverse voices to contribute to research and scholarship. Here we discuss the implications of this work, note some limitations of our study, and discuss future directions.

Implications

The learning experiences that occur in childhood and young adulthood can have direct and meaningful impact on the development of future researchers. Giving youth and early stage researchers opportunities to pursue their own research interests are a key way to make connections and build a love of research. For many of the participants in this paper, research ideas and agendas are seeded before post-secondary education; in other words, research agendas start young. Building on this, we identify a number of opportunities in regard to developing successful early research experiences and opening ways to include more diverse voices in the world of scholarship. The Connected Learning framework, which has served as an effective approach for designing learning experiences for youth, is a useful lens for understanding EREs and building bridges between research and libraries/librarians, especially considering the alignment between the experiences and perceptions of researchers with the foundational concepts of CL. Researchers, educators, and youth services providers should take seriously the opportunity of EREs in facilitating individuals' identity formation and persistence into research-oriented careers, as well as their potential for developing research skills and critical thinking abilities. Cultivating more opportunities for young people to engage in EREs will build CL opportunities and empower youth. Crucially, we argue that partnering with libraries to ensure that youth from a wide variety of backgrounds, including nondominant individuals, have exposure to early research experiences has the potential to help diversify the academy.

"Youth develop their interests and sparks through the support of adults," (Vaclavik et al., 2017, p. 907). Given the value of adult support and guidance broadly speaking, the impacts of it as described by the successful researchers in this study, and the unique role of youth services providers who are poised to provide this kind of relationship and support, it is key to develop ways to support those who work with youth to stoke connections to research. Following the trajectory of calls for extending teacher training (Murray et al., 2016b), we suggest that extending training in research to pre-service and practicing librarians who interact with youth is a fruitful direction for ensuring that more young people are exposed to research processes, meet individuals who can serve as mentors, and gain access to opportunities and key experiences that serve as signposts on the development of a research identity. Combining EREs, libraries, and the Connected Learning framework means that the resulting opportunities are remarkably well suited to provide youth with mentorship and support. There is also strong potential in this approach to provide youth opportunities for skills development and real world experience that enable youth to 1) critically engage with the research they interact with in everyday life and 2) to consider potential research careers.

Limitations

This study does include some limitations. In our work thus far, we have only recruited participants from R1 institutions. Given this, we are interested in broadening the scope of participation to researchers who have different levels of emphasis on research, and to researchers who work at non-academic institutions. Another limitation is that all participants who participated in the demographic survey identified as White. Some contributing factors that may help explain this. The general demographics of the academy in the United States are important to consider: as of 2016, 76% of full-time faculty across all ranks at U.S. institutions were White (National Center for Educational Statistics, 2018). Faculty from nondominant backgrounds are overburdened with issues like microaggressions and increased service expectations (Pittman, 2012), making the already hectic work of research more difficult to accomplish, much less discuss in an interview. Going forward, our work may require additional remuneration or an adjusted study design to account for these factors and support nondominant or underrepresented researchers in participating (Turner, Myers Jr., & Creswell, 1999).

We had less participants from the social sciences and professional disciplines. In retrospect, based on some communication from invited researchers who declined to participate, individuals from these disciplines may identify their work more as "scholarly" or "inquiry" than "research," and this may have affected the response rate overall. This is another area we will address with adjusted study design in our ongoing data collection. With the exploratory nature of this work and our emphasis on understanding the experiences and perspectives of participants, we needed to collect rich data and have the opportunity for rapport, conversation, and discussion, which necessitates a qualitative approach. It is also important to note that the use of a qualitative approach means that we do not contribute replicable findings, but given the saturation of these concepts and the fit of the Connected Learning framework to our participants' experiences, we consider it likely that this work is transferable to other contexts and populations.

Future Work

With the goals of diversifying the voices represented in scholarship and nurturing young people's skills and abilities for critical engagement with research in everyday life, our future work is currently focused on connecting with researchers from backgrounds that are underrepresented in this exploratory study. We are actively adjusting our recruiting strategies to enable us to learn from researchers from nondominant backgrounds, while recognizing that there are additional constraints on their time and availability. We are also working to recruit participants from academic fields and backgrounds that have lower participation in this study, specifically social sciences, professional studies, and other disciplines beyond STEM and arts & humanities. Continuing to engage with a wide variety of research and inquiry traditions will help ensure that these developing understandings of research incorporate diverse field perspectives and scholarly values. This will in turn help ensure that future EREs have broad potential to excite and inspire young people.

In addition to further exploring how successful early research experiences operate for nondominant researchers and continuing our work engaging researchers from a variety of areas, we are using these findings to inform the design of EREs for teens. Researchers have called for expanding opportunities for high school students to engage in research, framed through concepts of science and via "early college high school" courses that allow high school students to engage in college coursework (Murray, Obare, & Hageman, 2016a). While this is a welcome trajectory, the work presented here indicates there are additional opportunities to engage youth in broader concepts of research including not just traditional STEM fields but also professional studies, arts and humanities, and the social sciences, and to do so not just in formal settings.

The experiences of researchers interviewed in this study indicate that connections to research practices and areas of research interest are fruitful as early as elementary school. In addition to connecting youth to existing college curricula or emphasizing STEM research, we argue that developing new programs and opportunities specifically designed for youth, offered through informal settings, and informed by all kinds of research is a compelling direction for the future of early research experience development. Broadening what kinds of research are included in these conversations can pique the interests of students who may not have high levels of interest-driven engagement with STEM fields. Engaging youth in research outside of traditional academic contexts, including via public libraries, can also help to increase the reach of EREs, furthering the goal of ensuring that "all students across all demographics should be given the opportunity to engage in authentic hands-on research, early, often, and universally" (Murray et al., 2016a).

The EREs we are developing will be implemented in public libraries and a resulting model and supporting resources will be publicly available for libraries/library staff, researchers, and teens who are interested in making connections between teens and research in their own communities. We have opportunities to build on new understandings of EREs coupled with the Connected Learning framework in libraries to prompt the development of new researchers and young people who have the skills to critically engage with research. Other work in this project is focused on learning what youth services providers and teens look for in these kinds of informal and Connected Learning experiences, ultimately connecting the perspectives of various stakeholders to more effectively design early research experiences for youth.

CONCLUSION

In this paper we examined the experiences of academics who identify as researchers at a variety of career stages, identifying key elements in their development as researchers. We identified and described factors in successful early research experiences from researchers from professional, social science, arts and humanities, and STEM backgrounds. These factors for success included *key events, mentorship,* and *curiosity and joy*. We employed the Connected Learning framework as a lens for understanding EREs, and highlighted the opportunities in designing EREs that connect youth to research experience and skills, before they reach higher education institutions. This work also has implications for the design of EREs at all levels, including compulsory education as well as post-secondary education at undergraduate, graduate, and doctoral levels. Understanding what works for developing and supporting interest in original research activities and skills can help connect learners at all stages to early research experiences that are driven by their interests and which will prompt engagement for years to come, whether through the pursuit of research careers or through thoughtful interactions with research in everyday life.

ACKNOWLEDGMENTS

This project was made possible in part by the Institute of Museum and Library Services [RE-07-18-0054-18].

REFERENCES

Agosto, D. E., & Hughes-Hassell, S. (2006). Toward a model of the everyday life information needs of urban teenagers, part 2: Empirical model. *Journal of the American Society for Information Science and Technology, 57*(11), 1418–1426.

Alderton, E., & Manzi, M. (2017). Engaging Students: An authentic undergraduate research experience. *Professional Educator*, (1), 42.

American Association of School Librarians. (2018). *AASL Standards Framework for Learners*. Chicago, IL: American Library Association.

Bowman, N. A., & Holmes, J. M. (2018). Getting off to a good start? First-year undergraduate research experiences and student outcomes. *Higher Education, 76*(1), 17–33.

Braun, V., & Clarke, V. (2006). Using thematic analysis in psychology. *Qualitative research in psychology, 3*(2), 77–101.

Bruce, C. (1997). *The seven faces of information literacy*. Adelaide: Auslib Press.

Brunsma, D. L., Embrick, D. G., & Shin, J. H. (2017). Graduate students of color: Race, racism, and mentoring in the white waters of academia. *Sociology of Race and Ethnicity, 3*(1), 1–13.

Carnegie Classification of Institutions of Higher Education. (2018). *2018 Update public file* [EXCEL file]. Retrieved from: http://carnegieclassifications.iu.edu/downloads/CCIHE2018-PublicData.xlsx

Carpi, A., Ronan, D. M., Falconer, H. M., & Lents, N. H. (2017). Cultivating minority scientists: Undergraduate research increases self-efficacy and career ambitions for underrepresented students in STEM. *Journal of Research in Science Teaching, 54*(2), 169–194.

Case, D. O., & Given, L. M. (2016). *Looking for information: A survey of research on information seeking, needs, and behavior*. Bingley: Emerald Group Publishing.

US Census Bureau. (2000). *Census regions and divisions of the United States* [PDF file]. Retrieved from https://www2.census.gov/geo/pdfs/maps-data/maps/reference/us_regdiv.pdf

Chelton, M. K., & Cool, C. (2004). *Youth information-seeking behavior: Theories, models, and issues* (Vol. *1*). Scarecrow Press.

Chou, R. L., Pho, A., & Roh, C. (2018). *Pushing the margins: Women of color and intersectionality in LIS*. Library Juice Press.

Connected Learning Alliance. (2018). *The mentoring gap* [PDF file]. Retrieved from https://clalliance.org/wp-content/uploads/2018/05/mentorship_v8_small.pdf

Connected Learning Alliance. (n.d.-a). *About connected learning*. Retrieved from https://clalliance.org/about-connected-learning

Connected Learning Alliance. (n.d.-b). *Connected learning in libraries*. Retrieved from https://clalliance.org/about-connected-learning

ConnectedLib. (2019). *Our project*. Retrieved from https://connectedlib.ischool.uw.edu

ConnectedLib. (n.d.) *ConnectedLib home*. Retrieved from https://connectedlib.github.io

Cooke, N. A. (2016). *Information services to diverse populations: Developing culturally competent library professionals*. ABC-CLIO.

Cooke, N. A., Sweeney, M. E., & Noble, S. U. (2016). Social justice as topic and tool: An attempt to transform an LIS curriculum and culture. *The Library Quarterly, 86*(1), 107–124.

Craney, C., McKay, T., Mazzeo, A., Morris, J., Prigodich, C., & De Groot, R. (2011). Cross-discipline perceptions of the undergraduate research experience. *The Journal of Higher Education, 82*(1), 92–113.

De Abreu, B. S., & Mihailidis, P. (2013). *Media literacy education in action: Theoretical and pedagogical perspectives*. New York, NY: Routledge.

Dedoose (2018). *Version 8.0.35, web application for managing, analyzing, and presenting qualitative and mixed method research data*. Los Angeles, CA: SocioCultural Research Consultants, LLC. www.dedoose.com

Eisenberg, M. B., & Berkowitz, R. E. (1990). *Information problem solving: The big six skills approach to library & information skills instruction*. Norwood, NJ: Ablex Publishing Corporation.

Gazzaniga, M., Heatherton, T., & Halpern, D. (2016). *Psychological science* (5th ed.). New York, NY: Norton.

Gilmore, J., Vieyra, M., Timmerman, B., Feldon, D., & Maher, M. (2015). The relationship between undergraduate research participation and subsequent research performance of early career STEM graduate students. *The Journal of Higher Education, 86*(6), 834–863.

Guest, G., Bunce, A., & Johnson, L. (2006). How many interviews are enough? An experiment with data saturation and variability. *Field Methods, 18*(1), 59–82.

Guest, G., MacQueen, K. M., & Namey, E. E. (2012). Validity and reliability (credibility and dependability) in qualitative research and data analysis. In G. Guest, K. M. MacQueen, & E. E. Namey, *Applied thematic analysis* (pp. 79–106). Los Angeles, CA: SAGE Publications, Inc.

Hernandez, C. D. (2016). Project SEED: A catalyst for young scientists. In D. H. Murray, S. O. Obare, & J. H. Hageman, *The power and promise of early research* (pp. 71–81). Washington, DC: American Chemical Society Publications.

Hoffman, K., Subramaniam, M., Kawas, S., Scaff, L., & Davis, K. (2016). *Connected libraries: Surveying the current landscape and charting a path to the future*. College Park, MD; Seattle, WA: The ConnectedLib Project.

Hunt, S. L., & Bakker, C. J. (2018). A qualitative analysis of the information science needs of public health researchers in an academic setting. *Journal of the Medical Library Association: JMLA*, *106*(2), 184.

International Federation of Library Associations and Institutions & United Nations Educational, Scientific, and Cultural Organization. (1994). *Public Library Manifesto*. Retrieved from https://www.ifla.org/publications/iflaunesco-public-library-manifesto-1994

iSchool Inclusion Institute. (2017). *i3 news*. Retrieved from http://www.sis.pitt.edu/i3/about-i3/i3-news.html#

Ito, M., Gutiérrez, K., Livingstone, S., Penuel, B., Rhodes, J., Salen, K., … Watkins, S. C. (2013). Connected learning: An agenda for research and design. In *Digital media and learning research hub*. Irvine, CA.

Kuhlthau, C. C. (2010). Guided inquiry: School libraries in the 21st century. *School Libraries Worldwide*, *16*(1), 17–28.

Kumar, S., & Shukla, P. (2013). Information seeking pattern in electronic environment of sciences and arts researchers: a comparative study. *Brazilian Journal of Information Science: Research Trends*, *7*(1).

Little, D., Green, D. A., & Hoption, C. (2018). A lasting impression: The influence of prior disciplines on educational developers' research. *International Journal for Academic Development*, *23*(4), 324–338.

Lopatto, D. (2010). Undergraduate research as a high-impact student experience. *Peer Review*, (2), 12.

Martin, C. (2015). Connected learning, librarians, and connecting youth interest. *Journal of Research on Libraries & Young Adults*, *6*, 2–25.

Meyers, E. M., Fisher, K. E., & Marcoux, E. (2009). Making sense of an information world: The everyday-life information behavior of preteens. *The Library Quarterly*, *79* (3), 301–341.

Mraz-Craig, J. A., Daniel, K. L., Bucklin, C. J., Mishra, C., Ali, L., & Clase, K. L. (2018). Student identities in authentic course-based undergraduate research experience. *Journal of College Science Teaching*, *48*(1), 68–75.

Murray, D. H., Obare, S. O., & Hageman, J. H. (2016a). The future of early research. In D. H. Murray, S. O. Obare, & J. H. Hageman, *The power and promise of early research* (pp. 247–254). Washington, DC: American Chemical Society Publications.

Murray, D. H., Obare, S. O., & Hageman, J. H. (2016b). *The power and promise of early research*. Washington, DC: American Chemical Society Publications.

National Center for Education Statistics. (2018). *The condition of education 2018* (NCES 2018-144), Characteristics of postsecondary faculty.

National Science Foundation. (2017). *Inclusion across the nation of communities of learners of underrepresented discoverers in engineering and science (NSF INCLUDES)* (NSF 17-522). Alexandria: National Science Foundation.

Pittman, C. T. (2012). Racial microaggressions: The narratives of African American faculty at a predominantly White University. *The Journal of Negro Education*, *81* (1), 82–92.

Terry, G., Hayfield, N., Clarke, V., & Braun, V. (2017). Thematic analysis. In *The Sage handbook of qualitative research in psychology* (pp. 17–37).

Tracy, S. J. (2010). Qualitative quality: Eight "big-tent" criteria for excellent qualitative research. *Qualitative inquiry*, *16*(10), 837–851.

Turner, C. S. V., Myers, S. L., Jr., & Creswell, J. W. (1999). Exploring underrepresentation: The case of faculty of color in the Midwest. *The Journal of Higher Education*, *70*(1), 27–59.

Vaclavik, D., Sánchez, B., Buehler, K., Gray, T., & Rodriguez, E. (2017). How to support me in connected learning: Youth perspectives on adult supportive behavior and its benefits. *Journal of Community Psychology*, *45*(7), 906–921.

Van den Brink, M., & Benschop, Y. (2012). Slaying the seven-headed dragon: The quest for gender change in academia. *Gender, Work & Organization*, *19*(1), 71–92.

Wasserman, E. (2016). Perspectives from a New York high school science research enrichment program teacher. In D. H. Murray, S. O. Obare, & J. H. Hageman, *The power and promise of early research* (pp. 59–69). Washington, DC: American Chemical Society Publications.

Young Adult Library Services Association. (2014). *The future of library services for and with teens: A call to action*. Chicago, IL: American Library Association.

Young Adult Library Services Association. (2017). *YALSA national research agenda on libraries, learning, and teens*. Chicago, IL: American Library Association.

Zhang, C., & Swaid, S. (2017). Undergraduate research experience for STEM students: Efforts and outcomes. *Contemporary Issues in Education Research*, *10*(4), 213–218.

Considering "Atmosphere" in Facilitating Information Seeking by People With Invisible Disabilities in Public Libraries

Rebecca Muir
Charles Sturt University,
Wagga Wagga, NSW
rmuir@csu.edu.au

Kim M. Thompson
University of South Carolina,
Columbia, South Carolina
kimthompson@sc.edu

Asim Qayyum
Charles Sturt University,
Wagga Wagga, NSW
aqayyum@csu.edu.au

ABSTRACT

Twenty percent of Australians reported having a disability in 2015. Disability may occur at any time during the lifespan, however most disabilities are invisible. When a disability is invisible, or not immediately apparent to an outsider, individuals may need to self-identify to access inclusive services, or accommodation may never be offered at all. When the perceived number of information seekers with a disability is low, information organizations may deem services unnecessary. Considering information access is a human right, information service providers and researchers need to seek low cost and low effort ways to facilitate information access and information seeking behaviors. The research question was "how does the ambience, security, and mores (conceptualized as "atmosphere") of information services facilitate, or create barriers to, information seeking by people with an invisible disability?". Data from 23 semi-structured qualitative interviews were analyzed to explore the experiences of people with an invisible disability as current or prospective library users.

KEYWORDS

Invisible Disabilities; Hidden Disabilities; Latent Disabilities; Semi-Structured Interviews; Public Libraries; Information Services; Information Seeking Behavior

ASIS&T THESAURUS

Public Libraries; Information Science

INTRODUCTION

Based on the 2015 Survey of Disability, Aging and Carers, one in five Australians report having a disability (Australian Bureau of Statistics, 2016). It is a common misconception that disabilities are obvious or immediately recognizable (Ricci, 2016). While cues such as a wheelchair or white cane can assist in visualizing disability (Pilling, 2013), the iconographical person in a wheelchair, used to indicate disability services or facilities, is a graphical representation that represents only 4.4% of persons with a disability (Australian Network on Disability, 2019).

The library disability literature has predominately focused on visual disabilities such as vision loss; this is unsurprising considering the focus on text in libraries (Hill, 2013). In contrast, invisible disabilities such as learning disabilities are comparatively little researched. Invisible, hidden, or latent disabilities refer to any disability not immediately evident to another person such as acquired or traumatic brain injuries, physical disabilities such as spinal injuries, mental health disabilities, autism spectrum, chronic pain, chronic dizziness, and chronic fatigue (Autism Queensland, n.d.; Disabled World, 2018; House with No Steps, 2015).

While there is no official measure of the prevalence rates of invisible disabilities in Australia, disability organizations "House with No Steps" (2017) and "Attitude Foundation" (n.d.) suggest that between 70% and 90% of people with a disability have or experience an invisible disability. Goldberg and Steury (2001) note that by 2020, depression is expected to be the second most common disease and will account for 15% of the world-wide disease burden.

There are few circumstances where there is a legal obligation for an individual to disclose a disability in Australia (Ricci, 2016). An individual may decide not to disclose for several reasons, including the risk of stigma should the individual's experience of disability not meet an onlooker's expectation or experience (Brent, 2016; Feldman & Tegart, 2013; Invisible Disabilities Association, 2003). When an individual discloses a disability, the person disclosed to may believe that this opens the discussion to further questioning; an attempt to visualize the invisible through inquisition (Mullins & Preyde, 2013; Murphy, 2018).

The decision to disclose is a complex and personal one (Spirito Dalgin & Bellini, 2008). Yet people with a disability may be required to disclose to receive adjustments or services (e.g., Robertson, 2007). Non-disclosure may contribute to a sense that there is a low number of people with a disability in the community. Further, where services or staff may want

82nd Annual Meeting of the Association for Information Science & Technology | Melbourne, Australia | 19–23 October, 2019

DOI: 10.1002/pra2.00017

to provide tailored disability services, resources, staffing, or facilities; they may not know how to provide for the needs of people with a disability, or what is required (Equity Research Centre, 2007).

Information organizations such as public libraries are not immune from these considerations. Public libraries contribute to the possibilities of active citizenship across social, economic, and ethnic differences; increasing community efficacy and enabling communities to engage and participate in problem solving and local issues (Aabo, 2011; Homelessness Australia, 2013; Houghton, 2014). Public libraries provide access to critical information such as employment, education, and government resources (Jaeger, Bertot, Thompson, Katz, & DeCoster, 2012).

Yet as government expenditure tightens, library budgets tighten, and competition continues to be fierce for funding, there may be challenges in providing staffing, resources, or facilities (Equity Research Centre, 2007; Public Libraries Victoria Network, 2013). The wider literature on libraries and homelessness notes that funding for specialist staff such as social workers may require successful completion of funding applications (e.g., Kelley, Riggleman, Clara, & Navarro, 2017). Public libraries may struggle to balance the needs of patron groups, including homeless patrons with serious psychiatric disorders who may have limited services, health points, or places to go (Torrey, Esposito, & Geller, 2009). Library staff may not know how to engage with library patrons who are in crisis or in need of specialist advice (Williams, 2016). Lastly, traditional library systems such as fines may result in poor or socially excluded populations determining that the library isn't "for them" – self-excluding even before entry into the space (Working Together Project, n.d.).

Libraries may themselves be limited in the type of access or inclusion that they provide. While public libraries have improved physical access to buildings, they reflect less progress in the consumption of assistive or adaptive technologies or devices (Burke, 2009; Small, Myhill, & Herring-Harrington, 2015). Staff employed in school, academic, or council-controlled libraries may lack approval to make decisions around accessibility issues due to reporting and funding structures (Irvall & Nielsen, 2005). These reporting structures, funding, and knowledge limitations may limit what is focused on and developed in the library (Australian Human Rights Commission, 2011; Morley, 2000; Quinn & McCallum, 2012).

The "what" and "how" of services for people with a disability, particularly invisible disabilities, is further complicated by a limited disability research literature in Australia. While literature exists on disability and public libraries, it has been noted as being predominately American focused (Burns & Gordon, 2010; Hill, 2013). The University of Sydney's "Report of Audit of Disability Research in Australia" (2014, 2017) notes that there remain several research gap areas in the Australian literature; including, notably, that additional research is needed on the lived experiences of people with disabilities to bring these perspectives to policy.

Lastly, while overarching legislation exists such as the Disability Discrimination Act, this often makes no direct reference to public libraries (Fitzgerald, Hawkins, Denison, & Kop, 2015). In this absence, libraries may implement their own policies around services for people with a disability. The professional association that provides standards and accreditation within the Australian library community - the Australian Library and Information Association (ALIA) - provides guidelines by which libraries may benchmark their services to ensure that a minimum level of service is provided; however, there are no obligations to apply these.

This lack of legislation means that public libraries provide varying services across costing, resourcing, and knowledge lines, with the result that public expectations of access for people with a disability are not always high (Australian Human Rights Commission, 2011; Morley, 2000). This varied service may in turn impact on how people with a disability are served in libraries (Jaeger & Bowman, 2005).

Yet if the core of human rights holds that all individuals deserve equal rights as members of society, these rights are unattainable in the absence of free and equitable access to information (Hussain, 2000). It is not enough for public libraries to expect patrons to disclose the presence of a disability to provide services or resources. It is not practicable to wait on funding to provide services. Instead, libraries need to consider ways in which they may build upon their existing environment to facilitate information access and use by patrons with an invisible disability.

Information Seeking Behavior and Information Use

Information behavior explores how humans need, seek, manage, and use information in different contexts (Fisher, Erdelez, & McKechnie, 2005; Julien, 1992). Described by Spink (2010) as a critical evolutionary ability, information behavior may be active, such as through the direct foraging for information; or passive, such as watching television advertisements without any intention to act on the information (Beverley, Bath, & Barber, 2007; Todaro, 2005).

Understanding user information behaviors has practical implications in respect to the library policies, rules, and regulations (Mutula & Majine, 2016; Todaro, 2005). As a community information center, it is important that the public library responds to the changing information needs of their communities in a variety of formats (Irwin, 1995). This response includes ensuring that library collections, resources, services, and programs are accessible and meet the information needs of their communities (Craven & Booth, 2006; Gibson & Kaplan, 2017).

If public libraries are to utilize their potential to address social and educational inequalities within their communities (McKeown, 2016), all community members must have the same right to access information (Inglis & McAnelly, 2015). However, internal and external factors including the characteristics and needs of library users and the operating environments of the library may motivate and influence individual information needs and behavior (Day, 2007; Hepworth, 2007; Wellstead, 2010). As noted by Samure and Given (2004), marginalized groups may display different information behaviors than those viewed as "normal" seekers of information.

There is limited research on the information behavior of people with invisible disabilities in library settings. One study by Niedzwiedzka and Korycinska (2016) considered the information behaviors related to health information seeking by people with depression on online forums. The information need that prompted individuals to use this resource was shaped by the presence of a mental health condition in conjunction with the availability of an internet connection/knowledge of and access to the forum. The authors noted that participants "often have a problem with revealing their needs" (example: *I feel awful and the worst is that I can't stay that to anyone*) (p. 128). There were posts expressing social anxiety and shame related to disclosing their mental illness, or not feeling understood by their community. The manner in which anxious and depressed individuals process certain types of information and the impact of systematic bias, such as overestimation of threat and understatement of ability to cope, has been established in the literature (e.g., Beck & Clark, 1988).

Sambo, Rabiu, and Shaba (2016) note that physical disabilities shape information behavior through the paths of access into and through the information facility. Samure and Given (2004) undertook a pilot study on how blindness or partial sight influenced the information behavior of participants while completing university studies. The university library environment, structured to cater for "typical" information behavior, turned the straightforward task for a sighted individual of locating and copying a research article into an exercise of several days, spanning two locations. Due to this, participants in the study expressed a preference for internet resources and supported the value of adaptive technologies rather than undertaking this lengthy investigation and process into the library.

A significant portion of the autism spectrum research relevant to information behavior is focused on classroom learning and teaching environments; while not particular to the library setting, this knowledge translates across services providing a learning or education service. Individuals on the autism spectrum may not understand that questions can be used to gain information from others (Hurtig, Ensrud, & Tomblin, 1982), potentially limiting their information access. Gray and Garland (1993) recommend that autistic individuals may need to be taught specifically how to ask questions and be instructed that others may have information that could be valuable to them. Creating appropriate classrooms, or educative library environments, can also aid students on the autism spectrum, as low-stimulus surroundings have strong implications for feelings of safety, calm, and inclusion (McAllister & Maguire, 2012).

A theme that weaves its way through the information literature is the consideration of how the environment affects information behavior (e.g., Cordray & Romanych, 2005; Niu & Hemminger, 2012). The physical domain is the tangible world that surrounds us and in which information is provided, stored, used. This tangible world in turn possesses its own "atmosphere" – the ambience, sense of security, and mores of the space that themselves support, inhibit, or encourage the individual in their information pursuits. Public libraries are not immune from this influence; and as services available to all members of their community, libraries need to consider how their own "atmosphere" can contribute to information access and use by their community members.

The primary research question for this study was "how does the ambience, security, and mores (conceptualized as "atmosphere") of information services facilitate, or create barriers to, information seeking by people with an invisible disability?". The study explores and contributes to the existing literature base by exploring how "atmosphere" can provide support for, or create barriers to, information access for library users with invisible disabilities.

METHODOLOGY

Epistemology

An interpretivist epistemology was employed, holding that realities are multiple and individual, embedded in context (Pickard, 2013). Realities are socially based, local, specific and alterable (Guba & Lincoln, 1994). Using an interpretive framework, the researcher aims to describe, interpret, and understand (Ferguson, Ferguson, & Taylor, 1992).

Method

Qualitative semi-structured interviews were undertaken with people with an invisible disability. Semi-structured interviews permit a responsive exploration of the context and views of participants, permitting questions to be tailored to each interviewee (Babbie, 2005; deMarrais, 2003; Labuschagne, 2003). The data provide the researcher's understanding of the participant's understanding of a subject (O'Hara, 2006). Participant quotations are reflected in the discussion by indented paragraphs, with the participant number listed in closed brackets following.

Participants

Theoretical saturation was reached at the completion of 23 interviews. Seventy percent of interviews were conducted face to face; 17% by phone; and 9% via Skype. Eighteen participants were female; 5 were male. 12 participants were aged under 39 years; 10 were aged between 40 and 79. Most participants resided in a suburban area. Ten participants had completed, or were completing, a college or tertiary degree.

Interview Duration, Inclusion Criteria, and Confidentiality

Interviews averaged 29.4 min in duration and were conducted in public locations, including cafes and libraries. The inclusion criteria were that the participant resided in Victoria, was over 18 years old, and had an invisible disability. All participants indicated that they had visited a public library, however not all participants were current library users. Participants were recruited via promotion through disability advocacy organizations online through their social media and newsletters; through the researcher's Facebook account; via snowball sampling; and in the case of a supported workplace, through the employer. The interviewer did not seek disclosure apart from confirming that the participant identified as having an invisible disability. Of participants who self-disclosed, participants included people with mental health, intellectual or learning disabilities, acquired or traumatic brain injury, autism spectrum, and sensory disabilities.

Several interviews were undertaken at a supported workplace with the consent of the employer. Names were provided to the interviewer for participation in the study. The interviewer did not approach any person outside of this list for participation in the study; where approached by persons outside this list to participate in the study, the researcher declined the request. It was not possible to maintain confidentiality of participation from the employer or fellow employees. Instead, confidentiality of the interview was maintained by conducting interviews in an enclosed area and in pausing recordings and the interview if interrupted.

Data Collection and Analysis

Data was collected via interview and audio recorded. On the conclusion of the interview the recorded session was transcribed by the interviewer and analyzed establish themes, using NVivo software for data organization.

Written interviews were conducted with two participants at their request. One of these two participants also completed an audio interview, with some parts of this recording utilized in the data analysis; however, much of the information from this participant was drawn from the written interview. One participant attended the interview with a support person and provided consent for this person to be present.

Positioning of Researcher

The interviewer approaches the study as an insider, sharing a characteristic, role, or experience with participants (Dwyer & Buckle, 2009). While there are advantages to undertaking research in a field to which the researcher is already familiar, there can be perceived disadvantages such as a loss of objectivity or an illusion of sameness (Breen, 2007).

As noted by Alvesson (2003), when undertaking self-ethnographic research the researcher must be cautious to not see all things in only a specific light. It cannot be assumed that the researcher's experience is generic and identical to participants' (Nandhakumar & Jones, 1997). To reduce the possibility of assuming generic experiences, no identifying information was sought about the library services used by participants or about the nature of their invisible disability.

RESULTS AND DISCUSSION

Defining "Atmosphere"

The concept of "atmosphere" draws inductively from thematic analysis of the interview data. As defined by and conceptualized by the researcher from the interview data, "atmosphere" incorporates ambience; perceptions of safety; and staff behaviors and attitudes. These were often discussed by interview participants around their sense of welcome in the library and may in turn influence their information behaviors and seeking.

Each of these concepts also appears in the wider library literature, though not under the umbrella term of "atmosphere" and seldom in discussion around information behavior in libraries by people with invisible disabilities. Ambience, or sound and noise, has been both lauded and criticized in the library environment (Ashcroft, 2003; Schomberg & Cole, 2017; University Wire, 2018); while the psychological and ergonomics literature has debated the value of color therapy (Acking & Kuller, 1972; Kodama, 1990; Kuller, Ballal, Laike, Mikellides, & Tonello, 2006).

Perception of safety remains topical; particularly security in public places and the fear of crime (Bialek, n.d.; Johnson, 2012; Kovach, 2018; McBride, 2017; Yavuz & Welch, 2010). Library mores and staff and public attitudes have been considered in the literature around social policing and behavior in the wider community and in public libraries (Coldron, Cripps, & Shipton, 2010; Feldshuh, 2018; Ingraham, 2015; Shaffer, Vardaman, & Miller, 2010).

The previous section has emphasized the importance of considering how libraries can facilitate information behavior in low cost and low effort ways. "Atmosphere" is one way that libraries may be able to facilitate their whole community in their information behaviors, without requiring disability disclosure.

Ambience

Ambience encapsulated light, color, and sound. While participants did discuss temperature and lighting such as windows and overhead lights, the data analysis revealed additional thoughts on sound and color use.

Color was used by participants as a way of identifying how to use the library, or how the library perceived itself. Color referred both to wall paint and to furniture color as visible indicators of space utilization. Such choices did not need to include all furniture; the use of a red table or chairs to indicate a silent area was enough. Color was seen by some participants as a way of identifying what was allowed in an area (for example, children's areas using more vibrant and energetic colors then than those used in the calmer adult reading areas), what was permissible in the space, and how space could be utilized. Where libraries maintained the continuous use of the one color throughout, this monotony could cause confusion when individuals attempted to independently decode how to use the library space:

> [I]f everything's all the one colour and looks kind of the same and the desks are the same over here and over there, and I've been told that I can sit here, I'm not sure if I can sit there. That can retrigger and then I have to go ask the same 32 questions of the [staff]. (007)

Color could play a role in a participant's decision around which library branch to visit, and how long to stay in the library. The "reassuring suburban (council) color" scheme of mint green – colors that may be seen at hospitals and council offices – could subsume the identity of the library as a council, county, or city owned space; a place only to visit, as opposed to staying in. This was also the case with sound; participants recognized that sometimes they, as human beings, may make noise, incidentally drawing attention to themselves. The reverent silence of the library – not dissimilar to a church – could demand a suppression of the human to favor the pursuit of knowledge. For some, the quiet was calming:

> [If] I haven't visited [local library] in several years and I remember it being a very **quiet** – not dark but shadowed kind of place where I could go to relax and I walk in there several years later and have the same thing. A lot of things that mental illness sufferers look for is a constant [...] in their life (001, own emphasis)

For others, it led to anxiety:

> ... if you think about the way **silence** is used in films it is always to terrify. Tension, it's used to build tensions ... [i]f I'm in a space where I feel like you can't make a single noise, that builds and builds, and it's such a huge pressure on me to hold that in, and it's actually a cycle that makes it more likely that I'm going to tic – and then the embarrassment that follows, and that makes it a very uncomfortable position for me to be in. (007, own emphasis)

The distinction became evident in perception of the library as a quiet place, versus a silent place. Having quiet background noise permitted a return of humanity; a place of reflection and knowledge that people could stay in. This was not to say, however, that participants necessarily favored the contemporary version of the library as a "community living-room"; the noise of children screaming, jarring hold music, and people swearing were noted by participants as detrimental to their experiences in the library.

The data from this study suggested a rethink of the library as a silent space, or as a noisy space, to have a *spaces* model. In this library space, there would be areas set aside for different usage, with color-facilitated and signed user information behavior cues. Where an environment does not match needs, library users may take familiar paths to find known information and then leave the library; removing the opportunity to find different information, address other information needs, or to build information seeking skills. This model also impacts on individual's decisions to approach staff for information assistance.

In having discussed ambience, library practitioners or researchers might ask: How do we communicate to individuals what our spaces are for? How do we address the needs of our patronage for differing levels of sound? How do we communicate how library furniture may be used, as a social gathering space or a quiet study space? How do the colors of the library or wall art communicate to patrons, particularly with communication or mental health disabilities, what the library is and how both the library and its space can be used by individuals?

Perceptions of Safety

Safety covered the perception of security both internal and external to the library, the existence of mores or rules, and social policing.

There is a debate in the public library sector as to whether a security presence in the library is necessary (e.g., McBride, 2017). There can be a perception that security may make library visitors feel that the library is not "their" space; versus that security may make library users feel safer in the public sphere. Where security was mentioned by participants, either internal or external to the library space such as on roadways or carparks, it was spoken about in a positive manner: "And they also have a security guard there as well, so you feel safe. The security guard is just at the front door, when you walk in, it's one of those rotation door things" (018).

Establishing and enforcing clear mores was also discussed favorably. It was noted that people may choose to self-exclude themselves from the public library, and that this choice may derive from the individual. However, it was also noted that there was a practical aspect that exclusions were on occasion necessary to ensure the operation of the library:

I was talking before about reasons for visiting a library that were on the library side but on the personal side [...] you could be excluded by choice. That kind of self-exclusion. I acknowledge that there is that, people who will not visit and that's by choice [...] the practical aspect as well are that exclusions are sometimes necessary for the library to function. I wouldn't say harmoniously because it doesn't...harmony isn't always what you're striking (009)

Where there was an absence of understood rules, or where the cues of the environment may result in conflicting expectations of space usage, social policing became an issue. Social policing is the situation wherein the community is aware of rules or policies that apply to a given space or process and so members of the community keep on the lookout for violators of those policies. As humans, we seek predictable patterns and engage in normative behaviors (e.g., Chatman, 2000). Policies and rules inform the community of behavioral expectations of varying environments. Seeing others behaving in unexpected ways, that may be "breaking a rule" (using mobile phones, eating, speaking loudly, running, not wearing shoes, etc.) can lead to discomfort, annoyance, and even anger by other library users. Shushing of noisy library users (by other users) is a stereotypical library social policing activity. Even when the policy of imposed reverence is discontinued, not everyone is likely to be immediately aware of (or happy with) the policy change, and so may continue to feel justified in correcting the behaviors of others. This was a social concern and safety concern for some participants in this study:

[A] man came up and was excessively rude to us and very patronising and kind of yelled at us [...] I gave him my friendliest smile, and just said "look I'm so sorry, I asked the staff, this is where they told us to go, they've obviously made a mistake" [...] I remember thinking "there's a disconnect between the way the staff want this space to be used and the way it's being used" (007)

I have an anxiety disorder. At the moment I feel quite well but when something catastrophic goes wrong in my life [...] it would be really hard to use a library where I felt unsafe in. And so I think having places where you're not sort of looked at by staff as though you shouldn't be there, you're left to your own devices (005)

When this social policing occurs in a negative manner, and where there is not a security element such as a staff member to mitigate this occurrence, the desire of the individual to frequent social information spaces such as the public library can be unfavorably influenced. In having considered this, the library practitioner or researcher may ask: How are we maintaining and establishing the function of the library? How are we communicating our expectations for behavior? Do our social expectations still allow our users to feel this is a safe place? Can users choose different areas in the library; are there desks positioned where patrons can place their back to the wall or see out windows or doors? If there is a security guard, how do they demonstrate their presence? If there is not a security guard, do library staff fulfill this function? If so, how is this role enacted and how do library staff understand and communicate the mores of the space? Are there areas in the library that are regularly unmonitored?

While libraries should be inclusive to all, some exclusions that are communicated to individuals – such as around behavior and safety – can facilitate a library environment that is supportive of information seeking and information behavior around discovery.

Staff Behavior and Attitudes

Perceptions of staff behavior and attitudes can shape patron's information behavior around seeking and discovery. Some participants noted their invisible disability may impact on their communication patterns, or that staff attention could be difficult to either gain or to retain:

[F]or me with the brain injury, there's reading from a screen, I really have to print everything off, then again there's the concentration thing, the noise. Then there's aphasia, so if someone says "questions? Do you have any questions?" it might be in my head, coming out of my mouth could be a 24 hour delay, and they just think I'm an idiot (002)

I know I can be overly precise – which irritates people. But [...] it's like "I want this thing, and this is the one I need, and this is the edition I need, and this is where I need it from", and it's like – I think what autistic people find hard to understand is, "I'm giving you all the information you want, very clearly." That irritates people. They want to have small talk and kind of fluff all round those facts (003)

Imposed rules such as late fees could also be seen as a barrier:

It's just about getting there really [...] I read a lot so it makes a lot of sense to go to a public library, but it's just about getting there and then returning the books in a timely manner [...] it's just a bit of a challenge and I don't ever, I can't ever guarantee that I'll be able to do it (010)

Patrons can have a variety of information needs before they enter the library. When looking at staff attitudes and beliefs, information professionals might consider their own beliefs about their patron groups with questions including: Do we have our opening hours available online, and our busy or quiet periods? Do we have clear instructions on how to travel to the library via public transportation? Do we communicate to our community what our accessibility services include – and are we equipped to address the needs of community members in a thorough, meaningful way that is not tokenistic? Are library rules flexible, and are services available such as home delivery or quiet consultation rooms for staff and patrons? Are these services actively promoted to community members, or do we rely on community members to ask us? Are inclusive services created as a thoughtful and considered part of our programming, layout, and services, not an add-on?

Participants suggested that instead of requiring the individual to disclose their disability for assistance, staff indicate their disability awareness. This could be through an addition to staff name badges – such as "Ask me, I'm disability aware" or "Autism Ally". Libraries could also have posters or door signs indicating invisible disability awareness:

> Sometimes I've been in shops before, very, very rarely, but they'll have an "autism awareness" sticker or poster and you'll think "good, someone in this shop knows about autism", and it makes you feel - even if nothing happens and you don't need it and you don't find that person, it makes you feel a little bit better that people in that shop, somewhere, are thinking about autism and trying to understand it (003)

Signage could also be used to reduce the need for disability disclosure. Having signage indicating what an area was for, or where the toilets were, could reduce anxiety in visiting the public space. Tying back into the literature, signage could help users feel that they were able to ask for help:

> [I]f you had signage, like if you can't stand talk to our stuff, or this is a quiet area over here if you've got sensitivity. Just things to let people know that you can ask for help. I think if you ask for assistance, it can be a bit like a "well maybe this person's never thought of a healthy person asking for assistance before", like not healthy but looking healthy, do I have to do the whole education thing and is that even worth it for the support that I'll get? I think that even just something that lets you know that you can ask for help and it won't be seen as strange (010)

Libraries could also indicate invisible disability awareness and support via posters for support services for invisible disabilities in the toilet cubicles, such as for BeyondBlue or Black Dog--both free mental health services provided throughout Australia:

> When you have invisible mental illnesses like anxiety and depression you spend most of your time trying to believe that you actually have them and it's not just your fault. And I always, always love to see the reminder, any reminder, that depression is a real thing; that anxiety is a real thing; that chronic fatigue exists. It sounds really strange [...] I have absolutely no problem supporting, understanding, and acknowledging someone else with it but I cannot believe that of myself. So any reminder that it is a real thing that exists in the real world and that other people know it exists as well, just that sort of awareness that people do have it and visual signs of that are always helpful. (007)

Signage served three roles in the library; indicating staff awareness and knowledge, as an invitation to ask questions, and as a way to show library support for invisible disabilities. Confidence could therefore be generated by the environment, supporting the choice of the user to approach the library. Perceiving that staff were aware and experienced in invisible disabilities may positively influence the decision to consult.

CONCLUSION

Contemporary public libraries face several challenges when providing services to their communities. Invisible disabilities are prevalent in Australian communities; and as such, it is likely that a person with an invisible disability will at some time visit a public library. As one of the last free public services, libraries are increasingly serving a diverse demographic with a variety of needs, challenges, and expectations. As funding and staffing levels tighten, libraries need to consider how they can meet the information needs of their communities in low-cost, low-effort ways.

The paper has presented a variety of questions that library practitioners, researchers, and managers may ask themselves in considering how their library can contribute to information behaviors, including information seeking and information use. Additional questions that library managers may ask are: How does the library provide training in disability awareness to its staff, and what disabilities are considered? If the library has a disability inclusion or access plan, how does it discuss disability? How do libraries train new staff to understand accessibility and inclusion in the library? How are the voices of people with an invisible disability incorporated in strategic plans or in creating or revising library policy or mores?

Through these questions, the study has indicated ways that libraries can incorporate low-cost, low-effort means to enrich customer experiences of the library and better facilitate information seeking and discovery. As the experience of disability is personal these findings will not be applicable to all people with an invisible disability; however, this study aims to contribute to the field of library and information studies in several ways. First, the study contributes to the professional library literature on the experiences and needs of people with an invisible disability in the library sector. Second, the study contributes to the current literature on information behavior of people with a disability by exploring the little-documented area of people with an invisible disability. In view of the University of Sydney's Report on disability research, the predominate contribution of the study is in exploring the voices of people with an invisible disability as service users.

The study aimed to increase awareness for staff, practitioners, and researchers on how libraries may present barriers for information seeking and use that they may not necessarily experience themselves.

Libraries cannot solely expect patrons to identify if they have a disability. Libraries must provide a holistic service to all people in their communities, if they are to fulfill their stated purpose and mission of being truly inclusive to all.

ACKNOWLEDGMENTS

The authors acknowledge the support of Endeavour Foundation in the completion of this study. This research is supported by an Australian Government Research Training Program (RTP) Scholarship. The authors wish to thank the interviewees for their time and participation in this study, and the volunteers who provided helpful comments on previous versions of this document.

REFERENCES

Aabo, S. (2011). The value of public libraries: A socio-economic analysis. In M. Belotti, *Verso un'economia della biblioteca: finanziamenti, programmazione e valorizzazione in tempo di crisi* (pp. 169–176). Milano, Italy: Editrice Bibliografica.

Acking, C. A., & Kuller, H. (1972). The perception of an interior as a function of its colour. *Ergonomics, 15*(6), 645–654.

Alvesson, M. (2003). Methodology for close up studies - struggling with closenss and closure. *Higher Education, 46*, 167–193.

Ashcroft, L. (2003). Breaking the silence: The revolution in public libraries. *New Library World, 104*(4), 177.

Attitude Foundation. (n.d.). *What is invisible disability?* Retrieved from http://www.attitude.org.au/changing-attitudes/invisible-disability/

Australian Bureau of Statistics. (2016). *Disability, ageing and carers, Australia: Summary of findings, 2015.* Retrieved from https://www.abs.gov.au/ausstats/abs@.nsf/0/C258C88A7AA5A87ECA2568A9001393E8?Opendocument

Australian Human Rights Commission. (2011). *2010-2020: National Disability Strategy - an initiative of the Council of Australian Governments*. Canberra, Australia: Commonwealth of Australia.

Australian Network on Disability. (2019). *Disability statistics*. Retrieved from https://www.and.org.au/pages/disability-statistics.html

Autism Queensland. (n.d.). *Improving the employment participation of people with disability in Australia: Discussion paper*. Retrieved from https://submissions.employment.gov.au/empforms/Archive/Employment-Participation-of-People-with-Disability/Documents/Autism_Queensland.pdf

Babbie, E. R. (2005). *The basics of social research*. Belmont, CA: Thomson Wadsworth.

Beck, A. T., & Clark, D. A. (1988). Anxiety and depression: An information processing perspective. *Anxiety Research, 1*, 23–36.

Beverley, C. A., Bath, P. A., & Barber, R. (2007). Can two established information models explain the information behaviour of visually impaired people seeking health and social care information? *Journal of Documentation, 63*(1), 9–32.

Bialek, D. (n.d.). *The secret life of a public library security guard*. Retrieved from http://mentalfloss.com/article/72924/secret-life-public-library-security-guard

Breen, L. (2007). The researcher 'in the middle': Negotiating the insider/outsider dichotomy. *The Australian Community Psychologist, 19*(1), 163–174.

Brent, D. (2016). *But you don't look sick? Handicap parking and my invisible illness*. Retrieved from http://www.butyoudontlooksick.com/articles/guest-writers/handicap-parking-and-my-invisible-illness/

Burke, S. (2009). Perceptions of public library accessibility for people wth disabilities. *The Reference Librarian, 50* (1), 43–54.

Burns, K. K., & Gordon, G. L. (2010). Analyzing the impact of disability legislation in Canada and the United States. *Journal of Disability Policy Studies, 20*(4), 205–218.

Chatman, E. A. (2000). Framing social life in theory and research. *The New Review of Information Behaviour Research, 1*, 3–17.

Coldron, J., Cripps, C., & Shipton, L. (2010). Why are English secondary schools socially segregated? *Journal of Education Policy, 25*(1), 19–35.

Cordray, R., & Romanych, M. J. (2005). *Mapping the information environment*. IOSphere. Retrieved from http://www.au.af.mil/info-ops/iosphere/iosphere_summer05_cordray.pdf

Craven, J., & Booth, H. (2006). Putting awareness into practice: Practical steps for conducting usability tests. *Library Review, 55*(3), 179–194.

Day, R. (2007). Information connecting people with services: The information and referral role of community service organisations. *Australasian Public Libraries and Information Services, 20*(3), 103.

deMarrais, K. B. (2003). Qualitative interview studies: Learning through experience. In K. B. deMarrais & S. D. Lapan, *Foundations for research: Methods of inquiry in education and the social sciences*. New York, NY: Lawrence Erlbaum.

Disabled World. (2018). *Invisible disabilities: List and general information*. Retrieved from https://www.disabled-world.com/disability/types/invisible/

Dwyer, S., & Buckle, J. (2009). The space between: On being an insider-outsider in qualitative research. *International Journal of Qualitative Methods*, *8*(1), 54–63.

Equity Research Centre. (2007). *More than just equipment: Internet access and participation for people with a disability in Victorian public libraries*. Victoria, Australia: State Library of Victoria.

Feldman, S., & Tegart, G. (2013). Keep moving: Conceptions of illness and disability of middle-aged African-American women with athritis. In M. Banks & E. Kaschak, *Women with visible and invisible disabilities: Multiple intersections, multiple issues, multiple therapies* (pp. n.p). New York, NY: Routledge.

Feldshuh, H. (2018). Gender, media, and myth-making: Constructing China's leftover women. *Asian Journal of Communication*, *28*(1), 38–54.

Ferguson, P., Ferguson, D., & Taylor, S. (1992). *Interpreting disability: A qualitative reader*. New York, NY: Teachers College Press.

Fisher, K., Erdelez, S., & McKechnie, L. (2005). *Theories of information behaviour*. Medford, NJ: Information Today, Inc.

Fitzgerald, B., Hawkins, W., Denison, T., & Kop, T. (2015). Digital inclusion, disability, and public libraries: A summary Australian perspective. In P. Jaeger, B. Wentz, & J. C. Bertot, *Advances in librarianship: Accessibility for persons with disabilities and the inclusive future of libraries* (Vol. *40*, pp. 213–236). Bingley, England: Emerald Publishing Group Limited.

Gibson, A., & Kaplan, S. (2017). Place, community and information behavior: Spatially orientated information seeking zones and information source preferences. *Library and Information Science Research*, *29*, 131–139.

Goldberg, R., & Steury, S. (2001). Depression in the workplace: Costs and barriers to treatment. *Psychiatric Services*, *52*(12), 1639–1643.

Gray, C. A., & Garland, J. D. (1993). Social stories: Improving responses of students with autism with accurate social information. *Focus on Autistic Behavior*, *8*(1), 1–10.

Guba, E. G., & Lincoln, Y. S. (1994). Competing paradigms in qualitative research. In N. K. Denzin & Y. S. Lincoln, *Handbook of qualitative research* (pp. 105–117). Thousand Oaks, CA: SAGE.

Hepworth, M. (2007). Knowledge of information behaviour and its relevance to the design of people-centred information products and services. *Journal of Documentation*, *63* (1), 33–56.

Hill, H. (2013). Disability and accessibility in the library and information science literature: A content analysis. *Library and Information Science Research*, *35*, 137–142.

Homelessness Australia. (2013). *Homelessness and disability*. Retrieved from http://www.homelessnessaustralia.org.au/images/publications/Fact_Sheets/Disability.pdf

Houghton, K. (2014). The local library across the digital and physical city: Opportunities for economic development. *Commonwealth Journal of Local Governance*, *15*, 39–60.

House with No Steps. (2015). *Types of disability*. Retrieved from http://www.hwns.com.au/Resource-centre/Types-of-disabilities

House with No Steps. (2017). *5 things about invisible disabilities you need to know*. Retrieved from https://www.hwns.com.au/about-us/blog/5-things-about-invisible-disabilities-you-need-to-know/

Hurtig, R., Ensrud, S., & Tomblin, J. (1982). The communicatinve function of question production in autistic children. *Journal of Autism and Developmental Disorders*, *12*, 57–69.

Hussain, A. (2000). Preface. In S. Hick, E. Halpin, & E. Hoskins, *Human rights and the internet* (pp. x–xii). England: Macmillan Press Ltd.

Inglis, P., & McAnelly, S. (2015). Guiding principle 2: The importance of providing accessible information for people with learning disabilities. In S. McAnelly, S. Atkinson, J. Lay, & M. Richardson, *Intellectual disability in health and social care* (pp. 21–34). Oxon, England: Routledge.

Ingraham, C. (2015). Libraries and their publics: Rhetorics of the public library. *Rhetoric Review*, *34*(2), 147–163.

Invisible Disabilities Association. (2003). *Don't judge by appearances*. Retrieved from https://invisibledisabilities.org/ida-books-pamphlets/accessibleparking/dontjudgebyappearances/

Irvall, B., & Nielsen, G. S. (2005). *Access to libraries for persons with disabilities* (Vol. *89*). The Hague, Netherlands: International Federation of Library Associations and Institutions.

Irwin, M. (1995). Living in the community. In L. Walling & M. Irwin, *Information services for people with developmental disabilities: The library manager's handbook* (pp. 75–82). Westport, CT: Greenword Press.

Jaeger, P., Bertot, J. C., Thompson, K., Katz, S., & DeCoster, E. (2012). The intersection of public policy and public access: Digital divides, digital literacy, digital inclusion, and public libraries. *Public Library Quarterly*, *31*(1), 1–20.

Jaeger, P., & Bowman, C. (2005). *Understanding disability: Inclusion, access, diversity, and civil rights*. USA: Praeger Publishers.

Johnson, V. (2012). Security and libraries? *Incite, 33*(9), 18.

Julien, H. (1992). A content analysis of the recent needs and uses literature. *Library and Information Science Research, 18*, 53–65.

Kelley, A., Riggleman, K., Clara, I., & Navarro, A. (2017). Determining the need for social work practice in a public library. *Journal of Community Practice, 25*(1), 112–125.

Klauber, J. (1998). Living well with a disability: How libraries can help. *American Libraries, 29*(10), 52–56.

Kodama, A. (1990). The problems of environmental colour design in Japan. *Ergonomics, 33*(6), 763–774.

Kovach, J. (2018). *Still no security guards for Peterborough Public Library*. Retrieved from https://www.thepeterboroughexaminer.com/news-story/8346190-still-no-security-guards-for-peterborough-public-library/

Kuller, R., Ballal, S., Laike, T., Mikellides, B., & Tonello, G. (2006). The impact of light and colour on psychological mood: A cross-cultural study of indoor work environments. *Ergonomics, 49*(14), 1496–1507.

Labuschagne, A. (2003). *Qualitative research: Airy fairy or fundamental? The Qualitative Report, 8(1)*. Retrieved from http://www.nova.edu/ssss/QR/QR8-1/labuschagne.html

McBride, K. (2017). *Librarians in the 21st Century: We need to talk about library security*. Retrieved from https://lithub.com/librarians-in-the-21st-century-we-need-to-talk-about-library-security/

McKeown, A. (2016). *Overcoming information poverty: Investigating the role of public libraries in the twenty-first century*. Cambridge, MA: Elsevier Ltd.

Morley, J. (2000). *Mainstreaming disability services in Victorian public libraries - report, recommendations and key performance indicators*. Retrieved from http://www.libraries.vic.gov.au/downloads/Library_Network_Unit/disabrep.pdf

Mullins, L., & Preyde, M. (2013). The lived experience of students with an invisible disability at a Canadian university. *Disability & Society, 28*(2), 147–160.

Murphy, F. (2018). *Deciding to disclose an invisible disability*. Retrieved from https://www.eurekastreet.com.au/article/deciding-to-disclose-an-invisible-disability

Mutula, S., & Majine, R. (2016). Information behaviour of students living with visual impairments in university libraries: A review of related literature. *The Journal of Academic Librarianship, 42*, 522–528.

Nandhakumar, J., & Jones, M. (1997). Too close for comfort? Distance and engagement in interpreteive information systems research. *Information Systems Journal, 7*, 109–131.

Niedzwiedzka, B., & Korycinska, P. (2016). Are online forums a useful resource for the study of health needs and related information behaviour? Linguistic analysis of two online forums for people with mental disorders. *Public Health Management / Zdrowie Publiczne i Zarządzanie, 14*(2), 118–130.

Niu, X., & Hemminger, B. M. (2012). A study of factors that affect the information-seeking behavior of academic scientists. *Journal of the American Society for Information Science and Technology, 63*(2), 336–353.

O'Hara, A. (2006). The microskills of interviewing. In A. O'Hara & Z. Weber, *Skills for human service practice* (pp. 119–136). South Melbourne, Australia: Oxford University Press.

Pickard, A. J. (2013). *Research methods in information* (2nd ed.). London, England: Facet.

Pilling, M. (2013). Invisible identity in the workplace: Intersectional madness and processes of disclosure at work. *Disability Studies Quarterly, 33*(1).

Public Libraries Victoria Network. (2013). *Victorian public libraries 2030: Strategic framework*. Melbourne, Australia: State Library of Victoria.

Quinn, S., & McCallum, I. (2012). *Beyond a quality service: Strengthening the social fabric - standards and guidelines for Australian public libraries*. Canberra, Australia: ALIA House.

Ricci, C. (2016). *Disability discrimination and disclosure in recruitment and employment*. Retrieved from https://www.humanrights.gov.au/news/speeches/site-navigation-67

Robertson, L. (2007). *Access for library users with disabilities*. Retrieved from https://www.sconul.ac.uk/sites/default/files/documents/access_disabilities_0.pdf

Sambo, A., Rabiu, N., & Shaba, A. (2016). Physically challenged students and their information needs. *Library Philosophy and Practice*.

Samure, K., & Given, L. M. (2004). Digitally enhanced? An examination of the information behaviours of visually impaired post-secondary students. *The Canadian Journal of Information and Library Science, 28*(2), 25–42.

Schomberg, J., & Cole, K. (2017). *Hush...: The dangers of silence in academic libraries*. Retrieved from http://www.inthelibrarywiththeleadpipe.org/2017/hush-the-dangers-of-silence-in-academic-libraries/

Shaffer, C., Vardaman, L., & Miller, D. (2010). Library usage trends and needs of international students. *Behavioral & Social Sciences Librarian, 29*(2), 109–117.

Small, R. V., Myhill, W. N., & Herring-Harrington, L. (2015). Developing accessible libraries and inclusive librarians in the 21st Century: Examples from practice. In B. Wentz, P. T. Jaeger, & J. C. Bertot, *Accessibility for persons with disabilities and the inclusive future of libraries. Advances in librarianship* (Vol. *40*, pp. 73–88). Bradford, England: Emerald Publishing Group Ltd.

Spink, A. (2010). *Information behaviour: An evolutionary instinct*. Heidelberg, Germany: Springer-Verlag.

Spirito Dalgin, R., & Bellini, J. (2008). Invisible disability disclosure in an employment interview: Impact on employer's hiring decisions and views of employability. *Rehabilitation Counseling Bulletin*, *52*(1), 6–15.

Todaro, A. (2005). Library services for people with disabilities in Argentina. *New Library World*, *106*(1212/1213), 253–268.

Torrey, E. F., Esposito, R., & Geller, J. (2009). Problems associated with mentally ill individuals in public libraries. *Public Libraries*, *48*(2), 45–21.

University of Sydney. (2014). *Report of audit of disability research in Australia*. Sydney, Australia: Centre for Disability Research and Policy.

University of Sydney. (2017). *Audit of disabiltiy research in Australia update report 2017*. Sydney, Australia: Centre for Disability Research and Policy.

University Wire. (2018). *Concerns for library and noise issues*. Retrieved from https://search-proquest-com.ezproxy.csu.edu.au/docview/2132290751?accountid=10344

Wellstead, P. (2010). Delivery of everyday life information: Opportunities and challenges for the library and information profession in Australia. *The Australian Library Journal*, *59*(3), 95–107.

Williams, R. (2016). "We're not allowed": Public librarians' perspectives on providing health information to library users experiencing homelessness. *Computer Science*, *53* (1), 1–10.

Working Together Project, (n.d.). *Communities-led libraries toolkit*. Retrieved from https://www.vpl.ca/sites/vpl/public/Community-Led-Libraries-Toolkit.pdf?

Yavuz, N., & Welch, E. (2010). Addressing fear of crime in public space: Gender differences in reaction to safety measures in train transit. *Urban Studies*, *47*(12), 2491–2515.

Librarian Role-Playing as a Method for Assessing Student Information Literacy Skills

Soo Young Rieh
University of Texas at Austin,
Austin, TX, USA
rieh@ischool.utexas.edu

Doreen Bradley
University of Michigan Library,
Ann Arbor, MI, USA
dbradley@umich.edu

Emma Brennan-Wydra
University of Michigan,
Ann Arbor, MI, USA
ebwydra@umich.edu

Tori Culler
University of Michigan,
Ann Arbor, MI, USA
tculler@umich.edu

Elizabeth Hanley
University of Michigan,
Ann Arbor, MI, USA
hanleyel@umich.edu

Marley Kalt
University of Michigan,
Ann Arbor, MI, USA
marleyk@umich.edu

ABSTRACT

Researchers and practitioners alike have long investigated the effectiveness of information literacy instruction, addressing what to measure regarding student learning and how to measure it. The purpose of this paper is twofold. First, we review measures and methods that have been developed to assess student learning that results from information literacy instruction. We then present a study in which we employed a new research method of librarian role-playing to examine the extent to which college students are capable of demonstrating their information literacy skills while acting as an academic librarian. We also incorporated card-sorting exercises, asking about their perceived search difficulty before and after the role-playing exercise. Ten role-playing sessions were conducted by recruiting undergraduate students who had attended an information literacy instruction session 3–4 months prior as a part of their English writing course. Results showed that the librarian role-playing method provided opportunities for participants to recall and reflect upon what they learned from information literacy instruction effectively. Results also indicated that the role-playing method is potentially effective in developing students' meta-cognition about their search behavior.

KEYWORDS

Methods and Measures in Information Literacy Instruction; Method for Assessing Student Learning in Library Instruction; Role-Playing in Information Literacy

82nd Annual Meeting of the Association for Information Science & Technology | Melbourne, Australia | 19–23 October, 2019

DOI: 10.1002/pra2.00018

ASIS&T THESAURUS

Research Methods; Library User Instruction; Information Behavior

INTRODUCTION

There has been substantial discussion and research among library practitioners and library and information science researchers alike about what to teach and how to deliver information literacy instruction. Researchers and practitioners have also investigated the effectiveness of instruction, focusing on two research problems: *what to measure* regarding student learning in information literacy instruction and *how to measure it*. The first problem, what to measure, raises differing views concerning criteria and measurements of information literacy. Often this debate is related to how information literacy is defined: as a set of skills, or as concepts that enable critical thinking (Lloyd, 2010). Researchers and librarians have attempted to identify qualitative measures based on reflective narratives that can assess students' higher-level cognitive learning in ways that go beyond quantitative information literacy measurements (McKinney & Sen, 2012). In 2016, the Association of College and Research Libraries (ACRL) adopted the *Framework for Information Literacy for Higher Education*, taking a new direction in information literacy instruction as it moved away from its previous focus on locating, evaluating, and using information and began emphasizing meta-cognitive processes such as self-reflection and recognition of information value. To address the second research problem, how to measure student learning resulting from information literacy instruction, a number of research methods have been developed and employed over the years. Pre- and post-instruction surveys, individual interviews, focus group interviews, evaluation of student assignments or quizzes, and lab-based experimental studies have been widely used (Markey, Leeder, & Rieh, 2014).

Although there have been active discussions and studies regarding what to measure and how to measure student learning as a result of receiving information literacy instruction, many measures and methods have focused on investigating the impact of information literacy instruction through self-reports (e.g., surveys, questionnaires, interviews) or implicit indicators (e.g., quizzes, assignments, and lab-based experimental studies). However, these measures or methods may not offer sufficient evidence to demonstrate students' ability to conduct library research while also recalling, reflecting on, and articulating what they have learned from information literacy instruction.

This research problem led us to design an alternative research method that adopts *librarian role-playing* as a technique for investigating the extent to which students are capable of demonstrating their information literacy skills while acting as an academic librarian. Role-playing is an activity in which "participants act out a set of defined role behaviors or position with a view to acquiring desired experiences" (Sogunro, 2014, p. 356). Specifically, we asked study participants to act as librarians giving instructions to an incoming college student about how to use the academic library system in order to find scholarly articles to prepare for a writing placement test. We also incorporated card-sorting exercises, asking about the perceived difficulty of seven different types of search behavior before and after completing the role-playing task. We developed the librarian role-playing method to assess student learning in information literacy instruction because we believe that this method offers researchers and practitioners the potential to measure students' information literacy skills and perceptions of difficulty more accurately than other research methods used in previous work.

Role-playing has long been used as a training method for nurses, salespersons, and classroom teachers (Martinez Riera, Cibanal, & Mora, 2010) because of its ability to impart effective problem solving skills as well as insight, sensitivity, and awareness. Role-playing offers learners the opportunity to associate enacted roles, attitudes, and behaviors with real-life situations (Sogunro, 2004). From a teaching perspective, it emphasizes different points of view by enabling participants to examine their own behavior while experimenting with new attitudes (Carlomagno, Di Tore, & Sibilio, 2014).

In the field of library and information science, Mess (1994) introduced role-playing exercises as an instructional technique and discussed how "interactive modules" (p. 115) that adapt role-playing can be used for library instruction in a classroom setting. Sheets (1998) used role-playing to train student library assistants by placing a student assistant at the reference desk and having a librarian act as a patron by approaching the desk and asking a reference question. However, to the best of our knowledge, there has been no previous research on using role-playing as a method of assessing students' information literacy skills in conjunction with information literacy instruction.

The motivation for this research is our belief that it is important to develop a novel and performative research method to assess college students' abilities to search for and evaluate information in library systems that goes beyond studying the effectiveness of information literacy instruction programs. It is commonly understood that being able to teach a concept is a solid indicator of mastery of that concept. Therefore, evaluating how well students are able to take on the role of a librarian who teaches concepts involved in searching for and evaluating information is a creative and effective method.

The purpose of this paper is twofold. First, we review a variety of measures that have been developed and methods that have been employed to assess student learning that results from library instruction. We then present a study examining the benefits and drawbacks of librarian role-playing as a new research method that can be used to demonstrate students' information literacy skills. In this paper, we are particularly focused on students' information literacy skills with respect to searching for and evaluating information when using an academic library system. This paper addresses three research questions:

1. To what extent do college students recall and reflect on the learning they gain from an information literacy instruction session when they engage in librarian role-playing?
2. How do college students feel when they play the role of academic librarian to demonstrate their search behavior using an academic library system?
3. What are the benefits and drawbacks of using the librarian role-playing method to assess information searching and evaluation skills?

MEASURING LEARNING OUTCOMES IN INFORMATION LITERACY

Conceptualizing information literacy has long been a topic of discussion among librarians, faculty, and institutions of higher education. Notions of what constitutes *information literacy* continue to evolve, as do the methods used to measure student abilities. Information literacy is considered foundational to life-long learning. Cultivating the ability to find, understand, evaluate, and synthesize information is essential to learning within and beyond an academic curriculum. Information literacy is sometimes associated with competence in a set of skills, such as the *Information Literacy Competency Standards for Higher Education*, which can be discretely taught and measured (ACRL, 2000). The scholarly conversation shifts significantly with the discussion of information literacy in terms of a series of six frames through which students understand the theory and practice of information and its use (Bruce, Edwards, & Lupton, 2006).

Lloyd (2010) explores this dichotomy of whether information literacy is a skills-based literacy or a critical thinking process that serves as a catalyst for learning. Lloyd argues that context is a critical element of information literacy, lending more credence to the developing notion that information literacy is more conceptually based, rather than a set of independent skills. ACRL rescinded its original *Information Literacy Competency Standards for Higher Education* (ACRL, 2000) and replaced them with the highly conceptual *Framework for Information Literacy for Higher Education* (ACRL, 2016). With this framework, ACRL significantly moved the pendulum on the skills vs. conceptual debate on a national scale. Gone are the specific skills and in their place are *knowledge practices* and *dispositions* for each of six frameworks that information literate students should demonstrate. It suggests a framework within which librarians and faculty can collaborate to teach information literacy and firmly embeds information literacy in the scholarly process. While there are certainly skills that students should master, the core of the current information literacy debate is clearly centered in a conceptual model.

The *Information Literacy Competency Standards for Higher Education* (ACRL, 2000) presented an extensive list of skills that were incorporated into assessment projects. Assessing the construction of a search strategy or the selection of an appropriate database for a given topic are measurements that are easy to conduct and replicate. Many studies also seek to assess skills or factual knowledge at a very granular level, such as using the library catalog and academic databases to conduct searches (e.g., Bryan & Karshmer, 2013; Zhang, Goodman, & Xie, 2015). There are also numerous studies that assess students' skills in evaluating sources of information based on credibility (Bryan & Karshmer, 2013; Hess, 2014; Hufford, 2010; Zhang et al., 2015).

Studies investigating changes in *behavior* following library instruction have included questions about using library resources and conducting searches (Hess, 2014; Zhang et al., 2015), while commonly measured student *attitudes* include levels of research confidence or self-efficacy (Brennan-Wydra & Culler, 2019), comfort using or getting help from the library (Hess, 2014), and information anxiety (Halpern, 2016) before and after intervention.

With the adoption of the *Framework for Information Literacy for Higher Education* (ACRL, 2016), the road has been paved for many new methods that can assess information literacy at the conceptual level. In addition to quantitative measures, librarians may also look at qualitative measures using reflective evaluation measures and other processes that can assess students' higher-level reasoning and decision making. The *ACRL Framework for Information Literacy Sandbox* is designed to aid librarians in designing activities and assessments to measure student learning outcomes using the new framework (ACRL, 2017). As the ACRL Framework is adopted at institutions across the country, more studies will be designed to assess the conceptual approach to information literacy.

RESEARCH METHODS USED IN PREVIOUS WORK

Pre- and Post-test Surveys

Pe7rhaps one of the most widely used methods of measuring what students learn from library instruction is pre- and post-instruction surveys. Surveys are an appealing assessment tool because they allow researchers to collect data from a relatively large number of participants with little effort on the part of either the researchers or the participants, and because the quantitative data obtained from multiple-choice survey questions can be analyzed quickly and easily using appropriate statistical techniques. Administering surveys to students before (pre-test) and after (post-test) they attend library instruction sessions allows researchers to draw empirical conclusions about how student knowledge, behaviors, and/or attitudes changed across the period of data collection. These surveys may be administered across multiple modes, including online (Halpern, 2016; Hess, 2014), and on paper (Bryan & Karshmer, 2013). The amount of time between the administration of the pre- and post-test surveys varies widely among studies, from less than an hour to several months (Hufford, 2010).

Data collected from student surveys are most often analyzed using descriptive statistics, such as percentages and averages, to identify differences between students' responses before and after receiving library instruction. As noted by Walker and Pearce (2014), however, descriptive statistics can provide some insight into student learning but cannot determine whether or not changes in student responses were statistically significant. A smaller number of studies (Bryan & Karshmer, 2013; Halpern, 2016) have used inferential statistics in a formal hypothesis testing framework, such as *t*-tests and analysis of covariance (ANCOVA), to obtain more conclusive and generalizable results. Surveys have been used to assess not only the efficacy of single library workshops (Hufford, 2010) but also relative gains from different instructional formats (Bryan & Karshmer, 2013; Hess, 2014).

One major drawback of using surveys to understand and assess student learning is that the closed-ended, multiple-choice questions commonly employed may be too simplistic to accurately capture student learning. To combat this drawback, several studies have combined surveys with additional modes of data collection. For example, Mery, Newby, and Peng (2011) used a three-phase study design to assess the impact a library-based course had on students' information literacy skills: (1) collection of qualitative data via focus groups, reflection papers, and discussion forums; (2) collection of quantitative data through pre- and post-test surveys; and (3) evaluation of the quality of student work. In addition, Zhang et al. (2015) supplemented the quantitative data obtained from pre- and post-test surveys with qualitative data from two student focus group sessions consisting of open-ended questions about an online library instruction module. Combining quantitative survey data with other sources of information provides evidence of construct validity for home-grown survey instruments and provides a more complete picture of student experiences in information literacy instruction sessions.

Individual and Focus Group Interviews

Interviews and focus groups are more resource-intensive than other methods, meaning that the financial and time investments required to conduct interviews can be prohibitive. In some cases, researchers have attempted to conduct information literacy-related interviews but later abandoned the method due to time and resource constraints (Emmett & Emde, 2007). However, interviews and focus groups do provide additional insights into information literacy assessment that cannot be gained by static methods such as surveys. Interviews add an extra dimension to understandings of students' abilities, providing additional indicators of student knowledge (Dunn, 2002; Emde & Emmett, 2004). Asking students in person about search behaviors gives researchers the opportunity to witness meaningful steps that students take, which may reveal students' competencies beyond self-reports. In-person interactions can also be seen as a way to emphasize the importance of information literacy and cultivate relationships between students and librarians, thereby serving an educational purpose beyond that of assessment (Emmett & Emde, 2007).

A few studies have introduced a performance-based element into assessment interviews for information literacy. Dunn (2002) explored scenarios as part of a multi-year assessment of California State University core competencies, which mapped closely onto ACRL standards for information literacy. Depth and breadth of student understanding were found to be associated, and student proficiency was found to be relatively steady across competencies. In another performance-based interview, Emde and Emmett (2004) conducted a within-subjects study in which students were interviewed at the beginning and end of a semester. Students were presented with information seeking scenarios during the interviews, including how to navigate the library website and find items using the library catalog. Student performance at the beginning of the semester was compared to performance at the end and was overall found to have improved over the course of the semester.

Across studies, interview and focus group methodologies have proven valuable as means of dynamically assessing information literacy. The interpersonal nature of interviews and focus groups allows researchers to observe the process through which students reason about information, providing potentially richer insights than those provided by static surveys.

Student Assignments and Quizzes

Evaluation of student assignments completed in relation to library instruction sessions has been used as a technique for assessing student learning. Examples of student assignments include student research papers (Cooke & Rosenthal, 2011; Gamtso & Paterson, 2012; Luetkenhaus, Hvizdak, & Johnson, 2017), student worksheets administered as part of the instruction session (Matlin & Lantzy, 2017), and quizzes (Lowe, Boothe, & Tagg, 2014). Evaluation of student research papers is the most common way that this assessment technique has been implemented. Gamtso and Paterson (2012), for example, examined students' final papers written as part of a three-workshop series in which students were asked to solve a problem working as a group in collaboration with librarians, researchers, and instructors. Analysis of these final papers revealed students' ability to apply critical thought and provide well-crafted recommendations, indicating that this collaborative, active-learning exercise helped students move beyond merely learning information retrieval skills to learning how to analyze and apply information. Similarly, Luetkenhaus et al. (2017) used students' final research papers to measure the impact of library instruction for first-year students, having raters from across the library provide feedback on students' demonstration of information literacy skills. Cooke and Rosenthal (2011), on the other hand, took a slightly different approach to analyzing student research papers, examining the citation pages of the papers as opposed to the content. They found richer bibliographies among students who had received library instruction.

Another way student assignments have been integrated is by making them part of the library instruction session itself. Matlin and Lantzy (2017), for example, used a backwards instructional design process to identify learning outcomes and created library assignments accordingly to measure achievement of those outcomes from in-person vs., online library instruction. These assignments had students practice basic library skills, such as finding articles via library databases using relevant keywords and generating properly formatted citations, while also reflecting on the differences between scholarly literature and popular sources. The researchers found this method to be fruitful in eliciting student responses but did not find statistically significant differences between the online and in-person groups.

Researchers have also used testing and quizzes as a method for assessing student learning from information literacy instruction. Lowe et al. (2014), for example, developed a quiz that was integrated into an online information literacy tutorial at their library. They reported that this quiz provided valuable insights into first-year students' information literacy skills over time, which in turn increased librarians' ability to tailor student instruction.

Lab-based Experimental Studies

Experimental studies are not very prevalent in the literature assessing the impact of library instruction. When experimental studies appear in the library instruction literature, they often employ a pre-test and post-test design (e.g., responses are measured before and after the intervention and then compared) (Koufogiannakis & Wiebe, 2006; Van Scoyoc, 2003), but may also use a post-test only design (Mery, DeFrain, Kline, & Sult, 2014; Salisbury, Omolewu, & Smith, 2018). Experimental studies have been used in a variety of ways, including to test different library instruction methods (Mery et al., 2014), measure which type of instruction best alleviates library anxiety (Van Scoyoc, 2003), and quantify the effect of cell phone use during library instruction sessions (Salisbury et al., 2018).

Experimental studies can be difficult to implement in library instruction assessment because researchers usually only have access to participants who have already been formed into groups, such as university classes, rather than a subject pool of individuals who can be randomly assigned to different groups (Koufogiannakis & Wiebe, 2006). Due to these limitations, experimental studies in library instruction assessment typically apply randomization to entire groups of participants, for example, by randomly choosing which classes are in the control and which are in the treatment group, rather than randomly assigning individual participants to treatment or control groups (Koufogiannakis & Wiebe, 2006; Salisbury et al., 2018; Van Scoyoc, 2003).

ROLE-PLAYING AS A METHOD OF ASSESSING STUDENT LEARNING IN INFORMATION LITERACY INSTRUCTION

Data Collection

To investigate student learning in library instruction sessions, we designed our research in two phases. The students who participated in the study were undergraduate students in multiple sections of an English "writing and academic inquiry" course at a Midwestern research university in the Fall 2018 semester, the majority of whom were in their first year of college.

In Phase I, pre- and post-session online surveys were disseminated across eleven one-shot library instruction sessions taught by the same librarian. The pre-session survey was administered in class by displaying the survey link on-screen right before the library instruction was given, and the post-session survey was administered by contacting the students by email about two weeks later. Ten questions in the surveys focused on three areas of college-level information literacy: conducting searches, evaluating sources, and navigating the university library system. The results of paired *t*-tests for students who completed both surveys (N = 45) revealed areas in which respondents showed the greatest pre- and post- differences: how to get to articles using the library website (Mean change = +1.73, $t(36) = 10.07$, $p < .001$); how to use the library to do research (Mean change = +1.35, $t(36) = 7.40$, $p < .001$); and how to get research help from the library (Mean change = +1.27, $t(36) = 6.89$, $p < .001$) (Brennan-Wydra & Culler, 2019). The areas in which respondents did not report improvement were persistence in searching, credibility assessment, and relevance judgment (Brennan-Wydra & Culler, 2019). However, this method relied on gathering data about students' self-reported confidence levels. With pre- and post-session survey responses alone, we were not able to identify specific areas in which students struggled most in performing library research.

Being aware of the limitations in the results from Phase I, we decided to design another phase of the study that would allow us to supplement our quantitative data from student surveys with additional data coming from three different sources: (1) librarian role-playing; (2) card sorting exercises on perceived difficulty in various kinds of search behavior prior to role-playing and afterwards; (3) an opening interview and an exit interview. Figure 1 displays the procedures for each session.

In the Spring 2019 semester, we emailed 159 students who completed a pre-session survey in Phase I, inviting them to participate in the Phase II follow-up study. For the role-playing component, we began with a short exercise about finding the location of classrooms using the university website, which took 2–5 minutes. This exercise was included to make participants more comfortable in the interview environment and did not factor into the assessment outcomes. Once study participants completed this short exercise, the librarian role-playing session began. Note that while participants were asked to play the role of a librarian, the researcher pretended to be an incoming first-year student who needed help from the librarian to find scholarly resources using the library system.

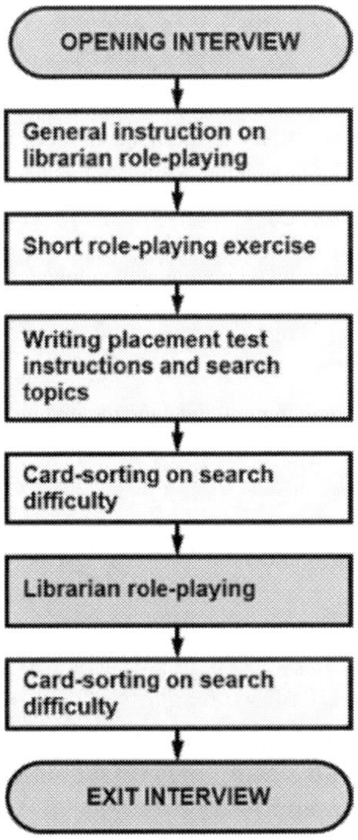

Figure 1. Data collection procedures.

The role-playing oral instruction given to study participants appears in Figure 2.

> Next, we will have a section where I ask you to put yourself in the shoes of a librarian. I'll ask you to imagine yourself as a librarian, and you'll have the chance to demonstrate how you might help an incoming student who needs your help finding scholarly sources. For this portion of the interview, you are now a librarian. I am an incoming first year student, and I have a couple of questions about navigating the University and my coursework.

Figure 2. Librarian role-playing script.

The researcher read the following script to participants: "I need to complete the placement test for writing before I start classes in the Fall, and have been given a few options for topics. I need to use scholarly sources, but am not sure where to start. Can you help me find at least 3-5 scholarly articles to use for my paper, on any one of these topics?" The researcher then gave out a paper copy of the "writing test instructions" to the participants. The instructions stated that all incoming students needed to write an academic essay in 1,200-1,500 words on one of four topics. The essay instructions read, "If you need any assistance completing your writing placement test, you are able to consult with a librarian to gain a better understanding of scholarly work and the research process."

Participants were asked to choose one topic out of four search topics for which they felt most comfortable finding information. All four search topics were real essay topics that one of the authors, who is a librarian at the university, received as reference questions from undergraduate students.

Topic 1: How does sleep deprivation among college students affect their academic achievement?

Topic 2: How does college students' use of energy drinks and/or ADHD medications affect their academic achievement?

Topic 3: How can childhood obesity rates be reduced in the U.S.? What are recommended best practices to reduce childhood obesity in the U.S.?

Topic 4: How effective are anti-homeless laws in reducing homeless rates in American cities?

Figure 3. Search topics given to study participants who played librarian role.

Another technique used in this study was card-sorting exercises (St. Jean, Taylor, Kodama, & Subramaniam, 2018), which were administered before and after the role-playing exercise. The card sorting method was employed to compare participants' perceptions of difficulty in conducting searches and evaluating sources when using the academic library system. Participants were instructed to rank the content of each card on a difficulty scale of 1-5 by placing each card onto a sheet of paper with the difficulty level: 1 = not at all difficult, 2 = a little difficult, 3 = somewhat difficult, 4 = difficult and 5 = very difficult. The seven cards were made using 3" X 5" cardstock. Before handing over the cards to a participant after the participant had selected a research topic, the researcher shuffled them to ensure they would be in random order. Each card contained a brief description of a different aspect of the search process:

- Figuring out where to start/where to look when beginning a search
- Thinking of keywords that will retrieve relevant information on my topic
- Judging the information with regard to its relevance
- Judging the information with regard to its trustworthiness/credibility
- Differentiating scholarly articles from non-scholarly ones
- Using the university library to get full-text articles
- Choosing the best sources on the topic

Once participants placed each card on one of the printed scales, the researcher took a picture to record the choices. After the participants completed the role-playing exercise, they were asked if they wanted to move any of the cards from one point on the scale to another to see if their perception of task difficulty had changed.

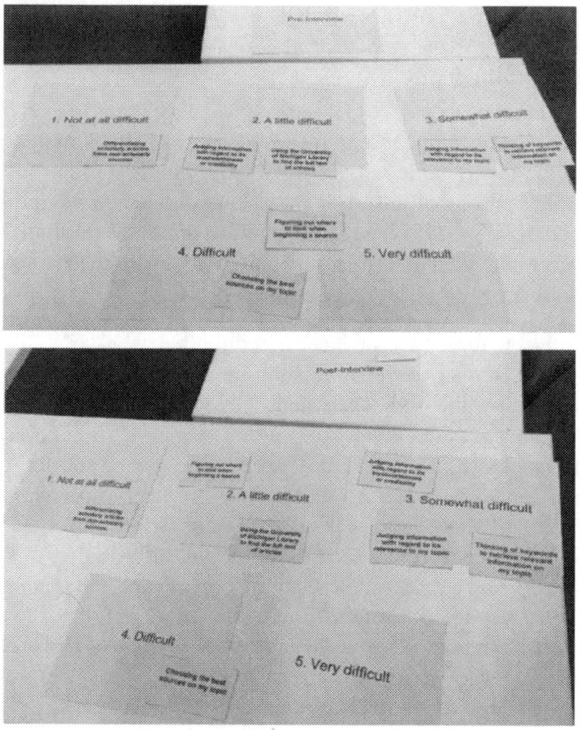

Figure 4. Card-sorting exercises.

Several interview questions were asked before and after the role-playing session. The opening interview included background questions about the year participants started at the university, their school/program, and their major. Two key questions asked at this stage were: (1) if they remembered anything from the library instruction session; (2) if the library instruction had changed the way they searched for information.

The exit interview questions included: (1) how did you feel during the search process? How did it feel to explain what you were doing to someone else?; (2) which part of the search process did you find most challenging to explain? Why?; (3) do you feel your searches were successful? Why or why not?; (4) is this how you typically would search? Did you do something differently because you played the role of librarian?; (5) after you've done this, is there anything else about library research that you wish that you had learned from the instruction session?; (6) are there any concepts or skills related to library research that you would like to improve?; (7) is there anything else you want to tell us, or do you have any questions for us before we finish the interview?

The entire session, including the opening interview, card-sorting prior to the role-playing, searching during the role-playing, card-sorting after the role-playing, and exit interview were audio-recorded and fully transcribed for data analysis. Each session took about 35 minutes, ranging from 20 to 45 minutes. The average length of audio recording was 30 minutes. Participants were compensated US $20.00 in cash for participation.

Data Analysis

The data were analyzed inductively through three phases. In the initial phase, we looked for ideas, issues, and patterns from the transcripts to develop codes. The initial codes included remembering library instruction session, takeaways from library instruction, reflection on library instruction, changes in search behavior after instruction, applying session content, demonstrating search skills, demonstrating information evaluation abilities, feeling during the search process, perception of successful search, confidence in searching, difficulty/challenges in role-playing, and general feeling about role-playing. In the second phase, we identified major categories by clarifying initial codes and merging some codes. The categories that emerged were recalling library instruction, reflection on library instruction, demonstrating/explaining search behavior, information literacy skills, role-playing experience, and value of role-playing. In the final stage, we aligned the categories with respect to our three research questions.

RESULTS

Out of 159 undergraduate students who completed a pre-library instruction session survey in Phase 1, 10 students volunteered to participate in the role-playing sessions. All participants except one reported that they began their undergraduate program in 2018 and were in their first year of college at the time of the session. One person began in 2017. Their major/interest areas were diverse: neuroscience, computer science, biology, political science, industrial design, music, and nursing. Eight participants were female and two were male. They all attended one-shot library instruction sessions taught by the same librarian in the Fall 2018 semester, which were offered as a part of a "writing and academic inquiry" course. For all participants, it had been about 3-4 months since they had attended a library instruction session. In terms of search topics used in the role-playing session (see Figure 3), seven participants (P01, P03, P04, P06, P07, P08, and P10) chose Topic 1 (sleep deprivation), two participants (P05 and P09) searched on Topic 2 (use of energy drinks and ADHD medications) and one participant (P02) selected Topic 3 (childhood obesity). No participant chose Topic 4 (anti-homeless laws).

Research Question 1: *To what extent do college students recall and reflect on the learning they gain from an information literacy instruction session when they engage in librarian role-playing?*

Most participants were able to recall a few things covered in the information literacy instruction, and some were able to reflect on the content in detail. P09 seemed to recall key takeaways very well: "I remember the instructor…walked through…what good sources to use, like what differentiates a good source from a bad source and how to validate your argument basically with supporting sources and how to find them through the library's website." P02 said that she remembered "going through different databases and libraries that we have access to online," saying "it definitely showed me new ways to do (things) such as accessing the libraries online and librarians here were able to help us so much." Likewise, P01 recalled that the session "was pretty much everything about the (library) website," including "how you can talk to a librarian right on the website, how to get documents, the different search (data)bases you can go to, (and) advanced search versus just one line search."

In terms of reflecting on whether the library instruction changed the way that they search for information, most participants were now less likely to rely on Google and more likely to turn to the academic library system and even use advanced search features. P10 responded that "I'm a lot less hasty now… and I delve more into, I don't pick the first one on the page…I like to go down and I know…what proper sources are." P02 reported that if she had not had the instruction, "probably I would have reached out to friends for advice versus talking to the librarians and using all the online resources they had." P06's reflection was that "it would have taken me longer to find sources if I were…either Googling them or not using the advanced searching techniques." P01 has been applying the content of the session to her other coursework, noting that she has been using library databases "probably daily, searching for things" as she works on a final paper for a women's studies class. When it comes to searching for scholarly articles, P01 said, "I would never just use Google. I always just use (the university library) database (because) I think it's way more successful (and) it's just so much easier for me to use."

In summary, participants of our study could recall what they learned from one-shot library session which they attended 3-4 months ago. Information literacy topics mentioned frequently by participants were source evaluation, accessing library databases, and navigating the university library system. Most participants reported that the library instruction made a difference in the ways that they search for information for academic purposes as they became more likely to use the library system.

Research Question 2: *How do college students feel when they play the role of academic librarian to demonstrate their search behavior using an academic library system?*

All participants, except P07, reported that they did not have difficulty in playing the role of academic librarian. P05's reaction was that "it was pretty easy. I felt like it was not very stressful" when he had to explain his search process to someone else. P04 said, "I personally love teaching, so it was just a thing I like to do." P01, on the other hand, said that "there was a lot of pressure to be sure that you're hitting on the points, and you're communicating well enough. But I feel like I mostly know what I'm doing." P07 was the only participant who found the role-playing difficult: "I mean it just felt weird because you're not actually a freshman." P07 also responded that "it was kind of difficult to be thinking about what to say next and, you know, helping that person."

One potential problem was that participants might change their search behavior because they were playing the role of a librarian. Most participants, except P08, responded that they did not search differently because of the role-playing. P03 and P09 were explicit about it, saying they would do exactly the same thing without having played the role. P01 said that aside from the choice of topic, "this was exactly how I would do my search." In the case of P08, she used the databases from the library a lot more because of the role given to her. Otherwise, she would have turned to Google and Wikipedia.

Some participants seemed to embrace the idea of being a librarian. P10 gave advice that sounded like what a real librarian would say: "Definitely don't be afraid to ask a librarian. I've asked a lot of times for help in finding good sources." P09 also encouraged students to find help in the library, saying "I would definitely tell an incoming student to ask questions if you're confused...because you don't want to write a paper that (is) either using articles that don't support your argument or worse comes to worse, plagiarizing because you don't know how to cite articles or what kind of articles to use and things like that." It was interesting to note that some participants seemed to internalize the librarian's experience when P01 somewhat jokingly stated, "Don't hire me as a librarian, okay?" when searching was not quite going as she initially planned and "I'm failing as a librarian right now" during the short role-playing exercise of finding classrooms on the university website. P02 was eager to promote librarians and the library during the role-playing exercise: "Good places to start are you can come to the librarians here and talk with them, you can email them, there is online chat so you don't even have to come in person, you can talk to the librarian there to ask them where to begin." P04 also pointed to the feature of getting help, saying "there's contact by email, call, text, but it looks like they make it pretty easy for you to contact them about anything."

The research design of librarian role-playing was well received by the vast majority of participants. These students seemed to feel comfortable acting as a librarian while demonstrating and explaining how to search information in the university library system. Further, they were able to take librarian's viewpoints and attitudes rather quickly.

Research Question 3: *What are the benefits and drawbacks of using the librarian role-playing method to assess information searching and evaluation skills?*

One of the benefits of this method was to give participants an opportunity to think more actively and critically about their own search behavior. According to P06, this method made him actively think throughout the whole session: "It definitely felt different just because, normally when I'm researching, it's not like I'm actively thinking about everything that I'm doing. I'm kind of just sort of clicking through...it's kind of like when you're driving on autopilot, and you don't really realize how you got somewhere, but you're there."

This method also gave participants opportunities to be conscious about making relevance and credibility judgments. P02 emphasized the importance of making relevance judgments when she said, "You can browse through (the source you found) a little bit to see if it's still relevant to your topic." Both P05 and P09 illustrated a difference between choosing "relevant" sources and "best sources." P09 explained her strategies of choosing "best sources" in detail by saying "I feel like most of the time you get a lot of evidence that you could use in your paper, but you need to pick which ones are going to validate your argument the most...That's a little bit difficult to differentiate." P05 was even more explicit about differentiating best sources from relevant sources than P09 when he engaged in the card-sorting exercise: "I think, sometimes, you'll just read information and as soon as you see something that's at all relevant, you're just gonna choose that, whereas you need to spend a little bit more time deciding which sources are gonna be your best."

The combination of the role-playing and repeated card-sorting exercises was useful in identifying challenging areas for students in their search process (Figure 4). For instance, P08 said that explaining whether a source is credible would be the hardest part because credibility assessment is something that people have to decide on their own. In contrast, P01 found that judging information with respect to credibility or trustworthiness was easier than she expected, while making decisions about which database to use and how to filter the results had been the most difficult aspects of the search process both to execute and to explain. To P10, "it's going to be so hard to figure out where to start" even after she completed the role-playing session. Likewise, P06 also responded that "figuring out where to look when beginning a search, I'd say that's still the hardest part. I kind of went down that path that I wasn't initially sure what to do the first time when I looked at the research guides and I decided that wasn't the right route for me, so I guess I'd keep that one as being somewhat difficult."

Another benefit of this method was that participants could get an accurate picture of how much they knew about searching in the library system. For instance, P03 acknowledged that she had "more of a surface level knowledge" about library databases than she initially thought, saying "it was harder (be)cause I think that I realized I didn't know as much as I thought about the databases." The role-playing method also revealed the misunderstandings that some participants had about how the library system and databases worked. As a result of doing the role-playing, P10 decided to lower her rating from 3 (somewhat difficult) to 2 (a little difficult) for the card which asked how difficult differentiating scholarly articles from non-scholarly ones because she felt she became "more familiar with the library resources." However, her reasoning was not necessarily accurate when she said, "I would think anything on the library website would be a scholarly article…If I were to just go there (the library system), that would be where I could find a lot of scholarly sources. So, it's much easier than like thinking how Google would do."

We found that role-playing offered our participants a unique opportunity to examine their own search behavior. As a result of role-playing, they became more aware of their knowledge, skills, and attitudes with respect to searching for and evaluating information in a library setting.

CONCLUSION

In this paper, we reported on the results of a study in which we investigated a proof-of-concept of a librarian role-playing method that could potentially be useful in assessing student learning resulting from information literacy instruction. The benefits of this method can be summarized as follows: First, the librarian role-playing method provided opportunities for participants to recall and reflect upon what they learned from an information literacy instruction session effectively. While acting as an academic librarian, some participants demonstrated behavior indicating that they internalized the experience of being a librarian and seemed to enjoy being in 'teaching mode.' Compared to a think-aloud method that asks people to articulate their action, thinking, and decision-making as they search (Kelly, 2009), role-playing seemed to make participants less "awkward and unnatural" (Kelly, p. 85) when performing searches and explaining what they were doing and how they were doing it because the researcher was also playing the role of an incoming college student. One of the significant findings is that this method offered participants an opportunity to pay attention to their own thinking process and searching strategies. As one participant explained, instead of "driving on autopilot" (P06), participants engaged in articulating their thoughts about search actions with detailed explanations. This finding indicates that the role-playing method is potentially effective in developing students' meta-cognition about their search behavior.

There are several limitations to this study. The study was conducted with students who were enrolled in the same English course at one university. The sample size of study participants was small (N = 10), and eight of them were female. We will need to collect and analyze more data using this method to be able to draw conclusive results regarding its benefits and drawbacks. There might be sampling bias as the 10 volunteers who agreed to participate in the follow-up study were students who might feel more confident about their information literacy skills than those who did not volunteer. In order to minimize that source of bias, we introduced our study in terms of interviews without specifying that there would be a role-playing component in the recruitment email. Another limitation of our research design is that it may have felt inauthentic to some participants as the role of an incoming college student was played by a graduate student research assistant. In a future study, we could recruit real incoming college students to fill this role so that participants who are acting as the librarian could feel more natural in the study setting.

In spite of the limitations of this study, we have made methodological contributions to the fields of library and information science, interactive information retrieval, and librarianship by developing a new method that could be used to assess college students' abilities to use library systems to search for and evaluate information, rather than relying on previous methods that tend to measure the effectiveness of an information literacy instruction program. Although we believe that librarian role-playing could be used as a stand-alone research method, we are confident that this method would be more effective when incorporated into a repertoire of data collection methods such as questionnaires, interviews, quizzes, and lab-based experimental studies. In our study, additional methods such as repeated card-sorting exercises as well as opening interview and exit interview questions strengthened the benefits of the librarian role-playing method.

ACKNOWLEDGMENTS

This project was made possible in part by the Institute of Museum and Library Services (RE-95-17-0104-17). We thank Angie Oehrli for her feedback on earlier drafts. We are also thankful to the anonymous reviewers for their thoughtful comments.

REFERENCES

Association of College and Research Libraries. (2000). *Information literacy competency standards for higher education*. Chicago, IL: American Library Association. http://hdl.handle.net/11213/7668

Association of College and Research Libraries. (2016). *Framework for information literacy for higher education*. Chicago, IL: American Library Association. http://www.ala.org/acrl/standards/ilframework

Association of College and Research Libraries. (2017). *Framework for information literacy sandbox*. American Library Association. http://sandbox.acrl.org/

Brennan-Wydra, E., & Culler, T. (2019, May). What first-year students learn from one-shot information literacy sessions and what (they think) they already know. Poster at LOEX Conference, Minneapolis, MN.

Bruce, C., Edwards, S., & Lupton, M. (2006). Six frames for information literacy education: A conceptual framework for interpreting the relationships between theory and practice. *Innovation in Teaching and Learning in Information and Computer Sciences, 5*(1), 1–18.

Bryan, J. E., & Karshmer, E. (2013). Assessment in the one-shot session: Using pre- and post-tests to measure innovative instructional strategies among first-year students. *College & Research Libraries*, *74*(6), 574–586.

Carlomagno, N., Di Tore, A., & Sibilio, M. (2014). Role playing and perspective taking: An educational point of view. *International Journal of Digital Literacy and Digital Competence*, *5*(2), 49–58.

Cooke, R., & Rosenthal, D. (2011). Students use more books after library instruction: An analysis of undergraduate paper citations. *College and Research Libraries*, *72*(4), 332–343.

Dunn, K. (2002). Assessing information literacy skills in the California State University: A progress report. *Journal of Academic Librarianship*, *28*(1-2), 26–35.

Emde, J., & Emmett, A. (2004). Assessing information literacy skills in the real world: The good, the bad and the literate. *Paper presented at the 4th Annual Brick and Click Libraries: An Academic Library Symposium*, pp. 83–89.

Emmett, A., & Emde, J. (2007). Assessing information literacy skills using the ACRL standards as a guide. *Reference Services Review*, *35*(2), 210–229.

Gamtso, C., & Paterson, S. (2012). Guiding students from consuming information to creating knowledge: A freshman English library instruction collaboration. *Communications in Information Literacy*, *5*(2), 117–126.

Halpern, R. (2016). Active learning works! Until it doesn't: Measuring the effectiveness of activity-based learning exercises on information anxiety. *Journal of Library & Information Services in Distance Learning*, *10*(3–4), 242–253.

Hess, A. N. (2014). Online and face-to-face library instruction: Assessing the impact on upper-level sociology undergraduates. *Behavioral & Social Sciences Librarian*, *33*(3), 132–147.

Hufford, J. R. (2010). What are they learning? Pre- and post-assessment surveys for LIBR1100, introduction to library research. *College & Research Libraries*, *71*(2), 139–158.

Kelly, D. (2009). Methods for evaluating interactive information retrieval systems with users. *Foundations and Trends in Information Retrieval*, *3*(1), 1–224.

Koufogiannakis, D., & Wiebe, N. (2006). Effective methods for teaching information literacy skills to undergraduate students: A systematic review and meta-analysis. *Evidence Based Library and Information Practice*, *1*(3), 3–43.

Lloyd, A. (2010). *Information literacy landscapes: Information literacy in education, workplace and everyday contexts*. Oxford, England: Chandos Publishing.

Lowe, S. M., Boothe, C., & Tagg, N. (2014). Integrating an information literacy quiz into the learning management system. *Communications in Information Literacy*, *8*(1), 115–130.

Luetkenhaus, H., Hvizdak, E., & Johnson, C. (2017). Measuring library impacts through first year course assessment. *Communications in Information Literacy*, *11*(2), 339–353.

Markey, K., Leeder, C., & Rieh, S. Y. (2014). *Designing online information literacy games students want to play*. Lanham, MD: Roman & Littlefield.

Martinez Riera, J. R., Cibanal, J. L., & Mora, M. J. P. (2010). Using role playing in the integration of knowledge in the teaching-learning process in nursing: Assessment of students. *Texto Contexto Enferm*, *19*(4), 618–626.

Matlin, T. R., & Lantzy, T. (2017). Maintaining quality while expanding our reach: Using online information literacy tutorials in the sciences and health sciences. *Evidence Based Library and Information Practice*, *12*(3), 95–113.

McKinney, P., & Sen, B. A. (2012). Reflection for learning: Understanding the value of reflective writing for information literacy development. *Journal of Information Literacy*, *6*(2), 110–129.

Mery, Y., Newby, J., & Peng, K. (2011). Assessing the reliability and validity of locally developed information literacy test items. *Reference Services Review*, *39*(1), 98–122.

Mery, Y., DeFrain, E., Kline, E., & Sult, L. (2014). Evaluating the effectiveness of tools for online database instruction. *Communications in Information Literacy*, *8*(1), 70–81.

Mess, J. A. (1994). Use of roleplaying in bibliographic instruction. *Science and Technology Libraries*, *14*(2), 105–118.

Salisbury, L., Omolewu, A. O., & Smith, J. J. (2018). Technology use for non-educational purposes during library instruction: Effects on students learning and retention of information. *Science & Technology Libraries*, *37*(3), 274–289.

Sheets, J. (1998). Role-playing as a training tool for reference student assistants. *Reference Services Review*, *26*(1), 37–41.

St. Jean, B., Taylor, N. G., Kodama, C., & Subramaniam, M. (2018). Assessing the health information source perceptions of tweens using card-sorting exercises. *Journal of Information Science*, *44*(2), 148–164.

Van Scoyoc, A. (2003). Reducing library anxiety in first-year students: The impact of computer-assisted instruction and bibliographic instruction. *Reference & User Services Quarterly*, *42*(4), 329–341.

Walker, K. W., & Pearce, M. (2014). Student engagement in one-shot library instruction. *Journal of Academic Librarianship*, *40*(3), 281–290.

Zhang, Q., Goodman, M., & Xie, S. (2015). Integrating library instruction into the course management system for a first-year engineering class. *College & Research Libraries*, *76*(7), 934–958.

Algorithmic Accountability and Digital Justice: A Critical Assessment of Technical and Sociotechnical Approaches

Howard Rosenbaum
Indiana University, Bloomington, Indiana, USA
hrosenba@indiana.edu

Pnina Fichman
Indiana University, Bloomington, Indiana, USA
fichman@indiana.edu

ABSTRACT

The concept of digital justice is intended to open up discourse about strategies for bringing relief to those who believe they have been discriminated against or harmed by algorithmic decision making. Digital justice has depended on algorithmic accountability, a means by which entities can be held accountable for the consequences of algorithmic decision making. This paper critically examines the concept of algorithmic accountability to assess its utility as a ground for digital justice and argues that it is fraught with difficulties. After discussing digital justice and algorithmic discrimination, algorithmic accountability is decomposed into two types, technical and sociotechnical. These approaches are critically assessed and a cautionary note is struck about the difficulty of enacting algorithmic accountability. If this argument is persuasive, it implies that the concept of digital justice also has difficulties. The paper concludes with suggestions for moving forward that do not use either version of algorithmic accountability.

KEYWORDS

Algorithmic Accountability; Digital Justice

ASIS&T THESAURUS

Information Science; Data Science

INTRODUCTION

Algorithms, as key components of algorithmic assemblages, are having an increasingly significant impact on our lives. From activities as mundane as online searching, using GPS directions, and seeking online recommendation to those as complex as making loan decisions, hiring, and making parole decisions, algorithmically mediated interactions are shaping our social and work lives in ways that are just beginning to come into focus. As Martin (2018, p. 1) explains, "[a]lgorithms can determine whether someone is hired, promoted, offered a loan, or provided housing as well as determine which political ads and news articles consumers see." Striphas (2015, p. 395) observes that "over the last 30 years or so, human beings have been delegating the work of culture – the sorting, classifying and hierarchizing of people, places, objects and ideas – increasingly to computational processes." This has, he argues (2015, 396) led to "the enfolding of human thought, conduct, organization and expression into the logic of big data and large-scale computation." Willson (2016, p. 140) suggests that this trend is important because "the ways algorithms are designed and implemented (and their resultant outcomes) help to influence the ways we conduct our friendships (Bucher, 2012), shape our identities (Cheney-Lippold, 2011) and navigate our lives more generally (Beer, 2009)." Put succinctly, "[a]lgorithms are not immaterial formulae, but practical expressions that that affect the phenomenal word of people" (Klett, 2016, p. 112).

Scholars working in such domains as critical data studies, legal scholarship, computer science, information science, anthropology, and sociology have begun to grapple with the complexities of the sociotechnical impacts of the integration and routinization of algorithmic assemblages into social and organizational life. Scholars critical of the potential for discriminatory outcomes of algorithmically-driven decision making in such domains as banking, insurance, college admissions, and criminal justice have begun to advocate for ways to hold the organizations that own and/or control algorithms accountable for these outcomes. In this move toward what some are calling "digital justice," (Couldry, Gray, & Gillespie, 2013; Jentile & Lawrence, 2016; Sabelli & Tallacchini, 2018; Taylor, 2017), the concept of algorithmic accountability has been introduced as a key component in the attempts to redress the problems created by reliance on algorithmic assemblages for decision making and support.

In this paper we critically examine the concept of algorithmic accountability to assess its utility as a ground for an approach to digital justice. After briefly describing the concepts of digital justice and algorithmic discrimination, algorithmic accountability is decomposed into two types, technical and sociotechnical. We provide a critical assessment of these approaches that strikes a cautionary note about the difficulty of enacting algorithmic accountability and the subsequent consequences for possibility of digital justice for those harmed by algorithmic decision making. The paper concludes with suggestions for moving forward that do not rely on either of these approaches.

82nd Annual Meeting of the Association for Information Science & Technology | Melbourne, Australia | 19–23 October, 2019

DOI: 10.1002/pra2.00019

DIGITAL JUSTICE

The concept of digital justice is, at the moment, variegated according to the lens that is used to examine it; data justice can be confrontational, distributive, or protective. In its confrontational form, it is a challenge to the uses of data to support and reinforce existing power asymmetries between those who gather and analyze the data and those who generated the data (Barnett, Koshiyama, & Treleaven, 2017, p. 1; Diakopoulos, 2016, p. 58; Martin, 2018, p. 3; McCarthy, 2016, p. 1133; Prins, 2018). According to this critique "data systems tend to have a disciplinary function because the way data are collected and structured constitutes a form of normative coercion" (Taylor, 2017, p. 6). Digital justice can also be oriented toward distributive uses of information with the goal of foregrounding groups disenfranchised by the effects of the big data divide (Barocas, Bradley, Honavar, & Provost, 2017, p. 3; McCarthy, 2016, p. 1131) that characterize the modern information environment. Finally, it can be protective, with the goal of mitigating the power of the surveillance state, which uses its ability to collect vast amounts of data about citizens (Fink, 2017, p. 13). This approach to digital justice emphasizes "resistance to government surveillance based on principles of social justice" (Taylor, 2017, p. 7).

One characteristic that is common to these approaches is that digital justice is not based on a foundation of individual rights because "data injustice increasingly tends to occur on the collective level" (Taylor, 2017, p. 8). Big data analytics aggregate data and generate insights about groups and populations meaning that digital justice is better seen as a structural concept that involves concern for preserving the privacy of groups in part by enhancing their ability to control their engagement with data and data organizations which, in turn, extends their capacity to control their data visibility, and their rights to non-discriminatory interactions with institutions that gather big data and make use of big data analytics. The positive dimension of digital justice involves a drive to develop ways to protect and enhance people's involvement with big data. This may involve a move toward algorithmic regulation (Mcquillan, 2017, p. 568). The negative dimension involves developing ways to redress people's grievances when they believe that they have been wronged by institutional algorithmically-mediated decision making. Because the problem of algorithmic discrimination is central to digital justice, the move to hold institutions responsible for these actions currently relies on a concept of algorithmic accountability.

ALGORITHMIC DISCRIMINATION

Algorithms can be used to enhance or hinder social progress and digital justice. The social life of algorithms is shaped in part by a pervasive technological frame that casts them as objective and neutral, meaning that their outputs are free from bias (Binns, 2018, p. 546; Iliadis, 2018, p. 3). This frame is supported by stakeholders with vested interests in preserving the status of algorithmic assemblages as neutral because it benefits them economically, legitimates them socially, and preserves power asymmetries. The frame masks what Martin (2018, p. 2) describes as a false tension - "algorithms as objective, neutral blank slates versus deterministic, autonomous agents;" when framed in this way, the discourse "absolves firms of responsibility for the development or use of algorithms" because the clean code is used in messy contexts with contaminated data by people who do not know how to use them. Those using algorithmic tools respond by claiming that the algorithms are too complex and opaque, so their responsibility for outcomes is mitigated.

Behind the veil of objectivity, critics argue that algorithms are value laden, have moral consequences and can reinforce or challenge power asymmetries (Ananny & Crawford, 2018, p. 978; Mccann, Hall, & Warin, 2018, p. 14). More specifically, they can support or undermine ethical qualities of the domain in which it is intended to operate this is due, in large part, to the decisions made by developers as they create the algorithms. The types of decisions that are relevant here are those that determine the roles the end users will play in the algorithmically-mediated decision; in simple terms, the decision can be left to the algorithm (with no human intervention), to the end users (with no algorithmic intervention), or to some combination of both (Martin, 2018, p. 2). In making these decisions, designers and developers are also are delegating accountability in the decision-making process.

Another important type of decision made by designers and developers is about the attributes of the data set that, in their opinions, are critical inputs to be taken into account as the algorithm generates its output. Two assumptions underlie big data collection that affect the training sets used to train algorithms. The first is that the training set is an accurate representation of the future populations to which the algorithm will be applied. The second is that the sample used in the training set is a good representation of the individuals constituting that population. However, "these assumptions are susceptible to error and bias, although that is precisely what they are intended to negate" (Haarkens, 2018, p. 22). Some subset of these attributes will be appropriate to the decision context while others may not; an example is the inclusion of attributes that are proxies for race in the algorithms used in the COMPAS system, which "wrongly labeled defendants as 'future criminals' when they did not commit a crime at twice the rate for black defendants as white defendants" (Martin, 2018, p. 4). In a sense, the developers are inscribing into the algorithms their assumptions about how the artifact will fit into the social context for which it is intended (Neyland, 2019, p. 32).

Just as there are legal prohibitions against discrimination by humans, there are restrictions against discrimination by algorithms (Kleinberg, Ludwig, Mullainathan, & Sunstein, 2019, p. 2). The challenge is to provide a level of proof that stands up to legal scrutiny. They argue against opening the algorithmic black box because it is a "mathematical impossibility" to understand what an algorithm will do by reading its code; the data it uses must be examined and the algorithm must be run and its outcomes observed (Kleinberg et al., 2019, p. 2). This allows an analyst to determine whether some input into the algorithm led to a discriminatory outcome or whether there is some other externality responsible for the observed disparity. There must be documentation of the decisions made during the development and training process, for example, the predictive goal used to train the algorithm affects the analysis of the training at a and the resulting outcome. The implication of this approach is that it is more important to regulate the person developing the algorithm than the algorithm itself.

Kleinberg et al. (2019, p. 21) describe four types of algorithmic discrimination. An algorithm may produce outcomes that lead to disparate treatment, predicting on the basis of gender or race. It may result in disparate impact, using a predictor variable that disadvantages a vulnerable population. It may use a predictor variable that is a result of prior discrimination, such as a credit score. Finally, it may produce a result that people find disturbing, such as giving preferential treatment to one gender over another; of the four, they point out that this last type of discrimination is not covered by law.

ALGORITHMIC ACCOUNTABILITY

A widespread and powerful technological frame has developed about algorithms and algorithmic assemblages over the last decade. It has taken the form of a decidedly utopian discourse about algorithms (and, by implication, the algorithmic assemblages in which they are embedded) that portrays them as objective, rational, and authoritative (Dourish, 2016; Gillespie, 2014; Lee, 2018). This technological frame is based, in part, on the way in which algorithms are thought of in their primary domain of origin, computer science. They are seen as code that becomes part of a software program that, when activated, can carry out sorting, optimizing, and prioritizing tasks quickly, efficiently, and without human intercession. Given this, algorithms are typically seen by computer scientists as tools that can be used to provide control plus logic (Lustig & Nardi, 2015, p. 744) in software. According to Gillespie (2014, p. 4):

> More than anything, algorithms are designed to be and prized for being functionally automatic, to act when triggered without any regular human intervention or oversight.

Despite the optimistic discourse about the power of algorithms to improve lives, Rainie and Anderson (2017, p. 1) report that "experts worry they can also put too much control in the hands of corporations and governments, perpetuate bias, create filter bubbles, cut choices, creativity and serendipity, and could result in greater unemployment." McCann et al. (2018, p. 14) argue that

> Although algorithms held out the promise of a more neutral decision making process, in reality it is more accurate to think of them as 'an opinion embedded in mathematics/

Willson (2016; p.145) foreshadowed this insight, claiming that the "combination of delegated everyday practices and algorithmic functions within social, cultural and political systems inescapably results in biases being enacted." Diakopoulos (2014, p. 2) states flatly that "[w]e're living in a world now where algorithms adjudicate more and more consequential decisions in our lives." In the domain of search engines, Willson (2016, p. 143) notes that "Google's Panda, Penguin and Hummingbird algorithms and recurrent updates are other examples where changes are made in order to encourage some outcomes, shift priorities: technical and social." O'Neil (2016, p. 12) describes the various ways that algorithmic assemblages, in her terms "weapons of math destruction," reflect and enact the biases, prejudicial beliefs, and misunderstandings of the people who developed them. She (2016, p. 10) argues that these math powered applications "define their own reality and use it to justify their results" and further, they tend "to punish the poor and oppressed in our society, while making the rich richer." O'Neil (2016, p. 12) details the negative impacts of algorithmic assemblages in higher education admissions, online, target advertising, criminal justice, the employment application process, surveillance in the workplace, and in the credit and insurance domains. According to Winter (2015, p. 132) "[i]n many cases, algorithmic discrimination unjustly harms individuals or groups who are already socially and economically disadvantaged."

In general, accountability is "the duty to justify a given action to others and be answerable for the results of that action after it has been performed" (Leonelli, 2016, p. 1). To what extent are the developers of algorithms responsible for the future actions of their creations? To what extent do the organizations that employ these developers bear any responsibility for the same? To what extent can the organizations that make use of the algorithmic assemblages (through lease, subscription, or purchase) be held responsible for the decisions made based on algorithmic analysis? These are some of the questions that underlie the concern for algorithmic accountability.

As the consequences of the pervasiveness of algorithmic assemblages in people's work and social lives become clearer, there have been calls to hold accountable the organizations that own, use and/or control these algorithmic assemblages. Such a call is clearly moving away from the utopianism of the dominant technological frame described above. One approach to algorithmic accountability is framed as a technical exercise and involves looking for (Dourish, 2016, p. 6):

> ... new ways to make algorithmic processes visible, to render algorithms accountable, and to find within the algorithmic process some opportunity for audit, external review, and examination.

Sandvig, Hamilton, Karahalios, and Langbort (2014, p. 3) similarly argue that "public interest scrutiny of algorithms is required [to] focus on subtle patterns of problematic behavior and that this may not be discernable directly or via a particular instance;" therefore, it is necessary to engage in auditing algorithms. This type of scrutiny would focus on such factors as uncovering the criteria that are coded into prioritization, ranking, sorting, and classification algorithms looking for the extent to which they are "politicized or biased in some consequential way;" the conditions under which algorithms fail; and the presence of bias in the training data (Diakopoulos, 2014, p. 9). It could also involve attempts to reverse engineer algorithms, because "[w]e don't necessarily need to understand the code of the algorithm to start surmising something about how the algorithm works in practice." (Diakopoulos, 2014, p. 14).

Problems quickly arise with this technical exercise approach to algorithmic accountability. For example, there is the opaque nature of algorithms, because if access is gained, as Seaver (2017) notes, algorithms are rarely straightforward to deconstruct. Within code, algorithms are usually woven together with hundreds of other algorithms to create algorithmic systems" (Kitchin, 2017, p. 7). Clearly specialist knowledge is required to unravel the mangle of code to first find the relevant algorithm (Dourish, 2016, p. 6), and second, to isolate and extract the code that is responsible for the biased or otherwise problematic outcome. There is also a question of whether the extracted excerpt of code is actually responsible for the outcome or whether the outcome requires the extracted code acting in concert with other components of the algorithmic assemblage. An additional complexity that may arise if the source of the bias or problem is thought to lie in the training set used to tune the algorithmic system. Assuming that it would be possible to gain access to the training dataset, finding specific evidence of biased data would be a difficult task.

There is also a problem of legal opacity where algorithms have patent or trade secret protection (Barnett et al., 2017, p. 7). Although some have proposed reverse engineering algorithms as a strategy to work around this type of protection, the problem here is that while it might show how the algorithm works in practice, reverse engineering results in little more than speculation about the inner workings of the algorithm (Kitchin, 2017, p. 11), making the attribution of accountability difficult. Algorithmic audits are another proposed method of determining accountability. The question here is whether this type of audit, which focuses on the forensic examination of an algorithm, can generate reliable evidence that bias or discrimination has taken place.

There is also a technical issue posed by the dynamic nature of algorithms. Willson (2016; 148) explains that:

> [a]lgorithms are dynamic processes designed and implemented by humans in conjunction with technical affordances and within broader political, social and cultural environments that are shaped by the continual interactions of strategies, structures and tactics."

What this means is that "algorithms are made and remade in every instance of their use because every click, every query, changes the tool incrementally." (Gillespie, 2014, p. 7). To make matters more challenging, this development takes place over time, as algorithms are coded, reviewed, and tested by teams whose composition changes over time and that do not typically create and maintain clear documentation of the process. Which version of the algorithm is the one for which the organization should be held accountable? If a person is denied a loan because of an algorithmically driven decision and seeks to challenge the outcome, how can the precise version of the algorithm be isolated and examined if it is changing as it is used?

Given the challenges of the technical exercise approach, an alternative approach has been proposed (Musiani, 2013; Neyland, 2019). The sociotechnical approach to algorithmic accountability recognizes that algorithmic assemblages are embedded in complex social, cultural, and organizational contexts where, in addition to the technical aspects of algorithms, the enactment of the algorithm involves the activities of individuals and groups. As Musiani (2013; p.3) explains, the questions on which accountability is based should subtly change:

> By asking questions such as: who are the arbiters of algorithms? Is algorithm design an assertion of authority over more than the algorithm itself? What is the autonomy of algorithms, if any? - it is the accountability and the responsibility of algorithms as socio-technical artifacts that is examined, that of their creators and users, and ultimately, of the balance of power facilitated or caused by algorithms.

At the center of this approach is the insight that there are a number of human influences embedded into algorithms, such as criteria choices, training data, semantics, and interpretation (Diakopoulos, 2014, p. 9; Haarkens, 2018, p. 25; Iliadis, 2018, p. 3). Any investigation must therefore consider algorithms as objects of human creation and take into account intent, including that of any group or institutional processes that may have influenced their design.

To assess algorithmic accountability in this approach would involve "[i]nterviewing designers and coders, or conducting an ethnography of a coding team" because it can provide "a means of uncovering the story behind the production of an algorithm and to interrogate its purpose and assumptions" (Kitchin, 2016, p. 11). Because the team is embedded in a complex organization, it would also be necessary to extent the scope of this research to include relevant stakeholders outside of the technical team as well as a dataset of relevant documentation related to the development of the algorithm.

However, there are a number of difficulties when moving from the technical exercise to the socio-technical approach, and when interviewing individuals and teams of coders to assess sociotechnical algorithmic accountability. In addition to focusing on the coding team, the sociotechnical frame would require extensive investigation of the social and organizational context involving, for example, the analysis of relevant company, advertising and marketing, and legal documents, interviews and observations of key stakeholders in the development, and implementation of the algorithm. This labor and time intensive process cannot happen quickly; Neyland (2019) conducted such an ethnography of a team developing an algorithmically based surveillance system and the work took 3 years. Particularly in the case of (particularly legal) attempts to hold organizations accountable for the outcomes of their algorithmic assemblages, the time required to collet relevant data that can serve as evidence means that the effort has less of a chance of being useful.

RETHINKING ALGORITHMIC ACCOUNTABILITY

A difficulty with the current state of algorithmically-mediated decision making is that according to Leonelli (2016), p. 1), it is:

> difficult to determine who is responsible for what output, and how such responsibilities relate to each other; what 'participation' means and which accountabilities it involves, with regard to data ownership, donation and sharing as well as data analysis, re-use and authorship

Barnett et al. (2017, p. 1) argue from a legal standpoint that algorithms are likely to be treated "as artificial persons: a legal entity that is not a human being but for certain purposes is considered by virtue of statute to be a natural person." The path to accountability then seems clear, meaning that if harm results from the actions of an algorithm, "just sue the humans who deployed the algorithm" (Barnett et al., 2017, p. 7). However, as Barnett goes on to argue, the reality may be more complex - for example, if a person suffers bodily injury as a result of a crash with an autonomous vehicle, who (or what) should be sued? To prove discrimination, it is necessary to demonstrate that the practice or requirement used in the process was chosen because it was likely to have an adverse effect on a person or group (Kleinberg et al., 2019, p. 8). This is an example of disparate treatment. Disparate impact, on the other hand, is discrimination based on an adverse effect against a protected group. In both cases, the person or organization charged with discrimination must justify the choices based on reasons such as "business necessity" or other "neutral" reasons.

One approach to accountability does not focus on the internal workings of the algorithm, thereby avoiding the problem of opening the "black box." In this view, attention should be turned instead to monitoring the outcomes of algorithmic decision making looking for instance of bias and discrimination, particularly when directed at vulnerable populations (Shah, 2018, p. 3). When considering algorithmic discrimination, in many cases there are two distinct types of algorithms at work; this is typically the case with prediction and selection algorithms. The first is the training algorithm, which analyzes a training dataset looking for patterns and making predictions on the basis of the choices made by the designers and developers. These choices involve the desired outcome to be predicted (hire this person) and the set of variables used to make the prediction (previous salary, education level, relevant experience). When the decision is made that the outputs of this first stage are within the desired parameters, the training algorithm "produces" a screening algorithm, which can then be used on specific cases to make specific predictions. This latter algorithm "cannot do "literally anything" – it is mechanically the result of whatever human decisions were made for the trainer" (Kleinberg et al., 2019, p. 16). Once the decisions have been made about the training data and the desired outcome, the statistical relationships among the variables in the training dataset determine which predictors will be used by the screener algorithm and the weights that they will have in the analysis. Predictions are then made on the basis of these historical data and variables. Therefore, accountability focuses on the social and organizational context of the training algorithm and the training dataset. For this to work, the algorithms and dataset must be "fixed, stored objects that can be inspected" (Kleinberg et al., 2019, p. 17).

Martin (2018, p. 1) advocates for an approach to algorithmic accountability that is tied to the decision; if the algorithm has the main responsibility for making the decision, then the developer should be held accountable. An implication of this approach is that organizations can be held accountable for ethical problems resulting from the operation of their algorithmic assemblages, even if they are working as designed.

In the case of algorithmic assemblages designed to act autonomously, Martin (2018, p. 9) argues that accountability lies with the organization that created and sold or leased the system; in his view, the "inscrutable defense ('It's too complicated to explain') does not absolve a firm from responsibility." Since the organization and its developers designed the algorithmic assemblage to play the major role in the decision context, they have inserted themselves into the context and have therefore taken on liability for the consequences of their system's operations. In this scenario, the end users are effectively cut out of the decision making and are simply delivering the algorithm's output, they cannot be held responsible for the negative consequences of the results.

The ACM (2017) has laid the groundwork for an approach to algorithmically-mediated decision making with its statement on algorithmic transparency and accountability. The seven principles described in the document call on stakeholders to be aware of potential harms that can occur and to provide a means by which affected groups can seek redress for harms that do occur. They suggest that organizations using algorithms should be able to explain to the affected groups how the algorithms work and should be held responsible for the outcomes of algorithmically-mediated decision making. Further, it is the organization's responsibility to provide. Clear documentation of the training, development and testing processes to provide an audit trail. It should be noted that, at this time, these are only guidelines.

CONCLUSION

Despite the technological frame that portrays algorithms and the assemblages in which they are embedded as objective, autonomous, and efficient, it has become increasingly clear that "… algorithms are not neutral but value-laden in that they (1) create moral consequences, (2) reinforce or undercut ethical principles, or (3) enable or diminish stakeholder rights and dignity." (Martin, 2018, p. 4). As algorithmically-mediated decision making becomes more pervasive in the public and private sectors, the potential for discriminatory outcomes also becomes more apparent. Barnett et al. (2017, p. 9) point out that "the lack of redress can have severe consequences affecting individuals as well as groups and whole societies."

Providing digital justice for people and groups who believe they have been harmed as a consequence of algorithmically-mediated decision making is a complex and difficult problem that is attracting the attention of scholars and researchers in many different fields. The main approach to digital justice has been to rely on algorithmic accountability. As a foundation for digital justice, the concept has promise, but as currently conceived, has problems of its own. Decomposed into technical and sociotechnical versions, algorithmic accountability is difficult to achieve. In the case of the former, deconstructing complex and dynamic algorithms, particularly when they are embedded in algorithmic assemblages where they interact with other algorithms, is a difficult and not likely to produce anything like a smoking gun, meaning the lines of code that provide evidence of discrimination (Kleinberg et al., 2019; Seaver, 2017). In the case of the latter, an ethnographic investigation is required that is time-consuming and expensive; it is made more difficult by the fact that algorithmic assemblages are developed and maintained by teams whose composition frequently shifts so again, finding the evidence of discrimination becomes a challenge.

Kleinberg et al. propose imposing a regime of accountability on the developers of algorithmic assemblages whereby they would be required to provide extensive documentation of their design and development processes that would make clear the decisions made when, for example, compiling the data set for training an algorithm. In fact, they would require that the training data set be reserved any be made available upon legal request. Martin (2017) also calls for all approach to algorithmic accountability the shifts the focus from the algorithm to the decision. If an organization provides an algorithm to a third party and has designed it in such a way as to remove the third party from the decision, the organization bears full responsibility for negative outcomes of the decision. Both of these approaches have been reinforced by the ACM, which recently proposes principles for algorithmic accountability and transparency.

Other approaches have also provided glimpses of ways forward. For example, Ananny and Crawford (2018) deconstruct the concept of transparency and in doing so, they provide an extended critique of a central concept in the technical approach to algorithmic accountability. Challenging the assumption that "observation produces insights which create the knowledge required to govern and hold systems accountable," they (2018; 294) argue that transparency is not a state of being able to see clearly, but is, in fact, a means of control that can be harmful, can be used to obscure, and can privilege seeing over understanding. They (2018; 983) also make the point that the central issue is not a matter of holding algorithms accountable - it is more an effort to figure out how to hold algorithmic assemblages accountable which requires "requires not just seeing inside any one component of an assemblage but understanding how it works as a system."

Binns (2018) offers a different way forward, bypassing the technical issues with accountability to move to the step where certain stakeholders are held publicly accountable for their actions. Drawing on political philosophy, he argues for a concept of algorithmic accountability based on the use of public reason, which amounts to a set of laws, beliefs, and regulations acceptable to all of the stakeholders involved in the decision making. The focus here is on the decision makers using algorithmic assemblages during the course of their work and not on the technical details of the algorithms themselves. In what Binns (2018, p. 544) considers the final stage of accountability, four questions must be asked. These revolve around the nature of an acceptable set of justifications about which decision makers and those affected by the decisions can agree, a means for resolving disputed should agreement not be forthcoming, the determinant of precedence when such disagreements occur (meaning, for example that the decision is imposed over the objections of the person affected by the decision), and a means to resolve "legitimate, epistemic and ethical standards to which algorithmic decisions are held." Binns (2018), p. 550) argues that

> public reason could act as a constraint on algorithmic decision-making power by ensuring that decision-makers must be able to account for their system's outputs according to epistemic and normative standards which are acceptable to all reasonable people.

Wong (2019) also focuses on the stage of accountability that occurs after the algorithmic assemblage has generated its output, arguing that the determination of algorithmic fairness is a political rather than a technical concern. This is due, in part, because the (Wong 2019, p. 4) the "idea of "fairness" in algorithmic fairness is in many ways contestable … [which] foregrounds the need to settle the meaning of fairness alongside, if not prior to, the technical tasks" involved in algorithm development. He proposes a different framework, Accountability for Reasonableness, adapted from decision making in health care, as a procedure for deliberating the fairness of any algorithm. Based on the assumption that in a liberal democracy there will always be disagreements between reasonable people, he offers criteria of publicity, relevance, revisions and appeals, and regulation as means by which algorithmic fairness can be ascertained. The rationales and justification for algorithmic decision making should be publicly available (publicity) and should make clear the reasons why the algorithmic assemblage works the way it does and why it is the best way to make decisions about the affected groups (relevance). There should be procedures for challenging these decisions and for dispute resolution that do not privilege either the decision makers or the affected groups ((revisions and appeals) that are monitored and regulated by appropriate entities (regulation).

Rahwan (2018) proposes a sociotechnical means of holding algorithms accountable based on a variation of social contact theory applied to a concept derived from HCI, human-in-the-loop (HITL), which is transformed into society-in-the-loop (SITL). An example of HITL is the case where interactive machine learning systems can speed the process of training when there is regular feedback from human users. Rahwan (2018, p. 7) describes more powerful applications of HITL in algorithmic assemblages; it can

> can also be a powerful tool for regulating the behavior of AI systems … The human can identify misbehavior by an otherwise autonomous system, and take corrective action … The human can be involved in order to provide an accountable entity in case the system misbehaves

To make the move from the human to society, Rahwan (2018, p. 9) proposes SITL, which is HITL and an algorithmic social contract between society and algorithmic assemblages that resolves tradeoffs between competing values on which assemblages can be based such as between privacy and security or different notions of fairness and determines who benefits and who pays the costs of the decisions made. The goal of this approach is to "to build institutions and tools that put the society-in-the-loop of algorithmic systems, and allows us to program, debug, and monitor the algorithmic social contract between humans and governance algorithms."

This paper has engaged in brush clearing to critically examine the concept of algorithmic accountability as a step toward providing a firm grounding for the concept of digital justice by moving away from a focus on the algorithm itself. The next steps involve a review of the range of alternatives that have been proposed.

REFERENCES

Ananny, M., & Crawford, K. (2018). Seeing without knowing: Limitations of the transparency ideal and its application to algorithmic accountability. *New Media & Society, 20*(3), 973–989.

Barnett, J., Koshiyama, A. S., & Treleaven, P. (2017). *Algorithms and the Law*. Legal Futures. Retrieved from https://www.legalfutures.co.uk/blog/algorithms-and-the-law

Barocas, S., Bradley, E., Honavar, V., & Provost, F. (2017). Big data, data science, and civil rights. arXiv preprint arXiv: 1706.03102.

Binns, R. (2018). Algorithmic accountability and public reason. *Philosophy & Technology, 31*(4), 543–556.

Bucher, T. (2012). Want to be on the top? Algorithmic power and the threat of invisibility on Facebook. *New Media & Society, 14*(7), 1164–1180.

Cheney-Lippold, J. (2011). A new algorithmic identity: Soft biopolitics and the modulation of control. *Theory, Culture & Society, 28*(6), 164–181.

Couldry, N., Gray, M. L., & Gillespie, T. (2013). Culture digitally: Digital in/justice. *Journal of Broadcasting & Electronic Media., 57*(4), 608–617.

Diakopoulos, N. (2014). *Algorithmic accountability reporting: On the investigation of black boxes*. Tow Center for Digital Journalism, Columbia University.

Diakopoulos, N. (2016). Accountability in algorithmic decision making. *Communications of the ACM, 59*(2), 56–62.

Dourish, P. (2016). *Algorithms and their others: Algorithmic culture in context*. Big Data and Society.

Fink, K. (2017). Opening the government's black boxes: Freedom of information and algorithmic accountability. *Information, Communication & Society*, 1–19.

Gillespie, T. (2014). The relevance of algorithms. In T. Gillespie, P. Boczkowski, & K. Foot, *Media technologies* (pp. 167–194). Cambridge, MA: MIT Press.

Haarkens, A. (2018). The ghost in the legal machine: Algorithmic governmentality, economy, and the practice of law. *Journal of Information, Communication and Ethics in Society, 16*(1), 16–31.

Iliadis, A. (2018). Algorithms, ontology, and social progress. *Global Media and Communication*, 1–12.

Jentile, C., & Lawrence, M. (2016). *How government use of big data can harm communities*. Ford Foundation.

https://www.fordfoundation.org/ideas/equals-change-blog/posts/how-government-use-of-big-data-can-harm-communities/

Kitchin, R. (2016). Thinking critically about and researching algorithms. *Information, Communication & Society*, 1–16.

Kleinberg, J., Ludwig, J., Mullainathan, S., & Sunstein, C. R. (2019). *Discrimination in the age of algorithms* (No. w25548). National Bureau of Economic Research

Klett, J. (2016). Baffled by an algorithm: Mediation and the auditory relations of 'immersive audio'. In R. Seyfert & J. Roberge, *Algorithmic cultures: Essays on meaning, performance, and new technologies* (pp. 111–127). London, England and New York, NY: Routledge.

Lee, M. K. (2018). Understanding perception of algorithmic decisions: Fairness, trust, and emotion in response to algorithmic management. *Big Data & Society*, *5*(1), 1–16.

Leonelli, S. (2016). Locating ethics in data science: responsibility and accountability in global and distributed knowledge production systems. *Philosophical Transactions of the Royal Society A, 374*(2083), 20160122.

Lustig, C., & Nardi, B. (2015, January). Algorithmic authority: The case of Bitcoin. In *Proceedings of the 48th Hawaii International Conference on the System Sciences* (pp. 743–752). IEEE.

Martin, K. (2018). Ethical implications and accountability of algorithms. *Journal of Business Ethics.*

McCann, D., Hall, M., & Warin, R. (2018). Controlled by calculations? Power and accountability in the digital economy. *New Economics Foundation.*

McCarthy, M. T. (2016). The big data divide and its consequences. *Sociology Compass*, *10*(12), 1131–1140.

McQuillan, D. (2017). Data science as machinic neoplatonism. *Philosophy & Technology*, 1–20.

Musiani, F. (2013). Governance by algorithms. *Internet Policy Review*, 2(3), 1–8.

Neyland, D. (2019). *The everyday life of an algorithm.* Springer International Publishing.

O'Neil, C. (2016). *Weapons of math destruction: How big data increases inequality and threatens democracy.* Crown.

Prins, C. (2018). Digital justice. *Computer Law & Security Review*, *34*(4), 920–923.

Rainie L., & Anderson J. (2017). *Code-dependent: Pros and cons of the algorithm age.* Pew Research Center. Retrieved from http://www.pewinternet.org/2017/02/08/code-dependent-pros-and-cons-of-the-algorithm-age/

Sabelli, C., & Tallacchini, M. (2018). From privacy to algorithms' fairness. In M. Hansen, E. Kosta, I. Nai-Fovino, & S. Fischer-Hübner, *Privacy and identity management. The smart revolution. privacy and identity 2017 IFIP advances in information and communication technology* (Vol. *526*, pp. 86–110). Cham, IL: Springer.

Sandvig, C., Hamilton, K., Karahalios, K., & Langbort, C. (2014). Auditing algorithms: Research methods for detecting discrimination on internet platforms. Presented at. In *Data and discrimination: Converting critical concerns into productive inquiry* (pp. 1–23).

Seaver, N. (2017). Algorithms as culture: Some tactics for the ethnography of algorithmic systems. *Big Data & Society*, *4*(2), 1–12.

Shah, H. (2018). Algorithmic accountability. *Philosophical Transactions of the Royal Society A, 376*(2128), 20170362.

Striphas, T. (2015). Algorithmic culture. *European Journal of Cultural Studies*, *18*(4-5), 395–412.

Taylor, L. (2017). What is data justice? The case for connecting digital rights and freedoms globally. *Big Data & Society*, *4*(2), 1–14.

Willson, M. (2016). Algorithms (and the) everyday. *Information, Communication & Society*, *20*(1), 137–150.

Leveraging Funds of Knowledge to Manage Privacy Practices in Families

Mega Subramaniam
College of Information Studies, University of Maryland, College Park, MD, USA
mmsubram@umd.edu

Priya Kumar
College of Information Studies, University of Maryland, College Park, MD, USA
pkumar12@umd.edu

Shandra Morehouse
College of Information Studies, University of Maryland, College Park, MD, USA
shandra@umd.edu

Yuting Liao
College of Information Studies, University of Maryland, College Park, MD, USA
yliao598@umd.edu

Jessica Vitak
College of Information Studies, University of Maryland, College Park, MD, USA
jvitak@umd.edu

ABSTRACT

Information and communication technologies play a critical role at home, school, and work for people of all ages. At the same time, use of these technologies can present challenges to privacy and security. In this study, we apply the concept of funds of knowledge to understand how families develop knowledge and skills around using technology and protecting personal information. Funds of knowledge explains how people gain knowledge and highlights how learning happens in a variety of environments beyond the classroom. Through interviews with 52 families living in economically disadvantaged communities in the United States, we develop a typology of privacy funds of knowledge in families. We also explore how privacy funds of knowledge inform families' privacy practices. We conclude the paper by identifying how these findings inform the development of resources for families to further enhance their digital practices.

KEYWORDS

Privacy; Security; Digital Youth; Digital Literacies; Funds of Knowledge; Youth Information Behavior; Family Learning

ASIS&T THESAURUS

Information Behavior; Communities; United States

INTRODUCTION

Families interact with a variety of information and communication technologies at work, home, and school. Smartphones and tablets are common and are increasingly used in public school systems as a part of formal education, while "smart" technologies like digital voice assistants and location-tracking devices are becoming more affordable for homes and more common in public spaces. Yet use of these technologies presents challenges to data privacy and security. How do people learn how to address these risks?

In addition to more formal educational settings, people turn to a variety of sources to develop digital competence, including through their interactions with family, friends, and their wider community.

A prominent concept for describing how young people gain and share knowledge from sources beyond formal education environments is *funds of knowledge* (Moll & Greenberg, 1990). Funds of knowledge recognizes that children, families, and communities gain valuable knowledge from life experience that can form the basis for—and supplement—formal learning practices.

In this paper, we investigate how families draw on funds of knowledge to learn about privacy and enhance their privacy practices. Specifically, we address the following research questions:

RQ1: What knowledge sources shape the privacy funds of knowledge in families?

RQ2: How do personal experiences contribute to the development of privacy funds of knowledge in families?

To answer these questions, we examine data we collected from 52 families (54 adults and 23 children) who live or work in the state of Maryland (USA). Our findings are part of a larger project funded by the Institute of Museum and Library Services (IMLS), with data collected in partnership with our

82nd Annual Meeting of the Association for Information Science & Technology | Melbourne, Australia | 19–23 October, 2019

DOI: 10.1002/pra2.00067

state's division of library services. In 2017, we partnered with four libraries across the state and a non-profit organization that works with Latinx[1] families to interview families from economically disadvantaged communities. We talked about their technology practices and challenges or barriers they faced when using technology. Specifically, we wanted to explore the privacy and security risks these families faced when using digital technology. Our project's goal is to develop resources to help families enhance their privacy practices and make better-informed decisions about their online data. We are also creating resources to help library staff address privacy and security concerns that may emerge when they assist patrons with online transactions that involve sensitive information. In this paper, we offer a typology of privacy funds of knowledge that low-income families draw on to inform their privacy practices. Our typology presents an alternative to the concept of privacy literacy and highlights the varied avenues through which knowledge acquisition happens across and within social networks.

RELATED FRAMEWORKS

In this section, we discuss the concept of funds of knowledge—its origin, the social contexts and networks that constitute funds of knowledge, and the importance of tapping into funds of knowledge for learning among underserved young adults. We then review the concept of privacy literacy and highlight how people and families develop related knowledge and skills.

Funds of Knowledge for Family Learning

Funds of knowledge, a concept from education literature, refers to the idea that children bring a diverse background of knowledge gained from their family and community into the classroom. Vélez-Ibáñez and Greenberg (1992), p. 313 define funds of knowledge as "the strategic and cultural resources…that households contain." Funds of knowledge come from a variety of social contexts and networks in a child's life. These include the child's own knowledge, the child's parents and relatives, other children and their family members, teachers' networks, school staff, and other community members (Moll & Greenberg, 1990). Moje et al. (2004) simplify this into four categories of funds of knowledge: family, community, peers, and pop culture.

In addition to gaining funds of knowledge through individual experiences (Moll & Greenberg, 1990), families access funds of knowledge from their immediate household, extended family, and friends. These social networks can "facilitate the development and exchange of resources, including knowledge, skills, and labor" (Moll, Amanti, Neff, & Gonzalez, 1992, p. 133). In their work with Mexican-American families in the Southwestern U.S., Vélez-Ibáñez and Greenberg (1992) found that a family's social network provides assistance and information regarding housing, jobs, and government services. Family social events (e.g., birthdays, weddings) also contribute to funds of knowledge (Barton & Tan, 2009; Vélez-Ibáñez & Greenberg, 1992).

Beyond their social networks, families also turn to community funds of knowledge, which can include formal groups (e.g., government agencies, labor unions, schools) that provide information and assistance (Vélez-Ibáñez & Greenberg, 1992). Community groups and organizations like churches, libraries, and after-school programs are a source of ethnic identity within communities; this ethnic identity plays a major role in developing an individual's funds of knowledge (Moje et al., 2004).

Students also acquire funds of knowledge from their peers. Moje et al. (2004) show how "hanging out" with peers in informal settings (i.e., spaces not mediated by adults), provides opportunities for students to teach each other skills or provide assistance (e.g., helping English language learners with their homework). Young people spend time online together, looking up their interests and refining their search strategies—skills that are also useful in classroom settings. Additionally, peers learn culture from one another, including popular music, fashion, and vernacular (Moje et al., 2004).

Connecting Funds of Knowledge and Learning

People need to make connections between the various types of funds of knowledge they encounter to actually learn a concept. Vygotsky's (1978) theory on the zone of proximal development (ZPD) identifies the space between what individuals can do with help and what they can do without help. Drawing on funds of knowledge can help someone move from needing support to fully understanding a concept (Moll & Greenberg, 1990).

Teachers play an important role connecting a student's funds of knowledge with classroom learning objectives (Kajamaa, Kumpulainen, & Rajala, 2018). Moll et al. (1992), p. 137 refer to teachers as "the ultimate bridge" to the student's world, their funds of knowledge, and the learning in the classroom. By allowing students to access their own funds of knowledge for learning, teachers put learning in students' hands, taking the role of facilitator rather than expert authority (Barton & Tan, 2009).

Family members make connections between funds of knowledge and learning as they interact with each other (Moll et al., 1992). Children also make these connections by asking family members questions, observing activities, and practicing learned behavior through play (Vélez-Ibáñez & Greenberg, 1992).

Leveraging Funds of Knowledge in Teaching and Learning with Underserved Families

Moll et al. (1992), p. 20 explain that classroom and research agendas usually assume that minority students come from "socially and intellectually limiting family environments, or

[1] This is a gender-neutral term referring to people from Latin American cultures.

that these students lack ability, or there is something wrong with their thinking or their values, especially in comparison to their wealthier peers." But, "funds of knowledge is an antithesis to this approach" (Mills, 2019, p. 7). Children, their families, and communities are assumed to be competent and possess valuable knowledge gained from life experience that forms the basis for education. Using funds of knowledge in the classroom for instruction is a way to legitimize and value students' out-of-school experiences in their home or community (Kajamaa et al., 2018).

Mills (2019) examines funds of knowledge in the context of science education. She identifies four settings for funds of knowledge—home, neighborhood, school, and after school. She explores how digital technology and other learning environments can supplement scientific funds of knowledge, particularly in underserved communities. Other researchers have explored how underserved students can draw on funds of knowledge to bring their cultural experiences into the classroom (Barton & Tan, 2009; Chen, Carger, & Smith, 2017).

Most of this work focuses on bringing funds of knowledge into formal education settings (Chen et al., 2017) or using it to improve school curricula (Mills, 2019). While studies on funds of knowledge have examined families as the unit of analysis, they typically focus on children learning from family members rather than on the different funds of knowledge each family member contributes to collective family learning. To the best of our knowledge, our study represents the first that considers how individuals integrate privacy-related funds of knowledge within their families and is not focused directly on school-based curricula.

Privacy Literacy

Privacy literacy refers to an individual's "level of understanding and awareness of how information is tracked and used in online environments, and how that information can retain or lose its private nature" (Givens, 2015), p. 58. Trepte et al. (2015), p. 339 further specify that privacy literacy encompasses "factual or declarative ("knowing that") and procedural ("knowing how") knowledge." In other words, it is not enough for someone to know *that* information is tracked online; they should also know *how* (if at all) they can limit such tracking.

Survey research highlights areas where privacy knowledge is low. For example, Americans consistently misunderstand the function of a privacy policy, with around half inaccurately believing that the existence of a policy means that companies do not share personal information with others (Turow et al., 2014). Most American internet users also lack understanding of relevant cybersecurity topics, such as encryption, private browsing, or VPNs (Smith, 2017). And while most American internet users recognize that companies track their online activities (Turow et al., 2014), many do not know that companies can legally sell consumer data to others or charge different prices based on such data (Turow, Hennessey, & Draper, 2015).

Researchers have also examined the factors that inform privacy literacy and the outcomes to which it contributes. People who spend more time on social media and who change their privacy settings frequently are more likely to have higher privacy literacy (Bartsch & Dienlin, 2016). Privacy literacy does not affect people's information sharing behaviors (Baruh, Secinti, & Cemalcilar, 2017), but those with higher privacy literacy and technical familiarity are more likely to take steps to control the flow of their information online (Bartsch & Dienlin, 2016; Park, 2013). Yet Park (2013) noted that overall levels of privacy literacy have remained low—even as access to technology increased—suggesting that the divide in digital skills encompasses privacy.

Indeed, recent research questions how digital literacy influences privacy behaviors. Researchers have observed that people increasingly approach online privacy with a sense of resignation (Turow et al., 2015). Hagendorff (2018) critiques the concept of privacy literacy, arguing that since people who have higher privacy literacy tend to have higher incomes and education, gaps in privacy literacy will persist while income and education remain unequally distributed.

Developing Privacy Knowledge

Privacy literacy research has explored *what* people know about online data flows, but more work is needed on *how* people develop this knowledge. In a representative survey of American adults, Redmiles, Kross, and Mazurek (2017) found that people primarily learn security-related information (e.g., passwords, antivirus programs, software updates, two-factor authentication) from media as well as family and friends. People also learn from their own negative experiences, from companies such as internet service providers or banks, and through their workplaces. They accept advice largely when they trust the source and reject advice that is inconvenient or contains too much marketing material (Redmiles et al., 2017). Different types of information also serve distinct purposes. Rader and Wash (2015) suggest that personal stories can help people care about security while expert advice can tell people how best to protect themselves online.

Indeed, Wash and Rader (2011) argue that people's security knowledge may matter less than their beliefs about online risk and how to mitigate it. They argue that security researchers should focus on getting people to make the right security decision rather than ensuring they have the right security knowledge. This approach makes sense in the security realm, where potential actions are less value-laden. For example, while people may find two-factor authentication confusing or inconvenient, there is little question that it makes a login process more secure. Privacy-related decisions, such as the disclosure of information, are often less clear cut and more context-dependent.

People's privacy beliefs and attitudes are informed by various sources, beginning with their families. As children spend more time in community institutions such as school, they gain awareness of group and social norms regarding interaction and information management (Petronio, 2002). And as digital technologies have embedded into families' everyday lives, extensive research has explored how children and families navigate online risks (e.g., Livingstone, Haddon, & Görzig, 2012). Parents of teenagers tend to more actively help their children navigate online privacy concerns (Wisniewski, Jia, Xu, Rosson, & Carroll, 2015), while parents of younger children may believe their children do not need such guidance until they are older (Kumar et al., 2017). Indeed, parents of younger children may be missing an opportunity to meet children in their ZPD and scaffold their development of online privacy management skills (Kumar et al., 2017). In addition to the home, schools and libraries are well-positioned to help children (and adults) develop privacy knowledge and skills (Agosto & Abbas, 2016; Givens, 2015; Kumar, Chetty, Clegg, & Vitak, 2019; Wissinger, 2017). Our work identifies the different funds of knowledge on which such efforts can build.

METHODS

Recruitment

At the start of the project, we identified four partner library branches in economically disadvantaged areas of the state. Table 1 includes general information about the partner libraries and the communities they serve, including their general location, unemployment rate, and poverty rate. Library branch managers and staff helped us recruit participants. We created fliers and shared details of the study with library staff, and they identified patrons who fit our recruitment criteria. We also partnered with a local non-profit organization that works primarily with disadvantaged Latinx families who are immigrants and speak English as a second language. We relied heavily on partners' knowledge of the local community and library patrons to help us identify likely participants. Going through these organizations to recruit families, rather than trying to recruit directly, helped us establish trust and rapport with community members and assuaged potential concerns about the research.

Branch	Location	Unemployment rate in the area	Poverty rate
A	Rural	14%	28%
B	Urban	12%	24%
C	Urban	17%	20%
D	Rural	11%	20%

Table 1. Descriptive details for partner library branches

Data Collection

From March–May 2017, we conducted face-to-face interviews with 46 families at the four partner libraries. In June 2017, we interviewed six additional families at a public center run by our nonprofit partner. In total, we spoke with 54 adults and 23 children from 52 families (13 identifying as Latinx). Our interviews lasted 25–75 min. We encouraged multiple family members to attend so we could obtain a variety of perspectives. When children were present, we asked them specific questions about their technology use at home and school and whether they had learned about online safety or security at school. Each family received US$75 cash as compensation.

Data Analysis

We had the interviews transcribed and imported the transcripts into the qualitative analysis software Dedoose. We created an initial codebook based on the existing interview protocol and broader research goals, and each member of the research team separately coded one interview. We then discussed the coding process and refined the codebook. We repeated this process with a second interview and finalized the codebook. Our final codebook included 24 codes regarding adults' and children's attitudes and behaviors related to privacy/security. Each interview transcript went through two rounds of coding. In the first round, a team member coded the transcript, and in the second round, a different team member reviewed the coding decisions. The team met and resolved coding differences through discussion (Lincoln & Guba, 1985).

To address the current study's research questions, we focus our analysis on six codes covering children's technology use, technology literacy, sources of technology knowledge, and privacy behaviors, as well as parents' technology oversight practices and privacy behaviors. Given that our primary project goal is to create privacy resources families can use together and/or individually, we conducted another round of analysis on these six codes to identify how and from where children and adults bring funds of knowledge to manage privacy online. Researchers who have studied children's funds of knowledge in the educational space have devised typologies to categorize the sources of funds of knowledge (e.g., community, culture, family). However, none of these existing typologies have categorized funds of knowledge for privacy-related learning. Using the lens of funds of knowledge, we further analyzed the excerpts from these six codes closely for evidence of sources and categories of privacy funds of knowledge that families draw from, including personal experiences that shape privacy practices. Additionally, wherever possible, we also highlight less-protective privacy practices that families obtain through funds of knowledge, which will inform the privacy-related resources we create for families.

When reporting findings, we use alphanumeric identifiers to indicate where the interview was conducted and whether the participant was an adult or child. The alphabet before participant number refers to the library where we interviewed them (see Table 1). Latinx participants recruited from the local non-profit are labeled as "LN". The "-A" or "-C" after the identifier indicates whether the speaker was an adult or child, respectively.

FINDINGS

RQ1: What knowledge sources shape the privacy funds of knowledge in families?

Privacy Funds of Knowledge through Formal and Informal Learning Settings

Formal schooling was the most salient context from which participants drew privacy knowledge, including both children's current experiences and adults' previous experiences. Children (and some adults) gained privacy knowledge in classes on computers, technology, financial literacy, and media. These included lessons on internet safety and instructions and/or strategies for protecting personal information online, such as creating strong passwords, being mindful of pop-ups, clearing caches and browsing history after using public computers, and using third-party services to monitor suspicious activities on one's accounts. For example, Participant A15-C said, *"They [the school] said do not ever put your personal information...they said not to click "accept" to anything that pops up, to let us know about it before you do anything for any pop-ups"*. Likewise, Participant A3-A took a financial literacy class and learned about using third-party services that will *"send me alerts...anything looks suspicious...So how I have my (bank) account set up now, where nobody can take anything out of my account without...being authorized by me first..."*.

School lessons often focused on creating strong passwords—*"They [school] taught...how to type in eight to 12-digit passwords"* (B15-C)—and safeguarding them—*"They do tell everyone to sign off their email when you're done using the computer because that's been an issue sometimes if people are logged in with their email and somebody can go inside their email and send out emails pretending to be that person..."* (C13-C). While this is encouraging, some parents also said their children receive pre-set passwords from the school systems that use their names and/or birthdates. In some cases, these children cannot change the password and use the same password for other systems. One parent (C6-A), observed how this affected her child's privacy practices: *"...Because you use your birthday for everything. So, we know, your sister and I know you use your birthday for everything...What about creating different codes that only you would know?"* The child confirmed that her school had not taught her anything about *why* or *how* to do that.

Parents said they obtained privacy-related knowledge through their children's school lessons. For example, Participant A5-A said, *"...my 11-year-old, he feels pretty comfortable because he knows more about how to use some of the stuff, than me. He knows more sites because they talk about it a lot in school. That's where I learn a lot of my information. Whatever he learns at school, that's where I find stuff out"*. These exchanges highlight how privacy-related information children obtain in school can contribute and transfer to become family funds of knowledge.

Beyond school, some parents we interviewed received on-the-job-training and attended short or semester-long courses in colleges. These ranged from basic instructions on how to use the computer and the Internet to more specific lessons on topics such as animation or creating and sharing movies. These courses involved brief conversations about privacy practices, such as protecting personal information when completing tasks like sharing videos online. Our participants also described informal training on privacy in the form of one-hour classes or tutorials at the library or short discussions on internet safety during an English-language-learning class at a community center.

Developing Privacy Funds of Knowledge through Family Interactions

Family members learn about privacy-related concepts and practices by sharing experiences with each other. These experiences and knowledge can be transferred from a child to a parent, from a parent to a child, between siblings, and can come from extended family members. We observed each of these in our analysis. We include any risky online practices participants discussed to highlight that such transfers that can be enriching or confusing.

Privacy Knowledge Shared from Child to Parent. Children assist parents in typical day-to-day practices such as finding information online, navigating social media, and completing essential transactions (e.g., shopping, submitting job applications). Regarding privacy, we found children imparting their knowledge about what features suggest trustworthiness on a website (i.e., lock icon next to a webpage URL), how to adjust social media settings (i.e., make a profile private), and how to configure phone settings (i.e., activating "Find my iPhone").

Privacy Knowledge Shared from Parent to Child. We found many instances where children follow parents' guidance. This included advice regarding tasks such as shopping from a trusted site. Participant A6-C said, "*...my mom does a lot of online stuff so I learned from her...I think she might do one clothing store that she really trusts. I even heard her say she hasn't had any problems with it*". Parents also gave advice more directly related to safety and security. Participant B18-C, whose mother lived outside the U.S., said, "*...my mom told me, since she lives in my country [of origin], 'you have to be very careful with what you do,' not so much because of my safety here but rather for their [family] safety over there [in the child's country of origin]. Then I went through my friends and I started, not deleting them [unfriending], but putting them on restricted access. Out of all the friends I have, it's just a few who can see my things. The rest are there, but they can't see it. It's a safety measure because of the violence in our countries*".

Privacy Knowledge Shared between Siblings. Children said they encountered websites that were not trustworthy and messages that could have been phishing attempts. They also helped—or were helped by—siblings in navigating difficult situations. Participant C5-C said his sister helped him avoid risk when responding to online prompts: "*My sister said, 'Don't. Just let me look at it first,' because she said sometimes it may appear to be secure like the actual site of Microsoft, but it might not be.*" He also said his older brother checked on him to see if he is *"downloading something that I should not"*.

Privacy Knowledge Shared Via Extended Family. Participants said that extended family members who experienced privacy violations warned relatives by sharing their stories. Participant A15-C said her uncle's debit card number was stolen and "*they stole his money out of his bank account. It was for the kids' Christmas presents and they stole his money. That's why I don't trust nothing on the internet.*" Relatives also shared other useful information. For example, participant D3-A said her cousin recommended an internet service provider that offered web filtering services that aligned with her values. "*I had to give up AOL because, I mean, it was just inappropriate spam coming in. I didn't like that, so I went to a Christian internet provider and that turned that [spam] down about 90%.*"

Friends as a Source of Privacy Funds of Knowledge

Friends' experiences also influence people's privacy practices. Participant B19-A wanted to purchase handbags from Facebook ads but explained why she refrained: "*They sell $50 or something but this is fake...My friends told me this is fake bags*". Participants also described instances when they hesitated because of privacy concerns and then were convinced by their friends to complete online transactions. Participant LN2-A said, "*This thing of sharing links is brand new to me and I'm still weirded out because I gave my address so that...just being able to do online jobs like they tell you, 'Oh, try to do this. Work at home. You just need the internet.' I don't trust those sites. She [my friend] did it and she said she got a check and we've known each other for 12 years so...okay, let me give it a try...Then when I started seeing the visits and the numbers and the numbers go up and the numbers go up every time you refresh the page, it'd be like, okay maybe. She's like, 'I wasn't very skeptical like you, but once I actually received a check with the amount that it showed on the computer and not a penny less, not a penny more, then I believed them.' I was like, wow. She said she made $800 in a month*".

Trusting Sources Deemed "Experts" Help Develop Privacy Funds of Knowledge

Participants described accepting information from individuals with affiliations that suggested they were trustworthy or reliable. Participant LN5-A said she looks for the lock icon next to URLs because "*the girl from the bank told my husband about it...be sure to check it whenever he wanted to purchase something*". Some interviewees said they ask librarians questions when they are completing online tasks in libraries "*...because if anything come up that's not right, they'll be notified. So, if I'm at home, on my own server I wouldn't even know. They [libraries] have all the right tools*" (A3-A). When participants had privacy questions, they often described asking someone who knows about the topic (without specifying who the "someone" was), hearing stories about negative experiences people had with certain websites (without specifying who the "people" were), and reading reviews for online services before engaging in online transactions to avoid being cheated or scammed.

Participants also described accepting information from well-established or popular organizations. They often referred to practices of larger companies as hallmarks of safe practices for dealing with sensitive information. Participant A4-A said, "*I know big businesses back up all their files and everything on the cloud. So, I guess it's safe. I'm sure all the big companies wouldn't put to cloud if it was not safe*". Participants considered shopping sites such as Amazon and Etsy "legit organizations" because many people use them. Participant D1-A said, "*I'll buy off of Amazon, but...I wouldn't feel comfortable buying off of some platform I've never heard of or anything like that*". On the other hand, our participants did not trust Facebook the way they did Amazon. For example, one participant (LN6-A) consciously decided not to use the site in a family emergency: "*...a year ago one of my nieces went missing while she was on her way here [U.S.] from El Salvador. In order to keep the smuggler from realizing that we were... looking for her, it was better to go to the center [a non-profit that helps immigrants and refugees] to get help...I know that I could have posted it on Facebook... [but] I seek help another way*". She was concerned that posting information on Facebook may have tipped off the smugglers and put her niece in greater danger.

RQ2: How do personal experiences contribute to the development of privacy funds of knowledge in families?

When we asked participants how they knew about a given privacy-related practice, the most common response was, as Participant C12-C put it, "*I figured it out on my own*". Personal experiences (in addition to the sources described above) are also a category of funds of knowledge (Moll & Greenberg, 1990).

Personal Encounters with Privacy Issues

Echoing Redmiles et al. (2017), our participants described how negative experiences led them to engage in protective behaviors. For example, Participant B5-A said, "*I had a strange guy come and knock on my door one time...This old white man...It was scary, and I shut the door real quick when I didn't know who it was...He tracked me on Facebook 'cause when I took a picture of me and my kids...posted it, it showed where I live, where I took the picture, the location. Everything... And when that guy comes to my house, I went on my Facebook and I turned the location off. 'Cause it was on. And then I turned the location off on my phone too*". Many of our adult participants said they avoided online banking (unless it was completely necessary) because they worried about their bank account information being compromised.

Others limited important online transactions to a single computer at home because they feared getting hacked, or they purchased third-party identity theft protection because their social security or credit card numbers had been stolen and used in the past. Many were wary of pop-ups and ads that took them to websites that asked for personally identifiable information because of past experiences losing control of their computers to hackers. Some did not respond to messages promising instant cash because they learned this was a scam.

Conversely, positive experiences reinforced participants' digital practices. Participant A3-A used Indeed.com for her job applications, and she said, "*...I've been using that for years and I feel a little bit more secure with that*". In addition to using services without any breaches or problems, many adults we interviewed looked for information before transacting with a company. Before buying something from a specific website, Participant A13-A did "*...a lot of research, pulling up a lot of websites, understanding where they're manufacturing it from. I've looked at them for some years, before I even purchased something from them. So, the consistency of their website, calling them up, and how their customer service is...*".

Personal Encounters with System-Programmed Privacy Measures

Some adults we interviewed relied on past experiences with their bank to flag questionable expenses in their account, and therefore protect them from being responsible for any purchases made that they had not authorized. Participant D1-A said, "*I've tried to buy things before from Etsy and it was going to New York state, and [my husband's] bank even flagged purchases coming from New York because at that time there had been a lot of, I guess, issues. So, it has flagged things before*". She further explained her complete comfort with her bank, saying, "*...we've gone to go pay gas and you're at the pump and something's wrong and we'll get a call from the bank like, 'You've had this many charges today, is this you?' Or we'll get text messages and stuff. So, I feel comfortable [with] all those security measures on there...*".

Participants described similar experiences with other companies. Participant D7-A said she had not experienced identity theft or hacking but had received related warnings: "*Either I think we've gotten warnings that people have attempted or like they've attempted to access the Facebook account, and I think maybe it was the email or banking account—I forget which it was—but we got a warning from the company saying change your password, this was attempted to be cracked*". Some participants said websites prompted them to change their passwords every three months, which got them into the habit of changing their passwords for every website they interact with. Some adults we interviewed described experiences receiving authentication codes, creating security questions, and interacting with Captchas. They considered these to be signals that websites protect their personal information and looked for them when interacting with new websites.

Participants paid attention to website prompts when setting up accounts, taking note of alerts about weak, medium, and strong passwords or alerts about logging into public WiFi. Participant LN2 said, "*to get to the McDonald's WiFi, it used to not let me go through and get it because they said it was not a trusted site*". Participants also relied on online platforms to protect their privacy. Participant D2 said, "*I leave a lot of the security up to the Google*". Similarly, participant LN3-A appreciated Google services that monitor for hacking and notify her through e-mails that say, "*You accessed your email on a certain computer, that was located at a certain place, let us know if that was you*".

We summarize the typology of funds of knowledge that we found through our study in Table 2.

DISCUSSION

Through our analysis of interviews with 52 families, this paper presents a typology of funds of knowledge related to digital privacy. Below, we explain how our findings extend the funds of knowledge framework and inform the potential form, process, and content of the privacy resources that we will develop for economically disadvantaged families—and the libraries/librarians that serve them.

Funds of knowledge	Examples of sources of funds of knowledge
Formal & informal learning experiences	School and educational lessons (e.g., computer/technology classes, financial literacy training), on the job training, short and semester-long college courses, classes and tutorials at libraries, classes at a community center
Family members	Learning from child, parent, sibling, extended family member
Friends	Friends' experiences, friends influence on privacy behavior
Sources deemed as Privacy "Expert"	*Individuals*: bank employees, librarians, "someone" (undefined), reviewers for services and websites *Organizations*: "big companies", "legit" organizations, Amazon, PayPal
Own experience	Experiences with privacy issues, experiences with system-programmed privacy measures

Table 2. Typology of funds of knowledge of digital privacy

Expanding Funds of Knowledge Framework to Privacy

Researchers have employed Moje et al.'s (2004) four categories of funds of knowledge—family, community, peers, and pop culture—in the context of science and language learning. We extend some of these categories to identify funds of knowledge related to privacy. While previous literature points to parents as sources of funds of knowledge for children (Moll & Greenberg, 1990), our research reveals that the flow of privacy knowledge can also move from children to parents, among siblings, and also across extended family members (e.g., cousins, uncles, aunts). Additionally, we highlight that while knowledge is shared within families, individual members also bring privacy-related knowledge gained from their own networks of peers and communities (RQ1) and through their own experiences (RQ2). A rich amalgamation of privacy knowledge flows among family members and forms privacy funds of knowledge within the family.

When it comes to privacy, community funds of knowledge go beyond schools and community centers to encompass workplaces and people or organizations deemed as "experts." Echoing Redmiles et al. (2017), the "someone" who supplies privacy tips and practices includes individuals who work in trusted organizations such as libraries; large companies such as Amazon and Etsy, banks, and internet service providers; and websites that provide visible signals that they protect the safety of their users. Particularly interesting are references to specific companies as sources of trusted funds of knowledge (e.g., trusting Amazon and Etsy, not trusting Facebook). This suggests possible influences of funds of knowledge from peers (family friends) and popular culture (media and television). The emergence of librarians as trusted sources of privacy funds of knowledge is particularly important to the growing literature that supports libraries as hubs for low-socioeconomic individuals to access support when completing essential tasks such as applying for housing, food assistance, etc. (Thompson, Jaeger, Taylor, Subramaniam, & Bertot, 2014; Vitak, Liao, Kumar, & Subramaniam, 2018). This suggests an important opportunity for libraries and librarians to consider new ways to support the growth and development of their patrons' privacy skills.

For children, school and formal education environments seem to be the most prominent "community" source of privacy funds of knowledge. While previous research has mostly studied out-of-school experiences with the goal of enhancing in-school learning, our findings reveal the reverse, where knowledge gained in school enhanced everyday privacy practices. It is imperative to consider school as a strong source of "community" funds of knowledge in future endeavors to facilitate learning of emerging digital literacies. Echoing Kumar et al. (2019), we argue that school systems should consider incorporating privacy-specific lessons into their curricula, since our findings suggest young adults are referencing such learning in their everyday practices.

Individuals' negative and positive experiences with technology inform their privacy perceptions and practices (Redmiles et al., 2017). Our finding that many participants said they developed privacy knowledge on their own aligns with previous education literature (Barton & Tan, 2009; Moll & Greenberg, 1990; Poole, 2017) on how one's own knowledge interacts and contributes to their own and their family members' funds of knowledge. These accrued funds of knowledge are picked up through experiences interacting with technology. To develop effective privacy skills, children need experience going online *and* support from parents and others to understand how to avoid risky situations or cope when they occur (Wisniewski et al., 2015). Our typology reveals how different sources of information and experiences inform people's privacy practices in a way that the concept of privacy literacy does not. By working with low-income families and considering how they collectively develop privacy skills and knowledge, we address some of Hagendorff's (2018) concerns with the concept of privacy literacy and offer privacy funds of knowledge as a complementary framework.

Prior literature has identified underserved families as having the most to gain from leveraging funds of knowledge, given their limited physical access to technology and inadequate access to digital literacy instruction (Davis & Fullerton, 2016; Subramaniam, Scaff, Kawas, Hoffman, & Davis, 2018). Our findings regarding some of the less-protective privacy practices families described imply that they may not have accumulated sufficient funds of knowledge to develop safe privacy practices. We believe they will need to tap all sources of funds of knowledge to fill this void. Identifying people who bridge these funds of knowledge is also crucial. While Moll and Greenberg (1990) identified teachers and family members as bridges to bring funds of knowledge to the classroom, more research should explore who can be an ideal bridge to connect the multiple privacy funds of knowledge we have identified in this research. Our participants referred to librarians, technology teachers, and media teachers (school librarians) as sources of funds of knowledge for privacy, and each offers unique strengths for facilitating learning and knowledge development.

Developing Privacy Resources for Families

The broader goal of this research is to create resources to help families enhance their privacy practices. Prior work has found that few people attend privacy or digital literacy classes offered at public libraries (Vitak, Liao, Kumar, & Subramaniam, 2018), and that low socio-economic populations face unique challenges in managing privacy and developing effective privacy practices (Vitak, Liao, Subramaniam, & Kumar, 2018). Our typology of privacy funds of knowledge can inform the development of privacy resources to help such families address these challenges. Our findings suggest a need to:

- Work closely with school systems and public libraries—which we identify as "community" funds of knowledge—to brainstorm ways to leverage technology lessons in schools and after-school library programs to help children enhance their privacy practices.
- Explore the potential of technology teachers, public librarians, and/or school librarians to serve as bridges that help generate privacy funds of knowledge in families. This could manifest as training on funds of knowledge and how they can be tapped to improve privacy practices.
- Develop strategic partnerships with local community experts in technology, banks, and libraries to co-develop

and co-facilitate privacy learning. Community partners—especially those who are familiar with the challenges local families face—will be able to build trust quicker than outside entities. Likewise, having multiple community groups involved in this process will encourage wider awareness and participation.

- Co-create privacy resources using participatory design methods (Muller, 2009) with families and other sources of privacy funds of knowledge, including family friends, extended family members, teachers, and librarians. Through participatory design, those who will use the resources will help design them, which allows the materials to better meet community needs.

LIMITATIONS

Since we did not design this study to explicitly identify privacy funds of knowledge, participants may have drawn on more sources than those they mentioned during the interview. Nevertheless, our data paints a rich picture of the variety of funds of knowledge that did emerge through our conversations with them. In addition, we specifically chose not to collect demographic information from participants to avoid asking invasive questions that may have prevented us from building rapport. Instead, we relied instead on the library branches' demographics as a proxy for socio-economic status and on the library staff to recruit families who fits the project's research goals. Finally, the interviews relied on self-reported data about participants' attitudes, opinions, and behaviors. We recognize that some participants may have been reluctant to share their experiences. We also recognize that family dynamics may have affected interviews. For example, children may have been less willing to discuss certain aspects of their technology use with a parent present; likewise, a parent might have been unwilling to talk about sensitive matters in front of their children.

CONCLUSION

This study extends the concept of funds of knowledge to privacy and explores how it can be used to enhance families' privacy practices. Researchers are investigating how children and families navigate and manage privacy and what challenges they face (Kumar et al., 2017); however, research on how and from where they develop privacy knowledge is still lacking. This study fills that void by illuminating the privacy funds of knowledge that inform families' privacy practices. Our findings can shape the pedagogical strategies used to help families better protect their privacy online and illustrate the positive roles that trusted community members can play in helping families do so. Future research is needed to design and develop these strategies in partnership with these community members.

ACKNOWLEDGMENTS

This research is funded by an IMLS National Leadership Grant, LG-81-16-0154-16. We thank the Maryland State Library Agency, as well as the coordinators at each library branch and at the Latino nonprofit for their assistance in recruiting participants and facilitating on-site interviews.

REFERENCES

Agosto, D. E., & Abbas, J. (2016). Simple tips for helping students become safer, smarter social media users. *Knowledge Quest, 44*(4), 42–47.

Barton, A. C., & Tan, E. (2009). Funds of knowledge and discourses and hybrid space. *Journal of Research in Science Teaching, 46*(1), 50–73.

Bartsch, M., & Dienlin, T. (2016). Control your Facebook: An analysis of online privacy literacy. *Computers in Human Behavior, 56*, 147–154.

Baruh, L., Secinti, E., & Cemalcilar, Z. (2017). Online privacy concerns and privacy management: A meta-analytical review: Privacy concerns meta-analysis. *Journal of Communication, 67*(1), 26–53.

Chen, Y., Carger, C. L., & Smith, T. J. (2017). Mobile-assisted narrative writing practice for young english language learners from a funds of knowledge approach. *Language Learning & Technology, 21*(1), 28–41.

Davis, K., & Fullerton, S. (2016). Connected learning in and after school: Exploring technology's role in the learning experiences of diverse high school students. *The Information Society, 32*(2), 98–116.

Givens, C. L. (2015). *Information privacy fundamentals for librarians and information professionals*. Lanham, MD: Rowman & Littlefield.

Hagendorff, T. (2018). Privacy literacy and its problems. *Journal of Information Ethics, 27*(2), 127–145.

Kajamaa, A., Kumpulainen, K., & Rajala, A. (2018). A digital learning environment mediating students' funds of knowledge and knowledge creation. *Studia Paedagogica*, (4), 49–66.

Kumar, P. C., Chetty, M., Clegg, T. L., & Vitak, J. (2019). Privacy and security considerations for digital technology use in elementary schools. *Proceedings of the 37th Annual ACM Conference on human factors in computing systems*. Presented at the CHI, New York.

Kumar, P., Naik, S. M., Devkar, U. R., Chetty, M., Clegg, T. L., & Vitak, J. (2017). "No telling passcodes out because they're private": Understanding children's mental models of privacy and security online. *Proceedings of the ACM on human-computer interaction, 1*(CSCW), 1–21.

Lincoln, Y. S., & Guba, E. G. (1985). *Naturalistic inquiry* (1st ed.). Beverly Hills, Calif: SAGE Publications.

Livingstone, S., Haddon, L., & Görzig, A. (2012). *Children, risk and safety on the internet: Research and policy challenges in comparative perspective*. Bristol: Policy Press.

Mills, K. (2019). *Illuminating children's scientific funds of knowledge through social media sharing*. (doctoral dissertation). University of Maryland, College Park.

Moje, E. B., Ciechanowski, K. M., Kramer, K., Ellis, L., Carrillo, R., & Collazo, T. (2004). Working toward third space in content area literacy: An examination of everyday funds of knowledge and discourse. *Reading Research Quarterly, 39*(1), 38–70 International Reading Association, Order Department, P.O. Box 6021, Newark, DE 19714-6021. Tel: 800-336-7323 (Toll Free); Tel: 302-731-1600; Fax: 302-737-0878; e-mail: customerservice@reading.org

Moll, L. C., Amanti, C., Neff, D., & Gonzalez, N. (1992). Funds of knowledge for teaching: using a qualitative approach to connect homes and classrooms. *Theory Into Practice*, *31*(2), 132.

Moll, L. C., & Greenberg, J. B. (1990). Creating Zones of Possibilities: Combining social contexts for instruction. In *Vygotsky and education: Instructional implications and applications of sociohistorical psychology*. Cambridge University Press.

Muller, M. (2009). Participatory design: The third space in HCI. In A. Sears & J. A. Jacko, *Human-computer interaction: Development process* (pp. 166–185). Boca Raton, FL: CRC Press.

Park, Y. J. (2013). Digital literacy and privacy behavior online. *Communication Research*, *40*(2), 215–236.

Petronio, S. (2002). *Boundaries of privacy: Dialetics of disclosure*. Albany, NY: State University of New York Press.

Poole, A. (2017). Funds of Knowledge 2.0: Towards digital funds of identity. *Learning, Culture and Social Interaction*, *13*, 50–59.

Rader, E., & Wash, R. (2015). Identifying patterns in informal sources of security information. *Journal of Cybersecurity*, tyv008.

Redmiles, E. M., Kross, S., & Mazurek, M. L. (2017). Where is the digital divide?: A survey of security, privacy, and socioeconomics. *Proceedings of the 2017 CHI conference on human factors in computing systems - CHI '17*, 931–936.

Smith, A. (2017). *What Americans knows about cybersecurity*. Retrieved from Pew Research Center website: http://www.pewinternet.org/2017/03/22/what-the-public-knows-about-cybersecurity/

Subramaniam, M., Scaff, L., Kawas, S., Hoffman, K. M., & Davis, K. (2018). Using technology to support equity and inclusion in youth library programming: Current practices and future opportunities. *The Library Quarterly*, *88*(4), 315–331.

Thompson, K. M., Jaeger, P. T., Taylor, N. G., Subramaniam, M. M., & Bertot, J. C. (2014). *Digital literacy and digital inclusion: Information policy and the public library*. Lanham, MD: Rowman & Littlefield.

Trepte, S., Teutsch, D., Masur, P. K., Eicher, C., Fischer, M., Hennhöfer, A., & Lind, F. (2015). Do people know about privacy and data protection strategies? Towards the "Online Privacy Literacy Scale" (OPLIS). In S. Gutwirth, R. Leenes, & P. de Hert, *Reforming European data protection law* (pp. 333–365).

Turow, J., Bleakley, A., Bracken, J., Carpini, M. X. D., Draper, N., Feldman, L., … Nir, L. (2014). *Americans, marketers, and the internet: 1999-2012*. Retrieved from https://papers.ssrn.com/abstract=2423753

Turow, J., Hennessey, M., & Draper, N. (2015). *The tradeoff fallacy: How marketers are misrepresenting American consumers and opening them up to exploitation* (pp. 1–24). Retrieved from Annenberg School for Communication website: https://www.asc.upenn.edu/sites/-default/files/TradeoffFallacy_1.pdf

Vélez-Ibáñez, C. G., & Greenberg, J. B. (1992). Formation and transformation of funds of knowledge among U.S.-Mexican households. *Anthropology & Education Quarterly*, *23*(4), 313–335.

Vitak, J., Liao, Y., Kumar, P., & Subramaniam, M. (2018). Librarians as information intermediaries: Navigating tensions between being helpful and being liable. In G. Chowdhury, J. McLeod, V. Gillet, & P. Willett, *Transforming digital worlds* (pp. 693–702). Cham: Springer International Publishing.

Vitak, J., Liao, Y., Subramaniam, M., & Kumar, P. (2018). 'I knew it was too good to be true": The challenges economically disadvantaged internet users face in assessing trustworthiness, avoiding scams, and developing self-efficacy online. *Proceedings of the ACM on human-computer interaction*, *2*(CSCW), 1–25.

Vygotsky, L. S. (1978). In M. Cole, V. John-Steiner, S. Scribner, & E. Souberman, *Mind in society: The development of higher psychological processes*. Cambridge: Harvard University Press.

Wash, R., & Rader, E. (2011). Influencing mental models of security: A research agenda. *Proceedings of the 2011 workshop on new security paradigms workshop - NSPW '11, 57*. https://doi.org/10.1145/2073276.2073283

Wisniewski, P., Jia, H., Xu, H., Rosson, M. B., & Carroll, J. M. (2015). "Preventative" vs. "Reactive": How parental mediation influences teens' social media privacy behaviors. *Proceedings of the 18th ACM Conference on computer supported cooperative work & social computing*, 302–316. https://doi.org/10.1145/2675133.2675293

Wissinger, C. L. (2017). Privacy literacy: From theory to practice. *Communications in Information Literacy*, *11* (2), 378–389.

U.S. State and State Capital Open Government Data (OGD): A Content Examination and Heuristic Evaluation of Data Processing Capabilities of OGD Sites

Rong Tang
School of Library and Information Science, Simmons University, Boston, USA
rong.tang@simmons.edu

Will Gregg
School of Library and Information Science, Simmons University, Boston, USA
willjgregg@gmail.com

Sandra Hirsh
School of Information, San José State University, San José, USA
sandy.hirsh@sjsu.edu

Elaine Hall
School of Information, San José State University, San José, USA
laynhall@gmail.com

ABSTRACT

This paper reports the results of a multi-phased investigation into Open Government Data (OGD) sites in the United States. Upon searching and examining OGD sites by state and state capital, we outlined current OGD practice in the US. An inventory of data processing capabilities of 50 OGD sites uncovered the most frequently occurring data categories, search and filter options, raw datasets, data visualization displays, data extraction formats, interactive and map tools, and help functions provided through the OGD sites. Heuristic evaluation of 15 sites containing "Transportation" datasets revealed that main usability problems were violations to the principles of "Flexibility and Efficiency of Use," "Help and Documentation," and "Help users to recognize, diagnose and recover from errors." Findings suggest that in order to sustain and achieve a good usage of OGD sites, a significantly better understanding of user populations, their data needs, and their data literacy levels is needed.

KEYWORDS

Open Government Data (OGD); Content Inventory; Data Processing Capability; Heuristic Evaluation; Violations to Usability Principles

ASIS&T THESAURUS

Data Science, Electronic Government; Systems Design; Content Analysis; United States

INTRODUCTION

Since the 2009 mandate of the Obama administration for transparency and open government (White House, 2009, 2013), there has been tremendous growth in open government data (OGD henceforth) portals and sites within the US. Around the world, parallel OGD efforts have been ongoing at about the same time. For example, New Zealand launched an open data catalog in 2009 (Nayek, 2018), followed by the UK and others in 2010 (data.gov.uk, n.d.). In 2011, Kenya became the first developing nation to launch a national open data site, an event which was regarded as a significant step toward advancing governance (Nayek, 2018).

Within the US, the proliferation of OGD sites extends to local government at both state and city levels. According to the opendata.gov site, there are 48 US states and 48 US cities/counties that have OGD sites. Even though it was mandated that high-level OGD datasets ought to be released to the public, the Obama guidelines did not contain criteria for assessing the quality of OGD sites (Bertot, McDermott, & Smith, 2012). In 2007, 30 OGD advocates gathered in Sebastopol, CA to establish eight principles for OGD: Complete, Primary, Timely, Accessible, Machine processable, Non-discriminatory, Non-proprietary, and License-free. Later on, seven additional principles including Online & Free, Permanent, Trusted, A Presumption of Openness, Documented, Safe to Open, and Designed with Public Input were offered (Tauberer, n.d.). Over the years, there have been empirical investigations on OGD portals (e.g., Xiao, Jeng, & He, 2018; Zhu & Freeman, 2019) with regard to metadata adoptions and user engagement framework. The majority of the investigative focus within the US has been on city OGD portals (e.g., Nahon, Peled, & Shkabatur, 2015; Thorsby, Stowers, Wolslegel, & Tumbuan, 2016; Xiao et al., 2018; Zhu & Freeman, 2019). Few studies have examined OGD sites at both city and state government levels. More importantly, existing studies that performed site inspection or evaluation have seldom examined the depth and specificity of the OGD data processing and extraction capacities, or usability.

In the present study, we performed a multi-phased investigation of the US OGD sites including sites sponsored by both state and state capital city governments. Our inspection of the content of OGD sites included not only the essential administrative features of 85 OGD sites in general but also the data processing functionality of 50 sites in particular.

82nd Annual Meeting of the Association for Information Science & Technology | Melbourne, Australia | 19–23 October, 2019

DOI: 10.1002/pra2.00020

Furthermore, we conducted a heuristic evaluation (HE henceforth) of 15 sites using Jakob Nielsen's 10 heuristic principles. Results of the study fill a gap in the systematic examination and evaluation of OGD websites developed by local governments in the US.

LITERATURE REVIEW

Definitions

There are a variety of definitions of open data or OGD provided in the literature. In seeking to define the parameters of OGD, Gonazlez-Zapata and Heeks (2015) find three "entry points": open government, open data, and government data. The definitions of these three terms, frequently offered by OGD literature, in turn comprise an understanding of OGD itself. According to Ubaldi (2013), government data "is any data and information produced or commissioned by public bodies," and open data "are data that can be freely used, re-used, and distributed by anyone, only subject to (at the most) the requirement that users attribute the data and that they make their work available to be shared as well" (p. 6). Similarly, opendefinition.com defines open data in the following manner: "Open data and content can be freely used, modified, and shared by anyone for any purpose." The principles of open government as declared by the Open Government Directive of the Obama Administration include "transparency, participation, and collaboration" which are "the cornerstone of an open government" (White House, 2009). From these definitions and statements, it seems that the essential aspects of OGD include its open and non-proprietary datasets and its accessibility by any member of a diverse public.

Needs of OGD users

On the national level, users of OGD are more frequently those with some expertise in the use of data, and less frequently members of the general public with no prior training (Dawes, Vidiasova, & Parkhimovich, 2016). Expert stakeholders of OGD may include politicians, public officials, public sector practitioners, international organizations, civil society activists, funding donors, ICT providers, and academics (Gonzalez-Zapata & Heeks, 2015). The degree to which local (municipal or state) OGD users differ from national OGD users is not fully explored. While a study of OGD users of Raleigh Open Data suggests that local users largely fit the profile of those who work in the tech industry (O'Conner, 2015, p. 28), interviewees in another study reported that "'a lot of people (from the community) were intimidated' when using secondary data" and that "publicly available raw data are often not user-friendly to community members" (Yoon, Copeland, & McNally, 2018, pp. 4–5). Further study of non-expert OGD users or citizens is needed to determine their motivations for accessing OGD (Wang, Chen, & Richards, 2018; Wang, Richards, & Chen, 2019).

Non-experts at the local level stand to benefit from the use of OGD (Yoon et al., 2018). The barriers they encounter when attempting to access open data were mainly in the form of a poor user interface and lack of help features (O'Conner, 2015; Thorsby et al., 2016). In a study of the fitness of data for policy analysis, Helbig, Nakashima, and Dawes (2012) find that simply making data available is not enough to make it informative or usable. Similarly, Vetro et al. (2016) find that "low-quality data provision increases the cost... of accessing and interpreting data" (p. 326). If the average citizen is to harvest the substantial benefits of open data, open data must be provided in a high-quality manner. Non-expert users of open data sites require platforms which are easy to navigate and readable, contain help documentation and rights information, and provide tools for displaying and manipulating data.

Evaluating OGD Platforms

Evaluations of OGD often focus on data quality instead of usability of OGD sites for the general public. For instance, Nayek (2018) evaluated metadata quality of six national OGD sites, whereas Kubler and their colleagues (Kubler, Robert, Neumaier, Umbrich, & Le Traon, 2018) established an Analytic Hierarchy Process (AHP) for comparing and ranking sites for the quality of their metadata from a user-centered perspective. In addition, there are notable studies that compared the content and features of US municipal OGD sites (Thorsby et al., 2016), developed 30 criteria for evaluating e-government services (Sá, Rocha, & Pérez Cota, 2016), created a framework for measuring OGD quality and applied it to two Italian datasets (Vetro et al., 2016), evaluated the effectiveness of platforms for promoting transparency (Lourenço, 2015), and presented (but did not apply) a framework to measure the overall quality of national OGD sites (Ubaldi, 2013).

Several recent studies, however, have evaluated OGD platforms directly in terms of their usability. Zhu and Freeman (2018) developed a "User Interaction Framework" that includes dimensions of Access, Trust, Understand, Engage-Integrate, and Participate, and applied it to the evaluation of 34 municipal OGD sites in the US. Meanwhile, Gill and Corbett (2017) employed usability heuristics to evaluate municipal OGD sites in British Columbia and also used the Open Data Barometer to monitor data quality dimensions with implications for usability. In summarizing previous research on open government transparency, Lourenço (2015) indicated that there is a dual meaning associated with usability when it comes to "web-based governmental transparency." On the one hand, usability "is closely related to interactivity" and the ease of access and use; on the other hand, usability should encompass "comprehensibility and timeliness" (p. 325). Lourenço (2015) further lists a set of key characteristics of desired data disclosure, with "usability and comprehensibility" as one among eight characteristics. These studies represent a valuable contribution toward reaching the potential of OGD by specifically addressing a main barrier for citizens using OGD: their usability. In focusing exclusively on municipal OGD sites, these studies leave an opportunity for research into the OGD platforms of US states.

Heuristic Evaluation

A substantial body of knowledge exists for evaluating web-based platforms and tools using HE. HE is defined as "An inspection method for finding certain types of usability problems in a user interface design. HE involves having one or more usability specialists individually examine the interface and judge its compliance with recognized usability principles" (usability.gov, n.d.). There are several well-regarded sets of heuristic principles including the 247 criteria compiled by David Travis (2016) for userfocus.co.uk, 10 principles by Jakob Nielsen (1994), and 10 cognitive-designs by Jill Gerhardt-Powals (1996), and seven dialog heuristics by the International Organization for Standardization (ISO) (2010).

Though there are limited studies which employ heuristics in evaluating OGD portals (see Gill & Corbett, 2017 for one example), Nielsen's heuristics have been incorporated into evaluations of similar services including e-commerce websites (Hasan, Morris, & Probets, 2013), e-government services (Delopoulos, 2015; Saeed, Malik, & Wahab, 2013), government mobile applications (Al-Khalifa, Al-Twaim, & AlHarbi, 2016), and e-learning platforms (Freire, Arezes, & Creissac, 2012). The present study recognizes that there is a gap for using usability principles to evaluate OGD from the perspective of the non-expert citizen. In addition, the majority of the evaluations of OGD sites were on city OGDs (e.g, Kassen, 2013; Throsby et al., 2016; Zhu & Freeman, 2018), including those outside the US (Gill & Corbett, 2017; Vetro et al., 2016). Within the US, there have not been any studies focused on the state OGDs, even though there was a study on Chinese city as well as province OGDs by Wang et al. (2018). Overall, comprehensive research on both city and state OGDs is lacking. Our efforts of performing a content inventory and HE of city and state OGD sites have enabled us to present insights into the missing areas in OGD research and identify usability problems in current OGD data provision to citizens who are not data experts.

RESEARCH QUESTIONS

The present study addresses the following research questions:

RQ1. What is the current state of practice with OGD sites by states and state capitals?

RQ2. What specific data processing capability do OGD sites offer?

RQ3. To what extent do OGD sites conform with usability heuristics? What are the most common violations of usability principles of OGD sites?

METHODS

A multi-phased and multi-method approach was employed for this study which involved Phase I inventory of OGD sites, Phase II content inventory and analysis in terms of datasets processing capability, and Phase III HE of the sites containing "transportation" data sets. Authors from two institutions formed teams to perform coding for Phase I and II. OGD sites selected for both phases' coding were divided evenly between the two teams. Specifically, during Phase I of the study, we performed an inventory that included searching for the OGD site for each state and its capital city. Once we identified the OGD site for a given state or state capital, we recorded the state/city, the name of the site, the site URL, the webmaster, whether the site had a mission statement, the copyright date, the date of the most recent dataset, and the platform. When needed, we added notes of our observation of the site.

Upon completing Phase I, we selected the 50 sites containing a mission statement for Phase II. A mission statement is a statement on the site describing what the site is, who the site is for, and how it is to be used. The Phase II content inventory focused on data processing capability. For each of the 50 sites, we collected information on data browsing categories, raw data sets, dataset search and filtering functions, data visualization display options, data extraction formats, interactive tools to engage with data, and help functions available.

With regard to data browsing categories, we used the groupings from Zhu and Freeman's (2018) results as our basis for coding. We subsequently added and modified those categories based on the actual data categories present on the homepage of the OGD sites in our study sample. For example, Zhu and Freeman (2018) had a category labeled "Finance;" based on our data, we changed that label to "Finance and Budget." For the data browsing categories, there were a total of 39 categories, ranging from "Health," "Recreation," "Housing," "Economy," "Arts, Culture, History," "Natural Resources," "Community," "Education," to "Quality of Life." The categories for visualization display, the subcategories were "Table View," "Chart View," "Line View," "Map View," "Raw Data," "Text," "Calendar," "Form," and "List." Meanwhile, there were 24 categories under data extraction formats, including "CSV," "XLSX/XLS," "PDF," "PNG," "Shapefile," "JSON," "RDF," "RSS," and "XML."

Following Phase II, we randomly selected 15 OGD sites that contained the "transportation" data category, and performed HE. These OGD sites included seven states and eight capital cities. The HE was conducted by following a set of task scenarios relevant to the transportation datasets. We then employed Nielsen's 10 principles of HE, and used a five-point rating scale to rate the severity of violations to each of the 10 principles. Figure 1 provides detailed information about the phases and the number of sites involved in each phase.

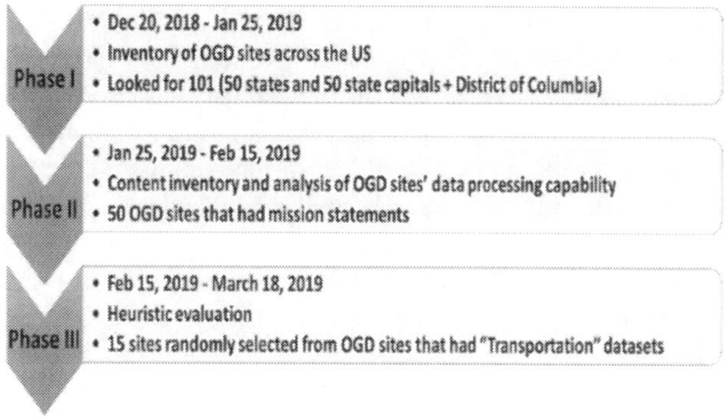

Figure 1. OGD sites analyzed and evaluated for each phase.

RESULTS

The results of the study are outlined below in three sections addressing each of our research questions.

State of Practice of OGD in the US

Our Phase I inventory search for OGD sites of 50 states and 50 state capitals revealed that 47 states and 37 state capitals had OGD sites. The District of Columbia (DC) also had an OGD site. The three states that did not have an OGD site were Arkansas, Idaho, and West Virginia. Table 1 lists the states and capital cities that had not yet developed their OGD sites. Even though a great majority of the states (94%) had open data sites, a much lower percentage of the capital cities had OGD sites (74%).

Among the 85 sites (including DC) that we examined, 79 (92%) had webmaster's information listed. Among those, 75 sites' webmasters (95%) were a part of city or state government. Of 85 OGD sites, over half (*n* = 51%, 60%) had a mission statement. These mission statements vary in terms of length, but their common focus tend to be promoting the openness and transparency of their government data. In fact, four sites included the term "transparency" in their site title. An example of a mission statement, from Sacramento Open Data, reads "As part of our ongoing commitment to promote transparency, accountability, and citizen engagement, the Sacramento Open Data Portal was designed for you to explore, visualize, and download our publicly accessible data. Developers can also use exported data to build new Web and mobile applications" (City of Sacramento, 2018).

Of 85 OGD sites, 23 did not incorporate a specific platform. Among those sites that had a platform, Socrata was the most common (*n* = 36%, 58%), followed by ArcGIS (*n* = 15%, 24%), CKAN (*n* = 5%, 8%), and OpenGov plus CKAN (*n* = 2%, 3%). The remaining platforms included DKAN, Granicus, REVIZE, and ESRI, among others. Of 85 sites, 31 (36%) did not list any copyright dates. Among 54 sites that had copyright dates, 2019 was the most frequently listed year. Table 2 contains copyright year information of the OGD sites.

State	Arkansas, Idaho, West Virginia
State capitals	Juneau (AK), Dover (DE), Springfield (IL), Frankfort (KY), Annapolis (MD), Concord (NH), Trenton (NJ), Harrisburg (PA), Pierre (SD), Montpelier (VT), Olympia (WA), Charleston (SC), Cheyenne (WY)

Table 1. States and state capitals that did not have an OGD site.

Copyright year	# (%)
2019	35 (65%)
2018	8 (15%)
2017	6 (11%)
2016	1 (2%)
2015	4 (7%)
2014	1 (2%)

Table 2. Copyright dates (*n* = 55).

With regard to the URL domains of the OGD sites, *.gov* was the most common domain (*n* = 59%, 69%), followed by *.com* (*n* = 15%, 18%), *.org* (*n* = 8%, 9%), *.edu* (*n* = 3%, 4%), and *.us* (*n* = 1%, 1%). In terms of the most recent dates for datasets, of 85 OGD sites, 15 did not have any information about their most recent datasets. Among 70 sites that listed their most recent datasets, 59 (84%) listed datasets from 2019, 10 from 2018 (14%), and 1 from 2011 (2%).

Data Processing Capacity of OGD

In Phase II, we examined the data processing capacity of 50 OGD sites that had a mission statement. The sections below outline the results of this examination.

Data Categories

The 50 OGD sites offered a total of 39 unique categories. The most common categories included government (*n* = 33%, 66%), finance/budget (*n* = 29%, 58%), public safety (*n* = 28%, 56%), transportation (*n* = 28%, 56%), and environment (*n* = 22%, 44%). Figure 2 displays those data categories that were equal to or higher than 10%.

Search and Filter Options

In terms of the ability to search and display retrieved datasets through filters, 92% (*n* = 46) of the OGD sites contained searchable datasets. The number of filters ranged from no filters to 8 filters. The average number of filters was 3.54. The most common type of filter available on OGD sites was the format filter (*n* = 39%, 85%). Other common types of filters included the text filter (*n* = 37%, 80%), topic filter (*n* = 28%, 61%), organizations filter (*n* = 23%, 50%), and authority filter

(n = 9%, 20%). Figure 3 includes all the filter types sorted in descending order by frequency.

Raw Datasets

On these OGD sites, an average of 1714.45 datasets were provided. The range was from as low as none to as high as 151,615 (Mass Data https://opendata.digital.mass.gov). The date range of the datasets were from 1997 to 2019.

Data Visualization Displays

All of the OGD sites examined had some form of visualization display. Some OGD sites had advanced visualization tools whereas others had minimal capacity for visualization. Figure 4 is a screenshot of the state of New York's open data site, using plot.ly for their visualization display. The most common visualization view was table view (n = 43%, 86%), followed by chart view (n = 41%, 82%), map view (n = 40%, 80%), line view (n = 34%, 68%), and text view (n = 31%, 62%).

Data Extraction Formats

All OGD sites offered some levels of data extraction capabilities, but the extraction format options provided varied by the number of formats available. The most common format was CSV (n = 42%, 84%), followed in a distant second by XML (n = 23%, 46%), then RDF (n = 22%, 44%). Figure 5 lists all the format types that were over 10% in frequency.

Interactive Tools

All sites featured interactive tools for their datasets. The most common tool available was an API viewer (n = 34%, 68%), followed by the ability to select chart type (n = 33%, 66%), the presence of a map tool (n = 21%, 42%), and an interactive timeline (n = 2%, 4%). Within the map tool, some sites offered tools for measuring (n = 8%, 16%) and drawing (n = 2%, 4%).

Map Tools

The 21 sites which included maps used five different web mapping tools, namely ArcGIS (n = 15%, 71%), Socrata (n = 12%, 57%), ESRI (n = 7%, 33%), Leaflet (n = 4%, 19%), and OpenStreetMap (n = 2%, 10%).

Help Tools

For help tools, we considered only those tools/texts available within the OGD sites. Help documentation made available on platform vendor sites was not viewed as a part of the OGD's own effort. Among the sites that provided help features, the most frequent type was email contact or contact form (n = 35%, 70%), followed by links to vendor help (n = 19%, 38%), how-to videos (n = 14%, 28%), and tutorials (n = 13%, 26%). Figure 6 provides information about help tools available on OGD sites.

Heuristic Evaluation of OGD Sites

HE was performed by two of four authors who have expertise in usability and UX. Fifteen randomly selected sites

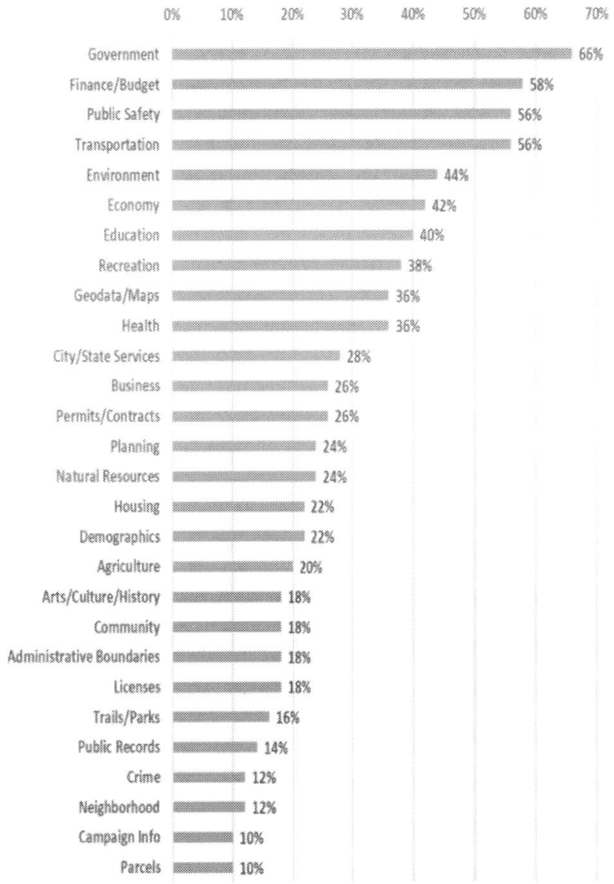

Figure 2. Top data categories on OGD sites (n = 50).

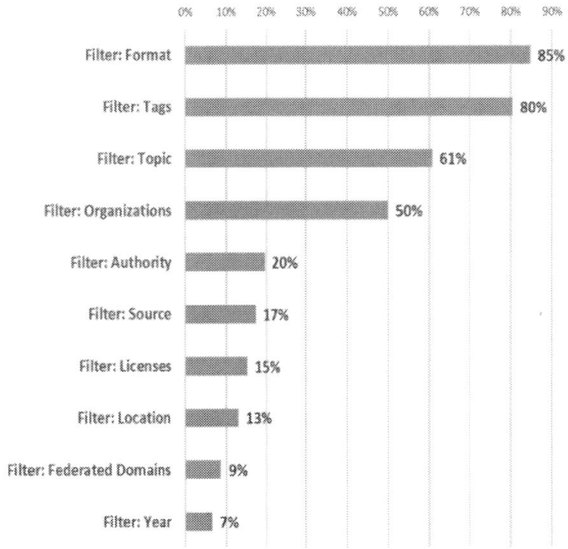

Figure 3. Top filter options on OGD sites (n = 46).

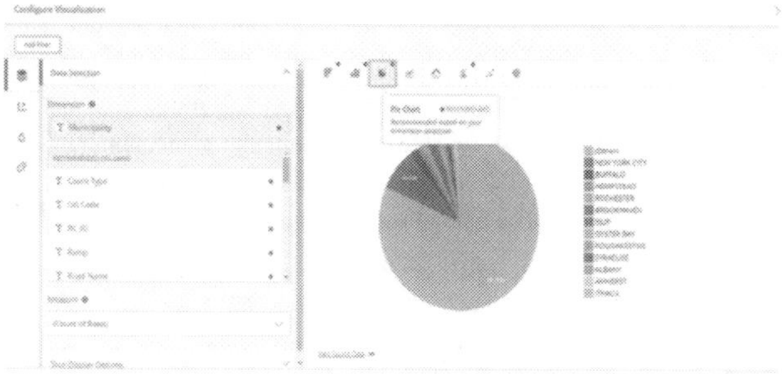

Figure 4. New York State OGD datasets visualization display.

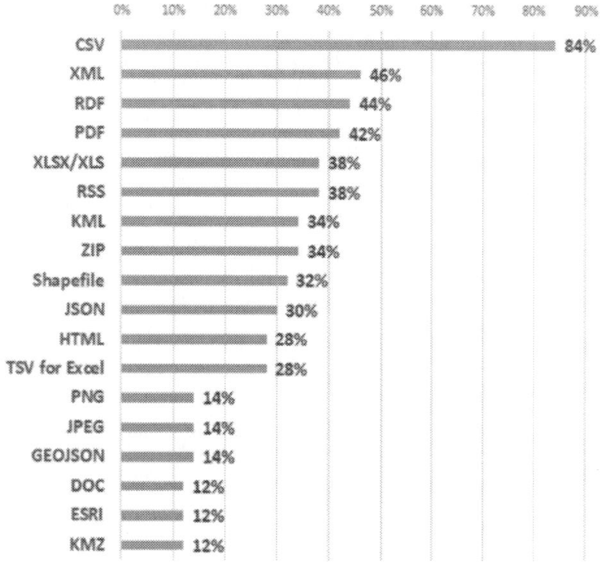

Figure 5. Top data extraction formats on OGD sites (n = 50).

containing the "Transportation" data category were evaluated. We selected the category of "Transportation" because it was one of the top categories on OGD sites, and the datasets in this category tended to have maps or other visualization features. Table 3 lists the OGD sites selected for Phase III evaluation. An HE worksheet was created to enable the researchers to identify and evaluate the violations of HE principles established by Nielsen (1994). Since two authors have had years of experience performing HE using Nielsen's principles, we decided to employ these principles for our Phase III OGD evaluation. We selected a five-point scale to rate the severity of the violations (0-no problem, 1-cosmetic problem, 2-minor problem, 3-major problem, 4-catastrophic problem).

One example for a site receiving a "4" (catastrophic problem) on the principle of "Help users recognize, diagnose, and recover from error" was, as commented by the researcher, "I

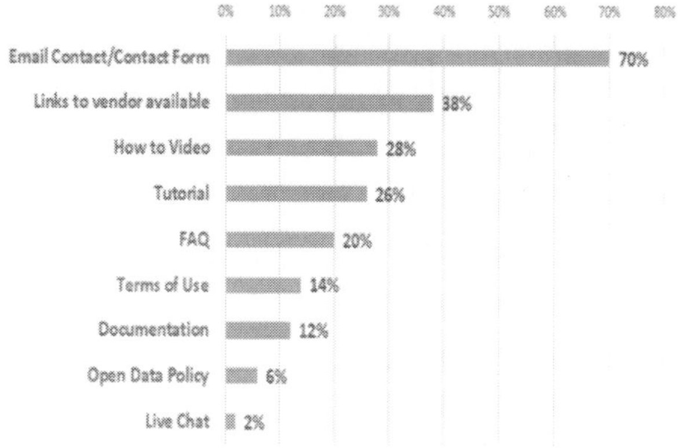

Figure 6. Top help tools available on OGD sites (n = 50).

received an error (loading error?) when I tried to click on Closure Intersection dataset. See 3 vertical blue lines. Also, when I tried to click on the Closures dataset (not Intersection), it did load a page but didn't show any data." Figure 7 is a screenshot of the problem encountered.

Site name	Site URL
City of Phoenix Open Data	https://www.phoenixopendata.com/
California Open Data Portal	https://data.ca.gov/
Sacramento Open Data	http://data.cityofsacramento.org/
My Florida	http://myflorida-floridadisaster.opendata.arcgis.com/
The State of Hawaii's Open Data Portal	https://data.hawaii.gov/
OpenIndy	http://data.indy.gov/
Mississippi Open Data	http://opendata.gis.ms.gov/
Open NY Data	https://data.ny.gov/
Raleigh Open Data	https://data-ral.opendata.arcgis.com/
data.ok.gov	https://data.ok.gov/
Open Data Portal City of Oklahoma City	https://data.okc.gov/portal/page/start/
Access Salem	https://city-salem.opendata.arcgis.com/
Nashville Open Data Portal	https://data.nashville.gov/
Austin's Open Data Portal	https://data.austintexas.gov/
State of Utah Open Data Catalog	https://opendata.utah.gov/

Table 3. OGD sites selected for Phase III HE (n = 15).

Usability Problem Areas as per HE Score Rankings

Based on our evaluation, the most frequently occurring usability problem area for OGD sites was the violation to the

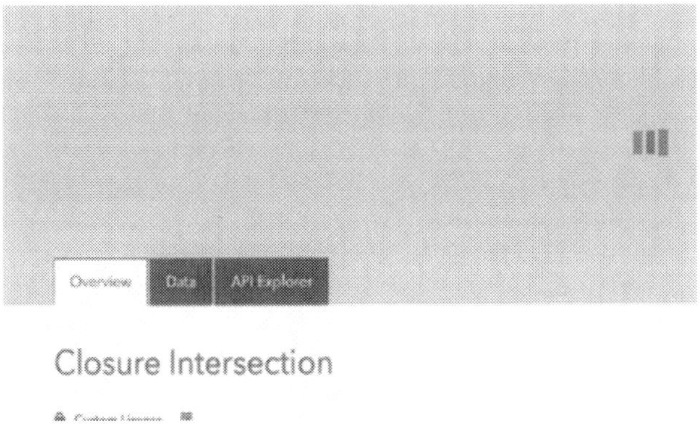

Figure 7. Loading error. Unable to diagnose and recover from errors.

principle of "Flexibility and Efficiency of Use" with an average score of 2.2. The next was "Help and Documentation" (average = 2.06), followed by "Help users to recognize, diagnose and recover from errors" (average = 1.73). Table 4 lists the violation scores of each principle and the number of 4s and 3s (highest level of problems) associated with a given principle. Note that even though "Flexibility and Efficiency of Use" had the highest average on violation scores, it only had one instance of 4. The principle of "Help and Documentation" received six 4s, indicating a serious deficiency in this area for OGD sites.

When looking at the scores received by each site, one of the state sites that received the highest score of violation received two 4s and four 3s. The most severe violations occurred in "help and documentation" and "help users recognize and recover from errors." One of the capital cities that was ranked high in violation of HE principles received two 4s and three 3s. The most severe violations were in "help users to recognize, diagnose, and recover from errors," and "visibility of system status."

Usability Problem Areas as per HE Evaluators' Comments

As researchers conducted the HE, they also included feedback and comments on the violation areas. Based on the comments, the most serious usability problem areas were outlined as follows:

Flexibility and Efficiency of Use. In this area, the most frequent complaints or violation to the principle included: Lack of flexibility (n = 5), lack of customization ability (n = 4), unable to create shortcuts (n = 3), and required to sign in to enjoy additional functionality (n = 3). An example comment about the lack of flexibility was "Flexibility is an issue when the map is stacked with other datasets display, and there is no way to have a popup screen to focus on the map."

Principles	Mean	# of 4s	# of 3s
Flexibility and efficiency of use	2.20	1	7
Help and documentation	2.06	6	1
Help users to recognize, diagnose and recover from errors	1.73	2	2
User control and freedom	1.47	1	3
Error prevention	1.40	1	3
Match between system and the real world	1.33	0	5
Recognition rather than recall	.73	0	0
Visibility of system status	.53	1	0
Consistency and standards	.33	0	0
Aesthetic and minimalist design	.07	0	0

Table 4. HE usability principles and their violation scores.

Help and Documentation. The violations in this area most frequently resulted from a lack of any help or documentation

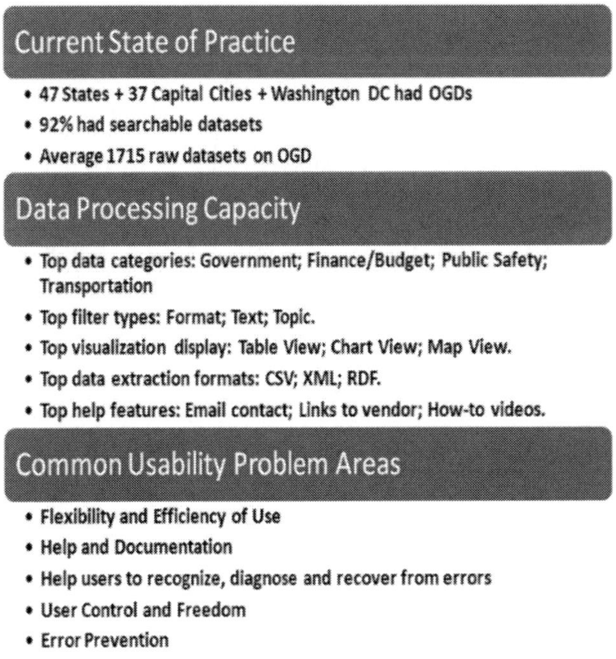

Figure 8. Summary of results.

($n = 7$). When help and documentation was provided, it was sometimes found to be inadequate ($n = 3$) and there was a lack of context-sensitive help ($n = 2$). In one case, the help page provided was inaccessible due to a 404 error. An example complaint about the lack of help functions was: "Lack of documentation and help in data filter or extraction pages."

Help users to recognize, diagnose and recover from errors. For this area, the most frequent violations included no help ($n = 3$), no error messages ($n = 3$), and no alternatives provided when encountering errors ($n = 2$). One comment about this principle was "I didn't receive any error messages but also didn't receive help when I couldn't find a legend or other supports."

Overall, OGD sites appeared to have the least level of violations in the area of "Aesthetic and minimalist design" with a very low score of .07 and none of the scores were in 4s or 3s. The principle of "Consistency and standards" appears to be confirmed as there was an average of .33 violation and no scores in 3s or 4s.

DISCUSSION AND CONCLUSION

The present investigation into OGD sites in the US through three phases has provided great insights into the current practices of OGD sites. Figure 8 presents a summary of the results from various phases.

Not all states or state capitals had OGD sites, with 13 state capitals missing in action with regard to their OGD. Therefore we recommend that all states/state capitals develop an OGD site. Furthermore, there are different levels of content depth and functionality provided through these existing OGD sites. Some were very minimal, based mostly on the state or capital's departments, and datasets were produced in ready-made files with pre-defined data categories and visual display. In these cases, users were unable to customize the data processing based on their needs. Some OGD sites offered more advanced levels of process/filtering capability and several visualization formats. These features might still be challenging for users with limited data literacy who are unable to fully take advantage of what is offered. These sites seem to assume that the target users are fluent with dataset processing and visualization tools. These findings confirm the previous results by O'Conner (2015) and Thorsby et al. (2016) regarding the poor user interface and the lack of help features on OGD sites.

In this study, the employment of Nielsen's HE principles provided useful discovery with regard to applying general principles toward evaluating specialized data-driven websites such as OGD sites. We did not use evaluation principles that are data portal specific (e.g., Zhu & Freeman, 2018) for this study, because, in part, some of these evaluative frameworks were made in a binary response format which does not allow granularity in assessing the degree of violation of usability principles. Even though there has been a growing number of research studies on the topic of OGD, the present study is one of the few that focused on both state and state capital OGD sites. In addition to examining the OGD sites from 47 states, 37 state capitals, and DC, and conducting content inventory of the data processing capacity of 50 OGD sites, we performed HE of randomly selected OGD sites and identified major gaps in areas of flexibility and efficiency, help and documentation, error diagnosis, and recovery. These gaps significantly impair non-expert users' ability to use OGD sites, which should be seriously addressed in future improvement of the site design. Given that citizens are considered as the primary target users and stakeholders of OGD sites (Ruijer, Grimmelikhuijsen, & Meijer, 2017; Wang et al., 2019), providing user friendly data processing capabilities and ample help and support for citizens' diverse data needs is the key to ensure the success of OGD services. The findings of this study confirmed previous research discovery on the lack of help and documentation (e.g., O'Conner, 2015; Thorsby et al., 2016), and it is essential for OGD sites to equip more support tools to help non-expert citizen users to navigate the site and use the datasets to inform themselves and their communities.

One of the challenges that we encountered during the coding for Phases I and II was that the understanding of how a given feature should be coded varied to some extent between the two teams who collaborated in data processing. During the Phase I coding, we discovered that there were two errors in the state capital cities list that we downloaded from the web. In addition, there was some misunderstanding of whether open data network sites could be qualified as an OGD. We corrected those mistakes, but there might still be inconsistency in the two teams' coding in the first two phases. The Phase III HE may also vary between the two evaluators. Nevertheless, the reliability of the data coding was achieved through two authors performing a final check and coding corrections of the entire dataset. The final coding was based on the consensus of the whole team.

The scope of this research is limited to the OGD sites within the US only; future research involving international OGD sites would yield meaningful insights into the global effort of open data movement. In addition, linking usability principles with established OGD principles (e.g., Tauberer, n.d.) or desired characteristics of open data release established by relevant communities and scholars (e.g., Lourenço, 2015), and contextualizing usability heuristics in the OGD ecosystem (Dawes et al., 2016) would enable a well-rounded assessment of OGD sites. Such an assessment would not only address particular data processing functions and features but also consider non-expert users' data needs, their data literacy level, and their participatory use of OGD data to fulfill their citizenry responsibilities and proactive contributions to communities and democratic societies.

REFERENCES

Al-Khalifa, H. S., Al-Twaim, B., & AlHarbi, B. (2016). A heuristic checklist for usability evaluation of Saudi government mobile applications. In *Proceedings of the 18th International Conference on Information Integration and Web-based Applications and Services* (pp. 375–378). https://doi.org/10.1145/3011141.3011189

Bertot, J. C., McDermott, P., & Smith, T. (2012). Measurement of open government: Metics and process. In *Proceedings of the 45th Hawaii International Conference on System Sciences* (pp. 2491–2499). https://doi.org/10.1109/HICSS.2012.658

City of Sacramento. (2018). *Sacramento open data*. Retrieved from http://data.cityofsacramento.org/

Dawes, S. S., Vidiasova, L., & Parkhimovich, O. (2016). Planning and designing open government data programs: An ecosystem approach. *Government Information Quarterly*, *33*, 15–27. https://doi.org/10.1016/j.giq.2016.01.003

data.gov.uk. (n.d.). *About find open data*. Retrieved from https://data.gov.uk/about

Delopoulos, H. (2015). A usability evaluation of e-government services: The case of e-deliberation service of Greece. *International Journal of Electronic Governance*, *7*(2), 93–112. https://doi.org/10.1504/IJEG.2015.069499

Freire, L. L., Arezes, P. M., & Campos, J. C. (2012). A literature review about evaluation methods for e-learning platforms. *Work*, *41*(1), 1038–1044. https://doi.org/10.3233/WOR-2012-0281-1038

Gerhardt-Powals, J. (1996). Cognitive engineering principles for enhancing human-computer performance. *International Journal of Human-Computer Interaction*, *8*(2), 189–211.

Gill, M., & Corbett, J. (2017). Downscaling: Understanding the influence of open data initiatives in smaller and mid-sized cities in British Columbia, Canada. *The Canadian Geographer*, *61*(3), 346–359. https://doi.org/10.1111/cag.12372

Gonazlez-Zapata, F., & Heeks, R. (2015). The multiple meanings of open government data: Understanding different stakeholders and their perspectives. *Government Information Quarterly*, *32*, 441–452. https://doi.org/10.1016/j.giq.2015.09.001

Hasan, L., Morris, A., & Probets, S. (2013). E-commerce websites for developing countries: A usability evaluation framework. *Online Information Review*, *37*(2), 231–251. Retrieved from https://dspace.lboro.ac.uk/2134/12422

Helbig, N., Nakashima, N., & Dawes, S. S. (2012). Understanding the value and limits of government information in policy informatics: A preliminary exploration. In *The Proceedings of the 13th Annual International Conference on Digital Government Research* (pp. 291–293).

International Organization for Standardization. (2010). ISO 9241-210:2010. Retrieved from https://www.iso.org/standard/52075.html

Kubler, S., Robert, J., Neumaier, S., Umbrich, J., & Le Traon, Y. (2018). Comparison of metadata quality in open data portals using the Analytic Hierarchy Process. *Government Information Quarterly*, *35*, 13–29. https://doi.org/10.1016/j.giq.2017.11.003

Lourenço, R. P. (2015). An analysis of open government portals: A perspective of transparency for accountability. *Government Information Quarterly*, *32*, 323–332. https://doi.org/10.1016/j.giq.2015.05.006

Nayek, J. (2018). Evaluation of open government data sites: A comparative study. *Library Philosophy and Practice (e-journal)*, 1781. Retrieved from: https://digitalcommons.unl.edu/libphilprac/1781

Nielsen, J. (1994). Heuristic evaluation. In J. Nielsen & R. L. Mack, *Usability Inspection Methods*. New York, NY: John Wiley & Sons.

Nahon, K., Peled, A., & Shkabatur, J. (2015). OGD heartbeat: Cities' Commitment to open data. *eJournal of eDecmocracy and Open Government (JeDEM)*, *7*(2), 116–136.

O'Conner, J. (2015). *Towards a profile of open government data users* (Master's Thesis). University of North Carolina, Chapel Hill. Retrieved from http://john.oconnorv.com/wp-content/uploads/2016/06/John-OConnor-Masters-Paper-Final.pdf

Ruijer, E., Grimmelikhuijsen, S., & Meijer, A. (2017). Open data for democracy: Developing a theoretical framework for open data use. *Government Information Quarterly*, *34*(1), 45–52. https://doi.org/10.1016/j.giq.2015.05.006

Sá, F., Rocha, Á., & Pérez Cota, M. (2016). Potential dimensions for a Local e-Government services quality model. *Telematics and Informatics*, *33*(2). https://doi.org/10.1016/j.tele.2015.08.005

Saeed, S., Malik, I., & Wahab, F. (2013). Usability evaluation of Pakistani security agencies websites. *International Journal of E-Politics (IJEP)*, *4*(3), 57–69. https://doi.org/10.4018/jep.2013070105

Saxena, S. (2018). Open government data (OGD) in six Middle East countries: an evaluation of the national open data portals. *Digital Policy, Regulation and Governance*, *20*(4), 310–322. https://doi.org/10.1108/DPRG-10-2017-0055

Travis, D. (2016). *247 web usability guidelines*. Retrieved from https://www.userfocus.co.uk/resources/guidelines.html

Thorsby, J., Stowers, G., Wolslegel, K., & Tumbuan, E. (2016). Understanding the content and features of open data portals in American cities. *Government Information Quarterly, 34*, 53–61. https://doi.org/10/1016/j.giq.2016.07.001

Tauberer, J. (n.d.). *The annotated 8 principles of open government data*. Retrieved from: https://opengovdata.org/

Ubaldi, B. (2013). Open government data: Towards empirical analysis of open government data initiatives. *OECD Working Papers on Public Governance, 22*. https://doi.org/10.1787/5k46bj4f03s7-en

usability.gov. (n.d.). *Glossary*. Retrieved from https://www.usability.gov/what-and-why/glossary/h/index.html

Vetro, A., Canova, L., Torchiano, M., Minotas, C. O., Iemma, R., & Morando, F. (2016). Open data quality measurement framework: Definition and application to open government data. *Government Information Quarterly, 33* (2), 325–337. https://doi.org/10.1016/j.giq.2016.02.001

Wang, D., Chen, C., & Richards, D. (2018). A prioritization-based analysis of local open government data portals: A case study of Chinese province-level governments. *Government Information Quarterly, 35*, 644–656. https://doi.org/10.1016/j.giq.2018.10.006

Wang, D., Richards, D., & Chen, C. (2019). Connecting users, data and utilization: A demand-side analysis of open government data. In N. G. Taylor, et al. (Eds.), *Proceedings of iConference 2019* (Vol. *11420*, pp. 488–500). *LNCS*. https://doi.org/10.1007/978-3-030-15742-5_47

White House (2009). *Memorandum on transparency and open government*. Retrieved from: https://obamawhitehouse.archives.gov/the-press-office/transparency-and-open-government

White House (2013). *Executive order — making open and machine readable the new default for government information*. Retrieved from http://www.whitehouse.gov/the-press-office/2013/05/09/executive-order-making-open-and-machine-readable-new-default-

Xiao, F., Jeng, W., & He, D. (2018). Investigating metadata adoptions for open government data portals in US cities. *Proceedings of the 81st Annual Meeting of the Association for Information Science & Technology (ASIS&T)*, 573–582.

Yoon, A., Copeland, A., McNally, P. (2018). Empowering communities with data: Role of data intermediaries for communities' data utilization. *Proceedings of the 81st Annual Meeting of the Association for Information Science & Technology (ASIS&T)*, 583–592.

Zhu, X., & Freeman, M. A. (2018). An evaluation of U.S. municipal open data portals: A user interaction framework. *Journal of the Association for Information Science and Technology, 70*(1), 27–37. https://doi.org/10.1002/asi.2408

"Computer What's Your Favourite Colour?" Children's Information-Seeking Strategies in the Classroom

Nicholas Vanderschantz
Department of Computer Science,
The University of Waikato, New Zealand
vtwoz@waikato.ac.nz

Annika Hinze
Department of Computer Science,
The University of Waikato, New Zealand
hinze@waikato.ac.nz

ABSTRACT

This research investigates children's information seeking in primary and intermediate school classrooms as seen by their teachers. We report the results of a series of semi-structured interviews with teachers of pre-teen children. The teachers discussed specific issues that children encounter during information search, including query construction and information triage difficulties. Further issues were identified during the interviews regarding motivation, frustration and poor strategies for overcoming barriers. We compare the results of our teacher interviews reported here with the results of an interview study with children. This paper concludes that even with significant advancements in technology, teachers and children still require further assistance in order to succeed in their inquiry practices.

KEYWORDS

Children's Information Seeking; Search Strategies; Interview Study; Digital Literacy; Information Literacy

ASIS&T THESAURUS

Search Behavior; Educational Technology; Interviews

INTRODUCTION

Information problem solving and information seeking is a common part of daily adult life. Information seeking is a complex process that necessitates using a range of technologies and techniques to locate, identify, collate, and organize information, and sources. During their education children are developing the skills they will need in adulthood and thus supporting both children and teachers in the development of information seeking skills is necessary. We used an interview study to reveal when and how information seeking is being conducted in children's education.

Children are known to have difficulties when using the information technologies that are available to them effectively. Barriers to successful information seeking by children have been well-documented, dating back to the early days of search engines and Web access (Bilal, 2000) as well as work with digital libraries (Hutchinson, Druin, & Bederson, 2007). However, contemporary strategies for information seeking as taught to, and practiced by children in the classroom are less understood and have little recent investigation. This paper contributes to the investigation into best practices and research to support children's digital information seeking; we focus on current information seeking teaching and practices in New Zealand (NZ) educational settings. We provide new insight into when and where do children engage in information seeking activities; what processes of information seeking children engage in; and what contemporary issues children encounter. We highlight in this paper that teachers themselves may not have received training or education to be successful information seekers, and yet, we require these overworked professionals to prepare children to be daily information seekers.

This paper is structured as follows; related work focuses on children's information seeking with details of the NZ education setting. We detail the *Study Method* for interviews with teachers. The *Results* section provides a snapshot of the information seeking practices of children. We next outline a model of the working process of children's online search for information. Our *Discussion* provides an analysis of our study results with comparison to related work. Finally, we summarize the identified information seeking issues encountered by children and provide recommendations.

BACKGROUND AND RELATED WORK

We outline existing work on the use of Information Communication Technology (ICT) in classrooms, as well as research on children's information seeking and use. Additionally, we describe the educational environment in which our investigation was undertaken so that readers may clarify any similarities to their own research environments.

ICT in Classrooms

Children are engaging in information seeking with contemporary ICT in both formal educational settings and in their daily recreational activities. In earlier work we observed how children in the NZ classrooms and homes used a broad range of technologies including digital whiteboards, laptops, and tablets and a range of child-targeted software for skill-

82nd Annual Meeting of the Association for Information Science & Technology | Melbourne, Australia | 19–23 October, 2019

DOI: 10.1002/pra2.00021

based learning (e.g. reading and maths) (Timpany & Vanderschantz, 2011; Vanderschantz, Hinze, & Cunningham, 2014a). This is similar to the situation globally with studies confirming that, worldwide, child-specific software is seeing significant use in primary education: for example, for reading and searching (i.e., Hutchinson et al., 2007), and novel teaching of mathematics and programming using tablets, software and haptic devices (i.e., Hegedus, 2013). Recent research also explores use of contemporary devices in the classroom including tablet and mobile devices such as iPods and iPads (Falloon, 2015), interactive whiteboards (Mellingsaeter & Bungum, 2015), and clicker classroom response systems (Moratelli & DeJarnette, 2014). While it is common to find a wide range of digital information seeking technologies in modern schools these technologies only enhance the learning through quality pedagogically driven implementation by teachers (Okojie, Olinzock, & Okojie-Boulder, 2006). Teachers require support to successfully implement technology into their teaching practice. This paper provides insight into what areas of support might be necessary for children and teachers.

Children's Information Seeking & Use

Early children's information seeking behaviour studies explored use of electronic databases (i.e., Spavold, 1990), OPACs (Online Public Access Catalogues) (i.e., Dinet, Favart, & Passerault, 2004) and digital libraries (i.e., Druin et al., 2001, 2003). Many researchers report the observation that children across a wide range of ages experience difficulties with many facets of digital information seeking and the findings of these numerous studies show that technological capability, searching, document selection, and triage all play a part in the issues experienced by children. Research has investigated the issues children experience when constructing search queries during Internet, library catalogue, and digital library search. These studies have included investigations of query formulation, miss-spellings, term repetition, and difficulties with text entry (Bilal, 2000; Large, Beheshti, & Rahman, 2002). Children experience many of the same difficulties with search that adults do: for example children struggle when using Boolean operators, choosing effective keywords, modifying queries, (i.e., Bilal, 2000; Kafai & Bates, 1997). Research of children's Internet use has examined children's evaluation of information when using the Internet as well as other digital resources (Hirsh, 1999; Kafai & Bates, 1997). McCrory Wallace, Kupperman, Krajcik, and Soloway (2000) noted that children poorly access the validity, authoritativeness or correctness of information and often attempt to simplify the complex task of information seeking to simply finding an obvious answer. Recent focus has been on youth health related information seeking (i.e. Kodama, Jean, Subramaniam, & Taylor, 2017; Subramaniam et al., 2015) where young people's digital literacy and their information-credibility and quality decisions have been explored. Similarly recent investigations explored children's mental models of information seeking interfaces and computers (Robertson, Manches, & Pain, 2017; Taylor, 2018).

Given the speed of technology evolution, much of the existing research into children's information seeking and use is somewhat dated, and very few investigations into children's information seeking have appeared in the last 5 years. Among the more recent works, we find researchers have investigated children's search performance on commercial search engine interfaces designed for children (Jochmann-Mannak, Huibers, Lentz, & Sanders, 2010; Vanderschantz & Hinze, 2017) as well as on research led search user interfaces for children (Gossen, Nitsche, & Nürnberger, 2012; Vanderschantz & Hinze, 2018), and in the home (e.g., Druin, Foss, Hutchinson, Golub, & Hatley, 2010), but little education or classroom based investigations of what and how children are interacting with technologies.

Overall, we found limited research explores the strategies used by children or the issues and successes encountered during online search for information, either in the classroom or at home. Therefore, where educational information seeking is happening, as well as what issues children are encountering during internet search, is still not fully answered by the related work.

The New Zealand Context

While roughly similar to the US and UK primary education systems we offer here a brief insight into the context in which these studies have been performed. NZ government-funded schools at pre-high school level (i.e., Years 1–8) are typically separated into *primary schools* (catering to new entrant Year 1–6) and *intermediate schools* (catering to Years 7 and 8). Our work presented in this paper focuses on teachers of Years 5 & 6 at primary level and Years 7 & 8 at intermediate level. Years 5 & 6 children are typically 9 to 10 years old while Years 7 & 8 students are 11 to 12 years. The Decile Rating System is the measure used to describe the socio-economic status of homes within a school's catchment zone (a Decile 1 rating indicates a high proportion of low socio-economic homes in the catchment zone).

Children in NZ are exposed to computer technology at home and in school very early in their education (Vanderschantz et al., 2014a). Information search is encouraged by the NZ school pedagogy through the "inquiry-based learning" framework. We have observed teachers set investigation tasks of broad topics that require the children to develop questions to explore independently. These investigations then take place inside and outside the school. Previous research has observed that children in NZ classrooms use this full range of technologies during their daily education (Vanderschantz et al., 2014a). These technologies have included digital books on CD-ROMs, eBooks, Internet resources, OPAC systems, along with specific educational software. No studies, have elicited the teachers' perspectives on the use of these technologies for information seeking.

STUDY METHOD

We conducted a series of semi-structured interviews with teachers of pre-teen children aged 9 to 12 years. The interviews took place in the teachers' classroom or in a space in the school selected by the interviewee. All interviews took place during the school day and therefore, the school was in operation while the interview was taking place. Interviews were audio recorded, and handwritten notes were taken.

Participants and Participant Recruitment

Our interview series was conducted in the Waikato School District, which is located in the central North Island of NZ. The participating teachers were recruited from two primary schools and one intermediate school. The three schools that participated in this study are the same as those that participated in our related study that investigated children's self-reporting of their information seeking (Vanderschantz, Hinze, & Cunningham, 2014b). The schools have Decile ratings of 4, 5, and 9. When inviting participant schools to contribute to our studies, the Decile Rating System has been taken into consideration in an attempt to fairly include a cross section of NZ schools in our research. While schools from across the full breadth of the rating system were approached to participate we were not able to gain participation from a school with a decile rating lower than 4.

We interviewed 10 teachers who had teaching experience ranging from 6 years to 25 years. We received only female participants, however this is in line with the Teacher Census 2016 that found almost 75% of NZ primary school teachers are female (Ministry of Education, 2016). Following our university ethics approval, we gained written consent from the school principal to conduct interviews with teaching staff at their school. The teachers were then invited and agreed without coercion to participate.

Interview Questions

Our interview questions (see Figure 1) were designed to allow comparison with the findings of our interviews with children reported in our corresponding paper (Vanderschantz et al., 2014b).

1) What types of topics did the students choose to investigate?
2) Where did the students investigate this topic?
3) What instruction or training did the students receive on how to investigate this topic?
4) What resources did you expect the students to use to investigate this topic?
5) What percentage of students used the following resources?
6) What issues did you notice children having when *searching* for digital information?
7) What issues did you notice children having when *using* digital information?
8) What issues did you notice children having when *searching* for printed books?
9) What issues did you notice children having when *using* printed books?
10) Do you have further observations regarding children's search for and use of information?
11) Can you describe the process when searching using printed material or books etc.?
12) Can you describe the process when searching using computers or iPads etc.?
13) What previous instruction or training did the students receive on how to investigate a task?
14) Do you have plans for further instruction or training on how to investigate a task?
15) How did the student submit a result of this?
16) What future topics will you set this year for investigation?

Figure 1. Teachers interview questions.

The interview questions were developed in consultation with tertiary teacher educators. Demographic information was also gathered. No probes were used. Our results are structured through answers to questions 1 to 4 and 12 to 15 reported in the section *Information Seeking in Classrooms*; while questions 5, 6 and 9 to 11 are reported in *Issues and Successes Observed During Search*; and questions 7 and 8 are reported in *Preference for Print Versus Digital Information*.

RESULTS

We report here the results of our interviews about teachers' observations of children's information search practices.

Information Seeking in Classrooms

Questions 1 to 4 and 12 to 15 (see Figure 1) were designed to explore children's information seeking as facilitated by these teachers. The answers to these questions give insight into the way that teachers structure modern classroom education in an inquiry-based learning environment.

What Types of Investigations are Children Undertaking?

The teachers reported a range of topics that the children had just completed investigating or that they were currently working on, with some teachers listing more than one topic (see Table 1). The topics reported by the teachers covered sectors of the NZ primary school curriculum, which included science, history, social studies, and English. It is common for multiple classes across a single school level, as well as across many school levels to be investigating the same topics. All 10 teachers stated that the investigations described in Table 1 were teacher or school-initiated topics of inquiry with five of the teachers stating that students were required to choose sub-topics for their personal investigation.

Environmental issues	3
Scientific investigations	5
Identity & culture	3
Human rights	1
Labour day	1
Book initiated	3

Table 1. Information seeking in classrooms.

Where are Students Undertaking these Tasks?

The 10 teachers stated that they expected all of their students to predominantly investigate these topics in the classroom. Nine of the teachers stated that typically all of the children in their class would conduct parts of their investigation in the school library, while five teachers stated that very few of their students would have explored the subject in a public library. Eight of the teachers stated that some children might investigate their topics at home and 1 teacher suggested some of their students would also use the school computer lab.

What Resources are Children Using?

Teachers reported that their students used a range of print and digital resources to complete the most recent inquiry task (see Table 2). All 10 teachers stated that some of their students used printed books, including school library books. Five teachers stated that their students used a dictionary during the last inquiry task. However, only T4 thought that students use an online dictionary. Five teachers assumed that their students used www.wikipedia.org, only two teachers thought that their students use an alternative digital encyclopaedia or printed encyclopaedia.

Digital searching was discussed as the most used or preferred source of information for children. For example, T8 stated that she "expected [the children] to use Google as their first port of call." All 10 teachers referred to the Google search engine when describing internet searching (no other search engine was discussed). Five teachers believed that students use the school library catalogue to conduct a search, but many of the teachers discussed that children were as likely to wonder the shelves and seek advice from the librarian. It was also discussed that the teachers regularly collected printed books from the school library for classroom use, which is likely why library and printed books were a feature of all 10 teachers' responses.

ID	Library catalog	Library books	Printed books	Printed dictionary	Printed encyclopedia	Digital books	Digital dictionary	Digital encyclopedia	Wikipedia	Google	Specific website	Videos
T1		✓	✓						✓	✓		✓
T2		✓	✓						✓	✓	✓	
T3		✓	✓	✓						✓		
T4	✓	✓	✓	✓	✓	✓	✓	✓	✓	✓	✓	
T5		✓	✓	✓					✓	✓	✓	
T6		✓	✓					✓		✓		✓
T7	✓	✓	✓	✓						✓	✓	
T8	✓	✓	✓							✓	✓	
T9	✓	✓	✓	✓	✓					✓		
T10	✓	✓	✓						✓	✓	✓	

Table 2. Expected resources used.

Students at all three schools had access to a small number of desktop computers in the classroom, and bookable class sets of laptop or tablet devices, and weekly class visits to a computer lab, as well as computer lab access during lunch periods. This multitude of internet-capable devices was regularly used by students of all 10 teachers for conducting internet searches for the students' inquiry tasks. All three schools had school libraries with full time or part time librarians. Classes visited the library on a weekly basis, and the libraries were also available outside of scheduled visits for student use. All school libraries have a digital library catalogue (OPAC) that is accessible by the children. Teachers also selected relevant books from the school and public libraries for in class resources for use during inquiries.

No teacher reported any use of digital libraries or child-specific search engines, and none of the schools explicitly provide or promote these for their students to use. T1 also listed photocopies of resources and material from books that the she has supplied as a resource the children in her class will have used. T2 reported children emailing and phoning experts as an enquiry technique that she had promoted during the present inquiry task. T5 discussed the NZ School Journal series as a potential resource for her students and T7 reported that students likely used apps on the schools and the students' mobile devices during the recent inquiry task.

Instruction or Training

The teachers were asked about the specific training that children were given this year and in previous years. We have tabularised the answers to these questions in two separate tables, Table 3 (teaching related to information search practice) and Table 4 (teaching related to internet search).

While search skills are not specifically a part of the curriculum, information search skills are taught as a part of the larger literacy competencies of the curriculum as well as during library or computer lab visits. Teachers described teaching inquiry practice and the necessity of asking and identifying a quality question. Three teachers reported teaching skimming and scanning of information sources to find information as well as the broader teaching of note taking, referencing and summarizing.

Inquiry practice	1
Good question	2
Skimming & scanning	3
Note taking	1
Referencing	1
Summarising	1

Table 3. Information search teaching.

Teachers noted that they must teach to the standards and the curriculum, which often does not allow time for teaching content that is outside of the scope of the curriculum. T8 noted that "we as educators could came up with specific search friendly things that should be taught within the curriculum. The problem is it doesn't really fit anywhere within the curriculum". T10 recommended that digital information literacy and search skills need to be integrated into the NZ curriculum within the ICT or Literacy units. All teachers reported that there was room for improvement with their own knowledge and what they were able to teach about information search. The teachers also felt that it would be helpful to have resources available for them. T8 stated "I think it needs to be age appropriate. Something that is designed as children go through the years, and through stages of intellectual development [i.e.] by year six you should be able to skim and scan and this is how you should teach it. Or this is a tool that you use to teach it".

Before listing the specific training, T10 said it was "not enough, in my opinion. I think I probably needed to teach them a little bit more about search engines and Google and that. Be more specific". There was indication of lack of confidence and knowledge in some of the finer details of the advances that are taking place around the teachers, with internet search being one of many areas of need. A further concern to the teachers was the pace at which information technology progresses and the difficulty for individuals to keep up to speed with the changes and processes for successful information search. T1 described the fact that she used to need to teach "a lot of 'who' / 'why' / 'when' / 'where' / 'what is,' [information problem identification techniques] but now Google is so good that doesn't seem to be a problem. They [the students] still seem to get to their result." Being aware of the changes in information search practices can be difficult for teachers who must also remain abreast of curriculum requirements, as well as the myriad of technologies that become a part of society and education.

When answering Q13 the teachers also offered a range of answers including many tools and techniques. For example, T5 stated "I do a big focus on keywords, because if they haven't got keywords, that's a problem." All 10 teachers discussed having given specific search instruction during the current search topic and in previous topics this year. Six teachers specifically reported teaching children how to use the Google search engine — naming Google specifically. Seven teachers discussed teaching concepts of search query creation, while five teachers specifically described teaching the use of keyword search query constructions. T1 discussed teaching students to omit "small words" (i.e., pronouns and conjunctions) from queries. T10 described teaching the use of query qualifiers such as "for kids" or "for children" at the end of a search query. This technique was described as a method for focusing the content of returned searches to websites that are written with children in mind. Similarly, three teachers [T3, T9, & T10] described encouraging the use of the (now defunct) Google Basic Reading Level Filter to return websites at a level appropriate for the reader. Three teachers discussed triangulation of information sources for confirmation of truthfulness.

Specific website	1
Google	6
Google advanced search	3
Search query creation	7
Keyword search	5
Query qualifiers	1
Triangulation / confirmation	3
Trust / truth	1

Table 4. Internet search teaching.

Issues and Successes Observed During Search

Questions 5 to 11 explored the information seeking processes that teachers have observed during inquiry and search tasks.

Snapshot of Children's Search Processes

When given a topic of inquiry, it was discussed that children look for information in digital format first. All 10 teachers described regular weekly school library sessions and in-class supply of books selected by the teacher for use during information search, and yet, all teachers listed Google as the primary tool for information seeking. Given this preference for digital search, the teachers still identified a number of issues the children experienced when searching for information on the Internet when answering Q7 (see Table 5).

Teachers identified an absence of effective skills in developing and identifying information need as being a fundamental issue for children when searching. They observed that when a child does not clearly identify their information need, they tend to use very broad searches in the hope of stumbling across information that they will be able to use. Teachers stated this was counter to what they considered best practice for children. All 10 teachers aimed for the children to be able to identify a need before conducting a search, and searching with intent and purpose with well-constructed search queries rather than the scattershot approach that was observed by the teachers.

The construction of sound queries was an issue that all 10 teachers identified. T10 stated, "they type in the whole question; they have no concept of breaking it down to key ideas." T2 suggested that: "[some students will use] keyword searching, some will still be putting questions and sentences." T10 also noted "they think that they can ask the computer 'Computer what's your favourite colour?' they really do think it is like a little brain that is going to talk back to them." T5 discussed further difficulties for query construction relating to the focus of a query believing that "if they [the students] narrow it too far they can miss vital information too." Three teachers also described the children's reading level as a barrier for identifying which websites to visit and for identifying useful results in the websites that Google returns.

Teachers noted issues that children encounter when they are looking through search engine results to identify potentially relevant Web pages. The teachers believed children would visit the first website in the search engine results page (SERP) list and then proceed sequentially down the list of SERP entries — stopping at the first website that they considered to include the relevant information. Over the preceding year(s), the teachers had taught a more formal approach, recommending that the children first review the SERP list and make relevance decisions to prioritize the websites to visit. The teachers also stressed the importance of reviewing multiple sources to validate the information found, rather than relying solely on a single source.

Six teachers observed that children struggle with comprehending the information presented on both SERPs and Web pages due to visual presentation and language level. Related to comprehension was children's ability to triage the information that they were presented in the SERP list and on the relating web pages. Seven teachers identified this difficulty with triage of information. If the presentation appears too difficult for a child to read and understand due to the lack of headings and images, or to the over-saturation of text on a page, the teachers hypothesized that the children would be discouraged from attempting to read the page. The ability to synopsise the content that has been read and the time required to read, comprehend and to synopsise were additional barriers to success that teachers identified. These barriers may lead to frustration, abandoned searches or searches that result in poor responses to the inquiry task.

Search terms	10
Reading level	3
Spelling	1
Technology access	1

Table 5. Issues searching for digital information.

Adult Intervention

Five of the teachers also discussed the importance of parents during information searching in the home. Teachers believed it to be standard practice for their students to work in close collaboration with parents to gain assistance with and guidance in search practices and search queries when conducting inquiry tasks at home. Teachers hypothesised that students whose parents have computer and information literacy skills and who use computers in the home are noticeably more proficient in searching the Internet. Librarians were also described as sources of assistance and information during the search process. T3 also described emailing experts as a potential resource in information seeking for certain tasks.

Child-Specific Search Engines

The teachers we interviewed did not observe any use of child-specific search engines. T7 suggested: "there are children's search engines, but they are too narrow." Six teachers mentioned child-specific search engines and the need for presenting search results that are tailored to the children's needs, but no teacher reported recommending or using child-specific search engines in the classroom.

Three teachers discussed the advanced search tools, including the basic reading level filter offered by Google. The Reading Level Filter that is available in Google (at the time of the interviews, but now defunct) is a tool that allows a searcher to specify search engine results at one of three reading levels (Basic, Intermediate, Advanced). At the time of writing this paper we are unaware of a similar feature in either of the other two major search engines, Bing or Yahoo!.

T9 also discussed the need for search engines and the websites the children visit to be well designed for young readers: "Websites cluttered with ads hinder them [the students] finding information. Visual presentation of information is needed for this young audience." Teachers also discussed that systems that aid children more specifically may be helpful, but these would need to be built into Google, rather than a browser designed specifically for children. For the teachers, Internet searching seemed to be synonymous with using the Google search engine with no other search engines discussed by children in our related study or teachers in this study.

Frustration

Frustration was a sentiment expressed by all 10 teachers throughout the interviews. T3 stated that "Google searches can be frustrating and can feel futile if the search is not working". T4 noted that "[students] often get frustrated and do not put all of the words correctly into the search engine" when describing difficulties encountered with query construction. T6 said children "will type in something and get frustrated when the specific thing they are looking for doesn't come up". While T8 could relate to the students and said "even myself when searching, I become overwhelmed sometimes by the amount that you receive back".

Preference for Print Versus Digital Information

We asked teachers about children's use of, and search for, printed information in Questions 7 & 8. All 10 teachers believed that, given the choice, children use the Internet as their primary information resource and that children will only search print resources if directed to do so. Teachers listed a range of issues that children encounter when using printed information (see Table 6). As was also reported in responses to previous interview questions, the teachers described the children's difficulty with spelling and a need for assistance by an adult, such as a teacher or librarian, when searching for information in a library. The schools' OPACs were seen to be a significant barrier in locating relevant print documents; one teacher suggested that children might use the OPAC more successfully (and so access print material more frequently) if the OPAC offered greater assistance in search and query construction. A major cause of difficulty in using OPACs is that the children do not understand how searching on OPACs differs from searching on Google. Three teachers believed that children use the same initial strategy on OPACs as on Google—i.e., natural language querying—and that they are then stymied when the OPAC returns few results. Even when a child successfully identified a potentially useful book in the school OPAC, it may not have been accessible because often the entire school would be focusing on the same topic (4 teachers). And, of course, print material is not as easily searched and browsed as digital documents; two teachers detailed children's difficulties utilizing the features of books such as tables of contents and indexes.

Comprehending	5
Ability to synopsise	3
Catalog	3
Dewey	3
Availability	6
Features	2

Table 6. Issues using and searching for print information.

A MODEL OF CHILDREN'S ONLINE SEARCH BEHAVIOUR AS OBSERVED BY TEACHERS

We offer here a model of children's online search behaviour as observed by teachers (see Figure 2). Teachers described children's searching for information on computers as beginning with a new search in Google by entering either a question or a set of keywords (Figure 2, process 1). Children then select a search result using one of three methods (Figure 2, process 2). Once the children have clicked through to a page, the children then attempt to locate information on the page visited by skimming and scanning the text, likely from top to bottom of the page (Figure 2, process 3). The child must then decide if an answer to the question has been identified (Figure 2, decision A).

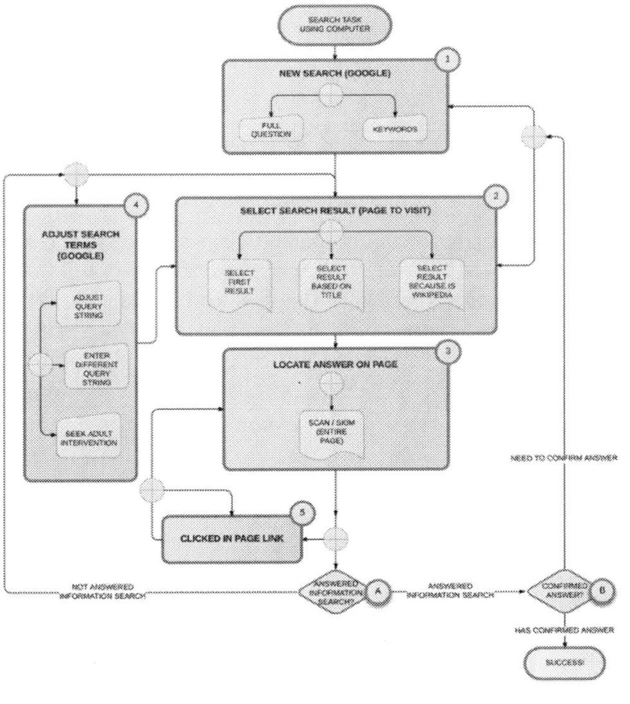

Figure 2. A model of children's online search behaviour as observed by teachers.

Decision A, requires the child confirm if they have answered their information need. If the student has confirmed their answers with a number of sources (Figure 2, decision B), the child would likely consider the search completed. If the child required further triangulation of their sources, they would likely either return to the SERP list to choose an alternative website or adjust their search terms (Figure 2, process 4).

Teachers described children as being easily distracted by in-page links, and tangents that may result in an infinite loop. Process 5 shows the potential for the student to delve deeper into the rabbit hole, losing track of time and sight of the task at hand. Teachers also discussed games and videos as distractions that could impede continued information search.

Comparison to Children's Self-Reported Search Process

Our related interview study (Vanderschantz et al., 2014b) proposed a model of children's online information search processes. That suggested model was based on children's self-reported recollections of their own processes during information search. When we consider the model as described by the children in comparison to the model described by the teachers, we find very similar processes. We discuss the development of our two models here as well as their relationship to the related work. The children were able to describe the process in more depth than the teachers, presumably because the children were recounting their own actions, or describing processes they believe they should be doing (which they may or may not actually be doing), while the teachers were recounting the actions that they observed.

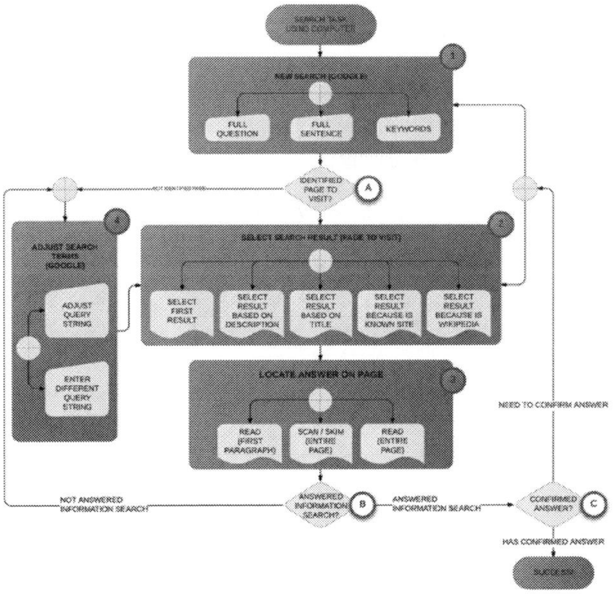

Figure 3. A model of children's online search behaviour (based on children's reports), from (Vanderschantz et al., 2014b).

As we explained in more detail in (Vanderschantz et al., 2014b) children described their search activities requiring three points of decision (labelled as A, B, and C in Figure 3) and four processes (labelled as 1, 2, 3, and 4 in Figure 3). Children described beginning a new search by constructing one of three types of the search query using Google (see process 1 in Figure 3). A child would then decide (Figure 3, decision A) if they could identify a page to visit from the SERP (Figure 3, process 2) or would adjust their query (Figure 3, process 4). The child would select a search result page from the SERP in one of five ways, most often reported was choosing the first entry or search for a specific web page (i.e. Wikipedia) from the SERP. The child would then locate their answer on the page by reading the first paragraph, skimming or scanning or reading the entire page (Figure 3, process 3). At this point, the child would be required to decide if the information search had been answered (Figure 3, decision B). The child would then either adjust queries (process 4 in Figure 3, decision C) or decide if the answer requires confirmation (Figure 3). If confirmation was required the child would revisit the previous SERP (Figure 3, process 2) or conduct a new Google search (Figure 3, process 1). Otherwise, the search was considered completed.

The robust model provided by students is a fuller picture than that observed by teachers. The model as garnered from teacher interviews does not significantly differ from the model proposed in (Vanderschantz et al., 2014b), however, the model presented in this paper does differ in Processes 1 to 4, with no Decision at A, and a new process labelled 5.

Query Construction

In Process 1 (Figure 3) children described using full questions, full sentences or keywords while teachers suggested children would use natural language as the very first query in most circumstances. Teachers observed students using keyword searches only if the keywords had been clearly identified in the inquiry task or work sheet; otherwise, the students used natural language question queries. T10 discussed children's search processes stating, "these kids, seriously, they turn on their computer 'ok I'm going to go look for this.' What do they do? They go 'Okay I'm going to look for Google.' They type their question in. They don't think about eliminating the smaller words."

Search Results List Triage

Teachers reported less information triage by children than children reported. Therefore, Process A is not included in Figure 2 because teachers did not discuss a decision at this point; instead, teachers believed that children move directly from a query to selecting a result from the SERP. Teachers stated that children are likely to a) click the first link in a SERP or b) read only the titles of the top few SERP entries or c) scour the SERP for Wikipedia (see process 2 in Figure 2). Teachers did not mention selecting a result based on a description or known website, which children did report.

Locating an Answer

While children interviewed in (Vanderschantz et al., 2014b) cited three ways that they locate information on a page (see process 3 in Figure 3), our teachers believed that students would skim and scan a significant portion if not the entire page looking for their answer (see process 3 in Figure 2).

In-Page Link Use

Teachers noted that students were easily distracted and would link from one web page to another in a sporadic tangential search. Teachers suggested students may not go back to a SERP, instead needing to re-enter or begin a new query after some time surfing deeper into the Web on a whim. Teachers noted that children would suffer from distraction by information that appears related, and equally by content that is off topic. This is included in Figure 2 as Process 5, yet was not discussed by children in our related study. This looping behaviour and confusion was discussed in early web use investigations (i.e. Bilal, 2000; Large et al., 2002) and is reinforced by our interviews.

Adjusting Search Terms

Adjusting search terms was something that teachers felt students lacked confidence and ability. Children described adjusting search terms or entering new search terms during Process 4 in Figure 3. Early work in children's Internet search has shown that query reformulation is a difficult task (Bilal & Kirby, 2002) and this remains the case with children's information seeking today. Additionally, teachers in this study described the need for input from teachers, parents, and peers to successfully adjust searches (see process 4 in Figure 2). T3 stated: "most children rely on asking a question. They would prefer to sit down and ask for help from a parent or teacher. They would prefer to have someone assist them with a search."

Confirming Sources

Teachers reported confirming sources was necessary for students and something that they specifically taught. Yet, teachers were sceptical as to if students were confirming sources as part of their processes. Students in (Vanderschantz et al., 2014b) claimed to confirm sources when searching. The decision to confirm sources is found at Decision B (Figure 2) and Decision C (Figure 3).

DISCUSSION

Our interviews with teachers confirm that information search issues persist for children using contemporary online information seeking systems. Search planning and mid-search assessment and development of search paths was discussed to be difficult for children. Teachers discussed a need to clarify the entire information search process for children so that they will fully understand the fundamentals of successful investigation strategies. Teachers believed that the search skills and information literacy of children in their classrooms was still very limited, even at Years 7&8. Children's difficulties in completely identifying their search questions and information needs were also seen to be impediments to successful information seeking. The children's most significant issues were reported to lie in search query construction, spelling, language level of websites, search query reformulation, and triaging of information. Correct spelling of search queries was identified to be difficult for children in both this study and (Vanderschantz et al., 2014b) as it has been in many studies of children's information seeking (e.g., Druin, 2009).

The teachers felt that adding information seeking strategies to the national curriculum would allow them to address these learning gaps formally; in the absence of recognition of information seeking as a legitimate topic of study, the teachers could only fold information literacy instruction into the recognized areas of the NZ curriculum. This situation was exacerbated by the fact that the teachers were not confident in their own information search skills; they were concerned that the resources and tools changed rapidly and they too could benefit from further professional development to update their own information search skills. These reported shortcomings in the curriculum, teachers own knowledge, and the difficulties experienced by children is evidence of the importance of both digital literacy and information literacy and the implications for both children and teachers.

Overcoming Frustration

Teachers reported a significant barrier to children's successful web searches were issues of confidence and frustration. We show in Figure 2 teachers reported Processes 1 to 4 were points in the search process that children have few strategies for overcoming barriers such as a search query returning poor results. Teachers believed this frustration is exacerbated when children are not able to identify for themselves what is not working or how to fix their issues. The teachers did not have solutions to assist the children when they encountered these points of frustration.

Bilal (2000) showed that successful keyword queries were difficult for children to create. Our findings differ from Bilal's in that we note that teachers and children describe difficulties with keywords and a preference for natural language queries. Query reformulation is a difficult task (Bilal & Kirby, 2002), as is knowing when a query reformation is necessary. We recommend search engine features that offers related searches in the form of search reformations or refinements along with improved visibility of Related Searches will assist users to evaluate their searches and to reformulate searches more successfully.

Teachers in this study, and children in (Vanderschantz et al., 2014b), discussed students seeking adult assistance at points of frustration or when they had given up on their own search. Adults serve as an integral tool in assisting children to overcome motivational and frustration issues that arise during Internet search. Systems that support self-reliance and assist with error correction during search require further investigation. Related to this is the importance placed on librarians by teachers and children alike. NZ school librarians are responsible for managing loans and acquisitions as well as collection maintenance, and can also be found to work with students and teachers in locating information sources and performing information seeking tasks. Certified teacher-librarians (as seen in the US American school system) who are involved in the teaching of information literacy are not typically found in NZ schools.

Digital Compared to Printed Information Seeking

Overall children appear to be less competent information seekers when using printed sources. Teachers even suggested that children "[only] turn to books for pleasure and leisure, not for information" [T2]. Teachers noted that books relevant to many of the inquiry tasks in NZ classrooms often become out of date very quickly or simply are unavailable when students require them. The language in the books is often not at the children's reading level, or is too shallow for the educational purposes. It seems from the interviews with teachers that children's print information search skills are diminishing and the perceived value of print information is also fading in today's educational environment.

Limitations

Our models (see Figures 2 and 3) were developed based on studies with comparatively small numbers of participants, using interviews with children that rely on children's self-reporting and on the posthoc recollections of teachers. However, our chosen methodology allowed us to tease out fine-grained insights into the difficulties experienced by children as well as the instruction given by teachers that would have been difficult to identify in large-scale studies. These models have been confirmed in subsequent observational studies.

CONCLUSION

Our study provides first-hand observations of the regular habits of young information seekers in NZ classrooms. We found that the inquiry-based model used in these classrooms often requires children to choose and investigate sub-topics of a class-wide area of investigation and for this reason development of good information problem-solving techniques and quality digital and information literacy is a requisite of modern education. We show that children require assistance to better understand the information seeking process, and teachers require assistance to teach children how to effectively conduct information searches. Our comparison of the children's perceived online search behaviour to the teachers perceived model of children's online search behaviour provides new opportunities for researchers to develop targeted investigations into children's information seeking in educational environments.

When/Where Do Children Search for Information

Our interviews have revealed that children engage in educational information seeking most predominantly in the school with only some conducted in the home. Children are given opportunities to work with digital and printed information seeking resources, yet given the choice will use Google to search the internet. The teachers reported that children do not choose to use print sources unless directed to do so and prefer the more easily accessed digital sources.

Further our interviews revealed that teachers desire to be better equipped to facilitate Internet searching and digital and information literacy. Teachers regretted the few opportunities to teach information seeking and information searching practices and skills—but also discussed their lack of confidence in their own skills. We recommend professional development support for teachers as well as clear identification of the appropriate space in the curriculum for inclusion of this type of learning for children.

Children's Information Seeking Processes

Teachers did not recommend search engines designed for children and discussed children's use of commonly available tools – i.e. Google. We compared our model of teachers' reports of children's information seeking to Vanderschantz et al. (2014b) model of children's self-reports. These two models identify areas of need for educational interventions and software interventions to support children's information seeking. We recommend software support for (1) topic expansion; (2) tailoring of typographic presentation of information to highlight details relevant to the triage phase of information seeking; and (3) specific tools for the three decision points identified in our models. Tools that support the complete inquiry process in the form of extended features of mainstream search engines, rather than dedicated children's search engines, are likely to be well received by both children and teachers.

Issues Children Encounter During Information Search

The teachers in our study confirmed three major difficulties: (1) constructing searches, (2) identifying potentially relevant information in search results lists, and (3) locating relevant information within a web page. These provide themes for future work in this area globally.

In summary, our study investigated issues for contemporary information search in an educational environment. Its results highlighted the concerning fact that many issues identified for digital search a decade ago are still prevalent showing opportunities for research and technology intervention. We therefore identify the need to support teachers with their pedagogy of technology integration and information literacy in today's rich digital information world.

REFERENCES

Bilal, D. (2000). Children's use of the Yahooligans! Web search engine: I. Cognitive, physical, and affective behaviors on fact-based search tasks. *Journal of the American Society for information Science, 51*(7), 646–665.

Bilal, D., & Kirby, J. (2002). Differences and similarities in information seeking: Children and adults as Web users. *Information Processing & Management, 38*(5), 649–670.

Dinet, J., Favart, M., & Passerault, J.-M. (2004). Searching for information in an online public access catalogue (OPAC): The impacts of information search expertise on the use of Boolean operators. *Journal of Computer Assisted Learning, 20*(5), 338–346.

Druin, A. (2009). *Mobile technology for children: Designing for interaction and learning*. Morgan Kaufmann.

Druin, A., Bederson, B., Hourcade, J. P., Sherman, L., Revelle, G., Platner, M., & Weng, S. (2001). *Designing a digital library for young children. In Proc 1st ACM/-IEEE-CS Joint Conference on Digital Libraries (pp. 398–405).*

Druin, A., Bederson, B. B., Weeks, A., Farber, A., Grosjean, J., Guha, M. L., … Zhang, L. (2003). *The International Children's Digital Library: Description and analysis of first use. Technical Report No. #CS-TR-4433 UMIACS*. University of Maryland.

Druin, A., Foss, E., Hutchinson, H., Golub, E., & Hatley, L. (2010). Children's roles using keyword search interfaces at home. In Proceedings of the SIGCHI Conference on Human Factors in Computing Systems (pp. 413–422).

Falloon, G. (2015). What's the difference? Learning collaboratively using iPads in conventional classrooms. *Computers & Education, 84*, 62–77.

Gossen, T., Nitsche, M., & Nürnberger, A. (2012). Knowledge journey: A web search interface for young users. In Proceedings of the Symposium on Human-Computer Interaction and Information Retrieval (pp. 1–10).

Hegedus, S. (2013). Young Children investigating advanced mathematical concepts with haptic technologies: Future design perspectives. *The Mathematics Enthusiast, 10* (1/2), 87–107.

Hirsh, S. G. (1999). Children's relevance criteria and information seeking on electronic resources. *Journal of the American Society for information Science, 50*(14), 1265–1283.

Hutchinson, H. B., Druin, A., & Bederson, B. B. (2007). Supporting Elementary-age Children's Searching and Browsing: Design and Evaluation Using the International Children's Digital Library. *Journal of the American Society for information Science and Technology, 58*(11), 1618–1630.

Jochmann-Mannak, H. E., Huibers, T. W. C., Lentz, L. R., & Sanders, T. J. M. (2010). Children searching information on the Internet: Performance on children's interfaces compared to Google. In *Proc of the 33rd ACM SIGIR (SIGIR 2010)*, Geneva, Switzerland (pp. 19–26). New York, NY: ACM.

Kafai, Y., & Bates, M. J. (1997). Internet Web-searching instruction in the elementary classroom: Building a foundation for information literacy. *School Library Media Quarterly*, *25*(2), 103–111.

Kodama, C., Jean, B. S., Subramaniam, M., & Taylor, N. G. (2017). There's a creepy guy on the other end at Google!: Engaging middle school students in a drawing activity to elicit their mental models of Google. *Information Retrieval Journal*, *20*(5), 403–432.

Large, A., Beheshti, J., & Rahman, T. (2002). Gender differences in collaborative web searching behavior: an elementary school study. *Information Processing & Management*, *38*(3), 427–443.

McCrory Wallace, R., Kupperman, J., Krajcik, J., & Soloway, E. (2000). Science on the Web: Students online in a sixth-grade classroom. *The Journal of the Learning Sciences*, *9*(1), 75–104. https://doi.org/10.1207/s15327809jls0901_5

Mellingsaeter, M. S., & Bungum, B. (2015). Students' use of the interactive whiteboard during physics group work. *European Journal of Engineering Education*, *40*(2), 115–127.

Ministry of Education. (2016). Ministry of Education - Education Counts. Retrieved October 31, 2018, from Education Counts website: http://www.educationcounts.govt.nz/

Moratelli, K., & DeJarnette, N. K. (2014). Clickers to the rescue. *The Reading Teacher*, *67*(8), 586–593.

Okojie, M. C., Olinzock, A. A., & Okojie-Boulder, T. C. (2006). The Pedagogy of technology integration. *Journal of Technology Studies*, *32*(2), 66–71.

Robertson, J., Manches, A., & Pain, H. (2017). "It's like a giant brain with a keyboard": Children's understandings about how computers work. *Childhood Education*, *93* (4), 338–345.

Spavold, J. (1990). The child as naïve user: A study of database use with young children. *International Journal of Man-Machine Studies*, *32*(6), 603–625.

Subramaniam, M., Taylor, N. G., St. Jean, B., Follman, R., Kodama, C., & Casciotti, D. (2015). As simple as that?: Tween credibility assessment in a complex online world. *Journal of Documentation*, *71*(3), 550–571.

Taylor, N. G. (2018). Youth information-seeking behavior and online government information: Tweens' perceptions of US federal government websites. *Journal of Documentation*, *74*(3), 509–525.

Timpany, C., & Vanderschantz, N. (2011). Learning outcome dependency on contemporary ICT in the New Zealand middle school classroom. In Proceedings 12th Sig-CHINZ (pp. 65–72).

Vanderschantz, N., & Hinze, A. (2017). A study of children's search query formulation habits. In *Proc of the 32nd International BCS Human Computer Interaction Conference* (p. 7). BCS Learning & Development Ltd.

Vanderschantz, N., & Hinze, A. (2018). Designing an internet search interface for children. In *Proc of the 32nd International BCS Human Computer Interaction Conference* (p. 30). BCS Learning & Development Ltd.

Vanderschantz, N., Hinze, A., & Cunningham, S. J. (2014a). Current Educational Technology Use for Digital Information Acquisition by Young New Zealand Children. In Proceedings of the Thirty-Seventh Australasian Computer Science Conference (Vol. 147, pp. 125–134).

Vanderschantz, N., Hinze, A., & Cunningham, S. J. (2014b). "Sometimes the Internet reads the question wrong": Children's search strategies & difficulties. In Proceedings of the Seventy-Seventh ASIST Annual Meeting (Vol. 51, pp. 1–10).

Searching Heterogeneous Personal Digital Traces

Daniela Vianna
DCS, Rutgers University
Piscataway, USA
dvianna@cs.rutgers.edu

Varvara Kalokyri
DCS, Rutgers University
Piscataway, USA
v.kalokyri@cs.rutgers.edu

Alexander Borgida
DCS, Rutgers University
Piscataway, USA
borgida@cs.rutgers.edu

Amélie Marian
DCS, Rutgers University
Piscataway, USA
amelie@cs.rutgers.edu

Thu Nguyen
DCS, Rutgers University
Piscataway, USA
tdnguyen@cs.rutgers.edu

ABSTRACT

Digital traces of our lives are now constantly produced by various connected devices, internet services and interactions. Our actions result in a multitude of heterogeneous data objects, or traces, kept in various locations in the cloud or on local devices. Users have very few tools to organize, understand, and search the digital traces they produce. We propose a simple but flexible data model to aggregate, organize, and find personal information within a collection of a user's personal digital traces. Our model uses as basic dimensions the six questions: what, when, where, who, why, and how. These natural questions model universal aspects of a personal data collection and serve as unifying features of each personal data object, regardless of its source. We propose indexing and search techniques to aid users in searching for their past information in their unified personal digital data sets using our model. Experiments performed over real user data from a variety of data sources such as Facebook, Dropbox, and Gmail show that our approach significantly improves search accuracy when compared with traditional search tools.

KEYWORDS

Personal Digital Traces; Personal Search; Data Model

ASIS&T THESAURUS

Information Discovery; Knowledge and Information

INTRODUCTION

Digital traces of our lives are constantly being produced and saved by users, either actively in files, emails, social media interactions, multimedia objects, etc., or passively via various applications such as GPS tracking of mobile devices, web search records or quantified self-sensor usage. These "personal digital traces" are different from traditional personal files; they are typically (but not always) smaller, heterogeneous, and accessible through a wide variety of different portals and interfaces, such as web forms, APIs or email notifications; or directly stored in files used by apps on our devices. These traces reflect a chronicle of the user's life, keeping record of where the user went, with whom the user interacted with, what the user did, and when. However, the large quantity of personal data available, and the fact that data is stored in multiple decentralized systems, in heterogeneous formats, makes it challenging for users to interact with their data and perform even simple searches.

Our goal is to give back to individual users easy and flexible access to their own data. Personal data is highly sensitive; consequently, privacy and ethical issues have to be considered while dealing with this type of information. The work discussed in this paper is developed as part of a series of tools to let user retrieve, store and organize their digital traces on their own devices (Kalokyri, Borgida, Marian, & Vianna, 2017a, 2017b; Vianna, Yong, Xia, Marian, & Nguyen, 2014), guaranteeing some clear privacy and security benefits.

Work in Cognitive Psychology (Brewer, 1988; Jones & Teevan, 2007; Schacter, 2001; Wagenaar, 1986) has shown that contextual cues are strong triggers for autobiographical memories. (Abowd et al., 1999) and (Dey, 2001) define context as any information that can be used to characterize the situation of an entity. This suggests that a natural way to remember and learn from past events is to include any pertinent contextual information when organizing and searching personal data. Personal information can be modeled, and indexed following six dimensions that mirror the basic interrogative words: what, who, when, where, why, and how. Each trace is a source of knowledge. For instance, a Facebook post may contain enough information to identify where a user went, what they did, who they interacted with, and when. Multiple traces, from the same or different sources, are often related to each other. The correlation between traces can be

82nd Annual Meeting of the Association for Information Science & Technology | Melbourne, Australia | 19–23 October, 2019

DOI: 10.1002/pra2.00022

identified through common information such as time and location. Even though multiple traces may share common information, they may have significantly different structures. This heterogeneity presents a major challenge. Thus, in this work, we are proposing a data model that can effectively represent this heterogeneous data, helping users find pieces of information again.

Search of personal data is usually focused on retrieving information that users know exists in their own data set, even though most of the time they do not know in which source or device they have seen the desired information. Current search tools such as Spotlight and Gmail search are not adequate to deal with this scenario as the user has to perform the same search multiple times on different services or/and devices rather than search over just a single service. Besides, traditional searches are often inefficient as they typically identify too many matching documents. In addition to the unified data model, we are proposing scoring and searching techniques that allow personal information search over data from multiple services and devices integrated in a unified data set.

In this paper, we make the following contributions: (1) a unified and intuitive multidimensional data model to link and represent heterogeneous personal digital traces; the model, called w5h, uses those six dimensions to unify features of each personal data object, regardless of its source (Section 3), (2) a frequency-based scoring methodology for searching personal digital traces; our scoring, named *w5h-f* is based on our multidimensional data model and leverages entities interactions within and across dimensions in the data sets (Section 4), (3) an implementation of our techniques, from data extraction, to entity recognition, classification and index structures, that will be used as the basis of our experimental evaluation (Section 5), and (4) a thorough qualitative evaluation of our proposed w5h scoring and search techniques, as well as comparison with two popular existing search tools, Solr (Apache Solr) and Spotlight (Apple, 2017), and techniques, TFIDF and BM25, on real data using both manually designed and synthetically generated search queries. Our results show that our scoring model results in improved search accuracy (Section 6). We discuss related work in Section 7 and conclude with future work directions in Section 8.

W5H DATA MODEL

We propose a data model that relies on the context in which personal data traces are created, produced and gathered to integrate heterogeneous traces into a unified data model that will support accurate searches. The proposed model, called w5h, was derived from the following observations: (1) personal digital traces are rich in contextual information, in the form of metadata, application data, or environment knowledge, and (2) personal digital traces can be represented following a combination of dimensions that naturally summarize various aspects of the data collection: *who, when, where, what, why and how*.

Our w5h model uses these six dimensions as the unifying features of each personal digital trace object, regardless of its source. Using these natural questions as the main facets of data representation will also allow the combination of our data representation with a natural and intuitive query model for searching information in digital traces. Listed below are some examples of dimensional data that can be extracted from a user's personal digital traces:

- **what:** messages, messages subjects, publications, description of events, description of users, list of interests of a user.
- **who:** user names, senders, recipients, event owners, lists of friends, authors.
- **where:** hometown, location, event venue, file/folder path, URL.
- **when:** birthday, file/message/event created-time, file/message/event modified-time, event start/end time.
- **why:** sequences of data/events that are causally connected.
- **how:** application, device, environment.

W5H SCORING MODEL

```
{
"message": "March for Science in Seattle.",                  (WHAT)
"from": "John Smith",                                        (WHO)
"place": "Seattle, Washington",                              (WHERE)
"with_tags": "Anna Smith",                                   (WHO)
"story": "John Smith and Anna Smith in Seattle, Washington", (WHAT)
"created_time": "2017-04-22T22:43:56+0000",                  (WHEN)
"data_type": "Facebook post"                                 (HOW)
}
```

Figure 1. Simplified Facebook post classified according to the w5h model.

Figure 1 presents a digital trace from a Facebook post with each piece of information identified as belonging to one of the six dimensions proposed (what, who, where, when, why and how). Even though multiple digital traces come from different sources and have their own data schema, they can be unified using the six dimensions proposed in our w5h model. For instance, two separate traces that have John Smith or/and Anna Smith under the same dimension who (for example a Facebook image tagging Anna Smith, or a tweet mentioning John Smith), can be linked by our unified model. Details on the implementation of the dimension classification and entity resolution are given in Sections 5.2 and 5.3. The w5h model is used both to unify heterogeneous digital trace data from different sources, and to link digital traces using the six proposed dimensions.

The why dimension is not explored in this paper, but is the topic of related work (Kalokyri et al. 2017; Kalokyri, Borgida, & Marian, 2018). This dimension can be derived by inference and could be used to connect different fragments of data that derive from a common real-life task, or episode. For instance, the why value "March for Science Demonstration" may be inferred for the Facebook post in Figure 1 and could be used to connect to other related traces such as a message thread.

As pointed in (Wagenaar, 1986), users tend to remember their actions using the six natural questions; thus, using them to guide search is a logical approach. We now evaluate the potential benefits of the w5h model for integrating and searching personal data. Specifically, we propose a search mechanism that supports queries containing conditions along each of the six interrogative dimensions. Our proposed search relies on a novel frequency-based scoring methodology over the w5h data model, called *w5h-f*, that will be detailed in this section.

Scoring Methodology

To illustrate our query and scoring methodology let us consider the following search scenario: the user is interested in message(s) from John Smith or/and Anna Smith about the 2017 March for Science. We consider each digital trace to be a distinct object that can be returned as the result to a query.

DEFINITION 1 (Object in w5h Dataset). An object O in the data set is a structure that has fields corresponding to the 6 dimensions mentioned earlier. Each of these dimensions contains 0 or more items (corresponding to text, entities identified by entity resolution, times, locations, etc). The fields of an object O are accessed using functions O.get("who"), O. get("what"), etc.

Formal queries have the same structure as objects in the unified data set. In the example above, the query has three filled dimensions: March for Science (**what**); John Smith, Anna Smith (**who**); 2017 (**when**).

Given objects Q and O, O is considered as an answer to object Q treated as a query if it contains at least one of the dimensions specified in Q. In looking for (partially) matching objects to a given query, each dimension will be searched separately, and the results will be combined according to a scoring function, generating a rank-ordered list of candidates. The choice of scoring function can be application dependent. We propose our frequency-based scoring function, *w5h-f*, below.

w5h-f Scoring

Because personal digital traces are byproducts of users' actions and events, they are not independent objects. Our intuition is that the correlation between traces (objects) can be leveraged to improve the accuracy of search results. For example, if the March for Science query from Section 4.1 returns several potential matches, one from Alice Jones, and one from Bob White, we may want to score the one from Alice higher if she communicates more frequently as a group with the user, Anna Smith, and John Smith, than Bob White.

Our *w5h-f* scoring scheme uses the correlation between users (or entities) and how they interact over time to rank an object. Because we are focusing on personal digital traces, all the data articulates around a user. By analyzing the data collected by our Extraction Tool (Vianna et al., 2014) (Section 5.1), we observed a strong correlation between the user (owner of the data) and multiple users (*who* groups), through times (*who, when*), location (*who, where*) and data sources (*who, how*). For instance, in one of the datasets, 94.9% of the objects have more than 2 users (*who*), 95.7% of objects have at least one date (*when*), 99.9% of objects have content (*what*) and only 1.5% of the objects have location (*where*). Our scoring exploits those interactions and correlations by way of a frequency score.[1] Frequencies can be computed for individual users or group of users. They can be associated with multiple times, multiple data sources, and also with a set of locations. For example, from a set of emails exchanged between a group of users, we can extract the frequency (number of interactions) with which those users communicated, and in which time period those interactions occurred. In short, frequency expresses the strength of relationships, based on users, time, location and data sources (*who, when, where, how*).

To compute the frequencies across multiple dimensions, the frequency algorithm starts by retrieving a list of objects for each data source. For each object, the algorithm extracts groups of users, times and locations. Then, the following frequencies are computed:

- Frequency of each individual user: number of objects that mention a user in the who dimension.
- Frequency of a group of users: number of objects mentioning a group of users. If {a,b,c} is the group mentioned, frequencies of subgroups of {a,b,c}, e.g. {a,b} and {b,c}, are not counted.
- Frequency of each individual user at specific times: number of objects that mention a user at matching times. Time is normalized, so variations are also considered. For instance, a query searching for June, will match objects with time June 2016 and June 2017.
- Frequency of a group of users at specific times: number of objects mentioning the group at a specific time.
- Frequency of a location: number of objects that mention a location.

In addition to computing the frequencies per source, we also compute the total frequency of a user, group of users, times and locations by combining the individual results obtained for each data source. For simplicity, every time a user or group of users has an interaction, the frequency is increased by one; however, in practice, the algorithm allows us to weigh differently distinct types of interactions. For example, likes or comments on a Facebook post could be weighed differently, giving more relevance to interactions coming from comments than likes. Different roles, e.g. From and To in an email, can also be weighed differently.

[1] Our model is focused around personal digital traces and as such we included this specific group of correlations in our scoring. Other application scenarios could also benefit from our w5h, with other group and pairwise correlations highlighted in a dedicated frequency-based scoring. For instance, traces from weather sensors could have strong pairwise (where, when), or (where, how) correlations.

DEFINITION 2 (Similarity Score). Given a query Q, an object O, and the frequencies above, we define:

$$fscore(Q,O) = f[g] + \sum_{u \in who} f[u] + \sum_{u \in who} fs[u] + \sum_{\substack{u \in who \\ dt \in when}} f[u][dt] + \sum_{\substack{u \in who \\ dt \in when}} fs[u][dt] + \sum_{\substack{u \in who \\ dt \in when}} f[g][dt] + \sum_{addr \in where} f[addr] + scorewhen(dt,O) + scorehow(s,O) + scorewhat(O)$$

where g is the group of users in the who dimension of O, u is each user in g, dt is each time in the when dimension, s is a data source, addr is each location in the where dimension, $f[g]$ is the frequency of a group of users in the same object, $f[u]$ is the total frequency of each user across all data services, $fs[u]$ is the frequency of each user in the data source s of the object, scorewhen(dt, O) = 1 when the date dt from query Q matches object O; otherwise, scorewhen(dt, O) = 0, $f[u][dt]$ is the total frequency of the user u in the time dt across all data sources, $fs[u][dt]$ is the frequency of the user u in the time dt and data source s of the object, $f[g][dt]$ is the total frequency of the group of user g in the time dt, $f[addr]$ is the frequency of each location addr, and scorehow(s, O) is the score of an object O for a given source s: scorehow(s, O) = 1 when the service s from query Q matches object O; otherwise, scorehow(s, O) = 0. Lastly, scorewhat (O) is a text-based score for object O, using any chosen scoring function (e.g., TFIDF, BM25, ...).

The equation in Definition 2 assumes that a query Q has all 4 dimensions *who*, *when*, *where* and *how*; if a dimension does not exist in a query, the equation term corresponding to that dimension will be 0.

Let us consider the query Q_0 (*what*: March for Science; *who*: John Smith, Anna Smith; *when*: 2017), and the object *O1* illustrated in Figure 1 (Section 3). According to the *w5h-f* methodology, the object *O1* will have the following score:

$$\begin{aligned} fscore(Q,O1) = & f[g = John\ S., Anna\ S.] \\ & + f[u = John\ S.] + f[u = Anna\ S.] \\ & + fs[u = John\ S.] + fs[u = Anna\ S.] \\ & + f[u = John\ S.][dt = 2017] \\ & + f[u = Anna\ S.][dt = 2017] \\ & + fs[u = John\ S.][dt = 2017] \\ & + fs[u = Anna\ S.][dt = 2017] \\ & + scorewhen(2017, O) \\ & + f[g = John\ S., Anna\ S.][dt = 2017] \\ & + scorewhat\ \text{"March for Science"} \end{aligned}$$

Where s = Facebook.

SEARCH IMPLEMENTATION

We now discuss our search implementation in details.

Data Retrieval

To create a data set of personal digital traces, we use the extraction tool proposed in (Vianna et al., 2014) to identify and retrieve data from current popular services and sources of digital traces. The data retrieved is stored in its original format to avoid mistakes that could lead to missing relevant data. All the data collected by the tool is stored in MongoDB, a NoSQL database that is already optimized for semi-structured data, with the data from each service stored in its own collection. We are constantly adding and revising sources of personal digital traces; the current implementation includes emails services (Gmail), social networks interactions (Facebook, LinkedIn, Twitter), location services (GPS, Foursquare), file management (Dropbox, Local File-system), browsing data (Firefox, Chrome), financial data (Mint, bank accounts), calendars (Google Calendar).

In the next section we will present how the raw data retrieved can be parsed and mapped into the w5h model proposed in Section 3.

Classification

Having defined the w5h model (Section 3), it is still necessary to find an effective mechanism to translate the heterogeneous set of personal data into the six dimensions. The dynamic nature of data sources, especially the rapid rate of change in the service APIs, and the fact that new sources can be added into the extraction tool, also pose a challenge.

Digital traces have their own structures but most are retrieved in a semi-structured data format (typically JSON through APIs), or are extracted along with some metadata. We implemented parsers to represent the raw data from each source in the w5h model, thus unifying the data downloaded into a single data collection. The identification of data according to the six dimensions is done by analyzing the data available to be retrieved for each data source implemented and then building a dictionary of words/labels for each w5h dimension. Much of the classification is intuitive, for instance, the words From and To should be classified under the who dimension, while words Subject and Body should be classified as what.

We designed a machine learning multi-class classifier that automatically maps the raw data from each source into the w5h dimensions. The input data to the w5h classifier is a set of sentences and w5h labels. For instance, in Figure 1 (Section 3) each line corresponds to a sentence/label pair. Each sentence is then transformed in embedding vectors by a Word2vec algorithm, and labels are reshaped into one-hot encoded binary matrices. Architectures were built combining LSTM (Long Short-Term Memory) and Dense layers. Dropout was used in some architectures to reduce the complexity of the model with the goal to prevent overfitting. Parameters were evaluated using a 5-fold cross validation process to estimate the performance of models. We use categorical cross-entropy as the training criterion (loss function); Adam optimization algorithm as the optimization algorithm for our models.

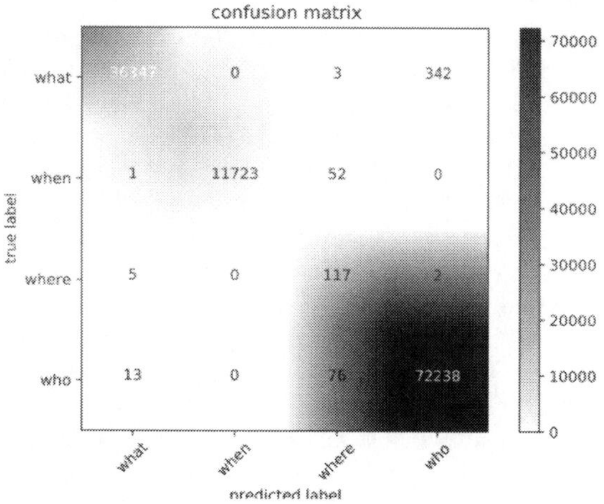

Figure 2. Confusion matrix with predictions for dataset *User 1*. The model was trained using dataset *User 2*.

The evaluation was conducted using the dataset *User 2* described in Table 1. The confusion matrix in Figure 2 shows the accuracy of the model for dataset *User 1* (Table 1), using the training data from *User 2*, with the true labels represented in the y-axis and predicted labels in the x-axis. All correct predictions are located in the diagonal of the table. The results indicate that a machine learning classifier can accurately translate dynamic and heterogeneous set of personal data into the w5h model. Our implementation uses the classifier to translate raw data into the w5h model and does not require user intervention.

Entity Resolution

Our scoring technique (Section 4) relies on frequency scoring of the same entity across objects. To make this possible, we need to identify separate instances of the same entity in data traces coming from the same sources, and across sources. For instance, the same person may appear in different services using variations of their names and email addresses. The impact of entity resolution on search performance will be discussed in Section 6.

Entity Resolution for the who Dimension

We use the Stanford Entity Resolution Framework (SERF), a generic open-source, infrastructure for Entity Resolution (ER) (Stanford), to identify entities. Using SERF person entities are identified and grouped in final entities that are stored in MongoDB in a separate collection.

Entity Resolution for the where Dimension

To disambiguate and match location data, we used Google Geocoding, Google Places API and SERF. We start by using Google Maps to disambiguate places that appear under different names and to augment the existing data, then we rank all addresses returned by a Google Maps search using a *tf* (term frequency) function computed based on the user's data set. When there are no results, we use location information from other related digital traces. We then use SERF for deduplication and record linkage for locations that have the same geo-coded address information or geographical coordinates (longitude, latitude).

EXPERIMENTAL EVALUATION

We now evaluate the efficacy of the *w5h-f* search approach by comparing its performance with two popular existing search tools, Solr (Apache Solr) (using different scoring methodologies: TFIDF, BM25, and field-based BM25), and Spotlight (Apple, 2017). In this section, we first describe our evaluation methodology. Then, we explore the accuracy of the search approach for a set of search scenarios manually designed to be representative of possible user queries. Finally, we explore the accuracy of the search approach using a much larger set of synthetically generated searches.

	User 1		User 2	
Data source	**#Objs**	**Size**	**#Objs**	**Size**
Facebook	1493	9Mb	2384	19Mb
Gmail	1136	107Mb	10926	1Gb
Dropbox	-	-	573	32Mb
Foursquare	-	-	55	59Kb
Twitter	-	-	2062	10Mb
Google Calendar	2	9Kb	209	389Kb
Google+	1	1Kb	102	343Kb
Google Contacts	157	158Kb	427	430Kb
Total	2789	116Mb	16738	1.4Gb

Table 1. Personal data sets for two users.

Methodology

Data Set

There is a dearth of synthetic data sets and benchmarks to evaluate search over personal data. This challenge has only been exacerbated by the recent explosion in the amount of personal digital traces, as well as the varied services that create, collect, and store them. Thus, we perform our evaluation using a real data set collected by our extraction tool (Vianna et al., 2014) for two users.

Table 1 shows two real user data sets along with the number and size of objects retrieved from different sources over different periods of time. These two data sets will be used to evaluate the w5h scoring approach proposed in Section 4.

Search approach	Query description	Rank
Scenario 1 – search target: a Google+ post about SIGIR 2013 posted by Ashley in 2013		
Spotlight	MDContent:SIGIR, MDAuthors:Ashley, MDCreationDate:2013	2 - 14
TFIDF	SIGIR, Ashley, 2013	11
BM25	SIGIR, Ashley, 2013	12
Field-based BM25	who:Ashley, what:SIGIR, when:2013	8
w5h-f	who:Ashley, what:SIGIR, when:2013	5
Scenario 2: search target: a photo of a cat posted on Facebook by Katie in March 2012		
Spotlight	MDContent:photo, MDContent:cat, MDAuthors:Katie, MDCreationDate:2012-03	2-2964
TFIDF	Photo, cat, Katie, 2012-03	5468
BM25	Photo, cat, Katie, 2012-03	9106
Field-based BM25	what:photo, what:cat, who:Katie, when:2012-03	65
w5h-f	what:photo, what:cat, who:Katie, when:2012-03	13
Scenario 3: search target: a Facebook photo of Anna taken in Campos		
Spotlight	MDContent:Photo, MDContent:Anna, MDContent:Campos	2 - 3169
TFIDF	Photo, Anna, Campos	17
BM25	Photo, Anna, Campos	43
Field-based BM25	what:Photo, who:Anna, where:Campos	1
w5h-f	what:Photo, who:Anna, where:Campos	1

Table 2. Representative search scenarios targeting information stored in a user's personal data set.

Evaluation Techniques

Solr. Solr (Apache Solr) is a popular open source full-text search platform from the Apache Lucene project. For the experiments in this section, we integrate all data retrieved by the extraction tool, from each different data source, in a unified collection. This approach allows user to search for information across the entire set of retrieved digital traces, which is already a significant step forward from the current state. We consider three different scoring methods in conjunction with Solr: TFIDF, BM25, and field-based BM25 where the fields correspond to the parsing into the w5h model.

Spotlight. We also compare our search approach to Spotlight, the desktop search platform in Apple's OS X. Spotlight allows users to search for files based on metadata (Apple, 2017). This approach also works using the integrated raw (original) data. Each object in the evaluation data set is stored as an individual file in a machine running OS X Yosemite version 10.10.5. When possible, the following metadata is added to the files: MDAuthors (authors), MDCreationDate (creation date), MDChangeDate (content change date), MDCreator (content creator), MDFroms (path of a file). It is important to mention that Spotlight only ranks one item that it views as most relevant to a query. All other matching items are returned without ranking, typically organized by type of documents (e.g., email, pdf, etc.).

w5h-f. Our proposed approach relies on the six memory cues (what, who, when, where, why and how) to guide search. The *w5h-f* approach uses the data parsed according to the w5h model. The correlation between users/entities and how they interact over time through different services, including the frequency users communicate, is used to rank objects, as described in Section 4. *w5h-f* uses entity resolution, as described in Section 5.3, to disambiguate/link entities from different sources (e.g. Facebook, Gmail, Twitter...) in the data set.

Case Studies

We begin our evaluation by studying three manually created search scenarios designed to be representative of realistic user searches targeting different personal digital traces from the data set *User 2* described in Table 1. For each scenario, we compose one query for each of Spotlight, Solr (TFIDF), Solr (BM25), Solr (Fieldbased BM25) and *w5h-f* using the same information. Query conditions are derived from information in the target objects, and all conditions are classified accurately along the dimensions within Spotlight, field-based Solr and *w5h-f*.

Table 2 describes the search scenarios, the corresponding queries, and the rank of the target object as returned by each search method. Note that the target objects are always found, since the queries are accurate, and all three search tools currently return all matching objects. When Spotlight does not return the target item as the 1st ranked result, we report the ranking as the range from 2 to the total number of returned items.

The results show that *w5h-f* achieves the best accuracy by always ranking the target object higher than or equal to Spotlight and Solr. The differences can be significant (e.g., scenarios 1 and 2), demonstrating that using memory cues to guide search can lead to improved search accuracy. We next discuss each of the search scenarios in more detail to show how differentiating between the dimensions, and using frequency information, helps to improve search accuracy.

In scenario 1, the user is searching for a data item containing information about the 2013 SIGIR Conference. The information was sent or posted by Ashley. In this scenario, identifying Ashley as who and 2013 as when allows *w5h-f* to rank the target object higher than all instances of Solr. When compared with Solr field-based BM25, using the same parsed data as *w5h-f*, the fact that *w5h-f* scoring function takes into consideration the frequency that Ashley communicated with the user during the year of 2013 using Google+, allows *w5h-f* to rank the target object higher than Solr. Spotlight was unable to leverage the same distinctions as *w5h-f* since the target object was not ranked number 1. Thus, Spotlight returned the target object as an unranked item among 13 other items.

Scenario 2 targets a photo of a cat sent or taken by Katie in March 2012. In this case, the classification of photo and cat as what and Katie as who allows *w5h-f* and Solr field-based BM25 to rank the target object much higher than Solr BM25, Solr TFIDF and Spotlight. Entity resolution in the who dimension and the scoring function based on frequency help *w5h-f* to rank the target object in the top 20.

Scenario 3 looks for a picture of Anna taken at a place called Campos. The good performance achieved by the w5h and Solr field-based BM25 approach is explained by the fact that those approaches were able to classify Anna under the dimension who and Campos under dimension where. Since Campos is a very common family name in the user database, the keyword search approaches ended up returning lots of documents matching Campos as location and also as a name.

Simulated Known-Item Queries

We now study a larger set of automatically generated known-item queries: search of personal data is usually focused on retrieving information that users know exists in their own data set. Considering the fact that personal data trace search is a known-item type of search, simulated queries can be automatically generated, using known-item query (Elsweiler & Ruthven, 2007) generation techniques such as the ones presented in (Kim & Croft, 2009), as detailed below.

For this set of experiments, we built two query sets, one using data set *User 1*, and one using data set *User 2* (Table 1). Both sets comprise 5 different groups of queries, each containing 1,500 queries for 250 different scenarios. Each scenario is automatically created by randomly choosing a target object from one of the evaluation data set. We then choose d dimensions, from which we randomly select v random values. We adapted the queries to each of our evaluation methods. The parameter d for each group is defined as following: Group 1, d = {what}; Group 2, d = {what, who}; Group 3, d = {what, who, when}; Group 4, d = {what, who, when, how}; Group 5, d = {what, who, when, how}. For Groups 1 to 4, v = 1. For Group 5, v = 2 to dimensions who and what, and v = 1 to dimensions when and how. We performed our experiments on both *User 1*, and *User 2* data sets and observed similar behaviors. For space reasons, we only report here on the results over the *User 2* data set.

Our evaluation resulted in the following observations on the impact of the multidimensional w5h data model, choice of text search function, entity resolution, and frequency scoring on the accuracy of the search results.

Methods	MRR	NDCG@10
Solr TF.IDF	0.2920	0.3384
Solr BM25	0.4742	0.5192
Solr Field-based BM25	0.4979	0.5428
w5h-f (no entity)	0.5632	0.5993
w5h-f	0.6119	0.6114

Table 3. MRR, NDCG@10 for Group 2 of queries.

Including pertinent contextual information when searching personal data can significantly improve accuracy. Tables 3 and 4 show the MRR (Mean Reciprocal Rank) and NDCG@10 (Normalized Discounted Cumulative Gain through position 10) of each approach, Solr TFIDF, Solr BM25, Solr field-based BM25, and *w5h-f*, for Group 1 - 5 of queries. If the target object has the same ranking as other matching objects, we report the median value of the range. Observe that all search implementations that use the data parsed according to the w5h model, Solr field-based BM25, and *w5h-f*, outperform the keyword-based approaches, Solr TFIDF and Solr BM25. These results show how valuable it is to use context (*w5h-f* and Solr field-based BM25) to find matching documents.

(a) Group 1

Methods	MRR	NDCG@10
Solr TF.IDF	0.1959	0.2304
Solr BM25	0.2127	0.2481
Solr Field-based BM25	0.2383	0.2712
w5h-f	0.2383	0.2712

(b) Group 3

Methods	MRR	NDCG@10
Solr TF.IDF	0.3580	0.4036
Solr BM25	0.5267	0.5619
Solr Field-based BM25	0.6117	0.6582
w5h-f	0.7072	0.7488

(c) Group 4

Methods	MRR	NDCG@10
Solr TF.IDF	0.3328	0.3925
Solr BM25	0.5357	0.5888
Solr Field-based BM25	0.6327	0.6765
w5h-f	0.7539	0.7931

(d) Group 5

Methods	MRR	NDCG@10
Solr TF.IDF	0.3772	0.4270
Solr BM25	0.5345	0.5924
Solr Field-based BM25	0.5769	0.6363
w5h-f	0.6514	0.7014

Table 4. MRR, NDCG@10 for groups 1, 3, 4, and 5 (Group 2 is in Table 3). Compared against w5h-f all the results are statistically significant (Wilcoxon signed-rank test).

The use of a more elaborated approach to search text data can positively impact the final results obtained by the w5h approaches. As previously mentioned, the what dimension in the w5h model is composed basically by content information comprising most of the text. *w5h-f* uses Solr field-based BM25 to score the what dimension. The impact of the text search using Solr field-based BM25 versus Solr TFIDF and Solr BM25, can be seen in Table 4 (a), which presents MRR and NDCG@10 for Group 1 of queries (queries have only the what dimension). We can observe that Solr field-based BM25 and *w5h-f* use a more efficient approach to search and score text data than Solr TFIDF and Solr BM25. Note that since Group 1 has only one textual dimension in the query, the *w5h-f* is equivalent to the underlying text-based scoring approach for the what dimension; field-based BM25 in our implementation. The results show that the adoption of a field-based text search for the what dimension leads to better results.

Being able to disambiguate/link people from different sources of data can significantly improve the accuracy of search. To analyze the importance of the entity resolution phase presented in Section 5.3, we created a group of queries (Group 2) composed by values from the who and what dimensions. The results, for the data set *User 2*, are illustrated in Table 3, with *w5h-f* approach being superior when using entity resolution, compared with an implementation of *w5h-f* that does not use entity resolution.

Including frequency information as part of the scoring results in significant improvements. Tables 3 and 4 show that *w5h-f*, which uses our proposed frequency scoring (Section 4), consistently outperforms Solr field-based BM25, which also relies on the w5h model (Section 3) but does not consider frequency. This shows that taking into consideration the correlation between dimensions while scoring an object improves the search accuracy.

Our evaluation shows that using a tailored frequency based multidimensional scoring approaches yields significant improvements in search accuracy over personal digital traces where the desired search outcome is a specific known object.

RELATED WORK

The case for a unified data model for personal information was made in (Karger, Bakshi, Huynh, Quan, & Sinha, 2005; Xu, Karlsson, Tang, & Karamanolis, 2003). deskWeb (Zerr, Demidova, & Chernov, 2010) looks at the social network graph to expand the searched data set to include information available in the social network. Stuff I've Seen (Dumais et al., 2003) indexes all of the information the user has seen, regardless of its location or provenance, and uses the corresponding metadata to improve search results. Most notably, Personal Dataspaces (Blunschi et al., 2007; Dittrich & Salles, 2006; Halevy, Franklin, & Maier, 2006) propose semantic integration of data sources to provide meaningful semantic associations that can be used to navigate and query user data. Our work is related to the wider field of Personal Information Management (Jones & Teevan, 2007), in particular, search behavior over personal digital traces is likely to mimic that of searching data over personal devices. Unlike traditional information seeking, which focuses on discovering new information, the goal of search in Personal Information systems is to find information that has been created, received, or seen by the user.

Bell has pioneered the field of life-logging with the project MyLifeBits (Gemmell, Bell, & Lueder, 2006) for which he has digitally captured all aspects of his life. While MyLifeBits started as an experiment, there is no denying that we are moving towards a world where all of our steps, actions, words and interactions will be recorded by personal devices or by public systems, and will generate a myriad of digital traces. Digi.me (digime) is a commercial tool that aims at extending Bell's vision to everyday users. The motivations behind digi.me are very close to ours; however, digi.me currently only offers a keyword- or navigation-based access to the data; search results can be filtered by service, data type or/and date.

Other file system related projects have tried to enhance the quality of search within the file system by leveraging the context in which information is accessed to find related information (Chen, Guo, Wu, & Xie, 2009; Gyllstrom, Soules, & Veitch, 2007) or by altering the model of the file system to a more object-oriented database system (Bowman, Dharap, Baruah, Camargo, & Potti, 1994). YouPivot (Hailpern et al., 2011) indexes all user activities based on time and uses the time-based context to guide searches. Social context (users' friends and communities) is leveraged in (Smith, Barash, Getoor, & Lauw, 2008) for information discovery; similarly (Derczynski, Yang, & Jensen, 2013) uses temporal and location context to aid discovery in social media data. Our work integrates all these sources of contextual information and provides a unified complete model of context-aware personal data.

Contextual information has been considered in various computer science applications. Context-aware applications dynamically adapt to changes in the environment in which they are running: location, time, user profile, history. Bolchini et al. provide a thorough survey of context-aware models in (Bolchini, Curino, Quintarelli, Schreiber, & Tanca, 2007). Truong and Dustdar survey context-aware Web-Service systems in (Linh Truong & Dustdar, 2009). Context-awareness has become increasingly popular with the wide adoption of mobile devices. While the types of context these systems consider overlap with ours, the overall approach is different from ours, for instance a contextually-aware Information Retrieval system will use the current context (e.g., user location and time of day) to adjust search results (Shen, Tan, & Zhai, 2005). In contrast, we consider context as information that can be queried and used to guide the search.

CONCLUSION AND FUTURE WORK

We proposed and implemented a multidimensional data model based on the six natural questions: *what, when, where, who, why* and *how* to represent and unify heterogeneous personal digital traces. Based on this proposed model we designed a frequency-based scoring strategy for search queries that takes into account interactions between entities across objects to assist in the ranking of query results. Experiments over personal data sets composed by data from a variety of data sources showed that our approach significantly improved search accuracy when compared with traditional search methods. In the future, we plan on investigating several extensions to our work on searching personal data traces: (1) including topic modeling approaches over the *what* dimension to be able to correlate objects based on their contents, (2) designing dedicated indexes and search algorithms for search efficiency, (3) adding query relaxation rules to allow for approximate query matching, and (4) designing an aggregate query model where groups of objects (traces) can be returned together as a query answer (e.g., all the social media messages and pictures relating to a party), integrating the why dimension (Kalokyri et al. 2017) into our scoring framework.

REFERENCES

Abowd, G. D., Dey, A. K., Brown, P. J., Davies, N., Smith, M., & Steggles, P. (1999). Towards a better understanding of context and context-awareness. In *Proceedings of the 1st International Symposium on Handheld and Ubiquitous Computing* (pp. 304–307). Springer.

APACHE SOLR. Retrieved from http://lucene.apache.org/solr/

Apple. (2017). *Spotlight*. Retrieved from https://developer.apple.com/library/content/documentation/Carbon/Conceptual/MetadataIntro/MetadataIntro.html

Blunschi, L., Dittrich, J.-P., Girard, O. R., Kirakos, S., Marcos, K., & Salles, A. V. (2007). A dataspace odyssey: The imemex personal dataspace management system. In *CIDR*.

Bolchini, C., Curino, C. A., Quintarelli, E., Schreiber, F. A., & Tanca, L. (2007). A data-oriented survey of context models. *ACM SIGMOD Record*, *36*(4), 19–26.

Bowman, C. M., Dharap, C., Baruah, M., Camargo, B., & Potti, S. (1994). A file system for information management. In *Proceedings of the International Conference on Intelligent Information Management Systems*.

Brewer, W. (1988). *Memory for randomly sampled autobiographical events* (pp. 21–90). Cambridge University Press.

Chen, J., Guo, H., Wu, W., & Xie, C. (2009). Search your memory! - an associative memory-based desktop search system. In *Proceedings of the 2009 ACM SIGMOD International Conference on Management of data* (pp. 1099–1102). New York, NY.

Derczynski, L. R. A., Yang, B., & Jensen, C. S. (2013). Towards context-aware search and analysis on social media data. In *Proceedings of the 16th International Conference on Extending Database Technology, EDBT '13* (pp. 137–142). New York, NY.

Dey, A. K. (2001). Understanding and using context. *Personal and Ubiquitous Computing*, *5*(1), 4–7.

digi.me. Retrieved from https://www.digi.me.

Dittrich, J.-P., & Salles, M. A. V. (2006). iDM: A unified and versatile data model for personal dataspace management. In *Proceedings of the 32nd International Conference on Very Large Data Bases*.

Dumais, S., Cutrell, E., Cadiz, J., Jancke, G., Sarin, R., & Robbins, D. (2003). Stuff I've seen: A system for personal information retrieval and re-use. In *Proceedings of the 26th ACM SIGIR Conference on Research and Development in Information Retrieval* (pp. 72–79).

Elsweiler, D., & Ruthven, I. (2007). Towards task-based personal information management evaluations. In *Proceedings of the 30th ACM SIGIR Conference on Research and Development in Information Retrieval* (pp. 23–30).

Gemmell, J., Bell, G., & Lueder, R. (2006). MyLifeBits: A personal database for everything. *Communications of the ACM*, *49*(1), 88–95.

Gyllstrom, K., Soules, C., & Veitch, A. (2007). Confluence: enhancing contextual desktop search. In *Proceedings of 30th ACM SIGIR Conference on Research and Development in Information Retrieval* (pp. 717–718). ACM Press.

Hailpern, J., Jitkoff, N., Warr, A., Karahalios, K., Sesek, R., & Shkrob, N. (2011). YouPivot: improving recall with contextual search. In *Proceedings of SIGCHI Conference on Human Factors in Computing Systems* (pp. 1521–1530). New York, NY.

Halevy, A., Franklin, M., & Maier, D. (2006). Principles of dataspace systems. In *Proceedings of 25th ACM Symposium on Principles of Database Systems* (pp. 1–9). New York, NY.

Jones, W., & Teevan, J. (2007). *Personal information management*. University of Washington Press.

Kalokyri, V., Borgida, A., & Marian, A. (2018). Yourdigitalself: A personal digital trace integration tool. In *Proceedings 27th ACM International Conference on Information and Knowledge Management, CIKM '18* (pp. 1963–1966).

Kalokyri, V., Borgida, A., Marian, A., & Vianna, D. (2017a). Integration and exploration of connected personal digital traces. In *Proceedings of the ExploreDB'17*, May 19, 2017, (pp. 3:1–3:6). Chicago, IL.

Kalokyri, V., Borgida, A., Marian, A., & Vianna, D. (2017b). Semantic modeling and inference with episodic organization for managing personal digital traces. In *Proceedings of 16th International Conference on Ontologies, DataBases, and Applications of Semantics (ODBASE'17)* (pp. 273–280).

Karger, D. R., Bakshi, K., Huynh, D., Quan, D., & Sinha, V. (2005). Haystack: A general-purpose information management tool for end users based on semi structured data. In *CIDR* (pp. 13–26).

Kim, J., & Croft, W. B. (2009). Retrieval experiments using pseudo-desktop collections. In *Proceedings of the 18th ACM Conference on Information and Knowledge Management* (pp. 1297–1306).

Linh Truong, H., & Dustdar, S. (2009). *A survey on context-aware web service systems* (Vol. *5*, pp. 5–31).

Schacter, D. (2001). *The seven sins of memory: How the mind forgets and remembers*. Houghton Mifflin.

Shen, X., Tan, B., & Zhai, C. (2005). Context-sensitive information retrieval using implicit feedback. In *Proceedings of the 28th ACM SIGIR Conference Research and Development in Information Retrieval* (pp. 43–50). New York, NY.

Smith, M., Barash, V., Getoor, L., & Lauw, H. W. (2008). Leveraging social context for searching social media. In *Proceedings of the 2008 ACM Workshop on Search in Social Media* (pp. 91–94).

Stanford, I. *Stanford entity resolution framework*. Retrieved from http://infolab.stanford.edu/serf/

Vianna, D., Yong, A.-M., Xia, C., Marian, A., & Nguyen, T. (2014). A tool for personal data extraction. In *Proceedings of the 10th International Workshop on Information Integration on the Web (IIWeb)* (pp. 80–83).

Wagenaar, W. A. (1986). My memory: A study of autobiographical memory over six years. *Cognitive Psychology*, *18*(2), 225–252.

Xu, Z., Karlsson, M., Tang, C., & Karamanolis, C. (2003). Towards a semantic-aware file store. In *Proceedings of the Workshop on Hot Topics in OS (HotOS'03)*.

Zerr, S., Demidova, E., & Chernov, S. (2010). deskweb2.0: Combining desktop and social search. In *Proceedings of Desktop Search Workshop, in Conjunction with ACM SIGIR 2010*, 23 July 2010. Geneva, Switzerland.

Improving Explicit Term Matching With Implicit Topic Matching for Short Text Conversation

Jianqiang Wang
Department of Information Science, University at Buffalo, Buffalo, NY 14260, USA
jw254@buffalo.edu

Ying Sun
Department of Information Science, University at Buffalo, Buffalo, NY 14260, USA
sun3@buffalo.edu

ABSTRACT
Short Text Conversation (STC) is the task of retrieving comments made to a post and reuse them as appropriate comments to a later post. Large vocabulary variations and very limited length of posts and comments pose great challenges to traditional retrieval techniques of matching terms. To address these problems, we propose a new technique of re-ranking comments initially retrieved through explicit term matching by using evidence of implicit topic matching gained from topic models of large collections of posts and comments. The key of our technique lies in (1) combining each post with the comments responding to it into a longer pseudo-document for topic modeling purposes, and (2) carrying out implicit topic matching by comparing the most probable topics contained in the topic composition of a comment and that of the query post. Experiments using the NTCIR-13 STC Chinese WeiBo collection showed that with properly tuned parameters, our technique can lead to improved retrieval effectiveness. The paper analyzes and discusses the results and outlines future work.

KEYWORDS
Short Text Conversation; Topic Models; Re-ranking

ASIS&T THESAURUS
Information Retrieval; Evaluation

INTRODUCTION
Natural language conversational systems use computer agents to converse with humans in a coherent manner. Such systems can be useful in many application areas, including education, healthcare, government, business, marketing, and social networking where fast and accurate responses to a potentially large number of user inquiries are desired. The user input and the system's output can be text, speech, graphics, haptics, etc. Such a system often consists of three key components, namely natural language understanding, dialog management, and natural language generation (Young, Gasic, Thompson, & Williams, 2013). The development of the system often requires techniques of natural language processing and understanding, machine learning, reasoning, dialog modeling, information extraction, knowledge base development, and in the cases of speech-based systems, automatic speech recognition and text-to-speech synthesis. While much success has been achieved with task-oriented dialog systems in constrained domains, it remains one of the fundamental challenges to build dialog agents for open-domain complex tasks (Gao, Galley, & Li, 2019).

82nd Annual Meeting of the Association for Information Science & Technology | Melbourne, Australia | 19–23 October, 2019

DOI: 10.1002/pra2.00023

A research focus in this area in recent years has been on social media interaction, thanks to the rapid growth of platforms such as Twitter and the Chinese Sina WeiBo that online users with shared interests use to connect to each other (Shang, Lu, & Li, 2015). Short posts are used for a variety of purposes, including broadcasting news of current events, releasing product information, marketing for business, promoting education, and sharing personal interests, opinions, and activities; users often respond with comments that are also very short. The research, known as "Short Text Conversation" (STC), aims at developing and studying computer systems that retrieve previous messages (known as *comments*) or automatically generate new messages in response to initial messages (known as *posts*). This task is on *short text* because it focuses on application areas like Twitter and WeiBo where posts and comments are usually very short. Ultimately, a STC system should support multiple turns of conversation between the user and the computer. As an initial but important step it is useful to build a one-turn STC system in which the user submits a post and the computer responds by either generating new comments (generation-based method) or retrieving comments from an existing collection (retrieval-based method).

In our study we focus on retrieval-based methods, using the Chinese WeiBo collection produced for the NTCIR-13 STC task. A key challenge of this task lies in the fact that posts and comments are very short, thus rendering traditional information retrieval (IR) techniques that are based on matching terms (i.e., words, word stems, phrases, character n-grams, etc.) less effective. Inspired by previous work in latent semantic analysis (e.g., Deerwester, Dumais, Furnas, Landauer, & Harshman, 1990), topic modeling (e.g., Blei, Ng, & Jordan, 2003), and neural IR (e.g., Mitra & Craswell,

2018) we view IR for STC as a task of combining evidence from two sources: (1) *explicit term matching*, which is what many traditional IR systems are built upon, and (2) *implicit topic matching*, which direct term matching could fail to capture but topic modeling can help.

As an example, here is a post with three relevant comments:

- Post: *Not sure if it is a good time to invest in the stock market.*
- Comment C_1: *This is perhaps the worst time to invest in the stock market.*
- Comment C_2: *Maybe you should consider investing in the real estate.*
- Comment C_3: *I would just hold my money and patiently wait.*

Comment C_1 will be retrieved reliably and ranked highly by term-matching techniques. This is where traditional IR techniques remain very effective. Unfortunately, term-matching will rank C_2 very low because only one word, *invest*, matches the query post and will not retrieve C_3 at all because no terms match (after stemming and stopword removal are applied). On the other hand, topic modeling may attribute the post and the comment C_3 to the same topic, because *stock, buy, invest, real estate*, and *money* are highly likely to appear in the word cluster for the same topic, resulting in a positive implicit topic match.

In this paper, we introduce a technique of re-ranking comments initially retrieved using explicit term matching for a query post by utilizing implicit topic matching information between each comment and the post, which is estimated using Latent Dirichlet Allocation (LDA) based topic modeling. This technique is simple because it has only two stages: initial retrieval and re-ranking. It does not use additional datasets other than a collection of existing post-comment pairs. Through experiments we demonstrate that with carefully tuned parameters, our technique can lead to improved IR effectiveness that is on par with some of the state-of-the-art techniques that require to use and combine much more similarity features and neural network models.

The rest of this paper is organized as follows. We first review related work on topic modeling as well as IR approaches to the STC task. We then introduce the techniques developed in this study. The next section provides a brief description of the test collection, IR system, and the retrieval effectiveness measures used in the experiments. That is followed by the section that reports our experiment results and analyses. We finally summarize our experiment findings and contributions and discuss future areas of improvement for our technique.

RELATED WORK

The problem of word mismatch has long been recognized in the community of information retrieval (Furnas, Landauer, Gomez, & Dumais, 1987). In the field of Library and Information Science, controlled vocabulary has been popularly used to address this problem. Controlled vocabulary based approaches, however, have their obvious limitations, including high demands for the skills by the cataloger and the searcher, challenges of full automation, and difficulties of being integrated with ranked retrieval. Latent semantic analysis (LSA) is a technique of analyzing relationships between a set of documents and the terms they contain by producing a set of concepts related to the documents and terms and hence can capture the semantic connections among terms (Deerwester et al., 1990). However, LSA can be computationally expensive and does not usually work well with short documents and polysemy.

In recent years, topic modeling has become a popular technique for inferring topics present in text collections since the first models were proposed by Deerwester et al. (1990) and Blei et al. (2003). Because topic models provide not only semantic relationships between words, but also associations between documents and words, they have been successfully applied to information retrieval (Boyd-Graber, Hu, & Mimno, 2017). For example, Lu, Mei, and Zhai (2011) and Wei and Croft (2006) applied topic models in document language modeling to improve information retrieval results. Other researchers used topic models for query expansion to further improve ranking results of information retrieval (e.g., Andrzejewski & Buttler, 2011 and Park & Ramamohanarao, 2009). Yi and Allan (2009) compared the effectiveness of different types of topic models for retrieval purposes. While providing valuable insights into the usefulness of topical models for IR, none of these studies were conducted with social media collections of short messages.

The problems of applying topic modeling to collections of very short documents, such as tweets, have been well recognized. Multiple researchers have looked into techniques of aggregating Twitter message based on whether they are written by the same person (e.g., Hong & Davison, 2010) or whether they belong to the same thread (e.g., Alvarez-Melis & Saveski, 2016). These studies generally showed that by combining multiple messages into a longer document, topic modeling results can be improved. However, these studies focus more on improving topic modeling rather than information retrieval.

Ji, Lu, and Li (2014) and Shang et al. (2015) are among the first to look into retrieval-based approaches as well as generation-based approaches for the task of STC. Their work led to the creation of a large Chinese WeiBo data set and the development of the NTCIR's STC task (Shang et al., 2016; Shang et al., 2017), which attracted many researchers to participate in the development of various methods for STC.

A careful review of the papers published in the NTCIR-13 conference proceedings reveals that most teams participating in the STC Chinese subtask used neural network approaches to the retrieval-based paradigm, thanks to the recent resurge of neural IR (Mitra & Craswell, 2018). Among the top performing teams, Zhao et al. (2017) utilized traditional web search features to produce an initial list of comments for a given query post, which was followed and refined by two ranking stages that used many similarity features as well as deep neural network models. Yang, Wu, Li, Wu, and Xu (2017) first generated candidate comments based on BM25 weights and named entity information, which were then re-ranked based on the combination of many similarity features, including tf-idf cosine, word overlap, word-to-word translation probability, word embedding cosine, and convolutional neural network models. Zhang, Li, and Shi (2017) also used BM25 to produce candidate comments and then ranked them by combining multiple features, including recall and precision of 2-g between the query post and each comment, longest common subsequence, word embedding, and deep learning models. Ni, Lin, & Xu, (2017) trained LSA and LDA for the degree of topic relatedness between a comment and a query post, used *word2vec* (Mikolov, Chen, Corrado, & Dean, 2013) for semantic similarity, and finally combined them to produce the relevance score.

While having some similarities with the techniques used in those studies, such as exploring the post-comment relationship included in the test collection and using BM25 weighting, our technique does not use any neural network features or additional training data. Instead, we compare the topic model of the query post and that of each initially retrieved comment using BM25 and use that information to re-rank the comment, as described in detail below.

OUR PROPOSED TECHNIQUE

Our analysis of earlier experiment results for the NTCIR-13 STC tasks revealed multiple cases in which relevant comments were ranked very low in the result set returned by our search system, which uses Okapi BM25 weighting. This is because these low-ranking comments share very few content-bearing words with the query post even though they are clearly talking about the same topic as the query post. Therefore, if we can manage to raise the ranks of such comments, IR effectiveness could potentially be improved. This led to two important considerations:

1. how to decide whether a comment and a post are about the same topic even if they do not share many content-bearing words and
2. how to use that information to improve the rank of the comment in response to the post.

In devising our techniques, the guiding idea is not to use external data sets nor manually labelled relevance data as these resources can be expensive to acquire or generate. Instead, we want to explore the given collection itself for the underlying topics. This naturally pointed us to topic modeling approaches.

The architecture of our system is illustrated in Figure 1. In that figure, rectangle boxes represent data or results while ovals represent functions performed by the system. The system takes a collection of post-comment pairs and a query post as inputs, processes these inputs through indexing, retrieving, topic modeling, estimating topic composition, and finally re-ranking to generate a hopefully improved ranked list of comments in response to the query post. In the following parts of this section, we describe these functional components of the system and the techniques behind them.

Generating Topic Compositions for Comments

Topic modeling techniques analyze large text collections to identify patterns in the use of words. A topic is constructed as a cluster of words that frequently occur together in the same document (McCallum, 2002), defined by probability distribution over words. Topic models can also offer the semantic relationships between documents and words. As a result, a trained topic

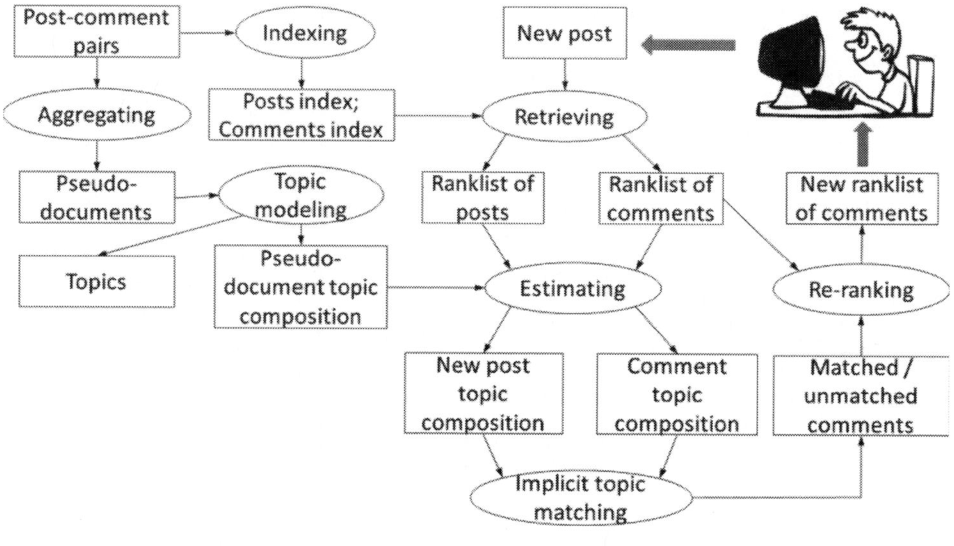

Figure 1. System architecture.

model of a document collection can provide a framework for us to understand the document collection directly by examining the topics as well as indirectly by using topics as input for future applications, such as information retrieval. Topic modeling usually generates two important outputs:

1. a list of underlying topics, each of which is represented by a set of words (topic keys) that often co-occur in documents, and
2. a topic composition for each document, which specifies a percentage value expressing the relative importance of a topic in a document. The percentage value can be roughly regarded as the likelihood of the document being about the corresponding topic.

Topic modeling requires input documents with reasonable lengths. Social media posts and comments are very short. For example, both Twitter and WeiBo used to have a 140-character limit for posts and comments. Although these constraints have been relaxed, studies showed that shorter messages tend to attract more engagements (e.g., Gligorić, Anderson, & West, 2018). Short documents do not provide sufficient word co-occurrence information for topic modeling tools to generate good topic models. To overcome this problem, we concatenate a post with all its responding comments to form a large pseudo-document (which is similar to treating an email thread as one document in email retrieval). The basic assumption here is that a post and all responding comments are on the same topic. Of course, there will be noise since not every responding comment is guaranteed to bear meaningful or appropriate content. For example, comments can be advertisements that are not necessarily related to the post; spamming and malicious comments also degrade the accuracy of topic models. Nonetheless, we are hoping that legitimate comments are prevalent and hence meaningful topic models can be generated using such longer pseudo-documents.

How do we get each comment's topic composition now that we have the topic models and the pseudo-document topic composition? If a comment responded to only one post, it would have appeared in only one pseudo-document. In this case, we can simply treat the pseudo-document's topic composition as the comment's topic composition. However, a comment may be linked to multiple posts and hence it would have appeared in multiple pseudo-documents. One way to estimate the percentage value of a topic for such a comment is to use the average percentage value of the topic of all pseudo-documents that the comment appears in.

We estimate the percentage p_i of Topic t_i for Comment c as:

$$p_i = \frac{1}{m}\sum_{j=1}^{m} p_{ij}$$

where p_{ij} is the percentage value of Topic t_i for Pseudo-document d_j while m is the number of pseudo-documents that Comment c appears in.

This estimation will guarantee all percentage values in the resulting topic composition add up to 100%. If a topic has higher percentage values in multiple posts that a comment responded to, we have a good reason to believe the comment is indeed about that topic.

Estimating Topic Compositions for Query Posts

We estimate a query post's topic composition based on the topic compositions of existing *posts* that are most relevant to the query post. Specifically, for a query post we first retrieve a ranked list of posts from the collection, which can be done by using the same IR system for retrieving comments. For each retrieved post above a certain rank, we take the topic composition of its pseudo-document. To estimate the percentage value of each topic for the query post, we simply use the average of the percentage values of that topic in the topic compositions of these pseudo-documents.

IR Re-ranking Based on Implicit Topic Matching

Once we have the topic composition of the query post and that of each comment in the collection, we can then use that information to re-rank initially retrieved comments for the post, which essentially is to combine evidence from explicit term matching, which is what most traditional IR systems do and implicit topic matching, which is based on comparing the topic composition of the query post with that of each retrieved comment. "Re-ranking" in this study specifically means promoting or demoting the initial rank of a comment according to its implicit topic matching with the query post. There are two key questions here:

1. how to perform implicit topic matching? and
2. how to use that result to re-rank?

The guiding idea for the answer to the first question is like this: if the comment and the post share any topic(s) in common according to their topic compositions, then their implicit topic matching is positive.

As we described earlier, a document's topic composition consists of n percentage values, each of which corresponds to one of the n topics generated by the topic modeling routine. Lower-percentage topics are not as important as higher-percentage topics for a given comment or post, so we should consider only the latter ones. Therefore, the key here is the selection of topics with higher percentage values, which is usually done by including only the m topics of highest percentage value or by using a percentage (i.e., probability) threshold.

Using only the top m topics can guarantee equal number of topics selected for each comment or post. However, there is a potential problem with this technique. That is, if a comment has a uniform or nearly uniform topic composition (and there are comments like that as we see from our experiment), it means it is difficult to tell which topic(s) the comment is about. In cases like this, it does not make much sense to select m topics and deem the comment to be about these topics. Our experiment results reported later also confirm this weakness of the technique.

The other method sets a percentage threshold such that any topics whose percentage values in a comment's topic composition are below that threshold are eliminated. The rationale behind this idea is that only if the percentage value of a topic is high enough do we have confidence that the comment is indeed about that topic. The same can be done for the query post, although the threshold does not need to be the same as that of its retrieved comments. Intuitively we think this is a better method, which is confirmed by our experiment.

For example, let us say there are five topics generated from topic modeling and the topic composition of Comment c is (0.1, 0.3, 0.1, 0.4, 0.1) - these values correspond to Topic 1 through Topic 5, respectively. If we set a percentage threshold of 0.3, then after the threshold is applied there will be only two topics (Topic 2 and Topic 4) left for Comment c. In other words, we believe the comment talks about these two topics only. Likewise, if we apply the same threshold for a query post p that has a topic composition of (0.15, 0.5, 0.1, 0.05, 0.2), there will be only one topic (Topic 2). Finally, when considering implicit topic matching between the post and the comment, since they share a topic (Topic 2) in common, we treat it as a positive match and hence the comment shall be re-ranked higher.

The first method of combining evidence that we considered works like this. We first set a percentage value threshold for both the post topic composition and the comment topic composition (e.g., 0.2) - any topics whose percentage value falls below the threshold are deemed to not have implicit topic matching with the query post. For example, if a comment has only one topic in its topic composition whose percentage value is equal to or larger than the set threshold, then we assume the comment talks about only that topic. Finally, for re-ranking, we can rank higher those retrieved comments that do have implicit topic matches with the query post than those that do not, while within each set the original relative rank of each comment is retained.

Here is an example to illustrate the idea. For the simplicity of discussion, let us assume only 10 relevant comments are needed for each query post. The 10 comments are represented in the following set in decreasing order of their relevance scores, which without considering implicit topic matching will be the final search result:

$(c_1, c_2, c_3, c_4, c_5, c_6, c_7, c_8, c_9, c_{10})$

Now let's assume after applying implicit topic matching as described above, we find that comments c_3, c_4, and c_7 do not share any implicit topic with the post while the rest seven comments do. Therefore, we demote the ranks of these three comments. The re-ranking result will be:

$(c_1, c_2, c_5, c_6, c_8, c_9, c_{10}, c_3, c_4, c_7)$

As implied here, the actual threshold is an important parameter because it decides whether a retrieved comment matches or not the query post in terms of the implicit topics and hence whether that comment's rank will be increased or decreased.

Tuning Parameters

The effectiveness of our above techniques depends on the actual parameter setting. Important parameters include:

The Number of Topics Generated by Topic Modeling

This is a parameter that is often decided and chosen by the user. Too many topics will result in too granular topics, which could incorrectly reject comments that actually talk about the same (broader) topic as the query post. On the other hand, too few topics will produce too broad topics, which could incorrectly include comments that actually do not talk about the same (more specific) topic as the query post. Nonetheless, we believe even a small set of topics can mimic common subject areas, which can be helpful for improving IR effectiveness. As described later, in this study we tried 20, 30, and 50 topics, respectively.

The Number of Top Relevant Posts

These are the posts used to estimate the topic composition of the query post. The basic assumption of using the topic compositions of top retrieved posts to estimate the topic composition of the query post is that those top-retrieved posts talk about the same underlying topic as the query post. Since retrieval can be inaccurate, however, how many of the top retrieved posts to use will affect the accuracy of the resulting topic composition of the query post. As described latter in the experiment section, we tried from top 1 to top 10 of the retrieved posts.

The Number of Most Probable Topics

This number refers to the most probably topics in a topic composition. That number is used to select a subset of topics for a given post or comment for consideration for implicit topic matching. Too large a number will likely include topics that a post or comment does not talk about while too small a number (like 1) will perhaps exclude topics that a post or comment indeed talks about (in the cases of multiple-topic posts or comments).

The Probability Threshold

A pre-set probability threshold can be used to select the most probable topics for a post or comment. In a document topic composition, each percentage value roughly indicates the likelihood that the document is about the corresponding topic. Similar to the above parameter, a too small threshold will include topics that the document does not actually talk about while a too large threshold could exclude topic(s) that the document indeed talks about and in some extreme case, may result in no topic being selected.

EXPERIMENT SETUP

In this section, we describe the nature of the test collection used in our study, processing of the collection, as well as the measures used for IR evaluation.

The Test Collection

To evaluate the effectiveness of our proposed techniques, we chose to use the test collection of the Chinese subtask of the NTCIR-13's STC task. To the best of our knowledge, this is the largest available test collection for research on the problems of short text conversation in the social media domain. It should be noted that in constructing the data set, the organizers chose to retain neither the context, history, date/time of conversations nor the poster's identity information. In other words, each post or comment is simply represented with a unique ID number and its text; comments with identical text are regarded as the same comment even though they responded to different posts.

Total number of post-comment pairs: 4,433,949		
Posts		
Total number	Avg. number of words per post	Avg. number of comments per post
219,174	13	20
Comments		
Total number	Avg. number of words per comments	Average number of posts per comment
4,305,706	10	1
Total number of query posts: 100		
Total number of relevance judgments: 61,743		

Table 1. NTCIR-13 STC Chinese WeiBo collection statistics.

Important statistics of this collection are shown in Table 1. As we can see, on average both posts and comments are very short and while each post has about 20 responding comments, most comments were made to one post only. Posts and comments in the collection are written in Chinese although sometimes foreign words (mostly in English) may be mixed with Chinese words in some comments; there are also a small number of comments that are entirely written in a language other than Chinese (e.g., Japanese or Korean).

Hundred query posts were provided as part of the collection for evaluation purposes. The NTCIR-13 STC task required for each query post, a ranked list of 10 comments to be retrieved from the collection. A total of 61,743 relevance judgments were made by the assessors on comments pooled from the officially submitted runs that used retrieval-based methods. Three levels of relevance judgments were used, with a score of 0 for "not relevant," one for "neutral or partial relevant," and two for "relevant." Each comment in the pool was judged by three independent assessors and the individual scores were added to give the final relevance judgment score of the comment, which can range from 0 to 6. This set of official relevance judgments can be used as the "grouthtruth" for evaluating future IR techniques, such as the one in our study.

Post/Comment Processing

Since we chose to use word-based IR, we had to segment the Chinese text into words. We used the Stanford NLP group's Chinese segmenter.[1] Manual inspection of a sample of posts and comments produced by this segmenter showed the result to be satisfactory. Additionally, we removed comments that contain only one word after segmentation, which would also eliminate most comments that were not written in Chinese. This resulted in 4,293,109 comments, which were then indexed by our IR system. We also created an index of all posts contained in the collection for the purpose of estimating each query post's topic composition, as described in previous section. We did not perform stopword removal as it generally does not have much effect on IR effectiveness. To formulate a query for a query post, we simply used all words contained in it. Our retrieval system uses Okapi BM25 weights with the default parameters setting (i.e., $k_1 = 1.2$, $b = 0.75$, and $k_3 = 7$). We did not run any experiments of tuning these parameters as that is not a focus of this study.

For topic modeling, we first created a pseudo-document collection following the aggregating technique described in previous section. We used the MALLET toolkit, which is an open-source topic modeling package.[2] Again, MALLET took the pseudo-document collection as its input and generated a list of topics and a topic composition representation for each pseudo-document in the collection.

We split the 100 query posts into two sets: a developing set for tuning parameters to find the optimal settings and an evaluation set for testing the generalizability of these settings. In creating these two sets of query posts, we did not use any randomized process. Instead, we simply put those query posts in the odd-numbered lines in the official file of the NTCIR-13 STC query posts into the developing set and the rest into the test set (note: each line contains only one post). For the baseline, we automatically retrieved a ranked list of 10 comments with our IR systems and then used the NtcirEval tool to compute IR effectiveness with the measures described below. Each re-ranked list of comments was evaluated in the same manner for comparison to the baseline.

Relevance and Effectiveness Measures

It is worth noting that the relevance or more precisely, the *appropriateness*, of a comment to a given post is defined in the NTCIR-13 STC task based on four criteria, namely (1) *Fluent*: the comment is acceptable as a natural language text, (2) *Coherent*: the comment should be logically connected and topically relevant to the original post (i.e., the comment makes sense in the eye of the originator of the post), (3) *Self-sufficient*: the assessor can judge that the comment is appropriate by reading nothing other than the post-comment

[1] The Stanford Chinese Segmenter is publicly available at: https://nlp.stanford.edu/software/segmenter.html\#Download.

[2] The open-source MALLET package is publicly available at: http://mallet.cs.umass.edu.

pair, and (4) *Substantial*: the comment provides new information in the eye of the originator of the post. The *fluent* criterion was largely for the generation-based STC task. As comments in this collection are all created by humans, this criterion should be easily satisfied. The *coherent* criterion is basically what *relevant* means in typical IR tasks. The last two criteria add to the challenge because, for example, merely repeating or echoing what the post said will not make a comment satisfy these criteria.

For this study, we used the three IR effectiveness measures that were used officially in the NTCIR-13 STC task. They are *nG@1* (normalized gain at cutoff 1), *nERR@10* (normalized expected reciprocal rank at cutoff 10), and *P+*. For space limit, we are not explaining these measures in this paper. Detailed definitions and explanations of them can be found in Shang et al. (2016).

RESULTS AND ANALYSES

In this section, we first present our experiment results of tuning the parameters with the set of 50 development posts. We then verify the optimal parameter setting with the other set of 50 evaluation posts. Finally, we briefly compare our results with the state-of-the-art results reported in the NTCIR-13 STC task.

Experiments of Parameter Tuning

We started our experiments with first producing a baseline run of searching the original collection of comments as described in the previous section. This baseline run represents the result of using the best-known classic probabilistic IR model. We then generated topic models for the pseudo-document collection using the MALLET toolkit, With the resulting topic compositions, we were able to estimate the topic composition of each comment in the collection. We then tried to use top 1 to 5 retrieved posts for each query post in the developing set to estimate its topic composition. For each of these settings, we tried top 1 to 5 most probable topics in the topic composition for implicit topic matching for re-ranking. Figure 2 shows the IR effectiveness in terms of *nG@1* or *nERR@10*.

We notice that despite variances among different parameter settings, our techniques of combining the two sources of relevance evidence helped in most cases, as compared to the

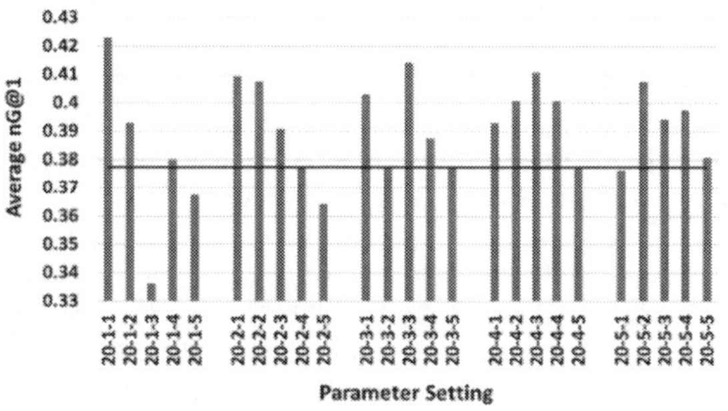

(a). IR effectiveness *nG@1* of different parameter settings.

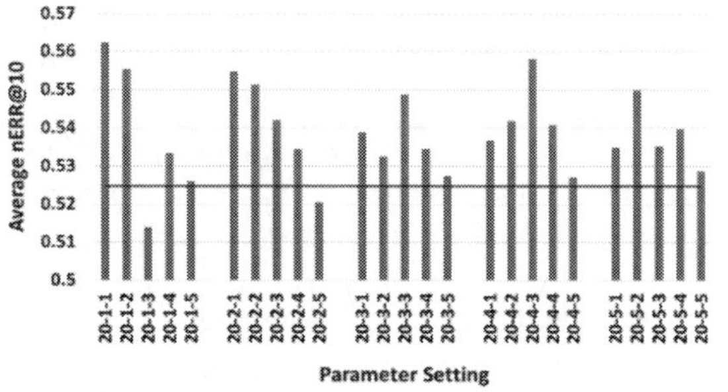

(b). IR effectiveness *nERR@10* of different parameter settings.

Figure 2. IR effectiveness of different parameter settings. Each setting is named in the form of "x-y-z" where x represents the number of topics generated by MALLET, y represents the number of top retrieved posts used to estimate the topic composition of the query post, and z represents the threshold for selecting the most probable topics in the topic composition considered for implicit topic matching. The horizontal line represents the baseline. (a) IR effectiveness *nG@1* of different parameter settings. (b) IR effectiveness *nERR@10* of different parameter settings.

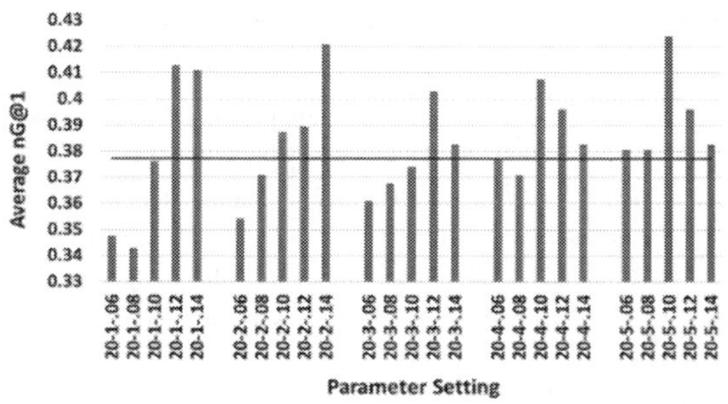

(a). IR effectiveness *nG@1* of different parameter settings.

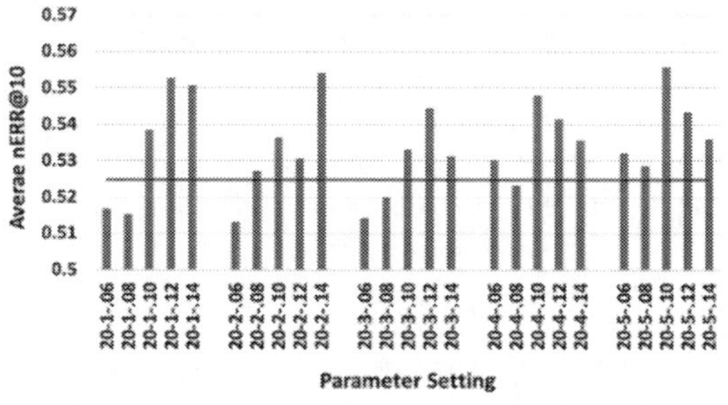

(b). IR effectiveness *nG@1* of different parameter settings.

Figure 3. IR effectiveness of different parameter settings. Each setting is named in the form of "x-y-z" where x represents the number of topics generated by MALLET, y represents the number of top retrieved posts used to estimate the topic composition of the query post, and z represents the probability threshold for selecting topics in the topic composition considered for implicit topic matching. The horizontal line represents the baseline. (a) IR effectiveness *nG@1* of different parameter settings. (b) IR effectiveness *nG@1* of different parameter settings.

baseline result. Specifically, when using a top *n* threshold, the best IR effectiveness was achieved with using top 1 retrieved post to estimate the topic composition of the query post and using the most probable topic in the post/comment topic composition (i.e., the first bar corresponding to the setting "20-1-1" in both Figure 2a, b), resulting in 15% (i.e., 0.4327 vs 0.3773) improvement of the average *nG@1* and 7% (i.e., 0.5621 vs 0.5248) improvement of the average *nERR@10* over the baseline, respectively. We ran a Wilcoxon signed-rank test to compare each optimal setting's results with the baseline results and found that the observed improvement of *nG@1* is not statistically significant whereas the observed improvement of *nERR@10* is statistically significant.

Further query-by-query comparisons indicate that with *nG@1*, which evaluates only the top 1 retrieved comment for each query post, re-ranking resulted in only nine queries with better results, four queries worse results, and the rest 37 queries did not have a difference. In the case of *nERR@10*, however, these numbers were 22, 7, and 21, respectively. Manual examinations on the initially retrieved comments and re-ranking results reveal that some of the more appropriate comments on the same topic as the query post were correctly promoted in most of the 22 cases; the comments promoted for the seven post with degraded *nERR@10* are mostly not much relevant.

Our second set of experiments were on the selection of topics in the topic composition of the post as well as that of each initially retrieved comment using a probability threshold. Since each post's or comment's topic composition contains 20 topics, on average the post or comment has 5% (or 0.05) chance of talking about each topic. Therefore, we tried a probability threshold of 0.06, 0.08, 0.10, 0.12, and 0.14, respectively. The IR effectiveness of these settings is displayed in Figure 3, in which the average *nG@1* values are included in Figure 3a and the average *nERR@10* values are included in Figure 3b. In terms of both measures, the optimal effectiveness was achieved with the setting of using top 5 retrieved posts to estimate the query post's topic composition and a probability threshold of 0.1 to select the topics contained in the post/comment's topic composition to be used in implicit topic matching (i.e., the parameter setting of "20-5-.10" in Figure 3). Specifically, this parameter setting led to 12% (i.e., 0.4240 vs 0.3773) increase of the average *nG@1* and 6% (i.e., 0.5556 vs 0.5248) increase of the average *nERR@1* over the baseline, respectively. Wilcoxon signed-rank tests on these results are consistent with the above cases of selecting top 1 topic, i.e., the difference between the baseline and our technique is statistically significant on *nERR@10* but insignificant on *nG@1*.

The effectiveness measured by *P+* is quite consistent with that of *nERR@10*. Due to space limit, we are not including the results of *P+* in this paper. Also, we did try 30 topics and 50 topics respectively generated by MALLET. However, the results were no better than using 20 topics. Therefore, we are not including those results in this paper either.

Verifying the Optimal Parameter Setting

With these parameter-tuning results, we moved on to use the two optimal parameter settings to test the other set of 50 query posts. Table 2 shows the evaluation results. The parameter setting that uses top 1 retrieved post to estimate the query post's topic composition and uses only the most probable topic turned out perform worse than the baseline, indicating that this parameter setting cannot be generalized.

	Avg. *nG@1*	Avg. *nERR@10*
Baseline	0.4433	0.5633
20_1_1	0.4167	0.5505
20_5_.10	0.4766	0.5985

Table 2. Evaluation results.

On the other hand, the other optimal parameter setting, which uses top 5 retrieved posts and a topic probability threshold of 0.1 did lead to statistically significant improvement (6%) of *nERR@10* over the baseline. The 8% gain of *nG@1* is not statistically significant, for the same reason that most query posts' *nG@1* did not change due to re-ranking.

As we discussed earlier, a weakness of using top *n* topics (with *n* being the same for all query posts and their retrieved comments) is that comments with uniform topic composition (i.e., they are really not strongly about any specific topics) will still "participate" in implicit topic matching with the query post. With the use of a probability threshold, however, such comments will be excluded, and hence their ranks are less likely to be boosted. This partly explains why the method of using a probability threshold performed more consistently in our experiments.

Comparison with the State-of-the-Art Results

To see where our proposed technique stands, we compare our experiment results with those reported for the NTCIR-13 STC Chinese task (Shang et al., 2017). A total of 64 retrieval-based runs by 14 teams were officially submitted to the NTCIR for evaluation. Our run reported here with the best parameter setting ranks the 12th among those 64 runs, or 5th among 15 teams, in terms of both *nG@1* and *nERR@10*. Table 3 shows the best run from each of four teams with a higher *nERR@10* value than ours, although only the top two runs are statistically better than ours. It should be noted that the values in this table are computed over all 100 query posts.

As we described in the "related work" section, the techniques that were used to produce these runs of other teams were all built upon neural networks and/or some features of machine learning. Specifically, SG01-C-R2 used many similarity features as well as two deep neural network models (Zhao et al., 2017). Furthermore, the team used about 11 K labeled post-comment pairs from previous year's STC task and additional 30 K post-comment pairs crawled from Sina.

	Avg. *nG@1*	Avg. *nERR@10*
SG01-C-R3	**0.5048**	**0.6663**
Beihang-C-R4	**0.4980**	**0.6105**
DeepIntell-C-R1	0.4323	0.5994
Nders-C-R2	0.4743	0.5882
Our	0.4493	0.5771

Table 3. Comparison with the best NTCIR STC results.

WeiBo website to enhance their training set. Candidate comments of Beihang-C-R4 were re-ranked based on the combination of features including tf-idf cosine, word overlap, word-to-word translation probability, word embedding cosine, and convolutional neural network models. DeepIntell-C-R1's BM25-weighted comments were re-ranked by combining multiple features, including recall and precision of 2-g between the query post and each comment, longest common subsequence, word embedding, and deep learning models.

In short, our experiment here seems to suggest that our technique of re-ranking comments retrieved with BM25 weights by matching the topic compositions of the query post and that of each comment can produce retrieval effectiveness that is on par with some of the top results reported in the official NTCIR-13 STC evaluation.

CONCLUSIONS AND FUTURE WORK

We presented a technique for combining two important sources of relevance evidence for improving the retrieval of old comments for query posts for the task of short text conversation in the open social media domain. The evidence of what we call *explicit term matching* is produced by an IR system that uses Okapi BM25 weighting. The evidence of what we call *implicit topic matching* is estimated using the topic models generated by LDA-based topic modeling approach. To overcome the problem of short comments and posts, we aggregated each post and all its responding comments in the collection to form a longer pseudo-document; such documents were the input to the topic modeling system. The topic composition of a comment is then estimated by summing up and normalizing the topic composition of all posts that it responded to. The topic composition of a query post is estimated in a similar fashion by considering top retrieved posts for the post. For parameter tuning, we tried different numbers of topics generated by topic modeling, different numbers of most probable topics for a given post or comment based on different number thresholds or different probability thresholds, and different numbers of top retrieved posts for estimating the query post's topic composition. Finally, those initially retrieved comments with positive implicit topic matching with the query post are ranked higher than those without, while within either set the original relative rankings are kept. Our experiments with the NTCIR-13 STC Chinese WeiBo collection showed that the techniques - with properly tuned parameters - can lead to improved IR effectiveness, which is on par with some of the best results achieved by using neural IR approaches.

The main purpose of this study is to demonstrate simple techniques of using underlying implicit topic information contained in the collection to re-rank and improve results returned by term-matching based IR systems. By no means we are claiming that the best parameter setting of the techniques has been found because there are many other settings that we did not try due to time and resource limit.

The effectiveness of our proposed techniques can be influenced by the appropriateness of the comments in the collection for their previously responded posts. As is not surprising to us, there are comments in the collection that are advertisements in nature or spamming messages. Including such comments in the process of topic modeling would inevitably affect the accuracy of topic models. The highly skewed distributions of comments per post resulted in pseudo-documents with quite different lengths, which can also negatively influence the accuracy of topic models.

There are different ways of using topic models to improve IR. Our proposed techniques merely re-rank search results from IR. In other words, they do nothing to recover relevant comments that are not returned by the IR system. As we discussed in the opening section, it is not uncommon that a relevant comment may not share any words with the query post. This limitation of our techniques suggests that in the future we should look into other ways of combining the two sources of relevance evidence. For example, a set of comments can be extracted from the collection based on their implicit topic matching with the query post; this set of comments can then be combined with the set returned by IR of term matching. Of course, how to score/rank the combined comment set will require careful consideration and experimentation.

The test collection used in this study, while being a unique and invaluable data set, can only represent an incomplete picture of interaction in the social media domain. Other important pieces of information, such as each poster's profile, are not included but can be extremely helpful for improving the techniques proposed in this paper. We look forward to test and improve these techniques with more information-richer data sets in the future.

ACKNOWLEDGMENTS

The authors would like to thank the NTCIR-13 Organizing Committee and the National Institute of Informatics (NII) of Japan for creating and making available the test collection used in this study and Dagobert Soergel and the anonymous ASIS&T reviewers for their valuable comments on earlier versions of this paper.

REFERENCES

Alvarez-Melis, D., & Saveski, M. (2016). Topic modeling in Twitter: Aggregating. In *Proceedings of International AAAI*

Conference on Web and Social Media Retrieved from https://www.aaai.org/ocs/index.php/ICWSM/ICWSM16/paper/view/13162.

Andrzejewski, D., & Buttler, D. (2011). Latent topic feedback for information retrieval. In *Proceedings of the 17th ACM SIGKDD International Conference on Knowledge Discovery and Data Mining* (pp. 600–608). New York, NY.

Blei, D. M., Ng, A. Y., & Jordan, M. I. (2003). Latent dirichlet allocation. *Journal of Machine Learning Research, 3*, 993–1022.

Boyd-Graber, J., Hu, Y., & Mimno, D. (2017). Applications of topic models. *Foundations and Trends in Information Retrieval, 11*(2-3), 143–296.

Deerwester, S., Dumais, S. T., Furnas, G. W., Landauer, T. K., & Harshman, R. (1990). Indexing by latent semantic analysis. *Journal of the American Society for Information Science, 41*(6), 391–407.

Furnas, G. W., Landauer, T. K., Gomez, L. M., & Dumais, S. T. (1987). The vocabulary problem in human-system communication. *Communication of the ACM, 30*(11), 964–971.

Gao, J., Galley, M., & Li, L. (2019). Neural approaches to conversational AI. *Foundations and Trends in Information Retrieval, 13*(2-3), 127–298.

Gligorić, K., Anderson, A., & West, R. (2018). How constraints affect content: The case of Twitter's switch from 140 to 280 characters. In *Proceedings of the International AAAI Conference on Web and Social Media* Retrieved from https://aaai.org/ocs/index.php/ICWSM/ICWSM18/paper/view/17895/17059

Hong, L., & Davison, B. D. (2010). Empirical study of topic modeling in twitter. In *Proceedings of the First Workshop on Social Media Analytics* (pp. 80–88). New York, NY.

Ji, Z., Lu, Z., and Li, H. (2014). *An information retrieval approach to short text conversation. CoRR*, Retrieved from https://arxiv.org/pdf/1408.6988

Lu, Y., Mei, Q., & Zhai, C. (2011). Investigating task performance of probabilistic topic models: An empirical study of PLSA and LDA. *Information Retrieval, 14*, 178–203.

McCallum, A. K. (2002). *Mallet: A machine learning for language toolkit.* Retrieved from http://mallet.cs.umass.edu

Mikolov, T., Chen, K., Corrado, G., & Dean, J. (2013). Efficient estimation of word representations in vector space. In *Proceedings of the ICLR 2013*, arXiv:1301.3781

Mitra, B., & Craswell, B. (2018). An introduction to neural information retrieval. *Foundations and Trends in Information Retrieval, 13*(1), 1–126.

Ni, H., Lin, L., & Xu, G. (2017). Nders at NTCIR-13 short text conversation 2 task. In *Proceedings of NTCIR-13* Retrieved from http://research.nii.ac.jp/ntcir/workshop/OnlineProceedings13/pdf/ntcir/03-NTCIR13-STC-NiH.pdf

Park, L. A. F., & Ramamohanarao, K. (2009). The sensitivity of latent dirichlet allocation for information retrieval. In W. Buntine, M. Grobelnik, D. Mladenić, & J. Shawe-Taylor, *Machine Learning and Knowledge Discovery in Databases* (pp. 176–188). Heidelberg, Germany: Springer Berlin Heidelberg.

Shang, L., Lu, Z., & Li, H. (2015). Neural responding machine for short-text conversation. In *Proceedings of the 53rd Annual Meeting of the Association for Computational Linguistics and the 7th International Joint Conference on Natural Language Processing* (pp. 1577–1586).

Shang, L., Sakai, T., Li, H., Higashinaka, R., Miyao, Y., Arase, Y., & Nomoto, M. (2017). Overview of the NTCIR-13 short text conversation task. In *Proceedings of NTCIR-13* Retrieved from http://research.nii.ac.jp/ntcir/workshop/OnlineProceedings13/pdf/ntcir/01-NTCIR13-OV-STC-ShangL.pdf

Shang, L., Sakai, T., Lu, Z., Li, H., Higashinaka, R., & Miyao, Y. (2016). Overview of the NTCIR-12 short text conversation task. In *Proceedings of NTCIR-12* Retrieved from http://research.nii.ac.jp/ntcir/workshop/OnlineProceedings12/pdf/ntcir/OVERVIEW/01-NTCIR12-OV-STC-ShangL.pdf

Wei, X., & Croft, W. B. (2006). LDA-based document models for ad-hoc retrieval. In *Proceedings of the 29th Annual International ACM SIGIR Conference on Research and Development in Information Retrieval* (pp. 178–185). New York, NY.

Yang, D., Wu, Y., Li, Z., Wu, W., & Xu, C. (2017). Beihang at the NTCIR-13 STC-2 task. In *Proceedings of the NTCIR-13* Retrieved from http://research.nii.ac.jp/ntcir/workshop/OnlineProceedings13/pdf/ntcir/06-NTCIR13-STC-YangD.pdf

Yi, X., & Allan, J. (2009). A comparative study of utilizing topic models for information retrieval. In M. Boughanem, C. Berrut, J. Mothe, & C. Soule-Dupuy, *Advances in information retrieval* (pp. 29–41). Heidelberg, Germany: Springer Berlin Heidelberg.

Young, S., Gasic, M., Thomson, B., & Williams, J. D. (2013). POMDP-based statistical spoken dialog systems: A review. *Proceedings of the IEEE, 101*(5), 1160–1179.

Zhang, C., Li, D., & Shi, H. (2017). DeepIntell at the NTCIR-13 STC-2 task. In *Proceedings of the NTCIR-13* Retrieved from http://research.nii.ac.jp/ntcir/workshop/OnlineProceedings13/pdf/ntcir/22-NTCIR13-STC-ZhangC.pdf

Zhao, H., Du, Y., Li, H., Qian, Q., Zhou, H., Huang, M., & Xu, J. (2017). SG01 at the NTCIR-13 STC-2 task. In *Proceedings of the NTCIR-13* Retrieved from http://research.nii.ac.jp/ntcir/workshop/OnlineProceedings13/pdf/ntcir/16-NTCIR13-STC-ZhaoH.pdf

Combine or Connect: Practical Experiences Querying Library Linked Data

David M. Weigl
University of Music and Performing Arts Vienna, AT & Oxford e-Research Centre, Dept. of Engineering Science, University of Oxford, UK
weigl@mdw.ac.at

Deren E. Kudeki
iSchool, University of Illinois at Urbana-Champaign, USA
dkudeki@illinois.edu

Timothy W. Cole
iSchool, University of Illinois at Urbana-Champaign, USA
t-cole3@illinois.edu

J. Stephen Downie
iSchool, University of Illinois at Urbana-Champaign, USA
jdownie@illinois.edu

Jacob Jett
iSchool, University of Illinois at Urbana-Champaign, USA
jjett2@illinois.edu

Kevin R. Page
Oxford e-Research Centre, Dept. of Engineering Science, University of Oxford, UK
kevin.page@oerc.ox.ac.uk

ABSTRACT

Linked Data provides a conceptual foundation for creating unified views across Digital Libraries, but implementation challenges must be overcome to realize the vision of computationally assisted cross-corpus research. We report practical experiences comparing two alternative workset building approaches across combined datasets: the HathiTrust Digital Library and the Early English Books Online Text Creation Partnership. In one experiment we combine both datasets within one triplestore using a single ontology and apply *consolidated* querying; in the other we build two distributed triplestores, each dataset conforming to its own ontology, and connected through *federated* querying. Each solution presents tradeoffs in complexity, system efficiency and responsiveness, and in the workload of configuring new methods providing access to Digital Libraries. We demonstrate that choosing a *consolidated* or *federated* approach fundamentally alters the dataset configuration process for cross-corpora workset building, so should be considered early in deployment specification and design. As both approaches provide equivalent functionality to the end-user, the practice and experience documented here inform design and development of distributed Linked Data Digital Libraries offering combined collection querying.

KEYWORDS

Digital library interoperability; federated SPARQL; Bibframe; Schema.org; EEBO

82nd Annual Meeting of the Association for Information Science & Technology | Melbourne, Australia | 19–23 October, 2019

DOI: 10.1002/pra2.00024

ASIS&T THESAURUS

Information architecture; databases; data set management

INTRODUCTION

Gathering digital resources into user-specific workbench collections and corpora remains a central task in the workflows of digital humanists. Because digital libraries (DLs) are increasingly adopting Linked Data format standards (e.g., through the application of RDF-based ontologies) suggests that old interoperability gaps (Haslhofer & Klas, 2010) between DLs using differing metadata vocabularies can be bridged, opening opportunities for humanities scholars to build research corpora across disparate, independently provided DL platforms. However, while Linked Data resources conform to a singular underlying data model, Nurmikko-Fuller et al. (2015) and Jett et al. (2016) demonstrate that large gaps still remain among the competing semantics of similar but non-equivalent domain models set forth by various ontologies and deployed by different DL and collections platforms.

In this paper we examine strategies available through Linked Data DL platforms to mitigate issues of semantic and lexical non-equivalence among different ontologies being applied to similar (or the same) data resources. We conduct this study in the context of striving to provide digital scholars with improved mechanisms by which they can create their worksets. Worksets are scholar-defined collections of digital materials drawn from one or more digital libraries/repositories brought together for the purpose of computational analyses (Page et al., 2018).

In Section 2 we consider approaches for managing ontological heterogeneity and the corpora at the focus of our study: the Early

English Books Online Text Creation Partnership (EEBO-TCP) and the HathiTrust Digital Library[2] (HTDL). Section 3 motivates our investigation through a unified viewer of worksets comprising items from across both datasets. In Section 4 we set out the general requirements and queries necessary to realize the viewer. Section 5 describes two alternative implementations of these queries representing a spectrum of trade-offs in terms of performance, reliability, and data fidelity: 1) a *consolidated* approach in which both catalogs are combined into a single RDF triplestore using a harmonized Schema.org ontology; and, 2) a *federated* approach where the HTDL and EEBO-TCP dataset remain in separate distributed triplestores abiding by their respective schemas, and are connected only at the point of query formulation. In Section 6 we reflect upon and compare our experiences implementing the two approaches, contrasting their applicability to particular uses depending on requirements according to the trade-offs listed above, and conversely on tolerance of overhead costs and on complexity of configuration.

BACKGROUND

Ontological Heterogeneity

Heterogeneities among ontologies cause interoperability issues. Various strategies including the development of metadata conversion specifications (St. Pierre & LaPlant, 1998), automated MATCH functions (Rahm, 2011; Rahm & Bernstein, 2001), and context-free lexical matching (Kitamura, Segawa, Sasajima, Tarumi, & Mizoguchi, 2008) have been developed to cope with these issues. Within library contexts, the crosswalk remains the preferred strategy for addressing these (see Chandrakar, 2002; Chandrakar, 2005; Godby, Smith, & Childress, 2008; Kondylakis, Doerr, & Plexousakis, 2006; among others). Chen (2015) provides an RDF-based crosswalk strategy for ontological heterogeneity problems.

In this paper, we take a different approach by focusing instead on achieving crosswalk-like mappings at query time through query normalization. We do this because our focus is on the creation of scholar-generated *worksets* – machine-actionable research collections supporting the requirements and information-seeking behaviors of scholars undertaking research in large-scale digital libraries (Weigl, Emsley, & Page, 2018; Weigl, Page, Organisciak, & Downie, 2017) – along with the metadata describing the objects contained within these collections. Inclusion of existing item-level metadata is helpful to scholars refining worksets and assessing others' worksets for reuse. Once a scholar gathers materials from different sources, any useful workset building tool must integrate metadata from multiple different sources.

Ontological heterogeneity problems can be divided into two broad categories (Lopes, Sacramento, & Lóscio, 2012)[2]:

1. Concept-based heterogeneity; and,
2. Restriction-based heterogeneity.

[2] https://www.hathitrust.org/

[2] Note that this categorization focuses Chan and Zeng's (2006) schema-level heterogeneity issues and does not necessary apply to the record and repository levels they name in their categorization of heterogeneity issues.

The first category describes cases where two ontologies are either using different lexical terms to describe the same conceptual class or property, or the same lexical term to describe different conceptual classes or properties.

The second category describes cases where either one or both ontologies are restricted to subsets of a specific class—a class restriction (Parundekar, Knoblock, & Ambite, 2010)—or use different levels of granularity with respect to class hierarchies (a subsumption restriction).

In response to these issues, Lopes, Sacramento, and Lóscio develop a 3-part query rewriting approach to alleviate problems of heterogeneity. This solution consists of:

1. Query normalization;
2. Generation of a SPARQLD tree, and,
3. Query rewriting and results restructuring.

Other researchers have approached this problem differently, such as Montoya (2015) who aggregates portions of RDF graphs using database views.

In this paper we focus on applying portions of Lopes, Sacramento, and Lóscio's method using SPARQL, an RDF query language analogous to SQL in relational databases that enables the retrieval and manipulation of data by specifying patterns of interlinked triples. We are not presently concerned with restriction-based interoperability issues, focusing instead on concept-based interoperability. The work below thus showcases only the first and third parts of their method:

1. Query normalization; and,
2. Query rewriting and results restructuring

and specifically, how they apply to the practical deployment of distributed DLs using Linked Data.

Figure 1. A collection viewed in HTDL.

Library Catalog Viewers & Linked Data

The HTDL has a tool (Figure 1) for browsing user-built collections made up of items from its corpus and which leverages existing MARC metadata. However, as Linked Data is steadily becoming more readily available efforts are being made to present library catalog records and their related data to consumers in Linked Data formats. ResearchSpace (Oldman & Tanase, 2018) is an example of one such tool designed to realize a Linked Data catalog environment.

The HathiTrust Research Center (HTRC) Analytics page[3] also supports Linked Data usages by mapping user-made collections for the HTDL to Linked Data ontologies through the concept of worksets. One of the HTRC workset's primary use cases is enabling researchers to mix in digital resources from multiple digital libraries by refining an existing collection that they have imported from the HTDL's collection building tools. The subsequent sections of this paper contrast two broad technical strategies for building digital infrastructure that accomplishes these user tasks through Linked Data.

Datasets

EEBOO-TCP

The EEBO-TCP is a partnership with ProQuest and over 150 libraries and universities, led by Michigan and Oxford, to generate highly accurate, fully-searchable texts tracing the history of English thought and learning from the first book printed in English in 1473 through to 1700. Between 2000-2009 EEBO-TCP Phase I converted 25,000 texts from the EEBO corpus into TEI-compliant, XML-encoded hand-transcribed texts, freely released in January 2015. In this paper we use an RDF version of the EEBO-TCP Phase I metadata, created from structured information in the EEBO-TCP TEI header data. The ontology terms chosen to encode this information—henceforth the EEBO Ontology (EEBOO[4])—include selections from MODS, Bibframe, and PROV, and custom elements encoding additional structures (e.g. dates). The RDF data was created using Python scripts manipulating the TEI P5 XML, then use of Karma Data Integration Tool[5] to map EEBO-TCP data structures into EEBOO. Links to author records in VIAF and the Library of Congress (LoC), and multimedia pages in the HTDL and "JISC Digital Books" website, were generated and added. The resultant EEBOO RDF was processed from 25,000 EEBO-TCP Phase 1 graphs (468,000 triples) and contains 713 unique places, 6,489 unique expressions of Person of which 3,588 have VIAF and LoC IDs.

HathiTrust Digital Library

The HathiTrust is another partnership involving nearly 150 university and research libraries. It provides a large-scale DL consisting of more than 16.8 million volumes of digitized text, of which about 50% are in English. The HathiTrust Research Center provides scholars with a suite of non-consumptive computational methods and workflows for them to use on subsets of the HT corpus (i.e., worksets). Worksets, which group together the identifiers for the digital objects and their metadata drawn from the HTDL, are a central feature of the HTRC's non-consumptive methods and workflows. Workset and volume-level metadata are stored in a triplestore using ontologies like the HTRC Workset ontology (Jett et al. 2016) and Bibframe[6] respectively. For this use case, a random subset of 500,000 English-language fiction-genre volumes (56 million triples) was selected from the HT corpus.[7]

MOTIVATION: MERGED WORKSET CONSTRUCTION

We have built a tool (Figure 2) for workset viewing and construction using two disparate (non-identifier-aligned) but mutually informative datasets: EEBO and HathiTrust (Section 2.3). Each describes early English literature but with different catalog characteristics: EEBO encompasses all known English texts from this period but exhibits limited coverage of metadata facets; HathiTrust describes a sizeable subset in richer detail, including genre, subject, and other metadata facets but with unknown coverage. Both provide access to digitized page images generated under different digitisation efforts. Although workset creation provides our immediate motivation for the work presented here, these considerations demonstrate the broader value and general

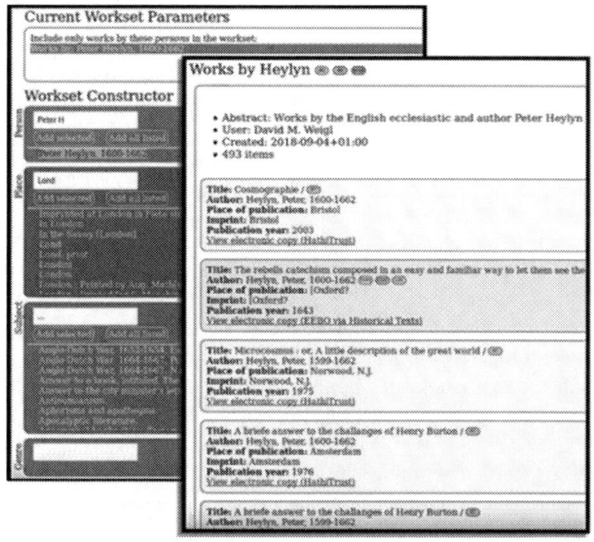

Figure 2. Queries specified using the tool's workset constructor retrieve references to works from across two datasets and insert them into a workset. The tool's workset viewer retrieves descriptions of these works from across the two sources, and displays them (EEBO in blue; HTDL in yellow) alongside workset provenance information.

---

[3] http://analytics.hathitrust.org
[4] http://eeboo.oerc.ox.ac.uk
[5] http://www.isi.edu/integration/karma

[6] http://www.loc.gov/bibframe/docs/index.html
[7] This random sub-corpus included approximately 17,000 pre-18th Century volumes which closely align with the Early English Books Online Text Creation Partnership (EEBO-TCP) corpus.

holistic benefit of providing unified access to the records within distinct DLs (henceforth *datasets*).

The HTDL data is grouped into worksets encoded using the HTRC Workset Ontology. The worksets function as a locus linking a group of scholar-selected works. Through Linked Data principles, the dataset is easily extended by reifying these links to aggregate additional data about each work. This individual work-level metadata for the HTDL dataset is encoded using the Bibframe ontology, whereas the corresponding data structures for EEBO are encoded using EEBOO.

To align these ontologically heterogeneous but semantically similar datasets, the tool provides simple, unified queries and exploration across the two datasets, and workset building comprising results from both datasets in response to a single query. Further, metadata available on one side informs retrieval on the other side—i.e., approximate genre and subject searches for EEBO can, for example, enable searches for books by authors with books on the subject of political science in HTDL. While somewhat imprecise (authors may be associated with multiple subjects or genres) this still usefully extends and enhances available avenues for search and retrieval.

Below, we detail the design of this tool, which aims to: enable users to search for works created by one or more authors specified in either dataset via a simple querying interface; create worksets gathering references (URIs) to these works; and provide unified views detailing the works constituting a workset, with descriptive information retrieved from both sources.

DESIGN

We now consider high-level requirements and design principles for the queries underpinning the tool outlined in the previous section. Queries are made across the complementary (but minimally aligned) datasets (Section 2.3) using SPARQL,[8] for which we contrast two different approaches (*consolidated* vs. *federated*) in the subsequent section on comparative implementations. We illustrate the need for this high-level design through a viewer in which datasets are offered in a combined view.

Requirements

To enable combined querying and exploration, we must first conduct domain-specific research to align the datasets (**dataset alignment**). We must then provide for a retrieval mechanism that identifies relevant results from both datasets in response to a single query (**retrieval to make workset**). The retrieved results must be stored within a workset housing constituents from heterogeneous sources (**workset creation**). In order to make this workset viewable (and to provide for exploration of results), descriptive details associated with workset constituents in either dataset must be retrieved (**retrieval to populate viewer**) and shown to the user in a unified presentation interface (**unified viewing**).

[8] https://www.w3.org/TR/sparql11-query/

Design: Dataset Alignment (Step A)

The datasets must first be aligned on a representational level to facilitate comparison and avoid implementational overhead (e.g. if we were to compare traditional and Linked Data representations). We choose a Linked Data representation for its schema flexibility and strengths in interlinking heterogenous data.

The datasets must then be aligned on an entity level. If existing identifiers, e.g., those published by the Virtual International Authority File (VIAF)[9] are shared between the sets, this step is straightforward. Where these do not exist, or their coverage is limited, further work is needed to reconcile entities across datasets and record their alignment through bridging structures. The EEBOO triples were prepared using a specialized Semantic Alignment and Linking Tool (*SALT*) for semi-automated entity alignment under supervision of a human expert (Weigl et al. 2017) for this step.

Finally, there must be some degree of schema alignment, either by transforming the datasets to a *consolidated* representation, or by establishing mappings between representations, to allow metadata descriptors associated with the aligned entities to be retrieved viewed uniformly. We implement and compare these two alternative approaches in later sections.

Design: Retrieval to Make Workset (Step B)

SPARQL is the primary query language for RDF and Linked Data, however its use requires significant expertise in Semantic Web technologies. To hide these complexities from the end user, we specify generic SPARQL templates, in a manner consistent with how SQL and similar query templates are developed for online public access catalogs (OPACs) so that library catalog users do not need expert knowledge of databases or query languages to meet their information needs. The query templates discussed here are instantiated in order to drive a collection building and refinement tool's user interface. This mechanism ensures that there are no constraints of SPARQL knowledge involved in the tool's use, freeing the user to apply their full attention to scholarly pursuits.

To fully benefit from unified querying, we want to capture the *union*, rather than the *intersection*, of the datasets. The generic query template has three conditions:

1. Sought-for entity (e.g. author) is represented in dataset 1
2. Sought-for entity is represented in dataset 2
3. Sought-for entity is represented in dataset 1 and 2

In SPARQL terms, each condition is represented by a UNION block within a query template, with parameters supplied via a VALUES clause:

```
SELECT ?author ?work WHERE {
  { (a) } UNION { (b) } UNION { (c) }
} VALUES (?author) { … }
```

[9] https://viaf.org

In blocks (a) and (b) the supplied author URI is connected to its work URIs according to the respective dataset's schema. Filtering conditions can also be specified according to the metadata available in each set—e.g., works in the HTRC dataset can be filtered according to their subject.

In block (c), the author URI is connected both to its work URIs in one dataset, and, via bridging triples identifying the same author entity in the other dataset, with work URIs available there. Filtering according to metadata specification can again be applied, and here, it can be done across datasets (e.g., "show me works by authors that have published a work on subject X in dataset Y").

Design: Workset Creation (Step C)

Work URIs retrieved via the templated SPARQL query mechanism (**Step B**) are inserted into worksets, alongside provenance metadata. These are published as further Linked Data structures.

Design: Retrieval to Populate Viewer (Step D)

Metadata about each constituent work must be retrieved to construct unified workset views, taking into account potential schema differences in work descriptions across datasets (as per the schema-level alignment in **Step A**). This is achieved with further SPARQL templates specifying a workset URI in the VALUES clause and retrieving metadata associated with each constituent work according to schema alignment decisions.

Design: Unified Viewing (Step E)

The information retrieved in **Step D** is used to parameterise HTML templates capable of showing descriptions of workset constituents from both datasets side by side. To do this, the HTML templates must also be informed by schema-level alignment (**Step A**).

COMPARATIVE IMPLEMENTATIONS: *CONSOLIDATED* AND *FEDERATED* APPROACHES

Having identified the five steps A-E in the previous section, here we consider implementation of each step using both *consolidated* and *federated* approaches.

Implementation: Dataset Alignment (Step A)

In either case, datasets must first be transformed to RDF if not already in this form, and entity alignment must be provided, either by shared identifiers if they exist, or by generating bridging triples if they don't. The *SALT* tool provides specialized bridging structures for this purpose which capture contextual information around each entity match decision. A simpler approach specifying `owl:sameAs` links between entities may suffice, depending on the use case.

Consolidated Schema Alignment

Taking a *consolidated* or *federated* approach has implications for the schema alignment process. In the *consolidated* case, one or both datasets must be transformed to an agreed-upon, shared ontology. After transformation, all data is housed in a single triplestore. Here, the Schema.org ontology was selected as the shared ontology. Like EEBOO, Schema.org exhibits a relatively flat structure. The transformation of EEBOO triples to Schema.org semantics preserved almost all data from the original and reduced the number of triples to 294,000. HTRC Bibframe metadata are richer and more hierarchical. In transforming Bibframe metadata (using SPARQL CONSTRUCT and JSON-LD Framing[10]), Work, Instance and Item were conflated, and some granules of metadata deemed unimportant for our purposes with no direct analog in the Schema.org ontology were discarded, resulting in a reduced set of 17 million triples. The resulting graphs derived from

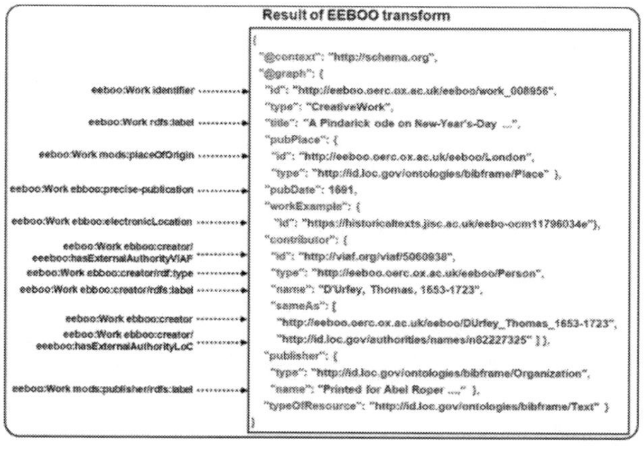

Figure 3. Mapping of EEBOO triples to Schema.org JSON-LD.

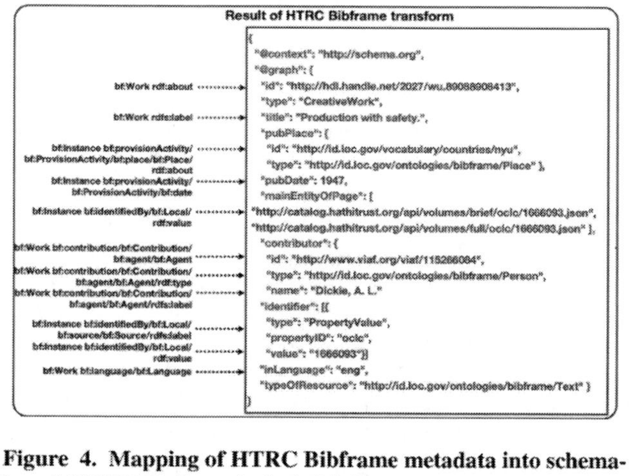

Figure 4. Mapping of HTRC Bibframe metadata into schema-based JSON-LD. Some included fields are the same as EEBOO results, but some new fields are added and others removed.

[10] https://w3c.github.io/json-ld-framing/

Bibframe remained qualitatively richer than the transformed EEBOO metadata, but the overlap supports our use case and the simultaneous querying of both sets.

This approach worked well for the EEBOO data, which included only around 25,000 graphs and a limited number of triples. The EEBOO transform (Figure 3) took about four hours. The HT-Bibframe sample dataset was much larger at around 500,000 distinct graphs. Because of the flattening necessary and the larger number of triples, it took close to a month on the same hardware to transform the HT-Bibframe into the consolidated schema (Figure 4). This demonstrated that our initial alignment approach is not as efficient for larger, more complex, HT-Bibframe graphs that require flattening.

Subsequent experiments suggest that a faster method for transforming the Bibframe metadata implements the transform using XSLT. This method is more than an order of magnitude faster, but it includes its own overhead of setting up a database populated during the transform to allow easy access to what has already been processed. The SPARQL method is easier to setup, but slower to run (although additional optimization of the SPARQL might improve performance).

Federated Schema Alignment

In the *federated* case, EEBO and HTRC triples live in separate stores using separate schemas (EEBOO and Bibframe respectively). This prevents significant schema transformation overheads (as above) by connecting and reusing the datasets in their native form, declaring mappings between descriptors and metadata facets within each query template. However, this results in significantly more complex queries.

For the Dataset Alignment stage (**Step A**), there is thus a trade-off between large-magnitude transformational overhead that only needs to be performed once, and smaller-scale mapping overhead that complicates query development and may impact retrieval efficiency.

Implementation: Retrieval to Make Workset (Step B)

Consolidated Retrieval

In the *consolidated* case, the query retrieving works associated with specified authors for inclusion within a workset is relatively straightforward, as both datasets are housed within the same triplestore and are expressed using the same schema. Therefore, only two cases apply: either the author is included in either one dataset; or, the author is included in both. In the latter case, we retrieve both works associated directly with the supplied author URI; and, works associated with the author URI in the other dataset (as per entity alignments produced in **Step A**):

```
SELECT ?work ?author WHERE {
 {
  ?author <...schema-connection...> ?work .
 } UNION {
  ?author <..bridged-with...> ?author2 .
  ?author2 <...schema-connection...> ?work .
 }
} VALUES ?author { <...list-of-author-URIs...> }
```

Federated Retrieval

In the *federated* case, we apply the schema mappings identified in **Step A** to specify distinct schema-specific connections in three blocks of the template query (accounting for authors described in the first, the second, or both datasets). We use SPARQL `SERVICE` calls to connect our local and remote triplestores. Compared to the consolidated approach, this case is characterized by additional complexities: schema differences require an additional clause to the `UNION` statement; `SERVICE` calls are required to combine triplestores over the network, potentially with associated issues of secured access (where each triplestore may adhere to a different authentication regime); and, the connections that must be specified in the query may be very different from one another (due to heterogeneity of schemas employed), complicating the creation of the template query.

Workset creation (**Step C**) is accomplished via a simple `SPARQL INSERT` query, specifying workset metadata, provenance information, and gathering references to the constituent works identified in **Step B**. As the works are included by reference (work URI), the process is identical in both the *consolidated* and *federated* approaches.

```
SELECT ?work ?author WHERE {
 { ?author <...schema1-connection...> ?work }
UNION
 { SERVICE <remote-endpoint> {
   ?author <...schema2-connection...> ?work . } }
UNION
 { ?author <...bridged-with...> ?author2 .
   SERVICE <remote-endpoint> {
    ?author2 <...schema2-connection...> ?work . } } }
VALUES ?author { <...list-of-author-URIs...> }
```

Implementation: Retrieval to Populate Viewer (Step D)

Consolidated Retrieval

In the *consolidated* case, the query retrieving descriptive information associated with works in a workset is simplified by the unified schema generated in Step A. Works from either dataset may be described using the same graph pattern. Any descriptors that are available in only one originating dataset (`?descX` in the example below) must be specified as OPTIONAL.

```
SELECT ?work ?desc1 ?desc2 ?descX WHERE {
 ?work <...consolidated-schema-prop1...> ?desc1 ;
       <...consolidated-schema-prop2...> ?desc2 .
 OPTIONAL {
   ?work <...consolidated-schema-propX...> ?descX . } }
```

Federated Retrieval

In the *federated* case, lacking a unified schema, our query must instead specify a `UNION` between works described with the local schema (and stored in the local triplestore) and works described using the remote schema (available from the remote endpoint via a `SERVICE` network connection). Any descriptors available in only one dataset (`?descX` below) will simply remain blank for works from the other dataset by virtue of the intended behavior of SPARQL `UNION`.

```
SELECT ?work ?desc1 ?desc2 ?descX WHERE {
 {
  ?work <...schema1-prop1...> ?desc1 ;
        <...schema1-prop2...> ?desc2 .
 } UNION {
  SERVICE <remote-endpoint> {
   ?work <...schema2-prop1...> ?desc1 ;
         <...schema2-prop2...> ?desc2 ;
         <...schema2-propX...> ?descX . } } }
```

Implementation: Unified Viewing (Step E)

As there are qualitative differences in the kind of descriptors available between the two datasets, the HTML templates of the viewer must accommodate these differences. If the viewer is to provide a hint as to a given work's source dataset (indicated by the different background colors in the workset viewer, Figure 2), this can be done by string matching the URI (against best practice); by checking for the existence of one-side-only descriptors and using these as a hint; or, by a special `?dataset` descriptor added to the retrieval in previous steps.

In the consolidated implementation, this must be added into the data and associated with works there (e.g. on ingest). In our federated implementation, this can be a bound variable populated in the individual query blocks, e.g.:

```
BIND(<dataset1> as ?dataset)
```

REVIEW OF QUERY COMPLEXITY

Having described the different implementation steps required to service equivalent query types for both consolidated and federated approaches, in this section we provide complete examples of realized queries as formulated by these two implementations, providing descriptions as highlighted comments within the query. We then reflect upon the differences in their complexity - and where that complexity falls – and implications for DL deployments.

Consolidated Approach

Retrieval to Make Workset: Works Authored by Peter Heylyn

```
PREFIX eeboo: <http://eeboo.oerc.ox.ac.uk/eeboo/>
PREFIX schema: <http://Schema.org/>
PREFIX owl: <http://www.w3.org/2002/07/owl#>
SELECT ?work ?author
WHERE { {
  ?viaf schema:sameAs ?author .
  ?work schema:contributor ?viaf .
} UNION {
  ?author owl:sameAs ?author2 .
  ?work schema:contributor ?author2 .
  }
} VALUES ?author {
  eeboo:Harvey_Christopher_1597-1663
}
```

Retrieve works originating from EEBOO. EEBOO creator ids are referred to via sameAs, while the VIAF URI is used as the contributor id

Retrieve works originating from HTRC. The bridging triples connect the EEBOO creator ids to the VIAF contributor ids used by HTRC

Inject author URI(s) for query. Both blocks will return works associated with the supplied EEBOO author

Retrieval to Populate Viewer

```
PREFIX ht: <http://hathitrust.org/htrc/workset#>
PREFIX dc: <http://purl.org/dc/elements/1.1/>
PREFIX schema: <http://Schema.org/>
SELECT
 ?workset ?creator ?mod_date ?title
 ?username ?work
 ?author ?publisher ?place ?pubdate
 ?worktitle
 ?loc ?elecLoc
WHERE {
 ?workset a ht:Workset ;
          dc:modified ?mod_date ;
          dc:title ?title ;
          dc:abstract ?abstract ;
          dc:creator ?username ;
          ht:gathers ?work .
 ?work schema:title ?worktitle ;
       schema:contributor ?creator ;
       schema:pubDate ?pubdate .
 ?creator schema:name ?author .
 OPTIONAL {
  ?work schema:publisher ?publisher_node .
  ?publisher_node schema:name ?publisher .
 }
 OPTIONAL {
  ?work schema:pubPlace ?place .
 }
 OPTIONAL {
  ?creator schema:sameAs ?alt_name .
  FILTER(regex(?alt_name,"id.loc.gov"))
  BIND(?alt_name as ?loc) }
 OPTIONAL {
  ?work schema:workExample ?elecLoc .
 }
}
VALUES ?workset { }
```

Workset metadata

Work descriptions potentially present in both datasets

EEBOO-specific descriptions - will be blank for HathiTrust results

Retrieve workset metadata and provenance information

Retrieve fields that every work will have

Retrieve fields that may be in either EEBOO or HTRC works, but are not guaranteed

Retrieve fields that are only in EEBOO works

Workset URI(s) injected here

Federated Approach

Retrieval to Make Workset: Works Authored by Peter Heylyn

```
PREFIX owl: <http://www.w3.org/2002/07/owl#>
PREFIX eeboo: <http://eeboo.oerc.ox.ac.uk/eeboo/>
PREFIX bib: <http://id.loc.gov/ontologies/bibframe>
SELECT ?work ?author WHERE { {
  ?work eeboo:creator ?author . }
UNION {
  SERVICE <https://REMOTE-ENDPOINT-HOST/sparql> {
   ?work bib:contribution ?contribution .
   ?contribution bib:agent ?author .
  } }
UNION {
  ?author owl:sameAs ?author2 .
  SERVICE <https://REMOTE-ENDPOINT-HOST/sparql> {
   ?work bib:contribution ?contribution .
   ?contribution bib:agent ?author2 . } } }
VALUES ?author {
  eeboo:Peter_Heylyn_1600-1662
}
```

Union block 1: retrieve works from local dataset associated with an EEBOO author via eeboo:creator predicate

Union block 2: retrieve works from remote dataset associated with a HTRC author via bib:contribution and bib:agent

Union block 3: retrieve works from remote dataset associated with a HTRC author (?author2) aligned with a supplied EEBOO author

Values block: inject author URI(s) for query. In this example, we supply an EEBOO author. This means our union block 1 will retrieve EEBOO works by Heylyn; block 2 will retrieve nothing, since HathiTrust does not contain EEBOO author entities; and block 3 will retrieve HathiTrust works by the HathiTrust author entity associated with the supplied EEBOO author (via owl:sameAs).

Retrieval to Populate Viewer

```
PREFIX ht: <http://hathitrust.org/htrc/workset#>
PREFIX dc: <http://purl.org/dc/elements/1.1/>
PREFIX mods: <http://www.loc.gov/mods/rdf/v1#>
PREFIX eeboo: <http://eeboo.oerc.ox.ac.uk/eeboo/>
PREFIX bf: <http://id.loc.gov/ontologies/bibframe/>
PREFIX rdfs: <http://www.w3.org/2000/01/rdf-schema#>
SELECT
?workset ?creator ?mod_date ?title ?abstract
?username ?work
?author ?publisher ?place ?pubdate ?worktitle
?viaf ?loc ?elecLoc
?instance ?item
WHERE {
 ?workset a ht:Workset ;
         dc:modified ?mod_date ;
         dc:title ?title ;
         dc:abstract ?abstract ;
         dc:creator ?username ;
         ht:gathers ?work .
 {
  ?work rdfs:label ?worktitle;
       eeboo:raw_pubplace ?place ;
       eeboo:creator ?creator .
  ?creator rdfs:label ?author .
  ?work mods:publisher ?publisherbnode .
  ?publisherbnode rdfs:label ?publisher .
  BIND(COALESCE(?publisher, "") as ?imprint).
  ?work eeboo:electronicLocation ?elecLoc .
  OPTIONAL {
   ?creator eeboo:hasExternalAuthorityVIAF ?viaf ;
           eeboo:hasExternalAuthorityLoC ?loc .
  }
  OPTIONAL {
   ?work eeboo:precise-publication ?precisepub . }
  OPTIONAL {
   ?work eeboo:approx-publication ?approxpub . }
  BIND(COALESCE(STR(COALESCE(?precisepub,
   ?approxpub)), "Unknown") as ?pubdate ).
 } UNION {
  SERVICE <https://REMOTE-END-POINT-HOST/sparql> {
   ?work bf:hasInstance ?instance ;
        bf:agent ?creator .
   ?creator rdfs:label ?author .
   ?instance bf:hasItem  ?item ;
            bf:agent  ?publisher ;
            bf:place  ?place ;
            bf:date ?pubdate .
   OPTIONAL { ?item  dc:title  ?worktitle . }
  }
 }
}
VALUES ?workset { }
```

Workset metadata

Work descriptions present in both datasets

EEBOO-specific descriptions - will be blank for HathiTrust results

HathiTrust-specific descriptions - will be blank for EEBOO results

Retrieve workset metadata and provenance information

Union block 1: Description of EEBOO works contained in the workset, retrieved from local endpoint

Union block 2: Description of HathiTrust works contained in the workset, retrieved from remote endpoint

Workset URI(s) injected here

Comparative Discussion

Here we compare retrieval complexity in the *consolidated* and *federated* approaches by reference to the example queries in the preceding subsections. Table 1 summarizes the highlights of this comparison.

The first queries in both preceding subsections (**retrieval to make workset**) illustrate the retrieval of works authored by Peter Heylyn from both the EEBO and HT datasets. In both examples, Heylyn is specified by virtue of his record in the EEBO corpus, with the identifier `eeboo:Peter_Heylyn_1600-1662`. In the *consolidated* case, we specify the relationship between a work and a contributor to its creation via the `schema:contributor` property. Since we want to find works associated in this way both with Heylyn's EEBO entry, and with the HT entity associated with this entry via `owl:sameAs`, we need to introduce the additional complexity of the `UNION` clause: the first block of which here retrieves EEBO-works associated with EEBO-Heylyn, but could just as well retrieve HT-works associated with HT-Heylyn; whereas the second block retrieves HT-works associated with HT-Heylyn via his `owl:sameAs` connection to the specified EEBO-Heylyn, or vice versa EEBO-works associated with EEBO-Heylyn via the connection to HT-Heylyn, as the case may be.

The *federated* **retrieval to make workset** query requires significant additional complexity to fulfill the same purpose. Without schema consolidation, EEBO-Heylyn is associated with EEBO-works via the `eeboo:creator` predicate, whereas HT-Heylin is associated with HT-works via an intermediary sch`?contribution` node for which he is the `bib:agent`. Due to these schematic differences, we need to spell out what needs to happen when an EEBO author is specified—as here, find EEBO-works associated with EEBO-Heylyn in the local triplestore (union block 1); and, connect to the remote triplestore endpoint to find works associated with HT-Heylyn *there*, via the connection from EEBO-Heylyn to HT-Heylyn *here* (union block 3). Had we specified HT-Heylyn instead, we would need to consult the remote endpoint directly (union block 2).

The second queries in the preceding subsections illustrate the retrieval of descriptive information associated with works gathered in a specified workset (**retrieval to populate viewer**)—perhaps the works of Peter Heylyn. In the *consolidated* case, this takes the form of a simple query that does not explicitly need to differentiate between source datasets at all—it must merely account for any cross-corpora differences in the availability of certain descriptors using `OPTIONAL` clauses (but note, this may just as well be a requirement because of within-corpus differences in metadata coverage). In contrast, the *federated* version of the query again requires a `UNION` clause to be specified in order to obtain both local and remote works, according to local and remote schema connections.

It should be noted that the additional complexity introduced by the *federated* over the *consolidated* queries comes at a continual cost; while the human complexity of writing the query occurs only initially during template development (and thereafter, the queries are generated through the viewer UI), the additional computational and network loads inherent in data joins across triplestore endpoints accumulate every time a user executes a query.

In addition to the query complexities, two approaches differ in the number of additional triples generated to run each version. The *federated* approach only needs the bridging triples which we use to map authors in the EEBOO sample to their VIAF IDs in HTRC. Based on our sample of 25,000 items in EEBOO, 370 bridging triples were generated. While the *consolidated* approach uses the same bridging triples, it also needs to generate new triples for the Schema.org mappings. The number of triples in the EEBOO sample of 25,000 items was reduced by about 40% when mapped to schema. For the HTRC sample of 500,000 items, the number of triples was reduced by around 90% when mapped to Schema.org.

CONCLUSIONS AND FUTURE WORK

The choice of a *consolidated* or *federated* approach fundamentally alters the schema alignment process required to

	Consolidated	*Federated*
Dataset alignment (Step A)	Significant complexity (human), full schema alignment and harmonization across both datasets. Significant complexity (computational) for data translation.	Scoped complexity (human) to terms needed by task at hand; and within dataset (no cross-corpora harmonization).
Retrieval to make workset (Step B)	Scoped complexity (computational) to accommodate entities originating in either dataset via bridging triples.	Significant complexity (computational) incorporating queries over heterogeneous schemas, entity-bridging triples, cross-corpora, and across query endpoints.
Workset creation (Step C)	Simple INSERT query recording workset metadata, provenance information, and gathering entity URIs as workset constituents.	Simple INSERT query recording workset metadata, provenance information, and gathering entity URIs as workset constituents (no additional complexity over *consolidated* approach)
Retrieval to populate Viewer (Step D)	Simple query with light additional complexity to account for descriptors associated with only a subset of the entities (e.g. because they are only available in one originating dataset) via OPTIONAL	Significant complexity (computational) incorporating queries over heterogeneous schemas across query endpoints -- this directly impacts (negatively) on the end-user's perception of system performance .
Unified viewing (Step E)	Simple HTML templating	More complex HTML templating accounting for different descriptors according to originating corpus and schema

Table 1. Comparison of *consolidated* and *federated* approaches.

configure datasets in preparation for cross-corpora workset building. While both approaches can provide equivalent functionality to the user of the workset builder, the choice of approach will impact on both the user's experience and on behind-the-scenes repository workflows.

Results to date suggest several qualitative trade-offs between the two approaches. The *federated* query approach obviates the need to transform the complete metadata to a (lowest) common denominator schema. This avoids significant computational effort and avoids the tendency toward lossiness when mapping from one ontology to another (e.g., as suggested by the reduction in the number of triples, especially when flattening and transforming from Bibframe to Schema.org). While this lossiness was not found to be an issue for our use case, other use cases could be more sensitive to the loss of information during the transform. Additionally, the consolidated approach can be less nimble as use cases evolve. When adjusting for changes in use case, it is quicker to adjust federated queries than it is to re-transform all metadata. On the other hand, we found that not only the query but also the authentication regime was more complex when implementing federated queries across distributed triplestores. Complex federated queries require more skill with SPARQL, and templates seem likely to be unique to each use case. Based on our experience federated queries are slower, and performance directly impacts user experience.

We conclude that the *consolidated* approach is particularly applicable where the **up-front costs** of consolidation are deemed acceptable, and where the datasets are static (to avoid **stale data** post-consolidation), offering better **performance** and better **reliability** (no dependency on remote servers). In contrast, the *federated* approach offers high **fidelity** to the source datasets (non-lossy schema alignment by connecting through queries; non-stale data) and lower initial investment, at the cost of added **complexity**, worse performance, and reliance on remote endpoint **availability**. Neither approach is thus straightforwardly recommendable above the other for all cases; rather, these tradeoffs must be weighed in choosing the approach most suitable to the particular use case.

Further, more systematic research is needed. Our work to date suggests several future directions. The goal of next steps should be to go from largely qualitative observations to more systematic and quantitative studies that can help repository managers better understand these tradeoffs. This means research to optimize both consolidated transforms and the federated queries. A broader and more systematically chosen set of use cases needs to be developed. We also anticipate based on our experiences that improvements in link densities and more consistencies in the use of authorities could affect tradeoffs. Although not necessary from a database design perspective, the derivation and addition of triples to facilitate federated queries (e.g., "bridging" triples) and less use of blank nodes would facilitate the implementation of federated queries. Nonetheless, the common foundational model of RDF suggests that DLs may need a fresh assessment of the tradeoffs between federation and aggregation.

ACKNOWLEDGMENTS

This work supported in part by the *Workset Creation for Scholarly Analysis + Data Capsules* (WCSA+DC) project, grant #41500672 from the Andrew W. Mellon Foundation; conclusions and opinions expressed are those of the authors and are not necessarily shared by the sponsor. We gratefully acknowledge our colleague Terhi Nurmikko-Fuller for her work on the original EEBOO ontology and triples during the *Early English Print in the HathiTrust* (ElEPHãT) project.

REFERENCES

Chan, L. M., & Zeng, M. L. (2006). Metadata interoperability and standardization: A study of methodology part I: Achieving interoperability at the schema level. *D-Lib Magazine, 12*(6) Retrieved from: http://www.dlib.org/dlib/june06/chan/06chan.html

Chandrakar, R. (2002). CCF and INFLIBNET standard metadata to Dublin core crosswalk. *Journal of Internet Cataloging, 5*(3), 33–57.

Chandrakar, R. (2005). An approach to mapping CCF to dublin core. *The Electronic Library, 23*(5), 577–590.

Chen, Y.-N. (2015). A RDF-based approach to metadata crosswalk for semantic interoperability at the data element level. *Library Hi Tech, 33*(2), 175–194.

Godby, C. J., Smith, D., & Childress, E. (2008). Toward element-level interoperability in bibliographic metadata. *Code4Lib Journal, 2* Retrieved from: https://journal.code4lib.org/articles/54

Haslhofer, B., & Klas, W. (2010). A survey of techniques for achieving metadata interoperability. *ACM Computing Surveys, 42*(2) [article 7]. DOI: http://doi.acm.org/10.1145/1667062.1667064

Jett, J., Cole, T. W., Maden, C., & Downie, J. S. (2016). The HathiTrust Research Center workset ontology: A descriptive framework for non-consumptive research collections. *Journal of Open Humanities Data 2*, e1. https://doi.org/10.5334/johd.3

Jett, J, Nurmikko-Fuller, T., Cole, T.W., Page, K.R., & Downie, J.S. (2016). *Enhancing scholarly use of digital libraries: A comparative survey and review of bibliographic metadata ontologies*. In Proceedings of the 16th ACM/IEEE Joint Conference on Digital Libraries (JCDL 2016) (pp 35-44). https://doi.org/10.1145/2910896.2910903

Kitamura, Y., Segawa, S., Sasajima, M., Tarumi, S., & Mizoguchi, R. (2008). Deep semantic mapping between functional taxonomies for interoperable semantic search. *Lecture Notes on Computer Science, 5367*, 137–151.

Kondylakis, H., Doerr, M., & Plexousakis, D. (2006). Mapping language for information integration. *ICS-FORTH Technical Report No. 385*, December 6. Retrieved from: https://www.ics.forth.gr/isl/publications/paperlink/Mapping_TR385_December06.pdf

Lopes, F.L.R., Sacramento, E.R., & Lóscio. B.F. (2012). *Using heterogeneous mappings for rewriting SPARQL queries*. Paper presented at 23rd International Workshop on Database and Expert Systems Applications (Vienna, Austria, 3-6 Sept. 2012).

Montoya, G. (2015). *Answering SPARQL queries using views*. In Proceedings of the Doctoral Consortium at the 14th International Semantic Web Conference (ISWC-DC 2015) (pp. 33-40).

Nurmikko-Fuller, T., Page, K.R., Willcox, P., Jett, J., Maden, C., Cole, T.W., Fallaw, C., Senseney, M., & Downie, J.S. (2015). *Building complex research collections in digital libraries: A survey of ontology implications*. In Proceedings of the 15th ACM/IEEE-CE Joint Conference on Digital Libraries (JCDL 2015) (pp. 169-172). https://doi.org/10.1145/2756406.2756944

Oldman, D. & Tanase, D. (2018). Reshaping the knowledge graph by connecting researchers, data and practices in ResearchSpace. *The Semantic Web - ISWC 2018 [proceedings part 2]* (pp. 325–340). DOI: https://doi.org/10.1007/978-3-030-00668-6_20

Page, K.R., Jett, J., Cole, T.W., Kudeki, D., Bainbridge, D., Organisciak, P., & J.S. Downie. (2018). *Worksets expand the scholarly utility of digital libraries*. In Proceedings of the 18th ACM/IEEE Joint Conference on Digital Libraries (JCDL 2018) (pp. 371-372). https://doi.org/10.1145/3197026.3203886

Parundekar, R., Knoblock, C., & Ambite, J. (2010). *Linking and building ontologies of linked data*. In Proceedings of the 9th International Semantic Web Conference (ISWC 2010) (pp. 598-614).

Rahm, E. (2011). Towards large-scale schema and ontology matching. In Z. Bellahsene, et al. (Eds.), *Schema matching and mapping: Data centric systems and applications* (pp. 3–27). Berlin: Springer-Verlag.

Rahm, E. & Bernstein, P. A. (2001). On matching schemas automatically. *Technical Report MSR-TR-2001-17*. Redmond, WA: Microsoft Research. Retrieved from: https://www.microsoft.com/en-us/research/wp-content/uploads/2016/02/tr-2001-17.pdf

St. Pierre, M. & LaPlant, W. P. (1998). Issues in crosswalking content metadata standards. [NISO white paper]. Retrieved from https://groups.niso.org/publications/white_papers/crosswalk/

Weigl, D. M., Emsley, I., & Page, K. R. (2018). Serendipity in context: Prioritised contextual browsing in large-scale digital libraries. *Proceedings of the Association for Information Science and Technology, 55*(1), 544–553 f.

Weigl, D. M., Lewis, D., Crawford, T., Knopke, I., & Page, K. R. (2017). On providing semantic alignment and unified access to music library metadata. *International Journal on Digital Libraries*, 1–23. https://doi.org/10.1007/s00799-017-0223-9

Weigl, D. M., Page, K. R., Organisciak, P., & Downie, J. S. (2017). *Information-seeking in large-scale digital libraries: strategies for scholarly workset creation*. In 2017 ACM/IEEE Joint Conference on Digital Libraries (JCDL) (pp. 1-4). IEEE.

"You Don't Feel That You're So Far Away": Information Sharing, Technology Use, and Settlement of International Student Immigrants

Adam Worrall
University of Alberta,
Edmonton, AB, Canada
worrall@ualberta.ca

Erin Ballantyne
University of Alberta,
Edmonton, AB, Canada
eballant@ualberta.ca

Jen Kendall
University of Alberta,
Edmonton, AB, Canada
and Parkland Regional Library,
Lacombe, AB, Canada
jlkendal@ualberta.ca

ABSTRACT

While immigrants and international students' information behavior and practices are known, less is understood of their online information sharing, associated use of information and communication technologies (ICTs), and the roles of these technologies in their settlement. We conducted semi-structured interviews with 20 international students to help fill this gap. We find international students' ICT use and information sharing shares similarities and differences with other students and immigrants; a set of settlement barriers and helps associated with ICTs; and clear roles for ICTs in supporting the informational, social, and emotional needs of international students. Transferable findings fill existing gaps in our knowledge of international student immigrants' use of ICTs and online information sharing; can inform LIS research and practice in facilitating their successful settlement through informational, sociotechnical, and emotional lenses; and encourage further work to confirm and expand on our findings.

KEYWORDS

Information Sharing; Information and Communication Technologies; Immigrants; Settlement; Helps and Barriers

ASIS&T THESAURUS

Information Science; Information Behavior; Information Sharing; Information Science; Informatics; Social Informatics; Countries and Regions; North America; Canada

INTRODUCTION

A historical average of 235,000 newcomers to Canada per year (Statistics Canada, 2016) is expected to rise to over 350,000 for 2021 (Hussen, 2018). These newcomers will include many of the over 572,000 international students who studied in Canada in 2018 (Canadian Bureau for International Education (CBIE), 2019), given that 60% intend to immigrate and settle in the country after graduation (CBIE, 2018). International student immigrants find online information sharing important and significant in their lives (Sin & Kim, 2013), just as other settling immigrants rely on online social networks, ties, media, and ICTs to find and share information and social support; connect their global and local lives; improve their social, emotional, and psychological well-being; and better understand information and settle into Canadian culture and communities (Caidi, Allard, & Quirke, 2010; Mehra & Papajohn, 2007).

While immigrants and international students' information behavior and practices are known, less is understood of their online information sharing, associated use of information and communication technologies (ICTs), and the roles of these ICTs in their settlement. Social media and ICTs may have significant impacts on international students' information sharing and settlement, their everyday and academic lives, and, in turn, our universities, communities, cultures, and society. This paper reports on a research study filling this gap, examining the online information sharing, ICT use, and settlement of international students in Canada. The study asked the following four research questions:

1. How do international students, as prospective immigrants to Canada, use ICTs in their academic and everyday lives?
2. What role(s) do ICTs play in their settlement process?
3. How do they choose to share everyday and academic information with others using technology?
4. Are there differences or similarities in ICT use and sharing based on their move from their home country to a new one, or in academic vs. everyday life uses?

BACKGROUND AND LITERATURE REVIEW

Online Communities

Online communities are social aggregations of people who, with the mediation of ICTs, interact and communicate with each other (Ellis, Oldridge, & Vasconcelos, 2004; Rheingold, 2000; Rosenbaum & Shachaf, 2010). These are social resources incorporating human emotion, personal and social ties, and emergent social constructions (Haythornthwaite,

82nd Annual Meeting of the Association for Information Science & Technology | Melbourne, Australia | 19–23 October, 2019

DOI: 10.1002/pra2.00025

2007; Tufekci, 2013; Wellman & Gulia, 1999; Worrall, 2015), and often information-centric with a focus on creating, sharing, and using information and knowledge as a primary activity (Worrall, 2019). Communities and ties reinforced online can serve informational and social purposes for international students as they study and settle, influencing their ICT use and settlement as we address through RQ1 and RQ2.

Information Sharing

People tend to seek the most accessible information, favor interpersonal sources over formal ones, and find emotional and affective needs important (Harris & Dewdney, 1994), making information sharing a common information behavior and practice (Case & Given, 2016). Information sharing in academic and everyday life contexts is influenced by individual, cultural, community, and societal contexts (Case & Given, 2016; Savolainen, 1995) and various social, emotional, and cultural support factors and social and community ties (Ardichvili, 2008; Choi, Kitzie, & Shah, 2014; Haythornthwaite, 2006; McLure Wasko & Faraj, 2000, 2005; Worrall & Oh, 2013), including altruism, communality and social interaction, difficulties in communicating or translating, empathy, enjoyment, perceptions of cultural or information values, reciprocity, reputation or status, self-efficacy, social cognition, social isolation, and social or cultural norms (Caidi et al., 2010; Jaeger & Burnett, 2010; Oh & Syn, 2015; Worrall, Cappello, & Osolen, 2018). These may motivate academic and everyday sharing, explored further through our RQ3.

Immigrants, International Students, and Settlement

Information sharing is important for new immigrants, taken here to mean those living outside the country they consider their original "home" (Caidi et al., 2010). Recent views of immigrants consider the varied "forces that drive immigration" and immigrants (Lee, 2009, p. 732) within complex, transnational contexts as immigrants move between countries for education, work, and everyday lives (Alba & Nee, 2003; Lee, 2009; Verdery, Mouw, Edelblute, & Chavez, 2018).

Immigrants, including international students, rely on online social networks, ties, media, and ICTs to find social and informational support and connect the global and local facets of their lives, improving their understanding of community, culture, and information and their psychological, emotional, and social well-being (Andrade & Doolin, 2016; Caidi et al., 2010; Dekker & Engbersen, 2014; Fisher, Durrance, & Hinton, 2004; Mehra & Papajohn, 2007; Verdery et al., 2018). Those who are part of information-centric online communities use them for informational and emotional reasons; sharing personal stories, information, and resources helps immigrants "settle in Canada successfully" (Chien, 2005, p. 157), satisfy informational and social support needs, and build relationships in their new country as they settle into true communities (Chien, 2005; Komito, 2011; Saw, Abbott, Donaghey, & McDonald, 2013; Sin & Kim, 2013).

Immigrants' and international students' general information behavior and practices are quite well understood (Caidi et al., 2010; Case & Given, 2016, pp. 341-345). However, we know less about their information sharing in online environments or—beyond Chien (2005) and Mehra and Papajohn's (2007) work—their use of ICTs and social media as part of their settlement process (Caidi et al., 2010). All four of our research questions help fill this existing gap.

METHODS

The first and third authors conducted semi-structured qualitative interviews (Kvale & Brinkmann, 2009) with 20 international students at a Canadian university. Participants were recruited through email and Facebook invitations sent to students via the university's international student services office, leading to a purposive sample of interested international students of all levels who were users of ICTs and/or social media. Interview questions asked were intended to address (a) the students' background, including their home country, how long they have been in Canada, and whether they intend to stay beyond their studies, (b) their adjustment and settlement process, (c) their use of technology including web sites, phone, apps, etc., and (d) their connections and sharing of information with others. The interviews focused on critical incidents (Fisher & Oulton, 1999) of the interviewees' experiences with their settlement, technology use, and information sharing, but also incorporated broader discussion. Interviews took place in person on the university's main campus, were audio recorded, and continued until the first and third authors agreed saturation of findings was reached, based on thoughts on and preliminary analysis of completed interviews.

After interviews were transcribed by the authors, the first and second authors analyzed the transcriptions using an open qualitative coding process similar but not identical to grounded theory and its constant comparative method (Bradley, Curry, & Devers, 2007; Strauss & Corbin, 1994). Each independently developed emergent codes based on the four research questions. After three interviews were analyzed, both coders came together and reviewed the coding as developed, discussing similarities and differences as part of an inductive and iterative process (Ahuvia, 2001). This led to the development of a master coding framework to ensure consistent categorization and to standardize key codes, while allowing for further emergent coding within the established categories. The first two authors continued analysis of the remaining interviews while discussing emerging findings and any minor discrepancies week by week (as informed by Bradley et al. (2007)). While subtle differences existed as coding was completed, no significant discrepancies were observed and analysis aligned with the third author's earlier thoughts. This process helped ensure the trustworthiness of the findings, an approach to validity best suited for qualitative research (Lincoln & Guba, 1985).

FINDINGS

Our coding and analysis process looked to answer the four research questions mentioned in the introduction. The following subsections report these findings in relation to ICT use; roles played, outcomes seen, and differences observed in ICT use relating to settlement; factors that served as helps or barriers for successful settlement; and sharing of everyday and academic information by participants.

ICTs Used (RQ1)

A list of ICTs in common use by participants can be found in Table 1, placed in emergent categories for ease of presentation but acknowledthat many ICTs and their use could fall into multiple categories. Interviewees use academic ICTs to complete coursework and assignments; access course materials; conduct academic research; learn about campus activities and resources; and register for courses and obtain final grades. Google Drive was used by interviewees to help organize their files and projects, especially in relation to academics. Many of these uses are typical (see e.g. Case & Given, 2016) of students' use of ICTs, as is the common use of Facebook Messenger and email as communications technologies; interviewees used these for academic and everyday interactions with fellow students, friends, and colleagues in their current and home countries. Many used WhatsApp, a messaging app in common use beyond North America, for everyday communication and in a few cases for academic purposes.

Everyday activities are represented by many financial, shopping, news, and entertainment apps and web sites used by interviewees, most commonly Amazon, banking apps, and grocery store apps. Many participants mentioned using mapping apps on their phones, frequently seen in prior reviewed literature for immigrants and others in a new environment (such as first-year students), alongside the municipality's train/bus transit app. Social media sites and apps, most commonly Facebook and Instagram, were used most for everyday information practices, although in many cases information sought or shared was associated with the university and student groups (e.g. events happening on or near campus). Other information exchanges took place with friends and family locally and in many home countries. A range of utilitarian web sites and apps, including Google Search, were used as one would expect of other students.

Our findings were somewhat mixed as to whether academic and everyday uses overlapped for international students. For some interviewees there were differences in the technologies they used in each context. "For academic [information]," P15 "would choose Facebook … and I kind of [use] Instagram," but "for more personal information, [they use] WhatsApp." P2 mentioned they and others they know "don't really, like, email friends … [and] not everyone sees your email or checks every 10 min. So it's just easier" to text friends instead of emailing them. Other interviewees would use ICTs across both academic and everyday life contexts. P9 stated "for things like Facebook, I do share stuff that's sometimes personal and sometimes academic." P10 would "use email but … also use texting" for communicating with their supervisor, even WhatsApp sometimes, because they did "not necessarily need to be that formal."

ICT type	Common examples
Academic	Google docs, Microsoft office, university web sites (home page, library, learning management system, course registration)
Communication	Facebook messenger, WhatsApp, email
File & project management	Google drive
Finance, shopping, news, entertainment	Amazon, banking apps, grocery store apps
Hardware	Computer / laptop, cell phone
Navigation	Maps (Apple, Google), municipal transit app
Social media	Facebook (including events, groups), instagram
Utility / Misc.	Google search

Table 1. List of ICT in common use by international student participants.

The ICTs our participants used in everyday life, while similar to other students, were somewhat different because of the adjustment and settlement process from one culture to another. For example, our participants made use of a greater variety of social media, communication, and utility apps and web sites, many stemming from common use in their home countries (e.g. Baidu Search, Vibr, WeChat, Weibo). Most participants with strong attachments to ICTs not popular in North America had adopted many social media and communication apps (e.g. Facebook, Facebook Messenger, Instagram) common in Canada alongside their existing apps.

Roles, Outcomes, and Differences (RQ2 and RQ4)

In preparing for the move, participants used ICTs they were familiar with to find information on the culture and environment. P7 "watched a lot of YouTube videos" about Canadian culture, feeling like they were "having a good idea about that" prior to the move. P11 provided another example of preparation via information available via social media:

> …before I came to Canada, some of the, like, previous students, like students who older than us, they would create social groups [on WeChat]. And then I get in one, invited in it, and they would tell us what you will face when you come here … and they kind of, like, it's kind of like 'tutorial 101,' like how, like, Canadian [city] looks like, how's the campus life look like. (P11)

Two participants, P1 and P17, already felt familiar with North American culture because of prior knowledge and experiences from study in the United States, and had some familiarity with what kinds of ICTs to expect and how they would use them before becoming students in Canada.

Once they moved to Canada, many participants mentioned ICTs played a more frequent role in their lives than when in their home country, using them to interact with friends and family, university services, and other social services such as the healthcare system. P5 stated they "use more of the social medias [*sic*] now … I'm not into social media, but I cannot leave it" due to connections with friends and family. P8 noted "this university uses a lot of social media to engage the students in different activities, which is great" and "does not happen" in their home country. P10 stressed "you have everything connected here. The healthcare, services, and social services and everything … So here I've used more [ICTs] myself."

The many different ICTs playing a role was of concern for a few, facing a potential overload of options. For example, P12 mentioned "everybody was just on one app" in their home country, "but here everybody's on, like, different apps, so then you have to make sure you have every single thing so you make sure you can maintain contact."

Others related fewer differences in their frequency of use of ICTs, but a change in the specific nature of ICTs playing a role in their lives since the move. P11 felt "the process [of ICT use] is basically the same, just what [specific apps and web sites] I use for my activity has been changed." P17 compared the provision of university-specific email addresses in Canada and a prior experience in a US university as "promoting a sense of belonging" that they liked, unlike the lack of such email addresses provided to students studying in their home country.

Some of the differences seen in ICT use could be ascribed to differences in culture, but these were not raised by our participants as frequently as we expected; while there was an initial adjustment period, many found ICTs were supportive towards settlement. Technologies changed and shifted nonetheless, as participants found themselves in a culture more supportive of certain ways ICTs could be used, mediate information sharing, and play a role in providing informational, social, and emotional support. As mentioned by P11, some of the most significant differences were between specific apps (e.g. Facebook Messenger and texting in Canada vs. WhatsApp or other options elsewhere).

The roles played by ICTs in international student immigrants' lives sometimes led to unfortunate negative outcomes, as participants' emotions came into play. P11 would "go through all the pictures that my friends post [and note] they were, like, so happy; they are travlling, and they have good food. At that moment and when I stay individually, I kind of, like, feel depressed." P2 would "get really anxious if I'm constantly receiving messages from people"; they stressed they "have a comfort zone" with communication and preferred to stay within it.

In contrast, ICTs were helpful and promoted positive outcomes for the emotional side of many participants' settlement. P3 stated "IT helps with [their] emotions, because otherwise [their parents] are like, when will you come to [our country]?" ICT allowed their parents to have "a feeling of satisfaction" about their health, making the student's "life easier. You won't be having tension…" P12 similarly stressed that "because I had more contact with my friends … I wasn't feeling completely lost and lonely, and when I did feel lonely I had people to talk to."

Settlement Helps and Barriers (RQ2 and RQ3)

Our analysis identified many factors either helping international student immigrants with their settlement, or serving as a barrier to successful settlement in their new country, which in turn impacted the roles of ICTs (RQ2) and information sharing (RQ3), which we focused on in our analysis. A summary can be seen in Table 2.

Culture

In moving from their home country to a new environment, many participants faced significant culture shock, with P11 a prime example of culture serving as a barrier in settlement:

> For example, I want to go to the [mall]? I have to, like, Google here, what's the bus I should take … but although I got the information, it's still hard for me to find the bus station. Yeah. And also when I get in the bus, and I do not know I have to push the stop button before my destination. … So it's a total difference from what I do in my country. (P11)

Other participants had prior experiences in other countries which diminished culture shock, but led to possible reverse culture shock if they returned to their home country, as P17 did. They "loved it" when in the US for a study year, but "when I went back [to my home country] … I did not do well in my third year [after returning] … because of the [reverse] culture shock." Much of this was due to different teaching and technology practices back "home," with P17 saying they asked themselves "Where am I? Why are these people teaching me this way? Where is the technology?"

Information

Given the importance of information across cultures and societies and its significance to students, it was not surprising to see information be both a help and a barrier to international student immigrants. Many expressed support for university resources, as accessed via ICTs, as part of settlement and their information behavior and practices for academic purposes. P3 had found the "online library portal" and its "chat option" useful in finding book chapters; they "just chatted with [library staff] and in a matter of minutes [they] just sent me the PDF. … That makes life easier, definitely." P18 had had similar luck with the international student services office about "a question about work on campus, like, requirements for international students … they answered me in, like, not even in two hours. They just got back to me and I was like, 'oh, that's really quick.'"

photos of the university's campus "that I think are really beautiful, and my friends are really interested in" them; as a result,

Factor	As help	As barrier
Culture	Learning more about new culture leads to a stronger feeling of "fitting in."	Not knowing intricacies of new culture can lead to confusion in ICT use and information sharing.
Information	ICTs and those who provide them help find academic and everyday information useful for studies, settling in.	Can be difficult if international students miss specific steps or information sources that would help, or lack access when available only via a specific ICT.
Information behaviour and practices	Sharing can help with relaxation, emotional support; information found can be crucial to settlement.	*Not seen as a barrier by participants.*
Students	Classmates and "senior" students can help mentor, be a first source for information, especially of an academic nature.	*Not seen as a barrier by participants.*
Support structure	Connections with new friends (especially when from same / similar home culture) or local family / family friends, in person and via ICTs, a huge help for many international students. Academic connections and information can help expose to new contacts and social ties.	If introverted, can be difficult to make new friends at first and feel sidelined from the "majority."
Language	*Not seen as a help by participants.*	Lacking knowledge of specific words and phrases can cause communication issues, culture shock.
Information and communication technologies	Technologies support informational and emotional connection to friends and family in home country, entertainment and academic study needs and desires.	Lack of use of specific ICTs not popular in one's home country can cause informational barriers.

Table 2. Summary of settlement helps and barriers identified.

Other participants found they lacked information, and this served as a barrier to their successful settlement. P5 found it "hard to find information sometimes," stating "as an international student, when you get here you don't know where to start. … I was missing, kind of, a list of different steps I was supposed to go through." P17 found "nobody told me about" there being "so much paperwork" for things like healthcare, and "because I also missed the [university] orientation, because I came in late, so I didn't know I had to do the identification card and like all of those things."

Information Behavior and Practices

Information behavior and practices were a significant help for participants, with an emphasis on information sharing. Many interviewees focused on the emotional support coming from their use of ICTs to share academic and everyday information with others. P9 shared "about every aspect of life" and found sharing helpful "because I got to relax and I got to share, like, not everything … But I feel like I'm sharing something and I feel like I'm not isolated. So yeah, it helps my emotions." P9 further stated they had a photo album on social media with "two friends [were] already planning to" attend the university in the next year. Another interviewee, P18, was offering similar support to "another cousin that [recently] came here. So, I'm almost like a mentor to him. … I just tell him everything that he doesn't know" about Canada.

Other participants had received informational support toward settlement through the processes of information seeking and sharing mediated by ICTs. P19's experience is illustrative. Before moving to Canada, they found out from "a group in Telegram" of students from their home country that an apartment was up for rent. So they "texted them [on Telegram] and so I went there and saw." Later P19 "found another place on, I think, [a rental search] web site. And I went there too … and I decided to stay there." Information seeking, mediated by Telegram and the rental search web site, had supported P19's successful settlement.

Students

As international student immigrants are students, their fellow classmates and other students they interacted with were supportive of their settlement. Fellow students helped P9 "learn a lot of things … not only about the culture outside of the campus, but also about specific things about the industry, about the program, about everything." P12 had a similar positive experience from a formalized peer mentoring program:

> ...they sort of team you up like a pair, bunch of international students with a senior peer who is also an international student. ... So if I had any questions, when I did have questions, usually my first place of contact would be [them]. So I would usually just ask [them] what to do, and then if [they] couldn't help me I would probably ask my friends, and then... yeah, so it was easy because I didn't really have any big issues. (P12)

Support Structure

As helpful as fellow international students were, participants would rely on their broader support structure and network of social ties to support their settlement. ICTs provided for connections with new friends (on and off campus) and local family or family friends, many of which provided emotional and informational support. P8 found events through the university's web sites and Facebook, and "used to go" with their friends; they used ICTs to "talk with my family ... not just [for] my adjustment but to be able to communicate with [my] family..." P9 "was lucky to have a family ... who were like my parents' friends living in [the same city]," which influenced their choice of university to attend; they considered themselves "really lucky ... 'cause I got to learn a lot about Canadian life, but I also was not really, like, being separated 100% from [their home country's] culture." P16 similarly found various communities "very helpful ... especially the people from [my country] too" since they "share the same culture and stuff, and they went through the same thing before me, so I can, like, lean a little [on] them." These friends led one participant to say they "felt like home when I was with my friends" and settlement became "kind of easy. It was alright" (P4). Academic connections, too, were helpful for some, such as P13, whose advisor was from a country near theirs and had connections there, "so I've already known them [back there] before I came here." Their department also had existing students from their home country, "so it was easy to make this transition."

For participants who had faced difficulties, at least at first, in making new social connections, their lack of social ties became a barrier to their settlement and to feeling like they "fit in," P2 said "it was really hard for me [to], like, find people that would, you know, like stuff that I do." They commented they were "really introverted ... [and] don't like big groups, like big crowds of people," finding this to be a barrier. P11, while less introverted, faced similar challenges:

> To be honest, I didn't really like [this city] when I came first. Like, I kind of feel depressed 'cause I don't have any new friends yet, and I have troubles with communications, and I, I just, like, can't get into, I don't know, the... majority? (P11)

Language

Given almost all of our participants did not speak English as their primary language, it was a bit surprising that language was raised as a barrier by only a few interviewees. They stressed lacking knowledge of specific words and phrases could lead to challenges "trying to communicate with people and make new friends" (P18) and to further "culture shock struggle[s]" as they learned "what words do you use, [and] are these words explaining what you mean the best" (P1).

Information and Communication Technologies

As has been illustrated by many of the comments above, ICTs often served in support of international students' informational and emotional connections to friends and family. "If I hadn't [had] all those technologies," P5 shared, "it would have been harder for me to make the decision to come here and leave my country." P12 found social media "made the entire transition easier. Because I had more contact with my friends." P5 summed this up: for an international student immigrant in a new environment, ICTs make it so "you don't feel that you're so far away."

ICTs supported emotional and informational connections to entertainment and academic needs, as with other students. As one example, P11 stated "'cause I live individually, if I don't have my laptop when I'm eating, when I'm studying, I kind of feel lonely." They found watching videos and listening to music (via Netflix and YouTube) important for their well-being, because "if I lost it or I don't have it, I will feel crap." Another participant stated:

> Well, I think they are really helpful. Like, they are much better than having to write long notes in your book. [Interviewer laughs.] ... access to online stuff is more like, it giving you more accessibility and also, like, you have more time, compared to having to write all that. ... Like, it's compact everything, to get it in the computer ... you can also upload it online and you can read it later or whatever. (P18)

Lack of access to, or use of, a specific ICT could become a barrier, such as in cases where a specific ICT was not as important in one's home country. P10's experience is perhaps most evocative of this barrier to settlement:

> ...it's because I don't have Facebook ... and it's something that I think that is important right now, because I didn't have any Facebook [prior to coming to Canada], so I didn't get to know all of the things ... People give away things [online], right? ... So I didn't know that, so I spent [time] living on the floor for two months instead of knowing that someone in, I don't know, they are giving [away] a bed or something, right, that they don't need. ... So the thing is that I realized that when my wife came [interviewer laughs] ... because my wife, she has a Facebook, and she starts to get involved in, those uh, how do you say, groups, on Facebook. So she gets to know a lot of things. So it was like, easier for my family than for me... (P10)

Information Sharing (RQ3)

Information sharing was significant in our international student interviewees' settlement and use of ICTs. Their methods and reasoning for sharing were not unexpected considering their status as both students at a North American university and immigrants and newcomers to Canada. They ask friends, family, mentors, and perceived experts such as senior students or faculty advisors for advice; they help out friends and colleagues by themselves sharing information on facts, events, activities, and locations they feel will be useful in academics and everyday life; and they seek, share, and use information for informational, social, and emotional reasons, often at the same time. Not all participants are frequent sharers of their social, everyday lives online, but many do either publicly or semi-privately; we saw a similar range in use of and information practices around social media and communications as seen in the student and general North American populations of around the same age. While not all participants talked at length about sharing academic information via ICTs, many discussed using tools like Google Drive, Slack, Skype, WhatsApp, texting, and email for private or semi-private information sharing relevant to courses being taken and research being conducted as part of their academic lives, as one would expect of many students.

For many participants, information and information sharing online, and the ICTs that support this, were key to their lives. P1 stated "not being able to have access to the world of information around me" would be problematic, since "our devices basically became an extension of our hands…" Others made express decisions to share and seek more via face-to-face means, perceiving a difference between information found via ICTs and experience obtained from talking to people face-to-face. For example, P15 commented "when you read, for example, on the website it said some information, but it's different when you talk to people and they share their experience." P7 stated they would "rather go outside and meet people and do things directly" than engage via Facebook or WhatsApp, feeling the latter did not inform them of culture. P14 "usually [tried] to meet once a week or every two weeks" with close friends, stating they "always have preferred face-to-face. Because I sometimes feel that technology makes everything more, like, not that personal."

P4 struck a middle ground between face-to-face and ICTs, stating they "share most just by talking" and when they see friends, but nonetheless used WhatsApp, Facebook, and Facebook Messenger to semi-privately share with friends and family. They further stated "you always need a phone, you always need to phone" for connections to family. P19 felt similar about sharing in public, but still valued Facebook, Instagram, and Telegram for semi-private sharing.

Some participants sought to bridge the gap between themselves and ICTs when they were less confident of how to look up information, where to look it up, or another barrier existed. P8 commented they "first of all … [tried] to look for help with people," and after "a year … I am more comfortable and I can find things online." P12 similarly had moved beyond having to talk to student support services to going to the university web site, and would "usually" find the answer. P14 echoed the helpfulness of people over ICTs when first getting settled: "My main advice, and I always tell this to everyone, is just to be proactive and ask for help. … And if you ask for help, especially here at the university you have resources for everything."

Still others would be selective, using certain platforms for sharing information and others for other information practices. For example, P7 used "Instagram … just for sharing purpose … and WhatsApp just for contacting. But Facebook, like, I would say that I'm learning things"; each ICT had a unique purpose for them that drove their motivation for using it. P8 chose the app to use for sharing dependent on which "I know they check more" and, akin to P4, did not share information publicly online with much frequency. Some related drawbacks to relying on face-to-face interactions; for example, P7 mentioned "[a] number of people are also lost" in their Canadian city and had found it less useful to ask people for directions, instead using Google Maps to navigate.

Supporting their settlement, social connections, and the needs and practices of others were big factors motivating many other participants to share publicly or privately using ICTs, as with P4. P15 found sharing "pretty great to feel more comfortable here, and because in [my home country] I was very connected and still am … So it helps me a lot." P11 found "when I'm sharing stuff, it strengthens my connections with my classmates, with my friends." P17 had an altruistic motive, sharing information "more" in Canada because "it's beneficial for everybody" and they felt Canadian culture did not enforce "survival of the fittest," unlike their home country where sharing seemed less beneficial. P2 offered a nuanced view stressing that sharing, and associated ICT use, should be useful: "Like using Facebook or Instagram to share important events that are happening and, like, that's really good. But sometimes when you just use it for useless stuff, it's just, like, that's when it starts getting bad."

DISCUSSION AND IMPLICATIONS

The international students we interviewed, as prospective immigrants to Canada, use ICTs in ways that share similarities with the ICT use of non-international students, in line with the marginal differences seen in social media site use by Saw et al. (2013). They use ICTs in ways similar to other immigrants (see Andrade & Doolin, 2016; Caidi et al., 2010; Dekker & Engbersen, 2014; Fisher et al., 2004; Komito, 2011; Mehra & Papajohn, 2007; Verdery et al., 2018), but with nuances that represent the unique challenges and situations they face in their dual student and immigrant roles. These ICTs, in turn, play roles in their settlement process beginning as early as their preparation for moving and increasing for many as they move to Canada. If their use does not increase, the specific nature of the ICTs playing a role in their lives changes, as they adopt new ICTs and adapt existing ones to new needs and desires for not just informational, but also social and emotional support. While behavior and practices online and face-to-face may remain information-centric sometimes, other needs go beyond the findings of Sin and Kim (2013) to include desires for the human emotion and personal and social ties found in online communities (Tufekci, 2013; Wellman & Gulia, 1999; Worrall, 2015), desired in sharing information (Harris & Dewdney, 1994), and often significant in successful settlement (Chien, 2005).

Our international student interviewees' use of ICTs can end up helping or hurting their settlement in connection with several factors including culture, information, information behavior and practices, fellow students, support structures and social ties, language, and their use of the ICTs themselves. Some negative impacts and outcomes occur on their settlement, and for a few ICTs go beyond barriers to settlement to actively presenting negative feelings and emotions. While rare in comparison to positive outcomes, such negative affective factors in ICT use should be considered in research and practice through sociotechnical perspectives, frameworks, and models incorporating the importance and significance of feelings and emotions as part of ICT adoption and use (e.g. (Toombs, Bardzell, & Bardzell, 2015; Zhang, 2013), alongside the study of affect in information behavior and practices (Case & Given, 2016, pp. 116-117; Nahl & Bilal, 2007). For most, ICTs act more often as a help to and in support of settlement than as a barrier. Many human, sociotechnical, affective, cultural, and critical issues impact on and influence international students' settlement and their relative success, as seen in our findings and the broader literature on immigrants' settlement processes (e.g. Andrade & Doolin, 2016; Komito, 2011; Sin & Kim, 2013).

Our interviewees share everyday and academic information using technology in ways that, as with their use of ICTs, echo the online information sharing of other students and immigrants. The primacy of interpersonal sources (Harris & Dewdney, 1994) and concerns over privacy (e.g. Marwick & Boyd, 2014) are not unfamiliar from the past 25 years of information behavior and practices research and the past 15 years of social media research, which in turn informed information systems and services. When they are coupled with the processes of settling and adapting to a new culture, community, and environment, they present unique challenges for how international students seek and share information and how LIS researchers and professionals can best support these behaviors and practices. Many participants have strong altruistic tendencies, and this may be transferable to other populations of international students, as it has been seen in other information sharing communities online (McLure Wasko & Faraj, 2000; Oh & Syn, 2015). A "share and share alike" mentality is one we believe LIS researchers and professionals should encourage and support as part of facilitating international students' information behavior and practices and use of ICTs, drawing on our findings and other studies of motivations for online information sharing (e.g. Ardichvili, 2008; Choi et al., 2014; Oh & Syn, 2015; Worrall et al., 2018; Worrall & Oh, 2013) to further inform information system and service design, implementation, and use.

Based on their move to a new country from their original home and academic vs. everyday life uses, some participants experienced different factors impacting their ICT use, information sharing, and settlement. Even with these differences, clear roles emerge for ICTs in supporting the informational, social, and emotional needs of our interviewees, a significance we believe has strong transferability to the broader populations of international students and immigrants across North America. The importance and significance of such roles echoes literature on social and emotional support factors in online information sharing among many other populations (Ardichvili, 2008; Choi et al., 2014; Haythornthwaite, 2006; McLure Wasko & Faraj, 2000, 2005; Worrall & Oh, 2013), further implying the potential trustworthiness of these findings. We encourage further research into the informational, social, and emotional roles of ICTs for international students and other immigrants to further confirm and expand on our findings. We advocate for continued and greater consideration of social and emotional contexts alongside informational ones in research on ICTs and information sharing and in the practical design, adoption, and use of ICTs and associated library and information services and systems.

CONCLUSIONS

Our study helps fill a gap in our knowledge of international student immigrants' online information sharing, use of ICTs, and the role these play in their settlement. Although our findings are limited to the experiences of 20 interviewees at one Canadian institution, we believe our findings have strong transferability to other populations of international students and immigrants, based on connections with the existing research literature. ICTs and information sharing often support immigrants' informational, social, and emotional needs and desires as they find themselves in a new context and environment. LIS researchers and professionals should look for ways to facilitate and support sharing and ICT use as helpful, not hurtful, to immigrants' settlement processes, information needs, and social and emotional well-being. Our own future work intends to continue to examine the online and offline communities of international students, immigrants, and expatriates, and the roles technology and information sharing play as part of their immigration, settlement, and transnational experiences. Through such research and practice work, our hope is international students and other immigrants will feel they are not "so far away" from successful experiences as they advance their education, career, and lives in new contexts and countries.

ACKNOWLEDGMENTS

Our thanks to our participants and to the University of Alberta International Student Services office for support and help in recruitment. This paper represents the findings of the authors, and not necessarily the views of the University of Alberta or its International Student Services office.

REFERENCES

Ahuvia, A. (2001). Traditional, interpretive, and reception based content analyses: improving the ability of content analysis to address issues of pragmatic and theoretical concern. *Social Indicators Research, 54*, 139–172. https://doi.org/10.1023/A:1011087813505

Alba, R. D., & Nee, V. (2003). Assimilation theory, old and new. In *Remaking the American mainstream: Assimilation and contemporary immigration* (pp. 17–66). Cambridge, MA: Harvard University Press.

Andrade, A. D., & Doolin, B. (2016). Information and communication technology and the social inclusion of refugees. *MIS Quarterly, 40*, 405–416.

Ardichvili, A. (2008). Learning and knowledge sharing in virtual communities of practice: Motivators, barriers, and enablers. *Advances in Developing Human Resources, 10*, 541–554. https://doi.org/10.1177/1523422308319536

Bradley, E. H., Curry, L. A., & Devers, K. J. (2007). Qualitative data analysis for health services research: developing taxonomy, themes, and theory. *Health Services Research, 42*, 1758–1772. https://doi.org/10.1111/j.1475-6773.2006.00684.x

Caidi, N., Allard, D., & Quirke, L. (2010). Information practices of immigrants. *Annual Review of Information Science and Technology, 44*, 491–531. https://doi.org/10.1002/aris.2010.1440440118

Canadian Bureau for International Education. (2018). *The student's voice: National results of the 2018 CBIE International Student Survey* (CBIE Research in Brief series, report no. 9). Ottawa, ON: Author. Retrieved from https://cbie.ca/wp-content/uploads/2018/08/Student_Voice_Report-ENG.pdf

Canadian Bureau for International Education. (2019, February 15). *Another record year for Canadian international education* [Press release]. Retrieved from https://cbie.ca/another-record-year-for-canadian-international-education/

Case, D. O., & Given, L. M. (2016). *Looking for information: A survey of research on information seeking, needs, and behavior* (4th ed.). Bingley, England: Emerald.

Chien, E. H. M. (2005). *Informing and involving newcomers online: Users' perspectives of Settlement.Org* (Master's thesis). University of Toronto, Toronto, ON. Retrieved from ProQuest Dissertations and Theses. (MR07290)

Choi, E., Kitzie, V., & Shah, C. (2014). Investigating motivations and expectations of asking a question in social Q&A. First Monday, 19(3). Retrieved from http://firstmonday.org/ojs/index.php/fm/article/view/4830

Dekker, R., & Engbersen, G. (2014). How social media transform migrant networks and facilitate migration. *Global Networks, 14*(4), 401–418. https://doi.org/10.1111/glob.12040

Ellis, D., Oldridge, R., & Vasconcelos, A. (2004). Community and virtual community. *Annual Review of Information Science and Technology, 38*, 145–186. https://doi.org/10.1002/aris.1440380104

Fisher, K. E., Durrance, J. C., & Hinton, M. B. (2004). Information grounds and the use of need-based services by immigrants in Queens, New York: A context-based, outcome evaluation approach. *Journal of the American Society for Information Science and Technology, 55*, 754–766. https://doi.org/10.1002/asi.20019

Fisher, S., & Oulton, T. (1999). The critical incident technique in library and information management research. *Education for Information, 17*, 113–125. https://doi.org/10.3233/EFI-1999-17203

Harris, R. M., & Dewdney, P. (1994). Theory and research on information-seeking. In *Barriers to information: How formal help systems fail battered women* (pp. 7–34). Westport, CT: Greenwood Press.

Haythornthwaite, C. (2006). Articulating divides in distributed knowledge practice. *Information, Communication and Society, 9*, 761–780. https://doi.org/10.1080/13691180601064113

Haythornthwaite, C. (2007). Social networks and online community. In A. Joinson, K. McKenna, T. Postmes, & U.-D. Reips, *The Oxford handbook of Internet psychology* (pp. 121–137). New York, NY: Oxford University Press.

Hussen, A. (2018). *2018 annual report to Parliament on immigration* (catalogue no. Ci1E-PDF). Ottawa, ON: Minister of Immigration, Refugees, and Citizenship. Retrieved from http://publications.gc.ca/collections/collection_2018/ircc/Ci1-2018-eng.pdf

Jaeger, P. T., & Burnett, G. (2010). *Information worlds: Behavior, technology, and social context in the age of the Internet.* New York, NY: Routledge.

Komito, L. (2011). Social media and migration: Virtual community 2.0. *Journal of the American Society for Information Science and Technology, 62*, 1075–1086. https://doi.org/10.1002/asi.21517

Kvale, S., & Brinkmann, S. (2009). *InterViews: Learning the craft of qualitative research interviewing* (2nd ed.). Thousand Oaks, CA: Sage.

Lee, C. (2009). Sociological theories of immigration: Pathways to integration for U.S. immigrants. *Journal of Human Behavior in the Social Environment, 19*, 730–744. https://doi.org/10.1080/10911350902910906

Lincoln, Y. S., & Guba, E. G. (1985). Establishing trustworthiness. In *Naturalistic inquiry* (pp. 289–331). Newbury Park, CA: Sage.

Marwick, A. E., & Boyd, D. (2014). Networked privacy: How teenagers negotiate context in social media. *New Media and Society*, *16*, 1051–1067. https://doi.org/10.1177/1461444814543995

McLure Wasko, M., & Faraj, S. (2000). "It is what one does": Why people participate and help others in electronic communities of practice. *The Journal of Strategic Information Systems*, *9*, 155–173. https://doi.org/10.1016/S0963-8687(00)00045-7

McLure Wasko, M., & Faraj, S. (2005). Why should I share? Examining social capital and knowledge contribution in electronic networks of practice. *MIS Quarterly*, *29*, 35–57.

Mehra, B., & Papajohn, D. (2007). "Glocal" patterns of communication-information convergences in Internet use: Cross-cultural behavior of international teaching assistants in a culturally alien information environment. *The International Information and Library Review*, *39*, 12–30. https://doi.org/10.1016/j.iilr.2007.01.001

Nahl, D., & Bilal, D.. (2007). *Information and emotion: The emergent affective paradigm in information behavior research and theory*. Medford, NJ: Information Today.

Oh, S., & Syn, S. Y. (2015). Motivations for sharing information and social support in social media: A comparative analysis of Facebook, Twitter, Delicious, YouTube, and Flickr. *Journal of the Association for Information Science and Technology*, *66*, 2045–2060. https://doi.org/10.1002/asi.23320

Rheingold, H. (2000). *The virtual community: Homesteading on the electronic frontier* (revised ed.). Cambridge, MA: MIT Press.

Rosenbaum, H., & Shachaf, P. (2010). A structuration approach to online communities of practice: The case of Q&A communities. *Journal of the American Society for Information Science and Technology*, *61*, 1933–1944. https://doi.org/10.1002/asi.21340

Savolainen, R. (1995). Everyday life information seeking: Approaching information seeking in the context of "way of life.". *Library and Information Science Research*, *17*, 259–294. https://doi.org/10.1016/0740-8188(95)90048-9

Saw, G., Abbott, W., Donaghey, J., & McDonald, C. (2013). Social media for international students – it's not all about Facebook. *Library Management*, *34*, 156–174. https://doi.org/10.1108/01435121311310860

Sin, S.-C. J., & Kim, K.-S. (2013). International students' everyday life information seeking: The informational value of social networking sites. *Library and Information Science Research*, *35*, 107–116. https://doi.org/10.1016/j.lisr.2012.11.006

Statistics Canada. (2016). *150 years of immigration in Canada* (Canadian Megatrends reportseries, catalogue no. 11-630-X). Ottawa, ON: Minister of Industry. Retrieved from http://www.statcan.gc.ca/pub/11-630-x/11-630-x2016006-eng.htm

Strauss, A., & Corbin, J. (1994). Grounded theory methodology: An overview. In N. K. Denzin & Y. S. Lincoln, *The handbook of qualitative research* (pp. 273–285). Thousand Oaks, CA: Sage.

Toombs, A. L., Bardzell, S., & Bardzell, J. (2015). The proper care and feeding of hackerspaces: Care ethics and cultures of making. In B. Begole & J. Kim, Co-Chairs) *Proceedings of the 33rd annual ACM Conference on Human Factors in computing systems* (CHI 2015 (pp. 629–638)). New York, NY: ACM. https://doi.org/10.1145/2702123.2702522

Tufekci, Z. (2013). The social Internet: Frustrating, enriching, but not lonely. *Public Culture*, *26*, 13–23. https://doi.org/10.1215/08992363-2346322

Verdery, A. M., Mouw, T., Edelblute, H., & Chavez, S. (2018). Communication flows and the durability of a transnational social field. *Social Networks*, *53*, 57–71. https://doi.org/10.1016/j.socnet.2017.03.002

Wellman, B., & Gulia, M. (1999). Virtual communities as communities: Net surfers don't ride alone. In M. A. Smith & P. Kollock, *Communities in cyberspace* (pp. 167–194). New York, NY: Routledge.

Worrall, A. (2015, 2015). "Like a real friendship": Translation, coherence, and convergence of information values in LibraryThing and Goodreads. In G. Olson, *iConference 2015 proceedings*, Newport Beach, CA, March 24-27. Champaign, IL: iSchools Retrieved from http://hdl.handle.net/2142/73641

Worrall, A. (2019). "Connections above and beyond": Information, translation, and community boundaries in LibraryThing and Goodreads. *Journal of the Association for Information Science and Technology*, *70*, 742–753. https://doi.org/10.1002/asi.24153

Worrall, A., Cappello, A., & Osolen, R. (2018). Balancing socio-emotional and informational considerations in social Q&A: The case of Academia Stack Exchange. In A. Shiri, S. Farnel, & S. Polkinghorne, (Co-Chairs) *Proceedings of the 46th Annual Conference of the Canadian Association for Information Science (CAIS/ACSI 2018): Diversities on the data landscape: Connecting information science with data studies*. Canada: CAIS/ACSI Retrieved from https://journals.library.ualberta.ca/ojs.cais-acsi.ca/index.php/cais-asci/article/download/995/888

Worrall, A., & Oh, S. (2013). The place of health information and socio-emotional support in social questioning and answering. *Information Research*, *18*(3) Retrieved from http://informationr.net/ir/18-3/paper587.html

Zhang, P. (2013). The Affective Response Model: A theoretical framework of affective concepts and their relationships in the ICT context. *MIS Quarterly*, *37*, 247–274.

Understanding the Peer Review Endeavor

Shenmeng Xu
University of North Carolina at Chapel Hill, United States
shenmeng@unc.edu

Guangyao Zhang
Dalian University of Technology, China
sdgyzhang@163.com

Yao Sun
Dalian University of Technology, China
sylviass11@163.com

Xianwen Wang
Dalian University of Technology, China
xianwenwang@dlut.edu.cn

ABSTRACT

Peer review plays an essential role in the scholarly publishing life cycle. Using the verified peer review records of researchers on Publons, this study investigated how this scientific endeavor was distributed throughout the world. In addition, we took an initial step toward understanding the length of reviews as a potential indicator of time and effort put into this "scientific gatekeeping" process. The proficiency of English, the scientific Lingua Franca, was found to have a significant effect on the length of reviews. In addition, there was a significant effect of a country's economic development level on review length. Furthermore, we explored a subgroup of reviewers – reviewers in Singapore – in more depth, and found that reviewers in different genders, disciplines, economic and cultural backgrounds wrote reviews of significantly different lengths.

KEYWORDS

Peer Review; Publons; Scholarly Communication; Scholarly Publishing; Global Science

ASIS&T THESAURUS

Informetrics; Scientometrics; Scholarly Communication

INTRODUCTION

The peer review we focus on in this study is the mechanism for quality control before the acceptance and publication of scholarly articles (Borgman & Furner, 2002; Rowland, 2002). In this process, normally two or three reviewers (in some cases also called referees) provide the author(s) and editor(s) with written evaluation and an overall recommendation of the submission through one or more rounds of review. Since Le Journal des Sçavans (Journal of Scholars) was published in 1665, the practice of peer review has had a history of more than 300 years and has become the internationally accepted practice (Crawford & Stucki, 1990). However, the specific forms and processes of peer review differ depending on the publishing venues, publishers, norms in different disciplines and areas, and other factors. Given the private nature of the peer review practice, it has been a challenge to gain a large picture of the peer review landscape throughout the world.

The peer review process is highly regarded by scholars and considered to be essential to the communication of scholarly research (Mulligan, Hall, & Raphael, 2013). Acknowledged as an effective instrument for self-regulation in the evaluation and selection of scientific contributions (Abelson, 1980; Goodman, Berlin, Fletcher, & Fletcher, 1994; Shatz, 2004), peer review has been playing an important role in the evolution of scientific knowledge. At the same time, peer review is recognized as a flawed process (Eysenck & Eysenck, 1992). The unreliability of peer review has been demonstrated (Ceci & Peters, 1982; Ernst, Saradeth, & Resch, 1993). The validity of judgments in the peer review process is also often questioned (Armstrong, Idriss, Kimball, & Bernhard, 2008; Chubin & Hackett, 1990). Overall, researchers have shown mixed attitudes toward the peer review practice (Mulligan et al., 2013). Researchers from all over the world nowadays participate in the peer review process in different roles (authors, reviewers, and editors), marking it even more difficult to understand the many facets of peer review.

Publons was launched in 2012 as a website for academics to record and present their peer review and editorial activities for academic journals. Publons partners with academic journals so that the peer review activities that researchers choose to claim and showcase can be verified. By 2018, more than 500,000 reviewers have joined the site, adding more than one million reviews across 25,000 journals (Publons, 2018). In 2018, Publons released a Global State of Peer Review Report (Publons, 2018), addressing several issues including the "supply and demand chain" of peer review and academic publishing, the reviewer fatigue phenomenon, the efficiency of the peer review process, as well as the quality of peer review.

Aiming to provide complementary understandings to the Publons global report, driven by the following research questions, this study aims to draw back the curtain of the peer review endeavor in more depth:

1. How are peer reviewers distributed all over the world?
2. How are peer reviews distributed all over the world?
3. How long are reviews written by reviewers throughout the world?

82nd Annual Meeting of the Association for Information Science & Technology | Melbourne, Australia | 19–23 October, 2019

DOI: 10.1002/pra2.00026

4. Is there an effect of language (English) proficiency of reviewers on the length of reviews?
5. Based on a smaller sample of researchers affiliated with a Singapore organization, as a preliminary exploration: Do factors including gender, discipline, academic position, economic background, and cultural background of reviewers affect the length of reviews?

In this study, the length of reviews is studied as an initial step toward understanding it as a potential indicator of time and effort researchers devote to the peer review process.

METHODS AND DATA

Data Collection and Cleaning

On Publons.com, a researcher's peer review contributions for scholarly journals are verified and displayed on their Publons homepage. We used a Python program to collect the researchers' identity and affiliation information, as well as the counts of their peer review activities and the average length of their review texts. Our data were collected in April 2018. Starting from the aggregated page of all the countries (https://publons.com/country/), we included all reviewers that had at least one verified review in our dataset. In total, we collected 82,798 data points.

To investigate the relationship between review length and language proficiency, we collected the EF English Proficiency Index (EPI) for each country. The EF EPI indicators were calculated aiming to rank countries by the average level of English language skills among those adults who took the EF test. After excluding the countries with no EF score data available, we had 77,859 data points.

We then manually cleaned the data by removing duplicates and comparing the information on the Publons website with our data wherever erroneous data were spotted. After data cleaning, we obtained 76,370 data points. These data points are not unique Publons reviewers. Instead, each of them represents one reviewer with a unique affiliation. Considering that it is impossible to accurately identify the main affiliations of the reviewers on a large scale if they had multiple affiliations listed, those with two or more affiliations are counted multiple times in our dataset. In other words, if one reviewer has two affiliations, he or she accordingly appears as two data points. In total, there are 74,785 unique Publons reviewers (out of the 76,370 data points mentioned above) in this dataset. This dataset is our final dataset for the analysis of the distribution of reviewers and reviews.

Further Data Preparation

After we had obtained the full final dataset described above, we further processed the data to prepare for the analyses of review lengths and the factors that would potentially affect the length of reviews.

For the analyses focusing on review length, first, we removed all data points that had a review length of 50 words or less. This was because these data were considered incomplete or erroneous data. More explanations and discussions will be provided in the Discussion section of this paper. This step excluded 4,374 (5.72%) of the total data points. Secondly, we excluded data points that had a review count of one, because in the process of data cleaning described above, we found many erroneous data among these relatively inexperienced reviewers (or reviewers who have relatively incomplete and erroneous records on Publons). In this step, we deleted 24,437 data points. Our final dataset for the analyses relevant to review lengths contained 47,559 data points.

To further explore the potential factors that would affect the review lengths, we extracted all reviewers who were currently affiliated with an organization in Singapore for further analyses. Singapore has a diverse population with people from diverse cultural backgrounds and economies. We manually collected their gender, title, discipline, country background, and cultural background information. Table 1 presents the coding scheme used in this "Singapore dataset".

Gender is determined by the combination of name classification and the reviewers' online profile photos (on websites including Publons, Google Scholar, LinkedIn, and ResearchGate). Discipline was determined based on the Research Fields of the reviewers on Publons, including two large categories: the humanities and the social sciences were categorized as "Social Science"; the hard sciences were categorized as "Natural Science". Country background and cultural background were determined based on the country where the reviewers completed their undergraduate level education. The reason for this was because although these reviewers were currently affiliated with a research institution in Singapore, they came from different economic and cultural backgrounds. The country background variable was labeled according to the World Bank's classification mentioned in the following section; Cultural background was classified into three categories: Confucianism influenced culture, Christianism influenced culture, and others. The more detailed rationales and interpretations of this classification are provided in the Discussion section.

We obtained 199 reviewers affiliated with Singapore institutes who have sufficient reliable information online for us to label the complete variables listed in Table 1. This process was conducted by two authors. After checking for agreement and further examination, a complete agreement was reached for all reviewers coded in this dataset.

Data Analysis

In the Global State of Peer Review Report (Publons, 2018), countries were categorized into established countries and emerging countries "based on the typical classification of emerging economies" (p17). We adopted a similar approach. We applied the World Bank's latest classification of countries and regions based on income (retrieved from http://databank.worldbank.org/data/download/site-content/CLASS.xls) to label all the countries in our dataset.

Variable	Values
Gender	Male, Female
Discipline	Social Science, Natural Science
Title/Position	Assistant Professor, Associate Professor, Professor, Researchers, Senior Researcher
Country Background	Emerging, Established
Cultural Background	Confucianism, Christianism, Others
h-index	The value collected from the reviewers' Google Scholar homepages
Scopus	The value collected from Scopus by searching for the reviewers' publications

Table 1. Coding scheme of Singapore reviewers.

We performed statistical analyses using Python packages NumPy, SciPy, Pandas, and Regressor. We calculated the descriptive statistics to understand the distribution of reviewers, reviews, as well as the length of reviews. The geographical distribution of reviewers and reviews (sum and average) in different countries were visualized using the Python packages GeoPandas and Matplotlib. Linear Regression was run to explore the effect of English language proficiency on the length of reviews by reviewers from different countries. In our further investigation of the Singapore dataset, we used One-way ANOVA to test if gender, discipline, academic position, economic background, and cultural background are factors that would affect the length of reviews. We additionally performed Kruskal–Wallis tests to confirm the ANOVA results.

RESULTS

Distribution of Reviewers

In our dataset, there are 74,785 unique reviewers who have verified peer review records on Publons. These reviewers are from 70 countries over the world. The descriptive statistics of the number of reviewers by country is presented in Table 2 below, including the minimum, maximum, 1st, 2nd (median), and 3rd quantiles, as well as the standard deviation and skewness. These data are highly skewed, indicating a large number of reviewers are affiliated with research organizations in a small number of countries.

The countries and regions with the top 30 largest numbers of reviewers are shown in Table 3 below. Approximately half of all the reviewers are affiliated with the top five countries in this list.

Min	Q1	Median	Q3	Max	Mean	Sd.	Skewness
2	69.5	342.5	915	16716	1091	2316	4.85

Table 2. Descriptive statistics of the number of reviewers by country.

Rank	Country	No. of reviewers	% of reviewers
1	United States	16716	22.35%
2	United Kingdom	6684	8.94%
3	Australia	5567	7.44%
4	Italy	4318	5.77%
5	China	3857	5.16%
6	Spain	3660	4.89%
7	Canada	3046	4.07%
8	Japan	2699	3.61%
9	Germany	2439	3.26%
10	India	2272	3.04%
11	Brazil	2062	2.76%
12	Turkey	1636	2.19%
13	France	1566	2.09%
14	Iran	1454	1.94%
15	Sweden	1405	1.88%
16	Portugal	1207	1.61%
17	New Zealand	999	1.34%
18	Belgium	924	1.24%
19	Malaysia	888	1.19%
20	South Korea	825	1.10%
21	Switzerland	795	1.06%
22	South Africa	662	0.89%
23	Taiwan	645	0.86%
24	Poland	634	0.85%
25	Mexico	615	0.82%
26	Egypt	594	0.79%
27	Ireland	581	0.78%
28	Norway	562	0.75%
29	Greece	561	0.75%
30	Denmark	538	0.72%

Table 3. Top 30 countries with the largest number of reviewers.

Considering the highly skewed nature of the counts of reviewers in different countries, we calculated the log value of the counts to normalize the data visualized in Figure 1. In this map, the darker color indicates the larger number of reviewers in a country. Countries with higher number of reviewers are mainly concentrated in North America, Western Europe, Australia, and East Asia. The majority of missing data are countries in Africa.

Figure 1. Choropleth map of reviewer distribution by country (log data).

Distribution of Reviews

In our dataset, 464,728 reviews have been verified on Publons. The descriptive statistics are shown in Table 4 below. The most productive reviewer in our dataset has reviewed 2,613 articles. On average, each reviewer has 6.09 verified reviews. The distribution is highly skewed. The median is one review with two verified review records.

Min	Q1	Median	Q3	Max	Mean	Sd.	Skewness
1	1	2	5	2613	6.09	18.79	47.51

Table 4. Descriptive statistics of the number of reviews by country.

After aggregating the counts of reviews by country, we ranked them according to the sum of reviews by reviewers in each country (3rd column). The average number of reviews in each country normalized by the number of reviewers are also included (4th column). The ranking of these values is different from the sum values. Out of the 30 countries in this list, Greece has the highest average number of reviews per reviewer, followed by Switzerland, Austria, and Portugal. However, Syria and Morocco have higher average numbers of reviews per reviewer, which is shown in Figure 3. but not in Table 5.

We calculated the log value of the total number of reviews by country and visualized them in Figure 2. Overall, this map shows a similar pattern to Figure 1. Countries with higher number of reviews are mostly located in North America, Western Europe, Australia, and East Asia.

Further, we mapped the average number of reviewers by country in Figure 3a. In Figure 3b, a different view is displayed. Syria and Morocco are two countries with significantly higher average number of reviews.

Rank	Country	Sum of reviews	Avg.	Median
1	United States	92303	5.52	2
2	United Kingdom	38263	5.72	2
3	Australia	33818	6.07	2
4	Italy	27056	6.27	2
5	Japan	21546	7.98	3
6	Spain	21321	5.83	2
7	Germany	19839	8.13	3
8	Canada	19562	6.42	2
9	China	16452	4.27	2
10	India	13052	5.74	2
11	Brazil	11594	5.62	2
12	France	11412	7.29	3
13	Portugal	10362	8.58	3
14	Sweden	9417	6.70	3
15	Turkey	8147	4.98	2
16	Iran	7702	5.30	2
17	Switzerland	7163	9.01	3
18	New Zealand	6934	6.94	3
19	Greece	6392	11.39	3
20	Belgium	5665	6.13	3
21	Egypt	4550	7.66	3
22	Malaysia	4524	5.09	2
23	Taiwan	4371	6.78	2
24	South Korea	4318	5.23	2
25	Austria	4276	9.00	3
26	Norway	4142	7.37	2
27	Denmark	4045	7.52	3
28	Poland	3688	5.82	2
29	South Africa	3450	5.21	2
30	Mexico	3394	5.51	3

Table 5. Top 30 countries with the largest number of reviews.

Length of Reviews

In this section, we mainly describe our exploration of the effect of language (i.e., English proficiency) on review length. The average length of reviews for each country was calculated. A linear regression was conducted using the EF EPI as the independent variable. A significant regression

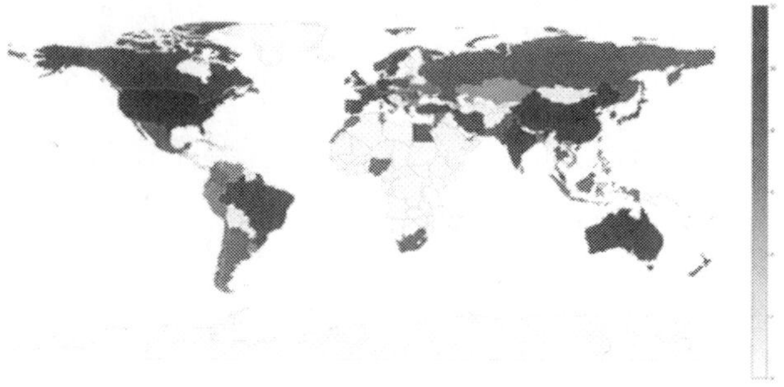

Figure 2. Choropleth map of review distribution (sum) by country (log data).

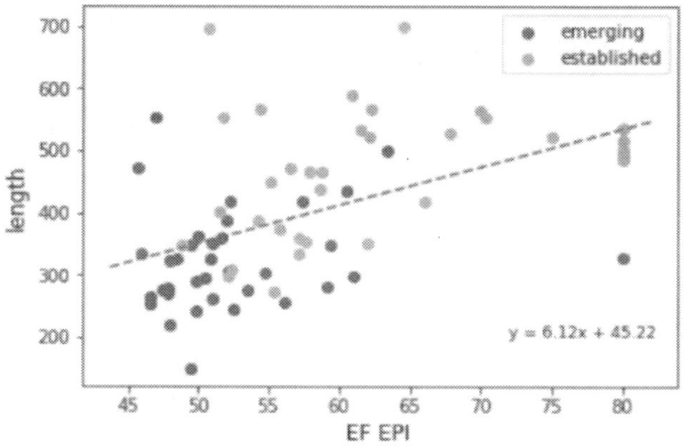

Figure 3b. Choropleth map of review distribution (average) by country (log data).

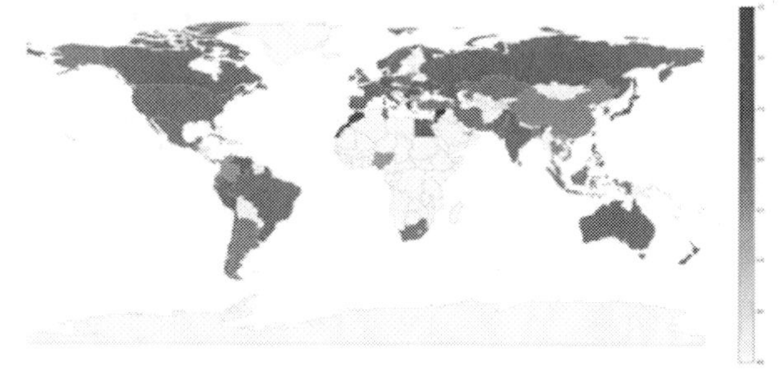

Figure 3a. Choropleth map of review distribution (average) by country (log data).

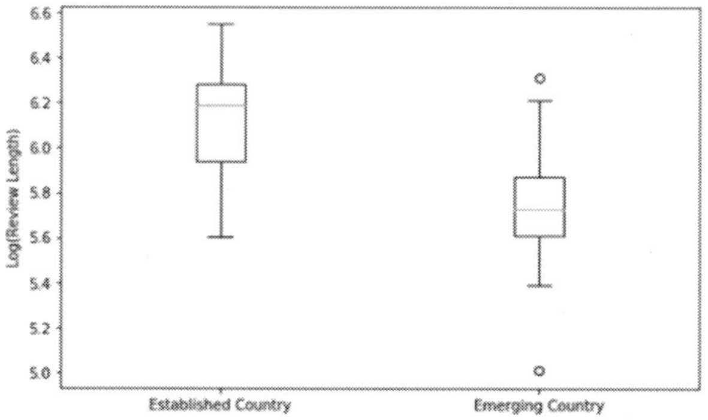

Figure 4. Boxplot of review length data in established and emerging countries.

equation was found (p = .00), with an R^2 of 0.26 and an adjusted R^2 of 0.25. The predicted length of reviews is equal to 45.22 + 6.12 (EF EPI).

According to the classification of World Bank described in the Data Analysis section, 35 countries out of these 70 countries were classified as established countries; The other 35 countries were classified as emerging countries. In Figure 3b, the established countries are labeled as orange dots and the emerging countries are labeled as blue ones.

To test if there existed a statistical difference between these two types of economies, a one-way ANOVA test was conducted to compare the effect of economy types on review length between established countries and emerging countries. After normalizing the length data for reviews, they met the normal distribution assumption (established countries p-value = .51, emerging countries p-value = .24) and the homogeneity of variance assumption (Levene's Test p-value = .91).

There was a significant effect of economy types on review length at the $p < .05$ level (p = .00). Nonparametric comparison also indicated that the mean length for the established countries was significantly different than that in the emerging countries (Kruskal–Wallis test p-value = .00).

Exploration of Factors in Review Length: Further Analyses Based on the Singapore Data

As described in the Data Analysis section, reviewers in Singapore were selected and further coded for our initial exploration of factors other than language that would potentially affect the length of reviews. This resulted in a complete dataset of 199 reviewers affiliated with Singapore organizations. The potential factors that we explored included gender, academic position, discipline, economic background, and cultural background. For each of the comparison, we visualized the different groups of data using boxplots (Figure 6, 8, 10, 12, and 14), and conducted one-way ANOVA tests and Kruskal–Wallis tests where appropriate.

Gender

Among these 199 reviewers affiliated with Singapore organizations, women are significantly underrepresented.

In order to test if there existed a statistical difference between male and female reviewers, a one-way ANOVA test was performed. After normalizing the length data for reviews by male and female reviewers, they met the normal distrbution

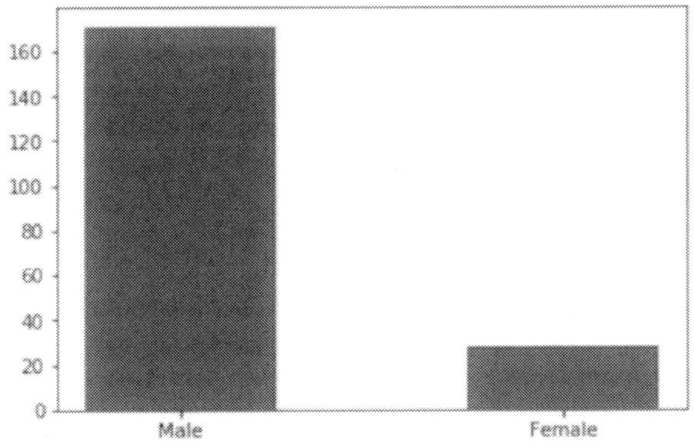

Figure 5. Distribution of gender.

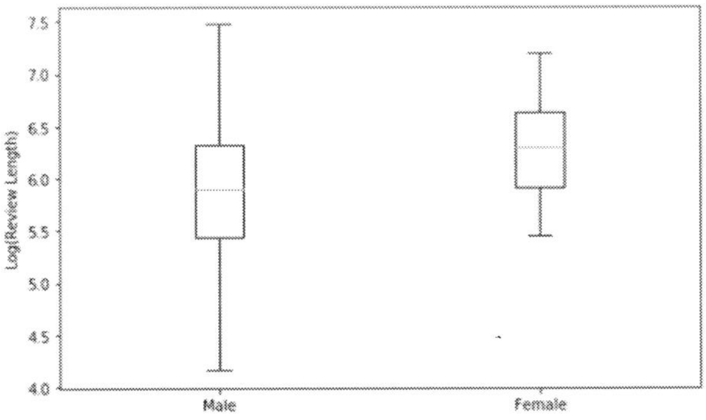

Figure 6. Boxplot of review length data by male and female reviewers in Singapore.

assumption (male p-value = .67, female p-value = .30) and the homogeneity of variance assumption (Levene's Test p-value = .07).

A significant difference was found in the lengths by male and female reviewers (p = .00). In addition, nonparametric comparison also indicated a significant differece (Kruskal–Wallis test p-value = .00).

Academic Position

Among these subgroups of reviewers, Assistant Professors and Associate Professors account for nearly 60% of all the reviewers.

A one-way ANOVA test was conducted to compare the effect of different academic positions on review length. After normalizing the length data for reviews by reviewers in a diverse range of academic positionss, they met the normal distrbution assumption (associate professor p-value = .53, assistant professor p-value = .29, professor p-value = .90, researcher p-value = .77, senior research p-value = .40). The homogeneity of variance assumption was also met (Levene's Test p-value = .34).

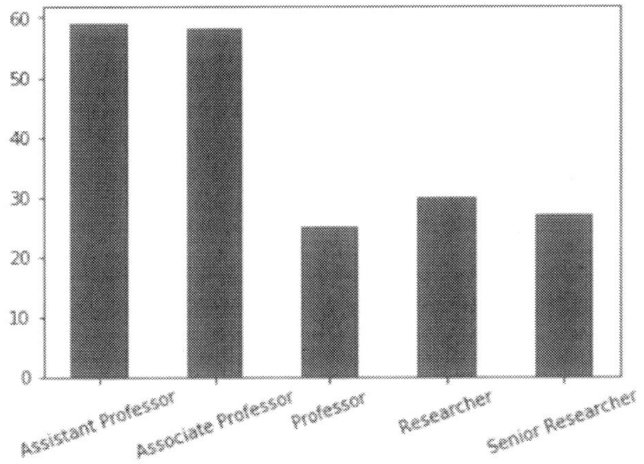

Figure 7. Distribution of academic positions.

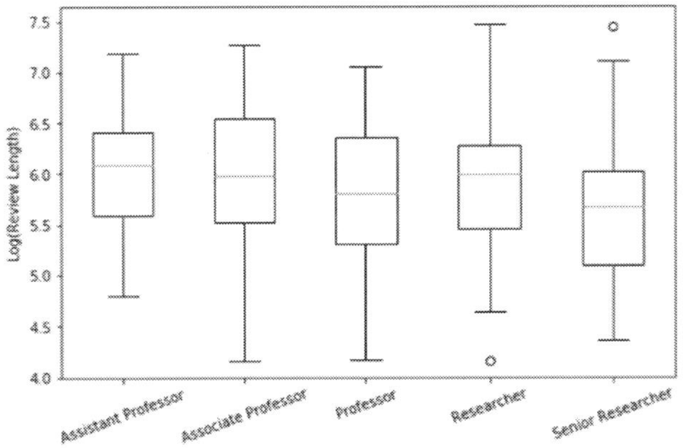

Figure 8. Boxplot of review length data by reviewers in different academic positions in Singapore.

There was no significant difference in the length of reviews by reviewers in different academic positions (p = .31). To confirm this result, we conducted a Kruskal-Wallis test, which indicated the same result (p-value = .19).

Discipline

Compared to reviewers in the natural sciences, i.e., Science, Technology, Engineering and Medical (STEM) disciplines, reviewers in the social sciences and humanities are underrepresented in this subgroup of reviewers.

Similarly, a one-way ANOVA test was conducted to investigate whether there was a difference between the length of reviews written by reviewers in natural science disciplines and the social sciences and humanities. After the length data was normalized, the length of reviews by social sciences and humanities reviewers was not in a normal distribution (p-value = .03), while review length data by natural science reviewers were normally distributed (p-value = .62). Because the normal distribution assumption was violated, we did not

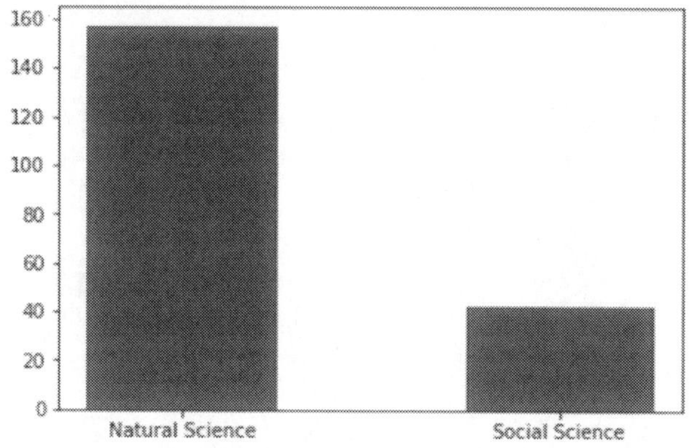

Figure 9. Distribution of disciplines.

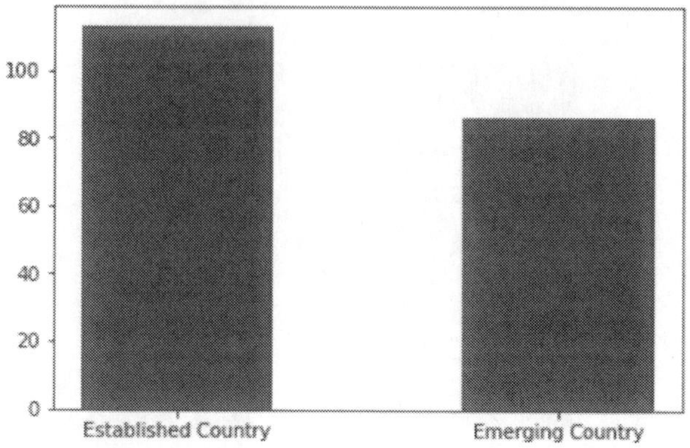

Figure 11. Distribution of economic backgrounds.

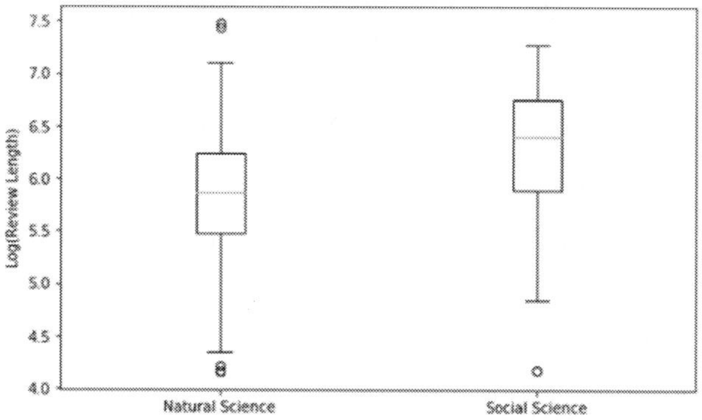

Figure 10. Boxplot of review length data by reviewers in different disciplines in Singapore.

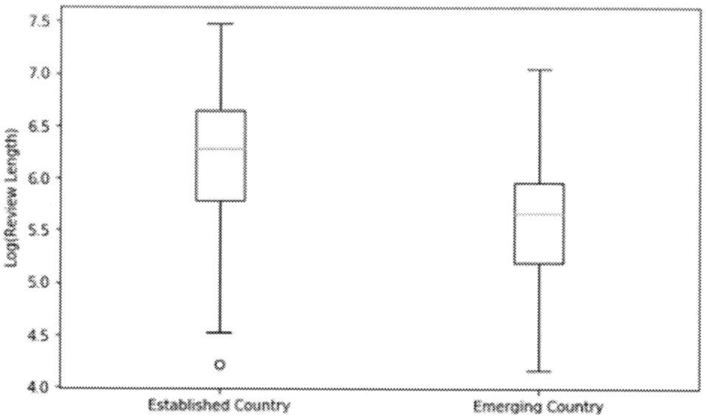

Figure 12. Boxplot of review length data by reviewers with different economic backgrounds in Singapore.

conduct the one-way ANOVA test. Instead, the nonparametric Kruskal–Wallis test p-value was .00, indicating a significant difference between the natural science disciplines and the social sciences and humanities, even if the social sciences and humanities length data were still skewed after being log-transformed. In fact, from the boxplot (Figure 7), it can be seen that a large number of reviews in social sciences and humanities tend to give relatively longer reviews, leading to the skewness.

Economic Background

The difference of review length between different economic backgrounds was then examined. The log data of the review length were normally distributed (established countries p-value = .07, emerging countries p-value = .18). The assumption of homogeneity of variance was met (Levene's Test p-value = .34). The result of the one-way ANOVA test indicated that there was a significant difference in the length of reviews written by reviewers from different economic backgrounds (p-value = .00). Similarly, the Kruskal-Wallis test also indicated a significant difference between these two groups of reviewers (p-value = .00).

Cultural Background

Reviewers from a Confucianism influenced cultural background take up the largest proportion of reviewers in Singapore.

Last, the difference of review lengths provided by reviewers in different cultural backgrounds were investigated. After normalizing the length data, the length of reviews written by reviewers from a Confucianism influenced cultural background and other background met the normal distribution assumption (Confucianism p-value = .44, Others p-value = .08), but the length data of reviewers from a Christianism influenced cultural background (p-value = .04) was not normally distributed. As a result, the nonparametric Kruskal–Wallis test was conducted. The result suggested that reviewers from a Christianism influenced cultural background wrote significantly longer reviews than Confucianism influenced and other cultural backgrounds.

DISCUSSIONS

Interpreting the Factors

In our exploration, we found several potential factors that might affect the length of reviews, including gender,

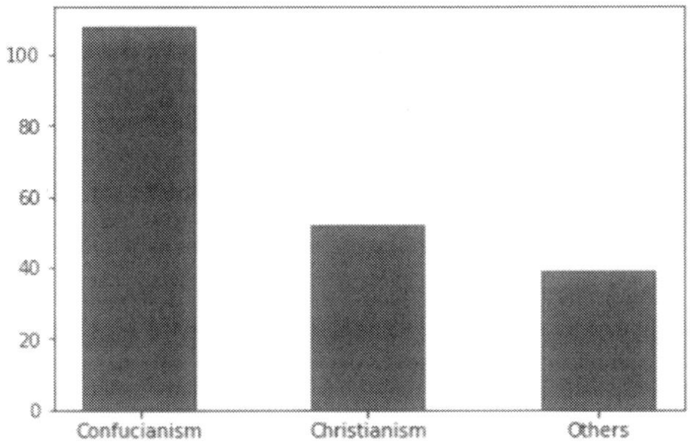

Figure 13. Distribution of cultural backgrounds.

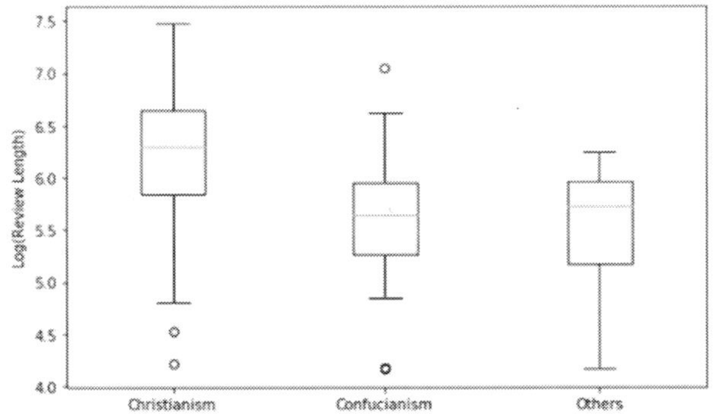

Figure 14. Boxplot of review length data by reviewers with different cultural backgrounds in Singapore.

discipline, English language proficiency, economic development level, and cultural background of a country. Among these factors, the latter three factors are relevant at the country level. They overlap with each other and might have compounding effects on each other. In terms of their effects on the length of reviews, each of these factors may play a role to a different extent that can hardly be measured.

The use of English has always been a complex issue over the world and in history. In Australia, New Zealand, United Kingdom, and United States, English is used as a de facto official language; In some other countries, English is used as a de jure official language. In these countries, English is in some cases the primary language, in some cases only used in official and educational uses, and in some cases used as Lingua Franca. In this Publons dataset, the peer reviews are typically performed for international journals, the majority of which are published in English. As a result, the so-called linguistic imperialism (Phillipson, 1992) phenomenon exists in this context. Considering some countries do not use English as their official languages or commonly used languages, it is likely that reviewers in those countries tend to write less in volume in a language that they are not proficiently familiar with (Hinkel, 2011). Empirical studies have also provided evidence that critical thinking is more difficult in a second language (e.g., Floyd, 2011).

Institutional factors relevant to the national scientific systems and norms should also be taken into consideration in the interpretation of our findings. The form of peer review is a relatively newer practice to researchers in the economically and scientifically emerging countries. For instance, even one decade ago, the main refereeing scheme for many Chinese academic journals was a system called "three-level review," which was carried out mainly by journal editors (Fang, Xu, & Lian, 2008). The three-level review is based on the hierarchy of Chinese publishing houses: the first review is done by the editor, the second review by the head of the editorial department, and the final review by the editor-in-chief of the publishing house (Fang et al., 2008). As a result, researchers who do not serve as editors might be less familiar with peer review guidelines and have less exposure to discussions and trainings about the scientific norms and best practices in the peer review process.

Publons' approach turning peer review into a visible and potentially measurable research output is a relatively new and not well received practice, probably particularly in the scientifically emerging countries where the focus of researcher evaluation is on the output and impact of scientific publications (King, 1987; King, 2004). In contrast, in western countries, it is more widely accepted that academics can use their review and editorial records as evidence of their standing and influence in their field (Bornmann, 2011). For instance, conducting peer review is not counted as research outputs or research impact in the current research evaluation criteria in the majority of Chinese research universities and institutions. This would result in researchers paying less time and effort in reviewing others' works as their time and effort are not recognized and rewarded.

In our hypotheses, culture also plays a role in peer review. For instance, east Asian countries' high-context culture prefers indirect communication over direct communication (Hall, 1976; Kim, Pan, & Park, 1998), which is believed to be contributed by the impact of Confucianism (Yum, 1988). Particularly, in the peer review process, providing criticism for authors involves issues relevant to modesty, politeness, and conflict management. The confrontation-avoiding disposition (Kim et al., 1998) in eastern cultures might lead to a shorter length of criticism.

In this section of discussion, we do not intend to provide speculations about the reasons behind the different lengths of review. Instead, we would like to bring more relevant factors into our horizon so that they will not be ignored in the interpretation of our findings or in future studies on peer review. It is also important to note that in this paper we do not intend to associate the length of reviews with the quality of reviews.

Limitations

There are several limitations in this study. First, the data in this study were collected in April of 2018. Given the increasing number of users and their records, these data need to be updated, potentially with more granularity. Ideally, we also hope to seek a way to confirm the data with Publons in the future. Currently, it is hard to compare our results to the Publons' Peer Review Report (Publons, 2018) due to different time frames.

The second limitation is in the length data and is rooted in the fact that the length data on Publons were calculated based on the review text submitted by reviewers themselves. This submission process was not mandatory. As a result, some reviewers do not submit review text onto Publons; Some reviewers submit the review text for some reviews but not others. In addition, the lack of a clear description about what should be submitted (i.e., the complete review, the first round of review, the last round of review, or the review decision sentence, etc.). This might lead to reviewers submitting different content to Publons. An additional concern about the length data is the ease of gaming. Unlike the review records, which are verified by Publons or the publishers, the actual review text does not need to go through any verification. This might provide an ease of gaming for researchers who would like to boost their review contribution by length data. Currently, the allegedly "average length" of reviews by one reviewer displayed on the Publons website is very likely to be calculated based on the total number of words divided by the total number of reviews that is not null in the "review text" field (instead of the total number of words in the reviews divided by the total number of reviews). We agree that this is the most optimal strategy based on the current constraint, but would like to point out that caution needs to be used when interpreting statistics based on these statistics.

Thirdly, as mentioned in the Methods and Data section, one reviewer might be affiliated with more than one organization. This is due to the difficulty in determining the main affiliation of reviewers. The strategy we adopted to handle this difficulty was that we treated reviewers with multiple affiliations as multiple reviewers. In total, 1,585 out of 76,370 datapoints in our dataset (2.08%) were duplicated reviewers due to multiple affiliations.

Fourthly, the classification of cultures can be improved and supported by more literature investigation. The reason we chose to classify the cultures into the current three categories was because we found the eastern/western classification of countries dichotomous. It is also not enough to simply classify them into for example, cultures that are directly or indirectly critical, or cultures with high or low context in communication (Hall, 1976; Kim et al., 1998). Since Confucianism is more commonly regarded as a social and ethical philosophy rather than a religion, we could not claim that this classification is based on religion either.

Fifthly, the gender information in our data is not self-reported and can be biased. Also, the binary classification is not inclusive enough to represent all genders.

Finally, this dataset is based on Publons data. It is possible that the self-reported review records are incomplete because of inactiveness of users. In addition, it is not clear to what extent can the verification process eliminate gaming. This is an important point when interpreting our data (for instance, 32% of the reviewers had reviewed only one article, and that the most productive reviewer had reviewed 2,613 articles.)

Future Works

In this study, reviewers in Singapore were studied as an initial step. In the future works, we plan to expand this in-depth analysis of the potential factors that would have effects on review length to a larger sample of reviewers from diverse backgrounds. This at the same time will help us better understand the meaning and indication of the length of reviews.

Another future direction of ours is to gain a more in-depth understanding of how Publons is used by scholars and researchers. This work would lay the groundwork for future research studies using Publons data because it is important to better understand if the data collected from Publons are representative of all peer reviewers.

CONCLUSION

Using the verified peer review records of researchers on Publons, this study investigated how this scientific endeavor was divided and distributed over the world. In terms of the absolute number of reviewers and the number of reviews performed, countries in North America, Western Europe, Australia, and East Asia played a primary role in this process. The data of average number of reviews performed by each reviewer in different countries displayed slightly different patterns.

On the global scale, the proficiency of English, the scientific Lingua Franca, was found to have a significant effect on the length of reviews. In addition, there was a significant effect of a country's economic development level on review length.

In our more in-depth explorations of reviewers in Singapore, we found that reviewers in different genders, disciplines, economic and cultural backgrounds wrote reviews of different lengths. Specifically, women, although underrepresented, write longer reviews. Secondly, although underrepresented, reviewers in social sciences and humanities write longer reviews than reviewers in the natural science disciplines. Thirdly, reviewers from economically established countries write longer reviews compared to those from economically emerging countries. Finally, peer reviewers in Western countries, which are countries with Christianism influenced cultures, write longer reviews than countries with Confucianism influenced cultures and other cultures.

To sum up, based on one of the largest sets of data about peer review so far, this study provided important complementary understandings to the Publons' Global State of Peer Review report (Publons, 2018). In addition to the detailed analysis of the global distributions of reviewers and reviews, we also took an initial step toward understanding the length of reviews as a potential indicator of time and effort researchers devote to the process of "scientific gatekeeping". Delving into the exploration of potential factors that would affect the length of peer review provided additional insight into how the endeavor of peer review is being accepted and performed.

ACKNOWLEDGMENTS

The authors would like to thank Dr. Bradley M. Hemminger for his feedback on improving this research. We thank Dr. Yuan Chong for his support in the data analysis process. We gratefully acknowledge the grant from the National Natural Science Foundation of China (71673038) and the Project of Fundamental Research Funds for the Central Universities (DUT18JC32).

REFERENCES

Abelson, P. H. (1980). Scientific communication. *Science, 209*(4452), 60–62.

Armstrong, A. W., Idriss, S. Z., Kimball, A. B., & Bernhard, J. D. (2008). Fate of manuscripts declined by the Journal of the American Academy of Dermatology. *Journal of the American Academy of Dermatology, 58*(4), 632–635.

Borgman, C. L., & Furner, J. (2002). Scholarly communication and bibliometrics. *Annual Review of Information Science and Technology, 36*(1), 2–72.

Bornmann, L. (2011). Scientific peer review. *Annual Review of Information Science and Technology, 45*(1), 197–245.

Ceci, S. J., & Peters, D. P. (1982). Peer review: A study of reliability. *Change: The Magazine of Higher Learning, 14*(6), 44–48.

Chubin, D. E., & Hackett, E. J. (1990). *Peerless science: Peer review and US science policy*. Suny Press.

Crawford, S., & Stucki, L. (1990). Peer review and the changing research record. *Journal of the American Society for Information Science, 41*(3), 223–228.

Ernst, E., Saradeth, T., & Resch, K. L. (1993). Drawbacks of peer review. *Nature, 363*(6427), 296.

Eysenck, H. J., & Eysenck, S. B. (1992). Peer review: Advice to referees and contributors. *Personality and Individual Differences*.

Fang, Q., Xu, L., & Lian, X. (2008). Peer-review practice and research for academic journals in China. *Journal of Scholarly Publishing, 39*(4), 417–427.

Floyd, C. B. (2011). Critical thinking in a second language. *Higher Education Research & Development, 30*(3), 289–302.

Goodman, S. N., Berlin, J., Fletcher, S. W., & Fletcher, R. H. (1994). Manuscript quality before and after peer review and editing at Annals of Internal Medicine. *Annals of Internal Medicine, 121*(1), 11–21.

Hall, E. T. (1976). *Beyond culture*. NY: *Dobleday & Company*.

Hinkel, E. (2011). What research on second language writing tells us and what it doesn't. In *Handbook of research in second language teaching and learning* (Vol. 2, pp. 523–538).

Kim, D., Pan, Y., & Park, H. S. (1998). High-versus low-context culture: A comparison of Chinese, Korean, and American cultures. *Psychology & Marketing, 15*(6), 507–521.

King, D. A. (2004). The scientific impact of nations. *Nature, 430*(6997), 311.

King, J. (1987). A review of bibliometric and other science indicators and their role in research evaluation. *Journal of information science, 13*(5), 261–276.

Mulligan, A., Hall, L., & Raphael, E. (2013). Peer review in a changing world: An international study measuring the attitudes of researchers. *Journal of the American Society for Information Science and Technology, 64*(1), 132–161.

Phillipson, R. (1992). Linguistic imperialism. *The Encyclopedia of Applied Linguistics*, 1–7.

Publons. (2018). *2018 Global state of peer review by Publons*. Retrieved from https://publons.com/static/Publons-Global-State-Of-Peer-Review-2018.pdf

Rowland, F. (2002). The peer-review process. *Learned publishing, 15*(4), 247–258.

Shatz, D. (2004). *Peer review: A critical inquiry*. Rowman & Littlefield.

Yum, J. O. (1988). The impact of Confucianism on interpersonal relationships and communication patterns in East Asia. *Communications Monographs, 55*(4), 374–388.

Performance of Citations and Altmetrics in the Social Sciences and Humanities

Siluo Yang
School of Information Management, Wuhan University, Wuhan, China
58605025@qq.com

Mengxue Zheng
School of Information Management, Wuhan University, Wuhan, China
1984367517@qq.com

ABSTRACT

It has always been argued that social sciences and humanities (SSH) impact evaluation calls for a broader range of indicators than only bibliometric indicators. This study analyzes the performance of scientific SSH publications using 1,327,924 records from the Social Sciences Citation Index (SSCI) and the Arts & Humanities Citation Index (A&HCI), and 629,586 records from Altmetric.com. The research covers a period of 5 years (2013–2017); three publication types (articles, reviews, and proceedings papers); four selected subject fields; three citation indicators; and 13 altmetric indicators. The comparative analysis of SSH performance is studied in both citation and altmetric pattern, and an attempt is made to interpret the results in both the metric and discipline contexts. Major contributions of this study include the extension of analysis methods for the SSH, as well as the validation of altmetric indicators.

KEYWORDS

Altmetrics; Citations; The Social Sciences and Humanities

ASIS&T THESAURUS

Altmetrics; Bibliometrics; Social Sciences

INTRODUCTION

Due to its objectivity, fairness, speed, and high efficiency, citation analysis has long been regarded as the primary method of research evaluation (Yang & Han, 2015). However, it has been proposed that citation analysis does not reflect knowledge dissemination adequately (Chen, Tang, Wang, & Hsiang, 2015). Since the channels of publication in the social sciences and humanities (SSH) are more diverse, using bibliometric analysis to evaluate academic performance in the SSH has proven to be more problematic than in natural sciences (Nederhof, Zwaan, De Bruin, & Dekker, 1988). Bibliometric analysis must be adapted to the peculiarities of SSH (Zhou et al., 2009). To evaluate SSH research performance, the same bibliometric methods can be applied as in the natural sciences, but a broader range of both publications and indicators is needed on the social sciences and humanities side (Nederhof, 2006). Evaluation indexes and methods need improvement, and the academic community is in consensus that, except for the number of publications and citations, scholarly evaluation should involve a multisource and multidimensional approach (Moed & Halevi, 2015).

Altmetrics—also called social web metrics—were first proposed in 2010 (Priem, Taraborelli, Groth, & Neylon, 2010), and have been regarded as the next generation of impact measurement in the new social media environment. Altmetric indexes refer to mentions, shares, and readers of academic outputs on social web platforms including Facebook, Google+, YouTube, blogs, etc. The purpose of altmetrics is to complete the impact metrics of both traditional and web-based analysis, as well as to give new insight into impact evaluation (Galligan & Dyas-Correia, 2013). The fact that SSH publications show a higher presence of altmetrics than their natural sciences counterparts (Costas, Zahedi, & Wouters, 2015) is confirmed. As the influence of SSH research outputs often exerts through non-academic-oriented platforms (such as Twitter, etc.), and the audiences for SSH scholars are extensive in society and the social network media, a close relationship exists between the SSH and altmetrics (Chen et al., 2015).

In this study, we evaluate and compare the performance of SSH publications by using citations and altmetrics. Compared with previous research, we use updated and large-scale data, aiming to reflect the current overall situation, considering the particularity of SSH, and evaluating the performance in the perspective of the field. These topics cover:

1. the evolution of publication output in the SSH;
2. a comparative citation analysis of SSH publications based on selected fields in 2013–2017;
3. a comparative altmetric analysis of SSH publications based on selected fields in 2013–2017;
4. the correlations between the indexes of citations and altmetrics in the SSH in 2013–2017.

82nd Annual Meeting of the Association for Information Science & Technology | Melbourne, Australia | 19–23 October, 2019

DOI: 10.1002/pra2.00069

RELATED STUDIES

Measure of Publications Impact

Evaluating the impact of academic publications has become a basis of necessary research for bibliometrics scholars, scientific institutions, scholarly journals, and countries (Cronin & Sugimoto, 2014). Citing other work is a natural part of scholarly writing, described by Yang and Han (2015) as the "on the shoulders of giants" phenomenon, so citation analysis plays a significant role in impact evaluation of academic publications; as such, citation indicators have received a lot of attention in bibliometrics (Waltman, 2016). Albarrán, Ortuño, and Ruiz-Castillo (2011) proposed a novel methodology for comparing the citation distribution of research units working in the same homogeneous field to rank the scientific performance of articles from around the world comprehensively, using a high- and a low-impact measure with citations. Bar-Illan (2012) suggested that scholars have been increasingly visible on the web, and they simply measured the social web impact of scholars and correlations between that impact and citation counts. Cronin and Sugimoto (2014) stated that the web has provided new data to measure scholarly performance, and that bibliometrics has been transformed from mere tracking of citations.

Social media platforms have been regarded as potential sources to evaluate scientific and social impacts, and altmetrics was proposed in 2010 as a new evaluation method under the social media environment (Costas et al., 2015; Sugimoto, Work, Larivière, & Haustein, 2017). According to Adie and Roe (2013), altmetrics is a generalization of article-level metrics, including quantitative or qualitative indicators of the impact that a single article has had, emphasizing the social aspect of altmetric data. Adie (2014) discussed the reasons to use altmetrics to measure the impact that a publication has on society. Sugimoto et al. (2017) argued that the adoption of altmetrics is more than a simple fad, and that the digitization of scholarly communication and tools allows for broader discussion outside the scientific community. Costas et al. (2015) confirmed that while the potential of altmetrics to replace traditional citation analysis is not very strong, altmetric indicators represent an interesting complement to traditional citations.

Similarities and Differences in the Evaluation of Natural Sciences and SSH

The quantitative evaluation of SSH and the investigation of the existing similarities between SSH and natural sciences represent the forefront of scientometrics research (Bonaccorsi, Daraio, & Fantoni, 2017). To evaluate SSH research performance, the same bibliometric methods can be applied as in the natural sciences, but a broader range of both publications and indicators is needed on the social sciences and humanities side (Nederhof, 2006). Bonaccorsi et al. (2017) tested a quantitative evaluation of SSH with scientific data produced by Italian academics between 2002 and 2012, and suggested that the quantitative evaluation method for natural sciences could also be applied in the SSH.

Hicks (1999) examined the main problematic factors in social bibliometrics, and confirmed them to be rooted in the national orientation in the SSH, and the centrality of books and their high citation rates. Archambault, Vignola-Gagné, Côté, Larivière, and Gingras (2006) pointed out that Thomson Scientific databases had a bias of English-language journals in the SSH, so it could not be used in isolation to evaluate output in the SSH. Zhou, Thijs, and Glänzel (2008) agreed with that English-language bias and suggested that bibliometric methods originally designed to analyze basic research in the natural sciences must be adapted to the particularities of the social sciences. Chen et al. (2015) explored alternative scholarly performance metrics in the SSH in Taiwan in an effort to better reflect SSH impact, and found that a closer relationship with altmetrics exists in the SSH than in the natural sciences. Similarly, Zahedi et al. (2013) and Costas et al. (2015) found that SSH publications exhibit higher altmetric activity than natural sciences publications.

Correlations between Altmetrics and Citations

Investigations such as Mohammadi et al. (2016) focused on measuring the correlations between citation and altmetrics in the SSH, and validated the new metrics partially.

Xia, Su, Wang, Zhang, and Ning (2016) presented a bibliographic analysis of *Nature* articles based on Twitter and Facebook altmetrics data, finding that tweets and citations were at least somewhat related. Zahedi, Costas, and Wouters (2014) found a moderate Spearman correlation ($r = 0.49$) between Mendeley readership counts and citations over the 19,772 Web of Science (WoS) publications published between 2005 and 2011.

Liu, Xu, Wu, and Chen (2013) confirmed that altmetric indicators complement—and most correlate significantly with—traditional citations, and suggested the consideration of active altmetrics and citations in future evaluations of the social impact of articles. Costas et al. (2015) studied the correlations between altmetric indicators and citations from a multidisciplinary perspective, and found that publications from the social sciences, humanities, and the medical and life sciences showed the highest presence of altmetrics. The analysis confirmed the positive correlations between altmetrics and citations. It also suggested that altmetric indicators could represent a complement to citations especially in SSH because these fields had a higher presence of altmetrics. However, Ortega (2015) found the correlations between altmetric and bibliometric indicators across academic social sites were poor, and this study also proposed that altmetrics could not be a proxy for research evaluation, but for the social impact of science.

In reviewing these related studies, it is clear that the application of traditional citations and new altmetrics in evaluation has been at the forefront of informetrics research (Bar-Illan, 2012; Sugimoto et al., 2017; Yang & Han, 2015). The academic community has been working to improve and complement analysis methods for SSH evaluation in the context of bibliometric methods originally designed for the analysis of natural sciences (Bonaccorsi et al., 2017; Nederhof, 2006; Zhou et al., 2008), with altmetrics—which have been proven to have a close relationship with SSH (Chen et al., 2015; Zahedi et al., 2013)—studied in particular. A mass of investigations have focused on measuring correlations between citations and altmetrics for the purpose of validating the new metrics (Costas et al., 2015; Liu et al., 2013; Ortega, 2015). Yet some conclusions are contradictory, and even the latest, larger data samples offer a lack of reliable conclusions. Thus, by using a mixed analysis of updated and large-scale SSH publication data to identify SSH's internal field difference, this paper aims to extend SSH analysis methods, as well as to validate altmetric indicators.

DATA AND METHOD

Data sources

We collected two sets of data. The first set is based on data from the Social Sciences Citation Index (SSCI) and the Arts & Humanities Citation Index (A&HCI) of Clarivate Analytics' Web of Science (WoS). The second set are publication records with altmetric indicators provided by Altmetric.com (http://www.altmetric.com/).

The WoS core collection has strict standards for the selection, evaluation, development, and management of journals, containing more than 18,000 globally authoritative and influential academic journals. The SSCI of WoS fully indexes more than 3,408 journals across 58 categories divided by the Institute for Scientific Information (ISI). The A&HCI of WoS fully indexes more than 1,829 journals across 28 ISI categories.

Altmetric.com is a website that collects and collates a vast amount of research output online and provides scholars with "a single visually engaging and informative view of the online activity surrounding … scholarly content" ("What does Altmetric do?" 2019). Altmetric.com offers an open application programming interface (API) that enables efficient downloading and makes it possible to collect large-scale altmetric indicator data.

The followings should be kept in mind while using the SSCI and the A&HCI data:

Social sciences and humanities are national oriented. Social sciences are oriented to the social surroundings which they study, including the political system, environment and so on. Humanities are related to history, language and culture that a social developed. Sometimes the concepts of SSH publications are difficult to translate or understand because it may require a piece of local knowledge, SSH scientists prefer to write in the original language (Hicks, 1999; Kyvik, 1988).

Differences exist between the social sciences and the humanities. Though compared to natural sciences, the social sciences and the humanities are both more affected by domestic conditions, the social sciences have a much stronger international impact while the domestic character of the humanities is much stronger (Chen et al., 2015).

The channels of SSH publication are more diverse. Compared to natural and life sciences, SSH publications are published in more types (Bourke, Butler, & Bigllal, 1996). And SSH relied much heavier on non-journal literature such as monographs (Chen, 2015; Hicks, 1999). However, Bonaccorsi (2017) shows that remarkable differences in the microstructure of scientific communication do not translate into different total statistical properties.

Data Processing

As shown in Figure 1, first, we downloaded a data set of SSCI and A&HCI articles from WoS in January 2019, using search string "PY = 2013-2017 AND DT= (Article OR Review OR Proceedings paper"; this search yielded a set of 1,327,924 records containing the three publication types for the 5-year period.

Second, we obtained the altmetric data from Altmetric.com by digital object unique identifier (DOI) search using API, which yielded 629,586 records.

Third, the data set of SSCI and A&HCI were matched to four main fields comprising four categories—Economics & business administration (E&B), Social, political & communication science (S,P&C), Psychology, and Humanities & Art (H&A)—with 67 subject categories (see the Appendix). This selection was based on the Global Institutional Profile Project (GIPP)-WoS subject map and the experience of SSH bibliometric application (Zhou et al., 2008).

Finally, the data set of Altmetric.com was matched to the data set of SSCI and A&HCI using the function formula "VLOOKUP" in Microsoft Excel, referring to DOI. Duplicates were removed, and a full-counting scheme was applied (i.e., a full count was recorded whenever a publication occurred in the text).

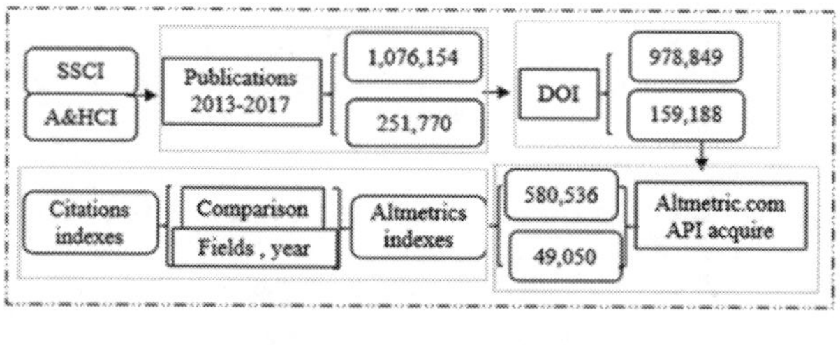

Figure 1. Data processing.

Citation and Altmetric Indicators

For all the publications finally selected, we calculated a series of citation and altmetric indicators. The citation indicators were calculated following the approach introduced by Glanzel, Debackere, and Meyer (2008) and considering a 2-year citation window. The altmetric indicators are provided by Altmetric.com.

The following citation indicators are calculated:

- Mean Observed Citation Rate (MOCR). MOCR means the ratio of citation count to publication count (Braun, Glanzel, & Schubert, 1985).
- Field-Expected Citation Rate (FECR) which expresses one expected citation rate of the corresponding fields. The expected citation rate of a paper equals the mean citation rate of all papers published in the same journal in the same year. FECR is calculated in the same manner as mean expected citation rate, but instead of journal citation rate, the average influence of corresponding fields is used. (Glanzel et al., 2008; Zhou et al., 2008).
- Normalized Mean Citation Rate (NMCR), which is a relative citation rate. NMCR = MOCR/FECR, NMCR has been used in the research of national publication strategy (Braun & Glanzel, 1996).

The altmetric indicators obtained through Altmetric.com and their details are following:

- cited_by_fbwalls_count. The count of the pages that have shared on Facebook.
- cited_by_feeds_count. The count of blogs that have mentioned the publication.
- cited_by_gplus_count. The count of the accounts that have shared on Google+.
- cited_by_msm_count. The count of the news sources that have mentioned the publication.
- cited_by_posts_count. A "post" is any online document that links to one or more research objects (i.e. a post is a mention or a group of mentions). This field contains the number of distinct posts that include one or more mentions of the research object in question (The Altmetric Details, 2019).
- cited_by_rdts_count. The number of Reddit threads posted about this publication.
- cited_by_tweeters_count. The number of the twitter accounts that have tweeted this publication.
- cited_by_videos_count. The number of the Youtube/ Vimeo channels that have tweeted this publication.
- cited_by_accounts_count. The sum of all "cited_by" entries (profiles per data source).
- Score. Current Altmetric score, which means a weighted count of all of the attention a research output has received and it is automated calculated by the algorithm. (How is, 2019).
- Mendeley. Readers in Mendeley.
- Connotea. Readers in Connotea.
- readers_count. Total Reader Counts.

Statistics

Spearman correlation analysis detects the linear correlation between ordered variables, suitable to non-normal distributions, when the type of distributions is frequent in large social network data (Ortega, 2015). If the correlation between the two variables is strong, the absolute value of the Spearman coefficient tends to be 1. In this case, this analysis allows to find statistical correlations between the indicators of citation and Altmetric (Bornmann & Leydesdorff, 2013; Zahedi et al., 2014).

RESULTS

Publication Output of the Selected Fields in SSH

The publication output of the subject field indicates the cumulation and dissemination of knowledge. Figure 2 depicts the slow but steady growth of publication output of all selected fields in the period 2013–2017, which, of course, led to the growth of SSH publication output.

However, the gaps among the number of publications across different fields did not decrease. The reasons are not only the different publication amount bases but also the different growth rates. The number of publications in the S,P&C category, which has the maximum base, increased by 16% from 2013 to 2017. And the number of publications in H&A, which has a minimum base, only increased by 15% from 2013 to 2017. Overall, the fastest-growing field of output is Psychology. It is reasonable to assume that S,P&C's leader position would maintain for a long period.

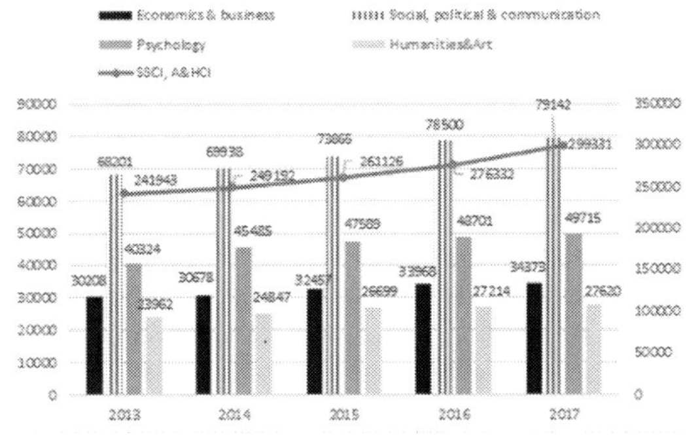

Figure 2. Evolution of publication output in SSH and selected fields in terms of publication years.

Traditional Citations

It is desirable for a scientific paper to include citation behavior. The practice of citing other work is almost second nature to anyone writing a scholarly or scientific paper because of the cumulative nature of science; Isaac Newton famously phrased this scenario as "on the shoulders of giants" (Yang & Han, 2015).

Table 1 presents the normalized mean citation rate (NMCR) values of the selected fields as well as the field expected citation rate (FECR) for the 2013–2017 period. First, the value of FECR, which equals the mean citation rate of all SSH publications for that year, predictably declined over time, because of the cumulative effect of citations (Leeuwen, 2006). Second, Psychology and E&B consistently showed relatively higher citation impact than the neutral value of 1.0 for the period 2013–2017, which indicates a higher-than-average citation rate than excepted. Third, Psychology ranks first and H&A ranks last according to the NMCR, suggesting that Psychology publications have more impact than H&A publications. This result could be explained by disciplinary differences that exist between the humanities and social sciences (Chen et al., 2015)—compared with humanities, social sciences tend to attract more attention by nature.

Year	E&B	S, P&C	Psycol -ogy	H&A	FECR
2013	1.17	0.98	1.32	0.30	12.23
2014	1.14	0.97	1.34	0.29	9.18
2015	1.15	0.99	1.32	0.28	6.39
2016	1.15	0.98	1.33	0.27	3.87
2017	1.12	1.00	1.32	0.29	1.81
All	1.16	0.98	1.32	0.29	6.48

Table 1. The NMCR of the selected fields and the FECR in different years.

Figures 3 and 4 demonstrate the citation distributions in the top 10 and top 100 publications in different disciplines in SSH according to the four selected fields. The share of top publications differed among the four fields in the 5-year period. First, Psychology had a relatively high share of top publications because of its size effect. Combining the higher-than-average citation rate in Psychology publications, it could be concluded that Psychology publications exert a significant influence. Second, the share of H&A publications was the lowest, perhaps because of the low publication output and the unique character of the humanities. However, there are three Humanities publications with very high citations, and one publication even got the highest number of citations—1,989—in 2013. Third, although the number of Psychology publications was always larger than that of S,P&C, the share of S,P&C was greater than or equal to that of Psychology both in the top 10 and the top 100. This result indicates the great influence of some publications in S,P&C, though many low-impact publications exist, referring to NMCR.

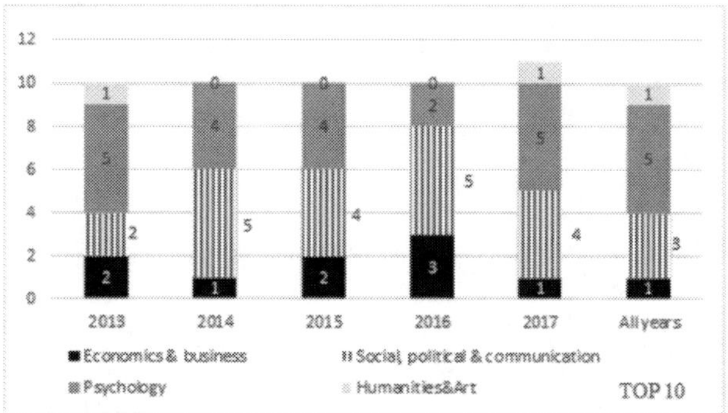

Figure 3. Distribution of citation top 10 publications in different disciplines in SSH.

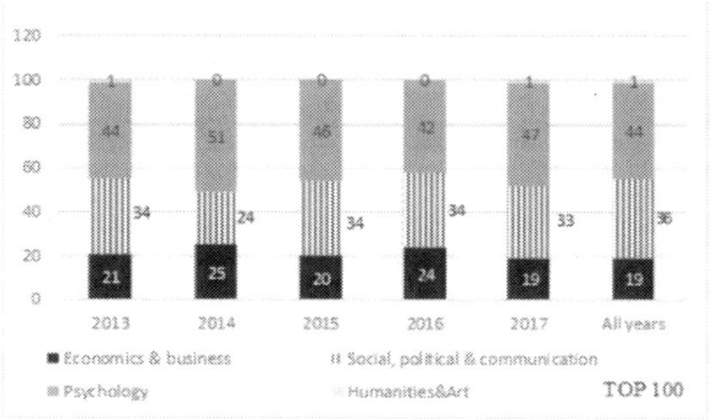

Figure 4. Distribution of citation top 100 publications in different disciplines in SSH.

Altmetric Impact

Presence of Altmetrics

As illustrated in Table 2, the coverage of SSH publications based on the SSCI and the A&HCI publications (2013–2017) reveals that 55.32% of the publications with DOI have altmetric data. 48.94% of these publications with DOI were mentioned on Twitter, followed by Facebook (14.81%), blogs (6.55%), news (6.4%), and Google+ (2.4%). The high Twitter share is consistent with the previous test (i.e., Costas et al., 2017). However, 85.7% of the articles in the collected data set did not use a DOI (1,138,037 out of 1,327,924) and could be mapped with altmetrics; a missing DOI is an inevitable limitation of altmetric studies. Concerning the large amount of data collected and the circumstances of aggregation, just 47.41% (n = 609,399) could be mapped to altmetric data, and the previous result that the publications from the SSH show a much higher presence of altmetrics than those from natural sciences (Costas et al., 2017) is evident. It is possible to conclude, regarding low presence of altmetrics, that altmetrics are not suitable to replace traditional citation analysis. Furthermore, it would be interesting to investigate whether natural science journals behave differently than SSH journals in terms of altmetrics, which we will examine in-depth soon.

Descriptive statistics including coverage rate, mean, and maximum and standard deviation are calculated for all 13 altmetric indexes for selected fields, Table 3 demonstrates a part. As the values of "cited_by_videos_count," "mendeley," and "connottea" are all 0.0 in this research (possibly the result of a server problem), these three indicators are not shown in this study. These statistics denote the amount of attention that a publication has received in each corresponding index (Yang, Xing, & Wolfram, 2018).

Here, coverage rate is defined as the percentage of publications with at least one mention on a given platform (Sugimoto et al., 2017). Score—an automatically calculated indicator given by Altmetric.com, which weights the count of the attention a publication has received—covered all SSH publications included in Altmetric.com. The coverage rates of "cited_by_posts_count," "readers_count," and "cited_by_tweeters_count" were also high, while those of nine others were low, possibly because different social web tools are popular in different contexts and have distinct characters. Besides, disciplinary differences exist in the use of the various platforms, and we have seen evidence that the populations in some academic social sites are thematically not homogeneous (Ortega, 2015). Additionally, it could be concluded that Psychology had better coverage performance than other fields mostly in terms of indexes, while E&B and H&A performed in reverse.

The mean value of mostly altmetric indexes varied significantly in different disciplines. In this study, the mean value was calculated as the ratio of mention count to publication, with at least one mention count. First, the mean values of "readers_count" were obviously higher than other indexes, logically because reading is one of the most basic links of knowledge dissemination. Second, the performance of mean value within the same field differed across altmetric indexes, perhaps because of the peculiarity of the index; further study is needed for to identify more specific causation. Finally, the mean value of reader counts in E&B was largest, showing the significant attention people paid to this field. What is interesting is that blog mentions of H&A publications were much higher than those of other SSH fields. This finding is likely due to blogs' suitability for expressing appreciation of H&A outputs on social media networks.

Maximum values show the most attention given to publications in a specific manner and subject field. The maximum values of different altmetric indexes showed significant differences. First, the altmetric indexes "readers_count," "cited_by_posts_count," and "cited_by_tweeters_count" had larger maximum values than other altmetric indexes, suggesting the significant academic influence of Twitter and online documents that link to research projects, which is consistent with previous studies (e.g., Bornmann, 2014). Second, S,P&C had the largest maximum values in mostly altmetric indexes, which indicates that publications in this field of SSH have received the most social web attention in the 2013–2017 period. Finally, the maximum values of H&A were less than other fields, combining coverage rates and mean values. It could be pointed out that H&A publications exert less impact than publications in other SSH fields, which could be affected by size, and the fact that the channels of H&A output seldom rely on journals (Nederhof et al., 1988).

Standard deviation is a statistic that reflects degree of dispersion. Each field had the largest standard deviation in "readers_count"—E&B at 143.74, S,P&C at 105.33, Psychology at 74.39, and H&A at 35.40. these results show that discretization existed in each field, as the publications received such different attention in the corresponding subject fields.

Year	All pub.	Pub. with DOI	Pub. with altmetrics (/DOI) (/All pub.)	Facebook	Blogs	Google+	News	Reddit	Twitter
2013-2017	1,327,924	1,138,037	609,399 (55.32%) (47.41%)	168,565 (14.81%) (12.69%)	74,521 (6.55%) (5.61%)	27,256 (2.4%) (2.05%)	72,806 (6.4%) (5.48%)	10,121 (0.89%) (0.76%)	556,959 (48.94%) (41.94%)

Table 2. Presence and density of altmetrics for the SSH publications in the SSCI and A&HCI (2013-2017).

Index	Coverage rate				Mean				Maximum			
	E&B	S, P&C	Psyc-	H&A	E&B	S, P&C	Psyc-	H& A	E&B	S, P&C	Psyc-	H&A
fbwalls	0.18	0.25	0.29	0.24	1.34	1.51	1.89	1.48	150	289	233	134
feeds	0.12	0.13	0.13	0.09	1.41	0.15	1.78	12.6	20	42	51	21
gplus	0.02	0.04	0.05	0.03	1.51	1.33	1.84	1.28	79	60	102	34
msm	0.1	0.1	0.13	0.04	3.64	4.48	5.96	3.01	111	228	257	92
posts	1	1	1	1	7.27	10.0	0.77	6.30	9739	25734	11039	5671
rdts	0.01	0.01	0.02	0.01	1.39	1.25	1.40	1.30	15	40	17	9
tweeters	0.88	0.91	0.91	0.88	5.79	7.72	8.24	5.24	8005	19907	10404	4543
videos	0.0	0.0	0.01	0.0	1.20	1.24	1.24	1.06	17	17	8	3
score	1	1	1	1	8.25	9.94	12.9	1	6403	6403	3575	1577
reader	0.99	0.99	1	0.93	59.61	39.07	49.57	18.1	13990	39803	12999	4613

Note. All indexes come from Altmetrics.com, and their values are the number of every indexes. Some values of indexes are 0.0 which represent they are less than 0.05 (rounding) and not equal to 0.

Table 3. Descriptive statistics of altmetric indexes.

Altmetric Score vs. Mean Citation Rate

Altmetric score, as mentioned above, means a weighted count of all the attention a research output has received, calculated by an algorithm (Altmetrics, 2019). Altmetric scores could have some added value for the analysis of humanities and social sciences (Costas et al., 2015).

Figure 5 shows the mean altmetric score and mean citation rate of SSH publications in different years and discipline fields; only publications with altmetric data are calculated in this comparison. First, the altmetric score in all selected fields presented a growth trend in various years. The altmetric score increased over time, and it is possible to conclude that altmetrics are valid for more recent publications (Costas et al., 2015). The cumulative effect did not influence the performance of altmetrics, but did influence the performance of citations, as the incidences of mean citations declined when looking at more recent publications. Second, the mean value of altmetric score and citation both varied visibly by subject field. Psychology had the highest mean altmetric score value, while H&A had the lowest; Psychology and E&B had the largest mean citation values, while H&A had the lowest. This phenomenon shows that the subject fields of SSH behave rather consistently between citations and altmetrics. It also contradicts what we already know about the performance of hard science (Bonaccorsi et al., 2017). To speculate, although citation is more scholarly whereas altmetric score is more multidimensional, SSH scholars and students use research-oriented social media more than those in the hard sciences. In other words, non-experimental disciplines favor discussion in forums and seminars to a greater extent than experimental disciplines (Liu, Hu, Tang, & Wang, 2015; Ortega, 2015).

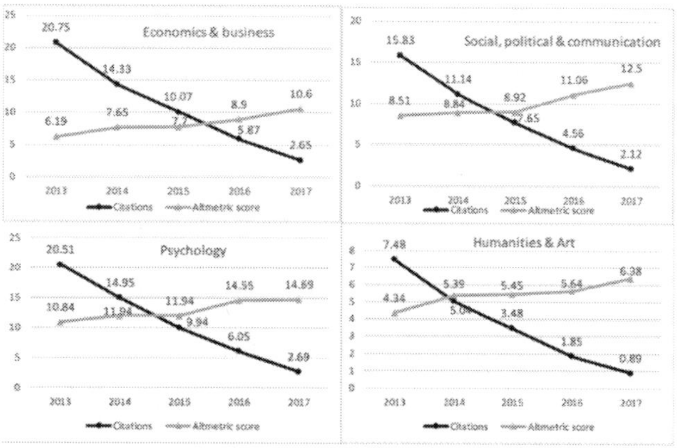

Figure 5. Mean altmetric score vs. MOCR in different disciplines in SSH.

Cumulative Distribution of Altmetric Score and Citation

Figure 6 demonstrates the cumulative distribution of citations and altmetric scores in SSH publications in 2013–2017. The Y-axis represents the values of corresponding metrics, and the X-axis represents the cumulative number of publications that had bigger values than the corresponding Y-value. The logarithmic transformation ln (x) was used for both metric counts and publication counts (Thelwall & Wilson, 2014).

It was found that the cumulative distribution trends of citation and altmetric score were visibly similar in each selected field. However, referring to the upper region of curves, the performance of citation and altmetric score was subtly different, especially in E&B and H&A, since the upper region of one curve is more inclined than the other one. Second, the number of highest H&A citations was quite fragmented compared with those of other fields, as was the number of highest E&B altmetric scores. These phenomena may partly be an effect of the specific distribution over the disciplines, which will be a focus of future research (Leydesdorff & Felt, 2012). Third, the difference performance of citation and altmetric score may indicate that altmetrics is more valid for the H&A discipline because of the huge gap seen in Figure 6. What's more, the similar trends in citation and altmetric score performance indicates consistency in their evaluation results, albeit with subtle differences, which seems to suggest that the altmetric indicators could represent a complement to citation in SSH.

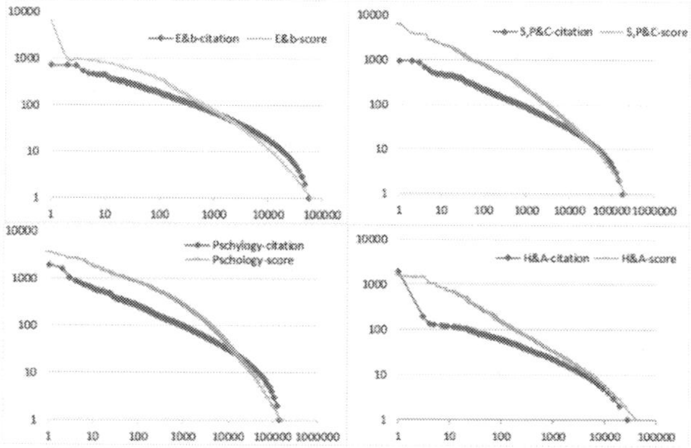

Figure 6. Cumulative distribution of citation and altmetric score of selected fields in SSH in 2013-2017 on log–log scale.

Correlation between the Indexes of Citations and Altmetrics

As mentioned above, SSH subject fields performed rather consistently in terms of citation and altmetric scores. Here, we analyze the correlations between citation and altmetrics indexes in SSH. Spearman correlation analysis is more suitable than Pearson correlation analysis, due to the data distribution of SSH publications (Bornmann & Leydesdorff, 2013; Zahedi et al., 2014). According to the coverage rate, 10 altmetric indexes were selected for this further analysis.

Table 4 exhibits the Spearman rank correlation coefficient among citation and altmetric indexes of SSH. For comparative purposes, Spearman correlations among citation and altmetric indexes of selected SSH fields are also shown. The table indicates clear but very weak correlations between the citation and mostly altmetric indexes in SSH. However, the correlation between "readers_count" and citation appears especially strong, the correlation between "altmetric score" and citation appears relatively strong. In terms of fields, the correlations between citation and "readers_count" in all selected fields appear especially strong, in agreement with overall SSH performance. Also, except for H&A, the correlation values of score and citation in all fields were relatively strong (>0.150). However, referring to the correlation between "cited_by_posts_count" and citation, the value was low in each field except for *Psychology*, different from the value of overall. In addition, the other altmetric indexes show very weak correlation with citation in all selected fields. As outlined above, altmetrics are not prepared to replace traditional citation analysis at present.

	E&B-citation	S,P&C-citation	Psyc-citation	H&A-citation	SSH-citation
fbwalls	-.146**	-.142**	-.085**	-.120**	-.112**
feeds	-.031**	-.006*	.024**	-.004	.007**
gplus	.008	-.036**	.057**	.017**	.012**
msm	.028**	.061**	.076**	.074**	.082**
posts	.123**	.126**	*.184***	.129**	*.154***
rdts	-.049**	-.025**	.025**	.014*	.002
tweeters	.030**	.076**	.126**	.079**	.095**
videos	.017**	.026**	.047**	.035**	.040**
score	*.180***	*.177***	*.223***	.120**	*.190***
readers	**.696****	**.664****	**.666****	**.634****	**.687****

Note. bwalls is the abbreviation of cite_by_fbwalls_count, and the rest of altmetric indexes show the same change.

*Correlation is significant at the 0.05 level (2-tailed).

**Correlation is significant at the 0.01 level (2-tailed).

Table 4. Spearman correlation analysis of the citation and altmetric variables (loadings > 0.250 are highlighted in bold characters and >0.150 in italics)in SSH and selected fields in 2013-2017.

DISCUSSION AND CONCLUSION

This study set out to better reflect scholarly performance in SSH, which is multifaceted (Chen et al., 2015). We investigated the performance of citations and altmetrics in the SSH by using 1,327,924 records from the SSCI and the A&HCI, and 629,586 records from Altmetric.com. The research covers a period of 5 years (2013–2017), three publication types (articles, reviews, and proceedings papers), four selected fields (Economics & business administration; Social, political & communication science; Psychology; and Humanities & Art), three citation indicators, and 13 altmetric indicators. The results are as follows:

Disciplinary Analysis

By using a mixed analysis of updated and large-scale SSH publication data, our results confirm that different discipline fields in SSH perform differently in terms of citations and altmetrics. Referring to the mean citation rate, Psychology publications had much higher values rate than those in other fields; H&A had the least mean citation rate. In terms of NMCR, Psychology and E&B had higher average citation rates than excepted on the basis of the average citation rates, while Humanities & Art and Social, political & communication science did not. Looking at altmetric score, Psychology and E&B have received the most attention, while H&A got the least attention. Cumulative distribution of citation and altmetric score also indicates the obvious dissimilarity between H&A and other fields. These disciplinary differences in SSH confirm that the social sciences have a different distinct character when compared with the humanities (Chen et al., 2015).

Citation Analysis

The FECR value of each field, which equals the mean citations of all the fields, and the mean citation rate of each field drop sharply when it comes to more recent published years, suggesting the hysteresis of citation (Costas et al., 2015) and the need for a citation window.

Altmetric Analysis

The presence of altmetrics is increasing over time, and more recent publications have better performance than earlier publications, according to altmetric score. The data indicate that contrary to citation analysis, altmetrics are valid for the most recent publications, though the exact publication time has not been confirmed (Costas et al., 2015; Ortega, 2015).

Correlations between the Indexes of Citations and Altmetrics

The correlations between reader count and citation are especially strong in SSH and in each selected field, and the correlation between "cited_by_posts_count" seems relatively strong, whereas there are clear but very weak correlations between the citation and other altmetric indexes. The reason could be that SSH has a wider reach across social media than natural sciences, so the number of readers and mentions online may reflects the scholarly impact somehow; the deeper reason should be studied. The weak correlations indicate that altmetrics is not suitable to replace entirely traditional citation analysis, and that the formation dimensions of altmetric indicators do differ from those of citation indexes (Costas et al., 2015; Ortega, 2015).

We already know that publications in the social sciences and humanities show a higher presence of altmetrics than natural sciences (Costas et al., 2015). Further research can aim to investigate the performance of natural sciences and SSH by traditional citations and altmetrics, and further, to improve and complete the evaluation methods. Further study may also examine the evaluation efficiency of each altmetric indicator in SSH regarding the distinct character of SSH discipline. Finally, further study may aim to gain a better understanding of the publication time for which altmetrics is valid, combining both quantitative analyses with more qualitative approaches.

In summary, the major contributions of this study include an extension of (1) the analysis method in the SSH context; (2) the validation of the altmetric indicators; and (3) the verification of claims that altmetrics works better as a complement to bibliometrics. Future research as outlined above will be telling in this area.

ACKNOWLEDGMENTS

We would like to thank Stacy Konkiel from Altmetric.com for data support. This research is funded by the National Social Science Fund Key Project of P.R. China (17ATQ009).

APPENDIX

List of fields selected for this study

Main field	Subfield	ISI subject category
Economics & business administration	Business, Economics, Planning	Business Business, Finance Management Industrial Relations & Labor Economics
Social, political & communication sciences	Policy, Planning and Development	International Relations Area Studies Political Science Public Administration Health Policy & Services Urban Studies Planning & Development
	Environmental Studies	Environmental Studies Geography
	Education & Information Science	Education & Educational Research Education, Scientific Education, Special Communication Information Science & Library Science
	Sociology & Anthropology	Anthropology Ethics/ Ethnic Studies Family Studies Hospitality, Leisure, Sport Archaeology/ Gerontology Women's Studies Sociology
	Community & Social Issues	Demography Social Issues Social Sciences, Biomedical Social Sciences, Interdisciplinary Criminology & Penology Social Work Law
Psychology	Psychology & Psychiatry	Psychology Psychology, Applied Psychology, Biological Psychology, Clinical Psychology, Developmental Psychology, Educational Psychology, Experimental Psychology, Mathematical Psychology, Multidisciplinary Psychology, Psychoanalysis Psychology, Social Psychiatry
Humanities & Art	Literature & Literary Reviews	Literature Literature, African, Australian, Canadian Literature, American Literature, British Isles Literature, German, Dutch, Scandinavian Literature, Romance Literature, Slavic Literary Reviews Literary Theory & Criticism
	Linguistics & Art	Language & Linguistics Linguistics Music Poetry Theater
	Humanities, Philosophy, History	Humanities, Multidisciplinary Medieval & Renaissance Studies Philosophy Religion History of Social Sciences History & Philosophy of Science

REFERENCES

Adie, E. (2014). Taking the alternative mainstream. *El Profesional de La Información*, *23*(4), 349–351.

Adie, E., & Roe, W. (2013). Altmetric: Enriching scholarly content with article-level discussion and metrics. *Learned Publishing*, *26*(1), 11–17. https://doi.org/10.1087/20130103

Albarrán, P., Ortuño, I., & Ruiz-Castillo, J. (2011). High- and low-impact citation measures: Empirical applications. *Journal of Informetrics*, *5*(1), 122–145.

Altmetric. (2019a). *The altmetric details page*. Retrieved from https://www.altmetric.com/about-our-data/altmetric-details-page/

Altmetric. (2019b). *What does altmetric do?* Retrieved from https://www.altmetric.com/

Altmetrics. (2019). *How is the altmetric attention score calculated?* Retrieved from https://help.altmetric.com/support/solutions/articles/6000060969-how-is-the-altmetric-score-calculated

Archambault, É., Vignola-Gagné, É., Côté, G., Larivière, V., & Gingras, Y. (2006). Benchmarking scientific output in the social sciences and humanities: The limits of existing databases. *Scientometrics*, *68*(3), 329–342.

Bar-Illan, J. (2012). *Beyond citations: scholars' visibility on the social Web*. arXiv: 1205.5611. Retrieved from http://arxiv.org/abs/1205.5611

Bonaccorsi, A., Daraio, C., & Fantoni, S. (2017). Do social sciences and humanities behave like life and hard sciences? *Scientometrics*, *112*, 607–653.

Bornmann, L. (2014). Do altmetrics point to the broader impact of research? An overview of benefits and disadvantages of altmetrics. *Journal of Informetrics*, *8*(4), 895–903.

Bornmann, L., & Leydesdorff, L. (2013). The validation of (advanced) bibliometric indicators through peer assessments: A comparative study using data from InCites and F1000. *Journal of Informetrics*, *7*(2), 286–291.

Bourke, P., Butler, L. & Bigllal, B. (1996). *Monitoring research in the periphery: Australia and the ISI indices*. Monograph Series Research Evaluation and Policy Project, No. 3.

Braun, T., & Glanzel, W. (1996). International collaboration: Will it be keeping alive East European research? *Scientometrics*, *36*(2), 147–254.

Braun, T., Glanzel, W., & Schubert, A. (1985). *Scientometric indicators. A32 country comparison of publication productivity and citation impact* (p. 424). Singapore and Philadelphia, PA: World Scientific Publishing Co. Pte. Ltd.

Chen, K., Tang, M., Wang, C., & Hsiang, J. (2015). Exploring alternative metrics of scholarly performance in the social sciences and humanities in Taiwan. *Scientometrics*, *102*, 97–112.

Costas, R., Zahedi, Z., & Wouters, P. (2015). Do "altmetrics" correlate with citations? Extensive comparison of altmetric indicators with citations from a multidisciplinary perspective. *Journal of the Association for Information Science and Technology*, *66*(10), 2003–2019.

Cronin, B., & Sugimoto, C. (2014). *Beyond bibliometrics: Harnessing multidimensional indicators of scholarly impact*. MIT Press.

Galligan, F., & Dyas-Correia, S. (2013). Altmetrics: Rethinking the way we measure. *Serials Review*, *39*(1), 56–61.

Glanzel, W., Debackere, K., & Meyer, M. (2008). 'Triad' or 'Tetrad'? On global changes in a dynamic world. *Scientometrics*, *74*(1), 59–76.

Hicks, D. (1999). The difficulty of achieving full coverage of international social science literature and the bibliometric consequences. *Scientometrics*, *44*(2), 193–215.

Kyvik, S. (1988). Internationality of the social sciences: The Norwegian case. *International Social Science Journal*, 163–172.

Leeuwen, T. V. (2006). The application of bibliometric analyses in the evaluation of social science research. Who benefits from it, and why it is still feasible. *Scientometrics*, *66*(1), 133–154.

Leydesdorff, L., & Felt, U. (2012). "Books" and "book chapters" in the book citation index (BKCI) and science citation index (SCI, SSCI, A&HCI). *Proceedings of the American Society for Information Science and Technology*, *49*(1), 1–7.

Liu, C., Xu, Y., Wu, H., & Chen, S. (2013). Correlation and interaction visualization of altmetric indicators extracted from scholarly social network activities: Dimensions and structure. *Journal of Medical Internet Research*, *15*(11), e259.

Liu, W., Hu, G., Tang, L., & Wang, Y. (2015). China's global growth in social science research: Uncovering evidence from bibliometric analyses of SSCI publications (1978–2013). *Journal of Informetrics*, *9*(3), 555–569.

Moed, H. F., & Halevi, G. (2015). Multidimensional assessment of scholarly research impact. *Journal of the Association for Information Science and Technology*, *66*(10), 1988–2002.

Nederhof, A. (2006). Bibliometric monitoring of research performance in the social sciences and the humanities: A review. *Scientometrics*, *66*(1), 81–100.

Nederhof, A. J., Zwaan, R. A., De Bruin, R. E., & Dekker, P. J. (1988). Accessing the useful of bibliometric indicators for the humanities and the social and behavioral sciences: A comparative study. *Scientometrics*, *15* (5–6), 423–435.

Ortega, J. L. (2015a). Relationship between altmetric and bibliometric indicators across academic social sites: The case of CSIC's members. *Journal of Informetrics*, *9*(1), 39–49.

Ortega, J. L. (2015b). Disciplinary differences in the use of academic social networking sites. *Online Information Review*, *39*(4), 520–536.

Priem, J., Taraborelli, D., Groth, P., & Neylon, C. (2010). *Altmetrics: A manifesto*. Retrieved from http://altmetrics.org/manifesto/

Sugimoto, C. R., Work, S., Larivière, V., & Haustein, S. (2017). Scholarly use of social media and altmetrics: A review of the literature. *Journal of the Association for Information Science and Technology*, *68*(9), 2037–2062.

Thelwall, M., & Wilson, P. (2014). Regression for citation data: An evaluation of different methods. *Journal of Informetrics*, *8*(4), 963–971.

Xia, F., Su, X., Wang, W., Zhang, C., & Ning, Z. (2016). Bibliographic analysis of nature based on twitter and facebook altmetrics data. *Plos One*, *11*(12), e0165997. https://doi.org/10.1371/journal.pone.0165997

Yang, S., & Han, R. (2015). Breadth and depth of citation distribution. *Information Processing & Management*, *51*(2), 130–140.

Yang, S., Xing, X., & Wolfram, D. (2018). Difference in the impact of open-access papers published by China and the USA. *Scientometrics*, *115*, 1017–1037.

Zahedi, Z., Costas, R., & Wouters, P. (2014). How well developed are altmetrics? A cross-disciplinary analysis of the presence of 'alternative metrics' in scientific publications. *Scientometrics*, *101*, 1491–1513.

Zhou, P., Thijs, B., & Glänzel, W. (2008). Is China also becoming a giant in social sciences? *Scientometrics*, *79* (3), 593–562.

Research on the Impact Evaluation of Academic Journals Based on Altmetrics and Citation Indicators

Rongying Zhao
School of Information Management, Wuhan University, Wuhan, China
zhaorongying@126.com

Xu Wang
School of Information Management, Wuhan University, Wuhan, China
xuwang@whu.edu.cn

Zhuozhu Liu
School of Information Management, Wuhan University, Wuhan, China
543193351@qq.com

Yongkang Qi
School of Information Management, Wuhan University, Wuhan, China
qiyongkang@whu.edu.cn

Zhaoyang Zhang
School of Information Management, Wuhan University, Wuhan, China
windboy727@vip.qq.com

Ruru Chang
School of Information Management, Wuhan University, Wuhan, China
changrr@whu.edu.cn

ABSTRACT

Taking international LIS journals as an example, combining 8 traditional citation indicators and 10 altmetrics indicators, we use the method of multi-indicator fusion to construct a comprehensive evaluation model of journal impact based on traditional citation indicators and altmetrics indicators. Through normalization processing, correlation analysis, reliability analysis, validity analysis, factor analysis, the paper evaluates the academic impact (F_A), societal impact (F_S) of LIS journals respectively. We get the following conclusion: (1) We get the 2-dimensional evaluation results and according to LIS journals impacts, we divide the roles into four categories: "Prestige journals", "Star journals", "Common journals" and "Expert journals". (2) It is found that 8 traditional citation indicators based on JCR, present strong positive correlations, and the indicators are highly consistent overall and internally. (3) There are moderate or high positive correlations among 10 altmetrics based on Altmetrics Explorer, and there are also significant consistency among the indicators as a whole and internally. (4) The correlation coefficient between F_A and F_S is 0.566, with a moderate positive correlation. It indicates that the evaluation of LIS journals' societal impact based on altmetrics indicators has a useful supplement to the evaluation of academic impact based on citation.

KEYWORDS

Journals Evaluation; Citation Indicators; Altmetrics Indicators; Academic Impact; Societal Impact

82nd Annual Meeting of the Association for Information Science & Technology | Melbourne, Australia | 19–23 October, 2019

DOI: 10.1002/pra2.00027

ASIS&T THESAURUS

Informetrics; Altmetrics; Bibliometrics

INTRODUCTION

The evaluation and ranking of academic journals have an important impact on scholar's publication and academic communication. Journals evaluation has a long history, and since the Journal Impact Factor was put forward (Garfield, 1955; Garfield, 1970), the researches on literature and scientific development trends from the perspective of citation have provided quantitative references for journals evaluation. Citation indicators play crucial roles in journal evaluation and have thus received much attention (Waltman, 2016). Nevertheless, due to the complexity, unpredictability of academic research and current bad academic ecological environment, the traditional quantitative evaluation methods of journals based on citation indicators such as impact factors have some shortcomings, including long time lag, single evaluation indicator system and subject, false, stack and anomalous citation, Matthew Effect and so on (Bornmann, 2014; Merton, 1988; Sud & Thelwall, 2014).

Meanwhile, traditional citation indicators have been questioned, and quite a few researchers are attempting to find new methods to evaluate academic papers and journals (Werner, 2015). Especially in the environment of web2.0, the traditional journals evaluation and measurement methods based on citation indicators have been unable to fully evaluate the impacts of academic journals. In order to make up for their limitations, Alternative Metrics (Altmetrics) came into being, and has become a research field of scientific evaluation (Priem, Taraborelli, Groth, & Neylon, 2010). Altmetrics is becoming increasingly important for researchers and journals wishing to demonstrate the impact of their work (Yu, 2017). In addition, Altmetrics, influmetrics, entitymetrics, usage metrics, article-level metrics, and other terms have been proposed for a full and comprehensive measurement of the impact of academic papers or journals (Gorraiz, 2015). Impact evaluation of journals cannot rely solely on citations, which has become the consensus in the academic community. However, the trend of journals' impact evaluation is moving toward multi-source and multi-dimensional measurements (Moed & Halevi, 2015; Yang, Xing, & Wolfram, 2018).

At present, researches on the theory, method and application of altmetrics mainly focus on the paper and journals, among which there are many research on the evaluation of academic papers (Thelwall, Haustein, Larivière, & Sugimoto, 2013; Costas, Zahedi, & Wouters, 2014a; Thelwall & Wilson, 2016; Sugimoto, Work, Larivière, & Haustein, 2017; Thelwall & Nevill, 2018; Mikhailov et al. 1984; Zhang & Wang, 2018; Torres-Salinas, Castillo-Valdivieso, Perez-Luque, & Romero-Frias, 2018), but there are several researches on journals evaluation. Costas, Zahedi, and Wouters (2014a) analyzed altmetrics and citation indicators of publications in various disciplines provided by Altmetric.com, and pointed out that altmetrics has potential value in journals evaluation. Bornmann and Haunschild (2016) tried to normalize Twitter counts based on journals in the Twitter indicator and found that Denmark, Finland, and Norway are the countries with the most tweeted papers. Luis Ortega (2017) found that journals with their own Twitter account obtain more tweets (46%) and citations (34%) than journals without a Twitter account. Akers (2017) illustrated how altmetrics may be better than traditional citations in reflecting the impact of Medical Library Association on the practice of health sciences librarianship.

To sum up, however, the current research on journals evaluation have the following shortcomings: firstly, there is a lack of a complete set of evaluation indicator system for multi-dimensional measurement for different data sources, and a lack of comprehensive evaluation by combining traditional academic impact indicators with social network impact indicators of journals. Secondly, each indicator has not been given a clear weight, and the research is relatively scattered. Thirdly, the correlations degree or mutual relations on journals' evaluation indicators between single database and multiple databases is not exceedingly clear. In order to comprehensively evaluate the impact of journals from a multi-indicators fusion perspective and on the basis of scholars' researches, this study attempts to further explore the following questions:

1. Is it feasible to evaluate the impact of journals by using altmetrics indicators and combining traditional citation indicators?
2. Are there any relations among the evaluation indicators of academic impact, the evaluation indicators of societal impact and the scores of the evaluation results of the two dimensions?
3. How can we use the two-dimensional rectangular coordinate system to evaluate the impact of journals?

CONSTRUCTION PROCESS OF COMPREHENSIVE IMPACT EVALUATION MODEL

In this paper, we divide the impact type of journals into academic impact and societal impact. The academic impact of journals is generated through formal (traditional) scientific communication processes. In the process of formal scientific communication, the realization of knowledge dissemination of journals is through the papers published in journals which are cited by other academic papers. At the same time, it reflects that the knowledge of journals is absorbed and utilized by other scholars, which is a one-way scientific communication. The societal impact of journals is generated in the informal scientific communication process of Web2.0 network environment. In the process of informal scientific communication, the realization of knowledge dissemination of journals is through the papers published in journals which are spread and used by online social media and website platforms. Moreover, it shows that the information of journals have attracted the attention of the public for being full of knowledge, topic or interest, which is a multi-directional informal scientific communication.

As shown in Figure 1, we use the method of multi-indicator fusion to construct the impact evaluation model of journals. In terms of the evaluation of academic impact of journals, first of all, we select 8 indicators to evaluate the academic impact of journals from the data source of Journal Citation Reports (JCR). Secondly, with Altmetric.com as the data source, 10 indicators are selected to evaluate the societal impact of journals. Then, the indicators data is normalized, and the correlation analysis, reliability analysis, validity analysis, factor analysis are used to evaluate the academic impact and societal impact of journals. After that, we analyze the correlation of the evaluation scores of two dimensions of journal impact. Then, we map the evaluation scores of journals' academic impact and societal impact to the two-dimensional rectangular coordinate system to evaluate and classify the sample journals.

Data and Processing

Data Collection

Clarivate Analytics' Journal Citation Reports (JCR) provides journal intelligence that highlights the value and contribution of a journal through a rich array of transparent data, metrics and analysis. Under the column of "Journals By Rank," we use "Select Categories: (INFORMATION SCIENCE & LIBRARY SCIENCE), Refined by: Select JCR Year: (2017), Select Edition: (SCIE, SSCI), Category Schema: (Web of Science)." We have retrieved 88 journals of Library and Information Science (LIS). Considering that the sample data can also be obtained in the following sections in the Altmetric.com, so, we selected 64 journals finally. The indicators used for evaluation in citation analysis are different according to the research content of each scholar, and the selected indicators are also different. In JCR, due to some journals' Cited Half Life and Citing Half-Life value are missing, so we remove the two indicators. Finally, eight indicators

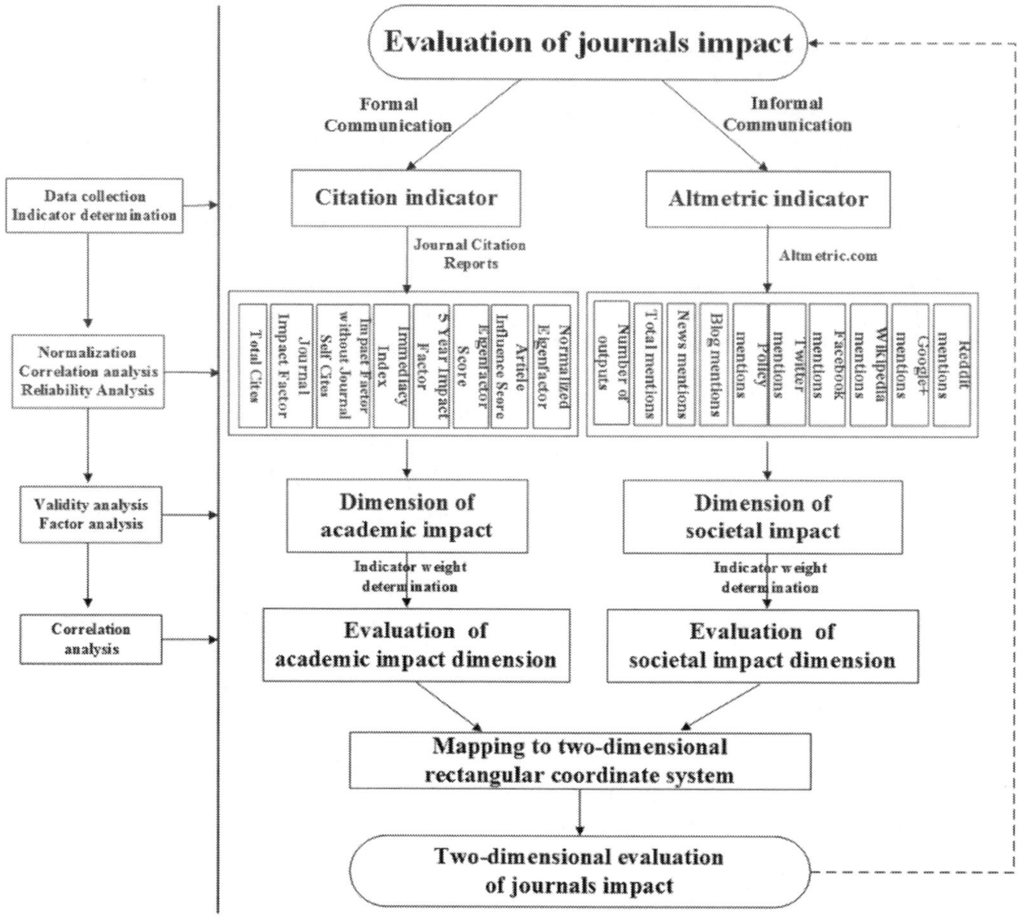

Figure 1. Construction process of impact evaluation model.

are selected, including Total Cites (TC), Journal Impact Factor (JIF), Impact Factor without Journal Self Cites (IFJSC), 5-Year Impact Factor (5YIF), Immediacy Index (IX), Eigenfacetor Score (ES), Article Influence Score (AIS), and Normalized Eigenfactor (NE).

In addition, we use the Altmetric Explorer platform of Altmetric.com to search ISSNs of 64 LIS journals in JCR, and use "Type of output: Articles, Publication Date: 2015-01-01 to 2016-12-31" (It is consistent with the data period of 2017JCR), Retrieval time: 2018-11-11." We obtain 10 relevant indicators of Altmetrics: Number of mentioned outputs, Total mentions, News mentions, Blog mentions, Policy mentions, Twitter mentions, Facebook mentions, Wikipedia mentions, Google+ mentions, Reddit mentions (since most of the remaining Altmetric indicator value is 0, the remaining indicator is temporarily not considered). Finally, 40617 Altmetric indicators data is retrieved.

Data Processing

Through data acquisition and statistics, we find that the gap between the numerical values of each indicator is very large. In order to eliminate the influence of statistical error and indicator difference, we normalize all the original indicators data. After processing, all the indicators data is distributed in the range of [0-1], and the calculation formula is:

$$y_{ij} = \frac{x_{ij}}{\max(x_j)}$$

Where i is the number of evaluation journals, j is the number of evaluation indicators, and x_{ij} is the original data value of each indicator. Then, y_{ij} is the normalized indicator data value.

RESULTS AND DISCUSSION

Evaluation of Academic Impact

The correlation analysis can be used to judge the relation between the indicators used in the dimension of academic impact and provide the basis for whether to use them for analysis in the next step. We analysis the correlation of eight indicators variables of journals obtained in JCR. Table 1 shows that all the correlation coefficients are very high which are in range from 0.624 to 0.978, and there are strong positive correlations among the indicators, and the indicators are consistent overall.

Spearman's rho	TC	JIF	IFJSC	5YIF	IX	ES	AIS	NE
TC	1.000	0.798**	0.784**	0.821**	0.624**	0.877**	0.808**	0.939**
JIF	0.798**	1.000	0.978**	0.967**	0.778**	0.862**	0.909**	0.875**
IFJSC	0.784**	0.978**	1.000	0.956**	0.747**	0.869**	0.917**	0.878**
5YIF	0.821**	0.967**	0.956**	1.000	0.724**	0.862**	0.943**	0.888**
IX	0.624**	0.778**	0.747**	0.724**	1.000	0.683**	0.717**	0.687**
ES	0.877**	0.862**	0.869**	0.862**	0.683**	1.000	0.879**	0.963**
AIS	0.808**	0.909**	0.917**	0.943**	0.717**	0.879**	1.000	0.903**
NE	0.939**	0.875**	0.878**	0.888**	0.687**	0.963**	0.903**	1.000

Note: **Correlation is significant at the 0.01 level (2-tailed).

Table 1. Correlation of academic impact indicators provided by JCR.

Reliability Statistics		Item-Total Statistics	
Cronbach's Alpha	**N of Items**		**Corrected Item-Total Correlation**
0.946	8	TC	0.795
		JIF	0.875
		IFJSC	0.889
		5YIF	0.898
		IX	0.643
		ES	0.803
		AIS	0.843
		NE	0.790

Table 2. Reliability analysis of academic impact dimension.

Reliability analysis performs a function in measuring the internal consistency of indicators. According to the analysis in Table 2, Cronbach's Alpha coefficient is 0.946, and the range of Corrected item-total Correlation is 0.643–0.898, indicating that there is a high degree of Correlation between each indicator and total indicators, and a high consistency within each indicator.

Meanwhile, the KMO (Kaiser-Meyer-Olkin) value is 0.801 and the significance value is 0 through KMO-Bartlett's Test. The selected indicators are of high validity, so they can be tested by factor analysis to evaluate academic impact of international LIS journals. In addition, principal component analysis is used as a factor extraction method, and the communalities extracted by each indicator are range from 0.802 to 0.954, with high values and little information loss. Therefore, the overall effect of factor extraction is ideal, which can reflect the original information of the indicator.

As shown in Table 3, it can be seen that the eigenvalue of component 1 is 5.992, which explains 74.898% ($74.898\% = 5.992 \div 8 \times 100\%$) of the total variance of the original 8 variables. The eigenvalue of component 2 is 1.094, which explains 13.674% ($13.674\% = 1.094 \div 8 \times 100\%$) of the total variance of the original 8 variables. The cumulative variance contribution rate of two component interpretation is 88.572%, while the characteristic value of latter component was small, and the contribution to explain the original variable is smaller and smaller. Therefore, it's appropriate to extract 2 common factor (dividing the 8 original indicators into two principal components).

Component	Initial Eigenvalues			Extraction Sums of Squared Loadings			Rotation Sums of Squared Loadings		
	Total	% of Variance	Cumulative %	Total	% of Variance	Cumulative %	Total	% of Variance	Cumulative %
1	5.992	74.898	74.898	5.992	74.898	74.898	3.597	44.958	44.958
2	1.094	13.674	88.572	1.094	13.674	88.572	3.489	43.614	88.572
3	0.546	6.822	95.394						
4	0.196	2.456	97.85						
5	0.117	1.459	99.309						
6	0.036	0.454	99.763						
7	0.016	0.195	99.959						
8	0.003	0.041	100						

Table 3. Total variance explained for each indicator.

The final factor score formula can be obtained from Component Matrix value:

F1 = 0.161*TC + 0.356*JIF + 0.320*IFJSC+0.222*5YIF + 0.385*IX−0.176*ES + 0.101*AIS−0.196*NE;

F2 = 0.371*TC−0.150*JIF−0.110*IFJSC−0.006*5YIF −0.227*IX + 0.386*ES + 0.110*AIS + 0.405*NE.

Meanwhile, according to Table 3, the proportion of variance contribution of principal components in "Rotation Sums of Squared Loadings" is taken as the weight. Then, we use the following formula:

$$F_A = \frac{\lambda_1}{\lambda_1 + \lambda_2} * F_1 + \frac{\lambda_2}{\lambda_1 + \lambda_2} * F_2$$

We can obtain evaluation model formula of the academic impact on international LIS journals:

$$F_A = \frac{44.958\%}{88.572\%} * F_1 + \frac{43.614\%}{88.572\%} * F_2$$

Finally, the results of academic impact evaluation of international LIS journals are obtained from the comprehensive evaluation scores (see Table 4).

Rank	Journal abbreviation	ISSN	Score	Rank	Journal abbreviation	ISSN	Score
1	MIS QUART	0276-7783	0.7175	11	J INFORMETR	1751-1577	0.3017
2	J AM MED INFORM ASSN	1067-5027	0.5800	12	QUAL HEALTH RES	1049-7323	0.3017
3	J COMPUT-MEDIAT COMM	1083-6101	0.4032	13	SOC SCI COMPUT REV	0894-4393	0.2958
4	INFORM SYST RES	1047-7047	0.3656	14	J ASSOC INF SCI TECH	2330-1635	0.2867
5	INFORM SYST J	1350-1917	0.3604	15	EUR J INFORM SYST	0960-085X	0.2860
6	INT J INFORM MANAGE	0268-4012	0.3582	16	TELEMAT INFORM	0736-5853	0.2828
7	J STRATEGIC INF SYST	0963-8687	0.3321	17	INT J GEOGR INF SCI	1365-8816	0.2823
8	SCIENTOMETRICS	0138-9130	0.3289	18	INFORM PROCESS MANAG	0306-4573	0.2727
9	GOV INFORM Q	0740-624X	0.3078	19	J MANAGE INFORM SYST	0742-1222	0.2671
10	J INF TECHNOL-UK	0268-3962	0.3043	20	J HEALTH COMMUN	1081-0730	0.2488

Table 4. Evaluation results of academic impact for international LIS journals (Top20).

Evaluation of Societal Impact

The evaluation of societal impact of international LIS journals is based on altmetrics indicators. Firstly, we analyze the correlation of 10 indicators variables of LIS journals (see Table 5). Table 5 shows that all the correlation coefficients are relatively high which are in range from 0.354 to 0.957.Therefore, there are moderate or high positive correlations among the indicators, and the indicators are consistent overall.

Secondly, according to the reliability analysis, we find that Cronbach's Alpha coefficient is 0.940, and the range of Corrected item-total Correlation is 0.432 to 0.972, showing a relatively significant consistency in each indicator. According to the validity analysis, we find that Approx. Chi-Square value is 1067.142, the KMO value is 0.799 and the significance value is 0 through KMO-Bartlett's Test. The selected indicators are of high validity, so they can be tested by factor analysis to evaluate the societal impact of LIS journals. Thirdly, using principal component analysis method as a factor extraction method, we find that the communalities extracted by each indicator are between 0.666 and 0.972, with high values and little information loss. Therefore, the overall effect of factor extraction is ideal, which can reflect the original information of the indicator.

Spearman	outputs	Total	News	Blog	Policy	Twitter	Facebook	Wikipedia	Google+	Reddit
outputs	1	0.957**	0.554**	0.851**	0.722**	0.924**	0.789**	0.692**	0.720**	0.479**
Total	0.957**	1	0.577**	0.890**	0.655**	0.975**	0.843**	0.638**	0.752**	0.541**
News	0.554**	0.577**	1	0.483**	0.357**	0.520**	0.462**	0.504**	0.395**	0.497**
Blog	0.851**	0.890**	0.483**	1	0.663**	0.883**	0.706**	0.579**	0.723**	0.575**
Policy	0.722**	0.655**	0.357**	0.663**	1	0.618**	0.388**	0.600**	0.436**	0.382**
Twitter	0.924**	0.975**	0.520**	0.883**	0.618**	1	0.838**	0.597**	0.725**	0.542**
Facebook	0.789**	0.843**	0.462**	0.706**	0.388**	0.838**	1	0.511**	0.712**	0.483**
Wikipedia	0.692**	0.638**	0.504**	0.579**	0.600**	0.597**	0.511**	1	0.468**	0.354**
Google+	0.720**	0.752**	0.395**	0.723**	0.436**	0.725**	0.712**	0.468**	1	0.441**
Reddit	0.479**	0.541**	0.497**	0.575**	0.382**	0.542**	0.483**	0.354**	0.441**	1

*Note: **Correlation is significant at the 0.01 level (2-tailed)*

Table 5. Correlation of societal impact indicators provided by Altmetric.com.

Component	Initial Eigenvalues			Extraction Sums of Squared Loadings			Rotation Sums of Squared Loadings		
	Total	% of Variance	Cumulative %	Total	% of Variance	Cumulative %	Total	% of Variance	Cumulative %
1	6.79	67.901	67.901	6.79	67.901	67.901	4.842	48.417	48.417
2	1.415	14.154	82.055	1.415	14.154	82.055	3.364	33.638	82.055
3	0.632	6.319	88.374						
4	0.512	5.122	93.496						
5	0.27	2.704	96.2						
6	0.188	1.882	98.082						
7	0.104	1.042	99.124						
8	0.068	0.682	99.805						
9	0.019	0.188	99.994						
10	0.001	0.006	100						

Table 6. Total variance explained for each indicator.

As shown in Table 6, it can be seen that the eigenvalue of component 1 is 6.79, which explains 67.901% of the total variance of the original 10 variables. The eigenvalue of component 2 is 1.415, which explains 14.154% of the total variance of the original 10 variables. The cumulative variance contribution rate of two component interpretation is 82.055%, while the characteristic value of latter component was small, and the contribution to explain the original variable is smaller and smaller. Therefore, it's appropriate to extract two common factor (dividing the 10 original indicators into 2 principal components).

The final factor score formula can be obtained from Component Matrix value:

F3 = −0.053*Number of mentioned outputs + 0.111*Total mentions + 0.299*News mentions + 0.043*Blog mentions-0.242*Policy mentions + 0.099*Twittermentions + 0.229*

Facebook mentions−0.117*Wikipedia mentions+.

0.211*Google+mentions+0.254*Reddit mentions;

F4 = 0.288*Number of mentioned outputs+0.094*Total mentions−0.208*News mentions+0.156*Blog mentions.

+0.438*Policy mentions+0.108*Twitter mentions −0.085*Facebook mentions +0.32*Wikipedia mentions −0.074*Google+mentions−0.16*Reddit mentions.

Meanwhile, according to Table 6, the proportion of variance contribution of principal components in "Rotation Sums of Squared Loadings" is taken as the weight. Then, we use the following formula:

$$F_s = \frac{\lambda_3}{\lambda_3+\lambda_4} * F_3 + \frac{\lambda_4}{\lambda_3+\lambda_4} * F_4$$

We can obtain evaluation model formula of the academic impact on international LIS journals:

$$F_s = \frac{48.417\%}{82.055\%} * F_3 + \frac{33.638\%}{82.055\%} * F_4$$

Finally, the results of societal impact evaluation of international LIS journals are obtained from the comprehensive evaluation scores (see Table 7).

Rank	Journal abbreviation	Score	Rank	Journal abbreviation	Score
1	J AM MED INFORM ASSN	0.7600	11	J LIBR INF SCI	0.0948
2	SCIENTOMETRICS	0.4066	12	J ACAD LIBR	0.0939
3	J ASSOC INF SCI TECH	0.3293	13	J MED LIBR ASSOC	0.0895
4	J COMPUT-MEDIAT COMM	0.2867	14	INFORM SYST RES	0.0888
5	QUAL HEALTH RES	0.2193	15	INFORM DEV	0.0765
6	LEARN PUBL	0.1923	16	SOC SCI COMPUT REV	0.0683
7	COLL RES LIBR	0.1717	17	INT J COMP-SUPP COLL	0.0664
8	J INFORMETR	0.1691	18	J MANAGE INFORM SYST	0.0583
9	J HEALTH COMMUN	0.1536	19	TELECOMMUN POLICY	0.0568
10	J INF SCI	0.1183	20	J INF TECHNOL-UK	0.0529

Table 7. Evaluation results of societal impact for international LIS journals (Top20).

Result Analysis of Impact Evaluation

Correlation Analysis of Two Evaluation Results

We conduct Spearman correlation analysis on the score of academic impact (F_A), societal impact (F_S) of 64 international LIS journals (see Table 8). According to Table 8, the correlation coefficient between F_A and F_S is 0.566 (SIG = 0) with a moderate positive correlation, which indicates that the evaluation of LIS journals' societal impact based on altmetrics

Spearman's rho	F_A	F_S
F_A	1.000	0.566**
F_S	0.566**	1.000

Note: N=64. **Correlation is significant at the 0.01 level (2-tailed).

Table 8. Correlations of the scores provided by 2 dimensions.

indicators has a good supplement to the evaluation of LIS journals' academic impact based on citation.

In the era of Web 2.0, open access movement is prevailing and online academic communication activities are frequent. Papers published in journals are shared on social media, often sparking interest in reading by other scholars in the field, and so achievements of higher academic value are easy to be concerned and cited. In addition, academic paper citations are lagging behind online browsing, sharing, comments and other behaviors, which also leads to lagging results for journals being cited. However, the timeliness of journals evaluated based on altmetrics is significantly better than citation indicators (Maflahi & Thelwall, 2018; Thelwall, 2017). At the same time, because of their strong positive correlation, it is known that the Altmetrics score has the certain predictability to the citation score. If a journal gets a higher Altmetrics score in the early stage, it will also get a higher citation score later. However, there are still some differences between the two evaluation dimensions, which cannot be completely replaced. This also shows that the combination of academic and societal impact for comprehensive evaluation has the certain value.

2-Dimensional Evaluation Results

The two-dimensional method is to select two classification dimensions, which can be used to comprehensively reflect the level and state of the evaluation object in the field. We take the score of academic impact (FA) and score of societal impact (FS) as the two dimensions of the international LIS journals' impact evaluation, and map them into the two-dimensional rectangular coordinate system for comprehensive evaluation. FA measures the academic contributions of LIS journals and the peer recognition of their achievements, which directly reflects the academic quality of LIS journals. Meanwhile, FS measures the impact of published papers in the society after they enter the network environment, reflecting the degree of social attention and the level of popularity of LIS journals.

Therefore, we take the abscissa as F_a and the ordinate as F_s. The mean values of the evaluation scores in two dimensions are calculated as 0.17 and 0.07 respectively, so this study determines the standard dividing of journals impact. At the same time, we divide the roles into four categories of journals (see Figure 3): "Prestige journals" ($x > 0.17$, $y > 0.07$), "Star journals" ($x < 0.17$, $y > 0.07$), "Common journals" ($x < 0.17$, $y < 0.07$), "Expert journals"($x > 0.17$, $y < 0.07$). From Figure 2, we can see that there is a great difference in the evaluation scores of international LIS journals, no matter in the academic impact level or in the societal impact level.

"Prestige journals": 9 journals, accounting for 14.06%.In this region, the LIS journals have higher academic and societal impact than average, including Journal of the American Medical Informatics Association, Scientometrics, Journal of the Association for Information Science and Technology, Journal of Computer-Mediated Communication, Journal of Informetrics etc.

"Star journals": 6 journals, accounting for 9.38%.In this region, the LIS journals have higher societal impact, but lower academic impact than average, Including Learned Publishing, College & Research Libraries, Journal of Librarianship & Information Science, Journal of Academic Librarianship, Journal of the Medical Library Association, Information Development.

"Expert journals":15 journals, accounting for 23.44%.In this region, the LIS journals have higher academic impact,but lower societal impact than average, including MIS Quarterly, Information Systems Journal, International Journal of Information Management, Journal of Strategic Information

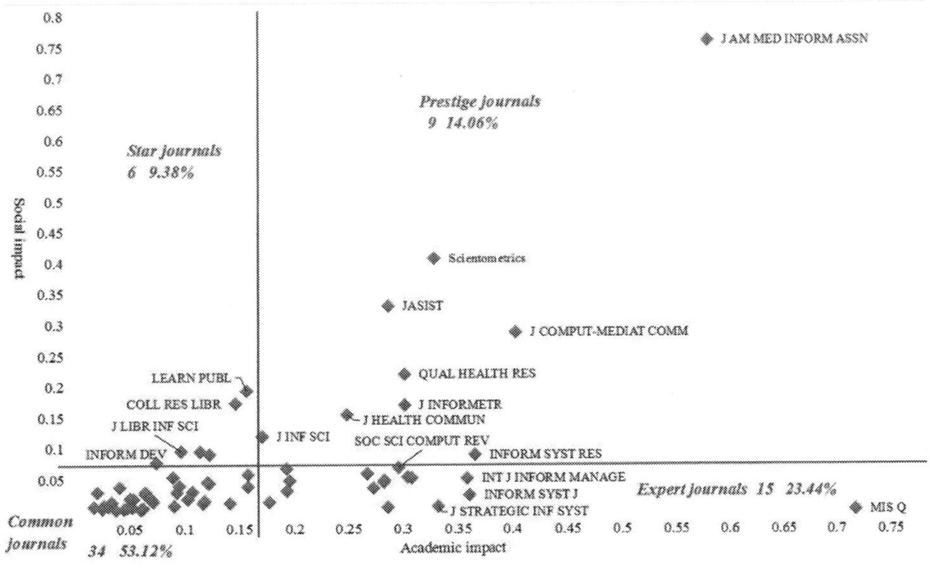

Figure 2. 2-dimensional evaluation of LIS journals impact.

Systems, Government Information Quarterly etc. While, "common journals" include the remaining 34 journals, accounting for 53.12%, which the academic and societal impact are below average

CONCLUSION

Taking international LIS journals as an example, combining eight traditional citation indicators and 10 altmetrics indicators, we use the method of multi-indicator fusion to construct a comprehensive evaluation model of journal impact based on traditional citation indicators and altmetrics indicators. We systematically construct the evaluation indicator system of LIS journals from two dimensions: academic impact dimension, societal impact dimension. Through normalization processing, correlation analysis, reliability analysis, validity analysis, factor analysis, the paper evaluates the academic impact, societal impact of LIS journals respectively. And then we get the 2-dimensional evaluation results and according to LIS journals impacts, we divide the roles into four categories: "Prestige journals," "Star journals," "Common journals" and "Expert journals." At the same time, through correlation analysis and reliability analysis, it is found that 8 traditional citation indicators, including TC, JIF, IFJSC, 5YIF, IX, ES, AIS and NE based on JCR, present strong positive correlations (range from 0.624 to 0.978), and the indicators are highly consistent overall and internally; There are moderate or high positive correlations among 10 altmetrics (range from 0.354 to 0.957), including Number of mentioned outputs, Total mentions, News mentions, Blog mentions, Policy mentions, Twitter mentions, Facebook mentions, Google+ mentions, etc. based on Altmetric Explorer, and there are also significant consistency among the indicators as a whole and internally; The correlation coefficient between F_A and FS is 0.566 with a moderate positive correlation. It indicates that the evaluation of LIS journals' societal impact based on altmetrics indicators has a good supplement to the evaluation of LIS journals' academic impact based on citation.

Merton R. K. believes that if the paper makes a significant contribution to scientific research in a field, it will be cited by more new literature after publication (Merton, 1973). Therefore, the citation evaluation method measures the contribution to scientific research, and the exchange of citation forms only exists in the scope of scientific community. The social function of science decides that science must step out of the ivory tower and step into the society. The communication activities of social network platforms directly lead academic literature to the public, and establish a direct connection between scientists and the public. As the altmetrics measure tool represented by Altmetric.com, which is more about scientists' impact in science communication (societal impact) and their contribution to the general public in science popularization and science education. Altmetrics indicators make up for the inability of traditional bibliometrics indicators to measure scientific communication. At the same time, due to the trend of scientific communication of social network platform communication, altmetrics indicators cannot fully measure the contribution of scientific research, and communication of social network platform has unique spatial and temporal characteristics, so altmetrics indicators cannot replace citation and other bibliometric indicators. To sum up, altmetrics is a powerful tool to measure the societal impact of journals, but it cannot replace the traditional bibliometrics at present.

ACKNOWLEDGMENTS

Thank Altmetric.com for providing the dataset. This research is funded by the National Social Science Found Major Project of China (18ZDA325), the National Social Science Found Project of China (16BTQ055) and the Fundamental Research Funds for the Central Universities (H&S Independent Research Projects of Wuhan University).

REFERENCES

Akers, K. G. (2017). Introducing altmetrics to the Journal of the Medical Library Association. *Journal of the Medical Library Association Jmla, 105*(3), 213.

Bornmann, L. (2014). Do altmetrics point to the broader impact of research? An overview of benefits and disadvantages of altmetrics. *Journal of Informetrics, 8*(4), 895–903.

Bornmann, L., & Haunschild, R. (2016). How to normalize Twitter counts? A first attempt based on journals in the Twitter Index. *Sc, 107*(3), 1405–1422.

Costas, R., Zahedi, Z., & Wouters, P. (2014a). Do "altmetrics" correlate with citations? Extensive comparison of altmetric indicators with citations from a multidisciplinary perspective. *Journal of the Association for Information Science & Technology, 66*(10), 2003–2019.

Garfield, E. (1955). Citation indexes for science; a new dimension in documentation through association of ideas. *Science, 122*(3159), 108–111.

Garfield, E. (1970). Citation indexing for studying science. *Nature, 227*(5260), 870.

Gorraiz, J. (2015). *Usage metrics versus altmetrics: confusing terminology?* New York, Inc: Springer-Verlag.

Luis Ortega, J. (2017). The presence of academic journals on Twitter and its relationship with dissemination (tweets) and research impact (citations). *Aslib Journal of Information Management, 69*(6), 674–687. https://doi.org/10.1108/AJIM-02-2017-0055

Maflahi, N., & Thelwall, M. (2018). How quickly do publications get read? The evolution of mendeley reader counts for new articles. *Journal of the Association for Information Science and Technology, 69*(1), 158–167. https://doi.org/10.1002/asi.23909

Merton, R. K. (1973). The sociology of science: theoretical and empirical investigations / Robert K. Merton; edited and with an introd. By Norman W. Storer. *Contemporary Sociology*, *5*(5), 52.

Merton, R. K. (1988). The Matthew Effect in Science, II: Cumulative Advantage and the Symbolism of Intellectual Property. *ISIS*, *79*(4), 606–623.

Moed, H. F., & Halevi, G. (2015). Multidimensional assessment of scholarly research impact. *Journal of the Association for Information Science & Technology*, *66*(10), 1988–2002.

Priem, J., Taraborelli, D., Groth, P., & Neylon, C. (2010). altmetrics: a manifesto.

Sud, P., & Thelwall, M. (2014). Evaluating altmetrics. *Scientometrics*, *98*(2), 1131–1143.

Sugimoto, C. R., Work, S., Larivière, V., & Haustein, S. (2017). Scholarly use of social media and altmetrics: A review of the literature. *Journal of the Association for Information Science & Technology*, *68*(9).

Thelwall, M. (2017). Are Mendeley reader counts high enough for research evaluations when articles are published? *Aslib Journal of Information Management*, *69*(2), 174–183. https://doi.org/10.1108/AJIM-01-2017-0028

Thelwall, M., Haustein, S., Larivière, V., & Sugimoto, C. R. (2013). Do Altmetrics Work? Twitter and Ten Other Social Web Services. *PLoS One*, *8*(5), e64841.

Thelwall, M., & Nevill, T. (2018). Could scientists use Altmetric.com scores to predict longer term citation counts. *Journal of Informetrics*, *12*(1), 237–248.

Thelwall, M., & Wilson, P. (2016). Mendeley Readership Altmetrics for Medical Articles: An Analysis of 45 Fields. *Journal of the Association for Information Science and Technology*, *67*(8), 1962–1972. https://doi.org/10.1002/asi.23501

Torres-Salinas, D., Castillo-Valdivieso, P., Perez-Luque, A., & Romero-Frias, E. (2018). Altmetrics at institutional level: Visibility on the web of the scientific production of Spanish universities from Altmetric.com. *Profesional De La Informacion*, *27*(3), 483–492. https://doi.org/10.3145/epi.2018.may.03

Waltman, L. (2016). A review of the literature on citation impact indicators. *Journal of Informetrics*, *10*(2), 365–391.

Werner, R. (2015). The focus on bibliometrics makes papers less useful. *Nature*, *517*(7534), 245.

Yang, S., Xing, X., & Wolfram, D. (2018). Difference in the impact of open-access papers published by China and the USA. *Scientometrics*, *115*(5), 1–21.

Yu, H. (2017). Context of altmetrics data matters: an investigation of count type and user category. *Scientometrics*, *111*(1), 1–17.

Zhang, L., & Wang, J. (2018). Why highly cited articles are not highly tweeted? A biology case. *Scientometrics*, *117*(1), 495–509. https://doi.org/10.1007/s11192-018-2876-6

Do I Own It? U.S. and Chinese College Students' Digital Ownership Perceptions

Xiaohua Zhu
University of Tennessee
Knoxville, USA
xzhu12@utk.edu

Tao Yang
South China Normal University
Guangzhou, China
yangtao@scnu.edu.cn

ABSTRACT
The notion of ownership of digital media content is complicated and fragmented, because of the interplay of intellectual property law, personal property rights, and contractual arrangements. Using a framework with multiple configurations of digital content ownership, we surveyed American and Chinese college students about their perceptions of ownership of digital media content—e-books, digital music, and digital movies—as well as their perceptions of the importance of various digital rights associated with digital media content. The results revealed many differences between the two groups. Overall, participants from China attributed more importance to most of the digital rights than their U.S. peers did, their variability was smaller, and they displayed a narrower, more uncertain conception of ownership than the Americans did. The study suggests directions and potential factors for future investigation, including familiarity with digital content, the sharing culture, and possession as a cultural dimension.

KEYWORDS
Digital Media Content; Ownership Perceptions; Digital Rights; Digital Youth

ASIS&T THESAURUS
Social Informatics; Digital Natives; Attitudes

INTRODUCTION
In 2009, Justin Gawronski, a high school student from Michigan, filed a class-action lawsuit against Amazon because the company deleted a kindle book, *1984*, from users' devices remotely (Albanesius, 2009). Justin not only lost the copy he was reading, but also his own work—notes and annotations he made for an assignment (Stone, 2009). This story makes us wonder whether content providers have too much control over their information products, at the expense of consumers' rights. Do consumers still "own" the copy of digital media content in the same sense in which they own a physical book or an album? Indeed, the notion of ownership is particularly problematic for digital content because content providers are increasingly reliant on contracts and digital rights management (DRM) technology, instead of copyright law and property laws, to regulate the behavior of users, regarding what they can and cannot do with the information products. Moreover, with the popularization of various subscription models, especially the freemium model (where free access leads to paid access), content providers seem to have successfully created an access culture, where information consumption is increasingly a "paid-for experience" and the idea of ownership may soon become outdated (Rifkin, 2000).

Young adults and teenagers, as early adopters of information technology and heavy consumers of digital information, often play a defining role in the development of digital media (Satofuka, Kantola, & Kono, 2009). Their notion of digital ownership and their acceptance of DRM, especially rights restrictions on digital media content—e-books, digital music, and digital movies—may shape the information/media market, policy making, and intellectual properties legislation in the near future. Tracking the evolution of these perceptions over time and comparing the perceptions of people from different cultures can help information scholars gain a better understanding of the interplay among users, technology, and policy.

China and the United States are usually perceived as having distinct institutions and cultures. China has been known for content piracy and is often accused by other countries of intellectual property (IP) theft. In recent years, however, the digital culture, as a global phenomenon, seems to have brought changes to China's IP and digital media consumption landscape. Similar to the U.S., media content providers have been experimenting with various business models since the early 2000s, and many have adopted the freemium model in the past few years. The most popular online music service, QQ Music, has over 20 million active users, many of whom are paying for their subscriptions (Wang & Niu, 2018). Privacy and illegal downloading are still quite common among college students, but the rapid changes in their media consumption/payment are also worth noting (Xu & Hua, 2018; Zhang, 2015). The differences and similarities between the

82nd Annual Meeting of the Association for Information Science & Technology | Melbourne, Australia | 19–23 October, 2019

DOI: 10.1002/pra2.00028

two countries make the cross-cultural research particularly interesting.

This paper focuses on the ownership perceptions of young adult users. Given these different rights arrangements for different information products and services, this study attempts to discern how the young adults in the two different countries perceive their ownership of digital content and the digital rights associated with the digital content. Using an online survey method with first-year and second-year university students (18–20 years old) in China and the U.S., we investigated the following questions regarding books, music, and movies in digital format:

RQ1: For each type of digital content, what ownership configurations are perceived as "owning" by participants?

RQ2: Are there significant differences between the two groups' ownership perceptions?

RQ3: What are users' perceptions of the importance of digital rights associated with different types of digital content?

RQ4: Are there significant differences between the two groups' perceived importance of digital rights associated with different types of digital content?

LITERATURE REVIEW AND FRAMEWORK

Digital Youth

Young consumers' utilization of technology and media has drawn the attention of information science, consumer science, and social science researchers since the early 2000s (Boyd, 2007; Hansen & Hansen, 2005; Venkatesh & Behairy, 2012). For example, the information science literature from the early 2000s to the present shows a trend of increased e-book usage among college students, in both leisure and academic settings (Gunter, Rowlands, & Nicholas, 2009; Littman & Connaway, 2004; Rainie & Duggan, 2012; Walton, 2014; Wong, Stelmaszewska, Bhimani, Barn, & Barn, 2010). A more recent survey found nearly 60% of millennials used two or more apps for streaming music (The Nielsen Company, 2017). Although scholars have gained deeper understandings of young adults' information use/adoption patterns and preferences, very few studies have directly examined these young users' perceptions of ownership or their attitude toward the digital rights that they do or do not have.

Psychological Ownership

The topic of individuals' perceptions of ownership has been discussed mainly in the consumer behavior and consumer psychology literature (e.g., the recently-published *Psychological Ownership and Consumer Behavior* (Peck & Shu, 2018)). Although the question of ownership versus access, specifically the shift from purchasing print materials to licensing e-resources, has been discussed for almost three decades in the library field, individual users' ownership/access notions have been largely overlooked (Miller, 2000; Monroe, 1992).

Psychological ownership is defined as a cognitive–affective state or a feeling of possession that can arise even in the absence of legal ownership, which "results from control, intimate association, or the immersion of the self into the target of ownership" (Pierce, Kostova, & Dirks, 2003, p. 102). Therefore, it is essential for the target objects to have certain characteristics for consumers to develop a sense of ownership, including being manipulatable and controllable, being attractive and relevant, and being open and accessible (Pierce & Peck, 2018). Scholars in consumer science observed a shift from the ownership to the access model for many types of commodities (Bardhi, Eckhardt, & Arnould, 2012; Belk, 2013; Moeller & Wittkowski, 2010). Some suggested digital media content as an example of short-term access in the "post-ownership economy" (Belk, 2014), a notion similar to "the age of access" (Rifkin, 2000).

In recent years, researchers began to ask questions about consumers' psychological ownership of digital technologies, in hope that answers to such questions can lead to predictions of consumer behaviors (Kirk & Sarstedt, 2016). Focusing on how consumers felt about intangible digital products compared to their tangible counterparts, some researchers used experiments to demonstrate that consumers experienced feelings of less psychological ownership for digital products because of lower perceptions of control over the product (Atasoy & Morewedge, 2018). Other researchers maintained that consumers could feel strong psychological ownership of digital technologies, e.g., the digital natives who have not encountered physical music media; however, their foci and motivations of ownership are different from the music consumers of the past (Kirk & Swain, 2018). In addition, quite a few researchers explored psychological ownership in terms of control from the perspective of digital affordances and appropriation, especially the functional interactivity (Kim, Spielmann, & McMillan, 2011; Kirk & Swain, 2015; Voorveld, Neijens, & Smit, 2011). Such research often shares similar approaches with social informatics researchers, but this common theme has not been examined in the LIS literature.

Legal Ownership

The concept of ownership or owning a property, as a legal term, is a complicated issue under frequent debate. A dominant, traditional view of law and economics scholars uses the "bundle of sticks" metaphor, explaining that property ownership is an aggregation of separable legal rights or incidents, namely, the right to physical possession, the right to use, the right to manage, the right to income, the right to capital, the right to security, the incident of transmissibility, the incident of absence of term, the prohibition of harmful use, liability to execution, and residuary character (Honoré, 1961). None of these rights and incidents is essential to ownership; if one of them is removed from the bundle, the remainder of them may still constitute property ownership (Honoré, 1961).

The ownership of media (tangible or intangible) is more complex than that of other objects, such as real estate property, because media content is also an intellectual property. Perzanowski and Schultz (2016) discussed the complicated issues around digital content ownership in depth. Starting with the question of whether consumers own the digital goods they pay for, they explored the conflicts between IP rights and personal property rights. The major conclusion of the book is that, while the norms about digital ownership and digital rights were still being shaped by various stakeholders, notions of ownership had already shifted in the digital market and it was imperative to protect consumers' rights (Perzanowski & Schultz).

Watkins, Denegri-Knott, and Molesworth (2016) pointed out that the relationship between psychological and legal ownership became very complex regarding digital virtual goods and was not adequately addressed, but their discussion of digital ownership mainly followed the legal ownership tradition, i.e., the bundle theory. They argued that users' possession of digital virtual goods cannot simply be explained by the dichotomy of access and ownership. Rather, ownership was "fragmented" and "partial," and there were different restrictions on rights (e.g., the right to use and the right to transform) associated with distinct configurations of ownership, namely, locally-created content, hosted content, non-transferable licenses, and subscription-based services (Watkins et al., 2016).

Expanding the framework of fragmented ownership configurations proposed by Watkins et al. (2016), Zhu and Cho (2018) proposed a more detailed framework for analyzing digital ownership from the perspective of legal rights, including the right to possess, the right to use, the right to manage, the right to transform, and transferability. They found that general American users' perceptions of digital ownership fell along a spectrum: most users felt that they owned their purchased, downloadable copies, even if these copies were software or hardware dependent, while few users felt they owned the subscribed or streaming-only content. They also observed that ownership was still important to media content consumers, especially with regard to books (Zhu & Cho, 2018).

Framework

The aforementioned literature provides a theoretical foundation for empirical research on digital content ownership. The current paper follows the legal ownership research stream, especially the partial ownership configuration framework proposed by Watkins et al. (2016) and expanded by Zhu and Cho (2018), by investigating the ownership perceptions of young adults in two different countries.

In this study, we modified and simplified Zhu and Cho's (2018) framework by combining some rights that have similar restrictions and by splitting "DRM-enabled copy" into two configurations—software dependent copy and hardware/device dependent copy (see Table 1). Simply put, we summarized the major ownership configurations in today's digital media content market into six typical categories: (1) purchased DRM-free digital copy, (2) purchased software-dependent copy, (3) purchased hardware/device-dependent digital copy, (4) purchased content hosted by the

<table>
<tr><th>Ownership legal rights</th><th>Specific digital rights</th><th colspan="6">Digital media content ownership configurations</th></tr>
<tr><td rowspan="2"></td><td rowspan="2"></td><td>(1) Purchased DRM-free digital copy</td><td>(2) Purchased, software dependent copy</td><td>(3) Purchased, hardware/device dependent copy</td><td>(4) Purchased, content hosted by content provider</td><td>(5) Subscription, allowing temporary download</td><td>(6) Subscription, hosting/streaming only</td></tr>
<tr><td>Mp3 purchase; O'Reilly eBooks*</td><td>Amazon e-books (AZM)</td><td>Nook e-books</td><td>Google Play movie purchase</td><td>Spotify Premium; Netflix</td><td>Scribd</td></tr>
<tr><td>Right to possess</td><td>Downloadability</td><td rowspan="2">Unrestricted</td><td>Unrestricted</td><td rowspan="2">Restricted</td><td rowspan="2">Denied</td><td rowspan="2">Restricted</td><td rowspan="2">Denied</td></tr>
<tr><td rowspan="3">Right to use</td><td>Format choice</td><td rowspan="2">Restricted</td></tr>
<tr><td>Device independence</td><td rowspan="2">Unrestricted</td><td rowspan="2">Denied</td><td rowspan="2">Restricted</td><td rowspan="2">Restricted</td><td rowspan="2">Restricted</td></tr>
<tr><td>Software independence</td><td rowspan="2">Denied</td></tr>
<tr><td rowspan="2">Right to manage</td><td>Format convertibility</td><td rowspan="4">Unrestricted</td><td rowspan="4">Restricted</td><td rowspan="4">Denied</td><td rowspan="4">Denied</td><td rowspan="4">Denied</td></tr>
<tr><td>Copying capability</td><td>Unrestricted</td></tr>
<tr><td rowspan="2">Right to transform</td><td>Modifiability</td><td rowspan="2">Restricted</td></tr>
<tr><td>Reusability</td></tr>
<tr><td rowspan="2">Transmissibility</td><td>Shareability</td><td>Restricted</td><td>Restricted</td><td>Restricted</td><td>Restricted</td><td>Restricted</td><td>Restricted</td></tr>
<tr><td>Resellability</td><td>Restricted*</td><td>Denied</td><td>Denied</td><td>Denied</td><td>Denied</td><td>Denied</td></tr>
<tr><td>Continuity</td><td></td><td>Permanent</td><td>Indefinite, requires software</td><td>Indefinite, requires device</td><td>Indefinite, requires account</td><td>Indefinite, requires active payment account</td><td>Varies, and requires active payment account</td></tr>
</table>

Table 1. Digital content ownership configurations.

content provider, (5) subscription allowing temporary downloads, and (6) subscription content hosted by the content provider. Although we provide example(s) for each configuration in Table 1 (the third row), it is important to point out that the specific configurations are still fluid and complex (for example, in the past few years, many service providers changed their policies from streaming only to allowing temporary download to mobile devices); and such categorization is more theoretical than factual. We also propose that five ownership rights/incidents are essential to the above-mentioned digital ownership configurations: the right to possess (embodied by downloadability), the right to use (embodied by format choice, device independence, and software independence), the right to manage (embodied by copying capability and format convertibility), the right to transform (embodied by modifiability and reusability), and transmissibility (embodied by shareability and resellability). Not all property rights apply to digital content because of the nature of intellectual properties. For example, only the IP right holders have the right to income from their work, as the copyright law gives the right holders this exclusive right for a certain period of time. In sum, the six ownership rights are embodied by 1 different specific digital rights, and the ownership configurations differ in the restrictions on these rights (displayed in Table 1). The only exception is (4) and (6), which have the identical rights configuration but differs in continuity.

It is worth mentioning that previous research by Attas (2006), Watkins et al. (2016), and Zhu and Cho (2018) considered transferability and continuity as another dimension—a form—of ownership rights. For example, the right to possess can be transferred to others. Therefore, the right to possess is the content of the right and the transferability is the form of the right. However, the aforementioned authors did not operationalize the "forms" specifically as another dimension of rights. In this study, we replace transferability with transmissibility, one of the incidents in the bundle theory (Honoré, 1961), to avoid complication. Regarding continuity, as indicated in Table 1, all five ownership configurations involve either permanent or indefinite use and access (even though the conditions vary). That is, continuity does not contribute much to the differentiation of ownership configurations, except differentiate two configurations, (4) and (6). Therefore, this study does not measure continuity.

Based on the different configurations of rights, we consider the six ownership configurations as a spectrum, from the least-restricted configuration on the left (purchased DRM-free copies), to the more restricted configurations on the right, such as the hosted-content only subscription. We anticipated that the configurations with more restrictions on the users' rights would be less likely to engender feelings of ownership. Because the configurations differ in the amount and pattern of restrictions, we look to the data to discover where the line falls, which demarcates ownership from non-ownership of digital content, among these young adult respondents.

RESEARCH DESIGN

This study used the online survey method. Both surveys were conducted in the spring and summer of 2018. We recruited U.S. college students from a research university in the southeastern United States with over twenty-two thousand undergraduate students, using a university research pool. The Chinese college students were recruited from a normal university in South China with over twenty-four thousand undergraduate students, using a university listserv. For both surveys, we recruited freshmen and sophomores ranging from 18 to 20 years old (born after 1997), from a variety of academic disciplines and socioeconomic backgrounds. The respondents fall within the age group often called Generation Z in the U.S. This post-Millennials demographic group is generally considered as digital natives who have grown up with digital information and communication technologies and social media, a status which holds true for both the American and Chinese students.

Qualtrics surveys in English and Chinese were administered to the U.S. and Chinese participants, respectively. Initially developed in English, the survey questionnaire was translated into Chinese by one of the authors and was edited by the other author. After several rounds of discussions, the authors reached consensus on the consistency/comparability of the English and Chinese versions. To further ensure the instrument's validity, we conducted a pilot study before finalizing the Chinese questionnaire for the actual survey.

After excluding incomplete surveys and those who failed the attention-check questions, 347 surveys from Chinese students and 327 surveys from U.S. students were used for the final analysis. As mentioned, the two groups were similar regarding age, academic class year, and diversity of socioeconomic background. However, in the U.S. survey, more males participated (56.3%) than females. In the China survey, there were more female participants (71.5%), which closely reflected the percentage of female students in the Chinese university (about 67%, typical for a normal university).

To measure participants' ownership perceptions of digital content, we asked participants to indicate whether they thought they owned a copy of the digital content in each of the six categories of ownership configuration identified in Table 1. Since configuration (4) "purchased content hosted by content provider" does not exist for digital music, only five categories were used for digital music. Three answer options were offered for each ownership configuration ("yes," "no," and "not sure").

To understand their perceptions of specific digital rights, we asked users to rate the importance of the ten digital rights associated with the digital content, for e-books, digital songs, and digital movies, respectively (see Tables 6–8), using a five-point Likert scale (1 = not important at all, 5 = very important). We also asked participants to rate their agreement with a number of statements regarding ownership and digital rights (Table 9). At the end of the survey, participants had opportunities to offer additional comments, which turned out to be very useful in explaining some of the results. The survey questions used user-friendly, explanatory language for all concepts.

FINDINGS

Comparing Two Groups' Ownership Perceptions

Aligning with the results of previous research (Zhu & Cho, 2018), users' perceptions of digital ownership, on the whole, look like a spectrum, along with the level of restrictiveness of users' rights in the different ownership configurations. Participants tended to agree that they owned the purchased, DRM-free copies, which is the least-restricted ownership configuration. Most felt that they did not own the hosted-content only subscription, which is the more restricted configuration, with some exceptions. However, there was great disagreement among participants regarding the ownership configurations in the middle, as to whether they own the DRM-enabled copies (software dependent or hardware dependent) and the purchased but hosted-only copies. Tables 2–4 list the configurations in the order of restrictiveness (per the authors' perceptions) and show the findings regarding RQ1 and RQ2.

Table 2 shows the percentage of each response for the six different ownership configurations of e-books, as well as the comparison of the two groups of students. For example, for a purchased DRM-free digital copy, most students (74.5% of the Americans or 72.9% of the Chinese) considered that they owned the copy. Meanwhile, 9.3% of the Americans and 17.6% of the Chinese did not think they owned the copy, while 16.1% and 9.5% of them were not sure. Chi Square tests showed that American and Chinese students had significant differences in their perceptions regarding e-book ownership configurations, with the exception of "subscription allowing temporary download" which had almost exactly the same

	(1) Purchased DRM-free digital copy		(2) Purchased content that requires dedicated software		(3) Purchased content that requires a dedicated device		(4) Purchased content hosted by content provider		(5) Subscription allowing temporary download		(6) Subscription content hosted by content provider only	
	US	CH	US	CH	US	CH	US	CH	US	CH	US	CH
Own	74.5	72.9	52.8	45.2	53.1	35.4	33.2	25.6	21.1	21.0	36.0	28.2
Do not own	9.3	17.6	24.8	37.8	27.3	45.5	46.0	58.2	60.6	60.8	43.5	53.0
Not sure	16.1	9.5	22.4	17.0	19.6	19.0	20.8	16.1	18.3	18.2	20.5	18.7
	$\chi^2 = 14.236$, $df = 2$, $p = .001$		$\chi^2 = 13.218$, $df = 2$, $p = .001$		$\chi^2 = 26.929$, $df = 2$, $p < .001$		$\chi^2 = 10.048$, $df = 2$, $p = .007$		$\chi^2 = 0.05$, $df = 2$, $p = .998$		$\chi^2 = 6.572$, $df = 2$, $p = .037$	

Table 2. Ownership perceptions toward e-books and comparison (unit %).

	(1) Purchased DRM-free digital copy		(2) Purchased content that requires dedicated software		(3) Purchased content that requires a dedicated device		(5) Subscription allowing temporary download		(6) Subscription content hosted by content provider only	
	US	CH	US	CH	US	CH	US	CH	US	CH
Own	83.9	78.7	62.4	43.5	60.2	31.1	43.5	50.1	23.0	14.7
Do not own	7.5	16.1	24.2	38.9	24.5	49.6	41.9	33.7	64.3	70.3
Not sure	8.7	5.2	13.7	17.6	15.2	19.3	14.6	16.1	12.7	15.0
	$\chi^2 = 14.076$, $df = 2$, $p = .001$		$\chi^2 = 23.946$, $df = 2$, $p < .001$		$\chi^2 = 60.892$, $df = 2$, $p < .001$		$\chi^2 = 4.826$, $df = 2$, $p = .090$		$\chi^2 = 7.645$, $df = 2$, $p = .022$	

Table 3. Ownership perceptions toward digital music and comparison (unit %).

	(1) Purchased DRM-free digital copy		(2) Purchased content that requires dedicated software		(3) Purchased content that requires a dedicated device		(4) Purchased content hosted by content provider		(5) Subscription allowing temporary download		(6) Subscription content hosted by content provider only	
	US	CH	US	CH	US	CH	US	CH	US	CH	US	CH
Own	82.3	73.8	58.6	33.7	68.0	33.4	52.5	28.5	39.1	53	19.6	15.3
Do not own	8.1	17.6	25.2	46.4	19.3	46.1	33.2	57.6	47.5	32.9	65.5	70.0
Not sure	9.6	8.6	16.2	19.9	12.7	20.5	14.3	13.8	13.4	14.1	14.9	14.7
	$\chi^2 = 13.337$, $df = 2$, $p = .001$		$\chi^2 = 82.146$, $df = 2$, $p < .001$		$\chi^2 = 44.418$, $df = 2$, $p < .001$		$\chi^2 = 45.628$, $df = 2$, $p < .001$		$\chi^2 = 16.028$, $df = 2$, $p < .001$		$\chi^2 = 2.777$, $df = 2$, $p = .320$	

Table 4. Ownership perceptions toward digital movies and comparison (unit %).

percentage distribution. We had assumed that the participants' ownership perceptions would align with the sequence of the configurations ordered by restrictiveness; that is, the more restrictive the configuration was, the fewer students would choose "yes." The results largely confirmed the assumption, but interestingly, in both groups, more students considered owning "subscription content hosted by content provider only"—the most restricting configuration—than the number who considered owning "purchased content hosted by content provider" and "subscription allowing temporary download." In addition, for most of the configurations, the percentage of the "not sure" answer was close to 20%, indicating a considerable level of uncertainty of the e-book ownership concept.

Table 3 shows participants' ownership perceptions of digital music. Similar to e-books, only the configuration of "subscription allowing temporary download" did not show a significant difference between the two groups. The ownership perceptions of the U.S. students aligned with the restrictiveness of these configurations completely. For the China group, however, it was very different from the case of e-books. Half of the participants claimed ownership to a "subscription allowing temporary download" copy, placing this category second only to the least restrictive configuration, "purchased DRM-free digital copy." This may indicate that whether an item can be downloaded was an important factor in this group's ownership perception.

Table 4 shows participants' ownership perceptions of digital movies. The configuration of "subscription content hosted by content provider only" was the only ones that did not display a significant difference between the two groups, based on Chi Square tests. Similar to the case of digital music, the U.S. group's perceptions largely aligned with the restrictiveness of the configurations, with the exception of software independence and hardware independence. More than half of the participants (53.0%) ascribed ownership to the "subscription allowing temporary download" copies, second only to the least restrictive configuration, "purchased DRM-free digital copy." Once again, this shows the importance of downloadability to the China group.

The Lines between "Own" and "Do not own"

We assumed that, as ownership configurations (1) to (6) ranged from the least restrictive to the most restrictive in terms of digital rights, most people's ownership perceptions of these configurations should follow a pattern of one or several "yes, I own it" for the first few configurations, followed by "no, I do not own it" for the rest. Then the line where "yes" stops and "no" appeared could be considered as the line between ownership and non-ownership for each participant. Findings reported in the previous section showed that both groups' perceptions, as a whole, largely reflected this pattern, but on the individual level, less than half of the participants' answers followed this pattern strictly. As Table 5 shows, the two groups of participants showed significantly different patterns as to where the line fell. The data for e-book configurations are especially scattered with no obvious line for both groups. In the cases of music and movies, the perceptions of around half of the US students did follow the pattern we had assumed, with the line fell between (3) and (4) for music and between (4) and (5) for movies. The perceptions of digital music of 122 Chinese was consistent with the pattern, highest among all three media for this group, but it is still difficult to draw a common line. These results indicate potential confusion and uncertainty about ownership within the Chinese group.

Perceived Importance of Digital Rights

Tables 6–8 show the mean values (out of 5) and the standard deviations of participants' perceived importance of the various digital rights associated with e-books, digital music, and digital movies, respectively. Each table ranks the rights by their importance, as perceived by the U.S. students. These tables also show the results of t tests that were used to reveal the differences between the two groups of young consumers.

Regard to e-books, both groups considered downloadability, device independence, and software independence as the three most important features, though the rankings were slightly different (Table 6). The China group also considered shareability, format choice, format convertibility, modifiability, reusability, and copying to be quite important (over 3.5). Reselling was the least important right to both groups. Except for the rights to download and to resell, all rights were considered more important by the China group than by the U.S. group. T tests showed that the two groups' perceptions differed significantly for all rights except downloading, using on multiple devices, and reselling.

The most important rights associated with digital music were also downloadability, device independence, and software independence, according to the survey results (Table 7). To American students, these rights were more important for digital music than for e-books. Sharing was also considered important (over 3.8) by both groups. In addition, the China group considered format convertibility important (over 3.5). T tests showed that the U.S. group attributed significantly more importance to downloadability and device independence than the China group did, and significantly less importance to format convertibility and reusability than the China group. The importance of resellability was marginally higher for the China group.

Table 8 shows downloadability, device independence, and software independence were still considered the most important rights by both groups, although the rankings were slightly different for each media type. In addition, the China group considered shareability, format choice, and format convertibility (over 3.5). With the exception of the top three rights, the Chinese students attributed significantly higher importance to all rights than the American students did.

	Before (1): none is owned		Between (1) and (2)		Between (2) and (3)		Between (3) and (4)		Between (4) and (5)		Between (5) and (6)		After (6): all is owned		Total		T test results
	US	CH	US	CH	US	CH	US	CH	US	CH	US	CH	US	CH	US	CH	
E-book	8	21	13	33	6	2	31	21	18	11	1	2	31	27	108	117	t (223) = 2.963, p = .003
Digital music	8	16	15	31	8	3	**61**	17	/	/	26	38	53	17	171	122	t (291) = 4.020, p < .001
Digital movie	9	21	19	23	10	1	18	2	**55**	9	22	10	41	26	174	92	t (264) = 3.305, p = .001

Table 5. The line between ownership and non-ownership perceptions.

Digital rights	**US**		**Chinese**		t	p
	Mean	**SD**	**Mean**	**SD**		
Downloadability	3.99	1.163	3.93	0.846	.759	.448
Device independence	3.94	1.280	3.95	0.887	–.117	.907
Software independence	3.75	1.283	3.96	0.884	–2.459	.014
Modifiability	3.48	1.281	3.67	0.872	–2.230	.026
Format choice	3.48	1.226	3.73	0.851	–3.052	.002
Shareability	3.38	1.155	3.86	0.828	–6.133	<.001
Format convertibility	3.31	1.222	3.71	0.870	–4.752	<.001
Reusability to create new content	3.25	1.248	3.64	0.903	–4.616	<.001
Copying capability	3.22	1.240	3.64	0.857	–5.016	<.001
Resellability	2.72	1.332	2.69	0.954	.350	.727

Table 6. Perceived importance of e-book digital rights.

Digital rights	**US**		**Chinese**		t	p
	Mean	**SD**	**Mean**	**SD**		
Downloadability	4.34	1.097	3.9	1.008	5.311	<.001
Device independence	4.28	1.183	3.97	0.886	3.902	<.001
Software independence	3.96	1.331	3.86	0.929	1.064	.288
Shareability	3.86	1.246	3.84	0.897	.222	.825
Copying capability	3.4	1.341	3.42	1.032	–.219	.827
Format choice	3.34	1.384	3.47	0.956	–1.381	.168
Format convertibility	3.17	1.396	3.54	0.938	–4.004	<.001
Reusability to create new content	3.06	1.435	3.4	1.005	–3.509	<.001
Modifiability	2.87	1.442	3.02	0.960	–1.545	.123
Resellability	2.45	1.487	2.65	0.985	–1.986	.047

Table 7. Perceived importance of digital music rights.

Digital rights	**US**		**Chinese**		t	p
	Mean	**SD**	**Mean**	**SD**		
Device independence	4.02	1.194	3.86	.908	1.903	.058
Downloadability	3.90	1.221	3.78	.931	1.451	.147
Software independence	3.80	1.303	3.84	.931	–.391	.696
Shareability	3.47	1.304	3.78	.902	–3.573	<.001
Format choice	3.23	1.366	3.54	.910	–3.386	.001
Copying capability	3.12	1.349	3.46	.968	–3.720	<.001
Format convertibility	3.08	1.362	3.52	.975	–4.781	<.001
Reusability to create new content	2.82	1.389	3.32	1.002	–5.274	<.001
Modifiability	2.81	1.366	3.07	.974	–2.830	.005
Resellability	2.56	1.444	2.83	.987	–2.812	.005

Table 8. Perceived importance of digital movie rights.

	US		Chinese		t	p
	Mean	SD	Mean	SD		
I would buy more digital content if it can be downloaded /shared	3.52	1.155	3.67	0.868	−1.923	.055
There are more and more restrictions on how to access and use digital information.	3.44	1.090	3.65	0.845	−2.695	.007
The different restrictions on digital content by different services are confusing.	3.26	1.107	3.64	0.826	−5.028	<.001
I'm concerned about the long-term access for digital content that I cannot download to my hard drive.	3.23	1.220	3.79	0.934	−6.592	<.001
There should not be any restrictions on how people use, share, and reuse information content	3.01	1.258	3.31	1.013	−3.401	.001
I would use software tools to remove the technical protection over digital content	2.64	1.238	3.11	0.951	−5.507	<.001

Table 9. General opinions about ownership and digital rights.

General Statements

Table 9 shows participants' degrees of agreement with the statements regarding ownership and digital rights (Table 9). Chinese students and American students' opinions were significantly different in most categories. Chinese students appeared to be more concerned about "ownership" rights than their U.S. counterparts. For example, more Chinese students agreed that DRM were confusing and they were concerned about the long-term access if downloading was not allowed. This once more shows the importance of downloadability to this group.

DISCUSSIONS

Limited by space, we only discuss several themes with the help of data collected from the open-ended questions in the survey, which was not reported in the previous section.

Uncertainty about Ownership

The analyses of survey results show a great amount of uncertainty about ownership from both groups of young adults, especially the China group, as indicated by our difficulty in drawing a commonly accepted line between owning and non-owning. This uncertainty is also reflected in the participants' responses to the general statement "The different restrictions on digital content by different services are confusing," to which Chinese students rated 3.64 (Table 9). Moreover, the additional comments made by the participants at the end of the surveys also demonstrated their uncertainty. Many said that the survey was interesting and made them think about matters they had not considered before, and therefore it took them much longer than expected. Some students commented that it was difficult to determine whether it was owning or not owning because it was more complicated than that. Indeed, ownership is more complicated than even before, as many researchers have pointed out (Kirk & Swain, 2018; Perzanowski & Schultz, 2016; Watkins et al., 2016). This theme echoes Perzanowski and Schultz's (2016) concern that social norms about digital ownership and digital rights were being shaped by different stakeholders and consumers' property/ownership rights may be increasingly restricted. Since the digital natives' perceptions may play an important role in the future digital landscape (Satofuka et al., 2009), it is imperative for them to have a good knowledge of rights-related issues.

Another cause of the uncertainty may be the confusion about intellectual property (IP) and personal property. In the survey, we clearly stated "[i]f you buy a book, you own it" before asking them to answer questions about whether they own a digital book with different right restrictions. However, a number of students were still thinking about the intellectual content, rather than the copy as a personal property, when answering the questions. Some students chose "not owning" for all instances because they did not think they could own the IP. A few Chinese students stated that they would not feel that they owned the copy until they had finished reading/watching it. In addition, although our study did not directly ask about the piracy issue or behavior, a number of students from both groups mentioned their attitudes to piracy in their comments, which is not directly related to the ownership perception but more about IP. Most of whom stated that they would not use pirated digital content because subscriptions were affordable; only a few of them said they would not pay for any digital content if free options were available. In this aspect, the young adults in both countries were not as different as the general public often suspects.

The uncertainty also shows in some of the contradictory answers. Whether an item could be downloaded appeared to be especially important for the Chinese participants' ownership perception, because "subscription allowing temporary download" was ranked ahead of those purchased but not downloadable configurations, for both music and movies (Tables 3 and 4). This was also supported by their answers to the questions in Table 9. Interestingly, however, when asked to rate the importance of specific digital rights, Chinese students gave lower importance to downloadability than their US counterparts did. Downloading was the most important right for all three media types according to the U.S. participants. For Chinese students, software/hardware independence was often more important than the ability to download (Tables 6–8).

Familiarity with Restrictions

The findings show many differences between the two groups of young adults, regarding their perceptions of ownership, the lines between ownership and non-ownership, and their perceived importance of digital rights. Although the survey results themselves cannot explain those differences, here we attempt to propose one possible factor in explaining the both cross-culture and within-culture differences—the familiarity with the various configurations and restrictions.

Previous research has hinted at the possible link between psychological ownership and previous (not) encountering of certain media (Kirk & Swain, 2018), and this study may have provided more evidence. For example, the participants' ownership perceptions varied by media type, with e-book perceptions being the most uncertain. This may be because the transition from book to e-book is different from the transition from CD/DVD (which are digital media too) to digital music/movies. Consumers may be more familiar and comfortable with the various ownership configurations of the digital media.

In general, Chinese students were less likely to report the perception that they owned the digital content than the US students (see Tables 2–4) and they often ascribed more importance to the specific digital rights (see Tables 6–8). One possible explanation is that the US was often one step ahead of China in developing new business models for digital media content, and therefore the US young adults were more familiar with the different ownership configurations and more used to the restrictions. The China group reported that they agreed more with the statement "The different restrictions on digital content by different services are confusing" than the U.S. group did (Table 9), possibly because subscription models and the subsequent digital media restrictions were relatively new to them. If this is true, that users' tolerance of restrictions on digital content increases with their familiarity, then we should be extra cautious because the young users' perceptions and attitudes will shape the future market, policy, and legislation (Hansen & Hansen, 2005; Satofuka et al., 2009). If restrictive rights become the norm, they could cause a deep impact on the fundamental social concepts of ownership and property. Longitudinal research is needed for us to gain a deeper, theoretical understanding of ownership, digital rights, and the possible mutual shaping.

Importance of Digital Rights

It is interesting that the participants from China often attributed more importance to the digital rights than their U.S. peers did, including the right to resell digital music and movies, even though there is no mature resale market for media content (digital or physical) in China. Their variability was also smaller than that of the U.S. group. In addition, they displayed a narrower conceptualization of ownership than the American students did. Qualitative research, such as interviews and cultural analysis, possibly from social, legal, and normative perspectives, should be used to find out the underlying reasons. Results of this study point to a few potential factors for future investigation. For example, sharing was more important for the Chinese students than for the American students (Tables 6–8). Since one could hardly share digital media, they tended not to think they own it. Possession may be another important cultural dimension—long-term access and possessing a copy were more important to Chinese students (Table 9).

CONCLUSION

Digital ownership is still in flux and even digital natives are often confused by the various configurations incurred by various business models. In this study, we explored the perceived importance of digital rights as an independent variable and did not find a clear relationship. Psychological, economic, and demographic factors may be explored in future studies. In particular, it may be feasible to combine psychological ownership and legal ownership by bridging technological affordances and specific digital rights.

A factor that may affect the external validity of the study is the representativeness of the samples. It included only two quite homogenous groups of students, and therefore the generalizability may be limited. The uneven gender distributions may also be problematic; however, we did not find significant gender differences regarding the variables in this study within each group. We hope to include more heterogeneous samples in future studies. In addition, as our participants pointed out correctly, the sense of ownership is often more than just yes or no, but about how strong it is, which was a good point to address in the future research.

REFERENCES

Albanesius, C. (2009, Aug 2). Kindle users sue Amazon over deleted Orwell book. Retrieved from https://www.pcmag.com/news/242815/kindle-users-sue-amazon-over-deleted-orwell-book

Atasoy, O., & Morewedge, C. K. (2018). Digital goods are valued less than physical goods. *Journal of Consumer Research*, *44*(6), 1343–1357.

Bardhi, F., Eckhardt, G. M., & Arnould, E. (2012). Liquid relationship to possessions. *Journal of Consumer Research*, *39*(3), 510–529. https://doi.org/10.1086/664037

Belk, R. W. (2013). Extended self in a digital world. *Journal of Consumer Research*, *40*(3), 477–500.

Belk, R. W. (2014). You are what you can access: Sharing and collaborative consumption online. *Journal of Business Research*, *67*(8), 1595–1600.

Boyd, D. (2007). None of this is real. In J. Karaganis, *Structures of participation in digital culture* (pp. 132–157). New York: Social Science Research Council.

Gunter, B., Rowlands, I., & Nicholas, D. (2009). *The Google generation: Are ICT innovations changing information seeking behaviour?* (1st ed.). Oxford, England: Chandos Publishing.

Hansen, F., & Hansen, M. H. (2005). Children as innovators and opinion leaders. *Young Consumers*, *6*(2), 44–59.

Honoré, A. M. (1961). Ownership. In A. G. Guest, *Oxford Essays in Jurisprudence* (pp. 370–375). London, England: Oxford University Press.

Kim, J., Spielmann, N., & McMillan, S. J. (2011). Experience effects on interactivity: Functions, processes, and perceptions. *Journal of Business Research*, *65*(2012), 1543–1550.

Kirk, C. P., & Sarstedt, M. (2016). Psychological ownership: A concept of value to the marketing field. In M. W. Obal, N. Krey, & C. Bushardt, *Let's Get Engaged! Crossing the threshold of marketing's engagement era*. New York: Springer.

Kirk, C. P., & Swain, S. D. (2015). Interactivity and Psychological Ownership in Consumer Value Co-Creation. In K. Kubacki, *Ideas in Marketing: Finding the New and Polishing the Old* (pp. 121–121). New York: Springer.

Kirk, C. P., & Swain, S. D. (2018). Consumer psychological ownership of digital technology. In J. Peck & S. Shu, *Psychological Ownership and Consumer Behavior*. New York: Springer.

Littman, J., & Connaway, L. S. (2004). A circulation analysis of print books and e-Books in an academic research library. *Library Resources & Technical Services*, *48*(4), 256–262.

Miller, R. H. (2000). Electronic resources and academic libraries, 1980-2000: A historical perspective. *Library Trends*, *48*(4), 645–670.

Moeller, S., & Wittkowski, K. (2010). The burdens of ownership: Reasons for preferring renting. *Managing Service Quality*, *20*(2), 176–191. https://doi.org/10.1108/09604521011027598

Monroe, W. S. (1992). Redefining the library: The year's work in collection development, 1991. *Library Resources & Technical Services*, *36*(3), 277–289.

O'Reilly (2017). Ebook usage, devices, and formats. Retrieved from http://shop.oreilly.com/category/customer-service/ebooks.do

Peck, J., & Shu, S. B. (2018). *Psychological ownership and consumer behavior*. New York: Springer.

Perzanowski, A., & Schultz, J. (2016). *The end of ownership: Personal property in the digital economy*. Cambridge, MA: The MIT Press.

Pierce, J. L., Kostova, T., & Dirks, K. T. (2003). The state of psychological ownership: Integrating and extending a century of research. *Review of General Psychology*, *7* (1), 84–107. https://doi.org/10.1037/1089-2680.7.1.84

Pierce, J. L., & Peck, J. (2018). The history of psychological ownership and its emergence in consumer psychology. In J. Peck & S. B. Shu, *Psychological Ownership and Consumer Behavior*. New York: Springer.

Rainie, L., & Duggan, M. (2012). E-book reading jumps. In *Print book readings declines*. Washington, DC: Pew Research Center.

Rifkin, J. (2000). *The age of access: The new culture of hypercapitalism where all of life is a paid for experience*. New York: Penguin.

Satofuka, F., Kantola, I., & Kono, Y. (2009). Explaining media choices; Theoretical discussion and empirical experiment. *AI & Society*, *24*, 135–150.

Stone, B. (2009, Jul 17). Amazon erases Orwell books from Kindle. Retrieved from https://www.nytimes.com/2009/07/18/technology/companies/18amazon.html?_r=1

The Nielsen Company. (2017). Millennials on millennials: Digital music and digital communication. Volume 2. Retrieved from https://www.nielsen.com/us/en/insights/reports/2017/millennials-on-millennials-digital-music-and-communication.html

Venkatesh, A., & Behairy, N. (2012). Young American consumers and new technologies. In M. Molesworth & J. Denegri-Knott, *Digital Virtual Consumption* (pp. 29–45). New York: Routledge.

Voorveld, H. A. M., Neijens, P. C., & Smit, E. G. (2011). The Relation between Actual and Perceived Interactivity. *Journal of Advertising*, *40*(2), 77–92.

Walton, E. (2014). Why undergraduate students choose to use e-books. *Journal of Librarianship and Information Science*, *46*(4), 263–270.

Wang, Y., & Niu, Y. (2018). The status quo and prospect of college students' digital music copyright consumption: The case of Shenyang. *Time Finance*, (5), 323–325.

Watkins, R. D., Denegri-Knott, J., & Molesworth, M. (2016). The relationship between ownership and possession: observations from the context of digital virtual goods. *Journal of Marketing Management*, *32*(1/2), 44–70. https://doi.org/10.1080/0267257X.2015.1089308

Wong, W., Stelmaszewska, H., Bhimani, N., Barn, S., & Barn, B. (2010). *JISC user behaviour observational study: User behaviour in resource discovery: Final report*. London, England: Joint Information Systems Council.

Xu, N., & Hua, J. (2018). College students' digital music consumption market in the context of copyright protection: An investigation in Nanchang. *Southeast Communication*, *2*, 1–3.

Zhang, L. (2015). Investigation and consideration of college students' copyright awareness in the digital environment. *Communication and Copyright*, *2*, 162–165.

Zhu, X., & Cho, M. (2018). The end of ownership? An investigation of users' preferences and perceptions of ownership configurations. Proceedings of the 81st ASIS&T Annual Meeting (634-643), Vancouver, BC, Canada, November 10-14, 2018.

Mapping Digital Information Security Management in the University Libraries of Pakistan

Maria Aslam
Institute of Administrative Sciences, University of the Punjab, Lahore, Pakistan
maria.ias@pu.edu.pk

Ayesha Khalid
Minhaj University, Lahore, Pakistan
ayeshamna@gmail.com

Syeda Hina Batool
Department of Information Management, University of the Punjab, Lahore, Pakistan
hina.im@pu.edu.pk

Ghulam Farid
Shalimar Medical and Dental College, Lahore, Pakistan
ghulam.farid@sihs.org.pk

ABSTRACT

Maintaining digital information and protecting data assets remains a principal concern in libraries. Digital information security awareness is a major tool in overcoming incidents about data loss in libraries. This paper focuses on the awareness level of librarians and current status of digital information security management (DISM) in academic libraries of Lahore, Pakistan. The results also highlight the policies at individual or institutional level about DISM in selected libraries. The data were collected through structured interviews from 15 public and private sector academic librarians. Findings revealed that presently, digital resources are the integral part of university libraries such as OPAC's, official records and digital resources. However, information professionals did not show interest in security management of digital resources, as they least considered this role as part of their jobs. Therefore, they attended limited training programs to update their knowledge. A general trend indicates that institutional information technology departments were responsible for maintaining library server, network and hardware.

KEYWORDS

Pakistan, University Libraries; Information Security Management; Digital Security; Information Professional; Digital Competencies

ASIS&T THESAURUS

Information Loss; Developing Countries

INTRODUCTION

Libraries are important social institutions that help the people to access various information resources. With the continuous development of information technologies, libraries have been evolving constantly, which greatly expanded library services and improved their efficiency. The concept of a digital library was proposed in the early 1990s and after years of practical application and development, digital libraries have gradually become an important aspect in the development of modern libraries. With emergence of digital libraries, Digital Information Security Management (DISM) issues are prevalent concerns for organizations or in libraries, specifically where issues directly impact upon regulatory, risk-based or reputational concerns resulting from intrusions and loss of data.

Currently, digital information is one of the most prominent assets for libraries and must be protected from security breach. Many data breaches continue to result from accidental, intentional or malicious human factors, leading to financial and data loss. One approach toward improving behaviors and culture is with the application of on-going awareness activities and trainings among users and librarians. The design of a fully functional and user customizable digital library service system involves technology and digital data sources. According to Al-Dhahri, Al-Sarti, and Aziz (2017) "Digital Information Security Management System provides requirements for establishing, implementing, maintaining and improving an information security management system" (p.3).

DISM continued to appear as an important concern in academic libraries all over the world. Academic libraries need to protect its soft assets from potential threats and should ensure the confidentiality and availability of secure digital information resources to its users. Literature indicates that mostly attention is given to digital threats (Ahmed & Siyal, 2005; Albrechtsen, 2007) that affect the performance of the libraries; however, DSIM is appeared less researched area with specific reference to Pakistan. Furthermore, little is available in context of academic libraries. Proper awareness about DISM among information professionals can minimize the risk of data loss in libraries. Security policy about DISM also helps in maintaining the Library data. Therefore, it is important to study the awareness level of library professionals regarding DISM. This study highlights the current status, measures as well as existing policies of DISM in selected academic libraries of Lahore city. This is an ongoing research project focusing on library's soft assets including

82nd Annual Meeting of the Association for Information Science & Technology | Melbourne, Australia | 19–23 October, 2019

DOI: 10.1002/pra2.00070

OPACs, official records, software, users' data, digital holdings (e-journals/e-books/e-resources) and only selected findings have been presented in this paper, qualitative research focusing on detailed practices and real time problems is in process. The findings of the study not only guide the university librarians to improve their digital information security management, but it will also provide help in designing policy in this fast- changing technological world. The findings will enable professionals to overcome the limitations in terms of loss of data. The results will indicate the level of awareness regarding DISM and therefore, will be beneficial for library schools and professional organizations.

RESEARCH OBJECTIVES

The present study will attempt to address the following research objectives:

- To know the existing status of digital information security management in selected academic libraries
- To investigate the present practices regarding digital information security management
- To ascertain the extent of information professionals' awareness regarding digital information security management
- To explore the existing policies about digital information security management in libraries

LITERATURE REVIEW

Previous studies have raised questions about digital content security violation though not specifically in the libraries' context. This section presents four major themes identified through literature.

Emphasis on DISM Policies & Training Programs

Hutchinson and Warren (2001) explored the policies and procedures of various organizations for securing data. They identified that users frequently face security threats yet very less of them are eventually prepared for such attacks. A study concluded that majority of the organizations use computer technology without protecting data or with minimum-security measures Webb White & Pearson, 2001.

Literature also emphasized on training programs regarding DISM, for example, Pérez-Freire, Comesana, Troncoso-Pastoriza, and Pérez-González (2006) focused on the policies, awareness programs, and security systems for effective secure information. Similarly, librarians need to acquire the essential skills and knowledge to protect library information assets from unauthorized access, loss, change and misuse (Pace, 2003). It is advised in studies that experienced professionals should customize software to the specific organizational context. It means automation requires expertise at first place to reduce the burden of security issues.

Library Soft Assets and Malware Agents

Susanto, Almunawar, and Kang (2012) highlighted the significant role of information in high-level decision making however, viruses, worms, hackers, social engineering could sometimes hurdle in providing information timely. Khan (2012) gave comprehensive details of the viruses and worms affecting the day-to-day goals of the librarian's computers within the library organization.

The main streams that concerns security in the library computers are physically vulnerable to attacks of malware agents, including Trojans, viruses, worms, adware, spyware, password stealers, pornware, keystroke loggers as well as to theft, damage and destruction. Hackers, viruses, worms and Trojan horses are referred as external threats that libraries should be able to handle (Afzal & Nasser, 2007; Zimerman, 2010). Other highlighting other weaknesses Boss (1984) mentioned poor security points (unsecure windows) and poor signage issues (cited as Maidabino & Zainab, 2011). Gritzalis, Iliadis, and Oikonomopoulos (2000) warns about freely distributed software despite their claims for protection they actually affect security of digital resources. Pace (2003) underlines users' confidentiality during library transactions such as browsing, database searching and librarians must use it in a professional way. The library needs to ensure access of material to authorized users timely, security also infers that contents of collection or information should not be altered through intentional or unintentional actions (Maidabino & Zainab, 2011).

DISM Requires a Great Deal of Attention in Libraries

Despite the major investments in technological infrastructures, not much have discussed regarding the actual digital Information Security Management (DISM) situation in libraries. The literature review exhibits that DISM is highly neglected area in libraries specifically in developing world. Subsequently, literature also indicates the difficulties that librarians face due to lack of IT knowledge and highly dependency on technical experts. Therefore, present study provides the insights of Pakistani public and private sector universities' librarians on DISM concerns, as this is one of the few of its kind on this topic in local context.

METHODS

The present study seeks to capture the DISM status and practices of academic libraries, therefore, the ICT librarians, of fifteen public and private completely automated or hybrid academic libraries, who either directly or indirectly responsible for maintaining library's information system or dealing with the libraries' digital content were interviewed. Lahore city is one of the modern and popular cities of Pakistan, therefore, it can be assumed that libraries must equip with modern DISM system. It was assumed that DISM concept is technical term and the terminologies used in questionnaire can be confusing for the respondents, therefore, researchers personally administered and conducted fifteen structured interviews. The questionnaire was based on literature and covered the aspects of DISM's present status in libraries, current practices, information professionals' awareness level and existing

DISM policies' status. This is an ongoing project based on structured and unstructured interview questions. In this paper we are presenting only structured interview data results which were analyzed manually and presented in the following paragraphs.

Data Analysis

Respondents were asked about their gender, qualification and status of universities in which they are working. Out of 15 respondents, majority (n = 12) were male while only two (n = 02) were female. Regarding qualification, results showed that majority (n = 08) were holding MPhil degree, Master's degree holders were five and only two hold PhD degree. Status of universities showed that more than half (n = 08) were working in private sector while others belong to (n = 07) public sector universities.

Libraries' DISM Status and Practices

In this section, respondents investigated about their present practices of securing library data. Data revealed that digital resources are the integral part of these selected libraries such as OPAC's, official records and digital resources for users (theses, reports, e-books, e-journals) In majority of the organizations the library professionals were using antivirus systems to protect the information resources (n = 13). Web server software, Anti-virus and firewalls were commonly used techniques to prevent the web server attacks (n = 10). To protect data and for uninterruptable power supplies, UPS and generators were commonly in practice to prevent data loss in case of power failures (n = 15). The respondents mentioned that data backup is their regular routine, few librarians (n = 6) took back up after 15 days and other took it after a month. Very few librarians (n = 3) mentioned that they do not take back up regularly. In practice, a large number of libraries (n = 11) were using Windows as an operating system; only few professionals mentioned that they are using Linux system.

However, some respondents mentioned that they are not aware of these security measures as their IT department is responsible for protecting digital content and library servers. Respondents mentioned that in case of data loss; disciplinary action can be taken by library and IT committee against those employees who violate the security policy.

Status of DISM Policies

Almost all public and private sector university librarians considered DISM policy necessary for their libraries. Data showed six libraries did not have any policy whereas nine libraries have digital content security policy. In most cases policy was written or designed by IT department (n = 7). Annual audit/ checkup policy of DISM exist in most of the libraries (n = 11). Library audit is conducted by library committee and by institutional IT committee. Access control policy is also existing in majority of the libraries (n = 14) which addresses the rules and rights for each user or a group of users. Controlled procedure exists in most of the libraries (n = 9) for implementation of changes to DISM and in few libraries it was totally controlled by IT department.

Librarians' Interest and Awareness Level

To investigate the interest and awareness level of information professionals regarding DISM, they were inquired about relevant trainings and seminars which they attended for learning purpose. Data showed that in last two years majority of the librarians (n = 11) attended information security management seminars, conferences and sessions, but only four information professionals said that they had proper trainings of DISM in their organizations. Therefore, they did not feel the need to attend outside their organization. Although, all respondents considered the importance of DSIM in libraries as they mentioned that sensitive information can be leaked, library's reputation was a major concern among all professionals in case of computer networks attack or in case of data loss. So, overall respondents strongly believed in the important role of DISM in libraries.

DISCUSSION

Based on the results the present study indicated that public and private sector university librarians oversee the DISM in their libraries. However, in the current scenario, ICTs are widely used for service provision to local and remote patrons digitally. Connecting a library to the outer world via internet increased the risks associated with control and security of information. Therefore, it is necessary for the university librarians to be aware of DISM as mostly university libraries are offering their services digitally.

Generally, majority of university librarians in Pakistan have been focusing on technology alone rather than security measures to protect it. Thus, it is necessary for these libraries to place and create awareness regarding DISM value and measures through active participation of librarians, top management support and trainings for adopting security measures. Webb White and Pearson (2001) mentioned that majority of the organizations are using computer technology without protecting data and very few provide minimum security measures.

Findings show that majority of the libraries were using free software to protect digital content, DISM or cyber security is observed one of the most neglected parts in budget allocation in both public and private sector selected libraries. The university librarians of Pakistan need to be aware about the value and importance of this sensitive issue. Breeding (2006) mentioned that this is one of the most important areas which can protect the library data from threats if properly implemented. Institutions also considered digital security threat as an important factor which can be minimized through proper budgeting and policies.

Findings, of the present research highlighted that data security threat was perceived as the least threatening concern as compare to hardware security threats in both sectors' libraries. Once the hardware, software, workstation, network, server and data have been implemented these are not reviewed on regular until any sudden technical mishap occurs. Maintenance negligence is viewed as the most prevalent threat to hardware and software security in selected university libraries.

University libraries in current study have configured their antivirus software and desktop security software to receive frequent updates. However, network security controls have not been revised regularly at these libraries.

University libraries in this study have regularly backed up the documents related to the server. However, never strictly follow the controls and disciplinary procedures such as suspension and dismissal in case a library staff or users breaches the digital security policies. Only verbal or written warning letters are issued without perusal. There is a dire need to strengthen DISM policies and security awareness initiatives in these university libraries.

CONCLUSION

This study found that implementing IT infrastructure in libraries is not enough without incorporating regular assessment of DISM toward better secured digital environments. It is necessary that information to be kept confidential when required, to be available when and where needed and protected from modification and loss of integrity. This requires proper policy and implementation of DISM in libraries. The policy must imply the technical, legal and ethical aspects with relevance to digital information. Furthermore, the policy must be prepared in order to link with cyber security, intellectual property, system implementation and internet policies. The study also pointed that information security is to be effective; and libraries need to be incorporated technical measures as well as information security policies, security procedures and awareness creation activities in their security programs. Presently, libraries are building more virtual collection than print, these steps reduce walk in users as well as physical theft of material, therefore, there is a dire need to improve and implement DISM systems in libraries. With ease, technology increased the intentional forgery of informational material, this made librarians to know more about technical requirements of access and security threats with the users' more demanding information needs. Therefore, information professionals need to play professionally and solve the dichotomy of serving users also safeguarding misuse of information resources.

Researchers anticipate further qualitative study to look into the following direction, DISM readiness among librarians for establishing a sound security policy and security control in libraries at Pakistan.

REFERENCES

Afzal, A. S. W., & Nasser, M. (2007). Digital age: Challenges for libraries. *Information, Society and Justice Journal, 1* (1), 43–48.

Ahmed, F., & Siyal, M. Y. (2005). A novel approach for regenerating a private key using password, fingerprint and smart card. *Information Management & Computer Security*, *13*(1), 39–54.

Albrechtsen, E. (2007). A qualitative study of users' view on information security. *Computers& Security*, *26*, 276–289.

Al-Dhahri, S., Al-Sarti, M., & Aziz, A. A. (2017). Information Security Management System. *International Journal of Computer Applications*, *158*(7).

Boss, R. (1984). Collection Security. *Library Trends*, *18*(1), 39–48.

Breeding, M. (2006). Protecting your library's data. Computers in libraries. Retrieved November 12, 2007, from http://www.librarytechnology.org/diglibfulldisplay.pl?SID=20110116654235839&ode=bib&RC=10343&Row=31&

Gritzalis, S., Iliadis, J., & Oikonomopoulos, S. (2000). Distributed component software security issues on deploying a secure electronic marketplace. *Information Management & Computer Security*, *8*(1), 5–13.

Hutchinson, W., & Warren, M. (2001). Attitudes of Australian information system managers against online attackers. *Information Management & Computer Security*, *9*(3), 106–111.

Khan, I. (2012). An introduction to computer viruses: Problems and solutions. *Library Hi Tech News*, *29*(7), 8–12.

Maidabino, A. A., & Zainab, A. N. (2011). Collection security management at university libraries: Assessment of its implementation status. *Malaysian Journal of Library & Information Science*, *16*(1), 15–33.

Pace, A. K. (2003). *The ultimate digital library: where the new information players meet*. Chicago, IL: American Library Association.

Pérez-Freire, L., Comesana, P., Troncoso-Pastoriza, J. R., & Pérez-González, F. (2006). Watermarking security: a survey. In *Transactions on data hiding and multimedia security I* (pp. 41–72). Berlin, Heidelberg: Springer.

Susanto, H., Almunawar, M. N., & Kang, C. (2012). Toward cloud computing evolution: Efficiency vs trendy vs security. *Available at SSRN*, 2039739.

Webb White, G., & Pearson, S. J. (2001). Controlling corporate e-mail, PC use and computer security. *Information Management & Computer Security*, *9*(2), 88–92.

Zimerman, M. (2010). Protect your library's computers. *New Library World*, *111*(5/6), 203–212.

Search Is the Future? The Young Search Less for Files

Ofer Bergman
Bar-Ilan University,
Ramat Gan, Israel
bergmao@mail.biu.ac.il

Tamar Israeli
Bar-Ilan University,
Ramat Gan, Israel
tamarisraeli@gmail.com

Steve Whittaker
UC Santa Cruz,
Santa Cruz, California
swhittak@ucsc.edu

ABSTRACT

There are two main ways to retrieve files: hierarchical folder *navigation* and query-based *search* using a search engine. Research consistently shows that users prefer retrieving files using folder navigation, rather than more flexible query-based search. But desktop search engines continue to improve, so does this mean that younger generations rely more on search as their usage habits were formed when experiencing more effective search? This study tested age effects on search use by asking 289 participants to retrieve 1,557 of their shared files. Counterintuitively, our results showed a positive correlation between age and search percentage, with participants over fifty searching over four times as much as participants in their twenties. Results were confirmed by an n = 653 combined data analysis. A possible explanation is that older participants forget the location of their files. We discuss the deep neuro-cognitive roots of navigation preference which may also explain our findings.

KEYWORDS

Files; Search; Navigation Preference; Age Effects

ASIS&T THESAURUS

Documents; Collections; Personal Collections

INTRODUCTION

Personal Information Management (PIM) is an activity in which people store information items (such as files and emails) in order to retrieve them later. The two main strategies by which these information items can be retrieved are *navigation* and *search*. When navigating, users manually traverse their organizational hierarchy until they reach the folder in which the target item is stored. For search, users first generate a query specifying an attribute of the target item, and when the search engine returns a set of results, they select the relevant item (Bergman, Beyth-Marom, Nachmias, Gradovitch, & Whittaker, 2008). Although search is more flexible than navigation and does not require creating or remembering a prior structure, research has consistently shown that users prefer navigation over search (Bergman & Yanai, 2017; Boardman & Sasse, 2004; Capra & Pérez-Quiñones, 2005; Fitchett & Cockburn, 2015; Kirk, Sellen, Rother, & Wood, 2006). Furthermore, well-documented improvements in search engine performance do not affect this preference, because search is used only as an infrequent last resort for situations where users forget file locations (Bergman et al., 2008).

However, to the best of our knowledge, the effect of age on retrieval strategy preference has never been systematically tested. We test the intuition that young people are more reliant on search. If young people do search more, then this can be interpreted as a move toward search domination, with navigation being just a legacy habit older people acquired through early exposure to primitive search technology. To test this, as part of a larger research project we asked 289 participants to retrieve 1,557 of their shared files, giving them a free choice regarding retrieval method.

BACKGROUND

When retrieving a file the user needs to choose between folder based *navigation* and query based *search*. There are obvious intuitive advantages of search for both retrieval and organization. Search seems to be more flexible and efficient for retrieval. It is flexible because it does not depend on users remembering the correct storage location; instead, in their query users can specify *any file attribute* they happen to remember (Lansdale, 1988). Search is also potentially more efficient as users can retrieve information by generating a single query, instead of using multiple operations to laboriously navigate to the relevant part of their folder hierarchy. Finally, search doesn't require careful organizational preparation in anticipation for future retrieval requirements (Cutrell, Dumais, & Teevan, 2006; Dourish et al., 2000; Lansdale, 1988; Russell & Lawrence, 2007). These arguments against navigation are bolstered by developments in web access, where initial use of navigational systems such as Yahoo categories has almost completely been superseded by search engines such as Google (Kobayashi & Takeda, 2000; Obendorf, Weinreich, Herder, & Mayer, 2007). These intuitive arguments have led many PIM researchers to propose that search engines should replace folders (Cutrell et al., 2006; Dourish et al., 2000; Fertig, Freeman, & Gelernter, 1996; Lansdale, 1988; Raskin, 2000; Russell & Lawrence, 2007).

In contrast, empirical research consistently shows that users prefer navigation over search (Bergman & Yanai, 2017;

82nd Annual Meeting of the Association for Information Science & Technology | Melbourne, Australia | 19–23 October, 2019

DOI: 10.1002/pra2.00029

Boardman & Sasse, 2004; Capra & Pérez-Quiñones, 2005; Kirk et al., 2006; Teevan, Alvarado, Ackerman, & Karger, 2004). Moreover, search engines have improved dramatically due to the use of indexing around 2005. For example, they work a thousand times faster than older search engines (Farina, 2005; Lowe, 2006). Nevertheless, people using such improved search engines do not search more than people using technically less developed ones. In fact, regardless of search engine quality, people consistently use search only as a 'last resort' for that minority of cases where they cannot remember file locations (Bergman et al., 2008; Fitchett & Cockburn, 2015).

But the search engine revolution occurred over a decade ago. So what happens in the new generation of tech-savvy users who grew up with high quality search? Do they break the 'rule' of searching only as last resort in contrast to the older generation who remain faithful to old navigation habits? We tested this and other research questions for shared files. We examine shared files as these have become an integral part of modern work process with the emergence of cloud based storage.

RESEARCH QUESTIONS

1. How do computer users prefer to retrieve their shared files – using search or navigation?
2. How does age affect search percentage?
3. Which method is more efficient – navigation or search?

RESEARCH METHOD

We used the Elicited Personal Information Retrieval (EPIR) technique described in (Bergman & Whittaker, 2016). Participants retrieved files requested by the tester. To increase ecological validity participants retrieved their own shared files from their own computers. Participants were free to choose their retrieval methods. *Search percentage* was calculated as the percentage of retrievals that included search from all retrievals conducted by the participant.

Participants

Although we gathered data from each participant individually, it was important for us to gather it from a large number of participants. This required considerable effort. However, our large scale data collection has the advantage of increasing external validity. We recruited 300 Israeli participants (non-random selection). Eleven participants were excluded because of a technical problem with their screen recording. Of the remaining 289 participants, 216 (75%) were women. Their age ranged from 19 to 77 years old (M = 36.99, SD = 12.7). All our participants used a Windows operating system, as this was required by our EPIR software. On a 1-5 Likert scale their average self-estimated computer literacy was 3.83 (SD = 0.87).

Procedure

Preparation for the Retrieval Task

The testers explained the study to potential participants and asked them to sign an informed consent form. The tester activated specially designed EPIR software to prepare the target file list. The software accessed the participants' 'Recent Items' folder and scanned for files where the author's name is different from the participants' user name (i.e., shared files). The files collected were document files because people typically share documents in order to collaborate on them.

The Retrieval Task

After the file retrieval list was created, participants were asked to retrieve up to ten files that were presented to them by the EPIR software. In each individual retrieval task, the participant was asked to retrieve a single shared file after the tester specified its name. Participants were instructed to retrieve the target file and click on it once, but not open it in order to retain their privacy. Each retrieval attempt continued until the file was successfully found, or the participant said they could not find it. Participants were not allowed to directly copy the file name into their desktop search box because this would not have been a realistic simulation of retrieval; real-life search processes are clearly cognitive in nature requiring participants to actively generate search terms (Ingwersen, 1996). Retrieval was video-recorded for later analysis.

RESULTS

RQ1: How do computer users prefer to retrieve their shared files – using search or navigation?

From a total of 1,557 retrievals, in 1,303 (84%) cases participants used folder navigation, in 134 (9%) retrievals participants navigated and then searched for the files using a search engine, only in 68 retrievals (4%) participants searched for the file as their first choice, and in 52 (3%) of the cases participants used other retrieval methods. These results indicate navigation preference over search.

RQ2: How does age affect search percentage?

A Pearson correlation revealed a significant positive correlation between age and search percentage $r(289) = 0.18$, $p < .001$. In addition, an independent t test indicated that the search percentages for participants over fifty (n = 56, M = 21.31%, SD = 27.21%) was significantly larger than those of participants in their twenties (n = 108, M = 4.61%, SD = 11.63%), $t(162) = 16.71$, $p < .001$. Note the large effect - participants over fifty years old searched more than four times as much participants in their twenties. A possible reason for these results is that older participants forget the locations of their files. However, greater reliance on search did *not* occur because older participants had larger collections. Contrary to our expectations, we found a negative correlation between age and the participants' overall collection size ($r = -0.26$, $p < .001$), and between age and participants' number of folders ($r = -0.22$, $p < .001$).

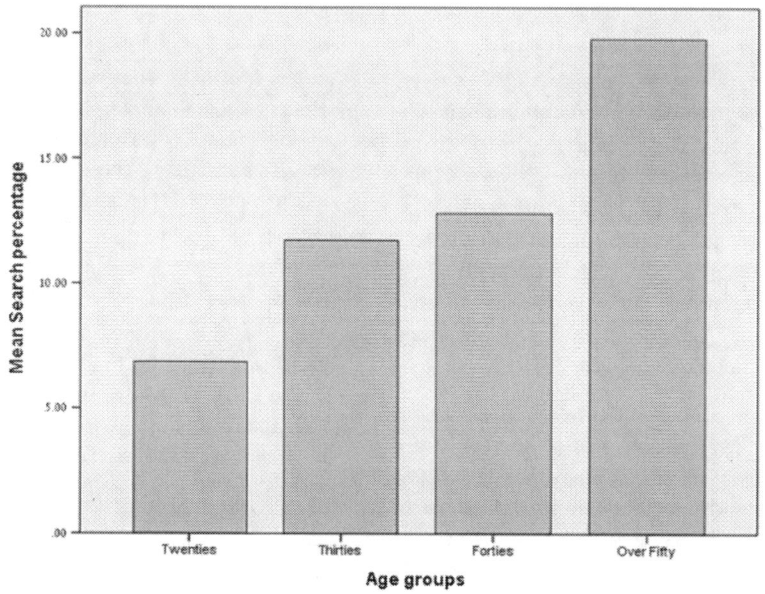

Figure 1. Search percentage of different age groups (n = 653).

As our results can be regarded as counterintuitive, we retested them by conducting a combined data analysis. We combined our data with the data from our previous studies which also tested shared files retrieval using EPIR (Bergman, Whittaker, & Falk, 2014; Bergman, Whittaker, & Frishman, 2019; Bergman & Yanai, 2017). Altogether, we examined data regarding the actual retrievals of 653 participants. Results indicate a significant correlation $r(653) = 0.20$, $p < .001$ between age and search percentage. Figure 1 shows age effects on search percentage for this combined data, revealing a consistent positive effect.

RQ3: Which method was more efficient – navigation or search?

In order to compare search and navigation effects on our dependent variables we assessed only *pure search* and *pure navigation*, and thus ignored combinations of the two that are trivially less efficient. An independent t test indicates that retrieval time for *pure search* retrievals (M = 41.59 s, SD = 26.02 s) was significantly longer than for *pure navigation* retrievals (M = 32.59 sec, SD = 26.27 s) $t(1243) = 2.31$, $p < .05$. Again, counterintuitively, these results suggest that search may be less efficient than navigation.

DISCUSSION

Our results confirm previous findings that navigation is the preferred file retrieval strategy (Bergman et al., 2008; Bergman & Yanai, 2017; Boardman & Sasse, 2004; Fitchett & Cockburn, 2015; Teevan et al., 2004) and that navigation is more efficient than search (Bergman, Tene-Rubinstein, & Shalom, 2013). Contrary to possible expectations, the younger generation whose computer habits were formed in over a decade of improved search engines usage did not search for their files more than the older generation. In fact we found quite the opposite: a positive correlation between age and search percentage, with participants over fifty searching more than four times as often as participants in their twenties. Furthermore, this cannot be attributed to bigger collections, because older people's collections were actually smaller. Results were confirmed when using a combined results analysis with 653 participants. We already know that people search for their files only as last resort when they cannot remember their location (Bergman et al., 2008). A possible reason for the increase in search with age is therefore that older people forget where they placed their files. This may result from well-documented age-related declines in memory (e.g., Deary et al., 2009; Salthouse, 2009; Verhaeghen & Salthouse, 1997).

Search allows users to flexibly retrieve an item using any attribute they happen to remember as opposed to navigation which requires users to remember the exact path to a specific information item. Why then do people prefer navigation to search, despite search being more flexible and over a decade of improved search technology use? It seems that navigation preference has deep neuro-cognitive roots that relate to cognitive processing demands: when navigating to their files, users deploy the same brain structures that they use when navigating in the physical world, requiring few verbal resources. In contrast, search uses Broca's area, commonly observed in attentionally demanding linguistic processing (Benn et al., 2015; Bergman et al., 2013). These neuro-cognitive findings may also explain our results as evolutionary changes in the brain cannot occur in a single generation.

ACKNOWLEDGMENTS

We thank our participants. This study was supported by the Israeli Science Foundation (Grant 1074/16).

REFERENCES

Benn, Y., Bergman, O., Glazer, L., Arent, P., Wilkinson, I. D., Varley, R., & Whittaker, S. (2015). Navigating through digital folders uses the same brain structures as real world navigation. *Scientific Reports*, *5*, 1–8.

Bergman, O., Beyth-Marom, R., Nachmias, R., Gradovitch, N., & Whittaker, S. (2008). Improved search engines and navigation preference in personal information management. *ACM Transactions on Information Systems*, *26*(4), 1–24. https://doi.org/10.1145/1402256.1402259

Bergman, O., Tene-Rubinstein, M., & Shalom, J. (2013). The use of attention resources in navigation vs. search. *Personal and Ubiquitous Computing*, *17*(3), 583–590.

Bergman, O., & Whittaker, S. (2016). *The science of managing our digital stuff*. Cambridge, MA: Mit Press.

Bergman, O., Whittaker, S., & Falk, N. (2014). Shared files – The retrieval perspective. *Journal of the American Society for Information Science and Technology*, *65*(10), 1949–1963. https://doi.org/10.1002/asi.23147

Bergman, O., Whittaker, S., & Frishman, Y. (2019). Let's get personal: the little nudge that improves document retrieval in the Cloud. *Journal of documentation*, *75*(2), 379–396.

Bergman, O., & Yanai, N. (2017). Personal information retrieval: smartphones vs. computers, emails vs. files. *Personal and Ubiquitous Computing*, 1–12.

Boardman, R., & Sasse, M. A. (2004). *"Stuff goes into the computer and doesn't come out": a cross-tool study of personal information management* Paper presented at the SIGCHI conference on Human Factors in Computing Systems, Vienna, Austria.

Capra, R. G., & Pérez-Quiñones, M. A. (2005). Using web search engines to find and refind information. *Computer*, *38*(10), 36–42.

Cutrell, E., Dumais, S. T., & Teevan, J. (2006). Searching to eliminate personal information management. *Communications of the ACM*, *49*(1), 58–64.

Deary, I. J., Corley, J., Gow, A. J., Harris, S. E., Houlihan, L. M., Marioni, R. E., … Starr, J. M. (2009). Age-associated cognitive decline. *British medical bulletin*, *92*(1), 135–152.

Dourish, P., Edwards, W. K., LaMarca, A., Lamping, J., Petersen, K., Salisbury, M., … Thornton, J. (2000). Extending document management systems with user-specific active properties. *ACM Trans Inf Syst*, *18*(2), 140–170.

Farina, P. A. (2005). A Comparison of Two Desktop Search Engines: Google Desktop Search (Beta) vs. Windows XP Search Companion 21st Computer Science Seminar, Hartford.

Fertig, S., Freeman, E., & Gelernter, D. (1996). Finding and reminding. *SIGCHI Bulletin*, *28*(1), 66–69.

Fitchett, S., & Cockburn, A. (2015). An empirical characterisation of file retrieval. *International Journal of Human-Computer Studies*, *74*, 1–13.

Ingwersen, P. (1996). Cognitive perspectives of information retrieval interaction: Elements of a cognitive IR theory. *Journal of documentation*, *52*(1), 3–50.

Kirk, D., Sellen, A., Rother, C., & Wood, K. (2006). *Understanding photowork SIGCHI conference on Human Factors in Computing Systems* (pp. 761–770). New York: ACM.

Kobayashi, M., & Takeda, K. (2000). Information retrieval on the web. *ACM Computing Surveys*, *32*(2), 144–173. https://doi.org/10.1145/358923.358934

Lansdale, M. W. (1988). The psychology of personal information management. *Applied ergonomics*, *19*(1), 55–66.

Lowe, M. (2006). *Evaluation of desktop search applications*. Sydney, Australia: Kalio.

Obendorf, H., Weinreich, H., Herder, E., & Mayer, M. (2007). Web page revisitation revisited: implications of a long-term click-stream study of browser usage. In *Proceedings of the SIGCHI conference on Human factors in computing systems* (pp. 597–606). New Yorks: ACM.

Raskin, J. (2000). *The humane interface: new directions for designing interactive systems*. Boston: ACM Press/-Addison-Wesley Publishing Co.

Russell, D., & Lawrence, S. (2007). Search everything. In W. Jones & J. Teevan, *Personal Information Management* (pp. 153–166). Seattle and London: University of Washington Press.

Salthouse, T. A. (2009). When does age-related cognitive decline begin? *Neurobiology of aging*, *30*(4), 507–514.

Teevan, J., Alvarado, C., Ackerman, M. S., & Karger, D. R. (2004). The perfect search engine is not enough: a study of orienteering behavior in directed search. In E. Dykstra-Erickson & M. Tscheligi, *SIGCHI conference on Human Factors in Computing Systems* (pp. 415–422). New York: ACM Press.

Verhaeghen, P., & Salthouse, T. A. (1997). Meta-analyses of age–cognition relations in adulthood: Estimates of linear and nonlinear age effects and structural models. *Psychological bulletin*, *122*(3), 231.

Exploration of Information Organization in Language Archives

Mary Burke
University of North Texas,
Denton, TX, USA
mary.burke@unt.edu

Oksana Zavalina
University of North Texas
Denton, TX, USA
oksana.zavalina@unt.edu

ABSTRACT

This submission reports preliminary results of the first stage of a research project that seeks to identify the information organization methods and techniques currently offered in the language data archives and the gaps between the tools and techniques available and the needs of actual and potential users of language data archives. We conducted an exploratory content analysis of the websites of the language archives (LAs) hosted by the institutions located in the United States and several other countries. The focus of our exploratory content analysis is on the information organization, including documentation on metadata standards, displaying of individual metadata records and availability of harvesting sets of metadata records, provision of advanced discovery and navigation options powered by metadata such as availability of adaptive and personalized search or social tagging functionality. Here, we report our preliminary findings and describe our plan for Stage 2 of the.

KEYWORDS

Language Archives; Information Organization; Metadata; Linked Data

ASIS&T THESAURUS

Digital Repositories; Archives

INTRODUCTION

Rich and unique digital language datasets have a potential to make a strong contribution in social science research and education (e.g., Language Science, Geography, History, Sociology) and Computer Science (e.g., natural language processing). However, this potential currently remains largely unrealized as the language data available in language archives are rarely accessed by linguists or indigenous language communities. One main reason for this lost opportunity is the confusing and cumbersome design of language archives (Wasson et al., 2018; Wasson, Holton, & Ross, 2016). For example, as depositors upload information with various levels of granularity, retrieval for educational or research purposes becomes untenable without much additional resorting and organization of the archived data.

Also, users of language archives cannot easily compare data across languages. Many theoretical breakthroughs in historical linguistics, syntax, phonology, and other areas would become possible if users could query archival data for cross-linguistic patterns. Currently, language archives place data on each language in a separate collection and do not function as databases (Al Smadi et al., 2016).

Current State of Language Archiving

Online language archives are a valuable tool to support language preservation and revitalization, and to providing data on lesser-known languages valuable for linguistic analysis (Henke & Berez-Kroeker, 2016).

Like most digital preservation activities in various knowledge domains, language data archiving initiatives started in late 1990s and early 2000s. To bring this rich language data together to facilitate access to it, an Open Language Archives Community (OLAC) was created, an international collaboration project sponsored by the US National Science Foundation in 2000-2010 and hosted by the University of Pennsylvania Libraries. OLAC's goal was to develop protocol for archiving language data and to create interoperable repositories for storing and making language data more widely accessible. OLAC put together the combined catalog of all resources from 60 participating language archives located throughout the world: in USA, Australia, Brazil, India, New Zealand, Taiwan, and several European countries. OLAC's combined catalog contains over 300,000 records, covering resources in many languages of the world.

In the 2000s, the language archiving community has been building awareness of metadata and working on designing metadata standards through projects such as Electronic Metastructure for Endangered Language Data (E-MELD, http://emeld.org/) which developed a metadata editor tool, a linguistic ontology, and a linguistic metadata standard (http://www.language-archives.org/OLAC/metadata.html) based on Dublin Core. Digital Endangered Languages and Musics Archive (DELAMAN) is another organization working

82nd Annual Meeting of the Association for Information Science & Technology | Melbourne, Australia | 19–23 October, 2019

DOI: 10.1002/pra2.00030

on standards, including metadata-related, for language data archives.

Language archiving research (e.g., Nathan & Austin, 2004) distinguishes between two kinds of metadata important for information organization in language archives: so called "thick" metadata that represents text encoding of the linguistic documents itself: transcriptions, commentary, and time-aligned annotations (e.g., TEI), and "thin" metadata that facilitates research discovery (e.g., Dublin Core, OLAC, MARC 21, etc.). In addition to item-level descriptions of individual objects in archives, collection-level metadata that describes the entire collection is important, with major standard examples including Encoded Archival Description (EAD), Dublin Core Collection Description Application Profile, etc.

In the past, language archives were primarily designed for and by linguists, described as a "one-way" model by Nathan (2014), p. 193), with limited communication between archivists and users. The current foci in language archiving are "expanding audiences for archives and breaking traditional boundaries between depositors, users, and archivists" (Henke & Berez-Kroeker, 2016, p. 412). The emerging adoption of participatory archives and self-depositing practices aims to rectify the previous lack of communication. Self-depositing is a key feature setting apart Endangered Languages Archive (ELAR) and Pacific and Regional Archive for Digital Sources in Endangered Cultures (PARADESIC), two of the largest language archives.

Scoping Definitions

For the purpose of this project, we define language data as any audio, video or textual material representative of authentic language use. A list of words, a speaker explaining how to cook a particular variety of rice, or a traditional song are examples of the various forms language data can take on. Language data should be accompanied by metadata describing its relevance and context (minimally, how and where it was collected, name of speaker, and a simple description of the content).

We define a language archive as containing at least one collection (two or more items) of language data. Crucially, language archives do not need to identify as such to be considered in this analysis. For example, many university repositories contain collections of language data (e.g., University of North Texas Digital Library's Lamkang Language Resource, Indiana University at Bloomington's Ethnomusicology Multimedia Materials Collection), but identify more broadly as digital libraries or university repositories. Language archives have materials available for public access with the intent of long-term preservation. For example, Kaipuleohone, housed at the University of Hawai'i at Mānoa (http://ling.hawaii.edu/kaipuleohone-language-archive/), exemplifies a language archive because it contains individual items, makes items available for public access, has structured metadata, and accept deposits of material (or has accepted in the past).

Resources not considered in this analysis, though in no way dismissed, are corpora and resource aggregators. The Language Data Consortium (LDC), a collection of corpora, does not organize corpora into collections, have structured metadata, or provide public access to its content. Resource aggregators, such as the Karuk Archives (http://karuk.org/) are also excluded from this definition. Such websites provide links to resources available on other websites and archives, but do not house language data itself, nor do they provide structured metadata. So, while these are platforms where language data is stored, they not considered a language archive for the purpose of this investigation.

LANGUAGE ARCHIVE ANALYSIS

In the first stage of our research project, we conducted exploratory content analysis of websites of language archives, with the goal to identify the information organization tools and practices currently employed by language data archives across the United States. We sought answers to the following specific questions:

- What item-level and (if applicable) collection-level metadata scheme(s) are used?
- To what extent metadata records are displayed to end users?
- Does the archive allow self-depositing and if so are metadata creation guidelines and/or documentation of a metadata application profile used in LAs available?
- How is authority control implemented? What data value standards are used?
- What options for advanced search against indexed metadata fields are available?
- Are metadata records available for harvesting/download?
- What Semantic Web applications are available? For example, is metadata available as Linked Data?

To investigate these aspects of information organization, a total of 20 language archives were considered, including 16 within the United States and 4 outside the United States for comparison (2 in Europe, 1 in Australia, 1 in Canada). Of the 16 US archives, 6 are collections housed in university libraries, 4 are standalone archives not affiliated with a university, and 6 are archives associated with universities.

FINDINGS

Preliminary findings from Stage 1 show a variety of information organization strategies in language archives.

Metadata Schemes Used

Though language archives make some information available on item landing pages, it is unclear which metadata schemes the elements belong to. See Figures 1–3 for examples of the variation in metadata records. It seems that many language archives are using locally developed schemes to suit their needs.

Identifier:	ANLC3234
Title	SLI De Reuse #3
Description:	Grammatical comments on text on singing. The morning of 4/12. Slow repeat of 2nd episode of 4/12
Comments	#3 WdR 3a+b. Tape is located in Annex. Tape 3 of 35.
Contributors	de Reuse, Willem Joseph (interviewer)
Date	1985-04-05
Type	Sound
Subject Language(s)	Siberian Yupik
Collection	SLI De Reuse

Figure 1. Metadata record, Alaska Native Language Archive (ANLA).

Another language archive, Kaipuleohone, makes two versions of each record available, a simple and full record, shown in Figures 2 and 3. "Simple item records" can be expanded by selecting "Show full item record." The full record seen in Figure 3 includes the namespace "dc" and qualifiers that clearly indicate the use of the Qualified Dublin Core metadata scheme. The ANLA record (Figure 1) contains many of the same elements, but does not include any other indications of the metadata scheme being used.

Title:	KH1-013
Contributors:	Kayho, Bryan (speaker) Openefa, Benas (speaker) Helgeson, Kirsten (recorder) Helgeson, Kirsten (depositor) several (participant)
Date Issued:	24 Aug 2015
Description:	Large group conversation about languages and language conservation; invitation to work on "pure" Bena
Pages/Duration:	00:16:57
URI/DOI:	http://hdl.handle.net/10125/36689
Appears in Collections:	House Cry for Paul Ine

Show full item record | Recommend this item | View Statistics

Figure 2. Simple metadata record, Kaipuleohone.

dc.date.accessioned	2015-08-26T00:52:07Z
dc.date.available	2015-08-26T00:52:07Z
dc.date.issued	2015-08-24
dc.identifier.uri	http://hdl.handle.net/10125/36689
dc.description	Large group conversation about languages and language conservation; invitation to work on "pure" Bena
dc.format	digital mov file recorded at 98 kHz/16 bit and HD1080/30 on Zoom Q3 HD recorder
dc.format.extent	00:16:57
dc.language.iso	gah
dc.language.iso	tpi
dc.title	KH1-013
dc.type.dcmi	Sound
dc.contributor.speaker	Kayho, Bryan
dc.contributor.speaker	Openefa, Benas
dc.contributor.recorder	Helgeson, Kirsten

Figure 3. Full metadata record, Kaipuleohone.

Most records include the following metadata elements: Identifier of some kind (local, doi), Title, Contributor/ Depositor/ Creator, Language (ISO code, plain text, or both), Date (deposited, created, or both), Description, Format, Notes, Rights, and Related items.

Availability of Records in Various Formats

Only 2 of the 20 archives, both collections within a university digital libraries, have metadata records available for download in RDF (i.e., University of North Texas Digital Library and University of British Columbia Open Collections). Few of the archives considered here had metadata records exposed using identifiable schemes.

Controlled Vocabularies

The use of controlled vocabularies is not consistent across language archives. Those used most frequently include ISO 639-2 Language Codes, DCMI Type Vocabulary, and Traditional Knowledge Labels. Language archives existing as collections within a digital library include Library of Congress Subject Headings, while other language archives do not include a Subject element. Dates are typically encoded using W3CDTF. Because most language archives make records available only on the object's landing page (see Figure 1), it is unclear whether additional metadata, including further use of controlled vocabularies, exists in a format inaccessible to users.

Advanced Search Capabilities

Eighteen of the 20 archives have advanced search capabilities, though not all fields are indexed for advanced search. Ten archives have only a subset of fields available for advanced search; minimally, Title, Author, and Language fields. None of the archives analyzed allow for personalized or adaptive searches, though PARADESIC and the Historical Books Collection at the University of British Columbia permit users to leave comments on items which are viewable to other users.

Metadata Creation Guidelines

Self-depositing is not allowed in most cases; only ELAR, the Tromsø Repository of Language and Linguistics (TROLLing), and Language Commons allow users to upload data without an intermediary. (The Archive of the Indigenous Languages of Latin America (AILLA) is developing this functionality now, but has not yet released it.) Few of the university repositories analyzed have information on depositing material. In these cases, it is unclear whether they are not open to deposits, or whether a potential depositor would have to contact the university library directly to discuss depositing. Similar to use of controlled vocabularies, the availability and level of detail of metadata creation guidelines vary widely. While some language archives (e.g., PARADESIC, AILLA, Kaipuleohone) provide detailed guidelines including examples, others require only a title and description.

STAGE 2 PLANS

In stage 2, we plan to assess the needs of depositors and various stakeholders for information organization functionalities in these archives. Stakeholders include:

- Linguistics researchers depositing or planning to deposit their datasets in language data archives and using or planning to use language data archives in their research
- Language and linguistics educators using or planning to use language data archives for teaching (K12 - higher education)
- Students who would benefit from using language data archives in their studies (linguistics students and information science students)
- Language community members interested in heritage language materials
- Language archiving practitioners and managers.

The team will conduct interviews and observations of a small selected sample of members of each user group. The semi-structured interviews will be conducted with the purpose of language data archive requirements analysis or user needs assessment, as well as to collect information on how these requirements are met by information organization in language archives based on the previous experience of respondents in using language archives. In addition to the users of these archives, we plan to interview archivists to learn about the use of metadata schemes and controlled vocabularies in these archives. Participants who already use language archives will also be observed by the project team:

- Depositing participants will be observed as they interact with information organization tools (including metadata) in language archives in the process of depositing.
- Participants who do not deposit themselves but use materials deposited by others in language archives will be observed searching and browsing language archives and interacting with metadata in the process.

Observations will represent the heuristic evaluation of information organization in a selection of language archives.

CONCLUSION

This project is the first step in a series of research and demonstration projects aimed at improving the information organization in language data archives around the country. The ability for libraries, archives, and museums to identify the most meaningful for users ways of information organization in language archives is an important first step in fully realizing the potential of language archives and digital libraries nationwide. As a result of this project, we will provide empirical data in support of planning the future large-scale collaborative project focused on development of more efficient and user-friendly tools for access to digital language archives.

ACKNOWLEDGMENTS

This research has been funded by the US Institute for Museum and Library Services through a planning grant IMLS LG-87-18-0197. We also thank our project team members for help in identifying language archives for analysis and interpreting results.

REFERENCES

Al Smadi, D. Barnes, S., Blair, M., Chong, M., Cole-Jett, R., Davis, A., ... Wasson, C. (2016). Exploratory user research for CoRSAL: report prepared for S. Chelliah, Director of the Computational Resource for South Asian Languages. University of North Texas. Department of Anthropology.

Henke, R., & Berez-Kroeker, A. (2016). A brief history of archiving in language documentation, with an annotated bibliography. *Language Documentation and Conservation, 10*, 411–457.

Nathan, D., & Austin, P. K. (2004). Reconceiving metadata: Language documentation through thick and thin. In P. K. Austin, *Language Documentation and Description* (pp. 179–187). London: SOAS.

Nathan, D. (2014). Access and accessibility at ELAR, an archive for endangered languages documentation. In D. Nathan & P. K. Austin, *Language Documentation and Description* (Vol. *12*: Special Issue on Language Documentation and Archiving, pp. 187–208). London: SOAS.

Wasson, C., Holton, G., & Ross, H. (2016). Bringing user-centered design to the field of language archives. *Language Documentation and Conservation, 10*, 641–671.

Wasson, C., Medina, M., Chong, M., Le-May, B., Nalin, E., & Saintonge, K. (2018). Designing for diverse user groups: Case study of a language archive. *Journal of Business Anthropology, 7*(2).

Automated Chat Transcript Analysis Using Topic Modeling for Library Reference Services

Xiaoju Chen*
Carnegie Mellon University, Pittsburgh, PA, USA
xjuliechen@cmu.edu

Huajin Wang*
Carnegie Mellon University, Pittsburgh, PA, USA
huajinw@cmu.edu

ABSTRACT

Chat reference service has been used in academic libraries to more efficiently serve patrons in the digital age. Identifying question topics on chat can help librarians understand patrons' needs and improve reference services. Researchers have used qualitative methods to understand question types in chat records; however, these methods are inefficient to analyze large chat datasets. Here, we conducted a novel research using Latent Dirichlet Allocation (LDA) topic modeling to automatically extract topics from chat transcripts generated in 5 years from a large university library. With little human intervention, the model identified major topics based on statistical distributions of terms-document relationships in chat transcripts. We also applied VOSviewer to analyze the same dataset and found consistent results. From these results, we found that the most prominent chat topics were about accessing various library resources. This finding can help libraries allocate resources, design educational materials, and provide trainings for future librarians.

KEYWORDS

Text Mining; Topic Modeling; VOSviewer; Chat Reference; Q&A

ASIS&T THESAURUS

Topic Models; Needs Assessment; Academic Libraries

INTRODUCTION

Chat virtual reference services have been used by academic libraries to provide real-time online reference services (Lee, 2004). Understanding questions frequently asked through chat can help librarians better understand patrons' needs and provide more timely and effective answers. To analyze question types and topics, researchers have traditionally used qualitative research methods to examine chat records, usually with a relatively small dataset collected. Diamond and Pease studied 450 reference transactions during a two-year period and concluded that standard reference questions were most frequently asked (Diamond & Pease, 2001). Lee measured questions asked through chat for a six-month period and found that accessing database and electronic resources and administrative questions represented over 60% of the questions asked (Lee, 2004). Recently, with the development of new technology, researchers began to use more advanced quantitative analysis methods to analyze much bigger datasets. For example, in a mix-method study to understand learning mechanisms on the chat platform used in an academic library (Schiller, 2016), a line-by-line open coding on 1% of the data were first conducted, before applying a text mining tool (QDA miner) to analyze the remaining records. These qualitative and mixed method studies are labor intensive and cannot keep up with the growing amount of data collected on electronic reference platforms nowadays. It is therefore necessary to explore automated methods using unsupervised probabilistic machine learning models that is more scalable.

In recent years, topic modeling methods have matured as useful tools to extract topics from documents, without the need to label the datasets or having predefined taxonomies. Latent Dirichlet Allocation (LDA) has been discussed as one of the best suited methods for finding topics and types in text document (Fu, 2017; Linares-Vásquez, Dit, & Poshyvanyk, 2013), and has been used to analyze topics on web-based question and answer (Q&A) platforms such as StackExchange and StackOverflow. Barua et al used LDA to analyze the main topics in the software developer discussions (Barua, Thomas, & Hassan, 2014). Allamanis and Sutton used a similar method to associate programming concepts with particular types of questions asked through StackOverflow (Allamanis & Sutton, 2013). Fu performed a LDA to understand music topics covered by questions and answers on StackExchange (Fu, 2017). These studies provided insights into how LDA can be used to analyze Q&A type of records and help to discover main topics and questions types. However, it has never been applied to understanding library reference Q&As.

Apart from topic modeling methods, network analysis tools such as VOSviewer are widely used to analyze topics and their relationships in large-size text records. VOSviewer was developed by Leiden University for analyzing bibliometric network data (van Eck & Waltman, 2011). It can cluster most important terms in a text input by finding noun phrases and their frequencies and co-occurrences. Due to its ability to show key phrases and their relationships, researchers have been using VOSviewer as both text mining and visualization tool to identify

*These authors contributed equally.

82nd Annual Meeting of the Association for Information Science & Technology | Melbourne, Australia | 19–23 October, 2019

DOI: 10.1002/pra2.00031

topics in scholarly outputs (Demeter, Szász, & Kő, 2019; Mahieu, van Eck, van Putten, & van den Hoven, 2018; Park & Nagy, 2018).

In this study, we built an LDA model to identify major topics occurred in library reference Q&As using chat transcripts in the last 5 years. The same dataset was also used in parallel to generate a term map using VOSviewer. Results generated from both methods were compared to provide further quality assurance for topics extracted from chat records.

METHODOLOGY

Data collection and preprocessing

The chat service offered by the university libraries has been provided using a third-party platform, LibraryH3lp. To generate the raw dataset, we exported all chat transcripts from January 1, 2013 to December 31, 2018 as CSV format. Each chat interaction often includes multiple rounds of questions and answers, and is considered as one record. After filtering out empty records and system generated offline messages, there were 5610 records with approximately 1.3 million words for our analysis. We used home-made Python (version 3.5.4) scripts to remove system-generated information and parse text. To further prepare the dataset for topic modeling, we used the Python NLTK Toolkit (version 3.2.5) to remove stopwords, tokenize, and lemmatize. To customize our model to the library services setting, we compiled a list of customized stopwords in addition to the standard English stopwords built-in with the Toolkit, e.g., greeting words.

Topic modeling with Latent Dirichlet Allocation (LDA)

Latent Dirichlet Allocation (LDA) is one of the most common probabilistic topic models used to automatically discover topics hidden in a collection of documents. It assumes that a document has a number of topics and these topics can be characterized by a distribution over words. By calculating document-topic and topic-word distributions using Dirichlet distribution as a prior, the model automatically generates topics and a set of keywords associated with each topic based on their probability distributions in the given text documents. The meaning of each topic is interpreted and determined by humans. Here, we implemented the LDA model using Python Gensim library (version 3.4.0) (Řehůřek & Sojka, 2010), which is based on the online variational Bayes algorithm of LDA implementation (Hoffman, Bach, & Blei, 2010). To train the model, we ran the LDA model for 20 passes, with random_state sets to 50 to enable reproducibility.

To determine the best number of topics K, we ran the LDA algorithm with K ranging from 2-20, and evaluated the quality of topics by calculating perplexity and coherence scores. Cv metric was used to compute coherence scores as it was reported to perform the best over many benchmark datasets (Röder, Both, & Hinneburg, 2015). Furthermore, we evaluated the quality of topics by visualization of topic clusters using pyLDAvis library (version 2.1.2), as well as by manually inspecting topics under each K. Based on these methods, we set the model to $K = 8$, which produced a perplexity score of -7.38 and coherence score (Cv metric) of 0.44. Labels of the topics were presented as serial numbers when generated by the LDA model, and later interpreted by human experience based on top keywords present in each topic.

Constructing distance-based maps with VOSviewer

One of the difficulties in using topic modeling for text mining is model evaluation. To gain further confidence in the topics generated from the LDA model, we ran the same preprocessed dataset with VOSviewer (version 1.6.10) to generate distance-based term maps. We used full-counting method (total numbers of occurrences in all documents) to analyze the 60% most relevant terms occurred at least 10 times within the entire dataset. Association strength was used for normalizing the strength of links between items, and resolution value was set to 1.2.

RESULTS AND DISCUSSION

Once model parameters were fixed as described in the METHODOLOGY session, we ran the LDA model multiple times to observe the stability of topics produced. Output from the model was presented as keywords for each topic and the weightage (importance) of each keyword. The content of each topic was determined by reference librarians based on the interpretation of the keywords in each topic. Results derived from a representative run is shown in Table 1, showing top 10 keywords in each of the eight topics identified by our LDA model. Topics were sorted by percentage of tokens of a given topic, with T1 accounting for the most percentage (22.3%) of total tokens (Figure 1, right). In each topic, keywords were arranged in descending order according to their weights. By running the model multiple times, we observed that most topics are very stable, including T1 (***physical book access***), T2 (***journal article access***), T3 (***off-campus access***), T4 (***interlibrary loan***), T6 (***guest access***), and T7 (***thesis and dissertation***). T5 represents a typical topic (***specialized reference***), in which specific subjects often co-occur with names of subject librarians in most runs, but in this specific run, those keywords were ranked lower. T8 (***http link to catalog item***) is the only topic that did not appear in every run.

To help intuitively assess the topics, we visualized the model output using Python pyLDAvis library (Figure 1). The result shows that for some topics, there are overlaps among each other, because terms can belong to more than one topic, while others are well separated from each other (Figure 1, left). It is worth noting, however, the visualization is a mapping of the multidimensional data into a 2-D plane through multidimensional scaling; the actual separation in higher dimensions are likely to be better.

To further verify the quality of the LDA model and the results, we analyzed the same preprocessed text with VOSviewer. VOSviewer uses a different text mining algorithm to analyze and visualize topics. Results generated by VOSviewer

ID	Topic	Keywords (top 10)
T1	Physical book access	book, library, check, available, see, help, hunt, get, hold, borrow
T2	Journal article access	article, journal, access, search, database, link, see, find, help, looking
T3	Off-campus access	access, library, id, vpn, link, campus, try, get, log, using
T4	Interlibrary loan	request, loan, get, ill, interlibrary, illiad, need, article, email, library
T5	Specialized reference	librarian, help, email, contact, information, find, question, know, liaison, looking
T6	Guest access	library, access, student, need, university, help, get, use, know, public
T7	Thesis and dissertation	dissertation, thesis, check, copy, help, online, find, title, looking, library
T8	http link to catalog item	citation, m, copy, author, style, volume, v, carnegie, j, vol

Table 1. The 8 topics and top keywords associated with each topic discovered by the LDA model. Names of the topics are generated based on human interpretation.

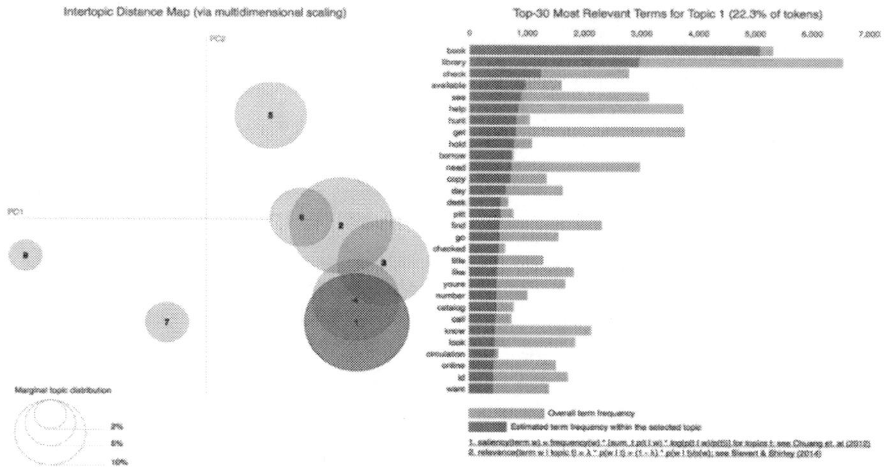

Figure 1. Screenshot of interactive visualization output from pyLDAvis. Left: distance map created based on keywords occurrence. Each cluster represents a topic generated by the LDA model. The index number of each cluster corresponds to the topic ID in Table 1. Right: distribution of the top 30 most relevant terms among topics. Red: the current topic; blue: other topics.

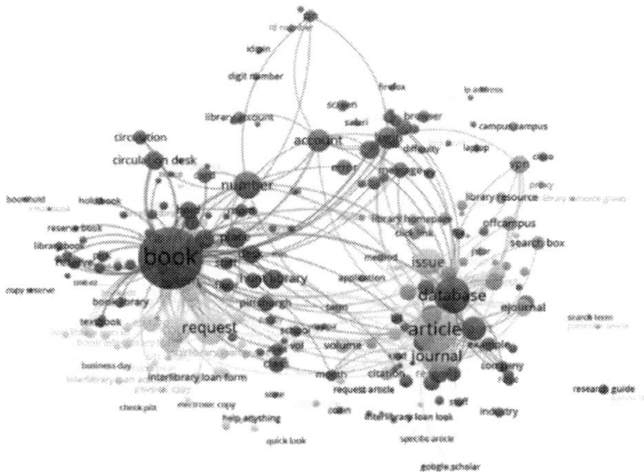

Figure 2. Screenshot of a representative distance map generated by VOSviewer, using the same preprocessed dataset used to build the LDA model. Colors show different clusters.

(Figure 2) show that the largest topic was ***physical book*** (dark blue circles), example terms include "book", "circulation desk", "hunt library". Additionally, ***journal article access*** (light green circles; key words: "e-journal", "volumn", "issue"), ***off-campus access*** (green circles; key words: "off-campus", "vpn", "proxy"), and ***interlibrary loan*** (yellow circles; key words: "request", "interlibrary loan", "business day") were also hot topics. These hot topics identified by VOSviewer were consistent with the those identified by the LDA model. VOSviewer also identified an additional topic, ***library account*** (sky blue circles; key words: "number", "account", "login"), that was not shown in one of the eight LDA topics. However, based on the keywords, the ***library account*** topic can be seen as an access question associate with electronic resource, which was captured in the LDA model.

Both LDA and VOSviewer results show that ***physical book access*** was the most mentioned topic in chat conversations (T1), followed by various ***access*** topics (T2, T3 T4, and T6). These topics also had more interconnections, reflected by the visualization in VOSviewer: terms in these hot topics such as ***book*** (dark blue) and ***interlibrary loan*** (yellow) were closely connected. This finding was consistent with the practice in real-life library services. Patrons often use the chat service for a fast and straightforward solution, for example, when they have problems accessing an electronic item. These problems are often caused by (1) the patron was not using campus network so they cannot use library resources, or (2) the library does not have subscription to the item. Therefore, ***off-campus*** and ***interlibrary loan*** were frequently mentioned topics in chat and these topics interconnect with ***book access*** and ***journal access***. Apart from the ***access*** topics, we found three isolated topics (T5, T7 and T8). In T5 (***specialized reference***), LDA keywords "librarian", "email", and "liaison" showed that patrons were referred to subject librarians for better assistance. T7 (***thesis and dissertation***) were questions related to locating thesis and dissertations published by graduate students in the university. T8 (***http link to catalog item***) included words and terms in the university library website's URL, inked to specific items in the catalog. In the eight topics discovered by the LDA model, most of the access questions can be answered by staff and students at the circulation desk; while T5 and T7 should be answered by more experienced and/or subject librarians.

CONCLUSION

We collected electronic chat transcripts from the past 5 years in the university library and used the dataset to build an LDA topic model. The model was able to identify 8 major topics related to Q&As using the chat reference service. Findings from this study will provide a data-driven approach for academic libraries to identify patrons' needs regarding the use of library resources, and help libraries to make informed decisions on how to allocate resources, design educational materials for patrons, and provide training for future librarians.

In the future, we will apply our model to analyze evolving trend in Q&As over the years, and extend this model to analyzing other electronic reference questions, such as emails and web forms.

REFERENCES

Allamanis, M., & Sutton, C. (2013). *Why, When, and What: Analyzing Stack Overflow Questions by Topic, Type, and Code*. 2013 10th Working Conference on Mining Software Repositories (MSR), 53–56.

Barua, A., Thomas, S. W., & Hassan, A. E. (2014). What are developers talking about? An analysis of topics and trends in Stack Overflow. *Empirical Software Engineering*, *19*(3), 619–654.

Demeter, K., Szász, L., & Kő, A. (2019). A text mining based overview of inventory research in the ISIR special issues 1994–2016. *International Journal of Production Economics*, *209*, 134–146.

Diamond, W., & Pease, B. (2001). Digital reference: a case study of question types in an academic library. *Reference Services Review*, *29*(3), 210–219.

Fu, H. (2017). *Categorization of Musicology Questions from Community-Based Q&A Site using Latent Dirichlet Allocation*. IConference 2017 Proceedings.

Hoffman, M., Bach, F. R., & Blei, D. M. (2010). Online Learning for Latent Dirichlet Allocation. In J. D. Lafferty,

Lee, I. J. (2004). Do virtual reference librarians dream of digital reference questions?: A qualitative and quantitative analysis of email and chat reference. *Australian Academic & Research Libraries*, *35*(2), 95–110.

Linares-Vásquez, M., Dit, B., & Poshyvanyk, D. (2013). *An Exploratory Analysis of Mobile Development Issues Using Stack Overflow*. 2013 10th Working Conference on Mining Software Repositories (MSR), 93–96.

Mahieu, R., van Eck, N. J., van Putten, D., & van den Hoven, J. (2018). From dignity to security protocols: a scientometric analysis of digital ethics. *Ethics and Information Technology*, *20*(3), 175–187.

Park, J. Y., & Nagy, Z. (2018). Comprehensive analysis of the relationship between thermal comfort and building control research - A data-driven literature review. *Renewable and Sustainable Energy Reviews*, *82*, 2664–2679.

Řehůřek, R., & Sojka, P. (2010). Software Framework for Topic Modelling with Large Corpora. In *Proceedings of the LREC 2010 Workshop on New Challenges for NLP Frameworks* (pp. 45–50). Valletta, Malta: ELRA.

Röder, M., Both, A., & Hinneburg, A. (2015). *Exploring the Space of Topic Coherence Measures*. Proceedings of the Eighth ACM International Conference on Web Search and Data Mining - WSDM '15, 399–408.

Rossum, G. v. (1995). *Python tutorial (No. CS-R9526)*. Amsterdam: Centrum voor Wiskunde en Informatica (CWI).

Schiller, S. Z. (2016). CHAT for chat: Mediated learning in online chat virtual reference service. *Computers in Human Behavior*, *65*, 651–665.

Sievert, C., & Shirley, K. (2014). LDAvis: A method for visualizing and interpreting topics. Proceedings of the Workshop on Interactive Language Learning, Visualization, and Interfaces, 63–70.

van Eck, N. J., & Waltman, L. (2011). Text mining and visualization using VOSviewer. *ArXiv:1109.2058 [Cs]*. Retrieved from http://arxiv.org/abs/1109.205

ReTracker: Actively and Automatically Matching Retraction Metadata in Zotero

Yi-Yun Cheng
School of Information Sciences, University of Illinois at Urbana Champaign, USA
yiyunyc2@illinois.edu

Nikolaus Parulian
School of Information Sciences, University of Illinois at Urbana Champaign, USA
nnp2@illinois.edu

Tzu-Kun Hsiao
School of Information Sciences, University of Illinois at Urbana Champaign, USA
tkhsiao2@illinois.edu

Ly Dinh
School of Information Sciences, University of Illinois at Urbana Champaign, USA
dinh4@illinois.edu

Janina Sarol
School of Information Sciences, University of Illinois at Urbana Champaign, USA
mjsarol@illinois.edu

Jodi Schneider
School of Information Sciences, University of Illinois at Urbana Champaign, USA
jodi@illinois.edu

ABSTRACT

Retraction removes seriously flawed papers from the scientific literature. However, even papers retracted for scientific fraud continue to be cited and used as valid after their retraction. Retracted papers are inadequately identified on publisher pages and in scholarly databases, and scholars' personal libraries frequently contain retracted papers. To address this, we are developing a tool called *ReTracker* (https://github.com/nikolausn/ReTrackers) that automatically checks a user's Zotero library for retracted articles, and adds retraction status as a new metadata field directly in the library. In this paper, we present the current version of *ReTracker*, which automatically flags retracted articles from PubMed. We describe how we have iteratively improved *ReTracker*'s matching performance through its initial two versions. Our tests show that the current version of *ReTracker* is able to flag retracted articles from PubMed with high precision and recall, and to distinguish retracted articles from articles about retraction. In its current state, *ReTracker* can actively and automatically bring retraction metadata into Zotero, and in future work we will test its usability with scholars.

KEYWORDS

Retraction; Scholarly Communication; Publishing Ethics

ASIS&T THESAURUS

Information Resources Management; Scholarly Publishing

82nd Annual Meeting of the Association for Information Science & Technology | Melbourne, Australia | 19–23 October, 2019

DOI: 10.1002/pra2.00032

INTRODUCTION

Retraction removes seriously flawed papers from the scientific literature. Reasons for retraction include honest error, scientific fraud, and plagiarism (Bar-Ilan & Halevi, 2017; Da Silva & Bornemann-Cimenti, 2017). The Committee on Publication Ethics, an industry group that develops best practices for scholarly publishing, says that "Prompt retraction should minimize the number of researchers who cite the erroneous work, act on its findings or draw incorrect conclusions" (COPE, 2009).

However, papers continue to be cited after retraction, sometimes at a higher rate than before retraction (Bar-Ilan & Halevi, 2017; Da Silva & Bornemann-Cimenti, 2017; Dong, Loh, & Mondry, 2005). Even fraudulent papers continue to accrue citations. For instance, in the 5 years following their retraction for fabricating data, 20 papers on fraudulent pain research by Scott Reuben were cited a total of 267 times in 122 different journals, yet only a quarter mentioned the retraction [Bornemann-Cimenti, Szilagyi, & Sandner-Kiesling, 2016].

Other studies have found that post-retraction citation is mostly positive, and rarely signals the retraction. For instance, bibliographies almost never indicated the retractions in Bar-Ilan & Halevi's study of 238 post-retraction citations to 15 papers across disciplines, and only 12 (5%) of these 238 post-retraction citations were negative [Bar-Ilan & Halevi, 2017].

In a print environment, medical librarians could disseminate information about retracted papers by flagging print copies and sharing lists of retracted papers [Snodgrass & Pfeifer, 1992], and many did so [Hughes, 1998]. Retracted papers are inadequately identified on publisher pages and in scholarly databases, and scholars' personal libraries frequently contain retracted papers [Da Silva & Bornemann-Cimenti, 2017; Davis, 2012]. In a 2012 study of 1,779 retracted articles in medicine, only 5% of PDFs indicated the retraction; this raised to only

26% when including landing pages. Of these articles, 75% were available in personal Mendeley libraries [Davis, 2012].

Systems to surveil personal PDF libraries (as well as bibliographies in pre-press manuscripts) have been suggested numerous times (e.g. [Bar-Ilan & Halevi, 2017; Davis, 2012]). A common recommendation from researchers in diverse fields is to flag retracted articles in bibliography management tools [Cosentino & Veríssimo, 2016; Granter & Papke, 2018].

To meet this need, this paper presents a tool called *ReTracker* that automatically detects retracted papers within the popular bibliography management tool, Zotero. *ReTracker*'s development began in 2018; its architecture [Dinh, Cheng, & Parulian, 2019] and open source code (https://github.com/nikolausn/ReTrackers) are publicly available. The goal of this paper is to demonstrate the reliability of *ReTracker*'s approach to matching retracted publications from PubMed, and to describe the development path for the project.

CURRENT TOOLS FOR IDENTIFYING RETRACTION

Retraction Watch Database

The Retraction Watch database[1] initially released in October 2018 [Brainard, 2018], contains the largest repository of retracted papers, reported at 19,303 articles from 1756 through mid-June 2019. The database allows any user to search various access points of retracted papers (including Author, Title, Reasons, etc), limited to 600 results. In our examination of the data, we have found articles that we could not confirm were retracted (e.g., withdrawn pre-press articles without issuing issue retraction notices). Bulk data is available for bibliometric analysis, but the licensing prohibits redistribution of the data.

re-cite

The re-cite website[2] highlights retracted papers in their database, given a list of APA or AMA references. Their database of 3,107 retracted articles published before 2016 was built by extracting articles from Web of Science with "retraction of" in the title, removing articles not categorized as corrections, and filtering out possible false positives. The database's inability to highlight the Wakefield paper Wakefield et al., 1998], retracted in 2010, suggests incomplete data even for the years covered. The database is not being consistently updated.

CrossMark

A CrossMark button[3] on an HTML, PDF, or EPUB paper enables the reader to "check for updates", when publishers have opted in to this paid CrossRef service. Clicking on the CrossMark button takes the reader to a landing page indicating any updates to the paper, including retractions. One limitation is that few publishers use CrossMark because they must pay fees for each record that is updated or corrected in CrossRef databases.

Open Retractions

Open Retractions[4] enables users to check whether a paper has been retracted, using the paper's DOI as a search query.

However, the tool requires a DOI and is highly dependent on finding the DOI and its retraction status in PubMed and CrossRef. The tool's inability to flag well-known retracted papers such as the Wakefield paper [Wakefield et al., 1998] warrants further improvements.

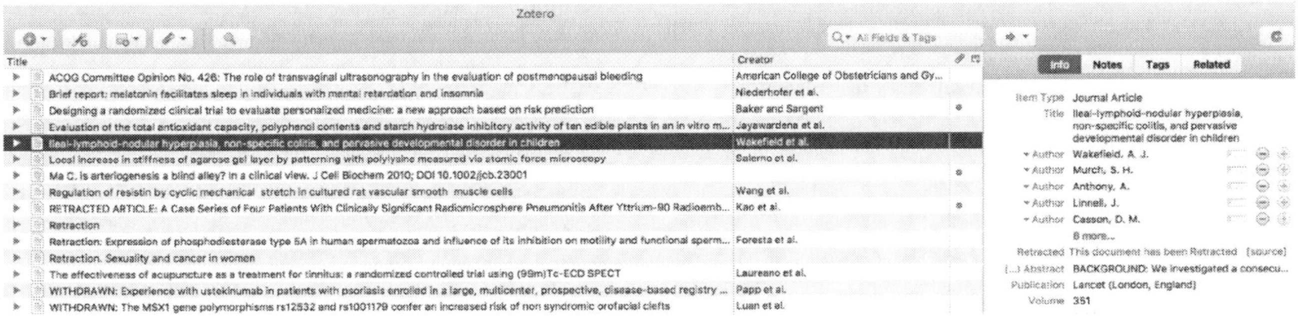

Figure 1. Interface of Zotero with *ReTracker* plugin showing a retracted article with retraction (in red) added by *ReTracker*.

Limitations of Current Tools

With most of these current tools, readers must check one paper at a time, by searching for its title, author, DOI, or reference, or by clicking on a "check for updates" button in the paper itself. The only tool that checks more than one paper at a time (re-cite) is not updating their records. By contrast, our approach actively and automatically adds the most current retraction metadata from PubMed into Zotero.

RETRACKER TOOL

We have developed a novel tool *ReTracker* that automatically detects retracted papers in the popular bibliography

[1] Retraction Watch database: http://retractiondatabase.org/

[2] re-cite: http://re-cite.org/ and https://github.com/recite/

[3] CrossMark: https://www.crossref.org/services/crossmark/

[4] Open Retractions: http://openretractions.com/ and https://github.com/fathomlabs/open-retractions/

management tool Zotero. Whenever the user downloads or syncs items in their Zotero library, *ReTracker* sends queries to PubMed to identify retracted articles, and flags the retracted ones. Retracted articles are flagged with retraction metadata in red, and users can click on the "[source]" button to navigate to the article's PubMed page (see Figure 1). This automatic design saves users' efforts in repetitively searching for and manually flagging retracted papers from external sources. The tool's infrastructure and features are described in [Dinh et al., 2019]. The current release of the tool and instructions on how to install ReTracker are freely available via our GitHub.[5]

We use PubMed as the data fetching point because: (1) It is freely, publicly available, with no restrictions on its redistribution; (2) It has been recognized as a reliable source for finding retracted articles, regardless of minor inconsistent retraction metadata [Bar-Ilan and Halevi, 2017; Schmidt, 2018]. Furthermore, unlike the tools mentioned above, ReTracker does not keep a local database of retracted articles. Our approach of directly querying data from PubMed gets the most up-to-date information on retractions.

ITERATIVE DEVELOPMENT AND TESTING

ReTracker Version One

The first version, *ReTracker v1*, queries the title of each article in users' Zotero library using PubMed's search box. It iterates the search until an exact match was found. To test the performance of *ReTracker*, we collect test sets in different stages. Our test sets were collected from March 29 to 30, 2019.

Test Set One: Retracted Articles (R)
To evaluate how well *ReTracker v1* flags retracted articles, we tested against Test Set One. Test Set One consists of a representative random sample of 1,250 retracted articles, from the 13,463 articles retrieved from PubMed with publication types "retracted publication" and "retraction of publication" with the following search:

```
"retracted publication" [Publication Type]
OR "retraction of publication"
[Publication Type]
```

Test Set one: Not-Retracted Articles (NonR + TopicR)
Similarly, not-retracted articles are also used to test *v1* to check whether *ReTracker* correctly *avoids* flagging these articles. These were identified by two means:

1. The not-retracted articles (**NonR**)

27,624,608 results are returned by the following query:

```
("journal article" [Publication Type]) NOT
("retracted publication" [Publication
Type] OR "retraction of
publication" [Publication Type])}
```

2. Articles About Retractions (**TopicR**)

Articles studying retractions often have the keyword "retraction" in the title and will be hard to distinguish from retracted articles. To identify articles that analyze retractions, we search the MeSH term *"Retraction of Publication as Topic" [MAJR]* in PubMed, and find 370 records on such articles.

We sampled 1,000 not-retracted articles from **NonR** and added the 370 articles in **TopicR** to form the test set of not-retracted articles (n = 1,370).

V1: Testing Result
ReTracker v1 identified 1,129 of retracted articles (**R**) as true positives, achieving a relatively high recall (0.903) in identifying retracted papers. *ReTracker v1*'s precision, at 0.806, was fair.

For the not-retracted articles, of the 1,000 **NonR** papers sampled, none were flagged as retracted. However, the precision fell short when *ReTracker* encountered articles *studying* retractions (**TopicR**). Out of the 370 papers that PubMed classified as **TopicR**, *ReTracker v1* falsely flagged 271 of them as "retracted" articles because the title or the abstract of the paper contained variations of the word 'retract'. Full results are shown in Table 1. Metrics for calculating accuracy, precision, and recall can be found in the Appendix.

Version	Test Sets	Accuracy	Precision	Recall
ReTracker v1	R, NonR+TopicR	0.850	0.806	0.903
ReTracker v2	R, NonR+TopicR	0.789	0.994	0.561
ReTracker v2	Precise R, NonR+TopicR	0.963	0.999	0.926

Table 1. The performance of the two versions of *ReTracker*.

Error Analysis
In our error analysis, we noticed two problems. First, for search queries that return multiple entries, *ReTracker v1* could not always find a single paper. Second, retraction notices were flagged along with retracted papers, because their titles are often similar, e.g. "Retraction Note:" followed by the name of the paper. This motivated us to improve the matching process.

ReTracker Version Two

To mitigate two matching issues—handling multiple search results, and falsely flagging papers studying retractions—we developed a second version of *ReTracker* with an improved matching process. *ReTracker v2 iterates* through results pages with multiple entries until it finds an exact match. *ReTracker v2* also stopped flagging retraction notices of articles.

Test Set One
To test the overall performance of *ReTracker v2* we first reused Testing Set One for both retracted and not-retracted articles.

[5] ReTracker Github repository: https://github.com/nikolausn/ReTrackers

V2: Testing Result 1

With the same testing sets as v1, high precision is reported at this stage (0.994), with only 4 of the not-retracted articles flagged as retracted (**NonR + TopicR**). After manual inspection, we found that 3 of these 4 articles (PMID 1471789, 25385480, 15495094) are in fact retracted articles misclassified into the MeSH term "Retraction of Publication as Topic". The remaining article, PMID 7854817, is titled "Fraudulent publication", but is a guest ed- itorial from 1994 that sought to define terms relating to scientific misconduct. *ReTracker v2* still flags it as retracted based on the title of the paper. However, results for this phase show that the accuracy (0.789) and recall (0.561) have significantly dropped from v1. Only 701 out of the 1,250 retracted articles were flagged by *ReTracker*.

Error Analysis

In our error analysis, we discovered that most articles that are *not flagged* were in fact *retraction notices*, suggesting that *ReTracker v2* can flag the original retracted article but avoid flagging the retraction notices. This led us to retest *ReTracker v2* against a more precise pool of retracted articles, (**PreciseR**).

Test Set Two: Retracted Articles (Precise R)

We develop a more optimal search strategy for precision retrieval of retracted articles in PubMed, with the following search:

```
(("retracted publication"[Publication
Type] OR"retraction of
publication"[Publication Type]) NOT
("Removal Notice"[TI] OR "TEMPORARY
REMOVAL"[TI] OR statement*[Ti] OR
editorial*[TI] OR retract*[TI] OR erratum*
[TI] OR withdraw*[TI]))
```

With the above search, **PreciseR** consists of a representative random sample of 1,250 articles, from the 7,399 articles retrieved from PubMed.For not-retracted articles, we reused Test Set One with **NonR + TopicR**.

V2: Testing Result 2

Testing *ReTracker v2* against Test Set Two helps us reflect the *true* positives of retracted articles (**PreciseR**). The results have improved substantially, compared to *ReTracker v1* and the testing result 1 of *ReTracker v2*. Out of the 1,250 retracted papers sampled, *ReTracker v2* was able to flag 1,158 of them as retracted. Again, *ReTracker* avoided flagging any of the **NonR**. When we update **TopicR** to only 1 article being flagged (PMID 7854817), the results reflect that *ReTracker v2* has higher accuracy (0.963), precision (0.999), and recall (0.926).

DISCUSSION AND CONCLUSION

The current version of *ReTracker* is able to flag retracted articles with high accuracy, precision, and recall, while not flagging articles that discuss retractions and not flagging retraction notices. *ReTracker*'s current matching process is based on an article's title, given that every article must have a title (whereas not all articles have metadata such as DOIs).

Some of our design choices for *ReTracker* are constrained by the tool development environment and the data licensing. Zotero was chosen not only because it is a popular bibliography management tool, but also since it allows plug-ins such as *ReTracker* to be integrated. For similar reasons, we chose PubMed as *ReTracker*'s external source because it is freely and publicly available for redistribution.

In future development, we would like to (1) expand the *ReTracker* plugin to other bibliography management tool environments (e.g. EndNote, Mendeley, etc.) and (2) incorporate additional external sources for *ReTracker*'s retraction metadata. We also plan to evaluate *ReTracker*'s usability through a user study with Zotero users.

In its current state, *ReTracker* can actively and automatically bring retraction metadata into Zotero. In future releases, when other external sources are aggregated, more rounds of iterative testing and development will be inevitable.

REFERENCES

Bar-Ilan, J., & Halevi, G. (2017). Post retraction citations in context: A case study. *Scientometrics*, *113*(1), 547–565.

Bornemann-Cimenti, H., Szilagyi, I. S., & Sandner-Kiesling, A. (2016). Perpetuation of retracted publications using the example of the Scott S. Reuben case: Incidences, reasons and possible improvements. *Science and Engineering Ethics*, *22*(4), 1063–1072.

Brainard, J. (2018). What a massive database of retracted papers reveals about science publishing's 'death penalty'. *Science*, 25. https://doi.org/10.1126/science.aav8384

COPE (2009). Guidelines for retracting articles. https://doi.org/10.24318/cope.2019.1.4

Cosentino, A. M., & Veríssimo, D. (2016). Ending the citation of retracted papers. *Conservation Biology*, *30*(3), 676–678.

Da Silva, J. A. T., & Bornemann-Cimenti, H. (2017). Why do some retracted papers continue to be cited? *Scientometrics*, *110*(1), 365–370.

Davis, P. M. (2012). The persistence of error: A study of retracted articles on the Internet and in personal libraries. *Journal of the Medical Library Association: JMLA*, *100* (3), 184–189.

Dinh, L., Cheng, Y.-Y., and Parulian, N. (2019). ReTracker: An open-source plugin for automated and standardized tracking of retracted scholarly publications. In Proceedings of the 2019 ACM/IEEE Joint Conference on Digital Libraries (JCDL 2019) (pp. 406–407).

Dong, P., Loh, M., & Mondry, A. (2005). The "impact factor" revisited. *Biomedical Digital Libraries*, *2*(1), 7.

Granter, S. R., & Papke, D. J. (2018). Opinion: Medical misinformation in the era of Google: Computational approaches to a pervasive problem. *Proceedings of the National Academy of Sciences*, *115*(25), 6318–6321.

Hughes, C. (1998). Academic medical libraries' policies and procedures for notifying library users of retracted scientific publications. *Medical Reference Services Quarterly*, *17*(2), 37–42.

Schmidt, M. (2018). An analysis of the validity of retraction annotation in PubMed and the Web of Science. *Journal of the Association for Information Science and Technology*, *69*(2), 318–328.

Snodgrass, G. L., & Pfeifer, M. P. (1992). The characteristics of medical retraction notices. *Bulletin of the Medical Library Association*, *80*(4), 328–334.

Wakefield, A. J., et al. (1998). RETRACTED: Ileal-lymphoid-nodular hyperplasia, non-specific colitis, and pervasive developmental disorder in children. *The Lancet*, *351*(9103), 637–641.

APPENDIX: METRICS*

$$Accuracy = \frac{R_f + NonR_{nf} = TopicR_{nf}}{Total\ Number\ Of\ Evaluated\ Subjects} \quad (1)$$

where R_f is the number of retracted articles flagged as retracted[2]; $NonR_{nf}$ is the number of not-retracted articles not flagged as re-tracted; $TopicR_{nf}$ is the number of articles about retractions *not* flagged as retracted.

$$Precision = \frac{R_f}{R_f + NonR_f + TopicR_f} \quad (2)$$

where $NonR_f$ is the number of not-retracted articles flagged as retracted; $TopicR_f$ is the number of articles about retractions flagged as retracted.

$$Recall = \frac{R_f}{R_f + R_{nf}} \quad (3)$$

where R_{nf} is the number of retracted articles not flagged as retracted.

* These metrics are written for Test Set One. To adapt to Test Set Two, which uses a different sample pool of retracted articles, all the $\boldsymbol{R_f}$ change to $\boldsymbol{PreciseR_f}$, and all the $\boldsymbol{R_{nf}}$ change to $\boldsymbol{PreciseR_{nf}}$.

Effects of Motivation and Tool Features on Online Photo-Sharing Behavior

Hyerim Cho
University of Washington,
Seattle, USA
chohr113@uw.edu

Josh Smith
University of Washington,
Seattle, USA
smith.josh.d@gmail.com

Jin Ha Lee
University of Washington,
Seattle, USA
jinhalee@uw.edu

ABSTRACT

Sharing photos online has become one of the most popular information sharing behaviors in recent years. Due to the plethora of online photo-sharing websites, applications, and other tools available, we share visual information easily, and quickly. In order to improve our current understanding of photo-sharing behaviors and identify the exhaustive list of online photo-sharing motivations, we analyzed 4,555 photos shared online. Seventeen interviewers interviewed 92 participants overall. Twenty photo-sharing motivations were identified in this study, including To share memory, To disseminate information, For amusement (humor, fun), To show off, and To appreciate beauty/cuteness.

KEYWORDS

Photo-Sharing Motivations; Photo-Sharing Behaviors; Image Information Behaviors; Online Photo-Sharing Behaviors

ASIS&T THESAURUS

Information Behavior; Information Sharing; Information Use

INTRODUCTION

Sharing photos has become a common activity in recent years due to the growth of photo-sharing applications and tools, such as Facebook, Instagram, Snapchat, and Flickr. At the end of 2015, there were more than 2,000 photo-sharing apps available, and in 2016 it was estimated that 2.5 trillion photos would be shared or stored online by the end of the year (Lee & Steward, 2016). Sharing photos with friends, family, or the public, and using a photo-sharing application have become part of our everyday life; 54% of adult Internet users share their original photos or videos online, and 47% of adult Internet users take photos or videos that they have found online and share them with others (Duggan, 2013).

Although several studies have investigated the motivations of sharing photos (Malik, Dhir, & Nieminen, 2016; Nov, Naaman, & Ye, 2010; Van House, Davis, Ames, Finn, & Viswanathan, 2005), many of the prior studies only focused on a single photo-sharing platform to analyze users' photo-sharing motivations, thus identifying and discussing only part of the existing user motivations. In addition, considering that many users, especially smartphone users, may be platform-agnostic and use different kinds of photo-sharing applications and services to share their photos with others, studying one specific photo-sharing tool might hinder our understanding of the overall picture of photo-sharing behaviors and their diverse motivations.

The objective of this study is to thoroughly understand the motivations of online photo-sharing behaviors and suggest necessary features of photo-sharing tools that could enhance users' overall visual information sharing experiences.

RQ1. What is the comprehensive list of primary motivations of online-photo-sharing based on the existing literature and current user investigation?

RQ2. Are there any differences between the uses of photo-sharing tools based on users' diverse photo-sharing motivations? If so, what are the differences?

RELEVANT STUDIES & IDENTIFIED MOTIVATIONS

Different Motivations for Photo-Sharing

Uses and Gratification theory is oft-cited in the literature seeking to explain motivations for Twitter users' need for a sense of connection to each other (Chen, 2011) and to the needs of self-presentation and belonging of Facebook users (Nadkarni & Hofmann, 2012). The use of Social Networking Sites (SNS) has provided a fertile ground for researchers exploring gratification factors in online behavior (Joinson, 2008), and SNS continue to become more prevalent in our everyday life. Photo-sharing behavior is a popular part of SNS: in 2013, Facebook's users were adding 350 million more photos per day, and Instagram users (90 million active users, monthly) were adding 40 million per day in 2014 (Etherington, 2013; Smith, 2013). In the context of photo-sharing on Facebook, Malik et al. (2016) rely on this theory to examine user behavior, identifying eight motivation factors relating to gratifications that users may seek from their sharing. Oeldorf-Hirsch and Sundar (2016) also drew on Uses and Gratification theory in their work, where they identified 42 distinct motivations organized into four motivation

82nd Annual Meeting of the Association for Information Science & Technology | Melbourne, Australia | 19–23 October, 2019

DOI: 10.1002/pra2.00059

factors, observed that "photo-sharing online meets higher-order needs, such as bonding, (2016, p. 628)" and found that photo-sharing is increasingly used to communicate, build relationships, and participate in a community. This supports Van House et al.'s (2005) earlier work, wherein the authors looked at the social uses of personal photography enabled by camera phones and predicted that the ease of sharing brought about by new technology would result in increased activity for the purposes of social engagement and self-expression. Similarly, Kindberg, Spasojevic, Fleck, and Sellen (2005a, 2005b) investigated how and why people use camera phones. The authors examined camera phone users' intentions at the time of image capture and broadly categorized the motivations into two groups: affective and functional, which can be again divided into social and individual purposes.

The idea of mundane activities being worthy of capturing in photographs is explored by Lasén and Gómez-Cruz (2009), who note that online photo-sharing capabilities change the relation between privacy and intimacy and engender complex behaviors around self-identity and self-knowledge, concepts which echo motivation factors like disclosure, seeking, and showcasing experience identified by Malik et al. (2016) and Oeldorf-Hirsch and Sundar (2016), respectively. Likewise, work by Hunt, Lin, and Atkin (2014) discusses user concern with self-expression, self-presentation, and social connection as motivation for sharing images.

A table which exhaustively synthesizes and provides a mapping of previously identified photo-sharing motivations, as well as motivations observed in this study is available publicly at http://hdl.handle.net/1773/43786.

METHODS

We conducted 60-minute semi-structured interviews with undergraduate and graduate students. Interviewers were provided a protocol which guided them though the data collection process with 8 specific questions to ask regarding their photo sharing behavior, and guidelines for taking field notes. Interviewees identified the last 50 photographs shared using applications on their smartphones—these photos were limited to those the interviewees had taken or created. In addition, interviewees were allowed to skip photos for privacy concerns, and an initial consent form notified participants that they were allowed to decline to answer questions. For the purpose of this research, 17 students from the University of Washington were recruited as interviewers. A total of 4,555 photo-sharing events were collected from 92 interviewees, in the summer of 2016. The group consisted of 82 undergraduate and 10 graduate students. There were 38 males and 54 females.

Since motivation was collected as an open answer, three authors coded and analyzed motivation types according to their operational definition, which is based on the motivation factors defined in the previous literature (Malik et al., 2016; Nov, Naaman, & Ye, 2009; Oeldorf-Hirsch & Sundar, 2016; Sung, Lee, Kim, & Choi, 2016; and Van House et al., 2005), using inductive thematic analysis (Corbin & Strauss, 2015). The first author read partial samples of survey responses and prepared the initial codebook. Afterwards, the survey data were divided among three different coders who read and coded different subsets of the survey responses using the codebook prepared by the first author. All the coders took and shared notes, and discussed memos related to the coding process in which the initial codebook was refined. We then used a deductive approach and mapped and grouped the themes that emerged from the inductive coding process with the categories of motivations discussed in previous literature. The final codebook was established by this combination of inductive and deductive approaches, and the three coders reviewed and revised the application of the codes to responses again with this final version of the codebook.

Snapchat brought us an interesting issue to discuss. When designing the method, we decided not to include Snapchat as one of our photo-sharing tools because interviewees and participants could not see the history of shared photos on Snapchat. However, many of the participants still answered that they used Snapchat to share photos with others, which caused the large number of *Other* in this study. Due to the application's feature that allows users to view shared photos and videos only for a few seconds before they disappear, users who share photos on Snapchat might have another distinguishable photo-sharing motivation compared to others, such as to share more sensitive photos. This issue will be further investigated in our future study.

FINDINGS & DISCUSSION

Among the motivations identified, *To share memory* (32.12%), *For amusement (humor, fun)* (9.15%), *To appreciate beauty/cuteness* (8.45%), *To show off* (7.51%), and *To disseminate information* (6.37%) were the most frequently mentioned codes by participants. The types of photo-sharing motivations identified in this study are aligned with previous studies (Hunt, 2012; Oeldorf-Hirsch & Sundar, 2010; Van House et al., 2005); there are affective vs. functional motivations and social vs. individual motivations (Kindberg et al., 2005a, 2005b; Van House et al., 2005), and self-presentation and social purposes are the main motivations of photo-sharing behavior (Hunt, 2012; Oeldorf-Hirsch & Sundar, 2010). Technological reasons identified by Oeldorf-Hirsch and Sundar (2010) also appeared in our study, in terms of sharing tool selection based on convenience.

Different Tools, Different Intentions

Participants have distinct intentions when using different types of photo-sharing tools. Regardless of whether a tool is private or public, the subject of the photos tends to differ as well, depending on the tools. Users were intentional in selecting which tool to use for which kinds of photos.

Motivations	Definitions	Examples (quotes)	Frequency
To share memory	To record a moment, such as an event or activity	*"Sharing photo of me and boyfriend on vacation"*	1463 (32.12%)
For amusement (humor, fun)	For comedic effect	*"To share with friend how funny he looked"*	417 (9.15%)
To appreciate beauty/cuteness	An occurrence of the abstract concepts, such as beauty and/or cuteness	*"Show everyone how cute my dog is with a haircut"*	385 (8.45%)
To show off	To seek the attention, approval, and/or affection of others	*"She wanted to show off the makeup she put on her sister."*	342 (7.51%)
To disseminate information	To share information with other people	*"give banking information for receiving money"*	290 (6.37%)
To honor/celebrate	To recognize and express appreciation for individual	*"Celebrating her university's basketball team's win"*	248 (5.44%)
To share/evoke certain emotions	To elicit feeling of happiness, love, etc.	*"Share excitement for end of school year"*	206 (4.52%)
To update status	For maintenance of one's social relations	*"Show what I was doing and who I was with"*	191 (4.19%)
Vague	Motivation is unclear	*"Sharing some of her photography"*	188 (4.13%)
To participate in an event	For proof of engagement	*"She wanted to show she went to a pool party."*	121 (2.66%)
To promote something	To spread awareness of an event or activity	*"To tell eveyone about the fundraiser"*	114 (2.50%)
For self-presentation/self-expression	To cultivate or express one's personality or image	*"A body selfie to show off my first tattoo"*	102 (2.24%)
To illustrate/use as evidence	To support an argument	*"to show that document was received"*	98 (2.15%)
To update profile	For maintenance of one's online presence	*"New profile picture for spring"*	56 (1.23%)
To make an inquiry	Request of response, information, and/or opinion	*"Asking opinion on purchasing a bike."*	43 (0.94%)
To suggest/persuade	To give recommendations or sway opinions	*"Wanted to show friend what she needed to buy"*	26 (0.57%)
To get confirmation	To establish the truth or correctness of something	*"Asking if the document is the correct one to take to a friend."*	17 (0.37%)
To say hello	To use as a greeting or to begin a conversation	*"wanted to say hi, wrote a message in the sand"*	9 (0.20%)
To recall/remind	To provide reference point for future activity	*"To remind friend of this event"*	6 (0.13%)
Other	Motivation does not fit any of the codes provided here	*"Commentary on life."*	233 (5.12%)
Total			4555 (100.00%)

Table 1. Definitions of motivations and overall frequency.

For example, when participants wanted to share photos *To appreciate beauty/cuteness*, they preferred Instagram (60.3%) over other tools. When the motivation was *For amusement (humor, fun)*, Facebook (35.7%) and Instagram (24.2%) were the most popular sharing tools among students. Overall, Instagram was the most frequently mentioned photo-sharing tool among participants (46.4%) followed by Facebook (42.7%).

"*Many of the surveyed participants used multiple messaging systems to privately send picture messages eg. LINE, messenger, sms text, etc. Depending on the nature of the application, the photos shared match the purpose of the application and may have been why the participant used the application. For example, text message was very commonly used to send pictures exclusively of directions and maps whereas FB messenger sent selfies and email was homework note pictures.*" (from the anonymous open-ended response from the student interviewers).

Presumably due to their different features, settings, and user groups, various photo-sharing tools seem to have evolved into culturally different photo-sharing communities. As an example, Facebook users are able to easily share their photos with longer textual descriptions so photos which illustrate discussion-worthy topics tend to be shared more frequently compared to the other tools. Similarly, participants are likely to share more food/drink or fashion/make-up related photos on Instagram, which is a tool that has a simple interface that emphasizes the photo itself.

Sharing Photos for Utility vs. Pleasure

Additionally, we noted the different viewpoints users had with regards to how they treated the photos; in some cases, they were mainly focused on aesthetic aspects of photos for pleasure, and in other cases, they were treated more like data for utility purposes, which also seemed to affect people's decision as to which tools they would use. This finding is aligned with Fidel's (1997) point of views on images, images as data and images as objects, and also with Kindberg et al. (2005a, 2005b).

"US graduate students were more likely to post less with more work/school related purposes. US undergraduate students on the other hand post much more frequently on multiple platforms but with more general, varied information." (from the anonymous open-ended response from the student interviewers).

Different Perceptions on Privacy

It was mentioned that when participants were older, their photo-sharing behavior tends to be more private compared to the younger participants. Privacy discourses on sharing photos has been conducted in a more cultural perspective in previous studies, such as Liu and Fan (2015) and Abokhodair, Hodges, and Vieweg (2017); but it seems that different age groups could be another factor to affect privacy related decisions on photo-sharing behaviors.

The older the person was, the more likely they are to not share photos with anyone, at least in a public sphere. They would rely on other people to share pictures of themselves for them instead." (from the anonymous open-ended response from the student interviewers).

Findings from this study indicate that subtle differences in the design of photo-sharing tools result in different user groups with different intentions of photo-sharing behaviors. Therefore, when designing tools for sharing photos online, considering what kinds of image uses the tool is aimed for would help to create better photo-sharing experiences for users.

CONCLUSION & FUTURE STUDIES

Overall, 19 photo-sharing motivations were identified based on a total of 4,555 photo-sharing instances from 92 participants. Some of the more frequently mentioned motivations were: *To share memory*, *For amusement (humor, fun)*, *To appreciate beauty/cuteness*, *To show off*, and *To disseminate information*, and Instagram and Facebook were the most frequently used photo-sharing tools among participants. The present study provides evidence of differences in user behavior with regard to tool choice depending on motivation and content. Given the wide array of factors affecting photo sharing behavior, developing a tool which satisfies all user needs appears unlikely or at least considerably challenging, but designing tools toward specific use cases may be a way to compensate for the breadth of need and improve user experiences.

This study is potentially limited in that the data only reflects photos that the participants were comfortable talking about with their interviewer. Thus, we may be missing data about personally sensitive photos.

REFERENCES

Abokhodair, N., Hodges, A., & Vieweg, S. (2017). Photo sharing in the Arab Gulf: Expressing the collective and autonomous selves. In *Proceedings of the ACM 2017 conference on computer supported cooperative work* (pp. 696–711). ACM.

Chen, G. M. (2011). Tweet this: A uses and gratifications perspective on how active Twitter use gratifies a need to connect with others. *Computers in Human Behavior, 27*(2), 755–762.

Corbin, J., & Strauss, A. (2015). *Basics of qualitative research: techniques and procedures for developing grounded theory* (4th ed.). Thousand Oaks, CA: Sage.

Duggan, M. (2013). Photo and video sharing grow online. *Pew Research Internet Project.*

Etherington, D. (2013). Instagram Reports 90M Monthly Active Users, 40M Photos Per Day And 8500 Likes Per Second. Retrieved from https://techcrunch.com/2013/01/17/instagram-reports-90m-monthly-active-users-40m-photos-per-day-and-8500-likes-per-second/

Hunt, D. S., Lin, C. A., & Atkin, D. J. (2014). Photo-messaging: Adopter attributes, technology factors and use motives. *Computers in Human Behavior, 40*, 171–179.

Joinson, A. N. (2008). Looking at, looking up or keeping up with people?: Motives and use of facebook. In *Proceedings of the SIGCHI* (pp. 1027–1036). ACM.

Kindberg, T., Spasojevic, M., Fleck, R., & Sellen, A. (2005a). An in-depth study of camera phone use. *IEEE Pervasive Computing, 4*(2), 42–50.

Kindberg, T., Spasojevic, M., Fleck, R., & Sellen, A. (2005b). I saw this and thought of you: Some social uses of camera phones. Paper presented at the Conference on Human Factors in Computing Systems, (April 2–7, 2005, Portland, Oregon, USA).

Lasén, A., & Gómez-Cruz, E. (2009). Digital photography and picture sharing: Redefining the public/private divide. *Knowledge, Technology & Policy, 22*(3), 205–215.

Lee, P. & Steward, D. (2016) *Photo sharing: trillions and rising*. Retrieved from https://www2.deloitte.com/global/en/pages/technology-media-and-telecommunications/articles/tmt-pred16-telecomm-photo-sharing-trillions-and-rising.html

Liu, Y., & Fan, J. (2015). Culturally specific privacy practices on social network sites: Privacy boundary permeability management in photo sharing by American and Chinese college-age users. *International Journal of Communication, 9*(20), 2141–2060.

Malik, A., Dhir, A., & Nieminen, M. (2016). Uses and gratifications of digital photo sharing on Facebook. *Telematics and Informatics, 33*(1), 129–138.

Nadkarni, A., & Hofmann, S. G. (2012). Why do people use Facebook? *Personality and Individual Differences, 52*(3), 243–249.

Nov, O., Naaman, M., & Ye, C. (2010). Analysis of participation in an online photo-sharing community: A multidimensional perspective. *JASIST, 61*(3), 555–566.

Oeldorf-Hirsch, A., & Sundar, S. S. (2010). Online photo sharing as mediated communication. In *Annual conference of the international communication association*. Singapore.

Oeldorf-Hirsch, A., & Sundar, S. S. (2016). Social and technological motivations for online photo sharing. *Journal of Broadcasting & Electronic Media, 60*(4), 624–642.

Smith, C. (2013). *Facebook users are uploading 350 million new photos each day*. Retrieved from http://www.businessinsider.com/facebook-350-million-photos-each-day-2013-9

Sung, Y., Lee, J. A., Kim, E., & Choi, S. M. (2016). Why we post selfies: Understanding motivations for posting pictures of oneself. *Personality and Individual Differences, 97*, 260–265.

Van House, N., Davis, M., Ames, M., Finn, M., & Viswanathan, V. (2005). The uses of personal networked digital imaging: an empirical study of cameraphone photos and sharing. In *CHI'05 extended abstracts on human factors in computing systems* (pp. 1853–1856). ACM.

Quality of Medical Advice for Chronic Pain on Social Platforms

Kaitlin Light Costello
Rutgers University, New Brunswick, NJ, USA
k.costello@rutgers.edu

ABSTRACT

Chronic pain is a stigmatized condition, and many patients report that it is difficult to get information from healthcare providers. As a result, some patients go online to exchange health information on social platforms, but the type and quality of this information is unknown. In this mixed-methods study, comments on a chronic pain platform were inductively analyzed and a typology of medical advice was developed. Subsequently, the alignment of this advice with evidence in the medical literature was assessed by systematically searching for relevant systematic reviews or meta-analyses. Five types of advice were present: over-the-counter remedies, prescription drugs, illicit substances, seeing a different healthcare provider, and lifestyle changes. No evidence was available for 33.9% of the advice, but 33% had at least low support in the literature. 7.8% was harmful. Contributions from this study include a general typology of medical advice online, a methodological approach for assessing the quality of such advice, and several recommendations for future research.

KEYWORDS

Health Informatics; Information Quality; Internet

ASIS&T THESAURUS

Credibility; Medical Science; User Generated Content

BACKGROUND

Chronic pain is experienced by over 50 million people in the United States, and the CDC notes that is one of the most common reasons for visiting the doctor in the country (Dahlhamer, 2018). Unlike acute pain, which acts as a signal, chronic pain has no apparent biological value, and its severity and evolution depend on multiple factors (Institute of Medicine, 2011) although it must persist for at least three months to be classified as chronic (IASP Task Force on Taxonomy, 1994). Chronic pain lowers quality of life and can cause depression, anxiety, job loss, social isolation, and in some cases, suicide (Institute of Medicine, 2011). Because its etiology is often difficult to pinpoint, it has historically been treated as a psychopathological issue (Katz, Rosenbloom, & Fashler, 2015). This is also because pain is inherently subjective, and its severity and impact is often difficult or impossible for people to articulate (IASP Task Force on Taxonomy, 1994). As a result, it can be difficult for patients to obtain treatment (Werner & Malterud, 2003). Stigma and disbelief from doctors are both commonly reported by patients (De Ruddere & Craig, 2016).

Stigma is an information problem (Goffman, 1963), and it is associated with information poverty (Lingel & Boyd, 2013). Information poverty is a theoretical framework wherein marginalized individuals are deprived of helpful sources of information; as a result, they may exhibit self-protective behaviors, such as secrecy, while interacting with information (Chatman, 1996). People with chronic pain are often information impoverished partly because healthcare providers, who work within a system that prioritizes objective indicators of illness, may discount patient narratives or label patients with pain as difficult or untrustworthy due to epistemic privilege (Buchman, Ho, & Goldberg, 2017). The resulting information poverty may lead some with chronic pain to seek out information online (Hasler & Ruthven, 2011). People with stigmatized conditions are more likely to use the Internet for health information, either in lieu of or to supplement information from providers (Berger, Wagner, & Baker, 2005). While surveys of patients in pain clinics indicate that up to 40% of them use the Internet for health information (Corcoran, Haigh, Seabrook, & Schug, 2010), this percentage is likely higher in the overall population of chronic pain patients.

People with chronic pain may use a variety of social platforms to exchange information and support (Newhouse, Atherton, & Ziebland, 2018). Social platforms allow those with chronic pain to connect with one another, exchange health information, and make sense of their illness experience (Merolli, Gray, & Martin-Sanchez, 2014). On Tumblr, for example, these discussions often include the difficulty of communicating about chronic pain with clinicians (Gonzalez-Polledo, 2016).

However, one long-standing concern about patients using the Internet for health information is the quality of that information (Eysenbach, 2005). On websites with no social component, information about chronic pain is generally of low quality (Bailey, LaChapelle, LeFort, Gordon, & Hadjistavropoulos, 2013). Such studies typically assess quality via readability scores, and may combine readability with scales that measure factors like formality of content and the site's design (Zhang,

82nd Annual Meeting of the Association for Information Science & Technology | Melbourne, Australia | 19–23 October, 2019

DOI: 10.1002/pra2.00033

Sun, & Xie, 2015). However, quality is not analogous with readability, and the quality of user-generated health information found on social platforms is often not directly addressed in the literature: "As more people began to contribute health information online, [there is an] urgent need to understand the quality of user-generated content" (Zhang et al., 2015, p. 2082). This article, therefore, addresses the following research questions:

RQ1: What medical advice is given for chronic pain on social platforms?

RQ2: Is this advice aligned with evidence in the medical literature?

METHODS

The data reported on in this article are part of a larger grounded theory study with multiple sources of data, including 3 separate interviews using semi-structured and structured techniques and 1 home visit observation session with seven individual participants, all diagnosed with chronic pain conditions, that took place in 2016-2017. During their interviews, almost all of the participants mentioned multiple online support groups that they visit for information about chronic pain. For theoretical sampling purposes, the 25 most popular posts from the forum mentioned most frequently were inductively analyzed over time in order to iteratively develop a codebook (Saldaña, 2015). These codes were refined and categorized progressively during three rounds of individual coding and peer-debriefing sessions (Lincoln & Guba, 1985). The six resulting codes are mutually exclusive and exhaustive. The codes were then applied to 1,346 comments made in 100 randomly-selected threads posted between 2014 and 2017; a second coder analyzed a subset of 237 of these comments in order to determine intercoder reliability using Cohen's kappa for each category. This article reports only on the comments offering medical advice ($\kappa = .86$), defined in the codebook as *information or advice about specific medications for pain, medical treatments for chronic pain, or alternative methods of treatment for pain.*

Each comment containing medical advice was assessed to determine the pain condition in question and the advice being offered for that condition (condition/advice pairs), in alignment with the PICO format commonly used in evidence-based medicine (Schardt, Adams, Owens, Keitz, & Fontelo, 2007). Comments that offered multiple pieces of advice were labeled with multiple pairs; for example, if a comment recommended the poster try pain relief cream or a TENS unit for back pain, it was labeled with both "Pain relief cream + back pain" and "TENS + back pain." These pairs were identified and inductively sorted into categories to develop a typology of advice by the research team, and disagreements were reconciled via discussion.

The Cochrane Library and MEDLINE (Ovid) databases were searched up to 15 February 2019 for systematic reviews or meta-analyses for each individual condition/advice pair. Only systematic reviews and meta-analysis were included as they represent the gold standard used for evidence-based medical practice (Munn, Stern, Aromataris, Lockwood, & Jordan, 2018). Systematic reviews typically report evidence quality ratings using the GRADE approach, which specifies the level of quality of the evidence and the effect of the treatment. In this study, the extended abstract, summary of findings, and/or plain language summaries were analyzed and the effect of the treatment or intervention in question and the quality of the evidence was recorded using the following scale: No review exists, Insufficient evidence available for recommendation, Harms outweigh benefits, Unsupported, Low support, Moderate support, and Supported. (Condition/advice pairs labeled as "insufficient evidence available for recommendation" returned relevant systematic reviews, but the reviews found that there was not sufficient literature available to make a recommendation.)

To address both research questions, percentages are reported to facilitate comparison, as in Byström (2002). Assessing the statistical significance of the findings was not appropriate due to the small sample size. Many threads contain multiple comments advising the same treatment; for example, a thread about trigeminal neuralgia, a facial nerve disorder, may contain five comments advising gabapentin, a nerve pain medication. Because repetition is one way that users form credibility assessments on social health platforms (Costello, 2016), redundant entries were counted multiple times when carrying out analyses.

RESULTS

RQ1: What medical advice is given for chronic pain on social platforms?

There are 173 comments containing medical advice, and 218 total instances of advice in the sample. Most comments contain only one piece of advice, but 45 comments present between two and five pieces of advice, with a mode and median of two per comment. There are 113 original condition/advice pairs in the data; 73 (64.6%) of these appear only once, and 40 (35.4%) are repeated. The mode of repeated advice pairs is two. Two pieces of advice are repeated nine times. Commenters rarely provide links to outside resources as evidence; instead, they discuss their personal experiences with treatments or simply offer advice without giving contextual information. The two most common pieces of advice are to ingest a cannabinoid product (n = 27) or to apply heat (n = 26). As it is against the rules of the forum to buy or sell products, no comments offering treatments for sale were present in the dataset.

There are five types of medical advice present; Table 1 reports their proportions.

Advice type	n (%)
OTC remedies	80 (36.7%)
Prescription drugs	63 (28.9%)
Illicit substances	33 (15.1%)
HCPs	21 (9.6%)
Lifestyle	21 (9.6%)

Table 1. Types of advice and their proportions.

Over-the-counter (OTC) remedies, such as using an anti-inflammatory drug; or applying heat or ice, muscle patches, a TENS unit, braces, or pain relief cream.

Prescription drugs or surgical treatments. Often, brand names (e.g., Lyrica, Gabapentin) are mentioned, but sometimes more general prescription treatments like "steroids" or "muscle relaxers" are advised. Surgical treatments mentioned include decompression surgery and gamma knife procedures.

Illicit substances. Marijuana and cannabinoid derivatives are overwhelmingly represented in this category, although other illicit substances are occasionally mentioned (e.g., kratom).

Seeing another type of healthcare provider, including those who practice "alternative medicine," such as acupuncture and chiropractic; physical therapists and massage therapists are also present in the data.

Lifestyle changes, including exercise, yoga, diet, meditation, and psychotherapy.

RQ2: Is this advice aligned with evidence in the medical literature?

Table 2 shows the proportion of types of evidential support for given advice. Percentages are reported out of the total instances of advice in the sample (n = 218). No systematic reviews or meta analyses were found for about a third of the advice instances (33.9%). Perhaps surprisingly, only 7.8% of the advice was harmful; a great deal more of it showed at least low support (33% total, combining low, moderate, and supported advice).

Evidential support	n (%)
No review exists	74 (33.9%)
Insufficient evidence	35 (16.1%)
Harms outweigh benefits	17 (7.8%)
Unsupported	20 (9.2%)
Low support	20 (9.2%)
Moderate support	30 (13.8%)
Supported	22 (10.1%)

Table 2. Evidential support for advice.

A contingency table (Table 3) showing the distribution of evidential support by evidence type suggests some findings for further exploration. For example, harmful advice given in this sample is either about prescription drugs or illicit substances, and, illicit substances are the only type of advice for which no strong support was found. There was also no unsupported advice regarding illicit substances.

	OTC	Drugs	Illicit	HCP	Life
No review	15.1%	10.1%	6.4%	—	2.3%
Insufficient	8.7%	1.8%	1.8%	2.8%	1.0%
Harms	—	3.7%	4.1%	—	—
Unsupport.	1.8%	4.1%	—	2.3%	1.0%
Low	3.7%	1.4%	1.8%	2.3%	—
Moderate	4.6%	4.6%	1.0%	.5%	3.2%
Supported	2.8%	3.2%	—	1.8%	2.3%

Table 3. Evidential support according to advice type.

DISCUSSION

This study makes several contributions to our understanding of advice quality in online social platforms for chronic pain. First, we provide a general typology of the type of advice offered; in future work, this typology could be tested for its transferability to other conditions. Future research could also assess differences in amount of advice types between different medical conditions in order to determine whether, for example, stigmatized conditions are more likely to garner advice about illicit substances when compared with non-stigmatized conditions, or if certain types of conditions have a higher likelihood of having low- or high-quality medical evidence available about them on social platforms.

Sixty-six percent of the advice on this platform has enough corresponding evidence for a systematic review or meta-analysis to exist; of these reviews, half of them have enough evidence for claims about treatment to be made. The level of harmful advice is lower than one might expect, especially given the level of pessimism regarding health misinformation on social platforms in both the popular media (e.g., Warraich, 2018) and the scientific literature (Lau, Gabarron, Fernandez-Luque, & Armayones, 2012). However, statistical analyses were not undertaken on this data due to the small sample size. A larger dataset would allow for more sophisticated statistical analyses to be carried out between and among the identified types of evidence and levels of evidential support, offering more robust conclusions.

This study also makes a methodological contribution by presenting a way to assess the quality of medical evidence on social platforms using measures of quality offered by evidence-based medicine. It may be possible to automate some or all of the techniques used in this study (e.g., identifying condition/advice pairs) in order to assess health information quality on social platforms in real-time. Similar efforts have been used to automatically identify users who are likely to share health misinformation (Ghenai & Mejova, 2018), but identifying the quality of advice itself in real-time has several advantages that are also worth pursuing.

CONCLUSION

In this study, comments on a chronic pain platform were inductively analyzed and a typology of five types of medical advice was developed. Advice quality was assessed by creating condition/advice pairs and searching for relevant systematic reviews. No evidence was available for 33.9% of the advice, and 33% had at least low support in the literature. 7.8% was harmful. Our findings offer a general typology of medical advice, methods for assessing health information quality on social platforms, and recommendations for future research.

ACKNOWLEDGMENTS

Thanks very much to the participants who spent time with me and who provided insight in the initial phase of this study. This research was partly made possible by a Rutgers SC&I Grant for Individual Faculty Research.

REFERENCES

Bailey, S. J., LaChapelle, D. L., LeFort, S. M., Gordon, A., & Hadjistavropoulos, T. (2013). Evaluation of chronic pain-related information available to consumers on the Internet. *Pain Medicine*, *14*(6), 855–864. https://doi.org/10.1111/pme.12087

Berger, M., Wagner, T. H., & Baker, L. C. (2005). Internet use and stigmatized illness. *Social Science & Medicine*, *61*(8), 1821–1827. https://doi.org/10.1016/j.socscimed.2005.03.025

Buchman, D. Z., Ho, A., & Goldberg, D. S. (2017). Investigating trust, expertise, and epistemic injustice in chronic pain. *Journal of Bioethical Inquiry*, *14*(1), 31–42. https://doi.org/10.1007/s11673-016-9761-x

Byström, K. (2002). Information and information sources in tasks of varying complexity. *Journal of the American Society for Information Science and Technology*, *53*(7), 581–591. https://doi.org/10.1002/asi.10064

Chatman, E. A. (1996). The impoverished life-world of outsiders. *Journal of the American Society for Information Science*, *47*(3), 193–206. https://doi.org/10.1002/(SICI)1097-4571(199603)47:3<193::AID-ASI3>3.0.CO;2-T

Corcoran, T. B., Haigh, F., Seabrook, A., & Schug, S. A. (2010). A Survey of Patients' Use of the Internet for Chronic Pain-Related Information. *Pain Medicine*, *11*(4), 512–517. https://doi.org/10.1111/j.1526-4637.2010.00817.x

Costello, K. L. (2016). Impact of patient-provider communication on online health information behaviors in chronic illness. *Proceedings of the Association for Information Science and Technology*, *53*(1), 1–10. https://doi.org/10.1002/pra2.2016.14505301060

Dahlhamer, J. (2018). *Prevalence of Chronic Pain and High-Impact Chronic Pain Among Adults — United States, 2016.* MMWR. Morbidity and Mortality Weekly Report, 67. Retrieved from https://doi.org/10.15585/mmwr.mm6736a2

De Ruddere, L., & Craig, K. D. (2016). Understanding stigma and chronic pain: a-state-of-the-art review. *Pain*, *157*(8), 1607–1610. https://doi.org/10.1097/j.pain.0000000000000512

Eysenbach, G. (2005). Patient-to-patient communication: Support groups and virtual communities, *Consumer health informatics: Informing consumers and improving healthcare*. Retrieved from. In D. Lewis, G. Eysenbach, R. Kukafka, P. Z. Stavri, & H. B. Jimison (Eds.). http://www.springerlink.com.content/v30740q33p124747

Ghenai, A., & Mejova, Y. (2018). *Fake Cures: User-centric Modeling of Health Misinformation in Social Media*. Proceedings of the ACM on Human-Computer Interaction, 2 (CSCW), 58.

Goffman, E. (1963). *Stigma: Notes on the management of spoiled identity* (1st ed.). New York: Simon & Schuster.

Gonzalez-Polledo, E. (2016). Chronic Media Worlds: Social Media and the Problem of Pain Communication on Tumblr. *Social Media + Society*, *2*(1). https://doi.org/10.1177/2056305116628887

Hasler, L., & Ruthven, I. (2011). *Escaping Information Poverty Through Internet Newsgroups*. Fifth International AAAI Conference on Weblogs and Social Media.

IASP Task Force on Taxonomy (1994). In H. Merskey & N. Bogduk (Eds.), *Classification of chronic pain: Descriptions of chronic pain syndromes and definitions of pain terms* (2nd ed.). Seattle, International Association for the Study of Pain Press.

Institute of Medicine. (2011). *Relieving pain in America: A blueprint for transforming prevention, care, education, and research*. Retrieved from http://www.ncbi.nlm.nih.gov/books/NBK91497/

Katz, J., Rosenbloom, B. N., & Fashler, S. (2015). Chronic Pain, Psychopathology, and DSM-5 Somatic Symptom Disorder. *Canadian Journal of Psychiatry. Revue Canadienne de Psychiatrie*, *60*(4), 160–167.

Lau, A. Y. S., Gabarron, E., Fernandez-Luque, L., & Armayones, M. (2012). Social Media in Health — What are the Safety Concerns for Health Consumers? *Health Information Management Journal*, *41*(2), 30–35. https://doi.org/10.1177/183335831204100204

Lincoln, Y. S., & Guba, E. G. (1985). *Naturalistic Inquiry* (1st ed.). Sage Publications, Inc.

Lingel, J., & Boyd, D. (2013). "Keep it secret, keep it safe": Information poverty, information norms, and stigma. *Journal of the American Society for Information Science and Technology*, *64*(5), 981–991.

Merolli, M., Gray, K., & Martin-Sanchez, F. (2014). Therapeutic affordances of social media: Emergent themes from a global online survey of people with chronic pain. *Journal of Medical Internet Research*, *16*(12). https://doi.org/10.2196/jmir.3494

Munn, Z., Stern, C., Aromataris, E., Lockwood, C., & Jordan, Z. (2018). What kind of systematic review should I conduct? A proposed typology and guidance for systematic reviewers in the medical and health sciences. *BMC Medical Research Methodology*, *18*. https://doi.org/10.1186/s12874-017-0468-4

Newhouse, N., Atherton, H., & Ziebland, S. (2018). Pain and the internet: Transforming the experience? In *Painscapes* (pp. 129–155). Springer.

Saldaña, J. (2015). *The coding manual for qualitative researchers* (3rd ed.). Los Angeles, CA: SAGE Publications Ltd.

Schardt, C., Adams, M. B., Owens, T., Keitz, S., & Fontelo, P. (2007). Utilization of the PICO framework to improve searching PubMed for clinical questions. *BMC Medical Informatics and Decision Making*, *7*(1), 16. https://doi.org/10.1186/1472-6947-7-16

Warraich, H. (2018, December 20). Opinion | Dr. Google Is a Liar. The New York Times. Retrieved from https://www.nytimes.com/2018/12/16/opinion/statin-side-effects-cancer.html

Werner, A., & Malterud, K. (2003). It is hard work behaving as a credible patient: encounters between women with chronic pain and their doctors. *Social Science & Medicine*, *57*(8), 1409–1419. https://doi.org/10.1016/S0277-9536(02)00520-8

Zhang, Y., Sun, Y., & Xie, B. (2015). Quality of health information for consumers on the web: A systematic review of indicators, criteria, tools, and evaluation results. *Journal of the Association for Information Science and Technology*, *66*(10), 2071–2084. https://doi.org/10.1002/asi.23311

Noticing the Unnoticed: Lines of Work in Everyday Life Information Practices

Nicole Dalmer
Trent University,
Peterborough, Canada
nicoledalmer@trentu.ca

Pam McKenzie
The University of Western Ontario,
London, Canada
pmckenzi@uwo.ca

ABSTRACT

This paper challenges the existing dichotomy between "everyday" and "workplace" information practices and uses an expansive understanding of *work* to make visible the often invisible and unpaid forms of work required to make everyday life possible. After an overview of existing understandings and applications of work within LIS, two studies that take up the information work of caring for a family member living with a chronic illness demonstrate that everyday life information practices transcend domestic and organizational contexts. The unpredictability of a chronic illness leads caregivers to undertake numerous and simultaneous lines of work in their everyday and every night lives, including information, document, affective, avoidance, and articulation work, among others. We argue that using the notion of work is a strategy to acknowledge, name, and count those everyday life information practices that are so commonplace they risk becoming unnoticed.

KEYWORDS

Information Work; Information Practices; Everyday Life; Work; Chronic Illness; Family Caregiving

ASIS&T THESAURUS

Information Behavior; Information Sharing; Information Seeking; Information Production; Human Information Resources; Sociocultural Aspects; Qualitative Analysis; Families

INTRODUCTION

Recent LIS scholarship has focused attention on contexts within which information practices are enmeshed (Courtright, 2007). Analysis of context within LIS, however, tends to remain unitary and to dichotomize "everyday" and "workplace" information practices. Such dichotomization is problematic for several reasons. First, what is "workplace" for one person is "everyday life" for another (e.g., a public library reference question counts as work for the librarian but as everyday life information seeking for the patron). Second, through the course of a single day an individual may take up roles and identities and engage in information practices in both workplace and domestic, as well as other, contexts. Third, "everyday" domestic life is not limited to domestic spaces, but is enacted in community spaces (DeVault, 2000). Conversely, work-related activities are not confined to work spaces (e.g., Thomson, 2013). That means that everyday life information practices (ELIP) are not, as is commonly assumed, unencumbered by organizational requirements. Rather, they are shaped by interactions with a myriad of organizations that exist outside of domestic life but touch on it and co-ordinate its work (McKenzie & Davies, 2010; Dalmer, 2018a; 2019).

Several LIS scholars have responded to and attempted to bridge this dichotomization. Savolainen (1995) showed that social capital and habitus developed through workplace participation shape non-workplace information practices. Hartel (2003) adopted Stebbins' (1992, p. 3) concept of serious leisure to explore the shades of meaning between the "work" and "leisure" poles. Ocepek (2018, p. 399) has recently advocated that LIS scholars draw on Lefebvre's (2008) theory of the everyday to consider everyday as "the totality of lived experience, so all aspects of life are represented in the everyday."

To date, these responses have focused on reconceptualizing and broadening the concept of "everyday" to facilitate an understanding of information practices that are so commonplace they become unnoticed. As everyday contexts become increasingly popular sites of study for information scholars, we wonder what comes to count in the everyday. How can information scholars study the unnoticed?

In this short paper, we seek to bridge the everyday life/paid work dichotomy through a different approach, one that takes up the notion of *work* to bring into view the often invisible forms of work required to make everyday life possible. Star (1991) notes that "work is the link between the visible and the invisible" (p. 265). We review several approaches to the study of *work* broadly conceived and its informational aspects. We then illustrate the possibilities of this approach with findings from two studies that consider information work related to caring for a loved one living with a chronic illnesses, a context that demonstrates that everyday life is not contained within particular hours or settings but reaches across and between domestic and organizational contexts.

LITERATURE REVIEW

Researchers in a variety of disciplines pay serious scholarly attention to the unwaged, unnoticed, and marginalized forms

82nd Annual Meeting of the Association for Information Science & Technology | Melbourne, Australia | 19–23 October, 2019

DOI: 10.1002/pra2.00034

of work required to carry out leisure, domestic, or other everyday activities. Feminist sociologist Dorothy Smith (1999, p. 7) defines *work* as "the ongoing concerting and coordinating of individuals' activities" and proposes that "life as usual" and the social order of any setting are the product of these activities. Defining work generously in this way brings into view *as work* activities that are otherwise invisible as work, even to those doing the activities (Smith, 2005).

Star and Strauss (1999, p. 12) argue that in order to understand cooperative work, it is necessary to understand "how work becomes visible or invisible, and then how negotiations about this status are structured." They use the term *articulation work* to refer to "work that gets things back 'on track' in the face of the unexpected, and modifies action to accommodate unanticipated contingencies. *The important thing about articulation work is that it is invisible to rationalized models of work*" (1999, p. 10, emphasis in original).

Within LIS, Trace's (2007) concept of *document work* – the situated understanding of how documents are and ought to be produced and used in a particular setting – reveals how documents make some things visible and others invisible, making order seem natural and erasing the articulation work done to achieve it. McKenzie and Davies (2012) showed that documents created and used in the home are embedded in both deeply meaningful interpersonal relationships and in the structures of the multiple organizations with which individuals interact. Huvila uses the term *information work* to refer to the information component of human activity more generally. According to him, "all work has an information component and presumes some degree of information processing whether the work is manual labor or highly abstract decision making" (Huvila, 2009, p. 697).

Corbin and Strauss (1985, 1988) took up the concept of work to better understand the management of chronic illnesses in the home. They focused on the social contexts, the relationships, and the many different, often invisible and taken-for-granted forms of action that people do to shape their experiences throughout the course of their or their spouse's illness. Corbin and Strauss identified *information work* as one type of work patients and their spouses undertake as they manage illness as part of their daily lives, and a small number of LIS scholars have taken this up. Hogan and Palmer (2005) conducted a nation-wide survey of people living with HIV/AIDS, and Souden (2008) considered information work related to a number of chronic illnesses. Kaziunas, Ackerman, and Veinot (2013) examined the mediating impact of individuals' everyday, local contexts on their information work as they navigate diabetes, hypertension, and kidney disease. Kaziunas et al. (2015) explored the relationship between pediatric bone marrow transplant caregivers' information work and emotion work. Büyüktür and Ackerman (2017) studied the impact of misaligned temporalities on the coordination between patients' and clinicians' information work. Dalmer (2018); Dalmer (2019) made visible the information work family members do while caring for an older adult living with dementia, uncovering how larger government and policy ideals ultimately impact how paid dementia care staff and family caregivers can engage with information.

In this paper, we apply Smith's generous understanding of work to make visible otherwise invisible forms of work in managing a loved one's chronic illness. Naming and acknowledging this work can have a ripple effect on understanding and valuing people's illness-related information work.

METHODS

To illustrate invisible forms of information work in everyday life, we present findings from two interview studies with 21 individuals (eight wives, one husband, six daughters, one son, one grandson, three mothers, one grandmother) living with one or more family member's chronic illnesses. Interviews ranged from 51 to 185 mins in length. Participants spoke about the information work needed to guide and support their care work.

Interviews took place in participants' homes, public cafés, or public library meeting rooms, depending on the participant's preference. The interviewers took handwritten notes throughout the interviews and wrote out impressions as soon as the interviews concluded. Interviews were audiorecorded and transcribed verbatim. Data collection and analysis conform to ethical guidelines on research on human subjects of the Social Sciences and Humanities Research Council of Canada. To maintain confidentiality, we identify participants by generic initials and do not associate demographic characteristics with any individual participant.

For this paper, we have selected findings that highlight the lines of work that participants made visible as they described how they create, find, use, make sense of, manage, and consider the implications of information related to their loved one's chronic illness.

FINDINGS

A number of participants spoke to the unpredictability of their loved one's chronic illness. This lack of a neat sequence or predefined trajectory implicates a number of intersecting lines of work that impact how information is conceptualized and used. As participants spoke about the patchwork pattern in which they received information, at different times from different places and people, they spoke of exercising constant vigilance; when or where they received information and whether or not the information may or may not be perceived as useful in the present or even in the future was not always certain. This necessitated ongoing work of managing and organizing information, in addition to the work of monitoring and scanning their loved one's bodily rhythms and routines or vocal utterances that they used as cues. This was especially so for caregivers of very young children or of adults in later stages of dementia, in which verbal communication can be difficult or fraught.

CG cared for a medically fragile toddler with several life-threatening chronic illnesses and allergies. The child had spent the first year of life in hospital and after discharge had weekly scheduled doctor's appointments and had required weekly trips to the hospital emergency department. CG engaged in a great deal of information creation and management work that reveals the close interconnections between home and hospital and work and everyday in her family's life. For example, the home had an alarm system: "It's connected to the hospital too. So I can hit a button and they send an ambulance."

> *I have a kind of small ... weekly calendar that stays in the diaper bag. So when I'm at appointments ... I have to write down [baby's] bowel movements, emesis for the day, any fevers that we had...-, if I was talking to [the hospital] they want me to do a follow-up with somebody else I have it all at my hands. I have an app on my phone that allows me to track just health stuff for the baby. So feeds, any increases in the rate on the pump, um, again, bowel movements, emesis, baths, uh, if I took [baby] to the playground to play, that kind of thing, so we can kinda see, um, if [baby] does get sick then I can go back and say, well we were in A, B, and C, right.*

The baby's changing and unpredictable condition necessitated a great deal of information, document, and articulation work to engage in even the most quotidian of activities, such as grocery shopping:

> *But with the baby having new allergies and stuff it's a learning process. And groceries takes a long time. We went grocery shopping the other day, it took six hours. I said, ok there's gotta be another way. So I contacted somebody at the hospital and she knows somebody who actually spent months coordinating this list [of products by brand name]. So it's broken down into dairy allergies, egg allergies, wheat allergies, gluten allergies and I said, "Just print it all off, 'cause [baby]'s allergic to a gamut of things." So she said, "Ok, 32 pages." I'll go through, highlight what I normally buy and then I'll know in the grocery store this is the product I can buy.*

CG was called on to collect data about her child and share it with the medical team. CG's work as an informal care provider therefore informed and was informed by the work of the paid hospital staff, and defied the unitary conceptualization of ELIP.

For example, CG needed to stop the interview to take a photograph of the baby's soiled diaper:

> *CG: K, I need to take a photo and send it off.*
> *Interviewer: Oh, so you have to take a picture of the stool each time, the diaper?*
> *CG: This time I do -- it has blood in it.*
> *Int: Ok, and then you send that to the-*
> *CG: Send it to the team. Say "Hey guys! What am I cutting back on [in baby's diet]?"*

A key source of participants' more abstract and cognitive work is made visible using Huvila's (2015) concept of situational appropriation. Participants creatively appropriated past information accrued in different situations (from their paid work, from formal education or training, or from decades of living with their spouse etc.), transforming that information based on the new situation at hand. SK, for example, explained how her searches about her husband's Alzheimer's disease were similar to the search strategies she developed when her daughter was first diagnosed with celiac disease. She went on to describe how she was able to adapt her past training as a school administrator and a primary school teacher to more fully engage with and support her husband:

> *I think that my background as an administrator but my background in the kindergarten was huge in preparing me for this. Absolutely huge because, and I was a Special Ed person as well, so I have a lot of knowledge about modifying programs, changing things to suit the pupils, the student. And a lot of those things like, story boarding with kids who can't follow instructions or can't handle verbal communication, that kind of thing – I use that with [husband] all the time now.*

SK's quote not only demonstrates the permeability of information accrued from paid work environs but also makes visible the work of transforming information received from "elsewhere and elsewhen" (Smith, 2005).

Finally, RV cared for her mother who was living with mixed dementia and, like a majority of dementia care providers interviewed, had difficulty dealing with any sort of information about long-term care placement. RV's quote below captures a number of caregivers' experiences, in that the lines of work that comprise her everyday, which include affective work, the work of organizing and managing, and strategic avoidance work, do not occur sequentially or in an orderly fashion, but instead happen simultaneously:

> *I learned right then that it scares the heck out of me to look too far ahead and I can't manage it. I can't manage stuff that isn't relevant. So a lot of the information that I got at the course, both courses, it was too far ahead. Like, I couldn't use it then. Like long-term care? I'm only now, 3 years later, ready to go back and look at that ... I'd file under L, but I wouldn't even look at it, you know?*

CONCLUSION

As information scholars increasingly recognize the everyday as an important site of study, we advocate for the integration of Smith's generous understanding of work as a means to acknowledge, name, and count the often invisible forms of work that make everyday life, including ELIP, possible.

Within the context of family caregiving, making caregivers' many lines of intersecting work visible can be a powerful act, particularly within current climates of austerity, in which responsibilities for care work, including information work, are increasingly shifted onto families. We prompt information scholars to ask *how is our understanding of people's information practices changed when we restore all of the work?* as an important step in more richly, realistically, and responsively studying and supporting individuals' intricate, messy, and workful everyday life information practices.

REFERENCES

Büyüktür, A. G., & Ackerman, M. S. (2017). *Information Work in Bone Marrow Transplant: Reducing Misalignment of Perspectives*. Proceedings of the SIGCHI Conference on Computer Supported Cooperative Work (CSCW '17). 1740-1752.

Corbin, J., & Strauss, A. (1985). Managing chronic illness at home: Three lines of work. *Qualitative Sociology, 8*(3), 224–247.

Corbin, J. M., & Strauss, A. (1988). *Unending work and care: Managing chronic illness at home*. San Francisco: Jossey-Bass.

Courtright, C. (2007). Context in information science research. *Annual Review of Information Science and Technology, 41*(1), 273–306.

Dalmer, N. K. (2018a). 'Add info and stir': An institutional ethnographic scoping review of family care-givers' information work. *Ageing & Society*, 1–27.

Dalmer, N. K. (2018b). *Informing care: Mapping the social organization of families' information work in an aging in place climate* PhD thesis. London, Ontario, Canada.

Dalmer, N. K. (2019). A logic of choice: Problematizing the documentary reality of Canadian aging in place policies. *Journal of Aging Studies, 48*, 40–49.

DeVault, M. L. (2000). Producing family time: Practices of leisure activity beyond the home. *Qualitative Sociology, 23*(4), 485–503.

Hartel, J. (2003). The serious leisure frontier in library and information science: Hobby domains. *Knowledge Organization, 30*(3/4), 228–238.

Hogan, T. P., & Palmer, C. L. (2005). "Information work" and chronic illness: Interpreting results from a nationwide survey of people living with HIV/AIDS. *Proceedings of the American Society for Information Science and Technology, 42*(1).

Huvila, I. (2009). Ecological framework of information interactions and information infrastructures. *Journal of Information Science, 35*(6), 695–708.

Huvila, I. (2015). Situational appropriation of information. *Aslib Journal of Information Management, 67*(5), 492–504.

Huvila, I., Lloyd, A., Budd, J. M., Palmer, C., & Toms, E. (2016). Information work in information science research and practice. *Proceedings of the Association for Information Science and Technology, 53*(1), 1–5.

Kaziunas, E., Ackerman, M. S., & Veinot, T. C. (2013). Localizing chronic disease management: Information work and health translations. *Proceedings of the American Society for Information Science and Technology, 50*(1), 1–10.

Kaziunas, E., Büyüktür, A. G., Jones, J., Choi, S. W., Hanauer, D. A., & Ackerman, M. S. (2015). Transition and reflection in the use of health information: The case of pediatric bone marrow transplant caregivers. In *Proceedings of the 18th ACM Conference on Computer Supported Cooperative Work & Social Computing* (pp. 1763–1774). New York, NY: ACM.

Lefebvre, H. (2008). In J. Moore, *Critique of Everyday Life* (Vol. *1*, 2nd ed.). London: Verso.

McKenzie, P. J., & Davies, E. (2012). Genre systems and "keeping track" in everyday life. *Archival Science, 12* (4), 437–460.

Ocepek, M. G. (2018). Bringing out the everyday in everyday information behavior. *Journal of Documentation, 74*(2), 398–411.

Savolainen, R. (1995). Everyday life information seeking: Approaching information seeking in the context of "way of life". *Library & Information Science Research, 17*(3), 259–294.

Smith, D. E. (1999). *Writing the social. Critique, theory, and investigations*. Toronto, ON: University of Toronto Press.

Smith, D. E. (2005). *Institutional ethnography: A sociology for people*. Lanham, MD: Altamira Press.

Souden, M. (2008). Information work in the chronic illness experience. In *Proceedings of the American Society for Information Science and Technology 45*(1), 1–6.

Star, S. L. (1991). The sociology of the invisible: The primacy of work in the writings of Anselm Strauss. In D. Maines, *Social Organization and Social Process: Essays in Honor of Anselm Strauss* (pp. 265–283). Hawthorne, NY: Aldine de Gruyter.

Star, S. L., & Strauss, A. (1999). Layers of silence, arenas of voice: The ecology of visible and invisible work. *Computer Supported Cooperative Work, 8*(1), 9–30.

Stebbins, R. A. (1992). *Amateurs, professionals, and serious leisure*. Kingston: McGill-Queen's University Press.

Thomson, L. (2013). When I've packed it in and they send me something: Information boundaries in professional home offices. *Proceedings of the American Society for Information Science and Technology, 50*(1).

Trace, C. B. (2007). Information creation and the notion of membership. *Journal of Documentation, 63*(1), 142–163.

Systematic Examination of Pre- and Post-Retraction Citations

Ly Dinh
School of Information Sciences, University of Illinois at Urbana-Champaign, USA
dinh4@illinois.edu

Janina Sarol
School of Information Sciences, University of Illinois at Urbana-Champaign, USA
mjsarol@illinois.edu

Yi-Yun Cheng
School of Information Sciences, University of Illinois at Urbana-Champaign, USA
yiyunyc2@illinois.edu

Tzu-Kun Hsiao
School of Information Sciences, University of Illinois at Urbana-Champaign, USA
tkhsiao2@illinois.edu

Nikolaus Parulian
School of Information Sciences, University of Illinois at Urbana-Champaign, USA
nnp2@illinois.edu

Jodi Schneider
School of Information Sciences, University of Illinois at Urbana-Champaign, USA
jodi@illinois.edu

ABSTRACT

Scientific retractions occur for a multitude of reasons. A growing body of research has studied the phenomenon of retraction through systematic analyses of the characteristics of retracted articles and their associated citations. In our study, we focus on the characteristics of articles that cite retracted articles, and the changes in citation dynamics pre- and post-retraction. We leverage descriptive statistics and ego-network methods to examine 4,871 retracted articles and their citations before and after retraction. Our retracted articles data was obtained from PubMed, Scopus, and Retraction Watch and their citing articles from Scopus. Our findings indicate a stark decrease in post-retraction citations and that most of these citations came from countries different from the retracted article's country of publication. Citation context analyses of a subset of retracted articles also reveal that post-retraction citations came from articles with disciplinary and geographical boundaries different from that of the retracted article.

KEYWORDS

Retraction; Post-Retraction Citation; Citation Networks

ASIS&T THESAURUS

Bibliometrics; Citation Analysis; Network Analysis; Scholarly Publishing

INTRODUCTION

Scientific retractions occur for a multitude of reasons, including minor problems such as publisher versioning mistakes, or major concerns such as plagiarism or fabrication of data.

82nd Annual Meeting of the Association for Information Science & Technology | Melbourne, Australia | 19–23 October, 2019

DOI: 10.1002/pra2.00035

Scientific misconduct was found to be the most prominent reason for retraction (Fang, Steen, & Casadevall, 2012), accounting for 94 of the 288 retracted articles identified. Thus, it is necessary that retracted articles are promptly retracted and publicly recognized to "minimize the number of researchers who cite the erroneous work, act on its findings or draw incorrect conclusions" (COPE, 2009).

The problem arises when retracted articles continue to be cited (Redman, Yarandi, & Merz, 2008), at times even at a higher rate than before retraction (see (Fukuhara et al., 2005)). As an example, a study of 315 retracted articles found that articles published in higher-impact journals remained highly cited even after they were found to have committed research misconduct (Redman et al., 2008). The reasons for these problematic citations are two-fold: (1) citing articles did not show awareness of the retraction statuses of the articles they cited (Da Silva & Bornemann-Cimenti, 2017), (2) retraction information is not consistently presented across platforms where citing authors obtain bibliographic records (COPE, 2009). Nevertheless, the continued circulation of retracted articles poses significant risks to the integrity of scientific research as honest and reliable works. (Bar-Ilan & Halevi, 2017; Da Silva & Bornemann-Cimenti, 2017).

To examine the citation dynamics of retracted articles in more detail, we analyze the citations of 4,871 biomedical articles from PubMed, leveraging both descriptive statistics and ego-network analysis methods. Our contributions are as follows: (1) we examine the characteristics of articles that cite retracted articles, and (2) we explore pre- and post-retraction citation ego-networks of 250 retracted articles using both citation context analysis and quantitative measures such as cited half-lives and time-lag. Ultimately, we hope to shed light on the potential reasons retracted articles continue to be cited and whether these citations can be considered as problematic.

RELATED WORK

There is a significant body of research about retraction of scientific publications. These articles analyze the characteristics of retracted articles such as retraction counts by disciplines and/or countries, reasons for retraction, cited half-lives, and self-citing dynamics (Bar-Ilan & Halevi, 2017; Bornemann-Cimenti, Szilagyi, & Sandner-Kiesling, 2016; Redman et al., 2008). While these studies examined characteristics of retracted articles at great lengths, more attention could be given to the characteristics of citing articles. (Budd, Sievert, & Schultz, 1998) and (Bar-Ilan & Halevi, 2017) have begun to look into citing articles and their reasons for citing retracted articles. Additional characteristics of citing articles, such as their scholarly discipline, country of affiliation, and publication type, are needed to fully understand the citation dynamics of retracted articles pre- and post-retraction.

Along with bibliometric statistics, network analysis is frequently adopted to examine the underlying citation structures of retracted articles (Lu, Jin, Uzzi, & Jones, 2013; Madlock-Brown & Eichmann, 2015). Specifically, ego-network analysis (Wasserman & Faust, 1994) where the retracted paper is the ego, is useful to reveal the dynamics between citing articles (alters) connected to a common ego. Analysis of ego-network data focuses on the composition of the alters, and posits that characteristics of both the ego (retracted article) and the alters (citing articles) will have an impact on the ego-network structure (Borgatti & Ofem, 2010). Therefore, we sought to explore characteristics of both retracted articles and their citing articles to understand how and why some retracted articles continue to be cited.

RESEARCH QUESTIONS

We examine citation dynamics of retracted articles by understanding the relationships between characteristics of retracted articles (*AR*) and citing articles (*AC*). Inspired by prior works, we operationalize characteristics in terms of citation counts, year of publication, and year of retraction. Hence, we address the following research questions:

RQ1: What are the characteristics of citing articles (*AC*) that cite retracted articles, pre- and post-retraction?.

RQ2: What are the citation dynamics of retracted articles (*AR*) pre- and post-retraction?.

DATA COLLECTION

Our list of *AR* comes from the intersection of three sources, PubMed, Scopus, and Retraction Watch. We collected a subset of biomedical *AR* verified to be retracted by PubMed (i.e. articles with publication type = "Retracted Publication") that were also available in Scopus. We then collected *AC* that cited *AR*, all of which were published in or before 2018. Using Scopus and Retraction Watch, we collected several characteristics of articles. For *AR*, we collected country and retraction date information from the Retraction Watch Database; citation and publication date information were collected from Scopus. For *AC*, we collected country, publication date, and *AC*'s citation counts from Scopus.

RESULTS AND DISCUSSION

Characteristics of Retracted Articles (*AR*)

Our dataset contains 4,871 *AR* published from 1959 until 2018. The distribution of citation counts of *AR* are shown in Table 1. The average citation count is 35 (Min = 0, Max = 1416, SD = 71.9). Average time from publication to retraction is about 3.9 years (46.8 months) (Min = 0, Max = 33 years, SD = 4.12). Our reported mean time is twice as long as the mean time of 25.8 months (Min = 2 months, Max = 197 months) found in (Budd et al., 1998), whose data consist of MEDLINE articles from 1966 to 1997.

The distribution of citation counts exhibits a power-law distribution ($\alpha = 2.933$, $R^2 = 0.831$), consistent with many prior studies of citation networks that found most articles are cited a several times, and very few articles are cited many times (Redner, 1998). Articles were by authors from 95 different countries of affiliations, with 16% of the articles being multi-country collaborations.

Citation count	*AR* count	*AC* count
0	307 (6.3%)	15,745 (10.5%)
1	237 (4.9%)	8,362 (5.6%)
2-10	1,566 (31.9%)	39,321 (26.3%)
11-20	889 (18.2%)	23,267 (16.2%)
21-100	1,514 (31.0%)	48,339 (32.3%)
101-1000	370 (7.6%)	13,108 (8.8%)
>1000	4 (0.1%)	326 (0.2%)

Table 1. Citation Counts of A_R and A_C in our dataset.

Characteristics of Citing Articles (*AC*)

We found 149,471 articles that cite one or more AR in our dataset. 1,086 of these *AC* are retracted as well. Author affiliations of *AC* were from 158 countries; country information was available in Scopus for all but 6,400 *AC* (4%). The top citing country of affiliation, the United States, accounts for 29% (n = 43,402) of these *AC*. China is second with 13% (n = 18,775) of the *AC*. 4% (n = 5,402) of the *AC* resulted from collaborations of 2 to 5 different countries.

Most of the citations (66%, n = 98,818) to *AR* came from journal articles. 22% of *AC* are review articles. This can be problematic as review articles sum up prior research and are usually highly cited. We found a notable decline in *AC* pre-retraction in 2010, yet there is an increasing trend in *AC* post-retraction that same year onwards. This trend is potentially problematic, and warrants further investigation.

Relationships between *AC* and *AR*

We partition the citations into pre-retraction and post-retraction. We define post-retraction citations as citations at least two years after the retraction date. Thus, if an article was retracted in 2013, we still consider a *AC* published in 2014 as pre-retraction. Articles published 2015 onwards are considered post-retraction. This two-year rule takes into account the delayed nature of journal publication and retraction process. We found 129,727 pre-retraction citations by 112,614 *AC* to 4,360 *AR*. 1,347 *AR* were not cited pre-retraction. The total number of post-retraction citations is substantially smaller, with 40,050 post-retraction citations by 38,134 *AC* to 3,223 *AR*. 210 *AR* were not cited post-retraction. We found that *AC*, on average, cite *AR*, post-retraction, that have been retracted about 5 years ago (Mean = 5.02, SD = 4.05). In addition, we conducted a one-tailed *Wilcoxon signed-rank test* for non-normally distributed data to determine difference between pre-retraction and post-retraction citation counts. We found that post-retraction citation counts were significantly lower than pre-retraction counts ($Z = -12.1$, $p < 0.001$). This finding is consistent with prior studies that report a decrease of citations rates after retraction (Chen et al., 2013).

Ego-Network Analysis

We also used ego-network analysis to examine the structural changes in each *AR*'s network pre- and post-retraction. We extracted a subset of 250 articles from the entire *AR* dataset with identical pre-retraction and post-retraction citation time-lag, i.e. identical time elapsed considering the pre-retraction timeframe for citation as publication to retraction +2 years, and the post-retraction timeframe for citation as retraction +2 years to 2018.

Out of these 250 *AR*, 8 articles had no change in pre- vs. post-citation counts, 240 experienced a decrease in citation counts, and 2 articles had increased (though minimal) citation counts after retraction. We also found that on average, articles experience a citation loss of 86.5% (Min = 0%, Max = 100%) after retraction. Our reported finding is much larger than what was found in (Pfeifer & Snodgrass, 1990), who found that articles lost about 35% of citations after retraction (their data consists of 82 articles retracted between 1977 and 1988, with 6-month washout period). One possible reason could be that retraction has received more attention and higher scrutiny (Steen, 2012).

To take into account natural citation decay, we compared each *AR* to its similar articles, which we defined as articles published in the same journal and on the same year. We compared the year when the *AR* reached half of its current citations (*YR*) to the average year similar articles received half of its citations (*YJ*). In 127 of the 250 retracted articles, *YR* is before *YJ*, indicating that the retracted articles receive fewer citations over time compared to their similar articles. In 91 retracted articles, *YR* = *YJ*, while in 22 retracted articles, *YR* is after *YJ*. 8 retracted articles either did not have citations or had an irretrievable set of similar articles.

We also compared the percentage of citations received after the year of retraction for both the *AR* and its set of similar articles. In 221 of out the 250 retracted articles, the percentage of citations received by *AR* after retraction (i.e. post-retraction citations) is smaller than the average percentage received by its similar articles. For instance, one article published in 2007 and retracted in 2013 received 4% of its citations post-retraction, while on average, its similar articles received 58% of citations after 2014. This analysis shows that the decrease in citations may be attributed to a retraction effect, rather than just a natural citation decay. We aim to extend this analysis to all retracted papers in our dataset to determine whether the retraction effect persists.

To capture structural changes of the ego-networks after retraction, we partitioned the networks into 3 equal sets (*low-medium-high*) based on their citation counts, and conducted ego-network analysis for each set. The *low* set, contains *AR* with citation counts of 0-7, *medium* set of 8-26, and *high* set of 27-1426. We picked an exemplar case from each set to do an in-depth ego-network and citation context analysis of the changes pre- and post-retractions.

Figure 1 shows the ego-networks extracted from an *AR* in the *high* set of citation counts (n = 382). The time-lag of this *AR* is

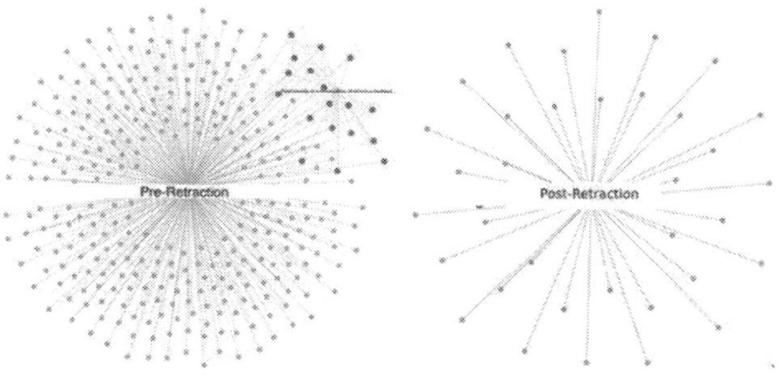

Figure 1. Ego-networks of *high* set example (PMID: 10514006) pre-retraction (left), post-retraction (right).

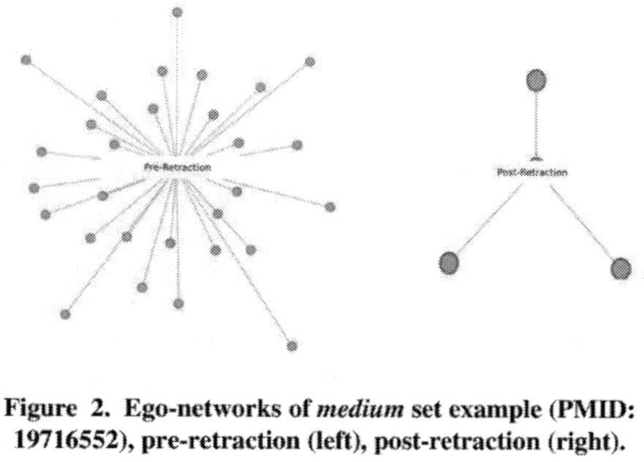

Figure 2. Ego-networks of *medium* set example (PMID: 19716552), pre-retraction (left), post-retraction (right).

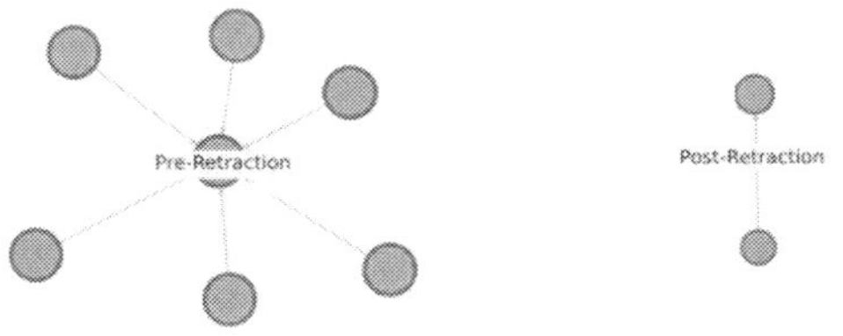

Figure 3. Ego-networks of *low* citation example (PMID: 21633303), pre-retraction (left), post-retraction (right).

10 years, and was retracted due to duplication of an image. The citation counts dropped from 347 to 35, reducing the size of the post-retraction ego-network by 90%. The cited half-life (i.e. years from publication until 50% of citations is reached) is about 5 years, and was reached 4 years before this paper was retracted. Interestingly, the pre-retraction network illustrates an *AR* citing another *AR*, and both were from the same group of authors. This is consistent with (Rubbo, Pilatti, & Picinin, 2018)'s finding that self-citations often occurred pre-retraction.

Figure 2's ego-networks are from an *AR* from the *medium* set (n = 33). This article has a time-lag of 5 years, and was retracted due to its manipulation of data. Its cited half-life is 4 years, and was reached 1 year before retraction. Post-retraction, the citation counts dropped from 29 to 3. These post-retraction citations were from Austria, Argentina, and Turkey, none of which were from the *AR*'s country of publication (United States). All 3 articles were published in areas only broadly related to *AR*'s field of neuroscience (e.g. genetics), and recognized the findings from the *AR* as legitimate. Citation context analysis reveals that these articles treated the experimental results in *AR* as reliable, indicating that they "have shown that calcineurin blockage increases depressive-like symptoms"[Turkish article], "induced depressive-like behavior" [Argentinan article] and "shown to cause neurotoxicity" [Austrian article].

Figure 3 shows the change in an ego-network of an *AR* in the low set of citation counts (n = 6). The article has a time-lag of 4 years, reached its cited half-life at 3 years, and was retracted due to manipulation of images. Pre-retraction, the article was cited 5 times by different articles broadly related to oncology, with 4 articles from China and 1 from the Czech Republic, none of which were from Japan (*AR*'s country of affiliation). After retraction, only 1 article from China cited *AR*, and the citation context was positive as it was used to affirm the authors' findings.

CONCLUSION AND FUTURE WORK

Our research sought to examine the characteristics of (1) citing articles (*AC*) that cite retracted articles, and (2) retracted articles' (*AR*) pre- and post-retraction citations, using descriptive statistics and ego-network analysis. Some of our statistical results differ from studies done about 20 years ago in terms of the citation loss rate post-retraction (our 86.5 %vs 35%) and the time-lag between pre- and post-retractions (our 46.8 months vs 25.8 months). These differences in findings suggest that the process of retraction, and the dynamics of citing *AR* have evolved.

Ego-network analysis shows decreasing trends in citations post-retraction (Bornemann-Cimenti et al., 2016), but also that these citations still recognized *AR* "positively" (Bar-Ilan & Halevi, 2017) as legitimate work. We also found that citations post-retraction came from articles affiliated with a different country than the *AR*. Although *AC* and *AR* are broadly related, they are not from the same specialized research areas (e.g. *AR*: neuroscience; *AC*: genetics). Consistent with (Pfeifer & Snodgrass, 1990) and (Bornemann-Cimenti et al., 2016), we suspect that the awareness of retractions may be lower as the *AR* disseminate across geographical and disciplinary boundaries.

Our study has several limitations. Our data only consists of retracted biomedical articles available in the intersection of PubMed, Scopus, and the Retraction Watch Database. Secondly, we only examined a subset of ego-networks and compared their pre- and post-retraction structures by their network degree counts.

In future work we plan to expand this dataset to research disciplines beyond biomedicine, in order to check for differences in citation dynamics across disciplines. We also aim to collect citation networks that extends beyond relations between retracted and citing articles, but also relations among citing articles.

REFERENCES

Bar-Ilan, J., & Halevi, G. (2017). Post retraction citations in context: A case study. *Scientometrics, 113*(1), 547–565.

Borgatti, S. P., & Ofem, B. (2010). Overview: Social network theory and analysis. In A. J. Daly, *Social Network Theory and Educational Change* (pp. 17–29). Harvard Education Press.

Bornemann-Cimenti, H., Szilagyi, I. S., & Sandner-Kiesling, A. (2016). Perpetuation of retracted publications using the example of the Scott S. Reuben case: Incidences, reasons and possible improvements. *Science and Engineering Ethics, 22*(4), 1063–1072.

Budd, J. M., Sievert, M., & Schultz, T. R. (1998). Phenomena of retraction: reasons for retraction and citations to the publications. *JAMA, 280*(3), 296–297.

COPE (2009). Guidelines for retracting articles. https://doi.org/10.24318/cope.2019.1.4

Da Silva, J. A. T., & Bornemann-Cimenti, H. (2017). Why do some retracted papers continue to be cited? *Scientometrics, 110*(1), 365–370.

Fang, F. C., Steen, R. G., & Casadevall, A. (2012). Misconduct accounts for the majority of retracted scientific publications. *Proceedings of the National Academy of Sciences, 109*(42), 17028–17033.

Lu, S. F., Jin, G. Z., Uzzi, B., & Jones, B. (2013). The retraction penalty: Evidence from the Web of Science. *Scientific reports, 3*, 3146.

Madlock-Brown, C. R., & Eichmann, D. (2015). The (lack of) impact of retraction on citation networks. *Science and Engineering Ethics, 21*(1), 127–137.

Pfeifer, M. P., & Snodgrass, G. L. (1990). The continued use of retracted, invalid scientific literature. *JAMA, 263*(10), 1420–1423.

Redman, B. K., Yarandi, H. N., & Merz, J. F. (2008). Empirical developments in retraction. *Journal of Medical Ethics, 34*(11), 807–809.

Redner, S. (1998). How popular is your paper? An empirical study of the citation distribution. *The European Physical Journal B-Condensed Matter and Complex Systems, 4*(2), 131–134.

Rubbo, P., Pilatti, L. A., & Picinin, C. T. (2018). Citation of retracted articles in engineering: A study of the Web of Science database. *Ethics & Behavior*. https://doi.org/10.1080/10508422.2018.1559064

Steen, R. G. (2012). Retractions in the medical literature: how can patients be protected from risk? *Journal of Medical Ethics, 38*(4), 228–232.

Wasserman, S., & Faust, K. (1994). *Social network analysis: Methods and applications*. Cambridge University Press.

"A Good Intention Gone Awry": Queering Makerspaces to Support Queer Creators

Diana Floegel
Rutgers University,
New Brunswick, USA
diana.floegel@rutgers.edu

ABSTRACT

Although library makerspaces encourage community-building and creativity, normative values in libraries may prevent queer individuals from using these spaces. Interviews with 11 adult queer entertainment media (EM) creators were analyzed using constructivist grounded theory to explore participants' perspectives on creating in libraries. Opportunities and obstacles related to physical spaces, community relationships, and resources demonstrate that makerspaces should be considered within overall contexts of library services in order to examine libraries' utility for queer people. Results support the idea that makerspaces need to be woven into library programs and services more broadly to make libraries more inclusive environments.

KEYWORDS

Queer; Makerspaces; Library Services; Creation; Qualitative Methods

ASIS&T THESAURUS

Information Production; Qualitative Methods; Persons

INTRODUCTION

Librarians and other information professionals should play a role in promoting equity of marginalized genders and sexualities (Mehra & Braquet, 2007). The American Library Association advocates for equal service to all patrons in its code of ethics (American Library Association, 2019) while the Gay, Lesbian, Bisexual, and Transgender Round Table (GLBTRT) offers tools meant to help libraries ameliorate queer individuals' marginalization through inclusive services and resources.

In practice, however, libraries' relationships with queer communities are mixed and often dependent on sociocultural circumstances and individual interactions. Though collections may provide vital information to queer people, they often fall short of meeting users' needs (Brendler et al., 2017; Chapman & Birdi, 2016), particularly in terms of representing intersectionally diverse identities (Sandy, Brendler, & Kohn, 2017). Including queer content in libraries may be controversial despite its benefits (Oltmann, 2015). Libraries' potential to function as safe spaces for queer individuals (Cooper, 2014; Oltmann, 2016) may be curbed by longitudinal injustices including discriminatory cataloging practices (Adler, 2012; Howard & Knowlton, 2018) and other stigmas (Floegel & Costello, 2019).

Libraries may be more supportive of queer individuals through makerspaces that allow users to explore and express their identities (Moorefield-Lang & Kitzie, 2018). However, scant literature incorporates queer individuals' perspectives into makerspace research. This paper uses queerness as a theoretical lens to examine how libraries can reorient (Ahmed, 2006) makerspaces and associated services to support adult queer entertainment media (EM) creators.

LITERATURE REVIEW

Library makerspaces foster community-building (Lille, 2016), increase users' access to technology, and offer opportunities for individuals to improve their creativity (Noh, 2017). Makerspaces may also increase users' satisfaction with libraries (Abbas & Koh, 2015).

Research on makerspaces tends to focus on information professionals who run them, while makerspace users are typically conceptualized as children or teenagers (e.g., Barniskis, 2016; Koh & Abbas, 2016). Work with information professionals finds that they may not be trained to manage a makerspace, particularly in terms of technical skills (Abbas & Koh, 2015; Moorefield-Lang, 2015). Though makerspaces can give users the ability to create things based on their interests (Barniskis, 2016), there are a number of equity issues tied to their implementation. For example, users tend to be white and male (Barton, Tan, & Greenberg, 2017).

Moorefield-Lang and Kitzie (2018) contend that inclusive makerspaces are beneficial for LGBTQ youth. However, a number of gaps remain in makerspace literature, particularly concerning their utility for marginalized populations. Literature often does not include users' voices, nor does it investigate why non-users may avoid library spaces. Makerspaces tend to be tied to science, technology, engineering, and mathematics (STEM) endeavors at the expense of other "making" activities (Li & Todd, n.d.). They are also primarily associated with youth. Investigating how adult queer EM creators

82nd Annual Meeting of the Association for Information Science & Technology | Melbourne, Australia | 19–23 October, 2019

DOI: 10.1002/pra2.00036

perceive library spaces and services as a phenomenon of interest helps address gaps related to inclusivity in makerspaces.

METHODS

Constructivist grounded theory (Charmaz, 2014) was employed to contribute to theoretical perspectives concerning how adult queer EM creators perceive library spaces and services. Data came from phone, Skype, and in-person interviews with 11 self-identified queer individuals who interact with and create EM. Here, EM broadly refers to fiction and creative non-fiction content such as television, zines, personal essays, and comics. Participants were recruited via convenience and snowball sampling and interviews took place between February and November of 2018. Ethics approval was obtained from the Rutgers University IRB. The sample includes white, white and Jewish, Indian, and Black participants whose ages range from 18 to 34 years old. Participants identify as queer, bisexual, asexual, male, female, and genderqueer. Two participants (Becca and Riley) are information professionals. Individuals both use and do not use libraries for their creative projects. Interviews were audio-recorded and lasted approximately 1 hour. Participants were compensated with $15 for their time and they selected their own pseudonyms. The author transcribed recordings verbatim, then qualitatively coded transcripts using the constant comparison method (Charmaz, 2014). Coding progressed from open coding to axial coding where theoretical constructs were formed from the data (Corbin & Strauss, 2008). The researcher was in constant dialog with the data and engaged in extensive memo-writing, peer-debriefing, negative case analysis, and member-checking to increase trustworthiness of findings (Corbin & Strauss, 2008).

FINDINGS

Two categories, opportunities and obstacles, were formed during analysis. Opportunities refers to potential areas for library support and makerspace use while obstacles refers to phenomena that keep participants from libraries. Axial coding was employed to develop constructs related to opportunities and obstacles: physical space, relationships between communities and institutions, and resources. Constructs are presented alphabetically, and their order does not imply primacy.

Physical Space

Libraries are valuable because they offer free spaces where participants can work. Mockingbird imagines their ideal library space: "a room and we have art supplied and just, like, go wild, have fun." Shirley can find "editing space" in a library, while Elyas can write collaboratively because a group of people can meet, exchange ideas, and quickly find reference materials. However, Jake suggests that library spaces may not be suited for all creative efforts because his work with comics makes it hard for him to "move any of my materials there."

Thus, library spaces may not be conducive to all participants' creative practices. Lea claims that "the layout of typical libraries…is not conducive to, like, creative work. They seem to be…the opposite." Library design is for "regimented activities" and studying things "in a very traditional way." Mockingbird notes that "there are queer disabled people" who may not be physically able to access libraries.

Relationships Between Communities and Institutions

Analysis suggests that while particular libraries may be welcoming to queer communities, institutional practices rooted in heteronormativity (e.g., Drabinksi, 2013) contribute to circumstances in which participants feel unsafe as members of queer communities. Becca says that libraries can be welcoming spaces where "a queer person who maybe feels like an outsider could feel welcome and at home." Mockingbird notes that libraries may be especially welcoming for sober queer creators because they provide alcohol-free spaces.

However, libraries are not universally welcoming to queer individuals. A library's ability to support a queer creator "depends on where you're living and where you're working, what the community is," says Becca. Riley points out that "some libraries can be much better or much worse" when interacting with queer people. Elyas notes that their positive library experiences do not apply "in the world at large," while Lea notes that libraries may be "super antagonistic toward queer people."

Such disparities relate to institutional barriers in libraries. Riley explains that attempts to remain neutral make libraries "a victim of their own snake-biting" because they are "forced to either be neutral or not spend money on anything." He says libraries need to operate in "a very different world" to be friendly to queer people. Participants indicate that policies around neutrality and ties to wider oppressive discourses limit opportunities in libraries because they often disadvantage users from marginalized populations.

Related to such barriers, participants recount feeling unsafe when considering using libraries for their creative work. Becca says a library would be useless to a queer person "if it didn't feel like a safe environment," while Elaine points out that libraries can be dangerous because staff "can't just say, 'Hey, you can't come in here if you're homophobic'… I wish people wouldn't, you know, follow someone out of something labeled queer and hurt them, but they might." Mockingbird says that they feel uncomfortable when surveilled in libraries by security guards and other law enforcement who may discriminate against queer people.

Resources

Current and potential library events are salient to participants' conception of how libraries may support their creative endeavors. Ideas include queer book clubs, writing workshops, queer poetry nights, and community programs. However, participants note that events need to be crafted and facilitated with care. Participants want events to be explicitly queer, have queer people involved, and be mindful of diverse experiences. Jake notes that it would be helpful to cover events like writing workshops online "for people to feel like they can observe or be involved without feeling so exposed" if they are uncomfortable being out or creating in public. Both Becca and Riley say that events should be regular rather than part of "special" programming that aligns with times like Pride Month.

In addition to formal events, participants need to find resources to orient their work within wider queer EM landscapes. Library holdings help participants like Elyas "figure out what queer media in 2018 looks like" and determine "what we can do next." Felix finds "some basic orienting stuff" in libraries that helps him "not repeat things that have been said," while Elaine finds sources of "dos and don'ts in queer writing." Shirley notes that libraries can offer technical equipment for podcasting and other endeavors that she cannot afford herself. Janet, however, says that "it's not always easy to find what you need" in a library. Her work focuses on Black queer experiences and she points out that library collections overrepresent white and straight perspectives (e.g., Howard & Knowlton, 2018).

In addition to finding resources specifically for their creative projects, participants use library resources to explore their own identities. Both Becca and Lia claim that libraries may allow queer youth to access content without having to come out to unaccepting parents. Elaine appreciates that she can use library e-resources because, when she's reading queer content, she does not "always like those covers to be visible" in case someone may judge her. Lia explains that biographies of queer people provide "access for people who might not have anyone in their life."

However, librarians who spearhead queer programming without knowledge of queer identities present a major issue for participants. Becca wants them to be "more sensitive" to queer identities and topics. Elaine says it would be "hard to show up" to an event "if it's not facilitated by somebody who is queer." Shirley claims that librarians can make or break a welcoming environment, while Janet finds that "people who are supposed to be helping you" may not be able to answer questions related to queer topics.

DISCUSSION

Findings suggest a number of implications for queer inclusion in makerspaces and associated library services. Participants discuss libraries in light of their EM creation practices; however, their responses cover library support beyond resources and spaces needed to create. Thus, makerspaces should not be framed as distinct from other library offerings. Instead, studies of makerspaces and their openness to marginalized individuals need to consider holistic library environments in order to better elucidate how libraries may both challenge and enact oppression on multiple levels.

Results also demonstrate that physical spaces, relationships between queer communities and institutions, and resources are fraught with opportunities and obstacles. Opportunities and obstacles are not binary concepts, nor are they universally applicable across all libraries. For example, while Felix, who is white, has the opportunity to find resources related to his identity, Janet, who is Black, faces obstacles because even queer collections are white-washed. While Mockingbird can imagine the opportunities created by an ideal library space, their actual experiences include obstacles related to surveillance and physical accessibility. The institutional barriers participants describe trickle down to other issues and are affected by processes outside library walls, given that libraries exist within wider social discourses (Adler, 2012). The constructs discussed here naturally impact and are impacted by each other. For example, Becca recounts an experience where a librarian misgendered a trans person who was using the women's restroom "and it was handled so poorly." This demonstrates that an institutional issue related to how library space is classified (e.g., binary-gendered bathrooms) may be compounded by inexperienced workers who ultimately make a queer person feel unsafe. To continue theoretical development in this area, interactive relationships between and among the identified constructs should be explored, and their theoretical salience should be further developed.

Despite concerns, data suggests that libraries do have the potential to reach queer individuals, particularly with opportunities afforded by events, resources, and spaces that can be facilitated through makerspaces. Participants' desires for creative spaces in which they can collaborate with others on EM projects with art and related supplies demonstrate makerspaces' potential to exist outside STEM contexts. Additionally, analysis suggests it's worthwhile to consider how adults use makerspaces. In addition to appealing to queer people, thinking about makerspaces in this way demonstrates a type of theoretical "queering" in which library spaces may be interrogated and reoriented to work outside of normative contexts.

This is particularly salient given that participants' perspectives reflect wider obstacles and stigmatization of queer identities that make it difficult for them to create and interact with EM in public spaces without risking their safety. If librarians are unaware of these issues, they may not be able to responsibly address concerns expressed by potential queer makers. Thus, "queering" makerspaces provides a useful way to further inclusivity in libraries given queer theory's aim to expose, critique, and reorient normativity (Ahmed, 2006).

CONCLUSION

Limitations to this work include the small sample size, the majority of which consists of white and highly educated individuals. Future work should employ different sampling strategies to be more inclusive and to examine the transferability of these findings. Results demonstrate the value of considering how marginalized individuals interact with makerspaces and associated library services, as well as how conceptions of makerspaces may be expanded beyond STEM contexts to include a broader range of creative endeavors. To that end, queering makerspaces is a valuable exercise in challenging normative assumptions that limit library services with often-negative implications for marginalized individuals, including queer people. Practitioners, scholars, and scholar-practitioners can benefit from queering makerspaces and incorporating queer people in powerful roles when designing programs meant for their benefit. Such efforts can further directions toward more equitable service and offer sustainable interventions to ameliorate institutional oppression in libraries.

ACKNOWLEDGMENTS

Special thanks to all participants and to Dr. Kaitlin L. Costello for peer-debriefing and revisions.

REFERENCES

Abbas, J., & Koh, K. (2015). Future of library and museum services supporting teen learning: Perceptions of professionals in learning labs and makerspaces. *The Journal of Research on Libraries and Young Adults*, *6*, 1–24.

Adler, M. A. (2012). Disciplining knowledge at the Library of Congress. *Knowledge Organization*, *39*(5), 370–376.

Ahmed, S. (2006). *Queer phenomenology: Orientations, objects, others*. Durham, NC: Duke University Press.

American Library Association. (2019). Code of ethics. Retrieved from http://www.ala.org/tools/ethics

Barniskis, S. C. (2016). Access and express: Professional perspectives on public library makerspaces and intellectual freedom. *Public Library Quarterly*, *35*(2), 193–125.

Barton, A. C., Tan, E., & Greenberg, D. (2017). The makerspace movement: Sites of possibilities for equitable opportunities to engage underrepresented youth in STEM. *Teachers College Record*, *119*(6), 1–44.

Brendler, B., Beckman, L., Adkins, D., Sandy, M., Wiggins-Prelas, N., & Adams, V. (2017). "Provide the highest level of service": Public library collections of LGBTQ* materials for adolescents in the United States. *The Journal of Research on Libraries and Young Adults*, *8*(1), 1–32.

Chapman, E. L., & Birdi, B. (2016). "It's woefully inadequate": Collections of LGBTQ* fiction for teens in English public library services. *The Journal of Research on Libraries and Young Adults*, *7*(1), 1–29.

Charmaz, K. (2014). *Constructing grounded theory* (2nd ed.). Los Angeles, CA: Sage.

Cooper, D. M. (2014). Rainbow flags and donor tags: Queer materials at the pride library. *InterActions: UCLA Journal of Education and Information Studies*, *10*(2).

Corbin, J., & Strauss, A. (2008). *Basics of qualitative research* (3rd ed.). Thousand Oaks, CA: Sage.

Drabinksi, E. (2013). Queering the catalog: Queer theory and the politics of correction. *The Library Quartlery: Information, Community, Policy*, *83*(2), 94–111.

Floegel, D., & Costello, K. L. (2019). Entertainment media and the information practices of queer individuals. *Library and Information Science Research*. https://doi.org/10.1016/j.lisr.2019.01.001

Howard, S. A., & Knowlton, S. A. (2018). Browsing through bias: The library of congress subject headings for American studies and LGBTQIA studies. *Library Trends*, *67* (1), 74–88.

Koh, K., & Abbas, J. (2016). Competencies needed to provide teen library services of the future: A survey of professionals in learning labs and makerspaces. *The Journal of Research on Libraries and Young Adults*, *7* (2), 1–22.

Li, X., & Todd, R. (n.d.). Makerspace opportunities and desired outcomes: Voices from young people. *The Library Quarterly* Forthcoming).

Lille, M. (2016). Evaluating the success of makerspace in a public library: The case of Narva City library MakerLab in Estonia. *New Library World*, *117*(9-10), 587–595.

Mehra, B., & Braquet, D. (2007). Library and information science professionals as community action researchers in an academic setting: Top ten directions to further institutional change for people of diverse sexual orientations and gender identities. *Library Trends*, *56*(2), 542–565.

Moorefield-Lang, H. (2015). When makerspaces go mobile: case studies of transportable maker locations. *Library Hi Tech*, *33*(4), 462–471.

Moorefield-Lang, H., & Kitzie, V. (2018). Makerspaces for all: Serving LGBTQ makers in school libraries. *First Monday*, *47*(1), 46–50.

Noh, Y. (2017). A study of the effects of library creative zone programs on creative thinking abilities. *Journal of Librarianship and Information Science*, *49*(4), 380–396.

Oltmann, S. M. (2015). Variables related to school media center LGBT collections. *Libri*, *65*(1), 25–33.

Oltmann, S. M. (2016). "They kind of rely on the library": School librarians serving LGBT students. *The Journal of Research on Libraries and Young Adults*, *7*(1), 1–21.

Sandy, H. M., Brendler, B. M., & Kohn, K. (2017). Intersectionality in LGBT fiction. *Journal of Documentation*, *73* (3), 432–450.

Topics of Example Questions and Discussion at the Early Stage of Community Building for Health Q&A: A Case Study of Health Stack Exchange

Hengyi Fu
School of Library and Information Studies,
University of Alabama
hfu4@ua.edu

Sanghee Oh
Department of Library and Information Science,
Chungnam National University
sanghee.oh@cnu.ac.kr

ABSTRACT

As one of the most significant examples of collective intelligence, online peer production communities, such as Wikipedia and Stack Overflow, have highly contributed to reshape the knowledge infrastructure on the Web. The current volume of peer production research is vast but empirical studies regarding the early stage of community building are in a very limited number. This empirical study, therefore, presents preliminary results of community building and user-driven issues associated with a Health Q&A site at its early stage, namely the ***Definition*** stage by the Q&A system. The method of content analysis was used to identify 4 categories with 20 subcategories of example questions and 8 categories with 23 subcategories of community building discussion threads. The example questions have shown, that the development of Health Stack Exchange was driven by cognitive instead of social or emotional motivations and social supporting questions were not much welcomed by early-stage community members. Findings also pointed to the importance of seeking consensus about the community's ultimate goal and target user group in the start-up stage, which could help to solve the scope definition problems.

KEYWORDS

Online Communities; Community Building; Community Survival; Peer Production; Social Q&A

ASIS&T THESAURUS

Information Science-Informatics-Social Informatics; Information Science-Information Behavior-Information Production-User Generated Content

82nd Annual Meeting of the Association for Information Science & Technology | Melbourne, Australia | 19–23 October, 2019

DOI: 10.1002/pra2.00037

INTRODUCTION

Online peer production communities, such as Wikipedia and Stack Overflow, have been popular for people to seek and exchange information and knowledge. In reality, however, most of them rarely get off the ground due to the unique characteristics of early-stage community building. For example, Arazy and Croitoru (2010) examined the activity pattern of 33,000 corporate wikis within IBM, and over 90% of them were closed or not sustainable. Studies on Sourceforge (English & Schweik, 2007; Hunt & Johnson, 2002) show that although 1000 of projects have been created, only 10.3% have more than three members; most projects were unable to maintain their status until to reach substantial levels of activity, with over half of the projects being classified as abandoned.

At a startup stage of community building, a community has more uncertainty, both in the community structure and membership, as well as less value, than it will after when being reached to a steady stage. The scope of the community, in terms of the breadth of topics to cover, the kind of people to attract as members, the activities it supports, and the purpose of the community as well as the norms and governance need to achieve that purpose, may still under a rough agreement among members in the startup stage. Due to the limitations to resource and interaction, the community could also experience difficulty in attracting potential members; a higher possibility of member loss could be expected since the switching costs to other similar communities of current members are much less. In addition, community members at the startup stage may seek a clear scope, purpose, focus of the community; a code of conduct could be extremely important compared to other social and technological components.

Findings from empirical studies about communities in general, however, may not fully discover which factor could highly influence community building at this early stage because members' needs and activities could change over through community evolution. To build successful online peer production communities, therefore, it is essential to have a good understanding of how a community has been developed to survive the initial growing pain at the early stage. To fill this research gap, this study examines community discussions and hypothetical example questions that have been posted in a health Q&A site—Health Stack Exchange (https://health.stackexchange.com/)--at its early stage, namely the ***Definition*** stage identified by Stack Exchange network (the first 40 weeks of the community building). We proposed and tested the following research questions:

1. What are the health questions that the early-stage members of the Health Stack Exchange expect to ask and answer on the site to promote the community?
2. What are the issues discussed among the early-stage members of the Health Stack Exchange about community building at this early stage?

PREVIOUS RESEARCH

Lifecycle of Online Peer Production Communities

Online communities go through different stages, and each stage may present distinct characteristics. In an online community, the needs of users and management evolve along with the community life cycle, and community building efforts must take into consideration the needs of community members in each stage of the life cycle (Andrews, 2002; Kling & Courtright, 2003). Wenger, McDermott, and Snyder (2002) specified five stages in building online communities, such as potential, coalescing, maturing, stewardship, and transformation stages; each stage identifies issues associated with different domains, communities, and practices. Iriberri and Leroy (2009) did a comprehensive review of community life cycle models and proposed a five-stage model, including inception, creation, growth, maturity, and death. They argued that matching social and technological design with each stage in the community life model could be highly essential in leading to the community success. For example, a clear scope, purpose, focus, and a code of conduct are the first priority at the community creation stage. Jullien, Crowston, and Ortega (2015) evaluated user efforts and participation in Wikipedia projects at different phases in the project life cycle. They suggested that three phases can be identified in the life of a collective action project: the initial phase, where the returns on investment are low but increasing; the diffusion phase, where it is increasingly rewarding to participate in the project; and the mature phase, when the returns on contributions are decreasing and thus fewer contributors are needed.

Social Q&A as Online Peer Production

Online Social Q&A sites are powerful tools for users to seek knowledge by posing questions and getting answers from peers. Prior research on social Q&A communities mainly falls into two groups. The first group of research focused on analyzing and identifying patterns of the content from the analyses of the posts on social Q&A communities to identify and understand the topics and trends of the questions (Barua, Thomas, & Hassan, 2014), evaluate and predict the quality of the questions and answers (Harper, Raban, Rafaeli, & Konstan, 2008; Zhu, Bernhard, & Gurevych, 2009), and identify the experts in social Q&A communities (Pal, Chang, & Konstan, 2012).The second group of research focused on examining social dynamics of the Q&A systems, such as what factors lead the social Q&A communities to thrive, how people interact with one another in these sites, and how the community design (reputation and badge system, user groups, governance mechanisms, etc.) could facilitate user contributions and community growth. For example, Mamykina, Manoim, Mittal, Hripcsak, and Hartmann (2011) claimed that productive competition, community credibility and feedback loop play important roles in Stack Overflow's initial and continuous fast growth. Tausczik, Kittur, and Kraut (2014) identified different collaborative acts in Math Overflow and evaluated their influences on the quality of solutions. Most pervious research addressing health Q&A communities also focused on either the nature of questions (Zhang, 2010), user motivations (Oh, 2012), or quality evaluation (Kim, Oh, & Oh, 2008; Oh & Worrall, 2013). There is few studies, however, that have addressed the dynamics and lifecycle of social Q&A communities in general or in health category.

METHODS

Stack Exchange (http://stackexchange.com/) is a network of more than 170 Q&A communities including Stack Overflow, the preeminent Q&A sites for programmers. Area 51(http://area51.stackexchange.com/) is the Stack Exchange network staging zone where groups of experts come together to build new Q&A sites. Anyone can propose a new Q&A site (called a proposal) in Area 51, reaching out to other experts and defining the type of questions that are wanted. A proposed Q&A site needs to go through four stages before it becomes a full member of the Stack Exchange network: ***Definition***, ***Commitment***, ***Private Beta***, and ***Public Beta***.

This study examines the community design process of the Health Stack Exchange Q&A site at its ***Definition*** stage. This health social Q&A site was proposed on March 9th, 2014 and graduated from the ***Definition*** stage on October 19th, 2014. It is run as a public beta site from Mar 31th, 2015 until now. In this short paper, we present preliminary results of content analysis based on data collected at its ***Definition*** stage, including: (1) 119 example questions and (2) 138 discussion threads on community building, both proposed by its early-stage members. We coded all the example questions using a scheme developed by Zhang (2010) to determine the types of questions that members would like to ask on health in the site. To determine the major themes of community building discussions, an open coding approach was used. Two researchers independently coded all of the example questions and the discussion threads to identify major themes pertaining to the research questions. After comparing, discussing, and resolving any differences in the coding, the researchers created a codebook and used it to recode all of the data. Some example questions and discussion threads were coded into more than one categories.

FINDINGS AND DISCUSSION

Table 1 shows an overview of major question types and the number of questions on each type. The example questions at the ***Definition*** stage set the tone of the community and represented early-stage members' information needs and expectations of community scope. The majority of questions were about a particular health condition, such as symptoms, causes, diagnoses, treatments, and prognoses. Other question categories include asking for what drugs to take, whether a particular drug works, how much to take, when to take, recommendations on diets or exercise routines to help lose weight, build muscle, stay healthy, or recover from a disease or a surgery. Unlike findings about questions in Yahoo! Answers' health category (Zhang, 2010), no example question was found seeking for successful stories and emotional support, no social or emotional motivations were observed from this health Q&A site, at least at this early stage. Additional questions that did not appear in Zhang's study included asking for Information about medical research and asking for information about health/medical devices. Question-answering activities on Health Stack Exchange were largely driven by cognitive motivation, recognizing the lack of knowledge on a particular subject. This may be due to early-stage members' preference to a 'personalized diagnosis' from this health Q&A site and reluctance to accept subjective comments or supports.

Categories (no. of questions)	Sub-categories (no. of questions)
Information about a particular disorder/disease (87)	Symptoms (9), Causes (16), Diagnoses (11), Treatment (28), Prognoses (8), General information (15)
Information about drugs or supplements (25)	Drug use (12), Side effects (3), Safety issues (9), Effects of stopping using a drug (1)
Information about lifestyle or habits (21)	Diet (10), Exercises (6), Stay healthy (3), Recovery from a disease or a surgery (2)
Others (80)	Information about medical professions (6), Interpretations of readings from medical tests (2), Health insurance and policies (5), Information about medical research (5), Information about health/medical devices (4), General health information (13)

Table 1. Topic categories of example questions.

Table 2 shows the frequency of each community building discussion category/subcategory. Similar to the talk pages on Wikipedia, discussion board on Stack Exchange allow for text-based interaction among Stack Exchange management team, moderators, and other users, to help guide and control open content creation and community governance. The most frequently occurring question category was about the scope development of the health Q&A site. Identifying an optimal scope for a community at the startup stage is essential to success-fully jumpstart and/or grow the community (Resnick, Konstan, Chen, & Kraut, 2012). At the ***Definition*** stage, there were ongoing discussion and debates on whether to restrict the scope of the site to a high level, including health-related questions for professionals only, or whether to allow personal health questions as well to increase traffic and recruit more users. This is similar to project scope/objective setting in open source software development research—while projects of large scope could attract more users, they are more likely to have high complexity and high task interdependence, need to be redefined, take longer to complete, require more resources, and involve increased lines of communication and potential conflicts, thus have less chance to succeed (Schmidt, Lyytinen, Keil, & Cule, 2001).

Discussions and debates about the site goal and target users helped form the consensus on site scope (what types of content should be included and what should not) among community members, especially regarding how to deal with questions about certain topics (e.g., sexuality questions). The effectiveness of such direct communication could have positive impact on conflict resolving and work coordination and minimize the potential harm, due to the "fair process effect" or the "voice effects" (Colquitt, Conlon, Wesson, Porter, & Ng, 2001) in group psychology. If users are involved in a certain community decision as having opportunity to express their opinions and learning the rationale behind the decision and the standard they are judged, they are more likely to accept the decision and negative effects of the decision can be controlled. Community building discussions at the ***Definition*** stage also highlighted the importance of weekly site status evaluation, content format, and interface design.

Categories (no. of discussion threads)	Sub-categories (no. of discussion threads)
Scope development (158)	Define scope (49), Clarify/Enforce scope (8), Site goal discussion (14), Specific question handing (42), Closed question discussion/dispute (4), Scope overlap (with other sites) discussion (5)
Community governance (65)	Site policy discussion (15), Site policy clarifications (3), Ask for explanations (2), Moderation discussion/expectation (2), Conflict mediation (2), Site status evaluation (14), Site promotion (9)
Membership/role management (12)	Target user group analysis (5), User recruiting (5), Expert recruiting (2)
Content development (9)	Content format requirement (3), Reference/source requirement (5), Management tool development (1)
Quality control/evaluation (6)	
Feature request/suggestion (1)	
Benchmarking with other communities (11)	Experiences from other sites (6), Site comparisons (5)
Site design (7)	Front page/dashboard design (3), Site name suggestion (4)

Table 2. Topic categories of community building discussion threads.

CONCLUSION FUTURE RESEARCH

The preliminary findings show various topics to discuss for the community building at Health Stack Exchange's first stage. A thorough and comprehensive review of the contents of the Health Stack Exchange in the ***Definition*** stage will be followed to identify early-stage members' motivations for proposing sites, the issues that they consider important for community building, and their expectation to obtaining health-related information from the site. More Data from the ***Commitment, Private Beta,*** and ***Public Beta*** stages will be analyzed in a similar manner, and compare to the results from the ***Definition*** stage—for example, if question types or community management concern change and how it could affect the community success. Giving the importance of peer production communities and the difficulties of actually building and maintaining a successful one, findings of this project could shed lights on theoretical understanding of the underlying mechanisms of successful peer production systems (especially theoretical claims of early stage community building) and provide practical guidelines to designers of existing peer production communities as well as individuals, groups, and organizations who intend to start or maintain a new community—for example redesigning or customizing reward policies/reputation system on social Q&A sites to encourage good community practices at different community stages.

REFERENCES

Andrews, D. C. (2002). Audience-specific online community design. *Communications of the ACM*, *45*(4), 64–68.

Arazy, O., & Croitoru, A. (2010). The sustainability of corporate wikis: A time-series analysis of activity patterns. *ACM Transactions on Management Information Systems*, *1*(1), 6. https://doi.org/10.1145/1877725.1877731

Barua, A., Thomas, S. W., & Hassan, A. E. (2014). What are developers talking about? An analysis of topics and trends in stack overflow. *Empirical Software Engineering*, *19*(3), 619–654. https://doi.org/10.1007/s10664-012-9231-y

Colquitt, J. A., Conlon, D. E., Wesson, M. J., Porter, C. O., & Ng, K. Y. (2001). Justice at the millennium: A meta-analytic review of 25 years of organizational justice research. *Journal of Applied Psychology*, *3*, 425.

English, R., & Schweik, C. M. (2007). *Identifying success and tragedy of FLOSS commons: A preliminary classification of Sourceforge.net projects*. Presented at the First International Workshop on Emerging Trends in FLOSS Research and Development. https://doi.org/10.1109/FLOSS.2007.9

Harper, F. M., Raban, D., Rafaeli, S., & Konstan, J. A. (2008). *Predictors of answer quality in online Q&A sites*. Proceedings of the SIGCHI Conference on Human Factors in Computing Systems, 865–874. https://doi.org/10.1145/1357054.1357191

Hunt, F., & Johnson, P. (2002). *On the pareto distribution of Sourceforge projects*. Proceedings of the Open Source Software Development Workshop, 122–129. Newcastle, England.

Iriberri, A., & Leroy, G. (2009). A life-cycle perspective on online community success. *ACM Computing Surveys*, *41*(2), 11.

Jullien, N., Crowston, K., & Ortega, F. (2015). *The rise and fall of an online project: Is bureaucracy killing efficiency in open knowledge production?* Proceedings of the 11th International Symposium on Open Collaboration, 13.

Kim, S., Oh, S., & Oh, J. S. (2008). Evaluating health answers in a social Q&A site. *Proceedings of the American Society for Information Science and Technology*, *45*, 1–6. https://doi.org/10.1002/meet.2008.14504503134

Kling, R., & Courtright, C. (2003). Group behavior and learning in electronic forums: A sociotechnical approach. *The Information Society*, *19*(3), 221–235.

Mamykina, L., Manoim, B., Mittal, M., Hripcsak, G., & Hartmann, B. (2011). *Design lessons from the fastest q&a site in the west*. Proceedings of the SIGCHI Conference on Human Factors in Computing Systems, 2857–2866. https://doi.org/10.1145/1978942.1979366

Oh, S. (2012). The characteristics and motivations of health answerers for sharing information, knowledge, and experiences in online environments. *Journal of the American Society for Information Science and Technology*, *63*(3), 543–557. https://doi.org/10.1002/asi.21676

Oh, S., & Worrall, A. (2013). Health answer quality evaluation by librarians, nurses, and users in social Q&A. *Library & Information Science Research*, *35*(4), 288–298. https://doi.org/10.1016/j.lisr.2013.04.007

Pal, A., Chang, S., & Konstan, J. A. (2012). *Evolution of experts in question answering communities*. Proceedings of the 6th International AAAI Conference on Weblogs and Social Media.

Resnick, P., Konstan, J., Chen, Y., & Kraut, R. E. (2012). Starting new online communities. In *Evidence-based social design: Mining the social sciences to build online communities*. MIT Press.

Schmidt, R., Lyytinen, K., Keil, M., & Cule, P. (2001). Identifying software project risks: An international Delphi study. *Journal of Management Information Systems*, *17*(4), 5–36. https://doi.org/10.1080/07421222.2001.11045662

Tausczik, Y. R., Kittur, A., & Kraut, R. E. (2014). *Collaborative problem solving: A study of mathoverflow*. Proceedings of the 17th ACM Conference on Computer Supported Cooperative Work & Social Computing, 355–367.

Wenger, E., McDermott, R., & Snyder, W. (2002). *Cultivating communities of practice: A guide to managing knowledge*. Boston, MA: Harvard Business Review Press.

Zhang, Y. (2010). *Contextualizing consumer health information searching: An analysis of questions in a social Q&A community*. Proceedings of the 1st ACM International Health Informatics Symposium, 210–219. https://doi.org/10.1145/1882992.1883023

Zhu, Z., Bernhard, D., & Gurevych, I. (2009). *A multi-dimensional model for assessing the quality of answers in social Q&A sites*. Darmstadt, Germany: UKP Lab, Technische Universität Darmstadt.

How Were Science Mapping Tools Applied? The Application of Science Mapping Tools in LIS and Non-LIS Domains

Jiangen He
Department of Information Science, Drexel University, Philadelphia, USA
jiangen.he@drexel.edu

Wen Lou
Department of Information Management, East China Normal University, China
wlou@infor.ecnu.edu.cn

Kai Li
Department of Information Science, Drexel University, Philadelphia, USA
kl696@drexel.edu

ABSTRACT

As a scientific field, scientific mapping offers a set of standardized methods and tools that can be consistently adopted by researchers in different knowledge domains to answer their own research questions. This study examined scientific articles that applied science mapping tools (SMTs) to analyze scientific domains and the citations of these application articles. To understand the roles of these application articles in scholarly communication, we analyzed them and their citations by classifying them into library and information science (LIS) and other fields (non-LIS) in terms of both publication venues and analyzed domains. Through our preliminary study, we found that science mapping, a topic that is deeply situated in the LIS field, has gained increasing attention from various non-LIS scientific fields over the past few years. The application articles within and outside of the LIS fields played different roles in advancing the application of science mapping.

KEYWORDS

Science Mapping Tools; Scholarly Communication; Scientific Software; Scientific Evolution

ASIS&T THESAURUS

Citation Analysis; Scientometrics; Citation Impact

INTRODUCTION

Software is the engine of the contemporary scientific system. It covers almost every aspect of the scientific practice that researchers are conducting on a daily basis in the increasingly more data-driven environment (Hey, Tansley, & Tolle, 2009). While data analysis is the focus of the majority of scientific software, many of software objects in scientific contexts are dedicated to represent scientific data and results in visual manners.

These visualization tools play important roles in the production of scientific knowledge, often more than they are credited. One of such examples is that they are a central part of the mechanism of science as "inscription device", i.e., the function to create inscriptions that can be used for scientific arguments (Latour & Woolgar, 1979). Another reason for the strong rhetorical abilities of scientific graphs are also reflected in their capacity as immutable mobile (Latour, 1987), i.e., objects that can maintain their identities and meanings across time and space. This is also consistent with the idea that scientific visualization method is a boundary object (Star & Griesemer, 1989) across different knowledge domains. As a highly standardized set of method and tools, scientific visualizations can be easily used on different research problems by researchers from various communities.

One type of scientific visualization that is strongly connected to the field of information science is science mapping. Science mapping is a generic process of domain analysis and visualization (Chen, 2017). The process utilizes various methods and techniques including scientometrics methods (Callon, Courtial, & Laville, 1991; Kessler, 1963; Small, 1973; White & McCain, 1998), visualization techniques (Chen, 2006; Herman, Melancon, & Marshall, 2000; Shneiderman, 1996), and research metrics (Hirsch, 2005). The data used for the analysis process are scientific publications reflecting the scientific knowledge of the analyzed domain, which are usually collected from scholarly databases, such as the Web of Science, Google Scholar, and Scopus. Thanks to the availability of methods, techniques, and data, various science mapping tools (SMTs) have been developed to facilitate the process. These tools have become a necessary component in the science mapping study.

The method and tools of scientific mapping are an important site to understand how the material and methodological practice of science are represented in literary outputs of science, which in return, moderates how science is communicated. Several studies have examined the role of science mapping in scholarly communication by literature review (Chen, 2017), comparing SMTs (Cobo, López-Herrera, Herrera-Viedma, & Herrera, 2011), and analyzing the usage of SMTs (Pan, Yan, Cui, & Hua, 2018). However, the domain analyzed by using SMTs in scientific articles and the impact of

82nd Annual Meeting of the Association for Information Science & Technology | Melbourne, Australia | 19–23 October, 2019

DOI: 10.1002/pra2.00038

science mapping studies that applied SMTs were rarely involved.

Understanding which domains have been analyzed in articles applied SMTs along with where these studies published can provide insights of the evolutionary patterns of science mapping. The citation analysis of these application articles can reveal the role of application articles for overcoming the domain boundary between library and information science (LIS) and non-LIS domains. In this study, we examined the different kinds of SMT application articles in terms of their analyzed domains and journal domains and mapped out the citation impact of application articles. Specifically, the following research questions are pursued in this work-in-progress paper.

What is the evolutionary pattern of SMT application articles in LIS domains and non-LIS domains?

What are the scientific impacts of the application articles?

RESEARCH DESIGN

SMTs and Articles

As described in Figure 1, we identified fourteen scientific mapping tools from literature (Cobo et al., 2011; Pan et al., 2018), after excluding ones which are not fit into our SMT definition, i.e., (1) data sources are scientific literature and (2) aim to understand and visualize the evolution of scientific science domains in whose original vision description. They are BiblioTool, CiteSpace, CitNetExplorer, CoPalRed, CRExplorer, HistCite, IDR Toolkit, ITGInsight, NEViewer, SciCurve, Sci2 Tool, SciMAT, VOSViewer, and VxInsight. Seventeen articles that are most highly cited individually and for establishing the SMTs were selected as tool articles.

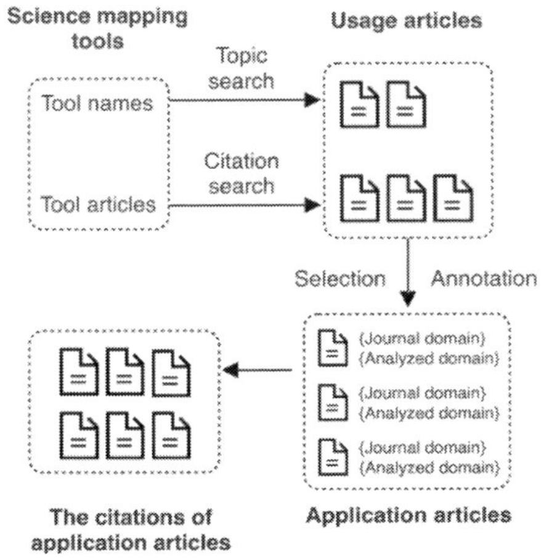

Figure 1. The procedure of data collection.

928 distinct articles were collected that mentioned or cited all fourteen SMTs through both citation and topic search in the Web of Science. They are classified as usage articles.

This study only focuses on SMTs being actually used in scientific research but not all the papers citing/mentioning these tools. Identifying articles (*application articles*) that used these tools to (1) model and analyze structure and dynamic of scientific collaborations, or (2) measure and analyze scientific contributions and impacts (Chen, 2017) is a must. Application articles were identified manually. We downloaded and read the abstracts (and full texts if necessary) of 928 articles and two collaborators asset if a tool is used to report scientific research independently. Cohen's kappa coefficient was used to measure the inter-coder reliability (IRR) and the result is 0.929 ($p = 0.000$). The cases of disagreement were assigned to the third collaborator. At last, 496 application articles were identified.

Annotating Application Articles

Researchers are more likely to use SMTs to conduct domain analysis. The applications in different domains, e.g., LIS and non-LIS domains provide different insights of the evolving role of science mapping as tools. Besides, the domains of journals where application articles published is another necessary dimension for our analysis.

Journal domains were identified by subject category field in data of Web of Science Core Collection. Journals that in the subject category "information science & library science" were annotated as "LIS journal", otherwise "non-LIS" journal. However, research domains in application articles analyzed by SMT cannot be determined by the subject category of journals. For example, a paper published in Scientometrics, a LIS journal may analyze nanotechnology or other non-LIS domains. Two collaborators manually identified domains studied in articles and then coded the domains as LIS or non-LIS domains. Two collaborators achieved an IRR of 0.951 ($p = 0.000$). The cases of disagreement were resolved by the third collaborator.

Four categories were annotated as below, which are combinations of LIS domains (LD), non-LIS domains (ND), LIS journals (LJ), and non-LIS journals (LJ).

- Articles studied a **LIS d**omain and published in a **LIS jour**nal (LD-LJ);
- Articles studied a **LIS d**omain but published in a **N**on-LIS **j**ournal (LD-NJ);
- Articles studied a **N**on-LIS **d**omain but published in a **LIS j**ournal (ND-LJ);
- Articles studied a **N**on-LIS **d**omain and published in a **N**on-LIS **j**ournal (ND-NJ).

Citations of Application Articles

To track the impact of application articles, the information of 4,178 articles that cited the application articles were downloaded from Web of Science Core Collection. We coded each article as a LIS or non-LIS article according to if it was published in a LIS journal.

RESULTS

A summary of application articles is shown in Table 1. We excluded the category of LD-NJ in our study, because it only covers six articles in our dataset, most of which are in the fields of health informatics and knowledge management. The rest of 490 application articles grouped in three categories (LD-LJ, ND-LJ, and ND-NJ) were used hereafter.

		Journal domain		Total
		LIS	Non-LIS	
Analyzed domain	LIS	57 (11.5%)	6 (1.2%)	63 (12.7%)
	Non-LIS	115 (23.2%)	318 (64.1%)	433 (87.3%)
Total		172 (34.7%)	324 (65.3%)	496 (100%)

Table 1. An overview of application articles.

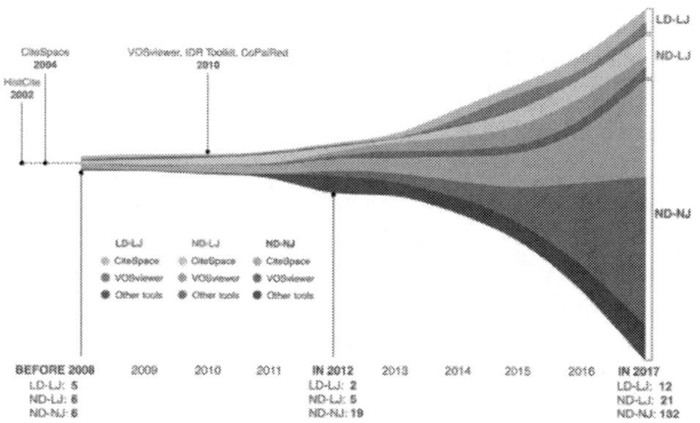

Figure 2. An evolution of SMT application articles in the three categories. The color is used to show the paper category and the shade of each color is used to depict tools in each category.

Evolution of Science Mapping Applications

Figure 2 shows the number of three kinds of application articles from 2008 to 2017. The majority of articles in our sample (481 out of 490) were publish during this period. Most of application articles were published in LIS journals (11 out of 17) that include 5 articles studied LIS domains and 6 articles studied non-LIS domains before 2008. At that time, LIS researchers contributed most application articles, which is reasonable as science mapping itself is a LIS domain. This situation greatly changed after 2012 when there was a burst in the number of articles published in non-LIS journals where 19 articles were published. The burst was followed by a rapidly increasing trend in publishing SMT application articles in non-LIS journals, which demonstrates the extended scientific impact of science mapping as a research method. It should be noted that various tools, including CiteSpace, IDR Toolkit, VOSViewer, and CoPalRed, have been used by in the articles published in non-LIS journals.

The number of articles published in LIS journals has also been increasing, but not as fast as those in non-LIS journals in recent years. SMTs were developed for analyzing various scientific domains. We believe publishing a SMT application articles in journals focusing on a domain can be beneficial for disseminating the knowledge created by using the SMT, since the article can get exposure to scientists in the domain.

Besides visualizing the evolving patterns of the three categories, we also addressed the articles that applied two most widely used SMTs, CiteSpace (197 articles, 40.2%) and VOSViewer (192 articles, 39.2%) respectively. The rest of SMTs following CiteSpace and VOSViewer are HistCite (38, 7.8%), IDR Toolkit (25, 5.1%), and CoPalRed (13, 2.7%). CiteSpace and VOSViewer were the leading tools in all the three kinds of application articles. In comparison with articles studied non-LIS domains (ND-LJ and ND-NJ), articles studied LIS domains (LD-LJ) tended to more commonly use CiteSpace and VOSViewer.

Citation Analysis

Table 2 shows an overview of the citations of applications articles. The articles in each category have a similar citation pattern in terms of their mean value and standard deviation. However, the citations of articles from the three categories are not comparable, as they were published in different disciplines and different years.

		Journal domain		Total
		LIS	Non-LIS	
Analyzed domain	LIS	585 (*M*=13.6, *SD*=20.7)	-	585 (*M*=13.6, *SD*=20.7)
	Non-LIS	1,077 (*M*=11.2, *SD*=14.1)	2,402 (*M*=9.6, *SD*=17.1)	3,479 (*M*=10, *SD*=16.4)
Total		1662 (*M*=12.0, *SD*=16.5)	2,402 (*M*=9.6, *SD*=17.1)	4,064 (*M*=10.6, *SD*=17.0)

Table 2. An overview of articles cited the applications articles. *M* = mean value, *SD* = standard deviation.

We focus on analyzing the citation flow of three kinds of application articles to unfold their roles in advancing the application of SMT in the scientific community. We mapped out the citation between the three kinds of application articles and the citations of application articles in Figure 3.

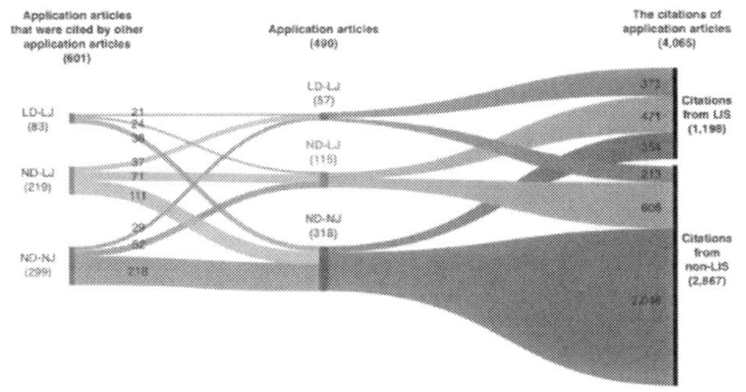

Figure 3. Citation flow of application articles. (#) represents the number of articles in a category. The numbers in the shades represent the citation/cited times toward a category.

On the left part of Figure 3, the composition of references of application articles in every category exist in all three categories. Articles published in non-LIS journals (ND-NJ) are less likely to be cited by articles in LIS journals. However, a considerable number of articles in LIS journal were cited by articles in non-LIS journals, especially articles studied non-LIS domains but published in LIS journals (ND-LJ). For instance, 115 articles in ND-LJ were cited 111 times by 318 articles in ND-NJ.

The citation patterns of application articles on the right part of Figure 3 are clear. The citations of articles in LD-LJ were from articles published in LIS journals, but also have some citations from non-LIS journals. Although articles in ND-LJ were published in LIS journal, they attracted even more attention from non-LIS communities who cited ND-LJ for 606 times which is larger than the citation from LIS journal (471 times). Relevantly, articles in ND-LJ which focused on non-LIS domains but published in non-LIS journals get much fewer citations from the LIS community.

Articles in ND-LJ, it seems, played an important role in advancing the wide application of SMT. For the LIS community, the articles validate the effectiveness of SMT for analyzing various domains. They also provided practical guidelines and successful showcases for non-LIS communities.

CONCLUSION AND FUTURE WORK

In this study, we investigated the application of fourteen SMTs by visualizing 490 articles that applied SMTs to analyze scientific domains. We examined the impact of these application articles by analyzing their citations. Both journal domains and analyzed domains were addressed in our study.

A few observations concerning the role-play of scientific mapping method and tools in the scholarly communication emerge in our approach. SMTs have been widely applied in various domains out of LIS. We have observed a rapid increasing of SMT application after 2012. CiteSpace and VOSViewer are the leading tools in both LIS and non-LIS domains. We have discovered the important role of articles, which studied non-LIS domains but published in LIS journals, in advancing the application of SMTs. In the future, we will investigate the effects of collaboration on the application of SMTs in non-LIS domains, especially the collaboration between domain experts and scientometrics researchers. Another direction is to investigate the citation context of application articles to improve our understanding of the scientific impact of science mapping.

ACKNOWLEDGMENTS

We wish to thank the support of the National Science Foundation (Grant Number: 1633286) and China Postdoctoral Science Foundation (Grant Number: 2019 T12035).

REFERENCES

Callon, M., Courtial, J. P., & Laville, F. (1991). Co-word analysis as a tool for describing the network of interactions between basic and technological research: The case of polymer chemsitry. *Scientometrics*, *22*(1), 155–205.

Chen, C. (2006). CiteSpace II: Detecting and visualizing emerging trends and transient patterns in scientific literature. *Journal of the American Society for Information Science and Technology*, *57*(3), 359–377.

Chen, C. (2017). Science mapping: a systematic review of the literature. *Journal of Data and Information Science*, *2* (2), 1–40.

Cobo, M. J., López-Herrera, A. G., Herrera-Viedma, E., & Herrera, F. (2011). Science mapping software tools: Review, analysis, and cooperative study among tools. *Journal of the American Society for Information Science and Technology*, *62*(7).

Herman, I., Melancon, G., & Marshall, M. S. (2000). Graph visualization and navigation in information visualization: A survey. *IEEE Transactions on Visualization and Computer Graphics*, *6*(1), 1–21.

Hey, A. J. G., Tansley, S., & Tolle, K. M. (2009). *The fourth paradigm: Data-intensive scientific discovery* (Vol. *1*). Redmond, WA: Microsoft Research.

Hirsch, J. E. (2005). An index to quantify an individual's scientific research output. *Proceedings of the National Academy of Sciences*, *102*(46), 16569–16572.

Kessler, M. (1963). Bibliographic Coupling between scientific papers. *American Documentation*, *14*(1), 10–25.

Latour, B. (1987). *Science in action: How to follow scientists and engineers through society*. Harvard University Press.

Latour, B., & Woolgar, S. (1979). In Princenton University, *Laboratory of life: The construction of scientific facts*.

Pan, X., Yan, E., Cui, M., & Hua, W. (2018). Examining the usage, citation, and diffusion patterns of bibliometric mapping software: A comparative study of three tools. *Journal of Informetrics*, *12*(2), 481–493.

Shneiderman, B. (1996). The eyes have it: A task by data type taxonomy for information visualizations. In Proceedings 1996 IEEE Symposium on Visual Languages (pp. 336–343).

Small, H. (1973). Co-citation in the scientific literature: A new measure of the relationship between two documents. *Journal of the American Society for Information Science*, *24*(4), 265–269.

Star, S. L., & Griesemer, J. R. (1989). Institutional ecology, translations' and boundary objects: Amateurs and professionals in Berkeley's Museum of Vertebrate Zoology, 1907-39. *Social Studies of Science*, *19*(3), 387–420.

White, H. D., & McCain, K. W. (1998). Visualizing a discipline: An author co-citation analysis of information science, 1972–1995. *Journal of the American Society for Information Science*, *49*(4), 327–355.

Modeling and Representation of Intangible Cultural Heritage Knowledge Using Linked Data and Ontology

Xilong Hou
School of Information Management, Wuhan University, Wuhan, China
houxilong2008@163.com

Xiaoguang Wang
School of Information Management, Wuhan University, Wuhan, China
wxguang@whu.edu.cn

ABSTRACT

Intangible cultural heritage (ICH) contains rich knowledge, and the effective organization and management of ICH knowledge is the foundation for the protection and inheritance of ICH. The development of semantic Web technology changes the way of knowledge representation and expression and provides new ideas and methods for the organizing and sharing of ICH knowledge. This paper describes a research project: to model and manage the ICH knowledge by publishing the knowledge as linked data. Firstly, a knowledge ontology was designed to reveal and standardize the concept, attribute and relationship of ICH knowledge elements. Then, we converted the knowledge to RDF data basted on the knowledge ontology and linked the entities with DBpedia and GeoNames. Finally, taking the ICH in Hubei province as an example, the methodology was used to create an RDF dataset which published as linked open data, and develop a knowledge service platform based on the linked data service. The research has promoted the standardization of knowledge management of ICH in China, which is of great significance for the protection and dissemination of ICH.

KEYWORDS

Intangible Cultural Heritage; Knowledge Representation; Knowledge Management; Linked Data; Ontology

ASIS&T THESAURUS

Cultural Heritage; Knowledge Management; Linked Data

INTRODUCTION

ICH refers to oral traditions, performing arts, rituals, and festive events that have been transmitted over generations and are thus recognized by communities as part of their cultural heritage (UNESCO, 2003) It is an important part of the excellent traditional culture of all ethnic groups, which highlights the regional characteristics and wisdom of the people. ICH has various forms of expression, and it covers a wide range of fields and contains a wealth of knowledge. The effective organization and management of ICH knowledge is the necessary requirement for the cultural protection and knowledge dissemination in the knowledge age. However, the knowledge elements of ICH lack rich semantic information. As a result, the relationship between knowledge elements cannot be fully expressed and revealed, and the knowledge of ICH is isolated and lost. Linked data and ontology technologies have brought innovative methods and applications that help to reduce the loss or waste of knowledge, and allow cultural heritage institutions to make the heterogeneous contents of cultural heritage data semantically interoperable, supporting wider exploration and use of data in digital humanities research. (Zeng, 2019) Candela, Escobar, Carrasco, and Marco-Such (2018) found that applying linked open data concepts to the cultural heritage domain has become an active and challenging field. In order to help managing this knowledge, researchers have been working in the construction of domain ontology, a host of ontologies and metadata standards exist in the cultural heritage domain: CIDOC CRM, DC, VRA core, Europeana Data Model (EDM), etc. (Hyvönen, 2012). Wijesundara and Sugimoto (2018) proposed a generalized metadata model called CHDE for organizing various digital cultural heritage information. Using instantiations of an ICH entity to connect tangible cultural heritage objects which are interrelation with the ICH. Although some research achievements of domain ontology of ICH, a unified, standardized and comprehensive ontology model of knowledge organization has not yet been formed. At the same time, most of the existing studies mainly focus on the aggregation and organization of ICH information resource, which lack analysis and research at the knowledge level. The knowledge of ICH is rarely organized and managed as linked open data and fail to build the connections between internal knowledge and external knowledge.

Starting from these considerations, this article works on two main aspects: (i) Designed and defined an ontology model for the knowledge organization of ICH. (ii) How to publish the knowledge as linked data based on the ontology. By applying these approaches to organize the ICH knowledge, the knowledge can be shared and understood, and then the ICH will be inherited and spread.

82nd Annual Meeting of the Association for Information Science & Technology | Melbourne, Australia | 19–23 October, 2019

DOI: 10.1002/pra2.00039

RESEARCH DESIGN

The Knowledge Ontology for ICH

Before starting processes of knowledge management, it is important to identify the knowledge that is to managed. For the protection and inheritance of ICH, China has established the catalogue of the representative items of ICH at national, provincial, municipal and county level. Each ICH item in the catalogue has its distribution areas or protection organization. The representative inheritors of ICH are determined in the category of oral literature performance, ritual, handicraft, traditional music, etc. In order to provide a unified and standardized knowledge representation model for the description and organization of ICH knowledge, a knowledge ontology was developed. The knowledge ontology of ICH is a formal, explicit specification of a shard conceptualization formed by highly abstracting and summarizing the content and components of ICH. We worked with domain experts to design the ontology on the basis of CIDOC CRM, FOAF, Relationship and GeoNames. It consists of six top classes (ICH Item, Agent, Category, Place, Batch and Level) and relationships between them. The knowledge ontology's structure is shown in the form of a graph in Figure 1.

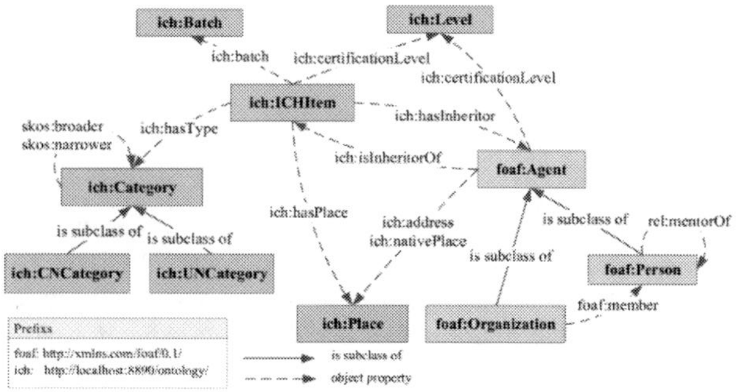

Figure 1. The knowledge ontology for ICH.

ICH Item

The ICH item class represents all the representative items in the ICH catalogue. The properties of ICH item class mainly include the introduction of the item and its inheritance situation, including the name, history, current conditions and value of the items, inheritance scope, the inheritance pedigree and other information and materials. Those properties were defined according to the main content of the *Application of the representative items of intangible cultural heritage (ICH) at national level.*[1] The item entities are linked with inheritor entities and place entities through object properties (*ich:hasInheritor, ich:hasPlace*).

Inheritor

The inheritors hold outstanding skills and have an influence on the community, they also play a key role in training the next generation and passing on technical skills, which is an important part of ICH. In the paper, we use agent class, which comes from the FOAF, to represent ICH inheritors. The agent class is divided into two subclasses: *Person* class and *Organization* class. For the *Person* class, its properties include the basic information, such as the inheritors' name, gender, appellation, nationality, date of birth, place of birth, what skills they have mastered and the situation of the inheritance about their skills, etc. In addition, reusing properties in the Relationship vocabulary to better express the intricate inheritance relationship and pedigree between the inheritors.

Category

The category class is used for the construction of ICH classification system. For the international universality of the classification, we subdivided it into two subclasses: *UNCategory* and *CNCategory*. The *CNCategory* subclass contains ten entities mainly used in China, including folk literature, traditional music, traditional dance, traditional opera, Chinese Quyi music, traditional sports, entertainment and acrobatics, traditional fine arts, traditional artistry, traditional medicine and folk-custom. The *UNCategory* subclass contains five entities defined by UNESCO, including oral traditions and expressions, performing arts, social practices, rituals, festive events, knowledge and practices concerning nature and the universe and traditional craftsmanship. By using the object properties that represent the conceptual hierarchy (such as *skos:broader* and *skos:narrower*, etc.), we can construct a multi-perspective and multi-level scalable classification system of ICH.

Place

ICH has distinct regional characteristics, and different regions give birth to the ICH with different characteristics. The place class in the ontology was defined to record the information about locations of items and inheritors. At the same time, each place individual was linked with the GeoNames to obtain more information, such as longitude, latitude and Wikipedia pages. And then, the regional distribution and evolution of ICH can be analyzed by using GIS spatial analysis technology with the spatial information.

Finally, according to the characteristics of ICH, the knowledge ontology was designed and constructed by reusing and extending the standard ontologies such as CIDOC CRM, FOAF, Relationship and other international ontology models. The knowledge ontology contains 10 classes, together with 26 object properties and 27 data properties. We used protégé tool to develop and realize the knowledge ontology for ICH.[2] The ontology acts as a comprehensive, standardized and unified model for the formal representation and organization of ICH knowledge.

Linked Data Set Construction

The construction of linked data set of ICH knowledge is a systematic project. First of all, it's necessary to clarify the scope of research and sort out the knowledge elements of ICH. Then,

[1] http://www.ihchina.cn/shenbaozhinan

[2] The ontology is available from github: https://github.com/houxilong/ichontology

the domain ontology was built in order to precisely define the complex and structured relationships between the knowledge. After that, following the four principles of linked data developed by Tim Berners-Lee (2006) and best practices for publishing linked data (Hyland, Atemezing, & Villazon-Terrazas, 2014), the data was converted to RDF according to the ontology, the entities were linked with external datasets, and finally the linked data was published and consumed.

RDF Data Conversion

As the number of Chinese ICH is quite large and the identification of ICH items and inheritors is changing dynamically, the construction process of the ICH knowledge base needs to be carried out in different levels and batches. This paper takes the ICH items in Hubei province as an example, collecting and sorting out the basic information of the ICH items and inheritors, and construct the linked data set of ICH knowledge on this basis. The data mainly comes from the provincial and local ICH protection centers, and also includes the Internet information from the ICH websites, such as Chinese ICH website (http://www.ihchina.cn) and Hubei ICH website (http://www.ihhubei.com/) obtained by using the web crawler method. We mapped relational database schemas to RDF vocabularies and ontologies by using D2RQ mapping language, and convert the relational database into RDF using D2R service. Then, the RDF data was stored in an RDF triplestore and published on the web using linked data technologies.

Entity Linking

The principles of linked data require that the resources should be linked with other resources, including making links within a data set and external data sources. In order to enhance the semantic enrichment of ICH knowledge, we linked the entities with DBpedia and GeoNames. By linked with DBpedia, the ICH items were linked to their corresponding terms in English language. Similarly, more information about the place entities can be obtained through linking with GeoNames. By using the *owl:sameAs* property, the entity is linked with the corresponding entity which is in the external dataset, which means that the two linked entities are the same resource. The diagram of linking with DBpedia and GeoNames is shown in Figure 2.

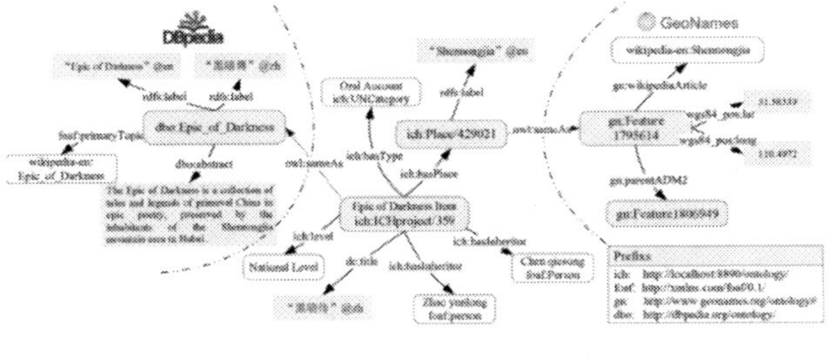

Figure 2. Linking with DBpedia and GeoNames.

Using the combination of automatic information retrieval and manual method, the entities of DBpedia were retrieved online by SPARQL query. Then, the retrieval results were filtered and checked manually. In the same way, we retrieved the GeoNames dataset by the SPARQL Endpoint of Factforge website. The place entities such as the residences of the inheritors and the locations of ICH items were linked to related GeoNames resources, by using the *owl: sameAs* property.

Through the above process, more than half of the ICH items were linked with DBpedia, and the place entities were all matched with GeoNames. Finally, Figure 3 shows the resource statistics of the RDF dataset of ICH in Hubei province. The dataset contains more than 9,600 RDF statements and 930 unique typed entities, including 370 ICH items entities and 310 inheritors entities. Among these, about 306 entities were linked to DBpedia or Wikipedia and 124 place entities linked to GeoNames.

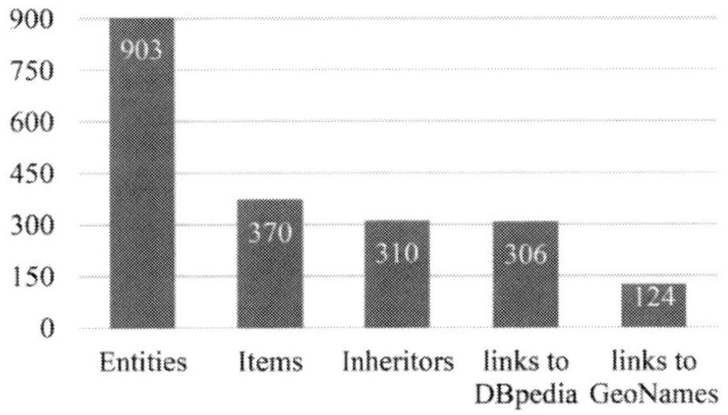

Figure 3. Resource statistics of the dataset.

Publishing Linked Data

The RDF data created above needs to be published before it can be utilized and shared. There are many patterns to store and publish linked data from structured data or textual content. (Heath & Bizer, 2011). We choose to use the native RDF triple store to store the RDF data, from where they are accessed using SPARQL endpoint and HTTP content negotiation for enrichment and consumption in general.All RDF statements were stored in an Openlink Virtuoso triplestore. Openlink Virtuoso is a tool designed for the integration of multimode data and supports heterogeneous view, stored procedures and text searches. All RDF data can be queried in SPARQL by making appropriate REST requests to the SPARQL endpoint. We used LodView (https://lodview.it/) to browse all RDF data directly in the triplestore, and used LodLive (http://en.lodlive.it/) to provide a user-friendly interface for browsing and navigating RDF resources based on data graph representation. Figure 4 shows an example of an ICH item's knowledge network using the LodLive application.

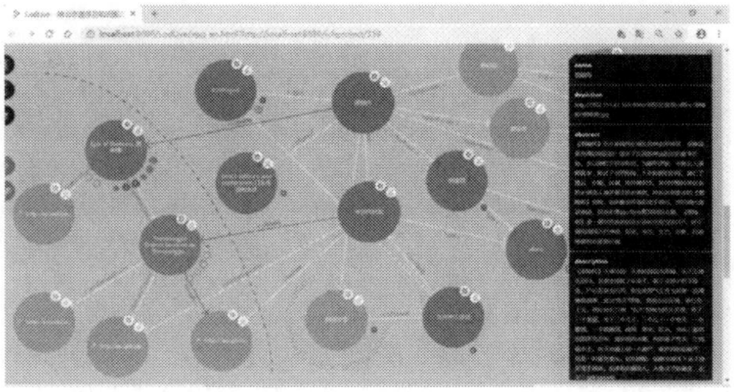

Figure 4. An ICH item's knowledge network using LodLive.

The Knowledge Service Platform

A domain specific knowledge service platform was developed based on the linked data set. It can provide users with visualization of ICH knowledge, as well as better organization and management of ICH knowledge content. With the GIS technology, geographical features in ICH knowledge base can be displayed in the form of online map as shown in Figure 5. In addition, the service platform's functions including linked data browsing, knowledge retrieval, knowledge mapping display and map query, entity relationship network and information visualization. The service platform provides downloadable semantic representations for the entity in RDF\XML, JSON, N-triples and Turtle formats, allowing the data to be passed between computer applications. The users can query the triplestore directly on the Web by means of SPARQL queries.

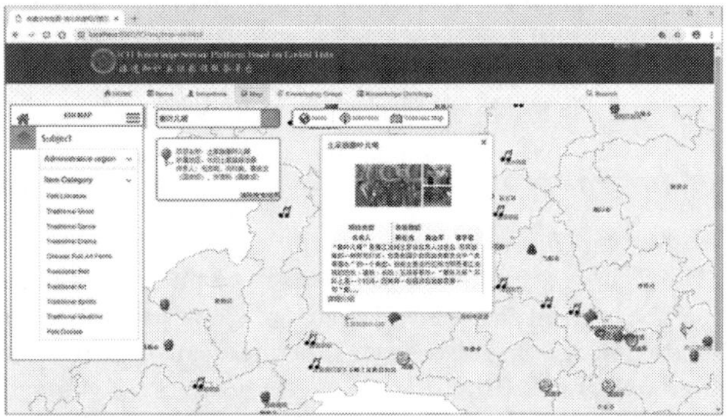

Figure 5. A knowledge query results with geospatial visualization.

With the help of domain experts and ICH conservation organizations, the knowledge base of ICH will be further supplemented and updated. Through standardized knowledge organization, we can enhance the semantic expression in the ICH domain and provide the society with knowledge sharing and reuse.

CONCLUSION

The thought and technology of ontology and linked data have great advantages in the domain knowledge organization of ICH. In the article, we addressed the semantic enhancement of ICH domain knowledge by means of semantic web technologies to make it easily discoverable, interchangeable, and interlinked with other relevant sources. In order to publish the ICH knowledge as linked data, we have constructed a knowledge ontology to reveal the abundant knowledge and its internal relationships. And then, according to the ontology above, the linked dataset was constructed after the process of RDF data conversion and entity linking. By using linked data technology to build the linked open dataset of ICH knowledge in China and linked with the international linked open data, the accessibility, interoperability and reusability of ICH knowledge can be improved. However, the granularity of knowledge organization still needs to be further refined and the knowledge ontology of ICH also needs to be further expanded and enriched. Finally, the practice of linked data project of ICH knowledge can promote the standardization and normalization of knowledge management of ICH. We believe that this research could be considered an exhaustive resource for cultural heritage institutions wanting to publishing their data as linked open data.

ACKNOWLEDGMENTS

This work was supported by Foundation of key Research Institute of Humanities and Social Science at Universities, Chinese Ministry of Education (No. 16JJD870002).

REFERENCES

Candela, G., Escobar, P., Carrasco, R. C., & Marco-Such, M. (2018). A linked open data framework to enhance the discoverability and impact of culture heritage. *Journal of Information Science*, 1–11.

Heath, T., & Bizer, C. (2011). Linked data: Evolving the web into a global data space. *Synthesis Lectures on the Semantic Web: Theory and Technology*, *1*(1), 69–83.

Hyland, B., Atemezing, G., & Villazon-Terrazas, B. (2014). *Best practices for publishing linked data: W3C Working Group Note 09 January 2014*. W3C. Retrieved from https://www.w3.org/TR/ld-bp/

Hyvönen, E. (2012). Publishing and Using Cultural Heritage Linked Data on the Semantic Web. *Synthesis Lectures on the Semantic Web: Theory and Technology*, *2*(1), 1–159.

UNESCO. (2003). Convention for the safeguarding of the Intangible Cultural Heritage. Retrieved from https://ich.unesco.org/en/convention

Wijesundara, C., & Sugimoto, S. (2018). Metadata Model for Organizing Digital Archives of Tangible and Intangible Cultural Heritage, and Linking Cultural Heritage Information in Digital Space. *LIBRES: Library & Information Science Research Electronic Journal*, (2), 28.

Zeng, M. L. (2019). Semantic enrichment for enhancing LAM data and supporting digital humanities. Review article. *El profesional de la información*, *28*(1).

Implications of the Embodied, Enactive Mind on Theorizing About Information Experience

Pamela Hoyte
Queensland University of Technology, Brisbane, Australia
pamela.hoyte@qut.edu.au

ABSTRACT

Information Experience is a recent and growing concept in Information Science that is proposed as a holistic approach to explicitly examine the human experience of information interactions, including an individual's perceptual, cognitive and embodied experience. Valuable to this discussion is setting out a suitable philosophical position about the conception of the mind. This paper proposes that the concepts of embodied cognition and the non-representational, enactive mind are necessary conceptions of mind for an adequate theoretical account of Information Experience. Furthering this discussion, the concept of information as an enactive cognitive phenomenon is explored, as constructed by the individual, embodied by their experience and contextually situated. These conceptions will provide a foundation for further development of the emerging field of information experience, and prove thought provoking for the Information Science field generally in the development of new approaches to the ways we use and share information in our communities and the future technologies we build for this.

KEYWORDS

Information Experience; Theory of Information; Embodied Cognition; Enactive Mind

ASIS&T THESAURUS

Information Behavior; Information Use

INTRODUCTION

Information Experience is a recent and growing concept in Information Science that is proposed as a holistic approach to explicitly examine the *human experience* of information interactions, including an individual's perceptual, cognitive and embodied experience.[1] Further examination of the underlying ontological and epistemological position is needed in order to clarify conceptual aspects and build toward a strong theoretical foundation of information experience. This includes the need for understanding the implications of embodied cognition, challenging the assumption of the mind as being inherently representational and critically examining the concept of 'information' in relation to this. That is, examining information as a cognitive phenomenon.

As has been shown through a vast body of information behavior and information practice research, everyday human information experience is commonly rather irregular, messy and disordered, and incorporates multifarious ways that people interact with information as they seek, avoid, serendipitously encounter, share, collaborate, appropriate, synthesize, and misunderstand. Conceptualizing these interactions from the perspective of information experience, enables a rich picture of how we as individuals live in the world, how we communicate with each other, and deepens the understanding we can build from these rich pictures. Valuing individual's information experiences, allows us to foreground understanding of these in the information technology we use and the communities we build.

Valuable to this discussion is setting out a suitable philosophical position about how the mind works. To this end, the concepts from Cognitive Science of *embodied cognition* and the *non-representational, enactive* mind are proposed as necessary conceptions of mind to provide the foundations for an adequate theoretical account of information experience.

EMBODIED COGNITION

A growing interest in embodiment in the Information Science field has seen a range of aspects being explored with regards to embodied information and knowledge.[2] Extending this understanding, this paper focuses on embodied cognition and on the way people think, the workings of the mind as being fundamentally connected to a person's interactions with the world. This perspective frames the phenomenon of experience as being the *present, in-the-moment, human experience from an individual's perspective*. Conceptualizing experience in this way fundamentally sets the scope of information experience to be a phenomenon accessed from the individual's subjective perspective and manifesting in an embodied, cognitive state. Embodiment locates the mind as essentially and inherently enmeshed with the experience of the body, such that "knowledge depends on being in a world that is inseparable from our bodies, our language, and our social history" (Varela, Thompson, & Rosch, 2017, p. 149).

82nd Annual Meeting of the Association for Information Science & Technology | Melbourne, Australia | 19–23 October, 2019

DOI: 10.1002/pra2.00040

[1] For example, see Bruce, Davis, Hughes, Partridge, and Stoodley (2014) and Gorichanaz (2019), Gorichanaz (2015).

[2] Such as in the recent double issue of *Library Trends* (2018).

While our bodies are sensual and physical intermediators of our experience, and the *senses* are a primary interface through which individuals experience, the concept of embodiment conveys that this experience of the lived body is not that of a "passive receiver of sensory stimuli or the locus of mechanical reflexes … [but that] from a first-person perspective, we *are* that body, and it is through our bodies that we are part of the world" (Aagaard, Friis, Sorenson, Tafdrup, & Hasse, 2018, p. xv). Perception is central to what and how we experience; it is the *means* by which we experience. The very concept of experience relies on the notion of something that is being "experienced" (Bitbol, 2016, p.3). Conscious and unconscious perception of this "something" then is the mechanism for this embodied experience, whether "it" is external to the individual (such as the information objects, context, other people) or the individual's own body (physical sensations), or of the mind itself (its states, emotions, and thoughts).

Moreover, "the phenomenal character of experience includes both the *qualitative character of what we experience* (e.g., sensory qualities of the world and our body) and the *subjective character of the mental acts whereby we experience* (e.g., perceiving, remembering, and imagining)" (Thompson, 2008, p. 401). In relation to our perceptions, these also have both sensory qualities and subjective characteristics, as "the perceived object is always contextualized, not just by its physical surroundings, but by the particular … perceiver" (Gallagher & Zahavi, 2012 p. 106).

Commensurate with the notion of the embodied mind, is that cognition is situated and contextual – in fact "it is situated because it is embodied" (Gallagher & Zahavi, 2012 p. 150). That is, what you experience you experience *here and now*, you experience wherever *you* are and that experience is specific to that context. Even if you are thinking about another place (by looking over holiday photos, or reading a historical drama), you are doing this, experiencing this, from the comfort of your armchair/train/office/place where you are. Similarly, embodied experience has a temporal dimension and is situated in the present. Experience is only now: "what we perceive, we perceive as *present*" (Le Poidevin, 2015).

As described above, the notion of embodiment is inseparable from a notion of mind where experience is subjective, spacio-temporal and culturally situated. In this conception, traditional views of the mind as information processor will not hold.

ENACTIVE MIND

Traditionally the mind is depicted as something like a computer processing information "bits" in response to external stimuli (Lakoff, 2012). In this framework, these 'information bits' are thought to be the internal, objective representations the external world that the mind holds, and the mind essentially processes "computations of symbolic representations, and that these representations are physically realized in the brain in a form of symbolic code" (Varela et al., 2017, pp. 40-1). This cognitivist mental framework lends itself to a conventional model of communication (such as Shannon & Weaver, 1949), in which information is given and the mind is like a receiver that collects and processes this information. This view is suited to and underlies the traditional information interface design described by Lueg & Twidale, as presuming the information seeker to be a patient, logical, rational robot (Lueg & Twidale, 2018, p. 409), and which relies on information being transferable as an objective commodity (Krebs, 2015, p. 30).

There are however points at which this reductive, realist representational model fails us. As Thompson states, cognitivist representationalism "neglects the subjective character of experience" (2008, p. 401), and therefore is inadequate to explain experience. This can be shown for example, when accounting for contextuality and the "many different worlds of experience" (Varela et al., 2017, p. 9) that are evident across the range of human experience. If we assume that an information experience is an experience, then cognitive representationalism is inadequate to explain information experience too.

An alternative approach is the concept of the *enactive* mind which captures the sense that "cognition is not the representation of a pregiven world by a pregiven mind but is rather the enactment of a world and a mind on the basis of a history of the variety of actions that a being in the world performs" (Varela et al., 2017, p. 9). The enactive mind is fundamentally embedded through embodiment in the perceptions of the world it inhabits, and also actively shapes that world through its actions and perceptions (Varela et al., 2017, pp. 172-173). In this way, it is a hybrid of interactions between the mind's intrinsic aspects and the extrinsic responses/interactions with external stimuli (Northoff, 2012, p. 356). Furthermore, the non-representational, enactive mind is characterized as being fundamentally non-reductive, and instead based in holism – that is, it is something different to and more than the sum of its parts.

Taking into account all these characteristics, the mind can be thought to operate as a complex, dynamic, self-organizing system. "It is thought that mental phenomena arise from the brain's self-organized and spontaneous, pattern-generating activity, and not simply from stimulus-driven processing" (Fazelpour & Thompson, 2015, p. 223).

The question arises then of how information experience can be understood in relation to the embodied, enactive mind. Of primary significance is conceptualizing information within the enactive mind.

INFORMATION AS AN ENACTIVE COGNITIVE PHENOMENON

As described above, human information experience is a phenomenon manifesting in an embodied, enactive cognitive state. It follows then that *information* is conceptualized as a phenomenon of human experience and cognition, and is instantiated within and arises as function of the human mind. This aligns well with Gorichanaz's depiction of information as needing to "be understood from the first-person perspective of the agent beholding that information, taking into account their lived situation" (Gorichanaz, 2019, p.3).

This conception disallows the idea that information exists independently of cognition, such as espoused by an information-as-thing conceptualization (Buckland, 1991). This is not to disregard that a range of documents and artifacts are commonly referred to as information in everyday life and in the field of Information Science. Instead, this conceptualization recognizes that an enactive mind experiences these artifacts in subjective ways, such that there is a variety of individual perceptions of what is actually informative (i.e. has the characteristic of "being information"), or indeed what information a given artifact imparts.

This foregrounding of the individual experience firmly extends the characterization of the information agent as the expert in their own life-world. Previously typified as a "needy user" – that is, someone who has a preconceived information need attempting to solve it through a course of guided seeking (Olsson, 2005) – in the modified position, the ways the individual perceives and interacts with information is therefore examined from their perspective. This incorporates a conceptualisation of individuals as socially complex agents interacting in valid, multifaceted and sophisticated ways, as they sift through/evaluate/ prioritize/discard/ignore information that is encountered by them through a variety of sources and contexts.

Furthermore, this enactive cognitive view of information enables a wide consideration of information sources without being constrained by socio-cultural preconceptions. That is, anything can be understood to be a stimulus for an information experience: from human generated symbols and communication, through to natural phenomena or individual thoughts, feelings, or beliefs (as has been explored, for example by Kari & Hartel, 2007). Also, it removes the privileging of formal information systems (e.g., books, reports, data systems) over informal sources (e.g., friends, co-workers) (Case & Given, 2016, p.59).

A consequence of the enactive mind is that, documents and information artifacts are not specifically information. They can be regarded as *representations* of information or *tools*, rather than information in and of themselves. Instead, it is proposed that these 'tools' with which we record our information (books, webpages, databases) have so closely been assimilated with the phenomenon of our information experience, that we have come to equate these objects as 'being information'. If we instead consider that highly frequent use of familiar "tools and technologies are characterized by experiential *transparency* in the sense that they withdraw from conscious awareness" (Aagaard et al., 2018, p. xiv), then it can be seen that through the very process of creating and using these 'information tools' in information ideation, they become experientially transparent to the individual. In this way, we can divest ourselves of being tied to the notion of 'information' as a captured characteristic of the physical texts (whether these be printed text, webpages, databases, music scores, art-works, or any other artifact).

Furthermore, this assumption that information is essentially an enactive cognitive phenomenon points to a special quality of information – that it is inherently individually defined, at the moment of being information – *as it is experienced* as information. This definition at the point of experience (or through the experience), necessitates that information is construed as such, it is *constructed* as such by the individual, embodied by their experience and contextually situated.

This shift in perspective then opens up a new way of conceptualizing an experientially-founded paradigm from the ways (behaviors/practices/activities) that we share and use information, the technologies we build for communicating and recording information, and the models we create to divine insights into the management and creation of data (systems architecture, process management and process mining, big data).

CONCLUSION AND FUTURE DIRECTIONS

This paper has provided a novel exploration of an embodied and enactive, non-representational view of the mind and its significance for theorizing about human information experience. It has argued that any theory of information experience needs to incorporate the notion of an enactive, embodied mind, rather than the more broadly received view of an object-oriented, representational mind founded on an assumption of realism, which is inadequate for holistically incorporating the subjective, situated and contextual characteristics of experience.

Furthering this discussion, this paper examined the significance of conceptualizing information within the enactive mind and as constructed by the individual in the moment of information experience.

These conceptions will be useful in providing a foundation for further development of the emerging field of information experience, and prove thought provoking for the Information Science field generally in the development of new approaches to the ways we use and share information in our communities and the future technologies we build for this.

REFERENCES

Aagaard, J., Friis, J. K. B., Sorenson, J., Tafdrup, O., & Hasse, C. (2018). An introduction to postphenomenological methodologies. In C. Adams, C. Aydin, L. Blond, J. Aagaard, J. K. B. Friis, J. Sorenson, et al., *Postphenomenological methodologies: New ways in mediating techno-human relationships* (pp. xi–xxv). Blue Ridge Summit: Lexington Books.

Bruce, C., Davis, K., Hughes, H., Partridge, H., & Stoodley, I. (2014). *Information experience: Approaches to theory and practice* (Vol. 9). Bingley, UK: Emerald Group Publishing Limited.

Buckland, M. K. (1991). Information as thing. *Journal of the American Society for Information Science*, *42*(5), 351–360. https://doi.org/10.1002/(SICI)1097-4571(199106)42:53.0.CO;2-3

Case, D. O., & Given, L. M. (2016). *Looking for information: A survey of research on information seeking, needs, and behavior*. Bingley, UK: Emerald Group Publishing.

Fazelpour, S., & Thompson, E. (2015). The Kantian brain: brain dynamics from a neurophenomenological perspective. *Current Opinion in Neurobiology*, *31*, 223–229. https://doi.org/10.1016/j.conb.2014.12.006

Gallagher, S., & Zahavi, D. (2012). *The phenomenological mind* (2nd ed.). London; New York, NY: Routledge.

Gorichanaz, T. (2015). Information on the run: Experiencing information during an ultramarathon. *Information Research*, *20*(4) Retrieved from http://InformationR.net/ir/20-4/paper697.html

Gorichanaz, T. (2019). Information experience in personally meaningful activities. *Journal of the Association for Information Science and Technology*. https://doi.org/10.1002/asi.24142

Kari, J., & Hartel, J. (2007). Information and higher things in life: Addressing the pleasurable and the profound in information science. *Journal of the American Society for Information Science and Technology*, *58*(8), 1131–1147. https://doi.org/10.1002/asi.20585

Krebs, J. (2015). Information transfer as a metaphor. In *Philosophy, computing and information science* (pp. 19–40). Taylor and Francis. https://doi.org/10.4324/9781315653938

Lakoff, G. (2012). Explaining embodied cognition results. *Topics in Cognitive Science*, *4*(4), 773–785. https://doi.org/10.1111/j.1756-8765.2012.01222.x

Le Poidevin, R. (2015). The experience and perception of time. In E. N. Zalta, *The stanford encyclopedia of philosophy (Summer 2015 Edition)* Retrieved from https://plato.stanford.edu/archives/sum2015/entries/time-experience/

Library Trends (2018). 66(3-4).

Lueg, C., & Twidale, M. (2018). Designing for humans, not robots (Or vulcans). *Library Trends*, *66*(4), 409–421. https://doi.org/10.1353/lib.2018.0010

Northoff, G. (2012). Immanuel Kant's mind and the brain's resting state. *Trends in cognitive sciences*, *16*(7), 356–359. https://doi.org/10.1016/j.tics.2012.06.001

Olsson, M. (2005). Beyond 'needy'individuals: Conceptualizing information behavior. Paper presented at the Annual Meeting of the American Society for Information Science and Technology

Shannon, C. E., & Weaver, W. (1949). *The mathematical theory of communication*. Urbana, IL.

Thompson, E. (2008). Representationalism and the phenomenology of mental imagery. *Synthese*, *160*(3), 397–415. https://doi.org/10.1007/s11229-006-9086-0

Varela, F. J., Thompson, E., & Rosch, E. (2017). *The embodied mind: Cognitive science and human experience*. Cambridge, MA: MIT Press.

Knowledge Transfer From Technology to Science: The Longevity of Paper-to-Patent Citations

Tzu-Kun Hsiao
School of Information Sciences, UIUC, Champaign, USA
tkhsiao2@illinois.edu

Vetle I. Torvik
School of Information Sciences, UIUC, Champaign, USA
vtorvik@illinois.edu

ABSTRACT

Citations between papers and patents reflect transfer of knowledge between science and technology. Patents commonly cite papers but papers rarely cite patents. Here, we identified 6,033 paper-to-patent citations in a collection of 1.5 million PubMed Central open access articles. These citing papers and cited patents contained 132,536 paper-to-paper, 200,339 patent-to-patent, and 36,342 patent-to-paper citations. These four citation datasets were used to model the temporal patterns of knowledge transfer within and across patents and papers. We found that the cited patents are generally much older than the cited papers, regardless of whether they are cited by papers or patents. Discipline, affiliation type, and self-citation also affect the age of the cited papers and patents. The recency of the citations partly explains the asymmetry in citations between papers and patents.

KEYWORDS

Knowledge Transfer; Time-Lag; Citation Analysis

ASIS&T THESAURUS

Scientometrics; Bibliometrics

INTRODUCTION

Although science and technology were once regarded as two complementary yet autonomous systems in de Solla Price [1965]'s study on the citations between scientific and technology journals, the following research on the linkage between science and technology discovered that the two realms had become interwoven and inseparable (Jaffe & Trajtenberg, 1996; Meyer, Debackere, & Glänzel, 2010; Narin & Noma, 1985). Among various approaches of studying knowledge transfer between science and technology, citation linkage is popularly adopted as the measurement of the dependence and connectedness between citer and citee (Narin and Noma,1985; Verbeek et al., 2002), and the time-lag of citations is used to capture the age distribution of the transferred knowledge (Van Vianen, Moed, & Van Raan, 1990).

82nd Annual Meeting of the Association for Information Science & Technology | Melbourne, Australia | 19–23 October, 2019

DOI: 10.1002/pra2.00041

In the past 30 years, patent-to-paper citations have been studied comprehensively to capture knowledge transfer from science to technology (Carpenter & Narin, 1983; Finardi, 2011; Narin & Noma, 1985), but how the knowledge transferred from technology to science has not been adequately studied yet (Glänzel & Meyer, 2003). Besides, although patents contain detailed methodological information about successful innovations (Narin & Noma, 1985), citations to patents are rarely seen in the scientific realm even in applied science (Glänzel & Meyer, 2003). Many reasons may lead to the uncitedness of patents such as the difference in the language used in patents and papers and the scientists' unfamiliarity with patent documents.

In this study, we focused on the age of knowledge transfer as reflected by the time-lag between the publication year and the cited year of a document. We first identified 6,033 paper-to-patent citations from the PubMed Central (PMC) open access (OA) articles; then, based on the patent-citing papers and paper-cited patents found in the collection, 132,536 paper-to-paper, 200,339 patent-to-patent, and 36,342 patent-to-paper citations were further collected. Using these four sets of citations, we built four models to measure the age of knowledge transferred within and across the scientific and technology realm.

RELATED WORK

Knowledge Transfer between Papers and Patents

Based on the direction of knowledge transfer, the linkage between papers and patents can be categorized as either patent-to-paper citations or paper-to-patent citation.

In the studies of patent-to-paper linkages, Carpenter and Narin [1983]'s pioneering study explored the possibility of using patent-to-paper citations to measure the science dependence of 24 technology fields. The following large-scale study conducted by Verbeek et al. (2002) showed that 35% of the U.S. patents granted between 1992 and 1996 had cited at least one scientific paper. The scientific dependence of the chemical and pharmaceutical patents reported in Verbeek et al. (2002) was also found in Carpenter and Narin (1983) and Callaert, Grouwels, and Van Looy (2011). As for the paper-to-patent linkages, Glänzel and Meyer (2003) reported that only about 0.98% of the papers published between 1996 and 2000 had cited U.S. patents, and the linkage between chemistry papers and chemical patents accounted for more than one-third of all the paper-to-patent citations. Huang, Yang, and Chen (2015)'s study on the cross-citations between fuel cell papers and patents showed 12.06% of the papers had cited patents.

The Age of Knowledge Transfer

Previous research showed that the age of knowledge transfer between papers was younger than the age between patents. Finardi (2014) mentioned that the cited peak of chemistry papers was about two to three years after being published while Hall, Jaffe, and Trajtenberg (2001) reported that the mean age of citations between patents was around 15 years, and 50% of the cited U.S. patents were more than 50 years old. On the other hand, the studies on the knowledge transfer between science and technology showed that the age of citations varied across different technology fields and countries. Van Vianen et al. [1990] found that 50% of the scientific papers cited in chemical patents were less than ten years old. Finardi (2011) reported that the age of European patent-to-paper citations varied from three to nine years, depending on the technology fields. Huang et al. [2015] reported that in the case of the fuel cell, the average age of patent-to-paper citations was about 11 years while the age of paper-to-patent citations was about 13 years.

METHOD

Data

Identifying Paper-to-Patent Citations

The paper-to-patent citations were identified from the PMC OA subset. The PMC OA subset provides part of the total collection of PMC articles which are under Creative Commons or similar licenses. The collection was retrieved on September 12, 2018. At that time, there were 5,286,115 articles in the PMC, and 1,643,140 articles were included in the PMC OA subset, in which 1,505,924 articles had at least one citation.

The paper-to-patent citations and the patent number of the cited patents were identified through matching the string patterns shown in the reference sections of the articles. Reference strings containing the patterns of "us", "unite state", "uspto", or "patent" and six to eight digits[1] were first identified as possible candidates of paper-to- patent citations. The matching process was performed by the regular expression module in *Python*. The identified citation strings were then manually examined to filter out false identifications.

Among the 1,505,924 articles having at least one citation, 6,033 paper-to-patent citations were found. It is worth noticing that a paper can cite multiple patents and vice versa; hence, the number of citing papers and the number of cited patents can be less than the number of paper-to-patent citations. In our case, 3,933 citing papers and 5,521 cited patents were found in the 6,033 paper-to-patent citations.

[1] According to USPTO, the length of the digits in a U.S. patent is six to eight (e.g. US 420179 and US 4544555).

The Linkage to Other Papers and Patents

For the purpose of understanding the age of the knowledge transferred within and across science and technology, we further collected three other sets of data: (a) 132,536 paper-to-paper citations in which 120,641 papers in PMC were cited by the 3,746 patent-citing papers; (b) 200,339 patent-to-patent citations in which 130,922 U.S. patents cited 4,725 paper-cited patents; (c) 36,342 patent-to-paper citations in which 2,333 paper-cited patents cited 29,924 papers. The paper-to-paper and patent-to-patent citations were collected from our local database in 2018. The patent-to-paper citations were identified in 2019 by using *Patci* [Agarwal, Lincoln, Cai, & Torvik, 2014]; the threshold of the match probability was set as no less than 0.9. Table 1 presents the summary of the four data sets.

Relation	# citations	# citing items	# cited items
Paper-to-patent	6,033	3,933 papers	5,521 patents
Paper-to-paper	132,536	3,746 papers	120,641 papers
Patent-to-patent	200,339	130,922 patents	4,725 patents
Patent-to-paper	36,342	2,333 patents	29,924 papers

Table 1. The Relationship between Four Sets of Data. Within the 3,933 patent-citing papers, 3,746 citedat least one paper. Within the 5,521 paper-cited patents, 4,725 were also cited by other U.S. patents, and 2,333 cited at least at least one paper.

Model

Explanatory Features

Each instance in the dataset captures a set of features about the citing document. The features used for modeling are listed in Table 2. The choices of features are based on the following reasons: (a) Publication year: the later the publication year, the longer the citing window could be, resulting in the longer age of citations. (b) Self-citations: it is known that self-citations might appear sooner than regular citations. (c) Chemistry: previous work had addressed the strong linkage between chemical patents and chemistry papers, yet its influence on the age of citations was unexplored. (d) Affiliation type: authors affiliated with commercial institutions might be more familiar with the patents and pay more attention to recent technical knowledge, resulting in younger citation age.

Feature	Description
PubYR-2006	is the difference in the publication year of a citing document and year 2006.
Self-citation	is 1 if the citing and the cited document shared at least one common author, 0 otherwise.
Chemistry	is 1 if the affiliation of the author of a citing paper belongs to chemistry discipline (e.g., chemistry departments in the universities or companies), 0 otherwise.
Affiliation Type	is the affiliation type of the first author/assignee of the citing documents. Each citing document can have one of following: *commercial, education, hospital,* or *others.*

Table 2. Descriptions of the Explanatory Features. *PubYR-2006* was the temporary change of the publication year of a citing document compared to year 2006, which was the starting point of the publication year of the citing papers in the model.

Modeling the Age

The age of the paper-to-patent citations was modeled using linear regression. The categorical features (e.g., self-citation, chemistry, and affiliation type) were set as dummy variables.

$$Log2(Age_i + 1) = \beta_0 + \beta_1 X_1 + \beta_2 X_2 + \cdots + \beta_n X_n$$

where

$$X_1, X_2, \ldots, X_n$$

denoted the explanatory features described in Table 2 and $Log2(Age_i + 1)$ was the log transformation of the age,[2] which was the difference in the publication year of the citing and cited document.

RESULTS

Descriptive Statistics

In the PMC OA subset, the patent-citing papers rarely appeared. Among the 1,505,924 articles having at least one citations, only 0.3% (3,933) of the articles had cited at least one patent. Figure 1 presents the number of citing papers, the number of cited patents, and the mean age of citations in each year. The paper-to-patent citations first appeared in 1993 and had increased to 906 cited patents and 672 citing papers in 2016. No paper-to-patent citation was found in 1994, 1998, and 1999.

The age of each citation varied from 0 to 168 years, and the mean was 17.7 years. Notably, because the number of paper-to-patent citations were too few before 2000, the age could easily be influenced by the outliers. For example, the age in 1993 and 1997 were both over 40 years because one of the papers cited a patent with an age of more than 60 years. Trending of the age was observed after 2005. From 2005 to 2010, the age has grown from 8.2 years to 16.6 years and remains around 17 to 18 years ever since.

The Model of Age

The paper-to-patent citations which happened earlier than 2006 were excluded from the model due to the following reasons. First, the data was too sparse before 2005. Second, the trending of age was observed from 2006. Third, the chemistry citing papers were first found in 2006 and appeared

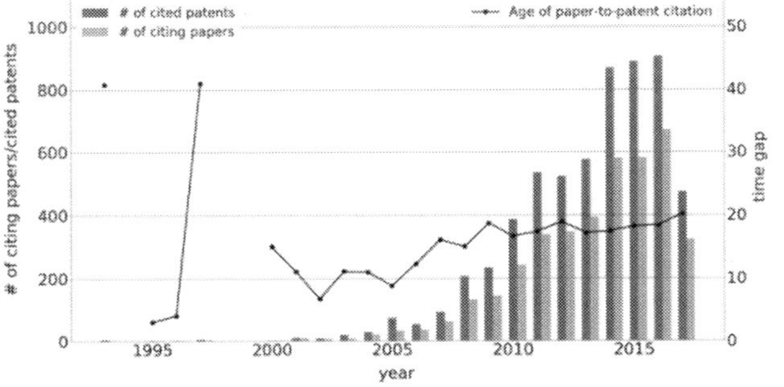

Figure 1. Number of citing papers, number of cited patents and the mean age of citations in each year.

[2] Because the N in $Log2(N)$ could not be zero, $Age_i + 1$ was set to cope with the condition of time-lag being zero.

consecutively in the following years. Since chemistry was one of the features in our model, the exclusion ensured that the influence of chemistry papers could be captured in each year. Moreover, the number of paper-to-patent citations found after 2005 was 5,882; accounting for 96.5% of all the paper-to-patent citations. Hence, we believed this subset was representative enough and fitted our research design better. Within the 5,882 paper-to-patent citations, 3,849 citing papers and 5,384 cited papers were found. Among the 3,849 patent-citing papers, 3,674 had cited 118,472 articles indexed in PMC. As for the 5,384 paper-cited patents, 4,597 were cited by other 128,475 U.S. patents, and 2,274 cited 29,556 PMC papers.

Table 3 presented the modeling results of the four pairs of citations. In each model, the coefficient of intercept represented the mean age of citations in year 2006. For the other features, the coefficient stood for positive or negative effect on age. The coefficient of each feature could be converted back to year or month by calculating the antilogarithm.[3]

Observation	Feature	Coefficient	Interpretation	SE
Paper-to-Patent Citations	Intercept	3.628 ***	11.36 years	0.077
	PubYR-2006	0.011	0.09 month	0.008
	Self-citation	-0.842 ***	-5.30 months	0.071
	Chemistry	0.376 ***	3.57 months	0.072
	Commercial	-0.362 ***	-2.66 months	0.085
	Education	0.065	0.55 month	0.058
	Hospital	-0.089	-0.72 month	0.102
Paper-to-Paper Citations	Intercept	2.818 ***	6.05 years	0.044
	PubYR-2006	0.031 ***	0.26 month	0.004
	Self-citation	-1.170 ***	-6.67 months	0.066
	Chemistry	-0.146 ***	-1.15 months	0.040
	Commercial	0.074	0.63 month	0.048
	Education	-0.084 **	-0.68 month	0.032
	Hospital	0.083	0.71 month	0.056
Patent-to-Patent Citations	Intercept	3.728 ***	12.25 years	0.008
	PubYR-2006	0.036 ***	0.31 month	0.000
	Self-citation	-0.811 ***	-5.16 months	0.010
	Commercial	-0.010	-0.08 month	0.009
	Education	-0.031 *	-0.26 month	0.013
	Hospital	0.057	0.49 month	0.031
Patent-to-Paper Citations	Intercept	3.490 ***	10.24 years	0.030
	PubYR-2006	0.012 ***	0.10 month	0.002
	Self-citation	-0.625 ***	-4.22 months	0.059
	Commercial	0.030	0.25 month	0.035
	Education	-0.022	-0.18 month	0.046
	Hospital	0.053	0.45 month	0.149

***$p<.001$, **$p<0.1$, *$p<.05$

Table 3. Models of Age.

The models showed that the age of knowledge transfer from patents to papers was almost twice as old as the age of knowledge transfer within papers. Besides, the age of the knowledge transferred from and within the technology realm was older than the age of knowledge transferred from and within the scientific realm as reflected by the older age of paper-to-patent and patent-to-patent citations.

Except for paper-to-patent citations, the positive effect of publication year on the age of citations was observed, and self-citation showed consistent negative effect on age across the four models. The results of the antilogarithm showed that the age of a self-citation would be about four to six months younger compared to the citations contributed by others.

[3] $Year = 2^{coefficient} - 1$; $Month = 12 \times (2^{coefficient} - 1)$

Chemistry authors showed different behaviors in citing papers and patents. In the case of paper-to-patent citations, the positive coefficient suggested that the age of patents cited by chemistry authors were about four months older than the other patents. However, in paper-to-paper citations, the negative coefficient indicated that the age of papers cited by chemistry authors was about one month younger. As for the effect of the types of affiliations, in paper-to- patent citations, the age of patents cited by authors affiliated with commercial institutions was about three months younger than patents cited by authors with other types of affiliations. This condition might be explained by positing that authors with commercial affiliations are more familiar with patents and technical knowledge.

DISCUSSION

This study implements the concept of using citation as the proxy of knowledge flow and uses the time-lag of citations to capture the temporal patterns of knowledge transfer. The results contribute to the understanding of the patterns as well as the influential factors of the age of knowledge transfer within and across science and technology.

In specific, we find that technical knowledge was rarely cited in scientific papers, and the age of knowledge transfer across science and technology is older than the age of knowledge transfer within science. Among the 1,643,140 articles in the PMC OA subset, 91.05% of articles have at least one citation, yet only 0.24% of articles have at least one citation to a patent. The age of paper-to-patent citations and patent-to-paper citations are both more than ten years, whereas the age of citations between papers is about six years. The longest age of citations between patents supports Hall et al. [2001]'s finding. As for the influence of discipline, our finding of the dominance of chemistry authors is aligned with Callaert et al. [2011] and Glänzel and Meyer [2003]. Within the 3,933 patent-citing papers, 8.85% (348 papers) are written by chemistry authors. Furthermore, compared to Van Vianen et al. [1990], in which the authors reported that chemical patents tended to cite recent scientific papers, we find longer age in paper-to-patent citations contributed by chemistry authors. Aside from the influence of discipline, we find younger patents are cited by authors with commercial affiliations, and the finding of the negative effect of self-citation on age is aligned with Hall et al. [2001].

As an exploratory study, we understand that there are limitations. First, our data is limited to the open access articles in the PubMed Central; hence our results might only capture the age of knowledge transfer happening in the biomedical discipline. We also cannot determine whether the patent-citing behaviors of the open-access articles are different from the general articles or not. Second, we understand that the mechanism of knowledge transfer is complicated, and we did not exhaustively consider every possible feature such as country mentioned in Jaffe and Trajtenberg [1996]. Third, we only discuss the time for patents to be cited in papers. The motives behind the paper-to-patent citations are not addressed in this paper. Being aware of the limitations, we plan to expand the scope of our research in the future to include more features and the text of the citing papers and cited patents. We hope that our following studies will provide more answers to the meaning and motives behind paper-to-patent citations.

ACKNOWLEDGMENTS

Research reported in this publication was supported by National Institutes of Health (Award Number P01AG 039347). The content is solely the responsibility of the authors and does not necessarily represent the official views of the NIH.

REFERENCES

Agarwal, S., Lincoln, M., Cai, H., and Torvik, V. I. (2014). *Patci-the citation matcher*. http://abel.lis.illinois.edu/cgi-bin/patci/search.pl

Callaert, J., Grouwels, J., & Van Looy, B. (2011). Delineating the scientific footprint in technology: Identifying scientific publications within non-patent references. *Scientometrics, 91*(2), 383–398.

Carpenter, M. P., & Narin, F. (1983). Validation study: Patent citations as indicators of science and foreign dependence. *World Patent Information, 5*(3), 180–185.

de Solla Price, D. J. (1965). Is technology historically independent of science? A study in statistical historiography. *Technology and Culture, 6*(4), 553–568.

Finardi, U. (2011). Time relations between scientific production and patenting of knowledge: The case of nanotechnologies. *Scientometrics, 89*(1), 37.

Finardi, U. (2014). On the time evolution of received citations, in different scientific fields: An empirical study. *Journal of Informetrics, 8*(1), 13–24.

Glänzel, W., & Meyer, M. (2003). Patents cited in the scientific literature: An exploratory study of reverse citation relations. *Scientometrics, 58*(2), 415–428.

Hall, B. H., Jaffe, A. B., & Trajtenberg, M. (2001). *The NBER patent citation data file: Lessons, insights and methodological tools*. Technical report. National Bureau of Economic Research.

Huang, M.-H., Yang, H.-W., & Chen, D.-Z. (2015). Increasing science and technology linkage in fuel cells: A cross citation analysis of papers and patents. *Journal of Informetrics, 9*(2), 237–249.

Jaffe, A. B., & Trajtenberg, M. (1996). Flows of knowledge from universities and federal laboratories: Modeling the flow of patent citations over time and across institutional and geographic boundaries. *Proceedings of the National Academy of Sciences, 93*(23), 12671–12677.

Meyer, M., Debackere, K., & Glänzel, W. (2010). Can applied science be 'good science'? Exploring the relationship between patent citations and citation impact in nanoscience. *Scientometrics*, *85*(2), 527–539.

Narin, F., & Noma, E. (1985). Is technology becoming science? *Scientometrics*, *7*(3-6), 369–381.

Van Vianen, B. G., Moed, H. F., & Van Raan, A. F. J. (1990). An exploration of the science base of recent technology. *Research Policy*, *19*(1), 61–81.

Verbeek, A., Debackere, K., Luwel, M., Andries, P., Zimmermann, E., & Deleus, F. (2002). Linking science to technology: Using bibliographic references in patents to build linkage schemes. *Scientometrics*, *54*(3), 399–420.

VR Creation Experience in Cultural Heritage Education: A Preliminary Exploration

Xiao Hu
Faculty of Education,
University of Hong Kong,
Pokfulam Road, Hong Kong
xiaoxhu@hku.hk

Jeremy Ng
Faculty of Education,
University of Hong Kong,
Pokfulam Road, Hong Kong
jeremyng@hku.hk

Jin Ha Lee
Information School,
University of Washington,
Seattle, WA, USA
jinhalee@uw.edu

ABSTRACT

Despite an increasing adoption of virtual reality (VR) in education, few studies have explored VR creation in cultural heritage education. This study aims to investigate students' experience of creating VR content featuring cultural heritage in an undergraduate general education course repurposed from a digital collection course. A survey was conducted with 87 students, collecting both close-ended and open-ended responses. A coding framework was designed to analyze students' open-ended responses. Preliminary findings show that students were largely satisfied with the experience, which helped learners from diverse academic backgrounds toward acquiring technological skills that are essential for the 21st century workforce. The VR creation experience also motivated the students to learn more about cultural heritage. Technical issues regarding spherical photo-taking and the online VR creation tool were identified, which may call for new alternative tools and devices. Findings offer empirical evidence on the value of integrating VR creation into cultural heritage education, as well as implications for pedagogical design and educational applications of VR creation.

KEYWORDS

Virtual Reality Creation; Cultural Heritage; General Education

ASIS&T THESAURUS

Information Technology; Education Technology; Humanities; Culture; Cultural Heritage

INTRODUCTION

Virtual Reality (VR) is defined as a complex technology which exploits existing technologies (e.g., 3D graphics, robotics, etc.) to create an immersive and interactive digital environment (Carrozzino & Bergamasco, 2010). It has been adopted as one of the various digital technologies (e.g., Augmented Reality) for documenting and preserving cultural heritages. While this technology has been increasingly adopted in education, VR creation in cultural heritage education is relatively new and under-explored. VR creation is usually perceived as an activity requiring professional devices and specialized technological skills (Feurstein, 2018). In this study, undergraduate students from diverse academic backgrounds in a general education course on cultural heritage used their smartphones and a free online VR creation tool to create VR stories of cultural heritage. This study targeted 124 students enrolled in this course in Fall 2018. Valid survey responses were collected from 87 students to understand their experience of VR creation. By analyzing the survey responses, this study aims to answer the following research questions:

RQ1: What are the benefits of creating a VR story of cultural heritage as perceived by students?

RQ2: What are the issues/challenges arising from students' experience of creating a VR story of cultural heritage?

The first research question sets out to understand students' opinions on the benefits of VR creation in the context of cultural heritage education, whereas the second research question aims at identifying possible issues/challenges encountered by students during the process of VR creation. Our findings will provide empirical evidence on the values and challenges of integrating VR creation into cultural heritage education and thereby shed light on pedagogical design and educational applications of VR creation.

RELATED WORK

VR for Cultural Heritage

VR technology has been rapidly adopted for conservation and restoration of cultural heritage. VR helps to reconstruct damaged or destroyed historic objects, buildings, and environments. VR also facilitates the presentation of heritage information via sensational means rather than linguistic codes, allowing apprehension by both expert and non-specialized users (Carrozzino & Bergamasco, 2010). In recent years, thanks to the availability of advanced software and hardware, museums are able to preserve and display artefacts digitally. Historic artefacts and architecture are made accessible online as interactive 3D models, giving rise to

82nd Annual Meeting of the Association for Information Science & Technology | Melbourne, Australia | 19–23 October, 2019

DOI: 10.1002/pra2.00042

Virtual Museum (VM) systems which are an effective solution for communication of cultural contents (Barbieri, Bruno, & Muzzupappa, 2017). Visitors can view digitized cultural objects and explore virtually reconstructed historical places by means of VM-hosted installations. VR technology in such features as mobile guides and interactive exhibits enhances visitors' experience with collections and exhibits, through engaging and educational methods available both inside and outside of the museums. VR is beneficial for both cultural preservation and visitors' experience (Alelis, Bobrowicz, & Ang, 2015).

VR for Education

VR enables students to interact with visualizations of abstract ideas and has been utilized as a medium for concept delivery, training, or skill application (Cheng & Wang, 2011). VR allows the creation of virtual environments and users' intuitive interaction via real-time natural manipulations (Mikropoulos & Natsis, 2011), leading to its pedagogical affordances in the classroom. Using VR not only encourages active participation, but also increases the interactivity and individualization of the learning process, contributing to effective learning (Mikropoulos & Natsis, 2011). The operation of the virtual environment offers a unique sense of engagement to the students as active learners via continuous interactions (Martín-Gutiérrez, Mora, Añorbe-Díaz, & González-Marrero, 2017; Baxter & Hainey, 2019). The immersion, interaction and imagination brought by VR experience are also shown to increase learners' motivation (Curcio, Dipace, & Norlund, 2016). However, most studies on VR for education to date focus on the learning experience where students are *consumers* of VR content. The creation of VR has been mostly discussed from the perspective of instructional designers and technicians (Feurstein, 2018). To the best of authors' knowledge, there is little empirical research that explores students' experience of VR content creation in cultural heritage education. This study aims to bridge the gap.

RESEARCH CONTEXT AND METHOD

Research Context

This on-going study was conducted in a large university in Hong Kong. This study involved an undergraduate general education course on digitizing cultural heritage, as a repurposed Digital Library course aiming to teach information science and technology as well as cultural heritage information to a broad audience (Hu, Yu, Alman, Renear, & Carbo, 2017). Students from any disciplines could enroll in the course. Two important learning outcomes of the course are to "demonstrate a good understanding of cultural heritages, their values and significance" and "apply digital technologies to promoting local cultural heritage to a global audience". The course was delivered through a 2-hour lecture given by an instructor and 1-hour small-class tutorial each week given by a teaching assistant.

In alignment with the two course learning outcomes, one of the course assessments was to create an individual VR story to showcase a cultural heritage of the student's own choice. One tutorial was designated for this assignment, with hands-on practices of taking a VR-friendly spherical photo (Figure 1) using a smartphone app *Google Street View* and creating a draft VR story using an online tool *Stories360* [http://stories360.org/].

Figure 1. Sample spherical photo.

VR Story-creating Procedures

These procedures were used to instruct the students how to create a VR story. First, the *Google Street View* smartphone app was used to take at least one spherical photo of the site of cultural heritage. Second, the photo was uploaded to the web interface of *Stories360* for generating a basic VR story. Different objects could then be added to the story, including text, image, interactive video, and background music or narration. The product was then saved online and could be viewed via any mobile devices. Both the regular and dual-lens views (Figure 2) are available where the latter can be activated when a pair of VR glasses is used.

Figure 2. Dual-lens view for VR glasses.

Data Collection

Adopting the mixed method approach, both quantitative and qualitative data were collected from an end-of-semester survey on students' overall experience of creating a VR story of cultural heritage. Consents were obtained from students prior to data collection. Besides demographic information (e.g., gender, handedness), the questionnaire contained both close-ended and open-ended questions, asking about students' satisfaction with and perceived benefits of the experience of VR story creation, issues arising from the experience, and suggestions for a similar experience in future courses. Their participation was entirely voluntary, and no compensation was provided.

RESULTS

A total of 87 responses were collected (responses rate = 70.2%). Among the survey respondents, 57% were female and 38% were male, leaving 5% not disclosing their gender. Half of the students (52%) were bespectacled, and a minority of them (5%) were left-handed.

The majority of respondents (90%) were satisfied with their VR story-making experience in the course. All of them deemed that they received enough instruction and resources on creating a VR story. A considerable portion of students (76%) were in favour of creating VR stories in their future courses, whereas 6% were not in favour and 18% were neutral.

Responses to the open-ended questions were coded with thematic content analysis. With the grounded theory approach (Strauss & Corbin, 1994), the codebook was developed from the data through an iterative coding process. An excerpt was defined as a unit with an independent meaning and was usually an utterance. The coding was done by two coders to calculate inter-rater reliability. Table 1 displays the coding framework with frequency information for each code.

Learning new technology, particularly spherical photo taking was mentioned frequently (37%) as a benefit of the VR creation experience:

> *"The best part of the experience was seeing how current technology could allow individual pictures to be pieced together in order to create a [spherical] photo"* – P57

VR creation was seen as a new and positive experience to many respondents (23%), being described as "fresh" (Participant 27(P27)), "meaningful" (P28), "comprehensive" (P11), and "magical" (P15). It was even more encouraging for students with less technical experience:

> *"Before making VR, it seemed like a big thing but now we know it's an easy thing and it makes me feel good about myself."* – P59

One third of the comments on benefits linked the VR creation to the subject matter, cultural heritage. 19 of them remarked that the respondents did physically visit the site of cultural heritage for collecting materials for the VR story:

> *"[The VR story-making experience] encouraged me to visit cultural heritages which I would not usually do so."* – P84

There were also 14 responses on how the experience enabled the students to learn more about and appreciate cultural heritage, in terms of their "current situation" (P43), "details" (P74), "importance" (P8), "interesting facts" (P64), and "aesthetic merits" (P21).

Code	Definition	Count
	Perceived Benefits of VR Story Creation	103
Spherical photos	Participant mentioned viewing, capturing, and/or creating spherical or 360-degree photos.	37
New or positive experience	Participant mentioned VR production as a new and/or positive experience	23
Visiting the heritage	Participant mentioned physically visiting the site of cultural heritage for making the VR story.	19
Appreciating the heritage	Participant mentioned learning something or more about and/or appreciating the cultural heritage via the VR story-making experience.	14
Ease of VR story-making	Participant mentioned the ease of creating VR stories.	10
	Issues / Challenges about VR Story Creation	79
Taking spherical photos	Participant mentioned issues regarding capturing, viewing, or other actions on spherical photos.	23
Operation	Participant mentioned issues arising when viewing, using and/or operating the VR story-making tool.	20
Features and functions	Participant mentioned the issues regarding features/functions of the VR story-making tool.	15
Alternative devices and tools	Participant mentioned and/or suggested alternative devices/tools for VR creation.	8
Need for sample work	Participant mentioned the need of sample VR stories for their reference.	5
Speed and stability	Participant mentioned issues regarding the speed and/or stability of the VR story-making tool.	4
Other issues	Participant mentioned other miscellaneous issues related to the VR story-making experience.	4

Table 1. Coding framework and code counts.

A total of 182 excerpts were extracted from the responses and 28% were double coded, with a Cohen's kappa coefficient of 0.93, implying a substantial to excellent level of agreement (McHugh, 2012). As shown in Table 1, there are 103 excerpts containing respondents' perceived benefits in their VR story creation experience and 79 about the issues arising from the experience.

As for issues arising from the VR story-making, the most mentioned one was dissatisfaction toward technical issues when taking spherical photos:

"I have spent nearly two hours on taking two [spherical] photos as there are too many slits and twists due to technical problems." – P29

Another commonly raised issue was related to the online tool used to create the VR story (i.e., *Stories360*):

"The loading speed of Stories360 [was an issue]." – P86
"Stories360 is in lack of different functions to create the ideal visual effects." – P58

Some students suggested alternative tools and devices such as the "360 Camera" to replace smartphones for taking spherical photos (P55) and a "more advanced platform" (P38) than Stories360 for creating VR story.

DISCUSSION

The results show that students were largely satisfied with their VR creation experience. The idea of VR creation in and of itself was deemed as a benefit, which to most students was a new experience from which they could learn new skills on "current technology" (P57). Given that students of this general education course were from diverse academic backgrounds including fields that are traditionally less technology-oriented, this benefit could be attributed to the ease and "simplicity" (P8) of making a VR story via a smartphone. In fact, some students who were anxious about making "technologically intensive" products became more confident in using digital technology through this VR creation experience. It is noteworthy that the tutorial session that taught and scaffolded the students how to use the tools was also indispensable for gaining this benefit Martín-Gutiérrez et al., 2017. As a good mastery of information technology is necessary for the 21st century workforce, this finding demonstrates the effectiveness of a "low tech-barrier" approach of VR creation in teaching current information technology in general education courses.

Another major benefit was students being more motivated to explore the cultural heritage of their choices. Students found it "enjoyable" (P31) to use their smartphones to take spherical photos of cultural heritage sites, which required students to make visits to the actual sites of cultural heritage, leading to their gains in knowledge regarding the status and significance (e.g., historic) of cultural heritages. Instead of merely capturing a digital representation of the site, students had to think about how to effectively present it as a story in VR which led them to pay attention to details and aesthetics of these sites. This shows the advantage of situating VR creation into the real world with authentic tasks and highlights the importance of a well-designed educational context in exploiting the pedagogical potential of VR technology Mikropoulos & Natsis, 2011.

The issues raised were mostly on technical aspects of the tools used, including difficulty in taking spherical photos using regular smartphones, slow loading speed, inflexible operation, and lack of advanced functions of the online VR creation platform, *Stories360*. In fact, some more tech-savvy students made suggestions for alternative tools/devices to mitigate these problems. However, these tools may involve steeper learning curves and/or financial cost. Whether or not they are suitable for general education courses will need further exploration. In sum, from the preliminary findings it seems that the benefits on learning new technologies and being motivated to delve into cultural heritage, the subject of the course, overweighed such technical issues.

CONCLUSION AND FUTURE WORK

The preliminary findings from this on-going study show that students were largely satisfied with their experience, particularly on the opportunity of learning VR technology and the process of visiting and taking spherical photos of the actual cultural heritage sites. Technical issues in spherical photo taking and the VR story-making tool were raised. These preliminary findings highlight the importance of a low-tech barrier approach in offering the experience of VR content creation in an educational setting and showcase the educational benefits in implementation of VR in the cultural heritage domain. As an ongoing study, we are conducting interviews with students to gather more in-depth data about their experience and opinions. To triangulate results on how VR creation impacts cultural heritage education, multiple sources of data including students' performance scores will also be collected and analyzed in our future study.

ACKNOWLEDGMENTS

This study is partially supported by a Common Core Teaching Development Grant in University of Hong Kong.

REFERENCES

Alelis, G., Bobrowicz, A., & Ang, C. S. (2015). Comparison of engagement and emotional responses of older and younger adults interacting with 3D cultural heritage artefacts on personal devices. *Behaviour & Information Technology*, *34*(11), 1064–1078.

Barbieri, L., Bruno, F., & Muzzupappa, M. (2017). Virtual museum system evaluation through user studies. *Journal of Cultural Heritage*, *26*, 101–108.

Baxter, G., & Hainey, T. (2019). Student perceptions of virtual reality use in higher education. *Journal of Applied Research in Higher Education*. https://doi.org/10.1108/JARHE-06-2018-0106

Carrozzino, M., & Bergamasco, M. (2010). Beyond virtual museums: Experiencing immersive virtual reality in real museums. *Journal of Cultural Heritage*, *11*(4), 452–458.

Cheng, Y., & Wang, S. H. (2011). Applying a 3D virtual learning environment to facilitate student's application ability–The case of marketing. *Computers in Human Behavior*, *27*(1), 576–584.

Curcio, I. D., Dipace, A., & Norlund, A. (2016). Virtual realities and education. *Research on Education and Media, 8* (2), 60–68.

Feurstein, M. S. (2018). Towards an integration of 360-degree video in higher education. *Proceedings of DeLFI Workshops, 2018*, 1–12.

Hu, X., Yu, B., Alman, S., Renear, A. H., & Carbo, T. (2017). Teaching information science and technology to the world? Practices, challenges and visions. *Proceedings of the ASIS&T, 54*(1), 566–569.

John, D., Shaw, L., Cheetham, P., Manley, H., Stone, A. A., Blakeburn, M., & Gosling, K. (2017). Educational virtual reality visualisations of heritage sites. *Eurographics Workshop on Graphics and Cultural Heritage*, 189–193.

Martín-Gutiérrez, J., Mora, C. E., Añorbe-Díaz, B., & González-Marrero, A. (2017). Virtual technologies trends in education. *Eurasia Journal of Mathematics Science and Technology Education, 13*(2), 469–486.

McHugh, M. L. (2012). Interrater reliability: The kappa statistic. *Biochemia medica, 22*(3), 276–282.

Mikropoulos, T. A., & Natsis, A. (2011). Educational virtual environments: A ten-year review of empirical research (1999–2009). *Computers & Education, 56*(3), 769–780.

Strauss, A., & Corbin, J. (1994). Grounded theory methodology. *Handbook of Qualitative Research, 17*, 273–285.

Investigating Users' Affective Load in Collaborative Search

Kun Huang
Department of Information Management, Beijing Normal University, Beijing, China
huangkun@bnu.edu.cn

Xin Yuan
Department of Information Management, Beijing Normal University, Beijing, China
hbuyuanxin@163.com

Lei Li
Department of Information Management, Beijing Normal University, Beijing, China
leili@bnu.edu.cn

Edwin Mouda Ye
School of Information Technology & Mathematical Sciences, University of South Australia, Adelaide, Australia
mouda.ye@mymail.unisa.edu.au

ABSTRACT

This paper draws on affective load theory to explore the characteristics of users' affective load in collaborative searching. In this experimental study, a total of 32 participants were recruited and divided into 16 pair-groups. Each pair-group collaboratively completed three search tasks in the Coagmento system. Users reported more irritation than anxiety, frustration, and rage. Moreover, the greater a task's perceived difficulty, the higher the irritation, anxiety and frustration felt by users. Users' affective load was higher when they spent more time on a search than they expected to. Conversely, their sense of retrieval success, self-motivation to search contributed to reducing users' perceived affective load, but not as much as satisfaction with collaborative search results, and satisfaction with collaborative task outcomes did.

KEYWORDS

Affective Load; Task Difficulty; Time Pressure; Collaborative Search

ASIS&T THESAURUS

Information Discovery; Information Seeking; Collaborative Information Seeking

INTRODUCTION

Due to the complexity and diversity of search tasks, people often resort to collaborative searching (Shah, 2014). Prior studies have actively explored the patterns of and factors influencing collaborative searching behavior (Mohammad Arif, Du, & Lee, 2015), among which the affective factors are receiving increasing attention (Shah, 2010). In her seminal work, Nahl (2004) conceived affective load theory (ALT) in the field of information behavior. Affective load (AL) is operationally defined as uncertainty feelings multiplied by perceived time pressure in the process of human-information interaction. Uncertainty is understood as the combination of irritation, frustration, anxiety, and rage, which are positively related to time pressure.

82nd Annual Meeting of the Association for Information Science & Technology | Melbourne, Australia | 19–23 October, 2019

DOI: 10.1002/pra2.00071

A series of empirical studies of AL has been carried out by Nahl and others in contexts such as a digital library, social media, and everyday information behavior (Nahl, 2010; Thatcher, Vasconcelos, & Ellis, 2015). However, prior research is mostly limited to individualistic environments, giving limited attention to how AL applies in collaborative settings. Users in collaborative settings could be affected by different factors compared to solitary environments, which might cause different searching experiences (González-Ibáñez, Shah, & Córdova-Rubio, 2011). As few studies have considered this question, this paper aims to investigate users' emotions during collaborative information seeking through the lens of ALT.

RELATED WORKS

Research has investigated users' emotional experience across different types of collaborative tasks. For example, Qiu and Wu (2013) studied user sentiments during collaborative information searching and found that users experienced more negative sentiments when facing more complex tasks. Yuan and Zhao (2015) conducted a similar study investigating users' perception of search tasks. They found that users exhibited a similar "positive–negative–positive" pattern of emotional states, and that positive emotional states enhanced seeking efficiency.

Some studies have also examined the relationships between user affects and group performance in collaborative information seeking. For example, Shah (2010) studied the impact of affective relevance on search performance. His results showed that the closer the distance among positive, neutral, and negative information judgements, the better the group performance.

Existing studies also explore the effects of affective states on performance. González-Ibáñez and Shah (2012) conducted an experimental study in which participants completed the same set of search tasks under different affective stimulations. They found that affective states had a significant impact on search performance.

Most prior studies adopted discrete and continuous emotion theory to describe emotion structure; few have applied ALT. Nahl (2004) first proposed the notion of AL to illustrate the uncertainty feelings mediated by time pressure in the process of human-information interaction.

ALT provides a basis for better measurement of and research into negative effects in the search process. Users engaging in collaborative searching are also affected by affects. Therefore, based on ALT, this study focuses on users' negative uncertainty feelings during collaborative searching, and how they interrelate with users' self-efficacy and search optimism feelings.

RESEARCH DESIGN

Research Questions

This study addresses the following research questions:

- How do users experience the four uncertainty feelings before and after a collaborative search? How are the four uncertainty feelings correlated with one another?
- How do perceived task difficulty and time pressure influence the four uncertainty feelings?
- How are user self-efficacy, optimism, satisfaction with the collaborative search results, and satisfaction with the collaborative task outcomes related to the four uncertainty feelings?

Task and Questionnaire Design

Three search tasks related to trip planning were designed. To distinguish task complexity, Task 1 required pair-groups to plan a trip to a destination at least one of them had previously visited, whereas Task 2 required the nominated destination to be one that neither of them had visited (Mohammad Arif et al., 2015). More constraints were added in Task 3 to further increase complexity (Byström & Järvelin, 1995).

The basic information common to all three tasks set the following constraints on destination, time, and budget:

- Create a plan to travel to the nominated destination over five days, including information on food, accommodation, transportation, sightseeing, activities, attractions;
- Budget of CNY 5000 per person.

As noted above, Task 1's description included the sole additional requirement that at least one pair-group member had been to the destination before, whereas Task 2's description included the sole additional requirement that no pair-group member had previously been to the destination. Task 3's instructions also stipulated that the accommodation should be close to the beach, the weather should be sunny, and the temperature should be around 20 °C. It was supposed that these constraints on location, weather, and temperature would make Task 3 the most complicated of the three.

To measure users' negative emotions, this study adapts ALT to measure affective variables, which include AL, the searcher's self-efficacy (SE), and the searcher's optimism (OP) (Nahl, 2004). The latter two are also called user coping skills. Nahl developed 11 statements to measure these variables and we adopted these 11 statements.

Data Collection

Participants were recruited randomly through student forum at Beijing Normal University. Sixteen pair-groups (32 individuals) participated in the experiment, comprising 5 males and 27 females. The sample also included 2 graduate students and 30 undergraduate students. The participants were from 11 different schools.

The experiment process was as follows. Participants were first instructed on the study objective and experiment process, after which they completed a questionnaire concerning their prior search experiences and travel experiences. Among the 32 participants, 28 indicated that they had previously conducted collaborative searching, while 27 reported that they travel frequently. Participants then performed the three collaborative search tasks in pair-groups on Coagmento. Before commencing each task, participants completed a questionnaire on AL to evaluate their four negative emotions (uncertainty feelings), self-efficacy, optimism, perception of task difficulty, and expected task duration time. On completing each task, participants completed another questionnaire that remeasured their AL and asked them to re-evaluate the search task difficulty and indicate their satisfaction with the search results and the travel plan they had made.

After the experiments, we calculated the Cronbach's α for the four negative emotions, three self-efficacy items, and three optimism items; the three scales' respective values of 0.794, 0.860, and 0.924 meet the requirements for reliability.

DATA ANALYSIS AND RESULTS

Characteristics of Affective Load

The mean values of the four negative affects measured before and after each collaborative search were calculated for the 96 total searches of the 16 pair-groups.

As Figure 1 shows, both before and after retrieval, levels of irritation were highest, followed in turn by anxiety, frustration, and rage. Using the paired-samples T test, no significant differences were found between users' perception of negative affects before and after searching.

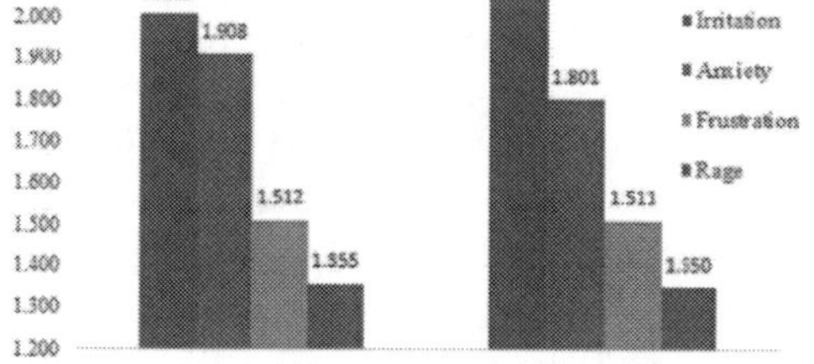

Figure 1. Changes in the degree of users' negative affects before and after searching.

We then analyzed the correlations between the four negative emotions, finding significant positive correlations between all four negative emotions perceived by users both before and after searching, as shown in Table 1. This indicates consistency in all four emotions.

Affective Load		Anxiety	Frustration	Rage
Before search	Irritation	.627**	.406**	.416**
	Anxiety	—	.561**	.459**
	Frustration	—	—	.796**
After search	Irritation	.473**	.398**	.492**
	Anxiety	—	.607**	.491**
	Frustration	—	—	.764**

Note: **: p<0.01

Table 1. Correlation analysis between four negative emotions before and after searching.

Effects of Perceived Task Difficulty on Affective Load

This section presents statistical analysis of ANOVA to detect significant differences in four negative emotions among different perceived task difficulty after searching. Perceived task difficulty was measured on a 5-point Likert scale, and we classified scores of 1 and 2 to indicate simple tasks, 4 to indicate medium difficulty, and 4 and 5 to indicate difficult tasks. As Table 2 shows, the higher the participants' perceived task difficulty, the higher their irritation, anxiety and frustration (all significant).

Task difficulty		Irritation	Anxiety	Frustration	Rage
After search	Simple (N=31)	1.480	1.642	1.287	1.222
	Medium difficulty (N=50)	2.167	1.789	1.522	1.357
	Difficult (N=15)	2.554	2.858	1.947	1.621
	F values	6.737	10.704	4.200	1.979
	P values	.002**	.000**	.018*	.144

Note: **: p<0.01; *: p<0.05

Table 2. Effects of perceived task difficulty on four negative emotions.

Effects of Time Pressure on Affective Load

ALT indicates that AL increases with time pressure. Time pressure is defined as "Expected Length-Felt Length" (Nahl, 2004). Expected length is measured at the beginning of the search and felt length is measured at the end of the task. If the difference in AL is positive, the participant's time pressure is classified as "low" If the difference in AL is zero, the participant's time pressure is classified as "medium" Otherwise, the participant's time pressure is classified as "high" which means that they spent much more time on the task than they had anticipated.

Using ANOVA, Table 3 reveals that time pressure had significant differences on anxiety, frustration and rage. When users felt that task completion took much longer time than they had expected, they reported feeling higher anxiety, frustration and rage.

Time pressure	Irritation	Anxiety	Frustration	Rage
Low (N=41)	2.097	1.842	1.319	1.181
Medium (N=30)	1.667	1.652	1.385	1.307
High (N=25)	2.262	2.324	1.982	1.697
F values	2.337	3.696	7.640	5.596
P values	.102	.029*	.001**	.005*

Note: **: p<0.01; *: p<0.05

Table 3. Effects of time pressure on four negative emotions.

Relationship between Self-efficacy, Optimism, and Post-task Affective Load

Correlation analysis between pre-task self-efficacy and the four post-task emotions is reported in Table 4. We found that the higher the user's perceived search success, the belief that they can become good at current task, and the luck in searching, the lower their anxiety, frustration, and rage. However, only the correlation between luck and frustration is significant negative ($r = -.234$, $p < .05$). The correlation analysis between pre-task optimism and the four post-task emotions is shown in Table 5. It indicates that the higher the user's search motivation, the lower their frustration, and rage (all significant).

Self-efficacy	Irritation	Anxiety	Frustration	Rage
How sure are you that you will succeed in this task?	.162	-.068	-.127	-.014
How likely is it that you will become good at this type of task?	.070	-.087	-.138	-.075
How much luck do you have in searching in comparison to other types of tasks?	-.015	-.181	-.234*	-.162

Note: *: p<0.05

Table 4. Correlation analysis between pre-task self-efficacy and four post-task emotions.

Optimism	Irritation	Anxiety	Frustration	Rage
How motivated are you to keep on trying today until you succeed?	-.026	-.137	-.252*	-.236*
To what extent do you believe that computers and search engines make it easy for people to find what they are looking for?	-.012	-.165	-.124	-.121
How likely is it that there will be something specific on what you are looking for?	.034	-.101	-.157	-.191

Note: **: p<0.01; *: p<0.05

Table 5. Correlation analysis between pre-task optimism and four post-task emotions.

Regarding users' satisfaction with the collaborative search results and their collaboration outcomes (i.e., travel plans), we found these two forms of satisfaction to be significantly positively correlated (r=0.560, p < =.01). As Table 6 shows, we also found that the higher each form of satisfaction, the lower users' anxiety, frustration, and rage.

Pearson Correlation	Irritation	Anxiety	Frustration	Rage
Satisfaction with collaborative search results	-.031	-.298**	-.296**	-.211*
Satisfaction with travel plans	-.098	-.241*	-.372**	.374**

Note: **: $p<0.01$; *: $p<0.05$

Table 6. Correlation analysis between post-task satisfaction and four post-task emotions.

DISCUSSION

The foregoing analysis demonstrates that the strongest affect both before and after the search task were irritation, followed by anxiety, frustration, and rage. These four negative emotions are almost all significantly positively correlated with one another. They are also related to the user's perception of task difficulty, self-efficacy, optimism, and satisfaction with the collaborative search results and collaboration outcomes.

Regarding negative affects after retrieval, the more difficult the user perceives the task to have been, the higher their irritation, anxiety and frustration. This finding is consistent with those of previous studies (e.g., Nahl, 2005). This study measured time pressure based on the degree of difference between the user's expected time and felt time of completing each task. When the user feels time pressure, their perception of anxiety, frustration and rage is stronger. On self-efficacy and optimism, we found that pre-task self-efficacy and optimism are not so helpful to decrease users' negative effects, differing from those of Nahl (2005). Although self-efficacy is regarded to be a strong motivational factor that could influence both users' cognitive and affective attributes Savolainen, 2012, it might not be as sufficient in explaining search behavior in collaborative settings. Users' affects are also influenced by the collaborative attributes (e.g., users' collaborative ability, partner's information literacy). Thus, it seems that users' coping skills in ALT need to involve more attributes in addition to self-efficacy and optimism. Nevertheless, we found another similar finding with previous study (Nahl, 2005) that the user's satisfaction with the collaborative search results and with the completed travel plan helps to alleviate negative effects, especially anxiety, frustration and rage.

This study strengthens the application of ALT in collaborative settings. It also provides a reference for further enhancing the affective support function of information retrieval systems. From the perspective of assisting individual retrieval, strengthening the system's context-sensitivity and intelligent pre-judgment and intervention can enable the provision of emotional support at the appropriate time. Meanwhile, for collaborative retrieval, the retrieval system can enhance interaction between team members through cross-device resource sharing and task collaboration (Morris & Horvitz, 2007), enabling users to receive more affective support. This will not only facilitate the achievement of high-quality collaborative results but also enhance users' affective experience.

CONCLUSION

This study employed ALT to empirically study the negative affective characteristics of individual users in a collaborative search context. We recruited 32 individuals and divided them into 16 pair-groups. Via Coagmento, they collaborated on three search tasks for making travel plans. The findings indicate how users' AL is related to task difficulty, time pressure, self-efficacy, and optimism. We found that users' AL was positively correlated with task difficulty and time pressure. The user's sense of retrieval success, self-perceived luck, satisfaction with collaborative search results, and satisfaction with collaborative task outcomes contributed limitedly to reducing negative effects.

The study's main shortcoming is that it only examines the impact of basic factors such as task and time on AL. Future studies should explore more issues such as the effects of team members' collaboration ability on AL, the relationship between collaborative behavior and AF, the difference of members' AL within the same group, need to be further explored. In addition, the findings need to be tested on a larger sample set to improve the universality of the findings.

REFERENCES

Byström, K., & Järvelin, K. (1995). Task complexity affects information seeking and use. *Information Processing & Management*, *31*(2), 191–213.

González-Ibáñez, R., Shah, C., & Córdova-Rubio, N. (2011). Smile! Studying expressivity of happiness as a synergic factor in collaborative information seeking. *Proceedings of the American Society for Information Science and Technology*, *48*(1), 1–10.

González-Ibáñez, R., & Shah, C. (2012). Investigating positive and negative effects in collaborative information seeking: A pilot study report. *Proceedings of the American Society for Information Science and Technology*, *49* (1), 1–4.

Mohammad Arif, A. S., Du, J. T., & Lee, I. (2015). Understanding tourists' collaborative information retrieval behavior to inform design. *Journal of the Association for Information Science and Technology*, *66*(11), 2285–2303.

Morris, M. R., & Horvitz, E. (2007). SearchTogether: An interface for collaborative web search. In *Proceedings of the 20th Annual ACM Symposium on User Interface Software and Technology* (pp. 3–12). ACM.

Nahl, D. (2004). Measuring the affective information environment of web searchers. *Proceedings of the American Society for Information Science and Technology*, *41*(1), 191–197.

Nahl, D. (2005). Affective and cognitive information behavior: Interaction effects in Internet use. *Proceedings of the American Society for Information Science and Technology, 42*(1).

Nahl, D. (2010). Affective load and engagement in Second Life: Experiencing urgent, persistent, and long-term information needs. *International Journal of Virtual and Personal Learning Environments (IJVPLE), 1*(3), 1–16.

Savolainen, R. (2012). Elaborating the motivational attributes of information need and uncertainty. *Information Research, 17*(2), 516.

Shah, C. (2014). Collaborative information seeking. *Journal of the Association for Information Science and Technology, 65*(2), 215–236.

González-Ibáñez, R. I., & Shah, C. (2010). Group's affective relevance: A proposal for studying affective relevance in collaborative information seeking. In *Proceedings of the 16th ACM international conference on Supporting group work* (pp. 317–318). ACM.

Thatcher, A., Vasconcelos, A. C., & Ellis, D. (2015). An investigation into the impact of information behaviour on information failure: The Fukushima Daiichi nuclear power disaster. *International Journal of Information Management, 35*(1), 57–63.

Yuan, H., & Zhao, Y. (2015). Tasks perception and emotional states of users in collaborative information retrieval behavior. *Library and information service, 59*(17), 89–98.

Everyday Life Information-Seeking Behaviors of Nomadic Pastoralists in Their Oral Culture

Hamid R. Jamali
Charles Sturt University, Wagga Wagga, Australia
h.jamali@gmail.com

Fariborz Foroutan
Ahvaz Branch, Islamic Azad University, Ahvaz, Iran
fariborz_foroutan@yahoo.com

ABSTRACT

Nomadic pastoralists, due to their lifestyle and the dominance of oral culture, have not received much attention from information service providers and little is known about their information behavior. This qualitative ethnographic study entailed twenty semi-structured interviews with Iranian Bakhtiari nomadic pastoralists using everyday life information seeking (ELIS) framework. Nomadic pastoralists' ELIS is dominated by reliance on human information sources including elders, chiefs (Khans) and family members. Most of their information needs relate to practical issues of daily life (e.g., animal husbandry, handicraft, and parenting) and therefore they prefer information sources that tap into their local and indigenous knowledge (e.g., elders) and value experience and skill over formal education when obtaining information from people. However, they purify their local knowledge through exposure to modern education. Relevance to daily life matters or practicality, previous successful utilization of information, and accessibility are among the factors they consider when choosing information sources.

KEYWORDS

Everyday Life Information Seeking; Information Needs; Information Sources; Information Use; Information Behavior; Trust; Nomads; Nomadic Pastoralists; Bakhtiari Tribe; Iran

ASIS&T THESAURUS

Information Behavior; Information Use; Human Information Resources

INTRODUCTION

Although information services focus primarily on recorded information and a lot of research related to information needs and behavior has focused on user groups that do not merely rely on oral communication, there are still groups of people around the world whose main means of communication and access to information are oral communication and word of mouth. Bakhtiari people (see Beck, 1991) in southwestern Iran are a group of people that include nomadic pastoralists. They migrate between summer quarters and winter quarters every year with their livestock. As a result, they do not settle in a single location as villagers do, and a part of their life is spent on the move each year. Nomadic people account for about 1.7 % of the Iranian population and they play a key role in the economy through livestock production. However, limited information services are provided for this part of the population and very little is known about their information needs and behavior.

Despite the rich information behavior literature, generally, there is not much research on the nomadic people. There is also a gap in our knowledge on the information behavior in communities with oral culture. Oral culture does not exclusively exist in remote rural areas; it can also exist in the heart of western societies, for instance, Somali women refugees in London (Olden, 1999).

In the case of nomadic people in Iran, there have been only two studies about them in the field of library and information science. One was a survey of nomadic students' information needs that showed the students mostly wanted print material, especially books and they needed cultural and health-related and non-educational books (Dehpadekani & Pourhamidi, 2011). The other study on the information needs of nomadic women showed that nomadic women had difficulties accessing health and educational information and that they usually needed health information to help their families have a healthy life. Radio was the only medium they used (Mohammadi, Sapidnameh, & Ebadallah-Amoghin, 2016).

Two other studies on nomads include a study that showed the effectiveness of camel mobile libraries for Kenyan pastoralists (Atuti, 1999), and another study that revealed how Ghanaian tribal leaders disseminated information in their oral culture and verified information by cross-checking with multiple sources (Buadi & Dzandza, 2015).

Given the lack of knowledge we have about everyday life information seeking (ELIS) (Savolainen, 1995) of nomadic people, this study investigate ELIS of Bakhtiari nomadic pastoralists and this short paper reports some of the findings related to their information needs, information sources and trust in information sources.

82nd Annual Meeting of the Association for Information Science & Technology | Melbourne, Australia | 19–23 October, 2019

DOI: 10.1002/pra2.00043

METHODOLOGY

This qualitative research used an ethnographic approach and entailed twenty face-to-face semi-structured interviews. Participants were 20 years old or above as the focus was people who were mature and independent and had some family/social responsibilities. Participants were from Babadi subdivision of Bakhtiari tribe in Lali area (southwest of Iran on the slopes of the Zagros mountain range). Participation in the study was voluntary. The research used a purposive sample to increase the diversity of the participants in terms of gender, age and social responsibilities. Participants included 13 male and 7 female; 15 married and 5 single; 5 illiterate, 6 with high school diploma, and one with an undergraduate degree.

Interviews were conducted by the second author who is originally from the Babadi tribe and can speak and understand the local dialect, which made it easier for the participants to communicate their experience. The interviews that continued until the point of theoretical saturation, included questions about participants' ELIS including their information needs, information seeking and sources of information, and trust in information sources.

The interviews were digitally recorded and transcribed verbatim. Thematic coding was used for the analysis without a formal pre-existing coding schema.

RESULTS AND DISCUSSION

Information Needs

The participants' ELIS was driven by information needs that could be categorized into seven major categories including: religious (e.g., burial rituals); political (e.g., voting times, their representative in parliament), health (e.g., illness of family members), parenting or child rearing (e.g., children's education), handicraft (e.g., weaving rugs or Kilim), economic (e.g., banking, cashing checks after selling livestock), and pastoralism and animal husbandry (e.g., right times for moving herds, cattle diseases).

Besides the desire to fill the gap in personal knowledge, there were a few triggers for these information needs as revealed from the interviews when the participants talked about their motivation for looking for information. They included improving the quality of life of themselves and their family (something also noted in the study by Mohammadi et al. (2016)), avoiding financial loss (e.g., through losing livestock to disease) and increasing income (e.g., by knowing which animal breed is more productive or favored in the market). The information needs and the motivation for looking for information show that information needs of nomadic people originate from very practical day-to-day living issues.

Sources of Information

In their ELIS, the participants almost exclusively relied on oral information and human information sources for the information they needed. Their sources of information included Khans or chiefs, elders, local officials, school teachers, technicians and experts of local public services, past personal experiences, educated members of the extended family, neighbors, and radio.

Apart from radio, which usually has a local station in each Iranian province that broadcasts programs related to the issues concerning local people, usually in local dialects, all other information sources in the list above are human information sources. A previous study (Mohammadi et al., 2016) also showed that the only medium used by nomadic pastoralists was radio. One should note that radio has no role in active information seeking and people passively receive information from the radio, which they might or might not need at the time.

Neighbors are not just those who live nearby, but also means the neighboring tribes. One participant said that "*when I have sick livestock I would check with the tribe in the neighborhood to see if the same disease is present in their livestock and what they have done about it.*"

School teachers are not usually local and are sent on a mission by the Education Ministry and are therefore seen as a source of information for certain issues. If they come from cities then they might know, for instance, more about banking than local nomadic people do. One participant stated "*I needed a loan to buy some sheep and increase my livestock. I asked the school teacher where to go and what to do and he gave me some instructions and I was able to expand my cattle.*" Participants relied on oral information even when they referred to local officials for information.

The reliance on the oral culture among nomadic people, even in the modern world, can be attributed to a number of reasons. In addition to low levels of education and literacy due to the lack of educational facilities and centers available to them, factors such as difficult roads that make access to the outside world difficult and the lack of electricity to use modern communication channels have contributed to this issue. Even mobile phones are not reliable as service might not be available when the tribe is moving through difficult roads on the mountains. Moreover, teaching information literacy in an oral culture requires different approaches to those used in the current formal education (Raseroka, 2006). Therefore, it is not surprising that little transition towards using modern media has occurred in this community.

Reliance on the oral culture goes hand in hand with the heavy reliance on the local and indigenous knowledge among nomadic people. As a result, the information sources such as chiefs, elders, family members, neighbors and past personal experiences play significant roles in meeting their information needs. Elders in oral cultures are usually considered as holders of knowledge and the local knowledge is considered as living knowledge (Whap, 2001). Local knowledge is specifically used for needs such as:

- Animal husbandry (e.g., knowing different types of weeds and plants for feeding animals);
- Handicraft (e.g., weaving techniques);
- Housework and production (e.g., producing dairy products, baking);
- Folk music and literature (e.g., music is used in all social ceremonies);
- Astronomy and astrology (e.g., for moving purposes, or knowing good and bad days for certain rituals);
- Traditional medicine and local medicinal plants;
- Genealogy, which is very important in tribal structure and drives how a tribe is subdivided.

Nomadic people take a few factors into account when choosing an information source to use. These factors are: credibility of the source; trustworthiness of the source; relevance of the information to daily life matters or practicality of information; successful application of the information in the past; timeliness of the information; and accessibility of the source.

For instance, participants trusted and used the radio for it belongs to the government and the perception was that it would not present false information. A mother-in-law or a grandmother would be considered trustworthy for her honesty and reliability. As mentioned above, the information needs of nomadic people are tied to their daily practical issues and therefore, a source of information is used if it can offer information that is perceived very relevant to the daily life matters of people. Another interesting factor in choosing and using information sources was if the information offered by that source has been successfully utilized in the past. If an elder's health advice was useful and worked in previous consultations, one might seek her advice again. Timeliness of information was another factor and finally, accessibility and ease of access played a role in using sources of information. This was particularly mentioned in the case of elders and chiefs (Khans) as they are always available to their community and people can access them for information when needed. In the case of an urgent need for access to information, elders and chiefs are usually the first source of information that nomadic people try to use. Some of the abovementioned factors (e.g., trustworthiness, timeliness and accessibility) have been found to be important in all kinds of contexts (e.g., Leckie, Pettigrew, & Sylvain, 1996; Lee, Shin, & An, 2018). However, the practicality of information and successful past utilization seem to be specific to the lives of nomadic people and similar contexts.

Trust in Information Sources

An interesting aspect of the nomadic people's ELIS is the trust mechanism. They used three main methods for verifying the information before using it and to establish trust in the information they wanted to use. While the first method is about the source of information, the other two methods deal with the information itself.

In the first method, users evaluate the source of information against a set of criteria that they consider critical for having trust in a person for his or her information. These included age, experience, and social reputation. Elders, chiefs and people who are well known for being skilled in certain tasks were trusted this way.

In the second method, users checked the validity of the information against their own prior knowledge and past personal experiences to see if the information made sense to them and was aligned with their previous experiences. This, of course, has the risk of suffering from cognitive biases such as "belief bias" (Cavojova, 2015) which means one might be influenced by one's knowledge about the world in evaluating information and accepting it.

In the third method, the information obtained was checked against another source to find out if the new source confirmed the information already obtained. This method includes, for instance, asking a second person. Cross-checking with multiple information sources was also used in the oral culture of Ghana (Buadi & Dzandza, 2015). Traditionally age is very important in nomadic culture for the social status of people. However, the older generation is not very educated while some of the younger people have a good level of education including, for instance, a higher education degree. This raises the question of what a person would do in cases when there are disagreements between two sources of information, an elder and a young educated person. Participants' answers to this question included a few strategies, and it appeared that in such cases, depending on the nature of the information and the context, different actions might be taken. However, overall the majority of participants were inclined to favor age and experience over formal education during their cross-validation of information. They tended to act based on the information obtained from an older or more experienced person rather than a young person who had a higher level of formal education. The reason participants expressed for this preference was that their information needs, as explained above, are mostly related to the practical aspects of daily life and they believe knowledge that accumulates through practice (in the case of elders and experienced people) is more relevant and valuable than what is taught at schools and universities. Generally, in Iran, the education system is known to be focused mainly on theory and lacks practical aspects. The following quotation from a participant is a good example of this perception. In this quote, the participant refers to the content of formal education as information that originates from cities, which is in a way true as the formal education is mostly oriented towards the lifestyle and needs of people living in cities.

> *"Although out of respect one should listen to what both [elder or experienced person and young educated person] have to say, and try to check with other people too, the information coming from civic societies mostly is not applicable to our nomadic life. Therefore, one should seek the advice of the elders and the experienced and skillful ones. If you have a question about how to handle livestock, you should ask a shepherd who has seen ups and downs of life"*

A positive outcome of the confrontation of the new knowledge originating from formal education and the local knowledge was the purification of the local knowledge. Local knowledge sometimes is mixed with superstition and incorrect information. Examples were given by some participants for instance about how their belief about certain traditional treatments for an illness, or the cause of a particular disease in livestock were incorrect. Exposure of some of the nomadic people to formal education and especially higher education has led some nomadic people to realize that not all of the local knowledge is correct. This happens through the cross-checking process and adverse outcomes of the utilization of some of the local knowledge. Past research has shown that indigenous knowledge, especially in the area of health, might include belief in supernatural causes (Maher, 1999). However, empirical validity of indigenous knowledge is something that is open to debate (Horsthemke, 2004).

CONCLUSION

The contribution of this study is in understanding the ELIS of an understudied community where oral culture is dominant and the use of human information sources who hold local knowledge is significant. In their ELIS, nomadic pastoralists of Bakhtiari tribe rely heavily on people within their community to meet their information needs. Their information needs are of a very practical nature related to their daily life and they usually find the information obtained through formal education to be inapplicable to their way of life. Therefore, they prefer their source of information to be experienced and knowledgeable in the context of their lifestyle rather than being formally educated. However, exposure to formal education sometimes helps them to purify their local knowledge by identifying incorrect information. Future studies should further investigate the confrontation of local knowledge with formal education in order to better understand what validation process is used and in what situations the knowledge originating from the modern education is accepted over local knowledge by nomadic pastoralists. Cross-checking with a second person is a common way of verifying information and trusting the source of information among Bakhtiri people. Besides trustworthiness, they want the information to be relevant to their daily life issues and prefer sources whose information has been successfully utilized in the past.

The government has done little to provide access to information for nomadic people. Improving access to telecommunications, radio programs tailored to the needs of nomadic people, mobile libraries, and especially equipping schools with reading materials would improve the access to, and use of, information among nomadic people.

ACKNOWLEDGMENTS

We thank all the participants from the Babadi subdivision of the Bakhtiari tribe in Lali who helped us in the study.

REFERENCES

Atuti, R. M. (1999). Camel library service to nomadic pastoralists: The Kenyan scenario. *IFLA Journal, 25*(3), 152–158.

Beck, L. (1991). *Nomad: A year in the life of a Qashqa'i tribesman in Iran.* University of California Press.

Buadi, D. W., & Dzandza, P. E. (2015). Information seeking behaviour of traditional leaders in the Shai Osudoku District of Ghana. *Library Review, 64*(8/9), 614–628.

Cavojova, V. (2015). Belief bias effect in reasoning of future teacher. *Social and Behavioral Sciences, 174*, 2211–2218.

Dehpadekani, H. S., & Pourhamidi, M. (2011). Investigating the information needs of nomadic students in Iran: Presenting a library service model. *IFLA Journal, 37*(3), 235–245.

Horsthemke, K. (2004). "Indigenous knowledge": Conceptions and misconceptions. *Journal of Education, 32*, 31–48.

Leckie, G. J., Pettigrew, K. E., & Sylvain, C. (1996). Modeling the information seeking of professionals: A general model derived from research on engineers, health care professionals, and lawyers. *Library Quarterly, 66*(2), 161–193.

Lee, M. A., Shin, C. N., & An, K. (2018). Trustworthiness, readability, and suitability of web-based information for stroke prevention and self-management for Korean Americans: Critical evaluation. *Interactive Journal of Medical Research, 7*(2), e10440.

Maher, P. (1999). A review of 'traditional' Aboriginal health beliefs. *Australian Journal of Rural Health, 7*(4), 229–236.

Mohammadi, M., Sapidnameh, Z., & Ebadallah-Amoghin, J. (2016). Barrasie niazhaye ettelaatie zanane ashayer koochneshin shahrestan Kohgiluyeh [Information needs of nomadic women of Kohgiluyeh city. *Human Information Interaction*, 2(4), 77–85.

Olden, A. (1999). Somali refugees in London: Oral culture in a western information environment. *Libri, 49*(4), 212–224.

Raseroka, K. (2006). *Information literacy development within oral cultures: Challenges and opportunities within a Southern African country.* In Proceedings of the 72nd International Federation of Library Associations Conference, 20-24 August 2006, Seoul, Korea.

Savolainen, R. (1995). Everyday life information seeking: Approaching information seeking in the context of "way of life". *Library & Information Science Research, 17*(3), 259–294.

Whap, G. (2001). A Torres Strait Islander perspective on the concept of Indigenous knowledge. *The Australian Journal of Indigenous Education, 29*(2), 22–29.

Empowering Citizens to Manage Their Chemical Exposures Step 1 - Identify Ingredients in Consumer Products

Jenna Kim
School of Information Sciences, University of Illinois at Urbana-Champaign, 501 E. Daniel St., Champaign, IL 61820-6211
jkim682@illinois.edu

Catherine Blake
School of Information Sciences, University of Illinois at Urbana-Champaign, 501 E. Daniel St., Champaign, IL 61820-6211
clblake@illinois.edu

Henry A. Gabb
School of Information Sciences, University of Illinois at Urbana-Champaign, 501 E. Daniel St., Champaign, IL 61820-6211
gabbiii2@illinois.edu

ABSTRACT

Our choices around consumer products directly influence our amount of chemical exposure. Although access to chemicals within individual products are available, we often use multiple products so ingredient names must be harmonized to accurately estimate cumulative exposure. We evaluated the accuracy and coverage of two strategies, PubChem and tmChem, with respect to a database of 55K products. More than half of the ingredients identified by PubChem were specific chemical names (55%), followed by natural or artificial colors (20%) and plants or plant derivatives (13%). The majority of ingredients identified by tmChem were chemical names (83.9%). Only 1,696 of the 8,247 (20.56%) were identified by both systems. Although tmChem had better coverage, ~70% of ingredients identified by tmChem need further work to align with a specific chemical. Both strategies are needed to provide an accurate, personalized, and cumulative measure of chemical exposure.

KEYWORDS

Chemical Entity Recognition; Knowledge Representation

ASIS&T THESAURUS

Information; Representations; Chemical Information

INTRODUCTION

In addition to making choices about diet and exercise, citizens make choices every day about their personal chemical exposure from the consumer products they use. The increased attention given to chemicals can be seen in updated product labeling where companies advertise that certain chemicals are not in their products. Similarly, retailors have introduced their own labeling such "Clean at Sephora" that is "… made without the ingredients you told us you'd most like to avoid." Citizens can access online information about chemicals within consumer products from Skin Deep (www.ewg.org/skindeep) and Work-group for Safe Products (www.safemarkets.org/ toxic-chemicals-in-products) that show ingredients from a variety of products, and in some cases provide hazard scores that evaluate products with respect to cancer, developmental and reproductive toxicity, allergies and immunotoxicity, and use restrictions.

Despite increased access to chemicals within a given product we often use more than one product in our personal care regimes such as a shampoo, conditioner, toothpaste, and deodorant. It is very difficult for a consumer to obtain a cumulative total for all their products when different manufacturers use different terms to refer to the same ingredient (synonymy) and the same term to refer to different ingredients (polysemy). These problems of synonymy and polysemy are key problems in the information sciences.

Given the long history of chemical nomenclature, you might assume that there exists an unambiguous list of chemical names that manufacturers could be encouraged to use; however, we provide two examples that highlight the challenges in unifying ingredient names. Methyl ether and dimethyl ether represent the same chemical even though these names could be misinterpreted as ether compounds with either one or two methyl groups. Someone with knowledge of organic chemistry understands why these names are synonyms in spite of the missing "di" prefix on methyl ether. By definition, an ether compound has two attached functional groups. Methyl ether would not be an ether compound without the second methyl group, so its presence is implied. The "di" prefix is simply dropped for convenience. PubChem lists over 400 synonyms for dimethyl ether, e.g., dimethylether, methylether, methyl ether, wood ether, methoxy-methane, methoxy methane, and methoxy-methane (the IUPAC systematic name). Chemists recognize the names in this truncated list as synonyms. For example, "wood" sometimes denotes methyl and methoxymethane is simply derived from a different naming scheme. Chemists perform this reasoning automatically and with certainty. Do the spaces matter (e.g., methylether vs. methyl ether)? Is the dash important (e.g., methoxy-methane vs. methoxymethane)? Without knowing the answers to these questions, non-chemists may conservatively treat these synonyms as different chemicals. Even the UMLS (Unified Medical Language System) treats methyl ether and dimethyl ether as different concepts

82nd Annual Meeting of the Association for Information Science & Technology | Melbourne, Australia | 19–23 October, 2019

DOI: 10.1002/pra2.00072

and although a relationship is captured, the UMLS assigns "relationship other" rather than a synonymous relationship.

The second example considers an analysis of consumer products, where the compound bucinal was listed as one of 55 endocrine disruptors and/or asthma-related chemicals (Dodson et al., 2012). Bucinal was identified as a synthetic fragrance but no other information was given. Searching for "bucinal" in the comprehensive chemical naming resources PubChem, ChemIDplus, ChEBI (Degtyarenko et al., 2007), and ChemSpider (www.chemspider.com) returned no matching compounds. Likewise, the UMLS Metathesaurus Browser returned no matching concepts. A PubMed search returned no articles with bucinal in the title or abstract. A Google search returned references to p–t-bucinal but no other identifying information like a molecular formula or Chemical Abstracts Service Registry Number (CAS-RN), and searching PubChem and UMLS for "p–t-bucinal" did not find any matches. Only the SciFinder Substance Identifier recognized bucinal and returned a CAS-RN (80-54-6) and a list of chemical synonyms including p-tert-butyl-α-methylhydrocinnamaldehyde and lilial. Either of these synonyms is readily matched in PubChem, ChemIDplus, UMLS, ChemSpider, or PubMed. Apparently, bucinal is an obscure synonym of a common fragrance chemical. This example illustrates that despite concerted efforts to establish comprehensive dictionaries of chemical names that obtaining complete coverage remains elusive.

The goal of this paper is to measure the utility of two automated approaches to identify and harmonize ingredient names listed in consumer products that were sold on a drug store website as an important step toward empowering citizens to manage their chemical exposures. The first strategy uses a dictionary of chemical synonyms which are aligned with ingredients (see Strategy 1). The second strategy leverages a long-standing tradition in chemistry nomenclature that dates back to 1782 when Louis-Bernard Guyton de Morveau proposed standards for naming inorganic chemicals. Since then International Union of Pure and Applied Chemistry (IUPAC) publishes naming standards for different chemicals including the Red Book for inorganic chemicals and the Blue Book for organic compounds (see Strategy 2). We applied each strategy to 55K consumer products containing about 2.4M ingredients (approximately 40K distinct ingredients) and then manually assessed the coverage and accuracy of the ingredients identified by each approach. Lastly, we characterize the types of ingredients that produce errors.

RELATED WORK

In addition to the public facing free resources mentioned in the introduction section, a database of consumer product ingredients was constructed by extracting data from the Material Safety Data Sheets (MSDS, (Goldsmith et al., 2014)). The database contains 1,797 unique chemicals from 8,921 products; however, MSDS are only required to include known toxicants so ingredients that have either unknown or limited evidence concerning toxicity may not be included.

From a text mining perspective, identifying chemicals is problematic because punctuation usage (in particular commas, hyphens, and brackets) in chemical names differs from punctuation usage in natural language. In addition, the standard IUPAC naming conventions are not uniformly employed in text. For this reason, several efforts have been underway to provide standardized corpora for testing. For example, the CHEMDNER corpus contains 10 K abstracts that have been manually annotated with trivial chemical names (30.36%) systematic names (22.69%), chemical abbreviations (15.55%), chemical formulas (14.26%) and chemical families (14.15%), along with chemical identifiers (2.16%) and text that captures more than one type of chemical entity (0.70%) (Krallinger et al., 2015). Table 1 summarizes how well some systems identify the entities in the CHEMDNER corpus.

Model	Precision	Recall	F1
ChemDataExtractor	89.1	86.6	87.8
tmChem	89.2	85.8	87.4
LeadMine	88.7	85.1	86.9
Chemspot	91.2	82.3	86.7
Becas	86.5	85.7	86.1
Banner-CHEMDNER	88.7	81.2	84.8

Table 1. Performance (%) of systems developed to identify chemical entities in the CHEMDNER corpus (modified from (Korvigo, Holmatov, Zaikovskii, & Skoblov, 2018)).

MATERIALS AND METHODS

Our approach is to first identify a large set of ingredients from consumer products and then to compare and contrast two strategies with respect to accuracy and coverage. The first strategy uses a dictionary approach that has the advantage of harmonizing the chemicals. The second strategy leverages both a dictionary approach and surface level characteristics of words that better recognize chemicals, but such an approach may not be able to unify the chemical name identified with other representations of the same concept. The same dataset of ingredient strings were used with each strategy and by focusing on where the approaches differ we can better identify strengths and weaknesses of each approach.

Consumer Products

This study uses a consumer product database that was collected from the online retailer, Drugstore.com (since acquired by Walgreens), in compliance with the site's terms of service and robot exclusion protocols, as described in (Gabb & Blake, 2016). After removal of duplicates (e.g., the same product retrieved from different branches of the retail hierarchy or different sizes of the same product) and products that do not typically provide an ingredient list (e.g., vinyl shower curtains, plastic storage containers, toothbrushes, makeup brushes), the final sample contained 55,209 unique products.

The ingredient lists from these products were converted to lowercase and parsed to remove extraneous (non-ingredient) text such as "may contain" or "certified organic," resulting in comma-delimited lists of ingredient names. Parsing these lists yielded 39,149 distinct ingredient names.

Strategy 1: Dictionary Approach (aka PubChem)

PubChem was launched in 2004 as a repository of information about the biological activity of small molecules. It is hosted by the National Center for Biotechnology Information (NCBI). "The primary aim of PubChem is to provide a public on-line resource of comprehensive information on the biological activities of small molecules accessible to molecular biologists as well as computation and medicinal chemists." (Bolton, Wang, Thiessen, & Bryant, 2008, p. 218). It consists of three distinct, community-supported databases: PubChem Substance, PubChem Compound, and PubChem BioAssay. Though distinct, these databases are interlinked through substance, compound, and assay identifiers. They are also integrated with other public knowledgebases (e.g., PubMed). The PubChem databases are supported by the user community. Users contribute the data but the actual database processing is highly automated. According to (Bolton et al., 2008), there is little manual curation or central control of input by the NCBI. The community of users is responsible for ensuring accuracy.

PubChem contains "247.3 million substance descriptions, 96.5 million unique chemical structures, contributed by 629 data sources from 40 countries, chemder, UMLS" (Kim et al., 2019). PubChem is available online and via an API, but experiments in this paper were based on a February 2019 download where each synonym string was converted to lowercase and processed (see Gabb and Blake (2016)).

Strategy 2: Dictionary + nomenclature (aka tmChem)

The tmChem system is a state-of-the-art tool developed to identify chemical named entities that combines independent machine learning models based on conditional random fields (CRF) which are combined into an ensemble (Leaman, Wei, & Lu, 2015). It has a built-in lexicon of chemical entities and their names with their unique identifiers that were collected from Medical Subject Headings (MeSH) and Chemical Entities of Biological Interest (ChEBI). In addition, chemical abbreviations can be recognized. Out of the two models available for use, we report the results of Model 1 because preliminary experiments showed that it had better performance than Model 2. Model 1 extends the BANNER named entity recognizer of (Leaman & Gonzalez, 2008) to identify chemical entities. The source code for Model 1 was downloaded from the NCBI web page as described in (Leaman et al., 2015). The default tmChem parameters were used to align tmChem with the product ingredients.

Evaluation

In addition, accuracy and coverage, we used the CHEMDNER definition of chemical entities that includes trivial (i.e., common) or systematic (i.e., formal) chemical names, chemical abbreviations, chemical formulas, chemical families, and chemical identifiers to characterize where each approach has limitations. We also expect the systems to identify colorants, plants or plant derivatives, and chemical mixtures. Thus, we expect the systems to identify all ingredients that meet at least one of these eight criteria.

RESULTS

Manual Evaluation

The 100 most frequent ingredient names for PubChem-only (A), tmChem-only (B), both PubChem and tmChem (C) and neither PubChem nor tmChem (D) were manually evaluated using the evaluation criterion defined in the methods section (see Figure 1). A "perfect match" occurs when an ingredient string from one of our eight target categories is exactly the same as the system output. A "partial match" occurs when the system can identify only a subset of words in the ingredient string. For example, ethylhexyl is identified for the ingredients ethylhexyl palmitate, ethyhexyl benzoate, and ethylhexyl acrylate. The "no match" label was used for text that either did not meet the criteria in the methods section and for extraneous text such as "organic" or "sunscreen". Table 2 shows that ingredients identified by PubChem were typically an exact match, whereas many of the ingredients identified by tmChem were chemical entities, but could not be aligned to a specific chemical, thus more work would be required to harmonize those chemicals.

Category	A	B	C	D
Perfect match	100	31	83	86
Partial match	0	69	17	5
No match	0	0	0	9
Total	100	100	100	100

Table 2. Manual Evaluation of the top 100 most frequent ingredients in each set.

More than half of the ingredients identified by PubChem were specific chemical names (55%), followed by colorants (20%) and plants or plant derivatives (13%). The remaining ingredients were chemical families, chemical abbreviations, and mixtures. None of the ingredients were chemical identifiers or formulas. The majority of ingredients that appeared only in tmChem are chemical names (83.9%) with the remainder being chemical families, plants or plant derivatives, and mixtures. As expected, most of the ingredients identified by both PubChem and tmChem are chemical names (94%) (Table 3).

Characterization	A	B	C	D
Chemical name	55	84	94	19
Chemical family	5	3	4	13
Plant or plant derivative	14	7	0	45
Colorant	20	0	1	14
Chemical abbrev iation	5	0	1	14
Chemical mixture	2	7	1	10

Table 3. Characterization of perfect match ingredient names. Categories are not mutually exclusive.

Among the ingredients that were not identified by either strategy, most were plants or plant derivatives (44.6%)

chemical names (18.5%), and colorants (14.2%), followed by chemical families (13%) and mixtures (9.8%). The eight categories are not mutually exclusive. For example, five ingredients in A were chemical names, abbreviations, families and colors and two ingredients were both chemical families and plants or plant derivatives. In D, there are seven ingredients showing overlap in the chemical families and mixtures, and nine ingredients do not fit into any of the classification groups because they are just extraneous texts in the ingredient list.

Coverage

Of the 2,439,392 total ingredient strings in the product database, PubChem identified 1,341,143 (55%) with 4,682 distinct ingredient names. The tmChem system identified 1,016,320 (42%) of the ingredients with 5,261 distinct strings (see Figure 1). Overall, 56.7% of the ingredients (1,383,123) were identified by either approach and 43.3% (1,056,269) were not recognized. Using both approaches resulted in 8,247 unique ingredient strings.

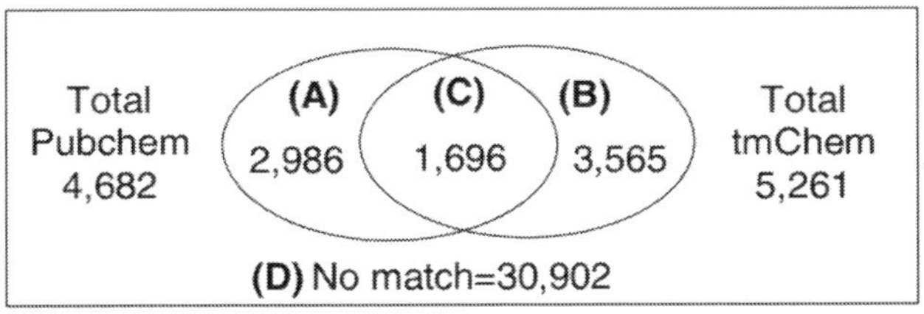

Figure 1. Coverage of the Pubchem and tmChem Approaches.

The dictionary + nomenclature approach (strategy 2) identified a greater proportion of unique ingredients than the dictionary approach (13.4% vs 12.0%). Although the proportion of both approaches may appear to be low, this reflects that many consumer product ingredients are not chemicals per se. For example, rose oil is a complex mixture, not a specific chemical. It is worth noting that the U.S. Food and Drug Administration (FDA) requires that manufacturers list ingredients in descending order of predominance. However, they are not required to list proprietary flavor/fragrance mixtures or trade secrets. Generic fragrance and flavor designations on product labels can hide many chemicals (Steinemann et al., 2011, 2015). In our consumer product database, fragrance was the second most common ingredient, second only to water.

Interestingly there was little redundancy in these two approaches where only 1,696 of the 8,247 (20.56%) chemicals identified were captured by both approaches (see Figure 1) that suggests multiple strategies are required to achieve the best coverage and accuracy.

Of the 100 most frequent ingredient strings that were not matched by either PubChem or tmChem, 79% were plants or plant derivatives, chemical names, families, colorants or mixtures. This suggest that more work is needed to ensure that chemical ingredients in consumer products are accurately detected. Neither tool was specifically designed to detect plants and plant derivatives so other approaches should be explored for those ingredients such as tools from the NCBI bioportal where there are now 13 plant ontologies.

CONCLUSION

Our findings show that neither PubChem nor tmChem provide complete and accurate coverage of chemical ingredients in consumer products. The biggest difference between these approaches is that ~70% of ingredient strings identified by tmChem do not align to a specific chemical. However, all of those chemical strings were missed by PubChem.

Both strategies should be employed, to maximize coverage which would account for 57.7% of all the ingredients using 8,247 distinct ingredient strings. More than half of the ingredients listed in consumer products are chemicals and further work is required to obtain better coverage for ingredients that are plants and plant derivatives.

The paper provides an automated approach to identify and harmonize chemicals from multiple consumer products that is critical to obtain an accurate, personalized, and cumulative measure of individual exposure. Such unification provides a critical first step in empowering citizens to make informed decisions about how their choices concerning consumer products impact their personal cumulative chemical exposure.

REFERENCES

Bolton, E. E., Wang, Y., Thiessen, P. A., & Bryant, S. H. (2008). Pubchem: Integrated platform of small molecules and biological activities. *Annual Reports in Computational Chemistry, 4*, 217–241.

Degtyarenko, K., De Matos, P., Ennis, M., Hastings, J., Zbinden, M., McNaught, A., … Ashburner, M. (2007). Chebi: A database and ontology for chemical entities of biological interest. *Nucleic Acids Research, 36*(suppl 1), D344–D350.

Dodson, R. E., Nishioka, M., Standley, L. J., Perovich, L. J., Brody, J. G., & Rudel, R. A. (2012). Endocrine disruptors and asthma-associated chemicals in consumer products. *Environmental Health perspectives, 120*(7), 935–943.

Gabb, H. A., & Blake, C. (2016). An informatics approach to evaluating combined chemical exposures from consumer products: A case study of asthma-associated chemicals and potential endocrine disruptors. *Journal Environmental Health Perspectives, 124*(8), 1155–1165.

Kim, S., Chen, J., Cheng, T., Gindulyte, A., He, J., He, S., & Bolton, E. E. (2019). Pubchem 2019 update: Improved access to chemical data. *Nucleic Acids Research, 47*(D1), D1102–D1109. https://doi.org/10.1093/nar/gky1033

Korvigo, I., Holmatov, M., Zaikovskii, A., & Skoblov, M. (2018). Putting hands to rest: Efficient deep cnn-rnn architecture for chemical named entity recognition with no hand-crafted rules. *J Cheminform*, *10*(1), 28. https://doi.org/10.1186/s13321-018-0280-0

Krallinger, M., Rabal, O., Leitner, F., Vazquez, M., Salgado, D., Lu, Z., & Valencia, A. (2015). The chemdner corpus of chemicals and drugs and its annotation principles. *J Cheminform*, *7*(suppl 1) Text mining for chemistry and the CHEMDNER track), S2. https://doi.org/10.1186/1758-2946-7-S1-S2

Leaman, R., & Gonzalez, G. (2008). Banner: An executable survey of advances in biomedical named entity recognition. *Pacific Symposium on Biocomputing*, 652–663.

Leaman, R., Wei, C. H., & Lu, Z. (2015). Tmchem: A high performance approach for chemical named entity recognition and normalization. *J Cheminform*, *7*(suppl 1), S3.

Objectives & Key Results for Active Knowledge Sharing in IT Consulting Enterprises: A Feasibility Study

Natthakan Klanwaree
Technopreneurship and Innovation Management Program Chulalongkorn University, Bangkok, Thailand
natthakan.klanwaree@gmail.com

Songphan Choemprayong
Department of Library Science, Faculty of Arts, Chulalongkorn University, Bangkok, Thailand
songphan.c@chula.ac.th

ABSTRACT

Objectives and Key Results (OKRs) have been utilized by numerous leading global enterprises for performance evaluation from a holistic perspective. Nonetheless, the applicability of OKRs for knowledge sharing has been rarely discussed. This paper aims to investigate the feasibility of the adoption of OKRs for active knowledge sharing in IT consulting organizations. As a case study, this project was conducted at an IT consulting organization in Bangkok, Thailand among thirty-three participants involved in a training session. Some of these participants volunteered to develop their team's OKRs. All participants were interviewed regarding the possibility of adopting OKRs for knowledge sharing based on Technology Acceptance Model (TAM). In general, participants tended to have positive perceptions regarding usefulness, ease of use, trust, and intention to use with some concerns surrounding compatibility with staff who lack creative and leadership personalities. The current study has shed some light on how OKRs may be adopted to support knowledge sharing within organizations.

KEYWORDS

Knowledge Sharing; Active Knowledge; Objectives and Key Results; OKRs; Consulting Enterprise

ASIS&T THESAURUS

Knowledge Management, Organizational Culture, Strategic Planning, Consultants, Information Technology Professionals

INTRODUCTION

Inefficient knowledge sharing contributes to productivity reduction, delayed product/service delivery, and frustration among employees. According to the results of one survey, most employees of large companies in the US feel that knowledge preservation and sharing is critical to organization success, but more than half have difficulty obtaining information essential to their jobs from their peers. (Panopto, 2018)

82nd Annual Meeting of the Association for Information Science & Technology | Melbourne, Australia | 19–23 October, 2019

DOI: 10.1002/pra2.00044

Despite the need for such cooperation, motivating employees to share knowledge is one of the grand challenges of knowledge management within organizations. Scholars from various disciplines have been attempting to discern influencing factors as well as develop interventions for stimulating knowledge sharing. (for instance, van den Hooff & de Ridder, 2004; Lin, 2007; Lam & Lambermont-Ford, 2010) A large body of literature concerns the influence of human resource development practices on knowledge sharing (e.g., Gagné, 2009). Performance and compensation systems seem to be, in particular, most commonly discussed. (e.g., Wang, Noe, & Wang, 2014).

A number of performance measurements have been utilized to promote knowledge sharing within organizations. (e.g., Dickel & de Moura, 2016; Minonne & Turner, 2009) These methods have been criticized for the difficulties they present in implementation (e.g., del-Rey-Chamorro, Roy, van Wegen, & Steele, 2003).

As an alternative measurement, Objectives and Key Results (OKRs) have been developed and utilized by numerous well-known global enterprises. This approach has been widely discussed in the media and scholarly communities (e.g., Steiber & Alänge, 2013; Yarow, 2014). OKRs aim to balance top-down and bottom-up approaches by encouraging clear communication, engagement, agility, and transparency as well as by allowing creative and visionary thinking. (Niven & Lamorte, 2016)

Niven and Lamorte (2016, p. 30) assert that OKRs should focus on peculiar issues encountered by the organization. This approach must be used to maximize cross-functional collaboration in which each team's objectives are aligned (2016, p. 7). Moreover, it should adhere to company strategy as such strategy is focused on the customer's point of view (2016, p. 57). They should also consider a dynamic and fluid approach that would help companies handle continuous changes (2016, p. 152).

Effective knowledge management can be considered key for information technology (IT) consulting businesses as these companies rely heavily on active knowledge and hands-on experience. Even more, an on-going consulting project involving staff from multiple teams demands a great deal of constant, active communication and clear direction. The nature of this business is, furthermore, customer-oriented, and the context is fast-changing. Thus, the approach of OKR seems promising in terms of supporting active knowledge sharing in these firms. Nonetheless, relevant literature on OKRs for active knowledge sharing remains scarce, particularly in the context of IT consulting businesses. The objective of this study is to examine the possibility of using OKRs to promote active knowledge sharing in IT consulting organizations.

RELATED LITERATURE

This section reports related studies on the adoption of OKRs for knowledge management and previous studies on roles of TAM in performance evaluation related to KM.

OKRs for Knowledge Management

While there are a number of studies on the adoption of OKRs, KM and/or knowledge sharing are included as part of an overall scheme in only a small number of papers.

Based on the OKRs approach, Steiber and Alänge (2013) reported Google's innovativeness in describing elements essential to each innovative rank. KM aspects are included in certain innovative ranks. For example, securing knowledge transfer is an attribute of the "leaders as facilitators" rank. Organizational learning also plays a critical role for virtual cross-functional or cross-product teams in facilitating knowledge exchange in order to reach the upper-level ranks. However, Steiber and Alänge (2013) did not address details on evaluation methods.

Lyle and Boulapha (2011) adopted the OKRs model to create a development plan for the Nam Ngum Basin in Indonesia. Knowledge management and research is considered here to lend itself well to capacity building. This work, nonetheless, does not address the feasibility or evaluation of the utilization of that plan.

Roles of TAM in Performance Evaluation Adoption

Developed by Davis, Bagozzi, and Warshaw (1989), the Technology Acceptance Model (TAM) is one of the most well-known models for measuring the adoption of technology. The original factors in the TAM model include perceived usefulness, perceived ease-of-use, and attitudes toward usage. Later, the model was further developed to include various additional factors, for instance, personal belief, perceived trust, and perceived compatibility (e.g., Ng, Shroff, & Lim, 2013).

TAM has been used to measure the possibility of adoption of knowledge management activities and tools. For instance, Money and Turner (2004) investigated the use of TAM to evaluate user acceptance of KM systems, finding that perceived usefulness, perceived ease-of-use, and behavioral intention each have a significant positive relationship with actual system usage. Another study conducted by Hwang, Lin, and Shin (2018) adapted TAM to evaluate knowledge system commitment and knowledge sharing intention. They introduced specific factors for such constructs including reasoned action and behavioral intention to share knowledge.

METHODS

The current study adopts a participatory single-case study approach (Choemprayong & Wildemuth, 2017) to gain a well-rounded, natural perspective on this phenomenon. A medium-size IT consulting company in Bangkok, Thailand was selected as a study site. With approximately 150 staff members, the company serves both local and international clients. Currently the company uses only KPIs to monitor knowledge acquisition following completion of a project. Thirty-three participants from four teams, including customer support, production and development, sales, and administration, were recruited to participate in the study. As well, participants were from various management levels including team managers, mid-level supervisors, senior consultants, and consultants.

Conducted between March and June 2019, the study protocol includes three stages including (1) OKRs training, (2) creating and reviewing objective and key results, and (3) collecting and analyzing interview data.

To begin, all participants attended training sessions on OKRs. Topics discussed included basic understanding of OKRs, rationales for choosing OKRs for active knowledge sharing, expectations of OKRs, and success stories from other organizations.

Participants were, then, asked to voluntarily develop OKRs related to active knowledge sharing for their teams. Three representatives from the customer support team and two from production and development team obliged by holding brainstorming sessions. Participants were asked to collectively review the company's vision, missions, and strategies before developing the OKRs. The outputs were, then, reviewed by the top-level manager of each team.

Lastly, all participants, after reviewing the prototype OKRs, were then interviewed using a semi-structured interview technique. The interviews were conducted face-to-face for participants located at the headquarters and via telephone for those working at client sites. The interview guidelines and data analysis were based on the six factors of TAM framework, including perceived usefulness, perceived ease of use, attitude toward using, behavioral intention, perceived trust and perceived compatibility. All interviews were partially transcribed. The data was, then, analyzed according to the deductive thematic analysis approach.

RESULTS

The results are divided into two sections. The first section gives the OKRs developed at the selected IT consulting company. The second section reports participants' responses on the feasibility of adopting OKRs for active knowledge sharing.

OKRs for Active Knowledge Sharing

Followings are the OKRs developed and reviewed by the team managers.

OKRs from the customer support team

Objective: To productively create knowledge assets to be used within the company.

Key Results:

1. Maintenance of manpower utilization rates of between 80% and 90% (Threshold Target Metrix)
2. Increase of 10% in resolved cases by service level agreement (Positive Metrix)
3. Delivery of first customer-inquiry responses by the milestone deadline (Baseline)

OKRs from the production and development team

Objective: To create practical knowledge assets.

Key Results:

1. Decrease of 10% in problematic cases from customer support team (Negative Metrix)
2. Decrease of 10% in time spent on knowledge transfer (Negative Metrix)
3. Requirement that at least 90% of new joiners pass job probation within the first 5 months (Baseline)

Feasibility of OKRs Adoption

Below are the responses from the participants regarding the possibility of adopting OKRs for knowledge sharing.

Perceived Usefulness

The participants addressed how OKRs may help remind the employees that the documents they are going to share need to be aligned with the objectives and that their activities will influence the pursuit of the key results. One participant commented that OKRs would help staff to envision the big picture and how their work is directly relevant to the company.

Moreover, one of the participants highlighted that OKRs allow employees to be creative and adopt a trial-and-error approach to achieving key results in an innovative manner.

> *I was taught that, to be successful, you may have to first fail several times. The more you fail, the closer you are to be successful. The idea of OKRs is reminiscent of this.* (Participant A)

Perceived Ease of Use

Due to an informal culture which fosters openness and promotes the flow of ideas and creativity, OKRs were perceived as easy to understand and use. However, a few participants expressed concern that using OKRs may make it difficult for management to monitor and control their subordinates and ensure productivity. Even if they were able to achieve the key results, employees may not work in compliance with company policy and regulations or may work beyond their responsibilities. Additionally, new employees may lack clear directions regarding their duties. During the development stage, one participant addressed the difficulty in expressing the desired objective, while key results are perceived to be easy to develop as they are based on day-to-day operations.

Attitudes Toward Using OKRs

All participants provided positive responses regarding their attitudes toward using OKRs. One participant said that OKRs made them feel a sense of belonging to the company. Another said they would share their knowledge of OKRs with other staff members in the company as well. One participant associated OKRs with morality.

> *I feel like I am a better person when using OKRs. There is a sense of connection to others and this could encourage everyone to support each other to achieve the team objective.* (Participant B)

Nonetheless, many participants said that employees, especially newcomers, may get lost along the way and, subsequently, fail to achieve the desired results.

Behavioral Intention

All participants said they would adopt OKRs as a performance evaluation of active knowledge sharing if the company allows provided that they remained confident that solutions could be found in effort alongside their team members when issues arose. The majority of the participants said that the implementation of OKRs should begin in their teams.

Several participants said that they would like to use OKRs as a framework while also keeping the current KPIs to give certain directions to team members. A couple of participants from the production and development team observed that OKRs are aligned with customer requirements. Some said they would introduce OKRs to their peers who did not participate in this study.

Perceived Trust

Many participants stated that they trust that OKRs can promote active knowledge sharing in their company given that the approach is result-oriented and quality-focused. They believe that sharing knowledge will lead to desired results, and many of the participants seemed confident in the outcomes of OKRs, particularly when compared with outcomes of the existing evaluation method.

Perceived Compatibility

All participants perceived that OKRs are compatible within their organization's culture. One of the participants asserted that OKRs would be especially useful in situations in which the company aims to foster a sense of acceptability of failure. Some observed that OKRs may only be applicable to teams with an informal culture and they may not work well among teams with a more formal working style that governs employees with a set of rules and regulations.

Additionally, they were also found to be suitable to the personalities of the employees (i.e., being active, enthusiastic, adventurous, and creative). The participants addressed that OKRs are suitable for employees who are confident, visionary, forward thinking, and unafraid of failure. One participant pointed out that OKRs would be appropriate for staff members who tend to plan before taking action.

DISCUSSION

The current study explores the possibility of developing and adopting OKRs for active knowledge sharing in an IT consulting enterprise. In general, the responses were quite positive in all TAM dimensions except that of ease of implementation regarding which certain caveats were raised as to compatibility with organization culture and staff personality.

Participants addressed the particular suitability of OKRs for visionary, forward-thinking employees as well as the ways in which this approach allows for greater creativity among employees. Participants also perceived that OKRs could promote awareness of the connection between employee activities and the achievement of key results and how their work is directly relevant to the company. These results are confirmed against those of by Niven and Lamorte (2016) and Yarow (2014).

While OKRs were perceived in a positive light, perceptions of current KM practice in the company seemed to play an important role. Participants tended to compare OKRs with the current single KPI on KM and referred to many KM issues they have experienced. For example, they reported that the documents shared are not of good quality and are not ready to use. A great deal of time and effort was then spent in seeking and locating the appropriate documents. It would be interesting to validate the results with organizations satisfied with their current use of KPIs for KM.

ACKNOWLEDGMENTS

The author would like to thank all participants in this study. This paper is also partially supported by the Arc of Memory Research Unit and the Behavioral Research and Informatics in Social Science Research Unit at Chulalongkorn University.

REFERENCES

Choemprayong, S., & Wildemuth, B. (2017). Case studies. In B. Wildemuth, *Applications of social research methods to questions in information and library science* (2nd ed., pp. 51–59). Westport, CT: Libraries Unlimited.

Davis, F. D., Bagozzi, R. P., & Warshaw, P. R. (1989). User acceptance of computer technology: A comparison of two theoretical models. *Management Science*, *35*(8), 982–1003.

del-Rey-Chamorro, F. M., Roy, R., van Wegen, B., & Steele, A. (2003). A framework to create key performance indicators for knowledge management solutions. *Journal of Knowledge Management*, *7*(2), 46–62.

Dickel, D. G., & de Moura, G. L. (2016). Organizational performance evaluation in intangible criteria: A model based on knowledge management and innovation management. *RAI Revista de Administração e Inovação*, *13*(3), 211–220.

Gagné, M. (2009). A model of knowledge-sharing motivation. *Human Resource Management*, *48*, 571–589.

Hwang, Y., Lin, H., & Shin, D. (2018). Knowledge system commitment and knowledge sharing intention: The role of personal information management motivation. *International Journal of Information Management*, *39*, 220–227.

Lam, A., & Lambermont-Ford, J. P. (2010). Knowledge sharing in organisational contexts: A motivation-based perspective. *Journal of Knowledge Management*, *14*(1), 51–66.

Lin, H. F. (2007). Effects of extrinsic and intrinsic motivation on employee knowledge sharing intentions. *Journal of Information Science*, *33*(2), 135–149.

Lyle, C., & Boulapha, C. (2011). *Scenario-based development planning for the Nam Ngum Basin*. Solo, Indonesia: Center for River Basin Organizations and Management.

Minonne, C., & Turner, G. (2009). Evaluating knowledge management performance. *Electronic Journal of Knowledge Management*, *7*(5), 583–592.

Money, W., & Turner, A. (2004). Application of the technology acceptance model to a knowledge management system. In R. H. Sprague, Jr., *Proceedings of the 37th Annual Hawaii International Conference on System Sciences* (pp. 1–9). Big Island, HI: IEEE Computer Society.

Ng, E. M., Shroff, R., & Lim, C. (2013). Applying a modified technology acceptance model to qualitatively analyse the factors affecting e-portfolio implementation for student teachers' in field experience placements. In Proceedings of the Informing Science and Information Technology Education Conference (pp. 355–365).

Niven, P. R., & Lamorte, B. (2016). *Objectives and key results: Driving focus, alignment, and engagement with OKRs*. Hoboken: John Wiley & Sons.

Panopto. (2018). Workplace knowledge and productivity report. Retrieved from https://www.panopto.com/everyday-expertise/

Steiber, A., & Alänge, S. (2013). A corporate system for continuous innovation: The case of Google Inc. *European Journal of Innovation Management*, *16*(2), 243–264.

van den Hooff, B., & de Ridder, J. A. (2004). Knowledge sharing in context: The influence of organizational commitment, communication climate and CMC use on knowledge sharing. *Journal of Knowledge Management*, *8*(6), 117–130.

Wang, S., Noe, R. A., & Wang, Z. M. (2014). Motivating knowledge sharing in knowledge management systems: A quasi–field experiment. *Journal of Management*, *40*(4), 978–1009.

Yarow, Y. (2014). This is the internal grading system google uses for its employees — and you should use it too. Business Insider. Retrieved from https://www.businessinsider.com/googles-ranking-system-okr-2014-1

One of a Kind: The Tail of Citizen Science Volunteers

Lo Lee
University of Illinois at Urbana-Champaign,
Champaign, USA
lolee2@illinois.edu

Peter Darch
University of Illinois at Urbana-Champaign,
Champaign, USA
ptdarch@illinois.edu

ABSTRACT

Online citizen science projects recruit members of the public (*volunteers*) to contribute to scientific research. Many projects involve volunteers donating processing capacity on their computers to process datasets. Retaining and motivating volunteers is a critical challenge. Existing studies of volunteers identify categories of volunteers, describing the main motivations and contributions of these categories. Based on case studies comprising surveys (n = 2031) and interviews (n = 39) with volunteers in two projects, Einstein@Home and Cosmology@ Home, we identify volunteers who do not fit easily into these categories. These volunteers exhibit non-typical motivations (e.g., getting acknowledgements in scientific publications, and accumulating Gridcoin) or non-typical contributions (e.g., successfully proposing new lines of work or projects, and conducting and presenting studies of subgroups of volunteers to teams running projects). These volunteers make vital contributions to projects. However, measures taken by project teams based on prior studies of volunteers may be ineffective in retaining and motivating these non-typical volunteers.

KEYWORDS

Astronomy; Citizen Science; Scientific Data; Volunteer Computing

ASIS&T THESAURUS

Astronomy; Big Data; Citizens

INTRODUCTION

Many scientific disciplines are becoming increasingly data-intensive. Some researchers have outsourced data collection and analysis tasks to members of the public, or volunteers, via online citizen science projects. Researchers in a range of disciplines, such as astronomy and bioinformatics, have successfully applied this methodology (Franzoni & Sauermann 2014).

For researchers who design and run these projects, motivating and retaining volunteers remain critical challenges (Raddick et al., 2013). Studies of these projects generally consider volunteers as a single group or identify specific categories of volunteers (Curtis, 2018a; Darch & Carusi, 2010; Nov, Arazy, & Anderson, 2014). Although these studies offer useful insights, classifying volunteers into a small number of groups can obscure the full range of motivations and abilities that can be found, and leveraged, in a project's volunteer community. Recommendations for practice drawn from these studies may be ineffective in retaining or motivating volunteers who do not easily fit into existing categories.

This paper presents case studies of two citizen science projects to argue that the heterogeneity of volunteers is a vital resource for citizen science projects. We identify volunteers whose motivations or behavior in projects mean they do not fit easily into any typology. We refer to these project participants as being in the *tail of citizen science volunteers*. We borrow the term *tail* from statistics, where it refers to the portion of a probability distribution a long way from its mode(s): events in the tail are expected to occur only very rarely. These volunteers can make vital, yet often unusual, contributions to projects. They exhibit a range of motivations and make use of a diverse range of skills.

LITERATURE REVIEW

To frame the discussion of volunteers, we briefly present an overview of online citizen science. Then, we discuss studies of volunteers, and how these studies are used to inform recommendations for practice.

Online Citizen Science

Online citizen science comprises a range of projects that differ considerably in terms of the tasks required of volunteers (Franzoni & Sauermann, 2014). Projects vary according to the amount of discretion afforded to volunteers in completing project tasks. In some cases, volunteers work on discrete, short tasks in a way rigidly defined by the project (*well-structured* tasks). Other projects involve tasks that are not well-defined by the project leadership. Given profound organizational and epistemological differences between types of projects, this paper focuses on those involving well-structured tasks.

Many of these projects use BOINC (the Berkeley Open Infrastructure for Network Computing), a piece of middleware that supports 49 other projects, as of April 2019 ("BOINCstats," 2019). BOINC provides projects with infrastructure for a website, containing forums where volunteers communicate

82nd Annual Meeting of the Association for Information Science & Technology | Melbourne, Australia | 19–23 October, 2019

DOI: 10.1002/pra2.00045

with each other, and news pages or blogs where project scientists give feedback on the project's progress. BOINC projects also include statistics systems that award credits to volunteers according to the quantity of processing performed by a volunteer's computer, and a table ranking volunteers according to their accumulated credits. Volunteers can also form teams, with a table ranking teams by their aggregated credits. Volunteer teams often have their own webpages and forums.

Volunteer Management: Motivations and Contributions

Projects face many challenges in achieving their goals. Some challenges are technological and are addressed elsewhere (Ivashko & Golovin, 2015). Other challenges are social, e.g., motivating volunteers to complete projects' scientific work (Curtis, 2018b).

Choices taken by teams who run projects about what policies and features to implement in their projects play a critical role in volunteer management. Different methods for recognizing volunteer contributions and reporting project progress can incentivize different types of volunteer behavior and contributions (Darch, 2014).

Many studies focus on what motivates volunteers to contribute to the core scientific task of a project. Some studies treat a project's volunteers as a single population. The most common motivations among volunteers as whole include contributing to science, learning about science, enhancing a volunteer's reputation within a project, and competing against other volunteers (e.g., ranking systems) (Nov et al., 2014).

Other studies identify different categories of volunteers, according to the nature of their contribution to projects, and ascertain the primary motivations for members of each category. Some studies categorize volunteers according to how they contribute directly to a project's core scientific tasks. One key category is the *overclocker*, identified by Curtis (2018b), who modifies their hardware to process large quantities of project data (see also Darch and Carusi (2010)). Overclockers are vital for a project because they complete a substantial portion of its work. They also share expertise with other volunteers on project forums. Overclockers are motivated by the prospect of contributing to science, learning about hardware, and sharing this knowledge with others.

Another important category of volunteers is those who join teams. Volunteer teams account for substantial portions of projects' overall work. Team members are motivated by a mix of competition with other teams and cooperation within their own team (Holohan, 2013).

Additional categories of volunteers prove valuable to projects in ways other than by directly contributing to the project's scientific tasks. One such category is those volunteers who share knowledge with other volunteers in forums, motivated by social interaction, enjoyment of project website features, and helping the project (Luczak-Roesch et al., 2014). Some contributors become forum moderators, motivated by enhanced social status (Holohan, 2013).

A final category of volunteers comprises those invited by project teams to test new features of projects before they are launched to the public (Curtis, 2018a; Darch & Carusi, 2010). The most common motivation identified among this group, the *alpha-* or *beta-testers*, is the status they derive from being part of a small group where membership is by invitation only.

Research Questions

Some studies identify common motivations among volunteers as a whole. Other studies categorize volunteers according to their contributions, with each category characterized by their most common motivations. Resulting recommendations for practice thus often focus on reinforcing the most common motivations of the volunteers who make a standard range of contributions.

Volunteers who are non-typical, or even unique, in terms of motivations or contributions may still be valuable to citizen science projects. This paper addresses the following research questions:

- What motivations do citizen science volunteers hold beyond those that are already well-characterized?
- What contributions do citizen science volunteers make beyond those that are already well-characterized?
- How are volunteers who hold non-standard motivations or make non-standard contributions valuable to citizen science projects?

CASE STUDY AND METHODS

We answer our research questions through case studies of two BOINC citizen science projects, Cosmology@Home and Einstein@Home ("Cosmology@Home," 2019; "Einstein @Home," 2019). Launched in 2007, Cosmology@Home has recruited over 74,000 volunteers (as of April 2019), with approximately 4,000 active at any one time. Einstein@Home has recruited over 460,000 volunteers (as of April 2019) since 2005, with approximately 19,000 active at any one time ("BOINCstats," 2019). Volunteer contributions to both projects have formed the basis of multiple peer-reviewed journals in physics and astronomy.

We employed online ethnographic methods (Hine, 2008). Methods comprised a short answer survey (n = 2,031), semi-structured interviews over Skype or instant messaging (n = 39), and observation of project forums.

We recruited participants via posts on the projects' forums. Survey questions covered topics such as length of participation and interactions with scientists and other volunteers. These survey responses enabled us to identify volunteers exhibiting non-typical motivations and/or making non-typical contributions to the projects. We selected 39 individuals, a mix of typical and non-typical volunteers, for follow-up interviews. Interviews lasted 30–45 min. Transcripts were coded iteratively using techniques informed by grounded theory (Glaser & Strauss, 1967).

FINDINGS

This section presents the profiles of three users. Each profile describes a real volunteer, identified by a pseudonym. Each volunteer, when compared to other volunteers we studied, makes distinctive yet highly valuable contributions to their project or is motivated by non-typical factors.

Juan

Juan has been involved in BOINC projects, including Einstein@Home, for more than 3 years and makes a range of contributions. First, he is a member of a volunteer team that is currently one of the top 10 in Einstein@Home rankings, and he actively advises teammates when they run into problems. However, it is his other contribution that is unique. Juan participated in the annual BOINC workshop. These workshops involve BOINC software developers. Juan was the only volunteer (of over 2,500,000 volunteers at the time) who attended the workshop. At the workshop, he made two presentations. One presentation involved leveraging his professional expertise to outline a proposed sub-project. As he said, BOINC developers responded well to his proposal:

> *"Because I'm a research scientist for the moment and occasionally I have research problems that need a lot of computational power, and because I'm familiar with the volunteer computing and I know several people, [...] I just asked them if they would like to do a sub-project out of this problem, and then they said yes."*

The other presentation gave an overview of the characteristics of BOINC volunteers in the same country as Juan. Through his team and forum activities, Juan has learned a great deal about behavior of these volunteers. In this way, Juan acts as a bridge between BOINC's developers (based mainly in the USA and Europe) and a large group of volunteers in a different country.

Joshua

Joshua, an Einstein@Home participant, has let BOINC run on his computer for more than 3 years and has also been involved in several other BOINC projects. Joshua is pursuing his doctoral degree in physics. At first, Joshua was motivated to improve his credits, so he started to run BOINC on multiple devices. However, after a few years, he stopped following the ranking tables because he could not compete with the highest-ranked volunteers:

> *"When I started the project, I remembered I was quite eager to get positions in rankings, and everything was installed in my computers in my house. But then I saw that some people, they got really, really more serious, so I couldn't really follow them just with a computer at home. [...] Today I don't really follow it anymore. I just leave the system running in the background of my computer."*

Today, he is motivated by the prospect of being mentioned by name in publications emanating from the project. Joshua enjoys reading Einstein@Home's publications and follows the project's Twitter account for announcements of new papers. Joshua is the only volunteer interviewed who expressed appreciation for the open availability of project publications. Joshua hopes 1 day to be mentioned in a paper, explaining, *"I definitely would like to make a contribution to see my name on one of the papers, or to find something that scientists could use for the future."*

Patty

Patty's primary motivation for participating in Cosmology@Home is accumulating gridcoins. Gridcoin is a cryptocurrency that serves as an electronic transaction method distributed to BOINC volunteers based on the amount of processing they contribute to projects. Patty joined Cosmology@Home because *"it gives out decent amount of credits."* Patty talks with other volunteers interested in accumulating gridcoins via multiple online forums. Volunteers motivated by gridcoins have formed a volunteer team, ranked number one in several BOINC projects, including Einstein@Home and Cosmology@Home. This team's contributions to Einstein@Home represents over 5% of all work completed by project volunteers.

DISCUSSION

The *Tail of Citizen Science Volunteers*

Studies of citizen science volunteers tend either to treat volunteers as a single population or to segment volunteers into categories. The volunteers discussed here do not fit into these existing categories. Juan, Joshua, and Patty either exhibit motivations or make contributions that are non-typical both for a project's volunteer population as a whole, and the categories of volunteers discussed elsewhere.

We refer to these participants as being in *the tail of citizen science volunteers*. Recommendations for practice derived from existing studies of citizen science projects have not been formulated with participants in the tail of citizen science volunteers in mind. Hence, these recommendations may be unsuited to, or even alienating for, them.

Typical motivation, non-typical contribution

Juan exhibits motivations commonly held by other volunteers, such as an interest in science and a desire to help advance science (Raddick et al., 2013). Some of his contributions are similar to those made by members of subgroups in categories identified in other studies, e.g., fostering a cooperative atmosphere in his volunteer team (Holohan, 2013), and helping other volunteers on forums (Luczak-Roesch et al., 2014).

However, Juan is unusual in interacting face-to-face with BOINC developers. Given BOINC projects have recruited over 4.6 million volunteers and at most a few have attended the annual BOINC workshop, our finding Juan is akin to locating a needle in a haystack. By relying on existing typologies and recommendations for practice, projects risk losing a valuable volunteer such as Juan.

Non-typical motivation, typical contribution

Both Joshua and Patty make contributions that are typical of volunteers, but their motivations are not typical. In common with the overclockers discussed by Curtis (2018b), Joshua has invested in hardware to contribute a substantial amount of processing. However, as Joshua is motivated by a mention or acknowledgment in published papers, he exhibits different motivations to those identified as typical for overclockers. Consequently, recommendations derived from these existing studies may not cultivate an important volunteer like Joshua.

Patty also makes substantial contributions to the core scientific work of the project, in this case via participation in a volunteer team. However, unlike the team members discussed by Holohan (2013), Patty's primary motivation is accumulating gridcoins. To date, other studies have not considered financial motivations as influential factors in citizen science participation. Actions taken by projects to motivate volunteers based on assumptions volunteers are motivated solely by non-financial motivations will do little to retain the involvement of Patty.

Unlike Juan and Joshua, Patty is likely an exemplar of a larger type of volunteers. However, volunteers motivated by accumulating gridcoins have not yet shown up in other studies of citizen science participants. This absence may be because this type of volunteer is still emergent in BOINC projects, or because the notion of making financial gain is so anathema to the concept of voluntarism that those studying citizen science have implicitly or explicitly not identified volunteers like Patty as a separate category.

CONCLUSION AND FUTURE WORK

Volunteers are crucial for citizen science projects. While prior studies provide typologies explaining contributions and motivations of typical volunteers, they have largely ignored non-typical volunteers, i.e., those in the tail of citizen science volunteers. Ignoring these volunteers means their contributions may be neglected and even jeopardized. Our study demonstrates the vital roles these volunteers can play in citizen science projects. We continue to analyze our survey and interview data to identify more volunteers in the tail and to characterize their motivations and contributions more sharply.

Project teams should learn what their research partners are thinking and engage them more effectively. A deeper and more holistic understanding of volunteers by citizen science projects will enhance these projects' abilities to make striking scientific discoveries in the future. We are continuing to develop recommendations for practice to help projects retain and motivate volunteers in the tail of citizen science volunteers.

ACKNOWLEDGMENTS

We would like to greatly thank Einstein@Home and Cosmology@home scientists and engineers for taking their time to speak with us. We are also deeply grateful to volunteers in these two projects for spending their time taking the survey and sharing their stories during interviews.

REFERENCES

BOINCstats. (2019). Retrieved from https://boincstats.com/en

Cosmology@Home. (2019). Retrieved from https://boinc.berkeley.edu/wiki/Cosmology@Home

Curtis, V. (2018a). *Online citizen science and the widening of academia*. https://doi.org/10.1007/978-3-319-77664-4

Curtis, V. (2018b). Patterns of participation and motivation in Folding@home: The contribution of hardware enthusiasts and overclockers. *Citizen Science: Theory and Practice*, *3*(1), 5. https://doi.org/10.5334/cstp.109

Darch, P. T. (2014). Managing the public to manage data: Citizen science and astronomy. *International Journal of Digital Curation*, *9*(1), 25–40.

Darch, P. T., & Carusi, A. (2010). Retaining volunteers in volunteer computing projects. *Philosophical Transactions of the Royal Society A: Mathematical, Physical and Engineering Sciences*, *368*(1926), 4177–4192.

Einstein@Home. (2019). Retrieved from https://einsteinathome.org/

Franzoni, C., & Sauermann, H. (2014). Crowd science: The organization of scientific research in open collaborative projects. *Research Policy*, *43*(1), 1–20.

Glaser, B. G., & Strauss, A. L. (1967). The discovery of grounded theory: Strategies for qualitative research. In *Observations*. Chicago: Aldine Pub. Co.

Hine, C. (2008). Virtual ethnography: Modes, varieties, affordances. *The SAGE Handbook of Online Research Methods*, 257–270.

Holohan, A. (2013). Community, competition and citizen science: Voluntary distributed computing in a globalized world. Retrieved from http://books.google.com/books?hl=en&lr=&id=UvpLJR6XSqUC&oi=fnd&pg=PP7&ots=uJlXAsCGit&sig=K26pKbuXyojsj2oudFFpN546ehg

Ivashko, E., & Golovin, A. (2015). Partition algorithm for association rules mining in BOINC–based enterprise desktop grid. International Conference on Parallel Computing Technologies (pp. 268–272). Springer.

Luczak-Roesch, M., Tinati, R., Simperl, E., Van Kleek, M., Shadbolt, N., & Simpson, R. (2014). Why won't aliens talk to us? Content and community dynamics in online citizen science. Retrieved from http://eprints.soton.ac.uk/363523/

Nov, O., Arazy, O., & Anderson, D. (2014). Scientists@ Home: What drives the quantity and quality of online citizen science participation? *PLoS One*, *9*(4), e90375.

Raddick, M. J., Bracey, G., Gay, P. L., Lintott, C. J., Cardamone, C., Murray, P., … Vandenberg, J. (2013). Galaxy Zoo: Motivations of citizen scientists. *Astronomy Education Review*, *12*(1), 010106.

Lack of the Normative Lens: Discussions on Research on Micro-Targeted Ads Explanation of Facebook

Yuanye Ma
University of North Carolina at Chapel Hill,
Chapel Hill, USA
yuanye1@live.unc.edu

ABSTRACT

This paper observes that studies on the explanation of recommender systems lack a *normative lens*. Specifically, it uses Facebook's micro-targeted advertisement explanations as a case for discussion, and shows how research mostly take a *descriptive* lens and focus on answering the what and how questions while the normative questions concerning how things should be are under explored. The paper argues that the normative and descriptive lenses are interdependent, and the lack of the normative lens contributes to inconsistent research suggestions. Explicitly putting on a normative lens is how researchers could avoid potential conflict among multiple normative goals.

KEYWORDS

Micro-Targeted Ads; Recommender System Explanation; Information Ethics

ASIS&T THESAURUS

Information Science; Research and Analytic Methods

INTRODUCTION

Information ethics makes a distinction between "the descriptive" and "the normative" (Capurro, 2008; Tavani, 2008), where "the normative refers to guidelines or norms, and normative assertions rest upon ethical commitments and behaviors to be prized, preferred, and valued; they are often called ought statements; on the other hand, … descriptive studies attempt to explain what is rather than what ought to be" (Smith, Dinev, & Xu, 2011, p.991). The normative and descriptive dichotomy can be useful to map out the researching of a topic. For instance, in the research of privacy, "descriptive privacy" concerns the status of privacy "as a matter of fact" (Mizutani, Dorsey, & Moor, 2004, p.121), while "normative privacy" concerns expectations a society holds regardless of the actual situation of privacy. The lack of descriptive privacy does not indicate the lack of normative privacy, and the study of the descriptive aspect cannot substitute the normative. In this paper, descriptive questions are about the current status of micro-targeted ads explanations, or the *what* and *how* questions; while normative questions are interested in the desired state of micro-targeted ads explanations, or how things should be and why. This paper leverages the descriptive and the normative framework to reflect on the current research of micro-targeted ads explanations of Facebook, and argues that research lacks a normative lens.

This paper is structured as follows: it starts with an introduction of micro-targeted ads explanations and the broader topic of recommender system explanation. Ting Fung Then, it moves on to discuss how current research takes mostly a descriptive perspective, and the lack of a normative lens not only renders research inadequate in dealing with the incompatibility between/among multiple goals of explanation (Tintarev & Masthoff, 2012), but also contributes to inconsistent suggestions. The paper then proposes two specific ways that future research could leverage to add the normative lens.

MICRO-TARGETED ADS & RECOMMENDER SYSTEM EXPLANATIONS

In recent years, a number of studies have looked into how Facebook provides explanations to its users regarding the micro-targeted advertisements. These ads appear just like the user's Facebook friend's updates and are called "micro-targeted ads" (Korolova, 2011), or "behavioral targeting" (Lee, Hosanagar, & Nair, 2018), or "personalized ads" (Tran, 2017). In 2014, Facebook started to provide explanations to its users regarding these ads. Micro-targeted ads have been drawing attention from information researchers because they differ from traditional ads placement in that they are constructed using a multitude of personal information provided by the social network site users, which could spark ethical concerns including privacy invasion (Ur, Leon, Cranor, Shay, & Wang, 2012). Facebook started to offer explanations about its micro-targeted advertisements in hopes that they would return a sense of control to users. Specifically, the explanatory information is provided through an additional information panel right next to the ad and is labeled "Why am I seeing this?" (Wasserman, 2014). Facebook has been updating this ads explanation feature; the most recent update in February 2019 claimed to reveal more information about the means by which a brand is distributing the ad (Hutchinson, 2019).

82nd Annual Meeting of the Association for Information Science & Technology | Melbourne, Australia | 19–23 October, 2019

DOI: 10.1002/pra2.00074

Providing explanations to help users gain some understandings about the inner workings of a complex information system is not new. Research on the explanation of recommender systems has attracted lot of attention in recent years (Nunes & Jannach, 2017). Explanations of a recommender system can be constructed for various purposes: to justify the recommendations (Bobadilla, Ortega, Hernando, & Gutiérrez, 2013), to inspire trust (Pu & Chen, 2007), to provide information for evaluation (Cleger, Fernández-Luna, & Huete, 2014). Despite the abundance of recommender system explanations work, "predicting which explanation strategies are best suited for achieving which explanation objectives", in other words, what explanations ought to be like under certain circumstances, remain as open research questions (Friedrich & Zanker, 2011, p.96). The lack of normative questions in micro-targeted ads explanations perhaps is not surprising for it is situated within the broader environment where ethical questions in recommender system research are overlooked (Paraschakis, 2016; Tang & Winoto, 2016, p.112).

RESEARCH OF MICRO-TARGETED AD EXPLANATION ON FACEBOOK

Research has endeavored to shed more light into the current operational details of the Facebook's micro-targeted ads. For example, Andreou et al. (2018) identified properties that can be used to understand the explanations, and specifically proposed two sets of measures that can be used to describe how advertisers target users ("ad explanations") and how Facebook infers data about users ("data explanations"). Other studies have turned to the users as a source of insights by seeking user input on micro-targeted ads explanations (Eslami, Krishna Kumaran, Sandvig, & Karahalios, 2018; Plane, Redmiles, Mazurek, & Tschantz, 2017; Ur et al., 2012). These works inevitably touched on some normative aspects of inquiry when they asked users' opinion of how ads explanations *should be like*. However, user input in general can be inadequate for the pursuit of normative questions for two reasons: it can be self-contradictory as a result of conflicting goals, and users could simply hold wrong knowledge about the system.

First, user input can be self-contradictory. Eslami et al. (2018) suggested a more immersive/embedded way of displaying ads explanations where explanations become *"an integral or central focus of the ad"* (p.432). This suggestion was directly inspired by one of the study participants, who, when asked to create their own ad explanation, suggested embedded design. Such user input might be reasonable; however, it could be problematic to be used directly as a design solution. In this case, immersive design could be a source of conflict between/among multiple normative goals: between the user's pleasure of experience and the invasion of privacy because immersiveness could dampen people's caution towards the intrusiveness of ads (O'Brolcháin et al., 2016), and users are likely not aware of these conflicting goals or even their own internal framework they rely on for coming up with certain suggestions. Furthermore, the conflict of normative goals could be between multiple interests that users have, or between user and Facebook's benefits. Since it is Facebook who currently provides explanations; therefore, for the company's own benefit, it might want to deliver the most possible immersive experience. While for the sake of safeguarding self-reflection on the user side, an immersive design might be not as desirable. The question remains what perspective shall the researchers take, which depends on what normative lens researchers put on.

The second reason that renders users' input inadequate for normative research is that it could be *inaccurate*. Ur et al. (2012) revealed that people misunderstood the intention of online behavioral advertising icons and how advertising networks work. In a word, when research lacks an explicit normative research agenda on their own, descriptive research could be bogged down by the conflicts between multiple normative goals within and across groups of stakeholders. Adding a normative research agenda could help researchers sort through their goals and make better use of user inputs and other descriptive findings about the system.

In light of potential conflicts among multiple goals, researchers not only need to consider normative questions, but also need to be explicit in their choice of focus on certain normative goals. In the case of Facebook micro-targeted ads explanation, even if the company is genuinely interested in promoting user privacy, it needs to be balanced among other goals. Researchers as the third-party independent of the potential conflict of interests of the system (unlike the users or the system provider), they might have a better position to advocate for certain normative goals for they are less entangled by the potential conflict of interest. But first of all, researchers need to be explicit with their own normative research agenda. And by being explicit, researchers not only need to attend to the chosen normative goal, but also need to recognize the connection with other potential goals. Though a normative lens will not eliminate conflicts, it can help with that these conflicts are properly acknowledge and then managed.

Research on micro-targeted ads of Facebook has selected privacy as their normative target of study. Korolova (2011) have leveraged experimental testing to reveal the potential privacy risks within the system by looking at how Facebook's targeted advertisement can potentially be used to infer personal information. Moreover, individuals and individual household can be effectively singled out using simple manipulations within the system's setting (Faizullabhoy & Korolova, 2018). For these studies setting privacy as their normative pursuit, the question remains regarding the conflict of achieving privacy and other normative goals, because Facebook users are not only or even mainly interested in privacy (Wisniewski, Xu, Lipford, & Bello-Ogunu, 2015).

The discussion here does not intend to say existing studies are not valuable. Instead, it aims to show how existing research overall lack a normative lens despite the could be engaging with normative questions. Privacy in the above example is just one of the normative goals that micro-targeted ads explanation research could pursue, but it is definitely not the only normative goal, and research could pursue multiple normative goals simultaneously. What's needed is to put on the normative lens, *explicitly*, especially for studies interested in multiple normative goals.

ADDING THE NORMATIVE LENS

To add the normative lens, this paper suggests two ways that researchers could do so. Firstly, to start selecting normative goals for their study, or for those already with normative goals, to start with reexamining normative principles that have been taken for granted. Referring to the immersive design suggestion discussed earlier, pleasure of use and privacy risk could be two normative goals that study could further explore. For micro-targeted ads explanation studies that already have a normative goal in mind (e.g., privacy), research could continue with revealing how privacy interact with other normative goals, and how privacy is affected by various assumptions of the micro-targeted ads system, as a closer look at taken for granted ideals might reveal *unexamined assumptions* about the *"ideal's benefits"* (Ananny & Crawford, 2018, p.977).

Another way to add the normative lens is to clarify how new norms emerge and old norms evolve as both are shaped/reshaped as users interact with the technology system. Reigeluth (2017) observed that the relationship between the recommender system and its users is a *"circularity"* (p.4), in that not just the system is influencing its users, but that users are also influencing the system; new "norms" (p.4) emerge out of continuous interactions. In the case of micro-targeted ads explanation on Facebook, user interactions with the ads and ads explanations might reveal that certain groups of people have more demand for explanations than the others, which could lead to more specific normative goals for these groups of people. In addition, observation of how users interact with the recommender system could reveal new characteristics of data-human relationship that has not been captured. Andreou et al. (2018)'s finding that *"the attributes inferred about users change quite often"* (p.12) revealed potentially a new temporal aspects interaction which deserve further research both descriptively and normatively.

CONCLUSION

This paper uses micro-targeted ads explanation on Facebook as a case for discussion, and calls for adding the normative lens when studying the explanations of recommender information systems. Adopting a normative agenda could not only help resolve the inconsistent research suggestions as a result of only taking a *descriptive* approach; furthermore, *explicitly* taking up a normative lens is necessary for independent research explorations. This paper is limited in its scope and studies included are not fully representative, however, its discussions can still be illustrative in revealing the lack of normative perspective in current studies. Consider the general shortage of the exploration of ethics questions in not only micro-targeted ads but also in recommender system, it will be particularly worthwhile for future work to continue exploring in a more systematic manner recommender system explanations related ethical issues. Lastly, since conducting both the descriptive and the normative inquiries will require expertise from multiple fields including but not limited to Information Science, Computer Science, and Ethics, future research could also explore the feasibility of integrating these inquiries into one study design.

REFERENCES

Ananny, M., & Crawford, K. (2018). Seeing without knowing: Limitations of the transparency ideal and its application to algorithmic accountability. *New Media & Society*, *20*(3), 973–989. https://doi.org/10.1177/1461444816676645

Andreou, A., Venkatadri, G., Goga, O., Gummadi, K. P., Loiseau, P., & Mislove, A. (2018). Investigating ad transparency mechanisms in social media: A case study of Facebook's explanations. Retrieved from http://www.eurecom.fr/publication/5414

Bobadilla, J., Ortega, F., Hernando, A., & Gutiérrez, A. (2013). Recommender systems survey. *Knowledge-Based Systems*, *46*, 109–132. https://doi.org/10.1016/j.knosys.2013.03.012

Capurro, R. (2008). Intercultural information ethics: Foundations and applications. *Journal of Information, Communication & Ethics in Society*, *6*(2), 116–126.

Cleger, S., Fernández-Luna, J. M., & Huete, J. F. (2014). Learning from explanations in recommender systems. *Information Sciences*, *287*, 90–108. https://doi.org/10.1016/j.ins.2014.07.031

Eslami, M., Krishna Kumaran, S. R., Sandvig, C., & Karahalios, K. (2018). Communicating Algorithmic Process in Online Behavioral Advertising. In *Proceedings of the 2018 CHI conference on human factors in computing systems* (pp. 432:1–432:13). New York, NY: ACM. https://doi.org/10.1145/3173574.3174006

Faizullabhoy, I., & Korolova, A. (2018). Facebook's advertising platform: New attack vectors and the need for interventions. ArXiv:1803.10099 [Cs], Retrieved from http://arxiv.org/abs/1803.10099

Friedrich, G., & Zanker, M. (2011). A taxonomy for generating explanations in recommender systems. *AI Magazine*; La Canada, *32*(3), 90–98. https://doi.org/10.1609/aimag.v32i3.2365

Hutchinson, A. (2019). Facebook's updating it's "Why Am I Seeing This?" Ad info with more specific detail. (n.d.). Retrieved March 14, 2019, from https://www.social

mediatoday.com/news/facebooks-updating-its-why-am-i-seeing-this-ad-info-with-more-specific/547859/

Korolova, A. (2011). Privacy violations using microtargeted ads: A case study. *Journal of Privacy and Confidentiality*, *3*(1). https://doi.org/10.29012/jpc.v3i1.594

Lee, D., Hosanagar, K., & Nair, H. S. (2018). Advertising content and consumer engagement on social media: Evidence from Facebook. *Management Science*, *64* (11), 5105–5131. https://doi.org/10.1287/mnsc.2017.2902

Mizutani, M., Dorsey, J., & Moor, J. H. (2004). The Internet and Japanese conception of privacy. *Ethics and Information Technology*, *6*(2), 121–128. https://doi.org/10.1023/-B:ETIN.0000047479.12986.42

Nunes, I., & Jannach, D. (2017). A systematic review and taxonomy of explanations in decision support and recommender systems. *User Modeling and User-Adapted Interaction*, *27*(3), 393–444. https://doi.org/10.1007/s11257-017-9195-0

O'Brolcháin, F., Jacquemard, T., Monaghan, D., O'Connor, N., Novitzky, P., & Gordijn, B. (2016). The convergence of virtual reality and social networks: Threats to privacy and autonomy. *Science and Engineering Ethics*, *22*(1), 1–29. https://doi.org/10.1007/s11948-014-9621-1

Paraschakis, D. (2016). Recommender systems from an industrial and ethical perspective. In *Proceedings of the 10th ACM conference on recommender systems* (pp. 463–466). New York, NY: ACM. https://doi.org/10.1145/2959100.2959101

Plane, A. C., Redmiles, E. M., Mazurek, M. L., & Tschantz, M. C. (2017). Exploring user perceptions of discrimination in online targeted advertising. In *Proceedings of the 26th USENIX Conference on Security Symposium* (pp. 935–951). Berkeley, CA: USENIX Association Retrieved from http://dl.acm.org/citation.cfm?id=3241189.3241263

Pu, P., & Chen, L. (2007). Trust-inspiring explanation interfaces for recommender systems. *Knowledge-Based Systems*, *20*(6), 542–556. https://doi.org/10.1016/j.knosys.2007.04.004

Reigeluth, T. (2017). Recommender systems as techniques of the self? *Le Foucaldien*, *3*(1), 7.

Smith, H. J., Dinev, T., & Xu, H. (2011). Information privacy research: An interdisciplinary review. *MIS Quarterly*, *35* (4), 989–1015. https://doi.org/10.2307/41409970

Tang, T. Y., & Winoto, P. (2016). I should not recommend it to you even if you will like it: The ethics of recommender systems. *New Review of Hypermedia and Multimedia*, *22*(1–2), 111–138. https://doi.org/10.1080/13614568.2015.1052099

Tavani, H. T. (2008). Floridi's ontological theory of informational privacy: Some implications and challenges. *Ethics and Information Technology*, *10*(2–3), 155–166.

Tintarev, N., & Masthoff, J. (2012). Evaluating the effectiveness of explanations for recommender systems. *User Modeling and User-Adapted Interaction*, *22*(4), 399–439. https://doi.org/10.1007/s11257-011-9117-5

Tran, T. P. (2017). Personalized ads on Facebook: An effective marketing tool for online marketers. *Journal of Retailing and Consumer Services*, *39*, 230–242. https://doi.org/10.1016/j.jretconser.2017.06.010

Ur, B., Leon, P. G., Cranor, L. F., Shay, R., & Wang, Y. (2012). Smart, useful, scary, creepy: Perceptions of online behavioral advertising. In *Proceedings of the eighth symposium on usable privacy and security* (pp. 4: 1–4:15). New York, NY: ACM. https://doi.org/10.1145/2335356.2335362.

Wasserman, T. (2014). Facebook will now tell you why you're seeing those ads. Retrieved March 14, 2019, from https://mashable.com/2014/06/12/facebook-explains-ads/

Wisniewski, P., Xu, H., Lipford, H., & Bello-Ogunu, E. (2015). Facebook apps and tagging: The trade-off between personal privacy and engaging with friends: Facebook apps and tagging: The trade-off between personal privacy and engaging with friends. *Journal of the Association for Information Science and Technology*, *66* (9), 1883–1896. https://doi.org/10.1002/asi.23299

Effects of a Gamified Learning Platform on Elementary School Students' Flow Experiences in Leisure Reading

Martin Ting Fung Mak
Hong Kong, China
martinmak@cantab.net

Meng Wang
Faculty of Education,
University of Hong Kong,
Hong Kong, China
ann625@connect.hku.hk

Kai Wah Samuel Chu
Faculty of Education,
University of Hong Kong,
Hong Kong, China
samchu@hku.hk

ABSTRACT

Reading is the basis of most learning but is regarded by students as a boring activity in Hong Kong. Therefore, schools in Hong Kong have launched different reading programs to promote reading. One of the successful examples is Reading Battle which gamifies the reading comprehension assessments with points, levels, e-badges and leaderboard on an interactive learning platform. This study looked into how gamification affected the flow experience of students and discussed to what extent the nine flow dimensions were experienced by them, especially the heavy users of the gamified learning platform. This case study chose nine students from four different elementary schools in Hong Kong and adopted a mixed method such as questionnaires and interviews. While many students first did it for external motivation such as getting more points and ranking high on the leaderboard, the study found that the heavy users of Reading Battle became committed to reading and many enjoyed the flow experiences where they seemed to forget about time and discomfort and truly enjoyed the reading process.

KEYWORDS

E-learning; Flow Theory; Gamification; Mixed Methods Research; Reading Motivation; Reading Enjoyment

ASIS&T THESAURUS

Educational Technology; Language Learning

INTRODUCTION

To elementary school children, reading is always considered important and has been heavily promoted by schools around the world. Research from around the world has found out that children who read immensely and extensively excel in not only their reading abilities but also their academic performance (Anderson, Wilson, & Fielding, 1998; Cox & Guthrie, 2001; Cunningham & Stanovich, 1997; Moats, 1999). To increase students' motivation in reading, many schools launch reading programs and among these programs, one of them is an e-quiz platform called 'Reading Battle' (RB) (Wu et al., 2014). RB makes use of various game design elements to engage primary school students to read more books and answer questions about the books read through post-reading activities. Research has shown that RB has been successful in stimulating students' reading motivation and interest, strengthening reading skills, and fostering self-directed learning (Chan, Chu, Mok, & Tam, 2016). Interestingly, many top achievers in that study in RB were first reluctant to read prior to the programme, but they were then committed to reading where they spent a long time carefully studying the books on RB to complete various kinds of challenges. The enjoyment brought by RB soon became an intrinsic motivation to read, and this has been demonstrated by the users who had "flow experiences" (Csikszentmihalyi, 1990, 1998, 2014) which is an optimal psychological state in which "people are so involved in an activity that nothing else seems to sheer sake of doing it" (Csikszentmihalyi, 1990, p. 4). This present study examines how this gamified learning platform, Reading Battle, affects the users' flow experience in their leisure reading.

82nd Annual Meeting of the Association for Information Science & Technology | Melbourne, Australia | 19–23 October, 2019

DOI: 10.1002/pra2.00075

LITERATURE REVIEW

Gamification in education and Reading Battle

Deterding, Khaled, Nacke, and Dixon (2011, p. 1) define the term *gamification* as "the use of game design elements in non-game contexts." In other words, it is the "intentional use of game elements for a game-like experience of non-game tasks and contexts" (Seaborn & Fels, 2015, p. 17). Writing from an education perspective, Kapp (2012, p. 66) defines gamification as the use of "game-based mechanics, esthetics, and game thinking to engage people, motivate action, promote learning, and solve problems." The learning platform, Reading Battle, is an example on how reading comprehension can be gamified to enhance students' learning and increase their motivation in reading. Similar to traditional reading programs, RB provides a book list for students to read and to do the reading challenges. RB turns the reading tests into challenges by introducing various game elements such as points, e-badges, levels and leaderboard onto the learning platform and makes the paper-based reading worksheets into an interactive challenging system with immediate feedback for users. Hakulinen and Auvinen's report (2014) showed that gamified elements such as achievement badges can change students' learning attitude. Other gamification literature (Barata, Gama, Jorge, & Gonçalves, 2013; de Byl & Hooper, 2013; Mitchell, Danino, & May, 2013; Leong & Yanjie, 2011) suggested that students deemed gamified courses to be motivating and engaging. This gamified learning platform has helped students internalize their external motivation such as getting more points and badges in RB into intrinsic motivation which can be understood by the flow theory.

Flow Theory

Flow theory originates from an attempt to understand a phenomenon observed by the psychologist Mihaly Csikszentmihalyi in a longitudinal study of creativity conducted in 1960s (Getzels & Csikszentmihalyi, 1976). In this phenomenon, Csikszentmihalyi noted that art students often became so engrossed in their creative processes, such as painting and sculpting, that they tended to forget time and discomfort. Csikszentmihalyi (1990) characterized this phenomenon as intrinsically motivated or autotelic (i.e. auto = self, telos = goal), where the reward of pursuing an activity lies in the hands-on experience itself. In describing a flow experience, Csikszentmihalyi (1990) pinned down nine characteristics, which are also referred to as flow dimensions, namely, autotelic, goal clarity, challenge-skill balance, sense of control, concentration, immersion, feedback, knowledge improvement, social interaction. In the field of education, flow has been found in elementary students' self-sponsored writing process (Abbott, 2000; Gute & Gute, 2008), in secondary school's foreign language classroom (Egbert, 2003; Judge, 2011; Kirchhoff, 2013), and in game-based learning (Buzady, 2017; Hamari et al., 2016; Inal & Cagiltay, 2007; Shernoff, Hamari, & Rowe, 2014). Similarly, top achievers in Reading Battle demonstrated a flow experience brought by this gamified learning platform.

AIMS & OBJECTIVES

To investigate the effects of a gamified learning platform on elementary school students' flow experiences in leisure reading, this study will answer two research questions:

1. Are there any major differences in the flow experiences between heavy users and light users on a gamified learning platform?
2. How does a gamified learning platform affect elementary school students' flow experiences in leisure reading?

METHODS

Participants

Nine students in four different elementary schools in Hong Kong who completed challenges of more than 60 books on RB within 5 months (across 2 school terms) from 2017 to 2018 and scored an average of 80 points or more per book were identified as the "heavy users." Another 17 students from those schools with comparable school grades but with records of completing just one book in RB within the same time frame were chosen as the 'light users'. It would be ideal to have the same number of heavy and light users, but based on the criteria in selecting participants, only 9 heavy users could be identified.

Research Methods

To answer the two sub-research questions, a mixed method with both quantitative and qualitative research methods was applied in this study (Creswell & Clark, 2017). Both the heavy users and light users were invited to participate in semi-structured interviews. The interview questions were written based on the flow theory (Csikszentmihalyi, 1990) and the EGameFlow (Fu, Su, & Yu, 2009) model. In the interview, items were divided into 9 sections with each section corresponding to a dimension of flow experience including autotelic, goal clarity, challenge-skill balance, and others. Students responded to the questions using a 5-point Likert scale regarding their experiences in leisure reading. As a semi-structured interview, open-ended follow-up questions were asked if necessary. To answer the second sub-research question, heavy users were also asked to self-report their flow experiences before and after joining RB as they had the most exposure to the gamification platform. All the interviews were done at the end of the 5-month program.

RESULTS

Differences in Flow Dimensions Between Heavy Users and Light Users

The following table shows the flow experience reported by both heavy-user and light-user groups.

Flow dimensions	Heavy users (n = 9)		Light users after joining for at least 2 school terms (n = 17)	Sig. Wilcoxon Signed Ranks[a]	Sig. Mann-Whitney[b]
	Before joining RB	After joining for at least 2 school terms			
Autotelic	4.00	4.63	4.16	0.017*	0.121
Goal clarity	3.59	4.19	3.82	0.024*	0.310
Challenge-skill balance	3.70	4.04	3.90	0.041*	0.495
Sense of control	3.93	4.22	4.18	0.057	0.869
Concentration	3.70	4.37	4.16	0.034*	0.891
Immersion	3.33	4.16	3.87	0.041*	0.254
Feedback	3.19	4.22	3.75	0.011*	0.146
Knowledge improvement	3.85	4.78	4.35	0.027*	0.037*
Social interaction	3.19	3.85	3.65	0.028*	0.604

a. Mann-Whitney Test: HU group versus LU group after joining RB for at least two school terms

b. Wilcoxon Signed Ranks Test: Heavy-User group before versus after joining RB for at least two school terms

* Statistically significant at $p < 0.05$

Note: In the 5-point Likert scale, 5 means students experienced the most flow and 1 being the least.

Table 1. The flow experience reported by both heavy-user group and light-user group.

Overall, statistical analysis indicated that RB could significantly help students in heavy-user group (HUs) achieve flow in leisure reading on all dimensions ($p < 0.05$) with the exception of "Sense of control" ($p = 0.057$). Before joining RB, HUs could only partially achieve flow on every dimension (total rating 3.01–4.00). After using RB on a regular basis for at least two school terms, students could achieve flow on every dimension in high level bracket of ratings (total rating 4.01–5) with Social Interaction (at 3.85) an exception. On the contrary, students from Light-User group (LUs) could achieve flow on four dimensions which were Autotelic, Sense of control, Concentration and Knowledge improvement.

Effects of RB on Flow Dimensions Experienced by Heavy Users

To further investigate how the heavy users experienced flow in leisure reading, qualitative data were also collected during the interviews.

(1) Autotelic

Students reported in the interview that they had a genuine interest in reading books in both and Chinese and English, and now they enjoyed their leisure reading more after their participation in RB. According to Csikszentmihalyi and Nakamura (2014), people need some kind of external goals as a motivation to start performing an activity. "With time, these goals might become intrinsic to the activity itself" (Csikszentmihalyi, 1990, p. 130). In addition, students developed a real passion in learning the two languages, one student (LTT_YYX) said "By doing the questions in RB, I can learn more Chinese idioms."

(2) Goal Clarity

In interviewing students, LTT_QEL pointed out that her goal was to "compete with others" and to "get points," but she eventually "realized that participating in RB was not just about competing with others… [one] should enjoy the book." Furthermore, students identified their goals in improving their literacy skills. For example, LTT_WGZ said "I didn't know any benefits from reading leisure books; but now I have read a lot, my goal was to increase my vocabulary." Students transformed their goals from external motivation into intrinsic motivation and experienced flow as a result.

(3) Challenge-Skill Balance

It was reported by most of the students that the levels of reading on RB could help them adjust to the appropriate level of challenge. As RB provided a levelled book list to students, students could find books suitable for their reading level (FSI_YZX). In order to find the most suitable level of appropriate challenge for themselves, students needed to proactively try the books on the book list. This challenge, in Csikszentmihalyi's words (1990, p. 128), was a "stimulus that attracts our attention, and demands some response on our part." Students challenged themselves to an appropriate level and eventually made progress academically.

(4) Sense of Control

RB promoted the idea of students taking an initiative to challenging themselves to read books from a higher level. LTT_YYX said, "Before using RB, all I read were easy books. Now, I spend all my free time on reading, RB books seemed very interesting to me."

(5) Concentration

One feature in flow experience is the psychological state that one tends to forget time and discomfort. Students were more focussed and their concentration level increased because they could enter an imaginary world brought by the novels. LTT_YYX said, "When I read, sometimes I feel as if I had entered the imaginary world brought by the book… and because I was focussed, I would not be easily distracted."

(6) Immersion

Similar to concentration, three students (LTT_YYX, FSI_YZX, LTT_WGZ) reported that they paid so much attention that they felt as if they were "immersed" in the world created by the novels. Furthermore, students stated that the level of immersion corresponded to the level of understanding of the story. The better they understood story, the easier they could feel that they were part of the story.

(7) Feedback

One of the prominent features of RB is that it gives students immediate feedback to their answers. Those feedback were usually the hints of where students could re-read the book and find out the answers on their own. In interviewing students, they really appreciated this feature and found that it was particularly useful. HCY_SRZ stated, "If my answer was wrong, RB would give me hints about which pages of the book that I should read more carefully." This promoted self-learning and their skills were developed as a result of the immediate feedback.

(8) Knowledge Improvement

Extensive reading developed students' language skills and knowledge of the world and this was reflected in the improvement in their academic performance. LTT_YYX said that "my academic performance has improved as I read more books."

(9) Social Interaction

Although the score in Table 1 for social interaction is not that high, students reported quite a few features of how RB has promoted their social interaction. LTT_YYX asked for help from their family members and friends when they encountered anything they did not understand. LTT_YYX would also share their recommendations of the books with their classmates and friends who also participated in RB.

CONCLUSION & IMPLICATIONS

In conclusion, the findings in this study showed that the gamified learning platform did make a difference in bringing students a better flow experience in all nine dimensions and students had a higher level of intrinsic motivation regarding reading after their participation in RB. Although the sample size was quite small in this study which only have an indicative value, this has a huge implication in the context of education, especially in Hong Kong. As mentioned in the introduction, traditional ways of reading have always been regarded as tedious and boring and students do not enjoy reading as much as they should. Therefore, to make reading interesting again, a gamified platform seems to be one of the solutions. Through an interactive platform with game elements, students can eventually discover the joy of reading and truly enjoy the reading process. Rather than assigning homework and reading tests, students take the ownership of their learning and read for joy.

REFERENCES

Abbott, J. A. (2000). "Blinking Out" and "Having the Touch", "Blinking Out" and "Having the Touch": Two Fifth-Grade Boys Talk about Flow Experiences in Writing, Two Fifth-Grade Boys Talk about Flow Experiences in Writing. *Written Communication, 17*(1), 53–92.

Anderson, R. C., Wilson, P. T., & Fielding, L. G. (1988). Growth in Reading and How Children Spend Their Time Outside of School. *Reading Research Quarterly, 23*(3), 285–303.

Barata, G., Gama, S., Jorge, J., & Gonçalves, D. (2013). *Improving participation and learning with gamification.* In Proceedings of the First Intl. Conference on Gameful Design, Research, and Applications (pp. 10–17). ACM.

Buzady, Z. (2017). Flow, leadership and serious games - a pedagogical perspective. *World Journal of Science, Technology and Sustainable Development; Brighton, 14*(2/3), 204–217.

Chan, M.Y.H., Chu, S.K.W., Mok, S.W.S. & Tam, F. (2016). *Fostering Interest in Reading and Strengthening Reading Comprehension Ability of Primary School Students Using a Children's Literature E-quiz Bank on the Cloud.* In Paper presented at Social Media 2016, The International Education and Technology Conference, Hong Kong.

Cox, K. E., & Guthrie, J. T. (2001). Motivational and Cognitive Contributions to Students' Amount of Reading. *Contemporary Educational Psychology, 26*(1), 116–131.

Creswell, J. W., & Plano Clark, V. L. (2017). *Designing and conducting mixed methods research* (3rd ed.). LA: SAGE Publications.

Csikszentmihalyi, M. (1990). *Flow: The psychology of optimal experience* (1st ed.). New York: Harper & Row.

Csikszentmihalyi, M. (1998). *Finding flow: The psychology of engagement with everyday life.* New York: Basic Books.

Csikszentmihalyi, M. (2014). *Flow and the foundations of positive psychology: The collected works of Mihaly Csikszentmihalyi.* Dordrecht: Springer.

Csikszentmihalyi, M., Abuhamdeh, S., & Nakamura, J. (2014). Flow. In M. Csikszentmihalyi (Ed.), *Flow and the foundations of positive psychology* (pp. 227–238). Dordrecht: Springer Netherlands.

Cunningham, A. E., & Stanovich, K. E. (1997). Early Reading Acquisition and Its Relation to Reading Experience and Ability 10 Years Later. *Developmental Psychology, 33*(6), 934–945.

de Byl, P. (2013). Factors at play in tertiary curriculum gamification. *International Journal of Games-Based Learning, 3*, 1–21.

Deterding, S., Dixon, D., Khaled, R., & Nacke, L. (2011). *From Game Design Elements to Gamefulness: Defining Gamification.* In Proceedings of the 15th Intl. Academic MindTrek Conference: Envisioning Future Media Environments, MindTrek 2011 (Vol. *11*, pp. 9–15).

Egbert, J. (2003). A study of flow theory in the foreign language classroom. *Modern Language Journal, 87*(4), 499–518.

Fu, F. L., Su, R. C., & Yu, S. C. (2009). EGameFlow: A scale to measure learners' enjoyment of e-learning games. *Computers & Education, 52*(1), 101–112.

Getzels, J. W., & Csikszentmihalyi, M. (1976). *The creative vision: A longitudinal study of problem finding in art.* New York: Wiley.

Gute, D., & Gute, G. (2008). Flow writing in the liberal arts core and cross the disciplines: A vehicle for confronting and transforming academic disengagement. *The Journal of General Education, 57*(4), 191–222.

Hakulinen, L., & Auvinen, T. (2014). *The Effect of Gamification on Students with Different Achievement Goal Orientations.* In 2014 Intl. Conference on Teaching & Learning in Computing and Engineering, 9–16.

Hamari, J., et al. (2016). Challenging games help students learn: An empirical study on engagement, flow and immersion in game-based learning. *Computers in Human Behavior, 54*, 170–179.

Inal, Y., & Cagiltay, K. (2007). Flow experiences of children in an interactive social game environment. *British Journal of Educational Technology, 38*(3), 455–464.

Judge, P. B. (2011). Driven to read: Enthusiastic readers in a Japanese high school's extensive reading program. *Reading in a Foreign Language, 23*(2), 161–186.

Kapp, K. M. (2012). Games, gamification, and the quest for learner engagement. *Training and Development, 66*(6), 64–68.

Kirchhoff, C. (2013). L2 extensive reading and flow: Clarifying the relationship. *Reading in a Foreign Language, 25* (2), 192–212.

Leong, B., & Luo, Y. (2011). Application of Game Mechanics to Improve Student Engagement. In Presented at the Proceedings of Intl. Conference on Teaching and Learning in Higher Education.

Mitchell, N., Danino, N., & May, L. (2013). Motivation and manipulation: A gamification approach to influencing undergraduate attitudes in computing. *European Conference on Games Based Learning*; Reading, 394–400.

Moats, L. C. (1999). *Teaching Reading Is Rocket Science: What Expert Teachers of Reading Should Know and Be Able To Do*. American Federation of Teachers, AFL-CIO, 555 New Jersey Ave.

Seaborn, K., & Fels, D. I. (2015). Gamification in theory and action: A survey. *International Journal of Human-Computer Studies*, *74*, 14–31.

Shernoff, D., Hamari, J., & Rowe, E. (2014). *Measuring flow in educational games and gamified learning environments*. In EdMedia: World Conference on Educational Media and Technology (pp. 2276–2281). Association for the Advancement of Computing in Education). AACE.

Wu, W. W. Y., Chu, S. K. W., Chan, H., Wong, J., Tse, S. K., Tavares, N., & Mok, S. W. S. (2014). *Strengthening students' reading comprehension ability (both Chinese and English) through developing children's literature equiz bank on the cloud*. In Presented at the The 19th International Education and Technology Conference, HK, China.

Transitions and Social Interaction: Making Sense of Self and Situation Through Engagement With Others

Pam McKenzie
The University of Western Ontario
London, Canada
pmckenzi@uwo.ca

Rebekah Willson
University of Strathclyde
Glasgow, Scotland
rebekah.willson@strath.ac.uk

ABSTRACT

This short paper examines social interaction (e.g. asking colleagues for help in the lunchroom) as an informative experience, a way to understand oneself and situation. The process of coming to an understanding is frequently hidden, but may be brought to light by examining the experiences of individuals undergoing a transition – a change that requires them to redefine their sense of self and situation. Using exemplars from previous research and drawing on Lave and Wenger's (1991) theory of situated learning, this paper explores the importance of social interaction to information practices. The role of social interaction will be discussed, including: information seeking to become part of a community, and social interaction as a source of information and as a site for information comparison (a type of information use) to situate oneself in a new environment. The paper proposes making social interaction a focus of study to better understand how individuals use information to change perception about and situate themselves.

KEYWORDS

Transitions; Information Practices; Information Behavior; Social Interactions; Sociocultural Research

ASIS&T THESAURUS

Information Behavior, Information Sharing, Information Seeking, Human Information Resources, Sociocultural Aspects

INTRODUCTION

The turn in LIS scholarship toward information seeking in context (Courtright, 2007) has focused researchers' attention on the nature of context and the information seeker's relation to it. Harris and Dewdney (1994) noted that people seek information first from others like them (i.e., in a similar context) and use methods that have worked before in that context. However, a transition, a "passage from one life phase, condition, or status to another" (Chick & Meleis, 1986, p. 239) may change the context and the information seeker's sense of identity sufficiently that they are no longer *like* their former self. By definition, transitions involve a substantive life change that can be developmental, situational, organizational, or health-illness related (Meleis, Sawyer, Im, Messias, & Schumacher, 2000). Therefore, the sources individuals formerly relied on may no longer be accessible, relevant, or authoritative.

Social interaction has been described as a primary activity where people meet, from which information is shared as a by-product (Fisher, Landry, & Naumer, 2007). Frequently in LIS research people are treated as information sources, analogous to a book or website. While this may be appropriate in some instances, social interactions are far more often complex, going beyond the simple provision of information. Social interactions in and of themselves can be seen as a source of information and a means to enter a community. This is particularly true – and particularly apparent – when individuals are undergoing a transition which requires them to "redefine their sense of self and redevelop self-agency in response to disruptive life events" (Kralik, Visentin, & van Loon, 2006, p. 321). Using transitions as the focus – and drawing on the work of Lave and Wenger (1991), this paper will explore what a "social interaction" focus can offer information practice research, discussing information seeking, interaction as a source of information, and a site for information comparison.

LITERATURE REVIEW

Transition has traditionally has been framed as a linear movement between settings or from one life phase or situation to another in relation to normative patterns and social or age-related expectations. However, an ecological perspective characterizes a transition as a change in role as a person moves "between and across systems," constituted by the relationships and connections that surround a person as well as individual experience (Dockett & Perry, 2007). Experiences of change and the meaning accorded to transition are personal and differ between individuals, and personal meaning alters the way that people perceive and respond to change (Meleis et al., 2000).

Importance is placed on the activities in which people participate as well as how participation changes over time (Dockett & Perry, 2007, p. 9), which attends to the ways that people develop socially-situated knowing. Resources – in the form of social, professional, or information support – play a key mediational role in transitions (Schumacher & Meleis, 1994). Beyond resources, information sharing in a community of

82nd Annual Meeting of the Association for Information Science & Technology | Melbourne, Australia | 19–23 October, 2019

DOI: 10.1002/pra2.00047

practice can create shared understandings, including shared understandings of how to enact work roles within a particular context (Pilerot, 2015). Lave and Wenger's theory of "situated learning", which attends to learning as "an evolving, continuously renewed set of relations" (1991, p. 50), is useful in this regard. In this theory, learning is a process of identification and belonging that depends on engagement in valued practices, and newcomers interact with communities of practice through "legitimate peripheral participation":

> *[R]ather than learning by replicating the performances of others or by acquiring knowledge transmitted in instruction, we suggest that learning occurs through centripetal participation in the learning curriculum of the ambient community. Because the place of knowledge is within a community of practice, questions of learning must be addressed within the developmental cycles of that community... (*Lave & Wenger, 1991, *p. 100).*

LIS scholars have examined biological transitions such as pregnancy, menopause, and illness (e.g., Genuis & Bronstein, 2017; McKenzie, 2003); geographic transitions, such as refugees in a new country (e.g., Lloyd, Pilerot, & Hultgren, 2017); migrant workers (Bronstein, 2019), students on international placements (e.g., Hicks, 2018); situational transitions such as between higher education and the workplace (e.g., Willson, 2016); and gender transition (e.g., Hawkins & Glesking, 2017). Within LIS, sociocultural approaches to research have considered the transition from novice to expert (Lloyd & Somerville, 2006) and the negotiation of meaning (Moring, 2012). This work is done in communities of practice, justification, and/or discourse. A major component of sociocultural approaches to the work of transition is coming to understand (or not) the information needs that are considered appropriate within the community, and the information sources, relevance, authority criteria the community values.

METHODS

At the 2018 ASIS&T Annual Meeting the authors began a discussion of transitions research, identifying it as a common area of interest. Through subsequent discussions, the role of social interaction in how individuals search for and use information was identified as an important area of study that requires further investigation. A sociocultural approach to transitions research sees transitions as centred in involvement in a community, rather than within a person or in their environment. Within this approach, transition may be characterized as "becoming somebody" in a personal, educational or occupational context (Ecclestone, Biesta, & Hughes, 2010, p. 7) and made visible through "people's changing participation in sociocultural activities of their communities" (Rogoff, 2003, p.52). Using a sociocultural lens, previously analysed interview data was reviewed for discussions of social interactions.

This paper discusses exemplars from the authors' previous qualitative analyses of interview and periodic check-in data. Willson conducted a constructivist grounded theory study of the information practices of early career academics as they transitioned from doctoral student to their first continuing academic position, following academics for 5-7 months within the first 2 years of their new position. McKenzie conducted a discourse analysis of the ways that pregnant women reconstructed cognitive authority through social interaction with experienced mothers of twins. Details of methods are addressed in Willson (2016) and McKenzie (2003).

FINDINGS

This section explores the various ways social interaction helps individuals undergoing a transition to redefine themselves and their situation. Using exemplars, social interaction is explored as a form of information seeking, a source of information, and a site for information comparison.

Information Seeking

In making a transition from one identity to another, individuals must navigate the prevailing forms of authoritative knowledge (Jordan, 1997) that are held as legitimate by participants in the context in which they are operating as novices. Social interaction with experienced individuals can both provide newcomers with authoritative information and enable them to develop new, context-appropriate strategies for determining what questions are legitimate and sources are authoritative (Hicks, 2018).

Participants in McKenzie's study consistently emphasized that they understood multiple pregnancy and parenting to be experiences quite distinct from bearing and rearing a single child. Experienced mothers of twins therefore took on an enhanced level of cognitive authority (Wilson, 1983) because of their ability to provide information situated in experiential knowledge "based on wisdom and know-how gained through reflection upon personal lived experience" (Schubert & Borkman, 1994, pp. 228-229). Participant "Karen" explained, "I need to connect with someone who gets it. I feel like I'm alone in the universe. You know, I'm in a lighthouse and everyone's going 'Wow' and waving but you know, nobody **gets** it."

Borkman (1990) argues that experiential knowledge constitutes a distinctive frame of reference and that it is commonly transferred through social interaction, particularly through the sharing of stories and through modeling of ways of coping. Both of these can be valuable to a newcomer. Participants sought out social interactions as sources of both information and reassurance. At a Multiple Birth Association meeting, "Gayle" found permission to feel overwhelmed, and received emotional support:

> *I needed somebody to talk to. [laughs] To know that I wasn't going psycho.... Like everybody was joyous and, "Oh twins, how wonderful, how wonderful, how wonderful!" And I didn't think that at all. And I wanted somebody to tell me that it was* ***okay****. And, thank God I found them.*

Interaction as an Information Source

While social interaction is an opportunity to seek information from experienced members of a community, the social interaction itself is source of information. Interaction requires response. Those in transition use the information conveyed in interaction to renegotiate their identity and/or position within a new community, a way of learning through participation (Lave & Wenger, 1991). This was the case for "Claire," an academic in business, who discussed having a meeting with a business owner, "I suppose my sense of who I was, it was changing because I sort of see him as the expert. He's the owner of the business but he obviously saw me as an expert of some sort or someone worth speaking about these issues." Treated as an expert, Claire's view of herself and abilities begin to shift. She uses the interaction to inform what she terms "rebranding of myself as the academic."

Making the transition from PhD student to early career academic included new roles, which required adjustment for many academics. "Evelyn," an indigenous academic in the social sciences, described others taking her more seriously:

> *Just losing the label student suggests that you've moved into a different role. In terms of my own identity, ... I've had quite a few students come to me and say they'd love to work with me in whatever capacity and even when I say I'm not quite sure what I'm doing, they're like, "It's okay, we want to be part of it." I mean at the same time that it's flattering, it's also very onerous and I guess I really am feeling that weight of responsibility ...*

New roles and responsibilities bring new pressures and feelings of uncertainty around identity. They also bring changes to others' perspectives. While Evelyn is "at the point of just getting comfortable saying I'm a professor", interacting with colleagues and students informs her she is viewed as a professor and pushes her to act in "professorial" ways (e.g., supervising PhD students). Extending the finding that information sharing is a way to reach a shared understanding of how to be a scholar in the field (Pilerot, 2015), for those undergoing a transition social interaction is a way to renegotiate their shifting identities with the community into which they are entering.

Interaction as a Site for Comparison

Information from social interaction and previous experience is frequently used by those undergoing transition in making comparisons – comparing the old and new situations and expectations to reality (Willson, n.d.). "Adam," an academic in the humanities, described an unexpected aspect of his transition from PhD student to academic within the same department:

> *I think I was surprised by the confidence I felt in response to people's, the other staff, my colleague's greater openness and recognition of getting the position and joining the staff. So that took me by surprise. In hindsight it made a lot of sense but, and in hindsight actually it makes me feel like the position of the casual academic is actually even harder than they realize.*

Adam describes an interaction in which his new role and status alters his colleagues' behavior towards himself, which, in turn, influences his own confidence. By comparing his current role and level of confidence to that of his previous experience, he is able to make sense of and situate himself more fully in his current context. His previous experience and interactions with his colleagues become a source of information against which to judge his current situation. His transition is a process of "reliving and integrating of past, present and future experiences" (Palmer, O'Kane, & Owens, 2009, p. 51). While comparison is part of a process of information use, the social interaction with his colleagues is the site where comparison begins and is played out.

CONCLUSION

This paper draws on Lave and Wenger's (1991) theory of situated learning to propose a more complex understanding of the role of social interaction in the information practices of those undergoing a transition. Beyond being an activity in which people engage when they meet, social interaction serves several functions when previously relied upon information and sources are no longer available. Social interaction is a means of information seeking, an information practice used by individuals undergoing a transition to engage with members of a community who have specialized information. More than information, community members can also offer help, support, and legitimize experiences. Social interaction is also a source of information in and of itself. By interacting with members in a community – by learning through participation – those undergoing a transition are given information about what it means to be and act as a member of a community. This is important information when renegotiating identity and position in a community. Social interaction is also important as a site of comparison. During a transition information is used to compare past and present experiences, which are used to make sense of new roles, identities, and contexts. By engaging with new members of a community, individuals in transition are able to test out and renegotiate their sense of self and situation. The implications of this research are to propose a focus on social interactions; by making these interactions a unit of analysis, the processes of renegotiation self and situation are better able to be seen and understood.

REFERENCES

Borkman, T. J. (1990). Experiential, professional, and lay frames of reference. In T. J. Powell, *Working with self-help* (pp. 3–30). Silver Springs, MD: National Association of Social Workers Press.

Bronstein, J. (2019). A transitional approach to the study of the information behavior of domestic migrant workers:

A narrative inquiry. *Journal of Documentation*, *72*(2), 314–333. https://doi.org/10.1108/JD-07-2018-0112

Chick, N., & Meleis, A. I. (1986). Transitions: A nursing concern. In P. L. Chinn, *Nursing research methodology: Issues and implementation* (pp. 237–257). Rockville, MD: Aspen.

Courtright, C. (2007). Context in information science research. *Annual Review of Information Science and Technology*, *41*(1), 273–306.

Dockett, S., & Perry, B. (2007). *Transitions to school: Perceptions, expectations and experiences*. Sydney, NSW: UNSW Press.

Ecclestone, K., Biesta, G., & Hughes, M. (2010). Transitions in the lifecourse: The role of identity, agency and structure. In K. Ecclestone, G. Biesta, & M. Hughes, *Transitions and learning through the lifecourse* (pp. 1–15). Abingdon: Routledge.

Fisher, K. E., Landry, C. F., & Naumer, C. (2007). Social spaces, casual interactions, meaningful exchanges: "Information ground" characteristics based on the college student experience. *Information Research*, *12*(2) Retrieved from http://informationr.net/ir/12-2/paper291.html

Genuis, S., & Bronstein, J. (2017). Looking for "normal": Sense making in the context of health disruption. *Journal of the Association for Information Science and Technology*, *68*(3), 750–761.

Harris, R. M., & Dewdney, P. (1994). Theory and research on information seeking. In *Barriers to information: How formal help systems fail battered women* (pp. 7–34). Westport, CT: Greenwood.

Hawkins, B., & Glesking, J. (2017). Seeking ways to our transgender bodies, by ourselves: Rationalizing transgender-specific health information behaviors. *Proceedings of the Society for Information Science and Technology*, *54*(1), 702–704. https://doi.org/10.1002/pra2.2017.14505401122

Hicks, A. (2018). *The theory of mitigating risk: Information literacy and language-learning in transition*. (Doctoral dissertation). University in Borås. Retrieved from http://urn.kb.se/resolve?urn=urn:nbn:se:hb:diva-15000

Jordan, B. (1997). Authoritative knowledge and its construction. In R. E. Davis-Floyd & C. F. Sargent, *Childbirth and authoritative knowledge: Cross-cultural perspectives* (pp. 55–79). Berkeley: University of California Press.

Kralik, D., Visentin, K., & van Loon, A. (2006). Transition: a literature review. *Journal of Advanced Nursing*, *55*(3), 320–329.

Lave, J., & Wenger, E. (1991). *Situated learning: Legitimate peripheral participation*. Cambridge, UK: Cambridge University Press.

Lloyd, A., Pilerot, O., & Hultgren, F. (2017). The remaking of fractured landscapes: Supporting refugees in transition. *Information Research*, *22*(3) Retrieved from http://www.informationr.net/ir/22-3/paper764.html

Lloyd, A., & Somerville, M. (2006). Working information. *Journal of Workplace Learning*, *18*(3), 186–198. https://doi.org/10.1108/13665620610654603

McKenzie, P. J. (2003). Justifying cognitive authority decisions: Discursive strategies of information seekers. *Library Quarterly*, *73*(3), 261–288.

Meleis, A. I., Sawyer, L. M., Im, E.-O., Messias, D. K. H., & Schumacher, K. (2000). Experiencing transitions: An emerging middle-range theory. *Advances in Nursing Science*, *23*(1), 12–28.

Moring, C. (2012). Newcomer information practice: Negotiations on information seeking in and across communities of practice. *Human IT: Journal for Information Technology Studies as a Human Science*, *11*(2) Retrieved from https://humanit.hb.se/article/view/66

Palmer, M., O'Kane, P., & Owens, M. (2009). Betwixt spaces: Student accounts of turning point experiences in the first-year transition. *Studies in Higher Education*, *34*(1), 37–54. https://doi.org/10.1080/03075070802601929

Pilerot, O. (2015). Information sharing in the field of design research. In Proceedings of ISIC, the Information Behavior Conference, 20(1). Retrieved from http://InformationR.net/ir/20-1/isic2/isic26.html

Rogoff, B. (2003). *The cultural nature of human development*. Oxford, UK: Oxford University Press.

Schubert, M. A., & Borkman, T. (1994). Identifying the experiential knowledge developed within a self-help group. In T. J. Powell, *Understanding the self-help organization: Frameworks and findings* (pp. 227–246). Thousand Oaks, CA: Sage.

Schumacher, K. L., & Meleis, A. I. (1994). Transitions: A central concept in nursing. *Image: Journal of Nursing Scholarship*, *26*(2), 119–127.

Willson, R. (2016). *Information in transition: Examining the information behavior of academics as they transition into university careers* (Doctoral dissertation). Charles Sturt University. Retrieved from http://primo.unilinc.edu.au/primo_library/libweb/action/dlDisplay.do?vid=CSU2&docId=dtl_csu85865

Willson, R. (n.d.). Transitions Theory and liminality in information behavior research: Applying new theories to examine the transition to early career academic. *Journal of Documentation* (In Press).

Wilson, P. (1983). *Second hand knowledge: An inquiry into cognitive authority*. Westport, CT: Greenwood.

Relations Among Participation, Fairness and Performance in Collaborative Learning With Wiki-Based Analytics

Jeremy Ng
Faculty of Education, University of Hong Kong, Pokfulam Road, Hong Kong
jeremyng@hku.hk

Xiao Hu
Faculty of Education, University of Hong Kong, Pokfulam Road, Hong Kong
xiaoxhu@hku.hk

Miyu Luo
Faculty of Education, University of Hong Kong, Pokfulam Road, Hong Kong
miuralaw@hku.hk

Sam K. W. Chu
Faculty of Education, University of Hong Kong, Pokfulam Road, Hong Kong
samchu@hku.hk

ABSTRACT

Utilizing data analytics for supporting collaborative learning is under-studied in secondary education. This study aims to evaluate the effectiveness of Wiki and Wiki-based learning analytics in facilitating collaborative learning in a junior secondary school, in terms of students' participation, contribution, performance, and perception. A Wiki-based learning analytic tool, Wikiglass, was employed for visualizing statistics of students' contributions and participation (e.g., revision counts) in Wiki, on both the group and individual levels. System log, student survey and performance data were collected from students involved in a Wiki-supported inquiry project assignment. An Unfairness Index is proposed to measure students' group work distribution. Results of statistical analyses show that fairness of group work distribution was positively related to active participation in revisions on Wiki on the group level, and the number of sentences with higher-order thinking was related to group performance scores. On the level of individual students, Wiki-based analytics increased the visibility of work distribution and peers' work progress and contributions which might have changed students' collaborative behaviors.

KEYWORDS

e-learning; Computer-Supported Collaborative Learning (CSCL); Wiki; Learning Analytics; Wikiglass; Work Distribution; Fairness

ASIS&T THESAURUS

Information Technology; Educational Technology; Humanities; Education; Schools; Middle Schools

INTRODUCTION

Wiki, as an online collaborative writing tool, has been used to support collaborative learning in different subjects and across all education levels (Chu, Siu, Liang, Capio, & Wu, 2013). While Wiki records rich student data along the process of learning (such as page revision history and student activity logs), the amount of data can be intimidating for teachers and often under-utilized (Kear, Donelan, & Williams, 2014). In recent years, data analytic methods have been increasingly used to assess, facilitate, and predict the process of teaching and learning, which fosters the rapid growth of learning analytics as a new research area. There is no exception for Wiki-supported learning, as analysis and visualization of learners' behaviorial data have been found to be effective in assessing their online collaborative learning (Rodríguez-Triana, Martínez-Monés, Asensio-Pérez, & Dimitriadis, 2015). However, most of these analytic tools were developed and exercised for higher education and online courses, while fewer studies focused on secondary education. In fact, school teachers and students might find such analytics complex or sophisticated (Dyckhoff, Zielke, Bültmann, Chatti, & Schroeder, 2012). Therefore, learning analytic tools that present straightforward and focused information tailored for school users are needed [Hu, Ip, Sadaful, Lui, & Chu, 2016]. Wikiglass is one of such tools especially designed for collaborative Wikis used in schools. It visualizes statistics of students' contributions, learning progress, and writing quality on both group and individual levels. This study aims to evaluate the effectiveness of using Wiki and Wikiglass to facilitate Computer-Supported collaborative learning (CSCL) for a Liberal Studies assignment in a junior secondary school in Hong Kong. System logs, student survey and performance data were collected and analyzed. Since the assessment of CSCL should be conducted on both group and individual levels [Strijbos, 2011], this preliminary study sets out to answer the following research questions:

RQ1: Can Wiki and Wiki-based learning analytics facilitate collaborative learning on the group level?

RQ2: Can Wiki and Wiki-based learning analytics facilitate collaborative learning on the individual level?

In this study, the effectiveness of Wiki and Wiki-based learning analytics is evaluated with regard to their support for collaborative learning. Specifically, a pair of metrics on (un)

82nd Annual Meeting of the Association for Information Science & Technology | Melbourne, Australia | 19–23 October, 2019

DOI: 10.1002/pra2.00048

fairness of work distribution on the group and individual levels are proposed. Statistical analysis is applied to reveal relationships between students' contributions, participation and work distribution on Wiki, usage of the learning analytic tool, learning performance, as well as self-reported perceptions.

RELATED WORKS

Wiki, an online tool for collaborative authoring, has been regarded as effective in improving group collaboration, quality of work, and knowledge construction and sharing [Naismith, Lee, & Pilkington, 2011; Chu et al., 2013]. Given that collaborative learning occurs when different learners interact and modify one another's work, Wiki is suitable for promoting collaborative learning, since it records all revisions and supports version comparison and reversion to an earlier version. Despite that rich information of student contributions and revision history are recorded by Wiki, it is mostly buried in the system and not readily used by learners or teachers. Tools for monitoring and assessing collaborative learning processes and products are either not available or under-developed [Strijbos, 2011; Rodríguez-Triana et al., 2015].

To assess the performance of CSCL in secondary education, quantitative analysis could be a robust approach for teachers and researchers to harvest empirical evidence of learning outcomes such as knowledge convergence in the collaborative work [Zheng, Chen, Huang, & Yang, 2014]. Although learning analytics (LA) has proved to be an effective instrument to collect, measure, and analyze the learners' behavior [Papamitsiou & Economides, 2014], the majority of existing studies on analytics for collaborative learning were conducted in tertiary education whereas scarce attention has been devoted to the case of secondary education [Hu, 2017]. Therefore, this study aims to fill the gap by employing Wiki and a Wiki-based analytic tool orchestrated for teachers and students in secondary schools.

RESEARCH DESIGN

Research Context

This study is part of a research project on developing inquiry-based learning with Web 2.0 and learning analytics in secondary and primary schools. Students from Secondary 1 to 3 (Grades 7 to 9 in the U.S.) in a government-subsidized junior secondary school in Hong Kong participated in this study. As an assignment of the academic subject Liberal Studies in the spring semester of 2017, students were required to work on a semester-long group inquiry project with a self-chosen topic related to current affairs (e.g., promotion of e-books, same-sex marriage, etc.). Each group had 4 to 5 students who collaborated using a Wiki and had access to analytics of their work on Wikiglass throughout the project period.

Wiki and Wiki-based Learning Analytic Tool

PBworks was adopted as the Wiki platform on which students collaboratively wrote their inquiry project report and edited content inputted from others within the same group. Each group shared a single Wiki, on which there were different pages corresponding to the sections of the project report, including literature review, data collection and so on. Students could only access their own group's Wiki.

On the other hand, Wikiglass was employed as the analytic tool that fetches data from Wiki and visualizes statistics of students' participation and contributions on Wiki, including revision counts, word counts, and thinking order of sentences (low vs. high) automatically recognized by machine learning algorithms [Hu, 2017]. It also supported flexible selection of date ranges in visualizing the statistics. Both visualizations of the statistics and their dynamic changes over time were available in the class, group and individual levels. In the group page, contributions from each group member were shown in pie charts (with one of the statistics shown in Figure 1), while in the individual page, the student's contribution (number of revisions, number of words amended) on each Wiki page was shown (with one of the statistics shown in Figure 2).

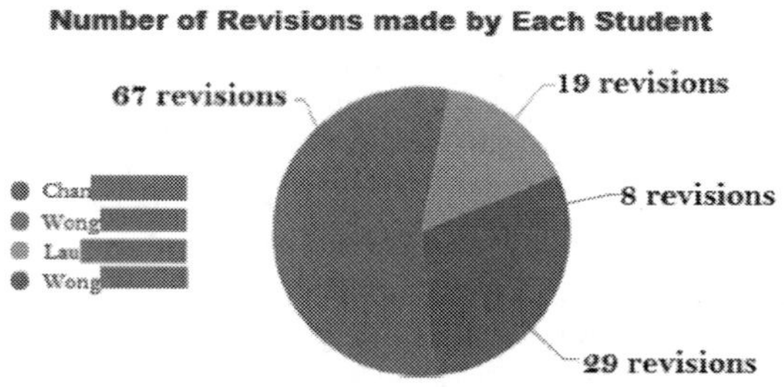

Figure 1. Visualization of revision counts in a group.

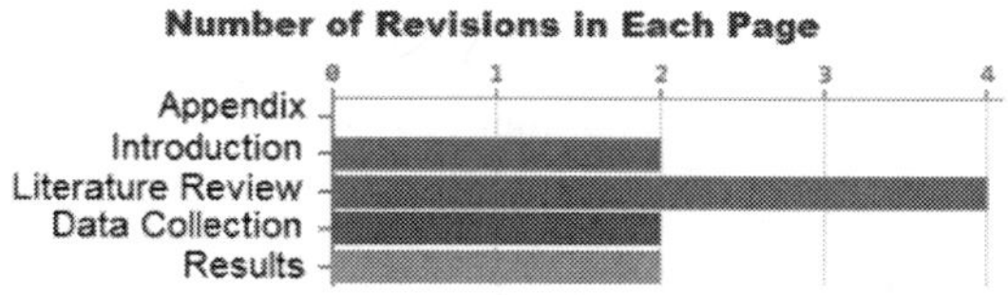

Figure 2. Visualization of revision counts of a student.

All visualizations and pages in Wikiglass were accessible to all students involved in the inquiry project. That is, a student could view work distribution among and work progress of his/her own group as well as those of other groups. Similarly, she/he could view her/his own statistics and progress on the individual page as well as those on any other student's individual page. All students used the Wiki platform whereas the use of Wikiglass was voluntary but encouraged.

Data Collection and Analysis

Ethical consent was sought from teachers and students prior to data collection. Table 1 displays the various measures and their corresponding metrics and data sources.

Measure	Metric	Data Source
Contribution	No. of words inputted	Wiki logs
Participation	No. of times a Wiki page has been revised	
Measure of writing quality	% of sentences with high-order thinking	
Usage of learning analytic tool	No. of times of viewing own individual and group's visualizations	Wikiglass logs
	No. of times of viewing other individuals' and groups' visualizations	
Perception	Opinions on Wiki, work distribution, and collaboration	Pre-survey, post-survey
Performance	Scores of inquiry project	Teachers

Table 1. Measures investigated in this study.

For the surveys, a 6-point Likert scale (1 = Strongly Disagree to 6 = Strongly Agree) was adopted for multiple-choice responses. In this paper, we only analyze data collected from students who used both Wiki and Wikiglass and the groups they were in, resulting in 53 groups and 119 students. Statistical tests including correlation analysis and Wilcoxon Signed-rank test were applied to compare student perceptions before and after the collaborative learning experience. Statistical significance of analysis in this study is indicated by * at $p < .05$ and ** at $p < .01$.

Proposed Measurement on Unfairness

The effectiveness of collaborative learning is often related to the fairness of students' group work distribution [Naismith et al., 2011]. A measurement of unfairness was proposed in this study to quantify work distribution. A group unfairness index (*UF*) will be calculated using this formula:

$$UF = \left(\sum_{i=1}^{n} | P_i - \frac{1}{n} \right) / n \quad (1)$$

P_i stands for the percentage of the individual contribution within a group in terms of word counts, whereas n refers to the number of students in the group. The absolute value of $|P_i - 1/n|$ is the individual unfairness index, indicating the deviation of an individual students' contribution from the "fairest" situation (everybody contributes 1/n). The average of the individual indexes in a group thereby yields the group unfairness index. The larger this index is, the more likely that the work distribution of the group would be unfair.

RESULTS AND DISCUSSION

RQ1: Effectiveness in the Group Level

To address whether Wiki and Wiki-based learning analytics facilitated collaborative learning on the group level, the correlations between the various statistics of group-level Wiki behavioral data and the group unfairness index were first explored. Results (Table 2) show that the group-level revision count and unfairness index had a moderate negative correlation (|r| > 0.3, [Akoglu, 2018]). This shows that fairness of group work distribution had a positive relationship with active participation of group members in making revisions on the analytics-supported Wiki.

Wiki statistics (group level)	Mean (Std Dev)	Unfairness index	Correlation coefficient r	Sig.
Word count	4784.91 (3942.29)	N = 53 groups	-.23	.10
Revision count	88.28 (24.07)		-.42	.00**
% of Higher-order Thinking sentences	.225 (.13)	Mean = .22 (.107)	.15	.29

Table 2. Pearson's correlations between group-level Wiki behaviors and group unfairness index.

Students' performance scores in the inquiry project serve as another indicator of the outcome of their collaborative learning. Correlations between students' group-level statistics of Wiki behaviors and the average scores of group members in the inquiry project were analyzed. As Table 3 shows, there was a moderate correlation (|r| > 0.3, [Akoglu, 2018]) between the percentage of sentences with higher-order thinking and the performance score. With reference to the thinking orders in secondary school students' writing [Hu, 2017; Krathwohl, 2002], this result implies that more creation and evaluation in collaborative writing would lead to a higher performance score. This validates the importance of higher-order thinking as a cognitive skill in computer-supported collaborative learning. On the other hand, there was no significant correlation between the score and either count, indicating that quantity of participation or contribution alone may not be sufficient in obtaining good performance scores in the inquiry project.

Wiki statistics (group level)	Mean (Std Dev)	Scores	Correlation coefficient r	Sig.
Word count	4784.91 (3942.29)	N = 53 groups	.23	.10
Revision count	88.28 (24.07)		.14	.31
% of Higher-order Thinking sentences	.225 (.13)	Mean = 29.69 (4.67)	.34	.01*

Table 3. Pearson's correlations between group-level Wiki behaviors and performance scores.

RQ2: Effectiveness in the Individual Level

On the individual level (N = 119 students), the correlations between the individual-level Wiki behavior statistics (word count, revision count, percentage of higher-order thinking sentences) and the individual unfairness index were computed. None of the statistics and the unfairness index on the individual level (UF = 0.231) was correlated ($p > 0.05$). This implies that fairness of group work distribution might not be related to students' individual contributions to the collaborative Wiki. It may be due to the two opposite situations of high individual unfairness index: either a student contributed a lot or very little. In this case no linear correlation could be found. Compared to results on the group level (Table 2), this result indicates that, in group work, collective participation of the group as a whole are more prominent in improving fairness than that of individuals.

Similarly, correlations between students' individual-level Wiki behaviors and their individual scores in the inquiry project were explored. Results show that there was also no significant correlation ($p > 0.05$). This suggests that neither quantity nor quality of individual contributions to collaborative work on Wiki bore relationship with a student's performance score in the inquiry project. Compared to the results on the group level (Table 3) where the quality of contributions of the group did correlate with the group's average score, this indicates that performances of individuals in a group work setting may not be directly related to individuals' contribution. Rather, dynamics of the group must have played a substantial role such as students' participation in editing each other's Wiki pages [Strijbos, 2011]. This also distinguishes collaborative work on Wiki from cooperative work [Kear et al., 2014].

A paired-samples comparison (Wilcoxon Signed-rank test) between the survey responses before and after the collaborative learning experience yielded an interesting finding. Students were less positive towards the level of fairness in their group work distribution (4.46 vs. 4.14, $p = .037^*$) after the project. This implies that the visualizations enabled by Wikiglass might have made students' work distribution more visible and it is therefore easier to detect unfair cases.

Table 4 displays the results of correlation analysis between various individual-level Wikiglass usage behaviors and the individual unfairness index. There was a weak correlation between the unfairness index and the frequency of viewing other groups' or one's own visualizations on the analytic tool. In other words, the more a student viewed other groups' or his/her own visualizations, the more deviation his/her contribution was from the norm of work distribution. This might imply that, in a Wiki-supported learning environment, the availability of peers' visualized progress and contributions might have stimulated comparison with one's own and thus influenced students' collaborative behaviors. For example, a student might have been curious about how much other groups) had written, and thus took a look at peers' progress in comparison to his/hers which might have provided him/her additional drive to contribute more.

Wikiglass statistics (viewing)	Mean (Std Dev)	Unfairness index	Correlation coefficient r	Sig.
Own group's visualizations	11.80 (13.33)	N = 119 students	.15	.09
Other groups' visualizations	5.95 (10.63)		.29	.00**
Own individual visualizations	2.67 (5.72)	.231 (.21)	.21	.02*
Other individuals' visualizations	3.87 (5.61)		.17	.06

Table 4. Correlation between individual-level Wikiglass usage behaviors and unfairness index.

CONCLUDING REMARKS AND FUTURE WORK

To evaluate the effectiveness of Wiki and Wiki-based analytics in facilitating collaborative learning, this study collected and analyzed system log, student survey and performance data in a junior secondary school in Hong Kong. In particular, the unfairness index was proposed as a measure of the fairness of work distribution in groups. Results of statistical analysis yielded a number of findings that show the evidence of effectiveness of Wiki and Wiki-based learning analytics in facilitating collaborative learning in terms of writing quality and work distribution on the group and individual levels.

A limitation of this study is that it captures only students' online learning behaviors from the platforms, leaving students' offline behaviors unconsidered such as brainstorming and discussion. Students' individual contributions, which only counted their words inputted and revisions on Wiki, might have been understated.

As an ongoing effort, interviews with students and teachers are being analyzed to triangulate with existing sources of data. Future work will evaluate the effectiveness of Wiki and Wiki-based learning analytics in primary education.

ACKNOWLEDGMENTS

This study is partially supported by an Early Career Scheme grant from the Research Grants Council of the Hong Kong Special Administrative Region, China (Project No. HKU 27401114).

REFERENCES

Akoglu, H. (2018). User's guide to correlation coefficients. *Turkish Journal of Emergency Medicine.*

Chu, S. K. W., Siu, F., Liang, M., Capio, C. M., & Wu, W. W. (2013). Users' experiences and perceptions on using two wiki platforms for collaborative learning and knowledge management. *Online Information Review, 37*(2), 304–325.

Dyckhoff, A. L., Zielke, D., Bültmann, M., Chatti, M. A., & Schroeder, U. (2012). Design and implementation of a learning analytics toolkit for teachers. *Journal of Educational Technology & Society, 15*(3), 58–76.

Hu, X. (2017). Automated recognition of thinking orders in secondary school student writings. *Learning: Research and Practice, 3*(1), 30–41.

Hu, X., Ip, J., Sadaful, K., Lui, G., & Chu, S. (2016). Wikiglass: A learning analytic tool for visualizing collaborative wikis of secondary school students. In *Proceedings of the 6th international conference on learning analytics and knowledge proceedings LAK '16.*

Kear, K., Donelan, H., & Williams, J. (2014). Using wikis for online group projects: Student and tutor perspectives. *The*

International Review of Research in Open and Distributed Learning, *15*(4).

Krathwohl, D. R. (2002). A revision of Bloom's taxonomy: An overview. *Theory into Practice*, *41*(4), 212–218.

Naismith, L., Lee, B. H., & Pilkington, R. M. (2011). Collaborative learning with a wiki: Differences in perceived usefulness in two contexts of use. *Journal of Computer Assisted Learning*, *27*(3), 228–242.

Papamitsiou, Z., & Economides, A. A. (2014). Learning analytics and educational data mining in practice: A systematic literature review of empirical evidence. *Educational Technology & Society*, *17*(4), 49–64.

Rodríguez-Triana, M. J., Martínez-Monés, A., Asensio-Pérez, J. I., & Dimitriadis, Y. (2015). Scripting and monitoring meet each other: Aligning learning analytics and learning design to support teachers in orchestrating CSCL situations. *British Journal of Educational Technology*, *46*(2), 330–343.

Strijbos, J.-W. (2011). Assessment of (computer-supported) collaborative learning. *IEEE Transactions on Learning Technologies*, *4*(1), 59–73.

Zheng, L., Chen, N.-S., Huang, R., & Yang, K. (2014). A novel approach to assess collaborative learning processes and group performance through the knowledge convergence. *Journal of Computers Education*, *1*(2-3), 167–185.

Introducing Orbis: An Extendable Evaluation Pipeline for Named Entity Linking Performance Drill-Down Analyses

Fabian Odoni
University of Applied Sciences Chur, Switzerland
fabian.odoni@htwchur.ch

Adrian M. P. Braşoveanu
Modul Technology GmbH Vienna, Austria
adrian.brasoveanu@modul.ac.at

Philipp Kuntschik
University of Applied Sciences Chur, Switzerland
philipp.kuntschik@htwchur.ch

Albert Weichselbraun
University of Applied Sciences Chur, Switzerland
albert.weichselbraun@htwchur.ch

ABSTRACT

Most current evaluation tools are focused solely on benchmarking and comparative evaluations thus only provide aggregated statistics such as precision, recall and F1-measure to assess overall system performance. They do not offer comprehensive analyses up to the level of individual annotations. This paper introduces Orbis, an extendable evaluation pipeline framework developed to allow visual drill-down analyses of individual entities, computed by annotation services, in the context of the text they appear in, in reference to the entities specified in the gold standard.

KEYWORDS

Named Entity Linking; Evaluation; Drill-down Analysis

ASIS&T THESAURUS

Evaluation (Term ID: 225)
Natural Language Processing (Term ID: 1246)
Entity Extraction (Term ID: 1152)
Data Visualization (Term ID: 3010)

INTRODUCTION

In order to measure and improve Named Entity Linking (NEL) performance, gold standards are used to evaluate the annotator predictions by using binary classification measures such as precision, recall and F1-measure. Projects and challenges like GERBIL and TAC-KBP provide researchers with powerful tools to determine aggregated performance metrics but do not supply any sophisticated means for visualizing individual results and performing drill-down analyses. They might provide options to inspect single annotations but do not offer intuitive, output formats that can be processed efficiently by humans. Instead, their output formats such as CSV files or spreadsheets contain not much more than the classification status of each annotation (recognized and linked correctly or not). Additional data to investigate the cause of a prediction, for example the context of the annotation in form of the full text or sentence, is not provided. Without this additional data, potential external error causes such as gold standard flaws that were introduced building the data set, Knowledge Base (KB) errors, or the use of different annotation guidelines are hard to detect (Brasoveanu, Rizzo, Kuntschik, Weichselbraun, & Nixon, 2018). Confronted with these problems we started to develop Orbis.

82nd Annual Meeting of the Association for Information Science & Technology | Melbourne, Australia | 19–23 October, 2019

DOI: 10.1002/pra2.00049

Orbis is a versatile framework for performing NEL evaluation analyses. It supports standard metrics such as precision, recall and F1-score and visualizes gold standard and annotator results in the context of the annotated document. Color coding the entities allows the experts to quickly identify correct and incorrect annotations and the corresponding links to the KB that are also provided by Orbis. Due to the modular pipeline architecture used by Orbis different stages in the evaluation process can be easily modified, replaced or added.

Results of our first Orbis based drill-down analyses efforts were presented at the SEMANTiCS 2018 Conference in Vienna (Odoni, Kuntschik, Braşoveanu, & Weichselbraun, 2018). Motivated by the positive feedback we received for our novel way for answering the why-question, we continued development, to be able to release Orbis as open-source software to a broader user base.

RELATED WORK

Most current evaluation systems focus on measuring performance and thus emphasize aggregated metrics such as precision, recall and F1-score. They offer little to no output to allow drill-down analyses or error analyses.

Tools like GERBIL can be used to evaluate different NEL systems on a large scale (Röder, Usbeck, & Ngonga Ngomo, 2017). GERBIL has been used in many NEL challenges (e.g., ESWC's Open Knowledge Extraction Challenges, ISWC's Semantic Web Challenges) providing more than 10 datasets in its online version, supporting NIF (Natural Language Processing Interchange Format) for gold standards, and multiple experiment types. GERBIL focuses on comparing results between different NEL systems and provides a comprehensive benchmarking system to do so.

The scorer (Hachey, Nothman, & Radford, 2014) used in the TAC-KBP challenges (Ji, Nothman, Dang, & Hub, 2016) provides the researcher with an option to inspect individual results and evaluation runs. It yields an output with each predicted entity and the corresponding score (correct, incorrect, missing or false positive) but not the context of the predicted annotation.

APPROACH

Orbis provides an extensible framework to create evaluation pipelines using YAML configuration files for individual evaluation runs. It offers multiple evaluation modes, parallel evaluation runs, resource versioning, and dataset normalization. A basic graphical drill-down analysis is provided by creating html files that can be viewed in the browser.

System Architecture

Orbis consists of two core components (see Figure 1). The first component is the "Orbis Control" component which handles the evaluation management. It loads the evaluation configuration files and executes the evaluations within the pipeline. Depending on the settings it will load all configuration files from a defined folder or just one specific file. Additional data used for multiple evaluation runs will be loaded and cached in order to avoid multiple and thus time consuming reloads.

The second component is the Orbis pipeline. The pipeline consists of three stages and multiple pipelines can be run simultaneously. The first stage is for the acquisition and normalization of the NEL annotations, the second stage handles the assessment of the annotations and the third stage concerns storage and display of the results.

In order to traverse the pipeline an object is created to store all the data and results needed for that evaluation run and provides methods for the separate stages to read and load data. This object is then passed from one stage to the next providing and collecting everything needed for the evaluation.

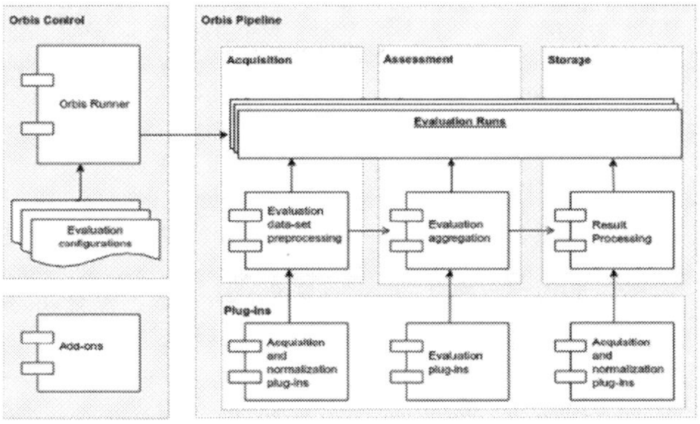

Figure 1. The Orbis system diagram.

The acquisition and normalization stage loads the evaluation corpus as well as its gold standard. Additionally it will search the specified annotation module defined in the YAML configuration file of that evaluation run, load it into Orbis and query the annotation service. A built-in caching framework can be used to speed up evaluations and reduce the load imposed on third party web services. At the time of writing, the following annotation tools are supported by Orbis: Spotlight,[1] AIDA[2] and Babelfly[3] as well as the Recognyze[4] annotation tools.

The assessment stage evaluates the predicted results against the gold standard. The predicted annotations are scored according to scoring rules and the resulting confusion matrix is used to calculate micro and macro precision, recall, and F1-measures.

In the storage and display stage the data is converted to storage and display formats. At this point the evaluation run object contains all the relevant data and the storage stage transforms this data into appropriate formats. Results can be saved as CSV, JSON or even sent to a Graphite server for time series visualization. For a detailed drill-down analysis, and one of the main drivers in developing Orbis, the storage stage can also convert the results into a detailed HTML based, per item view of the predicted entities, embedded in the corpus alongside the gold annotations (see Figure 2).

Plug-in System

Initially Orbis was only designed for internal use and thus was more of a compilation of scripts performing specific tasks. With time, more and more use cases arose and Orbis continually grew to a point where structuring Orbis into a pipeline made sense in order to keep Orbis maintainable. For this reason a modular system was developed to allow Orbis users to define the acquisition, assessment and storage stage components directly in the evaluation run configuration. By copy-pasting the configuration run files and merely changing the type of annotation service the same evaluation of two different annotator services can be run and compared with ease since Orbis would automatically search and load the necessary modules.

To fully utilize this pipeline extensibility, a modularization architecture, based on plug-ins, was implemented providing standardized data loading and storing methods, and devising rules on how a module should be built in order for Orbis to find and load a module. With this plug-in system third parties can develop and implement their own modules to provide Orbis access to additional web services, implement new scoring rules and metrics as well as new output formats.

[1] https://www.dbpedia-spotlight.org/
[2] https://www.mpi-inf.mpg.de/departments/databases-and-information-systems/research/ambiverse-nlu/aida/
[3] http://babelfy.org/guide#Disambiguateatext
[4] https://www.weblyzard.com/recognyze/

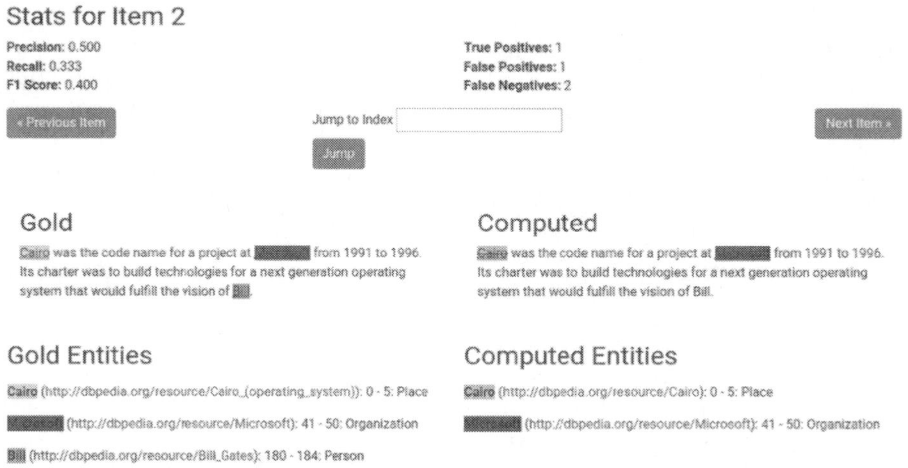

Figure 2. HTML view for drill-down analysis of predicted annotations compared to gold standard annotations.

Monocle

Monocle for Orbis provides a system to manage knowledge bases and evaluation corpora. This is done by using mappings, lenses, and filters.

Mappings

Most gold standard corpora use DBpedia as a knowledge source. Nevertheless, with the recent success of other linked data initiatives such as Wikidata, GeoNames and linked government data, named entity linking approaches have started to draw upon these other sources that even may surpass DBpedia's quality for same tasks. To compare the performance of such approaches, a mapping between these linked data sources and the DBpedia gold standard annotations needs to be established. Orbis provides a possibility to map KB links by providing a new link for a specific link found in the gold standard.

Lenses

Gold standard corpora are created based on a specific KB version available at the time of creation but are often not updated or rebuilt when the KB changes and evolves. Due to this, annotator services running on newer versions of a KB are likely to find entities that have not been annotated in the original gold standard because these entities can only be found in recent KB versions and have not been previously available. Lenses provide means for adjusting to such circumstances by letting Orbis only consider predicted annotations of entities found in the desired KB version.

Filters

Gold standard corpora often follow different annotation styles and guidelines. For instance, a location entity such as "Washington, DC" might be either annotated as one entity (Washington, the capital of the United States), or as two (once as the city of Washington and once as the District of Columbia). Filters provide means toward mitigating such differences and ensuring that NEL components that follow different guidelines are treated fairly by allowing researchers to manually exclude certain annotations from the evaluation process.

Gold Standard Link Equivalence

Modifying a gold standard is not considered good practice, however, replacing the existing links from a gold with the equivalent links from another KB (e.g., replacing DBpedia links with Wikidata links) should be a good scenario, otherwise the loss of gold standards due to links from KBs that are not maintained anymore could become a common issue. Modern KBs have a convoluted history as most of them start life as a research project that is than taken over by a private company or association. Due to this process, some KBs are discontinued (e.g., Freebase), others changed owners (e.g., DBpedia), while others are continuously updated (e.g., Wikidata). This also means that some corpora annotated with older KBs (e.g., Freebase, early DBpedia versions <3.9) might not be usable today. In order to update them, a mechanism to update these links is needed and lenses do enable this mechanism. A direct translation of the links involves simply collecting the corresponding links from the new KB (e.g., owl:SameAs, skos:exactMatch, skos:closeMatch) or checking that the old links are still okay in the current KB version (e.g., when converting DBpedia 3.7 links to DBpedia 2018 links). Such a translation is possible directly by using monocle, but it should only be used if the results are high quality, for example if (1) the number of correct annotations from the original corpora is high; (2) the number of missing annotations from the original corpora is small; and (3) the quality of the link alignment is high (e.g., over 90% of the entities have good equivalent links). If one wants to improve upon the original entities, then only by using the published annotation rules of the respective corpora.

Add-ons

Orbis provides an add-on infrastructure to auto detect add-ons and execute them. Unlike plug-ins that plug into the Orbis pipeline and are used for evaluation purposes, Orbis add-ons perform tasks outside of the Orbis evaluation runs. Orbis add-ons provided to date are a YAML configuration builder, an annotation comparison tool to view two evaluation runs next to each other and a corpus downloader to download corpora and the respective gold standard. A gold standard quality checking add-on is under development and will be released this year.

Corpus Downloader

In order to use or test Orbis, a corpus is needed to run these tests on. Orbis provides a corpus loader that downloads and converts gold corpus files into an Orbis corpus structure. NIF is supported to be used as corpus loading format, accessing the data from the NIF dataset and storing it in Orbis. This Orbis corpus structure also allows researchers to quickly access parts of the corpus for further analysis and can be saved with the annotation results and metrics in a single file for future reference.

Gold Standard Quality Check

Compiling gold standards is a very time and labor intensive task. We, therefore, plan to develop a gold standard quality checker add-on that provides heuristics for verifying the correctness of gold standard annotations.

These heuristics draw upon natural language processing methods that provide additional metadata by performing dependency parsing (e.g., Stanford, Spacy or custom components), part-of-speech tagging (e.g., to identify verbs between proper nouns) and named entity recognition (NER, i.e., to determine the entity's type such as location, organization and person).

The Orbis gold standard quality checker will then use these metadata to validate whether the gold standard annotations correspond to the expected usage of annotation types within the sentence and whether the named entity type determined by the NER component matches the gold standard annotation's entity type.

The Gold standard quality checker, can not only help (1) in illuminating issues with the original annotations, but also be adapted to (2) identify missing annotations (e.g., if the NER component identified an entity that has not been annotated),.

Methods for validating corpus quality are easily implemented with Orbis and should be used to ensure the validity of evaluation settings, since gold standards are expensive and rarely updated. We plan to further extend the capabilities of the gold standard quality checker to include more complex mechanisms for verifying gold standard quality.

CONCLUSION AND OUTLOOK

Orbis has proven to be useful for our research. It serves as a tool for NEL researchers to understand issues with their systems, and does not intend to rival or replace existing evaluation tools like GERBIL or TAC-KBP but is intended as an additional tool focusing on evaluation analyses. The pipeline architecture allows third party developers to utilize and extend Orbis. Further efforts are being made to not only allow NEL evaluations to be run but also other evaluation types for other tasks e.g., slot filling, POS tagging, sentiment analysis or dependency parsing.

A first public version of Orbis was released on Github[5] and future releases will be published to the same project account. We hope to not only provide researchers with a useful tool but also gain new Orbis developers that implement their own modules for various stages in the pipeline and help us to advance Orbis to become an evaluation tool for various tasks in the field of natural language processing.

REFERENCES

Brasoveanu, A., Rizzo, G., Kuntschik, P., Weichselbraun, A., & Nixon, L. J. B. (2018). Framing named entity linking error types. In *Proceedings of the Eleventh International Conference on Language Resources and Evaluation (LREC-2018)*.

Hachey, B., Nothman, J., & Radford, W. (2014). Cheap and easy entity evaluation. In *Proceedings of the 52nd Annual Meeting of the Association for Computational Linguistics (Volume 2: Short Papers)* (Vol. 2, pp. 464–469).

Ji, H., Nothman, J., Dang, H. T., & Hub, S. I. (2016). Overview of TAC-KBP2016 tri-lingual EDL and its impact on end-to-end cold-start KBP. In *Proceedings of TAC*.

Odoni, F., Kuntschik, P., Braşoveanu, A. M. P., & Weichselbraun, A. (2018). On the importance of drill-down analysis for assessing gold standards and named entity linking performance. *Procedia Computer Science*, *137*, 33–42. https://doi.org/10.1016/j.procs.2018.09.004

Röder, M., Usbeck, R., & Ngonga Ngomo, A.-C. (2017). GERBIL – benchmarking named entity recognition and linking consistently. *Semantic Web* (Preprint, 1–21.

[5] https://github.com/orbis-eval/Orbis

Exploring the Function of Citations in Ancient Chinese Literature

Fei Shu
Hangzhou Dianzi University, Hangzhou, China
fei.shu@hdu.edu.cn

Junping Qiu
Hangzhou Dianzi University, Hangzhou, China
jpqiu@hdu.edu.cn

Shibin Shu
Hangzhou Dianzi University, Hangzhou, China
shushibin@hdu.edu.cn

Vincent Larivière
Université de Montréal, Montréal, Canada
vincent.lariviere@umontreal.ca

ABSTRACT

Over the last 40 years, several studies have attempted to better understand the function of citations in scholarly communication. While the normative theory claims that researchers acknowledge the intellectual influence to their peers through citations, constructive theory suggests that authors cite to persuade their readers. This study explores this topic by analyzing citations found in ancient Chinese literature and finds that most ancient Chinese authors cite to convince their readers.

KEYWORDS

Function of Citation; Normative Theory; Constructive Theory; Chinese Ancient Literature

ASIS&T THESAURUS

Information Science History; Bibliometrics

INTRODUCTION

Citation analysis is at the heart of bibliometrics. It is used to evaluate the scholarly impact of journals based (Garfield, 1972, 1979), explore research networks through co-citation analysis (Small, 1973), and measuring the impact of research in their fields (Melkers, 1993). Although giving credit to other researchers and acknowledging their contributions to a piece of work in the form of referencing is a scientific tradition (Garfield, 1977), the reasons behind the act of citing remain poorly understood (Garfield, 1965; Smith, 1981; M. White & Wang, 1997).

Although several studies, based on different datasets, attempt to create a comprehensive theory of citations explaining the reason to cite, such comprehensive theory of citation still has not been formulated (Leydesdorff, 1998; Moed, 2005). The purpose of this study is to contribute to this topic by investigating a relatively peculiar atypical bibliometric dataset: citations in ancient Chinese literature.

82nd Annual Meeting of the Association for Information Science & Technology | Melbourne, Australia | 19–23 October, 2019

DOI: 10.1002/pra2.00050

LITERATURE REVIEW

Definition of Citation

Citations are generally regarded as rewards that grant scientists recognition for their distinctive contributions (Merton, 1973), as each citation represents a decision, from an author, that the work of another is relevant to hers or his (Liu, 1990). Garfield (1955, 1964) also suggested that a reference in a citing document can be viewed as an indexing term, better than traditional subject headings, labeling the cited document. Based on Garfield's idea, Small (1978) points out that each citation could be a concept symbol because it incorporates the citer's idea in a specific context. Price (1963) refers citations to a method in which each research is built on the foundation of previous works.

Gilbert (1977) proposes a different notion: citing is an aid to persuasion; it aims to convince an audience of the authoritative of research findings. Some scholars join the argument one after another and propose a variety of contexts for the definition of citations (Cozzens, 1989; Cronin, 1984; Martin & Irvine, 1993; van Raan, 1998; H. D. White, 2004; Zuckerman, 1987). A unified theory of citations has been called for a long time, but it is still lacking (Cronin, 1981; Leydesdorff, 1998; Small, 2004).

Function of Citations

The function of citations can be defined as the reason behind the act of citing a specific document (Bornmann & Daniel, 2008; Tahamtan & Bornmann, 2018; Teufel, Siddharthan, & Tidhar, 2006). Kochen (1974) believes that most authors arbitrarily select references for their bibliographies. Both Edge (1977) and Kaplan (1965) indicate that authors' decision to cite may be influenced by colleagues, peers, or journals' gatekeepers, such as editors and editorial boards members (Camacho-Minano & Nunez-Nickel, 2009; Cronin, 1982; Franck, 1999). Although a lot of studies regarding the function of citations have been conducted, we still do not know enough about why the authors cite or not cite (Smith, 1981; M. White & Wang, 1997). Indeed, there are two different theories of citations based on two different philosophy foundations: normative theory and constructive theory.

The normative theory of citations is based on Robert Merton's social theory of science and assumes that science is a social institution with values, norms and rewards (Merton, 1957, 1973). The normative theory suggests that scientists give credits to colleagues whose works they use by citing their works. Scientists are believed to exchange publications for recognition in the form of awards and citations (Hagstrom, 1965). Thus, citations can represent intellectual influence and contribution (Baldi, 1998). Kaplan (1965) points out that citing should be regarded as a normative behavior acknowledging the intellectual influence. It means that an author's reasons to cite are controlled by an internalized set of norms within this normative institution (Cronin, 1984).

Social constructivists challenge the normative theory based on socio-constructivists frameworks (Knorr-Cetina, 1981; Latour & Woolgar, 1979), they argue that knowledge is socially constructed through the manipulation of political and financial resources and the use of rhetorical devices (Bloor, 1976; Edge, 1977; Knorr-Cetina, 1981; Latour & Woolgar, 1979; Mulkay, 1979). Constructivists have different interpretations of authors' citing behavior. They believe that scientists have more complex citing motivations including social, political and financial issues than acknowledging the intellectual influence (May, 1967). In the socio-constructivist theory of citation, science is the art of persuasion (Latour & Woolgar, 1979), and is citation is its tool (Gilbert, 1977). In order words, to persuade authors and reviewers, researchers cite papers they consider their audience will consider as valid and important (Gilbert, 1977).

Dynasty	Period	Number of articles	Number of articles having citations	Total number of citations
Eastern Zhou including Warring States	771-221 BC	56	7	9
Qing	221-207 BC	17	3	3
Han	202 BC - 220 AD	31	19	46
Wei Jin Southern and Northern Dynasties	220-581 AD	5	1	1
Sui and Tang	581-907 AD	44	14	34
Song	960 -1279 AD	51	14	22
Ming	1368-1644 AD	18	4	8
Total		**222**	**62**	**123**

Table 1. Distribution of the citations retrieved from *Guwen Guanzhi.*

Functions	Description
Applied	The citing paper borrows or adopts a significant element from the cited paper and uses it in developing its own theme or study.
Contrastive	The citing paper contrasts its data, method, model, theory, findings, and so on with what was used, documented, reported, or found in the cited paper
Supportive	The citing paper refers to the cited papers to justify its algorithm, assumption, data, sample size, methodology, research purpose, or results.
Reviewed	The cited paper provides the readers with contextual information to understand the broad context of the study or the significance of the research questions or problems of the citing paper.
Perfunctory	The cited paper has little importance, significance, or contribution to the theme, analysis or results of the citing paper.

Table 2. Citation Scheme provided by Tabatabaei (2013).

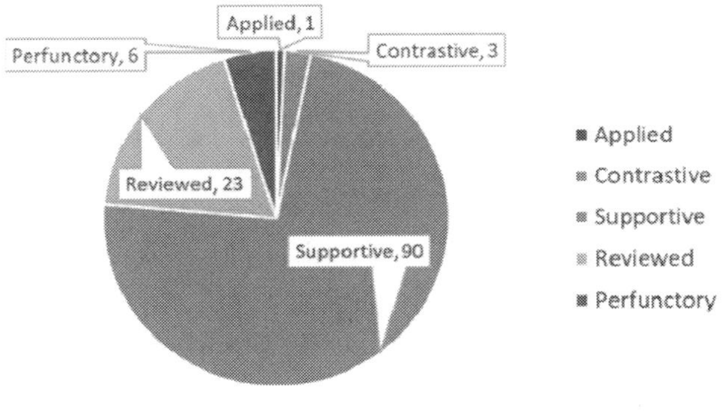

Figure 1. Distribution of citations by function.

Related Work

There are two approaches for investigating the function of citations. In the first approach, researchers aim to understand reasons behind the act of citing through what people say. Such approach focuses on citing authors and explore citation motivation or behavior through questionnaires or interviews. In the second approach, researchers use the full-text of scholarly documents and aim to find authors' citing intention by citation context analysis. Irrespective of the approaches, most previous research on the topic aim at validating either normative or constructivist approaches. Since either theory is supported or challenged by different research findings, it is difficult to say that one theory is better than another (Small, 1998).

Although there is no clear origin for the use of citations, historians of science believe that scientific authors started to cite and refer to earlier works (theories, methods, concepts, etc.) at the end of the sixteenth century (Nicolaisen, 2007). However, in China, it had been also a tradition in ancient Chinese literature for thousands of years that authors quote the classics and use the allusions (引经据典 in Chinese), which could also be another origin of citations. Unfortunately, no previous study investigates such citations found in ancient Chinese literature, which will be addressed by this study.

METHODS

Dataset

In this study, all references cited by the ancient Chinese anthology of essays written in literary Chinese, *Guwen Guanzhi* (古文观止 in Chinese), were retrieved. This anthology was first published during the Qing dynasty in 1694 as a textbook for Chinese literature. It includes 222 articles from Eastern Zhou dynasty (771–256 BC) to the Ming dynasty (1368–1644). This book is still widely used as reading material of ancient Chinese literature in secondary education in the Greater China Region, including the Mainland China, Hong Kong, Macao and Taiwan.

Ancient Chinese authors quote the classics and use the allusions (i.e., classic stories from ancient Chinese literature) but in different formats from modern citations. There is no in-text citation or bibliography in ancient Chinese literature, so the citations need to manually be identified by going through the text. In addition, most Chinese allusions are history stories, which are not regarded as intellectual contribution (Dolby, 2016); thus in this study, only quotations from these articles were collected while all allusions were excluded in the data collection. One hundred and twenty three citations were retrieved from 62 out of 220 articles in *Guwen Guanzhi* as shown in Table 1. However, due to the lack of the in-text citation and bibliography, 16 citations (13.0%) were recognized but missing the bibliographic information of cited sources.

Data Analysis

All 123 citations were categorized into five groups using the method developed by Tabatabaei (2013). This method which provides a citation scheme including five citation functions as shown in Table 2. Instead of exploring the citation motivation (reasons to cite), Tabatabaei (2013) develops a citation scheme by investigating the impact of cited papers on the citing papers. As there are no existing citation scheme for ancient Chinese literature, all citations were manually coded based on their impact on the citing papers using Tabatabaei (2013)'s citation scheme.

PRELIMINARY RESULTS

Of all the 123 citations, only five citations were contributed by articles while the rest were made to monographs or books. *Analects* was cited 20 times and is the most cited sources in this study, followed by *I Ching* (17) and *Book of Documents* (11). Confucius was the most cited individual contributing more than one third of citations (46/123) from five different sources: *Analects* (20), *Book of Documents* (11), *Spring and Autumn Annals* (6), *Book of Rites* (6), and *Classic of Filial Piety* (2). Two citations contributed by Mencius and King Wen of Zhou respectively were cited two times.

Although the cited sources vary, their functions were similar. As Figure 1 shows, 90 out of 123 citations were coded under "supportive" category while only 1 and 3 citations were coded under "applied" and "contrastive" categories respectively. In addition, 23 and 6 citations were coded under "reviewed" and "perfunctory" categories respectively. A difference was found before and after Wei Jin Southern and Northern Dynasties. All applied and contrastive citations were found in literature before this period while all perfunctory citations were retrieved from literature after this period. In addition, the ratio of supportive citations to all citations was 63.8% and 82.8% respectively in literature before and after this period.

DISCUSSION AND CONCLUSION

In this study, after investigating 123 citations from ancient Chinese literature from eighth century BC to seventeenth century, we found that ancient Chinese authors would like to quote the classics from Chinese saints such as Confucius, Mencius, and King Wen of Zhou to support their assertions or opinions. The findings partly confirm that authors would like to cite valid and important sources to convince their readers (Gilbert, 1977; Latour & Woolgar, 1979).

As a short paper, there are also several limitations in this study. The sample size is not big since only 123 citations are under investigation; some cited sources were not identified in the data analysis; literacy scholars may have different citing behavior from scholars in other disciplines, which was found by Frost (1979); the citation scheme used in this study may be inappropriate for ancient Chinese literature, which should be addressed in the future.

REFERENCES

Baldi, S. (1998). Normative versus social constructivist processes in the allocation of citations: A network-analytic model. *American Sociological Review, 63*(6), 829–846.

Bloor, D. (1976). *Knowledge and social imagery*. London, England and Boston, MA: Routledge & K. Paul.

Bornmann, L., & Daniel, H. D. (2008). What do citation counts measure? A review of studies on citing behavior. *Journal of Documentation, 64*(1), 45–80.

Camacho-Minano, M.-d.-M., & Nunez-Nickel, M. (2009). The multilayered nature of reference selection. *Journal of the American Society for Information Science and Technology*, *60*(4), 754–777.

Cozzens, S. E. (1989). What do citations count? The rhetoric-first model. *Scientometrics*, *15*(5-6), 437–447.

Cronin, B. (1981). The need for a theory of citing. *Journal of Documentation*, *37*(1), 16–24.

Cronin, B. (1982). Norms and functions in citation: The view of journal editors and referees in psychology. *Social Science Information Studies*, *2*(2), 65–77.

Cronin, B. (1984). *The citation process : The role and significance of citations in scientific communication*. London, England: T. Graham.

Dolby, W. (2016). *William Dolby* (2nd ed.). Edinburgh, England: Straightback Publishing.

Edge, D. (1977). Why I am not a co-citationist. *Society for Social Studies of Science Newsletter*, *2*, 13–19.

Franck, G. (1999). Scientific communication -- a vanity fair? *Science*, *286*(5437), 53–55.

Frost, C. O. (1979). The use of citations in literary research: A preliminary classification of citation functions. *The Library Quarterly*, *49*(4), 399–414. https://doi.org/10.1086/600930.

Garfield, E. (1955). Citation indexes for science: A new dimension in documentation through association of ideas. *Science*, *122*(3159), 108–111.

Garfield, E. (1964). "Science citation index" - A new dimension in indexing. *Science*, *144*(3619), 649–654.

Garfield, E. (1965). *Can citation indexing be automated*. In *Paper presented at the Statistical Association Methods for Mechanized Documentation, Symposium Proceedings*. Washington, DC.

Garfield, E. (1972). Citation analysis as a tool in journal evaluation. *Science*, *178*(4060), 471–479.

Garfield, E. (1977). To cite or not to cite: A note of annoyance. *Current Contents*, *35*, 5–8.

Garfield, E. (1979). *Citation indexing - its theory and application in science, technology, and humanities*. New York, NY: Wiley.

Gilbert, N. (1977). Referencing as persuasion. *Social Studies of Science*, *7*(1), 113–122.

Hagstrom, W. O. (1965). *The scientific community*. New York, NY: Basic Books.

Kaplan, N. (1965). The norms of citation behavior: Prolegomena to the footnote. *American Documentation*, *16* (3), 179–184.

Knorr-Cetina, K. (1981). *The manufacture of knowledge: an essay on the constructivist and contextual nature of science*. Oxford, England and New York, NY: Pergamon Press.

Kochen, M. (1974). *Principles of information retrieval*. Los Angeles, CA: Melville Pub. Co.

Latour, B., & Woolgar, S. (1979). *Laboratory life: The social construction of scientific facts*. Beverly Hills, CA: SAGE Publications.

Leydesdorff, L. (1998). Theories of citation? *Scientometrics*, *43*(1), 5–25.

Liu, M. (1990). *The citation process in scientific communication: An analysis of citer motivation and citation characteristics of Chinese physicists* (PhD ProQuest Dissertations & Theses Full Text database). University of Michigan.

Martin, B., & Irvine, J. (1993). Assessing basic research: Some partial indicators of scientific progress in radio astronomy. *Research Policy*, *22*(2), 106.

May, K. O. (1967). Abuses of citation indexing. *Science*, *156* (3777), 890–892.

Melkers, J. (1993). Bibliometrics as a tool for analysis of R&D impacts. In B. Bozeman & J. Melkers, *Evaluating R&D impacts : Methods and practice*. New York, NY: Springer Science+ Business Media.

Merton, R. K. (1957). Priorities in scientific discovery: A chapter in the sociology of science. *American Sociological Review*, *22*(6), 635–659.

Merton, R. K. (1973). *The sociology of science: Theoretical and empirical investigations*. Chicago, IL: University of Chicago Press.

Moed, H. (2005). *Citation analysis in research evaluation*. Dordrecht, England: Springer.

Mulkay, M. J. (1979). *Science and the sociology of knowledge*. London, England: G. Allen & Unwin.

Nicolaisen, J. (2007). Citation analysis. *ARIS Annual Review of Information Science and Technology*, *41*(1), 609–641.

Price, D. J. d. S. (1963). *Little science, big science*. New York, NY: Columbia University Press.

Small, H. (1973). Co-citation in the scientific literature: A new measure of the relationship between two documents. *Journal of the American Society for Information Science*, *24*(4), 265–269.

Small, H. (1978). Cited documents as concept symbols. *Social Studies of Science*, *8*, 327–340.

Small, H. (1998). Citations and consilience in science. *Scientometrics*, *43*(1), 143–148.

Small, H. (2004). On the shoulders of Robert Merton: Towards a normative theory of citation. *Scientometrics*, *60*(1), 71–79.

Smith, L. C. (1981). Citation analysis. *Library Trends*, *30*, 83.

Tabatabaei, N. (2013). *Contribution of information science to other disciplines as reflected in citation contexts of highly cited JASIST papers*. McGill University. Retrieved from http://digitool.Library.McGill.CA:80/R/?func=dbin-jump-full&object_id=116895

Tahamtan, I., & Bornmann, L. (2018). Core elements in the process of citing publications: Conceptual overview of the literature. *Journal of Informetrics*, *12*(1), 203–216.

Teufel, S., Siddharthan, A., & Tidhar, D. (2006). Automatic classification of citation function. In *Paper presented at the Proceedings of the 2006 Conference on Empirical Methods in Natural Language Processing*. Sydney, Australia.

van Raan, A. F. J. (1998). In matters of quantitative studies of science the fault of theorists is offering too little and asking too much. *Scientometrics*, *43*(1), 129–139.

White, H. D. (2004). Reward, persuasion, and the Sokal Hoax: A study in citation identities. *Scientometrics*, *60* (1), 93–120.

White, M., & Wang, P. (1997). A qualitative study of citing behavior: Contributions, criteria, and metalevel documentation concerns. *Library Quarterly*, *67*(2), 122–154.

Zuckerman, H. (1987). Citation analysis and the complex problem of intellectual influence. *Scientometrics*, *12* (5-6), 329–338.

Facilitating Open Access to Information: A Community Approach to Open Education and Open Textbooks

Adrian Stagg
University of Southern Queensland
Toowoomba, Australia
adrian.stagg@usq.edu.au

Helen Partridge
University of Southern Queensland
Toowoomba, Australia
helen.partridge@usq.edu.au

ABSTRACT

Access to information as a necessary precondition for human flourishing is recognized explicitly in the UNESCO Strategic Development Goals, and mirrored by the work of universities globally to reduce barriers to information, especially research outputs. Growing international attention has turned to learning and teaching resources, particularly textbooks as a key barrier to fully engaging with, and participating in, higher education. The affordances of open texts provide an alternative to commercially published and often exclusionary access practices; and empower educators and students in co-creation and open sharing of information and knowledge. This paper examines the design of an ongoing institutional grants program predicated on a facilitated community learning approach for academic staff seeking to adopt, or adapt open textbooks into the curriculum as one mechanism to increase access to information. The participants' experiences and personal learning were captured through a series of semi-structured interviews that inform the iterative design of the ongoing grants program that could be transferred to other institutions seeking to support educational change.

KEYWORDS

Open Educational Resources; Open Textbooks; Higher Education Access; Information Access; Theory of Educational Change

ASIS&T THESAURUS

Staff Development, Communities of Practice, Information Resources

INTRODUCTION

Open textbooks represent a significant lever to provide information resources free of cost to students and informal learners, and provide alternatives to traditional, proprietary sources of knowledge. Already well-established in the United States and Canada, open textbooks have begun to appear on the Australian higher education landscape in a response to costs that are exclusionary to parts of the student cohort, and antithetical to a university committed to broadening access to, and widening participation in, equitable higher education.

The University of Southern Queensland (USQ) is a regional university with a high proportion of students from low socio-economic backgrounds, from regional and remote communities, and those who are "first in family" to study at the tertiary level. Furthermore, it provides access to education to the largest incarcerated student cohort in Australia. It is recognized that textbook costs are a significant financial burden, and barrier to information access not only for these cohorts, but all students; from this an ongoing Open Educational Practice Grant Scheme was conceived in 2015.

OPEN EDUCATION AND OPEN TEXTBOOKS

Open educational resources (OER) "*can be defined as teaching and learning resources in any medium, digital or otherwise, that permit no-cost access, use, reuse, and repurposing by others with no or limited restrictions*" (McGreal, Miao, & Mishra, 2016, p. 1). The promise for higher education institutions engaging with OER include reduced costs for students, lowering barriers to tertiary education, exploring collaboration co-creative pedagogical practices, and the improvement in learning resources through reuse and co-construction of knowledge (UNESCO, 2016). While OER can include images, lesson plans, assessment, sound and video files, and entire courses, it is the textbook as OER that has generated international attention from both students and faculty.

Open textbooks provide flexibility for both students and educators, conceptualized as the "5 R's" (Wiley, 2014), namely the ability to *retain* (to store, print), *reuse* (to share freely for use in a variety of institutions and contexts), *repurpose* (to change format, for example converting text to audio), *remix* (to add to the resource, usually by incorporating other OER), and to *revise* (to update, and to make changes based on local teaching and learning needs). Many universities engaged with open text production include peer-review processes, and transparently publish the reviews alongside the

82nd Annual Meeting of the Association for Information Science & Technology | Melbourne, Australia | 19–23 October, 2019

DOI: 10.1002/pra2.00076

text (Ozdemir & Hendricks, 2017). Open textbooks provide affordances that are increasingly important as commercial publisher business models enclose knowledge, and privilege learners who can afford rising textbook costs. Increasingly, commercial textbooks include individual access codes to additional content (such as quizzes, case studies, and other value-add resources). This practice not only "locks out" students unable to afford the text, but removes second-hand texts as a viable information source as the codes are single-user only (Senack, Donoghue, Grant, & Steen, 2016). In an attempt to reduce student costs, other publishers instigated a rental scheme, reducing the overall cost of the text at the expense of perpetual access. Students are "locked out" of their text after semester concludes, unable to access the information, or use it post-graduation for professional purposes. The rising cost of textbooks was recognized by the Australian Student Union in 2016 (Jacobs, 2016), who responded with a petition for discussion in Federal Parliament, but no government action has been forthcoming, in direct contrast to international responses such as the Canadian provinces of British Columbia and Ontario committing to open text adoption after mounting student pressure (Barker, Jeffrey, Jhangiani, & Veletsianos, 2018).

In addition, fifteen years of research has yielded results that indicate awareness of OER (and in particular open textbooks) is still low, and that academic staff report the major barriers to use and reuse include a lack of time, and lack of sufficient skills to locate and appropriately interpret OER for localized contexts (McGreal et al., 2016). To realize the potential OER-empowered transformation of practice, therefore, requires time, support, and a meaningful context in which OER represent value to the curriculum. It should also be noted that while open texts are free to access and (re)use, they are not free to create and require institutional commitment to resourcing, reviewing, and integrating into existing practice, mirroring the experiences of institutional approaches to funding open access research publications (Pinfield, Salter, & Bath, 2016).

SUPPORTING OPEN TEXTBOOKS THROUGH GRANTS

In 2015, USQ committed funds to an Open Textbook Grants Scheme (later renamed the Open *Educational Practice Staff Scholarship Scheme*). The purpose of the T&L Grants generally is to construct an environment in which change to practice occurs in a structured, robust, repeatable (or transferable) manner resulting in innovation - relative to the institution or sector - that benefits students and develops the capabilities of educators. Developing leadership (especially practice-based, and thought leadership) may be explicit, implicit, or absent from the grants process, depending on the desired outcomes of the funding body. The emphasis on formal research publication and dissemination arising from the project is explicit in national grants schemes, but at the institutional level there may instead be a focus on enhancing practice within a Faculty (or other organizational unit). Linked to these principles were those of educational change, and the grant structure and processes needed to recognize the inherent challenges, especially as change is predicated on staff attitudes, beliefs, and values.

Engaging with the "beliefs, behaviors, attitudes, and values" of teaching is part of internal institutional change discourse; one intrinsically linked with open educational practice. A framework serves as a starting point, is viewed as an attempt to represent reality, and perspectives that interpret "framework-as-reality" are avoided. The framework is coupled with the realization that - as a construct - it provides the points of sameness or foundational consensus while simultaneously acknowledging the "subjective unknown" underlying individual paradigms that interpret reality.

Fullan and Stiegelbauer's *Theory of Educational Change* (1991) provides a lens to design and develop appropriate responses to these challenges; and to view ongoing engagement with the grant activities as situated professional learning. In this environment, de-contextualized, generic professional learning fails to reach its' full potential (Fullan & Stiegelauer, 1991) as the practitioner is incumbent to cognitively translate the generic skill set into a nuanced environment – often without dedicated support. Instead, Fullan's theoretical framework is predicated on four environment triggers namely that (1) staff need to actively participate in change seeking behavior usually starting in small groups and building in scope, (2) that pressure exists to change and that support exists to facilitate and navigate change, (3) that successful change requires attitudinal and behavioral change, and (4) that participants take ownership of the process as their confidence increases.

Staff agency and autonomy becomes a non-negotiable goal within the process and is achieved by providing a supportive, and supported environment in which they have the time and space to explore responsive approaches to their educational context, bounded by grant activities, and where the complexity of informational needs are acknowledged. The design supporting grant activity progress melded the *Theory of Educational Change* with Wenger's *Communities of Practice* (Wenger, 2010). In the CoP environment, the community is bounded by a domain of knowledge, committed to engaging with and building that domain collaboratively, underpinned by the consensus that the community space is "safe" for open discussion and practice. The designed community conceptually deviates from Wenger's original work (Dessne & Byström, 2015), however, the centrality of member autonomy was respected and the CoP leadership role was primarily focused on acting as a facilitator for the community, and intermediary between the CoP and the institution.

The resulting grants scheme developed to include a competitive call for proposals, supported by information sessions, and direct coaching to prepare submissions in the first phase, to a facilitated monthly community gathering of all successful grant awardees that focused on building professional networks and contacts, sharing emerging practice (and transferring practice across disciplines), peer-supported problem solving, and community celebration of individual successes. Most of the awardees were funded to author texts based on a mixture of original and open content; the remainder added value to curated OER by providing an explicit learning design that sequenced and aided students in "sense-making". From the outset, the facilitators strove to create an environment in which the community became responsible for charting their professional learning needs.

RESEARCH AND FINDINGS

Ongoing research has been conducted to understand the experience of the grant participants, especially in terms of the value ascribed to the support, and the types of mediated support that emerge during the completion of grant activities. Informed by a qualitative research approach, data is gathered through voluntary, semi-structured interviews, and subsequently organized in themes. Individual comments are isolated where statements illustrate the impact of strategies, or provide outcomes that are particularly valued by the participants. Over the 2015–2017 grants period, all successful grant awardees were invited to participate, seventeen out of twenty-four awardees agreed to be included in the research. They were interviewed at three key stages of the grant lifecycle; (1) three months after the grants were funded, (2) at seven months following the submission of an *Interim Report*, and (3) at thirteen months after the submission of the *Final Report*.

The predominant themes emerging from the interview analysis revealed *attitudes* to the experience of both the grant activities, and the community engagement; the *valued characteristics* of the community approach, and the *values, behaviors and attitudes* to open education.

Overwhelmingly, the participants described the community grant experience as *positive* experience, and an important *contributor* to their success, albeit an experience that was extremely *challenging*. The *regularity* of meeting intervals was valued, as a way of exploring *possibilities* for open textbooks, and as a forum to *generate, refine, and share ideas*. One participant [P01] noted:

> I think working with a team has been really good. Listening to other people, when we go to [] meetings... there are other people doing their own projects and the way they were doing them was a real eye-opener. It was something that gave me ideas, things to aspire to.

The role of the community was emphasized as highly *collaborative*, especially when related to *interactions with internal staff*, and the role of the facilitator was perceived as one of *guidance* and *connecting* – aligning with the original intent of a constructed CoP. The *approachability* of institutional staff, and willingness to *support* individual project was a key point of value, without which participants agree their projects would have been more challenging. The enduring nature of the networks beyond the grants is best encapsulated by reflections from one participant [P02]:

> There are other people there to help you see and just knowing that is really important. So that's another thing that it has changed for me with the openness, is knowing how many people are involved and sorts of things that they can help with, here at the uni particularly. But beyond the uni as well, you know through USQ's involvement with other organizations around openness, that all helps. I kind of feel like, if I wanted to do other stuff, I have more knowledge about who to go and ask.

When discussing open education, the experience of *authoring resources* dominated responses although *reflection on staff learning* was evident across the participants. Of particular note were concerns around staff knowledge of *copyright, and intellectual property policies* related to the creation of openly licensed content, and the need for pre-publication *quality assurance processes*. One participant described the need to recall Copyright and licensing with the following image, pointing to the need to reinforce concepts in practice:

> And so I go out there like, you know, like Little Red Riding Hood in the woods, with all my ideas in the basket and then suddenly come across the big bad wolf. What happened was, I had to really struggle to understand what creative commons licensing meant in practice. And I'm not very good with abstract figures and concepts unless they're embedded in a real experience that makes sense to me. So I kept forgetting what it meant and having to go back again and again.

Through the lens of policy influencing practice, copyright and intellectual property requires specific focus. Australian higher education institutions traditionally permit academic staff to retain ownership of research, while prevailing metrics of research prestige and impact are reliant (in some cases solely) on citation counts and Impact Factors. The underlying rationale espouses that research is valued when it reaches a wide readership, and is leveraged as the foundation (or contributor to) the creation or extension of new knowledge. By direct contrast, learning and teaching resources are traditionally closed to those outside of a course or unit, and ownership is retained by the university – the lecturer must seek policy approval to release course materials outside of the institution. This practice has ramifications for the perceived value of knowledge sharing, and the role of effective co-construction of knowledge across discipline fields. Policy misalignment between research output and learning resource construction was raised by a number of community participants; many of whom had not questioned the practice previously.

In cases where existing open content was (re)used in the grant project, participants expressed concern over the ability to locate sources of information *compatible with their local needs*, and the interaction of *existing license frameworks* (especially Creative Commons) with the university policy environment. *Ideological alignment* (that is to the extent to which an individual's personal beliefs about access to education drove engagement with openness) was not evident as a major theme, with a *student learning rationale* more common across participants. A post-grant reflection recorded in almost all interviews expressed a perception that open education was *poorly understood* across the institution (reflecting on the knowledge base of peers and colleagues) and that *baseline awareness* was low.

DISCUSSION

Based on the participant interviews, a supportive, community-based approach that provides regular space for discussion, the generation of new ideas, and testing of proposed activities is a valued approach to successfully developing staff learning concurrently with meeting the expectations of a funded grant process. The role of mediator and facilitator needs to be explicitly designed as a method of constructing a CoP, with a focus on structuring meetings as appropriate and connecting participant-identified needs with sources of information and expertise within the institution. Integrating open education with existing teaching and learning practices (especially in authoring or repurposing open textbooks) requires a deliberate and purposeful strategy and a focus on contextualized staff learning, driven by the participants and mediated by the CoP facilitator. The grants process also highlighted policy deficiencies, especially in the intellectual property area – that need to be addressed. Without this policy focus, open licensing of educational content remains the remit of funded grant activities only, instead of becoming normalized mainstream practice.

CONCLUSION

Open textbooks have the potential to reduce barriers to the creation, use, and dissemination of quality information resources that support authentic learning and teaching practices, and positively contribute to widening participation and increasing access to education globally. In order to engage with this agenda, staff require purposefully designed spaces (both physically and conceptually) that support staff learning, nurture relational approaches to learning resource design, and actively support the desired pedagogical outcomes.

REFERENCES

Barker, J., Jeffrey, K., Jhangiani, R., & Veletsianos, G. (2018). Eight patterns of open textbook adoption in British Columbia. *International review of research in open and distance learning*, *19*(3), 320–334. https://doi.org/10.19173/irrodl.v19i3.3723

Dessne, K., & Byström, K. (2015). Imitating CoPs: Imposing formality on informality. *Journal of the Association for Information Science & Technology*, *66*(11), 2277–2284. https://doi.org/10.1002/asi.23322

Fullan, M., & Stiegelauer, S. (1991). *The new meaning of educational change*. New York: Teachers College Press.

Jacobs, C. (2016). *National union of students launches campaign calling for cheaper university textbooks*, ABC news, February 20, Retrieved from https://www.abc.net.au/news/2016-02-20/call-for-cheaper-university-textbooks/7186214

McGreal, R., Miao, F., & Mishra, S. (2016). *Open educational resources: Policy costs, and transformation*. France: UNESCO and Commonwealth of Learning. Retrieved from https://unesdoc.unesco.org/ark:/48223/pf0000244365

Ozdemir, O., & Hendricks, C. (2017). Instructor and student experiences with open textbooks, from the California open online library for education (Cool4Ed). *Journal of computing in higher education*, *29*(1), 98–113. https://doi.org/10.1007/s12528-017-9138-0

Pinfield, S., Salter, J., & Bath, P. A. (2016). The 'total cost of publication' in a hybrid open-access environment: Institutional approaches to funding journal article-processing charges in combination with subscriptions. *Journal of the Association for Information Science & Technology*, *67*(7), 1751–1766. https://doi.org/10.1002/asi.23446

Senack, E., Donoghue, R., Grant, K., & Steen, K. (2016). *Access denied: The new face of the textbook monopoly*. Washington, DC: Student organizing Inc. Retrieved from www.studentpirgs.org/textbooks

UNESCO. (2016). *Study on international collaboration on Open Educational Resources (OER) (Commissioned study prepared under a consultant contract for UNESCO)* (pp. 1–15). Paris, France: UNESCO. Retrieved from http://en.unesco.org/sites/default/files/oer_study_march_2017.pdf

Wenger, E. (2010). Communities of practice and social learning systems: the career of a concept. In *Social learning systems and communities of practice* (pp. 179–198).

Wiley, D. (2014). The access compromise and the 5th R, *iterating toward openness* [blog], March 5, Retrieved from https://opencontent.org/blog/archives/3221

Open Access to Research Artifacts: Implementing the Next Generation Data Management Plan

Victoria Stodden
School of Information Sciences, University of Illinois Urbana-Champaign, Champaign, IL, USA
vcs@stodden.net

Vicki Ferrini
Earth Observatory of Columbia University, New York, NY, USA
ferrini@ldeo.columbia.edu

Margaret Gabanyi
Research Collaboratory for Structural Biology, Rutgers University, Piscataway, NJ, USA
gabanyi@rcsb.rutgers.edu

Kerstin Lehnert
Earth Observatory of Columbia University, New York, NY, USA
lehnert@ldeo.columbia.edu

John Morton
Earth Observatory of Columbia University, New York, NY, USA
jmorton@ldeo.columbia.edu

Helen Berman
Department of Chemistry and Chemical Biology, Rutgers University, Piscataway, NJ, USA
berman@rcsb.rutgers.edu

ABSTRACT

We describe a new vision for a Data Management Plan (DMP) that incorporates controlled vocabularies and semantic descriptions of the scholarly objects to be produced by the proposed project. We implement this vision in an open-source web-based DMP tool, called ezDMP, at ezdmp.org. The integrated use of structured information in ezDMP permits several important goals. First, with minimal additional effort, researchers can create DMPs with more complete information about the scholarly objects to be produced. Second, research funders can productively query this structured information to learn about repository use and other patterns of scholarly objects creation. Finally, ezDMP puts a structure in place that can support the integration of information about digital scholars objects, in an organized and systematic way, into research data management environments.

KEYWORDS

Data Management Plan; Data Sharing; Code Sharing; Cyberinfrastructure for Research; Data Policy; Code Policy; Reproducible Research; Digital Repositories; Open Access

ASIS&T THESAURUS

Computer Systems: Interfaces; Information Utilities; Public Policy; Government Agencies; Digital Repositories; Authors; Standards Developing Organizations

82nd Annual Meeting of the Association for Information Science & Technology | Melbourne, Australia | 19–23 October, 2019

DOI: 10.1002/pra2.00051

INTRODUCTION

Data Management Plans have been a required part of a National Science Foundation (NSF) proposal submission since 2011 and concern proposed artifact output of research grants. Artifacts can refer to datasets, software, workflow information, samples and other products of the research beyond the discoveries themselves. Reflecting on the 7 years that Data Management Plans (DMPs) have been required, we describe a next generation Data Management Plan structure that serves two principal DMP goals: first, to communicate and encourage awareness in the research community regarding priorities and modalities for artifact sharing, reuse, and research reproducibility; and second, to collect data to enable funders and stakeholders to learn about research artifact creation, archiving, and reuse practices by researchers and others.

The current NSF Data Management Plan guidelines limit its length to two pages. Each of the seven directorates within the NSF provide domain specific guidance for the content of these two pages (e.g., which research artifacts should be discussed). This guidance raises awareness in the community but does not give specifics on the factors the DMP should address regarding artifact sharing. This can leave many crucial questions unanswered such as artifact licensing and terms of use; artifact access, ownership, and stewardship; and repository use. We address this goal directly through the development of structured DMPs that prompt the researcher to (often optionally) address these pertinent issues. A DMP that is structured in this way permits machine readability and the automatic extraction of information. In this way, the next generation DMP permits funders to answer crucial questions such as: What are the patterns in repository use in research communities for the different types of artifacts? How do communities differ in archiving and sharing practices? Where are gaps in existing infrastructure and support for research artifact sharing? Do completed research projects meet the goals stated in their DMPs? Under current funding agency requirements answering these questions is challenging for the agencies, since DMPs are submitted as freeform text documents.

In this article we outline and motivate a next generation DMP that enables funders to meet the two goals articulated above, and we present an implementation of a web-based tool that facilitates the production of such DMPs.

OTHER DATA MANAGEMENT PLAN EFFORTS

Online tools that assist with the creation of the Data Management Plans that accompany research proposals are not a new idea. The DataONE project and the California Digital Library have created tools and many university libraries provide services in the creation of Data Management Plans for their researchers (Shreeves, 2014). There are DMP tool efforts in Europe, for example DMP Online (Sallans & Donnelly, 2012) and the DMPTuuli project in Finland (Ahokas, Kuusniemi, & Friman, 2017). These efforts, to our knowledge, do not use controlled vocabularies nor structured information in a template form, although in some cases the user can download and complete a template on their own. The IEDA DMP Tool (see https://www.iedadata.org/dmp/) is a structured webform geared toward earth and ocean scientists. We build on and extend the IEDA efforts by implementing a structured process for gathering information and completing the DMP using controlled vocabularies, as described below.

THE NEXT GENERATION DATA MANAGEMENT PLAN

Over the last decade computing has become central to the scientific research enterprise. Fields have embraced and leveraged data, computing power, and digital resources to advance and accelerate discovery (Donoho, Maleki, Shahram, Rahman, & Stodden, 2009). An early response to the increased need for transparency due to computation is described in (Buckheit & Donoho, 1995), and includes details on sharing data, software, and research tools that were used to generate research findings, This practice was called "really reproducible research." (Claerbout & Karrenback, 1992; Stodden, 2013). Since then, reproducibility has become a topic of great research and policy interest (National Academies, 2019). Recently steps toward enabling and rewarding the dissemination of the artifacts that underlie published findings have been taken by journals (Stodden et al., 2016) and institutions (AAU-APLU et al., 2017). The Data Management Plan is a key part of an overall strategy by many funding agencies to facilitate the production of reproducible and transparent research (see https://www.nsf.gov/bfa/dias/policy/dmp.jsp and https://science.energy.gov/funding-opportunities/digital-data-management).

Many disciplines do not have established and widely adopted domain repositories, nor broadly agreed-upon meta data definitions for artifacts such as data and software. This can create artifact interoperability issues and gaps in artifact provenance and data generation mechanisms. There is a wide range of possible artifact formats and a lack of community guidance on artifact release standards. In addition, there is little guidance is on appropriate workflow information and information needed to, for example, use artifacts to regenerate published scientific results (Gil et al., 2011; Santana-Perez et al., 2017). Therefore researchers may feel ill-equipped to meet DMP requirements.

Appropriate documentation for artifacts produced during the research along with a clear communication of how they underlie scientific results can enable reuse and accelerate discovery while reducing duplication of effort. The next generation DMP emerged via a community-driven NSF Advisory Committee Working Group.

Evolving the NSF Data Management Plan

A Working Group of the NSF Advisory Committee on Cyberinfrastructure (ACCI) called "Data and Code Access and Reproducibility" formed in 2015 under Victoria Stodden's Committee co-chairship and with Helen Berman serving as Working Group chair. The Working Group produced a detailed set of recommendations for a DMP consistent with the NSF Public Access Plan (see https://www.nsf.gov/pubs/2015/nsf15052/nsf15052.pdf) that both communicated of the importance of research artifact dissemination to the community, and enabled analysis of DMPs by funders to improve understanding of artifact sharing patterns.

These recommendations were then implemented into a prototype web-based interface in 2018. To do this, we examined more than 1,350 anonymized data management plans in the IEDA DMP Tool to understand gaps, successes, and patterns of use. The reported research products from these DMPs fell into five categories: Software, Data Products, Curriculum, Physical Specimens, and Workflow Information. From our sample, we compared and contrasted DMPs submitted to the different NSF Directorates. Finally, with the completion of a prototype ezDMP tool we surveyed potential users and presented the prototype to NSF program officers for feedback in 2018. The survey rubric is available at https://goo.gl/forms/CaEB3ddJ3iuUmpxS2.

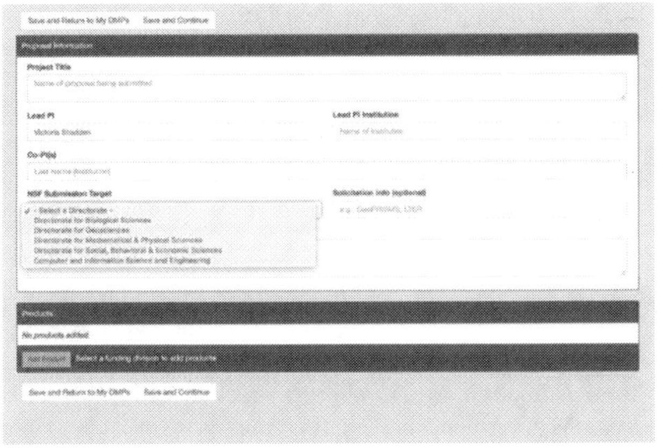

Figure 1. The ezDMP Data Management Plan is guided in the information it presents to the researcher guided by the DMP requirements specified by each NSF Directorate.

Communicating Artifact Dissemination Priorities

Prior to the completion of the prototype tool, the working group examined and collated information on all NSF DMP guidelines from the seven directorates. Although the high-level requirements are similar, the detailed requirements varied. As shown in Figure 1, the ezDMP tool gathers basic demographic and proposal information from the user. The user can click through to an NSF Directorate's current DMP guidance.

After completing demographic and solicitation information, the tool then presents the user with opportunities to enter information about each research artifact (dataset, software, curriculum materials, physical specimens, or workflow information) they expect to generate during the course of the project, as shown in Figure 2. A structured template is employed for the five research product categories.

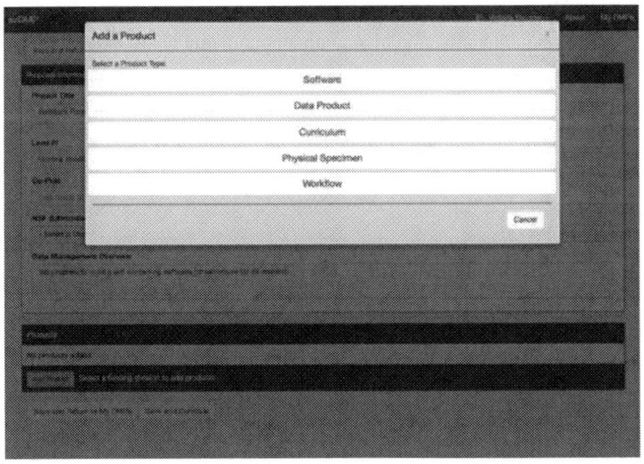

Figure 2. The addition of specific artifacts in ezDMP occurs in a structured way using controlled vocabularies.

For each artifact chosen, a structured set of choices are presented to elicit specialized information about the artifact with respect to attributes such as licensing, repository, stewardship, etc. As shown in Figure 3, at each stage the user has the ability to enter information that does not currently appear in the choices presented by the template.

After completing the modules for the appropriate artifacts, a two page pdf is returned to the author for inclusion in their funding proposal. An example of a Data Management Plan produced using ezDMP is available at https://zenodo.org/record/3247756#.XQfZbdM3nOQ (Gabanyi, 2019).

It is possible for users to contribute descriptions of artifacts that may not currently exist in ezDMP and for free text to be added to any drop-down menu that describes artifacts. A new repository can be included this way, using text boxes for artifacts or descriptions that do not fit the current template structure. ezDMP can update its templates in this way and funders can learn about artifacts and their requirements as they evolve over time. A novel contribution of the ezDMP tool is its communication to users a list of potential repositories based on the type of artifact they will be producing. The tool also makes a second novel contribution by communicating information that should travel with artifacts, such as licensing and access information, which adds to the evolving discussion on Data Management Plans and reproducibility in the community.

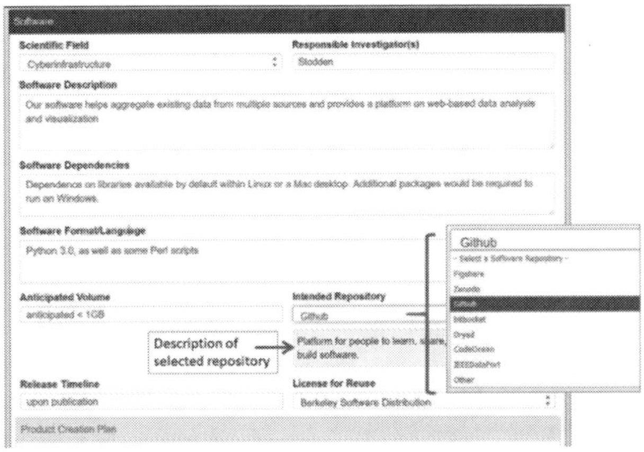

Figure 3. Repository choices for a software artifact. The interface also allows for information to be included in addition to that supplied in the drop-down menus, for example a repository not listed by the tool, so ezDMP can adapt to evolving community practices and funding agencies can learn about these changes in a systematic and timely way.

Enabling the Study of DMPs (Learning from the Community)

The specific fields in the DMP template generate data that can be used to understand community practices in artifact sharing. In the course of creating a DMP, information is collected on repository selection, licensing, NSF infrastructure and facility use, artifact formats and meta data, and information to use the artifacts and potentially reproducible the research results. The ezDMP tool also gathers information on planned artifact availability and retention. To do this, the ezDMP employs a controlled vocabulary specific to NSF Directorate and artifact type thereby enabling querying and information extraction.

EZDMP: A WEB-BASED IMPLEMENTATION OF THE NEXT GENERATION DATA MANAGEMENT PLAN

As shown in Figure 4, information is gathered by the ezDMP web interface in a systematic way that preserves relationships between the information types. The ezDMP application was developed in Node.js using the Express.js framework with a PostgreSQL backend connected via object-relational mapping (ORM) and the pg-promise library. The front-end is built in Angular.js with fully responsive Bootstrap UI elements for desktop, mobile, and tablet support.

Back-end work included developing the database schema, populating and refining all necessary controlled vocabularies based on community input, and building services necessary for desired functionality. The list of potential repositories is derived from curated repository lists we assembled. These repository lists are included in the back-end and enable the delivery of a menu of potential repositories to users based on division, product type, and scientific field chosen. The ezDMP schema also accommodates relating artifacts to one another, such as data products that will be derived from software that will be developed. Data collected by the tool is archived internally.

The web site with the prototype version of the ezDMP tool is https://www.ezdmp.org. The user interface source code is available at https://github.com/ezdmp/ezDMP-Site.

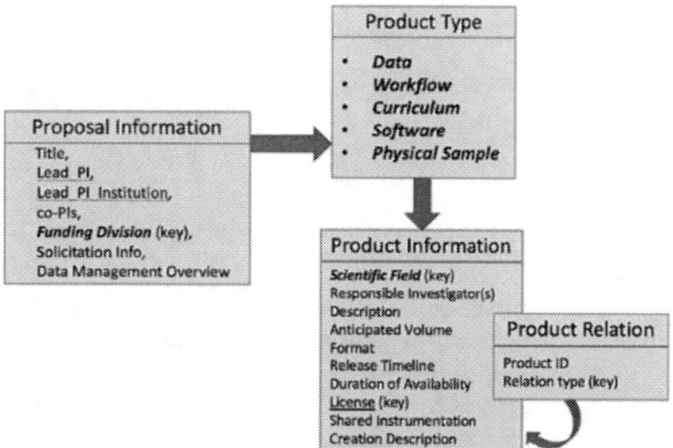

Figure 4. Conceptual schematic of the ezDMP Database Design showing the relationship between research artifacts and the use of controlled vocabularies when gathering information on artifacts produced by research grants. Fields in bold-italic control the options presented for underlined fields.

CONCLUSION

In this article, we have described the implementation of a next generation DMP and the motivation for the two key goals it addresses in facilitating greater access and transparency in research: To communicate policy priorities regarding artifact availability to the research community; and to enable funders and community stakeholders to learn about research artifact creation, archiving, and reuse practices by researchers and other stakeholders.

Funding agencies are continuing to implement Data Management Plans (see e.g., the October 2018 Request for Information by the National Institutes for Health entitled "Request for Information (RFI) on Proposed Provisions for a Draft Data Management and Sharing Policy for NIH Funded or Supported Research" https://grants.nih.gov/grants/guide/notice-files/NOT-OD-19-014.html). We anticipate extending the tool to accommodate other funding sources in a customized way in the future. Within NSF, data and artifact policies are advancing, especially with respect to enabling reproducibility of results (see e.g., https://www.nsf.gov/pubs/2019/nsf19022/nsf19022.pdf and https://www.nsf.gov/cise/oac/ci2030/ACCI_CI2030Report_Approved_Pub.pdf). Recommendation 6-5 of the recent National Academies report on reproducibility exhorts the NSF to "[c]onsider extending NSF's current data-management plan to include other digital artifacts, such as software" (National Academies, 2019).

We believe a next generation Data Management Plan, generated using a tool that produces structured, machine readable output using controlled vocabularies and semantic descriptions of the scholarly objects produced, will permit a greater understanding of practices regarding artifact creation, and availability, allowing for improved credit and recognition of these efforts. In addition, the approach pioneered by ezDMP will encourage greater development of artifact standards and interoperability and facilitate the incorporation of the Data Management Plan in future data management environments.

ACKNOWLEDGMENTS

We thank the stakeholders who provided feedback and completed our evaluation rubric. We also thank participants at RDA and other workshops for comments. NSF awards 1649555, 1649545, and 1649703 supported this work.

REFERENCES

AAU-APLU, Lynch, L., Nusser, S., Brown, S., Chasen, J., Dutta, D., … Wheeler, B. (2017). *AAU-APLU Public Access Working Group Report and Recommendations (White Paper)*. Retrieved from https://www.aau.edu/key-issues/aau-aplu-public-access-working-group-report-and-recommendations

Ahokas, M., Kuusniemi, M. E., & Friman, J. (2017). Tuuli Project: Accelerating data management planning in

Finnish Research Organisations. *International Journal of Digital Curation*, *12*(2), 107–115.

Buckheit, J. B., & Donoho, D. L. (1995). WaveLab and reproducible research. In A. Antoniadis & O. G, *Wavelets and statistics Lecture notes in statistics* (pp. 55–81). New York, NY: Springer.

Claerbout, J., & Karrenback, M. (1992). Electronic documents give reproducible research a new meaning. In *Proceedings of 62nd Annual International Meeting Society of Exploration Geophysics* (pp. 601–604).

Donoho, D. L., Maleki, A., Shahram, M., Rahman, I. U., & Stodden, V. (2009). Reproducible research in computational harmonic analysis. *Computing in Science & Engineering*, *11*(1), 8–18.

Gabanyi, M. (2019). *Example ezDMP output (Version 0.1)*. Zenodo. https://doi.org/10.5281/zenodo.3247756

Gil, Y., Ratnakar, V., Kim, J., González-Calero, P. A., Groth, P., Moody, J., & Deelman, E. (2011). Wings: Intelligent workflow-based design of computational experiments. *IEEE Intelligent Systems*, *26*(1).

National Academies of Sciences, Engineering, and Medicine. (2019). *Reproducibility and replicability in science*. Washington, DC: The National Academies Press. https://doi.org/10.17226/25303

Sallans, A., & Donnelly, M. (2012). DMP online and DMPTool: Different strategies towards a shared goal. *International Journal of Digital Curation*, *7*(2), 123–129. https://doi.org/10.2218/ijdc.v7i2.235

Santana-Perez, I., Ferreira da Silva, R., Rynge, M., Deelman, E., Perez-Hernandez, M. S., & Corcho, O. (2017). Reproducibility of execution environments in computational science using semantics and clouds. *Future Generation Computer Systems*, *67*, 354–367.

Shreeves, S. L. (2014). Presenting the new and improved DMPTool. In *Paper presented at Open Repositories* (p. 2014). Helsinki, Finland: http://hdl.handle.net/2142/49957

Stodden, V. (2013). *Resolving Irreproducibility in Empirical and Computational Research*. IMS Bull. Online. Retrieved from http://bulletin.imstat.org/2013/11/resolving-irreproducibility-in-empirical-and-computational-research/

Stodden, V., McNutt, M., Bailey, D. H., Deelman, E., Gil, Y., Hanson, B., & Taufer, M. (2016). Enhancing reproducibility for computational methods. *Science*, *354*(6317), 1240–1241.

Designing Feedback Information to Encourage Users' Participation Performances in Citizen Science Projects

Jian Tang
School of Information, Central University of Finance and Economics, Beijing, China
jiantang@cufe.edu.cn

Xinxue Zhou
School of Information, Central University of Finance and Economics, Beijing, China
zxxsnow1017@163.com

Meihua Yu
School of Information, Central University of Finance and Economics, Beijing, China
meihua_u@sina.com

ABSTRACT

Providing feedback is a design intervention that can enhance users' motivation and engagement in various contexts. Yet, prior research on citizen science has not specifically investigated how the design of feedback information can influence user experience and contribution. Furthermore, whether the presentation of feedback information may affect the quantity and quality of user contribution also requires further investigation. Drawing upon the feedback intervention theory, we propose a research model to depict the influence of feedback types (descriptive vs. evaluative) and feedback valences (positive vs. negative) on self-efficacy and enjoyment, which then affect the quantity and quality of contribution. We have developed an experiment website and will conduct an online experiment to validate our research model. The findings will provide the groundwork for feedback information design to enhance users' participation performance in citizen science projects.

KEYWORDS

Feedback; Citizen Science; Contribution Behavior; Motivational Design

ASIS&T THESAURUS

Information Behavior; Empirical Studies; Design

INTRODUCTION

In recent years, citizen science, a crowdsourcing approach for involving members of the general public in scientific inquiries, has gained increasing attention to help scientists address large-scale research investigation (Bonney, Phillips, Ballard, & Enck, 2016; Crall et al., 2013). In citizen science projects such as eBird, volunteers are recruited to collaborate and contribute to address scientific problems, through observation, data collection, and data analysis (Wiggins & Crowston, 2012). The proliferation of citizen science projects results in a large volunteer population, but researchers have also identified issues such as the lack of sustained user participation, that is, most participants quit after a few attempts. Participants become involved in citizen science projects for different reasons, including personal interest, altruism, or curiosity about new things. Researchers have noted that citizen science could be inherently interesting to some people, but might also be difficult, complex, or potentially tedious for others, thereby resulting in sharp decrease of participation after a few attempts (Prestopnik, Crowston, & Wang, 2017; Tang & Prestopnik, 2019). Therefore, how to effectively motivate user engagement and enhance their participation performance becomes a critical issue in citizen science research. More importantly, incorporating motivational design in citizen science projects is a more proactive approach when it comes to addressing challenges such as low user retention, participation, or contribution (Preece, 2016).

From the perspective of motivational design, providing feedback is a design principle that leads to positive user experiences and results in favorable attitudes toward information and communication technology use (Zhang, 2008). Previous research has also confirmed the positive impact of feedback information on users' immersive experience and their idea generation quantity (Jung, Schneider, & Valacich, 2010), but little attention has been paid to understand the effect of feedback information design. Therefore, this paper aims to address the following research question: how can feedback information design motivate users' engagement and influence their participation performances?

RELATED WORK

Citizen Science

Citizen science projects have become important outlets to promote science communication and education. Prior research has either focused on the stages of citizen science projects (Shirk et al., 2012; Wiggins & Crowston, 2012) or characterized the features of various citizen science projects (Prestopnik et al., 2017; Sauermann & Franzoni, 2015). Many of them have made efforts to improve the design of projects, such as the design of platforms (Newman et al., 2012) and the design of the tasks (Scheliga, Friesike, Puschmann, & Fecher, 2018), but very few studies have focused on the feedback information design.

82nd Annual Meeting of the Association for Information Science & Technology | Melbourne, Australia | 19–23 October, 2019

DOI: 10.1002/pra2.00052

The success of a citizen science project relies upon motivated crowds of participants, so exploring how to incorporate motivational design concepts into citizen science projects have become a key concern of citizen scientists, designers, and project initiators. Different types of motivation have been explored and studied, namely, altruism, activism, and tangible rewards (Curtis, 2015; Rotman et al., 2014). Besides the descriptive analysis of reasons for participation, researchers have specifically argued for the use of design intervention to motivate user participation (Preece, 2016).

Feedback Design

Feedback design is a key concept that draws continuous attention from researchers in the field of information science (Spink, 1997). Specifically in the context of citizen science, presenting feedback on users' performance has been found to encourage their extra-role behavioral contribution in an environmental monitoring citizen science projects (Nov, Laut, & Porfiri, 2016). Feedback intervention theory (Kluger & DeNisi, 1996) has been used to explain how feedback information can be purposely designed to induce individual motivation and thereby affect their behaviors (Pekrun, Cusack, Kou, Elliot, & Thomas, 2014; Steele-Johnson, Heintz, & Miller, 2010).

Prior studies have summarized three broad meanings of feedback, including motivational meaning, reinforcement meaning, and informational meaning (Kulhavy & Wager, 1993). Motivational meaning of feedback indicates its effect as a motivator to encourage user behavior; reinforcement meaning specifically refers to rewards or punishments regarding particular user behaviors; and informational meaning of feedback originates from information processing theories, indicating one can use information carried by feedback to change his or her performance to a particular direction (Nelson & Schunn, 2009). The reinforcement and information meanings of feedback indicate a dynamic human information interaction and are usually related to information processing, seeking, and retrieving models (Spink, 1997). The motivational meaning of feedback, however, signifies the its value in encouraging user behaviors (Harackiewicz, 1979) and affording possibilities to result in positive user experiences (Zhang, 2008).

CONCEPTUAL DEVELOPMENT AND HYPOTHESES

User participation performance is key to the success of citizen science projects, which is commonly measured with the quantity and quality indicators of user contributions. Several studies have used these measures and identified the existence of different user roles within citizen science communities (Prestopnik et al., 2017; Sauermann & Franzoni, 2015). Yet, little research has been done to uncover how feedback information design can be used to promote the quantity and quality of user contribution.

Drawing upon the feedback intervention theory, we proposed a research model (see Figure 1) to explain how feedback type and feedback valence affect participants' self-efficacy and enjoyment, which then influence their participation performances.

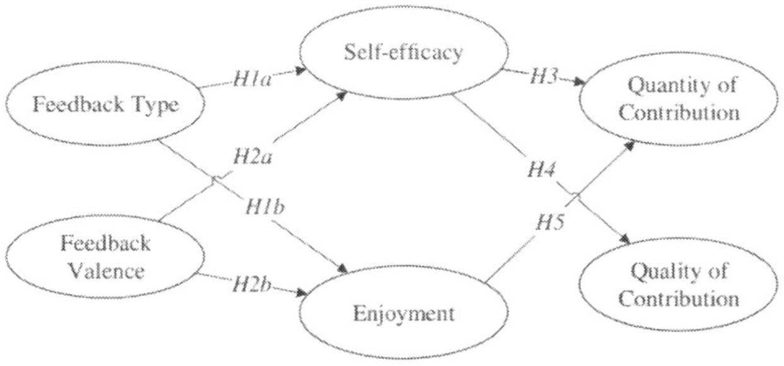

Figure 1. Research model.

Feedback Type

Feedback type refers to the focus of feedback information presented to receivers. Feedback can be evaluative or simply describe one's objective performance (Burgers, Eden, van Engelenburg, & Buningh, 2015). Descriptive feedback reports the summative information of user participation on the basis of observational data, whereas evaluative feedback adds a layer of subjective judgment to one's performance. Compared to descriptive feedback, evaluative feedback provides referent information of one's behavior and clearly states specific information of one's capability level (Johnson, 2013). Therefore, we hypothesize:

H1a: Evaluative feedback leads to a higher level of self-efficacy than descriptive feedback.

In addition, evaluative feedback is more persuasive than descriptive feedback and is more effective to satisfy intrinsic needs (Johnson, 2013), making one feel more fun and enjoyable while working on citizen science tasks. Therefore, we hypothesize:

H1b: Evaluative feedback leads to a higher level of enjoyment than descriptive feedback.

Feedback Valence

Feedback valence refers to the attributes of feedback that can be further divided into positive and negative information (Burgers et al., 2015). According to the feedback intervention theory, receivers of feedback often adjust their behaviors by comparing it to a standard or a goal (Kluger & DeNisi, 1996). Positive feedback usually compliments one's progress towards a designated goal, whereas negative feedback emphasizes a gap between the desired goal and one's actual behavior. Positive feedback makes one feel more confident about his or her capabilities of accomplishing a task, and therefore increases self-efficacy. However, negative feedback is very unlikely to satisfy one's confidence. Therefore, we hypothesize:

H2a: Positive feedback leads to a higher level of self-efficacy than negative feedback.

H2b: Positive feedback leads to a higher level of enjoyment than negative feedback.

Self-Efficacy

Self-efficacy indicates one's belief about his or her capabilities of controlling and organizing the courses of actions to produce given attainments (Bandura, 1997). If one has a higher degree of self-efficacy, he or she earns mastery experience and will be more confident about his or her capabilities of providing good performance (Santhanam, Liu, & Shen, 2016; Yi & Davis, 2003). Therefore, they are more likely to contribute well in both quantity and quality. Therefore, the hypotheses are:

H3: Self-efficacy positively influences the quantity of user contribution.

H4: Self-efficacy positively influences the quality of user contribution.

Enjoyment

Enjoyment refers to the hedonic state experienced by participants when working on citizen science tasks. Prior research has found that enjoyment can positively influence user participations in citizen science projects (Curtis, 2015; Tinati, Luczak-Roesch, Simperl, & Hall, 2017), and yet this hedonic experience may not be related to one's cognitive capability of addressing scientific problems. Therefore, we hypothesize:

H5: Enjoyment positively influences the quantity of contribution.

RESEARCH DESIGN

We plan to conduct our study in the context of a botanical classification citizen science project, which is one of the major application domains of citizen science. Photos of plants taken by nature enthusiasts are used as sources of classification. This project serves as our experiment setting, and we will collect data through an online experiment to validate our proposed model.

Experimental Treatments

We will conduct a 2 (feedback type: descriptive vs. evaluative) by 2 (feedback valence: positive vs. negative) online between-subject experiment. Subjects will be recruited via campus flyers and email invitations on crowdsourcing platforms. Table 1 shows our experimental treatments, showing four types of feedback information to be received by subjects in the experiment.

Feedback type	Feedback valence	
	Positive	**Negative**
Descriptive	Answering 3 photos correctly is regarded as qualified. You got xx photos correct in this set and achieved the bar.	Answering 2 photos wrong is regarded as NOT qualitied. You got xx photos wrong in this set and did NOT achieve the bar.
Evaluative	You performance was great in this set and had a satisfactory correct rate. Keep up the good work!	Your performance was poor in this set and had a unsatisfactory correct rate. Try to work better!

Table 1. Experiment treatment.

Experimental Procedures and Manipulation Check

Subjects who accept the invitation will go to the main page of experiment website. After a short welcome introduction of the botanical classification project, subjects will be randomly assign to one of the four experimental conditions. They will be requested to annotate the plant photos and then receive manipulated feedback information after they finish a fixed number of classification. When they click "quit", they will be directed to the questionnaire. They objective behavior data will also be record in our experiment database.

Measurements

In this research, we will triangulate both subjective and objective data. Constructs, including self-efficacy and enjoyment, are measured with subjective scales adapted from prior literature (Santhanam et al., 2016). User participation (quantity and quality) is measured with actual be behavioral data acquired from the experiment website. To validate whether experimental treatment is correctly perceived by subjects, we will conduct a manipulation check on feedback type and feedback valence.

EXPECTED CONTRIBUTION

This research will have both theoretical and practical implications. Theoretically, we developed a research model based on feedback intervention theory to enrich the understanding of feedback design, which then influence user experience and participation performance. Secondly, this research fills in the gap that little research has attempted to manipulate feedback information to enhance user experience and performance. Third, we present a two-dimensional perspective to understand feedback information design, and findings of this research help to promote active participation of the public and improve the quantity as well as quality of contribution. Methodologically, we use experimental research to compare the effects of feedback type and feedback valance. We will triangulate objective data with subjective data to validate our research model. Practically, our research has significant design implications for citizen science designers and scientists, providing guidelines for feedback information design to facilitate user contribution in citizen science practices.

ACKNOWLEDGMENTS

This research is supported by National Natural Science Foundation of China (71874215), the Social Science Fund Research Base Project of Beijing (18JDGLB020), the Ministry of Education, Humanities and Social Sciences Council in China (18YJCZH160), and the Program for Innovation Research in Central University of Finance and Economics.

REFERENCES

Bandura, A. (1997). *Self-efficacy: The exercise of control*. Macmillan.

Bonney, R., Phillips, T. B., Ballard, H. L., & Enck, J. W. (2016). Can citizen science enhance public understanding of science? *Public Understanding of Science*, *25*(1), 2–16.

Burgers, C., Eden, A., van Engelenburg, M. D., & Buningh, S. (2015). How feedback boosts motivation and play in a brain-training game. *Computers in Human Behavior*, *48*, 94–103.

Crall, A. W., Jordan, R., Holfelder, K., Newman, G. J., Graham, J., & Waller, D. M. (2013). The impacts of an invasive species citizen science training program on participant attitudes, behavior, and science literacy. *Public Understanding of Science*, *22*(6), 745–764.

Curtis, V. (2015). Motivation to participate in an online citizen science game: A study of Foldit. *Science Communication*, *37*(6), 723–746.

Harackiewicz, J. M. (1979). The effects of reward contingency and performance feedback on intrinsic motivation. *Journal of Personality and Social Psychology*, *37*(8), 1352–1363.

Johnson, D. A. (2013). A component analysis of the impact of evaluative and objective feedback on performance. *Journal of Organizational Behavior Management*, *33* (2), 89–103.

Jung, J. H., Schneider, C., & Valacich, J. (2010). Enhancing the motivational affordance of information systems: The effects of real-time performance feedback and goal setting in group collaboration environments. *Management Science*, *56*(4), 724–742.

Kluger, A. N., & DeNisi, A. (1996). The effects of feedback interventions on performance: A historical review, a meta-analysis, and a preliminary feedback intervention theory. *Psychological Bulletin*, *119*(2), 254–284.

Kulhavy, R. W., & Wager, W. (1993). Feedback in programmed instruction: Historical context and implications for practice. In G. C. S. J. V. Dempsey (Ed.), *Interactive instruction and feedback* (Vol. *3–20*). Englewood Cliffs, NJ: Educational Technology.

Nelson, M. M., & Schunn, C. D. (2009). The nature of feedback: How different types of peer feedback affect writing performance. *Instructional Science*, *37*(4), 375–401.

Newman, G., Wiggins, A., Crall, A., Graham, E., Newman, S., & Crowston, K. (2012). The future of citizen science: Emerging technologies and shifting paradigms. *Frontiers in Ecology & the Environment*, *10*(6), 298–304.

Nov, O., Laut, J., & Porfiri, M. (2016). Using targeted design interventions to encourage extra-role crowdsourcing behavior. *Journal of the Association for Information Science and Technology*, *67*(2), 483–489. https://doi.org/10.1002/asi.23507

Pekrun, R., Cusack, A., Kou, M., Elliot, A. J., & Thomas, K. (2014). The power of anticipated feedback: Effects on students' achievement goals and achievement emotions. *Learning & Instruction*, *29*(9), 115–124.

Preece, J. (2016). Citizen science: New research challenges for human–computer interaction. *International Journal of Human–Computer Interaction*, *32*(8), 585–612. https://doi.org/10.1080/10447318.2016.1194153

Prestopnik, N. R., Crowston, K., & Wang, J. (2017). Gamers, citizen scientists, and data: Exploring participant contributions in two games with a purpose. *Computers in Human Behavior*, *68*, 254–268.

Rotman, D., Hammock, J., Preece, J. J., Boston, C. L., Hansen, D. L., Bowser, A., & He, Y. (2014). *Does Motivation in Citizen Science Change with Time and Culture?* Paper presented at the 17th ACM Conference on Computer Supported Cooperative Work & Social Computing.

Santhanam, R., Liu, D., & Shen, W. C. M. (2016). Gamification of technology-mediated training: Not all competitions are the same. *Information Systems Research*, *27*(2), 453–465. https://doi.org/10.1287/isre.2016.0630

Sauermann, H., & Franzoni, C. (2015). Crowd science user contribution patterns and their implications. *Proceedings of the National Academy of Sciences*, *112*(3), 679–684.

Scheliga, K., Friesike, S., Puschmann, C., & Fecher, B. (2018). Setting up crowd science projects. *Public Understanding of Science*, *27*(5), 515–534.

Shirk, J. L., Ballard, H. L., Wilderman, C. C., Phillips, T., Wiggins, A., Jordan, R., … Krasny, M. E. (2012). Public participation in scientific research: A framework for deliberate design. *Ecology and Society*, *17*(2).

Spink, A. (1997). Information science: A third feedback framework. *Journal of the American Society for Information Science*, *48*(8), 728–740.

Steele-Johnson, D., Heintz, P., & Miller, C. E. (2010). Examining situationally induced state goal orientation effects on task perceptions, performance, and satisfaction: A two-dimensional conceptualization1. *Journal of Applied Social Psychology*, *38*(2), 334–365.

Tang, J., & Prestopnik, N. R. (2019). Exploring the impact of game framing and task framing on user participation in citizen science projects. *Aslib Journal of Information Management*, *71*(2), 260–280.

Tinati, R., Luczak-Roesch, M., Simperl, E., & Hall, W. (2017). An investigation of player motivations in Eyewire, a gamified citizen science project. *Computers in Human Behavior*, *73*, 527–540.

Wiggins, A., & Crowston, K. (2012). *Goals and Tasks: Two Typologies of Citizen Science Projects*. Paper presented at the 45th Hawaii International Conference on System Science (HICSS).

Yi, M. Y., & Davis, F. D. (2003). Developing and validating an observational learning model of computer software training and skill acquisition. *Information Systems Research*, *14*(2), 146–169.

Zhang, P. (2008). Motivational affordances: Fundamental reasons for ICT design and use. *Communications of the ACM*, *51*(11), 145–147.

Cultural Barriers to Intellectual Property Ethics: A Theoretical Model

Tao Jin
Louisiana State University,
Baton Rouge, USA
taojin@lsu.edu

Meihua Chen
Peking University,
Beijing, China
chenmeihua@pku.edu.cn

ABSTRACT

Numerous studies have revealed that cultural factors play an important role in intellectual property (IP) management in cross-national contexts. Although understanding the factors is currently recognized as an essential problem, little research has been done on systematically analyzing and modeling these cultural norms and values. This paper reports on a work in progress that aims to build a theoretical model to explain the differences of people's perceptions about IP infringement in different countries. In this paper, we introduce the background of the study and propose the theoretical model that was gleaned from a systematic review effort.

KEYWORDS

Intellectual Property; Intellectual Capital; Cross-national Research; Information Transfer; Ethics

ASIS&T THESAURUS

China; United States; Knowledge Management

INTRODUCTION

In the knowledge economy, intellectual property (IP), as a form of intangible asset, is closely related to an enterprise's or a society's core capabilities and innovation performances (Smith & Hansen, 2002). When an IP is properly maintained and well protected, the organization's competitive advantage on the marketplace will be gained and sustained. Otherwise, the IP will be vulnerable to counterfeiting and piracy, and the competitive advantage can be damaged or lost (Budde-Sung, 2013). The protection of IP rights (IPR), in both practical and ethical aspects, is not a new problem. Rather, it is an old and enduring complex that has been festering over the decades. In particular, when we consider it in a cross-national context.

Menou (1983) argues that information is hard to be separated from its cultural context, and information products and/or services are culture dependent. Thus, when transborder data flow occurs, different cultural traits in different societies will affect the perception, presentation, transfer and utilization of the information, and make it fly off the handle of its original creator and controller (Kim, 2013; Menou, 1983).

Likewise, an IP can be seen as an information product. When it travels across the borders, its original legal rights, use of intellectual contents therein, and semantic consistency will be limited by a series of cultural barriers. Prior research has documented rich evidence of significant variations in IP violation and protection in different countries (e.g., Husted, 2000; Whitman, Townsend, & Hendrickson, 1999). Specifically, while people in some nations are intolerant to IP infringement, those in others may see little evil even in plagiarism. In China, for example, there is an old saying: "All the writing is copied (*Tian xia wenzhang yi da chao*)" (Crook, 1990). Furthermore, the *shanzhai* phenomena (a Chinese term to describe massive imitation and knockoffs of branded products, most of which are foreign-owned, without permission or authorization) are so pervasive that ordinary Chinese there have taken it for granted (Beebe, 2014). These infringements and abuses have caused significant financial losses for IPR holders, high socio-economic impacts, as well as an immense and enduring challenge to IP management (European Commission, 2018).

Numerous previous studies have revealed that cultural factors play an important role in IP management in cross-national contexts (e.g., Ki, Chang, & Khang, 2006; Marron & Steel, 2000). Although understanding the factors is currently recognized as an essential problem, little research has been conducted to systematically analyze and model these cultural norms and values. This short paper reports on a work in progress that aims to build a theoretical model to explain the differences in people's perceptions about IP infringement in different countries. In this paper, we introduce the background of the study and propose the theoretical model that was gleaned from a systematic review effort. A central research question to guide this portion of the study is: Which cultural factors may affect people's perceptions about IP infringement in different countries?

The remainder of the paper will be organized as follows. The background section defines a few key concepts. The methods section describes the procedures of the systematic review. Finally, we report the review results, the status of this on-going project, and the conclusion.

82nd Annual Meeting of the Association for Information Science & Technology | Melbourne, Australia | 19–23 October, 2019

DOI: 10.1002/pra2.00053

BACKGROUND

This research project is framed in the theoretical and empirical literature on IP management. It is worth noting that IP-related issues are rarely discussed in the literature of information science and technology. Instead, the major knowledge domains that constitute this line of research are law and management. In this section, we concentrate on defining three concepts central to this endeavor: IP, IP ethics, and culture.

Intellectual Property

The World Intellectual Property Organization (WIPO, 2019) defines IP as "creations of the mind," such as "inventions, literary and artistic works, and symbols, names, and images used in commerce." Echoing that, Sullivan (2005, p. 118) sees IP as a subset of intellectual capital, and is "the legally protected and codified knowledge of its owners." Several meanings can be extrapolated from the above. Firstly, IP is by nature about knowledge. It comprises of technical *know-what* and *know-how* that may differentiate and distinguish the creation from others (Smith & Hansen, 2002). Secondly, the creation of intellect has been codified and articulated in a tangible form (Gajic, 2017; Kong & Thomson, 2009). Thus, it may face high risks of expropriation and misappropriation. Finally, IP is about the legally defined ownership. Under certain laws, IPR is granted to the owner of the IP. Also, such rights are legally protected by the law. Specifically, these major IPRs include: copyrights, patents, designs, trademarks, and trade secrets.

Intellectual Property Ethics

Ethics refers to those overarching moral principles that direct an individual's or a group of individuals' behaviors and decision-making about what is right or what is wrong. Thus, the notion of IP ethics can be defined as the moral principles that govern people's perceptions and judgments on what is right or wrong with regard to IP.

	Ethics	Level of acts
IP abuse	Wrong/Bad	Mostly acts of individuals
IP protection	Right/Good	Both acts of individuals and acts of government entities

Table 1. Dimensions of IP ethics.

As illustrated in Table 1, the notion of IP ethics has two sides. The wrong or bad side is represented by IP abuse (interchangeably used with IP infringement or IP violation), where counterfeiting, piracy, industrial espionage, plagiarism, and *shanzhai* are typical instances. At this level, most of such acts are conducted by individuals or a group of individuals (Yang & Sonmez, 2007). The right or good side of the ethics is reflected by IP protection, where relevant laws are in place and well enforced. At this level, individuals consciously abide by what the laws state, and additionally, the nation, through its government entities, uses its coercive power to safeguard IPR holders' interests (Himma, 2008). In contrast, if there is an absence or a lack of relevant laws, or a weak enforcement, the gap will invite IP infringements, abuses and violations.

Culture

Hofstede (2001, p. 9) defines culture as "the collective programming of the mind which distinguishes the members of one human group from another." Similarly, House, Hanges, Javidan, Dorfman, and Gupta (2004, p. 15) conceptualize culture as the "shared motives, values, beliefs, identities, and interpretations or meanings of significant events that result from common experiences of members of collectives that are transmitted across generations." In this paper, we treat the term *culture* as an all-inclusive umbrella notion to accommodate a family of political, economic, social and habitual factors. For instance, the regimes that govern and protect IPRs today are based on a Western culture. By the term *Western*, we essentially refer to those developed economies in Western Europe and North America, where John Locke's *property rights theory* are prevalent and the legal system is traditionally sound and well grounded. Western nations usually support and enjoy an individualist culture that embrace individual ownership of IP, whereas many non-Western nations value a collectivist culture that stresses sharing over individual ownership (Marron & Steel, 2000). Most Asian countries, for example, consider intellectual work as a communal good and copying them is to facilitate social learning (Kuanpoth, 2003).

METHODS

The research methodology used for this paper was a systematic review, including procedures and processes of comprehensive and extensive literature search, screening the studies to be included for review, extraction of major concepts from the selected studies, and analysis of the identified concepts.

We used two online search portals to locate qualified studies to be reviewed. The first portal was the EBSCO Discovery Service (EDS) subscribed by the institution where one of the authors works. The EDS allows users to access the institution's entire collection, including all major full-text databases, through a single entry point. The other search portal that we used was Google Scholar, a free search engine for scholarly research literature. On both portals, searches were conducted in January and February of 2019. We limited our search to English language items published between 1988 and 2018, and used phrases, wildcards, Boolean operators, and searching in specific fields. Removing duplications, overlaps, and irrelevant or unobtainable items, from nearly 1,000 retrieved results, we identified 184 items for further screening.

The abstracts of those 184 items were carefully examined. To complete a thorough screening process, three criteria were developed and employed. An item to be included in the final round of systematic review must be (1) about IP, (2) discussed in cross-national contexts, and (3) either an empirical study or a conceptual/theoretical research. These procedures resulted in a sample of 45 items that met all of the inclusion criteria.

After the included studies were finalized, the reviewers first started to read each of the studies independently and applied a reviewing grid, which was designed to identify the profile of the research, such as research question(s), conceptual or theoretical framework(s), methodology, key concepts or variables, and major findings and implications. Then the reviewers met and compared the results. After some mutual adjustment and alignment, the reviewers then moved to focus on further concepts extraction. In this step, each study was carefully read again by each reviewer, and the concepts were revisited, verified, or newly identified until a complete list was produced. Next, the reviewers worked together to examine, compare, and discuss what they have completed. Altogether, the reviewers identified 431 concepts, among which many were redundant. Therefore, they kept cleaning and clustering them into different hierarchical structures. In this paper, we decided to present 27 concepts.

RESULTS AND DISCUSSION

The results of this systematic review are presented in four parts.

Factor	Description
Regime type	Type of government or political system (e.g., democratic, autocratic, totalitarian)
Power structure	Characteristics of the political power structure (e.g., centralized totalitarian; separation of powers – three branches of the US government)
Legal system development	Level of development on legal infrastructure (e.g., highly developed; underdeveloped)
Political infrastructure	Characteristics of the political infrastructure (e.g., "rule of man"; "rule of law")
Economic system	Characteristics of economic institutions or systems (e.g., public ownership; private ownership; market or command economy)
Economic ideology	Characteristics of the economic ideology (e.g., capitalism, socialism)
Income inequality	Characteristics of income distribution and affordability (e.g., the size of the middle class)
GNP per capita	Indicator of the level of economic development

Table 2. Political & economic factors that may affect IP ethics.

Cultural Differences

As shown by Tables 2 and 3, we organized the cultural differences between nations in two clusters. One is a group of political and economic factors. The other is a group of social and habitual factors.

Factor	Description (Hofstede, 2001; House et al, 2004)
Uncertainty avoidance	The extent to which people strive to shy away uncertainty through formalized rules and order
Power distance	The extent to which people agree and support authority, power difference, and certain privileges
Individualism vs. collectivism	The extent to which an individual relates to others
Masculinity vs. femininity	The extent to which people value material success or quality of life
Future orientation	The extent to which people engage in future-oriented behaviors
Human orientation	The extent to which a society recognizes and facilitates people to be fair, nice, and altruistic
Assertiveness	The degree to which people in a society are assertive and aggressive
Performance orientation	The degree to which a society recognizes and facilitates people for career development, performance improvement and excellence
Social attitude	Characteristics of the general social attitude toward IP ethics (e.g., tolerant, intolerant)
Educational preparedness	Level of training received about IP knowledge
Religion	Religious beliefs (e.g., Confucianism, Christian)

Table 3. Social & habitual factors that may affect IP ethics.

Intellectual Property Awareness

Awareness is usually a precursor of behavior. Pitkethly (2012) develops the concept of IP awareness, which consists of three sub-concepts: (1) IP knowledge and understanding, (2) IP judgement, and (3) IP attitude.

Perception of Intellectual Property Infringement

Lastly, perception of IP infringement can be represented by one's perception about those five aforementioned types of IPRs: (1) copyright, (2) patent, (3) design, (4) trademark, and (5) trade secret.

A Theoretical Model

Based on these identified concepts, we postulate a theoretical model (see Figure 1). In that model, those political, economic, social and habitual factors are expected to affect an individual's level of IP awareness. Then, the IP awareness will influence the individual's perceptions about IP infringement.

THE WORK-IN-PROGRESS

Currently, we are fine-tuning those identified concepts and the theoretical model. Next, based on these concepts and

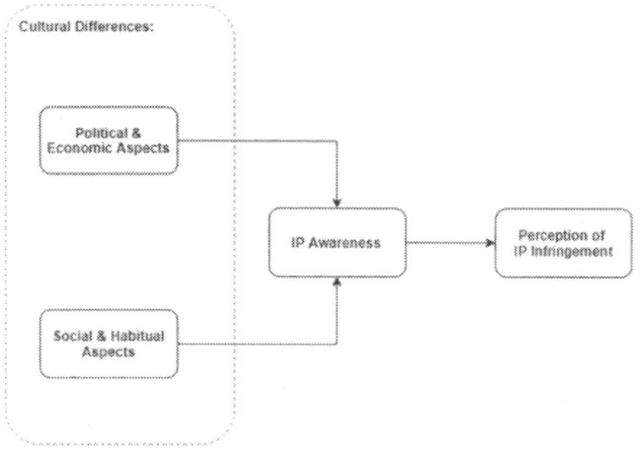

Figure 1. A proposed theoretical model to explain perception of IP infringement in a cross-national context.

the theoretical framework, we will identify objective items that can be used to represent and measure these concepts, so that the model can then be tested and validated. We plan to develop two similar questionnaires and administer them, respectively, in China and the United States, on two samples.

CONCLUSION

IP protection in a cross-national context is a deep and everlasting concern for both enterprises and government entities. As an information product, IP is culture dependent. That means people in different countries will differ in their economic development, as well as political, social and habitual values. Therefore, their perceptions about IP ethics cannot be identical. Findings of this study will potentially contribute not only to the IP and knowledge management communities, but also to companies and government agencies to help them formulate insightful policies and strategies in managing intellectual capital.

REFERENCES

Beebe, B. (2014). Shanzhai, sumptuary law, and intellectual property law in contemporary China. *UC Davis Law Review*, *47*, 849–874.

Budde-Sung, A. (2013). The invisible meets the intangible: Culture's impact on intellectual property protection. *Journal of Business Ethics*, *117*(2), 345–359.

Crook, D. (1990). *Hampstead heath to tian an men – The autobiography of David Crook*. Retrieved from http://www.davidcrook.net/simple/chapter13.html

European Commission. (2018). *Report on the protection and enforcement of intellectual property rights in third countries*. Retrieved from http://ec.europa.eu/transparency/regdoc/rep/10102/2018/EN/SWD-2018-47-F1-EN-MAIN-PART-1.PDF

Gajic, N. (2017). Intellectual property and intellectual capital: Defining a relationship. *Queen Mary Journal of Intellectual Property*, *7*(2), 242–255.

Himma, K. E. (2008). The justification of intellectual property: Contemporary philosophical disputes. *Journal of the American Society for Information Science and Technology*, *59*(7), 1143–1161.

Hofstede, G. (2001). *Culture's consequences: Comparing values, behaviors, institutions and organizations across nations*. Sage Publications.

House, R. J., Hanges, P. J., Javidan, M., Dorfman, P. W., & Gupta, V. (2004). *Culture, leadership, and organizations: The GLOBE study of 62 societies*. Sage Publications.

Husted, B. W. (2000). The impact of national culture on software piracy. *Journal of Business Ethics*, *26*(3), 197–211.

Ki, E.-J., Chang, B.-H., & Khang, H. (2006). Exploring influential factors on music piracy across countries. *Journal of Communication*, *56*(2), 406–426.

Kim, J.-H. (2013). Information and culture: Cultural differences in the perception and recall of information. *Library & Information Science Research*, *35*(3), 241–250.

Kong, E., & Thomson, S. B. (2009). An intellectual capital perspective of human resource strategies and practices. *Knowledge Management Research & Practice*, *7*(4), 356–364.

Kuanpoth, J. (2003). The political economy of the TRIPs agreement lessons: from Asian countries. In C. Bellman, G. Dutfield, & R. Meledez-Ortiz, *Trading in knowledge: Development perspectives on TRIPS, trade, and sustainability* (pp. 45–56). Sterling, VA: Earthscan.

Marron, D. B., & Steel, D. G. (2000). Which countries protect intellectual property? The case of software piracy. *Economic inquiry*, *38*(2), 159–174.

Menou, M. J. (1983). Cultural barriers to the international transfer of information. *Information Processing & Management*, *19*(3), 121–129.

Pitkethly, R. H. (2012). Intellectual property awareness. *International Journal of Technology Management*, *59* (3/4), 163–179.

Smith, M., & Hansen, F. (2002). Managing intellectual property: a strategic point of view. *Journal of intellectual capital*, *3*(4), 366–374.

Sullivan, P. (2005). An intellectual property perspective on intellectual capital. In B. Marr, *Perspectives on intellectual capital: multidisciplinary insights into management, measurement, and reporting* (pp. 137–151). New York, NY: Routledge.

Whitman, M. E., Townsend, A. M., & Hendrickson, A. R. (1999). Cross-national differences in computer-use ethics: A nine-country study. *Journal of International Business Studies*, *30*(4), 673–687.

WIPO. (2019). *What is intellectual property?*

Yang, D., & Sonmez, M. (2007). Economic and cultural impact on intellectual property violations: A study of software piracy. *Journal of World Trade*, *41*, 731–750.

How Do Students' Information World Maps Change While Developing Their Thesis Topics? A Longitudinal Study Using Arts-Based Elicitation Interviews

Tien-I Tsai
National Taiwan University,
Taipei, Taiwan
titsai@ntu.edu.tw

Hsuan-Ju Chen
National Taiwan University,
Taipei, Taiwan
r06126013@ntu.edu.tw

Chen-Hsuan Tai
National Taiwan University,
Taipei, Taiwan
r07126001@ntu.edu.tw

Yi-Ling Chen
National Taiwan University,
Taipei, Taiwan
r07126004@ntu.edu.tw

ABSTRACT

It is challenging for master's students, as novice researchers, to gather information throughout the process of thesis topic development. Information world mapping (IWM) provides a framework to depict a wide range of information activities and practices as well as the items, places, and relationships involved in a specific context from individuals' perspectives. The current study used IWM visual elicitation interviews to conduct a longitudinal study with 14 master's students at three iSchools. Since students typically develop their thesis topics throughout the first year in the master's program, each student was asked to draw an IWM during the interview after the first and second semesters ended. Situational analysis and qualitative content analysis were used to analyze the data. While students' IWMs remained similar in composition, their IWMs mainly changed in viewpoints of the world based on their work pace and relationships with various sources. Suggestions are provided based on the findings.

KEYWORDS

Information Behavior; Information World Mapping; Information Seeking; Visual Methods; Thesis Writing

ASIS&T THESAURUS

Information Behavior; Information Seeking; Information Resources

INTRODUCTION

Developing the research topic is a challenging task which involves many information activities with different sources at different places. Studies on students' topic exploration and development tended to focus on high school students (e.g., Cole et al., 2013; Kuhlthau, 1991), undergraduate students (e.g., Hulseberg & Twait, 2016; Wu et al., 2017), and doctoral students (e.g., Holliman & Jones, 2018; Isaac et al., 1989). Relatively few studies examined issues regarding topic development of master's students (e.g., Huang & Chen, 2014). While many professional master's programs do not require students to complete a thesis, as novice researchers, master's students in a program which requires to complete their theses have to gather information to develop their topic of the thesis. The required master's thesis is typically much more formal in style and longer in length than an honors thesis for high schoolers or undergraduate students. Students also have to finish the program within a much shorter time than doctoral students. Therefore, the process of developing a topic for master's thesis can last for a much longer time as compared to students' previous experiences but under time pressure as well. In order to help master's students to be prepared for this critical start, it is important to capture the information practices throughout the whole process of topic development.

While Kuhlthau's (1991) information search process (ISP) is important and can help identify students in different stages developing their project, the current study aims to capture what shapes students' information world throughout this process rather than focusing on the affective, cognitive, and physical aspects of information behavior. Based on Sonnenwald (1999), D. L. Greyson (2015), D. Greyson et al. (2017) proposed the information world mapping (IWM). It is an arts-based visual elicitation method to depict a wide range of information activities, behaviors, and practices of an individual, as well as the items, places, and relationships involved in the contexts. The broader scope of investigation with different focuses can help extend the understanding beyond what we have already learned based on Kuhlthau's ISP.

Although IWMs empirical studies have been mostly used in health information seeking contexts or with vulnerable populations (e.g., Dalmer, 2017; D. Greyson et al., 2017; Shankar et al., 2016), IWM is an innovative technique to be applied to other contexts. Drawing upon the framework of IWM, the current study used this visual elicitation interview technique to conduct a longitudinal study in academic contexts. Specific research questions include: 1. What items, places, and relationships do students use to shape their IWMs in the contexts of thesis topic development? And how do they present their

82nd Annual Meeting of the Association for Information Science & Technology | Melbourne, Australia | 19–23 October, 2019

DOI: 10.1002/pra2.00054

IWMs? 2. How do students' IWMs change during the process of thesis topic development?

METHODS

Participants

Fourteen first-year master's students in the iSchool program from three large research universities were recruited toward the end of their first semester in their master's program through email via the three programs. All three programs require students to complete their master's theses to obtain the degree. The proposal defense is also one of the requirements in all the programs. There are about 15 students in each cohort in a program. Fortunately, we retained all the voluntary participants in two stages. Among the 14 students who participated in the current study, most are female ($n = 11$) with an average age of 24.07 ($SD = 2.05$) in the first stage and 24.50 ($SD = 1.95$) in the second stage. Six students decided their thesis advisors prior to their first-stage interviews; eight had started to work on their proposals prior to their second-stage interviews. Nevertheless, four hadn't yet formally talked to their "thesis advisor in mind" at the second stage.

Data Collection

Two stages of individual interviews along with participant-drawn IWMs were conducted after each semester ended. Each interview lasted from nearly an hour to two hours, including 15–25 minutes for IWM drawing, with an average of one hour and 20 minutes. All the second-stage interviews lasted longer than first-stage interviews. Each interview in the two stages followed the same procedure by starting with asking students to recall what they have done in the past semester for their theses and what they did when needed information for developing their topics, and so on. After the major conversation was finished, students were then asked to draw their IWMs with a set of 12-color pens and a blank A4 paper provided by the researcher. Finally, they were asked to describe and explain the IWM to clarify things that may also covered earlier in the conversation. The researcher followed the procedure of D. L. Greyson (2015), D. Greyson et al. (2017) and provided a think-aloud option, but none of the participants chose to do so.

Data Analysis

Situational analysis and qualitative content analysis were used to examine the data as suggested by D. Greyson et al. (2019) for analyzing IWM data. The unit of analysis is individual participants. We transcribed all the interview recordings and investigated the verbal narrative together with the according participant-drawn IWMs. Following what Clarke (2005) emphasized in situational analysis, we focused on capturing the big picture and specific pictures of the relationships among people, places, and items. We especially investigated the human and non-human sources as well as what helped students develop their thesis topics. Qualitative content analysis was mainly used to identify different sources and the changes in the two stages. And consolidating what situational analysis and qualitative content analysis can help, we analyzed various information activities on the IWMs with extra attention to the compositions, elements/colors, viewpoints, and disciplinary cultures (here we look into the advisor's role). All the data collected were scrutinized by at least two researchers.

FINDINGS

Items, Places, and Relationships in Students' IWMs

As expected, advisors, other professors, peers, and major online sources such as Google and library databases appeared on most students' IWMs. A few students also included their significant others or family members (e.g., LIS04, LIS08). Physical spaces appeared on students' IWMs typically involved the classroom setting and office setting with a computer or laptop at the university or home/dormitory, and some also included the library; virtual spaces typically included cloud drives such as Google Drive or Dropbox. And students typically used directed links to show relationships and to express seeking information from sources, sources leading them to other sources, or exchange information with others. Some also used the links to present the sequential steps in the exploration process.

Depending on students' research interest, they may use different databases and consult people with different expertise. However, preferences of information sources and information organization style are somewhat similar. Before deciding their thesis advisors (e.g., LIS08, LIS10), many students consulted course instructors and relied on other senior fellow students working with the same professor (i.e., their "advisor in mind") (e.g., LIS5, LIS11). In general, most students' IWMs were densely populated with a wide range of sources, especially in stage one when they started to explore the topic for their theses. And most students relied on cloud-based systems to backup files, organize them, and take notes.

While most students used similar composition and ways of expression in both stages, after examining the IWMs along with their discursive narratives, we found that changes in the IWMs happened in several ways mainly based on their work pace and relationships change with various courses. The following discussions focus on the changes from stage one to two in composition, color, elements, and viewpoints.

Composition and Color of Students' IWMs

The major composition in most IWMs remained somewhat similar based on personal drawing style and preferences. Students tended to use links with categorical design to present their IWMs. However, the number of colors used was quite diverse. Students used one to twelve colors on their IWMs with an average of 4.71 ($SD = 3.15$) and 6.86 ($SD = 2.93$) in stage one and two, respectively. A few students prefer using simply black (Figure 1), others used colors to identify important sources, present different categories of sources, or present specific icons, etc. (Figure 2). Most students increased the number of colors used in their IWMs in their second stages. Only three remained the same (LIS08, LIS12, LIS14), and two of them were the ones who simply used black.

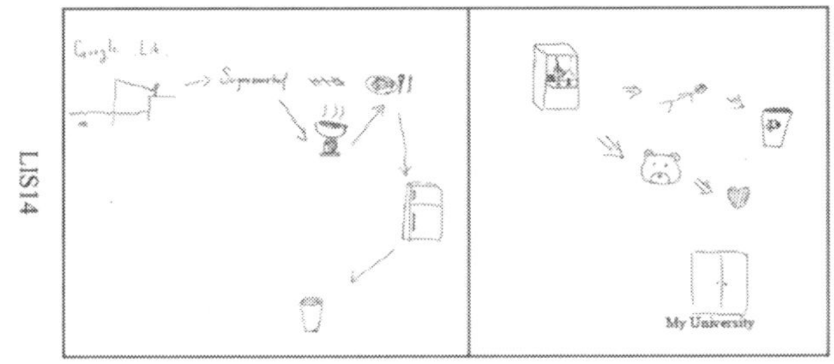

Figure 1. Sample IWMs using mostly black and showing more focused on specific sources from stage 1 to 2.
Note. "My University" was edited by the researcher to ensure confidentiality. The edges of each IWM were cut, if needed, in order to fit the layout.

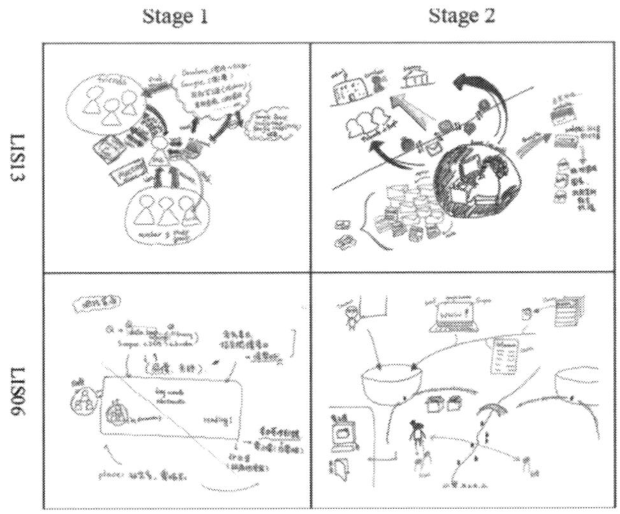

Figure 2. Sample IWMs showing role change in sources and being more isolated from stage 1 to 2.
Note. The edges of each IWM were cut, if needed, in order to fit the layout of the page.

Figure 1 presents a special case where the student used metaphor to present his IWMs. Even if the composition looks different than all the other IWMs, the thoughts are actually similar to many other students. In stage one, LIS 14 used "fishing in the ocean" as the starting point of developing the topic, and moved onto a cooking process of going shopping in the supermarket and make dishes. For things (information in any form) that he kept in the fridge (computer), he may later find it useless and throw it into trash. In stage two, he used "playing a claw machine/claw crane" to express the similar idea with a much-limited space and scope to get things (information). LIS14 believes that in the second stage he has a specific target to look for and acquire the item, but only when he gets into it will he learn whether or not it is his "favorite doll" or it is "merely trash."

Changes in Elements and Viewpoints of Students' IWMs

In general, students' IWMs typically changed in elements and viewpoints presented. Some students limited their sources to fewer types in stage two; others tended to include similar sources and spaces with different viewpoints in the two stages. Interestingly, changes in viewpoints typically happened when students' relationships with people or sources have changed between stages. Many students explicitly or implicitly presented more isolated relationships with others in stage two.

Viewing the information world with an isolated self can be identified in many IWMs and narratives. Some students used more two-way arrows or links to present interactions with various sources in stage one, and mostly one-way arrows in stage two (e.g., LIS13 in Figure 2). LIS13 also emphasized this isolation in stage two by drawing herself in black with a closed bubble with her laptop and a paper at hand. Other students expressed the isolation in other ways. For instance, LIS06 (Figure 2) used a red two-way arrow with a long line in stage two and emphasized his distance with others has become much farther at this stage.

As to the relationship change, when students explained why they stopped exchange ideas with other peers or family members, some students had a similar reaction with LIS08—"*I think maybe I'm gaining more expertise, so others may not understand what I'm talking about.*" Other examples are like:

"*Since my peers in the same cohort are doing all different things [topics in different areas], we don't have much to talk about……We still talk about topic selection issues, but we only share how things go and support one another.*" (LIS14).

Other typical relationship changes happened with professors and other sources. Important course instructors in the first stage may become advisors in the second stage (e.g., LIS04; LIS06); various databases may become specific databases (e.g., LIS08). However, the role change seems to be an interesting mechanism in students' IWMs. While students mostly agreed the important role of advisors and trusted their advisors, many students mentioned that since it's critical for them to talk to their advisors, they only consult their advisors when they feel prepared or after they have somewhat made their own decision. LIS 12 stated that "*Advisor is my last resort after I get ready because she is busy. And I don't consult my advisor before I am well-prepared because I'm afraid she will ask me if I really did my homework.*" And LIS07 explained that "*I'm afraid if I talked to my advisor what I think I'm going to do for my thesis, then I would really have to do this, so I need to make up my mind first.*"

However, similar to many other students who emphasized the critical role of the advisor, LIS13 explicitly highlighted advisors' role with a star on her IWM saying that "*Advisor is like the lighthouse guiding me the direction, and also making life decisions for me.*"

Students' work pace also played an important role in the changes of their IWMs. Fast-paced students tended to be more focused on sources consulted and emphasized advisors' role in the process. Fast-paced students who already decided their topics in the second stage became even more isolated and tended to emphasize the "inner space" other than the physical space or the virtual space on their IWMs. And therefore, similar sources may appear in both IWMs, but located differently. For instance, peers' role typically changed, but some students still kept other peers on the map but placed them in a distant location (e.g., LIS04, LIS13).

CONCLUSION

In the contexts of master's thesis topic development, students' IWMs tend to be densely populated with diverse sources. While the composition of students' IWMs remain somewhat similar in both stages, their sources consulted are more focused, and viewpoints of the world are more isolated in the second stage. Students who decided their thesis advisors earlier tended to work in a faster pace, and their IWMs tended to change more obviously due to relationship changes with professors and peers.

The current study applied IWM to academic contexts with a longitudinal design.[1] According to the findings, students' work pace and their relationship change are important drives to the IWM change. The rich IWM data can be further analyzed by examining the relationships change in many ways, especially investigating the role of peers and the style of advisors so that we can help provide implications for higher education institutions as well as faculty members who advise master's students. The isolation found in stage two is also worthy of notice. Future research can also further examine the relationships from affective and cognitive aspects. This way, the IWM in academic contexts may integrate with and extend Kuhlthau's ISP. It would help consolidate information behavior models and help us better understand information practices as a whole. Finally, the current study found the variation of color use and think aloud technique did not work for all the students. Future research can further experiment with the IWM procedure and tools provided with different populations to establish the protocol.

ACKNOWLEDGMENTS

We gratefully acknowledge the grant from the Ministry of Science and Technology, Taiwan (MOST#107-2410-H-002-202).

REFERENCES

Clarke, A. (2005). *Situational analysis: Grounded theory after the postmodern turn*. Thousand Oaks, CA: Sage Publications.

Cole, C., Behesthi, J., Large, A., Lamoureux, I., Abuhimed, D., & AlGhamdi, M. (2013). Seeking information for a middle school history project: The concept of implicit knowledge in the students' transition from Kuhlthau's stage 3 to stage 4. *Journal of the American Society for Information Science and Technology*, *64*(3), 558–573.

Dalmer, N. (2017). Information world mapping to explicate the information care relationship in dementia care. *Proceedings of the Association for Information Science and Technology*, *52*(1), 647–649.

Greyson, D., O'Brien, H., & Shankar, S. (2019). Visual analysis of information world maps: An exploration of four methods. *Journal of Information Science*. https://doi.org/10.1177/0165551519837174

Greyson, D., O'Brien, H., & Shoveller, J. (2017). Information world mapping: A participatory arts-based elicitation method for information behavior interviews. *Library & Information Science Research*, *39*(2), 149–157. https://doi.org/10.1016/j.lisr.2017.03.003

Greyson, D. L. (2015). *Health-related information practices and the experiences of young parents*. (Unpublished doctoral dissertation). University of British Columbia, Vancouver.

Holliman, A. J., & Jones, T. (2018). Identifying a topic for a psychology dissertation: A process map for students. *Psychology Teaching Review*, *24*(1), 82–90.

Huang, J., & Chen, C. (2014). A study of the information literacy of biomedical graduate students: Based on the thesis topic discovery process in molecular biology research. *Journal of Library and Information Studies*, *12*(1), 77–107. https://doi.org/10.6182/jlis.2014.12(1).077

Hulseberg, A., & Twait, M. (2016). Sophomores speaking: An exploratory study of student research practices. *College & Undergraduate Libraries*, *23*(2), 130–150. https://doi.org/10.1080/10691316.2014.981907

Kuhlthau, C. C. (1991). Inside the search process: Information seeking from the user's perspective. *Journal of the American Society for Information Science*, *42*(5), 631–371.

Shankar, S., O'Brien, H. L., How, E., Lu, Y. W., Mabi, M., & Rose, C. (2016). The role of information in the settlement experiences of refugee students. In *Proceedings of the 79th ASIS&T Annual Meeting: Creating Knowledge, Enhancing Lives through Information & Technology*. Copenhagen, Denmark.

Sonnenwald, D. H. (1999). Evolving perspectives of human information behaviour: contexts, situations, social networks and information horizons. In T. D. Wilson & D. K. Allen, *Exploring the contexts of information behavior: Proceedings of the second international conference on research in information needs, seeking and use in different contexts*. London, England: Taylor Graham.

Wu, D., Dang, W., He, D., & Bi, R. (2017). Undergraduate information behaviors in thesis writing: A study using the Information Search Process model. *Journal of Librarianship and Information Science*, *49*(3), 256–268. https://doi.org/10.1177/0961000616654960

[1] This paper is part of a larger project that traces students throughout their entire journey in the master's program. Stages 1 and 2 were reported in this paper. Stage 3 was mostly done by the time of submission, but stage 3 data analysis was underway.

An Analysis on Charitable Crowdfunding in an Authoritarian Regime

Shengnan Yang
Indiana University,
Bloomington, USA
yang290@iu.edu

Chenwei Zhang
Indiana University,
Bloomington, USA
zhang334@indiana.edu

Wenjuan Sang
Indiana University,
Bloomington, USA
wsang@iu.edu

ABSTRACT

This paper introduces the uniqueness of the Chinese online crowdfunding platform (CFP). The authors investigated national policies and 2,000 projects collected from the largest Chinese charitable CFP. The analysis shows that besides providing a channel to access the public, platforms partially facilitate the administration and supervision of online fundraising under the control of the government. Moreover, there is a great diversity among projects that are unevenly distributed by their category and geolocation.

KEYWORDS

Nonprofit; Online Donation; Crowdfunding Platforms

ASIS&T THESAURUS

Business Model; Social Informatics

INTRODUCTION

As a web 2.0-based phenomenon, crowdfunding (CF) relies on a collective effort to pool money together. Derived from crowdsourcing, this innovative financing solution enables collaboration and co-creation between fundraisers and backers (Haas, Blohm, & Leimeister, 2014). CF is also seen as challenging the traditional mechanism of financial resource distribution and influencing the power relations among financing intermediaries, capital-seekers, and capital-givers.

Current studies on crowdfunding are largely based on practices in Western countries, focusing on the reward model and the equity model (e.g., *Kickstarter* and *Fundable*). Little is known about this newly emerging phenomenon among nonprofits in non-Western countries. In China, for instance, the nonprofit sector is under tight state control and exercises limited autonomy. Here, CF serves not only to realize economic outcomes but also as a potential channel to mobilize public engagement and cultivate the development of civil society. This research introduces CCPs (charitable crowdfunding platforms) in China, which are different in some salient ways from their Western counterparts. In addition to explaining their particular operational model, we explore several important features of Chinese CCPs to reveal the broader nature of charitable CF in Chinese nonprofits. This research holds important implications for researchers, policy makers, campaign administrators and the designers of CFPs.

82nd Annual Meeting of the Association for Information Science & Technology | Melbourne, Australia | 19–23 October, 2019

DOI: 10.1002/pra2.00077

CROWDFUNDING

As an emerging phenomenon, CF has been broadly discussed in various fields. The fundamental consensus is that CF uses an open call format and relies on a collective effort from the crowd to pool money together without traditional and standardized intermediaries (Belleflamme, Lambert, & Schwienbacher, 2014). Scholars invariably classify CF into four categories, based on the forms of compensation that backers receive: donation-based, reward-based, lending-based, and equity-based (Haas et al., 2014). Donation-based CF mainly serves charitable projects or social causes, and capital givers receive no material compensation. The platforms focusing on crowdfunding services for nonprofit/charitable projects can be termed CCPs. Compared to profit-driven CF projects, charitable ones tend to adopt the lower-risk "Keep-it-all" (KIA) model under the motto "any money is welcome." This model also represents lower returns in terms of a decreased chance of obtaining the needed funds.

CF processes combine the efficiency and control of traditional, top-down processes with the benefits of bottom-up innovation and collaboration (Brabham, 2008). This crowd-based mechanism is usually interpreted as a form of equal participation by a large number of citizens. It is highly esteemed as a way to facilitate democratic participation, which is especially important in democratic deficit scenarios (Bott & Young, 2012; Hellström, Hämäläinen, Lahti, Cook, & Jousilahti, 2015).

CHINESE CHARITABLE CROWDFUNDING

In authoritarian regimes, crowdfunding is a double-edged sword, especially in the nonprofit sector. On the one hand, CF is seen as a threat to the government inasmuch as it presents social channels (Peng, 2017). On the other hand, CF may supplement or stand in for traditional means of participation in a positive direction (Hellström et al., 2015).

In China, nonprofits always face challenges when applying the traditional model of fundraising (Zheng, McKeever, &

Xu, 2016). The limited availability of traditional fundraising channels, such as point-to-point donation, reduces the effectiveness of funding. According to the Charities Aid Foundation, China ranked 144th out of 145 countries on the 2015 World Giving Index (CAF, 2015). This situation has changed in response to the enactment of administrative regulation and technology diffusion in 2016, when China's first ever Charity Law took effect and introduced a critical change of fundraising. On August 31, Chinese Ministry of Civil Affairs (MCA) approved 13 Internet fundraising platforms as "Public Fundraising Platforms." These platforms are also required by the government to verify the charitable status of their organizational users and to report illicit behavior; their status implies that these public platforms partially facilitate the administration and supervision of online fundraising.

In parallel with the implementation of "The Internet +" policy and the promulgation of the first Charity Law, there has been a sudden increase of social-media driven charitable crowdfunding campaigns in China (Marquis, Zhou, & Yang, 2015). Several charitable crowdfunding platforms, such as *Tencent Charity* and *Qingsongchou*, have emerged and demonstrated their great potential to pool resources from the public for nonprofit projects via the Internet. In 2018, 28 million individuals donated RMB 0.83 billion during the fourth "9/9 Philanthropy Day" which was an online campaign promoted by *Tencent Charity* (Zhang, 2018). According to the China Crowdfunding Industry Development Report (Tseeking, 2018), CFPs in China have received a great deal of social attention. The total amount of CF donations reached RMB 13.7 billion in the first half of 2018, a 24.46% increase compared with the previous year. Along with the increase in donations, the diversity of project types and the number of donors also show the expansion of CF in China, signaling a new area for researchers to study.

METHODOLOGY

Study Design and Data Sources

To investigate charitable CF in China, this research applies two main methods of data collection and analysis based on the online practices of the largest Chinese CCP—*Tencent Charity*. The first method is qualitative document analysis, in which formal policy statements issued by the Ministry of Civil Affairs and documents about the operation of *Tencent Charity* are considered as situated collective products produced in specific social settings (Prior, 2003). Analyzing those documents will yield a framework for understanding Chinese online fundraising, including its crucial actors, their relations, and the mechanism of the entire network in the political and social context of China.

The quantitative data used in the second part of the analysis was extracted from *Tencent Charity*. A PHP web scraping tool was designed and developed to collect all 3,000 available projects between July 2016 and February 2017 from the platform. To focus on the features and results of completed fundraising efforts, the researchers used data only from projects (n = 1,996) that had finished their fundraising campaigns.

Variables and Measurement

The factors associated with successful fundraising draw attention from both academia and industry. The most commonly used campaign project performance metrics include the project's goal, subject, geographical location, campaign duration, number of backers, amount funded (Fedor, 2015), and funding model (Cumming, Leboeuf, & Schwienbacher, 2015). Detailed factors affecting the probability of reaching the funding target include the purpose of the fundraising (Belleflamme et al., 2014), modes of communication (Beier & Wagner, 2015), frequency of information update [ibid], and the social capital of capital seekers (Giudici, Guerini, & Rossi Lamastra, 2013), as well as funding amount and duration. In China, the nonprofit sector is under tight state control with limited autonomy. The essential role of CF there is not only as a driver of economic outcomes but also as a potential channel to mobilize public engagement and cultivate the civil society. Thus, in this study, "success" is defined more broadly than the mainstream understanding through two aspects. First, success is about funding goal achievement—whether the fundraising target is accomplished or not. Second, success concerns project mobilization capability—the number of donors, which indicates the extent to which the project can mobilize the public's participation. A greater number of donors implies a larger-scale mobilization with more participants engaging in the project. The following essential characteristics are extracted for each project:

Target (project goal): Amount of money set by each initiator as the target of a crowdfunding project.

Donation (pledges): Total donation amount received.

Completion ratio: *Donation* divided by *Target*.

Funding status: Status of funding goal achievement.

Donors: Number of donors for each project.

Category: Theme of a project. Important categories include health, education, poverty, environment, among.

Region: Provincial location of a project.

FINDINGS

Online Fundraising Model in China and its Specialty

As in Hemer's model of the crowdfunding process (Hemer, 2011), CFPs, as the intermediary, play a crucial role in the charitable fundraising model. Functionally, they allow for pledge display, online transactions, payment, information distribution, and communication. Relationally, they effectively connect initiators, service providers (banks and payment service providers), and donors. A slight difference related to the fundraising framework is an additional factor—public foundation. The CFP-mediated charitable fundraising model is presented in Figure 1, with *Tencent Charity* as an example.

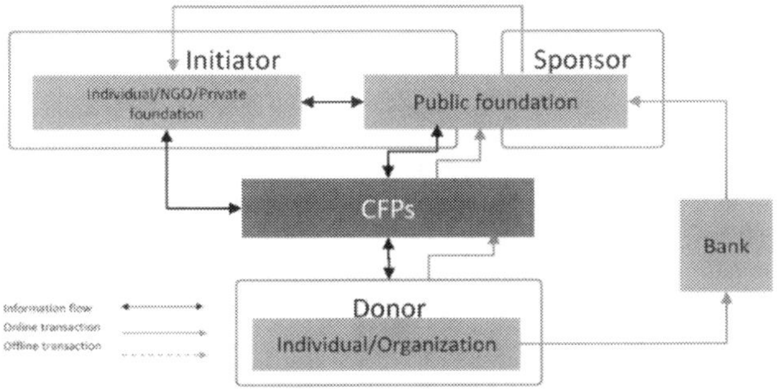

Figure 1. Free funding + KIA model on *Tencent* CFP.

Platform

Tencent CFP adopts a KIA plus "free funding" model, distinguishing it from most CFPs in other countries. In the KIA model, although initiators can keep all pledged money, they need to pay a high fee regardless of whether the fundraising goal is reached or not. Unlike other notable donation-based platforms which also adopt the KIA model, Tencent, as an Internet giant, takes advantage of its capital, technology, and products to provide free registration, online payment, and funding process operation.

Initiators

Different types of entities can launch charitable fundraising projects on CFPs, including individuals and nonprofits.

Donors

Multiple types of donors can engage in online giving, including individuals, corporations, and foundations.

Sponsors

Public foundations with government-granted credentials for public fundraising act as sponsors for the legitimacy of charitable fundraising. For each project initiated by individuals or nonprofits without public fundraising credentials, a sponsor is assigned to review the project for approval. Only approved projects are qualified to post their fundraising campaign on online platforms. Sponsors, rather than the projects' initiators, are in charge of receiving and allocating donations.

A Quantitative Snapshot of CF Projects

Among all projects, 36.7% have successfully achieved their funding goals. The aggregate completion ratio for all the projects is 26%. The average target is RMB 123,853, and the average donation amount received is RMB 32,371.5. For each project, an average of 2,879 donors participated, making an average donation of RMB 11.2 each.

Gaps between the successful and less-successful groups are obvious. For the 733 successfully funded projects, the average amount received was RMB 52,769, contributed by 5,416 donors on average. In contrast, the 1,263 less successful projects had an average donation of RMB 20,534, a little over one-third that of their successful counterparts. Goal setting and numbers of donors are the most prominent differences between successful projects and less successful ones. The average target in the unsuccessful group was twice that in the successful group, but the average number of donors showed the reverse trend: 1,406 donors for the unsuccessful group, or one-fourth the average count of a successful project. This enlarges the gaps in goal achievement.

Categorical Differences

Projects are distributed unevenly among different categories. By number of projects, the most active fields from the need side are health/illness (50.4%), poverty/disaster (24%), and education (14.3%). The majority of charitable donations goes to health (55%), education (20.8%), and poverty (11.1%). However, the distribution of completion ratio is considerably different. **Health** is the largest category, with the greatest demand and highest financial requirement. It absorbs the most donations but has the lowest percentage of success among the categories (21.7%). It may be that although the total number of successful projects is large and mobilization capacity is high, these small advantages are not altogether adequate to meet the category's high funding goals (RMB 155,284.5 on average). The **Education** category has a strong mobilization capability (3,509 donors/project on average) and a high giving efficiency (mean RMB 43 donation per donor), indicating that supporters are more generous to education-related projects. **Poverty**, having the lowest average funding target in monetary terms (RMB 49,921.3), is the most easily funded category: over 60% of these projects are fully funded. **Environment-related** projects have the largest mean donation amount (RMB 60,391.5) and a relatively high completion ratio (50%).

Geographic Difference

Geographic differences represent another dimension in the patterns of crowdfunding behaviors in China. As Figures 2-1 to 2-3 illustrate, crowdfunding projects and funding results are distributed unevenly across Chinese provinces. Central, South, and East China are more actively engaged in crowdfunding activities: they tend to initiate more projects and raise higher public attention, judging by the number of donors. However, more projects does not necessarily mean a greater chance of success. As Figure 2-4 shows, some less-developed provinces (e.g., Xinjiang and Tibet) with few projects have a higher likelihood of accomplishing their goals. These visualizations also reflect the potential relationship among donations, donors, and project location.

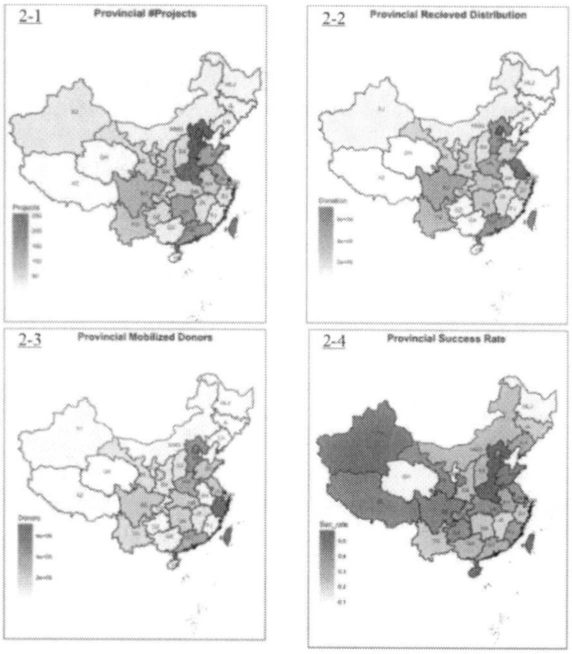

Figure 2. Free funding + KIA model on *Tencent* CFP.

The above descriptive analysis focuses on variations in received donation, target setting, donors' engagement, and giving intention by project category and region. The results briefly indicate that although all projects are equally presented on the same platform, donors tend to give more attention to specific types of projects. This observation should inspire further research to explore the potential factors influencing the amount of money a project receives and the public attention a project can draw during its fundraising campaign.

CONCLUSION AND IMPLICATIONS

This preliminary study investigates the characteristics of charitable crowdfunding projects in China. As with their Western counterparts, online crowdfunding platforms in China have, like other types of information and communication technology (ICT), empowered both individuals and nonprofits by presenting their needs to the public and therefore enlarging the funding pool. Additionally, the uniqueness of Chinese case has demonstrated the difference in underlying power relations: tight state regulation and control versus democratic governance and a market economy. The authoritarian context provides a comparative perspective from which to reconsider the relations among ICT, government, and the nonprofit sector.

The CCP operational model found in this research provides a comprehensive view of the dynamics of important actors engaged in crowdfunding. In particular, the introduction of public foundations to the game demonstrates the origin of the legitimacy accorded to CCPs and the entire activity of public fundraising in China. The platforms partially facilitate the administration and supervision of online fundraising. Moreover, various project features have been examined with a view to the success of the crowdfunding projects. It is found that, overall, failures occur more often than successes. Several findings reflect the particularities of the Chinese crowdfunding ecosystem, both academically and practically. Our results demonstrate great diversity among projects on Chinese crowdfunding platforms, but these projects are distributed unevenly among different categories, and the number of projects is inconsistent with the completeness ratio for each category. CF projects and funding results are also distributed unevenly with respect to geography.

Our study suggests the value of a deeper exploration of both CCPs and charitable CF projects based on richer data. More aspects will be incorporated into the analysis, such as platform features, narrative patterns of project description, initiators' social networks, specific donors' information and so on. Meanwhile, different regression models must be introduced to further understand the factors that influence charitable CF project success.

REFERENCES

Beier, M., & Wagner, K. (2015). Crowdfunding success: A perspective from social media and e-commerce.

Belleflamme, P., Lambert, T., & Schwienbacher, A. (2014). Crowdfunding: Tapping the right crowd. *Journal of Business Venturing*, *29*(5), 585–609.

Bott, M., & Young, G. (2012). The role of crowdsourcing for better governance in international development. *Praxis: The Fletcher Journal of Human Security*, *27*(1), 47–70.

Brabham, D. C. (2008). Crowdsourcing as a model for problem solving: An introduction and cases. *Convergence*, *14* (1), 75–90.

CAF. (2015). *CAF WORLD GIVING INDEX 2015*. Retrieved from https://www.cafonline.org/about-us/publications/2015-publications/caf-world-giving-index-2015

Cumming, D. J., Leboeuf, G., & Schwienbacher, A. (2015). Crowdfunding models: Keep-it-all vs. all-or-nothing. *Financial Management*.

Fedor, L. (2015). Success determinants of crowdfunding projects. *Review of Business and Economics Studies*, (4).

Giudici, G., Guerini, M., & Rossi Lamastra, C. (2013). Why crowdfunding projects can succeed: The role of proponents' individual and territorial social capital. *Available at SSRN, 2255944*.

Haas, P., Blohm, I., & Leimeister, J. M. (2014). *An empirical taxonomy of crowdfunding intermediaries*. Retrieved from http://aisel.aisnet.org/icis2014/proceedings/SocialMedia/13/

Hellström, E., Hämäläinen, T., Lahti, V. M., Cook, J. W., & Jousilahti, J. (2015). *Towards a sustainable well-being society*. Retrieved January 15, 2017.

Hemer, J., & others. (2011). *A snapshot on crowdfunding*. Retrieved from http://isi-lehre.de/isi-wAssets/docs/p/de/arbpap_unternehmen_region/ap_r2_2011.pdf

Marquis, C., Zhou, Y., & Yang, Z. (2015). The emergence of subversive charities in China. *Stanford Social Innovation Review*, *13*(4), 42–47.

Peng, L. (2017). Crisis crowdsourcing and China's civic participation in disaster response: Evidence from earthquake relief. *China Information*, *31*(3), 327–348.

Prior, L. (2003). *Using documents in social research*. London, England: Sage Publications.

Tseeking. (2018). *China crowdfunding industry development report*. Retrieved from http://www.zhongchoujia.com/data/31205.htm

Zhang, M. (2018). *9/9 Philanthropy Day: 28 million individuals donated RMB 0.83 billion*. Retrieved from http://www.ngocn.net/news/2018-09-11-e775388cf60949a0.html

Zheng, Y., McKeever, B. W., & Xu, L. (2016). Nonprofit communication and fundraising in China: Exploring the theory of situational support in an international context. *International Journal of Communication*, *10*, 24.

When Power Goes Wild Online: How Did a Voluntary Moderator's Abuse of Power Affect an Online Community?

Yukun Yang
University of North Carolina, Chapel Hill, Chapel Hill, USA
yukun@live.unc.edu

ABSTRACT

Online moderation is apropos to community curation as a way to fight against malicious behaviors bristling on User-Generated Content (UGC)-based Social Network Sites (SNS). Given the current research gap on voluntary moderation from the perspectives of power misuse, we investigate how power abuse by a moderator would affect the community dynamics in terms of participation indicators, linguistic characteristics, and network structure in a computational fashion. An event on Reddit is chosen for a case study. Using interrupted time-series analysis and social network analysis, we find moderation fueled short-term feuds and brought potential prolonged destruction to the community. People's linguistic patterns remained stable while the liberation from "tyranny" brought the community back to life and the power competition entailed negative repulsion. We also find an "Exodus" phenomenon as netizens voted with their feet and migrated to a mirror community when facing severe moderation. This preliminary research expands the connotation of moderation by addressing more forms of power abuse. We also refer to social movement and community choice theories in relevant fields and provide the insights of online moderation from interdisciplinary perspectives.

KEYWORDS

Online Moderation; Power Abuse; Reddit; Social Media; Interrupted Time-Series Analysis; Social Network Analysis

ASIS&T THESAURUS

Virtual Communities; Governance; Data Analysis

INTRODUCTION

Internet-based information and communication technologies trigger the emergence of digital spaces with the characteristics of public spheres. While democratic and decentralized virtual spaces promote the proliferation of user-generated content and stoke the participation of users, they also witness many malicious behaviors such as spam, vandals, trolls, and hate speech (Grimmelmann, 2015). As these problems are more ubiquitous across the platforms, online moderation, as a means to address these problems, becomes increasingly indispensable for community curation.

Approaches of online moderation could roughly fall into two categories: one is company-driven, which means the platform retains the privileges to regulate the forms and the moderation policy is designed by the company. This process usually involves outsourcing moderation tasks to paid workers or firms screening out the content (Roberts, 2016). This approach has drawn much attention as researchers try to understand this phenomenon from multiple perspectives (Klonick, 2017). Another type of online moderation is voluntary moderation. It is usually utilized by SNS that position themselves as content providers relying on UGC, such as Twitch, Wikipedia and Reddit (Lo, 2018). User-moderation is often characterized as bottom-up and user-run (Seering, Wang, Yoon, & Kaufman, 2019). Also, users gain the freedom to set and enforce the policy of the community (Massanari, 2017). Most research views voluntary moderation or moderators in a neutral lens. Main topics include how voluntary moderation would contribute to the community (Foerderer & Heinzl, 2018; Grimmelmann, 2015), while the negative outcome of moderation has not been exhaustively explored. Also, as most research focuses on content moderation, namely screening, modifying, removing comments, or banning users (Matias, 2016), little ink has been spilled on other types of moderation such as de-mod, the removal of one's moderator status.

Building on the literature review, we find "power" a good substitute for moderation and could serve as an umbrella term for all the forceful actions made by an online moderator. As a "basic force of social relationships" (Fiske, 1993), power accentuates the social and interactive nature of the online community. Also, it highlights the essence of moderation and thus leads the discussion of moderation into an interdisciplinary vision. Moderation boils down to power usage, the ability to "modify others' states by providing or withholding resources or administering punishments" (Keltner, Gruenfeld, & Anderson, 2003), since moderators can coercively control a user's rights in the virtual world. Under this scope, "power abuse" refers to the destructions made by moderators when they misbehave with their privileges. Based on the availability of data, we strive to answer these questions:

1. How does power abuse by user moderators affect community participation?
2. How does power abuse by user moderators affect a community's linguistic characteristics?

82nd Annual Meeting of the Association for Information Science & Technology | Melbourne, Australia | 19–23 October, 2019

DOI: 10.1002/pra2.00055

3. How does power abuse by user moderators affect a community's network structure?

In this preliminary research, we make contributions in the following ways. First, we contribute to research regarding voluntary moderation in a computational fashion using time-series analysis. Second, our research distinguishes from other voluntary moderation research for it focuses on the destructive side of moderator engagement. Finally, we enrich the connotation of moderation by adding other types of power usage neglected by previous research. On top of that, we link to relevant fields like sociology and provide new insights to study online moderation and online communities.

BACKGROUND & DATA

An infamous moderation event on Reddit is chosen for a case study. Subreddit r/xkcd was a placid comic forum until user u/soccer gained control of it in June 2011. After being the head moderator for 1.5 years, he began revising r/xkcd's sidebar by adding links to contentious subreddits like r/mensrights. Concurrently, he began repressing the voices of the opponents. In late 2013, user u/Wyboth was granted the permission to co-mod r/xkcd. However, after removing the inappropriate sidebar links, he was de-moded by u/soccer in January of 2014. This purge action attracted widespread reproof. The drama ended in August when the petition to remove u/soccer was agreed by the Reddit official. This scandal has been recognized as one of the worst moderation events that even made news headlines at the time. This historical event renders us opportunities to observe the wax and wane of the power usage in different phases. Unlike other intervention experiments (Matias & Mou, 2018), this event occurred without the researchers' intervention. Also, u/soccer is a "subreddit squatter", a person who maintains control of subreddits without active participation. It gives us new perspectives on moderator activities because of his non-typical nature. The de-mod action also set itself apart from other types of moderations as it is a form of power abuse toward colleagues, not the users.

Submissions and comments in r/xkcd are scraped using Google's Big Query (bigquery.cloud.google.com/dataset/fh-bigquery:reddit) and pushshift's API (pushshift.io/). Additionally, because of the online migrant pattern observed in the event, data of r/xkcdcomic is also obtained. In total, our dataset contains 5,259 submissions and 109,937 comments of r/xkcd, 387 submissions and 9,156 comments of r/xkcdcomic.

METHODOLOGY

Time-series analysis with intervention and outlier detection is used to answer RQ1 and RQ2. We use this method to avoid the over-simplification and auto-correlation issues which may produce problematic results. After filtering out variables with many missing values, we plot the time-series data, conduct the stationary test, and tune the ARIMA model by observing their ACF and PACF plots and comparing each model's BIC value. "tsoutliers" package in R is used to tune ARIMA model and detect novelties. Three common kinds of abnormal disturbances are examined in this research: additive outlier (AO), transitory change (TC), and level shift (LS) (Chen & Liu, 1993). An AO represents an isolated abnormal awry off the trend while a TC signifies a more influential disturbance that takes a few periods to disappear. An LS stands for an abrupt change in the mean level. After that, we also conduct model diagnostics using the Ljung-Box test. With iterative rounds of trials, we select the attributes that respond to RQs and are well-fitted for the model. For participation indicators, counts of comments, counts of submissions, the average score of the submissions, unique commenters, and unique submission posters are selected. For linguistic features, we merge all the texts from submissions and comments on a monthly basis, then calculate the number of unique words, number of sentences, average sentence length, and lexical diversity (MLTD).

Social Network Analysis is used for RQ3. We pick out 4 timings for network analysis: T1:1 month before the sidebar event, T2: the middle point between sidebar event and de-mod event, T3: the middle point between the de-mod event and dethrone event, and T4: 1 month after the dethroning.

RESULT

Participation Indicators

Figure 1 shows the effects of the outliers detected as interruptions in the time series. All three kinds of disturbance are captured in our dataset. While the inauguration of u/soccer did not translate to much influence, the forceful political indoctrination in mid 2013 stirred up controversies as we observe two AOs right after the sidebar event. Eliminationist action produces a similar result, since both submissions and comments have AOs around that time, and this effect also spread to the number of unique submission posters. However, the number of unique posters then plummet afterward, with a higher negative effect coefficient. The last momentous event, the dethroning of the moderator, proved to be the most influential one. All five metrics pertaining to participation have greatly increased, and most of them are LS and TC, the more intensive interruption.

In this section, we discern the transitory dispute induced by the power misuse, including the inappropriate use of the public sidebar and the removal of the other moderator; the latter one causes the decrease of thread posters. The emancipation from the authority intensively reinvigorates the whole community.

Lexical Features

Average sentence length and lexical diversity show no difference before and after the key event because the only AO is not detected around the time power abuse actions were executed. However, the number of unique words and the number of sentences do not keep stable over time. The sidebar event entailed a temporary increase on the

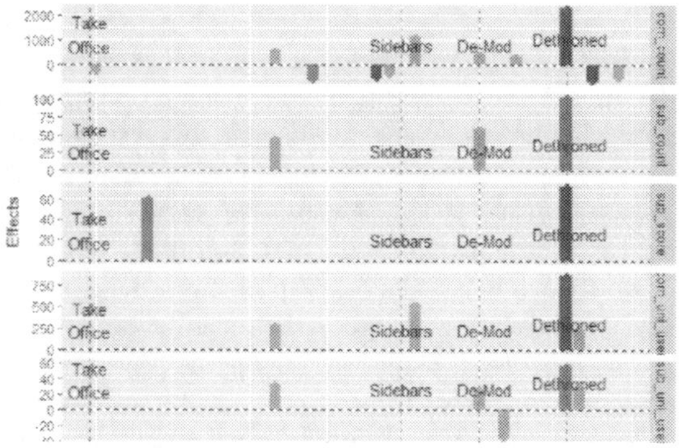

Figure 1. Outliers and their effects in community participation metrics from June 2011 to December 2014.

vocabulary of the corpus and number of sentences, which could be an indicator of activity intensity on the forum. Barring that, the dethronement of authority induced the highest impact on the user's linguistic pattern, as the abnormal effects all peaked right after August 2014. The influence is abrupt and intense and showed in the form of an AO in consecutive time sessions. In this part, we find that bad moderation only affects the vocabulary and the number of sentences. We also find the violent damaging effect of the power seizing event, since the only LS happened after that and lasted for 6 months.

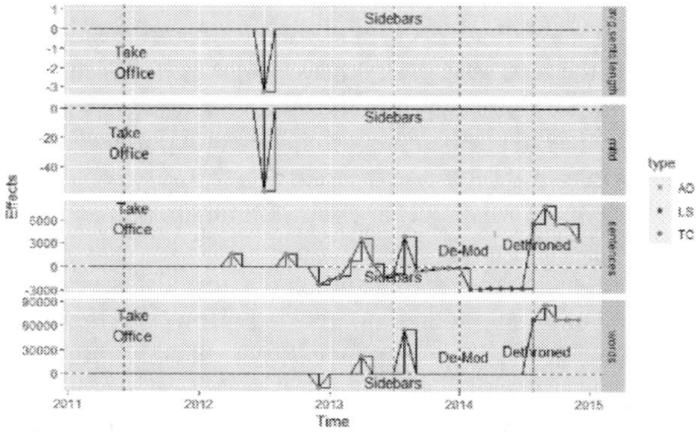

Figure 2. Outliers and their effects in lexical characteristics from June 2011 to December 2014.

Network Structure

We observe an interesting phenomenon that when people were undertaking severe moderation, they created another mirror subreddit. Based on this observation, r/xkcdcomic is also included for analysis in this part for comparison.

Figure 3 shows the social network of r/xkcd and r/xkcdcomic over time. We scale the size of the nodes based on their degrees and the width of edges based on their weights. The appearance of nodes with higher degrees indicated that the sidebar event, as a secretive action, slightly influenced the network. The brazen de-mod action aroused the controversies as the network was more stretched and more nodes were

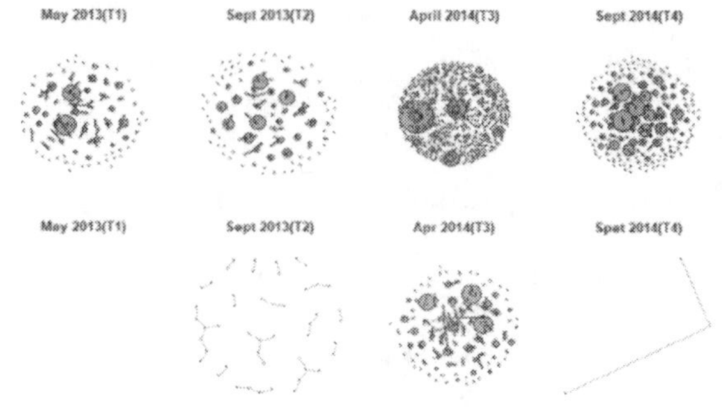

Figure 3. Network of r/xkcd(upper) and r/xkcdcomic(lower) in four chosen timings.

connected. The prevailing large nodes showed that dethroning produced many influential agents. We also witness the development of r/xkcdcomic from cradle to grave. As non-existence in May 2013, it began to flourish after the sidebar event and then evolved into a vigorous community after the de-mod event. It finally diminished after the dethroning event retaining with negligible users.

To better understand the evolution of networks, we calculate the network statistics of these networks as Table 1 shown. Nodes and edges numbers in r/xkcd kept dwindling and touched the floor after the de-mod event, while those of r/xkcdcomic peaked at that time. The dethroning produced a record high interaction between users within the r/xkcd, while the r/xkcdcomic barely being active at the same time. Density, the indicator for the network cohesiveness, is not informative as the numbers barely nudge. Centralization is a supplement of density, explaining the level of connectedness centered on a node (Chung, Piraveenan, Levula, & Uddin, 2013). Our dataset shows that the de-mod event saw a sudden increment in the r/xkcd, while the highest value of that in r/xkcdcomic occurred on the initial phase. Assortativity measures the homophily inside the group based on degree. We witness its steadiness in both subreddits. Modularity is also calculated after community detection. Its value stays stationary and high.

	r/xkcd				r/xkcdcomic			
	T1	T2	T3	T4	T1	T2	T3	T4
Nodes	1550	1390	925	2766	/	48	2090	3
Edges	1477	1304	864	2605	/	32	2010	2
Density	0.0012	0.0014	0.002	0	/	0.028	0.001	0.670
Centralization	0.021	0.016	0.067	0.013	/	0.037	0.014	1
Assortativity	0.099	0.155	0.135	0.150	/	0.077	0.110	1
Modularity	0.968	0.966	0.950	0.982	/	0.904	0.973	0

Table 1. Network statistics.

DISCUSSIONS & CONCLUSIONS

Based on the data analysis, we show that different forms of online power abuse indeed exert influence on the online community. Several implications stand out. In the participation indicators, we find that heated participation was evoked by power misuse that encompasses both covert misuses of the public sidebar and the overt power grab. The transitory dispute induced by the two kinds of power misuse aligns with the social movement theory proposed by Blumber, since the first stage "social ferment" also attracts great attention of "agitators" (Blumer, 1995). However, the number of unique posters plummeted after the event, with a higher effect coefficient, indicating a loss of the participants. This decrease potentially shows the hallmark of the fourth stage "the decline" as people choose a different community. Additionally, the uprooting of the absolute ruler has the most profound influence, as outliers are identified as LS and TC, not one-time additions, but longitude impacts. The dethroning event resembles the truth that a movement, in reality, could go back and forth. The huge volume of the participation, along with the chronological effects shares some similarity with the fourth stage that falls into the slot of the "establishment with the mainstream" (Macionis, 2000).

Although previous research indicates that lexical diversity is influenced by persuasion in an online forum (Tan, Niculae, Danescu-Niculescu-Mizil, & Lee, 2016), which is similar to the compelling nature of excessive moderation, it is not salient that lexical diversity has changed abnormally around the key events. On the other hand, the numbers of words and sentences are more sensitive and flow with the changes in almost every event. In these outliers, it is shown that the furtive scheme of adding hatred-provoking content is less long-lasting than the blatantly de-mod action. Also, the only LS in the linguistic features suggests the possible damage that excessive moderation could bring out.

The digital migration "Exodus" implies that the dynamics within social media resemble the real-world community choice when people are facing a social dilemma (Gürerk, Irlenbusch, & Rockenbach, 2009). The statistics of a network show the continual loss of users under moderation - the decreasing nodes and edges in the moderation period, signaled a loss of users. The short lifespan of r/xkcdcomic shows that it may primarily function as a hub of online social movement and a haven for online "refugees". As some researchers point out, the modularity bears the relationship to the network's robustness (Paranyushkin, 2012), so the success of the dethroning in the end, may have a relationship with the high modularity values in this event.

In conclusion, we explore the aftermath of different kinds of power abuses by a voluntary moderator. We might be wary of excessive moderation since it may bring potential long-term destruction on the community dynamics, especially the blatant action of eliminationism. Our analysis also echoes with other social theories. Additionally, an online "Exodus" phenomenon is observed as netizens' voting with their feet and migrating to a mirror community when facing severe moderation. The new community serves as temporary-use and drains the netizens from the repressed one. Liberation from tyranny is the most influential event as it brings the strongest positivity into all three aspects of the community dynamics. However, because this paper is based on a single case study, its anecdotal nature reduces the generality of the conclusions to some extent. Future studies could conduct similar case analysis for comparison. Also, the "Exodus" phenomenon could be selected to depict the user differences between the leavers and stayers.

REFERENCES

Blumer, H. (1995). Social movements. In S. M. Lyman, *Social movements: Critiques, concepts, case-studies* (pp. 60–83).

Chen, C., & Liu, L.-M. (1993). Forecasting time series with outliers. *Journal of Forecasting*, *12*(1), 13–35.

Chung, K. S. K., Piraveenan, M., Levula, A. V., & Uddin, S. (2013). Assessing online community-building through assortativity, density and centralization in social networks. In *2013 46th Hawaii International conference on system sciences* (pp. 1993–2002).

Fiske, S. T. (1993). Controlling other people: The impact of power on stereotyping. *American Psychologist*, *48*(6), 621–628.

Foerderer, J., & Heinzl, A. (2018). *Do online communities benefit from appointing volunteer moderators? evidence from a regression discontinuity design*. 12.

Grimmelmann, J. (2015). The virtues of moderation. *Yale Journal of Law and Technology*, *17*, 42.

Gürerk, Ö., Irlenbusch, B., & Rockenbach, B. (2009). *Voting with feet – Community choice in social dilemmas* (Vol. *46*).

Keltner, D., Gruenfeld, D. H., & Anderson, C. (2003). Power, approach, and inhibition. *Psychological Review*, *110*(2), 265–284.

Klonick, K. (2017). The new governors: The people, rules, and processes governing online speech. *Harvard Law Review*, *131*, 1598.

Lo, C. (2018). *When all you have is a banhammer: The social and communicative work of volunteer moderators*.

Macionis, J. J. (2000). *Sociology* (8th ed.). Bergen, NJ: Prentice Hall.

Massanari, A. (2017). #Gamergate and The Fappening: How Reddit's algorithm, governance, and culture support toxic technocultures. *New Media & Society*, *19*(3), 329–346.

Matias, J. N. (2016). *The civic labor of online moderators* (Vol. *10*). Oxford, England.

Matias, J. N., & Mou, M. (2018). CivilServant: Community-led experiments in platform governance. In *Proceedings of the 2018 CHI conference on human factors in computing systems - CHI '18* (pp. 1–13).

Paranyushkin, D. (2012). *Metastability of cognition in the body-mind-environment network!* 35.

Roberts, S. T. (2016). Commercial content moderation: Digital laborers' dirty work. *Dirty Work*, 12.

Seering, J., Wang, T., Yoon, J., & Kaufman, G. (2019). Moderator engagement and community development in the age of algorithms. *New Media & Society*, 1–27.

Tan, C., Niculae, V., Danescu-Niculescu-Mizil, C., & Lee, L. (2016). Winning arguments: interaction dynamics and persuasion strategies in good-faith online discussions. In *Proceedings of the 25th international conference on world wide web - WWW '16* (pp. 613–624).

Developing a Work-Identifier Allocation Algorithm to FRBRize KORMARC Records

Jaehyuk Yun
Department of Library and Information Science,
Sungkyunkwan University,
Seoul, Republic of Korea
seisiel89@gmail.com

ABSTRACT

Displaying search results by work requires clustering related works by assigning every Machine-Readable Cataloging (MARC) record a work-identifier. Although the manual assignment of work-identifiers may be unfeasible in some cases due to a high number of records, developing an instance-appropriate algorithm provides a convenient solution by enabling automated allocation. This study attempted to find a method to automatically convert the National Library of Korea (NLK) data to Functional Requirements for Bibliographic Records (FRBR) structure. However, there were some problems with the Korean MARC (KORMARC) records of the NLK. The NLK uses principally an added entry field (7XX) than a main entry field (1XX) and most 7XX fields do not have relator terms, and which makes us not to know the representative author of books when there are several contributors (multiple 7XX fields). Accordingly, this study seeks to maximize accuracy in cases of works with more than two contributors without using a main entry field or authority data by investigating the possibility of shifting from KORMARC to the FRBR.

KEYWORDS

FRBR; Korean MARC; FRBR Algorithm; FRBRization

ASIS&T THESAURUS

Cataloging; Cataloging Rules; Functional Requirements for Bibliographic Records; Digital Libraries

INTRODUCTION

In the age of big data, the amount of information resources is growing exponentially as are the relationships between them. However, existing Machine-Readable Cataloging (MARC) standards, which describe individual resources in a linear structure, have limited ability to represent relationships between resources. The Functional Requirements for Bibliographic Records (FRBR) is a set of recommendations issued by the International Federation of Library Associations and Institutions (IFLA) in 1998. This model is tailored to reflect the relationships between bibliographic resources and their range (IFLA, 1998). Through work-based clustering for bibliographic records, FRBR enables users to explore not only the sources that they search but also the information associated with those sources (i.e., translations or alternative editions).

Most libraries in South Korea still operate on a localized form of MARC called KORMARC (Korean MARC), but some Korean national institutions have begun to express an interest in FRBR-based user display services. Especially, the National Library of Korea (NLK) in South Korea has been attempting to develop a search system with RDA (Resource Description and Access) and FRBR models since 2014 (Kim, 2014). It aims to meet the diversifying information needs of users by providing them with the opportunity to explore various information related to resources. Since 1,107 public libraries in South Korea use the data management system of the NLK, improving the search system is expected to significantly affect institutions' abilities to meet the information needs of the South Korean people.

To apply the FRBR model to the search system, we must convert KORMARC records to the FRBR structure. An algorithm must be used to automatically convert records as manual conversions require significant financial and labor resources. Most previous studies on this subject did not conclude that extant records required revision because the NLK's incomplete bibliographic records will continue to invalidate attempts at FRBRization (Cho, 2004; Kim, Lee, & Lee, 2015; Lee & Chung, 2008; Rho, 2008). However, repairing records also requires significant labor and financial resources. Accordingly, this study aims to establish a method of converting incomplete KORMARC records to the FRBR structure as accurately as possible (Kim, Yoo, & Park, 2007).

FRBR ALGORITHM

Previous studies on converting KORMARC records to the FRBR structure are based on algorithms developed by the Library of Congress (LC) and the Online Computer Library Center (OCLC). A key aspect of these algorithms is that they

82nd Annual Meeting of the Association for Information Science & Technology | Melbourne, Australia | 19–23 October, 2019

DOI: 10.1002/pra2.00078

assign a unique identifier to each record in order to achieve work-based clustering. The OCLC algorithm uses authority records to automatically generate the representative form and variants of an author and title, matches the generated data with the author and title listed in the bibliographic records, and provides the representative form from the authority data as the work-set identifier. The LC algorithm extrapolates either the author and title or the title only from bibliographic records that are yielded by author or title queries. After the corresponding bibliographic records have been matched, the algorithm selects a representative form and assigns it as the identifier. OCLC provides various methods for cases such as those in which there is (1) a main entry field (1XX), (2) a uniform title, (3) no main entry field, and (4) a combination of the title and OCLC number. However, the LC algorithm organizes data depending on whether the main entry field (1XX) exists, and the added entry field (7XX) is not used when there is no main entry field.

LITERATURE REVIEW

Table 1 summarizes the fields used when generating the "author + title" key to identify a work in previous studies. Previous studies utilized main entry fields (1XX) and added entry fields (7XX) in order to extract authorship, but Lee (2010) attempted to use "$a - original title of translated book" of 507 field (now 534 field, original version note) as well. When extracting titles, researchers used uniform title fields (130, 240, and 730) and a title statement field (245). The input values of other fields such as series statement fields (440, 490), formatted contents field (505), and uncontrolled related/analytical title (740) mainly related to book series, and are thus suitable for extracting series titles, but not for individual books. Accordingly, the study focuses on main/added entry fields (1XX and 7XX) as author key, and the uniform title fields (130, 240, and 730) and title statement field (245) as title key.

Articles	Fields for identifying works	
	Author	Title
Cho (2004)	100, 110, 111, 700, 710, 711	245, 440, 490
Kim, Yoo, and Park (2007)	100, 110, 111, 700, 710, 711	130, 240, 243, 245, 730
Rho (2008)	100, 110, 111, 700, 710, 711	130, 240, 245, 505, 730, 740
Lee (2010)	100, 110, 111, 507, 700, 710, 711	130, 240, 245, 507
Kim et al. (2015)	100, 110, 111, 700, 710, 711	130, 240, 245, 246, 505, 730, 740

Table 1. Fields for identifying works in prior studies.

Prior studies on converting KORMARC records to FRBR have limitations in studying only records with main entry fields (1XX) or authority data (Cho, 2004; Kim et al., 2015). Moreover, there is a case in which the first 7XX field was used as the author name, when there were no 1XX fields but there were two or more 7XX fields (Kim et al., 2015). In other words, we do not know which 7XX field to use if there are multiple contributors. The study seeks to maximize the accuracy of selecting a representative author in cases of more than two contributors without using the 1XX field or authority record.

EXPERIMENT

The following challenges have been observed within the NLK records: (1) insufficient management of authority data and uniform titles, (2) limited usage of 1XX main entry fields, and (3) absence of relator terms in the 7XX added entry fields. Due to such issues, the OCLC algorithm, which relies on authority records and uniform titles, cannot be applied to KORMARC. Even with the LC algorithm, the lack of main entries and relator terms in KORMARC would lead to inaccuracies in cases of more than one contributor and therefore the need to designate a main author.

For this study, "Hamlet" was selected among works with various bibliographic types, derivations, and translations so that the algorithm could include the number of different cases. The experimental data consists of the 378 volumes in the results obtained from a keyword search using "Hamlet" in through the NLK database. According to Table 2, only 43 (11.4%) of 378 records have main entry field (1XX), and none have a uniform title. As already mentioned, the NLK records often do not have relator terms in the added entry fields (7XX). In experimental data, there are 1412 added entry fields, but only 59 (4.2%) have role terms. On the other hand, most title statement fields (245) have contributors and role terms. Considering this feature, we attempted to use the 245 field to identify authors through relator terms when there is no main entry field and multiple contributors are involved.

In 245 fields of MARC21 and KORMARC, subfields related to titles and contributors are composed as shown Table 3.

Fields	Description	Volume (%)
100, 110, 111	Single contributor (main entry)	43 (11.4)
130, 240, 730	Uniform title	0 (0.0)
700, 710, 711	Single contributor (added entry)	82 (21.7)
700, 710, 711	Multiple contributor (added entry)	253 (66.9)
Total		378 (100.0)

Table 2. "Hamlet" search results statistics.

Format	Guideline and example
MARC21	$aTitle (: or =)$bRemainder of title /$cStatement of responsibility1 ; Statement of responsibility2.
	Example - $aHamlet =$b햄릿 /$ccreated by William Shakespeare ; co-translated by A and B
KORMARC	$aTitle :$bRemainder of title =$xEquivalence title /$dStatement of responsibility1 (, or ;)$eStatement of responsibility2(R)
	Example - $aHamlet =$x햄릿 /$dcreated by William Shakespeare ;$eco-translated by A ,$eB

Table 3. MARC21 and KORMARC guidelines.

Unlike MARC21 expressing both sub-title and equivalence-title via $b, KORMARC separates the equivalence-title and expresses it at $x. There is also a big difference in the Statement of Responsibility. MARC21 describes all author information at $c (non-repeatable). However, KORMARC inputs all contributors' names into individual subfields by describing the first contributor name at $d and subsequent names at $e repeatedly.

Using KORMARC's 245 field helps identify a representative author when there are several contributors (multiple 7XX). When the roles of the contributors are different in the statement of responsibility ($d and repeatable $e), semicolons are used to distinguish them, and commas are used to separate the names of people who played the same role. The example in Table 3 can be expressed as "creator: William Shakespeare; Translator: A, and B," and from which we can extract a role term set like "creator; translator." Since the author of the translated edition is usually the original creator (creator > translator) in the FRBR model, we assign William Shakespeare as the representative author.

There are various expressions, such as those shown in Table 4, that are used in the statement of responsibility. To improve the algorithm's ability to distinguish between the role and name in the strings of the 245 field, we must create a dictionary that groups these synonym expressions into the same class. We constructed a relator term dictionary using metadata for representing the derivation type of ISTC (International Standard Text Code). Due to the possibility of linking to the ISTC later or to show the relationship with the original. For example, an adapted version has an adapter and an original creator. Since the author of the adapted resource is the adapter, "title + adapter name" is the representative key. At this time, if we match the original and adapted versions by using "title + original creator name" as the key, we can connect the two resources as follows: "Resource A is an adaptation of resource B."

"Translator" expressions		Normalized
공역	Co-translation (Korean)	Translation
共譯	Co-translation (Chinese)	Translation
공옮김	Co-translated (Korean)	Translation
번역	Translation (Korean)	Translation
역	Transl. (Korean)	Translation
譯	Transl. (Chinese)	Translation
역자	Translator(Korean)	Translation
옮긴이	Person who translated (Korean)	Translation
옮김	Translated(Korean)	Translation

Table 4. Normalization of various expressions of a translator shown in the 245 fields of "Hamlet" search results.

Figure 1 shows the sequence of processes.

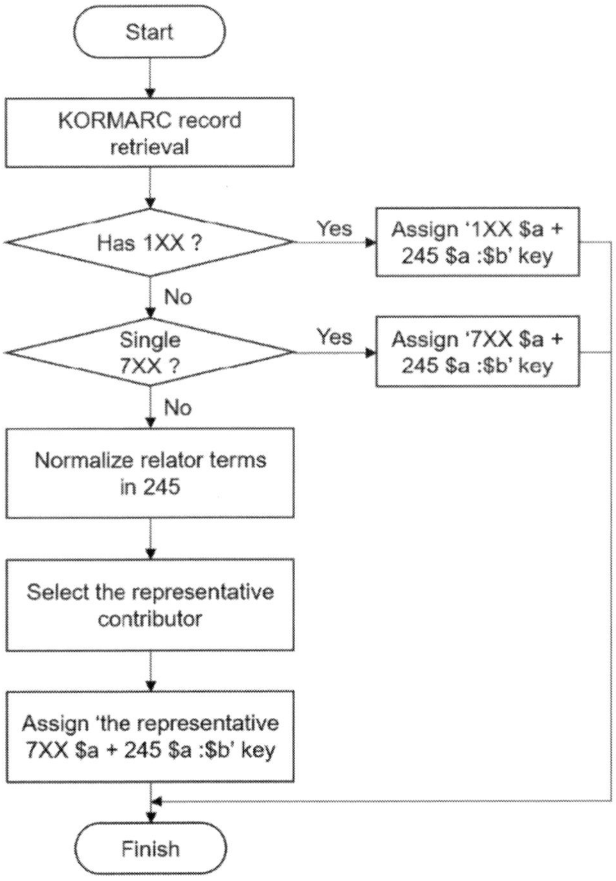

Figure 1. Algorithm for assigning a work identifier.

Using the 245 field leads to an issue if expressions of foreign names are different. Main/added entry fields (1XX and 7XX) describe the name as "First name, Last name." However, the title statement field (245) marks the contributor name differently such as "William Shakespeare," "W. Shakespeare," and "Shakespeare," because expressions of contributor names vary among publishers. If the author name is different, there is a risk of lowered accuracy when using the "author name + title." To solve this problem, the algorithm needs to connect and cluster author names (the variants) of the 245 field and corresponding author names (the representatives) of 7XX fields and group them into the same class, which enhances accuracy.

SUMMARY

When applying the FRBR structure to the KORMARC records, it is necessary to assign a work identifier to each record. Since the KORMARC usually uses the added entry field (7XX) instead of the main entry field (1XX), it is difficult to apply existing FRBR algorithms and choose the representative author when there are several contributors. A new algorithm using relator terms in the 245 field is expected to address these problems and improve the accuracy of assigning work identifiers. This method relies on patterning the relator term set and selecting a representative author for each pattern. However, there was no clear standard to select the representative author. Tillett's (2001) study on bibliographic relationships and subsequent studies are expected to help establish author selection criteria. Subsequent research will then assign work-identifiers to each bibliographic record according to the algorithm and assess its accuracy through expert interviews or surveys to determine if identifiers are properly designated.

REFERENCES

Cho, J. (2004). Study on the FRBR algorithm and application of KORMARC database. *Journal of the Korean Society for Library and Information Science, 38*(3), 5–21.

IFLA. (1998). *Functional requirements for bibliographic records: Final report*. Retrieved from https://www.ifla.org/files/assets/cataloguing/frbr/frbr_2008.pdf

Kim, H., Yoo, Y., & Park, S. (2007). An experimental study on the FRBR model adaptation to KORMARC database: Focusing on music materials. *Journal of Korean Library and Information Science Society, 38*(2), 185–202.

Kim, J. (2014). *A study on the FRBR model of national bibliographic data based on RDA*. Seoul, Korea: National Library of Korea.

Kim, J., Lee, S., & Lee, Y. (2015). A study on the development of FRBR algorithm for KORMARC bibliographic record. *Journal of Korean Library and Information Science Society, 46*(1), 1–23.

Lee, M. (2010). A study on suggestion for KCR and KORMARC by analyzing work and expression element of RDA in MARC. *Journal of Korean Library and Information Science Society, 41*(2), 251–272.

Lee, M., & Chung, Y. (2008). A study of FRBR implementation to catalog by using work clustering. *Journal of the Korean Society for Information Management, 25*(3), 65–82.

Rho, J. (2008). An application of FRBR model to KORMARC records. *Journal of Korean Library and Information Science Society, 39*(2), 291–312.

Tillett, B. (2001). Bibliographic relationships. In C. A. Bean & R. Green, *Relationships in the organization of knowledge* (pp. 19–35). Dordrecht, The Netherlands: Springer.

Listening to the User's Voice: A Temporal Analysis of Autism-Related Questions on Quora

Yuehua Zhao
Nanjing University, Jiangsu Key Laboratory of Data Engineering and Knowledge Service, Nanjing, China
yuehua@nju.edu.cn

Chao Min
Nanjing University, Nanjing, China
mc@nju.edu.cn

Xu Han
Nanjing University, Nanjing, China
me.hanxu@qq.com

Sanhong Deng
Nanjing University, Jiangsu Key Laboratory of Data Engineering and Knowledge Service, Nanjing, China
sanhong@nju.edu.cn

Hao Wang
Nanjing University, Jiangsu Key Laboratory of Data Engineering and Knowledge Service, Nanjing, China
ywhaowang@nju.edu.cn

Jiang Li
Nanjing University, Nanjing, China
lijiang@nju.edu.cn

ABSTRACT

Social question and answer (Q&A) platforms offer a new way for identifying information needs of people with certain diseases. Taking Quora as an example, we examine which health topics are of interest to autistic people and how these topics evolve over time. Experimental results reveal increasingly heavy and diverse attention to the condition, from diagnosis and treatment of autism itself to extended issues like social challenges, parenting, and education issues. We find that users tend to post clinical concerns about autism on Quora although traditionally such social Q&A platforms encourage more social and awareness-level questions. New concerns have appeared recently about autism's relations to other diseases like attention deficit hyperactivity disorder (ADHD) and obsessive–compulsive disorder (OCD). This study is beneficial for tracking and responding to autistic patients' and caregivers' information needs.

KEYWORDS

Social Q&A Platform; Health Informatics; Autism

ASIS&T THESAURUS

Information seeking; User Generated Content

INTRODUCTION

Autistic people's information needs sometimes be identified in time due to their difficulties in verbal communication. In this paper we address the question how temporal change of users' health concerns can be identified from crowdsourcing Q&A platforms. This is particularly beneficial for healthcare providers who are increasingly faced with the challenge of tracking and responding to patients' and caregivers' information needs.

LITERATURE REVIEW

Autism-Related Discussions On Social Media

Individuals with autism have been found to have a propensity toward the use of computers (Kientz, Goodwin, Hayes, & Abowd, 2013), which enables the emerging technologies to facilitate their communication. Roffeei, Abdullah, and Basar (2015) analyzed two autism support groups on Facebook using a deductive content analysis approach. They found that the highest percentage of messages were about informational support (30.7%) and emotional support (27.8%). A majority of the discussions were related to challenges and difficulties in caring and raising autistic children, as well as children's social life and self-care routines.

Health Information Seeking On Social Q&A Platforms

The major perspectives of research on social Q&A platforms include user satisfaction (Zhang, Deng, & Yang, 2014) and user behavior (Syn & Oh, 2011). In addition, user information needs analysis has become a popular research interest using social Q&A Websites. Both general health topics (Kim & Yoon, 2012) and specific diseases such as cancer, diabetes, eating disorders, sexually transmitted diseases, and smoking cessation (Bowler, Mattern, Jeng, Oh, & He, 2013), have attracted the attention of researchers.

Previous empirical studies suggest that social Q&A platforms provide a valuable opportunity for better understanding of users' information needs and concerns about various health issues (Westbrook & Zhang, 2015). In this study, our aim is

82nd Annual Meeting of the Association for Information Science & Technology | Melbourne, Australia | 19–23 October, 2019

DOI: 10.1002/pra2.00057

to explore, by answering the following two questions, the concerns and stated needs of users regarding autism.

RQ1: What are the topics of questions regarding autism on Quora?

RQ2: How do the topics of the questions evolve over time?

METHODOLOGY

Data Collection

Quora is a social Q&A platform where questions are asked, answered, edited, and organized by users. On Quora, questions can be organized by topics. Each question is assigned one or more topics by the original asker and can also be edited by other users later. To cover the majority of questions related to autism, in this study, we selected the following three autism-related user-assigned topics that contain the largest number of questions: Autism, Autism Rights, and Autism Spectrum Disorders.

The data collection process was performed with a crawler program developed by the authors in Python. Note that the first question under the above three topics was raised on October 6, 2016, on Quora. The dataset included 3,755 questions posted from October 6, 2010 to January 29, 2017. To reveal the most up-to-date change of the topics, we then gathered a second data collection from January 15, 2019 to April 2, 2019 that included 2,943 posted questions. For each autism-related record/item the question and corresponding answers were recorded separately along with a timestamp.

Data Analysis Process

After data collection, the data analysis process comprised four steps, as outlined in Figure 1. Each step will be addressed in more detail in the following sections.

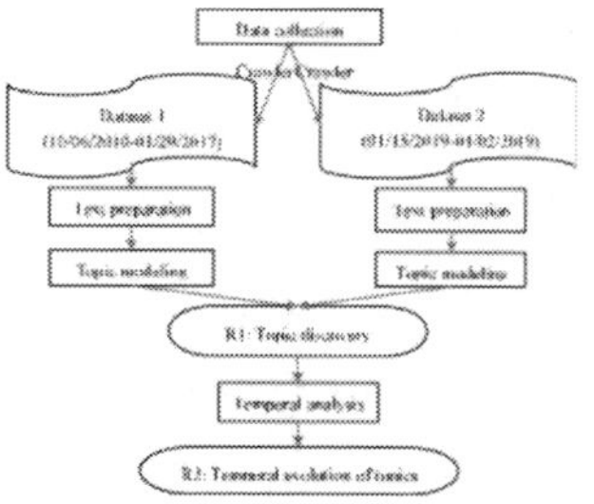

Figure 1. Data analysis process.

Topic Modeling

In this study, the text preparation process was performed by Python scripts using NLTK toolkits. The text preparation process consisted of the tokenization, stop-words removal and stemming of terms. We implemented a LDA model in Python with the *Sklearn* package using the Gibbs Sampling inference method. The hyperparameters α and β control the amount of smoothing in the model estimation process. The hyperparameters α was set to 50/K (K is the number of topics) while β equals 0.01. The number of iterations was set as 500.

LDAvis handles the model checking problem to aid topic interpretation by displaying the ranking of terms within topics and the relevance among topics. In this study, the *pyLDAvis* package was implemented in Python to visualize the models generated from the dataset, as well as assist the modeling checking process. Different values of K, or numbers of topics, were tested. The number of LDA topics was tuned until it reached a set of non-overlapping clusters that had sufficient distance between each other. After producing the appropriate LDA models, the revealed topics in each group were labeled manually according to the top terms in the topic-term distributions.

RESULTS

Topics of the Questions Being Asked on Quora

Through the model checking process, results indicated that the optimal number of topics for both datasets were four as the generated topics were distinctive to each other and the circles did not overlap anymore. The interpretation of a topic can be achieved by examining a ranked list of the most probable terms in that topic. Table 1 and Table 2 list the top 20 terms for each topic emerging during 2010–2017 and in 2019, respectively.

Topic 1	Topic 2	Topic 3	Topic 4
Diagnosis & treatment (34%)	**Social challenges (27%)**	**Parenting (22%)**	**Education (18%)**
Asperger	autism	autistic	autism
autism	spectrum	child	aspie
syndrome	disorder	feel	cure
diagnosis	affect	parent	skill
adult	function	neurotypical	talk
ASD	kid	aspie	social
child	treat	school	service
life	job	social	add
function	support	friend	learn
symptom	common	student	relate
test	relationship	learn	difficulty
woman	social	common	write
therapy	mild	function	speak
sign	mental	ADHD	hate
condition	issue	special	communicate
behavior	ADHD	understand	Asperger
disability	improve	girl	successful
develop	personality	normal	career
meltdown	sensory	hard	savant
bad	increase	individual	character

Table 1. Top 20 terms in each topic during 2010-2017.

The modeling evaluation process indicated that four topics emerged from the questions on Quora related to autism. The inter-topic distance map of the four topics (represented by the four circles) appearing during 2010–2017 and in 2019 are visualized in Figure 2. Each circle represents an

Topic 1	Topic 2	Topic 3	Topic 4
Diagnosis & treatment (68%)	**Related diseases (16%)**	**Social challenges (11%)**	**Education (5%)**
autism	Asperger	autistic	autism
autistic	syndrome	ASD	college
child	learn	neurotypical	notice
spectrum	ADHD	job	hurt
function	aspie	aspie	drug
disorder	common	meltdown	discriminati on
adult	hard	type	company
kid	neurotypical	human	product
parent	OCD	career	sound
diagnosis	read	affect	animal
feel	social	obsession	sign
ASD	book	hand	loud
friend	woman	play	anger
vaccine	intelligence	program	performanc e
social	ASD	easy	cultural
therapy	suffer	light	safe
school	relationship	character	scare
life	conversation	drive	IQ
experience	prevalence	Quora	diet
symptom	tend	autists	stim

Table 2. Top 20 terms in each topic in 2019.

individual topic. The size of the circles represents the popularity of the topic within the overall set of topics.

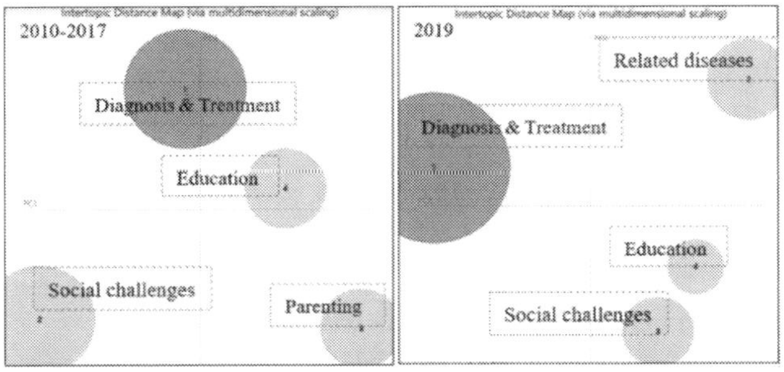

Figure 2. Visualization of the topics of the questions on Quora related to autism during 2010–2017 and in 2019.

Temporal Evolution of Autism-Related Topics

Armed with the topic labels for each question in the dataset, we conducted the following temporal analysis to take timestamps into account. The primary objective was to assess if users' concerns on autism have changed over time.

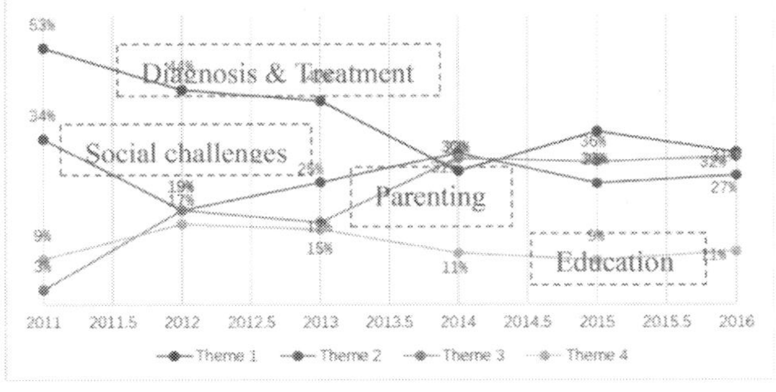

Figure 3. Temporal evolving patterns of revealed topics.

As shown in Figure 3, the proportion of the topics varied over time. Parenting was discussed increasingly from 2011 to 2016. Questions regarding diagnosis and treatment became the dominant topics in 2011, 2012, and 2013, and continued to be posted in the following years. From 2011 to 2016, parenting-related questions became increasing concerns. Users posted questions regarding education less commonly during the entire period, yet the topic evolved slowly over time.

DISCUSSION AND PRIMARY CONCLUSION

Growing Attention to Autism

Our findings concerning two research questions (topic discovery and temporal change) provide insights into the autism-related questions in the social question-and-answer environment. Undoubtedly, interests in autism have increased dramatically over the past ten years. Users' concerns have become increasingly diverse, from diagnosis and treatment of the disease itself to extended issues like social challenges facing the patients, how to raise autistic children, and especially education issues. Not only could autism patients use social Q&A platforms to facilitate their self-care routines and seek both informational and social support from others, but such platforms could also serve as an information source for neurotypical people with regards to the ways of interacting with autism patients and raising the public awareness about autism.

More Concerns about Clinical Information and Social Challenges

Through an investigation of cervical cancer-related queries on the Yahoo! Q&A platform, Westbrook and Zhang (2015) found that clinical subjects (including symptoms, diagnosis, prognosis, and treatment) received less attention. On the contrary, in this study we discovered that clinical information about autism (including diagnosis and treatment) was readily seen as a prominent concern (34% of all the questions) from 2010 to 2017 and still attracted the most attention (68% of all the questions) in 2019. Queries included diagnosis-related questions (e.g. "*Who can give a proper diagnosis for autism spectrum disorder?*") and information regarding specific therapies (e.g. "*If you are autistic and experienced ABA therapy, would you recommend it? Why, or why not?*"). It suggests that users tend to post clinical concerns about autism on Quora although traditionally such social Q&A platforms encourage more social and awareness-level questions.

Social challenges were another prevalent topic. Previous studies unveiled the social challenges of adults with autism including intense isolation, problems initiating interactions, communication difficulties, and a desire for facilitated social interactions and socially appropriate behavior, and alternative modes of communication (Burke, Kraut, & Williams, 2010). Therefore, on Quora, users could seek help from others regarding the approaches to deal with the social challenges (e.g. "*How do I handle my autistic meltdown so that I don't accidentally hurt people physically or emotionally?*"). With respect to autistic children, they generally require constant special care and attention from their parents, family, classmates, schoolteachers, and caregivers. Such difficulties present daily challenges for parents and/or caregivers of children with autism (Roffeei et al., 2015). Therefore, not only may the autism patients themselves seek help to deal with the social challenges on online Q&A platforms, but people surrounding them may also need information to face daily difficulties.

In particular, under the topic of social challenges, users frequently posted questions with respect to the job options for autism patients. Sample questions include "*What jobs do people with asperger have and what jobs are easiest to keep for someone with asperger?*" It implies that health-related organizations targeting autism patients should be encouraged to provide information and training for autism patients and their parents about job seeking in addition to the daily self-care information.

Major Concerns Become Stable

Users' major concerns shifted from clinical questions and social challenges to parenting issues as time progressed from 2010 to 2017. The proportions of the topics of the questions fluctuated from 2010 to 2013, and then the following three major topics become stable and almost equally distributed from 2014 to 2017: diagnosis and treatment, social challenges, and parenting. Education issues were less commonly posted but remained stable over time. This suggests that users' concerns have become more focused and stable as more information has become available and accessible on the Q&A platform.

New Concerns Appeared Recently

A large number and proportion of queries about the association between autism and other diseases (16% of all the questions) appeared in 2019. As shown in Table 2, attention deficit hyperactivity disorder (ADHD) and obsessive–compulsive disorder (OCD) were mentioned most. Users expressed their concerns about the relationships between different types of mental disorder and the commonly shared symptoms. Sample questions include "*Do ADHD/ADD and OCD accompany high-function autism?*" and "*Is it common for someone with ADHD to also receive a diagnosis of autism?*" From a research perspective, Anholt et al. (2010) claimed that the relationship between autism, ADHD, and OCD has scarcely been studied. Yet, users have requested information regarding the associations between those different types of mental disorder on the social Q&A platforms. It demonstrates that more research might be needed to examine such associations.

This study is limited by the data sampled and may not be applicable to all social question and answer platforms. Due to the data collection limitation of the Quora platform, the entire dataset consisting all questions and answers under the autism-related topics are not accessible.

ACKNOWLEDGMENTS

The authors thank Prof. Dietmar Wolfram for valuable comments and suggestions on this paper. The authors gratefully acknowledge the grant from the Fundamental Research Funds for the Central Universities (#010814370301), Tang Scholar program, and National Natural Science Foundation of China (# 71473114).

REFERENCES

Anholt, G. E., Cath, D. C., van Oppen, P., Eikelenboom, M., Smit, J. H., van Megen, H., & van Balkom, A. J. L. M. (2010). Autism and ADHD symptoms in patients with OCD: are they associated with specific OC symptom dimensions or OC symptom severity? *Journal of Autism and Developmental Disorders*, *40*(5), 580–589.

Bowler, L., Mattern, E., Jeng, W., Oh, J. S., & He, D. (2013). I know what you are going through: Answers to informational questions about eating disorders in Yahoo! Answers: A qualitative study. *Proceedings of the American Society for Information Science and Technology*, *50*(1), 1–9.

Burke, M., Kraut, R., & Williams, D. (2010). *Social Use of Computer-mediated Communication by Adults on the Autism Spectrum*. Proceedings of the 2010 ACM Conference on Computer Supported Cooperative Work, 425–434.

Kientz, J. A., Goodwin, M. S., Hayes, G. R., & Abowd, G. D. (2013). *Interactive Technologies for Autism* (1st ed.). San Rafael, CA, USA: Morgan & Claypool Publishers.

Kim, S., & Yoon, J. (2012). The Use of an Online Forum for Health Information by Married Korean Women in the United States. *Information Research*, 1–18.

Roffeei, S. H. M., Abdullah, N., & Basar, S. K. R. (2015). Seeking social support on Facebook for children with Autism Spectrum Disorders (ASDs). *International Journal of Medical Informatics*, *84*(5), 375–385.

Syn, S. Y., & Oh, S. (2011). Web resource selection behavior patterns of social media users in health: A comparison of Yahoo! Answers and delicious. *Proceedings of the American Society for Information Science and Technology*, *48* (1), 1–2.

Westbrook, L., & Zhang, Y. (2015). Questioning strangers about critical medical decisions: "What happens if you have sex between the HPV shots? ". *Information Research*, *20*(2).

Zhang, Y., Deng, S., & Yang, L. (2014). A tale of social Q&As in the United States and China. *Proceedings of the American Society for Information Science and Technology*, *51*(1), 1–4.

From Free to Fee: Exploring the Factors That Influence the Askers' Switching Behavior on Online Q&A Platforms

Yuxiang (Chris) Zhao
Nanjing University of Science & Technology, Nanjing, China
yxzhao@vip.163.com

Zhouying Liu
Nanjing University, Nanjing, China
liuzhouying0908@163.com

Si Chen
Nanjing University, Nanjing, China
si.chen@nju.edu.cn

Qinghua Zhu
Nanjing University, Nanjing, China
qhzhu@nju.edu.cn

ABSTRACT

More and more social Q&A platforms are launching new business models to monetize online knowledge. Many users of the traditional free Q&A are gradually adopting the payment-based Q&A services. Previous studies have focused more on askers' participation behaviors in the free Q&A context, while few of them explored the switching behavior of askers from free- to payment-based Q&A platforms. Based on the push-pull-mooring (PPM) model, this paper aims at exploring the influencing factors of askers' switching behavior using the critical incident technique. The classification scheme of the factors that influence the askers' switching behaviors includes 5 categories and 16 subcategories. We also use the entropy-weight method to calculate the weight of each factor. The findings suggest that the psychological characteristics, cognitive needs, and financial incentives have great impacts on askers' switching behavior in the Q&A context.

KEYWORDS

Switching Behavior; Payment-Based Q&A; Push-Pull-Mooring Model; Tri-lateral Q&A Platforms

ASIS&T THESAURUS

Information Sharing; Knowledge Management

INTRODUCTION

The view that "information wants to be free" on the Internet has been prevalent since the Internet could be accessed by public netizens (Lambrecht & Misra, 2016). However, the past few years have witnessed that many online content platforms, especially in China, start to charge consumers for access to the content (iResearch, 2018). This change from "free to fee" is visibly observed on online social question & answer (Q&A) platforms, which aims at facilitating knowledge contribution and diffusion as well as social interaction among askers and answers (iResearch, 2018). Traditionally, social Q&A service (e.g., Yahoo! Answers, Quora) was free and open to the public. Recently, these service providers have recognized the business value of social Q&A sites, and launched new business models to monetize online knowledge (Hsieh, Kraut, & Hudson, 2010; Lee, Kim, Yi, Sung, & Gerla, 2013). One of the most popular business models is the tri-lateral payment-based social Q&A platform (hereinafter called tri-lateral Q&A), which has drawn growing attention from both practitioners and researchers.

In the tri-lateral Q&A model, askers make payment to acquire professional knowledge from experts (i.e., answerers) directly, and answerers obtain the consultant fee only after they provide solutions before the deadline. In addition, askers are able to maintain social interaction with answerers during the Q&A process (Kitzie, Choi, & Shah, 2012). More importantly, this new model introduces a tri-lateral relationship by involving and activating traditional online lurkers as paid listeners (Jan, Wang, Zhang, & Wang, 2018; Zhao, Liu, & Song, 2018). The amount of listening fee is set by the platform and shared between askers and answerers. In this regard, the tri-lateral Q&A platform differs from traditional free Q&A services and thus, herein, the research question – why askers are willing to switch from the traditional free Q&A to the tri-lateral Q&A platform – is proposed.

So far, although several studies have been conducted to explore the askers' behavior in Q&A services, most of them mainly focused on the askers' participation behavior (e.g., Choi, Kitzie, & Shah, 2012; Choi & Shah, 2016; Jeon & Rieh, 2013) and little literature explores the askers' switching behavior from free to paid Q&A platforms. Investigating user switching behavior can help us better understand users' willingness and hindrance to adopt payment-based Q&A platforms. To fill the research gap, this exploratory study employs the critical incident technique to identify the relevant influencing factors based on the push-pull-mooring (PPM) model. Moreover, we also use the entropy-weight method to calculate the weights of the influencing factors. Our research findings may shed light on the design and evaluation of the payment-based Q&A platform.

RESEARCH DESIGN

Research Method

In this study, we used critical incident technique (CIT) to explore the factors that influence the askers' switching behavior. CIT was proposed as a qualitative research method and

82nd Annual Meeting of the Association for Information Science & Technology | Melbourne, Australia | 19–23 October, 2019

DOI: 10.1002/pra2.00056

applied to study the promoting/hindering factors of individual's behavior (Flanagan, 1954). In the field of library and information, this approach has been adopted to study the topics of human information behavior, such as information seeking failures (Wang & Shah, 2017) and online information encountering (Jiang, Liu, & Chi, 2015). The wide usage of CIT shows that this method has provided a systematic procedure to collect and analyze the incidents that influence the askers' switching behavior in our research context.

Data Collection

This research was supported by a well-known tri-lateral Q&A platform in China. The vendor selected the askers who have asked at least 10 questions on the tri-lateral Q&A platform from January 2017 to May 2018. After screening out the askers who used the free Q&A platforms more frequently than the tri-lateral Q&A platforms, 60 askers were selected by systematic sampling.

The interview included two parts. The first part was to guide the askers to recall the process and experience of their switching behavior from free- to payment-based Q&A platforms, and to provide as many detailed descriptions as possible. In the second part, we asked about the factors that influence askers' switching behavior and how these factors differ before and after the switch. The interviews were conducted from June to September in 2018. 51 askers were effectively interviewed and each interview lasted 40 to 60 minutes. Of these participants, 22 (43.14%) are male and 29 (56.86%) are female. Most of the participants' were in the age from 25-34 (21, 41.18%), and 94.12% of them held a bachelor or higher degree.

PRELIMINARY RESULTS

Classification of the Critical Incidents

We invited five doctoral students (Judges A, B, C, D, E) and introduced the push-pull-mooring (PPM) model to them. The PPM model, which is derived from the field of population geography (Moon, 1995), is a dominant paradigm to explore the users' switching behavior in information science (Wu, Vassileva, & Zhao, 2017; Ye, Seo, Desouza, Sangareddy, & Jha, 2008). The pushing factors are the negative factors that compel the users far away from the incumbent product/service. The pull factors are the positive factors that attract the user's switch to the alternative products/services. Mooring factors could hinder or facilitate user's switching intention and behavior, such as personal characteristics and social factors.

We asked students to code the 265 incidents that influenced askers' switching behavior based on the PPM framework. We divided the critical incidents into two parts, namely classification sample and confirmation sample. The classification sample consisted of two-thirds of the critical incidents, while the confirmation sample was the remaining one-third of the critical incidents. Five students sorted out the classification sample of critical incidents according to the way that Keaveney (1995) suggested. To begin with, A and B classified the critical incidents. The inter-judge reliability between A and B was 0.91, higher than 0.8, which has met the minimum reliability requirement (Holsti, 1969). After discussing the controversial results, A and B identified 5 categories and 12 subcategories. Then, C and D sorted and classified the critical incidents into the classification scheme as proposed by A and B. During the classification process, C and D found some incident could not be classified into the current scheme. Thereby, they added 1 and 3 new subcategories respectively. The inter-judge reliability between C and D was 0.90. Furthermore, E classified the critical incidents and did not add any new categories. A, B, C, D and E compared their classification schemes and resolved the controversies. Finally, Judges A-D sorted the remaining one-third critical incidents and no new categories were created, which showed that the categorization scheme was saturated. In addition, content validity was also acceptable in this study. To sum up, the high inter-judge reliabilities and content validity of the categorization scheme illustrate that the scheme reveals the influencing factors of the askers' switching behavior well.

As shown in Table 1, the final categorization scheme includes 5 categories and 16 subcategories. The pushing factors are the askers' dissatisfaction towards the information and system quality on free Q&A platforms. The pulling factors are the askers' satisfaction towards the information and system quality on tri-lateral Q&A platforms and financial incentives. In addition, mooring factors consist of social, personal and objective factors.

PPM framework	Category	Subcategory
Pushing factors	A. The relevant factors of free-based Q&A platforms	a1. Dissatisfaction with information quality
		a2. Dissatisfaction with system quality
Pulling factors	B. The relevant factors of tri-lateral payment-based Q&A platforms	b1. Satisfaction with information quality
		b2. Satisfaction with system quality
		b3. Financial incentives
Mooring factors	C. Social factors	c1. Social ties
		c2. Subjective norm
		c3. Network externalities
	D. Personal factors	d1. Cognitive needs
		d2. User experience
		d3. Information literacy
		d4. Psychological characteristics
		d5. Demographics
	E. Objective factors	e1. Time constraint
		e2. Question type
		e3. Switching cost

Table 1. The factors influencing askers' switching behavior.

Analysis of the Influencing Factors' Weights

We invited the former interviewees to rate the degree of influence of the factors before and after the switching behavior. The scoring standard was 8 points, with 0-point meaning that this factor had no effect on the switching behavior. As the value of rating goes up, the influence degree of this factor on the askers' switching behavior gradually increased. 7-point means that this factor greatly affects the askers' switching behavior. According to the results, we used the method of entropy-weight to calculate the factors' weights. The weight of the factor is determined by the value of the factor's information entropy (Shannon, 1950). The higher the value of the information entropy, the lower the relative weight of the factor.

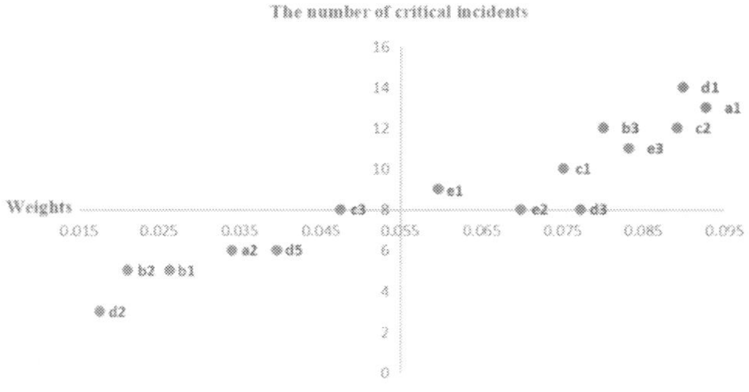

Figure 1. Scatter plot of the factors that influencing askers' switching behavior (before).

As shown in Table 2, before the switching, the 5 influencing factors with higher weights are psychological characteristics (d4), dissatisfaction with information quality (a1), cognitive needs (d1), subjective norm (c2) and switching cost (e3). After the switch, user experience (d2), cognitive needs (d1), satisfaction with the information quality (b1), psychological characteristics (d4) and financial incentives (b3) are the 5 factors that influence the askers' switching behavior more heavily.

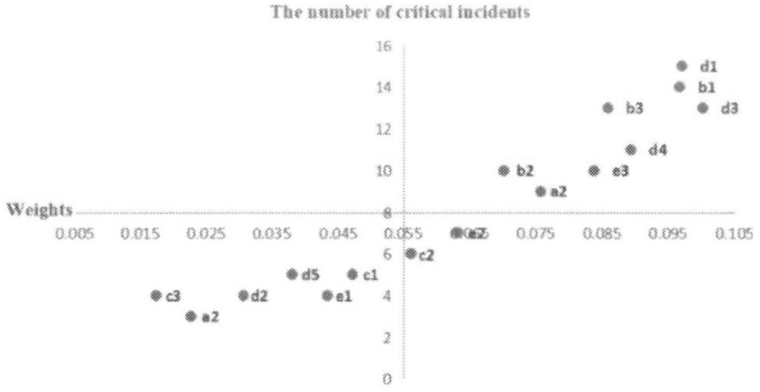

Figure 2. Scatter plot of the factors that influencing askers' switching behavior (after).

In addition, the weights of influencing factors and the number of critical incidents were taken as horizontal and vertical coordinates to draw scatter plots. As shown in Figures 1 and 2, the numbers of critical incidents of cognitive needs (d1), financial incentives (b3) and switching cost (e3) do not change a lot, and the weights of them are high both before and after the switching. In addition, after the switch, the weights of social ties (c1), subjective norm (c2) and network externalities (c3) on askers' switching behavior become lower and the number of critical incidents of these factors also become fewer than the weights of these factors before the switching. However, the impact of user experience (d2), satisfaction with information quality (b1) and system quality (b2) and the numbers of critical incidents of these factors both increase after the switch.

indicate that the askers pay more attention to the information quality on the Q&A platforms. The dissatisfaction with information quality on free-based Q&A platforms push the askers to switch away from the free-based Q&A platforms, while the satisfaction with information quality on payment-based Q&A platforms pull them to switch to the payment-based platforms. Meanwhile, askers also consider the financial benefit and cost during Q&A process. In addition, after having the experience of using the tri-lateral Q&A platforms, the effect

Factors	a1	a2	b1	b2	b3	c1	c2	c3	d1	d2	d3	d4	d5	e1	e2	e3
Before switch	0.09 26	0.03 40	0.02 63	0.02 11	0.08 00	0.07 51	0.08 91	0.04 74	0.08 98	0.01 75	0.07 72	0.09 75	0.03 96	0.05 96	0.06 98	0.08 32
After switch	0.07 57	0.02 27	0.09 67	0.07 02	0.08 59	0.04 71	0.05 62	0.01 75	0.09 70	0.10 02	0.03 07	0.08 94	0.03 80	0.04 33	0.06 32	0.08 38

Table 2. The weights of the influential factors of the askers.

PRELIMINARY DISCUSSIONS AND CONCLUSION

Based on the push-pull-mooring model, we finally classified 5 categories and 16 subcategories of the factors that influence the askers' switching behavior from free- to payment-based online Q&A platforms using the method of critical incident technique. Then, we calculated the weights of the influencing factors by using the entropy-weight method. The results

of user experience is greater on the askers' switching behavior. In terms of theoretical implications, this study contributes to the literature on askers' switching behavior in the context of online Q&A services and provides empirical support for future relevant researches. In terms of practical implications, according to these results, the vendor of tri-lateral payment-based Q&A platforms should take effective strategies to improve the information quality of the answers and design better price and reward mechanism to ensure the pleasant user experience on tri-lateral payment-based Q&A platforms.

This study has several limitations. First, when recalling the experience of their switching behavior, the interviewees may miss out some important details that influence their switching behavior. Second, due to space limitations, we are unable to provide rich quotes from the interviews to specify the qualitative findings. Third, the data was collected through the interview, therefore it lacks the analysis of the askers' actual usage behavior. In the future research, we will conduct in-depth interview to further understand the impacts of the influencing factors on the askers' switching behavior and model the askers' switching activities to reveal the switching process. Moreover, we will use the askers' objective behavioral data to analyze the askers' different behavioral characteristics on both Q&A platforms, such as the different preferences of question types, topics, etc.

ACKNOWLEDGMENTS

Gratefully acknowledge the grant from National Science Foundation of China (Nos. 71774083 and 71473114).

REFERENCES

Choi, E., Kitzie, V., & Shah, C. (2012). Developing a typology of online Q&A models and recommending the right model for each question type. *Proceedings of the ASIST, 49*(1), 1–4.

Choi, E., & Shah, C. (2016). User motivations for asking questions in online q&a services. *Journal of the Association for Information Science & Technology, 67*(5), 1182–1197.

Flanagan, J. C. (1954). The critical incident technique. *Psychological Bulletin, 51*(4), 327–358.

Holsti, O. R. (1969). *Content analysis for the social sciences and humanities*. Mass: Addison-Wesley.

Hsieh, G., Kraut, R. E., & Hudson, S. E. (2010). *Why pay?: Exploring How Financial Incentives are Used for Question & Answer*. In Proceedings of the SIGCHI Conference on Human Factors in Computing Systems, pp. 305–314.

iResearch. (2018). *Online Paid Knowledge Platforms Seek for More Business Model*. Retrieved from http://www.iresearchchina.com/content/details7_43746.html

Jan, S. T., Wang, C., Zhang, Q., & Wang, G. (2018). *Pay-per-Question: Towards Targeted Q&A with Payments*. In Proceedings of the 2018 ACM Conference on Supporting Groupwork, pp. 1–11.

Jeon, G. Y., & Rieh, S. Y. (2013). The value of social search: Seeking collective personal experience in social Q&A. *Proceedings of the ASIST, 50*(1), 1–10.

Jiang, T., Liu, F., & Chi, Y. (2015). Online information encountering: modeling the process and influencing factors. *Journal of Documentation, 71*(6), 1135–1157.

Jin, X. L., Zhou, Z., Lee, M. K., & Cheung, C. M. (2013). Why users keep answering questions in online question answering communities: A theoretical and empirical investigation. *International Journal of Information Management, 33*(1), 93–104.

Keaveney, S. M. (1995). Customer switching behavior in service industries: An exploratory study. *Journal of Marketing, 59*(2), 71–82.

Kitzie, V., Choi, E., & Shah, C. (2012). *To ask or not to ask, that is the question: Investigating methods and motivations for online Q&A*. In Proceedings of HCIR, pp. 1–4.

Lambrecht, A., & Misra, K. (2016). Fee or Free: When Should Firms Charge for Online Content? *Management Science, 63*(4), 1150–1165.

Lee, U., Kim, J., Yi, E., Sung, J., & Gerla, M. (2013). Analyzing Crowd Workers In Mobile Pay-For-Answer Q&A. In Proceedings of the SIGCHI Conference on Human Factors in Computing Systems, pp. 533–542.

Moon, B. (1995). Paradigms in migration research: exploring "moorings" as a schema. *Progress in Human Geography, 19*(4), 504–524.

Shannon, C. E. (1950). The mathematical theory of communication. 1963. *Bell Labs Technical Journal, 3*(9), 31–32.

Wang, Y., & Shah, C. (2017). Investigating failures in information seeking episodes. *Aslib Journal of Information Management, 69*(4), 441–459.

Wu, K., Vassileva, J., & Zhao, Y. (2017). Understanding users' intention to switch personal cloud storage services: evidence from the Chinese market. *Computers in Human Behavior, 68*, 300–314.

Ye, C., Seo, D. B., Desouza, K. C., Sangareddy, S. P., & Jha, S. (2008). Influences of it substitutes and user experience on post-adoption user switching: an empirical investigation. *Journal of the American Society for Information Science and Technology, 59*(13), 2115–2132.

Zhao, Y., Liu, Z., & Song, S. (2018). *Why Should I Pay for the Knowledge in Social Q&A Platforms?*. In International Conference on Information, pp. 577–582.

There Is a Method to It: Making Meaning in Information Research Through a Mix of Paradigms and Methods

Lynn Silipigni Connaway
OCLC,
Dublin, OH, USA
connawal@oclc.org

Ixchel M. Faniel
OCLC,
Dublin, OH, USA
fanieli@oclc.org

Bhuva Narayan
University of Technology Sydney,
Sydney, Australia
bhuva.narayan@uts.edu.au

Elham Sayyed-Abdi
University of Southern Queensland,
Toowoomba, Australia
elham.s.abdi@gmail.com

ABSTRACT

The current information environment provides many options for individuals in finding information and acquiring resources. It is increasingly necessary for Information Science (IS) researchers to employ user-centered research methods in order to better identify individuals' information behaviors within their contextual worlds. This panel will provide an overview of some of the novel user-centered research methods being used globally in information research within various contexts. Focusing on some recent innovative projects ranging from information discovery and access, refugee information behaviors, and cyberbullying, to personal health information management, the panel will examine the benefits, challenges, and implications for IS researchers. The panel will have an interactive component for participants to learn how to incorporate new methodologies in innovative ways within their research to make new meaning from their user studies.

KEYWORDS

Human information behaviors; information seeking behavior; information use behavior; information experience; experience sampling method; information research methodologies; qualitative information research; quantitative information research; mixed paradigm research

ASIS&T THESAURUS

User studies; Research methods; Data analysis

INTRODUCTION

In the current information environment, there are many options for individuals to get their information and resources. To identify individuals' information choice and access in order to develop more effective, relevant, user-centered, and ethical information environments, it is necessary to employ user-centered data collection and analysis techniques. These methods may include quantitative, qualitative and "mixed method" or "mixed paradigm" (Given, 2017) approaches, depending upon the specific research questions.

A review of the library and information science (LIS) literature indicates that survey research is one of the most widely used methods (Case & Given, 2016; Aytac & Slutsky, 2014; Chu, 2015; Luo & McKinney, 2015). Having said that, in a review of the information behavior research published between 2012 and 2014, Greifeneder (2014) reported that other methods, such as Delphi studies (Poirier & Robinson, 2014), eye-tracking (e.g. Balatsoukas & Ruthven, 2012; Wildemuth, 2009), log file analysis (Jiang, 2014), or participatory designs were used fewer than five times.

Connaway and Radford (2017) report that qualitative studies tend to use multiple methods including interviews, observations, or focus groups to gain insight into user needs and information-seeking and use behaviors. They also state that the development of new approaches for conducting qualitative research is welcome and necessary.

This panel will identify several underutilized research methods that could enhance user studies in LIS. The panelists in this session will discuss quantitative, qualitative, and mixed methods data collection techniques that can be used to investigate information behaviors of anyone, anywhere, anytime to derive a rich understanding of users' contexts, challenges, and constraints.

PANEL PROPOSAL

Each panelist contributes through her experiential insights based on her research and practice.

PANELISTS

Lynn Silipigni Connaway, PhD, is Director of Library Trends and User Research and leads the User Studies research at OCLC Research. She is the Past President of the Association of Information Science & Technology (ASIS&T). Connaway leads the digital visitors and residents project and currently is the co-principal investigator of an IMLS-funded project to investigate how late primary, secondary, and college and university STEM students judge credibility of digital resources. Lynn also was the project lead

82nd Annual Meeting of the Association for Information Science & Technology | Melbourne, Australia | 19–23 October, 2019

DOI: 10.1002/pra2.00080

on ALA ACRL "Action-Oriented Research Agenda on Library Contributions to Student Learning and Success."

In the panel Lynn will discuss a study that combined individuals' search behaviors documented in a discovery system's logs with semi-structured interviews to discuss how and why the individuals' conducted their searches and made the decisions they did for searching for information and sources. This mixed method approach is an update of a methodology developed by Connaway, Budd, and Kochtanek (1995). Search logs were used to reconstruct each participant's search session and create customized protocols for interview participants using the critical incident technique. The information from the semi-structured interviews was then used to inform a bulk log analysis to model how search sessions could result in the access of materials, and the features of the session that would make access more likely. The results of using this combined data collection method confirmed that user logs can contain incomplete or misleading evidence of user activity and provide only part of the user's search behavior and information on if and how they accessed the resources. It also indicates that interview protocols that are customized based on log analysis can elicit more detailed insights into user experience and behavior. This multi-method requires expertise in log analysis and in semi-structured interview data collection and analysis and can be resource intensive and time consuming. Using log data to inform semi-structured interviews of individuals' online searching behaviors and the ways they access resources can inform the development of information literacy instruction based on individuals' needs and behaviors and the development and enhancement of discovery systems.

Ixchel Faniel, PhD is Senior Research Scientist at OCLC. Ixchel's research interests include improving how people discover, access and use/reuse content. She is currently examining how academics manage, share, and reuse research data and librarians' experiences designing and delivering supportive research data management programs. She also is investigating how science, technology, engineering, and mathematics (STEM) students from grade school to grad school identify and judge the credibility of digital resources. Ixchel's research has been funded by the National Science Foundation (NSF), Institute of Museum and Library Services (IMLS) and National Endowment for the Humanities (NEH). Prior to joining OCLC Ixchel worked at the University of Michigan, School of Information, IBM, and Andersen Consulting (now Accenture).

Ixchel will discuss a simulation study that generated qualitative and quantitative data. The study was designed to examine students' information-seeking behavior, specifically how they identify and judge online information resources (Buhler et al., 2015-2018). Data were collected from a group of 175 students in six educational stages: 1) 4th-5th grade/year, 2) 6th-8th grade/year, 3) 9-12th grade/year, 4) community college/technical college, 5) undergraduate, and 6) graduate/postgraduate.

Pre-screen surveys were used to recruit participants for the in-person simulation sessions and to gather demographic data used for the sampling frames. The simulations were designed to examine students' point-of-selection behavior (i.e., the moment a user determines a piece of information potentially meets a research need) when starting work on a science inquiry assignment about Burmese pythons in the Everglades. Input was sought from the study's advisory board, comprised of local instructors and librarians to ensure assignments and resources were age appropriate. Working together they created a pool of online information resources and science assignments appropriate for each educational stage. The simulations employed a task-based methodology to observe student's cognition in action via think-aloud protocols that captured qualitative data about students' thoughts while deciding which resources were helpful, citable, and credible and deciding the container for resources (e.g. blog, book, conference proceeding, journal, magazine, news, preprint, website). In addition, quantitative data were collected as students clicked on resources to explore them further, chose which resources were helpful and citable, rated the credibility of the resources, and identified their containers. Simulations also included pre- and post- interviews to gather additional demographic data from the students, their experiences with libraries, and their research and information behavior.

Designing a mixed method simulation study across six educational stages enabled the creation of a realistic search experience for students without the challenges of a naturalistic setting (e.g. slow or unavailable websites, sudden changes in the user interface, different search results). Creating simulations where the search results were the same within each educational stage also enabled within group comparisons.

Bhuva Narayan, PhD, is a transdisciplinary researcher in the School of Communication at the University of Technology Sydney (UTS), Australia, and coordinates the Information and Knowledge Management (IKM) Program, including the Master of Digital Information Management. Bhuva holds degrees from Chatham University (BA Hons.), Columbia University Graduate School of Journalism (GradDip Publishing Procedures), University of Pittsburgh (MLIS), Queensland University of Technology (PhD), and University of Technology Sydney (GradCert Higher Education). Before moving to academia, Dr. Narayan spent over two decades in the book industry as a bookstore consultant, development editor, and publisher in the USA. Bhuva's research encompasses Library and Information Science, Social Informatics, Social Justice, HCI, Information Systems, Design Thinking, and Human Learning.

Bhuva will discuss some of the different user-centered methods used in her collaborative research around information behaviors including the diary method (Narayan, Case, & Edwards 2011; Narayan, 2014), experience sampling method or ESM (Narayan & Chowdhury, 2017), natural language processing (Narayan & Chowdhury, 2017), social media analysis (Fransen-Taylor & Narayan, 2018; Narayan & Preljevic, 2017; Fransen-Taylor & Narayan, 2016), discourse analysis (Booth & Narayan, 2017; Booth & Narayan, 2018), online ethnography (Talip et al., 2016; Pingo & Narayan, 2019a, 2019b), autoethnography (Campbell & Narayan, 2017; Latham, Narayan & Gorichanaz, 2019), design thinking (Luca & Narayan, 2016), conversation design (McKie & Narayan, 2019), and a mixed paradigm study (Luca & Narayan, 2016; Narayan & Luca, 2017; Narayan et al., 2018).

In discussing these studies that use a range of empirical methods, Bhuva will highlight the role of collaboration and cooperation with other researchers and practitioners as a key factor in the success of such interdisciplinary, transdisciplinary, and multidisciplinary research studies that investigate information behaviors in contexts as varied as diabetes information literacy, privacy literacy, conspiracy theories, cyberbullying, diversity and inclusion, young adult fiction, information inspiration, chatbot design, and library signage.

Elham Sayyad-Abdi, PhD, is an information researcher, a former Fulbright Scholar-In-Residence at the University of the Pacific, USA, and a Fellow of the Higher Education Academy, UK. From 2014-2018, Elham served as a lecturer (Assistant Professor) in the School of Information Systems, Queensland University of Technology (QUT), Australia. Elham's research interest lies in the application of information research within social settings to improve people's lives by empowering them for more engaged, informed, and inclusive citizenry. With an aim to address the pressing issue of social justice, and through leading a 1-year Library and Information Science Research Australia (LISRA)-funded study as well as managing a 3-year Australian Research Council-funded project, Elham has looked into the information world of immigrants to understand how their use of information could be enriched through more user- and information-centered interventions.

Elham will discuss the two-phase qualitative and participatory "information experience design" research approach which bridges theory to practice in the information use domain (Bruce et al. 2017, Sayyad Abdi, 2018, Sayyad Abdi et al., 2019). Elham will describe a qualitative investigation into immigrants' experience of "information use to learn" and how the analysis was used to inform the design of enabling interventions (e.g. services, programs) within the practice of resettlement service providers.

STRUCTURE OF THE PANEL

- The Moderator (Lynn Silipigni Connaway) will introduce the panel and discuss the need for new and innovative methodologies to understand information users (5 minutes);
- Each panelist will discuss the methods they have devised or used in their research and explain how these have enriched their findings (40 minutes total);
- The panelists will facilitate an interactive activity (e.g. pair and share, etc.) that focuses on methodological challenges attendees are experiencing in their current research, idea generation of potential solutions, and advice from the larger group of attendees who have experienced similar challenges (40 minutes);
- The Moderator will close the session by reviewing the results of the interactive session (5 minutes).

ACKNOWLEDGMENTS

Support for the research study, *Researching students' information choices: Determining identity and judging credibility in digital spaces*, was provided by the Institute of Museum and Library Services (IMLS). Support for the research study, *Digital Visitors and Residents: What Motivates Engagement with the Digital Information Environment*, was provided by Jisc.

REFERENCES

Aytac, S., & Slutsky, B. (2014). Published librarian research, 2008 through 2012: Analyses and perspectives. *Collaborative Librarianship*, 6(4). Paper retrieved from). https://digitalcommons.du.edu/collaborativelibrarianship/vol6/iss4/6.

Balatsoukas, P., & Ruthven, I. (2012). An eye-tracking approach to the analysis of relevance judgments on the Web: The case of Google search engine. *Journal of the American Society for Information Science and Technology*, *63*(9), 1728–1746.

Booth, E., & Narayan, B. (2017). Towards diversity in young adult fiction: Australian YA authors' publishing experiences and its implications for YA librarians and readers' advisory services. *Journal of the Australian Library and Information Association*, (3), 67.

Booth, E., & Narayan, B. (2018). "Don't talk about the gay character:" Barriers to queer young adult fiction and authors in schools and libraries. *English in Australia*, *53* (2), 40–48.

Bruce, C., Demasson, A., Hughes, H., Lupton, M., Sayyad Abdi, E., Maybee, C., … Mirijamdotter, A. (2017). Information literacy and informed learning: Conceptual innovations for IL research and practice futures. *Journal of Information Literacy*, *11*(1), 4–22.

Buhler, A., Cataldo, T. T., Faniel, I. M., Connaway, L. S., Valenza, J. K., Graff, R., Elrod, R., Putnam, S., Cyr, C., Towler, C., Hood, E., Fowler, R., Howland, S., Brannon, B., Langer, K., & Kirlew, S. (2015-2018). *Researching students' information choices: Determining identity and judging credibility in digital spaces*. IMLS Grant Project LG-81-15-0155. http://guides.uflib.ufl.edu/RSIC

Campbell, K., & Narayan, B. (2017). First-generation tertiary students: Access is not the same as support. *International*

Journal of Innovation, Creativity and Change, *3*(3), 43–60.

Case, D. O., & Given, L. S. (2016). *Looking for information: A survey of research on information seeking, needs, and behaviour*. Bingley, UK: Emerald.

Chu, H. (2015). Research methods in library and information science: A content analysis. *Library & Information Science Research*, *37*(1), 36–41.

Connaway, L. S., & Radford, M. L. (2017). *Research methods in library and information science*. Santa Barbara, CA: Libraries Unlimited.

Connaway, L. S., Budd, J. M., & Kochtanek, T. R. (1995). An investigation of the use of an online catalog: User characteristics and transaction log analysis. *Library Resources & Technical Services*, *39*(2), 142–152.

Fransen-Taylor, P., & Narayan, B. (2018). Challenging prevailing narratives with Twitter: An #AustraliaDay case study of participation, representation and elimination of voice in an archive. *Journal of Librarianship and Information Science*, *50*(3), 310–321.

Fransen-Taylor, P., & Narayan, B. (2016). #Homeless but at home in cyberspace. *Information Research: An International Electronic Journal*, *21*(4).

Given, L. M. (2017). It's a new year…So let's stop the paradigm wars. *International Journal of Qualitative Methods*, *16*, 1–2.

Greifeneder, E. (2014). Trends in information behaviour research. In *Proceedings of ISIC: the information behaviour conference, Leeds, 2-5 September* 2014*: Part 1*. Retrieved from http://InformationR.net/ir/19-4/isic/isic13.html

Jiang, T. (2014). A clickstream data analysis of users' information seeking modes in social tagging systems. In M. Kindling & E. Greifeneder (Eds.), *Proceedings of the 9th iConference* (pp. 314–328). Retrieved from). http://hdl.handle.net/2142/47288.

Latham, K., Narayan, B., & Gorichanaz, T. (2019). Encountering the muse: An exploration of the relationship between inspiration and information in the museum context. *Journal of Librarianship and Information Science*, Special Issue, 1-10.

Luca, E., & Narayan, B. (2016). Signage by design: A design thinking approach to library user experience. *Weave: Journal of Library User Experience*, *1*(5).

Luo, L., & McKinney, M. (2015). JAL in the past decade: A comprehensive analysis of academic library research. *The Journal of Academic Librarianship*, *41*(2), 123–129.

McKie, I. S., & Narayan, B. (2019). Enhancing the academic library experience with chatbots: An exploration of research and implications for practice. *Journal of the Australian Library and Information Association*, (2), 68.

Narayan, B. (2014). Information organising behaviours in everyday life: An exploration using diaries. In J. T. Du, Q. Zhu, & A. Koronios (Eds.), *Library and Information Science Research in Asia-Oceania: Theory and Practice* (pp. 24–44). Hershey, PA: IGI Global.

Narayan, B., Case, D. O., & Edwards, S. L. (2011). The role of information avoidance in everyday-life information behaviors. *Proceedings of the American Society for Information Science and Technology*, *48*(1), 1–9.

Narayan, B., & Chowdhury, G. (2017). The role of information avoidance in diabetes self-management: A mobile-based study using the experience sampling method. In *In i3 Conference: Information: Interactions and Impact, June 27-July 1, 2017*. Aberdeen: Robert Gordon University.

Narayan, B., & Luca, E. (2017). Issues and challenges in researchers' adoption of open access and institutional repositories: A contextual study of a university repository. *Information Research: An International Electronic Journal*, *22*(4).

Narayan, B., Luca, E., Tiffen, B., England, A., Booth, M., & Boateng, H. (2018). Scholarly communication practices in humanities and social sciences: A study of researchers' attitudes and awareness of open access. *Open Information Science*, *2*(1), 168–180.

Narayan, B., & Preljevic, M. (2017). An information behaviour approach to conspiracy theories: Listening in on voices from within the vaccination debate. *Information Research*, (1), 22.

Pingo, Z., & Narayan, B. (2019a). "My smartwatch told me to see a sleep doctor:" A study of fitness tracker use. Accepted for publication in *Online Information Review*.

Pingo, Z., & Narayan, B. (2019b). Privacy literacy and the everyday use of social technologies in information literacy in everyday life. In *Communications in Computer and Information Science* (Vol. *989*). Berlin: Springer.

Poirier, L., & Robinson, L. (2014). Informational balance: Slow principles in the theory and practice of information behavior. *Journal of Documentation*, *70*(4), 687–707.

Sayyad Abdi, E. (2018). Put information experience design to work in your library. *Incite*, *39*(7/8), 28.

Sayyad Abdi, E., Bruce, C., Partridge, H., & Watson, J. (2019). Understanding skilled migrants' information literacy: a qualitative study. *Journal of Documentation*, *75*(4).

Talip, B. A., Narayan, B., Watson, J. W., & Edwards, S. L. (2016). Digital ethnography as a way to explore information grounds on Twitter. *Qualitative and Quantitative Methods in Libraries*, *5*(1), 89–105.

Wildemuth, B. (2009). Direct observation. In B. Wildemuth (Ed.), *Applications of Social Research Methods to Questions in Information and Library Science* (pp. 189–198). Westport: Libraries Unlimited.

Exploring Card Sort Methods: Interaction and Implementation for Research, Education, and Practice

Lettie Y. Conrad
Queensland University of Technology, Brisbane, Australia
lettie.conrad@hdr.qut.edu.au

Andrew Demasson
Queensland University of Technology, Brisbane, Australia
a.demasson@qut.edu.au

Tim Gorichanaz
Drexel University, Philadelphia, PA, USA
gorichanaz@drexel.edu

Amy VanScoy
University at Buffalo, Buffalo, NY, USA
vanscoy@buffalo.edu

ABSTRACT

Exploring research methods can help scholars and professionals accurately answer questions and solve problems. Card sorting, which encompasses a variety of methods aimed at understanding participants' subjectivities, is not commonly used in information science research. This panel will familiarize attendees with the purpose and procedures of card sort methods and to allow for hands-on interaction with the artifacts and software using examples from different techniques. The opportunity to interact with the tools of card sorting methods will help to familiarize the method and allow them to better evaluate it for their research needs. Using a simple PowerPoint application, participants will have a chance to see how card sorting works as a reflective activity without significant expense or effort. Panelists, who have used these methods in industry and research, can discuss specific research questions with attendees and offer advice.

KEYWORDS

Card sorting; research methods; Q methodology

ASIS&T THESAURUS

Card sorting; Research design; Data collection; Data analysis

INTRODUCTION

Exploring research methods can help scholars and professionals accurately answer questions and solve problems. Card sorting, which encompasses a variety of methods aimed at understanding participants' subjectivities, is not commonly used in library and information sciences (LIS) research. From the techniques used in software and computer science fields, to academic variations across social science research, as well as therapeutic approaches and educational design, card sorting methods are used to generate diverse datasets for qualitative, quantitative, or mixed-method analysis. This panel intends to familiarize attendees with the purpose and procedures of card sort methods and to allow for hands-on interaction with the artifacts and software used by the methods.

82nd Annual Meeting of the Association for Information Science & Technology | Melbourne, Australia | 19–23 October, 2019

DOI: 10.1002/pra2.00081

During the first section of the presentation, the panelists will provide an overview of card sorting methods, so that attendees have a general understanding of the variety of procedures available. Following the overview, each participant will present a use case in greater detail, so that attendees also gain in-depth understanding of some specific methods and applications. These exemplars will include 1) Q methodology, 2) a hybrid variation used in qualitative interviews, 3) application of the method in industry, and 4) application of the method in professional education. A question and answer period will follow the presentation.

During the second section of the presentation, attendees will be invited to interact with tools typical of card sorting methods, such as card sorting software on tablets and paper cards on sorting mats. Panelists will demo the tools and answer questions about using them for study in LIS.

PRESENTATION SECTION

Conrad: Method Overview & Hybrid Case Sort Case Illustration

Card sorting is an interactive research method that aims to illuminate how participants understand and organize concepts. In the broadest context within the social sciences, sorting – or card sorting – is a participatory research method that aims to engage participants in co-development of conceptual categories and definitions, and to illuminate their approach to and organization of the topics at hand (Coxen, 2004; George, 2008).

These variations often guide the degree to which an investigator pre-defines the labels or values signified by the cards, and the headings or categories against which they are sorted. Where card-sort methods invite participant-defined labels and/or categories, resulting datasets are best managed via qualitative analysis, whereas card-sort studies that prescribe card labels and/or categories can numerically tabulate results for quantitative analysis, such as similarity matrices. While card sorting was initially developed for in-person research using physical cards, web-based tools now offer the option to conduct card sorting online, which offers benefits such as remote card-sort studies.

Whether open, fixed, or hybrid variations, conducted with digital or physical cards, "think-aloud" observation is a key component of card-sort activities, where participants can explain their decisions and actions as stream-of-consciousness thinking during the card labeling and sorting exercises. As noted by Nielsen (2004), para. 12), "much of the value from card sorting comes from listening to the users' comments as they sort the cards: knowing why people place certain cards together gives deeper insight into their mental models." The addition of think-aloud or interview discourse to explain participants' sorting rationale introduces an opportunity for mixed qualitative and quantitative analysis of card-sort research data. Card sorts within interviews allow for fluid integration of follow-up questions to contribute to answering the given research question.

Card sort exercises conducted within in-depth, qualitative interviews offer scholars another dimension to a study, increasing opportunities for an investigator's understanding and interpretation of the interview data and participant experiences. Card sorting is an approachable, object-based method to elicit deeper reflections and greater recall during interviews, build rapport during a research session, and can help engage other mental faculties and deepen participant reflection and recall, offering first-hand contact with abstract, sensitive, or rarely articulated concepts or feelings.

As demonstrated in a case illustration of a doctoral study currently in progress (Conrad & Tucker, 2019), hybrid card sorting within qualitative interviews offers added flexibility, allowing participants to reflect and respond at their own pace, to consider and revise sorting decisions. Whether adapting methods from computer science, psychology, or some intersection therein, card-sorting techniques within interviews are often cited as especially effective in examining individual conceptual frameworks and approaches to organizing concepts.

VanScoy: Case Illustration: Q Methodology

Q methodology is one type of card sort method that has been widely used in LIS and has a large, interdisciplinary community of support. Developed in 1935, the method aims to categorize points of view or opinions. Data is factored on clusters of opinions, rather than on individuals, allowing researchers to characterize perspectives about a phenomenon (Stephenson, 1935; Watts & Stenner, 2005). Procedures begin with the development a Q sample – a collection of statements that reflect the breadth of opinions about a topic. During data collection, participants sort the Q sample into a quasi-normal distribution based on which cards are most and least like the way they think. Following the card sort, participants elaborate on the cards they placed in the most extreme positions – this qualitative data is later used to inform the quantitative results.

Several apps are available to analyze data, such as PQ Method (http://schmolck.org/qmethod/) and Ken-Q Analysis (https://shawnbanasick.github.io/ken-q-analysis/). By comparing participants' card sorts, these apps identify factors, as well as statements from the Q sample that distinguish the factors. The researcher then describes each factor, drawing on the distinguishing statements and the qualitative data.

Q methodology is suitable for topics where there is literature covering a variety of approaches or opinions or where the research has a collected a large dataset of opinions on the topic. These form the concourse from which the Q sample is drawn.

Q methodology, in that it is inexpensive and portable (Durning & Osuna, 1994), forces participants to prioritize among competing values, and provides participants with an opportunity for reflection and learning. Drawbacks of Q methodology include researcher bias in the creation of the Q sample (Zabala, Sandbrook, & Mukherjee, 2018), concerns about language barriers, and the inflexible nature of the Q sample once it is developed.

Gorichanaz: Card Sorting in Web Design

In information architecture, card sorting is a human-centered design method used for improving the findability of information (Spencer, 2009). The method is simple, inexpensive, and reliable. It is often used in industry settings to understand users' needs and mental models. For example, card sorting can be used to inform the design of a website's navigational structure, including what content areas are grouped together and what labels are given to each group. Card sorting can be used as part of designing a new site, adding a new area to an existing site, or redesigning an existing site. While valuable, card sorting is best implemented as part of a fuller research-for-design program, including research on users' information needs (Rosenfeld, Morville, & Arango, 2015).

Card sorting for information architecture can be open- or closed-ended. Open-ended card sorting is best for exploration in the early stages of a project, while closed-ended card sorting is useful for validation later in the process. In open-ended card sorting, participants are given a stack of cards (generally about 20–25) labeled with categories of information (e.g., About, How it works, Blog, Recipes, etc.). Participants are asked to sort the pile into smaller stacks that make sense, and then to label each stack with a term of their choosing. The participant is asked to think aloud (Ericsson & Simon, 1993) while they work. Closed-ended card sorting is quite similar, except there the major labels are predefined and participants are asked to sort into those labels. A succinct guide is given by Spencer (2004).

Both qualitative and quantitative data can be captured in card sortings. Qualitatively, card sorting can help designers understand users' frustrations, reasoning and questions as they navigate a world of information. Quantitatively, designers can analyze the number of times that two cards are grouped together, or the number of times a particular card is placed in the same category. Both sorts of data can inform design choices.

Demasson: Broadly speaking, seeing and doing, the appeal of educational card sorting

When discussing the value of card sort within educational contexts it is typically proposed that it can beneficial in areas such as

- Identifying strengths and weaknesses
- Identifying values
- Reflecting on progress
- Developing linkages between ideas and concepts
- Building models of an area of knowledge/practice (Boyle & Jackson, 2009, p. 1, para 3)

That's all true. However, those benefits are more akin to learning outcomes than expressions of value to the student coming by way of their engagement with learning. Where card sort really shines is in its ability to allow for data collection and analysis by way of a process that is at once familiar, logical and sensory.

Where other methods may be difficult for a layperson to engage with, the idea of sorting cards based on value, preference or visual similarity is at once familiar and widely embedded across many cultures. That makes it a highly suitable instrument for educational and research practices. The immediate familiarity your audience or participants will have with the ethos of sorting cards reduces the amount of time necessary to explain the process of card sorting before introducing the learning component or data collection phase of your work. That sense of familiarity and simplicity (Fincher & Tenenberg, 2005) is also beneficial when dealing with cohorts who may require a delicate approach to data collection due to language, learning or personal factors.

What then is the logical component? That simply refers to the rationale behind grouping items based on a particular scale – similarity, preference, value, trust, etc. It is a process undertaken on a daily basis across any number of different contexts and requires little to no conceptual reframing in order for a participant group to be comfortable with its requirements. What we mean by sensory refers to the tangible component of card sorting. The cards must be moved in order to be sorted, which appeals to human physicality and provides a way in which to reach those who learn kinesthetically (Waite, 2011). The tactile nature of the card sort allows for direct physical engagement rather than relying on less interactive verbal or static presentations.

A similar value can also be had by those who are visual or spatial learners (Fleming & Baume, 2006). Within a classroom or educational setting, regardless of context, the need to engage with all types of learners – auditory, visual and kinesthetic – is key. However, it is equally important in a research setting where the aim is to extract the richest source of data. When the cohort is human there is almost certain to be diversity of learning styles. Therefore, a data collection instrument with broad appeal is invaluable and card sort method can be an ideal fit (if there is greater desire to engage auditory learners then 'think-aloud' method can be used so the participant thought process is brought to the fore).

INTERACTION SECTION

During the interaction portion of the event, attendees will participate in a trial demonstration of the card sort method. Led by Dr. Demasson, with the in-audience support of the other panelists, the group will experience the simplicity, tactility, and familiarity of card sort exercises. Using a simple PowerPoint application, participants will have a chance to see how card sorting works as a reflective activity without significant expense or effort.

A barrier to use of card sorting is researchers' lack of familiarity with these methods' procedures and tools. During the interaction section of the panel, attendees will have the opportunity to explore a digital variation for data collection and analysis. Panelists will provide demos and share advice from their experience.

Panelists will be available to answer questions and share advice related to card sort methods.

CONCLUSION

It is one thing to read about an unfamiliar method in an article or hear about one in a presentation, and another to actually use a method in one's research. This panel aims to move beyond simply describing procedures and advantages of a method, to encourage attendees to interact with the tools of the method and envision using them in their own research.

PANELISTS

The panelists have differing areas of experience with card sort techniques, as well as a broad awareness of the variations of this method.

Lettie Conrad is an Information Science Doctoral candidate at Queensland University of Technology via the San José State University's School of Information Gateway PhD Program. With more than 15 years of publishing experience, Conrad has led user-centered product research and development, leveraging creative design methods, such as card sorting. In both her professional and academic work, Conrad is dedicated to humanizing the development of digital resources to support the scholarly lifecycle. She has recently published a paper about card sort methods, and her use of a hybrid variation in her doctoral research, in the Journal of Documentation (DOI: JD-06-2018-0091).

Andrew Demasson is an Associate Lecturer in the Information Systems School, Science and Engineering Faculty at Queensland University of Technology. His research has focused on reconceptualising theoretical approaches to and understandings of information literacy as well as examining the area of information experience within community contexts. Works in progress include implementation of card sort as a reflective and evaluative tool in the ePortfolio framework and research outlining the information experience of aged persons after the loss of a spouse/partner.

Tim Gorichanaz is an assistant teaching professor at the College of Computing & Informatics at Drexel University, where he teaches courses such as *Introduction to Human–Computer Interaction* and *Design of Interactive Systems*. Previously, Gorichanaz worked in the digital department of Laughlin Constable, a full-service marketing agency in Milwaukee, Wisconsin, where he learned and used card sorting as a tool in web design.

Amy VanScoy is an associate professor in the Department of Information Science at the University at Buffalo. Her introduction to Q Methodology was participating in a study of subjectivities about homeschooling conducted by a doctoral student in education. VanScoy has recently completed a Q Methodology study of her own exploring conceptualizations of reference and information service, with participants from Slovenia, South Africa, and the United States.

ACKNOWLEDGMENTS

The panelists would like to express gratitude to their affiliate institutions and colleagues as key members of our academic communities and support networks. Many thanks to Dr. Abigail Winter, Information Coordinator at Queensland University of Technology, for her comments. Conrad would like to acknowledge the guidance of her doctoral supervisory team, in particular the expertise and insights of Dr. Virginia Tucker, Doctoral Supervisor and Professor at San José State University, http://www.virginiatucker.com/.

REFERENCES

Boyle, M., & Jackson, P. (2009). *Using card sorts*. UK Physical Sciences Centre -Briefing Paper. Retrieved from https://hydra.hull.ac.uk/assets/hull:4519/content

Conrad, L. Y., & Tucker, V. M. (2019). Making it tangible: hybrid card sorting within qualitative interviews. *Journal of Documentation*, *75*(2), 397–416.

Coxen, A. P. M. (2004). Sorting. In *Encyclopedia of social science research methods* (p. 1049). Thousand Oaks, CA: SAGE Publications, Inc.

Durning, D., & Osuna, W. (1994). Policy analysts' roles and value orientations: An empirical investigation using Q methodology. *Journal of Policy Analysis and Management*, *13*(4), 629–657.

Ericsson, K., & Simon, H. (1993). *Protocol analysis: Verbal reports as data* (2nd ed.). Boston, MA: The MIT Press.

Fincher, S., & Tenenberg, J. (2005). Making sense of card sort data. *Expert Systems*, *22*, 89–93.

Fleming, N., & Baume, D. (2006). Learning styles again: VARKing up the right tree! *Educational Developments*, *7*(4), 4–7.

George, C. (2008). Designing the website: Participatory design. In *User-centred library websites: Usability evaluation methods* (pp. 97–126). Witney, UK.

Nielsen, J. (2004), *Card sorting: How many users to test*. Retrieved from https://www.nngroup.com/articles/card-sorting-how-many-users-to-test/

Rosenfeld, L., Morville, P., & Arango, J. (2015). *Information architecture: For the Web and beyond* (4th ed.). Sebastopol, CA: O'Reilly.

Spencer, D. (2004). *Card sorting: A definitive guide*. Boxes and Arrows. Retrieved from http://boxesandarrows.com/card-sorting-a-definitive-guide/

Spencer, D. (2009). *Card sorting: Designing usable categories*. New York, NY: Rosenfeld Media.

Stephenson, W. (1935). Correlating persons instead of tests. *Journal of Personality*, *4*(1), 17–24.

Waite, D. (2011). A simple card trick: Teaching qualitative data analysis using a deck of playing cards. *Qualitative Inquiry*, *17*(10), 982–985.

Watts, S., & Stenner, P. (2005). Doing Q methodology: Theory, method and interpretation. *Qualitative Research in Psychology*, *2*(1), 67–91.

Zabala, A., Sandbrook, C., & Mukherjee, N. (2018). When and how to use Q methodology to understand perspectives in conservation research. *Conservation Biology*, *32* (5), 1185–1194.

Beyond the Data Management Plan: Expanding Roles for Librarians in Data Science and Open Science

Lisa M. Federer
National Library of Medicine
National Institutes of Health,
Bethesda, Maryland, USA
lisa.federer@nih.gov

Jian Qin
School of Information Studies
Syracuse University
jqin@syr.edu

ABSTRACT

Support for research data management (RDM) has become a popular focus for library services, and many training opportunities in RDM exist for librarians. However, fewer opportunities exist for librarians to develop the more advanced skills and expertise necessary to support data science and open science. To better understand how to develop a library workforce prepared to develop services in the emerging areas of data science and open science, the National Library of Medicine convened a workshop of 15 librarians and information professionals with a range of expertise in data and open science. This session will present the workshop's recommendations and use participatory facilitation methods to engage attendees in conversation about how to prepare information professionals to meet the evolving challenges of data science and open science.

KEYWORDS

Data science; open science; digital literacy; data analytics; education in information sciences; library education

ASIS&T THESAURUS

Data science; Library education

INTRODUCTION

The last decade has seen a rise in the number of libraries offering research data management (RDM) services (Miller, Miller, & Phillips, 2018; Yoon & Schultz, 2017). Librarians' skills and expertise in information management make them a natural partner for researchers who increasingly need assistance to manage, curate, and preserve datasets. As science becomes increasingly data driven, librarians and information professionals have further opportunities to take on new roles in support of data science and open science. Some libraries have been successful in developing such services, thanks to motivated information professionals with specialized expertise in topics like research reproducibility, data visualization, and clinical data collection (Brandenburg & Joque, 2016; Read & LaPolla, 2018; Sayre & Riegelman, 2018). However, this type of knowledge is not currently widespread in the field, nor do many iSchool curricula include comprehensive training to prepare information professionals to engage deeply with data science and open science.

82nd Annual Meeting of the Association for Information Science & Technology | Melbourne, Australia | 19–23 October, 2019

DOI: 10.1002/pra2.00082

In April 2019, the National Library of Medicine (NLM) held a 1.5-day workshop, entitled "Developing the Librarian Workforce for Data Science and Open Science," with 15 librarians, information professionals, and iSchool faculty with a range of expertise in data science and open science. The goal of this workshop was to gain insight into how to develop a library workforce that is prepared to move beyond RDM services to engage with researchers on the most pressing issues and challenges in the emerging areas of data science and open science. Participants reflected on topics such as challenges and opportunities for librarians in data science and open science, gaps in existing library services, and how to best prepare current and future librarians to provide such services. Underlying all of these topics was the central question of how to define core skills for librarians in data science and open science.

This session will provide an overview of the findings and recommendations of the NLM workshop. The presentation of the workshop outcomes will serve as a starting point for interactive and participatory discussion among participants. The rest of the session will be devoted to collaborative discussion, with feedback from session participants incorporated into a follow-up report.

CORE SKILLS FOR LIBRARIANS IN DATA SCIENCE AND OPEN SCIENCE

As this session will discuss in further depth, workshop participants identified a range of skills that can be considered core to librarianship in support of data science and open science. Since most workshop participants specialize in science, particularly biomedical research, the discussion primarily focused on the sciences, but many of these skills would be relevant for librarians working in digital humanities and other fields of computationally-driven research. The skills identified as core skills can be divided into six broad categories:

- Data skills, including:
  - Data management plans and workflows

- Data and metadata standards and curation
- Data citation
- Data policy and governance
- Data sharing and reuse
- Computational skills, including:
  - Familiarity with relevant coding languages, such as R and Python
  - Computational literacy
  - Database design
  - Machine learning and data or text mining
  - Data visualization
- Research and subject matter knowledge, including:
  - General understanding of the relevant science or subject matter
  - Research design and workflows
  - Statistics
  - Responsible conduct of research and research ethics
  - Methods for reproducibility
- Interpersonal skills, including:
  - Entrepreneurship
  - Logic and problem-solving
  - Team science skills
  - Project management
  - Community building
  - Advocacy skills to communicate the importance of the library to the institution
- Traditional library skills, including:
  - Consultation and reference
  - Scholarly communication
  - Training and instruction
  - Literature searching
  - Assessment and evaluation
  - Bibliometrics
- Skills for developing programs and services, including:
  - Interview and assessment skills to understand institutional needs
  - Leadership skills
  - Communication and marketing skills
  - Scoping and planning for sustainability
  - Willingness to embrace failure

Participants emphasized that a single librarian would not and need not have *all* of these skills to succeed in data science and open science work. Indeed, few institutions would need a librarian with all of these skills. Rather, libraries should carefully consider their institution's unique needs to determine how librarians can most meaningfully engage with their users. Developing successful services requires not only a librarian with the right mix of skills and knowledge, but also thoughtful assessment of the institution and users' needs, awareness of services within other units, and cultivation of relationships with relevant institutional partners.

Workshop participants also suggested that one of the most important skillsets for librarians working in data science and open science was a willingness to embrace life-long learning and adapt their skills over time. Given the rapidly evolving nature of data science and open science, skills related to specific programming language, software, or methods that are relevant today may soon be outdated. Computational literacy and the ability and willingness to learn new tools is therefore likely more important than deep experience with any one tool. Similarly, librarians will likely support researchers from a range of disciplines and will be well-served by adopting an "anthropological" mindset that will enable them to learn the language and research cultures of various groups with whom they work.

SESSION FORMAT

This session will begin with a brief presentation to familiarize attendees with the workshop setting and findings. The next 20-30 minutes will be devoted to panel discussion of questions from attendees with two workshop participants representing both library practitioners (Lisa Federer) and iSchool faculty (Jian Qin). The remainder of the session will utilize participatory group meeting activities to engage the audience and get feedback and input on developing the librarian workforce for data science and open science, which will be incorporated into future drafts of the report on the workshop. This discussion will encourage attendees to consider not only the skills that are needed for librarians specializing in data science and open science, but also what *all* librarians should know to enable them to work in an increasingly data-driven world.

SPEAKER BIOGRAPHIES

Lisa Federer is the Data Science and Open Science Librarian at the National Library of Medicine, focusing on developing efforts to support workforce development and enhance capacity in the biomedical research and library communities for data science and open science. Prior to joining the NLM, Lisa spent five years as the Research Data Informationist at the National Institutes of Health Library, where she developed and ran the Library's Data Services Program. Her research focuses on quantifying and characterizing reuse of publicly available biomedical research data. She holds a PhD in Information Studies from the University of Maryland and an MLIS from the University of California-Los Angeles, as well as graduate certificates in data science and data visualization.

Jian Qin is Professor at the School of Information Studies, Syracuse University. Her research areas include metadata and knowledge modeling, knowledge networks in biomedical data, research data management, and scholarly communication. Her ongoing projects include using GenBank metadata and associated patent and funding data to study the biomedical research enterprise as well as cyberinfrastructure-enabled collaboration networks surrounding molecular sequence submissions. She teaches courses in information organization, metadata, and digital curation. Dr. Qin holds a PhD degree from the University of Illinois at Urbana-Champaign and an MLIS from the University of Western Ontario.

ACKNOWLEDGMENTS

The authors thank the workshop participants who graciously offered their time and insights, and Sarah Clarke and Maryam Zaringhalam for their assistance in workshop planning and reporting. This work was carried out by staff of the National Library of Medicine (NLM), National Institutes of Health, with support from NLM.

REFERENCES

Brandenburg, M. D., & Joque, J. (2016). Contextualizing visualization in library services. In L. Federer (Ed.), *The medical library association guide to data management for librarians* (pp. 139–150). New York, NY: Rowman & Littlefield.

Miller, C., Miller, R., & Phillips, G. (2018). *Keeping up with...research data management*. American Library Association. Retrieved from http://www.ala.org/acrl/publications/keeping_up_with/rdm

Read, K., & LaPolla, F. (2018). A new hat for librarians: providing REDCap support to establish the library as a central data hub. *Journal of the Medical Library Association*, *106*(1), 120–126.

Sayre, F., & Riegelman, A. (2018). The reproducibility crisis and academic libraries. *College & Research Libraries*, *79* (1), 2–9.

Yoon, A., & Schultz, T. (2017). Research data management services in academic libraries in the US: A content analysis of libraries' websites. *College & Research Libraries*, *78*(7), 920–933.

Does Information Science Need History and Foundations?

Tim Gorichanaz
Drexel University,
Philadelphia, USA
gorichanaz@drexel.edu

Elliott Hauser
University of North Carolina,
Chapel Hill, USA
eah13@email.unc.edu

Yazdan Mansourian
Charles Sturt University,
Wagga Wagga, Australia
ymansourian@csu.edu.au

Joseph T. Tennis
University of Washington,
Seattle, USA
jtennis@uw.edu

Hilary Yerbury
University of Technology,
Sydney, Australia
hilary.yerbury@uts.edu.au

ABSTRACT

As ASIS&T looks to the future, all community members are invited to contribute to a shared vision for information science. As a program of the SIG for History and Foundations (SIG-HFIS), this alternative event focuses on developing a vision for conceptual, philosophical, theoretical and historical work in information science. This event will provide a participatory platform to investigate questions such as: What is the domain of history and foundations? How does it relate to other research areas in the information field? The event will involve panelist interviews with diverse scholars, small-group discussions of big questions for history and foundations, and the presentation of a new idea-sharing platform, the HFIS Wishlist. This event will be a locus for participation and inspiration regarding historical and foundations work in information science as part of formulating a future vision for SIG-HFIS, ASIS&T, and the information field more broadly.

KEYWORDS

Foundations research; philosophy of information; information science theory; information history

ASIS&T THESAURUS

Information science history; document theory

INTRODUCTION

Information science is a dynamic field of study, shifting in its focus and interests over time as well as in its relation to other fields, all while remaining attentive to its goals of stewarding the cultural record (Furner, 2015). This year's conference theme—*anyone, anywhere, any time, any way*—bears witness to that fact. As ASIS&T looks to the future, President Elaine Toms shared a number of concepts that may inform a future vision of the Association—and, moreover, of information science as a field (personal communication, May 8, 2019). Several of these concepts involve empowering special interest groups (SIGs) in terms of reach and impact. We take this opportunity to invite members of the SIG for History and Foundations (SIG-HFIS), as well as other interested ASIS&T members and conference attendees, to envision the role and future of historical and foundations work in information science.

SIG-HFIS exists to support and encourage historical and theoretical work in information science—including history, theories, fundamental concepts, and models (SIG HFIS, n.d.). Though SIG-HFIS is often styled "the history SIG," the SIG brings together a metatheoretically diverse group of ASIS&T members—including philosophers, conceptual thinkers, empirical researchers and reflective practitioners, in addition to historians. And indeed, "history" was added to the group's name and remit in 1995, before which its explicit mandate was to explore the conceptual foundations of information science. The name change acknowledged the importance of the history of ideas and practice to theoretical work, but has also seeded some of the issues precipitating this event. As we look to the future, many questions arise:

- What is the connection between history and foundations?
- How do we define the domain of history and foundations?
- What is the relationship between this domain and others within information science?
- How can history and foundations work inform other fields of research and practice?
- How does SIG-HFIS connect with other SIGs?
- How can history and foundations work inspire others, both within and beyond information science?

Such questions come up from time to time in the literature (e.g., Arafat & Ashoori, 2019; Buckland, 2012). In the service of moving forward and inspiring further work, this alternative event will serve to encourage reflection and discussion

82nd Annual Meeting of the Association for Information Science & Technology | Melbourne, Australia | 19–23 October, 2019

DOI: 10.1002/pra2.00083

on these and other questions. We will explore the work that the SIG has done while creating a vision for what a vibrant future for information science could be like. Specifically, the event will be comprised of three sections, in addition to a 5-minute welcome and 5-minute closing:

1. A panel of scholars at a range of career stages, whose work intersects with SIG-HFIS, share challenges and visions for history and foundations and ASIS&T in talk-show-style interviews with a discussant. (20 minutes)
2. Participants form small groups to discuss three big questions, followed by a large-group summarization. (45 minutes)
3. HFIS Wishlist, a new tool for sparking creative thinking and sharing research ideas, is presented. (15 minutes)

After the event, outcome deliverables will be prepared and communicated. All these activities and outcomes are described in detail below.

ABOUT THE PARTICIPANTS

Tim Gorichanaz (Co-Organizer, Panelist)

Tim Gorichanaz is Assistant Teaching Professor at Drexel University, as well as chair-elect of SIG-HFIS. He works on document theory and information experience, which he explores in domains of personally meaningful activities, such as religious practice and hobbies. His paper "Document Phenomenology" (Gorichanaz & Latham, 2016) was selected as Outstanding Paper in *Journal of Documentation*, and in 2017 he received the Litwin Books award for ongoing dissertation research in the philosophy of information.

Elliott Hauser (Co-Organizer, Discussant)

Elliott Hauser is a PhD candidate at the University of North Carolina School of Information and Library Science. His research examines the production of certainty in information systems.

Yazdan Mansourian (Panelist)

Yazdan Mansourian is a lecturer in the School of Information Studies at Charles Sturt University (CSU). He received his PhD in Information Science from the University of Sheffield. He has served as a faculty member, Director of the Central Library, and Head of LIS Department at Kharazmi University in Tehran. Yazdan joined CSU in 2017 and currently his main research interests are Human Information Behavior, Information Seeking and Sharing in the Context of Serious Leisure, and Whole Person Approach in LIS. Yazdan is interested in the philosophical and theoretical aspects of LIS and various methods that we can use to put these theories into practice.

Joseph T. Tennis (Panelist)

Joseph T. Tennis is Associate Professor and Associate Dean for Faculty Affairs at the University of Washington Information School. His research centers on classification theory and is primarily concerned with examining how classification systems change over time, how diverse design requirements are invoked by different communities, and how these systems can interoperate in a web environment. He is increasingly interested in the ethics of information organization.

Hilary Yerbury (Panelist)

Hilary Yerbury is Adjunct Professor in Information Studies at University of Technology Sydney. She has a longstanding interest in the relationships between information and civil society. Her background in European social and political cultures and information management has influenced her concern for "thinking tools," conceptual frames, which can guide research and also inform practice. More recently, she has brought her interest in the use of information in everyday decision-making and in social change to the exploration of human rights activism and of the role of local NGOs from small nations at risk from climate change in knowledge creation and dissemination.

OUTLINE OF THE SESSION

Welcome

To kick off the session, Elliott Hauser and Tim Gorichanaz will welcome the attendees, describe the agenda for the event, and introduce the panelists. This section will last 5 minutes.

Panelist Interviews

In this section, scholars at a range of career stages will share their experiences, including challenges they faced entering the field, what ended up working, and their vision for the future of history and foundations and ASIS&T. The purpose of this section is to elicit themes and background issues that will be taken up in the rest of the event. These will not be presentations, but rather brief, talk-show-style interviews led by Hauser as discussant. Each interview will last approximately five minutes, and as the conversation unfolds some questions may be directed at multiple panelists, and panelists may respond to each other. This section will last 20 minutes.

Discussion of Big Questions

Next, participants will form small groups of 6–8 people each to discuss three big questions, with a scribe designated to record the discussion. Each question will be discussed simultaneously for 5 minutes, timed and facilitated by Gorichanaz. After each question, groups will report back for a 10-minute whole-room discussion. Common findings and summaries of the discussions will be recorded by Hauser. The three big questions are:

1. In your view, what is the role of history and foundations work in information science?
2. What particular historical or conceptual works had a major influence on your own research or practice, and how?
3. What are the key outlets for this kind of work, and what impact do they have? (Publication venues, conferences, etc.)

Notes and other records will be then collected by Gorichanaz. This section will last 45 minutes.

Sparking Further Research: HFIS Wishlist

In this final section of the event, Gorichanaz and Hauser will introduce HFIS Wishlist, a tool for sparking creative thinking. The purpose of this section of the event is to catalyze participation in history and foundations work beyond this event, as well as spark creative thinking in research. It is expected that some will have a burning idea, while others will be interested in hearing and responding to what others have to say; HFIS Wishlist will appeal to both groups.

HFIS Wishlist is inspired by the Manuscript Wishlist movement (MSWL, see https://manuscriptwishlist.com) in the publishing industry. In MSWL, literary agents and editors post wishlists for works that they would consider representing or publishing—in short, things they'd like to see in the world—e.g., "a young-adult paranormal legal thriller." HFIS Wishlist will show a stream of submissions in the form: "I want to read a paper that…" (see Figure 1). Authors could elaborate, for instance describing why they are interested, how they would cite this work, etc. The HFIS Wishlist system is currently in development by Gorichanaz and Hauser, and it will be complete in Summer 2019. Prior to the conference, Gorichanaz and Hauser will publicize the system on the SIG-HFIS Community and other communications platforms with a handful of seeded examples (e.g., "I want to read a paper that proposes a field of critical bibliometrics") and invite others to submit their own examples. These may be ideas that the author hopes to pursue one day themselves, giving the chance to get feedback on the concept, or ideas that they would invite others to pursue.

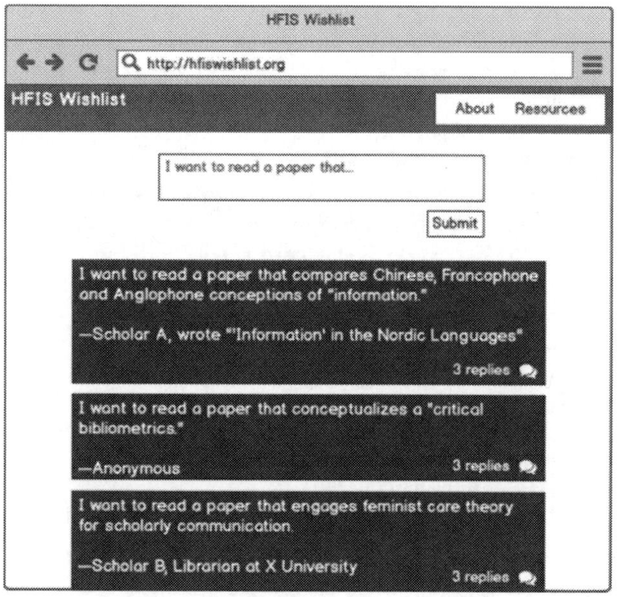

Figure 1. Mockup of HFIS Wishlist system.

It should be noted that HFIS Wishlist is only a beginning: The goal with the system will be to expand it to other research areas within information science, encouraging cross-, trans-, inter- and multidisciplinary thinking.

In this stage, Gorichanaz and Hauser will verbally present HFIS Wishlist and lead a discussion around the possibilities of the platform and in the research-domain specifics of some of the proposals therein. Considerations may include: How would I react to this as a potential reader/reviewer? Does this make me excited? How does this build on what we have discussed so far? I had a paper like this rejected—what am I doing wrong? This section will last 15 minutes.

Closing

In this final section of the event, major points will be summarized, and the outcomes (see below) will be explained. Participants will be invited to join SIG-HFIS. This section will last 5 minutes.

OUTCOMES OF THE EVENT

We expect that the event will inspire interest in history and foundations research, and perhaps spark some concrete ideas. Beyond this, we envision three immediate, concrete outcomes:

1. A white paper summarizing the session, functioning as a manifesto for future history and foundations work, to be published on the SIG-HFIS website and shared in the SIG-HFIS newsletter and other venues.
2. Updates to the SIG-HFIS website, including, e.g., a link to HFIS Wishlist, a list of the inspiring history and foundations works and publication outlets mentioned in the Discussion of Questions.
3. The development of *The Foundry*, a virtual working group on history and foundations work, to meet on an ongoing basis and discuss in-progress work in this domain, to be led by Hauser.

These outcomes will be communicated first and chiefly through the ASIS&T Community platform of SIG-HFIS, but the organizers will seek out other opportunities to bring these conversations to wider audiences.

CONCLUSION

This alternative event will be a locus for participation and inspiration regarding the role of historical and foundations work in information science. We hope to envision and model the future of SIG-HFIS, ASIS&T, and the field of information science more broadly by deeply engaging with our participant and panelist colleagues on these important issues.

REFERENCES

Arafat, S., & Ashoori, E. (2019). *Search foundations: Toward a science of technology-mediated experience (History and foundations of information science).* Cambridge, MA: The MIT Press.

Buckland, M. K. (2012). What kind of science can information science be? *Journal of the American Society for Information Science, 63*(1), 1–7.

Furner, J. (2015). Information science is neither. *Library Trends, 63*(3), 362–377.

Gorichanaz, T., & Latham, K. F. (2016). Document phenomenology: A framework for holistic analysis. *Journal of Documentation, 72*(6), 1114–1133.

SIG HFIS. (n.d.). *ASIS&T SIG HFIS: History & foundations of information science*. Retrieved from https://www.asist.org/SIG/SIGHFIS/

Data Science Education in Library and Information Science Schools

Loni Hagen
University of South Florida,
Tampa, Florida, USA
lonihagen@usf.edu

James Andrews
University of South Florida, Tampa, Florida, USA
jimandrews@usf.edu

Lisa Federer
National Library of Medicine, National Institutes of Health, Bethesda, Maryland, USA
lisa.federer@nih.gov

Gerald Benoit
University of California, Berkeley, California, USA
gbenoit@berkeley.edu

ABSTRACT

The need for data science education has grown recently among Library and Information Science schools to better prepare information professionals for the world of big data. However, there are many challenges to providing education on data science in Library and Information Science schools. For example, developing curricula and models for managing faculty resources (full-time teaching, buy-out, or specialized faculty) are some initial, common challenges. Participants will present their experiences and insights regarding data science education, which may include curricula, barriers, and best practices in the panel presentations. The panel session then will open up to an active discussion session with the audience, who will be encouraged to share their experiences and insights. This panel session is part of an ongoing effort by the organizers to establish sustainable data science education in Information Science schools. Developing a framework and curricula of data science education in Information Science schools, based on best practices and informed by experience, is the optimal goal of this ongoing effort. The success of this effort depends on active participation of the participants. This panel is sponsored by SIG ED.

KEYWORDS

Data Science; Education; Big Data

ASIS&T THESAURUS

Information science, Data Science, Library education, Big data

INTRODUCTION

Data science "encompasses a set of principles, problem definitions, algorithms, and processes for extracting non-obvious and useful patterns from large data sets" (Kelleher & Tierney, 2018, p. 1). The era of big data brought changes to the ways in which society operates at many levels, from government to business to entertainment and beyond. The implications for information professions are profound as decisions ranging from analyzing/purchasing collections to understanding user needs as they interact with large volumes of data, all require integrating data science perspectives and methods to support enhanced decision making.

While many agree that data science education is necessary for information professionals, what is less clear is how such training should be provided. Data science involves proficiency in technologies, programming, statistics, math, as well as communication and business insights (Berry, 2018). Infusing data science education in the curricula of information schools requires careful design considerations, for which best practices will be extremely helpful. As an initial effort to understand challenges of developing data science education in iSchools, some of the organizers of this panel held an interactive session regarding creating undergraduate data science education at the 2019 iConference held in April 2019. After active discussions among about 20 participants, we derived some core questions about initiating new undergraduate data science programs in iSchools. These questions include: 1) How to deal with political realities within universities? 2) Which models of faculty staffing would be most appropriate: teaching, buy-out, specialized faculty, etc.; and, 3) How should we develop/model curriculum?

The goal of this panel session is to continue the conversation on undergraduate education and to expand the conversation to graduate Library and Information programs.

The target audience would include faculty/administrators and students from schools that currently (or planning to) have undergraduate or graduate data science courses or formal programs. Additional participants include librarians and other information practitioners who can articulate the demands of data science skills in real world practices.

We hope to accomplish three goals through this panel session. First, to create a community of experts in data science education from various Library and Information Science schools. Second, to discuss curricula, challenges, and best practices for data science education, particularly from the

82nd Annual Meeting of the Association for Information Science & Technology | Melbourne, Australia | 19–23 October, 2019

DOI: 10.1002/pra2.00084

perspective of information science. Third, to develop a framework for successful data science education models within each program's unique institutional structure. We will continue pursuing this during future meetings at iConference and ASIS&T annual meetings in 2020 in order to develop a community for data science education in our discipline.

Each of the four panelists will give a short presentation (five to ten minutes each) reflecting their prior experience, which will be helpful in prompting discussion with the audience. For the second half, we will have an interactive discussion session with the audience. The following discussion questions and other follow-up questions will be discussed (for about 40 minutes).

- Gaps in education and opportunity across "information professions" – what's missing and why?
- Strategies for working across campus with other programs involved with data science.
- What are the available models of recruiting faculty to teach data science?
- Which data science courses are essential for information professionals?
- How data science programs can cope with incoming student body (strength and interests of students) in designing curriculum?

The final 20 minutes will be dedicated to wrapping up the discussions and planning for the discussion points in future forums (iConference and ASIS&T 2020). We will use ***#asist19_datascience*** for social media communication and to continue the conversation beyond the session. After the session, we will create a summary report and make it available in the ASIS&T community.

PANELISTS

Loni Hagen is an Assistant Professor at the School of Information at the University of South Florida. She received degrees in Law, Information Studies (specialized in Information Law), and earned her PhD in Information Science from University at Albany, SUNY. Prior to her current position, she worked for the Korean National Police Agency over ten years. Her current research interests are in finding novel ways of collecting, extracting information and using them for policy decision-making. She is also interested in privacy-aware practices of big data analytics and informing privacy protection policies with her study results.

James Andrews is Director of the School of Information at the University of South Florida. He is an active researcher in health informatics, particularly in the context of clinical research informatics, data standards, and information behaviors. Dr. Andrews helped design the BS in Information Science program at USF, including the concentrations in Data Science and Analytics, Health Informatics, and Information Security, and participated in the aforementioned panel discussion on undergraduate Data Science education at the last iConference.

Lisa Federer is the Data Science and Open Science Librarian at the National Library of Medicine, focusing on developing efforts to support workforce development and enhance capacity in the biomedical research and library communities for data science and open science. Prior to joining the NLM, Lisa spent five years as the Research Data Informationist at the National Institutes of Health Library, where she developed and ran the Library's Data Services Program. She holds a PhD in Information Studies from the University of Maryland and an MLIS from the University of California-Los Angeles, as well as graduate certificates in data science and data visualization.

Gerald Benoit teaches python for Data Science and Information Visualization courses in the Data Science program at UCB. Recent projects include a new monograph *Introduction to Information Visualization* (Rowman & Littlefield), applying expanded linguistic register and interactive visualization to medical resource retrieval, evidence-adaptive biomedical visualization, and critical theoretic perspectives of legitimacy of information institutions. Benoit received his MS from Columbia University, PhD from UCLA, and serves as an Adams House SCR faculty, Harvard University.

REFERENCES

Berry, A. (2018). *Data scientists are in-demand and well paid - so why is there a skills gap?* | Computing. Http://Www.Computing.Co.Uk. Retrieved from https://www.computing.co.uk/ctg/opinion/3034263/data-scientists-are-in-demand-and-well-paid-so-why-is-there-a-skills-gap

Kelleher, J. D., & Tierney, B. (2018). *Data science*. The MIT Press.

A Social Informatics Perspective on Misinformation, Disinformation, Deception and Conflict

Noriko Hara
Department of Information & Library Science, Indiana University, Bloomington, IN, U.S.A.
nhara@indiana.edu

Pnina Fichman
Rob Kling Center for Social Informatics, Indiana University, Bloomington, IN, U.S.A.
fichman@indiana.edu

Eric T. Meyer
School of Information, The University of Texas at Austin, Austin, Texas, U.S.A.
dean@ischool.utexas.edu

Yimin Chen
Faculty of Information and Media Studies, University of Western Ontario, London, Ontario, Canada
ychen582@uwo.ca

Soo Young Rieh
School of Information, The University of Texas at Austin, Austin, Texas, U.S.A.
rieh@ischool.utexas.edu

ABSTRACT

This panel will present and discuss the issues surrounding deception, misinformation, and disinformation using a social informatics perspective. The panel is sponsored by ASIST SIG-SI.

KEYWORDS

Misinformation; social informatics, social media

ASIS&T THESAURUS

Sociocultural aspects; social informatics

PANEL DESCRIPTION

In many ways, information serves as guidance for people to make decisions and to stay informed to be informed and make decisions. Traditionally, the types of information that people have acquired tend to come from vetted processes, such as experts' opinions and reputable media sources. In addition, information may derive from individuals' small social networks (Granovetter, 1973). More recently, however, the ease of distributing and accessing information through the Internet, including social media, began disturbing this information ecology. The spread of online deception, misinformation, and disinformation creates contentions and invites troubling behaviors, such as fake news (Greyson, 2019) and trolling (Shachaf & Hara, 2010).

Misinformation is defined as "incorrect or misleading information" (Merriam-Webster) whereas deception is defined as "a statement or action that hides the truth, or the act of hiding the truth." In other words, distortion is the introduction of bias, deception is such a statement or action, and misinformation is the result of distortion and deception.

82nd Annual Meeting of the Association for Information Science & Technology | Melbourne, Australia | 19–23 October, 2019

DOI: 10.1002/pra2.00085

These have major implications for a wide variety of areas including politics, academia, and science. While this kind of distortion of information is not novel (Alter, 2006), social media has amplified this phenomenon to the point that it deserves research attention (Menczer, 2016). A useful approach to study this phenomenon is through the Social Informatics perspectives, emphasizing context, using ideas such as mutual shaping of technology, and questioning the standard deterministic models of ICT impacts on society and individuals (Fichman & Rosenbaum, 2014). Therefore, the panel will explore the following questions:

- How have deception, misinformation, and disinformation changed the information ecology?
- What are theoretical and practical implications of deception, misinformation, and disinformation?
- What roles do deception, misinformation, and disinformation play in fake news, online trolling, vandalism, science communication, and public health?

The panelists will explore these problems using a social informatics perspective, discussing their research and drawing implications for theory and practice. They study a variety of socio-technical environments, using a wide range of methods, a variety of perspectives, and take critical approaches to the questions that drive their work. We expect a lively and interactive session as the panelists raise provocative issues and questions about the ways in which their work interacts with the issues of deception, misinformation, and disinformation. Furthermore, with this panel, we hope to attract participants who are new to or unfamiliar with the community of social informatics scholars.

The panelists will present various perspectives on the issues surrounding deception, misinformation, and disinformation by using individual studies, (which are informed by a social informatics perspective) on social media. First, Soo Young Rieh will provide a short introduction that will set the context for the panel, then she will moderate the panel. Second, using a social informatics perspective, the panelists will present four projects related to misinformation, disinformation, deception and conflict. Eric Meyer will discuss how social informatics provides a useful lens to examine the interaction between knowledge creators and misinformation. Noriko Hara will use her research on public engagement with science through social media to illustrate how misinformation about scientific controversies is legitimized by advocates of certain positions. Pnina Fichman will offer an insight into deception in online trolling across multiple social media platforms. Yimin Chen will describe his research on trolling in academia. After each presentation, the audience may briefly ask questions. Finally, the panelists will solicit questions from the audience for what we believe will turn into a lively discussion.

Knowledge creators in the misinformation age (Eric T. Meyer, University of Texas at Austin)

Most of us in the information field have matured during what has been widely referred to as The Information Age. We have generally taken for granted that the spread of information is good, positive, and democratizing, and serves to make the world a better and fairer place. While misinformation and propaganda have always been with us, we seem to be entering a time when the forces generating confusing, misleading, or false information are gaining an upper hand. It is becoming harder to know what to trust, who to trust, and who is a knowledge creator as opposed to a creator of misinformation. Charges of "fake news!", especially on social media, levied against honest actors are used by propagandists to further undermine the truth and to confuse the picture for everyone involved. Social informatics has long studied the unintended consequences of technological advances, and in this talk, I will discuss how we can understand the socio-technical interaction networks that have led us to where we are, and attempt to suggest ways forward for honest knowledge creators.

Misinformation in public engagement with science (Noriko Hara, Indiana University)

Presently, traditional models of scientific communication are giving way to new types of public engagement with science as the Internet becomes more ubiquitous. The general public—regardless of scientific background—can now take on the role of intermediary by writing and/or editing articles about scientific topics found on social media platforms. This new trend in sociotechnical environments offers both opportunities and challenges. On one hand, it provides more venues for lay people to voice their opinions. On the other hand, contentious topics such as climate change and vaccine are increasingly debated on social media platforms where experts and laypeople are both free to contribute. This kind of environment inevitably solicits misinformation and disinformation. Prof Hara will discuss her research about public engagement with science in the age of social media using a social informatics perspective.

Deception in online trolling (Pnina Fichman, Indiana University)

Online deception has been associated with trolling from the very early days of the Internet. This sociotechnical phenomena with its various manifestations ranges from individual trolls, who simply lie and deceive their targets, to state-sponsored trolling in recent years, where trolls are hired to flood social media platforms with propaganda, fake posts by fake accounts, and massive deception, to other instances of global trolling, where political satire unites dozens of countries across the globe. Prof. Fichman will showcase various tactics and processes of online deception that are utilized in ideological, satirical, and malevolent trolling, both by individuals and groups, drawing on trolling data from multiple social media platforms, and using social informatics lenses.

Trolls in the academy (Yimin Chen, University of Western Ontario)

Internet trolls have often been implicated as sources of misinformation, disinformation, and all manner of online abuse, but are the consequences of these actions always harmful? PhD candidate Yimin Chen presents a case of email trolling in a university setting that was arguably as amusing as it was disruptive—as friendly as it was divisive. Can transgressive trolling actions produce positive outcomes? What are the knock-on effects when knowledge producers create disinformation, no matter how humorous? This presentation will explore these and other questions at the intersection of trolling and academia, and will include implications for social media.

PANELIST BIOS

PANELISTS' BIOGRAPHIES

Yimin Chen is a PhD candidate in Library and Information Science in the Faculty of Information and Media Studies at the University of Western Ontario. His research examines the communicative practices of online communities and cultures, with a focus on Internet trolling behaviors and the controversy surrounding them. His previous projects range from fake news and deception detection, to library automation, to the impact of political memes on social media. His work has appeared in Library Hi Tech, Proceedings of the Association for Information Science and Technology, and the SAGE Handbook of Social Media Research Methods.

Pnina Fichman is a Professor of Information Science and the Director of the Rob Kling Center of Social Informatics in the School of Informatics, Computing, and Engineering at Indiana University, Bloomington. Her research in social informatics focuses the relationships between information technologies and cultural diversity; she studies processes and outcomes of crowds and online communities, as well as online trolling and its global manifestations. In addition to her most recent book *Online Trolling and its Perpetrators:*

Under the Cyberbridge (with Madelyn Sanfilippo), she has published four other books. Her articles have appeared in journals such as*: Information and Management, Journal of the American Society for Information Science & Technology, The Information Society*, and the *Journal of Information Science*. She earned her PhD from the School of Information and Library Science, University of North Carolina, Chapel Hill.

Noriko Hara is a Professor in the Department of Information & Library Science (ILS) in the School of Informatics, Computing, and Engineering at Indiana University. She is the Director of Master's of Information Science in ILS. Her research in Social Informatics emphasizes online knowledge sharing, communities of practice, and collective behaviors in mediated environments. Specifically, she examines the means by which collective behaviors are enabled and/or impeded by information Technology. She is currently investigating the role of technologies in public engagement with science. She is the author of *Communities of Practice: Fostering Peer-to-Peer Learning and Informal Knowledge Sharing in the Work Place* from Springer, and a co-editor of *Global Wikipedia: International and Cross-Cultural Issues in Online Collaboration* (with Pnina Fichman) from Rowman & Littlefied. She received a PhD in Instructional Systems Technology at Indiana University.

Eric T. Meyer is the Mary R. Boyvey Chair and Louis T. Yule Regents Professor at the University of Texas at Austin, where he serves as the Dean of the School of Information. He is also a Senior Fellow at the Oxford Internet Institute of the University of Oxford. His research looks at how the changing nature of knowledge creation in science, medicine, social science, arts, and humanities as technology is embedded in everyday practices, as described in his 2015 book with co-author Ralph Schroeder "*Knowledge Machines: Digital Transformations of the Sciences and Humanities*." His research has included both qualitative and quantitative work with marine biologists, genetics researchers, physicists, digital humanities scholars, social scientists using big data, medical doctors, theater artists, librarians, and organizations involved in computational approaches to research. More information is available on his website at https://dean.ischool.utexas.edu/.

Soo Young Rieh is Professor and Associate Dean for Education in the School of Information at the University of Texas at Austin. Over the past two decades, she has examined how people find credible information in online environments and how people's credibility assessments influence their information seeking strategies. She and her colleagues developed a *Unifying Framework of Credibility* in which they identified three distinct levels of credibility judgments: construct, heuristics, and interaction. She has also investigated content contributors' credibility constructs as well as strategies for establishing the credibility in content creation, and has used various research methods such as diaries, experience sampling methods, interviews, surveys, and lab-based user research.

REFERENCES

Alter, S. (2006). *Goals and tactics on the dark side of knowledge management*. In Proceedings of the 39th Hawaii International Conference on System Sciences (p. 144.1), Kauai, HI.

Cambridge Dictionary (2019). *Deception*. Retrieved from https://dictionary.cambridge.org/us/dictionary/english/deception

Fichman, P., & Rosenbaum, H.. (2014). *Social informatics: Past, present and future*. Cambridge Scholars Publishing.

Granovetter, M. S. (1973). The strength of weak ties. *American Journal of Sociology.*, *78*(6), 1360–1380.

Greyson, D. (2019). The social informatics of ignorance. *Journal of the Association for Information Science and Technology*, *70*(4), 412–415.

Menczer, F. (2016). *The spread of misinformation in social media*. In Proceedings of the 25th International Conference Companion on World Wide Web (p. 717), Montreal, Canada.

Merriam-Webster (2019). *Misinformation*. Retrieved from https://www.merriam-webster.com/dictionary/misinformation

Shachaf, P., & Hara, N. (2010). Beyond vandalism: Wikipedia trolls. *Journal of Information Science*, *36*(6), 357–370.

Information Behaviour and Practises Research Informing Technology and Service Design

Isto Huvila
Uppsala University, Uppsala, Sweden
isto.huvila@abm.uu.se

Heidi Enwald
University of Oulu, Oulu, Finland
heidi.enwald@oulu.fi

Kristina Eriksson-Backa
Åbo Akademi University, Turku/Åbo, Finland
kristina.eriksson-backa@abo.fi

Ying-Hsang Liu
Australian National University, Canberra, Australia
ying-hsang.liu@anu.edu.au

Noora Hirvonen
University of Oulu, Oulu, Finland
noora.hirvonen@oulu.fi

ABSTRACT

A common critique is that insights from information behaviour and practises (IBP) research have difficulties to find their way to inform the design of new technologies, systems and services. There is a certain seed of truth of these statements but the situation is much more complex as are the requirements to improve the relevance of empirical observations of information activities for design and development. This panel enquires into how different approaches to IBP research can inform technology and service development in different ways, how to support interdisciplinary dialogue between IBP and systems and service design, and what novel insights from the state-of-the-art of IBP research can be drawn to support technology and service development.

KEYWORDS

information behaviour; systems design; information service design; development; information practises

ASIS&T THESAURUS

Information behaviour; computer systems; information industry

INTRODUCTION

Several information science and technology researchers have criticised a posited disconnect between IBP literature and the development of information technologies and information services. There is no doubt that not all the insights from decades of meticulous studies of information activities have found their way to inform the design of new technologies, systems and services. A part of the problem can undoubtedly be traced back to a lack of communication between the two fields of inquiry and practise. To a degree, IBP research can also be criticised of being unnecessarily vague about the practical implications of its main findings. However, even if the exchange between the two communities could have been livelier, there are many examples of IBP researchers and technology and service developers working together, and fresh insights from the first mentioned field with prospects of informing the latter. Depending on the type and direction of IBP research, the insights can be different and applicable in distinct manner. There are also differences in technology and service design approaches, systems, services, their contexts and situations of design and use that entails different approaches to implement these recommendations.

This panel enquires into the intriguing nexus of IBP research and technology and service development to highlight 1) how different approaches to IBP research can inform technology and service development in different ways, 2) what novel insights from the state-of-the-art of IBP research can be drawn to support technology and service development, and 3) how to facilitate effective interdisciplinary communication for translating findings from IBP research to inform information systems and service design? The panellists represent information science researchers who have conducted empirical research on IBP in diverse contexts ranging from healthcare to archaeology and aerospace industry, and worked towards technology and service design as a part of their research work.

The relevance of discussing the links between IBP research and technology and service design relates to the long-established but still largely unresolved question of how to develop information technologies and services that match with the preferences and behaviours of their intended users. At the same time, as it has become increasingly apparent that the traditional focus on individuals and their use of specific systems and services in isolation is not enough, a more holistic understanding of their information landscapes and practises could provide novel insights into understanding systems and services in their lifeworld-wide context of use (Huvila & Ahmad, 2018). With its focus on information and people beyond specific (types) of technologies, IBP research has a potential to complement technology-oriented human-computer interaction (HCI) and technology studies research. Finally, it is apparent that the divergence of

82nd Annual Meeting of the Association for Information Science & Technology | Melbourne, Australia | 19–23 October, 2019

DOI: 10.1002/pra2.00086

epistemologies within IBP research and in development and design research mean that the findings of IBP studies need to be properly translated into the context they are expected to be informing.

INFORMATION BEHAVIOUR AND TECHNOLOGY USE

The critique of IBP research drifting away from systems and service design has been raised on several occasions (e.g. Fisher & Julien, 2009; Haider & Sundin, 2019; Ingwersen & Järvelin, 2005; Julien & O'Brien, 2014; Julien, Pecoskie, & Reed, 2011). The gap becomes especially apparent if compared to neighbouring fields such as human-computer interaction and information design with partly overlapping interests with IBP research and a very explicit interest in design.

In spite of the critique, there are exceptions to this tendency. Kuhlthau's seminal work on information seeking has had a broad and deep impact on library practises (Kuhlthau, 2016; Sonnenwald, 2016) and, for instance, research on (information) searching is constantly influencing the development of search systems (Järvelin & Wilson, 2003; White, 2016). Greifeneder (2014) notes that participatory design is increasing in popularity as a research method and remarks further that a partial reason to the seeming dearth of studies is that work-related information use, creation, saving and learning is not always included in surveys of the field. There are projects where the explicit focus is on eliciting and translating findings from IBP research to inform design and development (e.g. Huvila, Daniels, Cajander, & Åhlfeldt, 2016; Lin & Hertzum, 2018) and work that resides in the interface between systems design and IBP research (e.g. Blandford & Attfield, 2010; Dillon, 2016; Fidel & Pejtersen, 2004; Sonnenwald & Lievrouw, 1997). Further examples of systems and service design oriented IBP research include Huvila's and colleagues work in the context of archaeology (Huvila, 2008, 2012, 2018), Björneborn's work on library space (Björneborn, 2010), Du and colleagues' work on marketing professionals' information seeking in the workplace (Du, 2014; Du, Liu, Zhu, & Chen, 2013), and several recent studies related to health information and e-health technology with an aim of understanding IBP as a premise of systems use and design (e.g. Eriksson-Backa, Hirvonen, Enwald, & Huvila, 2018; Huvila et al., 2016; Moll et al., 2018; Nguyen, Eriksson-Backa, & Enwald, 2018) and broader user group specific health information acquisition patterns both in the wild (e.g. Lee, 2018; Oh & Kim, 2014; Oh, Zhang, & Park, 2016; Yoon, Huang, & Kim, 2017; Zimmerman, 2018) and in specific systems (e.g. Huvila et al., 2018; Rexhepi, Åhlfeldt, Cajander, & Huvila, 2015; Sabelli, 2014). Others have focused on providing more knowledge on individuals' health information related capabilities and their opinions towards technology (e.g., Enwald, Hirvonen, Kangas, & Keränen, 2018) and for instance on specific factors and their influence on information use and design (e.g. time in Tana, Kettunen, Eirola, & Paakkonen, 2018, gender in Rowley, Johnson, & Sbaffi, 2017 or diversity for Dali & Caidi, 2017).

In spite of the evidence of both more and less successful application of insights from IBP research in systems and service design, it is apparent that the exchange between the two fields could be livelier. There is no doubt that many different factors contribute to the present state of affairs. It is not a question of a lack of potential for mutual interests and potential (e.g. Beyene & Byström, 2017; Haider & Sundin, 2019) but something else. Many influential studies are focused on very specific contexts or activities (like information seeking processes in particular situations or searching specific types of information). The evidence of information activities is not always representative of larger populations due to diverse methodological shortcomings in research designs but possibly also because of the complexity of human experience as a whole (O'Brien, Dickinson, & Askin, 2017). The diversity of theoretical perspectives in IBP research (Haider & Sundin, 2019) does also mean that it can be difficult to extend insights from one study to another. Further, researchers in this particular field might not always be very good at communicating their findings in a way that is useful in systems and service design and all developers are not necessarily motivated to embrace them. Finally, especially the impact of the branch of IBP research that aims at understanding rather than explaining information activities (Haider & Sundin, 2019) can be difficult to trace and appreciate when it is conducted in context and close collaboration with practitioners.

LAYOUT OF THE PANEL

The panel starts with a short presentation by the moderator that introduces IBP research and its links to technology and service design underlining the pertinence of the issue in diverse contexts ranging from health to science, politics, engineering and heritage. After the 10 min introduction, all panellists give a 5 min lightning talk of how they have investigated IBP with a specific focus on its theoretical and empirical insights and implications to technology and service design. After the lightning talks, each of the panellists are asked to present a short commentary on their colleagues' presentations with a focus on pointing out commonalities and differences in the approaches and the relationship of their different takes on IBP research and technology and service design. After the commentaries the panellists are asked to give short, 1 min reflections of how they would push the state-of-the-art of IBP research in relation to technology and service design on the basis of their experience. During the final 30 min of the panel, the audience is asked to join the discussion with panellists on IBP research and its relation to technology and service design. The discussion is led by the moderator and facilitated by a set of questions based on the panellists' presentations. The panel closes with an invitation from the moderator to contribute to the discussion started at the panel and a short round of proposals and ideas for future work in the field from the panellists and the audience.

The presentations combine two parallel approaches to engage with technology and service design in the context of IBP research. All presentations explicate how IBP underpin user needs and preferences related to the availability, use and non-use of systems and services in specific contexts. At the same time, they also engage with individual, socio-cultural, and technico-material issues that obstruct and facilitate addressing users' needs, wants and preferences in the design, development and deployment of systems and services. By bringing these two parallel perspectives together, the panel explicates the disciplinary nexus of how IBP research can inform technology and service design and how it can inform future IBP research. Further, the panel delves into the practical and theoretical implications IBP research in and for technology and service development related research and practise.

PANELLISTS AND THEIR CONTRIBUTIONS

Isto Huvila, Uppsala University

Isto Huvila presents empirical findings of his research on archaeological and archaeology-related information work and practises, and the development of documentation and information management technologies and services in that particular domain. The presentation draws both on his earlier and ongoing empirical research on archaeological information work and information management in archaeology. Huvila shows how a better understanding of the information practises of both information producers and users and taking them holistically into account is a necessary precondition in the development of useful information systems and services. Considering the interdisciplinarity and societal impact of contemporary archaeological research, the implications of the findings discussed in the talk have implications to areas ranging from land development to digital humanities and community heritage.

Professor Huvila holds the chair in information studies at the Department of ALM at Uppsala University in Sweden. His primary areas of research include information and knowledge management, and social and participatory information practises.

Heidi Enwald, University of Oulu

Heidi Enwald presents the viewpoint of tailoring health information and communication in e-health services. She has been working in several multidisciplinary research projects and taken part into planning, design and testing of electronic behaviour change support systems relating, e.g., to improvement of wellness of young men and those in high risk for metabolic syndrome. Health IBP as well as health information literacy are aspects that could provide important information about the users. Furthermore, they can be used as basis for targeting or tailoring health information and communication. Tailoring health communication and services can improve the acceptance and effectiveness of the service and its content.

Enwald works as a university lecturer in Information Studies, the University of Oulu, Oulu, Finland. Her PhD thesis related to tailoring health information and her main research interests are health IBP, health information literacy, e-health literacy, e-health, health communication and open science.

Kristina Eriksson-Backa, Åbo Akademi University

Kristina Eriksson-Backa presents findings from recent qualitative and quantitative studies concerning IBP related to e-health technology especially amongst older adults in Finland. Group interviews with older adults about their experiences with a national patient-accessible electronic health record gave insights into how this type of service could be developed to meet users' expectations and needs, whereas quantitative data from a survey of online diabetes risk test users showed use of and potential benefits with online self-assessments and similar e-health services. Furthermore, results from a vast national survey carried out amongst a representative sample of older Finnish adults (aged 55-70 years) will add to the knowledge about IBP related to e-health services in general, and deepen the understanding of how to bridge the gap between such services and their users.

Dr. Eriksson-Backa is a university teacher and researcher in Information studies at Åbo Akademi University, Turku, Finland. She holds the title of docent (adjunct professor) in information studies with orientation on health information at the same university. Her main research interests are information about food and health in media, health IBP, health information literacy, and e-health.

Ying-Hsang Liu, Australian National University

Ying-Hsang Liu presents findings and on recent research cooperation with an international company in the aerospace industry. The project was designed to integrate professionals' information seeking research into the design, experimentation and implementation of interactive information retrieval systems in support of specific work/search tasks. Drawing from professionals' information seeking research, interactive information retrieval studies and how HCI theories are reused in practise, further reflections on different kinds of theories IBP and practise researchers have been developing and possible explanations for a posited disconnect between research and practise will be presented.

Ying-Hsang Liu is affiliated with the Research School of Computer Science, The Australian National University since 2012. He joined the School of Information Studies, Charles Sturt University in Australia after teaching at the Pratt Institute and Rutgers University. His research is concerned with human interactions of emerging technologies, such as modern search engines, with particular emphasis on human capabilities in terms of individual differences.

Noora Hirvonen, University of Oulu (Moderator)

Noora Hirvonen is a postdoctoral researcher at the University of Oulu, Finland. Her research interest focuses on empirical research on people's competencies and practises to acquire, evaluate, and use health information in varying settings and with different tools. She has experience in interdisciplinary research and has contributed to the design of a novel technological health application with IBP and literacy research.

ACKNOWLEDGMENTS

Huvila's work has received funding from the Swedish Research Council (Grant 340-2012-5751) and the European Research Council (ERC) under the European Union's Horizon 2020 research and innovation programme grant agreement No 818210. The studies presented by Eriksson-Backa were conducted within the project Taking Health Information Behaviour into Account: the implications of a neglected element for successful implementation of consumer health technologies on older adults funded by the Academy of Finland 2015-2020.

REFERENCES

Beyene, W. M., & Byström, K. (2017). *Rethinking information behavior in the context of universal design*. In IConference 2017 Proceedings (pp. 216–226).

Björneborn, L. (2010). Design dimensions enabling divergent behaviour across physical, digital, and social library interfaces. In T. Ploug, P. Hasle, & H. Oinas-Kukkonen (Eds.), *Persuasive technology* (pp. 143–149).

Blandford, A., & Attfield, S. (2010). *Interacting with information*. San Rafael, CA: Morgan and Claypool.

Dali, K., & Caidi, N. (2017). Diversity by design. *The Library Quarterly*, *87*(2), 88–98.

Dillon, A. (2016). Theory for design: The case of reading. In D. H. Sonnenwald (Ed.), *Theory development in the information sciences* (pp. 222–238). Austin: University of Texas Press.

Du, J. T. (2014). The information journey of marketing professionals. *Journal of the Association for Information Science and Technology*, *65*(9), 1850–1869.

Du, J. T., Liu, Y.-H., Zhu, Q., & Chen, Y. (2013). Modelling marketing professionals' information behaviour in the workplace: towards a holistic understanding. *Information Research*, *18*(1).

Enwald, H., Hirvonen, N., Kangas, M., & Keränen (2018). Relationship between everyday health information literacy and attitudes towards mobile technology among older people. In Kurbanoglu (Ed.), *Information literacy in the workplace* (pp. 450–459). Cham: Springer.

Eriksson-Backa, K., Hirvonen, N., Enwald, H., & Huvila, I. (2018). Opportunities and challenges with My Kanta: First results from a focus group study about user experiences and opinions on the National Archive of Health Information. *Informaatiotutkimus*, *37*(3), 20–24.

Fidel, R., & Pejtersen, A. M. (2004). From information behaviour research to the design of information systems: The cognitive work analysis framework. *Information Research*, (1), 10.

Fisher, K. E., & Julien, H. (2009). Information behavior. *Annual Review of Information Science and Technology*, *43*(1), 1–73.

Greifeneder, E. (2014). Trends in information behaviour research. *Information Research*, *19*(4).

Haider, J., & Sundin, O. (2019). *Invisible search and online search engine*. London: Routledge.

Huvila, I. (2008). Participatory archive. *Archival Science*, *8* (1), 15–36.

Huvila, I. (2012). Being formal and flexible: Semantic wiki as an archaeological e-science infrastructure. In M. Zhou, I. Romanowska, Z. Wu, P. Xu, & P. Verhagen (Eds.), *Revive the Past: Proceeding of the 39th CAA Conference, Beijing, 12-16 April 2011* (pp. 186–197).

Huvila, I. (Ed.). (2018). *Archaeology and archaeological information in the digital society*. London: Routledge.

Huvila, I., & Ahmad, F. (2018). Holistic information behavior and the perceived success of work in organizations. *Library & Information Science Research*, *40*(1), 18–29.

Huvila, I., Daniels, M., Cajander, Å., & Åhlfeldt, R.-M. (2016). Patients reading their medical records. *Information Research*, *21*(1).

Huvila, I., Enwald, H., Eriksson-Backa, K., Hirvonen, N., Nguyen, H., & Scandurra, I. (2018). Anticipating ageing: Older adults reading their medical records. *IPM*, *54*(3), 394–407.

Ingwersen, P., & Järvelin, K. (2005). *The turn*. Berlin: Springer.

Järvelin, K., & Wilson, T. D. (2003). On conceptual models for information seeking and retrieval research. *Information Research*, *9*(1), paper 163.

Julien, H., & O'Brien, M. (2014). Information behaviour research: Where have we been, where are we going? *Canadian Journal of Information and Library Science*, *38*(4), 239–250.

Julien, H., Pecoskie, J., & Reed, K. (2011). Trends in information behavior research, 1999-2008. *Library & Information Science Research*, *33*(1), 19–24.

Kuhlthau, C. C. (2016). Reflections on the development of a theoretical perspective. In D. H. Sonnenwald (Ed.), *Theory development in the information sciences* (pp. 68–86). Austin: University of Texas Press.

Lee, H. S. (2018). A comparative study on the health information needs, seeking and source preferences among mothers of young healthy children. *Information Research*, *23*(4).

Lin, Y.-T., & Hertzum, M. (2018). *Information seeking by service designers*. In Poster at the ISIC 2018 Conference, Krakow, Poland.

Moll, J., Rexhepi, H., Cajander, Å., Grünloch, C., Huvila, I., Hägglund, M., … Åhlfeldt, R.-M. (2018). Patients' experiences of accessing their electronic health records:

National patient survey in Sweden. *Journal of Medical Internet Research, 20*(11).

Nguyen, H., Eriksson-Backa, K., & Enwald, H. (2018). *Preliminary results of a survey on user opinions and experiences on an online diabetes risk test.* In PACIS 2018 Digital Proceedings (pp. 1–9).

O'Brien, H. L., Dickinson, R., & Askin, N. (2017). A scoping review of individual differences in information seeking behavior and retrieval research between 2000 and 2015. *Library & Information Science Research, 39*(3), 244–254.

Oh, S., & Kim, S. (2014). College students' use of social media for health in the USA and Korea. *Information Research, 19*(4).

Oh, S., Zhang, Y., & Park, M. S. (2016). Cancer information seeking in social question and answer services: Identifying health-related topics in cancer questions on Yahoo! Answers. *Information Research, 21*(3).

Rexhepi, H., Åhlfeldt, R.-M., Cajander, Å., & Huvila, I. (2015). *Cancer patients' attitudes and experiences of online medical records.* In 17th ISHIMR, York, UK 24-26 June 2015.

Rogers, Y. (2005). New theoretical approaches for human-computer interaction. *Annual Review of Information Science and Technology, 38*(1), 87–143.

Rowley, J., Johnson, F., & Sbaffi, L. (2017). Gender as an influencer of online health information-seeking and evaluation behavior. *Journal of the Association for Information Science and Technology, 68*(1), 36–47.

Sabelli, M. (2014). Health care information for youth in vulnerability contexts: designing a website with an interdisciplinary and participatory approach. *Information Research, 19*(4).

Sonnenwald, D. H. (2016). Exploring theory development: Learning from diverse masters. In D. H. Sonnenwald (Ed.), *Theory development in the information sciences* (pp. 1–18). Austin: Univ. of Texas Press.

Sonnenwald, Diane H., & Lievrouw, L. A. (1997). *Collaboration during the design process: A case study of communication, information behavior, and project performance.* In ISIC '96 (pp. 179–204). London: Taylor Graham.

Tana, J., Kettunen, J., Eirola, E., & Paakkonen, H. (2018). Diurnal variations of depression-related health information seeking: Case study in Finland using google trends data. *JMIR Mental Health, 5*(2).

Velt, R., Benford, S., & Reeves, S. (2017). *A survey of the trajectories conceptual framework: Investigating theory use in HCI.* In CHI'17 (pp. 2091–2105).

White, R. W. (2016). *Interactions with search systems.* Cambridge: Cambridge University Press.

Yoon, J., Huang, H., & Kim, S. (2017). Trends in health information-seeking behaviour in the U.S. foreign-born population based on the Health Information National Trends Survey, 2005 - 2014. *Information Research, 22*(3).

Zimmerman, M. S. (2018). Information horizons mapping to assess the health literacy of refugee and immigrant women in the USA. *Information Research*, (4), 23.

Lithium Hindsight 360: Increasing Access and Ensuring Preservation of Virtual Reality Narratives

Eugenia S. Kim
City University of Hong Kong
Kowloon Tong, Hong Kong
eugenia.kim@my.cityu.edu.hk

ABSTRACT

This alternative event combines a virtual reality (VR) demonstration and interactive discussion to brainstorm access and preservation strategies for individual VR creators. A specific challenge to address will be how to build these considerations into the creative process rather than after the work has been completed. The *Lithium Hindsight 360* medical humanities narrative will be used as the demo to raise additional questions about ethics that may not normally be present in a new media artwork.

KEYWORDS

Virtual reality; motion capture; narratives; dance; new media art; medical humanities; digital humanities; digital preservation

ASIS&T THESAURUS

Performing arts; Visual arts; Medical science

INTRODUCTION

The benefits of immersive environments to help induce embodiment and empathy means that various types of extended reality environments can be applied to a wide range of purposes. This may include showing the experience of having Alzheimer's, living in a refugee camp, being treated like a different race and a number of other perspectives that might be less effectively conveyed through traditional media. Although many advances in hardware, software, and technical skills have been made, there is one broad area in the creative workflow that has not been well-addressed: access (beyond exhibition) and preservation.

This is not to say that efforts to solve these problems have not been made at all over the past few years. One of the largest complications with this situation is the speed at which technologies evolve along with the cost of production. Access and preservation go hand in hand as the latter is needed to ensure the former – and both need to happen without extreme costs while being timely.

82nd Annual Meeting of the Association for Information Science & Technology | Melbourne, Australia | 19–23 October, 2019

DOI: 10.1002/pra2.00087

The author uses the *Lithium Hindsight 360* virtual reality (VR) experience as a case study for analyzing how independent creators can incorporate access and preservation into their creative process. As a hybrid creative/performing artist, information technologist and digital archivist/humanist, the author draws upon considerations from all fields equally to balance and map out at which points issues may arise. With this alternative event, the author will guide participants through a demo of *LH360* to help them consider how they might address access and preservation concerns for VR and other new media projects that they may encounter in the future.

BACKGROUND

The alternative event centers around use of the *LH360* VR experience as a starting point for discussion. *LH360* is an interactive real-time rendered animated experience using motion capture data that was produced on a relatively low budget (i.e. less than $5000USD) with a team of two individuals over several brief work periods. It falls under the category of medical humanities as it is a dance/movement-based illness narrative. These traits make *LH360* a relatively small VR work more representative of independent artists, academics starting pilot projects and home consumers. At the same time, given the types of data involved as well as ethical considerations, the structure of *LH360* raises a variety of access and preservation questions.

The following description of the *LH360* prototypes are focused on the technical structure and potentially generated data rather than the philosophical and artistic motivations behind its creation.

Overall Narrative

LH360 started as a data-driven concept based on patient narratives from medical reports. Six symptoms were selected for representation, a short dance was choreographed for each one, and then they were transposed into digital animations. While choreographing, the author realized that her own experiences were affecting movement choice. For Version 1a/b, the author split the experience into two sides. The first side consisted of dances based on six symptoms/feelings from the author's memories. The second side was a more linear narrative of a regular day in the author's teenage life. This allows the viewer to choose between an impersonal or personal telling of the same lived experience.

Versions 0 and 1ab

Version 0 was intended to primarily test whether it was feasible for a solo researcher to incorporate dance into a VR experience in a quick affordable manner. An HTC Vive-based system was used for motion capture (mocap), Autodesk Maya for modeling 3D figures, Adobe Audition and Audacity for sound design, and Unity for producing the actual VR experience. The project was produced over a 2-month period with the assistance of the MetaObjects company for mocap and then shown over 3 days to testers at City University of Hong Kong.

Figure 1. Screen capture from Version 0.

This user feedback was then used to produce Version 1ab the following year. Version 1ab is referred to as such because it was originally meant to be a comparison of two different types of work. The Raptor marker-based system at ACIM (Center for Applied Computing and Interactive Media) was used for mocap as well as Blender for clean-up. The rest of the software used was the same as Version 0.

Version 1ab was produced over a 3 month period, with additional programming by MetaObjects, and shown in private viewings at academic institutions in Australia, Hong Kong and the USA for technical feedback.

Figure 2. Screen capture from the "Symptoms" scene of Version 1ab.

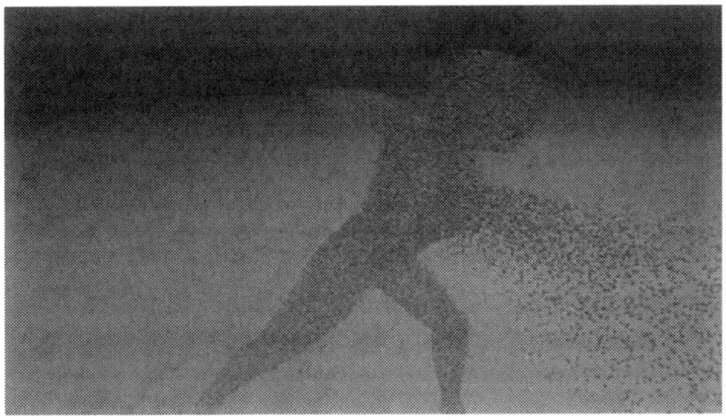

Figure 3. Screen capture from the "Coping" scene of Version 1ab.

Version 2: Release Version

Version 2 is the final exhibition version combining both sides of Version 1ab into a more structured experience. Although the hardware and software used for Version 2 is the same as Version 1ab, there is added consideration of the exhibition design plans and event documentation.

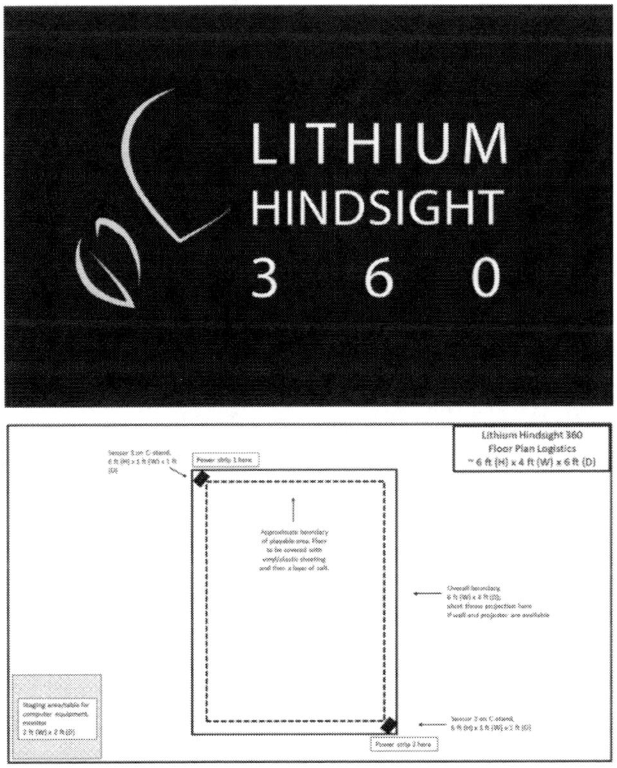

Figure 4. Logo/splashscreen and floorplan for *LH360*.

Proposed Framework/Guidelines

As a final step, the creative process for *LH360* will then be distilled into a set of guidelines for others to create their own dance/movement-based illness narratives for VR environments. Both the framework/guidelines and Unity builds will be disseminated through an online platform or other type of standalone website for reference by other creators.

Need for Preservation

There are thus far two categories of content to be preserved: artistic and contextual. The artistic content would be the components required for creating and assembling *LH360* as well as the finial output. The contextual content, aside from metadata, would include the user testing feedback, exhibition design and any other creator's notes.

One question that is carried over from performing arts archives is which iteration to preserve. While Version 2 is the final output being shown to the public, the previous versions give insight into the creation process and intentions. Another question would be whether information such as who provided the narrative and performance for the mocap should be protected. In the case of *LH360*, this is publicly known information, but in other instances, creators may be required to keep identities anonymous.

Challenges of Digital Stewardship for Virtual Reality

Although the concept of preserving new media art at the individual level is not new, common practices or well-known guidelines are still not in place. Narrowing down the focus to VR works and/or health-related artworks adds further complications in regards to human ethics.

What is known is that artistic content and metadata were considered important for new media art preservation (Ribeiro, David, & Calistru, 2007) as well as maintaining interactivity (Bruno, Puren, Riondet, Seillier, & Romary, 2010) and the actual user experience (Ng, Mikrovannidi, Ong, & Giaretta, 2009). Besides preserving multimedia components, Bruno et al. (2010) recommended considering additional components such as hardware and software. Post (2017) describes this issue as "complexity" in his user profiles of seven new media artists. This is a valid concern given that changes in file formats, hardware requirements and other technicalities could render an entire work inaccessible.

Several frameworks and models have been proposed over the years at both the institutional and individual levels. In the early 2000s, the PLANETS (Becker, Kolar, Küng, & Rauber, 2007) and the CASPAR frameworks (Ng et al., 2009) were developed in Europe with the participation of numerous academic and research institutions. During this time period, Rinehart (2007) proposed the MANS notation system for multimedia. More recently the Cultural Heritage Data Reuse Charter was developed for increasing access to cultural heritage content by digital means (Baillot, Puren, Riondet, Seillier, & Romary, 2017). The proposed strategies hold potential applications to other types of new media works.

On a more practical note, the Artists' Studio Archives published a workbook in 2016 (Ambrose-Smith, Beaudoin, Gendron, & Stroukoff, 2016) and the Artist's Legacy Toolkit was updated in 2017 (Sewell-Williams, Smith, Seltzer, & Bell, 2017). Both tools were aimed for use by individual creative and performing artists in preserving and maintaining access to their works. Although all these referenced frameworks are theoretically sound, the recommended procedures tend to apply to the post-creation phase.

EVENT FORMAT

The alternative event will center around a group viewing of the author's VR prototype and a subsequent discussion. A specific order of events and duration are as follows:

- The group will start with a self-introduction of each person's experience with VR, movement and mental health experience. This introductory discussion will include setting general discussion rules to ensure confidentiality and collegiality.
  (Approx. 15 minutes)
- Participants will then view the prototype collectively by taking turns in the headset while it is simultaneously projected for the group. The author will provide and set up the VR hardware.
  (Approx. 20 minutes)
- After the viewing, participants will use the prototype as a case study for looking at how the elite skillsets and technology required for VR affect access and preservation. Participants will also be asked to consider how current preservation trends do or do not support these kinds of multimedia works.
- The brainstorming discussion will start with a summary of the author's discoveries thus far, then the discussion will open up to the whole group. If there are more than 10 participants, smaller sub-groups will be made.
  (Approx. 30 minutes)
- Toward the end, a set of 3–5 considerations or potential solutions for each issue will be drawn up with follow up tasks for the author and general questions for the group to consider.
  (Approx. 25 minutes)

FUTURE PLANS

After the alternative event, the author will take the discussion content and incorporate it into a set of access and preservation guidelines. Participants will be asked if they would like to be notified of the results and will be encouraged to apply the brainstormed content to their own situations. The results will also be incorporated into the creation process for the derivative artworks based on *LH360*.

CONCLUSION

Although the topic and demo being used is very specific, the access and preservation issues raised apply to a wide range of projects. Given the rate of production of new media projects and their crossover into a variety of disciplines, there needs to be greater consideration about the lifespan of these projects and whether long-term preservation is relevant. If long-term preservation is actually necessary, then even independent creators need to do more to prepare their works for acceptance by a repository as most archival repositories already have a significant backlog of content. Conversely, if long-term preservation does not apply, then identifying an alternative preservation approach would be beneficial.

ACKNOWLEDGMENTS

Special thanks to ACIM for use of their mocap lab and to Andrew Crowe of MetaObjects for the technical collaboration.

REFERENCES

Ambrose-Smith, N., Beaudoin, J. E., Gendron, H., & Stroukoff, E. I. (2016). *Artists' studio archives: Managing Personal Collections & Creative Legacies*. Oak Creek, WI: Art Libraries Society of North America. Retrieved from: https://www.arlisna.org/publications/arlis-na-research-reports/1013-artists-studio-archives.

Baillot, A., Puren, M., Riondet, C., Seillier, D., & Romary, L. (2017). *Access to cultural heritage data. A challenge for digital humanities*. In Paper Presented at *Digital* Humanities 2017, Montreal, Canada, August 8–11, 2017. Retrieved from: https://hal.archives-ouvertes.fr/hal-01582176

Becker, C., Kolar, G., Küng, J., & Rauber, A. (2007). Preserving interactive multimedia art: A case study in preservation planning. In D. H. L. Goh, T. H. Cao, I. T. Sølvberg, & E. Rasmussen, *Asian digital libraries. Looking back 10 years and forging new frontiers. ICADL 2007. Lecture Notes in Computer Science* (Vol. *4822*, pp. 257–266). Berlin, Germany: Springer.

Bruno, F., Bruno, S., De Sensi, G., Luchi, M., Mancuso, S., & Muzzupappa, M. (2010). From 3D reconstruction to virtual reality: A complete methodology for digital archaeological exhibition. *Journal of Cultural Heritage*, *11*, 42–49.

Ng, K., Mikroyannidi, E., Ong, B., & Giaretta, D. (2009). *An ontology based framework for the preservation of interactive multimedia performances*. In 2009 Fifth IEEE International Conference on E-Science, December 2009, Oxford, United Kingdom (pp. 40-44).

Post, C. (2017). Preservation practices of new media artists: Challenges, strategies, and attitudes in the personal management of artworks. *LEONARDO*, *40*(2), 181–187.

Rinehart, R. (2007). *The media art notation system: Documenting and preserving digital/media art*. International.

Ribeiro, C., David, G., & Calistru, C. (2007). Multimedia in cultural heritage collections: A model and applications. In D. H. L. Goh, T. H. Cao, I. T. Sølvberg, & E. Rasmussen, *Asian digital libraries. Looking back 10 years and forging new frontiers. ICADL 2007. Lecture notes in computer science* (Vol. *4822*, pp. 186–195). Berlin, Germany: Springer.

Sewell-Williams, L., Smith, I., Seltzer, J., & Bell, K. (2017). *Artist's legacy toolkit*. Washington, DC: Dance. Retrieved from: https://danceusa.org/archiving-preservation-artists-legacy-toolkit.

Information Experience: A Domain and Object of Study

Clarence Maybee
Purdue University, West Lafayette, USA
cmaybee@purdue.edu

Elham Sayyad Abdi
Queensland University of Technology, Brisbane, AUS
elham.s.abdi@gmail.com

Kate Davis
University of Southern Queensland, Toowoomba, AUS
kate.davis@usq.edu.au

Lettie Conrad
Queensland University of Technology, Brisbane, AUS
lettie.conrad@hdr.qut.edu.au

ABSTRACT

Introduced into the field in 2014, "information experience" (IX) is a research domain that focuses on the ways that people derive meaning from engagement with information in the various aspects of their lives. IX is also an object of study comparable to other objects, such as information seeking or information literacy. This interactive panel will discuss aspects of IX, including the various ways it may be described in the field, and how it is manifest in a current IX research project. Two learning design models – informed learning design and information experience design (IXD) – will be introduced, exemplifying how theoretical understandings of IX can be applied in practice.

KEYWORDS

Information experience; information experience design; informed learning design

ASIS&T THESAURUS

Information theory; research and analytic methods

INTRODUCTION

Insights into people's experiences with information can inform the development of systems, services, and tools that support the needs of individuals and entire communities. However, "experience" has not typically been a lens through which information-centric research questions have been investigated. Drawing from their own research, this international panel of researchers will discuss "information experience" (IX), an emerging research domain and object of study that holistically focuses on socially contextualized human engagement with information (Bruce, Davis, Hughes, Partridge, & Stoodley, 2014). The panel will argue that information experience research reveals more of the complexity with which people experience engagement with information in the world.

82nd Annual Meeting of the Association for Information Science & Technology | Melbourne, Australia | 19–23 October, 2019

DOI: 10.1002/pra2.00088

INFORMATION EXPERIENCE

Introduced into the field in 2014 in the book, *Information Experience: Approaches to Theory and Practice* (Bruce et al., 2014), the domain of IX focuses on the ways that people derive meaning from engagement with information in the various aspects of their lives. Information behavior, broadly described as "human behavior in relation to sources and channels of information" (Wilson, 2000, p. 49), remains a prevalent domain in information science research. Information practice is another prevalent domain lens that highlights "practices" within a broader context (Lloyd, 2009; Tuominen, Talja, & Savolainen, 2005). Like information behavior, information practice has an emphasis on the things people do with information (Savolainen, 2007). Information practice researchers often adopt a socio-cultural framework to explore the socially and culturally situated ways in which people "deal with information" (Savolainen, 2007, p. 126). In contrast, IX offers an alternative lens by investigating how people interact with information and assign meaning to those interactions, with a contextual view of human experience. IX is an information-related aspect of what is referred to in phenomenology as people's *lived experience* that is part of their *life worlds* (Bruce et al., 2014).

IX is also an object of study, comparable to other bodies of research, such as information seeking, information literacy, or information sharing (Bruce et al., 2014). In contrast to research that seeks to identify trends, IX research recognizes and values each of the diverse and subjective experiences people may have when engaging with information. Assumptions are not made about the nature of information, but instead, IX research seeks to reveal contextualized understandings or experiences of information. Targeting what people experience as information, and how they experience using it in their lives, this object of study is approached through different research lenses, such as phenomenological, phenomenographic, or sociocultural. A variety of methods may be used in IX research, including phenomenography, grounded theory, phenomenology, or ethnography.

The panel session explores the IX domain by examining different aspects of research conducted from this perspective, including: 1) its varied depictions in research studies, 2) as the object of study in current research, and 3) ways that it has informed the development of research-based practices.

FORMAT OF THE PANEL

The panel will be interactive, allowing attendees to discuss and consider aspects of IX. It will begin with the moderator providing an overview of IX. Following the introduction, the panel will be broken into three parts.

Part 1 explores IX as an object of study, with brief presentations from two panelists (8 minutes each). Attendees will be invited to participate in an activity intended to help them consider research questions that can be answered through IX research.

Part 2 explores applications of IX research, with brief presentations from the other two panelists (8 minutes each). This will be followed by a second activity in which attendees will consider applications or implications of research in the IX domain.

The final thirty minutes of the panel (Part 3) will be allotted for panelists to address attendee questions, with prepared questions in reserve to round out the discussions.

PART 1: INFORMATION EXPERIENCE RESEARCH: IX AS OBJECT OF STUDY

To shed light on the nature of IX as on object of study, the various ways this object may be described in the field will be discussed. A current IX research project will be explored in some detail to further exemplify the nature of the object, along with more general discussion of a number of other studies.

Information Experience as an Object of Study (Davis)

Within the domain of IX research, researchers take an experiential view on a range of objects of study, including information literacy and IX (as object). As an object of study, IX attends to affect, cognition and behavior – it explores how people feel and think as they interact with information within their broader experience of the world, usually within a specific context.

To date, few studies have explored IX as an object of study, and as such, our understanding of IX as a phenomenon is in its infancy. With any new area of research endeavor, defining the boundaries of the phenomenon under study is critical. In information seeking and use research, there has been a lack of clarity around definitions of key objects of study. The differences between information behavior and information practice were explored in Savolainen's (2007) article on "umbrella concepts" in information-seeking research, with the suggestion that the boundaries of information practice and information behavior are ambiguous, and that discussion about the terms and their definitions needs to happen in "dialog within and between the… discourses" (p. 126). As interest in IX as an object of study grows, it would be useful to consider how we might arrive at shared ways of defining and describing IX, both in itself, and in relationship to other key concepts in information seeking and use research.

Drawing on a small number of studies, this presentation will identify the dimensions of IX. It will explore the way in which IX research findings have been presented, how the construct has been unpacked, and what we might take away about the structure of IX as an object of study. The intent is to initiate a discussion about how we might arrive at a shared definition of IX, and perhaps shared approaches to presenting IX research.

Student-Researcher Information Experience (Conrad)

The contexts and contours of student-researchers' management of academic information are often invisible and not well understood; prior research is largely behavioral, examining transactional aspects of academic information management, such as file storage. As a case illustration of IX research, where IX is the object of research, the doctoral study described here adopts a holistic perspective by asking: What is the student-researcher information experience with their management of academic information?

This study is the first of its kind to examine individual experiences with the management of academic information. Where IX research "responds to the complexity and change in contemporary society" (Bruce et al., 2014, p. 11), the goal of this study is to better understand how academic information is *individualized* – personally curated and orchestrated for individual reuse – by master's students in their social science research training and disciplinary emersion. Rooted in constructivist grounded theory, this study applies card sorting to enable interactive interviews, which offer rich, contextualized insights into how student researchers define what informs their academic work and how they relate to that information.

This study joins an emerging area of research focused on human IX, specifically the student experience (Maybee, 2015; Tucker, 2012). This doctoral research also focuses on IX in the research question and design, joining other efforts to demonstrate IX as the object of research. Preceding studies that have identified IX as the research object (e.g., Harlan, 2012; Lloyd, 2009) seek to characterize it in specific contexts and be open to defining the scope of information as "that which informs," (Lupton, 2014, p.71), allowing for a greater breadth of what participants may experience as information.

Early results illuminate the nature of student-researcher relationships with academic information and what values or meanings they assign to the information they are compelled to manage. A theoretical model that characterizes and explains this situated, contextualized IX will contribute relevant lessons for academics, instructors, librarians, and digital resource providers.

PART 2: INFORMATION EXPERIENCE RESEARCH APPLICATION

The IX research movement has gone beyond pure theoretical research to apply findings of IX research. This is done with the aim of enriching people's information experience in real world settings. So far, the two concepts of "informed learning design" and "information experience design" (IXD) have been developed and used to translate the theoretical understanding of IX research to practice.

Informed Learning Design (Maybee)

Informed learning design is a curriculum design model underpinned by IX that was developed for use in formal educational settings (Maybee, Bruce, Lupton, & Pang, 2018). The design model provides a process for enacting an informed learning pedagogic framework, which enables learners to experience new ways of engaging with information while simultaneously learning course content, such as disciplinary knowledge and practices (Bruce, 2008). Drawing from IX research identifying aspects of teacher and student experiences of using information to complete assignments in an undergraduate classroom (Maybee, Bruce, Lupton, & Rebmann, 2017), informed learning design recognizes that learning outcomes are influenced by how learners experience using information within the learning process.

Recognizing learners may have varied and partial experiences of information, informed learning design focuses on identifying goals for student learning and creating a learning environment that enables the students to build on their experiences of using information to understand new content (Maybee et al., 2018). Knowledge of students' information experience as it relates to various learning contexts, such as music, nursing, web design, etc., have been identified through IX research. In unexplored contexts, researchers may work with teachers to identity the information experiences they intend for their students. Learning activities designed using the model aim to allow students to become aware of aspects of using information that align with the teacher's more complex or multifaceted experience.

Informed learning design supports enabling learners to experience using information in highly contextualized learning environments (Maybee et al., 2018). The model enables the development of information-focused scholarly teaching that is guided by theory. Drawing from IX research to inform design responsive to varied student experiences, informed learning design may also act as a framework to guide new IX research in formal educational settings.

Information Experience Design (Sayyad Abdi)

IXD is a two-phase approach to translate information experience research to practice in informal learning settings. Rooted in variation theory (Marton & Booth, 1997), IXD starts with a research phase to identify variation in information experience of a target group. This is an in-depth investigation into how differently individuals within the target population understand information and information use, what information is for them, and how they engage with information.

The identified variation in information experience is then applied throughout the implementation phase. This includes designing interventions (such as guidelines, programs, services, systems, technologies, tools or spaces) that enable the targeted community to engage with information in more varied, sophisticated and powerful ways. As a result of this enhanced information experience, individuals become more effective information users, decision-makers and informed citizens.

The transformative nature of IXD allows it to act as an agent of change. When applied to social issues such as immigration (Sayyad Abdi, Bruce, Partridge, & Watson, in press), it has the potential to contribute to social progress in the form of social inclusion and when applied to organizational phenomena (Somerville, Chaudhary, Mirijamdotter, & Sayyad Abdi, 2019; Somerville, Imhof, Bruce, & Sayyad Abdi, 2017), it supports organizational change and innovation.

By bringing together research and practice, IXD aims to provide the most relevant, meaningful, and yet transformational solutions for real world problems. To ensure the maximum impact, IXD adopts a researcher-practitioner participatory approach, which involves both researchers and real-world beneficiaries in all phases of the process, from research design to enactment of findings.

IXD initiatives go beyond merely generating pure theoretical understanding and rather make the knowledge produced enacted. This simultaneous focus of IXD on research and its application makes it a translational approach that bridges IX theory to practice.

CONCLUSION

Although developing over many years, only recently has IX been identified as a research domain and object of study (Bruce et al., 2014). IX research provides new insights into contextualized experiences of engagement with information. Responsive to people's information needs, the insights gleaned from IX research inform the development of targeted applications.

PANEL MEMBERS

Clarence Maybee (moderator) is an associate professor of the Libraries and the School of Information Studies at Purdue University, United States. His research is on information literacy in theoretical and applied contexts. In 2018, he authored the book, *IMPACT Learning: Librarians at the Forefront of Change in Higher Education*, published by Chandos Publishing.

Elham Sayyad Abdi is an information researcher. Her research interest lies in the application of information research within social and organizational settings and through a participatory approach. In AY2018/19 Elham served as a Fulbright Scholar-In-Residence at the University of the Pacific, CA, United States.

Kate Davis is a Senior Research Fellow at the University of Southern Queensland, Australia. She is a human experience researcher with an interest in how people experience information and technology. Her doctoral study was the first to focus on IX as an object of study, exploring new mothers' information experience in social media.

Lettie Conrad is an information science doctoral candidate at Queensland University of Technology via the San José State University's School of Information Gateway PhD Program. Conrad's work is dedicated to humanizing the development of digital resources to support the scholarly lifecycle.

REFERENCES

Bruce, C. S. (2008). *Informed learning*. Chicago, IL: American Library Association.

Bruce, C. S., Davis, K., Hughes, H., Partridge, H. L., & Stoodley, I. (2014). *Information experience: Approaches to theory and practice*. Bingley, UK: Emerald Group Publishing Ltd.

Harlan, M. (2012). *Information practices of teen content creators: The intersection of action and experiences, a grounded theory study* (Doctoral dissertation). Queensland University of Technology.

Lloyd, A. (2009). Informing practice: Information experiences of ambulance officers in training and on-road practice. *Journal of Documentation*, *65*(3), 396–419. https://doi.org/10.1108/00220410910952401.

Lupton, M. (2014). Creating and expressing: Information as-it-is-experienced. In C. S. Bruce, K. Davis, H. Hughes, H. L. Partridge, & I. Stoodley (Eds.), *Information experience: Approaches to theory and practice* (pp. 69–83). Bingley, UK: Emerald Group Publishing.

Maybee, C. (2015). *Informed learning in the undergraduate classroom: The role of information experiences in shaping outcomes* (Doctoral dissertation). Queensland University of Technology.

Maybee, C., Bruce, C. S., Lupton, M., & Pang, M. F. (2019). Informed learning design: Teaching and learning through engagement with information. *Higher Education Research & Development*, *38*(3), 579–593.

Maybee, C., Bruce, C. S., Lupton, M., & Rebmann, K. (2017). Designing rich information experiences to shape learning outcomes. *Studies in Higher Education*, *42*(12), 2373–2388.

Marton, F., & Booth, S. (1997). *Learning and awareness*. Mahwah, NJ: Lawrence Erlbaum.

Savolainen, R. (2007). Information behavior and information practice: Reviewing the "umbrella concepts" of information-seeking studies. *The Library Quarterly*, *77* (2), 109–132. https://doi.org/10.1086/517840.

Sayyad Abdi, E., Bruce, C., Partridge, H., & Watson, J. (in press). Understanding skilled migrants' information literacy: A qualitative study. *Journal of Documentation*.

Somerville, M., Chaudhary, N., Mirijamdotter, A., & Sayyad Abdi, E. (2019). Informed systems: Designing together for learning together. *Journal of Library Administration*, *59*(1).

Somerville, M., Imhof, R., Bruce, C.S., & Sayyad Abdi, E. (2017). *Workplace information literacy: Co-designed information experience-centered systems and practices*. In Proceedings from the 2017 European Conference on Information Literacy (ECIL2017).

Tucker, V. M. (2012). *Acquiring search expertise: Learning experiences and threshold concepts* (Doctoral dissertation). Queensland University of Technology.

Tuominen, K., Talja, S., & Savolainen, R. (2005). The social constructionist viewpoint on information practices. In K. E. Fisher, S. Erdelez, & L. McKechnie (Eds.), *Theories on information behavior* (pp. 328–333). Medford, NJ: Information Today Inc..

Wilson, T. D. (2000). Human information behavior. *Informing Science*, *3*(2), 49–56.

The Convergence of Computational and Social Approaches for Unveiling Meaningful and Valuable Data

Angela P. Murillo
Indianapolis University-Purdue University Indianapolis, Indianapolis, U.S.A.
apmurill@iu.edu

Renata G. Curty
Universidade Estadual de Londrina, Londrina, Brazil
renatacurty@uel.br

Wei Jeng
National Taiwan University, Taipei, Taiwan
wjeng@ntu.edu.tw

Daqing He
University of Pittsburgh, Pittsburgh, U.S.A.
dah44@pitt.edu

ABSTRACT

The current data paradigm is seeking a more integrated and comprehensive framework to make sense of data and its derived issues. From the perspective of the data life cycle, we argue that *computational* and *social* approaches complement each other to confront data challenges. Computational approaches consist of ETL (extract, transform, and load), modeling, and machine learning techniques; social approaches include policy and regulations, data sharing and reuse behavior, reproducibility, ethical and privacy issues. In this panel, we frame these two approaches as *data acumen* and *data stewardship*. The merging of these two perspectives allows data not only to become discoverable, accessible, and interoperable, but also to further the value of revealing meaningful patterns and become supportive evidence for important decision making. In this panel, the opening facilitator and three panelists will report on their recent studies in terms of this convergence of both data acumen and stewardship while sharing their recent research insights on case studies in three disciplines: agriculture, biomedicine, and archeology.

KEYWORDS

Data acumen; data stewardship; agricultural data; biomedical data; archeological data

ASIS&T THESAURUS

Data Science; Cross Disciplinary Fertilization; Reproducibility

INTRODUCTION

As the world becomes increasingly more data-intensive, there is a need to examine how data-related work is impacting academia, the workforce, and society at large. The growing demand for data experts has been documented. In a Linked Workforce Report (2018), more than 151,000 data science jobs went unfilled across the United States. Additionally, there is an estimated shortage of 200,000 workers with deep analytics skills and 1.5 million employees who lack the knowledge to make data-driven decisions (Manyika et al., 2011). Despite the fact that Curty and Serafim (2017) observed a highly computational and business orientation in 93 data science/data analytics degrees offered by U.S institutions, and that these emphases were also found by Verma, Yurov, Lane, and Yurova (2019) in the majority of the job posts for data analysts, some research has shown that data knowledge is needed across all disciplines and domains (Börner et al., 2018).

Liberal arts and humanities students who pair their major with a data-related component qualify for additional jobs and increased salaries (Burning Glass Technologies, 2013). Additionally, studies have shown the need to incorporate "soft" social skills into the data fields, indicating the need for both social and computational approaches to data work (Börner et al., 2018). As a result, data-related job titles which were initially limited to data scientists or data analysts have been branching out. Lyon, Mattern, Acker, and Langmead (2015); Lyon and Mattern (2016) mapped iSchool curriculum to real-world job descriptions to examine the variety of data-related employer requirements and the current state of data science-related educational curriculum. In the series, six data science roles were compared in two articles: Data Archivist, Data Librarian, and Data Steward/Curator (Lyon et al., 2015), as well as Data Analyst, Data Engineer, and Data Journalist (Lyon & Mattern, 2016).

Grounded in the computational and social data approaches, for this panel, we consider that data acumen and stewardship are interconnected concepts that should be instilled in data practices and research. While the former relates to the capability to draw more informed and better decisions based on data, the latter is the capability which envisions the management of data among and between different data lifecycle stages (Baker, 2009), which allows decisions from data acumen to be readily available and accessible, respecting high-quality requirements.

This convergence of data acumen and data stewardship is impacting jobs, education, and how practitioners and researchers are responding to these computational and social knowledge domains. Both practitioners and academics are

82nd Annual Meeting of the Association for Information Science & Technology | Melbourne, Australia | 19–23 October, 2019

DOI: 10.1002/pra2.00089

seeking a more integrated and comprehensive framework to deal with data issues and challenges, by combining highly computational approaches (i.e., data gathering, extraction, modeling, etc.) for acumen analytics, with contributions from social perspectives, (i.e., data policy and regulations, data sharing and reuse behaviors, data stewardship, ethics and privacy, and so on). The merging of these two perspectives allows full compliance with the FAIR principles (Wilkinson et al., 2016) so that data becomes not only findable, accessible, and interoperable, but also reusable. Such integration facilitates the discovery of meaningful patterns and rules from data, as well as the investigation of questions which could not have always been anticipated by primary researchers. The panelists will provide examples of how data acumen and data stewardship are bound together while addressing data issues from case studies in clinical sciences, agriculture, and archeology.

OBJECTIVES OF THE PANEL

The objectives of this panel include:

- To introduce the framing perspectives of data acumen and data stewardship for the computational and social behavioral approaches, respectively;
- To examine how these two perspectives complement each other to solve data issues in different knowledge domains;
- To explore, as a result of the group interaction, some alternatives to strengthen the ties between data acumen and data stewardship.

STRUCTURE OF THE PANEL

The structure of the panel is as follows:

- The opening facilitator (He) will provide a framing introduction to the session and introduce the dynamics of the panel.
- Each one of the panelists (Murillo, Jeng, and Curty) will present their recent research findings on how both computational approaches and social and behavior-wise foci interplay in different knowledge domains.
- The facilitator and the panelists will host an interactive session which invites attendees to share their opinions and thoughts through the use of gamification and data visualization strategies.

PANELISTS AND TOPICS

Facilitator

Daqing He is a professor at the School of Computing and Information as well as has a joint appointment at the Intelligent Systems Program, an interdisciplinary academic unit focusing on research and education on Artificial Intelligence, both of which are at the University of Pittsburgh. He earned his PhD degree in artificial intelligence from the University of Edinburgh, Scotland. He has been the Principal Investigator (PI) and Co-PI for more than 10 research projects, funded by the National Science Foundation (NSF), United States Defense Advanced Research Projects Agency (DARPA), University of Pittsburgh, and other agencies. His current research projects include open corpus personalized learning, models for sentence simplification, and information access.

In this panel, He will serve as an opening facilitator and will provide an introduction to the panel theme and the basic structures of the panel. Equipped with a computer science background and years of teaching and service experience in the iSchool community, He is able to provide unique insights and identify promising research opportunities that can be achieved only through close integration of data acumen and stewardship.

Topic: Computational and Social Research in Agriculture

Angela P. Murillo is an Assistant Professor and the Program Director of the Applied Data and Information Science Program at the School of Informatics and Computing at Indiana University-Purdue University Indianapolis (IUPUI). Her dissertation investigated earth and environmental data sharing and reuse. More recently, her research has focused on the impacts of data science on LIS education (Murillo & Jones, 2018), and the impact of data science on earth and environmental science data management. Prior to joining IUPUI, she worked as a Research and Development Information Scientist at Novozymes, where she assisted with research and analytics in relation to Novozymes R&D, product development, and competitors.

For this panel, Murillo will share her recent research and perspectives of an ongoing research project related to agricultural data and new tools that are being used by farmers to gather data in the fields related to weather conditions, soil conditions, seed treatments, and other field data. This research is a collaboration between Murillo and data science faculty to produce predictive analysis to assist with the understanding of the return of investment of various treatments, field, and weather conditions in regards to agriculture and an understanding of farmers' use of new tools to gather agricultural data. In this study, the computational approaches will include ETL and modeling of field data provided by farmers and industry partners, and social approaches will include an analysis of farmers' data gathering processes, use of technological tools, and reproducibility considerations. Murillo will report on early research insights of this ongoing research project of data acumen and stewardship in agricultural.

Topic: Preserving the Research Workflow in Biology and Medicine

Wei Jeng is an Assistant Professor at the Department of LIS, as well as the Center for Research in Econometric Theory and Applications in the National Taiwan University, Taiwan. She completed her PhD studies at the School of Computing and Information, University of Pittsburgh. Her recent research interests involved research data sharing and reproducibility. While focusing on the social aspects of data research, Jeng frequently collaborates with computer science and biomedicine researchers practicing data acumen, and thus has first-hand experience in resolving tensions and identifying challenges when bridging the two worlds.

In this panel, Jeng will share her recent results and early research insights on an ongoing research project which explores better solutions for preserving the research work-flows for PIs. Jeng will discuss the context of reproducibility crisis recently raised in these fields, and review the most recent information services toward ensuring reproducibility and a potentially better solution--a decentralized, secure, and auditable infrastructure. Jeng will also report some early results about data gathering from a participatory design work-shop which is expected to be conducted in Summer 2019. Inviting a group of university faculty and researchers in biol-ogy and medical science, the design workshop aims to reveal PIs' strategies or techniques for data acumen (either standard-ized or "homegrown"), their data management practices for ensuring the reproducibility of their research around the data lifecycle, as well as potential challenges arose from the entan-glement between data acumen and stewardship.

Topic: The Role of Paradata in Digital Archeology

Renata G. Curty is an Assistant Professor in the Information Science Department at the Universidade Estadual de Lon-drina, in Southern Brazil. Her research relates to sociological aspects of science, digital scholarly communication and met-rics, data curation, and research data sharing and reuse.

In this panel, Curty will present her current findings of an ongoing study about paradata and its role in promoting more informed, responsible, and trustworthy data (re)use. She will first define paradata in relation to data documentation and its integration with contextual and descriptive metadata despite their conceptual and practical boundaries. Later, she will dis-cuss different types of paradata sources in the sciences, con-sidering the massive quantity of data which are gathered as a by-product of computer-mediated collection processes, such as web surveys. Taking a social approach, she will cover the need for paradata to be documented and easily accessible along with the structured dataset and its metadata in a consis-tent manner, and describe a few strategies for doing so. From a computational perspective, she will talk about how paradata can assist data interpretation and resignification in the context of digital archeology to increase scientificity, transparency, and reproducibility for digitally re-created environments and artifacts.

PANEL STRUCTURE

The structure of the proposed panel is as follows:

Introduction (5 minutes)

Dr. He will introduce the panel theme and objectives and talk briefly about how computational and social approaches are important for allowing excellence in data acumen and stewardship.

Presentations (30 minutes–10 minutes each)

The panelists (Murillo, Jeng, and Curty) will present their individual research projects and findings.

Q&A session (5–10 minutes)

A brief Q&A and discussion session regarding the content of panel presentations will be hosted.

Interactive Session (45 minutes)

The interactive session will be moderated by the panelists who will use a combination of gamification, visualization strategies, and team collaboration tools to better engage the audience. A set of situational-based data scenarios related to the fields panelists will cover on their presentations will be provided to attendees, and they will be asked to respond them both from a computational and social perspective.

We plan to use the Role Playing Game (RPG) as a methodo-logical technique to elicit and stimulate conversations, and promote retention of acquired knowledge and group discus-sion outcomes. Predefined archetypes will be provided to each participant in to guide discussions. The participants will be invited to "change hats" during the group discussion to address how they would approach data issues differently according to computational or social perspectives. Participant responses to questions elaborated by the panelists will be reg-istered through live poll tools, e.g., Sli.do (www.sli.do), and the results will be displayed to the audience to allow partici-pants to reflect about the responses provided. The responses will be discussed collectively, and the most salient remarks will be shared with the audience through a real-time online whiteboard. We will then, debrief and wrap up the session with all attendees.

EXPECTED CONTRIBUTION

This panel aims to raise attention to data issues and cultivate constructive conversations among scholars and practitioners from information science and data science communities, by integrating both computational and social perspectives to address data challenges in different knowledge domains. Through the interactive session, the panel expects to assist researchers and practitioners from both perspectives to con-sider the importance of understanding computational and social considerations of data, as well as potentially find areas of opportunity to expand their research frameworks, strength-ening the ties of researchers and practitioners from both perspectives.

We anticipate that this awareness will positively reflect on data-related initiatives and research endeavors that will not consider data acumen and data stewardship as antagonistic, but rather an opportunity to unify them to look at the data phenomenon. Through the sharing of experiences in the inter-active session, this panel expects to learn of others techniques in confronting data challenges both from a social and compu-tational perspective, to assist the panelists and participants in learning about practices, techniques, and tools when working with data. Ultimately, this panel will assist in examining how data acumen and data stewardship are complementary for unveiling meaningful and valuable data, as well as in allowing the collective development of more robust interconnected practices for both concepts.

ACKNOWLEDGMENTS

The panel of "Preserving the Research Workflow in Biology and Medicine" by Jeng was supported by Grant MOST108-2636-H-002-002 and MOST107-3017-F-002 -004, as well as under the Grant (#107L900204) received by CRETA at NTU, sponsored by the Ministry of Science and Technology and Ministry of Education (MOE) in Taiwan.

REFERENCES

Baker, K. S. (2009). Data stewardship: Environmental data curation and a web of repositories. *Digital Discourse*, *1*(1).

Börner, K., Scrivner, O., Gallant, M., Ma, S., Liu, X., Chewning, K., ... Evans, J. A. (2018). Skill discrepancies between research, education, and jobs reveal the critical need to supply soft skills for the data economy. *Proceedings of the National Academy of Sciences of the United States of America*, *115*(50), 12630–12637. https://doi.org/10.1073/pnas.1804247115.

Burning Glass Technologies. (2013). *The art of employment: How liberal arts graduates can improve their labor markets prospects*. Retrieved from http://www.burning-glass.com/wp-content/uploads/BGTReportLiberalArts.pdf

Committee on Envisioning the Data Science Discipline: The Undergraduate Perspective, Computer Science and Telecommunications Board, Board on Mathematical Sciences and Analytics, Committee on Applied and Theoretical Statistics, Division on Engineering and Physical Sciences, Board on Science Education, ... National Academies of Sciences, Engineering, and Medicine. (2018). *Data science for undergraduates: Opportunities and options*. https://doi.org/10.17226/25104

Curty, R. G., & Serafim, J. D. S. (2017). A formação em ciência de dados: Uma análise preliminar do panorama estadunidense. *Informação & Informação*, *21*(2), 307–331.

LinkedIn. (2018). *LinkedIn Workforce Report | United States | August 2018*. Retrieved from https://economicgraph.linkedin.com/resources/linkedin-workforce-report-august-2018

Lyon, L., & Mattern, E. (2016). Education for real-world data science roles (part 2): A translational approach to curriculum development. *International Journal of Digital Curation*, *11*(2), 13–26. https://doi.org/10.2218/ijdc.v11i2.417.

Lyon, L., Mattern, E., Acker, A., & Langmead, A. (2015). *Applying translational principles to data science curriculum development*. In IPRES 2015 Proceedings.

Manyika, J., Chui, M., Brown, B., Bughin, J., Dobbs, R., Roxburgh, C., & Byers Hung, A. (2011). *Big data: The next frontier for innovation, competition, and productivity | McKinsey*. Retrieved from https://www.mckinsey.com/business-functions/digital-mckinsey/our-insights/big-data-the-next-frontier-for-innovation

Murillo, A. P., & Jones, K. M. L. (2018). The development of an undergraduate data curriculum: A model for maximizing curricular partnerships and opportunities. In G. Chowdhury, J. McLeod, V. Gillet, & P. Willett (Eds.), *Transforming digital worlds* (Vol. *10766*, pp. 282–291). https://doi.org/10.1177/0165551517748149.

Ortiz-Repiso, V., Greenberg, J., & Calzada-Prado, J. (2018). A cross-institutional analysis of data-related curricula in information science programmes: A focused look at the iSchools. *Journal of Information Science*, *44*(6), 768–784.

Varvel, V. E., Jr., Bammerlin, E. J., & Palmer, C. L. (2012). Education for data professionals: A study of current courses and programs. *ACM International Conference Proceeding Series*, 527–529. https://doi.org/10.1145/2132176.2132275.

Verma, A., Yurov, K. M., Lane, P. L., & Yurova, Y. V. (2019). An investigation of skill requirements for business and data analytics positions: A content analysis of job advertisements. *Journal of Education for Business*, *94*(4), 243–250. https://doi.org/10.1080/08832323.2018.152068.

Data Science Education in the iSchool Context

Sam Oh	Il-Yeol Song	Javed Mostafa	Yin Zhang	Dan Wu
Sungkyunkwan University, Seoul, South Korea samoh@g.skku.edu	Drexel University, Philadelphia, PA, USA songiy@drexel.edu	University of North Carolina at Chapel Hill, Chapel Hill, NC, USA jm@unc.edu	Kent State University, Kent, OH, USA yzhang4@kent.edu	Wuhan University, Wuhan, China woodan@whu.edu.cn

ABSTRACT

The Data Science (DS) has grown in depth, breadth, and relevance in recent years as a prominent multidisciplinary field. iSchools have been among many contributing units in DS education; however, the question remains as to what unique characteristics and core curricula iSchools can best fit in and provide in the DS education landscape. This panel presents the iSchool Data Science Curriculum Committee (iDSCC)'s initiatives to address this question and report on related progress. It will also engage discussion with and seek input from the conference audience in an effort to uncover additional input on the unique characteristics of DS education in the iSchool context and core DS curriculum for iSchools.

KEYWORDS

Data science; iSchool; curriculum; education

ASIS&T THESAURUS

Data science; education; information science education

BACKGROUND

In recent years, most iSchools have started offering DS curricula to various extents (courses, specializations, and programs) at the undergraduate and/or graduate level. To better develop and advance DS education in the iSchool context, the Board of Directors of the iSchools decided in March of 2019 to create the iSchool Data Science Curriculum Committee (iDSCC) and charged the committee to complete with the following tasks during 2019-2021:

A. Gather information on data science courses from all iSchools that have such courses at the bachelor's and master's level and are willing to participate in the study.
B. Analyze provided information to propose common elements for a standard iSchool curriculum that member schools could build on and use as they see fit.
C. Propose key aspects of a standard iSchool data science curriculum that could potentially be used for accreditation processes.

The primary aim of iDSCC is to build and recommend a unique DS education model and framework for iSchools that reflects the core concepts, values, expertise, and strengths. For example, the human-centered systems analysis is an important and unique dimension for iSchools to approach data science. Since its inception, iDSCC has planned and initiated several projects to address the committee charges. Several imminent works the iDSCC will engage include:

- Identifying unique characteristics of iSchools that distinguish us from other related IT programs;
- Reviewing related literature and existing DS curricula proposed by different academic disciplines such as CS and business schools;
- Reviewing existing DS programs;
- Analyzing job market and job description; and
- Creating a draft DS curriculum for UG and MS programs.

The specific details of the ongoing projects are described below and will be reported during the panel session:

1. Gathering related literature and reviewing DS education models from various disciplines

   The iDSCC has been collecting and reviewing any published framework and recommendations for DS education for iSchools. In addition, there are already a few recommended DS curricula published by different academic disciplines such as ACM, Park City Models, EDISON Framework, National Academy's DS for UG programs, BHEA, and INFORMS. The committee will review these published models and frameworks created by peer disciplines. This helps establish the iSchool identity in a broad and multi-faceted DS education landscape.

2. Analysis of Master's Degree Curriculum in Data Science

   We have collected information from about 100 universities in the iSchools Alliance and 18 universities with a master's degree in data science and 25 master programs in data

82nd Annual Meeting of the Association for Information Science & Technology | Melbourne, Australia | 19–23 October, 2019

DOI: 10.1002/pra2.00090

science. Among the 362 colleges and universities in other schools, 114 have a master's degree in data science and 124 have master's programs in data science. We extracted the master's degree project description, talent training objectives, ability expectations, curriculum name, curriculum description, and other information in the school's official website using word frequency analysis method, content analysis method, and other methods to summarize the characteristics of the master's degree program of data science.

At first, courses with similar content are considered to be the same course by analyzing the course descriptions collected. These programs are then divided into five categories based on discipline background: information/information and other disciplines, mathematics and statistics, computer science and engineering, business and economics, and others (interdisciplinary or other disciplines). Next, we count the frequency of courses in each category to summarize unique courses with subject characteristics and the common courses in all categories. The result is part of the curriculum model. We also analyze and summarize the skills development and capacity development mentioned in the program, distinguish the background of the subject, describe the setting characteristics of the Master's degree in Data Science under different backgrounds, and differentiate curriculum features of the professional master's degree and the academic master's degree. Finally, with reference to the predecessor research model, combined with the course data analysis, the unique curriculum system model for the master's degree in Data Science is summarized. This model is applicable to the master's degree program of data science in the context of various disciplines.

3. Conducting a job market and job advertisements analysis

   This project identified a sample of DS job advertisements specifically targeted toward iSchool graduates during 2006-2018 and conducted detailed analyses to answer the following questions:
   - Who are the employers targeting iSchool DS graduates?
   - What are the job titles?
   - What are the qualifications of the DS jobs?
   - What are the requirements of the DS jobs?
   - What are the major job functions?
   - What are the core skill sets?
   - What are the DS job trends over time for iSchool graduates?

4. Gathering input and building consensus among educators on iSchool DS programs

   This project aims to seek input and build consensus among a group of DS educators on the major requirements for a data science program in two broad categories:
   - Program input: 1) theoretical and generalizable knowledge, 2) skills and competencies, and 2) practices.
   - Program output: a profile or two of the students whom iSchool DS programs wish to train in terms of careers or jobs that they may pursue.

   The Delphi method is chosen to engage iSchools faculty in identifying and rating the importance of critical curriculum elements and best practices in a multiple-round element-raising and consensus-building process via a Web-based survey instrument designed for this study.

5. Conducting an iSchool DS graduate survey

   This project aims to foster the success of iSchool DS programs by surveying graduates for important knowledge and skills that make iSchool DS graduates successful as DS professionals and/or researchers. It also helps identify potential employers as well as areas where iSchool DS programs need to improve.

PANEL ORGANIZATION AND FORMAT

iDSCC co-chair and representative members will first present an overview of the committee's activities, followed by progress reports on the committee projects. The panel will then engage the audience with an open dialog to seek feedback on the committee's current and future efforts.

PROMOTION

The panel will be advertised among the SIG/ED members and the iSchool community. The event will be publicized in listservs of ASIST and ALISE.

PANELISTS

Sam Oh, moderator and iSchools Chair, is Professor at Sungkyunkwan University LIS and Data Science. His expertise lies in the fields of metadata design, social/big data analytics, and data/ontology modeling.

Javed Mostafa, panelist and co-chair of iDSCC, is Frances McColl Distinguished Term Professor at the University of North Carolina at Chapel Hill. He is the Director of the Carolina Health Informatics Program (chip.unc.edu) and the Director of the Laboratory of Applied Informatics Research. He has current research engagements in biomedical data mining, analysis, visualization, user interface design, and multi-modal human-computer interaction. His research concentrates on information retrieval problems, particularly related to search and user-system interactions in large-scale document/data repositories.

Dan Wu, panelist, iDSCC member, is Professor at the School of Information Management, Wuhan University. She is the Chair of Library Science Department and the Director of Human-Computer Interaction Team. Her research interests include information retrieval, information behavior, human-computer interaction, and digital library.

Yin Zhang, panelist, iDSCC member, is Professor at the School of Information, Kent State University. Her research and teaching areas include user information-seeking behavior, information uses and services, informetrics, scientometrics, and information technology applications.

EXPECTED OUTCOMES

By the end of the panel's presentations and discussions, panelists and audience members will share a basic understanding of 1) the current status of DS education in general and in the iSchool context in particular; 2) job requirements and expectations for iSchool DS graduates; 3) some unique characteristics of DS education in the iSchool context; and 4) approaches to build iSchool DS programs.

Bridging the Library and Information Science Research – Practice Gap: A Panel Discussion

Helen Partridge
University of Southern Queensland, Toowoomba, Australia
helen.partridge@usq.edu.au

Lisa M. Given
Swinburne University of Technology, Melbourne, Australia
lgiven@swin.edu.au

Elham Sayyad Abdi
University of Southern Queensland, Toowoomba, Australia
elham.sayyadabdi@usq.edu.au

George Buchanan
University of Melbourne, Melbourne, Australia
george.buchanan@unimelb.edu.au

Kate Bunker
Australian Library and Information Association, Canberra, Australia
kate.bunker@alia.org.au

Edward Luca
University of Sydney, Sydney, Australia
edward.luca@sydney.edu.au

Dana McKay
University of Melbourne, Melbourne, Australia
dana.mckay@unimelb.edu.au

Bhuva Narayan
University of Technology Sydney, Sydney, Australia
bhuva.narayan@uts.edu.au

ABSTRACT
The panel will explore the challenges and opportunities for bridging the library and information science (LIS) research practice gap in Australia. The panel brings together participants from the Research Assistance and Development for Australian Researchers (RADAR) Grant, an initiative of the Library and Information Science Research Australia (LISRA) project. The LISRA project is a three-year project aimed at encouraging and enabling research culture and practice within the Australian LIS sector.

KEYWORDS
research practitioners; research engagement; library and information science research; research-led practice

ASIS&T THESAURUS
Australia; Research and Development

INTRODUCTION
It is frequently noted that there is a divide between research and practice in library and information science (LIS) (Booth, 2003; Crowly, 2005; Haddow and Klobas, 2004); McMenemy, 2010). LIS researchers lament that practitioners are not applying research findings, and LIS practitioners say research is too "ivory tower" and not relevant to practice. Although there may be some truth to these statements, there are many points of collaboration and application of research across the sector, worldwide.

82nd Annual Meeting of the Association for Information Science & Technology | Melbourne, Australia | 19–23 October, 2019

DOI: 10.1002/pra2.00092

The purpose of this panel is to explore how LIS practitioners and researchers, as well as professional associations, can work together to bridge the research practice gap, and in so doing continue to advance the LIS profession and its impact on the individuals and communities we support. To achieve this purpose, the panel will include key stakeholders from the Research Assistance and Development for Australian Researchers (RADAR) Grant, an initiative of the Library and Information Science Research Australia (LISRA) project. In addition, to reviewing the panelists' "lessons learned", a broader discussion with attendees will explore the current challenges and opportunities for practitioners and researchers working together in LIS contexts. Although situated in the Australian context, the RADAR initiative, and the experiences of its key stakeholders, can provide insights to the LIS sector internationally.

LIBRARY AND INFORMATION SCIENCE RESEARCH AUSTRALIA (LISRA)
Library and Information Science Research Australia (LISRA) is a three-year project funded by the Australian Research Council. The project aims to encourage and enable research culture and practice within Australia's library and information science (LIS) profession. LISRA is being led by the University of Southern Queensland and Swinburne University of Technology, in partnership with the Australian Library and Information Association (ALIA) and National and State Libraries Australia (NSLA). More details

on the project can be found at the website (http://lisresearch.org.au) or Twitter (@LISResearchAU).

Research Assistance and Development for Australian Researchers (RADAR) Grant

The Research Assistance and Development for Australian Researchers (RADAR) Grant was developed as part of the LISRA project to foster collaborative research in Australia's LIS sector. The RADAR grants were designed to provide: (i) research funding to teams of academics and practitioners to explore a research problem that will contribute to knowledge and practice in LIS; and (ii) a supportive network of academics and practitioners to foster engagement and build capacity in LIS research practice.

All LIS academics and LIS practitioners living in Australia were eligible to apply. Projects were required to have a minimum of two people (an LIS academic and an LIS practitioner) to serve as "team co-leads". Projects could include other team members, including those drawn from other disciplines or other professional contexts, as needed to meet the project goals. Successful applications received up to $15,000 AUD to support the research activities.

All applications were evaluated by the LISRA Advisory Board using the following evaluation criteria:

- Is the project clearly described, is the problem well defined and grounded in the relevant literature, and is the research aim clearly stated?
- Is the project designed to be successfully completed within one year?
- Is the proposed approach, including the methodology/method(s) appropriate, and are the investigative procedures clearly explained?
- What is the significance of the proposed research to the library and information science community?
- Are outcomes, impact and deliverables specifically identified?
- Are sufficient resources and expertise available?
- Is there institutional commitment as evidenced by cost sharing to support the project?

Thirteen applications were received with three funded. The projects were conducted during the 2017 calendar year. The successful applicants participated in a range of activities that would assist in building a community of practice, as well as promoting and sharing experiences, and the findings of the research, within the Australian IS sector. The activities included, but were not limited to:

- Regularly (virtual) meetings throughout 2017 to guide project development (e.g. workshops on project management, recruiting, dissemination)
- Three blog posts posted to the LISRA website during 2017
- Attendance at the August 2018 the joint Australian and New Zealand LIS conference to disseminate project findings.
- A full paper submission on the project to a scholarly LIS journal
- Participation in a free online seminar to disseminate project findings.

The Three RADAR Projects

The three research projects funded by the RADAR Grant scheme were:

Non-library user immigrants: How can libraries support their information experience?

An understanding of people's engagement with information in any specific context can inform the design and development of interventions (e.g. programs, services) that support individuals' information needs in that context. This project, in two (i) research and (ii) implementation phases, investigated (i) non-library user refugees' engagement with information, and (ii) how a case public library applied the findings to refine their services and program. The outcome was a set of recommendations for service and program refinement in the case library in order to enable it to more comprehensively address the identified ways of engagement with information among the target population. Future implementation of the recommendations ensures that the experience of non-library user clients from the refugee background is recognized, supported in more effective ways and therefore enhanced by the library. Such enhancement in refugees' information experience empowers them for more informed and inclusive citizenry and provides libraries with an opportunity to contribute to the realization of social inclusion within the society.

This project was undertaken by LIS researchers, Elham Sayyad Abdi, from the University of Southern Queensland and Kathleen Smeaton from the University of Queensland, in collaboration with Debra Cooper, an LIS practitioner from Logan City Council.

We're all in this together: investigations of a single presentation for books in all formats

Libraries invest heavily in ebooks, but these resources are often underutilized. One of the reasons for this lack of uptake is based on user preference for browsing physical shelves when information seeking. Making ebooks in some way 'visible' at the library shelves is likely to improve both the uptake of ebooks, and user experience of the library. The purpose of this project was to create a blended library experience at the library shelves: the project team created software that when a user scanned the barcode of a physical book with their mobile phone returned topically related ebooks held by the library. In testing, the users surprised the research team: while this software was used at the library shelves, it was also used in other locations such as bookshops and users' homes. In addition to providing a blended library, the software was repurposed by users to take the library to a range of locations in their lives.

This project was undertaken by George Buchanan an LIS researcher at the University of Melbourne, in collaboration with Dana McKay an LIS researcher practitioner from Swinburne University of Technology.

The Role of Academic Libraries in Promoting Scholarly Communication Literacy: An Exploration of Open Access, Researcher Identity and Social Impact

This project examined issues relating to the perceptions and adoption of open access (OA) and institutional repositories (IR). The team used a survey research design to gather data from academics and other researchers in the humanities, arts and social sciences (HASS). The findings suggest that HASS researchers are highly influenced by traditional measures of quality, such as journal impact factor, and are less concerned with making their work more findable or promoting it through social media. This highlights a disconnect between researchers' desired outcomes and their efforts toward promoting their work. The findings also suggest that institutional policies have the potential to increase OA awareness and adoption. The team recommend that academic librarians engage with faculty through outreach and workshops to change perceptions of OA and the institutional repository.

The project was undertaken by a team of LIS practitioners and LIS researchers from the University of Technology Sydney: Bhuva Narayan, Senior Lecturer; Edward Luca, Academic Liaison; Mal Booth, University Librarian; Belinda Tiffen, Director of Library Resources; and, Ashley England, Leader of the Arts and Social Sciences Team.

PANEL OVERVIEW

This panel brings together key stakeholders from the RADAR Grant scheme to discuss their experiences in the design delivery of a research project that involved both LIS practitioners and LIS academic researchers. Each team combined research and practice in their own way, bringing a diversity of perspectives to the challenge of combining research with practice. The panel will also involve audience members in an interactive discussion by exploring all attendees' experiences of the challenges and opportunities for bridging the research-practice gap in LIS. This panel aims to foster conversations that will continue well after the session has finished.

The Panelists

Each panelist contributes unique insights to the proposed panel based on their experience as members of the LISRA project, and the RADAR scheme, and their research and practice in the LIS context.

Dr Helen Partridge is Professor and Pro Vice-Chancellor (Education) at the University of Southern Queensland. She is an adjunct Professor in the School of Information Systems, Queensland University of Technology, Australia. Helen is an active member of the Australian and international library and information profession. She has twice been elected to the Board of Directors of the Australian Library and Information Association, and was appointed a Fellow of the Association in 2012. Helen has been the secretary for the Library Theory and Research Standing Committee of the International Federation of Library and Information Associations, and coordinated the committee's project, *Research Librarian Partnership*, a mentoring program aimed at helping new professionals in the library sector develop their knowledge, skill and experience in undertaking research. Helen has received over $2 million AUD in research funding; her work focuses on the interplay between information, learning and technology. From 2009 to 2011 she worked with 11 Australian educational institutions on a project that established a framework for the education of the information professions in Australia for the twenty-first century. She has been a visiting Fellow at the Oxford Internet Institute, University of Oxford (2011) and the Berkman Center for Internet and Society and Society, Harvard University.

Dr. Lisa M. Given is Professor of Information Science and Associate Dean, Research and Development, for the Faculty of Health, Arts and Design at Swinburne University of Technology, Australia. She is a Past-President of the Association for Information Science and Technology and has served on the College of the Australian Research Council. Lisa is an Adjunct Professor in the School of Information Studies, Charles Sturt University (Australia), as well as in the Faculty of Arts (Digital Humanities), University of Alberta (Canada). A former Director of the International Institute for Qualitative Methodology (Canada), Lisa has received numerous grants and awards. She is Lead Investigator of a current ARC Linkage Project exploring research adoption by the wine industry and of an ARC Discovery Project looking at knowledge management practices in non-profit organizations. Lisa is also co-investigator for the ARC Linkage Project "Library and Information Science Research Australia," where she co-developed the Research Assistance & Development Australian Researchers Grant Program to provide a series of supportive activities to foster research collaboration in library and information science. She is co-author (with Donald O. Case) of *Looking for Information: A Survey of Research on Information Seeking, Needs, and Behavior* (2016, 4th edition).

Dr Elham (Ellie) Sayyad-Abdi is an information researcher. She has served as an Australian Fulbright Scholar-In-Residence at the University of the Pacific, California (AY 2018/19) and a lecturer in the Master of Information Science, Queensland University of Technology, Australia. A former convenor of the LIS Education in Developing Countries Special Interest Group at IFLA, and the secretary of the ASIS&T Asia-Pacific chapter, Ellie is currently co-chairing the Research Advisory Committee at the Australian Library and Information Association (ALIA). Her research interests lie in information experience, information literacy, social justice and translation of research to practice.

Dr George Buchanan is Associate Professor and Director of the University of Melbourne iSchool. His research is focused on how technology can help people find information more effectively, and spans mobile usability, search technology and psychology. He previously led the Center for Human-Computer Interaction Design at City, University of London. He has made major contributions to the Greenstone Digital Library software, which is in use by over 200,000 organizations worldwide. His current interests include how physical and digital libraries can boost creative problem solving and how to improve privacy and security online.

Kate Bunker AALIA (CP) is Director of Learning at the Australian Library and Information Association (ALIA). In this role, she manages ALIA education and professional development policies and guidelines including ALIA course accreditation. Kate is also interested in assisting library and information science professionals become LIS practitioner researchers.

Dr Dana McKay recently finished her PhD in information interaction, looking at how people browse for books. This work was born of ten years' practical experience as a user experience professional in an academic library, where the project described in this submission took place. Dana worked on a range of challenges in her professional role, including making user-centric interface decisions while implementing web scale search, understanding how readers approached the shelves, and understanding how library users used the study space available in the library. Dana's current research is similarly information focused and industry-engaged; she is working on information seeking and use problems with GLAM sector industry partners.

Edward Luca is a library practitioner and researcher. He is currently Manager, Academic Services (Medicine and Health, Health Sciences) at the University of Sydney Library. He previously worked as an Academic Liaison Librarian, and before that was Communication Officer at the University of Technology Sydney (UTS) Library. Edward writes and speaks on topics including information literacy, scholarly communication and user experience.

Dr Bhuva Narayan is a Senior Lecturer and Discipline Head for the Information and Knowledge Management Program at the University of Technology Sydney (UTS), Australia. She completed an MLIS from the iSchool at the University of Pittsburgh and a PhD from the Queensland University of Technology (QUT), Australia. Her research interests are in information behavior, human learning, design thinking, social media, open access, and social justice.

Structure of the Panel

Time (in minutes)	Activity
5	Helen Partridge will introduce the panel and provide an overview of the LISRA project.
5	Kate Bunker will discuss why ALIA became involved in the LISRA project and how it benefits and impacts the work of ALIA and the Australian LIS profession.
5	Lisa Given will provide an overview of the RADAR scheme.
25	The members of the three RADAR funded projects will provide a brief overview of their projects, with particular focus on development and implementation of a collaborative team involving both LIS practitioners, and LIS researchers.
30	Together the panelists will facilitate an interactive discussion. In small groups of 5 to 6, attendees will consider the following three questions in the context of building a culture and practice of LIS practitioner and LIS research collaboration: (i) one thing that does not foster collaboration and should be stopped; (ii) one thing that needs to be started to increase collaboration; (iii) one thing that works well and should be kept.
15	Each group will report back stating the top 2 responses to each of the three questions.
5	Lisa Given will review key points from the presentations and discussion.

REFERENCES

Booth, A. (2003). Bridging the research-practice gap? The role of evidence-based librarianship. *New Review of Information and Library Research*, *9*(1), 3–23.

Crowly, C. (2005). *Spanning the theory-practice divide in library and information science*. England: Scarecrow Press.

Haddow, G., & Klobas, J. (2004). Communication of research to practice in library and information science: Closing the gap. *Library & Information Science Research*, *26*(1), 29–43.

McMenemy, D. (2010). Fostering a research culture in UK library practice: barriers and solutions. *Library Review*, *59*(5), 321–324.

Teaching Technology in Library and Information Science: Preparing Students With Diverse Needs for the Challenges of an Interconnected World

Danielle Pollock
Simmons University, Boston, MA
danielle.pollock@simmons.edu

Rachel Williams
Simmons University, Boston, MA
rachel.williams@simmons.edu

Catherine Dumas
Simmons University, Boston, MA
catherine.dumas2@simmons.edu

Naresh Kumar Agarwal
Simmons University, Boston, MA
agarwal@simmons.edu

Sanda Erdelez
Simmons University, Boston, MA
erdelez@simmons.edu

ABSTRACT

In an increasingly interconnected world, information professionals are expected to be at the forefront of implementing and instructing others in using information technologies. Yet, it is a challenge for educators to leverage library and information science students' varying interests and experiences to develop technology curricula that addresses diverse student needs and prepares them to engage actively with current and emerging technologies throughout the course of their careers. In this interactive event, technology instructors at Simmons University come together to share their experience in designing and teaching technology courses through interactive demos and case studies. This is followed by an interactive Q&A and small-group brainstorming to address issues related to technology education. The event will promote discussion around developing curricula and pedagogy to promote students' abilities to use and implement technology in professional practice.

KEYWORDS

Curriculum; Information Technology; Information Technology Education; Pedagogy

ASIS&T THESAURUS

Information Technology; Curricula; Information Science Education

INTRODUCTION

For educators in library and information science (LIS) programs, addressing information technology in the curriculum involves equipping students to acknowledge and anticipate technology needs in a diverse, increasingly interconnected and technology-dependent world. Both an awareness of trends in LIS and adjacent fields and the ability to understand and adopt emerging technologies are part of the American Library Association (ALA)'s Core Competences of Librarianship (ALA, 2008; Saunders, 2019) and information technology--including the design, evaluation, and implementation of technologies--is one of six general areas included the American Society for Information Science and Technology (ASIS&T) Educational Guidelines (ASIS&T, 2002).

It is not enough for LIS programs and their graduates to respond to technology changes: our students are expected to be at the forefront in implementing and instructing others in using emerging technologies and are expected to exhibit these skills in a global context (Maceli & Burke, 2013; Riley-Huff & Rholes, 2011). Further, they will be expected to be able to apply professional values--including those surrounding social responsibility, digital inclusion, information access, privacy, and intellectual freedom--to the design and provision of information technologies across a variety of connected information environments (Buschman, 2018; Wharton, 2018).

While information technology skills have been identified as crucial by librarians and archivists and those who hire them (Burke, 2016; Irons Walch et al., 2006; Schwartz, 2016), beginning LIS students' previous experiences, skills, and comfort with information technology vary (Kules & McDaniel, 2010). Understanding the technology skill sets currently in demand in LIS is important to developing a robust technology curriculum that prepares students to be future practitioners in a technology-rich, connected world (see Maceli, 2015; Singh & Mehra, 2013). However, equally important is ensuring that all students develop the self-efficacy and curiosity needed to continue to engage with a changing technological landscape throughout the course of their careers. With this in mind, how do we, as educators, ensure that students are capable of implementing existing and emerging technologies in LIS? Further, how do we leverage students' own interests and experiences as technology users and citizens in a digitally connected world to develop

82nd Annual Meeting of the Association for Information Science & Technology | Melbourne, Australia | 19–23 October, 2019

DOI: 10.1002/pra2.00091

technology curricula and course content that addresses diverse student needs?

GOALS OF THE EVENT: SIMMONS UNIVERSITY AS CASE STUDY

In 2018, the Simmons University School of Library and Information Science (SLIS) began redevelopment of its technology curriculum, starting with its core "Technology for Information Professionals" course, one of three required classes in the program. A group of educators from diverse backgrounds (event co-presenters) are working together to make this course one that prepares students in using and creating current and emerging technologies. Using the SLIS experience as a case study, this event addresses the following topics in the context of teaching technology:

- Current and emerging technology trends
- Strategies for curriculum development around various levels of technology expertise and varying career goals (e.g. breadth versus depth in an area, assignments that are useful beyond class, etc.)
- Encouraging self-efficacy and curiosity in beginning students with varying levels of comfort with technology
- Leveraging students' own interests and experiences
- Aspects of diversity, equity and inclusion impacting technology development and use
- Providing troubleshooting support to students

EVENT STRUCTURE

Ideally, the presenters will be assembled in a U-shape at the front, allowing for better interaction among the presenters. The audience will be seated in concentric U-shapes mirroring the presenters to catalyze conversation between the presenters and the attendees. A volunteer will tweet (#teachingTechnology #asist2019) the questions and answers for those who are unable to attend the event. Questions for the presenters will also be solicited prior to the conference on the ASIS&T Community Site and through SIG-ED, which is sponsoring the event. Attendees can transmit their questions electronically to the designated volunteer(s), who will share them with the event moderator, or submit them via index cards if they do not wish to use electronic media, in order to maintain the anonymity of the questions' source and promote the free exchange of ideas and perspectives. Additionally, we will use vevox.com for live polling and engage participants throughout the event.

Introduction (5 minutes)

The event moderator, Sanda Erdelez, will facilitate an introduction of the presenters, including highlights of their past experience.

Interactive Demo/Case Studies/Scenarios (40 minutes)

The four presenters will each provide a 10-min case study or demonstration centered around curriculum and technology teaching issues in their respective teaching experience, and address what they believe are the most important issues and priorities for course coverage when teaching technology in LIS.

Interactive Discussion & Q&A (35 minutes)

Thereafter, the moderator will ask presenters the questions transmitted by the volunteer(s). For more audience engagement, the presenters will also include an interactive poll and small group brainstorming.

Concluding thoughts (10 minutes)

Each of the presenters will be asked to provide a summary of one key challenge and its solution when teaching technology in today's information context. Finally, the moderator will ask each presenter to offer one final piece of advice for the attendees that was not covered previously during the discussion.

PRESENTERS

Sanda Erdelez (Moderator) is Professor and Director of Simmons SLIS. Erdelez earned her PhD at the School of Information Studies at Syracuse University while on a Fulbright scholarship. She received her LL.B. and LL.M. degrees from the University of Osijek Law School (Croatia) and PhD in information transfer from Syracuse University. Her research interests include human information behavior, human-computer interaction and usability evaluation in online environments. She has been internationally recognized for her pioneering research in the areas of information encountering and opportunistic discovery of information. Erdelez has over ten years of experience teaching *Introduction to Information Technology* for LIS professionals at the University of Missouri, and is currently engaged in XR@Simmons Usability Lab, which seeks to investigate usability of virtual and augmented reality information systems. She has been an active member of the Association for Information Science & Technology (ASIS&T) since 1987, and has served in numerous leadership roles.

Danielle Pollock is an Assistant Professor at SLIS. Dr. Pollock's research is centered on the drivers and consequences of changes in information behavior in research-intensive communities. Her most recent work has focused on research data management, team science, and innovation adoption in health care. Prior to receiving her PhD from the University of Tennessee, Pollock worked for a number of years as an information professional, most recently as a technical librarian for a national laboratory. Her background includes special, public, and academic libraries. Her teaching areas include technology for information professionals, metadata, and intersectionality and information technology.

HTML, CSS, and LIS - Applying What You Already Know Pollock will discuss teaching LIS students basic web coding skills and focus on the importance of guiding beginning technology students to make connections between these lessons and LIS core values, as well as providing an understanding of how a required technology course can benefit them as information professionals in real-world settings, even if they do not plan on pursuing technology-focused careers. Pollock will provide a brief demonstration of part of an introductory lesson from the required LIS 488 Technology for Information Professionals class, focusing on strategies for enabling all students, regardless of previous experience with technology, to leverage their existing skill sets and interests as they work to acquire new skills and master new concepts.

Rachel Williams is an Assistant Professor at SLIS. She earned her PhD from the University of Wisconsin-Madison's School of Library and Information Studies. Williams' research areas are rooted in issues of social justice, professionalization, and librarianship. Most recently, her work looks at how public library workers navigate issues of professionalization and work boundaries when providing consumer health and social services information to people in crisis. Her teaching areas are technology for information professionals, database design, and public libraries. Her professional background is in public and corporate librarianship.

Database Design and Teaching Tech to the Nontechie Underlying many of the technology based tools or resources information professionals rely on is a well designed database, made available by good programming and web design. Williams' presentation will describe the value of understanding database design, and how students can activate their own experiences and knowledge to successfully create databases for professional or personal use. Williams will discuss how she uses case studies to teach database design concepts and help students gain confidence in working with database tools. Finally, she will provide a brief demonstration from her Database Design course. The demo will highlight how these projects help students create connections with one another and how their own experiences and learning these technologies can lead to a variety of potential career paths.

Catherine Dumas is an Assistant Professor at SLIS. Dumas earned her PhD in Information Science from the University of Albany, an M.S. in Information Science from the University of Albany, and a B.A. from the College of Saint Rose in Albany, NY. Her research is motivated by data generated by platforms potentially used for online collective action or digital activism. Her teaching areas include technology for information professionals, introduction to programming, and systems analysis in information services. Dumas is very active in ASIS&T and its SIGs.

Why Program? Dumas will discuss why it is important for Information Science & Technology (IST) professionals to learn how to program. IST professionals work in a variety of information-centered organizations, including data processing centers, information centers, corporations, research centers, government, universities, libraries, archives and museums. Within these organizations, there is data that needs to be managed, organized, retrieved, stored, analyzed. Knowing a programming language like Python will enable IST professionals to work more efficiently with data. Dumas will also demo a lab from LIS 485, Introduction to Programming, and discuss her pedagogical strategies for teaching LIS graduate students how to write code in Python.

Naresh Agarwal is an Associate Professor at SLIS. He earned his PhD from the National University of Singapore (NUS)'s Department of Information Systems, School of Computing. Agarwal's research area is information behavior and knowledge management — the way people look for information and the contextual factors that impact their choice of information sources. His teaching areas are technology and web development, theories of information science, knowledge management, and evaluation of information services. He has held various leadership positions at ASIS&T. Prior to entering the doctoral program at NUS, Agarwal worked for six years in technology roles in the voice-over-IP, bioInformatics, and digital cinema industries.

User-centered Web Development - Teaching to Designers Versus Developers Agarwal will discuss the opportunities and challenges in teaching LIS 467 Web Development & Information Architecture, a course with rapidly changing best practices and developments across semesters, and the difficulty in deciding on what and how much to cover when students come with varying levels of comfort with technology, and those who are more comfortable with the design aspects versus the development aspects. He will go through the course syllabus, provide a brief demonstration of course content, and discuss and demonstrate challenges in teaching this class face-to-face versus online.

CONCLUSION

In this event, faculty members with diverse technology expertise will share their experiences and provide demos in designing and teaching technology courses in LIS. The interactive discussion between presenters and audience members will cover a range of issues exploring learning in a technology driven information context. The event should benefit participants by advancing curriculum development, pedagogy, and thinking as we prepare students to face a rapidly changing information technology landscape. The main takeaway will be initiating a conversation about how we, as LIS educators, should approach technology curricula development.

REFERENCES

American Library Association. (2008). *Core Competences.* Retrieved from http://www.ala.org/educationcareers/careers/corecomp/corecompetences

American Society for Information Science and Technology (2002). *ASIST Educational Guidelines.* Retrieved from http://www.asis.org/Board/educational_guidelines.html

Burke, J. J. (2016). Survey says…: How library staff members are using technology. In *Neal-Schuman library technology companion* (5th ed., pp. 15–27). Chicago, IL: Neal-Schuman.

Buschman, J. (2018). The new technocracy: Positioning librarianships' core values in relationship to technology is a much taller order than we think. In P. D. Fernandez & K. Tilton (Eds.), *Applying library values to emerging technology: Decision-making in the age of open access, maker spaces, and the ever-changing library* (pp. 35–54). Chicago, IL: Association of College and Research Libraries.

Irons Walch, V., Beaumont, N., Yakel, E., Bastian, J., Zimmelman, N., Davis, S., & Diffendal, A. (2006). A* CENSUS (Archival census and education needs survey in the United States). *The American Archivist*, *69*(2), 291–419.

Kules, B., & McDaniel, J. (2010). LIS program expectations of incoming students' technology knowledge and skills. *Journal of Education for Library and Information Science*, *51*(4), 222–232.

Maceli, M. (2015). Creating tomorrow's technologists: Contrasting information technology curriculum in North American library and information science graduate programs against Code4lib job listings. *Journal of Education for Library and Information Science*, *56*(3), 198–212.

Maceli, M., & Burke, J. J. (2016). Technology skills in the workplace: Information professionals' current use and future aspirations. *Information Technology and Libraries*, *35*(4), 35–62.

Riley-Huff, D. A., & Rholes, J. M. (2011). Librarians and technology skill acquisition: Issues and perspectives. *Information Technology and Libraries*, *30*(3).

Saunders, L. (2019). Core and more: Examining foundational and specialized content in library and information science. *Journal of Education for Library and Information Science*, *60*(1), 3–34.

Schwartz, M. (2016). Top skills for tomorrow's librarians. *Library Journal*, *38-39*.

Singh, V., & Mehra, B. (2013). Strengths and weaknesses of the information technology curriculum in library and information science graduate programs. *Journal of Librarianship and Information Science*, *45*(3), 219–231.

Wharton, L. (2018). Ethical implications of digital tools and emerging roles for academic librarians. In P. D. Fernandez & K. Tilton (Eds.), *Applying library values to emerging technology: Decision-making in the age of open access, maker spaces, and the ever-changing library* (pp. 35–54). Chicago, IL: Association of College and Research Libraries.

Technical and Policy Underpinnings of FAIR Data Principles

Jian Qin
Syracuse University,
Syracuse, NY, USA
jqin@syr.edu

Imma Subirats Coll
AIMS, Food and Agriculture Organization (FAO) of the United Nations
imma.subirats@gmail.com

Marcia Lei Zeng
Kent State University,
Kent, OH, USA
mzeng@kent.edu

Brian Dobreski
University of Tennessee,
Knoxville, TN, USA
bdobresk@utk.edu

ABSTRACT

At the trajectory of exponential data growth and FAIR (Findable, Accessible, Interoperable and Re-usable) requirements, organizations face the data management and publishing challenges in support of effective data discovery and publishing activities. This panel brings researchers and practitioners who have researched and practiced in managing datasets and providing discovery services to share their experience and expertise in addressing the challenges and proactively responding to trends in research data management, curation, sharing, and reuse.

KEYWORDS

Research Data Management; Data curation; Metadata interoperability; Knowledge representation for data

ASIS&T THESAURUS

Metadata standards; Knowledge and information; Knowledge organization systems

The FAIR Data Principles address the findability, accessibility, interoperability, and reusability of research data. The data mentioned in the FAIR principles include not only the data and supplementary materials such as algorithms, tools, and workflows that led to that data but also the metadata sufficiently rich and accompanied by persistent identifier (LIBRE, 2017; Wilkinson et al., 2016). Current data curation and management practices, however, face tremendous challenges in meeting the FAIR requirements and one of the grand challenges among all is "to improve knowledge discovery through assisting both humans, and their computational agents, in the discovery of, access to, and integration and analysis of, task-appropriate scientific data and other scholarly digital objects" (Wilkinson et al., 2016). In this panel, we will focus on the two key aspects of the grand challenge: technical and policy.

82nd Annual Meeting of the Association for Information Science & Technology | Melbourne, Australia | 19–23 October, 2019

DOI: 10.1002/pra2.00093

The technical challenge in providing FAIR data owes a large part to current metadata representation practices among repositories and the infrastructural support in performing metadata operations. Although different metadata standards and schemas have been developed in standardizing the description of datasets, the level of description is far from "sufficiently rich" or specific enough as the gene regulation and expression analysis example mentioned in Wilkinson et al. (2016). As the volume in data repositories grows at a fast pace, e.g., in Data.govalone, the number of datasets has increased from 949 in 2013 to 109,106 in 2018 (Data.gov, 2019), we face the dilemma that manual metadata description for datasets cannot keep up with the pace of data growth while the metadata generated by automatic methods have quality gaps. Part of such challenges are related to the intrinsic complexity and diversity of datasets, while others are broader issues related to the technical competencies of metadata systems and behavioral and cultural aspects of researchers' data practice.

The policy aspect of FAIR data principles refers to a wide range of issues related to how institutions react to the FAIR data requirements by institutionalizing support and practice guidelines for research data management, sharing, and reuse. There has been pressure on good data management rising from new requirements for publishing research results in journals, for example, the *Science* magazine requires data and other supplemental materials to be submitted at the time of manuscript submission, and has specific guidelines for preferred data repositories for depositing the data and supplemental materials when submitting manuscripts (AAAS, 2019). In addition, *Science* also requires authors to provide their Open Researcher and Contributor ID (ORCID) as part of the submission. Linking datasets with related publications for better data and knowledge discovery has been one of the goals since day one of data management. Most research data repositories such as GenBank, Dryad, and Dataverse offer this capability when authors submitting the data. By entering IDs for authors, datasets, and publications, the role of metadata in data management and publishing goes beyond describing individual datasets to establish links between datasets and publications, which extends to the links for authors and other resources.

At the trajectory of exponential data growth and FAIR requirements, how do organizations address the data management and publishing challenges in support of effective data discovery and publishing activities? What trends should we be aware of in relation to metadata standards for data management, curation, sharing, and reuse? What can and should we do as a community of practice for data management, curation, sharing, and reuse? How to ensure the interoperability of metadata that describing different types of resources such as bibliographic and research datasets? This panel will bring researchers and practitioners who have been engaged in FAIR data management and metadata deployment for research datasets to share their experience and expertise in addressing the above questions.

The panelists will present on the following topics:

Imma Subirats Coll (FAO) & Marcia Zeng (Kent State University): Ensuring AGRIS metadata framework's interoperability to support the management and access of bibliographic and research data

AGRIS, a global public service provided by the Agricultural Information Management Standards (AIMS) of FAO of the United Nations, has been providing access to bibliographic information resources on agricultural science and technology worldwide since 1975. This presentation reports the new efforts of the AGRIS on its metadata framework, addressing the interoperability of the metadata structure that unifies the management and access of bibliographic and research data. The new efforts have resulted a new function which enables users search for thousands open datasets through AGRIS since May 2019. Ensuring the interoperability of the metadata framework is the key when managing diverse resources crossing many boundaries such as resource types, languages, geographic regions, providers, and domains.

Brian Dobreski (UT-Knoxville): Placing Archival Items in the Web of Data

Linked data practices have opened new opportunities for archives for moving beyond collection-level records and representing, sharing, and leveraging metadata on individual items. This item-level metadata can facilitate innovative new topics and approaches in digital humanities research, but its preparation is far from easy. This presentation reviews the current technical challenges associated with representing and sharing item-level metadata from archives on the Semantic Web, and highlights ongoing work on the Linked Archives model, a modular, task-driven approach to supporting metadata availability, discovery, and reuse at the item level.

Jian Qin (Syracuse University): How well linked are biomedical data repositories? An assessment of data linkability of GenBank and related repositories.

This presentation reports a survey of linking mechanisms across the data repositories and databases for biomedical research data at the National Center of Biotechnology Information (NCBI) and their roles in meeting the FAIR data requirements.

The intended audience of this panel includes researchers and practitioners who are interested in learning about the FAIR principles and issues in supporting data discovery through good research data management.

Each panelist in this panel will give a 15-minute presentation and leave an half an hour at the end for the panel to interact with the audience.

BIOINFORMATION FOR THE PANELISTS

Imma Subirats has been working as senior knowledge and information management officer at the Food and Agriculture Organization of the United Nations (FAO) since 2006. She provides advice for standards, tools and good practices for the management and exchange of data to academic, research, private and governmental institutions worldwide. She is also actively promoting open access and open data in the agricultural research context. In recent years, she has been working on the facilitation of the AIMS community and portal, space for accessing and discussing information management standards, tools and methodologies with the objective to connect information specialists worldwide to support the implementation of structured and linked information and knowledge.

Marcia Lei Zeng is Professor at School of Information, Kent State University. Her major research interests include knowledge organization systems (taxonomy, thesaurus, ontology, etc.), Linked Data, metadata and markup languages, database quality control, multilingual and multi-culture information processing, and digital libraries for cultural objects. She has published more than 80 papers and five books and given 200+ national and international conference presentations, invited lectures and keynote speeches. She was the P.I. and Co-P.I. of two National Science Foundation's (NSF) National Science Digital Library (NSDL) projects. She currently is the P.I. of an IMLS funded Linked Data project. In 2014 she was elected inaugural chair of the Dublin Core Metadata Initiative (DCMI) Advisory Board. Zeng was recognized by Kent State University for Outstanding Research and Scholarship in 2014 and received the President's Faculty Excellence Award in 2016.

Brian Dobreski, PhD, is an assistant professor of iSchool at University of Tennessee-Knoxville. His research has centered around knowledge organization in various forms of systems, such as databases, classifications, catalogs, and archives. He specifically looks at knowledge organization in heritage settings, such as libraries, archives and museums. He is a recipient of the Eugene Garfield Doctoral Fellowship for his dissertation.

Jian Qin is Professor at the iSchool, Syracuse University. The areas of her research interest include metadata, knowledge and data modeling, scientific communication, research networks, and research data management. Her research has received support from Institute for Museum and Library Services (IMLS) and National Science Foundation (NSF) for projects in science data literacy, research data management, and big metadata analytics Jian Qin has published widely in national and international research journals and conferences. She was the co-author of the book *Metadata* and co-editor for several special journal issues on knowledge discovery in databases and knowledge representation.

REFERENCES

AAAS. (2019). *Science Journals: Editorial policies*. Data deposition. Retrieved from https://www.sciencemag.org/authors/science-journals-editorial-policies

Data.gov. (2019). *Data published per month*. Retrieved from https://www.data.gov/metric/federalagency/dataset-published-per-month

LIBRE. (2017). *Implementing FAIR data principles: The role of libraries*.

Wilkinson, M. D., Dumontier, M., Aalbersberg, I. J., Appleton, G., Axton, M., Baak, A., ... Mons, B. (2016). The FAIR Guiding Principles for scientific data management and stewardship. *Scientific Data, 3*, 160018. https://www.nature.com/articles/sdata201618

Digital Equity for Marginalised and Displaced Peoples

Anne Gilliland
UCLA, Los Angeles, USA
gilliland@gseis.ucla.edu

Sue McKemmish
Monash University, Melbourne, Australia
sue.mckemmish@monash.edu

Gregory Rolan
Monash University, Melbourne, Australia
greg.rolan@monash.edu

Barbara Reed
Recordkeeping Innovation, Sydney, Australia
b.reed@records.com.au

ABSTRACT

Upholding human rights – in particular for marginalised and displaced peoples – depends on exercising rights in data, information and records. In considering these information rights we face the challenge of designing ethical, adaptive, and inclusive information systems and technologies that support the actualisation of human rights, social justice, and Indigenous and First Nations sovereignty. Too often systems designed for an uncritical and generalised "happy centre" fail those on the margins, in all of their individualised complexity.

The purpose of this panel will be to introduce an international initiative aimed at addressing this challenge, and to explore a developing research agenda for tackling the broad range of socio-technical issues that comprise this wicked problem. It is hoped that this panel will galvanise the community towards action and engagement with this programme or its goals.

KEYWORDS

Records; recordkeeping; archives; data; rights; marginalised; displaced; social; informatics

ASIS&T THESAURUS

Social Informatics; Information Infrastructure; Persons

INTRODUCTION

Human rights for marginalised and displaced peoples include general human rights as well as those relating to specific peoples such as Indigenous human rights; and the rights of particular groups, such as refugees and children in out-of-home Care (note: we use the capitalised term "Care" to denote the ironic connotations of manifestly uncaring treatment, without the typographically heavy-handedness of continually enclosing the word in quotation marks – see Wilson & Golding, 2016). Such rights are articulated in international conventions and declarations, national instruments, and local jurisprudence. However, the actualisation of these rights depends on exercising rights in data, information and records.

82nd Annual Meeting of the Association for Information Science & Technology | Melbourne, Australia | 19–23 October, 2019

DOI: 10.1002/pra2.00094

For example:

- Refugees worldwide lack access to and control over their data, resulting in inability to exercise their rights under the United Nations (UN) Convention and Protocol Relating to the Status of Refugees 1951/1967; denial of asylum claims; return of displaced individuals into dangerous spaces; statelessness; separation of and difficulties in reuniting families; and heightened vulnerability for women and children (Gilliland, 2017).
- In the UK, Australia and Canada, many inquiries have highlighted the failure of information and recordkeeping systems to meet the lifelong identity, memory, cultural, accountability and information accessibility challenges for those caught up in child welfare and protection (for example, RCIRCSA, 2017). Care systems – including their operational and archival information systems – in the 20th and early 21st centuries often impede the exercise of their rights of the child as set down in the United Nations (1990) Convention.
- Throughout the world, colonisation has had and continues to have a devastating effect on Indigenous peoples (Ladner, 2017; Sherwood, 2009). Our information and recordkeeping systems continue as instruments of colonisation that often exacerbate rather than ameliorate the trauma of loss of knowledge, language and connection to Country. Indigenous peoples, UN rapporteurs, inquiries, and research findings frequently point to the failure of information and recordkeeping governance frameworks, policies and systems to support the actualization of rights under the UN Declaration on the Human Rights of Indigenous Peoples (2007). Too often they fail to support the recovery of Indigenous knowledge or provide evidence to support recovery of identity, family link-ups, and Native Title claims. Notably, such recommendations from the Australian Royal Commission into Aboriginal Deaths in Custody (RDADC, 1991) and Bringing Them Home report (Australian Human Rights Commission, 1997)) have never been implemented.

In contexts such as these, we face the challenge of designing ethical, adaptive, and inclusive information systems and technologies that support the actualisation of human rights, social justice, and Indigenous and First Nations sovereignty.

The purpose of this panel will be to introduce an international initiative aimed at addressing this challenge, and explore a developing research agenda for tackling the broad range of socio-technical issues that comprise this wicked problem.

ISSUES

Data, information, and records should be instruments for identity, memory, cultural heritage and safety, security, well-being, and accountability (Evans, McKemmish, & Rolan, 2017). However technological advances are (re)consolidating political and economic informational power at the centre, with divisive societal implications (Castells, 2010). Too often systems designed for an uncritical and generalised "happy centre" of use cases fail those on the margins, in all of their individualised complexity.

There is increasing evidence that embedded biases and values in data-driven software design and big data collection have particularly adverse impacts for marginalised and disempowered groups (Eubanks, 2018). In each of these instances, technologies and systems designed to support the "big-data" society are emerging as a root cause or exacerbating force of disenfranchisement of the most vulnerable.

The issues to be considered include:

1. Creating a platform of information rights to support enabling and actualizing human rights, and investigating whether information rights should themselves be recognised as fundamental human rights.
2. Developing innovative, people-centred data technologies that establish and maintain lifelong, rights-based information, identity, memory, cultural heritage, evidence and accountability needs of marginalised and displaced peoples in human rights, social justice and post-conflict societies.
3. Considering how marginalised and displaced peoples can be empowered through innovative, people-centred, culturally appropriate data technologies.
4. Investigating how to co-design trauma-informed data, information and records frameworks, reference models. Infrastructures, systems and technologies that embed people-centred values and principles
5. Exploring ways in which smart and secure information technologies may be designed to enable exercise of data sovereignties and rights in data, information and records, and provide crucial underpinning for the actualisation of human rights.
6. Developing equitable, transparent, accountable governance frameworks for data, information, recordkeeping and the deployment of AI, cybersecurity and optimisation technologies to support human rights, social justice and digital sovereignty.
7. Researching the cultural dimensions of complex transnational information ecologies in human rights, social justice and post-conflict societies, including translation strategies to mitigate against language colonisation.

PANEL AGENDA

The initiative will have convened a meeting of the foundation institutions (UCLA, UCL, U-Toronto, and Monash University) and other interested parties in July. The aim of this proposed panel is to introduce this programme to the broader community with a view to encourage participation. The panel will cover the forgoing material before opening up to the floor, and prompting discussion of the issues, goals, and methods for this research agenda.

The panel members and their contributions will be as follows:

Professor Sue McKemmish from Monash University has a proven track record of collaborative research partnerships with Care and Indigenous communities, the archival professional community, and archival institutions. She is engaged in major research and standards initiatives relating to the use of metadata in records and archival systems, information resource discovery and smart information portals, Australian Indigenous archives, and the development of more inclusive archival educational programmes that meet the needs of diverse communities. She, has published extensively on recordkeeping in society, records continuum theory, recordkeeping metadata, and archival systems, and is a Laureate of the Australian Society of Archivists.

Professor McKemmish will introduce the initiative, together with possible models for collaboration and governance. She will then provide a brief overview of the foregoing discussion of issues.

Barbara Reed from Recordkeeping Innovation is a long time records, archives and information professional with consulting experience in all levels of Australian government, private sector and not-for-profits. She is widely published in academic and professional journals and currently specialises in strategic advice, standards writing, digital archives and records. Her interests include strategic alignment, innovation in adopting new technologies for recordkeeping, recordkeeping metadata, standards writing, and digital records and archives.

Barbara Reed will develop this background by presenting a number of scenarios for discussion. It is expected that these scenarios may be used in the discussion to draw out the complexities, issues and challenges of working in this area.

Professor Anne J. Gilliland is Associate Dean for Information Studies in the Graduate School of Education & Information Studies, and Professor and Director of the Center for Information as Evidence, Department of Information Studies, and a faculty affiliate of the Center for Digital Humanities at the University of California Los Angeles (UCLA). She is the director of the Archival Education and Research Initiative (AERI), and a Fellow of the Society of American Archivists. Her research and teaching relate broadly to the history, nature, human impact and technologies associated with archives, recordkeeping and memory, particularly in translocal and international contexts. She has been instrumental in opening up a new field of human security informatics and currently co-directs a global project on Refugee Rights in Records (the R3 Project).

Professor Gilliland will outline the archival and information sciences research agenda with a view to obtain feedback, suggestions, and engagement in the programme.

Dr Gregory Rolan has had extensive experience in systems architecture and design, both in industry where he was a co-author of three patents, and in his current role as Research Fellow at Monash University. He has developed a domestic and international network of collaboration and support through involvement in various research networks, as well as the international archiving and standards-setting community.

Dr Rolan will introduce some technical challenges that have thus far been identified in this problem area. These include issues in recordkeeping informatics; data science; optimisation and reasoning; and cybersecurity.

CONCLUSION

This initiative promises to be a world-first international collaboration, tackling this significant problem domain. Whilst significant planning has been performed to draw together the foundation partners, the scope and scale of the challenges are such that buy-in will be needed from across the ASIS&T community to achieve the necessary transformational change on a global level. It is hoped that this panel will galvanise the community towards action and engagement with this programme or its goals.

REFERENCES

Australian Human Rights, Commission. (1997). *Bringing them home: National Inquiry into the Separation of Aboriginal and Torres Strait Islander Children from their Families*. Retrieved from https://www.humanrights.gov.au/sites/default/files/content/pdf/social_justice/bringing_them_home_report.pdf

Castells, M. (2010). *The information age: Economy, society and culture*. Chichester, West Sussex; Malden, MA: Wiley-Blackwell.

Eubanks, V. (2018). *Automating inequality how high-tech tools profile, police, and punish the poor*. New York, NY: St. Martin's Press.

Evans, J., McKemmish, S., & Rolan, G. (2017). Critical approaches to archiving and recordkeeping in the continuum. *Journal of Critical Library and Information Studies*, *1*(2).

Gilliland, A. (2017). A matter of life and death. A critical examination of the role of official records and archives in supporting the agency of the forcibly displaced. *Journal of Critical Library and Information Studies*, *1*(2).

Ladner, K. (2017). 150 years and waiting: Will Canada become an honourable nation? In K. Ladner & M. Tait (Eds.), *Surviving Canada: Indigenous peoples celebrate 150 years of betrayal* (pp. 398–413). Winnipeg: ARP.

RCIRCSA. (2017). *Final Report. Royal commission into institutional responses to child sexual abuse*. Retrieved from http://www.childabuseroyalcommission.gov.au/

RCADC. (1991). *Royal commission into aboriginal deaths in custody - Final Report*. Retrieved from http://www.austlii.edu.au/au/other/IndigLRes/rciadic/

Sherwood, J. (2009). Who is not coping with colonization? Laying out the map for decolonization. *Australasian Psychiatry*, *17*(1_suppl), S24–S27.

United Nations. (1990). *Convention on the rights of the child*. Retrieved from https://www.ohchr.org/en/professionalinterest/pages/crc.aspx

United Nations Commission on Human Rights. (2007). *United Nations declaration on the rights of indigenous peoples*. Retrieved from http://www.un.org/esa/socdev/unpfii/documents/DRIPS_en.pdf

Wilson, J. Z., & Golding, F. (2016). Latent scrutiny: Personal archives as perpetual mementos of the official gaze. *Archival Science*, *16*(1), 93–109. https://doi.org/10.1007/s10502-015-9255-3.

Data Science Research and Practice: High Time for Synergy

Abebe Rorissa
University at Albany, State University of New York, Albany, New York, USA
arorissa@albany.edu

Lisa Federer
National Library of Medicine, National Institutes of Health, Bethesda, Maryland, USA
lisa.federer@nih.gov

Loni Hagen
University of South Florida, Tampa, Florida, USA
lonihagen@usf.edu

Jeonghyun (Annie) Kim
University of North Texas, Denton, Texas, USA
jeonghyun.kim@unt.edu

James Andrews
University of South Florida, Tampa, Florida, USA
jimandrews@usf.edu3

ABSTRACT

Rapid increase in the rate of information and communication technology innovations resulted in the Big Data phenomenon and, in turn, led to challenges in data curation, management, processing, access, preservation, and dissemination. To effectively address these challenges, synergistic collaborations and partnerships between researchers and practitioners need to be established. For research to inform practice, and vice versa, the ASIS&T community, specifically those engaged in data science research and practice, need to regularly share their ideas, issues, findings, and best practices so that this young sub-discipline can grow and thrive. We believe a suitable time has arrived for all stakeholders to deliberate on how best to create synergy between researchers and practitioners in order to help set the agenda for the near and distant future. To that end, we are proposing an interactive panel where panelists will lead a discussion by researchers and practitioners to identify any gaps with respect to data science research and practice to collaboratively find ways to address them.

KEYWORDS

Big Data; Data Science; Research; Practitioner; Synergy

ASIS&T THESAURUS

Information Science; Big Data

INTRODUCTION

Because of an astronomical and unprecedented increase in the number and rate of information and communication technology innovations, massive amounts of data and information are being generated every day, creating what is often termed "big data." Big data enabled and necessitated businesses, governments, and other organizations to harness the power of data science to improve their competitiveness, effectiveness, and efficiency. In addition to being a technological opportunity (Boyd & Crawford, 2012), big data is an essential element of the information or digital age and is an integral component of information service provision by information agencies. In turn, this creates challenges for individuals, practitioners, and institutions involved in data capture, process, analysis, interpretation, management, preservation, dissemination, and access. These challenges span a variety of industries and fields, including marketing (Tirunillai & Tellis, 2014) and finance (Jie & Chen, 2015), and fundamentally affects the scientific, academic, and education realms (Gupta, Goul, & Dinter, 2015; Strawn, 2012). Importantly, these challenges require an understanding of the complexities inherent to big data, such as its size (Laney, 2001), breadth, depth (Lazer et al., 2009), and the technical limitations of the tools that are used to "capture, store and analyze" such data (Franks, 2012; Zicari et al., 2016).

The challenges can most effectively be addressed with synergistic collaborations between researchers and practitioners that can ultimately lead to maximizing the output and quality of each other's efforts. Therefore, if research is to inform practice, and vice versa, the ASIS&T community in general, and those engaged in data science research and practice in particular, need to regularly come together and share their ideas, discuss issues, implement solutions based on findings, and develop best practices so that this young sub-discipline can grow, thrive, and fulfill its potential. We believe a suitable time has arrived for all stakeholders to engage in discourse with a goal of creating synergies between communities of researchers and practitioners in order to set the agenda for the near and long-term future. To that end, we propose this interactive panel.

82nd Annual Meeting of the Association for Information Science & Technology | Melbourne, Australia | 19–23 October, 2019

DOI: 10.1002/pra2.00095

In this panel session, panelists will lead the audience in a discussion of the need for concerted efforts by both researchers and practitioners, among others. Panelists and members of the audience will identify any gaps with respect to data science research and practice and collaboratively find ways to address them so that the research community and all data-related professions could realize the potential benefits of the data science revolution.

Each of the four panelists and the panel moderator will give a short, 5 minute, presentation where they provide background information for the discussions based on their research and/or practical experience. Panelists will then engage the audience in an interactive discussion for about 50 minutes by posing the following discussion questions.

- How do we as information scientists/information professionals define and describe "data science"? Is it a subset of information science or a superset of information science?
- Is data science a threat or opportunity for the information science field?
- Governments, industry, healthcare, and academic institutions collect and store enormous amounts of data. How can researchers, information professionals, and data scientists collaborate to address common data management and analytics problems?
- Data science education: do we need to teach data science and data analytics to information professionals? If so, what should be our approach? What would be the core set of data science competencies for information professionals?
- If a data scientist and/or researcher wants to collaborate with other information professionals and practitioners, how can they go about it? What are the urgent research questions that need to be answered using data science approaches?
- What logistical impediments might there be to collaboration across disciplines or organizations (i.e. NDAs, deliverables, sharing of resources, political issues, etc.)? What are some strategies that seem to work for overcoming these?

The final 15 min will be dedicated to wrapping up the discussions and generating ideas for future topics in this area to be discussed at other similar forums.

PANELISTS

Abebe Rorissa is an Associate Professor at the University at Albany, State University of New York (SUNY). Prior to his current position, he worked in four countries as a lecturer and systems librarian for 17 years. He has consulted for academic institutions, national governments, and international organizations, including the United Nations. His research interests include multimedia information organization and retrieval, scaling of users' information needs/perceptions, use/acceptance/adoption and impact of information and communication technologies, and data analytics. Dr. Rorissa was a Member-at-Large on the ASIS&T Board of Directors and a member of its Executive Committee. He will be the moderator for this panel session.

Lisa Federer is the Data Science and Open Science Librarian at the National Library of Medicine, focusing on developing efforts to support workforce development and enhance capacity in the biomedical research and library communities for data science and open science. Prior to joining the NLM, Lisa spent 5 years as the Research Data Informationist at the National Institutes of Health Library, where she developed and ran the Library's Data Services Program. She holds a PhD in Information Studies from the University of Maryland and an MLIS from the University of California-Los Angeles, as well as graduate certificates in data science and data visualization.

Loni Hagen is an Assistant Professor at the School of Information at the University of South Florida. She received degrees in Law, Information Studies (specialized in Information Law), and earned her PhD in Information Science from University at Albany, SUNY. Prior to her current position, she worked for the Korean National Police Agency over 10 years. Her current research interests are in finding novel ways of collecting, extracting information and using them for policy decision-making. She is also interested in privacy-aware practices of big data analytics and informing privacy protection policies with her study results.

Jeonghyun (Annie) Kim is an Associate Professor at the University of North Texas (UNT). She has served as a director of digital curation and data management graduate academic certificate program since she developed the program through IMLS. In addition to coordination of this program, she developed and taught courses "Data Visualization and Communication" and "Digital Humanities" at UNT. Her research interests include digital libraries and archives, data management and curation, and workforce development for information professionals.

James Andrews is Director of the School of Information at the University of South Florida (USF). He has expertise in health informatics with particular interests in how data standards can support interoperability and data sharing, quality, and reuse in the context of the Rare Disease Clinical Research Network (RDCRN) distributed research network. He also has collaborated on national studies examining the outcomes and use of genetic testing by women at risk for or diagnosed with breast cancer, including their information behaviors.

REFERENCES

Boyd, D., & Crawford, K. (2012). Critical questions for big data: Provocations for a cultural, technological, and scholarly phenomenon. *Information, Communication & Society*, *15*(5), 662–679.

Franks, B. (2012). *Taming the big data tidal wave: Finding opportunities in huge data streams with advanced analytics* (Vol. *49*). John Wiley & Sons.

Gupta, B., Goul, M., & Dinter, B. (2015). Business intelligence and big data in higher education: Status of a multi-year model curriculum development effort for business school undergraduates, MS graduates, and MBAs. *Communications of the Association for Information Systems, 36*, 449–476.

Jie, S., & Chen, H. (2015). Internet finance innovation and traditional bank transformation based on Big Data. *Finance & Economics, 1*(2), 11–16.

Laney, D. (2001). *3D data management: Controlling data volume, velocity and variety*. META Group Research Note. Retrieved from https://blogs.gartner.com/doug-laney/files/2012/01/ad949-3D-Data-Management-Controlling-Data-Volume-Velocity-and-Variety.pdf

Lazer, D., Pentland, A. S., Adamic, L., Aral, S., Barabasi, A. L., Brewer, D., ... Van Alstyne, M. (2009). Life in the network: The coming age of computational social science. *Science (New York, NY), 323*(5915), 721–723.

Strawn, G. O. (2012). Scientific research: How many paradigms? *Educause Review, 47*(3), 26–34.

Tirunillai, S., & Tellis, G. J. (2014). Mining marketing meaning from online chatter: Strategic brand analysis of big data using latent dirichlet allocation. *Journal of Marketing Research, 51*(4), 463–479.

Zicari, R. V., Rosselli, M., Ivanov, T., Korfiatis, N., Tolle, K., Niemann, R., & Reichenbach, C. (2016). Setting up a Big Data project: Challenges, opportunities, technologies and optimization. In A. Emrouznejad (Ed.), *Big data optimization: Recent developments and challenges* (pp. 17–47). Springer.

Paradigm Shift in Information Research

Rong Tang
Simmons University,
Boston, USA
rong.tang@
simmons.edu

Bharat Mehra
University of Alabama,
Tuscaloosa, USA
bmehra@ua.edu

Jia Tina Du
University of South
Australia, Adelaide,
Australia
tina.du@unisa.edu.au

Yuxiang (Chris) Zhao
Nanjing University of
Science & Technology,
Nanjing, China
yxzhao@njust.edu.cn

ABSTRACT

In this panel, speakers will discuss a range of issues related to the evolution of theoretical frameworks employed in information research. It is in the view of this panel that there is a need for a paradigm shift, one that shakes the foundation of traditional information research. The new paradigm takes into account emergent information reality featuring ubiquitous access, contextual embeddedness, misinformation and its politicization, social justice and community outcomes, among others. Panelists will examine the history of information paradigms, explore the social responsibility of researchers, articulate actualities and potentialities of impact-driven shifts, outline community-based participatory research strategies, and discuss methodological innovations that advance information research. This panel calls for attention to a forthcoming special issue for JASIS&T which aims to open a forum for reconceptualization of the information field. It is hoped that this session will engage the audience and spark interest of potential contributors to this special issue.

AUTHOR KEYWORDS

Paradigm Shift; Social Responsibilities of Information Research; Impact-Driven Scholarship; Community-based Participatory Research; Methodological Innovations

ASIS&T THESAURUS

Information Behavior; Research and Development

INTRODUCTION

Information research went through its first significant paradigm shift in the late 1970s and early 1980s. The shift was marked by changing scholarly empirical attention on information retrieval research from a system orientation to a user-centered focus (Dervin & Nilan, 1986). Nardi and O'Day (2000) called for computer scientists and software engineers to design systems as information ecologies that connect people, information, technology, and their practices in context. In 2008, Marchionini (2008) indicated that information scientists should adopt an ecological view in their research. Fidel (2012) also advocated an ecological view to conceptualize the engagement between information behavior and information practice. Nevertheless, currently it remains questionable whether the transition to an ecological perspective of human information interaction in information research has successfully taken place. The existing key information retrieval or information behavior models are either general or context-specific, and they are mostly procedure oriented or based on flow-charts. They are also to a large extent individual-based, focusing less frequently on shared/distributed or embodied cognition (Allen, Karanasios, & Slavova, 2011). They tend to be centered on information seeking and typically do not take into account social, cultural, political, economic, and/or community-driven factors (among others) that influence human information behavior and shape people's use of socio-technical systems and services (Mehra, Bishop, Bazzell, & Smith, 2002). Furthermore, other significant issues have not been investigated in depth, such as ubiquitous access, user immersiveness (Robinson, 2015a, 2015b), contextual embeddedness of information, false information (misinformation or dis-information) and its politicization, social justice and community outcomes, digital readiness and online reasoning skills, or the fact that information seeking might no longer require the greatest effort, and new realms of information research (Mehra, 2017).

We believe that there is a need for a paradigm shift, the one that shakes the foundation of traditional information research, and takes into full account the emergent information reality (Tang, 2018). In this reality, information is manipulated and false information is produced without easy detection. Ubiquitous and mobile access to information enables users to have relatively less need to seek information as they already are overly-exposed to plentiful information from multiple sources and varying formats. Finally, there is more of a need to synthesize, assess, deselect, and make use of pertinent information. More importantly, such a shift embraces situational relevance and contextual factors (Höglund & Wilson, 2000; Pettigrew, Fidel, & Bruce, 2001; Solomon, 2002), social responsibility, action research and community engagement (Mehra & Rioux, 2016). Additionally, such a shift also presents an integration of impact/outcome in the theory-practice discourse (Mehra, Sikes, & Singh, 2018). This

82nd Annual Meeting of the Association for Information Science & Technology | Melbourne, Australia | 19–23 October, 2019

DOI: 10.1002/pra2.00096

integration will help expand the relevance of information research moving forward into the future and assist the information professions to make a difference in the lives of people immersed in a global, networked information society (Castells & Himanen, 2014).

We have proposed a special issue for JASIS&T which aims to open a forum for reconceptualization of information research. It will consist of a collection of articles that present a theoretical discourse and empirical evidence for a new thinking of information research. This will empower the information field to go beyond system-centered and user-centered design to new modes of conceptualization and practice more timely and pertinent to the emerging challenges and opportunities in the 21st century. We welcome submissions that address the theoretical and/or methodological innovation that effect a paradigm shift in information research. This also includes critical investigations into the general or specific outcome of paradigm shift in information behavior and practice.

PANEL FORMAT

This 90-minutes panel session will include following activities

- Introduction (5 minutes)
- Presentation and Lead Discussion: 4 panelists (15 minutes per panelist, 60 minutes total). Each presentation ends with two to three questions. Followed by Lead Discussion
- Overall discussion led by moderator (15 minutes).
- Summary and Next Steps (10 minutes)

PANELISTS AND PRESENTATION TOPICS

Panelists' biography, credentials and their presentation topics are outlined below:

Rong Tang

Dr. Rong Tang is an associate professor, Director of the PhD Program in School of Library and Information Sciences, Simmons University. Dr. Tang's areas of teaching and research include theories of information science, research methods, digital information services, usability & UX research, data science curriculum, and open data services. Dr. Tang was the PI of numerous funded research projects, including grants from American Psychological Association, OCLC Library & Information Science Research Program, and a NEH Subaward with WGBH. Dr. Tang is a co-leader of the RDMLA (Research Data Management Librarian Academy) project, which involves a partnership of seven academic research libraries, a LIS program, and Elsevier, which financially funded the project. Dr. Tang received her MLIS from Wayne State University, and her PhD from University of North Carolina at Chapel Hill.

In her presentation, Dr. Tang will provide an overview of the history and milestones of information behavior research. She will highlight the first paradigm shift from system-centric to user centric (Dervin & Nilan, 1986), outline the second paradigm shift as described by Marchionini in 2008 (Marchionini, 2008) as from investigating information objects, technology, and people as separate discrete entities to taking an ecological view to investigate them together as a part of an ecosystem. Dr. Tang will end her presentation by issuing a call for a new paradigm shift that addresses the ubiquity of information, manipulation of information, social responsibility of technological development, and community engagement. Dr. Tang will engage the audience to reflect on the following questions:

- To what extent are IB models (developed back in 1970s-1990s) still suitable to guide research investigation of information behavior in the new information reality?
- What social responsibilities that information science researchers should assume in an era where the advancement of technological solutions may be used to violate users' privacy, manipulate public's opinion for election or political powerplay, and endanger the wellbeing of communities and societies?
- What do you consider as the next paradigm shift? How do we build upon existing paradigms and integrate them into newer ways of conceptualizing information research paradigm shifts?

Bharat Mehra

From January 2019, Dr. Bharat Mehra joined the School of Library and Information Studies at the University of Alabama as Professor and EBSCO Endowed Chair in Social Justice. From January 2005 – December 2018, he was a faculty member in the School of Information Sciences at the University of Tennessee. His research focuses on diversity and social justice in library and information science (LIS) and community informatics or the use of information and communication technologies to empower minority and underserved populations to make meaningful changes in their everyday lives. He has applied impact-driven action research to further engaged scholarship and community engagement while collaborating with racial/ethnic groups, international diaspora, sexual minorities, rural communities, low-income families, small businesses, and others, to represent their experiences and perspectives in the design of community-based information systems and services. As principal investigator, over the past decade he has been awarded multiple grants from the Institute of Museum and Library Services totaling more than a million dollars to help train rural librarians in the Appalachian region as well as develop collaborative partnerships between rural libraries and other appropriate community stakeholders (e.g. small businesses).

Dr. Mehra will present on the actualities and potentialities of paradigmatic impact-driven shifts in information research and address contemporary efforts to integrate social justice and inclusion advocacy scholarship in information science research. He will further identify current challenges and opportunities related to the paradigm shift by extending the discourse surrounding traditional canons of knowledge domains, theories, and methods. He will also engage the audience to reflect on the following questions:

- How does the audience conceptualize impact-driven information-related research and scholarship? How do traditional paradigms serve as basis for impact-driven research?
- How does the audience implement (or plan to operationalize) impact-driven paradigm in their own research?
- What challenges and opportunities have the audience members encountered in this process in adopting this shift in their approach? [Or recognize that they will encounter in the future moving forward?].

Jia Tina Du

Dr. Du is a Senior Lecturer at the School of Information Technology and Mathematical Sciences, University of South Australia. She is awarded the Australian Research Council Discovery Early Career Researcher Award (ARC DECRA, 2017-20), a highly competitive national research fellowship, and visiting fellow at the University of Oxford's Internet Institute (2016-17). Dr. Du has published 80 papers in refereed journals and conference proceedings and obtained over AU$800,000 for research. Her research interests are interdisciplinary in nature, exploring online information search, human information behavior, marginalized communities and social innovation. Dr. Du has supervised 10 PhD students at UniSA (with 6 completions). She has served as co-chair and PC member for a number of national and international conferences. She is Fellow of South Australian Governor's Leadership Foundation program and the Chair-Elect for the Association for Information Science and Technology Asia-Pacific Chapter in 2018-19. She is the Winner of 2018 South Australian Winnovation Awards for "Maths and Data" Category.

In her presentation, Dr. Du will address another paradigm shift through applying the community-based participatory research (CBPR) framework to study information research projects with end users and communities. Different from traditional user-centered approaches to information seeking, the emphasis of the CBPR framework is on active participation and capacity-building of participants and improvement of local conditions for them. She will engage the audience to reflect on the following questions:

- Why engaging communities is important to information research?
- How to apply the community-based participatory research (CBPR) framework to study information research projects?
- How can this approach contribute to the move of information behavior research focus from study participants to co-researchers, and from process (e.g. information seeking) to outcomes (e.g. problem solving and social inclusion)?

Yuxiang (Chris) Zhao

Dr. Zhao is a professor at the School of Economics and Management, Nanjing University of Science and Technology, China. His research focuses on understanding social and managerial aspects of Information Technology and the Internet by qualitative & quantitative research methods. Specially, his research interests include: human information behavior, online collaboration (e.g., crowdsourcing, citizen science), health informatics, and macro level of human-computer interaction analysis. He has served as co-chair and PC member for a number of national and international conferences and workshops, and he has been involved in a wide range of research activities and research projects. He has been awarded the distinguished young scholars in Chinese Humanities & Social Science domain in 2016.

In his presentation, Dr. Zhao will address the methodological innovation in information behavior research in support of a paradigm shift, especially conducting the mixed methods research in the information studies. Mixed method research is an approach that combines qualitative and quantitative research methods in the same research inquiry (Venkatesh, Brown & Bala, 2013), which can help information behavior research extend from traditional exploratory questions to confirmatory cases. Specifically, more rigorous hypotheses are needed to propose on the basis of the solid literature, and more research design should be presented to examine the causal relationship and minimize the endogenous problems. In this regard, Dr. Zhao will engage the audience to reflect on the following questions:

- Which methods are often mixed in information behavior research?
- How to evaluate the appropriateness of a mixed methods approach and develop meta-inferences from such mixed methods research in information studies?
- What do you consider as challenges and opportunities when adopting some new tools and technologies (e.g., eye-tracking, EEG, mobile experience sampling method) to collect and analyze data in the domain of information behavior and practice?

Session Concluding Questions

Final questions that the panel will engage the audience to discuss are:

1. Will you be interested in contributing to this special issue of JASIST?
2. What themes should such a special issue contain?

REFERENCES

Allen, D., Karanasios, S., & Slavova, M. (2011). Working with activity theory: Context, technology, and information behavior. *Journal of the Association for Information Science and Technology*, *62*(4), 776–788.

Castells, M., & Himanen, P. (2014). *Reconceptualizing development in the global information age*. Oxford, UK: Oxford University Press.

Dervin, B., & Nilan, M. (1986). Information needs and uses. In M. E. Williams (Ed.), *Annual review of information science and technology* (Vol. 21, pp. 3–33). White Plains, NY: Knowledge Industry Publications.

Fidel, R. (2012). *Human information interaction: An ecological approach to information behavior*. Cambridge, MA: MIT Press.

Höglund, L., & Wilson, T. (Eds.). (2000). *Studies of information seeking in context The new review of information behaviour research 2000* (Vol. 1). London, UK: Taylor Graham Publishing.

Marchionini, G. (2008). Human-information interaction research and development. *Library and Information Science Research, 30*, 165–174.

Mehra, B. (2017). Mobilization of rural libraries towards political and economic change in the aftermath of the 2016 Presidential Election. *The Library Quarterly, 87*(4), 369–390.

Mehra, B., Bishop, A. P., Bazzell, I., & Smith, C. (2002). Scenarios in the Afya project as a participatory action research (par) tool for studying information seeking and use across the "digital divide,". *Journal of the American Society of Information Science and Technology, 53*(14), 1259–1266.

Mehra, B., & Rioux, K. (Eds.). (2016). *Progressive community action: Critical theory and social justice in library and information science*. Sacramento, CA: Library Juice Press.

Mehra, B., Sikes, E. S., & Singh, V. (2018). *Information technology use behaviors of community-engaged rural librarians: A future beyond the theory-practice discourse to integrate impact (short paper)*, In 2018 ASIS&T SIG-USE Symposium: Moving Toward the Future of Information Behavior Research and Practice, Vancouver, Canada, November 10, 2018.

Nardi, B. A., & O'Day, V. L. (2000). *Information ecologies: Using technology with heart*. Cambridge, MA: MIT Press.

Pettigrew, K. E., Fidel, R., & Bruce, H. (2001). Conceptual frameworks in information behavior. *Annual Review of Information Science and Technology, 35*(1), 43–78.

Robinson, L. (2015a). Immersive information behaviour: Using the documents of the future. *New Library World, 116*(3/4), 112–121.

Robinson, L. (2015b). Multisensory, pervasive, immersive: Towards a new generation of documents. *Journal of the Association for Information Science and Technology, 66*(8), 1734–1737.

Solomon, P. (2002). Discovering information in context. *Annual Review of Information Science and Technology, 36*(1), 229–264.

Tang, R. (2018). *Information behavior research in need of paradigm shift. (short paper)*. In 2018 ASIS&T SIG-USE Symposium: Moving Toward the Future of Information Behavior Research and Practice, Vancouver, Canada, November 10, 2018.

Information Seeking at the Intersection of Search, Learning, Inquiry, and Creativity: Sharing Stories to Inform Creative Research

Michael Twidale
School of Information Sciences,
University of Illinois at Urbana-Champaign,
Champaign, Illinois, USA
twidale@illinois.edu

Soo Young Rieh
School of Information,
The University of Texas at Austin,
Austin, Texas, USA
rieh@ischool.utexas.edu

ABSTRACT

This alternative event brings together researchers, practitioners, and students who are interested in developing new research ideas and methods by engaging in a series of activities around sharing stories about information seeking that helped their learning and inspired their creativity. Although storytelling is well established within Library and Information Science, it is not normally used to inform research about search. However we believe it has great potential in inspiring creative research about creativity.

KEYWORDS

Search as learning; search and inquiry; creativity in information seeking

ASIS&T THESAURUS

Information seeking; searching

INTRODUCTION

The goal of this alternative event is to bring together researchers, practitioners, and students who are interested in developing new research ideas and methods by engaging in a series of activities and sharing their own stories about information seeking that helped their learning and inspired their creativity. While participants could share their previous and current work related to searching, learning, and creativity, we invite any person who wants to learn about creativity, creative activities, and creative thinking processes in their everyday life.

Some people say the plural of anecdote is not data. Are they always right? What about in the world of information seeking at the intersections of search, learning, inquiry, and creativity? Are there creative ways we might prove them wrong? We have incredibly fast, powerful and effective systems for achieving known item search. But what about these situations: when you don't know exactly what you really want; when you want to be inspired; when you have no idea what the thing you vaguely want is even called; when you would like to do something to increase the rate of serendipity.

We often experience this kind of search in real life. We go to libraries, bookstores, farmers markets, craft fairs, museums and other inspirational places that we find trigger serendipities. Some of us even go to conferences for that reason. What do people do and why? What do you do? What have you seen others do? Maybe the best way to scope out a space of creativity is to creatively explore it by telling stories. Come to our event and share your stories.

Maybe it isn't science - yet. Does that matter if it helps us get to a different kind of truth about a certain kind of messy creativity? But we hope we can at least collect some stories to get a sense of the activity space and thereby inspire future analysis.

In collecting stories, maybe we can be inspired by Darwin collecting specimens on the Beagle voyage. Perhaps we are not yet at the stage of theory-building. Or perhaps our existing theories are at risk of locking us into a limited set of perspectives. Surely one kind of creativity involves breaking out from constraints – including constraints of what we define creativity to be. From the set of shared examples we hope to spot some interesting patterns that can inspire hypothesis creation and further study.

BACKGROUND

Since Guilford gave his presidential address at the 1950 American Psychology Association convention, creativity research has been advanced in social sciences such as psychology, education, and learning science and characterized the nature of creativity from diverse perspectives. Probably the best known definition is two-level creativity – big-C and little-c. Big-C creativity refers to a genius whose big-time creativity will be used by generations while little-c focuses on inquisitiveness, imagination, unconventionality, and freedom of thought in the layperson's everyday life (Sawyer, 2012). Sawyer developed a creativity framework which

82nd Annual Meeting of the Association for Information Science & Technology | Melbourne, Australia | 19–23 October, 2019

DOI: 10.1002/pra2.00097

identifies distinct cognitive processes across eight stages: finding the problem, acquiring knowledge, gathering related information, incubation, generating ideas, combining ideas, selecting the best ideas, and externalizing ideas. His framework has a number of implications for information science as he emphasizes that creative people actively seek out new information, solutions, connections, and problems and then engage in the critical thinking process by synthesizing information from multiple perspectives.

In the field of human-computer interaction, Shneiderman noted that information technologies would have profound effects in allowing people to be more creative. He advocated that "education could expand from acquiring facts, studying existing knowledge, and developing critical thinking, to include more emphasis on creating novel artifacts, insights, or performances" (p. 115). Shneiderman also characterized multiple perspectives on creativity research by identifying three kinds of creativity researchers: inspirationalists, structuralists, and situationalists. According to him, the inspirationalists emphasize the intuitive aspects of creativity, paying attention to "aha" moments. The structuralists emphasize orderly approaches to problem solving, studying previous work and using methods that explore various possible solutions. Situationalists are a group of researchers who consider the influence from teachers, peers, and mentors, stressing people's strong desire to create something new and pursuit a recognition. He then discussed how user interface designers can develop tools that could support these different creativity perspectives. For instance, he proposed tools that stimulate inspiration by linking to associate ideas, enable exhaustive exploration, and support social strategies.

In the field of information science, there is growing recognition in investigating the intersection of search, learning, and creativity from a variety of different perspectives. Lee, Theng, and Goh (2005) proposed a framework for creative information seeking in which they developed mappings between the creative process and information seeking activities. They then identified six stages for creative information seeking: (1) preparation for starting information seeking; (2) chaining information sources; (3) browsing and searching; (4) incubation for differentiating purposes; (5) monitoring and extracting for illumination; (6) verification of information sources.

Rieh, Collins-Thompson, Hansen, and Lee (2016) differentiated receptive learning, critical learning, and creative learning. Receptive learning is defined as remembering understanding facts and concepts while critical learning is about reviewing, criticizing and evaluating ideas gained from multiple sources. Creative learning refers to generating new ideas and designing new artifacts from what is learned. According to them, in the mode of creative learning, people engage in information behavior such as prioritizing and sense-making beyond obtaining, selecting, judging relevance, evaluating usefulness, assessing credibility, comparing, and differentiating. Zhang and Capra (2019) investigated what kinds of creative tasks people perform and how they conduct such tasks. Based on the results of an online survey, their research revealed creative task domains and activities, such as arts and crafts, visual arts, science and engineering, cooking, and literature. They also found out that while respondents used search engines when they need to look up information, they used videos to explore relevant information and images to help combine their ideas.

These previous studies demonstrate that creativity is closely associated with inquiry processes in which people pose questions and problems, stimulate their curiosity, engage in information seeking, connect with what they have learned, and generate ideas and themes.

WHY WE ARE COMBINING LEARNING, INQUIRY AND CREATIVITY

People often deal with unknown facts and information: you don't know what you don't know, or you don't know what it is called, so it is hard to search for. Even with the incredible informational abundance of the Web, we hit problems with these kinds of unknowns. In learning it especially applies in self-directed learning. If someone is teaching you, they are ideally giving you the informational nuggets, in just the right order, at just the right speed for you to assimilate. But if you are trying to learn on your own, then *managing* that learning is an extra problem on top of actually *doing* the learning.

With tasks involving creativity (and that includes research) there is the issue of being or feeling stuck (also very familiar when learning). There just does not seem to be a way to go forward. We may use metaphors of going around the problem, tackling it from another angle, or breaking it up into bite-sized pieces. These require creativity, and again acquiring information can help - assuming we can figure out how to acquire it.

PROCESS FOR THE ALTERNATIVE EVENT

In accordance with the call for alternative events, we intend the process to be "highly participatory, informal, engaging, and pluralistic" To enable this we have the following informal outline. We will of course creatively adapt this in the light of participation.

- Introduction to the event, the aims, the process
  - Examples of kinds of problems in learning, inquiry and creativity
  - Why such problems often do not involve straightforward information searching
  - Example problems from the facilitators
- Form into groups of three
  - Be inspired by trigger cards the facilitators hand out
  - Share stories of search-related learning, inquiry, and creativity
  - Personal stories, and those you have seen or heard about
- Plenary: share stories

- Collectively we try to spot themes and patterns, including dichotomies
- Second group of threes
  - Additional trigger cards, including those developed from issues emerging from the plenary
  - Share stories inspired by the discussed stories
  - Consider different kinds of stories unlike the discussed stories
  - Pay special attention to awkward stories that don't "fit"
- Second plenary: share stories
- Further assembly of themes and patterns
- Next steps, ideas and opportunities

SUMMARY

We are proposing an alternative event that aims in its structure to be a creative way to learn about creativity and learning issues in search by searching our memories for initial thought-provoking examples. We don't want to pretend that this is normal data collection. But it may be a way to search for ideas that can inspire refutable hypotheses for subsequent more careful regular searches for insight.

ORGANIZERS

Michael Twidale has investigated issues around the informal learning of technology in a range of settings, including those where searching online resources is a part of that learning process (Rutter, Blinzler, Ye, Wilson, & Twidale, 2019). He is also interested in exploring rapid, low cost, low stakes research methods, particularly as a way to scope out new research areas, inspired by agile software development methods as a reaction against Big Design Up Front methods (Twidale & Hansen, 2019). He is one of the co-editors for a special issue on Inquiry, Search, and Creativity for a journal, *Information and Learning Sciences* that will be published in 2020.

Soo Young Rieh has conducted several research projects on searching as learning. Rieh and her colleagues (Rieh et al., 2016) conceptualized searching as a learning process through the concept of comprehensive search which illustrates iterative, reflective, and integrative search sessions that facilitate individuals' critical thinking abilities (critical learning) and the development of new ideas directly (creative learning). She and her colleagues (Collins-Thompson, Rieh, Haynes, & Syed, 2016) also conducted a lab-based user study to develop methods, measures, and indicators that demonstrate learning experiences and outcomes in Web searching. In 2014, she co-organized a panel on Searching as Learning: Novel Measures for Information Interaction Research at the ASIST Annual Meeting (2014). She also co-edited a special issue on "Recent advances on searching as learning" for the *Journal of Information Science* (Hansen & Rieh, 2016). She is one of the co-editors for a special issue on Inquiry, Search, and Creativity for a journal, *Information and Learning Sciences* that will be published in 2020.

OUTCOMES AND NEXT STEPS

The outcomes of this alternative event will include: (1) a range of research topics to shape the field of creativity-supporting search behavior and inquiry learning; (2) characterization of designing tools and systems that could support creative activities; (3) identification of diverse research methodologies that enabling the intersection of search, inquiry, and creativity. At the end of this alternative event, participants are more likely to incorporate creative insights into their own research process and further being inspired to generate new research ideas about the intersection of inquiry, search, and creativity.

Participants of this Alternative Event will be encouraged to submit papers to the *Information and Learning Sciences* Special Issue on Inquiry, Search, and Creativity (co-edited by Preben Hansen, Soo Young Rieh, and Michael Twidale). The goal of this special issue is to bring together researchers from information science, information retrieval, learning science, education science, and design research and present a collection of contributions to our understanding of how inquiry, learning, and searching are interlinked with creativity. We expect to collect research that explores concepts, methodologies, interactive systems, and digital environments that support, facilitate, and promote creativity in the process of search and inquiry.

REFERENCES

Collins-Thompson, K., Rieh, S. Y., Haynes, C. C., & Syed, R. (2016). *Assessing learning outcomes in web searching: A comparison of tasks and query strategies*. In Proceedings of the ACM SIGIR Conference on Human Information Interaction and Retrieval (CHIIR '16) (pp. 163-172).

Guilford, J. P. (1950). Creativity. *American Psychologist*, *5*, 444–454.

Hansen, P., & Rieh, S. Y. (2016). Editorial: Recent advances on searching as learning: An introduction to the special issue. *Journal of Information Science*, *42*(1), 3–6.

Lee, S.-S., Theng, Y.-L., & Goh, D. H.-L. (2005). Creative information seeking part I: A conceptual framework. *Aslib Proceedings*, *57*(5), 460–475.

Rieh, S. Y., Collins-Thompson, K., Hansen, P., & Lee, H. J. (2016). Towards searching as a learning process: A review of current perspectives and future directions. *Journal of Information Science*, *42*(1), 19–34.

Rutter, S., Blinzler, V., Ye, C., Wilson, M. L., & Twidale, M. B. (2019). Search tactics used in solving everyday how-to technical tasks: Repertoire, selection and tenacity. *Information Processing & Management*, *56*(3), 919–938.

Sawyer, K. (2012). *Explaining creativity: The science of human innovation* (2nd ed.). New York, NY: Oxford University Press.

Shneiderman, B. (2000). Creating creativity: User interfaces for supporting innovation. *ACM Transactions on Computer-Human Interaction*, *7*(1), 114–138.

Twidale, M. B., & Hansen, P. (2019). Agile research. *First Monday*, *24*(1).

Zhang, Y., & Capra, R. (2019). *Understanding how people use search to support their everyday creative tasks*. In Proceedings of the ACM SIGIR Conference on Human Information Interaction and Retrieval (CHIIR '19) (pp. 153-162).

Information Science Education and Library and Information Studies Education: Transnational Conversations

Terry Weech
University of Illinois-Urbana-Champaign, Champaign, Illinois, USA
weech@illinois.edu

Clara M. Chu
University of Illinois-Urbana-Champaign, Champaign, Illinois, USA
cmchu@illinois.edu

Sandra Hirsh
San Jose State University, San Jose, California, USA
sandy.hirsh@sjsu.edu

Heidi Julien
University at Buffalo, Buffalo, USA
heidijul@buffalo.edu

Mary Anne Kennan
Charles Sturt University, Wagga Wagga, Australia
mkennan@csu.edu.au

Diane L. Velasquez
University of South Australia, Adelaide, Australia
diane.velasquez@unisa.edu.au

Bhuva Narayan
University of Technology Sydney, Sydney, Australia
bhuva.narayan@uts.edu.au

ABSTRACT

The panel/round-table will explore the status of the education of information professionals internationally, with a focus on a review of the status of Library and Information Studies, Information Science, and Information Professional education programs in the U.S., Canada and Australia. Similarities and differences between programs in each country specific to the information professions will be analyzed. The analysis will include a review of the quality assessment of programs, and specific issues related to their success, and concerns about the future of programs in each case. The impact of the iSchool movement will be examined.

KEYWORDS

Library and Information Studies Education; Information Science Education; Information Professions Education

ASIS&T THESAURUS

Information Science; Library Science; Information Science Education

INTRODUCTION

Library and information studies encompasses information and knowledge creation, communication, identification, selection, acquisition, organization and description, storage and retrieval, preservation, analysis, interpretation, evaluation, synthesis, dissemination, and management (ALA, 2008). The topic of Library and Information Science (LIS) education, and education of library and information professionals is relevant to information professionals globally, given that education for both information science and library studies have been an important topic for discussion in recent years with the rise of the iSchool movement internationally.

82nd Annual Meeting of the Association for Information Science & Technology | Melbourne, Australia | 19–23 October, 2019

DOI: 10.1002/pra2.00098

The iSchool movement originated in 1988 with three universities in the U.S., and today, the iSchools comprise a mix of over ninety information-centric academic departments and Schools, including Library and Information Science, Information Systems, and Computer Science across the U.S., Canada, Europe and Australasia. The iSchool members and their programs collectively encompass many facets of information science, including information systems, knowledge management, telecommunications, human-computer interaction, librarianship, archival studies, cultural heritage, media and journalism (Lyon & Brenner, 2015). More recently, iSchools have embraced the digital curation agenda, integrating various specializations within their curricula (Corrall, Kennan, & Afzal, 2013).

The International Federation of Library and Information Associations and Institutions (IFLA) has discussed and analyzed issues relating to the assessment of the quality of education for information professionals for more than twenty years, with IFLA's 2012 guidelines pointing to "the many issues and challenges, including the embedding of the Internet and other digital technologies and all they bring with them into the daily lives of many of our communities. This has brought a thrust by some library schools to adopt an iSchool philosophy in competition with the more traditional, yet still valid, library educational approaches of colleague schools, often in the same country" (Smith, Hallam, & Ghosh, 2012).

Globally, the Association for Library and Information Science Educators (ALISE) has provided a forum for library educators to share ideas, to discuss issues, and to seek solutions to common problems (Fitzgibbons, 2009).

In Australia, "the merging of previously independent LIS schools to form part of other, generally larger, academic units within their parent institutions…with other "information" fields such as computer science, information science, business, and communications …[has] resulted in a reduction of LIS educators as they share teaching with non-LIS educators in multidisciplinary or multi-field schools, …reducing the ability of LIS educators to advance LIS approaches in these areas of study. This limits most LIS programs to tightly serve a core curriculum that is generally based around the ALIA Core Knowledge, Skills and Attributes (ALIA, 2014), which Australian LIS courses must cover in order to achieve accreditation." (Kennan, Carroll, & Thompson, 2018).

PANEL PROPOSAL

The panel session will be highly participatory and will provide flexibility to explore topics that reflect the interests and expertise of those in attendance. The panel presentations will be focused to present contrasting viewpoints where appropriate.

The issues covered will include, but will not be limited, to the following:

- Certification or Accreditation for information professionals and the role of industry accreditation bodies in LIS education;
- Implications of stratification of the workforce through different levels of education (Diploma, Undergraduate Degree, and Master degree);
- Merging of previously independent LIS schools into larger academic units within their parent institutions (and in Australia the effects of fewer Schools);
- The "Academicization" of LIS education and educators, and resulting relationships with the LIS professions;
- Tensions between education focused on "learning to be" and that focused on "learning to do";
- How can LIS education reflect changes in the LIS professions?
- Potential synergies with other GLAM educators, disciplines and professions?
- Potential relationships with other "I" accreditation bodies e.g. in Australia ALIA (Australian Library and Information Association) ASA (Archivists Society of Australia), RIMPA (Records and Information Management Professionals Australia);
- Attracting potential students and ensuring employment for graduates;
- Succession planning within the profession and also within LIS education and research;
- Role of education for library and information studies programs in education for information science; and
- Whether there is a need for a form of international assessment of education for the information professions.

The panel will initiate a discussion on the iSchool movement and the traditional LIS education system, especially the positive and negative impacts of the former on the latter. Is library science education marginalized in the iSchool movement? Do the disciplinary identity vagueness of iSchool movement and its all-embracing research orientation in the information field undermine the position of LIS in iSchools? Mission, core values, faculty hiring, curriculum and other things have changed a lot during the transition from LIS school to iSchool; how do accreditation processes adapt to this new education system? What kind of changes should the accreditation systems make in the new environment from the perspectives of ALISE, ASIST and IFLA etc.? In what ways can these organizations collaborate to improve the education quality of iSchools? Another issue is the merging of LIS schools with larger academic units. This phenomenon is common in the UK, Australia and East Asia. It often leads to the loss of discourse power and stagnation or closure of LIS programs. How can LIS schools and iSchools survive and develop in the larger organization after school mergers?

The implications of the answers to these questions will inform how LIS educators approach their courses and programs, and the role of accreditation bodies in providing the flexibility for the same.

PANELISTS

The panel will consist of seven experts in the area of education of information professionals with expertise at both national and international levels. As a group, the panel represents current and prior International Federation of Library and Information Associations and Institutions (IFLA), Association for Information Science and Technology (ASIS&T), Association for Library and Information Science Education (ALISE), Australian Library and Information Association (ALIA), and American Library Association (ALA) members who hold or have held elected offices in one or more of these organizations. The panel includes an ASIS&T president-elect, an ASIS&T past-president, the current president, a past president, and a president-elect of ALISE, two prior chairs of the IFLA Education and Training Section and a current chair of the IFLA Continuing Professional Development and Workplace Learning Section, a current ALIA Research Advisory Committee Chair, the Secretary and Chair-elect of the Asia-Pacific Chapter of ASIS&T, and a prior chair of the ALA-Committee on Education.

Terry Weech is faculty at the iSchool at Illinois (School of Information Sciences), and Past Chair of ALA Committee on Accreditation, Past Chair of IFLA Library Education and Training Section, and researcher on Library and Information Science Education.

Terry will discuss the issues from the perspective of a member of an iSchool faculty and a former Chair of the ALA Committee on Accreditation, and review the benefits to iSchools of ALA Accreditation, noting an interest in exploring ALA accreditation by iSchools outside North America and exploring the reasons for this interest. Terry will also speak about the benefits of such accreditation to iSchools.

Clara M. Chu is Director and Mortenson Distinguished Professor, Mortenson Center for International Library Programs, University of Illinois at Urbana-Champaign, and Co-chair of IFLA Building Strong LIS Education Working Group, Past-President of ALISE, Past Chair of IFLA Library Education and Training Section, Former Chair of LIS Dept., UNCG, and External Review Panel Member for ALA accreditation, and ALA Task Force on accreditation.

Clara will discuss International LIS education issues as former ALISE President and ASIS&T President-Elect.

Sandra Hirsh is Director and Professor, School of Information, San Jose State University, and President-elect of the Association for Library and Information Science Education (ALISE), Past-President of the Association for Information Science & Technology (ASIS&T), Co-chair of IFLA Continuing Professional Development & Workplace Learning Section, Editor of *Information Services Today: An Introduction*.

Sandra will discuss the issues from the perspective of an iSchool director and from an ASIS&T and ALISE point of view.

Heidi Julien is Professor, Department of Information Science, University at Buffalo, and immediate past-president of the Association for Library and Information Science Education (ALISE).

Heidi will discuss the issues from the perspective of an iSchool department chair and also from the ALISE point of view. The iSchool movement has been an enormously successful branding initiative, providing schools, particularly in North America, a political opportunity to differentiate a range of information-focused programs from the traditional library science-focused programs. The result has been a significantly increased profile on campuses and a flourishing of programs unfettered by accreditation restrictions imposed by librarians.

Mary Anne Kennan is Associate Professor and Associate Head of School, School of Information Studies, Charles Sturt University, a past ALIA Research Advisory Committee member, and current Editor of the *Journal of the Australian Library and Information Association*, a flagship research journal of ALIA that addresses both research and practice within the LIS discipline.

Mary Anne will discuss the issues as Head of an iSchool and as LIS Educator, and as a researcher in LIS Education, also bringing an Australian perspective to the discussions. Mary Anne will also touch upon the emerging specialist knowledge and skills in LIS that could provide new opportunities for LIS professionals, employers, and educators, and researcher, and also emphasize the need for understanding the interdependency of all of these roles.

Diane L. Velasquez is Program Director of Information Management in the School of Information Technology and Mathematical Sciences at the University of South Australia, an iSchool.

Diane is a long-time LIS Educator who will bring a comparative Australian and American perspective, having taught on both continents.

Bhuva Narayan coordinates the Information and Knowledge Management Program at the University of Technology Sydney, and is the current Chair of the ALIA Research Advisory Committee and an Associate Editor *Journal of the Australian Library and Information Association*, a flagship research journal of ALIA that addresses both research and practice within the LIS discipline.

As an Australian LIS educator with an MLIS from the iSchool at the University of Pittsburgh, Bhuva brings a unique comparative perspective to the issues discussed. Additionally, as Program Director of an Australian LIS program, and as current Chair of the Research Advisory Committee for the Australian Library and Information Association, Bhuva will discuss current challenges in the Australian LIS landscape that have significant implications for research, education, and professional practice. Bhuva will also discuss why the small scale of most Australian LIS programs and the reality of being a small part of larger organizational units prevents most of them from taking advantage of the iSchool movement.

STRUCTURE OF THE PANEL

The audience will be engaged in the discussion of the panel's review of the education landscape in the countries covered across the panel and attendees, and be asked to contribute information from their local perspective that are relevant to the global issues identified by the panel. Each panelist will present a brief 5-minute summary of the educational issues that constitute the greatest concern to the discipline and profession in the future. A 3-minute period following each panel member's presentation will be open for discussion.

Terry Weech and Clara M. Chu will act as moderators for the session as well as present their own contributions as members of the panel. During the 90-minute period, approximately half will be dedicated to open discussion.

REFERENCES

American Library Association. (2008). *Standards for accreditation of master's programs in library & information studies*. Adopted by ALA Council. Retrieved from http://www.ala.org/educationcareers/sites/ala.org.educationcareers/files/content/standards/standards_2008.pdf

Australian Library and Information Association. (2014). *The library and information sector: Core knowledge, skills and attributes*. Canberra: ACT: Australian Library and Information Association. Retrieved from https://www.alia.org.au/about-alia/policies-standardsand-guidelines/library-and-information-sector-core-knowledge-skills-and-attributes

Fitzgibbons, S. (2009). Association for library and information science education. *Encyclopedia of Library and Information Science*, *1*, 192–204.

Kennan, M. A., Carroll, M., & Thompson, K. M. (2018, 2018). Letting go, holding on, or re-envisioning? Challenges and opportunities for lis education in Australia. In J. Percell, L. C. Sarin, P. T. Jaeger, & J. C. Bertot, *Re-envisioning the MLS: Perspectives on the future of library and information science education*. Emerald Publishing Limited.

Lyon, L., & Brenner, A. (2015). Bridging the data talent gap: Positioning the iSchool as an agent for change. *International Journal of Digital Curation*, *10*(1), 111–122.

Smith, K., Hallam, G., & Ghosh, S. B. (2012). *Guidelines for professional library/information educational programs-2012*. The Hague, Netherlands: IFLA Education and Training Section, IFLA. Retrieved from www.ifla.org/publications/guidelines-for-professional-libraryinformationeducational-programs-2012

Academic Social Networking: From Individual Acts to Institutional, Disciplinary, National, and Social Phenomena

Yin Zhang
Kent State University,
Kent, OH, USA
yzhang4@kent.edu

Weiwei Yan
Wuhan University,
Wuhan, China
yanww@whu.edu.cn

Sanghee Oh
Chungnam National
University, Daejeon,
South Korea
sanghee.oh@cnu.ac.kr

Jongwook Lee
Kyungpook National
University, Daegu,
South Korea
jongwook@knu.ac.kr

Keiko Kurata
Keio University, Tokyo, Japan
kei.kurata@keio.jp

Mamiko Matsubayashi
University of Tsukuba, Tsukuba, Japan
mamiko@slis.tsukuba.ac.jp

ABSTRACT

Academic social networking sites (ASNSs) are widely being adopted by individual academics. There has been an increasing research interest in this new phenomenon. This panel brings a group of researchers to share and discuss their recent research to address the research gaps in the following areas: (1) the institutional and disciplinary user structures and their behavior characteristics in ASNSs; and (2) how academics from non-English speaking countries use ASNSs and how the use may differ from their counterparts in U.S. Collectively, various studies presented in the panel will help achieve a better understanding of scholarly use of ASNSs in a broader scale.

KEYWORDS

Academic social networking; scholarly communication; ResearchGate

ASIS&T THESAURUS

Social web; communication patterns; collaboration

INTRODUCTION

In recent years, academic social networking sites (ASNSs) are being adopted as a new scholarly communication platform by individual academics that reflects a combination of academic capital and social networking skill (Gruzd et al., 2012; Thelwall & Kousha, 2015). Researchers have utilized ASNSs not only to discover, read, share, and archive publications, but also to seek and share research information, build networks, and present professional images (Arshad & Ameen, 2017; Bianchini, 2012; Dermentzi, Papagiannidis, Toro, & Yannopoulou, 2016; Lee, Oh, Dong, Wang, & Burnett, 2019; Xia et al., 2016).

Despite increasing research interest in this new phenomenon, there is little known about how academics from non-English speaking countries use ASNSs and how their use may differ from their counterparts in U.S., if at all. In addition, most research has focused on academics' individual activities, but very few reveal the institutional and disciplinary user structures and their behavior characteristics.

In this panel, a group of researchers will share and discuss their recent research to address the above research gaps using ResearchGate (RG) as an example. The various studies presented in the panel will provide a better and broader understanding of scholarly use of ASNSs and potential implications to global scholarly communication in the digital age.

PANEL ORGANIZATION AND FORMAT

Panelists will first present related background and their recent research, and then engage the audience with an open dialog on related issues, implications, and future research related to the presentations and panel themes.

PRESENTATION 1

U.S. research universities in ResearchGate: An Institutional level analysis

Presenters: Yin Zhang & Weiwei Yan

This presentation will highlight several recent studies based on data collected from 168,059 RG users in 61 U.S. research universities at different research activity levels, as categorized by the Carnegie Classification of Institutions of Higher Education (Yan & Zhang, 2018, 2019; Yan, Zhang, & Bromfield, 2018). Based on individual user RG metrics and the follower-followee relationships, an aggregated institutional level data

82nd Annual Meeting of the Association for Information Science & Technology | Melbourne, Australia | 19–23 October, 2019

DOI: 10.1002/pra2.00099

and networks based on individual users' affiliations is generated. The following areas are explored and summarized:

- Institutional differences, research activity level, and social networks formed;
- User behaviors and network characteristics of U.S. research universities on RG; and
- User characteristics and institutional participation differences among research universities on RG based on the follower-followee ratio.

We would like to discuss with the panelists and audience how ASNSs may be used for evaluating research activities among research institutions and how helpful and credible they are for acquiring resources, keeping informed about research, and promoting academic influence. Further discussion will involve how the social networks formed in RG may help promote a deeper understanding of the follower-followee relationship among users and institutions.

PRESENTATION 2

RG motivations for self-archiving and disciplinary differences

Presenters: Sanghee Oh & Jongwook Lee

This presentation will briefly introduce a recent study about researchers' motivations for self-archiving their information on ResearchGate. Self-archiving is defined as "the action of uploading any kind of academic work, material, or research data to personal websites or institutional or subject repositories to make them freely available to and accessible by the public online" (Lee et al., 2019). We proposed a motivational framework including 18 factors, including enjoyment, personal and professional gain, reputation, learning, self-efficacy, altruism, reciprocity, trust, community interest, social engagement, publicity, accessibility, self-archiving culture, influence of external actors, credibility, system stability, copyright concerns, and additional time and effort. We developed the framework mainly based on Kim (2010)'s and Oh and Syn (2015)'s studies as well as a comprehensive literature review of previous studies about motivations, ASNSs, researchers' information, and self-archiving behaviors, etc. We carried out a survey for collecting data from the RG users about their ratings on each motivational factors.

We will present the findings from the study about researcher's motivations by their demographic and background information of using RG. We also compared the motivations across different disciplines in two dimensions, such as (1) hard/soft and (2) pure/applied, which is initially proposed by Biglan (1973). A preliminary finding from these comparisons will be presented as well. Furthermore, we would like to discuss with the panelists and the audience about the opportunities and challenges of studying researchers in many different disciplines, to investigate their perceptions, attitudes, and behaviors of self-arching as well as other activities in research using ASNSs.

PRESENTATION 3

ResearchGate as a tool to develop a new style of scholarly communication in Japan: How do Japanese researchers use and recognize RG?

Presenters: Keiko Kurata & Mamiko Matsubayashi

We show the characteristics of the researcher's awareness and usage of ResearchGate (RG) in Japan from the results of the RG site survey and the questionnaire survey. We surveyed 100 RG sites randomly selected from RG registered researchers belonging to 13 large-scale research universities. Fifty five percent of them share the bibliographic data of their articles, and 51% of them uploaded full texts of articles. It is notable that all of the articles have been written in English. Fifty five percent of researchers had RG scores, with an average of 20.62, which was higher than 73% of all RG members. No researchers have uploaded any articles in Japanese to RG. It seems that Japanese researchers recognize RG as a tool for global communication in English.

We conducted a survey to investigate RG use and awareness of researchers who have accounts on RG, belonging to 13 large-scale research universities in Japan. We sent a questionnaire to 1,661 researchers by email and received 71 responses. Fifty five percent of the respondents "have shared bibliographic data of their articles on RG" in a year. Thirty five percent of them "have edited their profiles," 31% of them "have got other researchers' articles," 30% of them "have uploaded full-text of their articles." More than 60% of the respondents who shared bibliographic data of their articles answered the reason of RG use "to know the evaluation of their research by other researchers" and/or "to disseminate their research." More than 70% of the respondents highly valued RG as a useful tool "for disseminating their research" and "for getting the information of researchers who viewed their research."

Researchers in Japan have recognized and used RG as a new tool that can show the appeal of their research achievements to other researchers and receive feedback and evaluation from peers, which could only have been obtained from someone close to them in conventional scholarly communication.

PRESENTATION 4

Chinese top universities in ResearchGate: How are they compared to their U.S. counterparts?

Presenters: Weiwei Yan & Yin Zhang

This presentation will report on a study that compares and illustrates the differences in RG participation and scholarly influence between Chinese and U.S. research universities as measured by RG metrics and the institutional interaction networks formed by the users' follower-followee relationships.

We chose 21 Chinese top universities and 61 U.S. universities from 3 research activity levels for comparison. 284,093 members' RG metrics data were obtained in this comparative study. The study finds that the participation of top Chinese universities and their overall performance and publications are largely in line with those in a higher research activity level universities in the U.S., while scholarly influence and popularity are basically at the same level with those in a moderate research activity level universities in the U.S. A social network analysis of the sample universities reveals the top universities in both China and U.S. were well-connected on RG, while the other interactions between the two countries were limited. Moreover, Chinese users tend to follow their U.S. peers more than the other way around.

We would like to discuss with the panelists and audience how foreign users started to utilize RG for international academic reputation promotion, and the cultural/scholarly reasons and implications of the interaction characteristics in ASNSs between developed countries and developing countries.

PROMOTION

The panel will be promoted to SIG/SI, SIG/MET, and SIG/USE members.

PANELISTS

Keiko Kurata is Professor at the Department of Library and Information Science, Keio University, Japan. Her research interest is on the ecosystem of scholarly communication in the digital age, and now her research project, with funding from The Japan Society for the Promotion of Science, investigates the relationship among the social contexts of collaborative research such as the norm of the discipline, research practices, data practices, and scholarly communication such as articles. Her monograph *The System of Scholarly Communication and Open Access* received the Award for the best work of the year from Japan Society of Library and Information Science. She has also published articles on digital reading. Her research information can be accessible from https://keio.pure.elsevier.com/ja/persons/keiko-kurata.

Jongwook Lee is Assistant Professor in the Department of Library and Information Science at Kyungpook National University, South Korea. He earned a bachelor's degree in Library and Information Science from Kyungpook National University, South Korea, a master's degree in Information Science from Indiana University Bloomington, and a PhD in Information Studies from Florida State University. He is interested in conducting research on different aspects of scholarly communications, including creation, distribution, evaluation, and use of research. He studies researchers' information and collaboration practices using quantitative and qualitative research methods in cooperation with other researchers.

Sanghee Oh is Associate Professor in the Department of Library and Information Science, Chungnam National University, South Korea. She obtained her PhD in Information & Library Science from the University of North Carolina at Chapel Hill, and her Master of Library and Information Science from the University of California at Los Angeles. Prior to joining the faculty in March 2017, she served as Assistant Professor in the School of Information, Florida State University. Her areas of research interest are human information behaviors, social informatics, and health informatics. Sanghee has studied people's motivations, evaluations, and use of social media, utilizing the mixed methods of content analysis, data/text mining, and online surveys. Her research and teaching information is available on her website: http://shoh.cnu.ac.kr.

Mamiko Matsubayashi is Assistant Professor at the Faculty of Library, Information and Media Science, the University of Tsukuba, Japan. She earned a bachelor's and a master's degree in Library and Information Science from Keio University, Japan. She has been particularly interested in information practices among scientists and has studied information practices among scientists, students, and the general public using qualitative methods.

Weiwei Yan is Associate Professor in the School of Information Management, Wuhan University, China. He also obtained his PhD there. In August 2016 – August 2017, he came to Kent State University as a visiting scholar. His research interests include user information behavior and scientific collaboration. His research project, "Collaborative information behavior in scientific cooperation", has received a Chinese National Funding of Social Science. He has studied scientific cooperation motivations, collaboration behavior characteristics, collaboration networks, and is specifically interested in user behavior and scientific collaboration in ASNSs such as ResearchGate.

Yin Zhang is Professor at the School of Information, Kent State University. She received her PhD in Library and Information Science from University of Illinois at Urbana-Champaign, and her B.S. and M.S. in Information Science from Wuhan University, China. Her research and teaching areas include user information-seeking behavior, information uses and services, informetrics, scientometrics, and information technology applications. More information is available at: http://yinzhang.ischool.kent.edu/.

REFERENCES

Arshad, A., & Ameen, K. (2017). Scholarly communication in the age of Google: Exploring academics' use patterns of e-journals at the University of the Punjab. *The Electronic Library, 35*(1), 167–184.

Bianchini, L. (2012). *Social networks for scientists: What social media to use for your research activity*. Retrieved from https://www.mysciencework.com/omniscience/social-networks-for-scientists

Biglan, A. (1973). The characteristics of subject matter in different academic areas. *Journal of Applied Psychology, 57* (3), 195–203.

Dermentzi, E., Papagiannidis, S., Toro, C. O., & Yannopoulou, N. (2016). Academic engagement: Differences between intention to adopt social networking sites and other online technologies. *Computers in Human Behavior, 61*, 321–332.

Gruzd, A., & Goertzen, M. (2013). *Wired academia: Why social science scholars are using social media*. In 2013 46th Hawaii International Conference on System Sciences (pp. 3332-3341). IEEE.

Kim, J. (2010). Faculty self-archiving: Motivations and barriers. *Journal of the American Society for Information Science and Technology, 61*(9), 1909–1922.

Lee, J., Oh, S., Dong, H., Wang, F., & Burnett, G. (2019). Motivations for self-archiving on an academic social networking site: A study on ResearchGate. *Journal of the Association for Information Science and Technology., 70*(6), 563–574.

Oh, S., & Syn, S. Y. (2015). Motivations for sharing information and social support in social media: A comparative analysis of Facebook, Twitter, Delicious, YouTube, and Flickr. *Journal of the Association for Information Science and Technology, 66*(10), 2045–2060. https://doi.org/10.1002/asi.23320

Thelwall, M., & Kousha, K. (2015). ResearchGate: Disseminating, communicating, and measuring scholarship? *Journal of the Association for Information Science and Technology, 66*(5), 876–889.

Xia, F., Su, X., Wang, W., Zhang, C., Ning, Z., & Lee, I. (2016). Bibliographic analysis of nature based on Twitter and Facebook altmetrics data. *PLoS ONE, 11*(12), e0165997.

Yan, W., & Zhang, Y. (2018). Research universities on the ResearchGate social networking site: An examination of institutional differences, research activity level, and social networks formed. *Journal of Informetrics, 12*(1), 385–400.

Yan, W., & Zhang, Y. (2019). User behaviors and network characteristics of US research universities on an academic social networking site. *Higher Education*. https://doi.org/10.1007/s10734-018-0339-x

Yan, W., Zhang, Y., & Bromfield, W. (2018). Analyzing the follower-followee ratio to determine user characteristics and institutional participation differences among research universities on ResearchGate. *Scientometrics, 115*(1), 299–316.

Toward Effective Use and Balance: Investigating Pros and Cons of Smartphone Use in an Interview Study

Naresh Kumar Agarwal
Simmons University
Boston, USA
naresh.agarwal@simmons.edu

Wenqing Lu
Simmons University
Boston, USA
wenqing.lu@simmons.edu

ABSTRACT

A large number of people spend a major part of their days staring at their smartphone screens. The objective of this poster is to study smartphone use and its positive and negative effects, and to provide recommendations for balanced use. We interviewed 20 female and 4 male participants. Ease of communication and multitasking are the key benefits, and overuse and disconnect from real world are the detriments in smartphone use. We propose the Yin-Yang framework of smartphone use, and provide recommendations for effective usage.

KEYWORDS

smartphone use; pros; cons; being present; addiction

ASIS&T THESAURUS

Social Informatics; Information Behavior; Technology impact

INTRODUCTION AND LITERATURE REVIEW

A lot of people now spend their free time staring at their smartphones (Choi, 2016; Pew Research, 2017). Mobile communication can have both positive effects in improving subjective well-being (see e.g. Agarwal, 2014; Chan, 2015) and negative impacts upon excessive use, with smartphone addiction potentially leading to ill health, including physical, psychological, and social issues or affecting work-life balance (Dén-Nagy, 2014; Ding & Li, 2017; Haug et al., 2015). We investigate the following research questions: RQ1. What are the pros and cons of using smartphones? RQ2. What are the possible solutions for effective smartphone use? Yin-Yang has the dialectical thinking that all phenomena are shaped by the dynamic integration of opposite yet complementary elements, where these elements are partially conflicting and partially complementary, and that nothing is isolated and independent (Li, 2016). Using this, we propose the yin-yang framework of smartphone use.

82nd Annual Meeting of the Association for Information Science & Technology | Melbourne, Australia | 19–23 October, 2019

DOI: 10.1002/pra2.00100

RESEARCH METHOD

24 interviews were carried out from May–July, 2017 where participants responded to a call sent to a Simmons University mailing list. Data was gathered in person in 19 interviews of 1-2 hours each. 5 interviews were conducted online using Skype and Google hangouts. All the interviewees agreed to be recorded. The collected data was transcribed and summarized based on the answers to specific questions, and candidate categories arrived at to synthesize the findings.

RESULTS AND ANALYSIS

The 24 interviewees were in the age range of 22-64 years, with a mean age of 30.8 years, and a median of 27 years. The majority of the participants were women (20), while 4 men were interviewed. This skew represents the skew in the graduate student body at the School of Library and Information Science, Simmons University that has a majority of women. 87.5% of the participants were graduate/doctoral students, while the rest were working full-time. Most of the participants (19) identified as graduate students, with 11 of those indicating that they work as well. 2 were doctoral students, while 3 participants were working full-time.

RQ1. Pros and Cons of Using Smartphones

The pros and cons were identified in each of these 4 primary categories that emerged from the analysis. The number of responses for each argument are shown in brackets.

Communication. Pros (19) *"I'm able to keep in better touch with people that I don't necessarily see every day."* Cons (5) *"you can't really express your actual intention or emotion through text messages." "...if I just don't feel like talking to someone, it'd be easy to ignore*...[or say]...*'I'm in the shower' or something... it's easier to be deceptive."*

Multitasking. Pros (17) Participants reported being able to listen to music or audio books, and at the same time, doing other tasks on the phone such as texting, emailing, reading, or tasks outside of the phone such as walking or cooking, etc. Cons (7) Participants said multitasking can be distracting. *"I don't necessarily consider multitasking helpful; I know that I'm not as productive when multitasking."*

Heavy use / Overuse. Pros (7) Participants felt that using smartphones heavily is not necessarily a problem. "*It kind of creates a different reality for you...people use it for work and class, and everything...I really feel like it's an extension of my being.*"; Cons (11) "*I'm reading some stuff on my phone and walking to the train at the same time. I'm going to walk into a hole someday, I swear!*"; "*It's unhealthy because it's easy to waste your life.*"; No opinion (6).

Virtual over in-person Communication. Pros (7) Participants thought the online presence is more meaningful for them or didn't see it as a problem. "*I may not be in the moment where I'm living, but I'll be deeply involved... with something that's happening in Houston with some friends. So, I feel more to be present even though I might seem distracted. It's kind of hard to describe.*"; Cons (17) "*Our family gathering will be on smartphones. We actually made time to be at the same location together as a family; we should put our phones down.*"

Thus, smartphones enable people to communicate and to easily keep in touch with each other. However, that brings the problem of keeping a balance between virtual and in-person communications. Also, multitasking is powerful, but made some participants distracted from the work they needed to focus on. The opposite yet complimentary pros and cons perfectly fit in the Yin-Yang diagram showing a dynamic integration of pros and cons. In Figure 1, we see that there is a little black in the white, and a little white in the black. Thus, there are pros among the cons, and cons among the pros.

RQ2. Suggestions and Expectations for Better Use

For solving the problem of smartphones detracting them from "being present" in real life, participants suggested creating time to be with the real world, no matter how important the virtual contacts are. "*[Get] involved in your community... and go out and do something new.*" "*I suggest to take some 'self' time to put [the phone] aside for some time in a day.*" "*...unplugging for a little while can be beneficial*". Apple has introduced the 'screen time' feature for people to monitor their time using iOS devices.

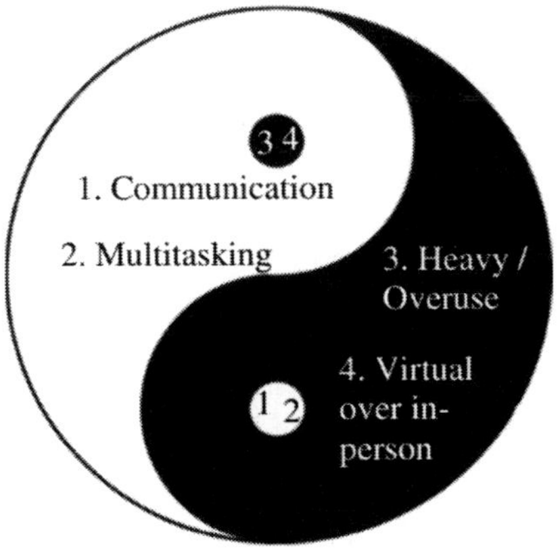

Figure 1. Yin-Yang (pros and cons) framework of smartphone use.

DISCUSSION AND CONCLUSION

While smartphones can inhibit people from being fully connected to "real life" (Turkle, 2017), however, as per Yin-Yang, there is a benefit hidden inside every detriment, and an opportunity within every difficulty. Given the right balance, overuse can be turned into effective use, and disconnect from real world into having many friends across the world. This sense of balance might differ based on individuals, households, situations and contexts (Agarwal, 2018). If the phones are used not as an end in itself, but an enabler for more facilitating deeper engagements, and more effective face-to-face communications (e.g. as a medium to plan a getaway to mountains; facilitating an online meeting of people who otherwise could not see each other; or connecting a distant mentee with a mentor), it can provide huge all-round benefits. Keeping the dynamic of Yin Yang in mind, we suggest to use the smartphones when needed, and put it away when presence in real life is needed. However, the generalizability of our findings are limited by the sample and its size.

ACKNOWLEDGMENTS

This is part of a larger study of non-response and information avoidance behavior, which was funded by the Hollowell grant 112-2435-20-211356 and the Presidents Fund grant 112-300-200000-UR_230000 by Simmons University. We thank Tenbit Mitiku and Nina Ferry for their contributions.

REFERENCES

Agarwal, N. K. (2014). Use of touch devices by toddlers and preschoolers: Observations and findings from a single-case study. In D. Bilal & J. Beheshti (Eds.), *New directions in children and adolescents' information behavior research* (pp. 3–38). Bingley, England: Emerald.

Agarwal, N. K. (2018). *Exploring context in information behavior: Seeker, situation, surroundings, and shared identities*. San Rafael, CA: Morgan & Claypool.

Chan, M. (2015). Mobile phones and the good life: Examining the relationships among mobile use, social capital, and subjective well-being. *New Media & Society*, *17*(1), 96–113.

Choi, S. (2016). The flipside of ubiquitous connectivity enabled by smartphone-based social networking service: Social presence and privacy concern. *Computers in Human Behavior*, *65*, 325–333.

Dén-Nagy, I. (2014). A double-edged sword?: A critical evaluation of the mobile phone in creating work–life balance. *New Technology, Work and Employment*, *29*(2), 193–211.

Ding, D., & Li, J. (2017). Smartphone overuse – A growing public health issue. *Journal of Psychology & Psychotherapy*, *7*(1), 289.

Haug, S., Castro, R. P., Kwon, M., Filler, A., Kowatsch, T., & Schaub, M. P. (2015). Smartphone use and smartphone addiction among young people in Switzerland. *Journal of Behavioral Addictions*, *4*(4), 299–307.

Li, P. P. (2016). Global implications of the indigenous epistemological system from the East: How to apply Yin-Yang balancing to paradox management. *Cross Cultural & Strategic Management*, *23*(1), 42–77.

Pew Research (2017). Mobile Fact Sheet. *Pew Research Center - Internet & Technology*. Jan 12. Retrieved from http://www.pewinternet.org/fact-sheet/mobile/

Turkle, S. (2017). *Alone together: Why we expect more from technology and less from each other*. London, England: Hachette.

Practice, Information and the Development of a Digital Platform

David K. Allen
Leeds University Business School, Leeds, UK
da2@lubs.leeds.ac.uk

Aleksandra Irnazarow
Leeds University Business School, Leeds, UK
a.irnazarow@leeds.ac.uk

Fiona McLaughlin
Leeds University School of Law, Leeds, UK
f.mclaughlin@leeds.ac.uk

ABSTRACT

This paper reflects upon the development of a digital platform using a theoretically informed, bottom-up approach to the co-production where the researchers were immersed in the design and development process. It draws upon three concepts from activity theory illustrating how each illuminates the development of the platform.

KEYWORDS

Activity theory; digital platform; co-production

ASIS&T THESAURUS

Qualitative analysis; Information sharing; Information infrastructure; Information behavior

INTRODUCTION

In this paper we focus on the development of a particular type of digital infrastructure: a digital platform developed for and by a heterogeneous group of public sector workers engaged in data science. The platform provides a variety of elements for the communities of practice including a systems to facilitate and agree data sharing between partners, a data observatory, training materials in data science and social media capability. The paper contributes our understanding of the development of digital platforms within the public sector and contributes to an established body of literature which explores the use of Activity Theory to understand people's interaction with information and technology (Karanasios, Allen, & Finnegan, 2018).

LITERATURE REVIEW

Organizational information is increasingly shared, used and managed in complex interconnected technological systems.

These have been described as configurations of the technical and social and are associated with significantly different degrees of challenge than stand-alone information systems. Much of the earlier work on these configurations has focused on how they accrete over time within organizational settings. An emergent body of literature, however, focuses on these as "digital infrastructures" exploring their evolution, formation as ecosystems, development (Constantinides & Barrett, 2014) and design. Digital platforms are one type of these new infrastructures and are seen as new and unique artifacts which necessitate conceptual and methodological innovation. We take a community-based approach viewing the infrastructure as a system of systems using Activity Theory. This allows us to go beyond the narrow conceptualisation of digital platforms as technical and digital artifacts and view them as comprising of both technical and social/organizational elements. This includes distributed actors and boundary resources, which are collectively used and created by the community of actors and which also regulate the relationships between them.

METHODOLOGY

The opportunity for the research came from a research project to support research activity between police services and universities around the topic of datification and data science. One element of this was the creation of a digital platform: the Data Analytics Digital Service (DADS). The researchers were engaged in both developing the DADS platform, building the community and undertaking research. The research involved three distinct communities: academics that were working or wished to collaborate with police services in the area of data analytics; police data analysts (including data scientists and business intelligence experts); individuals that play a role in data governance and management in these organizations. These groups were brought together in 'advisory groups' which formed communities of practice.

The digital platform was built over a period of three years as system of systems, each system offering different capabilities. At the time of writing the following four elements were being used: A systems to negotiate and agree data sharing between the eleven police services and the any academic who wishes to use police data. The output from this forms part of a data sharing agreement. A data observatory that provides a portal to a range of relevant data sources. A portal to relevant training and learning events and resources to be co-produced and developed by the academic and policing partners. This runs alongside a co-produced and delivered continual development program for Data Specialists in Policing. A

82nd Annual Meeting of the Association for Information Science & Technology | Melbourne, Australia | 19–23 October, 2019

DOI: 10.1002/pra2.00101

collaboration workspace for police and academic partners to share opportunities, develop new projects and share expertise.

Data was gathered in interviews, observation, and workshops to understand work practices, information behavior develop, test and implement elements of the systems over a three year period. In this paper we reflect on three concepts from activity theory and way in which they supported the development of the platform: congruence, contradictions and the object.

DISCUSSION

As contradictions arise, or are observed in a work activity system, they expose the dynamics, inefficiencies, and the structure of work, and importantly opportunities for enhancement. Congruencies can be seen as the corollary of contradictions in that they stabilize the work activity and can be used to understand inertia and resistance within systems to change. A contradiction identified early in the process of developing system one (a system to negotiate and agree data sharing) was between the norms and the rules associated with information practices undertaken when police services shared data with academics. The rules (internal rule and legal frameworks) which applied to such practices indicated that sensitive information could only be shared with academic partners using mandated digital tools. The norms of information practices (culturally accepted behavior), however, allowed practices which contravened these and led to the use of a different set of tools. Thus, for example, when there was a strong trust relationship between individuals or organizations the norm was that expedient information practices were often undertaken using tools which could allow data sharing rapidly. These practices were described as insecure and breaching organizational rules. Examples of such practices cited included the use of flash drives or e-mail to share large amounts of highly sensitive quantitative data. The concept of congruence provided a different view on this issue. During the analysis of the existing work activity system in system one we noted a congruence between the motivation and the norm. The motivation, held by some partners, to create a deep closed dyadic relationship with one university, group of academics or individual academic and the norm of information behavior based on informal inter-personal relationships and information sharing outside normal protocols. The focus on a limited but deeper set of organizational relationships facilitated trust and was seen as balancing the risks created by the contradiction between norms, rules and information practices. The congruence between these two elements of the existing system was a source of resilience in the existing system and can be linked to a resistance to change from existing patterns to adopt the new system. When understanding both current and future work and information practices the concept of the object took on particular importance. The object within an activity systems can be defined as that which is being acted upon and transformed. A core element of the development process was to recognize and engage with multiple fragmented understanding of the object (held by the different communities) and create a shared integrated view of the object for the new work activity system. For some, for example the object of the system was viewed in a wider or expansive way, such as the 'research relationship between academia and police services' in others it was seen in a much more limited way such as 'data access'. The different understandings of the object were also closely linked to differing motivations. Thus, for example the view of the object as a research relationship was linked, by some partners, to a set of expansive motivations, such as to develop more open and engaged scholarship partnerships with a wider group of organizations. This led to an expansive understanding of the platform and requirements. Others focused on the object of data as a something which mitigate risk and allow them to maintain control of data and the use of data.

CONCLUSION

In 2011 Allen et al., noted that a third opening is the needed to provide a language and models that will both reconnect information behaviour research with practice and allow us to communicate in a common language with disciplines that focus on design and development of systems. In this paper we present three concepts drawn from Activity Theory which illuminate the entwined nature of information behavior and practices in the development of new forms of digital infrastructure. Use of these concepts illuminates the significance of the resolution of deep socio-organizational issues for the longevity of the digital infrastructures. Equally, it also supports the view that information behavior in these platforms needs to be understood through heuristic frameworks (such as Activity Theory) which provide a holistic socio-organizational understanding of such technological tools.

ACHNOWLEDGMENTS

The authors would like to acknowledge funding provided by the N8 Policing Research Partnership.

REFERENCES

Allen, D., Karanasios, S., & Slavova, M. (2011). Working with activity theory: Context, technology, and information behavior. *Journal of the American Society for Information Science and Technology*, *62*, 776–788.

Constantinides, P., & Barrett, M. (2014). Information infrastructure development and governance as collective action. *Information Systems Research*, *26*, 40–56.

Karanasios, S., Allen, D. K., & Finnegan, P. (2018). Activity theory in information systems research. *Information Systems Journal*, *28*(3), 439–441.

Investigating Wisdom: Call for Research

Jeff Allen
University of North Texas,
Denton, USA
jeff.allen@unt.edu

Malak Khader
University of North Texas,
Denton, USA
mmkhader91@gmail.com

Amy Rosellini
University of North Texas,
Denton, USA
amy.rosellini@gmail.com

ABSTRACT

This study aims to address the gap in understanding "wisdom" as it relates to Data, Information, Knowledge, Wisdom (DIKW) Model/Hierarchy and the information science discipline. Disciplines like data science, information science, and knowledge management study wisdom without defining it. This study identifies the definition of the term wisdom within the information science discipline.

KEYWORDS

Knowledge management; wisdom; information science; DIKW

ASIS&T THESAURUS

Information science; knowledge management

INTRODUCTION

Wisdom has been an integral part of the information science field. Ackoff's Data Information Knowledge Wisdom (DIKW) Model/Hierarchy illustrates knowledge management as it starts with data, which leads to information that turns into knowledge, which then yields wisdom (Rowley, 2007). The DIKW model has been used since the mid-1950s and guides the field of information science to study critical components of and understand the hierarchy of needs within the field.

The aspects of data, information and knowledge of the DIKW model/hierarchy have been heavily studied and researched, while 'wisdom' has been neglected. Further, we have expanded the study of data, information and knowledge into degrees of study within data science, information science and knowledge management.

This paper serves as a call for research on a very prominent part the DIKW Model/Hierarchy and information science. An in-depth analysis of the last five years of JASIST publications reveals that only two publications focused on wisdom. However, the scope of the research was much broader than wisdom and the publications did not seek to define what wisdom entails. One of the publications was a research article which focused on "crowd wisdom" and the second publication was a book review which focused on leveraging wisdom from a crowd. Although both publications discuss wisdom, they are not focused on individual wisdom and what that entails.

The study of wisdom is difficult to both investigate and understand. This does not mean that there has not been any research conducted on wisdom; it simply implies that there is a lack of research concerning wisdom within the field of information science and especially in relation to the DIKW Model/Hierarchy. The fields of gerontology, psychology, and social science attempt to study the phenomena of wisdom with little significant impact on our understanding in the context of information science. Definitions of wisdom vary and mostly stem from a philosophical perspective (many of the definitions come directly from the discipline itself).

Rowley (2007) does well in comparing different interpretation of the DIKW Model/Hierarchy definitions, presented by Ackoff and Zeleny. Zeleny defines the hierarchy as follows: Data - know nothing, Information - know what, Knowledge - know how, and Wisdom - know why. While Ackoff presents the model as: Data - symbols, Information - data produced to use and answers the who/what/when/where/why questions, Knowledge - application of the data and information, and Wisdom - evaluated understanding of everything leading up to this point (as cited in Rowley, 2007). Through these definitions, wisdom, as a broad concept, has been explained, but what is lacking are knowing what lead to one being wise and what attributes "the wise" possesses.

ASPECTS OF WISDOM

Although there are main characteristics attributed to wisdom, those characters do not alone encompass the definition. Other, smaller attributes include: value relativism and tolerance; openness to new experiences; spirituality; and sense of humor (Bangen, Meeks, & Jeste, 2013). According to this definition, much of wisdom's characteristics are attributed to social factors and self-awareness, rather than information-knowledge factors. In other words, wisdom is not defined by the amount of information people know, but by the type of knowledge they have and how it is applied to the social contexts they experience.

82nd Annual Meeting of the Association for Information Science & Technology | Melbourne, Australia | 19–23 October, 2019

DOI: 10.1002/pra2.00102

A PATHWAY TO WISDOM

The pathway to creating wisdom allows for human experiences that develop within the individual. How can one be open to new experiences without experiencing them? How can one demonstrate spirituality or a sense of humor without deeper connection and meaning to their experiences?

Wisdom is a compilation of many human attributes. It requires a person to not only inherently have those attributes, but also demonstrate competency in building the characteristics of wisdom. The building of characteristics associated with wisdom - both social factors and self-awareness - may provide the pathway to wisdom. In order to create the path, a definition of wisdom will allow us to know what "wisdom" is, so we can determine how to attain it.

WISDOM IN INFORMATION SCIENCE

Information science provides a lack of research on wisdom while other social scientists see it as a great need in this information and technological age. With a wisdom-centric paradigm, information scientists are free to develop theories and understanding of how wisdom may contribute to the problems that arise over advances in technology (Dalal & Pauleen, 2019).

WISDOM DEFINED

There is an endless list of definitions for the other aspects of the DIKW Model/Hierarchy, but wisdom has been neglected. A proper and thorough definition of wisdom is needed for the field of information science because there is no known definition already attributed. Since wisdom is the pinnacle and goal of information seekers and managers, then it should be properly explained and understood.

Wisdom is the destination for information scientists and scientists of multiple disciplines. The call to study wisdom is the start to understanding it.

"Wisdom is a uniquely human quality demonstrated through an ability to apply self-insight, experience, and sound judgment in conjunction with applicable data, information, and knowledge to create a course of action leading to beneficial and productive decisions for both individuals and society." (Allen, Bracey, Gavrilova Aguilar, & Zimmerman, 2019). A definition of wisdom does not provide us a roadmap for creating wisdom, yet, it provides a definitional destination as we work with information professionals in a growing knowledge economy.

REFERENCES

Allen, J., Bracey, P., Aguilar, M., & Zimmerman, T. (2019). Supporting workforce wisdom in a global economy. In C. Hughes, *Handbook of research on attracting, maintaining, and balancing a mature workforce*. Hershey, PA: IGI Global.

Bangen, K. J., Meeks, T. W., & Jeste, D. V. (2013). Defining and assessing wisdom: A review of the literature. *The American Journal of Geriatric Psychiatry: Official Journal of the American Association for Geriatric Psychiatry, 21*(12), 1254–1266.

Dalal, N., & Pauleen, D. (2019). The wisdom nexus: Guiding information systems research, practice, and education. *Information Systems Journal, 29*(1), 224–244.

Rowley, J. (2007). The wisdom hierarchy: Representations of the DIKW hierarchy. *Journal of Information Science, 33* (2), 163–180.

Keeping the Human in the Data Scientist: Shaping Human-Centered Data Science Education

Theresa Dirndorfer Anderson
University of Technology Sydney (UTS),
Sydney, Australia
theresa.anderson@uts.edu.au

Nicola Parker
University of Technology Sydney (UTS),
Sydney, Australia
nicola.parker@uts.edu.au

ABSTRACT

Human-centered approaches are still relatively novel for data science practice, where data-driven analytics are often framed as ways to supersede human judgments. This poster presents core design principles devised by the authors to build a data science curriculum foregrounding ethics and valuing creative human capacities alongside strong data analytic skills. The curriculum design transforms human-centered principles into practice. The poster visually illustrates the trajectory of these principles in relation to three specific graduate attributes, using a selection of deep dives into the learning design. To illustrate the specific power information theory and practice has to shape data science training, the poster uses evocative quotes from information science theorists and displays how their work significantly influenced the overall philosophy of the program, student activities and assessments. Using 'gamestorming' techniques during the poster session, the audience is invited to contribute further insights about ways to nurture the deeply human capacities of the data scientists we train.

KEYWORDS

Data Science; Data Ethics; Human-Centered Approaches; Training & Education

ASIS&T THESAURUS

Data Science; Social Informatics

INTRODUCTION

In Australia, as in many other countries, there is a skills shortage in the data science fields. From startups through to large corporations, demand continues to outstrip the availability of talented professionals who can work with AI and autonomous decisioning tools to wrangle and analyze complex data (Guan, 2019; McKinsey, 2019). Alongside this increasing demand, however, concerns that data and AI-informed technologies truly serve humans (as individuals and collective groups) are also growing. Most recently, growing interest in AI as a strategic and commercial force is accompanied by increasing calls for better algorithmic governance and data/AI practices that more explicitly protect human rights (e.g.: AHRC, 2018). Attending to the human element in information and data practices has long been part of the training and study of members of the ASIS&T community. It is, however, still a relatively novel approach for data science practice, where data-driven analytics are often framed as a way to supersede human judgments.

82nd Annual Meeting of the Association for Information Science & Technology | Melbourne, Australia | 19–23 October, 2019

DOI: 10.1002/pra2.00103

CREATING ETHICAL CHANGE AGENTS

From 2014-2018 we collaborated on the design and delivery of the Master of Data Science & Innovation (MDSI) at UTS, a graduate data science program that foregrounded ethics and the necessity to develop creative human capacities alongside strong data analytic skills. As trained information professionals and social informatics educators, teaching human-centered approaches to tackle information and sociotechnical concerns has long been part of our own practice (e.g.: Kling & Star, 1998). Our curriculum design for MDSI therefore was able to draw on this experience to build a human-centered data science program.

Drawing on the core design principles we created to underpin our data science curriculum, the poster focuses on three particular MDSI graduate attributes (GA):

1. **Embracing ethical responsibilities:** interrogate and justify ethical responsibilities to create a framework for practice
2. **Making the invisible visible:** recognize, uncover and address the missing, underrepresented, or misrepresented
3. **Leading data science:** take a leadership role in promoting positive change in data science contexts

Examples from assessments, in-class and extra-curricular activities further articulate our design philosophy and illustrate the specific power information theory and practice have to shape data science training that embeds an ethical mindset in students from the outset.

HOW CURRICULUM DESIGN TRANSFORMS THESE PRINCIPLES INTO PRACTICE

The poster visually illustrates the trajectory of our design principles to these three specific GA using a selection of deep dives into our learning design for MDSI. Using evocative quotes from information science theorists, the poster displays how their work significantly influenced our curriculum, both in terms of overall philosophy and in terms of student activities and assessments. Two examples follow.

Data doesn't speak for itself, it's given a voice

From the first day of their training, we alert students to the challenges of fluidity and data variability in evolving contexts of data science practice. Our curriculum design was greatly influenced by sociotechnical explorations of classification, categorization and infrastructure studies, especially Bowker and Star (2000) and Star and Ruhleder (1996). The poster provides extracts of training using a Bowker (2006) quote as a springboard:

> *Raw data is both an oxymoron and a bad idea; to the contrary, data should be cooked with care.*

Through classroom activities and assessment, students learn not only about protecting personal data, but also how it feels to be represented in data used as a proxy for their behavior. In doing so we were able to foreground human values and make visible the limitations of assuming that data sets are complete representations of truth.

Embracing uncertainty as a necessary human condition

Being a program about data science for innovation, our MDSI curriculum design sought to deliberately disrupt assumptions about data objectivity and human subjectivity. We were especially inspired by Marcia Bates and her 1990 paper asking "Where should the person stop and the information search interface start?":

> *If we use, rather than ignore, the special traits of humans in the design of human-computer interfaces for information systems, we may find our abilities enhanced in unpredictable and creative ways (p 590)*

This insight was particularly compelling for promoting an augmentation approach to the students' computational work.

To raise students' (and thereby practitioner) awareness of the potential limitations of 'data-driven' decision making, the program design also drew on Anderson's work on creative ecologies of learning (2013) and approach to uncertainty as a delightfully human construct (2010). Opportunities for embracing uncertainty were deliberately embedded into classroom and extracurricular activities; assessments designed to reward students for taking intellectual risks.

WHEN IS THE HUMAN?

In the midst of contemporary conversations about the power of AI and autonomous decision tools to alter our work and everyday practices, our poster is intended to provide the ASIS&T community an opportunity to reflect on possible future implications of Don Swanson's observation:

> *Although the goal of much advanced IR research is to make computers do humanlike things, the possibility that people can be humanlike should not be overlooked (1988:98).*

Interpretation drawing on intuition and the insight born of lived experience is something humans do best. We see this as an invitation to frame data assemblages as computational capacity augmenting the human capacity to engage with and thrive in uncertainty and ambiguity.

Using 'gamestorming' techniques the poster invites the audience to share their thoughts on our approach, engage in conversation with us and contribute further insights about ways to nurture the deeply human capacities of the data scientists we train. In this way we hope to contribute to the growing network of human centered data science educators in our community.

ACKNOWLEDGMENTS

A heartfelt 'thank you' to all our MDSI students and teaching team, for their enthusiasm and trust as we sought to bring our vision of 'participatory curriculum' to life.

REFERENCES

Anderson, T. D. (2010). Kickstarting creativity: Supporting the productive faces of uncertainty in information practice. *Information Research, 15*(4), paper colis721. Retrieved from http://InformationR.net/ir/15-4/colis721.html

Anderson, T. D. (2013). The 4Ps of innovation culture: Conceptions of creatively engaging with information. *Information Research, 18*(3) paper C28. Retrieved from http://InformationR.net/ir/18-3/colis/paperC28.html

Australian Human Rights Commission (2018). *Human Rights and Technology Issues Paper* (July 2018). Retrieved from https://tech.humanrights.gov.au/consultation

Bates, M. J. (1990). Where should the person stop and the information search interface start. *Information Processing & Management, 26*(5), 575–591.

Bowker, G. C. (2006). *Memory practices in the sciences.* Cambridge, MA: MIT Press.

Bowker, G. C., & Star, S. L. (2000). *Sorting things out: Classification and its consequences.* Cambridge, MA: MIT Press.

Guan, L. (2019). Data boom creates demand for specialists, *CIO from IDG*, 3 May 2019. Retrieved from https://www.cio.com.au/article/661160/data-boom-creates-demand-specialists/

Kling, R., & Star, S. L. (1998). Human centered systems in the perspective of organizational and social informatics. *Computers and Society*, *28*(1), 22–29.

McKinsey & Company (2019). *Notes from the AI Frontier: Tackling Europe's Gap in Digital and AI*, Discussion Paper, February, 2019. Retrieved from https://www.mckinsey.com/featured-insights/artificial-intelligence/tackling-europes-gap-in-digital-and-ai

Star, S. L., & Ruhleder, K. (1996). Steps toward an ecology of infrastructure: Design and access for large information spaces. *Information Systems Research*, *7*(1), 111–134.

Swanson, D. R. (1988). Historical note: Information retrieval and the future of an illusion. *Journal of the American Society for Information Science*, *39*(2), 92–98.

Investigating the Productive Uses of Uncertainty in Knowledge Co-Creation Practices

Jean Archambeault
McGill University, Montreal, Quebec, Canada
jean.archambeault@mail.mcgill.ca

ABSTRACT

This poster presents results from an ongoing exploratory research study, which uses a participant observation methodology to investigate the productive uses of uncertainty in fostering knowledge emergence. Recent research suggests that introducing uncertainty can be a productive resource to facilitate the emergence of knowledge in co-creation practices. While recognizing productive traits to uncertainty is not new in information science, how uncertainty can be deliberately introduced, as a productive resource, remains generally unnoticed. This study extends previous research in this area by further detailing the use of uncertainty and by constituting a foray into investigating information practices in collective knowledge creation environments. Findings suggest that introducing uncertainty aims at inducing a state of unknowability to erode certainty, disrupt entrained thinking and processual constraints, and decompartmentalize disciplinary boundaries that inhibit knowledge emergence. The experiences of relational engagement, joint advantage and mutual transformation arose as conditions conducive to using uncertainty for knowledge emergence.

KEYWORDS

Uncertainty; co-creation; knowledge emergence; innovation

INTRODUCTION

The fostering of knowledge emergence is a significant research area in information science and a strategic challenge in learning, research-driven, and innovation environments. Co-creation practices, defined as the collaborative participation of "different social actors and articulation of multiple knowledge forms" (Phillips & Napan, 2016, p. 4) proliferate as a means to generate knowledge. Although the promises and key elements of co-creation practices are progressively documented (Beckett, Farr, Kothari, Wye, & le May, 2018), there is a need for more of an empirical understanding of informational processes facilitating knowledge emergence in those environments. Interestingly, recent research suggests that introducing uncertainty can foster knowledge emergence in co-creation practices (Hartner-Tiefenthaler, Roetzer, Bottaro, & Peschl, 2018; Wiltschnig, Christensen, & Ball, 2013).

While the productive traits of uncertainty are recognized in information science (Anderson, 2010), very little research proposes the deliberate introduction of uncertainty as a productive resource, or details methods for doing so. Most information science research and practices still negativize uncertainty, either seeking to reduce it through information provision or to manage it through probabilistic formalism (Kamal & Burkell, 2011). Furthermore, information behavior studies predominantly operationalize uncertainty as an individual, cognitive, and affective construct. Thus, there is a lack of research on the use of uncertainty in collective, non-individual information practices.

This study aims to extend previous research on uncertainty by exploring its productive function. The primary research question is: How and why is uncertainty introduced to foster knowledge emergence in co-creation practices? In the context, uncertainty designates an ambivalent state of unknowability and indetermination, experienced as threatening, uncomfortable (e.g., frustration, anxiety, anger) and/or pleasurable (e.g., stimulation, excitement). The poster presents empirical research findings, sketches an uncertainty landscape and proposes directions to guide the development of a conceptual framework. The intent is to raise awareness and stimulate discussions into appraising uncertainty as a complementary resource to information provision and data analytics methodologies.

METHODOLOGY

This qualitative research used a participant observation methodology. The observation site was VIA-Inno, a technological intelligence (TI) platform attached to a theoretical and applied economics laboratory (GREThA) from Université de Bordeaux in France. VIA-Inno operating model and TI practices (i.e. analytical, visualization, and interpretive methodologies on scientific, technological and financial datasets) exemplify a co-creation environment: VIA-Inno is grounded in social sciences and academia (i.e., economics, innovation management) while co-producing with industrial and territorial partners operating in science, technology and engineering. Participants were recruited through internal contacts, on a voluntary basis, using a non-probabilistic, purposive sampling method. Data collection took place in two phases.

82nd Annual Meeting of the Association for Information Science & Technology | Melbourne, Australia | 19–23 October, 2019

DOI: 10.1002/pra2.00104

The first phase was completed over a 5 1/2 months period, which included 30 individual and group interviews that were audio-recorded (N = 31 participants), reported in this paper. Interviewees were VIA-Inno practitioners, representatives from most of their partners, as well as associated researchers and PhDs, executives and stakeholders from Université de Bordeaux and the Center National de la Recherche Scientifique (CNRS). Interview transcripts were coded using Constant Comparative Analysis (CCA), an iterative, inductive coding technique. In the second phase (a few months later), preliminary results were presented to practitioners in a group setting first, then met individually to capture reactions, comments, and stimulate further discussions.

FINDINGS AND DISCUSSION

Findings indicate that introducing uncertainty served at least three purposes in the context of this study. First, to systematically erode certainty and challenge uninvestigated assumptions, most often at project proposal stage. Uncertainty is introduced to increase confidence in the robustness of decision-making processes by inquiring for biased information and unsupported expectations using TI generated informational evidences. Second, to guide attention toward neglected informational elements despite unknown outcomes. Practitioners reported that their partners often failed to recognize and explore intuitions, unarticulated insights, unexpected informational elements and unaddressed questions arising regularly in the course of co-creation projects. These marginal elements were often ignored, rejected upfront or may not have percolated seamlessly in the organizations, a potential loss in informational and strategic value. The third purpose was paradigmatic, motivated by a systemic need to decompartmentalize expertise, competence and specialization areas in knowledge production organizations. University executives and VIA-Inno stakeholders ascribe transformational value in co-creation activities' potential to induce productive uncertainty, in order to destabilize and reconfigure organizational and disciplinary boundaries.

Creating uncertainty to steer attention toward avoided, ignored or disregarded informational elements required the ability to lead partners into a state of unknowability. A key challenge is to create enough uncertainty in co-creating partners so that they bifurcate from conditioned expectations, processual constraints and entrained thinking. This entailed prompting experts to learn as novices, agree to share power or to let go of some control and reprioritize resource allocation to investigate. Provoking bodily, visceral reactions (i.e., surprises, suspense, contention) in partners evoked pleasure and excitement in practitioners and was the most sought-after tactic to introduce uncertainty. One explanation is that inducing unknowability or revealing ignorance may bring a gain in influence, credibility and power both for themselves and for their partners. Other strategies and tactics used to introduce uncertainty were the ability to insist and influence, to authorize oneself to take analytical risks and make decisions, to reveal one's own subjectivity and intuitions; and to apply offensive anticipation. Among conditions conducive to the deliberate introduction of uncertainty were relational engagement; joint advantage; methodological transparency and mutual transformation capacity (i.e., the willingness to challenge and be challenged).

CONCLUSION

While limited by its exploratory nature, this study makes several contributions and directs the development of a conceptual framework for further research into two areas. First, it expands uncertainty, a core concept in information science, as a potential resource that complements information provision and data analytics methodologies. Introducing uncertainty aims to deliberately disrupt influences that inhibit knowledge emergence. As co-creators, information and data analysts are knowledge partners assuming increased accountability and responsibility in revealing intuitions and in articulating unaddressed questions. This suggests that developing uncertainty self-tolerance (Anderson, 2010) may be insufficient in co-creation environments. To reap informational value potential in co-creation practices, introducing uncertainty requires the ability to entice attention, reveal, insist and use the fluidity of power to induce a state of unknowability. Secondly, findings position TI informational practices in a co-evolutive learning versus decision-making framework. This emphasizes the need to explore the collective experiences of relational engagement, joint advantage and mutual transformation as conditions conducive to knowledge emergence and innovation.

ACKNOWLEDGMENTS

The author is grateful to his thesis supervisor Dr. Max Evans and to Université de Bordeaux, GREThA, Via-Inno and their partners for their open participation. This research was made possible through a Mitacs Globalink Research Award (#IT08832GRA), support from National Research Council of Canada and McGill University.

REFERENCES

Anderson, T. D. (2010). Kickstarting creativity: Supporting the productive faces of uncertainty in information practice. *Information Research*, *15*(4).

Beckett, K., Farr, M., Kothari, A., Wye, L., & le May, A. (2018). Embracing complexity and uncertainty to create impact: Exploring the processes and transformative potential of co-produced research through development of a social impact model. *Health Research Policy and Systems*, *16*(1), 118.

Hartner-Tiefenthaler, M., Roetzer, K., Bottaro, G., & Peschl, M. F. (2018). When relational and epistemological uncertainty act as driving forces in collaborative knowledge creation processes among university students. *Thinking Skills and Creativity*, *28*, 21–40.

Kamal, A. M., & Burkell, J. (2011). Addressing uncertainty: When information is not enough. *Canadian Journal of Information and Library Science*, *35*(4), 174–186.

Phillips, L., & Napan, K. (2016). What's in the 'co'? Tending the tensions in co-creative inquiry in social work education. *International Journal of Qualitative Studies in Education*, *29*(6), 827–844.

Wiltschnig, S., Christensen, B. T., & Ball, L. J. (2013). Collaborative problem-solution co-evolution in creative design. *Design Studies*, *34*(5), 515–542.

Data for Development: The Case for Africa

Shimelis Assefa
University of Denver, Denver, USA
shimelis.assefa@du.edu

Daniel Gelaw Alemneh
University of North Texas, Denton, USA
daniel.alemneh@unt.edu

Abebe Rorissa
University at Albany, State University of New York, Albany, USA
arorissa@albany.edu

ABSTRACT

This study presents the results of a systematic review of data use practices by African countries to support the United Nations Sustainable Development Goals (UN SDGs) #2 – agriculture. Data use practices and existing data infrastructure are reviewed through the lens of the four big data value-chain - data generation, data acquisition, data storage, and data analysis. The findings show that – 1) national statistical offices are the primary institutions responsible for data collection and analysis at country level; 2) survey is the primary means for data generation and acquisition; c) the capability to transform data into actionable insight and knowledge is severely limited; 4) data is heavily used for reporting purposes.

KEYWORDS

Big data; Sustainable Development Goals; SDG #2; Africa; Data Collection; Agriculture

INTRODUCTION

The purpose of this study is twofold: 1) to review existing data use practices and data infrastructure by African countries to support activities geared to achieve the UN SDG #2, end hunger, achieve food security and improved nutrition and promote sustainable agriculture; and 2) to identify gaps in existing data use practices and capabilities with a view to recommend best practices. Africa is home to 1.2 billion population that is projected to double to 2.5 billion by 2050 (UNCTAD, 2018).

SDG #2, the focus of this poster is dubbed "Zero Hunger," and it includes 8 target areas ranging from ending malnutrition, doubling agricultural productivity, to maintaining genetic diversity (UNSD, 2018). Sustainable agricultural practice is a critical sector for Africa because recurring drought and food insecurity are the persistent challenges for the continent (FAOSTAT, 2017; Kogan, Guo, & Yang, 2019). Querying the FAOSTAT of the Food Agricultural Organization of the UN via the Kenya data portal (http://kenya.opendataforafrica.org/), the following graph shows how Africa compares with the rest of the world when it comes to total crop yield.

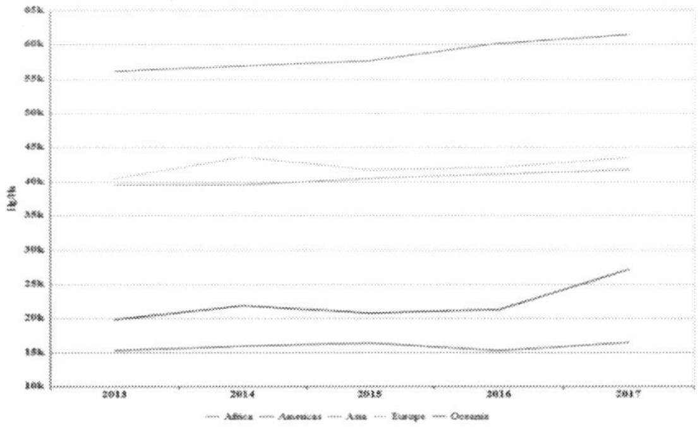

Figure 1. Cereals, total – yield.

Africa, a population of 1.3 billion has 16,433 hectogram per hectare (hg/ha) compared to Oceania that has 41.7 million population and 27,088 hg/ha.

BACKGROUND

The collection, analysis, and use of data (especially big data) has received substantial investment due to its promise as the next frontier for innovation and productivity (Manyika et al., 2011); as a capability to effectively optimize operations and create value in the agriculture sector– crop and livestock production (Chen, Mao, & Liu, 2014; Hilbert, 2016); as a key driver to improve supply chain linkages to enhance efficiency and effectiveness of the food production and distribution (Boehlje, 2016); as a resource to predict drought risk assessment (Skakun, Kussul, Shelestov, & Kussul, 2016); or in general good data collection and analysis is seen as a key driver to end malnutrition in Africa (Annan, 2018).

METHODS

A systematic review of scientific literature and technical reports on agriculture, food production, and data for development was conducted. Key resources include - The Africa Information Highway (AIH) - the African Development Bank's (AfDB) initiative that has linked the African countries through the Open Data Platform (ODP) (http://dataportal.opendataforafrica.org/); National Statistical offices of

82nd Annual Meeting of the Association for Information Science & Technology | Melbourne, Australia | 19–23 October, 2019

DOI: 10.1002/pra2.00105

African countries; PARIS21 (Greenwell, Kinyua, Klein, & Ranjan, 2016); UN SDG, Inter-agency and Expert Group on Sustainable Development Goal Indicators (https://unstats.un.org/sdgs/iaeg-sdgs/). PRISMA framework or Preferred Reporting Items for Systematic Reviews and Meta-Analyses (PRISMA) (Moher et al., 2009) together with the four value chain of big data - namely data generation, data acquisition, data storage, and data analysis (Chen et al., 2014) were used to guide the synthesis and presentation of the salient findings.

RESULTS

Big data value chain	Practices and data infrastructure in Africa
Data generation	Survey is the chief means for generating data. Very limited volume and variety. No IoT, no videos, no clickstreams, no web text generated. Data is largely generated by or for international development institutions.
Data acquisition	Methods for collection, acquisition and transportation are underdeveloped. Very few cases of network based communication and transportation to storage.
Data storage	Traditional data storage and management, few network based storage, legacy systems such as Excel and relational databases. Limited use of file systems such as Google GFS, databases such as NoSQL, and limited infrastructure for managing large scale data such as MapReduce.
Data analysis	Central statistical offices are the central organs for data collection, analysis, and dissemination. Very constrained socio-technical capability to transform data into actionable insights and knowledge. Limited use of advanced analytic methods such as R.

Table 1.Big data value chain and the state of data use practices and data infrastructure in Africa.

CONCLUSION

Data use practices and existing data infrastructure (technology, skill, processes, and policy) to support agriculture (the operation and effectiveness of crop and livestock production and distribution) in Africa is very limited. When this limitation is added to the existing social, political, and environmental bottlenecks, achieving the 'zero hunger' goal by 2030 could prove to be illusive for Africa. To bridge the existing gap in data use practices and capabilities, it is important to accelerate the efforts of PARIS21 and AfDB's AIH, most importantly to prepare data science professionals and a concerted effort to use open source tools, technologies, and frameworks.

REFERENCES

Annan, K. (2018). Data can help to end malnutrition across Africa. *Nature*, *555*(7694), 7.

Boehlje, M. (2016). How might big data impact industry structure and enhance margins? *International Food and Agribusiness Management Review*, *19*(A), 13–16.

Chen, M., Mao, S., & Liu, Y. (2014). Big data: A survey. *Mobile Networks and Applications*, *19*(2), 171–209. https://doi.org/10.1007/s11036-013-0489-0.

FAOSTAT. (2017). *FAO statistical databases*. Rome, Italy: Food and Agriculture Organization of the United Nations. Statistics Division. Retrieved from http://faostat3.fao.org/.

Greenwell, G., Kinyua, J., Klein, T., & Ranjan, R. (2016). *Making Data Portals work for SDGs: A view on deployment, design and technology* (Discussion Paper No. 8). PARIS21. Partnership in Statistics for Development in the 21st Century.

Hilbert, M. (2016). Big Data for Development: A Review of Promises and Challenges. *Development Policy Review*, *34*(1), 135–174.

Kogan, F., Guo, W., & Yang, W. (2019). Drought and food security prediction from NOAA new generation of operational satellites, Geomatics. *Natural Hazards and Risk*, *10*(1), 651–666. https://doi.org/10.1080/19475705.2018.1541257.

Manyika, J., Chui, M., Brown B., Bughin, J., Dobbs, R., Roxburgh, C., & Byers, A. (2011). *Big Data: The next frontier for innovation, competition, and productivity.*

Moher, D., Literati, A., Tetzlaff, J., Altman, D. G., & the PRISMA Group. (2009). Preferred reporting items for systematic reviews and meta-analyses: The PRISMA statement. *PLoS Medicine*, *6*(7), e1000097.

Skakun, S., Kussul, N., Shelestov, A., & Kussul, O. (2016). The use of satellite data for agriculture drought risk quantification in Ukraine. *Geomatics, Natural Hazards and Risk*, *7*(3), 901–917. https://doi.org/10.1080/19475705.2015.1016555.

UN Global Pulse (2016). *Integrating Big Data into the monitoring and evaluation of development programs*

United Nations Conference on Trade and Development (UNCTAD). (2018). *Economic development in Africa Report 2018 migration for structural transformation.* New York, NY: United Nations.

United Nations Statistics Division. UNSD. (2018). *The sustainable development goals report 2018.* New York, NY: Development Data and Outreach Branch Retrieved from https://unstats.un.org/sdgs/report/2018.

Everyday Health Information Seeking Among Millennials

Joan C. Bartlett
McGill University,
Montreal, Canada
joan.bartlett@mcgill.ca

Aaron Bowen-Ziecheck
McGill University,
Montreal, Canada
aaron.bowen-ziecheck@mail.mcgill.ca

Cynthia Kumah
McGill University,
Montreal, Canada
cynthia.kumah@mail.mcgill.ca

Jamshid Beheshti
McGill University,
Montreal, Canada
jamshid.beheshti@mcgill.ca

ABSTRACT

This research investigates the information behavior of millennial students in the context of everyday-life health information. Data was collected using a mixed-methods approach of a survey (3565 responses) followed by interviews. Results-to-date show that while the students make good judgements regarding the credibility of resources, that judgment is not always reflected in the resources they actually choose to use.

KEYWORDS

Everyday health information; information literacy; health information behavior

ASIS&T THESAURUS

Information behavior; information seeking

INTRODUCTION

Millennial students, those between the ages of 18 and 24, rely heavily on digital information and social networks to seek and share information for academic purposes, as well as for everyday life such as consumer purchases, health and finances (e.g., Head & Eisenberg, 2011; Kim, Sin, & Yoo-Lee, 2014). In particular, social media is used by 90 percent of young adults (Perrin, 2015) almost on a daily basis to ask and answer questions about everyday life activities such as entertainment and health information (Agosto, Purcell, Magee, & Forte, 2015), and to a lesser extent for academic information (Kim et al., 2014).

However, research shows that their ability to judge the validity and reliability of information, and to organize and synthesize the retrieved information for immediate and future use may be poor, in spite of their self-perception of competence (e.g., Gross & Latham, 2012). Likewise, recent studies indicate major gaps in students' knowledge and skills in evaluating the validity and reliability of information from social media (Kim, 2016) to the point of many students naively sharing misinformation (Chen, Sin, Theng, & Lee, 2015).

82nd Annual Meeting of the Association for Information Science & Technology | Melbourne, Australia | 19–23 October, 2019

DOI: 10.1002/pra2.00106

OBJECTIVES

This research is part of a larger study comparing information behavior and information literacy in both the academic and everyday-life domains. The research questions are: 1) what are the characteristics of student's information behavior in both domains? 2) what factors may impact students' information behavior in both domains? and, 3) are the characteristics and factors similar in both domains? The work-in-progress reported here is focused on the first two questions in the context of everyday-life health information.

METHODS

Data collection followed a two-phase mixed-methods approach, with an online survey followed by interviews. The survey was sent to all 22 900 undergraduate students of McGill University in October 2017; 3565 usable responses (response rate 15.6%) were obtained. Participants ranged in age from 18 to 24 years old, and represented all faculties within the university, and all years of study. 2396 identified as female, 1129 as male, with 38 preferring to gender self-identify. Survey questions included: how often specific resources were used to obtain information; how credible those resources were believed to be; the weight given to certain factors when judging the credibility of a resource; and which search tools or databases were used most often.

In the second phase of the research, semi-structured interviews with an additional 15 students are being used to further explore the survey responses. The focus of this phase is: how and why students choose resources; how students judge credibility and why; and why the credibility ranking of a resource does not necessarily correspond to how frequently it was used.

RESULTS

When looking for information regarding an everyday-health issue, the three resources most frequently used were family and friends, experts, and well-known websites (e.g., WebMD). While the survey presented family and friends as a single option, interview participants drew a distinction between them, reporting that they would rely on family (typically a parent) for health issues, but would not necessarily trust their friends. One caveat was a reluctance to discuss "private" or "sensitive" health concerns, such as mental or reproductive health with family.

"if it's something I just don't want my mom to know, like, for example birth control, no mom in that one. But if it's like 'Mom my tooth aches' ..." P1

When rating the credibility of the same set of resources, the three most highly rated resources were experts, scholarly books and journals, and government or university websites. Yet, these were not the most frequently used (Figure 1).

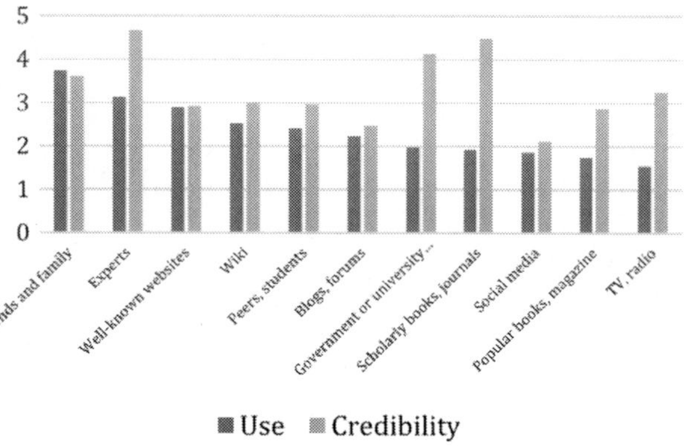

Figure 1. Frequency of use and rating of credibility of selected resources for everyday health information.

Interview participants reported that experts (defined as physicians and nurses) were difficult to access; other health professionals were not mentioned. Scholarly books and journals were reported to be inaccessible. One challenge was accessing the resources, either physically or digitally. The other was understanding the content, which was considered to be too detailed and high level for an everyday-health need.

"... like obviously they're credible but they're not necessarily applicable. you're not gonna look in some scholarly journal for some clear overview of like flu symptoms or anything ..." P2

Students were either unaware of government or university websites, or could not find or easily access them, reporting that they did not usually appear within the top Google results.

"... the first university website after 20 minutes of research I found was University of X's. I can't get access to it. And then it took another 10 minutes to find the correct corresponding website at Y University." P4

Survey participants rated the importance of various factors (e.g., up-to-date, matches other sources, quality of language) in judging credibility; the average scores for most factors were clustered around 4 on a 5-point Likert scale (5 being very important). While being in the top-5 Google hits scored slightly lower (3.4), interview participants reported that this was important to them, and their belief that the top-5 results were the most relevant and the "best".

Finally, the survey asked which tools or search engines were used most frequently, Google was the most frequently used, averaging 4.4 on a 5-point Likert scale (5 being "always"). All other resources (including YouTube, Facebook, Twitter, and the library website or catalog) had average scores below 2. Interview participants mentioned that they were aware of possible inaccuracies in self diagnosing with Google and the possibility of search results increasing anxiety, but that they still used Google regardless.

CONCLUSION

The results-to-date of this research show that while undergraduate students are able to identify credible information resources for everyday-health issues, they do not necessarily use them. In contrast to previous findings (Agosto et al., 2015), our participants did not use social media extensively for everyday-health information. Ongoing and future work will explore whether similar behaviors occur during academic information seeking, and also whether there is any overlap in information literacy skills (or lack thereof) from the academic domain to everyday-life.

ACKNOWLEDGMENTS

We would like to acknowledge the invaluable contribution of all the survey and interview participants. Research funding is from a SSHRC (Social Science and Humanities Research Council – Canada) Insight grant to the first author, and a SSHRC Insight Development grant to the last author. We thank research assistants Anna Couch, Kayley McLeod, and Amy Bergeron for their contributions.

REFERENCES

Agosto, D. E., Purcell, M., Magee, R. M., & Forte, A. (2015). Teens, libraries and social media: Myths and reality. *Public Library Quarterly, 34*(4), 318–327.

Chen, X., Sin, S. C. J., Theng, Y. L., & Lee, C. S. (2015). Why students share misinformation on social media: Motivation, gender and study-level differences. *Journal of Academic Librarianship, 41*(5), 583–592.

Gross, M., & Latham, D. (2013). Addressing below proficient information literacy skills: Evaluating the efficacy of an evidence-based educational intervention. *Library & Information Science Research, 35*(3), 181–190.

Head, A. L., & Eisenberg, M. B. (2011). How college students use the Web to conduct everday life research. *First Monday, 26*(4).

Kim, K. S., & Sin, S. C. J. (2016). Use and evaluation of information from social media in the academic context:

Analysis of gap between students and librarians. *Journal of Academic Librarianship*, *42*(1), 74–82.

Kim, K. S., Sin, S. C. J., & Yoo-Lee, E. (2014). Undergraduates' use of social media as information sources. *College & Research Libraries*, *75*(4), 442–457.

Perrin, A. (2015). Social Networking Usage: 2005-2015. *Pew Research Center, October 2015*. Retrieved from http://www.pewinternet.org/2015/10/08/2015/Social-Networking-Usage-2005-2015/

A Gap Analysis of Survivorship Terminology: Knowledge Resources Versus Literature Usage

Catherine Blake
School of Information Sciences,
University of Illinois at Urbana-Champaign
clblake@illinois.edu

Jenna Kim
School of Information Sciences,
University of Illinois at Urbana-Champaign
jkim682@illinois.edu

Milind Mathur
School of Information Sciences,
University of Illinois at Urbana-Champaign
milindm2@illinois.edu

Akanksha Aggarwal
School of Information Sciences,
University of Illinois at Urbana-Champaign
aa21@illinois.edu

ABSTRACT

Survivorship is arguably the most important endpoint in a cancer clinical trial. Our goal is to compare the extent to which survivorship concepts within existing medical knowledge resources adequately capture how authors describe survivorship when reporting the inclusion criterion and outcomes from studies of 5 breast cancer treatments. Results show that MESH and the NCI thesauri provide good coverage with respect to set of core survivorship concepts that appear frequently in text; further work, however, is required to account for modifiers used by authors so that noun phrases in literature are accurately aligned with the corresponding concept in a given ontology.

KEYWORDS

Information representation; knowledge management; biomedical and health informatics

ASIS&T THESAURUS

Information representations; information resources

INTRODUCTION

As with many medical conditions in medicine, the breast cancer community has been developing standard definitions for key outcomes, such as survivorship (Hudis et al., 2007). The goal is to improve consistency in how authors report clinical trial results. Such consistency also helps text mining systems to automatically identify endpoints from the literature in order to accelerate secondary analyses. Ontologies provide a bridge between the medical community harmonization efforts and informatics but ontologies will only produce improvements in text mining if (a) the concepts captured in the ontology reflect the concepts conveyed in the literature and (b) the specific words used in the literature can be automatically aligned to the ontological concepts. These considerations should be treated separately because an ontology might be complete with respect to the core concepts that are reported in the literature but lacking in terms of synonyms that authors use. For example, 'disease free survival' and 'relapse-free survival' are the same concepts, but if an ontology did not include both expressions, an automated system would be unable to provide an accurate estimate of the number of times this concept was reported.

The task of aligning text to concepts is difficult because authors use modifiers that may not be reflected in an ontology. For example, the noun phrase '5-year overall survival' may be better represented using the core concept 'overall survival' along with the time frame post-modification of '5-year' rather than capturing both the time frame and survivorship as a single concept.

Our goal is to compare survivorship concepts in the 2016 Unified Medical Language System with survivorship expressions that are frequently reported in studies of breast cancer treatments. We provide a summary of current survivorship concepts in existing knowledge resources and evaluate the coverage with respect to frequent survivorship noun phases used in the literature. To our knowledge, this is the first comprehensive overview of how survivorship is captured in existing knowledge resources.

MATERIALS AND METHODS

The Unified Medical Language System (UMLS) provides one of the most comprehensive knowledge resources in biomedicine. Eleven candidate ontologies that we thought would be most likely to capture survivorship were identified from a local copy of the 2016AB version of the UMLS. The ontologies were: the National Center for Biotechnology Information Taxonomy, Medical subject headings (MESH), US Systematized Nomenclature of Medicine - Clinical Terms (SNOMEDCT_US), normalized names for clinical drugs, National Cancer Institute (NCI), UMLS metathesaurus, Alcohol and Other Drug Thesaurus, Consumer Health Vocabulary, Metathesaurus Food and DXplain, Drug Administration Structured Product Labels, and Metathesaurus Source Terminology Names.

A two-step process was used to identify candidate survivorship concepts. In step 1, the Concept Unique Identifier

82nd Annual Meeting of the Association for Information Science & Technology | Melbourne, Australia | 19–23 October, 2019

DOI: 10.1002/pra2.00137

(CUI), string containing the relevant terms (STR), source vocabulary and unique identifiers were identified using the partial (case insensitive) string 'survi'. A second query was then issued to collect all other strings for each of the CUIs. Each concept was then manually reviewed.

Frequent survivorship phrases were obtained for abstracts in the 2016 version of MEDLINE that were retrieved for 5 breast cancer drugs (Tamoxifen, Raloxifene, Bazedoxifene, Doxorubicin, Docetaxel, and Trastuzumab), where search terms included both the generic drug and brand name. Abstracts were processed using the Stanford Core NLP (Manning et al., 2014) and noun phrases were then generated using the approach described in (Blake & Rindflesch, 2017). Noun phrases were aligned to the UMLS using MetaMap (Aronson, 2001).

RESULTS AND DISCUSSION

The UMLS contained 131 distinct survivorship concepts with 496 (437 distinct) phrases. Of the 131 concepts, 111 (85%) reflected the time-to-event sense of survivorship used in the literature and 20 (15%) were not aligned (i.e. were false positives). Figure 1 shows the frequent concepts that were produced using MetaMap (shaded) and the context of those concepts within the ontology by showing parent–child relationships (ISA) within a given ontology. The majority of concepts are in the NCI and MESH ontologies and very few of the concepts are found in SNOMEDCT_US. No matches were found in the other 5 ontologies. This suggests that there may be a difference between how survivorship is reported in clinical trials and endpoints that are reported from clinical data (e.g. death or cause of death).

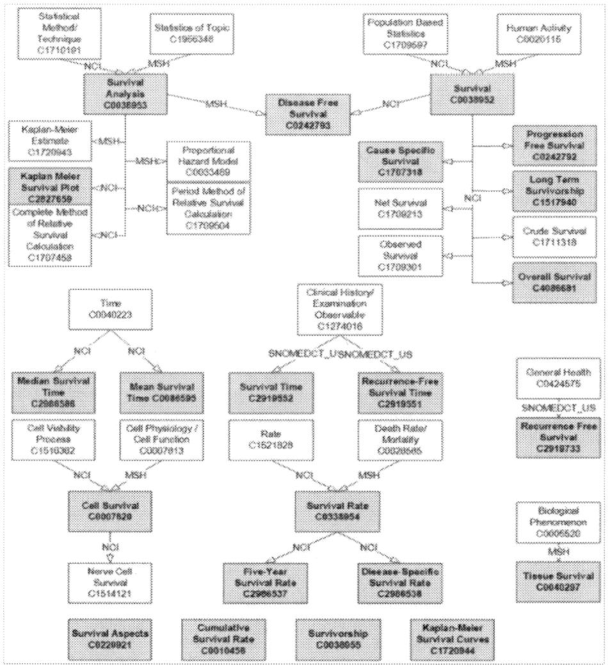

Figure 1. Summary of alignments between frequently occurring survivorship noun phrases used in the text and the corresponding survivorship term from knowledge resources. Highlighted concepts depict the MetaMap suggestions.

With respect to the literature, the search for breast cancer treatments resulted in a total of 89,613 abstracts and only 21,953 of the abstracts reported survivorship within a noun phrase or abbreviation. An iterative approach was used to identify frequent modifiers in survivorship noun phrases. We identified 4 key modifiers: time frame (e.g. 5-year), directionality (e.g. poor), measurement names (e.g. median), and scope (e.g. localized). These modifiers were removed from the noun phrases order to obtain a unified estimate of frequent survivorship terms which is shown in Table 1, where 'survival' was the most frequent unified expression. Overall survival, the most clinically relevant endpoint, is the second most frequent term in the literature and ranked 3rd with respect to MetaMap alignments.

Phrase	Frequency	%
survival	25,302	39.04
overall survival	17,390	26.83
progression free survival	7,761	11.97
disease free survival	7,905	12.20
event free survival	1,928	2.97

Table 1. Frequent unified survivorship expressions for abstracts related to Tamoxifen, Raloxifene, Bazedoxifene, Doxorubicin, Docetaxel and Trastuzumab.

As the unified survivorship terms in Table 1 show, the distribution of survivorship terminology is not even. The 40 most frequently used noun phrases account for 74% of all the survivorship noun phrases in this collection. However, modifiers such as time frame are used in the phrases ranked at 19, 22, 23, 31, 21, 33, 34 and 39 in the entire collection.

CONCLUSION

We have compared how survivorship is represented in existing knowledge resources with how survivorship is reported in studies of breast cancer treatments. Our key finding is that existing knowledge resources provide good coverage with respect to the survivorship terms that are frequently used in the literature, particularly in the NCI and MESH taxonomies. However, we did observe that some text expressions were not accurately aligned with the corresponding survivorship concept. Knowledge resources that capture key cancer concepts will never be complete and will never perfectly align with how authors express those concepts when reporting the results of their empirical studies. Despite this inevitability, ontologies can be leveraged to construct a database of outcomes reported in a collection of cancer clinical trials. Moreover, automated systems could play a role in identifying new survivorship expressions that should be considered for inclusion into existing ontologies.

REFERENCES

Aronson, A. R. (2001). Effective mapping of biomedical text to the UMLS metathesaurus: The MetaMap program. *American Medical Informatics Association.*

Blake, C., & Rindflesch, T. (2017). Leveraging syntax to better capture the semantics of elliptical coordinated compound noun phrases. *Journal of Biomedical Informatics, 72*, 120–131.

Hudis, C. A., Barlow, W. E., Costantino, J. P., Gray, R. J., Pritchard, K. I., Chapman, J. A., … Zujewski, J. A. (2007). Proposal for standardized definitions for efficacy end points in adjuvant breast cancer trials: the STEEP system. *Journal of Clinical Oncology, 25*(15), 2127–2132.

Manning, C.D., Surdeanu, M., Bauer, J., Finkel, J., Bethard, S. J., & McClosky, D. (2014). *The stanford corenlp natural language processing toolkit.* Paper presented at the Proceedings of the 52nd Annual Meeting of the Association for Computational Linguistics: System Demonstrations, Baltimore, MD.

An Integrated Framework of Patient Data Ownership

Aaron D. Bowen-Ziecheck
McGill University School of Information Studies, Montreal, QC, Canada
aaron.bowen-ziecheck@mail.mcgill.ca

Joan C. Bartlett
McGill University School of Information Studies, Montreal, QC, Canada
joan.bartlett@mcgill.ca

ABSTRACT

Patient data ownership is called for but not explicitly conceptualized in the literature. This proposal reports a framework of patient data ownership based which integrates literature from the fields of healthcare information systems, patient-centered care, and personal health information management. The 6 concepts identified are integrated, on-demand, access, control, security, and input. The framework is presented to combine and synthesize concepts which are found in disparate fields but are highly related.

KEYWORDS

Patient data ownership; healthcare data ownership; patient data; personal health information management; health data

ASIS&T THESAURUS

Medical informatics; personal information management

INTRODUCTION

Data ownership as a way to empower patients (referred to as "patient data ownership") is discussed in a diverse body of literature, from healthcare information systems to patient-centered care to personal health information management. Yet, patient data ownership is spoken about in a variety of ways. For instance, Bhuyan, Bailey-DeLeeuw, Wyant, and Chang (2016) discuss patient data in terms of affording patients the right to control who accesses their data. Meanwhile, Mikk, Sleeper, and Topol (2017) suggest a much more substantial level of patient control that readily incorporates patient engagement, notifications, and integrated data, among other factors. The objective of the conceptual framework reported in this paper was to identify the range of concepts inherent in the diverse and disparate definitions of patient data ownership, to understand the implicit commonalities and complementarity among them, and to propose a holistic conceptual framework that integrates and synthesizes the identified concepts.

METHODS

A literature review was performed to identify the key concepts of patient data ownership. PubMed, CINAHL, LISA, and LISTA were searched along with McGill University WorldCat and Google Scholar. In consultation with the university librarian, search terms included: patient data ownership, healthcare data ownership, health data ownership, and patient data. Articles discussing topics such as giving patients more rights and responsibilities over their data, or how patients use their data were analyzed. Notetaking focused on identifying definitions of patient data ownership, the key concepts inherent in each definition, and how concepts overlap between articles and research fields.

82nd Annual Meeting of the Association for Information Science & Technology | Melbourne, Australia | 19–23 October, 2019

DOI: 10.1002/pra2.00107

RESULTS

The concepts identified from the literature review have been integrated in the conceptual framework shown in Figure 1. Following the framework, each of the concepts is explained. The terminology used for the concepts was derived from terminology found in the literature.

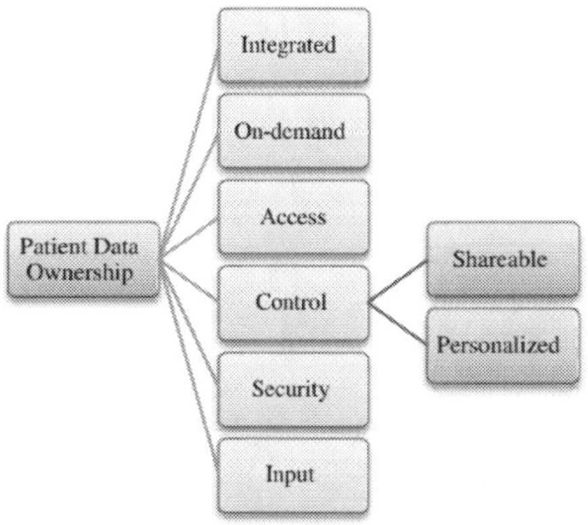

Figure 1. Conceptual framework of patient data ownership.

Integrated

This concept must not be confused with the literary disciplines which were integrated to form this framework. Instead, integrating patient data is combining personal and clinical health data. Integration has been advocated in personal health information management literature (e.g., Pratt, Unruh, Civan, & Skeels, 2006). Integrated data provides a holistic view of the patient's health and a better understanding of health conditions (Deverka et al., 2017; Mikk et al., 2017).

On-demand

Data should be accessible and retrievable within minutes by the patient. This could range from local data storage to online data storage. For instance, Deverka et al. (2017) suggest a cloud platform in which patients store, access, use, and control their data.

Access

Patients must decide who has access to their data within the healthcare organization. Leventhal, Cummins, Schwartz, Martin, and Tierney (2015) suggest a framework for patient decision over who has access to which type of data in their electronic health records. For instance, a patient may only want their primary care provider to see their health data while restricting access to other physicians.

Control

Control is concerned with what happens to the data when it leaves the healthcare organization. Control is broken into the two sub-categories of Shareable and Personalized. Patients should be able to share their data with people outside the healthcare organization. Patients often benefit from sharing health information with peers that have the same health problems (Hartzler & Pratt, 2011). Likewise, patients should be able to control whether their anonymized data is shared with researchers (Bhuyan et al., 2016). Patients must also be able to personalize their data (e.g., add labels, notes, and metadata, and choose storage location) so that it is easily retrievable and usable. Personalization is necessary because patients differ widely in their medical knowledge (Yeh, Wu, & Tung, 2018), data management practices (Ancker et al., 2015), and security concerns (Leventhal et al., 2015).

Security

Medical data is sensitive and subject to strict privacy regulations (Bhuyan et al., 2016). Any patient data ownership initiative needs to include technical security measures (e.g., encryption) to prevent cyber-attacks. Security must also address non-technical issues, such as ensuring patients do not erroneously share their data (Bhuyan et al., 2016). Zhou, Kankanhalli, Yang, and Lei (2016) recommend education and training to teach patients how to properly control their data.

Input

Patients should be able to directly change or request changes to their clinical data. A common issue when patients transition between care providers is erroneous data (Grimes, Delaney, Duggan, Kelly, & Graham, 2008). This erroneous data can cause care provider inconveniences, and even directly harm the patient's health. Furthermore, patients should be able to update their data, input personal data, and review new data when it is input by the care providers.

CONCLUSION

Patient data ownership is a concept used disparately in literature without a clear and consistent definition. The proposed integrated conceptual framework identifies 6 key concepts that are shared between healthcare information systems, patient-centered care, and personal health information management literature. The framework provides a holistic view of patient data ownership, which can be used to facilitate interdisciplinary discussions and research. Additionally, the framework presents key aspects that medical organizations, regulators, and advocates can focus on to institute patient data ownership policies and systems.

The proposed conceptual framework is the first phase of this ongoing research project. The next phase is to empirically evaluate the framework with the main users of patient data (i.e., patients and caregivers). Further research will focus on creating and testing a framework for implementing patient data ownership.

ACKNOWLEDGMENTS

This work forms part of the first author's PhD dissertation research; the second author is the supervisor. The first author also thanks the thesis committee.

REFERENCES

Ancker, J. S., Witteman, H. O., Hafeez, B., Provencher, T., Van de Graaf, M., & Wei, E. (2015). The invisible work of personal health information management among people with multiple chronic conditions: Qualitative interview study among patients and providers. *Journal of Medical Internet Research*, *17*(6).

Bhuyan, S. S., Bailey-DeLeeuw, S., Wyant, D. K., & Chang, C. F. (2016). Too much or too little? How much control should patients have over EHR data? *Journal of Medical Systems*, *40*(7), 174.

Deverka, P. A., Majumder, M. A., Villanueva, A. G., Anderson, M., Bakker, A. C., Bardill, J., … McGuire, A. L. (2017). Creating a data resource: What will it take to build a medical information commons? *Genome Medicine*, (84), 9.

Grimes, T., Delaney, T., Duggan, C., Kelly, J. G., & Graham, I. M. (2008). Survey of medication documentation at hospital discharge: Implications for patient safety and continuity of care. *Irish Journal of Medical Science*, *177*(2), 93–97.

Hartzler, A., & Pratt, W. (2011). Managing the personal side of health: How patient expertise differs from the expertise of clinicians. *Journal of Medical Internet Research, 13*(3), e62.

Leventhal, J. C., Cummins, J. A., Schwartz, P. H., Martin, D. K., & Tierney, W. M. (2015). Designing a system for patients controlling providers access to their Electronic Health Records: Organizational and technical challenges. *Journal of General Internal Medicine*, *30*(1), 17–24.

Mikk, K. A., Sleeper, H. A., & Topol, E. J. (2017). The pathway to patient data ownership and better health. *Journal of the American Medical Association*, *318*(15), 1433–1434.

Pratt, W., Unruh, K., Civan, A., & Skeels, M. M. (2006). Personal health information management. *Communications of the ACM*, *49*(1), 51–55.

Yeh, M.-Y., Wu, S.-C., & Tung, T.-H. (2018). The relation between patient education, patient empowerment and patient satisfaction: A cross-sectional-comparison study. *Applied Nursing Research*, *39*, 11–17.

Zhou, Y., Kankanhalli, A., Yang, Z., & Lei, J. (2016). Expectations of patient-centred care: Investigating IS-related and other antecedents. *Information & Management*, *54*(5), 583–598.

Machine Translation Literacy: Academic Libraries' Role

Lynne Bowker
University of Ottawa, Ottawa, Canada
lbowker@uottawa.ca

ABSTRACT

English is the main language of scholarly communication, but most researchers are not native English speakers. Machine translation (MT) technology is advancing, but such tools rarely produce high quality output of specialized text without human intervention. There is an emerging need for MT literacy, and academic librarians are well placed to deliver it. This poster reports the results of an MT literacy workshop delivered at Concordia University Library.

KEYWORDS

Scholarly communication; machine translation; machine translation literacy; digital literacy; HCI; academic libraries

ASIS&T THESAURUS

Social informatics; academic documents; published documents; multilingual information; information discovery

INTRODUCTION

Researchers around the globe are under pressure to interact with the scholarly literature—reading it and contributing to it—in English. English dominates scholarly communication though a small percentage of researchers are native English speakers. Where does this leave non-Anglophones who must read and write in English to participate in scholarly discourse? An issue of *Nature* interviews 7 researchers who discuss challenges posed by science's embrace of one global language. Some are turning to machine translation (MT) to assist them; however, as one interviewee – Tatsuya Amano – points out: "I suspect that a lot of native English speakers view language barriers as a minor problem. They probably think that Google Translate can solve everything. But the technology isn't there yet. You can't run a scientific paper through a translation programme and get a meaningful result." (Woolston & Osório, 2019, p. 267).

This observation is correct. While MT technology has advanced considerably, it rarely produces high quality output without human intervention. This raises questions such as how, when and why should scholars interact with MT systems in order to optimize their output? Answers to these and similar questions point to an emerging type of digital literacy: machine translation literacy. This poster describes work in progress at Canada's Concordia University Library, where we are developing and testing an MT literacy workshop for students and faculty.

82nd Annual Meeting of the Association for Information Science & Technology | Melbourne, Australia | 19–23 October, 2019

DOI: 10.1002/pra2.00108

ENGLISH AS THE LINGUA FRANCA OF SCHOLARLY COMMUNICATION

Numerous scholars have offered explanations for why English became the language of scholarly communication. (Delisle, 2008) explains that it dates to the industrial revolution, when English began to overtake French in science and technology. (Gordin, 2015) suggests this was extended by the military, economic and technological influence wielded by the US during World War II, and further entrenched due to the influence of the Internet and WWW, which developed mainly in the US, resulting in a cultural impact that made English the language of scholarly communication. Whatever the factors, English is now the most-widely used language in this context. For example, a bibliometric study of public health research published in Europe between 1995 and 2004 covered 210,433 publications found in the Science Citation Index and the Social Science Citation Index (with exclusions of overlap). Of these, 96.5% were published in English (Clarke et al., 2007). More recently, (Curry & Lillis, 2018) note that a vast majority of the 27,000 journals in Web of Science are almost entirely in English, while journals published in other languages are not included in prestigious indexes.

Options for non-Anglophone scholars to participate in scholarly communication include learning English (requiring time, money and effort), paying for translation services (over $100/page for specialized professional services), convenience editing (asking an English instructor to edit the text, or bringing an Anglophone 'co-author' on board just to get published). Given the drawbacks of such options, along with the ease of access to free online MT systems (e.g. Google Translate, DeepL), it is not surprising that more researchers are exploring the use of MT (Bowker & Buitrago Ciro, 2019). However, to get the most out of MT, users would benefit from MT literacy instruction.

INTERNATIONALIZATION OF HIGHER EDUCATION

Another trend is the number of university programs taught through English in places where English is not an official language. (Wächter & Maiworm, 2014) investigate English-taught programs offered across non-English-speaking Europe, noting the number rose from 725 in 2001 to 8089 programs in 2014. Also, universities in English-speaking countries are hosting growing numbers of international students. Data from (Citizenship & Immigration Canada,

2017) indicate that in 2017 there were 492,533 international students in Canada, up from 179,149 in 2007. China, India and Korea are the top 3 home countries of these students.

Universities also seek to attract top international faculty. On Canada's 150th anniversary, the government launched the 'Canada 150 Research Chairs Program' which gave funds to Canadian universities to attract top-tier international researchers (Canada 150 Research Chairs, 2017).

Such initiatives are increasing the number of international students and faculty on campuses, meaning there could be a role for academic libraries to provide new services like MT literacy instruction to these linguistically diverse groups.

TEACHING MACHINE TRANSLATION LITERACY: A ROLE FOR ACADEMIC LIBRARIES?

New 'literacies' emerge as societal needs evolve (e.g. computer, information, and media literacies). (Martin, 2006) describes digital literacy as the awareness, attitude and ability of individuals to appropriately use digital tools to identify, access, manage, integrate, evaluate, analyze and synthesize digital resources, construct new knowledge, communicate with others, and to reflect upon this process. This definition emphasizes that critical thinking, rather than technical competence, is the core skill of digital literacy. MT literacy is a new type of digital literacy.

Free online MT has been available for a decade, and recent approaches to MT use artificial intelligence and machine learning. Online MT systems are easy to use, but users may not apply the tools successfully to scholarly activities. Training in critical and effective use of MT can help.

A major role of academic librarians is to support scholarly communication. A way to do this is by providing different types of literacy instruction, including MT literacy. Researchers provide the focus and the purpose for scholarly communication, but outreach to scholarly community members is an important activity that academic librarians can undertake to promote positive change that will advance the scholarly communication system. Because the need for MT literacy exists in every discipline, academic librarians are well placed to develop and deliver a coherent program of MT literacy training to researchers across an institution.

MT LITERACY INSTRUCTION PROGRAM

In fall 2019, interactive MT literacy workshops were given at Concordia University Library that allowed scholars to:

- comprehend how MT systems process texts;
- understand how MT systems are or can be used (by oneself or by other scholars) to find, read, and/or produce scholarly publications;
- appreciate wider issues of MT use (e.g. privacy, ethics);
- evaluate how MT-friendly a scholarly text is;
- create or modify a scholarly text so that it could be translated more easily by an MT system;
- modify the output of an MT system to improve its accuracy and readability.

Initial participant feedback is encouraging and suggests that while MT works well for reading existing literature, it is less immediately successful as a writing aid and so more emphasis should be placed on both pre- and post-editing techniques, which may differ from one language to the next. This will be built more substantially into future iterations of the workshop. Information on privacy issues and ethics of MT use was also appreciated by participants.

ACKNOWLEDGMENTS

This work was carried out as part of Concordia University Library's Researcher-in-Residence program. Thanks to workshop participants and project research assistants Maria Kalsatos (Concordia U.) and Amy Ruskin (McGill U.).

REFERENCES

Bowker, L., & Buitrago Ciro, J. (2019). *Machine translation and global research*. Bingley, England: Emerald.

Citizenship & Immigration Canada (2017). *International students by top 50 countries of citizenship*. Retrieved from https://open.canada.ca/data/en/dataset/2bf9f856-20fe-4644-bf74-c8e45b3d94bd

Clarke, A., Gatineau, M., Grimaud, O., Royer-Devaux, S., Wyn-Roberts, N., Le Bis, I., & Lewison, G. (2007). A bibliometric overview of public health research in Europe. *European Journal of Public Health*, *17*(1), 43–49.

Curry, M., & Lillis, T. (2018). Dangers of English as lingua franca of journals. *Inside Higher Ed*. Retrieved from https://www.insidehighered.com/views/2018/03/13/domination-english-language-journal-publishing-hurting-scholarship-many-countries

Delisle, J. (2008). *La terminologie au Canada : Histoire d'une profession*. Montreal, Canada: Linguatech.

Gordin, M. D. (2015). *Scientific babel: How science was done before and after global English*. Chicago, IL: University of Chicago Press.

Government of Canada (2017). *Canada 150 research chairs program*. Retrieved from http://www.canada150.chairs-chaires.gc.ca/program-programme/index-eng.aspx

Martin (2006). Literacies for the digital age. In A. Martin & D. Madigan (Eds.), *Digital literacies for learning* (pp. 3–25). London, England: Facet Publications.

Wächter & Maiworm. (2014). *English-taught programmes in European higher education: The state of play in* (p. 2014). Bonn, Germany: Lemmens.

Woolston, C., & Osório, J. (2019). When English is not your mother tongue. *Nature*, *570*, 265–267.

The Impact of a Prescribed Journal List of Disciplinary Publishing

Jennifer Campbell-Meier
Victoria University of Wellington, Wellington, New Zealand
jennifer.campbell-meier@vuw.ac.nz

Allan Sylvester
Victoria University of Wellington, Wellington, New Zealand
allan.sylvester@vuw.ac.nz

Jacob Woods
Independent Researcher, Wellington, New Zealand
j.woods000101@gmail.com

ABSTRACT

In 2007, the Association for Information Systems created a basket of eight journals that claim to bound the discipline. A review of the literature found 41 studies discussing the impact of the basket on scholarly publishing. While the basket of eight has had a positive impact on the impact factors for Information Systems, an increase that has not appeared in the LIS journal set, a review of citations finds a steady increase in the number of basket of eight journals being cited within the basket of eight. This paper discusses the impact the basket of eight has had on cited references.

KEYWORDS

Scholarly publishing; Research Impact; Basket of eight; literature review

ASIS&T THESAURUS

Information associations; Evaluation; Citation analysis

INTRODUCTION

Information science, like information systems is a boundary spanning discipline that developed alongside the advent of computing as part of the fabric of daily life. However, unlike information science, scholarly publishing in information systems sought to develop the focus of publishing within the field in order to develop the perceived boundaries of the discipline and to increase the visibility of the field as a discrete disciplinary community.

During the 2000's, a group of "senior scholars" (later to become the college of senior scholars) within the Association for Information Systems conceived the "basket of eight" (initially six) information systems journals that sought to bound the discipline (Association of Information Systems, n.d.). The eight journals are: *European Journal of Information Systems, Information Systems Journal, Information Systems Research, Journal of AIS, Journal of Information Technology, Journal of MIS, Journal of Strategic Information Systems*, and *MIS Quarterly*. Deans, administrators and directors of information systems programs quickly accepted the list as the gold-standard and preferred outlets for scholarly publishing. Unsurprisingly, the basket of eight rapidly became the benchmark for decisions on hiring, tenure and promotion.

During informal discussions between information science and information systems researchers, we noticed an interesting contrast; information systems researchers discussed focusing within the basket of eight for literature reviews and publishing venues whereas information science scholars appeared to have a much broader church. With this in mind, we ask the following questions: *How has the development of a prescribed journal list impacted scholarly publishing in information systems? Are there differences between the citation patterns in information science and information systems?*

Several studies have examined scholar networks and subject coverage, none have investigated the relationships between journals in the basket of eight, nor have they compared the basket to a similar set of journals from sister discipline. Library and Information Science (LIS) was chosen as a sister discipline that has both theoretical and applied research but lacks a concrete preference for a specific set of journals.

METHODOLOGY

To identify any changes or impact in scholarly publishing, we compared citations used in articles in the basket of eight to a set of articles from LIS. The Excellence in Research in Australia (ERA) 2010 journals list was used to identify journals that held an A or A* rating in LIS (list archived by Lamp, 2010). 2010 was the most recent year LIS was included in the ABC ranking of journals for a "nationwide stocktake of discipline strengths and areas for development" within Australia (Australian Research Council, 2019). The basket of eight journals are identified as A or A* for Information Systems. From the list of thirty-six LIS titles, only nine were indexed in Web of Science with at least 10 years of coverage within the source. LIS journals include: *Journal of the American Society for Information Science and Technology, Journal of*

82nd Annual Meeting of the Association for Information Science & Technology | Melbourne, Australia | 19–23 October, 2019

DOI: 10.1002/pra2.00109

Documentation, Journal of Information Science, Knowledge Organization, Scientometrics, The Information Society, Library & information science research, Information Research: an international electronic journal, and *the Journal of Academic Librarianship*.

To focus this preliminary study, all articles with "Social Media" as a topic were fetched via the Web of Knowledge (WoK), API (TS = "Social Media"). The topic was chosen because both LIS and Information Systems have a shared definition of social media. Based on the raw data files downloaded from the WoK API, 129 basket of eight articles and 198 LIS articles were included in data sets for each discipline. A time series: 2000-2005, 2006-2010, 2011-2015, and 2016-2018, was used to bound the study and highlight changes. Cited references from the identified journal lists were used to construct graphs for each journal group per year from 2006 to 2018. The layout was produced and scaled by Cytoscape, a tool used to analyze network data (Shannon et al., 2003), using an edge-weighted spring-embedded model, meaning that journal/proceedings sharing more neighbors are closer on the display. In the resulting network, an identified journal is presented as the source and the journals it cites are targets, with the relationship weighted by the number of citations to that journal. Network node size was also mapped to degree, measure of quantity, not quality.

FINDINGS AND DISCUSSION

The citation networks from the basket of eight and the LIS Journals take on distinct patterns. The selected nodes from the journal lists appear to have the same general shape created from the edge weighted layout, the number and diversity of cited references is far more extensive in the LIS set. Central in both sets of images are cited references to the journals themselves.

There are cited references within each set, and journal sets appear frequently in the Top 5 cited references per year of the time series, the quantity of references in not identified. A review of citations finds a steady increase in the number of basket of eight journals being cited within the basket of eight, a self-citation metric that is not discussed in impact factors. For example, while reviewing cited references to MIS Quarterly, we found MIS Quarterly to be the most cited reference. Indeed, MIS Quarterly was the single journal to receive the most citations within our data set with 276 cited references from the set of 129 articles.

Informal discussions with colleagues point to a reliance on the basket of eight for the basis of the literature review scholarly publishing. Articles on "social media" did not appear in the journal sets until 2008 (LIS) and 2010 (basket of eight), the slow development of literature on the topic appears to support this presumption. Authorship was not examined in this exercise, it would shed light on the diversity of authorship within the journal sets.

The Journal Impact Factor (JIF) across the basket of eight journals has increased 842%, the median JIF for LIS journal group increased 174% (Clarivate Analytics, 2019). It is interesting to note that in 2000 the median impact factor of LIS journals was 0.532 up to 1.459 in 2017. The median impact for the basket of 8 was 0.396 increasing to 3.732 in 2017. All of the impact factors for basket of eight journals increased over time, the same is not true of the LIS set. The focus on publishing in and between the journals in the basket of eight does appear to have made an impact.

Reviewing cited references from within the basket of eight provided some insight into the inner workings of the journal citation process. The practice of citing both the source journal and content from the basket of eight is ongoing in Information Systems in a way that does not appear in sister disciplines like Library and Information Science. Despite discussions of the negative impact of the practice, the number of citations to basket of eight journals is increasing.

CONCLUSION

While the basket of eight has had a positive impact on the JIF for Information Systems, an increase that has not appeared in the LIS journal set. A review of citations finds a steady increase in the number of basket of eight journals being cited within the basket of eight. Over the years, the number of citations within the basket of eight journals increased, a self-citation metric that is not discussed in impact factors. However, the focus on the basket may be inhibiting new streams of research and may limit the diversity of research and researchers. Creating a disciplinary journal set has impacts for publishing as well as ramifications for authors. Disciplines wishing to enhance impact factors for journals in a specific discipline may wish to develop a collection, however, that collection may create areas of concern: such as self-citedness.

REFERENCES

Association of Information Systems. (n.d.). *Senior scholars' basket of journals*. Retrieved from https://aisnet.org/page/SeniorScholarBasket

Australian Research Council. (2019). *Excellence in research for Australia*. Retrieved from https://www.arc.gov.au/excellence-research-australia

Clarivate Analytics. (2019). 2017 Journal Impact Factor, Journal Citation Reports.

Lamp, J. (2010). *ERA Journal Rankings Access*. Retrieved from http://lamp.infosys.deakin.edu.au/era/?page=jmain

Shannon, P., Markiel, A., Ozier, O., Baliga, N. S., Wang, J. T., Ramage, D., ... Ideker, T. (2003). Cytoscape: a software environment for integrated models of biomolecular interaction networks. *Genome research*, *13*(11), 2498–2504.

Identifying the Contribution–Influence Gap in the Science and Technology Community

Yu-Wei Chang
Center for Research in Econometric Theory and Applications, National Taiwan University, Taipei, Taiwan
yuweichang2013@ntu.edu.tw

Mu-Hsuan Huang
Department of Library and Information Science, Taipei, Taiwan
mhhuang@ntu.edu.tw

Chung-Huei Kuan
Graduate Institute of Patent, National Taiwan University of Science and Technology, Taipei, Taiwan
maxkuan@mail.ntust.edu.tw

ABSTRACT

This study uncovered the gap between scientific and technological contributions and scientific and technological influence by tracking scientists who received two national awards that recognized their scientific and technological achievements. The results show that scientific and technological contributions can be made by the same intellectual ideas, indicating the complex relationship between science and technology. Only a few scientists had received a remarkable number of citations of their scientific publications and patents over decades. The contribution–influence gap indicates that quantifying the scientific and technological contributions of some scientists is difficult.

KEYWORDS

Scientific contribution; technological contribution; scientific influence; technological influence; citation

ASIS&T THESAURUS

Scientometrics; Science

INTRODUCTION

Numerous researchers have used citation analysis to measure the degrees of researchers' influence and contribution over time (Riikonen & Vihinen, 2008), indicating that "influence" and "contribution" are commonly regarded as exchangeable terms. However, we claim that these two broad concepts have different meanings. To explore the association between influence and contribution, this study investigated the scientific and technological aspects of influence and contribution. The main research question addressed in this study was as follows: can the contributions of scientists to science and technology be determined from their scientific and technological influence in terms of citations?

Scientific publications and patents are believed to indicate influence and contribution. The giving of distinguished academic awards aims to acknowledge scientists who have made substantial scientific and technological contributions. Therefore, we selected the winners of both the National Medal of Science (NMS) and National Medal of Technology and Innovation (NMTI) in the United States as the subject. NMS and NMTI awardees have made great contributions to science and technology. The NMS was first awarded in 1962 and the NMTI in 1985. Up to the most recently announced medals, those in 2004, only 12 individuals have received both the NMS and NMTI and thus made extraordinary contributions. Their outstanding contributions to science and technology make them suitable for exploring whether a scientist's influence, as indicated by his or her scientific publications and patents, is a measure of the scientist's scientific and technological contribution.

METHODOLOGY

We first collected the personal information and bibliographic records of scientific publications and patents of the 12 individuals receiving both the NMI and NMTI. Personal information including age, education, professional experience, honors, and awards was obtained from websites, social media, and online reference resources. Next, research papers were retrieved from the Scopus database, which is the largest multidisciplinary citation index database. Nonresearch papers such as interviews, editorial materials, and book reviews were excluded. The most recent publications and patents included were those from 2017. Because the 12 winners were Americans and due to information availability, the patents considered were limited to those issued by the United States Patent and Trademark Office (US patents). US patent information was retrieved from Google Patents. The research papers and US patents of each winner were identified on the basis of personal information such as work experience. Bibliographic records, including the number of citations, were collected in January 2019. The average number of citations per article, average number of citations per patent, h index for articles, and h index for patents were calculated for each winner.

RESULTS

Table 1 shows that the 12 winners, who were scientists and engineers, received the NMS between the ages of 46 and

82nd Annual Meeting of the Association for Information Science & Technology | Melbourne, Australia | 19–23 October, 2019

DOI: 10.1002/pra2.00110

89 years and the NMTI between 53 and 85 years. The youngest winner was aged 70 years in 2018, when the data for this study were collected. The 12 winners had retired and were at the end of their professional careers. Therefore, the scientific publications and patents almost represent the results of their entire professional careers. Not all the winners were productive authors and inventors, with one scientist not holding any US patents. In addition, some scientists had no influential articles and patents, as determined by their article and patent with the most citations.

Name	N (A/P)	C (A/P)	Year (A/P)	NMS Year (Age)	NMTI Year (Age)
R. S. Langer	1171 /479	7737 /590	1974-2018 1979-2018	2006 (58)	2011 (63)
J. D. Achenbach	376 /0	305 /0	1962-2018 0	2005 (70)	2003 (68)
H. W. Boyer	85 /3	3428 /319	1962-1992 1980-1988	1990 (54)	1989 (53)
N. Holonyak, Jr.	537 /61	521 /97	1955-2018 1966-2016	1990 (62)	2002 (74)
A. O. Beckman	13 /14	61 /31	1928-1953 1936-1966	1989 (89)	1988 (88)
S. N. Cohen	422 /29	2809 /319	1957-2016 1980-2018	1988 (53)	1989 (54)
P.C. Lauterbur	99 /4	626 /24	1956-2010 1992-2000	1987 (58)	1988 (59)
R. N. Noyce	4 /17	1837 /162	1956-1984 1959-1967	1979 (52)	1987 (60)
C. Djerassi	997 /102	1097 /31	1946-1990 1946-2013	1973 (50)	1991 (68)
H. E. Edgerton	56 /33	51 /32	1930-1997 1945-1978	1973 (70)	1988 (85)
J. St. C. Kilby	0 /58	0 /204	0 1953-1997	1969 (46)	1990 (67)
C. L. Johnson	7 /26	111 /30	1965-1972 1939-1971	1965 (55)	1988 (78)

Notes: N refers to the number of articles; C refers the number of citations; A refers to articles; P refers to patents.

Table 1. Productivity and influence of 12 NMI and NMTI winners throughout their professional careers.

The scientific and technological influence of the group of scientists—as measured by the average number of citations, maximum number of citations, and h index (Figure 1)—exhibited considerable variation. Two or three groups of winners could be identified on the basis of their locations in the plots presented in Figure 1. Three scientists had strong scientific and technological influence through both patents and articles (Langer, Holonyak, and Cohen), and this group is observed in each of the three citation measures. Four scientists were classified as article oriented with strong article influence—Achenhack, Boyer, Djerassi, and Lauterbur. Three engineers were patent oriented with strong patent influence—Noyce, Kilby, and Johnson. Finally, two scientists, Edgerton and Beckmen, had similar scientific and technological influence. Achenbach's technological contribution clearly originated from his scientific contribution because he did not produce any patents. In addition, Beckman published a limited number of articles and patents and received a limited of number citations. A large

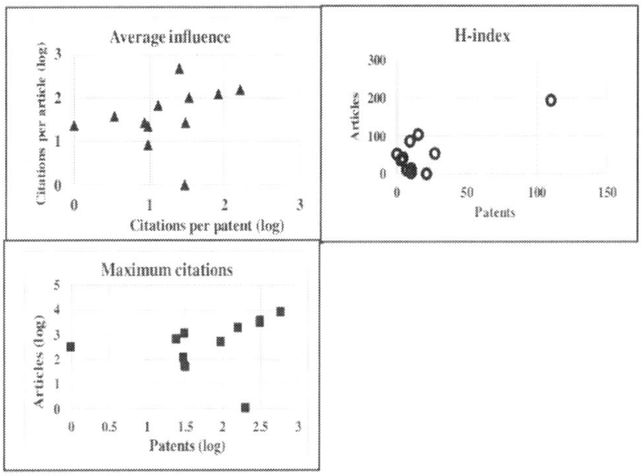

Figure 1. Scientific and technological influence of 12 winners.

difference indeed existed between scientific and technological contribution and scientific and technological influence.

CONCLUSION

This study confirmed the contribution–influence gap from the perspective of citations. Scientific and technological influence may not reflect scientific and technological contribution. The social contributions of scientists and inventors, such as their improvement of human life, may partially explain the contribution–influence gap, because social contribution cannot be identified from scholarly output and invention. In addition, scientific publications or patents can make contributions to both science and technology. Scientists who do not own patents can nevertheless make contributions to technology. The complex relationship between science and technology reflects that science leads whereas technology follows (Nelson & Rosenberg, 1993). The findings of this study suggest that a scientist's influence and contribution must be measured from various perspectives.

ACKNOWLEDGMENTS

This work was financially supported by the Center for Research in Econometric Theory and Applications (Grant no. 108L900204) from The Featured Areas Research Center Program within the framework of the Higher Education Sprout Project by the Ministry of Education (MOE) in Taiwan, and by the Ministry of Science and Technology (MOST), Taiwan, under Grant No. MOST 108-3017-F-002-003- and MOST 108-2410-H-002-219-.

REFERENCES

Nelson, R. R., & Rosenberg, N. (1993). Technical innovation and nation systems. In R. R. Nelson, *National invocation systems: A comparative study*. Oxford, England: Oxford University Press.

Riikonen, P., & Vihinen, M. (2008). National research contributions: A case study on Finnish biomedical research. *Scientometrics*, *77*(2), 207–222.

Understanding Interactions Among Citizens, Government Authorities, Media, and NGOs on Twitter During Natural Disaster

Sijing Chen
Wuhan University,
Wuhan, China
csj16912@whu.edu.cn

Jin Mao
Wuhan University,
Wuhan, China
maojin@whu.edu.cn

Xiao Wang
Central China Normal University, Wuhan, China
ray_wangx@mail.ccnu.edu.cn

Gang Li
Wuhan University,
Wuhan, China
ligang@whu.edu.cn

ABSTRACT

Social media has been adopted by various stakeholders to propagate information and communicate online for disaster-related discussions. This study aims to investigate the characteristics of interaction among multiple stakeholders on social media during natural disaster. Tweets related to Hurricane Harvey were analyzed. Four types of users reflecting the stakeholders of disaster were predicted by a supervised classifier. The communications among different user groups were formulated as an interaction network. Interaction characteristics of different user groups were compared through social network analysis. Preliminary results suggest that government authorities are frequently interacted and usually act as brokers in emergency communication. Individual citizens actively interact with others during the disaster. Media and NGO users have more external interaction. The findings of this study provide practical insights into emergency communication among different types of users.

KEYWORDS

Emergency Communication; Interactivity; Social Media; Social Network Analysis

ASIS&T THESAURUS

Information Sharing; Communication Patterns; Disasters

INTRODUCTION

Efficient information sharing and coordination among various stakeholders is critical for emergency management (Yates & Paquette, 2011). With the maturity and popularity of social media tools, social media has been increasingly adopted by various stakeholders, from the public to government agencies, across a variety of emergency scenarios, such as natural disasters, social movements, and terrorist attacks. Online communication among various stakeholders has been technically supported by social media. Current studies show that news media and journalism play an important role in propagating critical information from official actors to citizens (Ojala, Pantti, & Laaksonen, 2019) and enabling citizens to evaluate official actors' conduct. Non-government organizations (NGOs) often use social media to interact with citizens and are much more active than government agencies (Gálvez-Rodríguez, Haro-de-Rosario, & Caba-Pérez, 2019). However, in the situation of natural disasters, how different stakeholders interact with each other on social media has not been fully investigated.

In this study, we attempt to understand the characteristics of online interaction among multiple stakeholders during natural disaster through social network analysis. Four types of social media users reflecting the stakeholders of disaster were predicted by a supervised classifier. Based on retweet and mention relationships, we formulated interaction network among users, and compared the interaction characteristics of different groups of users through social network analysis.

METHOD

Data Source

We use the Hurricane Harvey Twitter Dataset (https://digital.library.unt.edu/ark:/67531/metadc993940/) provided by the University of North Texas Libraries, which collected twitter messages related to Hurricane Harvey and the subsequent flooding. A total of 7,041,866 tweets and 2,118,401 users were captured from August 18 to September 22, 2017. And 6,612,571 tweets in English were selected to be analyzed in this study.

User Classification

Four types of Twitter users are defined as individuals, governments, news media, and NGOs. The latter three are organizational users. We randomly sampled 7,342 users for manual labeling of user types. Three Information Science students were recruited for the work. In the first round, we did a pilot labeling on 1000 users, and obtained an inter-rater agreement of 0.87. In the second round, we labeled the remaining 6342 users based on the lessons learnt from the first round. Eventually, we obtained an improved agreement of 0.93. The labeled 7,342 users were used as training data.

82nd Annual Meeting of the Association for Information Science & Technology | Melbourne, Australia | 19–23 October, 2019

DOI: 10.1002/pra2.00111

We designed user classifier based on a bunch of features extracted from user profiles, including demographic features (verification, followers, friends, statuses, lists, and favorites), naming patterns (name, screen name, similarity of both name), and Google word2vec embeddings of profile descriptions. Seven classifiers were trained using Multi-nominal Naive Bayes, Random Forest, SGD, Logistic Regression, Support Vector Machine, MLPC, and Neutral Network. A 5-fold cross validation evaluation showed that Logistic Regression achieved the best performance (accuracy: 87.8%, F1-measure: 82.3%). Finally, this classifier was applied to predict the types of all users.

Interaction Network Construction

Interaction network of users is formulated as a directed network where the nodes denote the users and the edges are defined according to retweet and mention relations. For instance, we created a directed edge from account A to account B when B's post is retweeted by A or B is mentioned in A's tweet. Self-loop edges where users retweet themselves and isolated nodes were removed.

PRELIMINARY RESULT

Results of User Classification

The types of 2,118,401 users were first predicted by the selected classifier. Organizational users (i.e., government, news media, and NGOs) only take up a small portion of the users. To ensure the accuracy of organizational users for better subsequent analysis, we manually checked the predicted results of organizational users by examining their profiles. Eventually, 2,097,630 individual users, 1,271 government users, 3,949 media users, and 15,551 NGOs were obtained.

Network Analysis

The interaction network during Hurricane Harvey consists of 479,148 nodes and 3,924,126 edges. Since such large network requires higher computational cost and makes it challenging to gain an informative understanding of interaction structure, following Hagen, Keller, Neely, et al. (2017), we focused on the giant component and only kept the nodes with the degree greater than 30. This results in a subgraph with 782 nodes and 4,034 edges for the following interaction analysis, as shown in Figure 1. Included are 509 individuals, 72 government users, 80 media users, and 121 NGOs.

Figure 1. Interaction network among the four user groups.

Several network metrics of the four user groups were compared to understand the characteristics of their interactions, including average weighted in-degree centrality (AIC), average weighted out-degree centrality (AOC), average betweenness centrality (ABC), and External-Internal Index (E-I) that measures the dominance of external ties over internal ties with the score range from -1 to 1.

According to Table 1, government authorities are frequently retweeted or mentioned (high AIC) and usually act as brokers in emergency communication (high ABC). Individual citizens actively retweet or mention others on social media during the disaster (high AOC). For individuals, the E-I score is close to 0, while for the others, the E-I score is close to 1. It reveals that government, media, and NGO users have more external interaction, while individual users have similar external and internal links.

User Group	AIC	AOC	ABC	E-I
Individuals	7.33	11.91	0.0030	0.03
Governments	20.79	5.22	0.0035	0.74
News media	12.28	6.00	0.0031	0.93
NGOs	8.14	2.28	0.0015	0.87

Table 1. Network structures of the four user groups.

CONCLUSION

The interaction network during Hurricane Harvey was constructed to investigate the online interaction characteristics of citizens, government authorities, media, and NGOs. Preliminary results were obtained by analyzing on the giant component of the network. The results of this study may provide insights into the practice of emergency communication among different types of users. We will further analyze on the entire network to gain a more complete picture about interaction characteristics of all users. Further, we also plan to investigate the types of information that different user groups tend to communicate.

ACKNOWLEDGMENTS

The paper is supported by the National Natural Science Foundation of China (No. 71790612, No. 71804135 and No. 71603189).

REFERENCES

Gálvez-Rodríguez, M., Haro-de-Rosario, A., & Caba-Pérez, M. (2019). The Syrian refugee crisis: How local governments and NGOs manage their image via social media. *Disasters*, *43*(3), 509–533.

Hagen, L., Keller, T., Neely, S., DePaula, N., & Robert-Cooperman, C. (2017). Crisis communications in the age of social media. *Social Science Computer Review*, *36*(5), 523–541.

Ojala, M., Pantti, M., & Laaksonen, S. M. (2019). Networked publics as agents of accountability: Online interactions between citizens, the media and immigration officials during the European refugee crisis. *New Media & Society*, *21*(2), 279–297.

Yates, D., & Paquette, S. (2011). Emergency knowledge management and social media technologies: A case study of the 2010 Haitian earthquake. *International Journal of Information Management*, *31*, 6–13.

Analyzing Divergent Methodologies for Political Fact Checking: United States and South Korea

Wonchan Choi
University of Wisconsin-Milwaukee, WI, USA
wchoi@uwm.edu

Maria Haigh
University of Wisconsin-Milwaukee, WI, USA and Siegen University, Germany
mhaigh@uwm.edu

ABSTRACT

In this work in progress, we explore methods employed by professional journalists to fact-check political claims and debunk inaccurate ("fake") news stories. We content-analyzed 150 articles evaluating political claims and debunking fake news published by two media companies, the Washington Post (United States) and JTBC (South Korea), during the periods surrounding the recent presidential elections in their respective countries. Overall, the most common types of claims evaluated included false claims made by politicians or political groups about their opponents' positions and numerical and nonnumerical facts. The most frequently used methods for debunking such false claims included consulting with an independent expert in the given topic domain and checking government statistics or documents. There were some variations in the types of false claims focused and debunking methods used between the two fact-checking organizations.

KEYWORDS

Fake news; disinformation; misinformation; fact check

ASIS&T THESAURUS

Information behavior; knowledge and information

INTRODUCTION

Traditional fact checking assumes the accuracy of reporting and evaluates the accuracy of claims reported to have been made by politicians (Graves, 2016). This model of fact checking has been widely disseminated internationally, with many news organizations running fact-checking operations with a dedicated staff and their own sections on the organization's website. More recent events, most notably the Russian information offensive conducted around its 2014 invasion of Ukraine and the 2016 presidential election in the United States, posed a challenge to this model of fact checking. The widespread dissemination of entirely "fake news," primarily in online news outlets and via social media, created a different problem. Rather than accurately reporting suspect political claims, fake news stories propagated events, facts, and quotations that were fabricated or miscontextualized. For example, a picture said to illustrate child deaths in Ukraine might actually be taken in Syria. Or the report might claim to document the "Pizzagate" imprisonment of children as sex slaves by senior members of the Clinton campaign. As the product of journalistic process, fake news is defined as "*news articles* that are intentionally and verifiably false and could mislead readers," (Allcott & Gentzkow, 2017, p. 213). Traditional fact-checking services do not focus on analyzing fake news, although other groups such as Snopes.com specialized in evaluating and documenting the accuracy of widely shared online stories. Some groups, such as Ukraine's StopFake, applied aspects of journalistic fact checking to the debunking of fake news stories (Haigh, Haigh, & Kozak, 2018).

82nd Annual Meeting of the Association for Information Science & Technology | Melbourne, Australia | 19–23 October, 2019

DOI: 10.1002/pra2.00112

Our study looked at the work of two fact-checking services run by traditional media organizations. We content-analyzed fact-checking results produced by two fact-checking organizations in two countries—the Washington Post Fact Checker (U.S.) and JTBC Fact Check (South Korea)—to address the following research questions (RQs):

- RQ1: What kinds of political claims and suspect news stories did the organizations chose to evaluate?
- RQ2: What are the methods and evidence employed by fact checkers to evaluate the accuracy of political claims and of news reporting?
- RQ3: What was the balance of traditional fact-checking of political claims versus the evaluation of news reports themselves as real or fake.

METHOD

For this exploratory study, we selected two organizations with similar profiles according to Graves' (2016) framework for mapping the international fact-checking landscape. We looked at the fact-checking articles posted by each organization during a comparable time frame—2 months before and after the recent presidential elections in their respective countries: September through December 2016 for the Washington Post Fact Checker in U.S. ($N = 89$) and May through August 2017 for JTBC Fact Check in South Korea ($N = 61$). In terms of language, the Washington Post Fact Checker publishes in English and JTBC Fact Check publishes in Korean. We

Political claim or report evaluated	WP	JTBC	Evaluation methods	WP	JTBC
A claim made by a politician or political group about their own position or action	12 (13.5%)	12 (19.7%)	Checking government stats or documents	28 (31.5%)	45 (73.8%)
A claim made by a politician or political group about an opponent's position or action	26 (29.2%)	11 (18%)	Consulting with an independent expert evaluation of the claim in question	19 (21.3%)	30 (49.2%)
A claim about a number or percentage	32 (36%)	9 (14.8%)	Verifying original context of quoted source in the claim	12 (13.5%)	24 (39.3%)
Another kind of factual claim made by a politician or a political group	4 (4.5%)	15 (24.6%)	Relying on the external evaluation	14 (15.7%)	0 (0%)
Fake news	7 (7.9%)	11 (18%)	Referencing conclusions of trusted reports or credible news sources as an evidence	10 (11.2%)	3 (4.9%)
A flip-flop of a politician or political group	7 (7.9%)	5 (8.2%)	Checking the record of previous statements by the same politician	7 (7.9%)	5 (8.2%)
A causal claim made by a politician or political group (X happened because of Y)	17 (19.1%)	0 (0%)	Referencing a thinktank's or nonprofit's existing analysis	8 (9%)	3 (4.9%)
Summary or explanation of facts on a controversial issue	23 (25.8%)	28 (45.9%)	Referencing findings of other fact checkers as an evidence	8 (9%)	0 (0%)
			Checking the record of previous statements by other politicians as referenced in the claim	5 (5.6%)	0 (0%)

Table 1. Claims or reports examined (left) and evaluation methods (right) used by Washington Post and JTBC.

developed our coding scheme based on the fake news debunking methods identified by Haigh et al. (2018) and adapted the taxonomy to the context of the professional news organizations focused on fact checking. To test and refine our initial coding scheme, we recruited two third-party coders—one for English and the other for Korean articles. We used the refined coding scheme to code all the articles collected. The coders could assign more than one code for the types of claim being evaluated in each post and the evaluative methods used.

RESULTS

As presented in Table 1, the most common types of fake news debunked by the Washington Post fact checkers included claims made by politicians or political groups about the *positions and actions of their opponents* (n = 26, 29.2%) and *numerical facts* (n = 32, 36.0%). JTBC, however, focused more on debunking claims about *nonnumerical facts*, such as intentionally erroneous or biased interpretation of the law or juridical decisions (n = 15, 24.6%); also, JTBC more often evaluated the accuracy of internet reports to identify possible fake news (n = 11, 18%). Although the Washington Post often *summarized the facts on a controversial issue* (n = 23, 25.8%), it was even more common in the JTBC, occurring in almost half (n = 23, 49.5%) of posts examined. Looking at the evidence used to perform evaluations, we noted that fact checkers at the Washington Post were more likely to *consult with an independent expert about the claim in question* (n = 19, 21.3%) than any other method; this was done more routinely by the Korean fact checkers (n = 30, 49.2%). However, the JTBC's most frequent action was to *check official documents and statistics published by the governments or international organizations*, such as the United Nations, to evaluate political claims and reports (n = 45, 73.8%).

CONCLUSION AND FUTURE WORK

Both organizations focus on verifying and debunking politicians' or political groups' claims, although JTBC had begun to expand its remit to evaluate online reports as possible fake news. The results suggest that during the most recent presidential elections traditional fact-checking organizations in the United States and South Korea remained focused on subtle analysis of the degree of truthfulness of political claims and not the newer challenges of fake news.

Our immediate next steps will include: (a) expanding the dataset by including other types of fact-checking organizations (e.g., academic, political); (b) refining and validating the coding scheme as a research instrument; and (c) determining whether the new post-2016 focus on fake news has changed the balance of effort devoted by media organizations to checking the accuracy of political claims versus the veracity of news reports.

REFERENCES

Allcott, H., & Gentzkow, M. (2017). Social media and fake news in the 2016 election. *Journal of Economic Perspectives, 31*(2), 211–236.

Graves, L. (2016). Boundaries not drawn: Mapping the institutional roots of the global fact-checking movement. *Journalism Studies, 19*(5), 613–631.

Haigh, M., Haigh, T., & Kozak, N. I. (2018). Stopping fake news: The work practices of peer-to-peer counter propaganda. *Journalism Studies, 19*(14), 2062–2087.

Connective Power of the Twitter Networks: Discovering the Reverse Agenda-Setting Effects of Hashtag Activism Through Topic Modeling

Miyoung Chong
University of North Texas,
Denton, U.S.A
chongmiyoung@gmail.com

ABSTRACT

The extensive application of social media by the public may signify that the public can play a role in establishing the news media agenda. By rethinking the traditional agenda-setting theory, the purpose of this study is to investigate whether the public agenda of hashtag activism affected the traditional news media reports about the case of the Alton Sterling shooting. By applying topic modeling and qualitative content analysis, this study examined the agenda of the #AltonSterling Twitter network and concludes that reverse agenda-setting effects were identified within the one-day frame between the agendas of the #AltonSterling Twitter network and *The New York Times* based on high correspondence.

KEYWORDS

topic modeling; reverse agenda-setting; Alton Sterling; Latent Dirchlet Allocation (LDA); hashtag activism

ASIS&T THESAURUS

Data science, Qualitative analysis, Politics

INTRODUCTION

According to a report from the Pew Research Center, more than two-thirds of the US public acquire news through social media (Matsa & Shearer, 2018, September 21). In addition, social media has often functioned as a platform for online activism. Online activism researchers have primarily 1) explored the characteristics of connective and networked relationships enabled by social media and Web 2.0 technology (Bennett & Segerberg, 2013), 2) analyzed leading groups or leaderships of the network via social network analysis (Gerbaudo, 2018), and 3) examined socio-political dimensions of the online activism. However, the agendas of Twitter discussions and semantic aspects of the interpersonal conversations of online activism have not been fully discovered yet. One of the main interests of current reverse agenda-setting theory is whether the public agenda could affect the agenda of the traditional news media.

82nd Annual Meeting of the Association for Information Science & Technology | Melbourne, Australia | 19–23 October, 2019

DOI: 10.1002/pra2.00113

The purpose of this study is to examine reverse agenda-setting dynamics between public agenda and traditional news media agenda. This study argues that the US public used social media to express their thoughts and emotions about the Alton Sterling's death, and it influenced the agenda-setting role of the traditional news media outlet. To examine reverse agenda-setting effects, this study analyzed the #AltonSterling Twitter network applying topic modeling to identify the public agenda, and the content of nytimes.com was examined to identify the media agenda applying qualitative content analysis.

LITERATURE REVIEW

Agenda-setting theory is principally about transferring salience from the media agenda to the public agenda (McCombs & Shaw, 2002), which implies that the salience of components of the news agenda affects the public's awareness and prioritization of social events. Most agenda-setting research was mostly conducted in the pre-digital era. The evolution of online media, including social media, has fundamentally altered the media environments. Nair and Sharma (2017) claimed that it is not the media but the public who select issues on the agenda that could reversely influence the traditional media as public agenda, which is also one of the main interests of current reverse agenda-setting studies. The following research questions guided this study and answers to these questions can provide further evidence about reverse agenda-setting:

- RQ1: What are the agendas of the #AltonSterling Twitter network?
- RQ2: How did the agendas of the #AltonSterling Twitter network correspond with the agendas of *The New York Times* (nytimes.com)?

METHODS

Data Collection

Previous agenda-setting studies in online settings presented different findings about the agenda-setting cycle. This study examined both the one-day and the one-week time frame. Tweet data, including #AltonSterling, was collected using Twitter Application Programming Interface (API), and the dataset was collected on July 13, 2016 after Alton Sterling's death on July 5. A total of 9,670 edges were collected, which included tweets, retweets, mentions, and replied-to relationships between Twitter users. News media content was collected from a national newspaper,

The New York Times (*NYT*), in online form. Using the search term 'Alton Sterling', 32 news stories and opinion pieces were collected from *NYT* website, published from July 13 to 19 in 2016.

Data Analysis

This study claims that the extracted topics are the agendas of the #AltonSterling Twitter network. "Topics" are probability distributions across all terms in the dictionary (Blei, Ng, & Jordan, 2003). For example, the topic "police brutality" can be associated with terms such as "cop," "killed," etc., with high probability (Chong et al., 2018). Topics were extracted using the Latent Dirchlet Allocation (LDA) model applying the genism python library. LDA uses known priors to predict the occurrence of a term in a document and term in a topic. It is an iterative algorithm that begins with an initial prediction (guess) for the probability of a term appearing in a document and that same term appearing in a topic. Through each iteration, the predictions (guesses) are informed by the prior prediction and improve. This reiterative process will allow select a model that had a low perplexity score and high topic cohesiveness. A human analysis of topic interpretability also was applied to select the best model having the highest topic salience. To analyze news media content, content analysis was conducted with a qualitative approach. Content analysis is the first step in agenda-setting studies because it helps to discover the agendas demonstrated in the news media of interest for a selected time frame.

FINDINGS

The dataset represents how people felt and what the social media users were talking about regarding Sterling's death by including #AltonSterling in their tweets. The prominent topics from the dataset represent the public agenda. Figure 1 presents the top topics as the agenda of the #AltonSterling Twitter network. The two prominent issue agendas were identified: Cameron Sterling's media conference and protesters connecting Alton Sterling and Philando Castile's death to the Black Lives Matter movement.

Id	Count	Terms
16	1553	0.146*"#altonsterling's" + 0.141*"son" + 0.127*"today" + 0.124*"press" + 0.124*"conference" + 0.118*"speaking" + 0.018*"15" + 0.018*"po
17	382	0.126*"baton" + 0.125*"baton_rouge" + 0.125*"rouge" + 0.072*"shooting" + 0.066*"police" + 0.052*"meet" + 0.051*"detained" + 0.050*"fi
3	335	0.058*"time" + 0.054*"last" + 0.052*"talking" + 0.051*"father" + 0.051*"saw" + 0.048*"cameron" + 0.047*"cameron_talking" + 0.047*"saw_
2	266	0.113*"protest" + 0.083*"son" + 0.062*"everyone" + 0.058*"speaks" + 0.057*"right" + 0.055*"way" + 0.051*"want" + 0.051*"right_way" + (
12	258	0.111*"speaks" + 0.108*"death" + 0.103*"son" + 0.096*"15" + 0.095*"#altonsterling's" + 0.093*"father's" + 0.088*"year-old" + 0.088*"15_y
7	223	0.119*"peace" + 0.081*"violence" + 0.076*"gun" + 0.075*"son" + 0.068*"protest" + 0.065*"15" + 0.064*"drug" + 0.064*"alcohol" + 0.064*"j
9	217	0.075*"video" + 0.070*"police" + 0.059*"illegally" + 0.057*"felon" + 0.057*"firearm" + 0.044*"posted" + 0.043*"hour" + 0.041*"force" + 0.0
1	213	0.086*"#batonrouge" + 0.056*"rouge" + 0.056*"baton_rouge" + 0.056*"baton" + 0.054*"#blacklivesmatter" + 0.042*"cop" + 0.035*"turned
19	149	0.107*"life" + 0.105*"black" + 0.080*"matter" + 0.078*"#philandocastile" + 0.054*"justice" + 0.048*"black_life" + 0.048*"need" + 0.030*"li
8	126	0.254*"#23ways" + 0.251*"stand" + 0.084*"#blacklivesmatter" + 0.057*"#philandocastile" + 0.023*"read" + 0.021*"first" + 0.020*"think" + (
14	124	0.051*"must" + 0.045*"july" + 0.040*"arrested" + 0.037*"watch" + 0.031*"#philandocastile" + 0.030*"face" + 0.029*"day" + 0.026*"protest

Figure 1. The agendas of the #AltonSterling Twitter network.

As shown in Figure 1, the top topic (id 16) counted 1,553 times, which means the 1,553 tweets from the dataset had at least a 90% probability of being about that topic in this study. The 9,670 tweet relationships were entirely created on July 13. *NYT* also published 6 news stories, 1 editorial, and 1 video report on July 13. Among them, 3 news stories and the video reporting corresponded to the agenda of the #AltonSterling Twitter network. Therefore, within the one- day frame, 50% of the news media content published in *NYT* corresponded with the public agenda on Twitter.

The video reporting was about the media conference of Sterling's son, and the news stories were reporting details of Castile's death and protests against police brutality in relation to the Black Lives Matter movement. During the one-week frame from July 13 to July 19, many national news events occurred. For example, three Baton Rouge police officers were killed and three others were injured during the protest against Sterling's death on July 17, 2016. On July 6, 2017, five Dallas police officers were shot and nine others were wounded by a sniper during a protest in response to Sterling and Castile's deaths. In addition, 2016 was the year of the US presidential election. Some of these events, such as the police shootings, may have contributed to further media focus on Alton Sterling's case, but others, including the election, may have superseded this issue or directed the media's attention elsewhere. Thus, there was ultimately little correspondence between the Twitter agenda and *NYT*'s coverage for a week after July 13.

CONCLUSIONS

The top topics extracted by the topic modeling method using LDA were considered as the public agendas of the #AltonSterling Twitter network. The public agendas of the Twitter network were highly matched with the media agendas of *NYT* within the one-day frame. This study concludes that there are some evidences of potential reverse agenda-setting effects within the one-day frame cycle between the #AltonSterling Twitter network and *NYT*.

REFERENCES

Bennett, W. L., & Segerberg, A. (2013). *The logic of connective action: Digital media and the personalization of contentious politics*. Cambridge, England: Cambridge University Press.

Blei, D. M., Ng, A. Y., & Jordan, M. I. (2003). Latent dirichlet allocation. *Journal of Machine Learning Research*, *3*, 993–1022.

Chong, M., Habib, A., Evangelopoulos, N., & Park, H. W. (2018). Dynamic capabilities of a smart city: An innovative approach to discovering urban problems and solutions. *Government Information Quarterly*.

Gerbaudo, P. (2018). *Tweets and the streets: Social media and contemporary activism*. London, England: Pluto Press.

Matsa, K. E., & Shearer, E. (2018). *News Use Across Social Media Platforms 2018*. Retrieved from http://www.journalism.org/2018/09/10/news-use-across-social-media-platforms-2018/

McCombs, M. (2002, June). *The agenda-setting role of the mass media in the shaping of public opinion*. In Mass Media Economics 2002 Conference, London School of Economics.

Nair, P., & Sharma, S. (2017). Reverse agenda-setting: Politics in the time of facebook.

Examination of Online Information Search Stopping Behaviors and Stopping Rules by Task Type

Dedema
Peking University,
Beijing, China
dedema@pku.edu.cn

Chang Liu
Peking University,
Beijing, China
imliuc@pku.edu.cn

ABSTRACT

This poster aims to understand how task type could influence when people would stop searching and what stopping rules people would use in the following three stopping behaviors: query stopping, read stopping, and task stopping during online information search. We conducted a pilot user experiment with four participants; each performed two different types of search tasks. The results show two different patterns of stopping behavior on well-structured and decomposable tasks and poorly structured and indecomposable tasks: sequential mode, and simultaneous mode; and people use different stopping rules in three stopping behaviors.

KEYWORDS

Search stopping behavior; Stopping rules; User experiment; Interactive information retrieval

ASIS&T THESAURUS

Search behavior; Search strategies; Searching

INTRODUCTION

Online searching plays a significant role in people's daily life nowadays. People issue queries in search engines and click on webpages on search result page to get information they need. However, sometimes information overload makes them hard to decide when to stop searching. Better understanding when and how people stop searching on different search tasks could help system to guide people to stop at the right time to optimize their attention and get information more efficiently.

Prior studies on search stopping behaviors have indicated that users stopped searching when they got "enough" information (Zach, 2005). Researchers have tried to interpret what is "enough" by users through understanding what stopping rules people use to terminate their search behaviors. Some studies have pointed out that "enough" means satisficing information needs (Prabha, Silipigni Connaway, Olszewski, & Jenkins, 2007) and user characteristics are related to the stopping rule one may use (Pennington & Kelton, 2016).

82nd Annual Meeting of the Association for Information Science & Technology | Melbourne, Australia | 19–23 October, 2019

DOI: 10.1002/pra2.00114

Therefore, stopping rules are important to understand people's information stopping behaviors. The most widely used cognitive stopping rules for terminating information search in online tasks was proposed by Browne, Pitts, and Wetherbe (2007), including "mental list", "representational stability", "difference threshold", "magnitude threshold", and "single criterion". They also found the stopping rule people used was dependent on the type of task performed. The two types of task that they identified were well-structured/decomposition strategy tasks and poorly structured/holistic strategy tasks. As to stopping behaviors, Wu and Kelly (2014) focused on query abandonment (when people decide to stop their current query and issue a new one) and task stopping (when people decide to stop the search task), and found people used different rules on query abandonment and task stopping. Such results indicate that stopping rules may not only be related to the type of task but also related to different stopping behaviors. Therefore, this study aims to explore how task type could influence different stopping behaviors (query stopping, read stopping, and task stopping), in two types of tasks: well-structured and decomposable task, and poorly structured and indecomposable task, also what stopping rules people use during this process.

METHODOLOGY

User experiment

We conducted a lab-based user experiment in this study. Four undergraduate students were recruited in the pilot study. After signing the content forms, participants filled out a background questionnaire about their demographics. Among them, one is male and three are female; two are freshman and two are junior. Every participant needs to search for two assigned tasks. After reading the task description, participants started searching on the Internet using the same laptop. They were asked to bookmark all the webpages they read. During searching, their interactions with the computer were recorded by Morae Recorder. They filled out a post-search questionnaire about the stopping rules of each stopping behavior after each task.

Two tasks

Two types of search tasks were designed in this experiment. Task 1 is a well structured and decomposable.

You plan to buy a lamp for studying at night. Please search for the lamps and bookmark all the options you

are satisfied with, then add one of them as a final decision to your shopping cart.

Task 2 is a poorly structured and does not lend itself to a decomposition strategy.

Rembrandt was a great realistic painter of Netherlands in the 17th century. Please search for several representative self-portraits of Rembrandt in different periods and generalized the characteristics of them, then record it in a document.

Three stopping behaviors

In this study, we defined three types of stopping behaviors in the whole searching process to get detailed information on when and how people stop searching as follows:

Query Stopping: It means users stop issuing queries after the current query, which is actual the last query users issued.
Read Stopping: It means users have read enough information and they stopping reading more webpages, which is actual the last webpages they bookmarked.
Task Stopping: It means users have finished the whole search tasks as required and they closed the browser.

PRELIMINARY RESULTS

When to Stop?

To compare the sequence of each stopping behavior in a search session, we divided the elapsed time for each stopping behavior by the total elapsed time till task stopping as the time ratio for each stopping behavior. Since in the pilot study, we only have four participants, we also calculated the average time ratio for each stopping behavior in two tasks (shown as the vertical lines in Figure 1, and the scatter points horizontally were the time ratios of two stopping behaviors for each participant, and the y axis shows the participant id). It shows that 1) query stopping happens earlier in the well-structured and decomposable task than in the poorly structured and indecomposable task

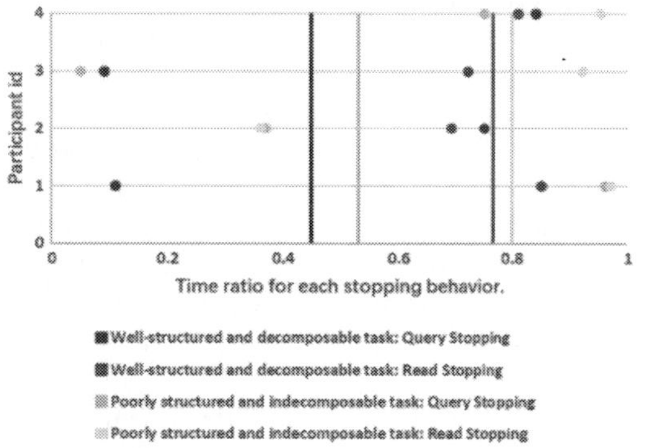

Figure 1. Demonstration of when three stopping behaviors happen (Task stopping is normalized as 1).

($0.45 < 0.53$); 2) read stopping happens nearly at the same time ratio during search process in the two types of tasks ($0.77 \approx 0.80$); 3) participants mainly have two stopping patterns: one is sequential, in which query stopping happens first, followed by read stopping and task stopping (e.g. participant #3); the other is simultaneous, in which query stopping happens simultaneously with read stopping till task stopping (e.g. participant #2).

How to Stop?

Participants described the stopping rules they used for different stopping behaviors for each task in an open-ended question in the post-search questionnaire. Then we coded their answers using cognitive stopping rules by Browne et al. (2007). We found there was no difference on stopping rules usage between two types of tasks, but participants used different stopping rules for the three stopping behaviors. For query stopping, 3 of 4 participants used mental list rule, which means they have specific query list to search for information. For read stopping, 2 of 4 participants used difference threshold role, which means they stop searching when the difference of change of search results are lower than the threshold. For task stopping, 2 of 4 participants use single criterion rule, which means they stopped task according to a specific single criterion. For example, participant #3 stopped task because he/she thought he/she had the expected length of document for the task.

DISCUSSION

Search stopping behavior is complex and is related to many factors. In this study, we found the time point that stopping behavior happened was different between two types of tasks. In particular, query stopping happens later in poorly structured and indecomposable task. It may because people are not clear about their information need at first in this task. But read stopping happens nearly at the same time ratio in two types of tasks, which may indicate that users usually leave similar ratio of time after they stop reading and before completing the task. Also, participants use different stopping rules on three stopping behaviors. What's more, we found two patterns of stopping behavior on search tasks, one is sequential mode, and the other is simultaneous mode. In the future study, we will consider more types of tasks, and increase the participant sample size to get more detailed search stopping behavior patterns which may shed light on how to guide people to search and stop online interactions with search engines.

REFERENCES

Browne, G. J., Pitts, M. G., & Wetherbe, J. C. (2007). Cognitive stopping rules for terminating information search in online tasks. *MIS Quarterly*, 89–104.

Pennington, R. R., & Kelton, A. S. (2016). How much is enough? An investigation of nonprofessional investors information search and stopping rule use. *International Journal of Accounting Information Systems*, *21*, 47–62.

Prabha, C., Silipigni Connaway, L., Olszewski, L., & Jenkins, L. R. (2007). What is enough? Satisficing information needs. *Journal of documentation*, *63*(1), 74–89.

Wu, W. C., & Kelly, D. (2014). Online search stopping behaviors: An investigation of query abandonment and task stopping. *Proceedings of the ASIS&T*, *51* (1), 1–10.

Zach, L. (2005). When is "enough" enough? Modeling the information seeking and stopping behavior of senior arts administrators. *Journal of the American Society for Information Science and Technology*, *56*(1), 23–35.

The Efficacy of Digital Literacy Training Initiatives Led by Local Community Organizations

Brian Detlor
McMaster University,
Hamilton, Canada
detlorb@mcmaster.ca

Mona Nasery
McMaster University,
Hamilton, Canada
naserym@mcmaster.ca

Heidi Julien
SUNY at Buffalo,
Buffalo, USA
heidijul@buffalo.edu

ABSTRACT

This paper describes an in-progress research study investigating the efficacy of digital literacy training initiatives led by local community organizations, including public libraries. The goal is to generate a theoretical model of factors affecting the efficacy of digital literacy training opportunities led by local community organizations, and to produce recommendations for practice for local community organizations to follow. The study adopts a constructivist grounded theory approach. Data collection is currently underway and involves interviews with administrators of local digital literacy training initiatives and users who participate in the training. As well, observations of the training and a review of documentation regarding the roll-out of the training are being conducted. Preliminary results will be communicated at the ASIS&T Annual Meeting in Melbourne.

KEYWORDS

Digital Literacy; Training; Grounded Theory; Community Organizations; Public Libraries

ASIS&T THESAURUS

User Training; Qualitative Analysis

INTRODUCTION

The purpose of this study is to understand the factors affecting the efficacy of digital literacy training initiatives run by local community organizations, including public libraries. Digital literacy is defined as "the set of skills, knowledge and attitudes required to access, create, use, and evaluate digital information effectively, efficiently, and ethically" (Julien, 2018). In this sense, digital literacy refers to the skills and know-how required by citizens to function and participate fully in today's digital society. Nowadays, people are surrounded by many different types of digital devices such as laptops and smartphones. As such, people need sufficient digital skills in order to: i) operate and utilize these digital devices; and ii) access and critically assess the information provided through these technologies. People who possess such skills are considered to be digital literate.

82nd Annual Meeting of the Association for Information Science & Technology | Melbourne, Australia | 19–23 October, 2019

DOI: 10.1002/pra2.00115

Such a study is important. People need to be digital literate today in order to fully participate and thrive in today's society. How best to offer such training is crucial to understand. This is especially true of local community organizations, such as public libraries, who wish to deliver such training to community members who may have no others means by which to receive such instruction. This training includes digital storytelling workshops, coding clubs for youth, and iPad training sessions for seniors, for example.

RESEARCH QUESTIONS

The overarching research question guiding this study is: "What factors affect the efficacy of digital literacy training led by local community organizations?" Lower-level research questions include:

- What constitutes a successful digital literacy training initiative within the local community context?
- What organizational factors (e.g., administrative factors) foster or challenge digital literacy training initiatives offered to local communities?
- What user considerations concerning digital literacy training initiatives influence community member uptake, lead to gains in digital literacy skills development, and foster greater digital literacy appreciation among community members?
- What design elements of a digital literacy training initiative foster or challenge digital literacy training initiatives offered to local communities?

The goal is to generate a theoretical model and produce recommendations for practice about how to run successful digital literacy training events for local communities.

METHODOLOGY

To investigate the phenomenon under study, semi-structured interviews are underway in the community in which the research team is based with administrators of local digital literacy training initiatives and users from the general public who participate in these training opportunities. Community organizations who have confirmed participation to-date include two local public libraries. Other local community organizations who deliver digital literacy initiatives and have expressed interest in learning how best to deliver such training include the local municipal (city) government and the city's industry education council. The Office of Community Engagement at the research team's university is offering support to help identify and rally participation in this research study from other local community organizations who deliver community-based digital literacy training programs to local residents.

Data collection includes a review of documents pertaining to the training initiatives being investigated (e.g., project charters; training materials, recruitment messages). Observations of the training sessions themselves are also being conducted.

Questions asked of participants who attend the training sessions include: What aspects of the training appealed to you? Why? What aspects of the training, in your opinion, was lacking? Why?

Questions asked of administrators of these training sessions include: What factors inhibit or promote the successful roll-out of these training sessions?

Constructivist grounded theory (Charmaz, 2014) forms the methodological basis for this study. This approach is inductive in nature. The idea is to generate theory and not test or validate pre-conceived notions. Further, this approach assumes that the opinions and reflections of the researcher and the people involved in the research study help constitute a shared understanding and interpretation of the phenomenon under investigation. In alignment with classic grounded theory (Glaser, 1978, 1998; Glaser & Strauss, 1967), no pre-conceived conceptual framework is proposed based on past literature, however sensitizing concepts based on previous research are used to structure interview questions as a means to start inquiry and not end it (Charmaz, 2014). With the approach adopted in this study, there are many iterative rounds between data collection and analysis. Data collection only stops when theoretical saturation has been reached. After results and interpretations have been made, outputs from the study will be compared with prior literature and findings.

This approach is appropriate. The lead researcher is well-versed in digital literacy concepts and has experience with the roll-out of digital literacy training initiatives in the local community. He has worked successfully with one of the local public libraries and his university's Office of Community Engagement (OCE) to deliver two digital literacy summits for the local community over the past two years. The first digital literacy summit coordinated between OCE and the local public library in 2017 yielded over 90 attendees; the second digital annual summit in 2018 yielded over 60 attendees. Monthly meetings between the city's local public library, the university's Office of Community Engagement, and the research team are on-going and speak well to the dedication and potential impact of the research investigation. This resulted in many useful insights which bode well.

Data collection and analysis methods for this study follow best-practice recommendations promoted by leading academics in the Information Systems field on how to conduct a grounded theory methodology: i) develop theory; ii) use constant comparison to analyze data from different standpoints; iii) ensure that developed theory is based on several iterations of data coding; iv) utilize theoretical sampling, with collection ceasing when data collection reaches theoretical saturation; v) ensure the study was not driven by existing theories; and vi) ensure that data collection and analysis activities were intrinsically related, done almost at the same time, in a recursive process, in which data analysis alternated with data collection until data saturation is reached (Birks, Fernandez, Levina, & Nasirin, 2013).

CONCLUSION

This paper outlines a research project currently underway that investigates the efficacy of digital literacy training initiatives run by local community organizations, including public libraries. Data collection is in-progress and preliminary results will be reported at the ASIS&T Annual Meeting in October 2019.

This research investigation promises both theoretical and practical contributions. There is little, if any, scholarly work on the efficacy of digital literacy initiatives run by local community organizations. The goal is to provide researchers interested in community-based digital literacy training with a theoretical model. On the practical side, this research has significant real-world implications for local community organizations wishing to deliver successful digital literacy training to members of their communities.

ACKNOWLEDGMENTS

This research is kindly supported by a Social Sciences and Humanities Research Council of Canada (SSHRC) Partnership Development Grant (#890-2018-0001).

REFERENCES

Birks, D. F., Fernandez, W., Levina, N., & Nasirin, S. (2013). Grounded theory method in information systems research: Its nature, diversity and opportunities. *European Journal of Information Systems*, *22*(1), 1–8.

Charmaz, K. (2014). *Constructing grounded theory* (2nd ed.). Los Angeles, CA: Sage.

Glaser, B. G. (1978). *Theoretical sensitivity: Advances in the methodology of grounded theory*. Mill Valley, CA: Sociology Press.

Glaser, B. G. (1998). *Doing grounded theory. Issues and discussions*. Mill Valley, CA: Sociology Press.

Glaser, B. G., & Strauss, A. L. (1967). *The discovery of grounded theory: Strategies for qualitative research*. Chicago, IL: Aldine Publishing Company.

Julien, H. (2018). Digital literacy in theory and practice. In M. Khosrow-Pour, *Encyclopedia of information science and technology* (4th ed., pp. 2243–2252). Hershey, PA: IGI Global.

In Memoriam Boleslaw Matuszewski: The Origin of Film Librarianship

Rubén Domínguez-Delgado
University of Seville,
Seville, Spain
rdd@us.es

María-Ángeles López-Hernández
University of Seville,
Seville, Spain
alhernan@us.es

ABSTRACT

In the current context of state policies characterized by hefty budget cuts affecting film preservation, thus seriously jeopardizing our film heritage and clashing with the pronouncements made by the UNESCO in 1980, our intention here is to analyze two texts published in Paris in 1898 by the eulogizing, but otherwise unknown, Pole Boleslaw Matuszewski: *A New Source of History* and *Animated Photography, What Is, What Should Be*. Although they have not received the recognition that they deserve, both works were crucial to the history of film insofar as they would play a vital role in film preservation as a cultural heritage.

KEYWORDS

Film librarianship; moving image librarianship; film archives; film preservation; Boleslaw Matuszewski

ASIS&T THESAURUS

Library Science; Librarianship

INTRODUCTION AND OBJECTIVE

Born in Pińczów (Poland) in 1856, Boleslaw Matuszewski left to study in Paris in the 1880s, where he was an active photographer and filmmaker working for the companies Lux and Lumière. In 1895, regarded as the year in which the film industry was officially born (Domínguez-Delgado & López-Hernández, 2016: 15), he returned to Poland to open the photographic studio Paryska Fotografia Lux - Sigismond & Co in Warsaw. Two years later, he accepted the position of official photographer and cameraman to the Russian Tsar Nicholas II, for whom he produced a film that would mark his life. As a matter of fact, Matuszewski's pioneering perception of the documentary value of moving images—beyond the predominant perception of film as a fair attraction during its initial years—was the result of a chance occurrence. In 1897, the footage that he obtained, with a Lumière camera, of the President of the French Republic Félix Faure's state visit to St Petersburg would have diplomatic repercussions. Thanks to this footage, a few years later the French were able to prove that the German Chancellor Otto von Bismarck's accusation that Faure had breached international protocol by failing to remove his hat before the Russian flag when disembarking was a malicious falsehood (Borde, 1991: 25).

One year later, in 1898, the Pole published two texts, *A New Source of History* and *Animated Photography, What Is, What Should Be*, with which he would sow the seeds of the first film archives created in the 1930s. Notwithstanding the fact that they are still little known, both gave rise to the scientific field of film librarianship, insofar as their definition of a film archive was very close to the current one. Thus, the main aim here is to analyze both of Matuszewski's works, with a view to highlighting their importance at a time when there is widespread pessimism and concern about film preservation.

A NEW SOURCE OF HISTORY

In Paris, on 25 March 1898, Matuszewski published the pamphlet entitled, *A New Source of History*, which he sent to newspapers, monarchs, ambassadors and scholars in an attempt to raise their awareness about the "documentary interest" of some actions and shows in the form of moving images, specifically those that represent "the scenes of public and national life" and not those "merely recreational, fantastic or curious life scenes" (Matuszewski, 1898a: 7). In this first text, he remarked that "the cinematographic test [...] makes the dead and the absent rise up and walk. That simple celluloid tape is not only a historical document, but a map of history". But he went even further and, given the interest of this type of document or "perhaps privileged historical sources", Matuszewski believed that it was appropriate and necessary to create a "museum or film repository" in Paris, bestowing on films "the same authority, the same official existence, the same access as other archives already known" (1898a: 9). Only three years after its advent, this was the first time in the history of film in which reference was made to the need for creating institutions to guarantee the preservation of films as historical documents forming part of the cultural heritage of humanity.

Matuszewski even envisaged the future archive, establishing the necessary human and material resources, the authority

82nd Annual Meeting of the Association for Information Science & Technology | Melbourne, Australia | 19–23 October, 2019

DOI: 10.1002/pra2.00116

that would be responsible for it—"one of the academies dealing with history"—and its possible locations in Paris— "the National Library, the Institute's Library, the Archives, or the Museum of Versailles". All of which can be understood as a clear and relatively early analogy between film and other preserved arts.

Lastly, he also referred to collection management and the different film-related tasks to be undertaken in this new archive: the selection of films after an appraisal of their historical value by a competent committee; a cataloging process of the camera film negative rolls accepted; and public access only to some of the positives under the conditions established by the committee.

WHAT MOVING IMAGES ARE, WHAT THEY SHOULD BE

Only some months later, Matuszewski published a new and more detailed study entitled, *Animated Photography, What Is, What Should Be*. With this, he broadened the possibilities of the future film archive to include roles that went beyond the purely conventional (such as its educational and military uses), foreseeing the creation of an "industrial film deposit", attached to the Arts and Crafts Department and to the Central School, a "military film deposit", administered by the Ministry of War, and a "medical film deposit" (1898b: 14-26). He also emphasized how useful it would be to preserve films about "local customs [...], family films [...], police investigations [...], dance and the art of the comedian [...], symphonic music and orchestra conductors" (1898b:40-53).

In order to give the archive a more authoritative and professional air, in this text Matuszewski also underscored that the collections had to be, first and foremost, of a public and official character—with frequent allusions to the state and its institutions. In his complete study, he also referred to the notion of legal deposit, proposing that, as with some printed documents, it should be obligatory for films. Finally, he also dwelt at length on how important it was that the public should have access to collections, suggesting the organization of screenings, the publication of a European newspaper to promote the creation of these official deposits, and laying the foundations of a policy of "voluntary donations, bequests, exchanges and purchases". Although he made it quite clear that priority should be given to film negatives, which would be kept "sealed in labeled cases" (1898b: 57).

AFTER MATUSZEWSKI'S TEXTS: FROM THE BOOM OF THE 1930s TO THE ALARMING CURRENT NEGLECT

The film archive project proposed by Matuszewski, who was pessimistic about the early transformation of his budding idea into reality (1898b: 60-61), would come up against the disinterest and ineffectualness of the film industry—in the main, only interested in box office business—and the public authorities, the only ones with sufficient means and power at the time to carry out such a project. Meanwhile, the global film heritage was hit by successive waves of destruction that reduced it considerably: in 1920, when 80 per cent of the global film production between 1895 and 1915 was destroyed, and in the early 1930s, when more than 75 per cent of all the films produced between 1919 and 1929 were lost in countries such as Italy and the United States (Domínguez-Delgado & López-Hernández, 2016: 22-23).

This situation would change drastically as from the 1930s thanks to a number of developments. The opening of Svenska Filmsamfundet, the first film archive in the world—with a similar concept to the current one—in Stockholm in 1933, was followed by the creation of film archives all over the world, including the Reichsfilmarchiv in Berlin in 1934, the National Film Archive in London in 1935, the Department of Film of the Museum of Modern Art of New York in 1935, the Cinémathèque Française in Paris in 1936 and the Filmoteca Nacional in Mexico in 1936, to name but a few. To these should be added the creation of the International Federation of Film Archives (FIAF) in 1938 and the publication of the "Recommendation for the Safeguarding and Preservation of Moving Images" by the UNESCO, which is tantamount to the official recognition of the heritage value of moving images and the first express request made to states to act to safeguard their audiovisual production (UNESCO, 1980: 168), 82 years after Matuszewski's pronouncements.

In the present century, however, we have been witnessing a progressive decline in film preservation. The World Cinema Foundation, created in 2007, has warned about the deterioration and loss of the world's film heritage, especially in less developed countries, but also in major powers such as the United States, where 90 per cent of the country's silent films have disappeared (Hermoso, 2009: 38). Equally alarming is that film preservation has suffered budget cuts in many countries, such as Spain where its main national film archive, Filmoteca Española, had its public funding slashed by 60 per cent between 2010 and 2014 (De Fontecha, 2014; Reviriego, 2016).

CONCLUSION

Matuszewski was a pioneer and a fundamental figure in film librarianship and the history of film, for his 1898 publications contributed enormously to the fact that film ceased to be considered as merchandize that once used—i.e. exhibited to the public—could be discarded, to be regarded as part of a documentary, cultural and historical heritage whose preservation is vital as a memory of humanity.

REFERENCES

Borde, R. (1991). *Los Archivos Cinematográficos*. Valencia, Spain: Filmoteca de la Generalitat Valenciana.

De Fontecha, R. (2014). "Un Laboratorio para Salvar el Legado del Cine". *El Confidencial.com*, 12 de agosto.

Domínguez-Delgado, R., & López-Hernández, M. A. (2016). Film Librarianship: historical contextual framework.

Documentación de las Ciencias de la Información, 39, 13–49.

Hermoso, B. (2009). "Scorsese, al Rescate del Cine Perdido". *El País*. Madrid, May 16, p. 38.

Matuszewski, B. (1898a). *Une Nouvelle Source de l'Histoire*. París, France. Retrieved from https://archive.org/details/unenouvellesourc00matu.

Matuszewski, B. (1898b). *La Photographie Animée, ce qu'elle Est, ce qu'elle Doit Être*. Paris, France: Noizette et Cie.

Reviriego, C. (2016). "La agonía de las filmotecas". *El Cultural.com*, July 21. Retrieved from http://www.elcultural.com/blogs/to-be-continued/2016/07/la-agonia-de-las-filmotecas-1/

UNESCO (1980). Recommendation for the safeguarding and preservation of moving images. In *Records of the General Conference, 21st session, Belgrade, 23 September to 28 October, Vol. 1, Resolutions* (pp. 156–161). París, France: UNESCO.

Are Invalid Patents Still Cited?

Huei-Ru Dong
Fu Jen Catholic University,
New Taipei City, Taiwan
141646@mail.fju.edu.tw

Dar-Zen Chen
National Taiwan University,
Taipei, Taiwan
dzchen@ntu.edu.tw

Mu-Hsuan Huang
National Taiwan University,
Taipei, Taiwan
mhhuang@ntu.edu.tw

ABSTRACT

Patents contain reference citations. However, unlike journal papers, patents may become invalid if they are not maintained or have expired. This study determines whether invalid patents are still cited. We collected telecommunications patents as a sample to compare the citations of valid and invalid patents. The results indicated that approximately 50% of cited patents were invalid. Furthermore, the citations per patent of invalid patents were fewer than those of valid ones. Nevertheless, the citations per patent of invalid patents were reduced 5.21, and nearly 5% of the patents were cited only after they became invalid.

KEYWORDS

Informetrics; patentometrics; citation analysis; patents

ASIS&T THESAURUS

Informetrics; Citation analysis; Scientometrics

INTRODUCTION

A patent is an information document containing details about the content and method of implementation of a novel technology. Patents are both technical and legal documents. Through a patent, a patentee discloses the patented technology to the public, and the government protects the patentee's rights to use this patented technology for a certain protected period. This period is limited. Typically, patents are protected for up to 20 years. During this 20-year period, the patentee can continue to maintain the patent or stop maintenance and let the patent expire. Once a patent is no longer maintained or the patent's maximum protection period of 20 years has lapsed, the patent becomes invalid. In this case, anyone can use the formerly patented technology to gain business benefits.

A patent, like an academic paper, can contain citations. Many studies have explored patent citation behavior and patent citation motivation (Azagra-Caro, Mattsson, & Perruchas, 2011; Bhattacharya, Kretschmer, & Meyer, 2003; Lai & Wu, 2005; Stock & Stock, 2006). Patent citations are often used to represent the quality of an innovation and are considered a manifestation of the patent's influence. The higher the number of citations, the better is the quality of the patent (Anderson, Duru, & Reeb, 2012; Bessen, 2009; Hall, Jaffe, & Trajtenberg, 2005; Hall, Thoma, & Torrisi, 2007; Lerner, Sorensen, & Strömberg, 2011). Patent citation analysis is considered suitable for analyzing the knowledge flow of patents (Criscuolo & Verspagen, 2008; Huang, Yang, & Chen, 2015).

Although many studies have investigated patent citations, few have conducted citation analysis to explore invalid patents. Therefore, the present study aims to explore whether patents are still cited after they become invalid. Further, we discuss how many citations an invalid patent attracts.

METHODOLOGY

Method

This study uses a patentometric method. Patentometrics, similar to bibliometrics, is a method for studying and characterizing bibliographic data. Patentometrics are often used to measure the value of patents, assist in the development of research plans, and analyze varied patent information (Lee, 2009). Depending on the level of analysis, patentometrics can be used to analyze national productivity, company productivity, invention productivity, and the development of patented technologies to reflect different levels of technological development in countries, companies, technologies, or individuals (Narin, 1994).

Data Collection

This study investigates utility patents from the United States Patent and Trademark Office (USPTO) because the United States remains the largest economy in the world. This study collected the field of telecommunications patents from 2005 to 2014 from the division of WIPO technology fields (USPTO, 2017). Then, the validity of a patent as of December 31, 2018, was estimated; most patents approved after 2015 remained valid.

From 144,339 patents, 86,587 (60%) were valid patents and 57,752 (40%) were invalid. Of the invalid patents, 11,260 (19.5%) were never cited by other patents. The remaining 46,492 (80.5%) had been cited at least once; these were selected as samples for analysis in this study.

82nd Annual Meeting of the Association for Information Science & Technology | Melbourne, Australia | 19–23 October, 2019

DOI: 10.1002/pra2.00117

RESULT

Comparison of Number of Citations of Invalid Patents

Of the patents granted between 2005 and 2014, 46,492 have been cited. Table 1 presents a comparison of the number of citations obtained by valid and invalid patents. Among the 46,492 patents, 2,058 (4.4%) were not cited when they were valid but were cited after. Further, 23,259 (50%) were not cited when they were invalid. In general, more patents were cited when they were valid than when they were invalid.

No. of citation	Valid	Invalid
0	2,058	23,259
1-5	27,948	15,170
6-10	7,119	3,076
11-20	4,805	2,314
21-30	1,831	930
31-40	898	453
41-50	556	296
51-100	972	637
>101	305	357

Table 1. Comparison of number of citations of invalid patents.

Change in Citations per Patent of Invalid Patents

The citations per patent for all telecommunications patents were 13.93. Figure 1 shows that the citations per patent were the highest in 2005, reaching 22.67. By contrast, the citations per patent were the lowest in 2014, being only 6.58. The citations per patent of valid patents were 8.71, but those of invalid patents decreased to 5.21. Figure 1 illustrates that the citations per patent of valid patents were higher than those of invalid patents. Although the citations per patent of valid patents were lower, it was still 1.65 times higher than those of invalid ones.

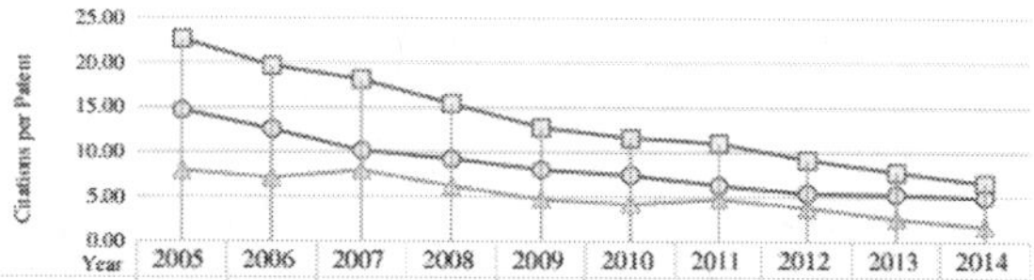

Year	2005	2006	2007	2008	2009	2010	2011	2012	2013	2014
Total	22.67	19.67	18.15	15.46	12.78	11.62	11.06	9.20	7.81	6.58
Valid	14.73	12.56	10.18	9.25	8.06	7.44	6.31	5.45	5.30	4.93
Invalid	7.95	7.11	7.97	6.21	4.72	4.17	4.75	3.75	2.51	1.65

Figure 1. Citations per patent of invalid patents.

CONCLUSION

This study investigated telecommunications patents to explore whether patents are cited even after they become invalid. The results indicated that approximately 50% of patents were not cited after they became invalid. In particular, 4.4% of patents were not cited until they became invalid. Furthermore, the citations per patent of valid patents were higher than those of invalid ones. However, the citations per patent for invalid patents still were high at 5.21. Thus, these preliminary results indicate that almost half of all patents were still cited after they became invalid and that the citations per patent remained high. These results need further confirmation; in a future study, we may discuss the perspective of time lag in detail.

ACKNOWLEDGMENTS

This work was financially supported by the Center for Research in Econometric Theory and Applications (Grant no. 108L900204) from The Featured Areas Research Center Program within the framework of the Higher Education Sprout Project by the Ministry of Education (MOE) in Taiwan, and by the Ministry of Science and Technology (MOST), Taiwan, under Grant No. MOST 108-3017-F-002-003- and MOST 107-2410-H-030-082-.

REFERENCES

Anderson, R. C., Duru, A., & Reeb, D. M. (2012). Investment policy in family controlled firms. *Journal of Banking & Finance*, *36*(6), 1744–1758.

Azagra-Caro, J. M., Mattsson, P., & Perruchas, F. (2011). Smoothing the lies: The distinctive effects of patent characteristics on examiner and applicant citations. *Journal of the American Society for Information Science and Technology*, *62*(9), 1727–1740.

Bessen, J. (2009). Estimates of patent rents from firm market value. *Research Policy*, *38*(10), 1604–1616.

Bhattacharya, S., Kretschmer, H., & Meyer, M. (2003). Characterizing intellectual spaces between science and technology. *Scientometrics*, *58*(2), 369–390.

Criscuolo, P., & Verspagen, B. (2008). Does it matter where patent citations come from? Inventor vs. examiner citations in European patents. *Research Policy*, *37*(10), 1892–1908.

Hall, B. H., Jaffe, A., & Trajtenberg, M. (2005). Market value and patent citations. *The RAND Journal of Economics*, *36* (1), 16–38.

Hall, B. H., Thoma, G., & Torrisi, S. (2007). The market value of patents and R&D: Evidence from European firms. *Academy of Management Proceedings*, *2007*(1), 1–6.

Huang, M.-H., Yang, H.-W., & Chen, D.-Z. (2015). Increasing science and technology linkage in fuel cells: A cross citation analysis of papers and patents. *Journal of Informetrics*, *9*(2), 237–249.

Lai, K.-K., & Wu, S.-J. (2005). Using the patent co-citation approach to establish a new patent classification system. *Information Processing & Management*, *41*(2), 313–330.

Lee, Y.-G. (2009). What affects a patent's value? An analysis of variables that affect technological, direct economic, and indirect economic value: An exploratory conceptual approach. *Scientometrics*, *79*(3), 623–633.

Lerner, J., Sorensen, M., & Strömberg, P. (2011). Private equity and long-run investment: The case of innovation. *The Journal of Finance*, *66*(2), 445–477.

Narin, F. (1994). Patent bibliometrics. *Scientometrics*, *30*(1), 147–155.

Stock, M., & Stock, W. G. (2006). Intellectual property information: A comparative analysis of main information providers. *Journal of the American Society for Information Science and Technology*, *57*(13), 1794–1803.

USPTO. (2017). *WIPO technology fields for all patents*. Retrieved from http://www.patentsview.org/download/

Tourists' Social Interactions on Social Media During a Group Trip Planning

Jannatul Fardous
University of South Australia,
Adelaide, Australia
jannatul.fardous@mymail.unisa.edu.au

Jia Tina Du
University of South Australia,
Adelaide, Australia
tina.du@unisa.edu.au

ABSTRACT

This paper explores the motivations for employing social interactions on social media during collaborative information seeking (CIS) in group trip planning. We conducted interviews with nine groups of tourists. The analysis identified three motivations for employing social interactions on social media while planning a group trip: finding and gathering information, scheduling the trip-related activities, and cross-checking of ideas. The findings also suggest that such interactions on social media contribute to group trip planning through improving the productivity of group information seeking and making better group trip planning.

KEYWORDS

Social interactions; social media; CIS; group trip planning

INTRODUCTION

With the increasing use of social media, social interactions on social media play an important role in many real-life situations. For example, planning a trip with families or friends can benefit from collaboration with other experienced tourists while they seek and gather information to make informed decisions (Fardous, Du, Choo, Huang, & Hansen, 2017). Social interactions may occur between an individual and their family members, friends, or peers in both the digital and physical worlds. Research has shown that when tourists search for information on holidays, they prefer to search for information shared by peers on social media over the information obtained from tourism websites, travel agents, and mass media advertising (Harrigan, Evers, Miles, & Daly, 2017). Information shared by experienced tourists on social media is perceived as similar to recommendations provided by friends, families or even like-minded people (Wang & Fesenmaier, 2002) and thus, considered as a trustworthy source of information. Tan and Goh (2015) found that individual tourist interacted with people around him/her to fulfill information needs; such social interactions with both immediate and extended social circles were found to affect tourists' decisions at the destination. However, these studies did not present an in-depth analysis of the contributions of social interactions on social media in group trip planning. In this study, we aim to address the following research question:

RQ1. Why does a group of tourists interact with other non-group members on social media during information seeking?

RQ2. How do social interactions on social media contribute to group trip planning?

RESEARCH METHOD

Semi-structured group interviews were conducted with tourists who had traveled with a group of people recently and organized trips on their own. We recruited graduate students and researchers working in a large IT school at a university in Australia, as well as professionals (e.g. engineers and IT professionals). Each interview lasted between 50-75 minutes, and AUD20 gift voucher and packets of chocolates were given as compensation to each participating group. The interviews were undertaken in different places (e.g. university campus, coffee shops, and library) depending on the convenience for the participants. A total of nine (9) groups of 25 participants took part in the interviews. The average group size was 4 people, and the average age was 31 years old. The interviews were audio recorded, and verbatim transcriptions of the recordings were used in the data analysis. Content analysis (Hsieh & Shannon, 2005) was started with reading the written transcripts across the nine groups; the phrases relevant to the aims of the study were chosen from the text, and then all condensed phrases were coded and grouped into categories. Eventually, the underlying connections and relationships were inferred. Some quotes from the participants were included in the results section to illustrate the interpretation.

RESULTS AND DISCUSSION

Motivations for using Social Interactions on Social Media

As reported, group members communicated with other non-group members to seek needed information which we called as social interactions via social media. Social interactions took place during trip planning to facilitate tourists' information gathering and validation. It is worthy to note that social interactions occurred on the occasions of individual information seeking to gather the information that subsequently used to compare, assess, validate and synthesize for facilitating

82nd Annual Meeting of the Association for Information Science & Technology | Melbourne, Australia | 19–23 October, 2019

DOI: 10.1002/pra2.00120

CIS and sharing tasks with group members. Details on the motives of employing social interactions for information seeking are reported below.

Finding and Gathering Information

Due to lack of relevant destination knowledge by the entire group, one motivation of interacting with other social media users is to finding out destination-related information, including must-see local places to visit, authentic restaurants serving local and traditional food, the appropriate time to visit, the best mode of transportation to travel, and roaming at the destination. The following quote exhibited such interactions:

> *"I [mem#1] contacted with my friend who visited Melbourne before to find the best way [by road or flight] to travel to Melbourne. I [memr#2] also contacted with my friend [another person] to have more information about best way, car renting and location of hotel so that we can compare our information [gathered by all] for making the right decision."*

Our finding confirms Tan and Goh (2015) that tourists interacted with people who had relevant experiences to seek a wide range of information in travel planning.

Scheduling the Trip-Related Activities

Arranging trip timeline and schedule of each event (e.g. how many sightseeing places can be visited per day) was usually tricky for the first time travelers. In such a scenario, participants wanted genuine knowledge about key travel sites and activities performed by experienced tourists in support of scheduling the trip event. As a group of tourists mentioned,

> *"We talked with two friends to know all details about their trip. For example, I [mem#1] asked about the time [taken] from Melbourne to Mount Buller, great ocean drive and Philip Island and things to do there. I [mem#2] also asked them how many days are enough to visit Melbourne and what are the main attractions we can cover in this time."*

Cross-Checking of Ideas

Last minute cross-checking of information and ideas was another critical reason for collaboration with the outside of the tour group on social media. In particular, participants interacted with experienced tourists to cross-check their itineraries such as verifying location and safety of the hotel, the frequency of tram, and distance of tourists' spots from the hotel. Also, they obtained information about the nearest food court and restaurants fulfilling special dietary requirements around the visiting places to include them in their trip plan. For example, a group stated that:

> *"I talked with my two friends to cross-check our travel plan like I told them our planned to go to Mount Baw Baw and great ocean drive on the same. Then they (two friends) suggested me to change the places and go to Mount Buller and a temple on the same day."*

Contributions of Social Interactions in Trip Planning

Participants described the ways how the information obtained from social interactions on social media helped their group trip planning. Follows are the contributions.

Improving the Productivity of Group Information Seeking

Individual members of a group relied on social interactions to find different ideas and adventures. These include group members contacted experienced tourists from their personal networks on social media (FB Messenger, WhatsApp, and WeChat) to obtain relevant information as suggestions and opinions on their trip. Afterward, they shared the information obtained from social interactions along with self-assessments with the group for discussions. A possible reason behind the sharing of obtained information within the group was to compare, assess and validate travel products together, which eventually assisted with their decision-making. Consulting with other experienced tourists helped to improve the productivity of information seeking for the tour group by quickly contributing authentic and proper information. As one group stated,

> *"We were looking for a mall which has indoor activities and decided the Mall of Emirates as per friend's suggestion. His suggestion directed us to find mall related information [route, time and distance] quickly otherwise we had to search for information first and then verify them, which could be a long process to make decision."*

Improving the Group Trip Planning

Trip planning is a complex and dynamic process during which information seeking via social media plays an important role in information searching and decision-making. Obtaining experiential tourism information based on experiences and reviews of other tourists on social media, group members found the information acquired via social interactions valuable which often impacted on their travel planning and resulted in the change of the original plan. In particular, social interactions on social media help a group of participants to plan a better holiday through practical knowledge of real tourists. For example, a group mentioned,

> *"His [participant's friend] information was beneficial for our trip. Because of his suggestions, we took the roadway to go to Melbourne and enjoyed the road trip otherwise we would take the flight to go there and would miss the natural beauty of roadways."*

CONCLUSION

The findings of this study add to the knowledge of CIS of understanding of using social interactions on social media during group trip planning. The identified motivations include finding and gathering information, scheduling the trip-related activities and cross-checking of ideas. Future research will investigate how social interactions and intra-group collaborations vary among different group characteristics, e.g. family group and friend group.

REFERENCES

Fardous, J., Du, J. T., Choo, K. K. R., Huang, S., & Hansen, P. (2017). Exploring collaborative information search behavior of mobile social media users in trip planning. In *Proceedings of iConference 2017* (pp. 435–444).

Harrigan, P., Evers, U., Miles, M., & Daly, T. (2017). Customer engagement with tourism social media brands. *Tourism Management*, *59*(Suppl. C, 597–609.

Hsieh, H.-F., & Shannon, S. E. (2005). Three approaches to qualitative content analysis. *Qualitative Health Research*, *15*(9), 1277–1288.

Tan, E., & Goh, D. (2015). A study of social interaction during mobile information seeking. *Journal of the Association for Information Science and Technology*, *66*(10), 2031–2044.

Wang, Y.,. Q., & Fesenmaier, D. R. (2002). Defining the virtual tourist community: implications for tourism marketing. *Tourism Management*, *23*(4), 407–417.

Usability Testing of LUI: A New Human-Computer Interface for Large Displays

Catherine Dumas
Simmons University,
Boston, USA
catherine.dumas2@
simmons.edu

Sanda Erdelez
Simmons University,
Boston, USA
sanda.erdelez@
simmons.edu

Jeffrey Pomerantz
Simmons University,
Boston, USA
jeffrey.pomerantz@
simmons.edu

Vik Parthiban
MIT, Media Lab,
Boston, MA
vparth@mit.edu

ABSTRACT

A usability study was conducted on a new human-computer web interface for large displays created by researchers from the Media Lab at MIT (Massachusetts Institute of Technology). Data was collected by observing 12 subjects who were asked interact with a large screen monitor using a set of gestures. The subjects were also asked to complete a survey after they participated. The purpose of the study was to discover new methods of how people interact with a large display using gestures. By understanding how people use this interface, novel applications that reflect user preferences can be designed. Our findings discovered usability and technology issues that were given to the creators of the web-interface that was evaluated in this study. We also created usability testing protocol that will be used in future studies of this gesture-based application.

KEYWORDS

usability testing; gesture-based technology; extended reality

ASIS&T THESAURUS

Information Science; Research methods; User studies

INTRODUCTION

LUI (Large User Interface) is a scalable, multimodal web-interface created by researchers from the Media Lab at MIT that uses a custom framework of non-discrete, free-handed gestures to control modular applications. The gestures are mapped to ReactJS web elements to provide a highly-responsive and accessible user experience. ReactJS is a JavaScript library for building user interfaces. This interface can be deployed on an augmented reality or virtual reality system, heads-up displays for autonomous vehicles, and every day large displays. Figure 1 is a screenshot of the LUI's website homepage.

Figure 1. Screen shot of home page of LUI website.

Integrated applications include media browsing for photos and YouTube videos. Viewing and manipulating 3D models for engineering visualization are in progress, with more applications to be added by the developers in the future.

The LUI menu consists of a list of applications which the user can "swipe" and "airtap" to select an option. Each application has its unique set of non-discrete gestures to view and change content.

The purpose of this research is to understand how people interact with a large display using gestures in order to design new applications that reflect user preferences. Twelve subjects were recruited to participate in this research study to evaluate the usability of LUI. The study took place in front

Figure 2. Screen shot of LUI's current applications.

82nd Annual Meeting of the Association for Information Science & Technology | Melbourne, Australia | 19–23 October, 2019

DOI: 10.1002/pra2.00118

of a large monitor. Subjects engaged with the display using their hand movements. After each subject finished a predefined set of tasks, they were asked to complete a survey. Figure 3 shows a subject interacting with LUI using hand gestures.

Figure 3. Subject interacting with LUI using hand gestures.

BACKGROUND

Gesture controlled systems are a combination of different tools and technologies like camera, graphics, vision etc. Research has shown that gesture controlled technologies are advanced enough to perform a diverse range of tasks and be widely useful (Bhuiyan & Picking, 2009; Bhuiyan & Picking, 2011; Li, 2016; Xun & Dai, 2017). Hand gesture-controlled games such the Wii and the Kinect sensor for the Microsoft Xbox360 are examples of hand gesture recognition (HGR) used for entertainment (Xu & Dai, 2017). However, HGR is also being researched and developed in medical systems and assistive technologies (Xu & Dai, 2017).

Leap Motion, Inc. manufactures a computer hardware sensor device that supports hand and finger motions as input, analogous to a mouse, but requires no hand contact or touching. Leap Motion technology is widely used by developers to create new augmented and virtual reality applications such as LUI, the application tested in this study.

METHODOLOGY

A large monitor and a Leap Motion controller (A small USB peripheral device which is the hardware for Leap Motion) were connected to a laptop. The Leap Motion software was installed on the laptop. The Leap Motion controller was placed at the correct appropriate for each user to move their hands above it. Subjects who participated in this study, were asked to do the following things:

1. Approach the monitor and stand in front of the table with the Leap Motion controller
2. Navigate the interface without instruction
3. Navigate the interface using a list of gestures
4. Unlock the screen with gestures
5. Enter an app with gestures
6. Browse the app with gestures
7. Exit the app with gestures
8. Navigate and explore another app with gestures
9. Fill out the survey

The total study took no more than 20 minutes per subject: 10 min for the experiment and 10 min for the survey.

USABILITY TESTING FINDINGS

Technology Support Issues

The application became laggy or slow to respond after several minutes of use. We recommend that it be restarted after each use.

Usability Issues

1. User must click with four fingers together, not index finger alone
2. Swipe up works best when gesture is smaller (in other words, smaller motion works better than larger motion)
3. Low level of sensitivity of app for opening/pausing videos
4. Hands get tired

Application Content & Features (Suggestions)

1. Include additional pages with photos and videos to allow users to practice left and right swiping and other hand gestures
2. Allow for photos to be enlarged since users expected this functionality
3. Have the videos play/pause by being tapped anywhere on the screen (when it is in full screen)

CONCLUSION

Future Usability Testing Protocol

1. Perform one-user-at-time testing after group introduction to prevent skill transfer and order effect
2. Identify main gestures (tap/open, swipe, exit/close, etc.) to be evaluated and provide short training for each gesture on a simplified version of LUI interface

The results of the survey are still being analyzed and will be included in the poster presentation.

FUTURE WORK

At the writing of this paper, several of the issues and suggestions from our usability testing findings have been addressed and implemented. In addition, LUI now has voice command. If the user wants to find a specific application, they can also say a voice command to search or directly go to that application. Future usability testing will be done with the new version of LUI and the usability testing protocol that we have developed as a result of this initial study.

REFERENCES

Bhuiyan, M., & Picking, R. (2009). Gesture-controlled user interfaces, what have we done and what's next. In *Proceedings of the Fifth Collaborative Research Symposium on Security, E-Learning, Internet and Networking (SEIN 2009)* (pp. 25–29). Darmstadt, Germany.

Bhuiyan, M., & Picking, R. (2011). A gesture controlled user interface for inclusive design and evaluative study of its usability. *Journal of Software Engineering and Applications, 04*(09), 513–521. https://doi.org/10.4236/jsea.2011.49059.

Li, X. (2016). *Hand gesture recognition Technology in Human computer interaction*. School of Computer Science, University of Birmingham.

Xu, Y., & Dai, Y. (2017). Review of hand gesture recognition study and application. *Contemporary Engineering Sciences, 10*, 375–384. https://doi.org/10.12988/ces.2017.7326.

Characteristics of Collaborative Information Seeking Activities During Group Trip Planning: A Preliminary Study

Jannatul Fardous
University of South Australia,
Adelaide, Australia
jannatul.fardous@mymail.unisa.edu.au

Jia Tina Du
University of South Australia,
Adelaide, Australia
tina.du@unisa.edu.au

ABSTRACT

Collaborative work among tourists is a topic of ongoing interest in information seeking area, and such activities are constantly evolving as technology advances. This paper explores the characteristics of a tourists group's activities during tourism information seeking. We conducted interviews with nine groups of tourists. The analysis identified four main characteristics of collaborative information seeking (CIS) activities in group trip planning process: initial co-planning on the trip, seeking and sharing of information, prioritization of choices, and collaborative decisions. The findings of CIS characteristics will help CIS developer and tourism service operators to integrate new customized features and strategies to support group trip planning.

KEYWORDS

Collaborative information seeking; tourism; trip planning

INTRODUCTION

Collaboration is necessary in many real-life situations. For example, planning a trip with families or friends requires collaboration while they seek and gather information, and make collective decisions to achieve a group holiday (Mohammad Arif, Du, and Lee, 2015). Collaborative information seeking (CIS) describes the process of searching for meaningful information performed by team members to accomplish their collaborative work (Hertzum, 2008; Shah, 2014). Collaborating with tour mates may facilitate the seeking and locating of relevant information and informing joint decision-making (Zhang, Sun, and Wagner, 2018). For example, Mohammad Arif, Du, and Lee (2015) reported that tourists in a travel group communicated with each other in order to learn personal preferences, to facilitate efficient completion of tasks, and to preserve team harmony. However, prior studies examined the reasons for intra-group collaboration in trip planning but did not examine the characteristics of tourism CIS activities of this phase. In this study, characteristics of CIS activities is defined as the collaborative activities performed by group members during a group trip planning. This study aims to address the following research question:

82nd Annual Meeting of the Association for Information Science & Technology | Melbourne, Australia | 19–23 October, 2019

DOI: 10.1002/pra2.00119

RQ. What are the characteristics of tourism collaborative information seeking activities during group trip planning?

RESEARCH METHOD

Qualitative semi-structured group interviews (Morris and Amershi, 2008) were conducted with holidaymakers who had traveled with a group of people recently and organized their trips on their own (free and independent travelers). We recruited graduate students and researchers working in a large IT school at a university in Australia, as well as professionals (e.g. engineer, teacher, and IT professionals) through snowball sampling. Each interview lasted between 50-75 minutes, and AUD20 gift voucher and packets of chocolates were given as compensation to each participating group. The interviews were undertaken in different places (e.g. university campus, coffee shops, and library) depending on the convenience for the participants. A total of nine (9) groups of 25 participants took part in the interviews. The average group size was 4 people, and the average age was 31 years old. The interviews were audio recorded, and verbatim transcriptions of the recordings were used in the data analysis. Content analysis (Hsieh and Shannon, 2005) was started with reading the written transcripts across the nine groups; the phrases relevant to the aims of the study were chosen from the text and then all condensed phrases were coded and grouped into categories. Eventually, the underlying connections and relationships were inferred. Some quotes from the participants were included in the results section to illustrate the interpretation.

RESULTS

Characteristics of a Group Trip Planning Activities

Initial Co-Planning on the Trip

At the initial stage of trip planning, participants reported that they communicated with group members to make a preliminary plan on the trip, including selecting destination, deciding on time, date and length of the trip, looking into possible transportation (by flight or by car), discussing weather and related suitable clothes, and security and safety issues at the potential destination. A possible reason for initial co-planning was to have a collective agreement on the upcoming group trip and conduct more research on particular tourism products relating to the destination. For example, one group mentioned,

> "*We discussed about the trip. Firstly, we chose Sydney as the destination because it is a famous international city. We discussed about airlines, hotel, scenic spots, transportation (taxi, bus or walk route). We also discussed about the date of travel and the length (4 days) we will stay in Sydney.*"

Seeking and Sharing of Information

Tourism is information demanding activity wherein communication plays an essential role in CIS in that it enhances the information seeking process by initiating common ground among the group members (Reddy, Bernard, and Rashmi, 2009). During group trip planning, group members are required to find a variety of information to resolve their shared information needs. Due to the lack of domain or search expertise, seeking and sharing of information is another key aspect of tourism CIS process. For example, individual group members collaborated with other members to seek from and share with different types of tourism information as well as updates on the progress of the trip planning, such as search results (reviews, and photos), links of websites, list of flights and hotels, and the details on attractions and activities at the holiday destination. To avoid future conflicts of preference, they used to notify the entire group about the progress of trip planning by sharing the findings of individual searches. A group stated,

> "*I [member #1] made a list after searching information on hotel and food and shared with the group to decide from the list. I [member #2] also made a list of attractions, transportation and shopping areas and shared with them [group] to know their opinions.*"

Therefore, information seeking from different sources on social media and sharing the gathered information with group members has a significant impact on synthesizing of information in a team setting otherwise they may have difficulties in decision-making due to the lack of sufficient information.

Prioritization of Choices

Prioritization of choices and making group decision is complicated because choices on tourism products vary over individuals, whereas every member's preferences need to be considered in the decision-making process. Moreover, the number of choices and options are more in the group trip planning in that choices and opinions provided by each group member. When group members perform CIS activities, they collaborated within the group to prioritize their choices through narrowing down the shared options (e.g. search results) as well as solving disputes on choices. Also, they share ideas and opinions on tourism products and services to make group decisions. The reason behind such collaboration was to ensure that everyone in the group could provide their opinions and was happy with the decisions made as a group. Another reason for collaborative prioritization was to show respect to everyone in the group otherwise every member of the group will not enjoy the entire trip equally. For example, a member of a group mentioned,

> "*We first compared our gathered info and made decisions together during group discussion because joint decision means everyone owns it. So, it's important for members to feel that ownership that we made the decision to come here and let's enjoy it.*"

Collaborative Decision

Making a collaborative decision on every aspect of a group trip is an important feature of tourism CIS activities since a group is formed with multiple members and each member has his/her own perceptions and experiences on the same subject. At the end of planning, the tour group makes decisions as well as changes on the prior decisions through verifying every detail of trip planning with all active members of the group. We found that during CIS activities, group members also negotiate with others via verifying different opinions and choices on tourism products like indoor or outdoor activities, bus or tram or taxi, and fast foods or local cuisines in order to avoid and resolve conflicts between them. Such coordination aided group members to plan the trip in harmony and avoid upcoming conflicts during the execution of the trip. A group mentioned,

> "*We used to verify with each other before confirming everything. For example, we shared every step of our planning specially places to visit in Italy and hotel to make sure that we agree with each other's planning and no conflict and arguments happen later.*"

CONCLUSION

This findings of the preliminary study add to the knowledge of CIS of understanding of the characteristics of tourism CIS behaviors performed by groups of tourists as they plan a group trip. The identified features include initial co-planning on the upcoming tour, seeking and sharing of information, prioritization of choices, and collaborative decisions. Future research will investigate how social interactions and intra-group collaborations vary among different group characteristics, e.g. different categories of groups, such as family group, friend group, or mixed.

REFERENCES

Hertzum, M. (2008). Collaborative information seeking: The combined activity of information seeking and collaborative grounding. *Information Processing & Management, 44*(2), 957–962.

Hsieh, H.-F., & Shannon, S. E. (2005). Three approaches to qualitative content analysis. *Qualitative Health Research, 15*(9), 1277–1288.

Mohammad Arif, A. S., Du, J. T., & Lee, I. (2015). Understanding tourists' collaborative information retrieval behavior to inform design. *Journal of the Association for Information Science and Technology, 66*(11), 2285–2303.

Morris, M., & Amershi, S. (2008). Shared sensemaking: Enhancing the value of collaborative web search tools. In *Proceeding of CHI 2008 sensemaking workshop*.

Reddy, M. C., Bernard, J. J., & Rashmi, K. (2009). The role of communication in collaborative information searching. *Proceedings of the American Society for Information Science and Technology, 45*(1), 1–10.

Shah, C. (2014). Collaborative information seeking. *Journal of the Association for Information Science and Technology, 65*(2), 215–236.

Zhang, L., Sun, X., & Wagner, C. (2018). Exploring the group holiday decision-making process with the support of technology. *Information Processing & Management*.

The False Trade-Off of Relevance for Safety in Children's Search Systems

Vanessa Figueiredo
University of British Columbia,
Vancouver, Canada
vanesfi@mail.ubc.ca

Eric M. Meyers
University of British Columbia,
Vancouver, Canada
eric.meyers@ubc.ca

ABSTRACT

Since the wide adoption of the Internet in public schools and libraries, parents, educators and caregivers have been concerned about the safety and efficacy of children's search practice, often willing to accept diminished information quality to ensure that young searchers do not encounter illicit materials. In this study, part of a broader examination of youth search practices in the early years, we demonstrate that "safe", child-oriented search engines provide less relevant results, while failing to keep children from the unfiltered Web, the narrow definition of safety proffered by the sites themselves. Based on our findings, we suggest that the rhetorics of these search tools present a false trade-off and may actually hinder inquiry practice, as opposed to supporting safe and developmentally appropriate access to online materials.

KEYWORDS

Search; youth; inquiry; safety; relevance; design

ASIS&T THESAURUS

Information discover; information seeking; search behavior; Product and service providers; search services

INTRODUCTION

Children's search engines are one solution among several designed to address the challenge of keeping children safe while enabling online inquiry activities. Such search portals are ostensibly designed to deliver safe, relevant information for novice Web users while supporting their cognitive and motor skills with child-appropriate interfaces (Gossen, Hempel, & Nürnberger, 2013). Over the past 20 years, online searching for children has evolved from curated collections of materials in portal- and catalogue-like interfaces to keyword-based search engines that more closely approximate how adult tools look and function (see earlier work, e.g., Bilal, 2000; Druin et al., 2009; Duarte Torres & Weber, 2011; Schacter, Chung, & Dorr, 1998). What many of these search systems implicitly or explicitly acknowledged was the essential trade-off of information quality and quantity in favor of safety. That is, walled garden approaches or filtered results present children a limited result set that may be less relevant or useful in exchange for being free of explicit material, or sites that were beyond the reading and comprehension level of young people.

Despite two decades of work in this area, children's search is still grappling with efficacious mechanisms for managing this essential trade-off. Current search engines billed as "child safe" make use of Google Custom Search (GCS) to provide a filtered search environment, ostensibly free of harmful information sources and focused on child-oriented and educational resources. This safe environment is achieved by customizing the GCS to filter out inappropriate information sources using keywords or prioritizing educational domain pages. This solution, which is far less time and labor-intensive than curating search results, has led to a proliferation of search engines marketed to parents and educators.

As part of a larger interrogation of youth search practices in the early years, we sought to test whether this new approach yielded an improved search experience for children. We were prompted by our observations that teachers regard these sites as "safe" alternatives to searching the open Web, yet can be frustrating and inhibiting for children, despite their bright colors and larger fonts. We ask: Do GCS-driven search engines for children return "safer" and more relevant results than open Web search via Google? The findings of this preliminary study will be used to understand to what extent GCS-based tools return efficacious search results for children. It provides a foundation for future research projects, as well as other scholars, in anticipating aspects of search that might be challenging for children and reinforces the need for additional user studies with children.

METHODS

For this analysis we examined the design and utility of six search engines for children that employ GCS (Kiddle, Kid Rex, Kids Search, Kidz Search, Kidtopia and Swiggle), and compared the search engine results to Google. We tested each search interface using three fact-checking queries retrieved from the TREC library, specifically: "How far away is the Moon?"; "Who invented the television?"; and "What do penguins eat?". Researchers have found children are likely to use

82nd Annual Meeting of the Association for Information Science & Technology | Melbourne, Australia | 19–23 October, 2019

DOI: 10.1002/pra2.00121

natural language and question-type queries when searching for information (Jochmann-Mannak, Huibers, Lentz, & Sanders, 2010; Kammerer & Bohnacker, 2012; Vanderschantz & Hinze, 2017). We examined 210 search results (the first 10 results from each search engine for all three queries) which yielded 104 unique pages. We assessed relevance on whether or not the page could answer the query posed. We acknowledge that this measure is different than how children might perceive the usefulness of these pages, which can depend on where in the page and how easily the answer is found. We classified the unique pages in three categories: 1) Child-oriented (C): targeted to youth, including characters, colorful features and a language easy for kids to understand; 2) Education (E): produced by research institutes, universities and educational sources but targeted to a broader audience; 3) General (G): no explicitly educational content and likely to be from commercial and news sources. Google was included in the analysis to compare whether the search results varied from those returned by the GCS search engines. We also evaluated whether the thumbnail images illustrated the search results, measured snippet length, and examined the presence and types of ads in the SERP.

FINDINGS

Of the 104 unique pages delivered by the seven search interfaces, there was a mix of educational, child-focused, and general sources (E = 42, C = 31, and G = 31). For the query "What do penguins eat?", 5 out 6 search engines returned the same first search result as Google, and the majority of high-ranking search results (ranks 1-3) overlapped with the top results for an unfiltered search. Beyond these top results there was more variation; however, it has been documented that youth tend to select the top results with greater frequency, and even adult searchers rarely venture "below the fold" or scroll for lower-ranked pages. While this poster abstract does not allow for a complete elaboration of our results, we identified the following themes in the analysis:

GCS Engines Delivered Lower Relevance Results

Nearly 30% of results (30 of 104 unique pages) returned by the six child-oriented search tools were deemed not relevant; that is, the answer could not be found in the suggested page. This did not compare favorably to Google (1 of 30 or 3%). Twenty-two of 30 not-relevant search results were either from child-oriented or educational sources.

Irrelevant or Redirecting Ads

Five of 6 search engines (only Swiggle was ad free) displayed paid advertisement or "promoted results" at the top of the SERP, which in some cases occupy nearly the entire top of the page, necessitating scrolling to see the non-promoted results. While search engines like Kiddle demarcated the ads with a shaded box, nearly all were irrelevant to the search, or redirected users to other GCS search portal results with the same keywords, misleadingly taking children from a "safe" set of results to one that offered no such filtering.

Not So Child-Friendly Designs

Many of the search engines used a thumbnail image from the result to increase interest or perceptions of usefulness. However, we found the majority of these (90 of 104) did not fulfill this purpose, or displayed images unrelated to the topic searched. The snippet length mean in lines was greater on Google ($M=\approx 2.46$) than the 6 search engines ($M=\approx 1.92$), which may affect the decision to select the search result or deem it useful.

DISCUSSION AND CONCLUSION

We argue from these results that the move from curated collections of resources for children to filtered search results using GCS has not resolved the challenges of child safe Web use. Rather, these search engines focus on a narrow and misleading narrative of safety while promoting results that are less relevant (and yet no more child friendly) than unfiltered Google, at least for the limited query set we used in this inquiry. This preliminary study will inform user studies with elementary age children to identify the extant barriers to novice information retrieval with the goal of informing more efficacious tools for inquiry.

REFERENCES

Bilal, D. (2000). Children's use of the Yahooligans! Web search engine: I. Cognitive, physical, and affective behaviors on fact-based search tasks. *Journal of the American Society for Information Science*, *51*(7), 646–665.

Druin, A., Foss, E., Hatley, L., Golub, E., Guha, M. L., Fails, J., & Hutchinson, H. (2009). How children search the internet with keyword interfaces. 89. https://doi.org/10.1145/1551788.1551804

Duarte Torres, S., & Weber, I. (2011). What and how children search on the web. *Proceedings of the 20th ACM International Conference on Information and Knowledge Management - CIKM '11*, 393. https://doi.org/10.1145/2063576.2063638

Gossen, T., Hempel, J., & Nürnberger, A. (2013). Find it if you can: Usability case study of search engines for young users. *Personal and Ubiquitous Computing*, *17*(8), 1593–1603. https://doi.org/10.1007/s00779-012-0523-4

Jochmann-Mannak, H., Huibers, T., Lentz, L., & Sanders, T. (2010). *Children searching information on the Internet: Performance on children's interfaces compared to Google*. 9.

Kammerer, Y., & Bohnacker, M. (2012). Children's web search with Google: the effectiveness of natural language queries. *Proceedings of the 11th International*

Conference on Interaction Design and Children, 184–187. https://doi.org/10.1145/2307096.2307121

Schacter, J., Chung, G., & Dorr, A. (1998). Children's Internet searching on complex problems: Performance and process analyses. *Journal of the American Society for Information Science*, *49*(9), 840–849. https://doi.org/10.1002/(SICI)1097-4571(199807)49:9<840::AID-ASI9>3.0.CO;2-D

Vanderschantz, N., & Hinze, A. (2017). A study of children's search query formulation habits. *Proceedings of the 31st British Computer Society Human Computer Interaction Conference*, *31*, 1–4. https://doi.org/10.14236/ewic/HCI2017.7

When the World Ends: Study of #FakeWesteros Twitter Fan Community During the Final Season of *Game of Thrones*

Eric Forcier
Swinburne University of Technology,
Edmonton, Canada
eforcier@swin.edu.au

ABSTRACT

#FakeWesteros is an online fan community that originated on Twitter when the worldwide blockbuster television series *Game of Thrones (GoT)* aired its first season in 2011. Fans from around the world live-tweeted episodes as a role-playing activity, assuming the identity of a character from the series in their tweets. This poster will present an analysis of this practice during the 2019 airing of the final season of *GoT*. Preliminary results reveal how fans responded to the controversial last episodes, demonstrating how Twitter was used to express their thoughts and feelings regarding the characters, the narrative and its creators. Findings indicate how this innovative use of the digital space represents evolving forms of information sharing. Findings inform ongoing research into the information-based practices of fans and provides new insights into the evolution of online communities, particularly how loyalty to a shared identity can extend bonds beyond fandom.

KEYWORDS

Fans; Game of Thrones; Twitter; Sentiment analysis; Qualitative analysis

ASIS&T THESAURUS

Entertainment; Popular Culture; Communities

INTRODUCTION

Online communities, open collectives of dispersed individuals operating within the virtual space, are important sources of knowledge (Faraj, Jarvenpaa, & Majchrzak, 2011). Fandom is the community or culture of fans of a popular media object, such as a narrative or celebrity; online communities of fans generate knowledge and develop virtual identities that represent evolving information practices within a fandom (Booth, 2008). As digital media and technologies increasingly converge and become embedded in everyday lives, the study of such practices is particularly valuable in providing key examples of how people's interactions with information is evolving (Forcier, 2017). This research-in-progress explores one such example in context. Relatively few studies have focused on the information-based practices of fans (e.g., Price & Robinson, 2016). This case study will further contribute to this new and growing thread in LIS research.

HBO's *Game of Thrones* (*GoT*) is a fantasy television series that has spanned eight seasons and 72 episodes, with an average viewership of 44.2 million viewers per episode (Pattern, 2019). Few television series have achieved the same pinnacle of mainstream success in the last decade and *GoT* has developed a global following as a result. Nevertheless, producers of the television series faced severe backlash following the final season, due to the perception that storytelling was rushed and inconsistent with quality fans had come to expect (Tefekci, 2019).

As a social media website, Twitter has transformed from a text based to a visual based platform, where over 275 million users worldwide can interact and share information online (statista.com). One particular community of fans on Twitter serves as a gauge for the severe reactions to *GoT* reported by journalists. #FakeWesteros is made up of over 100 Twitter users who have each taken on a *GoT* persona to interact with other fans online. In addition, a number of Twitter users follow the community, which has been boosted, over time, thanks to recognition from the television network Sky and various fan websites. For instance, #FakeWesteros member @NiceQueenCersei had over 58,000 followers at the time of the series finale.

What distinguishes #FakeWesteros members from other fans is that their interactions on Twitter are filtered through their *GoT* persona, responding to events in the show or comments in a way that readers would anticipate the character to respond. The use of externally hosted digital media, like memes, video clips and animated GIFs in addition to the text of tweets, increasingly, represents the most common form of information sharing for members. This example of virtual roleplay as information sharing demonstrates new ways of engagement and knowledge generation using digital media, which has implications for information researchers studying the creation and transmission of information in the digital realm. #FakeWesteros is also of interest to researchers studying the lifecycle of fan and leisure-based communities.

82nd Annual Meeting of the Association for Information Science & Technology | Melbourne, Australia | 19–23 October, 2019

DOI: 10.1002/pra2.00122

Specifically, what becomes of online communities once their original purpose for coming together is achieved.

METHODOLOGY

Twitter users identified with the hashtag #FakeWesteros in their profiles or in user-created lists were compared to generate a list of the top 50 most active community members during the airing of season eight from 12 April to 20 May 2019. Using the Twitter API, the timelines for 50 members during the above period were evaluated, including both textual and graphic content of tweets. Analysis of each timeline adopted a constructivist grounded theory approach, as defined by Charmaz (2014), which permits an inductive and recursive development of ideas and theoretical models through the empirical analysis of data. Themes were identified representing the reactions of community members to the conclusion of the show.

To further contextualize results, tweets were analyzed using natural language processing and the VADER sentiment analyzer in Python (Hutto & Gilbert, 2014).

EMERGING THEMES AND FINDINGS

A key theme of #FakeWesteros tweets was a keen awareness of the impending end to the series in relation to a concern for its impact on the community. This concern was expressed universally among members in their tweets, from earnest expressions of mourning for fallen characters and fear that real friendships might fade to entreaties that fellow members stay in touch after the end of the series. The use of humor and pastiche, involving the intertextual layering of information found in previous research (Forcier, 2017), served to "soften" what, for many members, was a deeply emotional experience.

An unexpected finding was that the criticism toward the show's producers was not reflected in members' tweets. Prior to the airing of the final episode, the negative mainstream reaction to the series had been covered extensively by journalists (Tefekci, 2019), suggesting that *GoT* fans were universally upset with the conclusion. However, while some members sympathized with the popular negative reaction, solidarity with *GoT*'s performers and producers is the common feeling that prevailed in #FakeWesteros. This result supports findings on the role of loyalty in multi-community engagement (Hamilton, Zhang, Danescu-Niculescu-Mizil, Jurafsky, & Leskovec, 2017), highlighting how members must weigh their loyalties within overlapping fan communities (e.g., #FakeWesteros vs. mainstream *GoT* fandom).

CONCLUSION

Days before the series finale, user @IronbornTheon wrote: "while I'm both excited, dreading it, and sort of not wanting to see it, I have realized that just because the show is going off the air, doesn't mean the community is going anywhere."

The activity of #FakeWesteros members aligns with previous findings on the negotiation of narrative information (Forcier, 2017). However, the multimedia content members produced and interactions they continue to have moves beyond the information behavior model developed in previous research. The data collected for this case study represents the negotiation of social identities and interpersonal relationships in the digital space.

The case study demonstrates how information is transmitted and transformed innovatively and multimodally in online fan communities. It further demonstrates how identity and loyalty shape collective practices and individual behaviors. All findings support ongoing research into the information behavior of transmedia fans.

ACKNOWLEDGMENTS

This research was supported by the Social Sciences and Humanities Research Council of Canada and by Swinburne University of Technology.

REFERENCES

Booth, P. (2008). Rereading fandom: MySpace character personas and narrative identification. *Critical Studies in Media Communication, 25*(5), 514–536.

Charmaz, K. (2014). *Constructing grounded theory: A practical guide through qualitative analysis* (2nd ed.). Thousand Oaks, CA: Sage.

Faraj, S., Jarvenpaa, S. L., & Majchrzak, A. (2011). Knowledge collaboration in online communities. *Organization Science, 22*(5), 1224–1239.

Forcier, E. (2017). Re(a)d wedding: A case study exploring everyday information behaviors of the transmedia fan. *Proceedings of the 80th Annual Meeting for the Association of Information Science and Technology*. https://doi.org/10.1002/pra2.2017.14505401011

Hamilton, W., Zhang, J., Danescu-Niculescu-Mizil, C., Jurafsky, D., & Leskovec, J. (2017). In *International AAAI Conference on Web and Social Media*. Retrieved from https://www.aaai.org/ocs/index.php/ICWSM/ICWSM17/paper/view/15710/14848

Hutto, C.J. & Gilbert, E.E. (2014). *VADER: A parsimonious rule-based model for sentiment analysis of social media text*. Eighth International Conference on Weblogs and Social Media (ICWSM-14). Ann Arbor, MI, June 2014.

Pattern, D. (2019). *'Game Of Thrones' Series Finale viewership burns HBO records with all-time high* [Deadline] Retrieved from https://deadline.com/2019/05/game-of-thrones-ratings-finale-season-8-hbo-viewers-1202618943/

Price, L., & Robinson, L. (2016). "Being in a knowledge space": Information behaviour of cult media fan communities. *Journal of Information Science, 43*(5), 649–664.

Tefekci, Z. (2019). The real reason fans hate the last season of *Game of Thrones. Scientific American*. Retrieved from https://blogs.scientificamerican.com/observations/the-real-reason-fans-hate-the-last-season-of-game-of-thrones/

Health Information at Intersections: Toward More Inclusive Personal Health Records for Marginalized Users

Amelia N. Gibson
UNC Chapel Hill,
Chapel Hill, United States
angibson@email.unc.edu

Kristen L. Bowen
UNC Chapel Hill,
Chapel Hill, United States
klbowen2@email.unc.edu

ABSTRACT

This paper highlights findings of two health information-seeking studies and applies them to the design of personal health library. Both studies focus on themes related to information marginalization and access – the first among Black and Latina tween and teen girls, and the second among autistic (Autistic Self-Advocacy Network, 2019) teens and young adults. The paper presents emergent findings related to common information values and defensive information behaviors among both study samples and examines implications for design of personal health records & libraries for groups traditionally marginalized in U.S. healthcare systems.

KEYWORDS

Medical informatics; Personal information management; information access

INTRODUCTION

Health care systems in the United States have long betrayed deep systemic biases against people of color and people with disabilities (Brooks, Smith, & Anderson, 1991; Centers for Disease Control and Prevention, 2013; Wong, LaVeist, & Sharfstein, 2015). Generally, user-centered design emphasizes the importance of designing information systems around the needs of specific groups of users (Norman, 1988), and requires some knowledge of user behavior. More specifically, designing racially-, gender-, and disability-inclusive health systems and services requires "a clear focus on specific communities at risk, a commitment to listen and collect meaningful data to understand local needs and priorities, a conviction to make progress, and ongoing assessment of health outcomes" (Wong et al., 2015).

Study Description

This paper compares findings of two qualitative information-seeking studies, applying them to initial design of a personal health library intended to support information literacy and seeking among traditionally marginalized groups. This comparison of information values as expressed within different contexts and different groups serves to further refine a working theoretical framework related to marginalization and health information seeking and management. Both qualitative studies employ small samples and focus on thick/rich data.

The Deconstructing Information Poverty – Autism (DIPS Autism study (Gibson & Hanson-Baldauf, 2019) is part of an ongoing study on information seeking and exchange among autistic people and their families in North Carolina. In this study, the researchers conducted thematic analyses of sixteen 60–90 min interviews with autistic individuals (ages 12–35) and their parents (n = 32) in North Carolina. Participants discussed a broad range of information seeking and sharing practices.

Study B (Healthy Girls Know) was a multimethod study following a group of 6 Black and Latina girls (ages 12–15) in Durham, North Carolina. Participants engaged in thirteen 1.5-hour focus group and Information world mapping (Greyson, O'Brien, & Shoveller, 2017) sessions over a 16-week period (total of 19.5 hours of focus group data). Participants discussed their experiences seeking information about specific health topics (one health topic per week). The researchers conducted inductive analysis of the data to determine the significant themes (Charmaz, 2014).

FINDINGS

Each of the themes in Table 1 represents an information value (Burnett & Jaeger, 2010) emergent from both data sets. Each value is expressed slightly differently within each group, but each has implications for the initial design of systems that support marginalized users.

DISCUSSION

While values are expressed differently by different groups, these differences highlight the need for attention to the needs of specific marginalized groups. Future work could incorporate this list into a heuristic framework for evaluation or design of personal health record or library systems.

82nd Annual Meeting of the Association for Information Science & Technology | Melbourne, Australia | 19–23 October, 2019

DOI: 10.1002/pra2.00123

Theme/Value	Study A: DIPS autism	Study B: Healthy girls know study	Implications for personal health record/library
Trustworthiness: Helping users make decisions about what information sources to trust	Relying on structured safety/security systems/community for safety; Trusting family but wary of overprotection; Wary of being taken advantage of by others.	Trust family for "important things"; Trust friends/self/professionals; Wary of unknown - strangers; "Testing behaviors" for untrusted information sources	Allow multiple means for judging authority/trustworthiness of sources, while allowing users to choose information sources. E.g.: Recommendations from friends/connected family/caregiver accounts; Verified non-commercial information sources (NLM, CDC, etc.).
Privacy: Actions taken to control access to personal information	Intentional disengagement - "hiding" (avoiding spaces/conversations); Avoiding potentially threatening situations	Intentional disengagement – Silence (choosing not to speak/respond); Progressive disclosure of information	Give users control over disclosure of personal information & user behavior on system. E.g.: Ability to send private questions to pediatrician/physician without parents having access to message logs.
Formatting and modality: User Needs **(Font, colors, size, brightness, contrast)**	Diverse (among group members) but strong, individually consistent user needs & preferences Video &short audio most popular. Written text least popular.	Expressed no explicit concerns about controlling formatting. Video, audio (music), and pictures were most popular.	Allow personalization re: formats and preferred mode of receiving information; ensure that information is readable. E.g.: Information presented as short video (with visual examples and captioning), in podcast format, and in transcript, written at 4th-grade level. Transcript should allow user to control font & background color.
Speed/Timeliness of information exchange	Once trust established, disclosed personal information freely. Trust based on sense of cognitive/administrative authority	Progressive Disclosure of Personal Information Berrypicking (Bates, 1989)	Should allow user to control personal information disclosure, and to revoke personal information if desired. Should encourage prompt and just in time responses from medical practitioners/other trusted information sources.

REFERENCES

Autistic Self-Advocacy Network. (2019). *Identity-first language*. Retrieved from https://autisticadvocacy.org/about-asan/identity-first-language/

Bates, M. J. (1989). The design of browsing and berrypicking techniques for the online search interface. *Online Review, 13*(5), 407–424.

Brooks, D., Smith, D., & Anderson, R. (1991). Medical apartheid: An American perspective. *JAMA, 266*(19), 2746–2749. https://doi.org/10.1001/jama.1991.03470190094036

Centers for Disease Control and Prevention. (2013). "*CDC health disparities and inequalities report: United States*." Retrieved from https://www.cdc.gov/mmwr/pdf/other/su6203.pdf

Charmaz, K. (2014). *Constructing grounded theory*. London, England: Sage.

Gibson, A. N., & Hanson-Baldauf, D. (2019). I want it the way I need it: Modality, readability, and format control for autistic information seekers online. *International Journal on Innovations in Online Education, 2*(4), 1–12.

Greyson, D., O'Brien, H., & Shoveller, J. (2017). Information world mapping: A participatory arts-based elicitation device for information behavior interviews. *Library & Information Science Research, 39*(2), 149–157. https://doi.org/10.1016/j.lisr.2017.03.003

Jaeger, P. T., & Burnett, G. (2010). *Information worlds: Social context, technology, and information behavior in the age of the Internet* (1st ed., p. 214). New York, NY: Routledge.

Norman, D. (1988). *The design of everyday things*. New York, NY: Doubleday.

Wong, W. F., LaVeist, T. A., & Sharfstein, J. M. (2015). Achieving health equity by design. *JAMA, 313*(14), 1417–1418. https://doi.org/10.1001/jama.2015.2434

Information and Communication Research in Promoting Workplace Safety and Health: A Topic Modeling Analysis

Dion Hoe-Lian Goh
Nanyang Technological University, Singapore
ashlgoh@ntu.edu.sg

Han Zheng
Nanyang Technological University, Singapore
han019@ntu.edu.sg

Edmund Wei Jian Lee
Nanyang Technological University, Singapore
edmundlee@ntu.edu.sg

Chei Sian Lee
Nanyang Technological University, Singapore
leecs@ntu.edu.sg

Yin Leng Theng
Nanyang Technological University, Singapore
tyltheng@ntu.edu.sg

ABSTRACT

This paper is a first step in understanding the role of information and communication research in promoting workplace safety and health practices, which is an important concern in any organization. We adopt topic modeling to identify the major issues discussed in the literature. Six diverse themes were identified, suggesting the importance of this body of work.

KEYWORDS

Topic modeling; literature review; workplace health and safety; information and communication research

ASIS&T THESAURUS

Topic models; organizational culture; academic documents

INTRODUCTION

Unsafe workplace conditions put employees at risk of injuries, occupational diseases, mental health issues or even fatalities. Research has demonstrated that an organization's safety culture facilitates or impedes the adoption of appropriate workplace safety and health (WSH) practices (Christian, Bradley, Wallace, & Burke, 2009).

Organizations have employed many methods to inculcate a strong safety culture. Over the years, there is a recognition that crafting and delivering timely and appropriate promotional messages, that is, employing information and communication strategies, are just as important in helping organizations achieve the goal of creating a safe workplace for its employees (Zanko & Dawson, 2012).

One of the key gaps in extant work is the dearth of studies that systematically map the research landscape. Hence, the present study is an initial step that summarizes existing literature on information and communication research and its role in safety culture. We employ topic modeling in our analysis of the literature, which allows for the discovery of latent topics or themes among a collection of unstructured documents (Richardson et al., 2014). We believe this study will contribute to the literature and help researchers and practitioners identify important WSH research topics, generating interesting research questions, as well as better implement changes in the workplace.

82nd Annual Meeting of the Association for Information Science & Technology | Melbourne, Australia | 19–23 October, 2019

DOI: 10.1002/pra2.00124

METHDOLOGY

The Scopus database was used because it offered a large number of publications across multiple disciplines on WSH research. A query was executed on the database to retrieve publications from 2000 to 2019 on culture and climate pertaining to workplace safety and health, as well as the use of information and communication strategies: (workplace OR occupational) AND (safety OR health) AND (climate OR culture OR environment) AND (message OR communication OR information OR content).

The search yielded 7,066 publications, which were analyzed using R statistical software. First, the text in each publication's abstract was extracted and preprocessed by removing stopwords and stemming the remaining terms. Next, to uncover latent core topics, we employed the Latent Dirichlet Allocation (LDA) topic modeling approach, which is one of the widely used statistical estimation for generating meaningful topics of given documents. Prior to building the LDA model, we calculated the perplexity score, which is an index of goodness-of-fit, to decide on the number of topics to set in the algorithm. Finally, we labeled the topics generated by the LDA model by interpreting their meanings and relevance to WSH research through the top-10 frequently occurring terms found in each topic.

RESULTS

Figure 1 shows the six topics that were derived from our LDA modeling. Each topic is represented by its 10 most frequently occurring stemmed terms.

Topic 1 was associated with *nurse occupational health*. This segment of literature focused on nurses and the health and safety issues they faced in the workplace. This includes stress, wellbeing, exposure to diseases or other contaminents, and workplace aggression. In addition, information sharing practices, interpresonal communication issues, as well as information needs and resources used were addressed.

Topic 2 was concerned with *health communication and information*. Issues researched included the development of WSH-related informational resources and promotional materials, WSH information seeking practices, devising communication strategies to target different segments of workers, as well as understanding the antecedents of the acceptance of WSH messages including individual differences and other characteristics.

Topic 3 covered *general WSH issues in the workplace environment*. The literature comprised a variety of areas such as causes of workplace injuries, and their impact on individuals, the organization and the economy, descriptions of the design of safety

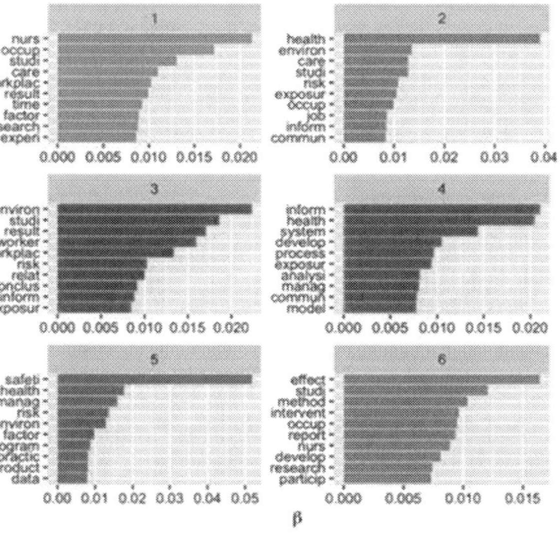

Figure 1. The top-10 terms in each LDA topic.

systems and workplaces, and research on WSH culture such as their influence on individual and organizational safety practices.

Topic 4 dealt with the *development and/or use of information systems for WSH*. Research included the design and implementation of systems across industries to monitor and manage WSH incidents, as well as systems for sharing knowledge about WSH practices. Studies of user perceptions and behaviors were also covered.

Topic 5 focused on *risk management for workplace safety and health*. The literature identified types of risks in the workplace and covered both mental and physical aspects. Characteristics of at-risk workers' were also investigated. Another major area involved the development of risk assessment processes and criteria. Finally, research was conducted on mitigating risks through practices such as educational programs and knowledge sharing systems.

Topic 6 covered *interventions for promoting WSH or to curtail unsafe practices*. This included the identification of requirements for intervention programs as well as the design of various types of WSH programs. Research under this topic also investigated success factors and barriers for implementation of intervention programs, including the perceptions of participants.

DISCUSSION AND CONCLUSION

The present study is a first step in understanding WSH and the role of information and communication research.

In terms of information research, our topic models revealed two broad areas. The first involves information seeking, sharing and use of WSH information. The second concerns the development of systems for collecting, monitoring and managing WSH issues. This suggests that both individuals and organizations play important parts in orchestrating the promotion of a strong safety culture. Individuals should be equipped with appropriate information skills to obtain and share relevant WSH content. While organizations should implement well-designed WSH information systems so that individuals can use them effectively.

From a communications perspective, one broad area involved the examination of communication strategies, comprising issues such as WSH message development and acceptance. Another area dealt with the development and evaluation of WSH campaigns or training programs. Here, the central theme investigated the factors that influenced effective communication to inculcate positive WSH attitudes and behaviors. Put differently, the creation and dissemination of WSH materials, such as posters, Web sites, and training programs, requires the consideration of a variety of factors including message characteristics, individual differences and the organizational context.

This study may be limited by the use of particular search terms and the database to obtain relevant publications. In future work, it would also be helpful to conduct a more extensive bibliometric analysis of the research publications to uncover patterns such as prominent authors/institutions, co-word/co-citation analyses, and impactful publications. Charting the evolution of topics would also be worthwhile.

ACKNOWLEDGMENT

This research project is funded by WSH Institute, Singapore and supported by WSH Council, Singapore.

REFERENCES

Christian, M. S., Bradley, J. C., Wallace, J. C., & Burke, M. J. (2009). Workplace safety: A meta-analysis of the roles of person and situation factors. *Journal of Applied Psychology, 94*(5), 1103–1127.

Richardson, G. M., Bowers, J., Woodwill, A. J., Barr, J. R., Gawron, J. M., & Levine, R. A. (2014). Topic models: A tutorial with R. *International Journal of Semantic Computing, 8*(1), 85–98.

Zanko, M., & Dawson, P. (2012). Occupational health and safety management in organizations: A Review. *International Journal of Management Reviews, 14*(3), 328–344.

Understanding the Information Landscape of Indigenous Elders' Knowledge and Cultural Practices

Jelina Haines
University of South Australia,
Adelaide, Australia
jelina.haines@mymail.unisa.edu.au

Jia Tina Du
University of South Australia,
Adelaide, Australia
tina.du@unisa.edu.au

Gus Geursen
University of South Australia,
Adelaide, Australia
geurseng@hotmail.com

Ellen Trevorrow
Camp Coorong,
Adelaide, Australia
ellen1955.et@gmail.com

ABSTRACT

This visual presentation is a timely topic while celebrating the year of Indigenous languages and cultures. However, the continuing impact of colonization, displacement, and oppression still lingers. Cultural traditions, once central to all knowledge practices, have been suppressed or subjugated by Western hegemony. This paper aimed to qualitatively articulate the importance of understanding the information landscape of Indigenous Elders, their role in the community and the correlation of Indigenous knowledge and health informatics. The informatic nature of Elders' knowledge was mapped and guided by two Indigenous Elders from the Ngarrindjeri community in South Australia. Video interviews were transcribed and coded using the Xmind mapping software. Limitations on articulating the knowledge map in its entirety were expected. Research implications will provide excellent opportunities for future research in both cultural, digital and health informatics.

KEYWORDS

Indigenous people; video ethnography; community-based participatory research

ASIS&T THESAURUS

Indigenous Elders; knowledge management; cultural informatics; health informatics

INTRODUCTION

Indigenous Elders' knowledge and cultural practices are tightly woven into the landscape, thus at the core of their knowledge lies the identity, culture, stories, and languages that are passed on from one generation to the next. These traditional practices are conveyed through storytelling, weaving, ceremonies, songs, dances, carvings, and paintings. However, global histories of the continuing impact of colonization, displacement, and oppression still destabilize and devalue the importance of Indigenous knowledge (Mazzocchi, 2006). In a sense, knowledge sharing of Elders' stories is integral to the preservation of Aboriginal cultures.

82nd Annual Meeting of the Association for Information Science & Technology | Melbourne, Australia | 19–23 October, 2019

DOI: 10.1002/pra2.00125

Elders' Role in the Community

Indigenous Elders hold crucial roles as gatekeepers of wisdom, knowledge and history. Elders who are chosen as knowledge keepers of stories are expected to pass on their knowledge to the future generation by imparting traditions, culture, values and practices for the continued preservation of stories (see Table 1).

Elders' role in the community	Elders' inherent knowledge
Knowledge keeper	Entrusted with generational knowledge
Storyteller	Passes on knowledge orally via cultural activities and ceremonies
Traditional teachers	Committed to sharing knowledge of traditional stories for the good of the people and the community
Bearer of wisdom	Knows the ways of the world and the land, and guides those in need
Herbalists	Knowledge of the traditional uses of a variety of Indigenous medicinal plants and work alongside medicinal people and seers
Facilitator	Lead without prejudice
Advisors	Provide specific cultural knowledge about the environment, cultural tradition and beliefs

Table 1: Recognizing the role of Elders in the community.

Table 1 displays some of the many roles that Elders have in any community. In a sense, Elders' knowledge is inherited from generational stories and the experiences of living on a particular land. Additionally, their experiences of living in contemporary Australian society have provided them with a new source of knowledge. Asserting that their personal history informs all aspects of Elders' knowledge and group histories facilitates reflection of their own collective cultural and national history. Elders' knowledge is not static but continuously evolving.

RESEARCH DESIGN

In this study, qualitative video interviews were employed, and directed by the principles of community-based participatory research, grounded by the video ethnography paradigm (Haines, Du, & Trevorrow, 2018). Video ethnography mediates the dynamic process of social interaction and allows us to record the storytelling accurately (Haines et al., 2018). The first author's 20 years of connection with the Ngarrindjeri Elders form the solid foundation of this research and the intent of the Elders' participation. Aunty Alice and Aunty Ellen's active role as co-researchers was crucial for the authenticity and integrity of stories gathered. Audio and video interviews were used to create the knowledge map and these were coded using the XMind mapping software (Figure 1). Using video format supported the author's objective of achieving accountability and reliable knowledge from the Elders. Accordingly, a new ethical method of conducting research involving Indigenous people was introduced. This was attained by quoting Aunty Ellen's statement as 'personal communication' (Figure 2). A cultural parameter applied to the community involved in this research. This approach encouraged co-learning and equal empowerment in the research process (Haines, Du, Geursen, Gao, & Trevorrow, 2017). Maintaining authenticity and integrity of the stories once published online was imperative (e.g. Aunty Alice's knowledge mapping).

FINDINGS: ELDERS INFORMATION LANDSCAPE

Indeed, the Elders' information landscape has changed dramatically. The term 'information landscape' in this context refers to textual knowledge mapping of individual cultural practices and experiences which constitute a holistic and dynamic knowledge system (Figure 1).

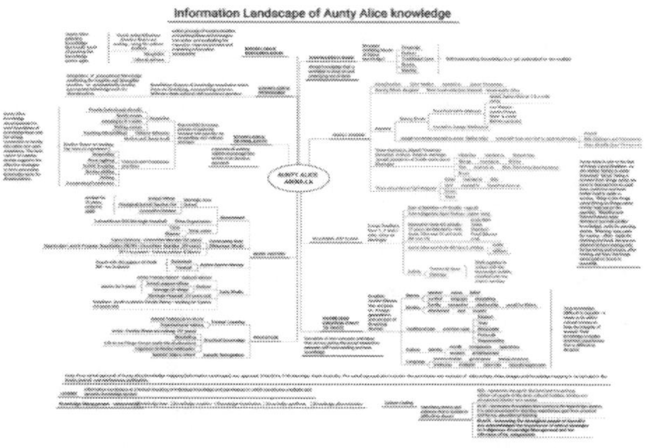

Figure 1. Information landscape of Aunty Alice's knowledge (link tolarger version: https://drive.google.com/file/d/18WdZd8B996ZItddzP0HHcxXyEKDsctkQ/view?usp=sharing).

Figure 1 provides a visual representation of text, stories, and experiences that Aunty Alice gained over 76 years of living on her community's traditional land. The informatics-oriented nature of Aunty Alice's oral knowledge map explores and conveys the pattern of information as it travels cyclically from the knowledge base, and with the support of family kinship, to the preservation of creation stories as they are translated, synthesized, and disseminated (Beitz, 1998). The knowledge map explicitly gathers the three epistemologies of knowledge: (1) self-transcending – not yet embodied; (2) tacit – uncodified and challenging to record; and (3) explicit – readily available. The knowledge map provides a holistic image of the facilitation of effective learning and provides a systematic approach toward presenting Aunty Alice knowledge.

EMERGENCE OF INDIGENOUS HEALTH INFORMATICS

Health informatics in the Indigenous Elders context correlates with utilizing knowledge acquisition, storage, retrieval, and use of information with the aid of technology (e.g. mobile phones). Hence, traditional knowledge of storytelling was central in mitigating shared findings of this research. As Aunty Ellen said:

Figure 2. Aunty Ellen checking messages on her mobile phone.

'Improving the quality and well-being of our people are important; access to modern technology is necessary. That's why the sharing of our stories needs to continue, and the teaching of our Elders need to be recorded for the future of our children to inherit.'

(Trevorrow, E., personal communication, 16 March. 2016)

Though Aunty Ellen relies on the oral transmission of her stories through weaving, she uses her mobile phone for all her everyday communication practices such as doctor's appointments, emails, calendars, sending texts/images, alarm clock, taking/storage of photos and keeping in touch with family (Figure 2). Thus, the role of information communication technology (ICT) in this context is the stability of infrastructure, affordability, and access to digital equipment to assist Aunty Ellen to further record her stories.

LIMITATIONS/CHALLENGES

This paper format was limited in articulating Aunty Alice and Aunty Ellen's involvement and the benefits of the knowledge map for the preservation of cultural stories. Challenges during the fieldwork were as follows: capturing the research participants engaging in activities; gaging the length of the recorded data; selecting those segments of the interview that would be allowed for publication; and moving between insider and outsider researcher perspectives without any preconceived ideas.

CONCLUSION

The research findings have illuminated the importance of the Elders' knowledge, indicating that storytelling is integral to the continuing preservation of such knowledge. In the most active sense, Elders are custodians of their culture, keepers of tradition, and teachers who disseminate knowledge.

The results provide valuable information on finding appropriate technology and frameworks that will underpin the preservation of Elders' knowledge, and both tacit and explicit stories.

ACKNOWLEDGMENTS

This research is supported by the University of South Australia Completion Scholarship. The author sincerely acknowledges the contributions of Aunty Ellen Trevorrow and Aunty Alice Abdulla for sharing their knowledge.

REFERENCES

Beitz, J. M. (1998). Concept mapping: Navigating the learning process. *Nurse Educator*, *23*(5), 3541.

Haines, J., Du, J. T., & Trevorrow, E. (2018). Video ethnographic documentation of stories and cultural practices with Indigenous Elders. In L. Freund (Ed.), *Proceedings of the association for information science and technology* (p. 821824). Hoboken, NJ: Wiley. https://doi.org/10.1002/pra2.2018.14505501132

Haines, J., Du, J. T., Geursen, G., Gao, J. & Trevorrow, E. (2017). A visual ethnographic exploration of knowledge creation in the context of indigenous elders: A dialogic inquiry. *iConference 2017 Proceedings*.

Mazzocchi, F. (2006). Western science and traditional knowledge. Despite their variations, different forms of knowledge can learn from each other. *EMBO Reports*, *7* (5), 463–466. https://doi.org/10.1038/sj.embor.7400693

Investigating the Impacts of Family Restriction Strategy on Chinese Children's Smartphone Use Behaviors

Leiqian Han
School of Information Resource Management,
Renmin University of China, Beijing, P.R. China
18810535600@163.com

Hui Yan
School of Information Resource Management,
Renmin University of China, Beijing, P.R. China
hyanpku@163.com

ABSTRACT

This study explores the attitudes, restriction strategies of parents toward children's smartphone use behaviors and their influencing factors in Chinese culture. Through the qualitative analysis from fifteen Chinese parents, the results show that Chinese family strategies with diversified restrictions are significantly influenced by children's behaviors and social environments. The findings of this study pave way for future large-scale quantitative studies.

KEYWORDS

Family smartphone restriction strategy; Attitudes; Factors

INTRODUCTION

As of July 31, 2018, the number of minor Internet users in China reached 169 million, with 89.5%, 99.4% and 96.3% of primary, middle and high school students respectively, and 92% of them using mobile phones (CNNIC, 2019). The mainstream view in Chinese society is children should not use smartphone too early and too much. However, there are few studies on family smartphone restriction strategies in China and the associated social and cognitive mechanisms. This study focuses on this practical problem. Adults always have ambivalence when children use smartphone. Children benefit from online opportunities while being exposed to online risks. (Livingstone & Helsper, 2013). Parental restriction is generally considered to be an effective risk prevention strategy (Álvarez, Torres, Rodríguez, Padilla, & Rodrigo, 2013).

METHODS

The data were gathered by semi-structured interviews from parents of fifteen Chinese students in January 2019 whose ages range from 7 to 19. They were carefully selected to represent students from elementary school through high school, with varying family structures, parental occupations, and so on. Two-thirds of the original data were randomly selected for encoding using grounded theory, and another 1/3 of the data was used as the theoretical saturation test.

82nd Annual Meeting of the Association for Information Science & Technology | Melbourne, Australia | 19–23 October, 2019

DOI: 10.1002/pra2.00126

RESULTS AND DISCUSSION

This section describes the attitudes, restriction strategies and the associated rationales of Chinese families.

Family Attitudes

Parents have double standards for using smartphone for themselves and their children. About 90% parents' own views on smartphone are positive. However, their attitudes to children are greatly divergent.

Support (proportion 5/15)

" Smartphone has become a necessity with the development of the times." said supportive parents. It brings many benefits for children, including "relaxation", "learning guidance", "convenient contact" and "all-round development", etc. Parents are happy to see their children master smartphone skills, and in some cases, children can help parents learn and use the Internet, such as online payment, booking, and so on.

Oppose (proportion 3/15)

Parents with opposing attitudes believe that "For young students, the disadvantages outweigh the benefits." Faced with the powerful temptation, children cannot solve the problems in the use process. For example, "waste time and money", "affect the body, study and life", and "addiction". Especially as the generation gap between parents and children becomes more and more obvious, such kind of misunderstanding deepens the opposition attitude.

Depend on situations (proportion 7/15)

These parents think that "children's use of smartphone is a double-edged sword." Parents especially emphasize children's self-control and parents' supervisory.

Influencing Factors of Family Restriction Strategy

24 initial concepts about the causes of family restriction strategy were extracted from open coding, and further abstracted into five categories and two main categories.

Subjective Judgment

Parenting style, value ranking and child's behavior are factors affecting family restriction strategies through parent's personal experience or external attribution. They are relatively subjective and flexible, influencing internally.

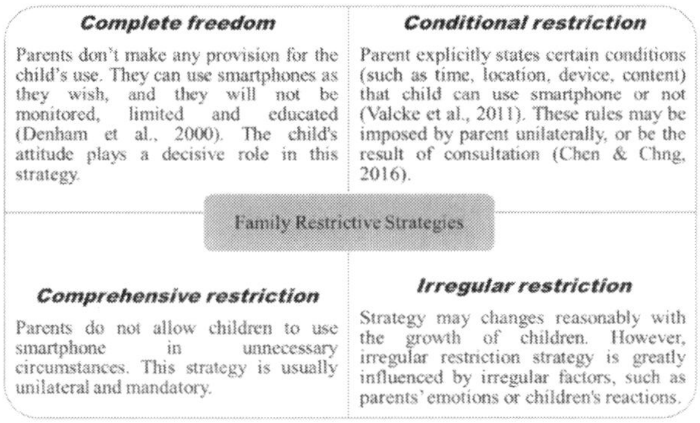

Figure 1. Four types of family restriction strategies.

- Parenting style is the way parents interact with their children, naturally applying to the management strategy of smartphone use (Rosen, 2008).
- The importance of smartphone in comparison with other things affects subjective judgment. Parents hope to make the best choice based on their experience. Smartphone, relatively unimportant, should be limited.
- Parents often attribute children's poor behavior to smartphone. For example, children's poor grades are due to playing mobile games. Children's myopia is caused by spending too much time on screen.

Objective Choice

Smartphone characteristics, basic conditions, social environment are factors affecting family restriction strategies through coercion and imperceptibility. They are relatively objective and fixed, influencing from the outside.

- The characteristics of smartphone (massive information, the complexity of the network, addiction risk, eye damage) are the reasons for parents to restrict.
- Whether the basic conditions (device, network or time) are satisfied or not can affect objective choice.
- In Chinese social customs, learning is the only thing that students need to do well. The emphasis on the college entrance examination also promotes the family restriction strategy to be stringent.

CONCLUSION

This study was well situated in Chinese context and found that family attitudes and strategies are diverse, mainly affected by two types of factors. It can serve as theoretical cornerstone for future large-scale quantitative research on similar topics. As for limitations, due to there are only 15 samples from Shanxi Province, China, so more data should be collected from all over the country. We also found other interesting questions worth studying. What is the impact of time? Do children and parents have different opinions?

ACKNOWLEDGMENTS

The research is funded by National Office for Philosophy and Social Science (Grant No. 18BTQ007). We would like to deliver our gratitude to all the volunteers who participated in the interviews, and the PhD candidate Jiqun Liu's help.

REFERENCES

Álvarez, M., Torres, A., Rodríguez, E., Padilla, S., & Rodrigo, M. J. (2013). Attitudes and parenting dimensions in parents' regulation of internet use by primary

Interview text (Part)	Conceptualization	Categorization	Main category
My son must be obedient. I think it's wrong to spoil children.	Authoritarian	Parenting style	Subjective judgment
I trust my child and I believe she can manage herself well.	Indulgent		
I will not restrict her use after the college entrance examination.	College priority	Value ranking	
I don't want him to indulge in the virtual world.	Real life priority		
He is crazy about mobile games. He plays anytime and anywhere.	Children addiction	Child's behavior	
He will get angry if he is not allowed to play mobile phones.	Children rebellion		
I'm afraid the children may be deceived.	Security issues	Smartphone characteristics	Objective choice
The screen is not good for the eyes. If the use of mobile phones is not restricted, children's myopia may be deeper.	Bad for eyesight		
My job requires mobile phones, so she has little chance to use.	No device	Basic conditions	
She has too much homework and pressure to use mobile phone.	No time		
School teachers repeatedly stress the dangers of mobile phones.	School regulations	Social environment	
Many people say don't buy mobile phones for children.	Surrounding		

Table 1. Text coding (part).

and secondary school children. *Computers & Education*, *67*, 69–78.

Chen, V. H. H., & Chng, G. S. (2016). Active and restrictive parental mediation over time: Effects on youths' self-regulatory competencies and impulsivity. *Computers & Education*, *98*, 206–212.

China Internet Network Information Center (2019). *Research Report on Internet Usage of Minors in China in 2018.*

Denham, S. A., Workman, E., Cole, P. M., Weissbrod, C., Kendziora, K. T., & Zahn-Waxler, C. (2000). Prediction of externalizing behavior problems from early to middle childhood: The role of parental socialization and emotion expression. *Development and Psychopathology*, *12*(1), 23–45.

Livingstone, S., & Helsper, E. J. (2013). Children, internet and risk in comparative perspective. *Journal of Children and Media*, *7*(1), 1–8.

Book or Screen? A Preliminary Study on Preschool Children's Reading and ICT Using Behaviors

Yanfang Han
School of Information Resource Management,
Renmin University of China,
Beijing, P.R. China
yf.han@foxmail.com

Hui Yan
School of Information Resource Management,
Renmin University of China,
Beijing, P.R. China
hyanpku@ruc.edu.cn

ABSTRACT

Question: Due to the ubiquity of various newly emerging information and communication technologies (ICT), numerous preschoolers have obvious preferences toward electronic devices and interfaces over printed books. Given that excessive exposure to screen usually result in problems in both physical and psychological aspects, it is essential to have a brief overview of the preschoolers' reading and ICT using behavior and a deeper understanding on how parental factors affect children with respect to their reading and ICT using behaviors.
Methods: In-depth interview is employed in this study, the sample of which includes forty parents of twenty preschool children aged from 1.5 years to 6 years. Then we analyzed the data with the means of text coding and correlation analysis.
Findings: There was a negative association between child's reading time and screen-viewing time. The same result occurred among parental reading and ICT behavior. Reading time duration of parents was correlated with that of preschool children. As for ICT using, preschool children frequently learnt from mothers' ICT activities, instead of fathers'.

KEYWORDS

Preschool children; ICT using; reading; parent–child information behavior

ASIS&T THESAURUS

Information behavior; Sociocultural aspects; Social informatics

INTRODUCTION

Reading benefits preschool children on several aspects. As various guidelines highlighted the importance of preschoolers' reading activities (IFLA Libraries for Children and Young Adults Section, 2017), their reading behaviors have been receiving more attention than ever before. The main reason is that reading can not only cultivate the preschool children's understanding abilities, but also help trigger children's interest in further reading. As a result, it is of great necessity to delve deeper into children's reading behaviors.

With the introduction of new technologies, digital devices are widely used in a variety of educational practices, including early education. A growing amount of research has studied the influence of screen-viewing on preschoolers and demonstrated that despite ICT usage benefited preschool children in some aspects, it still had multiple adverse impacts on children's health. A large body of quantitative research has demonstrated that excessive screen-viewing was associated with higher Body Mass Index (BMI), poor sleep and a series of physical and mental diseases (Lissak, 2018). So preschoolers' screen-using behavior needs specific attention and deep observation. In addition, there were still lots of factors affecting the amount of time children spent on screen, like parenting style and family type (Howe et al., 2017). Besides, another study has shown that parental screen time were positively associated with children's screen time (Lauricella, Wartella, & Rideout, 2015).

From prior studies, we learned that there was a negatively relationship between screen time and reading time duration (Wiecha, Sobol, Peterson, & Gortmaker, 2001; Poitras et al., 2017). Although numerous studies have found that screen time had an adverse impact on the alternative activities, such as reading and physical exercises, little is known exactly about the performance of the preschoolers and their parents regarding reading and ICT using, and the impact of parents on their children' reading and ICT using behaviors. So in order to have a better understanding of the relationship between preschool children's reading and ICT using behaviors and that of their parents, our study sought to answer the following three research questions:

1. How do preschool children read books and use electronic screen? Any conflict?

2. How do parents read books and use screen? Any relation pattern?

3. What are the impacts of parents' behaviors on their children in reading and screen using?

82nd Annual Meeting of the Association for Information Science & Technology | Melbourne, Australia | 19–23 October, 2019

DOI: 10.1002/pra2.00127

RESEARCH METHODOLOGY

Participants and Method

To answer the questions above, this study took the parents of preschool children as the interviewees and collected data through semi-structured in-depth interviews.

Data Collection and Analysis

The interview outline was designed to collect the following three groups of data for further study. We invited forty parents of twenty children aged from 1.5 to 6 years old from Beijing, Liaoning, Tianjin and Singapore. Considering the characteristics of preschool children including being less talkative and incapable of understanding and clearly communicating their own thoughts and surroundings, parents were the dominant participants of this research.

Demographic Data

The basic demographic data were collected firstly. Parents were asked to offer the demographic information, like gender and age of children, parents' age, identity, occupation, educational background, region, family power structure, degree of myopia.

Data Regarding Reading Behavior

Facts and attitudes on preschool children and their parents' reading habits, including the frequency, duration of reading, reading types, reading topics, were recorded.

Data on ICT Using Behavior

The variables related to ICT using behavior mainly include the media exposed to children, screen types, ICT using frequency and total time, ICT-related activities, the purposes and situations of ICT using. Besides, first using experiences especially the first time of child's screen touching and parental attitudes toward preschoolers' ICT using were also reported by the parents.

FINDINGS

ICT screening, instead of reading hard copy books, passively plays as the role of babysitter. According to our research, the earlier the child's first use time was, the longer time she/he used screen in everyday life settings. Besides, reading time and screen time by preschool children were negatively correlated in the 20 families. Especially in No.10 family, child spent totally two hours (the longest one) on screen but did not read at all, while child of the No.15 family was just the opposite.

As for their parents, reading time and screen time by parents were negatively correlated in the 20 families. For example, the mother of the No.12 family had the longest reading time and the shortest screen time. And in No.9 family, compared with two hours on screening, which was the shortest screen time among all families, parents spent large proportion of their time on reading.

When it comes to the relationships of parents' behavior and their children's, there are multiple findings to report. We found that reading time between parents and children were positively related. So it could be easily seen that preschool children had no reading experience in the families where parents did not read. In comparison, Parents who had heavy reading habits always promoted children's reading activities. In addition, screen time between parents and children were differently related: mother and child were slightly positively related, while father and child were negatively related. Take the No.10 family as an example, although the father had a lower level of screen dependence, his daughter had a heavy habit on TV-viewing, which was consistent with the mother's ICT behavior. Obviously, preschool children frequently learnt from mothers' ICT activities, instead of fathers'.

ACKNOWLEDGMENTS

We would like to express our gratitude to Ms. Na Wu, who interviewed the twenty families and collected in-depth textual data from Beijing, Liaoning, Tianjin and Singapore with the academic supervision of the second author.

REFERENCES

Howe, A. S., Heath, A. M., Lawrence, J., Galland, B. C., Gray, A. R., Taylor, B. J., … Taylar, R. W. (2017). Parenting style and family type, but not child temperament, are associated with television viewing time in children at two years of age. *PLoS One, 12*.

IFLA Libraries for Children and Young Adults Section. (2017). *Guidelines for Children's Library Services.* Retrieved from https://www.ifla.org/files/assets/libraries-for-children-and-ya/publications/guidelines-for-childrens-libraries-services-en.pdf

Lauricella, A. R., Wartella, E., & Rideout, V. J. (2015). Young children's screen time: The Complex role of parent and child factors. *Journal of Applied Developmental Psychology, 36*, 11–17.

Lissak, G. (2018). Adverse physiological and psychological effects of screen time on children and adolescents: Literature review and case study. *Environmental Research, 164*, 149–157.

Poitras, V. J., Gray, C. E., Janssen, X., Aubert, S., Carson, V., Faulkner, G., … Tremblay, M. S. (2017). Systematic review of the relationships between sedentary behavior and health indicators in the early years (0-4 years). *BMC Public Health, 17*(Suppl 5):868), 65–89.

Wiecha, J. L., Sobol, A. M., Peterson, K. E., & Gortmaker, S. L. (2001). Household Television Access: Association With Screen Time, Reading, and Homework Among Youth. *Ambulatory Pediatrics, 1*(5), 244–251.

Affording Cross-Cultural Access to Visualized Cultural Collections: A Preliminary Case Study of E-Dunhuang

Xiao Hu
University of Hong Kong, Hongkong, China
xiaoxhu@hku.hk

Jia Shan
University of Hong Kong, Hongkong, China
jiashan@hku.hk

Jing Chen
Nanchang University, Nanchang, China
chenjing@email.ncu.edu.cn

J. Stephen Downie
University of Illinois, Illinois, USA
jdownie@illinois.edu

ABSTRACT

E-Dunhuang is a visual material centered digital library of a UNESCO world heritage. This study aims to identify how users in different cultural backgrounds seek and use cultural heritage information on e-Dunhuang, as well as their perceptions and opinions toward that. As a preliminary report, this poster focuses on the visual content (i.e. images, panorama) of e-Dunhuang, which is arguably the most prominent component in this platform. Results of usability tests and follow-up interviews reveal that users had polarized opinions. The findings can inform cross-cultural access to cultural heritage collections dominant with visual content.

KEYWORDS

Cross-cultural access; Usability test; e-Dunhuang

ASIS&T THESAURUS

Humanities->Culture->Cultural heritage; Product and service providers->Libraries->Digital libraries

INTRODUCTION

Cultural heritage plays an important role in human life. The Mogao Caves are a UNESCO world-heritage located in a small city in northwestern China named Dunhuang. The Mogao Caves include nearly 500 caves constructed from about 300 A.D. to 1300 A.D., each decorated with plenty of statues and wall paintings reflecting the societal, cultural and spiritual themes of the time. As a means of preserving the unique heritage, the Caves are being digitized into high resolution images that support panorama views. E-Dunhuang (www.e-dunhuang.com) is a platform exhibiting digitized visual materials of 30 caves. Since its official launch in May 2016, e-Dunhuang has been evaluated with a group of Chinese users (Hu, 2018).

Similar to other heritage digital libraries worldwide (Reinecke & Bernstein, 2011), e-Dunhuang also aims to serve a global audience across countries and cultural backgrounds. However, e-Dunhuang has not yet been evaluated with non-Chinese users. This study therefore aims to fill this gap by conducting usability tests on e-Dunhuang with a group of non-Chinese users. Results were then compared with those of the previous study with Chinese users (Hu, 2018). As the Dunhuang cultural heritage is located in China and has been somewhat known among Chinese people, the two groups of users are deemed as representative in a cross-cultural comparison with regard to the e-Dunhuang heritage.

The most prominent content of e-Dunhuang is arguably the large amount of high-resolution visual materials, including digital scanning of wall paintings and sculptures. This study thus focuses on user perceptions of the visual materials and aims to answer the following research questions (RQs):

RQ1: To what extent does the visual content of e-Dunhuang facilitate or hinder user experience of accessing the heritage?

RQ2: How visual content related user experience concurs or differs between Chinese and non-Chinese users?

RESEARCH DESIGN

Usability tests were conducted with 24 non-Chinese users who were asked to conduct six pre-designed information seeking tasks on e-Dunhuang. The participants were also invited to join individual follow-up interviews probing their perceptions on the visual content presented in e-Dunhuang. A "think-aloud protocol" was applied for participants to verbalize their thoughts during each task. The semi-structured interview protocol was developed based on evaluation criteria in previous studies on user experience (Granić, Mitrović, & Marangunić, 2011; Hu, 2018).

In this paper, we focus on user responses to one interview question on the visual content of e-Dunhuang: "How do you like the visual content (i.e. images, panorama) in the e-Dunhuang platform? Why?". Furthermore, as visual content is the most prominent component of e-Dunhuang, we also summarize user responses to other questions on information presentation, organization, retrieval and user interactions if they mention the visual content and its related features. Last but not least, near the end of the interview, participants were asked to name and elaborate the strongest and weakest points of their experience while using e-Dunhuang.

82nd Annual Meeting of the Association for Information Science & Technology | Melbourne, Australia | 19–23 October, 2019

DOI: 10.1002/pra2.00128

RESULTS

Half of the 24 participants were female. Their age ranged from 19 to 49 with an average of 30. All of them had relatively high interests in cultural heritage, with an average rating of 4 in a 5-point Likert scale (1: not interested at all; 5: very much interested). Their places of origin were quite diverse, including South Asia (8), Europe (5), East Asia (4), Africa (3), Latin and South America (3), and Oceania (1).

Ratings on Visual Content

Nearly half of the participants rated the highest on the visual content of e-Dunhuang, in a 5-point Likert scale (1: Don't like it at all, 5: Like it very much), resulting in an average rating of 4.67. This indicates an overwhelmingly positive opinion on the visual content. In the interviews, users praised the stunning visual materials and a majority of them mentioned that they enjoyed the panorama view of the caves (Figure 1). The view was not only attractive, but also highly realistic, which truly placed users at the scene of the event.

The Strongest and Weakest Points

In responding to the question on the strongest and weakest points of e-Dunhuang, it is very interesting that the panorama feature was mentioned 7 times for the strongest and the weakest points, respectively. The other strongest points included the "zoom in" feature of all images shown in this platform, and the virtual reality feature provided in the panorama view. It is noteworthy that all the strongest points mentioned were related to visual content or functions.

Regarded as the strongest and the weakest by equal number of participants, the panorama feature deserves a close examination. It turns out that comments on the weak side mostly involve usability issues. A prominent one was the difficulty of using the panorama. Nearly half of the participants found it hard to control. Participants also complained about the operation buttons on the panorama view, as they did not understand the functions of the buttons. In addition, as the panorama view automatically rotated, the speed and direction of the rotations could intervene users' operations. Besides the panorama view, other weakest points mentioned by the participants included "lack of background/context information" (mentioned 5 times). For example, several participants mentioned that they could not find a definition of the word "Dunhuang", which is in the title of the platform. Such lack of context information might have hindered their understanding of the visual materials. The names and concepts closely related to the cultural heritage might be obvious for Chinese users, but for non-Chinese users, introductions to these concepts are necessary.

Figure 1. An example of panorama view in e-Dunhuang.

Comparisons with Chinese Users

A recent study (Hu, 2018) conducted similar usability tests with 16 Chinese users and their findings could be compared with those of this study. First, quantitatively, the Chinese users rated an average of 4.18 (out of 5) on "visual appearance" which refers to "the visual esthetics of the system" and is similar to the "visual content" criterion in this study. The median of the rating given by the Chinese users was 4, while it was 5 for non-Chinese users in this study. This may indicate that the non-Chinese users, having no prior knowledge with the cultural heritage, were even more amazed by the visual materials. Similar to this study, in (Hu, 2018), the panoramic function was mentioned as the favorite feature by 3/4 of participants who were also fans of the visuals, praising them to be "super cool" and "striking". On the other hand, both groups of users raised the needs for more introductory information on the background and context of the visual materials. For instance, the stories depicted in the paintings could be briefly presented in text or audio formats.

CONCLUSION AND FUTURE WORK

The splendid cultural heritage and high-quality visual materials contained in e-Dunhuang were well appreciated by users both with and without the cultural background of the heritage. However, there is still a long way toward cross-cultural access to the e-Dunhuang heritage. The panorama function was deemed as both the strongest and weakest aspects of the e-Dunhuang platform by the group of non-Chinese users. More obvious labeling of functional buttons was needed, so was textual description of the background and meanings of the cultural heritage. In addition, through a comparison with opinions from Chinese users reported in a previous study, common needs for high quality visual materials and descriptions were identified among users in diverse cultural backgrounds. Findings of this study could inform cross-cultural access to cultural heritage collections dominant with visual content. Future work will include analyzing other non-visual functions of e-Dunhuang and making suggestions on platform design for enhancing cross-cultural access.

REFERENCES

Granić, A., Mitrović, I., & Marangunić, N. (2011). Exploring the usability of web portals: A Croatian case study.

International Journal of Information Management, 31(4), 339–349.

Hu, X. (2018). Usability evaluation of E-Dunhuang cultural heritage digital library. *Data and Information Management, 2*(2), 57–69.

Reinecke, K., & Bernstein, A. (2011). Improving performance, perceived usability, and aesthetics with culturally adaptive user interfaces. *ACM Transactions on Computer-Human Interaction (TOCHI), 18*(2), 1–29. https://doi.org/10.1145/1970378.1970382

#Cyberbullying in the Digital Age: Exploring People's Opinions With Text Mining

Iman Tahamtan
University of Tennessee,
Knoxville, TN, USA
tahamtan@vols.utk.edu

Li-Min Huang
University of Tennessee,
Knoxville, TN, USA
lhuang23@vols.utk.edu

ABSTRACT

This study used text mining to investigate people's insights about cyberbullying. English-language tweets were collected and analyzed by R software. Our analysis demonstrated three major themes: (a) the major actions that needed to be taken into consideration (e.g. guiding parents and teachers to cyberbullying prevention, funding schools to cope with cyberbullying), (b) certain events that were important to people (e.g. the Michigan cyberbullying law), and (c) people's major concerns in this regard (e.g. mental health issues among students). Parents and teachers have an important role in educating, informing, warning, preventing, and protecting against cyberbullying behaviors. The frequency of negative sentiments was almost 2.45 times more than positive sentiments.

KEYWORDS

Cyberbullying; Social media; Human Information Behavior

ASIS&T THESAURUS

Latent semantic analysis; Co-occurrence analysis; Social media analytics; Text mining

INTRODUCTION

Cyberbullying has been a public concern in the past decade. According to Tokunaga (2010, p. 278), cyberbullying is defined as "*any behavior performed through electronic or digital media by individuals or groups that repeatedly communicates hostile or aggressive messages intended to inflict harm or discomfort on others*". Cyberbullying can negatively impact mental, physical, and behavioral health status of victims and their families (De Bourdeaudhuij, Jacobs, DeSmet, & Gunther, 2015).

The current study aims to reveal people's insights about cyberbullying from tweets. Twitter has become a valuable source of information to explore peoples' behaviors and viewpoints about various public health and social issues (Karami, Dahl, Turner-McGrievy, Kharrazi, & Shaw Jr, 2018). However, few studies (e.g., McHugh, Saperstein, & Gold, 2019) have used Twitter as a data source to explore people's viewpoints on cyberbullying. The present study will contribute to the literature by applying a textual analytics method to reveal people's cognition and perception about cyberbullying.

82nd Annual Meeting of the Association for Information Science & Technology | Melbourne, Australia | 19–23 October, 2019

DOI: 10.1002/pra2.00172

METHODS

Data Collection

Twitter's Application Programming Interface (API) was applied to collect English-language tweets that contained *#cyberbullying* and *cyberbullying*. Using R software (https://www.r-project.org/) we collected data on April 6th, March 24th, and June 2nd in 2019 and in total retrieved 8,079 tweets excluding re-tweets.

Data Cleaning and Analysis

We cleaned the data (numeric digits, URLs), and removed whitespaces, converted words to lowercase, filtered out stop words and stem the data. The screen names that (a) had posted more than one tweet, and (b) tweets with more than 5 hashtags were removed to avoid fake accounts or bots, which resulted in 6,050 tweets. We used Bing's lexicon approach to analyze and understand the negative and positive sentiments. We also performed correlation network analysis to identify which keywords in cyberbullying tweets occurred most often together (see Silge & Robinson, 2017).

RESULTS

The top 18 words are presented in Table 1. "Cyberbullying" (n = 5,932), "bullying" (n = 1,066), and "stop" (n = 585) were the top three words in the cyberbullying tweets. There were 163 terms in the category of positive sentiment and 391 terms in the category of negative sentiment (Figure 1). The frequency of negative sentiments (n = 3,257) was almost 2.45 times more than positive sentiments (n = 1,324).

Word	Counts	Word	Counts
Cyberbullying	5,932	Kid	214
Bullying	1,066	Student	210
Stop	585	Media	209
People	558	Social	206
Law	419	Michigan	198
Don't	389	Report	193
Online	362	Video	187
School	296	Internet	163
Call	233	Hate	60

Table 1. Most common words in cyberbullying tweets.

The correlation network analysis of keywords (Figure 2) revealed seven main clusters of keywords. For example, {experience, children}, {mental health}, {Michigan cyberbullying law}, {girl, photo, share, protect}, and {fund, adequate, school, bullying} were some of these clusters.

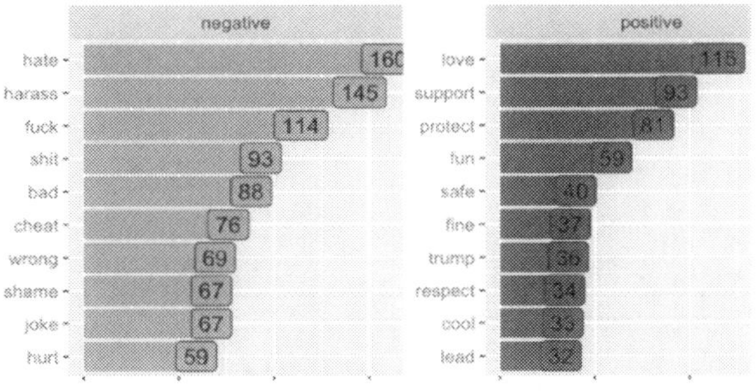

Figure 1. The frequency of positive and negative sentiments (The number in each chart represents the terms frequency).

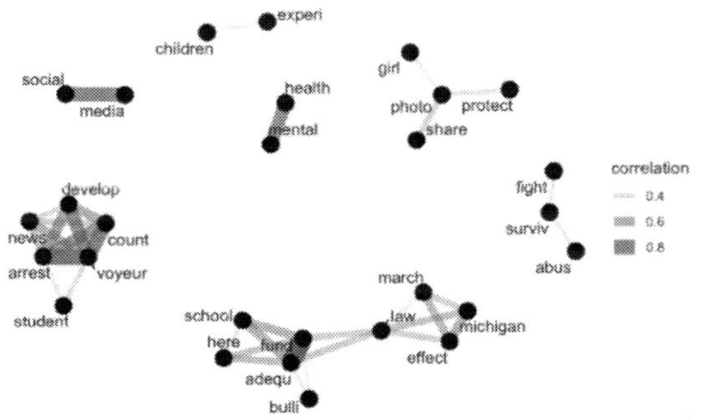

Figure 2. The correlation network of cyberbullying tweets.

DISCUSSION

Our analysis demonstrated that "people", "kids", "students", "schools", and "stop" were among the most frequently used words. This might indicate that people are mainly concerned about preventing and stopping cyberbullying behaviors among children and students. The results further revealed that parents and teachers should be trained about the different aspects of cyberbullying, in particularly about cyberbullying prevention in schools. One cluster in the correlation network included the terms {fund, adequate, school} which might indicate the importance of dedicating adequate funding to schools to take actions.

Another cluster included {girl, photo, share and protect} (Figure 2). This could be possibly an indication that gender differences exist in appearance-related cyberbullying. However, this finding needs further investigation. A previous study found that girls are more likely to experience appearance-related cyberbullying, because they tend to post photos or selfies on social media more often than boys. As a result, girls would receive more hurtful comments based on their appearance than boys (Berne, Frisén, & Kling, 2014). In this regard, a study among high school students indicated that female victims were more likely to have attempted suicide because of the depression caused by cyberbullying (Bauman, Toomey, & Walker, 2013).

In addition, many tweets were about the recently launched "Michigan cyberbullying law". This might be representative of the fact that the text mining of tweets could be used to learn certain (or the latest) events that have drawn people's attention. This is in line with Calvin, Bellmore, Xu, and Zhu's (2015) study, stated that the number of retweets may reflect certain important events. The correlation network analysis demonstrated that people concerned about the consequences of cyberbullying, mainly the "mental health" issues among kids and students. A few tweets had some suggestions about how to recognize the signs of cyberbullying. For example, a tweet expressed some of these signs: "*avoiding school or group gatherings, slipping grades, acting out in anger, wanting to stop using your computer or cellphone, and withdrawal from family members, friends and activities*".

CONCLUSION

Findings suggest that people use social media (Twitter) to share a rich content about cyberbullying-related information and coping strategies from different aspects, including (a) the actions that needed to be taken into consideration, (b) certain events that had drawn people's attention, and (c) people's major concerns in this regard.

REFERENCES

Bauman, S., Toomey, R. B., & Walker, J. L. (2013). Associations among bullying, cyberbullying, and suicide in high school students. *Journal of adolescence*, *36*(2), 341–350.

Berne, S., Frisén, A., & Kling, J. (2014). Appearance-related cyberbullying: A qualitative investigation of characteristics, content, reasons, and effects. *Body Image*, *11*(4), 527–533.

Calvin, A. J., Bellmore, A., Xu, J.-M., & Zhu, X. (2015). #bully: Uses of hashtags in posts about bullying on Twitter. *Journal of School Violence*, *14*(1), 133–153.

De Bourdeaudhuij, I., Jacobs, N. C., DeSmet, A., & Gunther, N. (2015). Comparing associated harm with traditional bullying and cyberbullying: A narrative overview of mental, physical and behavioural negative outcomes. In *Cyberbullying* (pp. 54–76). Routledge.

Karami, A., Dahl, A. A., Turner-McGrievy, G., Kharrazi, H., & Shaw, G., Jr. (2018). Characterizing diabetes, diet, exercise, and obesity comments on Twitter. *International Journal of Information Management*, *38*(1), 1–6.

McHugh, M. C., Saperstein, S. L., & Gold, R. S. (2019). OMG U# Cyberbully! An exploration of public discourse about cyberbullying on twitter. *Health Education & Behavior*, *46*(1), 97–105.

Silge, J., & Robinson, D. (2017). *Text mining with R: A tidy approach*. O'Reilly Media, Inc.

Tokunaga, R. S. (2010). Following you home from school: A critical review and synthesis of research on cyberbullying victimization. *Computers in human behavior*, *26*(3), 277–287.

How Is Knowledge Management Represented in Library and Information Science Research?

Md Anwarul Islam
University of Dhaka, Dhaka, Bangladesh
anwar@du.ac.bd

Naresh Kumar Agarwal
Simmons University, Boston, USA
agarwal@simmons.edu

ABSTRACT

Research published during the last two decades has frequently discussed how Knowledge Management (KM) is important for libraries. However, we do not know the extent to which KM forms a part of Library and Information Science (LIS) research. In this study, we looked for KM articles published in top LIS journals since 2000. We analyzed publication trends, and the distribution of articles by KM-related terms used, region/country and information-setting type. We also identified the top-cited KM articles published in these LIS journals. 672 KM-related articles (only 3.84%) were found within the 17,491 articles published in these LIS journals. This low percentage shows that while it might seem like LIS people are advocating for KM in libraries and other information settings, we find that despite the synergies, KM is yet to find a broader place within other LIS concerns.

KEYWORDS

Library and Information Science journals; Knowledge Management research; research publications; bibliometrics; Google Scholar journal ranking

ASIS&T THESAURUS

Information Science; Library Science; Knowledge Management

INTRODUCTION AND LITERATURE REVIEW

Knowledge management (KM) has gained much attention during the last three decades. Nonaka and Takeuchi (1995) define KM as the capability of 'a company as a whole to create new knowledge, disseminate it throughout the organization, and embody it in products, services and systems' (p. 3). Dalkir (2017) describes KM as a highly multidisciplinary field spanning organizational science, cognitive science, library and information science, anthropology, sociology, etc. Considering the multidisciplinary nature of KM, many researchers in the past two decades have worked on the intersection of LIS and KM fields and discussed how KM is important for LIS, LIS professional associations (Agarwal & Islam, 2016) and for libraries. While there have been many studies conducted on KM in libraries, we do not know the extent to which knowledge management forms a part of LIS research. Agarwal and Islam (2018) tried to ascertain the place of LIS in KM research and found that only 1.8 % of all articles in the top ten KM journals published since the year 2000 related to LIS. In this paper, we take an opposite lens and investigate the place of KM in LIS research. Even though we know that individual researchers and practitioners have called to incorporate KM in LIS settings because of the obvious benefits of KM for libraries, this research is important as it helps provide a benchmark on the overall level of acceptance of KM in LIS research. Librarians and other LIS practitioners stand to gain from the benefits of KM for service innovation and efficiency, should they have greater awareness about KM.

METHODOLOGY

We analyzed the top 20 publications from 2000 to 2018 as listed by Google Scholar Metrics (2019) in 'Library and Information Science' (as on January 6, 2019). The ranking can change over time. Of these, we excluded those that pertained to conference proceedings and were not journals. We excluded one journal (arXiv Digital Libraries – cs.DL), as it was specifically focused on digital libraries in different domains, including machine learning, physics, etc. This left us with a list of top 17 peer-reviewed journals among the 20 top publications identified by Google Scholar, where the Journal of the Association for Information Science & Technology (JASIST) was the top journal. From the journals identified, we accessed the individual issues of each journal from the years 2000 – 2018. For each issue, we scanned the title, abstract and keywords of articles looking for any relationship with knowledge management. We carried out the work of journal selection, combing of all articles and analysis of identified KM-related articles over a three month period from January – March, 2019.

DATA ANALYSIS AND FINDINGS

When analyzing the gathered data, we found that of the 17,491 articles published by the top 17 LIS journals from 2000-2018, 672 were KM-related. In total, since 2000, 3.84% of the LIS articles were KM related. The year 2017 had the most number of KM articles (4.7%) in LIS journals (see Figure 1).

From Figure 2, we can see that The Journal of Information Science published the most number of articles in the KM area (8.36%) from 2000-2018.

82nd Annual Meeting of the Association for Information Science & Technology | Melbourne, Australia | 19–23 October, 2019

DOI: 10.1002/pra2.00129

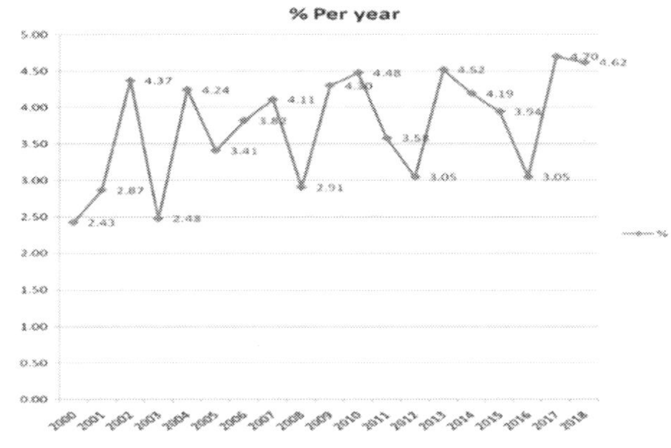

Figure 1. Percentage of KM related articles (among all LIS articles) per year across the top-17 LIS journals.

Among the 672 KM-related articles, a majority focused on key terms within the general knowledge management discipline. Most articles were from USA, followed by China, Taiwan and the UK. Majority of KM studies in LIS journals were either reviews of the literature, opinion papers or theoretical papers. 125 of the 672 studies described surveys carried out. The top 20 articles (based on citations) were analyzed for the journals in which they were published, and the years in which these articles were published. We found that Journal of Information Science (JIS) published most of these top-cited KM articles. Among the 672 KM articles, majority of the publications (36.46%) were written by 2 authors and the next largest (29.32%) was single authored. We found a declining trend in multiple authorship works over time from 2000 to 2018.

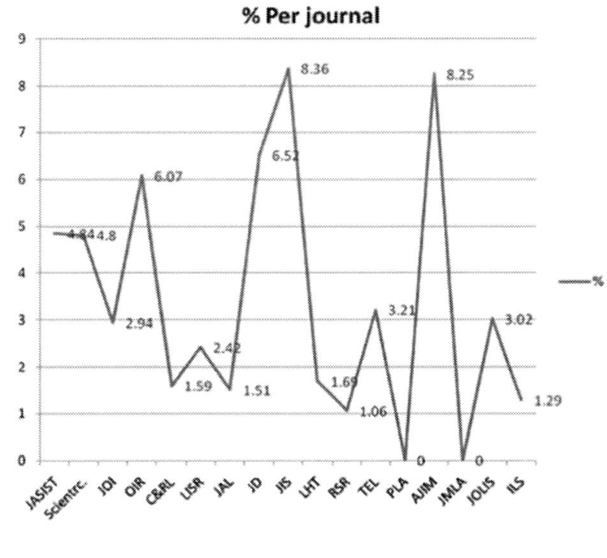

Figure 2. Percentage of KM related articles (among all LIS articles) per journal for 2000-2018.

DISCUSSION AND IMPLICATIONS

Of the more than 17,000 LIS articles published in top journals in the past two decades, only 672 (less than 4%) are KM-related. In a yearly analysis, the percentage of KM research in LIS journals went up and down since 2000, and went up to 4.7% in 2017. A reason could be that KM researchers in LIS are publishing more in KM journals, and less in LIS journals – where their research might get greater visibility. KM-researchers in LIS might be wanting to get to their primary KM audience for more practical usage and citation impact, as opposed to publishing in LIS journals, which other KM researchers may not read as much. Among the KM-related articles, a majority focused on key terms within the general KM discipline as their content area. This might be because of the limited inroads that LIS has made within KM, whereby a lot of authors still focus on the more popular terms/areas within KM. Most identified articles were theoretical and position papers. Limited work has been done on practical implementation of KM within libraries. In terms of citation impact, JIS and JASIST are good avenues for KM-researchers in the LIS area, as these two journals had most of the top-cited articles. Looking at the areas of focus in top 5 most-cited articles shows that knowledge management, knowledge sharing, knowledge integration, knowledge transfer and innovation are major areas of interest to other researchers citing KM-in-LIS-related work. These are all important areas when implementing KM within libraries and other information settings. The overall findings of this study revealed that KM has comparatively high visibility (3.84%) in the LIS field, as opposed to LIS within the KM field, where Agarwal and Islam (2018)'s study demonstrated a visibility of only 1.8%. Thus, LIS journals engage with KM more oftenthan KM journals engage with LIS. However, as such, less than 4% is still a low figure. The low percentage of KM articles within LIS articles may be due to the overall image of KM as something for businesses and for for-profit companies.

LIMITATIONS AND FUTURE WORK

This study has a few limitations. First, we determined the top LIS journals and publications based solely on Google Scholar. There were other scholarly databases e.g., SSCI, EBSCO, SCOPUS, and Web of Science, which might provide different listings of top LIS publications. Second, aboutness is a complex topic and we did not read the full papers to determine if they related to KM. Third, the research showed that despite the perceived synergies between the LIS and KM fields, KM research has had little impact within LIS publications. A qualitative study could be carried out to further delve into the reasons behind this scenario. Finally, while we seek to determine the place of KM within LIS research, the question still remains as to whether KM needs to have a place within LIS research, and what, if any, are the synergies within and between the fields.

REFERENCES

Agarwal, N. K. & Islam, A. (2018). *Ascertaining the place of library & information science in knowledge management research*. In Proceedings of ASIS&T AM, Vancouver, Canada, Nov 10-14 (Vol. 55(1), pp 1-9).

Agarwal, N.K. & Islam, M.A. (2016). *How can professional associations continue to stay relevant? Knowledge Management to the rescue*. In Proceedings of ASIS&T AM, Copenhagen, Denmark, Oct 14-18 (Vol. 53(1), pp. 1-10).

Dalkir, K. (2017). *Knowledge management in theory and practice*. Cambridge: MIT.

Google Scholar Metrics (2019). Top 20 publications matching library and information science. Retrieved from https://scholar.google.com/citations?view_op=top_venues&hl=en&vq=eng_libraryinformationscience

Nonaka, I., & Takeuchi, H. (1995). *The knowledge-creating company: How Japanese companies create the dynamics of innovation*. New York: Oxford Uni. Press.

Retrieval System Enhanced by Fine-Grained Knowledge Entities

Chuan Jiang
Nanjing Agricultural University, Nanjing, China
2018114013@njau.edu.cn

Dongbo Wang
Nanjing Agricultural University, Nanjing, China
db.wang@njau.edu.cn

Si Shen
Nanjing University of Science and Technology, Nanjing, China
shensi@njust.edu.cn

ABSTRACT

Along with the massive increase of academic full texts, users now have a growing need for fine-grained academic literature retrieval. However, few studies have attempted to build domain knowledge retrieval system for academic literature in information science. Compared with other disciplines, information science pays more attention to the domain knowledge entities sequence including data resources, models and software. To fill the gap, this paper use academic full texts from JASIST. Using SVM, Text-CNN, Bi-LSTM and BERT to extract the knowledge entities sequence including data resource, model, software. The highest Precision, Recall and F1 are 92.45%, 93.86% and 93.14%, respectively. And the knowledge entity sequence indexing system is built based on the extracted knowledge entities sequences. It was found that the MRR score of the knowledge entities sequence retrieval system was higher by 13% as compared with the full text retrieval system.

KEYWORDS

knowledge entities; full text; retrieval system; deep learning

ASIS&T THESAURUS

Informatics; Computing resource management

INTRODUCTION

Knowledge entities sequence is a carrier of knowledge units and mainly refers to sentences containing keywords, topics, key concepts, datasets, key methods and theories and domain entities (Ding et al., 2013). Recently, many studies have been published on retrieval system for deep mining of knowledge entities sequences in academic full texts and for constructing domain knowledge, including the acknowledgment retrieval system (Khabsa, Treeratpituk, & Giles, 2012) and algorithm retrieval system (Safder & Hassan, 2019; Tuarob, Bhatia, Mitra, & Giles, 2016).

For the discipline of information science, few studies have attempted to build domain knowledge retrieval system. Therefore, in this paper, JASIST data is used to identify the knowledge entity sequence, and based on the identified knowledge entity sequence, the corresponding retrieval system is constructed to meet the fine-grained retrieval needs of researchers.

DATA SET AND METHOD

The data are sourced from 892 openly published articles on JASIST from 2012 to 2016. A total of 281,035 sentences are obtained by paragraph segmentation and sentence segmentation. Knowledge entities sequences associated with data resources accounted for 4.22%, which is the highest of the three types of knowledge entities sequences, and the sample data related to it is that "We add all words in the Wikipedia corpus as vertices into the center concept graph." Knowledge entities sequences associated with model accounted for 4.16%, and the sample data related to it is that "LDA topic modeling is used to determine author relatedness for the topic-based approach." By contrast, knowledge entities sequences associated with software only accounted for 2.93%, and the sample data related to it is that "Automatic classification was performed using WordStat software of Provalis Research (v.5.1.10)." All these three types of knowledge entities sequences accounted for 11.31% of all sentences collectively. Sentences not containing knowledge entities sequences accounted for 88.69% of all sentences.

In this study, SVM, Text-CNN, Bi-LSTM and BERT models were respectively used to extract and recognize knowledge entities sequences from academic full texts of JASIST. The sequence segmented from the full text were identified by model to determine whether the knowledge entity is included. Academic full texts in JASIST were divided into training test and testing test in a 9:1 ratio, and the performance of above models was evaluated by calculating macro-average Precision, Recall and F1 value.

The text structure was first divided into 6 sections by artificial introspection, namely, introduction, literature review, method, experimental, conclusion and other. The reason for doing this is that the introduction and literature review sections may involve studies done by other scholars using relevant methods, data and software and is not the main contents of the present study. Lucene-based Elasticsearch framework was used for the indexing of knowledge entities sequences in the recognized sections of method, experimental and conclusion. If the current paper did not contain knowledge entities sequences, then the

82nd Annual Meeting of the Association for Information Science & Technology | Melbourne, Australia | 19–23 October, 2019

DOI: 10.1002/pra2.00131

keyword extraction algorithm RAKE (Rose, Engel, Cramer, & Cowley, 2010) was used to establish the index. The retrieval performance was evaluated based on reciprocal rank (PP) and MRR (mean reciprocal rank).

RESULT

The model recognition results are shown in Table 1. The Precision of SVM was the highest, which was 94.2%, but the recall rate was lower, which was only 84.9%. The Precision, Recall and F1 of Text-CNN、Bi-LSTM were all above 91%. Of all models, BERT model had the highest performance, its Precision, Recall and F1 being 92.45%, 93.86% and 93.14%, respectively.

Model	P	R	F1
SVM	0.942	0.849	0.8883
Text-CNN	0.9315	0.9123	0.9216
Bi-LSTM	0.9408	0.9089	0.9241
BERT	0.9245	0.9386	0.9314

Table 1. Comparison of the performance of knowledge entities sequence extraction among different models.

In order to ensure the scientificity and accuracy of retrieval effect evaluation, as shown in Table 2, two participants were asked to evaluate the same query simultaneously. If the two participants selected the most relevant documents to be different, the third participant is invited to make a judgment.

Query	P1	P2	P3
VOSviewer social network analysis	10.1002/asi.22680	10.1002/asi.23372	10.1002/asi.22680
opinion retrieval using TREC	10.1002/asi.22724	10.1002/asi.23111	10.1002/asi.22724
Application of K-means algorithm	10.1002/asi.23413	10.1002/asi.23413	

Table 2. Participant's evaluation sample of query.

As shown in Figure 1, 50 query examples were established by inviting three participants for the scoring. The dot represented RR scores of the knowledge retrieval system minus RR scores of the retrieval system based on knowledge entities. If the corresponding value is positive, it indicates that the performance of the knowledge retrieval system is better than the full-text retrieval system in the current query. It shown that the RR scores of the retrieval system based on knowledge entities were generally higher than those of the full text retrieval system. The solid line and dotted line in the figure represented the overall MRR scores. The overall MRR score was 0.721 with the retrieval system based on knowledge entities sequence, which was higher by 13% as compared with the full text retrieval system. Thus the retrieval system based on knowledge entities sequence better satisfied users' retrieval needs for specific knowledge as compared with the full text retrieval system.

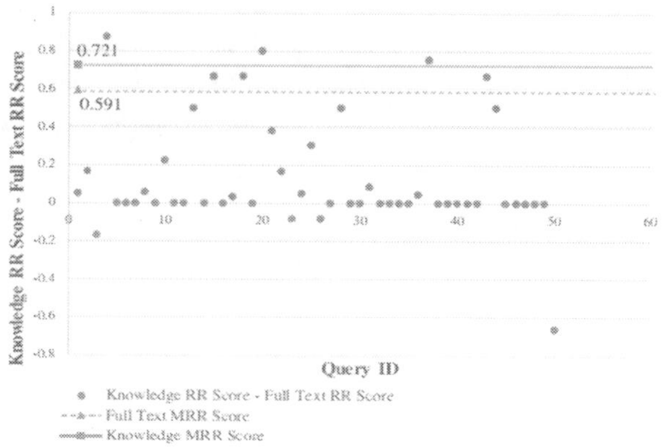

Figure 1. Performance comparison between retrieval system based on knowledge entities and full text retrieval system.

CONCLUSION

The present study conducted an extraction of knowledge entities sequences from the academic full texts in JASIST. The results showed that BERT model had the highest performance among all test models for knowledge entities sequence extraction. Moreover, a retrieval system was built based on the extracted knowledge entities sequences. It was found that the MRR score of this retrieval system was higher by 13% as compared with the full text retrieval system.

ACKNOWLEDGMENTS

Researches are supported by the National Natural Science Foundation of China (Grant Number: 71673143).

REFERENCES

Ding, Y., Song, M., Han, J., Yu, Q., Yan, E., Lin, L., & Chambers, T. (2013). Entitymetrics: Measuring the impact of entities. *PLoS One*, *8*(8), e71416.

Khabsa, M., Treeratpituk, P., & Giles, C. L. (2012). Ackseer: A repository and search engine for automatically extracted acknowledgments from digital libraries. In *Proceedings of the 12th ACM/IEEE-CS joint conference on Digital Libraries* (pp. 185–194). ACM.

Rose, S., Engel, D., Cramer, N., & Cowley, W. (2010). Automatic keyword extraction from individual documents. In *Text mining: applications and theory* (pp. 1–20).

Safder, I., & Hassan, S. U. (2019). Bibliometric-enhanced information retrieval: A novel deep feature engineering approach for algorithm searching from full-text publications. *Scientometrics*, 1–21.

Tuarob, S., Bhatia, S., Mitra, P., & Giles, C. L. (2016). AlgorithmSeer: A system for extracting and searching for algorithms in scholarly big data. *IEEE Transactions on Big Data*, *2*(1), 3–1.

A Clickstream Data Analysis of Users' Behavior on a Government WeChat Official Account

Tingting Jiang
School of Information Management, Wuhan University,
Hubei, China
tij@whu.edu.cn

Tianqianjin Lin
School of Information Management, Wuhan University,
Hubei, China
lintqj@whu.edu.cn

Lina Shangguan
School of Political Science and Public Administration, Wuhan University,
Hubei, China
sgln@whu.edu.cn

Ying Wang
School of Information Management, Wuhan University,
Hubei, China
wy1210@whu.edu.cn

ABSTRACT

This study took a user-oriented approach to investigating the effectiveness of a government WeChat official account in terms of service delivery. A transaction log file containing 42,188,760 clickstream records was obtained from an active account and analyzed at the footprint and movement levels. The current clickstream data analysis revealed the underutilization of the services provided by the account, the failure of the three navigational portals, and the poor completion rates of the tasks users performed on the account.

KEYWORDS

Government WeChat official account; user behavior; clickstream data analysis

ASIS&T THESAURUS

E-government; Web usage studies

INTRODUCTION

A popular type of social media, WeChat Public Platform enables individuals, enterprises, and organizations to reach target audiences through their official accounts. Subscription accounts and service accounts, respectively, focus on publishing information and providing services.

Useful practical implications for improving service delivery have been derived from the evaluation of WeChat official accounts which however depended heavily on expert opinions or user ratings (Li & Zhang, 2016). Experiential or subjective judgment might indicate account service quality to a certain extent, but never as persuasive as the actual usage data. This study is particularly interested in government accounts and aims to reveal their effectiveness based on real users' behavior. A clickstream data analysis was conducted on the transaction log file from an active account, to address the following research questions: (1) How do users visit the government account in general? (2) How do users utilize the services provided by the government account to complete their tasks?

The significance of this study consists in the introduction of unobtrusive data to the investigation of user behavior and the practical implications for interface and functionality design of government WeChat official accounts.

METHODS

The research data of this study was provided by an active WeChat official account owned by the Public Transportation Authority (PTA) of a capital city in central China. The PTA account has accumulated approximately 300 million followers since its establishment in 2013. The original data was a transaction log file containing 42,188,760 clickstream records generated on the server from 00:00:00 May 30th to 23:59:59 July 28, 2018. Each record has five basic fields: *User-IP* (IP address of the client who made the request), *Date/Time* (date and time when the request was made), *Request* (type of client to server request and URL of the resource requested), *Status* (HTTP status code), and *Referrer* (URL of the page where the request was made).

The log file was cleaned to eliminate corrupted and redundant records in the first place. The former were errors produced when the server performed logging incorrectly, and the latter were those irrelevant to the objective of this study. After data cleaning, 5,260,421 clickstream records remained in the log file. The next step was to identify sessions. Different users were identified with their IP addresses; and for the same user, if the time interval between any two records exceeded 5 minutes, they would be divided into different sessions. In this way, a total of 3,430,018 sessions were identified, involving 607,278 distinct IP addresses.

A data coding system was created based on the information architecture of the PTA account. There are seven major page categories: *home* (code "H", the three portals that provide access to various services), *user* (code "U", user's personal account), *appointment* (code "A", making appointments for offline services), *lookup* (code "L", looking up records, license plate number, and other information), *reporting* (code "R",

82nd Annual Meeting of the Association for Information Science & Technology | Melbourne, Australia | 19–23 October, 2019

DOI: 10.1002/pra2.00130

reporting accidents, road conditions, and illegal behaviors to the PTA), *online* (code "O", online services delivered directly on the PTA account), and *information* (code "I", news, notifications, and other information published by the PTA). Each category of pages enables users to perform a number of similar or related tasks.

This study followed a general framework of clickstream data analysis which has been successfully applied in the studies of users' information seeking behavior in social library systems and academic library OPAC systems (Jiang, Guo, Xu, Zhao, & Fu, 2019), and the above data was analyzed at the footprint and movement levels. When a user visits the PTA account, each click causes a movement, the changing of location from one page to another, and leaves a footprint, a mark showing the user's presence on a page. The footprint level analysis aimed to provide a basic understanding of traffic distribution within the PTA account, while the movement level analysis concerned whether and how users' goals are achieved.

PRELIMINARY RESULTS AND DISCUSSION

General usage of the PTA account

Figure 1 is a treemap showing the distribution of these footprints among the seven major page categories. Approximately 60% of the footprints were left on *home* pages (H), suggesting that most visits to the PTA account were limited to the three portals. They were followed by *lookup* pages (L, 15.52%), *user* pages (U, 9.67%), and *online* pages (O, 8.40%), while the other three age categories added up to merely 6.31%. It can be inferred that the PTA account was mainly used as a lookup tool. Users were promoted to manage their personal account, e.g. verifying identity and adding vehicle or driver license, to make more efficient use of the PTA account.

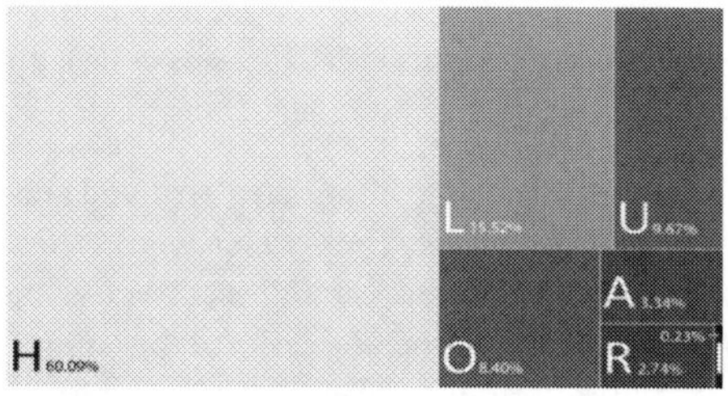

Figure 1. Footprint distribution among page categories.

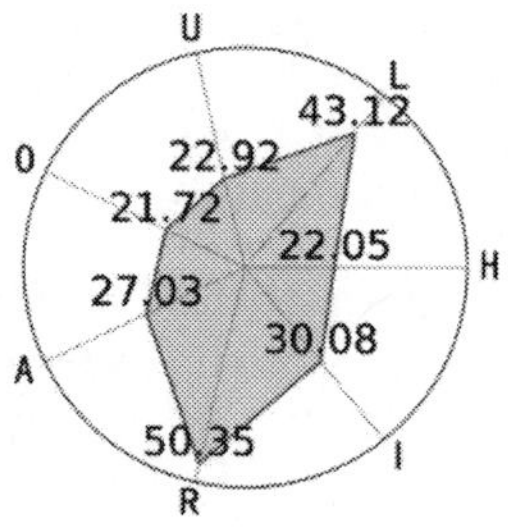

Figure 2. Footprint depths (in seconds) of page categories.

This study defined footprint depth as the time spent on a page. Figure 2 demonstrates the differences in footprint depth among the seven categories of pages. *Reporting* (50.35 seconds), *lookup* (43.12 seconds), and *information* pages (30.08 seconds) retained users for more than half a minute on average. It is understandable since the former two required a lot input from users whereas the latter displayed content for users to read. The other page categories featured less effortful interactions such as scanning and browsing, thus resulting in shallower footprints.

Task performing and completion on the PTA account

In Figure 3, the top 15 tasks performed the most frequently included 5 lookup tasks, which echoed the primary role of the PTA account as a lookup tool. In particular, LT5 (i.e. illegal driving record lookup) was performed 451,696 times, far exceeding the second most popular task, OT5 (i.e. paying a fine). If users want to pay a fine on the PTA account, they need to use WeChat Pay. It is likely that most people still preferred to pay a fine at the local PTA offices, which caused a remarkable drop in performing OT5.

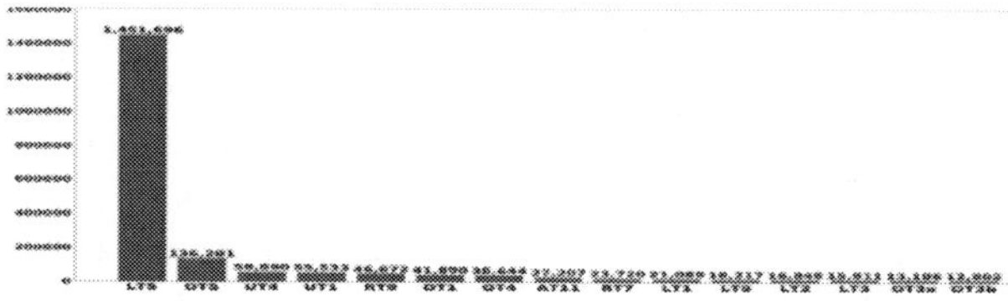

Figure 3. Top 15 tasks performed the most frequently.

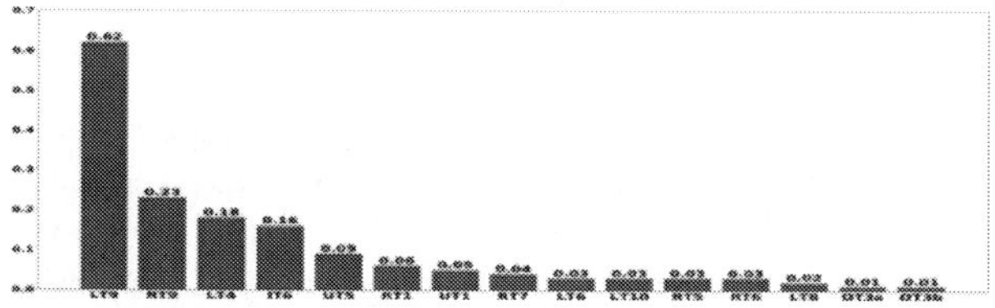

Figure 4. Top 15 tasks with the highest completion rates.

This study obtained unsatisfactory completion rates (frequency of performing divided by frequency of completion) for multi-step tasks, i.e. task completion involving two or more steps/pages, as seen in Figure 4. LT9 (i.e. electric bicycle license plate lookup) had a completion rate of 0.62, which stands out among all the tasks. This task and other tasks with relatively higher completion rates, e.g. RT9 (i.e. reporting a blocking vehicle), LT4 (i.e. electronic insurance policy lookup), and IT6 (i.e. traffic notifications), were either of higher urgency or easier to complete.

CONCLUSION AND FUTURE WORK

Overall, the PTA account was performing poorly. Despite the variety of services provided, the account was used mainly for lookup tasks, especially illegal driving record lookup. The three navigational portals failed to direct users to their desired tasks in most cases. It was not likely that the users would successfully complete the tasks they performed. This study plan to analyze the clickstream data at the pathway level in the near future, in order to reveal users' detailed behavioral patterns of their interaction with the PTA account. Also, a usability test will be conducted to identify the major deficiencies of the account that caused the poor performance.

REFERENCES

Jiang, T., Guo, Q., Xu, Y., Zhao, Y., & Fu, S. (2019). *What prompts users to click on news headlines? A clickstream data analysis of the effects of news recency and popularity*. In iConference (pp. 539–546).

Li, Z., & Zhang, X. (2016). Construction of evaluation index system and empirical research on the service quality of government WeChat official accounts. *Library and Information Science, 60*(18), 79–88.

"For the Benefit of All Students": Student Trust in Higher Education Learning Analytics Practices

Kyle M. L. Jones
School of Informatics and Computing,
Indiana University-Indianapolis (IUPUI),
Indianapolis, Indiana, United States
kmlj@iupui.edu

Tanisha Afnan
School of Informatics and Computing,
Indiana University-Indianapolis (IUPUI),
Indianapolis, Indiana, United States
tafnan@iu.edu

ABSTRACT

Learning analytics is a sociotechnical practice that seeks new insights from mining and analyzing student data. As new flows of student data emerge and granular information about student life becomes more accessible, there is a growing call to address student privacy and related issues. This poster reports emerging results from over 100 interviews with undergraduate students regarding their privacy perceptions especially with regard to trust.

KEYWORDS

Higher education; learning analytics; student privacy; trust

ASIS&T THESAURUS

Colleges and universities; educational technology; privacy

INTRODUCTION

Student privacy in higher education is becoming a significant concern among educational technology critics, information policy scholars, and the media. They argue that the use of data analytics and the data infrastructures that support analytic practice may negatively affect students' abilities to protect their privacy. Much of this analytic work falls under the banner of learning analytics (LA), and significant investments in LA among higher education institutions (HEIs) signal that the privacy concerns will need attention sooner rather than later as tools, methods, and practices mature. What students think of LA and related effects on their privacy is still a widely unanswered question. The project described below addresses student perceptions of their privacy specifically in relation to trust issues.

LITERATURE REVIEW

Learning Analytics in Higher Education

LA is defined as the the "measurement, collection, analysis, and reporting of (student and other data) for the purposes of understanding and optimizing learning and the environments in which it occurs" (Siemens, 2012, p. 4). With regard to learning, LA has been used to analyze learning behaviors, examine social networks, personalize learner content, adapt systems to student needs, and predict future success in a given course. The same data infrastructures that support learner analytics also help HEIs achieve other ends, such as: using descriptive and predictive analytics in addition to intervention algorithms to support admissions, streamlining advising, and nudging students to use library resources (Barnds, 2013; Jantti, 2016; Kraft-Terry & Kau, 2016).

Student Perspectives of their Privacy

On balance, the literature on student privacy perspectives is far less fleshed out than methods, tools, and possible outcomes associated with LA. What is known by this research suggests that students are unaware of LA (Roberts, Howell, Seaman, & Gibson, 2016), have granular opinions on what data should be shared and to whom (Ifenthaler & Schumacher, 2016), and want greater data controls (Slade & Prinsloo, 2014).

When asked whether or not students trust their institutions with the information they share, one study from the United Kingdom suggests that they do (Slade, Prinsloo, & Khalil, 2019). However, the authors caution that "(d)espite the apparent high levels of trust and low levels of privacy self-management strategies and capabilities shown in this study, HEIs should not underestimate the reputational value of bestowed trust, nor the need for transparency and good governance" (p. 242).

METHODOLOGY

Data Collection

The core team (see the acknowledgments) conducted IRB-approved interviews with undergraduate students at eight higher education institutions in the United States. Researchers used a combination of methods to recruit students, including e-mail lists and printed flyers. Researchers provided participants a $10 Amazon electronic gift card as an incentive. The researchers aimed to complete 120 interviews (15 per institution), but due to recruitment and quality control issues finished with 105 total interviews. Interviews were semi-structured and researchers conducted them face-to-face, on the phone, and using the web conferencing system Zoom. All interviews were digitally recorded and then professionally transcribed.

82nd Annual Meeting of the Association for Information Science & Technology | Melbourne, Australia | 19–23 October, 2019

DOI: 10.1002/pra2.00132

Data Analysis

The core team wrote case summaries for each transcription to summarize key findings and seed theoretical inquiry. One theoretical finding that emerged concerned the role of trust in student privacy. The authors began to explore the theme by 1) importing transcripts into MaxQDA (qualitative data analysis software), 2) conducting a lexical search for "trust*", 3) conducting separate open coding strategies on the retrieved segments, 3) merging and refining open codes, and 4) recoding the retrieved segments with the final code book. The lexical search retrieved 103 unique segments across 57 transcribed interviews. The final code book included seven families of codes with a count of 70 applicable codes. Thematic analysis is suggesting three significant themes that will be fleshed out in the poster.

THEMATIC FINDINGS

Inherent Trust in Educational Institutions

Matching findings in extant research, the data suggests that students have a high degree of trust in their university, and an even higher degree of trust in their university's library. It was evident that universities are seen as good institutions who employ trustworthy people whose work is aimed at improving the educational experience and serving student interests. In comparison, there was an expressed low degree of trust in social media and web services (e.g., Amazon) companies.

Certain Conditions must be Met

Even though trust was high, students expressed that conditions must be met to maintain their trust. Primarily, HEIs need to secure their data and information systems to protect against breaches and other informational harms. HEIs should also limit their data collection practices to information that is useful for LA but not personal, and additionally strictly control with whom the information is shared.

Forecasted Decreases in Trust

Students expressed what data and information practices in support of LA or otherwise would decrease their trust in their university. First, uses of identifiable information *without* informing students of such uses was viewed negatively. Second, there was a belief institutions could sell student data, and if this were a reality it would greatly decrease their trust. Attempting to make a profit off of student data was a clear red flag.

CONCLUSION

The emerging findings from this work are timely and have great potential to inform information practices and policies. Students place a significant amount of trust in their institutions, which allows HEIs significant leverage to use student data and information for LA and other purposes. If HEIs break this trust, the relationships between students and institutional actors (e.g., professors/instructors, advisors) will become limited. Consequently, students may not be as willing to open themselves up to educational experiences, put themselves in vulnerable situations, or seek, among other things, physical, mental, and emotional support when they most need it.

ACKNOWLEDGMENTS

This project was made possible in part by the Institute of Museum and Library Services (LG-96-18-0044-18). The views, findings, conclusions or recommendations expressed in this conference proceeding do not necessarily represent those of the Institute of Museum and Library Services. Additionally, the authors thank the core team who participated in participant recruitment, interviewing, and case summary writing portions of this project: Andrew Asher, Kristin Briney, Abigail Goben, Michael Perry, Brooke Robertshaw, and Dorothea Salo.

REFERENCES

Barnds, W. K. (2013, June 19). Does big data know best? NSA and college admissions. *The Huffington Post*. Retrieved from https://www.huffingtonpost.com/w-kent-barnds/does-big-data-know-best-n_b_3460096.html

Ifenthaler, D., & Schumacher, C. (2016). Student perceptions of privacy principles for learning analytics. *Educational Technology Research and Development*, *64*(5), 923–938. https://doi.org/10.1007/s11423-016-9477-y

Jantti, M. (2016). Libraries and big data: A new view on impact and affect. In J. Atkinson (Ed.), *Quality and the academic library: Reviewing, assessing and enhancing service provision* (pp. 267–274). Cambridge, MA: Chandos Publishing.

Kraft-Terry, S., & Kau, C. (2016). Manageable steps to implementing data-informed advising. *NACADA Clearinghouse*. Retrieved from http://www.nacada.ksu.edu/Resources/Clearinghouse/View-Articles/Manageable-Steps-to-Implementing-Data-Informed-Advising.aspx

Roberts, L. D., Howell, J. A., Seaman, K., & Gibson, D. C. (2016). Student attitudes toward learning analytics: "The Fitbit version of the learning world.". *Frontiers in Psychology*, *7*(1959), 1–11. https://doi.org/10.3389/fpsyg.2016.01959

Siemens, G. (2012). Learning analytics: Envisioning a research discipline and a domain of practice. *Proceedings of the 2nd International Conference on Learning Analytics & Knowledge*, 4–8. https://doi.org/10.1145/2330601.2330605

Slade, S., & Prinsloo, P. (2014). Student perspectives on the use of their data: between intrusion, surveillance and care. *Challenges for Research into Open & Distance Learning: Doing Things Better – Doing Better Things*, 291–300. http://oro.open.ac.uk/41229/

Slade, S., Prinsloo, P., & Khalil, M. (2019). Learning analytics at the intersections of student trust, disclosure and benefit. *Proceedings of the 9th International Conference on Learning Analytics & Knowledge*, 235–244. https://doi.org/10.1145/3303772.3303796

Put Relational Databases in Your Data Curation Toolbox

Jenna Jordan
University of Illinois at Urbana-Champaign,
Champaign, USA
jenna.jrdn@gmail.com

ABSTRACT

This poster paper makes a case for the use of relational databases as a data curation tool, especially for datasets that are published separately but can be used together due to a common identifier scheme and shared attributes. The Correlates of War datasets are used as an illustrative example to show how the normalization process results in a design with greater data reusability, while check constraints and foreign key constraints can improve data quality.

KEYWORDS

Digital data curation; digital humanities; information management; knowledge management; information design; information organization; knowledge organization

ASIS&T THESAURUS

Relational databases; data curation; international aspects

INTRODUCTION

This project began as an attempt to recreate the many disparate datasets in the Correlates of War (CoW) project[1] as one cohesive relational database. The CoW project is a collection of datasets that contains empirical data on large state conflicts, and "dominates the field of quantitative research into the onset of interstate military conflict" (Travlos & Rudkevich, 2016). It is currently maintained and hosted by several institutions in a system of "coordinated decentralization" that is designed to distribute the cost of curating and updating such a large collection of datasets (Izmirlioglu, 2017). In theory, the datasets are subject to strict rules to maintain data integrity and interoperability.

However, the CoW datasets have several organizational differences that makes successfully merging them together difficult (and in some cases impossible). The datasets required significant reorganization and transformation in order to fit the relational model. The process of transforming the datasets revealed unexpected issues with the data quality as well. The resulting database has greater data quality and the normalized structure allows all of the datasets to be used together; creating the potential for researchers to utilize this source of international conflict data in new ways and thus more fully realizing the goal of the Correlates of War project. The database file and data transformation code are publicly available on GitHub.[2]

The task of reorganizing the datasets ended up being an exploration of how the strict constraints and normalization standards of well-designed databases can be a useful tool for data curators. The same method – of taking a set of interrelated datasets, designing a relational model that can account for all of the information stored in the datasets, transforming the data to fit the database design, and then loading the data into the database with strict constraints in place – can be used to improve the quality and reusability of datasets in any field or discipline.

DATABASES AS A DATA CURATION TOOL

In the social sciences, it is becoming more common to share the data that research is based upon. However, this data usually comes in the form of a dataset, which may have been produced by hand – each value typed into a cell. Social scientists may be producing this dataset for one specific purpose or type of analysis, which affects their data design and formatting choices. This means that while the data may be shared, it is not necessarily easily re-usable.

Reusability is one of the areas of broad concern for data curation, and "repositories aiming to support future users may have to curate for data reuse by researchers in other communities" (Chao, Cragin, & Palmer, 2015). The relational database model is a valuable tool for data curators who wish to improve data quality and reusability.

The first step in designing a relational database is to normalize the data, so that the variables are organized into tables based on their functional dependences. For R users, normalized data is 'tidy' data – that is, data structured to facilitate analysis. Wickham's framework of tidy data (each observation a row, each column a variable, each table a type of observational unit) is essentially Codd's third normal form for relational databases, but framed for statisticians (Wickham, 2014). In other words, transforming datasets to fit the relational model results in datasets ready to be analyzed.

METHODOLOGY

In order to design the database, the first task was to identify the functional dependencies. In some cases, the documentation did not make this clear, and the database had to be redesigned several times when the data did not reflect the assumed

82nd Annual Meeting of the Association for Information Science & Technology | Melbourne, Australia | 19–23 October, 2019

DOI: 10.1002/pra2.00133

[1] https://www.correlatesofwar.org/data-sets

[2] https://github.com/jenna-jordan/international-relations-database

dependencies. Furthermore, many variables had a specific set of possible values which could be enforced through check constraints. This method of designing and filling a database forces the curator to identify and verify every assumption made about the data, without having to personally look through every cell in every table.

The CoW datasets were well-suited to this methodology for several reasons. First, they shared a common identifier scheme for important entities (states and conflicts). Second, the entities (mostly) shared the same attributes across datasets. Third, the datasets all had extensive documentation. All three of these traits are crucial for being able to safely reorganize the data in a meaningful way.

Data Quality

Unlike a spreadsheet, a (well-designed) database does not allow data to be entered that violates the specified constraints. Check constraints can be useful in catching data entry errors. For example, one row in the Intra-State War table lists a day as "-91866", while the following column (which is supposed to contain a year) is blank. Clearly, the person entering the data forgot to tab over to the next column. The day should have been "-9" (which means "unknown") and the year "1866". This mistake is easy to make in a program like Excel, and hard to detect after the fact. However, if the data were entered into a database, it would be found (and trigger an error) immediately. The "day" column could be specified to be a number with two digits, and a check constraint could further restrict that number to being between 1 and 31. While this method may not catch all such data entry errors, it will catch the most obvious.

Foreign key constraints can help catch errors that center on how different variables relate to each other. For example, the Territorial Change table has three columns (Gainer, Loser, TerritoryID) that relate to a single identifier column in the Polity table (PolityID). However, there is one territory present in the Territorial Change table that is not present in the Polity table – '822' – while the territories '8221', '8222', '8223', '8224', and '8225' are present in the Polity table. The original CoW documentation for the Territorial Change dataset makes clear that this is the pattern followed when a territory is broken up into component territories for an updated version of the dataset. So, this missing identifier '822' is evidence of a data versioning issue – a data quality issue revealed by the use of foreign key constraints.

Data Reusability

One of the advantages of relational databases is that they are self-describing: which combination of variables forms the primary key, which variables have relationships with other variables (thus creating variables to merge on), and even what the possible values for variables are.

Spreadsheets, however, are not self-describing – codebooks are required to understand what is happening in a table. However, most codebooks do not explicitly state the functional dependencies – that's up to the data curator to guess and check. Finding the functional dependencies and designing the CoW database was an iterative process.

The four War datasets (intra-, inter-, non-, and extra-state war) form the core of the CoW project – however, despite representing the same entity type (conflict), they are organized in one of three different ways: one row per war; one row per war and country; or one row per war, a side A country, and a side B country. These datasets cannot be used together as they are now, so researchers are limited to studying one type of war at a time. Furthermore, this difference in organization has resulted in other variables being inconsistent between tables. For example, the 'Outcome' column is either coded '1' for 'side A won' and '2' for 'side B won', or '1' for 'this side won' and '2' for 'this side lost'. These inconsistencies also prevent merging.

To solve these problems (and others), I designed a set of war tables – one for the wars (with a war ID primary key), one for the war participants (with a primary key of the war ID, polity ID, and start date), one for the multivalued region variable, and one for the recursive relationship of war transitions. This design is consistent with Codd's third normal form (Codd, 1970). The variables were standardized across tables, no information was lost, and the new format is both more flexible and space efficient, with the added advantage of allowing for analysis across war types.

CONCLUSION

During the process of transforming the CoW datasets into a single database, I caught and corrected data entry errors, discovered data versioning issues, and reconciled different organizational designs used for the same entity type across datasets. I used functional dependencies to reorganize datasets into normal (or 'tidy') form, with relationships maintained by foreign key constraints. The unforgiving nature of database management systems forced every assumption to be checked and verified. This process would be a useful addition to any data curation workflow.

REFERENCES

Chao, T. C., Cragin, M. H., & Palmer, C. L. (2015). Data practices and curation vocabulary (DPCVocab): An empirically derived framework of scientific data practices and curatorial processes. *Journal of the Association for Information Science and Technology*, *66*(3), 616–633.

Codd, E. F. (1970). A relational model of data for large shared data banks. *Communications of the ACM*, *13*(6), 377–387.

Izmirlioglu, A. (2017). The Correlates of War Dataset. *Journal of World-Historical Information*, *4*(1).

Rudkevich, G., & Travlos, K. (2014). Do we know too much about military conflict? A rapid evidence assessment of quantitative explanations of interstate conflict onset. In *International Studies Association Convention*.

Wickham, H. (2014). Tidy data. *Journal of Statistical Software*, *59*(10), 1–23.

Analyzing Public Opinion Toward the 2019 North Korea–United States Summit Through Mining Twitter

Jaewon Kim
Department of Library and Information Science,
Sungkyunkwan University,
Seoul, South Korea
finance1@skku.edu

Ji-young Kim
Department of Library and Information Science,
Sungkyunkwan University,
Seoul, South Korea
yes@kisti.re.kr

Yongjun Zhu
Department of Library and Information Science,
Sungkyunkwan University,
Seoul, South Korea
yzhu@skku.edu

ABSTRACT

The study aims to understand public opinion toward the 2019 North Korea–United States summit. Specifically, we investigate the changes in public opinion before and after the summit through comparing and analyzing networks of major keywords extracted from Twitter. We found a clear difference between public opinion before and after the summit. For example, we could see that the differences in public perception of End of war, peace, and freedom changed. The clear difference between Chinese and South Korean representatives can be interpreted as to how international relations and domestic situation lead to public opinion. This study shows that network analysis can be useful for quantitative public opinion analysis.

KEYWORDS

topic analysis; twitter; network analysis; opinion mining; North Korea

ASIS&T THESAURUS

Network analysis; Twitter; Social networking

INTRODUCTION

Many people express their opinions on twitter, and therefore, twitter is a rich data source of public opinion. Many studies have been conducted to mine public opinion from twitter. For example, Cram, Llewellyn, Hill, and Magdy (2017) analyzed the public opinion toward the UK general election 2017 and Wang, Hernandez, Newman, He, and Bian (2016) analyzed US Weekly Trends.

Undoubtedly, 2018 North Korea–United States Singapore summit is a recent big step toward world peace. Thanks to the summit, North Korea and the United States have been communicating with each other to find a way of cooperative development. South Korea is one of the most important key players in this change of international relations and people in the country are deeply concerned with any issues relate to North Korea. Therefore, investigating public opinion of South Korean is an effective way to understand how people perceive the summit and what are their matters of primary concerns. The study aims to investigate public opinion among South Korean by analyzing twitter data. Specifically, we analyze tweets posted by South Korean on the issues relate to the next summit that 2019 North Korea–United States Hanoi summit in a temporal manner to identify trends and primary concerns among them.

82nd Annual Meeting of the Association for Information Science & Technology | Melbourne, Australia | 19–23 October, 2019

DOI: 10.1002/pra2.00135

DATA COLLECTION AND METHOD

With "Kim Jung-un" and "Trump" as the keywords, we collected twitter texts for eight weeks, four weeks before and after the 2019 North Korea–United States Hanoi summit using Google Colaboratory and twitterscraper (Taspinar & Schuirmann, 2017). In total, we collected 79,773 tweets that mention the two keywords. After the data preprocessing and removal of duplicate tweets, we obtained 25,589 tweets created during the four weeks before the summit (Jan 31 ~ Feb 27) and 34,476 tweets during the other four weeks after the summit (Feb 28 ~ Mar 27). Konlpy (Park & Cho, 2014) was used to perform part-of-speech tagging and noun terms were extracted from the tweets. 69 noun terms that appeared more than 450 times were selected and used as the major keywords. Based on the selected keywords, we constructed co-occurrence matrix for each period.

RESULTS

Based on the co-occurrence matrix, we generated a public opinion network using gephi (Bastian, Heymann, & Jacomy, 2009). Public opinion networks consist of nodes that represents major keywords and edges that represents the co-occurrence values of pairs of keywords.

Label size of nodes is proportional to PageRank score (Brin & Page, 1998). The width of the edge is expressed by rescaling the maximum value to 25 and the minimum value to 0.1. Networks are clustered into communities by Modularity class (Blondel, Guillaume, Lambiotte, & Lefebvre, 2008). Color is used to differentiate each community. The name of

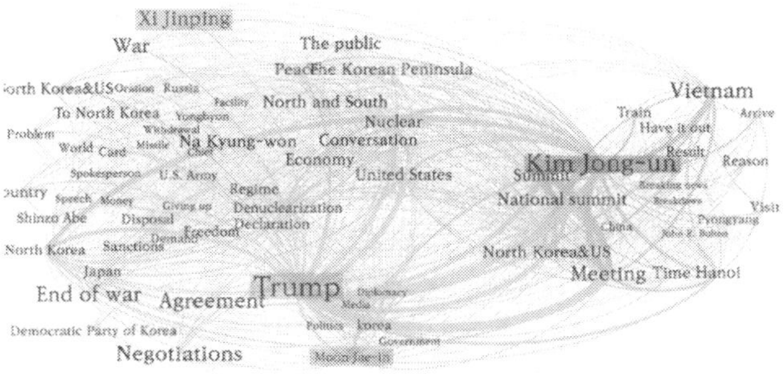

Figure 1. Public opinion network (before the summit).

each community is assigned with the name of the keyword that has the highest PageRank score in the community.

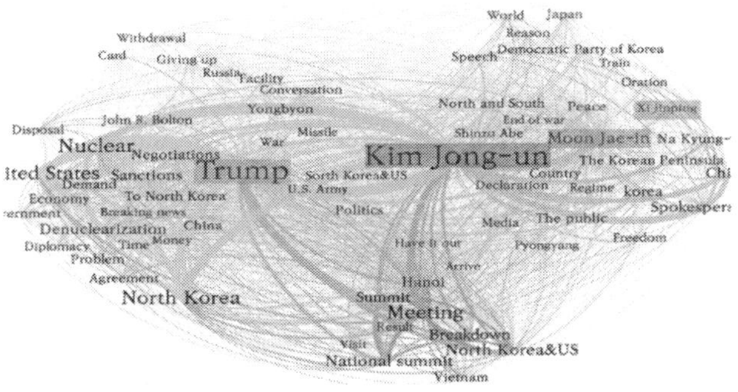

Figure 2. Public opinion network (after the summit).

From the two figures, we clearly see the following changes. The Kim Jung-un community increased from 19 to 26 nodes while the Trump community decreased from 50 to 32 nodes. We can see that people's interest in Kim Jung-un has increased after the summit. After the summit, a new community-meeting which has 11 nodes emerged. Overall, we see that the major keywords became more organized after the summit, from which we can tell that people had more clear understanding on the overall situation.

A few nodes that belonged to the Trump community in Figure 1 moved to the Kim Jung-un community in Figure 2. They include Moon Jae-in, Xi Jinping, Shinzo Abe, End of war, peace, and freedom. The change can be interpreted as the rise of Kim Jong-un's role after the summit and the importance of the relationship between Kim Jong-un and the Presidents of neighboring countries.

South Korea and China are the two countries that play important roles in the North Korea-U. S. relations. The two countries' presidents Moon Jae-in (South Korea) and Xi Jinping (China) are also two of the moved nodes. Xi Jinping made Kim Jung-un 's train pass through China and prepared for the summit with him. Moon Jae-in has acted as a facilitator since the summit and arranged a private meeting with Kim Jung-un. These might be part of the reasons for the two nodes' community movement.

CONCLUSION

The study showed changes in public opinion toward the 2019 North Korea–United States Hanoi summit through analyzing public opinion networks of twitter keywords. Through the network analysis of public opinion, major communities and the movement of keywords were identified. Before the summit, Trump was considered to play a more important role in improving the relationship between the two countries, but after the summit, people perceived the increasing role of Kim Jong-un. In addition, presidents of South Korea and China showed changes in community membership after the summit. It was possible to see public perception of the countries involved. The limitations of the study include the limited use of part of speech (i.e., nouns). Including other parts-of-speech may make it possible to identify more detailed changes. Future research may track changes in public opinion over a longer period to understand a broader impact of the summit. It is also worth studying in the future how much influence the media has had on public opinion during the same period.

REFERENCES

Bastian, M., Heymann, S., & Jacomy, M. (2009). Gephi: an open source software for exploring and manipulating networks. In *Third International AAAI Conference on Weblogs and Social Media*.

Blondel, V. D., Guillaume, J.-L., Lambiotte, R., & Lefebvre, E. (2008). Fast unfolding of communities in large networks. *Journal of Statistical Mechanics: Theory and Experiment, 2008*(10), P10008.

Brin, S., & Page, L. (1998). The anatomy of a large-scale hypertextual web search engine. *Computer Networks and ISDN Systems, 30*(1–7), 107–117.

Cram, L., Llewellyn, C., Hill, R., & Magdy, W. (2017). UK General Election 2017: A Twitter Analysis. *ArXiv* Preprint ArXiv:1706.02271.

Park, E. L., & Cho, S. (2014). KoNLPy: Korean natural language processing in Python. *Proceedings of the 26th Annual Conference on Human & Cognitive Language Technology, 6*.

Taspinar, A., & Schuirmann, L. (2017).*Twitterscraper 0.2. 7: Python Package Index*.

Wang, W., Hernandez, I., Newman, D. A., He, J., & Bian, J. (2016). Twitter analysis: Studying US weekly trends in work stress and emotion. *Applied Psychology, 65*(2), 355–378.

Toward Computational Reproducibility: A Doctoral Student's Story of Passing the Baton

Jenna Kim
School of Information Sciences,
University of Illinois at
Urbana-Champaign,
Urbana, IL, USA
jkim682@illinois.edu

Catherine Blake
School of Information Sciences,
University of Illinois at
Urbana-Champaign,
Urbana, IL, USA
clblake@illinois.edu

Peter T. Darch
School of Information Sciences,
University of Illinois at
Urbana-Champaign,
Urbana, IL, USA
ptdarch@illinois.edu

ABSTRACT

Computational reproducibility is a critical first step to supporting data reuse. Incentives that encourage data reuse within an academic setting are unlikely to be compelling for students who decide not to continue in academe. The goal of this work is to identify key barriers in the most likely of scenarios with computational reuse, when a doctoral student reproduces work done by another student from the same lab.

KEYWORDS

Reproducibility; data reuse; data curation

ASIS&T THESAURUS

Reproducibility; information reuse; data curation.

INTRODUCTION

Demand for reproducible research has become pervasive across research communities and funding agencies. For example, in the United States, the National Science Foundation requires researchers to submit data management plans with new grant application that will help to ensure that research data will be preserved and made openly available (Diekema, Wesolek, & Walters, 2014).

Researchers have attempted to reproduce published studies in their fields, often with discouraging results. According to a *Nature* survey of 1,576 scholars conducted in 2016, more than 70% of respondents had tried and failed to reproduce another researcher's experiments, and more than half had failed to reproduce their own experiments (Baker, 2016). Data on how much of scientific research is reproducible are rare. The *Nature* survey revealed that the best-known analyses from psychology and cancer biology found rates of around 40% and 10%, respectively.

Reproducibility can take a range of forms. One form, the focus of much research in information sciences, is *computational reproducibility (CR)*, which is characterized by the ability to rerun the computational analyses involved in original research. To test CR requires access to the raw data and code underpinning the original analysis. Many scholars and policymakers have formulated best practices for researchers to make their research computationally reproducible, such as open archiving of data and providing documentation for code (AlNoamany & Borghi, 2018); however, little work has been done to explore the extent to which these best practices improve reproducibility in practice. Moreover, many of the incentives around supporting CR are predicated in part on an author remaining in academe.

A new doctoral student will often reproduce findings to deepen their understanding of work described in a paper. When a student graduates, a good advisor will ensure that the code and data developed for their dissertation have been well documented. But as the student and advisor often share tacit knowledge, it can be difficult for either party to ensure that the depth of documentation is sufficient to provide to a new user.

We were provided with an opportunity to evaluate the computational reproducibility of a dissertation when a new student wanted to extend work that was developed by a graduating student who was leaving academia. During the process, gaps needed to repeat or extend the analysis from prior work were documented which allowed us to address the following questions: (1) What major challenges arise while testing computational reproducibility? (2) What underlying factors contribute to these challenges?

METHODOLOGY

A new doctoral student attempted to replicate software and data developed for a PhD dissertation (Gabb, 2019) and a journal article (Gabb & Blake, 2016). The goal of the initial research was to prioritize the chemical ingredients in consumer products and their most prevalent combinations for risk assessment based on likely exposure and retention.

As per good reproducibility practices, the dataset and source code from the doctoral work were provided by the graduating student via open access and thus publicly available for download. In addition, the processes used to collect and convert the raw data along with intermediate outputs and the final results

82nd Annual Meeting of the Association for Information Science & Technology | Melbourne, Australia | 19–23 October, 2019

DOI: 10.1002/pra2.00134

were described in 7 workflows such as that shown in Figure 1. A total number of 92 distinct files and scripts were tested on Amazon Web Services (AWS) EC2 instance running Linux, following the processing steps and workflows described in the dissertation.

RESULTS

Most of the code ran successfully, but despite good documentation and excellent code and data availability, about 10% of the workflows could not be immediately replicated. The issues were resolved via 62 email exchanges and 1 face-to-face meeting that took place over a 6-month period. There were 3 key reproducibility issues:

1. Software versioning differences: The majority of errors were caused by discrepancies between operating systems and versions of the software, which were not specifically described in the paper. For example, the initial work was run on Linux with Python 2.7, whereas the replication experiment was conducted in a Windows environment using Python 3.6. Windows and Linux have different file systems and the code in the paper was never tested on Windows. Lastly an external software package that was required was not mentioned and needed to be installed, specifically html2text that was used to extract the retail hierarchies from HTML.
2. Documentation discrepancies: Minor mismatches in file names and file formats prevented some of the workflow from running. In addition, some files were missing or located in a different folder which caused IOError messages.
3. Manual processes: The entire analytical process was not fully automated. For example, intermediate steps included manual evaluation and correction before moving to the next workflow. These steps that were necessary to ensure the validity of the research results remove the possibility of being computationally reproducible.

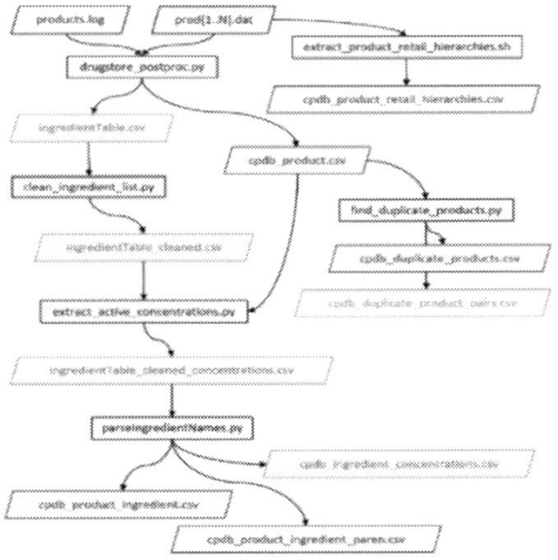

Figure 1. Example workflow (1 of 7) that extracts and cleans data from the raw consumer product HTML files.

DISCUSSION

Many factors can contribute to the lack of reproducible research such as difficulties in obtaining the original data, the availability of source code and good documentation. Both the student and advisor of the dissertation under investigation in this study had long histories in industrial software development and thus were very familiar with good practices surrounding documentation and software testing. We posit that the number and type of documentation errors would therefore be typical of most dissertations. The attempt to reproduce this work is consistent with Reproducibility Enhancement Principles (REP) where independent regenerations of the research results are enabled with the minimal components such as the input data, the computational steps that produce the findings, and the workflow describing how to generate the results using the data and code (Stodden et al., 2016).

However, the results show that simply sharing data and code is not sufficient. It is also critical to document the software environment and versions to ensure reusability and reproducibility of research results. There is little that can be done to ensure that code works on future in software versions, but identifying the versions can signal to the person reproducing the work which version to use. However, even software that is initially reproducible will degrade as new versions of software become available and old versions are no longer supported.

One of the biggest tensions we observed was between preserving, archiving, and releasing research products (data, code, and documentation) versus actually reusing those materials. For example, access to the intermediate files was necessary, but archiving those files is not well-supported by existing infrastructures and is not required by data management policies. Further, although comprehensive documentation was provided, it is extremely difficult to capture all of tacit knowledge necessary to ensure computational reproducibility. Lastly, not all research is completely computable. Any human effort employed within the research process to ensure accuracy falls outside the bounds of computational reproducibility.

REFERENCES

AlNoamany, Y., & Borghi, J. A. (2018). Toward computational reproducibility: researcher perspectives on the use and sharing of software. *PeerJ Computer Science*, *4*, e163.

Baker, M. (2016). 1,500 scientists lift the lid on reproducibility. *Nature News*, *533*(7604), 452.

Diekema, A. R., Wesolek, A., & Walters, C. D. (2014). The NSF/NIH Effect: Surveying the effect of data management requirements on faculty, sponsored programs, and institutional repositories. *The Journal of academic librarianship*, *40*(3-4), 322–331.

Gabb, H. A. (2019). In University of Illinois at Urbana-Champaign, *An informatics approach to prioritizing risk assessment for chemicals and chemical combinations based on near-field exposure from consumer products*. (Doctoral dissertation. Champaign, IL.

Gabb, H. A., & Blake, C. (2016). An informatics approach to evaluating combined chemical exposures from consumer products: a case study of asthma-associated chemicals and potential endocrine disruptors. *Environmental health perspectives*, *124*(8), 1155–1165.

Stodden, V., McNutt, M., Bailey, D. H., Deelman, E., Gil, Y., Hanson, B., … Taufer, M. (2016). Enhancing reproducibility for computational methods. *Science*, *354*(6317), 1240–1241.

A Study for Categorizing Relations Between Headword and Aliases

Jiyoun Kim
Department of German Linguistics and Literature, Sungkyunkwan University, Seoul, Republic of Korea
kite92@skku.edu

Youngeun Koo
Department of German Linguistics and Literature, Sungkyunkwan University, Seoul, Republic of Korea
sarah8835@skku.edu

Yongjun Zhu
Department of Library and Information Science, Sungkyunkwan University, Seoul, Republic of Korea
yzhu@skku.edu

ABSTRACT

In this study, we propose a method of categorizing relations between a headword and its aliases using Korean Wikipedia data. We propose orthographically similar types and orthographically different types. Orthographically similar types are divided into 5 types: Word space, Pronunciation difference, Omission, Abbreviation, and Word order change while different types are also classified into 4 types: Foreign word, Acronym, Paraphrased expression and Call name. We show examples to verify the proposed method.

KEYWORDS

Headword; Alias; Wikipedia

ASIS&T THESAURUS

Wikipedia; Written communication; Classification theory

INTRODUCTION

People use various language expressions to refer to a real-world entity. Although an entity can be expressed in many different ways, people can understand well about the entity. In written texts, however, term inconsistency may cause problems such as ambiguity. In this paper, we denote 'terms' as all expressions that represent a single unique object. Among the terms, we refer to 'headword' as the most common and representative expression and 'alias' as all the other terms except the headword.

To resolve ambiguity caused by term inconsistency, we need to correctly identify relations between headwords and aliases. Headword-alias relations are multi-faceted and different approaches are needed to tackle them. For example, terms such as 'United Nation' and 'UN', have orthographical similarity, while other terms such as 'water' and 'H2O', show no orthographical similarity.

This paper focuses on the categorization of the relations between headwords and aliases. Using Wikipedia's "redirection" information, we aim to identify criteria of categorizing the relations. Specifically, this study proposes approaches of pre-processing various terms in the written texts to solve the term-inconsistency problem.

82nd Annual Meeting of the Association for Information Science & Technology | Melbourne, Australia | 19–23 October, 2019

DOI: 10.1002/pra2.00136

METHOD

In this study, we use Korean Wikipedia's 'redirection' data, named 'Redirect', to get a list of pairs of headwords and their aliases where a headword has multiple aliases. Wikipedia provides 'Redirect', which is a function that guides visitors from one Wikipedia page to another. This function helps people locate more quickly the pages that they are searching for. One of the purposes of this function is to redirect alternative names of articles to the most appropriate article title ("Wikipedia: Redirection", 2019). Therefore, by analyzing the 'Redirect', we can identify the relation between headwords and their aliases.

To extract redirection data from Wikipedia, we performed the following steps. First, we download a Wiki dump files, named 'kowiki-latest-all-titles.gz', which contains titles of all Wikipedia pages ordered alphabetically. Titles are considered as 'terms' that comprise Wikipedia. In total, there are 1,015,928 terms in the Wiki dump file. Next, we use 'MediaWiki API' and the dump file to extract all 'Redirect' information from Wikipedia using Python. This step enables us to create a list of pairs of headwords and aliases. Through this step, pairs like [유엔-국제연합] and [유엔- UN] can be derived. Here, the title of a 'redirected page' is considered as a headword and titles of 'redirecting pages' as its aliases.

We classify the terms according to relation types between a headword and aliases in to orthographically similar ('TS') and orthographically different type ('TD'). Table 1 shows the types of the relations that we propose.

- TS_1 (Word space): multi word with or without space between words
- TS_2 (Pronunciation difference): orthographical difference resulted from different pronunciation
- TS_3 (Omission): leaving out insignificant part of word
- TS_4 (Abbreviation): short form of a word or phrase, made by leaving out some of the letters

- TS_5 (Word order change): multi word with change of the order
- TD_1 (Foreign word): corresponding, translated expression
- TD_2 (Acronym): a word composed of the first letters of the words
- TD_3 (Paraphrased expression): different form, but same/-similar meaning
- TD_4 (Call name): different form and less relevant meaning, but conventionally same/similar usage

Orthographically similar types of headword-aliases relation consist of 'Word space', 'Pronunciation difference', 'Omission', 'Abbreviation' and 'Word order change'. These are mostly affected by linguistic characteristic of Korean and frequent use of foreign expression in Korean. Especially, 'Word space(TS_1)' appeared a lot in our data. In principle, multi-word terms should be separated by space in Korean language. However, this principle is easily violated, when the multi-word-term is regarded to expresses one single concept. For this reason, 'Word space' type is easily observable with most types of terms. Also, due to frequent use of foreign expression in Korean, headword and aliases are 'Pronunciation difference(TS_2)' type in many cases. If the original term is not originated from Korean, this type of aliases are generated. Because Hangeul, the Korean alphabet, cannot match one to one to foreign alphabet, there are more than two terms that express one foreign term. Moreover, 'Omission(TS_3)' is also a commonly used type. Even if insignificant parts of terms are omitted, people can understand the term by the principle of economic usage of language. This principle effects the formation of aliases. This category is relevant to all kinds of terms, whether it is abstract or conceptual terms.

Next, orthographically different types of headword-aliases are 'Foreign word', 'Acronym', 'Paraphrased expression' and 'Call name'. These kinds of relations are caused by the other factors of the terms like presence of synonyms or the origin of terms. If the term is originated from another language and has translated form of Korean or vice versa, this causes 'Foreign word(TD_1)' type of relation. 'Acronym (TD_2)' type of relation occurs, when the single term has multiple words in other language. The acronym of the term can be another alias and the pronunciation of the acronym in Korean makes up another alias. In addition, 'Paraphrased expression(TD_3)' type can be found, if the headword is too expertise or abstract. These kinds of headwords tend to have paraphrased expressions as aliases. Lastly, 'Call name(TD_4)' type occurs when the term can be specifically and concretely designated This type of terms have aliased because of many external factors such as where speakers live(dialect), how old speakers are(baby talk), which style speakers use(polite expression).

RESULT

To examine validity of the proposed types, we provide example of each type found in Wikipedia data. For each example, first line is the original expression in Korean, second line is its translated expression in English, and the third line is its pronounced notation in Korean.

Type	Example		
	Original expression (H/A)	**Translated expression (H/A)**	**Pronounced form (H/A)**
TS_1	규슈대학/규슈대학	Kyushu University/ KyushuUniversity	(gyu-syutay-hak/ gyu-syu-tay-hak)
TS_2	그랜드캐니언/ 그랜드캐년	Grand Canyon/ Grand Canyon	(ku-layn-tukhay-ni-en/ ku-layn-tukhay-nyen)
TS_3	성라자로마을/ 라자로마을	St. Lazarus Village/Lazarus Village	(seng la-ca-lo ma-ul/ seng la-ca-lo ma-ul)
TS_4	동북아시아/동북아	Northeast Asia/Northeast Asia	(tong-pwuk-a-si-a/ tong-pwuk-a)
TS_5	동부인도/인도동부	East India/India East	(tong-pwu in-to/ in-to tong-pwu)
TD_1	염세주의/페시미즘	Pessimism/Pessimis m	(yem-sey-cwu-uy/ phey-si-mi-cum)
TD_2	성균관대학교/ SKKU	Sung Kyun Kwan university/ SKKU	(seng-kyun-kwan-tay-hak-kyo/SKKU)
TD_3	선헤엄/입영	Treading water/Egg Beater Kick	(sen-hey-em/ip-yeng)
TD_4	성룡/재키찬	ChéngLóng/Jackie Chan	(seng-lyong/cay-khichan)

Table 1. Headword-alias examples of each type.

LIMITATION & FUTURE WORK

We could find that there is a tendency between category and pairs that belong to each category. As mentioned above, 'paraphrased expressions' type and 'Call names' type have contrast definitions with regard to the relevance of the meaning. As we analyzed, paraphrased expressions tend to occurred with terms that are abstract and conceptual terms. On the contrary, objects that are concrete and specifics have tendency to have aliases that belong to 'Call names' type. It would be meaningful work, if we not only divide headword-alias pair into categories, but also examine the tendency between term's head-alias relation type and its semantic class.

REFERENCES

Wikipedia. Redirect. In *Wikipedia*. Retrieved from https://en.wikipedia.org/wiki/Wikipedia:Redirect

Wikipedia. Database download. In *Wikipedia*. Retrieved from https://ko.wikipedia.org/wiki/위키백과:데이터베이스_다운로드

Virtual Zenana: Reimagining Small World

Priya Kizhakkethil
University of North Texas,
Denton, United States
priyakizhakkethil@my.unt.edu

Gary Burnett
Florida State University,
Tallahassee, United States
gary.burnett@cci.fsu.edu

ABSTRACT

The concept of small world was used to study socio-economically and informationally poor communities, marked by norms and social types constraining information access. This poster presents a preliminary model of a reconceptualized small world designed to consider a world which is not information poor nor are its inhabitants purposively seeking information. The early stage research study looks at a diaspora small world, a gendered online community that coalesces around a shared interest in reading and writing fan fiction.

KEYWORDS

Information experience; context; small world; diaspora; leisure; fan communities

ASIS&T THESAURUS

Information behavior; Culture; Leisure activities

INTRODUCTION

Globalization has resulted in transnational movement of people creating diaspora communities and even though women have been a part of migratory flows, their perspectives and experiences remain largely underexplored. The transnational nature of immigrant networks underscore the necessity of taking into account the digital and online environments of immigrant and diaspora populations while studying their information worlds. Migration related literature also highlights the importance of leisure activities, including the consumption of ethnic media, in the everyday life of immigrant populations. The gendered nature of activities like fan fiction writing have been highlighted by studies of fan communities. The early stage research study covered by this poster looks at women belonging to the Indian diaspora and their participation in the leisure activity of fan fiction reading and writing, forming part of an online community. Long (2003) holds that reading groups may embody the concept of a deliberative space, a "counterhegemonic publics" (Fraser, 1989, p. 167), riding the boundary between public and private sphere. These diasporic environments which are "privately public and publicly private" (Papacharissi, 2010, p. 142) could be seen as online book clubs as well as small worlds and have been termed as "virtual zenanas". Zenana is a social or cultural practice seen across South Asia and across religions too, and refers to the part of a house or dwelling which belongs to girls and women. A reconceptualization of a small world in the form of a preliminary model is presented here.

SMALL WORLD

In Library and Information science, the concept of small world is associated with the work of Elfreda Chatman. Drawing on the work of Alfred Schutz and Manfred Kochen among others, Chatman used the concept of small world to study the everyday lives of communities that were socio-economically, as well as informationally poor. These worlds were described as been marked by a degree of predictability in their everyday happenings. People are seen to share "physical and/or conceptual space within a common landscape of cultural meaning" (Chatman, 2000, p. 3). A set of social norms and behaviors specific to its localized context, structures and defines the daily activities of the small world (Burnett & Jaeger, 2011). Chatman fully explicated the concept of small world in the theory of normative behavior, with its associated concepts of social norms, social type, world view and information behavior.

Savolainen (2008) noted Chatman's approach as that of functional sociology and her conception of a small world with its values and social norms is in line with the model of homo sociologicus which "explains action by pointing to collective norms and values, i.e., to rules which express a social 'ought'; social order is then guaranteed by a normative consensus" (Reckwitz, 2002, p. 245). The functional sociology approach places emphasis on group specific roles and norms that constrains information seeking. Chatman's work highlighted the importance of context, but Savolainen (2008) avers that a broader view of information seeking needs to be adopted for today's times marked by "increasing individualization characteristic of reflexive modernization" (p. 6) and the availability and use of extensive networked sources. People may be less prone to pressures induced by norms that direct the seeking of information. The efficacy of using the theory of normative behavior in studying virtual worlds, was noted by Burnett, Besant, and Chatman (2001), but Worrall (2014) who employed the framework of the theory of information world (of which the theory of normative behavior is a part) to study communities fostered by LibraryThing and

82nd Annual Meeting of the Association for Information Science & Technology | Melbourne, Australia | 19–23 October, 2019

DOI: 10.1002/pra2.00138

Goodreads, found social ties played a larger role, where "getting to know one another is more of a process of establishing social ties than socially typing others" (p. 209). A sense of community was another aspect noted by the aforementioned study forged around shared and common interests and values.

REIMAGINING A SMALL WORLD

The small world as a concept is useful to encapsulate a world which coalesces around a common interest, together with a common experience of being part of a diaspora, but it is felt that a reconceptualization of small world, especially a virtual one is required for the purpose of this study, the reason being; (1) the world looked at is not information poor, (2) the inhabitants of this world are not explicitly seeking or looking for information and (3) there is no institutional or organizational structure to impose some sort of order in the world, leading to establishment of norms. Putting information (and information behavior) aside, an attempt should be made to draw a picture of this world to understand it as a context in which people experience information and then identifying any associated practices surrounding that experience. In the words of Chatman (1996), "the process of understanding begins with research that looks at their social environment and that defines information from their perspective"(p.205).As a step toward a reconceptualization, based on the researcher's observation and understanding of the world under study and drawing on relevant literature, a preliminary model of a small world is presented below.

Primary Activity and Site of Activity

Social worlds have one primary activity and a site where these activities take place (Strauss, 1978). This is in line with the concept of an information ground, with Fisher and Naumer (2006) noting that people gather for a primary instrumental purpose and social interaction can be seen as a primary activity, with information flow as a by-product. This is also characteristic of Oldenburg's (1999) third place.

Social Ties

Social ties refer to the establishment of connections between people who inhabit a common space, through the process of interactions.

Sense of Community

According to McMillan and Chavis (1986) a sense of community has four elements; membership, influence, reinforcement and shared emotional connection.

World View

For this study world view has been defined as a common perspective arising out of shared ethnicity and culture, shared leisure interest, and even the experience of migration.

Mediated Practices

Virtual communities are characterized by the presence of mediated practices and following the approach adopted by Sköld (2013), the act of commenting, replying to comments, posting videos, gifs, etc., can be viewed as mediated practices.

The preliminary model would be used in the first stage of the study to address the question: How do the fanfiction blogs (or the spaces afforded by them) form and function as a small world? A content analysis of comments posted on five fan fiction blogs would be carried out followed by semi-structured interviews of at least twelve (12) participants and a focus group.

SIGNIFICANCE

Fisher and Naumer (2006) had noted the need for exploring how information grounds could form a part of small worlds, a point reinforced by Savolainen (2009) who argues for the research potential in viewing small world and information ground as complementary constructs. He notes that new attributes of social and spatial factors may be found if the phenomena of a small world were to be reconceptualized from the perspective of information ground and vice versa. This study is an attempt in this direction and thereby contribute toward conceptual and theoretical work in the field.

REFERENCES

Burnett, G., Besant, M., & Chatman, E. A. (2001). Small worlds: Normative behavior in virtual communities and feminist bookselling. *Journal of the American Society for Information Science and Technology*, *52*, 536–547.

Burnett, G., & Jaeger, P. T. (2011). The theory of information worlds and information behavior. In S. Amanda & J. Heinstrom, *New directions in information behavior* (pp. 161–177). Bingley, England: Emerald.

Chatman, E. A. (1996). The impoverished life-world of outsiders. *Journal of the American Society for information science*, *47*(3), 193–206.

Chatman, E. A. (2000). Framing social life in theory and research. *The New Review of Information Behaviour research*, *1*(December), 3–17.

Fisher, K. E., & Naumer, C. M. (2006). Information grounds: Theoretical basis and empirical findings on information flow in social settings. In A. Spink & C. Cole, *New directions in human information behavior* (pp. 93–111). Dordrecht: Springer.

Fraser, N. (1989). *Unruly practices: Power, discourse, and gender in contemporary social theory*. Minneapolis, MN: University of Minnesota Press.

Long, E. (2003). *Book clubs: Women and the uses of reading in everyday life*. Chicago, IL: University of Chicago Press.

McMillan, D. W., & Chavis, D. M. (1986). Sense of community: A definition and theory. *Journal of Community Psychology*, *14*(1), 6–23.

Oldenburg, R. (1999). *The great good place: Cafes, coffee shops, bookstores, bars, hair salons, and other hangouts at the heart of a community*. Cambridge, MA: Da Capo Press.

Papacharissi, Z. A. (2010). *A private sphere: Democracy in a digital age*. Cambridge, England: Polity.

Reckwitz, A. (2002). Toward a theory of social practices: A development in culturist theorizing. *European Journal of Social Theory*, *5*(2), 243–263.

Savolainen, R. (2008). *Everyday information practices*. Lanham, MD: The Scarecrow Press Inc.

Savolainen, R. (2009). Small world and information grounds as contexts of information seeking and sharing. *Library & Information Science Research*, *31*, 38–45. https://doi.org/10.1016/j.lisr.2008.10.007

Sköld, O. (2013). Tracing Traces: A document-centered approach to the preservation of virtual world communities. *Information Research*, *18*(3). Retrieved from http://www.informationr.net/ir/18-3/colis/paperC09.html

Strauss, A. (1978). A social world perspective. *Studies in Symbolic Interaction*, *1*(1), 119–128.

Worrall, A. (2014). *Roles of Digital Libraries as Boundary Objects within and Across Social and Information Worlds*. (doctoral dissertation). Florida State University.

Memory Making and Documenting in a Diaspora Small World

Priya Kizhakkethil
University of North Texas,
Denton, United States
priyakizhakkethil@my.unt.edu

ABSTRACT

Diaspora communities are known for the transnational nature of their information networks and it is imperative that information behavior research takes into account the global nature of their information worlds. This early stage research study looks at women belonging to a diaspora and part of an online community converging around a leisure activity, especially focusing on the role of memory making and documenting as part of their information and document experience.

KEYWORDS

Diaspora; fan communities; memory making; documentation

ASIS&T THESAURUS

Information behavior; Culture; Leisure activities

INTRODUCTION

Diaspora refers to ethnic communities which are dispersed around the globe and in the postmodern world, it is the result of transnational capitalism with its attendant movement of people, goods and capital. Migration studies note the role played by media in the acculturation process of immigrants (Raman & Harwood, 2016). Studies have also noted the role played by ethnic media in helping immigrants maintain ties with their home countries. Diasporas use ethnic media to provide scripts that enable them to enact and embody their "ethnicity in a transnational, transmedia global culture" (Ramasubramanian & Doshi, 2017, p. 183). Information and communication technologies allow diaspora communities to stay in touch with family and friends while enabling continued contact with their cultural roots, through the synchronous transnational participation in everyday life, altering the diasporic experience (Hegde, 2016). Pyati (2010) noted that diaspora are often part of a rich global information network and any information behavior research pertaining to them should take into account online diaspora information environments. There has been much research on the diasporic use of online communities as many view these as safe spaces, "enabling various kinds of identity formation" (Nikunen, 2013, p.1). Traversing distances and establishing connections with others around the world may not be limited to diasporic experience but virtual remembering may have particular significance in the context of diaspora and migration (Nikunen, 2013).

Cultural or collective memories refer to the collective memory of many which can span generations, unlike personal ones which are those of a person, experienced firsthand. Collective memories could be found in oral and written stories, as well as in gestures, rumors, cultural styles and in institutionalized cultural activities. Memory is considered cultural especially because it's mediated and uses symbols in communication, and the act of remembering is always socially and culturally situated, with material objects often supporting memory. Memories of a group is always social as it involves social interactions in discussions of the past. Worrall and Hyduk (2016) in a study of an online immigrant community notes that information sharing could lead to the invocation and sharing of cultural memories.

Women have always been a part of migratory flows, but their experiences and perspectives remain underexplored. Studies of fan communities overwhelmingly note the gendered natured of such communities with women said to write more of what is termed as fan fiction. Information studies have mostly looked at place based settlement and acculturation experiences of immigrant and refugee populations, especially information seeking surrounding such experiences. This poster covers an early stage research study which looks at women belonging to the Indian diaspora and who are part of an online community which converges around the shared interest of reading and writing fan fiction. The online spaces occupied by this community which are "privately public and publicly private" (Papacharissi, 2010, p. 142) has been termed "virtual zenanas", and they can also be viewed as small worlds. According to Appadurai (2003) the life of those belonging to diasporas are riddled with confusion about what needs to be remembered and recovered, often leading to what is a "deliberate effort to construct a variety of archives, ranging from the most intimate and personal (such as the memory of one's earlier bodily self) to the most public and collective, which usually take the form of shared narratives and

82nd Annual Meeting of the Association for Information Science & Technology | Melbourne, Australia | 19–23 October, 2019

DOI: 10.1002/pra2.00139

practices" (p. 21). Drawing on this idea of a memory archive, a purpose of this study is to see whether the communicative material, (textual and non-textual), that is generated, and which supports these spaces, can be conceptualized as a serendipitous memory archive.

BLOGS AS DOCUMENTS

Sköld (2013) studying virtual gaming communities, makes the point that placing the analytical focus on documents instead of on their latent information helps in bringing to light the important role played by them in the socio cultural life of virtual communities. This is because these virtual worlds are characterized by the pervasiveness of mediated practices enabled by new media technologies. Sköld (2013) draws on Levy (2001) who defines documents as 'talking things' and narrowing this further means that documents are primarily about speaking. Viewed in this manner a "document can be understood as a material object connected to an activity aimed at making it talk in some ways, to someone" (Sköld, 2013, p. 6) and by extension the blogs on which the fan fiction stories are hosted and the mediated practices supported by these sites like posting comments, replying to comments, liking comments, posting images, gifs and videos, etc., can be viewed as documents.

Figure 1 shows the framework of the study.

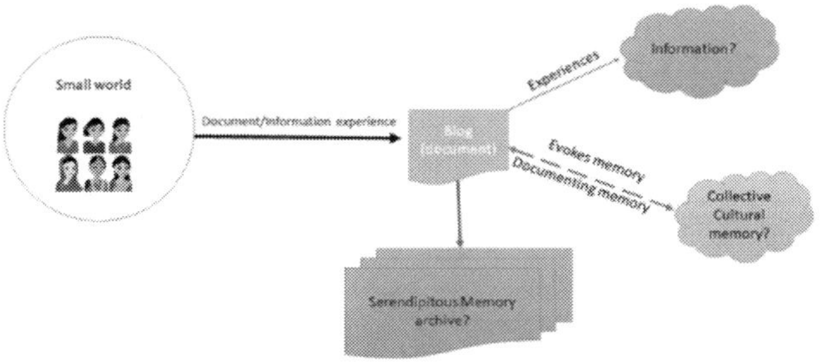

Figure 1.

THEORETICAL FRAMEWORK AND RESEARCH DESIGN

Based on the researcher's observation and understanding of this world and a literature review, a preliminary model of a small world has been drawn up and a theoretical framework combining information experience as a concept, Latham's (2014) model of document experience (from a user/reader perspective), Gorichanaz & Latham's document phenomenology, and Gorichanaz's (2018) first person model of documentation (creator/writer perspective) will be employed. Document experience has been termed as information experience from a document perspective. According to Bruce, Davis, Hughes, Partridge, and Stoodley (2014) researching information experience of people takes one "deeply into their existence, to explore what is experienced as information and how it is experienced, how information is present or appears and its role and influence" (p. 5). The broad research question is: How is the diasporic small world a serendipitous memory archive? With specific questions; a) How is collective memory making enacted in practice? b) How does the small world environment impact the collective memory making? c) What role does cultural knowledge play in memory making?

Adopting a qualitative research approach inspired by institutional ethnography along the lines adopted by Ocepek (2016), data will be collected through semi-structured interviews of at least 12 participants and content analysis of comments posted on five fan fiction blogs.

SIGNIFICANCE

The study hopes to address a gap in the information studies literature which has taken a diaspora perspective by looking at the transnational nature of these communities. It will also address a gap in literature which has looked at cultural memory invocation and documenting of the same, and as Sköld (2015) noted, there is a dearth of studies which have considered the interplay between memory making, documentary practices and affordances of new media in virtual communities and this is especially interesting in the context of migration and leisure.

REFERENCES

Appadurai, A. (2003). Archive and aspiration. In J. Brouwer, A. Mulder, & S. Charlton, *Information is alive* (pp. 14–25).

Bruce, C., Davis, K., Hughes, H., Partridge, H., & Stoodley, I. (2014). Information experience: Contemporary perspectives. In C. Bruce, K. Davis, H. Hughes, H. Partridge, & I. Stoodley, *Information experience: Approaches to theory and practice* (pp. 3–15). Bingley, England: Emerald.

Gorichanaz. T. (2018). Understanding self-documentation (doctoral dissertation). Drexel University.

Gorichanaz, T., & Latham, K. F. (2016). Document phenomenology: A framework for holistic analysis. *Journal of Documentation*, *72*(6), 1114–1133.

Latham, K. F. (2014). Experiencing documents. *Journal of Documentation*, *70*(4), 544–561.

Levy, D. M. (2001). *Scrolling forward: Making sense of documents in the digital age*. New York, NY: Arcade.

Nikunen, K. (2013). Re-imagining the past in transnational online communities. *Transit*, *8*(2), 1–17.

Ocepek, M. G. (2016). Everyday shopping: an exploration of the information behaviors of grocery shoppers (doctoral dissertation). University of Texas, Austin.

Papacharissi, Z. A. (2010). *A private sphere: Democracy in a digital age*. Cambridge, England: Polity.

Pyati, A. (2010). Information needs and behaviors of diasporic populations. In *Encyclopedia of library and information sciences* (3rd ed., pp. 2459–2466). https://doi.org/10.1081/E-ELIS3-120044049

Raman, P., & Harwood, J. (2016). Media usage and acculturation: Asian Indian professionals in Silicon Valley. *Journal of Intercultural Communication Research, 45*(5), 355–373.

Ramasubramanian, S., & Doshi, M. J. (2017). Ethnic performance, language proficiency, and ethnic media use among Indian American immigrants. *Journal of International and Intercultural Communication, 10*(3), 183–200.

Sköld, O. (2013). Tracing traces: A document-centred approach to the preservation of virtual world communities. *InformationResearch, 18*(3). Retrieved from http://www.informationr.net/ir/18-3/colis/paperC09.html

Sköld, O. (2015). Documenting virtual world cultures: Memory- making and documentary practices in the City of Heroes community. *Journal of Documentation, 71* (2), 294–316.

Worrall, A., & Hyduk, A. (2016). Information values, sharing, and cultural memory: interactions with ICT use in an online immigrant community. *IConference 2016 Proceedings*.

Argumentation Model of WeChat Group Chat: Evidence From Content Analysis With Inductive Coding

Jiyao Lai
Department of Information Management,
Peking University,
Beijing, China
laijiyao@pku.edu.cn

Yuzhe Han
Department of Information Management,
Peking University,
Beijing, China
hanyuzhe@pku.edu.cn

Pengyi Zhang
Department of Information Management,
Peking University,
Beijing, China
pengyi@pku.edu.cn

ABSTRACT

Argumentation, the act of defending one's inherent knowledge or views through speech expression, is a kind of widespread information expression and communication behavior. In this poster, we aim to explore the characteristics and patterns of argumentation in social media to examine basic rules the patterns follow by conducting content analysis of the transcript of a WeChat Group Chat. We build a theoretical model of argumentation behavior in mobile social media using the inductive coding and find that social media has a great influence on argumentation.

KEYWORDS

Argumentation; Information expression behavior; Mobile social media

ASIS&T THESAURUS

Information behavior; Qualitative analysis

INTRODUCTION

People use social networking services (SNS) to communicate with others frequently. Argumentation occurs in such online SNS settings as well. The expression behavior of argumentation has changed in online settings compared with traditional face-to-face communication. Schneider and others (2013) identified argumentation patterns that distributed ad-hoc online task groups use in evaluation and decision-making. Mao and others (2014) aim to extract one type of attack, the directive speech act formed as an imperative from Wikipedia Article for Deletion Discussions. In addition, the availability of the communication records in online communications offers opportunities to use computational techniques to automatically detect user opinions and rationales. In a variety of social media in China, a common phenomenon is that people express their opinions on Traditional Chinese Medicine (TCM) which often causes controversies. TCM practitioners use herbal medicines and various mind and body practices, such as acupuncture and tai chi, to treat or prevent health problems. TCM reflects the traditional Chinese cultural concept, such like Yin-Yang. Western medicine (or modern medicine) based on empirical science has various conflicts with TCM in theory, treatment and even medical policy. This poster chooses TCM as a topic of argumentation to study the pattern of people's argumentation behavior in online SNS communications.

82nd Annual Meeting of the Association for Information Science & Technology | Melbourne, Australia | 19–23 October, 2019

DOI: 10.1002/pra2.00140

METHODS

This poster conducted a qualitative content analysis using inductive coding method. We coded nearly 500 posts produced in a three-day discussion and argument on TCM in a WeChat group. All data was anonymized. This research used open coding, axial coding and selective coding to analyze and study the data.

Open Coding

Open coding refers to the conceptual labeling of any text segment recorded, and then the categorization of the initial concept is realized by further refining. Through this step, we obtained 12 categories: setting topic, constructing argument, deconstructing argument, rhetoric, catharsis, target stigmatization, opponent stigmatization, status, interpersonal relationship, experience, philosophical cognition, object cognition.

Axial Coding

Based on the 12 categories mentioned above, the axial coding resulted four fundamental categories, while the initial category becomes the support and corresponding category of the four fundamental categories. These four fundamental categories include "argumentation ", "emotional expression", "cognition" and "context".

Selective Coding

We used selective coding to analyze the connection between categories and describe the behavior patterns of the "story line". The so-called story line refers to the typical relationship structure between categories. In combination with the text, the typical relationship structure between the main categories is shown as following:

- Cognition ←→Argumentation: ndividual cognitive state, including philosophical knowledge, influences the content and behavior of argumentation and the evaluation of other's arguments.
- Emotional Expression←→Argumentation: The emotions expressed are influenced by the content of argument, they also affect the individual's argument behavior.
- Context←→Argumentation: Status in context influences the way and content of argument, and the latter also strengthens the construction of context.
- Context←→Cognition: "Personal experiences" in context always influence their perception of things (traditional Chinese medicine)

Finally, we built a theoretical model of argumentation behavior in mobile social media.

RESULTS

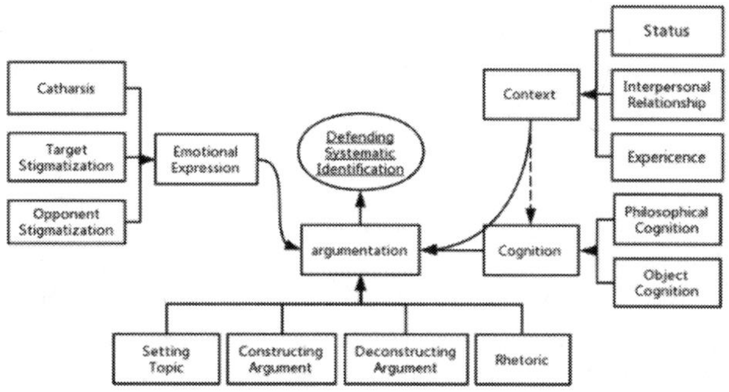

Figure 1. Theoretical model of argumentation behavior in mobile social media.

This model represents the ultimate goal and core pursuit of the whole expression behavior with "defending systematic identification". Specifically, this means the understanding of traditional Chinese medical is actually a kind of recognition (or disapproval) of a specific system (represented here as traditional Chinese medical or Yin-Yang system).And the four main categories of "demonstration expression", "emotional expression", "situation" and "cognition" respectively represent the main content of argumentation behavior, and there are corresponding support categories under each main category. Argumentation is affected by emotional expression, context and cognition. People's controversy about TCM is essentially due to their different cognition, such as gnosis and agnosticism. Emotional expression is more irrational but common in argument. Context, includes status, interpersonal relationship and experience affects both argumentation and cognition. It's not difficult to understand that a person who is cured by TCM will support TCM more. Besides, context affects argumentation directly. Status can be used as a means of attack or defense. Experiences about TCM can be evidence. Interpersonal relationship influences the way of expression.

At the same time, we find that social media has a great influence on argumentation. First, the expression is more fragmented and short. They respond quickly and emotionally. Second, because there are more people involved in the debate, the information in group chat is rich and the topic changes quickly. They often started arguing about the next problem before reaching consensus on the previous one. Third, the way of argumentation is multiplicity in social media.

CONCLUSION AND DISCUSSION

The purpose of argumentation is defending systematic identification. Based on the typical relationship structure, we can find that these relationships are essentially related to the core concept of "defending system identification". The understanding of TCM is a kind of recognition (or disapproval) of a specific system (represented here as TCM or Yin-Yang system). All the fundamental categories and related structures mentioned above are essentially the defense of one's own inherent system identity. Therefore, "defending system identification" is the core category. And the argumentation serves the fundamental purpose of defending system identification directly, all kinds of argumentation methods aim at this goal. Compared with previous studies, this poster builds a systematic model, and analyze the factors affecting argumentation. Further research can explore specific factors and situations of argumentation in mobile social media.

ACKNOWLEDGMENTS

The authors received supports from travel funds from Peking University and from NSFC Grant #71603012.

REFERENCES

Jodi Schneider, J., Samp K., Passant, A., and Decker, S. (2013). Arguments about deletion: How experience improves the acceptability of arguments in ad-hoc online task groups. *Proceedings of the 2013 Conference on Computer Supported Cooperative Work*, 1069–1080. ACM.

Mao, W. T., Mercer, R., & Xiao, L. (2014). *Extracting Imperatives from Wikipedia Article for Deletion Discussions, First Workshop on Argumentation Mining at the 52nd Annual Meeting of the Association for Computational Linguistics (ACL)*, June 22 – 27, Baltimore, MD.

Peldszus, A., & Stede, M. (2013). From argument diagrams to argumentation mining in texts: A survey. *International Journal of Cognitive Informatics and Natural Intelligence (IJCINI)*, *7*, 1–31.

Xiao, L., & Askin, N. (2014). What influences online deliberation? A Wikipedia study. *Journal of the American Society for Information Science and Technology*, *65*, 898–910.

Xiao, L., & Conroy, N. (2017). Discourse relations in rationale-containing text-segments. *Journal of the American Society for Information Science and Technology*. Retrieved from http://rdcu.be/v7s2

A Crowdsourcing Approach to Explore Helping Motives in a Smart City: A Preliminary Analysis

Chei Sian Lee
Nanyang Technological University, Singapore
leecs@ntu.edu.sg

Dion Hoe-Lian Goh
Nanyang Technological University, Singapore
ashlgoh@ntu.edu.sg

Sei-Ching Joanna Sin
Nanyang Technological University, Singapore
joanna.sin@ntu.edu.sg

Hamzah Osop
University of Sydney, Australia
hamzah.osop@sydney.edu.au

Yin Leng Theng
Nanyang Technological University, Singapore
tyltheng@ntu.edu.sg

ABSTRACT

Drawing from the functional approach to volunteerism, the aim of this preliminary study is to investigate the motives driving people's willingness to use a mobile crowdsourcing app to voluntarily help others in a smart city. Data were collected from 125 individuals. Preliminary results indicate that there are three categories of motives (i.e. Values, Protective and Professional) underlying helping behaviors in a smart city.

KEYWORDS

Crowdsourcing; Smart City; Helping; Motivations

ASIS&T THESAURUS

Collaboration; Social web; Information behavior; Information use

INTRODUCTION

A smart city leverages modern technologies to enable its efficient functioning to improve the everyday lives of its residents. With the proliferation of mobile devices, crowdsourcing apps for the smartphone have the potential to harness the power of the mobile crowd to help the community (Lee, Goh, Osop, Sin, & Theng, 2017). Crowdsourcing is an online distributed problem-solving and production model (Brabham, 2010). We advocate that through the participation of the local crowds, crowdsourcing uncovers solutions that could solve problems in a local community.

This study focuses on the underlying motives of helping behaviors of smart city residents. Fundamentally, crowdsourcing is community engagement and we deem that through crowdsourcing, city residents can make use of a collaborative digital platform to help the community. Drawing from the functional approach to volunteerism (Clary, Snyder, & Stukas, 1998), this study investigates the motives behind smart city residents' willingness to participate in voluntary acts via a mobile crowdsourcing app. Thus, this study seeks to answer the following research question: *What are the motives underlying helping behaviors on a mobile crowdsourcing app for a smart city?*

LITERATURE REVIEW

Smart cities promise to be a new frontier in city development, embracing new technologies including sensors, mobile technology, and big data analytics (Srivastava & Mostafavi, 2018). Besides technology, people and the community are equally critical in smart cities. Futher, the collaborative aspect between various city stakeholders (e.g. residents, government agencies, businesses) in a smart city suggests that crowdsourcing is well suited for smart city projects. Crowdsourcing is the practice of obtaining services, ideas or content as well as solutions to problems by soliciting contributions from a large group of people, often with the use of the Internet platforms (Zhao & Zhu, 2014).

In essence, smart cities are not just about connected smart sensors but they are also about connected people and communities. As such, smart cities are likely to provide the social conditions to allow residents to connect and help each other. Helping is a form of prosocial behavior and refers to behaviors that will benefit others (Eisenberg, 1986). Crowdsourcing in a smart city has potential to influence residents' helping behaviors as it facilitates participation in worthy endeavors that will benefit the community (Goh, Lee, & Guo, 2018). Relevant examples in the current context include volunteering to provide information (e.g. traffic, dengue fever) that will be useful to other residents in the community. Here, we examine woluntary helping behaviors from the functional approach to volunteerism (Clay et al., 1998). This approach suggests that people have different motives for participating in voluntary acts. When we dedicate time and effort to help others, we experience positive emotions and gain mental satisfaction. In the process, we also make new friends and reap other benefits (e.g. career, enhance self-worth) (Clary & Snyder, 1991).

METHDOLOGY

We developed a mobile crowdsourcing app prototype to be used by community residents in a smart city. The app

82nd Annual Meeting of the Association for Information Science & Technology | Melbourne, Australia | 19–23 October, 2019

DOI: 10.1002/pra2.00142

provides a platform to connect users through helping. Through the app, residents have access to volunteers in their vicinity to get help. They are also alerted to volunteering opportunities to help others through the platform (e.g. location based services). The unique design of the app is the integration of inputs from the community in a smart city. A total of 125 participants were recruited in Singapore to participate in the study. A demonstration of the app was first shown to the participants. Participants were given tasks to use and explore the app before answering a questionnaire. The participants' ages ranged from 21 to 54 years. Measures regarding assessing the helping behaviors for participation were drawn from prior research (Snyder, Clary, & Stukas, 2000).

ANALYSIS AND RESULTS

Principal components analysis with varimax rotation was used to assess the factor structure of the 12 items that comprised the scales used to evaluate the motives to help. Five items were dropped either due to low factor loadings or due to high cross factor loadings. The resulting three-factor solution accounted for 69.65% of the variance. The reliabilities for the three factors were all acceptable.

The first factor (**Values function**) refers to the motives to express or act on important values such as helping the less fortunate. The second factor (**Protective function**) refers to motives to help others to lessen negative feelings (i.e. stress, depression). The last factor is a combination of (**Career function**) and (**Social function**) which denotes the motives of gaining career-related experience through volunteering as well as the motives to strengthen one's social relationships. We labeled this factor as **Professional function.** The variance for the three factors were 27.97%, 24.53% and 17.15% respectively.

DISCUSSION AND CONCLUSION

Our results indicate there are three categories of helping motives (i.e. Values, Protective and Professional) driving people's willingness to use a mobile crowdsourcing app. The Values motive highlights that the mobile crowdsourcing app provides opportunities for residents to express values related to altruistic and humanitarian concerns for others especially the elderly and less fortunate in the community. The Protective motive explains that residents who help was trying to escape from negative feelings (e.g. stress in real life). The Professional motive reflects the motivations concerning enhancing professional connections which will create career related benefits. For instance, a person who volunteers to answer healthcare related questions on the app sees potential career related benefits in the healthcare sector.

This preliminary study shows that the app we developed supports helping in a smart city. While the motives to help may vary, we reason that the app through the exchanges creates a sense of shared responsibility among members. This study is still a work in progress. Extension to this study is to integrate the app with other relevant sensors to allow for a more comprehensive analysis of the motives underlying voluntary helping on the crowdsourcing app in a smart city.

The preliminary results highlight the important role crowdsourcing applications play in facilitating voluntary helping and problem solving in a smart city. Ultimately, this research provides insights on the design features that need to be incorporated on mobile crowdsourcing platforms to demonstrate commitment and social bonding through helping acts.

ACKNOWLEDGMENTS

This work was supported by NTU MOE/Tier 1 grant RG149/15. The authors would like to thank Anran Hao and Quan Zhou for providing research assistance.

REFERENCES

Brabham, D. C. (2009). Crowdsourcing the public participation process for planning projects. *Planning Theory*, *8*(3), 242–262. https://doi.org/10.1177/1473095209104824

Clary, E. G., & Snyder, M. (1991). A functional analysis of altrusim and prosocial behavior: The case of volunteerism. In M. Clark (Ed.), *Review of personality and social psychology* (Vol. *12*, pp. 119–148). Newbury Park, CA: Sage.

Clary, E. G., Snyder, M., & Stukas, A. A. (1998). Volunteer motivations: Findings from a national survey. *Nonprofit and Voluntary Sector Quarterly*, *25*(4), 485–505.

Eisenberg, N. (1986). *Altruistic emotion, cognition, and behavior.*

Goh, D. H.-L., Lee, C. S., & Guo, H. (2018). Finding trafficked children through crowdsourcing. *Proceedings of the Association for Information Science and Technology*, *55*(1), 811–812.

Lee, C. S., Goh, D. H.-L., Osop, H., Sin, S.-C. J., & Theng, Y. L. (2017). Public services or private gains: Motives behind participation on a mobile crowdsourcing application in a smart city. *Proceedings of the Association for Information Science and Technology*, *54*(1), 495–498.

Snyder, M., Clary, E. G., & Stukas, A. A. (2000). The functional approach to volunteerism. In G. R. Maio & J. M. Olson (Eds.), *Why we evaluate: Functions of attitudes* (pp. 365–393). Hillsdale, NJ: Lawrence Erlbaum Associates.

Srivastava, P., & Mostafavi, A. (2018). Challenges and opportunities of crowdsourcing and participatory planning in developing infrastructure systems of smart cities. *Infrastructures*, *3*(4), 51.

Zhao, Y., & Zhu, Q. (2014). Evaluation on crowdsourcing research: Current status and future direction. *Information Systems Frontiers*, *16*(3), 417–434. https://doi.org/10.1007/s10796-012-9350-4

Getting Creative in Everyday Life: Investigating Arts and Crafts Hobbyists' Information Behavior

Lo Lee
University of Illinois
at Urbana-Champaign,
Champaign, USA
lolee2@illinois.edu

Melissa G. Ocepek
University of Illinois
at Urbana-Champaign,
Champaign, USA
mgocepek@illinois.edu

Stephann Makri
City, University of
London, London, UK
stephann@city.ac.uk

George Buchanan
University of Melbourne,
Melbourne, Australia
george.buchanan@unimelb.edu.au

Dana McKay
University of Melbourne,
Melbourne, Australia
dana.mckay@unimelb.edu.au

ABSTRACT

While there has been increasing interest in how creative professionals find information to drive creative outputs, previous information behavior research has largely ignored how arts and crafts hobbyists look for information sources in their everyday lives. To fill this literature gap, we conducted interviews and observations with arts and crafts hobbyists to find out how they conceive potential DIY projects. The findings highlight three themes: the dearth of human sources, the prevalence of domain-specific information, and the use of self-curated information. In addition to empirical results, this work also broadens the understanding of information behavior in an arts and crafts context by studying populations beyond professional artists.

KEYWORDS

Information behavior; sources; arts and crafts; hobbyists

ASIS&T THESAURUS

Information seeking; information sources

INTRODUCTION

There has been increasing research interest in how creative professionals find information as both a driver and enabler of creative outputs (see, for example, Hemmig, 2009; Makri, Hsueh, & Jones, 2019). Moving beyond work contexts is important, as it allows for a fuller understanding of behaviors. Hartel (2003) has suggested the significance of studying information-rich hobbies to gain a broader understanding of information behavior. The arts and crafts hobby is one activity that has received little attention from previous information behavior research. Seeking creative inspiration usually is an information-heavy process, as sources of inspiration are varied, idiosyncratic, and exist everywhere (Hemmig, 2009). To this end, we investigate how hobbyists navigate information sources in the arts and crafts domain to motivate their creative practices.

82nd Annual Meeting of the Association for Information Science & Technology | Melbourne, Australia | 19–23 October, 2019

DOI: 10.1002/pra2.00141

BACKGROUND

Previous literature divides information sources into different categories. For instance, Savolainen (2008) classified six source types: human sources, printed media, networked sources, broadcast media, organizational sources, and other sources, and found human sources were the most favored approach. Another kind of source in everyday life, which does not fall into this classification, is domain-specific sources (Ocepek, 2016). Domain-specific information directly relates to the information environment unique to the activity and helps individuals in those spaces acquire information. For example, labels and in-store signs are domain-specific information in grocery stores which are likely to affect grocery shoppers' information interaction.

In the arts and crafts context, prior research has typically examined how professional artists interact with information (e.g., Gorichanaz, 2018; Hemmig, 2009). From their findings, it is apparent that artists rely on various sources, such as memories, conversations, and personal works, to seek inspiration. Moving beyond examining professionals can provide meaningful insights for information source development and provision.

METHODS

We examined the information behavior of arts and crafts hobbyists at two sites: one digital - Pinterest (pinterest.com), the other a brick-and-mortar crafts store. We recruited 20 participants in total (10 for each site) with self-declared interests in arts and crafts, through weekly university newsletters, flyers, and personal contact. Our study included semi-structured interviews and think-aloud observations. The study began with pre-interviews to learn participants' experiences with arts and crafts and their current interests. Next, the participants explored the sites for 30-minutes and were observed. During the observations, participants were asked to browse for 15 minutes and then seek a particular item for 15 minutes. We asked participants to verbalize their feelings and thoughts throughout the observations. After the observation, we conducted two post-interviews for participant debriefing and data validation. We audio-recorded each interview, observation, and took notes. A bottom-up Thematic Analysis of transcripts and field notes was conducted to identify sources of information used.

FINDINGS AND DISCUSSION

Between the data collected at both sites, we identified 27 information sources from interviews and observations. Within the 143 mentions of sources, domain-specific information—the top source of this study—was mentioned 72 times. These sources had slightly higher mentions from Pinterest participants likely due to the ability to organize information in the Pinterest setting. Networked sources were mentioned 50 times, with 41 and 9 mentions by Pinterest and store participants. Additionally, there were 10 mentions of human sources, 8 mentions of printed media, and 3 mentions of organizational sources. Based on empirical data, we identified three interesting themes.

The Dearth of Human Sources

The first theme we noted from the diversity of sources was the dearth of human sources. In our findings, human sources were mentioned 10 times, and there were two types of them: friends and store staff. Participants regarded friends as sources by meeting with them regularly. For example, one Pinterest participant described how she interacted with friends to seek ideas: "*We have like a club that we meet once a month, and we just kind of talk about ideas*." Store staff, not just those in the brick-and-mortar store in this study, became sources when participants questioned them and learned something new from them. For instance, one store participant mentioned he liked chatting with store employees: "*I feel in small stores, staff is more familiar with their products and are more passionate about introducing what they have. I like interacting with staff like that and learn from them.*" Unlike previous literature, human sources were less covered by our participants, possibly due to the explorative nature of seeking inspiration. Such tasks are not driven by knowledge gaps typically having exact answers. Instead, as ideas can be everywhere, arts and crafts hobbyists may try to discover numerous sources to optimize creativity.

Domain-Specific Information

The second theme we identified was the common uses of domain-specific information from participants. For Pinterest participants, when seeing pictures selected by Pinterest, they frequently considered them as potential projects they could work on. For store participants, many of them mentioned they liked the layout of the store and how products were displayed because they could spark their inspiration. One store participant said she would revisit the store in this study when seeking future craft ideas: "*I get a lot of ideas when I am walking around place like this, so I would definitely come here for things like that.*" Domain-specific information was found to be a popular source in grocery stores as individuals relied heavily on things such as price tags or expiration dates when selecting items (Ocepek, 2016). This research aligns with the previous finding on domain-specific sources and extends the literature into the arts and crafts context.

Self-Curated Information

The third interesting theme we saw was participants' habits of preserving useful information. For example, when participants found something engaging, they liked to collect and organize them for later use. We call this type of source self-curated information. One store participant shared how she used self-curated information found online in grocery stores: "*Sometimes I like to print pictures out because then when I go to the grocery store, I have a list of what I need. Sometimes I can just put it on my phone so I'm not gonna lose it.*" Self-curated information sources were more observed by Pinterest participants. This may be because of the special functions Pinterest has for individuals to save images ("pin it") and categorize them ("make boards"). One Pinterest participant explained how she used these tools when seeking craft ideas: "*When I get ready to do the project, I'll pull up the boards that I pin those to, and kind of look at them and get more inspiration.*" Here boards and pinned pictures were participants' self-curated information. We categorized these sources as domain-specific information.

CONCLUSION AND FUTURE RESEARCH

This work identifies the information sources arts and crafts hobbyists use when seeking ideas. We identified three interesting themes: the dearth of human sources, the prevalence of domain-specific information, and the use of self-curated information. Future work can determine whether these themes extend to other creative everyday life domains (e.g., photography, gardening). This study provides insight into the use of information sources for creative purposes and provides a more holistic understanding of information behavior in the arts and crafts domain that extends beyond the behavior of professional artists.

REFERENCES

Gorichanaz, T. (2018). Art and everyday information behavior: Sources of understanding. *Proceeding of the ASIS&T, Vancouver, Canada*, 143–150.

Hartel, J. (2003). The serious leisure frontier in library and information science: Hobby domains. *Knowledge Organization*, *30*(3-4), 228–238.

Hemmig, W. (2009). An empirical study of the information-seeking behavior of practicing visual artists. *Journal of Documentation*, *65*(4), 682–703.

Makri, S., Hsueh, T. L., & Jones, S. (2019). Ideation as an intellectual information acquisition and use context: Investigating game designers' information-based ideation Behavior. *JASIST*.

Ocepek, M. G. (2016). Shopping for sources: An everyday information behavior exploration of grocery shoppers' information sources. *Proceeding of the ASIS&T, Copenhagen, Denmark*, 1–5.

Savolainen, R. (2008). Source preferences in the context of seeking problem-specific information. *Information Processing & Management*, *44*(1), 274–293.

Disciplinarity of Software Papers: A Preliminary Analysis

Kai Li
Drexel University,
Philadelphia, USA
kl696@drexel.edu

Pei-Ying Chen
Indiana University,
Bloomington, USA
peiychen@iu.edu

Zhichao Fang
Leiden University,
Leiden, Netherlands
z.fang@cwts.leidenuniv.nl

ABSTRACT

The present study investigates the disciplinarity of papers describing scientific software (i.e., "software papers") as the first step to gain a deeper understanding of how science is operated in its material and practice bases. The preliminary analysis mapped 768 software papers in the *Journal of Statistical Software* and about 57,000 papers that cited them to the five knowledge domains in the CWTS classification system and traced how these papers are cited within and across disciplinary boundaries.

KEYWORDS

Scientific software; Software citation; Scientometrics

ASIS&T THESAURUS

Instrumentation; Informetrics

INTRODUCTION

Software has arguably become the engine for scientific discoveries nowadays. As software is increasingly integrated into the scientific system, a new type of publication, famously named "software paper" (Hong et al., 2013), gradually emerged over the past decades with the goal to describe a scientific software, rather than report empirical results. Since software papers are more likely to be cited and rewarded than other forms of software publications (Smith et al., 2018), the genre has been adopted by various disciplines with a growing number of journals dedicated to it. Initiated in 1996, the *Journal of Statistical Software* (*JSS*) has become one of the most famous software journals (Fox & Leanage, 2016) featuring statistical software and algorithms implemented in various environments.

Software, as a type of standardized scientific tool, is easy to travel across disciplinary boundaries (Fujimura, 1988; Li et al., 2019). However, software papers published in the same journal are often represented as mono-disciplinary in most citation databases. For example, *JSS* was classified into the categories of *Computer Science, Interdisciplinary Applications* and *Statistical Probability* in Web of Science (WoS), and thus all its articles were treated as such in the WoS-based analyses.

In this project, we plan to classify the disciplinarity of software papers and examine the distribution patterns of their citations as an indication of how software is involved in scientific activities. As the first step, we analyzed how software papers in *JSS* published between 2006 (the earliest year in which *JSS* is indexed in the WoS) and 2016 and their citations are distributed according to the classification system developed by the Centre for Science and Technology Studies (CWTS) at Leiden University. As a core component in the CWTS Leiden Ranking, the 2019 CWTS classification system categorizes research articles into five knowledge domains (see Table 1) and 4,535 research fields by using a clustering method based on citation relations between publications. Focusing on the disciplinary attributes of individual articles, the system has been proven to be a reliable instrument for article-level disciplinary information (Schneider & Costas, 2017) and offers a more fine-grained classification suitable for our project. We traced how software papers were cited across different knowledge domains and discussed future work in conclusion.

METHODS

In this study, we utilized (1) all software papers (excluding review papers) published in *JSS* between 2006 and 2016 and (2) all articles that cited the software papers between 2016 and 2018 ("citing articles" hereafter) indexed in WoS. The CWTS classification for all the papers was retrieved from the CWTS in-house database; papers without a field assigned in this system were removed. In total, 768 software papers and 57,299 citing articles were included in the final sample. About 90% of software papers received at least one citation, with small variations across domains. Table 1 demonstrates that software papers in *JSS* have diverse disciplinary backgrounds, which was not captured by the conventional journal-level classification.

RESULTS AND DISCUSSION

Figure 1 is a Sankey diagram showing how software papers and works citing them are distributed over different knowledge domains. Each line is a citation link between a software paper (left) and a corresponding citing article (right).

This figure reveals different patterns of domain distribution between software papers and citing articles. Among five domains, *Social Science and Humanities* (SSH) and

82nd Annual Meeting of the Association for Information Science & Technology | Melbourne, Australia | 19–23 October, 2019

DOI: 10.1002/pra2.00143

Mathematics and Computer Science (MCS) have higher shares in software papers cited than in articles citing them, indicating that they are more oriented toward software development than application. The reverse holds true for the other domains. While it is not surprising that MCS developed software to be later applied in other knowledge domains, the considerable share of SSH may be attributed, at least partially, to the inclusion of the highly-cited paper "Fitting Linear Mixed-Effects Models using lme4" in the category. The single paper has received more than 10,000 citations and has a strong connection to both MCS and LBS based on its authors and developers (Li et al., 2019).

CWTS category	Software papers	Citing articles
Biomedical and Health Sciences (BHS)	135 (17.5%)	17,103 (29.8%)
Life and Earth Sciences (LES)	74 (9.6%)	23,239 (40.6%)
Mathematics and Computer Science (MCS)	434 (56.5%)	6,424 (11.2%)
Physical Sciences and Engineering (PSE)	11 (1.4%)	1,667 (2.9%)
Social Sciences and Humanities (SSH)	114 (14.8%)	8,866 (15.5%)

Table 1. Distribution of software papers and citing articles in the CWTS classification system.

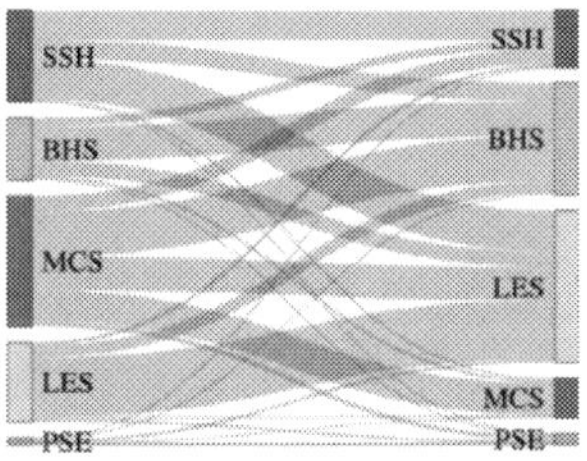

Figure 1. The five knowledge domains as the receiver (left) and giver (right) of software paper citations.

In addition to analyzing citation links, we also examined the disciplinarity of software papers by looking at the disciplinary composition of citations for an individual paper with two indicators: (1) the share of software papers primarily cited in its own category and (2) the mean share of citations software papers received in the same category. To avoid biases introduced by lowly-cited papers, we only included 341 software papers with at least 10 citations in the sample. Due to the small quantity that meets the criterion (n = 6), papers in *Physical Sciences and Engineering* (PSE) was excluded from the analysis.

Table 2 shows that software papers in MCS have much lower in-category citation rates by both measures than those in other domains. In other words, software papers in MCS are more likely to be cited in other domains but not vice versa. This finding conforms to the patterns of domain distributions in Figure 1, suggesting that disciplinarity is characteristic of the division between producer/developer (MCS) and consumer/user (application domains) of scientific software.

CWTS category	Paper w/ >10 citations	Ind. 1	Ind. 2
BHS	64 (47.4%)	75%	60.1%
LES	45 (60.8%)	93.3%	74.7%
MCS	187 (43.4%)	39%	34%
SSH	45 (39.5%)	80%	56.2%

Table 2. Summary of in-category citations across CWTS knowledge domains (n = 341). Ind. 1: Share of papers with most in-category citations. Ind. 2: Mean share of in-category citations by paper.

CONCLUSION

As part of our project to evaluate how software papers are cited in disciplinary contexts, the present study finds that disciplinarity is an important attribute of software papers and is manifested in the different patterns of domain distribution of software papers and their citations. Specifically, software is primarily developed in MCS and later applied in other domains. This study also points to the discrepancies of classifying software papers not only between systems (e.g., WoS vs. CWTS classification) but also between citation-based algorithms and author-based identification (e.g., the case of lme4 R package). Given the complexity of both disciplinarity and scientific software, future research should implement more fine-grained methods to quantify the disciplinarity of software papers and augment the citation-based classification with additional analyses (1) of social dimensions of disciplinarity and (2) at the semantic level of software papers. By doing so, we hope to gain more insights into the lifecycle of scientific software in the disciplinary context, including how it is developed, inscribed as software papers, and cited by researchers from different epistemic communities.

REFERENCE

Fox, J., & Leanage, A. (2016). R and the journal of statistical software. *Journal of Statistical Software*, *73*(2). https://doi.org/10.18637/jss.v073.i02

Fujimura, J. H. (1988). The molecular biological bandwagon in cancer research: Where social worlds meet. *Social Problems*, *35*(3), 261–283.

Hong, N. C., Hole, B., & Moore, S. (2013). *Software papers: improving the reusability and sustainability of scientific software*.

Li, K., Chen, P.-Y., & Yan, E. (2019). Challenges of measuring software impact through citations: An examination of the lme4 R package. *Journal of Informetrics*, *13*(1), 449–461.

Schneider, J. W., & Costas, R. (2017). Identifying potential "breakthrough" publications using refined citation analyses: Three related explorative approaches. *Journal of the Association for Information Science and Technology*, *68*(3), 709–723.

Smith, A. M., Niemeyer, K. E., Katz, D. S., Barba, L. A., Githinji, G., Gymrek, M., … Moerman, K. M. (2018). Journal of Open Source Software (JOSS): Design and first-year review. *PeerJ Computer Science*, *4*, e147.

Questions or Questioners: Factors Affecting Response Quantity on Academic Social Q&A Sites

Lei Li
Department of Information Management, Beijing Normal University, Beijing, China
leili@bnu.edu.cn

Kun Huang
Department of Information Management, Beijing Normal University, Beijing, China
huangkun@bnu.edu.cn

Edwin Mouda Ye
School of Information Technology & Mathematical Sciences, University of South Australia, Adelaide, Australia
mouda.ye@mymail.unisa.edu.au

Chengzhi Zhang
Department of Information Management, Nanjing University of Science and Technology, Nanjing, China
zhangcz@njust.edu.cn

ABSTRACT

With the continuous development of academic social network sites, academic social Q&A platforms have also become a venue for scholars to obtain academic information. This study explores the factors that influence the response quantity for questions on an academic social Q&A platform. Using 130 questions from the library and information services domain on ResearchGate Q&A, we adopt content analysis and multiple linear regression analysis to investigate the relationship between question characteristics and response quantity. We find that, for academic questions, the questioner's authority does not affect response quantity but questions that provide academic resources and contain fewer personal opinions from the questioner tend to attract more answers.

KEYWORDS

Response quantity; Academic social Q&A; Information seeking

ASIS&T THESAURUS

Information science; Information discovery; Information seeking; Searching; Social Q&A

INTRODUCTION

With the continuous proliferation of social media, various platforms are emerging, including academic social network sites (ASNSs). Increasing numbers of scholars are turning to ASNSs to access and share academic information (Van Noorden, 2014). One of the largest ASNSs is ResearchGate, which includes a Q&A platform through which scholars can communicate by posing academic questions and providing answers. However, prior studies have found that scholars' engagement with ASNSs is lower than that with other types of social media (Muscanell & Utz, 2017). This is reflected in the low response quantity for many questions on ResearchGate Q&A. To begin to tackle such low engagement on ASNSs, we undertook a study to explore what influences response quantity on academic social Q&A platforms.

Previous studies of response quantity have targeted other social media, such as Facebook (Teevan, Morris, & Panovich, 2011) and Weibo (Liu & Jansen, 2018). Furthermore, studies of generic social Q&A (e.g., Yahoo! Answers) have considered the number of responses to a question as a representation of question quality, and then explored the factors that influence question quality (Choi, Kitzie, & Shah, 2013). Although the factors influencing response quantity to requests on various types of social media are evidently important research topics, academic social Q&A platforms feature a new type of requests that the literature is yet to consider. This paper aims to fill this gap.

Prior research on the user's willingness to contribute knowledge in a Q&A community indicates that the knowledge exchange process therein is issue-driven. Specifically, questioner characteristics and question content may be two types of factors that specifically influence the user's knowledge contribution behavior (Lou, Fang, Lim, & Peng, 2013). Therefore, this paper takes a question dataset from ResearchGate Q&A (a representative academic social Q&A) as the research object and explores which characteristics of the question content and questioner affect response quantity. Its findings should provide guidance for scholars on how to ask questions on ASNSs to attract more answers.

METHOD

Dataset

To circumvent the influence of the questions' domain on this study's findings, we limited the question dataset of this pilot study to the "library information services" domain on ResearchGate Q&A. We collected 133 questions published over one year in this domain and got the number of responses received within one year of each question, aiming to control for

82nd Annual Meeting of the Association for Information Science & Technology | Melbourne, Australia | 19–23 October, 2019

DOI: 10.1002/pra2.00144

the impact of exposure time on the number of responses. Since a ResearchGate Q&A user can answer a question multiple times, we only counted responses from distinct answerers.

Question and Questioner Characteristics

To explore the factors influencing response quantity, we established a framework of characteristics based on our own experience and previous studies (Jeng, DesAutels, He, & Li, 2017; Li, He, Jeng, Goodwin, & Zhang, 2015; Li, He, Zhang, Geng, & Zhang, 2018). As Table 1 shows, the framework includes two categories: the questioner and question content. Each characteristic in the questioner category was crawled using the web crawler program from the responder's profile; Among the question content characteristics, question length was obtained by simply counting the number of words in each question, but the other characteristics were coded by two coders separately, with inconsistent coding results discussed to reach agreement. Since three questions in the acquired dataset did not contain questioner profiles, the following data analysis is based on the characteristics of 130 questions and their response quantity.

Data Analysis

Since this paper explores the independent effects of multiple independent variables (questioner/question characteristics) on the dependent variable (response quantity), multiple linear regression (MLR) was used to analyze these relationships. Before conducting MLR analysis, multicollinearity was checked to ensure that the dataset's suitability. In addition, we use log-transformation to normalize the continuous independent variables, thus reducing the right skewness of the dataset.

Question and questioner characteristics (n = 130, df = 1)			**Coeff.**	**Sig.**
Questioner	Questioner's history	Questions asked	0.190	0.762
		Answers provided	0.184	0.589
	Questioner's academic reputation	Questioner's publications	0.091	0.842
		Publication reads	0.313	0.310
		Publication citations	0.141	0.621
		Publication h-index	0.427	0.536
		Publication recommendations	0.257	0.376
		Questioner's followers	0.294	0.534
Question content	Academic-related content characteristics	Providing academic resources*	0.551	0.015
		Referring to basic theories	-2.576	0.489
		Providing research experience	0.006	0.997
	Non-academic content characteristics	Adding factual information	-0.585	0.711
		Providing opinions*	-1.877	0.040
		Question length	0.849	0.407

Note: *p<0.05

Table 1. MLR results for response quantity.

RESULTS AND DISCUSSION

As Table 1 shows, the questioner characteristics are not significantly correlated with response quantity. Previous studies on Weibo have found a significantly positive correlation between the questioner's followers (number) and response quantity (Liu & Jansen, 2018). Furthermore, we have previously found that content published on ResearchGate by scholars with high academic reputation is more likely to obtain user recommendations (Li, He, Zhang, Geng, & Zhang, 2018). However, in this study, response quantity on ResearchGate Q&A seemed unaffected by questioner characteristics.

By contrast, we found that questions providing academic resources, such as hyperlinks or citations, attracted more answers. We also found questions providing personal opinions were less likely to receive responses. This finding was consistent with our previous finding (Li, He, Zhang, Geng, & Zhang, 2018). We have found that the answers to the ResearchGate Q&A containing the answerer's opinions will result in fewer recommendations. From the above findings, it can be seen that scholars are evidently more willing to answer questions that provide objective information resources but do not express opinions. We consider this a meaningful finding on response quantity for academic questions, which can guide scholars on asking questions likely to receive more responses.

CONCLUSION

This paper analyzed the relationship between questioner/question characteristics and response quantity on a renowned academic social Q&A platform. In the future, we will investigate more comprehensive question characteristics to further identify which affect response quantity. In addition, the findings of this study may be affected by the question's domains or the questioner's demographic characteristics, so we will obtain question data from more disciplines to further confirm this paper's findings.

ACKNOWLEDGMENTS

This work was supported by National Social Science Fund Project (No. 19CTQ032).

REFERENCES

Choi, E., Kitzie, V., & Shah, C. (2013). A machine learning-based approach to predicting success of questions on social question-answering. *Iconference 2013 Proceedings*, 409–421).

Jeng, W., DesAutels, S., He, D., & Li, L. (2017). Information exchange on an academic social networking site: A multi-discipline comparison on ResearchGate Q&A. *Journal of the Association for Information Science and Technology, 68*(3), 638–652.

Li, L., He, D., Jeng, W., Goodwin, S., & Zhang, C. (2015, May). Answer quality characteristics and prediction on an academic Q&A Site: A case study on ResearchGate. In *Proceedings of the 24th international conference on world wide web* (pp. 1453–1458). ACM.

Li, L., He, D., Zhang, C., Geng, L., & Zhang, K. (2018). Characterizing peer-judged answer quality on academic

Q&A sites: A cross-disciplinary case study on ResearchGate. *Aslib Journal of Information Management*, *70*(3), 269–287.

Liu, Z., & Jansen, B. J. (2018). Questioner or question: Predicting the response rate in social question and answering on Sina Weibo. *Information Processing & Management*, *54*(2), 159–174.

Lou, J., Fang, Y., Lim, K. H., & Peng, J. Z. (2013). Contributing high quantity and quality knowledge to online Q & A communities. *Journal of the American Society for Information Science and Technology*, *64*(2), 356–371.

Muscanell, N., & Utz, S. (2017). Social networking for scientists: an analysis on how and why academics use ResearchGate. *Online Information Review*, *41*(5), 744–759.

Teevan, J., Morris, M.R., & Panovich, K. (2011). Factors affecting response quantity, quality, and speed for questions asked via social network status messages. *Proceedings of the Fifth International AAAI Conference on Weblogs and Social Media*. pp. 630–633.

Van Noorden, R. (2014). Online collaboration: Scientists and the social network. *Nature News*, *512*(7513), 126–129.

How Do University Data Services Present Their Collection and Reference Service Information on the Web?

Chi-Shiou Lin
Dept. of Library and Information Science, National Taiwan University,
Taipei, Taiwan
chishioulin@ntu.edu.tw

Yi-Yu Wang
Dept. of Library and Information Science, National Taiwan University,
Taipei, Taiwan
f03126027@ntu.edu.tw

ABSTRACT

This poster describes how 83 university data services in three English speaking countries present their collection and reference services information on their Web sites. The information on the Web constitutes the first step toward data awareness. Our analysis shows that both collection and reference services information can be further enriched to facilitate data visibility and data reuses.

KEYWORDS

Data services; data centers; data libraries

ASIS&T THESAURUS

Data science; research data sets

INTRODUCTION

The emergence of data science and advocacy of research data sharing and data curation have prompted universities to build on-campus data service units. Recent surveys of those university data centers have focused on how they support data curation (ARL, 2017) and research data management (ARL, 2013). However, data services can also serve as an intermediary that bridges data-seeking patrons and the existing datasets. That is, data services could be data libraries, providing services including data collection development, data search assistance and other reference services.

A dated survey conducted by the Association of Research Libraries showed that, in 2001, 66 of the 121 ARL member libraries (55%) have had provided some forms of intermediary services on numeric datasets. Their services ranged from dataset acquisitions, cataloging, preservation, and reference consultation. But at that time, only 1/3 of the responding libraries had established a data services unit for those tasks (ARL, 2001). As many universities have founded new data services unit on campus in response to RDM requirements, we are interested in understanding to what extent the existing university data services also serve as data libraries. Specifically, we focused on how they present their data collection information and reference services on their Web sites so as to understand how potential patrons may become aware of their datasets and services.

82nd Annual Meeting of the Association for Information Science & Technology | Melbourne, Australia | 19–23 October, 2019

DOI: 10.1002/pra2.00145

METHODOLOGY

We reviewed the recent data services surveys including the aforementioned ARL Spec Kit reports along with our additional manual searches to identify existing university data services in the major English-speaking countries, i.e., US, UK, and Australia. We identified 83 university data services with Web presence and conducted Web content analysis to compare their collection development and reference and access practices. The majority of the data services were located under the university libraries. A small number of the data services were under specific information centers, e.g., the Data Services under the Center for Sciences and Social Sciences Information in Yale University. A few other university data services were performed by a campus library, e.g., the Lamont Library of the Harvard University. We studied the data services' Web sites to see how they present their dataset collections and what types of reference and access services are provided to the patrons.

COLLECTION BUILDING IN THE DATA SERVICES

A rather large proportion of the data services provided little or no information on their data collections on their Web sites. Only 23 (27.71%) have described their collection focus and/or collection building policies. Other data information was presented as follow.

- **Data types**: the languages used to describe data collections varied among the data services. There is not a uniform way to describe data types. Here's what we found from those sites:
  - File types: when collection information is available, most of the data centers may describe the file types include in their data collection. The major file types included documents and spreadsheets in popular, standardized and open formats.
  - Data types: some data services may describe data by data content, e.g., experimental data, field study data, 3D

imaging data. Some data services focused highly on certain special data types. For instance, the Data Library Service in University of Toronto features geospatial datasets along with a maps collection.
  - Quantitative vs. qualitative data: some data services feature data collections of quantitative or qualitative nature. Examples of such services included the Data Library and Consultancy in University of Edinburgh, and the Research Data Services in the University of Illinois-Urbana Champaign.
  - Digital vs. tangible data: some data services have data stored in physical formats, including artifacts.
- **Collection size**: only twelve (14.46%) of the data services mentioned the size of their existing data collection. The units used included numbers of datasets or megabytes.
- **Data sources**: four data centers (4.82%) acquired data exclusively from outside the parent organizations; 21 (25.30%) obtained data exclusively from within the parent organizations; 9 (10.84%) collected both.
- **Acquisition methods**: 44 data services (53.01%) offered no information on their data acquisition. A few data services mentioned their data acquisitions including purchase, e.g., University of Southampton, King's College London, McGill University, Columbia University, etc.

REFERENCE SERVICES IN THE DATA SERVICES

We referenced Jacobs (1991), Bennet (2010), and Wang (2012) and categorized data library reference services into the following six categories:

- **[A] Data search assistance:** including search helps with the internal or external data search systems.
- **[B] Data recommendation:** assisting the patrons to discover and identify the needed data variables and to locate datasets with those variables.
- **[C] Referral services:** referring patrons to other data centers with datasets or services that meet their needs.
- **[D] Data reuse/analysis consultation:** assisting patrons to decipher and interpret datasets, including helps with data cleaning and other data processing and analysis assistance.
- **[E] Data reuse/analysis workshops or group instructions:** providing group courses on data search, data cleaning and processing, data interpretation and analyses.
- **[F] Research data management advisory:** providing consultations services regarding data management issues throughout the research lifecycles.

Based on the service type schemes, we identified the Web sites with related information, and the results were presented as Figure 1. As can be seen, more than half of the data services have provided certain reference services information on their Web sites. Understandably, slightly less data services were offering data reuse/analysis consultation because it involves in-depth engagement with a patron's research inquiry and thus requires more staff devotion and investment. But surprisingly, the mentions of research data management advisory were less than we expected. We had anticipated to see more research data management services on their Web sites as it was what drove the universities to build or expand the data service units, but it wasn't the case.

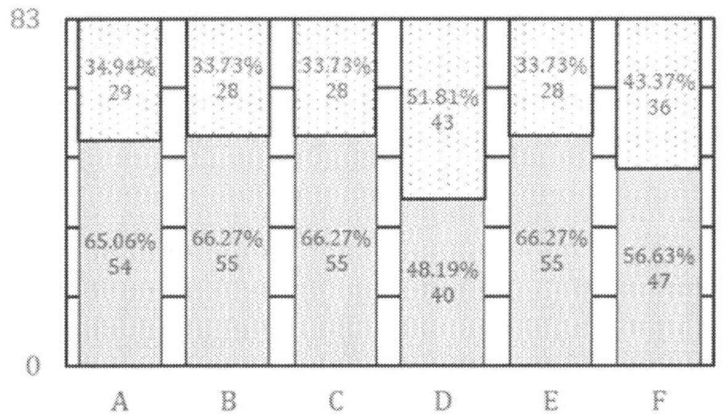

Figure 1. The distribution of the data library reference services as mentioned on the data services' Web sites.

CONCLUSION

The presentation of collection and reference information on Web provides the first impression for the potential data users to identify, access, and reuse the datasets. It also helps the peer data specialists to discover and locate existing available datasets for researchers outside the universities. This Web content analysis study shows that a lot more can be done to facilitate data awareness and exchange in the scholarly world. Our future research will continue to investigate the collection development and reference and access policies of the data centers so as to understand how we may build a rich and global network of research data.

ACKNOWLEDGMENTS

This study is supported by the Ministry of Science & Technology, Taiwan (Grant No. MOST 105-2410-H-002-120-MY2) & National Taiwan University (NTU108L8804).

REFERENCES

Association of Research Libraries. (2001). *Spec kit 263: Numeric data products and services*. Washington, DC: Association of Research Libraries.

Association of Research Libraries. (2013). *Spec kit 334: Research data management*. Washington, DC: Association of Research Libraries.

Association of Research Libraries. (2017). *Spec kit 354: Data curation*. Washington, DC: Association of Research Libraries.

Jacobs, J. (1991). Providing data services for machine-readable information in an academic library: Some levels of service. *Public Access-Computer Systems Review*, *2*(1).

Online News Sharing Among Taiwan's Middle-Aged and Elderly Populaces: Influencing Factors

Chieh Liu
National Taiwan University,
Graduate Institute of Library and Information Science,
Taipei City, Taiwan
d00126001@ntu.edu.tw

Tingyu Wu
National Taiwan University,
Graduate Institute of Library and Information Science,
Taipei City, Taiwan
d07126001@ntu.edu.tw

Wayland Chang
National Taiwan University,
Graduate Institute of Library and Information Science,
Taipei City, Taiwan
d07126009@ntu.edu.tw

ABSTRACT

Online news sharing has emerged as being influential in how certain news is targeted toward and received by certain audiences. Especially for the middle-aged and elderly populaces, online fake news' increased presence has made such sharing more complex. With much of Taiwan's middle-aged and elderly populaces with mobile phones, this study analyzes the influencing factors—namely motivation and willingness ones—of such populaces' online news sharing practices. analyses that were approached via a survey, an adapted questionnaire, and several quantitative analyses.

Motivation-wise, weighed more were communication exchange, knowledge sharing, and social interaction factors. Willingness-wise, the news' authenticity strength level was the most influential in such populaces' mindsets to share the highlighted online news or not. And differing education levels have differing social interaction plus knowledge sharing-based motivations. Overall, such results reflect the unique considerations of more information literacy education-related initiatives for Taiwan's middle-aged and elderly populaces in online news sharing practices.

KEYWORDS

Online news sharing and factors; middle-aged and elderly information literacy; global information literacy studies

INTRODUCTION & LITERATURE REVIEW

Since 1993, Taiwan has moved toward an "aged society" at roughly two times faster than that of the United States (Lin & Huang, 2015). About Taiwan's elderly and cellphones use: the elderly has had high access toward and frequency of such use. And Taiwan's elderly has had high receptions toward information technology (Chen, McGaughey, Zeltmann, Lu, & Lee, 2018).

In 2018, Taiwan's mobile internet access rate was nearly 90% with more and more mobile phone users in both the 50-59 and 60 plus age categories (National Communications Commission, 2018). Mobile internet access' convenience has let online news sharing be effective for certain news' sharing to certain audiences. Yet, online fake news' sharing has been more present among more middle-aged and elderly age groups than other ones (Guess, Nagler, & Tucker, 2019).

Taiwan has been more attentive to online fake news' increased sharing, but there has been little research—at the outset—on general online news sharing's influencing factors. With more Taiwan's middle-aged and elderly mobile phone users, all of these areas are worthy of more analyses. For future comparative global information literacy-related studies, this study thus could serve as a solid reference point.

Research Questions

This study wants to address the following research questions from the standpoints of Taiwan's middle-aged and elderly:

- What's their motivations in sharing online news?
- Do such motivations differ by certain demographics?
- In sharing online news, was the willingness due to the news' type or news' authenticity strength level?

RESEARCH METHODOLOGY

This study was based on a previous questionnaire model about fake news sharing attitudes and motivations (Chen, Sin, Theng, & Lee, 2015). For this study, such questionnaire was adapted into one—with three main parts—about online news sharing's willingness and motivations. From April to May 2019, distributed online were questionnaires for Taiwanese persons 50 years and older. Collected were 267 valid questionnaires in total. To analyze, applied were: descriptive statistics, factor analysis, independent sample t-test, single-factor variance analysis, and Pearson correlation analysis.

1. *Motivations to share online news*: With 29 factors categories and 7-point Likert scale applied – asked were motivations in sharing highlighted news.
2. *Willingness to share online news*: With 6 online news case studies and 7-point Likert scale – asked were to judge the authenticity of and willingness to share highlighted news.
3. *Basic personal information*: Namely included – age, education level, gender, or employment status.

82nd Annual Meeting of the Association for Information Science & Technology | Melbourne, Australia | 19–23 October, 2019

DOI: 10.1002/pra2.00146

RESULTS & DISCUSSION

For motivations to share online news: weighed more were the "communication exchange", "knowledge sharing", and "social interaction" premises. The below reflect the aforesaid 29 factors categories: not all are shown as some had no responses during the survey period.

Communication Exchange:

- M01: This message might help me open a topic.
- M05: I can share more personal opinions with message sharing.
- M03: Message is very attractive.
- M06: Message's sharing helps me interact with others.
- M10: More relevant information is received with message sharing.

Knowledge Sharing:

- M24: Message seems to be correct.
- M13: Message seems to be very useful.
- M26: Message's source is credible.
- M11: Message gives me more understanding of this event.
- M18: Message seems to be very important.
- M22: Message consistent with personal opinions.

Social Interaction:

- M20: Sharing messages is a great way to pass the time.
- M15: Sharing messages makes me not bored.
- M28: I want to be the first to share message among friends.
- M19: Sharing a message is a culture that everyone does.
- M25: Sharing information makes me feel influential.
- M17: Sharing the message makes me feel relaxed.
- M27: Sharing messages helps my personal image.
- M21: My interpersonal interactions are strengthened with information sharing.
- M29: Message may seem frightening.
- M16: Sharing the message makes me happy.
- M23: Message comes from my friend or family.

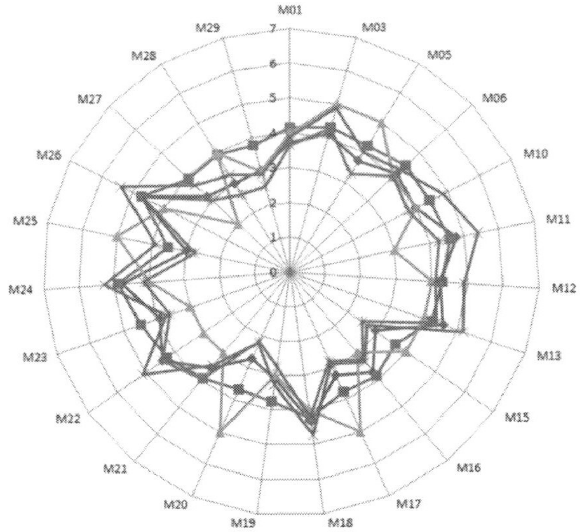

Figure 1. Education levels: average scores' distribution.

For willingness to share online news: Taiwan's middle-aged and elderly were more willing to do so per the news' authenticity strength level (moderate positive relation). Yet, there was no changes in willingness per the news' type.

For specific demographics: In the aforesaid motivations to share online news' premises: education levels variables are sizably different in the aforesaid "knowledge sharing" and "social interaction" categories. Figure 1 reflects the average scores' distribution. In Figure 1, to reflect the person's highest attained education level: green (middle school), red (high school), dark blue (bachelor's degree). Light blue (master's degree). Purple (doctorate degree).

CONCLUSION & LIMITATIONS

For online news sharing among Taiwan's middle-aged and elderly populaces, this study concludes some sizable factors in both willingness-to-share and motivations-for-sharing realms. Willingness-wise, such populaces are more likely to share per the particular news' authenticity's strength level and not news type. Motivations-wise, more likely to share are per the communication exchange, knowledge sharing, and social interaction premises altogether: with varying education levels as sizable variables. Limitations-wise, this study's smaller sample size does not fully reflect Taiwan's middle-aged and elderly populaces. And perhaps a lengthier longitudinal-based research would give a fuller picture.

Overall, this study perhaps provides and serves as a starting basis to meet the emerging information literacy resources needed for Taiwan's middle-aged and elderly populaces in the online news sharing-mobile phone use realm.

REFERENCES

Chen, A. N., McGaughey, R. E., Zeltmann, S. M., Lu, H. K., & Lee, M. R. (2018). How seniors in Taiwan use information technology: Computer and cell phones. *International Journal of Human–Computer Interaction, 34*(2), 166–176.

Chen, X., Sin, S. C. J., Theng, Y. L., & Lee, C. S. (2015). Why students share misinformation on social media: Motivation, gender, and study-level differences. *The Journal of Academic Librarianship, 41*(5), 583–592.

Guess, A., Nagler, J., & Tucker, J. (2019). Less than you think: Prevalence and predictors of fake news dissemination on Facebook. *Science advances, 5*(1), eaau4586.

Lin, Y. Y., & Huang, C. S. (2015). Aging in Taiwan: Building a society for active aging and aging in place. *The Gerontologist, 56*(2), 176–183.

National Communications Commission. (2018). *National Development Council's 2018 National Survey Report on Mobile Phone Uses [107年持有手機民眾數位機會調查報告]*. Retrieved from https://ws.ndc.gov.tw/

An Experimental Comparison on Reading Comprehension Effect of Visual, Audio and Dual Channels

Huiyun Liu
Sun Yat-sen University,
Guangzhou, China
liuhy39@mail2.sysu.edu.cn

Shujin Cao
Sun Yat-sen University,
Guangzhou, China
caosj@mail.sysu.edu.cn

Shiyu Wu
Sun Yat-sen University,
Guangzhou, China
shiyuwu51@foxmail.com

ABSTRACT

Audiobooks is booming audibly in the mobile age. According to Global Audiobook Trends and Statistics (2018), audio-book performed better than e-book, and US has occupied the largest market share, and the sales reached 21 billion dollars in 2016 and 23.5 billion dollars in 2017. Though previous researches show that the reading comprehension effect of audio channel is better than that on visual channel and the reading comprehension effect of dual channel combining visual and audio channel is better than the single channel. However, is that also established on the new mobile device? Using an experiment approach, we found that (1) The reading comprehension effect of the audio channel is better than that of the visual channel. (2) The reading comprehension effect of the dual channel is better than that of any single channel. That means listen to audiobooks through the audio channel and even the new reading format, like VR reading or AR reading should be encouraged in terms of the reading comprehension effect.

KEYWORDS

Reading Comprehension Effect; Audio Reading

ASIS&T THESAURUS

Digital audio files; Information technology

INTRODUCTION

Audiobooks is booming audibly in the mobile age. According to Global Audiobook Trends and Statistics (2018), audio books performed better than e-book, and US has occupied the largest market share, and the sales reached 21 billion dollars in 2016 and 23.5 billion dollars in 2017. In 2017, 26% of Americans listened to audio books, and listeners read an average of 15 books. *2017 China Digital Reading White Paper* (2018) also found that the market size of audio reading reached 4.06 billion Armbinder, Smart speaker, Himalaya and other companies have actively expanded the market of audio books. The mobile phone in is the most popular device in which people listen to audiobooks. Apps make accelerated listening easy too. In the past, most researchers focused on reading comprehension effect of e-books and printed books, few researches pay attention to the reading comprehension effect of audiobooks listening through audio channel. Compared with reading comprehension effect of e-books and printed books through our visual channel, is the effect of audiobooks through our audio channel better? Moreover, the comprehension effect through dual channel combined with visual and audio is better than any one of single channel? These are the research questions of this paper.

82nd Annual Meeting of the Association for Information Science & Technology | Melbourne, Australia | 19–23 October, 2019

DOI: 10.1002/pra2.00148

THEORETICAL BACKGROUND

Reading is a process dominated by readers to process complex information of reading materials. Reading comprehension effect depends on readers' ability to identify information. According to Dual Coding Theory in the theories of cognition (Paivio, 1986) and Working Memory Model (Baddeley & Hitch, 1974), human have visual channel and audio channel for information processing. They are independent, and have their own information processing method. Based on this, Mayer (2005) proposed Modality Effect, he claimed the learning effect of dual channel combining visual and audio channel is better than the effect of single channel. And later it was explained by Cognitive Theory of Multimedia Learning which believes visual channel and audio channel can cooperate with each other. Many clinical trials of memory physiology also showed it is not only difference between visual channel and audio channel, but also certain correlation between them (Macaluso & Driver, 2005; Meylan & Murray, 2007). Based on existing studies, we proposed: (1) The reading comprehension effect of audio channel is better than that of visual channel; (2) The reading comprehension effect of dual channel is better than that of any single channel.

EXPERIMENT DESIGN

Experiment Material

In order to avoid the cognitive load, we selected a short novel PIERROT as the experiment materials. PIERROT is rich in plot, cleverly conceived and short. We provided mobile phones (iPhone 6 s: screen size 4.7 inches, resolution 1334*750) and headphones (IPHONE 6 wire-controlled headphones, speaker parameters 6_copper ring horn, the type of socket is standard 3.5 socket, product length 120 cm), offline audio material from Himalayan APP.

Questionnaire Design

This study draws on the evaluation framework of Program for International Student Assessment, which is used to assess the skills and knowledge of international students (PISA, 2018). There are 20 items for each reading text, which were divided into three types. These three type items account for 9:6:5 respectively. The answers of type I items can be directly found in the texts; thus, the score only has two levels, 1 point (full score) or 0 point (no score). Type II and III items require deeply understanding to the materials, and are more subjective, thus there are three levels of the score, 2 points (full score), 1 point (partial score) and 0 point (no score). Reading time is limited within 20 minutes, and the questionnaire needs to be finished within 15 minutes.

Experiment Procedure

The 42 respondents were all undergraduates majoring in humanities and social sciences and they had not read the texts before this experiment. They were randomly assigned to three reading groups, and each group is 14. Before the experiment, they were told the purpose, procedure and time limitation of the experiment. After finishing the reading task, they were asked to finish the questionnaire.

EXPERIMENT RESULT

The study Used the SPSS software to test the significance of the sample. F = 3.307,P0.047 < 0.05, indicating that the reading of three different channels has significant differences (Table 1). Besides, the average score of visual reading, auditory reading and dual channel reading are respectively 20.071, 21.333 and 23.071, showing a gradual increase in scores. It can be seen that dual channel reading is superior to auditory reading, and auditory reading is superior to visual reading (Table 2).

	Sum of square	df	Mean square	F	Significance
Between Groups	64.714	2	32.357	3.307	.047
Within Groups	381.571	39	9.784		
Total	446.286	41			

Table 1. Significance test of different reading channels.

Reading channel	Visual channel	Audio channel	Dual channel
Average value	20.071	21.143	23.071
Maximum	25	25	27
Minimum	11	14	19
Variance	3.845	2.669	2.313

Table 2. Comparison on different reading channels.

DISCUSSION

According to the experimental results, the dual channel is better than audio channel and audio channel is better than visual channel on the reading comprehension effect. And the reading comprehension effect of the auditory reading is better than visual reading. This is consistent with previous research result that the memory efficiency of audio channel is better than that of visual channel. The reading comprehension effect of the dual channel reading is better than the reading comprehension effect of any single channel reading. This is also consistent with the dual channel theory. The information presented by dual channel is more conducive to promoting readers' knowledge memorization and understanding.

CONCLUSION

According to the experiment result, the two hypotheses are both established. That means the best reading comprehension effect can be achieved by using dual channel for creation on the mobile phone. Compared with the traditional visual reading, the audible reading is better on the mobile phone. Therefore, the reading comprehension effect of the audio channel is better than that of the visual channel on the mobile phone, so it is of great significance to popularize audio books. What's more, with the development of VR and AR technology, VR and AR reading through the dual channel should be encouraged in the future.

ACKNOWLEDGMENTS

We thank all the volunteers and National Social Science Fund of China (Grant No. 12&ZD222) support.

REFERENCES

Baddeley, A. D., & Hitch, G. (1974). Working memory. In *The psychology of learning and motivation: Advances in research and theory* (pp. 47–89). New York, NY: Academic Press.

China Youth International. (2018). *2017 China Digital Reading White Paper released: In 2017, Chinese read 10.1e-books per person.* Retrieved from http://news.youth.cn/gn/201804/t20180415_11598764.htm

Good e-Reader. (2017). *Global Audiobook Trends and Statistics for 2018.* Retrieved from https://goodereader.com/blog/audiobook/global-audiobook-trends-and-statistics-for-2018

Macaluso, E., & Driver, J. (2005). Multisensory spatial interactions: A window onto functional integration in the human brain. *Trends in Neurosciences, 28*(5), 264–271.

Mayer, R. E. (2005). Cognitive theory of multimedia learning. In *The Cambridge handbook of multimedia learning.*

Meylan, R. V., & Murray, M. M. (2007). Auditory–visual multisensory interactions attenuate subsequent visual responses in humans. *Neuroimage*, *35*(1), 244–254.

Paivio, A. (1986). *Mental representations: A dual coding approach*. Oxford Psychology.

PISA. (2018). *PISA 2018 Released Field Trial New Reading Items*. Retrieved from http://www.oecd.org/pisa/test/PISA_2018_FT_Released_New_Reading_Items.pdf

Does Citation Content of References From Different Disciplines Demonstrate Same Distribution Pattern?

Lifan Liu
Nanjing University of Science and Technology,
Nanjing, China
liulf@njust.edu.cn

Yuzhuo Wang
Nanjing University of Science and Technology,
Nanjing, China
wangyz@njust.edu.cn

Chengzhi Zhang
Nanjing University of Science and Technology,
Nanjing, China
zhangcz@njust.edu.cn

ABSTRACT

Citation in academic articles is an important expression of knowledge flow between different disciplines. Analysis of citation content of references from different disciplines can help scholars to understand the role of various disciplines in knowledge flow. This study identifies the discipline of references in academic articles, and then explores the distribution pattern, including cited frequency and cited position (different type of section), of citation content of these references from different disciplines. Finally, we conclude that distribution patterns of different disciplines are different in knowledge flow. Although most references come from natural science, the humanities and social sciences still play an important role in the introduction and background. Basic disciplines like Mathematics are the main providers of methods, and some disciplines relevant to the research topic, like Nursing and Medicine in PLOS, provide more support for the results part of articles.

KEYWORDS

Citation content analysis; discipline of reference; knowledge flow

ASIS&T THESAURUS

Bibliometrics; Content analysis

INTRODUCTION

Understanding the distribution pattern of references from different disciplines can discover the role that different disciplines play in scientific research. For complex research problems in a discipline, knowledge from other disciplines may provide new methods for the study, and knowledge from various disciplines can also solve the comprehensive problems together, so knowledge flow is important in promoting the development of scientific research (Bammer, 2012).

In existing research, scholars mainly describe the phenomenon of knowledge interflow through bibliographic information of cross-citation between different disciplines (Rinia, Van Leeuwen, Bruins, Van Vuren, & Van Raan, 2002). However, these studies do not reveal the roles that different disciplines play when cited.

In this study, we explore the distribution pattern of references from different disciplines and further to understand the feature of disciplines in knowledge flow. Different from the previous study only considered the amount of citation in different sections (Bertin, Atanassova, Gingras, & Larivière, 2016), we analyze the citation content of references from different disciplines in the full text and different sections respectively. This study is a basic work to explore the motivation and specific content of different disciplines in knowledge flow.

METHODS

Dataset Collecting

210,334 articles in XML format, which types are 'Research Article' and published from 2003-10-01 to 2017-12-31, are downloaded from PLOS (https://www.plos.org/). It should be noted that, we just research on the references from journals rather than conferences or other sources. Finally, we select 154,134 articles, in which the type 'journal' comprising more than 80% of its all references.

Dataset Preprocessing

Identifying Disciplines of References

We obtain a list about the discipline of journals from Scopus (https://www.scopus.com/). It includes 27 first-level disciplines and covers 23,359 journals.9,528,311 references, which types are 'journal', are extracted from the 154,134 articles. After removing duplicates, we get 409,728 kinds of journal titles (including the full name and various abbreviations). Then, we identify the discipline of references according to the name of the journals.

(1) Firstly, we obtain the full name of abbreviation through the journal title list from NLM (National Library of Medicine, https://www.nlm.nih.gov/). Then we identify the discipline of references by matching the full-name of journals in references with the journal list in Scopus, and 71.90% of references get the discipline.

82nd Annual Meeting of the Association for Information Science & Technology | Melbourne, Australia | 19–23 October, 2019

DOI: 10.1002/pra2.00147

(2) For the remaining journals with unknown discipline, we call them journal U. Edit Distance algorithm is utilized to calculate the steps of edits (e.g., delete, insert) that can convert the name of journals from journal U into the name of journals with known discipline. The discipline of journal which has the minimum number of steps is the discipline of journal U. After manual reviewing, we keep 91.98% of reference records (8,284,654) that have specific discipline.

Classifying Types of Sections

Based on the content of section title and the body text of articles, we formulate a rule manually and then use it to classify all first-level sections in articles into six types automatically: IMRaD (Introduction, Methods, Results and Discussion respectively) structure, MR (Methods and Results) and RD (Results and Discussion) (Bertin & Atanassova, 2018). Finally, we obtain 733,302 titles of first-level section, and 99.4% of these sections have exact type.

Citation Content Analysis of Distribution Pattern in Different Disciplines

We combine the cited frequency and cited position (different type of section) to analyze the distribution pattern of different disciplines in this research.

(1) Cited frequency in the full text. It shows the frequency of different disciplines cited in the full text, so we add all the number of times that each discipline appears in the citation content in whole paper separately.

(2) Cited frequency in different sections. We calculate it similar to the method of getting the cited frequency in the full text mentioned above. After classifying the types of first-level sections, we add the frequency of reference from each discipline in each type of section, not in the full text.

RESULTS

Cited Frequency of Different Disciplines

As shown in Figure 1, most of the top disciplines belong to the field of natural sciences. Medicine gets the highest frequency of citation, since most research in PLOS focus on Medicine and Biochemistry. Multidisciplinary ranks the second, which indicates the importance of Multidisciplinary articles in knowledge flow. In addition, basic disciplines like mathematics also provide a large proportion of citation.

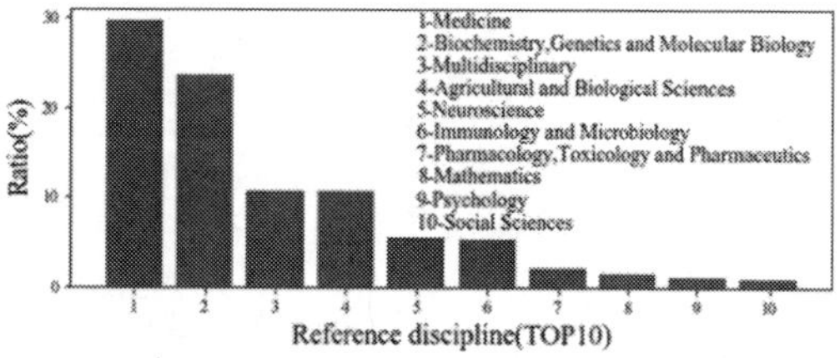

Figure 1. Proportion of cited frequency in TOP10 disciplines.

Highly Cited Disciplines in Different Sections

Table 1 illustrates the TOP3 highly cited disciplines in four sections: I, M, R, and D. Obviously, the distribution pattern of reference shows variety among different sections. In section I, disciplines in social science like Economics and Arts and Humanities are cited more frequently. In section M, TOP3 disciplines are basic (Mathematics) and fast-growing (Computer Science). Decision Sciences cited less in the full-text (not the TOP10 in figure 1), but it is more prominent in section M. However, in section D, disciplines relevant to the research topic about PLOS get higher citation, including Nursing and Medicine, which also indicates the disciplines cited in section D is more relevant to the topic of citing paper.

Section	TOP3 disciplines of reference cited frequency
I	Energy/Economics, Econometrics and Finance/Arts and Humanities
M	Decision Sciences/Mathematics/Computer Science
R	Social Sciences/Biochemistry, Genetics and Molecular Biology/Immunology and Microbiology
D	Nursing/Neuroscience/Medicine

Table 1. TOP3 disciplines of reference cited frequency in the section type I, M, R, D.

CONCLUSION AND FUTURE WORKS

Based on the full-text content of articles, we explore the distribution pattern of references from different disciplines and demonstrate different role played by various disciplines in knowledge flow. Disciplines in natural science are more popular in PLOS, but Humanities and Social Sciences are important in background. Computer Science and Mathematics provide more methods for research. Medicine and Biology are more valuable in results and discussion.

In general, this paper is a primary work to explore the role of reference from various disciplines. We only study the text in section- level and sentence-level. In the future, we will attempt to dig the text content of disciplines using citation content analysis, involving cited motivation, knowledge entities of different discipline when they are cited, and get an insight in knowledge flow between different disciplines.

ACKNOWLEDGMENT

This work is supported by Major Projects of National Social Science Fund (No. 17ZDA291) and Postgraduate Research & Practice Innovation Program of Jiangsu Province (No. KYCX19_0243).

REFERENCES

Bammer, G. (2012). *Strengthening interdisciplinary research: What it is, what it does, how it does it and how it is supported.* Report for the Australian Council of Learned Academies. https://i2s.anu.edu.au/wp-content/uploads/2014/04/bammer_2012.pdf

Bertin, M., & Atanassova, I. (2018). *InTeReC: In-text reference corpus for applying natural language processing to bibliometrics* (pp. 54–62). BIR@ ECIR.

Bertin, M., Atanassova, I., Gingras, Y., & Larivière, V. (2016). The invariant distribution of references in scientific articles. *Journal of the Association for Information Science and Technology*, *67*(1), 164–177.

Rinia, E. J., Van Leeuwen, T. N., Bruins, E. E., Van Vuren, H. G., & Van Raan, A. F. (2002). Measuring knowledge transfer between fields of science. *Scientometrics*, *54*(3), 347–362.

Understanding Formal Scholarly Communication in Information Science by Exploring Generational Evolution of Academic Writing Patterns

Wen Lou
East China Normal University
wlou@infor.ecnu.edu.cn

Jiao Chen
East China Normal University
cj97pro@outlook.com

Tim Gorichanaz
Drexel University
tjg68@drexel.edu

ABSTRACT

Professional academic writing skills can improve the validity of scholarly communication. Aiming to reveal the generational differences of academic writing patterns, by applying quantitative linguistic analysis to explore 53 information scientists in China and 2,328 papers of them, we found that (1) the writing pattern evolves smoothly, (2) sentences that scientists compose in a paper have become longer and longer, and syntax has become more and more complex as time goes by, and (3) scientists tend to be more and more cautious on choosing expression manners and norm words. This research will continue the matters of exact relationships between the age differences and writing patterns, and will be extended to other languages.

KEYWORDS

Scholarly communication; academic writing; NLP; content analysis

ASIS&T THESAURUS

Human communications; Sociometrics; Research and analytic methods

INTRODUCTION

Writing and publishing papers has been the mainstream of formal scholarly communication (FSC) without doubts (Ghiasi, Larivièr e, & Sugimoto, 2015), even though informal publishing has been challenging formal scholarly communication (Shehata, Ellis, & Foster, 2015). Thus, understanding the paradigms of FSC could improve the effectiveness of scientific communication and cohabitate senior and junior scientists with different culture background. Few studies have used quantitative analysis to examine writing patterns. We illustrate the differences in academic writing patterns among information scientists from different generations in China to explore the current most prevalent writing patterns in academic writing for information science in China and the possibility of the effect of age on writing style. Our novel idea of using quantitative linguistic analysis aims to propose a way to measure scholarly communication and even to improve academic writing patterns nowadays.

82nd Annual Meeting of the Association for Information Science & Technology | Melbourne, Australia | 19–23 October, 2019

DOI: 10.1002/pra2.00149

RESEARCH DESIGN

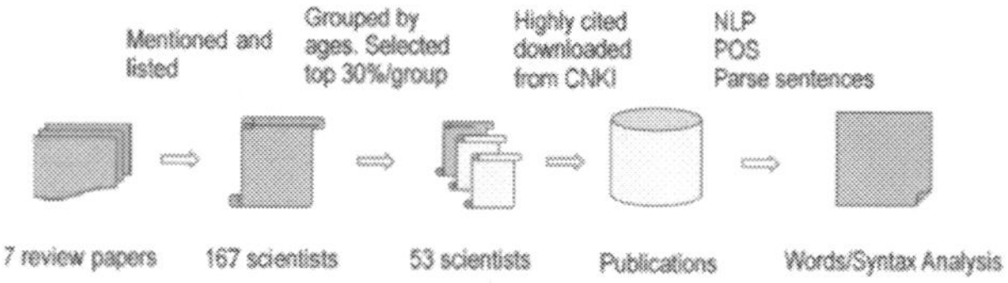

Seven literature reviews from literature retrieval listed 167 information researchers. We gathered their birth years and composed them into six groups: 1930s, 1940s, 1950s, 1960s, 1970s, and 1980s to understand the generational differences. The top 30% of researchers in each group in terms of their total number of appearances in the seven reviews were selected, which is composed of 53 researchers. The top 50 most highly cited papers by each author were collected from CNKI, the largest academic literature database in China; when one has fewer than 50 articles, all of them were collected. 2,328 papers were selected as the sample.

We classified the POS into six groups: noun, verb, adjective, adverb, conjunction, modal particle (uninflected words that convey an utterance's mood, e.g., 啊, 呢). The latest version of information science session in the Chinese Thesaurus was selected for terminology analysis. We used HanLP to parse sentence structure in individual sentences, i.e., subject-predicate ("sun/n comes out/v"), verb-object ("writing/v papers/n"), attributive-centered ("exciting/adj movie/n"), adverbial-centered ("very/adv careful/adj", "suddenly/adv find out/v"), coordination ("dog/n and cat/n").

FINDINGS

Overview

The total number of sentences maintained at around 30,000 in all generations, even as the total number of words increased generation after generation, especially from the perspective of the averages. So scientists tend to use fewer and fewer sentences but more and more words in each paper.

This implies that sentences have become longer, and that compound and complex sentences have become more popular than simple sentences. It reflects one possible evolution of Chinese writing patterns: Senior scientists' patterns tend to be concise and short, and junior generation's pattern appear to be abundant and long.

Generation	Total	1930s	1940s	1950s	Early 1960s	Late 1960s	1970s	1980s
# of scientists	53	7	8	9	7	9	9	4
# of papers in CNKI	5596	739	1502	908	707	1100	547	93
# of sampled papers	2328	319	376	434	313	434	364	88
# of sentences	189163	29443	32444	32868	24146	32037	31474	6751
# of words	7259210	929825	1157637	1328549	964736	1271412	1289289	317762
# of thesaural terms	317646	41470	58057	56457	49334	40464	59861	12003
Avg # of sentences		92.30	86.29	75.73	77.14	73.82	86.47	76.72
Avg # of words		31.58	35.68	40.42	39.95	39.69	40.96	47.07
Avg # of thesaural terms		130.00	154.41	130.09	157.62	93.24	164.45	136.40

Table 1. Statistics of our samples. Avg # represents the number of one indicator per paper per person.

Word level analysis

Nouns are the most frequently used (35%) in all generations, followed by verbs, adverbs, adjectives, and conjunctions in turn. The least commonly used type is the modal particle for all scientists. It is expectable to see the general phenomenon because the sequence frequency of using words' types is, in turn: noun, verb, adverb/adjective, conjunction, and modal particle in a single sentence (Tolley-Stokes, 2014).

The writing pattern in terms of types of words has notchanged dramatically over decades. Mild waves in Figure 1 show some minor generational differences. The 1980s generation use nouns the most often and frequently, and use fewer and fewer modal particle in academic papers, which we consider to be an improvement in writing technique.

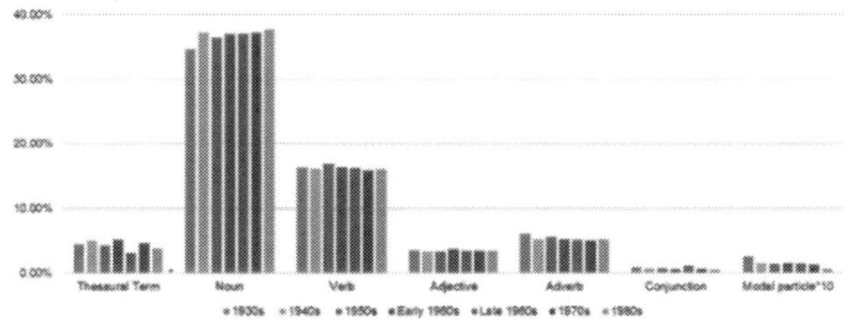

Figure 1. Ratios of the number of one type of words to the total number of words in a sentence. The ratio of modal particle is multiplied by 10 to see it clear.

Syntax analysis

In Figure 2, it is noticeable that junior generations preferred attributive-centered and coordination relations rather than subject-predicate and adverbial-centered relations, which senior generations would prefer. There could be a tendency that academic writing is becoming influenced by popular

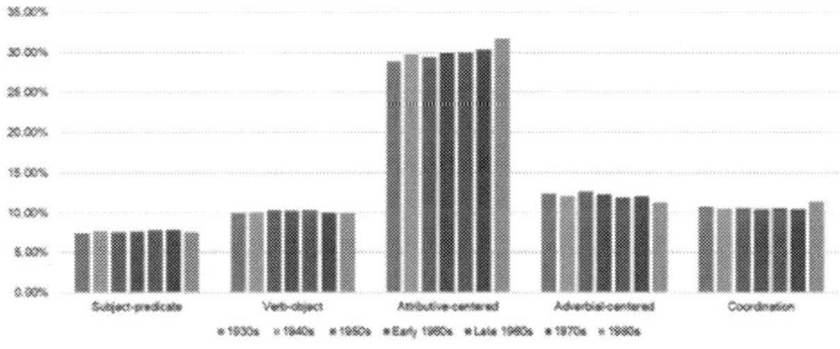

Figure 2. Ratios of the number of one type of sentence structure to the total number of sentence structures in a sentence.

writing. We consider that sentences containing subject- predicate relations as a writing pattern that puts the writers' ideas ahead of the objective experimental results. Compared to attributive-centered relation, which focus on what the results represent, adverbial-centered relation focus on describing what the writers do. We consider attributive- centered relation would be a more objective writing pattern than adverbial-centered relation (Cole, 2014).

DISCUSSION AND CONCLUSION

In this work in progress, we explored the academic writing patterns of Chinese information scientists and found that (1) the writing pattern has evolved smoothly, (2) sentences that scientists compose in a paper have become longer, with syntax becoming more complex as time goes by, implying formal scholarly communication would be more and more complex as well, and (3) writing patterns have become more standardized. Scientists are tending to be more cautious in choosing manners of expression and norm words. To contribute to formal scholarly communication, writing patterns ought to be precise and professional. It would be constructive to have a unified writing standard to correct the unprofessional and to influence the novice.

ACKNOWLEDGMENTS

This research is funded by the grant from China Postdoctoral Science Foundation [2019T12035].

REFERENCES

Cole, S. (2014). Beyond the topic sentence: Paragraph-level inductive rhetoric in humanities and social science writing. *2014 ELTU Conference*, 4.

Ghiasi, G., Larivière, V., & Sugimoto, C. R. (2015). On the compliance of women engineers with a gendered scientific system. *PLoS One*, *10*(12), e0145931.

Shehata, A., Ellis, D., & Foster, A. (2015). Scholarly communication trends in the digital age. *The Electronic Library*, *33*(6), 1150–1162.

Tolley-Stokes, R. (2014). A practical writing guide for academic librarians: keeping it short and sweet. *Serials Review*, *37*(2), 143–144.

Location Recommendation by Combining Geographical, Categorical, and Social Preferences With Location Popularity

Yaxue Ma
Center for Studies of Information Resources, Wuhan University, Wuhan, China
myx_vicky@whu.edu.cn

Jin Mao
Center for Studies of Information Resources, Wuhan University, Wuhan, China
maojin@whu.edu.cn

Gang Li
Center for Studies of Information Resources, Wuhan University, Wuhan, China
imiswhu@aliyun.com

ABSTRACT

Location recommendation could not only increase location visibility, but free users from information overload dilemma. We propose a novel location recommendation method, which first exploits geographical proximity of locations and check-in history of users' friends to measure geographical preference and social preference respectively, and innovatively estimates categorical preference by calculating semantic similarity between location tags based on category hierarchy. Then, all of three preferences are integrated, and location popularity is introduced as a coefficient to determine the priority of locations to be recommended. The preliminary result on a publicly available real-word dataset shows that the proposed method significantly outperforms two state-of-the-art baselines. This study expands the methods of location correlation measurement, and can meet user's personalized information needs.

KEYWORDS

Location recommendation; Check-in; Categorical hierarchy; Location popularity; Social correlation

ASIS&T THESAURUS

Information filteringUser generated content

INTRODUCTION

As one of the crucial features on location-based social networks, location recommendation has received extensive attention from industry and academia. Location recommendation aims to predict users' future movement by mining their check-in history or consuming behavior. The crucial problem to be solved is to precisely model preferences from exiguous visit records. Recent studies have applied collaborative filtering, content-based methods, and hybrid to extract useful information from multiple types of data for modeling user preferences. Simultaneously combining multiple information by some means may help alleviate the problems caused by sparse data, which however has proven to be a significant challenge (Geng, Jiao, Gong, Li, & Wu, 2019).

In this poster, we report our on-going project on how to identify locations that best meet users' multiple preferences. We propose a new location recommendation approach that measures users' personalized preferences to locations by geographical, categorical and social associations, as well as the popularity of locations (abbr. GCS-P). Although neither the three aspects of preferences nor location popularity are novel, we introduce a new way of integrating them into the model to improve the accuracy of location recommendation. This study, to our best knowledge, is the first to introduce category hierarchy and semantic similarity of tags to reveal potential connections and to exploit location popularity as a global attribute of locations for regulating overall recommendation ranking, which expands the relevant theories and methods of location recommendation.

METHODOLOGY

The Framework of GCS-P

Estimating Location Popularity

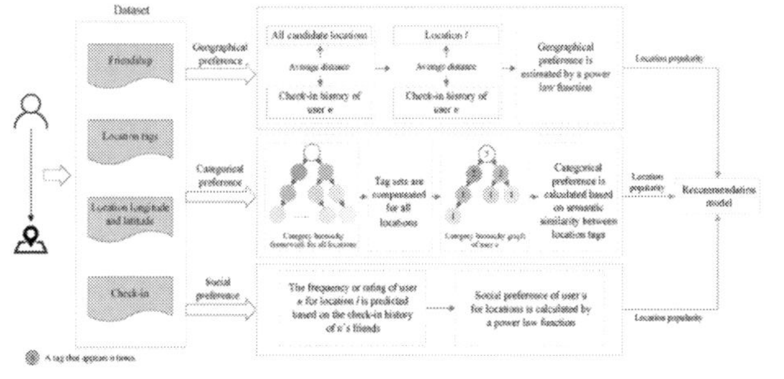

Figure 1. The framework of GCS-P.

In real-world datasets, location popularity score follows the power-law distribution, but users' check-in possibility should increase as location popularity rises. Thus, we estimate popularity preference with the same method of social preference using:

82nd Annual Meeting of the Association for Information Science & Technology | Melbourne, Australia | 19–23 October, 2019

DOI: 10.1002/pra2.00150

$$Pop_l = \int_0^n f_{pop}(z)dz = 1-(1+\mathrm{n})^{1-\gamma}$$

where, n is the number of check-ins in location l, $f_{pop}(x)$ is used to estimate the distribution of location popularity.

Location Recommendation

To comprehensively model user preference and predict locations for recommendation, we apply a linear fusion framework that has been widely used in previous studies to integrate the aforementioned three types of preference and location popularity. The final recommendation score $R(u, l)$ of location l to user u is combined as:

$$R(u,l) = \left(\alpha F_{Geo_{(u,l)}} + \beta F_{Ca_{(u,l)}} + (1-\alpha-\beta) F_{So_{(u,l)}}\right) * Pop_l$$

where, $F_{Geo_{(u,l)}}$, $F_{Ca_{(u,l)}}$ and $F_{So_{(u,l)}}$ represent the score of geographical, categorical and social preference respectively, all of which are normalized. Pop_l refers to the location popularity score of location l. And the two weighting parameters, α and β $(0 \le \alpha + \beta \le 1)$, are used to adjust relative importance of geographical preference, categorical preference, and social preference.

EXPERIMENTAL RESULTS

Dataset

A large scale dataset from Weeplaces is used to evaluate the proposed method. The dataset originates from Foursquare, involving 43,969 cities. Among them, four cities, Chicago, Los Angeles, New York, and San Francisco, are used in this paper. The location tags in the dataset were cleaned by correcting misspelling. Individuals with at least one friend and his/her friends have at least one check-in record were selected as test users, for whom recommendation results will be evaluated. The details of the dataset are shown in Table 1.

	Weeplaces
Number of users in samples	6,740
Number of categories	269
Number of cities	4
Number of POIs	65,621
Number of users' check-ins	1,336,958

Table 1. Basic information of the dataset.

Baselines

GeoSoCa (Zhang & Chow, 2015) and Item-based Collaborative Filtering (CF) (Sarwar, Karypis, Konstan, & Riedl, 2001) are implemented as baselines in our experiments.

Performance Comparison

We evaluate the top N (N = 1 and 5) recommended items for our proposed method and baseline algorithms. Best performance is achieved with the optimal parameters of each method. Table 2 presents the performance of the three techniques. For the dataset, GCS-P shows statistically better performance over the two baselines in terms of precision, recall, and F1 at every position. From the result, we can observe that the F1 score of GCS-P is nearly doubled on average compared to GeoSoCa and CF, which demonstrates the superiority of GCS-P.

Methods	Precision		Recall		F1	
	@1	@5	@1	@5	@1	@5
GCS-P	**0.045**	**0.035**	**0.009**	**0.023**	**0.014**	**0.028**
GeoSoCa	0.021	0.016	0.003	0.011	0.006	0.013
CF	0.029	0.023	0.003	0.012	0.006	0.015

Table 2. The performance @N (N = 1, 5) on Weeplaces.

CONCLUSION

This poster presents preliminary results on the study of location recommendation by combining geographical, categorical, and social preferences with location popularity. Experiments on a publicly available dataset, Weeplace, show that the proposed method outperforms two state-of-the-art baselines. The next step is to test GCS-P on other datasets to further verify the rationality of the algorithm. And further analysis will be conducted on the reason why the accuracy of recommendation is improved by analyzing the influence of information selection, method optimization, and data sparsity respectively. And we plan to conduct a case study to compare the specific recommended locations of different techniques for comprehensively studying what affects location recommendation quality, which may provide clues for better recommendation algorithms in future study.

ACKNOWLEDGMENTS

This study was funded by the NSFC (Nos. 71790612 and 71804135) and Young Elite Scientists Sponsorship Program by CAST (YESS, No. 2018QNRC001).

REFERENCES

Geng, B., Jiao, L., Gong, M., Li, L., & Wu, Y. (2019). A two-step personalized location recommendation based on multi-objective immune algorithm. *Information Sciences, 475*, 161–181.

Sarwar, B. M., Karypis, G., Konstan, J. A., & Riedl, J. (2001). Item-based collaborative filtering recommendation algorithms. *WWW '01 Proceedings of the 10th international conference on World Wide Web May 1–05, 2001*. 285-295.

Zhang, J. D., & Chow, C. Y. (2015). GeoSoCa: Exploiting geographical, social and categorical correlations for point-of-interest recommendations. *Proceedings of the 38th International ACM SIGIR Conference on Research and Development in Information Retrieval*. ACM. 443–452.

Understanding the Relevance Between Text and Images in Disaster-Related Social Media Posts

Jin Mao
Wuhan University,
Wuhan, China
maojin@whu.edu.cn

Ji Zhang
Wuhan University,
Wuhan, China
talentneptuner@163.com

Kun Lu
University of Oklahoma,
Norman, USA
kunlu@ou.edu

Gang Li
Wuhan University,
Wuhan, China
ligang@whu.edu.cn

ABSTRACT

Disaster-related social media posts are often attached with images, either relevant or irrelevant to the text. The relevance between text and attached images can be indicative of the quality of posts because relevant images bring enriched information beyond text. A relevance framework is proposed to depict four aspects of relevance between text and images. A dataset about Typhoon Mangkhut was collected from a microblog application in China. A random sample of 3,000 posts along with 6,217 images were independently annotated. In addition, an automated text and image similarity measure is introduced. Annotation results show that more images are relevant to text on the aspects of object and scene relevance than on literal and behavior relevance. Irrelevant images account for roughly 10% of all images. Text and image pairs with different relevance aspects show different similarity scores. The goal of this study is to improve our understanding of the relationship between text and images in disaster-related social media posts, which have implications for applications based on text and images integration.

KEYWORDS

Image annotation; Disaster information; Multimode information; Semantic similarity

ASIS&T THESAURUS

Data analysis; Image indexing; Disasters

INTRODUCTION

Images are widely used in social media posts. Relevant images can carry more information than text content does. In disaster-related discussions, images posted by users may reveal useful information for disaster response, e.g., infrastructure and utility damages (Imran & Castillo, 2015). However, not all posted images are relevant to the text, and there are different aspects of relevance between text and images. Thus, understanding the relationship between post text and images paves the way for applications based on the integration of text and images.

82nd Annual Meeting of the Association for Information Science & Technology | Melbourne, Australia | 19–23 October, 2019

DOI: 10.1002/pra2.00151

In this study, we extended a semantic model of image annotation to describe the aspects of relevance between text and images. A random sample of 3,000 posts were independently annotated. A similarity measure between text and image is introduced based on the state-of-the-art natural language processing and computational vision techniques. The distributions of the scores in different relevance groups were analyzed.

METHOD

Data Collection

Sina Weibo, the largest microblog application in China, was selected as the data source to collect posts related to Typhoon Mangkhut that was formed on Sept. 7, 2018, hit China mainland on Sept 16, and disappeared on Sept. 18. The query term "台风山竹 (Typhoon Mangkhut)" was used to search Sina Weibo (https://s.weibo.com/) from Sept. 5 to 31, 2019. Metadata of retrieved posts, including user name, text, and links of images, etc., were parsed and stored into a database. Images were downloaded according to the links. A total of 51,652 posts along with 107,328 images were obtained.

Relevance Annotation

Multiple aspects of relevance between text and images can be defined. We define four aspects of relevance between post text and images by referencing to the Eakins model (Eakins, 1996), a hierarchical model consisting of abstract attributes (behavior, emotion, scene, etc.), logical features (objects and their relationships), and primitive features (color, texture, etc.). Details of the relevance definitions are shown in Table 1. We incorporate literal relevance between text and an image in that an image can contains text.

Aspects of relevance	Definition
Literal	The semantic similarity between post text and text found in image (Applicable when the image contains text).
Object	The match between objects depicted in text and image.
Behavior	The same behavior of mobile objects described in text and image
Scene	The same scene described in text and image

Table 1. Aspects of relevance between text and images.

A total of 3,000 randomly selected posts along with 6,217 images were annotated by four Information Science students after training. Each pair of text and image was assigned to two students for independent manual annotation. A pair can be labeled with multiple aspects of relevance (e.g. literal relevance, object relevance, behavior relevance, scene relevance) or indicated as irrelevant.

Similarity Measure

To measure the similarity between text and images, we first used Google Cloud Vision API (https://cloud.google.com/vision) to automatically assign labels to the images. The labels are categories of entities, including objects, locations, activities, species, products, etc. A maximum of six labels with highest support scores that are greater than 0.5 were used for each image.

Then, we measure the semantic similarity between text and labels of the images using word embedding. Weibo posts are generally written in Chinese, while the labels assigned by Google API are in English. The Chinese text was segmented into words and the words were translated into English by Google Translation API after removing stop-words. The representations of text (Text2Vec) and images (Image2Vec) are obtained using word embedding as:

$$\text{Text2Vec} = \frac{1}{|T|}\sum_{w_i \in T}\vec{w}_i, \text{Image2Vec} = \frac{1}{|L|}\sum_{w_j \in L}\vec{w}_j$$

where T is the word set of the text, L is the label set of the image, and $\vec{w}_i$ is the word vector of a word, w_i. Pre-trained Glove word vectors (Pennington, Socher, & Manning, 2014) were used.

Cosine similarity between Text2Vec and Image2Vec was used to calculate the similarity between text and an image. It should be noted that the similarity measure is mainly based on the objects due to the functionality of Google API.

RESULTS

Annotation Results

We obtained 16,796 relevance annotations from 3,000 posts (each text and image pair can have multiple aspects of relevance) with an inter-rater agreement of 65.28%. Table 2 reports the annotation results for the four aspects of relevance.

Aspects	Freq. of text-image pairs	Distinct pairs	Agreed pairs (prop.)
Literal	2,645	1,546	1,099(71.09%)
Object	5,316	3,136	2,180 (69.52%)
Behavior	1,436	898	538(59.91%)
Scene	5,498	3,333	2,165(64.95%)
Irrelevant	1,901	1,249	652(52.20%)

Table 2. Annotation results of the 3000 posts with 6,217 images related to Typhoon Mangkhut.

As shown in Table 2, more images are relevant to text on the aspects of object and scene than literal and behavior. The agreements on literal and object relevance are higher than those on scene and behavior relevance. It suggests that scene and behavior in images are more difficult to determine even by human, which relies on reasoning. Among the 6,217 images, 5,378 have at least one aspect of relevance agreed by two annotators, which are treated as relevant images. And, 652 images (10.48%) are labeled as irrelevant by two annotators. For the above 6030 images (5,378 + 652), we further calculate the similarities between text and images.

Similarity Score Distributions

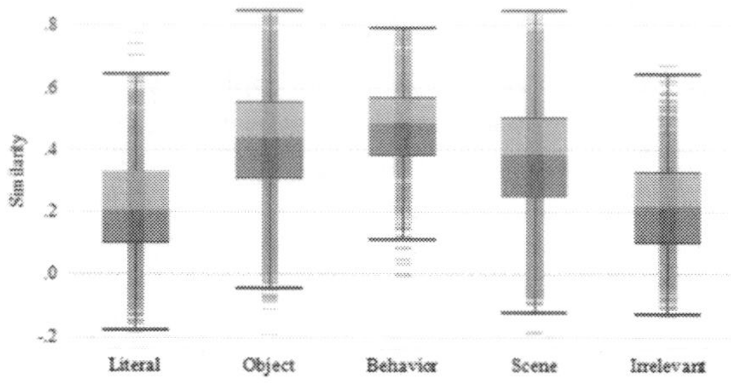

Figure 1. Similarity score distributions of 6,030 text-image pairs in different groups of relevance.

Figure 1 presents the distributions of similarity scores in different groups of text-image pairs. The similarity scores in the groups of behavior, object, and scene relevance are significantly higher than those of literal relevance and irrelevant groups based on Mann–Whitney U test. This shows the similarity score can differentiate object, behavior, and scene relevance groups from literal relevance and irrelevance groups. However, the score cannot distinguish among the literal relevance and irrelevance groups. Literal relevance is not well measured because the proposed similarity does not consider the text contained in the image.

CONCLUSION

This poster presents preliminary results on the study of the relevance between text and images in disaster-related social media posts. Four aspects of relevance are defined and 3,000 posts are annotated. The similarity score of text-image pairs can distinguish object, behavior and scene relevance from literal relevance and irrelevance groups. Future study will further analyze the relevance annotations. We also plan to use machine learning methods to automatically determine the relevance aspects between text and image.

ACKNOWLEDGMENTS

The paper is supported by the National Natural Science Foundation of China (No. 71790612 and No. 71804135) and the Chinese Postdoctoral Science Fundation (No. 2018M630885).

REFERENCES

Eakins, J. P. (1996). Automatic image content retrieval - Are we getting anywhere? *Aslib, De Montfort University, Milton Keynes*, 123–135.

Imran, M., & Castillo, C. (2015). Towards a data-driven approach to identify crisis-related topics in social media streams. *WWW – SWDM, ACM*.

Pennington, J., Socher, R., & Manning, C. (2014). Glove: Global vectors for word representation *Proceedings of the 2014 Conference on Empirical Methods in Natural Language Processing, Doha, Qatar*, 1532–1543.

A Comparative Study of Online News Use by Young Adults in Canada and Japan

Mamiko Matsubayashi
University of Tsukuba,
Tsukuba, Japan
mamiko@slis.tsukuba.ac.jp

Luanne Freund
University of British Columbia,
Vancouver, Canada
luanne.freund@ubc.ca

ABSTRACT

This paper reports on a comparative survey of online news use and perceptions of trust in Canada and Japan among young university educated adults. Results indicate that information use patterns are broadly consistent, with some differences by gender and country. Notably, young adults report heavy reliance upon social media channels as sources of online news, despite consistently low levels of trust for this type of content.

KEYWORDS

Online news use; trust; young adults; gender

ASIS&T THESAURUS

Information Use; News Media; World Wide Web

INTRODUCTION AND BACKGROUND

In the era of social media, people use a wide range of channels to access news, which we define broadly as information about what is going on in the world. Some prefer websites of news publishers or media companies and others prefer social networking sites (SNSs), such as Twitter, Facebook, and Reddit. This diversification of news media has affected patterns of news consumption. According to a Pew Internet Center study (2016), young adults show low levels of interest in the news and prefer to use SNSs rather than traditional news media. Public discourse about "fake news" and reports of bias and manipulation of the news via social media also have had some effect. A recent report (Reuters, 2018) indicated that while Canadians continue to be relatively trusting of the news media, levels of trust in the U.S. and Japan have dropped to low levels.

The purpose of this study is to investigate news use and perceptions of trust among young adults through a cross-cultural and gender-based comparison. We are interested in understanding the role and importance of news in the lives of young adults, what tools and channels they use to seek news, and whether levels of trust for news vary based on the news type. Given reported differences in news use in Canada and Japan (Reuters, 2018), we have chosen these countries for comparison.

82nd Annual Meeting of the Association for Information Science & Technology | Melbourne, Australia | 19–23 October, 2019

DOI: 10.1002/pra2.00152

There exists substantial prior research on online news consumption; far more than can be reviewed here. Given the important links between news use, civic and political engagement and media literacy skills among young adults, this study builds upon and contributes to current research focused on local and cross-national use of news media by young adults (e.g. Antunovic, Parsons, & Cooke, 2018; Elvestad, Phillips & Feuerstein, 2017).

METHODS

This survey was carried out through online questionnaires administered in parallel in Japan (Japanese) and Canada (English). The survey was exploratory, and these results focus on a subset of questions. Data have been examined using descriptive methods and non-parametric statistical tests, with the significance level set at $p < .05$.

The study population is undergraduate students in Canada and Japan and convenience samples were obtained through one major university in each country. Participants were recruited through listservs and social media channels. Valid data were gathered from 189 students. We restrict our analysis here to those in major gender groups (M/F), consisting of 77 (Canada) and 108 (Japan). Due to differences in local means of recruiting, the sample from Canada includes a wide range of nationalities and disciplines, while the sample from Japan is more homogenous in terms of nationality (Japanese) and discipline (social sciences).

RESULTS

Importance and Interests

Respondents rated how important it is to them to "keep up to date with what is going on in the world" (Table 1). The overall average was 7.35/10 and results were consistent across groups, suggesting that respondents considered it quite important. Non-parametric Mann Whitney U Tests found no significant differences by Gender or Country.

	Female	Male	All
Canada	7.5 (1.72)	7.5 (2.14)	7.5 (1.90)
Japan	7.1 (1.30)	7.6 (1.86)	7.3 (1.56)
All	7.2 (1.49)	7.5 (1.97)	7.4 (1.70)

Table 1. Mean (SD) importance of keeping up to date (10-point scale).

With respect to the topics they try to stay up to date with, politics was the most frequent response reported by 53% (n = 39) of the students in Canada. Meanwhile, Entertainment, including Arts, Culture, and Celebrities, was the most frequent response from students in Japan (35.1%, n = 34), which was followed close by politics (32%, n = 31).

Time and Tools

Most respondents reported using online content for more than 30 minutes per day (Figure 1). However, a Crosstab analysis shows that female students reported spending significantly less time than their male counterparts ($X^2(3) = 8.336$, $p = .04$). There is no difference by Country.

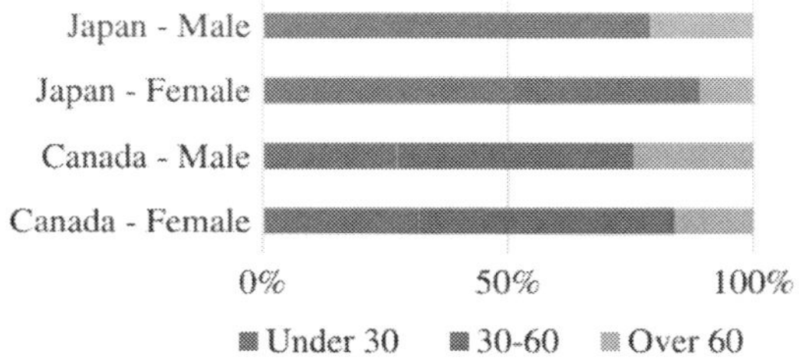

Figure 1. Time on online content per day (minutes).

Patterns of tool use for finding online content are similar across groups. In descending order, the most common methods are: browsing specific sites (86%), using search engines (40%), and receiving alerts or notices from email or other apps (30%). More than 80% of respondent across all groups reported reading news either daily or several times per week, suggesting that news plays an important role in their lives. Social media is consistently the most popular channel to access online news (Table 2). Group comparisons show significant differences by Country for Specific Sites, which are used more in Canada ($X^2(1) = 30.154$, $p = .000$), and for News Aggregators, which are used more in Japan (X^2 (1) = 8.667, $p = .003$). There are no differences by Gender.

	Canada		Japan		All
	F N=44	M N=33	F N=65	M N=43	N=185
Social media	82%	82%	79%	79%	80%
News aggregators' websites/apps	39%	58%	80%	54%	60%
Specific news websites/apps	66%	76%	28%	33%	46%
Print newspapers	18%	12%	15%	26%	18%

Table 2. Use of news reading tools/channels.

Trust in News

Respondents rated the trustworthiness of various categories of news (Table 3). The highest levels of trust were reported for "news they read regularly", and the lowest for "news found through social media". Students in Canada reported significantly higher levels of trust than in Japan, except for "news found through social media", where ratings were consistently low. Gender differences were significant only for "news in general", where female students reported higher levels of trust.

	Canada		Japan		Sig
News...	F (N=44)	M (N=33)	F (N=65)	M (N=43)	C=Country G=Gender
in general	6.4 (1.26)	6.1 (1.52)	6.0 (1.37)	5.2 (1.74)	C: *U*=3179; p=.007 G: *U*=3315; p=.024
they read regularly	7.0 (1.26)	7.0 (1.83)	6.5 (1.49)	6.0 (1.98)	C: *U*=3057.5; p=.002 G: *ns*
through search engines	6.3 (1.42)	6.0 (1.91)	5.1 (1.43)	5.0 (1.60)	C: *U*=2559.5; p=.000 G: *ns*
through social media	4.7 (1.78)	3.8 (1.70)	4.2 (1.39)	4.1 (1.71)	C: *ns* G: *ns*

Table 3: Mean (SD) trust in news (10-point scale).

DISCUSSION AND CONCLUSION

This study indicates that university educated young adults place substantial importance on keeping up to date through online content and are regular readers of news. This is in contrast with other reported results of low levels of interest (Pew, 2016). Paradoxically, across all groups, there is a heavy reliance upon social media, despite very low levels of trust for news sourced from social media. Trust in news is generally low, and likely reflects exposure to the "fake news" rhetoric and concerns over bias in social media. Some interesting within group differences arose, providing support for the notion that trust in news and social media is influenced both by gender and national context (Reuters, 2018; Elvestad, Phillips, & Feuerstein, 2018; Warner-Søderholm et al., 2018).

We acknowledge the limitations of self-report data and the potential impact of differences in these samples, such that these results are subject to further validation.

REFERENCES

Antunovic, D., Parsons, P., & Cooke, T. R. (2018). 'Checking' and googling: Stages of news consumption among young adults. *Journalism.*, *19*(5), 632–648.

Elvestad, E., Phillips, A., & Feuerstein, M. (2018). Can trust in traditional news media explain cross-national differences in news exposure of young people online? *Digital Journalism*, *6*(2), 216–235.

Pew Research Center (2016). *The modern news consumer*. Retrieved from www.journalism.org/2016/07/07/the-modern-news-consumer/

Reuters Institute (2018). *Digital News Report*. Retrieved from http://www.digitalnewsreport.org/

Warner-Søderholm, G., Bertsch, A., Sawe, E., Lee, D., Wolfe, T., Meyer, J., … Fatilua, U. N. (2018). Who trusts social media? *Computers in Human Behaviour*, *81*, 303–315.

Computational Analyses of the Relation of Theme and Genre in the Writing of Aphra Behn

Adam Mazel
Union College,
Schenectady, USA
mazeladam@gmail.com

Catherine Dumas
Simmons University,
Boston, USA
catherine.dumas2@simmons.edu

ABSTRACT

This poster displays the results of preliminary computational analyses of the writing of Aphra Behn, a Restoration-era woman of letters who wrote in a variety of genres. We analyze a selection of her diverse corpus via term frequency and topic modeling to consider how theme and genre relate in her writings: did Behn express similar themes in the many genres in which she wrote, or did she explore certain themes in certain genres, suggesting that her thematic interests determined the genres in which she wrote and vice versa?
Analyzing the relationship between theme and genre in her writing offers insight into whether Behn adhered to the long-standing classical aesthetic concept of *decorum*: the belief, widespread when Behn wrote, that certain genres require certain themes and vice versa. Our preliminary analysis suggests both that she adhered to decorum and that computational text analysis is useful for studying theme and genre in individual authors.

KEYWORDS

Aphra Behn; Topic Modeling; Digital Humanities; Text Analysis; Literature

ASIS&T THESAURUS

Fiction; Poetry; Quantitative Analysis

INTRODUCTION

In the last decade, humanist scholars have employed computers to derive the themes of large numbers of texts, creating a field known as the digital humanities. But while computational methods have been thought suitable for analyzing only large corpora, this digital humanities project hopes to show their validity for single author studies as well. Thus, this poster presents early findings from a computational analysis of the writing of Aphra Behn.

Behn (1640?–1689) was a Restoration-era woman of letters who wrote in a variety of genres: drama, narrative, and poetry; she also translated foreign works into English and edited anthologies of works by other writers. But despite her generic variety, she is often popularly characterized as a writer who was interested in only a single set of related themes: love and desire, sex and gender (Todd, 2004).

This characterization is tested by our digital humanities project, which computationally analyzes, via term-frequency analysis and latent dirichlet allocation (LDA) topic modeling, a representative sample of 11 texts from her collected works of approximately 50 texts. (This analysis of a sample of her texts was a preliminary step to determine whether further inquiry was warranted and how that analysis should be implemented.)

The purpose of this study is to explore how theme and genre relate in her writings and whether her thematic interests are complicated by differences of genre. Do her well-known erotic themes cut across the many genres in which Behn worked, or does eroticism cluster only in certain genres? Likewise, did Behn explore other themes in her writings, and if so, are those themes consistent throughout her formally diverse corpus or do those themes cluster in specific genres? In short, do her themes and genres determine each other?

Understanding how theme and genre relate in her writing offers insight into Behn's relationship to the classical aesthetic concept of *decorum*: the belief, widespread in the early Modern and neoclassical era when Behn wrote, that certain genres require certain themes and vice versa (Abrams, 43–44). Did Behn conform to convention and expectation by writing themes in the genres considered most suitable for them? Or did she break with propriety, thus showing herself to be just as radical in form and genre as she is in her salacious content?

METHOD

The computational analyses were carried out in the Python programming language (via the Gensim and Pandas libraries). LDA topic modeling computationally determines topics in texts by clustering words that frequently occur together in the analyzed text(s); these clusters, if they cohere semantically, are the corpus's topics (Blei, 2012).

The subset of 10 Behn texts, which we acquire from Northeastern University's Women Writers Project, were

82nd Annual Meeting of the Association for Information Science & Technology | Melbourne, Australia | 19–23 October, 2019

DOI: 10.1002/pra2.00153

preprocessed through tokenization, lemmatization, and the removal of stopwords and stopnames. Doing so removes "data noise," such as meaningless proper names and function words, which can drain the thematic coherence of word frequency analyses and topic models.

To reveal each text's themes, each processed text was analyzed for its 30 most frequent keywords and her excerpted corpus was topic modeled; the number of topics was set to 25.

The results were tabled in two spreadsheets: word frequencies and topic models. The former lists each text's most frequent keywords. The latter table (below) shows the percentage of each topic in each text: the columns were the topic names, the rows were the text metadata (title and genre), and each cell listed what percent of the text was comprised by that topic. Named topics in 9% or more of the Behn texts are highlighted (most of the topic percentages range between 1%–20%, suggesting 9% is an apt cut off). The table is sorted by genre. So doing reveals which genres contain which topics and vice versa.

each other; Behn is following classical models and thus adhering to convention. Likewise, Behn uses the Pindaric ode to celebrate and praise, perhaps because Pindar's odes, which created this poetic genre, were celebratory, which codified that the encomiastic tone was apt for the genre.

Thus, in Behn's writing, subject matter and genre may relate and be mutually co-determining—for Behn certain genres may have been appropriate for certain themes and vice versa, just as decorum demands. Thus, while Behn was scandalous via her erotic content, she may also have been conventional in her decorous equations of theme and genre, marking her as a woman ahead of her time in her pathbreaking content and of her time in her traditional uses of literary form.

FUTURE WORK

As this computational analysis of a subset of Behn's oeuvre was fruitful, these computational methods will be expanded to an analysis of her entire corpus so that firmer claims can be made about her aesthetics. Moreover, the insights of these expanded analyses will be put in conversation with the scholarship on both Behn's writing and literary decorum to show how our computational research contributes to those conversations.

Title	Year	Genre	Sacred, Beauty / Attraction / Appearance	War, Violence, Bravery / Cowardice	Justice, Trial, Judgment	Pastoral	nunnery	beauty, pleasure / pain, desire	desire?	women	martial honor	time, language, writing	glory, fame, triumph, power, impressive	virtue / judgment
Sir Patient Fancy	1678	Drama	1%	1%	5%	0%	1%	4%	3%	19%	0%	1%	0%	1%
The Widow Ranter, or, the history of Bacon in Virginia	1690	Drama	0%	11%	17%	0%	1%	4%	2%	2%	26%	1%	1%	0%
The Emperor of the Moon	1687	Drama	2%	2%	5%	1%	1%	3%	2%	2%	0%	0%	5%	2%
The Amorous Prince, Or, the Curious Husband	1671	Drama	1%	3%	1%	1%	1%	15%	1%	3%	0%	0%	0%	2%
Miscellany	1685	Anthology-Poetry	5%	9%	2%	7%	1%	9%	2%	0%	0%	0%	4%	9%
Poems upon Several Occasions	1684	Poetry	18%	5%	1%	14%	0%	13%	1%	0%	0%	0%	4%	2%
A Pindaric Poem to the Reverend Doctor Burnet	1689	Poetry	1%	2%	1%	11%	2%	12%	2%	2%	1%	5%	20%	7%
A Pindarick Poem on the Happy Coronation of ... [King] James II and ... Queen Mary	1685	Poetry	22%	6%	1%	2%	0%	9%	2%	0%	1%	1%	23%	0%
La montre, or, the lover's watch	1686	Translation-Mixed	10%	3%	0%	3%	0%	26%	17%	0%	0%	1%	3%	7%
A Discovery of New Worlds	1688	Translation-Narrative	0%	1%	3%	0%	1%	1%	3%	0%	0%	54%	1%	6%
The History of the Nun: or, the Fair Vow-Breaker	1688	Narrative	3%	1%	3%	0%	24%	10%	11%	2%	0%	0%	1%	0%

Table 1. Topics organized by genre to show how theme and genre relate in a selection of Behn's writing.

RESULTS AND CONCLUSION

These preliminary tables reveal clear trends, confirming that more complete research is warranted. While Behn is usually thought to be a writer interested in desire, this preliminary study shows that her literary interests may be as multifarious as the genres in which she wrote, spanning war, justice, and even language itself. Moreover, her supposed master-theme of eroticism is surprisingly largely absent from her dramas and to a certain extent her narratives; instead, in this sample eroticism concentrates in her poetry. Moreover, pastoral themes also saturate the poetry analyzed here, perhaps because the pastoral mode emerged from classical poetry wherein an urban speaker expresses nostalgia for idealized rural life. In other words, because the pastoral mode was originally poetic, the mode and genre were considered fitted for

REFERENCES

Abrams, M. H. (1993). *A glossary of literary terms* (6th ed.). Wadsworth Publishing.

Blei, D. M. (2012). Probabilistic topic models. *Communications of the ACM*, *55*(4), 77–84.

Todd, J. (2004). *Behn, Aphra (Aphara)*. Retrieved from https://doi.org/10.1093/ref:odnb/1961

An Exploratory GIS Prototype to Map Community Engagement in the Southern and Central Appalachian Rural Libraries

Bharat Mehra
University of Alabama,
Tuscaloosa, USA
bmehra@ua.edu

Everette Scott Sikes
University of Tennessee,
Knoxville, USA
esikes@vols.utk.edu

Vandana Singh
University of Tennessee,
Knoxville, USA
vandana@utk.edu

ABSTRACT

This poster highlights a work-in-progress prototype of a geographic information system (GIS4SCA-RL) to map rural libraries' community engagement with external stakeholders in the Southern and Central Appalachian (SCA) region. It presents a prototype visualization platform for the audience to apply its pilot framework/design for visually representing their own community-based information research in a geospatial context. The GIS4SCA-RL informs a globally networked information society of the efforts of SCA rural libraries via multi-media, web-based hyperlinked collections visually integrated to generate greater impact/relevance in the 21st century.

KEYWORDS

community engagement; GIS; prototype design; rural libraries; Southern and Central Appalachia

ASIS&T THESAURUS

communities; information mapping; multimedia

INTRODUCTION

This poster highlights a work-in-progress prototype (GIS4SCA-RL) of a geographic information system (GIS) to map rural libraries' community-engaged collaborations with external stakeholders in the Southern and Central Appalachian (SCA) region. Historically experienced poverty, illiteracy, unemployment, lack of access to information resources, and other unique political, cultural, social, and economic circumstances have sparked solely *deficit representations* of Appalachian people in the American psyche, news media, and public discourse, within a bigger pigeonholing marginalization of the "South" (Appalachian Regional Commission (ARC), 2015; Cooper Jr. & Terrill, 2009; Mehra, 2017). Identifying positive efforts of SCA libraries and their communities in the GIS4SCA-RL opens-up future possibilities of a *constructive approach* to include additional community assets of the region in such technology-use applications (Mehra, Bishop, & Partee II, 2018).

The structure of the GIS4SCA-RL demarcates eleven domains including agriculture, diversity, economy, education, environment, government, health, information technology, law, manufacturing, and social welfare. Rural community engagement activities in each domain describe their descriptive "aboutness," collaborating partners, debilitating challenges specific to the region, and resulting outcomes (Mehra, Sikes, & Singh, 2018). This web-based dynamic collection in GIS might inspire information agencies (e.g., public/private sectors, professional associations/organizations, etc.) to expand the prototype in developing applications that represent a larger set of rural libraries and other under-represented information entities.

DEFINITIONS

The ARC (1974) identifies *Central Appalachia* to include West Virginia's nine southernmost counties, eastern Kentucky, Virginia's southwestern tip, and the northwestern portion of Tennessee's Appalachian area (Bush, 2003), while *southern Appalachia* includes Appalachian Virginia and Tennessee, western Carolinas, and northern parts of Georgia, Alabama, and Mississippi. The U. S. Census Bureau (2010) defines "rural" as areas with less than 2,500 people and territory (Economic Development Research Group, 2007). *The Encyclopedia of Rural America* defines the related "nonmetropolitan" concept to include spread of housing developments outside metro area boundaries (Rathge, 1997), in addition to being non-urbanized (Office of Management & Budget, 1998).

DEVELOPMENT OF THE GIS4SCA-RL

The GIS4SCA-RL includes limited web-based examples of select community-engaged initiatives in SCA rural libraries and is available at URL: https://tiny.utk.edu/GIS4SCA-RL. We used "Story Map Journal" developed by the ArcGIS software produced by international supplier Environmental Systems Research Institute (Esri) to implement the GIS4SCA-RL and tailor user-centric and research-driven resources online (Esri, 2018). The GIS4SCA-RL structured as a "map journal" contains entries (called sections) on the left-side margin that users can scroll and/or click on

82nd Annual Meeting of the Association for Information Science & Technology | Melbourne, Australia | 19–23 October, 2019

DOI: 10.1002/pra2.00154

embedded hyperlinks, maps, images, or videos. Future usability studies will evaluate the effectiveness of the system, its functionality, navigation, structure, and esthetics, while expanding the content. The GIS4SCA-RL sections categorized according to an alphabetical ordering of the eleven domains with a list of relevant community-engaged initiatives in each domain spotlight the rural library where that activity took place. Users can also navigate by clicking on an SCA map on the right-hand side that has identified "hot spots" highlighting the location of the specific rural libraries (See Figure 1).

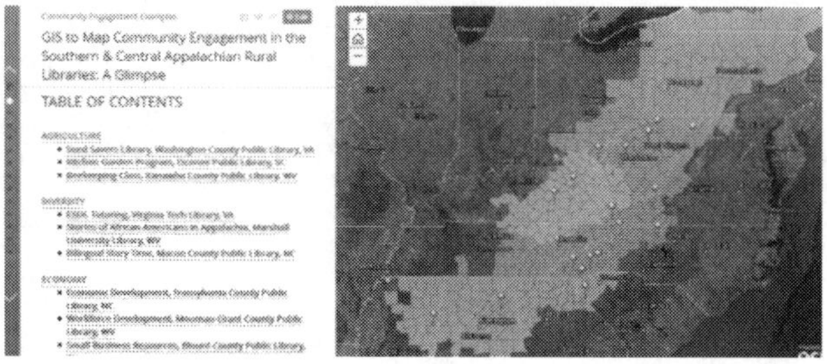

Figure 1. Visual representation of the information and structure of the GIS4SCA-RL.

Under each listed domain, clicking on the name of the community-engaged initiative provides the user a glimpse of analysis of the project represented as an online record with appropriate metadata descriptions. These contain fields that include the agency name and location, domain focus, project description, community partners, challenges, and outcomes (as relevant) (See Figure 2).

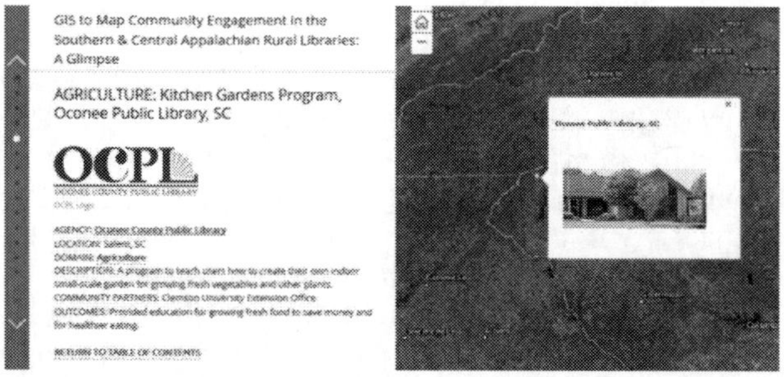

Figure 2. A snapshot of a record located in the GIS4SCA-RL of the Kitchen Gardens Program at the Oconee Public Library in South Carolina.

CONCLUSION

This poster gives a glimpse of an innovative GIS project that provided us an opportunity to explore visualization strategies to evaluate and represent community-engaged initiatives in select case examples of SCA rural libraries (Rinner & Bird, 2009). The GIS4SCA-RL served as an experimental test bed to further mapping the efforts of a larger set of rural libraries around the country based on availability of future funding.

The need to tell the story of the positive experiences of rural libraries and translate those through the medium of a potentially powerful visualized resource (such as the GIS4SCA-RL) is important to challenge past negative stereotypes about the SCA region. We hope such efforts inspire information researchers, educators, and practitioners as well as information-based organizations, professional associations, funding agencies, among others, to develop such tools to further social justice agendas in "making visible" and constructively representing the experiences of marginalized entities (e.g., SCA rural libraries) within the library and information science professions (Mehra & Rioux, 2016).

ACKNOWLEDGMENTS

The GIS4SCA-RL was developed as part a planning grant entitled "Assessment of Rural Library Professionals' Role in Community Engagement in the Southern and Central Appalachian Region: Mobilization from Change Agents to Community Anchors" (CA2CA@SCA-RL) recently awarded by the Institute of Museum and Library Services' (IMLS) Laura Bush 21st Century Librarian to the University of Tennessee, and subcontracted to the University of Alabama this year. The authors thank IMLS for their support and Chris Barrett, graduate student, for loaning his visualization skills.

REFERENCES

ARC. (1974). The new Appalachian subregions & their development strategies. *Appalachia, 8*, 11–27.

ARC. (2015). *Appalachia then and now: Examining changes…since 1965*. Washington, DC: ARC.

Bush, W. S. (2003). *Bridging the gap between culture & mathematics*. Athens, GA: Ohio State University.

Cooper, W. J., Jr., & Terrill, T. E. (2009). *The American South* (Vol. 2, 4th ed.). Lanham, MD: Rowman & Littlefield.

Economic Development Research Group. (2007). *Sources of regional growth in non-metro Appalachia*. Cambridge, MA: MIT.

Esri. (2018). *Story map journal: Create compelling multimedia narratives*. Redlands, CA: Esri, Inc.

Mehra, B. (2017). Mobilization of rural libraries. *The Library Quarterly, 87*(4), 369–390.

Mehra, B., Bishop, B., & Partee, R., II. (2018). A case methodology of action research to promote economic development. *JELIS, 59*(1-2), 48–65.

Mehra, B., & Rioux, K. (2016). *Progressive community action*. Sacramento, CA: Library Juice Press.

Mehra, B., Sikes, E. S., & Singh, V. (2018). *Information technology use behaviors*, In 2018 ASIS&T SIG-USE Symposium, Vancouver, Canada, November 10, 2018.

Office of Management & Budget. (1998). *Alternative approaches to defining*. Federal Register, 63.

Rathge, R. W. (1997). Rural demography. In *Encyclopedia of rural America* (pp. 1–19). Santa Barbara, CA: ABC-CLIO.

Rinner, C., & Bird, M. (2009). Evaluating community engagement. *Environment & Planning, 36* (4), 588–601.

U. S. Census Bureau. (2010). *2010 Census urban area facts*.- Washington, DC: U. S. Dept. of Commerce.

Toward Responsible Scholarly Communication and Innovation: A Survey of the Prevalence of Retracted Articles on Scholarly Communication Platforms

Shinji Mine
Mie University,
Tsu, Japan
mine.shinji@mie-u.ac.jp

ABSTRACT

Open scholarly communication benefits us with unprecedented open access to scholarly information and many innovations, but it requires adequate quality control. This study aims to identify the extent of online availability of retracted articles across all disciplines in early 2019. In all, 1,541 articles were identified in Web of Science, published between 2000 and 2018. Using Google, Google Scholar, and Sci-Hub, the full text of articles were searched on formal and informal platforms. The results showed that while even formal publishers could not comply with Committee on Publication Ethics (COPE) guidelines (e.g., the lack of retraction alerts and open availability), most copies on informal platforms were non-Version of Record, lacking any information of retraction. This preliminary study showed online propagation and inadequate quality control of the retracted articles by scholarly communication platforms, particularly by informal platforms.

KEYWORDS

Retraction; Electronic journals; Platform; Open access; Scholarly communication

ASIS&T THESAURUS

Publishers; Electronic journals; Open access publications

INTRODUCTION

For the last few decades, many stakeholders have engaged in a variety of initiatives to promote open scholarly communication. The implications of this open access (OA) / open science movement cause some ambivalence. While we benefit from unprecedented open access to scholarly information and innovations, illegal or "Black OA" sites (e.g., Sci-Hub, ResearchGate), predatory journals, and the posting of non-Version of Record (VoR) articles have endangered the quality control traditionally ensured by publishers. In particular, the online propagation of retracted articles without adequate control may harm the general public (e.g., patients) as well as the scientific community. Therefore, uncontrolled open access to retracted articles should be avoided, and monitoring and tracking them should be considered an important task (Chen, Hu, Milbank, & Schultz, 2013).

While there are several studies on open online availability of retracted articles in medicine (Davis, 2012) and radiology (Rosenkrantz, 2016), little is known about other fields in the recent scholarly communication landscape. This study aims to fill this gap by surveying the extent of online availability of retracted articles across all disciplines in early 2019.

METHOD

Sampling

For identifying retracted articles in all disciplines, Web of Science (SCI, SSCI, and AHCI) was searched, using the following limits: (Title: "See vol" OR "Retraction of vol" OR "Retracted article. See vol"; Document type: Retraction OR Retracted publication OR Correction OR Correction, Addition OR Article OR Review OR Letters; Language: English; Publication year: 2000-2018). After removing duplicates and irrelevant documents, a total of 5,194 records were identified. A random sampling, with a confidence level of 99% and a sampling error of 2%, yielded 2,500 retracted articles. Among the samples, this paper analyzed 1,541 articles from top 11 publishers.

Searching Retracted Articles on Platforms

Using Google, Google Scholar, and Sci-Hub, articles' DOI or title search were performed to find the full text of retracted articles on formal and informal platforms between March and June 2019. For each article, the author manually checked the abstract page and full text to identify 1) the style of retraction (heading, watermark, reason for retraction, and links to the retraction notice); 2) the full text's availability and OA/non-OA status; 3) the article version (VoR, old-VoR, proof/article in press/early view, author-accepted manuscript [AAM], preprint, retraction note [RN], unknown); and 4) its location (official publisher platform, Sci-Hub, academic social network services [ASNS], subject repository [SR], institutional/departmental website [IR], personal website [PW], and others).

82nd Annual Meeting of the Association for Information Science & Technology | Melbourne, Australia | 19–23 October, 2019

DOI: 10.1002/pra2.00155

Publisher	OA	No retraction information		Total
		abstract	full text	
ACS	43.5%	8.7%	2.2%	46
ASBMB	100.0%	0.0%	0.0%	47
BMC	100.0%	0.0%	16.7%	84
Elsevier	94.3%	1.9%	4.7%	528
LWW	54.7%	26.7%	34.7%	75
NPG	54.9%	1.4%	8.5%	71
OUP	83.1%	16.9%	37.3%	59
Sage	27.1%	10.2%	8.5%	59
Springer	38.4%	1.6%	4.0%	250
T&F	13.3%	6.0%	8.4%	83
Wiley	37.2%	9.6%	20.1%	239
Total	64.2%	5.4%	10.6%	100.0%
	990	83	164	1,541

Table 1. Summary of retracted articles on formal platforms.

	Sci-Hub	ASNS	SR	FSS	IR	PW	Others
VoR	34.8%	23.8%	63.7%	38.4%	19.6%	20.7%	27.3%
RN	1.4%	5.5%	0.3%	1.3%	0.0%	0.0%	0.6%
Total	36.2%	29.3%	64.0%	39.6%	19.6%	20.7%	27.9%
Old-VoR	55.4%	61.2%	14.2%	53.5%	48.6%	72.4%	65.1%
Proof/AiP/EV	4.8%	5.2%	2.2%	3.1%	7.5%	3.4%	4.8%
AAM	3.4%	2.5%	17.5%	2.5%	14.0%	0.0%	1.7%
Preprint	0.0%	0.8%	1.8%	0.6%	7.5%	0.0%	0.3%
Total	63.6%	69.7%	35.7%	59.7%	77.6%	75.9%	71.8%
Unknown	0.1%	1.1%	0.3%	0.6%	2.8%	3.4%	0.3%
	(n=1,528)	(n=366)	(n=325)	(n=159)	(n=107)	(n=29)	(n=355)

Table 2. Article version on informal platforms.

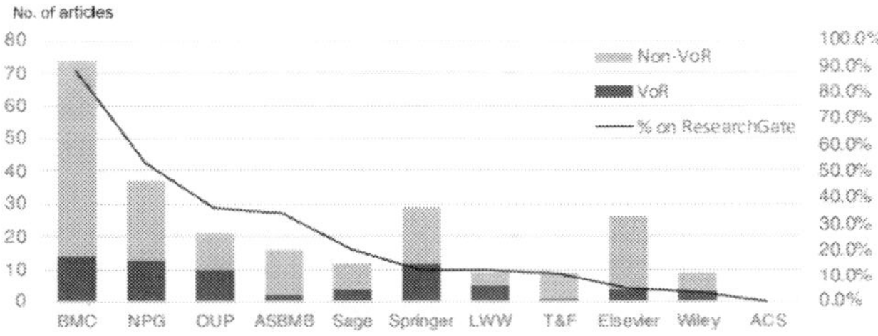

Figure 1. Article version and percentage of articles posted on ResearchGate.

PRELIMINARY RESUTS AND DISCUSSION

Formal Platforms

On formal platforms (official publisher, e.g., ScienceDirect), 99.2% of 1,541 retracted articles provided the full text (VoR), and 64.2% of them were OA. The ratio of OA availability largely varied among publishers (Table 1). About 10% of full text articles did not have any retraction information (heading/watermark/link). While the Committee on Publication Ethics (2009) guidelines recommend that publishers make retracted articles OA to all readers, most publishers could not thoroughly comply with those guidelines.

Informal Platforms

On informal platforms (non-publisher's websites), Sci-Hub contained 99.2% of the sample articles. With the exception of Sci-Hub, 45.9% of the articles were found on at least one or more informal platforms, providing a total of 1,341 files. Disciplinary differences did not significantly affect the extent of informal online availability. ResearchGate (245, 15.9%), PMC (240, 15.6%), Semantic Scholar (161, 10.4%), and Academia.edu (117, 7.6%) were the platforms most frequently hosting retracted articles. Of 1,341 files, 27.3% were available in ASNS (e.g., ResearchGate and Academia.edu); 24.2% were SR (e.g., PMC and CiteSeerX); 11.9% were on file sharing services (FSS) (e.g., kundoc.com and dokumen.tips); 8.0% were IR; 2.2% were PW; and 26.5% were available on other platforms.

The distribution of article versions shows a critical situation regarding quality control on informal platforms (Table 2). All types of informal platforms other than SR provided many more non-VoR copies (old-VoR is a no-heading/watermark VoR) than VoR. Publishers' actions regarding sharing on ResearchGate seemed varied (Figure 1). While articles by ACS, Wiley, and Elsevier (members of the Coalition for Responsible Sharing) had very low availability, BMC (an OA publisher) and NPG (a prime publisher for researchers) left more than half their retracted articles available to readers.

CONCLUSION

This preliminary study showed online propagation and inadequate quality control of retracted articles by scholarly communication platforms, particularly informal platforms. Given that all platforms have responsibility for quality control, it is suggested that all stakeholders, especially researchers, librarians, and publishers, need to take collective actions for retracted articles to ensure responsible scholarly communication and innovation.

ACKNOWLEDGMENTS

This work was supported by JSPS KAKEN-HI Grant Number JP17K00451.

REFERENCES

Chen, C., Hu, Z., Milbank, J., & Schultz, T. (2013). A visual analytic study of retracted articles in scientific literature. *Journal of the American Society for Information Science and Technology*, *64*(2), 234–253.

Committee on Publication Ethics. (2009). *Retraction guidelines*. Retrieved from https://publicationethics.org/files/retraction/guidelines_0.pdf

Davis, P. M. (2012). The persistence of error: A study of retracted articles on the Internet and in personal libraries. *Journal of the Medical Library Association*, *100*(3), 184–189.

Rosenkrantz, A. B. (2016). Retracted publications within radiology journals. *American Journal of Roentgenology*, *206*(2), 231–235.

Identification of Citation and Cited Texts for Fine-Grained Citation Content Analysis

Shiyan Ou
School of Information Management, Nanjing University, Nanjing, China
oushiyan@nju.edu.cn

Hyonil Kim
School of Information Management, Nanjing University, Nanjing, China
kimhyonil@126.com

ABSTRACT

Citation content Analysis is very useful to reveal the nature of citations among scientific papers. However, most of previous studies had been done only from the side of citing papers and ignored the side of cited papers. We proposed a similarity-based unsupervised citation text identification method and a ranking-based supervised cited text identification method. Based on the identified citation and cited texts, we performed a fine-grained citation analysis and found there was a difference in the cited texts between the citing papers in different disciplines.

KEYWORDS

Citation Content Analysis; Citation Text Identification; Cited Text Identification

ASIS&T THESAURUS

Citation analysis; Computer science

INTRODUCTION

Traditional citation analysis focuses mainly on citation frequency between documents, which makes it impossible to deeply discover the real value of a cited work. With the rapid growth of online full-text articles and the development of text processing techniques, it becomes possible to make fine-grained citation analysis and explore the meaning of each citation in depth. This new citation analysis method is called Citation Content Analysis and has obtained the interest of many researchers in the field of bibliometrics (Ding et al., 2004).

Most of previous related studies performed document-level citation content analysis from the side of citing papers to identify citation functions, citation sentiments and citation importance (Jha et al., 2017; Lu et al., 2017). They did not care which part of the content of the cited paper is cited by a cited paper and whether different citing papers cited the same content or not. In fact, a citation in academic papers not only globally refers to a link between a citing paper and a cited paper but also locally refers to a link between a citation text in the citing paper and its corresponding cited text in the cited paper. By identifying citation texts and cited texts, it is possible to perform sentence-level citation content analysis both from the side of citing papers and from the side of cited papers.

In this study, we proposed a similarity-based method for identifying citation texts from citing papers and then a ranking-based method for identifying cited texts from cited papers for each citation text. Based on the identified cited texts, we explored the difference of the cited texts between the citing papers in different disciplines.

METHODLOGY

For a target paper (i.e. cited paper), some of its citing paper were collected. For each citing paper, each citation text related to the target paper should be identified first. A citation text usually can be divided into two parts at sentence level: an explicit citation sentence that attaches a citation tag; and one or more implicit citation sentences that surround the explicit citation sentence and provide additional interpretation to the content of the cited paper. It is not a problem to identify explicit citation sentences in a citation text because an article usually has its own fixed citation format. Thus we focused on the identification of implicit citation sentences in the citing paper and proposed a novel unsupervised similarity-based method for it.

After identifying a citation text from a citing paper, its corresponding cited text in the target paper should be identified. A cited text refers to a piece of text fragments in the cited paper that usually contain one or more continuous sentences (called cited sentences) and have the most similar content with the citation text. We regarded cited text identification as a ranking problem and proposed a ranking-based method for identifying cited texts from the target paper.

Once the cited texts in the target paper for the different citations in various citing papers are identified, we can analyze the content of the cited texts to explore whether the citing papers in different disciplines have different preferences to the contents of the cited paper.

The process of the fine-grained citation content analysis based on the identification of citation and cited texts is shown in Figure 1.

82nd Annual Meeting of the Association for Information Science & Technology | Melbourne, Australia | 19–23 October, 2019

DOI: 10.1002/pra2.00156

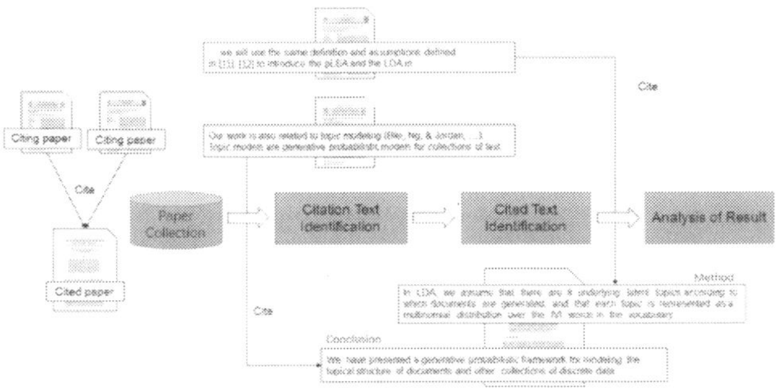

Figure 1. The process of the fine-grained citation content analysis based on the identification of citation and cited texts.

Identification of Implicit Citation Sentences

A citation sentence usually summarizes the main content of a cited paper or mentions some key points of the paper rather than focusing on the current work in the citing paper. It should be more similar to the cited paper than to the citing paper. Thus, we choose some sentences surrounding an explicit citation sentence as candidate sentences and then compared the similarity of each candidate sentence with the cited paper against the one with the citing paper.

As the classical document representation based on bag of words and the Vector Space Model (VSM) only considers word occurrences and ignores their meaning, we improved it using word embedding and thus used TFIDF-weighted average word vector to represent a text (i.e. document vector). Then we calculated the cosine similarity between a candidate sentence and a paper based on their document vector and then chose those candidate sentences that are more similar to the cited paper as citation sentences.

Identification of Cited Sentences

Our ranking-based method includes two stages of ranking: a similarity-based unsupervised ranking and a supervised listwise ranking. Since a cited sentence was deemed to contain more similar content with its corresponding citation text than other sentences in the same paper, we first ranked all the sentences in a cited paper according to each sentence's modified Jaccard similarity with a citation text. Then we choose top K sentences as candidate sentences for the second-stage ranking. In the second stage, a listwise ranking model was trained on the training corpus to rank the K candidate sentences according to the combination of 36 similarity measures and 11 location features, and finally top N sentences ($N < K$) were chosen as cited sentences.

EXPERIMENTS AND RESULTS

We selected and annotated 7 academic papers as well as their 84 references papers in computer science to evaluate our similarity-based citation text identification method. The experiment results showed the document representation based on the TFIDF-weighted average word vector outperformed the VSM-based document representation and Doc2Vec-based representation. Furthermore, using an abstract to represent a paper is better than using its full text while comparing the similarity between a candidate sentence and a citing or cited paper.

The CL-SciSumm Shared Task is a competition of extracting cited texts for scientific document summarization. Since it had the same purpose of identifying cited texts with our study, we used its 2017 dataset to evaluate our cited text identification method. The experiment results showed that our ranking-based method outperformed all the participant systems in the CL-SciSumm Shared Task 2017.

We selected a highly cited paper, Blei's 2003 LDA paper in Journal of Machine Learning Research, and its 556 citing papers as an example to explore whether there was difference in the cited texts between the citing papers from different disciplines. The experiment results showed that the papers in 'Business & Economics' mainly cited the texts in three sections—Title, Method and Experiment, in which 56.2% cited Method, 37.5% cited Title, and 6.3% cited Experiment. Meanwhile, the papers in 'Computer Science' cited all kinds of sections, in which 36.1% cited Method, 20.5% cited Introduction, 13.3% cited Conclusion, 12.1% cited Title, 10.4% cited Experiment and 7.5% cited Abstract.

CONCLUSIONS AND DISCUSSIONS

In this study, we proposed a similarity-based citation text identification method and a ranking-based cited text identification method. Compared against the previous studies, this method can precisely identify citation texts with different spans rather than regarding a citation text as a fixed window, and can flexibly identify cited texts according to sentences' similarity rank to the citation text rather than rigidly categorizing them into cited sentences or not.

A simple application demonstration showed that the identification of citation and cited texts made it possible to do fine-grained citation content analysis. In future, we will explore more in-depth applications.

ACKNOWLEDGMENTS

This paper is one of the research outputs of the project supported by the State Key Program of National Social Science Foundation of China (Grant No. 17ATQ001).

REFERENCES

Ding, Y., Zhang, G., Chambers, T., et al. (2014). Content-based citation analysis: The next generation of citation analysis. *Journal of the Association for Information Science and Technology*, *65*(9), 1820–1833.

Jha, R., Jbara, A. A., Qazvinian, V., & Radev, D. R. (2017). NLP-driven citation analysis for scientometrics. *Natural Language Engineering*, *23*(1), 93–130.

Lu, C., Ding, Y., Schnaars, M., & Zhang, C. (2017). Understanding the impact change of a highly cited article: A content-based citation analysis. *Scientometrics*, *112*(2), 927–945.

Mining Knowledge Entities in mHealth Literature

Min Sook Park
School of Information Studies, University of Wisconsin Milwaukee, Milwaukee, WI, USA
minsook@uwm.edu

Hyejin Park
College of Nursing, Florida State University, Tallahassee, FL, USA
hpark5@nursing.fsu.edu

ABSTRACT

This study introduces a work in progress project that demonstrates how research trends can be captured by mining domain knowledge entities in scholarly articles. From Web of Science, 5,600 mHealth related journal articles published between 2008 and 2018 were downloaded and analyzed. The preliminary results demonstrate how text mining techniques facilitate capturing knowledge transit in mHealth.

KEYWORDS

Entitymetrics; mHealth; Text mining

ASIS&T THESAURUS

Scientometrics, Medical informatics, Data analysis

INTRODUCTION

The purpose of the current project is to mine domain level knowledge entities using text mining techniques to capture knowledge usage and transit in mHealth. Knowledge entities are carriers of knowledge in scholarly literature that can be leveraged to understand knowledge usage and transfer. Unlike evaluative entities (e.g., authors, journals, and institutions) that can assist with measuring scholarly impact, domain knowledge entities facilitate knowledge discovery in a domain (Ding et al., 2013). Examples include entities like disease, drugs, and genes in biology.

As knowledge is being amassed rapidly, domain knowledge entities accumulate as data sets in scholarly documents. These scholarly documents have become huge reservoir of data that contain diverse information such as authors, references, and keywords (Khan, Liu, Shakil, & Alam, 2017; Xia, Wang, Bekele, & Liu, 2017). The data are encapsulated as strings in the literature (Ding et al., 2013). Analysis of such entities offers the opportunity to uncover latent knowledge, including overlay views of research trends, scholarly impacts, and latent scholarly communities.

Recent advancement of data analytic techniques enables us to effectively extract knowledge from scaled data. When it comes to scholarly data, data analytic approaches have recently started being utilized to either evaluate or trace knowledge structure (Ding et al., 2013; Song & Chambers, 2016). Particularly, text mining offers the opportunity for discovering hidden patterns, important concepts, or themes within scholarly literature, which are often text heavy (Song & Chambers, 2016).

Despite the strong potential of discovering latent knowledge embedded in literature, scholarly data is one of the lesser-explored application areas of data analytics (Khan et al., 2017). The primary focus of previous efforts was evaluative entities (Ding et al., 2013; Swanson, 1990). Knowledge entities at the domain level have been understudied, whereas the analysis on them may provide in-depth understanding of knowledge usage and transfer in a domain (Ding et al., 2013).

Therefore, this poster reports on preliminary findings of mining domain knowledge entities from published journal articles regarding mHealth with research questions: a) in what disease context, were mHealth studies conducted, listed by published year; b) what research methods were used in those studies, by published year; and c) what research methods were used to study which disease in mHealth intervention? This study uses mHealth as an example domain because a substantial amount of scholarly articles have been produced as the field attracted researchers from various fields.

METHODS

With the search terms "mHealth" and "mobile health," 5,600 journal articles were retrieved and downloaded from Web of Science (WOS). The search was restricted to English peer-reviewed journal articles published between 2008 and 2018. The titles and abstracts of the articles were used for analysis.

In the first step, 39, 292 terms were extracted using the text mining tool after removing stop words. Then, researchers of this study reviewed the terms to identify meaningful knowledge entities, focusing on diseases and research methods. Lastly, the identified entities were imported into the text mining tool to measure productivity and relationships among the entities.

An open source software, KHcoder3, was used for text mining. The relationships among the entities were measured using Jaccard coefficient index (Jaccard, 1901) and Betweenness centrality (Borgatti, 2005).

82nd Annual Meeting of the Association for Information Science & Technology | Melbourne, Australia | 19–23 October, 2019

DOI: 10.1002/pra2.00157

RESULTS & DISCUSSION

Preliminary findings of the knowledge entities regarding diseases and research methods used in mHealth studies are reported in this poster.

Table 1 shows the top five most frequently appearing diseases out of the 69 different identified diseases. Depression was found to be the most frequently studied, appearing approximately 9.5% (DF = 534) of the dataset (Table 1). When examining the publication productivity by year, depression appeared to have attracted researchers' attentions recently, whereas infection and cancer related studies were conducted more often in 2008, and their productivity has gradually decreased (see Figure 1).

Rank	Disease type	Num. of articles	%*
1	Depression	534	9.54
2	Diabetes	525	9.38
3	Infection	479	8.55
4	Obesity	430	7.68
5	Cancer	416	7.43

Table 1. Top 5 most frequently studied diseases in mHealth.

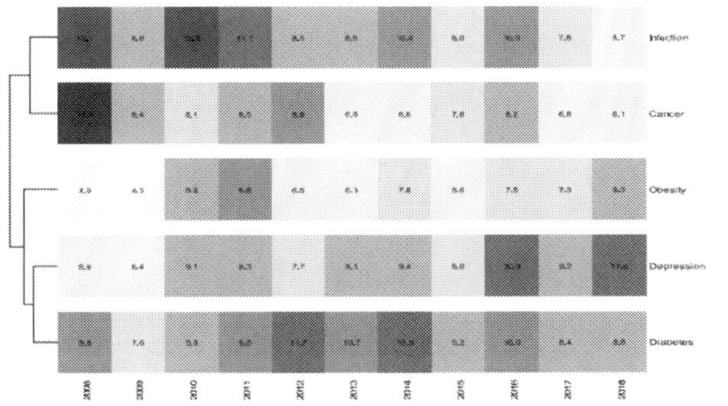

Figure 1. A heating map of top 5 most frequently studied disease types in mHealth by year.

A total of 23 research methods were found to be used in mHealth research. Randomized controlled trial (RCT) was the most prominent research method, appearing in 2,097 journal articles (37.45%). It was followed by survey (DF = 858, 15.32%), blind trial (DF = 577, 10.3%), placebo-controlled trial (DF = 472, 8.43%), and self-reporting (DF = 469, 8.38%). When examining the heating map by year, RCT appeared to be relatively more popular during last decade and gaining more popularity recently among mHealth researchers (Figure 2).

Co-occurrence analysis indicates RCT has been used to study many different diseases including depression, cancer, obesity, and diabetes. Depression was also studied using other popular methods like survey and self-reporting. On the other hand, infection appeared to be studied using the placebo-controlled trial method.

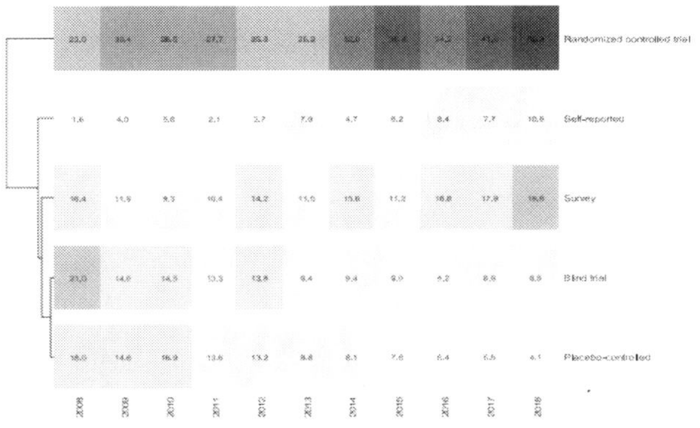

Figure 2. A heating map of top 5 most frequently used research methods in mHealth by year.

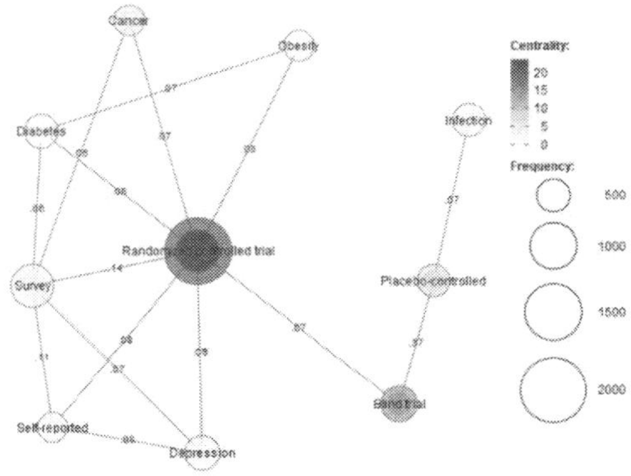

Figure 3. Co-occurrence network of diseases and research methods in mHealth.

The results presented in this study demonstrate how domain knowledge entities can be mined to capture research trends using text mining techniques. The current study used journal articles from only one database, WOS. The larger-scale data and different data analysis techniques may provide a more accurate and overlay view of what research has been conducted in a scholarly area than is currently available. From a practical point of view, findings will help mHealth researchers better understand research trends and find gaps.

REFERENCES

Borgatti, S. P. (2005). Centrality and network flow. *Social networks*, *27*(1), 55–71.

Ding, Y., Song, M., Han, J., Yu, Q., Yan, E., Lin, L., & Chambers, T. (2013). Entitymetrics: Measuring the impact of entities. *PloS one*, *8*(8), e71416.

Jaccard, P. (1901). Distribution de la flore alpine dans le bassin des Dranses et dans quelques régions voisines. In *Bulletin de la Société vaudoise des sciences naturelles* (Vol. *37*, pp. 241–272).

Khan, S., Liu, X., Shakil, K. A., & Alam, M. (2017). A survey on scholarly data: From big data perspective. *Information Processing & Management*, *53*(4), 923–944.

Song, M., & Chambers, T. (2016). Text mining with the Stanford CoreNLP. In Y. Ding, R. Rousseau, & D. Wolfram (Eds.), *Measuring scholarly impact: Methods and Practice*. Switzerland: Springer International Publishing.

Swanson, D. R. (1990). The absence of co-citation as a clue to undiscovered causal connections. In C. L. Borgman, *Scholarly communication and bibliometrics* (pp. 129–137). Newbury Park, CA: Sage.

Xia, F., Wang, W., Bekele, T. M., & Liu, H. (2017). Big scholarly data: A survey. *IEEE Transactions on Big Data*, *3*(1), 18–13.

The Role of Data & Synthesis Centers in Convergence Research

Danielle Pollock
Simmons University, Boston, MA, USA
danielle.pollock@simmons.edu

Suzie Allard
University of Tennessee, Knoxville, TN, USA
sallard@utk.edu

An Yan
University of Washington, Seattle, WA, USA
yanan15@uw.edu

Michelle Parker
University of Tennessee, Knoxville, TN, USA
mparke48@vols.utk.edu

ABSTRACT

The convergence of scientific disciplines poses many challenges for data integration and management. As part of ongoing research into the role of data in new emerging research communities, we examined the perspective of synthesis center directors, professionals with expertise in supporting cross-domain research using existing data to solve complex environmental challenges. Responses give insight into the roles data and synthesis centers play in the development of convergence research communities.

KEYWORDS

Data sharing; Convergence research; Environmental health; Synthesis; Emerging research communities

ASIS&T THESAURUS

Emerging disciplines; Research data sets; Information sharing

INTRODUCTION

Convergence research is "driven by a specific and compelling problem" involving "deep integration across disciplines," (NSF, 2017) going beyond the intermingling of knowledge, methods, and theory that characterize interdisciplinary or transdisciplinary research to encompass the emergence of entirely new research paradigms and communities. Convergence research often involves the integration of data from multiple domains; however, little is known about the role of data in shaping these collaborations.

This study is part of ongoing research to understand the role of data in new emerging research communities. We examine how these researchers understand and interact with scientific data sets, particularly those outside their primary discipline; how data is shared within convergence research teams; and how information professionals can help researchers with the interpersonal and technical challenges of reusing, integrating, and managing often very diverse data sets (Specht et al., 2015). Our study began with environmental health, an emerging research community focusing on the impacts of chemical, biological, and other factors in the environment on human health (WHO, 1993), due to the data-driven nature of the research and its potential high impact on human life.

Synthesis centers are institutions that support collaborative research involving the transdisciplinary synthesis of existing data to solve complex environmental problems (Baron et al., 2017; Specht et al., 2015). Personnel at the 13 synthesis centers worldwide have expertise in helping facilitate data-intensive interdisciplinary and transdisciplinary research, including helping assemble diverse teams, facilitating group collaboration, and providing resources and expertise for research support. In this study, we talked to four synthesis center directors who had worked with facilitating synthesis research projects in the environmental health domain. We had the following research questions:

- RQ1: What is the role of synthesis centers in supporting data usage for cross-domain research groups?
- RQ2: What are the data challenges that cross-domain researchers face?

METHODS

Participants were current or former synthesis center directors who were also members of the Data Observation Network for Earth (DataONE) community. Semi-structured interviews were conducted via web or phone at a time of participants' choosing between July and August of 2016.

No.	Center	Role
1	Synthesis Center 1	Director
2	Synthesis Center 2	Director
3	Synthesis Center 2	Director Emeritus
4	Synthesis Center 3	Director

Table 1. Interview Participants.

Interviews were transcribed. After an initial round of open coding to identify broad themes and develop a codebook, a second round of coding was done by at least two researchers

82nd Annual Meeting of the Association for Information Science & Technology | Melbourne, Australia | 19–23 October, 2019

DOI: 10.1002/pra2.00158

on each transcript; where coding differed, researchers came to consensus via subsequent discussion.

RESULTS

RQ1; What is the role of synthesis centers in supporting data usage for cross-domain research groups?

Baron et al. (2017) identified six "critical ingredients" for successful synthesis centers. Our participant responses focused on four of these:

- *Active management of social dynamics and intellectual space for teams*: Including provision of formal facilitators, dispute resolution support, and data experts to help with cross-domain vocabularies/practices.
- *Diversity of working-group participants*: Help gathering the appropriate disciplinary expertise together to address a particular challenge, including identifying relevant data creators.
- *The offering of time and environment for group associative thinking*: Including provision of time and space for in-person collaboration as well as opportunity for team building and socialization beyond the immediate scope of the project.
- *Computing, data management, and informatics support*: Including help with data analysis, provision of software and software/database specialists, and help using free tools such as R.

The remaining two critical ingredients—*organizational flexibility to accommodate the needs of working groups* and *support for students and postdoctoral and sabbatical fellows*—were less emphasized in this specific context. Synthesis centers do participate in outreach and education activities, including, in one case, working with cross-disciplinary teams and holding research conferences with students at the undergraduate level.

RQ2: What are the data challenges that cross-domain researchers face?

While synthesis center personnel may also help with the technical challenges of analyzing and managing data, in this study, respondents primarily discussed the interpersonal and disciplinary-level challenges of integrating and managing data of "very different types across different domains" (Interview 2). Beyond data heterogeneity, disciplines differ in the openness of their data. Restrictions on public health data were mentioned as particular challenges for environmental health research, as were social and political challenges related to making some environmental data open. The need for quality metadata and good data visualization was noted, and one respondent wished for a new cross-disciplinary journal "that allows a lot of metadata along with the article" (Interview 3) to aid scholars in interpreting synthesis research.

Synthesis centers helped with data challenges in a variety of ways, including:

- Help with data use agreements and intellectual property issues
- Supporting team discussion about data
- Providing online tools for data sharing
- Providing education on data interpretation
- Providing expert personnel "that are able to listen to people from different domains" (Interview 4).

When speaking of the skills required for managing cross-disciplinary data one respondent noted, "it's really important to have someone as the data manager who is open and interested in the way people from different domains come at data, and they find that fascinating" (Interview 4).

While synthesis centers provide support for individual research collaborations, challenges created by a lack of an overall culture of collaboration between health and environmental sciences at the disciplinary level remain, prompting one respondent to note "probably we need to stimulate more interactions between health sciences and environmental sciences" (Interview 2).

CONCLUSION

This study revealed a number of disciplinary challenges that exist for data-intensive collaboration, including data interoperability, data ownership, education, and scholarly publication. Researchers approach and interact with data differently because of diverse research cultures. Synthesis centers play an important role in understanding these differences and facilitating data usage across domains and the unique perspective their directors provide on cross-disciplinary data challenges will inform future information studies. Ongoing research examines scientists' perspectives on the role of data in convergence research teams and will go beyond environmental health to focus on other emerging research communities.

REFERENCES

Baron, J. S., Specht, A., Garnier, E., Bishop, P., Campbell, C. A., Davis, F. W., … Halpern, B. S. (2017). Synthesis centers as critical research infrastructure. *BioScience*, *67*(8), 750–759.

National Science Foundation. (2017). *Dear colleague letter: Growing convergence research at NSF (NSF 17-065)*. Retrieved from https://www.nsf.gov/pubs/2018/nsf18058/nsf18058.jsp

Specht, A., Guru, S., Houghton, L., Keniger, L., Driver, P., Ritchie, E. G., … Treloar, A. (2015). Data management challenges in analysis and synthesis in the ecosystem sciences. *Science of the Total Environment*, *534*, 144–158.

World Health Organization. (1993). *WHO | Public health, environmental and social determinants of health (PHE)*. Retrieved from http://www.who.int/phe/en/

Using Text Mining and Data Visualization to Trace the Disciplinary Boundaries of Collective Memory Studies

Ana Roeschley
University of North Texas,
Denton, USA
ana.roeschley@unt.edu

ABSTRACT

Halbwachs first coined the term "collective memory" in 1941 (Halbwachs, 1992). Since then collective memory has permeated a number of disciplines including history, psychology, political science, and information science. In applying the concept of collective memory to library and information sciences (LIS), it has been most widely used in archival science. The purpose of this study is to examine if collective memory scholarship translates across disciplinary boundaries. To examine the wider field of collective memory literature, this study employs text mining and visualization in an analysis of scholarly articles on the topic. This initial study shows that collective memory literature is overwhelmingly concerned with similar topics across disciplines and has further potential for archival scholars and other information scientists beyond disciplinary silos.

KEYWORDS

Collective memory; archival science; text mining; data visualization; cooccurrence analysis

ASIS&T THESAURUS

Archival Science; Cooccurrence analysis; Network analysis

INTRODUCTION

While we may have always known that our memories are affected and shaped by those around us, we did not clearly articulate this until close to the mid 20th century when the concept of collective memory was originated by sociologist Maurice Halbwachs in 1941 who argued that "there exists a collective memory and social frameworks for memory; it is to the degree that our individual thought places itself in these frameworks and participates in this memory that it is capable of the art of recollection" (Halbwachs, 1992, p. 38). Since then, collective memory has been researched in many disciplines including information science where the focus on collective memory has mainly been in the archives field. Collective memory also plays a part in other aspects of information science as well. In knowledge management, understanding collective memory could allow us to gain a deeper understanding of knowledge transfer. However, there seems to be little research on the role of collective memory in information science topics beyond archival science.

Furthermore, when Jacobsen, Punzalan, and Hedstrom (2013) systematically examined and mapped collective memory literature in the archival field they found archival literature on collective memory "insular and self-referential" (p. 233). To examine the wider field of collective memory literature, this project explores the scholarship on collective memory beyond the archival discipline through a text mining approach.

In order to help us understand whether scholarship on collective memory translates across disciplinary boundaries, the goal of this study is to map the knowledge structure of collective memory research from the 1970's to the present period. To identify and visualize the relationships between topics within the subject area, I applied the concept of co-word investigation to analyze cooccurrence of keywords derived from the abstracts in peer-reviewed journal articles on collective memory. Through this analysis, we can come to an understanding of whether literature and scholarship on collective memory translates across disciplinary boundaries and if collective memory scholars outside the archival field are researching aspects of collective memory that should hold appeal for archival and other information science scholars.

BACKGROUND

In information science, archivists and archival scholars have been the primary researchers of collective memory in the field. Notably, Jacobsen et al. (2013) explore the concept of collective memory and its place within archival literature. They stress that archivists and archival scholars are fascinated by this subject because so many of archival "professional activities are considered forms of memory preservation" (p. 218). Jacobsen, Punzalan, and Hedstrom express a "belief that collective memory research by non-archivists should be of interest to archivists" but that testing this belief is beyond the scope of their study (p. 234). However, they found that archival scholars did not stray far past archival literature when researching collective memory (p. 233).

While the bulk of the research on collective memory in information science is found within archival literature, there is further

82nd Annual Meeting of the Association for Information Science & Technology | Melbourne, Australia | 19–23 October, 2019

DOI: 10.1002/pra2.00159

potential for the concept within the field. Knowledge management can also be paired with the concept of collective memory easily. Dieng, Corby, Giboin, and Ribiere (1999) argue that the collective memory concept can be useful when dealing with organizational crises. The authors state that "the collective memory of past incidents can be useful for taking a decision in case of a new breakdown. The retrieval of a similar past case can be used to suggest a solution to a new problem" (p. 20). However, collective memory is not utilized frequently in the information sciences literature beyond the archival sciences.

METHODOLOGY

I searched both Library and Information Science-related databases, including Library and Information Science Abstracts and Library & Information Science Sources, as well as general databases including Academic Search Complete, ProQuest, Project MUSE, Web of Science, and Google Scholar for English language, peer-reviewed articles containing the phrase "collective memory" in either the title or abstract fields.

Once the data was collected, I exported the publication record for all peer-reviewed journal articles in a tab-delimited format from RefWorks. Two variables were then added to the spreadsheet including publication subject classification using journal subject classification and geographic location based on the first author's institution. Data visualizations based on these two variables and the publication year variable were created using Tableau.

The processed text file was also imported into WordStat where I could determine frequently occurring terms to create a dictionary for text mining. Words that stemmed from the same cognate were manipulated as synonyms of a single-word entry and abbreviation/acronyms were fixed to their formal version. Once the dictionary was created, I calculated high frequency keywords and created a co-occurrence matrix. Due to the complexity and density of the extracted keywords co-occurrence network, the words were drawn for the words and phrases that were found in four or more abstracts; thus, a total of 376 keywords were used as the basis for subsequent co-word analysis. The visualization map and its network characters were obtained by analyzing the co-occurrence matrix using betweeness centrality and modularity measures in Gephi.

RESULTS

This initial study of collective memory literature found 1756 scholarly, peer-reviewed articles from 51 disciplines and 75 countries. LIS/archival scholars are responsible for 3% of these articles. The top 55 terms include terms that are often found in archival science and wider information science. These include "archive," "knowledge," and "representation." The text mining analysis shows a graph density of .182 and a modularity .033. This indicates that the graph is considerably homogenous. However, three distinct concept communities were identified.

The largest and most dominant community is in purple and it consists of 50% of the nodes. This community includes the words and phrases such as "narrative," "memory," "history," and "national identity." This community can be interpreted as the building blocks of collective memory studies. The works belonging to this community are largely concerned with how narratives of the past impact collective memory.

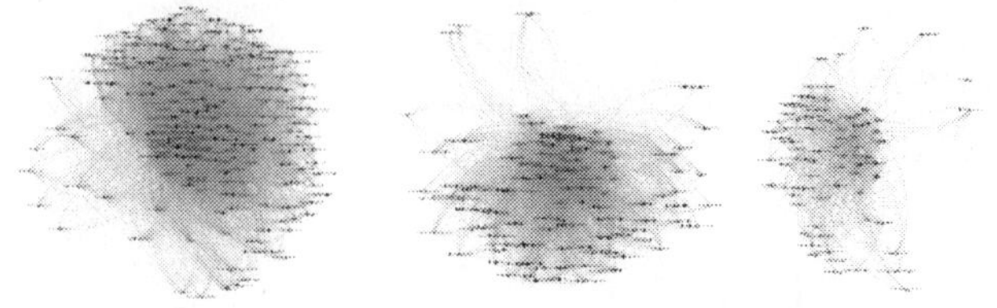

Figure 1. The text mining analysis shows a graph density of .182 and a modularity .033. This indicates that the graph is considerably homogenous. However, three distinct concept communities were identified.

The second largest community is in orange and it contains 30.32% of the nodes. This community, which includes the words "archive," "individual," "material," "theory," and "concept," can be seen as collective memory as theoretical concept. The literature in this community explores the theoretical underpinnings of collective memory scholarship.

The last community, in green, contains 19.68% of the nodes. This community contains phrases and keywords such as "personal," "truth and reconciliation," "trauma," and "experience." This community can be interpreted as impact of collective memory on individuals and communities. The works in this community are principally focused on how people and their lived experiences are shaped by collective memory.

DISCUSSION AND CONCLUSION

This study shows that the concept of collective memory is highly interdisciplinary and concerned with similar topics across disciplines. The lack of highly distinct communities suggests that rather than a concept that is used for disparate purposes throughout the disciplines, "collective memory" is used to discuss similar research topics.

While Jacobsen et al. (2013) found archival science scholars to be insular in their collective memory research, these findings suggest that archival studies scholarship could benefit from the influence of wider literature on collective memory. As was found in this study, archival studies and other LIS literature only accounts for 3% of the wider literature on collective memory. Wider collective memory studies are a rich field of literature that provides archival scholars and other information scientists opportunities to conduct wider interdisciplinary research on collective memory.

REFERENCES

Dieng, R., Corby, O., Giboin, A., & Ribiere, M. (1999). Methods and tools for corporate knowledge management.

International Journal of Human-Computer Studies, *51* (3), 567–598.

Halbwachs, M., & Coser, L. A. (1992). *On collective memory*. University of Chicago Press.

Jacobsen, T., Punzalan, R. L., & Hedstrom, M. L. (2013). Invoking "collective memory": Mapping the emergence of a concept in archival science. *Archival Science*, *13*(2-3), 217–251. https://doi.org/10.1007/s10502-013-9199-4

Identifying the Collaboration Styles of Research Students

Harry Rolf
Australian National University,
Canberra, Australia
harry.rolf@anu.edu.au

ABSTRACT

Today engaging in collaboration is an important factor affecting the success of research students. Having insight into the social dynamics of collaboration can enhance their decision making when engaging with researchers, projects and institutions. This poster reports on the results of a study that investigated collaboration by research students at the University of Tasmania using co-authorship information on research publications. The study applied a visual analytic method for exploring and interpreting the social dynamics of collaboration. Results demonstrate the effectiveness of this approach, providing insight into the roles of co-authors and revealing the presence of functional research teams with different styles of collaboration.

KEYWORDS

Collaboration; Social networks; Research students; Teams

ASIS&T THESAURUS

Scientometrics; Network analysis; Decision making

INTRODUCTION

Engaging in collaboration is an essential part of research that enhances the chances of impact, innovation and success (Fortunato et al., 2018). For research students and early-career researchers collaborations can give them and their work greater visibility and access to networks which can lead to information, new ideas and career opportunities (Horta & Santos, 2016). Collaboration also benefits the organizations involved by developing and sustaining networks for inter-organizational engagement and knowledge transfer – generating greater reputational value from the research training process (Thune, 2009). While bad collaboration can damage reputations and careers (Youtie & Bozeman, 2014).

Having insight into the social dynamics of collaboration can enhance reasoning and decision making by research students when engaging in collaborations with researchers, projects and institutions. However, information about collaboration is often not easy to access or interpret. This poster reports on the results of a study that applied a visual analytic method to explore and interpret collaboration by research students at the University of Tasmania using research publications.

82nd Annual Meeting of the Association for Information Science & Technology | Melbourne, Australia | 19–23 October, 2019

DOI: 10.1002/pra2.00160

DATA & METHOD

Inferring Collaboration from Co-authorship

To study research student collaboration, a co-author network was created from a sample of 1216 publications authored by research students at the University of Tasmania from 2007-2015, the publication metadata was retrieved from Elsevier's Scopus abstract and citation database. The Gephi software package (version 0.9.2) was used for the visualization and statistical analysis of the co-author network (Bastian, Heymann, & Jacomy, 2009).

Identifying Teams and Co-author Roles

To study the structural and functional characteristics of collaboration an information-theoretic clustering algorithm was used to decompose the co-author network into clusters of closely interconnected co-authors (Rosvall & Bergstrom, 2007). The algorithm was chosen because the clusters that it generates have been found to detect functional research teams (Velden, Haque, & Lagoze, 2010).

Co-authors were then categorized into a series of seven universal roles (Table 1) by comparing a co-author's within-cluster degree (that is the number of links between a co-author and other co-authors in the cluster) using a z-score (z) and the distribution of a co-author's degree to co-authors in other clusters using a participation coefficient (P) (Guimera et al., 2007).

Role	Name	z-score	Coefficient P
R1	Ultra-peripheral	$z < 2.5$	$P \leq 0.05$
R2	Peripheral		$0.05 < P \leq 0.62$
R3	Satellite connector		$0.62 < P \leq 0.8$
R4	Kinless		$P > 0.8$
R5	Provincial hub	$z \geq 2.5$	$P \leq 0.3$
R6	Connector hub		$0.3 < P \leq 0.75$
R7	Global hub		$P > 0.75$

Table 1. Summary of universal roles R1-R7 with z and P thresholds (Guimera et al., 2007, p. 6).

Type	R1	R2	R3	R4	R5	R6	R7
Student	490	249	35	0	3	2	0
Non	1434	688	66	2	22	31	2

Table 2. Frequency table of roles (R1-R7) and co-authors by type (research student or non-student).

RESULTS

The resulting co-author network contained 3024 co-authors (779 were research students) with 26414 links between them, the network was decomposed into 277 clusters. The network's giant component (the largest connected group of co-authors) contained 83% of all co-authors and 162 clusters, with an average clustering coefficient of 0.87 and a graph density of 0.007. Only 60 co-authors occupied hub roles on the network, 5 of which were research students (Table 2). The majority of the 277 clusters (80.5%) had no hubs, while 50 had one (18.1%) and 4 had two or three (1.4%). The low density and high level of clustering among co-authors reveals a dispersed network of many locally interconnected clusters.

The networks role-role link profile is indicative of a stringy-periphery class of network (Guimera et al., 2007). Ultra-peripheral (R1) co-authors were highly connected to one another (69.85% of all links), many Provincial (R5) and Connector (R6) hub co-authors were directly connected to one another forming cores of hubs and less connected to (R1) co-authors than would be expected by chance (only 2.48% of all links). The presence or absence of roles in a cluster and the variation of within-cluster degree (Figure 1) reveals different styles of collaboration. Within the clusters research students occupy the bonding (homophilic) non-hub roles (R1-R3) that act as local organizers while non-students tend to occupy the hub roles (R5-R6) that act as the bridges, brokers and gatekeepers to clusters on the network.

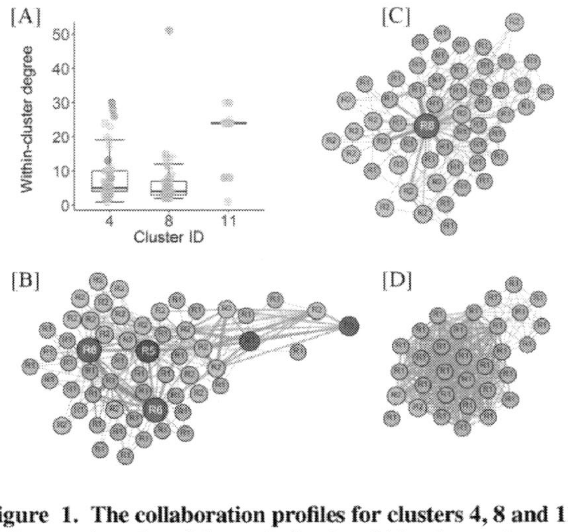

Figure 1. The collaboration profiles for clusters 4, 8 and 11. [A] Shows a boxplot of the variation in within-cluster degree for co-authors in the three clusters; [B] Shows Cluster 4 which has a distributed profile with multiple hubs; [C] Shows Cluster 8 which has an ego-centric profile with a single dominant hub; [D] Shows Cluster 11 which has an equal contribution profile with no hubs.

DISCUSSION

This poster demonstrates the effectiveness of a visual analytic method for exploring and interpreting the social dynamics of collaboration. The method was able to describe collaboration by research students at the University of Tasmania and reveal the presence of different styles of collaboration within clusters that represent functional research teams. Future work should investigate the extent to which collaboration styles identified by the visual analytic method are related to an institution's policies, physical research environment and the experience of co-authors.

ACKNOWLEDGMENTS

I want to thank the University of Tasmania for their assistance with the identification of publications by research students used in this study.

REFERENCES

Bastian, M., Heymann, S., & Jacomy, M. (2009). *Gephi: An open source software for exploring and manipulating networks*. In Third International AAAI Conference on Weblogs and Social Media.

Fortunato, S., Bergstrom, C. T., Börner, K., Evans, J. A., Helbing, D., Milojević, S., … Barabási, A.-L. (2018). Science of science. *Science*, *359*(6379), eaao0185. https://doi.org/10.1126/science.aao0185

Guimera, R., Sales-Pardo, M., & Amarl, A. N. L. (2007). Classes of complex networks defined by role-to-role connectivity profiles. *Nature Physics*, *3*(1), 63–69. https://doi.org/10.1016/j.jacc.2007.01.076.White

Horta, H., & Santos, J. M. (2016). The impact of publishing during PhD studies on career research publication, visibility, and collaborations. *Research in Higher Education*, *57* (1), 28–50. https://doi.org/10.1007/s11162-015-9380-0

Rosvall, M., & Bergstrom, C. T. (2007). An information-theoretic framework for resolving community structure in complex networks. *Proceedings of the National Academy of Sciences*, *104*(18), 7327–7331. https://doi.org/10.1073/pnas.0611034104

Thune, T. (2009). Doctoral students on the university-industry interface: A review of the literature. *Higher Education*, *58*(5), 637–651. https://doi.org/10.1007/s10734-009-9214-0

Velden, T., Haque, A., & Lagoze, C. (2010). A new approach to analyzing patterns of collaboration in co- authorship networks - mesoscopic analysis and interpretation. *Scientometrics*, *85* (1), 219–242. https://doi.org/10.1007/s11192-010-0224-6

Youtie, J., & Bozeman, B. (2014). Social dynamics of research collaboration: norms, practices, and ethical issues in determining co-authorship rights. *Scientometrics*, *101*(2), 953–962. https://doi.org/10.1007/s11192-014-1391-7

Library Shelf Signs Affect Users' Search Time Length: Evidence From an Experiment Using a VR Library System

Sho Sato
Doshisha University,
Kyoto, Japan
min2fly@slis.doshisha.ac.jp

Takashi Harada
Doshisha University,
Kyoto, Japan
ushi@slis.doshisha.ac.jp

Saki Itagaki
Doshisha University,
Kyoto, Japan
bkq0031@mail2.doshisha.ac.jp

Asuka Suehiro
Doshisha University,
Kyoto, Japan
bkq0109@mail2.doshisha.ac.jp

Tomoka Takamura
Doshisha University,
Kyoto, Japan
bkq0119@mail2.doshisha.ac.jp

Koji Yamashita
Hacoya.inc, Tokyo,
Japan
k.yamashita@hacoya.info

Ryuta Ichikawa
Hacoya.inc, Tokyo,
Japan
r.ichikawa@hacoya.info

Katsuhiko Sukoboshi
Hacoya.inc, Tokyo,
Japan
sco@hacoya.info

ABSTRACT

This study explores the effect of library shelf sign designs on users' search time length using a virtual reality (VR) library system that was developed by the authors to test library designs. An experiment was performed with 20 participants in 2018. The results showed that sign designs affected users' search time length. Signs featuring library classification reduced users' search time length by 80 seconds on average in comparison with signs featuring sequential shelf numbers that were not related to subjects. It was also revealed that the system is effective for testing library sign designs.

KEYWORDS

information behavior; library design; signs; virtual reality

ASIS&T THESAURUS

information behaviorlibrary science

INTRODUCTION

While library systems such as online public access catalogs or discovery tools have been improved as a result of user test methods, it is difficult to apply user test methods to library facilities such as buildings, shelves, and signs because of the high cost of constructing and preparing them for testing. That is why we developed a virtual reality (VR) library system to test library designs (Sato et al., 2019). Whether by eliminating the cost to make actual prototypes or reproducing the spatial experiences, VR has been attracting attention in the field of architecture and design education (Milovanovic, Moreau, Siret, & Miguet, 2017).

82nd Annual Meeting of the Association for Information Science & Technology | Melbourne, Australia | 19–23 October, 2019

DOI: 10.1002/pra2.00161

At the beginning of our study, we performed an experiment to reveal the effects of library signs on users' search behavior. Some studies carry out experiments assessing the use of signs to locate library sources (Mandel & Johnston, 2019). However, no study has used the control experiment method with intervention because of the cost problem mentioned above. Our VR system solved this problem and enabled us to conduct a control experiment as a method for assessing library signs.

We first studied the signs displayed on the bookshelves. It is generally agreed that bookshelf signs should indicate the subject area of the books on the shelves. However, many public libraries in Japan use signs that are not related to subjects. While a study has shown that signs of this kind have negative effects on user search behavior (Sato et al., 2018), the degree of actual impact has not been revealed. Our study addressed this issue.

METHODS

Materials and Settings

A VR library system developed by Hacoya, Inc. was used in the experiment. The system was created using Unity and Windows Mixed Reality software, and the Dell Visor was used in our experiment as a VR device. A virtual library with two floors and 426 bookshelves was constructed in the VR world, and sign boards featuring the books' library classification were displayed at each shelf. In addition, box signs indicating broader subject areas were displayed at each block of shelves. In this system, the broader subject signs could be switched between two patterns (see Figures 1 and 2). Figure 1 shows pattern A: signs with subject name and the first digit of the Nippon Decimal Classification (NDC) number. NDC is the most commonly used library classification in Japanese libraries, and the signs displayed at each shelf also featured NDC.

Figure 1. The VR library with sign pattern A: NDC signs.

Figure 2. The VR library with sign pattern B: shelf number signs.

Figure 2 shows pattern B: signs featuring subject name and shelf number. The shelf numbers are simply sequential numbers, and there are no relationships between these numbers and the subject areas of books placed on the shelves. Oddly enough, bookshelf numbers like these are displayed larger than NDC in many public libraries in Japan.

Subjects

Twenty undergraduate students participated in our experiment. Ten were male and ten were female. None had a visual impairment or impaired color vision. There were two experimental groups: ten subjects used the sign pattern A system (NDC signs) and another ten used the sign pattern B system (shelf number signs).

Protocol

The experiment was conducted in a laboratory at Doshisha University in Kyoto, Japan, from November to December 2018. After explanation of how to use the VR system and a training session performed outside the VR library building, subjects entered the VR library. The experiment consisted of two trials. In the first trial, subjects were requested to find the location of NDC 320 (law) books. In the second trial, they were requested to find the location of NDC 540 (electrical and electronic engineering) books. In both trials, subjects were presented with both NDC numbers and subject names.

RESULTS

Data from one subject who participated in the pattern B sign-type group were not recorded because of machine errors. Thus, 38 sets of trial data from 19 subjects were analyzed. Figure 3 shows the difference in search time length between

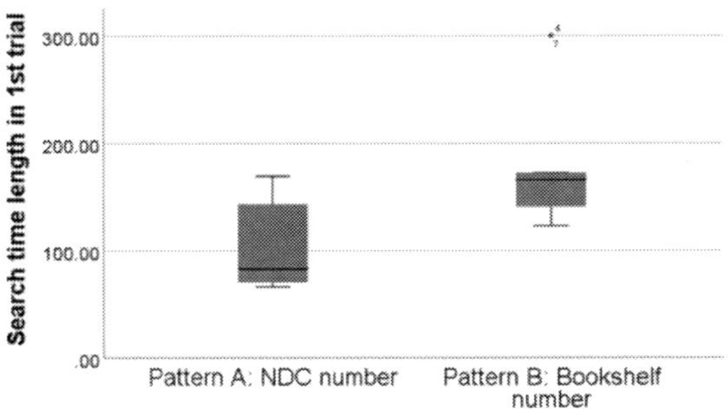

Figure 3. Box plots of search time length in the first trial.

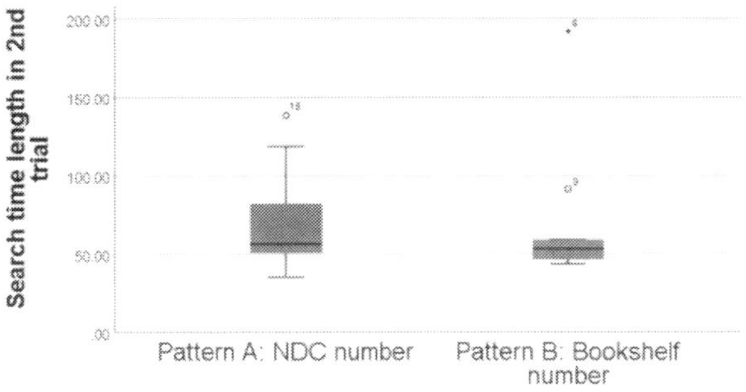

Figure 4. Box plots of search time length in the second trial.

sign patterns A and B in the first trial. The mean search time was 102.4 seconds (SD = 41.50) with pattern A and 185.5 seconds (SD = 67.24) with pattern B. The difference between sign patterns was significant ($t = 3.281$, $df = 17$, $p < 0.01$).

However, this effect of sign patterns was not observed in the second trial. Figure 4 shows the difference in search time length between sign patterns A and B in the second trial. The mean search time was 71.8 seconds (SD = 33.02) with pattern A and 70.4 seconds (SD = 47.89) with pattern B. There was no significant difference ($t = -0.075$, $df = 17$, $p > 0.05$).

DISCUSSION

The results showed that sign designs affected users' search time length in the first trial. Signs featuring library classification (NDC) reduced users' search time length by 80 seconds on average. On the other hand, no effect was observed in the second trial. One reason may be that subjects grasped the order of books in the VR library during the first trial and would have therefore known the location of the target bookshelf. Thus, our experiments suggested that signs with bookshelf numbers and without library classification may have a negative effect, particularly on first-time visitors' behavior.

It was also revealed that the system is effective for testing library sign designs. If we were to conduct experiments like ours in a real library situation, this would incur many costs, including the necessity of making many signs, changing them for experiments, and returning to the original setup for daily use. Our VR library system thus enables us to undertake such experiments more easily and with greater cost effectiveness.

ACKNOWLEDGMENTS

This work was supported by JSPS grant KAKENHI JP 18K18335.

REFERENCES

Al-Hakim, L. (2008). Modelling information flow for surgery management process. *International Journal of Information Quality*, 2(1), 60–74.

Mandel, L. H., & Johnston, M. P. (2019). Evaluating library signage: A systematic method for conducting a library signage inventory. *Journal of Librarianship and Information Science*, *51*(1), 150–161.

Milovanovic, J., Moreau, G., Siret, D., & Miguet, F. (2017). Virtual and augmented reality in architectural design and education. *Proceedings of the 17th International Conference, CAAD Futures 2017, Istanbul, Turkey*, July 2017.

Sato, S., Ikemoto, M., Koike, T., Matsubara, S., Yamanaka, A., Kawata, H., Miyazaki, N., Nagano, Y., & Nagao, R. (2018). Users' gaze behavior tendency in a public library and impact of library design on it. *Proceedings of the Spring Conference of the Japan Society of Library and Information Science, Tokyo, Japan*, May 12, 2018. pp. 35–38.

Sato, S., Itagaki, S., Suehiro, A., Takamura, T., Yamashita, K., Ichikawa, R., Sukoboshi, K., & Harada, T. (2019). Development of VR system for testing library designs. *Will be presented at IFLA WLIC 2019 Poster Sessions, Athens, Greece*, August 26–27, 2019.

Between Informative and Esthetic: A User Study of Content and Visualization on Government Data Dashboards

Liang-Yu Sie
National Taiwan University,
Taipei, Taiwan
b03106002@ntu.edu.tw

Wei Jeng
National Taiwan University,
Taipei, Taiwan
wjeng@ntu.edu.tw

ABSTRACT

This preliminary study aims to explore users' perceptions of and experiences with using government dashboards, accomplished by conducting experiments and interviews with eight participants. The results reveal that participants prefer information related to their lives and the government's performance on data dashboards. Confusing jargon on data dashboards is an obstacle that prevents users from understanding data visualizations. We also found that effective conveying of information does not always correlate with participants' preference of a data dashboard design. This study also suggests that participants are unclear about the role of government dashboards.

KEYWORDS

data dashboard; data visualization; open government data; open government; government data services

INTRODUCTION

According to Few (2006), a data dashboard is a visual pane that displays "the most important information needed to achieve certain objectives which fits on a single screen so it can be monitored at a glance" (Few, 2006, p. 34). Through graphic representation, dashboards display data to help audiences understand and make decisions, usually in a single page. An enterprise uses a data dashboard to track the company's performance, while a growing trend has shown that public sectors have also been adopting data dashboards in recent decades. Not only do data dashboards help governments monitor their internal performance, but they also engage the public to enhance transparency and accountability on office performance (Ganapati, 2011). Well-known cases include the IT Dashboard in the US and the Performance Dashboard in Australia. The former provides information about investments of information technology in the US; the latter displays the performance of Australian government services.

Despite data dashboards being used in the public sector recently, relatively little attention has been given to citizen's experiences with these dashboards. To bridge this gap, this preliminary study aims to investigate user perspectives (including perceived functions and preferred data visualization) of government dashboards by conducting a user study on existing government dashboards.

82nd Annual Meeting of the Association for Information Science & Technology | Melbourne, Australia | 19–23 October, 2019

DOI: 10.1002/pra2.00163

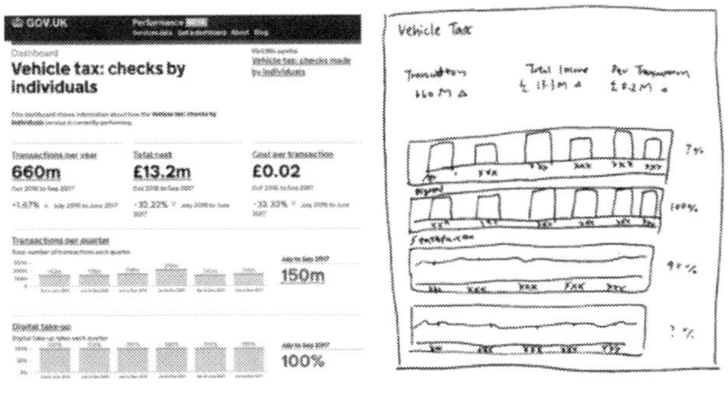

Figure 1. The screenshot of UK Performance and a participant's sketch.

USER STUDY DESIGN

Site selection. We designed an experiment to investigate user perspectives of and experiences with government data dashboards. When finding suitable sites for testing, we considered two criteria: relevance and sustainability, which led to the selection of two sites on a local level and a national level, respectively. Local policies such as public housing and transportation can be relevant to a citizen's everyday life. We thus selected the Public Housing Project Dashboard published by the Taipei City Government in Taipei, Taiwan. Secondly, considering the size and continuity of a dashboard, we selected the UK Performance Dashboard (Figure 1), which collects 780 government services and has run for more than four years.

User study design. In order to investigate user perspectives and experiences while interacting with the government dashboards, the user study comprises three sessions: the *sketch* session, *think-aloud* phase, and the *interview* phase.

Study procedure. In the sketch session, we aim to discover what overall impressions the participants form through charts or graphs displayed on the dashboard in a short period of time. Participants were instructed to explore the dashboard on a given website for 90 seconds, based on pre-test results. Participants were then asked to recall dashboard components by drawing or writing on a sheet.

In the think-aloud session, participants freely explored the dashboard without time limitations. While revisiting the functions of data dashboards, participants were asked to report interesting findings they encountered. The time spent on each site in this session varied from 2 to 11 minutes. We also conducted an accompanying interview with the think-aloud session to further gather participants' thoughts. ATLAS.ti was utilized for data analysis in the think-aloud and interview sessions.

PRELIMINARY RESULTS

When analyzing the data, we coded the elements of drawings into three categories. 1) Visualization (V): the participant recovered the shape of a certain visualization. 2) Text (T): the participant provided the text label of performance metrics. 3) Statistics (S): the participant recalled information about statistics or numbers. Table 1 below reveals the elements recalled by participants in the sketch session. It is not surprising that visualization was the most recalled, while text labels and statistics were rarely reported.

Feedback on Content on Dashboards

We found that participants expected to see highlights of government performance. Some participants (P01, P07) viewed government dashboards as propaganda tools, and suggested government performance should be highlighted. "*(A dashboard) should display data that helps people see the performance of government, then people may leave a good impression on government* (P01)." In addition, interviews reveal that participants are interested in data related to their daily experience. When exploring the Public Housing Project Dashboard, some participants tried to search the public housing projects in areas where they live and spent more time reading that information.

We also found that the text labels of performance metrics displayed on dashboards may be used by a professional group, but can be difficult for the general public to understand. For example, seven out of eight participants reported information they could not understand (e.g., digital take-up) in the interview.

Feedback on Data Visualization

Based on the think-aloud sessions, we found that participants' data visualization preferences varied, which may be influenced by previous experiences (familiarity with or exposure to a certain visualization) or graphic literacy. Three participants highlighted pie charts as effectively presenting the proportion of each subject, whereas three participants preferred line charts as they are more familiar with them and they contained much information. "*You can see the progress at a glance, and also the rise and fall between months.* (P06)" Not every visualization received positive comments; some participants (P05, P06) considered the gage graph "space-wasted" and "contains unnecessary visual embellishments." Contrarily, one participant considered the gage chart catchy.

Finally, our preliminary results found that the use of micro-animations in the visualizations raises participants' attention. Micro-animations are found in both the Public Housing Project Dashboard and the Performance Dashboard. Participants had positive attitudes about micro-animations. "*I like this because it pops up when I mouse-over it. It's interactive.*" (P08).

Elements	V	T	S
Projects (pie chart)	5	2	1
Project progress (line chart)	4	2	-
Public housing (gage chart)	3	1	-
Workers (weather icon)	2	1	-
Payment ratio (pie chart)	3	1	-
Audit (table)	3	-	-
Transaction per year (simple text)	4	2	3
Total cost (simple text)	4	2	3
Cost per transaction (simple text)	4	1	1
Digital take-up (bar chart)	6	4	3
User Satisfaction (line chart)	5	4	4
Completion rate(line chart)	5	2	2

Table 1. The occurrence of dashboard elements drawn by participants.

DISCUSSION

We found that users' preferences about dashboard design are not strongly associated with the design's effectiveness of conveying information. There is a long-standing debate over information design between minimalism (Tufte, 1983) and embellishment (Holmes, 1984). Perspectives adopted in the design of a government dashboard can achieve different objectives, but our study shows that, surprisingly, esthetics matter greatly to the participants.

Overall, we also observed that participants held different perspectives about the role of government dashboards: propaganda for policies, daily information gathering, and public supervision. The different roles that participants perceived can lead to different expectations or user experience. We also found that the role of government data dashboards is still unclear. While this study reveals that participants' perceptions are not fully aligned with the designer's viewpoint, a future study can examine the associations between citizens' different types of expectations of and their usage patterns with government data services.

ACKNOWLEDGMENTS

This work was financially supported by the Ministry of Science and Technology (MOST) and Ministry of Education (MOE) in Taiwan, under #MOST 108-2636-H-002-002- and MOST 108-3017-F-002-003-, and #108L900204.

REFERENCES

Few, S. (2006). *Information dashboard design: The effective visual communication of data*. Sebastopol, CA: O'Reilly Media.

Ganapati, S. (2011). *Use of dashboards in government*. Washington, DC: IBM Center for the Business of Government.

Holmes, N. (1984). *Designer's guide to creating charts and diagrams*. Watson-Guptill Publications.

Tufte, E. R. (1983). *The visual display of quantitative information*. Cheshire, CN: Graphics Press.

Linking the Thoughts Within Scientific Papers: Construction and Visualization of Argumentation Graph

Huimin Zhou
Wuhan University,
Wuhan, China
zhouhm@whu.edu.cn

Ningyuan Song
Wuhan University,
Wuhan, China
songny@whu.edu.cn

Wanli Chang
Wuhan University,
Wuhan, China
wanlichang@whu.edu.cn

Xiaoguang Wang
Wuhan University,
Wuhan, China
wxguang@whu.edu.cn

ABSTRACT

Argumentation structure within the content of scientific paper is the fundamental for proving scientific findings. Constructing the argumentation graph is an effective way to realize the visualization of argumentation structure and help users quickly understand the logical of papers. This study presents the method for constructing argumentation graph of scientific papers, includes an ontology for describing the scientific papers' argumentation structure, a process for deep semantic annotation and a mapping protocols for transforming the annotation results into graph structure by using Neo4J. The method was applied to construct an argumentation graph and the argumentation process retrieval was also realized. The result suggest that the argumentation graph could be benefit for the argumentation visualization and strategic reading of scientific papers.

KEYWORDS

Scientific Papers; Argumentation Graph; Neo4J

ASIS&T THESAURUS

Information science ~ Knowledge and information

INTRODUCTION

Scientific papers are the most essential manifestations of evolving knowledge in all scientific disciplines. The argumentation structures within scientific papers are considered as the important fundamental for constructing scientific theory, while also the essential clue for reading scientific papers (Walton & Zhang, 2013). Revealing and visualizing the argumentation structure, constructing the argumentation graph could accurately represent the argumentation process of scientific papers and help user quickly grasp the required reading content, so as to achieve the strategic reading (Renear & Palmer, 2009). In this study, a top-down construction method was adopted, firstly, an argumentation ontology was built, the argumentation graph was then constructed based on the results of deep semantic annotation approach, then related experiment which aimed for argumentation process retrieval was also carried out.

82nd Annual Meeting of the Association for Information Science & Technology | Melbourne, Australia | 19–23 October, 2019

DOI: 10.1002/pra2.00205

METHOD

Construction of Argumentation Ontology

In order to reveal the argumentation structure within the scientific content, the Scientific Paper Argumentation Ontology (SAO) was designed according to AMO, DoCO, DEO (Bagnacani, Ciancarini, Lorio, Nuzzolese, & Vitali, 2014) and mircopublication model (Clark, Ciccarese, & Goble, 2014). SAO included 19 Classes and 10 Properties, specifically defined two types of scientific evidence (the theoretical evidence and the factual evidence), which made the ontology more adaptable to the context of scientific papers. Figure 1 shows the structure of SAO.

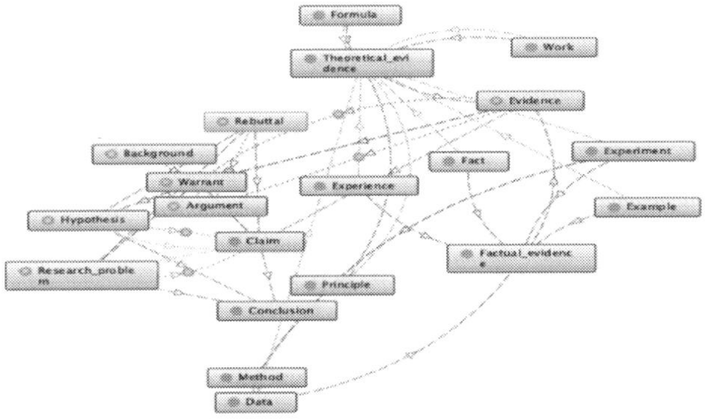

Figure 1. The structure of SAO.

Deep Semantic Annotation

Before the scientific argumentation graph's construction, deep semantic annotation approach was adopted following the steps shown in Figure 2. We used the XML editing tool,

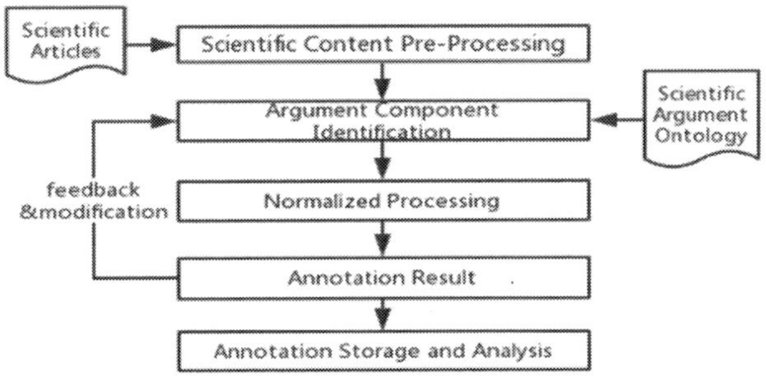

Figure 2. The deep semantic annotation steps.

the XML Spy, to annotate the scientific paper. The narrative scientific paper content was transformed and parsed into different text segments with semantic labels after the deep semantic annotation, which provided the fundamental dataset for the construction of argumentation graph.

Tool for Argumentation Graph Construction

By comparing the common graph database, like Cayley, Orientdb, and etc., this study used Neo4J, to construct argumentation graph. According to the data structure of Neo4J graph and the deep semantic annotation results, the mapping rules were set up to transform the annotation results into graph structure. Figure 3 presents the specific rules.

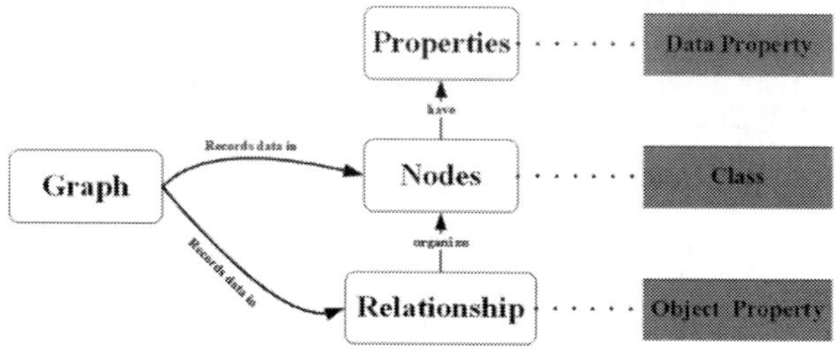

Figure 3. The mapping rules.

THE ARGUMENTATION GRAPH FOR SCIENTIFIC PAPER

Presentation and Storage of Argumentation Graphs

For better presentation of the argumentation graph structure, this study chose a scientific paper, named *Consumer Acceptance and Use of Information Technology: Extending the Unified Theory of Acceptance and Use of Technology*, (UTAUT2) which was published in MIS Quarterly, the top journal in Information System research area, as the example. Firstly, the semantic annotation experiment was based on SAO, then following the mapping rules, the argumentation graph was constructed by using Neo4J.

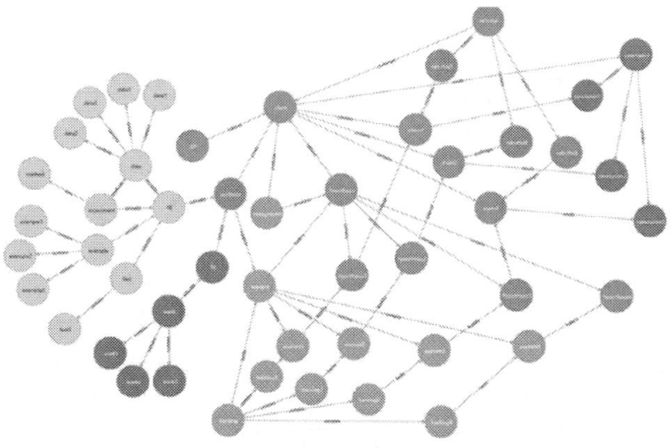

Figure 4. The argumentation graph of UTAUT2.

As shown in Figure 4, Different colors symbolize different concepts. The argumentation graph of UTAUT2 represented an argumentation process about the main claim *"we integrate hedonic motivation, price value, and habit into UTAUT in order to tailor it to the consumer technology use context"*, and three sub-claims, included *hedonic motivation, price value* and *habit*. It not only displayed the juxtaposing nodes such as background, hypothesis and conclusion, but also represented the argumentation relations between nodes.

The Argumentation Process Retrieval

The retrieval of argumentation process about one specific claim can be realized through argumentation graph. This study used match "*s=(n: work{name: 'work1'})-[*]->(m: conclusion{name:'conclusion1'}) return s*" as the query, which can get all the argumentation nodes contained in argumentation graph from Work1 to Conclusion1, as shown in Figures 5 and 6. The results indicated that the complete argumentation logic and the specific content were represented.

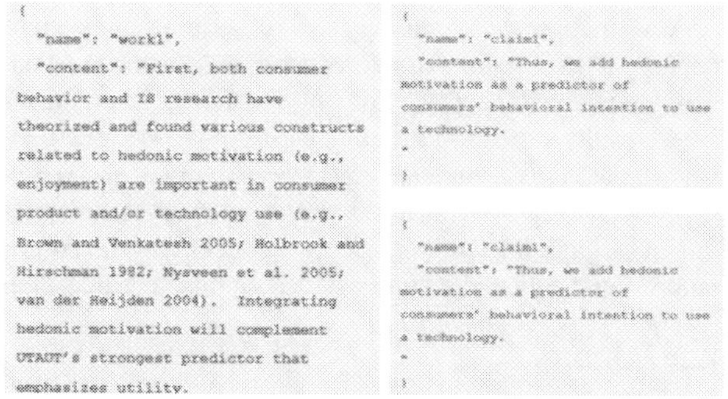

```
{
  "name": "work1",
  "content": "First, both consumer
behavior and IS research have
theorized and found various constructs
related to hedonic motivation (e.g.,
enjoyment) are important in consumer
product and/or technology use (e.g.,
Brown and Venkatesh 2005; Holbrook and
Hirschman 1982; Nysveen et al. 2005;
van der Heijden 2004). Integrating
hedonic motivation will complement
UTAUT's strongest predictor that
emphasizes utility.
```

```
{
  "name": "claim1",
  "content": "Thus, we add hedonic
motivation as a predictor of
consumers' behavioral intention to use
a technology.
"
}
```

```
{
  "name": "claim1",
  "content": "Thus, we add hedonic
motivation as a predictor of
consumers' behavioral intention to use
a technology.
"
}
```


Figure 5. The retrieval results of argumentation process 1.

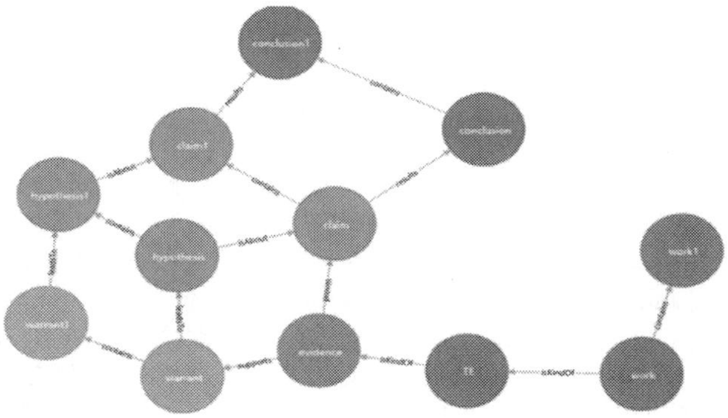

Figure 6. The retrieval results of argumentation process 2.

CONCLUSION

The argumentation graph presented in this study, not only stores the deep semantic annotation information of the argumentation structure within the scientific content, but also implements the straightforward visualization of the argumentation process. Besides, the results of this study also indicate that the multiple relation paths and property filtering can be used to query any relationship or node within the argumentation graph, which means the overall or local perspectives of the scientific papers' argumentation structure could be represented and the strategic reading could also be achieved. In the future, we aim to continue this study with a large-scale, cross-discourse scientific argumentation graph by using NLP techniques and semi-automatic annotation.

REFERENCES

Bagnacani, A., Ciancarini, P., Lorio, A. D., Nuzzolese, A. G., & Vitali, F. (2014). *The semantic lancet project: A linked open dataset for scholarly publishing*. In Proceedings of the 7th International Conference on Knowledge Engineering and Knowledge Management, Sibiu, Romania (pp. 101-105).

Clark, T., Ciccarese, P. N., & Goble, C. A. (2014). Micropublications: A semantic model for claims, evidence, arguments and annotations in biomedical communications. *Journal of Biomedical Semantics*, *5*(1), 28.

Renear, A. H., & Palmer, C. L. (2009). Strategic reading, ontologies, and the future of scientific publishing. *Science*, *325*(5492), 828–832.

Walton, D., & Zhang, N. (2013). The epistemology of scientific evidence. *Artificial Intelligence and Law*, *21*(2), 173–219.

The Role of Information Cues on Users' Perceived Credibility of Online Health Rumors

Xiaokang Song
Nanjing University,
Nanjing, China
sxksxk666@163.com

Yuxiang (Chris) Zhao
Nanjing University of Science and Technology, Nanjing, China
yxzhao@vip.163.com

Shijie Song
Nanjing University,
Nanjing, China
ssong@smail.nju.edu.cn

Qinghua Zhu
Nanjing University,
Nanjing, China
qhzhu@nju.edu.cn

ABSTRACT

There are a lot of health rumors on social media that can lead to misunderstandings, health risks, and negative health behaviors. Understanding what makes health rumors credible becomes an important research topic. Based on elaboration likelihood model (ELM), this study aimed to explore the impact of three information cues (quality cues, attractiveness cues, and affective polarity) on the credibility of health rumors, under different levels of health literacy and personal involvement. We conduct an online experiment and obtain data from 218 participants. The preliminary results show that the quality cues and attractiveness cues of health rumors have negative impacts on credibility. Dread health rumors are more credible than wish rumors. Health literacy has a significant negative moderating effect between quality cues and health rumor credibility, and personal involvement has a significant positive moderating effect between attractiveness cues and health rumor credibility. This study offers insights on the intervention of social media health rumors.

KEYWORDS

Information cues; Online health rumors; Information credibility; ELM

ASIS&T THESAURUS

Information use; Factor analysis

INTRODUCTION

With the rapid growth of online health information, the Internet has become an important channel for people to obtain health information. Online health information mixed with a huge amount of health rumors. Rumors are defined as "unverified and instrumentally related information statements in circulation" (DiFonzo & Bordia, 2007). Rumors may include unsubstantiated facts, biased interpretation of facts or deliberate deception results. According to the impact on people, rumors can be generally divided into dread and wish rumors (Chua & Banerjee, 2018).

82nd Annual Meeting of the Association for Information Science & Technology | Melbourne, Australia | 19–23 October, 2019

DOI: 10.1002/pra2.00165

In recent years, the credibility of health information has attracted great attention from IS scholars (Ma & Atkin, 2017). Information cues are a series of indicators reflecting the effect of information content, and their existence can be evaluated objectively (Hasley & Gregg, 2010). Because most health information posts on social media are UGCs and have similar styles (Gao, Tian, & Tu, 2015). It is necessary to take the information cues as the main indicator for internet users to judge the credibility of health information. Based on the elaboration likelihood model (ELM), this paper studies how information cues in health rumors affect Internet users' perceived credibility.

THEORETICAL MODEL AND RESEARCH HYPOTHESIS

ELM is a theory that focuses on how individuals respond to information content. It suggests that attitude and behavior changes among individuals may be caused by two kinds of influence routes: central route and peripheral route (Petty & Cacioppo, 1986). The theoretical model is shown in Figure 1.

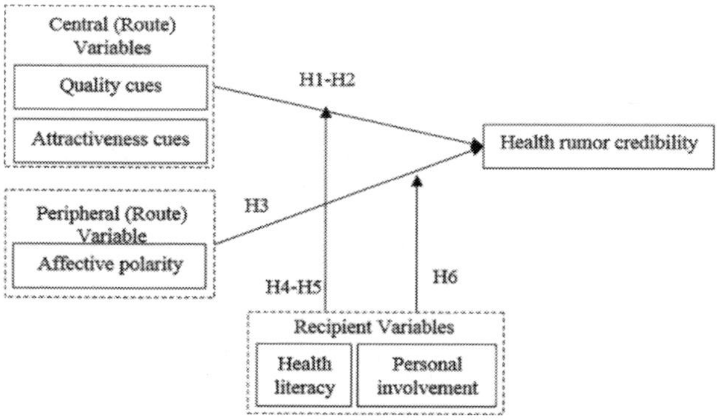

Figure 1. The theoretical model.

H1: Quality cues have positive effects on health rumors credibility.

H2: Attractiveness cues have positive effects on health rumors credibility.

H3: Dread health rumors are more credible than wish rumors.

H4: The effect of quality cues on health rumors credibility is stronger when both the recipient's health literacy (H4a) and personal involvement (H4b) are higher.

H5: The effect of attractiveness cues on health rumors credibility is stronger when both the recipient's health literacy (H5a) and personal involvement (H5b) are higher.

H6: Affective polarity's effect on health rumors credibility is stronger for recipients with lower levels of health literacy (H6a) and personal involvement (H6b).

METHODS

In this study, four health rumors were selected from China's Internet anti-rumor platform (piyao.org.cn), which spread widely on social media. Research assistants encoded health rumors as fear or hope based on information titles. They coded the number of scientific research institutions, scientific journals and statistics that appeared in the information content as quality cues. Expressions of exaggeration and inducement in information content were coded as attractive cues.

Furthermore, we conducted an online experiment. 230 participants were publicly recruited from the social media. Each participant was exposed to four health information. Participants were asked to report their age, gender, education, health literacy, personal involvement and perceived credibility through a questionnaire. Personal involvement and perceived credibility measurements are adapted from Chua and Banerjee (2018), and all items were measured on a 5-point Likert scale. Health literacy was measured by the NVS scale. The scale contains an ice-cream food label and six related questions, and with a score 1 for the correct answer and 0 for the wrong answer.

RESULTS

218 participants completed the experiment. Each of them was tested for perceived credibility of four health rumors. The data set contains 872 data cases. Table 1 presents the variables and their descriptive statistics.

Variable	Mean	s.d.	min	max
Credibility	3.62	1.00	1	5
Quality cues	3.25	1.09	2	5
Attractiveness cues	3	0.71	2	4
Affective polarity	0.5	0.5	0	1
Health literacy	4.68	1.47	0	6
Personal involvement	3.84	0.85	1	5

Table 1. Descriptive statistics of key variables.

We used multiple regression method to estimate the effect of each variable on credibility perception. In this study, variables were centralized. Meanwhile, moderated multiple regression was used to test the moderating effect of recipient variables. All calculations were finished via stata15. The results of regression analysis are shown in Table 2.

Table 2 suggested that when the recipient judges the credibility of health information, the quality cues and attractiveness cues in the information content have a negative impact. Consistent with previous studies (Chua & Banerjee, 2018), dread health rumors are more credible than wish rumors. Hypotheses 3 were supported. Health literacy has a significant negative moderating effect between quality cues and health rumor credibility. And personal involvement has a significant positive moderating effect between attractiveness cues and health rumor credibility.

	Model 1	Model 2	Model 3	Model 4
Quality cues	-0.22***	-0.39***	-0.22***	-0.23***
Attractiveness cues	-0.10†	-0.09	-0.12*	-0.12**
Wish rumor	-0.41***	-0.64***	-0.42***	-0.42***
Female	-0.10†	-0.05	-0.13*	-0.12*
Age	0.01**	0.02***	0.01**	0.01**
Education	-0.03	0.02	-0.05†	-0.02†
Health literacy (HL)	-0.09***	-0.10***		-0.09***
HL × Quality cues		-0.07**		-0.03
HL × Attractiveness cues		-0.00		-0.02
HL × Wish rumor		-0.11		-0.06
Personal Involvement (PI)	0.60***		0.59***	0.59***
PI × Quality cues			-0.02	-0.03
PI × Attractiveness cues			0.13†	0.13*
PI × Wish rumor			-0.05	-0.06
Constant	3.46***	2.78***	3.65***	3.47***
Adjusted R-squared	0.38	0.16	0.37	0.38

Note: † $p < 0.1$, * $p < 0.05$, ** $p < 0.01$, *** $p < 0.001$

Table 2. Results of regression analyses.

CONCLUSION

This study contributes to the online health rumor literature with the investigation of the effect of information cues on the credibility of health rumors. The findings of this study can help social media managers or policymakers intervene in health rumors to reduce the negative consequences.

REFERENCES

Chua, A. Y. K., & Banerjee, S. (2018). Intentions to trust and share online health rumors: an experiment with medical professionals. *Computers in Human Behavior*, *87*, 1–9.

DiFonzo, N., & Bordia, P. (2007). Rumor, gossip and urban legends. *Diogenes*, *54*(1), 19–35.

Gao, Q., Tian, Y., & Tu, M. (2015). Exploring factors influencing Chinese user's perceived credibility of health and safety information on Weibo. *Computers in Human Behavior*, *45*, 21–31.

Hasley, J. P., & Gregg, D. G. (2010). An exploratory study of website information content. *Journal of Theoretical and Applied Electronic Commerce Research*, *5*(3), 27–38.

Ma, T. J., & Atkin, D. (2017). User generated content and credibility evaluation of online health information: A meta analytic study. *Telematics and Informatics*, *34*(5), 472–486.

Petty, R. E., & Cacioppo, J. T. (1986). The elaboration likelihood model of persuasion. In *Communication and persuasion* (pp. 1–24). New York, NY: Springer.

What Will Influence Users' Knowledge Sharing Behavior in the Social Q&A Community?

Zhijun Song
Central China Normal University, Wuhan, China
zjsong@mails.ccnu.edu.cn

Qingxing Dong
Central China Normal University, Wuhan, China
qxdong@mail.ccnu.edu.cn

Gaohui Cao
Central China Normal University, Wuhan, China
ghcao@mail.ccnu.edu.cn

Ye Chen
Central China Normal University, Wuhan, China
cheny@mail.ccnu.edu.cn

ABSTRACT

The social Q&A community, as one of the most popular platforms of knowledge sharing, now faces user churn and slower growth in new active user numbers. To some extent, the main problem concealing in the decrease of growth is the lack of knowledge contribution from the users, which is the most attractive function of the social Q&A community. Thus the key point of tackling this problem is to explore which factors influence users' knowledge sharing behavior. Based on social capital theory and social exchange theory, this study constructs a regression model and collects empirical data to investigate the influencing factors of users' knowledge sharing behavior. It is found that the increment of users' centrality, harvest and users' trust toward the community lead to more and better shared-knowledge. However, the increase in users' reputation has a significant negative impact on the quantity and quality of their behavior. The theoretical and practical implications derived from the findings are further discussed.

KEYWORDS

Knowledge Sharing Behavior; Social Capital Theory; Social Exchange Theory

ASIS&T THESAURUS

Knowledge Management; Regression Analysis; Virtual Communities

INTRODUCTION

The social Q&A community has become an irreplaceable platform of knowledge sharing with the development of Web 2.0. Typical social Q&A communities represented by Zhihu (https://zhihu.com/), Quora (https://www.quora.com/) have gradually become common used tools for users from all walks of life to exchange industry information, professional knowledge, and life experience.

82nd Annual Meeting of the Association for Information Science & Technology | Melbourne, Australia | 19–23 October, 2019

DOI: 10.1002/pra2.00164

However, the social Q&A communities now face the dilemma where the number of users grows slowly, even shows a declining trend. One of the most famous social Q&A community in Japan, Qixil, failed to maintain the level of knowledge contribution after the loss of expert users, further lead to the abandon of more users, finally quit itself. In order to solve this problem, previous studies have centered on the influencing factors of knowledge sharing in the Q&A community. Nevertheless, most of them used questionnaire and interview methods to explore users' intention of knowledge sharing from the perspective of motivation mechanism (Berger, Hennig, Bocklisch, Herold, & Meinel, 2016; Moqri, Mei, Qiu, & Bandyopadhyay, 2018), and ignored the possible deviation between subjective intention and actual behavior. More specifically, users may have the intention to share knowledge, but in the community, due to the cost of time, personal ability or other reasons, users will not conduct actual knowledge sharing behavior. To fill in this gap, this study focuses on exploring the influencing factors behind users' knowledge sharing behavior based on users' behavioral data in the Zhihu. This study will address the following two research questions:

1. Which factors influence users' knowledge sharing behavior in social Q&A community?
2. How to promote users' knowledge sharing behavior in social Q&A community?

EMPIRICAL RESEARCH

Data

This study selected Zhihu, the largest Q&A community in China as the data sources. By using web crawler technology, the demographic data and behavioral data of 13,000 users during the period from Feb 12, 2019 to Feb 18, 2019(T_1), and from Feb 19, 2019 to Feb 25, 2019(T_2), were respectively crawled randomly. After eliminating the lost users and noise data, 5,069 users were included in this study.

Variables

From the view of characteristics of behavior, this study considered the quantity and quality of knowledge sharing behavior. Therefore, we used the number of answers users provided and

Theory	Variable name	Measure name	Description	Result of Model 1	Result of Model 2
	Dependent Variables				
	Quantity of knowledge sharing behavior	$Answer_{i2}$	The number of user i 's answers during period T_2.		
	Quality of knowledge sharing behavior	$Agree_{i2}$	The number of agrees user i gained during period T_2.		
	Independent Variables				
Social Capital Theory	Increment of centrality	$relative\_followee_{i1}$	The relative increment of user i's followees during T_1.	1.8045(n.s.)	-3.2969***
		$relative\_follower_{i1}$	The relative increment of user i's followers during T_1.	20.918***	33.222***
	Trust towards the community	$SelfExposed_i$	The number of personal-information items of user i.	0.3484***	0.0805***
Social Exchange Theory	Increment of harvest	$re\_followQuestion_{i1}$	The relative increment of user i's follows questions in T_1.	55.719**	10.915***
	Increment of reputation	$relative\_agree_{i1}$	The relative increment of agrees user i gained during T_1	-0.541*	-0.299***
	Inception	-	-	-2.900***	3.8680***

Table 1. List of variables.

Note: n.s. means not significant; $*$ means $p < 0.05$; $**$ means $p < 0.01$; $***$ means $p < 0.001$.

agreements users gained during the T_2 period to represent two dependent variables respectively. We also selected several typical behavior of Zhihu users and their demographic data as independent variables. The final list of variables is shown in Table 1.

Regression Model

When investigating the influence of independent variables on the quantity of knowledge sharing behavior, the regression model was as following:

$$Answer_{i2} = c_{1i} + \beta_{11} relative\_followee_{i1} + \beta_{21} relative\_follower_{i1} + \beta_{31} SelfExposed_i + \beta_{41} re\_followQuestion_{i1} + \beta_{51} relative\_agree_{i1} \quad \text{(Model1)}$$

When investigating the influence of independent variables on the quality of knowledge sharing behavior, the regression model was as following:

$$Agree_{i2} = c_{2i} + \beta_{12} relative\_followee_{i1} + \beta_{22} relative\_follower_{i1} + \beta_{32} SelfExposed_i + \beta_{42} re\_followQuestion_{i1} + \beta_{52} relative\_agree_{i1} \quad \text{(Model2)}$$

Results

Since the dependent variables are all count data and are overly dispersed, this study chooses the Negative Binomial regression model. The regression results of quantity and quality of knowledge sharing are shown in the 4th and 5th column of Table 1 respectively.

CONCLUSION

Based on social capital theory and social exchange theory, this study reveals which factors will influence the quantity and quality of knowledge sharing behavior. The regression results show that the increment of centrality in the network has a positive impact on the quantity and quality of knowledge sharing behavior, which illustrates that the more centrality a person enjoys in the community, the stronger connection s/he with other members in the community will be. Also, based on the social capital theory, users with higher trust in the community will have a more open mind with other users, then they will contribute more frequently with higher quality answers. Additionally, from the perspective of social exchange theory, the more users gain from the community, the more and better knowledge they will share to feedback the community out of the principle of reciprocity. On the contrary, after reputation promotion, users will be more cautious about their answers in order to maintain their existing reputation and further reduce their knowledge sharing behavior.

Referring to the results, this study provides some constructive suggestions for the development of the social Q&A community. First of all, recommend users "the users you may be interested in" individually, encourage users to pay closer attention to each other, strengthen the social connections among them. Secondly, invite users to complete their basic personal information and interests in order to create a safe and harmonious community atmosphere to increase the trust between users on the platform. Last but not least, timely and efficiently recommend high-quality and cutting-edge knowledge to users, so that users will have stronger reciprocity in the platform. These results advance the existing knowledge-sharing research and provide practical suggestions in community management.

REFERENCES

Berger, Philipp., Hennig, P., Bocklisch, T., Herold, T., & Meinel, C. (2016). A journey of bounty hunters:

Analyzing the influence of reward systems on stackoverflow question response times. *2016 IEEE/WIC/ACM International Conference on Web Intelligence (WI), IEEE*, 644-649.

Moqri, M., Mei, X., Qiu, L., & Bandyopadhyay, S. (2018). Effect of "Following" on contributions to open source communities. *Journal of Management Information Systems, 35*(4), 1188–1217.

An Initial Study of Information Behavior in Pokemon Go

Krishna Srinivasan
Nanyang Technological University, Singapore
krishna009@ntu.edu.sg

Marcus Lee Kiang Tan
Nanyang Technological University, Singapore
marc0045@ntu.edu.sg

Derrick Chin Kiat Peh
Nanyang Technological University, Singapore
chinkiat001@ntu.edu.sg

Dion Hoe-Lian Goh
Nanyang Technological University, Singapore
ashlgoh@ntu.edu.sg

Chei Sian Lee
Nanyang Technological University, Singapore
leecs@ntu.edu.sg

ABSTRACT

This paper presents a preliminary study of issues pertaining to the information needs, sources and behaviors of Pokemon Go players. Participants were found to be passive in the fulfillment of their information needs and they expressed a willingness to share information with others.

KEYWORDS

Information sources; information needs; information behavior; mobile games; Pokemon Go

ASIS&T THESAURUS

Information use; Information seeking; Information behavior

INTRODUCTION

Released in the summer of 2016, Pokemon Go has established itself as a popular mobile augmented reality game. By 2018, it had generated a revenue of $2 billion with 147 million active users in 2018 (Tassi, 2018).

To the exasperation of many players, there is little official information about how to play it except for basic descriptions of game features and mechanics. Consequently, crowd-sourced efforts have emerged where players share information to help others learn and master the game. Examples include Whatsapp chats and Facebook groups. Although helpful, problems are associated with these initiatives. First, users may not be aware of their existence, and thus miss important information. Second, the information offered may not be relevant, timely or accurate.

Arising from these issues, we aim to address the following research questions in this initial study of Pokemon Go: (1) What are players' information needs? (2) What are their sources of information? (3) What triggers these information needs? (4) What and why do people share with others?

82nd Annual Meeting of the Association for Information Science & Technology | Melbourne, Australia | 19–23 October, 2019

DOI: 10.1002/pra2.00166

It is important to address these questions because information is an essential resource to accomplish the objectives of many games. Thus, those who possess superior information literacy skills will likely succeed faster than those who do not (Harviainen & Savolainen, 2014). Further, these skills are transferable to other information seeking contexts in information intensive environments.

METHDOLOGY

A semi-structured interview was considered appropriate as this was an exploratory study. The interview schedule comprise three sections: (1) **Player profile**, which included questions on demographics and player characteristics; (2) **Information needs and sources**, which focused on type of information that were sought after and their sources; (3) **Information sharing**, which examined the types of information shared, reasons for doing so and outcomes.

A total of 35 adult Pokemon Go players were recruited using snowball and convenience sampling. Participants were the general public who were observed playing the game in parks, or friends and colleagues who played the game. The interviews averaged 16 minutes in length. All interview responses were transcribed and consolidated according to the questions asked. Each response was then individually analyzed and inductively coded to extract the information that could answer our research questions.

RESULTS

Participants averaged 40 years in age. There were 21 males and 14 females. Most were long-time players, with 68.6% playing for around two years, 17.1% playing for more than a year, and 14.3% playing for less than a year. Participants were also frequent players, with 45.7% of them playing more than 10 hours per week. The remaining 28.6% and 25.7% played up to 5 and 10 hours per week respectively.

Three triggers of information needs were uncovered. First, **in-game notifications** prompted users to find out more ("*notifications when app is turned on*"). Examples include new Pokemon releases or special in-game events. Second,

friends playing the game could trigger searches. This arose either through information sharing (*"friends tell me about new information"*) or through a sense of competition to know just as much as others (*"peer pressure, if your friends are also playing with you"*). Finally, **third-party application notifications** subscribed by participants prompted information needs. Examples include social media or messaging apps (*"When I receive notification from the whatsapp group"*).

Interestingly, for participants with information needs (74.3%), only 54.3% actually attempted to fulfill those needs. One possible reason for this gap could be a lack of time. Participants likely accumulated their information needs and deferred fulfilling them until a later time such as on a fixed schedule (e.g. *"every Sunday"*). Another reason was that some participants considered in-game notifications as sufficient and did not conduct further searches (*"don't actively check, mainly pop up notifications"*).

Participants' information needs fell into three categories: (1) **Pokemon information** such as where to find rare Pokemon; (2) **in-game events** such as extra spawns of specific Pokemon types during certain periods; and (3) **gameplay strategies** including battling and defending Pokemon gyms, and winning raid battles.

Surprisingly, 80% of our participants cited information about Pokemon as their primary need, suggesting that the other categories were less important. Comments included *"Important so it possible to complete the game"*, and *"Important to me because I want to complete my pokedex objective"*. Hence, catching Pokemon appeared to be the main focus of gameplay consistent with the Pokemon franchise's tagline of "Gotta Catch 'Em All".

Participants reported four sources that could fulfill their information needs: (1) **friends** (face-to-face or via messaging apps); (2) official information from the game developer **Niantic** through in-game notifications, Facebook page or its Web site; (3) **search engines** such as Google; and (4) **social media** sites created by users to share information (e.g. Facebook, YouTube and Reddit).

Few participants (25.7%) relied on singular sources. Instead, most (74.3%) used multiple. Of these, the majority relied on Niantic coupled with friends, search engines or social media. This would suggest either that the information Niantic provides was considered inadequate or participants used multiple sources as a means of triangulation.

All participants but one reported sharing information with others, indicating that players built a community around the game. The types of information shared closely mirrored players' information needs described above and included Pokemon information, events, gym battles and raids. Sharing was done near equally via face-to-face or messaging apps (e.g. Whatsapp). Surprisingly, very few participants reported sharing using social media.

The reasons for sharing fell into three categories: (1) **to help others** (*"update personal friends as it is a duty to do so"*,); (2) **build or maintain relationships** (*"plays an important role of forming the social bonds…"*); and (3) **reciprocate or receive help in return** (*"Win-win situation. Everyone benefits…"*). Regardless of these reasons, 80% of participants reported that sharing improved player relationships while the rest said that there was no impact.

DISCUSSION AND CONCLUSION

An interesting observation is that most of our participants' information needs appeared to be externally triggered through notifications or other players. In order words, participants' were passive (Wilson, 1997) in their search for information, preferring to rely on content to be pushed to them. However, the receipt of passively acquired information may trigger active searches. Specifically, Niantic and participants' friends were passive information sources while search engines were used to actively supplement information from the former two categories.

We were heartened to find that participants were willing to share information with others. The lack of official content that could meet information needs is one possible reason, as is the collaborative/competitive nature of some aspects gameplay (e.g. gym battles) that brings people together. Finally, the game's dynamic nature such as the appearance of rare Pokemon or raid battles means that information sharing is needed to accomplish in-game objectives.

In conclusion, the present study provides an initial overview of the information behavior of players of a popular augmented reality game. Two implications may be drawn from our results. First, because players seem to be passive consumers of in-game information, game developers need to carefully consider the types of content delivered to ensure an enjoyable user experience. Second, since players actively share information, sites that offer game-based content should design mechanisms to effectively promote content creation and dissemination.

The small sample size of the study may limit the generalizability of our findings. Future work may expand the number of participants and their diversity. Incorporating other data collection methods to triangulate the results such as via diary studies to record information behavior, and analyses of sites offering Pokemon Go information for content type and quality would be instructive. Finally, it would be worthwhile to investigate collaborative information seeking behaviors to obtain a richer picture of information behavior associated with gameplay.

REFERENCES

Harviainen, J. T., & Savolainen, R. (2014). Information as capability for action and capital in synthetic worlds.

Information Research, *19*(4), Retrieved from http://www.informationr.net/ir/19-4/isic/isic12.html

Tassi, P. (2018). *"Pokémon GO" is more popular than it's been at any point since launch in 2016*. Forbes. Retrieved from https://www.forbes.com/sites/insertcoin/2018/06/27/pokemon-go-is-more-popular-than-its-been-at-any-point-since-launch-in-2016/#2f16a3c4cfd2

Wilson, T. D. (1997). Information behavior: An interdisciplinary perspective. *Information Processing & Management*, *33*(4), 551–572.

Moving From Assumptions to Evidence: Assessing Quality in Online Courses in a Master of Information Program

Sharon Stoerger
Rutgers, The State University of New Jersey,
New Brunswick, NJ, USA
sharon.stoerger@rutgers.edu

Lilia Pavlovsky
Rutgers, The State University of New Jersey,
New Brunswick, NJ, USA
lilia.pavlovsky@rutgers.edu

ABSTRACT

Creating opportunities that encourage and support student learning is at the heart of what instructors do. At the same time, LIS programs are attempting to keep up with and navigate a rapidly changing educational landscape. The types of students who enroll in and graduate from our programs are becoming more diverse, as are their needs. This also is true of the employers who are hiring our graduates. Further, concerns have been raised about student debt and the value of the degree. Linking these issues to the quality of the program and more specifically the courses themselves is key. This poster discusses an attempt to develop a proactive structure to formally assess the quality of the online courses in the Master of Information program at Rutgers, The State University of New Jersey.

KEYWORDS

Distance education; e-learning; education in information sciences; learning improvement; quality control

ASIS&T THESAURUS

Distance learninge-learning; information science education

INTRODUCTION: A QUALITY EDUCATION

As education professionals, we know the importance of a quality education. Yet, research is often privileged at many institutions. In recent years, however, attention has been shifting to the importance of teaching and learning in higher education. Earning a degree from a higher education institution in the United States is an expensive investment. The growing number of students going into debt to finance their education poses many troubling challenges (Miller, 2018). The number of entities that are becoming a part of the higher education landscape is on the rise, which is giving students more options when it comes to degree- and non-degree baring learning opportunities (Schwartz, 2019).

Questioning the costs and proposing ways to "fix" higher education have become commonplace, as well (e.g., Kerr, 2019, Vander Ark, 2019).

82nd Annual Meeting of the Association for Information Science & Technology | Melbourne, Australia | 19–23 October, 2019

DOI: 10.1002/pra2.00167

These issues, coupled with concerns raised by employers who contend that today's college graduates do not have workplace-ready skills and the negative media coverage of higher education, have led to the public to lose trust in our institutions' ability to prepare people for life after graduation (Jaschik, 2018). If we are to regain the public's trust, we need to provide reliable evidence to illustrate the role of higher education and its value. In other words, we are obligated to deliver a high-quality education to students who attend our institutions.

For many years, determining the quality of instruction and the achievement of learning outcomes has been assessed through student evaluations. However, questions have surfaced about the reliability of the data obtained through student feedback alone. Many stakeholders – campus administrators, the public, parents, students, etc. – use this information to make important decisions. These range from determining to renew an instructor's contract to selecting a college to attend. Being able to obtain multiple forms of data to better evaluate the quality of our teaching is critical.

THE PROBLEM

This poster will describe the use of design-based research methodology to develop an online course audit structure and process for the Master of Information (MI) program in the School of Communication and Information at Rutgers.

The project began with reports from a few online students in the MI program who were expressing concerns associated with selected courses. Examples of concerns ranged from inaccurate assignment due dates to conflicting policies to the lack of content organization in the learning management system (LMS). While this form of feedback was recorded, it was not producing clear insights that could lead to change. Instead, these informal comments were producing assumptions – ones indicating that there might be room for improvement in the online courses. In order to effectively address any problems in these courses, more data were needed to understand their true nature.

Thus, we launched an analysis of formally collected data. At the end of every semester and for every course, the university provides students with the opportunity to complete a survey about their learning experience. The output that results from this part of the research are both qualitative and quantitative in nature.

In addition to the survey, every student in the MI program produces an e-portfolio as part of a required course. At the end of the e-portfolio creation process, students are asked to submit a reflection on their experience in program. The qualitative responses obtained through the reflection are routinely reviewed.

Through an analysis of these data, potential problems with selected courses were noted. A closer investigation revealed that the primary pain points were connected to online courses. The MI program prides itself on having a foundation that is built on integrity and student success. Thus, the concerns raised by students in the online courses prompted the need for further investigation.

THE ONLINE COURSE AUDIT APPROACH

Instead of reacting to problems, the objective of this project was to develop a proactive way to assess the quality of the MI online courses. The Director of the MI program and the Assistant Dean for Instructional Support and Assessment in the School of Communication and Information at Rutgers collaborated to develop an online course audit structure and begin the review process.

The result has been to employ design-based research methods to develop a systematic approach to identify and address the concerns noted by the students, as well as other problems that might not yet be articulated by that group.

Guiding Questions

To guide the development of the audit process and the review of courses in the LIS program, our work began by considering the following questions:

- How should we measure online course quality?
- What standards should we used to measure quality in our online courses?
- Do the online courses in the Master of Information program preparing our students to be information professionals?

The Solution

The following stages of the research were developed and implemented to review the online MI courses:

- Identify course quality standards to use as an assessment framework
  - General online standards include Quality Matters, Online Learning Consortium Scorecard, Open SUNY Course Quality Review Rubric
  - Standards that integrate MI practices
  - American Library Association Standards
- Determine key syllabi elements and conduct a review
- Aggregate data manually
  - Use EXCEL to analyze data obtained through the end-of-the-semester survey and e-portfolio reflections
- Aggregate data automatically
  - Use Canvas (LMS) Outcomes to track student outcomes in the online courses and map against the MI program goals
- Conduct interviews with students and instructors to review audit results and discuss next steps
- Establish a review cycle for online courses

We are currently in the early phases of this course audit process and plan to share results in Fall 2019.

CONCLUSION

Our goal is to insure the best possible outcomes for students in the MI program. The development of an auditing system to systematically assess the MI online courses is enabling us to address concerns raised through feedback obtained from the student data, along with those identified through this review process. By being proactive instead of reactive to course quality, the goal is to continue to offer students a learning experience that prepares them to be information professionals in a variety of contexts.

REFERENCES

Jaschik, S. (2018, October). *Falling confidence in higher ed.* Inside Higher Ed. Retrieved from https://www.insidehighered.com/news/2018/10/09/gallup-survey-finds-falling-confidence-higher-education

Kerr, E. (2019, June). *Is college worth the cost?* U.S. News & World Report. Retrieved from https://www.usnews.com/education/best-colleges/paying-for-college/articles/2019-06-17/is-college-worth-the-cost

Miller, B. (2018, August). *The student debt problem is worse than we imagined.* The New York Times. Retrieved from https://www.nytimes.com/interactive/2018/08/25/opinion/sunday/student-debt-loan-default-college.html

Schwartz, N. (2019, May). *Online directory of college alternatives launches.* Education Dive. Retrieved from https://www.educationdive.com/news/new-online-directory-of-college-alternatives-launches/554983/

Vander Ark, T. (2019, June). *How to fix higher education: Seven keys.* Forbes. Retrieved from https://www.forbes.com/sites/tomvanderark/2019/06/19/how-to-fix-higher-education/#49fe6c5a5310

How Socio-Culture Impact the Information Behavior of Chinese Urban Newcomers

Honglei Sun
Nanjing University,
Nanjing, P.R.China
sunhl@nju.edu.cn

Jianming Zheng
Nanjing University,
Nanjing, P.R.China
zhengjm@nju.edu.cn

Meng Wang
Jiangsu University,
Zhenjiang, P.R.China
wangm@smail.nju.edu.cn

Ya Chen
Nanjing University,
Nanjing, P.R.China
yachen@nju.edu.cn

ABSTRACT

Nowadays, migrants have become the majority population of some Chinese cities, rather than a vulnerable group in the coming information society. To gain a better understanding of urban newcomers' information behavior, we interviewed 13 newcomers in China and employed grounded theory to explore how socio-cultural factors impact their information behavior. The preliminary findings show that information behavior of urban newcomers may be influenced by a complex cultural framework involving cultural integration, social integration, and cognitive value. Based on the qualitative analysis, we propose a theoretical model to understand the inner relationship, which may also yield practical implications on Chinese urban newcomers' information practices.

KEYWORDS

Information behavior; Newcomer; China; Urbanization; Socio-culture

ASIS&T THESAURUS

Social informatics; Information behavior

INTRODUCTION & BACKGROUND

According to the latest statistical bulletin of Chinese National Economic and Social Development (2019), urbanization level of China had been 59.58% by the end of 2018, the population of urban residents had increased by 20.951 million over the past 10 years. As a result, many Chinese cities have experienced "population inversion", which refers to the phenomenon of migrants becoming the majority of the local population. Nowadays, the number of migrant urban newcomers in China has increased so rapidly that they can't be ignored anymore as a vulnerable group in the coming information society.

In recent few years, researches on the information behavior of migrant in China have increased dramatically in various disciplines in China, such as sociology, economics, library and information science (Wang & Chen, 2012). Yet, most of the literature refers to their information needs, information literacy and information barriers, research on influencing factors of Chinese newcomers' information behavior is in its infancy, specifically, it is unclear how socio-cultural factors may impact Chinese urban newcomers' information behavior. To address this gap in the literature, we collected data by face to face interviews and employed grounded theory approach to address how socio-cultural factors may impact Chinese urban newcomers' information behavior.

82nd Annual Meeting of the Association for Information Science & Technology | Melbourne, Australia | 19–23 October, 2019

DOI: 10.1002/pra2.00169

METHODS

Data Collection

We employed a judgment sampling strategy to recruit every single participant, who already migrated to a new urban in recent five years, resided in urban and self-identified as a newcomer. This judgment sampling method can include cases that have the most strategic position to provide the information needed (Sekaran & Bougie, 2010). Meanwhile, social ties are very important among the immigrants and the interview encounter required a sensitive interaction, it was important that participants knew and trusted the interviewers (Guttman, Lev, Segev, et al., 2018). Finally, 30 participants were recruited through the interviewers' social networks. Participants were from 15 cities located in 10 provinces of China, enabling geographical diversity.

A face-to-face interview was carried out from September 10th to October 12th, 2018. The interview began with describing the study and obtaining consent and personal information, including education, age, province, migrant purpose, where they come from, and where they reside now. Then, we asked questions in four aspects, including specific information behaviors (e.g., information-seeking behavior), information ground, information barriers, and how they deal with the barriers in the new environment. Each interview took about 60-90 minutes.

Data Analysis

We employed grounded theory approach to elicit concepts, categories, and core categories. During this process, two researchers coded the first 2/3(20) interview data respectively, then we used the remaining 1/3 (10) for the theoretical saturation test.

When we coded all interview data, we found socio-cultural factors were frequently referred by the participants, specifically, 13 of 30 mentioned socio-cultural factors impact their information behavior. Thus, to address how socio-cultural factors impact the information behavior of Chinese urban newcomers, we characterized it for further content analysis, and report here. The other interview data of 17 participants do not allude to the idea of this issue; these are not reported in this paper but have been analyzed in detail separately. The demographic information of the participants for this paper is shown in Table 1.

	Profile category	Count
Gender	Male	8
	Female	5
Age	18~30	5
	31~40	5
	>40	3
Education	Doctoral Degree/Master Degree	2
	Bachelor Degree	8
	Junior/Senior High School Degree	3
Region	Guangdong Province	2
	Jilin Province	4
	Beijing (equal to a Chinese province)	1
	Jiangsu Province	3
	Zhejiang Province	1
	Neimenggu Province	2

Table 1. Demographic information.

THE PRELIMINARY RESULTS

We identified 27 initial concepts, 11 categories, and corresponding 3 core categories after three coding stage - open coding, axial coding, and selective coding (Strauss & Corbin, 1990). The 3 core categories include cultural integration, social integration, and cognitive value. As Figure 1 shows, we then proposed a theoretical model based on the coding results.

Cultural Integration

Cultural integration is the aspect of urban newcomers from original culture adopt the essence of host society culture, such as its attitudes and ceremonies. Cultural integration interact with social integration and cognitive value, are mainly composed of the following four categories: (1) Acculturation, (2) Ease of communication, (3) Familiarity with local culture, and (4) Sense of belonging. 8 (62%) newcomers mentioned the assimilation to the host culture may impact their information behavior significantly, specifically, 5 interviewees said that the host culture was better than their original culture, and they were willing to adopt it, so they hoped to know more about host urban and would like to seek information from others in the host city. Meanwhile, 4 (31%) participants said that the ease of communication could also influence the way they seek information and the willingness to interact with other for sharing information (e.g., *I think you'd better not to ask local residents if you want to know something, since the dialects here is difficult to understand*). Furthermore, the familiarity with local culture and sense of belonging were also frequently mentioned by the participants.

Social Integration

Social integration refers to the process during which urban newcomers are incorporated into the social structure of the host society, including five categories in this study: (1) Social exclusion, (2) Frequency of social interaction, (3) Willingness to settle down, (4) Lifestyle, and (5) Living condition. Social exclusion is the most significant aspect of social integration in this study, 6 (46%) participants referred to this aspect and believed that it always affected their information needs or information-seeking behavior. Meanwhile, newcomers who liked to interact with residents and were willing to set down at the host city had more local friends, when they need to know something, they'd like to ask their local friends and appreciated this way. Furthermore, the way and the condition which newcomers live were also mentioned frequently by respondents.

Cognitive Value

Cognitive value is connected with the urban newcomers' perception of costs and benefits, including three categories: (1) Perceived cost, and (2) Expected benefit. Perceived cost mainly refers to the time and effort they need to spend, 5 (38%) interviewees said that if they thought they need to spend a lot of time or effort to get the information, they felt stressed. However, of which 2 (15%) participants explained that if the expected benefit can cover the cost, they would do it at last. Meanwhile, another 3 participants mentioned the expected benefit which is mainly reflected by emotional support and useful information urgently needed. For example, one newcomer said that "*It is difficult to join this Buddhist online community if no one recommends you, but after joining it, I gained a lot, especially emotional comfort...So, the effort is valuable.*"

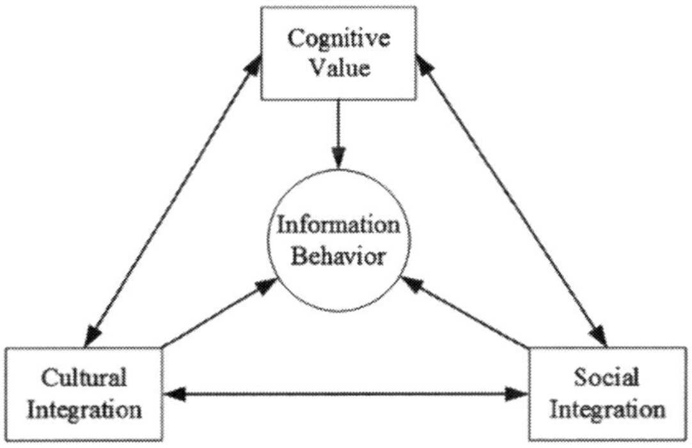

Figure 1. The theoretical model.

ACKNOWLEDGMENT

This research is supported by the National Social Science Fund of China Grant No. 19ATQ001, and the Ministry of Education of Humanities and Social Science Project Grant No. 19YJC870022.

REFERENCES

Guttman, N., Lev, E., Segev, E., et al. (2018). "I never thought I could get health information from the Internet!": Unexpected uses of an Internet website designed to enable Ethiopian immigrants with low/no literacy skills to browse health information. *New Media & Society*, *20*(7), 2272–2295.

Sekaran, U., & Bougie, R. (2010). *Research method for business* (5th ed.). John Wiley and Sons, Inc.

Strauss, A., & Corbin, J. M. (1990). *Basics of qualitative research: Grounded theory procedures and techniques*. Sage Publications, Inc.

Wang, F., & Chen, Y. (2012). From potential users to actual users: use of e-government service by Chinese migrant farmer workers. *Government Information Quarterly*, *29* (supp-S1), 98–111.

Service Mode Selection Strategy for Resource-Constrained Content Service Providers

Mengting Sun
Wuhan University,
Wuhan, China
ida_sun@foxmail.com

Jingjia Ding
Wuhan University,
Wuhan, China
jingjia_19@whu.edu.cn

Xiaoqun Yuan
Wuhan University,
Wuhan, China
yuan20030308@whu.edu.cn

ABSTRACT

This poster deals with the service schemes of Content Service Providers (CSPs) with limited service resources by proposing a service mode selection strategy. In this poster, content service modes of resource-constrained CSPs are roughly but practically separated into three categories according to their collaborative relationship with other resource providers: Self-service, Delegation service and Cooperation service. Then the service mode selection problem is formulated as a profit optimization problem from the service chain perspective, and the optimal service mode selection strategy is deduced. The experiment results show that compared with the fixed λ service strategy applied in real world, our strategy can improve the service profits significantly.

KEYWORDS

Content Service Providers; Service Mode; Collaboration Service; Profit Optimization Model

ASIS&T THESAURUS

Business Models; Management Operations; Computer Simulation

INTRODUCTION

Digital technologies have transformed content service from printed hard copies to online electronic files and data streams. But due to the financial and(or) technological constraints, most CSPs, especially the small and middle ones, may fail to serve the end users with guaranteed service quality (Wang, 2013). One intuitive solution for this problem is to collaborate and share the available content service resources with other CSPs. Through the collaboration, a resource-constrained CSP can delegate part or all of its services to resource-rich collaborators, reducing cost and scaling service footprints. What's more, the collaborators also can achieve extra profits with their idle resources. However, the determination of the optimal service mode can be complicated and challenging. Firstly, the competitive nature of all participant CSPs is at odds during the collaboration. Secondly, in addition to the profitability, there are many other variables, such as service quality, may influencing the service mode selection. Thirdly, enterprises' service modes have different characteristics in different development stages rather than static.

Previous works on the related topics of service resource pricing (Mitra, Wang, & Hong, 2017) and service market (Mao, Ma, Wang, & Xu, 2017) only took the interests of service resource providers (the resource-rich collaborative CSPs in this poster) into account, ignoring the interests of resource customers (resource-constrained CSPs in this poster). In fact, most CSPs delegate their services to their collaborators with idle resources due to economic constraints. Obviously, both the profitabilities of resource providers and resource customers should be considered carefully in developing a collaborative service mode.

This poster focuses on the problem by proposing a service mode selection strategy for resource-constrained CSPs. The proposed strategy is based on three kinds of service modes, which are identified according to the collaborative relationship of different CSPs: Self-service, Delegation service and Cooperation service. Then, the service mode selection is formulated as a profit optimization problem from the service chain perspective, which takes the service cost, service quality and profitability of CSPs into account and adapts to the CSPs' different development stages. The experiment results show that compared with the fixed λ service strategy, where the resource-constrained CSP shares the revenues of delegated service requests in a fixed percentage λ, our proposed strategy may achieve more service profits.

SERVICE MODE SELECTION STRATEGY

To simplify, this poster considers the case when only two CSPs (the target CSP T_p and the collaborative CSP T_c) are involved. According to the collaborative relationship be-tween T_p and T_c both serving T_p's end users, three kinds of service modes are identified: **1) Self-service**: T_p serves all end users. It may happen in the stage when T_p has enough resources to provide all its end users with content services of guaranteed quality. **2) Delegation service**: T_p delegates all of its services to T_c and shares a certain percentage of T_c's profits. It may happen in the stage when T_p is unable to set up its own online service infrastructures due to the economic and(or) technical constraints. **3) Cooperation service**: T_p and T_c co-serve T_p's end users, i.e., T_p delegates part of its services to T_c. T_p and T_c share the revenue in proportion to their respective contributions.

82nd Annual Meeting of the Association for Information Science & Technology | Melbourne, Australia | 19–23 October, 2019

DOI: 10.1002/pra2.00168

Then, it considers that T_p and T_c are operating independently, each attempting to maximize its profits. That is, when T_p receives the content service requests, it will choose one of these three service modes to achieve the maximum profit. Obviously, this service mode selection problem can be formulated as a profit optimization problem, described as follows:

$$\Gamma = \max(R_{1oS};R_{1oD};R_{1oC}) \tag{1}$$

St.

$$C_T \geq f_{cp}(D) + f_{cs_1}(D) \tag{2}$$

where R_{1oS}, R_{1oD} and R_{1oC} is the optimal profit of T_p with Self-service, Delegation service and Cooperation service mode correspondingly. C_T denotes the total available budget for content production and service of T_p, $f_{cp}(D)$ represents the actual production cost, $f_{cs_1}(D)$ denotes the actual service cost of T_p, and D means the total service demand, which can be described respectively as following:

$$f_{cp}(D) = CT + \vartheta D \tag{3}$$

$$f_{cs}(s) = \mu s \tag{4}$$

where μ is the service cost coefficient.

$$D = f_d(p_1, s_1, p_2, s_2) \tag{5}$$

Then, the optimal profit of T_p and T_c with these three service modes can be deduced as Equations 6–10, respectively.

$$R_{1oS} = \frac{\mu_1^2\overline{D}^2 + 2\mu_1(C_T - CT)(\theta_1\overline{D} - 22\mu_1 k_1 - 2k_1\theta_1\vartheta)}{4\mu_1 k_1(\mu_1 + \theta_1\vartheta)} - CT \tag{6}$$

$$R_{1oDS} = \frac{(C_T - CT)^2}{\vartheta^2 k_2} - \frac{\mu_2(C_T - CT)}{\theta_2\vartheta} - C_T \tag{7}$$

$$R_{2oDS} = \frac{\mu_2\overline{D}}{\theta_2} - \frac{\mu_2(C_T - CT)}{\theta_2\vartheta} \tag{8}$$

$$R_{1oc} = \mu_1\frac{\overline{D} + \theta(C_T - CT)}{\theta\vartheta + 2\mu_1}\left[\mu_1\frac{\overline{D} + \theta(C_T - CT)}{k(\theta\vartheta + 2\mu_1)} - \frac{2\mu_1 + \mu_2}{\theta} - \vartheta\right] + \mu_1\frac{\overline{D}}{\theta} - CT \tag{9}$$

$$R_{2oc} = \frac{\mu_2\overline{D}}{\theta} - \frac{\mu_2(\mu_1\overline{D} + \theta(C_T - CT))}{\theta(\theta\vartheta + 2\mu_1)} \tag{10}$$

where $\overline{D}$ is the expected number of service requests, CT is the static content production cost, θ is the service quality sensitive coefficient, and k is the price sensitive coefficient. Since the copyright fee is paid as a fixed percentage of the service price in China, let ϑ denote the percentage. The subscripts 1 and 2 represent T_p and T_c.

EXPERIMENT VALIDATION AND RESULT ANALYSIS

To evaluate the effectiveness of our strategy, the performances of this proposed strategy and the fixed λ service strategy are compared. With the fixed λ service strategy, the resource-constrained T_p delegates part of service requests to its collaborator T_c and shares the revenue of the delegated service in a fixed percentage λ. To ensure the maximum service profits of the fixed λ service strategy, the experiment lets $\lambda = 0.6$, which is the optimal value of λ among the various collaborative service platforms adopted by *Amazon Book*. The data used in the experiment is collected from two publishing content service platforms (called Platform 1 and Platform 2) of the Industry and Information Publishing Group, which is one of the biggest publishers of Information Science in China. Besides, this experiment lets $k_1 = 0.10$, $\theta_1 = 13$, $\mu_1 = 75$, $\vartheta = 2.27$, $k_2 = 0.14$, $\theta_2 = 3.5$, $\mu_2 = 100$, $C_T = 1000 * 10^4$ and $CT = 700 * 10^4$ according to our practical experience.

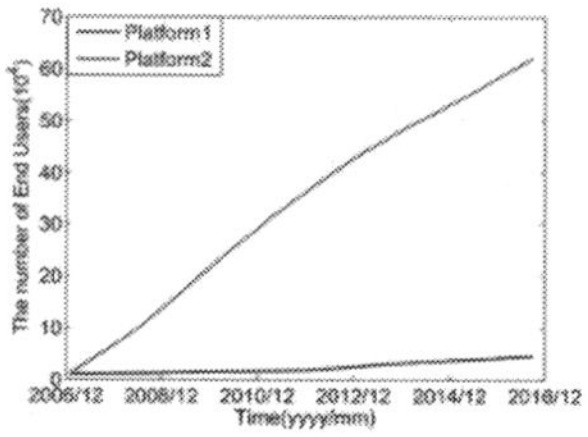

Figure 1. The end users' number of two platforms.

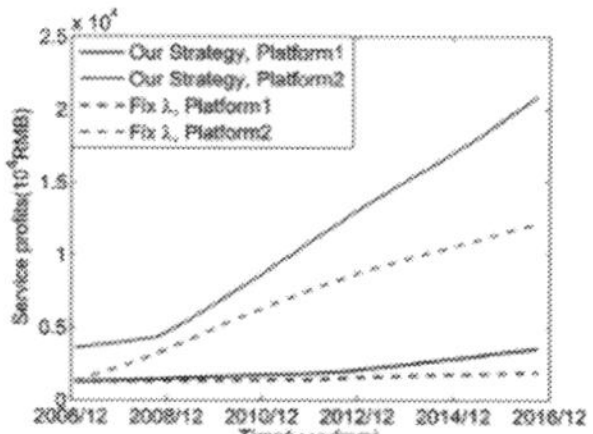

Figure 2. The service profits of different service strategies.

In Figure 1, the blue and red curves plot the number of end users of Platform 1 and Platform 2 from 2006.12 to 2016.10. In Figure 2, the blue and red curves denote the service profits of Platform 1 and Platform 2. Comparing our strategy with the fixed λ service strategy, it is clear that: 1) the service profits of both two strategies are increasing with the growth of end users' population; 2) our strategy can achieve more service profits than the fixed λ strategy, and the more the end users are, the more obvious this advantage is. Thus, compared with the fixed λ strategy which is commonly applied in real world, our service mode selection strategy may increase the service profits significantly and accelerate CSP's business growth.

CONCLUSION

Resource-constrained CSPs tend to collaborate with each other to improve their service profitability and expand the scope of services, but how to choose a suitable service mode is a dynamic and complicated problem with many factors involved in. This poster formulates the problem as a profit optimization problem, which takes the service cost, service quality and profitability of CSPs into account and adapts to the CSPs' different development stages. The experiment results show that the proposed service mode selection strategy may improve CSPs' service profits significantly and promote CSP's business growth, compared with the fixed λ strategy.

REFERENCES

Mao, Z., Ma, R. T. B., Wang, X., & Xu, Y. (2017). *On optimal service differentiation in congested network markets*. In IEEE INFOCOM - IEEE Conference on Computer Communications.

Mitra, D., Wang, Q., & Hong, A. (2017). *Emerging internet content and service providers' relationships: Models and analyses of engineering, business and policy impact*. In IEEE INFOCOM - IEEE Conference on Computer Communications.

Wang, W. (2013). The investigation on the current situation of university digital publishing service platforms. *Publishing Research*, *8*(6), 16–19.

Professional and Institutional Support for RDM: A Case of the National Institutes of Health (NIH)

Sue Yeon Syn
Department of Library and Information Science,
Catholic University of America
syn@cua.edu

Soojung Kim
Department of Library and Information Science,
Chonbuk National University,
Republic of Korea

ABSTRACT

This study explored biomedical researchers' Research Data Management (RDM) practices and investigated how institute and professional services support their practices through the RDM processes with a case of NIH. It was found that institutional information technology (IT) and library services are focused on certain stages of RDM processes. Also, it was found that having a close collaboration among service units within an institute is important to maximize their resources for services, reduce duplicated services, and publicize their services to a wider range of users.

KEYWORDS

Research data management; Information and data processes; Library services; Biomedical research data

INTRODUCTION

The explosive volume of research data and granting agency mandates for data management have spurred many libraries to initiate RDM services to meet the growing demand of researchers. For effective RDM services, libraries should understand researchers' data management needs and ensure their services align with those needs. As a case study, we analyzed biomedical researchers' RDM practices and institutional RDM services to identify where professional support can be improved.

Studies have introduced the current RDM practices and support needs of biomedical researchers (Federer, Lu, & Joubert, 2016; Wiley & Burnette, 2019). A common theme recurring in the literature is that researchers do not have a high level of data literacy skills, about how to organize, describe, process, store or preserve data, which confirms the urgent need for training researchers. Libraries can provide a variety of RDM services, for example, teaching RDM best practices, providing RDM consulting, helping with annotation/metadata creation, and managing an institutional repository (Creamer, Martin, & Kafel, 2014). Libraries are not the only actor in the RDM service landscape. IT or other actors can create an integrated institutional approach to RDM services.

82nd Annual Meeting of the Association for Information Science & Technology | Melbourne, Australia | 19–23 October, 2019

DOI: 10.1002/pra2.00170

Little has been done to identify gaps between researchers' RDM practices and RDM services implemented for them in the research process. This study aims to answer the research question: How can a research institution support biomedical researchers' research data management practices? The findings will provide opportunities for research institutions and libraries to assist researchers with RDM needs.

RESEARCH DESIGN AND FINDINGS

Interviews were conducted with biomedical researchers at the NIH during November and December, 2018. NIH was selected as it is the largest biomedical research agency in the world (About NIH, n.d.). Eleven researchers in various health-related fields were interviewed, including a Biologist, Physician, Biostatistician, and Computer Scientist. They worked at NIH for 7 years on average. The interview data was coded based on the RDM practices at each step of the RDM process. The RDM processes were identified as data generation, data organization, data storage, data analysis, data sharing, and data preservation.

Data Generation: Researchers collected data from various sources. Data generated from labs include blood samples, DNA sequencing data, RNA samples from mice, monkeys or patients. Data that researchers collected outside of the lab is usually shared data from other researchers, other institutions, or from public databases. Data formats also vary from numbers to images. The data consists primarily of digital formats, but also includes printed or hand-written data such as lab notes. Researchers tend to figure out data generation processes individually or within the lab, rather than relying on institutional or library services.

Data Organization: Researchers have their own ways of organizing folders, naming files, and describing data. This happens with little guidance or interference from principal investigators (PIs), which often leads to insufficient documentation as well as inconsistent data organization practices among researchers. These practices constrain the ability of researchers to track necessary data, impeding the effective preservation of research data. We found little evidence for the perceived support of professional services for data organization and management.

Data Storage: For personal data storage, most researchers use a lab computer or notebook. For the internal exchange of data with colleagues, researchers tended to rely on an institutional server.

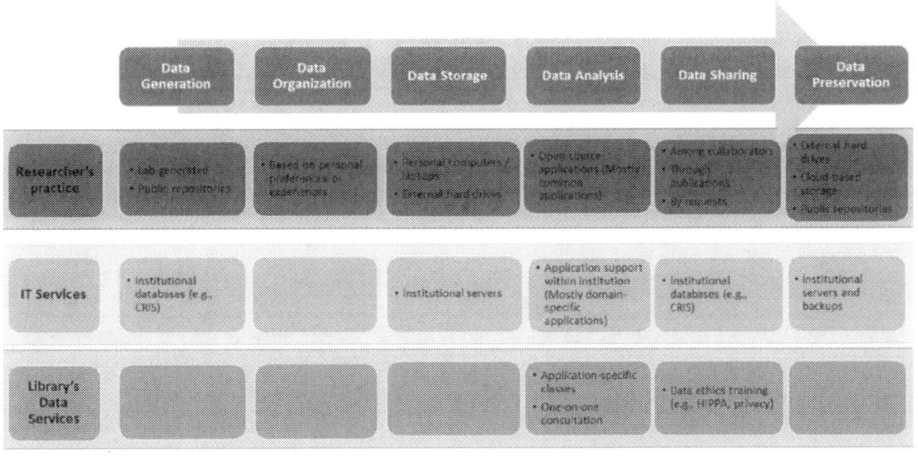

Figure 1. Biomedical researchers' RDM practices and institutional and library's professional services throughout RDM processes.

This happened especially when a lab deals with large size data such as a high volume of MRI data. In such cases, institutional IT support with high performance server spaces seem to be very helpful and well-used.

Data Analysis: Data analysis methods are dependent on the type of data. We found that researchers used the following types of applications for data analysis: (1) common applications (75%), such as office products, or (2), domain-specific applications (25%), such as microscope software or gene sequencing tools. The common applications were used for sharing (38%), documentation (19%), analysis (15%), or image processing (12%). Researchers tend to search widely for common applications that are provided by the institution or freely available tools. NIH Library's Data Services tend to be focused on training researchers for use of applications.

Data Sharing: Researchers share data among collaborators of the project team or within lab (53%), through publications (20%), to public repositories (19%), or to other researchers by request (6%). The interviewees mentioned that they have used shared data as part of their research (82%). Data sharing is becoming more common among biomedical researchers. However, we found that the reasons for sharing data are mostly related to disciplinary climate (35%) and institutional support (24%). Institutional support is often provided with established internal databases. Support on data ethics and the ethical use of data is provided at the institute level and also through NIH Library's educational programs.

Data Preservation: A variety of storage media are used for long-term preservation, including internal servers, external hard drives, public repositories, and cloud-based storage. Researchers regard internal servers as the most reliable storage solution because of automatic daily backups. A few researchers use public repositories and cloud-based storage as an additional preservation option. However, use is limited, due to security concerns.

Figure 1 provides an overview of the data management practices of biomedical researchers, and institutional and professional support at each stage of the RDM process.

DISCUSSION AND CONCLUSION

Using a case study of NIH and the NIH Library, this study explored biomedical researchers' RDM practices and investigated how institutional and professional services support their practices through the RDM process. It was found that IT and library's services are focused on certain stages of the RDM process. This is understandable as some RDM practices are very specific to a particular subject area or lab-practice. However, the review of the overall support also provides opportunities for librarians who provide support for data services. For example, at the NIH Library, support is mainly focused on data analysis and sharing stages. Librarians may be able to find ways to get involved in earlier stages of the RDM process such as data organization. It was also found that having a close collaboration among service units within an institution is important to maximize resources for RDM services, reduce duplicated services, and publicize services to a wider range of users. This study only examined one institution and one research domain as a case study, although the researchers interviewed were specialized in various areas within the biomedical field.

REFERENCES

About NIH (n.d.). Retrieved from https://www.nih.gov/about-nih

Creamer, A. T., Martin, E. R., & Kafel, D. (2014). *Research data management and the health sciences librarian*. University of Massachusetts Medical School. Library Publications and Presentations. Paper 147.

Federer, L. M., Lu, Y., & Joubert, D. J. (2016). Data literacy training needs of biomedical researchers. *Journal of the Medical Library Association, 104*(1), 52–57.

Wiley, C. A., & Burnette, M. H. (2019). Assessing data management support needs of bioengineering and biomedical research faculty. *Journal of eScience Librarianship, 8*(1), e1132.

"I'm in the Center of the Vortex": The Affective Chain of Social Media Trolling

Huixin Tian
Indiana University, Bloomington, USA
huixtian@iu.edu

Pei-Ying Chen
Indiana University, Bloomington, USA
peiychen@iu.edu

ABSTRACT

Dominant models for the conceptualization of trolling fail to address the subjective experiences of its victims. By bringing affect into perspective, this paper explores the negative impact of trolling on individuals, drawing on data from semi-structured interviews with 19 respondents who were trolled on popular Chinese social networks (e.g., *Weibo*, *Zhihu*, *Renren*), blogs, and forums (e.g., *Baidu Tieba*, *Tianya*). Our preliminary findings suggest that: (1) the affective chain of trolling is materialized by the social network platforms' affordability and human actors' desire for intensity, and (2) the victims of trolling were overwhelmed by the accumulated affective intensities in circulation to which they were exposed.

KEYWORDS

Trolling; Social media; Affect theory

ASIS&T THESAURUS

Social informatics; Information theory

INTRODUCTION

Trolling refers to a wide range of phenomena and behaviors that feature intentional "fishing for flames" in an online context (Phillips, 2016). Although trolling does not always contain hostile or harmful content (Sanfilippo, Yang, & Fichman, 2017), the sheer volume of information to which individuals are subjected during a trolling episode can overwhelm them irrespective of hostility. Moreover, while the mainstream conceptualization of trolling holds a strong rational assumption as to both the act and the actor (e.g., Fichman & Sanfilippo, 2016), the victims of trolling often experienced strong bodily reactions. For instance, Campbell (2017) described her own experience of being trolled on Twitter in this way: "My head feels warmer. My cheeks go numb. The space behind my eyes starts to ache … My body is reacting to the toxic nature of intimidating tweets. The sarcasm, the sneering, the mockery. The public shaming".

In contrast to previous research, where researchers assume that trolling is an outcome of the cognitive process and the actors involved are rational, the present study explores the non-rational aspect of trolling experiences by focusing on affect. On the one hand, affect is embodied in the strong bodily reactions to trolling, as it emphasizes the precognitive, bodily, and visceral forces or intensities that are associated with but also generally distinct from conscious knowing (Seigworth & Gregg, 2010). On the other hand, given that affect dwells in the world of relations, the online social networks where most trolling takes place are not only ideal sites for affect to be mediated, circulated, and translocated, but also part of the doing of affect via mediating, circulating and translocating information (Paasonen, Hillis, & Petit, 2015).

This study focuses on the personal experiences of individuals who self-identify as victims of trolling and elaborates on the mechanism by which trolling generates negative feelings through the affective network.

METHOD

We conducted 19 semi-structured interviews with individuals who have experienced online trolling in China. We used snowball sampling to recruit participants based on the first author's personal connections on *Zhihu*, a popular Q&A forum in China. The first author maintained a long-term personal account to build rapport with respondents and help facilitate participant recruitment. Subjective feeling about trolling was the main criterion for participation. Additional participants were actively sought during the interviews by asking the interviewees if they knew anyone else who had been trolled. Most of the interviews were carried out by instant messaging ($n = 15$); three took place in person and one by phone. All interviews were conducted in Chinese; only direct quotations have been translated to English.

We analyzed the interview data as well as supplementary materials (e.g., screenshots and links to the original trolling scenarios) data via qualitative coding (Miles, Huberman, & Saldaña, 2013). We adopted the grounded-theory approach to identify patterns based on the combination of open and thematic coding (Glaser & Strauss, 2000).

RESULTS

Among the 19 respondents, 17 reported themselves as victims of trolling; the remaining two described themselves as witnesses. Most of the self-identified victims ($n = 14$) described their experience as stressful, depressing, sad, or even threatening. The sites where trolling occurred ranged from Reddit-like forums (e.g., *Baidu Tieba* and *Tianya*) and

82nd Annual Meeting of the Association for Information Science & Technology | Melbourne, Australia | 19–23 October, 2019

DOI: 10.1002/pra2.00173

blogs to newer social networking sites similar to Facebook, Twitter and Quora (e.g., *Zhihu*, *Renren*, and *Weibo*).

Escalation of Affective Intensities

One means by which trolling generates negative feelings is the escalation of affective intensities afforded by the functionalities of social media platforms, including comments and retweets as well as follow, hashtags, and buzzword search. Most respondents ($n = 18$) described their trolling experiences as starting from small-scale, low-intensity incidents but quickly expanding in scope to include hundreds of comments on a personal timeline and retweets of controversial posts. The functionality of the platforms not only adhered the individuals involved in trolling to a gigantic circulation network, but also escalated the circulation of intensities—attentions, expressions, and revisits—that could easily overwhelm them. Half of our respondents described feeling surprised, unprepared, or even scared by the volume of messages made possible by social network platform functionality during the trolling events—for example, when they found more than 100 comments under a single post and hundreds of notifications of retweets.

The Vortex of Affect

Participants reported shutting down the commenting function on their posts as a common countermeasure against trolling. They did not, however, have an effective means of preventing retweeting. Compared to comments that directed accumulative intensities toward a single individual, retweets perpetuated trolling by bringing personal expressions to publicity and circulating those expressions in a network of affective intensities In this regard, retweets not only produced but also reproduced continuous affective intensities that trapped individuals "in the center of the vortex" (quote from respondent R3).

This vortex of affect is formed, at least partially, through people's desire to seek out the intensity found in trolling episodes, especially in hotspots harnessing massive attention (Paasonen, 2015). Once the affective chain of retweets starts, however, it can quickly deviate from the topic of the affective jolt, driven by the impulse to retweet instead. As exemplified by the stories of R3 and R20, the chains of trolling quickly spread from heated discussions surrounding an actor to irrelevant things, while trolls started to scan their personal timeline and retweet their previous posts. In this communication for its own sake, neither topic nor content mattered as much as communication itself, even though new elements (e.g., comments, links, screenshots, and new users) were constantly brought in to strengthen circulation. In other words, affective circulation itself empowered the affective apparatuses, including retweeted messages and buzzwords, as well as the accumulated attention from affect seekers who continuously brought in new fuel and heat. As long as the post was still in circulation, trolling, or the vortex of affects, showed remarkable endurance and trapped its victims.

CONCLUSION AND FUTURE WORK

Our findings suggest that the negative experiences of trolling victims were exacerbated by the accumulated affective intensities attached to them. It is the affective intensities constantly accumulated and attached in circulation that overwhelmed the individuals, whose effort to escape the vortex of affect was outrun by the endurance and efficiency of the affective network. Future work should account for the socio-technical variations of affective networks on different social media platforms and examine how individuals adapt their coping strategies to the different contexts in which trolling can take place.

REFERENCES

Campbell, E. (2017). "Apparently being a self-obsessed c**t is now academically lauded": Experiencing Twitter trolling of autoethnographers. *Forum Qualitative Sozialforschung / Forum: Qualitative Social Research, 18*(3). https://doi.org/10.17169/fqs-18.3.2819

Fichman, P., & Sanfilippo, M. R. (2016). *Online trolling and its perpetrators: Under the cyberbridge*. Lanham, MD: Rowman & Littlefield Publishers.

Glaser, B., & Strauss, A. (2000). *The discovery of grounded theory: Strategies for qualitative research.* New Brunswick, NJ: Routledge.

Miles, M. B., Huberman, A. M., & Saldaña, J. (2013). *Qualitative data analysis: A methods sourcebook* (3rd ed.). Thousand Oaks, CA: SAGE Publications.

Paasonen, S. (2015). A midsummer's bonfire: Affective intensities of online debate. In K. Hillis, S. Paasonen, & M. Petit (Eds.), *Networked affect* (pp. 27–42). Retrieved from https://ieeexplore.ieee.org/document/7087532

Paasonen, S., Hillis, K., & Petit, M. (2015). Introduction: Networks of transmission: Intensity, sensation, value. In K. Hillis, S. Paasonen, & M. Petit (Eds.), *Networked affect* (pp. 1–26). Retrieved from https://ieeexplore.ieee.org/document/7087714

Phillips, W. (2016). *This is why we can't have nice things: Mapping the relationship between online trolling and mainstream culture*. Cambridge, MA: The MIT Press.

Sanfilippo, M. R., Yang, S., & Fichman, P. (2017). *Managing online trolling: From deviant to social and political trolls.* In Hawaii International Conference on System Sciences 2017 (HICSS-50). Retrieved from https://aisel.aisnet.org/hicss-50/dsm/critical_and_ethical_studies/6

Seigworth, G. J., & Gregg, M. (2010). An inventory of shimmers. In M. Gregg & G. J. Seigworth (Eds.), *The affect theory reader* (pp. 1–25). Durham, NC: Duke University Press.

"I Don't Understand It So It Can't Be Good": Users' ACG Domain Expertise and Perceived Quality of Video Tags

Liuyi Tong
Department of Information Management, Peking University, Beijing, China
tly124@pku.edu.cn

Hui Lin
Department of Information Management, Peking University, Beijing, China
linhui16@pku.edu.cn

Pengyi Zhang
Department of Information Management, Peking University, Beijing, China
pengyi@pku.edu.cn

ABSTRACT

Tag quality is an important factor to the success of social tagging systems and platforms. Users' domain expertise may influence they perceive tag quality. This study aims to explore how users of different domain experience (frequent user, occasional user, and non-user) perceive the quality of the same tags. We examined an online video community, Bilibili, which specializes in Anime, Comic and Games (ACG) subculture. We asked 60 users to watch 15 videos and rate the 95 tags of these videos, and found that: 1) Users with more domain expertise give higher ratings for tags' relevance to the videos and their retrieval value; 2) Occasional users have the lowest understandability rating, followed by non-users, and frequent users; 3) users think high-frequency tags are less suitable for retrieval. These results may provide insights to high quality tag selection for personalized recommendation and retrieval.

KEYWORDS

Domain expertise; tag quality; user perception; folksonomy

ASIS&T THESAURUS

User generated content; organization of information

INTRODUCTION

Social tagging is widely used as a powerful tool to allow Internet users to manage online resources in many Web 2.0 applications, such as Delicious, Flicker, Movielens, BibSonomy, and so on (Shepitsen, Gemmell, Mobasher, & Burke, 2008). In social tagging system, tag quality is an important attribute of tags that directly determines the effects of information organization and retrieval.

Several factors may be indicators of a tag's quality. For example, three attributes could be used to measure the quality of tags: the centrality, frequency, and information entropy of the tags in tag networks (Zhang, Farooq, & Carroll, 2009). The higher the level of familiarity with tags, retrieval engines, web navigation, and social tagging system, the higher the validity of the tags they assigned (Lee, Goh, Razikin, & Chua, 2009). Tag co-occurrence, tag stability, and tag descriptive force to improve the tag quality (Belém, Martins, Almeida, Gonçalves, & Pappa, 2010). Domain experts assigned tags will be judged more relevant than non-experienced assigned tags (Darvish & Chin, 2010). However, little is known about whether users' expertise has any influence on the ability to recognize tag quality.

82nd Annual Meeting of the Association for Information Science & Technology | Melbourne, Australia | 19–23 October, 2019

DOI: 10.1002/pra2.00174

Therefore, this paper aims to study whether users of different domain familiarity have different perceptions of the quality of same tags. According to the related paper, we found usually users rate the tag quality in the three aspects: understandability, retrieval value (Zhang et al., 2009) and relevance (Belém et al., 2010) of tags. The RQs are:

1. Do frequent users, occasional users, and non-users of a video website have differences in their perception of tags quality?
2. Do users have different perception for tags of different frequency?

METHODS

Data Collection

We used a Python crawler to collect top-viewed 1,100 videos (top 100 videos from 11 topic categories and 3,934 tags from Bilibili in November, 2017. Random sampling was used to select a set of 15 videos and all 95 tags attached to these videos. We recruited 60 users (32 M and 28 F, between 18 to 25 years old) through snowball sampling: 20 non-users, 20 occasional users, and 20 frequent users depending on their registration time, frequency and duration of use.

User group	Registration time	Frequency per week	Duration per week
Non-user	Never use	Never use	Never use
Occasional user	Less than half year	Less than 1 time/week	Less than 0.5 hour/week
Frequent user	More than 2 years	More than 3 times/week	More than 2 hours/week

Table 1. Definition of different domain expertise users.

We asked each user to watch the 15 videos and rate the 95 tags by answering three questions related to each tag according to his/her perception on a five-point scale, 1 being lowest and 5 being highest. The three questions are:

1. Understandability: is the meaning of the tag clear to you?
2. Value for retrieval: do you think this tag is suitable as a retrieval term for finding videos?
3. Relevance: do you think this tag is relevant to the video?

Data Analysis

Since the ratings were not normally distributed, we conducted Kruskal-Wallis Tests compare whether the three user groups show any differences in the above three quality ratings with low, medium and high frequency.

RESULTS

We conducted Pearson's Correlation test between the three quality criteria. Understandability has a medium to strong correlation with relevance ($R = 0.575$, $p < 0.01$) and retrieval ratings ($R = 0.596$, $p < 0.01$). Relevance and value have a strong correlation ($R = 0.854$, $p < 0.01$). The more users think they understand a tag, the higher the perceived relevance and value for retrieval.

Understandability

In Table 2, frequent users have a significantly higher rating than both non-users and occasional users, suggesting that frequent users participating more can better understand tags. Interestingly, occasional users' rating is slightly lower than non-users, perhaps because the occasional users understand there is different meaning of the same tag in ACG subculture, which lowers their perceived understandability ratings.

User group	N	Mean rank	df	χ^2	p
Non-users	20	26.15	2	11.40	0.003
Occasional	20	24.15			
Frequent	20	41.2			

Table 2. Understandability rating by user group.

Value for Retrieval

In Table 3, frequent users have a significantly higher rating than occasional users, and occasional users higher than non-users. This suggests that users with more expertise in the domain are able to appreciate the search value of a tag.

User group	N	Mean rank	df	χ^2	p
Non-users	20	22.95	2	10.77	0.004
Occasional	20	28			
Frequent	20	40.55			

Table 3. Retrieval value rating by user group.

Relevance

Table 4 shows the result of the K-W Test on the ratings for relevance. There is a similar pattern in judging the relevance of tags to the value for retrieval. Frequent users have a significantly higher rating than occasional users, and occasional users higher than non-users. This suggests that users with more expertise in the domain think that the tags are more relevant to the videos than less experienced users.

User group	N	Mean rank	df	χ^2	p
Non-users	20	25.25	2	11.37	0.003
Occasional	20	25			
Frequent	20	41.25			

Table 4. Relevance rating by user group.

Tag Quality and Frequency

In Table 5, results show that users think high frequency tags are less suitable for retrieval. Tag frequency do not have any significant influence on understandability or relevance ratings and less frequent tags may be more specific and better search terms.

Tag frequency	N	Mean rank	df	χ^2	p
Low (=1)	37	58.23	2	11.463	0.003
Medium (2-6)	29	47.86			
High (≥7)	29	35.09			

Table 5. Retrieval value rating by tag frequency.

CONCLUSION AND DISCUSSION

This poster reports a study exploring the relationship between users' domain experience and their perceived quality ratings of video tags in ACG subculture. Results show that: 1) users with more domain expertise give higher ratings for tags' relevance to the videos and their retrieval value; 2) occasional users have the lowest understandability rating, followed by non-users, and frequent users; 3) users think that high-frequency tags are less suitable for retrieval.

These results provide some insights into better organizing recourses in video web sites in specific domain that use social tagging systems. System need to consider users' level of domain expertise and provide tag recommendation according to their appropriate domain experience.

ACKNOWLEDGMENT

We received support from NSFC Grant #71603012.

REFERENCES

Belém, F. M., Martins, E. F., Almeida, J. M., Gonçalves, M. A., & Pappa, G. L. (2010). *Exploiting co-occurrence and information quality metrics to recommend tags in web 2.0 applications*. In Proceedings of the 19th ACM International Conference on Information and Knowledge Management (pp. 1793-1796). ACM.

Darvish, S., & Chin, A. (2010). *Dealing with the video tidal wave: The relevance of expertise for video tagging*. In Proceedings of the 21st ACM Conference on Hypertext and Hypermedia (pp. 289-290). ACM.

Lee, C. S., Goh, D. H. L., Razikin, K., & Chua, A. Y. (2009). Tagging, sharing and the influence of personal experience. *Journal of Digital Information*, *10*(1).

Shepitsen, A., Gemmell, J., Mobasher, B., & Burke, R. (2008, October). *Personalized recommendation in social tagging systems using hierarchical clustering*. In Proceedings of the 2008 ACM Conference on Recommender Systems (pp. 259-266). ACM.

Zhang, S., Farooq, U., & Carroll, J. M. (2009, May). *Enhancing information scent: identifying and recommending quality tags*. In Proceedings of the ACM 2009 International Conference on Supporting Group Work (pp. 1-10).

An Analysis of Published Journals for Papers Posted on bioR$_X$iv

Hiroyuki Tsunoda
Tsurumi University,
Yokohama, Japan
tsunoda-h@tsurumi-u.ac.jp

Yuan Sun
National Institute
of Informatics, Tokyo, Japan
yuan@nii.ac.jp

Masaki Nishizawa
National Institute
of Informatics, Tokyo, Japan
nisizawa@nii.ac.jp

Xiaomin Liu
National Science Library, Chinese
Academy of Sciences, Beijing, China
liuxm@mail.las.ac.cn

Kou Amano
National Institute for
Materials Science, Tsukuba, Japan
amano.kou@nims.go.jp

ABSTRACT

This study investigated papers posted on bioR$_X$iv. In 2013–19, 17,818 papers were published in academic journals, accounting for 40.67% of the total publication. Among them, the Web of Science (WoS) Core Collection recorded journals of 16,525 published papers, accounting for 92.74% of the total. The following conclusions can be drawn. (1) Results indicate scientists' attention to the preprint system. (2) A large number of papers still use traditional publishing as the ultimate goal. (3) Because the posted papers scrutinized in this study were published in journals with a high impact factor, they have attracted the attention of many scientists. Nevertheless, we believe that the preprint platform will play a greater role from the academic exchange perspective.

KEYWORDS

Library and Information Science; Bibliometrics; Scholarly Communication; Preprint Archive; Open Access; bioR$_X$iv; Journal Impact Factor

ASIS&T THESAURUS

Bibliometrics; Electronic journals; Digital repositories

INTRODUCTION

The preprint platform in academic publishing has developed rapidly. Several studies have focused on preprint servers, such as arXiv (Ginsparg, 1997; Larivière et al., 2014; McKiernan, 2000) and bioR$_X$iv (Abdill & Blekhman, 2019). The increased availability of research results leads to a faster advancement of university performance (Tsunoda, Sun, Nishizawa, & Liu, 2016). bioR$_X$iv is a free online preprint archive and distribution service for unpublished papers. By posting papers on this archive, authors can make their findings immediately available to the scientific community and receive feedback on draft manuscripts from scientists worldwide. This study aims to analyze the status of published journals for posted papers by collecting metadata of all 43,812 papers posted on bioR$_X$iv since its launch till February 28, 2019.

82nd Annual Meeting of the Association for Information Science & Technology | Melbourne, Australia | 19–23 October, 2019

DOI: 10.1002/pra2.00175

METHODS

This study investigated papers posted on bioR$_X$iv. The web crawler that we developed for this purpose visited every page on bioR$_X$iv and downloaded metadata of the title, authors, published digital object identifier (DOI), posted date, and versions of a paper. If the paper was published, it would download the journal title and the published DOI. Next, the metadata was manually verified. The papers were matched with the Web of Science (WoS) Core Collection by Clarivate Analytics using the keywords of published DOIs.

RESULTS AND DISCUSSION

Published and Unpublished Papers

As seen in Figure 1, the number of papers on bioR$_X$iv has been rapidly increasing. Over a thousand papers have been posted every month since September 2017. Therefore, 43,812 papers were posted from November 7, 2013 to February 28, 2019. Among them, 17,818 papers were published in academic journals. The publication rate (P-Rate) was defined as the number

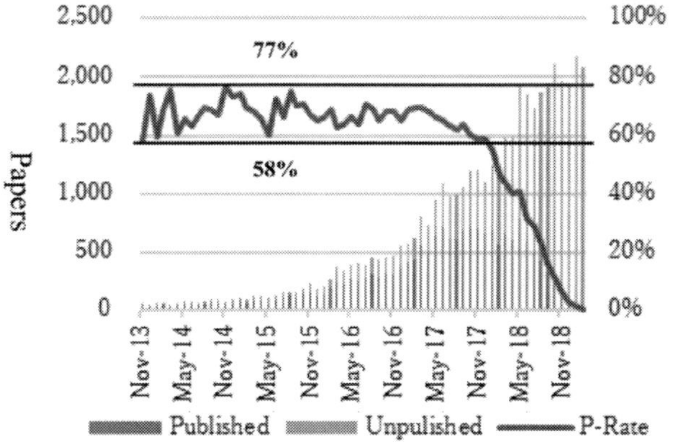

Figure 1. Number of papers published in journals.

of papers published each month divided by the number of papers posted each month. The average P-Rate accounts for 40.67% of the total. However, during 2013–2017, the P-Rate was higher: between 58% and 77%.

Publishing Journals

The total number of journals was 1,626. Although the top five journals received over 500 papers, 1,001 (61.56%) journals received only two or fewer. Figure 2 presents the number of papers published per journal.

Table 1 lists the top 20 journals. The weighted average of the 2017 journal impact factor (JIF) of these journals was 6.84.

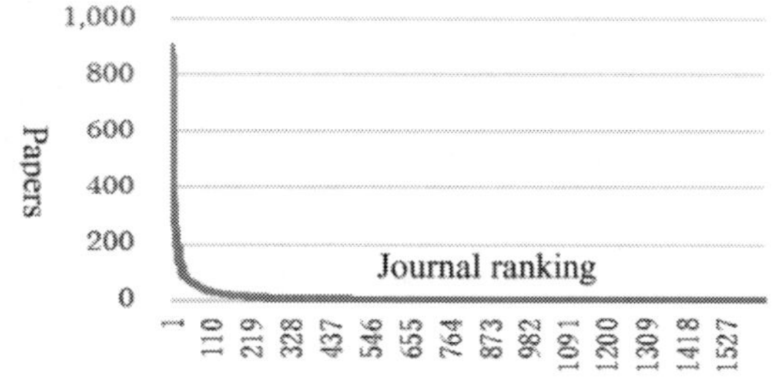

Figure 2. Papers published per journal.

JIF	Journals	Papers	JIF	Journals	Papers
2.77	PLOS ONE	920	2.74	G3: Genes | Genomes | Genetics	266
4.12	Scientific Reports - Nature	881	5.43	NeuroImage	238
7.62	eLife	866	3.73	BMC Genomics	203
12.35	Nature Communications	611	5.97	Journal of Neuroscience	197
5.48	Bioinformatics	509	13.21	Genome Biology	191
9.50	PNAS	487	10.10	Genome Research	189
3.96	PLOS Computational Biology	375	10.22	Molecular Biology and Evolution	175
5.54	PLOS Genetics	333	2.21	BMC Bioinformatics	157
11.56	Nucleic Acids Research	285	8.03	Cell Reports	149
4.08	Genetics	283	27.13	Nature Genetics	135
			6.84	**The weighted average**	

Table 1. Top 20 journals.

Core Collection

Among these, the journals of 16,525 published papers were recorded by the WoS Core Collection. These journals receive a high number of citations. The core collection rate (CC-Rate) was defined as number of papers in the WoS Core Collection divided by number of papers published each month. From 2013 to 2017, the CC-Rate was considerably high: between 90% and 100%. Therefore, the most published papers should evidence a high impact for research. Figure 3 demonstrates the status of papers in high-quality journals.

CONCLUSION

According to the statistics considered thus far and given the change in the open access environment, the following conclusions can be drawn. (1) The preprint system papers continue

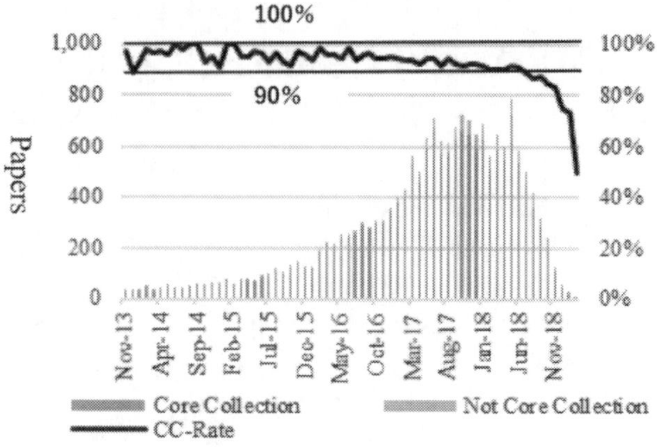

Figure 3. Number of papers in the Core Collection.

to grow and indicate scientists' attention to the system. (2) The publication of papers was around 70% from 2013 to 2017, which indicates that a large number of papers still use traditional publishing as the ultimate goal. (3) Because the papers examined in this study were published in high JIF journals, they have attracted the attention of many scientists worldwide. Thus, this study reveals that the flow of papers in the preprint server is highly important; we believe that preprint platform will play an even greater role from the academic exchange perspective. Certainly, the preprint systems of different disciplines reflect different situations; therefore, it is more convincing to compare the preprint systems of multiple disciplines.

ACKNOWLEDGMENTS

This work was supported by JSPS KAKENHI Grant Number JP19K12707, JP18005852, and ROIS NII Open Collaborative Research 2019-(19FS02).

REFERENCES

Abdill, R. J., & Blekhman, R. (2019). Meta-research: Tracking the popularity and outcomes of all bioRxiv preprints. *eLife*, *8*, e45133.

Ginsparg, P. (1997). Winners and losers in the global research village. *The Serials Librarian*, *30*(3-4), 83–95.

Larivière, V., Sugimoto, C. R., Macaluso, B., Milojević, S., Cronin, B., & Thelwall, M. (2014). arXiv E-prints and the journal of record: An analysis of roles and relationships. *Journal of the Association for Information Science and Technology*, *65*(6), 1157–1169.

McKiernan, G. (2000). arXiv.org: The Los Alamos National Laboratory e-print server. *International Journal on Grey Literature*, *1*(3), 127–138.

Tsunoda, H., Sun, Y., Nishizawa, M., & Liu, X. (2016). A study on the academic and research impact of shared contents in institutional repositories in related to performance indicators of university rankings. *Proceedings of the Association for Information Science and Technology*, *53*(1), 1–6.

Repurposing: Another R to Prioritize in Data Curation

Michael Twidale
School of Information Sciences, University of Illinois at Urbana-Champaign, Champaign, Illinois, USA
twidale@illinois.edu

Catherine Blake
School of Information Sciences, University of Illinois at Urbana-Champaign, Champaign, Illinois, USA
clblake@illinois.edu

Maria Souden
US Department of Veterans Affairs VA Information Resource Center (VIReC), Edward Hines, Jr. VA Hospital, Hines, Illinois, USA
maria.souden@va.gov

Jenifer Stelmack
US Department of Veterans Affairs VA Information Resource Center (VIReC), Edward Hines, Jr. VA Hospital, Hines, Illinois, USA
jenifer.stelmack@va.gov

Jenna Kim
School of Information Sciences, University of Illinois at Urbana-Champaign, Champaign, Illinois, USA
jkim682@illinois.edu

ABSTRACT

Data repurposing has great potential for innovative research. But there are distinct risks of researchers outside the group who originally collected the data misunderstanding the actual meaning of particular fields and values. These meanings may not be sufficiently well documented, as those within the collecting group know what is really meant in the context of the original purposes of collection.

KEYWORDS

Reuse; repurposing; metadata; tacit knowledge

ASIS&T THESAURUS

Information flow; Information loss

INTRODUCTION

Various researchers have proposed terms important in data use including rerun, repeat, replicate, reproduce, reuse and replicate, e.g. [Benureau & Rougier, 2017]. We propose another R: repurpose - a special kind of data reuse for a reason other than why it was originally collected. Data repurposing has great potential for innovative research, but there are risks of misunderstanding the meaning of particular fields and values. As part of a larger study [Blake, Souden, Anderson, Twidale, & Stelmack, 2015] we interviewed 18 researchers about their experiences of technical help-giving. Here we report issues arising from the reuse of data collected for clinical purposes being repurposed for research.

82nd Annual Meeting of the Association for Information Science & Technology | Melbourne, Australia | 19–23 October, 2019

DOI: 10.1002/pra2.00176

RESULTS

"*... the data don't necessarily mean what you think they mean. I think a lot of the researchers forget, or are not aware, or didn't even think of ways in which data that are collected for the primary purpose of taking care of a patient, may not fit snugly with their research agenda.*"

All groups use technical terms, jargon and specialist meanings of words. That enables efficient communication within the group, but can cause confusion for outsiders. The obvious case is where a group uses special terms and acronyms. But in that case the person outside the group is at least aware that they do not understand something and can try to find out what is actually meant. It is more problematic when a word or phrase is used in a way that has a particular meaning within the group but a subtly (or not so subtly) different meaning outside. In that case the person outside the group may not be aware that there is a different meaning and so may misinterpret the data. This is especially problematic in datasets. There is an understandable need to use rather terse terms for field names and values, and this terseness can hide subtle qualifications about the actual meaning of the field or what was actually collected.

Problems can occur even when two groups are very closely related. In our case; clinicians who had collected the data for the purposes of treating patients, and medical researchers doing subsequent data analysis, often longitudinal. This was shown by a researcher who happened to be in both groups:

"*I have operational privileges, which means that I learn tremendously from the operation work. And sometimes, I feel, I feel bad for those that are strictly on the research side. Sometimes because they're trying to look through a keyhole. They don't necessarily understand the data. ...*

being able to relay what's there, without handing over a hundred-page document that they're not going to read."

If you know how and why the data was originally created, you can make sense of things that otherwise look odd, or even wrong. There can be an implicit subjectivity in data repurposing, unconsciously assuming as a researcher that this data was created for your benefit and then being mystified why anyone would ever have created such peculiar values or measures (as illustrated by the first quotation). But it wasn't created for you and it wasn't created for what you want to do with it. It was created for another purpose, that you may not know about and under constraints you do not know or even care about.

"A lot of really helpful responses come from people that are actually in the environment where the data's generated or created. And they have more understanding of how the files are created or merged that might cause this thing that looks odd to us to appear. "

Fields and Values should not always be taken Literally

"... people just read the word 'in-patient' and think in-patient, which a lot of people just think is regular acute care"

Subtleties of the actual meaning of words may not be sufficiently well documented. It is especially problematic when the wording of a field or value has a meaning that is reasonable, perhaps by being taken literally, but actually this literal interpretation is an over-simplification, or indeed wrong.

Changes in Practice or Process Over Time

"prior to 2003 ..., in the VA you could only make, identify yourself as in one racial category. ... And then in post 2003 they implemented something that was mandated and so now people can make multiple race designations."

This was a useful and important change, aligning with practices in the US Census data. However in a longitudinal analysis, it can seem that a patient's self-reported race and ethnicity can change over time. This may not be because their self-perception of their race has changed, or be a data error, but just that after 2003 they were given different options to choose from and so they chose differently.

Retrospective Tidying Up

"And then embedded in those [outpatient records] is some patient level information, like what is the patient's race, what is the patient's zip code. And, that's really useful because if you're trying, ... to figure out how far the patient had to go to get their care. ... And so if you know the zip code at the time of the visit, that's really useful. ...
It turns out that only the data up to 2008 was populated with what that information was at the time of the visit. Anything pre-2008 was populated with 2008 values. So, the zip code that was populated in a 2004 outpatient visit was the zip code as it existed in 2008. Likewise it was what their, their race and ethnicity were at that point in time, and all their other variables or patient level variables. And that is something that no one would ever have known, that they had done that. If the question hadn't been asked. And, god, that makes me so nervous, you know, how much of that is going on."

Peculiarities of Automated Data Collection

"... instead of like adding another date if the medicine gets returned or something, actually the [pharmacy] software that they have, changes the date, which is not something that happens, like with ordinary, at all ... You shouldn't, that shouldn't happen, right? Cause now information is gone. ... That is a provenance thing. This is how the data got between there and then. If somebody, if it changed, they've erased the old data and put a new one in that spot."

In this case, a quirk of the pharmacy software used to generate the clinical data meant that dates may be updated as exceptions occur. That is important for future researchers to know about as they might otherwise assume (reasonably) that the date is the date the medicine was issued to the patient.

Peculiarities of Original Data Collection and its Purpose

"So, another example is, is for inpatient movements ..., we're on our third iteration and we still don't have it right because of the convoluted processes and logic that go into creating those, those movement records.
You know, when a patient is in a hospital and they move from one bed to another, you would think that that would be straightforward. Actually it's not. It's recorded in different processes that write to different files that then sometimes are duplicative and sometimes not. And so, you know, it's, it's not just defining the field that gives you the big picture. You have to know what the context, what the, what the process is, or the, you know, that feeds that file, what a record in that file represents. And, you know, often times, when, in the case of like the inpatient movements, it's so convoluted that you really can't describe what this record means in a concise way. So, you know, the best we do is try to understand it and then create a data model that makes sense from somebody using the data and somebody knowledgeable about the clinic practices.
So those are just a couple of examples of, of, you know, the problems that, that are not resolved by simply describing at the field level: what does this mean."

The data was originally collected for clinical and hospital administrative purposes, making use of what was feasible to collect, sometimes using available automated processes. Subsequent repurposing needs to allow for those processes, otherwise the data will be open to misinterpretation. In this case, an outsider repurposing the data may (reasonably) assume that a patient moving from one bed to another would be a simple single recorded piece of information in the database and be rather surprised that there are many logically interconnected records of the same event.

Even with considerable (and commendable) efforts to provide metadata, problems and confusions may persist.

CONCLUSION

Data repurposing has enormous potential to advance scientific insights, not just in medicine but across academia. However it raises significant concerns when done by researchers who are not sufficiently familiar with how and why the original data collection actually occurred. One risk is misinterpretation of understandably terse field names and values. Such errors are predictable and to a large extent reasonable, or at least understandable. There is a need for detailed metadata clarifying provenance, purpose, prior cleaning efforts, conversion processes and any modifications to protocols over time.

ACKNOWLEDGMENTS

This work was supported in part by the US Department of Veterans Affairs (VA).

REFERENCES

Benureau, F. C. Y., & Rougier, N. P. (2017). Re-run, repeat, reproduce, reuse, replicate: Transforming code into scientific contributions. *Frontiers in Neuroinformatics*, *11*, 69.

Blake, C., Souden, M., Anderson, C. L., Twidale, M., & Stelmack, J. E. (2015). Online question answering practices to support healthcare data re-use. *Proceedings of the Association for Information Science and Technology*.

The Use of Theory in Research Relating to Open Access: Practitioner Perspectives

Simon Wakeling
Charles Sturt University, Australia
swakeling@csu.edu.au

Stephen Pinfield
University of Sheffield, United Kingdom
s.pinfield@sheffield.ac.uk

David Bawden
City, University of London, United Kingdom
d.bawden@city.ac.uk

Lyn Robinson
City, University of London, United Kingdom
l.robinson@city.ac.uk

ABSTRACT

The relationship between theory and practice has long been considered problematic for many applied academic disciplines. In this short paper we report preliminary findings from a two-year research project investigating the ways and the extent that theory and practice have interacted in the development of open-access (OA) approaches to the publishing and dissemination of research outputs. Based on interviews with practitioners and researchers working on OA related issues, we explore the ways in which theory is (and isn't) of value to practice. We find that while practitioners acknowledge that theory has the potential to improve understanding, bestow credibility on work, and codify existing knowledge about OA, they also perceive it as "mood music" to the practical work of OA, lacking explicit links to action.

KEYWORDS

Open access; theory and practice; practitioner attitudes

ASIS&T THESAURUS

Library management; Access to resources

INTRODUCTION

"There is nothing so practical as a good theory." So goes the famous maxim by Kurt Lewin (1944, p. 27), who repeatedly called for action to address what he considered a problematic gap between theory and practice, and theorists and practitioners. While much has been written on the subject in the intervening years, it seems clear that the theory-practice gap is still a recognizable and troublesome issue in applied fields as diverse as management (Scapens, 1994), nursing (Corlett, 2000), education (Korthagen, Kessels, Koster, Lagerwerf, & Wubbels, 2001), and library and information science (Haddow & Klobas, 2004).

The broad brush arguments common to these debates will be familiar to many. Researchers using theory are often characterized by practitioners as remote and unhelpfully abstract. Practitioners, meanwhile, are perceived by researchers as too narrowly focused on their immediate working context, and unwilling or unable to engage with the broad picture. In this paper we present some preliminary results from a two-year project investigating the ways and the extent that theory and practice have interacted in the development of open-access (OA) approaches to the publishing and dissemination of research outputs. Based on a systematic review and analysis of the theoretically informed literature relating to OA, and in-depth interviews with 36 researchers and practitioners working on OA problems, we have attempted to better understand what the use (or non-use) of theory has meant for the development of OA, and what this tells us about the theory-practice gap in general. In this paper we focus on data generated from our interviews with OA researchers and practitioners, and in particular material relating to the value (or lack of value) of theory to the practical business of OA. These are among the most significant of our findings, which go to the heart of the theory-practice question.

82nd Annual Meeting of the Association for Information Science & Technology | Melbourne, Australia | 19–23 October, 2019

DOI: 10.1002/pra2.00177

METHOD

Detailed interviews were conducted with 36 participants (11 female, 25 male), selected through maximum variation sampling to ensure a broad range of perspectives and backgrounds. Of these, 12 were academic researchers working on OA related issues, and 24 were practitioners. This latter group was comprised of librarians (L) (9), publishers (P) (7), OA providers (Pr) (3), policy makers (Po) (3), and consultants (C) (2). Of these practitioners, seven had also published theoretically informed work on OA. The interview schedule covered three main areas: the participant's background and experience with OA; what they understood theory to mean, and how it had informed their understanding of OA; and their view of the theory-practice relationship, and how theory had informed their practical work. Interviews were recorded and transcribed, and thematic analysis used as a framework for organizing and interpreting the data, with a coding process following Braun and Clarke (2006).

RESULTS

Value of Theory to Practice

A number of participants acknowledged a link between theory and practice in OA, but in general they found the relationship vague and difficult to articulate. As one publisher put it: *"I do believe there is a golden thread, if you like, between theoretical work and practice ... Does theory influence and, ultimately, shape in some form practice? Yes. I just couldn't tell you how"* (Pu5). Theory was seen by some as a way to extend thinking *"beyond the day to day"* (L5), and by others as a means of avoiding trial and error. Theory was seen by some as a *"short-cut to understanding"* (C2), and a means of linking work to an established and robust intellectual base. Interviewees also spoke of theory bestowing *"academic credibility"* on research outputs, which in turn strengthened advocacy and policy positions. However the most commonly cited benefit of theory to practice was as a tool for understanding. As one librarian put it, *"I do love it when I get some theory that makes sense of things for me"* (L3). Several participants gave examples of specific theories that had helped them understand certain aspects of OA, particularly theories relating to innovation diffusion, and the concept of knowledge as a commons. Finally, and perhaps most interestingly, interviewees spoke of the capacity for theory to formalize and codify existing knowledge. As one librarian explained: *"I'm thinking of the, 'what was often thought but never so well expressed' thing. Where it's sort of there in my mind, but in a, kind of, random inchoate way. And I suppose one of the purposes of theory is to round up these sort of stray ideas and say, actually that is what you think is this"* (L3).

Lack of Value of Theory to Practice

A number of interviewees recognized the aversion of practitioners to theory, although, intriguingly, this tended to be reported of others rather than stated as their own view: e.g. *"there's a lot of practitioners that, I suspect, will say theory is nonsense, we don't need any of it"* (Pu5). Academics who had used theory echoed this point: *"I haven't found much acceptance of theoretical discussion in the area of practice that I'm familiar with"* (R9).

Several reasons were given for this. Some participants questioned the timeliness of theoretically informed work, in terms of both publication lag, and its ability to keep pace with a fast moving field. Many practitioners also saw the work of OA as unsuited to theory: *"I think of it more as more of a practical thing"* (L4), and there were numerous examples of participants positioning theory in opposition to practice. Theory was considered *"mood music"* (Po1) for the practical work of OA, creating an atmosphere but lacking value because it did not translate well into action. In this sense it was compared unfavorably to outputs such as toolkits, checklists, or case studies, which practitioners felt could be of immediate and direct use.

Is the Theory-Practice Relationship Harmonious?

Unsurprisingly, most interviewees believed that the relationship between theory and practice was not harmonious. Indeed, the language and imagery of conflict was often used to address the question, with participants describing *"a locking of horns"* (R2) or a *"struggle"*. It was also striking that the discussion often turned to individuals – *theorists* and *practitioners* – with academics engaged in theoretical work perceived as *"a bit sort of ivory-towerish. People that are actually trying to put this into practice are down in the trenches ... They're just trying to fill the repository"* (Pr2). In general most practitioners felt that academics were most to blame for the lack of a harmonious relationship, although a researcher noted that *"if one side were good at breaching the gap or divide, then it wouldn't be there"* (R9). One final point is relevant here, and that is the unconscious influence of theory on the practitioner community. As one librarian noted, echoing Keynes, *"every man who thinks he's just practical actually has a theory ... Every librarian who thinks he understands libraries practically is really the slave of some defunct library theoretician"* (L3).

DISCUSSION AND CONCLUSION

In many ways, the views expressed by our participants reflect general perceptions of the relationship between theory and practice. While they somewhat reluctantly acknowledged the value of theory to OA work in certain circumstances and for certain purposes, practitioners tended to view theory as mostly distinct from and only obliquely relevant to their practical work. There is, however, evidence that the issue may be more complex than this. Two points in particular stand out. First, the role of theory as a means of codifying existing knowledge represents a clear and fundamental way for theory to add value to practitioners. Second, the notion that theory serves as a silent and essential foundation to practical work undercuts the popular view of theory and practice as separate, and potentially reframes the theory-practice gap as an issue of perception rather than reality. Further work as part of this project will attempt to model the theory-practice relationship in the field of OA, and highlight the ways in which this gap might be bridged.

ACKNOWLEDGMENTS

We thank all our participants, and acknowledge the AHRC grant (AH/P014569/1) which funded the work.

REFERENCES

Braun, V., & Clarke, V. (2006). Using thematic analysis in psychology. *Qualitative Research in Psychology, 3*(2), 77–101.

Corlett, J. (2000). The perceptions of nurse teachers, student nurses and preceptors of the theory-practice gap in nurse education. *Nurse Education Today, 20*(6), 499–505.

Haddow, G., & Klobas, J. E. (2004). Communication of research to practice in library and information science: Closing the gap. *Library & Information Science Research, 26*(1), 29–43.

Korthagen, F. A., Kessels, J., Koster, B., Lagerwerf, B., & Wubbels, T. (2001). *Linking practice and theory: The pedagogy of realistic teacher education.* London, England: Lawrence Erlbaum Associates.

Lewin, K. (1944). Constructs in psychology and psychological ecology. *University of Iowa Studies in Child Welfare, 20,* 23–27.

Scapens, R. W. (1994). Never mind the gap: Towards an institutional perspective on management accounting practice. *Management Accounting Research, 5*(3-4), 301–321.

Assessing the Informativeness of User Reviews on Mobile Health Applications for Chronic Diseases

Shengang Wang
School of Information Studies, University of Wisconsin-Milwaukee, Milwaukee, USA
shengang@uwm.edu

Hyun Seung Lee
School of Information Studies, University of Wisconsin-Milwaukee, Milwaukee, USA
lee649@uwm.edu

Wonchan Choi
School of Information Studies, University of Wisconsin-Milwaukee, Milwaukee, USA
wchoi@uwm.edu

ABSTRACT
With advances in mobile health (mHealth) technology and growing ownership of smartphones, mHealth applications have great potential to support patients' self-management of chronic diseases such as diabetes and hypertension. Informative consumer reviews on app stores (e.g., Google Play) are a useful source of information for app developers to understand users' needs and for users to select a pertinent app over similar alternatives. This poster reports preliminary findings of a study that explores factors affecting the informativeness of consumer reviews using a feature-centered rating scale. The results show that consumer ratings and the length of consumer reviews are both correlated with informativeness. These findings will contribute to filtering informative reviews for future in-depth analyses of app features.

KEYWORDS
Mobile health applications; informativeness; app reviews; user generated content

ASIST&T THESAURUS
Mobile devices; content analysis; user generated content

INTRODUCTION AND RELATED WORKS
Chronic diseases, such as diabetes and hypertension, require regular self-management behavior (i.e., medications, dietary behavior, physical activity, and attendance at follow-up appointments) to follow recommended treatment regimens (Centers for Disease Control and Prevention, 2019). Advances in health information technologies have made self-monitoring or self-management possible for patients. In particular, with the growing ownership of smartphones, mobile health applications (mHealth apps) can provide customized healthcare services and self-management assistance to patients.

In the marketplace, such as Google Play and Apple App Store, hundreds and thousands of mHealth apps under health and fitness categories are available for users to download. Not surprisingly, mHealth app overload has become an issue for users when identifying a "best" app meeting their needs among other similar alternatives (van Velsen, Beaujean, & van Gemert-Pijnen, 2013). Although user-generated reviews may be an important source of information for understanding apps, the major obstacles in obtaining valuable information about an app are the large volume of reviews and the relatively low proportion of "informative" consumer reviews (Chen, Lin, Hoi, Xiao, & Zhang, 2014). In the information quality (IQ) literature, informativeness is considered an underlying dimension of IQ referring to "the extent to which the information is new or informative in the context of a particular activity or community" (Stvilia, Gasser, Twidale, & Smith, 2007, p. 1729). For the software engineers, an informative review "contains information that app developers are looking to identify and is potentially useful for improving the quality or user experience of apps" (Chen et al., 2014, p.769).

To our best knowledge, there is a lack of research on the informativeness of user reviews in the context of mHealth apps. This study, with a focus on the informativeness of user reviews on mHealth apps for chronic conditions, especially diabetes and hypertension, explores the potential factors affecting the informativeness of consumer reviews. A better understanding of their relationships will contribute to filtering informative reviews more efficiently so that app developers can improve associated features of the apps.

METHODOLOGY
We conducted a content analysis on 571 consumer reviews, which were selected based on two criteria. First, we identified apps for diabetes and hypertension in the Health & Fitness category on Google Play that had been rated more than 1,000 times—as of March 16, 2019, 19 out of 241 apps for diabetes and 26 out of 208 apps for hypertension were identified. Second, we selected three best and three worst apps for diabetes and hypertension based on average ratings (i.e., 6 apps for each disease). We downloaded all consumer reviews of target apps—as of March 16, 2019, the numbers of consumer reviews ranged from 1,223 to 24,754 (Mean = 8,146). We randomly selected 50 reviews from each of these apps. There was one app that had only 21 textual comments (My Glycemia Diabetes tracker) and we included them all. In total, a data set of

82nd Annual Meeting of the Association for Information Science & Technology | Melbourne, Australia | 19–23 October, 2019

DOI: 10.1002/pra2.00178

571 consumer reviews consisting of textual comments and star-ratings was used for further analysis.

Informativeness in the present study is defined as the degree to which an app review offers information about the existing features or those requested by users. Based on this definition, we developed a coding scale that has 5 anchors (1-5) to measure the informativeness of the collected consumer reviews (Table 1). First, we individually coded 50 consumer reviews from the sample data; the simple agreement percentage was 86. Then we resolved the differences in our codes, refined the coding scheme, and used this refined scheme to code the entire sample dataset.

Rating	Description and example
1	Pure emotional expressions or general comments without supporting evidence (e.g., "Best app ever!")
2	Comments on non-feature related factors such as perceived usability, services, and policies (e.g., "I find it to be very useful.")
3	Reviews identifying one existing feature in terms of either strength or weakness or requesting a new feature (e.g., "Works well, just wish there was printing option.")
4	Reviews identifying two or more existing features in terms of either strength or weakness or requesting multiple new features (e.g., "Works well. Track data and exports to excel files.")
5	Reviews identifying two or more features in terms of both strength and weakness or a combination of existing and requested features (e.g. "Very useful to keep my records especially the stats. Needs multi user support.")

Table 1. Feature-centered informativeness rating scale.

We counted the number of words used in each consumer review as an important intrinsic attribute of textual information. We examined star ratings as another potential factor associated with the informativeness of app reviews. We examined the correlations among these three variables using the Pearson correlation.

RESULTS

Results of independent sample t test revealed that there were no statistically significant differences in (a) rating score between diabetes-related (M = 2.96, SD = 1.07, N = 271) and hypertension-related apps (M = 2.99, SD = 0.93, N = 300), $t(569) = 1.796$, $p = .077$, (b) length between diabetes (M = 22.06, SD = 15.96, N = 271) and hypertension apps (M = 22.96, SD = 17.52, N = 1.01), $t(569) = -.650$, $p = .516$, and (c) informativeness between diabetes (M = 2.96, SD = 1.07, N = 271) and hypertension apps (M = 2.99, SD = 0.93, N = 300), $t(569) = -.362$, $p = .717$. Results of Pearson correlation indicated that both the start rating and length had a positive association with informativeness, but the association between length and informativeness was stronger, $r(569) = .44$, $p < .001$, than that of start rating with informativeness, $r(569) = .09$, $p = .04$.

CONCLUSION AND FUTURE RESEARCH

Informative consumer reviews play an important role in app development; they provide app developers with feedback on how they can improve existing features and identify missing features that could potentially be integrated in future updates. For users, informative reviews help select apps that satisfy their needs. Our findings suggest that length is an important cue associated with the informativeness of consumer reviews of mHealth apps. App developers and users, therefore, may focus on relatively lengthier consumer reviews to find more "informative" reviews for their needs. Another contribution of this study to be noted is the proposed rating scale for feature-centered informativeness of consumer reviews. The scale can be used as a knowledge resource in analyzing consumer reviews of mHealth apps, especially in understanding users' perceptions and experience with existing features as well as new requirements of the app. In the next phase of the study, we will use the length of reviews as a factor to filter reviews and analyze specific features of target apps.

REFERENCES

Center for Disease Control and Prevention. (2019). About chronic diseases. Retrieved from https://www.cdc.gov/chronicdisease/about/index.htm

Chen, N., Lin, J., Hoi, S. C., Xiao, X., & Zhang, B. (2014). *AR-miner: mining informative reviews for developers from mobile app marketplace*. In Proceedings of the 36th International Conference on Software Engineering, May and June 2014, Hyderabad, India (pp. 767-778).

Stvilia, B., Gasser, L., Twidale, M. B., & Smith, L. C. (2007). A framework for information quality assessment. *Journal of the American Society for Information Science and Technology*, *58*(12), 1720–1733.

van Velsen, L., Beaujean, D. J., & van Gemert-Pijnen, J. E. (2013). Why mobile health app overload drives us crazy, and how to restore the sanity. *BMC Medical Informatics and Decision Making*, *13*(1), 23.

Mapping the State of Community Libraries: An Empirical Study in Hubei Province

Chunying Wang
Wuhan University,
Wuhan, China
cywanglib@163.com

Zhenzhen Yuan
Nankai University,
Tianjin, China
1294114399@qq.com

Ruhua Huang
Wuhan University,
Wuhan, China
rhhuang@whu.edu.cn

Jiangping Chen
University of North
Texas, Denton, USA
jiangping.chen@unt.edu

ABSTRACT

This study aims to improve understanding of the state of the community library, to identify challenges in development, and to propose corresponding solutions. This paper uses questionnaires and semi-structured interviews to investigate the development status of 164 community libraries in Hubei Province. The survey results show that community libraries in Hubei province grow rapidly in recent years. And some them have established close interactions with residents. However, they still face a number of challenges, such as shortage of collections, lack of funding, Lack of qualified library staff, limited programs, insufficient rules and regulations, and poor infrastructure.

KEYWORDS

Public library; Community library; Library service; Empirical study

ASIS&T THESAURUS

Product and service providers; Libraries; Public libraries

INTRODUCTION

Community libraries (Branch libraries) are public libraries that serves nearby communities, streets, or township. Their mission is to motivate, engage and educate the community through high quality, creative and informative programs and services (Ziheng & Min, 2002).

Although community libraries have been developeed rapidly in recent years, there are still many problems in funding, staffing, collections, equipment, activities, institutions and so on. In order to help to better formulate relevant policies and effectively allocate resources, our team cooperated with the Hubei Provincial Press and Publication Bureau and conducted an empirical investigation of the community libraries in Hubei Province. The aim is to better understand the state of community libraries, discover problems in the development process, and propose corresponding solutions.

82nd Annual Meeting of the Association for Information Science & Technology | Melbourne, Australia | 19–23 October, 2019

DOI: 10.1002/pra2.00185

RESEARCH DESIGN

Research Questions

1. What is the status of the funds, personnel, collections, equipment, activities, and regulations in community libraries?
2. What problems have the community libraries encountered in the development process?

Research Object

The research team visited 164 community libraries, including 137 community libraries in Wuhan, 27 community libraries located in another cities of Hubei Province (such as Yichang, Ezhou, Shiyan). The survey started from August 2017 to April 2018.

Research Method

This study used an explanatory sequential mixed-methods research design (Creswell & Plano Clark, 2011, pp. 81-85). The survey began with the quantitative research phase, followed by the qualitative phase. At first, questionnaires were distributed to the community librarians. Questionnaire questions related to funds, personnel, collections, equipment, activities, and regulations. And the questionnaire was formed comprehensively based on previous studies (subject to length limitation, not described here). Then interviewed librarians selected by typical case. The purpose sampling strategy allows selection based on a set of typical values, or participants represent a broader group (Gerring, 2007; Williams, 2018).

FINDINGS

Table 1 lists the critical issues encountered in the development of community libraries.

Shortage of Books

1. **The number of books is insufficient.** There are only 15 libraries with more than 5,000 books. Most libraries have fewer than 2,000 books (see Figure 1).
2. **The types of books are not in demand.** Lack of children and health books that residents need; new books are very few, only 40% libraries update books every year.

Lack of Funding

Lack of funding is a common phenomenon, manifested in the absence of special funding, no other subsidies. Employees generally do not feel strong financial support.

Table 1. The critical issues.

Order	Category	Description	Frequency	Percentage
1	Books	Less variety, slower update, old version, no features	45	27.43%
2	Funding	Tight budget/finance, no special funds, no subsidies	40	24.39%
3	Staff	Part-time, less energy and enthusiasm, lack of business training	29	17.68%
4	Activity	Less activity, no borrowing	25	15.24%
5	Management	No catalog, inappropriate lending management and open hour	24	14.63%
6	Infrastructure	Not dedicated venue, poor infrastructure	17	10.37%

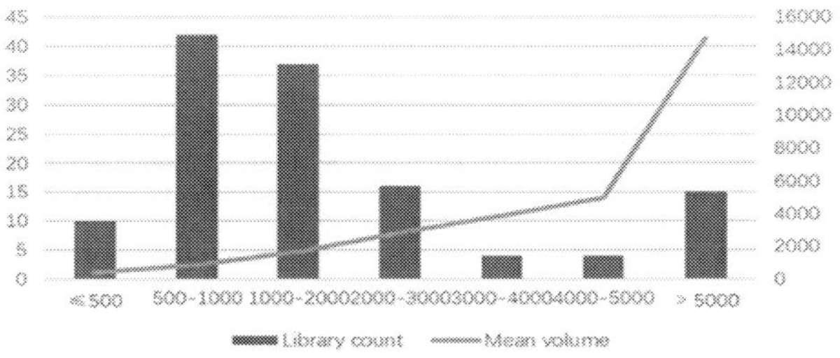

Figure 1. The number of books in community libraries.

Lack of Qualified Library Staff

More than 90% of community librarians are part-time by retirees. They have not received training and are not enthusiastic about their work.

Limited Programs

Library activities are not sustainable and are only held at festivals such as World Book and Copyright Day. 80% of the libraries hold fewer than five events a year (see Figure 2).

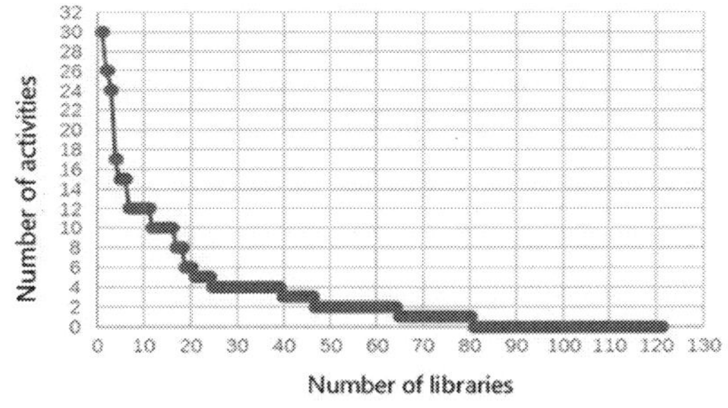

Figure 2. Number of activities held each year in community libraries.

Insufficient Rules and Regulations

(1) lack of infrastructure in terms of library cards (not borrow card); (2) rules about borrowing books are either missing or not enforced; (3) the mismatch between library hours and the schedule of patrons.

Poor Infrastructure

1. **Space.** About 70% of the libraries are less than 60 m^2, only 6.6% of the libraries' room area are over 120 m^2. More than 90% of the libraries do not have a reading room (see Figure 3).

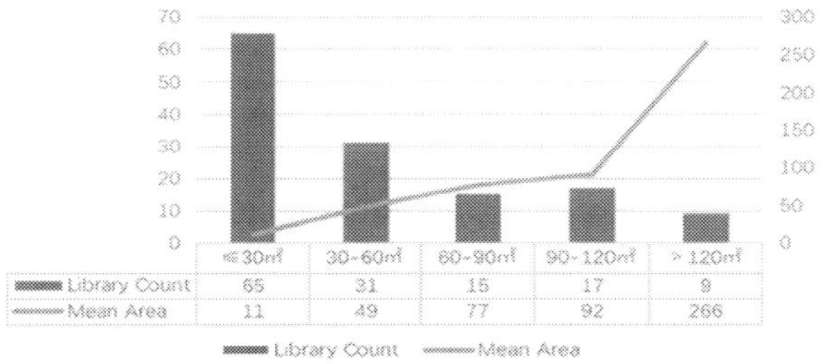

Figure 3. Area and number of community libraries.

2. **Infrastructure**. Ninety percent of the community libraries have WIFI coverage, but about 60% of the libraries do not have computers. About 55% of libraries do not have printers, and a few libraries do not even have air conditioning and hot water.

DISCUSSION

Our team visited the 164 community libraries in Hubei Province. We found that some problems in the community library of Hubei Province, such as shortage of collection, lack of funding, lack of qualified library staff, limited programs, insufficient rules and regulations, poor infrastructure.

The interviewees in this paper are the librarians of community libraries. In the future, we will investigate the users of community libraries and discover the service needs of users for community libraries. And then puts forward suggestions for promoting the development of community libraries

REFERENCES

Creswell, J. W., & Plano Clark, V. L. (2011). *Designing and conducting mixed methods research* (2nd ed.). Thousand Oaks, CA: Sage Publications. https://doi.org/10.5588/ijtld.10.0654

Gerring, J. (2007). *Case study research: Principles and practices*. Cambridge, MA: Cambridge University Press.

Williams, R. N. (2018). Future strategic considerations and development priorities for national museum libraries. *Journal of Documentation*, *74*(6), 1204–1225. https://doi.org/10.1108/JD-01-2018-0011

Ziheng, L., & Min, X. (2002). The functions, models and management mechanism of community libraries. *Journal of Library Science in China*, *28*(5), 32–35.

Detecting Opinion Evaluation Object Drift in Chinese Microblog Posts

Xiao Wang
Central China Normal University, Wuhan, People's Republic of China
ray_wangx@mail.ccnu.edu.cn

Chao Ma
Wuhan University, Wuhan, People's Republic of China
machao456@hotmail.com

Sijing Chen
Wuhan University, Wuhan, People's Republic of China
csj16912@whu.edu.cn

ABSTRACT

The drift of opinion evaluation object can reflect the evolution of online public opinion from a fine-grained level. By representing and calculating the distribution of opinion evaluation objects, we propose a method to detect its drift. A dataset of posts published by opinion leaders in social-events discussion is collected from a microblog application in China. The preliminary result on the dataset shows that when subject discussion changes, opinion leaders will focus on the identity characteristic of one person in most cases. By using our proposed method, the drift of opinion evaluation object can be clearly uncovered. Furthermore, by combining with opinion sentiment tendency drift, our research can enrich the perspective of public opinion evolution analysis and better the monitoring of public opinion crisis.

KEYWORDS

Opinion Drift; Opinion Evaluation Object; Social Media

ASIS&T THESAURUS

Data analysis; Social web; Disasters

INTRODUCTION

When people conduct a discussion on a subject, their opinion may change over time due to the effect of various factors. This kind of change is known as the Opinion Drift (Wang, Feng, Wang, & Yu, 2013). Based on real data recorded in social media, the detection of opinion drift helps to carry out the evolution analysis, discover the hotspot and early-warning the crisis of public opinion. The existing research on opinion drift mainly focuses on analyzing the change of opinion sentiment tendency (Durant, 2008). However, considering the complexity of language expression, a negative sentiment tendency does not necessarily mean a public opinion crisis, neither does a positive one necessarily mean a nice comment. That is to say, changes in opinion sentiment tendency cannot fully observe the public opinion or accurately reveal the crisis. And in a few studies that consider changes in opinion content, such as the drift of public opinion object, a method of manual judgment is used (Yang, 2018), which cannot be applied to a quantitative analysis of massive data in social media. Thus, it is necessary to propose a method to detect the opinion evaluation object drift and prepare for the automatic analysis.

In this poster, we report our on-going project on this topic. We propose a method to extract the opinion evaluation object from microblog posts and calculate its distribution. The drift is then detected on the basis of difference between its distribution probability over a series of adjacent time slices.

82nd Annual Meeting of the Association for Information Science & Technology | Melbourne, Australia | 19–23 October, 2019

DOI: 10.1002/pra2.00181

METHOD

Data Collection

A web crawler named GooSeeker was used for collecting data from Sina Weibo for this study. From June 2015 to June 2018, a total of 177,627 posts were collected in Chinese written by 20 users who act as opinion leaders in social-events discussion. After data pre-processing steps, 124,556 valid posts are obtained.

Opinion Evaluation Object Extraction

To detect the drift, words including common noun, name of person, name of place, name of organization, name of the work, denominal verb, other proper noun, and named entities as well, are used as the source of feature words for extracting evaluation objects. The part-of-speech tagging is completed by calling the lexical analysis function of Baidu AI. By representing these words into vectors, clustering by k-means algorithm and sort the results according to the frequency of being mentioned, a set of opinion evaluation objects that can be measured and observed is therefore determined.

Opinion Evaluation Object Drift Detection

To represent the distribution of opinion evaluation objects in a post, a tuple form is being used here, i.e. Target(post) = post $(ot_1, ot_2, \ldots, ot_n)$. It is also used in a subset consisting of several posts from same time slice, i.e. Target(P) = POST(OT_1, OT_2, …, OT_n). While ot represents the rate of mentions of evaluation object ob_i in a post, OT represents the average rate of mentions of evaluation object ob_i in a subset. Calculation formula as shown below.

$$\mathrm{ot}_i = \frac{Count(ob_i)}{\sum_{i=1}^{n} Count(ob_i)}$$

$$OT = \frac{\sum_{j=1}^{Count(C)} ot_j}{Count(C)}$$

$$i = 1, 2, \ldots, n; \; j = 1, 2, \ldots, Count(C)$$

To detect the opinion evaluation object drift, the difference between distribution probabilities of evaluation object ob_i of subsets from two adjacent time slices is calculated, and the result is recorded as $diff(OT_i)$. If the absolute value $|diff(OT_i)| > \alpha$ is established, the opinion evaluation object drifts, otherwise the opinion evaluation object does not drift. α is a given threshold.

RESULTS

Extraction Results

70 subjects were extracted in total by clustering the text vectors. We selected week as a unit time slice, and therefore divided the overall time interval into 161 time slices. According to the analysis, 10 evaluation objects were identified to observe the opinion drift in posts of durative subject as the label and description are shown in Table 1.

Num.	Opinion evaluation object	Description
1	Causation	Mainly discuss the causal relationship of things
2	Human body	Mainly discuss human body parts and organs
3	Identity	Mainly discuss the identification and title of individuals or a group
4	Food	Mainly discuss food material, dishes and catering brands
5	Job	Mainly discuss the job content of all walks of life
6	Tool	Mainly discuss tools used by people to carry out an activity
7	Behavior	Mainly discuss behaviors people take in different situations
8	Individual	Mainly discuss the public figures or characters in film , television or novel
9	Place	Mainly discuss countries, cities, regions in the world
10	Document	Mainly discuss various types of document used in all walks of life

Table 1. Label and description of opinion evaluation object.

Opinion Evaluation Object Drift Analysis

We found the opinion evaluation object drift in about one-third of the subjects. There are 3 opinion evaluation objects, which are Identity, Place and Document, drifted between different time slices in different subject discussion. Among them, the drift of Identity is the most frequent, with up to 7 times drift only in subject No.68, while the remaining opinion evaluation objects drifted only 1 or 2 times in a single subject.

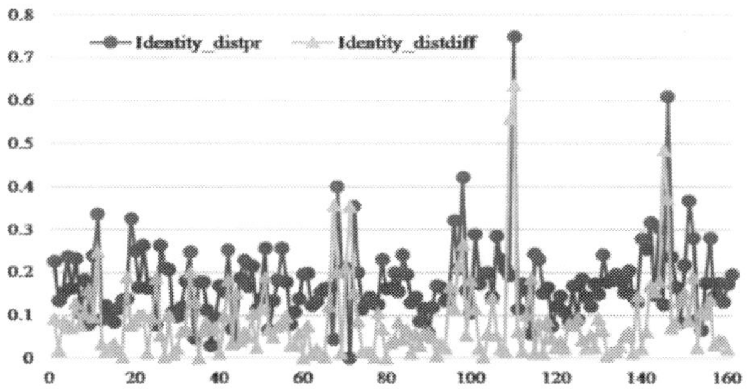

Figure 1. Distribution probability and difference of the Identity evaluation object in Topic 68.

Figure 1 presents the distribution probability (Identity_distpr) and the difference (Identity_distdiff) between them of the Identity evaluation object in Topic 68. The distribution probability reveals the popularity of the Identity object in the opinion expression of Topic 68, while the difference between distribution probabilities of two adjacent time slice subsets locates the drift.

CONCLUSION

This poster presents preliminary results on the study of the opinion evaluation drift detection in durative subject. The experiment on Sina Weibo posts shows that, by using our proposed method to extract the opinion evaluation object and calculate its distribution, the drift of opinion evaluation object can be clearly uncovered. Further analysis is planning to be conducted on the combination with opinion sentimental tendency drift, explore its application in monitoring public opinion crisis.

ACKNOWLEDGMENTS

This work is supported by NSF in China (No. 71790612 & No. 71804135).

REFERENCES

Durant K. T. (2008). *Sentiment drift and its effect on the classification of Web log posts* [Electronic version] (PhD dissertation). Harvard University, USA.

Wang, D., Feng, S., Wang, D., & Yu, G. (2013). Detecting opinion drift from Chinese web comments based on sentiment distribution computing. In X. Lin, Y. Manolopoulos, D. Srivastava, & G. Huang (Eds.), *Web information systems engineering – WISE 2013. WISE 2013 Lecture notes in computer science* (Vol. *8180*). Berlin: Springer.

Yang, L. (2018). *Research of network public opinion transfer in social media environment* (Master dissertation). Harbin Engineering University, P.R. China.

Gender Bias in Invention

Yukai Wang
Institute of Science of Science and S&T Management, Dalian University of Technology, Dalian, China
qingluchenhui@mail.dlut.edu.cn

Zhongkai Yang
Institute of Science of Science and S&T Management, Dalian University of Technology, Dalian, China
email@dlut.edu.cn

Xianwen Wang
Institute of Science of Science and S&T Management, Dalian University of Technology, Dalian, China
xianwenwang@dlut.edu.cn

ABSTRACT

Gender bias exists not only throughout society but also in inventing. In this study, we identify the gender of 15,752,108 inventor in USPTO to analyze gender bias in invent. There are 3,525,055 invent teams led by male inventors (who are named first on the patent), and 435,341 invent teams led by female inventors. Even through the invent teams led by male are more than those of female, gender bias is also in the invent teams led by female. Specifically, the proportion of the joint inventor of female (20.4%) is 8.4% higher than that of male (12.0%) in the invent teams led by female. Moreover, the actual proportion of the joint inventor of female (20.4%) is 7.5% higher than that of expected (12.9%). Besides, the average number of joint female inventors are 0.24 more than that of joint male inventors in the female-led invent teams.

KEYWORDS

Gender bias; Inventor; Patent; USPTO

ASIS&T THESAURUS

Society; Social sciences; sociology; Social discrimination; Gender

INTRODUCTION

As we all know, gender bias in academia and science has been acknowledged a lot (Frietsch et al. 2009; Jensen, 2018). Many scholars have studied gender bias in the output, peer review, cooperation, and dissemination of scientific papers. Not surprisingly, women continue to be underrepresented in peer reviewers of academic. The peer review process involves authors, reviewers, editorial board members. Gender bias is found in both the composition of editorial boards and the authors that are published. Similarly, there are gender biases among editors and reviewers. Editors reveal substantial gender biases (homogeneity) in their daily work, and this homogeneity could be explained as gender bias (Helmer, 2017). Moreover, gender and party bias in voting for female candidates. It offers evidence that female candidates gain marginally greater support from their own gender (Brians, 2016).

Is there gender bias for among female inventors? Clearly, gender bias are found among female inventors. Compared with male inventors, female inventors prefer to cooperate with others, which leads to a higher proportion of joint female (Mauleón, 2013).

In recent research, it is show that huge gender bias among male and female inventors. Since May 2018, female inventors only account for 10.7% in the USPTO. By comparing invent teams by different gender, we try to find gender bias in the invent teams.

DATA SOURCE AND METHODOLOGY

The data source extent the information of the inventors, linking the inventors' forename and gender. Collecting the data from multiple perspective, such as USPTO (the United States Patent and Trademark Office), SSA (the United States Social Security Administration), GitHub and other websites, which may ensure the authoritativeness of the data. From the massive patent data source, we combine the relevant fields in the full-text patent database provided by the USPTO; the data of gender collect from SSA and other websites. The steps of gender identification include preprocessing of raw data, matching with the name-gender thesaurus, and classifying with the Bayes algorithm.

Furthermore, invent teams could be defined as two types. The invent teams usually contains lead inventor (who is named first on the patent) and joint inventor (who is not named first on the patent). Invent teams-I is defined as that male inventor named first on the patent. Invent teams-II is defined as that female inventor named first on the patent.

RESULTS

Whether the choice of joint inventor's gender is related to the lead inventor's gender? As shown in Table 1, gender bias is obvious in inventing. The actual proportion of joint female inventors is 20.4% (218,052/1,071,346) in the invent teams led by female, while the proportion of joint female inventors is 12.0% (964,284/8,033,874) in the invent teams led by male. The expected proportion of joint female is 12.9% (1,182,336/9,105,220). The actual ratio of joint female is 7.5% higher than expected ratio. Comparing observed data

82nd Annual Meeting of the Association for Information Science & Technology | Melbourne, Australia | 19–23 October, 2019

DOI: 10.1002/pra2.00182

	Female-led (expectation)	Male-led (expectation)	Total
Female-joint	218,052 (139,117)	964,284 (1,043,219)	1,182,336
Male-joint	853,294 (932,229)	7,069,590 (6,990,655)	7,922,884
Total	1,071,346	8,033,874	9,105,220

Pearson $\chi2$ = 58,335; P value = 0.000.

H0: Testing whether the choice of joint inventor's gender is related to the lead inventor's gender?

Table 1. The number of joint inventors in different type of invent teams.

Team size	Pearson χ^2	Cramer's V	Significant
2	77.643	0.047	0.000***
3	445.277	0.038	0.000***
4	563.430	0.066	0.000***
5	510.901	0.070	0.000***
6	280.381	0.061	0.000***
>=7	22.090	0.011	0.000***
All	1424.031	0.080	0.000***

Table 2. One-test of hypotheses concerning the joint females of female-led and male-led invent teams.

with "expected" ones, we obtain a value of Pearson$\chi2$ (58,335), and a P_{value} (0.000), which confirm the statistical significance of the association between the two variables. We repeat the same analysis for the different sizes of invent teams in full sample. Results (Table 2) show a significant relation between the gender of joint and lead inventors of invent teams in full sample.

Furthermore, gender bias could be verified in invent teams led by female. Here we use Kruskal-Wallis test and means of joint female in invent teams to verify the gender bias. It is significant different for joint female inventors between male-led and female-led invent teams. And the average number of joint female inventor in the female-led invent teams are 0.24 more than those of male.

CONCLUSION

Gender of the inventors could make a great influence on the patent. There is a strong correlation between the gender of the lead inventors and the joint inventors. Among them, the lead inventors of female prefer to cooperate with joint inventors of female. As the results show, the gender bias in female-led invent teams is more obvious than in male-lead teams. From the perspective of proportion of male or female inventors on the patent, male inventors occupy the absolute majority proportion, which leads to more opportunities for male to become joint inventors than for female. Even if controlling the variable of invent team size, the number of male inventors is still far more than female inventors. Analyzing the bias in invent teams only by the number of inventors are not fully reliable. Therefore, we need to validate gender bias from multiple perspectives. And we should observe the proportion of joint inventors of female in different types of invent teams, such as in male-led or female-led invent team. The actual proportion of the lead inventor of female (20.4%) is 7.5% higher than that of expected (12.9%). The proportion of the joint inventor of female (20.4%) is 8.4% higher than that of male (12.0%). In addition, there is a significant gap between the joint inventor of female and male in the invent team led by female, with the invent team gap of 0.24 women on average.

With a fair view of gender bias, it will enrich the structure of the invent teams. Promoting the collaboration between the male and female inventors is conducive to play the advantages of gender diversity in the invent teams.

ACKNOWLEDGMENTS

This work was supported by the "National Natural Science Foundation of China" (71673038), the project of "Fundamental Research Funds for the Central Universities" (DUT18JC32), and "ISTIC-CLARIVATE ANALYTICS" Scientometrics Joint Laboratory Open Fund.

REFERENCES

Borsuk, R. M. (2009). To name or not to name: The effect of changing author gender on peer review. *BioScience*, *59*, 985–989.

Brians, C. L. (2016). Women for women? *American Politics Research*, *33*, 357–375.

Helmer, M. (2017). Gender bias in scholarly peer review. *eLife*, *6*.

Jensen, K. (2018). Gender differences in obtaining and maintaining patent rights. *Nature Biotechnology*, *36*, 307–309.

Mauleón, E. (2013). Assessing gender balance among journal authors and editorial board members. *Scientometrics*, *95*, 87–114.

Enhancing Scholar Supportive Data: Surveying the Landscape of Information Resources for Digital Dunhuang

Xiaoguang Wang
Wuhan University,
Wuhan, China
wxguang@whu.edu.cn

Xu Tan
Wuhan University,
Wuhan, China
txishuo@whu.edu.cn

Qingyu Duan
Wuhan University,
Wuhan, China
duanqingyu@whu.edu.cn

ABSTRACT

Cultural heritage informatics (CHI) has aroused great interest from libraries, archives, and museums (LAMs) in recent years. As an international project, the organization of digital Dunhuang resources is of typical significance. This study aims to explore the current situation of digital resources in Dunhuang, and discuss the digital Dunhuang in supporting of digital humanities (DH) research. (Methodology) 21 websites related to digital Dunhuang were accessed, and the subject, size, data type and organization of 8 arts & humanities databases were analyzed. (Finding) The study finds that digital Dunhuang resources are multi-source, multi-format, multi-topical, multi-lingual and multi-cultural. However, the information organization of digital Dunhuang is not yet at the "fine-grained" level. The interoperability and value density of the data is low, and only primary search and word frequency statistics can be used in these databases. (Conclusion) The lack of integration and relevance of resources are principal dimensions that hinder the research of DH, especially for the demand of data mining and analysis. Semantic enrichment may be an available chance for enhancing the data of digital Dunhuang and supporting DH research.

KEYWORDS

Cultural heritage informatics; Digital Dunhuang; Digital humanities; Arts & humanities database

ASIS&T THESAURUS

Humanities; Culture; Cultural heritage

INTRODUCTION

Dunhuang Mogao Grottoes is the largest site of Buddhist art in the world, as well as world cultural heritage listed by the United Nations Educational, Scientific and Cultural Organization (UNESCO). The concept of digital Dunhuang was put forward in the 1990s, aiming for preserving and promoting the precious Dunhuang heritage using digital tools (Hu, Ho, & Qiao, 2017). Digital Dunhuang has successively implemented a series of projects, and a large number of digital resources have been built through data collection, processing, storage and management. The knowledge system of Dunhuang is reconstructed in digital space by means of the methods and technologies of DH, which offers a new direction and environment for humanities research. In this study, we took digital Dunhuang resources as the main research object, and tried to analyze the current status of digital Dunhuang from the perspective of DH.

82nd Annual Meeting of the Association for Information Science & Technology | Melbourne, Australia | 19–23 October, 2019

DOI: 10.1002/pra2.00180

RESEARCH QUESTION AND METHODOLOGY

The goal of this study was to understand the overall characteristics and status of digital Dunhuang resources, organization methods and cultural computing service level of digital Dunhuang. Through literature research and database research, the study was guided by four research questions:

- RQ1: What is the status and characteristics of Dunhuang heritage resources?
- RQ2: What is the typical characteristics of digital Dunhuang resources?
- RQ3: What is the information organization status and problems of digital Dunhuang resources?
- RQ4: What extent of DH research can the digital Dunhuang resources support?

From June to December 2018, our team investigated 21 databases and extracted the basic information of data topics, types, quality and website addresses into a detailed list. In 2019, on the basis of consulting scholars of Dunhuang studies, our team selected 8 representative databases as the main research object in consideration of international research progress, completeness of resource topics, and usability of database (see Table 1).

RESULTS AND DISCUSSION

Dunhuang heritage resources is collected and maintained by different LAMs around the world, such as the Dunhuang Academy, the National Library of China, the British Library, the British Museum, Bibliothèque nationale de France, Musée Guimet, The Freer Gallery of Art, etc. These resources are rich in semantics with characteristics of heterogeneity, knowledge, artistry and environment dependence in content.

Digital Dunhuang resources are multi-source, multi-format, multi-topical, multi-lingual and multi-cultural. Table 1 shows the information of themes, types and volume. At the same time, because Dunhuang is located in the center of the ancient Silk

Information / Database	Building in	Theme	Data type	Volume
International Dunhuang project (IDP)	1994	Comprehensive type	Image	527,374 images
Mellon international Dunhuang archive (MIDA)	1998	Comprehensive type	Image, 2D and 3D record	2500 black-and-white photos, which cover sculptures, manuscripts and silk flowers in over 40 caves
Erudition Dunhuang manuscripts library	2010	Manuscript	Image, text	30,000 Chinese manuscripts
Dunhuang manuscripts database (built by Shanghai Normal University)	2012	Manuscript	Image, text	40% of the total area of manuscripts, 17,519 manuscripts numbers, 20,422 document numbers
Dunhuang manuscripts database (built by Zhejiang University)	2013	Manuscript	Image, text	554 Chinese and Tibetan manuscript; thousands of research literatures (the first stage)
Dunhuang manuscripts digital library	2016	Manuscript	Image	14 types of Dunhuang literature, more than 70,000 manuscripts numbers, 90,000 copies records; 510,000 images
E-Dunhuang	2016	Grotto art	Image, text, video and 3D record	30 typical grottoes, 4,430 m^2 murals
Dunhuang academic resources database	Update in 2019	Research literature	Image, text, audio, video	25 sub-libraries

Table 1. Information of 8 representative databases (Ending: 2019.4.13).

Road, the data content also involve different languages (such as Sanskrit, Tibetan, ancient Chinese, Tangut script, Mongolian and Uighur script) and different cultures (such as Buddhism and Taoism). Visual resource is the most important resources type and high-precision images, and 3D data are the main growth hot spots, but there exist some serious problems in current digital resources. When using the databases, we found that the overall image accuracy was very low, and the text content recognition sometimes offered wrong results.

Organizational problem may be a serious challenge. Reasons to support this are as follows: 1) In these databases, traditional organizational methods prevail, mainly metadata and classification. Dunhuang Manuscript Digital Library, for example, relies entirely on metadata for data description. 2) Interoperability challenge: metadata produced by different organizations is usually incompatible with each other in terms of metadata schemas and cataloging conventions. Moreover, the field of digital Dunhuang also lacks of theoretical research on thesaurus system and domain ontology. 3) Semantic problem: Data encoding is not yet structured, which makes the phenomenon of disordered organization prominent. Besides, there are only representation models for murals currently, the "blank space" of important heritage resources such as caves, statues, manuscripts impedes the construction of digital Dunhuang. 4) Digital Dunhuang resources are semantically highly interlinked, but data in the databases is sparsely correlated, especially the association based on knowledge content and the association of external resources. From what we have mentioned above, we can come to the conclusion that information organization of digital Dunhuang resources is still immature.

With the rise of digital humanities research, the data-driven approach to the humanities has shown new characteristics during recent years, such as quantitative, interdisciplinary, integrated and multi-dimension analysis. However, the databases related to digital Dunhuang only can offer service of primary search and word frequency statistics, digital Dunhuang is still in the early stages of DH. Take E-Dunhuang as an example, according to existing user experiments, it can only support simple information search tasks and has a very limited ability to promote knowledge understanding and discovery (Hu, 2018). In order to meet the demand of DH research, information organization of digital Dunhuang must go into the "fine-grained" level, overcome the interoperability challenge and solve the semantic problem. "Semantic enrichment" may be an appropriate strategy which has been used by LAMs during recent years (Zeng, 2019). For the main data types, such as semi-structured and unstructured data, ontology and linked data can be used to enhance digital Dunhuang resources' quality and discoverability. An interactive semantic enhancement platform should be established. Through integrating functions such as semantic search and browsing, semantic mediation, semantic annotation, semantic analytics and knowledge discovery (Damjanovic et al., 2011), academics and engineers of digital Dunhuang could maximize delivering the value density of data and the usability of the platform.

CONCLUSION

The study shows the current situation of digital Dunhuang and the key lessons are as follows: 1) We summarized the features of digital Dunhuang resources, including multi-source, multi-format, multi-topical, multi-lingual and multi-cultural. 2) We found that semi-structured and unstructured data are still mainly types, which increased the difficulty of data integration and relevance and led to resources disordering. 3) We make it clear that digital Dunhuang is still in the early stages of DH, there is imbalance between the rapid expansion of data demand and the lag of the research of information organization. 4) We hold the opinion that semantic enrichment could be the future for digital Dunhuang and more attention should be paid to. We believe this will help people to understand, rebuilt and disseminate digital Dunhuang as well as similar projects of LAMs.

REFERENCES

Damjanovic, V., Kurz, T., Westenthaler, R., Behrendt, W., Gruber, A., & Schaffert, S. (2011). *Semantic enhancement: The key to massive and heterogeneous data pools.*

In Proceeding of the 20th International IEEE ERK (Electrotechnical and Computer Science) Conference (pp. 413-416).

Hu, X. (2018). Usability evaluation of E-Dunhuang cultural heritage digital library. *Data and information management*, *2*(2), 57–69.

Hu, X., Ho, E. M. Y., & Qiao, C. (2017). Digitizing Dunhuang cultural heritage: A user evaluation of Mogao Cave panorama digital library, *2*(3), 49–67.

Zeng, M. L. (2019). Semantic enrichment for enhancing LAM data and supporting digital humanities. *El profesional de la información*, *28*(1).

A Survey of Data Science Programs and Courses in the iSchools

Yi-Yu Wang
Dept. of Library and Information Science,
National Taiwan University, Taipei, Taiwan
f03126027@ntu.edu.tw

Chi-Shiou Lin
Dept. of Library and Information Science,
National Taiwan University, Taipei, Taiwan
chishioulin@ntu.edu.tw

ABSTRACT

In this poster, we examined the current data science programs and courses in the 102 iSchools members. The result shows that the program distribution was unequal by region, and the courses offered by iSchools concentrated on data analysis skills. Research data management, which concerns data management throughout research life cycle and data curation, constituted less than 10% of the courses.

KEYWORDS

Data science education; data analysis; research data services

ASIS&T THESAURUS

Data science; Information associations

INTRODUCTION

Data science has been a popular subject in recent years. Information schools have introduced programs and courses in their curriculum. While data science encompasses a wide range of topics (Saltz & Stanton, 2017), Song and Zhu (2016) indicated that data analysis is usually the main component of the subject. For the data specialists who work in academia, research data service (RDS) is another important aspect in the emerging subject expertise.

To gain an overview of the current state of data science education in the worldwide information schools, we examined all iSchools members' website to analyze data-related curriculum. We conducted program-level and course-level comparisons to see how data science education have developed in different regions of the world.

METHODS

We employed a Web content analysis approach for the study purpose. We thoroughly reviewed the websites of all iSchools members as listed in the member directory. By May 30, 2019, 102 institutions have joined the organization. Located in five continents, the iSchools members formed three regional groups, i.e., Asia Pacific, Europe & Africa, and North & South America. We examined each member institute's website and identify if data science education has been offered and whether it is offered at the program level or course level.

82nd Annual Meeting of the Association for Information Science & Technology | Melbourne, Australia | 19–23 October, 2019

DOI: 10.1002/pra2.00184

Program-level Condition

By program-level condition we aimed to reveal to what extent data science education has been offered in degree programs either at the bachelor, master or doctoral level, also in non-degree programs such as minor programs or specialization certificate programs.

Course-level Condition

We examined each iSchools member's website and/or the parent university's course catalogs or graduated requirements in 2018-2019 to identify any data-related course. We identified course titles containing the word "data" and/or "digital curation" as data curation and digital curation are used interchangeably and has minor distinction. Some institutes offered several courses with an identical course title yet with different course numbers. They were counted as different courses.

Within the identified courses, we further examined courses that addressed data analysis (DA courses) and research data services (RDS courses). DA courses were those addressing computational analysis skills for big data, statistical methods and techniques, and/or data visualization. RDS courses were those concerning research data management, rules and policies, and data library services, including data/digital curation and data stewardship.

RESULTS

Data Science Programs in iSchools

Table 1 shows the distribution of data science programs in iSchools in the three regions. 28 of the current 102 members now offered DS programs. Some institutes offered more than one program. North & South America had the most iSchools (16 institutes) offering program-level education. Only three Asia Pacific iSchools have offered program-level education, and all were in Australia. No iSchools in Asia has provided program-level education.

In degree programs, the graduate degree programs were mostly at the master's level. Undergraduate programs were few in all regions. The Asia Pacific iSchools currently offered none undergraduate degree programs so far.

In non-degree programs (minor and certificate), while the American iSchools have been very active, their peer institutes in the other regions offered very little. Differences in educational systems as well as laws and regulations may have influenced the development of non-degree offering. For the European and African iSchools, master-level education seemed to be the major approach.

It should be noted that half of the programs, degree or non-degree, were offered by a small number of iSchools members. The iSchool at Indiana University-Purdue University Indianapolis offered eight DS programs (3 degree + 5 non-degree), followed by Drexel (2 degree + 5 non-degree), Indiana, Syracuse, and Universidade NOVA de Lisboa (each with 4 programs). Their programs together accounted for 43.55% of overall DS programs. In contrast, half of the schools offering DS programs (14/28) provided only one program. That means over 75% of the programs (48 programs) were provided by the other 14 schools.

	Asia Pacific	Euro. & Africa	N. & S. America	Total
N. of institutes	24	30	48	102
Institutes with DS program(s)	3 (10.71)* (12.50)**	9 (32.14)* (30.00)**	16 (57.14)* (33.33)**	28 (100.00)* (27.45)**
N. of DS programs	7 (11.29)**	14 (22.58)**	41 (66.13)**	62 (100.00)**
PhD	0	0	1	1
Master	4	12	15	31
Bachelor	0	2	4	6
Degree Program	4 (10.53)* (57.14)**	14 (36.84)* (100.00)**	20 (52.63)* (48.78)**	38 (100.00)* (61.29)**
Minor	1	0	8	9
Certificate	2	0	13	15
Non-degree Program	3 (12.50)* (42.86)**	0 (0.00)* (0.00)**	21 (87.50)* (51.22)**	24 (100.00)* (38.71)**

Table 1. The Distribution of Data Science Program founded by iSchools Member Institutions.

* Percentage of iSchools with DS program(s) globally.

** Percentage of iSchools with DS program(s) within that region

Distribution of Data Science Courses

Table 2 shows the distribution of all data science (DS) courses. We can now see that the majority of the Asian-Pacific iSchools (83.33%) have offered DS courses; the percentage was equivalent to its American peers. Further, we can see that the Asian Pacific iSchools have all emphasized greatly on data analysis. Not only have them all offered DA courses, DA courses also constituted the predominant majority of all courses offered in that region. Observing the distribution of the broad course topics, data analysis was indeed at the core of data science education globally in iSchools. However, the lower percentages in the Europe & Africa as well as in N. & S. America regions suggested that curriculum diversity was higher there.

In RDS education, while the topic was all a minor offering in the three regions, the percentage was particularly low in Asian Pacific and European and African iSchools. Whether this indicates the differences in job markets or a lack of attention or faculty expertise awaits further investigation.

	Asia Pacific	Euro. & Africa	N. & S. America	Total
N. of institutes	24	30	48	102
Institutes w. DS courses	20 (26.32)* (83.33)**	15 (19.74)* (50.00)**	41 (53.95)* (85.42)**	76 (100.00)* (74.51)**
N. of DS courses	114 (21.97)*	93 (17.92)*	312 (60.12)*	519 (100.00)*
Institutes w. DA courses	20 (28.99)* (83.33)**	14 (20.29)* (46.67)**	35 (50.72)* (72.92)**	69 (100.00)* (67.65)**
N. of DA courses	80 (24.77)* (70.18)**	52 (16.10)* (59.77)**	191 (59.13)* (60.06)**	323 (100.00)* (62.24)**
Institutes w. RDS courses	4 (16.00)* (16.67)**	4 (16.00) (13.33)*	17 (68.00) (35.42)*	25 (100.00)* (24.51)**
N. of RDS courses	5 (12.20)* (4.39)**	7 (17.07)* (7.53)**	29 (70.73)* (9.29)**	41 (100.00)* (7.90)**

Table 2. The Distribution of Data Science Course Offered by iSchools Member Institutions.

*Percentage of (1) iSchools with courses or (2) the course type globally

** Percentage of (1) iSchools within courses or (2) the course type in the region.

CONCLUSION AND DISCUSSION

Our analysis showed that less than one-third (27.45%) of the iSchools members were now offering DS degree programs; slightly over one-third (38.71%) offered non-degree programs. Yet globally, 3/4 (74.51%) have offered course-level education. Not surprisingly, the American iSchools were the most active in data science education. While DA constitutes the majority of the courses, it also had higher topic diversity in their curriculum. Future studies may explore factors underlying the course offering to identify needs and gaps in data science education.

REFERENCES

Saltz, J. S., & Stanton, J. M. (2017). *An introduction to data science*. SAGE Publications.

Song, I.-Y., & Zhu, Y. (2016). Big data and data science: What should we teach? *Expert Systems*, *33*(4), 364–373. https://doi.org/10.1111/exsy.12130

Thomas, C. V. L., & Urban, R. J. (2018). What do data librarians think of the MLIS? Professionals' perceptions of knowledge transfer, trends, and challenges. *College & Research Libraries*. https://doi.org/10.5860/crl.79.3.401

Order Effect on Relevance Judgment: An Exploratory Study on the Detection of Quantum Interference

Zhihong Wang
Sun Yat-sen University, Guangzhou, China
wangzhh38@mail2.sysu.edu.cn

Shujin Cao
Sun Yat-sen University, Guangzhou, China
caosj@mail.sysu.edu.cn

ABSTRACT

This poster explores the existence of order effect on relevance judgment, especially the interference of one document on the other while evaluating the relevance. A between-subject experiment with 78 undergraduate students was reported. The results demonstrated the statistically significant existence of order effect for some topics and spotted quantum interference while evaluating the relevance of documents. This preliminary study provides insights into how documents' evaluation is contextualized and interdependent with each other. It has some implications for future theoretical and practical research on the human cognitive aspect of relevance judgment in information retrieval.

KEYWORDS

relevance judgment; order effect; quantum interference; comparison effect; attraction effect

ASIS&T THESAURUS

Document retrieval; relevance

INTRODUCTION

In information retrieval practice, it is assumed that the evaluation of documents is independent with each other. However, it is commonly acknowledged that relevance is a dynamic and situational concept. Presentation order is one of situational factors influencing users' assessment on the search results (Bar-Ilan, Keenoy, Levene, & Yaari, 2009). This effect can be called order effect, which refers to the difference caused by the users' evaluation on relevance facing with different ranking lists (Xu & Wang, 2008). In other words, the evaluation of one document would interfere with that of the other because the document previously evaluated could change the context for the evaluation of the other subsequently. The interference between two documents is similar to that between two micro particles explained by quantum theory (Wang, Solloway, Shiffrin, & Busemeyer, 2014), which is unpredictable and incompatible. Comparing with the classical probability theory, the model based on quantum theory is more inclusive and has stronger explanatory power for both compatible and incompatible events by representing the vector spaces as orthogonal axes in a Hilbert space, rather than in the form of a set. (Uprety and Song, 2018; Wang et al., 2016)

There is not enough research of order effect on relevance judgment (Eisenberg & Barry, 1988; Huang & Wang, 2004; Xu & Wang, 2008). This exploratory research aims to explore this quantum-like phenomenon, especially to examine the existence of quantum interference in order effect on relevance judgment. The research questions are: 1) Does order effect exist in relevance judgment of two documents? 2) Can the quantum-like interference be detected in the order effect on relevance judgment? By addressing these questions, we mainly contribute to the future research via providing insights of the cognitive mechanism behind order effect on relevance judgment.

RESEARCH METHODS

We recruited 80 junior undergraduates in total by convenience sampling from School of Information Science, Sun Yat-sen University and conducted a between-subject experiment. The subjects were randomly divided into two groups. They were asked to complete the pre-questionnaire (including gender, English ability, topical familiarity etc.), assess 8 pairs of documents for 4 topics with four-point scales (1-4 for non-relevant, partially non-relevant, partially relevant, relevant) and answer the open-ended questions about the judgment criterion. The document pairs are swapped for two groups. The full texts were selected from Wikipedia and News sources, with 200-300 words as the average length. 2 subjects did not submit the questionnaire. Among the remaining 312, five of the questionnaires have missing value in the assessment. Thus, 307 questionnaires were left for the analysis (male:34, female: 44).

The Chi-square test, the Law of Total Probability (LTP) (Khrennikov, 2015) and the Quantum question test (QQ test) (Wang et al., 2014) are used to examine the order effect on relevance judgment. The LTP and QQ test equations can be found in Khrennikov (2015) and Wang et al. (2014).

RESEARCH RESULTS

Order Effect by Chi-Square Test

Using the non-parametric Chi-square test, we found the difference of document B's evaluation between two groups is statistically significant ($\chi^2 = 8.377$, $P = 0.039 < 0.05$) while

82nd Annual Meeting of the Association for Information Science & Technology | Melbourne, Australia | 19–23 October, 2019

DOI: 10.1002/pra2.00179

it is not for document A ($\chi^2 = 4.568$, $P = 0.206 > 0.05$) overall. The test by topics reveals that only the evaluation of document B in Topic 2 is statistically significantly affected by the order ($\chi^2 = 9.411$, $P = 0.024 < 0.05$).

Violation of LTP

Because of the left-skewed distribution of data, we merged the 1-3 categories of relevance into the irrelevant and the 4 into the relevant category in the later analysis. By applying LTP (See Table 1), we found that the independent probability of document A ($p(d_A)$) or B ($p(d_B)$) evaluated as relevant is not significantly larger or smaller than the conditional probability of document A ($p'(d_A)$) or B ($p'(d_B)$). Thus, LTP is not violated overall. However, document A in topic 1 and 4 and document B in topic 2 and 3 violate LTP, indicating the existence of quantum-like interference.

Topic	$p'(d_A)$	$p(d_A)$	$p'(d_A)-p(d_A)$	$p'(d_B)$	$p(d_B)$	$p'(d_B)-p(d_B)$
T1 (n = 78)	0.58	0.40	**0.18**	0.13	0.21	-0.09
T2 (n = 76)	0.43	0.41	0.02	0.33	0.22	**0.12**
T3 (n = 77)	0.39	0.41	-0.02	0.44	0.24	**0.20**
T4 (n = 76)	0.59	0.44	**0.15**	0.33	0.24	0.09
Overall (n = 307)	0.50	0.41	0.09	0.31	0.23	0.08

Table 1. The independent and total probabilities of documents.

Order Effect by QQ Test

Based on the QQ test's equation, q value for each topic and overall were calculated. Only topic 3 has a significant q value ($q = \mathbf{0.0135}$**†**, < 0.05) while other topics did not pass the QQ test (T1: $q = -0.1013$; T2: $q = -0.0963$; T4: $q = -0.1005$; Overall: $q = -0.0715$).

DISCUSSION AND CONCLUSON

By conducting a between-subject experiment, this study confirmed the partial existence of order effect and quantum interference on relevance judgment. The results are consistent with prior studies (Eisenberg & Barry, 1988; Wang et al., 2016). However, inconsistent with the findings from Wang and Huang (2004), we found that the order effect is also significant even when there are only two full-texts to be assessed. This indicates that the learning effect of full text is larger than that of snippet.

The data from the open-ended questions provides some supplementary evidences for the order effect, specifically comparative effect and attraction effect (Wang et al., 2016). For instance, one participant gave the reason for the second ranking document's evaluation that "*Generally speaking, it is more objective than the first document*". Another participant directly specified that "*According to the conclusion from the first document that global warming is caused by the carbon dioxide, this document mentioned that the cement production and use process release a lot of carbon dioxide*".

This research contributes to offer the evidence and deep insights on the order effect in relevance judgment and its mechanism although it has a limitation of small sampling. The progress work in the future is to testify the order effect in a large scale and under different situations, like considering the document relationships (e.g., complementary and contradictory) and types (e.g., full-text and snippet) as well as the characteristics of judges.

ACKNOWLEDGMENTS

This research is supported by the Major Project of National Social Science Fund (No. 12&ZD222) and China Scholarship Council. The authors would like to thank Pertti Vakkari and Jaana Kekäläinen who provided helpful comments on previous versions of this document.

REFERENCES

Bar-Ilan, J., Keenoy, K., Levene, M., & Yaari, E. (2009). Presentation bias is significant in determining user preference for search results—A user study. *Journal of the American Society for Information Science and Technology, 60*(1), 135–149.

Bruza, P., & Chang, V. (2014). Perceptions of document relevance. *Frontiers in Psychology, 5*, 612.

Eisenberg, M., & Barry, C. (1988). Order effects: A study of the possible influence of presentation order on user judgments of document relevance. *Journal of the American Society for Information Science and Technology, 39*(5), 293–300.

Huang, M. H., & Wang, H. Y. (2004). The influence of document presentation order and number of documents judged on users' judgments of relevance. *Journal of the American Society for Information Science and Technology, 55*(11), 970–979.

Khrennikov, A. (2015). Quantum-like modeling of cognition. *Frontiers in Physics, 3*, 77.

Wang, B., Zhang, P., Li, J., Song, D., Hou, Y., & Shang, Z. (2016). Exploration of quantum interference in document relevance judgement discrepancy. *Entropy, 18*(4), 144.

Wang, Z., Solloway, T., Shiffrin, R. M., & Busemeyer, J. R. (2014). Context effects produced by question orders reveal quantum nature of human judgments. *Proceedings of the National Academy of Sciences of the United States of America, 111*(26), 9431–9436.

Xu, Y., & Wang, D. (2008). Order effect in relevance judgment. *Journal of the American Society for Information Science and Technology, 59*(8), 1264–1275.

Extracting Method Knowledge Elements From Scientific Literature: A Rule-Based Approach

Zhongyi Wang
Central China Normal University, Wuhan, China
wzywzy13579@163.com

Xueying Shen
Central China Normal University, Wuhan, China
1244057668@qq.com

Rong Huang
Central China Normal University, Wuhan, China
748224206@qq.com

Jing Huang
Wuhan Polytechnic, Wuhan, China
6238477@qq.com

ABSTRACT

Knowledge elements are the basic unit of knowledge. Extracting knowledge elements from literatures enables granular knowledge organization and retrieval. This paper proposes a rule-based framework for extracting method Knowledge Elements (KEs) in scientific literature aiming to improve the accuracy and complete extraction of method KEs. The method is divided into two stages: semi-automated extraction of initial description rules of method KEs and automated derivation of additional description rules. In a preliminary evaluation on 415 papers, the precision and recall for the method KEs extraction are 0.77 and 0.84, respectively, indicating the effectiveness of our method.

KEYWORDS

method KEs; description clues; automated extraction

INTRODUCTION

With the increase of knowledge resource, the main purpose of user retrieval is to obtain the appropriate knowledge units of granular size that meet their needs, rather than the whole documents. As the smallest knowledge element, a KE is the basic element for generating knowledge of various granularities. It is necessary to identify the KEs to improve the accuracy of the user query. As we know, according to different knowledge content, KEs can be categorized into multiple types. Among them, the method KEs as dynamic procedural knowledge involve more content, including not only the logic of the method, but also the factual elements such as concepts, values, and facts. This makes the identification of method KEs more complicated than that of the numerical KEs, the factual KEs, etc. However, existing extraction methods fail to correlate the various parts of a method KE, making it difficult to guarantee the integrity of the extracted method KEs. In order to solve the problem, this study attempts to identify description rules/patterns of method KEs, to improve accurate and complete extraction of the method KEs.

82nd Annual Meeting of the Association for Information Science & Technology | Melbourne, Australia | 19–23 October, 2019

DOI: 10.1002/pra2.00183

PROBLEM SETTING

The KE refers to the smallest and integral knowledge unit that cannot be further divided. Method KEs Extraction refers to automatically identifying sentences describing the same method from a specified literature. Now, among the KE extraction: rule-based and statistical-based, the rule-based extraction method is to extract KEs with frameworks, models or symbols, so that the KEs are formalized and modeled (Ultsch, 1993. Engin, 2007). The research on rule-based extraction method achieves better recognition accuracy, but cannot avoid a lot of manual intervention. To reduce the participation of humans, scholars study the unsupervised method——the statistical-based approaches, using machine learning, deep learning algorithms for statistical calculations, to achieve the identification of knowledge (Kambhatla, 2004. Liu, Zhang, Wei, & Zhou, 2011. Nguyen & Grishman, 2015). The unsupervised algorithm reduces the domain dependence and the time spent on labor. However, the problem of parameter setting still exists, when it is applied to the text, the feasibility is not high.

METHOD

We present a method to extract method KEs in scientific literatures. The method is divided into two stages: semi-automated extraction of initial description rules, automated extraction of method KEs and its description rules.

Semi-automated Extraction of Initial Description Rules

In the first stage, a set of high-quality description rules of method KEs is generated semi-automatically. First, we download 1,000 literatures form NCBI with the MeSH Major Topic = "disease" as training corpus. Then sentences split, and use the Method Term as clue to identify the sentences about method. And then filter the domain subject words get the linear structure of the sentences. And then with the help of K-means algorithm, we clustered the linear structures to summarize the constitution dimensions of method KEs. After multiple data analysis, we set K = 8. Then, we analyze the content of the eight clusters and define the eight dimensions of the method KE: Definition, Pre-condition, Purpose, Function, Use, Process, Result, and Effect. Finally, we invite three scholars to review and summary to get the initial description rules of method KEs.

Automated Extraction of Method KEs and its Description Rules

According to the initial description rules of the method KEs, the system automatically extracts method KEs from the now literatures. (shown in Figure 1) The specific steps are as follows:

1. Document preprocessing. Convert the documents into plain text format, and remove irrelevant information, such as bibliography, images, etc.

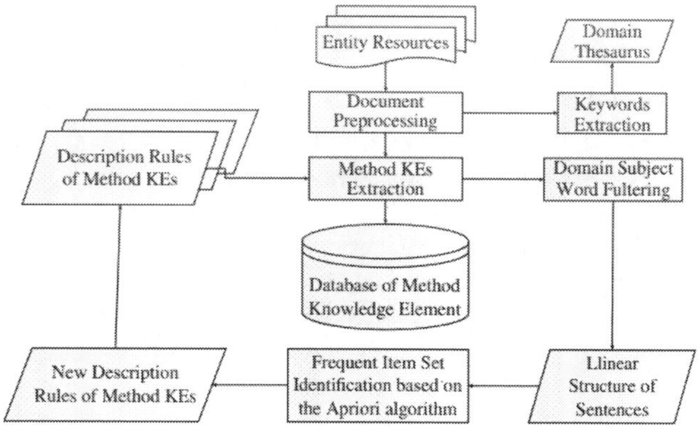

Figure 1. Automated Extraction of Method KEs and its Description Rules.

2. Method KE extraction. Regard initial description rules as clue, then use the regular expressions are matched with sentences in documents to automatically extract method KEs.
3. Keyword extraction. Based on the tf-idf algorithm, the keywords in the documents are extracted to update the previous domain subject words.
4. Domain subject words filtering. According to the domain subject words, the domain subject words in the method KEs are filtered out to form the sentence structures
5. Identifying frequent item sets in the sentence structures based on the improved Apriori algorithm. The algorithm steps are shown in Table 1.
6. The generated frequent item sets are reviewed and summarized to generate the new description rules of the method KEs which need to be stored in the rule database. According to this process, the loop is repeated to update the description rules of the method KE.

EXPERIMENTS AND RESULTS

First, we downloaded and selected 415 papers randomly from the medical databases with the MeSH Major Topic = "Disease". Then, we invite three annotators to extract method KEs from the 415 papers as the comparative data, and follow the principle of minority obeying majority. The experiment results were evaluated by recall R and precision P. We calculate each dimension of the method KEs, the P, R of some

Input: the sentence structures
Output: Frequent itemsets

1. The first pass of the algorithm counts item occurrences to determine large 1-itemsets L(1).

2. This process is repeat until no new large 1-itemsets are identified.

3. (k+1) length candidate itemsets C(k+1) are generated from length k large itemsets L(k). And attention the order when generating, data items {a b} and {b a} are different data items.

4. Candidate itemsets containing subsets of length k that are not large are pruned.

5. Support of each candidate itemset is counted by scanning the database

6. Eliminate candidate itemsets that are small.

Table 1. The algorithm steps of improved apriori.

	Definition	Pre-condition	Purpose	the Use	Result
P	0.50	0.80	0.50	0.87	0.65
R	1.00	0.63	0.63	0.80	0.81

Table 2. The P, R of extracted dimensions (part).

dimensions are shown in Table 2. Calculated by experimental results, the overall Precision and Recall are 0.77 and 0.84, respectively, showing that this method is effective.

CONCLUSIONS AND FUTURE WORK

We have investigated the approach of rule-based extraction of method KEs from scientific literatures by machine. The precision and recall for the method KEs extraction are 0.77and 0.84, respectively, indicating the effectiveness of the method. The findings of this study have implications for more granular knowledge organization and retrieval.

ACKNOWLEDGMENTS

This study is supported by "the Fundamental Research Funds for the Central Universities". "Research on multi-granularity hierarchical structure mining of digital library resources" (Project No. CCNU19TS043).

REFERENCES

Engin C. S. (2007). Extraction procedures from text(C)// *Proceedings of the 4th International Conference on Knowledge Capture, ACM 2007*, 177–178.

Kambhatla, N. (2004). Combining lexical, syntactic, and semantic features with maximum entropy models for extracting relations. In *Proceedings of the ACL 2004 on Interactive poster and demonstration sessions* (p. 22). Association for Computational Linguistics.

Liu, X., Zhang, S., Wei, F., & Zhou, M. (2011). Recognizing named entities in tweets. *Proceedings of the 49th Annual*

Meeting of the Association for Computational Linguistics: Human Language Technologies-Volume 1, Association for Computational Linguistics, 359–367.

Nguyen, T. H., & Grishman, R. (2015). Relation extraction: Perspective from convolutional neural networks. *Proceedings of the 1st Workshop on Vector Space Modeling for Natural Language Processing*, 39–48.

Ultsch, A. (1993). Knowledge extraction from self-organizing neural networks. In *Information and classification* (pp. 301–306). Heidelberg, Germany: Springer.

A Versatile Approach for Constructing a Domain Knowledge Graph for Culture

Jingzhu Wei
Sun Yat-sen University,
Guangzhou, China
weijzhu@mail.sysu.edu.cn

Rui Liu
Sun Yat-sen University,
Guangzhou, China
liur76@mail2.sysu.edu.cn

ABSTRACT

[Question] The construction of cultural knowledge base in digital library is in progress with the development of information technology. However, traditional cultural knowledge bases are facing the problems of high participation of manual operation and monotonous data source. This paper combines knowledge graph, a frontier technology of artificial intelligence, to explore a new method of building high-quality, automated cultural knowledge base. [Method] Using the experimental method, we selected the knowledge of the Hundred Schools of Thought in ancient China. Because these knowledges are clearly interrelated, it is suitable to construct the knowledge graph of them. The knowledge graph can provide experience for the construction of other cultural knowledge bases. [Conclusion] At present, this paper has preliminarily completed the experimental design of the knowledge graph of the Hundred Schools of Thought, and provided the flowchart of the construction of cultural domain knowledge graph.

KEYWORDS

cultural knowledge base; knowledge graph; information extraction

ASIS&T THESAURUS

China; Culture values; domain knowledge

INTRODUCTION

In 2012, Google first introduced the concept of knowledge graph, its core knowledge graph system is Freebase and WikiData. Google's knowledge graph is based on Wikipedia. The main characteristics of knowledge graph based on encyclopedia website are with huge scale and relatively low precision requirement. It is necessary to modify the data sources to construct the knowledge graph especially suitable for domain of culture, not only extract relevant information from Wikipedia, but also combine the cultural digital resources of digital libraries to form a special construction process of knowledge graph in domain of culture. We take The Hundred Schools of Thought as an example to test this special construction of knowledge graph. The Hundred Schools of Thought is the phenomenon that lots of philosophers belong to different schools flourished in thousand years ago in China. It's an explosion of culture and wisdom which still influence on social consciousness in China today. The Schools mainly consist of Confucianism, Legalism, Taoism, Mohism, School of Yin-yang, Logicians and others. The classification of these schools is clear, but there are many potential semantic relations between them we do not know. We need knowledge graph to represent these nformation and their relations.

82nd Annual Meeting of the Association for Information Science & Technology | Melbourne, Australia | 19–23 October, 2019

DOI: 10.1002/pra2.00186

THE CONSTRUCTION OF KNOWLEDGE GRAPH FOR DOMAIN OF CULTURE

At present, the main knowledge graph is open general knowledge graph, such as DBpedia, which emphasizes the breadth and integration of more entities. Compared with domain knowledge graph, its accuracy is not high enough. However, in the construction of knowledge graph in domain of cultural, we can take use of the basic framework from DBpeida, and then through the information extraction methods to obtain knowledge from text to perfect cultural domain knowledge graph. This method can address three limitations of traditional cultural knowledge base.

Beyond Manual Construction

The construction of traditional cultural knowledge base depends largely on the manual method of compiling case data by library experts, and the scale is very limited. In the Internet era, the interaction between people and society will produce huge amounts of data. These data exist in the form of text, pictures, videos, audio and other isomerism forms. We must rely on computers to automatically read and analyze massive data and acquire the cultural knowledge we need from it.

Beyond Monotonous Source of Knowledge Acquisition

The cultural knowledge base of traditional libraries is mainly composed of structured data stored in relational databases, and the data sources are relatively single. Therefore, the cultural knowledge base project websites in digital libraries are relatively single and cannot update knowledge with time. This paper argues that knowledge acquisition should be consist of structured data from library's database, structured data from general knowledge graph and unstructured data from text.

Beyond using Relational Databases

The traditional data source of cultural knowledge base is generally structured data from relational database. Graph-based storage can be very flexible in design, generally requiring only local changes. Therefore, this paper argues that high-performance graph databases, such as neo4j, should be used to store cultural knowledge graph instead of traditional relational database storage.

THE FLOWCHART OF CULTURE KNOWLEDGE GRAPH CONSTRUCTION

According to the steps of creating knowledge graph in cultural field, this paper constructs the flowchart of knowledge graph in the domain of culture (see Figure 1).

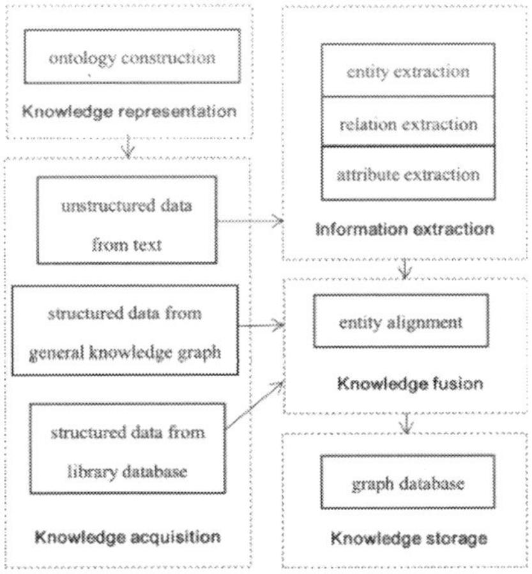

Figure 1. The flowchart of knowledge graph in the domain of culture.

The flowchart is validated by experiments using the knowledge of the hundred schools of thought about Chinese traditional cultural knowledge. The main contents of knowledge graph flowchart include four parts: knowledge representation, knowledge acquisition, knowledge fusion and knowledge storage. Among them, information extraction is the most important part to make the cultural domain knowledge graph with various semantic relations, and we are focusing on this part now.

Knowledge Acquisition

Based on ontology construction, the categories of special data are decided. The three main aspects of cultural data sources are as follows. Firstly, structured data in digital libraries are derived from special relational databases in libraries, and obtaining these data requires library permission. Secondly, using DBpedia can obtain main entities and their properties. Thirdly, unstructured data from text need to use information extraction technology to acquire knowledge.

Information Extraction

With structured data, we can only obtain basic relations between entities. We have finished the basic knowledge graph of the hundred schools of thought, which can show different schools are subsets of the hundred schools of thought, and different representative person is the element of different schools (see Figure 2). But now, we are trying to use the technology of natural language process to do information extraction from text, such as some professional papers.

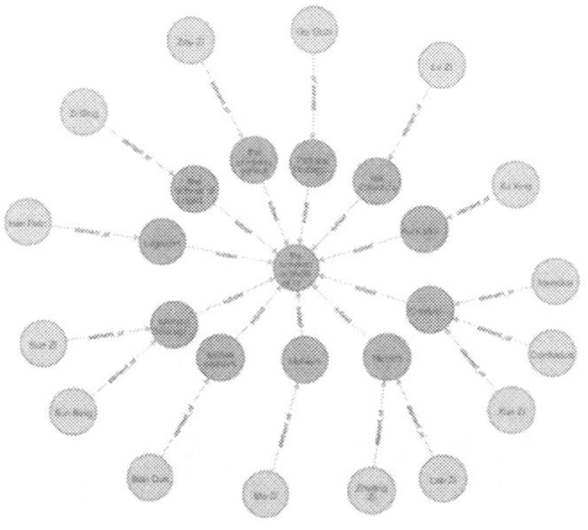

Figure 2. The basic knowledge graph of the hundred schools of thought.

Because there are still many potential semantic relations between these people not be represented. Such as mentoring relationship. In some articles and sentences, we can find some mentoring relationship between them. For example, Xunzi is one of representatives of Confucianism, and Xunzi's disciples were numerous. Because of his open-minded thinking, emphasis on practice and encouragement of independent thinking, his disciples did not stick to one thought. Han Feizi, the representative of legalism, and mozi, the founder of mohism, were all disciples of Xunzi. Through this example, there are mentoring relationship between Xunzi and others.

Information extraction mainly includes entity extraction, attribute extraction and relationship extraction. Entity extraction, refers to the automatic recognition of named entities from raw data corpus. Such as Xunzi, Han Feizi and Mozi above. The goal of relation extraction is to solve the problem of entity semantic linking. In this sentence, disciple is the trigger word of their relationship.

REFERENCES

Barbosa, D., Wang, H., & Yu, C. (2013). Shallow information extraction for the knowledge web. In *Proceedings of international conference on data engineering* (p. 1264). Washington DC: IEEE Computer Society.

Ernst, P., Siu, A., & Weikum, G. (2015). KnowLife: A versatile approach for constructing a large knowledge graph for biomedical sciences. *BMC Bioinformatics*. https://doi.org/10.1186/s12859-015-0549-5

Suchanek, F., & Weikum, G. (2013). Knowledge harvesting from text and web 25. sources. In *Proceedings of International Conference On Data Engineering* (p. 1250). Washington, DC: IEEE Computer Society.

Vulnerability and Meeting the Needs of People Experiencing Homelessness in Public Libraries

Rachel D. Williams
SLIS, Simmons University,
Boston, MA, United States
rachel.williams@simmons.edu

ABSTRACT

This study examines how public library workers navigate professional boundaries when providing information services to people experiencing homelessness. Relying on interviews with twenty-four library staff at three public library systems in the Midwest United States and Gieryn's (1983) boundary work theory, this project focuses on the information public librarians provide to people experiencing homelessness. It also argues that public librarians navigate tensions in professional and personal boundaries, and that some of these tensions can be attributed to perceptions of vulnerability in both themselves and in the patrons they assist. The paper concludes by making arguments to consider the importance of self-care and building resilience in the profession of public librarianship. It also suggests the value of partnerships that enable public library staff to re-conceptualize what their professional roles entail.

KEYWORDS

Information services; people experiencing homelessness; public librarianship; boundary management

ASIS&T THESAURUS

Public libraries; Information workers; Underserved users

INTRODUCTION

Patrons in crisis often turn to the public library as a space for support in finding information resources, social support, and a safe space. Public libraries actively meet the needs of a variety of people in crisis, including those experiencing homelessness, people suffering from substance use disorders, and survivors of domestic violence, for example. To address these needs, public libraries have taken various approaches, including everything from hiring security guards to partnering with social services agencies. Regardless of the strategies used to address these concerns, public libraries are seeking ways of further expanding services, addressing service challenges, and identifying ways in which staff can engage with people in crisis. Several studies centered on public library services for people in crisis have focused on understanding and meeting the needs of people experiencing homelessness or survivors of intimate partner violence (Hersberger, 2005; Terrile, 2009; Westbrook, 2014). Other scholars have explored public libraries as places that support public health, particularly to vulnerable populations [Morgan et al., 2016]. Additional work has examined how public libraries provide consumer health education and wellness programming (Lenstra, Rubenstein, Smith, Flaherty, & Gibson, 2018).

As Whiteman et al. (2018) explain, public libraries often serve the most vulnerable within a community, particularly those experiencing homelessness, mental illness, immigration challenges, and trauma or disasters. Walsh (2018), for example, considers how the public library serves as a space for homeless LGBTQ youth to find information, poignantly noting the complexity of the public library as an invaluable but overtly public space that may make it difficult for these youth to satisfy their information needs. Meeting the needs of vulnerable individuals requires empathy, as Birdi, Wilson, and Cocker (2008) describe. As recent literature suggests, providing access to information and services is a difficult and critical aim for public libraries, particularly in assisting people experiencing homelessness.

In this paper, I consider boundary work to be the activities one does to create, demarcate, manage, redefine, or cross the boundaries associated with one's professional role (Gieryn, 1983). In the context of this work, the term vulnerability means those "who are economically insecure, who may not have stable housing, and who may not have regular access to computers and the internet beyond that provided by the library or a mobile device" (Jacobs, 2018). Vulnerable can also refer to those with unstable living situations, poor health, or those with any other life situations that put them at risk in some way. This project's analysis builds on previous work by examining public library services for people experiencing homelessness and explores the following research question:

What role does one's perception of vulnerability play in the context of managing boundaries?

METHODS

Participants were part of a voluntary sample recruited by email at three library systems throughout the Midwestern

82nd Annual Meeting of the Association for Information Science & Technology | Melbourne, Australia | 19–23 October, 2019

DOI: 10.1002/pra2.00187

United States. The library systems were selected because they were all suburban communities which had varying populations of people experiencing homelessness. In Library System A, 3 library staff agreed to participate, 9 library workers participated in Library System B, and 12 in Library System C. Interviews were about an hour, and they were held in quiet offices in the library. All interviews were audio-recorded and transcribed. The transcripts were analyzed by employing an inductive thematic approach to identify concepts related to identify the types of information provided, information sources, and boundary work activities, along with any emergent themes that could not be accounted for through the boundary work framework. The analysis also uncovered a few major themes related to perceptions of vulnerability and boundaries, which is the focus of this study.

FINDINGS

The results of the analysis to be presented in this study will center on examining how the boundary work practices of public library staff are often related to perceptions of vulnerability. In addition to describing the resources public library staff use in aiding people experiencing homelessness, the study will discuss boundary management practices and their role in the work of public librarians. Library staff use boundary management activities to:

- Justify their roles and explain why they do or do not complete a work activity
- Reiterate and/or redefine their professional identity amidst challenges, changing practices, or organizational structures
- Identify new areas of knowledge/practice to claim, or to use to bound one's profession and thus one's practices

Furthermore, the analysis will describe how feeling vulnerable can be related to specific kinds of boundary management activities. While public library staff did not often explicitly discuss issues of vulnerability, they pointed to situations that made them feel vulnerable, as well as the risks associated with experiencing homelessness within their communities. These comments centered on medical emergencies and emergency department visits, the public library as the only space option, and the power dynamic between reference staff and individuals experiencing homelessness.

The results of this study will demonstrate that feeling as though one is vulnerable—while helping someone that is vulnerable—can create barriers to providing information and services to those individuals. Many participants wanted to be of assistance but did not know how to be. They were afraid of placing themselves in what could be a vulnerable or unsafe situation, but recognized that the people they were helping were vulnerable as well.

CONCLUSION

This study will show that addressing the vulnerable nature of experiencing homelessness suggests a need to reflect on existing policies to identify where they stem from, and how those policies may marginalize these individuals. Having a select number of concrete policies while identifying those that can be flexible empowers librarians to make more decisions and provide more tailored services to people experiencing homelessness. Which rules can be changed, and when? Focusing on building trusting relationships with people experiencing homelessness is also fundamental to meeting the needs of people experiencing homelessness. Much of this work involves what Moxley and Abbas (2016) argue for—moving beyond providing traditional information resources toward collaboration with social services agencies and the provision of health services.

The study also makes the argument that as public library staff are expected to do more to meet the needs of people experiencing homelessness (and people in crisis, more broadly), there is a need to build support for library staff. This may include finding ways to foster self-care and building resilience in the workplace. These changing roles and responsibilities also result in a need to develop strategies to deal with burnout. Finally, adjusting curriculum and continuing education opportunities for public library staff can help prepare them to meet the needs of people experiencing homelessness more effectively, which may empower staff to foster healthy boundaries with their patrons.

REFERENCES

Birdi, B., Wilson, K., & Cocker, J. (2008). The public library, exclusion and empathy: A literature review. *Library Review*, *57*(8), 576–592.

Gieryn, T. F. (1983). Boundary-work and the demarcation of science from non-science: Strains and interests in professional ideologies of scientists. *American Sociological Review*, 781–795.

Gieryn, T. F. (1999). *Cultural boundaries of science: Credibility on the line*. University of Chicago Press.

Hersberger, J. (2005). The homeless and information needs and services. *Reference & User Services Quarterly*, *44* (3), 199–202.

Jacobs, G. (2018). Advancing digital equity in public libraries: Assessing library patrons' problem solving in technology rich environments. *Roundtable presented at the Adolescent, Family, and Community Literacy: Mobilizing Strength Based Pedagogies conference, Tucson, AZ.*

Lenstra, N., Rubenstein, E. L., Smith, C. A., Flaherty, M. G., & Gibson, A. N. (2018). How does health happen in public libraries? Ethical and emerging issues. *Proceedings of the Association for Information Science and Technology*, *55*(1), 704–707.

Moxley, D. P., & Abbas, J. M. (2016). Envisioning libraries as collaborative community anchors for social service provision to vulnerable populations. *Practice*, *28*(5), 311–330.

Terrile, V. C. (2009). Library services to children, teens and families experiencing homelessness. *Urban Library Journal*, *15*(2).

Westbrook, L. (2015). "I'm Not a Social Worker": An information service model for working with patrons in crisis. *The Library Quarterly*, *85*(1), 6–25.

Whiteman, E. D., Dupuis, R., Morgan, A. U., D'Alonzo, B., Epstein, C., Klusaritz, H., & Cannuscio, C. C. (2018). Peer reviewed: Public libraries as partners for health. *Preventing Chronic Disease*, 15.

How Do Consumers Acquire Health Information? A Pattern Analysis on Online Health Consultation

Dan Wu
iSchool, Wuhan University,
Wuhan, China
woodan@whu.edu.cn

Hao Xu
iSchool, Wuhan University,
Wuhan, China
josephxu@whu.edu.cn

Shu Fan
iSchool, Wuhan University,
Wuhan, China
fanshu@whu.edu.cn

ABSTRACT

Nowadays, consumers can conveniently access and use health information from online health consultation platforms. It is important to identify the patterns of consumers' multi-source health information acquisition in the circumstance of online health consultation. However, little research has been done in this area. Focusing on such a target, data from an online health consultation platform was taken as an example. 869 cases from the platform were crawled, and a grounded theory research methodology was adopted. According to the coding results, the author found eight patterns of consumers' health information acquisition. This study broadens our understanding of the behavioral pattern of attaining multi-source health information, enriching the field of health information search behavior.

KEYWORDS

Online health consultation; health information; health information acquisition; health information seeking

ASIS&T THESAURUS

Information use; Information resources

INTRODUCTION

Nowadays, health information is available from many different sources. The Internet (online communities, Wikis, social Q&A, and social networking sites), medical institutions, mass media (TV, newspapers, magazines, and radio) and interpersonal sources (friends, family) are all sources of health information (Zhang, 2014). In China, online health consultation (OHC) is an important online source of health information. Doctors can directly provide online disease and health counseling to users on the cyber health consultation platform.

In the area of health information seeking, existing studies mainly focus on the factors that influence consumers' choice of a certain source of information and the evaluation of the quality of that source. For online health information, current studies suggest that similar to assessments of traditional print sources, users rely on various source cues, such as layout and appearance, disclosures, advertisements, references provided, editorial processes, and picture of the site owner, to evaluate web-based health information (Zhang, 2014). However, it is worth noting that the reliability and integrity of health information from different sources vary greatly. Instead of obtaining information through one or two sources to develop a coping strategy, consumers tend to use a combination of sources that change over time to meet their health information needs (Greyson, 2018). On this condition, when multiple health information sources are combined, a systematic understanding of patterns of consumers health information acquisition is necessary. The purpose of this study is to elucidate the pattern of consumers' health information acquisition in multi-source health information circumstance.

DATA COLLECTION AND PROCESSING

In this study, Python was used to collect the data for 20,000 cases from Haodaifu (https://www.haodf.com/) in December 2018. Haodaifu is a leading OHC platform in China, providing four services: *doctor-seeking, hospital-seeking, online consultation*, and *health guidance*. In each case, data including doctors' information (*name, title, practice experience, recommended index, thank-you letters, gifts*), case information (*ID, disease description, purpose, disease course, allergy, anamnesis, hospital, inspection*) and all *Q&A* data are available.

Previous studies have found that friends and family were important sources of information and emotional support (Bernhard et al., 2017). In many cases, users exposed their offline experience, but very few exposed their interpersonal sources (friends, family, etc.). In order to study the pattern of consumers' health information acquisition in the multi-source health information circumstance, the data were screened by keywords 'friend' or 'friend recommend' or 'family' or 'family recommend' to gain exposure to interpersonal sources (family or friends) case data. After screening and cleaning, 869 sample cases were obtained.

In order to ensure the rigor and completeness of the research, this study followed a strictly grounded theoretical research paradigm and basic process. Using NVivo 11 content

82nd Annual Meeting of the Association for Information Science & Technology | Melbourne, Australia | 19–23 October, 2019

DOI: 10.1002/pra2.00189

analysis software, the case data were encoded and analyzed by the grounded theory coding method. The specific process of coding was done by two MA students in Library Science. The index of category agreement CA = 0.84 (> 0.5) was obtained by coding consistency test, which concluded that the coding had a good consistency.

RESULTS ANALYSIS AND DISCUSSION

After encoding 869 cases, the four categories (symptoms, purposes, patterns, and results) were finally obtained. Three health information sources, OHC, medical institution, and interpersonal source (friends/family) were also identified.

In the category of pattern, when the three information sources, OHC, medical institution, and interpersonal source (friends/family), are combined into the consumer's health information sources, there are eight patterns of consumers' health information acquisition, as shown in Figure 1.

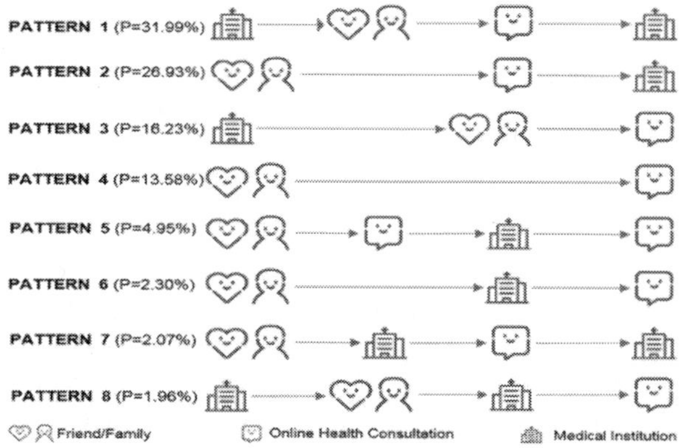

Figure 1. The eight patterns of consumers' health information acquisition. *Note*. P=Percentage (total = 869).

Pattern 1: In this pattern, medical institutions, friends and family are more reliable health information sources for consumers. They regard OHC as their second opinion for medical help. Moreover, since the inability of OHC to provide the necessary examinations and equipment for diagnosis or treatment, consumers still need to go to medical institutions after OHC. *"My mother was diagnosed with...lung cancer. She was treated at ...Hospital. Friends said that...is more effective ..." "I can't...online... bring your mother to my hospital." (Case 802, disease description and Q&A).*

Pattern 2: After family and friends' consultation, consumers would go online as their first choice for medical help. Similarly, due to the above limits, consumers still have to go to medical institutions for help after OHC. *"I had a sore ..., I didn't go to the hospital. My friend said ..." "You need dermoscopy to ..." (Case 16, disease description and Q&A).*

Pattern 3: Similar to Pattern 1, consumers choose medical institutions as their first choice of help, treating OHC as a second source of health information.

Pattern 4: Similar to Pattern 2, consumers choose online health consultation as the first option to meet their demand for medical information.

Pattern 5: In this pattern, OHC is the first choice. After the diagnose from the medical institution, consumers would go back to OHC for more information. This happens mainly because the doctors that the consumers previously met also provides online consultation, providing convenient follow-up medical help. *"Hello, Dr. Zhou, ... had an operation before." (Case 192, Q&A).*

Pattern 6: Consumers are more willing to acquire health information from their family, friends and medical institution, treating OHC as a secondary medical help.

Pattern 7: After OHC, consumers continue to go to medical institutions for help.

Pattern 8: In this pattern, consumers often have complicated health problems, they have to toss around medical institutions before turning to OHC.

As a supplement to traditional health information sources, OHC has broadened the channels for consumers to acquire health information. At the same time, OHC has its limitations. It cannot provide more information for doctors' decision-making through other means such as observation, physical examination, laboratory examination, image examination, etc. In half of the eight identified patterns, consumers still need medical institutions to complete the relevant examination or treatment after OHC. This study enables us with an in-depth understanding of the sequence, role, and limitations of OHC in the consumers' health information acquisition, which has not been studied before.

CONCLUSIONS AND FUTURE WORK

In this study, eight patterns of consumers' health information acquisition were identified and discussed. This work greatly expands our understanding of consumers' multi-source health information acquisition behavior, which is conducive to research on health information search behavior. Due to the limitation of the case data, in future research, questionnaire and semi-structured interview will be adopted to obtain more comprehensive behavioral data to interpret consumers' complete health information acquisition process.

ACKNOWLEDGMENTS

This work was supported by the project "HCI & Collaboration Team (whu2016020)", Wuhan University.

REFERENCES

Bernhard, G., Ose, D., Baudendistel, I., Seidling, H. M., Stützle, M., Szecsenyi, J., … Mahler, C. (2017). Understanding challenges, strategies, and the role of support networks in medication self-management among patients with type 2 diabetes: A qualitative study. *The Diabetes Educator*, *43*(2), 190–205.

Greyson, D. (2018). Information triangulation: a complex and agentic everyday information practice. *Journal of the Association for Information Science & Technology*, 69 (2), 869–878.

Zhang, Y. (2014). Beyond quality and accessibility: Source selection in consumer health information searching. *Journal of the Association for Information Science and Technology*, *65*(5), 911–927.

Users' Visual Attention Flow on the Search Result Page of Digital Cultural Heritage Collection

Dan Wu
iSchool, Wuhan University, China
woodan@whu.edu.cn

Shuang Xu
iSchool, Wuhan University, China
xs2277@126.com

Xiaoyun Xu
iSchool, Wuhan University, China
376187825@qq.com

Xi Chen
iSchool, Wuhan University, China
chenxi7776@qq.com

ABSTRACT

Cultural heritage breathes a new life with digital technologies and the internet. Digitization of cultural heritage artifacts do represent new materials and new contexts for research and practice. It is important to know how the public access and browse online collections of digital cultural heritage. This paper presents an eye-tracking experiment on Digital Dunhuang, which is the most famous digital cultural heritage project in China, and identifies users' visual attention in search engine results pages (SERP). The results show how visual attention allocates in each area of interest (AOI), and the AOIs are browsed back and forth until the information needs are satisfied.

KEYWORDS

visual attention; eye-tracking; digital cultural heritage; digital humanities; web interaction; SERP

ASIS&T THESAURUS

Cultural heritage; Information seeking; Eye tracking

INTRODUCTION

With the development of culture and education in various countries of the world, museums, libraries, archives, art galleries and other cultural institutions are increasingly being used as carriers to disseminate, preserve and display humanities knowledge with online resources and interactive or visual additions to the exhibit. This is what we called digital cultural heritages. Today, information technology offers new approaches and tools for digital cultural heritage to break the existing limitations of physical cultural institutions, making the extension of cultural heritage broader, and maximizing the function to meet the needs of public cultural services (Marcella, 2019).

SERP is often attached great importance in information retrieval field, because it allows finding and arriving detailed pages based on the users' interest and attention. Users interact with digital cultural heritage such as digital museum website through visual channel mostly, where there are plenty of visual resources such as photos, videos, panorama etc. Visual signals embody users' search choice and attention. This allows to use eye-tracking to capture users' visual attention. Previous works studied visual attention or gaze behavior on the website or SERPs mainly for the design of website, information retrieval system, and the launch of the advertisement. Therefore, the purpose of this paper is to identify how users' visual attention flow on SERP, acquire user behavior's intention, optimize the layout of SERP and enhance user's search efficiency, so as to make the interested users find their own path to cultural heritage collection and knowledge enlightenment, and enhance the system as well.

82nd Annual Meeting of the Association for Information Science & Technology | Melbourne, Australia | 19–23 October, 2019

DOI: 10.1002/pra2.00188

EXPERIMENT DESIGN

Website

Digital Dunhuang is a brilliant digital humanities project in China, which pursues overall digitization and virtualization, including collection, processing and storage of Dunhuang Grottoes and related cultural relics. Taking it as an experimental website helps it make efforts for permanent preservation and sustainable use of Dunhuang's cultural heritage. Text-based visual search is used in the website.

Tasks

The experiment was a controlled user experiment, including preparation, training, testing and interview which lasted about 30 minutes. The search task was to search Mogao Grottoes Cave 194, and observe SERP for 30 seconds, try to find the best result, then answer questions about the cave.

Participants

40 students were recruited from a University in China, with 20 males and 20 females from 32 majors in 19 schools, distributed evenly from undergraduate to graduate. Everyone got ¥50 labor fee after finishing the experiment.

Data Collection and Cleaning Methods

There were two main methods in data collection. One was eye-tracking data recorded by Tobii Studio. In our lab we used Tobii Pro X3-120 with a 120 Hz sampling frequency. 31 participants were selected, whose weighted gaze sampling rate reached 85% to eliminate the interference. The other method was the interview after all the tasks were finished. Participants were asked by two questions: 1) Which result did you choose in SERP? 2) Which area did you have interest in? The questions were open-ended, all the interview data were collected, recorded and transcribed.

RESULT AND DISCUSSION

We divided SERP into 9 AOIs as Figure 1: Search box, Result title, Result fragment, Thumbnail, URL, Search results and time consuming, Search page number, Related search and Historical search.

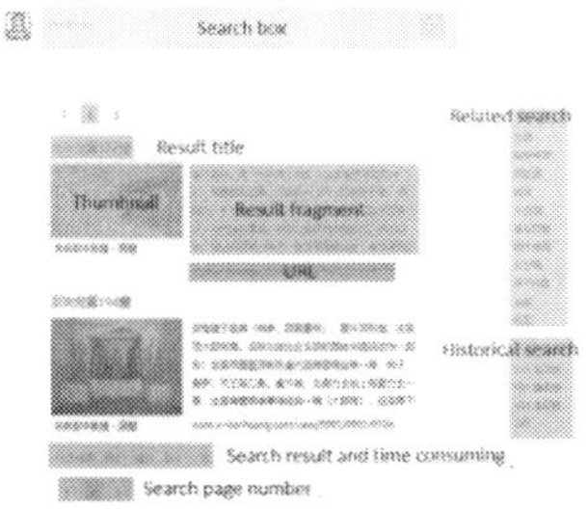

Figure 1. The Divided AOIs in SERP.

Two kinds of eye-tracking data were recorded, which were fixation duration and fixation number for analyzing the attention users paid to the SERP (shown in Figure 2). Fixation is maintaining the visual gaze on a single location or the slight eye movement in a certain spatial and temporal range. The more fixation duration and the more fixation number, the more attractive the AOI was to users. It could be seen that both two metrics of result fragment and thumbnail were much bigger than other AOIs, which meant these two AOIs gathered most visual attention of users.

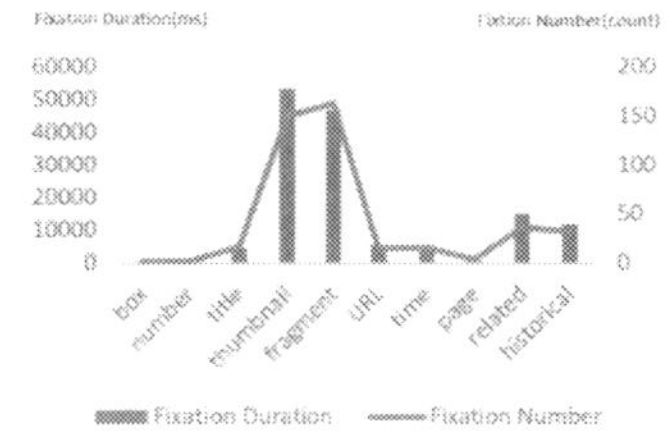

Figure 2. Fixation Duration and Fixation Number of AOIs.

We visualized eye movement sequence of AOIs of users in same SERP with same query. Some sequences were deleted when the fixation duration was too short (less than 200 ms). The final result was shown as a Sankey diagram in Figure 3. 10 different colors represented different AOIs. However, the search box did not appear in anyone's eye movement sequence and it didn't have a corresponding color. Gray color meant eye movement stopped in the last area. The number in each color block indicated the user number who had noticed the AOI, and the curve between color blocks indicated visual attention flow.

In Figure 3, the red blocks (result fragments) and yellow blocks (thumbnails) account for a large proportion in every sequence, which means that the two AOIs were more attractive to users. Based on later interview, we found users thought that result fragment might include most useful information in daily search habits, and thumbnail was more intuitive and interesting in vision because of the presented picture. It's consistent to Djamasbi Soussan's suggestion that participants enjoyed presence of images on webpages and didn't like to read "long boring text" (Djamasbi, Siegel, & Tullis, 2010).

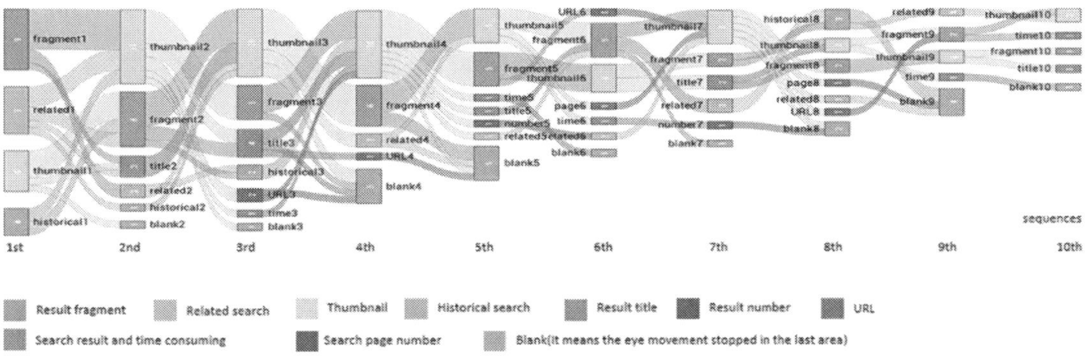

Figure 3. The Sankey Diagram of Eye Movement Sequence of AOIs in SERP.

As time went by, the number of users has decreased in every sequence, indicating that more people left from SREP after finishing the task with their visual attention shifted. The curve between color blocks showed that users browsed AOIs back and forth until they found enough information.

CONCLUSION

In this paper, eye-tracking experiment on Digital Dunhuang was conducted to explore how visual attention flow and shift on SERP. We found result fragment and thumbnail gathered most visual attention, most users would browse AOIs back and forth until they found enough information. Therefore, web designers should optimize the layout of AOIs for higher retrieval efficiency. The limited sample is not representative of all users, which will be improved in future work.

ACKNOWLEDGMENT

This work was supported by a key project of School of Information Management, Wuhan University.

REFERENCES

Djamasbi, S., Siegel, M., & Tullis, T. (2010). Generation y, web design, and eye tracking. *International Journal of Human-Computer Studies*, *68*(5), 307–323.

Idris, J., Alex, A., Kevin, H., & Azevedo, R. (2019). Are visual search patterns predictive of hazard recognition performance? Empirical investigation using eye-tracking technology. *Journal of Construction Engineering and Management*, *145*(1), 1–13.

Research on Voice Search Behavior in the Last 10 Years

Zhaopeng Xing
University of North Carolina,
Chapel Hill, U.S.
zhaopeng@live.unc.edu

Fei Yu
University of North Carolina,
Chapel Hill, U.S.
feifei@unc.edu

Xiaojun Yuan
University at Albany, State
University of New York,
New York, U.S.
xyuan@albany.edu

ABSTRACT

Voice search enables users to issue spoken information requests and retrieve desired information on web/mobile search interfaces. We conducted a literature review to examine the extent to which existing studies have addressed voice search behavior, with a focus on the employed methodologies and the focused topics in these studies. Fourteen relevant studies conducted since 2008 were identified from four publication databases. These studies were mainly focused on three aspects of search behavior: voice query characteristics, reformulation strategies, and users' perception/satisfaction. Our results provide a snapshot of how users perform and perceive voice search in order to inform future research and design of voice search systems.

KEYWORDS

Voice search; literature review; search behavior

ASIS&T THESAURUS

Natural language interfaces; information behavior

INTRODUCTION

Voice search has become prevalent since the release of google voice search in 2008 (Schalkwyk et al., 2010). This increases information accessibility by presenting an alternative to traditional typing modality. Voice is useful in hand/eye off scenarios and for those having difficulties with typing. To understand how users perform voice search can guide the design and evaluation of voice search systems. Some recent studies have investigated and revealed users' voice search behavior, interactions and experience. However, the evidence regarding how voice search is performed was rarely systematically synthesized. We thus filled this gap by examining research conducted since 2008 and summarizing what have been studied on voice search behavior to inform future studies.

METHODS

A systematic search strategy was employed with 34 terms regarding voice interaction (e.g., "voice interface", "spoken interface") and 22 terms regarding search interaction (e.g., "search behavior", "mobile search", "web search"), combined with "and." The publication data were retrieved from four electronic databases: Scopus (N = 1229), Web of Science (N = 478), and Association for Computing Machinery Digital Library (N = 518), PubMed (N = 40). Duplicate studies were excluded (N = 541). The search terms were validated by a librarian and a domain expert. The eligibility criteria included: 1) Full-text English paper published since 2008; 2) Primary research findings should have been reported. Thus, the conference proceedings and journal papers were considered while editorials, letter, reviews, and brief communications, talk, lecture, tutorial, conceptual papers, design papers, study protocols, and opinion papers were excluded; 3) A study should explicitly express interests in understanding users' voice search behavior and interactions with voice-based interfaces. This type of behavior-centered studies typically collect searchers' behavioral data, from search activity logs and/or experimental user studies where users issue queries and examine results in assigned search tasks (Kelly, 2009). These data are then used to interpret users' needs, search behavior and interaction patterns, rather than as human gold standards to assess the goodness of systems (e.g., speech recognition accuracy, retrieval precision and recall); 4) In user studies, queries and results should be visually available for users. We are interested in multimodality with visual feedbacks, which is considered richer and more efficient in information delivery than speech-only modality (Schalkwyk et al., 2010); 5) collaborative search studies, where two or more users perform search tasks collaboratively, were excluded because it is out of our research focus.

RESULTS

Given the eligibility criteria, this review identified a total of 14 publications[1], which included two types 1) large scale query log analysis (N = 7) (Figure 1) and 2) user studies in lab settings (N = 7) (Figure 2). It should be noted that three pairs of studies (#1&2, #8&9, #10&11) were based on three log analysis/experiments respectively. Three aspects of voice search behavior were deductively identified in these studies, 1) Query characteristics (QC), 2) Query reformulation strategy (QRS); 3) User perception and/or satisfaction (UPS).

[1] See details about the included studies at https://docs.google.com/document/d/1VhdBGCzKuHaFdWOns9_5qYxVE-_DxiPaisih65bc_AA/edit?usp=sharing

82nd Annual Meeting of the Association for Information Science & Technology | Melbourne, Australia | 19–23 October, 2019

DOI: 10.1002/pra2.00190

The log analysis studies were conducted using larger datasets and longer data collection duration to answer what and how users searched by voice (i.e., QC and partly QRS) while user studies, in contrast, drew attention to individuals' behavior and primarily explicated how they searched and why in such manners (i.e., QRS and UPS). The adopted data collection methods included: 1) Content analysis (CA) (N = 3); 2) Focused group interview (FGI) (N = 6); 3) Questionnaire (QTN) (N = 6); 4) Small-scale retrospective log analysis (RLA) (N = 6). Wizard of OZ (WO) was used in two lab experiments where the researchers simulated voice search interfaces to reveal user behavior without considering the effects of the system limitations (N = 3). Next, we presented review results organized by the three deducted aspects of voice search behavior.

Voice Search Behavior

Query Characteristics

Voice query characteristics typically refer to query topical contents, structural (e.g., query length (in words and/or character)), and linguistic (i.e., lexical, syntactic and semantic) features. These characteristics were examined in comparison with those of textual queries, to identify users' unique information needs and distinct query features in voice search interfaces. Some agreements were achieved in the prior findings: 1) voice queries were linguistically closer to natural language than textual queries (N = 3); 2) voice queries were more likely to occur in mobile scenarios, such as local business, and less in sensitive situation such as health-related questions and adults website name (N = 4); 3) Voice search was also preferred for quick answer tasks and less for ones involving complex interaction (N = 5). However, a controversy existed over the voice and textual query length, where four studies found that voice queries in average were significantly longer than textual queries whereas another study reported the opposite.

Query Reformulation Strategy

It has been shown that users employed similar query reformulation strategies for both voice and textual search when they were unsatisfied with retrieved results. In general, the most frequently used reformulation strategies, in both voice and textual search, were term addition and removal, by which users generalized or specialized query topics (N = 3). However, users also adapted the strategies according to the occurrence of speech recognition errors (SREs). They tended to reorder error terms and/or substituted them with the ones in similar meanings. In addition, users tended to use phonetics tactics, such as repeating and partially emphasizing the erroneous part of queries, which yet was not as effective as expected (N = 1). When textual and voice modality were both available, users were prone to resort to textual input (N = 1) and to perform partial query reformulation as SREs occurred (N = 3). It has been suggested that query reformulation support be provided in future voice information retrieval for query refinement purpose (N = 5).

User Perception and Satisfaction

As voice search is in its early stage, it is indispensable to investigate users' perception and satisfaction to enhance its usability. Five studies have examined this aspect. FGI and QTN were commonly used in user studies to collect users' preference and perceived challenges. Overall, users considered voice search more intuitive and interesting (N = 3), and showed the preference to voice search in the similar scenarios identified in the log analysis studies. The perceived challenges increased when iterative interactions occur, especially due to SREs (N = 5). SREs imposed additional workload which further hurt user satisfaction. Users demonstrated a preference to the provision of textual input modality for SREs recovery (N = 6). Furthermore, age-induced difference led to the older participants' dependence more on conventional input for refining queries and on the visual cues to detect the occurrence of SREs (N = 1).

#	Year	Platform	Collection session	Voice query log size (User counts)	Topic
1 2	2010	Google mobile	1 month 2009	1M (75K)	QC
3	2011	Yahoo mobile	2 months 2010	79K	QC
4	2014	Bing mobile	1 month 2013	7.67M (706.76K)*	QRS
		Bing desktop	2 months 2013	N/A	
5	2015	Bing (N/A)	7 months 2014	14.64K	QRS
6	2017	Bing Cortana desktop	1 month 2016	6M (over 3.6M)	QC
7	2018	Yahoo mobile	6 months 2015	500K	QC

Figure 1. Study with large scale log analysis. #: The number of each study. *: The study did not specify query type. K: Thousands; M: Millions.

#	Year	Study methods	Platform	Subject counts (mean age (sd))	Voice query log size	Topic
8	2013	FGI, QTN & RLA	Google mobile	20 (23.7 (4.72))	1650	QRS, QC & UPS
9	2016					
10	2016	CA, FGI, RLA, & QTN	Self-designed and WO	48 (28.41)	N/A	QC & UPS
11	2017					
12	2016	QTN	Cortana mobile	60 (25.53 (5.42))	2040	UPS
13	2018	CA, FGI, RLA & QTN	Google mobile	15 (>85)	N/A	UPS
14	2019	FGI & RLA	Self-designed and WO	32 (26.69)	607	QRS & UPS

Figure 2. User study. #: The number of each study.

DISCUSSION AND CONCLUSION

This review presented a preliminary systematic portrayal of users' voice search behavior and has implications to inform future research and voice search system design. Compared with conventional search, voice search has distinct behavioral characteristics and patterns, which should be considered and adapted properly to the design and evaluation of voice search systems. The "on the go" and "less interaction" nature of voice search requires efficient result presentation and its unique linguistics features require appropriate interpretation for better understanding of user intents. Also, users' behavioral changes may indicate a "misunderstanding" due to SREs, such as the phonetic emphasis, the changes of reformulation patterns and/or the transitions to textual query. To help users recover from SREs, especially older users, some search supports should be provided in users' preferred way, such as enabling multimodal input and giving sufficient visual cues. This preliminary review is limited in the breadth and depth of the reported findings. Our future work will continue to examine users' voice search behavior and perceptions by extending the analysis of the above-mentioned three main themes to speech-only interfaces for a broader coverage of voice search studies.

REFERENCES

Kelly, D. (2009). Methods for evaluating interactive information retrieval systems with users. *Foundations and Trends® in Information Retrieval*, *3*, 1–224.

Schalkwyk, J., Beeferman, D., Beaufays, F., Byrne, B., Chelba, C., Cohen, M., … Strope, B. (2010). "your word is my command": Google search by voice: A case study. In A. Neustein, *Advances in speech recognition* (pp. 61–90). Boston, MA: Springer US.

Using Crowdsourcing to Construct Special Collection Resources Under the Perspective of Digital Humanities

Xiaojuan Xu
School of Management,
Anhui University,
Hefei, China
xuxiaojuan@ahu.edu.cn

Manli Wu
School of Journalism and Information
Communication, Huazhong University
of Science and Technology,
Wuhan, China
wmanli2-c@my.cityu.edu.hk

ABSTRACT

This paper builds on the Fogg behavior model to explore the factors that drive users' participation in special collection resources crowdsourcing. Factors underlying the dimensions of motivation, ability and triggers are identified. This paper further explores the changes of the role of motivation, ability and trigger in initial and sustained participation. The results show that motivation and trigger are high in initial participation, and motivation and ability are high in sustained participation. The reasons for such change are further discussed. This study concludes with a discussion of theoretical and practical implications.

KEYWORDS

Digital humanities; Fogg behavior model; Special collection resources; participation

INTRODUCTION

Special collection resources (SCRs) are the basis for the sustainable development of libraries. Crowdsourcing is an effective way to construct SCRs. The SCRs crowdsourcing in library has some features that make it distinct from the existing crowdsourcing modes. First, crowdsourcing tasks tend to allow users to participate in voluntary. Second, it has educational functions. Third, participants are familiar with a specific humanistic knowledge domain. Their interests and familiarity in the specific SCRs entail them to develop social relationships and build knowledge community. Therefore, a crowdsourcing project under the perspective of digital humanities should not only be concerned with finishing tasks on the platforms, but also need to pay attention to users' knowledge absorption. In addition, taking a digital humanities perspective to construct SCRs contributes to the understanding of their role in promoting the development of the library.

At present, the crowdsourcing mode of SCRs under the perspective of digital humanities has attracted researchers' attention (Terras, 2015). Nevertheless, research that pertinent to the crowdsourcing participation of SCRs is not enough, which motivates our further investigation. In practice, participation in crowdsourcing tasks is not ideal due to the nature of voluntary participation. The literature tends to use motivation to understand participation, but research on voluntary participation is somewhat lacking. In addition, the division of motivation in existing research is more random and lacks corresponding theoretical support, which lays the research gap to be filled. In this study, we adopt the Fogg behavior model to investigate the antecedents of users' initial and sustained participation in SCRs crowdsourcing.

82nd Annual Meeting of the Association for Information Science & Technology | Melbourne, Australia | 19–23 October, 2019

DOI: 10.1002/pra2.00191

THEORETICAL BACKGROUND

SCRs Crowdsourcing

The literature pointed out that crowdsourcing modes change with the contexts (Doan, Ramakrishnan, & Halevy, 2011). Thereafter, the research on the crowdsourcing modes of SCRs under the perspective of digital humanities needs further exploration.

At present, some scholars have explored user behavior of the SCRs crowdsourcing. For instance, Ridge (2013) and Carletti, Giannachi, Price, et al. (2013) held seminars on the digital humanities crowdsourcing projects, and they carried out discussions on public participation motivation and users' knowledge exchange. They further used case study to summarize the factors that lead to the success of crowdsourcing. However, their works did not produce scientific research results. Zhang et al. (2018) interviewed the volunteers of Sheng Xuanhuai's archive transcription project. They based on the grounded theory to explore the motivational factors that influence the volunteers' sustained participation. However, their work has a coarser granularity in dividing motivational factors and lacks the theoretical support.

Fogg Behavior Model

Fogg behavior model is concerned with using persuasive design to create persuasive techniques (Fogg, 1999; Hamari, Koivisto, & Pakkanen, 2014). Since Fogg behavior model can clarify the composition, the classification and the effects of the factors in antecedent of users' behavior, it is appropriate to explain the crowdsourcing of SCRs.

At present, the Fogg behavior model is mainly used to analyze the antecedents of user behavior and uncover their transformation across time. The model clarifies that behavior is caused by three antecedents: trigger, motivation, and ability, and the occurrence of behavior has a critical value. When the motivation and ability exceed certain thresholds, the behavior will occur, and the two can be converted to each other in certain situations. Motivation refers to users' reasons for participation, and it mainly has three dimensions: joy and pain, hope and fear, social identity and social rejection. Ability includes two dimensions: user-defined ability, product usability and ease of use. Trigger deals with the way in which an actor is reminded of a certain behavior, which involves sparks, leader, signals. We build on the three elements of Fogg behavior model to conduct the following research.

RESEARCH METHODOLOGY

The interviews were conducted between July 29, 2018 and August 29, 2018. Semi-structured interviews were conducted on 21 interviewers via face-to-face or WeChat. Participants who participated in the Sheng Xuanhuai file transcription project via Shanghai library crowdsourcing system were recruited. Interviewees need to fulfill two conditions. First, they are official registered users of the investigated platform. Second, they have participated in the task of the crowdsourcing platform. Using the sampling method of snowballing, we finally got 20 valid responses.

The interview is divided into two parts: initial participation and sustained participation. The process of motivational factors selection includes: (1) using NVIVO content analysis software to extract the processing text; (2) conducting frequency accumulation based on the extracted elements.

RESULTS ANALYSIS

Based on the Fogg behavior model, the elements in each antecedent factor are identified.

- Motivation: curiosity, interest, learning, get positive feedback, confidence, feedback seeking, give help, peer recognition, mission, achievement, responsibility, social interaction, friends making.
- Ability: time, physical ability, IT knowledge level, domain knowledge level.
- Trigger: material reward, honorary reward, interface reminder, signal.

The antecedents of initial participation: high motivation, high trigger, and low ability. The antecedents of sustained participation: medium or high motivation, high ability, and low trigger. In both initial and sustained participation, the motivation keeps high, while the level of ability changes largely. (see Figure 1).

We discuss the results further. The elements of trigger remain unchanged in the two stages. The high-frequency elements of motivation and ability are quite different in the two stages. In the early stage, the elements of motivation are mainly influenced by physiological and psychological primitive dynamics

Initial Participation Sustained Participation

Figure 1. Effects of MAT.

such as interest and curiosity. The elements of ability are mainly influenced by knowledge related IT. In the late stage, motivation is mainly influenced by social attributes such as responsibility and sense of achievement. The elements of ability are mainly influenced by domain knowledge, such as Classical Chinese ability.

IMPLICATIONS

This paper has theoretical implications. First, this paper identifies a combination of the antecedents and builds time series model of digital humanities crowdsourcing tasks, which extends the Fogg behavior model and provides a theoretical basis for subsequent research. Second, the theoretical model proposed in this study can be used to discriminate the participation stages, based on which interventions can be given to promote further participation.

This study has practical implications. First, social interactions and incentives should be encouraged to foster participants' social responsibility and sense of belonging, which is conducive for their sustained participation. Second, for platform designers, the feedback function should be added in order to promote social interactions and build knowledge communities. Third, since motivation, ability and trigger act differently in initial and sustained participation, different strategies should be taken to improve the three factors in order to increase initial and sustained participation in crowdsourcing tasks.

ACKNOWLEDGMENTS

This work is supported by National Social Science Youth Foundation in China (Grant No. 17CTQ001).

REFERENCES

Carletti L, Giannachi G, Price D, et al. (2013). *Digital humanities and crowdsourcing: An exploration*. Museums and the Web, Portland, Portland, OR.

Doan, A., Ramakrishnan, R., & Halevy, A. Y. (2011). Crowdsourcing systems on the world-wide web. *Communications of the ACM, 54*(4), 86–96.

Fogg, B. J. (1999). Persuasive technologies. *Communications of the ACM, 42*(5), 27–29.

Hamari J., Koivisto J., & Pakkanen T. (2014). *Do persuasive technologies persuade? A review of empirical studies*. In International Conference on Persuasive Technology, May 2014, Padua, Italy (pp. 118-136).

Ridge, M. (2013). *Designing successful digital humanities crowdsourcing projects*. Lincoln, NE.

Terras, M. M. (2015). *Companion to digital humanities—Crowdsourcing in the digital humanities* (pp. 420–439). Oxford: Blackwell.

Xuanhui, Z., Yuxiang, Z., & Xiaokang, S. (2018). Exploring participants' motivations in sustained stage of citizen science projects in digital humanities domain: A case study on transcribe sheng. *Document, Informaiton & Knowledge*, (3), 16–25.

Disciplinary Comparisons of Academic Social Networking Site Use by Chinese Researchers

Weiwei Yan
Wuhan University,
Wuhan, China
yanww@whu.edu.cn

Yin Zhang
Kent State University,
Kent, OH, USA
yzhang4@kent.edu

ABSTRACT

This poster showcases recent research on disciplinary comparisons within the academic social networking site ResearchGate (RG). It aims to depict how users from top Chinese universities utilize the site across disciplines and how researchers from a non-English speaking country embrace the academic social networking platform for scholarly communication.

KEYWORDS

Social web; communication patterns; collaboration; China

INTRODUCTION

Discipline differences have already been examined as widely existing in online user behavior (Bosman & Kramer, 2016). Previous studies have found that disciplinary distributions are the most unbalanced aspect of academic social networking sites (ASNSs), but also the most distinguishing aspects of these academic platforms (Li, He, Zhang, Geng, & Zhang, 2018; Martín-Martín, Orduna-Malea, Ayllón, & López-Cózar, 2016; Ortega, 2017). For example, ResearchGate (RG), one of the leading ASNSs, was used more than Academia.edu in all areas except the arts & humanities (Kim, 2018; Mikki, Zygmuntowska, Gjesdal, & Al Ruwehy, 2015; Ortega, 2015). However, previous research has rarely investigated cultural differences; it is also unclear how researchers from non-English speaking countries embrace and use RG and whether there are any differences across disciplines. The study in this poster chooses top Chinese universities for empirical analysis and aims to fill these research gaps.

METHODS

This study collected data using a website crawler (train crawler) from public RG user profile pages from 21 Chinese research universities based on a combination of top 20 universities from Wu Shu-lian Chinese University Research Ranking (Tencent Education, 2016) and Chinese First-Class University Ranking (NSEAC, 2016). The data collection and processing procedure is illustrated in Figure 1. The data collection took place in September 2016 and included 116,034 users affiliated with the sample Chinese universities, of whom 49,827 (42.94%) were seen as active on RG (i.e., RG score ≥ 0.01). Web of Science research areas (Arts & Humanities, Life Sciences & Biomedicine, Physical Sciences, Social Sciences, and Technology) and a cross-disciplinary category (Multiple Disciplines) were used for

82nd Annual Meeting of the Association for Information Science & Technology | Melbourne, Australia | 19–23 October, 2019

DOI: 10.1002/pra2.00192

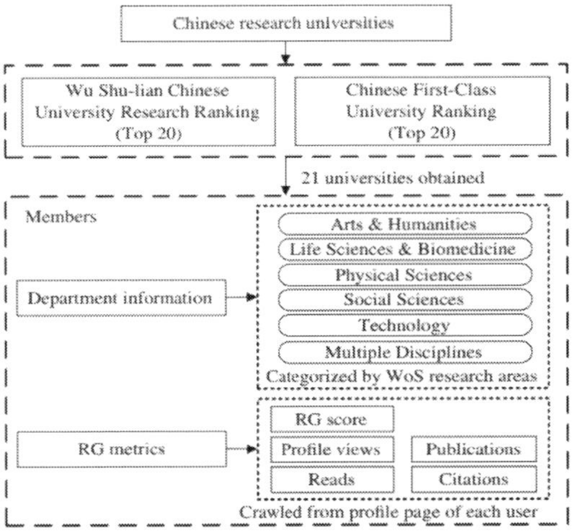

Figure 1. The data collection and processing process.

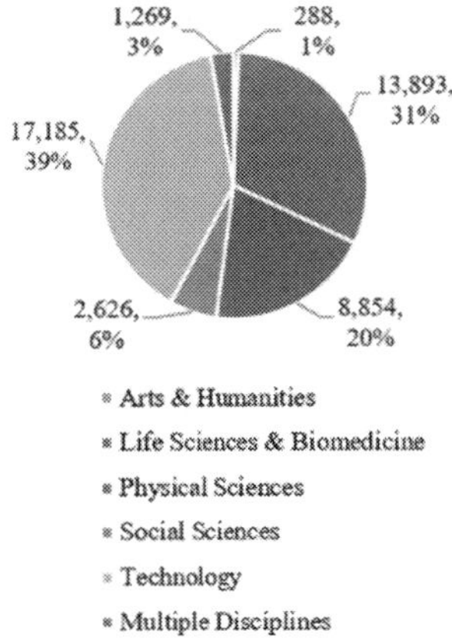

Figure 2. Sample structure (users by discipline).

Discipline	RG score		Profile views		Publications		Reads		Citations	
	Mean	SD	Mean	SD	Mean	SD	Mean	SD	Mean	SD
Arts & humanities	10.64	10.27	112.66	242.65	22.14	45.65	31.43	61.17	6.21	9.15
Life sciences & biomedicine	15.90	10.27	151.77	353.53	22.13	43.03	36.27	88.29	9.54	24.38
Physical sciences	**16.09**	11.31	**185.56**	354.58	**28.79**	62.00	31.61	44.97	8.51	13.48
Social sciences	10.10	9.11	132.68	287.94	16.75	46.51	**41.11**	57.93	**11.49**	203.26
Technology	13.46	10.52	160.21	307.53	27.13	58.75	32.14	46.47	6.37	19.57
Multiple disciplines	16.01	11.24	181.60	268.69	25.84	45.00	38.60	41.91	9.33	16.14
Total	14.61	10.68	161.31	330.22	25.20	53.95	34.05	63.12	8.19	53.31
Between group Sig.	.000***		.000***		.000***		.000***		.000***	

Table 1. The overall statistics of the disciplinary comparisons.

the discipline categorization according to the department information of each user's RG profile. After excluding users without department information, the final sample of 44,145 (38.04%) users was formulated for disciplinary analysis. The discipline distribution of the sample is shown in Figure 2. Finally, the disciplinary comparison was conducted using the crawled RG metrics from each user's public RG profiles, including RG score, profile views, publications, reads per publication, and citations per publication.

FINDINGS

The preliminary results show noticeable and significant discipline differences among RG users from top Chinese universities. As shown in Figure 2, Technology and Life Sciences & Biomedicine are the two disciplines with the most users in RG. Table 1 highlights the main RG metrics comparisons by discipline. Physical Sciences users tend to have a higher reputation score, more profile views, and publications in RG, while Social Sciences users receive more reads and citations. It is also worth noting that compared to the metrics of their U.S. counterparts reported in a previous study (Yan & Zhang, 2018), these metrics of the Chinese top universities are mostly lower except the "reads" metric from Chinese Social Sciences.

CONCLUSION

The study found discipline differences in RG use by researchers from Chinese universities. For example, application-oriented disciplines such as Technology tend to embrace the international ASNS. The higher degree of internationalization in Physical Sciences also encourages researchers to better utilize RG to reach a wider audience for scholarly communication, collaboration, and reputation promotion. This study contributes to research efforts in discipline characteristics in ASNSs such as RG, especially by top Chinese research universities. The findings have practical implications for Chinese universities to promote ASNS use with considerations for the disciplinary context, as well as how they can stimulate digital scholarship and facilitate cross-disciplinal and cross-national interactions and collaborations. Future research directions will be discussed at the presentation.

REFERENCES

Bosman, J., & Kramer, B. (2016). Swiss army knives of scholarly communication - ResearchGate, Academia, Mendeley and others. *Figshare*. https://doi.org/10.6084/m9.figshare.4290428.v1

Kim, Y. (2018). An empirical study of biological scientists' article sharing through ResearchGate: Examining attitudinal, normative, and control beliefs. *Aslib Journal of Information Management, 70*(5), 458–480.

Li, L., He, D., Zhang, C., Geng, L., & Zhang, K. (2018). Characterizing peer-judged answer quality on academic Q&A sites: A cross-disciplinary case study on ResearchGate. *Aslib Journal of Information Management, 70*(3), 269–287.

Martín-Martín, A., Orduna-Malea, E., Ayllón, J. M., & López-Cózar, E. D. (2016). *The counting house: measuring those who count: Presence of bibliometrics, scientometrics, informetrics, webometrics and altmetrics in the Google Scholar Citations, ResearcherID, ResearchGate, Mendeley & Twitter.* (EC3 Working Papers No. 21). Retrieved from https://arxiv.org/ftp/arxiv/papers/1602/1602.02412.pdf

Mikki, S., Zygmuntowska, M., Gjesdal, Ø. L., & Al Ruwehy, H. A. (2015). Digital presence of Norwegian scholars on academic network sites—where and who are they? *PloS ONE, 10*(11), e0142709.

Ortega, J. L. (2015). Disciplinary differences in the use of academic social networking sites. *Online Information Review, 39*(4), 520–536.

Ortega, J. L. (2017). Toward a homogenization of academic social sites: A longitudinal study of profiles in Academia.edu, Google Scholar Citations and ResearchGate. *Online Information Review, 41*(6), 812–825.

Yan, W., & Zhang, Y. (2018). Research universities on the ResearchGate social networking site: An examination of institutional differences, research activity level, and social networks formed. *Journal of Informetrics, 12*(1), 385–400.

Designing Effective Knowledge Presentation Techniques for Large Digital Collections

Yejun Wu
School of Library and Information Science,
Louisiana State University,
Baton Rouge, Louisiana, USA
wuyj@lsu.edu

Seungwon Yang
School of Library and Information Science,
Center for Computation & Technology,
Louisiana State University,
Baton Rouge, Louisiana, USA
seungwonyang@lsu.edu

ABSTRACT

We are developing a prototype knowledge presentation system for enhancing the access to, and use of, large digital document collections. We have started a preliminary user interface design for our prototype system which will employ the state-of-the-art knowledge visualization techniques. The techniques, which will be based on knowledge extraction and interactive visualization, will also be tested on open digital text document collections.

KEYWORDS

Knowledge presentation; visualization; large text collection

ASIS&T THESAURUS

Knowledge organization systems; Prototypes

INTRODUCTION

We are developing a knowledge presentation prototype system for enhancing access to digital document collections. We have started a preliminary UI design for our prototype system which will be based on knowledge extraction and interactive visualization techniques. In this study, we attempt to address the following questions: Can a knowledge presentation tool better support users access and use digital document collections than the regular browsing and searching systems? If the answer is yes, what features of the knowledge presentation tool may be most desired?

NOVELTY AND SIGNIFICANCE OF STUDY

Libraries are building and providing access to more digital repositories. Digital collections in libraries are expanding as the "idea of [a] 'collection' has expanded from the library and catalogue-bound holdings…to a concentric collection model which situates discovery and access within the entire biblioblogosphere, which are merging through mass digitisation and open discovery" (Booth, McDonald, & Tiffen, 2010, p. 2). These digital collections are mainly accessed by browsing and/or searching. Current discovery layer interfaces of digital collections are equivalent across major vendors (e.g., EBSCO, SirsiDynix Enterprise, and WorldCat) as all vendors have adopted a keyword searching interface. However, libraries may not rely only on a catalogue as an end-user discovery tool, since there is a belief "that the OPAC is dead" and that they should "not encourage users to start their search in a local library catalogue" (Kortekaas & Kramer, 2014, p. 248).

Fortunately, text/data mining and visualization can be used to facilitate access to information (Julien, 2015). The main benefit of information visualization is in "its ability to visualize data, communicating information clearly and effectively" and "in a more intuitive way" (Friedman, 2008). In the current interfaces for digital collections in libraries, the knowledge content contained in the digital collections are not revealed, and the relationships between topics/keywords and their associated topics/keywords are ignored. We aim to design a knowledge presentation system to reveal the knowledge content of a potentially large digital document collection, and hypothesize that it will improve the access and use of the document collections.

BRIEF LITERATURE REVIEW

Scholars in Library and Information Science have demonstrated the usefulness of information visualization techniques for managing digital collections in libraries (Chen, 2017). In Computer Science, multiple studies investigated more effective presentations of topics. For example, Hall, Jurafsky, and Manning (2008) emphasized that it is important for human analysts to be able to identify and validate the latent topics discovered within a large collection of text documents more efficiently through the use of visualizations. The visualization of topic structures for browsing (Julien, 2015) and the challenges of visualizing knowledge structures were also studied as well (Lin & Ahn, 2013). However, only a few have studied the usefulness of visual presentation for the *knowledge* extracted from a digital collection. It is still not known whether and to what extent a knowledge presentation (i.e., topics and their relationships) may help browsing, searching, and using large digital collections in libraries. Thus, it is necessary to study effective

82nd Annual Meeting of the Association for Information Science & Technology | Melbourne, Australia | 19–23 October, 2019

DOI: 10.1002/pra2.00193

knowledge presentation techniques for enhancing the access to and use of digital collections.

DESIGN AND DISCUSSIONS

The knowledge nuggets (i.e., topics and their relationships) will be extracted from documents using techniques such as Named Entity Recognition, POS-tagging, etc. They can be presented in both tabular and graphical formats (Wu, 2016) so that users could effectively identify what knowledge can be found in the collection. The knowledge nuggets can be displayed together with retrieved documents. Regarding knowledge browsing, we can apply the famous principle in visual information seeking—the Shneiderman's mantra of "overview first, zoom and filter, then details-on-demand" (Shneiderman, 1997). Our UI shows an overview network graph of all the knowledge nuggets first (Figure 1), and then users can expand any entity (node) on the graph to zoom (Figure 2) and further select the entities of their interest. The details of the selected knowledge nuggets are then presented on the UI. Cluttering of nodes may force the users to repeatedly zoom-in and -out in multiple areas of the large knowledge graph to identify and have a clear view of entities of their interests.

Figure 3 shows an initial UI design of our prototype. The components of the UI include a search box, and the four views to present the search results in multiple ways: (A) Network View presents the knowledge nuggets in a collection as a network graph; (B) Tabular View lists data as a spreadsheet visualization; (C) List View lists knowledge nuggets found from searching in the order of their significance; and (D) Content View presents the textual content of a document which is associated with a selected knowledge nugget.

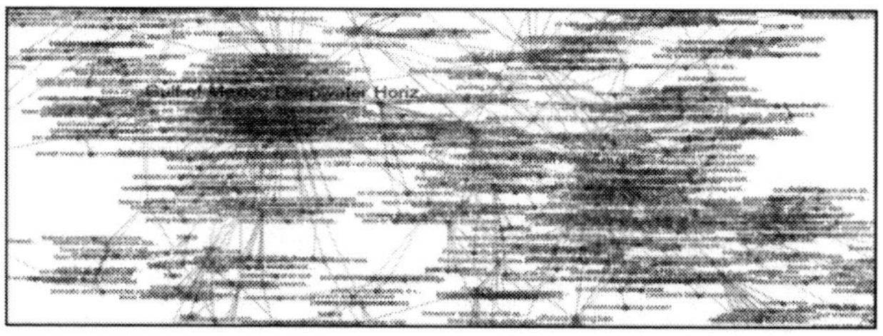

Figure 1. Visualization of 5,000 oil spill related topics and their relations (Source: Wu and Bai 2017).

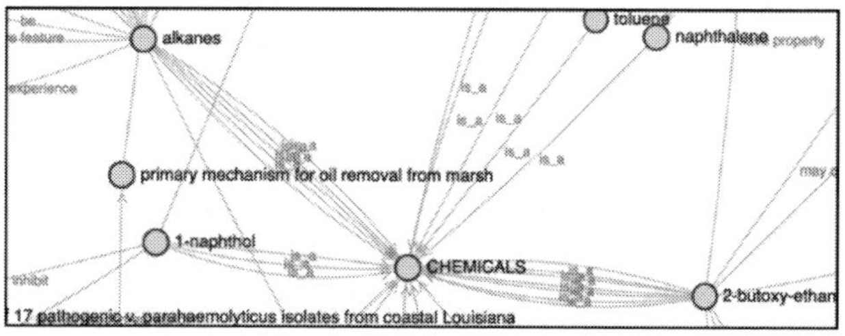

Figure 2. Chemicals and associated concepts and relations (Source: Wu, Lehman and Dunaway 2015).

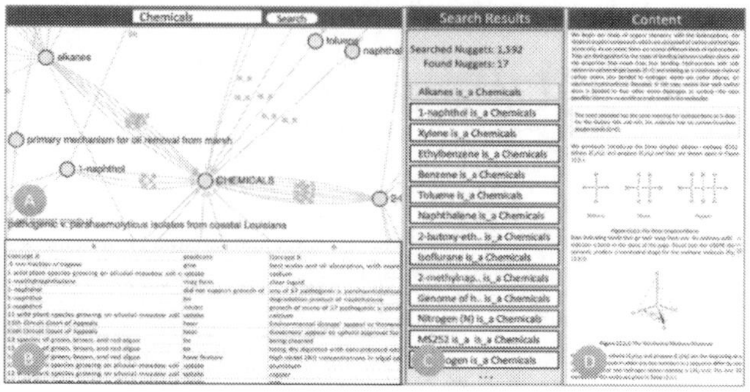

Figure 3. User interface design of the prototype system: (A) network view; (B) tabular view; (C) list view; and (D) content view. Note: "is_a" is a normalized relation type.

JavaScript libraries and MongoDB databases will be used for implementing the prototype.

CONCLUSION, IMPLICATION AND FUTURE STUDY

This research aims to develop an open-source prototype system of knowledge presentation to support access to, and use of, digital collections. Our prototype system will be further developed to incorporate not only text but also multimedia content as well. It will also be tested on various digital library collections. The fully developed system may potentially have a significant national impact on the capacities of libraries to provide enhanced access to digital document collections to diverse users.

REFERENCES

Booth, M., McDonald, S., & Tiffen, B. (2010). *A new vision for university libraries: Toward 2015*. In VALA 2010.

Chen, H. M. (2017). Information visualization. *Library Technology Reports*, *53*(3).

Friedman, V. (2008, January). Data visualization and infographics. Smashing Magazine.

Hall, D., Jurafsky, D., & Manning, C. (2008). *Studying the history of ideas using topic models*. In EMNLP 08.

Julien, C.-A. (2015). Navigating large topic structures: the metaphor of exploring physical space. In R. P. Smiraglia & H. Lee (Eds.), *Ontology for Knowledge Organization* (pp. 107–132). Ergon-Verlag.

Kortekaas, S., & Kramer, B. (2014). Thinking the unthinkable – doing away with the library catalogue. *Insights*, *27*(3), 244–248.

Lin, X., & Ahn, J. (2013). *Challenges of knowledge structure visualization*. In Proceedings of the Int'l UDC Seminar (The Hague, 24-25, October 2013) (pp. 73-87).

Shneiderman, B. (1997). A grander goal: A thousand-fold increase in human capabilities. *Educom Review*, *32*(6), 4–10.

Wu, Y. (2016). *Oil spill impacts: Taxonomic and ontological approaches*. CRC Press.

"Active Followers": An Emerging Role of Information Behaviour Among Group Holiday Makers

Edwin Mouda Ye
School of Information Technology & Mathematical Sciences, University of South Australia, Australia
mouda.ye@mymail.unisa.edu.au

Jia Tina Du
School of Information Technology & Mathematical Sciences, University of South Australia, Australia
tina.du@unisa.edu.au

Helen Ashman
School of Information Technology & Mathematical Sciences, University of South Australia, Australia
helen.ashman@unisa.edu.au

Preben Hansen
Department of Computer and Systems Sciences, Stockholm University, Sweden
preben@dsv.su.se

Songshan (Sam) Huang
School of Business and Law, Edith Cowan University, Australia
s.huang@ecu.edu.au

Marianna Sigala
School of Management, University of South Australia, Australia
marianna.sigala@unisa.edu.au

ABSTRACT

In an era of information overload, people often work together on information-intensive projects. Group holidaying is such an example where people plan and conduct trips together. In this poster paper we present preliminary findings from an ongoing investigation of collaborative information behaviour of group holidaymakers. Through a grounded-theory approach, preliminary findings show that not all members of the travel group engage equally in the information search. A role labelled "active followers" is identified and the role-taker's contribution to the group's information seeking and decision-making is discussed. This paper calls for attention to heterogeneity within collaborating groups and invites further discussion of research into this topic in information science community.

KEYWORDS

Collaborative information behaviour; information seeking; tourism; role

INTRODUCTION

Information behaviour is increasingly studied from a collaborative perspective. While working in groups, people often assume various roles in contributing to the overall team performance. Factors including search competence, domain expertise have been identified to impact role designation within collaborative search tasks. Accordingly, several team role configurations have been proposed to help with team performance (Shah, Pickens, & Golovchinsky, 2010) However, there is a lack of understanding of how different roles are assumed voluntarily by members of a collaborating group in an unsupervised environment. In addition, other possible factors such as relationships among the members and dominance in the team remain understudied in exiting research. Furthermore, existing studies have not sufficiently addressed how these roles shift across search sessions (Tamine & Soulier, 2015). To achieve personalised support for heterogeneous group members on information seeking and decision-making, it is important to understand what team role collaborator take in real-life situations beyond search tasks but larger information-intensive projects (Elbeshausen, Mandl, & Womser-Hacker, 2019).

Trip-planning and travelling is an obvious example of collaborative information behaviour (CIB), where travel mates need to work together in information searching, sensemaking and decision-making while planning and conducting their holiday (Karunakaran, Reddy, & Spence, 2013; Ye et al., 2019). This leisure activity provides a rich context for researchers to investigate the various roles of collaborative information behaviour in non-work situations and everyday life.

In this paper, we highlight one interesting role "active follower" from our ongoing study on group dynamics of collaborative information behaviour during group holidays from China to Australia. We seek to address the research question: *What is the role of "active follower" in CIB for group holidays?* The poster will illustrate the role of "active followers" in travel groups and invites discussion on the contribution and influence of such roles in a group in leisure situations.

METHODS

This study applied a grounded theory approach to explore the understudied leisure situations of CIB. Semi-structured interviews were conducted with eight travel groups of Chinese

82nd Annual Meeting of the Association for Information Science & Technology | Melbourne, Australia | 19–23 October, 2019

DOI: 10.1002/pra2.00194

tourists to Australia. The participants were asked to explain their roles in the group holiday, detailing their actions and responsibilities during the trip, and reflect on the contribution of the remainder of the group. Two interview sessions were conducted one week before their trips and one week after they return respectively, with the aim of catching the nuances of CIB across time and space.

Data reported in this paper were generated from 23 individual interview sessions, each lasting 30-60 minutes. All adult participants were aged between 25 and 35 years old, with 58% males and 42% females. At least one traveller from each travel group participated in two interview sessions, during which actions and thoughts of their travel mates were also reported.

Group	Group composition	Group size	"Active followers"
A	Couple	2	Yes
B	Couple	2	No
C	Family with one child	3	Yes
D	Two families each with one child	6	Yes
E	One couple with three colleagues	5	Yes
F	Friends	2	No
G	Friends	2	Yes
H	Couple	2	Yes

Table 1. Profile of the participating travel groups.

All interviews were first audio-taped, then fully transcribed into over 200 A4 pages of text. A constructivist point of view of grounded theory (Charmaz, 2006) were applied in data analysis.

RESULTS

Only 2 out of 8 travel groups exhibited highly collaborative searching behaviour, in which much of the searching activities were conducted by all members of the group. In the other 6 groups, at least one member remained idle in retrieving information, hence tagged "followers". However, they were not irrelevant in sensemaking and decision-making during the trip. This role is thus labelled "active followers" and their engagement in CIB during the group holiday is reflected in the following aspects.

Enlisting Information Search Tasks of Travel Mates

Through expressing their 1) personal constraints or 2) travel preferences, "active followers" influence their travel mates' information search. This could be done explicitly through communication, or implicitly through knowing each others' circumstances from previous travel experiences. For instance, while choosing accommodation for their trip to Melbourne, participant H1 mentioned she was looking particularly for hotels with gym facilities as her partner normally exercised in the morning regardless of holidays or work.

Choosing from Alternatives Generated in the Group

Often during the planning of the trip, a pool of alternatives will be generated on a certain topic. It is observed that in this situation, "active followers" can end up as the one making the choice, as a way of reaching consensus, despite the absence of their input into the search. C1 described such a scenario when choosing a restaurant in which to dine.

> *He asked first what I wanted for dinner, after I said 'whatever', he started searching on his own. A while later he showed me a list of must-eats in Sydney on his computer display and asked me to check if I fancy any of those. I made the choice and we went for dinner at that Korean barbeque.*

Approving Proposed Ideas in Decision-Making

When those who performed most of the search proposed ideas within the groups, approval from "active followers" appeared appreciated and sometimes even important. For example, based on extensive research, participant D1 proposed not to visit Brisbane due to the tight schedule. He noted that although many of his mates travelling with him did not search or know much about the destination, he felt more certain to exclude Brisbane from the trip after the others gave their consent.

CONCLUSION AND FUTURE WORK

In tourism studies, research has noted the phenomenon of "social surrogate" (Stone, 2016), where members of travel groups delegate their mates to choose where to dine or visit. Despite seldom being involved in active searching for tourism information, "active followers" identified in this study are not completely idle in the group's information seeking and decision-making process. From a marketing standpoint, it is suggested that when providing tourism information, both searchers and the "active followers" need to be impressed to reach successful purchase persuasion. Furthermore, it is important in future research to explore how different roles differ in information processing, sensemaking and decision-making as well as details of group dynamics where "active followers" are present. With an enhanced understanding of how they work with the rest of the group, specific guidelines can be provided to assist in personalised collaborative information behaviour in similar situations, such as family purchases.

ACKNOWLEDGMENTS

This research work is supported by the Australian Research Council DECRA Grant and the University of South Australia Research Themes Investment Scheme Development Fund.

REFERENCES

Charmaz, K. (2006). *Constructing grounded theory: A practical guide through qualitative analysis*. Sage.

Elbeshausen, S., Mandl, T., & Womser-Hacker, C. (2019). Role-specific behaviour patterns in collaborative information seeking. *Information Research, 24*(1) isic1831.

Karunakaran, A., Reddy, M. C., & Spence, P. R. (2013). Toward a model of collaborative information behavior in organizations. *Journal of the American Society for Information Science and Technology*, *64*(12), 2437–2451.

Shah, C., Pickens, J., & Golovchinsky, G. (2010). Role-based results redistribution for collaborative information retrieval. *Information Processing and Management*, *46*, 773–781.

Stone, M. J. (2016). Deciding not to choose: Delegation to social surrogates in tourism decisions. *Tourism Management*, *57*, 168–179.

Tamine, L., & Soulier, L. (2015). *Understanding the impact of the role factor in collaborative information retrieval.* In Proceedings of the 24th ACM International on Conference on Information and Knowledge Management (pp. 43–52).

Ye, E. M., Du, J. T., Hansen, P., Ashman, H., Sigala, M., & Huang, S. S. (2019). *Young Chinese tourists' motivations to engage in collaborative information behaviour for group holidays.* In Proceedings of the 23rd Pacific Asia Conference on Information Systems.

Stages of Change in Smoking Cessation and Health Information Behavior

Yong Jeong Yi
Library and Information Science,
Sungkyunkwan University,
Seoul, South Korea
redpapa01@skku.edu

Seo Jin Nam
Library and Information Science,
Sungkyunkwan University,
Seoul, South Korea
namsj0327@gmail.com

ABSTRACT

The study aimed at investigating the health information behavior of consumers who attempt to quit smoking and analyzing the effects of the information obtained on health behavior changes. The researchers interviewed 35 college students who were in different stages of smoking cessation for seven months. The study participants in precontemplation or contemplation stages tended to demonstrate passive information-seeking modes, whereas the participants in more advanced stages tended to perform active and direct information-seeking. The participants in these stages tended to search more for professional information or firsthand experiences related to pros and cons as well as strategies for smoking cessation. The findings identified the different cognitive or affective effects of the information on individuals at the discrete stages. In particular, the study bridges the gaps of the research that focuses on information behavior related to changes of addictive health behavior by applying the transtheoretical model (TTM) to the concepts of health information behavior.

KEYWORDS

Health Information-Seeking Behavior; Transtheoretical Model; Stages of Change; Smoking Cessation; Consumer Health Information; Health Behavior Change

ASIS&T THESAURUS

Information behavior; Longitudinal studies; Qualitative analysis

INTRODUCTION

One of the biggest challenges to modify addictive behaviors, such as smoking, is that it is difficult for individuals to identify their particular needs to cope with related temptations (Hirvonen, Huotari, Niemelä, & Korpelainen, 2012). Despite the importance of information intervention for needs of consumers in modifying addictive behaviors, there is limited research on how individuals interact with health information to change their behavior. The present study, thus, aims at investigating the health information behavior of consumers who attempt to quit and the effects of the information on health behavior changes.

82nd Annual Meeting of the Association for Information Science & Technology | Melbourne, Australia | 19–23 October, 2019

DOI: 10.1002/pra2.00195

THEORETICAL FRAMEWORK

The study employed the transtheoretical model (TTM), also called Stages of Change (Prochaska & Diclemente, 1983), to understand health information behavior of consumers who attempt to stop smoking. TTM is composed of five key constructs: 1) five stages of change (precontemplation, contemplation, preparation, action, maintenance), 2) 10 processes of change, 3) decisional balance, 4) self-efficacy, and 5) temptations. Five stages of change depict the progress that individuals move through to modify their health behavior. The 10 processes of change are interventions that involve cognitive and affective mechanisms classified into two categories, experiential processes (consciousness-raising, self-reevaluation, dramatic relief, environmental reevaluation, social liberation) and behavioral processes (self-liberation, counterconditioning, stimulus control, reinforcement management, helping relationships).

METHODS

The study recruited a total of 35 college students in their 20s; Precontemplation (N = 6), contemplation (N = 4), preparation (N = 9), action (N = 11), and maintenance (N = 5). For seven months (December 2017~ July 2018), researchers used semi-structured intensive interviews, each of which took about 30 minutes; one interview for participants in each of the the precontemplation, contemplation, and preparation stages, and six monthly interviews with participants in each of the action and maintenance stages. To analyze the textual data obtained from the interviews, the study conducted content analysis employing open coding, axial coding, and theoretical notes.

FINDINGS

Most of the study participants in the precontemplation or contemplation stage passively obtained information about negative health effects of smoking, whereas the participants in preparation, action, and maintenance stages performed active and direct information-seeking utilizing diverse information sources. The 10 processes of change and the other constructs were identified as the *effects* of information obtained, as presented in Table 1.

Information/*Effects*	**Sources**
Precontemplation stage	
Anti-smoking campaign: testimony of celebrity who died from lung cancer *[consciousness-raising]* Severe health issues of a friend who smokes *[dramatic relief]*	Internet/Social media Traditional media (TV, radio, newspaper) Family/Friend Campus, army service, cigarette box
Contemplation stage	
Testimony of a friend who suffered from pneumothorax *[consciousness-raising, dramatic relief]* Pros & Cons of SC • Health/financial benefits • Withdrawal symptoms *[decisional balance]*	Internet/Social media (news, research article, YouTube) Family/Friend Campus, cigarette box Firsthand experience
Preparation stage	
Causal relationships between health issues and smoking • Ulcerative colitis, Impotence, Rhinitis, Cancer or lung damage *[consciousness-raising, dramatic relief]* Advice on reducing smoking *[self-liberation, self-efficacy]* Pros/cons of e-cigarettes *[self-liberation]* • SC programs *[social liberation, helping relationships]*	Internet/ Social media (news, research article, medical encyclopedia, community, blog, social Q&A) Healthcare expert, SC program, SC counseling websites Family, friends using e-cigarettes Army service, Campus
Action stage	
Behavior guidelines for coping with temptation *[counterconditioning, helping relationships, self-efficacy]* Socio-emotional support *[helping relationships]* Withdrawal symptoms *[consciousness-raising]* Health, financial, or social benefits *[consciousness-raising; environmental reevaluation]*	Internet/Social media (news, community, blog, healthcare center) Healthcare expert, SC program Family/Friend who attempted to or succeeded Poster
Maintenance stage	
Quantitative or visual data of health outcomes *[consciousness-raising]* Self-development, Introspection of one's state *[self-efficacy, counterconditioning]* Addiction *[self-reevaluation]*	Internet/Social media (news, blog, YouTube) Traditional media (book) Friend Counselor/SC program

Table 1. Health information and its effects.
***Note*. SC=Smoking cessation. Information is followed by the related processes of change (in italics).**

DISCUSSION & CONCLUSION

The study identified dynamic health information behavior and different effects of information on smoking cessation in individuals at the discrete stages. The findings support information acquisition as a motivator of health behavior changes (Hirvonen et al., 2012), and that five stages of change need particular information or techniques for smoking cessation at each stage (Prochaska, DiClemente, & Norcross, 1992). Regarding theoretical implications, the study extends the discussion of information-seeking to health behavior changes and bridges the research gap caused by lack of longitudinal or qualitative methods in the field of health information behavior. Furthermore, it provides practical insights into effective health information services or smoking cessation programs by suggesting information intervention strategies that meet the particular information needs at each smoking cessation stage.

ACKNOWLEDGMENTS

Authors gratefully acknowledge support by the Sungkyun Research Fund from Sungkyunkwan University (#S20172474000).

REFERENCES

Hirvonen, N., Huotari, M. L., Niemelä, R., & Korpelainen, R. (2012). Information behavior in stages of exercise behavior change. *Journal of the American Society for Information Science and Technology*, *63* (9), 1804–1819.

Prochaska, J. O., & Diclemente, C. C. (1983). Stages and processes of self-change of smoking: Toward an integrative model of change. *Journal of Consulting and Clinical Psychology*, *51*(3), 390–395.

Prochaska, J. O., DiClemente, C. C., & Norcross, J. C. (1992). In search of how people change: Applications to addictive behaviors. *American psychologist*, *47*(9), 1102–1114.

An Analysis of Physical Characteristics of Joseon Dynasty Books Using Statistical Approaches

Jaehyuk Yun
Department of Library and Information Science,
Sungkyunkwan University,
Seoul, Republic of Korea
seisiel@g.skku.edu

Yongjun Zhu
Department of Library and Information Science,
Sungkyunkwan University,
Seoul, Republic of Korea
yzhu@skku.edu

ABSTRACT

The study analyzes physical characteristics of Joseon Dynasty books using statistical analysis of cataloging metadata. ANOVA and Scheffe tests are used to understand the differences among books published in three different periods of Joseon Dynasty. The study reports statistical evidences on physical differences of Joseon Dynasty books and contributes to our understanding of the history of Joseon Dynasty books.

KEYWORDS

Joseon Dynasty; Book analysis; Analytical bibliography

ASIS&T THESAURUS

Bibliographic records; Descriptive metadata; Rare materials

INTRODUCTION

Human beings have been communicating knowledge and information through records for a long time. As one of the representative recording instruments, books are a physical form that includes the intellectual outcomes expressed in letters, and bibliography is a field of investigating, analyzing, and criticizing books (Carter & Barker, 2004). Especially, analytical bibliography plays an important role in finding the original form or text of literature and understanding the process of change through analyzing the characteristics and transitional process of the physical form of the book (Bowers, 1959).

Different from the general library cataloging metadata developed for the contemporary books, the old book cataloging metadata describes the physical form of old books in detail. In the case of Jon'gyeong'gak library, which is originated from the first university library of Joseon dynasty, 13 elements (40.6%) of the 32 metadata elements are related to various aspects of books' physical form. This enables us to analyze the old books quantitatively to identify characteristics of old books written in different times. Most studies on old books focus on analyzing limited number of books through the content analysis, and therefore, we have a limited understanding on the general characteristics of old books. Accordingly, this study aims to examine old books by analyzing their rich metadata and provide empirical evidence on physical characteristics of old books.

82nd Annual Meeting of the Association for Information Science & Technology | Melbourne, Australia | 19–23 October, 2019

DOI: 10.1002/pra2.00196

METHOD

The study analyzes cataloging metadata to investigate the physical characteristics of Joseon Dynasty books. Among the 14,246 books in Jon'gyeong'gak library, the analysis includes 3,696 books published during the Joseon Dynasty. The Joseon dynasty has more than 500-year history (1392-1910), which can be classified into various periods according to political and social situations: 3 periods by ruling forces, 3 periods by modernity, 4 periods by Japanese Invasion of Korea in 1592 and opening a port, and 5 periods by each century. In this study, we divide the data into three categories: early modern (1,275 books before 18th century), politics by in-powers (1,551 books in 19th century), and the Korean Empire (870 books in 1897-1910).

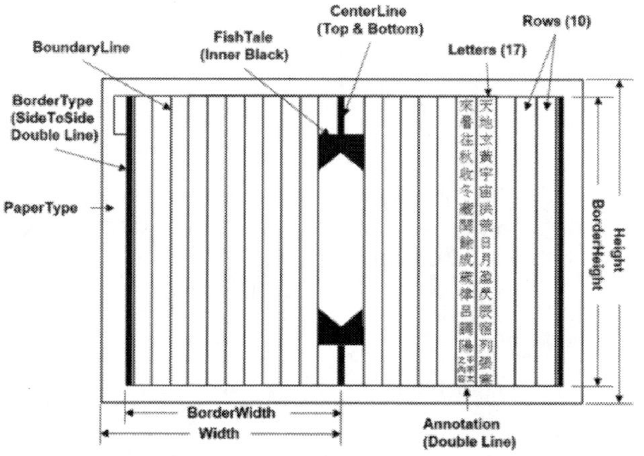

Figure 1. An example of metadata elements related to physical characteristics.

There are 13 metadata elements about physical characteristics, and we can divide them into two categories based on their value types: nominal scale and ratio scale. Boundary Line, Border Type, Center Line, Fish Tale, Annotation, and

Paper Type (see Figure 1) have nominal scale values. For example, there are three kinds of Annotation and their proportions are as follows: Double line (96.4%), Single line (3.2%), and Double line with headnote (0.4%). We can see that the frequency difference is extreme, and in the experimental data, most of nominal scale variables shows the same pattern. Therefore, it is difficult to obtain significant results, so the study focuses on the variables of ratio scale such as Chapter & Volume, Border Size, Rows & Letters, and Total Size, and subdivided the variables. We performed ANOVA (Analysis of Variance) because the publication period of the independent variable includes three categories and the physical characteristics corresponding to the dependent variable are suitable to compare the mean. Table 1 summarizes the variables used in the analysis.

Variables		Description
Independent	Age	Early Modern (EM)
		Politics by in-powers (PBI)
		Korean Empire (KE)
Dependent	Volume	Ratio Scale
	Border Height	Ratio Scale
	Border Width	Ratio Scale
	Rows	Ratio Scale
	Letters	Ratio Scale
	Total Height	Ratio Scale
	Total Width	Ratio Scale

Table 1. Independent and dependent variables.

RESULTS

To check whether the physical characteristics of the ancient books differ by time, we conducted ANOVA and Scheffe tests and the results are shown in Table 2. According to Table 2, the volume shows a significant difference only between PBI and KE, and the others showed significant differences in every pairs at the significance level of 0.05.

The volumes of books published in Korean Empire were fewer than those published earlier ($F = 4.097$, $p < 0.05$). The number of rows ($F = 21.337$, $p < 0.001$) and letters ($F = 60.735$, $p < 0.001$) differed by three periods, and especially there was a difference of 0.9 letters on average. The total height ($F = 86.557$, $p < 0.001$), total width ($F = 131.560$, $p < 0.001$), and the height of border ($F = 53.701$, $p < 0.001$) generally became smaller along with the time. The horizontal size of border ($F = 30.540$, $p < 0.001$) was also the smallest in 'Korean Empire' period, but it was larger in 'Politics by in-powers' period than in 'Early Modern' period.

VAR	Age			AVG	F value
	EM	PBI	KE		
Volume	3.81ab	3.92b	3.22a	3.72	4.097*
Rows	9.94 a	10.19 b	10.40 c	10.17	21.337 ***
Letters	19.165 a	20.024 b	20.942 c	20.0	60.735 ***
Border Width	16.216 b	16.669 c	15.920 a	16.341	30.540 ***
Border Height	22.514 b	22.963 c	21.555 a	22.469	53.701 ***
Total Width	33.620 c	23.659 b	20.062 a	26.248	131.56 0***
Total Height	36.562 c	33.570 b	29.525 a	33.648	86.557 ***
*p<.05, ***p<.001, Scheffe: a < ab < b, Scheffe: a < b < c					

Table 2. ANOVA-Scheffe results.

We can compare the average size differences for each period as shown in Figure 2.

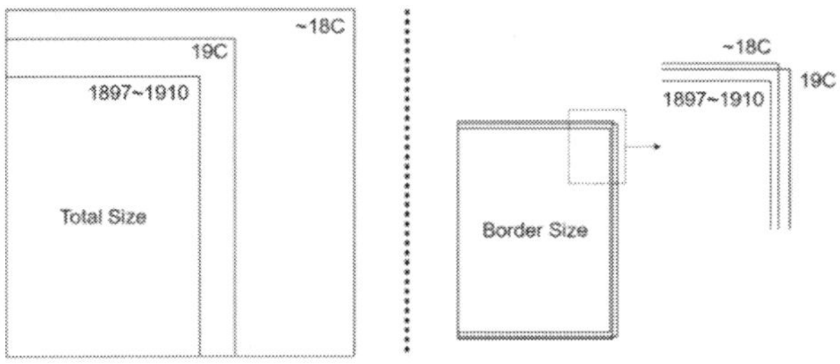

Figure 2. Average book size and border size.

CONCLUSION

The study investigated the differences of physical characteristics among the Joseon Dynasty books of different periods by performing statistical analysis on cataloging metadata. The results indicate that Volume, Rows, Letters, Border Size, and Total Size are significantly different for each period. In particular, there is a notable difference when we express the average total size by a figure. These results suggest that statistical and data-based analysis can be applied to the bibliographical study on old books.

REFERENCES

Bowers, F. (1959). The function of bibliography. *Library Trends*, *7*(4), 497–510.

Carter, J., & Barker, N. (2004). *ABC for book collectors* (8th ed.). New Castle, DE: Oak Knoll Press London: British Library.

The Antecedent and Consequence of Users' Satisfaction and Dissatisfaction With Information Seeking in Online Health Communities

Jinchao Zhang
School of Information Management, Wuhan University, Wuhan, China
jczhang@whu.edu.cn

Bo Luo
School of Information Management, Central China Normal University, Wuhan, China
luob@mail.ccnu.edu.cn

Fenfang Cao
School of Information Management, Wuhan University, Wuhan, China
fenfangcao@whu.edu.cn

ABSTRACT

With the improvement of individuals' health consciousness and health literacy, online health communities are employed as complementary sources by them to seek health-related information. Given dominant information seeking behavior focuses exclusively on satisfiers, although dissatisfiers may not simply be their opposites, the purpose of this study is to investigate the antecedent and consequence of individuals' satisfaction and dissatisfaction with information seeking in online health communities. A research model was developed based on information quality and two-factor theory. Information quality is the antecedent of users' satisfaction and dissatisfaction with seeking health information in online health communities. Individuals' continuance health information seeking behavior is taken as the consequence.

KEYWORDS

Satisfaction; Dissatisfaction; Online health communities; Continuance health information seeking behavior

ASIS&T THESAURUS

Internet information resources; Information behavior

INTRODUCTION

Online health communities (OHCs) are online communities that adopt the Web 2.0 model, leverage community wisdom, and organize information exchange in the form of asking and answering health-related questions (Gazan, 2011; Harper et al., 2008; Jin, 2009). They have become important sources of health information for general public and changed health information seeking behavior (Kanthawala, Vermeesch, Given, et al., 2016). Users can freely participate in OHCs to browse and seek for help to address their health-related issues. In practice, with the improvement of users' health consciousness and health literacy, users are capable of switching among different OHCs to maximize their benefits which might discontinue users' health information seeking in a specific OHC.

Users' satisfaction and dissatisfaction with health information seeking are their subjective perceptions which determine the subsequent behavior. Despite the increasing quality of information contributed to OHCs, the considerable variance in the quality of health information poses a significant challenge to effectively satisfy users' needs (Agichtein et al., 2008). Given the importance of information quality as a determinant of user satisfaction (DeLone & McLean, 2003), the relationship between information quality and users' satisfaction and dissatisfaction which in turn govern the continuance health information seeking behavior in OHCs will be investigated.

The research questions are (1) based on two-factor theory and the dimensions of information quality, how are these dimensions related to users' satisfaction and dissatisfaction? (2) do users' satisfaction and dissatisfaction mediate the relationship between the dimensions of health information quality and continuance health information seeking behavior?

THEORY BACKGROUND

Two-Factor Theory

The two-factor theory posits that an individual's motivation derives from satisfiers and dissatisfiers (Herzberg et al., 1959). According to this theory, satisfaction comes from motivational factors referring to the characteristics of working itself or content features. On the other hand, dissatisfaction is caused by hygiene factors referring to environment or contextual features. That is to say, satisfaction and dissatisfaction come from separate sets of factors, and they are not opposite concepts. What affects satisfaction does not directly associate with dissatisfaction, and vice versa. An individual can simultaneously be satisfied and dissatisfied with a service (Herzberg et al., 1993).

In recent years, the two-factor theory has been applied in many areas and activities such as library instruction, consumer motivation, web services, and knowledge sharing. Although not largely used in information seeking behavior research, the two-factor theory gives a considerable

82nd Annual Meeting of the Association for Information Science & Technology | Melbourne, Australia | 19–23 October, 2019

DOI: 10.1002/pra2.00200

explanatory power to understand the disconnection between factors leading to seeking or not seeking information in an online health community.

Information Quality

Users can benefit from OHCs participation only when an online health community provides information valued by them (Butler, 2001). High-quality information plays an important role in making better decisions for users. Low-quality information is distracting because it increases users' search and information processing costs (Gu et al., 2007), and then leads users to discontinue their seeking activities and withdraw from the communities (Stvilia et al., 2005). Information quality is considered as a multi-dimensional concept by researchers (Arazy & Kopak, 2011; Hilligoss & Rieh, 2008; Knight & Brun, 2005; Wang & Strong, 1996) in various context, including both subjective and objective aspects, i.e., completeness, accuracy, format, currency, reliability, relevancy and understandability (Lu, Zhang, Wu, et al., 2018; Wixom & Todd, 2005). They are also highly vital factors affecting users' information seeking behavior in OHCs.

RESEARCH MODEL

Given that user participation is voluntary in OHCs, it is a challenging issue to attract users to perpetuate ongoing health information seeking behavior. High-quality health information enhances the reputation of an online health community and user satisfaction, and can serve as a competitive tool to attract and retain users (Lin, 2008). This study investigates how the dimensions of information quality affects users' satisfaction and dissatisfaction in terms of completeness, format, accuracy, reliability, currency, relevance and understandability which in turn influence continuance health information seeking behavior.

The aim of this study is to develop a research model integrating the information quality and two-factor theory to study which dimensions of information quality drive users' satisfaction and dissatisfaction in OHCs and the consequence of these two factors in further. The proposed model identifies multi-dimensional information quality as predictors of users' continuance health information seeking behavior. The relationships between the constructs are depicted in the research model (see Figure 1.). The continuance health information seeking behavior expresses the likelihood that users will continue to seek health information in OHCs. Users' satisfaction and dissatisfaction are their subjective perceptions influenced by different dimensions of health information quality.

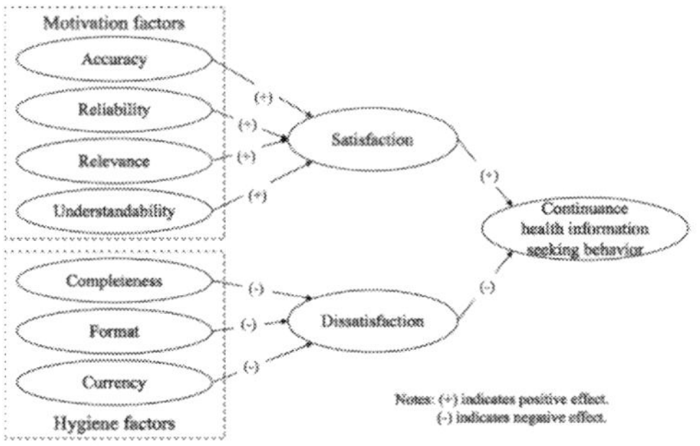

Figure 1. Research model.

CONCLUSION

Dominant health information seeking behavior focuses exclusively on motivation factors, although hygiene factors may not simply be their opposites. Two major research contributions can be made from this study. First, this study contributes to the existing literature on the continuance health information seeking behavior in OHCs by integrating users' satisfaction and dissatisfaction. Second, the dimensions of health information quality are classified as motivation factors and hygiene factors, which will advance our understanding the different effects of multi-dimensional information quality. A further research will be conducted to verify the relationships in this research model.

ACKNOWLEDGMENTS

This study is supported by the National Natural Science Foundation of China (Grant Numbers 71804136, 71874124, 71774126, 71573195) and the National Social Science Foundation of China (Grant Number 18CTQ025).

REFERENCES

Arazy, O., & Kopak, R. (2011). On the measurability of information quality. *Journal of the American Society for Information Science and Technology, 62*(1), 89–99.

DeLone, W. H., & McLean, E. R. (2003). The DeLone and McLean model of information systems success: A ten-year update. *Journal of Management Information Systems, 19*(4), 9–30.

Kanthawala, S., Vermeesch, A., Given, B., et al. (2016). Answers to health questions: Internet search results versus online health community responses. *Journal of Medical Internet Research, 18*(4), e95.

Lu, X., Zhang, R., Wu, W., et al. (2018). Relationship between internet health information and patient compliance based on trust: Empirical study. *Journal of Medical Internet Research, 20*(8), e253.

Wixom, B. H., & Todd, P. A. (2005). A theoretical integration of user satisfaction and technology acceptance. *Information Systems Research, 16*(1), 85–102.

Developing Community Phenotype Ontologies: Understanding Users' Preferences

Limin Zhang
University of Arizona, Tucson, AZ, U.S.A
liminz@email.arizona.edu

Zuleima Cota
University of Arizona, Tucson, AZ, U.S.A
zcota@email.arizona.edu

Hong Cui
University of Arizona, Tucson, AZ, U.S.A
hongcui@email.arizona.edu

Hsin-liang Chen
Missouri University of Science & Technology, Rolla, MO, U.S.A.
chenhs@mst.edu

Bruce Ford
University of Manitoba, Winnipeg, Canada
bruce.ford@umanitoba.ca

Joel Sach
Agriculture Agri-Food Canada, Ottawa, ON, Canada
joel.sach@aaf.ca

Jocelyn Pender
Agriculture Agri-Food Canada, Ottawa, ON, Canada
jocylin.pender@aaf.ca

James Macklin
Agriculture Agri-Food Canada, Ottawa, ON, Canada
james.macklin@aaf.ca

Anton Reznicek
University of Michigan, Ann Arbor, MI, U.S.A.
reznicek@umich.edu

Julian Starr
University of Ottawa, Ottawa, MB, Canada
julian.starr@uottawa.ca

ABSTRACT

This poster reports preliminary user-testing results on four different methods to add terms to a phenotype ontology. A total of 31 graduate students from UA iSchool and three senior botanists participated in two different experiments. Results suggest the Quick Form and WebProtege are preferred by biologists and WikiData and Wizard are not preferred for different reasons.

KEYWORDS

Ontology construction; user studies; phenotype data management; biodiversity informatics

ASIS&T Thesaurus

Knowledge organization systems, bioinformatics, user generated content

INTRODUCTION

Phenotypes are critical for describing species, studying function, and understanding organismal evolution, but only a very small amount of descriptive data are provided with clear semantics via ontological annotations. The lack of such computable data is due to the high cost of manual annotation, incomplete phenotype ontologies, and high inter-curator variations. We are investigating ways to enable biologists to directly contribute to ontology construction with the purpose of producing semantically clear computable phenotype data for large scale biological projects. Here we report preliminary findings on users' preferences for adding terms to their research community. Ontologies. Four methods were evaluated, Quick Form, Wizard, WikiData, and WebProtege. These methods cover the full range of the ontology construction landscape, from simple web-based forms, to a set of guided questions, an open knowledge base used by some biology ontologies, and a well-known editor designed for an ontology engineer.

Graphic-based ontology editors were not selected for this user study because our biologist collaborators had ruled out these options in our first project meeting.

RELATED WORK

Several other projects share the same goal as ours – to enable biological authors to produce computable data. These include TaxonWorks (http://taxonworks.org/) and Morph*D*Base (https://www.morphdbase.de/), but neither conducted usability research. Prior work that compared the usability of different ontology editors (e.g., Norta et al., 2010; Khondoker et al., 2010; Alatrish, 2013;) either tested only ontology experts or used tasks unconnected to phenotypes.

RESEARCH QUESTION

What are biology users' relative preferences among Quick Form, Wizard, WikiData, and WebProtege, in terms of the usability, the support for recording the full semantics of a

82nd Annual Meeting of the Association for Information Science & Technology | Melbourne, Australia | 19–23 October, 2019

DOI: 10.1002/pra2.00199

term, and biology users' confidence in their ability to use t method(s)?

RESEARCH DESIGN

The user interface of the four methods evaluated are at http://shark.sbs.arizona.edu/add2ontologymodular/public/leaf/hong/carex.

Thirty-six participants were recruited from a required graduate-level course in the UA iSchool and assigned arbitrarily into a Latin Square with four groups. Only completed the experiment. Participants first filled out a survey regarding their experience with controlled vocabulary editors and wikis. After watching a 3-6 minute video demo of each method, they rated them using a 5-point Likert-Scale in terms of their usability, their support for recording full semantics of a term, and the user's confidence in her ability of use the methods. Around three days later, they completed a hands-on task adding the term "leaf blade" to an ontology with over 2000 terms, followed by rating these methods again using the same scale. This task involved adding leaf blade's synonym, part of, and has part relationships with other existing terms or new terms.

In addition to the student experiment, three botanists at different career stages also participated in a group think-aloud experiment using the same "leaf blade" task to rate the four methods.

This usability study employs common biological knowledge that is familiar to the general public. More studies will be conducted to involve more advanced biology knowledge with biology students and other botanists as participants. Participants with diverse backgrounds help reveal different usability issues.

RESULTS

The sum of scores (ranks) of all 31 participants on the three aspects of the four methods are reported in Table 1. The "*" indicates a statistically significant Friedmann test at 99.9% confidence level on the ranks, meaning the ranks of the four tools were significantly different.

	Easy to use*	Helpfulness	Confidence*
Rankings after watching the video			
Quick form	108	80	112
Wizard	98	77	109
WebProtege	57	81	74
WikiData	47	72	69
Rankings after hands-on task			
Quick form	115	75	130
Wizard	90	88	110
WebProtege	65	86	93
WikiData	42	71	70

Table 1. Sum of student participants ranks.

The think-aloud session with botanists revealed similar preferences, but new interesting observations. Botanists agree that WikiData is the most challenging method. While agreeing that Quick Form is the easiest method, they recognize that it does not record computer consumable semantics of the terms and relationships. And for the latter task, all three botanists agree that a WebProtege-like tool has the potential. While students liked Wizard, botanists find the questions asked by Wizard too detailed.

User-method interaction logs recorded by the experiment platform and other questions in the surveys on the specific features of different methods will be analyzed in more depth in the near feature and discussed at the poster session during the ASIST meeting.

DISCUSSION

In terms of ease of use, the two rounds of ranking by student participants produced a similar result: Quick Form is the easiest, followed by Wizard and WebProtege, and WikiData was deemed the most difficult. The hands-on experience resulted in a slight adjustment in the scores of WebProtege (scored a bit higher) and Wizard (scored a bit lower), but did not change the overall ranking.

In terms of the methods' support/helpfulness for recording the full semantics of the terms, the scores are similar across different methods and the ranking is not statistically significant.

In terms of the user's confidence in applying the methods to add terms to ontologies, participants felt equally confident using Quick Form and Wizard, either before or after the hands-on task.

The three botanists' observation on the tools covered the ease of use, like the student participants, but went beyond. They acknowledged that WikiData's page-based organization schema does not provide the user with a full picture of all the terms in an ontology, and the process of adding a term could become rather involved (need to add several other terms and visit several other pages). While the users are guided by Wizard's questions, the detailed questions have the potential of inviting the user to over-think, thus rising the introduction of errors to the ontology. For many botanists, Quick Form is the preferred one, however, it cannot fulfill some botanists' demands to to convert the information collected by Quick Form to machine consumable semantics. They are also fond of WebProtege for several reasons: (1) WebProtege's class hierarchy shows all terms in an ontology upfront and this familiar set of the terms makes botanists feel at home right away. (2) WebProtege makes adding terms that are needed in asserting a new relationship easy – typing the needed term and it is added right on the spot.

CONCLUSION

Usability studies involving iSchool students and botanists show that Quick Form and WebProtege are preferred methods for users with limited knowledge of ontology construction.

ACKNOWLEDGMENTS

National Science Foundation Award 1661485.

REFERENCES

Alatrish, E. S. (2013). Comparison some of ontology. *Journal of Management Information Systems*, *8*(2), 018–024.

Khondoker, M. R. et al. (2010). *Comparing ontology development tools based on an online survey*. In WCE 2010, London, England.

Norta, A., et al. (2010). *Utility evaluation of tools for collaborative development and maintenance of ontologies*. In 14th IEEE IEDOCConference Workshops (pp. 207–214). https://doi.org/10.1109/EDOCW.2010.30

Investigating Roles of Social Value Orientation and Domain Knowledge in Crowdsourced Manuscript Transcription

Xuanhui Zhang
Nanjing University,
Nanjing, China
zhangxhdo@163.com

Yuxiang (Chris) Zhao
Nanjing University of
Science & Technology,
Nanjing, China
yxzhao@vip.163.com

Shijie Song
Nanjing University,
Nanjing, China
ssong@smail.nju.edu.cn

Qinghua Zhu
Nanjing University,
Nanjing, China
qhzhu@nju.edu.cn

ABSTRACT

Although prior literature has presented some attempts on crowdsourcing transcripts, research on how individual differences affect the cooperation level and the quality of crowdsourcing transcripts is limited. Drawing on theories of social value orientation and domain knowledge, the study proposes that participants' social value orientation and domain knowledge will have significant effects on the cooperation level and the quality of transcription in crowdsourced manuscript transcription. Meanwhile, an interaction effect will exist between social value orientation and domain knowledge.

KEYWORDS

Crowdsourced manuscript transcription; social value orientation; domain knowledge; cooperation level; the quality of transcription

ASIS&T THESAURUS

Humanities→Culture→Cultural heritage

INTRODUCTION

In the cultural heritage domain, the digitizing of historical manuscripts collected by various galleries, libraries, archives, and museums (short by GLAMs) is playing an extremely important role in the long-term preservation, dissemination and effective use of cultural heritage. Although advanced technologies such as optical character recognition (OCR) and deep learning have brought breakthroughs in the digitization of manuscripts, in many cases, performances are not satisfied due to some inevitable limitations, such as the paper oxidation, illegible handwriting, and the great variability in calligraphic style, etc.

Crowdsourced manuscript transcription is a typical crowdsourcing initiative in digital humanities, which harness the wisdom of crowds to do the knowledge-intensive tasks. However, traditional online crowdsourcing projects on manuscript transcription rely primarily on the individual efforts of volunteers rather than through collaborative approaches (Daniels, Holtze, Howard, & Kuehn, 2014). Prior work suggests that manuscript transcription is not an easy job and usually requires a lot of time, effort, and intellectual input from the public (Causer & Terras, 2014). Especially when the complexity of transcribing tasks is increasing, it is difficult to find sufficient and qualified volunteers to engage with the cultural heritage projects. To the best of our knowledge, so far there is no relevant research to examine the impact of individual differences on the performance of crowdsourcing projects in the cultural heritage domain. In this paper, a field experiment is conducted to explore the role of social value orientation and domain knowledge on the performance of Transcribe-Sheng project, a well-known crowdsourced manuscript transcription initiative in China. The study may shed light on recruiting qualified participants for crowdsourcing projects.

RELATED WORK AND HYPOTHESES

Crowdsourcing initiatives provide a convenient, efficient, and inexpensive way to digitize manuscripts through volunteer engagement. Crowdsourcing approach has been widely adopted in the context of manuscript transcription. Among them, quality control (or assessment) constitutes a central concern of manuscript transcription in crowdsourcing context (Moyle, Tonra, & Wallace, 2011).

So far, few researches have explored the characteristics of participants, for example, what types of transcribers are more likely to contribute high quality transcripts in such projects? Prior work has shown that social value orientation is an individual difference construct that is often examined in collaborative information studies. Specifically, social value orientation can reliably explain cooperative behavior in a variety of mixed motivation situations (Van Lange, De Bruin, Otten, & Joireman, 1997).

Meanwhile, manuscript transcription is an intellectually intensive task that requires some specific skills, such as the understanding of historical knowledge and various types of calligraphy. Domain knowledge can be defined as the degree of subject familiarity with participants (Ju, 2010). Previous research indicated that participants with relevant domain

82nd Annual Meeting of the Association for Information Science & Technology | Melbourne, Australia | 19–23 October, 2019

DOI: 10.1002/pra2.00197

knowledge usually provide high quality transcripts (Granell & Martinez-Hinarejos, 2017). Thus, we believe that domain knowledge plays an important role in affecting the task completion of crowdsourced manuscript transcription. The cooperation level and the quality of transcription will be examined as the proxy of task completion. We propose the related hypotheses as below:

H1: Participant's social value orientation will have a significant effect on their cooperation level (a) and the quality of transcription (b) in crowdsourced manuscript transcription.

H2: Participant's domain knowledge will have a significant effect on their cooperation level (a) and the quality of transcription (b) in crowdsourced manuscript transcription.

H3: The interaction effect is significantly different between social value orientation and domain knowledge on the cooperation level (a) and the quality of transcription (b).

METHOD

Experimental Design

In this study, we selected Transcribe-Sheng project (http://zb.library.sh.cn), a well-known crowdsourced manuscript transcription initiative in China, as our research object. In the field experiment, participants were recruited through online and offline advertisements and were requested team up with two to four members. We controlled the complexity and quantity of the tasks among various teams. After the experiment, experts checked all the tasks and rated them with one to five points.

Experimental Procedure

The study included two between-participants factors, namely the participant's social value orientation (prosocial vs. proself) and domain knowledge (high vs. low). In addition, two dependent measures were assessed: the cooperation level and the quality of transcription.

Assessment of Social Value Orientation

The Triple Dominance Measure (Van Lange et al., 1997) was used to assess participants' social value orientations.

Assessment of Domain Knowledge

The domain knowledge of participants was investigated through pre-task questionnaires.

Measuring the Cooperation Level and the Quality of Transcription

We measured the cooperation level of each participant by counting the percentage of tasks completed in the team, and used the equation (1), where j indexes each participant, k indexes each team, and jk indexes participant j in team k, to calculate the value of the cooperation level. At last, the quality of transcription depended on the participants' performance, which graded by two experts from one to five.

$$f(Cooperation\ Level) = \frac{PersonalVolume_{jk}}{GrossVolume_k} \times TeamMembers_k. \tag{1}$$

PRELIMINARY RESULTS

Analyses were performed on 45 participants (27 prosocials and 18 proselfs). 23 had high domain knowledge and 22 had low domain knowledge. Table 1 shows the descriptive statistics of the four variables.

Variable	Mean	Std. dev	Min	Max	N
Social value orientation	0.60	0.50	0	1	45
Domain knowledge	0.51	0.51	0	1	45
Cooperation level	1.01	0.59	0.12	2.92	45
Transcription quality	3.78	0.85	1	5	45

Table 1. Descriptive statistics.

A 2(prosocial vs. proself) × 2(domain knowledge: high vs. low) between-subjects analysis of variance (ANOVA) was conducted on the cooperation level. First, we obtained a main effect of social value orientation on the cooperation level, $F(1, 41) = 9.84$, $p < 0.01$. Prosocials ($M = 1.23$, $SD = 0.10$) showed more cooperation than proselfs ($M = 0.74$, $SD = 0.12$). Second, a main effect of domain knowledge on the cooperation level, $F(1, 41) = 5.14$, $p < 0.05$, revealed that high domain knowledge ($M = 1.16$, $SD = 0.10$) produced significantly more cooperation than low domain knowledge ($M = 0.81$, $SD = 0.11$). However, the two-way interaction between social value orientation and domain knowledge had no significant effect on the cooperation level.

For transcription quality, an ANOVA revealed a significant main effect of domain knowledge on the transcription quality, $F(1, 41) = 37.58$, $p < 0.001$. Participants with high domain knowledge ($M = 4.26$, $SD = 0.13$) performed better in transcribing than those who with low domain knowledge ($M = 3.09$, $SD = 0.14$). In addition, we also found a main effect of social value orientation on the quality of transcription, $F(1, 41) = 9.52$, $p < 0.01$. In total, prosocials ($M = 3.97$, $SD = 0.11$) got higher scores on transcription quality than proselfs ($M = 3.38$, $SD = 0.14$). Furthermore, an interaction effect of social value orientation and domain knowledge, $F(1, 49) = 5.40$, $p < 0.05$, was identified.

Thus, hypothesis 1 and 2 were confirmed. For hypothesis 3, the interaction between social value orientation and domain knowledge had a significant effect on the quality of transcription, but no significant effect on the cooperation level.

REFERENCES

Causer, T., & Terras, M. (2014). Crowdsourcing Bentham: Beyond the traditional boundaries of academic history. *International Journal of Humanities and Arts Computing*, *8*(1), 46–64.

Daniels, C., Holtze, T. L., Howard, R. I., & Kuehn, R. (2014). Community as resource: Crowdsourcing transcription of an historic newspaper. *Journal of Electronic Resources Librarianship*, *26*(1), 36–48.

Granell, E., & Martinez-Hinarejos, C. D. (2017). Multimodal crowdsourcing for transcribing handwritten documents. *IEEE/ACM Transactions on Audio, Speech, and Language Processing*, *25*(2), 409–419.

Ju, B. (2010). Does domain knowledge matter: Mapping users' expertise to their information interactions. *Journal of the American Society for Information Science & Technology*, *58*(13), 2007–2020.

Moyle, M., Tonra, J., & Wallace, V. (2011). Manuscript transcription by crowdsourcing: Transcribe Bentham. *Liber Quarterly*, *20*(3/4), 347–356.

Van Lange, P. A., De Bruin, E., Otten, W., & Joireman, J. A. (1997). Development of prosocial, individualistic, and competitive orientations: Theory and preliminary evidence. *Journal of Personality and Social Psychology*, *73*(4), 733–746.

Influence of Course Type and Assignment Features on Students' Information Seeking Behaviors

Yao Zhang
Peking University, Beijing, China
zhangyao_im@pku.edu.cn

Chang Liu
Peking University, Beijing, China
imliuc@pku.edu.cn

ABSTRACT

Exploring students' information seeking behavior and its influencing factors during assignment completion process can help promote teaching and learning performance. In this study, we collect college students' assignment information and their information seeking behaviors during assignment completion process through questionnaires. In total we have data of 162 courses ranging from a variety of majors. We analyzed the relationship among course type, assignment features and information behaviors during assignment completion process. We found students' information sources election is closely related to course type and assignment cognitive complexity, and their preferred information type is also related to assignment type. Results also indicate that assignments from professional compulsory courses emphasize more on basic cognitive learning, while other courses more on advanced cognitive learning. These findings are useful for course instructors to improve students' information literacy through assignments.

KEYWORDS

Information Seeking; Course Type; Assignment Features; Time Management; Learning-Related Search

ASIS&T THESAURUS

Information Seeking; Information Behavior

INTRODUCTION

Studies have examined college students' information seeking behavior, especially credibility judgment for online sources (Rieh & Hilligoss, 2008), but very few studies have examined how assignment features affected information behaviors. Assignments provide practical feedback for learning, enabling students to work purposeful during the teaching and learning cycle (Eleanor, 2012). In this study, we examined the relationship among course types, assignment features, and students' information behavior during assignment completion process. Such investigation could better reveal how college students seek information for academic work, and how search systems could help students with their assignments and improve their learning performance. In studies on academic information searching behavior, information source and information resource have received much attention. Meyers and Eisenberg (2008) found students used multiple information sources for assignments, including interpersonal sources, search engines, and mass media, but library portals were not welcome. The process of completing learning-related tasks or assignments is also the focus of such studies, for Kuhlthau (1991) proposed the ISP model about the six stages that students experienced for one type of assignment, project-type of assignment. Studies on college students' information source behaviors showed students often turned to the Internet (e.g. search engines or Wikipedia) before the library, and they had different preferences for study versus for project-type of research (Biddix, Chung, & Park, 2011); and students' use of Wikipedia differs by gender, year of study, culture difference and subject area (Selwyn & Gorard, 2016). Research showed that the consultation of professional academic sources (e.g. databases) could separate low-achieving from high-achieving students (Weber, Becker, & Hillmert, 2019). Researchers often design search tasks varying different cognitive complexity in empirical studies (e.g. Jansen, Booth, & Smith, 2009). The most widely used is the revised Bloom, Engelhart, Furst, Hill, and Krathwohl (1956)'s taxonomy of *Remember, Understand, Apply, Analyze, Evaluate, and Create* (Krathwohl, 2002). However, it's not clear how cognitive complexity level relates to students' assignments, and few studies on academic information seeking have considered course types or assignment features. This study aims to explore the relationship among course type, assignment features, and students' assignment completion behavior, including time management and information seeking behaviors.

METHODOLOGY

Data in this study were collected through questionnaires during the last month of the fall semester of 2018-2019. We recruited 99 undergraduates from departments of *Humanities*, *Social Science*, and *Information and Engineering Sciences* in Peking University. Each subject was allowed to submit multiple questionnaires, one for each assignment, and finally we collected 206 questionnaires, with 205 valid for data analysis containing assignment information from 162 courses. In the questionnaire, four groups of variables were examined: course type, assignment features, time management, and information seeking behaviors (details are shown in Table 1). We provided definition and example of some abstract variables in the questionnaire, such as

82nd Annual Meeting of the Association for Information Science & Technology | Melbourne, Australia | 19–23 October, 2019

DOI: 10.1002/pra2.00198

Groups of variables	Variable	Value
Course type		Professional compulsory course, professional elective course, others
Assignment features	Assignment type	Research paper, system implementation/experiment, reading notes, presentation, others
	Cognitive complexity	Understand, apply, analyze, evaluate, create
Time management variables	Preparation time	The period of time from starting doing assignment to the deadline of this assignment (days)
	Completion time	The actual time student used to finish the assignment (hours)
Information seeking behavioral variables	Information source	Professional literature, encyclopedic site, personal site, news site, social Q&A, online education site
	Information type	Factual information, subjective information, procedural information, others

Table 1. Variables examined in this study.

assignment cognitive complexity. We hypothesize that course type and assignment features have influence upon information seeking behaviors and time management for assignment completion.

RESULTS

Firstly, Chi-square test showed course type and assignment cognitive complexity were significantly related to student's information sources selection ($p < 0.05$). Students use less professional literature and fewer encyclopedia sites in professional compulsory courses than in other courses, while their usage of other types of information sources (e.g. statistics websites) was higher. Students tended to use search engines (e.g. Google) as their first information source for low cognitive complexity (*understand* and *apply*) assignments (40.6%), and were more likely to turn to online academic search systems (e.g. Google Scholar) as their first information source for high cognitive complexity (*analyze, evaluate* and *create*) assignments(37.6%).

Secondly, with respect to the type of information sought for assignments, Chi-square showed a significant relationship between assignment type and information type ($p < 0.01$). Students tend to find factual and subjective information for research paper, subjective information for reading notes, factual information for presentation, and procedural information for system implementation/experiment.

Thirdly, assignment type was significantly related to students' time management for assignment completion. Students' preparation time and completion time of research paper and reading notes were longer than that of other types of assignments ($p < 0.05$). T-test showed students' preparation time and completion time of low cognitive complexity assignments were shorter than that of high cognitive complexity assignments ($p < 0.01$). Besides, Chi-square test showed significant difference in assignment cognitive complexity of different courses ($p < 0.05$). Among the professional compulsory course assignments, 60% were at low cognitive complexity level, while only 40% were on a high level. However, for other types of courses, more percentage required students to analyze, evaluate or create.

CONCLUSION

In this paper we explore the relationship among course type, assignment features, students' time management and information seeking behaviors. The findings indicate that students' information seeking behaviors are closely related to the type and the cognitive complexity of assignment and course type. Teachers can lead students to use more professional and credible information sources by adjusting assignment's type and requirements to improve students' information literacy during information seeking process. This study also suggests that teachers can help students develop good time management habit by changing the ways of issuing assignments, such as breaking big projects into small tasks to encourage students to start working earlier. This study helps us better understand students' information seeking behavior in an educational context and shed lights on how instructors could guide students in their information source selections for different courses and assignments.

REFERENCES

Biddix, J. P., Chung, C. J., & Park, H. W. (2011). Convenience or credibility? A study of college student online research behaviors. *The Internet and Higher Education, 14*(3), 175–182.

Bloom, B. S., Engelhart, M. D., Furst, E. J., Hill, W. H., & Krathwohl, D. R. (1956). *Taxonomy of educational objectives: The classification of educational goals. Handbook I: Cognitive domain.* New York, NY: David McKay Company.

Eleanor, D. (2012). *Assignments matter: Making the connections that help students meet standards.* ASCD.

Jansen, B. J., Booth, D., & Smith, B. (2009). Using the taxonomy of cognitive learning to model online searching. *IP&M, 45*(6), 643–663.

Krathwohl, D. R. (2002). A revision of bloom's taxonomy: An overview. *Theory Into Practice, 41*, 212–218.

Kuhlthau, C. C. (1991). Inside the search process: Information seeking from the user's perspective. *JASIS&T, 42* (5), 361–371.

Meyers, E. M., & Eisenberg, M. B. (2008). *Information seeking and use by Grade 9 students: More and less savvy than you might think*. In Paper presented at IASL'08, Berkeley, CA.

Rieh, S. Y., & Hilligoss, B. (2008). College students' credibility judgments in the information-seeking process. In *Digital media, youth, and credibility* (pp. 49–72).

Selwyn, N., & Gorard, S. (2016). Students' use of Wikipedia as an academic resource—Patterns of use and perceptions of usefulness. *The Internet and Higher Education*, *28*, 28–34.

Weber, H., Becker, D., & Hillmert, S. (2019). Information-seeking behaviour and academic success in higher education: Which search strategies matter for grade differences among university students and how does this relevance differ by field of study? *Higher Education*, *77*(4), 657–678.

Exploring Older Adults' Health Information Seeking Behavior: Evidence From Urban China

Dongxiang Zhao
Wuhan University, Wuhan, China
zhao_dongxiang@163.com

ABSTRACT

In order to achieve health self-management and healthy aging, it has become an obvious trend for older adults to seek health information. The purpose of this poster is to present the results of a study implemented with thirty-five older adults in urban China, designed to explore their health information seeking behavior. Semi-structured interview and qualitative analysis were employed. The research results revealed the different preferences of older adults in urban China on the popularity and credibility of health information sources. The obstacles to their health information seeking behavior were mainly manifested in individual factors and social support. Additionally, the conceptual model was established, which described the factors influencing older adults' health information seeking behaviors and their relationships.

KEYWORDS

health information seeking behavior (HISB); older adults; interview; urban China

ASIS&T THESAURUS

Information behavior; Qualitative analysis; China

INTRODUCTION

The world's population is rapidly aging. In 2017, an estimated 962 million people or 13% of the global population were ages 60 or older (United Nations Department of Economic and Social Affairs, 2017). China's subpopulation over 60 has exceeded 249 million, now accounting for 17.9% of the national population. How to achieve successful aging, active aging, and healthy aging is becoming a global challenge. Moreover, due to poor health condition and chronic disease, older adults arguably have the greatest need for health information and service (Mayoh, Todres, & Bond, 2011). However, human beings are facing imbalanced socio-economic development and limited health care resources, which is particularly evident in China. Nowadays, an increasing number of older adults have begun to seek and acquire health information so as to achieve effective health self-management (Manafo & Wong, 2012; Tennant et al., 2015; National Network of Libraries of Medicine, 2019). Given the cost and convenience of research, Wuhan, where the author lives and works, was selected as the research site. The purpose of this study was to investigate: 1) health information source preferences of older adults, 2) the obstacles to health information seeking behavior of older adults, and 3) the factors influencing older adults' health information seeking behavior.

82nd Annual Meeting of the Association for Information Science & Technology | Melbourne, Australia | 19–23 October, 2019

DOI: 10.1002/pra2.00203

METHODS

The author employed individual, semi-structured in-depth interview to gather data. A total of thirty-five participants were recruited through flyers and the university for the elderly located in local community, which provides the elderly with sports and recreational facilities, as well as educational courses in photography, music, computer, etc. The inclusion criteria of participants were: a) age over 60, b) living in the urban area of Wuhan, c) having rich experience of searching for health information in daily life, and d) having certain health status and cognitive ability to participate in the interview (for example, the elderly with Alzheimer were excluded). The interviews took place in a quiet room of the university for the elderly, and lasted about 30 to 50 minutes each. The interviews were recorded by voice recording equipment and then transcribed into text for further qualitative analysis.

RESULTS

Research Question 1: health information source preferences of older adults

Overall speaking, interpersonal networks, such as family, friends, relatives and neighbors, were the most frequently used health information source among the participants (35/35). In addition, the television programs related to healthcare are the most popular media sources of health information for older adults. Almost all of the participants (31/35) had the experience of searching for health information through television programs. The main reasons mentioned include: visual presentation, reliability and lifestyle. Interestingly, the Internet is playing an increasingly important role in searching for health information for older adults (Tennant et al., 2015). Most participants (29/35) said they had used WeChat, search engines, online health websites or mobile apps to search for health information in the past month. Among them, WeChat is the most popular and even the only source of online health information. Participant C said, "*WeChat is the first mobile app I have learned and used. There are lots of articles and discussions about health in WeChat Moments and groups*." The printed materials such as books, newspapers and magazines are also important sources for some older adults (21/35) to seek health information. The important advantages of printed materials are that they are more suitable for the reading habits of the elderly, and they are easy to organize, preserve, manage and use health information. Finally, unless there is an emergency such as illness, the elderly usually does not prefer to seek health information from medical institutions and health professionals (that means the utilization frequency is relatively low), but this source is the most trusted.

Research Question 2: the obstacles to health information seeking behavior of older adults

Next, participants were asked to share the difficulties and obstacles they had encountered in searching for health information. Qualitative method was employed to analyses the interview text and the sub-concepts and concepts were extracted (see Table 1). The obstacles mainly include two aspects: individual factor and social support.

Concept	Sub-concept	Quotes/Examples
Individual factor	Degraded physiological function	*"I'm old and my eyesight has dropped a lot." "I have poor memory and I forgot it soon after reading it."*
	Lack of health literacy	*"Due to lack of basic health knowledge, I was deceived and bought many ineffective health products." "Sometimes I have difficulty in understanding health information."*
	Lack of information search skills	*"I can't search by typing or voice. When entering search requests, the only thing I can do is handwriting." "I usually just look at the first few results and don't know if it's true."*
Social support	Inadequate support from adult children	*"My son works away from home and can't take care of us in daily life. Last time he came back and installed Wi-Fi at home, making it convenient for us to surf the Internet."*
	Limited professional healthcare services	*"Seeking medical advice from healthcare providers is expensive and time consuming." "Some hospitals have poor service, and some health indicators are not explained clearly."*
	Lack of library health information services	*"I once worked in a library. Some librarians from the U.S. visited China and said that American libraries started health information services very early. We should learn from them."*
	Inadequate control of health information quality by the government	*"I saw TV advertisement about weight-loss tea. Later, I searched online and the results showed that weight-loss tea can help loss weight. Then I bought it, but it didn't work." "Some health information is misleading." "Many health-related advertisements are exaggerated."*

Table 1. The obstacles to HISB of older adults.

Research Question 3: the factors influencing older adults' health information seeking behavior

Similar to the analysis method in research question 2, the sub-concepts and concepts, regarded as variables or factors that affect the HISB of older adults, were extracted from the interview text. The conceptual model of older adults' health information seeking behavior is shown in Figure 1.

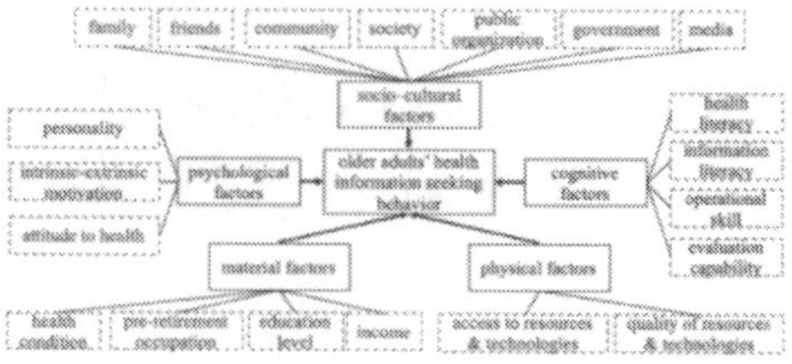

Figure 1. The factors influencing older adults' HISB.

DISCUSSION AND CONCLUSION

The findings contribute to product & service design, system development and policy making related to health information services for older adults. First, the health needs of the elderly should be paid enough attention to by the government, media, public organization, community, family and the general public. Second, older adults' information preferences, search barriers, behavioral factors and their life world should be incorporated into the design, deployment and optimization of health information services for the elderly, for example, providing high quality, easy-to-understand health information and the training related to information search and health literacy. Finally, the development and application of ICTs should be more friendly to the elderly so as not to create a greater gap. Since all the samples were from a metropolitan city in central China, the results and conclusions may not be applicable to all regions and situations (given the imbalance of regional development). The health information seeking behavior of older adults in rural China or from different social and cultural background will be the future work.

ACKNOWLEDGMENTS

This work was supported by National Natural Science Foundation of China (No. 71661167007) and China Scholarship Council (CSC) (No. 201806270054).

REFERENCES

Manafo, E., & Wong, S. (2012). Exploring older adults' health information seeking behaviors. *Journal of Nutrition Education & Behavior*, *44*(1), 85–89.

Mayoh, J., Todres, L., & Bond, C. S. (2011). Exploring the online health information seeking experiences of older adults. *Indo-Pacific Journal of Phenomenology*, *11*(2), 1–13.

National Network of Libraries of Medicine (2019). *Healthy aging: Connecting older adults to health information.* Retrieved from https://nnlm.gov/class/healthy-aging-jan19

Tennant, B., Stellefson, M., Dodd, V., et al. (2015). eHealth literacy and Web 2.0 health information seeking behaviors among baby boomers and older adults. *Journal of Medical Internet Research*, *17*(3), e70.

United Nations Department of Economic and Social Affairs (2017). *World population prospects.* Retrieved from https://esa.un.org/unpd/wpp/Publications/Files/WPP2017_KeyFindings.pdf

How Did People Feel During the Zika Virus Breakout? A Sentiment Analysis of Zika Virus Related Posts on Yahoo! Answers

Yue hua Zhao
Nanjing University,
Nanjing, China
yuehua@nju.edu.cn

Ye Chen
Central China
Normal University,
Wuhan, China
cheny@mail.ccnu.edu.cn

Jin Zhang
University of Wisconsin-
Milwaukee, Milwaukee, USA
jzhang@uwm.edu

Qingxing Dong
Central China
Normal University,
Wuhan, China
qxdong@mail.ccnu.edu.cn

Gaohui Cao
Central China
Normal University,
Wuhan, China
ghcao@mail.ccnu.edu.cn

Zhaoyang Zhang
Wuhan University,
Wuhan, China
windboy727@vip.qq.com

ABSTRACT

A sudden outbreak of the Zika virus led to public panic and discussion on social Q&A forums. Most research studies concentrated on what the public discussed about the Zika virus. However, how they felt during the Zika virus outbreak reflects the emotional stability of the public, which has a positive significance in public health monitoring, intervention and service. For this paper, we conducted a sentiment analysis of Zika-related posts on Yahoo! Answers during the outbreak of the Zika virus to investigate how emotions of the public changed overtime and if users' emotions could be influenced by others. It was found that significantly more negative emotions appeared when an outbreak started in Brazil, yet people's reactions became milder afterwards. Besides, a small positive correlation between the sentiment characteristics of the questions and the received answers implies the exchanges of emotions between questioners and answerers.

KEYWORDS

Sentiment analysis; Zika virus; Social media

ASIS&T THESAURUS

User generated content; Information seeking

INTRODUCTION

A sudden outbreak of the Zika virus happened in Brazil just before the 2016 Summer Olympics Games in Rio de Janeiro. Due to the character of infectivity and lethality (Hennessey, Fischer, & Staples, 2016), it is not surprising that the outbreak of the Zika virus led to public panic and discussion on social Q&A forums, such as Yahoo! Answers.

82nd Annual Meeting of the Association for Information Science & Technology | Melbourne, Australia | 19–23 October, 2019

DOI: 10.1002/pra2.00202

How the public's emotions changed during the outbreak of the Zika virus and if users' emotions could be influenced by others attracted public health officials' attentions for monitoring the emotional stability of the public, intervening the public panic, and providing emotional support for the public. Investigating the emotional differences among different topics about the Zika virus could help public health organizations to pick out sensitive topics and then initiate intervention mechanism in case of emotional out of control. Therefore, the following research questions were investigated in this study:

RQ1. Do people's emotions regarding Zika virus change over time on the Yahoo! Answers?

RQ2. Do people's emotions regarding Zika virus vary depending on the topics of the questions on the Yahoo! Answers?

RQ3-1. Do positive questions regarding Zika virus receive more positive answers on the Yahoo! Answers?

RQ3-2. Does the best answer express different emotions compared to other answers to questions regarding Zika virus on the Yahoo! Answers?

METHODOLOGY

An exhaustive search on Yahoo! Answers was conducted to include all questions relevant to the Zika virus. As a result, 209 questions were included in this study. After the data collection, the data analysis process comprised 4 steps, as schematized in Figure 1.

The entire period of the data collection was set from December 25, 2015 to January 1, 2017, and was then divided into the following 4 periods: Period I- December 25, 2015 to

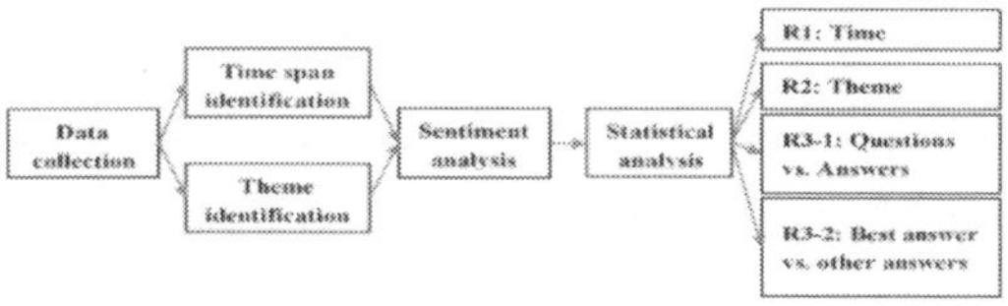

Figure 1. Data analysis process.

March 31, 2016, Period II- From April 1 to June 30, 2016, Period III- From July 1 to September 30, 2016, and Period IV- October 1, 2016 to January 1, 2017.

Following the steps proposed by Braun and Clarke (2008) for the thematic analysis, questions related to the Zika virus were classified into 3 themes: About the Zika virus, Social impact of the Zika virus, and Consumer concerns about the Zika virus. In this study, the sentiment characteristics of each question/answer was measured by the calculated sentiment scores and the classified sentiment categories produced by Lexalytics. A series of parametric tests were performed to examine the null hypotheses.

RESULTS

An Overview

The question and answer frequencies of the three themes and the four periods are summarized in Figure 2. In the table "Q" and "A" represent the number of questions and the number of answers, respectively.

Comparison among Periods and Themes

The results of an *ANOVA* test showed that there were significant differences across the defined 4 periods ($F(3, 1338) = 3.999$, $p = 0.008 < 0.05$). It suggested that the sentiment characteristics of the questions related to the Zika virus on the Yahoo! Answers varied across different periods. A*Turkey HSD* test identified that there were very strong evidences of differences between Period I and Period II with an effect size $r = 0.467$.

Figure 2 describes the distribution of four types of sentiments which appeared during the four defined periods and the three themes. Negative sentiments circulated across the whole period. In line with the results from the statistical analysis, positive sentiments were expressed more in the Period II, whereas negative sentiments appeared more in the Period I. Considering the themes of the questions as a factor, the results of an *ANOVA* test showed no significant difference among the defined 3 themes ($F(2, 1338) = 0.679$, $p = 0.507 > 0.05$).

Comparison between Questions and Answers

A small positive correlation between the sentiment characteristics of the questions and the received answers ($rho = 0.141$, $n = 209$, $p = 0.041 < 0.05$) suggested that positive questions tended to receive answers which expressed more positive sentiment, while negative questions tended to obtain more negative responses.

Comparison between Best Answers and Other Answers

A paired-samples *t-test* Indicated that there was a statistically significant difference between the sentiment characteristics of the best answer and the other answers ($t(1129) = 4.658$, $p = 0.000 < 0.05$ (two-tailed)). The eta squared statistic (0.02) indicated a large effect size. It suggests that the best answers delivered significantly more negative sentiment than the other answers.

DISCUSSION AND PRIMARY CONCLUSION

In order to provide a reflection of public sentiment toward the breakout of the Zika virus, we mined, filtered and analyzed questions and answers that related to the Zika virus on Yahoo! Answers. Armed with a lexicon-based sentiment analysis approach, it was found that negative reactions of people toward such a public health crisis remained predominantly negative during the whole time span.

Yet, sentiments expressed by users changed significantly over time. Significantly more negative emotions appeared during the first time period when an outbreak started in Brazil. It suggests that the outbreak of the Zika virus, at the beginning, led to public panic and resulted in a vast majority of negative reactions appearing on social Q&A forums. People's reactions became milder as more information about prevention and treatment were released by official organizations.

The best answers contained significantly more negative sentiments than the other answers to the same questions. It coincided with Chmiel et al. (2011)'s finding that negative emotions can drive Internet discussions. In addition, a small positive correlation was found between the sentiment characteristics of the questions and the received answers. The results were also in line with the findings from Chmiel et al. (2011), which revealed that negative threads in an online discussion forum can be followed by negative comments. Exchanges of negative emotions between questioners and answerers might raise the average emotional temperature of the discussion and may encourage other users to adopt a similar tone, creating a generally negative emotional content related to a certain topic on the social Q&A forum.

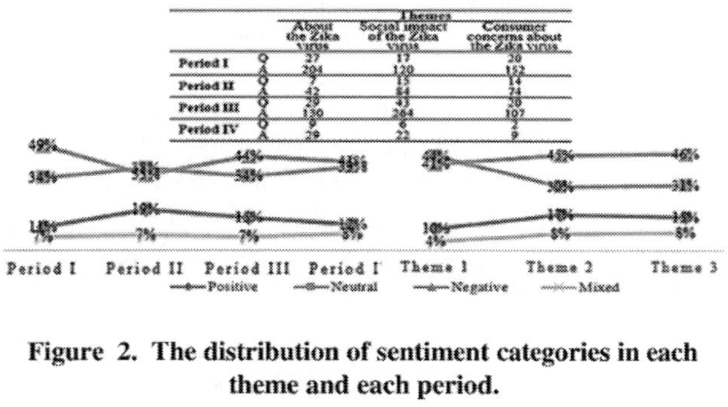

Figure 2. The distribution of sentiment categories in each theme and each period.

ACKNOWLEDGMENTS

Authors gratefully acknowledge the grant from CPSF (#2018M642884) and NSFC of China (#71420107026).

REFERENCES

Braun, V., & Clarke, V. (2008). Using thematic analysis in psychology. *Qualitative Research in Psychology*, *3*(2), 77–101.

Chmiel, A., Sobkowicz, P., Sienkiewicz, J., Paltoglou, G., Buckley, K., Thelwall, M., & Hołyst, J. A. (2011). Negative emotions boost user activity at BBC forum. *Physica A*, *390*(16), 2936–2944.

Hennessey, M., Fischer, M., & Staples, J. E. (2016). Zika virus spreads to new areas—region of the Americas, May 2015–January 2016. *American Journal of Transplantation*, *16*(3), 1031–1034.

Scientists' Academic Disruptiveness Significantly Increased After They Moved to China

Zhenyue Zhao
Nanjing University,
Nanjing, China
njujack@163.com

Jiang Li
Nanjing University,
Nanjing, China
lijiang@nju.edu.cn

Chao Min
Nanjing University,
Nanjing, China
mc@nju.edu.cn

Yi Bu
Indiana University,
Bloomington, U.S.A.
buyi@iu.edu

Lele Kang
Nanjing University,
Nanjing, China
lelekang@nju.edu.cn

Yiyang Bian
Nanjing University,
Nanjing, China
bianyiyang@nju.edu.cn

ABSTRACT

This paper investigates the relationships between scientists' international mobility and their academic disruptiveness, by using data collected from the ORCID website and the Web of Science database (2008-2017). Specifically, our observations contain 1,388 scholars who joined "brain gain" and "brain drain" and moved to China in the past decades. Results illustrate that scientists' disruptiveness significantly increased after they moved to China.

KEYWORDS

International mobility; disruptiveness; academic performance; China

ASIS&T THESAURUS

China; bibliometrics

INTRODUCTION

Mobility of scientists has a long history and is becoming an increasingly common phenomenon worldwide (Li & Tang, 2019). Most of the early studies reported a better academic performance of returnees than their local counterparts in terms of research productivity, international visions, and career advancement (e.g., Jonkers & Cruz-Castro, 2013; Lawson & Shibayama, 2015). One potential reason is the transnational capital accumulated in international mobility like global vision, advanced knowledge, and academic network, as pointed by Li and Tang (2019). Academic disruptiveness refers to the degree to which each work disrupts the field of science or technology to which it belongs by introducing something new that eclipses attention to previous work upon which it has built (Wu, Wang, & Evans, 2019). This paper examines the relationships between scholars' international mobility and their academic disruptiveness.

82nd Annual Meeting of the Association for Information Science & Technology | Melbourne, Australia | 19–23 October, 2019

DOI: 10.1002/pra2.00201

DATA AND MEASUREMENT

The dataset of this study is collected from two sources, the ORCID website and the Web of Science database. The ORCID, i.e. the Open Researcher and Contributor ID, disambiguates author names by providing a unique 16-digit ID code for each registrant. From all ~2.8 million scholars in the ORCID website, we filtered 2,127 scholars who moved to China from other countries/territories at least once during 2008-2017, based on their CVs. Their complete working experiences were divided into two phases, W_a (working abroad before moving to China, only considering the latest time they moved to China if more than once) and W_c (working in China after this move). Researchers who had no publication records found in the WoS database (limited to SCI, SSCI and A&HCI subsets) by the end of 2018 were excluded, and our dataset contains the remaining 1,388 scholars. Then, we matched each paper published between 2008 and 2017 to the exact affiliations of the authors during W_a and Wc, and 26,977 articles were successfully matched. This study follows Wu et al. (2019) in the definition for the disruptiveness d_p of a certain paper:

$$d_p = \frac{i-j}{i+j+k}, \tag{1}$$

where i is the number of citations given to the focal paper from papers that did not cite the references of the focal paper; j is the number of citations given to the focal paper from papers that cite at least one of the references of the focal paper; and k is the number of citations given to the reference(s) of the focal paper from papers that did not cite the focal paper. For a certain paper, if d_p is positive, it is considered to be a disruptive study and, elsewise, a developing study (developing existing work). To measure the disruptiveness of a set of publications, e.g., of scholars, in certain periods, we propose $d_s(t)$ instead of d_p by giving up the calculation of k, because it caused inconsistence of d_p (Wu & Wu,

2019). The simplified measurement of disruptiveness we used in this study is:

$$d_s(t) = \frac{N_{d_p>0}(t)}{N(t)}, \quad (2)$$

where $N_{d_p>0}(t)$ indicates the number of disruptive articles published in a period t, and $N(t)$ represents the total number of articles published in t. For example, if a scholar published ten papers in 2008 (among which four are disruptive by the time we accessed their citation data), he/she then has $d_s(2008) = 0.4$.

PRELIMINARY RESULTS

Disruptiveness is dependent on the length of citation windows. We first examined the proportion of disruptive articles among the 1,388 scholars' publications in each year between 2008 and 2017. As shown in Figure 1, along with the shrinkage of citation windows, the proportion of disruptive articles in each year appears decreasing.

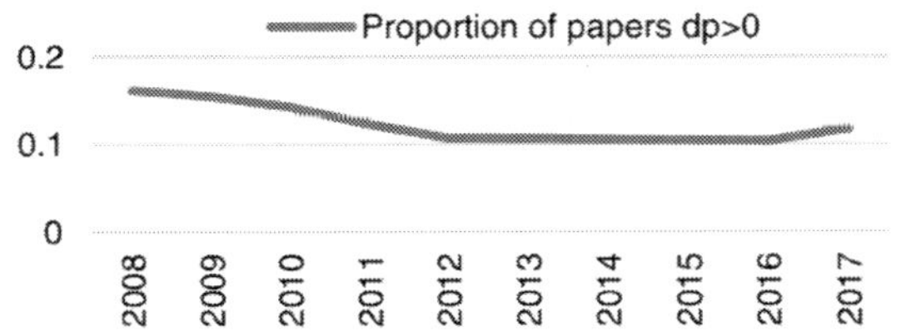

Figure 1. Disruptiveness of the 26,977 articles with different citation windows.

We calculated each year's disruptiveness of each of the 1,388 scientists, for a ten-year period since his/her very first publication. By averaging sampled scientists' disruptiveness, Figure 2 shows that in general scientists' academic disruptiveness does not increase in their later career stage, no matter how we counted their publications (marked in different colors in the figure) in order to exclude the disturbance of the outliers in the number of scientists' yearly publications. Interestingly, the tendency is similar to that in the purple curve in Figure 1. Both figures are consistent with the finding in Bornmann and Tekles (2019) that the disruptiveness depends on the length of citation windows.

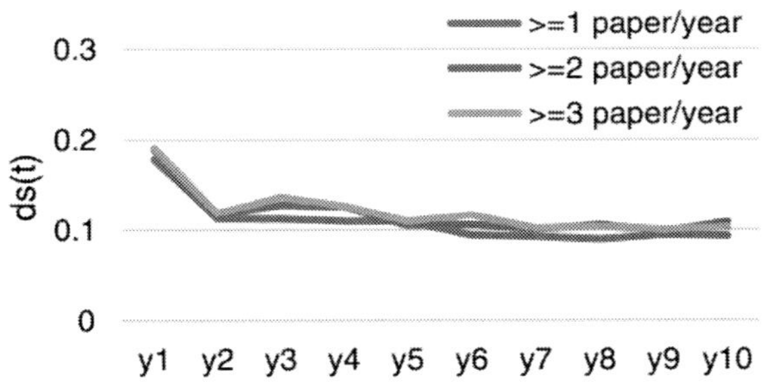

Figure 2. Evolution of scientists' disruptiveness in the first ten years of their career (522 scientists for the blue curve, 349 for red, and 219 for green).

Scientists' disruptiveness significantly increased after they moved to China. We explored whether the law that scientists' disruptiveness does not increase in their later career stage is disturbed with scientists' abrupt mobility. First, we compared scientists' $d_s(t)$ values before and after they moved to China. For the 1,388 scholars who moved to China from abroad, their average $d_s(W_c)$ was 0.104, which is significantly higher than 0.064, the average $d_s(W_a)$ ($p < 0.01$, paired-samples t-test). After eliminating scholars who had no publication in W_a or in W_c, 779 scholars remained. This difference was still significant where $d_s(W_c) = 0.111$ and $d_s(W_a) = 0.093$ ($p < 0.05$, paired-samples t-test).

Second, we examined whether mobility led to leaping in scientists' disruptiveness curve. We plotted values of $d_s(t)$ for 365 scientists who published at least one paper per year during the period from the fourth previous year of c (the year they moved to China), i.e., c-4, to the third subsequent year of c, i.e., c + 3. Similar to the trend in Figures 1 and 2, a general downward trend emerged in Figure 3, except for a significant increase ($p < 0.05$, paired-samples t-test) between $d_s(c)$ and $d_s(c + 1)$.

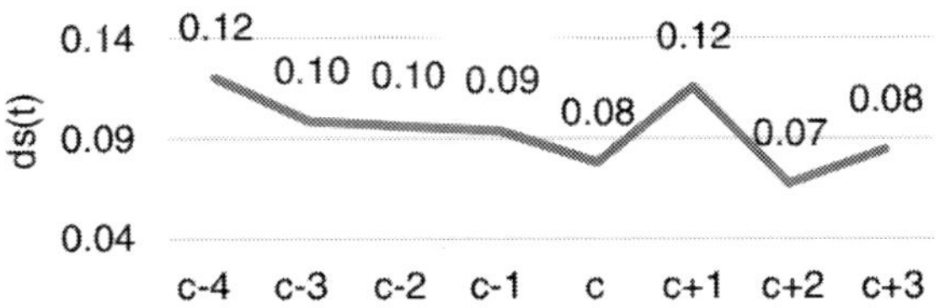

Figure 3. The annual change of scientists' disruptiveness before and after they moved to China.

Both approaches came to the same conclusion that mobility to China leads to growth of scientists' disruptiveness.

SUMMARY

One finding shows that scientists' disruptiveness significantly increased after they moved to China. The other is that our improved measure of disruptiveness, $d_s(t)$, is also dependent on the length of citation windows, similar to d_p. In another word, recently published articles are less likely to be disruptive, probably because an article is more likely to be cited together with its reference(s) when it is newly published, but as time goes by, it is more likely to be cited alone. These findings provide practical implications for the debate on the effects of "brain gain" policy in China. Further studies will focus on the reasons why mobility leads to the increase of disruptiveness.

REFERENCES

Bornmann, L., & Tekles, A. (2019). Disruption index depends on length of citation window. *El profesional de la información, 28*(2).

Jonkers, K., & Cruz-Castro, L. (2013). Research upon return: The effect of international mobility on scientific ties, production and impact. *Research Policy, 42*(8), 1366–1377.

Lawson, C., & Shibayama, S. (2015). International research visits and careers: An analysis of bioscience academics in Japan. *Science and Public Policy*, *42*(5), 690–710.

Li, F., & Tang, L. (2019). When international mobility meets local connections: Evidence from China. *Science and Public Policy*. https://doi.org/10.1093/scipol/scz004

Wu, L., Wang, D., & Evans, J. A. (2019). Large teams develop and small teams disrupt science and technology. *Nature*, *566*(7744), 378.

Wu, S., & Wu, Q. (2019). *A confusing definition of disruption*. Retrieved from https://osf.io/preprints/socarxiv/d3wpk/

Argument Ontology for Describing Scientific Articles: A Statistical Study Based on Articles From Two Research Areas

Huimin Zhou
Wuhan University,
Wuhan, China
zhouhm@whu.edu.cn

Ningyuan Song
Wuhan University,
Wuhan, China
songny@whu.edu.cn

Hanghang Cheng
Wuhan University,
Wuhan, China
chhang@whu.edu.cn

Xiaoguang Wang
Wuhan University,
Wuhan, China
wxguang@whu.edu.cn

ABSTRACT

The research provides (1) an account of the construction of a new Scientific Argument Ontology (SAO), (2) a statistical analysis of 40 articles from both fields of Library and Information Science and Biomedical Research, and (3) a summary of important differences between the article structures common to each respective field of study and characteristics of their contents as revealed by applying SAO to conduct qualitative analysis. Ontology coverage ratios as well as the ratios of different classes and evidence types were calculated in the analysis. The results show a comprehensive coverage of SAO, while also indicate that the ontological construction of scientific arguments should fully consider the characteristics of their disciplines and fields in order to better facilitate extraction, discovery and retrieval.

KEYWORDS

Scientific Articles; Argument Structure; Ontology Construction

ASIS&T THESAURUS

Information science ~ Knowledge and information

INTRODUCTION

Scientific articles form the foundation of scientific communication. Within every scientific article an argument structure exists to provide the bases to organize content. Argumentation mining in scientific articles is benefit for knowledge extraction, discovery and retrieval. Due to the complexity of scientific articles, formally representing the structure of scientific content is necessary. Recent studies have come up with different ontologies (Shotton & Peroni, 2015; Constantin & Peroni, 2016) and models (Teufel, Carletta, & Moens, 1999), defining the components of scientific content from a rhetorical perspective. Other studies designed to formally define the basic argument process have put forward argument-based models (Clark, Ciccarese, & Goble, 2014; Vitali & Peroni, 2011). In contrast, Scientific Argument Ontology (SAO) was designed to enable a science communication ecosystem in which semantic context of scientific discourse can be created, stored, accessed, integrated and exchanged along with unstructured or semi-structured digital scientific information. In this study, SAO was used to annotate 40 articles from two different domains (Library and Information Science & Biomedical). The results showed a comprehensive coverage of SAO.

82nd Annual Meeting of the Association for Information Science & Technology | Melbourne, Australia | 19–23 October, 2019

DOI: 10.1002/pra2.00204

DEVELOPMENT OF THE ONTOLOGY

Process of the Ontology Construction

The seven-step method of Stanford university was adopted to construct SAO. We began our design with reusing existing ontologies. The core classes employ AMO and Mircopublications reference to represent the basic argument structure of scientific articles. Then based on the DEO, CoreSC and Discourse Segment, we emphasized theoretical and factual evidences which can support divergent viewpoints. SAO was developed in OWL through Protégé 5.1.

Elements of the Ontology

SAO includes 6 core classes and 14 extended classes, The core classes include: *Background, Claim, Evidence, Warrant, Backing* and *Conclusion*. Within the context of scientific articles, the extend classes provide deep definitions and representations of the Evidence, include two parts: the theoretical evidence and the factual evidence. The *Theoretical Evidence* category includes: *Work, Principle* and *Formula*. The *Factual Evidence* category includes: *Experience, Example, Data* and *Fact*. Our ontology also defined *Research Problem* and *Hypothesis*, to make it more suitable for scientific articles. In addition, the classes of *Rebuttal, Conclusion* were also defined to fully represent arguments. All of these elements provide a model of the claims, questions and hypotheses in

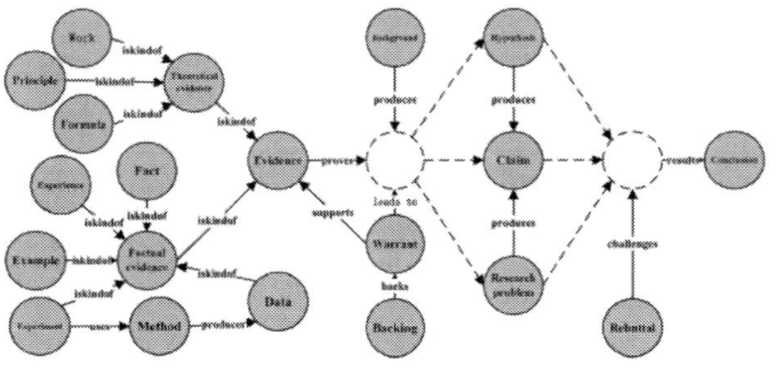

Figure 1. The class graph of SAO.

scientific discourse, their supporting evidence, and the argumentation relationships among them. As shown in Figure 1.

METHOD

Library and Information Science (LIS) and Biomedical research, were selected as the two distinct knowledge domains for use in this study, and the Top 10 journals of each area were chosen as ranked by the Impact Factor. Next, two articles published between 2008 and 2018 were randomly selected from each journal, while the review articles were excluded. Then we followed an iterative process to identify the reliability testing, and the Cohen's Kappa was 67.50%. This statistic can be interpreted in the middle range of substantial agreement [0.61-0.80; (Cohen, 1960)].

RESULTS

The Coverage Ratio of the Ontology

Based on the two fields, the coverage ratio of each SAO class was calculated to evaluate the ontology applicability. The ratio was calculated by using the number of articles with the labels divided by the number of total articles. The following radar chart was generated according to the results (Figure 2). From these results, we found SAO to be more suitable for LIS. Also, the coverage ratio showed both of the articles in two areas have the same fundamental elements. The publication of each contain *background, claim, method, research problem* and *conclusion*. Some different focuses had also been found through these results, like *backing, experience, example*, etc.

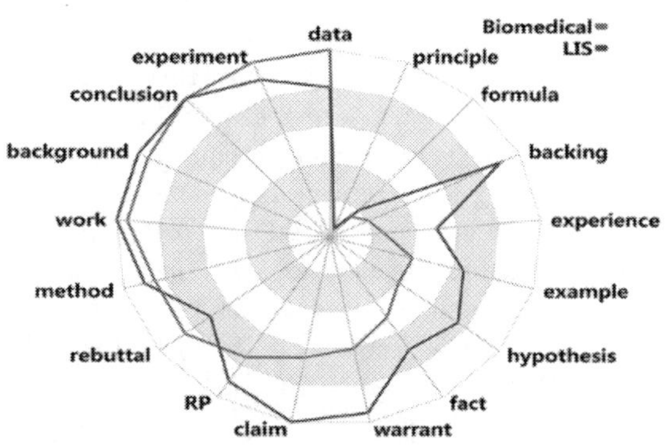

Figure 2. Coverage ratio of each class in SAO.

The Ratio of Different Ontology Class

The ratio of different ontology classes was calculated in Figure 3. The *data* (29.36%) and *experiment* (20.8%) were the most important argumentation unit in Biomedical articles. While in LIS, *work* (14.62%), *background* (8.11%), *backing* (7.32%) were the most significant components. This indicates a difference in argumentation due to the two research patterns in different domains. As for other classes, like *warrant, rebuttal and claim*, both two types of articles had relatively same proportion, meaning even if there are some differences, the fundamental argument structure remains the same in the scientific publications of both knowledge domains.

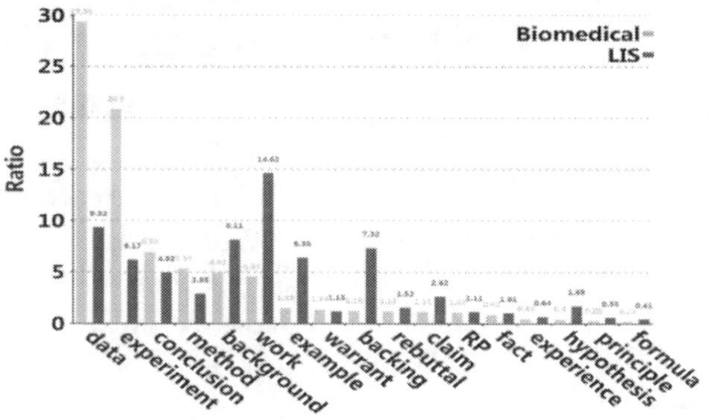

Figure 3. Different class ratio of two types articles.

Two Types of Evidence

In order to clearly explain the difference between the argument within each knowledge domain, the ratio of two types of evidence was calculated. As illustrated by Figure 4, the ratio of theoretical evidence in the articles from LIS was 15.58%, and the ratio of factual evidence was 26.37%. In contrast, in biomedical articles, the proportion of theoretical evidence was only 4.98%, but the ratio of factual evidence reached up to 58.24%. The results showed a clear difference in the argumentation between two knowledge domains.

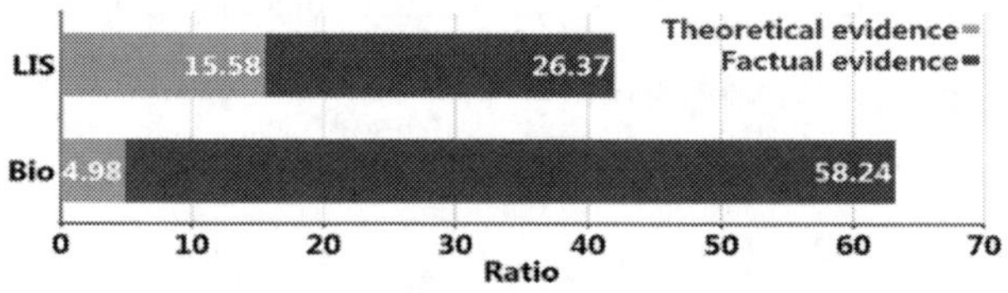

Figure 4. The ratio of two types evidence in different areas.

CONCLUSION

This study has the following findings: (1) we designed a general ontology SAO oriented to the argumentation structure of scientific articles; (2) 20 articles in LIS and 20 in Biomedical were selected to test SAO, the results showed a comprehensive applicability to both two fields. So, SAO can be used to represent and extract argument structure from scientific content, the deep indexing could also be realized to further support knowledge discovery and retrieval; (3) By analyzing and comparing the proportion of the classes in the ontology, we find that data and experiment account for a relatively high proportion of articles in the Biomedical, while work, example and backing in the field of LIS have the greatest occurrence. The proportion of other classes is relatively balanced. Furthermore, The Biomedical field pays more attention to experimental and data-oriented empirical research, while LIS tends toward reasoning and deduction according to facts. Through SAO it is possible to achieve automatic semantic annotation for scientific papers, thus realize knowledge connection among different research fields further.

REFERENCES

Clark, T., Ciccarese, P. N., & Goble, C. A. (2014). Micropublications: A semantic model for claims, evidence, arguments and annotations in biomedical communications. *Journal of Biomedical Semantics*, *5*(1), 28.

Cohen, J. (1960). A coefficient of agreement for nominal scales. *Educational & Psychological Measurement*, *20* (1), 37–46.

Constantin, A., & Peroni, S. (2016). DoCO: The document components ontology. *The Semantic Web*, *7*(2), 167–181.

Shotton, D., & Peroni, S. (2015). *The discourse element ontology (DEO)*. Retrieved from https://sparontologies.github.io/deo/current/deo.html

Teufel, S., Carletta, J., & Moens, M. (1999). *An annotation scheme for discourse-level argumentation in research articles*. In Proceedings of the 8th Meeting of the European Chapter of the Association for Computational Linguistics (EACL-99), June 1999, Bergen, Norway (pp. 110-117).

Vitali, F., & Peroni, S. (2011). *The argument model ontology (AMO)*. Retrieved from http://www.essepuntato.it/2011/02/argumentmodel

Recognizing Sentences Concerning Future Research From the Full Text of JASIST

Zihe Zhu
Nanjing Agricultural University, Nanjing, China
2018114012@njau.edu.cn

Dongbo Wang
Nanjing Agricultural University, Nanjing, China
db.wang@njau.edu.cn

Si Shen
Nanjing University of Science and Technology, Nanjing, China
shensi@njust.edu.cn

ABSTRACT

In the conclusion part of an academic paper, sentences concerning future research provide an outlook about future focus of research and reflect the latest development trend in a specific topic or field. These sentences are of high value for further investigation. However, very little has been done on sentences talking about future research in academic full texts. Here, papers in JASIST were studied with respect to these sentences. Deep learning model was trained on articles containing sentences annotated as relating to "future research" by BERT model. The model capable of automatic extraction of such sentences from academic full texts was obtained. Later this model was verified on the unannotated corpus, which demonstrated good performance. Finally, clustering was performed for the extracted sentences. It was found by cluster analysis that the sentences concerning future research were divided into four types. Our findings provide support for classification of sentences concerning future research.

KEYWORDS

BERT; academic full text; future research; text mining; deep learning

ASIS&T THESAURUS

Scientometrics; Computer science

INTRODUCTION

The conclusion section of an academic paper usually contains a prospect for future research. Although these sentences are placed in the last section of an academic paper and not the part under intense discussion, they are of high importance for having a glimpse of future trend and also for pinpointing the next mission of research. But given the sparsity of sentences concerning future research and the time-consuming nature of reading bulky volume of scientific literature, it is of particular importance to recognize and analyze sentences concerning future research. So far, studies on extraction of sentences concerning future research have only reached the stage of using regular expression for the extraction (Hu & Wan, 2015). To fill this gap, deep learning was performed to extract sentences concerning future research from academic full texts in the present study. This was followed by clustering experiment on academic full texts and four types of sentences concerning future research were identified.

82nd Annual Meeting of the Association for Information Science & Technology | Melbourne, Australia | 19–23 October, 2019

DOI: 10.1002/pra2.00206

DATA SET AND METHOD

The data were sourced from 2,849 published articles full text on *JASIST* (2006-2016). A total of 1579 papers from JASIST were retrieved between the year 2006 and 2016. The specific information of the corpus is shown in Table 1.

Num.	Type	Count
1	Papers	1,579
2	Total Sentences	73,120
3	Future research sentences	3,647
4	Marked sentences in each article average number	2.50
5	Average words number in each sentences	29.17
6	The longest sentence words number	232

Table 1. Basic information of our corpus.

In this paper, a deep learning model - BERT - was used. With BERT, pre-training is already performed on linguistic representation before the training begins (Devlin, Chang, Lee, & Toutanova, 2018). Our experiments were conducted based on the BERT pre-training model (multi-language version).

Sentences were clustered by using the hierarchical clustering algorithm. Zhou, Xu, and Liu (2016) proposed an agglomerative hierarchical clustering (AHC) method to deter-mine the optimal number of clusters, which proved to be of high performance. By reference to the above, a BERT-based pre-training model was used to generate representation vectors for sentences, which further improved the clustering performance.

RESULT

In the training of BERT model, the pre-training model with 11 layers, 748 hidden units and 12 self-attention heads was chosen. Then 10-fold cross-validation tests were performed of the BERT model, and assessed by P, R and F value. Results are summarized as shown in Table 2.

Num.	Non-future sentence F-value	Future sentence F-value	micro-AVG F-value	Macro-AVG F-value
1	98.49%	64.77%	97.11%	81.63%
2	98.20%	64.59%	96.58%	81.40%
3	98.35%	66.95%	96.85%	82.65%
4	98.15%	60.43%	96.47%	79.29%
5	98.15%	67.01%	96.50%	82.58%
6	98.07%	60.61%	96.32%	79.34%
7	98.19%	64.80%	96.57%	81.50%
8	98.26%	66.76%	96.69%	82.51%
9	98.32%	63.89%	96.80%	81.11%
10	98.12%	62.57%	96.42%	80.35%
MAX-F	98.49%	67.01%	97.11%	82.65%
AVG-F	98.23%	64.24%	96.63%	81.24%

Table 2. Results of 10-fold cross-validation on BERT.

In our previous experiment using bidirectional LSTM model, the maximum F-value for the classification result was 81.71%, which was lower than that of BERT. Then, the model trained in the above section was used to extract sentences concerning future research from the academic full texts in JASIST in 2018. A total of 131 sentences concerning future research were extracted. To further mine the information of future research sentences that were automatically extracted, hierarchical clustering was performed for the sentences. Then by using the pre-trained BERT model, each sentence was translated into a 768-dimensional vector, for which the dimensionality reduction process could reduce errors in the vector. The result was plotted as shown in Figure 1.

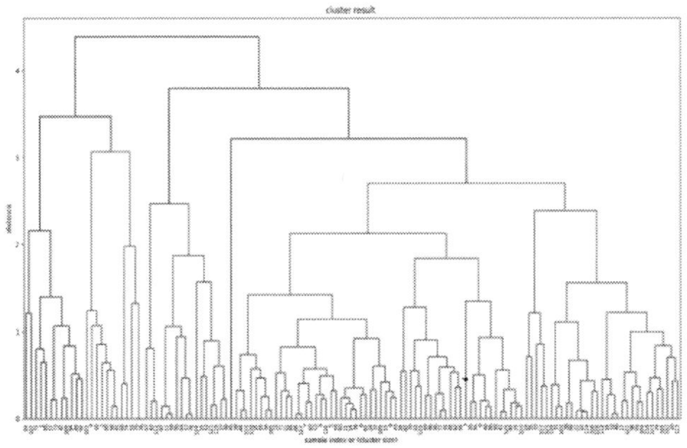

Figure 1. Dendrogram of sentence clusters extracted from academic full texts in JASIST in 2018.

It's easy to see that the sentences concerning future research extracted from the academic full texts were divided into four types, each of which was represented with a different color. The sentences were classified based on their function, namely, supportive, methodological, high-lighting potential influence factors and presenting future target. Examples of sentences of each type and their sources are provided in Table 3.

Type	Description	Example	Reference
Supportive	Explaining the support and contribution of the current study to future research.	Accordingly , it provides empirical evidence helpful for future decisions regarding corpus delineations and	10.1002/asi.23913
Methodologic	Explaining the use of certain method or algorithm for improvement in future research.	We will also explore other potential applications ...	10.1002/asi.23929
Identifying potential influence factors	Pointing out the prospect of discussing potential influence factors of experimental result in future research.	In future work , we will investigate the impact of product category on user requirement modeling...	10.1002/asi.23932
Presenting future target	Future plan, goal and measures.	Our future work will include the creation of a larger multilingual parallel data set using a postdating approach .	10.1002/asi.23925

Table 3. Descriptions and examples of cluster result.

CONCLUSION

Here a case study was performed on the corpus of academic full texts. BERT model was used for automatic extraction of sentences concerning future research, and the maximum harmonic mean was up to 82.65%. The model with the best effect was employed to extract sentences concerning future research from all academic full texts in JASIST in 2018. Then, on the semantic level, hierarchical clustering was applied to classify these sentences into four clusters, which were further divided into four types based on function, namely, supportive, methodological, identifying potential influence factors and presenting future target. The present study filled the gaps in the research of methods to extract sentences concerning future research from academic full texts. We proposed that these sentences can be divided into four types, which provides support for further classification of such sentences.

ACKNOWLEDGMENTS

Researches are supported by the National Natural Science Foundation of China (Grant Number: 71673143).

REFERENCES

Devlin, J., Chang, M. W., Lee, K., & Toutanova, K. (2018). Bert: Pre-training of deep bidirectional transformers for language understanding.arXiv preprint. arXiv:1810. 04805v1.

Hu, Y. & Wan, X. (2015). Mining and analyzing the future works in scientific articles. arXiv:1507.02140.

Zhou, S., Xu, Z., & Liu, F. (2016). Method for determining the optimal number of clusters based on agglomerative hierarchical clustering. *IEEE Transactions on Neural Networks and Learning Systems*, *PP*(99), 3007–3017.